Oxford Dictionary of
National Biography

Volume 41

Oxford Dictionary of National Biography

IN ASSOCIATION WITH

The British Academy

From the earliest times to the year 2000

Edited by

H. C. G. Matthew

and

Brian Harrison

Volume 41
Norbury–Osborn

OXFORD

UNIVERSITY PRESS

OXFORD
UNIVERSITY PRESS

Great Clarendon Street, Oxford OX2 6DP

Oxford University Press is a department of the University of Oxford.
It furthers the University's objective of excellence in research, scholarship,
and education by publishing worldwide in

Oxford New York

Auckland Bangkok Buenos Aires Cape Town
Chennai Dar es Salaam Delhi Hong Kong Istanbul Karachi
Kolkata Kuala Lumpur Madrid Melbourne Mexico City Mumbai Nairobi
São Paulo Shanghai Taipei Tokyo Toronto

Oxford is a registered trade mark of Oxford University Press
in the UK and in certain other countries

Published in the United States
by Oxford University Press Inc., New York

© Oxford University Press 2004

Illustrations © individual copyright holders as listed in
'Picture credits', and reproduced with permission

Database right Oxford University Press (maker)

First published 2004

All rights reserved. No part of this material may be reproduced,
stored in a retrieval system, or transmitted, in any form or by any means,
without the prior permission in writing of Oxford University Press,
or as expressly permitted by law, or under terms agreed with the appropriate
reprographics rights organization. Enquiries concerning reproduction
outside the scope of the above should be sent to the Rights Department,
Oxford University Press, at the address above

You must not circulate this book in any other binding or cover
and you must impose this same condition on any acquirer

British Library Cataloguing in Publication Data
Data available

Library of Congress Cataloging in Publication Data
Data available: for details see volume 1, p. iv

ISBN 0-19-861391-1 (this volume)
ISBN 0-19-861411-X (set of sixty volumes)

Text captured by Alliance Phototypesetters, Pondicherry
Illustrations reproduced and archived by
Alliance Graphics Ltd, UK
Typeset in OUP Swift by Interactive Sciences Limited, Gloucester
Printed in Great Britain on acid-free paper by
Butler and Tanner Ltd,
Frome, Somerset

LIST OF ABBREVIATIONS

1 *General abbreviations*

AB	bachelor of arts		BCnL	bachelor of canon law
ABC	Australian Broadcasting Corporation		BCom	bachelor of commerce
ABC TV	ABC Television		BD	bachelor of divinity
act.	active		BEd	bachelor of education
A$	Australian dollar		BEng	bachelor of engineering
AD	*anno domini*		bk *pl.* bks	book(s)
AFC	Air Force Cross		BL	bachelor of law / letters / literature
AIDS	acquired immune deficiency syndrome		BLitt	bachelor of letters
AK	Alaska		BM	bachelor of medicine
AL	Alabama		BMus	bachelor of music
A level	advanced level [examination]		BP	before present
ALS	associate of the Linnean Society		BP	British Petroleum
AM	master of arts		Bros.	Brothers
AMICE	associate member of the Institution of Civil Engineers		BS	(1) bachelor of science; (2) bachelor of surgery; (3) British standard
ANZAC	Australian and New Zealand Army Corps		BSc	bachelor of science
appx *pl.* appxs	appendix(es)		BSc (Econ.)	bachelor of science (economics)
AR	Arkansas		BSc (Eng.)	bachelor of science (engineering)
ARA	associate of the Royal Academy		bt	baronet
ARCA	associate of the Royal College of Art		BTh	bachelor of theology
ARCM	associate of the Royal College of Music		*bur.*	buried
ARCO	associate of the Royal College of Organists		C.	command [identifier for published parliamentary papers]
ARIBA	associate of the Royal Institute of British Architects		*c.*	*circa*
ARP	air-raid precautions		c.	*capitulum pl. capitula*: chapter(s)
ARRC	associate of the Royal Red Cross		CA	California
ARSA	associate of the Royal Scottish Academy		Cantab.	Cantabrigiensis
art.	article / item		cap.	*capitulum pl. capitula*: chapter(s)
ASC	Army Service Corps		CB	companion of the Bath
Asch	Austrian Schilling		CBE	commander of the Order of the British Empire
ASDIC	Antisubmarine Detection Investigation Committee		CBS	Columbia Broadcasting System
ATS	Auxiliary Territorial Service		cc	cubic centimetres
ATV	Associated Television		C$	Canadian dollar
Aug	August		CD	compact disc
AZ	Arizona		Cd	command [identifier for published parliamentary papers]
b.	born		CE	Common (*or* Christian) Era
BA	bachelor of arts		cent.	century
BA (Admin.)	bachelor of arts (administration)		cf.	compare
BAFTA	British Academy of Film and Television Arts		CH	Companion of Honour
BAO	bachelor of arts in obstetrics		chap.	chapter
bap.	baptized		ChB	bachelor of surgery
BBC	British Broadcasting Corporation / Company		CI	Imperial Order of the Crown of India
BC	before Christ		CIA	Central Intelligence Agency
BCE	before the common (*or* Christian) era		CID	Criminal Investigation Department
BCE	bachelor of civil engineering		CIE	companion of the Order of the Indian Empire
BCG	bacillus of Calmette and Guérin [inoculation against tuberculosis]		Cie	Compagnie
			CLit	companion of literature
BCh	bachelor of surgery		CM	master of surgery
BChir	bachelor of surgery		cm	centimetre(s)
BCL	bachelor of civil law			

Cmd	command [identifier for published parliamentary papers]		edn	edition
CMG	companion of the Order of St Michael and St George		EEC	European Economic Community
			EFTA	European Free Trade Association
Cmnd	command [identifier for published parliamentary papers]		EICS	East India Company Service
			EMI	Electrical and Musical Industries (Ltd)
CO	Colorado		Eng.	English
Co.	company		enl.	enlarged
co.	county		ENSA	Entertainments National Service Association
col. *pl.* cols.	column(s)		ep. *pl.* epp.	*epistola(e)*
Corp.	corporation		ESP	extra-sensory perception
CSE	certificate of secondary education		esp.	especially
CSI	companion of the Order of the Star of India		esq.	esquire
CT	Connecticut		est.	estimate / estimated
CVO	commander of the Royal Victorian Order		EU	European Union
cwt	hundredweight		ex	sold by (*lit.* out of)
$	(American) dollar		excl.	excludes / excluding
d.	(1) penny (pence); (2) died		exh.	exhibited
DBE	dame commander of the Order of the British Empire		exh. cat.	exhibition catalogue
			f. *pl.* ff.	following [pages]
DCH	diploma in child health		FA	Football Association
DCh	doctor of surgery		FACP	fellow of the American College of Physicians
DCL	doctor of civil law		facs.	facsimile
DCnL	doctor of canon law		FANY	First Aid Nursing Yeomanry
DCVO	dame commander of the Royal Victorian Order		FBA	fellow of the British Academy
DD	doctor of divinity		FBI	Federation of British Industries
DE	Delaware		FCS	fellow of the Chemical Society
Dec	December		Feb	February
dem.	demolished		FEng	fellow of the Fellowship of Engineering
DEng	doctor of engineering		FFCM	fellow of the Faculty of Community Medicine
des.	destroyed		FGS	fellow of the Geological Society
DFC	Distinguished Flying Cross		fig.	figure
DipEd	diploma in education		FIMechE	fellow of the Institution of Mechanical Engineers
DipPsych	diploma in psychiatry			
diss.	dissertation		FL	Florida
DL	deputy lieutenant		*fl.*	*floruit*
DLitt	doctor of letters		FLS	fellow of the Linnean Society
DLittCelt	doctor of Celtic letters		FM	frequency modulation
DM	(1) Deutschmark; (2) doctor of medicine; (3) doctor of musical arts		fol. *pl.* fols.	folio(s)
			Fr	French francs
DMus	doctor of music		Fr.	French
DNA	dioxyribonucleic acid		FRAeS	fellow of the Royal Aeronautical Society
doc.	document		FRAI	fellow of the Royal Anthropological Institute
DOL	doctor of oriental learning		FRAM	fellow of the Royal Academy of Music
DPH	diploma in public health		FRAS	(1) fellow of the Royal Asiatic Society; (2) fellow of the Royal Astronomical Society
DPhil	doctor of philosophy			
DPM	diploma in psychological medicine		FRCM	fellow of the Royal College of Music
DSC	Distinguished Service Cross		FRCO	fellow of the Royal College of Organists
DSc	doctor of science		FRCOG	fellow of the Royal College of Obstetricians and Gynaecologists
DSc (Econ.)	doctor of science (economics)			
DSc (Eng.)	doctor of science (engineering)		FRCP(C)	fellow of the Royal College of Physicians of Canada
DSM	Distinguished Service Medal			
DSO	companion of the Distinguished Service Order		FRCP (Edin.)	fellow of the Royal College of Physicians of Edinburgh
DSocSc	doctor of social science		FRCP (Lond.)	fellow of the Royal College of Physicians of London
DTech	doctor of technology			
DTh	doctor of theology		FRCPath	fellow of the Royal College of Pathologists
DTM	diploma in tropical medicine		FRCPsych	fellow of the Royal College of Psychiatrists
DTMH	diploma in tropical medicine and hygiene		FRCS	fellow of the Royal College of Surgeons
DU	doctor of the university		FRGS	fellow of the Royal Geographical Society
DUniv	doctor of the university		FRIBA	fellow of the Royal Institute of British Architects
dwt	pennyweight		FRICS	fellow of the Royal Institute of Chartered Surveyors
EC	European Community			
ed. *pl.* eds.	edited / edited by / editor(s)		FRS	fellow of the Royal Society
Edin.	Edinburgh		FRSA	fellow of the Royal Society of Arts

FRSCM	fellow of the Royal School of Church Music	ISO	companion of the Imperial Service Order
FRSE	fellow of the Royal Society of Edinburgh	It.	Italian
FRSL	fellow of the Royal Society of Literature	ITA	Independent Television Authority
FSA	fellow of the Society of Antiquaries	ITV	Independent Television
ft	foot *pl.* feet	Jan	January
FTCL	fellow of Trinity College of Music, London	JP	justice of the peace
ft-lb per min.	foot-pounds per minute [unit of horsepower]	jun.	junior
FZS	fellow of the Zoological Society	KB	knight of the Order of the Bath
GA	Georgia	KBE	knight commander of the Order of the British Empire
GBE	knight or dame grand cross of the Order of the British Empire	KC	king's counsel
GCB	knight grand cross of the Order of the Bath	kcal	kilocalorie
GCE	general certificate of education	KCB	knight commander of the Order of the Bath
GCH	knight grand cross of the Royal Guelphic Order	KCH	knight commander of the Royal Guelphic Order
GCHQ	government communications headquarters	KCIE	knight commander of the Order of the Indian Empire
GCIE	knight grand commander of the Order of the Indian Empire	KCMG	knight commander of the Order of St Michael and St George
GCMG	knight or dame grand cross of the Order of St Michael and St George	KCSI	knight commander of the Order of the Star of India
GCSE	general certificate of secondary education	KCVO	knight commander of the Royal Victorian Order
GCSI	knight grand commander of the Order of the Star of India	keV	kilo-electron-volt
GCStJ	bailiff or dame grand cross of the order of St John of Jerusalem	KG	knight of the Order of the Garter
		KGB	[Soviet committee of state security]
GCVO	knight or dame grand cross of the Royal Victorian Order	KH	knight of the Royal Guelphic Order
GEC	General Electric Company	KLM	Koninklijke Luchtvaart Maatschappij (Royal Dutch Air Lines)
Ger.	German	km	kilometre(s)
GI	government (*or* general) issue	KP	knight of the Order of St Patrick
GMT	Greenwich mean time	KS	Kansas
GP	general practitioner	KT	knight of the Order of the Thistle
GPU	[Soviet special police unit]	kt	knight
GSO	general staff officer	KY	Kentucky
Heb.	Hebrew	£	pound(s) sterling
HEICS	Honourable East India Company Service	£E	Egyptian pound
HI	Hawaii	L	lira *pl.* lire
HIV	human immunodeficiency virus	l. *pl.* ll.	line(s)
HK$	Hong Kong dollar	LA	Lousiana
HM	his / her majesty('s)	LAA	light anti-aircraft
HMAS	his / her majesty's Australian ship	LAH	licentiate of the Apothecaries' Hall, Dublin
HMNZS	his / her majesty's New Zealand ship	Lat.	Latin
HMS	his / her majesty's ship	lb	pound(s), unit of weight
HMSO	His / Her Majesty's Stationery Office	LDS	licence in dental surgery
HMV	His Master's Voice	*lit.*	literally
Hon.	Honourable	LittB	bachelor of letters
hp	horsepower	LittD	doctor of letters
hr	hour(s)	LKQCPI	licentiate of the King and Queen's College of Physicians, Ireland
HRH	his / her royal highness	LLA	lady literate in arts
HTV	Harlech Television	LLB	bachelor of laws
IA	Iowa	LLD	doctor of laws
ibid.	*ibidem*: in the same place	LLM	master of laws
ICI	Imperial Chemical Industries (Ltd)	LM	licentiate in midwifery
ID	Idaho	LP	long-playing record
IL	Illinois	LRAM	licentiate of the Royal Academy of Music
illus.	illustration	LRCP	licentiate of the Royal College of Physicians
illustr.	illustrated	LRCPS (Glasgow)	licentiate of the Royal College of Physicians and Surgeons of Glasgow
IN	Indiana	LRCS	licentiate of the Royal College of Surgeons
in.	inch(es)	LSA	licentiate of the Society of Apothecaries
Inc.	Incorporated	LSD	lysergic acid diethylamide
incl.	includes / including	LVO	lieutenant of the Royal Victorian Order
IOU	I owe you	M. *pl.* MM.	Monsieur *pl.* Messieurs
IQ	intelligence quotient	m	metre(s)
Ir£	Irish pound		
IRA	Irish Republican Army		

m. *pl.* mm.	membrane(s)		ND	North Dakota
MA	(1) Massachusetts; (2) master of arts		n.d.	no date
MAI	master of engineering		NE	Nebraska
MB	bachelor of medicine		*nem. con.*	*nemine contradicente*: unanimously
MBA	master of business administration		new ser.	new series
MBE	member of the Order of the British Empire		NH	New Hampshire
MC	Military Cross		NHS	National Health Service
MCC	Marylebone Cricket Club		NJ	New Jersey
MCh	master of surgery		NKVD	[Soviet people's commissariat for internal affairs]
MChir	master of surgery		NM	New Mexico
MCom	master of commerce		nm	nanometre(s)
MD	(1) doctor of medicine; (2) Maryland		no. *pl.* nos.	number(s)
MDMA	methylenedioxymethamphetamine		Nov	November
ME	Maine		n.p.	no place [of publication]
MEd	master of education		NS	new style
MEng	master of engineering		NV	Nevada
MEP	member of the European parliament		NY	New York
MG	Morris Garages		NZBS	New Zealand Broadcasting Service
MGM	Metro-Goldwyn-Mayer		OBE	officer of the Order of the British Empire
Mgr	Monsignor		obit.	obituary
MI	(1) Michigan; (2) military intelligence		Oct	October
MI1c	[secret intelligence department]		OCTU	officer cadets training unit
MI5	[military intelligence department]		OECD	Organization for Economic Co-operation and Development
MI6	[secret intelligence department]		OEEC	Organization for European Economic Co-operation
MI9	[secret escape service]		OFM	order of Friars Minor [Franciscans]
MICE	member of the Institution of Civil Engineers		OFMCap	Ordine Frati Minori Cappucini: member of the Capuchin order
MIEE	member of the Institution of Electrical Engineers		OH	Ohio
min.	minute(s)		OK	Oklahoma
Mk	mark		O level	ordinary level [examination]
ML	(1) licentiate of medicine; (2) master of laws		OM	Order of Merit
MLitt	master of letters		OP	order of Preachers [Dominicans]
Mlle	Mademoiselle		op. *pl.* opp.	opus *pl.* opera
mm	millimetre(s)		OPEC	Organization of Petroleum Exporting Countries
Mme	Madame		OR	Oregon
MN	Minnesota		orig.	original
MO	Missouri		OS	old style
MOH	medical officer of health		OSB	Order of St Benedict
MP	member of parliament		OTC	Officers' Training Corps
m.p.h.	miles per hour		OWS	Old Watercolour Society
MPhil	master of philosophy		Oxon.	Oxoniensis
MRCP	member of the Royal College of Physicians		p. *pl.* pp.	page(s)
MRCS	member of the Royal College of Surgeons		PA	Pennsylvania
MRCVS	member of the Royal College of Veterinary Surgeons		p.a.	per annum
MRIA	member of the Royal Irish Academy		para.	paragraph
MS	(1) master of science; (2) Mississippi		PAYE	pay as you earn
MS *pl.* MSS	manuscript(s)		pbk *pl.* pbks	paperback(s)
MSc	master of science		*per.*	[during the] period
MSc (Econ.)	master of science (economics)		PhD	doctor of philosophy
MT	Montana		pl.	(1) plate(s); (2) plural
MusB	bachelor of music		priv. coll.	private collection
MusBac	bachelor of music		pt *pl.* pts	part(s)
MusD	doctor of music		pubd	published
MV	motor vessel		PVC	polyvinyl chloride
MVO	member of the Royal Victorian Order		q. *pl.* qq.	(1) question(s); (2) quire(s)
n. *pl.* nn.	note(s)		QC	queen's counsel
NAAFI	Navy, Army, and Air Force Institutes		R	rand
NASA	National Aeronautics and Space Administration		R.	Rex / Regina
NATO	North Atlantic Treaty Organization		*r*	recto
NBC	National Broadcasting Corporation		r.	reigned / ruled
NC	North Carolina		RA	Royal Academy / Royal Academician
NCO	non-commissioned officer			

RAC	Royal Automobile Club		Skr	Swedish krona
RAF	Royal Air Force		Span.	Spanish
RAFVR	Royal Air Force Volunteer Reserve		SPCK	Society for Promoting Christian Knowledge
RAM	[member of the] Royal Academy of Music		SS	(1) Santissimi; (2) Schutzstaffel; (3) steam ship
RAMC	Royal Army Medical Corps		STB	bachelor of theology
RCA	Royal College of Art		STD	doctor of theology
RCNC	Royal Corps of Naval Constructors		STM	master of theology
RCOG	Royal College of Obstetricians and Gynaecologists		STP	doctor of theology
RDI	royal designer for industry		*supp.*	supposedly
RE	Royal Engineers		suppl. *pl.* suppls.	supplement(s)
repr. *pl.* reprs.	reprint(s) / reprinted		s.v.	*sub verbo* / *sub voce*: under the word / heading
repro.	reproduced		SY	steam yacht
rev.	revised / revised by / reviser / revision		TA	Territorial Army
Revd	Reverend		TASS	[Soviet news agency]
RHA	Royal Hibernian Academy		TB	tuberculosis (*lit.* tubercle bacillus)
RI	(1) Rhode Island; (2) Royal Institute of Painters in Water-Colours		TD	(1) *teachtaí dála* (member of the Dáil); (2) territorial decoration
RIBA	Royal Institute of British Architects		TN	Tennessee
RIN	Royal Indian Navy		TNT	trinitrotoluene
RM	Reichsmark		trans.	translated / translated by / translation / translator
RMS	Royal Mail steamer		TT	tourist trophy
RN	Royal Navy		TUC	Trades Union Congress
RNA	ribonucleic acid		TX	Texas
RNAS	Royal Naval Air Service		U-boat	*Unterseeboot*: submarine
RNR	Royal Naval Reserve		Ufa	Universum-Film AG
RNVR	Royal Naval Volunteer Reserve		UMIST	University of Manchester Institute of Science and Technology
RO	Record Office		UN	United Nations
r.p.m.	revolutions per minute		UNESCO	United Nations Educational, Scientific, and Cultural Organization
RRS	royal research ship			
Rs	rupees		UNICEF	United Nations International Children's Emergency Fund
RSA	(1) Royal Scottish Academician; (2) Royal Society of Arts		unpubd	unpublished
RSPCA	Royal Society for the Prevention of Cruelty to Animals		USS	United States ship
			UT	Utah
Rt Hon.	Right Honourable		*v*	verso
Rt Revd	Right Reverend		v.	versus
RUC	Royal Ulster Constabulary		VA	Virginia
Russ.	Russian		VAD	Voluntary Aid Detachment
RWS	Royal Watercolour Society		VC	Victoria Cross
S4C	Sianel Pedwar Cymru		VE-day	victory in Europe day
s.	shilling(s)		Ven.	Venerable
s.a.	*sub anno*: under the year		VJ-day	victory over Japan day
SABC	South African Broadcasting Corporation		vol. *pl.* vols.	volume(s)
SAS	Special Air Service		VT	Vermont
SC	South Carolina		WA	Washington [state]
ScD	doctor of science		WAAC	Women's Auxiliary Army Corps
S$	Singapore dollar		WAAF	Women's Auxiliary Air Force
SD	South Dakota		WEA	Workers' Educational Association
sec.	second(s)		WHO	World Health Organization
sel.	selected		WI	Wisconsin
sen.	senior		WRAF	Women's Royal Air Force
Sept	September		WRNS	Women's Royal Naval Service
ser.	series		WV	West Virginia
SHAPE	supreme headquarters allied powers, Europe		WVS	Women's Voluntary Service
SIDRO	Société Internationale d'Énergie Hydro-Électrique		WY	Wyoming
			¥	yen
sig. *pl.* sigs.	signature(s)		YMCA	Young Men's Christian Association
sing.	singular		YWCA	Young Women's Christian Association
SIS	Secret Intelligence Service			
SJ	Society of Jesus			

2 Institution abbreviations

All Souls Oxf.	All Souls College, Oxford
AM Oxf.	Ashmolean Museum, Oxford
Balliol Oxf.	Balliol College, Oxford
BBC WAC	BBC Written Archives Centre, Reading
Beds. & Luton ARS	Bedfordshire and Luton Archives and Record Service, Bedford
Berks. RO	Berkshire Record Office, Reading
BFI	British Film Institute, London
BFI NFTVA	British Film Institute, London, National Film and Television Archive
BGS	British Geological Survey, Keyworth, Nottingham
Birm. CA	Birmingham Central Library, Birmingham City Archives
Birm. CL	Birmingham Central Library
BL	British Library, London
BL NSA	British Library, London, National Sound Archive
BL OIOC	British Library, London, Oriental and India Office Collections
BLPES	London School of Economics and Political Science, British Library of Political and Economic Science
BM	British Museum, London
Bodl. Oxf.	Bodleian Library, Oxford
Bodl. RH	Bodleian Library of Commonwealth and African Studies at Rhodes House, Oxford
Borth. Inst.	Borthwick Institute of Historical Research, University of York
Boston PL	Boston Public Library, Massachusetts
Bristol RO	Bristol Record Office
Bucks. RLSS	Buckinghamshire Records and Local Studies Service, Aylesbury
CAC Cam.	Churchill College, Cambridge, Churchill Archives Centre
Cambs. AS	Cambridgeshire Archive Service
CCC Cam.	Corpus Christi College, Cambridge
CCC Oxf.	Corpus Christi College, Oxford
Ches. & Chester ALSS	Cheshire and Chester Archives and Local Studies Service
Christ Church Oxf.	Christ Church, Oxford
Christies	Christies, London
City Westm. AC	City of Westminster Archives Centre, London
CKS	Centre for Kentish Studies, Maidstone
CLRO	Corporation of London Records Office
Coll. Arms	College of Arms, London
Col. U.	Columbia University, New York
Cornwall RO	Cornwall Record Office, Truro
Courtauld Inst.	Courtauld Institute of Art, London
CUL	Cambridge University Library
Cumbria AS	Cumbria Archive Service
Derbys. RO	Derbyshire Record Office, Matlock
Devon RO	Devon Record Office, Exeter
Dorset RO	Dorset Record Office, Dorchester
Duke U.	Duke University, Durham, North Carolina
Duke U., Perkins L.	Duke University, Durham, North Carolina, William R. Perkins Library
Durham Cath. CL	Durham Cathedral, chapter library
Durham RO	Durham Record Office
DWL	Dr Williams's Library, London
Essex RO	Essex Record Office
E. Sussex RO	East Sussex Record Office, Lewes
Eton	Eton College, Berkshire
FM Cam.	Fitzwilliam Museum, Cambridge
Folger	Folger Shakespeare Library, Washington, DC
Garr. Club	Garrick Club, London
Girton Cam.	Girton College, Cambridge
GL	Guildhall Library, London
Glos. RO	Gloucestershire Record Office, Gloucester
Gon. & Caius Cam.	Gonville and Caius College, Cambridge
Gov. Art Coll.	Government Art Collection
GS Lond.	Geological Society of London
Hants. RO	Hampshire Record Office, Winchester
Harris Man. Oxf.	Harris Manchester College, Oxford
Harvard TC	Harvard Theatre Collection, Harvard University, Cambridge, Massachusetts, Nathan Marsh Pusey Library
Harvard U.	Harvard University, Cambridge, Massachusetts
Harvard U., Houghton L.	Harvard University, Cambridge, Massachusetts, Houghton Library
Herefs. RO	Herefordshire Record Office, Hereford
Herts. ALS	Hertfordshire Archives and Local Studies, Hertford
Hist. Soc. Penn.	Historical Society of Pennsylvania, Philadelphia
HLRO	House of Lords Record Office, London
Hult. Arch.	Hulton Archive, London and New York
Hunt. L.	Huntington Library, San Marino, California
ICL	Imperial College, London
Inst. CE	Institution of Civil Engineers, London
Inst. EE	Institution of Electrical Engineers, London
IWM	Imperial War Museum, London
IWM FVA	Imperial War Museum, London, Film and Video Archive
IWM SA	Imperial War Museum, London, Sound Archive
JRL	John Rylands University Library of Manchester
King's AC Cam.	King's College Archives Centre, Cambridge
King's Cam.	King's College, Cambridge
King's Lond.	King's College, London
King's Lond., Liddell Hart C.	King's College, London, Liddell Hart Centre for Military Archives
Lancs. RO	Lancashire Record Office, Preston
L. Cong.	Library of Congress, Washington, DC
Leics. RO	Leicestershire, Leicester, and Rutland Record Office, Leicester
Lincs. Arch.	Lincolnshire Archives, Lincoln
Linn. Soc.	Linnean Society of London
LMA	London Metropolitan Archives
LPL	Lambeth Palace, London
Lpool RO	Liverpool Record Office and Local Studies Service
LUL	London University Library
Magd. Cam.	Magdalene College, Cambridge
Magd. Oxf.	Magdalen College, Oxford
Man. City Gall.	Manchester City Galleries
Man. CL	Manchester Central Library
Mass. Hist. Soc.	Massachusetts Historical Society, Boston
Merton Oxf.	Merton College, Oxford
MHS Oxf.	Museum of the History of Science, Oxford
Mitchell L., Glas.	Mitchell Library, Glasgow
Mitchell L., NSW	State Library of New South Wales, Sydney, Mitchell Library
Morgan L.	Pierpont Morgan Library, New York
NA Canada	National Archives of Canada, Ottawa
NA Ire.	National Archives of Ireland, Dublin
NAM	National Army Museum, London
NA Scot.	National Archives of Scotland, Edinburgh
News Int. RO	News International Record Office, London
NG Ire.	National Gallery of Ireland, Dublin

NG Scot.	National Gallery of Scotland, Edinburgh
NHM	Natural History Museum, London
NL Aus.	National Library of Australia, Canberra
NL Ire.	National Library of Ireland, Dublin
NL NZ	National Library of New Zealand, Wellington
NL NZ, Turnbull L.	National Library of New Zealand, Wellington, Alexander Turnbull Library
NL Scot.	National Library of Scotland, Edinburgh
NL Wales	National Library of Wales, Aberystwyth
NMG Wales	National Museum and Gallery of Wales, Cardiff
NMM	National Maritime Museum, London
Norfolk RO	Norfolk Record Office, Norwich
Northants. RO	Northamptonshire Record Office, Northampton
Northumbd RO	Northumberland Record Office
Notts. Arch.	Nottinghamshire Archives, Nottingham
NPG	National Portrait Gallery, London
NRA	National Archives, London, Historical Manuscripts Commission, National Register of Archives
Nuffield Oxf.	Nuffield College, Oxford
N. Yorks. CRO	North Yorkshire County Record Office, Northallerton
NYPL	New York Public Library
Oxf. UA	Oxford University Archives
Oxf. U. Mus. NH	Oxford University Museum of Natural History
Oxon. RO	Oxfordshire Record Office, Oxford
Pembroke Cam.	Pembroke College, Cambridge
PRO	National Archives, London, Public Record Office
PRO NIre.	Public Record Office for Northern Ireland, Belfast
Pusey Oxf.	Pusey House, Oxford
RA	Royal Academy of Arts, London
Ransom HRC	Harry Ransom Humanities Research Center, University of Texas, Austin
RAS	Royal Astronomical Society, London
RBG Kew	Royal Botanic Gardens, Kew, London
RCP Lond.	Royal College of Physicians of London
RCS Eng.	Royal College of Surgeons of England, London
RGS	Royal Geographical Society, London
RIBA	Royal Institute of British Architects, London
RIBA BAL	Royal Institute of British Architects, London, British Architectural Library
Royal Arch.	Royal Archives, Windsor Castle, Berkshire [by gracious permission of her majesty the queen]
Royal Irish Acad.	Royal Irish Academy, Dublin
Royal Scot. Acad.	Royal Scottish Academy, Edinburgh
RS	Royal Society, London
RSA	Royal Society of Arts, London
RS Friends, Lond.	Religious Society of Friends, London
St Ant. Oxf.	St Antony's College, Oxford
St John Cam.	St John's College, Cambridge
S. Antiquaries, Lond.	Society of Antiquaries of London
Sci. Mus.	Science Museum, London
Scot. NPG	Scottish National Portrait Gallery, Edinburgh
Scott Polar RI	University of Cambridge, Scott Polar Research Institute
Sheff. Arch.	Sheffield Archives
Shrops. RRC	Shropshire Records and Research Centre, Shrewsbury
SOAS	School of Oriental and African Studies, London
Som. ARS	Somerset Archive and Record Service, Taunton
Staffs. RO	Staffordshire Record Office, Stafford

Suffolk RO	Suffolk Record Office
Surrey HC	Surrey History Centre, Woking
TCD	Trinity College, Dublin
Trinity Cam.	Trinity College, Cambridge
U. Aberdeen	University of Aberdeen
U. Birm.	University of Birmingham
U. Birm. L.	University of Birmingham Library
U. Cal.	University of California
U. Cam.	University of Cambridge
UCL	University College, London
U. Durham	University of Durham
U. Durham L.	University of Durham Library
U. Edin.	University of Edinburgh
U. Edin., New Coll.	University of Edinburgh, New College
U. Edin., New Coll. L.	University of Edinburgh, New College Library
U. Edin. L.	University of Edinburgh Library
U. Glas.	University of Glasgow
U. Glas. L.	University of Glasgow Library
U. Hull	University of Hull
U. Hull, Brynmor Jones L.	University of Hull, Brynmor Jones Library
U. Leeds	University of Leeds
U. Leeds, Brotherton L.	University of Leeds, Brotherton Library
U. Lond.	University of London
U. Lpool	University of Liverpool
U. Lpool L.	University of Liverpool Library
U. Mich.	University of Michigan, Ann Arbor
U. Mich., Clements L.	University of Michigan, Ann Arbor, William L. Clements Library
U. Newcastle	University of Newcastle upon Tyne
U. Newcastle, Robinson L.	University of Newcastle upon Tyne, Robinson Library
U. Nott.	University of Nottingham
U. Nott. L.	University of Nottingham Library
U. Oxf.	University of Oxford
U. Reading	University of Reading
U. Reading L.	University of Reading Library
U. St Andr.	University of St Andrews
U. St Andr. L.	University of St Andrews Library
U. Southampton	University of Southampton
U. Southampton L.	University of Southampton Library
U. Sussex	University of Sussex, Brighton
U. Texas	University of Texas, Austin
U. Wales	University of Wales
U. Warwick Mod. RC	University of Warwick, Coventry, Modern Records Centre
V&A	Victoria and Albert Museum, London
V&A NAL	Victoria and Albert Museum, London, National Art Library
Warks. CRO	Warwickshire County Record Office, Warwick
Wellcome L.	Wellcome Library for the History and Understanding of Medicine, London
Westm. DA	Westminster Diocesan Archives, London
Wilts. & Swindon RO	Wiltshire and Swindon Record Office, Trowbridge
Worcs. RO	Worcestershire Record Office, Worcester
W. Sussex RO	West Sussex Record Office, Chichester
W. Yorks. AS	West Yorkshire Archive Service
Yale U.	Yale University, New Haven, Connecticut
Yale U., Beinecke L.	Yale University, New Haven, Connecticut, Beinecke Rare Book and Manuscript Library
Yale U. CBA	Yale University, New Haven, Connecticut, Yale Center for British Art

3 Bibliographic abbreviations

Adams, *Drama* W. D. Adams, *A dictionary of the drama*, 1: *A–G* (1904); 2: *H–Z* (1956) [vol. 2 microfilm only]

AFM J O'Donovan, ed. and trans., *Annala rioghachta Eireann / Annals of the kingdom of Ireland by the four masters*, 7 vols. (1848–51); 2nd edn (1856); 3rd edn (1990)

Allibone, *Dict.* S. A. Allibone, *A critical dictionary of English literature and British and American authors*, 3 vols. (1859–71); suppl. by J. F. Kirk, 2 vols. (1891)

ANB J. A. Garraty and M. C. Carnes, eds., *American national biography*, 24 vols. (1999)

Anderson, *Scot. nat.* W. Anderson, *The Scottish nation, or, The surnames, families, literature, honours, and biographical history of the people of Scotland*, 3 vols. (1859–63)

Ann. mon. H. R. Luard, ed., *Annales monastici*, 5 vols., Rolls Series, 36 (1864–9)

Ann. Ulster S. Mac Airt and G. Mac Niocaill, eds., *Annals of Ulster (to AD 1131)* (1983)

APC *Acts of the privy council of England*, new ser., 46 vols. (1890–1964)

APS *The acts of the parliaments of Scotland*, 12 vols. in 13 (1814–75)

Arber, *Regs. Stationers* F. Arber, ed., *A transcript of the registers of the Company of Stationers of London, 1554–1640 AD*, 5 vols. (1875–94)

ArchR *Architectural Review*

ASC D. Whitelock, D. C. Douglas, and S. I. Tucker, ed. and trans., *The Anglo-Saxon Chronicle: a revised translation* (1961)

AS chart. P. H. Sawyer, *Anglo-Saxon charters: an annotated list and bibliography*, Royal Historical Society Guides and Handbooks (1968)

AusDB D. Pike and others, eds., *Australian dictionary of biography*, 16 vols. (1966–2002)

Baker, *Serjeants* J. H. Baker, *The order of serjeants at law*, SeldS, suppl. ser., 5 (1984)

Bale, *Cat.* J. Bale, *Scriptorum illustrium Maioris Brytannie, quam nunc Angliam et Scotiam vocant: catalogus*, 2 vols. in 1 (Basel, 1557–9); facs. edn (1971)

Bale, *Index* J. Bale, *Index Britanniae scriptorum*, ed. R. L. Poole and M. Bateson (1902); facs. edn (1990)

BBCS *Bulletin of the Board of Celtic Studies*

BDMBR J. O. Baylen and N. J. Gossman, eds., *Biographical dictionary of modern British radicals*, 3 vols. in 4 (1979–88)

Bede, *Hist. eccl.* *Bede's Ecclesiastical history of the English people*, ed. and trans. B. Colgrave and R. A. B. Mynors, OMT (1969); repr. (1991)

Bénézit, *Dict.* E. Bénézit, *Dictionnaire critique et documentaire des peintres, sculpteurs, dessinateurs et graveurs*, 3 vols. (Paris, 1911–23); new edn, 8 vols. (1948–66), repr. (1966); 3rd edn, rev. and enl., 10 vols. (1976); 4th edn, 14 vols. (1999)

BIHR *Bulletin of the Institute of Historical Research*

Birch, *Seals* W. de Birch, *Catalogue of seals in the department of manuscripts in the British Museum*, 6 vols. (1887–1900)

Bishop Burnet's History *Bishop Burnet's History of his own time*, ed. M. J. Routh, 2nd edn, 6 vols. (1833)

Blackwood *Blackwood's [Edinburgh] Magazine*, 328 vols. (1817–1980)

Blain, Clements & Grundy, *Feminist comp.* V. Blain, P. Clements, and I. Grundy, eds., *The feminist companion to literature in English* (1990)

BL cat. *The British Library general catalogue of printed books* [in 360 vols. with suppls., also CD-ROM and online]

BMJ *British Medical Journal*

Boase & Courtney, *Bibl. Corn.* G. C. Boase and W. P. Courtney, *Bibliotheca Cornubiensis: a catalogue of the writings … of Cornishmen*, 3 vols. (1874–82)

Boase, *Mod. Eng. biog.* F. Boase, *Modern English biography: containing many thousand concise memoirs of persons who have died since the year 1850*, 6 vols. (privately printed, Truro, 1892–1921); repr. (1965)

Boswell, *Life* *Boswell's Life of Johnson: together with Journal of a tour to the Hebrides and Johnson's Diary of a journey into north Wales*, ed. G. B. Hill, enl. edn, rev. L. F. Powell, 6 vols. (1934–50); 2nd edn (1964); repr. (1971)

Brown & Stratton, *Brit. mus.* J. D. Brown and S. S. Stratton, *British musical biography* (1897)

Bryan, *Painters* M. Bryan, *A biographical and critical dictionary of painters and engravers*, 2 vols. (1816); new edn, ed. G. Stanley (1849); new edn, ed. R. E. Graves and W. Armstrong, 2 vols. (1886–9); [4th edn], ed. G. C. Williamson, 5 vols. (1903–5) [various reprs.]

Burke, *Gen. GB* J. Burke, *A genealogical and heraldic history of the commoners of Great Britain and Ireland*, 4 vols. (1833–8); new edn as *A genealogical and heraldic dictionary of the landed gentry of Great Britain and Ireland*, 3 vols. [1843–9] [many later edns]

Burke, *Gen. Ire.* J. B. Burke, *A genealogical and heraldic history of the landed gentry of Ireland* (1899); 2nd edn (1904); 3rd edn (1912); 4th edn (1958); 5th edn as *Burke's Irish family records* (1976)

Burke, *Peerage* J. Burke, *A general* [later edns *A genealogical*] *and heraldic dictionary of the peerage and baronetage of the United Kingdom* [later edns *the British empire*] (1829–)

Burney, *Hist. mus.* C. Burney, *A general history of music, from the earliest ages to the present period*, 4 vols. (1776–89)

Burtchaell & Sadleir, *Alum. Dubl.* G. D. Burtchaell and T. U. Sadleir, *Alumni Dublinenses: a register of the students, graduates, and provosts of Trinity College* (1924); [2nd edn], with suppl., in 2 pts (1935)

Calamy rev. A. G. Matthews, *Calamy revised* (1934); repr. (1988)

CCI *Calendar of confirmations and inventories granted and given up in the several commissariots of Scotland* (1876–)

CClR *Calendar of the close rolls preserved in the Public Record Office*, 47 vols. (1892–1963)

CDS J. Bain, ed., *Calendar of documents relating to Scotland*, 4 vols., PRO (1881–8); suppl. vol. 5, ed. G. G. Simpson and J. D. Galbraith [1986]

CEPR letters W. H. Bliss, C. Johnson, and J. Twemlow, eds., *Calendar of entries in the papal registers relating to Great Britain and Ireland: papal letters* (1893–)

CGPLA *Calendars of the grants of probate and letters of administration* [in 4 ser.: *England & Wales, Northern Ireland, Ireland*, and *Éire*]

Chambers, *Scots.* R. Chambers, ed., *A biographical dictionary of eminent Scotsmen*, 4 vols. (1832–5)

Chancery records chancery records pubd by the PRO

Chancery records (RC) chancery records pubd by the Record Commissions

CIPM	*Calendar of inquisitions post mortem*, [20 vols.], PRO (1904–); also *Henry VII*, 3 vols. (1898–1955)
Clarendon, *Hist. rebellion*	E. Hyde, earl of Clarendon, *The history of the rebellion and civil wars in England*, 6 vols. (1888); repr. (1958) and (1992)
Cobbett, *Parl. hist.*	W. Cobbett and J. Wright, eds., *Cobbett's Parliamentary history of England*, 36 vols. (1806–1820)
Colvin, *Archs.*	H. Colvin, *A biographical dictionary of British architects, 1600–1840*, 3rd edn (1995)
Cooper, *Ath. Cantab.*	C. H. Cooper and T. Cooper, *Athenae Cantabrigienses*, 3 vols. (1858–1913); repr. (1967)
CPR	*Calendar of the patent rolls preserved in the Public Record Office* (1891–)
Crockford	*Crockford's Clerical Directory*
CS	Camden Society
CSP	*Calendar of state papers* [in 11 ser.: *domestic, Scotland, Scottish series, Ireland, colonial, Commonwealth, foreign, Spain* [at Simancas], *Rome, Milan,* and *Venice*]
CYS	Canterbury and York Society
DAB	*Dictionary of American biography*, 21 vols. (1928–36), repr. in 11 vols. (1964); 10 suppls. (1944–96)
DBB	D. J. Jeremy, ed., *Dictionary of business biography*, 5 vols. (1984–6)
DCB	G. W. Brown and others, *Dictionary of Canadian biography*, [14 vols.] (1966–)
Debrett's Peerage	*Debrett's Peerage* (1803–) [sometimes *Debrett's Illustrated peerage*]
Desmond, *Botanists*	R. Desmond, *Dictionary of British and Irish botanists and horticulturists* (1977); rev. edn (1994)
Dir. Brit. archs.	A. Felstead, J. Franklin, and L. Pinfield, eds., *Directory of British architects, 1834–1900* (1993); 2nd edn, ed. A. Brodie and others, 2 vols. (2001)
DLB	J. M. Bellamy and J. Saville, eds., *Dictionary of labour biography*, [10 vols.] (1972–)
DLitB	Dictionary of Literary Biography
DNB	*Dictionary of national biography*, 63 vols. (1885–1900), suppl., 3 vols. (1901); repr. in 22 vols. (1908–9); 10 further suppls. (1912–96); *Missing persons* (1993)
DNZB	W. H. Oliver and C. Orange, eds., *The dictionary of New Zealand biography*, 5 vols. (1990–2000)
DSAB	W. J. de Kock and others, eds., *Dictionary of South African biography*, 5 vols. (1968–87)
DSB	C. C. Gillispie and F. L. Holmes, eds., *Dictionary of scientific biography*, 16 vols. (1970–80); repr. in 8 vols. (1981); 2 vol. suppl. (1990)
DSBB	A. Slaven and S. Checkland, eds., *Dictionary of Scottish business biography, 1860–1960*, 2 vols. (1986–90)
DSCHT	N. M. de S. Cameron and others, eds., *Dictionary of Scottish church history and theology* (1993)
Dugdale, *Monasticon*	W. Dugdale, *Monasticon Anglicanum*, 3 vols. (1655–72); 2nd edn, 3 vols. (1661–82); new edn, ed. J. Caley, J. Ellis, and B. Bandinel, 6 vols. in 8 pts (1817–30); repr. (1846) and (1970)
DWB	J. E. Lloyd and others, eds., *Dictionary of Welsh biography down to 1940* (1959) [Eng. trans. of *Y bywgraffiadur Cymreig hyd 1940*, 2nd edn (1954)]
EdinR	*Edinburgh Review, or, Critical Journal*
EETS	Early English Text Society
Emden, *Cam.*	A. B. Emden, *A biographical register of the University of Cambridge to 1500* (1963)
Emden, *Oxf.*	A. B. Emden, *A biographical register of the University of Oxford to AD 1500*, 3 vols. (1957–9); also *A biographical register of the University of Oxford, AD 1501 to 1540* (1974)
EngHR	*English Historical Review*
Engraved Brit. ports.	F. M. O'Donoghue and H. M. Hake, *Catalogue of engraved British portraits preserved in the department of prints and drawings in the British Museum*, 6 vols. (1908–25)
ER	*The English Reports*, 178 vols. (1900–32)
ESTC	*English short title catalogue, 1475–1800* [CD-ROM and online]
Evelyn, *Diary*	*The diary of John Evelyn*, ed. E. S. De Beer, 6 vols. (1955); repr. (2000)
Farington, *Diary*	*The diary of Joseph Farington*, ed. K. Garlick and others, 17 vols. (1978–98)
Fasti Angl. (Hardy)	J. Le Neve, *Fasti ecclesiae Anglicanae*, ed. T. D. Hardy, 3 vols. (1854)
Fasti Angl., 1066–1300	[J. Le Neve], *Fasti ecclesiae Anglicanae, 1066–1300*, ed. D. E. Greenway and J. S. Barrow, [8 vols.] (1968–)
Fasti Angl., 1300–1541	[J. Le Neve], *Fasti ecclesiae Anglicanae, 1300–1541*, 12 vols. (1962–7)
Fasti Angl., 1541–1857	[J. Le Neve], *Fasti ecclesiae Anglicanae, 1541–1857*, ed. J. M. Horn, D. M. Smith, and D. S. Bailey, [9 vols.] (1969–)
Fasti Scot.	H. Scott, *Fasti ecclesiae Scoticanae*, 3 vols. in 6 (1871); new edn, [11 vols.] (1915–)
FO List	*Foreign Office List*
Fortescue, *Brit. army*	J. W. Fortescue, *A history of the British army*, 13 vols. (1899–1930)
Foss, *Judges*	E. Foss, *The judges of England*, 9 vols. (1848–64); repr. (1966)
Foster, *Alum. Oxon.*	J. Foster, ed., *Alumni Oxonienses: the members of the University of Oxford, 1715–1886*, 4 vols. (1887–8); later edn (1891); also *Alumni Oxonienses … 1500–1714*, 4 vols. (1891–2); 8 vol. repr. (1968) and (2000)
Fuller, *Worthies*	T. Fuller, *The history of the worthies of England*, 4 pts (1662); new edn, 2 vols., ed. J. Nichols (1811); new edn, 3 vols., ed. P. A. Nuttall (1840); repr. (1965)
GEC, *Baronetage*	G. E. Cokayne, *Complete baronetage*, 6 vols. (1900–09); repr. (1983) [microprint]
GEC, *Peerage*	G. E. C. [G. E. Cokayne], *The complete peerage of England, Scotland, Ireland, Great Britain, and the United Kingdom*, 8 vols. (1887–98); new edn, ed. V. Gibbs and others, 14 vols. in 15 (1910–98); microprint repr. (1982) and (1987)
Genest, *Eng. stage*	J. Genest, *Some account of the English stage from the Restoration in 1660 to 1830*, 10 vols. (1832); repr. [New York, 1965]
Gillow, *Lit. biog. hist.*	J. Gillow, *A literary and biographical history or bibliographical dictionary of the English Catholics, from the breach with Rome, in 1534, to the present time*, 5 vols. [1885–1902]; repr. (1961); repr. with preface by C. Gillow (1999)
Gir. Camb. opera	*Giraldi Cambrensis opera*, ed. J. S. Brewer, J. F. Dimock, and G. F. Warner, 8 vols., Rolls Series, 21 (1861–91)
GJ	*Geographical Journal*

Gladstone, *Diaries* — *The Gladstone diaries: with cabinet minutes and prime-ministerial correspondence*, ed. M. R. D. Foot and H. C. G. Matthew, 14 vols. (1968–94)

GM — *Gentleman's Magazine*

Graves, *Artists* — A. Graves, ed., *A dictionary of artists who have exhibited works in the principal London exhibitions of oil paintings from 1760 to 1880* (1884); new edn (1895); 3rd edn (1901); facs. edn (1969); repr. [1970], (1973), and (1984)

Graves, *Brit. Inst.* — A. Graves, *The British Institution, 1806–1867: a complete dictionary of contributors and their work from the foundation of the institution* (1875); facs. edn (1908); repr. (1969)

Graves, *RA exhibitors* — A. Graves, *The Royal Academy of Arts: a complete dictionary of contributors and their work from its foundation in 1769 to 1904*, 8 vols. (1905–6); repr. in 4 vols. (1970) and (1972)

Graves, *Soc. Artists* — A. Graves, *The Society of Artists of Great Britain, 1760–1791, the Free Society of Artists, 1761–1783: a complete dictionary* (1907); facs. edn (1969)

Greaves & Zaller, *BDBR* — R. L. Greaves and R. Zaller, eds., *Biographical dictionary of British radicals in the seventeenth century*, 3 vols. (1982–4)

Grove, *Dict. mus.* — G. Grove, ed., *A dictionary of music and musicians*, 5 vols. (1878–90); 2nd edn, ed. J. A. Fuller Maitland (1904–10); 3rd edn, ed. H. C. Colles (1927); 4th edn with suppl. (1940); 5th edn, ed. E. Blom, 9 vols. (1954); suppl. (1961) [see also *New Grove*]

Hall, *Dramatic ports.* — L. A. Hall, *Catalogue of dramatic portraits in the theatre collection of the Harvard College library*, 4 vols. (1930–34)

Hansard — *Hansard's parliamentary debates*, ser. 1–5 (1803–)

Highfill, Burnim & Langhans, *BDA* — P. H. Highfill, K. A. Burnim, and E. A. Langhans, *A biographical dictionary of actors, actresses, musicians, dancers, managers, and other stage personnel in London, 1660–1800*, 16 vols. (1973–93)

Hist. U. Oxf. — T. H. Aston, ed., *The history of the University of Oxford*, 8 vols. (1984–2000) [1: *The early Oxford schools*, ed. J. I. Catto (1984); 2: *Late medieval Oxford*, ed. J. I. Catto and R. Evans (1992); 3: *The collegiate university*, ed. J. McConica (1986); 4: *Seventeenth-century Oxford*, ed. N. Tyacke (1997); 5: *The eighteenth century*, ed. L. S. Sutherland and L. G. Mitchell (1986); 6–7: *Nineteenth-century Oxford*, ed. M. G. Brock and M. C. Curthoys (1997–2000); 8: *The twentieth century*, ed. B. Harrison (2000)]

HJ — *Historical Journal*

HMC — Historical Manuscripts Commission

Holdsworth, *Eng. law* — W. S. Holdsworth, *A history of English law*, ed. A. L. Goodhart and H. L. Hanbury, 17 vols. (1903–72)

HoP, *Commons* — *The history of parliament: the House of Commons* [*1386–1421*, ed. J. S. Roskell, L. Clark, and C. Rawcliffe, 4 vols. (1992); *1509–1558*, ed. S. T. Bindoff, 3 vols. (1982); *1558–1603*, ed. P. W. Hasler, 3 vols. (1981); *1660–1690*, ed. B. D. Henning, 3 vols. (1983); *1690–1715*, ed. D. W. Hayton, E. Cruickshanks, and S. Handley, 5 vols. (2002); *1715–1754*, ed. R. Sedgwick, 2 vols. (1970); *1754–1790*, ed. L. Namier and J. Brooke, 3 vols. (1964), repr. (1985); *1790–1820*, ed. R. G. Thorne, 5 vols. (1986); in draft (used with permission): *1422–1504*, *1604–1629*, *1640–1660*, and *1820–1832*]

IGI — *International Genealogical Index*, Church of Jesus Christ of the Latterday Saints

ILN — *Illustrated London News*

IMC — Irish Manuscripts Commission

Irving, *Scots.* — J. Irving, ed., *The book of Scotsmen eminent for achievements in arms and arts, church and state, law, legislation and literature, commerce, science, travel and philanthropy* (1881)

JCS — *Journal of the Chemical Society*

JHC — *Journals of the House of Commons*

JHL — *Journals of the House of Lords*

John of Worcester, *Chron.* — *The chronicle of John of Worcester*, ed. R. R. Darlington and P. McGurk, trans. J. Bray and P. McGurk, 3 vols., OMT (1995–) [vol. 1 forthcoming]

Keeler, *Long Parliament* — M. F. Keeler, *The Long Parliament, 1640–1641: a biographical study of its members* (1954)

Kelly, *Handbk* — *The upper ten thousand: an alphabetical list of all members of noble families*, 3 vols. (1875–7); continued as *Kelly's handbook of the upper ten thousand for 1878* [1879], 2 vols. (1878–9); continued as *Kelly's handbook to the titled, landed and official classes*, 94 vols. (1880–1973)

LondG — *London Gazette*

LP Henry VIII — J. S. Brewer, J. Gairdner, and R. H. Brodie, eds., *Letters and papers, foreign and domestic, of the reign of Henry VIII*, 23 vols. in 38 (1862–1932); repr. (1965)

Mallalieu, *Watercolour artists* — H. L. Mallalieu, *The dictionary of British watercolour artists up to 1820*, 3 vols. (1976–90); vol. 1, 2nd edn (1986)

Memoirs FRS — *Biographical Memoirs of Fellows of the Royal Society*

MGH — Monumenta Germaniae Historica

MT — *Musical Times*

Munk, *Roll* — W. Munk, *The roll of the Royal College of Physicians of London*, 2 vols. (1861); 2nd edn, 3 vols. (1878)

N&Q — *Notes and Queries*

New Grove — S. Sadie, ed., *The new Grove dictionary of music and musicians*, 20 vols. (1980); 2nd edn, 29 vols. (2001) [also online edn; see also Grove, *Dict. mus.*]

Nichols, *Illustrations* — J. Nichols and J. B. Nichols, *Illustrations of the literary history of the eighteenth century*, 8 vols. (1817–58)

Nichols, *Lit. anecdotes* — J. Nichols, *Literary anecdotes of the eighteenth century*, 9 vols. (1812–16); facs. edn (1966)

Obits. FRS — *Obituary Notices of Fellows of the Royal Society*

O'Byrne, *Naval biog. dict.* — W. R. O'Byrne, *A naval biographical dictionary* (1849); repr. (1990); [2nd edn], 2 vols. (1861)

OHS — Oxford Historical Society

Old Westminsters — *The record of Old Westminsters*, 1–2, ed. G. F. R. Barker and A. H. Stenning (1928); suppl. 1, ed. J. B. Whitmore and G. R. Y. Radcliffe [1938]; 3, ed. J. B. Whitmore, G. R. Y. Radcliffe, and D. C. Simpson (1963); suppl. 2, ed. F. E. Pagan (1978); 4, ed. F. E. Pagan and H. E. Pagan (1992)

OMT — Oxford Medieval Texts

Ordericus Vitalis, *Eccl. hist.* — *The ecclesiastical history of Orderic Vitalis*, ed. and trans. M. Chibnall, 6 vols., OMT (1969–80); repr. (1990)

Paris, *Chron.* — *Matthaei Parisiensis, monachi sancti Albani, chronica majora*, ed. H. R. Luard, Rolls Series, 7 vols. (1872–83)

Parl. papers — *Parliamentary papers* (1801–)

PBA — *Proceedings of the British Academy*

Pepys, *Diary*	*The diary of Samuel Pepys*, ed. R. Latham and W. Matthews, 11 vols. (1970–83); repr. (1995) and (2000)
Pevsner	N. Pevsner and others, Buildings of England series
PICE	*Proceedings of the Institution of Civil Engineers*
Pipe rolls	*The great roll of the pipe for . . .*, PRSoc. (1884–)
PRO	Public Record Office
PRS	*Proceedings of the Royal Society of London*
PRSoc.	Pipe Roll Society
PTRS	*Philosophical Transactions of the Royal Society*
QR	*Quarterly Review*
RC	Record Commissions
Redgrave, *Artists*	S. Redgrave, *A dictionary of artists of the English school* (1874); rev. edn (1878); repr. (1970)
Reg. Oxf.	C. W. Boase and A. Clark, eds., *Register of the University of Oxford*, 5 vols., OHS, 1, 10–12, 14 (1885–9)
Reg. PCS	J. H. Burton and others, eds., *The register of the privy council of Scotland*, 1st ser., 14 vols. (1877–98); 2nd ser., 8 vols. (1899–1908); 3rd ser., [16 vols.] (1908–70)
Reg. RAN	H. W. C. Davis and others, eds., *Regesta regum Anglo-Normannorum, 1066–1154*, 4 vols. (1913–69)
RIBA Journal	*Journal of the Royal Institute of British Architects* [later *RIBA Journal*]
RotP	J. Strachey, ed., *Rotuli parliamentorum ut et petitiones, et placita in parliamento*, 6 vols. (1767–77)
RotS	D. Macpherson, J. Caley, and W. Illingworth, eds., *Rotuli Scotiae in Turri Londinensi et in domo capitulari Westmonasteriensi asservati*, 2 vols., RC, 14 (1814–19)
RS	Record(s) Society
Rymer, *Foedera*	T. Rymer and R. Sanderson, eds., *Foedera, conventiones, literae et cuiuscunque generis acta publica inter reges Angliae et alios quosvis imperatores, reges, pontifices, principes, vel communitates*, 20 vols. (1704–35); 2nd edn, 20 vols. (1726–35); 3rd edn, 10 vols. (1739–45); facs. edn (1967); new edn, ed. A. Clarke, J. Caley, and F. Holbrooke, 4 vols., RC, 50 (1816–30)
Sainty, *Judges*	J. Sainty, ed., *The judges of England, 1272–1990*, SeldS, suppl. ser., 10 (1993)
Sainty, *King's counsel*	J. Sainty, ed., *A list of English law officers and king's counsel*, SeldS, suppl. ser., 7 (1987)
SCH	Studies in Church History
Scots peerage	J. B. Paul, ed. *The Scots peerage, founded on Wood's edition of Sir Robert Douglas's Peerage of Scotland, containing an historical and genealogical account of the nobility of that kingdom*, 9 vols. (1904–14)
SeldS	Selden Society
SHR	*Scottish Historical Review*
State trials	T. B. Howell and T. J. Howell, eds., *Cobbett's Complete collection of state trials*, 34 vols. (1809–28)
STC, 1475–1640	A. W. Pollard, G. R. Redgrave, and others, eds., *A short-title catalogue of . . . English books . . . 1475–1640* (1926); 2nd edn, ed. W. A. Jackson, F. S. Ferguson, and K. F. Pantzer, 3 vols. (1976–91) [see also Wing, *STC*]
STS	Scottish Text Society
SurtS	Surtees Society
Symeon of Durham, *Opera*	*Symeonis monachi opera omnia*, ed. T. Arnold, 2 vols., Rolls Series, 75 (1882–5); repr. (1965)
Tanner, *Bibl. Brit.-Hib.*	T. Tanner, *Bibliotheca Britannico-Hibernica*, ed. D. Wilkins (1748); repr. (1963)
Thieme & Becker, *Allgemeines Lexikon*	U. Thieme, F. Becker, and H. Vollmer, eds., *Allgemeines Lexikon der bildenden Künstler von der Antike bis zur Gegenwart*, 37 vols. (Leipzig, 1907–50); repr. (1961–5), (1983), and (1992)
Thurloe, *State papers*	*A collection of the state papers of John Thurloe*, ed. T. Birch, 7 vols. (1742)
TLS	*Times Literary Supplement*
Tout, *Admin. hist.*	T. F. Tout, *Chapters in the administrative history of mediaeval England: the wardrobe, the chamber, and the small seals*, 6 vols. (1920–33); repr. (1967)
TRHS	*Transactions of the Royal Historical Society*
VCH	H. A. Doubleday and others, eds., *The Victoria history of the counties of England*, [88 vols.] (1900–)
Venn, *Alum. Cant.*	J. Venn and J. A. Venn, *Alumni Cantabrigienses: a biographical list of all known students, graduates, and holders of office at the University of Cambridge, from the earliest times to 1900*, 10 vols. (1922–54); repr. in 2 vols. (1974–8)
Vertue, *Note books*	[G. Vertue], *Note books*, ed. K. Esdaile, earl of Ilchester, and H. M. Hake, 6 vols., Walpole Society, 18, 20, 22, 24, 26, 30 (1930–55)
VF	*Vanity Fair*
Walford, *County families*	E. Walford, *The county families of the United Kingdom, or, Royal manual of the titled and untitled aristocracy of Great Britain and Ireland* (1860)
Walker rev.	A. G. Matthews, *Walker revised: being a revision of John Walker's Sufferings of the clergy during the grand rebellion, 1642–60* (1948); repr. (1988)
Walpole, *Corr.*	*The Yale edition of Horace Walpole's correspondence*, ed. W. S. Lewis, 48 vols. (1937–83)
Ward, *Men of the reign*	T. H. Ward, ed., *Men of the reign: a biographical dictionary of eminent persons of British and colonial birth who have died during the reign of Queen Victoria* (1885); repr. (Graz, 1968)
Waterhouse, *18c painters*	E. Waterhouse, *The dictionary of 18th century painters in oils and crayons* (1981); repr. as *British 18th century painters in oils and crayons* (1991), vol. 2 of *Dictionary of British art*
Watt, *Bibl. Brit.*	R. Watt, *Bibliotheca Britannica, or, A general index to British and foreign literature*, 4 vols. (1824) [many reprs.]
Wellesley index	W. E. Houghton, ed., *The Wellesley index to Victorian periodicals, 1824–1900*, 5 vols. (1966–89); new edn (1999) [CD-ROM]
Wing, *STC*	D. Wing, ed., *Short-title catalogue of . . . English books . . . 1641–1700*, 3 vols. (1945–51); 2nd edn (1972–88); rev. and enl. edn, ed. J. J. Morrison, C. W. Nelson, and M. Seccombe, 4 vols. (1994–8) [see also *STC, 1475–1640*]
Wisden	*John Wisden's Cricketer's Almanack*
Wood, *Ath. Oxon.*	A. Wood, *Athenae Oxonienses . . . to which are added the Fasti*, 2 vols. (1691–2); 2nd edn (1721); new edn, 4 vols., ed. P. Bliss (1813–20); repr. (1967) and (1969)
Wood, *Vic. painters*	C. Wood, *Dictionary of Victorian painters* (1971); 2nd edn (1978); 3rd edn as *Victorian painters*, 2 vols. (1995), vol. 4 of *Dictionary of British art*
WW	*Who's who* (1849–)
WWBMP	M. Stenton and S. Lees, eds., *Who's who of British members of parliament*, 4 vols. (1976–81)
WWW	*Who was who* (1929–)

Norbury. For this title name *see* Toler, John, first earl of Norbury (1745–1831).

Norbury, George (*fl. c.*1586–1634), legal writer, was the son of Thomas Norbury (*d.* 1598) of Flamstead, Hertfordshire, and his wife, Barbara, daughter of Robert Gooche of Diss, Norfolk. He was a clerk in a six clerk's office of the court of chancery from about 1586 at least until 1621. Against the background of the fall of Lord Chancellor Bacon, and an attack upon the chancery in the parliament of 1621, Norbury assisted a parliamentary committee established to investigate complaints about the chancery, and deposed in parliament 'concerning such grievances as he has observed to be in the court of Chancery of late years' (Norbury, 'Depositions', fol. 342), including among them a failure to ensure that vexatious litigants paid costs, the dilatory proceedings of the court, the recent creation of needless offices, and the immoderate fees taken by the officers and clerks. Also in 1621 Norbury was examined with others concerning the conduct of Lord Chancellor Bacon, and in August of the same year presented to Bacon's successor, Lord Keeper Williams, a tract entitled 'The abuses and remedies of the high court of chancery'. Shortly before his appointment, Williams had himself presented to the king a detailed plan for reform of the chancery. In his own subsequent tract, which enjoyed a wide circulation in manuscript and was printed in 1787 in Francis Hargrave's *A Collection of Tracts Relative to the Law of England*, Norbury referred to his deposition in parliament, expressing the hope that Williams might 'reform the disorders of your own court, and ease that honourable and high house from being any further troubled therewith' (Norbury, 'Abuses and remedies', 428). Norbury grouped the abuses of the court under three headings, concerning respectively the scope of its jurisdiction, its lenient treatment of litigious persons, and its dilatory proceedings, setting out the difficulties under each head and suggesting remedies based upon his experience as a clerk and in advising clients. The limits to the court's jurisdiction were compassed, he said, by 'matters of fraud, trust, extremity, or casualty; or else not lightly to be dealt in here' (ibid., 431). He saw no value in the use of precedent in chancery, 'which I cannot conceive to what purpose it should be' (ibid., 446), while accepting that 'the common wealth is best governed where least is left to the direction of the judge' (ibid., 431) and arguing for the establishment of 'ordinances, rules, and instructions' (ibid.) to restrain idle suits in chancery and to direct the conduct of the lord chancellor. He supposed that only three in ten chancery suits had any merit, and argued that multiplicity of suits might be reduced by prescribing time limits or by dismissing suits in which the plaintiff failed to proceed quickly, these remedies to be accompanied by ensuring that frivolous litigants were 'well lashed with costs' (ibid., 434). A series of bills for chancery reform were introduced into parliament in 1621, much of their thrust being directed at abuses identified by Norbury. Norbury subsequently lost his position in the chancery, perhaps because of his tract, and in 1629–30 was involved in a quarrel with the six clerks, giving evidence against them to the commission on fees.

Norbury married first Ann, daughter of William Drue of Great Marlow, Buckinghamshire. They had four daughters and two sons. He subsequently married Ann, daughter and coheir of Stephen Geffrey of Canterbury, Kent. They had at least one son.

John Norbury (*bap.* 1601, *d.* 1658), judge, eldest son of George Norbury and his wife, Ann Drue, was baptized at Great Marlow, Buckinghamshire, on 22 March 1601. He was admitted to Gray's Inn on 6 August 1621. At one time, like his father, a clerk in a six clerk's office, he was apparently dismissed at the time of his father's quarrel with the six clerks in 1629–30. He was appointed second justice of Brecknockshire, Glamorgan, and Radnorshire on 16 March 1649, holding the office until 18 June 1653. On 25 June 1651 he was added to the high court of justice in response to a report of insurrection in Wales. In March 1655 he signed a petition to the council of state by the cursitors in chancery, complaining about loss of income through the abolition of fines on original writs and describing himself as principal of the society of cursitors. In August of the same year he was summoned by the council to answer questions on a printed petition to the protector 'for the freeholders and well-affected' (*CSP dom.*, 1655, 277), which asked for the suppression of arbitrary power or ecclesiastical censures and the reform of legal procedure, expressing a desire to enable the achievement of these aims by taking Cromwell 'as our chief magistrate in place of the late king' (ibid., 278). Though Norbury told the council that he had composed the petition merely 'as a lawyer for his clients', he was 'sharply reproved' (ibid., 281), and the petition's suppression was ordered. After the death of his first wife, he married on 1 September 1627 Elizabeth, daughter and coheir of George Symcotts of London, and subsequently married Frances, daughter of William Clifton of Chesham Bury, Buckinghamshire, who survived him. He had at least four sons and two daughters. George Norbury, a son by his third marriage, who was admitted to Gray's Inn on 13 August 1639, became, like his father and grandfather, a clerk in the chancery. John Norbury died between 6 and 22 February 1658.

N. G. JONES

Sources *The visitation of London, anno Domini 1633, 1634, and 1635, made by Sir Henry St George*, 2, ed. J. J. Howard, Harleian Society, 17 (1883) · G. Norbury, 'The abuses and remedies of chancery', *A collection of tracts relative to the law of England*, ed. F. Hargrave, 1 (1787), 427–48 · depositions of George Norbury in parliament, 1620, CUL, MS Gg.2.31, fols. 342–343v · W. Notestein, F. H. Relf, and H. Simpson, eds., *Commons debates, 1621*, 3, 7 (1935) · W. R. Williams, *The history of the great sessions in Wales, 1542–1830* (privately printed, Brecon, 1899) · W. J. Jones, *Politics and the bench* (1971) · R. Zaller, *The parliament of 1621: a study in constitutional conflict* (1971) · J. L. Chester and J. Foster, eds., *London marriage licences, 1521–1869* (1887) · will of John Norbury, PRO, PROB 11/273 q 102 · *CSP dom.*, 1651; 1653–5 · A. H. Cocks, ed., *The earliest register of the parish of Great Marlow, Buckinghamshire, 1592–1611* (1904) · D. Veall, *The popular movement for law reform, 1640–1660* (1970) · Holdsworth, *Eng. law*, vol. 5 · J. Foster, *The register of admissions to Gray's Inn, 1521–1889, together with the register of marriages in Gray's Inn chapel, 1695–1754* (privately printed, London, 1889) · R. J. Fletcher, ed., *The pension book of Gray's Inn*, 1 (1901) ·

G. W. Thomas, 'James I, equity, and Lord Keeper John Williams', *EngHR*, 91 (1976), 506–28 · parish register, Hertfordshire, Flamstead, Herts. ALS

Norbury, John (d. 1414), soldier and administrator, derived from Norbury near Marbury, Cheshire. The son of Thomas Norbury, a Cheshire gentleman descended from the Bulkeleys, another gentry family in the same county, Norbury maintained few links with his native county, and made his reputation elsewhere as a soldier in the lean years of the Hundred Years' War after the peace of Brétigny in 1360, serving as a *routier* in Brittany in 1368, as captain of Libourne in 1377, and as lieutenant of Brest at intervals between 1382 and 1397. Repeated accusations that he profited from piracy and subjected the countrysides round his garrison towns to ransoms and other extortions provide a glimpse of his growing wealth from a military career. In the early 1380s these were said to amount to a self-awarded bonus of £3000, and in 1397 John de Montfort, duke of Brittany, complained of even greater peculation during the final year of the English occupation. The commercial basis of much freebooting gave Norbury links to the London merchant community and the financial resources to grant loans to the crown. In 1388 he had purchased the manor of Bedwell, later adding other lands in its vicinity which made him a prominent landowner in southern Hertfordshire and secured his parliamentary election in 1391.

Norbury was evidently a man of considerable military ability, as Froissart shows in his account of the victory of João I of Portugal at Aljubarota in 1385, telling how Norbury, who had arrived with a group of English mercenaries from Calais, Brest, and Cherbourg, advised the employment of English tactics to fight using hedges and bushes. But his continuing advancement was also partly due to the patronage of noble captains, notably William Windsor, John, Lord Neville and, importantly, Henry Percy, earl of Northumberland, and his brother, Sir Thomas Percy. In July 1390 Norbury joined Henry, earl of Derby, on his crusade to Prussia, thereby cementing a connection that would transform his success from that of the archetypal careerist soldier to that of a prominent Lancastrian civil servant. He was retained by both Henry and John of Gaunt, duke of Lancaster, and married a daughter, born of an apparently unendowed but companionate first marriage to an otherwise anonymous Petronilla, to Nicholas Usk, the duke's treasurer. Like others, he repaid such patronage with considerable loyalty, going into exile with Henry in 1399 and playing what seems to have been an important role in the deposition campaign, since he received rewards at Leominster on 10 July and appointment as treasurer of England on 3 September. In 1399 he was keeper of Leeds Castle, the site of Richard II's captivity, and in the 1400 rising was entrusted with the escort, rendered unnecessary by their summary execution at Cirencester, of the earls of Kent and Salisbury to Oxford.

Such prominence attracted favours from elsewhere, and gave Norbury an independent status. He was retained by Ralph Neville, earl of Westmorland, and (his first wife having died some time after 1399) before 1410 married

again, taking as his second wife Elizabeth, daughter of Sir Thomas Butler and widow of William Say, Lord Heron. Norbury's connection with Henry IV seems to have been essentially a personal one; his eldest son, Henry, was the king's godson, he witnessed the king's will in 1409, and in the king's last year received grants of Henry's 'special grace and own motion' (*CPR, 1408–13*, 404–5). Norbury's position as a permanent councillor also placed him at the centre of political affairs, and in 1405 he was recalled from a proposed tenure of the captaincy at Guînes in order to accompany the king in Wales. His Breton experience also recommended him as a go-between to Henry's new wife, Joan of Navarre, the widow of the duke of Brittany.

Norbury's role in the government's response to petitions for clerical disendowment in the parliament of 1410, almost his final involvement in public affairs, reveals a man of conservative piety, although his attack on the 'pseudo-knights' who drew up the petition may also have been politically inspired. Walsingham lionized him as 'one man in a thousand … powerful in lay affairs and with a heartfelt devotion to the church' (*St Albans Chronicle*, 56). Norbury died some time after March in 1414, and the chronicler's judgement is echoed in the description of the lost alabaster tomb in the now destroyed but then still highly fashionable Greyfriars Church in London of 'John Norbury valens armiger, strenuus ac probus vir' ('a valiant esquire, a vigorous and virtuous man'; BL, Cotton MS Vitellius F. xii, fol. 289). PHILIP MORGAN

Sources M. Barber, 'John Norbury (c.1350–1414): an esquire of Henry IV', *EngHR*, 68 (1953), 66–76 · Chancery records · BL, Add. charters 5829–5836, 43237, 43466 · HoP, *Commons, 1386–1421*, 3.843–6 · exchequer, king's remembrancer, accounts various, PRO, E101/181/1, no. 24 · M. Jones, ed., *Recueil des actes de Jean IV, duc de Bretagne*, 1 (Paris, 1980), 331–2; 2 (1983), 357–8, 654–6 · K. Fowler, 'Les finances et la discipline dans les armées anglaises en France au xivᵉ siècle', *Les Cahiers Vernonnais*, 4 (1964), 55–84 · M. D. Legge, ed., *Anglo-Norman letters and petitions from All Souls MS 182*, Anglo-Norman Texts, 3 (1941) · T. Walsingham, *The St Albans chronicle, 1406–1420*, ed. V. H. Galbraith (1937) · BL, Cotton MS Vitellius F.xii, fol. 289 · *Chroniques de J. Froissart*, ed. S. Luce and others, 15 vols. (Paris, 1869–1975) · *Inquisitions and assessments relating to feudal aids*, 6, PRO (1921), 460, 475, 488, 523

Archives BL, Add. charters 5829–5836

Wealth at death £294 p.a. in 1412: *Feudal aids*, 6, 460, 475, 488, 523

Norbury, John (bap. 1601, d. 1658). See under Norbury, George (fl. c.1586–1634).

Norcome, Daniel. See Norcum, Daniel (1570x85–1653).

Norcott, William (1770?–c.1820), satirist, was educated at Trinity College, Dublin, where he graduated BA in 1795, proceeding LLB in 1801, and LLD in 1806. He was called to the Irish bar in 1797, and practised with some success for a time, but was not entirely committed to a career in law, preferring instead various kinds of social amusements.

During the viceroyalty of the duke of Richmond, Norcott became very popular for a time at Dublin Castle, and endeared himself to much of Dublin society, particularly on account of his excellent mimetic and satiric talents. He and his friend John Wilson Croker subsequently had a brief career as popular poetic satirists, particularly in the years following the Act of Union. He anonymously published attacks on various Dublin institutions, poetical satires such as *The Metropolis* (1805) and *The Seven Thieves* (1807). His works usually went to at least two editions in their first year of publication, and had as their dedicatees a variety of influential nationalist and political figures including Henry Grattan and George Ponsonby, then lord chancellor of Ireland. Because of their anonymity, however, Norcott's works were at first frequently attributed to other writers including Thomas Grady, Croker, and Richard Frizelle.

Despite his brief period of celebrity, Norcott quickly fell into debt and out of social favour since he was a reckless, and generally dissipated gambler. Croker, however, loyally stood by him, obtaining for him in 1815 an excellent appointment in Malta, but Norcott failed to hold it for long, and fled entirely discredited.

After a period of wandering, Norcott reached Turkey, where he supported himself by selling opium and rhubarb in the streets. On arriving in Constantinople, he initially lived in destitution, before converting to Islam. About 1820, having recanted his faith, Norcott attempted to escape from Constantinople, but was pursued, captured, and mutilated. His decapitated body was finally thrown into the sea.

D. J. O'DONOGHUE, *rev.* JASON EDWARDS

Sources pamphlets, 1805–7, Royal Irish Acad., Haliday pamphlets · [J. H. Todd], ed., *A catalogue of graduates who have proceeded to degrees in the University of Dublin, from the earliest recorded commencements to … December 16, 1868* (1869), ongoing · *The Gentleman and Citizen's Almanack for …* (1800–15) · J. Barrington, *Personal sketches of his own times*, rev. T. Young, 3rd edn, 1 (1869), 445–51 · *N&Q*, 8th ser., 1–12 (1892–7) · D. J. O'Donoghue, *The poets of Ireland: a biographical dictionary with bibliographical particulars*, 1 vol. in 3 pts (1892–3), 177–8 · 'Stray leaves of Irish satire', *Dublin University Magazine*, 58 (1861), 714–32, esp. 725 · R. L. Sheil, *Sketches, legal and political*, ed. M. W. Savage, 2 vols. (1855)

Norcum [Norcombe], **Daniel** (1570x85–1653), musician, was born in England. Nothing is known either about his parents or about his education, but it is conceivable that this subject was the Daniel Norcombe who, born in 1576, was court lutenist and perhaps also viol player to Christian IV of Denmark from 1599 to 1601, before absconding with Johan Meinart (John Maynard) to Venice (1602) and then disappearing. Driven or encouraged into exile because of his Roman Catholic faith (Brussels, Algemeen Rijksarchief, Raad van Financiën, 198, fol. 46), in 1602 or 1603 he appeared in Brussels, probably aged between his late teens and early thirties. Here he took a post as instrumentalist of the 'royale chapelle' at the archducal court of Albrecht and Isabella, and later of the Cardinal Infante. His name appears on a list of 1611, in two account books covering the period 1612–18, in a book of pensions for rendered services of 1634, where a pension is granted to him from 1631 onwards for a term of six years, on a list of personnel of 1637, and on a payment list of 1642 (for May–December 1641). From Norcum's high position on the payment lists, from the amount of his fee, and from the way this was calculated per annum and not per day, one can deduce that he had an important position in the chapel, but there is no mention of the instrument he played.

Daniel Norcum of Brussels is often assumed to be the composer of two dances for lyra viol and thirty-five divisions for bass viol preserved in a number of seventeenth-century English manuscripts, although this cannot be proved conclusively. It may seem surprising that the compositions of an Englishman living abroad for such a long time are widely known in English sources, to the extent that Christopher Simpson, in *The Division Viol*, praised 'Mr. Daniel Norcome' as one of the 'excellent men of this our Nation, who (hitherto) have had the preheminence for this particular instrument; observing and noting in their *Divisions*, what you find best worthy to be imitated' (Simpson, 57). There are, however, similar cases like that of Henry Butler, an English Catholic viol player, employed at the Spanish court in Madrid. That there was an English bass viol virtuoso in Brussels is indicated by the inclusion of three viola da gamba divisions, showing some English influence, in the *Symphoniae … op. 4* (1642) by the Brussels organist Nicolaus a Kempis. Norcum's divisions seem to have been written by someone who was primarily a virtuosic player rather than a gifted composer. They are technically demanding and bustling, but rather weak in melodic invention and counterpoint, and lack a sense of structure and contrast.

A request of 1643 asked for a prolongation of Norcum's pension, and described him as 'very old and without any means of living'. He was living at the 'lovensche wegh' ('road to Leuven') opposite the 'roscam' ('curry-comb') when he died in Brussels, apparently unmarried and without children, in 1653. After a funeral mass in the main church of Brussels, St Michiel and St Goedele, on 26 June, he was buried in the St Goedele churchyard.

PIET STRYCKERS

Sources C. Simpson, *The division viol: the art of playing ex tempore upon the ground*, 2nd edn (1665) · J. Hawkins, *A general history of the science and practice of music*, 3 (1776), 405 · S. Clercx, 'Le dix-septième et le dix-huitième siècle', *La musique en Belgique*, ed. E. Closson and C. van der Borren (1950), 145–233 · F.-J. Fétis, *Biographie universelle des musiciens, et bibliographie générale de la musique*, 2nd edn, 8 vols. (Paris, 1860–65); repr. (1877–8), vol. 6, p. 474 · E. van der Straeten, *La musique aux Pays-Bas*, 2 (Brussels, 1872), 9 [list of 1611] · E. van der Straeten, *La musique aux Pays-Bas*, 5 (Brussels, 1880), 133–40 [list of 1641] · *DNB* · J. A. Stelfeld, 'Johannes Ruckers de Jongere en de Koninklijke Kapel te Brussel', *Hommage à Charles van den Borren* (1945), 283–91 [list of 1637] · T. Dart, 'Norcombe', Grove, *Dict. mus.* (1954) · H. Hoppe, 'John Bull in the Archduke Albert's service', *Music and Letters*, 35 (1954), 114–15 · J. Richards, 'A study of music for bass viol written in England in the seventeenth century', BLitt diss., U. Oxf., 1961 · P. Stryckers, 'Philippus Van Wichel (1614–1675), violist aan het hof van Brussel, en zijn "Fasciculus Dulcedinis"', diss., University of Leuven, 1976, 13, 16 · M. Urquhart, 'Was Christopher Simpson a Jesuit?', *Chelys*, 21 (1992), 3–26 · D. Brown, 'Norcombe', *New Grove* · G. Dodd, *Thematic index of music for viols* (1980–)

Archives Archives Départementales du Nord, Chambre des Comptes, Lille, recette générale des finances, list of 1641, B 3035 · National State Archives, Brussels, Rekenkamer, accountbook, 1837/38 · National State Archives, Brussels, Raad van Financiën, book of pensions, 234, fol. 25 · National State Archives, Brussels, Raad van Financiën, request of 1643, 198, fol. 46 · State Archives, Antwerp, Gilden en Ambachten, 4820; list of 1637 · State Archives,

Brussels, Parochieregisters, 155 (St Michiel en St Goedele, overlijdens 1650–1655), fol. 127, nr. 2644 (burial)
Wealth at death most likely died in poverty, as was without means of living in 1643: National State Archives, Brussels, Raad van Financiën, 198, fol. 46

Norden, Frederik Ludvig (1708–1742), traveller and artist, was born on 22 October 1708 at Glückstadt, Holstein, the fourth of five sons of Jørgen Norden, a Danish lieutenant-colonel of infantry (*d.* 1728) and his wife, Cathrine Henrichsen (*d.* in or after 1728), both of Rendsburg. In 1722, at fourteen, Norden entered the naval academy in Copenhagen, where, among other subjects, he was taught shipbuilding, languages, and drawing. He showed a talent for drawing maps, and was employed to restore Christian VI's collection of charts and plans. In 1732 King Christian gave Norden, by then a lieutenant, an allowance to study fortifications abroad. In Amsterdam he was instructed in engraving by Jan de Ryter, and sent drawings home. He spent 1734–7 in France, Italy, and Malta, looking at fortifications and ship construction. In Florence he met the German diplomatist and archaeologist Philippe, Baron de Stosch, who introduced him to artists and scholars and stirred his interest in ancient Egypt, and the Nuremberg engraver Carl Marcus Tuscher, whom he later chose to prepare his drawings for publication. Norden was made an associate of the Florence Academy of Drawing.

In 1737 King Christian dispatched an expedition, including a reluctant Norden, to Egypt to establish commercial relations with 'the Emperor of Ethiopia' and also 'with the design of enriching the learned world' (Norden, viii). The expedition was led by a strange French adventurer, Pièrre Joseph le Roux, Greve d'Esneval, but, to Esneval's displeasure, Norden was the king's official representative. The expedition reached Alexandria in June 1737. There Norden observed and drew the ancient and modern cities and the catacombs. They travelled on to Cairo on camels, and planned to travel to Upper Egypt, but unrest upriver and Norden's ill health kept them in Cairo, where he made drawings and measurements of buildings. He entered the pyramid of Cheops, and his measurement of the interior is now known to be 'astonishingly accurate' (Buhl, 17).

In November the whole expedition—some sixteen people, including two Franciscan monks recruited by the devious Esneval without Christian's knowledge to establish missionary activity in Ethiopia, a physician, interpreters, servants, and Esneval's wife, Anna Barbara—set off up the Nile. Norden's records contain finely drawn maps and observations of the towns and villages they passed, and drawings of hydraulic machines, ploughs, and canal systems. He made unique drawings and plans of the monuments, of local life, and of the fauna and flora. He also made a study of the obelisks, which he described as 'entitled to rank among valuable curiousities and majestic ornaments', and he took a careful record of hieroglyphic texts. He did all this despite continuous trouble both with robbers and with local people at the monuments.

The party reached Aswan on 18 December where Norden sketched at Elephantine. In Nubia hostile people, turbulent waters, and ill health forced them to turn back on 6 January 1738 before the second cataract. On the return journey Norden surveyed and sketched by moonlight at Philae, completing a series of drawings of the capitals. He landed at Luxor, Gurna, and Karnac to sketch the temples, then half buried in the sand. On 3 February 1738 the party reached Cairo, where Norden revisited the pyramids, made drawings of ships, and helped the Catholic priests with plans for new churches and monasteries. He also recorded light-hearted advice to future travellers.

Back in Denmark, Norden had a mixed reception but King Christian asked him to prepare his work (more than 200 drawings, twenty-nine detailed maps of the Nile, and two survey maps) for publication. He finished the greater part by 1739 and translated his notes into French. He was promoted captain and worked at the royal dockyard in Copenhagen. He and other Danish officers were invited to serve in the English navy, and went to London. In 1740 they were called up as 'volunteers' and served in the War of the Austrian Succession at the siege of Cartagena in April 1741.

Norden's interest in Egypt continued and his comments on John Greave's treatise on the pyramids resulted in his election to the Royal Society while he was serving in the West Indies. On his return to England he was admitted to the Society of Antiquaries through which he met Richard Pococke whom he had narrowly missed on the Nile. Together in 1741 they and others, including another Nile traveller, the fourth earl of Sandwich, formed the Egypt Society with the purpose of examining Egyptian antiquities. In the same year Norden published his *Drawings of some Ruins and Colossal Statues at Thebes in Egypt* (with two engravings by Marcus Tuscher), which attracted great scholarly interest.

Norden suffered from consumption and his health was failing. He set off with a Danish naval friend to southern France. Having reached Paris, Norden was unable to continue the journey and he spent his last days there planning for the future of his work. He died in Paris on 22 September 1742 and was buried in Paris in an unknown grave. At Norden's request all his drawings and notes were handed over to the Danish navy with the hope that the engravings would be executed by Tuscher. Tuscher moved to Copenhagen in 1743 and over the next seven years completed all but one plate before he died. The Royal Danish Academy published Norden's *Voyage d'Egypte et de Nubia* (2 vols., 1750–55) with 159 plates. The English edition was published in 1757 for the Royal Society, and since then there have been further German, French, Danish, and English editions. Sixty years before the French expedition to Egypt, Norden had made excellent maps, precise descriptions, detailed topographical drawings, and panoramas of the landscape and monuments of Egypt. His drawings and comments on contemporary Egypt, its government, and peoples, also supply valuable historic and ethnographic information.   DEBORAH MANLEY

Sources F. Norden, *Travels in Egypt and Nubia*, trans. P. Tempelman (1757) • M.-L. Buhl, ed., *The Danish naval officer, Frederik Ludvig Norden*

(1986) • F. A. H. Kjølsen, *Rokokogreven Pierre d'Esneval og Christianns etiopiske projekl* (1968) • H. C. Bjerg, 'Norden, Frederik Ludvig', *Dansk biografisk leksikon*, ed. C. F. Bricka and others, 3rd edn, ed. S. Cedergreen Bech (Copenhagen, 1979–84) • I. Hilmy, *Literature of Egypt*, 2 (1886) • F. A. H. Kjølsen, *Capitain F. L. Norden og hans rejse til Ægypten*, 1737–38 (Copenhagen, 1965) • Nichols, *Lit. anecdotes*, 2.590
Archives Kongelige Bibliotek, Copenhagen • Royal Dansk Academy of Sciences and Letters, Copenhagen
Likenesses J. Richardson, portrait, 1718 • J. Smith, mezzotint, 1719 • J. Vanderbank, oils, 1736 • J. A. Dassier, medal, 1740 • J. Faber junior, mezzotint, 1741 (after J. Vanderbank) • W. Hogarth, oils, 1741, RS • M. Folkes, medal, 1742 • Barrett, line engraving, pubd 1793, NPG • line engraving, 1793, NPG • T. Cook (after mezzotint by J. Faber junior, 1742), repro. in J. Nichols, *Biographical anecdotes of William Hogarth* (1810), vol. 2, p. 156 • T. F. Dibdin, woodcut (after portrait repro. in *Portraits des Hommes Illustres de Denmark*, 1746, 7 parts), repro. in T. F. Dibdin, *Bibliomania, or, Book madness*, 2nd edn (1811) • M. Tuscher, etching (after portrait by J. M. Preisler, 1751), repro. in F. Norden, *Travels in Egypt and Nubia*, 2 (1757)

Norden, John (*c*.1547–1625), cartographer, a native of Somerset, entered Hart Hall, Oxford, in 1564, and graduated BA in 1568 and MA in 1573. William Ravenhill suggested that John Norden of Milverton near Taunton was his father (Ravenhill, 1), but nothing else is known of his parentage except he was 'of a genteel family' (Wood, *Ath. Oxon.*, col. 279). No authentic portraits of him exist but in the eighteenth century Hearne reported a tradition that one of the two figures engraved on the title-page of Norden's *Speculum Britanniae: Middlesex* represented Lord Burghley, Queen Elizabeth's first minister, and that the other was Norden—upright, bearded, and dressed in the fashion of a gentleman, with a collection of surveying instruments above his head.

As a surveyor Norden necessarily led a peripatetic life, but for most of the time he lived near London: in 1592 he was at Walham Green, Middlesex; and by 1607 he was signing his works from Hendon, Middlesex, where he stayed until 1619 when he moved to St Giles-in-the-Fields, a village on the outskirts of London. He was married and had at least two sons: John Norden junior, who co-signed some of Norden's later surveys, and Josias.

Surveying Norden's fame came from his cartography, but surveying was always the mainstay of his career. His earliest work was in the service of Lady Anne Knyvett, but after her death in 1582 he took other commissions while campaigning for a government position. In 1600 he was successful, being appointed surveyor of crown woods and forests in southern England, and in 1605 he added the surveyorship of the duchy of Cornwall. Although he was always ready to undertake large and important private surveys for senior figures at court and for City magnates, including a description and maps of Ireland made for the earl of Salisbury, Norden came to devote his time mainly to the duchy. From 1611 until 1623 he travelled throughout England, surveying incessantly. His notebook of 1623 listed 176 manors that he had surveyed, many more than once. The duchy estates had been neglected during Elizabeth's reign and Norden's work was instrumental in putting the duchy's affairs into profitable order. Duchy records show attempts to retire him in 1623, but the poor quality of surveys being made by his successors led to his recall. After

his death the duchy council paid a considerable sum to his son for 'a book of surveys and other workings concerning his Majesties revenues, left by his father' (Duchy of Cornwall RO, letters and warrants, vol. 6). Norden's surveys remained a valued tool for the management of the duchy estates for the next 150 years.

It was from this position of eminence that in 1607 Norden published *The Surveyor's Dialogue* as a text to educate the landowner and tenant in the usefulness and trustworthiness of his profession. Surveyors were often considered the landowner's creature and were accordingly distrusted by tenants. A popular work, the *Dialogue* shows Norden as a compassionate man, in sympathy with the respectable and hard-working of every class; the book ran to three editions in his lifetime.

Devotional writing *The Surveyor's Dialogue* also reveals Norden as a pious and faithful follower of the reformed Elizabethan church. Between 1582 and his death he published twenty-four volumes of devotional writings; some proved very popular and one, *A Pensive Mans Practice*, went to more than forty editions in his lifetime. While there is no need to doubt Norden's sincerity, these works were written mostly in periods when his surveying career was slow and money short, as in 1613 when he and his son Josias were injured by robbers on the highway. In the early years of his career his books not only provided a small income but also served as a tool in the search for preferment. Advancement in place or position in early modern England needed the seeker to find a patron and Norden's devotional books were dedicated with this in mind, being addressed, along with letters of petition, to Burghley, Sir Christopher Hatton, the earl of Essex, and other leading political and social figures including Elizabeth herself.

One set of dedications seems to have led Norden into a political storm and his attempt to extricate himself from this controversy has left a problem for posterity. In the late 1590s he dedicated several works to the earl of Essex, one of Elizabeth's favourites. The political party surrounding Essex was in conflict with that round Sir Robert Cecil, son of and successor in office to Burghley. In 1599 it seems that, because of the devotional books, Norden was assumed to be of the Essex party and so fell out of favour with the Cecil party. Norden wrote a letter to Sir Robert explaining:

> And the more to throw me down … I was by some unfortunately mistaken for another of my name, and her Majesty (upon surmise) informed against me, I being innocent, under colour of a Norden, I know not in what guilty. The Norden pretender was a Kentishman, I, born in Somersetshire. By which mistaking I have sustained much wrong, ignorant how to save it. (Hatfield House, Cecil MSS, 103/27, 2)

The letter has led some scholars to suppose that there were two Nordens—one the surveyor, the other the devotional writer—but this cannot be sustained because both share interests, backgrounds, written expression, everyday circumstances, and style: one as shown in the devotional works, the other as shown in the comments and advice given in the surveys, the descriptions of the *Speculum*, and *The Surveyor's Dialogue*. Further, in the relevant years the two series of works were prefaced from 'my poor house at Hendon'.

Norden's poverty was a subject that he often mentioned in his dedications and petitions for office. Doubtless this was so in his early career but 'my poor house at Hendon' in 1664 was recorded as having sixteen hearths; in 1691 it was inhabited by the commissioner of the great seal, and in the eighteenth century, before its demolition, it was described as a mansion (*VCH Middlesex*, 5.6). Fees for surveys could vary greatly: on one occasion £5, and on another £150. Fees could also be augmented by irregular gifts, such as the £200 that Norden received from James I in 1608, probably for a survey of Windsor Park. As well as cash, grants of land could be used as a stipend and Norden received a number of these from the duchy of Cornwall for 'good and faithful service heretofore done and hereafter to be done'. In his surveying business Norden also had travelling expenses and assistants to pay. In 1610 the duchy allowed him £1 6s. per day for expenses and extra for the tools of his trade (substantially above the normal rate). Norden could also be instructed to pay himself from the sales of timber. Such irregular circumstances make firm computation difficult, but conservative calculations suggest that between 1607 and 1624 Norden's income was at least £200 a year, four times the income typical for a lesser merchant or lower gentry.

Topographical work including maps Norden also turned to topographical projects when finances were tight. In the difficult years of his seeking place under Elizabeth, he produced a very large (1251 x 368 mm) panorama of London—*Civitas Londini*—showing the Thames and London as if from the air over the south bank. This view was widely imitated by others during the next fifty years. In his retirement Norden republished a work begun in 1597 but embezzled from him: *A View of London Bridge from East to West* (1624). In the following year he produced *An Intended Guyde, for English Travailers*, an innovative book of triangular distance tables, arranged by county, showing the distances from one town to another. His *Guide for Countrymen in the Famous City of London* (1623) consisted of a leaflet map of London with a key to places of interest. It proved very popular and was republished many times in the next thirty years. Like the view of London Bridge, it was a reworking of an earlier project, the map being taken from his first published topographical work, the 1593 *Speculum* of Middlesex.

Norden conceived the *Speculum Britanniae* in 1583, when he fell into the company of Portugal's King Antonio, who, exiled by the annexation of his country by Philip of Spain, came to England looking for support. In the preface to his *Speculum* of Cornwall, Norden told how he fell to travelling with the followers of 'Don Anttonie', 'for the most part very learned', and how they questioned him about the names of the places through which they passed and the nature of things they saw. Culturally and administratively the county was the dominant social unit in early modern England, and inspired by the Portuguese visitors Norden next wrote in 1591 a small guidebook to Northamptonshire (where he was surveying at the time), containing some historical and antiquarian background and a résumé of the economic and social life of the county. To complete the description he included a map of the county. This, his first county map, was not very innovative, being based closely on an earlier map by William Saxton, and it and the guide remained unpublished until 1720. In 1593, however, Norden produced the next part of the *Speculum*, a guide to Middlesex. The text followed the formula established by the description of Northamptonshire but the map of the county and its two plans of Westminster and the City of London were, like all his later maps, his own, and not based on Saxton's work. Norden's 'Middlesex' was the first English county map to mark roads, and his inclusion of a characteristic sheet, giving a key to symbols used on the map, introduced this practice to English cartography.

A manuscript copy of the 'Middlesex' description was presented to Burghley, and the privy council granted Norden permission but not funds to continue with the project. In 1594 Norden produced descriptions and maps of Surrey and Essex and in 1595 descriptions and maps of Sussex, Hampshire, the Isle of Wight, Jersey, and Guernsey. None of these descriptions was published in his lifetime, despite his sumptuous presentation volume for Elizabeth (BL, Add. MS 31853). However, the maps were published, as were the *Speculum* and map of Hertfordshire made in 1597. The *Speculum* as a whole seems to have been critically received, because in 1596 Norden felt he had to write *Speculum Britanniae: a Preparative to this Work*, explaining in the preliminary text that he 'intended a reconciliation of sundrie propositions by divers persons, critics wise and otherwise tendred, concerning the same'. After the description of Hertfordshire, Norden produced only one more part for the *Speculum*: a description of Cornish maps made and presented to James I in 1604 as part of his campaign to seek a position. The text and maps of Cornwall, a county map and a set of nine maps of the county's hundreds (an administrative unit), remained unpublished until 1728. Norden died in St Giles-in-the-Fields in the late summer of 1625.

Despite the failure of the county descriptions, Norden's maps of Middlesex, Surrey, Essex, Sussex, Hampshire, and an otherwise unknown map of Kent were included in the 1607 edition of William Camden's *Britannia*. There is no evidence of a personal relationship with John Speed, but in 1611 Speed used Norden's maps of Surrey, Sussex, Middlesex, Cornwall, and Essex in his *Theatre of the Empire of Great Britaine*, the first published atlas of the British Isles. Most maps of these counties published in the following 150 years were based on Norden's work, and so he can be credited not only with key innovations in English cartography such as marking roads, administrative units and hierarchies of place, a grid-reference system, and the characteristic table, but also with producing enduring images of English landscape that must have shaped the views which generations had of their homelands.

FRANK KITCHEN

Sources F. Kitchen, 'Cosmo-choro-poly-grapher: an analytical account of the life and work of John Norden, 1547?–1625', DPhil diss., U. Sussex, 1992 · F. Kitchen, 'John Norden (*c*.1547–1625), estate surveyor, topographer, county mapmaker and devotional writer', *Imago Mundi*, 49 (1997), 43–61 · W. Ravenhill, *John Norden and his maps of Cornwall and its nine hundreds* (1972) · Wood, *Ath. Oxon.*, new edn, 2.189, 279–81
Archives BL, Cotton MS Aug. I, ii, 44 · BL, Egerton MS, 2644, fol. 49 · BL, Harley MS 3749 · BL, 'chorographicall discription', Add. MS 21853 · BL, description of Essex, Add. MSS 31853, 33769 [copies] · BL, surveys, Add. MS 42508 · Bodl. Oxf., surveys · CUL, MS Dd viii, 9 · CUL, MS Mm 315 · Duchy of Cornwall office, London, acts of council, letters and warrants, enrolments, receivers-generals' accounts, Prince Henry's patent rolls · Duchy of Cornwall office, London, surveys, S58, 59, 61, 62, 63, 64, 67 · Essex RO, Chelmsford · GL, bishop's court act books, 9168/17 · Hatfield House, Hertfordshire, Cecil papers, 103/27 (2) · LMA, MJ/SR 526: 161, 163 · Norfolk RO, description of Norfolk · PRO, MPF 65, 67, 117 · PRO, SP 14 12/43
Likenesses portrait, repro. in J. Norden, *Speculum Britanniae: Middlesex* (1593), title-page
Wealth at death £29 14*s*. 4*d*.: GL, bishop's commissary court act books, 9168/17

Norfolk. For this title name *see* Bigod, Hugh (I), first earl of Norfolk (*d.* 1176/7); Bigod, Roger (II), second earl of Norfolk (*c*.1143–1221); Bigod, Roger (III), fourth earl of Norfolk (*c*.1212–1270); Bigod, Roger (IV), fifth earl of Norfolk (*c*.1245–1306); Thomas, first earl of Norfolk (1300–1338); Brotherton, Margaret, *suo jure* duchess of Norfolk (*c*.1320–1399); Mowbray, Thomas (I), first duke of Norfolk (1366–1399); Mowbray, John (V), second duke of Norfolk (1392–1432); Neville, Katherine, duchess of Norfolk (*c*.1400–1483); Mowbray, John (VI), third duke of Norfolk (1415–1461); Howard, John, first duke of Norfolk (*d.* 1485); Howard, Thomas, second duke of Norfolk (1443–1524); Mowbray, John (VII), fourth duke of Norfolk (1444–1476); Richard, duke of York and duke of Norfolk (1473–1483); Mowbray, Elizabeth, duchess of Norfolk (*d.* 1506/7) [*see under* Mowbray, John (VII), fourth duke of Norfolk (1444–1476)]; Howard, Thomas, third duke of Norfolk (1473–1554); Howard, Agnes, duchess of Norfolk (*b.* in or before 1477, *d.* 1545); Howard, Elizabeth, duchess of Norfolk (1497–1558); Howard, Thomas, fourth duke of Norfolk (1538–1572); Howard, Mary, duchess of Norfolk (1539/40–1557); Howard, Thomas, fourteenth earl of Arundel, fourth earl of Surrey, and first earl of Norfolk (1585–1646); Howard, Henry Frederick, fifteenth earl of Arundel, fifth earl of Surrey, and second earl of Norfolk (1608–1652); Howard, Henry, sixth duke of Norfolk (1628–1684); Howard, Henry, seventh duke of Norfolk (1655–1701); Howard, Mary, duchess of Norfolk (1658/9–1705); Howard, Mary, duchess of Norfolk (1692–1754); Howard, Mary, duchess of Norfolk (1701/2–1773); Howard, Charles, tenth duke of Norfolk (1720–1786); Howard, Charles, eleventh duke of Norfolk (1746–1815); Howard, Bernard Edward, twelfth duke of Norfolk (1765–1842); Howard, Henry Charles, thirteenth duke of Norfolk (1791–1856); Howard, Henry Granville Fitzalan-, fourteenth duke of Norfolk (1815–1860); Howard, Henry Fitzalan-, fifteenth duke of Norfolk (1847–1917); Howard, Bernard Marmaduke Fitzalan-, sixteenth duke of Norfolk (1908–1975); Howard, Lavinia Mary Fitzalan-, duchess of Norfolk (1916–1995) [*see under* Howard, Bernard Marmaduke Fitzalan-, sixteenth duke of Norfolk (1908–1975)].

Norford, William (1715–1793), physician and surgeon, was apprenticed to John Amyas, a surgeon in Norwich 'of the first character and in full business' (Norford). He began practice at Halesworth, Suffolk, as a surgeon and man-midwife. In 1753 he published in London *An Essay on the General Method of Treating Cancerous Tumours*, dedicated to John Freke, senior surgeon to St Bartholomew's Hospital, London. He had been encouraged to write by some remarks of Freke, and by the example of Dale Ingram, also a country practitioner. He endeavoured to establish rules for the treatment of cancer, which had, he believed, been successful in several cases. Some of his supposed cures were, however, followed by recurrence and death, and in others of his cases it is clear that abscesses or inflamed glands, but not cancers, were present. He discussed the views of H. F. Ledran, G. Van Swieten, and R. Wiseman, and stated his own cases with fairness. He believed in a sulphur electuary and an ointment of his own.

Norford married the daughter of a surgeon, and after some years moved to Bury St Edmunds. He became an extra-licentiate of the Royal College of Physicians on 26 November 1761, and began practice as a physician. He had a quarrel with Edward Sharpin of East Dereham over a case of intestinal obstruction, and defended his own conduct in a sixpenny pamphlet entitled *A letter to Dr. Sharpin in answer to his appeal to the public concerning his medical treatment of Mr. John Ralling, apothecary, of Bury St. Edmund's in Suffolk*. On the strength of his licence he styles himself 'doctor'. The letter is dated 'Bury, Oct. 9, 1764', and the case, which is fully described, has considerable medical interest. In 1780 he published at Bury St Edmunds *Concisae et practicae observationes de intermittentibus febribus curandis*. He died in 1793. NORMAN MOORE, rev. MICHAEL BEVAN

Sources P. J. Wallis and R. V. Wallis, *Eighteenth century medics*, 2nd edn (1988) · W. Norford, *A letter to Dr. Sharpin in answer to his appeal to the public concerning his medical treatment of Mr. John Ralling, apothecary, of Bury St. Edmund's in Suffolk* (1764) · Munk, *Roll*
Likenesses J. Singleton, stipple, pubd 1788 (after portrait by G. Ralph), BM · G. Ralph, portrait

Norgate, Edward (1581–1650), miniature painter, musician, and writer on art, was born in Cambridge, the son of Robert *Norgate (*d.* 1587), master of Corpus Christi College, Cambridge, and vice-chancellor of that university in 1584, and Elizabeth, daughter of John Baker of Cambridge. His father having died Norgate was brought up by his stepfather, Nicolas *Felton (1556–1626), bishop of Ely. He left Cambridge without a degree, supported by his stepfather, who, 'finding him inclined to Limning and Heraldry, permitted him to follow his fancy therein; for parents who cross the current of their children's genius (if running in no vicious chanells) tempt them to take worse courses to themselves' (Norgate, 2). In London he entered the service of both James I and Charles I, and became intimate with the great art connoisseur Thomas Howard, second earl of Arundel.

Norgate first benefited from royal patronage with his

appointment in 1611 as tuner, and then keeper, of the king's virginals, organs, and other instruments. This was no sinecure, since there is evidence that he was actively involved in repairing and restoring the organs at the royal palaces at Greenwich and at Hampton Court. His fame as an organist spread to the continent, where the eminent Dutch statesman Constantijn Huygens heard of his skills. It was probably through Norgate's royal appointment that he first travelled to the Low Countries, where many of the best instrument makers in Europe then worked. Later, unusually among his English contemporaries, he became acquainted with the culture of the Netherlands in its golden age.

On 24 April 1613 Norgate was paid £10 by the treasurer of James I's chamber 'for his paynes taken to write and Lyme in Gold and Colours certain Letters written from his Majesty to the King of Persia, and the King of Mager' (Norgate, 2). His calligraphic skills and his finesse as an illuminator led him to write *Miniatura* (manuscript, 1627–8 revised, 1649; first printed, 1919), the fundamental treatise on Tudor and Stuart miniature painting. Norgate himself indicates that the treatise on the techniques of miniature painting was written for the benefit of his friend Sir Theodore Turquet de Mayerne, virtuoso of the arts and gynaecologist to Queen Henrietta Maria. Besides enjoying the support and friendship of Mayerne, who was himself an assiduous collector of information on the techniques of the visual arts, Norgate's 'Cousinell' was the English limner Peter Oliver, with whom he was associated in playing music for Charles I. In addition, on 22 September 1613 Norgate married, as his first wife, Judith Lanier (1590–1618), whose brother Nicholas was responsible ten years later for undertaking the negotiations between Charles I and the dukes of Mantua for purchase by the English crown of the Gonzaga collection. Thus Norgate's connections with the Laniers and the Olivers probably directed him towards the visual arts; indeed it may have been Peter Oliver who first taught him the rudiments of miniature painting. His second wife, whom he married at St Margaret's, Westminster, on 15 October 1619, was Ursula, daughter of Martin Brighouse of Coleby, Lincolnshire, with whom he had three sons and two daughters.

Over a period of roughly thirty years Norgate prepared illuminated state letters dispatched to all parts of the world by way of tribute and greeting from Charles I to monarchs of kingdoms stretching from Russia to the East Indies. He was a clerk of the signet as from 1625, when he was granted the monopoly for writing and ornamenting with gold and colours 'letters to the Emperour and Patriarch of Russia, the Grand Signior, the Great Mogul, the Emperor of Persia, and Kings of Bantam, Macassar, Barbary, Siam, Achien, Fez, Sus, and other far distant Kings' (Norgate, 3).

In 1633 Norgate was appointed Windsor herald at the College of Arms by the earl marshal, his patron, the earl of Arundel. He often illuminated letters patent and other heraldic documents, of which one of the most splendid is the grant of an augmentation of arms to William Alexander, first earl of Stirling, of 1634 (Audley End, Essex). Here the landscape vignettes suggest how sensitively he had responded to the Netherlandish tradition of landscape painting.

Norgate was with the king during the first bishops' war, of 1639, when he was signet clerk; his letters testify to the anxiety felt by royalists at the unprepared state of the king's cause. He wrote of Charles I 'I think none who do love him but must wish the army ten times doubled, and those fifteen times better accommodated' (K. Sharpe, *The Personal Rule of Charles I*, 1992, 803). He wrote to his friend Robert Read on 12 May 1639 that 'I am commanded from the King to make certain patternes for 4 new Ensignes with devises for the gard of his person' (Norgate, 3).

Norgate was a man of many talents. Besides his skill in music and calligraphy he had an exceptional eye, which gave him access to the studios of famous painters. He was involved in trying to acquire drawings by Rubens for his patron, Arundel, as early as 1618, and in 1632 Van Dyck lodged with him at 15 s. per diem until grander accommodation was provided. Norgate's versatility was nicely epitomized when in February 1638 he acted for one of the two secretaries of state, Sir Francis Windebanke. Windebanke acquired a virginal, once the property of the Infanta Isabella, which included a *Cupid and Psyche* attributed at the time to Rubens, declaring during the negotiations 'I will advise wᵗʰ yʳ good frende and myne Mr. Norgat, whose skill in these businesses is excellent' (Sainsbury, 209). From November 1639 Norgate was responsible for the negotiations over a commission to Jacob Jordaens for a cycle of Cupid and Psyche for the Queen's House, Greenwich (unexecuted).

Norgate was with the king at Oxford during the civil war, and there acted as clerk of the upper house at the opening of parliament on 22 January 1644. In 1646 he left for the Netherlands, where he revised his *Miniatura* in 1648–9. Thereafter he accepted employment from the parliamentary side, being confirmed as Windsor herald in November 1648. He died at the Herald's College, London, and was buried in St Benet Paul's Wharf on 23 December 1650. In his will of 5 October 1649 he left his Latin, French, and Italian books to one of his sons, Thomas, while in effect disinheriting another, Arthur, for his 'manie disorders'. Thomas who was ordained, was for a time chaplain to Sir Thomas Glemham, governor of Oxford during the civil war.

Norgate seems to have been related to Sir Balthazar Gerbier who had been Charles I's agent in Brussels in 1631. Norgate acted as Gerbier's factotum while Gerbier spent ten years in the Spanish Netherlands. There is a mass of letters from Gerbier to Norgate in the Public Record Office: 'The entry books of Sir Balthazar Gerbier' (PRO, SP 105). 'Miniatura' survives in two manuscripts—one in the Bodleian Library, Oxford, and the other at the Royal Society, London. Both are copies, differing in significant details, of a lost original. 'Miniatura' was first edited by Martin Hardie and published in 1919; that edition has recently been superseded by *Miniatura, or, The Art of Limning* (1997), edited by Jeffrey Muller and Jim Murrell.

DAVID HOWARTH

Sources E. Norgate, *Miniatura, or, The art of limning*, ed. J. M. Muller and J. Murrell (1997) · W. N. Sainsbury, ed., *Original unpublished papers illustrative of the life of Sir Peter Paul Rubens, as an artist and a diplomatist* (1859) · *CSP dom.*, 1610–50 · *DNB*
Archives Arundel Castle, West Sussex, corresp. with William Boswell, John Coke, Richard Plumleigh, and John Quarles

Norgate, Frederick (1817–1908). *See under* Norgate, Thomas Starling (1772–1859).

Norgate, Kate (1853–1935), historian, was born in St Pancras, London, on 8 December 1853, the only child of Frederick Norgate, bookseller, later a partner in the firm of Messrs Williams and Norgate, and his wife, Fanny, daughter of John Athow, stonemason and surveyor of the Norwich city pavements. Her grandfather Thomas Starling *Norgate, a friend of William Taylor (1765–1836), gave her a link with the active literary group that throve in Norwich in the first half of the nineteenth century. When Norgate became the protégée of the historian John Richard Green, she was ready to use to the full the opportunities that he gave her. Green encouraged her to devote herself to a history of the Angevins. By 1877 she had already made some progress with her first book. Her mother is said to have accompanied her to the British Museum and to have sat by her in the reading-room. *England under the Angevin Kings*, in two volumes, was published in 1887, four years after Green's death. Its merits were recognized at once: E. A. Freeman wrote a long appreciation of it in the *English Historical Review* (vol. 2, 1887). Norgate's mastery of the original sources showed critical skill and found expression in a clear narrative. If she was influenced by Green's strong preference for the chronicles and avoided unpublished material, including the generally uncatalogued manuscript sources in the Public Record Office, she did not share his deliberate indifference to records and used them assiduously in her later studies. Her work reveals her extensive knowledge and accurate rendition of the printed sources then available for a history of the twelfth and thirteenth centuries. In addition, Norgate stressed the importance of topography and travelled extensively, especially in Anjou, in support of her work. Self-trained, yet scholarly in her approach to research, Norgate represented a transition point in the professionalization of women historians.

England under the Angevin Kings carried her narrative to 1206. It was continued in *John Lackland* (1902) and *The Minority of Henry the Third* (1912). In *Richard the Lion Heart* (1924) Norgate retraced her steps to follow the life of Richard I, as a hero of the Christian West. All three books are well-arranged, spirited narratives. At the time, they were the best available history of the Angevin empire, and were well received by contemporaries. They are still occasionally cited by scholars today. Steeped in the historical controversies of her day, Norgate joined with her friend Thomas Andrew Archer in a passionate defence of Freeman against the attacks of J. H. Round (*English Historical Review*, 9, 1894). Of her critical studies, the most important are her defence of the authenticity of Adrian IV's bull *Laudabiliter* (*English Historical Review*, 8, 1893), and her consideration of the alleged condemnation of King John by

the French court in 1202 (*Transactions of the Royal Historical Society*, new ser., 14, 1900). Her work elicited critical attention from historians such as Round, another indication of the growing importance of women in the historical field.

In these early years Norgate was very active: she contributed forty-four entries to the *Dictionary of National Biography*, collaborated with Alice Stopford Green in the preparation of the illustrated edition of Green's *Short History of the English People* (1892–4), and worked on her next book in the society of learned friends such as William Hunt. Her historical contributions were later recognized by Somerville College, Oxford, which in 1929 elected her an honorary fellow. She died unmarried at her home, Jasmine Cottage, 2 Church Lane, Gorleston, Great Yarmouth, on 17 April 1935, and was fittingly described in her *Times* obituary as the 'most learned woman historian of the pre-academic period' (*The Times*, 6 May 1935).

F. M. POWICKE and P. MILLICAN, *rev.* JANICE GORDON-KELTER and ELLEN JACOBS

Sources *The Times* (6 May 1935) · *Letters of John Richard Green*, ed. L. Stephen (1901) · A. Brundage, *The people's historian: John Richard Green and the writing of history in Victorian England* (1994) · W. Rye, *Norfolk families*, 2 vols. in 5 pts (1911–13) · private information (1994)
Archives BL, corresp. with Macmillans, Add. MS 55078
Wealth at death £2857 16s. 2d.: probate, 21 June 1935, *CGPLA Eng. & Wales*

Norgate, Robert (d. 1587), college head, was born at Aylsham in Norfolk. He matriculated as a pensioner at St John's College, Cambridge, at Michaelmas 1550 and graduated BA in 1565. He was admitted to a fellowship of Corpus Christi College in 1567 and proceeded MA in the following year. Norgate married Elizabeth, daughter of John and Katherine Baker of Cambridge. John Baker was a half-brother of Archbishop Parker, who made Norgate one of his chaplains and presented him to the rectory of Latchingdon, Essex, where he was instituted on 27 January 1573.

Parker's influence was soon afterwards even more profitably deployed in Norgate's favour. When Norgate took up his fellowship Corpus Christi was still under the aged John Pory, but continuing discipline problems at the college led to his replacement in 1570 by Thomas Aldrich, then senior proctor of the university. Aldrich soon revealed himself as a supporter of Thomas Cartwright and neglected college affairs. Parker sought his resignation and urged his replacement by Norgate, then the oldest of the fellows. This was resisted both by Aldrich himself and five of the fellows. Parker sought to force the issue by summoning the master before ecclesiastical commissioners at Lambeth. Presented with the choice between resignation or deprivation, Aldrich chose the former.

In these highly inauspicious circumstances, on 22 August 1573 Robert Norgate was admitted as the new master of Corpus Christi College. Not until 1575 did he take his BTh degree. He was appointed university preacher in 1576 and was awarded the doctorate in 1581. During his mastership Norgate acquired many benefices and honours. He gave up the rectory of Latchingdon before 10 November 1584, but in that year became rector of Little Gransden, Cambridgeshire, by royal presentation. He was instituted to two Norfolk rectories, that of Marsham in 1575 and Forncett in 1578. On 29 January 1578 he was installed as prebendary of Decem Librarum in the cathedral of Lincoln, and on 8 May 1579 he was instituted as canon of the second prebend of Ely, of which the patron was John Baker.

Norgate expected much from the undergraduates of his college, if a timetable drawn up by him in the 1570s may be relied on. Morning prayer between five and six in the morning was followed by an hour-long lecture on Aristotle's natural philosophy; then came two lectures in Greek, followed at 3 p.m. by a lecture on Cicero. Norgate's sensitivity to attacks upon his dignity seems sometimes to have affected his judgement. In 1582 a fellow of Corpus named Tobias Bland had penned an 'infamous libel, blasphemous to the dishonour of God, directed manifestly against Mr D. Norgate, master of that college and now vice-chancellor of the university'. The vice-chancellor saw to it that Bland was 'put to the shame of sitting in the stocks, and then expelled and banished the college', a decision 'made known to all colleges in the town by the particular bills of Mr Doctor Norgate, sent to every master of a college … lest any of them ignorantly might receive him into their colleges' (Heywood and Wright, 1.392). In 1584, against strong opposition, Bland was admitted MA; in 1602 he became a canon of Peterborough.

During Norgate's time and in large part on his initiative, a new chapel was built at Corpus Christi to accommodate the increasing numbers at the college. The work began in 1578 and was partly financed by the lord keeper, Sir Nicholas Bacon, who donated more than £200 for the purpose; the queen provided timber, the earl of Bedford stone, and there were many lesser benefactors. However, the total cost of more than £650 was not fully met by donations, and the college found itself in debt: several tradesmen brought suits against it. In an effort to remedy the situation Norgate bought lands at Stow cum Qui, Cambridgeshire, which, it was hoped, would provide a substantial income. But the title was challenged, and the legal costs incurred gave rise to further financial difficulties.

There may have been an element of misfortune in this, but Norgate appears to have been a poor administrator. His financial stewardship brought many complaints and there were reports of irregularities. His successor, John Copcot, wrote to Lord Burghley that 'the college was undone in respect of wealth, [meaning by the last Master, Dr Norgate, who had run the college deep in debt]' (Strype, *Whitgift*, 2.522). It seems that Norgate had acted as bursar and borrowed from the college to spend both on its behalf and on his own account. He certainly did not become a rich man as a result: after his death on 2 November 1587 the college authorities found that he owed about £600, more than half of it to the college, but that his assets amounted to only £86. 6s. 8d. Most of this was distributed to various creditors, but £4. 12s. 8d. was set aside for 'Mrs Eliz Norgate his late wife for a bed for her and children'

(*Masters' History*, 135). Daughter of John Baker of Cambridge, she had borne Norgate a son, Edward *Norgate, in 1581. Elizabeth escaped destitution by marrying Nicholas Felton, later master of Pembroke College, Cambridge, and bishop of Ely. Norgate was buried at the church of St Benedict in Cambridge.   STEPHEN WRIGHT

Sources *Masters' History of the college of Corpus Christi and the Blessed Virgin Mary in the University of Cambridge*, ed. J. Lamb (1831) · H. C. Porter, *Reformation and reaction in Tudor Cambridge* (1958) · Venn, *Alum. Cant.* · H. P. Stokes, *Corpus Christi* (1898) · *Fasti Angl., 1541–1857*, [Ely] · *Fasti Angl., 1541–1857*, [Lincoln] · J. Strype, *Annals of the Reformation and establishment of religion … during Queen Elizabeth's happy reign*, new edn, 4 vols. (1824) · J. Strype, *The life and acts of Matthew Parker*, new edn, 3 vols. (1821) · J. Strype, *The life and acts of John Whitgift*, new edn, 3 vols. (1822) · J. Heywood and T. Wright, eds., *Cambridge University transactions during the puritan controversies of the 16th and 17th centuries*, 1 (1854), 392–7
Wealth at death £86 6s. 8d.; but debts of about £600: *Masters' History*, 135

Norgate, Thomas Starling (1772–1859), writer, was born in Norwich on 20 August 1772, the eldest child of Elias Norgate (1727–1803), surgeon, and his wife, Deborah (1733–1801), the daughter of Thomas Starling, from a family of coach-painters and ironmongers. Elias Norgate was a member of the Presbyterian and later Unitarian congregation at the Octagon Chapel in Norwich. Thomas Norgate was educated first by John Baxter and then at the Norwich Free School, where until 1785 the headmaster was the famous classical scholar Samuel Parr, to whom Norgate later attributed 'my present great ignorance of classical literature' (Norgate). In 1788 he entered New College, Hackney, a dissenting foundation headed by Thomas Belsham, newly recruited to Unitarianism from Independency. On leaving Hackney, Norgate was apprenticed to a firm of solicitors, Kinderley and Long, in Chancery Lane and was entered at Lincoln's Inn. He kept his terms but disliked the practice of law and returned to Norwich. In London he had often visited William Beloe, also from Norwich, and on his advice began to write essays and pamphlets and to review for the *British Critic*. In 1795 he inherited the estate belonging to his maternal grandmother at Hethersett, Norfolk, and retired there. On 4 August 1797 he married Mary Susan Randall (1774–1857), the daughter of Benjamin Randall, a bankrupt East India merchant. They had eight sons and four daughters. The eldest son, Elias, died in 1833, aged thirty-five.

Norgate was an intimate of the Norwich literary circle, whose best-known member was William Taylor (1765–1836). Through William Enfield, minister of the Octagon Chapel, he regularly contributed to the *Analytical Review* until its demise in 1799, and wrote for other periodicals connected with the Unitarian intelligentsia, notably the *Monthly Magazine*, for which between 1797 and 1807 he wrote a semi-annual review of literature published in England, and the *Annual Review* (1802–8) of Arthur Aikin, to which Norgate contributed about a seventh of the contents. He also wrote for the *Monthly Review*.

Norgate opened a fire insurance office, the Anchor, in Norwich, but claims exceeded capital and a clerk, William Calthorpe, proved to be a swindler, so after three years he sold the business. In 1809 Norgate became a partner of Benjamin Dowson (1763?–1843), a corn and coal merchant at Geldeston, near Norwich; this venture also failed, and a later determination to emigrate to either France or the Netherlands was frustrated by the return of Napoleon from Elba. He returned to Hethersett, where he again combined farming and a literary career. He contributed the sections on agriculture and horticulture to the *General History of the County of Norfolk* (2 vols., 1829) and in the same year founded the Norfolk and Norwich Horticultural Society. He also helped to found and, assisted by his son Elias, edited a weekly paper, the *East Anglian*, published from 1830 to 1833. He died at Hethersett on 7 July 1859.

Norgate's fourth son, **Thomas Starling Norgate** (1807–1893), was born at Hethersett on 30 December 1807. He was educated at Norwich grammar school under Edward Valpy (1764–1832) and at Gonville and Caius College, Cambridge, where he matriculated in 1827 and graduated BA in 1832. He was curate successively of Runton, Briningham, Cley next the Sea, and Banningham, all in Norfolk, and was collated rector of Sparham, Norfolk, in 1840. He married Caroline Roxalana, daughter of Francis Cremer Woodrow; they had five children. He was the author of three translations of Homeric poems; *Batrachomyomachia: an Homeric Fable Reproduced in Dramatic Blank Verse* (1863); the *Odyssey* (1863); and the *Iliad* (1864). He died at Sparham on 25 November 1893.

The youngest son, **Frederick Norgate** (1817–1908), born at Hethersett on 20 or 21 November 1817, was admitted to St John's College, Cambridge, in 1835, moved to Clare College the next year, and graduated BA in 1839. Intended for the church, in 1843 he became a bookseller and a partner in the publishing firm of Williams and Norgate. After two decades he retired to devote himself to his scholarly interests, especially the poetry of William Caxton. In 1850 he married Fanny, daughter of John Athow, stonemason and surveyor of the Norwich city pavements; their only child was the historian Kate *Norgate (1853–1935). Frederick Norgate died at his home in Ashchurch Grove, Shepherd's Bush, London, on 10 August 1908.　　　　R. K. Webb

Sources T. S. Norgate, 'Horae otiosa', Norfolk RO [autobiography] · *DNB* · W. Rye, *Norfolk families*, 2 vols. in 5 pts (1911–13) · Venn, *Alum. Cant.* · Crockford (1890) · *The Times* (13 Aug 1908) · d. cert. · d. cert. [Mary Susan Norgate] · *Norfolk Genealogy*, 6 (1974) [s.v. Cremer] · *Norfolk Genealogy*, 13/3 (1981) [s.v. Norgate] · private information (2004) [J. Creasey]
Archives Norfolk RO, autobiography
Wealth at death under £16,000: probate, 9 Sept 1859, *CGPLA Eng. & Wales*

Norgate, Thomas Starling (1807–1893). *See under* Norgate, Thomas Starling (1772–1859).

Norie, John William (1772–1843), hydrographer and writer on navigation, was born at 39 Burr Street, Wapping, London, on 3 July 1772, the eldest of the eight children of James Norie (1737–1793), a Scot who had trained for the Presbyterian church and kept a school in Burr Street, and his wife, Dorothy Mary Fletcher (1753–1840).

Norie's first work, *The Description and Use of Hadley's Quadrant*, was published in 1796 by William Heather, the chart

John William Norie (1772–1843), by Adam Buck (after Solomon? Williams, *c.*1803)

and instrument seller. By early 1797 Norie was drawing charts for Heather and teaching navigation. In 1800 he was 'keeper of a nautical academy' at Heather's address, 157 Leadenhall Street. Soon after this his two best-known works were published, *A Complete Set of Nautical Tables* in 1803 and *A Complete Epitome of Practical Navigation* in 1805. Editions of the *Epitome*, many of them with the *Tables* included, were published for over a century, and editions of the *Tables* to the present day.

In 1813, after Heather's death, Norie, with a partner, George Wilson, who provided most of the capital, bought Heather's business. The copyright of his own books and the nautical academy remained Norie's personal property. The partnership traded as J. W. Norie & Co. and was managed by Norie. It grew steadily and published large numbers of charts and sailing directions, the majority drawn and written by Norie himself. The Leadenhall Street premises, which were decorated by the trade sign of the Wooden Midshipman, were immortalized by Charles Dickens in *Dombey and Son* as the shop kept by Sol Gills. Norie's charts and books, particularly the *Tables* and *Epitome*, made his name well known among seamen for nearly two centuries, a success due to his teaching ability, prolific output, and commercial shrewdness.

On 25 April 1797 Norie married Elizabeth Hill, who died in 1824; they had four daughters and a son. In 1840 he sold his share of the business and retired to Edinburgh, where he died at his home, 3 Coates Crescent, on 24 December 1843, and was buried in St John's Episcopal Church.

Susanna Fisher

Sources S. Fisher, *The makers of the blueback charts: a history of Imray, Laurie, Norie and Wilson Ltd* (2001) · private information (2004) · *Catalogue of the … charts, pilots and navigational books … sold by J. W.*

Norie & Co. (1816) • *BL cat.* • *British Library map library catalogue* (1998) [CD-ROM] • *Caledonian Mercury* (30 Dec 1843) • P. C. F. Smith, 'The little men: carved shop signs of the navigational instrument sellers', *American Neptune*, 34 (1974), 197–210 • parish register (baptism), London, St Botolph without Aldgate, 19 July 1772 • *DNB*
Likenesses A. Buck, watercolour drawing (after miniature by S? Williams, *c.*1803), NPG [*see illus.*] • oils, priv. coll.
Wealth at death £735 3*s.* 8*d.*: administration, 1843, Scotland

Norman, Barak (1651–1724), musical instrument maker, was born in London. Archival apprenticeship and later records refer to him as a member of the Weavers' Company. Perhaps this was for family reasons and because it would have conferred a status that could not be derived from the loose association of violin makers working in the City of London established to meet the increased demand of the Restoration period. The earliest identified instrument of Norman's is a bass viol of 1689, and by 1692 his labels show the sign of 'the Bass Viol' in St Paul's Alley, a street then adjacent to St Paul's Cathedral but since destroyed by bombing during the Second World War. His neighbours and occasional collaborators included the talented violin maker Edward Lewis and the Hare family of makers and music publishers.

A little is known of Norman's family life. On 24 February 1685 he married Mary Turner at All Hallows, London Wall. She had died by 12 September 1701, and on 14 October 1701 he married Sarah Watts, again at All Hallows, London Wall. She died the next year; and on 24 August 1703, at the same parish church, he married Elizabeth Seale. From 1706 he was churchwarden at All Hallows.

Norman's fame stems partly from his place as the last in London's pre-eminent line of viol makers. At this time the cello was beginning the long process of superseding the bass viol, and Norman can claim to have founded a line of English cello makers that is now much esteemed. He also made violins and violas, and it was on one of his 'tenors' that Henry Hill gave the first London performance of the solo viola part in Berlioz's 'symphony' *Harold en Italie* in 1848. Berlioz referred to it as an 'incomparable instrument' (W. H. Hill, A. F. Hill, and A. E. Hill, *Antonio Stradivari: his Life and Work*, 1963, viii). About 1713 Norman started to work with the more youthful Nathaniel Cross, and from then until his death a number of instruments were jointly labelled. Stylistically, Germanic influence can be detected, for example in the purfled and elaborately drawn patterns sometimes decorating the backs of his instruments. There is some Brescian influence too, and inevitably some of his instruments have been rebaptized 'Italian'. The varnish and many other features are in fact characteristic of the best of the 'Old English' school. Norman died, presumably in London, in 1724; his widow, Elizabeth, took over the Norman workshop. There are no children known from any of his marriages.

In their *History of the Violin* William Sandys and Simon Forster relate that the eminent cellist John Crosdill had a particularly favoured Barak Norman cello at a time when Crosdill was providing tuition for the prince of Wales, later George IV. The prince borrowed it and failed to return it, though Crosdill was presented with an Amati cello, costing 70 guineas, in lieu and given a sinecure worth £100 a year to soothe his disappointment. Norman's instruments are in various museum collections, including ones in London, Paris, and at the Shrine to Music in Vermillion, South Dakota.

BRIAN W. HARVEY

Sources T. Baker and others, *The British violin*, ed. J. Milnes (2000) [exhibition catalogue, Royal Academy of Music, London, 31 March – 11 April 1988] • B. W. Harvey, *The violin family and its makers in the British Isles: an illustrated history and directory* (1995) • *IGI*
Archives Horniman Museum, London, specimens • Musée de la Musique, Paris, specimens • Royal College of Music, London, specimens • Shrine to Music, Vermillion, South Dakota, specimens

Norman, Conolly (1853–1908), psychiatrist, was born on 12 March 1853 at All Saints' Glebe, Newtown Cunningham, co. Donegal, Ireland, the fifth of six sons of Hugh Norman, rector of All Saints', and his wife, Anne, daughter of Captain William Ball of Buncrana, co. Donegal. Several members of the Norman family served as mayor of Londonderry and two represented the city in parliament. Conolly Norman studied at Trinity College, Dublin, the Carmichael medical school, and the House of Industry hospitals. He received the licences of the King and Queen's College of Physicians in Ireland and the Royal College of Surgeons in Ireland in 1874. Four years later he became a fellow of the Royal College of Surgeons and in 1890 he was elected fellow of the Royal College of Physicians. He worked at the Bethlem Hospital in London before returning to Ireland in 1882 to take up the post of medical superintendent at Castlebar Asylum, co. Mayo (1882–5) and then at Monaghan Asylum (1885–6).

Norman was appointed medical superintendent of the largest psychiatric hospital in Ireland in 1886. This was the Richmond District Asylum in Dublin, later St Brendan's Hospital. At that time conditions within the asylum were very primitive and it was described as being more like a prison than a hospital. Norman was committed to reform and he strove consistently to introduce more humane practices. He also sought to incorporate a scientific approach in psychiatry. He published several papers in the *Journal of Mental Science* and in the *Transactions of the Royal Academy of Medicine of Ireland*. These papers included reports on the mental state in aphasia, an unusual case of brain tumour, an account of senile dementia, and medication trials. He also published in *The Lancet* and the *British Medical Journal* and was for very many years joint editor of the *Journal of Mental Science*.

In 1899 Norman reported an epidemic of beriberi in the Richmond Asylum in the *Transactions of the Royal Academy of Medicine in Ireland*. Beriberi is a condition caused by a deficiency of vitamin B1 (thiamine), and it is found mainly in rice-eating communities where polished rice is the staple diet. Norman's description was the first account of the condition in a temperate climate in the Western world and within a short period it was followed by similar accounts from other institutions around the world, including one from the state asylum in Little Rock, Arkansas. Norman's subsequent reports referred to these epidemics as well as to an obscure earlier account of an outbreak of beriberi in northern Japan. The condition is still found in Western countries particularly in malnourished alcoholics.

In the course of his regular visits to European centres of psychiatry Norman became aware of the tradition at Gheel, near Antwerp in Belgium, where the tradesmen and peasants cared for people with psychiatric disabilities in their own homes. Over 80 per cent of asylum patients were boarded out in this way at Gheel where they worked in the houses and fields. Norman became an advocate of this form of care which he claimed was more humane and which avoided the partial dementia which resulted from the institutionalization of patients. He also argued that it would be more cost effective. His efforts to introduce this enlightened approach in Dublin were frustrated by the authorities at the time.

On 6 June 1882 Norman married Mary Emily (d. 1933), daughter of Dr Randall Young Kenny of Killeshandra, co. Cavan. There were no children of the marriage. Norman had a deep interest in English literature and he was a keen student of French, German, and Italian. He was valued by his friends for his wisdom and integrity and for his humour. He collected art and old books and he was a practical botanist. In 1907 the honorary degree of MD was conferred on him by the University of Dublin. He died suddenly on 23 February 1908 while out walking in Dublin and was buried in the city's Mount Jerome cemetery. A memorial was erected by public subscription in the north aisle of St Patrick's Cathedral, Dublin. It was unveiled by the lord lieutenant, the earl of Aberdeen, on St Luke's day, 18 October 1910. The Conolly Norman medal, presented annually to the best student in psychiatry in the final medical examinations in Trinity College, Dublin, commemorates his name.   DAVIS COAKLEY

Sources BMJ (29 Feb 1908), 541 · Journal of Mental Science, 54 (1908), 203–6 · Medical Press and Circular (4 March 1908) · M. Webb, 'What's Irish about psychiatry', Irish Journal of Psychological Medicine, 7 (1990), 7–16 · DNB · J. Reynolds, Grangegormon (1992) · Irish Times (21 Oct 1933)
Likenesses J. M. S. Carré, memorial with medallion, 1910, St Patrick's Cathedral, Dublin · Miss Harrison, oils, 1910, Royal College of Physicians of Ireland, Dublin · photograph, repro. in Journal of Mental Science
Wealth at death £5230 15s. 11d.: probate, 10 March 1908, CGPLA Ire.

Norman, Sir Francis Booth (1830–1901), army officer, was born on 25 April 1830 in London, the second son of James Norman (d. 1853) (of Calcutta) and Charlotte (d. 13 Sept 1902), eldest daughter of Henry Wylie; he was the younger brother of Sir Henry Wylie *Norman. He attended Addiscombe College from 1846 to 1847, and obtained his commission in the 14th Bengal native infantry of the Bengal army on 8 December 1848. In 1852 he married Eliza Ellen, daughter of Lieutenant Nisbett, Bengal army, who died at Rawalpindi in 1870.

On the mutiny of his regiment in 1857 Norman was attached to the Ferozepore Sikh regiment, and remained at Ferozepore during subsequent operations. In 1863 he took part in the second expedition against the Yusufzais at Ambela, and was present at the storming of the conical hill and the destruction of Laloo. He was mentioned in dispatches. In the three following years he was engaged during the Bhutan campaign in the capture of Dewangiri and of the stockades in the Gurgaon Pass, serving as assistant quartermaster-general and receiving a brevet majority. In 1868 he took part in the Hazara campaign as second in command of the 24th (Punjab) regiment.

In the Second Anglo-Afghan War (1878–80) Norman commanded the 24th in the Bazar valley and the defence of Jagdalak, marching with Robert's force from Kabul to Kandahar and taking part in the battle of Kandahar. Mentioned in dispatches, he received a CB and brevet colonelcy. During the war with Burma in 1885–6 he commanded the Bengal brigade of the Upper Burma field force, assisting in the occupation of Mandalay and Bhamo. He was promoted KCB in 1886, attained the rank of major-general on 1 September 1889, and left India in 1891. He became lieutenant-general on 25 April 1892.

In March 1892 Norman married Caroline Matilda, daughter of the Revd W. W. Cazalet and widow of Major E. F. J. Rennick, Bengal staff corps, who survived him. He died on 25 June 1901 at Dulwich and was buried in Norwood cemetery. He left three sons and three daughters; one of the latter, Edith, was the wife of Sir Louis W. Dane (1856–1946), lieutenant-governor of the Punjab.

WILLIAM LEE-WARNER, rev. JAMES FALKNER

Sources Indian Army List · Hart's Army List · The Times (27 June 1901) · WWW · H. M. Vibart, Addiscombe: its heroes and men of note (1894)
Archives BL OIOC, diary and papers, MS Eur. D 659 [copy]
Wealth at death £5016 4s.: probate, 14 Sept 1901, CGPLA Eng. & Wales

Norman, George Warde (1793–1882), financial writer and merchant banker, was born on 20 September 1793 at Bromley Common, Kent, the eldest of the nine children of George Norman (1756–1830), timber merchant, and his wife, Charlotte (1766–1853), third daughter of Edward Beadon DD, rector of North Stoneham, Hampshire. He was educated at home, and locally in Eltham from about 1801 to 1805. He attended Eton College from 1805 to 1810 but his wish to go to Cambridge University was frustrated by family necessity. Instead, he joined his father's firm which specialized in the Baltic timber trade but was also involved in banking and insurance.

Norman's commercial training left him time for cricket (he founded the West Kent cricket club in 1812) and for a variety of literary and historical pursuits, which he developed in a close intellectual companionship with George Grote, a family friend. However, throughout his life he was subject to recurrent nervous depression, which struck in 1816 and led to a severe breakdown in 1822. Travel in Europe (in 1817 with Grote to Germany, and in 1822 to Italy with J. W. Cowell) assisted his recovery. He also developed his lifelong interest in political economy, forming a strong bond with the banker Samuel Jones Loyd, Lord Overstone and becoming a founder member of the Political Economy Club in 1821. Unusually for a man who was not yet a partner in a mercantile firm, he was elected a director of the Bank of England in 1821, the result of his father's connections with the City of London. In 1824 he took over the family firm, paying several visits to Norway (he became well versed in its history, language, and literature) but also acquiring new interests as a director of the Sun assurance group (1830–64) and an investor on various American and Australian ventures. In 1830, with an ample fortune (some £200,000), he retired from the family business; in the same year, on 12 October, he married Sibella (1808–1887), the daughter of Henry Stone, a former Bengal civil servant and a partner in Stone and Martin, bankers.

In the 1830s, with his keen interest in political economy and as a leading director of the bank (in 1826 he had promoted its new policy of establishing provincial branches), Norman became one of the most important exponents of what he first termed 'currency principles'. Having given evidence to the Bank Charter select committee in 1832, in 1833 he circulated privately his *Remarks upon some Prevalent Errors with Respect to Currency and Banking* (revised edn, 1838) setting out his beliefs that banknotes and deposits were by their nature distinct, that the Bank of England should regulate notes in accordance with specie, and that the bank should be divided into issuing and banking departments; he also held out as desirable, if not practicable, a monopoly of issue for the Bank of England. Such views tended to replace the discretion which the bank had traditionally exercised with a more self-regulating management of note-issue, hoping thereby to avoid the monetary instability prevalent in the 1820s and 1830s. While unwelcome to many directors, this view won influential recruits inside and outside the bank, with Norman and Overstone forming a mutually reinforcing partnership. They won over the future whig chancellor Sir Charles Wood, who chaired the select committee on banking in 1840 to which Norman gave lengthy evidence, and to whom he addressed an important *Letter on Money and the Means of Economising the Use of It* (1841). Here were largely foreshadowed the principles upon which the Bank Charter Act of 1844 was based. In subsequent financial crises, Norman was an active and influential defender of this act, consulted daily by Wood in 1847, combining powerfully with Overstone in 1857, and in 1866 dissenting strongly from Walter Bagehot's views of the bank as the lender of last resort. Norman remained a director of the bank until 1872, though his nervous disposition led him to decline to become governor by rotation, the normal practice in the 1830s and 1840s; interestingly, in the crisis of 1847 he strongly urged the need for a permanent governor, which his grandson Montagu Collet *Norman (1871–1950) later became.

Besides monetary policy Norman took a consistent interest in taxation, urging (unusually) that Britain was a lightly taxed nation, and in free trade, publishing in 1864 the best contemporary refutation of Robert Torrens's case for reciprocity. Politically he was a keen Liberal, active in the City of London and in West Kent where he regularly marshalled campaigns, though he declined several opportunities to enter the Commons. A friend of N. W. Senior, he took a close interest in the formulation of the new poor law, acting locally as an overseer of the poor, and after 1836 as chairman and deputy chairman of the Bromley Union for over forty years. In London he remained active in the Political Economy Club, served as a public works commissioner (1831–76), and for many years was a governor of Guy's Hospital. At Bromley he cultivated a range of friendships (Charles Darwin was a neighbour) and intellectual pursuits. He often wrote for *The Economist*, published his *Papers on many Subjects* in 1869, and later wrote on the Saxon archaeology of Kent. Melancholic and introspective by nature, in 1857–8 he composed a candid autobiography revealing with great honesty his nervous disorders, his wrenching quarrel with Grote in 1832, his religious quandaries (he had been brought up a Unitarian), and his love of cricket. He also remodelled the family home, The Rookery, developed his sizeable landed and urban estates, presided over the West Kent Agricultural Association, and acted as a magistrate.

An archetypal patriarch within his extensive family circle, Norman was deeply influenced by the loss of his eldest son, Herman (1831–1855), in the Crimean War; his second son, Charles Loyd (1833–1889), became a partner in Barings, and his sixth son, Philip (1842–1931), a prolific artist, author, and antiquary. His fourth son, Frederick Henry (1839–1916), having married the daughter of Norman's bank colleague Mark Wilks Collet, was the father of Montagu Norman, governor of the Bank of England from 1920 to 1944. In later life Norman continued to travel frequently in England (he regularly fished at Stockbridge and often visited Overstone) and Europe. After contracting a cold, he died at Bromley Common on 4 September 1882 and was buried at Bromley Common church on the 8th.

A. C. HOWE

Sources CKS, Norman papers [incl. autobiography] · *The correspondence of Lord Overstone*, ed. D. P. O'Brien, 3 vols. (1971) · Borth. Inst., Hickleton MSS · J. Clapham, *The Bank of England: a history*, 2 (1944) · F. W. Fetter, *Development of British monetary orthodoxy, 1797–1875* (1965) · P. Norman, *Scores and annals of the West Kent cricket club, originally the Prince's Plain club* (1897) · *South-Eastern Gazette* (11 Sept 1882) · Mitchell L., NSW, Macarthur MSS · *The Economist* (9–30 Sept 1882) · Mrs Grote, *The personal life of George Grote* (1873) · DNB · Burke, *Gen. GB*

Archives Bromley Central Library, Kent, corresp., diaries, and papers · CKS, autobiography; corresp. and papers | Borth. Inst., letters to Lord Halifax · Borth. Inst., Hickleton MSS · LUL, Overstone MSS · Mitchell L., NSW, Macarthur MSS

Likenesses portrait, *c*.1830, repro. in Clapham, *Bank of England*, frontispiece · E. U. Eddis, portrait, *c*.1840, priv. coll.; repro. in O'Brien, ed., *Correspondence of Lord Overstone*, 2, facing p. 592 · T. Woolner, plaster cast of medallion, 1859, NPG · G. F. Watts, portrait, *c*.1875, priv. coll.; repro. in O'Brien, ed., *Correspondence of Lord Overstone*, 3, facing p. 1272 · F. Wilkin, oils, Bank of England, London

Wealth at death £126,131 6s. 1d.: resworn probate, April 1883, *CGPLA Eng. & Wales* (1882)

Norman, Sir Henry, first baronet (1858–1939), journalist and politician, was born on 19 September 1858 in Leicester, the only son and first of two children of Henry Norman (1814–1877), merchant, and his wife, Sarah Edna Riddington (1833–1887). The family were Unitarians; Norman's father was a small-time radical politician who had once sheltered the Chartist leader Thomas Cooper. Educated at Leicester collegiate school (1865–9) and Grove House School (1870–75), he was talent-spotted at the age of fifteen by a visiting American clergyman, and sent to Harvard University and the University of Leipzig, taking a BA degree in divinity from Harvard. Although staunchly religious as a young man, he gave up his faith and a career as a preacher when he returned to England in 1883.

Norman joined the staff of the *Pall Mall Gazette* under the editorship of the celebrated W. T. Stead, and became a prominent and prolific journalist in the heyday of the 'new journalism'. He maintained his links with the United States, working as a London correspondent for the *New York Times*. An astute networker, Norman reported on literary, theatrical, and political matters, and came to know such figures as Robert Louis Stevenson, William Archer, Walter Pater, Henry Irving, George Bernard Shaw, and Walt Whitman. In 1887 he set off on a four-year world tour on behalf of several international newspapers, reporting from places as far apart as Canada, Siberia, the Philippines, Siam, and Japan. The trip gave him material for his successful travel books *The Real Japan* (1892) and *The Peoples and Politics of the Far East* (1895).

In 1891 Norman married Ménie Muriel *Dowie (1867–1945), the intrepid 24-year-old author of *A Girl in the Karpathians*. They formed a precocious literary double act, travelling and reporting together on long journeys through the Balkans and north Africa. Norman joined the *Daily Chronicle*, where he became in 1895 the assistant and literary editor, while Dowie contributed to *The Yellow Book* and published books including the controversial 'modern girl' novel *Gallia*. They went through a bitter divorce in 1903, on the grounds of her adultery with their friend the climber Edward Arthur Fitzgerald, author of *The Highest Andes*. Norman was given custody of their child, Henry Nigel St Valéry Norman, and refused to let Dowie see the boy until he reached adulthood. on 8 May 1907 he married (Florence) Priscilla ('Fay') McLaren (1884–1964), the vigorous and opinionated daughter of the wealthy industrialist and Liberal MP, Sir Charles Benjamin Bright *McLaren, later Lord Aberconway. The marriage brought Norman three more children, a life of moneyed luxury divided between London, Surrey, and Cap d'Antibes, and a degree of personal tranquillity that had previously eluded him.

Norman obtained several scoops during his years as a journalist, including revelations on the truth behind the Dreyfus affair and a border clash between Venezuela and British Guiana, averting a serious rupture in American–British relations in the latter case. His quasi-diplomatic role, acting as a conduit between the British and foreign governments, provoked some envy among his colleagues. W. T. Stead referred to him in the *Review of Reviews* of April 1896 as 'Plenipotentiary Extraordinary to the Universe', and wrote that:

> If you waked him up at midnight with a telegram announcing the assassination of the Prime Minister of Timbuctoo, he would hardly have learned the exact locality of the crime before he would begin recounting, with the sang froid of a phonograph, the last conversation he had enjoyed with the deceased statesman as they went gorilla stalking in the Great Forest.

Norman was elected to parliament in 1900 as the Liberal member for Wolverhampton South, and was tipped as a future foreign secretary. Despite announcing that he had given up journalism, he started a magazine called *The World's Work*, secured interviews with both the tsar of Russia and President Theodore Roosevelt, and published a travel book called *All the Russias* (1902). His political career did not flourish, and he never progressed beyond the post of assistant postmaster-general which he held briefly in 1910, although he gained a reputation as a back-room fixer.

In the 1890s Norman had been a strong press ally of Lord Rosebery during his brief term as prime minister, and shared his brand of Liberal Imperialism. He now became closely identified with David Lloyd George, and organized the budget league in support of the Liberals' radical reforming budget of 1909. Norman lost his seat in the first general election of 1910, but was returned as MP for Blackburn in the second general election of the same year. As a parliamentarian he chaired a select committee on patent medicines and was involved in legislation on broadcasting, women's suffrage, and daylight saving. He remained a supporter and confidant of Lloyd George, acting as a personal envoy to France for him several times during the First World War. He was awarded the cross of the Légion d'honneur by the French government in January 1917. He retired from parliament in 1923, having helped to run the coalition government's campaign in the 'coupon election' of December 1918. Knighted in 1906, he was created a baronet in June 1915.

Henry Norman had a restless and inquisitive mind, which spanned matters as diverse as air navigation, Japanese typography, motorized scooters, and developments in the science of wireless telegraphy. He was a private man, whose life was marked by a willingness to change direction at key moments and cauterize the past. He died at his country house, Ramster, near Chiddingfold, in Surrey, on 4 June 1939.   PATRICK FRENCH

Sources P. French, *The life of Henry Norman* (1995) · M. M. Dowie, *Gallia*, ed. H. Small (1995) · private information (2004)
Archives British Medical Association, London · Inst. EE, corresp. and papers · IWM, corresp. and papers · National Motor Museum, Beaulieu, Hampshire · priv. coll. · Sci. Mus., scientific and technical corresp. and papers · U. Nott. L., letters | BL, corresp. with Lord Gladstone, Add. MS 46042 · BL OIOC, letters to Lord Reading, MSS Eur. E 238, F 118 · CAC Cam., corresp. with Sir E. L. Spears
Likenesses portraits, repro. in French, *Life of Henry Norman*
Wealth at death £6393 13s. 8d.: probate, 27 June 1939, *CGPLA Eng. & Wales*

Norman, Sir Henry Wylie (1826–1904), army officer and colonial governor, was born on 2 December 1826 in London, only son of James Norman, a businessman who had been at sea and at Havana, and Charlotte, *née* Wylie, of Dumfries. His father subsequently moved to Calcutta, where he died in 1853; his mother died at Sandgate, near Folkestone, on 13 September 1902.

Early career While his parents were overseas Norman was educated indifferently at three private schools in England, under the supervision of his maternal grandparents. He joined his father in Calcutta in 1842, where he worked as a clerk for eighteen months. In March 1844 he received a direct appointment to the Bengal army and joined the 1st Bengal native infantry as ensign in April 1844, transferring in March 1845 to the 31st Bengal native infantry. He served with his regiment in the First Anglo-Sikh War in 1846, becoming adjutant in 1847 and serving through the Second Anglo-Sikh War, being present at Ramnagar, Sadulapur, Chilianwala, and the final victory at Gujrat in February 1849. In 1849 he became brigade major to Sir Colin Campbell at Peshawar. He had already begun to create a reputation as an able, immensely hardworking staff officer, with a prodigious memory and a natural aptitude for work. He served in the 1850 Kohat Pass expedition under Sir Charles Napier and in expeditions against the Afridis, the Mohmands, and the Utman Khel, and was mentioned in dispatches in April 1852. He was made deputy assistant adjutant-general and aide-de-camp to Lieutenant-General Sir Abraham Roberts, commanding the Peshawar division, in 1853, where he became friendly with Sir Abraham's son, Frederick. Also in 1853 he married Selina Eliza Davidson, daughter of Dr Alexander Davidson, inspector of hospitals in India, and they had four daughters and a son, Henry Alexander, who died in 1858. In 1855 he rejoined his regiment in the suppression of the Santal uprising in Bihar, moving in May 1856 to the post of assistant adjutant-general at army headquarters in Calcutta and Simla.

Service in the mutiny Norman was at Simla in May 1857 when news arrived of the Meerut mutiny and the mutineers' occupation of Delhi. Norman accompanied the force assembled for the siege of Delhi as assistant adjutant-general and became acting adjutant-general when Colonel Chester was killed at the battle of Badli-ki-sarai on 8 June 1857. He served throughout the siege and the recapture of the city at the end of September 1857, being superseded as adjutant-general to the force by Neville Chamberlain in June, but standing in again when Chamberlain was severely wounded in July 1857. He left Delhi with Greathead's column five days after the city fell and took part in the actions at Bulandshahr, Aligarh, and Agra before joining the new commander-in-chief, Colin Campbell, for the second relief of Lucknow, as deputy adjutant-general to the force. He took a direct part in the fighting at the Shah Najafmosque in November 1857, having his horse shot underneath him. He was present at the final capture of Lucknow in March 1858, and subsequently in the operations in Rohilkhand and the battle of Bareilly on 5 May,

Sir Henry Wylie Norman (1826–1904), by unknown photographer

where he was wounded, and finally in the operations in Oudh in the winter of 1858–9. When the mutiny ended he had been mentioned in dispatches or general orders twenty-three times. He published *A Narrative of the Campaign of the Delhi Army* (1858), and subsequently pamphlets and articles in reviews.

Later career Norman received a CB in August 1859 and was appointed to the new Bengal staff corps (which he had largely designed) in December 1860, when he also received a brevet lieutenant-colonelcy. The mutiny had consolidated his reputation as one of the most able staff officers in India.

In October 1860, after leave in England, Norman was appointed assistant military secretary to the commander-in-chief of the British army, the duke of Cambridge, a post which was effectively the link between the commander-in-chief and the authorities in India on all matters of personnel appointments. It was a post of high influence and responsibility, in view of the duke's keen interest in Indian army matters, and required tact and discretion. He held that post only until 1861, when he was sent back to India as secretary to the government in the military department to assist in the massive task of post-mutiny reorganization. It was a tribute to his abilities but also effectively the end of active soldiering, the rest of his career being in administrative posts.

As a key figure in the reorganization, Norman attracted the wrath of the many vested interests affected, but he was rewarded by being made aide-de-camp to the queen in September 1863. His wife had died on 3 October 1862, and in September 1864 he married Jemima Anne (Minnie)

Temple, the daughter of T. Knowles and widow of Captain A. B. Temple, but she died in 1865 at sea, *en route* with her husband for leave in England. Throughout 1866 Norman was on sick leave in England, following a prolonged bout of fever, but he resumed his post in India in 1867 and was promoted major-general in March 1869. In March 1870 he married Alice Claudine Sandys, the daughter of Teignmouth Sandys, a Bengal civil servant. They had two sons and a daughter, and she survived her husband.

In June 1870 Norman was promoted to the post of military member on the governor-general's council and head of the military department. He was a prominent supporter of the policy of 'masterly inactivity' associated with the governor-generalships of Lord Mayo and Lord Northbrook, of friendly relations with Russia, non-interference in Afghanistan, and retrenchment and reform in India. He was made a KCB in May 1873, but with the arrival of Lord Lytton as governor-general in 1876 Norman's views became out of tune with the 'forward policy' espoused by Lytton, Colley, Roberts, and others, and he resigned in March 1877, becoming a lieutenant-general shortly afterwards. In 1878 he joined the secretary of state for India's Council of India in London, playing a major part in the decision in 1881 to withdraw from Kandahar at the end of the Second Anglo-Afghan War.

Final years Norman's military career was over, his lack of recent service and command experience militating against him. He was promoted full general by seniority on 1 April 1882. Later that year he was employed in settling financial questions arising from the Indian contingent in Wolseley's Egyptian expedition. In November 1883 he resigned from the Council of India on taking up the governorship of Jamaica. He arrived to face a constitutional crisis over non-official representation on the governor's council. He brought with him new proposals which through his tact and discretion he succeeded in introducing without uproar, thus defusing the issue. By the time his tenure ended, he had become respected and popular. His reward was the GCMG and a military GCB in 1887.

In 1889 Norman became governor of Queensland, succeeding Anthony Musgrave after Sir Henry Blake's nomination proved unacceptable there because of his Irish connections. Norman faced constitutional problems and financial difficulties. He defused the situation in his usual tactful and wise way, characteristically offering to accept a reduction in his own pay to assist in the financial crisis. He travelled much, was public-spirited and supported colonial rights, and was generally liked and respected. On issues such as the partition of Queensland and Australian federation he was cautious, but he was keenly in favour of the principle of imperial defence, although unable to do much because of Queensland's financial difficulties. His successful governorship ended in 1895, and he left Queensland in November for London, where he acted for a year as agent-general for the colony.

In September 1893 Norman had been offered, and initially accepted, the governor-generalship of India, the highest post in the empire. It was a great tribute to his abilities and reputation, but within a few days he realized that the strain of such an arduous office would be too much for him at the age of nearly sixty-seven, and he withdrew; Lord Elgin was subsequently appointed.

In 1896 Norman was appointed chairman of the royal commission on the economic conditions of the sugar-growing colonies in the West Indies. It enabled him to indulge his lifelong recreation of cruising, but his views on sugar duties were not shared by his fellow commissioners.

In 1901 Norman accepted the pleasant post of governor of the Royal Hospital, Chelsea, and was raised to field marshal in June 1902. He was vice-president of the Royal Geographical Society and of the Royal Colonial Institute, and director of the Commercial Union Assurance Company. His last public service was as a member of the royal commission on the war in South Africa. His health was already failing and he died at the Royal Hospital, Chelsea, on 26 October 1904, and was buried in the Brompton cemetery, London. Memorial tablets were installed at the Royal Hospital, in Calcutta, and in the crypt of St Paul's.

Character and appearance Norman was slightly below medium height and slender. During the mutiny he had shown his personal courage, presence of mind, and coolness, and there is no reason to suppose that he could not have gone on to be a successful commander; but it was as a staff officer and administrator that he excelled—lucid, penetrating, immensely industrious, holding his views firmly, but always modest, friendly, and tactful. He did not possess the charisma of a Roberts but he was the quiet man to whom others instinctively turned for wise counsel and to whom difficult problems could be presented with the expectation that they would be handled sensibly and without fuss—the epitome of 'a safe pair of hands'.

BRIAN ROBSON

Sources F. Lee-Warner, *Memoirs of Field Marshal Sir Henry Norman* (1908) · *DNB* · H. W. Norman, *A narrative of the campaign of the Delhi army* (1858) · J. W. Kaye, *A history of the Sepoy War in India, 1857–1858*, 4th edn, 3 vols. (1880–81) · Lord Roberts [F. S. Roberts], *Forty-one years in India*, 2 vols. (1897) · G. B. Malleson, *History of the Indian mutiny, 1857–1858: commencing from the close of the second volume of Sir John Kaye's History of the Sepoy War*, 3 vols. (1878–80) · *WWW* · G. W. Forrest, *Field-Marshal Sir Neville Chamberlain* (1909) · P. D. Wilson, 'Norman, Sir Henry Wylie', *AusDB*, vol. 11

Archives BL, corresp. with Lord Ripon, Add. MS 43560 · BL, letters to Lord Strathnairn, Add. MS 42807 · BL OIOC, letters to Lord Elgin, MS Eur. F 83 · Bodl. Oxf., letters to Lord Kimberley · CKS, letters to Edward Stanhope · NAM, letters to Lord Roberts

Likenesses T. J. Barker, oils, 1859, NPG · Garnett, photograph, c.1860, NPG · Shepherd & Bourne, group portrait, photograph, c.1864 (with Viceroy's council), NPG · L. Dickinson, oils, exh. RA 1879, Calcutta Corporation · engraving, c.1893 (after photograph by Fradelle & Young), NPG · Vandyk, photograph, c.1902, NPG · G. Nicolet, oils, 1905 · W. & D. Downey, woodburytype photograph, NPG; repro. in W. Downey and D. Downey, *The cabinet portrait gallery*, 5 (1894) · Spy [L. Ward], chromolithograph caricature, NPG; repro. in *VF* (25 June 1903) · photograph, NPG [*see illus.*]

Wealth at death £11,574 4s. 5d.: probate, 29 Nov 1904, *CGPLA Eng. & Wales*

Norman, John (*c*.1489–1553/4), abbot of Bindon, is probably identical with the monk who as 'John Sarisbury' of Bindon, Dorset, was ordained deacon on 5 June 1512 and priest on 12 March 1513. Presumably he had attained the canonical minimum age of twenty-four by the latter date, so he was probably born about 1489, in Salisbury. Nothing else is known of him until he was elected abbot by his brethren in 1534, the duke of Richmond having petitioned the king for a free election on behalf of the monks in return for a promise that the abbey would care for his deer. In early 1535 the abbot of Ford received a royal commission to undertake a visitation of Bindon Abbey, but no record survives to indicate the spiritual or temporal condition of the house under Norman's short rule. In the same year the abbey was assessed as having an income of less than £200 per annum, thereby bringing it under the terms of the act passed in 1536 to dissolve the lesser monasteries. Norman was able to negotiate with the crown to have his monastery exempted from suppression, and upon payment of the large fine of £300 the abbey was restored by letters patent of 16 November 1536. This reprieve was short-lived, however, and Norman and his brethren were finally forced to surrender the abbey on 14 March 1539. Norman was granted a pension of £50 per annum which he continued to receive until September 1553. He probably died in late 1553 or early 1554.　PETER CUNICH

Sources VCH Dorset, 2.86 · A. Miller, The monasteries of Dorset (1999), 49, 68 · LP Henry VIII, 7, no. 821; 8, no. 74; 13/2, no. 457(1.3); 14, nos. 509, 1355 · auditors of land revenue, receivers' accounts, ser. 1, PRO, LR6/104/4, m.52v · E. Audley, bishop's register, Wilts. & Swindon RO, D1/2/14, fols. 19v, 22 · DNB

Norman, John (1622–1669), clergyman and ejected minister, was baptized on 15 December 1622, the son of Abraham Norman of Trusham, Devon. He matriculated aged fifteen on 16 March 1638 from Exeter College, Oxford, and graduated BA on 21 October 1641. His movements during the civil war are unknown, until 1645, when he appears as vicar of Frampton, Dorset. On 1 June 1647 he was nominated to the vicarage of Bridgwater, Somerset, vacant through the expulsion of George Wotton. Norman signed the presbyterian Attestation (1648) urging more effective religious discipline, and with nine others of the Taunton, Bridgwater, and Dunster classis signed a letter dated from Taunton 13 June 1649, concerning the propriety of administering the sacrament without a settled church government. On 1 July 1651, following the receipt of a petition from the mayor and inhabitants of Bridgwater against his 'malignity and disobedience' (CSP dom., 1651, 277), the council of state directed the mayor to demand that Norman take the engagement, and in the event of refusal, to instruct him to leave the town within ten days or face committal. Nevertheless, Norman's Family Governors Perswaded to Family-Godliness, signed from his study at Bridgwater on 6 April 1657, contained much advice to godly magistrates. He acted as an assistant to the Somerset commission into the ministry up to December 1657, and preached the ordination sermon at Somerton on 9 June 1658, published as Christ's Commission-Officer (1658). Norman remained at Bridgwater until ejected under the Act of Uniformity in 1662.

A close friend of Joseph *Alleine (bap. 1634, d. 1668), the ejected vicar of Taunton, Norman had married, perhaps about 1650, Alleine's sister Elizabeth (d. 1664); a son, John,

matriculated from Exeter College, Oxford, on 8 May 1669 aged seventeen. Norman and Alleine briefly shared prison accommodation at Ilchester in May 1663. He was probably the Pylades to whom Alleine, under the signature Orestes, wrote from Bath on 12 October 1668. In August 1663 Norman was fined £100 by the assizes at Taunton for preaching; since he could not pay he was sent to Ilchester gaol, where he remained for eighteen months, until Sir Matthew Hale reduced the amount of his liability. Norman is reported to have been terrified by threats of banishment, fearing that he would end his life as an indentured labourer on one of the plantations of the West Indies. Such treatment appears to have had an effect. In 1665 the authorities in the diocese of Bath and Wells were informed that in 'Weston Zoyland there resideth one Mr. Norman sometimes Lecturer in Bridgwater who is a Non-Conformist yet often times cometh to the parish church aforesayd to the Sermon but not to Divine Service' (Calamy rev., 367). Norman's second wife was a daughter of Humphrey Blake (brother of the admiral), but they cannot have been married long before he died, at Bridgwater, early in 1669. He was buried at St Mary's, Bridgwater, on 9 February. His Cases of Conscience Practically Resolved appeared posthumously in 1673.　STEPHEN WRIGHT

Sources Calamy rev., 367 · C. Stanford, Joseph Alleine: his companions and times [1861] · Foster, Alum. Oxon. · E. Calamy, ed., An abridgement of Mr. Baxter's history of his life and times, with an account of the ministers, &c., who were ejected after the Restauration of King Charles II, 2nd edn, 2 vols. (1713) · R. Baxter, T. Alleine, and G. Newton, The life and death of that excellent minister of Christ, Mr Joseph Alleine (1822) · W. A. Shaw, A history of the English church during the civil wars and under the Commonwealth, 1640–1660, 2 vols. (1900) · F. W. Weaver, ed., Somerset incumbents (privately printed, Bristol, 1889) · J. Hutchins, The history and antiquities of the county of Dorset, 3rd edn, ed. W. Shipp and J. W. Hodson, 4 vols. (1861–74)

Norman, Montagu Collet, Baron Norman (1871–1950), banker, was born on 6 September 1871 in Kensington, London, the eldest of the three children of Frederick Norman (1839–1916), barrister and banker, and Lina Susan Collet (1851–1950). He had a sister, and a brother, Ronald Norman (1873–1963), who became chairman of London county council (1918–19) and of the British Broadcasting Corporation (1935–9). Montagu Norman gained little stimulus from formal education: after four unhappy years at Eton College he spent only a year at King's College, Cambridge (1889–90).

Norman's real education was obtained during the next twelve years. In 1890 he lodged in Dresden to improve his German, later travelling around central Europe before perfecting his French in Switzerland. His values, aspirations, and early career were shaped by membership of two dynasties of City merchants and bankers. His father became a partner in Martin's Bank. His maternal grandfather, Mark Collet, to whom he was particularly close, was senior London partner in the Anglo-American merchant bank Brown, Shipley & Co. and was also, like Norman's paternal grandfather George Warde *Norman (1793–1882), a long-serving director of the Bank of England with much influence in defining its developing functions; he acted as its governor in 1887–9. Norman began

Montagu Collet Norman, Baron Norman (1871–1950), by
Augustus John, 1931

work at his father's bank in 1892, moving two years later
to his Collet grandfather's firm. In 1895 he was sent to
complete his training with its partners, Brown Brothers of
New York. Over the next four years he learned much about
Anglo-American financial relationships and American
commerce and industry, travelled to many parts of the
United States, and acquired important friends—knowledge and friendships renewed and expanded by frequent
visits in later life. Norman's family traditions also
included admiration for the army: he joined the 4th Bedfordshire and Hertfordshire militia in 1894, returned
annually from the USA for its training camps, and was promoted captain. He served with distinction in the Second
South African War in 1900–01, earning the DSO before
being invalided home with persistent gastritis. Confidence in exercising leadership under stress had been
added to an extensive financial apprenticeship.

Appointed a Brown Shipley partner before he left for
South Africa in 1900, on his return to England, Norman
soon became its most energetic member. He revealed
great skills in assessing financial propositions, expanded
the area of the bank's acceptance business, and acquired a
close understanding of the bill and exchange markets. His
tenacious grasp of orthodox banking principles led, however, to disagreement with partners seeking to diversify
the business in what he considered an unsound manner.
This, together with an absorption which fostered overwork, aggravated nervous troubles he had suffered periodically since childhood and undermined his health.
From 1911 to 1913 he was unable to work, and he suffered
further distress when the Zürich psychiatrist Carl Jung

bizarrely misdiagnosed his condition as general paralysis
of the insane (a late consequence of syphilis), and he was
given only months to live (Boyle, 90–95).

During this period Norman drifted apart from his
Brown Shipley partners, but the First World War presented alternative activities as adviser to various government departments on financial censorship and blockade,
and especially at the Bank of England. As early as 1907 his
qualities had been recognized by election to its court of
directors; now, his American expertise was invaluable in
the bank's tasks of war finance and exchange control. In
December 1915 he finally retired from Brown Shipley and
became assistant to the bank's deputy governor. He was
soon appointed to its policy-making body, the committee
of treasury, and was much involved in the sterling–dollar
exchange crises of 1916–17 and the 1917 dispute over the
powers of the governor, Walter Cunliffe. He was elected
deputy governor in late 1917 and governor in 1920.

Norman's governorship was frequently renewed, to
become the longest in the Bank of England's history. It
was also the most controversial, as the effort to cope with
immense post-war difficulties increased the impact and
public awareness of the bank's activities. He understood
the extent to which the British economy depended not
just on international trade and services but also on international systems of payment which the war had dis-
located and which remained distorted by war debts and
reparations. Consequently he believed that the recreation of an international monetary system based on
the pre-war gold standard and the revival of the international capital market would provide the necessary
framework for industrial prosperity, high employment,
and social progress, and should therefore take priority
over other economic claims. Working closely with the
League of Nations financial committee and European and
American bankers, he was prominent in successive efforts
to revise, and arrange the smooth transfer of, German
reparations, which led to the Dawes plan of 1924 and the
Young plan of 1929. In the early 1920s he also helped
orchestrate, where necessary with the aid of Bank of England loans, the re-establishment of sound currencies and
central banks in much of central Europe. This experience
was later applied to the establishment of central banks in
the dominions, and to advising upon recurrent problems
of Indian finance. By the mid-1920s Norman was the
accepted international authority on central banking practice. One of his leading principles was that monetary and
banking matters should be conducted independently of
governments, ever prone to sacrifice long-term interests
to political pressures and national rivalries. This was also
an important feature in domestic stabilization. Contrary
to Bank of England advice, in 1919 the coalition government suspended the gold standard and thereby allowed
wartime levels of inflation and public expenditure to continue. But after the brief but alarming post-war boom of
1919–20, the bank and Treasury were allowed to reimpose
financial disciplines and to work towards restoring the
gold standard, with its supposed 'automatic' mechanisms

for economic adjustment under autonomous Bank of England supervision. Norman accompanied the chancellor of the exchequer, Stanley Baldwin, at the Washington negotiations in 1923 which arranged the funding of the British war debt to the United States and helped clear the way to stabilizing the pound against the dollar. Conservative ministers and Treasury officials finally sanctioned restoration of the gold standard at the pre-war parity in April 1925.

This decision was famously criticized by J. M. Keynes, and as the British economy failed to recover significantly in the later 1920s a belief that sterling had been overvalued, unnecessarily imposing a damaging burden of high interest rates, became one of the propellants of the Keynesian revolution. Norman himself came to be regarded as bearing much of the responsibility for the inter-war mass unemployment, by putting the interests of the financial sector before those of manufacturing industry. He was sometimes represented as an archetype of the arrogance of irresponsible power, as not just misguided but dictatorial, reactionary, insensitive, and mysterious in ways linked to his supposed psychological instability. Later opening of the archives went some way towards qualifying such interpretations. For most of the 1920s the objectives of 'sound money' were supported by almost all political leaders, irrespective of party. Norman certainly dominated the bank, but he proceeded more collectively and upon wider advice and information than his predecessors. Always careful to consult his fellow directors, he implemented organizational reforms, creating a properly professional senior staff and from 1928 appointing expert economic, industrial, and foreign advisers; internal debate was encouraged, and he did not always prevail in the committee of treasury. Himself aware that the restored gold standard was not producing all the expected benefits, he presided over major innovations in practice and policy. Seeking to neutralize the effect of what were believed to be abnormal international money flows, he promoted close co-operation between the major central banks, building upon his already good relations with the Federal Reserve Bank of New York. When, with Norman's support, the Bank for International Settlements was formed in 1930 under the Young plan, he hoped it would provide a forum for even closer co-ordination. In defending sterling, the Bank of England also devised techniques which minimized the use of high bank rate and credit restriction; by 1928 Norman was writing of 'a more or less managed Currency' (Clay, 310). As the manager of the now huge government debt and through informal control of capital issues, the bank's supervision of the money markets and financial institutions was greatly extended. Norman became the father confessor to the City, accumulating unrivalled knowledge of its many activities and offering advice which individuals and institutions generally thought it best to accept. From the late 1920s the difficulties of basic industries—and a desire to forestall Labour Party demands for nationalization—drew him into mobilizing the City to help finance industrial rationalization, creating the Securities Management Trust (1929) and the Bankers' Industrial Development Company (1930), which initiated and supervised large-scale restructuring in the cotton, engineering, iron and steel, and shipbuilding industries. Norman even tried to boost consumer demand, encouraging the development of institutions to finance hire purchase. Nevertheless, the attempt to reimpose the pre-war gold standard upon transformed post-war conditions proved to be mistaken, with Norman and the Treasury underestimating the financial nationalism of other central banks and overestimating the flexibility of British industry and wage-levels.

Norman's influence owed something to an impressive presence. Tall, with a broad forehead and pointed beard, wearing his hat at a rakish angle, and seductively courteous, he reminded some of a Spanish grandee. His real power lay in tremendous grasp of complex detail, feel for the mood of the financial markets, and skilful deployment of his information and the authority of his office. Secretiveness—characterized by his occasional use of 'Mr Skinner', his secretary's name—seemed prudent to a man bearing so many secrets, and whose very movements might affect market behaviour. His understanding and powers of exposition should not be judged solely by a calamitous appearance before the (Macmillan) committee on finance and industry (1929–31), when defensiveness before his chief critics, Keynes's deployment of a newly minted theoretical model—so alien to Norman's concrete and intuitive thinking—and refusal to accept largely monetary explanations for unemployment, reduced him to monosyllables and silent gestures. Nor is it surprising that as governor he suffered one or two further nervous collapses: he bore great responsibilities and heavy workloads for a longer period than any other modern public figure.

The burdens increased sharply from 1928, when the American stock market boom threatened the sterling exchange. The 1929 Wall Street crash and the growing effects of the world depression then disrupted the work of industrial rationalization, required rescues of important financial and commercial institutions, and destabilized the international monetary system. In early 1931 Norman sponsored an impressive plan for international reflation, but it met insurmountable American and French opposition. From May there were central European banking collapses, which he struggled to contain by arranging loans to Austria and standstill agreements on funds lent to Germany. But a European liquidity crisis had begun, which from mid-July focused upon London. Since late 1930 Norman had been aware of declining foreign confidence in sterling, and he warned Labour ministers of the damaging impression created by an unbalanced government budget. Now he undertook defensive measures in co-operation with the American and French central banks, while looking to the (May) report on national expenditure to persuade the British politicians to act. But in late July the strain broke his health, and during a long convalescent visit to Canada the emergency National Government was unable to keep sterling on the gold standard.

The remarkable, but patchy, recovery of the British economy between 1932 and 1937, once free trade and the high interest rates required under the gold standard had been abandoned, helped to undermine public confidence in the orthodoxies which Norman had championed; and as the Treasury became partners in the conduct of monetary policy the Bank of England's traditional independence was reduced. But despite the collapse of much of Norman's earlier work, his knowledge and experience still seemed invaluable. He remained prominent in industrial restructuring and helped repair the damage to some City institutions and to central European finance. During 1932 the establishment of the Exchange Equalisation Account enabled the sterling exchanges to be stabilized, and the long-planned conversion of war loan brought cheap money. After the 1933 World Economic Conference failed to agree upon a new international monetary regime, Norman accepted the informal creation of a sterling area and encouraged negotiations which in 1936 produced the tripartite monetary agreement for co-operation with the Americans and French. As the European diplomatic crisis unfolded in the late 1930s, he was principally responsible for preparing the battery of controls which ensured that the outbreak of war did not bring the financial chaos experienced in 1914. From 1939 his advice helped prevent wartime inflation, and during 1943 he began organizing City support for post-war industrial reconstruction. But in early 1944 illness forced his retirement. A privy councillor since 1923, he now accepted a peerage (having declined one twenty years earlier), and became Baron Norman of St Clere.

In 1933 Norman married Priscilla Cecilia Maria, *née* Reyntiens (1899–1991), the divorced wife of Alexander Koch Worsthorne. A London county councillor from 1925 to 1933, after Norman's death she became chairman of the National Association for Mental Health, and was made CBE in 1963. Her two sons—Norman's stepsons—were Simon Towneley (surname adopted by royal licence, 1955), appointed lord lieutenant of Lancashire in 1976, and Sir Peregrine Worsthorne, editor of the *Sunday Telegraph* and writer. Norman himself had no children, and his peerage became extinct when, after a stroke, he died at his home, Thorpe Lodge, Campden Hill, London, on 4 February 1950.   PHILIP WILLIAMSON

Sources H. Clay, *Lord Norman* (1957) · M. Moss, 'Norman, Montagu Collet', *DBB* · R. S. Sayers, *The Bank of England, 1891–1944*, 3 vols. (1976) · D. E. Moggridge, *British monetary policy, 1924–1931: the Norman conquest of $4.86* (1972) · S. V. O. Clarke, *Central bank co-operation, 1924–31* (1967) · P. Clarke, *The Keynesian revolution in the making, 1924–1936* (1988) · A. Boyle, *Montagu Norman* (1967) · *The Times* (6 Feb 1950) · S. Howson, *Domestic monetary management in Britain, 1919–38* (1975) · I. M. Drummond, *The floating pound and the sterling area, 1931–1939* (1981) · R. W. D. Boyce, *British capitalism at the crossroads, 1919–1932* (1987) · P. Williamson, *National crisis and national government: British politics, the economy and empire, 1926–1932* (1992) · Venn, *Alum. Cant.* · d. cert.
Archives Bank of England Archive, London [photocopies] · CKS, scrapbook · priv. coll. | Bank of England, Bank MSS · Bank of England, Governor's MSS · BL OIOC, corresp. with Sir Basil Blackett, MS Eur. E 397 · BLPES, letters to Edwin Cannan · Federal Reserve Bank of New York, archives · Federal Reserve Bank of New York, George Harrison MSS · Federal Reserve Bank of New York, Benjamin Strong MSS · NA Scot., corresp. with Lord Lothian · SOAS, letters to Sir Charles Addis
Likenesses P. A. de Laszlo, portrait, 1919, Bank of England, London · A. K. Lawrence, group portrait, mural, c.1927–1930 (*Committee of Treasury, 1928*), Bank of England, London · A. K. Lawrence, oils, c.1928, Bank of England, London · J. Guthrie, oils, 1929, Bank of England, London · W. Stoneman, photograph, 1930, NPG · A. John, portrait, 1931, Bank of England, London [*see illus.*] · K. Kennet, bronze head, c.1937–1938, Bank of England, London · H. Coster, photograph, 1942, Bank of England, London · Karsh, photographs, 1942, Bank of England, London · C. Wheeler, bronze bust, c.1945–1946, Bank of England, London · C. Wheeler, Portland stone statue, 1946, Bank of England, London
Wealth at death £253,316 4s. 1d.: probate, 1 March 1950, *CGPLA Eng. & Wales*

Norman, Sir Richard Oswald Chandler (1932–1993), scientist and university teacher, was born on 27 April 1932 in Norbury, London, the only child of Oswald George Norman (1890–1941), bank manager, and his wife, Violet Maud, *née* Chandler (1901–1981). He was educated at Durston House preparatory school in Ealing, and St Paul's School, London. It was there that he became interested in science and caught an infectious enthusiasm for chemistry from Jack Strawson, who taught him in the upper school. He played cricket for the first eleven and subsequently became captain of the school. He won a Brackenbury scholarship in chemistry to Balliol College, Oxford, and matriculated in 1951. His career at Oxford was meteoric: he won the Gibbs scholarship in 1954 and obtained a top first in 1955. He then studied for his doctorate under W. A. (Alec) Walters, using continuous flow mixing techniques to study rapid free radical reactions. It was the influence of Walters and also of his other tutor, R. P. (Ronnie) Bell, that determined the course of much of the subsequent work that he did, both at Oxford and York.

In 1957, despite opposition from the chemical establishment, Norman was made a fellow of Merton College and rapidly built up a high-class research team. He also became a brilliant lecturer and an inspiring tutor. His abilities were recognized by Eric James, who persuaded Norman to start the chemistry department at the newly founded University of York. There Norman established an international reputation for the quality of his work on the mechanisms of organic reactions. This was further enhanced by his publication (with Roger Taylor) of *Electrophilic Substitution in Benzenoid Compounds* (1964) and (as sole author) *Principles of Organic Synthesis* (1968); the latter became a standard undergraduate text for the next two decades.

Norman was always intensely keen on teaching, both in the department at York and in the wider field of education in schools. *Modern Organic Chemistry* (1972), written in collaboration with David Waddington, brought an up-to-date rigour to A level school chemistry and helped to make the chemistry department at York one of the most sought after in the country. He consolidated this interest by his work with the Salters' Company, who set up research grants for teachers and financed the new A level courses, first in chemistry and subsequently in all three major sciences. Nor were his interests restricted to York: he was

Sir Richard Oswald Chandler Norman (1932–1993), by unknown photographer

president of the Royal Institute of Chemistry, and of the Royal Society of Chemistry, formed after the amalgamation of the institute with the Chemical Society in 1980. On 30 December 1982 he married Jennifer Margaret Tope (b. 1942), a university administrator whom he met at the University of York. It was characteristic that they married quietly when on holiday in Jerusalem. There were no children. She proved to be an ideal companion for the extensive entertaining associated with Norman's work. Her wide interests, particularly in music, also provided a contrast to Norman's scientific work and helped make him accessible to a wider range of people.

In 1983 Norman became chief scientific adviser to the Ministry of Defence and it was there that his capacity for getting the best results out of committee work became apparent. For him the role of the committee was publicly to endorse a consensus that had been arrived at by detailed and persuasive discussion with the main protagonists. In this way he cut through unnecessary red tape, quickly produced results, and alienated few people. A colleague emphasized the even-handed and impartial way he treated everyone; he was not a prime mover and shaker but if there was a consensus for change he speedily brought it to fruition. After five years as a civil servant Norman returned to Oxford as rector of Exeter College. He loved being close to students and took personal responsibility for them as tutor for graduates. He and his wife offered hospitality to every student every year, a quite remarkable achievement. He was made a fellow of the Royal Society in 1977 and appointed KBE in 1987.

Norman was of an athletic build. The large horn-rimmed glasses that he wore throughout his life gave him an owlish appearance and contributed to his aura of scholarly wisdom. He was warm-hearted and friendly, a convivial host who always found time to talk to everyone, making each of them feel individually valued. Apart from being a stylish cricketer and an accomplished bridge player, he was a keen gardener and an expert photographer, particularly in portraiture. When asked how he managed to become competent in so many fields he replied that after *reading* chemistry at Oxford, he could find out anything he wanted by using a book. His ability to digest large quantities of material, for example *Chemical Abstracts*, was phenomenal, and yet he tempered his intellectual powers with a humanity which made him accessible to a wide variety of people. He was a man of absolute

integrity based on the Christian principles he learned early in his life. He had the happy knack of being at the right place at the right time, and could count on support from family, colleagues, and friends whenever he needed it. He had a happy and varied life, marred only by the shortness of time he had as rector of Exeter. He had an operation for cancer of the bile-duct in 1987 and this may have been the cause of the pulmonary embolism that struck him in June 1993. He died at the John Radcliffe Hospital, Oxford, on 6 June 1993. The chapel was so crowded at his funeral that many stood in the antechapel. He was cremated at Oxford on 14 June. On 27 September a memorial service was held in St Mary's, the university church, which was packed with friends, many going back to his schooldays.   D. E. P. HUGHES

Sources personal knowledge (2004) · private information (2004) [R. Barrow, R. Farrow, N. Hughes, J. M. Norman] · D. Waddington, *Memoirs FRS*, 43 (1997), 335–47 · D. Waddington, Memorial service address, 27 Sept 1993 · *The Times* (19 June 1993) · *Daily Telegraph* (22 June 1993) · *The Independent* (12 June 1993) · *The Guardian* (16 June 1993) · *WWW* · b. cert. · d. cert.
Archives University of York | FILM Open University, Milton Keynes, videotape, ESR spectroscopy
Likenesses photographs, 1957–66, Hult. Arch. · T. Coates, oils, Exeter College, Oxford · photograph, News International Syndication, London [*see illus.*] · photograph, repro. in *The Independent* (16 April 1993)
Wealth at death £380,465: probate, 15 July 1993, *CGPLA Eng. & Wales*

Norman, Robert (*fl.* 1560–1584), maker of mathematical instruments, whose origins are unknown, spent, by his own account, eighteen or twenty years at sea before settling down as a compass maker and self-styled 'hydrographer' at Ratcliff, London. Most of what is known about him comes from his own publications, in particular *The Newe Attractive*, which appeared in London in 1581. The title-page announced Norman's discovery of magnetic inclination or dip; in his terminology this was called the 'declining' of the needle from the horizontal. He made variation compasses, as well as common steering compasses, and designed the first dip circle for measuring inclination. He judged that any theory of magnetic variation, a measurement he considered useful for position finding as well as necessary for the management of the steering compass, would have also to take account of inclination; from reports and observations of both these variables he drew general conclusions regarding the contested explanations of the earth's magnetism. Norman added astronomical and calendaric tables to his book, including daily values for solar declination over four years, calculated by himself and essential for finding latitude from the noonday altitude of the sun. He was encouraged in his magnetic work by William Borough, comptroller of the navy, to whom he dedicated *The Newe Attractive*; Borough's own *Discourse of the Variation of the Cumpas* was published with it as an appendix.

Norman's second work, *The Safegard of Sailers, or, Great Rutter*, was published in London in 1584. It is a manual of coastal navigation, for the most part translated by Norman from Dutch sources, but containing some additions of his own. It was dedicated to Charles Howard, earl of Nottingham and lord high admiral of England. Norman may have been the editor of a 1607 London edition of an English translation of Jean de Cartigny's *The Voyage of the Wandering Knight*. The dedication to Sir Francis Drake, signed by R. N., is sometimes attributed to the gunner Robert Norton, but it is closer to the style of Norman, and he is identified by an early hand in a copy in Cambridge University Library. One chart by Norman, of the outer Thames estuary, was preserved at Hatfield House. Nothing is known of his later life or of his death.

Norman has attracted considerable interest on account of his self-conscious adoption of an experimental approach and his unusual application of instruments. He was deploying his dip circle at a time when instruments were associated not with natural philosophy but with applications of mathematics to practical arts. He was sensitive that, as an 'unlearned mechanician', he would scarcely have been expected to concern himself with an area of practical mathematics relevant to natural philosophy, but he vigorously asserted the worth of investigations by practical men, who had the relevant art 'at their fingers ends', while their more learned critics were 'in their studies amongst their bookes'. Norman saw himself and his fellow mechanics as heirs to the vernacular tradition of mathematical publication, exemplified by the works of Robert Recorde and Billingsley's English translation of Euclid.   J. A. BENNETT

Sources E. G. R. Taylor, *The mathematical practitioners of Tudor and Stuart England* (1954); repr. (1970) · D. W. Waters, *The art of navigation in England in Elizabethan and early Stuart times*, 2nd edn (1978) · *An Elizabethan in 1582: the diary of Richard Madox, fellow of All Souls*, ed. E. S. Donno, Hakluyt Society, 2nd ser., 147 (1976) · R. Norman, *The newe attractive* (1581)

Norman, Tom [*real name* Thomas Noakes] (1860–1930), showman and freak show proprietor, was born on 7 May 1860 at the Manor House, Dallington, Sussex, the eldest of the seventeen children of Thomas Noakes (1835–1903), master butcher and farmer, and his wife, Eliza Haiselden (1840–1911). According to his own manuscript autobiography he left home at fourteen and found employment as a butcher's assistant in London. He first became involved in showbusiness in 1878 when he went into partnership with a showman who had a 'penny gaff' or freak show shop in Islington, exhibiting Mdlle Electra. Records are unclear about when Tom Noakes started exhibiting under the name Norman, as a freak show proprietor also named Norman was a regular visitor to the World's Fair held annually at the Royal Agricultural Hall in Islington from 1873 onwards (Connell, 1973). That show, which probably became his, included Norman's Performing Fishes—which could reputedly not only talk but play the pianoforte—and Norman's French Artillery Giant Horse. In addition Norman's Panorama was a regular attraction at fairs around the country and at the Royal Agricultural Hall.

By 1882 the young aspiring showman had been involved in exhibiting Eliza Jenkins, the Skeleton Woman, and the Balloon Headed Baby in shop premises throughout London. Such was the popularity of these shows that by the mid-1880s Norman claims to have operated thirteen shop shows in Hammersmith and five shops in Nottingham and exhibited freak shows at fairs and shop venues throughout the United Kingdom. His motto was 'It was not the show, it was the tale that you told', and such was his oratorical skill and 'silver tongue', that in 1882 P. T. Barnum is said to have named him the Silver King after attending his show at the Royal Agricultural Hall.

By 1883 Norman had penny gaff shops throughout London in such locations as Whitechapel, Hammersmith, Croydon, and in the Edgware Road. In November 1884 he exhibited Joseph *Merrick—the Elephant Man—at his shop at 123 Whitechapel Road, London, on behalf of a consortium of London showmen. This episode in Norman's life is shrouded in controversy; in his autobiography published in 1923 Sir Frederick Treeves blackened the showman's character by portraying him as a ruthless drunkard; this was rebutted by Norman in a letter published in the *World's Fair* newspaper in the same year.

Over the next decade Norman managed a troupe of midgets, as well as exhibiting the famous Man in a Trance show at Nottingham goose fair in 1892; Mary Anne Bevan, the World's Ugliest Woman; John Chambers, the Armless Carpenter; and also Leonine, the Lion Faced Lady. In January 1893 he advertised his travelling concerns and living carriage for sale in *The Era* as he was leaving for Chicago (although he did not in the event go). Items for sale included a flea circus, novelty booth, and oilcloth banners advertising the Skeleton Girl and fat women (*The Era*, 28 Jan 1893). By 1893 he had become actively involved in both the temperance movement and the newly formed United Kingdom Van Dwellings Association, the trade association of travelling showpeople; he served as the latter's vice president. In 1894 he appeared at Nottingham goose fair with a Midget Show and in 1895 with Norman's Varieties. Other ventures included the Bear Lady at Nottingham in 1899 and the famous Electrograph Show.

In 1896 Norman married Amy Rayner (d. 1943), a theatrical performer at the Royal Agricultural Hall. They had six sons and four daughters, and their marriage lasted until his death in 1930. By 1900 Norman had also become an auctioneer, and the first show he sold belonged to Fred and George Ginnett. He advertised in both *The Era* and *The Showman* newspapers as the recognized showman's auctioneer and valuer. Early clients included in 1902 W. T. Kirkland who had concessions at Southport, Morecambe, and New Brighton. Norman subsequently instituted the annual showman and travellers' auction sales in London, Manchester, and Liverpool from 1903 onwards. One of his most famous auctions was the disposal of Lord George Sanger's zoo at Margate in 1905. This was followed by what Tom Norman described 'as the crowning point in my life as regards the auctioneering business', when he was called upon by Sanger to offer in auction the whole of his travelling circus effects.

By 1915 the Norman family was firmly based in Beddington Lane, Croydon, but the business was inevitably affected by the onset of the First World War. Norman began to dispose of some of his business concerns when his eldest son enlisted. The shops for sale included 'Tom Normans New Exhibition' with waxworks and novelty museum, and also the Croydon Central Auction Rooms. He gradually retired from the travelling business to concentrate on supplying horses for circuses and pantomimes. However, in 1919 he returned to showbusiness and appeared at the Olympia circus with Phoebe the Strange Girl, and also exhibited at Birmingham and Margate in 1921. Throughout the 1920s he still put on shows at the Christmas fair held at the Royal Agricultural Hall. He died in Croydon Hospital, on 24 August 1930, while making plans to travel with a large auction show around the country. His funeral at Mitcham Road cemetery three days later was attended by many leading showmen. A fitting tribute—'All his life he has been a showman and as such he died' (*World's Fair*, Aug 30, 1930)—appeared in the trade press.   VANESSA TOULMIN

Sources Tom Norman MSS, University of Sheffield, National Fairground Archive, Norman family collection · *The penny showman: memoirs of Tom Norman 'Silver King'* (privately printed, 1985) · Goose Fair, programme of amusements with a map of the city, 1899, Nottingham Central Library, L38.93 · Goose Fair handbills, Nottingham Central Library, L38.93 · S. Race, diary, Notts. Arch., M24.480/A/8 · M. Howell and P. Ford, *The true history of the Elephant Man*, rev. edn (1983) · J. Connell, *The Royal Agricultural Hall* (1973) · *The Showman* (11 Jan 1901) [advert for Tom Norman, auctioneer] · *The Era* (28 Jan 1893) [for sale advertisements] · *The Era* (23 Oct 1915) [for sale advertisements] · 'Silver King: the passing of Mr Tom Norman', *World's Fair* (30 Aug 1930) · K. Scrivens and S. Smith, *The travelling cinematograph show* (1999) · F. Treeves, *The Elephant Man and other reminiscences* (1923) · PRO, Ref. RG11, piece 1035, fol. 31, p. 11 · T. Horne, ed., *The United Kingdom and Van Dwellers Protection Association Yearbook, 1900* (1900)
Archives University of Sheffield, National Fairground Archive, MSS | Nottingham Central Library, Goose Fair handbills, L38.93
Likenesses photographs, University of Sheffield

Normanbrook. For this title name *see* Brook, Norman Craven, Baron Normanbrook (1902–1967).

Normanby. For this title name *see* Phipps, Constantine Henry, first marquess of Normanby (1797–1863); Phipps, George Augustus Constantine, second marquess of Normanby (1819–1890).

Normand, Sir Charles William Blyth (1889–1982), meteorologist, was born on 10 September 1889 in Edinburgh, the youngest of four sons of John Hodge Normand, pharmaceutical chemist, and his wife, Mary Baxter, the daughter of a ship's captain; both parents were natives of Fife. He entered the Royal High School in Edinburgh in 1901. He was awarded a Heriot bursary to Edinburgh University in 1906, and in 1911 took his MA degree with first-class honours in mathematics and natural philosophy, and also the BSc with advanced chemistry, based on research supported by a Hope prize. In 1913 he was offered the post of imperial meteorologist in India. When he reported for duty in Simla, then the headquarters of the meteorological department, he had no knowledge of the subject; he had to learn it by reading, guided by senior staff.

In 1916 Normand joined the Indian army reserve of officers and was posted to Mesopotamia as meteorological officer; he was mentioned in dispatches. The effects of the severe climate on his fellow soldiers caught his attention. He was able to develop his consequent ideas on atmospheric humidity after April 1919 when he resumed his post in Simla. This work formed the content of his first meteorological papers (1921), and also of his Edinburgh DSc thesis (1921). With related problems of atmospheric thermodynamics, it interested him for the rest of his life. In 1920 he married Alison (d. 1953), daughter of James MacLennan of Nairnshire. They had two sons, the elder of whom died in a motor accident in 1960.

In 1927 Normand was appointed director-general of observatories in India, and in the same year the meteorological department moved to its new headquarters in Poona. During the next seventeen years Normand presided over massive and almost continuous expansion. He saw the department totally Indianized. After his retirement in 1944 he stayed on in the department as officer on special duty for maintaining liaison with military organizations. He left India in 1945. In the spring of 1946 Normand received an unexpected invitation from Professor G. M. B. Dobson at Oxford to join in his work on atmospheric ozone. The two men were congenial and complementary partners, and Dobson's small private laboratory on Shotover Hill became a centre of international importance. In 1948 the International Ozone Commission was formed, with Dobson as president and Normand as secretary (until 1959). The spectrophotometer designed by Dobson in the 1920s was greatly improved (with the assistance of R. H. Kay), so that by the start of the International Geophysical Year in 1956 there were about fifty instruments in action, almost all of which had been to Shotover to be checked, calibrated, and compared with Dobson's own instrument. Normand undertook the bulk of the extensive and often tedious calculations (which Dobson detested) produced by all this work.

In 1931 and 1938 Normand was president of the mathematics and physics section of the Indian Science Congress. He was a founder member of the Indian Academy of Sciences and in 1938 was appointed CIE. He was awarded the Symons gold medal of the Royal Meteorological Society in 1944. He was knighted in 1945 and in 1953 the American Meteorological Association elected him an honorary member. From 1951 to 1953 he was president of the Royal Meteorological Society, which made him an honorary fellow in 1976. After a severe attack of bronchitis in 1959, he moved to Winchester, where he died on 25 October 1982.   C. D. WALSHAW, *rev.*

Sources *Hundred years of weather service, 1875–1975* (1976) [pubd by India Meteorological Department] · G. M. B. Dobson, 'Forty years' research on atmospheric ozone at Oxford', *Applied Optics*, 7 (1968), 387–405 · D. Walshaw, 'G. M. B. Dobson — the man and his work', *Planetary and Space Science*, 37 (1989), 1485–1507 · personal knowledge (1993) · *CGPLA Eng. & Wales* (1982)
Likenesses photograph, repro. in *Quarterly Journal of the Royal Meteorological Society*, 79 (1953), facing p. 463 [pl. 5]
Wealth at death £43,718: probate, 9 Dec 1982, *CGPLA Eng. & Wales*

Normand, Wilfrid Guild, Baron Normand (1884–1962), judge, was born at Aberdour, Fife, on 16 May 1884, the youngest son of Patrick Hill Normand (1843–1910), linen merchant and manufacturer, and his wife, Ellen Prentice (d. 1900). He followed four brothers to Fettes College, and in 1902 went on to Oriel College, Oxford, where he obtained a first in *literae humaniores* in 1906; he then went to Paris University and, finally, to Edinburgh University, where he graduated LLB in 1910. So reserved and scholarly was Normand at this stage that few would have predicted for him exceptional success in high office. In 1910 he was admitted to the Faculty of Advocates, and quickly established a busy junior practice. On 22 July 1913 Normand married Gertrude, daughter of William Lawson, banker, of New York, they had a son and a daughter.

Normand's legal career was interrupted by service as an officer in the Royal Engineers from 1915 to 1918. On his return to the Scottish bar after the war he developed a substantial practice, particularly in the shipping and commercial field, and took silk in 1925. As editor of the *Juridical Review* in the early 1920s he contributed also to legal scholarship. His wife having died in 1923 he married, on 27 April 1927, Marion Bell Gilchrist (d. 1972), daughter of David Cunningham, farmer, of Aberdour.

In 1929 Normand was solicitor-general for Scotland for a few weeks, and he resumed that office after the general election of 1931, when he was elected Unionist member of parliament for West Edinburgh. His was the responsibility as solicitor-general to pilot through parliament the important Administration of Justice (Scotland) Act of 1933, which still basically regulates procedure in the Court of Session. He was appointed lord advocate and sworn of the privy council in 1933, and in 1934 was elected an honorary bencher of the Middle Temple. He vacated his parliamentary seat in 1935, when he succeeded Lord Clyde as lord justice-general and lord president of the Court of Session. He presided in the highest courts in Scotland until 1947, when he was appointed a lord of appeal-in-ordinary, an office from which he retired in 1953—although he continued to sit from time to time thereafter both in House of Lords appeals and in the judicial committee of the privy council. In January 1947 he was created a life peer.

Normand's high reputation as an appellate judge in London and Edinburgh is assured, and it was as such that he was happiest in his professional career. The administrative duties of lord president he did not find very congenial. Moreover he preferred dealing with legal principles rather than with the weaknesses and shortcomings of men and women. Thus as lord advocate he did not relish his responsibilities for criminal prosecutions, nor did he enjoy the earthier aspect of practice at the bar; his was a specialist rather than a general purposes practice. On the other hand he was keenly interested in the art of pleading, himself favouring clear, unemotional, and concise exposition. He often quoted the advice of a well-known dean of the Faculty of Advocates, Condie Sandeman: 'If you have thought of anything good to say the night before your speech, don't say it.' A typical example of Normand's style was *Cantiere San Rocco, S.A.* v. *Clyde Shipbuilding and Engineering Co. Ltd.* (1923), a case of unjustified enrichment,

where Normand was led by Sandeman. English authorities might have been fatal to this case and Normand therefore argued the appeal in the House of Lords on Scottish and Roman law authorities, translating the *Digest* with successful effect. It was painful to Normand, but characteristic, that as lord advocate he refused to recommend his friend Sandeman for elevation to the bench after the latter had allowed his name to be used by a company, the administration of which had been criticized judicially in England.

As a judge in the House of Lords, Normand employed his grasp of principles and his powers of reasoning to expound Scots law and English law with authority so as to influence substantially the course of foreseeable legal development. The House of Lords having since 1966 reclaimed its earlier freedom to depart from its own precedents, the quality of individual decisions rather than the fact that the House of Lords has spoken has greater importance. Normand fulfilled admirably the special responsibility of a Scottish lord of appeal in recognizing the areas in which Scottish and English solutions may or must be harmonized and areas in which divergences must be stressed. No legal nationalist, he was vigilant for the best interests of Scots law in a United Kingdom setting. Thus he accepted reluctantly (and with sympathy for the Court of Session, whom he overruled) the statutory anomaly that for fiscal purposes Scottish charities must conform to the requirements of a statute of the Tudor Elizabeth. On the other hand, in *A.G.* v. *Prince Ernest Augustus of Hanover* (1957) judicially (but more vehemently extrajudicially) he deplored the attitude of the attorney-general, who was apparently prepared to accept that pre-union English statutes could confer British nationality while pre-union Scottish acts could not; the anomalous outcome was apparently that the prince became British in England only.

Normand was distinguished in appearance and bearing, and had a fine head of white hair to the end. Throughout his life he was recognizably a Scot in speech and outlook. Although he might on first impression seem reserved and austere he could be most courteous and charming in public and in private, and warmed in scholarly circles. During his six years' sojourn in London he was always happy to return home to Scotland, and it was there that he spent nearly a decade in retirement. These years enabled him to pursue those many scholarly interests that he had always maintained. He was an active trustee of the National Library of Scotland from its foundation in 1925 until his death, and in 1950–53 was a trustee of the British Museum. He was active as chairman of the trustees of the Scottish Museum of Antiquities and of the Carnegie Trust for the Scottish Universities. He served in the capacity of president of the Classical Association of Scotland, of the International Law Association, of the Stair Society, and of the Scottish Universities Law Institute—which he conceived to revive contemporary Scottish legal literature. His scholarship did not lack official recognition: he was an honorary LLD of Edinburgh, and an honorary fellow of Oriel College, Oxford, and of University College, London, which he served as chairman of its college committee during the era of post-war reconstruction. Somewhat fastidious in extrovert society, he enjoyed the company of scholars old and young. At his death he was working with Dr J. C. Corson, of Edinburgh University, on notes to the legal references in the works of Sir Walter Scott; these are deposited in the National Library of Scotland. He died in Edinburgh on 5 October 1962.　　　T. B. SMITH, *rev.*

Sources *The Times* (8 Oct 1962) · *Scots Law Times* (1935), News, 113 · *Scots Law Times* (1947), News, 1 · *Scots Law Times* (1962), News, 148 · *Glasgow Herald* (6 Oct 1962) · personal knowledge (1981, 2004) · private information (1981, 2004) · *CGPLA Eng. & Wales* (1962)
Wealth at death £67,098 18s. 0d.: confirmation, 13 Nov 1962, CCI

Normandy, Alphonse René Le Mire de (1809–1864), chemist, was born at Rouen on 23 October 1809. The name de Normandy, indicating his country of origin, was probably added to his surname after he moved to England, though his children dropped the use of 'de'. He originally trained for the medical profession but during these studies he became attracted to chemistry, and on the completion of his medical course he went to Germany and studied under Leopold Gmelin. He took out a British patent in 1839 (no. 8175) for indelible inks and dyes, and in 1841 he patented a method of hardening soap made from what were known as 'soft goods' by the addition of sulphate of soda (no. 9081). However, for some years he was prevented from using the process by the excise, who regarded the addition of sodium sulphate as an adulteration. The restriction was at length removed, and the patent was prolonged by the privy council in 1855 for three years to compensate him for the difficulties which had been thrown in his way. In the two patents Normandy was described as 'MD, of Rouen', with a temporary residence in London, but he seems to have moved to England permanently about 1843, taking up his residence at Dalston, and subsequently at 67 Judd Street, Brunswick Square, London, where he lived until 1860.

Normandy had a complicated and probably painful family life, about which little is known with certainty. In his will of 20 October 1860 he formally recognized three children, Alphonse Louis Le Mire Normandy (*b.* 1838), Louise Isabelle Le Mire Normandy (*b.* 1841), and Frank Normandy (*b.* 1850), stating that the need for this arose 'owing to my ignorance of the formalities to be accomplished' in the particular circumstances of their birth; national registration came into effect at that time, and as a consequence only the third child was properly registered as his. He named their mother as Miss Louise Taynton; from the domestic details given it seems that she was either no longer alive or not living as part of the Normandy family. It is not clear if he was ever formally married to her—she is referred to throughout by her maiden name. However, from the fact that his children were apparently known by the surname Le Mire Normandy it would seem that they were not generally regarded as illegitimate. He admonished his children not to have anything to do with their mother's family, the Tayntons, whom he described as 'dangerous persons' who had been 'the cause of intense

misery to their mother and me'; and begged of them, somewhat pathetically, that after his death they should move in together and live as one household, 'in peace and harmony', together with his own mother, who was then still alive.

Normandy invented an apparatus for distilling sea water to obtain drinking water which was commonly used on board ship, and which formed the subject of a patent granted in 1851 (no. 13714); between 1852 and 1861 six further patents were taken out for improvements to the device. Its merit lay in conducting the operation at a low temperature and causing the condensed water to absorb a large quantity of atmospheric air, which rendered it more palatable. A medal was awarded to him for this apparatus at the exhibition of 1862. The manufacture of these stills became an important business, which was carried on near the Victoria Docks by Normandy's Patent Marine Aerated Fresh Water Company.

Normandy wrote a number of important textbooks on analytical chemistry. Although he only produced one scientific paper, 'The spheroidal state of water in steam boilers' (*Philosophical Magazine*, 7, 1854, 283), he made significant contributions to the subject, reported via his texts. His *Guide to the Alkalimetric Chest* (1849) was one of the first texts on volumetric analysis *per se*. In the influential text *Commercial Hand-Book of Chemical Analysis* (1850) he described some of the earliest quantitative colorimetric assays of products of commerce (indigo, madder, and saffron or crocus) using apparatus based on the design of J. J. Houton de Labillardière, and one of the first applications of microscopy for the detection and description of adulteration of starches (such as potato flour in wheat flour).

Normandy was an intimate friend and associate of Andrew Ure and contributed to the fifth edition of *Ure's Dictionary of Arts, Manufacturers and Mines*; his last literary work was to produce material for the sixth edition (1867). For some years he had a considerable practice as a consulting and analytical chemist. In 1855 and 1856 he gave some then startling evidence before a committee of the House of Commons on the adulteration of food with particular reference to the use of alum in the manufacture of bread. He was elected a fellow of the Chemical Society on 20 May 1854. He died at his home, Odin Lodge, King's Road, Clapham Park, London, on 10 May 1864.

R. B. PROSSER, *rev.* D. T. BURNS

Sources *JCS*, 18 (1865), 345 · J. C. Poggendorff and others, eds., *Biographisch-literarisches Handwörterbuch zur Geschichte der exacten Wissenschaften*, 2 vols. (Leipzig, 1863) · 'Normandy's soap patent: before the judicial committee of the privy council', *Mechanics' Magazine*, 63 (1855), 56–7 · *Mechanics' Magazine*, new ser., 11 (1864), 347 · *The Lancet* (21 May 1864), 598–9 · will, 20 Oct 1860 · d. cert.
Likenesses wood-engraving, NPG; repro. in *ILN* (23 July 1864), 105
Wealth at death under £9000: administration, 24 June 1864, *CGPLA Eng. & Wales*

Normanton. For this title name *see* Agar, Charles, first earl of Normanton (1736–1809).

Normanton, Helena Florence (1882–1957), barrister and feminist campaigner, was born on 14 December 1882 in

Helena Florence Normanton (1882–1957), by Elliott & Fry, 1945

London, the eldest of two daughters of William Alexander Normanton (1853–1886), pianoforte manufacturer, and his wife, Jane Amelia (1850–1900), daughter of Thomas William *Marshall and his wife, Harriet. When Helena was aged four, her father was found dead in mysterious circumstances with a broken neck in a railway tunnel. Her mother sought respectable ways to support her daughters, letting rooms of the family home at 30 Willington Street, Woolwich, to the wives of officers, but soon moved to Brighton where she ran a small general (grocery) store and later turned the family home at 4 Clifton Place into a modest boarding-house.

Education and admission to the bar Helena Normanton excelled at school and in 1896 won a scholarship to York Place Science School in Brighton, the forerunner of Varndean School for Girls. In July 1900 she left as a pupil teacher, and after her mother's death she helped to run the family's boarding-house before leaving Brighton to accept a place at a teachers' training college at Edge Hill, Liverpool (1903–5). She lectured, predominantly in history, at both Glasgow and London universities, and was for a time tutor to the sons of the baron de Forest, a Liberal MP.

During the period up to 1918 Helena Normanton appears to have combined a teaching career with a developing interest in the position of women, becoming a prolific writer and public speaker on feminist issues, and furthering her own education, reading for a history degree at London University (passing with first-class honours), and

holding a diploma in French language, literature, and history from Dijon University. Described by her niece Elsie Cannon as a 'suffragette—though not of the ultramilitant kind', she was active in the campaign to extend the franchise to women. Perhaps drawing on her own childhood experiences she recognized that many women and children could not rely, as society then expected, on a morally responsible male capable of providing financial security. On 1914 she published a pamphlet entitled *Sex Differentiation in Salary* arguing for equal pay for equal work. On the front cover a 'Special War Notice' challenged readers to consider the plight of female headed households: 'During and after a war, many soldiers' wives and widows become the breadwinners for families. Should they be paid according to their sex or their work?' Pamphlets advertising public meetings organized by the Women's Freedom League throughout 1919 list Helena Normanton as a speaker and she was also an ardent and practical supporter of the Indian National Congress and editor of its London-based organ *India* (1918–20).

In the preface to her book *Everyday Law for Women* (1932) Normanton wrote that she conceived the ambition of becoming a barrister at the age of twelve during a visit to a lawyer with her mother. Her first application to be admitted to the Middle Temple, in 1918, was presented immediately after the enfranchisement of women became law but was unanimously refused. Undeterred, and supported by the Women's Freedom League, she lodged a petition against the benchers' decision at the House of Lords. However, before the date fixed for its hearing, the Sex Disqualification (Removal) Bill (1919) was introduced which allowed women entry to the legal profession; the press attributed its enactment in large part to her campaign. On Christmas eve 1919, within forty-eight hours of the passing of the new act, she made a second application to the Middle Temple, and was successful. She became the first woman to be admitted to the Middle Temple as a student to the bar. Unusually, she took the three compulsory parts of the bar examination simultaneously, passing with first-class marks in one part and second-class marks in the other two. She was called to the bar on 17 November 1922, a few months after Ivy Williams had become the first woman to do so.

The pioneering barrister On 26 October 1921, while a bar student, Helena Normanton married Gavin Bowman Watson Clark (1873–1948), son of the Scottish politician Gavin Brown Clark, and her application to retain her maiden name after her marriage attracted considerable public interest. Helena deplored the loss of a woman's identity on marriage and its disadvantageous legal results. While she believed in the respectability of retaining the title Mrs she also wished to maintain continuity of identity in her professional career. She was the first married British woman to be issued a passport in her maiden name (1924) and also fought for the right of women who married foreigners to retain their British nationality. Later in life she quipped, 'Anne Boleyn did not change her name even though she married the King. He at least had the decency to leave her with her own name even though he took her head' (*Yorkshire Post*, 26 March 1954). The couple had no children.

Despite the many barriers Helena forged a successful legal career that included some notable 'firsts'. She was the first woman to obtain a divorce for a client and to lead the prosecution in a murder trial (May 1948). She was the first female counsel in cases in the High Court of Justice (1922), the Old Bailey (1924), and the London sessions (1926). In a breach of promise case she obtained for her client the highest damages in such a case obtained by a woman up to that date—£1250 and costs. In 1925 she became the first woman to conduct a case in the United States, appearing in the test case in which a married woman's right to retain her maiden name was confirmed. In 1949, with Rose Heilbron, she became the first female king's counsel.

Despite these achievements, Normanton felt betrayed by members of the legal profession who fabricated myths that were damaging to her career. Charges of advertising (forbidden by legal etiquette) were made against her, as the notoriety she had gained from her writing, public speaking, and feminist activities ensured that as one of the first women to be admitted to the bar she was a focus of (unwanted) attention. Believing that these rumours had led to the rejection of her application to practise on the western circuit, in April 1923 she requested the bar council to hold a full inquiry into whether she had ever advertised herself. She called attention to the way in which male barristers used their relatives as vehicles for self-promotion, and supplied documents indicating the great trouble she had taken in trying to minimize public scrutiny. She curtailed her public speaking engagements, forfeited a handsome income writing for the daily press, and resigned from all the organizations and committees of which she was then a member. No notification of the outcome of the inquiry was given to her and she continued to complain of the inequity of treatment of male and female barristers by the bar council. A further incident arose in 1933 when she was referred to in the press as the 'senior practising woman barrister in England'; the general council of the bar urged her to make clear that she was 'in no way responsible for the description'.

Conscious of the difficulties women faced, Normanton did what she could to support other women pursuing a legal career. Of particular importance was her role as a mentor and sponsor to female students whom she accepted into her chambers. Women still found it difficult to obtain positions in chambers, as male barristers often refused to sponsor them. She protested that this informal segregation of men and women seriously disadvantaged women who were denied the opportunity to develop contacts that would be important for the progression of their career.

Normanton's relatively low earnings from the law compelled her to supplement her income. She let rooms in her house in Mecklenburgh Square, Bloomsbury, and advised enquirers of her need to charge fees 'on the rare occasions when I in fact accept speaking engagements' (Helena Florence Normanton Archive). Under the pseudonym Cowdray Browne she published *Oliver Quendon's First Case* in 1927, a romantic detective novel. A contributor to the thirteenth edition of the *Encyclopaedia Britannica* she also published two books on famous cases, *The Trial of Norman Thorne* (1929) and *The Trial of Alfred Arthur Rouse* (1931). She wrote several titles published under the Books of Our Time series and numerous articles and studies on topics as diverse as Shakespeare, buying a house, and (following Edward VIII's abdication) a study on the succession to the throne.

Fighting for divorce reform Between the wars Helena's experience of the English divorce courts led her to reflect on perceived deficiencies of the current statute. She fought hard to equalize and extend the grounds on which a petition of divorce could be made between husband and wife. However, her desire was not to challenge the sanctity of marriage but rather to standardize what she termed in 1934 'irregular' partnerships (*Huddersfield Daily Examiner*, 3 Oct 1934). She argued that the tremendous cost of divorce and limited grounds on which a petition could be filed ensured separated partners could not divorce but remained legally married while they formed separate unions unrecognized by the state and to which illegitimate children were often born. She highlighted how difficult it was to maintain the ideal of a single monogamous marriage for life where couples were separated by drunkenness, imprisonment, or psychiatric confinement. At the annual meeting of the National Council of Women in October 1934, her resolution to reform matrimonial law was strongly opposed by the Mothers' Union, and was passed only with the addition of a clause disallowing divorce during the first five years of marriage. She publicly declared that its inclusion represented a 'cowardly capitulation to reactionary ecclesiastics, who would rather never see young people free to marry' (Helena Normanton Archive). In 1938 she resigned the chairmanship of the Married Persons Income Tax Reform Council, frustrated with those who failed to keep pace with her, and she urged women to 'press forward to open the Church, the Stock Exchange, the House of Lords, the Diplomatic and Consular Services, the Press Gallery in the House of Commons, and the Overseas Civil Services to women'. Her historical reading convinced her that the limitations and restrictions placed on women of her day were a recent phenomenon, and she referred to women's past achievements in her arguments supporting the extension of women's rights.

Normanton's resignation as president of the Married Women's Association over the submissions which she presented on the association's behalf to the royal commission on marriage and divorce in 1952 highlighted the complexity of feminist responses to these questions. She proposed that husband and wife should have a fairer financial partnership, principally effected by 'paying' a wife an allowance from the family income voluntarily agreed on between the spouses or adjudicated by the courts, and she proposed that wives who were guilty of 'wilfully negligent housekeeping should become amenable to law whether by way of remedial training or penalty' (*Manchester Guardian*, 25 Nov 1952). The Married Women's Association complained that the memorandum had been submitted to the royal commission by her 'without previous circulation to executive or members'. The association felt Helena's proposal of a housekeeping allowance for wives equated to 'pocket money given to a child', particularly as the housekeeping money was to remain the absolute property of the husband. It was felt to represent a complete departure from the association's policy of standing for a 'true partnership in marriage based on joint responsibility and mutual aid'. In a scathing attack the association stated 'this is a middle-class Victorian approach to the problem. The underlying attitude in this evidence is that a wife is an employed subordinate, and not a partner' (*Manchester Daily Dispatch*, 3 April 1952). Helena, who argued that neither spouse was entitled to the resources of the other, felt the association's proposal to pool the resources of husband and wife was 'nonsensical rubbish', which negated the work of previous feminists in obtaining the Married Women's Property Acts and was thus 'dangerous for a wife … and unfair to the husband' (*Beckenham Advertiser*, 26 Nov 1952). She withdrew the report and founded a breakaway organization, the Council of Married Women, with other former senior members of the Married Women's Association. However, the legislation eventually enacted followed from the stance of the association: the principle of marriage as a partnership was maintained and the complementary and equally necessary contributions of both husband and wife were recognized in the legal joint ownership of the matrimonial home and the incomes of both spouses.

The controversy surrounding this issue highlights how Helena's strong notion of social duty and responsibility and her desire to equalize relationships between the sexes could combine to support a position which some women perceived as anti-feminist. While seeking to ensure wives were protected from husbands whose sense of duty did not extend to providing adequately for partners whose primary occupation was maintaining the family, she also felt wives who misappropriated funds should be admonished or punished. She was concerned that without maintaining the separation of property between husbands and wives, feminist agitation and protest would be lost as women, who were the prime instigators of such action, would find themselves without access to the tremendous amount of money required to finance particular protests (*Beckenham Journal*, 28 Nov 1953).

Character and interests Among her various interests, Normanton founded the Magna Carta Society and served as its honorary secretary for many years (1921–53). She learned Italian and paid several visits to the country, meeting Mussolini in 1935. After the Second World War she remained active in feminist circles as a member of the Six Point Group and the Council of Professional Women. Her irrepressible activism continued and, maintaining her long standing pacifist beliefs, in 1953, aged seventy, she marched in a women's demonstration against the atom bomb.

Although she lived in Bloomsbury with her husband, Helena Normanton maintained her links with the Brighton area. She was a passionate supporter of the proposed university for Sussex, making the first donation to the Sussex University appeal in 1956; she followed this gift of £5 with a larger donation of £45 and bequeathed the capital of her trust to the university. She requested that part of the university be named after her 'because I was the first subscriber to the project and because I make this gift in gratitude for all that Brighton did to educate me when I was left an orphan' (last will and testament).

In her lifetime of activism, Helena Normanton challenged the social norms of her generation while simultaneously being careful to conform to strict etiquette and make the most of feminine wiles. During her tour of America in 1925 a reporter for *The World* (7 January) commented:

> Mrs. Normanton is tall and stout of build. She is in every respect the typical matron. Distinctly feminine in appearance and manner and also in inclination, as was proved when she left the group of reporters cooling their heels in her hotel while she walked up and down Fifth Avenue 'to look at the shops'.

She was remembered by close relatives as an imposing character who dressed in black from head to toe. Her niece Elsie Cannon wrote of her:

> controversy often surrounded Helena Normanton, sometimes, I fancy, deliberately fostered to attract attention for some cause for which she was fighting, or perhaps to stimulate demand for her articles and talk … life near her could on occasion be like having a volcano as a neighbour, but it's quite true, it wasn't dull!

She was careful to ensure that she was correctly known as the first female barrister *to practise* in England, and not as the first female barrister. The distinction was important to her, having suffered from the charges of self-promotion made against her throughout her long and successful career. She died in a nursing home at 44 Sydenham Hill, Sydenham, London, on 14 October 1957, and was buried, after cremation, with her husband in Ovingdean churchyard, Sussex.   JOANNE WORKMAN

Sources Women's Library, London, Helena Florence Normanton archive · private information (2004) · *Daily Telegraph* (16 Oct 1957) · *Daily Mail* (16 Oct 1957) · *The Times* (16 Oct 1957) · *WWW*, 1951–60 · will, 1956 · m. cert. · m. cert. [parents] · newspaper cuttings, Library of the Honourable Society of the Middle Temple · M. Pugh, *Women and the women's movement in Britain, 1914–1959* (1992) · C. Law, *Suffrage and power: the women's movement, 1918–1928* (1997) · CGPLA Eng. & Wales (1958) · E. Sussex RO

Archives Women's Library, London, corresp. and papers

Likenesses Elliott & Fry, photograph, 1945, NPG [*see illus.*] · D. Miller, double portrait, photograph, 1949 (with Rose Burstein), Hult. Arch. · photographs, Women's Library, London, Helena Florence Normanton archive

Wealth at death £23,104 1s. 9d.: probate, 2 Jan 1958, CGPLA Eng. & Wales

Normanton, John (*b.* 1605/6), Roman Catholic convert, was born in London, the son of Alexander Normanton, a cutler. He was educated at a London school run by Mr Best and admitted sizar at Gonville and Caius College, Cambridge, on 9 January 1620, at fourteen. He remained a scholar until 1627, graduating BA in 1624 and proceeding MA in 1627, when he became a fellow of the college.

In 1633 Normanton was questioned by the vice-chancellor's court for a sermon that he preached in the university church arguing that grace is resistible; he was made to recant this Arminian position. In 1636 he was again examined for a university sermon, this time 'extolling of the Romish religion' (CUL, MS Com. Ct I.18, fol. 130). He confessed denying that the pope is Antichrist, praising Catholic theologians including Bellarmine and Baronius, and impugning authority by preaching on controverted issues; however, he denied the remaining charges against him—disparaging the doctrine of justification by faith alone, clerical marriage, the earliest protestant reformers, the government of the university, and sabbath observance. Evidence provided by auditors indicated that he had in fact criticized solifidianism, clerical marriage, Luther, Calvin, and their 'pew fellow precisians' (Sidney Sussex College, MS Ward F, fol. 28 from the back). He had in addition praised auricular confession, penance, contemplatives, and flagellants and had castigated vernacular scriptures, the dissolution of the monasteries, and the antipapal myth of Pope Joan—a favourite protestant story. Naturally suspected of popish sympathies he was vigorously prosecuted by Calvinist members of the university court but was defended by John Cosin and dismissed by the anti-Calvinist majority.

The suspicions of the Calvinists were borne out in 1638 when Normanton renounced his clerical orders, 'pronounced himself a papist' (BL, Harley MS 7019, fol. 56), and left the country. Refusing to return as ordered, in 1639, he was deprived of his fellowship for 'contumacy'. The circumstances of his later life are unknown; however, his case became a *cause célèbre* for the Long Parliament's committee on religious abuses in the universities, and grounds for prosecuting the Arminian heads of Cambridge colleges.   MARGO TODD

Sources M. Todd, '"All one with Tom Thumb": Arminianism, popery, and the story of the Reformation in early Stuart Cambridge', *Church History*, 34 (1965), 563–79 · CUL, MS Com. Ct I.18, fols. 82, 129v–131v, 134–5 · Sidney Sussex College, Cambridge, MS Ward F, fols. 22–36 from the back · BL, Harley MS 7019, fols. 55–6, 66 · Venn, *Alum. Cant.*, 1/3.263 · J. Venn and others, eds., *Biographical history of Gonville and Caius College*, 1: 1349–1713 (1897), 248 · CUL, CUR 20.1, no. 6.21 · CUL, CUR 18.6(8) · CUL, Mm I.44 (Baker 33), vols. 225–6 · BL, Harley MS 7033, fol. 79

Normanville, Thomas de (d. 1295), administrator, was the son of Sir Ralph de Normanville, lord of the manor of Empingham in Rutland, and his wife, Galiena. When his father died in 1259, Thomas was said to be only two and a half years old; the course of his career makes so young an age impossible, but he was certainly a minor, and his wardship was sold to his mother for 300 marks. It is not known how he came into royal service, but on 13 November 1275, as part of a scheme for improved fiscal administration, he was appointed one of three stewards to whom

the custody of the king's demesnes and the more significant functions previously exercised by the escheators were entrusted; Normanville's responsibility was the counties north of the Trent and also Kent (the home county of Ralph Sandwich, another steward), and like his colleagues he was to receive a salary of £50 per annum. The reform was only moderately effective, and did not add greatly to the king's revenue. The less important tasks formerly entrusted to the escheators were to be performed by the sheriffs, who did not always co-operate with the stewards; consequently in May 1279 Normanville was empowered to manage lesser marriages and wardships, and on 4 November 1281, in a reversion to former practice, he was addressed as escheator north of the Trent. He held that office for the rest of his life.

As well as being concerned, as either steward or escheator, with the royal lands and rights entailed upon his office, Normanville was a very active royal servant who conducted a large number of inquests and was appointed to many individual custodies. Thus in 1276 he was commissioned to hear complaints about the assessment and collection of the previous year's fifteenth. In 1279 he was appointed keeper of the archbishopric of York after the death of Archbishop Walter Giffard. In 1281 he inquired into poachers in Sherwood Forest. In 1283 he was a collector of a subsidy in the diocese of Durham. In 1285 he was a commissioner to settle a dispute over whether land at Carham on the Tweed was in England or Scotland. In 1288 he was appointed keeper of the liberty of Alston in Cumberland. Three years later he was directed to sell houses formerly belonging to Jews in York.

In 1288 Normanville was summoned to a meeting of the royal council, and he was also appointed several times in the 1280s to act as a forest justice in the northern counties. He had some experience as a justice of assize—in 1288, for instance, he was appointed to take two assizes in Lancashire—so when a purge of the bench in 1290 resulted in a shortage of justices for the eyres that began in 1292, Normanville was chosen to serve on the circuit in the west midlands and home counties headed by John Berwick. But he was not appointed a justice in one of the central courts, and in any case his career was cut short by death, in the early summer of 1295. He left a will, whose provisions were still being administered in May 1297. In 1290 Normanville had been pardoned 100 marks of a fine for licence to marry Alice, widow of Ralph of Everingham. They appear to have had two children. Their son, Edmund, who was aged four at his father's death, must have died soon afterwards, since by February 1297 their daughter, Margaret, had become a royal ward and her marriage was disposed of accordingly, being granted to Robert Basing. She married Robert's son William, who still held Empingham in the right of his wife in 1316.

HENRY SUMMERSON

Sources *Chancery records* · *CIPM*, 1, no. 3 · patent rolls, PRO, C 66/107, mm. 8d, 12d · M. Prestwich, *Edward I* (1988) · S. L. Waugh, *The lordship of England: royal wardships and marriages in English society and politics, 1217–1327* (1988) · E. R. Stevenson, 'The escheator', *The*

English government at work, 1327–1336, ed. W. A. Morris and J. R. Strayer, 2 (1947), 109–67 · R. M. T. Hill, ed., *The rolls and register of Bishop Oliver Sutton*, 2, Lincoln RS (1950); 5, Lincoln RS, 60 (1965) · *Calendar of the fine rolls*, PRO, 1 (1911), 353 · *CPR, 1281–92*, 356–94 **Wealth at death** see *CIPM*, 3, no. 253 · Hill, ed., *Rolls and register*, vol. 5, p. 194

Norreis [Norris], **Roger** (*d.* 1223), abbot of Evesham, appears to have been of Norse origins and is referred to as 'from the North'. He became a monk of Christ Church, Canterbury, at an unknown date, and first comes to notice as treasurer of that monastery in 1187, when he was sent to Henry II by the convent to put their case against the archbishop, who was proposing to establish a college of secular clerks, thus threatening the cathedral priory. The king was abroad, at Alençon, where it appears that Archbishop Baldwin (*d.* 1190) succeeded in engaging the support of Norreis by making him cellarer of the convent. In September 1187 the convent refused to accept Norreis, and appealed to the pope on the grounds that the appointment was against the Benedictine rule and 'reasonable custom'. The monks deposed him as cellarer and imprisoned him, informing messengers from the king that he was sick in the infirmary.

Early in 1188 Norreis escaped down the great conventual drain, a departure punningly recorded at Canterbury— 'Roger Norreis, who, since he was not necessary to us, exited, filthy, by the sewer [*necessaria*]' (Stubbs, 193)—and arrived the next day at the archbishop's house at Otford. Here he was believed by the convent to have revealed the secrets of the chapter to the archbishop, their sworn enemy. From his exit down the drain, he acquired the nickname of Roger Cloacarius (the Drain-Cleaner). These events are recorded in the remarkable collection of conventual letters known as the *Epistolae Cantuarienses*, and in the chronicle of the Christ Church monk, Gervase.

With singular insouciance, Archbishop Baldwin now proposed to make Norreis prior of Dover, Christ Church's dependency. During 1189 the quarrel between the archbishop and the monks of his cathedral church dragged on, the archbishop maintaining that the convent would not obey him, the monks complaining of his seizure of their possessions and of the intended college. Following the coronation of Richard I on 3 September, the priorate of Christ Church having been vacant since the previous year, the archbishop came into the chapter at Canterbury on 6 October and appointed Norreis the new prior. Baldwin then put a guard on the convent so that they could not reach either the king or the legate to complain, gave certain conventual manors to the prior, and sent to Rome to have Norreis confirmed. In November the monks demanded the deposition of Norreis. They succeeded on 30 November. But, before the year was out, Norreis had been given the abbacy of Evesham by the king.

From this point the main source for Norreis's career is another chronicle, that of an Evesham monk, Thomas of *Marlborough. His first comment on Norreis is that he 'was not a monk of any monastery' (*Chronicon abbatiae de Evesham*, 102). At Evesham Norreis behaved exactly as he

had done at Canterbury, appropriating the convent's manors and revenues, despoiling the monks of their property, 'everywhere condemned as the manifest enemy of God' (ibid., 103). He was frequently drunk, seduced women, wore secular clothing, cloaks, and shirts, advanced his own relatives, and was violent. Affairs were brought to a head by the attempt of Bishop Mauger of Worcester to visit the monastery. Not only did the monks appeal to Rome to uphold their exemption, but it was also agreed that they would stand by the abbot if he stood by them. Norreis also set out for Rome, fearing what the convent might do. There was complete mistrust between abbot and convent, and Thomas of Marlborough feared that Norreis might kill him. In April 1205, when the abbot returned, Mauger excommunicated him, and tried to conduct an inquiry into the abbot's character, but the monks remained loyal. However, once the judgment had been given, at Christmas 1205, declaring the abbey exempt, then an inquiry began.

With this exemption, Norreis thought himself safe from prosecution, but he reckoned without a legatine visitation. In 1206 the legate, Giovanni, cardinal-deacon of Santa Maria in via Lata, came to Evesham, but left without completing the investigation. Now the abbot tried to expel the monks: monastic life was virtually suspended. But in 1213 a full legatine inquiry began before Nicolò, cardinal-bishop of Tusculum, who visited Evesham and forced Thomas of Marlborough to speak out against Norreis. Thomas's speech lasted from early morning until 3 p.m. It outlined the monks' persecution and deprivations, inadequate food and clothing, monks leaving the cloister, buildings in disrepair. Four main charges were presented: that Norreis had intruded himself on the monastery, that he had been guilty of simony, and of murder, and that he had plundered the church's possessions. Thomas would not have spoken about the abbot's flagrant disrespect of the monastic vow of chastity but for the legate's insistence. On 22 November 1213 Norreis was deposed, forced to restore the conventual property, and escorted from the chapter house at Evesham. He was given the priorate of Penwortham, Evesham's dependency in Lancashire, so that he should not become a wandering monk, but five months later, in April 1214, he was again deposed because of his delinquent behaviour. He set out for Rome and tried his influence in various quarters, but this time to no avail. However, the legate Pandulf took pity on him, and restored him to Penwortham in 1218. He died on 19 July 1223 and was buried at Penwortham.

There is strong evidence pointing to the conclusion that there were two monks called Roger Norreis at Canterbury roughly contemporaneously. The second Roger Norreis was sent as part of a delegation to the king by the convent, when they were trying to oust his namesake as prior, and went into exile with the convent from 1207 to 1214. He is likely to be the Roger Norreis who had over sixty books, mainly of sermons, but also on medicine, one of which survives (Canterbury, Dean and Chapter Library, Lit. MS B.13). Knowles saw the Roger Norreis who became abbot of

Evesham as a man of practical ability, but there is no archival evidence to substantiate this. There are only the accounts of the chroniclers, who leave no doubt as to what they thought. JANE E. SAYERS

Sources W. D. Macray, ed., *Chronicon abbatiae de Evesham, ad annum 1418*, Rolls Series, 29 (1863) [Bod. MS Rawlinson A.287] · *The historical works of Gervase of Canterbury*, ed. W. Stubbs, 2 vols., Rolls Series, 73 (1879–80) · W. Stubbs, ed., *Chronicles and memorials of the reign of Richard I*, 2: *Epistolae Cantuarienses*, Rolls Series, 38 (1865) [Lambeth MS 415] · *Gir. Camb. opera*, vol. 4 · G. G. Coulton, *Five centuries of religion*, 2 (1927), 347–78; 4 (1950), 549–53 · D. Knowles, *The monastic order in England*, 2nd edn (1963), chap. 19 · C. R. Cheney, *Innocent III and England* (1976), 196–9 · M. R. James, *The ancient libraries of Canterbury and Dover* (1903), 102–4 · J. Greatrex, *Biographical register of the English cathedral priories of the province of Canterbury* (1997), 244 · W. G. Searle, ed., *Christ Church, Canterbury*, 2: *List of the deans, priors, and monks of Christ Church Monastery*, Cambridge Antiquarian RS, 34 (1902), 172

Norreys, John. *See* Norris, Sir John (*c*.1547x50–1597).

Norrington, Sir **Arthur Lionel Pugh** (1899–1982), publisher and university administrator, was born on 27 October 1899 at Normandy Villa, Godstone Road, Kenley, Croydon, Surrey, the only son and elder child of Arthur James Norrington, an iron merchant in the City of London, and his wife, Gertrude Sarah Elizabeth, daughter of William Pugh, a merchant in China, from Montgomeryshire, Wales. In 1913 he went to Winchester College as a scholar, where his general scepticism of received lore earned him the nickname Thomas, which remained with him for life. In 1918 he joined the Royal Field Artillery; the end of the war meant that he did not see active service, but he lost a little finger in an accident. In 1919 he went to Trinity College, Oxford, as a scholar and achieved a first class in classical honour moderations (1920) followed by a second in *literae humaniores* in 1923. He then joined Oxford University Press (OUP) in London and was forthwith sent to India; in later years he would recall his life there in almost Kiplingesque phrases. In 1925 he returned to Oxford as junior assistant secretary to the delegates of the press. Henceforward Oxford was his home. On 15 September 1928 he married Edith Joyce (1902/3–1964), daughter of William Moberly Carver, electrical engineer. Theirs was a happy marriage, rooted in their Christian faith. They had two sons, one of whom, Roger, was to become a conductor, and two daughters.

In 1942 Norrington became assistant secretary to the delegates of Oxford University Press, when Kenneth Sisam succeeded R. W. Chapman as secretary, and in 1948 he followed the former as secretary to the delegates—what was, in practice, the post of senior administrative officer of OUP. His old Oxford college, Trinity, at once elected him a professorial fellow. Norrington was deeply concerned with the expansion of the range of the press's educational books. In particular he was closely associated with the great wartime series Oxford Pamphlets on world affairs and on home affairs, which ultimately sold almost 6 million copies. He also made OUP better known in the outside world, and his devotion to and knowledge of music contributed much to the press's music publishing.

Sir Arthur Lionel Pugh Norrington (1899–1982), by John Ward, 1967

A member of the Oxford Bach Choir since 1919, he became chairman of its committee in 1949.

To his classical learning Norrington added a wide knowledge of English literature, and a quick capacity for mathematical evaluation. His manner was kindly and he established friendly contacts everywhere. His searching blue eyes and quizzical glance would confront a problem and then a ready smile would enliven his taut, almost arid skin, and an apt solution or verdict would appear. He also loved gardening, and he was a keen ornithologist. He served as a JP and rose to be chairman of the Oxford bench, but his innate sense of justice was also manifested in college and university affairs.

In 1952 the fellows of Trinity invited Norrington to become their next president and he took up office in 1954, in time to preside over the quatercentenary celebrations in 1955. These were followed by a fund-raising appeal, and also by an extensive and successful programme of refacing the crumbling walls of the college. Norrington was an admirable head of house, and also played a full part in the affairs of the university—both on council and on the general board. Further afield, he was on the revising committee for the *New English Bible*, and from 1960 was the first chairman of the government committee for the publication of cheap books abroad. His name also survives in Oxford as a result of his devising the 'Norrington table', a system of assessing the performance of the various Oxford colleges in final examinations. The table is compiled by assigning a certain number of points to each candidate at each college, depending on his or her degree result. It acts as a kind of league table of the performance of candidates from different colleges. It has never been given any official sanction by the colleges or the university, but has been compiled over the years unofficially, and reservations over the accuracy of the picture it portrays have been voiced. Members of congregation voted in the early 1990s to discontinue publishing a candidate's college against his or her name in class lists of finals results as a way of seeking to stop its compilation, but this failed, and the candidate's college affiliation was restored to the lists. The Norrington table continues to be compiled, and the results appear regularly in the national press.

In 1960 Norrington succeeded T. S. R. Boase as vice-chancellor of the University of Oxford. He devoted much attention to the status of dons who were not fellows of colleges, and to the need for planning the future development of the science area. His college was delighted to welcome him back in 1962, and he resumed his close contacts with its members at all levels. In 1968 he received a knighthood. The early death of his wife in 1964 had been a shattering blow to Norrington, but on 9 December 1969 he married again; his second wife was Ruth Margaret (b. 1921/2), the widow of (Peter) Rupert Waterlow, and daughter of Edmund Cude, architect, surveyor, and estate agent. There were no children.

About this time Blackwells were enabled to create a large room of their bookshop under Trinity land, which was given, and continues to bear, his name. His more private interests were reflected in the publication (with professors H. F. Lowry and F. L. Mulhauser) of an edition of the poems of A. H. Clough in 1951, and in his *Blackwell's 1879–1979: the History of a Family Firm*, which was published posthumously in 1983. In 1970 he retired from Trinity, but became warden of Winchester College until 1974, a position which he filled with distinction and zest. He was an honorary fellow of Trinity, St Cross, and Wolfson colleges, Oxford, and an officer of the Légion d'honneur (1962). Norrington died in the John Radcliffe Hospital, Oxford, on 21 May 1982.   MICHAEL MACLAGAN, rev.

Sources *The Times* (24 May 1982) · *The Bookseller* (5 June 1982) · personal knowledge (1990) · private information (1990) · b. cert. · m. certs. · d. cert. · 'Commission of inquiry report', University of Oxford, www.admin.ox.ac.uk/coi, 1994 [information on the Norrington table]
Archives Bodl. Oxf., letters to O. G. S. Crawford · Bodl. Oxf., corresp. with Gilbert Murray · Harvard University, near Florence, Italy, Center for Italian Renaissance Studies, letters to Bernard Berenson and Nicky Mariano
Likenesses J. Ward, portrait, 1967, Trinity College, Oxford [see illus.]
Wealth at death £84,718: probate, 26 July 1982, *CGPLA Eng. & Wales*

Norris, Antony (1711–1786), antiquary and lawyer, was born on 17 November 1711 in the parish of St George's Tombland, Norwich, the third but second surviving son, and subsequently heir, of Stephen Norris (1678–1749), rector of Felthorpe, Norfolk, vicar of Felmingham, and perpetual curate of St Mary and St Michael in Thorn, Norwich, and his wife, Bridget (1680–1743), the only daughter and heir of John Graile, rector of Blickling and Waxham and minister of St George's Tombland. He was educated at Norwich grammar school under John Reddington before

proceeding to Gonville and Caius College, Cambridge, where he was admitted pensioner on 4 April 1727. On 3 November 1729 he was admitted to the Middle Temple, taking up residence on 27 April 1730; he was called to the bar on 29 November 1735. He subsequently served as deputy lieutenant of Norfolk and was one of the four chairmen of the general quarter sessions between 1761 and 1781. However, throughout his life much of his time and resources were devoted to topographical and antiquarian researches: 'Nature having given him an almost irresistible propensity for inquiries after the ancient state and inhabitants of Norfolk' (*DNB*).

On 18 May 1737 Norris married Sarah (d. 1787), daughter of John Custance, alderman and former mayor of Norwich. The couple settled at the Norris family home at Barton Turf, where Norris had moved in 1736 after the death of his elder brother, Stephen, and his widow. There their only child, John, was born on 28 January 1738. John Norris followed his father to Gonville and Caius and to the Middle Temple but died of consumption on 19 March 1762. Thereafter Antony Norris remained on good terms with two of his son's college friends, John Fenn and John Frere, both of whom were later to become noted antiquaries.

Between 1730 and 1733 Norris collected six volumes of church notes and other historical materials relating to various towns and villages in Norfolk. On the publication of Francis Blomefield's proposals for a topographical history of the county in July 1733, Norris wrote to offer his substantial collections, many of which were transcribed and incorporated in the work. He likewise secured several subscribers for this publication, the first volume of which appeared in 1739. His 'great labour and uncommon exactness' were acknowledged in Blomefield's introduction to the work. After Blomefield's death in 1752 the history was completed in a somewhat more cursory manner by Charles Parkin between 1755 and his death in 1765. Parkin's manuscript was acquired by the publisher William Whittingham in 1767. Over the next seven years Norris, together with John Fenn, assisted Whittingham in seeing the remaining volumes through the press. In particular Norris was able to correct the many errors and to fill the gaps in those hundreds to the east of the county which were furthest from Parkin's home, and so were less accurately covered. Although he recognized the deficiencies of Parkin's work, Norris nevertheless refused to condemn it, as he was well aware of the scale of the task that had been undertaken.

In later years Norris completed detailed and largely accurate histories of the eastern hundreds of Norfolk that had been most neglected by Parkin. His accounts of East and West Flegg, Happing, and Tunsted were ready for publication, and he was working on the hundred of North Erpingham when ill health forced him to abandon his task. He also compiled and transcribed extensive collections of genealogical and heraldic materials relating to the county, some of which were published by Walter Rye in 1886. Other significant manuscripts compiled by him concerned ancient customs and ceremonies, excerpts from will registers, and a glossary of ancient words used by Old English writers.

In 1782, conscious of his declining mental powers and in the absence of an heir, Norris arranged to leave his extensive manuscript collections to John Fenn after his death. However, the gradual onset of senile dementia meant that he could have no further use for them, and his wife gave them to Fenn in August 1785. Norris survived until 14 June 1786, when he died at Barton Turf, and his wife died a year later; both were buried in Barton church. In 1788 Fenn compiled a biography of Norris which he appended to the manuscript history of East and West Flegg. Norris's considerable abilities as a topographical historian have never been fully recognized because of his own and his successors' failure to publish his excellent works.

DAVID STOKER

Sources J. Fenn, biography of A. Norris, appended to A. Norris, 'An history of the hundreds of East and West Flegg in the county of Norfolk', Norfolk RO, Rye MS 3 · *The correspondence of the Reverend Francis Blomefield, 1705–52*, ed. D. Stoker, Norfolk RS, 55 (1992) · F. Blomefield and C. Parkin, *An essay towards a topographical history of the county of Norfolk*, [2nd edn], 11 vols. (1805–10) · A. Norris, ed., *Three Norfolk armories: a transcript* (now in the library of Mr Walter Rye) made in 1753 (1886) · G. A. Stephen, *Walter Rye: memoir, bibliography, and catalogue of his Norfolk manuscripts in the Norwich public libraries* (1929) · Venn, *Alum. Cant.* · H. A. C. Sturgess, ed., *Register of admissions to the Honourable Society of the Middle Temple, from the fifteenth century to the year 1944*, 3 vols. (1949) · *IGI* · *DNB* · M. Riviere, 'The Rev. William Gunn, B. D. a Norfolk parson on the grand tour', *Norfolk Archaeology*, 33 (1965–6), 351–406

Archives Norfolk RO, Norfolk historical compilations · Norfolk RO, corresp., antiquarian, genealogical, and linguistic notes | Bodl. Oxf., Gough Norfolk MSS · Norfolk RO, Norfolk and Norwich Archaeological Society deposit

Likenesses W. C. Edwards, line engraving (after portrait by Smissen), BM, NPG

Norris, Charles (1779–1858), topographical artist, born on 24 August 1779, was the younger son of John Norris of Marylebone, Middlesex, a wealthy merchant. His older brother was called John. His parents died when he was a child and he was left a considerable estate, which enabled him to be educated at Eton College and at Christ Church, Oxford, where he matriculated on 26 October 1797. He afterwards obtained a commission in the King's dragoon guards, but resigned this in 1800, when he married Sarah, daughter of John Saunders, an Independent minister at Norwich, and a descendant of Laurence Saunders, martyr (d. 1555). They bought a yacht called *The Nautilus* and subsequently lived in Milford Haven, Pembrokeshire, for about ten years, moving in 1810 to Bridge Street, Tenby, Pembrokeshire, where Norris researched Welsh architectural antiquities. With Sarah he had thirteen children, four sons and nine daughters, of whom only two outlived him. He remarried on 25 January 1832 and had three further children, two sons and one daughter, with his second wife, Elizabeth Harris of Pembrokeshire. On 22 December 1810 Joseph Farington recorded in his diary that a Miss Byrne

> spoke of a Young Man, Mr. Norris, who resides at Tenby in South Wales. He has devoted much time to making sketches from nature particularly the remains of Abbeys, Castles, &c. She said His outlines are very neatly executed, but that He

> has no knowledge of light & shade. (Farington, *Diary*, 10.3830)

In 1810 Norris issued two numbers of an ambitious work, entitled *The Architectural Antiquities of Wales*. Each number was to contain six oblong folio plates from his own drawings, for which he also provided the letterpress. Although an attractive publication, the expense of production meant that the work did not proceed beyond the third instalment in 1811. In the same year the three numbers were reissued in one volume, under the title *St. David's, in a series of engravings illustrating the different ecclesiastical edifices of that ancient city*. For economic reasons, Norris taught himself to engrave, and in 1812 published *Etchings of Tenby*, which contained forty engravings both drawn and etched by himself. These accurate depictions of the medieval town remains were invaluable records of archaeological interest to scholars and historians. Five drawings of Pembroke Castle by Norris, engraved by J. Rawle and originally intended to form a fourth number, were published in 1817. In 1818 he wrote *An Historical Account of Tenby*, which contained six plates of local views and a map. In addition to these he left unpublished a large collection of architectural drawings, many of which were in the possession of his son, R. Norris, of Rhode Wood House, Saundersfoot, Pembrokeshire.

Norris was of average size, strong, and good at hill walking. The poet Walter Savage Landor wrote to his sister from Paris in 1802, commenting on Napoleon's likeness in 'figure and complexion [to] Norris' (Laws, 310). Norris remained good friends with Robert Landor, younger brother of the poet. He always exhibited a spirit of cynical independence, verging often upon eccentricity. Norris died at his home, Waterwynch, near Tenby, on 16 October 1858 and was buried in Tenby cemetery. His wife Elizabeth survived him.

D. L. THOMAS, rev. L. R. HOULISTON

Sources E. Laws, *Journal of the Cambrian Archaeological Association*, 5th ser., 8 (1891), 305–11 · Bryan, *Painters* (1903–5) · Foster, *Alum. Oxon.* · Farington, *Diary*, vol. 10 · *CGPLA Eng. & Wales* (1858)

Likenesses J. Linnell, oils, 1837, NMG Wales

Wealth at death under £800: probate, 1 Dec 1858, *CGPLA Eng. & Wales*

Norris, Sir Edward (c.1550–1603), soldier and administrator, was the third son of Henry *Norris, first Baron Norris (c.1525–1601), courtier and diplomat, and Margery (or Margaret) *Norris (d. 1599) [see under Norris, Henry], daughter and coheir of John *Williams, first Baron Williams of Thame. Edward was the third of six brothers, all soldiers, but the only one to live past 1599. Their mother, an old friend of Elizabeth I, got the queen to recall him from the Netherlands in that year. As he was governor of Ostend, which only two years later (1601–4) endured the greatest siege of the century, in which several governors were killed or badly wounded, there could easily have been six dead sons out of six, all before the decease of either parent. Instead, he was rusticated in Berkshire, a fate he may not have appreciated—Norris's career shows him to have been a natural-born fighter.

Little is known of Norris's early life, but in early 1582 Fulke Greville and he were sent to carry Elizabeth's best wishes to William, prince of Orange, who was recuperating after a failed assassination attempt. J. S. Nolan suggests that, while in the Netherlands, Norris intrigued with his elder brother John *Norris for a commission as colonel of one of the regiments being raised by the duke of Anjou, the newly installed governor-general in the Netherlands. In fact, the brother for whom 'Black Jack' sought a colonelcy may have been Henry Norris, who, albeit younger than Edward Norris, had been serving as captain in John Norris's regiment for at least the previous year. Still, Edward Norris was almost certainly interested in his brothers' military activity and had probably served previously in the Netherlands as a gentleman volunteer. When John Norris transferred to Ireland in 1584, he accompanied and served under him, along with Henry Norris.

Edward Norris was elected MP for Oxford in 1572 and Abingdon in 1584 and 1589, thanks to his father's influence, but does not appear to have been an active MP. He returned to the Netherlands as captain of a foot company in the army commanded by John Norris on 12 August 1585. His choleric nature soon revealed itself. One indication that he did have previous experience in the Netherlands is that in October he was appointed lieutenant-governor of the cautionary town of Flushing under Sir Philip Sidney. Sidney did not arrive until November and Norris governed tactlessly in his absence: English soldiers and diplomats alike protested to William Cecil, Baron Burghley, the lord treasurer about his hot-tempered and ill-judged conduct of affairs. Yet he worked well with Sidney, helping to reorganize the garrison effectively, and he was knighted in April 1586. Moreover, his combativeness had its good side: in May 1586 he won praise for his part in the operations around Schenken Schans, in the eastern Netherlands.

Norris's temperament soon caused problems again. In August 1586 he and Sidney were guests at Geertruidenberg of the count van Hohenlohe, one of the leading Dutch generals, together with other senior officers. There was much drinking after dinner, and when William Pelham, marshal of the field, made slighting remarks about Sir John Norris (who had fallen out with Robert Dudley, earl of Leicester, the new governor-general), Edward Norris upbraided him and was rebuked in turn by Hohenlohe, for insolence to a senior officer. He replied insultingly, the count 'hurled a cup at his face [which] cut him along the forehead' (*Correspondence*, ed. Bruce, 301), and the party broke up in drunken disarray. The next day Norris challenged Hohenlohe to a duel, with Sidney acting as his second. Leicester stopped the duel on the grounds that a junior officer could not challenge a superior, and all those involved fought together in the battle at Zutphen in September. Norris still resented Hohenlohe and renewed his challenge after Leicester went home in November; however, Hohenlohe was 'sicke at Delfte of his hurte receyved at Zutphen' (*Correspondentie*, ed. Brugmans, 2.428). Although things were said to be settled between them by

April 1587, when Leicester returned to the Netherlands in the summer with a reinforcing army he found the dispute was still a cause of ill feeling and that Hohenlohe had accused him of urging Norris to maintain the quarrel. As Robert Devereux, earl of Essex, a guest at the original dinner, observed, such 'private warres' were 'more dangerous then the annoyaunce of any enemy' (Hammer, 50).

Perhaps to keep him away from Hohenlohe, Norris was transferred to Ostend to act as deputy to the new governor, Sir John Conway, in 1587. Although not one of the cautionary towns, it was strategically important for England and a strong, mostly English, garrison was maintained there at Elizabeth's insistence. Norris may have been passed over by the Dutch as governor owing to his dispute with Hohenlohe. In 1589 he once again fought alongside his brothers, though for the last time, commanding a regiment in the expedition led by 'Black Jack' and Sir Francis Drake to Spain and Portugal. Early on, in fighting near La Coruña, Norris, who was commanding the army's vanguard, was 'hurt in the head with a sword' and might have been killed, but Sir Robert Sidney killed his assailant and rescued him (Wernham, *The Expedition*, 159). The campaign was a failure and Norris returned to Ostend, where he remained most of the subsequent ten years. He eventually replaced Conway as governor on 7 September 1590, with a commission from the states general, not the queen. Elizabeth seems to have regarded Norris as one of her favourites while he served as sewer in the household and was not too keen for her 'Ned' to go, at least until a satisfactory replacement had been found (HoP, *Commons, 1558–1603*, 3.135). Burghley assisted in his suit. This suggests that Norris could be charismatic and personable with Elizabeth at least, despite his quarrelsome nature. However, the queen could be critical of his handling of the Dutch.

Ostend's security became an obsession with Norris. His virtual paranoia is demonstrated by the fate of an English page in 1595, caught by the Spanish when out fowling, and interrogated and released on condition of participating in a conspiracy. He immediately told the governor all of what had taken place, but Norris had the boy flogged anyway. Unfortunately, his bad relations with the Dutch, dating back to 1586, combined with his anxiety about Ostend's security, led him to accuse his employers (who paid him £480 per annum as governor) of undermining his authority and not caring about the town's defences. In 1592 he was called to court and reprimanded by the queen, but was allowed to return. He threw his energies into building new fortifications, and in 1593, facing a likely Spanish attack, Elizabeth wrote urging 'Ned' to encourage his men to 'be so much bolder of heart as their cause is good and their honour must be according' (Motley, 3.268). By 1595 he was once again at daggers drawn with the Dutch. They commissioned as lieutenant-governor Captain Oliver Lambert, whom Norris did not want. He wrote to Burghley that Lambert was in a conspiracy with the Dutch—a wild and divisive accusation. Norris was summoned before the Dutch council of state to satisfy them 'as well of old matters as of new'; for this, he blamed Hohenlohe's 'spleen' (Wernham, *List and Analysis*, 6.85, 89–90). The old dispute still rankled.

Norris was able to placate the Dutch somehow; Elizabeth's favour (due to her long-standing friendship with his mother) no doubt helped. He remained in office in Ostend until, after the deaths of three brothers in two years, the queen wrote to console her 'own Crow', Margery, and her husband, for the 'bitter accident lately befallen you' (*Letters*, ed. Harrison, 250, 268). In response, Margery Norris apparently asked for her last son back, and he was recalled in 1599. His vigilance for the town's safety had at least been appreciated by the local citizens, who provided the rare gift of an ornate damask tablecloth 'representing the story of the prophet Jonah [with] the arms of Sir Edward' on it (van Ysselsteyn, 64, 212).

Norris lived in some comfort at Englefield in Berkshire, which his mother had settled on him. He was JP for the county from 1598. Elizabeth appointed him third clerk of the office of the petty bag in 1600 and he took an interest in building up his estates. His marriage between 1599 and 1602 to a distant cousin, Elizabeth Webb, a widow and daughter and heir of John Norris of Fifield, Berkshire, may have been to this end. They had no children. Norris's local consequence was enhanced by his promotion to the office of *custos rotulorum* for Berkshire and his appointment of the quorum in Oxfordshire in 1601. He oversaw the quarter sessions and was responsible for the records and the clerks as *custos rotulorum*. He had been popular with younger gentlemen at court and became patron of several captains or men of action, including Dudley Carleton, formerly his secretary at Ostend, and eventually James I's ambassador to the United Provinces. Norris maintained a keen interest in military affairs, both in Ireland and the Netherlands, but visitors and correspondents thought he pined for the old life of action. He died intestate and was buried on 15 October 1603 at Englefield. His estates passed to his nephew Francis Norris, second Baron Norris of Rycote. D. J. B. TRIM

Sources BL, Harley MS 1411, fol. 59*r* · PRO, SP 83/15 · PRO, SP 84/49–51 · *CSP for.*, 1584–6 · R. B. Wernham, ed., *List and analysis of state papers, foreign series, Elizabeth I*, 7 vols. (1964–2000) · BL, Egerton MS 1694 · BL, Harley MS 168 · Bodl. Oxf., MS Tanner 78 · J. Bruce, ed., *Correspondence of Robert Dudley, earl of Leycester*, CS, 27 (1844) · *Correspondentie van Robert Dudley graaf van Leycester en andere documenten betreffende zijn gouvernement-generaal in de Nederlanden, 1585–1588*, ed. H. Brugmans, 3 vols. (Utrecht, 1931) · Nationaal Archief, The Hague, Raad van State 1524 · Nationaal Archief, The Hague, Staten Generaal 8040 · PRO, Audit Office, AO 1/292/1096 · PRO, Exchequer, E 351/240–241 · J. S. Nolan, *Sir John Norreys and the Elizabethan military world* (1997) · R. B. Wernham, ed., *The expedition of Sir John Norris and Sir Francis Drake to Spain and Portugal, 1589*, Navy Records Society, 127 (1988) · J. L. Motley, *History of the United Netherlands: from the death of William the Silent to the Twelve Years Truce, 1609*, 4 vols. (New York, 1879–80) · P. E. J. Hammer, *The polarisation of Elizabethan politics: the political career of Robert Devereux, 2nd earl of Essex, 1585–1597* (1999) · T. Birch, *Memoirs of the reign of Queen Elizabeth*, 1 (1754) · *The letters of Elizabeth I*, ed. G. B. Harrison (1968) · A. Stewart, *Philip Sidney: a double life* (2000) · G. T. van Ysselsteyn, *White figurated linen damask: from the 15th to the beginning of the 19th century* (1962) · *The letters of John Chamberlain*, ed. N. E. McClure, 1 (1939) · *DNB* · H. A. Napier, *Historical notices of the parishes of Swyncombe and Ewelme in the county of Oxford* (1858) · HoP, *Commons, 1558–1603*, 3.135–6
Archives PRO, state papers Holland, SP 84 | BL, Cotton MSS, letters
Likenesses statue, Westminster Abbey
Wealth at death not known, but owned considerable amount of real estate

Norris, Edward (1583/4–1659), minister in America, was the son of Edward Norris, vicar of Tetbury, Gloucestershire. He matriculated at Balliol College, Oxford, on 30 March 1599, aged fifteen, moved to Magdalen Hall, graduated BA on 23 January 1607, and proceeded MA on 25 October 1609. According to John Traske he lived successively at Tetbury and Horsley, Gloucestershire, serving as a minister and teacher. During this period he married, and he and his wife, Eleanor, had a son, Edward (1615–1684), who was a schoolmaster at Salem, Massachusetts, from 1640 to 1676, and a daughter, Mary. Norris became rector of Anmer, Norfolk, in 1624. About 1630 a friend, Rice Boye, discussed his belief that the godly could rely on divine providence to provide all daily necessities, including good health, the lack whereof was the result of inadequate faith. Norris subsequently circulated five arguments against this view and a collection of Boye's writings he called 'Prosopopeia'. Responding in *The Importunate Begger* (1635), Boye denounced Norris's 'slanderous misconstructions and false reports' (A2r). Norris replied in *A Treatise Maintaining that Temporall Blessings are to bee Sought* (1636), averring that divine promises of goods and health are not absolute. In a postscript he refuted Traske's antinomian tenets, likening him to a Familist. Boye's retort, *A Just Defence* (1636), accused Norris of 'abusive carriages' and referred to him as a nonconformist, an early indication of his puritan tendencies. Dismissing Boye's 'Rhapsodie of falsities' in *The New Gospel Not the True Gospel* (1638), Norris focused much of his attention on the twenty-one reputed doctrinal errors of Traske, the 'seducing Impostor', as espoused in the latter's *True Gospel Vindicated* (1636). Heading the list was Traske's repudiation of the law's role in conversion and Christian living.

Seeking a friendly environment in which to pursue his nonconformist convictions, Norris emigrated to New England, where he joined the Boston church in July 1639 and obtained permission in September to settle at Salem as Hugh Peter's assistant. He was inducted as a teacher in the Salem congregation on 18 March 1640, for which he received 100 acres of upland, sixteen of meadow, and a stipend of £60 p.a. After Peter returned to England, Norris served as the church's pastor; John Whiting became his assistant in 1656. He defended the standing council against Richard Saltonstall in 1646, was one of seven ministers appointed to draft a confession of faith in 1647, declined to adopt the 1648 Cambridge platform of church discipline in his congregation, and published *A Short Catechisme* in 1649. He avoided the campaigns against Baptists, Gortonists, and reputed witches, but he did urge commissioners of the united colonies in May 1653 to prosecute the war against the Dutch of New Amsterdam or risk their existing good relations with the English parliament. Rendered mute while preaching in 1658, apparently by a stroke, he lingered in poor health until his death on 23 December 1659. In John Winthrop's estimation he was 'a grave and judicious elder' (Winthrop, 2.65).

RICHARD L. GREAVES

Sources Foster, *Alum. Oxon.*, *1500–1714*, 3.1076 · J. Winthrop, *The history of New England from 1630 to 1649*, ed. J. Savage, 2 vols. (1825–6); repr. (1972) · E. Hazard, *Historical collections: consisting of state papers*, 2 vols. (Philadelphia, PA, 1792–4) · 'Town records of Salem, 1634–1659', *Essex Institute Historical Collections*, 2nd ser., 1 (1868), 5–242 · *DAB* · W. Bentley, 'A description and history of Salem', *Collections of the Massachusetts Historical Society*, 6 (1800), 212–77 · R. Boye, *The importunate begger* (1635) · R. Boye, *A just defence* (1636) · J. Traske, *True gospel vindicated* (1636) · *DNB*

Norris, Edward (*bap.* 1665, *d.* 1726), physician, was baptized at Childwall, Lancashire, on 19 April 1665, fifth son of Thomas Norris (*c.*1618–1686) of Speke, Lancashire, and his wife, Katherine (*b.* 1632), daughter of Sir Henry *Garway (Garraway). Edward was the younger brother of Thomas *Norris (1653–1700) and Sir William *Norris (1658–1702). He graduated BA from Brasenose College, Oxford, in 1686, and proceeded MA in 1689, MB in 1691, and DM in 1695. He practised medicine at Chester, and in 1698 he was elected a fellow of the Royal Society. In 1699 he accompanied his brother Sir William as secretary of his embassy to the Mughal emperor Aurangzeb from April to November 1701. He returned home in 1702, taking with him a cargo valued at Rs 147,000, partly his brother's property. The journey took its toll on Norris's health, but after an interval he resumed the practice of medicine at Utkinton, Cheshire, and was elected a fellow of the Royal College of Physicians in 1716. In 1705 he had married Ann (1675/6–1729), daughter of William Cleveland of Liverpool; they had one son. Norris died on 22 July 1726, and was buried at St Michael's Chapel, attached to Garston Hall, a manor of the Norris family, near Speke. On the death of his son, which occurred some time before 1736, the family of the Norrises of Speke in the male line became extinct.

STANLEY LANE-POOLE, *rev.* MICHAEL BEVAN

Sources T. Heywood, ed., *The Norris papers*, Chetham Society, 9 (1846) · *IGI* · *The record of the Royal Society of London*, 4th edn (1940) · Munk, *Roll*

Norris, Edwin (1795–1872), linguist and Assyriologist, was born on 24 October 1795 in Taunton, Somerset, the son of a printer from a prominent local family that migrated from Devon in the sixteenth century. He was educated at a local school where the headmaster was his uncle Henry Norris, noted for his mastery of twenty-four languages. After leaving school Norris may have worked as a printer for a time, but in 1814 or 1815 he went to the continent as tutor in an English family. He spent much of this period in Naples, and became so familiar with the local dialect that he served as an interpreter even for other Italians; by this time he had also learned French, modern Greek, Hebrew, and Armenian. He returned to Taunton in 1821 and taught languages there until, in 1825 or 1826, he was appointed a

junior clerk in the East India Company's London headquarters, where he acquired a knowledge of south Asian languages.

In 1836 Norris retired after changes in the company's structure and then became assistant secretary to the Royal Asiatic Society, of which he remained an officer for the rest of his life, as secretary from 1856 and librarian and honorary secretary from 1861. His most important achievement in this connection was his contribution to the decipherment of cuneiform. His duties included editing the society's journal and corresponding with scholars abroad, so it fell to him to deal with the reports sent by Henry Creswicke Rawlinson from 1838 onwards about his work on the trilingual inscription at Behistan in Persia. Since Rawlinson could not return to Britain until 1849 Norris played a vital role in keeping him informed of the important progress made by scholars in Europe, especially Edward Hincks; he also contributed useful suggestions of his own, and studied related languages such as Avestan and Sanskrit. As an incidental result he demonstrated his own talents as a decipherer when in 1845 the society received copies of an inscription at Kapur di Giri, near Peshawar. By noting similarities with Bactrian script he was able to analyse the alphabet used and identify the text as a proclamation of the ancient Indian king Asoka (*Journal of the Royal Asiatic Society*, [1st ser.], 8, 1846, 293–314). Norris was thus the person best qualified to supervise the publication of Rawlinson's decipherments of the Old Persian and Babylonian (Akkadian) texts from Behistan; he not only designed a cuneiform typeface for this, but was able to make necessary corrections. The results filled the society's journal volumes 10 (1847) and 14 (1851). He himself also made substantial progress on the third (Elamite) text, published in his 'Memoir on the Scythic version of the Behistun inscription' (*Journal of the Royal Asiatic Society*, 15, 1855, 1–213). From 1857 to 1866 he assisted Rawlinson on his monumental publication of the British Museum collection, *Cuneiform Inscriptions of Western Asia* (2 vols., 1861–6), undertaking much of the work in Rawlinson's frequent absences. Norris was the first to recognize the importance of the sign lists designed for teaching scribes to write, many of which he copied for volume 2. After 1866 deteriorating eyesight prompted him to abandon text copying and his official duties in order to concentrate on his *magnum opus*, the first ever *Assyrian Dictionary*, covering the letters *aleph* to *nun* in three volumes (1868, 1870, 1872). Although unfinished at his death, and long since superseded, it was of great value at the time.

Norris's experience of both European and 'exotic' languages was extremely wide (he joked that he beat his uncle's score by two) and much consulted. From 1830 he was regularly used by the British and Foreign Bible Society as editor or adviser on translation projects, in languages including Berber, Maori, Persian, Arabic, and little-known languages of Africa and the Pacific. From 1847 to 1866 he was translator to the Foreign Office, and so was chosen to edit the linguistic papers of the African explorer James Richardson, from which he also compiled a grammar of the Bornu language (1853); he also wrote or edited other books on African languages. He was equally interested in the societies of the peoples whose speech he learned; he founded a series called the Ethnographical Library, of which only two volumes came out (1853, 1854), and edited the fourth edition (1855) of J. C. Pritchard's *Natural History of Man*. His most enduring legacy, however, concerns a subject much nearer home: in 1859 he published *The Ancient Cornish Drama*, which is the standard edition of the most important relic of Cornish literature—the trilogy of plays now known as the *Ordinalia*—and includes one of the earliest modern accounts of the by then extinct language.

Norris died on 10 December 1872 at his home, 6 Michael's Grove, Brompton, London, and was survived by his wife, Anne. He was remembered for his constant readiness to help others at the expense of his own work and for his great modesty, which partly explains why 'the value of [his] help to Rawlinson has never been fully recognised' (Budge, 77)—except for an honorary PhD from Bonn—and why 'Assyriologists have forgotten how much they are indebted to [his] infinite patience and never-ceasing labour' (ibid., 96). R. S. SIMPSON

Sources bishop of St Davids [C. Thirlwall], 'presidential address, 30 April 1873', *Report of the Royal Society of Literature* (1873), 24–51 · 'Annual report for 1873', *Journal of the Royal Asiatic Society of Great Britain and Ireland*, new ser., 7 (1875), xix–xxii · E. A. W. Budge, *The rise and progress of Assyriology* (1925) · Boase, *Mod. Eng. biog.* · *CGPLA Eng. & Wales* (1873) · J. A. Bakere, *The Cornish 'Ordinalia': a critical study* (1980), 2–4
Archives Som. ARS, MSS | BL, corresp. with Sir A. H. Layard, Add. MSS 38978–39119
Likenesses bust, Shire Hall, Taunton, Somerset
Wealth at death under £5000: probate, 17 Jan 1873, *CGPLA Eng. & Wales*

Norris, Francis, earl of Berkshire (1579–1622), nobleman and politician, was born on 6 July 1579 at Wytham, Berkshire, son of Sir William Norris (d. 1579) and Elizabeth, née Morrison (d. 1611). He was the grandson of Henry *Norris, first Baron Norris (c.1525–1601), and succeeded to the barony on the death of his grandfather on 27 June 1601. Norris's family were noted for their loyal service, five of his uncles having served in Ireland or on the continent, four of them dying of wounds. In February 1598 Norris went to France on diplomatic service with Sir Robert Cecil. In 1599 he served in the fleet to repel a threatened Spanish invasion. Shortly after 28 April the same year he married Lady Bridget de Vere (1584–1630/31), daughter of Edward *Vere, seventeenth earl of Oxford. They had one daughter, Elizabeth (1600?–1645), but by 1606 he and Bridget were living apart. An illegitimate son, Francis *Norris (d. 1669), was born of his union with Sarah Rose.

With considerable wealth and much landed property in Oxfordshire and Berkshire, Norris determined about 1600 on an active life in politics. He was summoned to parliament on 17 October 1601 and took his seat on 21 November. He proclaimed the accession of James I at Oxford in March 1603 and journeyed to Scotland to receive the queen consort. In 1605 he was made knight of the Bath at the creation of Prince Charles as duke of York on 6 January, and on 26 February, like his father before him, he was

admitted to Gray's Inn, London. The same year he travelled to Spain with the earl of Nottingham, the English ambassador; he returned to England late the following year.

Norris retained an interest in his locality, providing Sir Thomas Bodley with oak trees for building the Bodleian, helping him provide an endowment for the library, and giving Shotover, Oxford, to Prince Henry. His preferment advanced. He was present at the creation of Henry as prince of Wales in 1610, and later of Charles as prince of Wales in 1616.

Norris readily made enemies, however, and his quick temper began to affect his public life. He quarrelled with Peregrine Bertie, son of Lord Willoughby, and seriously wounded him in a duel in 1610. Three years later they almost fought again. In 1615 an affray in a churchyard in Bath resulted in the death of one of Lord Willoughby's servants, and Norris was found guilty of manslaughter but pardoned by the king. He was created Viscount Thame and earl of Berkshire on 28 January 1621, reputedly through the influence of Buckingham, who wanted his friend Edward Wray to marry Norris's daughter, Elizabeth. Shortly afterwards, on 16 February 1621 while in the House of Lords, he insulted Lord Scrope in the presence of the prince of Wales and was sent to the Fleet prison. Seriously humiliated, almost a year later on 29 January 1622, Norris shot himself with his crossbow at his home in Rycote, Oxfordshire, and he died two days later. His will directed that he should be buried at Dorchester, Oxfordshire, but that his heart should be buried at Watford, Hertfordshire, with his grandmother, the late countess of Bedford. His daughter and heir, Elizabeth, became Baroness Norris on his death. F. D. A. BURNS

Sources DNB · GEC, *Peerage*, 1.45–50, 9.643–9 · *Memorials of affairs of state in the reigns of Q. Elizabeth and K. James I, collected (chiefly) from the original papers of … Sir Ralph Winwood*, ed. E. Sawyer, 3 vols. (1725), vol. 2, p. 50; vol. 3, pp. 154–5 · *GM*, 1st ser., 67 (1797), 654 · J. Foster, *The register of admissions to Gray's Inn, 1521–1889, together with the register of marriages in Gray's Inn chapel, 1695–1754* (privately printed, London, 1889), 53, 108
Wealth at death no value given: will, proved 1624

Norris, Sir Francis (d. 1669), politician, was the illegitimate son of Francis *Norris, earl of Berkshire (1579–1622), and Sarah Rose, afterwards wife of Samuel Haywarde; he was also known as Francis Rose. In 1613 the earl settled on the boy Francis the manors of Weston on the Green, Oxfordshire, and of Yattendon, Chilswell, and Hall Court in Thatcham, all in Berkshire. To this property Francis succeeded following the suicide of his father on 29 January 1622. Probably in 1629 Norris married Hester (d. 1672), daughter of Sir John Rous of Rous Lench, Worcestershire. On 27 August 1633 he was knighted at Abingdon, and in 1635–6 he served as high sheriff of Oxfordshire. In that capacity he was responsible for the collection of ship money; he collected about three-quarters of the backlog left by his predecessor, Sir Peter Wentworth, but was then told to levy £4000 for the current year.

Nothing is known of Norris's activities during the civil war and under the Commonwealth, but he seems to have acquired office under Cromwell's protectorate. He was elected MP for Oxfordshire in September 1656, and on 10 October wrote that 'I am in my old lodging in Old Palace Yard', which was 'near the parliament' (*CSP dom.*, 1656–7, 130). During the next two years Norris wrote often to Joseph Williamson, tutor and chaperone to his second son, Edward (*bap.* 1634), then travelling in Europe, a venture which seems to have inspired both enthusiasm and high anxiety in the father. In December 1658 he stood again for Oxfordshire in the elections to Richard Cromwell's parliament. On 29 December it was reported that:

> yesterday our election was for the county: My lord Falkland and Mr Jenkinson stood, and upon the poll Mr Jenkinson carried it by 13 voices. This day the competition stands between the said Lord and Sir Francis Norris, and tis thought my Lord will carry it.   (*Mercurius Politicus*, no. 548, 135)

A double return was made, one for Henry Lucius Cary, fourth Viscount Falkland and Robert Jenkinson, and the other for Falkland and Norris. On 5 February, however, the house resolved that the second was invalid, and declared Falkland and Jenkinson elected.

At the Restoration, Norris was nominated to the proposed order of the Royal Oak, having at that time an income of £1500 a year. He died on 15 July 1669 at Weston on the Green, where he was buried and where there is a monument to him in the church. His will, initially dated 9 August 1663, named five daughters and five sons, of whom the eldest, John, seems either to have predeceased him or to have been in some way incapacitated. His son Edward followed him into politics. Knighted on 22 November 1662, he was MP for Oxfordshire in six parliaments (1675, 1679, February 1701, December 1701, 1702, and 1705), and for Oxford in four (1689, 1690, 1695, and 1698).   STEPHEN WRIGHT

Sources GEC, *Peerage* · *Diary of Thomas Burton*, ed. J. T. Rutt, 4 vols. (1828), vol. 3, pp. 23, 84 · *VCH Oxfordshire*, vol. 6 · *VCH Berkshire*, vol. 4 · Davenport [R. (?) Davenport], *Lords lieutenant and high sheriffs of Oxfordshire, 1086–1886* (1886) · W. H. Turner, ed., *The visitations of the county of Oxford … 1566 … 1574 … and in 1634*, Harleian Society, 5 (1871) · *Mercurius Politicus* (29 Dec 1658) [Thomason tract E 760(2)] · *Mercurius Politicus* (6–13 Jan 1659) [Thomason tract E 760(4)] · *Mercurius Politicus* (3–10 Feb 1659) [Thomason tract E 761(13)] · *CSP dom.*, 1656–8 · will, PRO, PROB 11/330, sig. 106 · L. Naylor and G. Jagger, 'Norreys, Sir Edward', HoP, *Commons, 1660–90*

Wealth at death substantial; £1500 bequeathed to one daughter; £1000 to each of two others; £1000 settled on a fourth beneficiary: will, PRO, PROB 11/330, sig. 106

Norris, Henry (*b.* before **1500**, *d.* **1536**), courtier, was apparently the second son of Richard Norris and an unidentified mother, and the grandson of Sir William Norris of Yattendon (*d.* 1506) and his first wife Jane, daughter of John de Vere, twelfth earl of Oxford. Henry's date of birth is not known, but his subsequent career suggests the late 1490s. He was born into a long-serving court family. His great-grandfather Sir John Norris (*d.* 1466) had kept the great wardrobe, while his grandfather was a knight of the body to Edward IV. Attainted after the Buckingham rebellion, Sir William escaped to Brittany, probably fought at Bosworth, was reappointed knight of the body, and held a command at Stoke; from 1488 until his death he was lieutenant of Windsor Castle.

Henry Norris received his first royal grant in 1515, suggesting that he was already one of Henry VIII's 'minions', the group of half a dozen or so courtiers somewhat younger than the king who made up his immediate circle. From at least 1517 he was serving in the privy chamber, and he became a key figure around which its as yet inchoate establishment was forming. By 1518 he was handling money for Henry and by September that year he probably held one of the newly designated posts of gentleman of the privy chamber. He was granted an annuity of 50 marks in January 1519 and in the following May escaped the temporary disgrace of some of the other minions. Throughout his career he was prominent in court revels and he was clearly more than competent in the tilt yard. In 1520 he attended Henry at the Field of Cloth of Gold and in 1526, when under the Eltham Ordinance William Compton surrendered the posts of groom of the (close) stool and keeper of the privy purse, Norris took his place.

As groom Norris alone had the right of entry to the king's 'bed-chamber and other privy places' ('Eltham Ordinances', 156) and for the rest of his life he remained the king's most intimate servant and confidant—perhaps the nearest thing Henry had to a friend: 'du Roy le mieulx ayme' (Crapelet, 184). As such he alone was in attendance when Henry and Anne went to inspect the newly surrendered Whitehall; he accompanied them to Calais in 1532 and was probably one of the handful of witnesses at their pre-dawn marriage about 25 January 1533. By then the privy chamber staff had become more organized, with Norris combining the post of groom with that of chief gentleman, which gave him responsibility for all staff in close attendance on the king.

Cavendish's *Life of Wolsey* preserves several revealing vignettes of Norris in action. When Wolsey (with his fate still in the balance) arrived at court at Grafton in September 1529, he found no lodgings provided. Norris remedied the deliberate slight by allowing the cardinal to change in his own room. This could have been calculation—he knew that Henry still nurtured warm feelings for his old minister. But Norris had previously been on good terms with Wolsey, and the action was typical of his emollient style. He is often described as gentle, and was clearly very well liked at court. As well as having the ideal personality, he was also discreet, as a groom/chief gentleman needed to be, especially when undertaking private missions for the king. On the cardinal's journey to Esher after his fall Norris intercepted him at Putney Hill, with confidential words of reassurance from Henry. Another element in Norris's posts was monitoring, indeed sometimes censoring, access to the king. When after Wolsey's death Cavendish was ordered to Hampton Court and Henry forgot to call him into the privy apartments, it was Norris who caught him before he left.

A corollary of Norris's position was that it guaranteed him a central role in royal patronage. The key in that was securing the king's signature to a grant, and Norris was perfectly placed either to obtain or to frustrate it. In consequence he became the focus of a network of clientage. The correspondence of Viscount Lisle, the deputy at Calais, exemplifies this in great detail. Lisle relied on Norris to promote and protect him and his interests, and he kept the groom sweet by suitable *douceurs*. After Norris's death a servant wrote to Lisle: 'if your friends were now as earnest in your suits to the king as Mr. Norris was, your matters had not slept so long' (*Lisle Letters*, no. 729). Of course as Thomas Cromwell rose in royal service, the groom stood in the way of his wish to control the patronage machine. There was no major friction, but although the two did sometimes rub against each other, it is unlikely that the secretary managed to reduce significantly Norris's role in patronage. It was otherwise with national finance. Between 1529 and 1532 Norris, as keeper of the privy purse, had taken over many payments previously the responsibility of Brian Tuke, treasurer of the chamber. However, once Cromwell acquired financial responsibilities he began to make these payments direct, leaving Norris to manage only the king's immediate expenditure.

Staff of the privy chamber were also ideally placed to advantage themselves and each other, and Norris clearly led a group of colleagues who acted together. He himself obtained a steady stream of rewards over twenty years, including many held by William Compton, his predecessor as groom; he received his latest—the house and manor of Minster Lovell—only six weeks before calamity struck. In all he held from the crown annuities worth £542, fees of offices of £328 12s. 3d., and farms and grants valued at £370 10s., a total of £1241 2s. 3d. Income from private sources raised this to £1327 15s. 7d., and gratuities in addition made him wealthier than many leading nobles.

Norris's good fortune crashed to the ground on 1 May 1536. When leading a team in the May day jousts at Greenwich he was called away to accompany the king, who had suddenly decided to leave for London. On the way Norris was accused of committing adultery with the queen. He fiercely denied this, even though Henry promised to pardon his offence if he confessed, and he was committed to the Tower. He was indicted for high treason and convicted on 12 May despite a plea of not guilty, although he said little before the sentence (commuted to beheading) was carried out on Tower Hill on 17 May. His body was buried that day outside St Peter ad Vincula, Tower Green.

Norris's first loyalty had been to Henry, but his place at court had necessarily brought him into frequent contact with Anne. He played the game of courtly flattery with her and also clearly admired her. He shared her reformist religious views, placing his son with the refugee evangelical teacher Nicholas Bourbon. Yet although one of her circle, the charges of adultery are demonstrably false and Norris died rather than make a false confession. The crown, however, also claimed that Anne and he had agreed to marry and so did intend the king's death. The basis for this was a distortion of a very public quarrel between them on or just before 30 April. Norris was a widower and a second marriage to Margaret Shelton, one of Anne's ladies and a relative of hers, was under consideration. Anne accused

him of holding back on this, something which she, faced with the threat of Jane Seymour, may have interpreted as a sign of weakening loyalty. She said, 'You loke for ded mens showys; for yf owth came to the king but good, you wold loke to have me', to which Norris replied that 'yf he should have ony soche thought he wold hys hed wer of' (BL, Cotton MS Otho C x, fol. 225). This, of itself, could only be used to incriminate Anne, so the fact that the charges were extended to Norris suggests there was a deliberate wish to bring him down. The king was clearly not the instigator—his sudden departure from Greenwich on May day suggests that he had no prior knowledge of allegations against Norris; so too his offer of pardon, which was wholly exceptional. The probability, therefore, is that the attack on Anne was seized as an opportunity to destroy Norris too, and most historians place the responsibility for this on Thomas Cromwell. With Norris gone, Cromwell would be unchallenged.

Norris's wife, Mary, the daughter of Thomas Fiennes, eighth Baron Dacre, was dead by 1530. They had three children. The son and heir, another Henry *Norris (c.1525–1601), was corrupted in blood following his father's conviction. Restored in 1539, he went on to a distinguished career and a peerage under Elizabeth I, who considered that his father had died for loyalty to Queen Anne. Another son, Edward, had died in 1529 and Norris's daughter, Mary, married Sir George Carewe, who died in 1545 as the captain of the ill-fated *Mary Rose*, and then Sir Arthur Champerdowne. E. W. IVES

Sources LP Henry VIII, vols. 1–11 · M. St C. Byrne, ed., *The Lisle letters*, 6 vols. (1981) · D. R. Starkey, 'The king's privy chamber, 1485–1547', PhD diss., U. Cam., 1973 · E. W. Ives, *Anne Boleyn* (1986) · HoP, *Commons, 1509–58*, 3.19 · J. C. Wedgwood and A. D. Holt, *History of parliament, 1: Biographies of the members of the Commons house, 1439–1509* (1936) · G. Cavendish, *Life of Wolsey*, ed. R. S. Sylvester, Early English Text Society, original series, 243 (1958) · G. A. Crapelet, *Lettres de Henri VIIIème à Anne Boleyn* (1835) · Cotton MS, BL, Otho C x · special collections, rentals and surveys, portfolios, PRO, SC12/23/51 · 'Eltham Ordinances', *A collection of Ordinances*, Society of Antiquaries (1790) · DNB · D. Starkey, 'Court and government', *Revolution reassessed*, ed. C. Coleman and D. Starkey (1986), 29–58 · G. Walker, 'The "expulsion of the minions" of 1519 reconsidered', *HJ*, 32 (1989), 1–16 · W. H. Rylands, ed., *The four visitations of Berkshire*, 2, Harleian Society, 57 (1908), 184–8

Wealth at death £1327 15s. 7d.: LP Henry VIII, 10.878 (ii)

Norris, Henry, first Baron Norris (c.1525–1601), courtier and diplomat, was the only son and second child of Henry *Norris (b. before 1500, d. 1536) and Mary (d. in or before 1530), daughter of Thomas Fiennes, eighth Baron Dacre. His father was a gentleman of the privy chamber, groom of the stool and keeper of the privy purse, who in May 1536 was accused of adultery with Anne Boleyn and executed for treason. Before Anne's fall, Norris had been tutored in her household by Nicholas Bourbon, a French evangelical reformer. Thereafter he apparently remained at court as a ward of the king. The act of parliament condemning his father had allowed him to supplicate Henry VIII for the restoration of the family estates. Accordingly, in 1539 all his lands were returned except those which had been forfeited to the crown or were part of his maternal grandmother's estate. In 1544 he was granted new holdings in Southampton, Oxfordshire, and Berkshire, including extensive lands of the former monastery in Reading.

Under Henry VIII, Norris held minor office at court. In 1544 he was described as the king's servant; he was an official of the royal stable, and may also have been an attendant of Prince Edward. In the next reign he was a gentleman of Edward VI's privy chamber and sat in the parliament of 1547 as MP for Berkshire. In 1553 he was one of the witnesses to Edward's letters patent assigning the throne to Lady Jane Grey.

By 1544 Norris had married Margery (Margaret) [**Margery Norris**, Lady Norris (d. 1599)], the younger daughter and coheir of Sir John *Williams and Elizabeth Edmonds; Sir John was created Baron Williams of Thame in 1554. This family connection became very important to Norris during the reign of Mary I. A strong partisan of the new queen, Williams acted as the protector and patron of his son-in-law, who had been an adherent of Northumberland and was out of sympathy with Catholicism. In 1553 Norris withdrew from court and retired to Wytham in Berkshire, one of Williams's manors. In 1556 the queen jointly granted the two men monastic land around Little Marlow in Buckinghamshire. Also thanks to Williams, Norris and his wife came to know Princess Elizabeth. As one of the princess's two guardians during her period of house arrest at Woodstock, Williams entertained her more than once at his house at Rycote in Oxfordshire, almost certainly while the Norrises were present. In May 1554 she was royally entertained there when stopping overnight on her way from the Tower to Woodstock. There is some evidence that over the next year, occasional short visits to Williams's house provided some relief from her otherwise isolated existence at Woodstock. In July 1555, on her return to London, she again stopped at Rycote. The memory of these visits and Williams's kindness to her during her period of confinement possibly prompted Elizabeth's warm feelings towards the Norrises at the beginning of her reign.

Immediately on her accession, Elizabeth removed the restrictions on Norris's inheritance. He inherited further landholdings in Berkshire and Oxfordshire on the deaths of his father-in-law and of his uncle Sir John Norris; with Williams's decease in 1559 he and his wife took possession of the family's primary seat at Rycote, Oxfordshire; and in 1565 he secured Yattendon, his uncle's property in Berkshire. His influence in these two counties proceeded apace: from 1559 he was JP for Berkshire, and for Oxfordshire from at least 1562.

Between 1563 and 1565 the Norrises spent much time at court. Although Margery was not appointed to the privy chamber, she was an intimate of the queen with the nickname Crow because of her dark complexion. In 1560 she was the chief mourner at the funeral of Lady Amy Dudley, probably because of her rank in the county of Oxfordshire where the death occurred. In September 1562 Norris had his first diplomatic experience when he was sent as special envoy to Paris, apparently with instructions to protest at the persecution of the Huguenots. In November 1565 he participated in a tournament in the queen's presence on the occasion of the marriage of the earl of Warwick. In September 1566 he was knighted when the queen visited him at Rycote on her return to London from Oxford. It has been suggested that his elevation was a preliminary to his appointment soon afterwards as ambassador to France.

Norris arrived in France in January 1567, and lived with his family outside Paris in a house chosen for its suitability to receive visitors without observation. His messages home were full of rumours of international conspiracies as well as detailed description of the military manoeuvres of both sides in the second and third French civil wars. He took the lead in requesting the return of Calais in the spring of 1567 in accordance with the treaty of Cateau Cambrésis—a request that was quickly rebuffed by the French. Besides writing regularly to the queen, Cecil, and Leicester (through whose influence he had probably secured the position of ambassador), Norris's recipients included Sir Nicholas Throckmorton, the duke of Norfolk, the earl of Pembroke, and Sir Walter Mildmay. One of his informants was Daniel Rogers, the son of the first Marian martyr. Norris was impressed with Rogers's lineage and learning, and appointed him tutor to his children as well as steward and secretary in his household. Another of his secretaries was Edmund Mather who came under suspicion of treason in 1571.

Norris found his stay in Paris difficult. Cecil criticized him for exceeding his allowances in the pursuit of low value intelligence. Elizabeth chided him for being 'somewhat too partial' towards the prince of Condé, especially in exaggerating his successes in the military conflicts (*CSP for.*, 1566–8, 401). The French royal family did not trust him because of his sympathy for the Huguenots and consequently his post was seized on several occasions, his servants were arrested, and attempts were made to search his house. Worn down by these indignities and wanting to return to England where he faced several legal suits, Norris requested a recall in the spring and summer of 1569, or at the very least the return of his wife and family, but he had to wait until December 1570 before Francis Walsingham arrived in France as his successor.

After his return home in March 1571, Norris sat as MP for Oxfordshire in the parliament which opened on 2 April 1571. There he spoke on the Bill to Preserve the Queen's Safety and served on various committees. In May 1572 he was called to the House of Lords as Baron Norris of Rycote. In February 1576 he petitioned parliament for his restoration in blood and honours, and an act was passed to this effect. In 1585 a statute went through parliament to settle a lengthy law suit with Lord and Lady Dacres.

After 1572 Norris carried out a few ceremonial duties for the queen and gave her advice on martial matters. In November 1581 he participated in the trial of Lord Vaux (for harbouring Edmund Campion), and in April 1589 was summoned to hear the trial of Philip, earl of Arundel. For the most part, however, Norris served Elizabeth at a local level. From 1578 he was the keeper of the armoury and porter of the outer gate of Windsor Castle. He probably became high steward of Abingdon on Leicester's death, though the evidence is not clear, and definitely succeeded the earl as high steward of Wallingford in 1588. In July 1588 he was appointed captain of the light horse in the queen's bodyguard. He acted as joint lord lieutenant of Oxfordshire and Berkshire between 1585 and 1599 (an office shared with first Sir Francis and then Sir William Knollys). In this post, he was responsible for home defence and for mustering men for service abroad during the Spanish war. Although Sir Robert Naunton suggested that Norris competed aggressively with the Knollys family for local influence, later historians believed the factional conflict had been exaggerated and point to evidence of co-operation between them over parliamentary patronage and the protection of puritans.

In 1586, while carrying out his duty as a leading magistrate, Norris was physically attacked by a group of students from Magdalen College, Oxford, after their peers had been imprisoned for poaching royal deer. In 1596 his house was targeted for attack by a group of Oxfordshire men planning a rising against enclosures. They had heard that the house was full of munitions and timed their action for St Hugh's day, when most of the local gentry would be in London to celebrate Elizabeth's accession day. The rising, however, proved abortive and Norris was made responsible for interrogating its leaders, one of whom was his own carpenter, Bartholomew *Steer.

From the 1570s onwards the Norrises' six sons fought as soldiers in the Netherlands, France, and Ireland. Norris and his wife supported their exploits financially and politically. They sold some of their manors, mortgaged their lands to the queen, and ran into debt to help pay the costs of their sons' martial careers. Both petitioned Burghley on John *Norris's behalf, first when he was banished from court in 1587 over his quarrels with Leicester during the Netherlands campaign, and again in 1589 when he was in trouble for his part in the disastrous Portugal campaign. In the 1590s both wrote to Robert Cecil to request their sons' return from Ireland.

In September 1592 Norris took advantage of the queen's visit to Rycote to present his children in a favourable light. In a courtly pastime, Elizabeth was offered gifts, ostensibly from a messenger sent by four of Norris's five surviving sons who were then serving her abroad. Each gift was an expensive token designed to remind the queen of their individual military service. In addition, Elizabeth was presented with a jewelled daisy supposedly sent by Norris's daughter Catherine who was married to Sir Anthony Poulett, governor of Jersey. Norris's sons tried in their turn to promote their father but without success. In September 1585 John suggested him as governor of Flushing, and in October 1598 Edward *Norris reminded Essex of his 'promise touching my aged father when any councillors shall be named' (*Salisbury MSS*, 8.405). All but one of Norris's sons died in royal service abroad: the eldest, William, in Ireland in December 1579; Maximilian in Brittany, 1593; John in Ireland in September 1597; and two years later both Henry and Thomas *Norris also died in Ireland. On the death of John, Elizabeth wrote Margery a personal letter of condolence addressed to 'Mine own Crow'. When Henry and Thomas died within weeks of each other in the summer of 1599, she again tried to comfort Margery and immediately relieved Margery's only surviving son, Edward, of his post as governor of Ostend, sending him home to be with his parents. Grief-stricken, Margery died soon afterwards, in December 1599. On her death, a court of wards commission was set up to inquire into her property and Elizabeth wrote off £2000 of debt to relieve Norris. He remained in good health until his death in June 1601. On 5 August he was buried in the chapel at Rycote, having been briefly interred at Englefield church, Berkshire. His heir was his grandson Francis *Norris, the son of William.   SUSAN DORAN

Sources N. J. O'Conor, *Godes peace and the queenes: vicissitudes of a house* (1934) • CSP for., 1566–71; 1584–5 • Report on the Pepys manuscripts, HMC, 70 (1911) • CSP dom., 1547–90; 1595–1601 • J. Nichols, *The progresses and public processions of Queen Elizabeth*, new edn, 3 (1823), 163–72 • HoP, Commons, 1558–1603 • Calendar of the manuscripts of the most hon. the marquis of Salisbury, 24 vols., HMC, 9 (1883–1976), vols. 4–9 • *Scrinia Ceciliana: mysteries of state and government … a … supplement of Cabala* (1663) • BL, Cotton MSS, Caligula IX, fol. 226 • letters from Lord Norris to Lord Treasurer on his sons' behalf, BL, Harley MSS 6993, article 26; 6994, article 5 • CPR, 1558–60; 1580–82 • APC, 1588, 1591–2, 1600–04 • LP Henry VIII, vols. 9/2, 17, 19/2, 21/2 • J. S. Nolan, *Sir John Norreys and the Elizabethan world* (1997) • G. M. Bell, *A handlist of British diplomatic representatives, 1509–1688*, Royal Historical Society Guides and Handbooks, 16 (1990) • Fuller, *Worthies* (1840), vol. 3 • PRO, PROB 11/98, fols. 93r–94 [will dated 24 Sept 1599]
Archives Magd. Cam., corresp.
Likenesses monument, Westminster Abbey, St Andrew's Chapel • portrait, priv. coll.; repro. in O'Conor, *Godes peace and the queenes*

Norris, Henry (1661×5–1731), actor, was the son of Henry Norris and his wife, both of whom were actors in Davenant's company. No record of the younger Henry Norris's birth has been discovered, but according to Chetwood he was 'born in Salisbury Court, Fleet Street, 1665' (Chetwood, 196)—the theatre there was destroyed in the great fire of 1666—but Chetwood also said, incompatibly, that Norris was sixty-nine when he died. His mother was acting until 1684 and his father until 1687. He had a sister, Mall (Mary?), of whom the *Satyr on the Players* said: 'she must f—k to get her father clothes'; she is not noticed on the stage.

The first records of Norris are at Smock Alley Theatre, Dublin, in 1693, but since he took significant roles he must have had prior acting experience. By then he had married Sarah Knapton (*fl.* 1693–1715), whose younger sister Elizabeth married Robert *Wilks. Their father, Captain Ferdinando Knapton, was town clerk of Southampton. Henry and Sarah's son Robert was baptized in Dublin at St John the Evangelist on 5 May 1694, and another son, James, on 20 November 1695. A third son, Henry, became an actor, but his date of birth is not known. Chetwood also mentions 'Females' who died comparatively young. Sarah was an actress, and a Mrs Norris sent in accounts for washing costumes to Drury Lane in 1714 and 1715. She is not heard of later, so she may have retired or died at that time. In contrast to her diminutive husband, she is described as a handsome and well-made woman.

Norris, Wilks, and George Farquhar were in Dublin under Ashbury in the 1690s. During the period Norris wrote a farce, *The Deceit*. The trio was in London in 1699, when Farquhar's *The Constant Couple, or, A Trip to the Jubilee* opened at Drury Lane on 28 November. It was a great success, with, according to Farquhar, fifty performances in five months. Wilks established himself as the type of the good-natured young gallant with Sir Harry Wildair, and Henry Norris was ever after known as Jubilee Dicky, from his performance as the servant. They took the same roles in the play's sequel, *Sir Harry Wildair*. Although he often played the comic servant—Handy in George Etherege's *The Man of Mode*, Scrub in Farquhar's *The Beaux' Stratagem* (Wilks was Archer), Lory in John Vanbrugh's *The Relapse*, and Setter in William Congreve's *The Old Bachelor*—Norris's repertory was much wider. He also played Fondlewife in *The Old Bachelor*, Pearmain in Farquhar's *The Recruiting Officer*, and Sir Jasper Fidget in William Wycherley's *The Country Wife*. In Dublin he played other Etherege parts, Sir Nicholas Cully in *Love in a Tub* and Sir Oliver Cockwood in *She Would if she Could*. At the Haymarket he played Old Bellair and Gomez in John Dryden's *The Spanish Fryar*. He was compared with James Nokes for comic female roles, such as the Old Woman in Beaumont and Fletcher's *Rule a Wife and Have a Wife*, First Trull in Thomas Shadwell's *Humours of the Army*, Mrs Fardingale in *The Funeral*, Duenna in John Dennis's *Gibraltar*, or the Nurse in *Gaius Marius* (Thomas Otway's version of *Romeo and Juliet*).

In other Shakespeare plays and adaptations Norris played the dim-witted drawer, Francis, in *1 Henry IV*, the braggart soldier Pistol in *2 Henry IV*, Caliban (and other parts) in *The Tempest*, Osric in *Hamlet*, the First Witch in *Macbeth*, and the Poet in *Timon of Athens*. In Jonson's plays he was Sir Politic Would-Be in *Volpone*, Cutbeard in *The Silent Woman*, Dapper in *The Alchemist*, and Littlewit in *Bartholomew Fair*.

Norris spent most of his career at Drury Lane. In 1706 he went to the Haymarket with Owen Swiny, but he returned when the two companies were reunited. In later years he played at the summer fairs. He was Sir Roger in John Gay's *The What d'ye Call it* with William Pinkethman at Bartholomew fair in 1716, and the following year he was at Tottenham Court fair with Leigh and at Southwark with Pinkethman; their collaboration continued (with a break in 1722) until 1725, when Norris played Spider in *Semiramis* at Bartholomew fair shortly before Pinkethman's death. In the summer of 1710 Norris was at Pinkethman's Greenwich Theatre and added Roderigo in *Othello* to his repertory. There on 11 September he played Old Moneytrap in Vanbrugh's *The Confederacy*, with his son Young Jubilee Dicky in the juvenile role of Jessemin. At Pinkethman's Richmond Theatre, in 1719 just after Addison's death, Norris played the title role in a burlesque of *Cato*. Chetwood comments, 'a blind Man might have borne with *Norris* in the *Roman Patriot*, for he spoke with all the Solemnity of a suffering Hero', while the rest of the cast made it 'ridiculous by Humour and Action' (Chetwood, 198), and suggests that Norris had a wider range than he could exercise in the theatre. 'He never performed any part of a serious cast: for

notwithstanding his judgment … his figure must have made the sentiments ridiculous' (ibid., 197).

There are not many descriptions of Norris's acting, but it is clear that he was a brilliant mime and frequently deployed the ad lib: 'Our celebrated Norris had introduc'd a thousand occasional pleasantries into every one of the ridiculous characters he was famous for playing … and if the author rav'd at the abuse, the audience never failed to be pleased with it' (Hill, 215).

Norris continued working into December 1730; he then became sick, and his death, at his house in Brownlow Street, on 10 February 1731, was reported in the *Daily Post* of 16 February 1731: 'That celebrated Comedian … who has entertained the Town near Forty years with general Applause and always followed Nature … was decently and privately interred (according to his own desire) near the body of his late wife … at Paddington' on 13 February 1731.   F. H. MARES

Sources Highfill, Burnim & Langhans, *BDA* · W. Van Lennep and others, eds., *The London stage, 1660–1800*, pt 1: *1660–1700* (1965) · E. L. Avery, ed., *The London stage, 1660–1800*, pt 2: *1700–1729* (1960) · W. R. Chetwood, *A general history of the stage, from its origin in Greece to the present time* (1749), 196–9 · W. S. Clark, *The early Irish stage: the beginnings to 1720* (1955) · J. Doran, *'Their majesties' servants', or, Annals of the English stage*, another edn (1897), 160–65 · J. Downes, *Roscius Anglicanus*, ed. J. Milhous and R. D. Hume, new edn (1987) · Genest, *Eng. stage* · [J. Hill], *The actor: a treatise on the art of playing* (1750) · *The Spectator* (6 Oct 1712)

Norris, Sir Henry George (1865–1934), property developer and football promoter, was born on 23 July 1865 at 23 Royal Terrace, Kennington, London, the son of John Henry Norris, warehouseman, and his wife, Georgiana Sarah Shaw. Educated privately, he was articled at the age of thirteen to a firm of solicitors.

Norris's great leap forward came in 1896 when he joined W. G. Allen in the firm of Allen and Norris, auctioneers and estate agents, builders, and joiners, of 298 Wandsworth Bridge Road (which was still extant in Fulham Palace Road in 1976). Under the auspices of this firm, he became a successful property developer in the London of the 1890s, building some 2000 flats and houses on what had been farmland and market gardens in Fulham. Many of the houses were divided into two flats with separate sculleries and a staircase leading from the upper flat to the back garden. They were designed for lower middle class and better-off working people. Norris also built larger houses of self-contained flats with bathrooms off the Fulham Palace Road. He later became a director of several companies including Kinnaird Park Estates and the Municipal Freehold Land Co. In 1901 he married Edith Anne *née* Featherstone; they had three daughters.

An energetic and ambitious man, Norris also played prominent roles in the worlds of politics and professional football. Having served for six years as a member of the Battersea vestry, in 1906 he was elected to the Fulham borough council for the Sands End ward. He was elected mayor in 1909, an office he retained until 1919. He was on the London county council from 1916 until 1919. The war provided an ideal opportunity to fuse energy and entrepreneurialism with patriotism. Norris had formerly held commissions in the 3rd Middlesex artillery volunteers and the 2nd Tower Hamlets volunteers. He was a member of the committee which raised the footballers' battalion of the Middlesex regiment and he personally raised three brigades of artillery from the Fulham area, where he was recruiting officer with the rank of colonel. A later wartime appointment was as director of recruiting for the south-eastern counties. In recognition of his role during the war he was knighted in 1917. The following year he was elected Conservative MP for East Fulham, but as a staunch free-trader retired in 1922 when the government adopted tariff reform. A leading freemason, he held high masonic office in the Kent and London mayors' lodges, and also in the grand lodge of England.

In addition Norris made a significant impact on professional football in London. He became a director in 1906, and later chairman, of his local club, Fulham, and helped it to reach the second division of the Football League in 1907–8. However, when Woolwich Arsenal appeared on the brink of bankruptcy he took it over and tried to amalgamate it with Fulham, but the Football League rejected the plan. He subsequently retired from Fulham and became chairman of Arsenal. The Arsenal was the capital's oldest professional club and Norris realized that it had to move from Plumstead if it was to realize its potential, and in 1913 £20,000 was spent on 6 acres of land belonging to St John's College of Divinity at Highbury in north London. There was opposition from local residents and from Clapton Orient and Tottenham Hotspurs who disliked the idea of a competitor only 4 miles away, but the Football League felt the market was far from glutted and Arsenal played the first match at Highbury on 6 September 1913.

English league football had been suspended in 1915 because of the war, with Arsenal in the second division, to which it had been relegated in 1912. However, in 1919 the Football League decided to expand the number of clubs in the first division from twenty to twenty-two. It was expected that the two teams who would have been relegated in 1915, Chelsea and Tottenham, would keep their places but Norris pulled off an audacious and ruthless coup, the full details of which remain unclear to this day. He persuaded the AGM of the Football League to keep Chelsea but to relegate Tottenham and further claimed that Arsenal should take its place on the dubious grounds of having been a member of the league for longer. Arsenal thus returned to the first division, not by virtue of performance on the field but as the result of apparently shady deals.

Norris was never again to be so influential in the corridors of Football League power, noticeably failing to persuade the league to place an upper limit on the amounts which could be paid in transfer fees when a player moved from one club to another. In 1927 he was suspended from all football and football management for making illegal payments to obtain players. Two years later he lost a libel action against the members of the FA commission which had convicted him. This was his third libel action in nine years, but the first he had lost.

A combative character, Norris was clearly a man used to exercising power and getting his own way. One Arsenal manager said that everyone in the club was frightened of him. Tall and thin, with pince-nez and white walrus moustache, he must have found it very frustrating to watch the success of Arsenal in the early 1930s under the management of Herbert Chapman, whom he had appointed in 1925. Norris died at his home, Sirron Lodge, Barnes Common, on 30 July 1934 and was buried in East Sheen cemetery on 2 August. TONY MASON

Sources S. Inglis, *League football and the men who made it: the official centenary of the Football League, 1888–1988* (1988) · B. Joy, *Forward, Arsenal!* (1952) · P. Soar and M. Tyler, *Arsenal, 1886–1986* (1986) · S. Studd and H. Chapman, *Football emperor* (1981) · W. T. Pike, ed., *Mayors of England and Wales* (1911) · *WW* (1935) · *Athletic News* (28 April 1913) · *Athletic News* (5 June 1917) · *Athletic News* (5 June 1922) · *Athletic News* (11 Feb 1929) · *Fulham Chronicle* (8 Aug 1934) · *Fulham Chronicle* (27 Aug 1976) · *The Times* (6 Feb 1929) · *The Times* (7 Feb 1929) · *The Times* (31 July 1934) · *The Times* (3 Aug 1934) · *CGPLA Eng. & Wales* (1935) · b. cert.
Likenesses C. Hall, oils, 1927, Fulham Town Hall, London
Wealth at death £72,051 4s. 1d.: resworn probate, 11 Jan 1935, *CGPLA Eng. & Wales*

Norris, Henry Handley (1771–1850), Church of England clergyman, was born on 14 January 1771 in the parish of St Andrew Undershaft, London, only son of Henry Handley Norris of Hackney and of West Ham, Russian merchant, and his wife, Grace, daughter of the Revd T. Hest, vicar of Warton, Lancashire. He was educated at Dr Newcome's school in Hackney, and was admitted as a pensioner at Pembroke College, Cambridge, in 1788, migrating to Peterhouse in 1789. He graduated BA in 1793 and MA in 1796. In 1817 he was admitted *ad eundem* at the University of Oxford (Pembroke College).

Norris's meeting with Joshua Watson in June 1794, when both organized a subscription for a company of Shropshire militia stationed at Hackney, proved to be the most significant event of his life. Norris and Watson became inseparable lifelong friends and allies; both sons of wealthy London merchants, they were to dedicate their lives and wealth to the service of the Church of England. Unlike Watson, Norris took holy orders (1796) and became a curate in Hackney to his brother-in-law, the Revd John James Watson (1767–1839), rector of Hackney and brother of Joshua Watson. Having succeeded to the property of his father in 1804, Norris used his considerable private means to contribute towards the endowment of a new chapel of ease erected by subscription in Lauriston Road, South Hackney, and dedicated to St John of Jerusalem. On becoming the perpetual curate of the chapel in 1806, he further endowed it at an annual rate of £21 and erected, at his own expense, a minister's residence in Well Street, Hackney. In 1831 the perpetual curacy became a rectory, and Norris remained rector until his death. In 1816 he was appointed a prebend of Llandaff Cathedral, and in 1825 he became a prebend of St Paul's Cathedral. He also acted as chaplain to the sixth earl of Shaftesbury. He had married on 19 June 1805 Henrietta Catherine, daughter of David Powell and sister of Baden Powell.

Norris was a pre-Tractarian tory high-churchman. His

high-church principles were partly shaped by reaction to what he regarded as the subversive forces unleashed by the French Revolution. Like many of his generation, he developed a deep-rooted horror of Jacobinism or 'French principles' from an early date. His first publication, *The Influence of the Female Character upon Society* (1801), contained much colourful invective against the immodesty of the 'poisoned garments' then being imported and copied from the 'Grecian' female fashions of late revolutionary France. He was not, however, a merely 'high and dry' or political churchman. In the tradition of the Caroline divines, the early nonjurors, and later eighteenth-century high-church mentors such as William Jones of Nayland and William Stevens, he held an exalted view of the dignity of the Christian priesthood and sacraments, and of the power and authority of the church as a divine institution. A diligent pastor, Norris was the author of *A Manual for the Parish Priest* (1815) and *A Pastor's Legacy* (1851). In 1805 he personally financed the establishment of a new school, and later also built and endowed a school for girls. Norris's zeal was partly a response to the strength of the dissenting interest in the Hackney area, and to the dissenting academy, Homerton College, which was situated in the vicinity. He became the acknowledged leader of the so-called Hackney Phalanx, the label bestowed on a group of high-church friends who exerted a dominant influence in the counsels of church and state in the period of Lord Liverpool's ministry from 1812 until 1827. During Liverpool's long premiership Norris gained the title of 'Bishopmaker'; it was said by Thomas Mozley that every see was offered to Norris, with the request that if he could not take it himself, he should be so good as to recommend someone else (Mozley, 1.338).

Norris exerted a potent influence through the medium of various Phalanx-dominated church organizations. With Joshua Watson he helped found the National Society for Promoting the Education of the Poor in the Principles of the Established Church (1811). He was also active in both the Society for the Propagation of the Gospel (SPG) and the Society for Promoting Christian Knowledge (SPCK), the proceedings of which he largely dominated from 1793 to 1834. A great patron of public charities, he helped organize relief for German refugees from the Napoleonic War, and was indefatigable in the initial promotion and later support of the colonial churches, whose earliest bishops, Thomas Fanshawe Middleton (Calcutta), John Inglis (Nova Scotia), and William Grant Broughton (Australia), were his intimate friends. Norris's missionary concerns earned him the title of Patriarch from his friend Charles Lloyd, bishop of Oxford, (1784–1829), 'for your care for all the churches is more than an Archbishop's' (Churton, *Memoir*, 1.281)—a playful and only slight overstatement of the truth. His personal sympathies with various colonial churchmen could overcome his political prejudices, as when he championed the cause of John Henry Hobart, bishop of New York, on Hobart's fund-raising tour of England in 1823. Norris's toryism was offended by Hobart's patriotic American republicanism, but Hobart's energetic high-church orthodoxy and personal character led Norris

warmly to defend his friend when he was criticized by other English high-churchmen. When another American churchman, Dr Hawks, visited England in 1838 for a similar purpose, Hawks reported that none took a deeper interest in his cause than Norris. Nearer home, Norris was a keen patron of the disestablished Scottish Episcopal church, while in England his missionary instincts found an outlet in his support for Anglican efforts to convert individual Jews to Christianity.

Norris also exerted a literary influence through the medium of the *British Critic*, the high-church periodical founded in 1793 by William Jones of Nayland, which Norris and Watson acquired in 1811–12. Under their management and the editorship of their friends William Van Mildert, Thomas Fanshawe Middleton, and Thomas Rennell, junior, the *British Critic* became a 'house journal' for the Hackney Phalanx.

Norris's high-churchmanship was characterized by a rigidity and narrowly anti-evangelical animus which his friend the eirenic Irish high-churchman John Jebb (who owed his preferment to the see of Limerick to Norris) privately lamented. Norris regarded both Anglican evangelicals and dissenters as heirs to the seventeenth-century puritans, whom he believed in the 1820s posed as much of a threat to the security of church and state as had their forebears in the time of Charles I. His suspicion of evangelical irregularities found expression in public opposition to the activities of the British and Foreign Bible Society. His *A practical exposition of the tendency and proceedings of the British and Foreign Bible Society* (1813; 2nd edn, 1814), provoked by an attempt to form an auxiliary Bible society in Hackney, instigated a pamphlet war with the Unitarian Robert Aspland and the Anglican evangelical William Dealtry. On the other hand, Norris allowed contributions to the *British Critic* from moderate and liberal churchmen such as Baden Powell, and even enlisted later liberal bogey figures of the Tractarians, such as Samuel Hinds and R. D. Hampden, to act as his curates at Hackney in the 1820s. Before 1830 the paramountcy of resisting the challenge from dissent helped blur theological differences between high-church and moderate liberal churchmen.

The waning of Norris's influence over ecclesiastical affairs (symbolized by the successful revolt against his management of the SPCK in 1834) coincided with the emergence of a whig political ascendancy and of a Tractarian theological ascendancy in the 1830s. The Hackney Phalanx, Norris included, was instrumental in the formation of the Association of Friends of the Church in 1833, but the group was ill-equipped to inspire the rising generation, many of whom embraced Tractarianism from an evangelical background. Norris was ever ready to add 'his name and authority to the good designs of younger men' (Churton, *Christian Sincerity*, 22), and initially welcomed the Oxford divines as much-needed allies in support of an embattled Anglican orthodoxy. It was uneasiness with the liberal tendencies of two editors of the *British Critic* between 1829 and 1836, Archibald Campbell and James Shergold Boone, that prompted Norris and his Hackney friends to enlist Newman and other Tractarians as contributors in 1836. Though Newman sometimes dined with Norris in Hackney, the two were never close. Norris became alarmed at the manner in which Newman and his friends assumed sole proprietorship of the *British Critic* in 1838 and made that journal an exclusive organ of Tractarian views. Norris retained a deep-seated horror of 'popery', which found ungainly expression in his polemical publication *The Principles of the Jesuits Developed in a Collection of Extracts from their Own Authors* (1839), and which put him at odds with the softening of Tractarian attitudes towards Rome. His misgivings increased with the publication of Hurrell Froude's *Remains* (1838). He repudiated Newman's 'catholic' interpretation of the Thirty-Nine Articles in Tract 90. Unlike some older high-churchmen, he even approved of the formal condemnation and suspension from preaching of Pusey for a heterodox sermon on the eucharist in 1843. Norris became convinced of a close analogy between the later history of the nonjurors and that of the Tractarian movement; in 1838 he gained the loan of a collection of papers on the nonjurors, the investigation of which inspired him to prophesy that the Oxford Movement would follow a similar path of sectarian self-destruction.

Norris supported the efforts in the early 1840s of high-church bishops such as Henry Phillpotts of Exeter and Charles Blomfield of London to enforce a stricter observance of the rubrics of the Book of Common Prayer. He was an advocate of greater decorum and a moderate ceremonial in public worship long before the foundation of the Cambridge Camden Society. Norris's adherence to the Laudian ideal of uniformity in public worship, however, made him critical of the ceremonial innovations of the later Tractarians and early ritualists. In an influential publication, *Ritual Conformity, a Divinely-Appointed Means of Preserving Christian Unity* (1842), he insisted that the liturgy was a bond of Christian unity and that only by 'uniformity in all our public devotions' could unity be preserved (12). Norris was appalled by the trend engendered by the more advanced phase of the Oxford Movement towards liturgical licence and diversity.

Norris's final years were marked by growing frustration at the dual threat to traditional high-church principles posed by the rival extremes of advanced Tractarianism and of its evangelical and low-church opponents. Having once been centre stage, Norris had become increasingly sidelined. Thomas Mozley (1.338) described him as 'the deposed monarch of a mighty spiritual empire'. The Gorham judgment in 1850, by which the judicial committee of the privy council ruled that it was allowable for an Anglican clergyman to hold that the grace of regeneration in baptism was not unconditional, dismayed Norris, but he was equally depressed by the agitation inspired by what he called 'Dr Pusey and his *junto*' (Norris to Watson, 22 Oct 1850; Bodl. Oxf., MS Eng. lett. C. 790, fol. 163).

Norris lived in semi-rural seclusion in his large parsonage house in Hackney, having done much to keep potential invasions of builders at bay during his lifetime. Although he could be stern and inflexible in manner, he was legendary in his generosity in supporting many students in their university and professional careers. He was also a hearty and amiable host at Hackney rectory, with an engaging propensity to fall into a deep sleep at the dinner table. Mozley, who once observed him closely in such circumstances in his later life, gave a vivid portrait of him as having 'very well-formed and well-chiselled features', with a striking resemblance to Cardinal Wolsey, 'finer, though not so powerful' (Mozley, 1.339). Norris remained active in his ministry until his death on 4 December 1850, at Grove Street, Hackney. His posthumous publication, *A Pastor's Legacy, or, Instructions for Confirmation* (1851), comprised a manual prepared from prayers which he had composed during the last year of his life. He was survived by a son, Henry Norris (1810–1889), of Swalcliffe Park, Oxfordshire.   PETER B. NOCKLES

Sources GM, 2nd ser., 35 (1851), 437–8 · Venn, *Alum. Cant.* · E. Churton, *Christian sincerity: a sermon on the death of the Rev. Henry Handley Norris* (1851) · Bodl. Oxf., Norris MSS · Pusey Oxf., Norris papers · W. Robinson, *The history and antiquities of the parish of Hackney, in the county of Middlesex*, 1 (1842), 173–8 · D. Lysons, *Supplement to the first edition of 'The environs of London'* (1811), 163–75 · E. Powell, *Pedigree of the family of Powell* (1891) · E. Churton, ed., *Memoir of Joshua Watson*, 2 vols. (1861) · T. Mozley, *Reminiscences, chiefly of Oriel College and the Oxford Movement*, 2 vols. (1882) · W. Gibson, 'The tories and church patronage, 1812–30', *Journal of Ecclesiastical History*, 41 (1990), 266–74

Archives Bodl. Oxf., collections relating to nonjurors · Pusey Oxf. · St John's College, Oxford, account books

Norris, Isaac (1671–1735), colonial official and merchant, was born on 26 July 1671 in Southwark, Surrey, to Thomas Norris (d. 1692), a Quaker carpenter, and Mary Moore (d. 1685). The Norris family migrated to Port Royal, Jamaica, about 1678. Isaac journeyed to Philadelphia in May 1692 where he met many prominent Quakers and his future wife, Mary (1674–1748), daughter of the president of the council of Pennsylvania, Thomas *Lloyd. On his return to Port Royal he learned that on 7 June 1692 an earthquake had caused the death of his father, sister, and brother. Only his stepmother survived. After making further voyages for trade to Philadelphia and Bermuda, Norris married Mary in March 1694 and, thereafter, made Pennsylvania his home. They had fourteen children, including Isaac *Norris (1701–1766).

Norris engaged in trade, probably using the contacts of his father-in-law, and within ten years had become wealthy. He exported tobacco, furs, and foodstuffs, and imported manufactured goods. As early as 1699 he was building ships. He also imported slaves, though complaining that this trade was troublesome because of the quality and frequent illness of Africans sent to Philadelphia. Even so, he continued to accept slaves on consignment, never voicing any moral qualms about slavery in spite of his Quaker faith and vocal Quaker protest against the trade. Norris presided as clerk in 1715 when the Philadelphia yearly meeting weakened a proposal from Chester Quakers to require Friends not to buy slaves. He advocated treating slaves humanely, but was also willing to allow miscreants to be whipped or sold abroad as a means of discipline.

Norris's success at trade enabled him to become a large landowner after 1704. He ultimately purchased at least 16,000 acres in Pennsylvania, plus many lots in Philadelphia—some of which he resold. He lived in the city until 1709 when he purchased a country estate at Fairhill in what is now Germantown, building a mansion there in 1718. He acted the country gentleman, planting an English garden and building a library. He purchased works of Locke, Pope, Addison, and Milton in addition to classical authors.

Norris's Quakerism seems to have played a prominent role in helping him to cope with the tragedy of the Port Royal earthquake, and he remained a strong supporter of this faith for his entire life. He engaged in a wide variety of tasks for Friends: investigating to make sure there was no impediment to a couple's desire to marry; arbitrating business disputes; and becoming a delegate from the Philadelphia monthly meeting to the quarterly meeting in 1701 and the yearly meeting in 1709. From 1712 to 1729 he was clerk of the Philadelphia yearly meeting. His service as delegate and clerk was a testimony to the high regard of other Quakers, because the clerk who presided over the annual business sessions of all Friends in Pennsylvania, West New Jersey, and Delaware occupied the most responsible position of any lay Quaker. Beginning in 1709 Norris also served as an overseer of the press, the agency responsible for approving all Quaker religious publications, and on several occasions wrote the epistles of the Philadelphia yearly meeting to London Friends. In the debates over Quaker participation in government and particularly over their refusal to take oaths, Norris defended the Friends' principles as compatible with political power but worried that their demands might compromise other denominations' religious liberty. Above all he sought moderation and peace with non-Quakers and eventually advised William Penn to sell his right of government. Norris typified the conservative and accommodating Quakerism which dominated Pennsylvania in the aftermath of the Keithian controversy of the 1690s until the reforms of the 1750s.

Norris was equally active in the political life of Pennsylvania. Beginning in 1699 he served sixteen terms in the Pennsylvania assembly, most occurring before 1720, and he was elected speaker in 1712 and 1720. He was a provincial councillor from 1709 to 1734 and served as justice of the peace from 1715 until his death. He was also appointed tax assessor, commissioner of land, and was elected mayor of Philadelphia in 1724. As land commissioner, he accompanied governors William Keith and Patrick Gordon in negotiations with Native Americans.

Norris remained an active supporter of the proprietor's interests throughout his career and worked hard to balance the Penns' interests with those of the Pennsylvania colonists. As a member of the assembly Norris worked with Penn for a new constitution, land rights, and financial support of the government. He opposed the separation of Delaware's assembly from Pennsylvania and feared the appointment of a royal governor. During the governorship of John Evans (1704–9), Norris opposed the attempts of David Lloyd to undermine proprietary authority and send a remonstrance against Penn to England without the approval of the assembly. Norris regarded Lloyd as an unprincipled opponent of Penn, but on occasion managed to work with him. While in England on business from 1706 to 1708, Norris worked on Penn's behalf in reaching a settlement over the proprietor's debts owed to the family of Philip Ford.

Upon his return to Pennsylvania in 1708 Norris viewed with dismay the disputes between Governor Evans, whose false rumours of a French attack in 1706 disgusted Friends, and the assembly, dominated by Lloyd. The resulting impasse meant that the colony could pass few laws. In 1710 Norris, on behalf of the Philadelphia yearly meeting, wrote *Friendly Advice to the Inhabitants of Pensilvania*, which criticized the actions of Lloyd and the assembly. In the following election all members of the assembly were replaced and Norris became speaker. The 1712 assembly provided financial support for the government, passed many new laws, and even voted £2000 for Britain's use in the War of the Spanish Succession. This last measure proved unpopular and led to Lloyd's return to power.

After 1711 Pennsylvania's political disputes revolved less around the powers of the assembly than around taxation and, in the 1720s, paper money. Initially favourable to the appointment of William Keith in 1717, Norris opposed this governor's bypassing of the council and attempt to create a circulating medium of paper money. After Keith was replaced as governor and sought to retain power through the assembly, Norris campaigned actively against Keith's stirring up of the common people and may have published a pamphlet about his debts. Norris also viewed with dismay the increasing migration to Pennsylvania of Germans and Scots-Irish.

In 1728 Norris's political career came to an end, except for a pamphlet war with Andrew Hamilton which began over the unsuccessful courtship by his son, and namesake, of Hamilton's daughter, Mary. Norris probably wrote some of the political attacks on Hamilton which appeared in Philadelphia newspapers. He was surprised when he was returned by Philadelphia county to the assembly in 1734, but felt he was too old to be of much service.

While attending a Germantown meeting on 9 March 1735, he had a stroke and died the next day at Stenton, the home of his friend James Logan near Germantown. His will left bequests of about £17,000, plus lots in Philadelphia and 620 acres of land.   J. WILLIAM FROST

Sources Proceedings of Pennsylvania Assembly, *Pennsylvania Archives*, 8th ser., 1–3 (1931) • minutes of provincial council, *Council Records*, 2–3 (1832) • J. W. Jordan, ed., *Colonial and revolutionary families of Pennsylvania*, 1 (New York, 1911), 81–3 • *The papers of William Penn*, ed. M. M. Dunn, R. S. Dunn, and others, 3–4 (1986–7) • 'Norris, Isaac', *Lawmaking and legislators in Pennsylvania: a biographical dictionary*, ed. C. W. Horle and others, [2 vols.] (Philadelphia, 1991–)
Archives Hist. Soc. Penn., family papers incl. letter-books
Likenesses W. Cogswell, painting (after painting by unknown artist), Hist. Soc. Penn.

Wealth at death £17,000 plus land in Philadelphia and 620 acres in neighbouring counties

Norris, Isaac (1701–1766), landowner and politician in America, was born on 3 December 1701 in Philadelphia, Pennsylvania, one of fourteen children of Isaac *Norris (1671–1735), and his wife, Mary (1674–1748), daughter of Thomas *Lloyd, president of the council of Pennsylvania. A lifelong resident of Philadelphia, he entered the Pennsylvania assembly at a pivotal time, when pacifist principles caused many Quakers to withdraw from active participation in politics. Norris's father was born in London but his grandparents moved to Jamaica in 1678 and were involved in the slave trade. After some doubts about this traffic the elder Isaac Norris moved to Philadelphia; there, if still ambivalent, he remained involved in the use of slaves and became an extremely successful and wealthy merchant, and one of the most extensive landowners in Pennsylvania. His marriage secured his place in the Quaker establishment. He built a splendid home, Fairhill, north of Philadelphia, and there he established an elegant lifestyle and a fine library. Next to James Logan, secretary to William Penn, he was the chief representative of Penn's interests in the Pennsylvanian colony and an executor of Penn's will.

The younger Isaac Norris attended a Friends' school in Philadelphia but also had private tutoring, which meant that he had 'an excellent classical education' ('Norris, Isaac'). He could read and write French, Latin, and some Hebrew and, as a final polish to his education, he was sent to England in 1722 and later made a tour of Europe. Perhaps chastened by criticisms of his own conspicuous lifestyle, his father advised him: 'Thou must remember that the more frugal thou art the more will be thy stock … Come back plain. This will be a reputation to thee and recommend thee to the best and most sensible people' (Norris papers, letter-book, April 1719).

On 6 June 1739 Norris married Sarah (d. 1744), daughter of Penn's secretary James Logan, a union that further secured his own standing in the Philadelphia Quaker aristocracy. Sarah was an accomplished mistress of Fairhill, to which the couple moved in 1741; they had four children, of whom two daughters survived them.

In political terms the period 1736 to 1756 was a troubled one that witnessed the rise of strong anti-proprietary feeling among the Friends. William Penn's successor as proprietor, Thomas Penn, managed his father's affairs from 1732 to 1741 but, as a tory and an Anglican, he was a bitter disappointment to the Quakers. In 1737 he violated the spirit of previous agreements with the Native Americans. Alienated by these and other actions, radical and conservative Friends joined forces to create a united political party—the 'Quaker party'—of which Isaac Norris emerged as a leader, with John Kinsey. The party, fiercely critical of the Penn family, embodied whig devotion to liberty and property.

Like his father, Norris entered the Pennsylvania assembly as representative (from 1735) for Philadelphia county; he was also speaker from 1750 to 1764. These were years during which reform-minded Quakers such as John Woolman and John Churchman were worried about conspicuous Quaker affluence, some of it based on the slave trade. At the Philadelphia yearly meeting of 1758 Woolman began a process that involved Friends in the abolition of the trade. More troubling for commercially active Quakers like Norris was Friends' perfectionist attitude towards war and the defence of the colony. Caught between these two views, on 18 May 1755 Norris wrote to an English Friend that '[we] have very much Thrown our Disputes from being a Quaker cause to a Cause for Liberty' (Norris papers, letter-book). Like his father and father-in-law, James Logan, Norris was not a strict pacificist, being 'satisfied [that] the Law of Nature and perhaps the Christian system leaves us a right to defend ourselves as well against the Enemies who are within the reach of our Laws, as those who owe no subjection to them' (ibid.).

Unlike his good friends James and Israel Pemberton (and many other Quakers), who resigned from the assembly because of their pacifist principles, Norris remained as speaker of the assembly until two years before his death. In this role he attempted to reconcile Quaker convictions with actions that most Friends considered warlike. Like his father he also steered clear of moves toward the abolition of slavery. In the end he remained the product of a family whose wealth had originated in slave commerce.

Alongside his political career Norris, in common with his father-in-law, was a noted book collector. Following his wife's death in 1744 he found consolation in the development of his library; in 1750–1, for example, he purchased 335 volumes, many bought from the London bookseller Thomas Osborne. Norris died on 13 July 1766 at Fairhill, of heart failure, and was buried at the Quaker burial-ground in Philadelphia. By the end of the decade his library had become the sole property of his last surviving daughter, Mary, who in 1770 married John Dickinson, the benefactor of Benjamin Rush's Dickinson College, Carlisle, Pennsylvania. Housed at Fairhill the collection, described by John Adams as 'very grand' (Korey, 8), survived the destruction of Norris's residence by the British in 1777. In 1784 some 1902 titles in 1750 volumes were donated by Mary Dickinson to the college that bore her married name. This gift, which formed only part of Norris's total collection, comprised a large number of heavily annotated Latin and French texts; it remains a testimony to the broad intellectual interests, energy, and wealth of an influential Quaker politician and businessman.

DAVID SOX

Sources 'Norris, Isaac (1701–1766)', RS Friends, Lond. [draft biography] · E. Digby Baltzell, *Puritan Boston and Quaker Philadelphia* (1980) · Hist. Soc. Penn., Norris papers · M. E. Korey, *The books of Isaac Norris, 1701–1766, at Dickinson College* (Carlisle, Pennsylvania, 1976) · H. Thomas, *The slave trade: the history of the Atlantic slave trade, 1440–1870* (1997) · F. B. Tolles, *Meeting house and counting house: the Quaker merchants of colonial Philadelphia, 1682–1763* (1948) · J. D. Marietta, *The reformation of American Quakerism, 1748–1783* (1984) · R. M. Jones, *The Quakers in the American colonies* (1911) · *The journal and essays of John Woolman*, ed. A. Mott Gummere (1922)
Archives Dickinson College, Carlisle, Pennsylvania · Hist. Soc. Penn.

Likenesses portrait, Hist. Soc. Penn.; repro. in Tolles, *Meeting house and counting house*, 82

Wealth at death very considerable; property; £5600 in notes and bonds; £1500 in mortgages; £18,000 in consolidated annuities: Tolles, *Meeting house and counting house*, 97

Norris [Norreys], **Sir John** (*c*.1547x50–1597), military commander, was the second son of Henry *Norris, first Baron Norris (*c*.1525–1601), courtier and diplomat, and his wife, Margery or Margaret *Norris, *née* Williams (*d.* 1599) [*see under* Norris, Henry, first Baron Norris (*c*.1525–1601)], younger daughter and coheir of John *Williams, first Baron Williams of Thame (*c*.1500–1559), administrator, and his first wife, Elizabeth. He was one of six brothers, all soldiers, including William Norris (*c*.1545x50–1579), Sir Edward *Norris (*c*.1550–1603), and Sir Thomas *Norris (1556–1599), all but one of whom died while on active service. Of them all, it was 'Black Jack', as he became known, who won the greatest renown, eventually becoming celebrated throughout Europe, particularly for his campaigns in the Netherlands. By the time he died he was 'renowned through the world' (Stowe, 805). Although his surname is usually rendered as Norris, he himself, his mother, and at least one brother always spelt it Norreys. Since his death Norris has been largely forgotten. He has recently been rediscovered to an extent, appearing prominently in histories of Elizabeth I's reign and foreign wars and has finally attracted a biographer in John Nolan (1997). Yet much of his career remains obscure. Norris's monument in Yattendon church in Berkshire states that he was born in 1529, but this is impossible; an intimate servant later asserted that he was aged fifty at his death in 1597, and 1547 has usually been given as the year of his birth. However, given Lord Norris's age and the probable dates of birth of his first and third sons, a later year of birth for Norris is likely.

Youth and early military career on the continent, *c*.1547x50–1573 Norris's father was heir of one of Henry VIII's favourites, Henry Norris of Bray (*b.* before 1500, *d.* 1536), who was caught up in the downfall of Anne Boleyn and executed on 17 May 1536. In addition to this association with Elizabeth's mother, during Mary I's reign Norris's parents befriended Princess Elizabeth. Henry Norris, protestant in his sympathies, lived quietly at Rycote in Oxfordshire, one of the manors of his father-in-law, a co-guardian of Elizabeth, who was sometimes kept there under house arrest. During those early years she would also have met the Norris children.

John Williams died on 14 October 1559 and Norris's parents inherited the best part of his estates. They made their seat at Rycote. Elizabeth stayed on close terms with them after her accession. Norris was brought up surrounded both by comfort and a feeling of familiarity with the court. However, little definite is known about his childhood and adolescence. There are indications that he may briefly have attended Magdalen College, Oxford. His later correspondence demonstrates that he was comfortable in both Latin and French, and had a working knowledge of Italian and Portuguese, all of which is indicative of a good education.

A soldier's life attracted Norris from an early age. In autumn 1566 his father was appointed resident ambassador to France—always a sensitive post, but even more so at this time because confessional tension was building there between Huguenots and Catholics. It was not uncommon for young English aristocrats to spend time in the household of a great French noble to finish their education and Norris, still in his late teens, was placed by his father in the household of Gaspard de Coligny, admiral of France. The choice of Coligny, one of the Huguenots' leaders, reflects the reformed religious sympathies of the Norris family, but Henry Norris was presumably embarrassed when his sons were not content to sit on the sidelines when the second war of religion broke out in 1567. Norris and his elder brother, William Norris, fought in the Huguenot ranks at the battle of St Denis on 10 November 1567 and drew a 'spirited' sketch of the action, which their father enclosed with one of his dispatches (*CSP for.*, 1566–8, 374).

The second civil war was officially ended by the edict of Longjumeau (March 1568) and both sons returned home, where they entered the household of Sir William Cecil, the principal secretary. The two youths sowed wild oats during this time. William Norris (who may already have been party to a scandal in France) was probably a bad influence, and his father summoned him back to the French court in autumn 1568, at about the time of the outbreak of the war of religion. Norris was left in England for the moment, though he may have served with William of Orange against the Spanish in the Low Countries during summer 1568. If so, he returned home and by July 1569 his father called him to France as well, fearing that he was living 'as idly as his eldest brother' (*CSP for.*, 1569–71, 96). From autumn 1569 until the end of the third civil war in August 1570 Norris again fought for the protestants, though details are not known. Two years later he may well have served in a mixed Huguenot and English force in the southern Low Countries, during the renewed outbreak of the Dutch revolt.

In these years Norris made contacts that he exploited to good effect later in his career. The protestants of France and the Low Countries maintained close contact, exemplified in 1583 by Orange's marriage to Louise de Coligny, Coligny's daughter. A memorandum to Elizabeth on military aid to continental protestants (undated, but probably from 1575), observed that Norris 'has always been friendly with the French' (*CSP for.*, 1575–7, 223). This reflects that he served his apprenticeship with them in the difficult days of 1569–70. In addition, he learned vital lessons, witnessing at first hand the results of inadequate arrangements for wages and logistics. He mastered the intricacies of the financial and logistical sides of war to a remarkable extent and became one of the great military entrepreneurs of the era.

Service in Ireland, France, and the Netherlands, 1573–1584 His early experiences evidently confirmed Norris's taste for a military life. In August 1573 his career took a new turn, when he and William Norris accompanied Walter Devereux, first earl of Essex, on his expedition to Ulster.

Norris commanded a troop of horse in which Norris was a gentleman volunteer. Norris saved his brother's life in a skirmish in October 1573 and in the following month carried home dispatches from Essex to the queen, in which the earl singled out the brothers for their good service, but also asked for reinforcements. These were authorized, and in January 1574 Norris returned in command of a company of 100 foot, raised from the family estates in Oxfordshire and Berkshire—his first independent command.

The Irish wars were full of brutal incidents perpetrated by both sides and Norris showed himself as ruthless as anyone. In October 1574 he had over 200 followers of the rebellious Brian Mac Phelim O'Neill killed, 'men, women, youths and maidens' (Nolan, 26). In July 1575, with the then little-known Francis Drake, he attacked the stronghold of Sorley Boy MacDonnell on Rathlin Island in co. Antrim. After a siege of four days the island surrendered on 26 July, but Norris put the soldiers to the sword and routed out their families from the caves where they were sheltering. Some 300–400 women and children were slain, including MacDonnell's own family. His actions were acclaimed by his superiors, but by autumn 1577 he had left Ireland.

The European wars of religion continued to rage in France and the Low Countries. In 1577 Norris raised his own battalion of infantry to serve the protestant cause. He was probably initially planning to serve in the Netherlands, but a truce there and the outbreak of the sixth war of religion in France directed him back to the Huguenots. In late summer 1577 he led a force of English troops in the defence of the Île de Ré, which commanded the approaches to La Rochelle, the key protestant portstronghold. Norris and his men 'hazarded themselves so well of danger they … honoured their country'—and helped to save the strategically vital island (*CSP for.*, *1577–8*, 201). He had now demonstrated that he was not only a brave soldier; he was in addition adept at both the complex business of raising, and the difficult art of commanding, military units or formations.

Peace between the Dutch rebels and Spanish was short-lived and by the end of 1577 war had resumed in the Netherlands. Elizabeth and Cecil (now first Baron Burghley) were wary of openly intervening in the Dutch revolt, as some privy councillors such as Robert Dudley, earl of Leicester, and Sir Francis Walsingham (*c*.1532–1590) advocated. Norris sympathized with them more than with Burghley, his family's long-standing patron. Walsingham was a distant cousin; Leicester a notable patron of military men. At some point in the mid-1570s Norris had become a client of Leicester, though he stayed on good terms with Burghley. In 1578 the government came close to sending a royal army under Leicester to the Low Countries, but eventually the queen decided instead to subsidize a mercenary army, part German and part English. Although frustrated, Leicester and Walsingham endorsed several English captains to Orange and the states general of the United Provinces, who promptly hired them.

Norris was one of these officers and commanded the largest regiment. The Dutch were very short of funds and some English regiments went unpaid and unsupplied. Yet Norris's regiment was different—his knack for military finance and organization revealed itself. The states were late in paying, but Norris filled the gap with credit obtained from a variety of English merchants and nobles. On 1 August 1578 the states' army was attacked by the feared Spanish army at Rijmenam: the bulk of the fighting was done by the English and Scottish regiments. Norris marched for an hour to come to the relief of the main army and took effective command; he led from the front, fighting furiously, and had four horses killed under him. The Spanish were forced to retreat, having lost 1000 dead: their first defeat in pitched battle. The English 'carried awaie the whole praise and commendation of this victorie' (T. S[tocker], trans., *A Tragicall Historie of the Troubles and Civile Warres of the Lowe Countries*, 1583, 4.31v). The Dutch commander-in-chief praised Norris for having 'borne himself in such manner that a Cæsar could not have done better'; a fellow English soldier compared Norris to 'a new Hector, another Alexander, or rather a second Cæsar' (*Correspondance*, 4.57; Churchyard, *True Discourse*, 32).

It is unsurprising that the English government soon afterwards tried 'to perswade [the] ynglyshe kaptaynes to the good acceptation of John Norrys for theyre onely coronell' (Lettenhove, 10.713). However, the English colonels and captains were all proud men, who, being in Dutch pay, were reluctant to accept the authority of another Englishman. Although Norris commanded the largest English regiment in the states' service until England openly went to war with Spain in 1585, he never achieved primacy over other English colonels in Dutch employ and the feuds among them often made co-operation in the common cause difficult.

For much of 1579 the English troops operated in Flanders, as part of an army under the celebrated Huguenot general François de La Noue. Norris no doubt learned from the Frenchman, but also further advanced his reputation and, increasingly trusted by his Dutch employers, he successfully sought Leicester's 'license to stay heer a whyll tyll it may be better seen what wyll become of thes warres' (BL, Harley MS 6992, fol. 110r). Norris became heir to his father when his older brother died of fever at Newry in Down on 25 December 1579. In spring 1580 he led his men in storming the important city of Mechelen. A friar swinging a halberd wounded him, but the city fell in a day—unusual in an era in which war was dominated by long sieges. That summer Norris and his regiment were shifted to Friesland, in the north-east of the Netherlands, where the war was going badly. In December he was appointed commander of the states' army in Friesland, with the rank of colonel-general. He achieved signal success there over the next two years, despite one close-run defeat at Nordhorn in 1581 where he was wounded.

The campaign in Friesland, especially his relief of the siege of Steenwijk, left Norris high in the estimation of his Dutch employers. It was probably at this time that he was nicknamed 'Black Jack' by his troops—partly because of the dark hair and features that were characteristic of his family, but perhaps partly because of his own black temper (Nolan, 9, 12). However, veterans declared that the desire of true honour and glory in Norris inspired his men, and between them there was 'a naturall love and inclination that the best mindes are stirred therewith' for him (Blandy, 25). He did face defiance from time to time, but this was the fruit of the Dutch inability at this time to pay and feed their troops adequately. Norris was solicitous for his soldiers' pay and welfare throughout his time in the states' service. His men were not always conscious of his efforts on their behalf with the various Dutch authorities, but when, at one point in 1582, they confronted him over rumours that he was keeping back money owed to them, he 'so cleared himself of the slander … that not one man … charge[d] him' (CSP for., May–Dec 1582, 258).

In February 1582 François, duc d'Anjou, the brother of Henri III of France, arrived in the Netherlands. He had been chosen by the states as their new sovereign with the backing of the French king, of Orange, and of Elizabeth, and Leicester escorted him with a large party of English nobles and gentlemen. The number of English regiments in the states' service doubled, as Anjou awarded new contracts. He and Norris were mutually suspicious, however, because Anjou, who was a Catholic (although he had a reputation for religious tolerance), had commanded the royal army during the sixth war of religion, in which Black Jack had of course fought for the Huguenots. One of Norris's great moments came in summer 1582. The allied army, commanded by Anjou and Orange, had been out-manoeuvred by the Spanish army under Alessandro Farnese, prince of Parma, and was in retreat to Ghent. Norris commanded the rearguard and covered the main army's withdrawal with great success:

> In continuall fight, from the Sunne rising untill the Sunne setting … about foure of the clocke in the afternoone Monsieur Rochpot [Antoine de Silly, comte de Rochepot], the Duke of Anjowes Lieutenant, and Monsieur Byron [Armand de Gontaut, baron de Biron] Marshall of the same Dukes Campe, came forth unto [Norris and] said unto him: the Duke of Anjow … hath sent us … to give you the honour of … this day as most worthie thereof above all other. (Churchyard, True Discourse, 47)

Orange and Anjou watched the latter part of the retreat from the city walls. By this action (in which he was wounded again), Norris 'got the renowne of a valorous and most judicious Warriour', not only in the Netherlands and England but right across Europe (W. Camden, Annales, trans. A. Darcie, 1625, 2.20).

Anjou's fecklessness eventually led him to fall out with the Dutch in early 1583. Norris was appointed general of all the states' forces in Flanders until the crisis was resolved. Anjou withdrew to France in June, and Norris returned home to brief Elizabeth and the privy council on the new situation in the Netherlands. In his absence, Thomas Morgan tried to lure Norris's captains into his own regiment. On Black Jack's return a duel with Morgan was avoided only through the mediation of Walsingham, and the fissures within the English contingent naturally deepened. Things were made worse by the general decline in Dutch military circumstances in 1583–4, thanks to the

prince of Parma's strategic brilliance and inadequate Dutch financial resources. A miasma of despair started to suffuse the Netherlands, and among the troops—foreign and native—in the states' army.

In February 1584 Norris resigned his commission in the Netherlands and returned to England. He did not regard this as permanent and probably wanted to lobby the queen for official English intervention, but he was greatly frustrated with the inadequate pay and supply arrangements for his men, and his parents, who had always had great influence on him, thought his current service too dangerous and wanted him (and his two brothers, Edward and Henry Norris, who were serving under him) to return home. The Dutch wanted him to stay. Most of their generals valued his abilities in the field, he was popular with many common folk in the Netherlands, and Orange wrote to Elizabeth of his wish that Norris would remain in Dutch pay and continue

> the good service which he has hitherto rendered to these countries, for in so many places and ways he has proved his fidelity and his valour, that we cannot but regret his absence, and feel the loss that it will be to us. (CSP for., July 1583 – July 1584, 352)

General in Ireland and the Netherlands, the Spanish Armada, and after, 1584–1594 Norris took some time for rest and recreation on his return to England but, in July 1584, he accepted an appointment as president of Munster. Once in Ireland, he again demonstrated a knack for ruthless efficiency. He took his troops all the way north to Ulster to participate in another government campaign against the Scots, in which he seized no less than 50,000 head of cattle. He also laid out a scheme for the plantation of Munster, which he initiated. However, Norris was uncomfortable in Ireland, for he was unable to get on with the local political factions. He also wanted to return to the Netherlands, for about the time Norris arrived in Ireland a Catholic fanatic assassinated Orange (10 July 1584).

Norris's younger brother, Thomas Norris, had served in Ireland the whole time that John, Edward, and Henry Norris were in the Netherlands. Norris was MP for co. Cork in the parliament that opened at Dublin on 26 April 1585 and spoke out strongly in favour of extending the queen's power in Ireland. In spring 1585, having been in Ireland only a few months, Norris left Thomas Norris to carry out the scheme for the plantation of Munster, while the three brothers with experience of the Netherlands returned east across the narrow seas. Norris secured Thomas Norris's appointment as vice-president of Munster in December 1585, thereby ensuring that he himself kept his salary as president (an office he retained, albeit mainly as an absentee, until his death).

The Dutch had decided at last to ask Elizabeth for direct military assistance. By the end of May 1585 Walsingham had agreed with envoys from the two wealthiest provinces, Holland and Brabant, to send 2000 men to relieve the siege of Antwerp—the greatest city in the Low Countries, now closely invested by Parma. The Dutch wanted Norris to command them: his reputation had not diminished in the year since his departure. Even while negotiations were still going on, Walsingham wrote on 12 May to Norris in Ireland, telling him that Elizabeth 'hath resolved … to take uppon hir the protection' of the Netherlands, and that she knew 'no body more fit to be employed in some honorable charge in the entreprise then you' (Bodl. Oxf., MS St Amand 8, fol. 67r). On 21 June, although no decision had yet been taken to enter the war outright, the privy council ordered Norris to prepare troops to serve in the Netherlands. However, negotiations between England and the United Provinces moved on apace as the danger to Antwerp increased, and eventually it was agreed that Elizabeth would aid the Dutch republic with a royal army. On 12 August Norris was commissioned 'colonel-general and governor of the Queen's forces' (*Draft Calendar of Patent Rolls, 1584–1585*, List and Index Society, 241, 1990, 194). In addition, that same day the Dutch delegation commissioned him to raise and command an extra 3500 men in their pay, rather than Elizabeth's.

At this time Norris already had nearly 3000 men in the Netherlands, raised in expectation of both the queen's commission and the states' contract. By mid-September he commanded a force of over 7000 English troops, with 1000 more following. Only half of this army was in the queen's pay—but all were under his command, and within weeks he had successfully led his men into battle with the Spanish. Elizabeth, meanwhile, had written to the states that while she knew they already valued Norris because of his past services, 'we want to tell you now that we hold him dear and that you should hold him likewise' (Algemeen Rijksarchief, regerings archieven, I.92). In many ways, this was the apogee of his career; but it was to be short-lived.

In October 1585, even while Norris held Parma at bay near Arnhem, Leicester was appointed lieutenant-general of the queen's forces with full diplomatic and political powers to go with his military rank. There was a delay in leaving England, but after Leicester's arrival in the Netherlands in January 1586, Norris ceased to be commander of the army and instead became colonel-general of the foot, with the young Robert Devereux, second earl of Essex, as colonel-general of the horse—both under the new lieutenant-general. Leicester, in turn, swiftly accepted the post of governor-general, offered by the desperate states and so Norris continued to hold a states' as well as a royal commission, but there was no question that he was now part of the English military hierarchy.

Norris was resentful at being supplanted, even by such a great nobleman as Leicester. It did not help that Leicester showed little ability either in military operations or local politics, yet was unwilling to take Norris's advice. Leicester was self-confident and found constant contrary advice from his subordinate irksome, not least because he regarded Norris as a client, who should know his place. Several officers, including Rowland Yorke, from England's small permanent military establishment who had not fought as mercenaries for the Dutch hoped to hold

high office in the army sent to the continent; to counteract Norris's standing with the states, they sought to undermine Leicester's confidence in him. All the English captains (many of them his followers from the early 1580s) took sides, for or against Norris. Consequently, English efforts were undermined by dissension within their own ranks. Yorke and Sir William Stanley even eventually went over to the Spanish side, defecting with their garrisons on 18–19 January 1587.

The English army did enjoy some success. Norris resupplied the besieged stronghold of Grave in February 1586, despite being wounded himself by a pike-thrust in the chest on 15 April, and on 23 April, Leicester knighted both Norris and his brother Henry Norris. In May, Norris defeated a Spanish force near Nijmegen. On 22 September he was effective commander when the army clashed with Parma outside Zutphen; the English 'won her Majesty at this day as much honour as ever … men did their Prince' (Bruce, 417). In January 1587, after officers of the Leicester faction betrayed two strongholds to Parma, Norris (whose warning that the treachery was likely had been ignored) shored up the front and prevented a major Spanish advance. However, the United Provinces' territory had diminished throughout 1586 and Leicester made Norris a scapegoat. In 1587 Norris was increasingly marginalized. That summer the queen, who initially had backed her Black Jack, was finally persuaded by her favourite, Leicester, that Norris was to blame for the divisions in the army and had to go. In July he returned to England, never to hold a military command in the Netherlands again.

Norris immediately faced charges of corruption and malfeasance, but was able to clear his name, partly because of the enduring support of his oldest patron, Burghley. He forswore Leicester and thereafter he and his brothers were very much the Cecils' men. It was presumably thanks to their influence that he was created MA on 11 April 1588 at Oxford University (he was not the John Norris who matriculated entry on 11 December 1576, because he would have been too old at the time).

Meanwhile Norris had been given high responsibilities for preparing England's defences against the expected onslaught of the Armada. He was on a special committee established for national defence planning and was given particular charge for bringing the militia, on which the country would depend, up to the expected standards. This was a thankless task, made difficult by entrenched local interests and bureaucracy, but Norris and his hand-picked subordinates worked manfully and all was in readiness when the Armada arrived in the channel on 27 July 1588. While the main army under Leicester guarded the approaches to London, Norris was in command of a force in Kent, the county where a Spanish landing was most likely, and remained there almost until the enemy fleet had been driven into the North Sea after 9 August. He escorted Elizabeth to the main army at Tilbury, where he was one of only four gentlemen (Essex and Leicester were two of the others) to accompany her when she made her famous review of, and speech to, the army on 8 August.

During 1587–8 Norris again worked with Drake—both

men were ardently Calvinist and champions of the war against Spain. Norris also had a long-standing friendship with Dom Antonio, pretender to the Portuguese throne, which Philip II of Spain had recently annexed. Elizabeth was keen to strike against Spanish naval power, so that the threat of another armada would be removed and Drake and Norris came up with a bold plan. They promised to raise the astonishing sum of £40,000 towards the cost of an attack on Portugal: Drake would command the fleet and Norris the army. They would attack Spanish ports *en route* for Lisbon (itself a major naval base), where they would proclaim Dom Antonio king of Portugal. The rich Spanish shipping in Lisbon would be captured, and Dom Antonio agreed to let English merchants enter the vastly profitable East Indian trade (dominated by Portugal). At one stroke the expedition could destroy Philip's naval capacity, carry the war to the Iberian peninsula, and also, it was expected, turn a tidy profit. The first two goals were what chiefly interested the queen and her privy councillors. Profit, however, was what chiefly interested the many backers whom Drake and Norris relied on to raise their contribution. Norris had built up a range of contacts who underwrote the costs of his aid to the Dutch in the early 1580s and he called on them now. In consequence, the two commanders always had different priorities from Elizabeth, who had, however, committed royal ships, troops, and large sums of money to the venture.

The fleet sailed from Plymouth in April 1589, with over 20,000 men embarked. The expedition made landfall at La Coruña on 20 April. Norris and the army captured its harbour and seized the shipping there, but they were unable to take the castle, though he utterly defeated a Spanish army that attempted to relieve the siege. The expedition moved on to Lisbon, but it failed to take the city, chiefly because Drake preferred to capture shipping in the Tagus River rather than take the fleet upstream to support the army's attack on the city. The English meanwhile suffered severely from sickness. In late May the fleet returned home, having failed to capture its main objective, Lisbon, and having lost between 4000 and 11,000 men, most of them dead from disease. They arrived in Plymouth on 2 July. The 'Lisbon voyage' is usually accounted a disastrous failure and the worst blot on Norris's record. Yet it had been a very successful large-scale raid into enemy territory: the problem was that this was not the expedition's avowed aim. There was a great gulf between what was expected and what was achieved. Had Norris and Drake not talked up the possible outcomes in the first place (in order to get the private financial backing they needed) they would have been regarded both at the time and since as more successful. Norris worked wonders to get the expedition mounted in the first place and handled the tactical side of land operations well, but while he was let down by Drake (who undoubtedly prioritized personal profit), he made a number of misjudgements and his strategic vision was flawed.

In 1590 Norris was sent back to Munster, charged with constructing a series of fortifications there along Dutch lines, to ensure that if a Spanish armada was sent to Ireland instead of England, any army it disembarked would not find an easy target. He was not pleased, but with his brother, now Sir Thomas Norris, carried out the job efficiently. By winter 1590–91 his mother's influence had left the queen once again well disposed to him. In addition, the threat of Spanish invasion fleets still occupied the minds of Elizabeth and Burghley. The Spaniards were now seeking to obtain bases closer to England and were therefore pouring resources into Brittany, where the new and protestant king of France, Henri IV, was hard-pressed. When the government decided to send an army to Brittany, Norris was the obvious man to command it, but Essex (Leicester's political and military heir) connived unsuccessfully in an attempt to get the command for himself. Throughout the years 1591–4 Norris commanded a small English army in Brittany. Essex's clients defamed him, hoping he would be replaced by one of them (if not by Essex), but Henri and his generals wanted Norris and so he maintained command throughout.

The English army took several towns in these years but the campaign was generally very indecisive; by the end of 1594, as Norris's biographer observes, 'his finances, his career and his once-mighty reputation had all been ruined', or so it seemed (Nolan, 203). In fact, simply by keeping an English army in being, Norris had done a great service, preventing the Spanish from winning control of the province, whose ports were the ideal embarkation point for an invasion of England. The turning point in the campaign occurred in 1594. In a brilliant operation Norris captured the Spanish base of operations at El Léon which threatened the great port of Brest. In the final assault, carried out at his insistence, against the advice of the French general, Norris himself was wounded (again). He was 'widely hailed, and once again … enjoyed a moment of international renown' (ibid., 217). Having essentially achieved its ends the army was withdrawn back to England early in 1595, but Norris had preceded it. His health was increasingly poor and Henri had converted to Catholicism in 1593—Norris had finally had enough of France.

Final service in Ireland and death, 1594–1597 Norris was in favour with the queen in spring 1595, or so the description of Elizabeth's court by a visiting German ambassador suggests. Nevertheless, he remained a controversial figure: old accusations of financial irregularities continued to be raised by Essex and his protégés. Despite this, he was, again, the obvious man to send to Ireland, where the great rebellion of Hugh O'Neill, second earl of Tyrone, was under way and the lord deputy, Sir William Russell, was unable to cope. Recognizing his own limitations, Russell asked for an experienced officer to command the army in Ireland. Norris's health was still poor and he made great efforts to avoid the command, but the privy council insisted that he go—testimony to the esteem in which he was held.

Unfortunately, this last command proved an inglorious one for Norris. He arrived in Waterford on 4 May 1595. Russell, an old enemy from the Netherlands in 1586 (and also Essex's man), was not happy at the appointment of Norris, who was independent of the lord deputy while in Ulster. Norris also had to fend off attempts by Essex to have his clients made Norris's subordinate officers. Despite these difficulties and persistent attacks of fever, Norris joined Russell's hosting against Tyrone from 26 June to 13 July. On 22 August, Tyrone made overtures to Norris for a pardon. Norris ignored this and invaded Ulster on the same day, campaigning there until 5 September. He still led from the front, was twice wounded, and was frustrated by the caution of the Old English establishment, complaining he 'would fayne have foughte with the Rebells' (St John's College, Cambridge, MS I.29, fol. 7r). Tyrone and Hugh O'Donnell were concerned enough to submit on 18 October, agreeing with Norris to a truce on 27 October (to last until 1 January 1596), but each side recognized that the other was playing for time, and Elizabeth was unimpressed. She reproached Norris for retiring back to his base in Munster too quickly and ruefully observed that she only ever received bad news from Ireland—though she added 'our meaning is not nowe to taxe yourself' (CUL, MS Kk.1.15, pt 1, fols. 124r, 177r).

Norris took advantage of the brief cessation of hostilities to go to Connaught to resolve local disputes there, hoping he could then concentrate all the crown's military resources on Ulster. The president of Connaught was an old comrade from the Netherlands, Sir Richard Bingham, but the two men (both of black temper) had long since fallen out. Norris now dismissed Bingham, on the grounds that his ruthless policies only excited opposition. Bingham accused him of wanting to appoint his younger brother Sir Henry Norris in Connaught, and Russell used Bingham's case to attack Norris. Soon the quarrel between the crown's two chief officers in Ireland was open knowledge, even on the continent. By late 1596 Norris was spending as much of his failing energies quarrelling with other English officers as fighting the Irish and he asked to be recalled.

Soon after, in early 1597, war broke out again across Ireland. Norris was needed too much to be allowed home, but his commission of 1595 was superseded and he was left with only his office as president of Munster. Crushed, Norris retired there and though he kept the Munster Irish in check he lost the will to resist illness. His many old wounds had been troublesome for some time and his mother appealed to the principal secretary, Sir Robert Cecil, for her son's recall, but it was too late. Norris was staying at the home of Sir Thomas Norris, Norris Castle in Mallow, co. Cork. On 3 September 1597, he died there, clasped in his brother's arms.

The story spread among the Irish that Black Jack's military successes had come only because he 'had sold himself to the devil, who carried him off unexpectedly' (AFM, 5–6. 2021 n. i). The story of contemporary English chroniclers, including Thomas Churchyard, that Norris died of exhaustion and disappointment seems likely to be closest to the truth. On hearing of his death Elizabeth wrote to his mother, full of sympathy for her old friend and perhaps feeling a trifle guilty: it is one of the most oft-quoted of the queen's letters, because of the glimpse of humanity it provides. The queen added a salutation in her own hand— 'mine own Crow'—and continued:

> Harm not thyself for bootless help; but show a good example to comfort your dolorous yokefellow … we have … resolved no longer to smother either our care for your sorrow, or the sympathy of our grief for his love, wherein … we do assure you … that nature can have stirred no more dolorous affection in you as a mother for a dear son, than gratefulness and memory of his services past hath wrought in us, his Sovereign, apprehension of our miss of so worthy a servant. (*Letters*, ed. Harrison, 250–51)

It was a fitting tribute to the greatest English soldier of her reign.

Character and posthumous reputation Norris lived a passionate life, as befitted a man of his time. He placed above all else the reformed religion, personal honour, and the service of his queen and country. The Norris and Williams families had been supporters of, or at least were sympathetic to, protestantism since the 1530s, but Norris himself was Calvinist. He urged the queen to help the Dutch because they were not just fellow protestants fighting Catholics: they had 'no other relygion but the Reformed', by which he meant Calvinism (Bodl. Oxf., MS Rawl. C. 836, fol. 6r). Before embarking on the Lisbon voyage Norris asked a group of Calvinist clergymen whether or not 'a professor of the true Reformed Religion may without offence aid a Popish king to recover his kingdom'—even against the king of Spain (Wernham, *Expedition*, 28). He was not just a Calvinist: he was devout, with a 'personal iconoclastic hatred of Catholicism … evident from the conduct of troops under his command' (Trim, 303). Indeed, he attracted iconoclastic soldiers, or at least encouraged them. Thus, in 1583, when Norris's troops were serving with an army under Anjou's general, they insulted its mostly Catholic troops by publicly profaning sacred objects plundered from Catholic churches, and his men attacked Catholic churches in Brittany in 1594. It is no wonder that a senior Spanish officer once told an English prisoner that Norris was 'the mortallest enemy they had' (*CSP for.*, 1579–80, 467).

Norris also had the sixteenth-century gentleman's passionate regard for his honour, which was best established by deeds of martial prowess. This came through in his sometimes reckless bravery. Norris had a penchant for leading from the front—at times he deliberately discarded armour. He was wounded at least nine times in his career, and a ballad about the queen's appearance at Tilbury sang of how his

> colours were carried there, all rent and torn
> The which with bullets was so burned when in Flanders he
>   sojourned.
> (A. F. Pollard, ed., *Tudor Tracts, 1532–1588*, 1964, 493–4)

It is worth stressing, however, that Black Jack was more than just a firebrand; if an ability to inspire his men was an important explanation of his military success, he was also exceptionally energetic and a very skilled battlefield tactician, while his careful management of logistics marks him out from most of his contemporaries. Concern for whether he was being treated honourably goes a long way towards explaining the number of fierce disputes Norris had with fellow officers. This temper, reinforced by his Calvinistic certainty that he was among the elect, was perhaps his greatest weakness.

Between religion and honour there was room for little else. Norris was not even very interested in his estates. His uncle, Sir John Norris, left him lands in Yattendon and Hampstead Norris in Berkshire. He possibly even sold off land in Buckinghamshire in April 1585 to supplement his income. Norris got most of his revenue, however, from his military offices, both from the wages paid and from plunder. The nature of state finance in this period, though, was such that military officers usually paid their troops' wages and expenses out of their own pockets in the hope of later reimbursement—which in practice was very risky. Norris may have successfully manipulated the system during his brief presidency of Munster (1584–5), but any profits thus made were very small. Generally, his personal salary and emoluments were paid well in arrears, if at all, and he was only able to keep going through a complex credit network.

The private man is something of an enigma. Orange was among those who enjoyed pleasant evenings with Norris in the early 1580s, and one contemporary called him a man of 'excellent wit' (Stowe, 805). He seems to have had a sardonic sense of humour. He was once said to be on the verge of marrying, but did not. However, he was very close to his family. Lord Norris and his wife were always solicitous of all their sons' welfare. Norris's mother wrote to Sir William Cecil in 1569 to thank him for being 'more like a father than otherwise' to her son (*CSP for.*, 1569–71, 70). In 1583 Norris asked Burghley to try to arrange for Norris to stay in England and not return to the Netherlands, because he and his wife felt it was too dangerous. Although Norris turned to his family for support throughout his career he was single-minded enough to ignore his parents' concerns for his safety.

Norris's fame arose from his martial ability and honourable personal conduct, which were widely recognized and praised. When Leicester requested in May 1578 that Norris be appointed commander of all the English troops in the Netherlands, it was because his 'birthe, skyll, courage, wisedome, modestye and faithfullnes' put 'him above all englishmen yet there' (PRO, SP 83/6, fol. 173*r*). William Blandy spent a summer fighting under Norris and not only praised him 'for his valiant actes' but also characterized him as a 'fountayne of fame, a welspring of vertue [and] a river of royaltye' (Blandy, 25*v*). In 1585 Elizabeth declared that he and his men had 'won our nation honour and themselves fame', while in 1596 she wrote to Norris that 'noe man, then yourself' knew better 'what is true honour' (Harrison, 178–9; CUL, MS Kk.1.15, pt 1, fol. 177*r*). This admiration was not restricted to his countrymen: the states of Utrecht praised him and Henri IV valued his abilities highly. Edmund Spenser made Norris one of the dedicatees of *The Faerie Queene* (1596), at the beginning of which he declared him 'the honor of this age' (E. Spenser, *Poetical Works*, ed. J. C. Smith and E. de Selincourt, 1970, 412).

Later writers, including George Chapman, himself a veteran of the war with Spain, also praised Norris. In recording Norris's death John Stowe wrote of his numerous 'excellent services', though 'many and singular exployts hee performed which are not here mentioned … he was excellent, either to plant a siege, or raise a siege, and could pitch a battell bravely'. Stowe concluded that 'an honourable remembrance' was appropriate for Norris's 'noble dedes, true valour, and high worth' (Stowe, 805). Early historians, like Sir Robert Naunton and Thomas Fuller, generally shared these sentiments. Gradually, however, Norris and his family dropped out of sight. Subsequent generations regarded Elizabeth's reign anachronistically, as the dawn of England's turning away from Europe and towards the Atlantic. This was not at all how most English people at the time saw matters. For centuries England had been allied with Burgundy and fought against the French. The war with Spain was not a contest to win control of the Americas or transoceanic trade routes, but a struggle for the domination of Europe, with Catholicism as the enemy. However, the heroes of later historical narratives were sailors like Sir Walter Ralegh, Drake, Sir Martin Frobisher, and Sir John Hawkins, who apparently presaged the era of British naval victories and maritime exploration, rather than the Elizabethan soldiers whose attitudes seemed to hark back to the medieval, rather than to prefigure the modern.

In his own time Norris was as famous as Drake. He was also arguably more significant in terms of English policy. Norris made a greater contribution to international history, for he played an important role in the Dutch struggle for nationhood and was an active participant in the process by which the French absolutist state was created. His role was not as significant as that of Leicester or Essex, for unlike them Norris was largely an executor, rather than a framer, of policies, yet he was indubitably their superior in military matters. Norris played a pivotal, positive role in ensuring the survival of the United Provinces until financial and military reform in the 1590s paved the way for counter-offensive and national independence. The first modern historian of the Netherlands observed that Norris 'combined much of the knight-errantry of a vanishing age with the more practical … spirit of … the new epoch' (Motley, *United Netherlands*, 1.334). Norris played an important role on a European stage during a great historical drama. His international renown will never be recaptured, but he deserves recognition for his chivalry, courage, and capability, as great as possessed by any Englishman of his era.

D. J. B. TRIM

Sources J. S. Nolan, *Sir John Norreys and the Elizabethan military world* (1997) • D. J. B. Trim, 'Fighting "Jacob's wars": the employment of English and Welsh mercenaries in the European wars of religion; France and the Netherlands, 1562–1610', PhD diss., U. Lond., 2002 • T. Churchyard and R. Ro[binson], *A true discourse historicall of the succeeding governors in the Netherlands and the civil wars there with the memorable services of our honourable English generals, captaines and souldiers, especially under Sir John Norrice, knight, there performed and in Portugale, France, Britaine and Ireland* (1602) • T. Churchyard, *A generall rehearsall of warres* (1579) • Bodl. Oxf., MSS St Amand 5–10 • Bodl. Oxf., MS Tanner 79 • Bodl. Oxf., MS Rawl. C. 836 • *CSP for.*, 1566–71;

1575–88 · state papers foreign, Elizabeth, PRO, SP 70 · state papers Holland and Flanders, PRO, SP 83 · audit office, PRO, AO 1/292/1096–7 · exchequer, PRO, E 351/240 · R. B. Wernham, ed., *List and analysis of state papers: foreign series, Elizabeth I, preserved in the Public Record Office* (1964–), 1589–95 · Nationaal Archief, The Hague, Archief van de staten-generaal, 5880–5882, 11095–11906, 12576 · Nationaal Archief, The Hague, Archief van de Raad van State, 1–3, 1524 · Regerings-Archieven van de Geünieerde en van de Nader-geünieerde Nederlandse Provinciën, Nationaal Archief, The Hague, I.90, 92, 197; III.28 · Nationaal Archief, The Hague, Collectie Ortell, 49–50 · Nationaal Archief, The Hague, Archief van de Staten van Holland, 15–20 · BL, Add. MSS 5753, 48084, 48116 · BL, Harley MSS 1411, 1529, 6992–6993 · J. Stowe, *Annales of England*, ed. E. Howes (1631) · Baron Kervyn de Lettenhove [J. M. B. C. Kervyn de Lettenhove] and L. Gilliodts-van Severen, eds., *Relations politiques des Pays-Bas et de l'Angleterre sous le règne de Philippe II*, 11 vols. (Brussels, 1882–1900) · *Correspondance de Guillaume le Taciturne, prince d'Orange*, ed. M. Gachard, 6 vols. (1850–57) · W. Blandy, *The castle, or, Picture of pollicy* (1581) · J. Bruce, ed., *Correspondence of Robert Dudley, earl of Leycester*, CS, 27 (1844) · *The letters of Elizabeth I*, ed. G. B. Harrison (1968) · J. L. Motley, *The rise of the Dutch republic*, 3 vols. (1855) · J. L. Motley, *History of the United Netherlands: from the death of William the Silent to the Twelve Years Truce, 1609*, 4 vols. (New York, 1879–80) · R. B. Wernham, *Before the Armada: the growth of English foreign policy, 1485–1588* (1966) · R. B. Wernham, *After the Armada: Elizabethan England and the struggle for western Europe, 1588–1595* (1984) · R. B. Wernham, ed., *The expedition of Sir John Norris and Sir Francis Drake to Spain and Portugal, 1589*, Navy Records Society, 127 (1988) · *APC*, 1571–89 · J. A. Dop, *Eliza's knights: soldiers, poets and puritans in the Netherlands, 1572–1586* (1981) · M. C. Fissel, *English warfare, 1511–1642* (2001) · Berks. RO, D/EBN/T1, D/ED/T37, D/EN 04/1 · HoP, *Commons, 1558–1603*, 3.135–40

Archives BL, report relating to security of Dorset coastline, Add. MS 69907A | BL, corresp. and papers, Cotton MSS · BL, Harley MS 6992 · BL, Egerton MS 1694 · Bodl. Oxf., letters, MSS St Amand 5–10 · Bodl. Oxf., private papers, MS Rawl. C. 836 · CUL, MSS KK.i.15, MM.1.32 · Nationaal Archief, The Hague, Liassen Engeland · Nationaal Archief, The Hague, Loketkast Engeland, esp. SG 12576 · PRO, state papers foreign, SP 70 · PRO, state papers France, 78 · PRO, state papers Holland and state papers Irish, SP 63 · PRO, state papers Flanders, SP 83 · PRO, state papers Holland, SP 84

Likenesses portrait, 16th cent., Knole, Kent; repro. in G. Mattingly, *Defeat of the Spanish Armada* (1959), pl. 12 · portrait, *c.*1630 (after Zucchero), repro. in Nolan, *Sir John Norreys and the Elizabethan military world*, frontispiece

Norris, John (1657–1712), Church of England clergyman and philosopher, was born on 2 January 1657 at Collingbourne Kingston, Wiltshire, the third surviving child of John Norris (*bap.* 1614, *d.* 1682) and his wife, Elizabeth (*d.* 1696). His father was vicar of Collingbourne Kingston under the Commonwealth and he moved to the living of Aldbourne, Wiltshire, in 1660. Norris was educated at Winchester College and entered Exeter College, Oxford, in 1676. A keen student at both Winchester and Oxford, he early abandoned his inherited Calvinism and concentrated his reading on Platonist authors. On graduating BA in 1680 he was appointed a fellow of All Souls by Archbishop Sancroft on the recommendation of Thomas Jeames, the warden, during a dispute with the fellows over the filling of the vacancies in the college. Norris always retained a great esteem for All Souls, and the college in turn erected a bust of him in the Codrington Library when this was built in the following century.

It was at All Souls that Norris formed his basic ideas and began his literary output. His early publications began in 1682 and included a correspondence with the Cambridge Platonist Henry More in 1685–6, published in 1688. His early writings show him to have been at that time a strong tory and high-churchman, but also show that he deliberately turned aside from political involvement. All the writings that he considered to be worth preserving were included in *A Collection of Miscellanies*, which appeared in 1687. His thought at this period already shows a combination of Platonist and Cartesian elements, which was always to be characteristic of him, and several of the essays in the *Miscellanies* express ideas that he developed further in his later writings. The *Miscellanies* also includes almost all of Norris's poetry. In the final poem he bids farewell to his muse, but he later composed two further poems, one in each part of his *Theory of the Ideal World*. The *Miscellanies* was to prove the most lastingly popular of all Norris's writings with the general public, and even in the nineteenth century it was reported that 'this is the most popular of all his works, and affords the picture of a truly amiable mind' (Watt, *Bibl. Brit.*, 2.710). Norris's last years at Oxford saw the publication of *The Theory and Regulation of Love* (1688) and *Reason and Religion* (1689). These are the first of his writings to show the influence of Malebranche, whom he clearly began to study at this time.

In 1689 Norris married and left Oxford. Little is known of Elizabeth Norris, whom Norris named in affectionate terms as executor of his will in 1706 and who survived him. They had three sons and a daughter: John, Edward, Elizabeth, and Thomas; John and Edward were later ordained and Elizabeth married a clergyman. Norris's love for his children can be seen from the little book that he wrote for their use, *Spiritual Counsel, or, The Father's Advice to his Children* (1694), and all the evidence suggests that the Norrises were a united and strongly Christian family. On leaving Oxford Norris accepted the living of Newton St Loe, near Bath, Somerset. His years there were marked by intense literary activity. *Discourses upon the Beatitudes* (1690) was followed in 1691 by a further volume of sermons. Two more were to follow later. *Reflections upon the Conduct of Human Life* (1690) was to become one of his most popular works. It was also at Newton St Loe that Norris wrote his *Cursory Reflections upon a Book called, 'An Essay Concerning Human Understanding'*—the first detailed critique of John Locke's *Essay* to be published—and that he became involved in a controversy with the Quakers, who detected a similarity between Norris and Malebranche's theory of knowledge and their own doctrine of the inner light.

Early in 1692 Norris was presented to the more valuable living of Bemerton, near Salisbury, Wiltshire, to which he was recommended by Locke, with whom he had a mutual friend in Lady Damaris Masham. When he discovered this Norris wrote to Locke to express his gratitude, but these good relations did not last. Later in the same year a quarrel occurred, based it seems on a misunderstanding, which left Norris with a feeling of injured innocence and Locke and Lady Masham with a bitter resentment that coloured all their later references to Norris. Although his friendship with Lady Masham ended in this way, Norris always remained close to several of the learned ladies of his time. Lady Mary Chudleigh, poet and author, used to visit him at Bemerton, and it is she who provides the only extant description of Norris's appearance. Writing to Elizabeth Thomas, who was also a friend of Norris and who corresponded with him and his family for many years without ever meeting them, Lady Chudleigh wrote:

> He is a little man of a plain complexion, but he has a great deal of sweetness and good humour in his face, attended with an extraordinary modesty and a more than common air of humility: there seems to be a reservedness in his temper, but when you are acquainted with him you will find it only the result of thoughtfulness. In a word, he is a man whose conversation is very agreeable as well as instructive. (Gwinnet, 2.250)

Norris advised and encouraged Elizabeth Thomas in her studies, and she in turn reported to him what people were saying about his books. But his closest collaboration was with Mary Astell, whose correspondence with him was published in 1695 as *Letters Concerning the Love of God*. Mary Astell later defended Norris's views more generally in *The Christian Religion as Professed by a Daughter of the Church of England* (1705).

In 1697 Norris published *An Account of Reason and Faith*, the first full-length book of his Bemerton period, which became a standard work on the subject throughout the eighteenth century and into the nineteenth. Norris's principal metaphysical work, *An Essay Towards the Theory of the Ideal or Intelligible World*, appeared in two parts, in 1701 and 1704. The first part of the *Theory* is largely an expansion of ideas contained in his earlier writings and it deals with the 'Ideal World' in itself, the eternally valid ideas and truths that, Norris argues, can only subsist in the mind of God, while the second part is concerned with our knowledge of this world of ideas and leans heavily on Malebranche. Norris was convinced that necessary truths can only be known 'in God', but his theory of empirical knowledge was confused by his not fully understanding Malebranche's theory of 'intelligible extension', which he was attempting to follow. Norris himself considered his theory of the knowledge of necessary truths as certain, but regarded his theory of empirical knowledge as no more than probable. The *Theory* was not one of Norris's most successful writings, though it did not lack enthusiastic supporters. It seems to have provided the main starting point for Arthur Collier's *Clavis universalis* (1713), in which Collier moved from Norris's theory of knowledge to an immaterialism not unlike that of George Berkeley. It also seems to be envisaged in some passages of David Hume's *Dialogues Concerning Natural Religion*.

After the *Theory* and a thoroughgoing revision of the *Miscellanies* for the fourth edition in 1706 Norris intended writing a series of studies on the Christian virtues. The first of these, *A Practical Treatise Concerning Humility*, appeared in 1707, but Norris's interest was then distracted by the controversy on the immortality of the soul, in which he intervened with two books, published in 1708 and 1709, both occasioned by the writings of Henry Dodwell. Norris then returned to his previous plan, but his health was now beginning to fail, and he felt that he could only write on one fundamental virtue; *A Treatise Concerning Christian Prudence* appeared in 1710 and was the last of Norris's works. After a long illness whose nature is unknown Norris died at Bemerton rectory and he was buried at Bemerton on 5 February 1712.

Norris's writings have tended to be neglected by historians of philosophy, partly perhaps because of Locke's dismissive attitude and partly because many of his theories are so close to those of Malebranche that it is difficult to disentangle their influence. He has been better treated by historians of literature, who see his poetry, much of which continues to be republished, as marking especially clearly the transition from the spirit of the Renaissance to that of modern times. Much of Norris's poetry, which has its roots in the metaphysical tradition, is somewhat laboured. At his best, however, he has a lyrical spirit, often inspired by Horace's ideal of rural retreat, and his last poems, in the *Theory of the Ideal World*, seem to foreshadow the hymns of Isaac Watts and Charles Wesley. Norris's sober evaluation of the relative certainties of reason and faith anticipates the views of Joseph Butler, while his 'practical' and religious writings are noted for their combination of fervour with reasonableness, and they were highly esteemed by John Wesley, who reprinted several of them in shortened form. Norris's works formed a considerable part of Wesley's own reading while at Oxford. Writing in 1756 to a Samuel Furly, Wesley complained of

> your not loving and admiring that masterpiece of reason and religion, the Reflections on the Conduct of Human Life with regard to Knowledge and Learning, every paragraph of which must stand unshaken (with or without the Bible) till we are no longer mortal.   (*Letters*, 3.173)

He later told the same correspondent that 'I have followed Mr. Norris's advice these thirty years, and so must every man that is well in his senses' (ibid., 175). In private life Norris seems to have been a kindly person, a devoted parish clergyman, and the friend and supporter of several of the learned ladies of his time. In the history of English thought he is a transitional figure. In contrast to the Cambridge Platonists he adopted wholeheartedly the Cartesian dualism of mind and matter. His theory of knowledge was a Cartesian Platonism similar to that of Malebranche, to whose more developed theories he was at times too inclined to defer. In the history of English philosophy, religion, and literature he deserves to be remembered.

RICHARD ACWORTH

Sources R. Acworth, *La philosophie de John Norris, 1657–1712* (1975) [incl. comprehensive bibliography] · R. Acworth, *The philosophy of John Norris of Bemerton* (1979) [incl. comprehensive bibliography] · J. Hoyles, *The waning of the Renaissance, 1640–1740* (1971) · M.-S. Røstvig, *The happy man: studies in the metamorphoses of a classical ideal*, 2 vols. (1954–8) · R. Gwinnett and E. Thomas, *Pylades and Corinna*, 2 vols. (1731–2) · *The letters of the Rev. John Wesley*, ed. J. Telford, 8 vols. (1931) · Watt, *Bibl. Brit.* · V. H. H. Green, *The young Mr Wesley* (1961) · C. Johnston, 'Locke's *Examination of Malebranche* and John Norris', *Journal of the History of Ideas*, 19 (1958), 551–8 · [J. Norris], *Where's my memorial? The religious, philosophical and metaphysical poetry of John Norris of Bemerton*, ed. P. D. E. White (1991) · parish register, Collingbourne Kingston, Wiltshire, 12 Jan 1657 [baptism] · parish register, Bemerton, Wiltshire, 5 Feb 1712 [burial]

Archives Bemerton church, Wiltshire, memorial tablet | Bodl. Oxf., MSS Locke c.16 and c.24

Likenesses H. Cheere, bronze bust, *c.*1756, All Souls Oxf.

Wealth at death lands at Collingbourne Kingston and Collingbourne Ducis to eldest son; also £400 in legacies to daughter and younger sons: will, Wilts. & Swindon RO

Norris, Sir John (1670/71–1749), naval officer, details of whose parentage and upbringing are unknown, came from 'a very respectable family in the Kingdom of Ireland' according to John Campbell (J. Campbell, *Lives of the Admirals*, 4 vols., new edn, 1818, 4.469). However, evidence of property dealings recorded in the Dublin register of deeds, especially those between the admiral and a son-in-law, John Ambrose of co. Dublin, in 1733 and 1740 (deed nos. 73 272 51039, and 100 234 70873), implies that his origins lay either in Dublin or Newcastle, co. Down. That his mother's Christian name was Mary can be established from the pay book of the *Dover* for March 1689 (PRO ADM 33/138) where she is entered as the recipient of her son's pay. Norris's consistent public stance upon the protestant, and Hanoverian, succession strongly suggests he was of the Anglo-Irish establishment; and following his knighthood in November 1705 his Norris of Speke arms were confirmed, though now impaled (through his marriage) with those of Aylmer of Balrath.

Early career Similarly unknown is how Norris, at the age of nine or ten, came to be entered as a servant in the *Gloucester* in September 1680 preparatory to joining Captain Cloudesley Shovell in the *Sapphire* (28 guns) at Tangier in February 1681. However, Shovell's patronage of Norris when a scantily educated boy was of profound importance. He served with Shovell almost uninterruptedly until promoted captain in July 1690. The years spent on the Tangier–Lisbon station, during which Norris became known to Arthur Herbert (later earl of Torrington), Edward Russell (member of the whig junto and later earl of Orford), Admiral George Byng (later first Viscount Torrington of the second creation), and not least Matthew Aylmer of Balrath, co. Meath—Norris was to become his son-in-law in May 1699 when, aged twenty-eight, he married Elizabeth Moore, *née* Aylmer (1682–1763)—were wholly formative, and still influential in Norris's strategic thinking in 1734. While it is possible that Norris had first been brought to Shovell's notice by Aylmer, frequent marriages between Norris and Aylmer cousins well into the eighteenth century do not themselves disclose an earlier family link. What is certain is that all these seniors of Norris were intimately involved in 1688 in ensuring that the navy deserted James II for the cause of William of Orange. No less plain is Norris's continuing association with Shovell, for he became the latter's flag captain in the *Britannia* (90 guns) in January 1703, and served under him with distinction at the capture of Barcelona in 1705. Having been promoted to flag rank as rear-admiral of the blue in March 1707, for which Norris was indebted to the whig junto leader Lord Somers, Norris was detached ashore in June by

Shovell to liaise with the troops of Savoy on their westwards coastal march to attack Toulon supported by the Anglo-Dutch fleet. This amphibious operation, warmly canvassed by Shovell and at longer range, the duke of Marlborough, was abortive but Norris here acquired an expertise in such operations which was valuable in his Baltic years and by 1740 had long gained him high repute. It was during the return home of Shovell's fleet on 23 October 1707 that three of his ships, including his flagship, *Association*, were lost in the Scillies, Norris with his flag in the *Torbay* only narrowly escaping the same fate. Shovell's memory was revered by Norris, and Lady Shovell, who died in 1735, appointed him her executor.

Of a different and contentious kind was Norris's association with the admiral and whig grandee, Edward, earl of Orford, over some twenty-two years from January 1695 to April 1717 when Orford resigned the first lordship of the Admiralty for the third and last time. Norris had first gained distinction when in command of the *Sheerness* (28 guns) during the Smyrna convoy action of May–June 1693, but it was his dramatic capture of the French warship *Content* in January 1695 in the Mediterranean—a ship which he himself then commanded for two years—which brought him Russell's approbation. Although political animosities at the end of the war in 1697 caused Orford's stewardship as treasurer of the navy to come under severe parliamentary censure, he was able to protect Norris after a command in Newfoundland, which had been hobbled by its being shared with the army commander, was then seriously compromised by a violent feud between Norris and Desborow, one of his captains. Subsequently both officers were suspended but reinstated in March 1701, a fortunate time for Norris because Orford himself now stood in such peril of impeachment that he would have been unable to afford Norris further assistance. The rise in Norris's fortunes in the earlier years of the War of the Spanish Succession was demonstrably owing to Shovell, rather than Orford who, until he became first lord for the second time in 1709, played little part in Norris's career. During 1710 and 1711 Norris's Mediterranean command was chiefly concerned with sustaining the allied base in Catalonia, and escorting back to the Austrian Habsburg dominions the titular Charles III of Spain who had become the emperor Charles VI following the death of his brother Joseph I in March 1711. Until the death of Queen Anne in August 1714 gave promise of a fair deal from her whig-inclined successor George I, Norris and other whig officers appear to have suffered financially. Yet Norris himself was now not ill placed in view of his long-standing whig-junto affiliations and his impressive retention of his parliamentary seat at Rye since 1708. George I, though a soldier, was under some constraint to familiarize himself with senior naval officers, owing to British regents' pleas for him to use his good offices with Charles XII so that Sweden might moderate its interruption of Britain's Baltic commerce. Norris, backed by his influential father-in-law, appeared professionally and politically sound to the new king. But he had other, and possibly crucial, qualifications for a future Baltic command: he had been to the Sound of Copenhagen in 1709; in 1711 he had been rewarded by Emperor Charles VI for his services to the imperial court, a move looked on favourably by a Hanover solicitous of imperial compliance with incipient territorial changes in north Germany now that Swedish power was receding; and in 1707 Norris had maintained cordial relations with Prince Eugene of Savoy, an imperial councillor known to share in Vienna's distrust of Hanoverian territorial aspirations, and hence that electorate's prospective dynastic union with Great Britain.

Baltic command While there is no evidence that such qualifications resulted in Norris's receiving the 1715 Baltic command, it is certain that his seniors—Byng and Sir John Jennings—had a prior option to take it up but did not do so. What appeared formally to be a convoying command could have delicate, though as yet ill-defined, political implications. The increasing number of seizures of British and Dutch Baltic shipping by Swedish privateers and the blockade of the staple ports of the east Baltic under Charles XII's orders after 1710 made a naval showing by the maritime powers inevitable by 1715. Hanover also hoped, despite British constitutional restraints on George I as king, that Norris's ships by their very presence might contribute to Sweden's military collapse in north Germany. Hanover's hand would thus be strengthened, with Denmark and Prussia then dividing up the spoils of war. Above all, Hanover was determined to prise Denmark out of the duchy of Bremen, and so wrest it and Verden from Sweden as a rich territorial acquisition for the electorate. Equally significant was Hanover's aim to win Tsar Peter of Russia's friendly compliance in such a gain. The presence in London over the winter of 1714–15 of the tsar's roving ambassador, Prince Kurakin, could have alerted Orford and his intimates that British neutrality in the northern war might be at risk the following summer. In 1715 Norris's squadron broke the Swedish blockade of the east Baltic ports, and he and his Dutch confederate eased the courses set by the largest assembly of merchant shipping to enter the Baltic in any one month between 1700 and 1729. The task, in a largely uncharted sea, precluded any involvement in amphibious operations against Sweden, though Norris may have been more disposed to act aggressively than the Dutch commander. What was to be of real consequence to Norris after his three weeks at Reval in July–August 1715 was that he quickly won a warm liking and respect from Tsar Peter.

Norris's Baltic season of 1716 was one he spent mainly in Copenhagen, implementing contingent instructions designed to gain Charles XII's ear and, failing that, to countenance a Dano-Russian invasion of south Sweden, an equivocation made the easier by later revelations of indirect Swedish support for the 1715 Jacobite rising. But in September a major crisis erupted when the invasion plan was abandoned and the full extent of Russia's design to render the duchy of Mecklenburg a western entrepôt was revealed. Norris had been unable to persuade the tsar to continue the invasion plan, and the Danes to assist in moving the Russian army further east, to Poland. These developments profoundly affected future relations with Russia, and Hanoverian policies through the closing years of the Northern War. Back home Orford's sustained opposition to George I's expectations for the navy severely embarrassed Norris, who now found himself a victim of the related collapse of the king's first British ministry in the spring of 1717. He refused to serve under Byng in the Baltic that season, for Byng's enjoyment of Orford's solid support would have rendered Norris's position intolerable. Instead, in 1717 he was sent on a mission to Tsar Peter in the United Provinces, in partnership with the diplomat Charles Whitworth in an attempt to restore George I's relations with the tsar and so forward a coveted commercial treaty for Britain with Russia. Not unpredictably, Russian prevarication rendered the mission abortive from the start, and from this time forward Norris became a convinced Russophobe. In late 1718 he evaded undertaking another mission to the tsar in Petersburg, proposed by Lord Stanhope.

During the remaining four seasons of his Baltic commands Norris was concerned (1718) with preventing a Russo-Swedish fleet junction, the product of a possible accommodation between Tsar Peter and Charles XII which was ended by the latter's death in December of that year. In 1719, 1720, and 1721 Norris observed the spirit rather than the letter of the revived Anglo-Swedish alliance of 1700, since Sweden was now irreversibly defeated and any defensive stance taken by Norris's ships, which could lead to British hostilities with Russia, must at all costs be avoided. The Swedes were also left in no doubt, since Norris was accorded diplomatic powers in 1720 and 1721, that he was now in the Baltic to act mediatorily, with the hope of accelerating a final peace between Sweden and Russia. But in the summer of 1721 Tsar Peter excluded Britain and Hanover from any role in the peace he dictated to Sweden. It was also a calculated exclusion not lost on Norris, a snub to British seapower represented by his ships off the Stockholm coasts. In 1727, the year of Norris's final return to the Baltic, he went no further than Copenhagen in order to honour a defensive convention with Denmark, fearful as she was of an impending challenge from Russia over her possession of Schleswig and Holstein. This did not materialize owing to the death of Tsarina Catherine I.

Later career The obfuscations of policy and the international import of Norris's Baltic commands, which had called forth peculiar resources from him personally, largely escaped contemporaries beyond the bounds of the northern department of the Foreign Office. Where credit might be imputed to him it was the more difficult to accord because of his known reputation for short temper and expletive opinion. Ministerial power was in itself sufficient to shield him from unfavourable exposure, just as it overcame an opposition in the Lords over the winter of 1721–2 which fiercely queried the size of the navy debt when the navy had obviously failed to succour Sweden after 1718. Furthermore it was freely alleged that it had been Hanoverian interest which had undermined the navy's effectiveness, so causing government to be in breach of the constitution. One tangible outcome from these years was Norris's *Book of Baltic Charts* (1723), notable in eighteenth-century British cartography and a tribute to the officers of the various squadrons who made detailed observations when opportunity offered. During the 1720s, when he was an MP for Portsmouth (elected in 1722), Norris was active in the affairs of Trinity House; but his tenure of a lordship of the Admiralty since 1718 was terminated in 1730 when he clashed with Robert Walpole's government over its failure to press France over the demolition of Dunkirk's defences.

In 1734 Norris was again elected to a seat at Rye, in preference to Rochester, and also became admiral of the fleet. His old rival, Torrington, had died in 1733 but the new first lord, Sir Charles Wager, was, in his turn, a potential new rival to Norris because of his prestige and greater popularity. In fact the two were to work together quite effectively before Wager's death in 1743, though initially some strains may have been avoided through Norris's absence at Lisbon (1735–7), when he commanded a squadron in earnest of Britain's support of Portugal against the Bourbon powers. Norris's papers from this time disclose a stickler for all shipboard measures for battle-readiness 'which every officer knows but may sometimes neglect as not seeing the accident near' (BL, Add. MS 28147, fol. 128). In 1739 with the outbreak of war against Spain he attended meetings of a privy council committee advising on flag officers' appointments and on the logistical problems in planning a campaign in the West Indies, though he himself had never served there. He was also an active commissioner for prize appeal (1742–8). A convinced but unregarded canvasser of blockade tactics against Spanish trade, in the campaigning seasons of 1740 and 1741 he commanded in the western approaches and Biscay in circumstances of uncertainty whether France would remain neutral in the Anglo-Spanish war. Following Walpole's resignation in 1742, Norris refused a place on the Admiralty board unless he was able to head it himself; George II in turn did not accept Norris's consequent request to resign. In February 1744 his last command, in the channel, was a bitter event due in part to heavy weather and a planned French invasion from Dunkirk. In fact the weather destroyed French preparations, and shortly afterwards George II accepted Norris's plea to retire on the grounds that 'he had served the crown longer as an admiral than any man ever did, and as zealously and faithfully as any man ever can do' (PRO SP 42/87, fol. 414). His correspondence with the duke of Newcastle during his last command indeed reveals a 74-year-old commander of impressive pertinacity. Norris died on 13 June 1749 at his country house, Hempsted Park, Benenden, Kent, and was buried in Benenden church. He was survived by his wife, Lady Elizabeth, who died in November 1763.

J. K. LAUGHTON, rev. D. D. ALDRIDGE

Sources DNB · D. D. Aldridge, 'Admiral Sir John Norris and the British naval expeditions to the Baltic Sea, 1715–1727', PhD diss., U. Lond., 1971 · D. D. Aldridge, 'Admiral Sir John Norris 1670 (or 1671)–1749: his birth and early service, his marriage, and his death', Mariner's Mirror, 51 (1965), 173–83 · F. Genzel, 'Studien zur Geschichte des nordischen Krieges 1714–1720 unter besonderer Berücksichtigung der Personalunion zwischen Gross Britannien und Hannover', PhD diss., University of Bonn, 1951 · R. M. Hatton, Diplomatic relations between Great Britain and the Dutch republic, 1714–1721 (1950) · C. J. Nordmann, La crise du nord au début du XVIIIe siècle (1962) · J. J. Murray, 'Anglo-French skirmishing in Newfoundland, 1697', Essays in modern European history, ed. J. J. Murray (1951), 71–84 · P. Le Fevre and R. Harding, eds., Precursors of Nelson: British admirals of the eighteenth century (2000) · J. F. Chance, George I and the Northern War (1909) · J. J. Murray, George I, the Baltic, and the whig split (1968) · R. C. Anderson, Naval wars in the Baltic during the sailing-ship epoch, 1522–1850 (1910) · J. H. Owen, War at sea under Queen Anne, 1702–1708 (1938) · H. W. Richmond, The navy in the war of 1739–48, 3 vols. (1920) · G. Hinchcliffe, 'Some papers of Sir John Norris', Mariner's Mirror, 56 (1970), 77–84 · R. R. Sedgwick, 'Norris, Sir John', HoP, Commons, 1715–54 · F. Aylmer, The Aylmers of Ireland (1931)

Archives BL, letter-books, journal, and papers, Add. MSS 28126–28157 · NMM, orders and letters received · Port Eliot, Saltash, corresp. | BL, corresp. with duke of Newcastle, Add. MSS 23627–23628, 32690–32791, passim · BL, corresp. with Charles Whitworth, earl of Sunderland, Earl Cadogan, Add. MSS 37365–37397, 37425, passim · East Riding of Yorkshire Archives Service, Beverley, letters and orders to Henry Medley · NA Scot., Campbell MSS · NA Scot., corresp. with Lord Polwarth

Likenesses G. Kneller, oils, 1711, NMM · G. Knapton, oils, 1720, NMM · T. Burford, mezzotint, 1741 (after unknown portrait) · P. Scheemakers, marble bust, 1749–50, Benenden church, Kent · T. Hudson, oils, Gov. Art Coll.

Norris, John (1733/4–1777), benefactor, was the only son of John Norris (d. 1734), lord of the manor of Witton, Norfolk, and his wife, Anna (Anne) Carthew, daughter of Thomas Carthew of Benacre Hall, Suffolk. Norris had one sister, Anna, who later married Anthony Aufrere and was the mother of the antiquary Anthony Aufrere (1756–1833). He was educated at Eton College and then at Trinity College, Cambridge, where he was admitted as a fellow commoner on 6 July 1752, aged eighteen; he did not graduate. In 1758 he married Elizabeth Playters (c.1741–1769), only daughter of John Playters of Yelverton. The couple, whose only child died in infancy, settled at Great Witchingham, Norfolk, where Norris built a house, which he partly demolished following Elizabeth's death on 1 December 1769. He then moved to Witton, where in 1770 he began building Witton House and laying out the grounds. On 12 May 1773 he married Charlotte Townshend, daughter of Edward Townshend, dean of Norwich; they had one daughter, Charlotte Laura, who married (17 November 1796) John Woodhouse, later second Baron Woodhouse. About 1773 Norris was introduced to the young Richard Porson, the future Greek scholar, who lived in the neighbouring village of East Ruston. Impressed by Porson's extraordinary feats of memory, Norris established a fund for the young man to be educated at Eton. A man of reserved and often gloomy disposition, Norris was said to be 'respected by all' though 'these were few who were easy and chearful in his society' (European Magazine).

Norris died of a fever on 5 January 1777 at his house in Upper Brook Street, London, and was buried at Witton. By his will, dated 26 June 1770, he made a charge against the Abbey Farm in the parish of Bacton, Norfolk, for an annuity of £120, free of all taxes or deductions, for the foundation of a professorship of divinity at Cambridge, and of an annual prize of £12 in a medal and books for an English essay on a sacred subject; for a Good Friday sermon at the university church; and for the distribution of books at the town's gaol. Norris's bequest may have been prompted by Beilby Porteus's call in 1767 for the promotion of theology as an integral part of the university curriculum. The gift carried with it certain stipulations in keeping with Norris's belief in the orthodox doctrine of the Trinity, which holders were prohibited from questioning. Despite these good intentions, the establishment of the Norrisian chair 'did little to alter the prevailing state of Cambridge education', in part because attendance at lectures remained voluntary (Gascoigne, 265). The £105 annually assigned to the professorship was afterwards augmented from other sources, and regulations for the prize were altered.

Norris's will, made before his second marriage, was accompanied by a manuscript explaining his intentions about the annuity in a curious style full of religious observations, and concluding 'Hallelujah'. It is the will of a sane but singular man. His daughter's guardians contested it but the lord chancellor finally ruled in favour of the university, which had already fulfilled Norris's directions for several years. The first incumbent, John Hey, took up the position in 1780, and a list of subsequent professors and prizewinners can be found in the *Historical Register of the University of Cambridge* and its supplements. In addition, Norris's will bequeathed £10 per annum to the vicar of Witton for the performance of service on every Sunday during Lent (rather than twice every three weeks), and endowed two small schools at Witton and Witchingham. He was survived by his second wife, who married Thomas Fauquier in 1779; the remainder of his estate of nearly £4000 per annum passed to his daughter.

W. W. WROTH, rev. JOHN D. PICKLES

Sources J. W. Clark, *Endowments of the University of Cambridge* (1904) · [University of Cambridge], *Trusts, statutes and directions* (1876) · Venn, *Alum. Cant.* · *European Magazine and London Review*, 5 (1784), 333–4 · *N&Q*, 2nd ser., 8 (1859), 286 · *GM*, 1st ser., 47 (1777) · Burke, *Gen. GB* (1882), 52–3 [Aufrere pedigree] · J. Gascoigne, *Cambridge in the age of the Enlightenment* (1989) · Nichols, *Lit. anecdotes*, 8.456
Likenesses W. C. Edwards, line engraving (after Smissen), BM, NPG
Wealth at death less than £4000 p.a. after bequests: *European Magazine*, 334

Norris, John Pilkington (1823–1891), Church of England clergyman, born at Chester on 10 June 1823, was the son of Thomas Norris, a physician of Chester. Educated first at Rugby School under Thomas Arnold, he proceeded to Cambridge, where he gained an open scholarship at Trinity College, matriculating in 1842. He came out in the middle of the first class of the classical tripos in 1846, and in the same year graduated BA. He became MA in 1849, BD in 1875, and DD in 1881. Norris obtained a fellowship at Trinity in 1848, and in the same year carried off one of the members' prizes for the Latin essay. He was ordained deacon by the bishop of Ely in 1849, and priest in the following year.

In 1849 Norris accepted one of the newly created inspectorships of schools. The high traditions of that office owe much to the spirit in which Norris and others entered upon the work. His own district comprised Staffordshire, Shropshire, and Cheshire. His enthusiasm was unbounded; his thoroughness and mastery of detail so great that he was said, by a pardonable exaggeration, to know not merely all the teachers, but all the children who came under his eye. In 1858 Norris married Edith Grace, daughter of Sir Stephen *Lushington (1782–1873) and his wife, Sarah; they had several children. Norris's work began to tell upon him, and in 1863 he moved to a smaller district in Kent and Surrey. But, finding himself unequal to this, he resigned his inspectorship in 1864, and became curate-in-charge of Lewknor, a small Oxfordshire parish.

In 1864 Norris was appointed a canon of Bristol, and incumbent of Hatchford, Surrey, where he remained until 1870. In that year there fell vacant the vicarage of St George, Brandon Hill, Bristol. The parish was large, the people poor, the income small. The dean and chapter were the patrons, and Norris felt it his duty to take the parish himself. He therefore moved permanently to Bristol. His own church and people were admirably cared for, and he also threw himself zealously into diocesan work. In 1876 he became rural dean of Bristol, and in 1877 vicar of the historic church of St Mary Redcliffe. In 1881 the bishop made him archdeacon of Bristol, a post which led in the following year to the resignation of his incumbency.

Norris filled other positions with unvarying success. He was a friend and confidential correspondent of Bishop James Fraser of Manchester, whose examining chaplain he was from 1870 to 1885, and was inspector of church training colleges from 1871 to 1876. He served as a member of convocation, as proctor for the chapter of Bristol from 1879 to 1881, and afterwards as archdeacon. Towards the end of December 1891 he fell ill with bronchitis. On 29 December his appointment to the deanery of Chichester was announced, but he died on the same evening. His wife survived him. He was buried in the graveyard adjoining Bristol Cathedral, and a tablet was erected within its walls to bear testimony to his worth. More than £5000 was subscribed as a memorial to him to be devoted to the augmentation of the Bristol bishopric.

Norris was a hard and successful worker for the restoration of the cathedral, the nave of which must always be associated with his name. He was one of the first to move for the revival of the former see of Bristol, as distinct from that of Gloucester; he gave at least £10,000 to this cause. He was also a vigorous promoter of church extension in and around the cathedral town. Norris's most important literary works were his popular handbooks for students in theology and two volumes of notes on the New Testament. He published widely on theology, wrote a handbook to Bristol Cathedral (1882), and edited John Keble's theological remains (1877). He published lectures on Joseph Butler in 1886.

A. R. BUCKLAND, rev. H. C. G. MATTHEW

Sources *The Times* (29 Dec 1891) · *The Times* (30 Dec 1891) · *Guardian* (6 Jan 1892) · *The Record* (8 Jan 1892) · Crockford (1890) · J. Gott, *Bristol bishoprick endowment fund* (1894) · T. Hughes, *Life of James Fraser* (1887)
Archives Bristol RO, corresp. and papers · U. Reading L., annotations to 'Theocriti Bionis et Moschi idylls' | BL, corresp. with W. E. Gladstone, Add. MSS 44449–44510 · Bucks. RLSS, letters to J. C. Ramsden · LPL, letters to A. C. Tait

Likenesses wood-engraving, NPG; repro. in *ILN* (9 Jan 1892)
Wealth at death £6724 9*s*. 10*d*.: probate, 15 Feb 1892, *CGPLA Eng. & Wales*

Norris, Margery, Lady Norris (*d.* **1599**). *See under* Norris, Henry, first Baron Norris (*c.*1525–1601).

Norris, Philip (*c.***1400–1465**), theologian, was probably born in Dundalk. On 31 July 1427 he was presented to the parish church of St Nicholas in Dundalk and granted leave of absence for seven years' study at a university. At Oxford he regularly witnessed documents and acted as principal of the Little University Hall from 1427 to 1429. By then he must have been MA: he was BTh by 1431 and DTh by 1435. On 26 August 1433 Pope Eugenius IV presented him to a canonry in St Patrick's Cathedral, Dublin, together with the prebend of Mulhuddart, Dublin, allowing him to retain his benefice in Dundalk. On 11 October 1435 the University of Oxford thanked the dean and chapter of St Patrick's for Norris's promotion and on 12 March 1436 the university recommended him to the archbishop of Dublin, Richard Talbot (*d.* 1449), as preacher, 'sonora sancte predicacionis tuba' ('the resounding trumpet of sacred eloquence'). In November 1435 proceedings were started against Norris for non-residence in Dundalk under the statute of Richard II of 1394 against Irish absentees, as he had exceeded his seven-year leave of absence, and in 1438 the archbishop of Armagh, John Swayne, acknowledged receipt of letters from the king's lieutenant in Ireland compelling Norris to personal residence in Dundalk.

At Oxford, Norris had already begun to criticize the four orders of mendicant friars with arguments similar to those of Richard Fitzralph, who as archbishop of Armagh had also used the church of St Nicholas in Dundalk. Presumably because of this criticism the university granted Norris letters testimonial on 20 June 1431 and again on 11 October 1435, to protect him against 'calumpnancium invidia' ('the jealousy of false accusers'). The University of Cambridge protested on 8 May 1438 about his campaign against the friars. The Dominican Thomas Hore had already appealed against him to the papal curia, and the Augustinian friar William Mussilwike had him cited for heresy in 1438 before John Stafford, chancellor of England and bishop of Bath and Wells. This initiative was a failure, as the university supported Norris and briefly suspended Mussilwike for breach of university privilege. The friars were equally unsuccessful when the matter came before the convocation of Canterbury, whereupon the provincials of the four orders appealed to the Roman curia.

In October 1437 the grand penitentiary Domenico Capranica, bishop of Fermo and cardinal-deacon of Santa Maria in via Lata in Rome, was commissioned by Eugenius IV to investigate the charges. Norris was cited to appear in Rome but failed to do so. He afterwards claimed that his enemies had secured his detention in England by royal order, furthermore that because Capranica was unaware of this he regarded the accused as insubordinate. On the basis of Capranica's investigations Eugenius IV condemned and excommunicated Norris in a bull of 24 August 1440 to the archbishops of Armagh and Dublin,

which contains a detailed statement of Norris's accusations and of the case for the defence. Norris questioned the friars' right to exercise priestly office, and insisted that penitents who confessed to a friar were obliged to repeat the same sins to their own parish priest. Finally Norris's claim that he would submit to judgment only before a general council was used against him, and he was ordered to pay the costs of the trial. This is presumably the document to which the friars referred, when they complained in August 1441 that Thomas Walsh, bachelor of laws, had obstructed the archbishop of Dublin and prevented him from publishing bulls obtained in their favour.

Norris appealed against this condemnation to the Rump Council of Basel in May 1443, and obtained a revocation of the papal sentence of excommunication. This judgment was subsequently confirmed by Nicholas V in a bull, no longer extant. Norris clearly continued to enjoy the confidence of the crown: from a bull of 5 February 1452 issued by Nicholas V it emerges that Henry VI had presented Norris to the parish church of St Patrick in Trim, Meath, despite the fact that the former holder had received a papal dispensation to retain it after becoming bishop of Meath. Norris was cited to appear before the archbishop of Armagh, John Mey (*d.* 1456), on 21 October 1454 or as soon as possible thereafter. On 22 December 1455 Calixtus III granted Norris a dispensation to receive—in addition to the rectory in Trim, which was wealthy by Irish standards—another compatible benefice. On 18 March 1456 the same pope confirmed the rehabilitation of Norris pronounced by Nicholas V, and further absolved him from the offence of having adhered so long to the schismatic Council of Basel. He ordered the friars not to molest Norris in future, but to help restore his reputation for orthodoxy. The archbishops of Canterbury and Dublin were to ensure that Norris—now advanced in age—enjoyed his benefices in peace. These benefices then included the prebend of Iago, Kildare, in the chapter of St Patrick's Cathedral, of which Norris became dean in 1457. He died in 1465, having for the previous seven years been too ill to make a will. John Bale ascribes to him the following works: *Declamationes*, *Lecturae scripturarum*, *Sermones ad populum*, and a tractate *Contra mendicitatem validem*, but no surviving manuscripts have been located. He donated to Lincoln College, Oxford, a codex containing *Speculum philosophiae* and other items. KATHERINE WALSH

Sources *CEPR letters*, 8.464–5; 10.233–4; 11.85, 100–02 · E. Monsignano, ed., *Bullarium Carmelitanum plures complectens summorum pontificum constitutiones ad ordinem fratrum beatissimae*, 1 (Rome, 1715), 198–200 · L. Wadding, *Annales minorum*, ed. J. M. Fonseca and others, 3rd edn, 11 (1932), 104–7, 119–23 · D. A. Chart, ed., *The register of John Swayne, archbishop of Armagh and primate of Ireland, 1418–1439* (1935), 63, 163–4, 174, 206 · E. F. Jacob, ed., *The register of Henry Chichele, archbishop of Canterbury, 1414–1443*, 3, CYS, 46 (1945), 275, 278 · Emden, *Oxf.* · Bale, *Cat.*, 2.246–7 · Tanner, *Bibl. Brit.-Hib.*, 549 · *The whole works of Sir James Ware concerning Ireland*, ed. and trans. W. Harris, 2/2 (1746), 89 · H. Anstey, ed., *Epistolae academicae Oxon.*, 1, OHS, 35 (1898), 64, 124 · W. M. Mason, *The history and antiquities of the collegiate and cathedral church of St Patrick, near Dublin* (privately printed, Dublin, 1820), 133–5 · E. Tresham, ed., *Rotulorum patentium et clausorum cancellariae Hiberniae calendarium*, Irish

Record Commission (1828), 262b · R. Weiss, 'The earliest catalogues of the library of Lincoln College', *Bodleian Quarterly Review*, 8 (1935–8), 350 · W. G. H. Quigley and E. F. D. Roberts, eds., *Registrum Iohannis Mey: the register of John Mey, archbishop of Armagh, 1443–1456* (1972), 376–7, no. 359 · R. B. Dobson, 'The religious orders, 1370–1540', *Hist. U. Oxf.* 2: *Late med. Oxf.*, 539–79, esp. 573

Norris, Robert (*bap.* 1724?, *d.* 1791), trader and author, was the brother of William *Norris, secretary to the Society of Antiquaries. He most probably was baptized on 5 May 1724 at St Mary Colechurch, London, the son of Selfe Norris (*d.* 1740), and his wife, Mary Pead. The statement in the *Dictionary of National Biography* that he was the son of John Norris of Nonesuch, Wiltshire, appears to be erroneous. As a ship's captain in the slave trade, Norris made at least five voyages to Dahomey in west Africa between 1770 and 1777, on four of which (1770, 1772, 1773, and 1775) he also travelled inland, to visit the king of Dahomey's court. In 1779, with the disruption of shipping to Africa by the American War of Independence, he found himself unemployed, and set up as a blacksmith. In 1788, when a committee of the privy council was appointed to inquire into the slave trade, in response to agitation for its abolition, Norris was delegated to lay before it the views of the Liverpool trade; and his evidence was published as a pamphlet, *A Short Account of the African Slave Trade* (1788). He also published *Memoirs of the Reign of Bossa Ahadee, King of Dahomy* (1789); besides a history of the reign of the Dahomian king Bossa Ahadee (now known as Tegbesu, reigned 1740–74), this contained an account of Norris's visit to the king's court in 1772, including a description of ceremonies there involving the offering of human sacrifices, and a revised version of his 1788 pamphlet. Norris subsequently revised the *Memoirs* and his account of the 1772 visit for incorporation into the *History of Dahomy* of Archibald Dalzel (1793), although Norris himself died before this was published. Norris depicted Dahomey as a barbaric society, with especial emphasis on the practice of human sacrifice, as the basis for a moral defence of the slave trade, which was supposedly rescuing slaves from a worse fate within Africa. Despite its pro-slavery bias, his book is of major historiographical significance as one of the earliest studies of the history of an African society. Norris's manuscript journal of his voyage to Dahomey and thence to Jamaica in 1769–71 is preserved in the Merseyside Maritime Museum; and a map by him of the west African coast, dated 1789, is in the British Museum. Norris died on 27 November 1791 in Liverpool, from what the obituary in the *Gentleman's Magazine* described as 'the effects of a damp bed on his journey from London' (*GM*, 1791). ROBIN LAW

Sources R. Norris, *Memoirs of the reign of Bossa Ahadee, king of Dahomy* (1789) · R. Norris, *A short account of the African slave trade* (1788) · A. Dalzel, *The history of Dahomy* (1793) · R. Law, 'The slave trader as historian: Robert Norris and the history of Dahomey', *History in Africa*, 16 (1989), 219–35 · I. A. Akinjogbin, *Dahomey and its neighbours, 1708–1818* (1967) · R. Norris, 'A journal of a voyage in the ship Unity of Liverpool bound to Holland, Africa and Jamaica, 1769–71', Merseyside Maritime Museum, Liverpool, Earle MSS · review of Norris's *Memoirs of the reign of Bossa Ahadee*, *GM*, 1st ser., 59 (1789), 433 · *GM*, 1st ser., 61 (1791), 1160–61 · *GM*, 1st ser., 62 (1792), 88 [obit. of William Norris] · E. Brydges, *Censura literaria: containing titles, abstracts, and opinions of old English books*, 5 (1807) · catalogue

[BM] · *IGI* · parish register, London, St Mary Colechurch, 5 May 1724 [baptism]
Archives Merseyside Maritime Museum, Liverpool, a journal of a voyage in the ship *Unity of Liverpool*, bound to Holland, Africa, and Jamaica

Norris, Roger. *See* Norreis, Roger (*d.* 1223).

Norris, Samuel (1875–1948), journalist and political reformer, was born on 11 July 1875 at 3 Schofield Street, Tyldesley, Lancashire, the fifth of six children of James Norris, coalminer, and his wife, Martha Dennerly. He was reticent about his childhood and youth; he attended elementary school but was otherwise self-educated. In 1894 he went to the Isle of Man as a reporter on the *Manx Sun*, and stayed for the rest of his life. In 1898 he became the Manx correspondent of the *Liverpool Mercury*, and later of the *Manchester Guardian*, papers which then paid considerable attention to Manx affairs. On 10 October 1901 he married his childhood sweetheart, Margaret Ellen Pearson (1875–1955), daughter of a paper mill manager, with whom he had four children.

In 1903, an election year for the Manx House of Keys, Samuel Norris wrote a series of five articles in the *Liverpool Mercury* under the pen-name Verax on 'Manxland's Home Rule Parliament'. These articles, reprinted as a pamphlet, described the state of Manx political life: the arbitrary power exercised by the governor and the unelected legislative council, the limited role of the elected House of Keys, an archaic legal and judicial system, reliance on indirect taxation instead of income tax, and the urgent need for reform. Norris's politics were radical Liberal, and shortly before the election he inaugurated the Manx National Reform League. Branches were formed throughout the island, and all except one or two of the twenty-four members of the new House of Keys claimed to support the reform programme.

Probably because of his political activities, Norris was dismissed by the *Liverpool Mercury* in 1904. He went into business, initially with a partner in the Norris-Meyer Press, from 1913 on his own as the Norris Modern Press. The firm flourished, diversifying from printing and publishing into picture postcards and the sale of stationery and newspapers. Norris was now able to produce his own political publications, such as the annual Manx Year Books from 1906 on, essential handbooks containing information on Manx finances, official salaries, and all aspects of national and local government. From 1906 to 1909 his monthly free sheet, the *Manx Patriot*, campaigned for reform.

However, the dilatory Manx political system, the reactionary views of the ultra-Conservative governor, Lord Raglan, and the low priority given to Manx affairs by British governments, ensured that little changed before 1914. By 1911 when, in response to a petition from the Keys, the Macdonnell committee of inquiry arrived on the island, the Reform League had faded away, as Norris had to admit when giving evidence. The Liberal reforms of 1906–14 left the Isle of Man even further behind UK norms.

The First World War gave Norris another opportunity to

organize public opinion. In 1915 the collapse of the holiday industry led to acute distress among boarding-house keepers. Norris set up the War Rights Union, with himself as organizing secretary, to campaign for rate rebates and aid from the Manx government. This was not forthcoming, so the War Rights Union embarked on passive resistance and rate refusal. In 1916 this broadened into the Redress, Retrenchment and Reform Campaign. Norris's 'Manifesto to the Manx People' called for income tax and a new governor. Several labour leaders joined the campaign, and a demonstration demanding 'Raglan must go!' disrupted the annual open-air Tynwald day ceremony. Norris organized another petition to the home secretary, and used his connection with the *Manchester Guardian* and the Manchester Liberals to good effect.

Later, Norris led the disruption of a coroner's sale of goods distrained from rate refusers. With eight others he was summoned before the High Court, over which Raglan himself presided, and was singled out for imprisonment until he had purged his contempt. A month's incarceration in Douglas gaol was ended by his apology, but brought more bad publicity for the Manx government in the UK, and he emerged from prison a symbol of resistance to arbitrary power.

The great bread strike of July 1918 (in which Norris played no part), the end of the war, and Raglan's enforced resignation, changed the political landscape. In the Manx election of 1919, Norris was elected a member of the House of Keys for North Douglas, and piloted the introduction of old-age pensions through the legislature. In 1921 he was responsible for the Married Women's Property Act. As an independent he took many other progressive initiatives, and consistently argued the case for responsible self-government, increasing the power of the Keys and diminishing the power of the governor. He was re-elected in 1924, lost his seat in 1929 by four votes, but returned to the Keys in 1934. In 1938 he published *Manx Memories and Movements*, an autobiography which largely focuses on his political activities between 1903 and 1919 and has ensured his posthumous fame.

From 1939 to 1942 Norris was a member of the governor's war cabinet, but he resigned in order to campaign for further reform, as outlined in his book *This Manx Democracy!* (1945). In 1943 he was appointed to the legislative council. He was not reappointed by the new House of Keys elected in 1946, so at the age of seventy-one his political career was over. He continued to run his business, and in 1947 published *Two Men of Manxland*, a dual biography of T. E. Brown and Hall Caine. He died in Noble's Hospital, Douglas, on 4 December 1948, and was buried in Douglas borough cemetery on 7 December.

Norris was a man of great integrity, a lifelong teetotaller and devout Congregationalist, a self-made Liberal journalist, businessman, and politician, and a strict Victorian paterfamilias. He left the considerable sum of £34,000, including a bequest of £100 for Douglas borough council to provide fruit and flowers, and Salvation Army concerts, for inmates of the island's prison. He was not modest, and could be difficult to work with, but his consistent advocacy of reform undoubtedly had considerable effect. He was described by the speaker of the House of Keys after his death as 'the fearless leader of Manx democracy' (*Tynwald Debates*, 14 Dec 1948), and almost all his aspirations came to pass, if not in his lifetime, then in the second half of the twentieth century.   ROBERT FYSON

Sources S. Norris, *Manx memories and movements* (1938); repr. (1994) · *Manx Patriot* [monthly] (1906–9) · *Manx Year Book* (1906–16) · *Manx Year Book* (1920–42) · *Manx Year Book* (1944–9) · *Douglas Weekly Diary* (1928–48) · War Rights Union file, Manx Museum Library, Douglas, Manx government office papers, 9845 · Samuel Norris prison file, Manx Museum Library, Douglas, Manx government office papers, 9673 · *Isle of Man Examiner Annual* (1903–48) · *Tynwald Debates* (1919–29) · *Tynwald Debates* (1934–48) · *Tynwald Debates* (1948) · W. Cubbon, *Bibliography of the Isle of Man*, 1–2 (1933–9) · D. Kermode, *Offshore island politics: the constitutional and political development of the Isle of Man in the twentieth century* (2001) · S. Norris; will, general registry, Douglas, Isle of Man · private information (2004) [family members] · D. Kelly, ed., *Manx worthies* (2003) · b. cert.
Archives priv. coll., family papers
Likenesses photograph, repro. in Norris, *Manx memories* (1994) · photograph, repro. in *Isle of Man Examiner Annual* (1920), 71
Wealth at death under £34,000: will, general registry, Douglas

Norris, Sylvester (1572–1630), Jesuit and religious controversialist, was born at Milverton, Somerset, the son of Hugh Norris and Joan Clarke. Two brothers of his, Richard and Hugh, became secular priests. In spite of a letter written on 24 July 1584 to Sir Francis Walsingham by the spy Nicholas Parker, warning him against the boy, Sylvester managed to flee from England to Rheims on 24 March 1585, shortly followed by his brother Richard. After receiving minor orders at Rheims on 18 August 1590 Norris proceeded to the English College, Rome, where he was ordained priest on 29 January 1595. That year he joined a group of disaffected students who unsuccessfully petitioned the pope to remove the Jesuits from control of the college.

In the following year Norris, after receiving his DD, left Rome for England. Soon after his arrival, on 28 January 1597, he wrote to his former fellow students at Rome expressing appreciation for 'the more than ordinary kindness' he had received from the Jesuits in England. This did not, however, prevent him from siding with the appellant priests in their dispute with the archpriest and his Jesuit supporters over the structure of the English Catholic church and from giving his signature to the two appeals they sent to Rome, first from Wisbech on 17 November 1600, and second from Paris on 3 May 1603.

After the discovery of the Gunpowder Plot, Norris was arrested in Northamptonshire and imprisoned in Bridewell, whence he wrote a letter to Robert Cecil, earl of Salisbury, on 1 December 1605, declaring his ignorance of the plot and his readiness to go to Rome and urge the pope to make due satisfaction (Foley, 3.301). The outcome of this letter was his banishment from England in 1606 with forty-seven priests. After his arrival at Douai on 24 July 1606 he went to Rome, where, in spite of his anti-Jesuit activities both as a student at Rome and as one of the appellant priests, he entered the Society of Jesus in October. He subsequently appears at the English College, Louvain, lecturing on scripture and theology, being 'held in great esteem as a preacher' (Foley, 3.302) and 'as a polemical writer ranked among the best of his time' (Gillow, *Lit. biog. hist.*, 5.190).

Notable among Norris's controversial writings is a work in three parts entitled *An Antidote* against the protestant and puritan writers of the time. The first part was published in 1615, the second in 1619. In 1622 a further edition of these two parts together was published as 'a treatise of thirty controversies'. The third part, which appeared in 1621, was entitled *The Guide of Faith*, devoted to specific criticism of Francis Mason's important treatise, *Of the Consecration of Bishops in the Church of England* (1613). Also in 1621 Norris brought out *An Appendix to the Antidote*, with 'A catalogue of the visible and perpetuall succession of the catholique professors of the Roman Church', similar to one already compiled by his fellow Jesuit John Fisher (*vere* Percy) in 1614. Another controversial work by Norris appeared in 1623 with the title *Pseudo-Scripturist*, arguing that the scriptures were 'not to be the sole judge of controversies' (Dodd, 2.402).

From about 1621 Norris was back in England as Jesuit superior of the Hampshire district. In May 1623, under the name of Smith, he held a disputation with the puritan divine George Walker. Walker published his account of the conference in 1624, prompting Norris to bring out his version as *A True Report of the Private Colloquy between M Smith, alias Norrice, and M Walker* in the same year. Norris died in Hampshire on 16 March 1630.   PETER MILWARD

Sources H. Foley, ed., *Records of the English province of the Society of Jesus*, 3 (1878), 301–2; 6 (1880), 184; 7 (1882–3), 552 • C. Dodd [H. Tootell], *The church history of England, from the year 1500, to the year 1688*, 2 (1739), 402 • G. Anstruther, *The seminary priests*, 1 (1969), 255–7 • G. Oliver, *Collection towards illustrating the biography of the Scotch, English and Irish members of the Society of Jesus* (1845), 151 • *Menology S.J.* (1902), 1.132–3 • P. Milward, *Religious controversies of the Jacobean age* (1978), 175–6, 181–3 • T. M. McCoog, *English and Welsh Jesuits, 1555–1650*, 2 vols., Catholic RS, 74–5 (1994–5)

Norris, Sir Thomas (1556–1599), soldier, was the fifth son of Henry *Norris, first Baron Norris (*c*.1525–1601), and Margery *Norris (*d*. 1599) [*see under* Norris, Henry], younger daughter of John *Williams, Baron Williams of Thame. He matriculated at Magdalen College, Oxford, in 1571 and graduated BA on 6 April 1576. He married Bridget, daughter of Sir William Kingsmill of Sydmonton, Hampshire. Norris came to Ireland in December 1579 as a captain of horse, serving under Lord Justice Sir William Pelham. His arrival coincided with the outbreak of a major rebellion in Munster, and Norris campaigned with Pelham against Gerald Fitzgerald, earl of Desmond, throughout the following year. In winter 1580–81 he was temporarily appointed governor in Connaught, a responsibility granted largely on the advice of his influential elder brother John *Norris. On his return to Munster he continued the assault on Desmond, pushing him back into Kerry and eventually forcing him to raise his siege of Dingle (December 1581). The weak state of his force ruled out

further action, but his initiative earned him praise from Pelham and he was made colonel of the forces in Munster on the retirement of Captain John Zouche (August 1582). Norris's appointment was not universally popular. Complaints of abuses committed in Munster by his captains and soldiers were a cause for concern, and many of the older administrators felt he was too young for such a responsibility. In December 1582 the government rebuked him when they heard that innocents had been murdered in 'rash revenge' when a trunk of his clothes was left behind.

In December 1583 the earl of Ormond took over the command of Munster and Norris travelled to England carrying a letter of recommendation from the under-treasurer, Sir Henry Wallop. He returned the following summer and was sent north to arbitrate in a dispute between Hugh Oge O'Neill and Shane MacBrian O'Neill over possession of the castle of Edendougher. Norris decided in favour of the latter as captain of the lower Clandeboye, and the government commended him for his tactful handling of the matter. In the autumn he accompanied the new lord deputy, Sir John Perrot, on his progress through Ireland. News that Sorley Boy MacDonnell and a large contingent of Scots had landed at Lough Foyle diverted them to Ulster; during the pursuit of Sorley Boy, Norris was wounded in the knee.

In Perrot's parliament (1585–6) Norris represented Limerick and in December 1585 was appointed vice-president of Munster during the absence of his brother John in the Netherlands. It was a difficult undertaking. The presidential force was in a weak state, and observers commented on a noticeable increase in lawlessness in the province. In March 1587 Norris arrested John fitz Edmund Fitzgerald, steward of Imokilly, Patrick Condon, and certain others whose loyalty he considered doubtful. He also complained that his fellow undertakers and their unruly settlers were causing unrest by attempting to take over land and castles that had not been forfeited. The undertakers replied by accusing the soldiers of fomenting trouble and Sir William Herbert, a prominent English planter, complained that Cork citizens were constantly harassed by Norris's own band. Some of the original undertakers became disillusioned, one of whom was Sir John Popham. In December 1587 he withdrew from the plantation and Norris was granted his seigneury of 6000 acres at Mallow. In December 1588 Norris was knighted by Lord Deputy Sir William Fitzwilliam.

In 1586 Norris was appointed to the commission for surveying the forfeited Desmond lands. Its activities included inquiries into concealed land (land unknown to the crown but legally belonging to it) and in some cases stretched beyond the forfeited land to include ancient concealments. Fear of an insecure title, a major source of grievance in early modern Ireland, produced a sense of insecurity among landowners and strong objections were raised against the commission. Disquiet also arose over promises made by Sir John Perrot that those pardoned before the acts of attainder would remain undisturbed in their land. Eight individuals were actually named, but Norris took a more generous view and assumed the proviso extended to any persons undeniably pardoned before the acts. Accordingly he restored Fitzgerald's heir in 1589.

The secret marriage of Ellen, the daughter and sole heir of Donald MacCarthy, earl of Clancare, to her cousin Florence MacCarthy in 1588 created a further problem for Norris. The marriage meant the union of the Kerry and west Cork MacCarthys, a situation the government would have liked to avoid. In July 1589 Norris had MacCarthy arrested but was unable to find proof that he had committed any crime, and so suggested he would be less dangerous if he were sent to England. This advice was primarily driven by the fear of a Spanish invasion and the suspicion that MacCarthy and other 'doubtful persons' would support a landing in Munster. From 1589 to 1590 Norris and an English engineer, Edmund Yorke, worked on improving the fortifications in Limerick, Waterford, and Dungannon but Norris warned Sir Francis Walsingham that they would fall without strong garrisons. To augment the defence of the province he suggested using loyal noblemen 'armed in the Irish fashion'. Norris constantly complained that his own force was too small and poorly equipped. It was also poorly and infrequently paid. In 1590 his band mutinied and marched to Dublin, and Norris was forced to petition the lord deputy for some of the arrears of pay and for fresh supplies of munitions.

In the winter of 1592–3 Norris went to England to give a detailed report of the proceedings of the plantation commissioners. Burghley had demanded the amplification of a number of points, and the commissioners were now forced to admit that they could only return figures for twelve undertakers. Norris was an exception to this trend as he was one of the few resident undertakers. He was building a new castle on the site of an earlier one, had restocked his land with English sheep, and was operating a small iron foundry. His wife claimed after his death that he had invested £5000 in his Munster undertaking. Norris also owned at least one privateer which operated out of Munster during the Anglo-Spanish war of the 1590s.

Norris was absent from Munster in the summer of 1594, when he accompanied the new lord deputy Sir William Russell on his journey through Ulster, and again in 1595, when the growing tension in the north led to his return to serve under his brother John. He was wounded in the thigh, and during his absence the first attacks on English settlers were recorded. Norris returned to Munster in the spring of 1596 but Russell, who had become involved in a serious dispute with Sir John Norris, now also criticized Thomas and accused him of neglecting his charge there. On his return to Munster in 1596 Norris was engaged in repelling raids by the MacSheedys and the O'Briens, and in August he reported he had hanged more than ninety of them in ten days.

Sir John Norris died in July 1597, and the queen appointed Thomas president of Munster in his brother's place in September. But a month later the sudden death of the lord deputy, Lord Burgh, led to his being chosen lord justice of Ireland by the Irish council. Norris did not welcome the appointment and the queen, fearing a Spanish landing in Munster, decided not to continue it.

Tyrone's victory at the Yellow Ford on 28 August 1598, markedly increased the danger of a full-scale rising in Cork. Norris's position was particularly precarious. Fearful of arming the Irish, unable to rely on the settlers whom he said were unwilling to look to their own defence, and with his own band seriously under strength, he reported that he had no hope of repelling a rebel incursion into Munster. When the rising began on 4 October Norris was forced to withdraw to Cork, and the settlers who tried to flee to the walled towns were in many cases killed or mutilated. An alarmed English government promised Norris munitions, victuals, and 2000 foot soldiers as soon as they could be mustered and transported. Norris's own estate at Mallow was attacked and, although Sir Robert Cecil assured him of his support, complaints had already reached the court that Norris had not provided enough protection for the settlers and had given encouragement to the enemy by a premature retreat to Cork. The queen appeared to have lost confidence in him and even suggested that he had acted out of cowardice.

The promised reinforcements arrived in Munster at the beginning of December. Norris, although beaten back at first, was eventually able to relieve Kilmallock and the following March, Ross Carbery. But by now Norris had lost control of the greater part of Munster and was short of basic supplies. He was offered some respite by the arrival in April 1599 of the new lord lieutenant, the earl of Essex, with fresh forces, and in May Norris went to meet him. On his way he unexpectedly met with a party of the Burkes, and in the ensuing skirmish he was wounded in the jaw. At first the wound did not appear serious and Norris recovered enough to proceed to Limerick. He revictualled the army there and then went on to Kilmallock where he joined Essex, accompanying him until his departure from Munster on 20 June. But by this time his wound was much more painful and he was taken to his house at Mallow. He died there on 20 August 1599. His body was brought to Bristol, possibly to be buried at Rycote.

Thomas Norris was one of six brothers, three of whom died in the Elizabethan army in Ireland. He was highly regarded by the English government, and although foremost a soldier he was also an educated and literary gentleman. An English protestant, he served on several ecclesiastical commissions and in 1596 was criticized for trying to enforce compulsory attendance at divine service. In other respects, however, he appears to have tried to deal fairly with both natives and newcomers. He was on the original commission for the plantation of Munster but had most influence on the commission of 1592 which he was appointed to lead. The commission of 1588 had been very accommodating to the settlers, but Norris had since been critical of their aggressive behaviour, and the commission of 1592 reversed many of the judgments made in 1588. Although Norris was rebuked for not providing enough resistance during the first wave of the rising, Fynes Moryson, a contemporary observer, blamed the undertakers who should have had 2000 men in arms in October 1598, whereas Norris could find only 200 men.

After Norris's death, his widow Bridget, a strong-minded and independent woman, constantly harassed Sir George Carew, president of Munster, to protect her property and interests, and in 1602 she became a Catholic. Norris had one daughter, Elizabeth, who became his sole heir. She also married a captain in the Irish army, Sir John Jephson of Froyle in Hampshire.   JUDITH HUDSON BARRY

Sources CSP Ire., 1574–1608 · J. S. Brewer and W. Bullen, eds., Calendar of the Carew manuscripts, 2–3, PRO (1868–9) · M. MacCarthy-Morrogh, The Munster plantation: English migration to Ireland, 1583–1641 (1986) · F. Moryson, An itinerary containing his ten yeeres travell through the twelve dominions, 2 (1907), 172–3, 219 · GEC, Peerage, new edn, 9.643–5 · D. Lloyd, State worthies (1670), 617–20 · Foster, Alum. Oxon. · F. H. Berry, 'The manor and castle of Mallow in the days of the Tudors [pt 2]', Journal of the Cork Historical and Archaeological Society, 2 (1893), 41–5, esp. 44 · H. G. Leask, 'Mallow Castle, co. Cork', Journal of the Cork Historical and Archaeological Society, 2nd ser., 49 (1944), 19–24 · DNB

Norris, Thomas (1653–1700), politician, the eldest son of Thomas Norris of Speke Hall, Lancashire (c.1618–1686), and Katherine (b. 1632), daughter of Sir Henry *Garway (or Garraway), lord mayor of London in 1639–40, was born on 30 May 1653. Sir William *Norris (1658–1702) and Edward *Norris (bap. 1665, d. 1726) were his brothers. Little is known of Thomas's early life, apart from his admittance to the Inner Temple in 1669, until in 1685 he was appointed to the council of Liverpool, the Lancashire borough closest to the family seat. Norris was following in the footsteps of his father, who had served as a common councillor of Liverpool since the early 1660s. Though Norris was removed from the borough élite in 1689, when the corporate charter of 1676 was restored, his standing in the borough remained high, as is evidenced by his election to serve for Liverpool in the Convention Parliament of 1688–9.

During the convention Norris voted against declaring that the throne had become vacant following the flight of James II, but this apparent unease with the consequences of the revolution of 1688 contrasts with Norris's otherwise staunch whiggery, both in the House of Commons and in Lancashire, where during the early 1690s he became one of the county's leading whigs. In 1693 Norris was appointed a commissioner to discover lands given over to the use of the Catholic church, and in the following year he assisted in the prosecution of those suspected of involvement in the Lancashire plot, allegedly a plan for a Jacobite rising in the north-west; that his motives for pursuing this matter lay, at least in part, in the hope of undermining Lancashire's tories was made clear when he wrote of his hope that a successful prosecution would put it 'in our power to choose (even in this county) much better Members of Parliament in case of a dissolution' (CSP dom., 1694–5, 355). On 18 October 1694 Norris served as foreman of the grand jury that indicted eight alleged Jacobite conspirators, but later that same month the prosecution collapsed. At the general election of the following year Norris stood down at Liverpool to allow the return of his younger brother William, but Thomas's retirement

from parliament did not indicate a desire to withdraw from the political arena. In 1695 he was one of the prime movers behind the successful campaign to obtain for Liverpool a new charter restoring the right of the freemen to elect the borough's mayor, efforts that were rewarded when the new charter named Norris to Liverpool's common council.

It became apparent in January 1696 that Norris's contemporaries were well aware of his staunch whiggery when, in the aftermath of the discovery of the plot to kill William III, a loyal supporter of the revolution settlement was needed to serve as Lancashire's high sheriff. It was Norris who was 'prickt at Kensington, by the King' to assume this office (Kenyon MSS, 395), and it was in this capacity that Norris accompanied the county's lord lieutenant, Charles Gerard, second earl of Macclesfield, when Lancashire's association oath rolls were presented to the lords justices in May of the same year.

Little more is known of Norris until his death at Harrogate in June 1700; he was buried at Childwall, near Speke on 6 July. Shortly after retiring from the Commons, Norris had married, on 31 December 1695, Magdalen, the daughter of Sir Willoughby Aston, second baronet, of Aston, Cheshire, with whom he had one son and one daughter. The former had died in infancy, but Norris was survived by the latter, who upon the death of the last of her uncles in 1730 succeeded to the Speke estates.

RICHARD D. HARRISON

Sources T. Heywood, ed., The Norris papers, Chetham Society, 9 (1846) · HoP, Commons, 1690–1715 [draft] · HoP, Commons, 1660–90, 3.148 · IGI · The manuscripts of Lord Kenyon, HMC, 35 (1894)
Archives Lpool RO, family papers
Wealth at death estates valued at £700 p.a. in 1695: HoP, Commons, 1690–1715 [draft]

Norris, Thomas (bap. 1742, d. 1790), singer and organist, was baptized at St Michael's, Mere, Wiltshire, on 15 August 1742, the son of John Norris. A chorister at Salisbury Cathedral from 1752 under John Stephens, he sang as Master Norris in concerts at Oxford in 1759 and 1760 and at Hickford's Room, London, in March 1761. He sang in oratorios at Covent Garden in Lent 1761 and made his stage début at Drury Lane on 9 October 1762 as the singing-master in Steele's The Conscious Lovers. In Salisbury he had sung with success in Daphnis and Amaryllis, a pastoral written and arranged by James Harris, a wealthy local musical amateur, and David Garrick mounted this as a vehicle for Norris, entitling it The Spring (22 October 1762). It had seven performances, but sections of the audience hissed, displeased by the 'Italian' nature of Norris's falsetto soprano voice. He sang again at Drury Lane in the oratorio The Cure of Saul (27 April 1763) and in George Rush's opera The Royal Shepherd (24 February 1764), but after the first night his part was taken by Elizabeth Dorman, a contralto. With Harris's support he moved to Oxford, where he matriculated at Magdalen College and, after submitting his anthem 'The lord is King', obtained the MusB degree in November 1765. Norris was appointed organist of St

Thomas Norris (*bap.* 1742, *d.* 1790), by John Taylor, pubd 1777

John's College in December 1766; he also became a lay clerk of Christ Church and of Magdalen College and, from 1776, organist of Christ Church Cathedral.

Norris had been a soprano soloist in the Three Choirs meetings of 1761 and 1762 and was tenor soloist there almost every year from 1766, when Stephens was the conductor, to 1788. He sang regularly at the Salisbury festival, in Oxford concerts, and at many other provincial festivals. In London he was a soloist in the Drury Lane oratorio seasons (1771–85) and the Handel commemoration concerts of 1784–7 and 1790. His contemporaries admired his 'fine full tenor' in Handel recitatives, which he delivered with 'manly dignity, and unaffected tenderness', but alcoholism undermined his career so that 'he at last excited pity instead of applause' (*GM*, 60, 1790, 863). Although rather lazy, Norris was a good teacher of promising choristers and retained the affection of his friends. He published some instrumental music (*Six Simphonies*, 1774) and composed several anthems and glees. Eight of his solo songs appeared in a posthumous collection. He died on 3 September 1790 at Himley Hall, Staffordshire, the seat of his patron Lord Dudley, shortly after singing in Handel's *Jephtha* and *Messiah* at the Birmingham festival. He was buried on 5 September at St Michael's, Himley.

OLIVE BALDWIN and THELMA WILSON

Sources *GM*, 1st ser., 60 (1790), 862–3 · G. W. Stone, ed., *The London stage, 1660–1800*, pt 4: 1747–1776 (1962) · C. B. Hogan, ed., *The London stage, 1660–1800*, pt 5: 1776–1800 (1968) · *Music and theatre in Handel's world: the family papers of James Harris, 1732–1780*, ed. D. Burrows and R. Dunhill (2002) · S. McVeigh, *Calendar of London concerts, 1750–1800* [unpublished computer database, Goldsmiths' College, London] · *The letters of David Garrick*, ed. D. M. Little and G. M. Kahrl, 1 (1963) · *Theatrical Review* (1763), 20–22, 38 · J. H. Mee, *The oldest concert room in Europe* (1911) · D. Lysons and others, *Origin and progress of the meeting of the three choirs of Gloucester, Worcester and Hereford* (1895) · D. J.

Reid, 'Some festival programmes of the eighteenth and nineteenth centuries [pts 1–2]', *Royal Musical Association Research Chronicle*, 5 (1965), 51–79; 6 (1966), 3–23 · B. Pritchard and D. J. Reid, 'Some festival programmes of the eighteenth and nineteenth centuries [pt 4]', *Royal Musical Association Research Chronicle*, 8 (1970), 1–22 · *The Director*, 2 (1807), 19 · A. Seward, 'Verses on the sudden death of Mr Norris', *GM*, 1st ser., 60 (1790), 841 · *ABC dario musico* (privately printed, Bath, 1780) · J. R. Bloxam, *A register of the presidents, fellows … of Saint Mary Magdalen College*, 8 vols. (1853–85), vol. 2 · *The John Marsh journals: the life and times of a gentleman composer*, ed. B. Robins (1998) · parish register, St Michael's, Mere, Wiltshire, Wilts. & Swindon RO [baptism, transcript] · parish register, Himley, Staffordshire, St Michael, Staffs. RO [burial] · records of Salisbury Cathedral, Salisbury Cathedral Library · R. J. Bruce, 'Norris, Thomas', *New Grove*, 2nd edn · *Public Advertiser* (14 March 1761)

Likenesses J. Taylor, mezzotint, pubd 1777 (after J. Taylor), BM, Harvard TC, NPG [*see illus.*]

Norris, William (1522/3–1591), courtier, was born in either 1522 or 1523, being sixty-eight in 1591, the eldest of two sons of John Norris (*b.* in or before 1502, *d.* 1577), courtier, of Fifield, Berkshire, and his wife, Mary, daughter and coheir of Henry Staverton of Bray, Berkshire. He had five sisters. John Norris was a gentleman usher of the privy chamber by 1536, principal gentleman usher from 1553 to at least 1558, keeper of Foliejon Park, Windsor, from 1536 to 1577, comptroller of works at Windsor Castle from 1538 to 1577, and gentleman usher of the black rod and the Order of the Garter from 1554 to 1577. William Norris was admitted to Gray's Inn in 1544. In 1547 or 1548, he married Mary, daughter of Sir Adrian *Fortescue (*c.*1481–1539), landowner and alleged traitor, of Shirburn and Stoner Place, Oxfordshire, and his second wife, Anne. They had six sons, including the MP John Norris (*c.*1550–1612/13), and six daughters. William Norris was a gentleman usher of the privy chamber by 1553 but was dropped by Mary I. In May 1554 Mary granted him the reversion of his father's offices of steward of Foliejon Park and comptroller of works and he was MP for New Windsor in November. Elizabeth I confirmed Mary's decision.

Norris was again MP for New Windsor in 1555 and 1558. In 1557 he was sent as herald to France to declare war against Henri II. He was a gentleman pensioner by May 1558, holding office until his death. In May 1567 he was appointed steward of the royal estates of Bray and Cookham, Berkshire, in recognition of his loyal service to the crown. However, more or less immediately, he surrendered these stewardships to the constable of Windsor Castle, Robert Dudley, earl of Leicester. His father died at Fifield on 30 January 1577 and Norris received the reversion of the Windsor offices. He also succeeded his father as gentleman usher of the black rod and the Order of the Garter, remaining in post until his death. The antiquarian Elias Ashmole described William Norris as a man of 'honest Behaviour and good reputation' (Ashmole, 3.11).

Norris died at Fifield on 16 April 1591 and was buried in St Michael's Church, Bray. He left the bulk of his property, including land in Berkshire and Oxfordshire, to Sir John Norris, who succeeded him as comptroller of works. The Norris family is a good example of the dynastic interest in minor offices, the use of such offices as sinecures, and the tension between the power of head officers over appointment of subordinates and direct grants of subordinate offices by the crown.   J. ANDREAS LÖWE

Sources *CSP dom.*, 1553–8 · E. Ashmole, *The antiquities of Berkshire*, 3 (1719) · *Discours de ce qu'a faict en France le héraut d'Angleterre et de la réponse que lui a faite le roi le 7 juin 1557* (Rheims, 1841) · H. M. Colvin and others, eds., *The history of the king's works*, 6 vols. (1963–82) · HoP, *Commons, 1509–58*, 3.19–20 · A. Harding, 'Norris, John', HoP, *Commons, 1558–1603*, 3.138
Likenesses brass plate, St Michael's Church, Bray, Berkshire

Norris, Sir William, baronet (1658–1702), politician and East India Company servant, was born on 3 February 1658, the son of Thomas Norris (*c.*1618–1686) of Speke Hall, Lancashire, and Katherine (*b.* 1632), daughter of Sir Henry *Garway (or Garraway), lord mayor of London (1639–40). Norris was the second of seven brothers including Thomas *Norris (1653–1700) and Edward *Norris (*bap.* 1665, *d.* 1726). As a younger son with little prospect of succeeding to the family estates he forged for himself an academic career. After a spell at Westminster School, to which he was admitted in 1672, he entered Trinity College, Cambridge, in 1675, was nominated a scholar the following year, and graduated BA in 1679. Two years later he was elected to a fellowship at Trinity, from where he graduated MA in 1682, and it was in his capacity as a fellow that in the later 1680s he opposed James II's attempts to force the college to acquiesce in the admission of Roman Catholics. Shortly after the revolution of 1688 Norris's prospects were transformed by his marriage (licence dated 13 December 1689) to a wealthy widow, Elizabeth, daughter of Robert Reade of Cheshunt, Hertfordshire, and the widow of both Nicholas Pollexfen of St Stephen Walbrook, London, and Isaac Meynell of Lombard Street, London. His financial position secured, Norris left his university post and moved to London. Once there he took a keen interest in political developments, demonstrating whig sympathies, and he also became active in the politics of Liverpool, the parliamentary borough nearest to his family's Lancashire seat, most notably assisting in the campaign of 1695 to obtain a new charter for the borough. Such efforts bore fruit at the election of 1695, when he replaced his elder brother Thomas as Liverpool's MP.

During the 1695 parliament Norris was an active member and proved himself a zealous whig, playing a significant role in assisting the passage of the supply legislation necessary to finance the Nine Years' War. He also took a keen interest in the related topic of trade, a matter of particular concern to the rapidly growing port which he represented in the Commons. In consequence Norris soon became an important whig man of business in the house, evidenced by his moving the address at the start of the 1697–8 session and by his appointment as chairman of the committee of privileges and elections during this session. Norris also began to harbour ambitions of public office, and the disappointment of such pretensions may explain his opposition in December 1697 to the maintenance of a standing army during peacetime. Though he remained loyal to the ministry on all other issues, continuing his active promotion of supply legislation, Norris's antipathy

towards a standing army cost him an appointment as a commissioner of excise in summer 1698. However, his disappointment was ameliorated when in October of the same year he was named as the New East India Company's ambassador to India, a post carrying a salary of £2000 p.a. Shortly afterwards, on 3 December 1698, Norris was created a baronet, and in January 1699 he set sail for the East. Though he remained Liverpool's member of parliament until November 1701 he never returned to England.

Norris's primary task as the New East India Company's envoy was to obtain trading concessions for this company, but his endeavour was always likely to be difficult and ultimately proved to be fruitless. On his arrival at Masulipatam on 20 September 1699 he faced the considerable challenge of persuading the Mughal authorities to grant protection and privileges to a newly established company. His task was made more difficult by determined opposition from the agents of the old company, who immediately attempted to undermine his mission by declaring that Norris was 'no ambassador from the King, but employed only by a company of merchants to rob them of their trade and privileges' (BL, Add. MS 34348, fols. 88–90). There is no doubt that advocates of the old company were indeed partly successful in influencing some Mughal officials against Norris, and the ambassador's position was further weakened when in 1700 the English parliament passed an act confirming the old company's right to trade as a separate entity until the end of its current charter in 1714. Norris had previously assured the Mughal authorities that the demise of the old company was imminent, and consequently his credibility was somewhat undermined. He also faced worsening relations between himself and officers of the new company, principally John Pitt, the new company's consul at Masulipatam. Disagreements centred on how to proceed, with Norris suspecting the consul of having been influenced by the old company's representative in Masulipatam, Pitt's cousin Thomas Pitt. Norris went so far as to report these suspicions to the directors of the new company. Such problems continued even after Norris had left Masulipatam, on 23 August 1699, for Surat, where he arrived on 10 December. Old company representatives continued to undermine Norris's embassy, largely provoked by the determination of Norris and Sir Nicholas Waite, the representative in Surat, to assert the position of the new company. None the less Norris's mission was again undermined by Waite's writing to the Mughal emperor Aurangzeb with an incautious offer to suppress piracy on the Indian seas in return for a grant of trading privilege. Norris left Surat on 27 January 1701 and set out for the emperor's camp at Burhanpur, a 470-mile journey which took thirty-eight days. The emperor had in fact left Burhanpur, so Norris proceeded to Panalla to meet Aurangzeb himself. After nearly a month of negotiations he was finally granted an audience on 28 April, but following the state procession to the emperor and the presentation of numerous gifts, the ambassador found that Aurangzeb was only willing to grant the new company's requests for trading privileges if the company confirmed Waite's earlier promise to suppress all piracy. Norris, however, only felt able to offer a limited, qualified pledge on this matter. This was to prove the crucial stumbling block to his embassy's success. Unable to persuade Aurangzeb to moderate his demands, Norris was eventually forced to refuse this request and, having been dismissed from the emperor's presence, left his camp on 5 November 1701.

Norris's failure can largely be explained in terms of the many obstacles placed in the way of his mission, but there is no doubt that his own lack of diplomatic experience exacerbated the problems he encountered. The historian of his embassy has described Norris as 'somewhat tactless and impatient', as having a 'tendency to pomposity', and noted the ambassador's 'unfamiliarity with Indian customs and languages [which] often betrayed him into … blunders', but concluded that 'success would have been difficult even with a more experienced and tactful ambassador' (Das, 326–8). Having failed in his mission, Norris encountered further indignities on his journey to Surat, being detained for two months at Burhanpur. He did not set sail for England until 5 May 1702, and it was during this journey that he suffered an attack of dysentery from which he died on 10 October 1702.

RICHARD D. HARRISON

Sources DNB · HoP, Commons, 1690–1715 [draft] · T. Heywood, ed., *The Norris papers*, Chetham Society, 9 (1846) · H. Das, *The Norris embassy to Aurangzib, 1699–1702*, ed. S. C. Sarkar (Calcutta, 1959) · R. Dickinson, ed., *The registers of the parish of Childwal, 1557–1680*, Lancashire Parish Register Society, 106 (1967), 87 · BL, Add. MSS 31302, 34348

Archives BL, corresp., embassy to the Great Mogul, and register of papers, Add. MS 31302 · Bodl. Oxf., account of embassy, MSS Eng. hist. c. 341–342 [typescript] · Lpool RO, MSS · W. Yorks. AS, Leeds, account of his meeting with the Great Mogul

Norris, William (*c*.1670–1702), composer, was brought up as one of the children of the Chapel Royal under John Blow and was among those who sang at the coronation of James II in Westminster Abbey on 23 April 1685. A year later he left the chapel, his voice having broken, and was appointed a lay vicar of Lincoln Cathedral in September 1686. These dates suggest a date of birth about 1670, or possibly a year or two earlier. In October 1686 he became, in addition, a poor clerk, and in 1690 master of the choristers. He was confirmed in the latter post the following year, and appointed steward of the choristers in 1693, serving in all these offices until his death in July 1702.

Partbooks in the cathedral library contain more than twenty incomplete anthems by Norris, nine of which are also found in score in the British Library (Add. MSS 17840 and 31444). They are capably written, transitional in style between those of Purcell and Croft in terms of their movement structure and expanding tonal range. He also composed two 'chanting services'; one each for morning and evening prayer (on the model of those by James Hawkins of Ely) with canticles comprising a harmonized chant alternating with freely composed verse sections. An ode for St Cecilia's day, *Begin the Noble Song*, for soloists, chorus, two trumpets, and three-part strings, is in the Bodleian Library (MS Mus. C. 28). The words, by Samuel Wesley, were printed in the *Gentleman's Journal* for April 1694, without further details other than that the ode had been 'written sometime since' though not yet 'seen in Town'. This may suggest a performance the previous November, possibly in Lincoln since both Norris and Wesley were connected with the city.

IAN SPINK

Sources A. R. Maddison, 'Lincoln Cathedral choir, A.D. 1640–1700', *Lincoln and Nottinghamshire Architectural Society*, 20 (1889), 41–55 · N. Thistlethwaite, 'Music and worship, 1660–1980', *A history of Lincoln Minster*, ed. D. Owen (1994), 77–88 · I. Spink, *Restoration cathedral music, 1660–1714* (1995), 282–5 · Lincs. Arch., Lincoln Cathedral archives

Norris, William (*bap.* 1718, *d.* 1791), antiquary, was the brother of Robert *Norris. Almost certainly his parents were Selfe Norris (*d.* 1740) and Mary Pead whose son William was baptized in London on 20 December 1718 (as was their son Robert in 1724). The statement in the *Dictionary of National Biography* that the father of William and Robert was John Norris of Nonesuch, Wiltshire, appears to be erroneous. William was educated at Westminster School from 1729. He is styled MA of Trinity College, but there is no corroboration of his university career at Oxford, Cambridge, or Dublin. He was evidently an ordained Church of England minister but appears never to have held a benefice.

The Society of Antiquaries received its royal charter in 1751 and occupied its first 'permanent' premises, in Chancery Lane, in 1753 (moving to Somerset House in 1780). Norris was elected a fellow of the Society of Antiquaries on 4 April 1754, while living in the parish of St Mary-le-Strand, Westminster. In May 1754 he was appointed to assist Joseph Ames as secretary and became sole secretary following Ames's death in October 1759. He lived on the society's premises from 1754 until his retirement; Jeremiah Milles, the society's president, wrote in 1773: 'I suppose Mr. Norris no longer uses the Library as a dressing room' (Evans, 162). Norris retired in 1790 through advanced age and ill health, whereupon the society voted him an annuity of £100 for life and he moved to Camden Street, Islington. There were differing opinions as to Norris's personality and his competence as secretary. Richard Gough composed a commendatory epitaph for him, but his mention of Norris's 'dragon-like vigilance' (Nichols, *Lit. anecdotes*, 6.128) is not an unambiguous compliment, and other comments by Gough, Milles, and Samuel Pegge the elder suggest that he could be a difficult and uncooperative character. There is a 1763 reference to Norris as corrector of the press to the king's printer, a post he apparently held for some years. In a letter of 1781 Michael Lort makes a somewhat derogatory remark about Norris's (unspecified) 'Dialect' (S. Antiquaries, Lond., MS 447/2, fol. 192v.). Norris died, unmarried, at his lodgings in 1791, following several paralytic strokes, and was buried on 29 November, aged seventy-two, in the churchyard of Pentonville Chapel. He left no writings apart from letters.

PETER W. THOMAS

Sources J. Evans, *A history of the Society of Antiquaries* (1956) · Nichols, *Lit. anecdotes* · Nichols, *Illustrations* · *GM*, 1st ser., 62 (1792),

88 · M. Noble, 'The lives of the fellows of the Society of Antiquaries of London', vol. 2, 1818, Getty Research Institute for the History of Art and the Humanities, Special Collections, 87–A742, fol. 52 [microfilm copy and print-out from it (shelf mark ref. 5h) at Society of Antiquaries, Burlington House] · parish register, St James's Church, Pentonville, 1790–1812, LMA, Microfilm X27/23 [burial] · minutes, 1754–90, S. Antiquaries, Lond. · *IGI* · S. Lewis, *The history & topography of the parish of St. Mary, Islington* (1842), 357 · R. Bruce-Mitford, *The Society of Antiquaries of London* (1951) · *DNB* · parish register, St Mary Colechurch, London, 20 Dec 1718 [baptism] · parish register, St Mildred Poultry, London, 6 Feb 1740 [burial, Selfe Norris] · *Old Westminsters*, vol. 2

Archives S. Antiquaries, Lond., corresp. | BL, Lansdowne MSS 165–167, 841 · priv. coll., Reginald Cholmondeley MSS

Norrish, Ronald George Wreyford (1897–1978), physical chemist, was born at Panton Street, Cambridge, on 9 November 1897, the elder son (there were no daughters) of Herbert Norrish, pharmacist, and his wife, Amy Norris, who came from the Isle of Wight. His father had settled in Cambridge after periods of residence in the Isle of Wight and Oxford. His mother died in 1905 and in 1908 his father married Susan Duff. In the same year Norrish won a scholarship to the Perse School, Cambridge, where he was encouraged by two able teachers to develop his natural inclination to chemistry. His father, recognizing his talent for experimental chemistry, allowed him to set up a small laboratory in the garden shed of the family home in Panton Street. The apparatus he used was later housed in the Science Museum at South Kensington, London.

In 1915 Norrish was awarded a foundation scholarship to Emmanuel College, Cambridge, but did not begin his studies until four years later after war service in the Royal Field Artillery and six months as a prisoner of war. His undergraduate studies, from which he gained a first class in both parts of the natural sciences tripos (1920 and 1921) were compressed into two years, after which he began research under the supervision of E. K. Rideal. In 1924 he obtained his PhD degree and was elected a research fellow of Emmanuel College. In 1926 he became university demonstrator in the physical chemistry department. Two years later he was promoted to H. O. Jones lecturer. In 1936 he was elected FRS and awarded the ScD degree. The following year he was appointed professor and head of the department of physical chemistry and elected by his college to a professorial fellowship, a post he held until his retirement in 1965.

In 1926, when he had secured his first university post, he married Anne, daughter of Albert E. Smith, of Heaton Mersey, near Manchester, departmental manager in a cotton mill in Stockport. She was a lecturer in child psychology at University College, Cardiff, and was not in the least overawed by her argumentative husband. Shortly after the birth of their twin daughters, the Norrishes moved from 48 Kimberley Road, Cambridge, to a handsome semi-detached house at 7 Park Terrace, which was convenient for the large parties that Norrish liked to give.

Norrish was one of the founders of modern photochemistry and also made significant advances in the field of chain reactions, especially those exemplified by combustion and addition polymerization processes. His forte was not in theory, where his understanding was often rudimentary, but in his quite remarkable flair and feel for the way molecules might react, and then for devising and executing, with great precision and reliability, experiments conclusively to establish (or demolish) the reaction mechanisms under consideration. His first work in classical photochemistry, which attracted international attention, was his demonstration that the decomposition of nitrogen dioxide did not begin until the wavelength of the incident light reached a value at which fluorescence ceased; this was also the point at which the absorption spectrum ceased to show fine structure. This was followed by equally important work on the photodecomposition of compounds containing the carbonyl group (such as aldehydes, ketones, esters, ketenes, and amides) and on the photocombination of hydrogen with chlorine. The main conclusions of this work have not been falsified by later investigations. His major innovation, with George Porter, for which he won a share of the Nobel prize for chemistry in 1967 (announced two days before his seventieth birthday) was flash photolysis. In this method a very brief flash of intense light is used to cause photochemical change and immediately after the flash the absorption spectrum of the unstable, short-lived, intermediate species (excited states or free radicals) thereby formed can be measured and used to identify the intermediates and the reactions they subsequently and very quickly undergo. This technique proved to be the most powerful in discerning the nature of the primary photochemical act in fluid systems. The last two decades of Norrish's scientific life were spent in exploiting this new method.

Norrish was of medium height and strong physique, always neatly dressed and with a carefully trimmed military moustache. In sport and in work he was combative and competitive, being much more impressed by a good experimental result than by closely reasoned argument. He had fierce loyalties to his town, university, and college. He worked hard and drove his students equally hard. In later years when he had given up tennis and squash his major pleasure was in post-prandial conversation in college or the Savage Club. He had little sympathy with administrators and was not a good one himself.

Norrish received honorary doctorates from a number of British and other universities. He also received the Meldola medal of the Institute of Chemistry (1928), the Davy medal of the Royal Society (1958), the Liversidge medal of the Chemical Society (1958), and the Faraday (1965) and Longstaff (1969) medals of the Chemical Society. He was the Bakerian lecturer of the Royal Society (1966). He was elected an honorary member of a large number of foreign scientific societies, and in 1974 he was awarded the knight's cross of the order of Polonia Restituta and the order of Cyril and Methodius of Bulgaria.

Despite his extensive travels, especially in Germany and eastern Europe, Norrish was essentially a Cambridge man. Like his contemporary (and fellow student both of Perse School and Emmanuel College) F. R. Leavis, he spent his entire life in the town of his birth, and closely identified with its history, in which he had a keen interest. He died after a stroke at Addenbrooke's Hospital, Cambridge, on 7 June 1978.

FRED DAINTON

Sources F. Dainton and B. A. Thrush, *Memoirs FRS*, 27 (1981), 379–424 · 'A light on life: an interview with Ronald Norrish', *Chemistry in Britain*, 11 (1975), 168–70 · private information (1996) · m. cert. · d. cert.
Archives CUL, corresp. and papers · Sci. Mus., artefacts
Likenesses W. Stoneman, photograph, 1945, NPG · W. Evans, oils, 1969, Emmanuel College, Cambridge · G. Argent, photograph, 1970, NPG · G. Argent, photograph, RS · W. Bird, photographs, RS · W. Stoneman, photograph, RS · photograph, repro. in *Memoirs FRS*, facing p. 379 · photographs, RS · photographs, Emmanuel College, Cambridge
Wealth at death £37,846: probate, 4 Aug 1978, *CGPLA Eng. & Wales*

Norsa, Hannah (d. 1784), singer and actress, was the daughter of Issachar Norsa (d. 1748?), a Jewish tavern keeper. She made her stage début as Polly in John Gay's *The Beggar's Opera* on 16 December 1732 in the newly opened Covent Garden Theatre and was an immediate success, the revival having a continuous run of twenty nights. Miss Norsa remained a leading singer and actress at Covent Garden, appearing in numerous ballad operas and musical afterpieces. In February 1733 she created the heroine, Deidamia, in Gay's posthumously produced ballad opera *Achilles*, and in Johann Ernst Galliard's *Nuptial Masque* she sang Cupid, 'the first Time of her appearing in Boy's Cloaths' (*Daily Journal*, 16 March 1734). Her non-singing roles included Dorinda in George Farquhar's *The Beaux' Stratagem* and Serena in Thomas Otway's *The Orphan*. Hannah's brother, Master Norsa, appeared with a children's company, the Lilliputians, in May 1734. The following spring he was joined by his younger sister, 'Little Miss Norsa', who then danced at Hannah's Covent Garden benefit on 29 April. Brother and younger sister made their final appearances in June and July 1736 at the Haymarket Theatre.

Hannah Norsa remained at Covent Garden until early May 1736, when she was taken off the stage by Robert Walpole, first Baron Walpole and later second earl of Orford (c.1701–1751), son of the prime minister Sir Robert Walpole and elder brother of Horace Walpole. Lord Walpole's marriage in 1724 to an heiress had proved unhappy; they were living apart and eventually obtained a legal separation. Hannah Norsa remained Walpole's mistress until his death, staying with him at Houghton Hall, Norfolk, after he became earl of Orford in 1745. Mrs Kerrich, the wife of a local rector and daughter of an archdeacon, was favourably impressed, despite earlier misgivings about the propriety of visiting:

> She is a very agreeable Woman, & Nobody ever behav'd better in her Station, She have every body's good word, and bear great Sway at Houghton, She is every thing but Lady, She came here in a Landau & Six horses & one Mr Paxton a young Clergyman with her. (Pyle, 244)

Orford was in debt when he died, and according to William Cooke, Hannah lost the £3000 legacy from her father which she had lent him. However, when she made her will in 1766 she owned about £3000 in stocks, together with diamond jewellery and gold and silver plate, so Cooke's report may have been unfounded. Hannah's sister Rachel had married Edward Wilford, the brother of Priscilla, wife of the theatre manager John Rich, and after Orford's death she lived for a time with the Riches. In August 1766 Hannah Norsa was resident in Rotterdam, on friendly terms with the family of Benjamin Sowden, the minister of the English Presbyterian church there; she left him her Bible and Thomas Tillotson's *Works* and made generous bequests to his children, while leaving the bulk of her estate to her sister and nephews. She was living in the parish of St Margaret, Westminster, in 1771, when she added a codicil to her will. She died at her lodgings in Queen's Row, Brompton Road, Kensington, and was buried at St Mary Abbots, Kensington, on 28 August 1784.

OLIVE BALDWIN and THELMA WILSON

Sources A. H. Scouten, ed., *The London stage, 1660–1800*, pt 3: 1729–1747 (1961) · *Daily Journal* (16 March 1734) · E. Pyle, *Memoirs of a royal chaplain, 1729–1763*, ed. A. Hartshorne (1905) · W. Cooke, *Memoirs of Samuel Foote*, 3 vols. (1805) · Walpole, *Corr.*, vols. 9, 18–19 · A. Rubens, 'Jews and the English stage, 1667–1850', *Transactions of the Jewish Historical Society of England*, 24 (1970–73), 151–70 · GEC, *Peerage*, new edn · will, PRO, PROB 11/1122, sig. 564
Likenesses R. Clamp, stipple, 1794 (after S. Harding, after etching by B. Lens), BM, Harvard TC; repro. in F. G. Waldron, *The Shakespearean miscellany* (1802) · B. Lens, etching (after portrait by B. Lens), BM · Worlidge, drawing, repro. in Highfill, Burnim & Langhans, *BDA*
Wealth at death £3400 in stocks; plus gold and silver plate; gold watch and chain and other jewellery; books; furniture: will, PRO, PROB 11/1122, sig. 564

North, Brownlow (1741–1820), bishop of Winchester, was born in London on 17 July 1741, and baptized on 9 August, the elder son of Francis *North, first earl of Guilford (1704–1790), and his second wife, Elizabeth (1707–1745), only daughter and heir of Sir Arthur Kaye, third baronet, and widow of George Legge, Viscount Lewisham. North was educated at Eton College as an oppidan between 1752 and 1759 and he matriculated on 10 January 1760 as a fellow-commoner of Trinity College, Oxford, the college founded by his ancestor Sir Thomas Pope in 1556. He graduated BA from Trinity in 1762 and was elected fellow of All Souls College as founder's kin on 3 November 1763, from where he proceeded MA on 4 July 1766 and DCL in 1770.

After his ordination North was appointed rector of Lighthorne, Warwickshire, by his brother-in-law, John, sixth Lord Willoughby de Broke. Thanks to family influence with the king, North accumulated preferment rapidly. His father was a courtier, appointed treasurer of Queen Charlotte's household in 1773, and his half-brother, Frederick, Lord North, was in government for much of the 1760s and was first minister from 1770 to 1782. On 28 April 1768 Brownlow North was presented with a canonry of Christ Church, Oxford, by the crown, which he held for two years before being installed as dean of Canterbury on 6 October 1770. He was in office for only eleven months, having little time to make much impact on either cathedral or diocese beyond securing for himself

Brownlow North (1741–1820), by Henry Howard, exh. RA 1818

the vicarages of Lydd—'full as good as Christ Church in point of profit' (North to Lord Guilford, 16 Oct 1770, Bodl. Oxf., MS North 49401, fol. 60)—and Bexley in Kent. North retained both *in commendam* with his first bishopric, Lichfield and Coventry, which he received on the recommendation of his half-brother, being consecrated on 8 September 1771.

Brownlow North continued to be given priority in the episcopal promotions of Lord North's premiership. In 1774 he was given the see of Worcester even before the then bishop, James Johnson, had expired after falling from his horse—'incontinently given' as Walpole archly reported to General Conway (Walpole, 39.220)—and in 1781 he succeeded John Thomas at Winchester, where he remained for the rest of his life.

After 1782 Bishop North generally supported the government in the upper house but took minimal interest in active politics. He told Lord Malmesbury that county politics was 'a great deal too like the Game of Snap-dragon, which I dislike, because it burns my fingers' (26 Aug 1807, Malmesbury MSS, 9M73/190/220). Instead North put some of his energies into diocesan work—a major visitation was held in 1788—though recurrent ill health limited his effectiveness. North was accessible and possessed of a basic fairness and a dry sense of humour. Generosity was one of his traits. At Worcester in 1778 he founded a society for the relief of distressed widows and orphans of clergymen in connection with the Three Choirs festival; he also organized other clerical charities. As bishop of Winchester he improved Farnham Park and in 1817 he spent over

£6000 on the castle. Although no institutional reformer, North did what he could at diocesan level to make the existing machinery of the church work more effectively: from 1804 to 1820 he consecrated eight new churches in the Winchester diocese and he took a strong interest in Channel Island church affairs throughout his episcopate.

North married Henrietta Maria (*d.* 1796), daughter and coheir of John Bannister, a West India merchant, on 17 January 1771; she acquired a reputation in society for her extravagance and gambling. By the late 1780s both the bishop and Mrs North were suffering poor health enough to justify a four-year expedition to Italy and southern Germany, travelling from court to court with their family. They were at Regensburg in 1794–5 where Betsy Wynne described the invalid Mrs North as 'the devil on Earth—and a nasty proud fool. She plagues her husband and Children to death' (*Wynne Diaries*, 2.4). Mrs North finally died on 17 November 1796 and was buried in Winchester Cathedral with a monument by Flaxman.

After a long illness North expired at home at Winchester House, Chelsea, London, on 12 July 1820, and he was buried in Winchester Cathedral on 21 August. He published nine sermons and took an interest in literary matters. Edward Hasted dedicated the fourth volume of his *History of Kent* (1778–99) to North, who had offered financial help to William Bingley to try and publish his history of Hampshire. When he was bishop of Winchester, North used his influence to protect Thomas Warton as visitor of Trinity College when Warton faced expulsion from his fellowship in 1788. A cultivated man, the bishop collected 'all kinds of antiquities' (Jenkins, 457), including Greek vases, while in Italy during the 1790s, and he was a major promoter of the Three Choirs festival and a friend of the Worcestershire Burneys. He was both FSA (elected 1773) and honorary member of the Linnean Society (elected 1800); the latter recognized his keen interest in botany, which he had shared with his wife.

Bishop North extracted maximum familial advantage from his long episcopate. He left three surviving daughters and two sons, both of whom took holy orders. The elder, Francis, succeeded his cousin as sixth earl of Guilford in 1827 and was rector of St Mary's, Southampton, 1797–1850. He was also master of St Cross Hospital, presented by his father, from 1808 to 1861, a tenure that was the subject of a judicial investigation in 1853 and the inspiration for Trollope's *The Warden*. Charles Augustus, North's younger son (*b.* 1785), was made prebendary of Winchester in 1812, and his grandson, Brownlow North, was named registrar of the diocese while still an infant. Apart from North's immediate family, his stepchildren and in-laws all benefited from his patronage; it has recently been calculated that twenty-six individuals received about seventy appointments to fifty churches through North's influence between 1785 and 1820.

NIGEL ASTON

Sources T. Kipling, 'Brownlow North, bishop of Winchester', *Winchester Cathedral Record*, 65 (1996), 32–41 · *GM*, 1st ser., 90/2 (1820), 183 · *Hampshire Chronicle* (17 July 1820) · Nichols, *Lit. anecdotes*, 5.658; 9.668–9 · C. J. Abbey, *The English church and its bishops*,

1700–1800, 2 (1887), 218–19 • [B. Buckler], *Stemmata Chicheleana*, 1 (1765), 125 • *Fasti Angl., 1541–1857*, [Bristol], 96 • *Fasti Angl., 1541–1857*, [Canterbury], 14, 83 • J. Gregory, 'Canterbury and the ancien régime: the dean and chapter, 1660–1828', *A history of Canterbury Cathedral, 598–1982*, ed. P. Collinson and others (1995), 204–55 • *Fasti Angl., 1541–1857*, [Ely], 109 • Walpole, *Corr.*, 39.220 • *The historical and the posthumous memoirs of Sir Nathaniel William Wraxall, 1772–1784*, ed. H. B. Wheatley, 5 vols. (1884), vol. 1, pp. 376–7 • V. Green, *The history and antiquities of the city and suburbs of Worcester*, 1 (1796), 217 • I. G. Smith and P. Onslow, *Diocesan history of Worcester* (1863), 337 • W. Benham, *Diocesan history of Winchester* (1884), 228 • M. W. Welman, *Farnham Castle, Surrey* (1961) • J. Ingamells, ed., *A dictionary of British and Irish travellers in Italy, 1701–1800* (1997), 711–12 • *The Wynne diaries*, ed. A. Fremantle, 2 (1937), 4 • I. Jenkins, 'Adam Buck and the vogue for Greek vases', *Burlington Magazine*, 130 (1988), 448–57 • *VCH Hampshire and the Isle of Wight*, 2.99 • *The correspondence of Thomas Warton*, ed. D. Fairer (1985), appx F, 674–7 • R. K. Pugh, 'Post-Restoration bishops of Winchester as visitors of Oxford colleges', *Oxoniensia*, 43 (1978), 170–87 • B. North, letter to Lord Guilford, 16 Oct 1770, Bodl. Oxf., MS 49401, fol. 60 • B. North, letter to Lord Malmesbury, 26 Aug 1807, Herts. ALS, Malmesbury papers, 9M73/190/220 • will, PRO, PROB 11/1634

Archives Bodl. Oxf., accounts, corresp., and schoolboy Latin exercises, MSS 49692, 49399, fols. 69–171; 49400–49402 *passim*; 41606, pp. 747–52 • Winchester Cathedral, MSS | Hants. RO, corresp. with William Bingley • Linn. Soc., letters to Sir James Smith

Likenesses T. Kettle, oils, 1762, Baltimore Museum of Art, Maryland • G. Romney, portrait, 1776, The deanery, Canterbury • H. Robinson?, portrait, *c.*1785–1792, Wolvesey, Winchester • H. Howard, portrait, 1798 • W. M. Bennett, pencil drawing, 1813, NPG • H. Howard, oils, exh. RA 1818, All Souls Oxf. [*see illus.*] • F. Chantrey, monument, 1825, Winchester Cathedral, Lady Chapel • J. Bond, engraving (after H. Howard, 1798) • H. Howard, oils; copy, Trinity College, Oxford

Wealth at death see will, PRO, PROB 11/1634

Brownlow North (1810–1875), by John Moffat, *c.*1870

North, Brownlow (1810–1875), preacher, was born on 6 January 1810 at Winchester House, Chelsea, the only son of Charles Augustus North (1781–1825), rector of Alverstoke, Hampshire, and prebendary of Winchester, and his wife, Rachel Jarvis. His grandfather was Brownlow *North, bishop of Winchester, whose half-brother was Frederick, Lord North, second earl of Guilford, the prime minister. In 1817 Brownlow North was appointed registrar of the diocese of Winchester, a lifelong sinecure. Educated at Eton College from the age of nine until 1825, he was then sent to a theological college on Corfu founded by his cousin, Lord Guilford. North, however, proved unmanageable, and he was dispatched on the European grand tour in the company of a tutor, whom he blackmailed into leaving their books behind in Paris. On returning, he lived at Cheltenham with his devout mother, and on 12 December 1828 he married Grace Anne, second daughter of Thomas Coffey, a Galway clergyman. Of their three children, Charles Augustus, Brownlow, and Frederic, the last two predeceased North.

North was at this time heir to the Guilford title, but the second marriage of an uncle produced an heir who was nearer in succession. He turned to gambling, but this proving disastrous, he moved to Boulogne to escape his debts. His family was sent back to Cheltenham upon his volunteering in 1832 for the liberal cause of Don Pedro's attempted conquest of Portugal. A bold horseman and accurate shot, from 1835 North rented various sporting estates in Scotland. Disturbed in mind after a conversation with the pious Elisabeth Brodie, wife of the fifth duke of Gordon, he consulted with his Cheltenham friend F. W. Robertson, later incumbent of Brighton, who was then in his evangelical phase, and on the latter's advice he entered Magdalen College, Oxford, intending to be ordained in the Church of England. However, upon graduating BA in 1842 a troubled conscience prevented him taking orders.

North returned to Scotland and resumed the sporting life, again renting various estates, mainly in the northeast. In November 1854, while playing cards at his house in Dallas, Moray, he was struck by a sudden illness and, convinced he was dying, he had a conversion experience. Intense spiritual distress followed, during which he consulted with Edward Blackwell, the evangelical rector of Amberley, Sussex. Having moved to Elgin, where he later built his house, The Knoll, he began, with considerable trepidation, to distribute religious tracts. In November 1855 he preached his first sermon to some shoemakers. During the latter part of 1856 he toured northern Scotland and, early in the following year, he extended his preaching activities to Edinburgh and Glasgow. He preached in Ulster during the revival of 1859 and was instrumental in spreading revivalism to Scotland through his missions. He claimed that 'instead of a shooter of grouse and catcher of salmon, I have become a fisher of men' (B. North, *Yes! or No!*, 1867, 193).

North had an athletic physique, a large head, and lively eyes. His dress in the pulpit was unconventional. One newspaper noted that 'in spite of his short shooting-coat, and the negligent tie, and the gold eye-glass dangling on the breast of his tightly buttoned coat, there is tremendous energy and force in his preaching' (Moody-Stuart, 106). He dispensed with the convention of sermon subdivisions and preached in popular language. His voice often broke under the force of his emotion, and through the logic of simple religious propositions he appealed to his hearers' minds. In Scotland he had an important role in making lay preaching more acceptable: exceptionally the Free Church of Scotland recognized him as an evangelist in 1859. He was a significant representative of contemporary interdenominational, non-institutional, lay evangelicalism.

After 1866 North spent more time preaching in England and he moved to London in 1871. From 1858 onwards he wrote in excess of fifty tracts and six short evangelistic books, including his first, *Ourselves* (1865), an interpretation of Israelite history as a type of the individual's salvation which reached ten editions. While holding a mission in Alexandria, Dunbartonshire, he fell ill, and died at nearby Tullichewan Castle on 9 November 1875. He was buried in the Dean cemetery, Edinburgh.

NEIL DICKSON

Sources K. Moody-Stuart, *Brownlow North, BA (Oxon): records and recollections* (1878) · J. Kent, *Holding the fort: studies in Victorian revivalism* (1978) · D. W. Bebbington, *Evangelicalism in modern Britain: a history from the 1730s to the 1980s* (1989), 114–20
Likenesses J. Moffat, cabinet photograph, c.1870, NPG [see illus.] · Caldesi, Blanford & Co., carte-de-visite, NPG · photograph, repro. in Moody-Stuart, *Brownlow North*, frontispiece

North, Charles Napier (1817–1869), army officer, born on 12 January 1817, was eldest son of Captain Roger North (d. 1822), half pay 71st regiment, who had served in the 50th foot under Sir Charles James Napier. His mother was Charlotte Swayne (d. 1843). On 20 May 1836 he obtained an ensigncy by purchase in the 6th regiment, became lieutenant on 28 December 1838, and served with that regiment against the Arabs at Aden in 1840–41. He exchanged to the 60th King's Royal Rifle Corps in 1860, in which he got his company on 28 December 1848, and served in 1849 with the 1st battalion in the Second Anglo-Sikh War at the second siege of Multan, the battle of Gujrat, and the pursuit of the enemy to the Khyber Pass.

North landed at Calcutta from England on 14 May 1857, two days before the arrival of the news of the mutinies at Meerut and Delhi. He started to join his battalion, which had been at Meerut, and in which he got his majority on 19 June 1857, but on the way, on 11 July, obtained leave to join the column under Henry Havelock. With it, first as a volunteer with the 78th highlanders, and from 21 July as deputy judge-advocate of the force, he was present in all the operations ending with the relief of the residency of Lucknow on 25 September 1857, and the subsequent defence until the arrival of Sir Colin Campbell's force. North was thanked by the governor-general in council and by General Outram for establishing and superintending the manufacture of Enfield rifle cartridges, and received a brevet lieutenant-colonelcy in 1858 and a year's additional service for Lucknow. North wrote a *Journal with the Army in India* (1858), a narrative of personal observation from May 1857 to January 1858, when he was invalided home. He became colonel by brevet on 30 March 1865 and sold out of the army on 26 October 1868. He was married and had a son. He died at Bray, co. Wicklow, on 20 August 1869, aged fifty-two, and was buried in the cemetery at Aldershot, Hampshire.　　　H. M. CHICHESTER, rev. JAMES FALKNER

Sources *Army List* · *Hart's Army List* · *Army and Navy Gazette* (Aug 1869) · *King's Royal Rifle Corps Chronicle* (1921) · CGPLA Eng. & Wales (1869)
Likenesses photograph, c.1865, repro. in *King's Royal Rifle Corps Chronicle*, 151
Wealth at death under £1500: administration, 27 Dec 1869, CGPLA Eng. & Wales

North, Dudley, third Baron North (*bap.* 1582, *d.* 1666), nobleman and poet, was born in London and baptized on 18 September 1582 at St Gregory by Paul, London. His parents were Sir John *North (c.1550–1597), eldest son of Roger *North, second Baron North, and Sir John's wife, Dorothy (d. 1618), daughter of Dr Valentine *Dale, master of requests. Sir John predeceased his father, dying in June 1597, and consequently Dudley inherited his grandfather's title on the latter's death in 1600. He was educated at Cambridge, matriculating fellow-commoner from Trinity College about 1597, though he took no degrees there. His relationship with his mother, who controlled part of his property, was difficult. Between 22 and 28 November 1600, over his mother's objections—'without her consent, or almost privity'—but very likely under pressure from his grandfather, he married Frances (1583/4–1677), the sixth and youngest daughter of Sir John Brocket, or Brockett (*Salisbury MSS*, 10.410). North denied his mother's claims, but petitioned the queen for control of his lands while still a minor. Although Frances was an heiress, in later years North complained that he had married too young, 'in a short fortune', and he blamed many of his later troubles upon his hasty action (D. North, 125). After his marriage, 'I was set to seek how to live, where to live: my birth and breeding was in the city, my affection and chief seat in Cambridgeshire' (ibid., 132). He postponed making this choice, however, leaving Frances and embarking upon an extended tour of the continent. In June 1601 he was a volunteer at the siege of Berck in the Low Countries, and in the summer of 1603 he wrote to Robert Cecil of his plans to visit the 'hither reaches of Germany' and return to England via France (*Salisbury MSS*, 17.293). North had returned to England by summer 1604, when he wrote from Portsmouth complaining of the officiousness of Sir Benjamin Bury, lieutenant-governor of the town, who was delaying his departure on another continental trip. At some point during these expeditions North dosed himself with treacle as a preventative for the plague, a precaution which he later asserted ruined his health: 'physic, instead of relieving me, was my bane' (D. North, 214). His travels in Europe left him with a well-developed artistic sense; he collected Italian and Flemish art and became an accomplished musician as well as a poet.

His later recollections notwithstanding, North was healthy enough to be an active participant at the court of James I. His grandson Roger *North said that in his youth North was 'a person of spirit and flame' (North, *Lives*, 1.5). He was a frequent performer in court masques, and often joined tournaments celebrating courtly milestones, such as the 1610 investment of Prince Henry as prince of Wales. In 1612 he had 'the flesh and sinews of his arm badly torn' in a tournament when the earl of Montgomery's lance went awry (Akrigg, 162). He acted in a masque honouring Queen Anne in 1613, and, in the same year, another celebrating the earl of Somerset's wedding. But North's career as a courtier was never very successful. In May 1620 he found himself imprisoned in the Tower of London, suspected by the king of encouraging his brother Roger *North to undertake an unauthorized voyage to the Amazon. He was never appointed to any office at court, and by the mid-1620s he had nearly ruined himself. Having, as he said, inherited an estate of only £600 a year, his position was precarious to begin with, but he worsened matters by building in Cambridgeshire and spending far too much money at court. Much of this extravagance, he said, was therapy for depression, his constant companion: 'Many things, which appeared in me affected courses of pleasure and vanity, were in truth laid hold on by me for diversions against the violence of my disease' (D. North, 119). It is certain that throughout much of his life North suffered extended bouts of ill health. 'My whole life hath been but a conflict with the worst of diseases and a wearisome seeking for contentment, plunged in an irretrievable gulf of all misery' (ibid., 121). It was during one of these periods of poor health, in 1606, that, while recuperating at Lord Abergavenny's estate at Eridge House, Kent, he stumbled across the mineral springs at Tunbridge Wells. He popularized the waters there, and also touted the benefits of Epsom, though they seem to have done relatively little to restore his health in the long term.

By the late 1620s North had largely withdrawn to his Cambridgeshire house at Kirtling, avoiding the city, where, as he put it, 'the purse falls into a dysentery' and recouping his fortunes (D. North, 68). His daughter-in-law, Anne Montagu, who married his son and heir Dudley *North in 1632, later commented bitterly that he oppressed her husband, forcing him to live at Kirtling, for which privilege he charged the young couple £200 a year—a sum he increased to £300 in 1637. He economized further by requiring his son and daughter-in-law to keep a coach at their own expense.

North spent most of his time in the country dabbling in music and composing poetry. His slender purse notwithstanding he kept a composer, John Jenkins, in his house, and according to his grandson Roger the servants were chosen more for their musical talents than their efficiency or honesty. North organized concerts at home with his children, servants, and grandchildren playing instruments and singing. He himself played the double viol. In 1645 he published *A Forest of Varieties*, a collection of verse

and autobiographical essays which he had composed over the previous decade. North was a demanding patriarch. He insisted that his family entertain him with the latest London gossip and games of backgammon in addition to his musical productions, and had little patience with any signs of independence among them. He quarrelled with his grandson Francis *North, a lawyer whom he accused of overcharging him, and finally cut him out of his will for presuming to advise against the employment of a dishonest steward.

Having no offices in the state, North's only political role until the outbreak of the civil wars was as a member of the House of Lords, where he seems to have done little before Charles I's accession. When he attended he generally followed a moderately sceptical line towards royal policy: in 1627 and 1628, for example, he was associated with Lord Saye and Sele in controversies surrounding the persecution of Buckingham's enemy Sir Dudley Digges. He also favoured the petition of right. It was not until the crisis of 1639–42 that he began to occupy a position of any importance. In 1639 he was described as the 'least-estated lord of the kingdom', but he promised six horsemen for the king's army against the Scots (*Buccleuch MSS*, 1.279). In the Short Parliament he advocated peace with the Scots, and at the great council of peers called by Charles in the autumn of 1640 he spoke passionately in favour of a parliament. During the early months of the Long Parliament he favoured moderate reform of the church, but wanted to avoid conflict: 'I would be sorry to see the cutting of throats for discipline and Ceremonie' (D. North, 235). In 1640 he complained to a correspondent about the difficulty of maintaining a middle course in the midst of growing conflict: 'The truth is, Carriages have been so Caballistical of all sides, so unpleasant and inconvenient to participate or comply with … I found enough to doe to look to myself' (ibid., 237). Despite these sentiments, however, parliament named him lord lieutenant of Cambridgeshire in March 1642, though his grandson said that after the outbreak of war he retired to Kirtling to 'grow his beard' (North, *Lord Keeper*, 174).

Lord North did not remain in retirement. His grandson says that parliament, noting his absence, tendered him the covenant, which he accepted. 'Thereupon he shaved off his beard, and turning beau, went up to London and became a declared advocate for the Cavaliers' (North, *Lord Keeper*, 174). In fact North's conversion to royalism did not come so soon. In December 1644 parliament named him one of its negotiators with the king. He served on a number of parliamentarian committees between 1644 and 1648, including one to manage the admiralty and the important Derby House committee. In the summer of 1648 he was speaker pro tem of the Lords. The king's trial was the turning point for North. On 28 December 1648 he joined a delegation of several other peers to Cromwell pleading against such a drastic step, and was one of the peers present on 2 January 1649 when the Lords rejected the Commons' resolution for Charles's trial. He returned to Kirtling after the regicide, where he remained throughout the interregnum, living as 'a retired old fantastical courtier' and avoiding politics, pursuing his private interests (North, *Lives*, 3.67).

North was seventy-eight when George Monck recalled parliament to London in early 1660, and despite his age and infirmity he travelled to Westminster, where on 11 February he voted for the readmission of royalist peers to the Lords. His fervent royalism continued unabated well into his eighties, when he set up a monument at Kirtling, which featured his arms and the motto 'Gratia Dei, et Carolo Secundo Vivo' ('Thanks to God and Charles II I live'; North, *Lord Keeper*, 174). He died on 16 January 1666, aged eighty-three, at Kirtling, where he was buried. His successor was his eldest son, Dudley, fourth Baron North.

VICTOR STATER

Sources GEC, *Peerage* · D. North, third Baron North, *A forest of varieties* (1645) · R. North, *The life of the Lord Keeper North*, ed. M. Chan (1995) · R. North, *The lives of … Francis North … Dudley North … and … John North*, ed. A. Jessopp, 3 vols. (1890) · *Calendar of the manuscripts of the most hon. the marquis of Salisbury*, 24 vols., HMC, 9 (1883–1976), vols. 10, 16–17 · J. Nichols, *The progresses, processions, and magnificent festivities of King James I, his royal consort, family and court*, 4 vols. (1828) · G. P. V. Akrigg, *Jacobean pageant* (1962), 162 · *Report on the manuscripts of his grace the duke of Buccleuch and Queensberry … preserved at Montagu House*, 3 vols. in 4, HMC, 45 (1899–1926), vol. 1, p. 279 · *Report on the manuscripts of Lord De L'Isle and Dudley*, 6, HMC, 77 (1966), 563, 577 · S. R. Gardiner, *History of England from the accession of James I to the outbreak of the civil war*, new edn, 6 (1886); repr. (1965), 111, 282 · C. Russell, *The fall of the British monarchies, 1637–1642* (1991), 112, 114, 159, 440 · Venn, *Alum. Cant.*
Archives BL, corresp. and papers, Add. MS 61873 · Bodl. Oxf., personal and estate papers
Likenesses line engraving, pubd 1783 (after oils), BM, NPG · oils, The Vyne, Hampshire
Wealth at death estate was much straitened

North, Dudley, fourth Baron North (1602–1677), politician and author, was born in October or November 1602, probably at the Charterhouse, the London mansion of his father, Dudley *North, third Baron North (*bap.* 1582, *d.* 1666), and mother, Frances (1583/4–1677), who was the youngest of the six daughters of Sir John Brocket or Brockett. He was reared 'after the best manner' (North, *Lives*, 1.6), and on 3 November 1616 was created a knight of the Bath in honour of Prince Charles's creation as prince of Wales. About that time Sir Dudley moved on to Cambridge. Matriculation records for his college, St John's, have not survived and he never took a degree, but he was certainly a fellow-commoner there as late as 1619. His earliest dated verses were included that year in *Lacrymae Cantabrigienses*, published on the occasion of Queen Anne's death. Cambridge was not enjoying its finest hour, however, and he later reflected that 'In the prime of my youth I past (or rather lost) some few years at the University'. Although he was admitted to Gray's Inn on 10 August 1619, Sir Dudley omits mention of this fact in his few sentences of autobiography, recording elliptically that 'I came to have a tast of the Court'. He lived with his parents at their London house, 'and having no employment I surfeited of Idlenesse, taking my pastime with some of the most corrupt young men of those dayes' (D. North, *Observations*, sig. A3v–A4r).

In 1620, with the rank of lieutenant, Sir Dudley joined

Dudley North, fourth Baron North (1602–1677), by John Hoskins, *c.*1628

Sir Horace Vere's expedition to recover the Palatinate. Upon returning home he registered at the Inner Temple about 12 May 1622, but soon asked his father's permission to return abroad, this time as a private traveller. On 26 December the privy council granted a pass for Sir Dudley and two servants to travel for three years—but not to Rome; he later recalled touring Italy, Spain, and France, the latter two during the wedding negotiations for Prince Charles. In 1624, returning to military service abroad, Sir Dudley was authorized by Henry Vere, earl of Oxford, to raise troops for the United Provinces. Now a captain, he commanded 'a Foot Company in our Sovereigns Pay' in the Netherlands (D. North, *Observations*, sig. A4).

On 24 April 1632 Sir Dudley married Anne Montagu (1613/14–1681), second daughter and coheir of Sir Charles Montagu of Cranbrook (near Ilford, Essex) and his second wife, Mary, daughter of Sir William Whitmore of London. He later assured Anne that she could assume herself 'to bee the person intended' in his early love poems addressed to a mistress named Serena (Randall, 128). Although the vast North fortune had shrunk badly during the previous thirty years, the newly-weds both proved to be careful housekeepers, and, according to their son Roger, 'If ever perfect Congugall amity were Intirely preserved with out the least interruption, it was there' (BL, Add. MS 32523, fol. 6r). Of their fourteen children, ten lived to adulthood, including six sons: Charles, (eventually fifth Baron North), Francis *North (1637–1685), Dudley *North (1641–1691), John *North (1645–1683), Roger *North (1651–1734), and Montagu, who became a Levant and London merchant. Of the girls, Anne married Robert Foley of Stourbridge, Worcestershire; Christian married Sir George Wenyeve of Brettenham, Suffolk; Elizabeth [see Wiseman, Elizabeth], Sir Robert *Wiseman (first) and William *Paston, earl of Yarmouth [see under Paston, Robert] (second); and Mary, Sir William Spring of Pakenham, Suffolk.

In his middle years Sir Dudley had to pay rent to his father in order to live at the family's main seat, Kirtling (or Catlidge), in Cambridgeshire. Even after he and Anne had purchased their own home at Tostock in Suffolk in 1638, Lord North, having turned over many of his affairs to his son, sometimes insisted that Sir Dudley and his family return to Kirtling to stay. By 1634 Sir Dudley was also serving in the public sphere as a JP for Cambridgeshire. In 1637 and 1638 he was involved in fen drainage projects in Lincolnshire.

Having first represented the borough of Horsham (Sussex) in the 1628–9 parliament, Sir Dudley subsequently sat as member for Cambridgeshire in both the Short and the Long parliaments; he eventually described the latter as 'that fatal Parliament which set the whole Kingdom on fire' (D. North, *Observations*, sig. A4v). Long a supporter of monarchy, he decided somewhat reluctantly to support parliament on the grounds that he might thus serve best the interests of both his country and his family. On one occasion in February 1642, as he later recorded in *A Narrative of some Passages in … the Long Parliament* (1670), he dared to express displeasure at the Commons' support of certain adverse comments made by Pym on the king, and in reprisal was quickly assigned to a delegation named to deliver the Commons' resolution to Charles at Hampton Court. In September that same year, when he, as deputy lieutenant, and Cromwell were sent down to Cambridge to keep the peace, Sir Dudley 'found all full of terror' there (D. North, *Narrative*, 36). In 1643 he found himself ordered to oversee the sequestering of delinquents' property, and was even put in charge of collecting money from the county of Cambridge for the purchase of pistols and armour for Cromwell's regiment. In 1648 he was secluded from parliament following Pride's Purge.

Once he had returned to the country, Sir Dudley resumed his earlier interest in draining the fens, an enormously complex project whereby he hoped—ultimately in vain, it appears—to better the North family's finances. In 1649, having made himself knowledgeable on fenland matters, he was named by parliament as one of the commissioners to assist with adjudicating fenland questions. Also in these years he resumed his duties as a justice, now also for Ely and Suffolk, concerning himself with local problems such as tippling, gaming, and swearing, and for a time after 24 August 1653 he also performed civil marriages.

Owing to his refusal to commit himself unconditionally to the Restoration, North failed to gain the county seat in the 1660 election, but he was returned as MP for the borough of Cambridge, which made him a freeman. However, he proved an inactive member and did not seek re-election in 1661. Meanwhile, on 5 June 1660 he had petitioned Charles II for a pardon, which was granted on 3 September. He reached his mid-sixties before his father died and he himself was summoned to the House of Lords (24 January 1667). Having long subordinated himself to the difficult old lord, he had cautiously expressed his frustration in a private poem of 1663:

> Past youth and strength yett under guardian still.
> I have my own, but serve anothers will.
> (Randall, 152)

Two years after his father's death the new Lord North published his *Observations and Advices Oeconomical* (1669), in which he suggested that the master of a large household should concern himself not only with private 'Rules of frugality' and public service as a justice but also with personally assuming 'a kind of Pastoral charge' on his estate for the 'Service of God … twice a day' (D. North, *Observations*, 81, 63). As for 'Countrey delights', he wrote, 'Study may deserve the first place' and music the second (ibid., 116, 119). Even in difficult times, the Norths had a resident composer (most notably John Jenkins) and a considerable library. Toward the end, when reading and writing became hard for him, Sir Dudley, according to his posthumously published *Light in the Way to Paradise* (1682), chose divinity as the study 'fittest for the farewell of my Pen' (sig. A3v), and he set down his view that 'the Fundamentals of Religion are neither many, nor abstruse' (p. 6). Long a 'speculatively orthodox' believer (North, *Lives*, 1.6), he finally came to think it impossible for a faithful servant of God not to achieve everlasting joy. Along with his *Light* the family published North's 'occasionals' (essay-like short prose pieces) and, dated 1658, his *Notes Concerning the Life of Edward Lord North*.

Having suffered much from the 'stone'—in one late poem he mentions his 'nephritick tortures' (Randall, 163)—North died on 24 June 1677 at Kirtling, and was buried privately on 27 June in the chancel of Kirtling church. A decent, decorous, thoughtful man who laboured long and diligently under difficult circumstances, public and private, he knew many of the great ones of his day and wrote on various subjects in both prose and verse, but perhaps may be remembered best as the strict yet nurturing father of outstanding sons. DALE B. J. RANDALL

Sources D. North, fourth Lord North, *Observations and advices oeconomical* (1669) • D. North, *A narrative of some passages in or relating to the Long Parliament* (1670) • will, PRO, PROB 11/354.69, fols. 205v–206v • R. North, *The lives of … Francis North … Dudley North … and … John North*, ed. A. Jessopp, 3 vols. (1890); repr. as *The lives of the Norths* (1972) • D. B. J. Randall, *Gentle flame: the life and verse of Dudley, fourth Lord North* (1983) • C. H. Firth and R. S. Rait, eds., *Acts and ordinances of the interregnum, 1642–1660*, 3 vols. (1911) • J. Foster, *The register of admissions to Gray's Inn, 1521–1889, together with the register of marriages in Gray's Inn chapel, 1695–1754* (privately printed, London, 1889) • Bodl. Oxf., MS North a.2, no. 272 • R. North, BL, Add. MS 32523 [on family] • M. W. Helms, E. R. Edwards, and G. Jagger, 'North, Sir Dudley I', HoP, *Commons, 1660–90* • Keeler, *Long Parliament*

Archives BL • Bodl. Oxf., official and estate papers • University of Kansas, Lawrence, Kenneth Spencer Research Library

Likenesses J. Hoskins, miniature, *c.*1628, NPG [*see illus.*] · C. Johnson, oils (as a young man), Waldershare Park, Kent

Wealth at death £1500 in debt, possibly counterbalanced by assets: Anne's notebook, transcribed in North, *Lives*, vol. 3, p. 313

North, Sir Dudley (1641–1691), merchant and economist, was born in London (probably at the Charterhouse) on 16 May 1641. He was the fourth (third surviving) son of Dudley *North, fourth Baron North (1602–1677), landowner, and his wife, Anne (1613/14–1681), second daughter of Sir Charles Montagu of Cranbrook and his second wife, Mary Whitmore. He distinguished himself first as a successful businessman who parlayed his small provision into a substantial fortune, second as a public servant in the customs, and third as an original analyst of the market economy.

North's life and character were recorded in depth by his youngest brother, Roger *North, a polymath and founder of the art of biography. In his *Examen* (published posthumously in 1740) Roger sought to vindicate the political careers of his elder brothers, Dudley and Francis *North, first Baron Guilford, and to challenge the whig version of history. In his classic *Lives of … Francis … Dudley … and … John North*, written between 1709 and 1720 but edited and published by his son Montague in 1744, Roger commemorated the personality and achievements of his beloved brother Dudley, who had been his constant companion during the 1680s.

Business Because the fourth baron inherited the family estate late in life and had fourteen children he could not afford to endow his younger sons, who were all given a solid education and were then expected to make their own way. Dudley North was sent to Bury St Edmunds grammar school, where he displayed little liking for scholarship or for the schoolmaster, Dr Stevens. Consequently he was not directed towards a university or an inn of court and a professional career, but was sent, in 1657, to a writing school in London in preparation for a business career. After taking advice Dudley's father selected the Levant trade, which had a high quotient of younger sons of gentlemen because it offered the prospect of economic advancement for a modest outlay. On 28 May 1658 Dudley was bound apprentice to Thomas Davis, a mercer free of the Russia Company and the Levant Company, who agreed to take on Dudley for £350 plus clothing, but without additional sureties.

After three years in London, Dudley North was sent abroad in the spring of 1661 with £400 of his own capital. He first travelled as supercargo to Archangel in Russia and then continued, via Italy, to Smyrna in the Ottoman empire, where he took up residence as a factor in January 1662. In 1666 he returned briefly to London to take his freedom, to settle disagreements with his master, and to borrow £1000 additional capital from his brother Francis. In 1669, when he was invited to join the *ragion*, or commission house, of William Hedges, he moved from Smyrna to Constantinople. In 1675 he set up his own *ragion*, bringing in as partners his younger brother Montague (who had also been apprenticed and sent out to Aleppo) and Richard Hampden. On 30 December 1679 Dudley finally left Constantinople, arriving in London in April 1680. The main

Honble Sr
Dudley North Kt
3d Son of Dudley Ld
North & Ann his Wife

Sir Dudley North (1641–1691), by unknown artist, *c.*1680

business of North's *ragion* was providing commercial and financial services for London principals. He bought and sold goods on commission, took delivery and arranged shipment, supplied market advice and credit facilities, exchanged currency and repatriated funds to England. He also traded on his own account and combined dealing in precious stones with high-risk loans to Turkish officials. When he returned to London, North branched out into silk manufacturing with his partner, Jacob Turner, and he invested in syndicated ships, occasional ventures to India and the West Indies, and in iron manufacture with his brother-in-law Robert Foley. But the core of his business remained the export of English cloth, the import of Levantine silk, the re-export of raw materials, bullion, and finished goods, and the carrying trade of the Mediterranean. Dudley North discontinued his speculative financial dealings after he left Turkey, but he continued to provide marine insurance for clients and banking services for his friends and relatives. Increasingly, however, he moved from active into passive investment, naming as his bankers first Benjamin Hinton and then Sir Francis Child. In 1681 he acquired 500 shares in the Royal African Company and he provided short-term funds for that company, the East India Company, and the crown. Most of his lending was, however, directed towards private individuals. He also assumed responsibility after his marriage in 1683 for his wife's landed estate at St Briavels and for her urban estate in Bristol, although most of the work was undertaken by the Bristol attorney and estate agent Thomas Edwards.

When North returned to England after twenty years in the Levant he had by his own efforts raised his initial capital of £1400 to £22,320—an achievement that few of his associates were able to emulate. Although the commission trade generated a steady return, capital accumulation on this scale would not have been possible without the exceptional profits of usury. Over the next eleven years his fortune increased further to reach £33,388, excluding £18,137 personalty brought in by his wife and £360 per annum from her real estate. But, after 1680, half of Dudley's income came from office and only 28 per cent from trade; even though loss of office prompted some reinvestment in the Levant, only half of his capital was in active commerce at his death.

Public life By accident rather than by design Dudley North became an instrument of the tory reaction of the 1680s. In 1682 Charles II needed a loyal sheriff to further his design of breaking the power of the whigs in London and Dudley seemed to be a perfect candidate. Dudley was no partisan tory, like his brothers Francis and Roger, but whig opposition to his candidacy was intense. Although formally an Anglican, his years in Turkey had made him sceptical and open-minded about religion; he disliked fanaticism of any kind, including the persecution of dissenters. But he was still tempted by office and he was finally persuaded by Francis that both interest and duty required him to serve the king.

In 1682, under pressure from the court, the mayor Sir John Moore used his customary (but disputed) power to nominate North as one of the sheriffs and to invalidate the votes of the livery for the whig candidates, Papillon and Dubois, in a riotous election. When in office Dudley had not only to spend £2000 of his own money, but to suffer ostracism and abuse. As sheriff he was expected to ensure the election of a tory mayor and he had to select the jury that tried and found guilty the conspirators in the Rye House plot. The charge that Dudley had undermined the liberties of the City acquired some force when the court initiated *quo warranto* proceedings against the City charter in 1683. Consequently Dudley was at risk after the revolution of 1688 and was in fact investigated by the Lords committee appointed to review the trial of William, Lord Russell. Dudley North also sat in the 1685 parliament as member for Banbury and he was active on several committees. He can be credited with single-handedly steering through the controversial new impositions on tobacco and sugar, which he rightly considered would raise revenue without hurting trade. What was fiscally defensible may still, however, have been politically unwise, since an enlarged revenue from customs gave James II the ability to rule without parliament and to pursue his personal agenda. After 1688 Dudley stayed in London but he kept a low profile and avoided contact with Jacobites. Although he was a political realist who realized that he had backed the wrong side, he was not prepared, like some of his associates, to turn his coat.

North was always better suited to administration than to politics. He was made an assistant of the Levant Company on his return to London, having acquired nine years' administrative experience as treasurer of the company in Constantinople, and he took part in the famous debate between the Levant Company and East India Company before the privy council in 1681. Although he played a major role in the renegotiation by Sir John Finch in 1675 of the 'capitulations' (the treaty articles under which the English traded in Turkey), he was never seriously considered for the ambassadorship. He was, however, elected governor of the Russia Company by a narrow majority in 1683—a post which he then held until his death. In addition he was an assistant of the Royal African Company from 1681 to 1686, as well as deputy governor, 1682–3, and sub-governor, 1684. As sheriff of London he was elected master of his livery company (though the Mercers refused to attend his installation), and he was alderman for the ward of Farringdon Without from 14 December 1682 until he resigned his seat on 26 September 1689.

North's major and most lucrative appointments were in the revenue departments. Although he was supremely well qualified for high office, his public appointments, like the knighthood which he received on 11 February 1683, were primarily a reward for loyalty to the king. From 26 March to July 1684 and from March 1685 to April 1689 Dudley was appointed one of the commissioners of the customs. From 21 July 1684 to 16 February 1685, when it was dissolved, he was in the Treasury commission, where his most notable task was to review for the king the farm of the hearth tax and excise. At the customs North favoured fiscal over protective duties and, as a poacher turned gamekeeper, he visibly improved the efficiency of collection by reducing fraud, rationalizing procedures, and streamlining management. His impact can be measured by the complaints of several merchants who submitted depositions to the Commons committee which, in July 1689, investigated alleged abuses by the commissioners. Dudley emerged from the inquiry as an honest, zealous, and professional commissioner, who had the practical ability to solve problems.

Writings Although his formal education was limited to grammar school and a writing school, and although he appears to have had no library, Dudley North still harboured strong intellectual interests and he was an accomplished linguist who wrote lucid, economical, and robust prose. None of his writings was published in his lifetime, but several were collected and edited by his brother Roger and they subsequently appeared in print. His detailed travelogues, presumably written as letters to his family while he was abroad, were reproduced in Roger's *Lives*. Some of his economic writings, which began as notes for a speech to the 1685 parliament with the probable intention of subsequent circulation as a tract, were edited and printed by Roger (with a new Preface) in 1692 after Dudley's death as the *Discourses upon Trade*. Other writings were collapsed into works by Roger that were ultimately printed; Dudley's notes on the poor law, for example, were partially reproduced in Roger's *Discourse of the Poor* published in 1753. Dudley North always wrote in response to specific problems of his own day, such as the level of interest rates, the condition of the currency, or the reform of the poor law. In his economic writings as in his scientific experiments he adopted the inductive method, basing his theories on practical experience of business in both Turkey and England. But Dudley also sought to compose an abstract (though not mathematical) theory by logical deduction from general propositions that was objective and universal. Many of North's ideas had been anticipated by other writers and his general theory is subject to all the criticisms that can be levelled at classical economics. Nor do his writings seem to have had any impact on his contemporaries or on later political economists, though Locke and Massie had copies of the *Discourses* in their libraries. But Dudley still stands out from his contemporaries. A businessman with a limited formal education, he succeeded in translating a commentary on specific problems into a coherent, systematic, and original economic theory.

Dudley North was the first economic writer to construct a complete equilibrium analysis. In his monetary theory bullion flowed where it was needed and the money supply adjusted automatically to the volume and direction of trade without human intervention. Dudley proposed, like Locke, to call in the clipped coin by weight, restore its silver content and reimpose seignorage charges at the Royal Mint. He argued against Sir Josiah Child that the rate of interest could not be reduced by legislative action and that it would not increase the value of land. The rate of interest was a dependent variable determined by the productivity of capital and by supply and demand in relation to risk. Because North placed more trust in market forces than in government policy he argued strongly for a free market in commodities and labour. Unlike most of his contemporaries he made no distinction between domestic and international trade and he argued that the global market was capable of infinite expansion. Consequently he wished to maximize the mobility of labour by repealing the Settlement Acts, and to increase the mobility of capital by the free export of bullion. His *laissez-faire* approach was most striking in relation to the poor, since he proposed to abandon public assistance and to rely on private charity and individual resourcefulness. Although his optimism was probably misplaced, he grasped the importance of demand and of the work ethic, that production could not be expanded without a corresponding increase in consumption.

Private life Dudley North certainly indulged himself sexually in his youth, but his absence abroad forced him to delay marriage, which finally occurred at Chelsea on 12 April 1683, when he was nearly forty-two. His bride, Ann (*d.* 1715), was the rich widow of Sir Robert Gonning and the daughter of Sir Robert Cann, tory merchant, alderman, and MP for Bristol. The belligerent, socially ambitious, and suspicious Sir Robert at first opposed the match, influenced by whig rumours that Dudley was a penniless rogue. Since Ann was worth £22,767 Sir Robert insisted that Dudley provide a jointure of £500 per annum and that Francis North give surety for £20,000.

In fact Ann very probably threw her marriage settlement into the fire and North was never obliged to fulfil his marriage articles. In the same trusting spirit he left his whole estate to his widow without settlement. It was a happy marriage that produced three sons—Dudley (*b.* 1684), the sole heir who acquired a country estate at Glemham, Suffolk, in 1708; Roger (*b.* 1686), who became a rake and died young; and Robert (*b.* 1688), who predeceased his father by twenty days. Although North sustained a close relationship with his wife's stepmother and sister, he usually avoided his Bristol in-laws, who were notoriously quarrelsome. On the other hand, with the exception of his eldest brother, Charles, he maintained very close relations with all his siblings and acted as their counsellor and executor.

North was at the same time a gentleman and merchant with the prejudices and manners of both. He always lived according to his means and was content with a modest diet and few servants as a young factor. In his prosperous later years, on the other hand, particularly when he had to maintain the dignity of an office, he lived more sumptuously, spending over £800 per annum on his household, more than many gentry families. His only real extravagance, however, was the acquisition of a splendid coach and four Flanders horses. While in Constantinople, North designed and built a grand house, though he thought it prudent not to own it directly. In London, after lodging for two years while a bachelor, he leased the house of Sir William Hedges in Basinghall Street in 1682. A year later, while sheriff and under pressure from his wife, he leased a great mansion, Camden House in Maiden Lane, but he never owned a house or a landed estate in his own right, despite his love of the countryside and his efforts to find a suitable property. He had to content himself with visiting his wife's estate and spending his summers at Wroxton, seat of the Guilfords.

North impressed his contemporaries with his force of intellect, his physical presence, and his principled character. His portrait, painted late in life, suggests a tall, round-faced, corpulent man with large piercing eyes. He had been athletic in his youth and he always liked outdoor pursuits—walking, swimming, and sailing. If he did not share his family's taste for music, he compensated with a profound interest in architecture and in both theoretical and applied science. He studied buildings and physical phenomena both to discover their underlying principles and to acquire practical knowledge, whether this involved forging iron, laying bricks, or measuring barometric pressure. North was fortunate to enjoy good health and a favourable political and economic environment within which to develop his business. But his fortune was still largely self-made. He not only acquired the practical and technical skills, but he mastered the art of business, which he pursued with pleasure. Although he swore, wagered, and whored, he was still parsimonious, self-disciplined, hard-working, self-sufficient, and single-minded. Above all he earned a reputation for honesty and demonstrated the courage to persevere.

While outspoken, rational and strong minded, North was also genial, spontaneous, and gregarious with a robust sense of humour and a gift for telling stories. He knew how to persuade and bargain and how to handle personal relations with the Islamic Turks. Despite his expatriate life and his individualism, he was not unduly acquisitive and he had a strong sense of family. A risk taker and entrepreneur, he kept both feet firmly on the ground. In many ways he was the classic younger son, anxious to outshine his eldest brother, to make his own fortune and thereby to prove himself and acquire his own identity.

Dudley North slowed down in middle age, but his death from respiratory failure at Roger's house in the piazza of Covent Garden on 30 December 1691 still happened rather suddenly. After a modest, but well-attended, funeral, he was buried in St Paul's, Covent Garden, on 2 January 1692. His body was transferred to Little Glemham church on 4 September 1715 to lie next to his widow, when she died on 27 August 1715.   RICHARD GRASSBY

Sources R. Grassby, *The English gentleman in trade: the life and works of Sir Dudley North, 1641–1691* (1994) • R. North, *The life of the Honourable Sir Dudley North …*, ed. M. North (1744) • R. North, *Examen, or, An enquiry into the credit and veracity of a pretended complete history* (1740) • N. Luttrell, *A brief historical relation of state affairs from September 1678 to April 1714*, 6 vols. (1857) • W. Letwin, *The origins of scientific economics* (1963)
Archives Bodl. Oxf., MSS • East Kent Archives Centre, Dover, U.471 • Suffolk RO, Ipswich, papers as sheriff of London and Middlesex, HA 491/Acc331 • V&A NAL, letters and papers | BL, Add. MSS 32500–32541 • Herefs. RO, letters to Robert Foley and Anne Foley • PRO, Levant Company MSS, SP 105–110
Likenesses oils, *c*.1680, NPG [*see illus.*] • T. Hawker, portrait, 1683–91, NPG • G. Vertue, line engraving, 1743 (after T. Hawker), BM, NPG; repro. in North, *Lives* • line engraving, 1743 (after G. Vertue), NPG
Wealth at death £50,000: Grassby, *English gentleman*

North, Dudleya (1675–1712). *See under* North, William, sixth Baron North, second Baron Grey of Rolleston, and Jacobite Earl North (1678–1734).

North, Sir Dudley Burton Napier (1881–1961), naval officer, was born at Great Yarmouth on 25 November 1881, the fourth of the five sons of Colonel Roger North of the Royal Artillery and adjutant in the 1st Norfolk artillery volunteers, and his wife, Fanny Ellen, the daughter of Stephen Beeching, of Tunbridge Wells. He entered the *Britannia* as a naval cadet in 1896 and then served in cruisers, destroyers, and battleships as a midshipman. He became sub-lieutenant in 1902 and lieutenant in 1903.

In the battle cruiser *New Zealand* North took part in the battle of Heligoland (1914). As commander, and in the same vessel, from 31 December 1914 he took part in the battles of the Dogger Bank (1915) and Jutland (1916). After a short period of shore service in the Admiralty, where he was naval assistant to Captain Lionel Halsey, he returned to sea in the battle cruiser *Australia*. Promoted captain and appointed CMG in 1919, he embarked on a series of world tours by various members of the royal family as naval equerry. In 1919 he was also appointed MVO, in 1920 CVO, and in 1922 CSI. In 1922–4 he commanded C class cruisers before taking another royal tour with the prince of Wales in 1925.

North was then successful in various important posts as captain, being flag captain in the flagship of the Atlantic

Fleet in 1926–7, and subsequently flag captain and chief of staff in the Reserve Fleet. In 1930 he became director of operations at the Admiralty, being promoted to rear-admiral in 1932. He then became chief of staff to Admiral Sir John Kelly, the commander-in-chief, Home Fleet. There his tact and courtesy combined well with the unconventional attitude of Kelly, who was determined to make the fleet forget the Invergordon rising of 1931. In 1934 North was appointed to the command of the royal yachts at Portsmouth, a post for which he was well qualified after his experiences as equerry and his friendship with the royal family, whom he accompanied to Canada in 1939. When war came in September 1939, North, CB since 1935, a vice-admiral since 1936, and KCVO since 1937, had been too long out of touch with the fleet to be appointed to a sea-going command. Instead, he was made flag officer commanding the north Atlantic station and admiral superintendent at Gibraltar, taking up his post in November 1939. He was promoted to admiral in May 1940. The bombardment of Oran, by the British fleet under Admiral Sir James Somerville on 3 July 1940, distressed him considerably. He wrote an official letter to the Admiralty in which he criticized the operation and explained how repugnant it had been to all who took part. The letter was ill-received and the first lord, A. V. Alexander proposed that he should be relieved, but Sir Dudley Pound, the first sea lord, did not agree that the case was strong enough, whereupon a sharp reprimand was sent instead. This was the start of a lack of confidence in North by the Admiralty which was to have serious consequences.

In September 1940 occurred the incident of the French squadron passing the Strait of Gibraltar and steaming on to Dakar where it played a part in repelling the attack of the Franco-British force, an operation of which North was aware unofficially. He had received previous intelligence reports of the French movements, but expected instructions from the Admiralty which were not sent, owing to mistakes in the handling of signals. In the event, he took no action to stop the French and this was regarded by the Admiralty as an unforgivable lack of initiative. The first sea lord proposed, and the first lord agreed, that he should be relieved, and this was done on 31 December 1940, despite North's violent protests and demands for an inquiry. On arrival in London in mid-January, North saw Pound, the first sea lord, but the interview, and subsequent letters, achieved no inquiry. North joined the Home Guard and in 1942 was appointed flag officer, Yarmouth, as a retired rear-admiral.

In appearance North was of medium height and stocky, with a cheerful round face which usually had a twinkle. He married, in 1909, Eglantine, daughter of William R. Campbell of Sydney, New South Wales. She died in 1917 and he married, in 1923, Eilean Flora, daughter of Edward Graham JP of Charminster, Dorset. There were a son and three daughters of the second marriage.

After the war North was still convinced that he had been treated unjustly, and so apparently was George VI, who appointed him admiral commanding royal yachts, a post which lasted a year only because economies were made.

North became GCVO in 1947. The post-war years saw a succession of efforts, some by North personally, some by others, to secure an inquiry. The Admiralty was criticized in several books and articles and North again wrote to Whitehall. In 1953 five admirals of the fleet took up the case with the first lord, J. P. L. Thomas, but without result. In 1954 the publication of the official history appeared to clear North, and a bitter argument took place in the House of Commons, in which the first lord emphasized the loss of confidence in North by the Admiralty board and refused to act. A fiery debate also took place in the House of Lords. Whereas it cannot be disputed that the Admiralty could relieve any officer in whom confidence had been lost, the method used was clumsy and the subsequent handling bungled.

When Lord Mountbatten of Burma, who had been a friend of North's for many years, became first sea lord in 1955, he at once investigated the affair and came to the conclusion that an inquiry would serve no purpose. However, in 1957 the publication of a book by Noel Monks, strongly criticizing the Admiralty, revived the matter yet again, and another debate took place in the Commons. Mountbatten, Lord Selkirk, the new first lord, and Harold Macmillan, the prime minister, spent many hours considering the documents and also met the five admirals of the fleet. The prime minister then produced a carefully balanced statement in which he stressed that North's honour and professional integrity had not been impugned but refused an inquiry into such a well-documented incident. The public generally were satisfied that the statement ended the affair with a vindication of North's honour. North himself was not so content. He died on 15 May 1961 at Herrison House, Dorchester, Dorset, a sad and bitter man. He was survived by his second wife.

PETER GRETTON, *rev.*

Sources *The Times* (16 May 1961) · S. W. Roskill, *The war at sea, 1939–1945*, 3 vols. in 4 (1954–61) · N. Monks, *That day at Gibraltar* (1957) · A. J. Marder, *Operation Menace: the Dakar expedition and the Dudley North affair* (1976) · C. Plimmer and D. Plimmer, *A matter of expediency: the jettison of Admiral Sir Dudley North* (1978) · WWW · CGPLA Eng. & Wales (1961)
Archives CAC Cam., naval papers · CAC Cam., papers relating to his removal from North Atlantic Command |FILM BFI NFTVA, news footage · IWM FVA, news footage
Likenesses W. Stoneman, two photographs, 1932–42, NPG
Wealth at death £17,743 6s.: probate, 12 July 1961, CGPLA Eng. & Wales

North, Dudley Long (*bap.* 1748, *d.* 1829), politician, was baptized Dudley Long on 14 March 1748 at Saxmundham, Suffolk, the younger of two sons of Charles Long (1705–1778), landowner, of Hurts Hall, Suffolk, and his wife, Mary (1714/15–1770), daughter and coheir of Dudley North of Little Glemham, Suffolk, and granddaughter of Sir Dudley North (1641–1691). He was educated at Bury St Edmunds grammar school from about 1758 and Emmanuel College, Cambridge, from 1766, whence he graduated BA (1771) and MA (1774). He entered Lincoln's Inn in 1769, but was not called to the bar. His father left him £25,000 and a joint interest in his Jamaican plantations. In 1780 he entered parliament as MP for St Germans on the Eliot interest, at Lord Rockingham's instigation. His kinsman Lord North was then still premier, but Long was discouraged from speaking in the Commons by a speech impediment. Despite inheriting the family's corrosive wit, his shyness, even in private, if the company was unfamiliar, led Dr Johnson to dismiss him as a man 'of genteel appearance, and that is all' when they were introduced in 1781 (Boswell, *Life*, 4.81). Long nevertheless offered silent support to the premier, and was mentioned as a possible secretary of embassy at Paris in 1783.

At the general election in 1784 Long switched to Great Grimsby, a more expensive constituency under the patronage of Charles Anderson Pelham. He was in opposition together with Lord North, and aligned himself with North's ally Charles James Fox. Already a member of Brooks's, Long joined the Whig Club in 1785, and Fox relied on him for political counsel, and as a dinner host to strengthen party unity. He was a manager of Warren Hastings's impeachment. On 2 May 1789 he changed his surname to North in order to inherit Little Glemham from his aunt Anne Herbert. The contested Grimsby election of 1790 being eventually voided on 11 February 1793, he secured re-election on 17 April. He had briefly joined the Friends of the People before seceding on 4 June 1792, but refused to join the subsequent desertion of Fox by conservative whigs, and backed the subscription to pay Fox's debts in 1793. He was thought unlikely to succeed at Grimsby in 1796, and found another seat, for Banbury, on the North family interest, which he held unopposed until 1806. A supporter of parliamentary reform in 1793 and 1797, he regretted Fox's decision to secede from the house in the latter year; he returned to oppose Pitt's taxes and Irish policy, and attended the Commons regularly from 1800. He voted with the government on the peace of Amiens and the war in Ceylon, but otherwise opposed Addington, and Pitt in his second term of office. On 6 November 1802 he had married Sophia (1775–1856), daughter of his former patron at Grimsby, Charles Anderson Pelham, by then first Baron Yarborough, and his wife, Sophia Aufrère. They had no children.

In 1806 North was involved in a surprise defeat at Banbury, a one-seat constituency with only eighteen electors, even though his friends were in office in Grenville's administration. In the 1807 election he tied with the usurper, William Praed, and regained the seat, by 5 votes to 3, in a fresh election, on 16 February 1808. He then vacated Newtown, Isle of Wight, where he had been returned on the Yarborough interest. These elections had cost North £5000, which he had expected his patron Lord Guilford to pay for, especially as he had promised to bequeath his own estate to Guilford. He justifiably felt let down when Guilford asked him to relinquish Banbury in favour of his nephew at the dissolution in 1812. He acquiesced none the less. Yet in 1811 he declined Grey's offer of a sinecure if the whigs returned to office, a hope dashed by the prince regent's desertion. After a protracted search North came in for Richmond, Yorkshire, on the Dundas interest, which was obtained for him by Earl Fitzwilliam in 1812. In December that year he resumed his former surname, thereby becoming Dudley Long North, on succeeding his elder brother Charles to the family estate of Hurts Hall. In parliament he voted with the opposition in favour of Catholic relief, against the resumption of war with Bonaparte in 1815, and for financial retrenchment. To Fitzwilliam's dismay, however, he also opposed the suspension of civil liberties and supported parliamentary reform in 1817. In the next parliament he sat on his friend Lord Lauderdale's interest for Jedburgh burghs (1818–20). He voted for Francis Burdett's critical motion of 1 July 1819, and supported George Tierney's move to lead the whigs in the Commons, though he did not attend the last session of that parliament. He reverted to representing Newtown, Isle of Wight, in 1820, but resigned his seat on 9 February 1821.

Unwarranted dejection about the state of his finances exacerbated the ill health which dogged Long North's later years. He died at Brompton, London, on 21 February 1829, and was buried at Little Glemham church where his widow erected a full length Italian marble statue of him. A pallbearer at Edmund Burke's funeral, a mourner at Sir Joshua Reynolds's, and a patron of the poet George Crabbe, Long North was a popular member of both literary and political circles, but few of his witticisms are preserved: they were for the most part confined to his friends.   ROLAND THORNE

Sources M. H. Port, 'Long (afterwards North), Dudley', HoP, Commons, 1754–90 · M. H. Port and R. G. Thorne, 'North, Dudley (formerly Long, afterwards Long North)', HoP, Commons, 1790–1820 · DNB · GM, 1st ser., 99/1 (1829), 208, 282 · Venn, Alum. Cant. · S. H. A. H. [S. H. A. Hervey], Biographical list of boys educated at King Edward VI Free Grammar School, Bury St Edmunds, from 1550 to 1900 (1908), 239 · Walpole, Corr., 33.420n. · W. A. Copinger, The manors of Suffolk, 7 vols. (1905–11), vol. 5, pp. 129, 163 · Baron Glenbervie [S. Douglas], The Glenbervie journals, ed. W. Sichel (1910), 151 · Collins peerage of England: genealogical, biographical and historical, ed. E. Brydges, 9 vols. (1812), vol. 8, p. 398 · Boyle's Court Guide (1792–1829)

Archives Blair Adam, Fife, Blair Adam MSS, letters · Sheff. Arch., Wentworth Woodhouse MSS, corresp. with Edmund Burke · U. Durham, Fitzwilliam Grey MSS, corresp.

Likenesses W. Lane, group portrait, chalk drawing (Whig statesmen and their friends, c. 1810), NPG · group portrait (after chalk drawing by W. Lane), Hampton Lodge, Surrey · marble statue, Little Glemham church, Suffolk

Wealth at death under £18,000: Society of Genealogists, Bank of England wills, vol. 32 (K–Z), no. 6795

North, Edward, first Baron North (c.1504–1564), administrator, was born in the London parish of St Michael-le-Querne, sole son of the merchant and haberdasher Roger North, a native of Nottinghamshire, and of his wife, Christian (or Christina), daughter of Richard Warcup of Sinnington, Yorkshire. Edward's father died in November 1509, and soon after he entered St Paul's School, where his contemporaries included future fellow councillors William Paget and Thomas Wriothesley, as well as the antiquary John Leland (who later addressed to North a Latin poem recalling their studies together). A tradition that North was a student at Cambridge (based upon his later bequest to Peterhouse) cannot be corroborated, but he may have matriculated at the university before beginning his legal training in the inns of court. North was admitted

to Lincoln's Inn on 1 July 1522, and he served as steward there from 1528 to 1530. About 1525 he was appointed counsel to the corporation of London (perhaps through the influence of his brother-in-law, the alderman William Wilkinson), and two years later he became a freeman of the Mercers' Company. North secured his economic and social status in 1528 by marrying Alice (d. 1560), daughter of Oliver Squire of Southby, Hampshire, and widow of the wealthy London merchant Edward Murfyn and of John Brigandine. They had at least two sons—Roger *North and Thomas *North—and two daughters. Although no surviving portraits of North are known, his descendant and biographer Sir Dudley North described him as 'of moderate stature, somewhat inclining to corpulency, and of a reddish hair' (North, 33).

Some time during the later 1520s North came to the attention of Sir Brian Tuke, treasurer of the chamber, to whom he had addressed a verse treatise on the evils of the realm and their remedies (BL, Lansdowne MS 858). In February 1531 the young lawyer joined Tuke as clerk of parliaments, but owing to the treasurer's many responsibilities and chronic ill health, he performed much of the work himself (although the absence of enrolled statutes in chancery during his tenure suggests that North was somewhat negligent). He also worked for Thomas Cromwell, and it was probably the minister's influence which enabled him in March 1539 to succeed Sir Thomas Pope as treasurer of the court of augmentations, handling the substantial revenue accruing to the crown from the dissolution of the monasteries. This appointment prompted him to surrender his parliamentary clerkship in September 1540, in order to devote his full energies to his new duties. In January 1542 he was knighted, and by April 1544 Sir Edward had been appointed joint chancellor of augmentations together with the incumbent Sir Richard Rich, whom he succeeded three months later as sole chancellor of augmentations. Now head of the largest of the royal revenue courts, during the 1540s he was also regularly employed auditing accounts of royal treasurers, and was a member of the commissions appointed to sell crown lands. On 1 January 1547 administration of crown lands was consolidated through the amalgamations of the courts of augmentations and of general surveyors; North was named chancellor of the reformed (second) court of augmentations.

Although a native of London, in 1533 North purchased the Cambridgeshire manor of Kirtling (and had his title subsequently confirmed by a private act: 28 Hen. VIII c. 40), and from 1536 was a JP in his adopted county. Rapidly establishing himself as one of the leading gentlemen in the shire, in November 1542 he was pricked as sheriff of Cambridgeshire and Huntingdonshire, and he was a knight of the shire for Cambridgeshire in the parliaments of 1542, 1547, and March 1553. In addition to his East Anglian estates, he acquired the Charterhouse in London in April 1545, and profited handsomely from his augmentations office by actively speculating in monastic properties. On one occasion he was suspected of peculation and summoned to defend his financial dealings to Henry VIII in person, but managed to clear himself, albeit with the help of an exchange of lands favourable to the king.

Appointed an executor by Henry VIII (who bequeathed him £300), in March 1547 North was admitted to the privy council by Protector Somerset. Relations between the two men soured, however, and it seems to have been under pressure from Somerset that in August 1548 North was bought out of his augmentations post by the protector's friend Sir Richard Sackville. He seems to have resented his displacement, and though not closely associated with either the conservative or reform faction at the council board, his loss of his chancellorship helped to ensure North's support for the earl of Warwick's successful coup the following year. Under the new regime he remained an active councillor; for example in May 1550 he was appointed to a committee to oversee crown finances, and was sent to Princess Mary to obtain her answer to an offer of marriage from the duke of Brunswick.

In common with his colleagues on the council, North initially backed the attempt by the duke of Northumberland (as Warwick now was) to place Lady Jane Grey on the throne in July 1553, but soon joined the defectors to Mary's cause. Despite his initial disloyalty Mary elevated him to the peerage in April 1554 as first Baron North, and restored to him the Charterhouse, which had passed briefly to the duke of Northumberland. He paid a political price for his earlier support of Northumberland, however, for he did not return to the privy council. Nevertheless he remained active as a commissioner examining (and torturing) prisoners on the council's orders, and although his sister Joan *Wilkinson was a committed protestant, in February 1557 he was included in the important commission to investigate heresies. As well as regularly attending the House of Lords, he continued to participate in court life, as in July 1554 when he escorted Prince Philip to Winchester for his wedding. Mystery surrounds one other service to the crown: Foxe recounts (with scepticism) how, during the queen's phantom pregnancy in June 1555, North allegedly approached a poor London woman on behalf of the council to purchase her new-born son to pose as the desperately desired prince.

Upon her arrival in London following her accession in November 1558, Elizabeth lodged for five days at the Charterhouse as the guest of Lord North, before moving to the Tower. Although later appointed to several legal commissions and to one to advise on the coinage, his opposition to the Elizabethan settlement in the Lords during the 1559 parliament ruled out any possible return to the council board. In August 1560 his wife, Alice, died and was buried at Kirtling; he then married the thrice-widowed Margaret Broke (d. 1575), daughter of Richard Butler of London. Apart from regular visits to the Charterhouse (as when he entertained the queen for several days in July 1561), he lived his last years in retirement at Kirtling.

On 20 March 1564 North drew up his will, to which he added a codicil on 30 December 1564, the day before he died at the Charterhouse. In 1563 he had been reported to be 'quite comfortable' in religion, but the preamble to his will (PRO, PROB 11/48, fols. 49–55), expressing his hope for 'the fruition of everlasting lief withe our blessid Lady sainct Marie mother of our Saviour Jesu Christe virgine immaculate and all the hollie companie of heaven', shows that at heart he had remained staunchly Catholic. He asked to be buried at Kirtling 'besides my welbelovid wief decessed', but showed his regard for her successor by leaving her £500 and a share of his impressively large store of plate. Children, grandchildren, and servants were also remembered, with bequests of cash alone totalling nearly £1400. North made elaborate provision for the descent of his lands, and left the rectory of Ellington in Huntingdonshire to Peterhouse, Cambridge. Sir William Cordell, master of the rolls, and Sir James Dyer, chief justice of common pleas, were named as executors, while the duke of Norfolk, the earl of Leicester, and Sir William Petre were asked to act as supervisors of the will, which was proved on 23 February 1565. North's elder son, Roger, succeeded to the title.   P. R. N. CARTER

Sources D. North, Some notes concerning the life of Edward, Lord North (1658) • W. C. Richardson, History of the court of augmentations, 1536–1554 (1961) • LP Henry VIII • HoP, Commons, 1509–58, 3.21–3 • CPR, 1547–58 • will, PRO, PROB 11/48, fols. 49r–55r • The acts and monuments of John Foxe, ed. G. Townshend, repr., 8 vols. (1965) • The diary of Henry Machyn, citizen and merchant-taylor of London, from AD 1550 to AD 1563, ed. J. G. Nichols, CS, 42 (1848) • D. E. Hoak, The king's council in the reign of Edward VI (1976) • APC, 1547–54 • C. Wriothesley, A chronicle of England during the reigns of the Tudors from AD 1485 to 1559, ed. W. D. Hamilton, 2, CS, new ser., 20 (1877) • M. A. R. Graves, The House of Lords in the parliaments of Edward VI and Mary I (1981) • CSP Spain, 1547–52

Archives Bodl. Oxf., papers • Bodl. Oxf., personal, estate, and official papers | BL, Lansdowne MS 858 • PRO, court of augmentations records

Likenesses stipple, 1802, BM, NPG; repro. in F. G. Waldron, The biographical mirrour, 3 vols. (1795–1810) • H. Meyer, stipple, 1817 (after Lord Guilford), BM, NPG; repro. in E. Lodge, Portraits of illustrious personages (1817) • oils, Peterhouse, Cambridge

Wealth at death very rich; cash bequests totalled nearly £1400; had large quantity of plate: will, PRO, PROB 11/48, fols. 49r–55r

North, Francis, first Baron Guilford (1637–1685), judge, was born on 22 October 1637, second son of Dudley *North, fourth Baron North (1602–1677), politician and author, of Kirtling, Cambridgeshire, and Anne (1613/14–1681), daughter of Sir Charles Montagu. He studied in a school in Isleworth run by 'a rigid Presbyterian' (North, 1.10) and later at Bury St Edmunds. He then moved to St John's College, Cambridge, in 1653, which he left without a degree to begin his legal education in the Middle Temple in November 1655. While he was still a student, his grandfather made him steward of his Cambridgeshire manors, where he learned some law and earned a good income too.

Early career, 1661–1671 In June 1661 North was called to the bar, his father having paid for his chambers before leaving his son henceforth to his own means. While his practice grew, North remained a diligent student, as testified by his notebook of case reports from the 1660s in his small, careful hand. North possessed great ability, but his rapid advance was aided by his close working relationship with Attorney-General Sir Geoffrey Palmer, whose late son had

Francis North, first Baron Guilford (1637–1685), by David Loggan

been North's friend. Throughout the 1660s Palmer sent business to his protégé, especially as the attorney-general's health declined. The great barrister Sir William Jones derisively called North 'Mr. Deputy Attorney' (North, 1.63), but North was gaining important experience, especially by pleading in king's bench.

In 1667 the young barrister represented his father before the lord chancellor, who told North privately 'that he did not take me to be old enough to advise my father and it would not be fit for me to take it upon me' (MS North c.4, fol. 151). North's letters suggest that he ignored this advice. North's youth proved little obstacle to his progress. He was asked to help in prosecuting the king's case against the 'bawdy house' rioters in early April 1668. The duke of York, who saw North argue in defence of the decision of 1629 against the five members around the same time, was so impressed that he convinced Charles II to appoint North as king's counsel. Perhaps to honour this important occasion, North sat for a portrait by his friend Peter Lely. But the benchers of the Middle Temple were not impressed: when North asked to be admitted to their number on the strength of his recent royal appointment they refused, saying he lacked age and eminence. North suggested that while he took no affront, their refusal of honour might be viewed as an affront to the king who promoted him. North was supported by the justices in Westminster Hall, who refused to listen to the pleas of the Middle Temple's benchers until they relented and made North one of them.

Despite such opposition North's renown grew. He was put into a fen drainage commission and a forest eyre and was made the judge of the royal franchise of Ely. In these roles, and by riding the Norfolk circuit, he frequently impressed more senior members of his profession. Thus on 20 May 1671 North became solicitor-general, to the great disappointment of Sir William Jones, who increasingly became North's rival. On the following day the king knighted North, and later that spring North gave his reading in the Middle Temple.

Having established himself professionally, North began to cast about for a wife. The daughter of another lawyer first caught his eye, but his ardour cooled when he learned of the modesty of her estate. He next fixed his attention on the widow of his old friend Edward Palmer. But according to his brother Roger North, Francis's inability to dance or to dress the part ended his suit. A third attempted match failed in the negotiations over the bride's portion. North then turned to Lady Frances (bap. 1647, d. 1678), third daughter of Thomas *Pope, third earl of Downe [see under Pope, Thomas, second earl of Downe], and coheir of her brother, the fourth earl. They married on 5 March 1672 in the church at Wroxton, Oxfordshire, her father's seat, before moving into a handsome house in Chancery Lane, London, that previously belonged to Chief Justice Sir Robert Hyde. They had three sons and two daughters. In the 1670s North made Wroxton his country seat, eventually buying out the interests of the fourth earl of Downe's other heirs in 1681.

Politician and judge, 1672–1682   North now directed his efforts to politics. Having been made a freeman of King's Lynn and, in return, having done the town good services with secretary of state Sir Joseph Williamson, North stood at a by-election in January 1673 to represent it in parliament. Corporation members eagerly supported him, but many townsmen were less enthusiastic, though North ultimately prevailed in the contest. On 12 November 1673 North advanced to the attorney-general's place. Questions now arose about the propriety of his remaining in the Commons since his new office required assisting the House of Lords, but he retained his seat in the lower house. North's rapid rise did not slow, and on 23 January 1675 he was made chief justice of common pleas, which now required his departure from the Commons.

Though total rates of litigation in the courts at Westminster declined in the decades after 1660, common pleas had been particularly hard hit by lost business, king's bench having poached much of the litigation that once belonged to common pleas. As chief justice, North tried to stem the tide by accepting new usages in his court, though with only limited success. As a justice offering advice on legislation in the House of Lords, North played an important role in writing the 1677 Statute of Frauds and in the making of the Habeas Corpus Act of 1679 as well as numerous other statutes that modified the workings of the law.

Roger North's biography of his brother tried to place him above the political fray during these years, but North could not avoid political combat, fought as so much of it was at law. As chief justice of common pleas his normal caseload concerned only civil matters. But on assizes or in the Old Bailey, North necessarily dealt with criminal matters too, and in this period the most sensational crimes concerned 'popish' plotting and other politically charged wrongs. Thus he sat on the bench of the Old Bailey with Chief Justice Sir William Scroggs in the trial of five Jesuits convicted of treason in June 1679. North returned to the Old Bailey the next month for the trial of Sir George Wakeman on charges, of which he was acquitted, of plotting to poison the king. More controversial was the August 1681 trial of Stephen College at Oxford. Upon the jury's return of a guilty verdict on the charge of treason, North lashed out at College's dissenting brand of protestantism, which North said only promoted 'popery'. North sat again in the Old Bailey in November 1681 for the trial of the earl of Shaftesbury.

North also joined the privy council in April 1679. As a councillor, North was necessarily concerned in developing the crown response to the political situation of the late 1670s and early 1680s. Thus North assisted in drafting the royal proclamation that condemned petitions calling for a meeting of parliament. For this his former Commons colleagues impeached him in November 1680, though the charge died with the end of the session. Not long thereafter North helped to draft another royal pronouncement: the king's declaration explaining his reasons for dismissing the third Exclusion Parliament of 1681, one of the most effective works of royal propaganda of Charles II's reign. It was also Sir Francis who recommended that his brother Dudley, recently returned from decades as a merchant in Turkey, should stand for election as sheriff of London. Dudley North was chosen after a highly questionable contest. This enabled him to appoint the juries that ultimately returned guilty verdicts against Lord Russell and other crown opponents. Contrary to the portrait drawn by his brother Roger, Sir Francis—as both judge and privy councillor—had proved quite incapable of avoiding entanglement in the political conflict that roiled England in the 1680s.

Lord keeper, 1682–1685 On 20 December 1682 the king named North lord keeper of the great seal, thus putting him in charge of the chancery, its court, and the passing of all royal charters and commissions. It was probably in the early 1680s, especially after this appointment, that North made his extensive and fascinating notes on the royal prerogative and the place of the king in creating and controlling all lesser jurisdictions. His observations reveal a coherent view of politics that placed the king's prerogative at the heart of law and government. Given that all jurisdictions arise from the king, North reasoned, all jurisdictions are the king's to terminate or to reconfigure when and how he sees fit. In the circumstances then prevailing, in which urban corporations were seen by North and others as dens of anti-royal agitation, North promoted the use of commissions of association by which more politically reliable county justices of the peace could be added to urban benches, even where urban charters normally prevented county justices from acting within town limits. As

North reasoned, all jurisdictions, including urban ones, are 'granted out of the Crown upon this trust, that there be justice done' (BL, Add. MS 32518, fol. 156). If justice was not done—for instance, at Berwick, where dissenters allegedly received too much consideration—North recommended that the king should intervene by sending in new justices of the peace by commissions of association.

Or the king might do more. In the case of urban corporations, the king could revoke their charters and then recast their governments in whatever form he might choose. North concluded that town charters might be 'forfeit for the least misfeasance or fault in government' (BL, Add. MS 32520, fol. 32v). Notes in North's papers on the nature of corporate franchises, on franchises' dependence on the king's grace for their existence, and on informations in the nature of *quo warranto* by which those franchises might be inspected in court point to North as the chief legal strategist behind the decision in 1681 to sue a *quo warranto* against London, which resulted in the city losing its charter in 1683. As a privy councillor and as lord keeper, North had become the indispensable legal mind behind the so-called 'tory reaction' from 1681 to 1685. Under his leadership commissions of the peace were remodelled and corporations were rechartered by the score to ensure that local government rested in the hands of those the crown could trust.

While North argued for the king's extensive power over government in all its institutional forms, he did not believe that the king possessed an absolute authority. He hoped that by reforming local government in a limited way, 'faction' might be destroyed and popular politics—which he abhorred—might be constrained. But North rejected the more extreme measures of Sir George Jeffreys, who now used threats of *quo warranto* to compel dozens of corporations to surrender their charters. As Roger North put it, under Jeffreys, 'this trade of charters ran to excess' (North, 2.15). Jeffreys promoted the very factional conflict that North hoped to settle by more moderate measures. Perhaps for this reason one finds the prominent whig-inclined lawyers William Williams and Sir Francis Winnington among recipients of North's annual new year's gifts in the 1680s.

On 27 September 1683 North was ennobled as Baron Guilford; days later, word surfaced of a plot to kill various London leaders and North too. But it was conflict with the often bombastic Jeffreys that plagued North most. Late in 1684, when Jeffreys proposed in the privy council that all Catholic recusants might receive a general pardon, North opposed him. A few months later, after the Catholic James II had become king, North continued to argue that it would be illegal to appoint Catholics to the army. North was clearly unhappy with the direction in which the new king was moving, and he refused to use the great seal to pass *non obstantes* by which Catholics might be allowed to take office contrary to statutory restrictions meant to bar them. By May 1685 rumours abounded that he would be removed from office. According to Roger North, his brother had long been weary of high office, but it must have rankled Lord Guilford that those same rumours suggested that Jeffreys himself would replace him if he retired.

Nature, not politics, intervened. By July North had retreated to Wroxton, hoping that country air might restore his declining health. Instead, he died in great pain at Wroxton on 5 September 1685. The next day his brothers, as his executors, took the great seal to Windsor where the king gave it to Jeffreys. On 9 September North was laid to rest at Wroxton next to his wife, who had died on 15 November 1678.

North was fortunate among the many lawyers prominently engaged in the partisan conflict of the last years of Charles II in having a thorough and sympathetic biographer: his brother Roger. Roger's long and loving account, constructed out of his extensive transcripts of North's private papers, is balanced by the less favourable views offered by Gilbert Burnet and others. Burnet called North 'a crafty and designing man', who 'died despised and ill thought of by the whole nation' (Burnet's History, 3.83–4). But to his brother, North was a prudent, quiet man, always above the political contest in which self-interest deformed the actions of others.

North's tidy mind—so evident in his papers—placed the prerogative at the centre of his conception of law and politics. This thinking provided the foundation on which the case against London and other corporations was built, thinking which would be vindicated by judgments and statutes concerning corporate law in the generations after 1688. North rejected majoritarian political principles as productive of 'faction'. But his commitment to royal authority was surpassed only by his commitment to the established church. Thus he baulked at James II's religious policies. Presiding in chancery as lord keeper, North added little to the body of law developed in that court, though he did reverse the famous judgment of Lord Nottingham in the duke of Norfolk's case; North's own decree was in turn overridden by the House of Lords less than three months before he died.

North's brother and others testify to the fact that there was more to the lord keeper than law and politics. He was a serious musician, having begun his study of the bass viol at Cambridge; he continued to play and to compose throughout his life. Evelyn called him 'a most knowing, learned, ingenious gent., and besides an excellent person, of an ingenuous sweet disposition, very skillful in music, painting, the new philosophy and politer studies' (Evelyn, 4.299). His interest in music, as well as mathematics and physics, revealed themselves in a short treatise, *A Philosophical Essay of Musick* (1677). He also had a keen appreciation for painting, though perhaps his finest quality was the consistent loyalty he displayed toward his brothers.

PAUL D. HALLIDAY

Sources R. North, *The lives of … Francis North … Dudley North … and … John North*, new edn, 3 vols. (1826) · E. Cruickshanks and B. D. Henning, 'North, Sir Francis', HoP, *Commons, 1660–90* · M. W. Helms, E. R. Edwards, and G. Jagger, 'North, Sir Dudley I', HoP, *Commons, 1660–90* · *Bishop Burnet's History of his own time: with the suppressed passages of the first volume*, ed. M. J. Routh, 6 vols. (1823) · BL, Add. MSS 32511, 32518–32521 · Bodl. Oxf., MSS North b.8, c.4, c.5, f.16 · Bodl. Oxf., MSS Rawl. A. 183, 185 · parish register, Kirtling, Cambs. AS, 2 Nov 1637 [baptism] · *State trials*, vols. 6–9 · P. D. Halliday, *Dismembering the body politic: partisan politics in England's towns, 1650–1730* (1998) · *CSP dom.*, 1671–5; 1677–8; 1680–5 · *Seventh report*, HMC, 6 (1879) · *Report on the manuscripts of Allan George Finch*, 5 vols., HMC, 71 (1913–2003), vol. 2 · *The manuscripts of the House of Lords*, 4 vols., HMC, 17 (1887–94) · *The manuscripts of the marquess of Abergavenny, Lord Braye*, G. F. Luttrell, HMC, 15 (1887) · *The manuscripts of S. H. Le Fleming*, HMC, 25 (1890) · *Calendar of the manuscripts of the marquess of Ormonde*, new ser., 8 vols., HMC, 36 (1902–20), vol. 6 · N. Luttrell, *A brief historical relation of state affairs from September 1678 to April 1714*, 6 vols. (1857) · Wood, *Ath. Oxon.*, new edn · J. B. Williamson, *The history of the Temple, London* (1924) · Sainty, *King's counsel* · Sainty, *Judges* · Evelyn, *Diary* · *VCH Cambridgeshire and the Isle of Ely*, vol. 2 · E. M. Thompson, ed., *Correspondence of the family of Hatton*, 2 vols., CS, new ser., 22–3 (1878) · will, PRO, PROB 11/380, fols. 379v–81v · *Le Neve's Pedigrees of the knights*, ed. G. W. Marshall, Harleian Society, 8 (1873) · GEC, *Peerage*, new edn · Foss, *Judges*, 7.260

Archives BL, Add. MSS 32500–32520 · Bodl. Oxf., account book as lord chancellor; MSS · Hunt. L., corresp. and papers | BL, notes of cases temp. Charles II, Add. MS 35521

Likenesses P. Lely, portrait · D. Loggan, line engraving (after his earlier work), BM, NPG [*see illus.*] · attrib. J. Riley, oils, NPG · J. Riley, oils, Harvard U., law school

Wealth at death house in Wroxton; also extensive but unspecified properties: will, PRO, PROB 11/380, fols. 379v–81v

North, Francis, first earl of Guilford (1704–1790), politician, was born on 13 April 1704, the eldest son of Francis North, second Baron Guilford (1673–1729), and his second wife, Alice (1684–1727), the second daughter and coheir of Sir John Brownlow, bt, of Belton, Lincolnshire. He entered Eton College in 1718, and matriculated at Trinity College, Oxford, on 25 March 1721, but does not appear to have taken any degree. At the general election in August 1727 he was returned to the House of Commons for Banbury. On 17 June 1728 he married Lady Lucy Montagu (d. 7 May 1734), the daughter of George Montagu, first earl of Halifax, with whom he had a son, Frederick *North, who became prime minister as Lord North, and a daughter. He succeeded his father as third Baron Guilford on 17 October 1729, inheriting the family estate at Wroxton Abbey, Oxfordshire, and took his seat in the House of Lords on 13 January 1730.

On 17 October 1730 Guilford was appointed by George II as a gentleman of the bedchamber to Frederick, prince of Wales. He became close enough to the prince to act as intermediary between father and son; he shared the prince's interest in architecture, marked by the erection of an obelisk at Wroxton by the prince in 1739. On 31 October 1734 Guilford succeeded his second cousin William, Baron North and Grey, as seventh Baron North of Kirtling in Cambridgeshire. Following the death of his first wife he married Elizabeth (b. 1707, d. 21 April 1745), the widow of George Legge, Viscount Lewisham, and the only daughter of Sir Arthur Kaye, bt, of Woodsome, Yorkshire, on 24 January 1736. The couple had three daughters and two sons, one of whom, Brownlow *North, became bishop of Winchester. On 30 September 1750 Guilford was appointed governor to Prince George and Prince Edward, but was superseded on the prince of Wales's death by Earl Harcourt, a nominee of the Pelhams, who wished to control the education of the young princes. A third marriage, on

13 June 1751, to Katherine (*d.* 17 Dec 1766), the widow of Lewis Watson, second earl of Rockingham, and the daughter of Sir Robert Furnese, brought him the house and estate of Waldershare in Kent. He was created earl of Guilford on 8 April 1752. In September 1763 Grenville's proposal that Guilford should succeed Bute as lord privy seal was rejected by George III, who considered that 'it was not of sufficient rank for him' (*The Grenville Papers*, ed. W. J. Smith, 4 vols., 1852–3, 2.208–9). Ten years later, at the age of sixty-nine, he was appointed treasurer to Queen Charlotte (29 December 1773).

An intimate personal friend of George III and Queen Charlotte, Guilford sympathized with the king's dislike of the Fox–North coalition in 1783. On the fall of the Shelburne ministry he attempted to persuade his son to form an alliance with Pitt, with the king's knowledge; when this failed to prevent the coalition with Fox, Guilford still hoped that Pitt could be induced to join the coalition and that in time Fox could be excluded. Although he was a wealthy man, and on affectionate terms with his son, he would never make Lord North an adequate allowance. Investigations by John Robinson on behalf of George III revealed that North received only £2500 a year from his father, whereas his debts, in 1777, stood at £18,000. Guilford died at his residence in Henrietta Street, Marylebone, Middlesex, on 4 August 1790, and was buried at Wroxton, Oxfordshire, on 18 August.

G. F. R. BARKER, *rev.* MATTHEW KILBURN

Sources GEC, *Peerage*, new edn, vol. 2 · E. Cruickshanks, 'North, Hon. Francis', HoP, *Commons* · P. D. G. Thomas, *Lord North* (1976) · C. D. Smith, *The early career of Lord North the prime minister* (1979) · A. Valentine, *Lord North*, 2 vols. (1967)
Archives Bodl. Oxf., corresp. and papers · East Kent Archives Centre, corresp. · Keele University Library, papers as executor | BL, corresp. with Lord Hardwicke, Add. MSS 35586–35597 · BL, corresp. with duke of Newcastle, Add. MSS 32696–33082 · CKS
Likenesses T. Gainsborough, portrait, Courtauld Inst.
Wealth at death wealthy; owned Wroxton estate, Oxfordshire, and Waldershore estate, Kent

North, Francis, fourth earl of Guilford (**1761–1817**). *See under* North, Frederick, second earl of Guilford (1732–1792).

North, Frederick, second earl of Guilford [*known as* Lord North] (**1732–1792**), prime minister, was born on 13 April 1732 in Albemarle Street, Piccadilly, London, eldest son of Francis *North, then third baron and later first earl of Guilford (1704–1790), politician, and his first wife, Lady Lucy Montagu (*d.* 1734), daughter of George, first earl of Halifax. He may have taken his given name from his godfather, Frederick, prince of Wales, a man reputed by later scandalmongers to have been his actual father; that is not a view supported by historical opinion. His mother died in 1734, and by his father's marriage to Elizabeth Legge, widow of Viscount Lewisham, in 1736 Frederick acquired a stepbrother, William *Legge (1731–1801), politician, who as the second earl of Dartmouth was his lifelong friend.

Education, marriage, and entry into the Commons After attending Eton College (1742–8) and Trinity College, Oxford, North completed his education by a grand tour

Frederick North, second earl of Guilford [Lord North] (1732–1792), by Nathaniel Dance, 1773–4

with Dartmouth, one that lasted from 1751 to 1754. At the age of twenty-two North was an intelligent young man of high moral character, excellent manners, and an engaging personality, a compound of urbanity, wit, and good humour. Such attributes offset his physical disadvantages. Already plump in face and figure, indeed with a heavy countenance conveying the impression of dullness, he possessed an indistinct but loud voice, defective eyesight, and a clumsiness of behaviour. He had returned for the general election of 1754, and entered parliament for the single-member family pocket borough of Banbury, 3 miles from the family seat of Wroxton in Oxfordshire. He represented Banbury without opposition until he succeeded his father as second earl of Guilford on 4 August 1790.

Before he cut a figure in politics North married, on 20 May 1756, the sixteen-year-old Anne (1739/40–1797), daughter and heir of George Speke of White Lackington, Somerset, and his third wife, Anne. They had seven children. It was a happy union, despite the financial strain that dogged the early years, when North's expenses were considerably more than his private income of some £2000: his wife's Somerset estate of Dillington, inherited from her father in 1753, probably yielded about £750 a year and not the much larger income of contemporary rumour. Such comparative poverty may have spurred North's political ambitions. He enjoyed useful connections in the government: his uncle, the second earl of Halifax, was president of the Board of Trade, Dartmouth's uncle was chancellor of the exchequer, and North claimed a distant kinship with the prime minister himself, the duke of Newcastle.

But North first had to prove himself in parliament, and this he did when seconding the address on 1 December 1757. This maiden speech was much praised as full of promise, displaying two of his debating assets, self-possession and a powerful voice. By 1759 his parliamentary prowess enabled him to leap-frog minor offices by appointment on 2 June as a lord of the Treasury, with a welcome salary of £1400. Six years at the Treasury board were to enable him to acquire the financial skill and knowledge that, allied to his parliamentary expertise, proved the foundation of his political success.

Political apprenticeship North retained that post through the political vicissitudes of the next few years. When government supporters had to decide whether to follow the duke of Newcastle into opposition when he resigned in May 1762, or stay on to back the king's favourite, Lord Bute, as the next prime minister, North was among those to retain office. It was a decision about which he was uneasy, his personal inclination to resign being outweighed by his father's pressure and his uncle Halifax's appointment as a secretary of state. It was an unhappy time for North, who did not get on well with Bute, and who resisted his attempts to move him from the Treasury board to a court office. A year later North found matters more to his liking when Bute was succeeded by George Grenville, a man he respected. It was during the Grenville ministry (1763–5) that North moved into the front rank of parliamentary debaters, making some fifty recorded speeches during the next two sessions. What established his reputation was the leading role he took for the ministry in the *North Briton* case involving MP John Wilkes. It was North who moved on 15 November 1763 that the paper was a seditious libel, on 24 November that parliamentary privilege did not cover seditious libel, and on 19 January 1764 that Wilkes should be expelled from the house. In the 1765 session he spoke in support of the Stamp Act's imposing taxation on the American colonies, a measure doubtless familiar to him at the Treasury board.

North was a loyal servant of Grenville's ministry, but did not develop any personal rapport with him. On Grenville's dismissal in July 1765 the incoming ministry under Lord Rockingham, Newcastle's political heir, therefore did not remove him from office, and, even after he resigned, offered him the post of joint vice-treasurer of Ireland, worth £2000 a year. North refused, went into opposition, and in 1766 criticized the conciliatory American policy of the new ministry. He was nevertheless keeping his options open, owing no allegiance to any political leader. In May 1766 he rejected another offer from Rockingham before in July accepting from his successor, Lord Chatham, a lucrative post as joint paymaster-general. His political role soon became more important than this office denoted. On 10 December 1766 he was sworn of the privy council, an honour that was followed by occasional summonses to cabinet early in 1767. On 4 March 1767 he was offered the post of chancellor of the exchequer, for the incumbent Charles Townshend was proving a difficult colleague. North declined, and proved

diffident even when the unexpected death of Townshend on 4 September reopened the prospect of such an appropriate post, without now facing an angry predecessor. North again refused the post when offered it on 9 September by the king and the duke of Grafton, who was acting on behalf of the unwell Chatham. He made the pretext of his father's illness, but accepted by post the next day after consulting his father. It meant more work for less pay, the salary of £2500 being lower than his income of some £3500 from the pay office. Both Townshend and Grenville are reputed to have already forecast that North was a future prime minister (Thomas, *Lord North*, 20).

Leader of the house The duke of Grafton, already acting head of the ministry before he formally succeeded Chatham in October 1768, found North an asset at the exchequer: experienced, competent, and, unlike Townshend, utterly reliable. Financial business could safely be left to him, and from early in 1768 Grafton seldom attended the Treasury board. At the king's behest North was now a regular member of the cabinet, both on account of his office and because he was ministerial spokesman in the Commons, having succeeded to the unofficial role of leader of the house in January 1768. Within a year or so he was master of the Commons as a result of the second Wilkes case, which arose from that demagogue's election for Middlesex in 1768. The ministry decided on his expulsion, ostensibly as a persistent libeller. North was strongly in favour of this, regarding the behaviour of Wilkes as unconstitutional and a threat to law and order. North's participation in the episode was twofold: management of the campaign, concerning motions, tactics, and speakers, and the leading debating role for government, even though he did not himself now move the resolutions against Wilkes. In a parliamentary battle from January to May 1769, which included four expulsions of Wilkes and the eventual award of the seat to an opponent, Henry Luttrell, North argued that his exclusion was the logical consequence of his initial expulsion. The ministerial majority fell to fifty-four, and North was in 'low spirits', talking about resignation, even though George III sought to boost his morale by commending 'the spirit and good conduct you have shown during the whole of this unpleasant business' (*Correspondence of George III*, 2.90–91). Such a scenario between king and minister was often to be repeated. The session had laid the foundation for North's long ministry. Grafton later recalled that 'if Lord North did not rise in popularity, without doors, he rose greatly in the estimation of those who were the best judges of distinguished Parliamentary abilities' (*Autobiography … of Grafton*, 227).

The Middlesex election case did not end with the parliamentary session. During the summer of 1769 a nation-wide petitioning campaign was launched by the opposition, with Chatham, now well again, joining in the attack on the ministry he had himself created. It was tottering even before the new session began in January 1770. Anticipating the possibility that Grafton might resign, the king interviewed North on 20 December 1769 and seemingly offered him the reversion of the prime ministership, for

North told his father that 'my pride … has by the late offer been gratified to the utmost of its wish' (Thomas, *Lord North*, 33). This presaged the course of events. Grafton's nerve failed under the combination of parliamentary attacks and the defections of his fellow Chathamites from the ministry. On 28 January 1770 North agreed to become first lord of the Treasury, after the king had seen him on 22 and 27 January, and three days later he faced a virtual vote of confidence when the Commons once again debated the Middlesex election. 'Lord North with great frankness and spirit, laid open his own situation, which, he said, he had not sought, but would not refuse, nor would he timidly shrink from his post.' So recorded Horace Walpole, who noted that North spoke 'with spirit but good-humour, and evidently had the advantage, though it was obvious how much weight the personal presence of a First Minister in the House of Commons carried with it' (Walpole, *Memoirs*, 4.50–52). North surpassed expectations by securing a majority of forty, and his evident determination to stay rallied support. At the next major clash, on 12 February, he defeated by seventy-five votes an opposition attack on government corruption, and by the Easter recess the political crisis was over. North was to be prime minister for the next twelve years; it was a title he eschewed and forbade his family to use.

Prime minister The post of prime minister was by now a demanding one. Since North was an MP, not a peer, it included being chancellor of the exchequer, with responsibility for national income and expenditure, involving considerable administrative work. The Treasury board met usually twice a week, and this demand on North's time became burdensome during the American War of Independence: between 1775 and 1782 he missed only 23 of 670 such meetings. In the House of Commons, three days a week were set aside, in form at least, for the two finance committees, supply to decide expenditure, and ways and means to meet the cost by taxes and duties. Budget day was already an annual occasion for the presentation of the nation's accounts, and in the early 1770s North made it a great political occasion, and an opportunity for a review of the year's events.

North also presided over the cabinet, the small group of ministers that decided policy: this met irregularly, but usually about twice a week. Other calls on his time were a multitude of individual tasks, political and administrative, such as frequent interviews with the king. Especially was he perpetually harassed by patronage applications. Although he endeavoured to be systematic, keeping records of applications and favours in indexed recommendation books, he sometimes worsened his own problems by carelessness, failure to reply, or by weakly yielding to importunate or influential claimants. In any case he was quite unable to meet more than a small proportion of requests, and so mastered the art of refusal without giving offence that he was sometimes misunderstood. In 1772 he gave the Commons this explanation of his technique, in reply to a complaining MP:

> It was the etiquette of the Minister, if he could not grant the favour asked of him, at least to send home the person refused in good humour. This was well understood by courtiers; but for such ignorant honest country gentlemen as the Honourable Member, he thought it right to explain, that, when he only nodded, or squeezed the hand, or did not absolutely promise, he always meant No; which produced a great and long laugh. (*London Evening-Post*, 25 Feb 1772)

That incident exemplifies how well North went down in the House of Commons, the basis of his political power, and for much of the year the centrepiece of his daily routine. During the parliamentary session he was expected to be in his seat on the Treasury bench every day from mid-afternoon until the house rose. This was more than mere form. That North was the ministerial spokesman was the true significance of his unofficial position as leader of the house. During his first five sessions as prime minister, from 1770 to 1774, he made about 800 speeches and interventions in debate. Later sessions are less well reported, but on a pro rata basis it is probable that he spoke some 2000 times in the Commons as prime minister. He was the leading administration speaker on government business, whether or not he moved the proposals himself, for he was 'the minister', and many of these major speeches lasted an hour or more.

North never prepared formal orations and seldom spoke from notes, for his prodigious memory enabled him to put the government case and refute points made against it. His speeches were distinguished by clarity. When he spoke every squire understood the subject of debate, whether foreign policy, the national finances, or the constitution, or at least thought he did. Equally important was his part in the cut and thrust of debate, as on opposition motions, and that was a role that suited his spontaneity and sharpness. To technique North added temperament. His imperturbable good humour was symbolized by his propensity for nodding off during debates. In 1770 he fell asleep when George Grenville was speaking on the national finances. Nudged awake to hear Grenville talking about 1689, he convulsed the house by the loud complaint 'You have wakened me nearly one hundred years too soon' (*Diaries of Sylvester Douglas*, 1.237–8). Humour was the most characteristic of his weapons, to the indignation of serious-minded opponents like Edmund Burke, who complained that 'it is not sufficient when the first minister shall make you laugh' (*Cavendish's Debates*, 2.85). Much of it was disarming self-mockery, and never did he give offence. George III commented in 1801 that nobody then possessed 'that easy natural flow of genuine good-natured wit which distinguished Lord North and forced a smile from those against whom it was exercised' (*Diaries of Sylvester Douglas*, 1.149, 326). North's political opponents did not become his personal enemies.

As prime minister North retained for twelve years the general support of the House of Commons. But in the context of the contemporary political scenario, that did not mean endorsement of all his policies and opinions. Such approval was obtained by his personal reputation and parliamentary skills, usually sufficient to win over independent opinion in the house, but also by his care to temper measures to the mood of the Commons, as in the biggest issue of all, the American colonies. Occasional defeats in the Commons upset North far more than the king, and often triggered resignation threats. His requests to be relieved of the burden of office punctuate the whole period from 1767 to 1782, and contemporaries and historians have differed as to their sincerity. Certainly the chief political question soon became whether he would stay, rather than whether he could. The parliamentary opposition disintegrated within a year. Grenville's death in November 1770 led to most of his group's defecting to the ministry, while the other two opposition groups, led by Rockingham and Chatham, disagreed on many topics.

North soon became the dominant figure in the cabinet as a result of the major issue of his first year, the Falkland Islands crisis, which arose out of the seizure by Spain in June 1770 of Britain's Port Egmont military base there. It enabled North to reshuffle to his advantage the cabinet he had inherited from Grafton. The bellicose southern secretary, Lord Weymouth, resigned when he could not get his way. The northern secretary, Lord Rochford, took his place, and was himself succeeded by North's uncle, Lord Halifax. The former Grenvillite Lord Suffolk took Halifax's post as lord privy seal, and the Admiralty went to Lord Sandwich, a man long marked out by North for that task. By January 1771 North had a cabinet united behind him, and withstood a parliamentary attack on the settlement he had made with Spain. Since the British base would be returned without a war, apparently because of Britain's mobilization of her navy, his opponents could complain only about lack of compensation and about suspected French mediation. North claimed that a war with both France and Spain had been the alternative, and won a crushing majority of 275 votes to 157 on 13 February 1771; kept a close secret was his verbal promise of future British evacuation, which took place quietly in 1774. Other ministerial changes soon consolidated his hold on the cabinet. When Halifax died in June 1771, Suffolk moved up to be northern secretary, and the duke of Grafton became lord privy seal but refused to sit in cabinet, doubtless to North's relief. A year later North failed to prevent the resignation of American secretary Lord Hillsborough when his veto on an Ohio valley colony was overruled by his colleagues, but North filled the post with his own stepbrother, Dartmouth.

The king and the Garter The political triumph of North, now supreme in the Commons and dominant in cabinet, was completed by a close personal relationship with the king. The latter in 1771 bestowed on Lady North the post of ranger of Bushy Park, a mark of royal favour that provided the use of a house just outside London that North found convenient, especially at weekends. A notable honour came in 1772, the Garter, bestowed only once before that century on a commoner, Walpole. In Lord North, charming and deferential in personal contact, conservative in political attitudes, George III had found the prime minister he had been seeking since his accession, and he would not willingly part with him. North knew his duty, as in his determination to carry the Royal Family Marriage Act of 1772, even though he himself disliked the measure. George III always gave him full political support in policy decisions and choice of colleagues alike, and in 1777 paid off from the royal purse personal debts North had accumulated to the tune of some £16,000. The next year the king put North's finances on a sounder basis by appointing him for life as lord warden of the Cinque Ports, whereby he secured a salary of £1000 when prime minister and a nominal £4000 thereafter.

A generation of war and a decade of political confusion had led to the postponement of some imperial problems, as in Ireland and America, and the creation of others, as in Canada and India. Now it was both possible and necessary to resolve them. Within Britain there was a stable ministry, and in western Europe there was peace, with the wisdom of Britain's foreign policy of isolation apparently confirmed by the outcome of the Falkland Islands crisis. Britain in the 1770s gave up a search for allies, Russia having been the main target, and decided to rely on her own naval power. With few internal or external distractions, North could turn his attention to Britain's own problems, and above all he concerned himself at first with a subject close to his heart, finance.

Finance In peacetime there was little need for new taxation, since the normal government expenditure of some £7 million was more than met by traditional sources of revenue, mainly customs and excise duties. There was often a budget surplus that North could use in his tactic of reducing the national debt, the capital burden of which at some £140 million alarmed many contemporaries. His chief weapon was an annual lottery. The demand for the limited number of tickets enabled him not only to raise money directly but also to induce government stockholders to accept repayment on terms favourable to the Treasury: they were offered tickets if they sold back their stock at below par. In 1775 North informed parliament that the national debt had been reduced by £10 million, nearly all while he had been chancellor of the exchequer. Such redemptions, and conversion of other stock to lower interest rates, had cut the annual interest burden by £500,000.

Unfortunately these achievements were undone by the outbreak of the American War of Independence that same year, for government expenditure rose steadily to over £20 million by 1780. The extra money had to be borrowed each year, for all new taxes went to meet the additional interest burdens. Seeking to keep both this interest and the new debt as low as possible, North made use of dated annuities, and further exploited the demand for lottery tickets. These were now distributed only to subscribers of government loans. Utilizing these two devices, he contrived to issue stock at par, despite the steady fall in the market price of government 3 per cent stock, from 86 in 1776 to 52 in 1782. Until 1780 his wartime finance was deemed a success, but his reputation for fiscal ingenuity was damaged by his 1781 loan, which increased the capital debt by £21 million to raise a £12 million loan. He then frankly admitted that he did not think the national debt would ever be repaid and that his concern was rather with the annual interest burden, a realistic appraisal of conflicting objectives, but one that exposed him to criticism. For his final loan, in 1782, he therefore changed his method from the customary one of bargaining with possible lenders to the device of inviting competitive secret tenders, a mode his successors were to adopt, since there were no political implications of corruption, a charge sometimes levied at North. In his seven wartime loans he increased the national debt by £75 million in raising £57 million, and the extra interest burden was £3.2 million, including the dated payments which would begin to end from 1787. Despite the disaster of 1781 his clever use of annuities and lotteries had undoubtedly held down the size of the capital debt in difficult borrowing circumstances.

Extra taxation was needed to pay the interest on these new debts. North, influenced by Adam Smith, favoured direct taxation, and his sole attempt to launch a productive new tax was a house tax of 1778, analogous to the existing window tax. But evasion and incompetence reduced the yield of any new taxes then, and he had to fall back on increasing such old sources of revenue as customs and excise duties. His years at the Treasury had already made him aware of the inefficiency of a revenue system where most taxes were appropriated to specific purposes, and where many officials retained cash balances until their accounts were passed by the exchequer. Reform was impelled by the now pressing need for money. In 1777 North ordered the preparation of schemes for the consolidation of revenue from the customs, excise, and stamp duties, and in 1780 he set up a commission on public accounts. He lacked the time and opportunity to remedy the defects revealed, but many of his ideas were carried out by the younger Pitt. Awareness of the need to overhaul the financial structure of government, belief in direct taxation, and realistic acceptance that the national debt would never be paid off: these attitudes reveal North as a finance minister prepared to discard traditional practices and attitudes. This perception was complemented by practical competence.

Ireland Apart from the recurrent issue of America, Ireland was the first imperial problem facing the North ministry. By 1760 effective control had passed from British lord lieutenants, more often absent than present, to 'undertakers', Irish magnates who managed the Dublin parliament on behalf of Britain. A decision to recover direct power for the British government by the appointment of resident viceroys had been taken in 1765, but the vicissitudes of British politics delayed its implementation, until in February 1770 North promised the current lord lieutenant, Lord Townshend, full support in his contest with the Irish politicians. With North's assistance, notably in the field of patronage, Townshend and his successors were able to secure a working majority in the Irish parliament for their 'Dublin Castle party'. This frequently overlooked achievement of North polarized Irish politics until the Union of 1800. That dénouement was a goal that North himself had aspired to. He is on record as favouring the

idea in 1777, and by 1779 union was the preferred Irish policy of most members of his cabinet, but one then deemed impracticable in the face of Irish hostility. North was later to speak in favour of union during the 1785 debates on Pitt's Irish trade proposals.

Earlier North, when prime minister, had been faced with Irish discontent arising out of the economic depression caused by the American war. Long-standing British commercial restrictions began to hurt as Ireland lost markets in America and Europe, and their abolition was demanded in a campaign for 'free trade'. North strongly sympathized with the Irish grievance, but was unable to grant more than permission in 1778 to export Irish goods to the colonies until, late in 1779, an Irish boycott of British goods silenced the opposition of British merchants and manufacturers, who were fearful of Irish competition. By North's legislation, enacted early in 1780, Ireland was allowed to export woollen goods, and to trade freely both ways with British colonies, a generous concession in defiance of current mercantilist principles. He had solved an Irish problem that in some opinions had threatened to develop into another American situation, but the protracted crisis had generated a political consciousness in Ireland that now found expression in resentment at the constitutional subordination of the Dublin parliament to London. The issue did not develop into a storm until near the end of his ministry, and he bequeathed it to his successor.

India India was a problem that forced itself on North's attention. It was an obvious anomaly that, for the last decade or so, the private trading East India Company should have been ruling vast territories there, especially as both distance and the internal structure of the company rendered such control difficult. Company servants in India often ignored orders from London, and the return home of many as wealthy 'nabobs' focused public opinion on the abuses and misrule there of the company. But the North ministry's intervention was caused by the company's financial weakness, not by such public concern. In the early 1770s the company faced both rising costs, of military and administrative expenditure, and declining income. Territorial revenue was falling, and so was the sale of tea, the basis of the company's profitability. In the summer of 1772 the company asked the ministry for help. North himself always took the view that the Indian territories rightfully belonged to the crown, but he was dissuaded by his colleagues from acting on that principle. He nevertheless decided that financial aid would be given only in return for reform of both the company's constitution and its administration in India.

North granted the company's requests for a loan of £1.4 million and for customs concessions to ease the sale of tea, the intended market being changed from Europe to America, with fateful consequences. But the Loan Act and Tea Act of 1773 were accompanied by the East India Company Regulating Act. At home this strengthened the company structure by extending the service of its directors from one year to four, and by tightening the voting qualifications for their election, thereby reducing the company's hitherto chronic instability of management. In India a governor-general and council were to rule the main province of Bengal, and British judges were to constitute a supreme court. The company was coerced into accepting this first government intervention in the management of India, one company politician, Laurence Sulivan, describing North as 'the boldest minister this realm has been blest with since the days of Oliver Cromwell' (BL, Add. MS 29194, fols. 84–5).

Nor was that the end of the story. The North ministry now sought, by direct political interference, to control the London end of the East India Company, with the long-term intention to review the whole Indian question when the company's charter came up for renewal in 1780. North's motive in all this was to ensure good government in India, and not, as some suspected, to extend ministerial patronage there. But the onset of the American war and a vigorous parliamentary opposition that asked whether, having lost America, he now intended to destroy Britain's position in India, deterred him from taking any further measures. In 1781 the charter was renewed for ten years without any remedy for the defects of the 1773 act, the lack of effective London control over India and the need both to strengthen the authority of the governor-general and to extend it over all British India. Sulivan now complained of 'the timidity of Lord North' (BL, Add. MS 29149, fol. 243).

Canada The Quebec Act of 1774 has long been seen as a feather in North's cap, traditionally portrayed as one thing he got right. Posterity acclaimed its statesmanlike provisions, establishing French civil law and a Roman Catholic church in defiance of contemporary prejudices, and attributed to it the retention of Canada within the British empire. In truth North deserved little credit for any of this. Successive British ministries from 1763 had intermittently considered the problem of France's former colony, where British settlers constituted 1 per cent of a population that was otherwise French and Catholic. The principles of accepting French civil law and Catholic worship there had been accepted years before North became prime minister. But it was the North cabinet that from 1771 rejected the idea of an elected assembly, previously a matter under favourable consideration, if for obviously sound reasons: an assembly based on the tiny minority of British settlers would be unfair, and one based on a Catholic electorate a dangerous experiment. By 1773 the ministry had decided to introduce legislation for Canada in the following year, and proceeded to enact it at the end of the 1774 session, despite the flood of American business generated by the Boston tea party. There is no evidence that the Quebec Act was intended or timed to retain the loyalty of that colony, and neither did it have that consequence.

A late decision was the incorporation within Quebec of the western areas north and south of the Great Lakes, down to the Ohio river, a wilderness hitherto left to the Native Americans. This tacked on to the original measure an attempt to solve the problem of 'the west'. The decisions of the North ministry, the absence of an assembly and the boundary clause, formed the main targets of parliamentary criticism, and North himself spoke seventy-two times in defence of the measure. Outside parliament popular prejudice in both Britain and the colonies detested also the concessions to Catholicism and the tyranny allegedly implicit in French law.

In Canada itself only the small class of *noblesse*, who had been consulted on the measure, were pleased with the Quebec Act. It alienated not merely the small number of British settlers, denied both an assembly and many customary legal rights, but also the mass of French peasantry, for whom the measure confirmed the burden of church tithes and feudal dues they had hoped to escape. Both groups gave assistance to the American invasion of 1775. Canada was saved for Britain not by the loyalty of its inhabitants but by the large military force sent there early in 1776, which found only the town of Quebec itself in British hands. Since American colonists were alienated by the alleged creation of a papist absolutism in Quebec, and also by the boundary clause, a symbolic and actual curb on their expansionist aspirations, the Quebec Act does not now appear the statesmanlike measure it was once assumed to have been.

The American crisis In the earlier 1770s contemporaries, unaware of what lay ahead, deemed North a successful prime minister. 'North serves the Crown more successfully and more efficiently upon the whole than any other man could be found to do' was the private opinion of Chatham in 1773 (Valentine, 1.306). He had solid achievements to his credit, with regard to finance, Ireland, India, and even, apparently, America. Britain was prosperous and at peace. North, in favour with both Commons and crown, seemed destined to enjoy power for the foreseeable future: in 1775 he was forty-three years of age, younger than Sir Robert Walpole when he had begun his long premiership. Yet even before the Boston tea party astute observers must have been uneasily aware that the American question was merely dormant and not solved. The colonial policy North had inherited as prime minister was one he had supported in the fateful cabinet meeting of 1 May 1769, summoned to resolve the problem caused by Charles Townshend's 1767 duties on a limited range of goods imported into America. Americans deemed that indirect method of revenue collection to be as much a tax as the Stamp Act of 1765, and gradually adopted another trade boycott. By the spring of 1769 this impelled the Grafton ministry to formulate a policy decision. Grafton favoured complete repeal, but was outvoted in his own cabinet, by five to four, over retention of the duty on tea imports. North was one of the majority, in accordance with his earlier hardline attitude on America over the Stamp Act. The tea duty was not a mere symbol but the only productive tax, and North was to use it to implement Townshend's plan for the payment of British salaries to colonial governors, judges, and other officials, thereby depriving the colonial assemblies of their financial weapon against royal officers.

North was prime minister by the time this American policy was presented to parliament on 5 March 1770. Anxious that it should not appear a surrender to American resistance, he denounced the trade boycotts as illegal, but then said that anger at American behaviour should not mislead parliament into retaining taxes harmful to the British economy. For whereas tea was simply imported from Asia, and would yield an adequate revenue, the other goods taxed by Townshend were British manufactures. In the ensuing debate this policy was attacked on both sides. An opposition amendment to include the tea duty was matched by hardliners who would support neither the motion nor the amendment, and who left before the vote. That confirmed the ministerial decision by a majority of 62, 204 to 142, and the compromise policy then seemed to be a masterly success. The trade boycotts collapsed by the end of 1770, and sufficient revenue came from the tea duty to enable the North ministry to commence payment of colonial salaries, notably in Massachusetts, which was regarded as the most refractory of the colonies.

It is now evident that this period of calm was deceptive. The quarrel over the tea tax lapsed mainly because large-scale tea smuggling nullified its impact. Most of the scanty tax collected came, ironically, from Boston. Colonial opinion never lost sight of the underlying conflict that had surfaced in the earlier quarrels over taxation. Whereas the Americans regarded their assemblies as mini-parliaments, comparable in status to that at Westminster, the British interpretation of the imperial structure was that parliament had overall sovereign authority. That conflict of opinion was the basic cause of the American War of Independence, not any dispute over royal power. It surfaced again early in 1773 after the Massachusetts assembly complained about the British salary payments of local officials, and the ensuing public debate in that colony on the imperial constitution drove the ministry into a hardline stance, signified by North's refusal to cancel the Townshend tea duty when the Tea Act otherwise eased the prospective sale of East India Company tea to the American colonies. The result was the Boston 'tea party' of 16 December 1773.

When news of this public defiance reached London in January 1774, retributive action by North's ministry was inevitable, and the decision to take action through parliament raised the constitutional stakes. The cabinet was led into this course of action not only by inability to identify individual miscreants, such direct action being the first preference, but also by a sense of propriety, a reluctance to close Boston harbour merely by royal edict. Hence the Boston Port Act, which did so until compensation was paid for the tea, and which, North told the Commons, could be enforced by a few frigates, a remark later misinterpreted into over-confidence about the American rebellion. The prime minister was well aware that the whole American legislation of 1774 was a calculated risk, notably the Massachusetts Government Act, which altered the colony's constitution. The ministerial hope was that the other colonies would not rally round Massachusetts if

that colony resisted. North obtained a massive vote of confidence in government policy, by 239 to 64, when the opposition staged the main debate on 2 May. The parliamentary opposition argued for some conciliatory measure to balance the coercion of Boston, but that option was not open to North, such was the intransigent mood of British political opinion: nor is there any evidence he contemplated it. For North was not a moderate trapped by events, and he discounted another colonial trade boycott, rightly confident that it would not harm the buoyant British economy. Even before any news came from America he privately told former Massachusetts governor Thomas Hutchinson that in such an eventuality Britain would retaliate: 'Great Britain would take care they should trade nowhere else. And if any colonies stood out, all encouragement should be given such colonies' (*Diary and Letters*, 1.245). North already had his future policy in mind. Meanwhile he cleared the political deck by bringing forward the general election due in 1775 to the autumn of 1774, so that a new parliament would deal with any colonial crisis. He secured a comfortable Commons majority, conservatively estimated at about eighty, and very much more than that on America.

By the end of 1774 the magnitude of the American problem had become evident. Massachusetts was ungovernable, and the other colonies rallied round her in the continental congress which imposed a trade ban to force a reversal of British policy. At this point North's realization that Britain was on the verge of a civil war against her colonies caused him to change tack. Hitherto he had been a consistent advocate of colonial taxation. Now he offered a measure of conciliation on that point. Although more soldiers were to go to Massachusetts, and legislation would be introduced to prohibit the colonies from trading and fishing, as North had forecast to Hutchinson, in January 1775 he persuaded the cabinet to allow individual colonies to tax themselves, to cover the cost of their own defence and administration. This was his own personal initiative and was accepted by his more hardline colleagues. It was an attempt to produce a practical solution acceptable to both Britain and the colonies, but one doomed to failure. North's assumption that taxation was the root cause of the dispute had been overtaken by events. The response of the American congress to the British legislation of 1774 had been to deny the right of parliament to legislate for the colonies at all. Since North's conciliatory proposition, put to parliament in February 1775, did not concede even the right of taxation, merely the practice of it, his plan would have been deemed unacceptable in America even if news of it had arrived before the outbreak of war. And the mixed reception his proposal met at Westminster demonstrated that he would not have been able to offer more, even had he been so inclined. The offer was to be repeated the next year, as the terms the 1776 peace commission was empowered to concede, and remained the basis of British policy during the war. North intended, in the event of victory, to impose by force his offer of 1775, not a return to the *status quo*.

The American war The second part of the historical condemnation of Lord North as 'the minister who lost America' concerns Britain's defeat in the American War of Independence. But North was not the man who conducted the
war: that responsibility lay primarily with Lord George
Germain, who was appointed American secretary late in
1775 for that very purpose. It is not too fanciful an analogy
to suggest that he was to North what Pitt had been to Newcastle in the Seven Years' War, albeit with a different outcome. North himself had a threefold role: at the Treasury
to raise money and ensure supplies for the war, in the
Commons to act as chief government spokesman, and as
prime minister to hold together a disunited administration. As chancellor of the exchequer he had to raise
money for the war, while the Treasury was responsible for
organizing material supplies for the army in America.
There were occasional blunders over pricing, punctuality,
and storage, but the war was not lost because of administrative defects and supply problems. Nor can North be
held personally responsible for any shortcomings of strategy. He merely shared cabinet endorsement of Germain's
plans. Modern analyses of Britain's defeat, indeed, tend to
discount the issue of blame and to question whether Britain could ever have won the conflict in circumstances of
such geographical and logistical problems, even before
foreign intervention worsened the situation.

North's chief personal initiative was an attempt to salvage what he could after the disaster of Burgoyne's surrender of Britain's northern army at Saratoga in October
1777, by sending out another peace commission with an
offer of virtual home rule under the British flag. But by
then America would accept nothing except complete
independence. North thereafter could himself see no purpose in continuing the war, arguing that the cost even of
victory would be financially disastrous. 'Great Britain will
suffer more in the end than her enemies … not … by
defeats, but by an enormous expense, which will ruin her,
and will not in any degree be repaid by the most brilliant
victories': so he told the king, who always dismissed that
line of argument as 'weighing such events in the scale of a
tradesman' (*Correspondence of George III*, 4.77, 350). Neither
George III nor British opinion would accept such pusillan-
imity.

The intervention of France in 1778 and Spain in 1779
forced Britain into a more limited war strategy in America, of fighting only in the southern colonies and in the
West Indies. It was in North's eyes a war of attrition aiming at a stalemate, and he argued in parliament that the
avoidance of defeat might lead to an honourable peace.
The surrender of Cornwallis with Britain's southern army
at Yorktown in October 1781 ended such hopes. When told
the news by Germain, Lord North said, 'Oh God! It is all
over' (Wraxall, 2.435).

Ministerial decline and fall During these closing years of
the conflict North was so busy with the political and financial consequences of the war that he often excused himself from its conduct. At first the outbreak of the rebellion
had rallied popular support behind the king's government, but news of Saratoga led to a significant drop in the
Commons majority, from about 150 to about 80. Thenceforth the parliamentary opposition was back in business.
For much of 1779 North, who defeated a censure motion
on the Admiralty by only 34 votes in March, was rendered
despondent by a combination of circumstances: the
adverse course of the war, which that year saw a Franco-
Spanish invasion fleet parade in the English Channel;
cabinet vacancies and divisions caused by death and resignation; and widespread Irish discontent. Despair begat
inaction, a period of indecision which long coloured the
image of his entire ministry. By the end of the year North
had roused himself to solve the problems of both Ireland
and the cabinet, and he held his own in 1780 during one of
the great parliamentary battles of the century, over economic reform. That was an opposition campaign to take
advantage of public concern over government expenditure, by seeking abolition of such methods of political
corruption as sinecures. North stole much of the opposition thunder by creating his own investigative commission of accounts, and all the reform proposals were narrowly defeated during a Commons battle of several
weeks, though the passage on 6 April of Dunning's
motion about the influence of the crown led North vainly
once more to offer his resignation. The king would not let
him go, and nor did parliament yet want to replace him by
opponents who would concede American independence.

These parliamentary shocks led North to think of an
early general election, a decision confirmed by two subsequent events: good war news from America, notably the
capture of Charles Town, and the anti-Catholic Gordon
riots that beset London in June 1780, which would enable
him to reap the political dividend of reaction against such
disorder. North himself displayed personal courage when
a crowd threatened 10 Downing Street on 7 June. Although
he spent the record election sum for a minister of £50,000
in negotiations with patrons and candidates, his administration suffered a small net loss of seats. Nevertheless, his
majority was 82 in the first vote of the new parliament on
6 November 1780, and the fate of his ministry evidently
depended on the war. It was sealed when news came on 25
November 1781 of Yorktown. North himself promptly
accepted the need to concede American independence,
and so did most of his cabinet colleagues, despite George
III's obduracy. But no public statement could be made, for
that would be against the national interest and also would
bring down the ministry. North could make gestures, as
when on 14 December he deliberately left the Treasury
bench as Germain was advocating continuation of the
American war, 'mute eloquence', as diarist Wraxall commented (Wraxall, 2.468). Beyond such a parliamentary
charade he could not go. There followed the irony of his
defeat and resignation over a policy that he had abandoned but could not publicly disavow.

The last act of North's ministry was played out on the
appropriate stage of the House of Commons, during February and March 1782. Only once, on 27 February, was the
ministry defeated, over a motion to end offensive war in
America. The vain hope that George III would allow North
to negotiate peace kept him from resigning, but he now

lost the backing of MPs who had supported his stand against American independence. After his majority fell to nine on 15 March, a group of independent MPs informed him they were withdrawing support, and, facing defeat on the next vote of confidence on 20 March, he thereupon informed the king that he must resign:

> The Parliament have altered their sentiments, and as their sentiments whether just or erroneous must ultimately prevail, Your Majesty, having persevered, as long as possible, in what you thought right, can lose no honour if you yield at length, as some of the most renowned and most glorious of your predecessors have done, to the opinions and wishes of the House of Commons. (*Correspondence of George III*, 5.395)

Only with ungracious reluctance on 20 March itself did George III accept this constitutional lesson, accusing North of desertion. He, by contrast, in his Commons resignation speech that day, behaved with 'equanimity, suavity and dignity', diarist Wraxall recalled, thanking the house for its long and steady support, and declaring his readiness to answer for 'his public conduct' (Wraxall, 2.600–07).

The Fox–North coalition To many observers North's resignation must have seemed only a temporary setback to his career. Long years of patronage, esteem for his personal character, and calculation about his future prospects as an excellent parliamentarian and administrator still in favour with the king: these factors ensured that he took into opposition with him a party estimated in the autumn at 120 MPs. He then held the balance between the ministry of Lord Shelburne, Chatham's political heir, with 140 MPs, and the 90-strong party of Charles James *Fox, Rockingham's successor, who after a coalition ministry on North's fall had broken with Shelburne in July. The other 200 MPs were independent, undecided, or absentee, and it was evident that any two of these three parties would control parliament. The ministerial assumption that North would support the king's government overlooked two factors: the peace settlement Shelburne made with the American colonies failed to provide adequate safeguards for the loyalists, a matter over which North was naturally sensitive, and North's belief that George III had behaved unfairly towards him over the 1780 election debt. In May 1782 the king had thrown on his former minister personal responsibility for £17,000 of the cost. North could not possibly pay such a debt. His private income was £2500 a year, and the wardenship of the Cinque Ports yielded less than £3000. Not until late in 1784 did George III reluctantly accept that situation and honour the commitment, and the whole unhappy episode soured their relationship. But North's attitude did not matter, for William *Pitt, Shelburne's 23-year-old leader of the house, vetoed any approach to the man whom he, too young to know the real story, deemed responsible both for the American war and for allowing the king unconstitutional influence. Pitt had also become the main victim of North's raillery in the Commons, and henceforth his enmity was the dominant factor in North's political life.

North therefore allied with Fox to defeat the peace terms and bring down the Shelburne ministry in February 1783. Contemporary criticism of the Fox–North coalition was hypocritical or naïve, yet it was long echoed by historians. Since July 1782 it had been apparent that some coalition was inevitable, and alliances between former opponents were common during the period. But although Fox and North had never been personal enemies, their long parliamentary duel was too fresh in the memory. After several weeks of negotiation, during which George III vainly put personal pressure on North to break with Fox, the king surrendered and accepted the Fox–North coalition ministry in April 1783, headed in name by the duke of Portland. But he signified his displeasure by refusing to allow the creation of any peerages, and thereby blocked the ministerial plan for North to go to the House of Lords as spokesman there. Instead he resumed a place on the Treasury bench and became home secretary, a new post created in 1782, with son George as under-secretary, Fox being foreign secretary. Northites took only three of the seven cabinet places, despite their numerical superiority, and North was very much the sleeping partner in the ministry, literally in the Commons as well as metaphorically. But the fag-end of the session was notable for his refutation on 7 May 1783 of Pitt's charge that his own ministry had been in some way unconstitutional:

> I trust the candid and discerning part of the House will see that the attack is most unjust. I was not, when I was honoured with office, a minister of chance, or a creature of whom Parliament had no experience. I was found among you when I was so honoured. I had long been known to you. In consequence, I obtained your support; when that support was withdrawn, I ceased to be a minister. I was the creature of Parliament in my rise; when I fell I was its victim. I came among you without connection. It was here I was first known, you raised me up, you pulled me down. (Cobbett, *Parl. hist.*, 23.847–61)

The king was merely biding his time for an opportunity to strike, and his chance came with Fox's India Bill, intended to remedy North's 1773 act. North took no part in its formulation, but it sealed his political fate, when George III virtually coerced the House of Lords into rejecting it, on 15 December 1783. Two days later in the Commons, North attacked such royal interference as threatening 'the privileges of Parliament and the rights of the people' (Cobbett, *Parl. hist.*, 24.199, 203–5), and, along with Fox, was dismissed from office that evening by a royal message, the king deeming the customary personal interview too unpleasant.

Pitt formed what was a minority ministry, denounced repeatedly as such by North, until a general election was called in the spring of 1784. The coalition then lost nearly 100 seats, North's personal following being reduced from 112 to 69 MPs. He had behaved well during this political crisis of 1782–4 as both a politician and a person. He never wavered in his view of the constitution, that in the end the king should bow to the will of the Commons. He had left and returned to office on this principle, and was genuinely indignant when George III and Pitt broke the constitution as he saw it. His character matched his political integrity, for he bore no grudge for past Foxite attacks, refused to desert his new ally, and behaved correctly to an ungrateful sovereign. It is a paradox that this creditable behaviour left him with a tarnished reputation and a ruined career.

Opposition to Pitt It was not obvious that North's political career was over by 1784. Realization that he was the only possible alternative prime minister acceptable to George III helped to prompt Pittite attacks on him, centred on the political millstone of the American War of Independence, 'their favourite hobby-horse' he complained in 1786 (Cobbett, *Parl. hist.*, 29.1044). In the first year of the new parliament he showed himself to be still an effective debater, playing a major role in the successful attack on Pitt's Irish trade proposals of 1785, and making on 16 June 1784 what some thought his best ever speech, against parliamentary reform. He was the most formidable critic of Pitt's Reform Bill of 1785, denouncing it on 18 April as 'a direct attack on the British constitution', and scornfully pointing out the lack of public support for the idea: 'What horrid sound of silence doth assail my ear' (Wraxall, 5.294).

This year, 1785, was the end of the high plateau of North's political life. In the 1780s he suffered from bad health, which greatly reduced his weight, and his weak eyesight deteriorated into virtual blindness by 1787. Such physical infirmities, coupled with the realization that he had no political future, caused him to withdraw increasingly into private life and appear in parliament only for subjects of particular interest to him. His personal following in the Commons, weakened by deaths and desertions, dwindled within a few years to about a dozen. He did exert himself to attack Pitt's Regency Bill at the time of the king's illness of 1788–9, on the constitutional ground that parliament alone had no right to pass laws. North's conservative instincts, shown in his hostility to parliamentary reform and later characterized by his opinion that nothing good would come out of the French Revolution, were also demonstrated by his defence of the privileged position of the Church of England. He had the prejudices of a devout Anglican, and when prime minister had permitted only token concessions to dissenters. Now, in 1787 and 1789, North opposed motions for repeal of the Test Act that barred dissenters from public office, claiming on 28 March 1787 that the constitution would be endangered if the Church of England were deprived of its monopoly position. A similar declaration on 8 May 1789 marked what, on doctors' orders, was his last appearance in the Commons. But he did make several speeches in the House of Lords after succeeding his father as second earl of Guilford in 1790. Believing from his own experience when prime minister that Russia should be cultivated as an ally, he attacked Pitt's proposed support of Turkey in 1791, and a year later, on 20 February 1792, offered this piece of wisdom as his last public political pronouncement: 'It was the interest of this country, to keep up a good understanding with Russia' (Cobbett, *Parl. hist.*, 29.855–60).

A family man Although North remained politically active to the end, a happy family environment was the keynote of his last decade. In a sense the wheel had turned full circle, for North, with a father who married three times,

had grown up in a large family, comprising six children even after death had taken its toll. They included a stepbrother, Lord Dartmouth, later his cabinet colleague for a decade, and a half-brother, Brownlow *North (1741–1820), whose career in the church prospered under North's patronage; in 1781 he became bishop of Winchester. Such a family setting fostered North's amiability and happy gift for friendship. Also already apparent in his youth were indolence and carelessness, traits that presumably explained the financial problems that beset him even when, as from the 1770s, his income ought to have sufficed for his needs. Another legacy from childhood was respect for authority, inculcated by a strict father. North was dutiful not only to his sovereign but also to his miserly, domineering parent even when he himself was a paterfamilias.

There were four sons, one of whom died young. The other three, George [see below], Francis [see below], and Frederick *North (1766–1827), colonial governor and philhellene, were all successively earls of Guilford. There were also three daughters: Catherine Anne (1760–1817), Anne (1764–1832), and Charlotte (1770–1849), all of whom made politically important marriages. Catherine married in 1789 the politician and diarist Sylvester Douglas, Lord Glenbervie; Anne became the third wife of John Baker Holroyd, first earl of Sheffield, in 1798; and Charlotte married the Hon. John Lindsay (d. 1826) in 1800.

North's resignation in 1782 freed him for enjoyment of social and family life that not even blindness could spoil, as Horace Walpole noted after a visit to Bushy Park in 1787:

> Lord North's spirits, good humour, wit, sense, drollery are as perfect as ever—the unremitting attention of Lady North and his children, most touching. Mr North leads him about, Miss North sits constantly by him, carves meat, watches his every motion … If ever loss of sight could be compensated, it is by so affectionate a family. (*Letters of Horace Walpole*, 14.27)

The happy dinner party North gave on the evening of his resignation set the tone. Contemporary memoirs and family recollections portray his London home in Grosvenor Square as a hive of social activity. Edward Gibbon had already written, in 1775, 'If they turned out Lord North tomorrow, they will still have him one of the best companions in the kingdom.' And he later recalled of the 1780s, 'The house in London which I frequented with the most pleasure was that of Lord North; after the loss of power and of sight, he was still happy in himself and his friends' (Whiteley, 15).

Not until the death of his father in 1790, when he inherited estates in five counties worth well over £10,000 a year, did North become a rich man. The second earl of Guilford did not long enjoy his new status and wealth. Early in 1792 symptoms of dropsy became obvious, and by July he knew his end was near. On 5 August 1792 he died quietly at his home, 41 Grosvenor Square, London, after taking leave of his family. He was buried at All Saints' Church, Wroxton, on 14 August. His widow died on 17 January 1797.

Historical reputation 'The worst prime minister since Lord North' was for long a ritual insult in British politics. This simplistic condemnation stems from his role as the man responsible for Britain's greatest disaster in modern history, the loss of the American colonies. His reputation also suffered, in a more sophisticated and somewhat contradictory fashion, as a main target of the long-fashionable whig interpretation of history, wherein he featured as the dummy prime minister whose passive acquiescence permitted George III to restore direct royal power. Modern historians eschew such prejudices. North is now perceived as a prime minister in the mould of Walpole and Pelham: head of the king's government, chairman of the cabinet, ministerial spokesman in the House of Commons, financial expert as chancellor of the exchequer, and altogether the man ultimately responsible for policy decisions, 'the Minister' or 'the Premier' in contemporary parlance. It was a heavy load to bear, in troubled times, and in many respects North was the success belied by his reputation. He was one of Britain's greatest parliamentarians, and perhaps the most popular prime minister ever within the House of Commons itself. He showed great skill as a financier and administrator. He coped well with imperial problems in Ireland, India, and Canada. His ideas and policies show that he might have achieved more here, and also in reshaping the administrative structure of British government, but for the American war. In that regard North is in the position of a captain whose ship sank under him, and who, whether fairly or not, must pay the ultimate historical penalty.

Successors North's first son, **George Augustus North**, third earl of Guilford (1757–1802), was born on 11 September 1757. He was educated at Eton College (1766–74) and at Trinity College, Oxford, and was an MP from 1778 until he succeeded to his father's peerage on 5 August 1792. A supporter of his father's ministry, he sat for the Treasury borough of Harwich (1778–84) and was given court office as secretary and comptroller of the queen's household on 13 January 1781. Many of his personal friendships, however, were with Foxite whigs, and he played a key role in arranging the Fox–North coalition, the new allies first meeting at his house on 14 February 1783. In the coalition ministry he was under-secretary to his father at the Home Office, and was named as one of the seven commissioners in the East India Bill. He lost both his offices when the coalition was dismissed in December 1783, and his seat at the 1784 general election. But he was then returned by a friend for Wootton Bassett, and sat briefly for Petersfield in 1790 before taking the family seat at Banbury, when his father went to the Lords, being known himself as Lord North between 1790 and 1792. He was a recognizable if lesser version of his father, good-natured and easy-going, with a sense of humour and a loud voice. He blossomed as a parliamentary speaker after 1790 in both Commons and Lords, and became a Foxite as his father faded from the scene. Pitt, however, saw him as a potential recruit, and offered him the governor-generalship of India in July 1792, the month before he succeeded his father. But the new Lord Guilford stayed with Fox and sometimes led for the opposition in the Lords, until ill health ended his political career about 1797. He married, on 24 September 1785, Maria (d. 1794), daughter of George *Hobart, MP and later third earl of Buckinghamshire. This marriage met with family disapproval, since the bride was dowerless, but his grandfather continued the £800 allowance he was already paying. Only one of their four children survived infancy, Maria (1793–1841), who married in 1818 the second marquess of Bute. After his wife died on 23 April 1794, Guilford married on 28 February 1796 Susan (d. 1837), daughter of banker Thomas Coutts, who brought a dowry of £150,000; they had two surviving daughters. Guilford died on 20 April 1802 at Stratton Street, Piccadilly, London, of a long-term injury caused by a fall from a horse. He was buried at Wroxton. His widow survived until 24 September 1837.

North's second son, **Francis North**, fourth earl of Guilford (1761–1817), was born on 25 December 1761. After attending Eton College he entered the army as a cornet in 1777: he became a major in 1783 and a lieutenant-colonel in 1794, when he retired. He was interested in the theatre, and wrote a play, 'The Kentish Baron', performed at the Haymarket in 1791. On 20 April 1802 he succeeded his brother as earl of Guilford. On 10 July 1810, when he was described by Lady Charlotte Bury as 'an old drunken man' (GEC, *Peerage*, 6.211), he married Maria (d. 1821), fifth daughter of Thomas Boycott of Rudge Hall, Shropshire. He died childless at Pisa on 11 January 1817, and was buried, probably at Wroxton, on 28 March. His widow died on 30 December 1821.

                      PETER D. G. THOMAS

Sources P. D. G. Thomas, *Lord North* (1976) · P. Whiteley, *Lord North: the prime minister who lost America* (1996) · A. Valentine, *Lord North*, 2 vols. (1967) · W. B. Pemberton, *Lord North* (1938) · C. D. Smith, *The early career of Lord North the prime minister* (1979) · HoP, *Commons, 1754–90* · P. D. G. Thomas, *Tea party to independence: the third phase of the American Revolution, 1773–1776* (1991) · J. Cannon, *The Fox–North coalition: crisis of the constitution, 1782–4* (1969) · P. D. G. Thomas, *The House of Commons in the eighteenth century* (1971) · GEC, *Peerage* · J. E. D. Binney, *British public finance and administration, 1774–92* (1958) · BL, Warren Hastings papers, Add. MSS 28973–29236 · *Autobiography and political correspondence of Augustus Henry, third duke of Grafton*, ed. W. R. Anson (1898) · *The diaries of Sylvester Douglas (Lord Glenbervie)*, ed. F. Bickley, 2 vols. (1928) · Cobbett, *Parl. hist.* · *The correspondence of King George the Third from 1760 to December 1783*, ed. J. Fortescue, 6 vols. (1927–8) · *The diary and letters of His Excellency Thomas Hutchinson*, ed. P. O. Hutchinson, 2 vols. (1883–6) · *The letters of Horace Walpole, fourth earl of Orford*, ed. P. Toynbee, 16 vols. (1903–5) · H. Walpole, *Memoirs of the reign of King George the Third*, ed. G. F. R. Barker, 4 vols. (1894) · N. W. Wraxall, *Historical memoirs of his own time*, new edn, 4 vols. (1836) · N. W. Wraxall, *Posthumous memoirs of his own time*, 2nd edn, 3 vols. (1836) · *Sir Henry Cavendish's Debates of the House of Commons during the thirteenth parliament of Great Britain*, ed. J. Wright, 2 vols. (1841–3)

Archives BL, corresp. and papers, Add. MSS 61860–61876, 61979–61987 · Bodl. Oxf., corresp. and papers · Bodl. Oxf., financial papers · East Kent Archives Centre, Dover, papers · PRO, papers, T 49 · U. Mich., Clements L., papers relating to America | BL, corresp. with Lord Auckland, Add. MSS 46490–46491, 46519 · BL, corresp. with marquess of Buckingham, Add. MSS 40177–40178 · BL, letters to Francis Drake, Add. MS 46834 · BL, letters to Sir Frederick Haldimand, Add. MSS 21705, 21732, 21735 · BL, letters to Lord Harwicke, Add. MSS 35424, 35614–35620, *passim* · BL, letters to Charles Jenkinson, loan 72 · BL, corresp. with duke of Newcastle, etc., Add. MSS 32729–33101, *passim* · BL OIOC, corresp. with Philip Francis, MSS Eur. C 8, D 18, E 12–22, F 5–6 · Bodl. Oxf., letters to first

earl of Guilford · CKS, corresp. with Sir Jeffrey Amherst · CKS, letters to first earl of Guilford · E. Sussex RO, letters to first earl of Sheffield · JRL, letters to Thrale Piozzi · L. Cong., letters to third duke of Portland · N. Yorks. CRO, corresp. with Lord Bolton · NA Scot., Adam MSS · NMM, corresp. with Lord Sandwich · NRA, priv. coll., corresp. with William Adam, etc. · NRA, priv. coll., letters to Sir Ralph Payne and Lady Payne · PRO, corresp. with Sir Jeffrey Amherst · PRO, corresp. with Lord Stafford, PRO 30/29 · Royal Arch. · Sheff. Arch., corresp. with Edmund Burke · Staffs. RO, letters to Lord Dartmouth · Suffolk RO, Bury St Edmunds, letters to duke of Grafton · U. Nott. L., corresp. with duke of Newcastle
Likenesses P. Batoni, oils, 1752–6, NPG · J. Reynolds, oils, c.1756, priv. coll. · N. Dance, oils, c.1773, NPG · line engraving, pubd 1773, BM, NPG · N. Dance, pastel drawing, 1773–4, NPG [see illus.] · J. S. Copley, crayon drawing, c.1779, Library of the Boston Athenaeum, Boston · J. Downman, watercolour drawing, 1780, V&A · Wedgwood medallion, c.1782 (after M. Gosset), Wedgwood Museum, Stoke-on-Trent · J. Sayers, stipple, pubd 1783 (*The mask*), NPG · J. Jones, stipple, pubd 1787 (after A. Ramsay, 1761), BM, NPG · J. Flaxman, bust, 1806, Examination Schools, Oxford · J. Bacon, marble bust, Bodl. Oxf. · W. Behnes, bust, Eton · J. S. Copley, drawing, Metropolitan Museum of Modern Art, New York · J. S. Copley, group portrait, oils (*The collapse of the earl of Chatham in the House of Lords, 7 July 1778*), Tate collection; on loan to NPG · N. Dance, oils, NPG; version, Bodl. Oxf., Trinity College, Oxford · studio of Reynolds, oils, Petworth House, Sussex · J. Sayers, etchings, NPG · caricatures (political satires), BM · plaster medallion (after J. Tassie), Scot. NPG · prints, BM, NPG
Wealth at death in 1790 inherited father's estates, value over £10,000 p.a.: Valentine, *Lord North*; Whiteley, *Lord North*

North, Frederick, fifth earl of Guilford (1766–1827),

colonial governor and philhellene, was born on 7 February 1766, the youngest of the three surviving sons of Frederick *North, second earl of Guilford (1732–1792) (who as Lord North was prime minister), and his wife, Anne (d. 1797), daughter of George Speke. His health was always poor and much of his childhood was spent in southern Europe, acquiring a lifelong facility for languages. He was educated at Eton (1775–82) and Christ Church, Oxford, where his classical abilities were soon recognized. He was elected a student of Christ Church but was in residence only for one term (Michaelmas 1782) before taking indefinite leave of absence, resigning his studentship in 1786. He was created DCL by Oxford in July 1793, and again by diploma in October 1819, sharing with the second Earl Granville the curious distinction of twice being awarded the same degree.

After leaving Oxford, North's exact movements are uncertain, though in May 1788 he was in Madrid, where the ambassador, Lord Auckland, encountered him attired in the dress of a Spanish mule-driver. His philhellenism developed during a tour of the Ionian Islands and Greece, probably in 1791. He lived among the inhabitants of Ithaca, where his imagination was stirred by his recognition of scenes from Homer's *Odyssey*. Crossing to the mainland he visited Tiryns, Mycenae, Athens, and Mount Athos, before going on to Smyrna, Cyprus, Alexandria, Jerusalem, and Constantinople. He is known to have given money to assist a school at Preveza on the Greek mainland. He composed a Pindaric ode in honour of the Empress Catherine of Russia following the treaty of Galatz (August 1791), which concluded the war between Russia and Turkey. But his philhellenic enthusiasm was not

Frederick North, fifth earl of Guilford (1766–1827), by Jean-Auguste-Dominique Ingres, 1815

limited to the classical Greek heritage. He was already familiar with the ritual of the Orthodox church when he visited Corfu, then under Venetian rule, early in 1792. On 23 January 1792 (some sources give 1791) he was received into the Orthodox church at the residence of the protopope of Corfu, Dimitrios Petrettinos; North enjoined strict secrecy for fear of alienating his family, though an eye-witness account of the baptism, recorded by North's sponsor, George Prosalendis, was published in 1879. He then spent Lent in a monastery on the island of Levkas before returning to England, arriving hours after his father's death in August.

In September 1792 North succeeded to his father's parliamentary seat, the pocket borough of Banbury, and was identified with the Portland whigs, opposing recognition of the revolutionary regime in France. He was possibly the only member of the Orthodox church to have sat in the House of Commons, though his conversion was not publicly known. He was a reluctant speaker in debate and vacated the seat without regret in March 1794 on being appointed to the controllership of customs in the port of London. He was elected FRS and became a member of the Eumelian Club, which met at the Blenheim tavern in Bond Street. In 1795 he went to Corsica as secretary to Sir Gilbert Elliot, the viceroy during the British occupation of the island. His amiable manners impressed both Pope Pius VI and Maria Caroline, queen of the Two Sicilies. Corsican patriots found him conciliatory, and Elliot recommended him for further promotion.

In 1798 Henry Dundas appointed North the first British

governor of Ceylon, which had been captured from the Dutch two years earlier. On arriving there in October 1798 he immediately set about implementing the programme of administrative reforms recommended by a committee chaired by Brigadier-General Pierre Frederick de Meuron in 1797. He reorganized the executive and judiciary but was resented by the existing Madras civil servants, who ran the island until 1801, when he cracked down on their malpractices. In his drive against corruption he clashed with his chief secretary, Hugh Cleghorn, who returned to England in 1800 following allegations of fraud in the government pearl fisheries. He enforced the abolition of slavery. After the island became a crown colony in 1801 he took part in establishing the Ceylon civil service, which gained a reputation for probity. He created a medical department, which organized vaccinations, and a system of orphanages and poor relief, and was responsible for setting up a postal service on the island. He extended the system of schools set up by the Dutch. His major administrative failure was his attempt at land tenure reform. Both his humane policies and his entertainments in the governor's residence made him a popular figure, whose benevolent rule was referred to by the chaplain, James Cordiner, in his *Description of Ceylon* (1807).

North's governorship was blighted by his attempt to secure control over the independent kingdom of Kandy in the interior of the island. In 1800 his embassy, under the command of Major-General Hay MacDowall, failed to overawe the younger ruler of Kandy, Sri Wikrama Raja Sinha. He then imprudently encouraged intrigues against the king by the latter's chief adviser, Pilima Talauya. When these, too, were unsuccessful he allowed himself to be dragged into hostilities, declaring war on 29 January 1803, a decision for which he was later rebuked by Lord Hobart. MacDowall, with whom North enjoyed a good working relationship, occupied Kandy in February 1803, but his supply lines were cut and his army was severely weakened by jungle fever. Most of the army was forced to make a humiliating withdrawal in April 1803, leaving a small garrison in the capital of Kandy under the command of Major Adam Davie. Surprised by a Kandyan assault during the night of 23–4 June 1803, the garrison force surrendered and was massacred. MacDowall was replaced by Major-General David Douglas Wemyss, who quarrelled both with North, over financial matters, and with the island's judiciary. During his last months in office, which were bedevilled by recriminations between the military and civil authorities, an inconclusive war was waged, leaving him near to breakdown. His pleas to London to be relieved on health grounds were finally granted in July 1805 with the arrival of Sir Thomas Maitland as a replacement. Maitland's subsequent dispatches, critical of North's administration, further undermined his reputation. North himself was uncertain 'whether I have acted like a good politician or a great nincompoop' (Hulugalle, 16).

On returning to Europe, North resumed his travels, crossing the continent in a diagonal route from Spain to Russia. He settled in Italy, but revisited Greece, where at Patras in July 1810 he met Byron, who was dismissive of his philhellenism. Some of the hostile accounts of him originated among Byron's circle. In 1812 J. C. Hobhouse recorded with glee a story that at Algiers North had asked the dey for permission to see some of the women in his harem; 'He is so ugly, let him see them all', the dey reputedly replied (J. C. H. Broughton, *Recollections of a Long Life: by Lord Broughton*, ed. Lady Dorchester, 1, 1909, 36). His appearance was said to be ramshackle, and a surviving engraving (reproduced in Powell, opposite p. 128) indicates his tendency to corpulence, though it also suggests his genial countenance. He was an excellent linguist and conversationalist, always willing to adopt the customs and usages of whichever country he was living in. After dining with him in 1819 in the company of professors and waiters of various nationalities, Charles James Napier recorded, 'Lord Guilford was very pleasant, addressing every person in a different language, and always in that which the person addressed did not understand' (Ferriman, 94).

In 1814 Guilford was elected president of the Philomousos Society of Athens, founded in that year to encourage the spread of education among the Greeks. In his statement of acceptance, composed in Attic Greek, he styled himself 'an Athenian citizen' (Ware, 254 n.). In the following year, when the treaty of Vienna confirmed the British protectorate over the Ionian Islands, North had had discussions with Ioannis Kapodistrias, later the prime minister of Greece, who urged the foundation of an institution of higher education on the islands. The Ionian University, or Ionian Academy, with modern Greek as its medium of instruction, was to act as a centre of learning for all Greeks, the mainland still being under Turkish rule.

Though of frail health North outlived his elder brothers, succeeding to the title fifth earl of Guilford on 11 January 1817, and with it property worth £18,000 a year and a seat at Wroxton Abbey, Oxfordshire. This placed him in a position to further the establishment of the Ionian Academy, for which provision was made in the constitutional charter for the Ionian Islands (1817). He was created GCMG in 1819 by the prince regent who, in the following year (and by then George IV), felt aggrieved by the evidence in favour of Queen Caroline which Guilford and his sister Lady Charlotte Lindsay gave at her trial. In 1820, through the influence of his cousin, Lord Bathurst, secretary for the colonies, he was made director of education in the Ionian Islands and set about bringing to fruition his scheme for a Hellenic university, initially favouring a site on Ithaca, where there was no town with temptations to distract the students from their books. Guilford, who had brought his own secretary, Spiridon Trikoupes (later a Greek foreign minister), to be educated in England, paid to send promising Greek students to universities in Europe so as to train up a staff of Greek-speaking professors. Some were lost to the war for Greek independence: 'Three hundred pounds worth of my theology carried off by a cannonball' was his reflection on one of his intended professors who fell in battle against the Turks (Ferriman, 99). He renewed his own studies, being admitted as a nobleman at Downing College, Cambridge, and received the degree of honorary LLD in 1821.

Sir Thomas Maitland, the high commissioner, with whom North resumed an uneasy relationship, was determined to maintain the neutrality of the Ionian Islands during the Greek war of independence, and obstructed the proposed university. Its foundation was delayed until after his death. The university's eventual location on Corfu, was at Maitland's insistence, though proximity to hospitals and courts there was an undoubted asset for students of law and medicine. In November 1823 the legislative assembly appointed Guilford *archōn* (or chancellor) of the university, which was constituted with four faculties (theology, law, medicine, and philosophy) on 17 May 1824. The opening ceremony of the Ionian Academy, 'the first Greek university' (Henderson, ix), was notable for the costumes worn by the professors and students, designed by Guilford himself from the example of ancient Athenian statues. His insistence on this peculiar academic dress attracted much ridicule when news reached England, Napier remarking 'He goes about dressed like Plato, with a gold band around his mad pate and flowing drapery of a purple hue' (Ferriman, 94–5). He presided over admissions examinations, sat in on lectures, subsidized the stipends of professors, and supported students with bursaries. His own extensive collections of books and manuscripts, notable for their works in modern Greek, formed the nucleus of the library. After three academic sessions Guilford's poor health forced him to return to England, where he died at the house of his sister Anne, the countess dowager of Sheffield, in Portland Place, London, on 14 October 1827. On his deathbed, to the disapproval of his relatives, he received communion according to the Greek rite from Father Smirnov, chaplain to the Russian embassy. A memorial service was held in the church of the Speliotissa, Corfu.

Controversy surrounded Guilford's will, dated 25 September 1827, and codicil added on 13 October 1827, bequeathing his books and manuscripts to the Ionian Academy on condition that the Ionian government endowed the university with a specified annual income. His personal heir, the second earl of Sheffield, took the failure to meet this condition as a cause to demand the return of Guilford's library, which was sold at auction in London. The mortification of Andreas Papadopoulos Vretos, whom Guilford had brought to Kerkyra to be librarian, at the loss of so large a part of the academy's library was evident in his *Biographical-Historical Recollections Concerning Frederick, Earl of Guilford*, published in Greek and Italian at Athens in 1846. Guilford's executors also stopped payment of the stipends and bursaries to members of the Ionian Academy, which declined after his death (the University of Athens was founded in 1837) and finally ceased to exist in 1864 when the islands were united with Greece. Guilford's enduring achievement was his part in the re-establishment of modern Greek as a language of scholarship and in the education of a generation

of Greek-speaking lawyers, doctors, scholars, and civil servants. On this account he was revered by Greek writers, though his own family and fellow countrymen were more inclined to dismiss him as an eccentric.

M. C. CURTHOYS

Sources DNB · GEC, *Peerage* · Z. D. Ferriman, *Lord Guilford* (1919), vol. 6 of *Some English philhellenes* (1917–20) · HoP, *Commons, 1790–1820*, 4.676–7 · K. Ware, 'The fifth earl of Guilford (1766–1827) and his secret conversion to the Orthodox church', *The Orthodox churches and the West*, ed. D. Baker, SCH, 13 (1976), 247–56 · C. R. De Silva, *Ceylon under the British occupation, 1795–1833*, 2 vols. (1942); repr. (1953–62) · H. A. J. Hulugalle, *British governors of Ceylon* (1963) · G. Powell, *The Kandyan wars: the British Army in Ceylon, 1803–1818* (1973); repr. (New Delhi, 1984) · P. D. Kannangara, *The history of the Ceylon civil service, 1802–1833* (1966) · G. P. Henderson, *The Ionian Academy* (1988) · Foster, *Alum. Oxon.* · Venn, *Alum. Cant.* · E. A. Smith, *A queen on trial: the affair of Queen Caroline* (1993) · J. Ingamells, ed., *A dictionary of British and Irish travellers in Italy, 1701–1800* (1997)

Archives American School of Classical Studies, Athens, Gennadius Library, corresp. · BL, family corresp., Add. MSS 61981–61983 · BL, MSS, Add. MS 61985 · Bodl. Oxf., corresp. and papers; travel journal · Corfu Literary Society, Corfu, corresp. and papers relating to Ionian Islands · East Kent Archives Centre, Dover, corresp. and papers | BL, MSS relating to Guilford's library, Add. MSS 61984–61985 · Bucks. RLSS, letters to Lord Hobart · E. Sussex RO, letters to first earl of Sheffield · JRL, letters to Sir Codrington Carrington · NL Scot., corresp. with Robert Liston; corresp. with William Robertson · NL Wales, corresp. with Lord Clive · NMM, letters to first earl of Minto

Likenesses T. Hickey, drawing, 1799, Stratfield Saye, Hampshire · J.-A.-D. Ingres, drawing, 1815, Art Gallery of New South Wales, Sydney, Australia [*see illus.*] · J.-A.-D. Ingres, lithograph, 1815, BM, NPG · Calosgouros, bust, *c*.1827, Corfu · Prosalendis, bust, *c*.1827, Corfu · bust, *c*.1860; formerly in the Palace Gardens, Athens, 1919 · W. T. Fry, stipple (after J. Jackson, 1817), NPG

North, George (*fl.* 1561–1581), translator, about whose early life nothing is known, was an enterprising writer, who exploited the flurry of public interest in Scandinavia, spurred by the courtship of Queen Elizabeth by Erik XIV of Sweden, with his first publication, *The Description of Swedland, Gotland, and Finland* (1561), dedicated to Thomas Stukeley, whose hospitality he had enjoyed. The first work in English devoted solely to these countries, the book claims to be 'collected out of sundrye authors', although close inspection shows it to be almost entirely a verbatim translation from Sebastian Münster's *Cosmographia*. Nevertheless, North feels licensed to enliven his translation with occasional creativity. At one point, for example, the single word 'consenescens' ('growing old') is rendered thus: 'as crooked age, with creeping pace overtook her (whose stalking steps none can over run)'. Nor does he omit his sources' more fanciful declarations: paraphrasing Joannes Magnus's *Historia*, North begins a list of the ancient kings of the Goths and Swedes with Magog, a nephew to Noah's son Japhet. In a special dedication copy for Gyllenstierna, Erik's ambassador, North calls himself 'unlettered but well-meaning' (see Swann).

Having apparently taken service with John, count of Tenczin, North was dispatched to Princess Cecilia of Sweden in February 1564, but their amicable relationship soured after various monetary dealings, and Cecilia later wrote to Elizabeth calling North 'a wicked man'. An angry lady-in-waiting to Cecilia claimed that when in Sweden

North masqueraded as 'a fine gentleman' (he describes himself as 'gentleman' on the title-pages of his books), yet when the Swedish entourage reached England he proved to be 'a tailor's son in London' (corroborative evidence for this is unavailable; see Swann). In 1569 North crossed to La Rochelle and, joining the prince of Orange in the hope of booty, was involved in various marches and skirmishes. His second book, *The Philosopher of the Court* (1575), translated from Philbert of Vienne, inveighs in its prologue against 'foolish and brutish youth' at court, 'wild and rash till the scum and filth of youthful heat be boiled out of them'. Dedicated to Sir Christopher Hatton, it contains 'the delightful instructions of philosophy and manner how to live', as well as infrequent verse translations from Latin authors. A third translation, from Henricus Stephanus's 'Apology on Herodotus', entitled *The Stage of Popish Toyes*, was also dedicated to Hatton and printed at London in 1581.   ROSS KENNEDY

Sources M. W. S. Swann, 'Introduction', in G. North, *The description of Swedland, Gotland, and Finland*, Scholars' Facsimiles and Reprints (1946) · Tanner, *Bibl. Brit.-Hib.*, 549

North, George (1707–1772), numismatist, was born on 26 May 1707 in Aldersgate Street, London, the second son and third of seven surviving children of George North (d. 1754), pewterer, and Elizabeth, whose surname was probably Morris. He was educated at St Paul's School and, in 1725, entered Corpus Christi College, Cambridge, where he graduated BA in 1728, MA in 1744. He was ordained deacon in 1729 and officiated as curate at Codicote and nearby Welwyn in Hertfordshire. In 1743 he was presented to the vicarage of Codicote and lived there, a bachelor, for the rest of his life. He became chaplain to Lord Cathcart in 1744. His widowed father spent his last years living with him in the vicarage, where he died in 1754.

North was a keen student and collector of English coins. He corresponded on English numismatics and antiquities with a wide circle of antiquaries, including Andrew Coltee Ducarel, whom he encouraged to travel to Normandy in 1754. North was the 'friend' to whom Ducarel addressed his subsequent *Tour of Normandy*. He first attracted the attention of Francis Wise and other antiquaries with *An answer to a scandalous libel intituled The impertinence and imposture of modern antiquaries displayed*, published anonymously in 1741 in response to a pamphlet probably written by William Asplin, vicar of Banbury. North, who was described by John Nichols as a 'well-looking jolly man … much valued by his acquaintance' (Nichols, *Lit. anecdotes*, 5.469), was elected a fellow of the Society of Antiquaries of London in 1742. He took an active part in the society's affairs and was opposed to its seeking a royal charter in 1750, as it would lead to greater costs and an increased membership. He did much research into the Elizabethan origins of the society, but in 1765, believing himself to be dangerously ill, he gave orders that most of his papers 'be indiscriminately burnt … from a conviction how ungenerously such things are commonly used after a person's decease' (ibid., 5.466).

North compiled a number of catalogues of coin collections, including that of Ducarel in 1744. According to

Nichols, North's notes on Joseph Ames's *Typographical Antiquities* (1747) were used by William Herbert in his extensive revision of Ames's work. North published a brief monograph on Arabic numerals in *Archaeologia* (10, 1748, 360). He was a member of the Spalding Gentlemen's Society. In 1750 he toured the west of England, visiting Dorchester, Wilton, and Stonehenge, and in 1751 he went to Bath in search of a cure for his ailments. He died on 17 June 1772, aged sixty-five, at his vicarage at Codicote, and was buried at the east end of Codicote churchyard. In addition to his cabinet of coins, he left his fine library, which included a number of his unpublished tracts, to Anthony Askew and his executor, Michael Lort. The help and encouragement he gave to fellow antiquaries gave him a greater claim to fame than his published work.

                                        W. W. WROTH, *rev.* ROBIN MYERS

Sources Nichols, *Lit. anecdotes*, 5.426ff., 468ff. · Nichols, *Illustrations* · J. Evans, *A history of the Society of Antiquaries* (1956) · parish register, Christchurch Greyfriars, Newgate Street, London, 7/6/1707 [baptism] · will of George North senior, PRO, PROB 11/811/256 · Venn, *Alum. Cant.*
Archives Bodl. Oxf., catalogue and letters | BL, letters to Robert Masters, Egerton MS 2166
Wealth at death see will, PRO, PROB 11/979/267

North, George Augustus, **third earl of Guilford** (1757–1802). *See under* North, Frederick, second earl of Guilford (1732–1792).

North, Sir John (*c*.1550–1597), soldier and traveller, was the eldest son of Roger *North, second Baron North (1531–1600), of Kirtling, Cambridgeshire, and Winifred (d. 1578), daughter of Richard *Rich, first Baron Rich, and widow of Sir Henry Dudley. The second Lord North, courtier, diplomat and soldier, was one of the most prominent puritan nobles, *éminence grise* of the earl of Leicester (leader of the so-called political puritans). However, as it turned out, John inherited neither his father's subtlety, nor his maternal grandfather's ability to conceal his opinions.

North was probably born about 1550 and was admitted to Peterhouse, Cambridge, in 1562, despite being 'of immature age'. He was put in the charge of John Whitgift, later archbishop of Canterbury; when the latter became master of Trinity in 1567, North also changed colleges. He took his MA in May 1572. Later that year he was admitted to Gray's Inn, where his father had also gone as a young man. Three years later, he went to Italy to finish his education. He was granted a licence to pass beyond the seas for two years in May 1575. North did not leave until September, but still arrived in Italy in October 1575. He stayed exactly two years, finally arriving back home in November 1577. The entries in his interesting journal of the trip are initially in English, but by the end are entirely in Italian (Bodl. Oxf., MS Add. C.193). He had passed through the Netherlands and the Palatinate on his outward journey, where he met veterans of the Dutch revolt. The spring following his return, North crossed the North Sea again, this time to fight with the Dutch as a gentleman volunteer. How long he served at this time is uncertain, but by 1580 he was back in England. It was probably in this year that he married Dorothy (d. 1618), daughter of Sir Valentine

*Dale, master of requests. A son was born in 1582 and named Dudley [see North, Dudley, third Baron North], after his godfather, the earl of Leicester. There were five more children: Elizabeth, who married William Hussey; Sir John; Gilbert; Roger *North, the well-known navigator; and Mary, who married Sir Francis Coningsby.

In February 1582 North was among the large number of English nobles and gentry, led by Leicester, who accompanied the duc d'Anjou to the Netherlands for his installation as governor-general. Over the next two months North attracted much comment by his 'great pursuit of a commission for an English regiment' (PRO, SP 83/15, fol. 232). However, his determination got him a commission from Anjou in May 1582 for a regiment of 1000 foot (though its actual strength never exceeded 400). North intended his lieutenant-colonel to be the veteran Thomas Cotton, but when he obtained his own regiment, North was left without an experienced deputy's advice: his senior captain, Ralph Cromwell, lacked Cotton's social status and probably felt obliged to defer to a future baron.

North quarrelled with the other English colonels in Dutch service, refusing to accept John Norris's claim to seniority, despite the latter's experience. However, he assisted Norris in his celebrated covering action at Ghent in late 1582 and, after Anjou's failed attempt at a *coup d'état* in Antwerp in early 1583, joined the force under him which pursued the duke. North's regiment remained in service until spring 1584. One company was in the garrison that betrayed Alost to the Spanish in October 1583, but though the rest of the regiment remained faithful to the cause, in April 1584 the states general ordered 'no monthly payment be made' to it and it disappears (MS North b. 25, fol. 64).

North returned to England in time to be elected to parliament for Cambridgeshire in 1584. He also served in the parliaments of 1586 and 1588, but had made another trip to the Netherlands in 1587. The reasons are uncertain, but it was probably not he but his uncle, Thomas, who commanded a company of foot in Leicester's expedition to Sluis in summer 1587. North was JP for Suffolk from about 1591. He went to Ireland in 1595, as the earl of Tyrone's uprising began to cause real problems, and was knighted there in April 1596. The following year he returned to the Low Countries, where he died on 5 June 1597. John Chamberlain claimed that North left his wife 'but a meane widow' (*Letters of John Chamberlain*, 1.31), but she erected a monument to his memory in the church of St Gregory by Paul's, London.

North was prickly and combative. At one stage in his dispute with Norris he quarrelled with three of his rival's captains in five days, drawing a knife on one. In Dordrecht in autumn 1587 he lost his temper when one (Thomas?) Webbe spoke slightingly of Leicester; North violently assaulted Webbe, yet was genuinely surprised when arrested by the local authorities, calling this a 'harde and reprochefull measure' (Cotton MS Titus B. vii, fol. 79). Nor was North a competent military leader: in October 1583, the celebrated Welsh soldier Roger Williams wrote of North's 'simplicity' (*CSP for.*, 18.124) and in winter 1583–4

the experienced Cromwell joined another regiment. North's prosecution and humiliating imprisonment that winter for a debt of just 10 livres (having incurred debts of some 1200 livres with Dutch merchants in 1582–4) reveals how ill he managed his finances, and how readily he rubbed people up the wrong way. John North showed admirable devotion to his cause, but his zeal and ambition outstripped his perspicacity and charm. D. J. B. TRIM

Sources *CSP for.*, 1581–3 and addenda; 1583–4 · Bodl. Oxf., MS Add. C. 193 · Bodl. Oxf., MSS North b. 25, c. 27 · BL, Add. MS 32502 · BL, Cotton MS Titus B. vii · GEC, *Peerage*, new edn, vol. 10 · *DNB* · Nationaal Archief, The Hague, Collectie van Dorp, liassen 971, 986 · W. Camden, *Annales: the true and royall history of the famous Empresse Elizabeth*, trans. A. Darcie (1625) · T. Churchyard and R. Ro [Robinson], *A true discourse historicall of the succeeding governors in the Netherlands and the civil wars there begun in the yeere 1565, with the memorable services of our honourable English generals, captaines and souldiers, especially under Sir John Norrice, knight, there performed from the years 1577 until the year 1589, and afterwards in Portugale, France, Britaine and Ireland, untill the yeere 1598* (1602) · *The letters of John Chamberlain*, ed. N. E. McClure, 2 vols. (1939) · PRO, E 157/1 · PRO, SP 83/15 · H. H. Davis, 'The military career of Thomas North', *Huntington Library Quarterly*, 12 (1948–9), 315–21 · W. A. Shaw, *The knights of England*, 2 (1906) · S. L. Adams, 'The protestant cause: religious alliance with the west European Calvinist communities as a political issue in England, 1585–1630', DPhil diss., U. Oxf., 1973 · J. S. Nolan, *Sir John Norreys and the Elizabethan military world* (1997), chap. 4

Archives BL, family papers, Add. MS 32502 · Bodl. Oxf., accounts and travel diaries · Bodl. Oxf., papers

Likenesses Crainus the younger, portrait; known to be at Waldershare, Kent, in 1894 · oils, The Vyne, Hampshire · portrait; known to be at Wroxton Abbey, Oxfordshire, in 1894

North, John (1645–1683), college head, was born in London on 4 September 1645, the fifth of the seven sons of Dudley *North, fourth Baron North (1602–1677), and his wife, Anne (1613/4–1681), daughter of Sir Charles Montagu. Along with his brothers Francis *North (1637–1685), Dudley *North (1641–1691), Montagu, and Roger *North (1651–1734), he attended King Edward VI School, Bury St Edmunds. The headmaster, Thomas Stephens, was a defiant royalist, and paraded his boarders in scarlet cloaks as worn by the cavaliers. A portrait of John North in this outfit was commissioned by Stephens from Blemwell. North was a sickly child, and retained a frail physique and soft complexion together with a mop of blond hair; he was consequently not without admirers. His poor health and studious disposition marked him out for a clerical career. After leaving Bury he spent some time at home in further study. In 1661 he matriculated at Jesus College, Cambridge, as a fellow-commoner (advancing to the status of nobleman when his father inherited the barony of North in 1666). His tutor was William Cook. He graduated BA in 1664 and proceeded MA in 1666. By royal mandate of 28 September 1666 he was nominated to a fellowship at Jesus, with dispensation from ineligibility because the place vacant was reserved for a northerner. By this time North was already accumulating a substantial library; in this he was helped by the London bookseller Robert Scot, whose sister was in service with North's family.

North never cared much for social recreation. An early enthusiasm for playing the organ came to an end when his lucubrations upset a neighbour, who retaliated with a cacophony of pots and pans. Thereafter North's only real interests were cerebration and arachnophilia. By way of preparing for the ministry he gave sermons in churches around Cambridge which lay in his college's gift, deputizing for ordained fellows who had the duty of preaching there. In 1668, while still a layman, he preached before Charles II at Newmarket, and was said to have made a good impression. He was made deacon by Bishop Benjamin Laney of Ely on 18 December 1669. In July 1670 he told his father he had no immediate intention of proceeding to the priesthood, and indeed had been advised by his own bishop and Henry Compton, later bishop of London, to bide his time until a suitable benefice came along. Despite his rehearsals, he felt that preaching was 'not [his] best course' (Trinity College MS o.11a.3/36). However, by October Archbishop Gilbert Sheldon had promised him a sinecure worth £500 a year; this was the rectory of Llandinam, Montgomeryshire. North was duly ordained priest on 30 October 1670.

Having accepted preferment, North was obliged to vacate his fellowship at Jesus. Instead he moved to Trinity, where for the present he lived as a resident MA, without college stipend. His chief study was in Greek, and in 1671 he contributed to a collection of texts put out by the regius professor, Thomas Gale. On Gale's retirement in 1672 North succeeded him, holding the chair for two years. In 1673 he published extracts from Plato as *Dialogi selecti*, of which no copy survives. On 9 January 1673 he was appointed by the king to a canonry of Westminster, which he held to his death. In 1674 it was said that he was to be made clerk of the closet, and perhaps also bishop of Bristol. The mitre he never had, and although there are subsequent references to his clerkship (including in the memoir by his brother Roger), there is no mention of him in the formal records of that office. He was, however, a royal chaplain and regular court preacher; John Evelyn heard him on Easter eve 1676 and judged him 'a very young, but learned, & excellent person' (Evelyn, 4.87). In the following summer he was made DD at Cambridge on the occasion of a visit by the duke of Lauderdale, whose patronage North enjoyed.

On 5 May North was nominated master of Trinity in succession to his friend Isaac Barrow. It proved to be an unwelcome honour. North's preferences had always been for the company of younger men of good family (and the more ancient the family the better) or older men of superior learning. For the generality of academic society he had no liking, and the feeling was reciprocated. Recent masters of Trinity had allowed the direction of affairs to pass to a clique of eight seniors, and North's determination to assert his authority (especially over fellowship elections) generated much bitterness. The most satisfactory aspect of his mastership was the progress in building the Wren Library, which had been begun in 1676. In North's time the ceiling and plumbing works were completed, and carvings were executed by Gabriel Cibber. In July 1677 the college issued an appeal for funds, envisaging the extension of Neville's court to achieve 'a decent and beautiful space' (J. North, over North's signature).

North's health, which had never improved, was enfeebled by inadequate diet and excess of study—the latter to no lasting purpose, since he had no capacity for sustained composition. He died on 14 April 1683. By his will he directed that no escutcheon or other ceremony should accompany his funeral service, and that all his literary manuscripts should be destroyed. His grave is marked by a simple slab in the paving of the ante-chapel at Trinity, immediately behind Roubiliac's towering statue of Isaac Newton, who had been North's closest friend in life at the college.   C. S. KNIGHTON

Sources R. North, *The lives of … Francis North … Dudley North … and … John North*, ed. A. Jessopp, 2 (1890); repr. as *The lives of the Norths* (1972), 266–342 · Venn, *Alum. Cant.*, 1/3.266 · S. H. A. H. [S. H. A. Hervey], *Biographical list of boys educated at King Edward VI Free Grammar School, Bury St Edmunds, from 1550 to 1900* (1908), 278 · *CSP dom.*, *1664–5*, 18–19; *1673–5*, 359; *1677–8*, 113 · *Fasti Angl., 1541–1857*, [Ely], 85 · G. M. Trevelyan, *Trinity College: an historical sketch* (1946), 47–8 · R. Willis, *The architectural history of the University of Cambridge, and of the colleges of Cambridge and Eton*, ed. J. W. Clark, 2 (1886), 540, 542 · Evelyn, *Diary*, 4.87, 97, 107 · Trinity Cam. · J. North, *Concerning the new library now building in Trinity College* (1677) · will, PRO, PROB 11/372, fols. 366v–367

Archives Bodl. Oxf., letters and papers | Trinity Cam., letters to his parents and brothers

Likenesses Blemwell, oils, *c.*1660, Rougham Hall, Norfolk · Miss North, oils (after Blemwell), Trinity Cam.

Wealth at death a few small cash bequests: will, PRO, PROB 11/372, fols. 366v–367

North, John Dudley (1893–1968), aircraft designer, was born at 18 Kinver Road North, Peak Hill, Sydenham, on 2 January 1893, the only child of Dudley North, solicitor, and his wife, Marian Felgate. He was educated at Bedford School where he learned the elements of the mathematics which he applied so skilfully until the end of his days. After leaving school he became an apprentice in marine engineering. While still an apprentice he won two competitions in *The Aeroplane*, edited at that time by Charles Grey. It was through Grey's advice that his apprenticeship was transferred to Horatio Barber's Aeronautical Syndicate at Hendon, and when that venture ended he joined the Grahame-White company. He was still only nineteen when he became its chief engineer. Between 1912 and 1915 he designed and supervised the construction of a number of aeroplanes, one of which was the first British aeroplane to loop the loop. The best-remembered product of this period of extraordinary precocity was the Grahame-White Charabanc which in 1913, piloted by Louis Noel, took nine passengers, including the youthful designer, into the air.

In 1915, North joined the Austin motor company as superintendent of its aeroplane division. In this post he was responsible not for design but for constructing the large numbers of RE7 and RE8 aircraft which the company produced for the Royal Flying Corps. At the end of 1917 he joined Boulton and Paul Ltd, of Norwich. As a consequence of the aircraft production work it had taken up during the war the company had decided to start a design department, and North was put in charge.

The first machine North designed was the Bobolink, a fighter. It was followed by the Bourges, a bomber–reconnaissance aircraft of attractive design and remarkable performance. This aeroplane, of which there were several versions, was the first of a series of high-performance bombers. It was followed by the Bolton and the Bugle and, in 1927, by probably the most famous of North's aeroplanes, the Sidestrand. Towards the end of the 1920s there followed two single-seater fighters, the Partridge, which was a single-engine biplane and the Bittern, a twin-engine monoplane with a number of original features. The Air Ministry appeared to decide, however, that the forte of Boulton and Paul, and its successor (1934) in the aircraft field, Boulton Paul Aircraft Ltd, was the bomber, and the next selected for service was the Overstrand. Towards the end of the series came the remarkable turret-fighter, the Defiant, which was used in the early days of the Second World War and aided the Dunkirk evacuation. The last aircraft production run, which came after the war ended, was on the Balliol, an advanced trainer for the Royal Air Force and Fleet Air Arm. Thereafter the only aircraft of note were the delta research aircraft P111 and P120, the first to use Boulton Paul power controls. Few designers have to their credit a more remarkable series of aircraft, a testimony to North's outstanding fertility in invention and skill in engineering.

North was one of the first to move away from the wood and fabric of the First World War to the tubular and monocoque constructions of the later years. He was always close to the latest development in metal and plastic materials. His particular genius for design in metal was given an excellent opportunity in 1924 when Boulton and Paul became intimately associated with the design and construction of the R101 airship. Its sad fate should not be allowed to obscure the ingenuity of its structure. The overall design of the skeleton was the work of the Royal Airship Works, but the design of the individual girders, in some parts of the ship a matter of most complicated three-dimensional geometry, was the work of North and his team.

An outstanding characteristic of North's last bombers was their gun-turrets. As Boulton and Paul became famous for making powered turrets for a variety of aircraft, its work moved progressively away from complete aircraft to the increasingly complex parts thereof. In his last phase as a designer North concentrated more on powered controls—including those of Concorde—and on other powered devices within and without the aeronautical field.

It was North's ideas on control which led to his deep interest in control mathematics and cybernetics. He developed a wide-ranging knowledge of operational research, ergonomics, and statistics, on which he published several profound and imaginative scientific papers. North was a member of the council of the Society of British Aircraft Constructors from 1931 to 1962. It was as the society's nominee that he joined the council of the Air Registration Board and the governing body of the College of Aeronautics at Cranfield, on both of which he worked with characteristic dedication.

As engineer, as designer, and as applied mathematician, North was a great professional. As horticulturalist, gastronome, and cook, he was a great amateur, yet equal in skill to many professionals. He was an honorary fellow of the Royal Aeronautical Society and in 1967 he became an honorary DSc of the University of Birmingham. In 1962 he was appointed CBE. Although he seemed indifferent to fame and his course was determined only by logic, he did not scorn recognition and when he was honoured he was greatly pleased. When his years of service to the Air Registration Board were appreciated by a modest presentation he was deeply touched. Perhaps, in his great modesty, he never felt neglected, but to those who knew him best he stood out as a person of distinction whose merit in his lifetime was comprehended by too few. This may have been because his integrity was complete and in things which mattered he could not compromise. North was a tall, heavily built man, bespectacled from youth. His voice was deep, his manner deliberate. On first meeting he could be a little frightening, but it was usually not long before his humour and kindliness came through.

North married in 1922 Phyllis Margaret, daughter of Edward Huggins, clerk to the Norwich board of guardians. They had two daughters. He died at his home, Eversley, in Oldbury, Bridgnorth, Shropshire, on 11 January 1968.

KINGS NORTON, *rev.*

Sources H. F. King, *Flight International* (7 Oct 1965) · Lord Kings Norton, *Journal of the Royal Aeronautical Society*, 72/696 (Dec 1968), 1055–7 · private information (1981) · personal knowledge (1981) · *The Times* (12 Jan 1968), 10f · d. cert.
Wealth at death £70,103: probate, 20 Aug 1968, *CGPLA Eng. & Wales*

North, John Thomas (1842–1896), engineer and nitrate entrepreneur, was born on 30 January 1842 in Holbeck, Leeds, the second child in the family of two sons and one daughter of James North, coal merchant of Leeds, and his wife, Mary Gambles of Batley. North's basic education at a local school was followed, when he was fifteen, by an engineering apprenticeship at Shaw, North, and Watson of Hunslet, millwrights and shipwrights. In 1865 North joined Fowler & Co. at their well-known steam-plough works in Leeds and in 1869 they sent him to Peru to supervise the running of two of their steam ploughs there.

North was to remain in Peru for thirteen years, and soon found scope for his natural business acumen. He left Fowlers, and in 1871 settled in the port of Iquique, which was growing rapidly through its trade in nitrates. This natural fertilizer was present in abundance in the desert hinterland, and mining works were rapidly being developed there, though they were totally dependent on imported machinery and supplies. In partnership with Maurice Jewell, another expatriate, North established an import and trading business to supply the mines, and the partners also soon became local agents for steamship lines. North himself then moved into water supply, buying in

1875 an old hulk to use as a tanker, and when in 1878 an English group founded the Water Company of Tarapacá in Iquique to bring water from Arica, he rented the carriage business and storage tanks on a service contract and ran it well.

But North's fortune was really made with the war of the Pacific (1879–83) between Chile on one side and Peru and Bolivia on the other. Before the war, in 1875, Peru had sought to nationalize the nitrate fields, issuing bonds 'payable to bearer' to their owners; the fields were to become government property when the bonds were redeemed. This never happened, and the war in 1879 cut their value, many holders selling them off for a pittance. The chief buyer was North, together with the British inspector-general of nitrate to Peru, Robert Harvey, and John Dawson, agent of the Chilean Bank of Valparaiso in Iquique. Harvey gave advice, Dawson advanced funds, and North, then in Lima, bought the bonds—effectively title-deeds to the properties. Chile acquired Peruvian Tarapacá (including Iquique) and Bolivian Antofagasta, rich in nitrates, and returned the industry to private hands, leaving the trio with title to many major deposits.

North returned to England in 1882 to float several nitrate companies on the stock exchange. The first of these, formed with the aid of certain Liverpool merchant houses, was established in 1883, and thousands of investors were infected by the fever for nitrate shares. North was a born promoter, and one critical report noted: 'Put Colonel North's name on a costermonger cart, turn it into a limited company, and the shares will be selling at 300 per cent premium before they are hours old' (*Financial News*, 23 May 1888). The raging bull market was fuelled by North's extravagant lifestyle. *The Economist* commented that 'his great notion of hospitality was to drown his friends in champagne', and those whom he so entertained at his vast mansion at Avery Hill in Kent included the Rothschilds (who became his bankers at the end of 1888).

North's popular sobriquet was 'the Nitrate King', and this image was enhanced by his sporting interests. He kept a stud of racehorses, and his expensive greyhounds (especially Fullerton and Troughend) won a number of major races. He became an honorary colonel of a regiment of volunteers at Tower Hamlets, funding it himself, and was an important figure in the county establishment of Kent. Yet North never forgot his origins, and the city of Leeds benefited from his munificence: he bought Kirkstall Abbey for £10,000 and presented it as a civic monument. He gave £5000 to Leeds Infirmary, and in 1889 he was made the first honorary freeman of the city. In 1895 he also contested West Leeds as a Conservative against Herbert Gladstone and was defeated by only ninety-six votes. North married Jane Woodhead of Leeds in 1865, and they had two sons and a daughter.

North had many critics, especially in Chile, where his name was a byword for ambition and greed. The basis of his fortune, however, lay not so much in share dividends, as in the sale of assets to the nitrate companies he founded, most of which were grossly over-capitalized.

The *Financial News* had long predicted a crash, and the boom in nitrate shares collapsed in the early 1890s; but North must have envisaged this, as he had already transferred the greater part of his own investment into gold and silver, and his own fortune was not affected. He died on 5 May 1896, while presiding at a company meeting at 3 Gracechurch Street in the City of London. His popularity continued to the end: his funeral was attended by huge crowds, and letters of sympathy came from the prince of Wales, the king of the Belgians, and the khedive of Egypt. He was buried at Eltham parish church.

H. BLAKEMORE, *rev.*

Sources H. Blakemore, *British nitrates and Chilean politics, 1886–1896: Balmaceda and North* (1974) · H. Blakemore, 'John Thomas North, the nitrate king', *History Today*, 12 (1962), 467–75 · D. Kynaston, *The City of London*, 1 (1994), 398–400 · Boase, *Mod. Eng. biog.* · *Leading men of London: a collection of biographical sketches* (1895)
Likenesses P. May, portrait, Leeds City Art Gallery
Wealth at death £575,535 10s. 11d.: probate, 2 July 1896, *CGPLA Eng. & Wales*

North, John William (1842–1924), illustrator and water-colour painter, was born in Walham Green, Fulham, on new year's day 1842, the son of Charles North (*d.* 1890), a linen draper, and his wife, Rosemary Knight (*d.* 1880). His father failed in business as a draper in 1852 and then moved with his family to Worthing. Two years later North's parents emigrated to Canada, taking his younger brother but leaving North with his uncles, Alfred and John North, who lived in Brixton and Dartford. He spent school holidays with a great-uncle who was a farmer in Hertfordshire. Early drawings by North, dating from the mid-1850s, are of agricultural and rustic subjects.

It seems that North left school at a young age, having already decided to follow a career as an artist. Following a short period of study at the Department of Science and Art's school at Marlborough House, in 1857 or 1858 he was apprenticed to the wood-engraver Josiah Wood Whymper, and so met among his fellow employees Fred Walker (1840–1875) and George John Pinwell (1842–1875). From 1862 to 1866 North worked principally as an illustrator for the Dalziel Brothers, and rapidly gained a reputation for his sensitive interpretation of landscape subjects in the medium of black and white woodblock engraving. He made designs for periodicals including *Good Words* (in 1863 and 1866), *Once a Week* (between 1864 and 1867), and the *Sunday Magazine* (between 1865 and 1867). In addition, he contributed to *A Round of Days* (1866), *Wayside Posies* (1867), and Jean Ingelow's *Poems* (1867).

In 1860 North made a walking tour of Somerset in company with Edward Whymper (1840–1911), his employer's son who was to become a distinguished alpinist and who in 1865 was to make the first ascent of the Matterhorn. The two came across a rambling and decrepit old house—originally built as a hunting lodge by Cardinal Beaufort, half-brother of Henry IV—called Halsway Manor, on the western flank of the Quantock hills. Over the following few years North made several long stays at Halsway, lodging with Mrs Thorne, wife of the tenant farmer, and being accompanied on occasions by Walker and Pinwell (although not together as the two were not themselves friends). Gradually the house itself, with nearby Little Halsway Farm and the surrounding countryside, became North's principal motif and inspiration. About 1868 Halsway changed hands and the easy arrangement with the Thornes ended. By 1869 North settled at Woolston Moor, a village closer to Williton and where he was to remain until 1884, the year of his marriage (on 19 February) to Selina (1862/3–c.1898), the daughter of a Somerset farmer, Abraham Weetch.

North also maintained a studio in London, from the early 1870s onwards in Charlotte Street, and later at Wynchcombe Studios on Haverstock Hill. He visited Scotland on at least one occasion in the early 1870s, probably as a guest of William Graham MP, and painted views on the River Tay at Stobhall. In 1874–5 he travelled with Walker to Algeria—for the sake of the latter's health. North remained in Algeria after Walker returned to England, and in due course he had a house built there where he often stayed in the winter months until the time of his marriage. From 1884 to 1898 North and his wife lived (along with North's father, a widower since 1880) at Beggearn Huish House, at Nettlecombe between the sea and the Brendon hills. Eight children were born to them there, although at least two did not survive infancy, and Selina North herself died about 1898. As a widower North lived at Bilbrook and then, from 1904 to 1914, at Withycombe.

North loved the Somerset countryside and knew it well. Although agriculture itself is seldom represented in his art, he cared about the men and women whose lives were spent working the soil: he wrote articles about their living conditions and campaigned against the game laws. That North was a true countryman is witnessed by his friendship with the writer and naturalist Richard Jefferies (1848–1887), to whose landscape accounts North's watercolours make a pictorial equivalent. Jefferies stayed with North in 1883 when gathering material for his book *Red Deer*; his memoir of this stay appeared as the essay 'Summer in Somerset' (published in *English Illustrated Magazine* in 1887 and accompanied by drawings by North). In August 1887 North wrote an obituary of Jefferies for *Pall Mall Gazette*, and organized a subscription to provide for the writer's widow.

North's watercolours of the 1860s owe something to his experience as a designer of illustrations, retaining a coherent and linear compositional structure, matched with intense colour and careful observation of detail. According to Walker, writing in December 1868, 'each inch [of North's drawings was] wrought with gem-like care' (Marks, 165). A personal and artistic sympathy existed between North and both Walker and Pinwell, each of whom occasionally introduced figures to his landscape compositions, and he felt a great loss when in 1875 both died. North's later subjects are freer and more abstract; a classic North composition might consist of an entangled thicket or a marshy valley, with dense textures of vegetation forming a predominant foreground and all sense of perspectival distance sacrificed to effects of hazy atmosphere. In 1880 his work was characterized in a review in the *Spectator* as:

> a manner which gives the effect of wandering from place to place in his picture, working now here, now there, and finally, that seeing so much more beauty than he can compass, he stays his hand altogether, and sends his picture out to exhibition as little finished or as much so, as one of Turner's wilder fancies.   (*Spectator*, 8 May 1880, 594)

Herbert Alexander explained how determined North was to capture the particular aspect of places he cared about, for:

> he did not sit down, like the average painter, in picturesque scenery and arrange it improvingly; but ... waited until an entrancing moment in the passage of light or some human episode happily related to its surroundings awoke in his heart the ecstasy which is the poetic state. Then no sacrifice of time or labour was too great in the searching of nature to aid his revelation. The production of a picture was one long agony, and so little was he satisfied with his achievement that it was always painful to him to view his works again. (Alexander, 48)

North's watercolour *The Old Pear Tree* (exh. Royal Society of Painters in Water Colours 1892; Southampton Art Gallery)—in which a ravaged tree is weighed down by golden fruit—was admired as an evocation of a season that brings both fecundity and decay. Alexander described the technique devised by North to suggest the constant variety of nature: 'In water colour and oil an effect of intricate detail is found on examination to be quite illusive—multitudinous form is conjured by finding it and losing it in endless hide-and-seek till the eye accepts infinity' (ibid.). In the last years of his life North painted pure landscapes that commented ironically upon the destruction of war, titles of which include *England in September 1914 (an Allegory)* and *England's Green and Pleasant Land*.

North exhibited at the Dudley Gallery from the late 1860s until 1871, the year of his election as an associate member of the Old Watercolour Society and to which he then transferred his main allegiance as an exhibitor (he became a full member of the society in 1883). From 1869 he occasionally exhibited at the Royal Academy, and in 1893 he was elected as an associate member. He exhibited at the Grosvenor Gallery between 1880 and 1887, later transferring to the New Gallery on the exhibition committee on which he sat. The purchase by the trustees of the Chantrey Bequest in 1891 of North's sad and symbolical painting *The Winter Sun* (Tate collection), a work which Herbert Alexander claimed was influential on the rising generation of landscape painters, was said to have been due to the influence of Frederic Leighton. Hubert Herkomer, in his 1892 Slade lecture, sought to identify North as the originator of the idyllist style of landscape. This campaign to raise public awareness of North was an embarrassment and irritation to him, and a final rift occurred when it emerged that he had opposed Herkomer's candidacy for the presidency of the Royal Watercolour Society.

From 1895 North devoted time and money to a business making drawing papers, and particularly one called

O.W. Paper. Its failure left him virtually destitute and he depended in old age on a small pension from the Royal Academy. North died on 20 December 1924 at Stamborough, Old Cleeve, Somerset, the farmhouse high in the Brendon hills that was his last home. He was buried in Nettlecombe cemetery, Somerset.

CHRISTOPHER NEWALL

Sources H. Alexander, 'John William North', *Old Water-Colour Society's Club*, 5 (1927–8), 35–52 · S. Wilcox and C. Newall, *Victorian landscape watercolors* (1992) [exhibition catalogue, New Haven, CT, Cleveland, OH, and Birmingham, 9 Sept 1992 – 12 April 1993] · P. Goldman, *Victorian illustrated books, 1850–1870: the heyday of wood-engraving, the Robin de Beaumont collection* (1994) · P. Goldman, *Victorian illustration: the Pre-Raphaelites, the idyllic school and the high Victorians* (1996) · A. Staley and others, *The post-Pre-Raphaelite print* (1995) [exhibition catalogue, Miriam and Ira D. Wallach Art Gallery, Columbia University, New York, 10 Oct – 16 Dec 1995] · R. M. Billingham, 'A Somerset draw for painters: Victorian artists at Halsway Manor', *Country Life*, 162 (1977), 428–30 · H. von Herkomer, 'J. W. North, painter and poet', *Magazine of Art*, 16 (1892–3), 297–300, 342–8 · J. G. Marks, *The life & letters of Frederick Walker* (1896) · b. cert. · m. cert. · d. cert.

Likenesses double portrait, photograph, 1868 (with Frederick Walker), repro. in Alexander, 'John William North' · F. C. Cowper, watercolour, Bankside Gallery, London · H. Herkomer, watercolour, priv. coll.

Wealth at death £523 2s.: probate, 30 June 1925, *CGPLA Eng. & Wales*

North, Marianne (1830–1890), painter and traveller, was born at Hastings on 24 October 1830, the second child and elder daughter of Frederick North MP, descendant of Roger North, and his wife, Janet, eldest daughter of Sir John Marjoribanks and widow of Robert Shuttleworth of Gawthorpe Hall, Lancashire. Marianne's sister, Catherine married John Addington Symonds, and her half-sister Janet married John Kay Shuttleworth.

Marianne North's early days were spent between Hastings, Rougham (where the North family had property), her half-sister's house at Gawthorpe, and school in Norwich. In 1847 she and her family began three years of travel in Europe. Hating school and despising governesses, she had little formal education, but possessed a wonderful capacity for concentrating on what she enjoyed, which, at this point, was mainly music. When, on the family's return to England, her fine contralto voice failed, she turned with equal enthusiasm to painting, making flowers her special subject. Among her father's many influential scientific and artistic friends were several—including Sir William and Sir Joseph Hooker, successive directors of the Royal Botanic Gardens at Kew—who gave support and recognition to Marianne in the travels on which her fame rests. After her mother's death in 1855, her father took the flat at 3 Victoria Street, London, which was to be her home when in England during her travelling years. She declared her father 'the one idol and friend of my life' (North, *Recollections*, 1.5) and they journeyed together as far afield as Turkey and Egypt in the years following Catherine North's marriage in 1864. His death in 1868 hit her hard, but, instead of indulging in grief, she revived an old dream 'of going to some tropical

Marianne North (1830–1890), by unknown photographer

country to paint its peculiar vegetation in its natural abundant luxuriance' (ibid., 1.39). She was eventually to go further, but never into cold climates, as she found that cold weather crippled her with rheumatism and made her teeth ache.

Encouraged by Kew and armed with introductions from her own and her father's friends, Marianne embarked on her quest. In 1871–2 she visited Canada, the United States, Jamaica, and Brazil. Between 1873 and 1877 she journeyed to California, Japan, Borneo, Java, and Ceylon. In 1878–9 she made an extensive tour of India. After a successful showing of her work, she presented her collection to Kew, for display in a gallery designed, furnished, and financed by herself. In 1880, while this was being built, she took Darwin's advice and sailed via Borneo for Australia and New Zealand. She returned to England via California in 1881 and, after a year's work arranging the pictures and compiling the catalogue, the gallery opened on 9 July 1882. It was set 'far from the usual entrance gate as I thought a resting place and shelter from rain and sun were more needed there, by those who cared sufficiently for plants, to have made their way through all the houses' (North, *Recollections*, 2.86). To fill gaps in the collection she went to South Africa and the Seychelles in 1882–3. Her last journey was in 1884–5 on a stormy passage through the Strait of Magellan to Chile to paint the monkey-puzzle tree in its natural surroundings.

Marianne North travelled alone, laden with palettes and easels, sometimes staying at government houses and embassies, sometimes fending for herself. In Jamaica she rented a derelict house in a wilderness of flowers, painting all day in happy independence, refreshing herself from a bunch of bananas hung like a chandelier from the ceiling. Eight months were spent in Brazil up country with the family of a Mr Gordon, manager of a goldmine at Morro Velho. At a 'capital' little inn among the Californian redwoods she enjoyed 'a most adorable iced mixture and a straw to suck it through' (North, *Recollections*, 2.197). She ate her 1880 Christmas dinner with settlers in the Australian outback. She cared little what impression she made, attending a viceregal occasion in India clad in an 'old hooped-up serge gown and a shabby hat' (ibid., 2.7).

Miss North was a painter who travelled, rather than a traveller who painted. She was not much interested in the people whose lands she passed through or in the conditions under which some of them lived. Complacent about the lot of domestic slaves in Rio and caring little for the plight of dispossessed Indians in America, she was single-minded in her adoration of nature, watching with infinite patience the skill of a caterpillar weaving its cocoon, revelling in the botanic gardens she found on her way. She was also a botanist with six species registered in her name, notably the pitcher plant *Nepenthes northeana*, which she found in Borneo while staying with the raja of Sarawak. The rani, roused from her customary siesta to go on a jungle ramble, describes her energetic guest 'with skirts kilted up to the knees and heel-less Wellington boots as though born for Borneo jungles' (Ranee of Sarawak, 175). And in a boat on the way back,

'How unusual, how lovely', said Miss North seating herself beside me with her high boots and undraped knees *en évidence* … For the first time that day her topee came off, and I admired her thick fair hair with hardly a touch of grey. 'What a divine country! How I love it all!'   (Ranee of Sarawak, 177)

Her last two journeys severely damaged Marianne's health and in 1886 she retired to Mount House, Alderley, Gloucestershire, where she died, unmarried, on 30 August 1890. She was buried in Alderley.

DOROTHY MIDDLETON

Sources M. North, *Recollections of a happy life: being the autobiography of Marianne North*, ed. Mrs J. A. Symonds, 2 vols. (1892) · M. North, *Further recollections … from the journal of Marianne North*, ed. Mrs J. A. Symonds, 2 vols. (1893) [chiefly between 1859 and 1869] · L. Ponsonby, *Marianne North at Kew Gardens* (1990) · Ranee Margaret of Sarawak [M. Brooke], *Good morning and good night* (1934) · M. North, *A vision of Eden* (1980) [ed. version of *Recollections*]
Archives McGill University, Montreal, McLennan Library, corresp. and papers · Rougham Hall, King's Lynn | RBG Kew, letters to Burnell; letters to Shaen family · Somerville College, Oxford, letters to Amelia Edwards, travel diary
Likenesses M. Hall, portrait, 1860, repro. in North, *Vision of Eden* (1980) · Williams, drawing, c.1864, Somerville College, Oxford · C. Dressler, bust, RBG Kew, North Gallery · W. J. Newton, portrait (as a girl) · photograph, RBG Kew [*see illus.*] · wood-engraving, NPG; repro. in *ILN* (24 June 1882)
Wealth at death £39,329 1s. 3d.: probate, 28 Oct 1890, *CGPLA Eng. & Wales*

North, Nathaniel (*d.* in or after **1709**), pirate, was born in Bermuda, the son of Nathaniel North (*fl.* 1680), a descendant of an indentured servant, living on crown lands at Tucker's Town. The earliest record of the younger North, who initially followed his father's trade of sawyer, or carpenter, is of his being one of those fitting out Thomas Tew's sloop *Amity* for a privateering cruise in 1691.

As with most outlaws and common seamen, especially those who were never put on trial, many of the details of North's career remain somewhat conjectural. From the best sources available, however, it would seem that he first went to sea, aged seventeen or eighteen, as cook in a privateer, from which he was pressed into a British man-of-war bound for Jamaica, reputedly the *Reserve*, under Captain John Moses. This would have been between 1695 and 1698, and if his subsequent (admittedly apocryphal) experience in the Caribbean is to be believed, presumably towards the beginning of that period. Having escaped from the *Reserve* he is supposed to have made two privateering-cum-trading voyages with Captain Reesby to the Spanish main, to have been pressed into the *Mary* at Jamaica, to have escaped to the privateer *Neptune*, and to have been pressed into another man-of-war, the *Assistance*. On the run again, he may have made a number of voyages in Dutch or Spanish vessels before signing up at Rhode Island for the privateer *Pelican*, presumably in 1696 or 1697.

This leaky old vessel had a letter of marque to cruise against Spanish vessels in the East Indies (although some sources imply French vessels off west Africa were her intended prey). Instead the captain and crew turned pirate, probably because the end of King William's War in 1697 deprived them—paid no wages and only a share of the prizes—of any legitimate recompense for their voyage. North was elected quartermaster, and in the *Pelican* he headed for the Indian Ocean. In the Red Sea in September 1698 the *Pelican*, in company with two other pirate vessels—the *Mocha* (Captain Robert Culliford) and the *Resolution*, or *Soldado* (Captain Dirk Shivers, or Chivers)—took the *Great Mahomet*, a large and richly-laden vessel, and returned to their base at St Mary's Island, off the east coast of Madagascar. There, in 1699, they were tracked down by three British warships under Captain Burgess in the *Margaret*, and many of North's fellows accepted the pardon that was periodically offered to pirates who would quit their lives of crime. Apparently North, however, was suspicious, since the deadline for acceptance of the pardon had already expired, and he escaped to the mainland of Madagascar.

In April 1700 North was with a gang of pirates who seized the *Speaker*, in which he served as quartermaster to Captain Bowen until that ship was lost in December 1701. He continued cruising in the Indian Ocean, at first with George Booth and then with Bowen in the *Speedy Return* and with Captain Howard in the *Prosperous*; in March 1703 they took the *Pembroke* (Captain Woolley). North succeeded Bowen as captain of the *Speedy Return* in 1703 or 1704, and after spending some months on Mauritius he settled for a few years with some of his crew on the east coast of Madagascar, where he intervened in local tribal wars to secure slaves and women, cattle and other supplies. Early in 1707 he joined the brigantine *Charles* as quartermaster under Captain John Halsey and went cruising again in the Red Sea, but he was apparently back at Madagascar by 1709, when the crew of the wrecked *Neptune* came across him. Some time after that, reputedly, North was murdered in his bed by Madagascans.

RANDOLPH COCK

Sources D. Defoe, *A general history of the pyrates*, ed. M. Schonhorn (1972) · H. C. Wilkinson, *Bermuda in the old empire* (1950) · H. C. Wilkinson, *The adventurers of Bermuda: a history of the island from its discovery until the dissolution of the Somers Island Company in 1684*, 2nd edn (1958) · J. Rogoziński, *The Wordsworth dictionary of pirates* (1997)

North, Roger, second Baron North (1531–1600), nobleman and administrator, was born on 27 February 1531 in the parish of St Thomas the Apostle in London, the first child in the family of two sons and two daughters of Edward *North, first Baron North (c.1504–1564), administrator, and his first wife, Alice (d. 1560), daughter of Oliver Squire of Southby, Hampshire, and widow of Edward Murfyn of London and of John Brigandine of Southampton. As the leading nobleman in late sixteenth-century Cambridgeshire, North carved out an energetic and successful career as a soldier, courtier, and diplomat that was primarily bound up in the politics of the county rather than the politics of the court.

Early career, 1531–1575 Little is known of North's early days. There is no evidence that he was a student at Peterhouse, Cambridge, like one of his younger brothers, the translator Sir Thomas *North (d. 1603?). However, as his father was a benefactor to the college and he sent his own sons there, it is possible that he spent some time at Peterhouse. On 4 November 1542 he was admitted to Lincoln's Inn, London. A special admission to the inn recorded two years later, on 16 July 1544, probably reflects his social status. He appears to have been introduced early to the court, perhaps serving as a page of honour and learning to joust, a sport at which he excelled. There is a portrait of the youthful North dressed, unusually, for a tournament with a scarf of red silk tied around his left arm, which Princess Elizabeth is traditionally said to have affixed. About 1547 he married Winifred (d. 1578), sixth daughter of Richard *Rich, first Baron Rich (1496/7–1567), and his wife, Elizabeth, and widow of Sir Henry Dudley, eldest son of John Dudley, earl of Warwick. The couple had three sons and one daughter, the eldest son dying in infancy. The younger sons were the soldier Sir John *North (c.1550–1597) and the MP Sir Henry North (1556–1620).

North's father's position, as well as his own ambition and ability, explains how he came at the age of twenty-four to be elected senior knight of the shire for Cambridgeshire to the parliament of 1555. He voted against a government bill during the session, which may account for his absence from the next parliament, but he was

returned again for Cambridgeshire in 1559 and 1563. Created a knight of the Bath at the coronation of Elizabeth I on 15 January 1559, he spent much of the first five years of the reign at court. In May 1559 he received a licence for the export of 2000 woollen cloths and kerseys, and two months later he was one of the challengers at the grand tournament held in Greenwich park, Kent. He was appointed to the chamber in 1558 and named JP for Cambridgeshire for the year 1558–9. On 29 December 1561 he was admitted to Gray's Inn, London. When his father died on 31 December 1564, North, who succeeded him, apparently took to heart the paternal warning to avoid pride and profligacy, settling down to manage his considerable estates and proving 'a most industrious and provident man' (North, 30). North had inherited lands in Cambridgeshire and Suffolk, with property in Harrow, Pinner, and other parts of Middlesex as well as the Charterhouse, which he sold in May 1565 to Thomas Howard, fourth duke of Norfolk. In May 1577 he increased his Suffolk property with the purchase of the house and estate of Mildenhall, which he eventually bequeathed to his younger son Sir Henry North.

As the only resident peer in late sixteenth-century Cambridgeshire, North dominated county politics and threw his energies into local administration. He attended quarter sessions regularly after his appointment as JP, and in 1568 was elected alderman and free burgess of Cambridge. He became lord lieutenant of Cambridgeshire in 1569 and high steward of Cambridge in 1572. Throughout the 1570s his local influence grew, as he was named *custos rotulorum* of the Cambridge bench in 1573 and JP for Suffolk and the Isle of Ely in 1579. He proved an active and efficient administrator, whether organizing county musters, serving as a subsidy commissioner, supervising schemes for draining the fens, or investigating matters brought to his attention by the privy council. He cultivated a warm relationship with the town authorities in Cambridge and in the course of his duties not infrequently clashed with the university. In May 1569 he alarmed the university with his attempt to muster the servants of students, and in December he pilloried a student for slandering and insulting the mayor.

Elizabeth used North on two, and possibly three, diplomatic missions. In 1567 he was sent as special ambassador with Thomas Radcliffe, third earl of Sussex, on an embassy to Vienna to invest Emperor Maximilian II with the Order of the Garter on 4 January 1568. The mission lasted from 20 May 1567 to 14 March 1568 and included an audience on about 15 August; the objective was to make a last attempt to negotiate marriage terms for the Archduke Charles. It is possible that North accompanied Francis Walsingham, who was sent as resident ambassador to France in 1570 in an attempt to secure greater toleration for the Huguenots. His final embassy was carried out from 3 October to 6 December 1574, when, on the death of Charles IX, he was sent to Lyons as special ambassador with letters of congratulation to Henri III on his accession. He was to assess the political changes, negotiate a renewal of the treaty of Blois, first concluded in 1572, and urge for greater toleration for the Huguenots. North impressed his hosts with his charm, presence, and command of Italian (this was why he was chosen for the mission), but when a fool dressed in imitation of Henry VIII was paraded before the court in the presence of the English visitors, he angrily broke out, 'the tailors of France ought to know how that great King was accustomed to dress, for he came over the sea divers time with banners flying, and made some noise among men here' (Bushby, 70–71). The French king was regarded with suspicion in England, and the matter, once reported, caused a minor stir in the always delicate relationship between France and England at this time, but by April 1575 Henri agreed to renew the treaty.

Dudley connection and privy councillor, 1575–1600 North cultivated his old friendship with Elizabeth with care. He entertained the queen lavishly towards the end of her progress through East Anglia in late summer 1578 and calculated that the visit, which lasted two days, cost him £762, including a gift of jewellery worth £120. His household books often record the amounts that he lost to Elizabeth playing cards—'Lost at play with the Queen £32'—and he never failed to present her with a new year's gift of £10 in gold in a silken purse (Bushby, 105). Lady North was still alive in November 1578 but appears to have died shortly afterwards. Although North was a suitor for the hand of the second of three coheirs of Sir Thomas Rivett, writing to William Cecil, Baron Burghley, in October 1582 about the matter, he apparently did not marry again. He was on close terms with Robert Dudley, earl of Leicester, and Francis Russell, second earl of Bedford, and supported the godly preachers of the counties where puritanism tended to find expression in nonconformity. There is little detailed evidence of North's religious views, but there can be little doubt of his stout support for protestantism. He complained bitterly in 1584 to Burghley about the behaviour of Sir Edmund Anderson, chief justice of the court of common pleas, who had no sympathy for puritan ministers, calling him 'the hottest man that ever sat in judgment', and he mused on the tension he felt between spiritual and worldly desires in verse:

> my inward mane [man] to heavenly thyngs would trade me
> And styll thys fleash doth evermere dyssuade me.
> (ibid., 89, 109)

Leicester's Commonwealth (1584) claimed that North converted Leicester to puritanism. The two men were close friends from the late 1560s, and Leicester described North in a letter to Burghley of 17 October 1578 as 'my very friend & one I love well, howsoever heretofore there was little friendship between us' (PRO, SP 12/126/21). On 9 July 1574 North appointed Leicester steward of his Middlesex estates; he was with him at Kenilworth in Warwickshire in 1577 and took the waters with him at Buxton, Derbyshire, in 1578, and Bath, Somerset, in 1587. He joined him on his tour to Chester in 1584. Leicester trusted him implicitly, asking North to witness his marriage to Lettice Dudley, dowager countess of Essex at Wanstead in Essex in September 1578; North also had custody of Leicester's illegitimate son by Douglas Sheffield, dowager Baroness Sheffield, for a time, and was godfather to Robert Dudley,

Baron Denbigh. North's loyalty to Elizabeth and a hot temper brought him into conflict with others, most notably Sussex during the royal progress of 1578, and Richard Cox, bishop of Ely, who from 1574 onward tenaciously refused to grant him a lease on Somersham in Huntingdon. The quarrel with Cox is quite famous. The bishop refused to part with Somersham, saying he was duty-bound to protect the property he had inherited with the see. This provoked North into producing in December 1575 a bill of complaint against him that claimed he had ignored the queen's instructions, mishandled local justice, mismanaged the diocesan estates, and favoured his family. A compromise was eventually reached, but North's pursuit of the issue reflected his distaste for a powerful and wealthy episcopate. However, his main aims were to consolidate the family estates and to acquire a more impressive seat than Kirtling.

Late in 1585, at the age of fifty-four, North, together with his eldest son, John North, accompanied Leicester to the Netherlands with the English forces sent to assist the Dutch rebels in their fight against Philip II. The queen actually ordered him to go, despite the fact that Leicester did not have a post for him, and he was forced to serve without pay. Ill health and a sense that he was not given enough to do seem to have dogged North, who was regarded by some as one of Leicester's chief cronies there, but at the beginning all attempts to obtain some office for him, whether as governor of Brill or as a member on the commission for the states general of the United Provinces, failed. He served as governor of Flushing in June 1586 and of Utrecht and Harlingen the following month, fighting in the campaigns that summer and behaving with great courage at the battle of Zutphen on 22 September; there, despite a wound to the knee from a musket shot which subsequently left him 'bedde-redde', hearing that the enemy was engaged, he had himself carried to his horse and lifted to the saddle, and 'with one boot on and one boot off, went to the matter very lustily' (Bushby, 121). His courage was rewarded by Leicester with promotion to knight banneret. He was back in London in February 1587 for the funeral of Sir Philip Sidney but returned with Leicester in June to campaign in the Netherlands. Following Leicester's recall in October, North served for some months under Peregrine Bertie, thirteenth Baron Willoughby de Eresby, who formed so high an opinion of his abilities that he named North as one of the four best fitted to succeed him as captain-general. By April 1588, however, North was summoned back to Cambridgeshire as lord lieutenant to attend to the defence of the realm in preparation for the coming Spanish invasion. Back in the county, he called on the assistance of the privy council in his drive to obtain the necessary contributions for soldiers and armour from the local gentry and clergy, and during the Armada commanded part of the queen's bodyguard, accompanying her to Tilbury. Later that year he failed to persuade Burghley to secure for him the governorship of Berwick.

Perhaps kept from high office in the wake of Leicester's

death by privy councillors, North found that his friendship with his old card-playing companion, the queen, finally brought him promotion. Despite failing health and increasing deafness, following the death of Sir Francis Knollys he was made a privy councillor and treasurer of the household on 30 August 1596. Although he claimed to have achieved great economies as treasurer, his remaining years were marked by declining health and personal sadness. His elder son died on 5 June 1597, leaving as heir his grandson Dudley *North (*bap.* 1582, *d.* 1666), whom he tried unsuccessfully to marry to a relation of Burghley's. North died at his London house in Charterhouse Square on 3 December 1600. The funeral service took place on 22 December at St Paul's Cathedral, and he was buried at Kirtling on 12 February 1601. His will, drawn up on 22 October 1600, detailed annuities and bequests totalling £1300 to a number of grandchildren and £100 in gold to the queen, 'in acknowledgment of my love and duety to her Majesty from whom I have receaved advauncement to honor and many and contynuall favours' (PRO, PROB 11/97, sig. 6).

JOHN CRAIG

Sources F. Bushby, *Three men of the Tudor time* (1911) · *DNB* · E. J. Bourgeois, *A Cambridgeshire lieutenancy letterbook, 1595–1605*, Cambridgeshire Records Society, 12 (1997) · E. J. Bourgeois, 'The queen, a bishop and a peer: a clash for power in mid-Elizabethan Cambridgeshire', *Sixteenth Century Journal*, 26 (1995), 3–15 · HoP, *Commons, 1558–1603*, 3.140–43 · G. S. Thomson, *Lords lieutenants in the sixteenth century* (1923) · T. A. Walker, *A biographical register of Peterhouse men*, 2 vols. (1927–30) · W. P. Baildon, ed., *The records of the Honorable Society of Lincoln's Inn: admissions*, 1 (1896) · P. S. Allen, 'The birth of Thomas North', *EngHR*, 37 (1922), 565–6 · will, PRO, PROB 11/97, sig. 6 · D. North, *Some notes concerning the life of Edward, Lord North* (1658) · F. Heal, 'The bishops of Ely and their diocese, c.1515–1600', PhD diss., U. Cam., 1972 · HoP, *Commons, 1509–58*, 3.21–5 · GEC, *Peerage* · R. North, *The lives of … Francis North … Dudley North … and … John North*, ed. A. Jessopp, 3 vols. (1890)

Archives BL, household accounts, Stowe MS 774 · Bodl. Oxf., papers · 'Booke of household charges' [at Wroxton Abbey, Oxfordshire, in 1904] | BL, Harley MSS, papers

Likenesses M. Gerards, portrait; formerly in possession of earl of Guilford at Waldershare, 1904 · portrait (as a youth); formerly in possession of Lord North at Wroxton Abbey, Oxfordshire, 1904 · portraits, repro. in Bushby, *Three men* · two portraits; known to be at Wroxton, 1904

North, Roger (1588–1652/3), soldier and projector of the Amazon Company, was the third child of Sir John *North (*c*.1550–1597), of Kirtling, Cambridgeshire, soldier and politician, and his wife, Dorothy, daughter of Sir Valentine Dale. Roger *North, second Baron North, was his grandfather, and Dudley *North, third Baron North, his elder brother. North matriculated as a fellow-commoner from Peterhouse, Cambridge, in Michaelmas 1607. He is next heard of in 1616 when, probably fired by glowing reports from the River Amazon, he joined the expedition under Sir Walter Ralegh, in search of the goldmines which Ralegh and his lieutenant Laurence Keymis claimed to have discovered in Guiana in 1595. North was related to Keymis through his sister-in-law Frances Brockett, wife of his brother Dudley.

The expedition sailed in 1616 and anchored off the mouth of the Orinoco in December, where Ralegh remained, while Keymis proceeded up river with five small ships, carrying 150 sailors and 250 soldiers, North being one of their commanders. Three of the ships reached the settlement of Santo Tomé, beyond which lay one of the supposed mines. Keymis's orders had been to approach the mine without fighting the Spaniards, but this was not to be. It is unclear if Keymis had secret orders to take the town, or if he hoped that malcontents within the town would admit his troops; it is more likely that he endeavoured to blockade it while he gained access to the mine. The English approached the defences in darkness, the Spaniards fired, and the English responded by storming the town, Ralegh's son Walter being killed in the confusion. Following this disaster, which brought only modest pillage, and harried by the Spaniards, Keymis made token searches for the mine before retreating back to the coast where he had to face Ralegh with the fateful news. He committed suicide the same day. In the inquiry that took place in London, North testified that Keymis had said that they would not discover the mine until they had taken the town, and that it would be folly to open a mine in full view of the enemy.

Despite the disastrous end to North's first expedition, he was attracted by the region. He was a prime mover behind the foundation of the Amazon Company, set up to establish a colony on that river, where there were already several Dutch, English, and Irish plantations. North's proposals attracted many influential and titled subscribers, but the company found itself blocked by an earlier patent granted to Robert Harcourt in 1613. North complained to the privy council that Harcourt, though his interest centred on the area of the River Oyapoco, had refused to come to an accommodation regarding the River Amazon. The privy council thereupon cancelled Harcourt's patent and reissued separate grants to Harcourt and to North, and on 10 September 1619 a charter was issued for the 'Governor and companie of noblemen and gentlemen of the Cittie of London: adventurers in and about the river of the Amazons'. By this time there were fifty subscribers and regular meetings were held at Arundel House to organize the first plantation. The sum raised, probably not more than £5000, was almost exhausted by the first outfit. North was keen to enlist merchants, druggists, dyers, and carpenters who had gained experience of the region at Sir Thomas Roe's settlement of 1611 and who would be able to exploit the area's natural products, rather than follow other colonists who were raising tobacco, annatto, and cotton. Matthew Morton, who had been with Roe on the Amazon, was to accompany North in a pinnace.

The Amazon Company's influential subscribers made it a powerful supporter of the anti-Spanish faction at court, which sought to weaken James I's attachment to Catholic Spain and his pursuit of a Spanish marriage. Opposition to the Amazon Company's proposals was voiced by Lord Digby, ambassador to Spain, who engaged in angry words with North across the table at court, but principally by the Spanish ambassador Diego Sarmiento de Acuña, better known as Count Gondomar. Gondomar reminded James of Ralegh's broken promise not to attack Spanish settlements, while the agent Julian Sanchez de Ulloa claimed that none of the 400 men North intended to take with him were merchants. He was countered by Sir George Calvert who wrote to Ulloa that, unlike Ralegh, North was a loyal and upright gentleman who had no reason to offend the king of Spain and that his adventurers and promoters were similarly minded, a claim that Ulloa would have known to be untrue. In fact there were then no Spanish settlements on the Amazon, only a Portuguese settlement at Belém, on the Pará River.

While protestations and counter-protestations flew back and forth, matters came to a head with the return of Gondomar from the continent in March 1620. North's departure was postponed to allow Gondomar to put his case to the privy council, which he did on 14 April before a packed audience that included many who were resentful of Spanish interference in a region with a long-established English presence. Gondomar repeated Spain's claims and threatened a breakdown of the friendship between the two countries. Uncertain of James's feelings and divided among themselves, the council further delayed North. Gondomar reported to his monarch that James had assured him that North's scheme would not be allowed to proceed, but Gondomar's fears that the Amazon settlers would go anyway were proved correct. North, who had been permitted to send two ships to Plymouth while he petitioned James to lift the embargo, went down to Devon and sailed without permission. John Smith in his *True Travels* (1630) wrote:

> Whereupon accompanied with 120 Gentlemen and others, with a ship, a pinnace, and two shallops, to remaine in the Countrey, hee set saile from Plimouth the last of April 1620 … and within seven weekes after hee arrives well in the Amazones … some hundred leagues they ran up the River to settle his men, where the sight of the Countrey and people so contented them, that never men thought themselves more happie.

The plantation was probably on the River Okiari, a northern tributary of the Amazon, entering close to the delta and close to Roe's settlement of Tourege.

James denounced North, cancelled the Amazon Company's patent, and issued a proclamation calling for the return of North and his companions. Leaving Thomas Painton in charge, North returned in January 1621. He was arrested, and committed to the Tower, and the 28,000 lbs of Roe's tobacco and other merchandise that he had brought back were seized as the property of the king of Spain. Negotiations between James, who wished to appease the powerful Amazon Company supporters, and Gondomar, who felt that Spain would be best served if North was pardoned, along with an undertaking not to revive the project, led to North's release on 28 February, but in April he petitioned the grand committee of the House of Commons during the recess to relieve his settlers or bring them back. The committee questioned James's powers to dismantle the company and asserted North's right to sue the Spanish government for the return of his tobacco, which he had earlier been denied. James was furious; North was rearrested, but Gondomar's

wish to see him executed or at least sentenced to a long term of imprisonment was refused and he was freed in July, on condition that he made no further attempt to contact his settlers. North's share of the tobacco was then released, but immediately made subject of a further restriction, being claimed by the crew in lieu of wages. A third dispute, with customs over the duty payable, delayed the release of the tobacco until the end of October, by which time it had spoiled and was worthless. North continued to find supporters in court and in parliament. The tobacco dues were remitted and, for the next few years, despite the dissolution of the company, North maintained contact with the settlers and continued to receive goods.

Anglo-Spanish relations cooled with the death of James and the accession of Charles I, prompting North and his former Amazon Company supporters to revive their plans. Harcourt surrendered his patent and joined North; the Guiana Company was chartered in May 1627, with George Villiers, duke of Buckingham, as first honorary governor and North as deputy governor. The company's rights extended over a vast territory, combining Harcourt's grant of the coast from the Essequibo to the Oyapoco with the former Amazon Company's grant of land from the Oyapoco to 5° S of any part of the Amazon. The subscribers were, however, gentlemen rather than merchants, who were now more inclined to invest in the West Indies, and North had difficulty in raising enough cash to equip his settlers. Harcourt sailed for the Amazon in November 1628, but ignored his orders and returned to the Oyapoco where he allocated land for sugar production.

Unaware of Harcourt's actions, a syndicate of the company consisting of Sir John North and others dispatched a second ship with at least 100 men to the Amazon in January 1629, but by this time the situation there was becoming confused. Many of the earlier English and Irish settlers were joining new plantations set up by the Dutch West India Company, while the Portuguese were beginning to oust the northern Europeans from the delta region. The men were settled at North Fort, just down river of the Okiari confluence with the Amazon. The next two years brought only assorted disasters; no merchandise was sent to England, and the company found itself with two colonies on the coast to be relieved. North insisted that both should be uprooted and transplanted to the Amazon, and his supporters seem to have won the argument in council. Further difficulties ensued, aggravating the split between North and Harcourt; the settlers likewise became divided among themselves, and North Fort fell to the Portuguese in February 1631.

In 1632 North was drawn into a chancery suit over his administration of the estate of his brother-in-law Sir Francis Coningsby and his actions as executor to Coningsby's widow, Lady Mary Coningsby. In 1634 North petitioned the king for a speedy settlement of these troublesome affairs, which had by then lasted for seventeen years. There was talk in 1635–7 of North's patent being renewed, and Sir John North expressed a wish that his brother could captain one of the king's ships, but nothing came of these proposals. North was unmarried; much of his later years was spent with his brothers at Kirtling, the Cambridgeshire home of Dudley, third Baron North. By October 1652, when he composed his will, North declared himself 'sick and weak in bodie' (PRO, PROB 11/231). He was then residing in his house in Princes Street, in the parish of St Giles-in-the-Fields, London, where he died shortly afterwards, his will being proved on 2 May 1653. After various cash gifts to his brothers and their wives, all his property and his lands in the fens and elsewhere in England were bequeathed to his brother Gilbert North.

ANITA McCONNELL

Sources J. Lorimer, ed., *English and Irish settlement on the River Amazon, 1550–1646*, Hakluyt Society, 2nd ser., 171 (1989) · V. T. Harlow, *Ralegh's last voyage* (1932) · J. A. Williamson, *English colonies in Guiana and on the Amazon, 1604–1668* (1923) · 'Examination of Captain Roger North taken before the Lords at Whitehall, 17 Sept 1618', BL, Harleian MS 6846, fol. 63 · *CSP dom.*, 1634–5, 413 · will, PRO, PROB 11/231, sig. 326 · M. Strachan, *Sir Thomas Roe, 1581–1644: a life* (1989)
Wealth at death exact sum unknown: will, PRO, PROB 11/231, sig. 326

North, Roger (1651–1734), lawyer, politician, and writer, the sixth and youngest son, and the youngest of the ten surviving children, of Dudley *North, fourth Baron North (1602–1677), and Anne (c.1613–1681), daughter of Sir Charles Montague, was born at Tostock, Suffolk, on 3 September 1651. Until recently there has been some uncertainty about North's date of birth. Jessopp (in his edition of the autobiography) gives this as 3 September 1653 (Jessopp, 3.286). Scholars since have favoured 1651: Grassby (appendix F) gives 3 September 1651.

Early life and education North's early childhood was spent between Tostock and the house of his grandfather Dudley, third Baron North, at Kirtling, where his parents were often summoned to amuse the old Lord North and to help defray his household expenses. North's first schooling was at Kirtling with the Revd Ezekial Catchpole and a year later he was sent to the free school at Bury St Edmunds where his older brothers Francis *North, Dudley *North, and John *North had received their education. Roger was sent home after a year because of illness—what he later referred to as 'an acute feavour' (BL, Add. MS 32506, fol. 12v)—returned to study with Catchpole for two or three years, and then was sent with his brother Montagu to the free school at Thetford.

In 1666 North spent a year at home reading with his father in preparation for the university and studying music with John Jenkins. On 30 October 1667 he entered Jesus College, Cambridge, as a fellow-commoner. He shared a room with his brother John, a fellow of the college, whom North regarded as his tutor. His brother took little trouble to direct his studies and North 'followed [his] owne appetite, which was to naturall philosophy … and particularly D[es] Cartes' and also to mathematics (BL, Add. MS 32506, fols. 18v–19, 20v). After about a year he fell ill and returned home; on 21 April 1669 he went to London with his father to be admitted to the Middle Temple to

Roger North (1651–1734), by Sir Peter Lely, 1680

study the common law. His brother Francis, already a distinguished lawyer, helped him materially and was to be his supporter and patron until his death in 1685.

Lawyer and politician, 1674–1689 On 29 May 1674 North was called to the bar of the Middle Temple and after Francis North became chief justice of the common pleas in 1675 and a circuit judge Roger regularly accompanied his brother. In February 1679 he was appointed steward to the see of Canterbury by Archbishop Sancroft. On 26 October 1682 North was made one of the king's counsel, one month later a bencher of the Middle Temple, and later a Lent reader. In October 1683 he was elected as treasurer of the Middle Temple. These positions brought him into contact with leading politicians: he frequently attended meetings of the privy council and became personally known to Charles II and the duke of York. North was one of the counsel for the prosecution against Lord Russell and Algernon Sidney, the two main defendants in the Rye House plot trials of 1683. On account of his work for the crown, on July 21 1683 he was chosen free burgess of Dunwich in Suffolk and in January 1684 he was appointed solicitor-general to the duke of York; on James's accession to the throne in February 1685 he became solicitor-general to Queen Mary of Modena. On 19 January 1686 he was appointed as her attorney-general and member of the queen's council, a post which required him to take charge of the queen's financial affairs. In March 1685 North was elected member of parliament for Dunwich. On 20 November 1685 he was elected recorder of the city of Bristol, a city with which he was familiar from frequent visits with his brother Francis as circuit judge. He held the post until 1688. Henning says that North was a 'very active member of James II's Parliament', that he was 'appointed to twenty committees ... and carried three bills to the upper house' (HoP, *Commons, 1660–90*, 3.154). He opposed the bill to naturalize all protestant refugees, introduced a bill for the improvement of tillage, and was among those 'instructed to draft a clause forbidding any motions in either House to alter the succession to the throne' (ibid., 3.155). He was involved with promoting ship-building and with a bill for registering births, deaths, and marriages, and issue of the nobility and gentry.

Because he refused to take the oath of allegiance to William and Mary in 1689, North was a nonjuror. After the rev-olution he was a regular legal adviser to Sancroft and the other six bishops who had refused to take the oath and who were, as a consequence, threatened with suspension and subsequent deprivation. North refused to present himself to Sancroft's successor, Archbishop Tillotson, who had been installed in May 1691, and he refused to give up his post as steward to the see of Canterbury until, in April 1692, he was officially replaced by William Baber. After William and Mary were offered the crown on 13 February 1689 committees of both houses of parliament were set up to review what the whigs regarded as illegal meas-ures under the reigns of Charles II and James II. On 13 December 1689 North appeared before the House of Lords committee (called the 'Murder-Committee') to answer for his role in these trials. From 1689 he considered moving from London and began negotiations to purchase the Rougham, Norfolk, estate of Yelverton Peyton, a property over which both his brother Francis and his sister Eliza-beth Wiseman had held mortgages. The purchase was finalized on 26 December 1690.

Marriage and family On 26 May 1696 North married Mary Gayer (c.1666–c.1729), daughter of Sir Robert Gayer of Stoke Poges in Buckinghamshire. Sir Robert had been a courtier and friend of Charles II and of William Sancroft. As a Jacobite he was implicated in the duke of Berwick's plot in 1696 and he fled to the continent until 1698. It may have been because of his wife's connections that North was regarded with suspicion by the authorities, and his house was three times searched for weapons: in 1696, dur-ing the Jacobite rising of 1715, and at the time of the Atter-bury plot in 1722.

The Norths had seven children: Anne (b. 1697), who mar-ried Thomas Wright of Downham; Elizabeth; Christian; Catherine; Mary, who married Sir Henry L'Estrange; Roger (1703–1771), who married, first, his cousin Mary, daughter of Sir George Wenyeve of Brettenham in Suffolk, then Jane, daughter of William Lake of Flitcham in Norfolk; and Montagu (1712–1779), who later became canon of Windsor and married Elizabeth, daughter of the Revd Francis Folkard.

North spent the rest of his life at Rougham. There he devoted himself to music, philosophical interests, mech-anical pursuits, legal work for family, friends, and neigh-bours (including his brother-in-law, William Gayer, Sir Nicholas L'Estrange, the Walpoles, and the Beddingfields), and to the development and management of his estate. He maintained his rooms in the Middle Temple until his death, leasing them to his nephew, North Foley, until 1717, and then to Arthur Onslow, to 1724. On his death he bequeathed them to his elder son, Roger.

Political and legal writings North claimed to have been always indebted to his brother Francis, who was fourteen years his elder and who in many ways took on the role of the eldest son in default of the eldest, Charles, who seems not to have been on good terms with any of the younger members of the family. It was Francis on whom their father also leaned—for both legal and financial advice and assistance. It was on Francis's advice that Roger North studied the common law, and it was Francis who helped him set up his rooms in the Middle Temple. Roger North went on the circuit with him and he lived with him, even after Francis married in 1672, until the latter's death in 1685.

Nevertheless, despite his expressed feelings of depend-ence on his brother, his writings show that well before his brother's death North had made major contributions to both the legal and political life of the late 1670s and early 1680s. Furthermore, after Francis's death it was North's turn to protect his brother from the slanders of the whig party opposed to his judgments in some law cases of the early 1680s, including the Rye House plot trials and the case of Soame and Bernardiston. After William and Mary came to the throne in February 1689 not only was North required to answer for his own and Francis's role in the prosecution of the 'martyrs' of the Rye House plot, but the whigs also wished to restore the corporations and to deprive all those who had taken part in the surrender of charters of the right to vote. North wrote a pamphlet against the Corporation Bill, which would have made pos-sible charges against the estates of prominent tories, including that of Francis North. At this time the whigs attempted to introduce the bill of pains and penalties, in January 1690. North wrote also against this bill 'A letter in answer to an inquiry touching an act of paines and penaltys ... Jan. 1689' (BL, Add. MS 32524, fols. 1–12). He began his *Life of the Lord Keeper North* partly in response to what he saw as continued misrepresentation of Francis, and in the early years of the eighteenth century, when these criticisms became part of whig history, he wrote the *Examen* in order to refute at length the claims made against Francis as well as against his brother Dudley, one of the commissioners of the customs (1684, 1685–9) and sheriff of London (1682).

North's political and legal writings survive mainly in BL, Add. MSS 32520, 32523, and 32524 and date from the time he became politically prominent, playing an active part in parliament during the reign of James II from 1685. One bill of which he was proud was for a general registry of estates and titles, a project which Francis North had been keen to pursue ('About a registry', BL, Add. MS 32518, fols. 51–6; Rougham MSS, Box 23/C.5), which, although finally rejected by parliament, North nevertheless published in 1698: *Arguments and Materials for a Register of Estates*. One work, 'Discourse on the study of the laws' (BL, Hargrave MS 394, fols. 2–17v, transcription with additions in North's hand, published in 1824), is a general treatise on the requirements of legal study in the late seventeenth century.

There is no doubt that under James's rule North felt that his position was more and more compromised. While strongly loyal to the Stuart kings, he believed James's political and legal decisions were wrong. For instance, in 1686, when James wished to waive the provisions of the Test Act for military officers, Roger North was required, as attorney-general to the queen and as one of the king's counsel, to deliver his opinion, which was against the waiving (BL, Add. MSS, 32520, fols. 35–37v; 32523, fols. 47–53v; Add. MS 32520, fols. 38–41v is North's account of the lawsuit against Sir Edward Hales on this same issue). When Samuel Parker, bishop of Oxford, a strong supporter of James, wrote his *Reasons for Abrogating the Test Imposed upon All Members of Parliament* (1687) North wrote an answer to it, claiming that the king had no right nor precedent for abrogating the test ('Matter of Fact', BL, Add. MS 32523, fols. 47–53v).

The universities were also subject to James's plans to promote Catholics to high posts and in July 1686 he reintroduced the ecclesiastical commission (defunct since 1641) to enforce his own way in ecclesiastical matters. Sancroft was appointed to this commission, although he refused to sit on it. It was at Sancroft's instigation that North wrote his paper on the high commission and the prerogative (BL, Add. MS 32520, fols. 48–61v; Add. MS 32506, fol. 115v). *Quo warranto* proceedings were to be used against the universities, and although North, with Francis, had approved of the *quo warranto* proceedings against municipal charters he now disapproved of them against ecclesiastical corporations ('An account of franchises', BL, Add. MS 32520, fols. 66–73). He wrote in support of Magdalen College, Oxford, where James tried to influence the election of a new master in 1687 (BL, Add. MS 32520, fols. 106–119v). Sancroft consulted North not only on the ecclesiastical commission but also on his position under *praemunire* in case he (Sancroft) refused to confirm bishops who had not taken the tests (BL, Add. MS 32520, fols. 74–105; Add. MS 32506, fol. 116r–v).

When the declaration of indulgence was reissued in 1688 and clergy were required to read it in all churches, the question of resistance to the king's command arose. After James had fled the country (December 1688) and while England still had no monarch (January 1689), North wrote a pamphlet, 'The present state of the English government considered' (BL, Add. MS 32520, fols. 132–57). He believed that James's flight did not alter the continuity of the constitution and that the convention (which North called the 'pretended parlement') could not alter hereditary monarchy ('Of parlements', BL, Add. MS 32520, fols. 120–31).

In his role as legal adviser to Sancroft and the nonjuring bishops, North set out the legal implications of their position (BL, Add. MSS, 32520, fols. 158–165v; 32523, fols. 70–72v, 78–81v; 32506, fol. 116v). After Sancroft retired, North 'constantly visited him', just before his death settling his legal affairs for him (BL, Add. MS 32506, fol. 117r–v). Sancroft gave North his bass viol when he left Lambeth Palace and on his death North was to have £20 for a memorial ring. At the time (November 1693) North was setting up his parochial library at Rougham and 'thought a memoriall of him there would be more lasting of him then a ring. And I bought a sett of law books, had 'em bound after his manner and wrote in them' (BL, Add. MS 32506, fol. 118; Rougham MSS, Box 23.F.2). Another prominent nonjuror, the antiquarian divine George Hickes, also took legal advice from North when he was forced to surrender his post of dean of Worcester, and at that time he took refuge, disguised, in North's chambers in the Middle Temple. North's ideas on the effect of Queen Mary's death (1694) on the parliament and on allegiance after the death of James II (1701) are expressed in letters to unidentified friends (BL, Add. MS 32524, fols. 14–29, 82v–87).

Life interests Along with his writings on law and politics, North's writings on other subjects are included in some 50,000 manuscript leaves surviving in both public and private libraries and some printed books, published anonymously. His surviving writings, ranging in topic from mechanics to music, from biography to perspective, from etymology to the management of fish ponds, provide an insight into his wide-ranging interests, and into the intellectual issues which concerned not only him but others of his contemporaries. One of the best sources for understanding his early life and interests is his autobiography, 'Notes of me' (BL, Add. MS 32506), which he began in the late 1680s and probably worked at spasmodically until the late 1690s when he abandoned it, incomplete. There he writes of his interest in applied mathematics and in music—both performed and theoretical; of his design for the building of the Middle Temple gateway after the fire in January 1679 (completed 1683–4, when North was treasurer); of his work with Sancroft; and as one of the executors of the estate of Sir Peter Lely, who died in 1680. There, too (fols. 176v–180 and 184–93), he describes his method for disposing of Lely's pictures by lottery and his efforts as one of the legal guardians of his two children. After Francis North's death in 1685, North lived in Lely's house in Covent Garden until he moved to Rougham. Shortly before his death Lely painted North's portrait, which survives in the private collection of the Norths of Rougham.

Although most of North's writing was accomplished after he moved to Rougham, during his time in London he began to develop his ideas about art, mechanics, architecture, and music by his friendship and discussion with many of the virtuosi then living in London. He was an avid frequenter of concerts. During the rebuilding of St Paul's Cathedral he and his brother Dudley spent Saturday mornings talking to Sir Christopher Wren about the building. After the fire at the Middle Temple, North was involved in the plans for rebuilding, and in 1684 he designed and supervised the building of the new gateway (BL, Add. MS 32540, fol. 37v). During 1684 and 1685 North with his brother Dudley tried to divert Francis, then in declining health, with plans for rebuilding and extending his property at Wroxton in Oxfordshire. North designed his own house at Rougham and even attempted to make the bricks on the site. The experience led him to write his treatise on architecture, 'Cursory notes of building'. This work is 'probably the most detailed account of the planning and building of a seventeenth-century house in English architectural literature' but it was written primarily to show general principles and thus stands beside other major seventeenth-century architectural treatises in significance (Colvin and Newman, xv–xxi).

North maintained a long friendship with George Hickes, whom he had met through Francis in 1679 and whose political opinions he shared. After he moved to Rougham, he and Hickes corresponded on several matters including their common interest in etymology and North's plans to write the *Examen*, a history of the 1670s and 1680s and in answer to White Kennett's *Compleat History*. Hickes also donated some books to the parochial library which North set up at Rougham.

North wrote biographies of three of his brothers, his most ambitious being that of his brother Francis. This *Life*, his first attempt at biography, was written partly with the aim of defending his brother's reputation in the late 1680s, but also for Francis's son, the young Lord Guilford (BL, Add. MS 32520, fols. 208–210v). As Francis's reputation continued to be attacked in the first two decades of the eighteenth century, North continued to revise and rewrite his *Life*, completing the last surviving extant version in the late 1720s. During the 1700s and 1710s he began writing lives of John and Dudley North, and about 1715 he completed an essay on biographical writing which he obviously intended to preface all three lives—'Praeface, by way of essay upon the usefullness of private biografie' (BL, Add. MS 32525, fols. 43–63v; Chan, xx–xxi). North's son Montagu published the three lives after his father's death, that of Francis in 1742 and those of John and Dudley in 1744. While he heavily edited his father's manuscripts of the two latter, the version which Montagu produced for publication of Francis's *Life*, the longest of the three, grossly distorts both the form and content of his father's final version. North's theory of biography, discussed in his 'general preface' (published in 1984 as *Roger North: General Preface and Life of Dr John North*, edited by Peter Millard), is among the earliest in English, and his longest biography—that of Francis North—demonstrates not only his theoretical concerns but, in its innovative form, his ideas of combining chronological and thematic structure.

North spent a good deal of his time with his brother Dudley in the 1680s after Dudley's return from the east. Through Dudley he became interested in the laws appertaining to trade and it was he, not Dudley, who was the author of the preface to Dudley's 'Discourses of trade' (BL, Add. MS 32522, fols. 1–4), an essay of significance in the history of economics. The two brothers also discussed their ideas on the poor laws and both wrote on them (Dudley in BL, Add. MSS, 32512, 124v–130v, and 32522, 29v–32v; Roger in BL, Add. MS 32523, 82–101v, published by Montagu in 1753).

In 'Notes of me' North describes his two passions as mathematics and music. His passion for mathematics inclined to 'the practique which is much easyer [than the mastery]' (BL, Add. MS 32506, fol. 27), that is what is now called applied mathematics, and for North included geometry, arithmetic, dialling, mechanics, and particularly sailing. He was given a present of a yacht by John Windham which Windham himself had made, and which North kept four years in the Thames during the early 1680s. North includes his account of his role in rebuilding the Middle Temple and his interest in perspective (BL, Add. MSS 32538, 32539) as part of his mathematical interests. His practical bent included his love of making what he called 'gimcracks' (BL, Add. MS 32506, fol. 15), a love he passed on to his younger son and which is reflected in his bequeathing to Montagu his 'iron turning lathe and maundrill and what turning and other tools he shall think fit to choose out of my workhouse for his own use'. He also bequeathed to Montagu his 'walnut case of mathematical instruments', and another, better set, he bequeathed (in the second codicil of his will) to Jesus College, Cambridge, where it is now housed in the library.

Music was North's dominant passion and one which he pursued all his life. He had been early introduced to the performance of it because both his father's and his grandfather's households included a resident music master, to teach the North children and to provide music for family performance. His father's account book details payments to John Lilly, Henry and George Loosemore, and to John Jenkins, with whom Roger North studied the viol. North was interested not only in performance. His many manuscript treatises on music and their preliminary essays deal with both the science and the art of music. Kassler points out how North's writings on music are innovative: in his attempts to understand the production of sound in wind instruments; in his elaboration of a 'physics of beauty'; in his development of 'a theory of harmony as individual chords that function in relation to a chord root and within a key'; and in his theory of the origins and history of music. North's theory of music is also important to his understanding of the operations of sense perception and the role of memory in these. His essays on mechanics, air, sensation, and teaching and learning were also part of his attempt to understand both the production of sound and its reception.

North was also an accomplished bass violist and at Rougham he had the famous organ builder Bernard (Father) Smith build him a chamber organ. North had first become acquainted with Smith when, as a bencher, he was involved in the competition at the Middle Temple to see whether Smith or Renatus Harris could provide the better organ. The 'battle of the organs' began in 1682 and it was not until 1688 that the Middle Temple finally decided to buy Smith's. On his death North had several musical instruments to leave his children: two harpsichords, two violins, two bass viols, and his organ, which was to remain at Rougham Hall, and a large collection of music books, which he originally intended his children to choose from as they wished but which he bequeathed entirely, by a second codicil to his will, to Montagu.

Death and historical significance Besides being guardian of Sir Peter Lely's children, North was also guardian of Francis North's three children (Francis, Charles, and Anne), of the two sons (Dudley and Roger) of his brother Dudley (d. 1691), and of the four children (William, Charles, Katherine, and Dudleya) of his eldest brother, Charles, Lord North and Grey (d. 1691). When his sister Anne (who married Robert Foley of Stourbridge in Worcestershire) died in 1717 he was involved in a lengthy correspondence with her son Philip and daughter Anne about the will and their living arrangements (BL, Add. MS 32501). His nephew Francis, Lord Guilford, gave some trouble after he went up to Trinity College, Oxford, in 1689 and North spent energy setting him right (Bodl. Oxf., MS Ballard 10, fols. 131, 133, 135r–v, 137r–v, 139r–v, 145). His involvement in the education of his wards was possibly the impetus for his interest in the moral essay genre including topics of social behaviour (BL, Add. MSS, 32523, fols. 122–141v; 32526, fols. 48–87v; 32549, fols. 36–38v).

North died at Rougham on 1 March 1734 and was buried in St Mary's Church there. A plaque in the church, erected in the early twentieth century, celebrates his life. He died owning not only his estate at Rougham but also those at Ashwicken, Leviat (Leggit), and Methwold, all in Norfolk. His will with two codicils was proved at London on 19 October 1734. The two codicils imply a falling-out between North and his eldest son, Roger, for in the first he bequeathed the surplus of his estate to both his sons, altering his original intentions to Roger in favour of Montagu. In the second codicil, besides the bequest of his best case of mathematical instruments to Jesus College (originally bequeathed to Roger), he gave his portrait painted by Lely to his daughter Mary L'Estrange, for life, afterwards to return to his family.

Although few of his works were published during his lifetime and therefore were relatively unknown, North was important to his contemporaries as a lawyer and politician and is significant to historians for his study of, and writing on, many of the topics exercising scholars of his own time in a number of disciplines. While his writings are a major source for details of the political and intellectual life of the late seventeenth and early eighteenth centuries, the genre and purposes of his writing must be taken into account when using the *Examen* and his *Life of the Lord Keeper North*, in particular, for historical source material. In these, North has been criticized for 'gossiping inaccuracies' and for what some modern historians have seen to be sometimes exaggerated claims he makes for his brother the lord keeper (Keeton, 492, 102). In the case of the *Examen*, North was writing in defence of two of his brothers, Francis and Dudley, who he believed had acted scrupulously in their public offices, and whom he believed later historians had maligned. In the case of the *Life*, his purpose was both to defend his brother and to present his life as in many respects exemplary. Neither was written for publication (although North gave a manuscript copy of the *Examen* to Jesus College, Cambridge). Rather, it seems that North's intention was to write for his own family. Modern scholars have been too ready to take

him at his own, heavily ironic, assessment—as in 'Notes of me' (BL, Add. MS 32506, fols. 23v–24) where he appears to devalue what is revealed elsewhere in his writings as an enormous capacity for intellectual enquiry, for advancing public and political ideals about which he felt passionately, for giving assistance and sound advice, and for entering into and relishing the physical details of day-to-day life. His writings on the theory and philosophy of music were in advance of those of other writers in many areas. He was a major theorist and writer of extended biography. His writing on architecture is among the most important in the seventeenth century. Additionally, the survival not only of his finished treatises in these and other subjects, but also of his numerous essays in preparation for writing these treatises, lays bare the process of composition and refinement of ideas—a process common but rarely surviving for writers of his period—making it possible to understand how one man, at any rate, reacted to, read, and made use of the published writings, the scientific experiments, the music, and the art and architecture of his time.

MARY CHAN

Sources BL, Add. MSS 32500–32551 [incl. 'Notes of me', Add. MS 32506] • MSS, priv. coll. of Thomas North, Rougham, Norfolk • F. J. M. Korsten, *Roger North (1651–1734) virtuoso and essayist* (Amsterdam and Maarssen, 1981) • M. Chan and J. C. Kassler, *Roger North: materials for a chronology of his writings, checklist no. 1* (1989) • M. Chan, ed., *The life of the lord keeper North by Roger North* (1995) • *Roger North: general preface and life of Dr John North*, ed. P. Millard (1984) • J. C. Kassler, 'North, Roger', *New Grove*, 2nd edn • *Roger North's Cursory notes of musicke (c.1698–c.1703)*, ed. M. Chan and J. C. Kassler (Kensington, NSW, 1986) • *Roger North's The musicall grammarian, 1728*, ed. M. Chan and J. C. Kassler (1990) • M. Chan, J. C. Kassler, and J. D. Hine, *Roger North's 'Of Sounds' and Prendcourt Tracts* (Kensington, NSW, 2000) • *Of building: Roger North's writings on architecture*, ed. H. Colvin and J. Newman (1981) • Bodl. Oxf., MS Eng. hist. b.2; MS Ballard 10; MS Tanner 104; MS North c.10, fol. 104 • CUL, Baker MS Mm. 1.48, fols. 114–117v • R. Grassby, *The English gentleman in trade: the life and works of Sir Dudley North, 1641–1691* (1994) • A. Freeman and J. Rowntree, *Father Smith, otherwise Bernard Schmidt* (1977) • Dudley North's account book, Rougham MSS, Rougham, Norfolk • D. B. S. Randall, *Gentle flame: the life and verse of Dudley, fourth Lord North (1602–1677)* (Durham N.C., 1983) • W. Letwin, 'The authorship of Sir Dudley North's *Discourses on trade*', *Economica*, new ser., 18 (1951), 35–56 • A. Jessopp, ed., *The lives of the Norths*, 3 vols. (1890); repr. with a new introduction by E. Mackerness (1972) • *CSP dom.*, 1682 • G. W. Keeton, *Lord Chancellor Jeffreys and the Stuart cause* (1965) • HoP, *Commons, 1660–90*, vol. 3 • *Notes of me: the autobiography of Roger North*, ed. P. Millard (2000) • will, PRO, PROB 11/667, sig. 223

Archives BL, corresp. and papers, Add. MSS 32500–32551 • Bodl. Oxf., corresp. • priv. coll., family MSS | Bodl. Oxf., MSS Eng. hist. b.2, Ballard 10, Tanner 104 • Herefs. RO, letters to Robert Foley and Anne Foley • St John Cam., MS James 613

Likenesses P. Lely, oils, 1680, priv. coll. [*see illus.*] • oils, 1680 (after P. Lely), NPG • G. Vertue, line engraving (after P. Lely, 1680), BM, NPG; repro. in R. North, *Examen* (1740)

North, Sir Thomas (1535–1603?), translator, was born on 28 May 1535 in London, the younger son of the four children of Edward *North, first Baron North (c.1504–1564), and his first wife, Alice Murfyn, formerly Brigandine, and *née* Squire (d. 1560). It has been thought likely that he attended Peterhouse, Cambridge, to which his father left a benefaction on his death, but his name does not survive among the college records (Walker, 1.204–5). He was admitted on 9 February 1556 as a member of Lincoln's Inn; North's manucaptors, or sureties, were his elder brother, Roger *North, and Richard Allington. On the following day North's special admission was recorded: it brought with it certain privileges, such as exemption from keeping vacations and serving certain offices. Average age on admission to an inn of court in the period immediately preceding North's entry was twenty or twenty-one. Whether North's special admission also exempted him from undertaking the legal exercises is unclear; in any event, he did not proceed to be called to the bar.

Some indication, however, of how North's time was spent at Lincoln's Inn can readily be inferred from the publication in 1557, by John Waylande, of his translation of Bishop Antonio de Guevara's *The Diall of Princes*. North's dedication to Queen Mary, dated 20 December, sought the queen's encouragement, the author 'beinge yonge, to attempt the like enterprise' on further occasions. North's translation, though it advertises itself as 'Englyshed oute of the Frenche', also involved recourse to the Spanish original, since it closes with a section of letters absent in the French translation 'conferred with the originall Spanishe copye' (sig. X5r). The volume's title-page, showing an elaborately staged scene of a monarch taking advice from his counsellors, and its spacious, double-columned folio format, certainly give evidence of North's ambition that his translation should (as he described it in the dedication) 'serve to hygh estates for counsell, to curious serchers of antiquityes, for knowledge, and to all other vertuous gentlemen for an honest, pleasaunte, and profitable recreation' (sig. A1r–v). As a bid for patronage, however, *The Diall*—for all that its title-page emphasized North as 'second sonne' to Mary's counsellor Lord North—was ill-, or at least unfortunately, timed. It seems likely, moreover, from comments made by North in the second, revised edition, *The Diall* (1568), that the first edition was not altogether well received for more literary reasons: 'detracting tongues', he wrote, had given out that the translation 'was no woork of myne, but the fruit of others labor' (sig. R1v). An existing translation, from an abridged French translation of Guevara by Jean Bouchier, Lord Berners, had been published in 1535 (it reached its ninth edition in 1557), but North does not seem indebted to it. How long North remained as a student is not known, though in 1568 he recalled with apparent fondness 'the woorshipfull, and my beeloved compaignyons, and fellow students of our house of Lyncolnes Inne' (ibid.).

North's father died on 31 December 1564; the will (20 March 1563) bequeathed him 'the patronage and Advowsons of the Churche Personage and Vicaredge' of Melton, Suffolk (PRO, PROB 11/48, fol. 54v). Whatever the disappointments of the reception afforded his first translation, in the years following his father's death North worked to expand its fourth book (entered to Thomas Marsh in the Stationers' register between July 1566 and July 1567), and to defend himself in the second edition, printed by Richard Tottell and Marsh in 1568 (Marsh and Tottell registered 'the hole boke of the Dyall of prynces' at some point between July 1567 and 1568). In the same year North was presented with the freedom of the city of Cambridge.

North had signed his defensive 'Epistle to the Reader' in 1568 'From my lord Norths house nere London' (sig. R1v). He seems intermittently to have been resident with his elder brother, Roger, for much of the rest of his life, and for the periods covered by 'The booke of the howshold charges and other paiments laid out by the .L. North and his commandement', January 1575 to February 1581 and April 1582 to December 1589, he was in receipt of an annual pension of £40, paid quarterly, of his brother's 'fre gift' (BL, Stowe MS 774, fols. 18r, 42v). Numerous other, smaller irregular payments are also recorded: they contribute to an impression that North was never independently financially secure. His next publication, *The Morall Philosophie of Doni*, published by Henry Denham in 1570, sought explicitly to draw on his brother's connections in its fulsome dedication to Robert Dudley, earl of Leicester. North translated the much-travelled *Morall Philosophie* from the Italian; Leicester himself spoke Italian, and North attempted to turn this to his advantage, suggesting that 'your L: that understandeth, maye at your pleasure and leysure … be judge of the matter, as I have made your Lordship patrone and my only Mecenas' (sig. A4r). Roger North, a close friend of Leicester, had earlier, in 1566, solicited the earl's patronage for his sister; here Thomas North delivered his own work to Leicester's 'honorable protection', and himself, 'Your Lordships humbly to commaunde' (sig. a1r). Fifteen years later Leicester was paying £5 to those who dedicated books to him—as valuable must have been his influence about court.

Between October 1573 and December 1574 Roger North was appointed and then dispatched as ambassador-extraordinary to the French court of the new king, Henri III, then resident at Lyons. He was accompanied by Thomas, whose early return from the embassy in November was greeted with eager curiosity at the English court: he reported 'plusieurs propos de fort grande satisfaction, du lieu d'où il venoit' ('many very highly satisfying reports of the place from which he came'), recorded the French ambassador, de la Mothe Fénélon (*Correspondance*, 6.292). The Norths' facility with European languages (Roger North discoursed in Italian with the French court) must have recommended them to the queen and her council (*CSP for.*, 1572–4). Bodl. Oxf. MS North a. 1 contains Roger North's official papers relating to the embassy.

On 10 December 1576 Roger North recorded the payment of £46 11s. 15d. for the purchase of 'the Lease of A howse & houshold stuff for Mr Tho: North', and a further £7 spent on 'preparacions' of the house. The location of this residence is not specified. None the less, North is likely to have been (at least temporarily) resident with his brother at Kirtling in September 1578 when Queen Elizabeth spent three days there on progress, and in March 1579 Roger North's note of 'persons lieng in my house ordinary' records (without punctuation) 'my brother his wif daughter man maid' among those present (BL, Stowe MS 774, fols. 29r, 89r). North was twice married: first to Elizabeth Rich (*née* Colville) of London, and second to

Judith, daughter of Henry Vesey of Isleham, Cambridgeshire, and widow of Robert Bridgwater. His second marriage may be connected to the payment recorded in July 1582 by Roger North: 'geven my brother iij^{li} goeng a woeng'. The dates of birth for the children of his first marriage, Edward and Elizabeth, are not known; payments by Roger North of £66 13s. 3d. to 'm^r stutvile for Bess Norths marriaeg' and a further £23 6s. 8d. 'geven hir to aparrel hir self w^t all', between June and October 1587, perhaps date his daughter's wedding (BL, Stowe MS 774, fols. 11r, 118r). There were no children of North's second marriage.

North's next publication is likely to have had its roots in a purchase made during the 1574 embassy, since his translation of Plutarch, *The Lives of the Noble Grecians and Romanes*, is taken from the third edition of Jacques Amyot's French translation, printed at Lausanne by François le Preux in 1574. North's translation was entered to the French refugee stationer Thomas Vautrollier on 6 April 1579; Vautrollier had earlier registered a privilege 'for .viij yeres. of PLUTARCH *de vitis imperatorum*' first granted to Lodwyck Lloyd in April 1573 (Arber, *Regs. Stationers*, 2.351, 886). North's dedication to Queen Elizabeth, dated 16 January 1579, rhetorically 'presumed to present' her with the translation, and her subjects with examples of 'honor, love, obedience, reverence, zeale, and devocion to Princes' (sig. *2r). North also took steps to orchestrate a real presentation of the book. Leicester, at the request of Roger North, wrote to William Cecil, Lord Burghley, in August 1580, to seek his favour towards the translation: Leicester found Thomas North, he wrote, 'a very honest gentleman & hath many good things in him, wch are dround only by pov^{er}tie' (Hatfield MSS 162/9; *Salisbury MSS*, 2.339). Burghley's reply on August 25, as well as confirming Leicester's assessment of North, 'whom I thynk truly well of for manny good partes in hym', cautiously announced an intention 'to mak his portion more by x^l by yere, then hir Ma^{ty} did assent, hopyng th^t she will not mislyk it' (PRO, SP 12/141/39; *CSP dom.*, 1547–80, 672). Unfortunately notice of the initial rate at which the portion was set does not survive.

The earl of Desmond's escalating rebellion in Ireland later in the year offers tangible proof of North's usefulness to his patrons. In October 1580 North was one of five captains embarking with troops at Chester to sail to Dublin, where they arrived on 11 November; later in the month, 200 of North's footmen were sent to Dundalk. He returned to England in March 1582, bearing with him a letter from Loftus to Burghley praising his 'faithful and chargeable service' and hoping that the queen would have 'consideration' of it and him (*CSP Ire.*, 1574–85, 264–70, 352). North seems at least briefly to have considered returning, for Roger North recorded payment of £37 'geven my brother to goe in to yrland' in early April 1582; his wooing in July perhaps put paid to the intention. Five years later North was again in military service, on this occasion embarking at Yarmouth in June 1587 with 150 men from Cambridge and Ely for the Low Countries; Sir Thomas Shirley's accounts record payment to North for service until 10 October 1587 (*CSP for.*, 1587–9). On 24 June

1588 the privy council wrote of him to his brother as 'a very meet person for the trayninge' of men in Ely against the threat of the Armada (*APC*, 1588, 134).

North probably continued to circulate in and about the court. On 9 January 1591 he provided for Sir Julius Caesar, perhaps as a paid legal opinion or possibly on behalf of the earl of Oxford, a statement of 'his exceptions against the sute of Surveyor of the gagers of baer & ale', the latest of Caesar's schemes for a money-making monopoly; he signed himself, with an Italianate flourish, 'Divotiss^{mo} & affectionatiss^o' (BL, Add. MS 12497, fols. 411–12). In March 1591 North purchased for 5s., secondhand, a copy of the third edition (1582) of his *The Diall of Princes* and set about revising it towards a (never published) fourth edition (CUL, Adv.d.14.4). About this time he was knighted; in February 1592 he was given a commission as a justice of the peace in Cambridge, and he was present again in the rolls in 1597 (*CSP dom.*, 1591–5, 191).

Between September and December 1596 North served again in Ireland as captain of 100 footmen from Cambridge and Huntingdonshire stationed in Dublin (*CSP Ire.*, 1596–7, 108, 139–40; *Salisbury MSS*, 6.543, 558). His conduct there was perceived by others as less than exemplary: an anonymous report accuses him of having left his men, some of 'whose feet and legs rotted off for want of shoes', 'uncared for and unrelieved', but all the while continuing to demand their pay. It was also alleged that before leaving Ireland he sold his company, now a 'piteous, forlorn band', to his son, Edward North (*CSP Ire.*, 1596–7, 194–5). Whatever the truth, his reputation does not seem to have suffered: he was given a grant of £20 by the city of Cambridge in 1598.

Roger North's will (20 October 1600) requested that, once all debts, legacies, and charges had been settled, 'out of the Remaynder with some portion my brother Sr Thomas Northe, his sonne Edward Northe, his daughter my neece Stutfeyld be reteyned' (PRO, PROB 11/97, fol. 45r). However, delaying tactics on the part of Roger North's executor, George Calfield, kept back legacies not only from North but also from the will's prime beneficiary, Roger's grandson Dudley; legal recourse having failed them through the summer of 1601, the beneficiaries petitioned the queen (BL, Add. MS 61873, fols. 1–44). In February 1600 North was charged with the watch of the Tower in a jurisdictional dispute with the City of London, and in March 1601 was paid £10 for his part in putting down 'the late attemptes made by the late Earle of Essex and his adherentes' (*APC*, 1600–01, 153–4, 239–40). The references to 'my great unkle Sr Tho: North (whose poore estate yor Mat^{ie} hathe so gratiously pitied & relieved)' (BL, Add. MS 61873, fol. 39r) in Dudley North's petitions recognize the annual pension of £40 bestowed by the queen in 1601, as did North in the dedication to *The Lives of Epaminondas* and others printed by Richard Field in 1602, and reprinted with the Plutarch, again by Field, in 1603. There North praised the queen's comfort and support for his 'poore old decaying life' (sig. a2r), and, though some minor corrections were made to the text of his Plutarch in the edition of 1603, it is likely that he died in 1603 or soon afterwards. No will is extant.

In 1658 Dudley North described his great-uncle as 'a man of courage, a man learned … and endued with very good parts otherwise', yet suggested that he had never possessed 'a steadines comparable to his brother' (CUL, MS Ee.V.3, p. 46). North's fame, since Samuel Johnson's contention that Shakespeare had read Plutarch in North's translation (verified by Richard Farmer in 1767), has rested in the dramatist's having, among very much else, thrown (as Farmer had it) 'the very words of *North* into blank verse' (Farmer, 14). Shakespeare's acquaintance with North's translation probably derived from the printing house of Richard Field, whose presses may have been at work on a 1595 edition of Plutarch at the same time that they were printing Shakespeare's *Lucrece* in 1594 (entered 9 May; Arber, *Regs. Stationers*, 2.648). North's translation influenced profoundly not only the larger narrative structures of Shakespeare's Roman plays but innumerable local shapings of their language; though criticism now more strongly emphasizes Shakespeare's activity, creativity, and competitiveness as a reader of North than his passive indebtedness, the importance of this single work is unargued. In 1579 North, Englishing Amyot, wrote of translation as an accommodation of voices: 'the office of a fit translater, consisteth not onely in the faithfull expressing of his authors meaning, but also in a certain resembling and shadowing out of the forme of his style and the maner of his speaking' (*Lives*, sig. *7r*). If the manner of his own speaking is muffled, and his identity overlaid, in his literary work, it is none the less tempting to think that a (now cropped) side note added in manuscript by North to his copy of *The Diall* may have had for him a personal biographical application: 'want of mone[y] maketh a goo[d] scoller, and makes him fa[ll] to his booke' (sig. A4r).

TOM LOCKWOOD

Sources BL, Stowe MS 744 · BL, Add. MSS 12497 and 61873 · Bodl. Oxf., MS North a. 1 · CUL, MSS Ee.V.3 and Adv.d.14.4 · will, PRO, PROB 11/48 [Edward North, father] · will, PRO, PROB 11/97 [Roger North, brother] · S. Adams, *Household accounts and disbursement books of Robert Dudley, earl of Leicester, 1558–1561, 1584–1586* (1995) · APC, 1588, 1600–01 · CSP dom. · CSP for. · CSP Ire. · *Calendar of the manuscripts of the most hon. the marquis of Salisbury*, 24 vols., HMC, 9 (1883–1976) · W. P. Baildon, ed., *The records of the Honorable Society of Lincoln's Inn: admissions*, 2 vols. (1896) · P. S. Allen, 'The birth of Thomas North', *EngHR*, 37 (1922), 565–6 · Arber, *Regs. Stationers* · *Correspondance diplomatique de Bertrand de Salignac de la Mothe Fénélon*, ed. A. Teulet, 7 vols., Bannatyne Club, 67 (1838–40) · H. H. Davis, 'The military career of Thomas North', *Huntington Library Quarterly*, 12 (1948–9), 315–21 · R. Farmer, *An essay on the learning of Shakespeare*, 2nd edn (1767) · J. Nichols, *The progresses and public processions of Queen Elizabeth*, new edn, 3 vols. (1823) · K. A. Quinn, 'Sir Thomas North's marginalia in his *Dial of princes*', *Papers of the Bibliographical Society of America*, 94 (2000), 283–7 · T. A. Walker, *A biographical register of Peterhouse men*, 2 vols. (1927–30)

Archives BL, document in his hand, Add. MS 12497 · Bodl. Oxf., family papers · CUL, annotated copy of *The diall of princes*, Adv.d.14.4

North, Thomas (1810/11–1868), coal owner, was born probably at the Toll House, London Road, Nottingham. He was the son and heir of Thomas North (d. c.1833), a toll-gate keeper and mining contractor, but little else is known about his early life. He married twice; following the death of his first wife, Hannah Laycock (1811/12–1865), North married Catherine Sarah Stanley (d. 1920); they had a son, also called Thomas, born in 1867. In the 1820s the population of Nottingham was growing under the impetus of a fast-expanding demand for the machine-wrought lace in which the town specialized. North's father embarked on brick making at Mapperley, near Nottingham, and the production of coal from small mines at Babbington village, near Ilkeston. He is known to have borrowed £800 from Thomas Nunn, a chemist, in 1826; but apart from this the source of his capital can only be guessed at.

Between 1832 and 1841 (when he moved to The Park, Nottingham) North lived at Babbington Cottage, and was in overall control of the mining enterprise in that village. These mines were run by sub-contractors called 'butties', who hired the labour and provided the working capital. Mining methods and equipment were primitive and working conditions harsh. In 1835 North was joined by Thomas Wakefield (1791–1871), a member of a prosperous family engaged in textiles, who injected substantial capital funds into the partnership. In 1839 James Morley of Sneinton (third son of Richard Morley, a partner in the textile firm of I. and R. Morley) also joined the partnership; he contributed capital and worked full time without salary. About this time North and Wakefield were taking out mining leases over a wide area to the north of Nottingham, and were busily engaged in widening and deepening old shafts and sinking new ones. Between 1835 and 1844 they also constructed 18 miles of private railway, linking all their mines with canals, landsale wharves, and, subsequently, main-line railways, which gave them access to a substantial market at minimal cost. In July 1845 a fourth partner, Samuel Parsons, was admitted by agreeing to pay £18,000, in instalments, for a one-fifth share of the firm.

North and his partners then embarked on a new and risky venture. Up to this point all coalmines in Nottinghamshire and Derbyshire had been sunk into the exposed coalfield, where the seams outcropped onto the surface. The new Cinderhill colliery (about 3 miles north of Nottingham) was to work coal in the east of the coalfield, where the seams were concealed below magnesian limestone. The general belief was that either there was no coal beneath the limestone or, if there was, it was of no value. However, relying on the advice of his mining engineer, J. T. Woodhouse of Moira, North sank two shafts into the top hard seam in 1841–3; production commenced using the most up-to-date methods and equipment—the true longwall system, a powerful winding engine, iron wire ropes, shaft cages held rigid in the shafts by guide rails, mechanical haulage underground, efficient furnace ventilation, and pumping equipment. Also the shafts were lined with wrought iron 'tubbing' to keep them dry. All these were new to the district. Unfortunately a major fault to the east of the shafts brought production almost to a halt in March 1845, and pessimists were certain that this marked the limit of the coalfield. But North decided to drive a stone heading through the fault, and though by the middle of September 1847 he was in dire financial straits and had almost given up, coal was once more reached and production recommenced. Unfortunately the chief capital provider, Wakefield, had been bankrupted, losing his own money, that of his late father's estate, and funds entrusted to him by various charitable institutions. To add to North's difficulties, Morley felt cheated also, and consequently the partnership came to an end; North carried on as sole proprietor with the backing of Wright's Bank. For his share in the enterprise, Wakefield received from North only £2000, a mere fraction of the amount he had invested.

Thomas Wakefield had been leader of the whig Liberal group that dominated the Nottingham borough council. It was owing to his influence that North became a councillor in 1837 and mayor in 1844-5. In 1859 North was elected alderman, a position he held until his death in 1868. However, unlike Wakefield, he played no active part in politics and rarely spoke in council. Although coming from a Baptist background, North became an Anglican and was for some years a churchwarden at Basford parish church, Nottinghamshire. At a cost of £2000 in 1856 he provided a daughter church at Cinderhill, close to Basford Hall, the substantial mansion he leased in 1851 and in which he resided until his death. He also provided a Baptist mission hall at Cinderhill and a General Baptist chapel in Babbington village, along with houses for his workers.

North sank several new collieries similar to Cinderhill in the 1850s and 1860s. He also owned Nottinghamshire's largest brickworks, adjacent to his Cinderhill mine. He built a gasworks which supplied gas lighting to his mines as well as to chapels and workmen's houses. Without doubt he over-extended himself financially, and he and his agent spent much time and energy fending off creditors. When he died he owed Wright's Bank over £190,000. Ironically, the period 1871-4 was one of high prosperity in the coal trade, and had North lived his debts would have been cleared and his massive investment would have shown a handsome return.

North's pioneering venture at Cinderhill induced others to invest in large, well-equipped collieries to exploit the concealed coalfield in Nottinghamshire, which became the most profitable coalmining district in Britain. Despite his flawed character, North's enterprise and vision brought prosperity to what had been a poverty-stricken agricultural and framework-knitting district. He died at Basford Hall, Nottinghamshire, on 28 January 1868, from haematuria and congestion of the lungs, and was buried at Old Basford cemetery. He was survived by his second wife, and left an estate valued at under £120,000. ALAN R. GRIFFIN

Sources A. R. Griffin, 'Thomas North: mining entrepreneur extraordinary', *Transactions of the Thoroton Society*, 76 (1972), 53-73 · A. R. Griffin and C. P. Griffin, 'The role of coal owners' associations in the east midlands in the nineteenth century', *Renaissance and Modern Studies*, 17 (1973), 95-121 · A. R. Griffin, *Mining in the east midlands, 1550-1947* (1971) · *Nottingham Daily Guardian* (2 March 1868) · *Nottingham Review* (6 March 1868) · d. cert.
Archives Notts. Arch., collection

Wealth at death under £120,000: probate, 13 March 1868, *CGPLA Eng. & Wales*

North, Thomas (1830-1884), antiquary, was the son of Thomas North of Burton End, Melton Mowbray, Leicestershire, a butcher and grazier, and his wife, Mary Raven. He was born at Burton End on 24 January 1830 and was educated at Melton grammar school, but left to work for a local firm of solicitors. He presently gave up any ideas of a career in the law and moved from Melton to Leicester, where he took up a post at Paget's Bank.

From an early age North was drawn to the study of archaeology and antiquities. In 1861 he was elected honorary secretary of the Leicestershire Architectural and Archaeological Society, and he edited all its transactions and papers from that time until his death. He contributed more than thirty papers of his own and wrote on a variety of subjects, including tradesmen's tokens, ancient stained glass, and the letters of Robert Heyricke. Eight of these papers relate to his native town, of which he planned to write a history, although he did not live to complete it.

North's earliest book was a scholarly history of the church of St Martin in Leicester, published in 1866. In later life he became an authority on campanology and brought out in remarkably quick succession a series of monographs on the church bells of Leicestershire (1876), Northamptonshire (1878), Rutland (1880), Lincolnshire (1882), and Bedfordshire (1883); further volumes, on Hertfordshire, Essex, and Shropshire, were in preparation at the time of his death. North was elected a fellow of the Society of Antiquaries in 1875.

On 23 May 1860 North married Fanny, daughter of Richard Luck of Leicester; they had a son. In 1872 North resigned his post with Paget's Bank on the grounds of ill health and retired to Ventnor on the Isle of Wight. In 1881 he moved to the Plas, Llanfairfechan; he died there from lung disease on 27 February 1884. He was survived by his wife. In 1885 the Leicestershire Architectural and Archaeological Society erected a brass to his memory in St Martin's Church, Leicester.

W. G. D. FLETCHER, *rev.* MICHAEL D. RAFTERY

Sources W. G. Dimock Fletcher, 'The late Thomas North FSA', *Transactions of the Leicestershire Architectural and Archaeological Society*, 6 (1885) · *Church Bells* (8 March 1884) · private information (1894)
Wealth at death £11,222 0s. 7d.: probate, 19 May 1884, *CGPLA Eng. & Wales*

North, William, sixth Baron North, second Baron Grey of Rolleston, and Jacobite Earl North (1678-1734), army officer and Jacobite conspirator, was born at Caldecote, Cambridgeshire, on 22 December 1678. He was the eldest son of Charles, fifth Baron North (*d.* 1690), and Katherine (1644?-1694), the only daughter of William, Lord Grey of Wark. Following her husband's death Katherine married the governor of Barbados and left her son Charles and his sister Dudleya [*see below*] to young William's care. Raised and educated together, a 'deep and romantic affection' (North, 3.295) developed among the siblings, characterized by the brothers' virtual worship of their intellectual older sister. Perhaps inspired by her, William and Charles entered Magdalene College, Cambridge, in October 1691. Charles graduated MA in 1695. William, however, was distracted by the promise of military glory, and left Cambridge without a degree in 1694 so he could enter the newly established Foubert's military academy in London. To avoid mounting debts the aspiring officer was advised by his uncle Roger North to live abroad for what ultimately amounted to a three-year period. As his father had done in 1673, when he came of age in 1699 Lord North took his seat in the House of Lords as Baron Grey of Rolleston.

Known thereafter as Lord North and Grey, he was commissioned in March 1702 as captain of the foot guards. In January 1703 he received the colonelcy of the 10th regiment of foot. At Blenheim on 13 August 1704 he was wounded and lost his right hand. North accompanied the duke of Marlborough on his return to England in December. Soon promoted brigadier-general, in October 1705 North married Maria Margaretta (1690?–1762), daughter of the Vryheer van Ellemeet, treasurer of Holland. Maria was a woman of substantial fortune whom contemporaries described as attractive. Although some historians have described their childless marriage as unaffectionate, North's papers reveal numerous love letters presumably addressed to Maria. After North's death she married Patrick Murray, Lord Elibank, and resided with him in Scotland.

During the campaign season North spent the next six years in Flanders, but he also became an important figure in parliamentary debates. Extremely active in crucial votes, divisions, and protests in the House of Lords from 1706 to 1723, North was an eloquent, impassioned orator whose provocative speeches defiantly taunted whig opponents. North played a prominent role in debates over the union with Scotland and argued against impeachment of Henry Sacheverell. In November 1710 North opposed voting thanks to Marlborough for the campaign that year. In 1712 he entertained Prince Eugene during his visit to London. He was sworn a privy councillor and created lord lieutenant of Cambridgeshire in 1711 and governor of Portsmouth the following year. North's political inclinations were staunchly tory throughout his career, and his Jacobite tendencies only increased as Queen Anne's reign neared its end. When in June 1713 a motion was made for the queen to influence European powers to deny sanctuary to the Pretender (James Stuart, Stuart claimant to the throne), North insisted it suggested distrust of her majesty and that, since most of Europe was favourably inclined toward Britain, the Pretender had few choices for a country of residence. Similarly, in April 1714 North made defiant protests against the 'barbarity' of imposing a bounty on the exiled Pretender's head during debates on the question of whether or not the protestant succession was in danger. In addition to estate income from lands in Kent and Essex he received after his mother's death, North's military fortunes flourished. Promoted major-general in 1709 and lieutenant-general by 1710, he was present at the battle of Malplaquet and at such major sieges as Lille (1708), Béthune (1710), and Bouchain (1711). With the Hanoverian succession North exhibited his Jacobite zeal more openly. Suspected by Hanoverian ministers in early 1714, North was described by Lord Bolingbroke as a 'brave honest man by principles' (*Stuart Papers*, 1.444), one of few inclined to support the Stuarts for reasons other than mere self-interest. North received a commission from Rome, but apparently took no active part in the rising of 1715. None the less, government suspicion motivated his arrest by the authorities at Brussels in 1715.

North was indisputably involved in Jacobite and political plotting following the South Sea Bubble's collapse. He and other tory peers were members of a core group of vehement ministerial opponents who protested against measures in the Lords in the early 1720s as sheer acts of defiance. North was also one of a small group of eminent English Jacobite conspirators traditionally associated with the plot named after Francis Atterbury, bishop of Rochester. They contrived plans for an armed uprising to be launched early in 1722. North was commissioned by the Pretender as lieutenant-general and commander-in-chief for London and Westminster; therefore he was to play a crucial role in the takeover of the capital. North was given the Jacobite title of Earl North and also designated lord regent for the Pretender's restoration. North was the principal Jacobite leader who had extensive contacts with Christopher Layer, a Norfolk barrister who journeyed to Rome in 1721 and met the Pretender. After his return Layer sought proxy godparents to represent the exiled monarch and his queen *in absentia* for the christening of Layer's infant daughter. North eventually served as the Pretender's proxy when Charles Boyle, fourth earl of Orrery, refused the privilege. After the April 1722 christening North's friendship with Layer apparently blossomed. Detailed, sophisticated plans for the conspiracy referred to as 'the scheme' and recovered after Layer's apprehension later that year exhibited obvious signs of North's influence and military experience. During a deposition in October 1722 Layer admitted meeting North at his house in Epping, Essex, and drawing up these plans with his permission. Layer's interrogations made repeated damaging allegations about North's programme for instigating a rebellion incited initially among army officers. North's arrest order was issued on 26 September and soldiers were dispatched to his London house, which was thoroughly searched for incriminating papers. Captured instead of North was Orrery's secretary, sent there to warn of the danger, as Layer had done after his own earlier short-lived escape from the authorities. Realizing his imminent apprehension, North had meanwhile engineered an escape plan that nearly succeeded. Embarking for France at midnight on a smuggler's yacht, he reached the Isle of Wight before he was apprehended.

In October 1722 North was committed to the Tower of London for complicity in 'Atterbury's plot'. He was examined by lords of the council but never tried, yet Layer's interrogations left little doubt as to the extent of North's guilt. At his own trial Layer begged permission to subpoena Orrery and North. North made one brief appearance but, interestingly, strict limits were placed on the subject matter of his testimony. Other revelations described how North had arranged to purchase over 5000 muskets from a London gunsmith to be distributed throughout the city. The full extent of co-operation between Layer and North is difficult to determine, since Layer probably assumed primary responsibility for the conspiracy in order to minimize North's involvement. There were clearly several overlapping conspiracies rather than a single unified plot directed by Atterbury. Layer himself admitted emphatically that Orrery and North 'had different schemes' ('Report from the committee', 139, 144).

North was bailed on 25 May 1723 for £20,000 for himself and four sureties of £10,000 each. He appeared on his recognizance and was discharged on 28 October 1723. Shortly thereafter he retired to a life of exile, arriving in the Low Countries in 1724. He called on Atterbury regularly and met other leading Jacobites such as Orrery and Philip, duke of Wharton, in Brussels and Paris throughout 1725–8. In 1727 North was a strong contender for the vacant position of Jacobite secretary of state, but it was hastily awarded instead to James Graeme, Jacobite agent in Vienna. Exactly why he was denied the post is unclear, but his criticism of James during the latter's separation from his wife and Atterbury's hostility are likely factors. Thus, threatened with attainder if he returned to Britain, denied use of funds from his estates, and refused resources from his wife Maria's fortune to pay debts and enable him to maintain a lifestyle commensurate with his rank, North undertook, as a fellow Jacobite exile explained, 'the best 2d hand game' available (Lockhart, 2.338). After years of solicitations North, aided by the Jacobites' most prominent military exile, James, duke of Ormond, received a Spanish army commission in 1728. The same year he embraced Roman Catholicism, as his fellow exile Wharton had done, in what perhaps was perceived as an ultimate demonstration of loyalty. Their actions, however, severely alienated them from leading Jacobites such as Atterbury, who bitterly reproached North for his conversion. Consequently, North spent his remaining years commanding Spanish troops in and around Barcelona. Like Wharton, he unsuccessfully sought a government pardon in 1731. In North's last correspondence with James he was rather curtly informed that he could not obtain some favour North had requested. North died an embittered exile at Madrid on 31 October 1734. His second title of Lord Grey expired; the barony of North devolved upon his second cousin Francis, first earl of Guilford, who had succeeded his father, Francis, on 17 October 1729. North left a provision in his will for a ten-year-old illegitimate son named William Grayson, whose mother may have been Catherine Vanderline. She was North's mistress during a portion of his exile and reputedly became pregnant with his child after she had 'made his Guineas speak for the Sincerity of his Heart' (Argens, 95). She was married to a wealthy older man, but

followed North to Spain where he broke off their relationship.

Lord North's sister, **Dudleya North** (1675–1712), orientalist, was born at her father's house in Leicester Fields, London. Educated privately along with her brothers by their tutors, her natural facility as a linguist was obvious and she quickly gained fluency in Latin and Greek. She then began studying Hebrew, and after a 'long and severe course of study' had mastered 'a competent share of knowledge in the whole circle of Oriental learning' (Ballard, 357). The fact that non-western language works comprise the majority of books in a small personal library she amassed confirms her proficiency. Devotion to her brothers and her studies being the salient features of her life, we know little else about her. Lord North made plans for her marriage, but Dudleya evidently had little interest in the prospect of matrimony. On 25 April 1712 she died of consumption, supposedly brought on by her diligent studies and 'sedentary distemper', at her sister-in-law's house in Bond Street, London. Dudleya's uncle Roger North attended to her affairs and established a parochial library at Rougham, Norfolk, which contained her books and manuscripts. She was buried in the North family vault at Kirtling, Cambridgeshire.   LAWRENCE B. SMITH

Sources DNB · MSS of William, Lord North and Grey, Bodl. Oxf., MSS North a. 3, a. 7, b. 2, c. 8, c. 9–11, d. 1 · R. North, *The lives of … Francis North … Dudley North … and … John North*, ed. A. Jessopp, 3 (1890) · 'The report from the committee appointed by order of the House of Commons to examine Christopher Layer, and others', *Reports from Committees of the House of Commons*, 1 (1722–3), 99–350 · PRO, state papers domestic, 1714–27, SP 35 · Royal Arch., Stuart papers · E. Cruickshanks, 'Lord North, Christopher Layer and the Atterbury plot, 1720–23', *The Jacobite challenge*, ed. E. Cruickshanks and J. Black (1988) · S. Lambert, ed., *House of Commons sessional papers of the eighteenth century* (1975), vol. 3 · G. Ballard, *Memoirs of several ladies of Great Britain*, ed. R. Perry (1985) · GEC, *Peerage* · G. Lockhart, *The Lockhart papers: containing memoirs and commentaries upon the affairs of Scotland from 1702 to 1715*, 2 vols. (1817) · *Calendar of the Stuart papers belonging to his majesty the king, preserved at Windsor Castle*, 7 vols., HMC, 56 (1902–23) · M. Reynolds, *The learned lady in England, 1650–1760* (1920) · Marquis D'Argens, *Memoirs of the count du Beauval, including some curious particulars relating to the dukes of Wharton and Ormond, during their exiles*, trans. Mr Derrick (1754)

Archives Bodl. Oxf., personal, military, and estate papers | PRO, state papers domestic, SP 35 · Royal Arch., Stuart MSS

Likenesses G. Kneller, oils, Phillimore Ives Memorial Gallery, Stellenbosch, South Africa · G. Kneller, portrait, AM Oxf., Sutherland Collection; repro. in R. Sharp, *The engraved record of the Jacobite movement* (1996), 186 · J. Simon, mezzotint (after G. Kneller), repro. in J. C. Smith, *British mezzotinto portraits*, 4 vols. in 5 (1878–84), 111

Northalis, Richard (d. 1397), archbishop of Dublin and administrator, was perhaps the son of John Northale (John Clerk), who was sheriff of London in 1335–6, and died in 1349. Richard Northalis entered the Carmelite friary in London, and is said to have been chaplain to Richard II. He was made bishop of Ossory in November 1386, but does not appear to have gone to Ireland immediately, as he was engaged from 1387 in diplomatic negotiations with Urban VI. He was at the papal court in July 1388, in England in February 1389, and again at Rome from June 1389.

In that month he obtained leave to receive all the temporalities of his see while he was absent on the king's business but in November 1390 he complained that in spite of this order two-thirds of the revenues had been kept back by the king's officers. During his absence serious disturbances took place in the diocese, and in September 1389 the bishop's representatives were commissioned to treat with the rebels. At the end of 1390 Northalis was appointed one of the custodians of the temporalities of the vacant see of Dublin. In February 1391 he was licensed by the king to export various goods from Ireland to England.

Northalis's first significant role in the administration of the Irish lordship came with his commission on 27 October 1390 to inquire into the government and retinue of John Stanley, the justiciar. On 20 February 1391 his powers were extended to a more general inquiry into the state of Ireland, the behaviour of Stanley, with particular reference to his capture and ransom of Niall Óg Ó Néill, and the revenues of the lordship. He was commissioned to scrutinize the records of all courts and investigate the behaviour of the lordship's officials. Although some inquiry did take place, the required report from Northalis to the English chancery does not survive and the extent of his involvement in the investigation is unclear. He had from March 1391 licence for a further three years to receive his rents in his absence. Although he may have been further employed by the king outside Ireland, he was in the lordship in August 1391, when he was appointed to act as joint deputy justiciar in the county of Kilkenny and to negotiate with the Irish. In the winter of 1392–3 he apparently attended meetings of the council. He was appointed chancellor of Ireland on 29 May 1393.

The degree of personal initiative exerted by Northalis in the duties of his office during his brief appointment is not recorded. The period was one of renewed attention to the problems of the Irish lordship, perhaps already anticipating the royal expedition in 1394. On 1 June 1393 he was commissioned to inquire into the concealment by the king's officers in Ireland of old debts and revenues. In July he was among the officials ordered to ensure the observation of earlier measures for good government, including the ordinances of 1357. As chancellor he was heavily engaged in the defence of the lordship, negotiating frequently with English and Irish in the absence of the justiciar, James Butler, third earl of Ormond, and attending the latter in a military expedition to Munster. With the approval of the Irish council he received (April 1394) a reward of £20, having petitioned that the fees of the chancellorship did not cover a third of his expenses. The circumstances during his last months in office are obscure, as are the reasons for his replacement on 1 July 1394 by Robert Sutton as keeper of the great seal. On 13 August 1394 his action when he had been chancellor in making a presentation to Rosclare was declared invalid on the grounds that he had not had authority to present to prebendal churches.

Northalis undoubtedly participated in the events of Richard II's first expedition to Ireland (1394–5), although his role is recorded only in the last stages of the settlement, when he acted in April as witness to the submissions of Ó Díomnsaigh, and of Ó Conchobhair Donn with other chiefs of Connacht, and, most significantly, of the final confirmation by Art Mac Murchadha of his submission. Mac Murchadha agreed for the future to submit himself to the decisions and demands of the bishop of Ossory as well as the archbishop of Dublin and their successors. In April, before Richard left Ireland, Northalis apparently attended him at a council in Kilkenny. He was translated on 25 October 1395 by papal bull to the archbishopric of Dublin, and obtained restitution of the temporalities on 4 February 1396. On 1 April 1396 he obtained licence to be absent from Ireland for five years. Northalis died in Dublin on 20 July 1397, and was buried a few days later in St Patrick's Cathedral.

Northalis is said by John Bale to have written *Sermones* and *Ad ecclesiarum parochos*, but neither is extant. The statement that he wrote a hymn on St Canute involves two mistakes: it was Richard Ledred who composed a hymn in honour of St Cainnech, patron saint of Ossory Cathedral.

A. G. LITTLE, rev. D. B. JOHNSTON

Sources The whole works of Sir James Ware concerning Ireland, ed. and trans. W. Harris, rev. edn, 2 vols. in 3 (1764) · Chancery records · E. Tresham, ed., Rotulorum patentium et clausorum cancellariae Hiberniae calendarium, Irish Record Commission (1828) · J. Graves, ed., A roll of the proceedings of the King's Council in Ireland… AD 1392–93, Rolls Series, 69 (1877) · Rymer, Foedera, 1st edn, vol. 7 · exchequer accounts various, PRO, E101/247/1 · E. Curtis, ed., Richard II in Ireland, 1394–1395, and submissions of the Irish chiefs (1927) · R. R. Sharpe, ed., Calendar of wills proved and enrolled in the court of husting, London, AD 1258 – AD 1688, 2 vols. (1889–90) · Bale, Cat.
Wealth at death died in debt to Richard II: Tresham, ed., Rotulorum patentium, 160

Northall, John (1723?–1759), army officer and travel writer, entered the service as a gentleman cadet in the Royal Regiment of Artillery on 1 July 1741 and was promoted to lieutenant fireworker on 1 April 1742. He served under Thomas Pattison with the Royal Artillery in Flanders in 1742, and was promoted second lieutenant on 1 April 1744. He was at the battle of Fontenoy on 11 May 1745, and became first lieutenant on 3 October 1745, captain-lieutenant on 24 March 1752, and captain on 1 October 1755. In February 1752 he went to Minorca, and thence to Livorno. He was recorded in Capua on 1 April 1752. Instead of making the usual tour of Italy, he visited the principal cities of Tuscany and, after a cursory visit to Rome, went to Naples. Then, after a more lengthened stay in Rome, he went to Loreto, Bologna, Venice, Mantua, Parma, Modena, and returned to Livorno, whence he sailed for Genoa. From Genoa he went by sea to Villafranca, and on by land to Marseilles. He died in 1759. An account of his Italian tour was published posthumously in July 1766, *Travels through Italy; Containing New and Curious Observations on that Country …* (1766), but the work has been criticized as following closely J. G. Keysler's *Travels* (1740; Eng. trans. 1756).

B. H. SOULSBY, rev. ROGER T. STEARN

Sources F. Duncan, ed., History of the royal regiment of artillery, 1 (1872) · J. Kane, List of officers of the royal regiment of artillery from the year 1716 to the year 1899, rev. W. H. Askwith, 4th edn (1900) ·

J. Northall, *Travels through Italy; containing new and curious observations on that country* (1766) · J. Ingamells, ed., *A dictionary of British and Irish travellers in Italy, 1701–1800* (1997)

Northall, William of. *See* Northolt, William of (d. 1190).

Northampton. For this title name *see* Senlis, Simon (I) de, earl of Northampton and earl of Huntingdon (d. 1111x13); Senlis, Simon (II) de, earl of Northampton and earl of Huntingdon (d. 1153); Bohun, William de, first earl of Northampton (c.1312–1360); Parr, William, marquess of Northampton (1513–1571); Howard, Henry, earl of Northampton (1540–1614); Gorges, Helena, Lady Gorges [Helena Parr, marchioness of Northampton] (1548–1635); Compton, Spencer, second earl of Northampton (1601–1643); Compton, James, third earl of Northampton (1622–1681); Compton, Spencer Joshua Alwyne, second marquess of Northampton (1790–1851).

Northampton, Henry of [Henry fitz Peter] (*fl.* 1189–1215), justice, was the son of Peter, son of Adam of Northampton, who was the first of forty burgesses of Northampton responsible for recording the town's laws; such a background in local legal knowledge is most notable. He was a justice itinerant for Lincolnshire, Cambridgeshire, and Huntingdonshire in 1189 and sat as one of the king's justices at Westminster and in the country from 1202, while in 1203–4 he was involved in exacting a tallage from Gloucestershire. In 1205 he was joint sheriff of Northamptonshire and in the same year King John granted Henry fitz Peter of Northampton licence to make a park at Little Linford in north Buckinghamshire. Northampton was again on eyre in 1208–9 with Adam de Port, Simon of Pattishall, and others in the north of England. In 1210/11, however, he was amerced 500 marks for an unspecified trespass. He was pardoned 200 marks, and had paid off the rest by Michaelmas 1212, but the exaction may be the reason why he apparently joined the baronial party, for in November 1215 his lands and houses in Northampton were given away by the king. He received letters of protection in the following March, while the pipe roll of the seventeenth year of John's reign records a Henry fitz Peter owing a fine of £100, perhaps to be allowed back into the king's peace.

The date of Northampton's death is unknown. The Henry discussed here should almost certainly be distinguished from the Master Henry of Northampton, who was a canon of St Paul's in the late twelfth century.

WILLIAM HUNT, *rev.* JOHN HUDSON

Sources Pipe rolls · court of common pleas, feet of fines, PRO, CP 25/1 · D. M. Stenton, ed., *Pleas before the king or his justices*, 4 vols., SeldS, 67–8, 83–4 (1952–67) · A. Morey and C. N. L. Brooke, *Gilbert Foliot and his letters* (1965) · D. M. P. Stenton, *English justice between the Norman conquest and the Great Charter, 1066–1215* (1965) · D. Crook, *Records of the general eyre*, Public Record Office Handbooks, 20 (1982) · T. D. Hardy, ed., *Rotuli chartarum in Turri Londinensi asservati*, RC, 36 (1837) · T. D. Hardy, ed., *Rotuli de oblatis et finibus*, RC (1835)

Northampton [Comberton], **John** (d. 1398), draper and mayor of London, was occasionally also called Comberton, a family name taken up by some chroniclers in a play upon the 'comber', or trouble, that his policies were supposed to have caused in London. The son of Thomas and Mariota Northampton, he had two brothers, William and Robert, and two sisters, Petronilla and Agnes.

Northampton's erratically brilliant career placed him in the forefront of city politics in later fourteenth-century London. At times he represented the general interests of the ruling oligarchy in its troubled dealings with the crown. At other times he dealt with the crown, on behalf of a sectional grouping of drapers, mercers, goldsmiths, and others, in opposition to the policies of an increasingly influential body of wealthy merchants who were making fortunes in the wool trade. Some of his policies appeared to reach beyond the immediate concerns of the ruling oligarchy, to address the interests of lesser citizens and less fully enfranchised Londoners. His motives have been debated, and one recent and influential analysis presents him as a manipulator of both crown and populace on his own behalf. Yet some of his initiatives nevertheless suggest an attempted use of the mayoralty to alleviate the daily problems of less prosperous Londoners, and of people resident or working in London who did not enjoy rights of full citizenship.

Appropriately for a London tradesman, Northampton enters the city records on 24 February 1361 as one of four 'upholders' of the Drapers' Guild. A sign of the times was his early involvement in city broils, giving sureties to keep the peace and refrain from affrays in 1365, 1369, and 1371—when arrested, with several of his future political allies, he was released on promise of refraining from assemblies, confederacies, or congregations. By 1375–7, when he was elected alderman for Cordwainer Street, he was ready to assume a substantial role in city government.

In the wake of the Good Parliament (1376), he was among a broad-based coalition of influential Londoners (though without the participation of such wealthy merchants as Nicholas Brembre, William Walworth, or John Philipot) that ousted Richard Lyons (d. 1381) and others from city offices and agreed that the common council should be chosen according to craft guild affiliation rather than city ward. In 1376 he was chosen sheriff, and in 1378 he was MP for London. After several relatively inactive years, in which he and his supporters may have suffered for supporting John of Gaunt, duke of Lancaster, in a quarrel over legal jurisdictions, he returned to major prominence when he served for two successive terms as mayor of London, in 1381–3.

Northampton's controversial mayoral programme—for which he was extensively criticized by the city oligarchs, their supporters, and conservative chroniclers—involved a number of initiatives to alleviate financial pressures on Londoners of all ranks and conditions. His most celebrated measures were aimed at the powerful London fishmongers and their monopoly, opening markets to non-resident tradesmen and forbidding wholesale purchase of fish for profitable resale. Similar measures were directed at resale of ale, wine, bread, and poultry, and—by logical extension—usury and false contracts. A piece of early legislation, indicating the popular side of his programme, required bakers to produce farthing measures of bread, reminted £80 sterling into 76,800 pieces of this low-denomination coin, and insisted that traders, mass priests, and others accept and employ farthings in transactions or else provide their services without charge.

Some elements of a 'moral agenda' may be discerned in his initiation of ordinances and enforcements bearing on misrepresentation, false practice, and prostitution. This aspect of Northampton's activities, and insinuations by Thomas Walsingham and other contemporary chroniclers, together with the fact that he and John Wyclif (d. 1384), at different times and for different short-term motives, enjoyed occasional encouragement by John of Gaunt, have encouraged unfounded speculations about possible Lollard influence. Northampton's will reveals him as a person of an intense and imaginative, but ultimately orthodox, piety, which included the maintenance of a chantry; burial before the altar of St John the Baptist in the church of the hospital of St Mary de Elsyngspitel, Cripplegate; entry of his name on the prayer roll of the church of Holy Trinity, Cheshunt, Hertfordshire; and benefactions to the London Charterhouse, with gifts of dates, figs, and raisins for the monks during Lent.

Because much of the evidence for Northampton's intentions is drawn from accusations and indictments from his later trial, a balanced view is difficult to achieve. Overall, he appears to blend extreme traditionalism and sporadic innovation in ways characteristic of late medieval radicalism. Elements of his programme included support for previously enacted but subsequently ignored or superseded measures (such as one-year terms for aldermen); less principled manoeuvres against the fishmongers' right to hold judicial office; and experiments with new methods of electioneering, caucusing, and political strategy.

The king had backed Northampton for re-election in 1382, but withheld support in 1383, when Northampton's adversary Nicholas Brembre stole a march by packing the Guildhall with armed supporters and won easy election. Northampton and his followers engaged in fruitless protests and demonstrations, without the support of their former patron, John of Gaunt, who seems to have interested himself sporadically in Northampton as a counterforce to Brembre's royalist party within the city, but chose not to contest this issue. Northampton was arrested on suspicion of sedition by Brembre on 7 February 1384, a step supported by the crown on 9 February. His arrest provoked an unsuccessful 'insurrection' (which seems mainly to have involved closing of shop windows, but which led to the execution of Northampton's kinsman John Constantine) on 11 February, and, ultimately, his trial on charges of sedition before king and council at Reading on 15 August 1384. He and his close associates John More and Richard Norbury were sentenced to hang at Tyburn, but the sentence was quickly modified to ten years' imprisonment, in separate locations, 100 leagues distance from London.

Manoeuvres over the terms of a possible pardon ensued, with the Brembre and Exton administrations of the next five years resisting any compromise (and even calling in 1385 for enforcement of the original death penalty), and

with John of Gaunt and other patrons seeking modification. In 1386 the king pardoned Northampton by letter patent, but still on condition of his banishment from the city. Finally, pressures on the city government in the wake of the rising of the lords appellant, and of the execution of Brembre in 1388, encouraged a new alignment, in which previous rivals for ascendancy co-operated in defence of city privileges. Faced with Richard II's displeasure and his exactions of 1391–5, all segments of city leadership co-operated to arrange for the payment of fines and to seek the restoration of city liberties. During this period Northampton finally received a full royal pardon in December 1390, and was restored to full citizenship in January 1395.

Northampton was married twice—to Johanna, who was still alive in 1371, and by 1375 to Petronilla, daughter and coheir of John Preston and Margaret Constantine; he left a son, James, from one of these marriages. Northampton died in 1398; his legacy to London was equivocal. If measured by its durability, his political programme can hardly be considered successful; all its salient elements were repealed by the Brembre–Exton administrations of 1383–8. Brembre and Northampton were well remembered, but, at least on the part of city leaders, as sowers of discord. Attempting to promote civic unity in 1390–91, the London authorities issued an ordinance 'forbidding any one whatsoever to express opinions about Nicholas Brembre or John Northampton, former mayors of the city, nor show any sign as to which of the two parties they favored', since 'the men of the City are to be of one accord' (*Calendar of Letter-Books*, H.364).   PAUL STROHM

Sources R. R. Sharpe, ed., *Calendar of letter-books preserved in the archives of the corporation of the City of London*, [12 vols.] (1899–1912), vols. G–H · A. H. Thomas and P. E. Jones, eds., *Calendar of plea and memoranda rolls preserved among the archives of the corporation of the City of London at the Guildhall*, 2–3 (1929–32) · R. R. Sharpe, ed., *Calendar of wills proved and enrolled in the court of husting, London, AD 1258 – AD 1688*, 2 (1890) · R. Bird, *The turbulent London of Richard II* (1949) · P. Nightingale, 'Capitalists, crafts, and constitutional change in late fourteenth-century London', *Past and Present*, 124 (1989), 3–35 · S. L. Thrupp, *The merchant class of medieval London, 1300–1500* (1948) · T. Usk, 'Appeal', *A book of London English, 1384–1425*, ed. R. W. Chambers and M. Daunt (1931) · E. Powell and G. M. Trevelyan, eds., *The peasants' rising and the Lollards* (1899) · L. C. Hector and B. F. Harvey, eds. and trans., *The Westminster chronicle, 1381–1394*, OMT (1982) · *RotP*, vol. 3 · P. Nightingale, *A medieval mercantile community: the Grocers' Company and the politics and trade of London, 1000–1485* (1995) · City of London RO, hustings rolls, wills, and deeds, 130 (69)
Wealth at death £5000?

North Berwick. For this title name *see* Dalrymple, Sir Hew, first baronet, Lord North Berwick (1652–1737).

North Berwick witches (*act.* 1590–1592) were a group of about sixty people accused of witchcraft in Haddingtonshire, Scotland. Of this group, most is known about the five men and women of relatively high status: **John Cunningham** [*alias* Fian, Sibbet] (d. 1591), schoolmaster, **Agnes Sampson** (d. 1591), midwife, **Barbara Napier** (c.1554–1592x1600), former lady-in-waiting to the countess of Angus, **Euphame MacCalzean** (d. 1591), daughter of a senator of the college of justice, and **Ritchie Graham**

(*d.* 1592), magician. They were tried in central courts in the course of perhaps the most extensive outbreak of witch-craft prosecutions in Scotland (1591–7), for an alleged conspiracy to assassinate King James VI, described in the pamphlet *Newes from Scotland* (1591). They were supposed to have raised by witchcraft a magical storm in an attempt to sink the king's ship as he and his bride, Anne of Denmark, returned from their Scandinavian honeymoon to Scotland in 1590. According to their confessions these deeds were done at witches' conventions attended by the devil. One of these took place at the Old Kirk in North Berwick—hence the naming of the group as the North Berwick witches, when in fact none of them lived there.

In fact the outbreak centred geographically on Tranent, Haddingtonshire, where Fian was schoolmaster. Tranent, an inland village between Edinburgh and North Berwick, featured in all the major witch-hunts of the period, and was the scene of a significant case as late as 1659. As elsewhere in the county, there was an uneasy co-existence of Catholicism and protestantism across all social groups, and tensions had been increased by dearth and by outbreaks of plague, including a prolonged epidemic between 1584 and 1588. The village also provided the most zealous local witch-hunters of the 1590–92 episode: David Seton, bailie to the recusant Lord Seton, and Bailie Seton's son David Seton the younger. Bailie Seton was the employer of a maidservant, Geillis Duncan, whom he tortured privately on suspicion of witchcraft. It was Geillis who implicated Agnes Sampson, a respected local midwife and magical healer, as a witch. Barbara Napier was one of Agnes's higher status clients—which later led to her implication. At a later stage Geillis also seems to have implicated Euphame MacCalzean, Seton's own much richer sister-in-law. There is some evidence that family tension may have led to this accusation; perhaps it was done in the hope of seizing Euphame's considerable estates of Cliftonhall. It is about these two high-status female accused witches that we know most. Of the others we know little beyond their confessions.

Euphame MacCalzean was born before 9 November 1558, the illegitimate daughter of Thomas MacCalzean, Lord Cliftonhall (*c.*1520–1581), senator of the college of justice and from a famous Edinburgh legal family. Her life seems to have been characterized by riches and friction. She was legitimated by her father in 1558 and inherited estates and money worth thousands of pounds Scots. As a condition of marriage in 1570, her husband, Patrick Moscrop, adopted her surname, becoming Patrick MacCalzean. The relationship was unhappy and she was later accused of trying to kill him. The marriage produced three heiress daughters but apparently no surviving sons. Euphame's attempts to marry her daughters into the local élite created conflicts with Sir James Sandilands, a royal favourite. She also had to go to court against relatives to protect her estates. These factors may have been crucial in her accusation as a witch in a hunt started by her brother-in-law.

Barbara Napier, daughter of Alexander Napier of Inglistoun (*b.* before 1529, *d.* 1572) and Isobell Litill (*d.* in or after 1578), came from a family of Edinburgh burgesses. She had married her first husband, George Ker, an overseas book dealer, about 1572. After his death at La Rochelle in September 1576, she married, probably in 1578, Archibald Douglas, brother to the laird of Corshogill. She and her husband had been in service to the countess of Angus, Lady Jean Lyon, at Smeton, Dalkeith. Anxieties over the health of her husband and children and the favour of her mistress led her to consult Agnes Sampson for charms. In consequence of a dispute with her employer, Barbara was dismissed and there was a wrangle over a pension. She thus lacked high-level support from that quarter when Sampson denounced her. It may be, however, that when accused she sought alternative patronage from Francis Stewart, fifth earl of Bothwell, who had just been made lord lieutenant of the borders. She knew Bothwell's wife and had met the earl himself while she was in service to Lady Angus.

The initial accusations against the lower ranking men and women seem to have been part of a local witch-hunt which had begun in early 1590, but at some point treason accusations were made, which led to central involvement by the king himself in late November 1590. Once the accusations reached the royal court, they became part of a power struggle in which factions tried to persuade the tortured witch-suspects to incriminate political rivals. This finally led in April 1591 to the earl of Bothwell being called before the privy council to answer accusations of being the ringleader of the witches' conspiracy. His connections with two of the accused witches, Barbara Napier and Ritchie Graham, were used in evidence against him. Bothwell was warded in Edinburgh Castle but escaped. Those mentioned above, however, were not so lucky. All were tried and, despite MacCalzean's lawyer kin, all were executed in 1591 or 1592 (Ritchie Graham) with the possible exception of Barbara Napier.

Barbara was tried on charges of witchcraft, treason, and consulting with witches. She was found guilty only of the last charge and was sentenced to death for it at the king's behest. This was the first time the crime, though theoretically a capital one, had ever been punished by execution. The king then launched an assize of error—a legal move to cancel her acquittal on the other charges by establishing that the jury of Edinburgh burgesses had wilfully erred in finding her innocent. It is not known what happened to Barbara but the existence of a second escheat for her estate in 1594 may point to her death by then; her husband was described as deceased. She was certainly dead by 1600 when her daughter tried to establish rights to her pension. It is likely that she was burnt, but where is unknown.

The trials of the North Berwick witches had marked a watershed. It was last instance of such prosecutions being subordinated to a political intent, the first major trial of witchcraft under criminal law, and the first occasion on which continental witch theory was deployed. The wave of prosecutions came to a sudden end in 1597 when the king, whose interest in the phenomenon of witchcraft had helped to stimulate them, published his attack on sceptics, *Daemonologie*, but also revoked witchcraft commissions.   L. A. YEOMAN

Sources L. Normand and G. Roberts, *Witchcraft in early modern Scotland* (2000) · R. Pitcairn, ed., *Ancient criminal trials in Scotland*, 3 vols., Maitland Club (1883), vol. 1 · NA Scot., CC 8/8/6, 14 October 1578; CC 8/8/35, 6 Feb 1601 [Moscrop] · NA Scot., GD 16/41/112 · NA Scot., RH 6/2262 · NA Scot., PS 1/63, fol. 23 · NA Scot., PS 1/67, fol. 16 · G. Brunton and D. Haig, *An historical account of the senators of the college of justice, from its institution in MDXXXII* (1832) · *Register of the great seal*, 4, no. 1313 · C. Larner, *Enemies of God: the witch-hunt in Scotland* (1981) · J. Wormauld, *Court, kirk and community: Scotland, 1470–1625* (1981) · *Scots peerage*

Northbourne. For this title name *see* James, Walter Charles, first Baron Northbourne (1816–1893).

Northbrook. For this title name *see* Baring, Francis Thornhill, first Baron Northbrook (1796–1866); Baring, Thomas George, first earl of Northbrook (1826–1904).

Northbrooke, John (*fl.* 1567–1589), Church of England clergyman and author, was born in Devon. Said to have been imprisoned under Mary by the bishop of Exeter, he was one of the first clergy to be ordained in the diocese of Bath and Wells during Elizabeth's reign. By 1567 he had moved to Bristol, where he was curate and preacher of St Mary Redcliffe, the city's largest parish church; he probably retained this post until 1576. In 1568 he joined James Calfhill in attacking the support expressed by Richard Cheyney, bishop of Gloucester, for the doctrine of free will. Calfhill had been a proto-puritan precisian in the convocation of 1563 along with Arthur Saule, a former Marian exile who was now a canon of Bristol Cathedral. Saule almost certainly had a role in placing Northbrooke at St Mary Redcliffe. While opposition to free will reflected the mainstream Calvinism of the Elizabethan church, of which the puritans formed part, Northbrooke's connections nevertheless emphasize his puritan leanings, the more so as he also had the support of a faction of the godly among Bristol's leading citizens, who shared his distaste for the doctrine maintained by the bishop.

Like most other puritans Northbrooke sought to conform to established church doctrine. This emerged explicitly in a controversy over the descent of Christ into hell, a doctrine that he had opposed. Disputed in the convocation of 1563, it had nevertheless remained among the Thirty-Nine Articles (as no. 3). In 1571, when the articles were finally ratified, Northbrooke refuted the charge that he denied this one in the preface to his book *Spiritus est vicarius Christi in terra: a breefe and pithie summe of the Christian faith, made in fourme of confession, with a confutation of the papistes objections and argumentes in sundry pointes of religion, repugnant to the Christian faith*. He carefully asserts his orthodoxy while positing a Calvinist view of the doctrine, that is, belief in the spiritual rather than literal descent of Christ into hell. He nevertheless implies that it should not have been included in the articles, even though his later career indicates that he conformed by subscribing to them himself.

Proctor for the clergy of Bristol diocese in convocation at least five times between 1571 and 1589, Northbrooke

published another treatise in 1573. Like its predecessor, its title begins with an anti-papal flourish, appropriate to works both of which attack the Catholic convert and controversialist Thomas Harding—*Spiritus est vicarius Christi: the poore mans garden, wherein are flowers of the scripture, and doctours, very necessary and profitable for the simple and ignoraunt people to read*. His best-known treatise, published in 1577, constitutes a wide-ranging critique of behaviour, albeit one squarely in the protestant mainstream. *Spiritus est vicarius Christi in terra: a treatise wherein dicing, dauncing, vaine playes, or enterluds, with other idle pastimes, &c., commonly used on the sabboth day, are reproved by the authoritie of the word of God and auntient writers*, published as part of the controversy over the formal opening of public theatres in London, has been described as marking the 'first wave of concentratedly antitheatrical tract-making' (Freeman, 5). It includes what may be the first written notice of London's playhouses, The Curtain and The Theatre. It may also have constituted an attack on Bristol's magistrates, who—unlike those of London—continued to support theatrical performances in their own guildhall. The treatise also expresses views on church music characteristic of a more puritan-inclined protestantism, emphasizing the primacy of the words (which must be scriptural) in congregational singing, while placing the sermon at the heart of public worship.

In 1576 Northbrooke became vicar of Henbury, just outside Bristol. He appears to have been living there in 1579. He may have held the living of Walton, in the diocese of Bath and Wells, from 1570 until 1577, and been presented to the vicarage of Berkeley, Gloucestershire, in 1575. It is not known whether he married, or when and where he died.   MARTHA C. SKEETERS

Sources 'Introduction', *A treatise against dicing, dancing, plays and interludes, with other idle pastimes, by John Northbrooke, minister, from the earliest edition, about A.D. 1577*, ed. J. P. Collier (1843) · P. Collinson, *The birthpangs of protestant England: religious and cultural change in the sixteenth and seventeenth centuries* (1988) · P. Collinson, *The religion of protestants* (1982) · A. Freeman, introduction, in J. Northbrooke, *A treatise*, ed. A. Freeman (New York, 1974) · M. Skeeters, *Community and clergy: Bristol and the Reformation, c.1530–c.1570* (1993) · Tanner, *Bibl. Brit.-Hib.* · *DNB* · M. C. Pilkington, ed., *Records of early English drama: Bristol* (1997)

Northburgh, Michael (*c.*1300–1361), diplomat and bishop of London, was a nephew of Roger Northburgh, bishop of Coventry and Lichfield (*d.* 1358). He studied at Oxford, proceeding MA by 1329 and DCL by 1336; in old age he was one of three bishops who witnessed the royal grant of privileges to the university on 27 June 1357.

Bishop Roger set him on the ladder of patronage, collating him to the archdeaconry of Chester on 30 January 1341, although owing to a papal provision he was forced to resign. His career provides a classic example of an ambitious, well-qualified lawyer–clerk, who was able to amass a substantial income by virtue of ecclesiastical, royal, and papal patronage without undertaking higher orders. As late as 1350–51 he acquired papal dispensation while absent in royal service to hold the archdeaconry of Suffolk—which he had assumed in 1347, and from which he took more visitation procurations than were lawful—together with the rectory of Pulham. At the time he had not proceeded to the priesthood; indeed, he apparently remained in minor orders until his promotion as bishop. Apart from other benefices, several of them in Lichfield diocese, he soon aggregated canonries and prebends in the cathedral churches of Lichfield (where he later held the precentorship), Salisbury, Hereford, and Lincoln. In 1343 he was granted papal provision to a Chichester canonry, notwithstanding his canonries and prebends in Lichfield, Hereford, Lincoln, and Pontefract. In 1349 a further provision of a canonry in St Paul's with reservation of a prebend permitted him to retain his archdeaconry and prebends at Lichfield, Hereford, and Chichester, together with the mastership of St John's Hospital, High Wycombe. He added the deanship of St Stephen's Chapel, Westminster, in 1351, and two years later canonries of Ripon, Beverley, and York. With the death of Ralph Stratford in 1354 the see of London fell vacant. Licence to elect was issued on 21 September, but as was usual by this date the pope issued a provisory bull, dated 7 May, naming Northburgh, who was clearly the royal candidate. His temporalities were released on 23 June, the spiritualities on 3 July. Consecrated on 12 June in St Mary's, Southwark, by Bishop William Edington (d. 1366), he made his profession of obedience on 2 December.

Northburgh may have travelled abroad in 1331, and was at Avignon in 1336. Two years later, in February 1338, there is a chance mention of him as an advocate in the court of arches, but soon afterwards he gravitated to royal service. He was appointed king's councillor in 1346, with a fee of 100 marks a year when abroad, 50 marks when in England. The chronicler Robert Avesbury regarded Northburgh as a powerful clerk, and in 1349, and from time to time thereafter, he is termed king's 'secretary'. By September 1350 he was appointed keeper of the privy seal, an office he held until 26 August 1354. Although diplomatic missions meant that he was often abroad, his household continued without him, his subordinates performing the duties of the office. During these years he also served as a diplomat. In 1345 he was at the curia, along with John Offord (d. 1349) and Bishop William Bateman (d. 1355), to secure marriage dispensations for Richard (II) Fitzalan, earl of Arundel, and Isabella Despenser, and for the prince of Wales and a daughter of the duke of Brabant. The following year saw Northburgh in the entourage of Edward III during his expedition to France—Murimuth describes him as having been the king's confessor. He sent back newsletters detailing the campaign from the landing at La Hogue on 12 July until the capture of Caen at the end of the month, and from the arrival at Poissy in August until the encampment before Calais on 4 September. He gives an account of the battle of Crécy on 26 August, with a list of the French casualties. In October he was once again engaged in implementing the royal policy of building up continental alliances against the French, and in 1348 was negotiating with the Flemings. Annually between 1349 and 1355 he was engaged in diplomatic missions: arranging truces

with France, treating with Louis, count of Flanders, negotiating terms for the liberation of Charles de Blois, captured at La Roche-Derien on 20 June 1347, and, most important, attempting to conclude a definitive peace. In 1353 letters of truce under the various seals were entrusted to his keeping.

Northburgh died on 9 September 1361, apparently from plague, at Copford, Essex. In his will, dated 23 May, for which probate was granted on 13 December 1361, he asked to be buried outside the west door of his cathedral. Although John Stow, in noting the 'residue of the monuments' in the cathedral, records that of 'Michael Norborow', he does not mention its precise location. Northburgh bequeathed a *Concordantia legum et canonum*, his *magnum opus* as he described it, to his younger namesake, Michael Northburgh (or Free), a canon of Chichester (who was apparently illegitimate), together with an entire suit of armour, a missal without musical notation, a small Bible, various silver dishes, a *byker* (probably a type of goblet or chalice) called 'Katherine', an amice, and a cope. Another beneficiary was Free's brother, Thomas Northburgh. Their precise relationship to the bishop is not clear. His best mitre and pontifical ring he left to his episcopal successor—despite the traditional claim of the metropolitan. To maintain poor scholars in canon and civil law for four years at Oxford he left £100, plus £20 for their master. St Paul's treasury was to have 1000 marks for a loan chest, from which money was to be advanced against security, the amounts graded according to the status of the borrower. He endowed a chantry in his cathedral church and was effectively joint founder, with Sir Walter Mauny or Manny (d. 1372)—'his first associate after himself'—of the London Charterhouse, dedicated to the Annunciation, or Salutation, of the Virgin Mary, to which he bequeathed £2000, as well as divers silver vessels, service books, vestments, and his rents and tenements in London. Mauny had originally planned a secular college adjacent to a burial site for victims of plague, but was persuaded to alter his plan by Northburgh. The latter's death slowed down the proceedings, so that the foundation of the Charterhouse was not effected until 1371, the year of Mauny's death. Northburgh's episcopal register is not extant, but his mandates as dean of the province can be recovered from other registers.   ROY MARTIN HAINES

Sources register of Archbishop Simon Islip, LPL · *Chancery records* · *CEPR letters* · W. Dugdale, *The history of St Paul's Cathedral in London*, new edn, ed. H. Ellis (1818), 24–5, 32 · *Hemingby's register*, ed. H. M. Chew, Wiltshire Archaeological and Natural History Society, Records Branch, 18 (1963) · Tout, *Admin. hist.*, vols. 3–6 · R. R. Sharpe, ed., *Calendar of wills proved and enrolled in the court of husting, London, AD 1258 – AD 1688*, 2 (1890), 61–2 · R. R. Sharpe, ed., *Calendar of letter-books preserved in the archives of the corporation of the City of London*, [12 vols.] (1899–1912), vol. F–G · E. M. Thompson, *The Carthusian order in England* (1930) · M. D. Knowles and W. F. Grimes, *Charterhouse* (1954) · I. J. Churchill, *Canterbury administration: the administrative machinery of the archbishopric of Canterbury*, 2 vols. (1933) · J. Stow, *A survey of London*, rev. edn (1603) · D. M. Smith, *Guide to bishops' registers of England and Wales: a survey from the middle ages to the abolition of the episcopacy in 1646*, Royal Historical Society Guides and Handbooks, 11 (1981), 136, n.3 · *Fasti Angl., 1300–1541*, [Lincoln; Hereford, Salisbury; Mon. cath. (SP); St. Paul's, London; York;

Chichester; Coventry; Introduction] • Emden, *Oxf.* • Rymer, *Foedera* • A. Sapiti, notebook [transcript], PRO, Roman transcripts MS 31/9/17A, fols. 86v–87r
Wealth at death see will, Sharpe, ed., *Calendar*

Northburgh, Roger (*d.* 1358), administrator and bishop of Coventry and Lichfield, seems to have been a founder member of an influential administrative family, supposedly taking its name from Norbury, Staffordshire, although this has been questioned. The family included his nephew Michael Northburgh (*d.* 1361), whom he was to appoint archdeacon of Chester in 1340. Other Northburghs—Peter, Master Roger, and William—obtained Lichfield prebends during Roger's episcopate, but their relationship to him is unknown. His later interest in Cambridge suggests that he could have been a student there, but there is no evidence that he proceeded to the degree of MA despite the fact that some royal letters entitle him *magister*. In July 1315 Edward II, who was to be assiduous in furthering his promotion, granted him the prebend of Farndon in Lincoln. He did not obtain it, but was successful in November of the same year in securing that of Stoke in the same cathedral. Papal provision pre-empted his appointment as dean of St Paul's in 1317, but for a short time he held the prebend of Newington there. Further royal presentations in that year brought him a prebend in St David's, and also the archdeaconry of Richmond—he had been granted the prebend of Wistow in York two years previously. His prebend in Hereford Cathedral, also granted in 1317, he exchanged the following year for one in Salisbury.

Northburgh was a clerk in the wardrobe in 1310–11, and became keeper of the privy seal in 1312, possibly in March, certainly by September. He held this office until 1316, when the king by word of mouth appointed him keeper of the wardrobe (1 February). He remained keeper until 30 April 1322. During and after March 1312 he was constantly at the king's side, the chancery rolls recording the issue of many writs on his information. Tout considered him to be 'a prudent and moderate man, who seems gradually to have drifted into the confidence of the barons' (Tout, *Admin. hist.*, 2.292). For the six months after November 1312 Northburgh was regularly absent from the court. Tout thought that this was because the ordainers were deliberately keeping him away from the king and endeavouring to separate the wardrobe from the privy seal, a policy that led to the latter's development as a state rather than a household office. And he pointed out that at this time, when Edward may not have been in agreement with the council, many writs of privy seal were endorsed as having been issued on the latter's authority. It was during one of Northburgh's absences that a clerk embarrassingly forged the privy seal.

In the summer of 1314 Northburgh was in attendance on the king at Bannockburn, but was captured in the rout, together with the privy seal and many of the wardrobe records. He seems to have recovered his liberty by November. Present as keeper of the wardrobe at the important parliament held at York in 1318—at which time he was drawing expenses for negotiations with the Scots—he was among those responsible for devising ordinances for the reform of the household. At times during 1320 and 1321 he was one of the clerks entrusted with custody of the great seal. When in 1320 the king formally protested against the provision of Rigaud d'Assier to the see of Winchester, Northburgh witnessed the notarial instrument. Towards the end of that year he was again engaged in negotiations with the Scots.

It used to be thought that between 1321 and 1326 Northburgh was chancellor of Cambridge University, an office for which in truth he would have had little time. The confusion possibly arose from the fact that he was instrumental in securing a royal licence, dated 5 July 1321, enabling the university to acquire advowsons of churches for the maintenance of students of theology and logic in halls that were to be founded for the purpose. He did not pursue the project.

The see of Coventry and Lichfield fell vacant in 1321, and licence to elect was granted on 22 November. Edward asked the pope to provide Robert Baldock (*d.* 1327), but Pope John XXII (*r.* 1316–34) declined. The election was complicated by a dispute between the regular and secular chapters of the see. On 14 December Northburgh was provided. As bishop elect and confirmed, he appointed Master Ralph Holbeach from Pontefract, Yorkshire, his commissary-general on 12 April 1322—the temporalities were restored on the same day. A further commission to Holbeach was issued at Bosworth, Leicestershire, on 7 May—the day after he appointed Geoffrey Blaston his vicar-general until 27 June. On 20 April from Rothwell, Northamptonshire (where he was in attendance on the court), he deputed Stephen Blound to act as steward and two days later commissioned Bishop Gilbert of Annaghdown to celebrate orders and perform other episcopal functions. Northburgh was consecrated on 27 June in the choir of Halesowen Abbey by the Worcester diocesan, Thomas Cobham (*d.* 1327), assisted by five other bishops. To mark the occasion he granted a forty-day indulgence to all who visited the head of St Barbara, the abbey's principal relic. On 31 August he performed obedience to Canterbury. It would appear from the justification by John Stratford (*d.* 1348) of his activities as royal envoy on his return from Avignon in 1323, and from royal letters, that Northburgh was Edward II's candidate for a cardinalate, but nothing came of this.

It would be hard to determine his political sympathies during the king's struggle with the ordainers. Tout regarded him as their nominee in 1312, and in 1318 as a member of what he considered to be a 'middle party'. Modern scholarship has repudiated a concept as rigid as a definable 'party', but it is clear that a strong core of bishops was pursuing a policy of mediation between the king and disaffected barons, and that after the battle of Boroughbridge, on 16 March 1322, they were anxious to secure the rehabilitation of those of their number who had incurred the king's anger. In this context it is clear that despite papal provision to his see—in disregard of Baldock's candidature—Northburgh retained Edward's confidence, and in 1323 was one of those ordered to sequestrate the property of the newly provided bishop of Winchester, John Stratford. He remained *persona grata* even during the turbulent final years of the reign, for in February 1326 he was directed to assist the commissioners of array in his diocese.

A wholesale abandonment of the king by senior administrators occurred in the autumn of 1326, and it is probable that initially Northburgh had no difficulty in accepting the regime of Queen Isabella and her adherents. He is named among the bishops who took the first, and apparently also the second, Guildhall oath (13 and 20 January 1327) to uphold the city's privileges, and to maintain the queen's cause and that of the young king. Between 2 March and 20 May 1328 he acted as treasurer, resigning the office to accompany Bishop Adam Orleton (*d.* 1345) to France where, following the death of Charles IV in that year, Philippe VI (*r.* 1328–50) was proclaimed his successor. At the end of May the envoys were in Paris to press Edward III's claims through his mother Isabella, the sister of the late king. John Stratford was later to urge that this was the main cause of the war that ensued.

It is not clear where Northburgh stood in relation to Roger Mortimer after Henry of Lancaster's bid for power collapsed in January 1329, but he became politically active following Edward III's assumption of personal rule in 1330. In the parliament of 1333 he was among the bishops and nobles specifically appointed to discuss the king's affairs, and early in the following year was witness to a writ dated from York allowing merchants of Coventry to be quit of certain tolls. He was specially summoned to a council at Stamford in May 1337, where measures were considered for financing the king's war expenses through the creation of a royal monopoly on the English wool crop. At the parliament of March 1340 he was one of those authorized to fashion petitions into statutes in return for the grant of a ninth, and was deputed to act as a trier of English petitions. Appointed treasurer on 21 June 1340, he entered office five days later. Inevitably he fell victim to the king's irritation at the failure of John and Robert Stratford (*d.* 1362), successive chancellors, to provide him with the sinews of war. Consequently, he was one of those summarily dismissed on 1 December 1340, following Edward's unheralded return from the continent. The king imprisoned a number of officials but the bishops, Northburgh and Robert Stratford, stood their ground and retained their freedom. When the Stratfords were excluded from parliament during the crisis of 1341, Northburgh was among those who stood by them in the interests of ecclesiastical liberty, and subsequently joined with others to intercede with the king on the archbishop's behalf. This affair marked the end of Northburgh's political career, although he attended the parliament of 1343, which saw the peremptory repeal of the 1340 statutes, and that of 1344, when he was one of the bishops who petitioned the king to end the war.

To all appearances an efficient and conscientious diocesan, Northburgh began by holding an ordination in Southam on 15 September 1322, and on the 27th he visited the cathedral priory of Coventry. The Lichfield chapter received him on 4 October, despite the canons' objection to a clause in his citation. On 8 October, while still at Lichfield, he appointed Master William Weston to act as his official and proceeded to the visitation of Stafford archdeaconry. He had subsequently to order the excommunication of parishioners of Abbots Bromley, who failed to respond to his citation, and he took similar action against the attackers of his apparitor at Cheswardine. He was forced, however, to suspend his visitation of the deanery of Stafford and Newcastle, owing to an incursion of the Scots which prompted a royal summons. A document in his register promised vigorous action against arsonists, thieves of sacred property, infringers of the liberties of his see, apostate nuns and canons, and monks guilty of misbehaviour. He deposed the prior of Arbury, Warwickshire, but subsequently made provision for him. Careful about the appointment of penitentiaries, he saw to it that some were Welsh speakers. There is evidence of further visitations, for instance in 1331, 1338, and 1347–8, and his register has quaternions containing injunctions issued to a number of religious houses, including the abbeys of Burton upon Trent, Staffordshire; Lilleshall, Shropshire; and St Werburgh, Chester. He maintained his connection with Lincoln, had recorded (perhaps as a model) a bull respecting certain statutes of that church which entailed conflict between bishop and chapter, and wrote to the pope urging the canonization of Bishop John Dalderby (*d.* 1320). Northburgh died on 22 November 1358 and was buried under a marble slab next to the magnificent tomb of his predecessor, Walter Langton, in the south aisle of the choir of Lichfield Cathedral. ROY MARTIN HAINES

Sources register of Bishop Langton, containing Northburgh's ordination quire, Lichfield Joint RO · Lichfield Joint RO, Northburgh MSS, B/A/1/1–3 · Reg. Islip, LPL · wardrobe books 10–11 Edward II, Society of Antiquaries, MSS 120, 121 · *Chancery records* · *RotP*, vols. 1–2 · A. H. Thomas and P. E. Jones, eds., *Calendar of plea and memoranda rolls preserved among the archives of the corporation of the City of London at the Guildhall*, 1 (1926) · R. R. Sharpe, ed., *Calendar of letter-books preserved in the archives of the corporation of the City of London*, [12 vols.] (1899–1912), vols. E–F · 'Thomae Chesterfeld … Coventrensibus', *Anglia sacra*, ed. [H. Wharton], 1 (1691), 423–43 · Osberno, 'Continuatio historiae Lichfeldensis', *Anglia sacra*, ed. [H. Wharton], 1 (1691), 448–59 · E. Hobhouse, ed., 'The register of Roger de Norbury, bishop of Lichfield and Coventry', *Collections for a history of Staffordshire*, William Salt Archaeological Society, 1 (1880), 241–88 · *The register of Thomas de Cobham, bishop of Worcester, 1317–1327*, Worcester Historical Society, 40 (1930) · F. J. Baigent, ed., *The registers of John de Sandale and Rigaud d'Asserio, bishops of Winchester*, Hampshire RS, 8 (1897) · W. Stubbs, ed., 'Annales Paulini', *Chronicles of the reigns of Edward I and Edward II*, 1, Rolls Series, 76 (1882), 253–370 · J. C. Davies, *The baronial opposition to Edward II* (1918) · Tout, *Admin. hist.*, vols. 2–6 · R. M. Haines, *Archbishop John Stratford: political revolutionary and champion of the liberties of the English church*, Pontifical Institute of Medieval Studies: Texts and Studies, 76 (1986) · N. M. Fryde, 'Edward III's removal of his ministers and judges, 1340–1', *BIHR*, 48 (1975), 149–61 · Venn, *Alum. Cant.* · H. Rashdall, *The universities of Europe in the middle ages*, ed. F. M. Powicke and A. B. Emden, new edn, 3 (1936) · Emden, *Cam.* · *Fasti Angl., 1300–1541*, [St Paul's, London] · *Fasti Angl., 1300–1541*, [Hereford] · *Fasti Angl., 1300–1541*, [Salisbury] · *Fasti Angl., 1300–1541*, [Chichester] · *Fasti Angl., 1300–1541*, [York] · *Fasti Angl., 1300–1541*, [Coventry] · *Fasti Angl., 1300–1541*, [Welsh dioceses]

Northchurch. For this title name *see* Davidson, (Frances) Joan, Viscountess Davidson and Baroness Northchurch (1894–1985).

Northcliffe. For this title name *see* Harmsworth, Alfred Charles William, Viscount Northcliffe (1865–1922).

Northcote, Henry Stafford, Baron Northcote (1846–1911), colonial governor, born on 18 November 1846 at 13 Devonshire Street, Portland Place, London, was the second son of Stafford Henry *Northcote, first earl of Iddesleigh (1818–1887); his mother was Cecilia Frances (1823–1910), daughter of Thomas Farrer and sister of Thomas Farrer, first Lord Farrer. He went to Eton College in 1858 and to Merton College, Oxford, in 1865, graduating BA in 1869 and proceeding MA in 1873. After leaving Oxford he was appointed to a clerkship in the Foreign Office on 18 March 1868.

In February 1871 Northcote was attached to the joint high commission, of which his father was one of the members and which sat at Washington from February to May 1871, to consider the 'Alabama claims' and other outstanding questions between Great Britain and the United States. He became secretary to the British member of the claims commission consequent on the treaty of Washington of May 1871, and assistant to the British claims agent in the general business of the commission. The commission sat at Washington from September 1871 to September 1873. In November 1876 Northcote became an acting third secretary in the diplomatic service. When Lord Salisbury went as British plenipotentiary to the Constantinople conference at the end of 1876, Northcote accompanied him as private secretary. In February 1877 he was made assistant private secretary to his father, who was then chancellor of the exchequer, and he was private secretary from October 1877 to 15 March 1880. In 1880 he retired from the diplomatic service and was elected tory MP for Exeter, his family's city. He held the seat until 1899.

From June 1885 to February 1886, during Lord Salisbury's short first government, Northcote was financial secretary to the War Office. In Lord Salisbury's second government he held the post of surveyor-general of the ordnance from August 1886 to December 1887, when he resigned his appointment in order to facilitate changes at the War Office. He had been created CB in 1880, and on 23 November 1887, after his father's death, he was made a baronet. He was a charity commissioner in 1891–2, and in 1898 was appointed a royal commissioner for the Paris Exhibition of 1900. He was also for a time chairman of the associated chambers of commerce, and became well known and much trusted in business circles. In 1899 he was appointed to be governor of Bombay, and in January 1900 he was raised to the peerage with the title of Baron Northcote of Exeter, next month being made GCIE.

On 17 February 1900 Lord Northcote landed at Bombay, where he served as governor for three and a half years. His tenure of office was marked by 'a famine of unprecedented severity, incessant plague, an empty exchequer, and bad business years generally' (*Times of India*, 5 Sept 1903). Famine did not completely disappear until 1902–3, and

plague was still rife when Northcote left India. He began an energetic programme of reform, and especially land reform, and his Bombay Land Revenue Code Amendment Act (intended to protect small cultivators from moneylenders by wiping out arrears) proved highly controversial. He took other steps in the direction of land revenue reform, doing much to bring the somewhat rigid traditional policy of the Bombay government into harmony with the views of the government of India. In municipal matters, too, he made improvements, although the most important municipal act passed in his time—the District Municipalities Act, by which local self-government in the *mofussil*, the rural hinterland, was much enlarged—was a legacy from his predecessor Lord Sandhurst. Northcote travelled widely through the Bombay presidency, and he also visited Aden. He was a strong supporter of schools and hospitals, but his efforts were hampered by the impoverished state of the public finances. 'So far as he was able, Lord Northcote drew on his privy purse for money which the state should have furnished, and especially in the administration of relief and in the assistance of charitable undertakings was he able to take a more personally active part than any of his predecessors' (*Bombay Gazette Budget*, 29 Aug 1903). He was present in 1903 at the coronation durbar which celebrated the accession of King Edward VII. When he left India on 5 September 1903 the viceroy, Lord Curzon, expressed the general feeling in the message 'Bombay and India are losing one of the most sympathetic and sagacious governors that they have known'.

On 29 August 1903 Northcote had been appointed governor-general of the commonwealth of Australia. On 21 January 1904, when he was made a GCMG, he was sworn in at Sydney, and he remained in Australia for nearly four years and eight months. Northcote's task in Australia was no easy one. The commonwealth had come into existence on 1 January 1901, and Northcote had had two predecessors (lords Hopetoun and Tennyson) in three years. He was thus the first to hold his office for an appreciable length of time, and it fell largely to him to establish the position of governor-general, and to create traditions. He worked well with Alfred Deakin, and much better than he expected with the Labor leader J. C. Watson.

In Australia, as in India, he travelled widely. He was determined, as the head of a self-governing commonwealth, to identify himself with the inhabitants of every part of Australia. During his term of office he travelled through the greater part of every state; visited most county towns, every mining centre, and the great pastoral and agricultural districts; and succeeded in obtaining a grasp of the industrial work and life of the people. He travelled an average of over 10,000 miles a year by land and sea. Particularly important was his tour of the Northern Territory, which called public attention to this little-known and somewhat neglected part of the continent. In Sydney and Melbourne he visited every factory of importance, while in social life, and through his support for institutions and movements for the public good, he won respect and affection. He laid stress on the importance of defence and of encouraging immigration for the development of the land. He was a vigorous governor-general, delaying royal assent to the Arbitration Act in 1904 and controversially supervising federal and state honours (*AusDB*). His personal wealth enabled him to entertain generously and his popularity was enhanced by his amiable and clever wife, Alice, the adopted daughter of George, Baron Mount Stephen, whom he had married on 2 October 1873.

Northcote returned from Australia in 1908. In 1909 he was sworn of the privy council and at the coronation of King George V he carried the banner of Australia. He was a strong defender of the privileges of the Lords in 1911. He died childless at Eastwell Park, Ashford, Kent, on 29 September 1911, and was buried at Upton Pynes, near Exeter. His wife died in London on 1 June 1934.

C. P. LUCAS, rev. H. C. G. MATTHEW

Sources *The Times* (30 Sept 1911) · *FO List* (1880) · L. Fraser, *India under Curzon and after* (1911) · H. G. Turner, *First decade of the Australian commonwealth* (1911) · C. Cuneen, *Kings' men* (1983) · *AusDB* · *Times of India* (5 Sept 1903) · *Bombay Gazette Budget* (29 Aug 1903)
Archives BL, corresp., Add. MS 50033 · NL Aus., corresp. and papers relating to retirement · University of Exeter Library, letterbooks and papers | BL OIOC, corresp. with Lord George Hamilton, MSS Eur. C 125–126, D 508–510, F 123 · Bodl. Oxf., corresp. with Lord Selborne · CAC Cam., corresp. with Alfred Lyttelton · NL Aus., corresp. with Alfred Deakin · NL Scot., corresp. with *Blackwood*'s · PRO, Elgin MSS
Likenesses B. Stone, photograph, 1898, NPG · A. S. Cope, oils, priv. coll. · S. P. Hall, pencil sketch, NPG · London Stereoscopic Co., photograph, NPG · Spy [L. Ward], chromolithograph caricature, NPG; repro. in *VF* (3 March 1904)
Wealth at death £177,073 19s. 3d.: probate, 28 Nov 1911, CGPLA Eng. & Wales

Northcote, James (1746–1831), artist and author, was born on 22 October 1746 in Market Street, Plymouth, one of seven children of Samuel Northcote (1709–1791), watchmaker, and his wife, whose name is unknown, but who died, according to Northcote, on 3 September 1778 aged sixty-seven. Of the seven Northcote children, three reached adulthood: James; his elder brother, Samuel; and his sister, Mary. The other four children, all boys, died in infancy. According to his autobiographical memoir, Northcote's great-great-grandfather Samuel Northcote settled in Plymouth, where he was elected mayor in 1658. Although he came from an artisan background, Northcote proudly traced his lineage back to the Norman conquest, claiming descent from one Galfrid Miles who had his seat at Northcote in the parish of East Down, Devon, and whose family subsequently took on the name de Northcote (BL, Add. MS 47790, fols. 15–18).

Youth and apprenticeship Northcote's paternal grandfather was a painter, albeit unsuccessful—one reason, Northcote asserted, why his father was reluctant to encourage his son's artistic ambitions. Northcote's father, who intended him to enter the family watchmaking business, was apparently unconcerned about his sons' education, and by his own account Northcote could not read or write until he was thirteen. Even so, an autobiographical reference to a volume of drawings of birds executed in watercolour by his father and brother suggests that the

James Northcote (1746–1831), self-portrait, 1784

male members of the family shared an abiding interest in art (BL, Add. MS 42524). In 1759 a family friend, Henry Tolcher, showed a specimen of Northcote's drawing to Joshua Reynolds and to the engraver James MacArdell, probably the landscape drawing now contained in Northcote's manuscript memoir (BL, Add. MS 47790, fol. 32). Northcote first caught sight of Reynolds in 1762, when he was visiting Devon with Samuel Johnson—the fifteen-year-old managing merely to touch the hem of Reynolds's coat as he passed through the crowd. In December 1762 Tolcher arranged for Northcote to be apprenticed to the engraver Edward Fisher who, like MacArdell, engraved prints after Reynolds. Northcote's father turned down the offer. Determined to pursue an artistic career, Northcote saved 10 guineas earned in part from the sale of a print made from one of his drawings. At five in the morning on Whitsunday, May 1771, he set out for London with his brother Samuel, who was then apprenticed to a watchmaker in Fleet Street. Northcote took with him a painting he had made of a duck, 'which had met with much commendation at home' (Northcote, *Artist's Book of Fables*, xvii). Once in London, Northcote presented letters of introduction to Reynolds from Tolcher and the physician John Mudge, a boyhood friend of Reynolds from Devon. Reynolds, who was already acquainted with his brother Samuel, received Northcote warmly, permitting him to make copies in oils from works in his collection. In order to make money, Northcote—then lodging with a grocer in the Strand—coloured prints of flowers for a printseller on Ludgate Hill at 1s. per sheet. Shortly afterwards Reynolds took him on as a pupil, providing board and lodging in exchange for his services.

Northcote's various accounts of his five-year apprenticeship under Reynolds, including a series of letters written at the time to his brother in Devon (RA), provide a vivid insight into these formative years of his career, and to Reynolds's ménage. Northcote quickly became adept at painting drapery and other incidental details in Reynolds's portraits, including *James Calthorpe* (exh. RA, 1773; priv. coll.), *Miss Sarah Child* (exh. RA, 1773; priv. coll.), *Henry Frederick, Duke of Cumberland* (exh. RA, 1773; des.), *James Beattie* (exh. RA, 1774; University of Aberdeen), and *Archbishop Robinson* (exh. RA, 1775; Birmingham University). He also painted a study of one of Reynolds's housemaids, which, to the amusement of family and friends, became the object of repeated attacks by Reynolds's pet macaw. Northcote himself served as a model to Reynolds, including as one of the young men in *Ugolino and his Children in the Dungeon* (priv. coll.). Although initially polite about his professional situation, Northcote became disenchanted at Reynolds's personal indifference to him, at his unwillingness to provide training, and even at his own studio space, which he described in 1775 as a 'dismal hole' (Gwynn, 111). According to Northcote, Reynolds 'was not the master to produce good scholars, as most of his could never get a decent livelihood, but lived in poverty and died in debt, miserable to themselves and a disgrace to the art. I alone escaped this severe fate' (ibid., 225–6). Northcote later made much of his association with Reynolds and his circle. Yet there is no evidence that he was ever regarded as a close friend. Indeed, Henry Fuseli cruelly stated that, while he was on close personal terms with Reynolds, Northcote was 'considered as little better than his pallette cleaner' (*The Collected English Letters of Henry Fuseli*, ed. D. H. Weinglass, 1982, 12). Sometimes Northcote was invited to join Reynolds at table. However, much of the gossip he relayed in later years was clearly obtained by eavesdropping and through his conversations with Reynolds's sister, Fanny, who took him under her wing.

On 25 October 1771 Northcote enrolled as a student at the Royal Academy Schools, where he drew from the antique cast and the living model. At the time he told his brother excitedly that the 'information concerning the drawing from the naked woman is really true'. He added that the practice was 'much disapproved of by some good folks and Miss Reynolds says it is a great pity that it should become a necessary part in the education of a painter' (Whitley, 2.286). Of the female models themselves he remarked that they 'looked upon it as an additional disgrace to what their profession imposed upon them, and as something unnatural. One in particular ... always came in a mask' (*Conversations*, ed. Swinnerton, 83). In 1773 Northcote exhibited his first portrait, *Dr John Mudge*, at the Royal Academy. He exhibited two further works in 1774, *A Lady in the Character of St Catherine* and a 'portrait of an old gentleman'. In 1775 he showed a fancy picture of a 'girl sleeping' and in 1776 a character study of an old man's head. In the same year, about 12 May, he left Reynolds's service to pursue an independent career.

Italy and Germany, 1776–1780 From May to September 1776 Northcote worked as a portraitist in Portsmouth, lodging with Edward Hunt, master builder at the dockyard. In August he also spent a fortnight on the Isle of Wight, and in the autumn he moved on to Plymouth, where he continued to paint portraits. Altogether, over seventy portraits from this period are recorded. The money he earned, between £400 and £500, was sufficient to finance a visit to the continent. On 31 March 1777 he sailed from Brighton to Dieppe, and then travelled on to Paris, where he spent ten days, including a visit to the palace of Versailles. From Paris he travelled to Lyons, and across the Alps to Turin. It was a miserable journey, Northcote being temporarily short of money and quite unable to speak any foreign language. For the journey from Turin to Genoa he equipped himself with a large pair of horse-pistols—much to the vexation of his fellow passenger, who told him that they were likely to increase the possibility of being attacked by bandits. From Genoa he travelled by mule to Florence, and straight on to Rome, where he arrived on 23 May 1777. There, assisted by the Scottish landscape painter Jacob More, he found lodgings in the strada della Croce. In February 1779 he took apartments in the Palazzo Zuccaro, noting that his rooms were the very same used by Reynolds nearly thirty years earlier.

In Rome Northcote made sketches from the old masters. However, he painted few pictures, complaining to his brother about 'those cursed antiquaries' who controlled patronage and the Italian artists who would 'work for the meanest trifle' (4 Feb 1778, RA, Nor/40MS). Northcote painted three self-portraits in Italy: the first in the summer of 1778 for the director of the Uffizi; the second in 1779 for the Accademia del Disegno, Florence, of which he became a member on 27 September 1778; and the third for the Accademia Etrusca at Cortona, to which he was elected on 9 August 1779. He was also elected to the Accademia dei Forti at Rome on 4 November 1779. Northcote's friends in Rome included the miniaturist Maria Hadfield (later Mrs Richard Cosway), the sculptor Thomas Banks, and the painters Prince Hoare and Henry Fuseli, whose drawings he copied (Yale University). Northcote and Hoare frequently explored the Vatican together, once managing to penetrate as far as the pope's bedroom, a cause of consternation to the palace guards, since the pope was still in bed. He also made the acquaintance of the painters Anton Raphael Mengs, Pompeo Batoni, and Jacques-Louis David. Northcote, perhaps with the benefit of hindsight, recalled that David always carried secret-pocket pistols and that 'all his conversation was tinctured with blasphemy in respect to religion, and licentiousness in regard to government, interspersed with many ludicrous anecdotes of the late unfortunate King of France' (Gwynn, 155).

With the exception of a visit to Naples in April 1779 Northcote continued to reside in Rome until June 1779, when he and Hoare left for Florence. After three months they travelled to Bologna, Modena, and Parma, where Northcote made a copy of 'the famous Magdalene in the well-known picture by Correggio' (Gwynn, 6), then in the academy at Parma (Louvre, Paris). After wintering in Venice, Northcote and Hoare travelled to Augsburg via Padua, Verona, and Mantua. In Germany Northcote once more encountered the language barrier, prompting Hoare to attempt conversation with the locals in Latin. Travelling by way of Munich, Frankfurt, and Cologne, they arrived at Düsseldorf, where they saw *Hamlet* performed in Flemish, 'which to us had a very droll effect' (ibid., 188). The final leg of the journey took them to Antwerp and to Ostend, from where they took the packet to Margate, arriving on 2 May 1780. Northcote headed for London.

Paintings, 1780–1825 Confident of attracting patrons, Northcote immediately rented expensive apartments in Old Bond Street, although lack of business soon forced him to retreat to Plymouth, where he painted portraits at 8 guineas a head. Again he took up residence in London, this time in nearby Clifford Street. Still unable to make a living, he once more returned to Plymouth, where suspicions that he had failed in the capital evidently led to estrangement from local patrons. Returning to London for a second time, he was informed by Reynolds of the arrival of John Opie, who, according to Northcote, now monopolized the attention of his own potential allies and patrons. In 1781 and 1782 Northcote exhibited several portraits of naval officers at the Royal Academy, commissions derived no doubt from his Plymouth contacts. Among these was probably the dashing bust-length of Lieutenant George Dyer of the Royal Marines (priv. coll.). By now Northcote's living was derived principally from small-scale fancy pictures and illustrations of popular works of literature, including Laurence Sterne's *Sentimental Journey* and Goethe's *The Sorrows of Young Werther*, which were sold as prints. In 1784 he exhibited his first modern history painting, *The Wreck of HMS Centaur*, painted for Henry Noel, sixth earl of Gainsborough (des.), which Northcote acknowledged as 'the grandest and most original thing I ever did' (Gwynn, 201). The success of this painting helped launch Northcote's career as a history painter, which began in earnest in 1786.

On 13 November 1786 Northcote was elected associate member of the Royal Academy, achieving full membership the following year, on 10 February. By this time he was committed to producing a series of works for Boydell's Shakspeare Gallery, the idea for which he claimed came from his painting *The Murder of the Princes in the Tower* (Petworth House, Sussex), which Boydell had exhibited at his house in Cheapside. Other works for Boydell included *The Death of Wat Tyler* (exh. RA, 1787; des. 1940), *The Meeting of Edward V and his Brother* (exh. RA, 1787), *Last Scene in Part Three of 'Henry VI'*, *Last scene in 'Romeo and Juliet'* (1791; priv. coll.), and *The Death of Mortimer in Prison* (1791). He also painted for Woodmason's Shakespeare Gallery, a rival of Boydell's, including *The Death of John of Gaunt from 'Richard III'* (ex Phillips, 30 April 1991, lot 29). More successful than these rather lugubrious *grandes machines* were his fancy pictures, such as the *Beggar Boy with a Monkey* of 1784 (ex Christies, 5 June 1953, lot 96), and *The Flower Girl Sleeping*, painted for the Polygraphic Society in 1791. A large number of Northcote's paintings were engraved, Northcote presenting a volume of 190 prints after his work to the Royal Academy in 1823. In 1796 Northcote painted a series

of ten narrative pictures, *Diligence and Dissipation*, featuring a 'modest girl' and her 'wanton fellow servant', along the lines of William Hogarth's 'modern moral subjects', although lacking Hogarth's humour, invention, or technical skill.

Northcote exhibited each year at the Royal Academy from 1781 to 1825 (with the exception of 1790). He also showed works at exhibitions in Carlisle, Birmingham, Liverpool, Manchester, Newcastle, and Exeter. His account book, listing many works from the mid-1770s until his death, is in the National Portrait Gallery. Throughout Northcote's career portraiture remained a staple; he relied heavily on the patronage of Devon and Cornish families, although later significant patrons included Sir John Leicester, Thomas Lister Parker of Browsholme, and Charles Townley. Among his more celebrated portrait subjects were Master Betty, 'the young Roscius', as Hamlet (exh. RA, 1805; Royal Shakespeare Company Gallery, Stratford upon Avon), the infant John Ruskin (1822; NPG), Samuel Taylor Coleridge (1804; Jesus College, Cambridge), and Napoleon (1801; ex Sothebys, 16 November 1983, lot 82). During the 1790s Northcote also began to specialize in portraits of dogs, as well as narrative paintings involving monkeys, tigers, lions, vultures, and snakes. He painted numerous self-portraits, especially from the early 1800s. One of the more unusual of these depicts him as a falconer with two hawks and a dog (1823; Royal Albert Memorial Museum, Exeter).

Character and appearance Northcote was small and lean with angular features; Fuseli described him memorably as resembling 'a rat that had seen a cat' (Gwynn, 12). Peter Patmore, who knew him in old age, observed 'His figure is small, shadowy, emaciated; but you think only of his face, which is fine and expressive. His body is out of the question' (ibid., 21). As early as the 1780s he had earned a reputation for miserliness. When his historical painting *The Death of Wat Tyler* was counted a success at the 1787 Royal Academy exhibition, Fuseli observed wryly: 'Now Northcote will go home, put an extra piece of coal on the fire, and be almost tempted to draw the cork of his one pint of wine when he hears such praise' (ibid., 12). In 1789 Northcote moved from Clifford Street to 39 Argyll Street. He lived there until 1822, when he moved to 8 Argyll Place. Northcote never married, living from the 1790s with his sister, Mary, in an increasingly dilapidated household. Northcote's eccentricity and sharp tongue earned him the nickname the 'walking thumb-bottle of aqua fortis' (*Conversations of James Northcote*, 21). These attributes were made forcibly apparent to the young Benjamin Robert Haydon, who paid him a visit in 1804, armed with a letter of introduction from Prince Hoare. Northcote greeted him in an old blue striped dressing-gown.

> Looking keenly at me with his little shining eyes, he opened the letter, read it, and in his broadest Devon dialect said, 'Zo, you mayne to bee a peintur, doo ee; and whaat zort of peintur?' 'Historical painter, sir.' 'Hees-torical peintur!' raising his eyebrows; 'why, yee'll staarve—with a bundle o' streaw under yer heead'. (B. R. Haydon, *Correspondence and Table-Talk*, 1876, 1.21)

Literary career In 1807 Northcote was invited to contribute to Prince Hoare's short-lived periodical *The Artist*, among his first efforts being an obituary of John Opie, who had died earlier that year. His essays on the fine arts included 'The dream of a painter', 'The painter and the philosopher', and a pretentious piece entitled 'The slighted beauty, or, The adventures of an unfortunate lady; including a concise view of the progress of the fine arts in various parts of Europe'. Of limited literary merit, but more historically interesting, are his essays 'On originality, imitators, and collectors', 'On the independence of painting on poetry', his semi-autobiographical 'Second letter from a disappointed genius', and his 'Advice to a young artist'. In 1809 he composed a brief memoir of Reynolds for John Britton's *Fine Arts of the British School* and about 1810 began to write his own memoirs, initially couched in the third person, although he subsequently amended parts to the first person. The manuscript, now in the British Library (Add. MSS 47790–47793), was bequeathed to Sir William Knighton, on the understanding that he should publish it. Knighton did not, but allowed C. R. Leslie access to it in writing his own *Life of Reynolds*, published in 1865. It was eventually published in 1898, edited by Stephen Gwynn.

Northcote incorporated some of the early material in his memoirs into a biography of Sir Joshua Reynolds which was published in 1813 as *Memoirs of Sir Joshua Reynolds, knt. … comprising original anecdotes of many distinguished persons, his contemporaries; and a brief analysis of his discourses*. It received poor reviews, James Prior in his *Life of Oliver Goldsmith* even asserting that the book was not Northcote's own work. There was a grain of truth in the accusation for, as Northcote later told William Hazlitt, he had employed a certain Mr Laird to edit the book and see it through the press. Moreover, the publisher, Henry Colburn, employed researchers to gather anecdotal material relating to Reynolds, which was incorporated unacknowledged and verbatim in Northcote's text. As the *British Critic* noted, 'these anecdotes are so artificially strung together, or rather have so little connection, that the performance assimilates much more to a bundle of bonmots, or witticism, or "felicities in *ana*", than to the character of regular composition' (February 1814, 150). In 1815 Northcote published a *Supplement to the memoirs of the life, writings, discourses, and professional works of Sir Joshua Reynolds, knt., late president of the Royal Academy* which, as well as supplying additional material on Reynolds, contained a compilation of Northcote's own essays for *The Artist* entitled 'Varieties on art'. In 1818 Henry Colburn published *The Life of Sir Joshua Reynolds*, an expanded version, in two volumes, of Northcote's *Memoirs* of 1813.

Northcote's most deeply held opinions on art, life, and politics did not emerge in his own writings but via a compelling series of 'conversations' published by William Hazlitt. Hazlitt, who had known Northcote since 1802, published their conversations from 1826 to 1829 in various journals, including the *New Monthly Magazine*, the *Court Journal*, the *London Weekly Review*, and *The Atlas*, using the pseudonym Boswell Redivivus. A compilation of his essays was published in book form in 1830 as *Conversations of James Northcote, R.A.* Northcote fascinated Hazlitt, not merely as a relic from another age, but by the sheer force and venom of his monologue:

> His thoughts bubble up and sparkle like beads on old wine. The fund of anecdote, the collection of curious particulars, is enough to set up any common retailer of jests that dines out every day; but these are not strung together like a row of galley-slaves, but are always introduced to illustrate some argument, or bring out some fine distinction of character. (Gwynn, 13)

Hazlitt freely paraphrased and even invented, introducing 'little incidental details that never happened; thus, by lying, giving a greater air of truth to the scene—an art understood by most historians!' (*Conversations*, ed. Swinnerton, xii). At times Northcote was angered at Hazlitt's revelations, not least those concerning the Mudge family, who protested to the *New Monthly Magazine* (Gwynn, 23). And when the book was published in 1830 Northcote told John Ruskin's father that he had tried to prevent its publication (*Conversations*, ed. Swinnerton, xiii). In later years Northcote was also courted by a young painter, James Ward, whose manuscript notes (RA) pertaining to their conversations were eventually published in 1901 by Ernest Fletcher. Although they lack the flair of Hazlitt's *Conversations*, they are an invaluable, and more trustworthy, source of information.

Late works Northcote's final years were taken up by two further literary projects, *One Hundred Fables, Original and Select*, first published in 1828, and in 1830 *The Life of Titian, with Anecdotes of the Distinguished Persons of his Time*, both written with the assistance of Hazlitt. Northcote's *Fables* were illustrated with woodcuts based on illustrations from old prints onto which Northcote pasted his own designs. The text is uninspired and, as it has been remarked, 'neither Hazlitt nor any one else could have redeemed them from dullness' (Gwynn, 25). In 1828 Northcote painted a portrait of Sir Walter Scott, who described the artist as looking like 'an animated mummy' (Simon, 112). Although he neglected his house and his personal appearance, Northcote indulged his hobbies, principally the purchase of memorabilia connected with an ennobled branch of the Northcote family from which he claimed descent. He died at 8.30 p.m. on 13 July 1831 at his home in Argyll Place. In his will he stipulated that his body should remain uninterred 'as long as it can be suffered' to ensure that he was not accidentally buried alive. He also gave three choices for his place of burial, including St Paul's Cathedral, 'as near as possibly may be to the remains of my late lamented Friend and Master Sir Joshua Reynolds'. In the event he was buried in St Marylebone Church. His estate was estimated at about £25,000. In his will he left a sum of up to £1400 to pay for a second edition of his *Fables*, to be edited by Edward Southey Rogers. His Northcote family memorabilia he left to Sir Stafford Northcote of Upton Pyne, Devon, also his various portraits of the Northcotes, his bust by Joseph Bonomi, and his two-volume manuscript account of the Northcote family. He left £1000 to the sculptor Francis Chantrey for his monument to be placed in St Andrew's Church, Plymouth, and a further £200 for a memorial to his brother, who had died intestate on 9 May 1813. His brother's monument was placed in St Andrew's, although his own was erected in Exeter Cathedral. His sister remained in Argyll Place until her death on 25 May 1836. MARTIN POSTLE

Sources S. Gwynn, *Memorials of an eighteenth century painter* (1898) · *Conversations of James Northcote esq., R.A. by William Hazlitt*, ed. F. Swinnerton (1952) · *Conversations of James Northcote R.A. with James Ward on art and artists*, ed. E. Fletcher (1901) · J. Northcote, *Memoirs of Sir Joshua Reynolds*, 2 vols. (1813–15) · J. Northcote, *The life of Sir Joshua Reynolds*, 2nd edn, 2 vols. (1819) · J. Simon, ed., 'The account book of James Northcote', *Walpole Society*, 58 (1995–6), 21–125 · N. Surry, 'James Northcote at Portsmouth', *Burlington Magazine*, 136 (1994), 234–7 · J. Northcote, *The life of Titian, with anecdotes of the distinguished persons of his time*, 2 vols. (1830) · J. Northcote, *The artist's book of fables*, ed. E. S. Rogers (1845) · W. T. Whitley, *Artists and their friends in England, 1700–1799*, 2 vols. (1928) · *The diary of Benjamin Robert Haydon*, ed. W. B. Pope, 5 vols. (1960–63) · J. Northcote, autobiographical memoir, BL, Add. MSS 47790–47793 · RA, MS NOR 1–61 · will, PRO, PROB 11/1788, sig. 411 · *GM*, 1st ser., 101/2 (1831) · *Library of the Fine Arts*, 2 (1831), 1–8

Archives BL, corresp., memoirs, and papers, Add. MSS 42424, 47790–47793 · BL, letters and MSS, Add. MS 42524, fols. 1–48b · Bodl. Oxf., notebook · Devon RO, corresp. · Plymouth City Museum and Art Gallery, corresp. · Westcountry Studies Library, Exeter, MS tables · Yale U., Sterling Memorial Library, corresp. | Ches. & Chester ALSS, letters to Sir John Leicester · NL Scot., letters to Archibald Constable · RA, letters to his brother Samuel

Likenesses J. Northcote, self-portrait, oils, 1779, Uffizi Gallery, Florence · J. Northcote, self-portrait, oils, 1784, NPG [see illus.] · G. Dance, drawing, 1793, RA · J. Northcote, self-portrait, oils, 1802, priv. coll. · J. Northcote, self-portrait, oils, 1807; ex Sothebys, 8 April 1992 · F. Chantrey, original model for bust, exh. RA 1812, AM Oxf. · J. Northcote, self-portrait, oils, exh. Walker Art Gallery, Liverpool 1812 · Prince Hoare, pencil and crayon drawing, 1813, Victoria Art Gallery, Bath · G. H. Harlow, oils, *c.*1817, NPG · J. Northcote, self-portrait, oils, 1823, Royal Albert Memorial Museum, Exeter · W. Brockedon, pencil and chalk drawing, 1825, NPG · J. Northcote, self-portrait, oils, 1826; Christies, 11 November 1983 · J. Northcote, self-portrait, oils, 1827, NPG · F. Chantrey, marble statue, exh. RA 1840, Exeter Cathedral · G. H. Harlow, pencil and chalk drawing, BM · Prince Hoare, pencil and watercolour drawing (as an old man), V&A · J. Northcote, self-portrait, oils, Frans Hals-museum, Haarlem · J. Northcote, self-portrait, pencil and watercolour drawing, V&A · G. Shepheard, pencil drawing, NPG · H. Singleton, group portrait, oils (*The Royal Academicians, 1793*), RA

Wealth at death left several thousand pounds to family and friends; bequeathed £1000 for monument to himself by Chantrey: will, PRO, PROB 11/1788, sig. 411

Northcote, James Spencer (1821–1907), college head and historian, born at Feniton Court, near Honiton, Devon, on 26 May 1821, was the second son in the family of two sons and four daughters of George Barons Northcote (1796–1875), landowner, of Feniton Court and his wife, Maria (*d.* 1836), daughter and coheir of Gabriel Stone of South Brent, Somerset. Educated at Ilmington grammar school (1830–37), he entered Corpus Christi College, Oxford, in 1837, was awarded a scholarship, and graduated BA in 1841 with a first class in the classical school. While at Oxford he came under the influence of J. H. Newman and E. B. Pusey. On 10 December 1842 he married his cousin Susannah Spencer Poole (*d.* 1853), the daughter of Joseph Ruscombe Poole, solicitor, of Bridgwater, Somerset. Having been ordained deacon at Exeter Cathedral on Trinity Sunday 1844, he served as a supernumerary curate at Ilfracombe,

but his doubts about the Anglican position steadily increased.

In 1845 Northcote's wife, with three of her sisters, joined the Church of Rome. After resigning his curacy, Northcote himself followed her example and was received at Prior Park, Bath, on 7 January 1846. The move caused a lasting rift with his father. He set out his position in *The Fourfold Difficulty of Anglicanism*, published in 1846. A French translation by Jules Gondon appeared the next year. From 1847 to 1850 he resided at Rome and there developed a close friendship with G. B. De Rossi, the historian of the catacombs—a subject which he now made his lifetime study. His stay at Rome coincided with the first years of the pontificate of Pius IX, and he witnessed the dramatic events attending the assassination of the papal prime minister and the pope's flight to Gaeta.

Northcote spent the years 1850–53 at Clifton, devoting himself to literary work. From June 1852 to September 1854 he was acting editor of *The Rambler*, to which he had been a contributor since its inception by his friend John Moore Capes in January 1848. Following the death of his wife on 3 June 1853 he began studies for the priesthood, first at the Birmingham Oratory (1854) and then at the Collegio Pio in Rome (1854–5). Having been ordained priest on 29 July 1855 at St Dominic's Convent, Stone, Staffordshire, he was in charge of the mission at Stoke-on-Trent until his appointment in January 1860 as vice-president of St Mary's College, Oscott, near Birmingham. He became president the following July.

Northcote's seventeen-year presidency came to be regarded as the golden age of the college. He modernized the studies and the regime in line with the principles established by Thomas Arnold, and Oscott gained the status of the leading Catholic public school, attended by the sprigs of the aristocracy. During his later years in office, however, Northcote had to contend with competition from the Oratory School, Birmingham, and with two severe epidemics, one of which led to the death in 1867 of his only surviving son, then a pupil at the college. In February 1865 he was involved in a highly publicized court case which came before the lord chief justice, Sir Alexander Cockburn, at the queen's bench. The case revealed some tension at the college between the fee-paying students and the clerical students, supported by charity, who went on to study divinity. David Fitzgerald, the son of an Irish appeal judge, was expelled by Northcote for leading a campaign of derision against the church students, as being 'of inferior extraction', and took an action against him for technical assault. The plaintiff was awarded damages of only £5 but Northcote had to pay costs of £800—a sum which was raised by his supporters. Another of the many Irish pupils at the college was the future novelist George Moore, who in his memoirs recalled Northcote, unflatteringly, as 'a great-bellied, big, ugly fellow, whom we used to call the Gorilla. He was almost as hairy, great tufts starting out of his ears and out of his nostrils' (Moore, 421–2).

Northcote retired through ill health in 1877, and twelve years later the college at Oscott was converted to exclusive use as an ecclesiastical seminary. He was parish priest at Stone from 1877 to 1881, and of Stoke-on-Trent from 1881 to 1887, when creeping paralysis forced his retirement from active work. He died at the presbytery in Stoke on 3 March 1907 and was buried at Oscott cemetery. His three sons and three daughters all predeceased him. The only one who survived into adulthood became a Dominican nun at Stone.

Northcote's most lasting literary legacy was his work on the Roman catacombs, first adumbrated in articles for *The Rambler* (January and July 1860). His most substantial scholarly publication, *Roma sotteranea, or, An Account of the Roman Catacombs* (1869), based on G. B. De Rossi's *Roma sotteranea*, was revised for a much expanded edition in 1879, which took account of De Rossi's important later work. De Rossi himself contributed a preface in which he praised Northcote for having 'remodelled' his own work to produce 'a new and partly an original book'. Northcote also published some popular guides to the catacombs as well as other devotional and controversial volumes. He was awarded the degree of DD by Pope Pius IX in January 1861.   G. MARTIN MURPHY

Sources 'Memoir', *The Oscotian*, 3rd ser., 7 (1907), 111–70 [unsigned] · J. F. Champ, *Oscott* (1987) · *Fitzgerald v. Northcote* (1865), 4 Foster and Finlason 656, 176 ER 734 · *The Tablet* (9 March 1907) · *The Times* (9 March 1907) · *Birmingham Daily Post* (9 March 1907) · G. Moore, *Hail and farewell: ave, salve, vale*, ed. R. A. Cave, 2nd edn, 2 vols. (1925); repr. in 1 vol. (1976) · W. Barry, *The Lord my light* (1907) · Burke, *Gen. GB*
Archives Oscott College, Birmingham, corresp. and papers | Birmingham Oratory, letters to J. H. Newman · CUL, letters to Lord Acton
Likenesses photographs, *c*.1860–1875, repro. in *The Oscotian*, 142 · J. R. Herbert, oils, 1873, Oscott College, Birmingham
Wealth at death £5063 1*s*. 2*d*.: resworn probate, 16 May 1907, *CGPLA Eng. & Wales*

Northcote, Sir John, baronet (1598/9–1676), politician, was the eldest child of the twelve sons and six daughters of John Northcote (1570–1632) of Newton St Cyres, Devon, long-serving JP, and his second wife, Susan (*d*. 1654), daughter of Sir Hugh Pollard of King's Nympton, Devon. He matriculated at Exeter College, Oxford, on 9 May 1617 and became a student at the Middle Temple on 26 November 1618. He married Grace (*d*. 1675), daughter and heir of Hugh Halswell of Wells, Somerset; they had seven sons and four daughters. Northcote's seat of Hayne in Newton St Cyres was substantial enough to accommodate Charles I in 1644 and his estate was valued at £1500 per annum in 1660. He became a baronet on 16 July 1641. Unlike his father, who was an active JP from 1599 to 1632 and sheriff in 1626–7, he played little part in county government until after the civil war. His only significant service was as a militia captain, at least from 1627. In 1640 he was at York with the army assembled against the Scots, probably on the staff of the lord general, the earl of Northumberland.

Northcote was elected to the Long Parliament when the Ashburton seat was restored on 26 November 1640 and kept a notebook of the Commons proceedings until 28 December. He aroused the Commons, on 14 January 1642, when he mentioned the rumour that it was intended to crown the prince and make him king. On 20 June 1642 the Commons required him to return to Devon and aid the deputy lieutenants in raising the militia. By 12 July he was fulfilling this order and on 4 August was present at a muster on Haldon Common. Serving with parliament's forces, he took part in the siege of Sherborne and was Bedford's envoy to the royalist marquess of Hertford to request that their army might withdraw peaceably to prevent bloodshed: Hertford refused. Northcote retreated with Sir George Chudleigh towards north Devon where, on 28 September, they ordered the arrest of the earl of Bath, leader of the commission of array. These activities led to Northcote's being one of the four Devonians excluded from a royal pardon on 9 November and protected by a parliamentary declaration of 31 December. He was back in the Commons in December and served on the committee for the western parts. In January he returned to Devon, helped raise an army for the relief of Plymouth, and resisted a royalist attack at Chagford. He took part in negotiations to secure a local truce, which lasted until 22 April, and then served with the army defeated at Stratton on 16 May. He retreated to Exeter where, in July, he was shot through the arm by a besieging soldier. When Exeter surrendered he became a prisoner, ignoring the offer of a royal pardon. He was allowed to seek an exchange in October 1644 but was not readmitted to the Commons until 7 May 1645 because of doubts of his loyalty. He took the covenant on 21 May and on 3 June was one of those members allowed £4 weekly while his lands were occupied.

Northcote's activities as JP and as a militia commissioner in Devon suggest that he was seldom, if ever, present in parliament in 1647 and 1648. This evidence is supported by his being named as one of the MPs absent without leave on 9 October 1647. He never dissented from continued negotiations with the king to secure a settlement, and absented himself from parliament following Pride's Purge in December 1648. He was dropped from the county bench until 1658, but he continued to be elected MP for Devon to the protectorate parliaments. He was not active in 1654 and was excluded by the council of state in 1656 but was elected again in 1659 when his speeches showed his longing for rule by three estates of unquestionable legality. Later that year he was approached as one likely to support a rising in favour of Charles II. In January 1660 he advocated the restoration of the secluded members of the Long Parliament and was among those arrested for inciting riots in Exeter. Sent to London, he was imprisoned only until 21 February when the secluded members were restored to parliament. When the Convention Parliament was elected he was again the member for Devon. He spoke frequently on a variety of subjects and was appointed to sixty-seven committees. He was chiefly concerned with the religious settlement and agreed there should be bishops, while criticizing deans and chapters. He was not elected to the Cavalier Parliament in 1661 but became the member for Barnstaple at a by-election in 1667. In Devon he continued on the bench and also served as a colonel of the militia and as a deputy lieutenant. Northcote showed little activity in parliament or Devon during the last five years of his life. The language of his will of 1675 showed his puritanical leanings. He died aged seventy-seven, and was buried at Newton St Cyres on 24 June 1676.

MARY WOLFFE

Sources *Notebook of John Northcote*, ed. A. H. A. Hamilton (1877) · Devon RO, QS 1/1–6, 8–11, QS boxes 24–35, 51–53, QS28/3–12, DRO 1392M/L1645/32, Seymour MSS · *JHC*, 2 (1640–42) · *JHC*, 3 (1642–4) · *JHC*, 5 (1646–8) · S. K. Roberts, *Recovery and restoration in an English county: Devon local administration, 1646–1670* (1985) · Thomason tracts: *True newes from Devonshire and Cornwall* (1642) [E 83(43)]; *A true relation of the late victory obtained by the Right Honourable the Earle of Stanford* (1643) [E 91(25)]; *Some late occurrences in Shropshire and Devonshire* (1641/2) [E 121(4)]; *The protestation taken by the commissioners of Cornwall and Devon* (1642) [E 94(21)]; *By the king: a proclamation of his majesties grace, favour, and pardon to the inhabitants of his county of his citty of Exeter* [1642] [669.f.5(99)]; [see also E 61(16) and E 89(17)] · M. W. Helms, 'Northcote, Sir John', HoP, *Commons, 1660–90* · J. L. Vivian, ed., *The visitations of the county of Devon, comprising the herald's visitations of 1531, 1564, and 1620* (privately printed, Exeter, [1895]) · Cobbett, *Parl. hist.*, 3.1429, 1479, 1486–7, 1531, 1579; 4.5, 75, 79, 82–3, 94, 100, 102, 115, 144, 155, 162 · militia details, 1627, PRO, SP16/17/18 · militia details, 1629, PRO, SP16/150/76i · militia details, 1633, PRO, SP16/241/55 · Crown office docket books, PRO, C231/5,6 · W. H. Coates, A. Steele Young, and V. F. Snow, eds., *The private journals of the Long Parliament*, 1: *3 January to 5 March 1642* (1982) · Som. ARS, 56/6/52.2,3 · CKS, U269 C276 (56); C290/5 · E. A. Andriette, *Devon and Exeter in the civil war* (1971) · *Diary of Thomas Burton*, ed. J. T. Rutt, 4 vols. (1828), vols. 3–4 · *Bellum civile: Hopton's narrative of his campaign in the West, 1642–1644*, ed. C. E. H. Chadwyck Healey, Somerset RS, 18 (1902) · *Diary of the marches of the royal army during the great civil war, kept by Richard Symonds*, ed. C. E. Long, CS, old ser., 74 (1859) · D. Underdown, *Pride's Purge: politics in the puritan revolution* (1971) · J. T. Cliffe, *Puritans in conflict* (1988) · J. T. Cliffe, *The puritan gentry besieged, 1650–1700* (1993) · *Fourth report*, HMC, 3 (1874) [Earl De La Warr] · *The manuscripts of his grace the duke of Portland*, 10 vols., HMC, 29 (1891–1931), vols. 1–4 · *Fourteenth report*, HMC (1896) · *The letter-book of John, Viscount Mordaunt, 1658–1660*, ed. M. Coate, CS, 3rd ser., 69 (1945) · parish register, Devon, Newton St Cyres [marriage, burial] · *Devon and Cornwall Notes and Queries*, 18 (1934–5), 316 · parish register, Devon, Crediton [birth, father] · Wood, *Ath. Oxon.* · Admissions to Middle Temple, vol. 1

Likenesses portrait, 1662, priv. coll. · A. Wivell, stipple, pubd 1817, BM, NPG · Bowes, portrait (as a young man), priv. coll. · A. Wivell, wash drawing, AM Oxf. · portrait, priv. coll.

Wealth at death substantial; estate valued at £1500 p.a. in 1660: *Devon and Cornwall Notes and Queries*

Northcote, Stafford Henry, first earl of Iddesleigh (1818–1887), politician, was born at 23 Portland Place, London, on 27 October 1818, the eldest of three sons (there were also two daughters) of Henry Stafford Northcote (1792–1850), himself the eldest son of Sir Stafford Henry Northcote, seventh baronet (1762–1851), of The Pynes, Upton Pyne, Exeter, a descendant of Sir John *Northcote. Stafford Northcote's mother was Agnes Mary, only daughter of Thomas Cockburn of the East India Company's service and then of Bedford Hill, Surrey. Through his mother, who died on 9 April 1840, Northcote inherited Scottish border ancestry. The Northcotes were a family of Devon landowners of great antiquity who could trace their lineage back to 1103. Nevertheless they were not particularly wealthy, owning an estate of only 5700 acres in Devon which yielded an annual income of about £6000 in 1883. Throughout his career Northcote was considerably poorer than many leading politicians of his time, and accepted a

Stafford Henry Northcote, first earl of Iddesleigh (1818–1887), by Elliott & Fry

variety of professional and business positions (such as chairman of the Hudson's Bay Company) to improve his circumstances.

Education As a child Northcote displayed precocity, writing a supernatural romance for his brother and sister at the age of six. From his mother he absorbed considerable Anglican religious piety, as well as a lifelong love of reading, and what she described in her diary as 'a very strong imagination', the last, however, not being a quality for which he was renowned in public life. From 1826 to 1831 he was a pupil of the Revd Mr Roberts at a school in Mitcham which was subsequently transferred to Brighton, where he wrote much precocious verse. In 1831 he was sent to Eton College, to the house of the Revd Edward Coleridge. At Eton he was nicknamed Tab by his circle of friends, which included Arthur *Hobhouse and Thomas Henry *Farrer, both later his brothers-in-law. Although initially indolent (and frequently flogged), he acquired a reputation for versification and rowed for the Eton eight in 1835. In October 1836 he went into residence at Balliol College, Oxford, and was elected to a scholarship in the following month. Contemporaries noted his extraordinary feats of memory.

Northcote entered university life at the height of the crisis engendered by John Henry Newman and his circle. He appears to have been affected only marginally by the Oxford Movement; although he was sometimes labelled a

Puseyite (a pejorative description in tory circles) he demonstrated sympathy with both the evangelical and high-church wings of Anglicanism. Northcote also found himself at this time in the midst of a family religious dispute between his mother, who had been attracted to the revivalism of Edward Irving, and his father's more conventional views; in letters to his parents he noted himself to be a critical but essentially orthodox supporter of the Church of England. In the late 1830s he felt that a protestant Englishman travelling in a Catholic country should attend Catholic services, a view he later abandoned. Northcote graduated BA in 1839 with a first class in classics and a third in mathematics. He proceeded MA in 1840, and in June 1863 was created DCL.

Early career and marriage On deciding to read for the bar, Northcote took chambers at 58 Lincoln's Inn Fields, and entered the Inner Temple in 1840. This was a period of especial importance in Northcote's life, for in the early 1840s both his domestic and his career circumstances changed significantly. The death of his mother in 1840 led to an increase in his religious earnestness, and Northcote spoke in Exeter on behalf of the Society for Promoting Christian Knowledge and other evangelical bodies. On 5 August 1843 he married, at Holy Trinity Church, Marylebone, Cecilia Frances (1823–1910), daughter of Thomas Farrer of Lincoln's Inn Fields, a solicitor, and his wife, Cecilia, daughter of Richard Willis of Halsnead, Lancashire. The Northcotes had seven sons, including Walter Stafford Northcote, second earl of Iddesleigh, Henry Stafford *Northcote, Baron Northcote, John Stafford Northcote, chaplain to Queen Victoria, and Arthur Francis Northcote, a parish priest; they also had three daughters, the eldest of whom, Agnes Mary Cecilia, married Sir Reginald MacLeod and was mother of Dame Flora *MacLeod (born in 11 Downing Street during her grandfather's chancellorship).

Gladstone's secretary Meanwhile, in June 1842, while Northcote was engaged in a career at the bar, there occurred an event which was to alter his life. William E. Gladstone, then vice-president of the Board of Trade, wrote to Edward Coleridge, the Eton housemaster, asking him to recommend a private secretary from among his former pupils. Coleridge suggested Northcote and two others, and Gladstone chose Northcote. His duties included opening all letters addressed to Gladstone, making notes of their contents, and, after receiving instructions, responding to them, as well as accompanying Gladstone throughout the country. Gladstone was chiefly engaged in carrying out the policies of Sir Robert Peel of reducing tariffs. Although Gladstone resigned over the Maynooth grant in 1845, Northcote continued to serve as his private secretary until about 1850, assisting Gladstone in his election for Oxford University in 1847 and in 1852 (he declined to help in 1859). He also held the position of legal assistant at the Board of Trade from February 1845 until August 1850, despite the fact that he was not called to the bar until 19 November 1847. In January 1850 he was appointed one of the secretaries of the Great Exhibition, a position requiring much application and one which frequently brought him into contact with Prince Albert. Gladstone specifically denied that this appointment was made on his recommendation, noting that Northcote's reputation stood high with whig leaders such as Lord Taunton and Lord Granville. Prince Albert greatly admired Northcote, dissuading him from resigning following his succession to the baronetcy on his grandfather's death in March 1851. On 17 October 1851 Northcote was created a CB for his efforts on behalf of the Great Exhibition, and he also demonstrated the first signs of the chronic heart ailment to which he was prone until his death.

Northcote's own political views now began to move in a more Conservative direction. In 1849 he had published a pamphlet on the navigation laws which showed him to be a convinced free-trader. In April 1851, however, he noted in a letter to his wife that he was moving 'towards the Protectionist side', and it is known that Northcote's increasingly orthodox views on the Church of England precluded him from joining the whig party, which was anxious to have his support. Gladstone was, of course, moving in the opposite direction, but relations between the two were still excellent, to the extent that Gladstone was godfather to Northcote's son John Stafford in 1850, and in April 1852 asked Northcote to be an executor of his will (Northcote did not live long enough to discharge this obligation). In 1850–52 Northcote had thought of standing for parliament as a Conservative in the seats of Totnes, Taunton, and Exeter, issuing an address to the last place in May 1852, although he eventually declined to stand. At this time he stated that he was 'a warm supporter of Lord Derby's Government'. In December 1852, when Gladstone entered the Aberdeen coalition as chancellor of the exchequer, Northcote wrote to him to say that 'I am rather a stiff Conservative, and do not feel at all sure that the next Administration will be one that I can work under', but also was careful to point out that 'though you form a leading element in it I can scarcely imagine my having any doubts'.

The Northcote–Trevelyan report It was at this time that Northcote became associated with the matter for which, perhaps, his name is now best remembered. In conjunction with Sir Charles Trevelyan, Northcote was invited to serve on eight commissions inquiring into various aspects of civil service department reform. One of these was on the Treasury. By a Treasury minute of 12 April 1853 Northcote and Trevelyan were instructed to draw up a general report on the civil service with especial reference to its means of selection and promotion. The Northcote–Trevelyan report (with an approving appendix by Benjamin Jowett), dated 23 November 1853 and published in the parliamentary papers in 1854 (*Parl. papers*, 1854, 27), is one of the most famous and typical of mid-Victorian reforms, recommending the widespread use of the examination system and recruitment on merit in place of patronage and 'old corruption'. These proposals anticipated the movement for administrative reform which was so striking a consequence of the Crimean War and affected the rising importance of the middle classes and the 'career open to talent'. It is perhaps superficially somewhat ironic that Northcote should have been the co-author of this report at a time when he was moving from Peelism to 'stiff Conservatism', but the Conservative Party which emerged some decades later, usually electorally victorious, was one which was increasingly preferred by the middle classes. In 1854 Northcote published a paper in a volume entitled *Suggestions under which university education may be made available for clerks in government offices, for barristers, for solicitors* for the Oxford Tutors' Association, in which he pointed out the suitability of a classical education as a preparation for senior positions in the civil service.

Early years in the House of Commons On 9 March 1855 Northcote was returned as a member of parliament at a by-election in the seat of Dudley. He is recorded in *McCalmont's Poll Book* as a 'Liberal Conservative', and the seat was largely owned by Lord Ward, a strong Peelite, who agreed to Northcote's standing upon Gladstone's recommendation. Northcote took his seat on 16 March, and delivered his maiden speech, on civil service reform, only a week later, on 23 March. He noted in a letter that the speech was 'very well received, especially considering that … the subject of Civil Service reform, and particularly of the competition system, is exceedingly unpopular in the House', and pointedly noted that 'Dizzy did me the honour to turn round and look very attentive' (Lang, 1.116). Northcote spoke in the following session on civil service superannuation, but he was chiefly occupied, somewhat curiously, on the question of reformatory schools. From about 1850 the question of the establishment of reformatory schools, to be used for delinquents in place of prison terms, became much debated (drawing on long previous discussion). In 1854 an act was passed authorizing judges and magistrates to commit children under sixteen years to schools duly licensed for this purpose. This act led to the foundation of many such schools, one of which, at Brampford Wood, near Pynes, was established by Northcote in April 1855. This school operated on the model of Barwick Baker's farm schools in Gloucestershire and continued to be one of Northcote's foremost interests. It was established against the wishes of the local inhabitants, who feared the escape of youthful criminals, but proved to be a considerable success. Northcote took a personal interest in the welfare of reformatory students which often persisted long after they were adults. He read a paper on this subject to the first meeting of the Reformatory Union at Bristol in August 1856. In December 1855 Northcote drafted a bill, enacted in 1856, providing for the establishment of industrial schools, to which vagrant and truant children might be sent.

On 3 March 1857, when Palmerston's government was defeated, Northcote voted with the opposition, to Lord Ward's chagrin. Northcote was anxious to be free of his Dudley connections. On 6 April 1857 he stood as a liberal conservative for the seat of North Devonshire, but came in third for the two-member seat, incurring very great expenses. The costs of the election were such that Northcote and his family were forced to live in France for purposes of economy until the middle of 1858.

In June 1858 Northcote received a letter from Ralph Earle, Disraeli's private secretary, suggesting a meeting, at which it was proposed, on Disraeli's suggestion, that Northcote contest Stamford as a Conservative, with the strong possibility of his securing a ministerial position in the Conservative government formed in February 1858, as financial secretary to the Treasury. Northcote was genuinely vexed in knowing how to deal with this offer, for, as he wrote to his wife, he would 'mark myself as Dizzy's man' (Lang, 1.152), while 'I fear it would be disagreeable to Gladstone. I would much rather give up all thoughts of Parliament and office than do anything that would give him the impressions I was deserting him'. Nevertheless, by 6 July Northcote had written to his wife 'three cheers to Dizzy!', and that 'Dizzy talked as if he had always had my interests in the centre of his heart'. Not surprisingly Northcote also wrote that 'I feel as if I were reading a novel about myself, the whole thing is so queer' (Lang, 1.153).

For the next twenty-three years Northcote served as Disraeli's most loyal and trusted deputy on financial matters, a relationship which worked to the advantage of Disraeli no less than to Northcote. The close association between the Devon baronet and the London-born Jewish intellectual, though superficially curious, is best explained by the fact that each respected and needed the other. Disraeli relied upon Northcote for his utter respectability, soundness, and competence in debate; Northcote admired Disraeli's brilliance and the fact that Disraeli had plucked him out of near obscurity to be his lieutenant. That Northcote had been Gladstone's private secretary gave their relationship an especially piquant flavour. Disraeli referred to Northcote as 'my right hand', and promoted him to the most senior of cabinet positions, arguably beyond his objective merits. Additionally, Disraeli's own fiscal policies, as recent research has revealed, were surprisingly moderate and orthodox, differing from Gladstone's chiefly in eschewing a doctrinaire notion of 'retrenchment' and in much greater sympathy for the landed interest; Northcote's views, admired by Gladstone, served equally well for Disraeli.

On 17 July 1858 Northcote was returned unopposed for Stamford at a by-election, McCalmont now denoting him as a 'Conservative' pure and simple. He was again returned, on 29 April 1859, at the general election, standing unopposed in this two-member seat with Lord Robert Cecil (afterwards third marquess of Salisbury and prime minister). True to Disraeli's promise, Northcote was appointed to office shortly after his election at Stamford, holding the position of financial secretary to the Treasury (under Disraeli's chancellorship) from 21 January 1859 until the fall of the government later that year. At Disraeli's request Northcote wrote a long note on the reform question, advocating a moderate extension of the franchise but without the redistribution of parliamentary seats. In his advice on foreign and defence policy Northcote consistently advocated caution and economy in military expenditure.

In opposition for the next seven years, Northcote now found himself a leading spokesman for the Conservative

Party, although attracting some criticism, even then, that his attacks upon the government were never full-spirited. On 21 February 1860 he spoke on the commercial treaty with France, approving the bill as a whole while voicing criticism of some details. On 8 May 1860 he moved an amendment, defeated by only nine votes, to Gladstone's motion for the repeal of the paper duties. His reputation in the financial area was enhanced by a number of fine parliamentary speeches on taxation in 1861, one of which (delivered on 2 May 1861) was considered by Disraeli to be 'one of the finest he ever heard', and was deemed by Lord Stanley to be 'the most complete parliamentary success' he had heard in twelve years. Stanley also wrote to Northcote, prophetically, 'you are marked out for a Chancellor of The Exchequer' (Lang, 1.177). In 1862 Northcote produced a book, *Twenty Years of Financial Policy*, dedicated to his old friend Edward Coleridge, which criticized the government's excessive reliance on the income tax coupled with excessive government expenditure. At this time he also spoke again on reformatory schools and on civil service reform. Northcote, an opponent of slavery, also did much to keep Conservative sentiment from overtly supporting the South in the American Civil War, and hence to keep Britain neutral. Throughout this period Northcote was also heavily concerned with financial policy, advocating retrenchment and a broadening of the tax base.

Educational royal commissions in the 1860s and further political career In 1862–4 Northcote served on the important Clarendon commission on the future of the public schools, named for its head, the fourth earl of Clarendon. This commission visited the nine old public schools and met 127 times. Here Northcote was no radical reformer, claiming that 'the English mind did not want *lycées* and *gymnasia*, but schools for the moral, physical, and intellectual training of boys between twelve and eighteen, which should make of these boys young men,—men in every sense of the word', and recommended that such schools 'accommodate the new studies … to the old learning' (Lang, 1.205–6)—in other words, advocating much the same regime which actually emerged in Britain's public schools over the next fifty years. He did, however, advocate as proper the reform of school endowments, the restructuring of governing bodies, and the removal of restrictions. Northcote also served, in 1864, on the School of Art committee, and in December 1865 was appointed to the royal commission on endowed schools. During these years Northcote was a frequent and lengthy correspondent to Disraeli (whom he continued to address as Mr Disraeli) on many political matters, again consistently advocating the avoidance of foreign entanglements, as well as retrenchment and fiscal moderation.

After debating and rejecting, out of residual deference to Gladstone, one of its sitting members, the idea of standing for Oxford University at the 1865 general election, Northcote again stood for Stamford, where he was again returned unopposed with Lord Robert Cecil (now Viscount Cranborne). On 9 May 1866, after the sitting member, the Hon. C. H. R. Trefusis, succeeded to the Clinton peerage, Northcote was elected unopposed as member for

North Devonshire, his local seat. Northcote retained his place in this two-member constituency until he accepted a peerage, and was unopposed at all subsequent elections except that of 1868, when he finished first ahead of the Liberal candidate, Sir Thomas Dyke Acland, bt, and the sitting Conservative member for Tiverton, J. W. Walrond, who also contested the seat.

At the Board of Trade and the India Office, 1866–1868 Upon the formation of Lord Derby's third government, in 1866, Northcote entered the cabinet for the first time, taking office as president of the Board of Trade on 6 July 1866. At the same time he was sworn of the privy council, together with five other new ministers, at Windsor Castle. Disraeli had made Northcote's appointment to this position a condition of his own assumption of office as chancellor of the exchequer. Little is recorded of Northcote's tenure of this post, although he made a speech at Liverpool on 30 August to celebrate the departure of the *Great Eastern* to lay the Atlantic telegraph cable. When, in March 1867, Lord Cranborne resigned as secretary of state for India, Northcote was appointed in his place, officially taking up the position on 6 March 1867.

As Indian secretary Northcote entered a world of the greatest importance to a tory government, but one which required knowledge, tact, and wisdom. Of these virtues Northcote possessed the first in least measure, for he had no previous experience whatever in Indian affairs. Northcote agreed with Lord Lawrence on the wisdom of non-intervention in Afghanistan, and opposed the annexation of Mysore. He advocated a large measure of financial decentralization for the subcontinent, and also a separate government for Bengal, eventually carried out by Lord Mayo. On 23 April 1868 he introduced the Government of India Amendment Bill (which was eventually withdrawn), and on 12 August 1868 an Indian budget. Northcote was an advocate of the Abyssinian expedition, on which he spoke on 27 November 1867, but could not convince Lord Lawrence, the governor-general, that India ought to pay for its contingent. He was also concerned with a wide variety of other issues, such as the status of missionaries, the question of the place of Indians in the Indian Civil Service, and the question of Indian public works. Northcote's tenure of the Indian office generally received praise, although after he had left office (on 8 June 1869) he was challenged for the fact that costs exceeded the original budget by £3.3 million. Just before leaving office, and although not a rich man, he gave £1000 to hospitals and other useful institutions in India, the only Indian secretary to that point to have made so large a contribution to Indian charities.

In opposition and in North America Northcote found himself again in opposition with the resignation of Disraeli's government on 1 December 1868. In January 1869 he was elected to the rather improbable position of chairman of the Hudson's Bay Company. Northcote had previously declined a number of lucrative City directorships but accepted the Hudson's Bay position at a time when, generally viewed as an anachronism, it was engaged in transferring its huge estate in Rupert's Land to Canada, just after the formation of the dominion of Canada in 1867. On 24 March 1869 he persuaded the company to transfer this land to the Canadian government for £200,000. In April–May 1870 he visited Canada and the United States on behalf of the company, touring Montreal, Ottawa, New York, and Niagara Falls, seeing at first hand the operation of the ballot in American politics and the operations of the Fenians against Britain in Canada. Northcote saw the necessity for attracting new, permanent settlers to Canada in place of the *voyageurs* and for a more enlightened attitude by the company. In November 1869 Northcote visited Egypt, and he was present at the opening of the Suez Canal, a guest on Sir George Stucley's yacht the *Deerhound*.

Rather unexpectedly, on 13 February 1871, Northcote was asked by Lord Granville, the foreign secretary, to join the commission which had already been dispatched to Washington to arrange a number of outstanding disputes between the two countries, especially the *Alabama* claims, Canadian fisheries, and the San Juan boundaries. After the signing of the treaty of Washington on 8 May 1871, a dispute arose over interpretation of a clause in the treaty concerning the indirect claims arising from the negotiated settlement, and in 1872 and 1873 Northcote was forced to defend the British commissioners from charges that they failed to do justice to Canadian interests. Shortly before leaving for America, on 14 January 1871, Northcote had been appointed by H. A. Bruce, the home secretary, to chair the commission which was to inquire into the workings of the friendly societies. Both of these appointments, made by senior Liberals of a leading Conservative politician, indicated the esteem in which Northcote was held, as well as suggesting, perhaps, some residual hope of wooing him back; the expertise gained in this area was useful to Northcote, and to the Conservative Party generally, when Disraeli's government came to legislate on friendly societies four years later. The commission found that many friendly societies were fraudulently or incompetently managed, a conclusion reached after taking evidence throughout the country.

In January 1872 a group of leading Conservatives, including Gathorne Hardy, Lord Cairns, Sir John Pakington, and Northcote, met at Lord Exeter's Burghley House to discuss the possibility of replacing Disraeli with the fifteenth earl of Derby as leader of the Conservative Party. Northcote and Lord John Manners were, apparently, the only Disraeli loyalists present, although the proposal was never acted upon.

Chancellor of the exchequer, 1874–1880 Northcote's life was comparatively quiet until the formation of the second Disraeli government on 20 February 1874, when he was appointed chancellor of the exchequer, a position he held during the whole period of this government until it resigned on 21 April 1880. Northcote's position in this famous administration will be discussed with respect first to his stance on social questions and second to his financial policies. The relatively active policy on social reform of the government of 1874–80 has long been viewed as founding the modern Conservative Party's commitment to 'one nation' toryism, embodying a rapprochement with the working classes, a view which has, however, been questioned by some recent historians who view its growing alliance with the urban middle classes as a more salient feature of this period. Northcote's attitude illustrates the difficulties of coming to any firm opinion on this question. Although it is clear that he was no radical reformer, Northcote was one of the few leading Conservatives who had sat for an industrial seat—Dudley, in 1855–7—and he had a long record of interest in the welfare of the poor. Yet he was also a former disciple of Gladstone and an orthodox financier who was, if anything, less likely to embrace extravagant notions of costly social reform than a romantic like Disraeli. In a letter to G. J. Holyoake, written on 30 October 1875, Northcote stated:

> the three things to which I attach importance in efforts to assist the working classes [are] to get a clear insight into their wants and feelings from their own point of view, … to assist them to obtain an equally clear insight into … other classes, … [and] … to get them to work out their own improvement for themselves. (Smith, 205)

These principles, emphasizing both sympathy and self-help, animated Northcote's attitude toward social questions. Northcote was the author of the Friendly Societies Bill, introduced on 8 June 1874 then withdrawn on 22 July after passing its second reading. Brought in again, it passed its second reading without division (25 February 1875) and became law on 11 August. The aim of this bill was moderate, providing model actuarial tables to the societies and offering such information to the public as to enable them to judge their soundness. The revised bill of 1875 actually lessened the powers granted to the registrar of friendly societies in the 1874 bill, although it did limit infant insurance, often seen as an invitation to child murder. Northcote's bill was criticized as inadequately weak by some Conservatives, but also as improperly increasing the powers of the state by others. Northcote's attitude—a perceptible, but minimal, acquiescence in the extension of state powers in the interest of social reform—was evident in his stance on the other social legislation of Disraeli's government, such as that regulating merchant shipping and artisans' dwellings. In a speech at Manchester on 8 December 1875 Northcote noted that fuller government control was inexpedient in such cases.

Northcote's first budget was introduced on 16 April 1874. In it he abolished sugar duties (worth £2 million) and a tax on horses, took a penny off the income tax, applied £500,000 to the reduction of the national debt by terminable annuities, and applied another £500,000 to the relief of local taxation. He thus much reduced the surplus of £5.5 million bequeathed to him by Gladstone. One Liberal described Northcote's first budget as 'the Liberal budget watered down to the standard of Conservative finance' (Lang, 2.62), and in his budget speech Northcote both congratulated and defended the previous Gladstone government's finance. On 25 January 1877 at Liverpool he defended his whittling down of the surplus by claiming that it was 'got up to a certain extent by putting off a great many claims and charges which would ultimately have to be met' (Lang, 2.63).

On 15 April 1875 Northcote introduced his second budget, which was remarkable for the creation of a 'new' sinking fund based upon the concept of a permanent annual charge of £28 million which would cover both the servicing of the national debt and debt redemption; under this scheme, as the size of the debt became smaller, a proportionately higher amount of the fixed sum could be applied each year to debt redemption. During his term as chancellor Northcote came under pressure to direct the sinking fund to other purposes, especially at the time of the Anglo-Zulu War in July 1879, when the cabinet attempted to get him to suspend the fund (which he refused to do). In 1880 he was forced to make a small raid on the fund in order to keep a pledge that there would be no new taxation in an election year. Successive late Victorian chancellors, even orthodox ones, were compelled to whittle down the sum set aside for debt redemption, G. J. Goschen decreasing it to £25 million. As the size of the British budget grew through ever-increasing imperial, military, and social commitments, both the sinking fund and its aim of eliminating the national debt became increasingly irrelevant. Northcote's sinking fund would seem to have been an example of Gladstonian finance *par excellence*, but it was attacked by Gladstone as having 'taken a flight into the empyrean' (Lang, 2.71). The proposal for a sinking fund was, however, passed by a majority of 189 to 122. Northcote's second budget also showed a much smaller surplus than his first, of only £497,000.

In 1875 Northcote also carried a Savings Bank Bill, which he was forced to defend against Liberal charges that he had made such deposits less secure. A series of blunders over the handling of the Merchant Shipping Bill led to an offer (25 July 1875) by Northcote to Disraeli to take up a lesser position, which was, of course, declined. At this time, in fact, Northcote's stocks were higher than ever and many now saw him as Disraeli's successor in the leadership of the House of Commons. Northcote was also privately opposed to the purchase of the Suez Canal shares on the grounds that 'suspicion will be excited that we mean quietly to buy ourselves into a preponderating position, and then turn the whole thing into an English property' (Lang, 2.84). He also stated to Disraeli 'I know so little of the actual state of our foreign policy'. Disraeli's strategy toward the recalcitrant chancellor was sometimes guileful. In November 1877, just before Northcote was due to have an audience with Queen Victoria, Disraeli wrote to Victoria that 'it would be as well to intimate that our military and naval preparations should be adequate for emergencies'. This strategy evidently worked, for Disraeli wrote a month later that he was now 'pleased' with Northcote's 'tone'.

In 1876 Northcote encountered a different situation from the previous years, for he was faced with an estimated budget deficit of £774,000. Northcote's solution in his budget speech of 3 April was to place an extra penny on the income tax, but he also raised the lower limit on liability to taxation from £100 to £150 and added a deduction of £80 on incomes of up to £300. The extra penny on the income tax, however, compensated for this, producing what Northcote estimated as a surplus of £368,000. Northcote's 1877 budget (introduced on 12 April 1877) was more routine, but showed that the amount applied by the sinking fund to the reduction of the national debt was £176,000 greater than had been foreseen. In April 1878 Northcote was again faced with a less than rosy financial position due to an extraordinary supplement of £6 million for military preparations against Russia, met by issuing exchequer bonds for £2.75 million. His 1878 budget (introduced on 4 April) acknowledged a deficit of £2.6 million, causing income tax to be raised to 5*d*. in the pound and other new taxes to be added. In 1879 Northcote was faced by another deficit of £2.3 million, brought about by commercial depression and the Anglo-Zulu War. In his budget (introduced on 3 April 1879) Northcote chose to extend the repayment of the debt over an additional year rather than raise taxes again. The deteriorating financial situation in 1879 gave rise to an unusual volume of Liberal criticism. Northcote's last budget, introduced on 10 March 1880, saw yet another deficit of £2 million, chiefly occasioned by the £5 million cost of the Anglo-Zulu War. The floating debt stood at £8 million, which Northcote proposed to deal with by the creation of a terminal annuity, lasting until 1885, which would extinguish £6 million of this sum. He was also compelled to appropriate £600,000 of his new sinking fund to this annuity, leading to Gladstone's charge that he was 'immolating' his creation.

There is general agreement that Northcote was an able and innovative chancellor, one whose policies, while similar to those of a Liberal treasurer, were more flexible and less orthodox. He was not without his critics, Lord Carlingford observing in his journal that Gurdon, the Treasury civil servant and another of Gladstone's former secretaries, described Northcote and H. C. E. Childers, chancellor from 1882 to 1885, as 'weak'. Sir Reginald Welby, later under-secretary at the Treasury, believed that Northcote 'left great discretion' to his financial secretaries (successively W. H. Smith, F. A. Stanley, and Sir Henry Selwin-Ibbetson), while Northcote once admitted to Lord Salisbury that 'I am terribly soft-hearted about money, and your note comes at a time when the two vigilant guardians of the public purse, Smith [financial secretary] and Lingen [permanent secretary] are both away'. Yet Lord Esher's summary of Northcote, made in 1876 in his journal, that 'there is no genius in him, but much capacity for sheer hard work' (*Journals and Letters of Reginald Viscount Esher*, ed. M. V. Brett, 4 vols., 1934–8, 1.37), while just, probably understated the novelty of Northcote's position as the first Conservative chancellor with a parliamentary majority since Peel's time, and hence one bound to adopt a course which was both politically original and yet, of necessity, financially orthodox.

Northcote was involved in other matters at this time. On 16 March 1876 he vigorously defended the Royal Titles Bill, obtaining the defeat of Lord Hartington's amendment by a majority of 105 votes. On the Eastern question, which arose at this time, Northcote believed that the British government, in refusing to accept the Berlin memorandum of 18 May 1876, should have put forward an alternative policy, and implicitly criticized the flippancy of Disraeli's response to the 'Bulgarian atrocities'. In late 1876 he also set out, in two speeches, the government's principles on the Eastern question: strict neutrality, provided the route to India was neither blocked nor stopped. On 31 March 1879 he accepted full responsibility, on behalf of the government, for Sir Bartle Frere's activities in Zululand, which led to war.

On 12 August 1876 Disraeli was created earl of Beaconsfield and Northcote succeeded him as leader of the House of Commons, at the time an unofficial position but indicative of his standing in the government. It carried with it the duty of writing the daily letter to the queen on the progress of business in the house. He officially became leader with the resumption of parliament on February 1877 and remained in this position until his elevation to the Lords in July 1885. Northcote's term as leader coincided with the beginning of the policy of parliamentary obstruction, led by C. S. Parnell and J. G. Biggar, in the debates on the South African Confederation Bill. Northcote was instrumental in adopting several rules to deal with obstruction. Two resolutions adopted on 27 July 1877 altered the rules of the house in matters of 'naming' and suspending a disorderly member and in the suppression of delaying motions. His motion of 24 February 1879 prohibited preliminary debate upon going into committee of supply, while his proviso of 28 February 1880 permitted a member to be summarily suspended after being named by the chair. None of these measures, however, materially checked the problem of obstruction. As his last measure as leader of the house Northcote also carried the Irish Relief of Distress Bill, which became law on 18 March 1880.

Conservative leader in the Commons, 1880–1885 The Conservative government was soundly defeated in the general election held in April 1880. Upon the reassembling of parliament on 20 May 1880 the Conservatives numbered only 243 as against 349 Liberals and 60 home-rulers; Northcote himself had been returned unopposed. In this period Northcote led the opposition, first as Beaconsfield's lieutenant and, after his death in April 1881, as joint leader of the party with Lord Salisbury. As opposition leader in the House of Commons, however, Northcote's position was, in the words of Robert Rhodes James, 'invidious and unenviable'. The Liberal front bench contained at least six men of the highest parliamentary talent while the Conservatives were dispirited and bewildered. Northcote, now sixty-two, showed signs of the chronic heart ailment which brought about his sudden death seven years later. His failure to treat Gladstone as an opponent, rather than his former master, so marked a feature of Northcote's parliamentary career, now became even more widely noted than before; Northcote was one of several reputed to have coined the term 'GOM' (Grand Old Man). Even so, Gladstone formed a contempt for his former secretary and colleague so powerful that, most unusually, he openly commented on what he saw as Northcote's 'flabby weakness'.

Even more seriously, however, Northcote was faced with the articulate and memorable animosity of some of the brightest younger members of his own back benches, especially Lord Randolph Churchill, Sir Henry Drummond Wolff, John Gorst, and, occasionally, Arthur James Balfour, who were studiously impatient with Northcote's lack of vigour in attacking the government. Over the next few years the 'Fourth Party', as it quickly became known, achieved national renown as much for its daily sallies aimed at the courteous but helpless Northcote as for its baiting of the government. Northcote emerged from this experience widely perceived as the butt of a particularly talented group of 'young Turks', and his modern reputation for what might be termed pompous incompetence, obviously unfair, largely grew out of these events. At this time Northcote gained his nickname, 'the Goat', and was identified as one of the 'Old Gang', whom Churchill hoped to displace. He was also paired by Churchill with W. H. Smith, the wholesale newsagent turned tory cabinet minister, as 'Marshall and Snelgrove', a most inappropriate description of Northcote, whatever his Hudson's Bay Company connections, whose family had been landowners far longer than even Churchill's. Nevertheless, this description has become one of the memorable catchphrases of late Victorian politics.

That the reputation Northcote acquired was unfair is shown by the damaging defeats he was able to inflict on the government in connection with the claim made by Charles Bradlaugh to affirm the oath, notably on 4 May 1883, when the Affirmation Bill was rejected by a majority of three. Northcote also resisted Gladstone's closure resolution of 20 February 1882, and the twelve resolutions for the curtailment of debate were postponed until the autumn session of 1882. Northcote also spoke on the Irish question at this time, in a speech at Brecon on 19 May 1881 describing 'the three Fs' in the Irish Land Bill a 'force, fraud, and folly', and recommending 'the confidence which produces capital' as the solution to what 'Ireland requires' (Lang, 2.191). He supported the Prevention of Crime Bill introduced by the Liberals after the murder of T. H. Burke and Lord Frederick Cavendish in Dublin, and in other respects moved to join the Conservative mood of opposition to home rule, presaging a policy which became central to tory philosophy from 1886 on. He also attacked the Liberals over their lack of a 'stable, and farsighted, and consistent policy' towards the empire, predicting (25 June 1881) that if the Liberals were in power for twenty years 'at the end of that period there will be very little of the British Empire left for them to govern' (Lang, 2.198). In this, too, he reflected the growing place of the empire in post-Disraelian tory thought. On the other hand, he discouraged the fair-trade movement, describing protection (at Newcastle on 12 October 1881) as a 'pious opinion'. Northcote was closely involved in the inter-party discussions on the 1884 Representation of the People Bill, speaking frequently during the campaign which followed the measure's initial rejection by the House of Lords. In conjunction with Lord Norton (Sir Charles Adderley) he helped to arrange the compromise by which the measure extending the franchise would be passed if the government agreed to produce the Redistribution Bill and communicate their details to the opposition. Together with Lord Salisbury, Northcote represented the Conservative Party in a series of conferences in November 1884 with Gladstone and Sir Charles Dilke.

Northcote also spoke frequently on foreign affairs, discussing the Transvaal (25 June 1881), Egypt (27 June 1882), and the Sudan (12 February 1884). Over the last issue he moved a vote of censure against the government, lost by a vote of 311 to 262. Another vote of censure, moved by Northcote on 23 February 1885, was defeated by only fourteen votes, 302 to 288. Its terms, however, were considered too mild by the majority of Conservatives.

Earl of Iddesleigh By the time Gladstone's government fell in June 1885 much dissatisfaction was manifested throughout the Conservative Party in Northcote's leadership, the almost inevitable result of his decades at the top but unquestionably increased by the impatience of the Fourth Party and Northcote's own lack of vigorous partisanship. On the formation of Lord Salisbury's first government, which took office on 23 June 1885, Northcote was offered the office, high in seniority but lacking in real power, of first lord of the Treasury, but with a peerage. On 6 July 1885 Northcote took his seat in the House of Lords as earl of Iddesleigh and Viscount St Cyres, titles taken from places on Northcote's Devon estate. His appointment as first lord of the Treasury was a curious one. While W. H. Smith and Arthur Balfour later also held this position separately from the premiership when Lord Salisbury, the prime minister, sat in the Lords, Iddesleigh anomalously occupied this office only after he had been elevated to the upper house. On 29 August Iddesleigh was made president of the royal commission to inquire into the trade depression, issuing a series of reports, the last dated 21 December 1886. This commission was notable for being one of the first to acknowledge Britain's disadvantages as the earliest industrial country at a time of intense foreign competition. Its recommendations were moderate, and Iddesleigh's chairmanship ensured that it did not stray from free-trade orthodoxy despite the growing calls for protection from many tories.

Foreign secretary, 1886–1887 Salisbury's government fell at the end of January 1886, and was replaced by Gladstone's ill-fated third government, which took office on 1 February 1886 and itself fell, in momentous circumstances, on 20 July. On 8 March 1886 Iddesleigh's political friends from both parties entertained him at Willis's Rooms, where he was presented with a handsome testimonial. On the formation of Salisbury's second government in July 1886, to Queen Victoria's regret but with Gladstone's support, Iddesleigh was appointed foreign minister, a post for which he was obviously well suited; he took office on 3 August 1886. He had to deal with the complications in the Balkans of the kidnapping of Prince Alexander of Bulgaria on 21 August, and was outspoken in his remarks to the Russian ambassador to Britain. His stance was amplified on 17 December when he expressed strong objections to

the candidature of Prince Nicholas of Mingrelia for the vacant Bulgarian throne, terming him 'a vassal, or rather a subject, of Russia' (quoted in *DNB*). In the dispute which arose between Canada and the United States over the rights of American fishermen in Canadian waters he advocated (30 November) a settlement based on mutual concessions.

In retirement Iddesleigh's period as foreign minister proved to be his final office. On 23 December 1886 Lord Randolph Churchill suddenly resigned as chancellor of the exchequer, and when Salisbury then entered into negotiations with Lord Hartington and the Liberal Unionists Iddesleigh unselfishly, but unwisely, placed his seat in the cabinet at the premier's disposal. On 4 January 1887 he learned, by reading a morning newspaper, that his offer had been accepted, a telegram in cipher from Lord Salisbury not reaching him in Devon until that afternoon. Salisbury appointed himself to the Foreign Office and W. H. Smith to the post of first lord of the Treasury. Salisbury made no proposal of another position to Iddesleigh, and he accepted the arrangement as final with his usual good grace. Some days later Salisbury offered him, by telegram, the position of lord president of the council, which he declined as he was anxious not to 'have more political bother' (Lang, 2.280). He reiterated his refusal to accept this position after a second letter from Salisbury. Iddesleigh seems to have decided, at the age of sixty-eight, that his active years were behind him, although the view widely put at the time, that he was conscious of failing health, is inaccurate.

Character and non-political activities In mature life Iddesleigh had a white beard, was rather overweight, and was avuncular in appearance. He was never a narrow politician. He was elected lord rector of Edinburgh University in November 1883, defeating G. O. Trevelyan and Professor J. S. Blackie. He delivered his address on 29 January 1884, deploring the tendency of men of letters to abstain from political life. On 16 April 1884 he spoke at the celebration of the tercentenary of the university as a civic institution, and on 3 November 1885 he again lectured to students, his subject being 'The pleasures, the dangers, and the uses of desultory reading'; the lecture was subsequently published. His reprint for the Roxburghe Club of *The Triumphes of Petrarch* appeared after his death in 1887, as did *Lectures and Essays*, edited the same year by his widow. He wrote humorous poetry and plays for his family, and was also the author of several articles published in journals of the times, including 'Schools of design' (*Edinburgh Review*, July 1883), 'Conservative and liberal finance' (ibid., Jan 1884), and others noted in this entry. Iddesleigh was a diarist, and his journals for the years 1869–71, 1875, and 1882 were privately printed in 1907. Anthony Trollope cast him as Sir Warwick West End in *The Three Clerks* (3 vols., 1858).

An unusual death After retiring from political life Iddesleigh remained extremely active in a variety of national and local projects, especially in the post of lord lieutenant of Devonshire, a position he held from January 1886, and in speaking on behalf of the prince of Wales's scheme for an imperial institute. On 11 January 1887 he returned to London from his estate at Pynes, where he was to speak at the Mansion House on the prince of Wales's scheme. On the morning of 12 January he visited the Foreign Office, where he had a long talk with Sir James Fergusson MP, the under-secretary for foreign affairs, and then walked across the street to 10 Downing Street to visit Lord Salisbury. On reaching the anteroom he suffered a heart attack, and was found by two secretaries of the prime minister to be very ill and breathing with great difficulty. He never spoke again, and died at 3.05 p.m. in the presence of two doctors, Lord Salisbury, and his secretary, Henry Manners. Iddesleigh's sudden and dramatic death, coming closely upon his resignation and the reconstruction of the government, naturally caused a national sensation, and there was universal regret at the passing of a figure who had held so many high offices without rancorous partisanship. On 18 January he was buried, at his request, at Upton Pyne, Exeter, while memorial services were simultaneously conducted at Westminster Abbey, Exeter Cathedral, and St Giles's Cathedral, Edinburgh. Statues of him by Sir Joseph Edgar Boehm were placed after his death in the vestibule of the House of Commons and at Northernhay, Exeter.

Reputation and assessment Stafford Northcote is not an easy figure with whom to come to terms, even after more than a century. As Lang astutely noted in 1890, when Northcote first entered parliament he was both a Conservative and a free-trader, and was one of the few Conservative free-traders who ultimately failed to join the Liberal Party. Additionally he was a country gentleman of the old school. Northcote's uncommon position but undoubted competence helped him to rise high during the mid-Victorian period, when party politics was relatively fluid; indeed, the very rareness of his stance helped him to do so. With the coming of mass democratic politics in the 1880s, founded in very real ideological differences between the parties and constantly observed by a popular press, Northcote appeared increasingly antiquated; to younger partisans he seemed a ridiculous figure, easily mocked. The qualities remarked upon most often by observers—his caution, virtual non-partisanship, and incapability of long resenting an injury—were similarly regarded as increasingly reminiscent of a bygone age. Northcote 'carried conviction by force of his character' rather than by oratorical skills. Yet his competence as a financier and an administrator was acknowledged by virtually all.

Posterity has not been particularly kind to Stafford Northcote. Though Andrew Lang's biography (1890) is surprisingly good, Northcote is almost alone among Victorian politicians of his stature in lacking a modern biography, and he normally appears in accounts of late Victorian politics as the hapless victim of the superior cleverness of Lord Randolph Churchill and others; he is almost always depicted by modern historians in terms of his inadequacies. To Lord Blake, Disraeli 'perceived Northcote's defects—a lack of vigour and an excessive respect for Gladstone' (Blake, *The Conservative Party*, 134). While

noting that Northcote was 'an excellent financier' and 'the incarnation of common sense', Robert Rhodes James stated that he was 'without a spark of dangerous genius' (James, 73). To be sure, these recent verdicts build upon the judgement most often voiced by contemporaries, for example Lord Rosebery, who concluded, after enumerating Northcote's virtues, that 'where he failed was in manner. His voice, his diction, his delivery were all inadequate … he had not the spice of devil which is necessary to rouse an Opposition to zeal and elation' (*Lord Randolph Churchill*, 1906, 169). While there is much justice to these views, it is also the case that he was jointly responsible for one of the best-known and most typical social reforms of the century, was a financier of note, and loyally served two great tory leaders, being responsible in some measure for the success they enjoyed. Although no 'tory democrat' in social policy, he was a genuine philanthropist. In retrospect it is clear that the very solidity Northcote represented did much to facilitate the growth of the Conservative Party at that time and its evolution into the normal British party of government. As much as any well-known tory leader, Northcote personified the mainstream of the Conservative Party which, under leaders like Stanley Baldwin and Harold Macmillan, has regularly been preferred by the electorate. Another judgement of Lord Blake's, that Northcote 'was a born second in command' (Blake, *Disraeli*, 545), seems especially apt, although this may understate his true contribution to the success of his party.

W. D. RUBINSTEIN

Sources A. Lang, *Life, letters and diaries of Sir Stafford Northcote*, 2 vols. (1890) · R. Shannon, *The age of Disraeli, 1868–1881: the rise of tory democracy* (1992) · R. Blake, *Disraeli*, another edn (1967) · P. Smith, *Disraelian Conservatism and social reform* (1967) · R. Blake, *The Conservative Party from Peel to Thatcher* (1985) · S. Buxton, *Finance and politics: an historical study, 1783–1885*, 2 vols. (1888) · J. B. Conacher, *The Aberdeen coalition, 1852–1855* (1968) · E. Hughes, 'Civil service reform, 1853–1855', *Public Administration*, 32 (1954) · Gladstone, *Diaries* · H. C. G. Matthew, *Gladstone, 1875–1898* (1995) · *Dod's Parliamentary Companion* · Burke, *Peerage* (1939) · D. Kynaston, *The chancellor of the exchequer* (1980) · *The letters of Queen Victoria*, ed. A. C. Benson, Lord Esher [R. B. Brett], and G. E. Buckle, 9 vols. (1907–32) · R. R. James, *Lord Randolph Churchill* (1977) · N. Gash and others, *The Conservatives: a history from their origins to 1965*, ed. Lord Butler [R. A. Butler] (1977) · M. Bentley, *Politics without democracy* (1984) · GEC, *Peerage* · DNB

Archives BL, corresp. and papers, Add. MSS 50013–50064 · Devon RO, corresp. and papers · Queen's University, Kingston, Ontario, corresp. and papers · University of Exeter Library, letter-books and papers | Balliol Oxf., corresp. with Sir Robert Morier · BL, corresp. with Lord Carnarvon, Add. MS 60767 · BL, corresp. with Lord Cross, Add. MS 51265 · BL, corresp. with Sir Charles Dilke, Add. MS 43893 · BL, corresp. with W. E. Gladstone, Add. MSS 44216–44217 · BL, corresp. with Florence Nightingale, Add. MS 45779 · BL, corresp. with Augustus Paget, Add. MS 51230 · BL, corresp. with Lord Ripon, Add. MS 43519 · Bodl. Oxf., letters to Lord Kimberley · Bodl. Oxf., corresp. with J. E. Thorold Rogers · Bucks. RLSS, letters to Lord Cottesloe · CAC Cam., corresp. with Lord Randolph Churchill · CKS, letters to Aretas Akers-Douglas · CKS, letters to Edward Stanhope · CUL, letters to Lord Hardinge · CUL, corresp. with Lord Mayo · Devon RO, letters to Sir Thomas Dyke Acland · Glos. RO, letters to Sir Michael Hicks Beach · HLRO, letters to Lord Ashbourne · HLRO, corresp. with Lord Hampden · ICL, letters to Sir Lyon Playfair · Lincs. Arch., corresp. with Edward

Stanhope · LPL, corresp. with A. C. Tait · Lpool RO, letters to four-teenth earl of Derby · Lpool RO, corresp. with fifteenth earl of Derby · NRA, priv. coll., letters to Sir Richard Temple · PRO, corresp. with Sir Evelyn Baring, FO633 · PRO, letters to Lord Cairns, 30/51 · PRO NIre., letters to Lord Crichton · PRO NIre., letters to Lord Erne · PRO NIre., letters to James Emerson Tennent · Suffolk RO, Ipswich, letters to Lord Cranbrook · UCL, corresp. with Sir Edwin Chadwick · W. Sussex RO, letters to duke of Richmond · W. Yorks. AS, Leeds, letters to Lord St Oswald

Likenesses G. Richmond, portrait, 1836 · M. Carpenter, oils, 1840?, Eton · A. S. Lumley, oils, 1876, Hughenden Manor, Buckinghamshire · E. Long, oils, 1882, NPG · E. Long, oils, 1883, University of Exeter; replica, 1889, NPG · J. E. Boehm, statue, 1887, Palace of Westminster, London · J. E. Boehm, statue, 1887, Northernhay, Exeter · W. Tyler, marble bust, 1887, Royal Collection; related plaster bust, Balliol Oxf. · Ape [C. Pellegrini], chromolithograph caricature, NPG; repro. in VF (8 Oct 1870) · A. Beau, carte-de-visite, NPG · H. Edwin, drawing, silhouette, NPG · Elliott & Fry, carte-de-visite, NPG [see illus.] · H. Furniss, caricature, pen-and-ink sketch, NPG · M. Gales, group portrait, watercolour drawing (The Derby cabinet of 1867), NPG · W. Hole, etching, NPG; repro. in Quasi cursores (1884) · W. Holl, stipple (after G. Richmond), BM · Lock & Whitfield, woodburytype photograph, NPG; repro. in T. Cooper, Men of mark: a gallery of contemporary portraits (1877) · Maull & Polyblank, carte-de-visite, NPG · G. Pilotell, etching, BM · T [T. Chartran], chromolithograph caricature, NPG; repro. in VF (5 July 1881) · lithograph, BM; repro. in Civil Service Review (Dec 1876) · prints, NPG · woodburytype photograph, NPG

Wealth at death £24,717 16s. 9d.: resworn probate, July 1887, CGPLA Eng. & Wales

Northcote, William (d. 1783?)

Northcote, William (d. 1783?), naval surgeon, of Camelford, Cornwall, passed an examination for naval surgeons at the Company of Surgeons in London on 20 October 1757, and was declared to be fit to act as a surgeon's second mate on ships of war of the fourth rate. Progressing through the ranks, in February 1771 Northcote was certified by the Company of Surgeons as qualified to serve as surgeon to a ship of the first rate. His first warrant is dated 11 February 1771 and he is said to have served on the *Dublin*.

Northcote's professional works, written for the guidance of naval surgeons, show that he experienced active service in many parts of the world, and he claimed to be especially skilled in the treatment of tropical diseases. While a surgeon's mate, in 1770 he published his chief work, based on his personal experiences at sea and titled *The Marine Practice of Physic and Surgery*. A comprehensive work published in two volumes, this contained an appendix of 'Some brief directions to be observed by the sea-surgeon previous to and in an engagement', which hinted at the difficulties posed by medical practice at sea when under fire.

In 1772 Northcote published *The Anatomy of the Human Body*, which was intended for use by naval practitioners. In the same year he published *A Concise History of Anatomy*. This was later denounced as a plagiarism of the lectures of Alexander Monro (*Primus*) on the history of anatomy. Northcote continued to serve with the navy after 1772, but he published no more works on medical matters.

While serving in America during the War of Independence in 1774–83, Northcote wrote to the first lord of the Admiralty, requesting supplies of orange and lemon juice as a 'grand specific' against scurvy, in place of elixir of vitriol. This he regarded as a matter of 'national concern' (Lloyd and Coulter, 3.129).

The date of Northcote's death is uncertain, though he is marked as dead in the Admiralty list for 1783.

D'A. POWER, *rev.* CLAIRE E. J. HERRICK

Sources K. F. Russell, *British anatomy, 1525–1800: a bibliography of works published in Britain and America and on the continent* (1987), 142, 151–2 · J. J. Keevil, J. L. S. Coulter, and C. Lloyd, *Medicine and the navy, 1200–1900*, 3: 1714–1815 (1961), 20, 34, 57–8, 129, 367 · P. J. Wallis and R. V. Wallis, *Eighteenth century medics*, 2nd edn (1988) · private information (1894)

Northesk. For this title name *see* Carnegie, John, first earl of Northesk (1578/9–1667); Carnegie, William, seventh earl of Northesk (1756–1831).

Northey, Sir Edward (1652–1723)

Northey, Sir Edward (1652–1723), lawyer and politician, was born on 7 May 1652, and was baptized two days later at St Mary-le-Bow, London, the son of William Northey (c.1620–1683), a barrister of the Middle Temple, and his first wife, Elizabeth Garrett (d. in or before 1666). Northey was educated at St Paul's School, under Samuel Cromleholme, and matriculated at Queen's College, Oxford, on 4 December 1668. He entered the Middle Temple the same year and was called to the bar on 29 May 1674. He appeared as counsel before the House of Lords and represented Edward Godden in 1686 in the *Godden v. Hales* case, which was a collusive suit brought to give legal colour to James II's use of the dispensing power exempting individuals from the Test Act. His eligibility in the marriage market was increased when he inherited one-third of Lady Wentworth's estate, and on 1 December 1687 he was licensed to marry Anne (c.1662–1743), daughter of John Jolliffe of St Martin Outwich, London, and Woodcote Green, Surrey. They had two sons and three daughters, one of whom married Lord Chief Justice Robert *Raymond.

Northey was appointed attorney-general of the duchy of Lancaster in 1689 and as early as 1693 was seen as a possible solicitor-general. He became a bencher of his inn in 1697. One of his most controversial legal opinions was to deny that convocation could condemn as heretical John Toland's *Christianity not Mysterious* because ultimately convocation had no licence from the king to do so. When Sir Thomas Trevor was made a judge, Northey succeeded him as attorney-general on 29 June 1701, an appointment in keeping with William III's strategy of employing moderates, rather than out-and-out tories. He was reappointed at the beginning of Queen Anne's reign and knighted on 1 June 1702. Northey prosecuted at many state trials including that of David Lindsay for high treason, and John Tutchin for publishing *The Observator* in 1704. Northey was replaced on 25 April 1707 by Sir Simon Harcourt, although on 2 May he was accorded precedence in the courts after king's counsel. There were rumours of his reappointment as solicitor in 1708, but Sir James Montagu was given the post.

Northey appears to have declined to defend Dr Sacheverell, but this seems to have been no bar to his advancement when a tory ministry came to power later in 1710. He was reappointed attorney-general on 19 October 1710, and on 16 December he was elected to parliament in a by-election for Tiverton. He spoke out against the duke of Marlborough during the attack on the general at the beginning of 1712, but the division lists of the period reveal that he was difficult to assess politically. Thus he was able to survive the Hanoverian succession, being reappointed attorney-general on 14 October 1714. As Lord Cowper put it in his advice to George I, Northey 'is an excellent lawyer and a man of great abilities in the law, a moderate Tory, and much respected by that party, and no further blameable than by obeying those who could command him if he kept his place' (Holmes and Speck, 66). Northey was finally replaced on 13 March 1718 and was given a pension of £1500 p.a. provided that he did not accept an office of equal value. He was also accorded precedence in the courts on 25 April, this time after the attorney- and solicitor-generals. While in office Northey had supported the government in the division lobbies, including voting for the Septennial Bill in 1716. Out of office, Northey was more critical, voting against the government over the repeal of the Occasional Conformity and Schism Acts and the Peerage Bill. Northey retired as an MP at the 1722 election, already it would seem afflicted by 'a paralytic distemper whereby he was deprived of the use of his right hand and became unable to write' (PRO, PROB 11/592/170). He died at Epsom on 16 August 1723, 'a very eminent lawyer' (Boyer, 237), and was buried in Epsom churchyard. His wife died on 14 August 1743.

STUART HANDLEY

Sources 'Northey, Sir Edward', HoP, *Commons, 1690–1715* [draft] · HoP, *Commons, 1715–54,* 2.300 · *Le Neve's Pedigrees of the knights,* ed. G. W. Marshall, Harleian Society, 8 (1873), 478–9 · Sainty, *King's counsel,* 47–8, 276–7 · J. L. Chester and J. Foster, eds., *London marriage licences, 1521–1869* (1887), 983 · H. A. C. Sturgess, ed., *Register of admissions to the Honourable Society of the Middle Temple, from the fifteenth century to the year 1944,* 1 (1949), 176 · R. Somerville, *Office-holders in the duchy and county palatine of Lancaster from 1603* (1972), 22 · Bishop Burnet's History, 4.525 · *The Genealogist,* new ser., 6 (1889–90), 22 · Foster, *Alum. Oxon.* · GM, 1st ser., 13 (1743), 443 · PRO, PROB 11/592, sig. 170 · G. Holmes and W. Speck, eds., *The divided society: parties and politics in England, 1694–1716* (1967) · A. Boyer, *The political state of Great Britain,* 26 (1723)
Archives Harrowby Manuscript Trust, Sandon Hall, Staffordshire, his opinion on the Bubble Act · Lincoln's Inn, London, legal notebooks · LUL, legal opinions · S. Antiquaries, Lond., papers as attorney-general

Northington. For this title name *see* Henley, Robert, first earl of Northington (*c*.1708–1772); Henley, Robert, second earl of Northington (1747–1786).

Northleigh, John (1656/7–1705), physician and pamphleteer, was the eldest of three surviving sons of John Northleigh (*d*. 1669), merchant of Hamburg and Exminster, Devon, and his wife. It is unclear whether he was born in Hamburg, where his father was based as a merchant, or in the family's native Devon: relevant baptismal records are not sufficiently complete to resolve the matter. It is equally unclear where he spent his early childhood but at twelve he was orphaned, though not apparently left in want. In later life he claimed to have sufficient private

means to be above having to write in support of the government for money. Five and a half years later, on 23 March 1675, he matriculated at Exeter College, Oxford, aged eighteen, and six years after that graduated as a BCL. The same year (1681) he published *Exercitationes philologicae tres,* a scholarly work entirely in Latin. Having failed to win a fellowship at All Souls he left Oxford and on 8 November 1682 he was admitted to the Middle Temple and in the same year incorporated LLB, apparently as of Magdalene College, Cambridge, though he was a fellow-commoner of King's College from 1681 to 1683.

Northleigh's interests were by no means confined to his studies, for on 6 February 1682 he emerged as an effective and influential tory propagandist with the publication of his anonymous work *The Parallel.* This was part of a tory propaganda offensive against the whig leader, the earl of Shaftesbury, who had recently been controversially cleared of treason. A plan for an association to prevent a Catholic succession, found among his papers, appeared to confirm tory accusations of preparations for rebellion. Northleigh not only drew a parallel between the association and the solemn league and covenant of 1643 but also between the whigs and the Catholic league in the French wars of religion of the sixteenth century, enabling him to be both loyal and anti-Catholic at the same time. This was a propaganda point which Northleigh's friend John Dryden admired and emulated in the play *The Duke of Guise,* which he co-wrote with Nathaniel Lee in 1682. A further tract, *A Gentle Reflection,* which claimed to be by the author of *The Parallel,* also appeared in 1682.

By the time Northleigh's next political work appeared, *The Triumph of our Monarchy,* in 1685 he was happy to be known as the author of *The Parallel* and was celebrated as such in a verse preface by Dryden. This was a massive work, running to 765 pages besides dedications and an introduction. It was a blow-by-blow refutation of the views of Algernon Sidney, Henry Neville, and other whigs and republicans. Appearing as it did in the wake of the suppression of Monmouth's rebellion, it was indeed a highly triumphalist work. Another edition appeared in the same year.

Over the next three years Northleigh continued his studies at Cambridge, obtaining his LLD in 1687. Unlike many other tories, he continued to support James II, even after the king embarked upon his tolerationist religious policy. Indeed, his next work, *Parliamentum pacificum,* argued strongly in its favour, although it appeared anonymously as '[b]y a True Protestant and no Dissenter'. It was approved by the earl of Sunderland on 15 February 1688 and the king paid for 20,000 copies of it to be produced. A second English edition appeared; it was translated into French and Dutch and elicited three replies in Dutch alone. Gilbert Burnet replied to it in English, having been strongly criticized within it. Northleigh replied in turn in *Natural Allegiance* (which ran to more than 100 pages) and also in *Dr Burnet's Reflections ... Answered* (July 1688), but again anonymously. The revolution must have come as a severe blow to Northleigh. He published nothing else for fourteen years. When he did go into print again, in 1702, it was in the guise of a travel writer in *Topographical Descriptions*, being a tour through Europe originally intended to run to three volumes, although only one appeared. It was not devoid of political comment: the old polemic against republicanism rumbles on in its pages.

In or after 1688 Northleigh settled in Exeter and worked as a doctor, having obtained the further degree of MD from Cambridge in 1687. He was married to Frances (d. 1715) and produced one son, John (1701–1726), before his death in Exeter on 17 January 1705. He was buried on 24 January in Exeter Cathedral, where he is commemorated along with his wife and son in a terse Latin inscription.

ANDREW M. COLEBY

Sources P. Harth, *Pen for a party: Dryden's tory propaganda and its contexts* (1993) · J. R. Jones, *The revolution of 1688 in England* (1972) · Wood, *Ath. Oxon.*, new edn, 4.502 · *Devon and Cornwall Notes and Queries*, 14 (1926–7) · Venn, *Alum. Cant.* · Foster, *Alum. Oxon.* · C. W. Boase, ed., *Registrum Collegii Exoniensis*, new edn, OHS, 27 (1894) · Bodl. Oxf., Tanner MSS 25, 28, 340 · O. Murray, collection of will abstracts, Devon RO, 8/36 · memorial, Exeter Cathedral · private information (2004)
Archives Bodl. Oxf., Tanner MSS
Wealth at death £234 6d.—inventory; incl. money and apparel £10; also plate and other items £30: Murray, abstracts

Northmore, Thomas (*bap.* 1766, *d.* 1851), geologist and writer, was born at Fulham, Middlesex, and was baptized on 24 November 1766 at St Luke's, Chelsea, the eldest of three surviving sons of Thomas Northmore (1735–1777) of Cleve House, Devon, and his wife, Elizabeth (d. 1770), daughter and heir of Richard Osgood of Fulham. He was educated at Blundell's School, Tiverton, and Barnstaple School, before entering Emmanuel College, Cambridge, in 1785; he graduated BA in 1789 and MA in 1792. He was elected to the Society of Antiquaries in 1791, and was also a fellow of the Royal Society of Arts. There was a brief marriage to Penelope (d. 1792), eldest daughter of Sir William Earle Welby, bt, of Denton Hall, Lincolnshire, with the birth in 1791 of a son, Thomas Welby Northmore, who predeceased his father. On 9 November 1809 he married Emmeline (d. 1850), fifth daughter of Sir John Eden, bt, of Windlestone Park and Beamish Park, Durham, with whom he had one son and nine daughters.

On leaving college Northmore took up permanent residence at Cleve House, dividing his time between politics—in 1818 he unsuccessfully contested Exeter in the Liberal interest, and Barnstaple, with similar lack of success—literature, and geology. An early interest in chemistry led him to experiment with the compression of gases, first with Humphry Davy at the Royal Institution, and subsequently alone. He compressed oxygen, hydrogen, and nitrogen mixtures, which yielded various vapours, water, and acids, but his results, published in 1805 and 1806, were criticized as vague and inconclusive. Northmore's reaction was to accuse the scientific fraternity of suppressing his name as an original discoverer of gases, and to abandon the subject. His *Triplet of Inventions* (1796), reissued as *A Quadruplet of Inventions* (1799), was a collection of three, then four, short articles claiming improvements on such recent inventions as the semaphore telegraph, the unsinkable lifeboat, and a scheme

for renaming the bones in the body. His other minor writings continued the interest in communication and dealt with utopian societies and matters of philosophy.

In geology Northmore turned out to be more successful. He had already traversed the county in search of druidical and Roman antiquities, and in September 1824 he took his family to Torquay hoping to find within Kent's Cavern signs of Mithraic or druidical worship, perhaps cave paintings. Looking at the available sparse literature concerning the cavern, he was fired with geological enthusiasm and decided to search for organic remains. Accompanied by two labourers and a draughtsman, he excavated down through the stalagmite flooring and underlying mud and uncovered bones of carnivores and human artefacts. He also detected what he decided was evidence for a Mithraic temple, and was therefore disappointed that there were no human bones indicating sacrifice. Northmore seems to have been the first to discover fossils in Kent's Cavern, and he made the important observation that four of the animals represented now existed only in tropical regions. Subsequent excavations, undertaken by William Pengelly, helped to open the way to an understanding of climatic change and the antiquity of man in Britain. Northmore died at Furzebrook House, near Axminster, on 29 May 1851.

ANITA MCCONNELL

Sources Burke, *Gen. GB* (1882) · Venn, *Alum. Cant.* · W. Pengelly, 'The literature of Kent's Cavern, Torquay, prior to 1859', *Report and Transactions of the Devonshire Association*, 2 (1867–8), 469–522 · d. cert.
Likenesses C. Turner, mezzotint, pubd *c.*1818 (after oil painting by W. Brockedon), BM, NPG

Northolt, William of (*d.* 1190), bishop of Worcester, took his name from Northolt, formerly Northall, in Middlesex, where the chapter of St Paul's held property. Nothing is known of his family or education. He is never called *magister*, and in later life he was described as wise as a result of experience rather than of learning. He spent most of his working life in the service of three archbishops of Canterbury. He became a clerk of Archbishop Theobald (d. 1161), and bought property on the archbishop's fee in London in 1145–50. He was a canon of St Paul's, holding the prebend of Neasden, from about 1163, and was parson of Hanwell in Ealing, in the gift of the bishop of London, by 1177. In 1181 he was farming the chapter's manor of West Drayton. He was evidently sufficiently prosperous to be worth asking for money for the exiled archbishop in the 1160s; it is not known whether he responded. He did not serve Archbishop Thomas Becket but he respected Becket's authority when the announcement was made in his presence in St Paul's on Ascension day 1169 that Becket had excommunicated the bishop of London—as a canon of St Paul's Northolt was taking part in the service, and had read the gospel, but proceeded no further. Subsequently he entered the service of Archbishop Richard (d. 1184), probably soon after the archbishop's return to England in August 1174, and became his seneschal. He was in constant attendance on Richard, and Richard's successor, Archbishop Baldwin (d. 1190), until his own election to Worcester. In 1177 Northolt became archdeacon of

Gloucester, possibly after a request to Roger, bishop of Worcester (d. 1179), from Gilbert Foliot, bishop of London, but he is seldom recorded in the diocese of Worcester. He also served the king, acting as custodian of the vacant bishopric of Rochester in 1184–5, and of Worcester in 1185–6.

Northolt was elected bishop of Worcester on about 25 May 1186, and consecrated at Westminster on 21 September. Trusted by the king and the archbishop, he was one of three bishops chosen to negotiate with the monks of Canterbury about the archbishop's much disputed proposal to build a new church in honour of St Thomas. The monks suspected them all, and Gervase of Canterbury calls Northolt 'a snake in the path' (*Works of Gervase of Canterbury*, 1.349). In 1188 Northolt was again one of those sent to try to reach a settlement, but there is no indication of his separate activity. In his own diocese Northolt's practical ability led to successful action against the bishop of Hereford, who claimed to hold the manor of Inkberrow of the bishop of Worcester for half a knight's fee, instead of for a whole fee. The case came before the king at Kempsey, a manor of the bishop of Worcester, probably in March 1188; the bishop of Hereford withdrew his claim rather than face the verdict of the twenty-four knights who had been summoned. Gerald of Wales relates that Northolt banned a certain English love song, by announcements in synods and chapters, because a priest had accidentally sung the refrain in church. It is doubtful whether a particular song was forbidden, but the prohibition may be an early example of the ban on singing, dancing, and games in churchyards, which appears in synodal statutes from about 1214 onwards. The Worcester chronicle records the death of William of Northolt on 3 May 1190; he was commemorated on 4 May at Osney.   M. G. CHENEY

Sources *Fasti Angl., 1066–1300,* [St Paul's, London] · A. Saltman, *Theobald, archbishop of Canterbury* (1956) · *The historical works of Gervase of Canterbury,* ed. W. Stubbs, 2 vols., Rolls Series, 73 (1879–80) · C. R. Cheney and B. E. A. Jones, eds., *Canterbury, 1162–1190,* English Episcopal Acta, 2 (1986) · M. G. Cheney, ed., *Worcester, 1066–1212* [forthcoming] · R. C. van Caenegem, ed., *English lawsuits from William I to Richard I,* SeldS, 2, 107 (1991), no. 574 · *Gir. Camb. opera,* vol. 2 · *Ann. mon.,* vol. 4 · *The letters of John of Salisbury,* ed. and trans. H. E. Butler and W. J. Millor, rev. C. N. L. Brooke, OMT, 2: *The later letters, 1163–1180* (1979) [Lat. orig. with parallel Eng. text] · *Letters and charters of Gilbert Foliot,* ed. A. Morey and others (1967) · R. R. Darlington, ed., *The cartulary of Worcester Cathedral Priory (register I),* PRSoc., 76, new ser., 38 (1968)

Northumberland. For this title name *see* Henry, earl of Northumberland (c.1115–1152); Ada, countess of Northumberland (c.1123–1178); Puiset, Hugh du, earl of Northumberland (c.1125–1195); Percy, Henry, first earl of Northumberland (1341–1408); Percy, Henry, second earl of Northumberland (1394–1455); Percy, Henry, third earl of Northumberland (1421–1461); Percy, Henry, fourth earl of Northumberland (c.1449–1489); Percy, Henry Algernon, fifth earl of Northumberland (1478–1527); Percy, Henry Algernon, sixth earl of Northumberland (c.1502–1537); Dudley, John, duke of Northumberland (1504–1553); Dudley, Jane, duchess of Northumberland (1508/9–1555) [*see under* Dudley, John, duke of Northumberland (1504–

1553)]; Percy, Thomas, seventh earl of Northumberland (1528–1572); Percy, Henry, eighth earl of Northumberland (c.1532–1585); Percy, Henry, ninth earl of Northumberland (1564–1632); Percy, Algernon, tenth earl of Northumberland (1602–1668); FitzRoy, George, duke of Northumberland (1665–1716); Wharton, Philip James, duke of Wharton and Jacobite duke of Northumberland (1698–1731); Percy, Hugh, first duke of Northumberland (*bap.* 1712, *d.* 1786); Percy, Elizabeth, duchess of Northumberland and *suo jure* Baroness Percy (1716–1776); Percy, Hugh, second duke of Northumberland (1742–1817); Percy, Hugh, third duke of Northumberland (1785–1847); Percy, Algernon, fourth duke of Northumberland (1792–1865); Percy, Alan Ian, eighth duke of Northumberland (1880–1930).

Northumbria. For this title name *see* Erik of Hlathir, earl of Northumbria (*fl.* 995–1023); Siward, earl of Northumbria (*d.* 1055); Tostig, earl of Northumbria (c.1029–1066); Copsi, earl of Northumbria (*d.* 1067); Cumin, Robert, earl of Northumbria (*d.* 1069); Gospatric, earl of Northumbria (*d.* 1073x5); Waltheof, earl of Northumbria (c.1050–1076); Walcher, earl of Northumbria (*d.* 1080); Morcar, earl of Northumbria (*fl.* 1065–1087); Mowbray, Robert de, earl of Northumbria (*d.* 1115/1125).

Northwell, William de. *See* Norwell, William (*fl.* 1311–1352).

Northwick. For this title name *see* Rushout, John, second Baron Northwick (1769–1859).

Northwold, Hugh of (*d.* 1254), bishop of Ely, took his name from the Norfolk parish of Northwold. The son of Peter and Emma, in 1202 he was professed a monk at Bury St Edmunds, and was subsequently appointed sub-cellarer there. Abbot Samson having died at the end of 1211, on 25 July 1212 King John ordered the monks to send delegates to elect a successor in his own presence. But the community then proceeded by the way of compromise to elect Hugh of Northwold, ignoring the king's traditional rights. Not only was John furious, but the monks became almost evenly divided into two bitterly opposed factions on the issue. The consequent dispute, recorded in what has been described as 'the most detailed eyewitness account of an English monastic election dispute extant' (Thomson, xxv), lasted for nearly three years, and involved the archbishop of Canterbury, the papal legate, and the pope, as well as the king and his advisers. Although Northwold's supporters showed a greater awareness than their opponents of trends in canonistic doctrine identifying papal authority with the cause of ecclesiastical freedom, both sides sent delegates to Rome, while Hugh himself left England for a while, though apparently only for Poitou, where he began to achieve reconciliation with John in 1214. The abbot-elect won the support of Innocent III (*r.* 1198–1216) at an early stage, and appears later to have gained the backing of the king's baronial adversaries as well. John's political difficulties may well have been influential in causing him finally to accept Northwold's election, on 10 June 1215.

As abbot Hugh of Northwold was only occasionally

involved in public business, though in November 1218 he was a witness to the decision that the king should have his own seal. He was an assize justice at Thetford, as well as at Bury itself, and in 1227 headed a judicial eyre in Norfolk. However, he became more closely concerned in affairs of state after 1231, when he was elected bishop of Ely. Bishop Geoffrey de Burgh had died on 17 September 1228; the prior of Ely died at about the same time, causing some delay in the election of a new bishop, but the monks were soon able to proceed by way of compromise, choosing Hugh of Northwold on about 3 February 1229. The temporalities were restored on 26 May, and he was consecrated at Canterbury on 10 June. He became bishop at a time when Henry III was increasingly anxious to have episcopal support. Northwold received gifts of deer in 1232, while in 1233 he ended years of disputes with the sheriff of Cambridgeshire by obtaining a widespread confirmation of Ely's liberties (for a payment of 500 marks). In 1235 he was sent to Provence to escort Eleanor, the king's bride, to England, and in 1237 he was named as an ambassador to Frederick II (r. 1212–50), though in the end no embassy went. In the same year he sued Henry III for the advowson of Thorney Abbey, given to Ely by King John.

In the following decade Northwold was little at court (though he is recorded at Westminster in October 1241), but he attended parliament in February 1248, and in October that year complained to Henry III of the deleterious effects of the king's new fair at Westminster on the bishop's own fair at Ely. Fobbed off with fair words, he exasperated the king in the following year by refusing to present Henry's half-brother Aymer de Lusignan (d. 1260) to the church of Dereham, Norfolk. In 1251 he was one of the bishops who resisted Archbishop Boniface's plan for a provincial visitation. He was present at the feast held by Henry III at Westminster on St Edward's day (5 January) 1252, but in October resisted the king's efforts to gain his consent to a tax on the clergy; according to Matthew Paris, Henry invited Northwold to a private interview, at which he dwelt upon his own needs, appealed to the bishop for assistance, and promised future rewards, but Hugh remained firm, and was finally driven away with insults by the angry king. Perhaps the fact that during 1252 Northwold was appointed a collector of the crusading tenth granted to the king helped to appease the latter, for the bishop was present when Henry reissued Magna Carta on 3 May 1253, and attended a banquet given by Queen Eleanor on 5 January 1254.

The most distinctive feature of Northwold's diocesan administration was his reorganization of episcopal property; in this he followed the policy he had already adopted at Bury, where even before he had been consecrated abbot he ordered a survey of the monastery estates. At Ely (where he had the assistance of an advisory council) he had a survey of the bishop's demesne manors carried out in 1251, and where possible he added to his demesnes, by buying out free tenants, and to his revenues, by increasing, sometimes to the extent of doubling, rents. This went hand in hand with a systematic programme of fen reclamation, in which he co-operated with Thorney Abbey, and which resulted in the intake of extensive new lands between Thorney, Wisbech, and Leverington. Individual groups of the bishop's subjects benefited markedly from Northwold's administrative efficiency. The convent of Ely, for instance, received the rectories of Witcham, Hauxton, and St Mary, Ely. The two hospitals in Ely were united and given new statutes, and the hospital of St John in Cambridge was also reorganized. He gave a good deal of attention to Cambridge, partly as a result of the growth of the university—in May 1231 he was ordered to take part in measures to discipline the students. He appears to have begun to provide lodgings for some scholars ('his own' scholars), the house or houses he set aside being part of the rectory of St Peter at Trumpington Gate (later known as Little St Mary's).

Northwold was a notable builder. He carried out large-scale works on his central manors, constructing new halls and extending old ones, particularly at the palace at Ely, and at Downham, Wisbech Castle, and Hatfield. But it is within Ely Cathedral that his greatest architectural memorial is to be found, in the presbytery that he had built at the east end of the choir, primarily to house a new shrine for St Etheldreda. On 16 August 1235 Henry III gave him sixteen oaks for work on the cathedral, at the beginning of a campaign that was to last for seventeen years, and cost £5350 18s. 3d. The cost is at least partly to be explained by the fact that it entailed the construction of the church's first high vault to be made of stone, and by the exceptional lavishness of the carved decoration of the architectural elements. Work on the presbytery was complemented by the building of a wooden spire above the stone tower which crowned the galilee at the cathedral's east end. Presbytery and spire were dedicated on 17 September 1252, in the presence of the king and a great company of lay and ecclesiastical magnates.

Hugh of Northwold died at Downham, on 6 August 1254, and was buried in the new presbytery, between the high altar and St Etheldreda's shrine. Upon his tomb, which supports a handsome marble effigy of the bishop, is carved the martyrdom of St Edmund, doubtless in allusion to Northwold's abbacy of Bury. Some time before 1248 he had bought the manors of Totteridge, Hertfordshire, and Bramford, Suffolk, to endow prayers for his soul, and he also built and endowed a chantry house ('the chantry on the green') for the priests who were to celebrate for his own soul, and for the souls of his family and of members of the monastic community. Moreover, he bequeathed a number of sumptuous copes and other vestments to the convent. A Benedictine before he became a bishop, a prelate who stood up to the king, it was perhaps inevitable that Northwold should have been greatly admired by Matthew Paris, who at his death describes him simply as 'the good bishop Hugh of Ely' and hails him as 'hospitable, pleasant and serene. At his death there passed the flower of the black monks; as he had been the abbot of abbots in England, so he shone forth as the bishop of bishops' (Paris, Chron., 5.454–5). DOROTHY M. OWEN

Sources R. M. Thomson, ed., *The chronicle of the election of Hugh, abbot of Bury St Edmunds and later bishop of Ely* (1974), appxs. 4 and 5 ·

M. Gibbs and J. Lang, *Bishops and reform, 1215–1272* (1934) · M. B. Hackett, *The original statutes of Cambridge University* (1970), 38–40 · E. Miller, *The abbey and bishopric of Ely*, Cambridge Studies in Medieval Life and Thought, new ser., 1 (1951), 77–9 · [H. Wharton], ed., *Anglia sacra*, 1 (1691), 635–6 · S. J. A. Evans, ed., 'Ely chapter ordinances and visitation records, 1241–1515', *Camden miscellany, XVII*, CS, 3rd ser., 64 (1940), v–xx, 1–74, esp. 1–3 · J. Bentham, *The history and antiquities of the conventual and cathedral church of Ely*, ed. J. Bentham, 2nd edn (1812), 146–8 · Paris, *Chron.*, vols. 3–6 · *Chancery records* · *Ann. mon.*, vols. 1, 3 · N. Vincent, *Peter des Roches: an alien in English politics, 1205–38*, Cambridge Studies in Medieval Life and Thought, 4th ser., 31 (1996) · P. Draper, 'Bishop Northwold and the cult of St Etheldreda', *Medieval art and architecture at Ely Cathedral*, British Archaeological Association Conference Transactions, 2 (1979), 8–27
Archives BL, Cotton MS Tiberius B.ii · CUL, Ely dean and chapter, cartularies and charters (EDC)
Likenesses effigy on tomb, Ely Cathedral

Northwold, John of (*d.* 1301). *See under* Luton, Simon of (*d.* 1279).

Northwood, John, first Lord Northwood (1254–1319), soldier and administrator, the son of Roger of *Northwood, was born on 24 June 1254 and succeeded his father in December 1285. In 1291–2 he was employed on a commission of oyer and terminer in Kent; he was also sheriff of Kent in 1291–3, 1299–1300, and 1304–6. He was summoned in 1297 for service in Flanders, but there is no conclusive evidence that he sailed with Edward I on 22 August; and on 30 July 1297 he was appointed assessor of the fifth and eighth in Sussex. In 1298 and 1301 he was summoned for the Scottish war and he may have been present at the siege of Caerlaverock in 1300. There is evidence that he also served in Scotland in 1303 and 1306. On 24 December 1307 and on 17 March 1308 he was appointed a keeper of the peace for Kent; in 1308–9 he was justice for gaol delivery in Kent, where during 1308 and the two following years he was a commissioner for the survey of bridges. On 18 December 1309 he was nominated a justice to receive complaints of prises and on 15 October 1310 he was appointed to investigate disorders caused by army recruits on their way to Scotland. He was nominated a supervisor of array for Kent on 20 May 1311; his son John [*see below*] led the arrayed foot soldiers to Roxburgh. About that time he is spoken of as lately employed to inquire concerning forestalments in Kent, and in March 1312 was one of the justices appointed to settle the complaints of the Flemings.

Northwood was regularly summoned to serve in Scotland from 1309 until 1319; in 1301 he proffered the service of two sergeants for his lands and he (or his son) had letters of protection for personal service in 1314 and 1317. In August 1315 he had orders to stay in the north until 1 November, and then to join the king at York. He was first summoned to parliament on 8 January 1313, and specifically as a baron on 23 May of the same year. After this he was regularly summoned until 20 March 1319. On 8 June 1318 he is styled one of the 'majores barones'. In June 1317 Northwood and his son John were two of those deputed to receive at Dover the two cardinals coming to treat for peace between England and Scotland.

With his wife, Joan Badlesmere, Northwood had six

John Northwood, first Lord Northwood (1254–1319), memorial brasses, *c*.1330 [with his wife, Joan]

sons. He died on 26 May 1319, and his wife a week later; they are represented in two fine brasses in Minster church, Isle of Sheppey (*c*.1330). His arms (ermine, a cross engrailed gules) and those of his son John (differenced with a label azure) appear on the parliamentary roll of arms *c*.1312.

John Northwood (*d.* in or before 1318), the eldest son of the above, served several times in the Scottish war. He married in 1306 Agnes (*d.* 1348), daughter of Sir William Grandison, and with her had six sons, of whom two, John and Otto, were successively archdeacons of Exeter and Totnes from 1329 to 1360, during the episcopate of their uncle John Grandison; William, a third, was a knight hospitaller. John Northwood died before 8 September 1318. Roger (1307–1361), his eldest son, married in 1322 Juliana (*d.* 1329), daughter of Sir Geoffrey de Say, and after her death had four other wives, the last of whom, Agnes, widow of Sir John Cobham, outlived him. He served in the king's army at Sluys in 1340 and in Brittany in 1342, but missed the battle of Crécy. He was summoned to parliament on 3 April 1360, and died on 5 or 6 November 1361. His son John from his first marriage served in France in 1359; he was summoned to parliament from 1363 to 1376.

He married Joan, daughter of Robert Here of Faversham, Kent, and on his death, on 27 February 1379, left a son, Roger, born about 1356. This last Roger was never summoned to parliament, and at the death of his son John in 1416 without offspring, the title fell into abeyance.

C. L. KINGSFORD, rev. ANDREW AYTON

Sources GEC, Peerage · C. Moor, ed., Knights of Edward I, 3, Harleian Society, 82 (1930), 272-4 · L. B. Larking, 'Genealogical notices of the Northwoods from the Surrenden collection', Archaeologia Cantiana, 2 (1859), 9-42 · F. Palgrave, ed., The parliamentary writs and writs of military summons, 2 vols. in 4 (1827-34) · Chancery records · CDS · G. Wrottesley, Crécy and Calais (1897); repr. (1898) · CIPM, 2, no. 582 · N. H. Nicholas, A roll of arms of the reign of Edward the Second (1829) · J. G. Waller, 'On the brass of Sir John de Northwode, and lady, in Minster church, Sheppey', Archaeologia Cantiana, 9 (1874), 148-63

Likenesses memorial brasses, c.1330, Minster church, Isle of Sheppey [see illus.]

Northwood, John (d. before 1318). See under Northwood, John, first Lord Northwood (1254-1319).

Northwood, Roger of (d. 1285), administrator, was of Kentish origins, the son of Stephen Northwood, and grandson of Jordan Sheppey. A minor at his father's death in 1231, he was of age by 1247. In 1257 he was given licence to hold his lands in Northwood, Milton, Sheppey, and Upchurch (all in Kent), whether inherited from his father or otherwise acquired, by knight's service rather than gavelkind. In 1265, in addition to a lease of the manor of Shorne, north-west of Rochester, he possessed houses in London and in Southwark, Lambeth, and Camberwell, in Surrey, and held an interest in the manors of Littlebrook, Harrietsham, Newton, and Littlehoe, and lands at Beckenham, all in Kent. His marriage to Bona, daughter of Henry of Waltham, brought him the manor of Thornham as her inheritance from Ralph Fitzbernard; hence she was also known as Bona Fitzbernard.

Northwood was an executor for Reginald Cobham, a Kentish magnate, in 1258. In 1265 he became the archbishop of Canterbury's steward, and was commissioned to take into the king's hand lands held by rebels in Kent. By 1274 he was a baron of the exchequer. In November 1275 Northwood was ordered to scrutinize chests belonging to the Jews in Canterbury; two years later he was instructed to have the chests unsealed and the charters transcribed. He occasionally heard pleas at the Jewish exchequer. In 1277 he was ordered to hold an inquest concerning the collection of wharfage at the quay by Rochester Bridge, and three years later to inquire who was responsible for repairing the bridge and quays at Rochester.

Northwood died on 9 November 1285. In 1303 Master Henry Northwood was allowed to alienate to the nunnery of Minster, in Sheppey, 2½ acres of land and 100 acres of marsh in Iwade, to provide in perpetuity for a chaplain and a daily celebration for the souls of Roger and his wife, buried there. During his lifetime Northwood had restored the nunnery, which had fallen into a ruinous condition. His generous benefaction may have engendered the erroneous belief (dating from the seventeenth century) that

the two brasses in the chancel of Minster church depicted Roger and his wife. The cross-legged knight, 'restored' over the years, has early fourteenth-century armour and may have been his son, John *Northwood.

A. J. MUSSON

Sources Chancery records · L. B. Larking, 'Genealogical notices of the Northwoods from the Surrenden collection', Archaeologia Cantiana, 2 (1859), 9-42 · GEC, Peerage · C. Moor, ed., Knights of Edward I, 3, Harleian Society, 82 (1930), 272 · R. Griffin, 'Minster in Sheppey: notes on two brasses in the church', Archaeologia Cantiana, 36 (1923), 43-7 · J. Cave-Browne, 'Minster in Sheppey', Archaeologia Cantiana, 22 (1897), 144-68 · J. M. Rigg, ed., Select pleas, starrs and other records from the rolls of the exchequer of the Jews, AD 1220-1284, SeldS, 15 (1902), 1220-84 · CIPM, 2. no. 582

Wealth at death manors and lands mainly in Kent; also houses in London: CIPM, 2, no. 582

Norton. For this title name see individual entries under Norton; see also Adderley, Charles Bowyer, first Baron Norton (1814-1905).

Norton, Bonham (1565-1635), printer and bookseller, was born in Onibury, Shropshire, the only son of William *Norton (1526/7-1593), printer and bookseller, and his wife, Joan (d. in or after 1593), daughter of William Bonham (1497-1557), printer and bookseller. On 15 December 1590 he married Jane (c.1566-1640), daughter of Sir Thomas Owen of Condover, Shropshire, with whom he had nine sons and four daughters. Upon his father's death in 1593, Norton received the bulk of the estate, which included not only a significant amount of money but also large landholdings in Shropshire, Middlesex, and Kent. His wealth and connections quickly allowed him to become one of the most important and powerful stationers of the period. Freed by patrimony of the Stationers' Company on 4 February 1594, he was chosen into the livery five months later, elected as an assistant on 6 June 1597, and served as master of the company for 1613, 1626, and 1629. He served briefly as an alderman for Aldgate in London in 1607, was elected sheriff of Shropshire in 1611, received a grant of arms in 1612, and was elected a governor of Christ's Hospital in 1613. He also developed his property holdings in the Shropshire town of Church Stretton. He helped with the rebuilding of the town after a fire in 1593, providing a school and a court house as well as a large town house for himself, known as The Hall. By 1616 he held nine or ten copyholds in the manor (probably along with the local demesne wood of Bushmoor) and in that year, as 'lord of the larger part of the lands and possessions' in the town, he was granted the right to hold a Thursday market (VCH Shropshire, 10.93).

For most of his publishing career Norton dealt with privileged works, classes of valuable texts protected as monopolies by royal letters of patent. Between 1597 and 1599 he was a partner in the law book patent with Thomas Wight, who had acquired the privilege upon the death of its previous holder, Charles Yetsweirt. During that time they printed such profitable works as William West's general treatise on English law, Of Symboleography, and Sir Anthony Fitzherbert's La nouvelle natura brevium, a manual of legal procedure. In 1605 Norton and his cousin John

Norton, along with fellow stationer and Shropshire native John Bill, established the Officina Nortoniana, a house that dealt primarily in scholarly books printed in London and on the continent. Two years earlier John had succeeded in wresting away the patent for Latin, Greek, and Hebrew printing from John Battersby, and the privileged titles that went with the office also became part of the Nortoniana business. Holding onto the right to print those titles, however, proved difficult. Both Battersby and his assignees brought court actions in an attempt to regain control over publishing rights, and in the middle of the fray Robert Barker, who held the office of king's printer, managed to acquire the reversion for John Norton's patent. It was not until 1606 that a working compromise agreeable to all parties was reached.

When John Norton died in 1612, Bonham Norton was named principal heir and executor of his cousin's estate. He immediately brought suit in the court of exchequer, asserting that the previous agreements were now void and claiming the sole right to exercise the privilege. Although the suit was denied, in January 1613 he obtained the royal patent for Latin, Greek, and Hebrew, to take effect when the existing patent expired. Further court actions followed, and it was not until Battersby's death in 1618 that he gained clear control over the materials. He then turned around in late 1619 and sold the patent to the Stationers' Company, who folded it into the newly formed Latin stock. Unfortunately the Latin stock venture proved unsuccessful, and Norton bought back the patent in 1624, holding it until his death.

Norton was an aggressive businessman, frequently using the law and company courts in an attempt to gain an advantage over his fellow stationers. Perhaps the most important series of the legal fights that Norton pursued concerned the important office of king's printer. For a number of years Norton had dealings with Robert Barker, and at some point he and John Bill apparently became partners with Barker in the king's printing office, perhaps as part of an investment arrangement to pay for the so-called Authorized Version of the Bible in 1611. Early in the partnership things went smoothly, so smoothly in fact that Barker's eldest son, Christopher, and Norton's eldest daughter, Sarah, were married in 1615. As was so often the case with Norton, the arrangement turned sour, and the constantly changing imprint formulae on books printed by the office from 1617 to 1629 bear witness to the legal imbroglio that followed.

Barker began the exchange in 1618 by filing suit in the court of chancery to evict Norton and Bill from the business. Barker claimed that he had placed his son Christopher in the establishment with the understanding that Norton and Bill would 'ayde and direct [Christopher] for his best advantage in the execution of the said office of printinge' (Plomer, 'King's printing house', 356). Earlier in the decade Barker, tired of the squabbles and deeply in debt, had determined to sell the patent. Norton and Bill set their sights on this prize, and according to Barker's statement, they 'did cunningly devise & practise how to obteyne & get the said office of printing wholly into their own hands' (ibid., 357), even using Christopher against his father. A complicated sales agreement ensued, one that included a clause whereby Barker had the option after a year and a day to buy back the operation. Barker claimed that all the sales documents were destroyed in a fire shortly after the deal was signed, and that Norton and Bill had subsequently refused to turn over the office or to render an account of the business. Norton responded in his own statement to the court that he and Bill had reluctantly bought the patent only after it had become clear that there were no other potential buyers, that the option to buy back the business claimed by Barker had never been part of the deal, and that he was in no way bound to give an account of the office.

On 7 May 1619 the court found for Barker, holding that the transaction had not been a sale but only security for a loan. Norton was ordered to surrender the office, although Bill's right to the office was upheld and he continued to operate the establishment along with Barker. The court also ordered Barker to repay Norton his initial investment, which he apparently failed to do, for some time in 1620 Norton reoccupied the office. Again Barker sued, and for the rest of the decade he attempted to regain the patent while Norton employed all manner of evasions and subterfuges. Finally, on 20 October 1629, the court of chancery settled the matter, awarding the office of king's printer to Barker and Bill. Norton's response was unwise. His agents broke into the office immediately after the decree and carried off stock and equipment. Norton refused to divulge the whereabouts of one of the agents (his son Roger) and was imprisoned. He also publicly accused the lord keeper of taking a bribe to decide in Barker's favour. After a trial in Star Chamber in July 1630, Norton was fined £6000 and again imprisoned 'during his majesties pleasure' (Plomer, 'King's printing house', 366). Whether at this point Norton remained in prison or retired to his family home in Shropshire is unclear. Perhaps signalling his withdrawal from the trade, in 1632 the rights to a number of popular titles were transferred to Joyce Norton, the widow of his cousin John, and her partner Richard Whitaker.

Norton died intestate on 5 April 1635, and the administration of his estate was granted to his son John, a lawyer, on 28 May 1636. He was buried in St Faith's under St Paul's, under the choir of St Paul's Cathedral in London, where his widow erected a monument next to those of his father and three of his sons.   DAVID L. GANTS

Sources H. R. Plomer, 'The king's printing house under the Stuarts', *The Library*, new ser., 2 (1901), 353–75 • W. A. Jackson, ed., *Records of the court of the Stationers' Company, 1602 to 1640* (1957) • *STC, 1475–1640* • H. G. Aldis and others, *A dictionary of printers and booksellers in England, Scotland and Ireland, and of foreign printers of English books, 1557–1640*, ed. R. B. McKerrow (1910) • N. Mace, 'The history of the grammar patent, 1547–1620', *Papers of the Bibliographical Society of America*, 87 (1993), 419–36 • H. R. Plomer, *Wills of English printers and stationers* (1903) • Arber, *Regs. Stationers* • E. G. Duff, *A century of the English book trade* (1905) • W. Dugdale, *The history of St Paul's Cathedral in London* (1658) • *VCH Shropshire*, 10.76, 79, 85, 92–4, 101, 108, 115, 118 • A. Hunt, 'Book trade patents, 1603–40', *The book trade and its customers, 1450–1900*, ed. A. Hunt, G. Mandelbrote, and A. Shell (1997), 27–54

Archives BL, drawing of arms granted February 1612, Harley MS 6095, fol. 17*v* · BL, drawing of arms, Harley MS 6140, fol. 40*r*

Norton [*née* Sheridan]**, Caroline Elizabeth Sarah** [*other married name* Caroline Elizabeth Sarah Stirling Maxwell, Lady Stirling Maxwell] **(1808–1877)**, author and law reform campaigner, was born in London on 22 March 1808, the second of the three daughters of Thomas *Sheridan (1775–1817), colonial official, and his wife, Caroline Henrietta Callender (1779–1851) [*see* Sheridan, Caroline Henrietta], novelist. She had four brothers. The Sheridan inheritance was a flamboyant one: her paternal grandparents were the dramatist, politician, and sometime friend of the prince regent Richard Brinsley *Sheridan and his first wife, the celebrated singer Elizabeth Linley. But the family finances were perilous, especially after the destruction by fire in 1809 of the Drury Lane theatre, which R. B. Sheridan owned, and in 1813 Caroline's parents and her eldest sister, Helen [*see* Hay, Helen Selina], went to the Cape of Good Hope, where her father was colonial treasurer. He died at the Cape, of consumption, and the rest of the family was reunited in England. Mrs Sheridan's small pension was enhanced by the royal gift of a grace-and-favour apartment in Hampton Court Palace, but the overwhelming sense of poverty narrowly averted, together with the need to keep up an aristocratic lifestyle on a tiny income, was, along with a clannish sense of family loyalty, the defining characteristic of Caroline's childhood.

A 'passionate and self-willed child' (Acland, 22), Caroline Sheridan was considered plain and difficult by her mother. She displayed early literary tendencies, at the age of eleven writing and illustrating *The Dandies' Rout* (a pastiche on the popular series of 'Dandy' books), which was published by John Marshall in 1820. In 1824, finding her sixteen-year-old daughter too difficult to manage, Mrs Sheridan sent her to a boarding-school at Shalford, Surrey. Through family connection the girls at the school were invited to Wonersh Park, the seat of the local landowner, Lord Grantley. Caroline, whose early plainness had blossomed into a dark-eyed, dark-haired, southern European style of flamboyant beauty, caught the eye of Grantley's brother George Chapple Norton (1800–1875), and he informed her governess of his intention to propose marriage to her. Caroline was speedily returned to her mother.

Marriage à la mode Caroline Sheridan was brought out into London society in 1826 with her elder sister, Helen. But though all three Sheridan sisters were popular, witty, beautiful—and slightly shocking to the staid—there were no queues of suitors waiting to marry the portionless girls, who were nicknamed the 'Three Graces'. At the end of their first season Helen married the equally penniless Captain Price Blackwood, heir to Lord Dufferin, against his family's wishes, but Caroline remained unattached. Her second season drawing to a close without matrimonial success (and with her younger, more beautiful sister Georgiana about to make her own début), she accepted the renewed proposals of George Norton, and they were married on 30 June 1827 at St George's, Hanover Square.

Caroline Elizabeth Sarah Norton (1808–1877), by London Stereoscopic Co.

The marriage was a disaster from the outset. Two less compatible individuals would have been hard to find. Norton was slow, rather dull, jealous, and obstinate; Caroline was quick-witted, vivacious, flirtatious, and egotistical. Moreover the Sheridans were convinced whigs, the Nortons tories. Soon after returning from their honeymoon Caroline found that her slower-tongued husband resorted to physical violence to end their disputes. Money was to be the cause of frequent arguments between the couple. Norton, although an MP and a barrister, lived mostly on his expectations of inheriting the family property from his childless brother, and was both indolent and mean. He was a desultory commissioner in bankruptcy under the tory administrations of the 1820s, but having lost his seat in parliament in 1830, he resigned his commissionership in the following year in the expectation that it would fall victim to the retrenchment plans of the new whig government. He then permitted his wife to solicit an appointment for him from her friends in the new ministry; in 1831 Lord Melbourne, the home secretary, made him a stipendiary magistrate, with a salary of £1000 a year. To supplement the family budget Caroline sought a publisher for *The Sorrows of Rosalie* (1829), a lengthy narrative poem about the tragic downfall of a seduced and abandoned woman, written some years earlier; it was highly praised in *Blackwood's Magazine* (vol. 48,

April 1830) and the profits met the expenses incurred by the births of her first son, Fletcher, in 1829. Two further sons, (Thomas) Brinsley and William, were born in 1831 and 1833, respectively. Caroline began to write in earnest, but though Norton was willing to accept his wife's income he resented the imputation that he could not provide for his family, disliked the social prominence that her literary work gave to his wife, and came to loathe her Sheridan family connections. Caroline in turn, bored by her husband, frustrated by their financial limitations, disliking and disliked by his family, threw herself into literary society.

'The Byron of our modern poetesses' Caroline followed up the success of The Sorrows of Rosalie with another lengthy narrative poem, based on the legend of the wandering Jew, The Undying One and Other Poems (1830), which also was favourably received. Her The Dream and Other Poems (1840) was in a similar, high-Romantic vein, and in reviewing it H. N. Coleridge described her as 'the Byron of our modern poetesses. She has very much of that intense personal passion … She also has Byron's beautiful intervals of tenderness, his strong practical thought, and his forceful expression' (Quarterly Review, 66, June 1840, 374–418).

A Voice from the Factories (1836) and The Child of the Islands (1845) showed Norton writing a very different type of poetry, in the condition-of-England genre. In obvious reference to her own difficulties these volumes focused on the plight of working-class children, whose desperate lives were portrayed in realistic detail and contrasted with the callous greed of the factory owners and upper classes. The later narrative poem (almost a verse-novel) The Lady of La Garaye (1862) continues the strategy of comparison and contrast: a fine lady, injured in an accident, devotes herself to philanthropy and finds joy in relieving the sufferings of others.

Norton published her first novels in 1835, as her marriage was deteriorating. The Wife and Woman's Reward were issued together anonymously. Both were autobiographical and address the themes of women's powerlessness in marriage and men's abuse of domestic power. The narrator of the latter, observing that the heroine's eventual consolations may seem insufficient to the reader, remarks despondently: 'I do not recollect any instances of poetical justice in real life' (vol. 3, p. 213). Norton's poetry and prose were well received, but she derived most of her income from contributions to magazines and periodicals (including Fraser's Magazine, the New Monthly Magazine, and Macmillan's Magazine), and from editing several annuals, beginning with La Belle Assemblée and Court Magazine (1832–7) and including The Keepsake (1836) and Fisher's Drawing Room Scrapbook (1846–9). She wrote prolifically, and her output included children's fiction, short stories, song adaptations, and a play, The Gypsy Father, produced at Covent Garden in May 1831. Her financial need was pressing, and if quality was sacrificed to quantity there can be no doubting the seriousness of her labours. Hers was, she wrote, 'a life of incessant occupation: I have written day after day, and night after night, without intermission; I provided for myself by means of my literary engagements; I provided for my children by means of my literary engagements' (Acland, 99).

It was not all work, however. Norton's literary and artistic circle included Benjamin Disraeli, who based the character of Berengaria Montford in Endymion on her; Fanny Kemble, the actress, whose later marital difficulties resembled Caroline's; and Charles Dickens, whose Pickwick Papers contains references in its trial scene to the more ludicrous episodes of George Norton's subsequent legal action against Lord Melbourne. A frequent house guest of the poet Samuel Rogers and a regular correspondent of Mary Shelley, Caroline Norton was also the reputed literary model for Alfred Tennyson's Princess Ida in The Princess (1847) and for several of William Thackeray's heroines. Thomas Moore's poem 'Summer Fete' (1831) was dedicated to her.

Lord Melbourne and criminal conversation Caroline Norton was too flamboyant to integrate fully into aristocratic society: her background was too eccentric, her personality too dramatic, her literary activities too unusual for women of her class. Women in particular were suspicious of her, and she never escaped the damning charge of vulgarity, of deliberately seeking to shock, 'affecting to be so much more wicked than there is the slightest call for' (Mitchell, 221). But she entranced men, among them Lord Melbourne, whom she had first approached at the behest of her husband in his quest for a patronage appointment. With the acquiescence of Norton, Melbourne—prime minister from 1834—became a regular visitor at their house in Storey's Gate. The public humiliations of Melbourne's marriage with Lady Caroline Lamb had ended with her death in 1828, but he was left with a dubious reputation where women were concerned. By 1834 Caroline's own reputation was thoroughly compromised, while her husband was regarded by society as complaisant towards her affairs provided that her lovers were in a position to advance his own interests. Her friendship with Melbourne was probably platonic but it was certainly unwise: Norton's brother and his tory associates were keen to make political capital out of it, and Norton himself came to see it as a potential source of income. The relationship between the Nortons had deteriorated rapidly; in 1835 Caroline was refused access to their house and her children were sent away. A private separation was discussed but Norton insisted on custody of the children and refused to make a financial settlement with his wife. Over the next few years he regularly offered access to the children in exchange for reducing or removing his financial liabilities towards Caroline. In June 1836 Norton brought a case for criminal conversation between Melbourne and his wife to the courts, suing Melbourne for £10,000 in damages for adultery. (Such a case was a necessary preliminary for a successful action for divorce.) The case, which naturally generated great interest, was dismissed in a matter of hours; the jury, asked to put the worst possible construction on the most innocent of written communications from the prime minister, found that Norton's witnesses were unreliable. Melbourne was not called to give evidence; as a married woman Caroline was legally disbarred from doing so, even in her own defence. The trial over, Melbourne offered Caroline financial support but disengaged himself from the friendship as quickly and as completely as possible. Without the protection of husband or lover she found herself in a precarious position—childless and penniless. Only the kindness of Harriet, duchess of Sutherland, who took her for a drive in her carriage in London in a public display of support, prevented her from being completely ostracized by respectable society.

The custody of infants The Nortons' marriage was effectively ended in 1835 but, the action for criminal conversation having failed, there was no possibility of a divorce. George Norton, activated less by interest in his children's welfare than by a desire to cause his wife pain and to secure the least onerous financial settlement, took full advantage of the law, which vested custody of children in their father, and took his three sons away to Yorkshire. Enraged and distraught, Caroline began a campaign to change the law, using the political contacts that she had made in the preceding decade. She published a pamphlet, *Observations on the natural claim of the mother to the custody of her infant children: as affected by the common law rights of the father* (1837), and Sergeant (Thomas Noon) Talfourd was persuaded to introduce a child custody bill in the House of Commons. The bill failed but Caroline kept up her lobbying (three further pamphlets on the subject are attributed to her pen), and in 1839 the Infant Custody Act was passed, with the support of Talfourd in the Commons and Lord Lyndhurst in the Lords. This act gave custody of children under seven to the mother (provided she had not been proven in court to have committed adultery) and established the right of the non-custodial parent to access to the child. The act was the first piece of legislation to undermine the patriarchal structures of English law and has subsequently been hailed as the first success of British feminism in gaining equal rights for women. But Caroline Norton was no feminist: in 1838 she wrote to *The Times* that 'The natural position of woman is inferiority to man … I never pretended to the wild and ridiculous doctrine of equality' (Stone, 363). She did not seek 'women's rights' but rather to redress a grievous wrong: 'in proportion to the inferiority and helplessness of their [women's] position towards men, should be the generosity and forbearance exercised towards them by men' (*The Times*, 19 Aug 1838). But the change of law brought no relief for Caroline; it applied only in England and Wales, and Norton promptly removed the children to Scotland. Disputes over access to the children were only resolved in 1842, after the youngest son, William, died in Scotland, having contracted blood poisoning after a fall from a pony. Thereafter the two remaining sons, Fletcher and Brinsley, spent half the year with their mother in London.

Years of respite The issue of custody more or less resolved, the Norton feud slipped into abeyance during the 1840s. After July 1845 Caroline lived alone, without female companionship or chaperonage, at 3 Chesterfield Street, London, where she continued to entertain guests and to wield her ready pen; this unusual arrangement kept gossip swirling about her. She had been received at court in the summer of 1839, which ostensibly restored her good name and position in society, but she remained a slightly dangerous person to know. Caroline had apparent freedom but her tie to Norton ultimately isolated her. It is impossible to establish the nature of her relationship with the Peelite politician Sidney Herbert between 1841 and 1845 but it seems likely at least that she was in love with him and that he was fascinated by her; gossips linked their names more closely. When in December 1845 *The Times* informed its readers that Sir Robert Peel's cabinet had changed its mind about the corn laws the source of the leak was widely believed to have been Caroline Norton, indiscreetly passing on information received from her lover. In fact Lord Aberdeen had been the source. This slander was famously repeated by George Meredith in *Diana of the Crossways* (1884), a novel that bore many resemblances to the details of Caroline's life. The affair with Herbert—if that is what it was—ended with his marriage in August 1846.

With their eldest son launched on a career in the diplomatic service Norton demanded a revision of his and Caroline's deed of separation. Once more under pressure, Caroline agreed to his terms, which were for a reduced annual allowance to her of £500 and, crucially and unenforceably, an agreement that she should be liable for her own debts for the preceding ten and all subsequent years. She spent 1849 abroad with Fletcher, who had become ill during his posting to Lisbon, and returned home in 1850 to nurse her mother. In this year she also met William Stirling of Keir (1818–1878) [*see* Maxwell, Sir William Stirling], a noted book collector and art historian, who in 1865 succeeded his uncle in a Scottish baronetcy. They formed a close friendship that was not interrupted by his marriage in 1865 and the births of his two sons.

Caroline Norton's main literary venture of this period was her second novel, *Stuart of Dunleath: a Story of Modern Times* (1851). The tribulations of its heroine, Eleanor Raymond—who marries a man she does not love to provide for herself and her mother, and suffers brutish behaviour under him that includes the deaths of her sons in an avoidable accident—owed much to incidents in Caroline's own life; in particular the heroine's refusal of the nobleman who encourages her to divorce her husband and marry him carries wistful echoes of Caroline's relationship with Sidney Herbert. It proved popular with audiences and reviewers.

Married women's property In June 1851 Caroline's mother died. By her death George Norton became possessed of a life interest in Caroline's share of her father's small estate, while Caroline was left £480 a year by her mother. Norton immediately reduced—almost stopped—his own annual payments to Caroline, telling her that the settlement of 1848 was not binding. She had no redress but to break her own side of that agreement by referring her creditors to her husband. She was abroad in 1852 and early 1853, but on her return home she was flung once more into public warfare with him. Their children grown up, this time the source of contention was explicitly financial, and the full injustice of the laws of property as applied to married women was brought home to Caroline.

As the law stood in 1853 a married woman had no legal right to own property in her own name at all. She had no legal identity, which meant she could neither sue nor be sued. She could not make contracts. She could neither receive legacies nor make a will. She had no right to any earnings that she might acquire. The complicated law of trusts had been devised in part to allow wealthy women to retain some independent income after marriage, but trusts had to be specifically drawn up. Deeds of separation had weight in law, allowing an officially separated wife an income and relieving the separated husband from liability for his wife's debts, if they were signed by guarantors. But, as Caroline discovered in 1853, the deed of 1848 that she had agreed with Norton had not been guaranteed. As such he was entitled to her mother's legacy and indeed to the money that she had made by her writing. Caroline took legal advice and allowed her creditors to sue Norton. The case *Thrupp v. Norton* (in which Thrupp was suing for the costs of repairs to Caroline's carriage) was heard in Westminster court on 18 August 1853. Norton had subpoenaed all his wife's financial papers, among which he discovered that Melbourne had left her a small legacy in 1848. He made great play of this in court, bringing forward again all the old slander about Caroline's relationship with Melbourne. She defended herself vigorously, to cheers in the courtroom, but the court found for Norton on a technicality. Caroline's verdict, 'I do not ask for my rights. I have no rights; I have only wrongs' (Acland, 198), was greeted with renewed applause.

Incensed by the reporting of the case, which emphasized once more the Melbourne connection, Caroline wrote to *The Times* on 20 August to correct Norton's courtroom statements. He replied, and for some weeks the dirty linen of their marriage and financial affairs dominated the letter columns of the paper. It was an unedifying spectacle, which aroused some sympathy for Caroline, but it was a more profound embarrassment that the issues should be discussed in public at all. Caroline did not confine herself to bemoaning her lot and airing past wrongs (though she did both). She was able to see beyond her own situation to the legal position of married women in general, and began to campaign for changes in the law relating to married women's property rights. Her first salvo was a privately printed pamphlet, *English Laws for Women in the Nineteenth Century* (1854). In it she rehearsed her own grievances at exhaustive length; the public, grown weary of her tribulations, paid it little heed. Shortly after its publication Lord Cranworth brought a bill forward in the House of Lords to reform the marriage and divorce laws; Caroline responded with *A Letter to the Queen on Lord Cranworth's Marriage and Divorce Bill* (1855), which argued the case for property rights for divorced and separated women. Many of her proposals and arguments were accepted and embedded in the Matrimonial Causes Act (1857), which relieved many of the wrongs to which Caroline had been subjected.

Caroline Norton was not the only campaigner for women's property rights but she had little contact with the emergent organizations that were concerned with women's rights. The predominantly middle-class campaigns of Barbara Leigh Smith Bodichon and Lydia Becker were aimed at property rights for all women, and they themselves considered Caroline's campaign a selfishly motivated distraction from the real goal of establishing property rights for all married women. They were further embarrassed by her doubtful reputation for sexual propriety, while Caroline had no time for a general assault on the relations between men and women; the distancing between them was mutual.

Lost and Saved Alongside the anxieties induced by Caroline's battles with Norton were worries about her sons. Brinsley had inherited the Sheridan taste for excess and, having left Oxford in debt, married an Italian peasant girl whom he met on Capri. They had a son and daughter, who lived for much of the time with their grandmother, perhaps compensating her in some measure for the lost childhoods of her own sons. Fletcher, like Brinsley, had poor health, and in 1859 died in the British embassy at Paris, of consumption. Caroline continued to write, publishing the poem *The Lady of La Garaye* in 1862 and her third novel, *Lost and Saved*, in 1863. The latter, with its theme of the sexual morality—and immorality—of the upper classes, was found too frank by many reviewers at the time but by the end of the twentieth century it was generally considered Norton's best work, showing her considerable skill in portraying believable characters and a grim, satirical humour. Her last novel, *Old Sir Douglas* (1867), continued the semi-autobiographical line, this time concentrating her attack on the sisters and other female connections of her heroine's husband; Norton had always been fortified in his attacks on his wife by his sister Lady Menzies and his relative Margaret Vaughan.

This was Caroline's last really creative flurry. She continued her literary hack-work, reviewing and writing for magazines and periodicals, but her energy was flagging. She had after a fashion won the long struggle against Norton, who was at last compelled by law to make her regular maintenance payments, but it had left her embittered and contentious, liable to depression, fits of rage, and constant harping on old grudges. Her beauty had lasted well, and into late middle age she retained her lustrous black hair and elegant neck: 'I shall be handsome, even in my coffin,' she remarked (Chedzoy, 255). The Sheridans remained faithful to her to the last: she spent much of her time travelling between the houses of her sisters, Lady Dufferin and the duchess of Somerset, and her brother Brinsley Sheridan; she visited her son and his family in Capri as often as she could; and she made an annual visit to Sir William Stirling Maxwell and his family at Keir, in Stirlingshire, Scotland.

Death continued to take its toll of her family and friends: in 1867 her sister Helen died, and in May 1875 she received word that George Norton died at Wonersh Park. Even in death he managed to spite his wife, narrowly predeceasing his brother and thus denying her the title

Lady Grantley. Grantley himself died in August, and Caroline's invalid son, Brinsley, succeeded as fourth Baron Grantley. Caroline became seriously ill and was virtually confined to a wheelchair in her home in Chesterfield Street for eighteen months. It was there that Sir William Stirling Maxwell (whose wife, Lady Anna, had died tragically in an accident in 1874) proposed to her in February 1877 and married her on 1 March 1877. The marriage was greeted with surprise in many quarters: Mrs Norton, who had spent her whole life battling against the restrictions of marriage, was willingly entering that state again. But conditions in 1877 were vastly different from those of fifty years earlier, thanks in no small part to her own efforts, while she and Maxwell had a long history of friendship as the basis of their relationship. And marriage would free Caroline from the burden of her over-famous name: as Lady Stirling Maxwell she had anonymity, a release from the past. With her new husband she made plans to visit Scotland and Capri, but in the fourth month of her marriage she was suddenly taken ill, and died at her new London home, 10 Upper Grosvenor Street, on 15 June 1877. She was buried in the Stirling Maxwell vault at Lecropt church, near Keir. She was soon joined by her husband, who died in Venice on 15 January 1878, on his way home from Capri; Brinsley Norton had died five weeks after his mother, leaving his son, John Richard Norton, to become fifth Baron Grantley.

Caroline Norton was an extraordinary woman by any account. Fascinating, beautiful, witty, intelligent, and charming, she was also temperamental and difficult to live with. As a writer her natural talent was perhaps overwhelmed by the financial pressures on her to produce quantity rather than quality. Lady Eastlake wrote 'her talents are of the highest order, and she has carefully cultivated them ... She still has only talents; genius she has nothing of, or of the nature of genius' (Perkins, 254). Of her copious short poetry 'The Arab's Farewell to his Steed' (1830), 'Bingen on the Rhine', and 'I do not love thee' (1829), among others, were consistently anthologized, and at the end of the twentieth century Norton benefited from the general flowering of interest in women writers and poets. Her public admission of the failure of her marriage and her campaigns for legal reform led to her adoption by twentieth-century feminists as one of their early forebears, a designation that she strenuously rebutted in her own lifetime: she sought to redress wrongs, not to assert rights.　　　　K. D. REYNOLDS

Sources A. Acland, *Caroline Norton* (1948) · J. G. Perkins, *The life of Mrs Norton* (1909) · A. Chedzoy, *A scandalous woman: the story of Caroline Norton* (1992) · J. O. Hodge and C. Olney, *The letters of Caroline Norton to Lord Melbourne* (1974) · L. Mitchell, *Lord Melbourne, 1779–1848* (1997) · L. Stone, *The road to divorce: England, 1530–1987* (1990) · L. Holcombe, *Wives and property* (1983) · M. Poovey, *Uneven developments: the ideological work of gender in mid-Victorian Britain* (1988) · Blain, Clements & Grundy, *Feminist comp.* · P. R. Feldman, ed., *British women poets of the Romantic era: an anthology* (1997) · O. Banks, *The biographical dictionary of British feminists*, 1 (1985) · Burke, *Peerage* (1939) · GEC, *Peerage* · H. J. Spencer, 'Norton, George Chapple', HoP, *Commons, 1820–32* [draft]

Archives BL, corresp. with her brother, Richard Brinsley Sheridan, Add. MS 42767 · BL, letters, prob. to Agatha Cowell (copies) ·

BL, letters [microfilm: M/593] · Bucks. RLSS, corresp. · Harvard U., Houghton L., papers · King's AC Cam., corresp. and literary MSS · Mitchell L., Glas., Glasgow City Archives, corresp. and papers · Mitchell L., Glas., letters, poem, and story · Morgan L. · PRO NIre., family corresp., literary MSS, and papers · UCL, letters to Lord Brougham · Women's Library, London, letters · Yale U., Beinecke L. | BL, letters to Lord Holland and Lady Holland, Add. MSS 51837–51843, 51851–51856, 52065, 52126 · BL, corresp. with Charles Jennings, Add. MS 42767 · BL, corresp. with Macmillans, Add. MS 54964 · Bodl. Oxf., letters to Sir Robert Hay · Bodl. Oxf., letters to Mary Shelley and Lady Shelley · Bodl. Oxf., corresp. with Sir Henry Taylor · Carl H. Pforzheimer Library, New York, letters, probably to Agatha Cowell [copies in BL, RP5154] · CUL, letters to A. W. Kinglake · Herts. ALS, letters to Lord Lytton · Herts. ALS, letters to Lord Melbourne · Hunt. L., letters, mainly to James Hain Friswell · News Int. RO, letters to J. T. Delane · NL Scot., letters to Edward Ellice · NRA, priv. coll., corresp. with Lord Wemyss · Trinity Cam., letters to Lord Houghton · U. Nott. L., corresp. with fifth duke of Newcastle

Likenesses H. W. Pickersgill, oils, possibly exh. RA 1829, Beaverbrook Art Gallery, Fredericton, Canada · I. W. Slater, lithograph, pubd 1829 (after drawing by J. Slater), BM · G. Hayter, oils, 1832, Chatsworth House, Derbyshire · E. Landseer, pen and wash caricature, *c.*1835, NPG · W. Etty, oils, *c.*1845, Pollok House, Glasgow · F. Stone, group portrait, oils, *c.*1845, NPG · W. Etty, oils, *c.*1847, Man. City Gall. · D. Maclise, group portrait, fresco, 1848–9 (*Justice*), House of Lords, Palace of Westminster, London · attrib. Mrs Ferguson of Raith, watercolour drawing, 1860, Scot. NPG · F. J. Williamson, plaster bust, 1873, NPG · J. C. Bromley, mezzotint (after E. T. Parris), BM · T. Carrick, portrait · Mrs Ferguson of Raith, portrait, Scot. NPG · Lord Gifford, marble bust (as young woman), Pollok House, Glasgow · F. Grant, portrait, repro. in Acland, *Caroline Norton* · J. Hayter, chalk drawing, NG Ire. · J. Hayter, drawing, repro. in Acland, *Caroline Norton* · E. Landseer, oils, Nottingham College of Art · F. C. Lewis, engraving (after drawing by E. Landseer), repro. in Perkins, *Life* · London Stereoscopic Co., photograph, NPG [*see illus.*] · D. Maclise, lithograph, BM, NPG; repro. in *Fraser's Magazine* (1831) · A. Miles, engraving (with Lady Blessington and Eliza Cook), repro. in *Reynolds's Miscellany* (13 Feb 1847) · Mrs Munro-Ferguson, drawing, repro. in Acland, *Caroline Norton* · H. Robinson, stipple (after T. Carrick), BM, NPG · J. H. Robinson, engraving (after portrait by T. Carrick), BL · F. Stone, NPG · J. Thomson, stipple (after J. Hayter), BM, NPG; repro. in *New Monthly Magazine* (1831) · G. F. Watts, oils, NG Ire. · engraving (after crayon drawing by Swinton) · group portrait (with Samuel Rogers and Mrs Phipps), NPG · photograph (of bust), repro. in Perkins, *Life* · portrait (after portrait by J. Hayter), Hult. Arch.; repro. in Perkins, *Life*

Norton, Chapple (1746–1818), army officer and politician, was born on 2 April 1746, the third son of Fletcher *Norton, first Baron Grantley (1716–1789), and his wife, Grace (1707/8–1803), the daughter of Sir William Chapple. His siblings included William (1742–1822), Fletcher (1744–1820), and Edward (1750–1786), all of whom pursued parliamentary careers. Chapple Norton entered the 19th foot, in which regiment, then serving at Gibraltar, he became captain in June 1763. In 1769 he was promoted major in the 1st Royal foot, and in 1774 he became captain and lieutenant-colonel in the Coldstream Guards. He served with this regiment during the American War of Independence and distinguished himself in February 1780 by the capture of Young's House, near White Plains, an important American post. He became brevet colonel in the November of the same year. In 1784 he was elected MP for Guildford, which he represented as an independent until 1790, voting against William Pitt during the Regency crisis. He was promoted regimental major (1786), major-general (1787), lieutenant-general (1797), and general (29 April 1802), and was appointed colonel of the 81st regiment (1795) and of the 56th (24 January 1797). His last regiment, the 56th (West Essex) foot, was raised to three strong battalions towards the close of the French revolutionary wars. Norton continued to represent Guildford in the parliaments of 1796, 1802, 1806, and 1807–12, and took an active interest in all matters relating to Surrey, where the Grantley estates and residence, Wonersh, were located. Noted for his amiableness, Norton was a close friend of his commander-in-chief, the duke of York. He died, unmarried, at Wonersh on 19 March 1818.

H. M. CHICHESTER, rev. PHILIP CARTER

Sources J. Brooke, 'Norton, Chapple', HoP, Commons, 1754–90 · B. Murphy and R. G. Thorne, 'Norton, Chapple', HoP, Commons, 1790–1820 · GM, 1st ser., 88/1 (1818), 472

Norton, Christopher (1738?–1799), engraver, painter, and antiquary, may have been the son of John and Susanna Norton baptized on 26 March 1738 at St Anne's, Soho, Westminster. From about 1755 he was a pupil of Peter Charles Canot, and in the later 1750s did the preliminary etching on several of Canot's plates and completed others, including fine interpretations of drawings by Jean Pillement, such as Le petit pont de pierre (1759). He studied at the St Martin's Lane Academy and in 1760 won a premium from the Society for the Encouragement of Arts, Manufactures, and Commerce. He exhibited 'a sea piece' in the inaugural exhibition that May, but later in 1760 he went to Rome and by 1762 he was living with the Catholic Jacobite antiquary James Byres, and the painter and antiquarian Colin Morison, by the strada Paolina. In 1766 he was engraving plates for James Byres's Etruria, and he also etched several plates for Views in Italy by Peter Stephens, published in 1767.

Norton became closely associated with Byres, who was the principal guide to English tourists in Rome: in 1780 he was described as Byres's partner as an antiquarian guide and a dealer. He exported old masters and modern paintings from Rome and visited England frequently. In 1776 the landscape painter Thomas Jones, about to make his first visit to Rome, took the opportunity to travel from London to Italy with Norton, who had engaged to accompany a Mr Hardwick from Paris to Rome. The three travelled to Lyons and over Mont Cenis to Milan, where they visited the Academy of Arts; Jones was not amused to find afterwards that Norton had waggishly introduced him as an eminent figurista or historical painter. Jones found him somewhat ceremonious and haughty, and did not very much enjoy the various jokes Norton played on him in the course of their journey. Norton's portrait was painted by Hugh Douglas Hamilton and by Nathaniel Dance, and both pictures used to hang in Byres's house. Norton also appears with Byres in two group portraits and he was drawn by Pichler. He returned from Italy with Byres in July 1790. In 1792 he married Janet Moir, Byres's niece, in Scotland, where he may have settled for the last few years of his life. He died in 1799.

TIMOTHY CLAYTON and ANITA MCCONNELL

Sources Dodd's manuscript history of engravers, BL, Add. MS 33403, fol. 141 · Redgrave, Artists · J. Ingamells, ed., A dictionary of British and Irish travellers in Italy, 1701–1800 (1997), 715–16 · G. Vaughan, 'Byres, James', The dictionary of art, ed. J. Turner (1996) · A. P. Oppé, ed., 'Memoirs of Thomas Jones, Penkerrig, Radnorshire', Walpole Society, 32 (1946–8) [whole issue]

Norton, Sir Clifford John (1891–1990), diplomatist, was born on 17 July 1891, the son of the Revd George Norton and his wife, Clara, daughter of John Dewey. He was educated at Rugby School and Queen's College, Oxford, from where he graduated with a third-class degree in literae humaniores in 1914, before joining the Suffolk regiment. He served with the regiment at Gallipoli and in Palestine, being promoted captain in 1917. At the end of the war, he served as a political officer in Damascus, Deraa, and Haifa, before entering the Foreign Office in May 1921. He began his career as a third secretary and obtained his promotion to second secretary in January 1925. On 27 March 1927 he married Noel Evelyn Hughes (d. 1972), only daughter of Sir Walter Charleton Hughes, civil engineer and member of the Bombay legislative council. There were no children of the marriage.

Norton had a lengthy period in the under-resourced Foreign Office news department before being appointed private secretary to the permanent under-secretary, Sir Robert Vansittart, in January 1930. This was an important promotion and Norton remained in this post until December 1937, being promoted first secretary in April 1933 and appointed CMG in 1933 and CVO in 1937. As Vansittart's private secretary, Norton was 'involved in all the vagaries of what came to be known as the policy of appeasement' (The Times), yet later his role was oddly ignored by his long-standing chief. In his memoirs Vansittart made just one reference to 'a fond Private Secretary Clifford Norton' (Vansittart, 399). Norton claimed in later years to have warned the British ambassador in Berlin, Nevile Henderson, not to anger Vansittart by talking of the need to understand the Nazis, but the record shows that he shared Henderson's concern that the British press was too hostile to Nazi Germany.

Norton had to wait until December 1937 for his first foreign posting, as acting counsellor in the Warsaw embassy under Sir Howard Kennard. He was chargé d'affaires in Poland in 1938–9 before becoming counsellor in October 1939, after the German invasion. While in Warsaw he was sympathetic to the Polish cause, and dined with the foreign minister, Beck, as well as going hunting with him. Beck was an unpopular figure in the Foreign Office, but Norton told the foreign secretary, Lord Halifax, that Beck and Smigly-Rydz, the Polish president, were 'extremely prudent and moderate men' (Gilbert and Gott, 252) and were unlikely to authorize a pre-emptive move into Danzig, to head off German aggression. When Nevile Henderson, whose telegrams Norton criticized, said that Britain had deceived Poland with its promises of assistance, Norton told the Foreign Office that such a view was 'rubbish' (Documents on British Foreign Policy, Norton to Sargent, 3 July 1939). He assured Halifax that the British guarantee of March 1939 would not encourage the Poles to act recklessly, and reminded the new permanent under-secretary, Sir Alexander Cadogan, that 'from the British point of view, our record in protecting victims of aggression has not recently been impressive' (ibid., Norton to Cadogan, 10 July 1939). When Poland fell to the Nazis in September 1939, Norton and his embassy colleagues were evacuated from the country via Romania. He was then transferred back to the Foreign Office, in January 1940.

Norton's next foreign posting was to the Swiss capital, Bern, in April 1942, where he remained as envoy-extraordinary and minister-plenipotentiary until posted as ambassador to Athens in March 1946. In the same year he was promoted KCMG. The situation he inherited in Greece from his predecessor Reginald Leeper was a difficult one. Civil war had broken out between the communists and the royalists in 1943, and British troops had been sent in by Churchill in 1944 to prevent a communist takeover. Norton, who, according to one source, had 'no special pretensions to either force or finesse' (Watt, 117), was instructed by the Foreign Office to avoid interfering in Greek politics in the way Leeper had done. He did his best to obey this almost impossible injunction, but could 'not escape the vortex of Athenian politics' (Iatrides, 198). His suggestion that the regency of Damaskinos be extended to 1948, for example, resulted in accusations that he opposed the return to Greece of King George of the Hellenes. This was not the case. King George returned after a plebiscite in 1946, but it became increasingly clear that Britain was unable to bear the military burden of defeating communism in Greece. Norton was depressed by the ignorance about Greek affairs in Britain, deploring to the Foreign Office the fact that 'a newspaper of the standing of "The Times" should continue to depend on an unintelligent and unreliable Greek for its news from this country' (Norton to the Foreign Office, 9 May 1946, R 7098/1/19, PRO). But he realized that the USA would eventually have to take the lead in the defence of both Greece and Turkey. He therefore worked in tandem with his American colleague MacVeagh to reshape the Greek government along pro-western, democratic lines. Before he left Greece, in 1951, he was made an honorary citizen of Athens, and the communist threat had been defeated.

Norton retired from the foreign service on 31 December 1951, but continued to be employed as a UK alternate delegate to the United Nations in 1952 and 1953. In retirement, he was made president of the Anglo-Swiss Society, and was elected honorary fellow of Queen's College, Oxford. Writing of his role in the Polish tragedy, he said: 'We were actors in a moving tragedy, not proud of our roles, but saying our lines with conviction' (Gilbert and Gott, 370). He lived into great old age; he died at his home, 21A Carlyle Square, London, on 6 December 1990, just short of his hundredth year. PETER NEVILLE

Sources E. L. Woodward and R. Butler, eds., *Documents on British foreign policy, 1919–1939*, 3rd ser., 6 (1949) · M. Gilbert and R. Gott, *The appeasers* (1963), 252–60 · N. Clive, *A Greek experience* (1985), 175–8 · H. Richter, *British intervention in Greece* (1986) · J. O. Iatrides, 'Britain, the United States and Greece, 1945–9', *The Greek civil war, 1943–1950*, ed. D. H. Close (1993) · *The diaries of Sir Alexander Cadogan*, ed. D. Dilks (1971) · *The diplomatic diaries of Oliver Harvey, 1937–40*, ed. J. Harvey (New York, 1971) · D. Watt, 'Withdrawal from Greece: the end of balance-of-power diplomacy, the beginning of the cold war', *Age of austerity*, ed. M. Sissons and P. French (1963), 101–25 · Lord Vansittart [R. G. Vansittart], *The mist procession: the autobiography of Lord Vansittart* (1958) · *The Times* (14 Dec 1990) · *FO List* · *WWW, 1981–90* · Burke, *Peerage* · N. Rose, *Vansittart: study of a diplomat* (1978) · C. Norton to the foreign office, PRO, R 7098/1/19
Archives IWM, papers relating to service in Syria, Palestine, and Bern | PRO, FO 800 · PRO, Halifax MSS; Nevile Henderson MSS
Likenesses photograph, repro. in *The Times*
Wealth at death £1,631,629: probate, 12 March 1991, *CGPLA Eng. & Wales*

Norton, Edward (*bap.* **1654**, *d.* **1702**), conspirator, was the second son of Sir George Norton (*d.* 1677) of Abbots Leigh, Somerset, and Ellen, daughter of Sir William Owen of Condover in Shropshire. Norton's father, the ward of Sir John Strangeways, remained neutral during the civil war but did conceal Prince Charles at his house during the battle of Worcester, for which he was rewarded with a knighthood following the Restoration. In the late 1670s and early 1680s Edward Norton was active in London whig circles. He joined the notorious Green Ribbon Club and signed the May 1679 whig petition presented to the court of aldermen, which affirmed belief in the Popish Plot and called for a parliament to preserve the king and the protestant religion. He also stood for Westbury, Wiltshire, in 1679 on the interest of his brother-in-law, William Trenchard, unseating a court supporter on petition.

In September 1681 Norton was summoned before the privy council along with the whig barrister John Ayloffe on charges of suborning a government informer. In November 1681 he led a noisy demonstration in London celebrating the earl of Shaftesbury's acquittal by a Middlesex grand jury in which the mob shouted, 'no Popish successor, no York, a Monmouth, a Buckingham' and 'God bless the earl of Shaftesbury' (*CSP dom.*, 1680–81, 581). Norton was part of the lower circle of Rye House conspirators in 1682–3 along with Nathaniel Wade, Robert West, Robert Ferguson, and John Rumsey. Secretary Jenkins believed that Norton had a 'very deep hand in that treason' (*CSP dom.*, Jan–June 1683, 353). Following the plot's discovery in June 1683 Norton hid in London, where he lay wounded from 'a Whig and Tory brawl' and eventually escaped to the Netherlands (*CSP dom.*, July–Sept 1683, 11). On 26 June Secretary Jenkins issued a warrant for his arrest; his estate at Ashe, Dorset, was searched and some arms were discovered. Norton's estate was declared forfeit on 14 June 1684. While in exile Norton took the alias 'Mr Willoughby' and associated with the various whigs and dissenters gathered around the duke of Monmouth and the earl of Argyll. At one point Norton was sent back to England to inform the earl of Macclesfield of Monmouth's coming and to tell his brother Sir George Norton to prepare in Cheshire. Fellow conspirator Elizabeth Gaunt was responsible for his safe travel to and from London.

Following the failure of Monmouth's rebellion (in

which he did not participate), Norton was seen in the company of Robert Ferguson, Monmouth's army chaplain, and was supposedly lodging with him in Amsterdam. At one point Norton was joined by his brother Sir George, who had been in France. In 1686 Norton returned to England; he received a pardon on 10 June on the petition of his brother and on 12 November the outlawry against him was reversed. In November 1688 he readily joined the prince of Orange and received a commission in Captain Lord Mordaunt's regiment. Norton remained in the army from 1691 to 1699 as a major of marines. He was buried at Highgate in November or December 1702. He never married. In his will, dated 8 November 1702, he left 40s. to his sister Ellen. She had married William Trenchard of Cutteridge, and they eventually inherited the Norton family property. Their eldest son was John Trenchard, who co-authored *Cato's Letters* and the *Independent Whig*.

MELINDA ZOOK

Sources CSP dom., 1680–81, 302, 432, 483, 583; Jan–June 1683, 321, 314, 353; July–Sept 1683, 11, 39, 70, 119, 137, 151, 155, 158, 164, 183; 1684, 227–8; 1684–5, 13, 28; 1686–7, 615, 653, 1143 · N. Luttrell, *A brief historical relation of state affairs from September 1678 to April 1714*, 1 (1857), 267 · J. Collinson, *The history and antiquities of the county of Somerset*, 3 (1791), 153 · DNB · W. A. Shaw, ed., *Calendar of treasury books*, [33 vols. in 64], PRO (1904–69), vol. 7, pp. 1163, 1378 · *Condover register*, Salop Parish Register Society, Lichfield diocese, vol. 6, p. 108 · R. L. Greaves, *Secrets of the kingdom: British radicals from the Popish Plot to the revolution of 1688–89* (1992), 133, 172, 174, 178, 180, 193, 197, 230, 256, 258, 415, 296–9, 307–8, 412 · M. Zook, *Radical whigs and conspiratorial politics* (1999), 10, 103, 145n., 170, 199 · Burke, *Peerage* · PRO, PROB 11/469, sig. 72

Archives PRO, SP 44/54, p. 319 | BL, Middleton collection, corresp. of James Middleton, Add. MS 41818, fols. 77r–77v, 83r, 84, 108, 112v, 187r, 207v, 248r; 41817, fol. 218

Norton, Edward Felix (1884–1954), army officer and mountaineer, was born on 21 February 1884 at San Isidro, Argentina, the second son of Edward Norton, a director of the Royal Mail and Union Castle shipping lines, and his wife, Edith Sarah, the daughter of Sir Alfred Wills, judge of the Queen's Bench Division. His father established the Estancia la Ventura on wild pampas some 300 miles south of Buenos Aires, but Norton was taken back to England as an infant. He was educated at Charterhouse School and the Royal Military Academy, Woolwich, and was commissioned in 1902. In 1907 he was posted to Meerut, India, first with the Royal Field Artillery, then from 1910 with the Royal Horse Artillery. During this period he was aide-de-camp to the viceroy.

In 1914 Norton went to France, where he served throughout the First World War, some of the time as staff officer, Royal Artillery, to the Canadian corps and from 1917 as commander of D battery, Royal Horse Artillery. He was three times mentioned in dispatches, was appointed to the DSO, and was awarded the MC. After the war he commanded D battery in India and later served on the staff at Chanak at a time when British relations with the Turks called for much diplomacy and tact. On 18 December 1925 he married (Isabel) Joyce, the daughter of William Pasteur CB CMG, a physician, with whom he had three sons. Having attended the Staff College and later the

Edward Felix Norton (1884–1954), by H. Ruttledge, 1924

Imperial Defence College, he returned to India as senior instructor at the Staff College at Quetta (1929–32). He then became commander, Royal Artillery, to the 1st division at Aldershot, and subsequently brigadier-general staff to the Aldershot command. In 1937 he was appointed aide-de-camp to King George VI, in 1938 he commanded the Madras district, and in 1939 he was appointed CB.

As acting governor and commander-in-chief, Hong Kong (1940–41), Norton took a firm lead in bringing the inadequate air-raid shelter system up to scratch, so saving many lives when Japan invaded a few months later. While there he was severely injured in a riding accident, from which he never fully recovered. It forced his retirement in 1942, at which time he was holding command of the western independent district in India. He was granted the honorary rank of lieutenant-general. After returning to England he became commander of the north Hampshire sector of the Home Guard (1942–4); when the Home Guard was disbanded he went on to serve as Hampshire's county Army Cadet Force commandant (1944–8). In 1947 he was appointed colonel commandant of the Royal Horse Artillery.

Norton began alpine climbing at the Eagle's Nest above Sixt, in the Haute-Savoie, a chalet built by his grandfather Sir Alfred Wills, who was founder and third president of the Alpine Club. There, with his brother, Norton stalked chamois over ground which was so bad that even the local men kept off it. During his long service abroad he climbed wherever the opportunity offered, and in 1922 he was selected for the second British Mount Everest expedition. With George Leigh Mallory and (Theodore) Howard Somervell he reached the then record height of 26,985 feet. They were the first to pass the critical level of 8000 metres, and this without supplementary oxygen. In 1924, when the leader, Charles Granville Bruce, was taken ill, Norton took charge of the difficult third Everest expedition. After many crushing setbacks, and hazards owing to blizzards and ferocious winds, Norton led the first serious summit attempt. Again he climbed without oxygen, an aid for which he had little respect. At 28,000 feet his companion, Somervell, was stopped by severe throat trouble and Norton continued alone to a height of 28,126 feet. He reached the great couloir on the north face, which later became popularly known as Norton's couloir. This, too, was an altitude record, and it was fifty-four years before anyone climbed higher without oxygen. Another summit bid was undertaken a few days later by Mallory and Andrew Comyn Irvine, from which neither man returned. Norton handled this tragedy and the publicity it engendered with impeccable dignity, and his dispatches from Mount Everest after the loss are among the most lucid and moving examples of mountain writing. He also wrote the greater part of the official expedition book, *The Fight for Everest, 1924*.

In 1922 Norton was elected to the Alpine Club, of which in later years he twice refused the presidency on health grounds; he was a founder member of the Himalayan Club and an original member of the Mountain Club of India. In common with other members of the 1922 Everest expedition, he was awarded an Olympic silver-gilt medal (the prix d'Alpinisme, presented at the 1924 winter Olympics), and in 1926 he received the founder's medal of the Royal Geographical Society. In 1953 he was consulted by Brigadier John Hunt, who led the first successful Everest expedition and who was always quick to acknowledge Norton's useful strategic advice.

Tall and athletic in figure, Norton was a fine horseman, a keen shot, and an enthusiastic fisherman. His service years offered him plenty of scope for adventurous sports, but he was interested, too, in natural history, and on his trips to Everest made collections of birds and flowers for the British Museum (Natural History). He was a skilled draughtsman and watercolourist, with a preference for painting landscapes, several of which have been reproduced in the Everest literature. He also had a talent for quick and often witty sketches of his companions. A man of many interests, he was widely read, well informed, and a charming companion. Integrity was the essence of his character. He was a born leader and, in the army, popular with all ranks; he understood and got on well with Indians and with the Gurkhas, Sherpas, and Bhotias on Everest. Norton died at his home, Morestead Grove, Morestead, Winchester, on 3 November 1954, survived by his wife, Joyce. T. G. LONGSTAFF, rev. AUDREY SALKELD

Sources personal knowledge (1971) · private information (1971) · T. H. Somervell and T. G. Longstaff, *Alpine Journal*, 60 (1955), 157–60 · *GJ*, 121 (1955), 123 · E. Shipton, 'Norton of Everest', *GJ*, 121 (1955), 84–5 · R. C. W. and T. G. Longstaff, *Himalayan Journal*, 19 (1955–6), 183–6 · m. cert. · d. cert.

Archives King's Lond., Liddell Hart C., MSS incl. some relating to service as acting governor of Hong Kong · priv. coll., Norton Everest archive, letters, diaries, paintings, sketches, and photographs | Alpine Club, London · RGS, Everest expedition archives | FILM BFI NFTVA, record footage | SOUND priv. coll.

Likenesses H. Ruttledge, photograph, 1924, RGS [see illus.] · W. Stoneman, photograph, 1952, NPG · photograph, repro. in *Alpine Journal*, facing p. 158 · photographs, RGS, Alpine Club, John Noel photographic collection · photographs, priv. coll.

Wealth at death £51,385 7s. 7d.: probate, 2 July 1955, *CGPLA Eng. & Wales*

Norton, Fletcher, first Baron Grantley (1716–1789), speaker of the House of Commons, was born at Grantley, near Ripon, Yorkshire, on 23 June 1716, the eldest son of Thomas Norton (*d.* 1719) and his wife, Elizabeth, daughter of William Serjeantson of Hanlith, near Skipton, Yorkshire. His father died when he was less than three years old. He was educated at school in Ripon under Mr Stephens and was admitted to St John's College, Cambridge, in 1734. He was admitted a member of the Middle Temple on 14 November 1734, called to the bar on 6 July 1739, and was for many years leader of the northern circuit. In 1754 he became a king's counsel and was elected a bencher of his inn. On 21 May 1741 he married Grace (1707/8–1803), eldest daughter of Sir William Chapple and Treherne Clifford; they had five sons, including Chapple *Norton, and two daughters, but a son and a daughter died in infancy.

In 1756 Norton was elected to the House of Commons for the borough of Appleby, Westmorland. He was elected one of the members for Wigan, Lancashire, in 1761, and in 1768 he was returned for Guildford, Surrey, the seat he held until his elevation to the peerage in 1782. On 25 January 1762 he was appointed solicitor-general under the Bute administration. He was knighted on the same day and created DCL of Oxford University on 20 October. From 1763 to 1765, under the Grenville administration, he was attorney-general, a post he lost on the formation of a new administration by the marquess of Rockingham. On 19 February 1769 he was appointed chief justice in eyre south of the Trent, a sinecure paying a salary of £3000 per annum which he admitted years later was too great a reward for the duties involved. He was sworn of the privy council on 22 March. In 1763, while solicitor-general, he took part in the prosecution of John Wilkes for publishing no. 45 of the *North Briton* and *Essay on Woman*. In 1765, while attorney-general, he took part in the prosecution before the House of Lords of William, Baron Byron, for the murder of William Chaworth.

On 22 January 1770 Norton was elected speaker of the House of Commons following the resignation of Sir John Cust. The election was contested, Norton being the administration's candidate, proposed by Lord North and seconded by Richard Rigby. His opponent, Thomas Townshend, was proposed by Lord John Cavendish and seconded by Lord George Sackville on behalf of the opposition, even though Townshend himself had declined to be nominated. Norton was elected by 237 votes to 121. It is said he

Fletcher Norton, first Baron Grantley (1716–1789), by Sir William Beechey

accepted the speakership with reluctance and only on condition he could keep his sinecure and resign in order to be appointed lord chief justice if a vacancy arose. In respect of the latter condition he was to be disappointed.

Norton's political career both before and after becoming speaker was highly controversial. On 17 February 1764, during the debate on the illegality of general warrants, he told the house that if he were a judge he would pay no more regard to the resolution than to the opinion of a drunken porter. During the debate on the repeal of the Stamp Act on 27 January 1766 he crossed swords with the elder Pitt, accusing him of having sounded the trumpet to rebellion. In 1769 he fiercely attacked George Grenville for his defence of John Wilkes's claim to take his seat as the lawfully elected member for Middlesex.

Norton's choleric disposition regularly involved him in arguments with other members after he became speaker. At the same time there is ample evidence that he came to the chair determined to maintain order and enforce the rules of procedure. On the very first day of business following his election to the chair he called certain members of the opposition to order because he objected to their language and was commended by Lord North for his intervention. He had been in the chair less than a month when, on 16 February 1770, he offended Sir William Meredith during a debate on a resolution relating to the irrepressible John Wilkes. Meredith had proposed that the question, being a complicated one, should be separated into two parts and asked the speaker for a ruling. Norton angrily rebuked Meredith, saying 'it would have been but

candid in Sir William to have appraised him of his intention … that he might have been prepared' (Cobbett, *Parl. hist.*, 16, 1765–71, 808). Meredith protested that 'the Speaker had used him very ill' (ibid.), upon which Norton repeated his reproach in even stronger language. At this point several members demanded that Norton's words should be taken down as disorderly. The words alleged to have been used by Norton were written down by a protesting member and handed to the clerk, who read them out, upon which Norton declared these were not the words he had used. Matters immediately became worse, but in the course of the angry exchanges which ensued Norton was moved to concede that he had had no intention of reflecting on Sir William's character. Several members seized this opportunity to suggest that the speaker had effectively apologized, but Norton angrily repudiated any such interpretation. The undignified wrangle dragged on for six hours until even the offended parties desired to have done with it. The matter was settled when a motion critical of the speaker was negatived without a division.

Norton was speaker at a time when the reporting of debates was still considered a breach of parliamentary privilege and the agitation for press freedom was at its height. On 8 May 1771 an angry mob broke the windows of his house in consequence of the committal to the Tower of Brass Crosby, the lord mayor of London, and Alderman Richard Oliver, who had fallen foul of the Commons by protecting the printers of offending newspapers. As speaker it was Norton's duty to sign the warrants for committal in execution of the orders of the house.

In the year that he became speaker Norton angered the king by supporting Grenville's bill for the determination of election petitions by select committees rather than on the floor of the house, thus lessening somewhat the influence of the crown over the process. The representative system was an important source of court patronage and the king was opposed to any attempt to reform it. Another brush with royalty occurred in March 1772, resulting from Norton's interventions in the committee stage debates on the Royal Marriage Bill. His objection was to the penalty clause, but it has been surmised that his real motivation was to embarrass the administration for denying him favours. Provocative and unmannerly though he was, the Commons did not hesitate to vindicate Norton when a letter by John Horne (later Horne-Tooke) was published in the *Public Advertiser* denouncing his conduct as speaker. A unanimous resolution was adopted on 11 February 1774, declaring the letter to be 'a false, malicious and scandalous libel' (Cobbett, *Parl. hist.*, 17, 1771–4, 1016). He was re-elected speaker without opposition on 29 November of the same year.

Norton gave far more serious offence to the king on 7 May 1777 when presenting for the royal assent a money bill relating to the civil list debt. This event marked a crucial turning point in his relations with the administration and his rising popularity with the opposition who were able to make political capital out of it. In the course of his speech he said that the Commons 'have not only granted to your Majesty a large present supply, but also a great additional revenue, great beyond example; great beyond your Majesty's highest expense' (Cobbett, *Parl. hist.*, 19, 1777–8, 213). Two days later he was violently condemned for this speech by Richard Rigby; but Charles James Fox, seizing his opportunity, declared that since the speaker had been charged with misrepresenting the view of the house it was necessary to take the sense of the house. He therefore moved a motion in vindication of the speaker, and Norton, appreciating Fox's strategy, made it clear he could not remain speaker unless the motion was adopted. The ministry had no wish to provoke a crisis over the speakership and Fox's motion was carried without a division, followed by a vote of thanks to the speaker. The event also earned Norton the approval of the corporation of the City of London, who on 14 May 1777 conferred on him the freedom of the City.

Norton's breach with the ministry was now beyond repair and during the remaining years of his speakership he showed a continuing disposition to be the darling of the opposition. He supported Edmund Burke's Establishment Bill and on 13 March 1780 he was called upon by Fox when the bill was in committee to give his opinion on the competence of the house to enquire into and control the civil list expenditure. He gave a lengthy speech in the bill's favour, in the course of which he said that 'Parliament had an inherent right vested in it of controlling and regulating every branch of the public expenditure, the civil list as well as the rest' (Cobbett, *Parl. hist.*, 21, 1780–81, 267–8). He concluded by launching a bitter attack against Lord North, largely induced by the rumoured appointment of attorney-general Wedderburn as chief justice of the common pleas. He maintained this was a violation of the agreement made when he was first elected speaker, a claim Lord North denied. Norton subsequently apologized for his outburst but maintained the truth of what he had asserted. It was during this speech that he acknowledged the unwarranted generosity of the emoluments attached to the sinecure office of chief justice in eyre south of the Trent.

On 6 April 1780 Norton supported Dunning's famous resolution 'that the influence of the Crown has increased, is increasing and ought to be diminished'. The substance of the resolution, carried by 233 votes to 215, had been foreshadowed by Norton himself during the debate in committee on Burke's bill. On 1 May he denounced a government bill for the appointment of commissioners to examine the public accounts on the ground that it would simply create new placemen at the nomination of the minister.

The king and the ministry were determined that Norton should not remain speaker, and the new parliament which met on 31 October 1780 gave them their opportunity. Their candidate was Charles Wolfran Cornwall, the excuse given for supplanting Norton being the state of his health. John Dunning rose to propose Norton's re-election, expressing mock surprise that Lord North had not risen to do so himself. Norton was seconded by Thomas Townshend, after which Norton spoke himself,

declaring that only an idiot would believe that the reason for removing him was the state of his health. Cornwall was elected by 203 votes to 134. On 20 November a resolution of thanks to the late speaker was moved by Townshend and carried by 136 votes to 96. On 1 February 1781 the new speaker conveyed to Norton the thanks of the house as ordered by the resolution. It is recorded that he did so in a few cold words, to which Norton returned a curt acknowledgement.

Norton remained a member of the Commons on ceasing to be speaker and continued as a vigorous opponent of the administration. He spoke in support of the opposition in a number of important debates, notably on 12 December 1781 when he supported Sir James Lowther's motion for bringing the American war to an end. Ever a consistent defender of the right of the Commons to unfettered control over public expenditure, he declared 'that until this was done not a single shilling should be voted as supply to his Majesty' (Cobbett, *Parl. hist.*, 22, 1781–2, 814).

The installation of the second Rockingham administration in 1782 paved the way for Norton's elevation to the peerage. The king, of course, had no wish to confer any kind of honour on Norton, and would not have done so without Rockingham's insistence. John Dunning had already been elevated to the peerage without Rockingham's knowledge on the recommendation of Secretary of State Lord Shelburne, and Rockingham, being first lord of the Treasury (and effectively prime minister), was incensed at not having been consulted. Supported by Fox, Burke, and other members of the new administration, he insisted that another peer should be created on his personal recommendation without delay. The choice fell on Norton as being the only available candidate with claims comparable to those of Dunning, and on 9 April 1782 he was created Baron Grantley of Markenfield. Although his peerage was not bestowed in direct recognition of his service as speaker, the tradition that a retiring speaker is automatically entitled to a peerage probably derives from his ennoblement.

In the House of Lords Grantley was not very active, although he gave some signs of reverting to his former allegiance. He opposed Fox's East India Bill in 1783 and voted for that of Pitt in 1784. The last time he spoke in the Lords was on 19 March 1788 when he opposed the third reading of the East India Declaratory Bill.

Norton lacked the qualities of an ideal speaker and did not pursue the high standards set by Arthur Onslow, who was speaker from 1734 to 1761. He was coarse, tactless, ill-tempered, and careless of whom he offended. On the other hand he was bold, able, outspoken and certainly nobody's lackey. He was firm in his control of the house and there is no evidence that his partisanship influenced his duties as speaker. He was disliked by many of his contemporaries and his reputation for greed earned him the unflattering nickname of Sir Bull-Face Double Fee, a slur on both his appearance and his integrity. He died on 1 January 1789, aged seventy-two, at his house at 63 Lincoln's Inn Fields, London, probably from complications associated with asthma. He was buried at Wonersh, Surrey, on 9 January. He was survived by his widow, who died on 30 October 1803, said to be aged ninety-five.

PHILIP LAUNDY

Sources P. D. G. Thomas, *The House of Commons in the 18th century* (1971), esp. 312–62 · J. Brooke, 'Norton, Fletcher', HoP, *Commons, 1754–90* · P. A. C. Laundy, *The office of speaker* (1964), 275–82 · A. I. Dasent, *The speakers of the House of Commons* (1911), 276–82 · E. Porritt, *The unreformed House of Commons*, 1 (1903), 280, 453, 458–60 · M. Macdonagh, *The speaker of the house* (1921), 31, 47, 278–84 · J. A. Manning, *The lives of the speakers of the House of Commons* (1850), 445–56 · Cobbett, *Parl. hist.*, 16.807–11; 17.422–3, 1006–16; 19.213, 224, 227–34; 21.258–69, 270–73, 355–9, 561–3, 793–807, 1106, 1144; 22.813–15; 27.245–7 · N. W. Wraxall, *Historical memoirs of his own time*, new edn, 4 vols. (1836) · N. W. Wraxall, *Posthumous memoirs of his own time*, 2nd edn, 3 vols. (1836) · H. Walpole, *Memoirs of the reign of King George the Third*, ed. D. Le Marchant, 4 vols. (1845) · Walpole, *Corr.* · *The last journals of Horace Walpole*, ed. Dr Doran, rev. A. F. Steuart, 2 vols. (1910) · *DNB*
Archives BL, letters and legal opinions · Harvard U., law school, legal notebooks and papers
Likenesses J. Sayers, caricature, etching, pubd 1782, BM, NPG · J. Sayers, caricature, etching, pubd 1783, NPG · W. Beechey, oils, Palace of Westminster, London [*see illus.*] · Ingoldsby, caricature, repro. in Dasent, *Speakers of the House of Commons* · stipple, NPG · stipple and line engraving, NPG; repro. in *Town and Country Magazine*

Norton [*née* Freke], **Frances, Lady Norton** (1644–1731), religious writer, was born on 22 May 1644 in Oxford, the third of five daughters of Ralph Freke (*bap.* 1596, *d.* 1684) of Hannington, Wiltshire, and his wife, Cicely (*bap.* 1610, *d.* 1651), daughter of Sir Thomas Culpepper, of Hollingbourne, Kent, and his wife, Elizabeth. After the death of their mother, Frances and her sisters, Elizabeth *Freke (1642–1714), Cicely, Judith, and Philippa, were brought up by their father and an aunt, Frances, a sister of their mother who married their father's brother William Freke and who also lived at Hannington.

About 1672 Frances married her first husband, Sir George Norton (1647/8–1715), of Abbots Leigh, Somerset. Sir George Norton is said in several sources to have been a royalist who concealed Charles II in his house; however, the king's protector was his father, also Sir George and a documented royalist. They had three children: George and Elizabeth (who both died young), and Grace [*see* Gethin, Grace, Lady Gethin].

George Ballard, writing in 1752, gives Lady Norton credit for Grace's education, in particular for 'observing in her daughter a capacity capable of great improvement' and 'giving her all the advantages of a liberal education' (Ballard, 363). Grace Gethin's untimely death at the age of twenty-one in October 1697 prompted her mother's entry into print: Gethin's *Reliquae Gethinianae* was published in 1699 'at the Request and Desire' of her mother (unpaginated prefatory page) and Norton then published two works of her own in 1705, bound together in a small quarto volume and entitled *The Applause of Virtue* and *Memento mori, or, Meditations on Death*. She dedicated these essays and meditations to her cousins 'Madam Freke, of Shroten' (sig. A2r) and Elizabeth Hambleton, both of whom had suffered losses of their own and had been of support to her in 'Seven Years' of 'sharp Tryal'

(unpaginated prefatory page). Norton describes the volumes' content: 'your self can witness (Dear Cousin) the several Methods I try'd to paliate that Grief, which could not be extinguished but by the common Fates of Mortals' (unpaginated prefatory page). The two volumes contain prose deliberations on virtue and on death, weaving together the wisdom of biblical figures, church fathers, ancient philosophers, and others. Norton describes her method in the dedicatory epistles to the volumes, insisting that she is not a drone 'eating the Honey which the Bees gathered', but rather that the wisdom of her essays and meditations is 'taken from, and is grounded upon, the best Orthodox Writers of our True and Pure Religion; as my Quotations prove' (unpaginated prefatory pages). *Memento mori* concludes with a poem entitled 'A Short Ejaculation, or Hymn, Preparatory for Death' (p. 108).

Norton also published *A miscellany of poems, compos'd, and work'd with a needle, on the backs and seats & c. of several chairs and stools* (1714). The volume is now extremely rare, one copy being held in the Central Library, Bristol. It is of interest in the context of this volume that Ballard knew in 1745 of 'several pieces of furniture of her own working, with many devout sentences wrought on them' extant at Abbots Leigh (Ballard, 435–6).

Norton's first husband died aged sixty-seven on 26 April 1715, and while it is reputed that she had already been living separately from him for several years, there is no evidence of this. On 23 April 1718 at the Chapel Royal, Whitehall, she married her second husband, Colonel Ambrose Norton (*c.*1646–1723), who was her first husband's cousin. After his death, on 10 September 1723, she married her third husband, William Jones, at the Somerset House chapel on 24 September 1724. In addition to the house at Abbots Leigh, she is known to have had residences in London on Brownlow Street and Ormond Street. Norton died on 20 February 1731. She was buried in the south aisle of Westminster Abbey on 9 March 1731. William Jones had predeceased her.

SARAH ROSS

Sources 'A pedigree or genealogy of ye family of the Frekes', Bodl. Oxf., MS Eng. misc. c. 203 · J. Hutchins, *The history and antiquities of the county of Dorset*, 4 (1873) · J. Cave-Browne, *The story of Hollingborne, its church and clergy* (1890) · Kent church notes, BL, Add. MS 11259 · parish register, Hollingbourne · parish register, Hannington · Elizabeth Freke's remembrances and miscellaneous papers, BL, Add. MSS 45718–45721 · J. L. Chester, ed., *The marriage, baptismal, and burial registers of the collegiate church or abbey of St Peter, Westminster*, Harleian Society, 10 (1876) · G. Gethin, *Reliquae Gethinianae* (1699) · BL, Harrington MSS, 11, Add. MS 46373B · *Le Neve's Pedigrees of the knights*, ed. G. W. Marshall, Harleian Society, 8 (1873) · G. Ballard, *Memoirs of several ladies of Great Britain* (1752) · D. F. Foxon, ed., *English verse, 1701–1750: a catalogue of separately printed poems with notes on contemporary collected editions*, 2 vols. (1975) · F. A. Crisp, *Abstracts of Somersetshire wills* (1890) · will, PRO, PROB 11/642, fols. 316r–317r
Wealth at death £2000; plus £500 p.a. jointure from first husband, plus other small rents, and payments made to her on annual basis: will, PRO, PROB 11/642, fols. 316r–317r

Norton, Frederic [*real name* George Frederick Norton] (1869–1946), singer and songwriter, was born at 1 Sun Terrace, Great Cheetham Street, Broughton, Salford, Lancashire, on 11 October 1869, the son of George Norton, a cheese factor, and his wife, Ann Hunstone. He had at least one sister. Having worked originally as a clerk in insurance, he later became a professional singer, touring as an operatic chorister with the Carl Rosa Opera Company and making occasional appearances in the musical theatre. At the same time he wrote the music for a number of parlour songs, which he performed in recital with 'an agreeable voice and pleasing delivery' (*The Era*, 22 Nov 1902), and had the occasional number performed in West End musical comedies. In 1903 he was invited to Sandringham to entertain the king and queen with his songs at the piano ('Mama's Baby Boy', 'The Camel and the Butterfly', 'Madcap Marjorie', 'Tatters and Tucks', 'Oh Mr Moon', 'Naughty Little Maid', and so on). In 1908 he was introduced by Mrs T. P. O'Connor to the artist and writer W. Graham Robertson, and the two composed the words and music to a musical fairy play, *Pinkie and the Fairies*, which, thanks to Robertson's high-theatrical connections, was produced as a Christmas entertainment at His Majesty's Theatre, with Ellen Terry and Mrs Patrick Campbell among its cast.

Norton later returned to His Majesty's Theatre to help Herbert Beerbohm Tree with his organization of Offenbach's score for *Orpheus in the Underground* (1912), but thereafter he worked as a singer in the Musketeers concert party and as an intermittent composer of songs for revue and music hall until he was once again recalled to work with Tree. This time the commission was a larger one, to provide the score for Oscar Asche's fairy-tale spectacular *Chu Chin Chow* (1916). *Chu Chin Chow* was a record-breaking wartime success in London, and went on to be seen in America and Australia and also on the cinema screen before returning for several revivals on the British stage and even as an ice show. Norton's score threw up the two most popular songs he had ever written—the duet 'Any Time's Kissing Time', introduced by Courtice Pounds and Aileen d'Orme, and the baritone 'Cobbler's Song', which would remain a concert standard for more than half a century. It also included some rather more appreciable music from a composer whose usual produce was of the lightest kind, with such pieces as the lament 'I Long for the Sun', where the long phrased soprano lines seem to reach out in front of the singer. Norton made the most of his big hit, going on at various times in several of *Chu Chin Chow*'s principal parts, notably in Pounds's star role of Ali Baba.

Norton never wrote another piece of the scope of *Chu Chin Chow*. On the back of his hit he was hired to do the score for Lilie Elsie's pale and not very lingering comeback piece *Pamela* (1917), but thereafter he returned to the same kind of work he had always done, providing the occasional song for interpolation in scores by others and writing little tunes for such pieces as the amateur *The Willow Pattern Plate* or the children's Christmas show *Teddie Tail* (1920). *Chu Chin Chow*, however, ensured that his name appeared regularly on theatre bills right up to the end of his life. Norton never married. He died at his home, Hare Knap, Holford, near Bridgwater, Somerset, on 15 December 1946.

KURT GÄNZL

Sources K. Gänzl, *The encyclopedia of the musical theatre*, 2 vols. (1994) · K. Gänzl, *The British musical theatre*, 2 vols. (1986) · W. G. Robertson, *Time was: the reminiscences of W. Graham Robertson* (1931) · b. cert. · *CGPLA Eng. & Wales* (1947) · will of Frederick Norton · 'Mr F. Norton's song recital', *The Era* (22 Nov 1902), 12
Wealth at death £623 19s. 3d.: probate, 31 March 1947, *CGPLA Eng. & Wales*

Norton, Sir Gregory, first baronet (*c*.1603–1652), politician and regicide, was the eldest surviving son of Henry Norton of Charlton, in Wantage, Berkshire, and Elizabeth, daughter of William Nelston of Challeworth in the same county. He probably grew up in Ireland, possibly in Dublin, where his family was prominent in administrative affairs. Although he acquired an estate in Sussex upon his marriage, some time before 1621, to Martha (*d*. in or before 1671), daughter of Bradshaw Drew and widow of John Gunter, Norton was in Dublin in April 1624 when he was awarded a baronetcy. By 1626 he appears to have settled in Densworth, Sussex, although after a brief spell at Gray's Inn (to which he was admitted in August 1629) he probably spent much of his time in London.

In 1634 Norton was appointed to the band of gentleman pensioners but this court position did not prevent his parliamentarian allegiance becoming apparent upon the outbreak of civil war. As such his career mirrored that of another gentleman pensioner, Humphrey Edwards, to whom Norton was evidently close and with whom he secured compensation from parliament for the loss of his office. Norton was an assiduous member of the local administration in Sussex and the Isle of Wight, where he was proposed for military service. He was returned to parliament in October 1645 as a recruiter MP for Midhurst in Sussex, and he soon emerged as an energetic supporter of the independent faction. He was particularly active in relation to Ireland and on the committee for Irish affairs, to which he was appointed as part of a manoeuvre by independents in May 1646. In January 1647 he was proposed as a privy councillor for Ireland, although he remained in England. He also played a prominent part in independent attempts to undermine the influence of the Scots, and his London interests ensured that he became involved in independent attempts to raise money from the City, and to secure control of its militia in early 1647. Norton was one of the independents who fled to the army after the presbyterian 'counter-revolution', and he signed the declaration of protest issued on 4 August. Although he returned to Westminster in September 1647 he was one of many independents who appear to have been absent from the Commons for much of the second half of 1648, prior to Pride's Purge on 6 December.

When Norton returned to Westminster, however, his status as a leading independent was confirmed by his nomination to a host of important committees. His rapid taking of the 'dissent' on 20 December 1648 affirmed his opposition to negotiations with the king, and his position among the most radical MPs. He was involved in proceedings against Charles I from 23 December, and as a commissioner for the high court of justice attended every session of the trial before signing the death warrant [*see also* Regicides]. He remained a prominent member of the Rump after the execution and appears to have shared the political radicalism of Henry Marten and some of the religious enthusiasm of Thomas Harrison. A probable advocate of the abolition of kingship, he also helped to organize the sale of property belonging to both the crown and delinquents, although the latter concern was not disinterested and his own gains from such sales led to suspicions of corruption.

Once the impetus for radical reform became dissipated in the second half of 1649, Norton became less active at Westminster. He may have been encouraged by the imposition of the engagement oath in January 1650, and by the wave of republican enthusiasm after the battle of Worcester in September 1651, but he failed to resume a leading role in the Commons and died in 1652; he was buried on 26 March of that year. His wife, from whom he may have been estranged, returned from France to settle the estate, the bulk of which had already been settled on Norton's trustee, Humphrey Edwards, while Norton's 'unnaturally disobedient son' Henry was effectively disinherited (PRO, PROB 11/223, fol. 202v). Henry succeeded to the baronetcy, however, and later sat in parliament in 1659. In October 1655 Norton's widow married Robert Gordon, Viscount Kenmure, a leading Scottish royalist. At the Restoration, Norton's estate, which included the royal manor of Richmond, was forfeited to the crown.   J. T. PEACEY

Sources GEC, *Baronetage* · *JHC*, 2–7 (1640–59) · C. H. Firth and R. S. Rait, eds., *Acts and ordinances of the interregnum, 1642–1660*, 3 vols. (1911) · *CSP dom.*, 1637–61 · *CSP Ire.*, 1633–60 · D. Underdown, *Pride's Purge: politics in the puritan revolution* (1971) · B. Worden, *The Rump Parliament, 1648–1653* (1974) · J. G. Muddiman, *The trial of King Charles the First* (1928) · will, PRO, PROB 11/223, fol. 202v · R. K. G. Temple, 'Norton, Sir Gregory', Greaves & Zaller, *BDBR* · M. Noble, *The lives of the English regicides*, 2 vols. (1798) · Badminton House, Beaufort archives, FM H2/4/1 · valuation of regicides' estates, 1660, PRO, LR 2/266, fol. 1v

Wealth at death £400 p.a. from estates: LR 2/266, fol. 1v; will, PRO, PROB 11/223, fol. 202v

Norton, Humphrey (*fl.* 1655–1660), Quaker missionary and author, first appears in the records in March 1655 when he was briefly imprisoned for his beliefs at Durham; he was also noted as preaching in Essex the same year. From September 1655 to May 1656 he lived in London, where he served as the accredited agent for the 'Public Friends' (travelling Quaker preachers). In April 1656 he offered himself 'body for body' in lieu of George Fox, then imprisoned in Cornwall. In June, he was preaching in Ireland in Leinster, Munster, and Connaught. He was driven violently from Galway only to be seized at Wexford while conducting a meeting. Committed to gaol until the next court of assizes, he wrote *To All People that Speakes of an Outward Baptisme; Dippers, Sprinklers and Others* (published in 1659), in which he responded to the objections to Quakerism raised by Thomas Larkham, a minister at Wexford.

Norton returned to England by early 1657, and on 1 June he sailed with ten other Friends for Boston, as part of a concerted campaign to bring Quakerism to colonial North America. A brief account of the voyage of this 'Quaker Ark' (as one scholar described it) by their captain, Robert Fowler, was published in 1659 as *A Quakers Sea-Journal being a True Relation of a Voyage to New-England*. The ship landed at Rhode Island on or about 12 August. In October Norton proceeded to Sandwich, Massachusetts, where he was arrested for being an 'extravagant person', thought 'guilty of divers horred errors', and detained without examination (Norton and Rous, 25; Shurtleff, 123). He presented a paper that set forth his purpose in coming, and required that he be 'publikely punished, if not, cleared' (Norton and Rous, 25). Unable to convict him of heresy, the colonial court banished Norton for vagrancy on 6 October 1657.

The following February Norton travelled to Southold, Long Island. He was promptly arrested and taken to New Haven, Connecticut, where he was imprisoned for three weeks in shackles. A special court was convened on 10 March and Norton was charged with trying to spread heretical beliefs and disturbing the peace by interrupting church services. When Norton attempted to reply to the charges made by John Davenport, a puritan clergyman, a 'great Iron Key' was bound over his mouth (Norton and Rous, 50). After two days of trial he was recommitted for ten days; he was then whipped, branded with an 'H' for heresy on his right hand ('to hinder him from Writing' he later claimed), heavily fined (the sum was met, without Norton's consent, by a sympathetic Dutch colonist), and banished from New Haven (ibid., 105). Shortly afterwards, partly it seems to justify their treatment of Norton, the authorities drew up anti-Quaker legislation modelled on that recently passed by the Massachusetts government.

Norton returned to Rhode Island, where the presence of Quakers was tolerated. There he met up with a fellow missionary from Barbados, John Rous, and together they journeyed to Plymouth for that colony's general court in order to protest against the treatment of Quakers. They arrived on 1 June and were summarily incarcerated, during which time Norton presented a written list of complaints against the local government. Despite two examinations and a trial (at which the two men behaved 'turbulently'), the authorities were unable to secure a conviction for heresy; instead, when Rous and Norton refused to swear an oath of allegiance, they were flogged (Shurtleff, 139). On 10 June they were released and returned to Rhode Island. On 16 June Norton wrote a caustic rebuke to Thomas Prince, charging false accusations, 'aspersions', and other actions 'contrary to law, equity, and justice and judgement'. Prince had defrauded poor Friends through fines and hindered Norton's effort to 'speak in the people's hearing striving what thou could to stain the truth of God with thy envious tongue'. In crescendo, Norton promised Governor Prince 'vengeance' from God 'if thou repent not' (Cadbury, 294). Not surprisingly the colonial authorities considered the letter as 'horrible railing contempt and pernicious wickedness' and ordered him apprehended (ibid., 293).

In July Norton and Rous headed for Boston but upon their arrival were warned by a local inhabitant not to stay; the previous day one of their fellow missionaries had been nearly whipped to death. Moreover, Norton had 'been expected certain moneths' by the authorities (Norton and Rous, 79). Undaunted the two publicly clashed with the puritan minister John Norton, a leading persecutor of the Quakers. They were presented to the magistrates, imprisoned for three days, whipped, and returned to prison. On 18 July Boston authorities ordered that Quakers in prison be flogged twice a week. By now, however, public opinion expressed weariness of the repeated cruelties and a subscription was made to pay prison fees and forward the prisoners to Providence, Rhode Island. This was not the last clash that Norton would have with the Boston authorities. The following month Rous and two other Quakers had their right ears cropped following a trial at Boston. Norton responded to this punishment with a fierce letter to Endecott, listing a series of curses against the governor and the colony; the letter was made public and gained Norton a great deal of further notoriety, to which he responded in an open letter to Endecott and John Norton.

In January or February 1659 Norton travelled to Barbados where he met up again with Rous. About April they sailed to England, co-writing *New-England's Ensigne*, 'Written at Sea, by us whom the Wicked in scorn calls *Quakers*', a catalogue of all they and their associates had endured in New England, including several of their oral and written rebuttals of magistrates and ministers. Norton set the tone for the work with his opening declaration that:

> Greater hypocrites are not under the Sun then they are in word, and in shew they appear beautiful unto men, but in covetousness and deceitful dealing, secret lust, and dissimulation, they flow; Penitency nor Mercy, Justice nor Righteousness in reality, is not in the least amongst them. (Norton and Rous, 1)

In its concluding summary of the Quaker sufferings, Norton's were enumerated as four imprisonments, four banishments, twenty days in irons, four whippings, one £10 fine, and one branding. Norton and Rous also collaborated on the similarly spirited *The Secret Workes of a Cruel People Made Manifest*, published in London the same year. Little is known of Norton's life after his return, although he was back in Rhode Island by 1660. According to Fox, Norton later became disaffected from, and disowned by, the Society of Friends he had previously so ardently defended. The date and place of his death are uncertain.

STEVEN C. HARPER and I. GADD

Sources 'Dictionary of Quaker biography', RS Friends, Lond. [card index] • W. C. Braithwaite, *The second period of Quakerism*, ed. H. J. Cadbury, 2nd edn (1961) • *The journal of George Fox*, ed. N. Penney, 2 vols. (1911) • J. Besse, *A collection of the sufferings of the people called Quakers*, 2 vols. (1753) • F. B. Tolles, 'A Quaker's curse—Humphrey Norton to John Endecott, 1658', *Huntington Library Quarterly*, 14 (1950–51), 415–21 • H. J. Cadbury, 'Humphrey Norton and the court at Plymouth', *Huntington Library Quarterly*, 15 (1951–2), 291–6 • N. B. Shurtleff and D. Pulsifer, eds., *Records of the colony of New Plymouth in New England*, 12 vols. (1855–61), vol. 3 • J. Bowden, *The history of the Society of Friends in America*, 1 (1850) • C. J. Hoadly, *Records of the colony or jurisdiction of New Haven* (1858), 232–3 • A. J. Worrall, *Quakers in the colonial northeast* (1980) • H. Norton and J. Rous, *New-England's ensigne* (1659) • F. Howgill, *The dawning of a brighter day* (1676) • *The Mayflower descendant, 1620–1937*, 18 (1916), 71–7 • *The secret workes of a cruel people made manifest* (1659) • F. Howgill, *The popish inquisition newly erected in New-England* (1659) • DNB **Archives** Plymouth, Massachusetts, county registry of deeds, book 2, pp. 85–8

Norton, James Lansdowne (1869–1925), motor cycle designer and manufacturer, was born at 37 Spon Terrace, Aston, Birmingham, on 8 January 1869, the son of James Norton, a journeyman cabinet-maker, and his wife, Elizabeth Chinn. The family were members of the Salvation Army, in which Norton remained active throughout his life. He demonstrated mechanical aptitude at an early age, being apprenticed as a toolmaker and working on bicycle chains. In 1888 he suffered a severe attack of rheumatic fever; a transatlantic voyage helped him to recuperate, but he was prematurely aged, earning the nickname 'Pa', in honour of his white hair and beard.

In 1898 Norton set up the Norton Manufacturing Company in Bromsgrove Street, Birmingham. On 30 October that year he married Sarah, daughter of Charles Henry Saxelby, a clockmaker, at the Salvation Army Citadel. There were five children of the marriage. Norton's small company, employing only a few men and boys, initially made bicycle chains but he was quick to see the potential of the motorized bicycle. In 1902 his friend Charles Garrard began to import French Clement engines for Clement-Garrard machines. Norton built Garrard's frames and advertised his own Clement-engined machine. The following year he expanded the manufacturing capacity of the company and in 1904 adopted larger engines when the Garrard work ended. Although initially committed to lightweight machines, Norton responded to public demand for more powerful engines.

Norton motorcycles reflected the fact that the designer and manufacturer was also an active competition rider. Norton's experience was reflected in machines that relied on simple proven systems, light weight, and good roadholding. The emphasis on competition and improvement came at the expense of production and profit, but brought its own pay-off with a win at the inaugural Isle of Man Tourist Trophy (TT) races in 1907. Norton used the resulting orders and publicity to fund the design of his own engine, the single-cylinder type that would be the basis of Norton production until 1963. This engine demonstrated a practical appreciation of metallurgical problems and the need to dissipate heat from the exhaust port. Nortons competed in the TT every year from 1907, but without success. By 1910 Norton was seen as the father figure of the industry, despite the small size of his company.

Unfortunately poor financial management forced Norton in 1913 to sell the company to his major component suppliers, R. T. Shelley. Recognizing that Norton was the company, Shelley retained him as managing director, with a nominee finance director. Competition remained the basis of development and several world records were secured at Brooklands. As a result the simple Norton side-valve machine was faster than its more complex, and apparently more advanced, rivals, reflecting Norton's design philosophy. He was the last manufacturer to fit a conventional gearbox, in 1915.

In 1914 the Norton company was too small for direct sales to the armed forces, so it was able to continue supplying the civilian market, where greater profits could be made. By 1919 the company had a reputation for fast and reliable machines. Norton, anticipating the roller-coaster trading conditions of the early 1920s, and fearful that trade unions and restrictive practices would destroy business, suffered a nervous breakdown in mid-1919. In 1920 the company moved to Bracebridge Street, its home for the next forty-three years. Second place in the 1920 TT encouraged Norton to pursue another win, which he realized would be the key to strong sales. To this end he developed an overhead-valve engine and experimented with mechanically closed valves, the desmodromic system, for which he patented a design in 1924. The simple overhead-valve engine proved adequate, breaking the 500 cc world speed record on its first outing in 1922.

Over the winter of 1921–2 Norton spent six months in South Africa, where he visited his brother and rode 3000 miles on a sales trip. Shortly after his return to England terminal cancer of the bowel was diagnosed. His machines, however, continued to perform well: two second places at the 1923 TT on standard machines boosted sales. Finally in 1924 the company, prompted by Castrol Oils, agreed to hire a professional racer, Alec Bennett, who secured the elusive win. Bennett also won the other major events that year, the Belgian and French grands prix. In July Norton was the guest of honour at a civic reception in Birmingham, his last public appearance. His machines were now acknowledged to be the best in the world.

Norton died from cancer at his home, 24 Sampson Road, Birmingham, on 21 April 1925, aged fifty-six. He was buried at Lodge Hill cemetery, Birmingham, on 24 April. Within days Norton Motors marked the passing of a man loved and respected by all who knew him, and of whom *Motor Cycling* could say, in its obituary notice of 29 April 1925, 'the advanced design of motorcycles of today has been largely due to his skill and knowledge', by sacking his eldest son and cutting off all connection with the Norton family. Norton had an enormous influence on the development of motor cycles and the industry that built them, an area where Britain was the world leader for fifty years. His name still commands worldwide recognition.

ANDREW LAMBERT

Sources M. Woollett, *Norton* (1992) · *Motor Cycling* (29 April 1925) · b. cert. · m. cert. · d. cert. · *CGPLA Eng. & Wales* (1925) · B. Holliday, *Norton story*, 2nd edn (1976)
Likenesses photographs, repro. in Woollett, *Norton*
Wealth at death £5306 4s. 2d.: probate, 12 June 1925, *CGPLA Eng. & Wales*

Norton, John (d. 1521/2), Carthusian author and prior, was of the armigerous family of Norton of Bilbrough, near Tadcaster in Yorkshire. Although he is not named as the son of John Norton of Bilbrough, esquire, and his wife, Margaret, whose wills of 1494 and 1506 refer to only one son, William, Margaret's will nevertheless directs that he should act with William as her executor, and share with him the residue of her estate. John was the brother of 'Sir'

Robert Norton of Bilbrough, who was probably the chantry priest named as an executor in the wills of Sir Ranulph Pigot in 1503 and Jane Stapleton in 1508, and whose attempts to grant land to the Charterhouse of Mount Grace were frustrated by his family c.1522.

According to Norton's own *Devota lamentatio*, he became a Carthusian in 1482 or 1483. A copy of another short treatise by him states that he had been a monk of the Coventry Charterhouse and experienced the communal life of the cloister before seeking the solitary life of the 'desert'. This suggests that he had been a member probably of a less strict order, but possibly of a university; a John Norton was admitted BA at Cambridge in 1480 and incepted as MA in 1484. It is not known when he transferred from Coventry to Mount Grace, but he was procurator of the latter house before he was prior there from 1509 until his death in 1521 or 1522.

Among Norton's works the earliest is probably a short treatise, most likely written while he was a monk of Coventry, and surviving only in a late fifteenth-century mystical miscellany (Bodl. Oxf., MS Lat. theol. d. 27, fols. 200r–200v), in which he defends those who progress from the coenobitic to the eremitic life. Three other treatises survive only in an early sixteenth-century collection (Lincoln Cathedral, chapter MS 57, now in Nottingham University) compiled after his death by Robert Fletcher, a monk of Mount Grace, who described him as 'devout and venerable' and as having written the first two treatises while he was procurator of Mount Grace (fols. 1, 27). Fletcher also copied, as prefaces to the three treatises, three letters to Fletcher himself from William Melton, chancellor of York, in which the works are highly recommended for Carthusian (but maybe by implication not for non-Carthusian) readers. All three works describe Norton's dialogues with an angel, Christ, or the Virgin Mary, and visions which he believed to be divinely inspired. The first, the *Musica monachorum* (fols. 1–27), is chiefly concerned with obedience, illustrated with many examples from both the Old and New testaments, because although 'neither the tongues of men nor angels can adequately describe the virtues of pure obedience', 'in pure obedience all the virtues are acquired and nurtured' (ibid., fols. 8v, 10). The Carthusians are frequently praised for excelling the other earthly orders as the seraphim excel the other heavenly orders. The second work, the *Thesaurus cordium vere amantium* (fols. 28–76v), deals with the difficulties facing Carthusians and how they are to overcome them. The third work, the *Devota lamentatio* (fols. 77–95v), narrates a heavenly vision which Norton had in his cell after mass on the Friday before Whitsunday (20 May) 1485 (his third year as a Carthusian). Among other wonders, he saw 'in spirit' the Virgin Mary and other heavenly virgins dressed as Carthusian nuns, and the salvation won by a Carthusian monk.

According to Maurice Chauncy and Hugh Taylor, two sixteenth-century monks of London and Sheen Anglorum, Norton also had a vision in which Christ told him that there would eventually be thirty-three Charterhouses in England. This vision has, however, also been attributed to John Wilson, prior of Mount Grace from 1521 or 1522 to 1539. Although Norton's highly affective devotion represents only one strand of Carthusian spirituality in the later middle ages, he stands in the same tradition as his more highly regarded contemporary colleague, Richard Methley, who dedicated two translations to him. The ecstatic experiences of both monks are compared to those of Margery Kempe in the margins of the sole surviving manuscript of her *Book*, originating from Mount Grace. At Norton's death in 1521 or 1522 Mount Grace was attracting more applicants than it could accommodate and building new cells funded by Henry, tenth Lord Clifford (*d.* 1523). As author and prior Norton had contributed to the distinguished reputation that his house continued to enjoy until its dissolution in 1539. W. N. M. BECKETT

Sources Lincoln Cathedral chapter, U. Nott. L., MS 57 (A.6.8) · R. M. Thompson, *Catalogue of the manuscripts of Lincoln Cathedral Chapter Library* (1989) · Bodl. Oxf., MS Lat. theol. d.27 · J. Hogg and others, eds., *The chartae of the Carthusian general chapter*, Analecta Cartusiana, 100/1–24 (1982–94) · A. G. Dickens, ed., *Clifford letters of the sixteenth century*, SurtS, 172 (1962) · [J. Raine], ed., *Testamenta Eboracensia*, 4, SurtS, 53 (1869) · J. Hogg, ed., *Mount Grace Charterhouse and late medieval English spirituality*, [1] (Salzburg, 1980), 1–43 · Emden, *Cam.* · L. Hendriks, *The London Charterhouse: its monks and its martyrs* (1889) · L. Le Vasseur, *Ephemerides ordinis cartusiensis*, 3 (1891) · *The book of Margery Kempe*, ed. S. B. Meech and H. E. Allen, EETS, 212 (1940) · A. G. Dickens, 'The writers of Tudor Yorkshire', *TRHS*, 5th ser., 13 (1963), 49–76 · J. Hogg, 'The pre-Reformation priors of the *Provincia Angliae*', Analecta Cartusiana, new ser., 1 (1989), 25–59
Archives Bodl. Oxf., MS Lat. theol. d.27, fols. 200–200v · U. Nott. L., Lincoln Cathedral chapter MS 57 (A.6.8)

Norton, Sir John (*d.* 1534), soldier, was the eldest son of Reginald Norton of Sheldwich, Kent, and Katherine, daughter of Richard Dryland. This John Norton should not be confused with his namesake of Norton Conyers, Yorkshire, who was knighted in 1501, served as sheriff of that county in 1514, and died in 1520. His Kent origins explain Norton's prominence in the expedition to Gelderland in 1511 under another leading Kentishman, Sir Edward Poynings. Despite failing to take the town of Venlo, the English acquitted themselves with honour and Norton was among those knighted by the future Charles V. In 1513, for the invasion of France, Poynings asked for Norton to be allowed to accompany him as his lieutenant and in the following year Norton's contingent of 123 men was the third largest in the retinue of Baron Bergavenny for the 'army-by-sea'.

In November 1513 Norton was chosen sheriff of Kent, serving again in 1522. He lived at Middleton, Kent, from about 1514. He was one of the mainstays of the government of the county during the first two decades of Henry VIII's reign. He was a member of the reception party for Charles V at Dover in 1522 and was also one of the commissioners organizing the transport of the English army for the French campaign; in 1523 and 1524 he was one of the subsidy commissioners for Kent and was a regular member of the commissions of the peace. Norton, like many of the Kent gentry, was also a member of the royal household; he was a gentleman usher of the king's chamber at the funeral of Henry VII, accompanied Henry VIII to the Field of Cloth of Gold in 1520, and at his death was a knight of the body. As such he participated in some of the important political and ceremonial events of the 1520s, including membership of the Kent grand jury that indicted the duke of Buckingham in 1521 and acting as a leading mourner at the funeral of Sir Thomas Lovell in 1526.

Norton married, first, Jane, daughter and coheir of John Northwood of Northwood, and, second, in 1528, Jane, widow of Sir Richard Fitzlewis. He had a son, also named John, and a daughter, Frisewide, with his first wife. His son was vice-admiral for Kent in 1550 and MP for Rochester in March 1553. He married Alice, daughter and heir of Edward Cobbe. Frisewide married William, son of the chief justice, Sir John Fyneux. Norton died on 8 February 1534, leaving disposable wealth worth over £800, and was buried in Middleton church beside the tomb of his first wife. His second wife survived him.

DAVID GRUMMITT

Sources will, PRO, PROB 11/25, fols. 75–7 · *LP Henry VIII* · E. Hall, *The triumphant reigne of Kyng Henry the VIII*, ed. C. Whibley, 2 vols. (1904) · HoP, *Commons, 1509–58*, 2.140; 3.26–7 · W. A. Shaw, *The knights of England*, 2 vols. (1906)
Archives PRO, letter from the commissioners to defend Kent coast signed by Norton, SP 1/29, fols. 315–16
Wealth at death over £800 in disposable wealth: will, PRO, PROB 11/25, fols. 75–7

Norton, John (1556/7–1612), bookseller, was the son of Richard Norton (*d.* before 1578) of Billingsley, Shropshire; he was probably not the John Norton who was baptized at Berrington, Shropshire, on 15 July 1561. He may have been the John Norton who matriculated as a pensioner from Queens' College, Cambridge, at Michaelmas 1570, only to leave without taking a degree. He was bound as an apprentice to his uncle, the London bookseller William *Norton (1526/7–1593), on 8 January 1578. He was freed on 18 July 1586. He was active in Edinburgh from 1587 and was, he claimed, importing books from Germany with the Scottish bookseller Andro Hart. In 1589 the two men were granted the right to import books duty free into Scotland by the Scottish privy council, a licence renewed two years later. He was apparently resident in Edinburgh in 1590, and in June 1591 the Stationers' Company listed a series of books 'which camme out of Scotland to master William Nortons house for his Cozen John Norton', which Arber claimed had been seized by the company (Arber, *Regs. Stationers*, 2.38). Norton and Hart, however, evidently fell out, because in February 1593 Norton lost a legal case brought against him by Hart and other Edinburgh booksellers over his retailing of books in the city. When his servant Edmond Wattes—who had been a fellow apprentice under William Norton—died in 1596 Norton sold his Edinburgh business to Hart and Edward Cathkin.

The infrequency of Norton's name on imprints belies his eventual significance in both the domestic and international book trade, and over the next two decades he became one of the wealthiest booksellers in England. He published his first work (a tract by Beza) in 1590 while his second publication, *A Discoverie of the Unnaturall and Traitorous Conspiracie of the Scottish Papists*, appeared only in 1593. In 1592 he began a long and fruitful relationship with John Bill when he bound the younger man as his apprentice. Norton was living in St Paul's Churchyard, near Paul's School, from 1594, remaining there until at least 1605, if not until his death. His wealth and connections evidently enabled him to take over the large debt that John Dee had amassed with the international bookselling Birckman family in 1595. In 1597 Norton published John Gerard's *Herball*, a presentation copy of which was given to Bodley's library in 1601. Norton was evidently still travelling between London and Edinburgh as, according to Henry Cuffe, a supporter of the earl of Essex, Norton had been entrusted with a secret letter from Essex to James VI just a few months before Essex attempted an ill-fated coup against Elizabeth in February 1601. Cuffe was promptly executed for his part in the uprising and his will included a legacy of £40 to 'my honest friend Jhon Norton the bookeseller' partly to clear a debt 'as allsoe to give him recompence for the trouble which this great tempest (I feare) is like to bringe uppon him' (Bruce, 92). However, Cuffe's fears proved groundless, as no government action seems to have been taken against the bookseller.

As his experiences in Scotland indicate Norton was an important English player in the international book trade, regularly selling works at the Frankfurt fair. Bill, who was freed in early 1601, became Norton's international agent—travelling to France, Germany, Spain, and Italy. Norton's activities with Hart (the two men having evidently been reconciled) in printing English bibles at Dort prompted a successful petition of complaint from the queen's printer, Robert Barker, to the privy council in 1601. Two years later, in a shrewd commercial move, Norton was one of six senior members of the trade who entered James VI's *Basilicon doron* in the Stationers' register just four days after the Scottish king acceded to the English throne in March 1603; a month later, however, they were fined by the company for selling the work at inflated prices. Later that year Norton was granted the office of king's printer of Latin, Greek, and Hebrew (which included the right to print Lily's *Grammar* and other school texts), although his grant may have been delayed as a patent of his was 'stayed' at chancery that year despite having passed the privy seal (Collier, 373–4). In 1605 Norton, his cousin Bonham *Norton (1565–1635), and John Bill formed a publishing partnership under the imprint of Officina Nortoniana. The exact purpose of the partnership is unclear: in certain cases the imprint was used for scholarly publications (some of which were imported) but it may also have been used as a marketing device for works sold at the Frankfurt fair. Norton's most notable publication in these years was Sir Henry Savile's Greek edition of Chrysostom printed in eight volumes on a press specially set up by Melchisidec Bradwood at Eton between 1610 and 1612. Norton was involved in this project from as early as 1601, seeking out on Savile's behalf both an appropriate font of Greek typeface and a suitably skilled printer.

Norton was elected to the livery of the Stationers' Company on 15 May 1598, and was appointed to the company's court in January 1602. In 1605–6 he bought the manor at Billingsley from Sir Thomas Aston, which was sold to Bonham Norton seven years later, and in 1607 he purchased the manor of Longnor and Blackhurst in the same county. He served for two successive terms as upper warden between 1604 and 1606, and as master for 1607–8 and 1611–12. He acted briefly as a London alderman for Bread Street ward in October 1611. He was re-elected master of the company in 1612, but died on 19 December that year. According to the family monument in St Faith's under St Paul's, where Norton was buried, he was fifty-five at his death. He left a widow, Joyce (*d.* 1643), who was later active in the trade in the 1630s, but no children.

Norton's will, dated 21 May 1612 and proved on 12 January 1613, demonstrated how wealthy he had become. The smallest bequest was £5 (to each of London's prisons), with numerous gifts to relatives of £50 (including to Jane Norton, Bonham's wife, 'to buye hir a diamond'; PRO, PROB 11/121, fol. 38v). A sum of £150 was given to Norton's local parish of St Faith's in order to buy property, with the yearly rents to be shared between the Stationers' Company and the parish, while a further sum of £1000 was bequeathed to the company to buy land and use the rents to lend money to young or poor members of the company. Bonham was executor and principal individual benefactor. Bonham also took over the Officina Nortoniana imprint and although Robert Barker had secured a reversion of Norton's privilege as the king's printer in Latin, Greek, and Hebrew in February 1604 this right seems to have been passed on to Bonham, who was confirmed in the office on 6 January 1613.   I. GADD

Sources STC, 1475–1640 · W. W. Greg and E. Boswell, eds., *Records of the court of the Stationers' Company, 1576 to 1602, from register B* (1930) · Arber, *Regs. Stationers* · H. R. Plomer, *Abstracts from the wills of English printers and stationers from 1492 to 1630* (1903) · private information (2004) [J. Barnard, M. Treadwell] · P. W. M. Blayney, *The bookshops in Paul's Cross churchyard* (1990) · H. G. Aldis and others, *A dictionary of printers and booksellers in England, Scotland and Ireland, and of foreign printers of English books, 1557–1640*, ed. R. B. McKerrow (1910) · *DNB* · *IGI* · W. C. Ferguson, *The loan book of the Stationers' Company with a list of transactions, 1592–1692* (1989) · *Patricius Junius (Patrick Young), Bibliothekar der Könige Jacob I und Carl I. von England: Mitteilungen aus seinem Briefwechsel*, ed. J. Kemke (Leipzig, 1898) · *Correspondence of King James VI of Scotland with Sir Robert Cecil and others in England during the reign of Elizabeth*, ed. J. Bruce, CS, old ser., 78 (1861), xxv–xxvi, 90–92 · W. Dugdale, *The history of St Paul's Cathedral in London* (1658) · will, PRO, PROB 11/121, sig. 5 · E. Lloyd, *Antiquities of Shropshire*, ed. T. F. Dukes (1844) · J. P. Collier, ed., *The Egerton papers* (1840) · Venn, *Alum. Cant.* · PRO, E112/99/1005, membrane 1

Norton, John (1606–1663), minister in America, was born on 6 May 1606 in Bishop's Stortford, Hertfordshire, the son of William Norton and his wife, Alice Browest. As a youth he was tutored by Alexander Strange at Bunningford School, and he matriculated as a pensioner at Peterhouse, Cambridge, in 1620 at the age of fourteen, graduating BA in 1624 and proceeding MA in 1627, having earned a reputation as an excellent Latinist. Cotton Mather claimed that family financial difficulties prompted him to leave the university rather than continue as a fellow. Mather also reported that as a youth Norton had been addicted to card-playing, but that once chastised for the practice by one of the family servants he henceforth adopted a strong lifelong opposition to the practice. After returning home he accepted a post as usher at the Stortford grammar school and also served as the local curate. Although he was exposed to puritan ideas at Cambridge, it was his attendance to the preaching of Jeremiah Dyke and other local puritans that effected his conversion. Because he was unwilling to compromise his new convictions he turned down a church benefice to become chaplain to Sir William Masham of High Lever, Essex. He likewise declined Richard Sibbes's efforts to procure him a fellowship at St Catharine's College, Cambridge.

After their attempt to leave England in 1634 was thwarted by bad storms, the following year Norton migrated to New England in the company of his wife, about whom nothing is known, and of his fellow clergyman Thomas Shepard. They landed at Plymouth, and he initially preached in that colony before moving to Boston in 1636. There he took a lead in opposing Anne Hutchinson, who preached a mystical apprehension of spiritual election and accused most of the region's clergy, including Norton, of preaching an Arminian-style covenant of works. He was a member of the synod of 1637 which defined religious errors said to be maintained by Hutchinson and her followers, and supported her exile. In 1638 Norton accepted the ministerial post of teacher in the church at Ipswich, Massachusetts, where Nathaniel Rogers was pastor.

In England in 1643 the unity of the puritans in the Westminster assembly splintered when the dissenting brethren issued their *Apologetical Narration* calling for toleration within a projected presbyterian settlement for independent congregations of orthodox believers. English congregational Independents such as Thomas Goodwin and Philip Nye cited the example of the New England way in defence of congregational polity while the presbyterian majority, led by the assembly's Scottish observers, sought to discredit that position. Among other strategies the presbyterians sought to engage respected continental theologians to write in support of their position. One such important work was produced by William Apollonius, pastor of the church in Middleburg. The congregationalists turned to their New England allies for a response and the colonial clergy selected Norton. His Latin *Responsio ad totam questionum …* (1648) was an answer to Apollonius that was published in London with a preface by Nye, Thomas Goodwin, and Sidrach Simpson. It spelt out in great detail congregational church polity and sought to demonstrate the affinity of congregational practice with continental reformed belief and polity. Like most New Englanders, Norton strongly supported the dissenting brethren but was concerned about the alliance with the sects into which they were forced in the 1640s. As he wrote to the former New Englander Giles Firmin, he thought 'better of many Presbyterians' than he did of some of the sects, 'for I distinguish between Independents and Congregational men' (*New England Historical and Genealogical Register*, 20, 1886, 229).

With his answer to Apollonius behind him, Norton served in 1648 as a member of the colonial assembly that prepared the Cambridge platform, which expressed the structural character and the faith of the churches of New England. When, prior to the assembly, members of the Boston church questioned whether such an endeavour would interfere with congregational autonomy, Norton preached to that congregation a guest sermon which was credited with gaining their participation. He also wrote to John Dury a letter, signed by forty-three other ministers, which expressed support for that reformer's eirenic efforts to unite Christians.

In 1645 Norton was invited to deliver the election sermon for the colony and was considered as a possible agent to represent Massachusetts in England until that plan was postponed. He came to the assistance of the magistrates in 1650 when one of their number, Springfield's William Pynchon, published *The Meritorious Doctrine of our Redemption* (1650), a tract which denied the doctrine that man's sins were imputed to Christ and that the Saviour suffered to redeem them. At the request of the colony's general court Norton wrote and published a refutation of Pynchon's *A Discussion of that Great Point in Divinity, the Sufferings of Christ* (1653).

John Cotton was said to have recommended Norton to succeed him as teacher in the First Church of Boston, and following Cotton's death in 1652 the churches of Ipswich and Boston entered into a protracted struggle for his services. After a council of twelve churches intervened the Ipswich congregation relented and Norton was ordained at Boston on 23 July 1656, the New England churches maintaining that ordination was specific to a particular congregation. In 1654 he published *The Orthodox Evangelist*, a critical exposition of puritan faith and theology which strongly asserted the inefficacy of man's work in the process of salvation while maintaining that the pietistic love that results from God's election of the saints was expressed within their lives. He also published *A Brief and Excellent Treatise Containing the Doctrine of Godliness* (1648), a *Brief Catechism* (1660), and a biography of his friend and predecessor John Cotton, *Abel being Dead yet Speaketh* (1658). The last work is credited as being the first biography written in America. In 1659 he wrote *The Heart of New England Rent*, in which he expounded on the threat posed by Quaker missionaries to New England and justified the application of the death penalty to Quakers who defied banishment to return to the colony. Appointed an overseer in 1654 he also devoted attention to the affairs of Harvard College, and in addition he tutored children in his home, the most notable of whom was the young Increase Mather. By 1656 his wife had died, and on 23 July that year he married Mary Mason, who outlived him.

New Englanders had supported the English puritan regimes of the Commonwealth and protectorate and feared the consequences of the restoration of the Stuarts in 1660. Though he continued to urge the prosecution of the puritan errand, Norton's 1661 election sermon, 'Sion the Outcast Healed of her Wounds', called for reconciliation with the crown. Consequently in 1662 Norton and Simon Bradstreet were sent to England by the Massachusetts general court to seek reassurances regarding their charter and to respond to criticism about the colony's harsh treatment of Quakers. While the charter was upheld for the time, the royal government insisted on changes in the Massachusetts franchise, demanded adherence to the Navigation Acts, and required toleration of dissenters. Norton and Bradstreet were generally blamed by their fellow colonists for conceding too much and their mission was judged a failure. Shortly after returning from England, on 5 April 1663, Norton appeared to suffer a stroke after preaching at the morning service and died that same day; he was buried in the King's Chapel burialground, Boston. His contemporary Nathaniel Morton characterized Norton as 'singularly endowed with the tongue of the learned, enabled to speak a word in due season' and 'not only a wise steward of the things of Christ, but also a wise statesman' (N. Morton, *New England's Memoriall*, 1669).

John Norton (1651–1716), minister in America, was the son of William Norton of Ipswich, Massachusetts, and his wife, Lucy, daughter of Emmanuel Downing (1585–1660) and Lucy Winthrop. He was thus the nephew not only of John Norton but also of George Downing, and greatnephew of Governor John Winthrop. He was a pupil at Ipswich School and then matriculated at Harvard, where he received his BA in 1671. Ordained at Hingham, Massachusetts, in 1678, he became the colleague and then successor of Peter Hobart; his ministry was undistinguished. He published an election sermon, *An Essay Tending to Promote Reformation* (1708), and delivered a funeral elegy on Anne Bradstreet. Having proceeded MA from Harvard in 1716, he died in the same year.   FRANCIS J. BREMER

Sources C. Mather, *Magnalia Christi Americana*, 7 bks in 1 vol. (1702) · F. J. Bremer, *Shaping New Englands: puritan clergymen in seventeenth-century England and New England* (1994) · S. E. Morison, *The founding of Harvard College* (Cambridge, MA, 1935) · J. Durbin-Dodd, 'Norton, John', *ANB* · E. Elliott, ed., *American colonial writers, 1606–1734*, DLitB, 24 (1984) · J. Savage, *A genealogical dictionary of the first settlers of New England*, 4 vols. (1860–62) · *The answer to the whole set of questions of the celebrated Mr. William Appolonius by John Norton*, ed. D. Norton (Cambridge, MA, 1958) · 'John Norton to Giles Firmin, c.1658', *New England Historical and Genealogical Register*, 20 (1866), 299
Archives Mass. Hist. Soc., religious MSS
Wealth at death library of 729 volumes

Norton, John (1651–1716). *See under* Norton, John (1606–1663).

Norton, John (b. 1661/2?), spelling reformer, was supposedly born in London. In 1674, when he claimed to be only twelve, he published a small volume, *The Scholar's Vade Mecum, or, The Serious Student's Solid and Silent Tutor*. It comprised four parts: his 'new mode of spelling, founded on derivation' (Norton, title-page); his paraphrase translation of the poems of Marcus Antonius Flaminius, using this spelling; instances of the different figures of speech from the hymn of Flaminius, with Norton's Latin commentary; and 163 pages of an ingenious and painstaking collection of idioms, which included introducing and displaying parts of the Latin verb 'facere' and its English equivalent 'to make' in such idioms. Norton's declared aim was to spell words in a manner which more closely resembled the (mainly) Latin words from which his examples were drawn—for instance, 'vaie' rather than 'way', from 'via'; 'paur' rather than 'poor', from 'pauper'—but his efforts in this direction betrayed his lack of learning. He also sought generally to exclude letters that were superfluous (for example the second 'l' in 'all') or silent (the 'u' after 'q', or the 'g' in 'light').

The book was dedicated to Margaret Arnold, wife of the Monmouthshire JP John Arnold, urging, in a sentence which neatly embodies his reformed spelling, that:

> The deie of smal things wil not (I hope) be despised bi you so much a cgnoun and cgnoing Christian, since evn the Juæs are wont proverbialy to acgnoledg and avouch that the young in Years sometimes are as the Aged in al gravitie and wisdom of carriage.   (Norton, sig. A2v)

The book was prefaced by an engraving of the serious young scholar and by four congratulatory verses; his age and origins are taken from these and from his dedication. A broadside in verse, by a John Norton and published in 1674, entitled *The King's Entertainment at Guild-Hall, or, London's Option in Fruition*, may be his, as the author has appended *aet suae* ('aged') at the bottom of the text; the actual figure has, however, been lost in trimming on the surviving copy in the British Library. Nothing else is known of him.

FOSTER WATSON, *rev.* ANITA McCONNELL

Sources J. Granger, *A biographical history of England from Egbert the Great to the revolution*, 5th edn, 6 vols. (1824), vol. 5, p. 295 · J. Norton, *The scholar's vade mecum* (1674)
Likenesses W. Sherwin, line engraving, BM, NPG; repro. in *Scholar's vade mecum*

Norton, John [called Teyoninhokarawen] (1770–1831?), leader of the Mohawk Indians, was born on 16 December 1770 at Crail, Fifeshire, the son of John Norton (b. c.1750, d. before 1809), printer and soldier. His father was most likely a Cherokee from North Carolina who had been adopted by a soldier in 1760 and taken to Scotland. There he became a printer and married a Scottish woman from Salen, Christian Anderson.

The younger John Norton probably grew up in the Crail–Salen–Dunfermline area, then moved to Edinburgh about 1781, either to advance his education or to learn the printing trade. In 1784 he joined the 65th foot. His father enlisted in 1786 and both men were posted to Canada. Norton's mother came with them and worked as a servant. In 1787 Norton deserted from Fort Niagara, but received a discharge in 1788, apparently with the help of his mother's employer. His father deserted in 1789. Norton

John Norton (1770–1831?), by Thomas Phillips, 1816

subsequently lived in the aboriginal–white middle ground of the lower Great Lakes region; learned several Native languages; worked as a schoolteacher, trader, and interpreter; and became 'at once as perfect an Indian as ran in the woods, having his ears cut & his nose bored' (*Missouri Gazette*, 15 June 1816).

Norton impressed the Mohawk leader Joseph Brant, who adopted him as his 'nephew' about 1798. Shortly afterwards he was given the Mohawk chiefly name Teyoninhokarawen. He settled on the Six Nations Iroquois tract on the Grand River in Upper Canada, became a diplomatic and war chief, and had at least two successive marriages to now unknown aboriginal women with whom he had two children. In July 1813 Norton married again, this time to Karighwaycagh or Catherine (*c*.1797–1827), who probably was a Delaware.

Norton was active in the pro-British party on the politically-divided Grand, and succeeded Brant as its principal leader when the latter died in 1807. Norton favoured good Anglo-Iroquois relations, but wanted to ensure that the Six Nations Mohawks, Oneidas, Tuscaroras, Onondagas, Cayugas, and Senecas enjoyed as much freedom from unwanted European and American influence as possible, in order to make the transition on their own terms, to plough agriculture from traditional horticultural and forest subsistence patterns. His demand for full Native control over Grand River land in particular annoyed colonial officials, who sought to undermine his authority by claiming that he had no aboriginal ancestry (a view that some modern scholars have accepted). The historical record,

however, suggests that Norton was half Cherokee; nevertheless Native origins were not necessary for him to have been adopted as a Mohawk.

Frustrated by internal Grand River politics and by the hostility of government officials, Norton journeyed to England in 1804–5 to seek a commission in the army and to represent Iroquois interests at the imperial centre. He failed on both missions. Yet, because of his interest in promoting Christianity and European and American agricultural practices among the tribes, he was befriended by a number of prominent Quakers and evangelical Anglicans, as well as by the duke of Northumberland. During this visit Norton, an Anglican, translated the gospel of St John into Mohawk for the British and Foreign Bible Society. He returned to Canada in 1805, and then travelled to Tennessee and neighbouring regions in 1809–10 to visit his Cherokee relatives and honour his father's grave.

When the United States declared war on Britain in 1812, most Grand River people chose to remain neutral, while others favoured an alliance with the Americans. Norton's pro-British party had difficulty mustering support because of long-standing problems in crown–Iroquois relations and because many people assumed the Americans would conquer Canada quickly. However, the king's forces won some unexpected early victories, which helped bring most of the Grand River community into the war on the British side. Norton, with considerable support from the army, worked to recruit warriors and maintain the Iroquois–crown alliance. As 'captain of the Confederate Indians' he regularly saw action and proved to be an outstanding combat commander. Perhaps his most important contribution to Canadian defence occurred at Queenston Heights in 1812, where his badly outnumbered warriors helped keep the American army pinned down in a precarious position for several hours until the British could deploy their troops to repel the invaders. However, his political and diplomatic aspirations were frustrated because of both the divisions on the Grand and the animosity of civil officials, especially in the Indian department. Consequently, he retired from public life at the end of the war.

In 1815 Norton and his family sailed to England where he sought preferment (being given the local Canadian rank of major). In Britain, he finished a manuscript he had been working on for a number of years, which now is housed at Alnwick Castle. Although intended for publication, it was not published until 1970, as *The Journal of Major John Norton*. It describes his journey to the Cherokee country, recounts his adventures in the Anglo-American War, assesses aboriginal–white issues in the period between 1783 and 1815, and presents a history of the Six Nations based on published European and American, and oral Iroquois, sources. It is a rare and extensive aboriginal-centred document, containing detailed ethnographic information presented by a reliable observer.

Norton returned to Canada in 1816 to farm his land. In 1823 he mortally wounded a man in a duel to protect his wife's honour. After the courts fined him £25 for manslaughter, he left Karighwaycagh and travelled to the

Cherokee settlements in Arkansas. He is known to have been in Laredo, then in Mexican territory, in 1825, but afterwards he disappeared. A nephew thought he lived until October 1831.

CARL BENN

Sources The journal of Major John Norton, 1816, ed. C. F. Klinck and J. J. Talman (1970) · C. Benn, The Iroquois in the war of 1812 (1998) · C. M. Johnston, ed., The valley of the Six Nations: a collection of documents on the Indian lands of the Grand River (1964) · E. A. Cruikshank, ed., Documentary history of the campaign on the Niagara frontier, 9 vols. (1902–8) · Newberry Library, Chicago, Ayer Collection, J. Norton letter-book, 1805–13, MS 654 · Archives of Ontario, Toronto, J. Norton MSS, 1796–1842, MS 94 · W. N. Fenton, 'Cherokee and Iroquois connections revisited', Journal of Cherokee Studies, 3 (1978), 239–49 · R. D. Fogelson, 'Major John Norton as ethno-ethnologist', Journal of Cherokee Studies, 3 (1978), 250–55 · Z., letter, Missouri Gazette and Public Advertiser (15 June 1816) · Headley [C. A. Winn?], 'Account of the descriptions, given by Mr. Norton concerning his country customs and manners', 12 March 1805, New York State Library, Albany, MSS 13350–13351 · D. W. Boyce, ed., 'A glimpse of Iroquois culture history through the eyes of Joseph Brant and John Norton', Proceedings of the American Philosophical Society, 117 (1973), 286–94 · C. F. Klinck, 'Norton, John', DCB, vol. 6 · IGI
Archives Archives of Ontario, Toronto, MSS · Newberry Library, Chicago, letter-book · University of Western Ontario, London, Ontario, D. B. Weldon Library, MSS
Likenesses S. Williams?, oils on paper, c.1804, Canadian War Museum, Ottawa · M. A. Knight, miniature watercolour on ivory, 1805, NA Canada; repro. in Benn, Iroquois in the war of 1812 · T. Phillips, oils, 1816, Syon House, Brentford, Middlesex [see illus.]

Norton, John (1823–1904), architect, was born on 28 September 1823 at Bristol, the son of John Norton and his wife, Sarah, née Russell. In 1846, after attending Bristol grammar school, he became a pupil in the London office of Benjamin Ferrey; he also attended the classes of Professor Thomas Leverton Donaldson at the University of London, where he won a first prize in 1848. In 1857 he married Helen Mary, the only daughter of Peter Le Neve Aldous Arnold; they had eight daughters and two sons.

Norton became an associate of the Royal Institute of British Architects in 1850 and a fellow in 1857; he was for a time a member of its council, and became president of the Architectural Association for the 1858–9 session. He was honorary secretary of the Arundel Society (which produced printed copies of paintings by old masters) throughout its existence (1848–98) and a council member of the Artists' General Benevolent Institution.

Norton was for some time in partnership with Philip Edward Masey and quickly built up a large and lucrative architectural practice which handled both domestic and ecclesiastical commissions. He worked for a number of wealthy patrons, including the maharaja Duleep Singh (for whom he built Elveden Hall, Suffolk, 1863–70), William Gibbs (who commissioned the rebuilding of Tyntesfield, Somerset), and Alexander Acland-Hood, first Baron St Audries (for whom he designed a house and church at St Audries in Somerset in c.1856). His other principal works were: Badgemore, Oxfordshire, for Richard Ovey; Ferney Hall, Shropshire (after 1856), for W. Hurt-Sitwell; Horstead Hall, Norfolk, for Sir E. Birkbeck; Nutfield Priory, Surrey (1858–9), for H. E. Gurney; Monkhams, Essex, for H. Ford Barclay; Euston Hall, Suffolk, for the duke of Grafton; public works and buildings of the new boulevard, Florence;

International College, Isleworth; the Winter Gardens at Great Yarmouth and Tynemouth; Langland Bay Hotel, south Wales; South Western Terminus Hotel, Southampton (1872); Fickle Castle, Estonia; Framlingham Hall, Norfolk; Brent Knoll, Somerset (1862–4); Summers Place, Sussex (now an outpost of Sothebys); Chew Magna Manor House, Somerset (1864); the town hall and constitutional club, Neath; and a training college for the diocese of Gloucester and Bristol. He also won the Bombay public markets competition.

Among Norton's London commissions were the Turf Club, Piccadilly; the Submarine Telegraph Company's office, Throgmorton Avenue; the Canada government buildings and Victoria Mansions, Westminster; as well as mansions in Mandeville Place and several hotels, business premises, and residential flats elsewhere in London.

Norton did not work exclusively in Gothic, though this was the norm for his church designs, the most important of which was Christ Church in Finchley (1870). His other church commissions included those at Stapleton, Stoke Bishop, and Frampton Cotterell in Gloucestershire; St Matthew's, Brighton, Sussex; St John's, Middlesbrough, Yorkshire; those at Bourton, High Bridge, and Congresbury in Somerset; and St Luke's, St Matthias, Emmanuel (Clifton), and the parish church of Bedminster in Bristol. He designed a number of churches in Wales and Monmouthshire, including those at Pontypridd and Llwynmadog. He was responsible for the church on Lundy island and others at Powerscourt, Wicklow; Chevington, near Howick, Northumberland; Bagnères de Bigorre in the French Pyrenees; and Bishop Hannington's Memorial Church, Frere Town, Kenya.

Norton acted as architect to the Crystal Palace Company, for the Ascot Land Company, and for several London clubs. He was also responsible for the Church Missionary Society children's home at Limpsfield and the Royal Normal College for the Blind at Norwood, Surrey; the county courts at Williton, Dunster, and Long Ashton in Somerset; and the High Cross at Bristol. He died at Casalini, his home in Bournemouth, on 10 November 1904, and was buried there. He was survived by his wife. His son Charles Harrold Norton (1867–1942) succeeded him in his practice.

PAUL WATERHOUSE, rev. JOHN ELLIOTT

Sources The Builder, 87 (1904), 526 · RIBA Journal (1905), 66–8 · Building News (6 March 1891) · Dir. Brit. archs. · CGPLA Eng. & Wales (1904)
Archives RIBA · RIBA, biographical file
Likenesses photograph, repro. in Building News, 330
Wealth at death £3596: probate, 19 Dec 1904, CGPLA Eng. & Wales

Norton, John Bruce (1815–1883), judge in India, was born, probably in London, on 8 July 1815, the eldest son of Sir John David Norton (d. 1843), of St Pancras, London, and afterwards Madras supreme court judge, and his wife, Helen Barrington, daughter of Major-General Bruce of the Madras army. He was educated at Harrow School and Merton College, Oxford, where he graduated BA in 1838. In November 1841 he was called to the bar at Lincoln's Inn.

In 1842 Norton accompanied his father to India when the latter took up an appointment to the Madras supreme court. In 1845, after two years as the sheriff of Madras, Norton was appointed clerk of the crown in the supreme court, a post he retained until the court's abolition in 1862. He also practised as a barrister. In 1853 he published a stinging critique of the local legal system, *The Administration of Justice in Southern India*, in which he berated the judges of the East India Company's courts for their incompetence and ignorance and accused the Madras government of failing to provide justice to all its subjects. This attack, which provoked a storm of counter-claims, initiated a long process of legal reform in Madras in which Norton himself was often prominent.

In 1852 Norton's wife, Zélie Marie Brittam, gave birth to a son, Eardley John. Three daughters followed: in 1857 Helen Mary; in 1860 Sophie Isabel; and in 1864 Charlotte Alice Zélie.

In 1855 Norton was appointed the first professor of law at Presidency College and thus became the architect of formal legal education in south India. In the absence of sufficient textbooks, he published his first set of lectures, of which *The Law of Evidence Applicable to the Courts of the East India Company* (1858) became a standard text and reappeared in numerous editions.

In 1859, with the East India Company now abolished, the governor of Madras, Sir Charles Trevelyan, chose Norton as one of two barristers to sit on a four-man committee to study ways of unifying the old bifurcated structure of crown and company courts. Norton was the most radical contributor to the inquiry and argued that it would be neither fair nor necessary to exclude Indian lawyers from the new High Court, an opinion endorsed by Trevelyan. In 1862 Norton was appointed public pleader and shortly thereafter acting advocate-general of Madras, an appointment which was confirmed on 2 June 1863 and carried with it a seat in the Madras legislative council. He was also patron of Pachaiyappa's high school at Madras.

In 1871 Norton resigned as advocate-general and returned to England. In January 1873 he became the first lecturer on law to Indian students at the Temple. He died at his home in London, 11 Penywern Road, Earls Court, on 13 July 1883. His wife survived him. His only son, Eardley John Norton, who was educated at Rugby School, Merton College, Oxford, and Lincoln's Inn, became coroner of Madras and practised at the bar in Calcutta. He was a member of the early Indian National Congress.

KATHERINE PRIOR

Sources J. P. Paul, *The legal profession in colonial south India* (1991) · C. E. Buckland, *Dictionary of Indian biography* (1906) · *The Times* (16 July 1883), 1, 10 · *DNB* · Foster, *Alum. Oxon.* · ecclesiastical records, BL OIOC · J. J. Cotton, *List of inscriptions on tombs or monuments in Madras* (1905) · J. Foster, *Men-at-the-bar: a biographical hand-list of the members of the various inns of court*, 2nd edn (1885) · M. G. Dauglish and P. K. Stephenson, eds., *The Harrow School register, 1800–1911*, 3rd edn (1911) · *CGPLA Eng. & Wales* (1883)
Archives BL OIOC, corresp. and papers, MS Eur. D 968 | PRO, Ellenborough MSS
Likenesses portrait, 1905; at Patcheappah's Hall, Madras, in 1905

Wealth at death £1650 7s. 6d. in England: probate, 12 Nov 1883, *CGPLA Eng. & Wales*

Norton, Katherine. *See* McLoughlin, Katherine (*fl.* 1671–1679).

Norton [*née* Pearson], **(Kathleen) Mary** (1903–1992), children's author, was born at 48 Mildmay Park, Highbury, London, on 10 December 1903, the only daughter of Reginald Spencer Pearson, a surgeon, and Minnie Savile, *née* Hughes. She had four brothers. When she was still young, the family moved to Leighton Buzzard, Bedfordshire, to live at The Cedars, a rambling Georgian house that became the setting for Mary's most famous work, *The Borrowers*. She was educated at St Margaret's Convent, East Grinstead, and attended art school for a short course, before joining the Old Vic Shakespeare Company in the season for 1925–6. There she understudied for Edith Evans, and later described this period as the most memorable of her life. At this time Mary was 'as thin as a wasp and very pale and quiet and gentle' (*The Times*).

On 4 September 1926, at St Mary's, Lambeth, London, Mary Pearson married Robert Charles Norton (*b.* 1892/3), an engineer who came from a wealthy shipowning and trading family from Portugal. They moved to Portugal on their marriage, to a country estate several miles from Lisbon. At the outbreak of the Second World War Robert joined the navy, and Mary and their children, two boys and two girls, moved first to England, and then to New York, where Mary worked for the British Purchasing Commission. She rented a house in Connecticut, where she began to write essays, translations, and children's stories. Her first children's book, *The Magic Bed-Knob, or, How to Become a Witch in Ten Easy Lessons*, was first published in America in 1943. In that same year Mary and her family returned to England, where she briefly resumed her stage career—including a part in a two-year run of *The Guinea-Pig* at the Criterion Theatre, London. *The Magic Bed-Knob* was published in England in 1945, and two years later was followed by a sequel, *Bonfires and Broomsticks*. John Betjeman described the work as 'quite the best modern fairy story I have read' (Stott, 199). The two books were combined into one volume, *Bed-Knob and Broomstick*, in 1957. A successful Disney film, *Bed Knobs and Broomsticks*, a mixture of live action and animation, was released in 1971.

Once back in England, Norton had begun work on *The Borrowers*. Published in 1952, the work was immediately hailed as a classic of children's fiction, and won the Carnegie medal for that year. The story concerned the life and adventures of a race of tiny people tucked away under floorboards and in the crevices of houses, and living parasitically off the 'human beans'. Part of the thrill of the book is the ingenuity with which the borrowers recycle their 'borrowings' into their own domestic sphere. A knight from a chess piece, sawn in half, becomes the pedestal for the dining-room table and a statue for the hall. But the wider story was equally gripping: the Clock family—Pod, Homily, and their daughter Arietty—so called because their front door is under the grandfather clock—are the last of the borrowers to survive in the old house. As

(Kathleen) Mary Norton (1903–1992), by unknown photographer

the adolescent Arietty rebels against the narrow boundaries imposed on her, and makes contact with a human boy, their whole way of life is threatened. They are discovered by the adults, and at the end of the book have to flee from the house into the open fields beyond.

Norton later wrote of the origin of these characters. Short-sighted from childhood, she remembered peering close up into banks and tree roots, wondering what life would be like so close to the ground, when ordinary things became obstacles and dangers. The first book was followed by several sequels: *The Borrowers Afield* (1955), *The Borrowers Afloat* (1959), *The Borrowers Aloft* (1961), and 'Poor Stainless' (a short story about a borrower published in 1971). These sequels follow the Clocks as they try to find some stability in a series of hostile environments, with increasingly predatory humans on the scene.

Norton's first marriage was dissolved, and on 24 April 1970, at the Chelsea register office, London, she married the writer (Arthur) Lionel Bonsey (1911/12–1989). In 1972, encouraged by the Irish government's offer of tax concessions for writers and artists, they moved from their old Essex farmhouse to co. Cork, where they bought and restored a Queen Anne rectory in Kilcoe, Aughadown, Ballydehob. There Norton wrote *Are All the Giants Dead?* (1975), a dream adventure which explores what happens to the characters of fairy tales after the ends of the tales. She also wrote the last of the borrowers books, *The Borrowers Avenged* (1982), in which the Clock family is finally rewarded with the possibility of a stable future. *The Borrowers Omnibus* was published in 1990. There have been a

number of television series based on *The Borrowers*, both American and British, and films in 1973 and 1997.

For her publisher Vanessa Hamilton, there were few authors 'quite so charming and distinguished as Mary, so vital, and with such a marvellous sense of humour' (*The Independent*). Norton died of a heart attack on 29 August 1992, at 102 West Street, Hartland, Bideford, Devon.

ELERI LARKUM

Sources   *The Independent* (4 Sept 1992) · *The Times* (7 Sept 1992) · b. cert. · m. certs. · d. cert. · J. C. Stott, 'Mary Norton', *British children's writers, 1914–1960*, ed. D. R. Hettinga and G. D. Schmidt, DLitB, 160 (1996), 197–206 · H. Carpenter and M. Prichard, *The Oxford companion to children's literature* (1984)
Archives   Book Trust, London, corresp. with Diana Stanley | SOUND BL NSA, oral history interview
Likenesses   photograph, repro. in *The Independent* · photograph, repro. in *The Times* · photograph, priv. coll. [*see illus.*]
Wealth at death   £16,052: probate, 26 Oct 1992, *CGPLA Eng. & Wales*

Norton, Matthew [*name in religion* Thomas] (**1732–1800**), prior of Bornhem, born at Roundhay, near Leeds, was converted to the Roman Catholic faith during a visit to Flanders. He enrolled as a student in the English Dominican college at Bornhem, near Antwerp, in 1751. He entered the order at Brussels and was professed as a Dominican on 23 October 1754 at Bornhem. He went on to study at the English Dominican college at Louvain, and was ordained priest there in 1757. He was designated to serve under the direction of Patrick Bradley (1705–1760), an Irish Dominican assigned to the English province since 1748, on a mission in the Caribbean island of Santa Cruz. The Caribbean mission was to be under the financial sponsorship of Robert Tuite, a West Indian merchant of Portman Square in London. Permission for Norton to go to the West Indies was refused by the master of the Dominican order on 2 December 1758, on the grounds that he had not yet completed his theological studies. The scheme foundered with Bradley's death in 1760. On 29 June 1759, after a brilliant academic career in the Low Countries, Norton was sent to Aston Flamville, a Leicestershire mission sponsored by the Turville family. In August 1759 he moved to Sketchley, and six years later bought a piece of ground in Hinckley, Leicestershire, for £200.

The move from a rural mission to an urban setting marked the beginning of a change in English Catholicism from a dependence on the squirearchy to a closer association with the middle and poorer classes. In the spring of 1765 Norton set up a Catholic chapel in Hinckley and ministered there until elected prior of Bornhem in November 1767, where in 1769 he began the rebuilding of the priory and the college attached to it somewhat in the style of an English country house, expanding it to accommodate 150 pupils. The chief benefactors of the project were Lord Stourton, Lord Dormer, the earl of Fingall, Sir Henry Englefield, and a Mr John Wade, a merchant of Leeds. In March 1771 he returned to Hinckley and was appointed preacher-general in September of the same year. In early 1774 he was once more elected prior of Bornhem but resigned, and was instituted rector of the college at Louvain on 17 February 1775. From 1774 to 1778 he was vicar provincial in the Low Countries, having under his jurisdiction the priory and college at Bornhem, the college at Louvain, and the monastery of English Dominican nuns at Brussels. In 1783 he was granted the degree of DD by the University of Louvain. He returned to Hinckley in October 1780 and was created master of sacred theology by the master of the order on 10 May 1785. He laboured intensively in Leicestershire and the surrounding area. He served the Leicester mission from Hinckley from October 1783 to August 1785, and also began the mission at Coventry around the same time. He was a familiar figure as he walked between his various cures.

Norton maintained a keen interest in farming and was affected by the dynamics of the agricultural revolution of the eighteenth century. While in the Low Countries he won three medals offered by the Brussels Academy for dissertations respectively upon raising wool, keeping bees, and the use of oxen rather than horses by farmers. These works were published by the Académie Impériale des Sciences et Belles-Lettres de Bruxelles in 1776, 1777, and 1779 respectively. On his return to England he sustained his interest in methods of cultivation and hoped to encourage the use of oxen rather than horses among the farmers of Leicestershire. He was greatly respected as a priest and as an agronomist by his Catholic and protestant neighbours, many of whom attended his funeral following his death at Hinckley on 7 August 1800. He was buried in Aston Flamville churchyard, where a monument to him was erected. ALLAN WHITE

Sources profession register, English Dominican Archives · W. Gumbley, *Obituary notices of the English Dominicans from 1555 to 1952* (1955), 80–81 · D. A. Bellenger, ed., *English and Welsh priests, 1558–1800* (1984), 92 · J. Nichols, *The history and antiquities of the county of Leicester*, 4/2 (1811); facs. edn (1971), 473 · J. Monk, *General view of the agriculture of the county of Leicester: with observations on the means of their improvement* (1974), 40–41

Norton, Richard (*d.* 1420), justice, was the son of Adam Conyers, of the bishopric of Durham, who adopted the name Norton on marrying the heiress of Norton in Yorkshire. He is mentioned as an advocate in 1399, and was created a serjeant-at-law in 1401. On 4 June 1405 he was included in the commission appointed for the trial of all concerned in Archbishop Scrope's rebellion; his name was, however, omitted from the fresh commission appointed two days later. In 1406 he was a justice of assize for the palatinate of Durham, and is recorded as one of the king's serjeants in the same year. Appointed a justice of the common pleas by Henry V on 23 May 1413, he became chief justice a month later, on 26 June. Around the same time he became chief justice of the palatinate of Lancaster. From November 1414 to December 1420 Norton appears regularly as a trier of petitions in parliament.

A lawyer of distinction, Norton served frequently on government commissions during the reigns of Henry IV and Henry V, notably as a judicial commissioner of oyer and terminer in counties ranging from Durham and Yorkshire to Norfolk, Suffolk, and Devon, and as an agent charged to bring to justice felons and fugitives in Northumberland, Yorkshire, Norfolk, Suffolk, and elsewhere. Besides

his role in the task of inquiring into lands forfeited by the rebellious archbishop of York in June 1405, he was involved in similar investigations concerning Henry Percy, earl of Northumberland, in July 1407, and in July 1408 was charged to investigate 'divers conspiracies among certain stone-cutters and other evil-doers of the county of York and elsewhere' not only 'to hinder work on the fabric of the church of St Peter, York' but also 'to maim William Colchestre, mason' and the men employed by him (*CPR, 1405–8*, 482). He served as a justice of the peace, initially for the North Riding of Yorkshire, from November 1399, and thereafter for varying periods of time in several counties.

Norton married Elizabeth, daughter of Sir John Tempest of Studley. They had several sons. He died on 20 December 1420 and was buried at Wath in Yorkshire, and following his death a licence was granted to his trustees for the founding of 'a perpetual chantry of one chaplain to celebrate divine service daily in the chapel of St Cuthbert, Norton Conyers' (*CPR, 1416–22*, 392–3).

C. L. KINGSFORD, *rev.* KEITH DOCKRAY

Sources Chancery records · Foss, *Judges*, 4.207–8 · R. Surtees, *The history and antiquities of the county palatine of Durham*, 4 vols. (1816–40) · Baker, *Serjeants* · R. Somerville, *History of the duchy of Lancaster, 1265–1603* (1953) · RotP · N. H. Nicolas, ed., *Proceedings and ordinances of the privy council of England*, 7 vols., RC, 26 (1834–7), vols. 1–3 · J. H. Wylie, *History of England under Henry the Fourth*, 4 vols. (1884–98)

Norton, Richard [*called* Old Norton] (*d.* 1585), rebel, was the eldest son of John Norton (*d.* 1557) of Norton Conyers in Allertonshire, near Ripon, and the heiress Anne Radcliffe (*d.* before 1557) of Rylstone in Craven, Yorkshire. The Nortons were a leading Yorkshire family whose heads were commonly JPs, sheriffs, and knights. John Norton was treasurer of the household to Henry Percy, fifth earl of Northumberland (*d.* 1527), where Richard was brought up. Of age by 1524 and probably already married to Susan Neville (1501–*c.*1560), daughter of Richard, second Lord Latimer, Richard Norton had close relations with her brother John, Lord Latimer (*d.* 1542). He was parker of the Percy lordship of Topcliffe near Thirsk in 1538. The Nortons' free warren in Rylstone conflicted with the forest of Borden belonging to the Clifford earls of Cumberland, and Nortons and Cliffords clashed violently in 1531, for which John was indicted. In October 1536 John and Richard diverted the Pilgrimage of Grace into besieging Cumberland's castle of Skipton in Craven, from which Robert Aske called them to Doncaster and to the Pontefract council. Neither was involved in the 1537 uprising, when John was a juror at the rebels' trials.

Perhaps it was his Percy connections that introduced Richard Norton to border warfare. He led 100 men on the 1544 campaign when his son Francis was captured at Ancram Moor and ransomed for £40. Next year, on the recommendation of Bishop Tunstall and Archbishop Holgate, Norton was appointed to the constableship of Norham Castle, Northumberland, and to the council of the north; in 1549 he was in constant attendance on Lord President Shrewsbury. In 1558 he was criticized by Queen

Mary for first subletting and then selling the constableship for £300 to Sir Henry Percy. Pleading ill health, inadequate munitions, the suitability of Percy, and especially the debts of himself and his father that left him unable to afford the responsibility, he offered to buy out Percy, if necessary by selling land, assuring the queen: 'I wish to serve you with all my sons and friends; no poor man intends truer to you'. Mary ordered him to serve or resign, 'as the contrary would not be to our contentation' (*CSP dom.*, *1547–65*, *addenda*, 468–9). He was not reappointed to the council of the north by Queen Elizabeth.

Richard Norton had good reason to be in debt. The Nortons were very long-lived and fertile. Richard's Norton grandparents did not die until 1520 and his father John lived until 1557. Long overshadowed by his father and resident at Hartforth near Ripon, Richard became a JP for Ripon only in 1538 and sheriff of Yorkshire in 1568–9. He was already old when he entered his inheritance, from which John had carved life estates for Richard's brothers Thomas and William. Richard's twenty children also had to be provided for. Francis, the eldest, was married in 1542 to Albreda Wimbish, eventually and unexpectedly an heiress. Further jointures were hived off for them, for Edmund (1553), John (1555), George (1559), Sampson (1570), and Francis's son John (1565) on their marriages. Respectable husbands were found for Richard's four sisters by 1538 and for his seven daughters, portions presumably being funded from the estate. Two daughters, Elizabeth and Mary, were married to Richard's wards Henry Johnson and John Green. Three sons, described as 'of Norton' or 'of Hartforth', were still dependants in 1569. No wonder that Richard married by 1563 the rich Philippa Trappes (*d.* 1593), widow of Sir George Gifford (*d.* 1557) of Middle Claydon, Buckinghamshire, nor that the fair appearance of Richard's house and park, 'where he had pleasure', concealed 'all out of order within' (*CSP dom., 1566–9*, 299).

The Nortons were plotting from 1568, when Richard's son Christopher planned to remove Mary, queen of Scots, from Lord Scrope's custody, and in November 1569 Richard's brother and seven sons, several middle-aged, joined Old Norton (Richard Norton) in the northern rising. So did his brother-in-law Thomas Markenfeld, and his nephew the seminary priest Nicholas Morton. Two sons and several daughters were to be recusants. 'Although an old gentleman with a reverend grey beard' (Camden, 121) and sheriff, Richard was a prime mover in what he saw as a Catholic uprising. He pushed Northumberland forward against his better judgement, resurrected the banner of the five wounds from the Pilgrimage of Grace, led the rebels into Durham and helped strip the cathedral of its protestant symbols, and may have created rumours of Spanish support to raise morale. Francis checked whether Mary could be freed.

The rising was disastrous for the Nortons, their friends, and tenants, many of whom were executed, dispossessed, and exiled. Edmund (*d. c.*1610) and Thomas escaped involvement and John (*d.* 1585) escaped punishment. Richard Norton, his five sons Francis, George, Christopher,

Marmaduke (*d.* 1594), and Sampson, and his brother Thomas were attainted. Two sons surrendered at once, and soon four Nortons were in custody. Richard's brother Thomas and son Christopher were executed at Tyburn on 27 May 1570: their exemplary Catholic deaths were celebrated in verse and prose by protestants as a warning to papists and traitors and lamented as martyrdom by Catholics. William and Marmaduke were spared and eventually released. Richard himself, Francis, George, and Sampson fled first to Scotland and onwards in 1572–6 to the Low Countries and France, where they were pensioned and whence Francis sought a pardon. Sampson died by 1574 and Francis in 1576. Richard and George visited Rome, returning to Paris in 1577 with a recommendation for George from Gregory XIII to Don John of Austria, who passed him on to the duke of Guise. Elizabeth Johnson, in the Gatehouse prison in 1580 but with Richard at his death, may have been his daughter. Richard occurs at Brussels in 1577–8 and in France in 1581–4. He plotted endlessly and communicated with relatives, friends, and co-religionists at home, where they were feared and persecuted as 'a tribe of wicked people … most of them in effect traitors, rebels, fugitives, and intelligencers against her Majesty' (BL, Lansdowne MS 27, no. 26). George visited Scotland in 1581, Rheims in 1582, and Scotland again in 1584, whence he went as an English agent to Richard in the hope of earning a pardon. Despite reports to the contrary, it was not George who was the very old man captured and wounded by a caliver blow to the head by English soldiers in Flanders in April 1585; probably it was Richard himself, who died at sea on 9 April, *en route* perhaps for an English prison. Richard's will the same day bequeathed garments to George and Marmaduke, referred to a servant Leonard and to assets in Italy, France, and Flanders, and urged his widow to repay his debts. Elizabeth Johnson, his executor, applied from Edinburgh for a pardon, probably successfully. George was still living in 1594.

MICHAEL HICKS

Sources *CSP dom., 1547–1625* · *CSP for., 1547–* · *CSP Scot. ser., 1509–1603* · *CSP Scot., 1547–97* · *CSP Spain, 1558–1603* · *CSP Rome, 1558–78* · C. Sharp, ed., *Memorials of the rebellion of 1569* (1840) · [J. W. Clay], ed., *North country wills*, 2, SurtS, 38 (1912) · S. Davie, *The end and confessions of Thomas Norton and Christopher Norton* (1570) · R. Bristow, *A briefe treatise of diverse plaine and sure wayes to finde out the truthe in this time of heresie* (1599) · J. Morgan, *Phoenix Britannicus*, 5 (1731) · R. R. Reid, *The king's council in the north* (1921) · R. R. Reid, 'The rebellion of the earls, 1569', *TRHS*, new ser., 20 (1906), 171–203 · W. Camden, *The history of the most renowned and victorious Princess Elizabeth*, [new edn], ed. W. T. MacCaffrey (1970) · *Dugdale's visitation of Yorkshire, with additions*, ed. J. W. Clay, 2 (1907) · M. Bush, *The Pilgrimage of Grace: a study of the rebel armies of October 1536* (1996) · T. D. Whitaker, *The history and antiquities of the deanery of Craven, in the county of York* (1805) · J. Fisher, *History and antiquities of Masham and Mashamshire* (1865) · BL, Lansdowne MS 27, no. 26 · PRO, E 164/38

Likenesses double portrait (with T. Norton); formerly priv. coll.

Wealth at death £186: PRO, E 164/38

Norton, Richard [*nicknamed* Idle Dick] (1615–1691), army officer and politician, was born on 19 November 1615, the second but first surviving son of Sir Daniel Norton (1568–1636) of Southwick, Hampshire, and Honor (*d.* 1648), daughter of Sir John White of Southwick. His father was a leading member of the county's Calvinist gentry, who opposed Arminian innovations in the church and claims for the divine right of monarchy. Richard was educated at Brasenose College, Oxford (1631–4), and Gray's Inn (1634), before travelling on the continent until 1636, when he returned to England upon succeeding his father, and in the same year on 4 July married Anne (*b.* 1617, *d.* in or before 1650?), daughter of Sir Walter Erle of Charborough, Dorset.

Despite his standing in the county Norton was not returned to parliament in 1640, and initially made his mark during the civil war as a colonel of horse, and as one of the leading members of the parliamentarian administration in Hampshire. He quickly became a hate figure for royalists, who repeatedly emphasized his plundering, his military cowardice, and the dominance of his mother. Parliament, however, had sufficient confidence in his abilities to appoint him governor of Southampton in late 1643, a task which he undertook zealously, as he did his role in the siege of Basing House. Like many local commanders his concern with the safety of his own county provoked tension with his superiors, and his status as an increasingly controversial figure is evident from the opposition raised in the House of Lords to his nomination as sheriff of Hampshire in December 1643. Norton evidently supported the creation of the New Model Army, and in May 1645 was made governor of Portsmouth, and played a leading role in countering the threat from local clubmen.

Norton was returned to parliament for Hampshire in December 1645, and although naturally concerned with military matters soon emerged as a figure of national stature. On religion he favoured a presbyterian settlement, albeit one which was firmly Erastian, and he opposed both the divine right presbyterianism of the Scots and the views of sectarians. Although he was personally close to leading presbyterians such as William Jephson and Sir Philip Percival, Norton's political inclinations lay with the Independent grandees who opposed the political influence of the Scots, but who also resisted pressure from the army. Norton was a close friend of Oliver Cromwell, who dubbed him Idle Dick, and during late 1648 Norton was perceived to be an important ally of those Independents, such as Viscount Saye and Sele and his son Nathaniel Fiennes, who led negotiations with the king at Newport. Indeed all three men were reported to be possible beneficiaries of a negotiated settlement with the king and the creation of a new royal court. The strength of Norton's connection to the Fiennes family is evident from his marriage, after the death of his first wife, to Saye's daughter, Elizabeth (*b. c.*1612, *d.* in or after 1655), probably in 1650, and his involvement in negotiations for Nathaniel Fiennes's marriage in 1653. Norton warned parliament not to provoke the army into revolutionary action in December 1648, but he himself was targeted by the more radical elements within the New Model and was a victim of Pride's Purge. He was readmitted to the Rump Parliament in November 1651, however, probably at Cromwell's behest, and although not a prominent member he was

able to secure election to the council of state in November 1652. Cromwell's influence may also have ensured Norton's nomination to the Barebone's Parliament in July 1653, and his reappointment to the council.

Norton supported the creation of the protectorate, was returned to parliament for Hampshire in 1654, and was reappointed as governor of Portsmouth in 1655. Although he remained willing to serve the Cromwellian regime in later years he was less enthusiastic about the rule of the major-generals, and during the second half of 1656 his loyalty came into question, particularly during preparations for the second protectorate parliament, when it became clear that he refused to support the candidacy of Major-General William Goffe. Although Norton was not prevented from taking his own seat he played little part in the proceedings, and by early 1658 was in contact with royalist agents. By March 1658 Charles II had solicited his support, although it was clear that he remained committed to the agenda of his father-in-law, Viscount Saye and Sele, and the Newport peace proposals in particular. Norton refused to sever his relations with the Cromwellian government, and sat in the 1659 parliament for Hampshire, but he declined to take his seat in the restored Rump in May 1659, when suspicions regarding his loyalty prompted his removal from the governorship of the strategically important garrison at Portsmouth. In the months which followed he avoided commitment to either the civilian republicans or the army, and returned to parliament only after the readmission of the secluded members (21 February 1660).

That Norton had distanced himself from the interregnum regimes is evident from his re-election to the council of state, his reappointment as governor of Portsmouth, and his election to the Convention Parliament, and he was able to make his peace with the royalists through the help of his kinsman William Legge. He remained in parliament until his death in May 1691, either for the county or Portsmouth, and although he was largely inactive, he nevertheless remained a powerful figure within the region. He sheltered an ejected minister at his house, was listed as a friend by Lord Wharton, and was later allied with the earl of Shaftesbury, whom he reportedly told in 1676 that 'the Church of England is the greatest schismatical church in the world' (*Fourth Report*, HMC, 231). Nevertheless he avoided active opposition on the issue of exclusion in 1679, and in 1685 protested his loyalty to the king during Monmouth's rebellion. In December 1688, indeed, he commented of James II's departure from England: 'Oh unhappy man to follow such counsel, the like was never or will be in story, a king with a great army driven out of his kingdom by a lesser army without fighting' (*Dartmouth MSS*, 3.135).   J. T. PEACEY

Sources *CSP dom.*, 1644–61 · *JHC*, 2–7 (1640–59) · M. W. Helms and P. Watson, 'Norton, Richard', HoP, *Commons, 1660–90*, 3.160–61 · C. H. Firth and R. S. Rait, eds., *Acts and ordinances of the interregnum, 1642–1660*, 3 vols. (1911) · *Fourth report*, HMC, 3 (1874) · *Fifth report*, HMC, 4 (1876) · *Sixth report*, HMC, 5 (1877–8) · *Seventh report*, HMC, 6 (1879) · *The manuscripts of his grace the duke of Portland*, 10 vols., HMC, 29 (1891–1931), vol. 1 · BL, Add. MS 24860 · *The writings and speeches of Oliver Cromwell*, ed. W. C. Abbott and C. D. Crane, 4 vols. (1937–47);

facs. edn (1988) • Thurloe, *State papers*, vols. 4–6 • *The manuscripts of the earl of Dartmouth*, 3 vols., HMC, 20 (1887–96) • *Calendar of the Clarendon state papers preserved in the Bodleian Library*, 5: 1660–1726, ed. F. J. Routledge (1970) • G. N. Godwin, *The civil war in Hampshire, 1642–45, and the story of Basing House*, new edn (1904) • A. M. Coleby, *Central government and the localities: Hampshire, 1649–1689* (1987)
Archives BL, Maijor MSS, Add. 24860–24861

Norton, Robert (*c*.1540–1587?), Church of England clergyman, was the son of Thomas Norton of Norwich. Admitted scholar of Gonville Hall, Cambridge, in 1556, he graduated BA in early 1560 and was a resident fellow in 1561. Dr John Caius described him at this time as 'bashful of nature', adding that he regarded this as 'a token of grace' in a young man (Venn, 43). Norton commenced MA in 1563, was university preacher in 1569, and was granted the degree of BTh that year.

On 11 February 1570, at the petition of the godly Norfolk magistrate Dru Drury among others, Norton was granted letters patent for the vicarage of Endgate (Beccles), by the lord keeper, Sir Nicholas Bacon. During his metropolitical visitation of Norwich diocese in 1572, Archbishop Parker suspended the aged Dr John Willoughby, rector of Aldeburgh, committing the cure of souls to Norton on the grounds that he was a learned man and a good preacher. After Willoughby's subsequent deprivation Norton was presented to Aldeburgh by letters patent dated 7 July 1572, and instituted on 11 October.

In 1573 Norton published his only known work, *Certaine godlie homilies or sermons upon the prophets Abdias and Jonas, conteyning a most fruitefull exposition of the same, made by the excellent learned man Rodolph Gualter of Tigure, and translated into English by Robert Norton, minister of the word in Suffolk*. The epistle dedicatory, to William Blennerhasset, was signed by John Walker from Leyton, Essex: Walker had in 1571 left the ranks of the godly Suffolk clergy to become archdeacon of Essex.

Norton proceeded DTh in 1575, and in 1577 was appointed town preacher of Ipswich at a salary of £50. In 1580 he resigned Beccles but was instituted rector of Sproughton, contiguous to Ipswich, in 1581. His preacher's salary was nevertheless raised in 1582 to a remarkable £73 6s. 8d.

Following William Negus's appointment as assistant preacher in 1584 Ipswich was riven by faction, probably because Negus objected to Norton's holding the preachership in plurality. So serious did the situation become that on 1 February 1585 the town authorities offered a reward of £40 for information leading to the apprehension of the authors or disseminators of certain 'libels and seditions' recently spread abroad against 'the governors and preachers' of the town. At the same meeting they were obliged to make up the balance of Norton's salary from the treasury, contributions from the townsmen 'failing in the collection'. A month later a committee was convened 'to conclude' with Norton and Negus 'for the departure or continuance of them, or either of them' (Richardson, 341–2).

The result was the resignation of both men. On 27 April the committee reported back that Norton was prepared to go at Michaelmas, with financial compensations. He finally departed with letters testimonial to the effect that

his resignation was the result of his scruples about non-residency and that otherwise his life was blameless, his doctrine orthodox, his family well governed, and his ministry diligent and industrious.

A successor at Aldeburgh was instituted on 30 June 1587 and although the episcopal register gives no reason for the vacancy Norton's death must be assumed since he likewise vacated Sproughton in 1587 and is not heard of again.   BRETT USHER

Sources J. Venn and others, eds., *Biographical history of Gonville and Caius College*, 1: 1349–1713 (1897) • BL, Lansdowne MS 443, fol. 181v • J. Strype, *The life and acts of Matthew Parker*, new edn, 3 vols. (1821), vol. 2, pp. 157–8 • Norfolk RO, DN Reg 13/19, fol. 184v • Norfolk RO, DN Reg 14/20, fol. 150r • N. Bacon, *The annalls of Ipswche*, ed. W. H. Richardson (1884) • CPR, 1569–72, nos. 345, 2691

Norton, Robert (*d*. 1635), army officer and writer, was the third son and fifth child of Thomas *Norton (1530×32–1584) and his second wife, Alice Cranmer, daughter of Edmund Cranmer, archdeacon of Canterbury, and niece of Archbishop Thomas Cranmer. Robert was to publish his own tribute to his father, 'Master Norton the Parliament man, [who] hath left even to this day a pleasing impression of his wisedome and vertues in the memory of many good men' (Graves, 1). His mother survived his father by many years, but never recovered from the severe mental breakdown she suffered in 1582; twenty years later, when she was living in the care of her eldest daughter, Anne, she was described as a 'Lunatike' (ibid., 403).

Robert Norton prospered. He benefited from the misfortunes of his eldest brother, Henry, bought up the family estate of Sharpenhoe, and acquired another Bedfordshire property in Markyate Cell in the parish of Caddington, near Dunstable. He married Anne Hare, daughter of Robert Hare, a minor gentleman from Lincolnshire, with whom he had three sons and two daughters. He also established himself in royal service, where he was made a gunner through the influence of John Reynolds, master gunner of England, under whom he had studied engineering and gunnery. On 11 March 1624 he received the grant of a gunner's room in the Tower of London. On 26 September 1627 he was sent from Lambeth to Plymouth in the capacity of engineer to await the arrival of the earl of Holland in order to accompany him on the expedition to the Île de Ré. Three weeks later, on 18 October, he was granted the post of engineer of the Tower of London for life. In 1628 Norton published two works on artillery whose dedications cast a light on the ambitions and frustrations which went with his post and with the pursuit of patrons. He initially dedicated *The Gunners Dialogue, with the Art of Great Artillery* to the duke of Buckingham, seeking his favour and leave 'to publish my Treble Architecture, Civill, Military and Marine, almost ready for the Presse' (Norton, *Gunners Dialogue*, sig. K2v). However, the duke's assassination cut that off, and the copy of the book in the Bodleian Library bears a second, hand-written dedication to Horace Vere, Baron Vere. Norton recalled how Buckingham had appointed him 'chief Comander of the Ordinance then designed for the Landservice in the late intended Expedition for Rochell'. Norton now sought the endorsement of the veteran Vere for the book, since Buckingham's 'sodaine & unfortunate End so soone succeeding, and his E[x]perience in this Ellement, then but in the Blossom, I have conceived to be the cause it hath not found the Entertainment (if I mistake not) it deserveth, among *English Gunners* for whose sakes it was first composed' (ibid., facing sig. K2v). Norton dedicated *The Gunner Shewing the Whole Practise of Artillerie* to the king, begging him to redress 'my wrong and discouragements' which had hindered the publication of the book, 'which if your Maiestie would be pleased to referre to be examined and relieved accordingly; It will then appeare I had cause to speake' (Norton, *The Gunner*, sig. A3v). Given the undistinguished conduct of the wars of the 1620s, he was perhaps somewhat tactless in how he expressed his patriotic protestantism:

> Gunners your Maiesty hath, but want Gunners, because they want Respect and Encouragement: let Occasions be ruled with Reason, Warrs managed with Displine, Iudgement, and Pollicie: Let Stubborne Offenders be punished, Deserving Men preferred, Eminent Places not granted for Favour to insufficient Men and Strangers, having honest Subiects farre more able to performe the Service: So we shall all make Holiday to serve our God, obey our King, and enjoy Gods blessings bestowed upon us. (ibid., sig. A3r–v)

There is one final glimpse of Norton as gunner from the last months of his life, when he was offered £5 by an ironmonger to intercede with Lord Newport and the officers of the store of the Tower in order to force one Thomas Browne, who had taken a contract to scrap old ordnance from the Tower and replace it with new, to make use of the furnace that the ironmonger had taken at Brenchley.

In his encomium to his father Norton referred to the many 'pretty bookes he wrote … tending to the promoting of religion, the safety of his Prince and good of his Country, to the advancement whereof, he applied his uttermost studies and endeavours' (Graves, 1), and in this the son emulated the father; his books on artillery form only part of this output, by no means untypical in their combination of patriotism and useful knowledge. He produced a series of works of practical mathematics. *A mathematicall apendix, containing many propositions and conclusions mathematicall, with necessary observations both for mariners at sea, and for cherographers and surveyors of land* (1604), which he claimed was based upon both the work of others and his own observations, sought to provide a reliable means of calculating longitude. His other mathematical publications were *Disme, the Art of Tenths, or, Decimall Arithmetike* (1608), a translation of the work of Simon Stevin; *A table of boorde and timber measure, more perfect than ever hath beene made shewing also the root between 4 and 31 from quarter to quarter* (1615?); and tables of interest and measurement and instructions in decimal arithmetic for the 1623 edition of Robert Record's *Ground of Arts*. He is probably the Robert Norton whose verses are printed at the beginning of Captain John Smith's *Generall Historie of Virginia* (1626). In 1630 he published his translation into English of William Camden's work, under the title *Historie of the most Renowned and Victorious Princesse Elizabeth, Late Queene of England*, and it was in the third edition (1635) that his panegyric to his father was published.

Norton died in 1635, between 28 January, when he made his will, and 19 February, when it was proved in the prerogative court of Canterbury. His wife had evidently died before him; his will mentions three sons and two daughters. M. R. GLOZIER

Sources CSP dom., 1623–5; 1627–8; 1636–7 • M. A. R. Graves, *Thomas Norton: the parliament man* (1994) • *Herald and Genealogist*, 3 (1866), 278–80 • will, PRO, PROB 11/167, sig. 19 • R. Norton, *The gunners dialogue, with the art of great artillery* (1628) [annotated copy with MS dedication, Bodl. Oxf., Savile G 27 (1)] • R. Norton, *The gunner shewing the whole practise of artillerie* (1628) • DNB

Norton, Sir Sampson (*d.* 1517), administrator, is first recorded on 18 October 1485, when with the designation of 'king's servant' he was appointed chief customer of Southampton—a post he held for at least fifteen years, also representing the town in parliament in 1487. Suggestions that he belonged to the Norton family of Yorkshire lack substantiation, though the unusual name of Sampson did occur among its members. In 1486 Henry VII granted him the manor of Tarrant Launceston, Dorset (worth £80 per annum); he became sheriff of Somerset and Dorset in 1494. In 1497 he was still 'of Southampton', but later lived mainly at Fulham, Middlesex.

Norton held a geographically disparate selection of offices. He was master porter and councillor at Calais from at least 1500 until 1505, under Sir Richard Nanfan (*d.* 1507). In 1500 he helped receive the Archduke Philip of Burgundy; he also witnessed the disloyal talk of the Calais treasurer, Sir Hugh Conway, which was denounced some time between 1502 and 1506 by John Flamank (perhaps the mayor of Southampton 1503–4, who seems also to have captained a king's ship). After a commission to inquire into Shropshire disorders in 1491 came the stewardship of Denbigh (1495), surrendered after two years, as perhaps was the constableship of Flint Castle, though Norton was reappointed to Flint in 1509 (after leaving Calais). Following the condemnation of Sir William Stanley for treason in 1495 Norton became chamberlain of north Wales in January 1496 and a titular chamberlain of the London exchequer in February 1495, holding these offices until 1503 and his death in 1517 respectively. He also became a knight of the body in this period. He was made Henry VII's master of the ordnance in 1494, though he seems to have been replaced four months later (on receipt of the Denbigh and Flint grants); but he had resumed the office by 1511, apparently without further patent. He 'played an important part in the major rearmament of 1509–15' (Ashley, 177).

Norton had long been involved in French affairs, as well as those of Calais. He was employed on a mission to Brittany in 1490, for which he was knighted on 20 June, and attended the reception given to a French embassy in 1492. These threads of his career combined in the French war of 1512–14, when he soon left the ordnance office to deputies. He was probably based at Calais in the summer of 1512, when his capture of some Frenchmen in Artois—then neutral territory, as part of the Holy Roman empire—led to a brief imprisonment at Arras. When Henry VIII invaded France in 1513, Norton was master of the ordnance in the army 'beyond the seas' and certainly spent the next winter at Calais. In February 1515 he was made marshal of English-occupied Tournai—a post he held for precisely one day before the news that he was to cashier much of the overmanned garrison brought a mob of soldiers calling for his hanging. A speedy departure proved expedient. Within three months of this fiasco he had been succeeded in the ordnance office by Sir William Skeffington (d. 1535).

In 1516 Norton was regranted the constableship of Flint Castle jointly with his cousin John Norton; a man of that name had served under him as an ordnance clerk. Sampson also had a Calais namesake, vintner there at least between 1528 and 1540. Sir Sampson Norton died on 8 February 1517. He was buried at All Saints' Church, Fulham, alongside his wife, Elizabeth (said to be an illegitimate daughter of John, Lord Zouche); he left no male children eligible to inherit his Dorset entail.   JULIAN LOCK

Sources *LP Henry VIII* · *Chancery records* · W. Campbell, ed., *Materials for a history of the reign of Henry VII*, 2 vols., Rolls Series, 60 (1873–7) · J. Gairdner, ed., *Letters and papers illustrative of the reigns of Richard III and Henry VII*, 2 vols., Rolls Series, 24 (1861–3) · C. G. Cruikshank, *The English occupation of Tournai, 1513–1519* (1971) · J. G. Nichols, ed., *The chronicle of Calais*, CS, 35 (1846) · P. T. J. Morgan, 'The government of Calais, 1485–1558', DPhil diss., U. Oxf., 1966 · J. Hutchins, *The history and antiquities of the county of Dorset*, 3rd edn, ed. W. Shipp and J. W. Hodson, 4 vols. (1861–74); facs. edn (1973) · PRO, ministers' accounts (Henry VIII), SC6 Hen. VIII · privy seals and signed bills (Henry VIII), Bodl. Oxf., MS Rawl. B. 238 · H. W. Gidden, ed., *The book of remembrance of Southampton*, 3 vols., Southampton RS, 27–8, 30 (1927–30) · *N&Q*, 7th ser., 8 (1889), 9, 133, 215 · W. E. Hampton, *Memorials of the Wars of the Roses: a biographical guide* (1979), 114–15 · R. Ashley, 'The organization and administration of the Tudor office of the ordnance', BLitt diss., U. Oxf., 1973, 36, 44–5, 96–7, 117–20, 149

Wealth at death main estate (Tarrant Launceston, Dorset) valued at £80 p.a.: Hutchins, *History*

Norton, Samuel [*pseud.* Samuel Rinvill] (1548–1621), alchemist, was the son of Sir George Norton (d. 1584) of Abbots Leigh in Somerset and his wife, Elizabeth, daughter of Thomas Grey, second marquess of Dorset, and widow of Thomas Audley, Baron Audley of Walden. He was the great-grandson of the alchemist Thomas Norton (1433?–1514) of Bristol. Norton's writings indicate that he was in residence at St John's College, Cambridge, in 1577 but it appears that he took no degree. He succeeded to his father's estates in 1584, by which time he was already active in the administration of the county of Somerset. Norton served in the Somerset commission of the peace, and, in 1586, sought the post of lieutenant-general of the Somerset horse. He appears to have been unsuccessful in winning patronage, however, and was removed from the commission of the peace for a time. Nevertheless, his loyalty to the crown and to the Church of England was not in doubt, and he was reappointed as a justice of the peace on the recommendation of Thomas Godwin, bishop of Bath and Wells, in the difficult days of the autumn of 1587. He acted as sheriff of Somerset in 1589, and thereafter as the county's muster master, in which capacity he helped to raise troops for the campaigns in Ireland in 1599. His service as muster master continued until at least 1615, despite difficulties in raising the rates for his pay which, by then, had fallen into arrears totalling £112.

Norton was proud of his descent from one of the greatest English alchemical writers of the fifteenth century and was eager to reinterpret the chemical discoveries of his great-grandfather in the light of the writings of Paracelsus. He distinguished between the work of Thomas Norton and his teacher and that of the other leading English alchemist of the late fifteenth century, George Ripley. Despite this, his own alchemical writings owed much to Ripley as well, and his earliest surviving alchemical manuscript consists of an English translation of Ripley's 'Bosome booke', which is dated 5 February 1574. This work provided the foundation for Norton's own, more wide-ranging exposition of alchemical practice, 'The key of alchimie' (Bodl. Oxf., MS Ashmole 1421, fols. 165v–220v), which was composed at Cambridge in July 1577. Norton dedicated the manuscript of his 'Key' to Elizabeth I, but failed to win the royal patronage which he sought. Awareness that his work fell under the prohibitions of the statute against the multiplication of metals may have prevented Norton from publishing any of his writings, which nevertheless urged both the usefulness and the simplicity of the alchemist's art and stressed that it need not bankrupt its practitioners in a fruitless search for unattainable riches. Norton claimed that the alchemical equipment and processes described in the 'Key' had cost him a little over £68, and that they promised to develop the perfect medicine.

Norton's early alchemical writings displayed an unusual degree of simplicity of style. This commitment to clarity was manifested in the increased use of diagrams outlining chemical processes in Norton's later writings which continued to reinterpret the native English alchemical tradition in a Paracelsian vein. Norton became particularly interested in processes involving mercury and sulphur, demonstrating his familiarity with the alchemical tradition of Geber (Jabir ibn Hayyan) and Avicenna, and distinguished between the preparation and action of three 'stones' (vegetable, mineral, and animal) in the purification and transmutation of metals. He also concentrated on the description of recipes for 'lac virginis', a liquid for the dissolution of metals whose alchemical importance he stressed. Norton did not neglect the practical aspects of his art, however, and continued to furnish his work with diagrams of chemical equipment and glossaries intended to simplify the arcane terminology of alchemy.

Most of these aspects of Norton's alchemical practice were displayed in an illustrated manuscript which he composed between November 1598 and May 1599, but which drew on writings dating back to 1586. This work, by 'Samuel Rinvill, alias Norton' and entitled 'Libri tres tabulorum arboris philosophicalis sive ramorum' (Bodl. Oxf., MS Ashmole 1478, 6, fols. 42–104; BL, MS Sloane 3667, fols. 17–21, 24–8, 31–90), replaced the structure of the 'Key of alchimie', which was divided into eight sections, with one of three books. Norton planned to supplement the manuscript with further books at a later stage, but none seems to have been composed by him. His writings circulated in manuscript during his lifetime, copies coming into the possession of the adept Thomas Robson, and, through him, reaching the library of the astrological and chemical physician Richard Napier, and eventually that of Elias Ashmole.

Norton's manuscripts also came to the attention of Edmund Deane (1572–c.1640), a chemical physician who, after being educated at Merton College and St Alban's Hall, Oxford, practised medicine in his native York. In 1630 Deane published editions of Norton's writings in Latin with the Frankfurt house of William Fitzer. Closely based on Norton's 'Libri tres', despite Deane's claims to have perfected an incomplete text, the eight tracts were entitled: 1, 'Mercurius redivivus'; 2, 'Catholicon physicorum, seu, Modus conficiendi tincturam physicam et alchymicam'; 3, 'Venus vitriolata in elixer conversa'; 4, 'Elixer, seu, Medicina vitae, seu, Modus conficiendi verum aurum, et argentum potabile'; 5, 'Metamorphosis lapidum ignobilium in gemmas quasdam pretiosas'; 6, 'Saturnus saturatus dissolutus, et coelo restitutus, seu, Modus componendi lapidem philosophicum tam album, quam rubeum e plumbo'; 7, 'Alchymiae complementum, et perfectio seu modus et processus augumentandi, sive multiplicandi omnes lapides, et elixera'; and 8, 'Tractatus de antiquorum scriptorum considerationibus in alchymia'. Deane's major addition to Norton's writings consisted of the composition of a dedication for each of the eight published tracts. Deane aimed high in his search for patronage through these dedications, the first three of which were addressed to William Laud, Samuel Harsnett, and Thomas Wentworth, respectively, but his efforts at winning support do not appear to have been fruitful. Perhaps as a consequence, Norton's alchemical works do not seem to have reached a particularly wide audience, although a German translation by the pseudonymous Vigilantius de Monte Cubiti appeared at Nuremberg in 1667 as part of the *Dreyfaches hermetisches Kleeblat*, and was reprinted in 1757.

Norton continued to live at the manor of Abbots Leigh until his death in 1621. His will, which was proved in February 1621, bequeathed his estates to his son, George, and his granddaughter, Grace, and mentioned a further two sons and two daughters, but nothing is known of his wife. SCOTT MANDELBROTE

Sources S. Norton, [Alchemical works], ed. E. Deane (Frankfurt, 1630) [8 tracts, each with sep. title] · S. Norton, 'The key of alchimie', 1577, Bodl. Oxf., MS Ashmole 1421, fols. 165v–220v · S. Norton, Bodl. Oxf., MS Ashmole 1478, pt 6, fols. 42r–104v · BL, MS Sloane 2175, fols. 148r–172r · *CSP dom.*, 1547–80, 635; 1581–90, 146, 364; 1598–1601, 167, 414; 1603–10, 126 · J. Strype, *Annals of the Reformation and establishment of religion … during Queen Elizabeth's happy reign*, 2nd edn, 3 (1728), 177–8 · Bodl. Oxf., MS Ashmole 1424, pt 2, 49–89 · Bodl. Oxf., MS Ashmole 1432, pt 8, fol. 10r–v · J. Collinson, *The history and antiquities of the county of Somerset*, 3 (1791), 152–3 · BL, MS Sloane 3667, fols. 17–21, 24–8, 31–90 · J. Ferguson, ed., *Bibliotheca chemica*, 2 (1906), 141–4 · T. G. Barnes, *Somerset, 1625–1640: a county's government during the personal rule* (1961), 263 · will, PRO, PROB 11/137, sig. 16

Archives BL, Sloane MSS 2175, 3667 · Bodl. Oxf., Ashmole MSS 1421, 1478
Wealth at death wealthy; bequests of £21; annuity of £10 p.a.; plus substantial estates at Abbots Leigh; debtors more than £100: will, PRO, PROB 11/137, sig. 16

Norton, Thady. *See* Ó Neachtain, Tadhg (*c*.1670–*c*.1752).

Norton, Thomas (*d.* 1513), alchemist, was the son of Walter Norton, merchant of Bristol and Worcester. His grandfather Thomas Norton represented Bristol in parliament six times between 1399 and 1421 and established his family in an imposing residence on the site later occupied by St Peter's Hospital.

In 1466 Walter Norton settled his lands in Worcestershire and the majority of his estate in Bristol on a younger son, also called Thomas, possibly the child of a later marriage. The older Thomas received only half the Bristol house, a silver cup, and a few household furnishings devised by will. On his father's death he may also have inherited lands at Stache and Kingston Seymour in Somerset. These estates, passed to Walter on the death of his brother and not included in the 1466 settlement, are later found in Thomas's possession. This partial disinheritance probably encouraged Thomas to seek his fortune in royal service and in the practice of alchemy, which was known to interest Edward IV. During the 1470s he represented himself as a member of the king's household. In 1479, when Norton was in dispute with the common council of Bristol, doubt was cast on the veracity of this claim, which is unsupported in contemporary records, but the council did accept that he had been among those commissioned to receive the lands of rebels following Edward IV's resumption of the throne in 1471. In 1475–6 he was sheriff of Gloucestershire and in the next year held the same office in Somerset and Dorset. In 1477 he was certainly employed as a crown agent, commissioned to seize the goods of John Stacy, condemned for practising necromancy against Edward IV.

In Bristol, Norton suffered from an unsavoury reputation, which culminated in March 1479 when he charged the mayor, William Spencer, with treason, apparently as a result of Spencer's earlier endorsement of Walter Norton's controversial property settlement. Among the welter of counter accusations made by the common council was the claim that Norton had deprived his younger brother Thomas of his estates, engineered his imprisonment in the Savoy, and driven him to seek refuge in Spain, on the voyage to which he drowned. The council also asserted that Norton had coerced his father-in-law, John Shipward, a former mayor, into supporting his claims. There is some truth in this story, as between 1494 and 1504 Norton held lands at King's Norton in Worcestershire which had previously been settled on his brother. The council also claimed that Norton was a riotous haunter of taverns and that he avoided religious observance. But this conflicts with the conventional piety of his will, which left instructions for burial before the high altar of St Peter's Church in Bristol, and made bequests for the singing of masses and for the local cult of St James. It is most plausible that the dispute between Norton and the council resulted from shifts in Bristol's internal politics. Shipward had been mayor of Bristol during the Lancastrian readeption of 1470–71, and when Edward IV regained the throne an order was made for his arrest, making him vulnerable to pressure from Norton, as described by the council. In turn, Shipward's death in 1473 and the power vacuum created by the fall in 1478 of Bristol's chief aristocratic patron, the duke of Clarence, must have left Norton exposed to his enemies.

Both Norton and the recorder of Bristol argued their cases personally before Edward IV with the result that the king sought to appease the quarrel by intimidating Norton into silence. This suggests that while Norton may have had a connection with the crown, he cannot be considered part of the king's close circle. Thomas Norton's boastfulness and the exaggeration of his enemies make it difficult to separate the realities of associations and alchemical activities from the accretion of myth after his death. There are no apparent grounds for the story related by Thomas's descendant and fellow alchemist Samuel Norton that Thomas had gone into exile with Edward IV in 1470. Similarly, the story that he learned alchemy from the Bridlington monk George Ripley originates from a misreading of a passage in Norton's *Ordinal of Alchemy*.

The *Ordinal*, the verse alchemical manual, for which Norton is principally known, was his only work, though it has been known by several titles, sometimes leading to the false belief that he wrote others. Within the text he states that it was begun in 1477 and he identifies himself in an acrostic deciphered by Elias Ashmole from the first word of the proem, the initial letters of the first six chapters, and the first line of the seventh:

> Tomais Norton of Briseto
> A parfet master ye maie him call trowe.
> (Norton, xlii)

This encryption typifies the obscurantism of the entire work, a characteristic justified on the grounds that it was only through moral perfection and divine revelation that the student could gain full access to the secrets of what Norton called 'the subtile science of holi Alchymye' (Norton, 6). While this appears to be at odds with the accusations about Norton's personal life, as a professional alchemist it identifies him with the contemporary vogue for ideas attributed to Roger Bacon and Ramon Lull, which were highly moralized in their approach and bore overtones of gnosticism. At the same time Norton stressed the importance of experiment, again reflecting the ideas of Roger Bacon, and continuing a trend towards systematic enquiry, which had begun under Henry VI. 'With due proofe and discreet assaye', he wrote, 'Wise men may learn new things every day' (Norton, 19). However, no efforts would reveal the philosophers' stone to those who sought it through greed. On the other hand, revelation might be granted to Edward IV to aid his search for social stability at the end of the Wars of the Roses. Thus, Norton commented that if the alchemical secret had been revealed before, the king would have been able:

> To have ceased taxes and tallages of this londe;
> Whereby much love and grace would have be
> Between knighthood, priesthood and commonalty.
> (Norton, 34)

Several expensive illuminated versions of the *Ordinal* were made in Norton's lifetime, suggesting that it reached a prestigious readership. Elias Ashmole, who produced the first printed English edition in his *Theatrum chemicum* of 1652, saw three of these manuscripts, one of which survives as BL, Add. MS 10302, and another, now lost, which bore the arms of the Neville family. The third, also lost, Ashmole describes as 'Henry the Seavanth's owne book', suggesting that Edward IV, while not necessarily commissioning the *Ordinal*, did own a presentation copy which he passed on to his successors. Norton's verse has an openness and vivacity which contrasts starkly with the opacity of alchemical instructions. His readability, combined with his fondness for moral axioms, sustained the popularity of the *Ordinal* through the sixteenth century and beyond, a point reflected in the numerous English manuscript versions which antedate Ashmole's 1652 printing. At the same time, the *Ordinal*'s influence reached Germany, where interest in alchemy was particularly intense, and it was in Frankfurt in 1618 that it was first printed by Michael Maier in a Latin translation. Norton lived long enough to see the beginnings of his book's success. He died on 30 November 1513; his heir, Andrew, the son of Thomas and his wife, Joan Shipward, was already forty years old.   ANTHONY GROSS

Sources T. Norton, *Ordinal of alchemy*, ed. J. Reidy, EETS, 272 (1975) · E. W. W. Veale, ed., *The Great Red Book of Bristol*, [pt 2], Bristol RS, 8 (1938) · E. W. W. Veale, ed., *The Great Red Book of Bristol*, [pt 3], Bristol RS, 16 (1951) · E. W. W. Veale, ed., *The Great Red Book of Bristol*, [pt 4], Bristol RS, 18 (1953) · J. Latimer, 'Some curious incidents', *Bristol History*, 22 (1899), 272–85 · inquisition post mortem, PRO, C142/29/123 · T. P. Wadley, *Notes or abstracts of wills*, Bristol and Gloucestershire Archaeological Society (1986), 27–8 · G. Roberts, *The mirror of alchemy* (1974) · E. J. Holmyard, *Alchemy* (1957) · A. F. C. Baber, ed., *The court rolls of the manor of Bromsgrove and King's Norton*, Worcestershire Historical Society, new ser., 3 (1963) · F. A. Crisp, *Abstracts of Somersetshire wills*, 5th ser. (1890), 73 · F. B. Bickley, ed., *The Little Red Book of Bristol*, 2 vols. (1900) · *Calendar of the fine rolls*, PRO, 21 (1961), 102 · *CClR, 1468–76*, 438 · will, PRO, PROB 11/17, sig. 30

Archives BL, Add. MS 10302 · BL, Sloane MSS 1873, 2174

Wealth at death lands at Stache; manor of Kingston Seymour, Somerset; estates in Bristol and King's Norton, Worcestershire; probably other Worcestershire estates: PRO C 142/29/123 (Somerset only); will, PRO, PROB 11/17, sig. 30

Norton, Thomas (1530×32–1584), lawyer and writer, was born in London, the first son (and heir) of Thomas Norton, grocer of London, and his first wife, Elizabeth, daughter of Robert Merry of Northall, Hertfordshire. Norton senior had roots in Bedfordshire and through fortunate purchase amassed substantial property there: Sharpenhoe, and the rectory, church, and advowson of Streatley which after his death in March 1583 passed to his eldest son. Thomas had two stepmothers. With the first, said to have been the widow of a Mr Osborne, his father had at least three sons. Of her suicide by drowning, William Fleetwood reported (7 December 1581) that 'she was ledd by evell spirettes some tyme to hange herselff and some tyme to drowne herselff'. He warned Walsingham that she 'hath left half-brothers [to Thomas Norton] the which are shrewdlie geven'. This malice and the stepmother's 'nicromancia' Fleetwood blamed on her upbringing in the household of Sir Thomas More, where she learned 'idolatrous toyes … conference and speaches had (as she thowght) with dead bodies being of her old acquayntans' (BL, Lansdowne MS 32, no. 9). Luke Norton of Sharpenhoe is almost certainly Thomas's half-brother; his education (some thirty years later) at Cambridge and the Inner Temple matches that of Thomas (Venn, *Alum. Cant.*, 3.269). Thomas's inheritance was sufficiently threatened for Fleetwood to ask Walsingham to alert the remembrancer of the exchequer, Peter Osborne, who was also a friend, possibly a relative, of Norton's. Thomas's father promptly married his third wife, Elizabeth Marshall, widow of Ralph Ratcliff of Hitchen, Hertfordshire, the schoolmaster–dramatist.

Education and early years Young Thomas matriculated fellow-commoner from Michaelhouse, Cambridge, in 1544 and again in Easter 1545; he took his MA in 1570 'after 12 years study' (Venn, *Alum. Cant.*, 3.269). By 1550 he was in the service of Edward Seymour, duke of Somerset, as tutor to his children with some secretarial duties. This was shortly after the duke had been shorn of the protectorship. Notably in Norton's first employment, as in his first marriage (*c*.1556 to Margaret Cranmer, daughter of the martyred archbishop), he allied himself openly and courageously with the two principal architects of the Edwardian reformation just as they fell from power. It was probably in Somerset's household that Norton met Cranmer, as well as English reformers newly returned from rustication or from continental exile: John Hooper, Thomas Becon (chaplain), and the duke's physician, the herbalist William Turner. In this company Norton made the first of his many translations: of a work by Pietro Martire Vermigli, rendered as *An epistle unto the right honorable … the duke of Somerset written in Latin and translated by T. Norton* (1550). Opportunities for contact with protestant reformers may have come before this, if the duke's support for the senior Norton's private bill in parliament of 1547 is taken as a favour to the son (Graves, 88–9).

Norton's literary publications in the following decade declare his moderate but unshakeable protestant loyalties. In 1552 he joined a team of translators led by Nicholas Udall, and provided an index for *The Paraphrases of Erasmus upon the Newe Testament*. This volume was the work of Miles Coverdale, Lennard Cox, and J. Olde. Udall indexed his own and translations by Thomas Key, Princess Mary, and Francis Malet. Their New Testament text was that of the Great Bible, their printer Edward Whitchurch, who together with Richard Grafton had published the first edition of the Great Bible in 1537 under Cranmer's guidance. In the first year of Elizabeth I's reign *The Paraphrases*, together with a Bible in English, were ordered to be placed in every church.

At Somerset House Norton probably met not only Cranmer, his future father-in-law, but his future patron, William Cecil, who was in service with the duke in 1547 and was imprisoned with him in October 1549. Cecil may have frequented the household as late as October 1551 (Graves, 27). Norton's first commendatory poem was prefixed to a tract by the duke's physician, Dr Turner, *A preservative, or treacle, agaynst the poyson of Pelagius latlie renued by the furius secte of the annabaptistes* (1551); the volume was dedicated to Hugh Latimer. Norton remained in post after the duke's execution (22 January 1552), living with his pupils, who were wards of the king, at the house of Lord Treasurer William Paulet, marquess of Winchester. In a letter of 13 November 1552 answering John Calvin's enquiry about the family of Somerset, Norton struck a note of solemn compassion for those 'cast down from the pinnacle of prosperity' (H. Robinson, ed., *Original Letters Relative to the English Reformation*, 2 vols., Parker Society, 37–8, 1846–7, 1.339). 'Philip Gilgate, a worthy gentleman, is their governour, and I retain my old office of instructing them' (ibid., 341).

Inns of court, translator, and man of letters Norton was twenty-one or twenty-two when Edward VI died in July 1553. He may have continued as tutor to the late king's cousins until his admission to the Inner Temple on 28 June 1555. While learning common law at the Temple he found time to translate some of the psalms. On Mary I's accession the printer Edward Whitchurch went into exile, probably in Germany. Whitchurch had published the first edition of thirty-nine psalms 'drawn' into English verse by Thomas Sternhold in 1549, the year of Sternhold's death. Some time between Whitchurch's last edition of the metrical *Psalms* in 1553 and the publication in 1562 by John Day of *Psalms of David in Englishe Metre by T. Sterneholde and Others*, Norton provided twenty-four psalms for the growing collection. It is likely that Norton was drawn into this enterprise through his domestic alliance with Whitchurch. The exact date of Norton's marriage to Margaret Cranmer is not known. Whitchurch married Cranmer's widow probably late in 1556.

Norton's poetic skill was praised in 1560 by Jasper Heywood (son of John, the poet and dramatist); his 'Ditties' are said to be worthy of those by fellow Templars Thomas Sackville and Christopher Yelverton (J. Heywood, *The Seconde Tragedie of Seneca Entitled Thyestes Faithfully Englished*, 1560, sig. A7v). When Sackville resolved to turn from love to holy poetry later in the decade, he was following William Baldwin and Norton who had already put 'their pen to paynt His honour and His praise' (Zim and Parkes, 20, 25). Some of Norton's original poems survive. 'Epitaphe of Maister Henrie Williams' appeared in Richard Tottel's edition of *Songes and sonettes written by the right honourable Lorde Henry Howard late erle of Surrey and other* (1557). In rhyming iambic pentameter Norton maintains that Williams (*d*. 1551) will triumph over death by his recent conversion to protestantism. The same conviction drives some unambitious octosyllabic quatrains: 'Stay gentel frend that passest by' (BL, Cotton MS Titus A.xxiv, fol. 79v). Also ascribed to 'norton' is a witty octosyllabic sonnet in Shakespearian form 'A Man may Live Thris Nestors Lyfe' (ibid., fol. 80v). Such experiments with verse were characteristic of students at the inns at this time, as Heywood notes.

For his prose translation of Calvin's final edition of the *Institutiones* (1559), *The Institution of Christian Religion* (1561), Norton used a dignified iambic pentameter blank verse to render Calvin's quotations from Virgil's *Aeneid*, vi, and from *Georgics*, iv. In this he may have been prompted by Surrey's experiments with two books of the *Aeneid*. For Calvin's borrowings from Horace, *Satyre I*, Norton chose fourteeners. Calvin's prose was most difficult because he packed 'great plentie of matter in small rome of wordes … so circumspectly and precisely ordered, to avoid … cavillations … in this matter of faith and religion'. In translating Calvin and drawing the psalms into English verse Norton observed 'howe perilous it was to erre in matters of doctrine' (*Institution of Christian Religion*, 1582, sig. A2r). Every sentence in his translation was read against the Latin by David Whitehed before printing. The second and subsequent editions set from printed copy were recompared with Norton's manuscript and purged of 300 printing errors due to 'the evill maner of my scribling hand, and interlining of my Copy' (ibid., sig. A2v–A3r).

An anonymous translation of four *Orations of Arsanes agaynst Philip the Trecherous Kyng of Macedone*, published by J. Day (*c*.1560), has been attributed to Norton (Graves, 41–2). The preface praises the usefulness of orations to 'the common weale' because they convey truths 'in the names of those persons whom they make to speake them … sometime for appeasing troubles, sometime for councell for mater of justice or of policie' (*Orations*, sig. A1r, A4v). More specifically, the concluding prayer for Queen Elizabeth exhorts her to 'destroy the rod of foreine and Popish tyrannye' to prevent the 'thraldome of Mariane crueltie' (ibid., sig. A6v–A7r).

In 1558 Norton was sworn a freeman of the Grocers' Company (his father's guild). Called to the bar in 1563 he thenceforth earned his living as a lawyer. On 22 January 1563 (shortly after the death of Edward Whitchurch) Norton was appointed standing counsel to the newly incorporated Stationers' Company with a yearly annuity of 20s. and paid 40s. 'for his counsell in Drawynge our ordenaunces' (Arber, *Regs. Stationers*, 1.189, 192–3). This association lasted all Norton's life and may have stemmed from Whitchurch's interest and influence. Norton and his wife, Margaret, lived with her mother and stepfather at Greyfriars until Whitchurch's death. Norton was one of his executors. He describes his stepfather-in-law affectionately in the last edition of the *Institutions* before his own death:

> her Maiesties Printer of the bookes of common Prayer … a man well knowen of upright hearte and dealing, an auncient zealous Gospeller, as plaine and true a friend as ever I knewe living and as desirous to doe any thing to common good, specially by the advancement of true religion. (Norton, *Institutions*, 1582, sig. Π2r)

In his preface to Grafton's *Chronicle at Large* (1569) Norton praised Whitchurch's courageous printing partner for his part in the Reformation. There were no children from Norton's first marriage. After the death of Margaret, some time before 1568, Norton married her cousin Alice (*d.* after

1602), daughter of Edmund Cranmer, archdeacon of Canterbury. They had six children: Anne, Elizabeth, Thomas, Henry, William, and Robert *Norton.

Norton's growing expertise as counsel for the stationers, for whom he also vetted books as early as 1571, brought him to the notice of Bishop Aylmer of London, with whom he was joined (27 November 1581) as licenser of books. Together with Dr John Hammond, Norton was appointed by the privy council as a commissioner to investigate privileges of the London stationers, as well as the privilege to print bestowed by Henry VIII on Cambridge University. On 18 June 1581 Norton was made solicitor to the Merchant Taylors' Company.

Gorboduc In collaboration with Thomas Sackville, Norton wrote the first Senecan tragedy in English blank verse. Its five acts unfold the story of one of Geoffrey of Monmouth's most unfortunate British kings: Gorboduc, in old age, divides his realm between his sons, Ferrex and Porrex; goaded by ambition the younger kills his brother; in revenge the queen murders the remaining son, whereupon the people rise up and kill both king and queen. The duke of Albany, the first of many Elizabethan stage overreachers, takes advantage of the power vacuum to make an unsuccessful but bloody bid for the crown. The tragedy of *Gorboduc* was praised by Sir Philip Sidney in his *Apologie for Poetrie* (1595) as 'full of stately speeches, and well sounding Phrases, clyming to the height of Seneca his stile, and as full of notable moralitie, which it doth most delightfully teach; and so obtayne the very end of poesie'. A significant aspect of the play's 'notable moralitie' was its classicization of English political history. Gorboduc sees himself as the last of the ill-fated Trojan survivors:

> GORBODUC: O cruel fates, O mindful wrath of Goddes,
> Whose vengeance …
> Ne slaughter of unhappie *Pryams* race,
> Nor *Illions* fall made levell with the soile
> Can yet suffice but still continued rage
> Pursues our lynes and from the farthest seas
> Doth chase the issues of destroyed *Troye*.
> (*The Tragedie of Gorboduc*, 1565, III. i, sig. D4r)

Equally innovative are the play's formal aspects. Each act is preceded by music and a dumbshow and followed by a chorus. Four Ancient Britons relate a mime of furies to the British story in rhymed pentameters.

The literary éclat of this 'new' form was heightened by performance in the solemn revels honouring the queen's favourite, Lord Robert Dudley, as patron of the Inner Temple on 27 December 1561. A second performance was given before Queen Elizabeth at Whitehall on 18 January 1562. A firsthand report of the performance of the tragedy survives bound in a manuscript which also contains Norton's holograph letter-book, his 'Devices', and other working papers mixed with papers of Robert Beale, later clerk of the council (BL, Add. MS 48023, fols. 358–359v). The anonymous viewer calls the tragedy 'Ferrex and Porrex'; so too does the authorized edition of 1570, thus focusing blame for dynastic tragedy on the king's unruly sons. After summarizing the plot, the viewer recalls three of the dumbshows and goes on to interpret the meaning: 'wherby was ment that yt was better for the Quene to marye with the L. R. knowen then with the k of Sweden' (ibid., fol. 359*v*). 'Many thinges were handled of mariage, and that the matter was to be debated in Parliament … but that hit ought to be determined by the councill … And many thinges were saied for the Succession to putt thinges in certenty' (ibid., fol. 359).

Until recently *Gorboduc* was thought to favour the succession claims of the English-born Catherine Grey, wife of Edward Seymour, earl of Hertford. But, although these revels were certainly favourable to Lord Robert Dudley's marriage suit, Norton was not a client of Dudley's. The Inner Temple–Dudley connection was probably suggested by the father of Norton's collaborator, Sir Richard Sackville, a privy counsellor and senior bencher of the Inner Temple (Wingfield, *Vitae Mariae Angliae reginae*, Camden *Miscellany*, 4.28, 1984, 267).

Parliament man and pamphleteer Norton's first parliament, as burgess for Gatton, was Queen Mary's last (1558). In Elizabeth's second parliament (1563) he sat for Berwick upon Tweed. His skill in the common law and his eloquence made him an obvious draftsman, though it is not known whether his numerous readings were all of his own making. In the Commons of 1563 he read a draft report of the committee 'to draw Articles of Petition for the Queen's Marriage and Succession' (Graves, 103). At William Cecil's request he worked loyally to detect and discourage pamphleteering about the succession. Norton's political discretion is notable during the 1560s, as is his alignment with Cecil's moderating tactics in the Commons.

The first printing of *The Tragedie of Gorboduc* in 1565 was almost certainly not authorized. Printer William Griffith recorded that: 'three Actes were written by Thomas Nortone and the two laste by Thomas Sackvyle'. However, this attribution of labours is not endorsed by the second, authorized, edition of 1570. Although act-by-act collaboration was sometimes practised by inns of court dramatists, modern attributions to Sackville or to Norton on the evidence of style have been conflicting and inconclusive. Acts 4 and 5 of the tragedy are larded with the most explicitly political advice; perhaps this is why the piratical printer wished to attribute these 'two laste' to the well-connected courtier Thomas Sackville. Norton himself oversaw the second edition, whose title *Ferrex and Porrex* refocuses responsibility for the tragedy on the king's ill-advised sons, and claimed that the imprint of 1565 was 'exceedingly corrupted' (sig. A2). In fact the texts are virtually identical, except for eight lines omitted in 1570 urging non-resistance to tyrants. Norton's prefatory complaint probably concerns the changed title and impolitic timing of the first edition, which appeared in the year that Mary, queen of Scots, married her cousin Henry Darnley (July 1565). Subsequent events made such caution unnecessary: Darnley's murder (10 February 1567), Mary Stewart's remarriage (May 1567) and subsequent deposition (July 1567), her flight and imprisonment in England, and the death of Catherine Grey (February 1568). In September

1569 Leicester revealed to Queen Elizabeth the duke of Norfolk's plans to marry Mary Stewart; the pope excommunicated Elizabeth (*Regnans in excelsis*, 1570) and the Ridolfi plot (1570–71) was unravelled soon after. This course of events convinced Norton that there was a papal conspiracy to depose Elizabeth I; hereafter his political counsel became overt and public.

Norton turned pamphleteer with *A discourse touching the pretended match betwene the duke of Norfolke and the queene of Scottes* ([1569]). Five further political pamphlets were printed by John Day and bound together with the authorized text of the tragedy by Thomas Norton and Thomas Sackville, now Lord Buckhurst: *All such treatises as have been lately published by Thomas Norton: to the queenes maiesties poore deceived subiectes of the north countrey drawn into rebellion by the earles of Northumberland and Westmerland*; *A warning against the dangerous practices of the late rebellion*; *A bull graunted by the pope to Doctor Harding etc. and other … to undermine faith and alleageance to the queene*; *A disclosing of the great bull, and certaine calves that he hath gotten, and specially the mou[n]ster bull that roared at my Lord Bishops gate*; *An addition declaratorie to the bulles with a searching of the maze*; *The tragedie of Ferrex and Porrex written by the L. Buckherst and Thomas Norton*.

With the battle lines now clearly drawn, Norton's next project had an educational thrust: the instruction of a protestant clergy and promotion of English as the language of the faith. His translation of Alexander Nowell's *Catechismus* is dedicated to the archbishops of Canterbury and York, the bishop of London, and 'all the other reverend Fathers my Lordes the Bishops … in England'. *A Catechism* was printed in 1570 by John Day 'under the protection of their names for the use of such as understand no latine at all, as also for their commodities who having a litle sight in the language desire some more perfection therin' (*A Catechism*, sig. A2r–v). Norton claims to have denied himself 'that libertie in rendering the sense at large, which the order of translation doth permitt' and 'tyed myselfe very much to observing of the wordes themselves, but so yet that I had alway regard to the natural properties and easinesse of our native tong'. From Day he 'procured that the English print answereth the Latine, page for page' (ibid., sig. A2v), as in his earlier translation of Calvin's *Institutiones*.

With his appointment in February 1571 as remembrancer to the lord mayor of London, Norton gained one of London's four seats in the House of Commons. At first the job entailed merely indexing city records, but Norton soon became in effect the mayor's personal secretary; in reporting the proceedings of parliament the remembrancer was increasingly expected to identify and advance the city's interests. By 1581 he handled all correspondence between the queen's government and the court of aldermen.

In the parliament of 1571 Norton introduced a comprehensive review of the canons for church government. From Cranmer's library he supplied an incomplete manuscript of a code of ecclesiastical law drafted in 1551 by a committee which had included the young William Cecil.

It was compiled by Walter Haddon and John Cheke under the direction of Cranmer, whose annotations it bears (BL, Harley MS 426). Christened *Reformatio legum ecclesiasticarum* by John Foxe, who gave it a preface and saw it through the press in time for the opening of parliament, the *Reformatio* proposes a more uniform administration for church courts and reform of ecclesiastical discipline (Freeman, 132). Although Archbishop Parker lent Foxe his own complete manuscript of *Reformatio* it now seems unlikely that he knew that it would be used in making the edition of 1571 (ibid., 138). Foxe and Norton, perhaps with a nod from Burghley, seem to have taken the initiative to find a broad consensus, including the bishops, for making moderate reforms to the prayer book and settling the dispute about vestments within the Church of England. If this interpretation is correct then the parliament of 1571 shows Norton, Foxe, and John Day actively moving for moderate reform; Norton is no longer Neale's 'hot puritan reformer' nor the grey 'man of business', the pawn of his patron (ibid., 144). Neither Foxe nor Norton challenged an episcopal role in church government. Nor did they look for support from members of the council in the Commons. In the event, Cranmer's *Reformatio* sank without trace. Such a comprehensive model of church government was not discussed again in any of Elizabeth's parliaments.

The moderate thrust of Norton's activities seems to have been misunderstood by Archbishop Parker who reprimanded him during the *Admonition to Parliament* controversy. Norton replied that his views on episcopacy had long been known to Parker (letter, 16 Jan 1573, cited in Graves, 319; PRO, SP 12/148, no. 37). Norton had advised Whitgift (Parker's choice for the reply to the presbyterian pamphleteers) that a published counterblast would merely add notoriety to *Admonition*'s attack on episcopacy.

Arguably Norton's most effective initiative in the parliament of 1571 was the treasons bill which he drafted in accordance with the sturdily loyal sentiments expressed in his pamphlets. This too was weakened by successive redrafting in committee. Norton originally called for the exclusion of any claimant who challenged the present queen's right. He defended such retrospective provisions in words reminiscent of his British tragedy: 'where ambition hath once entered such is the nature of the same that it never will bee satisfyed, and the thirst for a kingdome is unquenchable' (12 April 1571, Hartley, 1.214).

The consistency and toughness of Norton's position are exemplified by his attitude during the 1572 parliament to the duke of Norfolk's treason. Having been pardoned by the queen in 1569 Norfolk had persisted in his marriage plans and was tried by his peers in the Lords and found guilty of treason (16 January 1572). Norton was the scribe and 'wrote down the Trial upon the scaffold' at Westminster (*State Trials*, 1.957). Subsequently in parliament Norton argued implacably for petitioning the queen to have Norfolk executed. Even after this had happened (2 June 1572) Norton continued to argue, to no avail, for similar measures against Mary Stewart.

A range of issues occupied Norton in the parliament of 1576, where he sat on committees for aliens' children (3 March), and the queen's marriage (12 March). He served again in 1581, but there is no record of any of his parliamentary speeches. Asked whether 'there be few of the acts which either you have not drawn or travailed about penning them at committees' he replied 'all that I have done I did by commandment of the House, and specially of the Queen's Council there'. He admitted, however, that he had 'written many a bill of articles that the House did not see' (HoP, *Commons, 1558–1603*, 3.147). The diversity of this legal and administrative activity is unrivalled: parliamentary records reveal that in 1572, 1576, and 1581 Norton was a member of at least eighty-four committees.

Commissioner Between 1578 and 1583 Norton served as a commissioner to examine Catholic prisoners. The activities of the English mission had increased the presence of seminary priests, encouraged lapsed Catholics, and made new converts; from 1580 onwards Jesuit missionaries swelled the number. Pope Gregory XIII financed two expeditions to support Irish rebels in 1578–80. Norton took part in the examination of Cuthbert Mayne, a priest who was tried and executed for bringing a papal bull to England contrary to the statute of 1571. He also drafted questions put to the Jesuit Edmund Campion. When the council ordered a theological dispute between Campion and Anglican divines, Norton, although he had advised against it, organized the disputations, acted as scribe, and saw to it that Campion was provided with books. By such means he sought to counter reports of Campion's unjust treatment. He was present and in commission with John Hammond, the civilian, was questioned at Campion's trial in November 1581; though he was not present at the execution on 1 December 1581. He interrogated conspirator Francis Throckmorton and consequently wrote *A Discoverie of Treasons* (1584). Late in 1583 Norton drafted a private paper for the council, 'Chaine of treasons', in which he argued the similarities between Throckmorton's plot and Norfolk's.

The appellation 'Rackmaster' was given to Norton by Robert Parsons in *A defence of the censure gyven upon two bookes of William Charke and Meredith Hanmer … against M Edmond Campion* (1582). Parsons and other Catholic pamphleteers gloated that Norton's own brief imprisonment, following immediately after Campion's sentence, was punishment for persecution of Catholic 'martyrs'. Norton defended himself in a letter to Walsingham dated 27 March 1582 (PRO, SP 12/152/72) which may be a draft for the anonymous *A declaration of the favourable dealing of her Maiesties Commissioners … and of tortures, unjustly reported to be done upon them for matters of religion* (1583). As he later wrote in his 'Devices':

> Touching tolerations to papistes, I have ever holden, and have published this opinion, that her subjectes holding popish heresies upon persuasion of conscience were to be borne withall and releved by instruction and the leysure of Gods spirit to be attended, so long as they did not desturbe the church, and held them within the allegeance and loyal affections to the *Queene* for her crowne. (BL, Add. MS 48023, fol. 48v; Graves, 203)

Notoriety and the idiom of religious polemic have obscured the variety of service to church, crown, and parliament in Norton's life. His skills as a peacemaker were employed in the Channel Islands between 1580 and 1583. As the last remnant of the crown's duchy of Normandy, the islands were thought vulnerable to attack by Catholic powers. In the governorship of Sir Thomas Leighton deep conflicts emerged between his own military authority and those of the crown commissioners who regranted lands in the bailiwick of Guernsey. English common law clashed uneasily with Guernsey's elusive mixture of Norman customary law and unwritten island precedents. In response to this a royal commission was appointed on 27 July 1579; it reported by 9 October 1579, requesting a written codification of Guernsey's Norman customary law. Norton was paired with one of the 1579 commissioners, Dr John Hammond, civil lawyer, and their brief was to examine the island's code in relation to the Extentes made by the English crown confirming the rights and privileges of the Channel Islanders. While Guernsey's royal court prevaricated about producing a written code, as required by order in council, Hammond and Norton had to resolve several appeals connected with the matter (Report, 6 Aug 1580: 'The opinion of D. Hammond & Mr. Norton … for reformation of the Isle of Gernsey'; BL, Add. MS 48001, fols. 400v–401r). In 1583, when the documents were finally produced, the pair were given a new commission within the bailiwick of Guernsey. This concerned a conflict of authority between Governor Leighton and the newly enfiefed seigneur of Sark, Philippe De Carteret. Norton and Hammond were to 'content the two parties', which with further urging by Walsingham and Leicester they eventually did. (*Second Report*, 242–4, prints the order in council setting up Sark's new jurisdiction and constitution.)

Final years and reputation On 5 December 1581 Roger Manners (esquire of the body to Elizabeth I), wrote to his nephew Edward, third earl of Rutland, that 'Mr Norton, the great Parliament man is committed for his overmuch and undutiful speaking touching this [Monsieur's] cause' (*Rutland MSS*, 1.130). The circumstances of Norton's 'undutiful speaking' about the queen's last marriage proposal are not directly known. 'This cause' was the political courtship of Elizabeth and François, begun by the duc d'Anjou in the mid-1570s, soon after he inherited that title from his brother, King Henri III. By the queen's personal displeasure Norton spent three months in the Bloody Tower and a month under house arrest at his home in the Guildhall. Aspects of the episode remain puzzling. If Norton made his offending speech in parliament (which ended in March 1581) why was punishment delayed eight months? Were the events of early December mere coincidence? Campion was hanged on the 1st. Norton was imprisoned by the 5th. His Catholic stepmother was reported drowned by the 7th. Did she report her stepson's 'undutiful speaking' against a Catholic marriage for the queen? Although Norton bombarded his patrons with letters from the Tower the only cause mentioned is the queen's displeasure. Walsingham, Hatton, Mildmay, and

Burghley were unable, or unwilling, to obtain a release for Norton until after the duc's departure on 7 February 1582 (Graves, 393–4). The Tower took its toll. Norton's wife, Alice, suffering from menopause-related melancholia sank into permanent dementia (letter, 11 April 1582, Norton to Walsingham, PRO, SP 12/153/5). At the same time, his learned son and heir, Thomas, died in Cambridge.

Norton's own health was not yet in question and he resumed a heavy schedule of work, not entirely interrupted by his imprisonment. At Walsingham's request (BL, Add. MS 48023, fol. 41v), Norton began while still in prison what are now his best-known works: 'The devices' (white papers on reforming the universities, public schools and private schoolmasters, the inns of court, and chancery: BL, Add. MS 48023, fols. 45–58). Although 'Devices' was never printed in his lifetime its usefulness is attested by survival in contemporary copies among Walsingham's and Burghley's papers. In a second project requested by Walsingham (BL, Add. MS 48023, fol. 44v) Norton reviewed the reigns of the earliest monarchs. He chronicled first 'What warres'; second 'What good lawes have been made in eache time that have renued the public state?'; and third 'What rebellions have growen in eche princes time and what hath been the cause at issue?' Walsingham had asked for a review of a mere 500 years since the Norman conquest. Characteristically, the unfinished 'Norton of the v periodes of 500 yeares' is a prolegomena (owing something to Bale) to a much larger undertaking (see BL, Cotton MS Titus F3, fols. 271–275v).

There was not to be time for such a massive project. Norton's father died in March 1583 (HoP, *Commons, 1509–58*, 3.27; PRO, C142/203/12). At the family house in Sharpenhoe, Norton made a nuncupative will shortly before his death on 10 March 1584; this suggests a sudden, not a lingering illness. He was buried in St Margaret's Church in Streatley. His will was proved in London by his executor Thomas Cranmer (his brother-in-law) on 15 April (PRO, C142/203/38). He was succeeded as counsel to the stationers on 26 March 1584 by Richard Grafton; and as remembrancer in 1586 by Giles Fletcher. Although he described himself as early as 1551 as 'Thomas Nortonis Sharpenhavius' he was proprietor of Sharpenhoe, and the rectory, church, and advowson of Streatley for barely a year. The property passed to the eldest surviving son, Henry. Robert Norton became an engineer, the author of works on artillery and mathematics, and translator of Camden's *Annals*. Elizabeth married Miles Raynsford, a groom of the privy chamber. Anne, the eldest of the children, married George Coppyn, who was knighted at the accession of James I and became a clerk of the crown in chancery. The Coppyns were still caring for Alice Norton in 1602 (*Diary of John Manningham of the Middle Temple and of Bradbourne, Kent, Barrister-at-Law, 1602–1603*, CS, 99, 1868, 19).

Views have changed since J. E. Neale's seminal studies of Elizabeth's parliaments. Norton is no longer one of the 'hotter' protestants. His initiative in the *Reformatio* could have ushered in a period of moderate reform of prayer book and ritual. In the brief period before positions polarized it might have achieved a workable consensus of bishops and reforming protestants. But when the code sank in 1571 Norton accepted a procedural defeat. The view that he did not actively question the necessity for bishops or royal supremacy in church government is supported by recent historians. His ideals thus remained close to those of his father-in-law, Cranmer. But as a man of law and letters he actively continued to promote his ideas—drafting ordinances, clarifying common and customary law. His translations of key texts into English did much to educate the laity and non-Latinate clergy.

Robert Parsons's caricature of 'rackmaster' Norton has now been largely deconstructed. The 'spy's' diary long attributed to Norton is correctly listed in the posthumous catalogue of Norton's books and papers as 'Notes delivered by Charles Slade ... touching practices of the pope and thinglishe traitors and fugitives at Rome' (Hatfield House, Cecil papers, MS 140/5, fol. 51r, item 41). Sledd (or Slade) carried out espionage for Walsingham from Rome between July 1579 and May 1580 (Read, 2.323). The *Dictionary of National Biography* followed early pamphleteers in having Norton imprisoned for zeal in pursuit of Catholic recusants. Norton demurs in a letter to Walsingham:

> for my part I was never the Rackmaister but the meanest of all that were in commission and as it were clerk unto them, and the doing was by the handes only of the quenes servauntes, and by Mr. Lieutenant [of the Tower] (27 March 1582; PRO, SP 12/152/72)

His most recent biographer refines the evidence. Norton devised questions to determine treason, but did not take any part in decisions to administer torture (Graves, 276). It seems likely that Norton was a selected target because of his own skill in the pamphlet war. Patrick Collinson detects a strain in Norton's final years, when he lacked support of prelates of the quality of Grindal and Parker. He suggests that if Norton had lived ten years longer under the conservative Archbishop Whitgift and his queen he would have despaired of reforming the English church from inside; he would have questioned the need for episcopacy and moved closer to the puritan position (Collinson, 202). Norton himself must have the final word:

> I do not in this labour thrust in my self uncalled, and as I acknowledge and honor the continuance of Gods work in the hartes of her majestie and you all to the reparation of Gods church, which hath ben and shalbe her majesties defense and upholding for ever, so [God] will blesse me and my poore hod upon my back among the mortarbearers in the work of God, or rather the caryers away of dung and rubish to make roome for workmen and bylders in the house of Jesus Christ the church of England committed to his Salomon our gracious Quene. ('Devices': BL, Add. MS 48023, fol. 45v)

MARIE AXTON

Sources M. A. R. Graves, *Thomas Norton: the parliament man* (1994) · T. E. Hartley, ed., *Proceedings in the parliaments of Elizabeth I*, 1 (1981) · HoP, *Commons, 1509–58* · HoP, *Commons, 1558–1603* · P. Collinson, 'Puritans, men of business and Elizabethan parliaments', *Parliamentary History*, 7 (1988), 187–211 · *The manuscripts of his grace the duke of Rutland*, 4 vols., HMC, 24 (1888–1905), vol. 4/1, p. 130 · T. S. Freeman, '"The Reformation of the Church in this Parliament": Thomas Norton, John Foxe and the parliament of 1571', *Parliamentary History*, 16 (1997), 131–47 · G. R. Elton, *The parliament of England, 1559–1581* (1986) · H. James and G. Walker, 'The politics of *Gorboduc*', *EngHR*, 110 (1995), 109–21 · M. Axton, 'Entertainments of the 1560s ... and the inns of court', *The queen's two bodies* (1977) · C. Read, *Walsingham*, 3 vols. (1925), vol. 2, p. 323 · A. J. Eagleston, *The Channel Islands under Tudor government, 1485–1642*, ed. J. Le Patourel (1949), chap. 8 · W. H. Whitmore, 'Norton of Sharpenhoe, co. Bedford', *Herald and Genealogist*, 3 (1866), 276–81 · H. R. Plomer, *Wills of English printers and stationers, 1492–1630* (1903), 14 · R. Zim, *English metrical psalms: poetry as praise and prayer, 1535–1601* (1987) · R. Zim and M. B. Parkes, '"Sacvyles olde age": a newly discovered poem by Thomas Sackville, Lord Buckhurst, earl of Dorset (c.1536–1608)', *Review of English Studies*, new ser., 40 (1989), 1–25 · H. Baker, 'Blank verse before *Gorboduc*', *Modern Language Notes*, 48 (1933), 529–30 · S. Adams, 'The Dudley clientèle, 1553–1563', *The Tudor nobility*, ed. G. W. Bernard (1992), 241–65 · L. C. John, 'Roger Manners, Elizabethan courtier', *Huntington Library Quarterly*, 12 (1948–9), 57–84 · 'Royal commission to inquire into the state of the criminal law in the Channel Islands: second report', *Parl. papers* (1847–8), 27.242–3, no. 945 [Guernsey] · BL, Harley MS 426 · G. L. Bray, ed., *Tudor church reform: the Henrician canons of 1535 and the Reformatio legum ecclesiasticarum*, Church of England Record Society, 8 (2000) · Arber, *Regs. Stationers*, vol. 1 · W. W. Greg, *Licensers for the press ... to 1640* (1962) · W. W. Greg and E. Boswell, eds., *Records of the court of the Stationers' Company, 1576 to 1602, from register B* (1930) · Venn, *Alum. Cant.* · BL, Add. MS 33271, fol. 32 · inquisition post mortem, PRO, C/142/203/38

Archives BL, Add. MS 33271 · BL, Add. MS 32379 · BL, Add. MS 48001 · BL, Add. MS 48023 · BL, Add. MS 48027 · BL, Add. MS 48029 · BL, Cotton MSS · BL, Lansdowne MS 155 · BL, M 485/34 · Hatfield House, Hertfordshire, Cecil MSS · PRO, C 142/203/12 · PRO, SP12/152/72 · PRO, SP12/177/59 · PRO, 1584, 35

Norton, William (1526/7–1593), bookseller, was almost certainly not the son of Andrew Norton of Bristol, as asserted in the *Dictionary of National Biography*. IGI's claim that he was born in Onibury, Shropshire, the son of Richard Norton and his wife, Jane Pyeres, seems more convincing, as William's own son was later born in that parish and the parish was also remembered in William's will. He was an apprentice of the London bookseller William Bonham, whose daughter, Joan (d. in or after 1593), he later married. The date of his freedom as a member of the Stationers' Company is unknown, but he bound an apprentice on 13 October 1556 and was listed in the Stationers' Company's charter of incorporation in May 1557. He was elected to the company's livery in the summer of 1561, and during 1561–2 he entered his first title in the Stationers' register. He served as a renter warden for the company for two successive terms between 1563 and 1565; in the latter year he and Joan had a son, Bonham *Norton (1565–1635), born at Onibury. Norton's name does not appear frequently on imprints: the first surviving work to bear his name dates from 1570, by which time he had already risen to the office of under warden in the company. He also served as upper warden twice during the 1570s. His device showed a barrel (a 'tun') displaying the letters 'Nor' with a Sweet William growing out of it.

Few of Norton's imprints bear an address; this may mean, as Peter Blayney has suggested for other London booksellers, that he operated more than one bookshop. However, he took up a lease for a property from the bishop of London in St Paul's Churchyard on 25 May 1573, which was renewed for twenty-one years a decade later. This was the Queen's Arms in the north of the churchyard, first identified in a Norton imprint in 1580, and was presumably a continuation of the King's Arms that was used by his former master, William Bonham, during the 1540s. He was a partner with the bookseller George Bishop in the publication of at least six books. Norton's publications included works by Horace, Cicero, Erasmus, Calvin, Thomas Palfreyman, Thomas Cogan, Paolo Manuzio, and Dionis Gray, as well as a Latin psalter and the Bible in Latin and in English. His publication of John Browne's *The marchants avizo verie necessarie for their sonnes and servants when they first send them beyond the seas* (1589) is interesting given the later foreign commercial interests of his nephew John *Norton, whom Norton freed in July 1586.

With the death of the printer Reyner Wolfe in 1573 his lucrative printing patent as the queen's typographer for Latin, Greek, and Hebrew (most notable for including the rights to Lily's *Grammar*) was granted in December for life to Francis Flower, a non-stationer. Flower promptly appointed six members of the book trade, including Norton, as his assigns to exercise the patent in return for an annuity. One of the assigns, Christopher Barker, later commented that while the *Grammar* was 'the most profitable Copie in the Realme', the assigns had been heard to grumble that 'they would willingly geve two, or three hundred pound, to be rid thereof' (Arber, *Regs. Stationers*, 1.115). Later in the decade the patent was cited in a list of other privileges in a petition of complaint from members of the book trade, despite every one of its assigns being among the signatories. The terms of the patent were evidently much infringed: not only did John Wolfe pirate works protected by the patent, but the assigns were forced to go to Star Chamber twice during 1585 and 1586 to defend their rights. Norton remained an assign until his death.

Norton served as master of the company for 1581–2 and 1586–7, and was a common councilman for the city from 1583. He was also the treasurer of Christ's Hospital from 1581 or 1582 until 1593. In October 1590 he and George Bishop were involved in a scheme to buy a house belonging to one Bland—presumably the Adam Bland who had purchased premises adjacent to Stationers' Hall in the 1550s—in order to sell it on to the company. In an unusual gesture on 6 March 1592 Norton arrived at the meeting of the company's governing body (of which he was a member) carrying a 'wrytinge Roled up cov[er]ed w[i]th paper bound w[i]th packthred and sealed up w[i]th his seale' which he described as his will; this was solemnly deposited in the company's chest and was ordered not to be unsealed without the unanimous consent of the court (Greg and Boswell, 40). In July of the following year Norton was elected master of the company for a third time but never completed his term: he attended his last meeting on 3 December but was dead by 14 December, when the court reconvened to open his will. According to the family monument in St Faith's under St Paul's, where he was buried, he was aged sixty-six at his death.

Norton's will was an important document, but because the version granted probate on 1 January 1594 was dated 27 August 1593 this copy evidently superseded the one deposited in Stationers' Hall in 1592. He died a wealthy man, with his wife and son each receiving a third of his estate (Bonham also inherited his property interests in Shropshire, Middlesex, and Kent), and the will included bequests to members of Christ's Hospital who had gone on to the universities of Oxford or Cambridge and to no fewer than nine parishes both in London and elsewhere. Its most lasting legacy, however, was of land to the governors of Christ's Hospital who were to pay annuities to the Stationers' Company and to the churchwardens of Onibury; Norton requested that the bulk of the annuity to the company be used to make interest free loans to members of the company.

Norton is to be distinguished from a member of the Merchant Taylors' Company of the same name who was active in London in the 1580s.   I. GADD

Sources STC, 1475–1640 · DNB · IGI · W. W. Greg and E. Boswell, eds., *Records of the court of the Stationers' Company, 1576 to 1602, from register B* (1930) · E. G. Duff, *A century of the English book trade* (1905) · P. W. M. Blayney, *The bookshops in Paul's Cross churchyard* (1990) · will, PRO, PROB 11/83, sig. 8 · private information (2004) [J. Barnard; M. Treadwell, Trent University, Canada] · W. C. Ferguson, *The loan book of the Stationers' Company with a list of transactions, 1592–1692* (1989) · P. Blayney, 'William Cecil and the Stationers', *The Stationers' Company and the book trade, 1550–1990*, ed. R. Myers and M. Harris (1997), 11–34 · H. R. Plomer, *Abstracts from the wills of English printers and stationers from 1492 to 1630* (1903) · Arber, *Regs. Stationers* · W. Dugdale, *The history of St Paul's Cathedral in London* (1658) · C. K. Manzione, *Christ's Hospital of London, 1552–1598: 'a passing deed of pity'* (1995)

Norway, Nevil Shute [*pseud.* Nevil Shute] (**1899–1960**), novelist and aeronautical engineer, was born in Ealing, London, on 17 January 1899, the younger son of Arthur Hamilton Norway CB (1859–1938), who became an assistant secretary at the General Post Office and wrote erudite travel books, and his wife, Mary Louisa Gadsden (d. 1932). At the age of eleven Norway played truant from his first preparatory school in Hammersmith, spending inquisitive days among the model aircraft at the Science Museum. On being detected in these precocious studies he was sent to the Dragon School, Oxford, and thence to Shrewsbury School. His brother, Fred, was killed in action in 1915. Norway was on holiday in Dublin, where his father was then secretary to the Post Office in Ireland, at the time of the Easter rising of 1916 and acted as a stretcher-bearer, winning commendation for gallant conduct. He passed into the Royal Military Academy, Woolwich, with the aim of being commissioned into the Royal Flying Corps; but a bad stammer led to his being failed at his final medical examination, and he returned to civil life. In August 1918 he enlisted in the Suffolk regiment as a private and was posted on the Isle of Grain.

In 1919 Norway went to Balliol College, Oxford, where he took third-class honours in engineering science in 1922 and rowed in the college second eight. During the vacations he worked, unpaid, for the Aircraft Manufacturing Company at Hendon, then for Geoffrey de Havilland's own firm, which he joined as an employee on coming down from Oxford. He fulfilled his thwarted wartime ambition of learning to fly in 1923 and gained experience as a test observer by 1924. During the evenings he wrote novels and short stories, unperturbed by publishers' rejection slips. He wrote under his forenames only, as he felt authorship would compromise his reputation as a serious engineer. His first book, *Marazan*, was published in 1926.

In 1924 Norway took the post of chief calculator to the Airship Guarantee Company, a subsidiary of Vickers Ltd, to work on the construction of the R100. In 1929 he became deputy chief engineer under Barnes Wallis and in the following year he flew to and from Canada in the R100. He had a passionate belief in the future of airships but his hopes foundered in the crash of its government rival, the R101, wrecked with the loss of Lord Thomson, the minister of aviation, and most of those on board. He had watched with mounting horror what he regarded as the criminal inefficiency with which the R101 was constructed. His experience in this phase of his career left a lasting bitterness; it bred in him an almost pathological distrust of politicians and civil servants.

In 1931 Norway married Frances Mary Heaton, a doctor. They had two daughters. It was in the same year that, having recognized that airship development was a lost cause, he founded Airspeed Ltd, aeroplane constructors, in an old garage; he remained the company's joint managing director until 1938. The pioneering atmosphere of aircraft construction in those years suited his temperament. He revelled in individual enterprise and doing things by improvisation on a financial shoestring. When the business grew and was becoming one of humdrum routine, producing aircraft to government orders, he decided to get out of the rut and live by writing. He had by 1938 enjoyed some success as a novelist and had sold the film rights of *Lonely Road* (1932) and *Ruined City* (1938).

On the outbreak of war in 1939 Norway joined the Royal Naval Volunteer Reserve as a sub-lieutenant in the miscellaneous weapons department. Rising to lieutenant-commander in 1941, he found experimenting with secret weapons a job after his own heart. But his growing celebrity as a writer caused him to be in the Normandy landings on 6 June 1944, for the Ministry of Information, and to be sent to Burma as a correspondent in 1945. Soon after demobilization in 1945 he emigrated to Australia and made his home in Langwarrin, Victoria. High taxation and what he felt to be the decadence of Britain, with the spirit of personal independence and freedom dying, led him to leave the old country.

As a writer Norway had an unaffectedly popular touch which made his books best-sellers throughout the Commonwealth and the United States; his success lay in his skill in combining loving familiarity with technicalities and a straightforward sense of human relationships and values. He conveyed to readers his own zest for making aircraft and flying them, and he sympathetically portrayed the hazards and rewards that were the lot of backroom boys. His briskly moving plots were superior to his characterizations, and he retained to the last the outlook of a decent, average public-school boy of his generation. Although he lived into the James Bond era he never made concessions to the fast-growing appetite in the mass-fiction market for sadism and violence.

No Highway (1948), dealing with the drama of structural fatigue in aircraft, set in human terms of those responsible for a competitive passenger service, gave full scope to both sides of Norway's talent. Machines and men and women share in shaping the drama. *A Town Like Alice* (1950), describing the grim odyssey of white women and children in Japanese-occupied Malaya, captured cinema audiences in 1958 as completely as it had the reading public. This novel was also produced as a television serial in 1981. *Round the Bend* (1951) was thought by Norway himself to be his most enduring book. It told of an aircraft engineer of mixed Eastern and Western stock who taught his men to worship God through work conscientiously and prayerfully performed and came to be regarded as divine by people of many creeds. *On the Beach* (1957) expressed Norway's sensitive appreciation of the frightful possibilities of global nuclear warfare and annihilation by radioactive dust. It was very popular and was filmed in 1959. Other novels, several of them also filmed, were *What Happened to the Corbetts* (1939), *An Old Captivity* (1940), *Landfall* (1940), *Pied Piper* (1942), *Pastoral* (1944), *In the Wet* (1953), and *Requiem for a Wren* (1955).

In *Slide Rule* (1954), subtitled *The Autobiography of an Engineer*, Norway told, candidly and racily, of his life up to 1938, when he left the aircraft industry. His stammer, which was as much a stimulus as a handicap, did not prevent him from being good company, and he was always welcome at the social gatherings of his many friends. An enthusiastic yachtsman and fisherman as well as an air pilot, he delighted in outdoor life, and his gaiety was not dimmed by the heart attacks from which he suffered. He died in Melbourne on 12 January 1960.

A. P. RYAN, *rev.* SAYONI BASU

Sources *The Times* (13 Jan 1960) · N. Shute [N. S. Norway], *Slide rule* (1954) · J. Smith, *Nevil Shute* (1976) · J. Bennet, 'Nevil Shute: exile by choice', *A sense of exile*, ed. B. Bennet (1988) · W. H. Wilde, J. Hooton, and B. Andrews, *The Oxford companion to Australian literature*, 2nd edn (1994), 696 · WWW
Archives BL, corresp. with Society of Authors, Add. MS 56763
Likenesses photographs, 1953, Hult. Arch. · photograph, repro. in *The Times*

Norwell [Northwell], **William** (*fl.* 1311–1352), administrator, came from Norwell, near Southwell in Nottinghamshire. He is first recorded as clerk of Queen Isabella's kitchen in 1311–12, before serving in a similar post in the king's household from 1312 to 1314. By 1324 Norwell was surveyor of all royal purveyors, but then transferred once more to Isabella's service. He spent the next two years with her in France, and on his return was entrusted with the treasures of Edward II stored at Caerphilly. He went overseas with Henry Burghersh, bishop of Lincoln (*d.* 1340), in 1329 and was attorney for Richard Bury (*d.* 1345), the keeper of the privy seal, in April and May 1331. In addition to the prebend of Freeford in Staffordshire, he held from 1332 the rich prebend of Norwell Overhall in Southwell Minster. Although this was a royal living reserved for household clerks, his presentation to Norwell Overhall was initially disputed by Archbishop William Melton of York (*d.* 1340), delaying his installation for almost a year.

Norwell was cofferer of the wardrobe under Robert Tawton (1331–4) and on the latter's death rendered account in person for him. From April 1335 to September 1337 he was keeper of the great wardrobe, now an independent office accounting directly to the exchequer. During that period he rented quarters for the office while it was at York, and in 1336 was reimbursed for spending money on repairing and improving the houses and chambers of the wardrobe's London office in Lombard Street. He became controller of the wardrobe (1337–8) before being once more appointed keeper of the wardrobe on 12 July 1338. In 1338 he settled by fine on Henry, son of Richard Graving, lands in North and South Clifton, Norwell Woodhouse, Ossington, Holme, North Muskham, Sutton, and Kelham.

Norwell remained in office for two years and directed the financial transactions underpinning operations in France at that time. His surviving account (PRO, E 36/203) covers the early campaigns of the Hundred Years' War and is important for the light it sheds on the role played by the wardrobe in the administration of the war, exemplifying in particular the widened scope, responsibility, and considerable autonomy it possessed. On William de la Pole's retirement, Norwell became second baron of the exchequer (21 June 1340). In 1342 he was appointed to audit the account of Bartholomew Burghersh (*d.* 1355) for payments to the emperor and Edward III's German allies and creditors. Norwell remained at the exchequer until 1352. It is not known how much longer he lived, but he was dead by 1357.

He is not to be confused with another **William Norwell** (*fl.* 1345–1362), who served Edward, the Black Prince, as keeper of his wardrobe from 1345 to 1349, and was still acting as keeper in 1354. Concerned with financial administration both in the duchy of Cornwall and in Aquitaine, he was eventually appointed chief baron of the Black Prince's exchequer in 1362. Like his namesake he became prebendary of Norwell Overhall, succeeding John Norwell in 1353. This William rather than his namesake may have been a canon of Lichfield *c.*1342–1358.   A. J. MUSSON

Sources Chancery records · Tout, *Admin. hist.*, vols. 3–6 · D. M. Broome, 'The exchequer in the reign of Edward III, 1327–1377: a preliminary investigation', PhD diss., University of Manchester, 1922 · E. Andre, 'Die Reise Eduards III auf dem Kontinent, 1338–1340', doctoral diss., University of Bonn, 1993 · G. L. Harriss, *King, parliament and public finance in medieval England to 1369* (1975) · B. Wilkinson, *The chancery under Edward III* (1929) · R. Thoroton, *The antiquities of Nottinghamshire*, rev. J. Throsby, 2nd edn, 3 vols. (1790–96), vol. 3 · *The wardrobe book of William de Norwell*, ed. M. Lyon and others (1983) · M. C. B. Dawes, ed., *Register of Edward, the Black Prince*, 4 vols., PRO (1930–33) · W. H. Bliss, ed., *Calendar of entries in the papal registers relating to Great Britain and Ireland: petitions to the pope* (1896), 300
Archives PRO, wardrobe account, E 36/203

Norwell, William (*fl.* 1345–1362). *See under* Norwell, William (*fl.* 1311–1352).

Norwich. For this title name *see* individual entries under Norwich; *see also* Denny, Edward, first earl of Norwich (1569–1637) [*see under* Denny, Sir Anthony (1501–1549)]; Goring, George, first earl of Norwich (1585–1663); Cooper, (Alfred) Duff, first Viscount Norwich (1890–1954); Cooper, Diana Olivia Winifred Maud, Viscountess Norwich (1892–1986).

Norwich, Benedict (*fl.* 1340), prior of Norwich and theologian, was probably born in Norwich at the beginning of the fourteenth century. He entered the Augustinian order at the Norwich convent, and later became its prior. He probably studied at Oxford in the 1320s or 1330s, and was one of a number of scholars in the early fourteenth century who applied the teaching of the university arts faculties, on grammar, logic, and philosophy, to the study of theology. He was the author of an *Alphabetum Aristotelis*, some rhetorical letters, and a collection of sermons, none of which survives. The character of his work is unclear. Bale describes him vaguely as 'a man well-versed both in rhetoric and theology' (Bale, *Cat.*, 481), but it is probable that he was a follower of William Ockham (*d.* 1349). As a result of his work he became embroiled in controversy, and may have been accused of heresy. He was probably one of the English Augustinian friars attacked in a decree issued by the order's general chapter at Pavia in 1348. Issued at the instigation of the chapter's president, the theologian Thomas of Strasbourg, it outlawed the study of the works of Ockham in the friars' English studia. Under the patronage of Antony (II) Bek, bishop of Norwich (*d.* 1343), Benedict Norwich was appointed bishop of 'Sardica' with suffragan duties in Norwich (under Bek himself), and in Winchester under bishops Adam Orleton (*d.* 1345) and William Edington (*d.* 1366). The date of his death is unknown.   JAMES G. CLARK

Sources Bale, *Cat.*, 1.481 · Tanner, *Bibl. Brit.-Hib.*, 96 · A. Gwynn, *The English Austin friars in the time of Wyclif* (1940), 45–53 · F. M. Powicke and E. B. Fryde, eds., *Handbook of British chronology*, 2nd edn, Royal Historical Society Guides and Handbooks, 2 (1961), 267

Norwich, Isaac of (*c.*1170–1235/6), moneylender and patron of rabbinic scholarship, was the only known son of Eliab (or Jurnet) of Norwich (*c.*1130–1197) and his wife, Muriel. His father, also a moneylender and scholarly patron, was the dominant figure in the twelfth-century Jewish community of Norwich, and was one of the half-dozen or so wealthiest Jews in England. Although Eliab suffered serious losses in 1177, in a failed consortium to lend money to the crown, and was briefly exiled from England during the 1180s, he returned from the continent in 1186 on promise of a fine of 2000 marks, and resided thereafter in Norwich until his death in 1197.

Isaac of Norwich first appears in the records in 1194, as a partner with his father and mother in a small loan contract. Three years later, on his father's death, he paid a fine of 1000 marks to accede as heir to his father's estate. He appears to have been immediately successful. In 1199 his personal wealth amounted to more than 10 per cent of the total taxable wealth of the English Jewish community. His financial transactions extended throughout the eastern counties, and although the bulk of his fortune almost certainly came from moneylending, his six houses in Bishop's Lynn and the quay attached to his own stone house in Norwich suggest that he also had interests in trade.

Like his father, Isaac became the leading figure in the Jewish community of Norwich, carrying on a family tradition of financial support for rabbinical study, which earned Eliab, Isaac, and Isaac's own sons Moses and Samuel the honorific title *HaNadib* ('the Generous'). Under the family's patronage Norwich became one of the two leading centres in England for Hebrew learning in the half-century after 1190. Isaac and Samuel may have been rabbinical teachers themselves, as well as patrons of other teachers.

Along with other prominent English Jews, in 1210 Isaac fell victim to the wholesale confiscations and imprisonments ordered by King John in connection with the Bristol tallage of that year. Isaac avoided execution by promising the king a fine of 10,000 marks, and in 1213 was transferred from Bristol to the Tower of London. But he may not have been released from the Tower until 1217, when his remaining bonds were returned to him, and he and the rest of the Jews of Norwich were given letters of royal protection. Even so, Isaac continued to come under pressure in the early years of Henry III's reign, especially from the papal legate, Pandulf (d. 1226). In his last years he featured in a number of important legal cases, and also became the subject of a famous caricature drawn on a tallage roll of 1233. A rumour of his death circulated in 1230, but in fact he did not die until late 1235 or 1236.

Isaac had two sons, Moses (b. before 1200) and Samuel (b. before 1204), and a sister, Margalita, who was active on her own account in 1201. Moses moved to London, but was dead by October 1238. Samuel, Isaac's second son, thereupon became the head of the family and the leader of the Norwich Jewish community. Moses had three sons: Abraham, who returned to London in 1252 or early 1253 but died in 1255; Isaac, who converted to Christianity in 1253 after being accused of coin-clipping; and Eliab (or Jurnet), who was also dead by 1255. All were frequent business partners with their uncle Samuel. Samuel himself had no known children, however, and with his death in 1273 the line of Eliab and Isaac of Norwich came to an end.

ROBERT C. STACEY, *rev.*

Sources Exchequer, lord treasurer's remembrancer, originalia rolls, PRO, E 371 · Exchequer, lord treasurer's remembrancer, pipe rolls, PRO, E 372 · Chancery, fine rolls, PRO, C 60 · V. D. Lipman, *The Jews of medieval Norwich* (1967) · H. G. Richardson, *The English Jewry under Angevin kings* (1960) · N. Vincent, *Peter des Roches: an alien in English politics, 1205–38*, Cambridge Studies in Medieval Life and Thought, 4th ser., 31 (1996), 177–80 · Exchequer, exchequer of receipt, receipt rolls, PRO, E 401/1565 m1
Likenesses caricature, 1233, PRO; repro. in J. Gillingham, *The life and times of Richard I* (1973), 54–5

Norwich, John, first Lord Norwich (c.1299–1362), baron and soldier, was the eldest son of Sir Walter *Norwich (d. 1329), and of Katherine (d. c.1343), the daughter of John

of Hethersett. He had two brothers, Sir Roger (d. 1371) and Sir Thomas, both distinguished in arms, and two sisters, Cecily and Margaret (d. 1358), the latter of whom married Robert *Ufford, earl of Suffolk (d. 1369), establishing an important family alliance. Norwich married Margery (d. 1366), of unknown family, and had a son, Sir Walter (d. 1360). His heir was Sir Walter's son, Sir John (1351–1373), whose death marked the end of the direct family line.

Norwich was close to the household of Edward II despite his modest family background in the eponymous town, because of his father's rise to the offices of chief baron of the exchequer and treasurer. In 1319 Norwich was described as a king's yeoman when he received the manors of Dilham and Bradfield in Suffolk for a farm of £50 per annum. The following year he was knighted with the assistance of a gift of £100 from the king's wardrobe. The extent of his service in these years is unclear, but he campaigned with the king against the Scots in 1322. At his father's death he inherited considerable estates in Norfolk and Suffolk, including Great Massingham, Norfolk, where he secured the grant of a weekly market and annual fair in 1334.

In the 1330s there began an extended period of military service. In late 1334 Norwich prepared to join the king in Scotland, but instead was appointed admiral from the Thames northwards on 2 January 1335. This appointment was short-lived and he was replaced on 4 April 1335. He then went to Scotland serving as a banneret with twenty-six men-at-arms alongside the earl of Suffolk at Perth, and with Edward Balliol at the attack on Dumbarton. On 10 April 1336 he was reappointed admiral and was stationed at Great Yarmouth. He remained in office until November 1336. In 1337 Norwich intended to accompany a substantial force to Gascony. In July the expedition was scaled down and he was appointed as its commander. Following delays he departed in August with a force of perhaps between 300 and 500 men. His arrival meant that the immediate threat to the duchy from the French was reduced and Norwich was appointed lieutenant to Sir Oliver Ingham, seneschal of Gascony. The following March Sir Roger Norwich, his brother, arrived from England with promises of more men and money. That summer Ingham and Norwich successfully raised the French siege of Blaye. This brought an end to French campaigning at much the same time as Edward III cancelled the planned expeditionary force.

Norwich returned to England but remained on active service in the years that followed. He was rewarded with a pension in November 1339, which was increased in value to £40 per annum in April 1340. In 1343 he gained a licence to crenellate his properties in Mettingham, Suffolk, and Blackworth and Lyng, both in Norfolk. Norwich served with Henry of Grosmont, earl of Lancaster (d. 1361), in the French campaigns of 1345–7. In a spectacularly successful raid at the end of 1345, Norwich led a small force and seized Angoulême, which he retained until the following February: Froissart records that he obtained a day's truce at Candlemas from the French forces besieging the town under the leadership of the duke of Normandy. He took this opportunity to escape with his spoils. He went on to fight alongside the earl at Crécy and, having returned briefly to England thereafter, he was urgently summoned with the earl and about thirty others to assist the king when the siege of Calais was threatened by French forces in May 1347. Described as the king's sergeant-at-arms and being about fifty years old, he seems to have retired from active military service in the late 1340s.

Since 1329 Norwich had on occasions served on various judicial commissions. In 1343 he had received a general exemption from onerous local offices, but from 1349 was regularly involved in commissions of the peace. He also served on special commissions of oyer and terminer and in February 1359 was appointed to investigate the dilapidated state of Norwich Castle. Having attended great councils in 1342, 1358, and 1359 he was personally summoned to the parliament of April 1360 and hence became a peer of the realm. He died on 15 August 1362.

Norwich was a man of conventional piety. During the 1330s he and his mother seem to have planned various donations of rent and advowsons to religious houses, but these were frustrated by legal impediments and, once his mother had died, Norwich turned to founding a college with a master and eight priests at the church at Raveningham, Norfolk. In June 1345 a licence was granted for the college to acquire £20 per annum in land. Following periods at churches at Raveningham and at Norton Subcourse (which Norwich had partially built and where he had willed that he be buried) in 1394 the college moved to occupy the castle at Mettingham, Suffolk. The tall gatehouse built by Norwich to show his wealth and power, and which later formed part of the home of his religious foundation, still survives. It is a monument to a family which, during Norwich's own lifetime, had sought to conceal its origins by fabricating a pedigree tracing its ancestry back to a fictitious companion of William the Conqueror.

ANTHONY VERDUYN

Sources Chancery records · J. Sumption, The Hundred Years War, 1 (1990) · GEC, Peerage, new edn · R. Nicholson, Edward III and the Scots: the formative years of a military career, 1327–1335 (1965) · G. Wrottesley, Crécy and Calais (1897) · Chroniques de J. Froissart, ed. S. Luce and others, 15 vols. (Paris, 1869–1975) · Suffolk, Pevsner (1961) · CEPR letters · K. B. McFarlane, The nobility of later medieval England (1973) · Norwich cartulary, Bodl. Oxf., MS Top. Gen. c.62 · CIPM, 7, no. 235; 10, no. 396; 12, no. 72
Wealth at death substantial: CIPM, 10, no. 396

Norwich, Julian of. See Julian of Norwich (1342–c.1416).

Norwich, Ralph of (d. 1258/9), administrator and royal clerk, was perhaps a native of Buckinghamshire. He was sent to Ireland as the king's messenger in May 1216, and having returned to England with a message from Geoffrey de Marisco, the justiciar, was on the accession of Henry III detained by the government in order that he might give information as to Irish affairs, and in December was forgiven a debt to the crown of 100s. He was sent back to Ireland on the king's business in February 1217, and was employed there on exchequer affairs in 1218. Probably in 1219 he was sent by Peter des Roches, bishop of Winchester, and the justiciar, Hubert de Burgh, on a message to the archbishop of York, Walter de Gray, whom he found at Scrooby, Nottinghamshire, and was paid 2 marks for his expenses. He was that year sent back to Ireland with another messenger, 10 marks being paid to the two. Stormy weather delayed his return to England in the spring of 1220. When he returned he was granted a yearly salary of 20 marks until the king should bestow on him a benefice of greater value. He was employed in managing the duty on wool, and received the guardianship of the lands of certain great lords, but these guardianships appear to have been nominal, for in each case the lands seem to have passed almost at once out of his hands. Returning again to Ireland in September, Norwich was engaged in exchequer business there in 1221, and on his arrival back in England received 7 marks over and above the 5 marks usually allowed him for expenses.

In 1217 Norwich became dean of the royal chapel at Wallingford and in 1221 was presented to the rectory of Oakley in Buckinghamshire. In 1225 and 1226 he was acting as a justice of the Jews. He held a canonry in St Patrick's Cathedral, Dublin, in 1227, and in 1229 received the custody of the bishopric of Emly, with instructions to use the revenues in the king's interest in the dispute between the king and John Collingham, who claimed to be bishopelect. In 1229 he was commissioned to advise the archbishops and bishops of Ireland with reference to the collection of the sixteenth levied on ecclesiastical benefices, and to bring the sum collected over to England. He accordingly brought 2000 marks to the king from Richard de Burgh.

On 29 April 1230 Norwich was appointed a justice of the bench, and was one of the judges who heard the case between the burgesses and the prior of Dunstable. Notices of him as justice in England occur until February 1237. In 1231 it was reported that he was dead, and his death is wrongly recorded under that year in the annals of Dunstable. In order to protect his lands in Ireland from sequestration he obtained a writ from the king declaring that he was alive and well. In 1232 he attested the king's statement of the proceedings taken against Hubert de Burgh, and in 1233 was one of the justices appointed to receive Hubert's abjuration of the kingdom. He may have returned to Ireland in 1237 and served in the Irish exchequer. On 9 July 1249 the king appointed him his chancellor in Ireland, with an allowance of 60 marks a year until a more liberal provision should be made for him. Geoffrey de Cusack, bishop of Meath, had exercised his rights as bishop without having previously obtained the royal assent to his promotion, and Norwich, who had accepted a benefice from him in 1254, received the king's command to vacate it. The king having granted the lordship of Ireland to his eldest son, Edward, in 1256, Norwich sent back the seal of his office. Another chancellor was appointed shortly afterwards. He was in this year elected archbishop of Dublin, and although the election was approved by the king, it was quashed by Pope Alexander IV. By late 1257 Norwich was back in England, still in the king's service as one of his clerks.

Matthew Paris describes Norwich as 'a witty man, of

sumptuous habits, and from his youth more skilled in the affairs of the king's court than in the learning of the schools' (Paris, *Chron.*, 5.560). He was the founder of a small Augustinian priory at Chetwode in Buckinghamshire. He was still alive in June 1258 but was dead by June 1259.

WILLIAM HUNT, *rev.* PAUL BRAND

Sources C. A. F. Meekings and D. Crook, eds., *The 1235 Surrey eyre*, 1, Surrey RS, 31 (1979), 224 • R. V. Turner, *The English judiciary in the age of Glanvill and Bracton, c.1176–1239* (1985) • V. D. Lipman, *The Jews of medieval Norwich* (1967), 228 • *Chancery records* • Rymer, *Foedera*, 1st edn, vol. 1 • H. S. Sweetman and G. F. Handcock, eds., *Calendar of documents relating to Ireland*, 5 vols., PRO (1875–86), vol. 1 • W. W. Shirley, ed., *Royal and other historical letters illustrative of the reign of Henry III*, 2 vols., Rolls Series, 27 (1862–6) • Paris, *Chron.*, vol. 5 • *Ann. mon.*, vol. 3 • J. T. Gilbert, ed., *Chartularies of St Mary's Abbey, Dublin: with the register of its house at Dunbrody and annals of Ireland*, 2 vols., Rolls Series, 80 (1884) • H. M. Chew and M. Weinbaum, eds., *The London eyre of 1244*, London RS, 6 (1970)

Norwich, Sir Robert (d. **1535**), judge, may have been connected with the Norwich family of Brampton, Northamptonshire. His arms, as displayed in the windows of Serjeants' Inn Hall, Fleet Street, in 1599, were exactly the same as those borne by that family, though it is not known for certain that they were painted contemporaneously. He seems himself, however, to have been associated with Essex, where he served as a commissioner from 1518 and became a justice of the peace in 1525. Norwich was admitted to Lincoln's Inn in 1503, at the instance of Sir Robert Drury of Halstead, Suffolk, and seems to have been a somewhat disorderly student. In the very year of his admission he was mainprized to appear in chancery, probably as a result of some commotion, and two years later was fined for frequenting a bawdy house. In conjunction with his Lincoln's Inn contemporary John Tyrell of Essex, he took part in a common recovery of lands to the use of Tyrell's brother-in-law Edmund Norris (son of Sir Edward), who died in 1508. Norwich himself then married Norris's widow, Juliane, whose son John was less than a year old, and thereafter his life seems to have been more restrained.

Norwich is mentioned as practising in the court of requests in 1516, and was frequently engaged in chancery during Wolsey's chancellorship. In 1518 he became a bencher of his inn, on giving his first reading, and served as treasurer from 1519 to 1520. A mere three years after his readership, in the summer of 1521, he was created a serjeant-at-law, and the next year was appointed one of the king's serjeants. From this time onwards his name occurs regularly in the surviving year-books, and he was constantly employed in legal commissions, sitting as an assize judge on the western circuit until 1525 and thereafter on the midland circuit. In 1529 he was knighted. In the same year Norwich was appointed, jointly with Sir Thomas Nevill, as surveyor of the liveries, an office that he held until his death, and on 22 November 1530 as chief justice of the common pleas in succession to Sir Robert Brudenell. Although his judicial opinions were reported in the year-books, and by Spelman, he seems to have left little mark on the law. Nor is much known of his later

character. A reference to him as 'false Norwyge' by a madwoman in 1533 may deserve little credit (*LP Henry VIII*, 6, no. 923), though the advice given by a solicitor in 1534 to Lady Lisle that 'yf ye send the sayd Lord Norwich a fyrkyn of sturgeon that wyll not be lost' (PRO, SP 3/13, fol. 74) does suggest a reputation for corruptibility.

Norwich died shortly before 8 April 1535, when his widow and executor was directed to hand over his records. He asked to be buried in St Nicholas's Chapel in the Whitefriars, adjoining Serjeants' Inn, 'under the grate there where I am wounte to sytt and hire masse' (PRO, PROB 11/25, fol. 172). Sir Robert left no issue, and the only estate specifically mentioned in his brief will was at South Ockenden, Essex. Letters written to Cromwell in the 1530s indicate that he lived not far from Waltham Forest. One is dated from Porters and one from Gosest, which is perhaps Gooshays in the liberty of Havering. He left an annuity of 40s. to his sister Isabel, a nun in the priory of 'Kempsee' in 'Sussex', presumably a mistake for Campsey, Suffolk. Dame Juliane survived until 1556.

J. H. BAKER

Sources Baker, *Serjeants*, 167, 269, 529 • introduction, *The reports of Sir John Spelman*, ed. J. H. Baker, 2, SeldS, 94 (1978) • *LP Henry VIII*, vols. 2–7 • Sainty, *Judges*, 48 • W. Dugdale, *Origines juridiciales, or, Historical memorials of the English laws*, 3rd edn (1680), 328 • PRO, C244/153/137, 149 • PRO, REQ 1/4, fols. 14v, 34v • *CIPM, Henry VII*, 3, no. 514 • writ to executor 8 April, PRO, CP 40/1085 (1), m. 353d • PRO, PROB 11/25, sig. 24

Norwich, Sir Walter (d. **1329**), administrator, was probably the son of Henry of Norwich, a minor Norfolk landowner recorded in 1285, and his wife, Katherine. Walter is recorded as a clerk in February 1297, and again in December 1299, but presumably only took minor orders, since he was able to marry—his eldest son was born about 1299. His wife was Katherine Hedersete, the widow of Piers Braunche and daughter of John of Hethersett. Walter Norwich is recorded as a king's clerk in June 1304, and at Michaelmas that year became the treasurer's remembrancer, in the service of Walter Langton, being subsequently described as the latter's clerk. Following the death of Edward I, Langton was dismissed, and Norwich fell with him, but his expertise had clearly made him indispensable, for he was restored to his post on 19 November 1307. The rest of his career was based upon the exchequer, of which he was made a baron on 29 August 1311; on 30 September 1312 he is recorded as the spokesman for the barons in dealings with the Londoners. Norwich was also the treasurer's lieutenant between 23 October 1311 and 23 January 1312, and again from 17 May to 4 October 1312. From July 1311 he was regularly among the justices and senior officials summoned to councils and parliaments. By 21 September 1312 he had been knighted.

On 26 September 1314 Norwich ceased to be a baron and was made treasurer of England, an office he held until 27 May 1317. Although he was appointed by a government dominated by Edward II's adversaries, he remained on good terms with the king, attending the funeral of Piers Gaveston on 3 January 1315, while on 6 July Edward gave him 1000 marks 'on account of his good service', with the promise of 100 marks per annum 'to maintain his state more honourably in the king's service' (*CPR, 1313–17*, 280). Nearly two years later, on 30 May 1317, Norwich received a further accolade, when Edward II, 'being unwilling to lose the services of so useful and faithful a minister', appointed him to be chief baron of the exchequer, as a 'place with moderate labour', and ordered that whenever possible he should be 'present at the king's councils, both secret and other' (*CPR, 1313–17*, 655). Having been described as chief baron when he was briefly replaced in 1312, Norwich was now the first official to be given that title in his letters of appointment.

Although the burdens of office provided the ostensible reason for his stepping down, the fact that he was replaced as treasurer by the staunchly royalist John Hotham indicates that Norwich's discharge was an essentially political measure. But he continued to be involved in affairs of state. Late in 1318 he was a member of the committee set up to reform the royal household, and on 6 November 1319 he was once more appointed lieutenant to the treasurer, an office he held until 18 February 1320, and which he occupied again from 25 August 1321 to 9 May 1322. His incomparable knowledge of the workings of the exchequer led to his being closely involved both in the 'array' of that department's records which Walter Stapledon began in 1320, and then in the removal of the exchequer to York in 1322. He was also present at the controversial and unpopular London eyre of 1321, headed the commission that passed sentence of death on the two Roger Mortimers on 2 August 1322, and conducted many surveys of lands forfeited by rebels against the king. Yet his implementation of royal policy may sometimes have been less than wholehearted, for in November 1323 the king complained bitterly of the way he was being served by the exchequer in general, and by Norwich in particular. When the exchequer was divided in the following year, Norwich, who perhaps disapproved of the scheme, was placed in control only of the poorer, northern, half.

Whatever his reservations, Norwich continued to serve the king. On 28 August 1326 he was yet again appointed treasurer's lieutenant, and when Edward II fled from London on 2 October, Norwich was a member of the privy council that he left behind there, and tried to raise troops for the king. As the government disintegrated, he stayed at his post, and was present in the exchequer on 14 November when the bishop of Winchester arrived to take over as lieutenant. Norwich did not suffer from Edward II's deposition. He was reappointed chief baron on 2 February 1327, while on 18 August he was summoned to York, 'to hold the exchequer' there at the end of September (*CClR, 1327–1330*, 161). On 5 November 1328 he was appointed to mediate between the abbot and townsmen of Bury St Edmunds. His death, on 20 January 1329, may therefore have been sudden. He was buried in Norwich Cathedral.

Throughout his career Norwich was frequently active in government service outside the exchequer, often in London, but above all in East Anglia, where he was many times a commissioner of oyer and terminer, and at least once a justice of assize. His rewards included a number of custodies of lands, wardships, and marriages of heirs, which he used to benefit his family. He had three daughters, all of whom were married to wards in his charge. He also accumulated lands by purchase and exchange in Norfolk and Suffolk, and especially in and around Stoke Holy Cross, a few miles south of Norwich. He may, however, have been more than just another acquisitive civil servant. He appears to have been a pious man, since in 1317 he acquired a faculty for a portative altar, and at about that time received the thanks of Pope John XXII for what he had done for the church; the pope also urged him to work for peace in the realm. He was probably a friend of Bishop John Salmon of Norwich, whose executor he became. Norwich may therefore have owed his ability to remain acceptable to successive regimes to personal qualities more positive than a capacity for survival. His widow, who died between 1341 and 1343, was still commemorating the anniversary of her husband's death eight years after the event. Norwich had three sons, of whom the eldest, John *Norwich, enjoyed a distinguished career as a soldier, culminating in his being summoned to parliament as a peer in 1360; John's death without an heir in 1362 led to his father's estates passing to Robert Ufford, earl of Suffolk, who had married Walter Norwich's daughter Margaret.

HENRY SUMMERSON

Sources *Chancery records* · F. Palgrave, ed., *The parliamentary writs and writs of military summons*, 2/3 (1834), 1237–9 · Tout, *Admin. hist.*, vols. 2–3, 6 · GEC, *Peerage* · *CIPM*, 6, nos. 518, 727; 7, no. 235 · *CEPR letters*, 2.148, 415–16 · [R. E. Latham], ed., *Calendar of memoranda rolls (exchequer) …: Michaelmas 1326 – Michaelmas 1327*, PRO (1968) · W. Stubbs, ed., *Chronicles of the reigns of Edward I and Edward II*, 1, Rolls Series, 76 (1882), 218–19 · H. M. Cam, ed., *The eyre of London, 14 Edward II, AD 1321*, 1, SeldS, 85 (1968), 70 · Sainty, *Judges* · W. R. Childs and J. Taylor, eds., *The Anonimalle Chronicle, 1307 to 1334: from Brotherton collection MS 29*, Yorkshire Archaeological Society, 147 (1991), 127 · C. M. Woolgar, ed., *Household accounts from medieval England*, 1, British Academy, Records of Social and Economic History, new ser., 17 (1992), 177–227 · A. Beardwood, ed., *Records of the trial of Walter Langeton, bishop of Coventry and Lichfield, 1307–1312*, CS, 4th ser., 6 (1969), 125–6 · F. Blomefield and C. Parkin, *An essay towards a topographical history of the county of Norfolk*, [2nd edn], 11 vols. (1805–10), vol. 5, pp. 522–3; vol. 8, pp. 25, 183 · V. H. Galbraith, 'The Tower as an exchequer record office in the reign of Edward II', *Essays in medieval history presented to Thomas Frederick Tout*, ed. A. G. Little and F. M. Powicke (1925), 231–47 · D. M. Broome, 'Exchequer migrations to York in the thirteenth and fourteenth centuries', *Essays in medieval history presented to Thomas Frederick Tout*, ed. A. G. Little and F. M. Powicke (1925), 291–300 · J. R. S. Phillips, *Aymer de Valence, earl of Pembroke, 1307–1324: baronial politics in the reign of Edward II* (1972) · J. R. Maddicott, *Thomas of Lancaster, 1307–1322: a study in the reign of Edward II* (1970) · N. Fryde, *The tyranny and fall of Edward II, 1321–1326* (1979)

Wealth at death wealthy: *CIPM*, 7, no. 235

Norwood, Charles Morgan (*bap.* 1825, *d.* 1891), shipowner and politician, was baptized on 27 December 1825 at Ashford in Kent; he was the eldest son of Charles Norwood (*d.* c.1840), a surgeon, and his wife, Catherine (c.1799–1870), daughter of Charles Morgan of Archangel, Russia. He was educated at the collegiate school at Wye, Kent. Around

1840, after the death of her husband, Catherine removed with her children to Hull, where Norwood went in to business as a Russia merchant, firstly with his mother's relatives J. T. and N. Hill, then as manager for John Beadle & Co. It was at this time that he moved into shipowning, acquiring minority holdings in some of his employer's vessels. On 20 December 1855 he married Anna Maria Jane, youngest daughter of John Henry Blakeney of Abbert Castle, co. Galway, and set up home at Wyton House, near Hull. By this time he was trading on his own account in partnership with his brother. They expanded into shipowning in 1858 and Norwood became an active member of the Hull chamber of commerce and shipping, serving as director, treasurer, and, for the two years 1859 and 1860, president.

Norwood was thus well placed to play a leading role in a new phase of the continuing struggle between the monopolist Hull Dock Company and the wider commercial interests of the town by becoming chairman of a new company set up in 1860 to build a dock in competition with the existing company. This venture failed to obtain the necessary parliamentary powers and by 1862 Norwood had removed to London. He remained in partnership with his brother until 1868 when he severed his business connections with Hull. In February 1865 he served as the first chairman of the Associated Chamber of Commerce of the United Kingdom. Later he became a director of the London and St Katherine Dock Company.

The move to London made Norwood an ideal choice—metropolis-based with local connections—when the Hull Liberal Party was seeking a new candidate to contest one of the two parliamentary seats at the 1865 general election. Norwood's success on this occasion led to twenty years in the House of Commons. But by 1885 he had clearly lost touch with local opinion, and in December of that year was defeated in the first election to be fought in single member constituencies, having been opposed by a radical who secured enough votes to give the seat to the Conservative.

There were two occasions when Norwood became involved in national events. In 1873 Samuel Plimsoll published *Our Seamen: an Appeal* in which he attacked the malpractices of shipowners. One of his examples was the case of Norwood's ship the *Livonia* whose engines had failed 6 miles out of Sunderland on a voyage to Kronstadt. Norwood brought proceedings for criminal libel. The court found against him because the *Livonia* had been overloaded but made no award as to costs on the grounds that a single example did not justify a generalized defamation. His readiness to sue suggests that Norwood had been let down by his subordinates while he was out of the country. Certainly he was responsible for devising the compromise load line plan which proved to be sufficiently acceptable to all parties to become law in 1875. In 1889 it fell to Norwood, as chairman of the London and India Docks joint committee, to consider and refuse the demands of the London dock labourers, thereby precipitating the dock strike which by its success became a landmark in the development of the new unionism. After a long illness Norwood died at his London home, 11 Ennismore Gardens, on 24 April 1891; he was survived by his wife.

G. W. OXLEY

Sources *The Times* (27 April 1891), 9 · Boase, *Mod. Eng. biog.* · J. J. Sheahan, *History of Kingston upon Hull*, 2nd edn (c.1866) · 'Hull and East Riding elections, 1830–95', scrapbook, Hull Central Library, L324.075(5) · The queen on the prosecution of Charles Morgan Norwood against Samuel Plimsoll, affidavits, etc., Hull Central Library · Ashford, parish registers, CKS · trade directories, Hull and Kent · census returns for Hull · *Sculcoates' monumental inscriptions*, EYFHS (1991) · G. Alderman, 'Samuel Plimsoll and the shipping interest', *Maritime History*, 1 (1972), 73–95 · Hull shipping registers, Hull City Archives, DPC · *The Criterion* [Hull] (14 April 1877) · *CGPLA Eng. & Wales* (1891) · d. cert.
Likenesses drawing, 1885, Hull City Archives, DMX176 · drawing, Hull City Archives, DMT20 · photograph, repro. in *The Criterion* · portrait, repro. in G. Alderman, 'Samuel Plimsoll and the shipping interest', 68 · portrait, repro. in *ILN* (2 May 1891), 563 · portrait, repro. in *Pictorial World* (9 May 1891), 598
Wealth at death £38,891 12s. 11d.: probate, 13 June 1891, *CGPLA Eng. & Wales*

Norwood, Sir Cyril (1875–1956), educationist, was born in Whalley, Lancashire, on 15 September 1875, the only child of the Revd Samuel Norwood and his second wife, Elizabeth Emma Sparkes. His father was head of the local grammar school at Whalley, but when this closed in 1880 the family moved to Leytonstone in Essex. Home life was marred by Samuel's drink problem; this experience left a lasting impression on Cyril, who was always deeply reserved and later became a teetotaller. He managed to support himself and his mother through his own efforts at school and university. In 1888 he entered the leading day school Merchant Taylors', in London, where he showed ability especially in classics and cricket, and became head monitor in 1893. He won a scholarship to St John's College, Oxford, and gained firsts in classical moderations (1896) and *literae humaniores* (1898). One of his classics tutors described him as being 'among the most eminent Oxford students of his day' (A. T. Barton, letter of reference, 1 April 1902, Norwood MSS). In 1899 he headed the list for entry to the civil service by a considerable margin, and was the only candidate in his year who attained more than half marks in every subject.

Norwood entered the secretary's department of the Admiralty in October 1899 but he left in January 1901 to take up a teaching post at Leeds grammar school. Despite the shortness of his stay at the Admiralty, he was already highly regarded there, as he apparently showed a 'very considerable aptitude for administrative work', as well as 'a power of concentration and a sanity of judgment which, if he had remained in His Majesty's service would certainly have marked him out for promotion to the highest rank' (letter of reference, 2 Feb 1905, Norwood MSS). Later in 1901 he married Catherine Margaret Kilner, daughter of Walter John Kilner, medical practitioner, of Kensington. They were married for fifty years until her death in 1951, and had three daughters.

At Leeds, Norwood found his vocation as a teacher. He became sixth-form classics master and took an active part in sports, especially cricket. In 1906, at the age of thirty, he

Sir Cyril Norwood (1875–1956), by Walter Stoneman, 1945

was appointed headmaster of Bristol grammar school, which was experiencing major difficulties in forging a new identity and role for itself following the Education Act of 1902. During the following decade, under Norwood's headship, pupil numbers trebled, the facilities and grounds were extended, and a boarding-house was created. In 1907 he was commissioned as captain of the Territorial Force, and he commanded a company in the 4th battalion of the Gloucestershire regiment. In recognition of his achievement the University of Bristol awarded him an honorary doctorate in 1912.

In 1916 Norwood was appointed master of Marlborough College in Wiltshire, a traditional boys' boarding-school. In many respects this marked an important departure in his educational career, which had hitherto been spent at day schools in large cities, and his lack of boarding-school experience was the subject of criticism. He encouraged Marlborough to develop a relationship with the expanding educational agencies of the state and to make use of the opportunities offered by new developments such as the school certificate and higher school certificate examinations, while being careful at the same time to emphasize 'the building of character and the training for citizenship which at Marlborough must be the first considerations' (application for headship, April 1916, Norwood MSS). During his headship Marlborough enjoyed considerable academic success. By this time he had also become a national figure, and he was invited in December 1917 to become a member of the new Secondary Schools Examinations Council (SSEC), which had been created by the Board of Education. Board officials were worried that Norwood might be 'too engrossed with his reforms at Marlborough which are said to be extensive', but the president of the board, H. A. L. Fisher, insisted on Norwood, who struck him as being 'the most interesting Head Master I have yet met' (PRO, ED.12/246). Norwood became chairman of the SSEC in 1921 and was to continue in this role for a quarter of a century until his retirement (encouraged by a less sympathetic minister of education, Ellen Wilkinson) in 1946.

In 1926 Norwood cemented his reputation by accepting the headship of Harrow School, having been urged to take up the appointment by Randall Davidson, the archbishop of Canterbury and chairman of the Harrow governors. There his characteristic reforms to raise standards of work and discipline met with sterner resistance on the part of some staff and students, and his period there was not altogether successful or happy. Masters who resisted his authority were gradually removed. Nevertheless, his position did allow him a platform from which to seek influence in public debate about education. He had always been active in putting across his views, writing regularly on education for a wide range of newspapers and journals. In 1909 he had jointly edited (with Arthur H. Hope) a book entitled *The Higher Education of Boys in England*. In 1929, while head of Harrow, he produced his major published work, *The English Tradition of Education*. This celebrated the tradition of the boys' independent schools, which he regarded as being based on the historical ideals of knighthood, chivalry, and the English gentleman. He emphasized in particular the importance of discipline, the chapel, culture, athletics, and the ideal of service in promoting the training of character, public spirit, and leadership. This was a strongly conservative message, especially in the case of girls, who he insisted should be educated in a different way from boys. At the same time Norwood was anxious to spread the benefits of the 'English tradition' to pupils in state secondary education, and with this in view he also advocated radical reforms in the curriculum and examinations of secondary schools. His book attracted widespread and largely admiring notices from, among others, C. W. Valentine and Michael Sadler.

In the 1930s Norwood's educational influence was extensive. He took a leading role in international conferences, for example in Canada, Australia, and New Zealand, most notably under the auspices of the New Education Fellowship. He inspired the personal loyalty of many of his colleagues and followers such as Thorold Coade, who became headmaster of Bryanston School in Dorset in 1932, and Ronald Gurner, who held headships at boys' day schools. A distinguished and tall man with a piercing gaze, Norwood was a commanding presence at the pulpit, in the school, or in the committee room, although he was often reserved in company and tended to appear remote. An Anglican layman, he was devout in his theologically undogmatic Christianity, which he saw as fundamental to education, and was active in the Modern Churchmen's

Union, of which he was president. He was no less resolute in his admiration for the ideals of Plato, which formed the grounds for so much of his hierarchical ideals as well as for his notion of citizenship.

Norwood left Harrow in 1934 to become president of his old Oxford college, St John's, and was knighted in 1938. His long and distinguished public career culminated during the Second World War in his central involvement in the major educational debates that led to the Education Act of 1944. He was a staunch defender of the public schools at this time, when they were at their most vulnerable and most unpopular, but he also made enemies from among the public schools themselves by proposing that they should forge a new accommodation with the state. Even more controversial was his role as chairman of a committee established in 1941 to consider the secondary school curriculum and examinations. The Norwood report, as it became known, reported in July 1943, soon after the major white paper *Educational Reconstruction*. At first, this attracted less attention than the white paper, but its argument and ideals, clearly stemming in large part from Norwood himself, soon became highly contentious. Part one of the report identified 'three kinds of mind', and proposed that these should comprise the basis for three different kinds of secondary school—grammar, technical, and modern—in a new era of 'secondary education for all'. This report was far from alone in its Platonic ideals, and in its rejection of multilateral (comprehensive) schools, but it was later held responsible by many critics for the failures of the so-called 'tripartite system' that developed after the Second World War. The Norwood report also fell foul of established educational interests because of its call for the abolition of the school certificate examination in its existing form.

After his retirement to Iwerne Minster in 1946 Norwood faded from the scene, although he maintained a role in the Allied Schools, a group of schools of religious outlook founded after 1920, including Stowe and Canford, which sought to embody the tradition of the English public schools. He died in the Warneford Hospital, Oxford, on 13 March 1956 having, as the *Times Educational Supplement* (16 March 1956) expressed it, 'outlived his fame'. His ideas appeared outdated and even irrelevant for the future of education. In the end he was regarded as too radical and unsound for the public schools, but too traditional and conservative for state secondary education in a more socially mobile, if not egalitarian, age. In the inter-war years, however, he had been among the foremost educators of his time, of conservative stamp but with the passion of a reformer. He was a successful and highly regarded scholar and headmaster. He was also among the most influential educational thinkers of the period, alongside such figures as R. H. Tawney and Fred Clarke in his public impact. He was surely unique in his capacity to operate successfully within the closed worlds of both the Board of Education and the public schools, across the contested frontiers of private and state education.

GARY McCULLOCH

Sources DNB · *The Times* (14 March 1956) · *The Harrovian* (3 May 1956) · G. McCulloch, *Philosophers and kings: education for leadership in modern England* (1991) · G. McCulloch, *Educational reconstruction: the 1944 Education Act and the twenty-first century* (1994) · R. Curner, *I chose teaching* (1937) · CGPLA Eng. & Wales (1956) · University of Sheffield, Norwood MSS
Archives University of Sheffield, corresp., diaries, notebooks, and papers | PRO, Board of Education papers
Likenesses O. Birley, oils, c.1934, St John's College, Oxford · W. Stoneman, photograph, 1945, NPG [*see illus.*] · R. G. Eves, oils, Marlborough College, Wiltshire · G. Harcourt, oils, Marlborough College, Wiltshire
Wealth at death £33,479 3s. 7d.: probate, 12 May 1956, CGPLA Eng. & Wales

Norwood, Richard (1590–1675), surveyor and mathematician, was born in October 1590 in Stevenage, Hertfordshire, and baptized on 15 November 1590 at St Nicholas Church, Stevenage, the son of Edward Norwood, a gentleman farmer at Cannix, Stevenage, and his wife, whose maiden name was Mathew. When he was ten the farm, having become unprofitable, was abandoned and the family moved to Berkhamsted where Norwood attended the grammar school for two years. They next moved to Shutlanger, Northamptonshire, at which time his formal education ceased, and thence to Stony Stratford, Buckinghamshire.

When he was fifteen Norwood was apprenticed to a London fishmonger. After meeting mariners, he was allowed to join a coastal trading ship and studied mathematics and navigation. None the less, sailing proved unfulfilling: he abandoned his apprenticeship (resulting in a brief imprisonment) and returned to London after about a year. In late 1608 he visited the Netherlands with soldiers he had met on the *Anne Royal* and spent eighteen months in continental travel. He returned to England in early 1610, initially to his maternal uncle at Cornbury Park, Oxfordshire, as Norwood's inclination towards papistry caused a family rift.

Reunited with his parents in London, Norwood became bound to a master's mate of Limehouse, with whom he twice went through the Strait of Gibraltar. He again studied mathematics and navigation, but suffered from seasickness and bought his freedom on return to England in March 1612. He became navigation tutor to Captain Henry Mainwaring, who was planning a journey to Persia, and joined Sir Henry Thynne at Lymington, Hampshire, but the plan was abandoned on the death of the voyage's patron, Prince Henry, in November 1612. At Lymington, Norwood successfully constructed a crude diving bell to lift a piece of ordnance lost overboard and earned a reputation as an expert diver.

After a spell during which Norwood taught mathematics in London—initially with John Goodwin—this expertise took him to Bermuda at Christmas 1613 to exploit oyster beds for pearls and help the Adventurers for the Bermudas finance the settlement. Subsequently diving was abandoned owing to a paucity of pearls. His plans to return home by the next ship changed when it brought orders for surveying and mapping the country and Norwood was employed, with two others. An initial survey in

1614–15, followed by a survey and division of the land in 1616–17, resulted in Norwood's correctly reducing the Adventurers' allotment per share. This led to a surplus which, when Somerset Island was surveyed out of turn, fell in an attractive location. The governor endeavoured to be assigned this land and Norwood had to defend himself from accusations of conspiracy. The survey complete, he sailed for London in April 1617. While in Bermuda, Norwood abandoned his Roman Catholic inclinations, having been converted by evangelical protestants.

Norwood had earned a reputation for accuracy, and was appointed surveyor to the Virginia Company in May 1621. (Disagreements over pay meant he did not go then, although in 1623 he went there briefly and then to the Netherlands for the company.) He married Rachel Boughton on 9 May 1622, and his map of Bermuda was published in the same year. He then became a mathematics teacher and author in London. Many of his mathematical books reached several editions and remained in print in the 1690s. The preface to *Trigonometrie, or, The Doctrine of Triangles* was written from Tower Hill, on 1 November 1631. *The Seaman's Practice* (1637) was a major help to navigators and at least eighteen editions were published. Norwood's calculation of the length of a nautical mile made during 1633–5 by determining the latitude near the Tower of London and in York, and pacing and measuring by chain between them, was only 40 feet too long. He was also one of the first to calculate the length of a degree of the meridian with approximate accuracy, exceeding the true distance by 646 yards. He published methods for checking closure and declination of magnetic compasses, which were significant theoretical developments for traverse surveys by angle measurement.

The dedicatee of *The Seaman's Practice* was the earl of Warwick, whose cousin, Sir Nathaniel Rich, died in 1636 and endowed a school in Bermuda. Norwood had returned to Bermuda by early 1638 as schoolmaster, escaping religious persecution in England. In 1639, he published *Fortification, or, Architecture Military*. Controversy with the Bermudan clergy led him to resign as schoolmaster in 1649 and he refused an invitation to return to the post in 1658. But in 1661 he briefly returned to it, and he then moved to land he had acquired, and became a private teacher. His influence led to the growing of olive trees in Bermuda for their oil. His new survey, map, model, and valuation of the island's land (1663) formed the basis for future colonial laws. He also wrote some religious works as well as further mathematical works, including *Norwood's Epitome* (1659) and *A Triangular Canon Logarithmicall* (1669).

Norwood died in Bermuda in October 1675 and was buried there. He left much of his property to his four children, his grandchildren, and his brother-in-law.

SARAH BENDALL

Sources *The journal of Richard Norwood, surveyor of Bermuda*, ed. W. F. Craven and W. B. Hayward (1945) · J. H. Lefroy, *Memorials of the discovery and early settlement of the Bermudas or Somers Islands*, 2 vols. (1878–9) · G. L. Evans, 'Richard Norwood, surveyor, of Stephnage', *Hertfordshire Past and Present*, 8 (1968), 29–31 · S. S. Hughes, *Surveyors and statesmen* (1979) · A. Brown, ed., *The genesis of the United States*, 2 vols. (1890) · [N. Butler?], *The historye of the Bermudaes or Summer Islands*, ed. J. H. Lefroy, Hakluyt Society, 1st ser., 65 (1882) · A. W. Richeson, *English land measuring to 1800: instruments and practices* (1966) · marriage record, GL, MS 10091/8 · parish register, 15 Nov 1590, Herts. ALS, D/P 105/1/1 [baptism]

Wealth at death £487 13s. 11½d.; plus c.50 acres of land, house, school house, storehouse, outbuildings: probate, 4 Feb 1676, inventory of goods and chattels

Norwood, Robert (c.1610–1654), parliamentarian army officer, is of obscure origins: as yet no trace has been found of his father and mother. The family name was not uncommon and is found in Buckinghamshire, Gloucestershire, Hertfordshire, Lincolnshire, Middlesex, Yorkshire, and particularly in Kent, from where it may have originated. Robert Norwood was put apprentice to Thomas Stocke of the Grocers' Company on 19 March 1628, and gained his freedom on 6 April 1636. In December 1639 Norwood began living at the sign of the Chequer in the parish of All Hallows, Bread Street, London. Some years later he claimed that before the calling of the Long Parliament he suffered imprisonment, seizure of goods, and long, tedious suits at the hands of Charles I and his privy council. He seems at this time to have shared mutual business interests with his elder brother (or perhaps cousin) the presbyterian John Norwood (b. c.1602, d. in or after 1662), and to have acted on behalf of his kinsman Richard *Norwood of Bermuda. In September 1642 he signed the petition in favour of the appointment of Lazarus Seaman as rector of All Hallows, Bread Street. On 15 November 1642 Norwood was appointed a commissary of horse, and in the same month an assessor (Bread Street ward) for raising money for the defence of the kingdom. By the following summer he was commissioned as captain of a troop of horse in Colonel Edmund Harvey's regiment. His banner, taken from Zechariah 4: 7, carried the motto of Zerubbabel's encouragement to finish the Temple. Norwood's nominally sixty-strong troop of horse was mustered in London on 18 August 1643 and thereafter probably saw heavy fighting at the first battle of Newbury in September that year. In December, after further encounters with royalist troops, Norwood was stationed at the garrison town of Newport Pagnell with a nominally 48-strong troop of horse, besides officers. In May 1644 the troop was mustered again at Colnbrook. Norwood probably served with Colonel Harvey until June 1644, perhaps even later.

Following the new modelling of Harvey's regiment under the command of Colonel John Hurrey, Norwood was sent to the west of England as part of the spring campaign of 1645. Thereafter, he appears to have temporarily returned to civilian life. It was during this time that, by his own account, Norwood was 'threatned' for publicly opposing 'the Scotish interest then on foot' (Norwood, *Case and Trial*, 20). In April 1648 he was one of several men appointed to bring in the arrears of the assessments for the army, and in February 1649 one of sixty-four men appointed to sit on the court for the treason trials of the five lords—Norwood was one of the thirty-five men who on 6 March 1649 signed the warrant for the execution of James, earl of Cambridge (the duke of Hamilton). Norwood's services were also required as a cavalry officer in the Irish campaign of 1649. His troop seems to have been mustered in the spring of 1649, quartering at Chester before landing at Dublin on 26 July 1649. Commanding a nominally eighty-strong troop of horse, besides officers, Norwood may have supported Colonel Michael Jones's forces in their victory over the earl of Ormond at the battle of Baggotsrath. Four days later, on 6 August 1649, Norwood and his cavalry troop repulsed Sir Thomas Armstrong's forces in a skirmish outside Dublin. It is possible that Norwood was wounded in these engagements. In November 1649 it appears that he returned to England, perhaps docking at Liverpool. The following year, on 26 March 1650, Robert Norwood was made a member of the high court of justice. Despite incurring, by his own account, a 'just debt' of about £3000 in the state's service, Norwood at this time still appears to have been a relatively wealthy merchant (Norwood, *Form of an Excommunication*, sig. A2v). He had committed himself to a millenarian scheme to establish a utopia in the Bahama Islands, and seems also to have had interests in foreign trade. In common with a number of London merchants, Norwood was a congregant of Sidrach Simpson's gathered church that met at St Mary Abchurch.

On Thursday 25 April 1650 TheaurauJohn Tany, the self-proclaimed prophet and Lord's high priest of the Jews, issued a broadside. Its title was *I Proclaime from the Lord of Hosts the Returne of the Jewes*, and it is possible that Norwood may have helped pay towards its printing. Norwood was, at any rate, to contribute an epistle to another of Tany's works, *His Aurora in Tranlagorum in Salem gloria* (1651). In April 1651 Tany addressed a large gathering at Norwood's house in the parish of St Mary Aldermary; similar concourses apparently followed. In March that same year members of Sidrach Simpson's gathered church, troubled by Norwood's 'erroneous opinions', had spoken with Norwood at his home (Norwood, *Case and Trial*, 1). The following month, on 21 April 1651, Robert Norwood made a public profession of faith at St Mary Abchurch before the whole assembled church. Simpson, implacable, admonished Norwood for failing to repent his 'blasphemous Errors' and excommunicated him from his church in early May (Norwood, *Form of an Excommunication*, 2).

Afterwards, by his own account, Norwood was summoned before Oliver Cromwell, and there entreated by Joseph Caryl and John Owen to retract his errors. Evidently he was setting a bad example. Norwood, however, remained unrepentant. In June 1651 he was brought by warrant of Thomas Andrewes, lord mayor of London, before the bench at the sessions house in the Old Bailey. At the next sessions an indictment was prepared jointly against himself and Tany. The principal charges were that the two maintained that 'the soul [of men and women] is of the essence of God' and that 'there is neither hell nor damnation' (Norwood, *Case and Trial*, 9–10; Norwood, *Brief Discourse*, title-page, 3–4). On 20 June 1651 Norwood was removed from his place on the high court of justice by order of parliament. Five days later Norwood and Tany appeared at the Old Bailey and pleaded not guilty to the charges presented against them. Proceedings continued.

Then on Wednesday 13 August 1651, after adjournments the two previous days, at 7 o'clock in the morning Tany and Norwood again appeared at the Old Bailey to answer the charges presented against them in the indictment. Norwood at the last wavered, and seems to have been ready to recant—to no avail. The two were convicted of blasphemy by a jury of twelve men and sentenced to six months' imprisonment each in Newgate. Norwood was to intimate that his conviction owed much to the plotting of Thomas Andrewes, a long-time member of Sidrach Simpson's church, and another merchant, Alderman Stephen Estwick (*d.* 1657). Even so, it was on the charge of blasphemy that he became notorious.

Following their conviction for blasphemy, Tany and Norwood were committed to Newgate. The conditions for those that could not afford the services of the gaoler were intolerable. Norwood, it appears, was nearly financially drained by the experience. There followed a series of legal proceedings in the court of upper bench as Norwood brought forward a writ of error in an attempt to overturn the guilty verdict found against himself and Tany. The cardinal points of error in the writ were that two persons were not to be joined in one indictment—'their charge being severall', that judgment should not be given jointly, and that the defendants' alleged opinions fell outside the ambit of the Blasphemy Act: Norwood and Tany had been convicted for supposedly saying that 'there is no hell nor damnation', whereas the act condemned only those that maintained that 'there is neither Heaven nor Hell, neither Salvation nor Damnation' (Norwood, *Brief Discourse*, 1, 4). Moreover, even though Norwood and Tany avowed that the soul of man is of the essence of God, none the less the theological leap that the pair thus professed the mere creature to be very God had been provided by the framers of the indictment. On Tuesday 10 February 1652 the judges of the upper bench appear to have made their judgment. Chief Justice Rolle rejected the writ.

On Monday 16 February 1652 Robert Norwood and TheaurauJohn Tany, having served their terms of six months' imprisonment, were each released upon £100 bail—pending good behaviour for one year. In Easter term 1652 Robert Norwood prosecuted a new writ of error in the court of upper bench. After several hearings the judges deferred proceedings until the following law term. And then on Monday 28 June 1652, in Trinity term, after two more hearings, the judges ordered that 'the Judgement' against Norwood be reversed and the 'p[ar]tie restored' (PRO, KB 21/13, fol. 212r). Wary of setting a precedent, the judges of the upper bench had adhered to the strict letter of the law. Indeed, their decision to reverse the guilty verdict pronounced upon Norwood at the Old Bailey made manifest the discontiguous relationship between the Act against Atheistical, Blasphemous and Execrable Opinions and the supposed errors of doctrine propagated on the streets and public places of London: Tany and Norwood were convicted by inferring and taking out of context the true sense and meaning of their words, thereby making their opinions rigidly conform to the strictures of the Blasphemy Act of August 1650.

Following their release from Newgate, relations between Tany and Norwood appear to have cooled. Norwood, it seems, may have believed that the spirit of God had deserted Tany. During this period he wrote one pamphlet in which he advocated the readmission and toleration of the Jews and two other works, both published in the summer of 1653. These last two tracts, the one entitled *A Pathway unto England's Perfect Settlement*, the other *An Additional Discourse*, were concerned with constitutional theory, and in part derived from John Sadler's *Rights of the Kingdom, or, Customs of our Ancestours* (1649). They were censured in turn by John Spittlehouse, a former member of the army, and a group of six presbyterian booksellers. John Lilburne, however, commended Norwood's *An Additional Discourse*, calling it 'one of the excellentest pieces that lately I have read in England, for clearing up the ancient fundamental laws, rights, and liberties', and thought its author a 'sober and rational man' (J. Lilburne, *The Upright Mans Vindication*, 1653, 29–30). On 8 June 1654 Norwood was back with Tany, witnessing his claim under the name ThauRam Tanjah to the seven crowns of England, France, Reme, Rome, Naples, Sissiliah, and Jerusalem. It may have been about this time that Norwood became acquainted with Roger Crab (*c*.1616–1680), a former army agitator who had taken to a hermit's life. Crab subsisted on a vegetarian diet consisting of bread, bran, herbs, roots, dock leaves, mallows, and grass. It was said that Norwood, 'enclining' to his 'opinion, began to follow the same poore diet till it cost him his life' (R. Crab, *The English Hermite, or, Wonder of this Age*, 1655, 'To the reader'). Robert Norwood died at one Mr Manning's house, in Enfield, on 17 September 1654. His place of burial is unknown.   ARIEL HESSAYON

Sources R. Norwood, *A declaration or testimony given by Captain Robert Norwood* (1651) · R. Norwood, *The form of an excommunication* (1651) · R. Norwood, *The case and trial of Capt. R. Norwood* [n.d., 1651?] · R. Norwood, *A brief discourse made by Capt. Robert Norwood* (1652) · R. Norwood, *A pathway unto England's perfect settlement* (1653) · R. Norwood, *An additional discourse* (1653) · A. Hessayon, 'Gold tried in the fire': the prophet Theaurau John Tany and the puritan revolution [forthcoming] · PRO, KB 21/13, fol. 212*r* · PRO, KB 27/1743, mems i–ii · GL, MS 11571/11, fol. 233*v* · GL, MS 11571/12, fol. 146*r* · PRO, C5/404/129 · PRO, E179/252/4 · PRO, SP28/131, pt 3, fols. 19*v*, 101*v* · parish registers, St Andrews, Enfield, LMA

Norwych, George (*b.* before **1405**, *d.* **1469**), abbot of Westminster, entered the monastery in 1423–4 and said his first mass in 1428–9. His origins are unknown. As warden of the lady chapel (1445–6) he was responsible for the chapel itself and its extensive properties in Westminster and London. Until he became abbot, this was his only experience of the care of property, and he held no office at all for the next five years. In 1447, when he accidentally set fire to the monks' dormitory in the early hours of the morning, he was evidently living as a cloister monk. As a long-serving archdeacon (for at least ten years after 1451), however, he acquired some knowledge of legal matters, and this may help to explain his surprising election as abbot in 1463. A disastrous abbacy, characterized by great personal extravagance, ended effectively with his resignation of powers into the hands of three senior monks on 24

November 1467. He was said on this occasion to have accumulated debts amounting to £2025 under the common seal of the monastery (a sum approaching the monastery's total net income for a year) and, in addition, further debts under his own seal. Moreover, he had wasted the abbot's manors through sales of wood, and, with the connivance of Bro. Thomas Ruston, who was concurrently keeper of the new work, sacrist, and cellarer, pledged precious objects belonging to the monastery. Norwych was given a pension of 100 marks (£66 13*s*. 4*d*.) per annum and urged to spend his retirement in some other Benedictine house; he may have done so. He died in 1469, on an unknown date between 26 August and 14 November. His place of burial is unknown. He had flouted checks on the abbot's use of the monastery's seal and control of its property which dated from an earlier, more democratic, phase in Benedictine history and succeeded only in demonstrating that they were still needed in the fifteenth century, when democracy was in decline.

BARBARA F. HARVEY

Sources E. H. Pearce, *The monks of Westminster* (1916), 141–2 · R. Widmore, *An enquiry into the time of the first foundation of Westminster Abbey* (1743), appx 7 · Westminster Abbey, muniments, 5668, 5898–5899, 5901–5902, 28159–28162, 28166–28167 · B. Harvey, *Westminster Abbey and its estates in the middle ages* (1977) · B. Harvey, *The obedientiaries of Westminster Abbey and their financial records, c.1275 to 1540* (2002)
Archives Westminster Abbey, muniments, 5668, 5898–5899, 5901–5902, 28159–28162, 28166–28167

Nossiter, Maria Isabella (**1735–1759**), actress, was the daughter of a housekeeper of George Cholmondeley, third earl of Cholmondeley (1703–1770), and was probably Cholmondeley's illegitimate child; the comic actor West Digges later described her mother as 'a *favourite* housekeeper!' (*Letters*, 17). The George Robert Nossiter baptized at Richmond, Surrey, on 9 September 1739, son of Thomas Nossiter, was probably the brother mentioned in her will. Little is known of her early life, save that she 'was possessed of a handsome fortune and genteel education' (Wilkinson, 180), until her triumphant first theatrical appearance, at the age of eighteen, when she played Juliet to the Romeo of Spranger *Barry (*bap.* 1717, *d.* 1777) at Covent Garden on 10 October 1753. According to Digges, she had been tutored by Barry and the instructor and actor L. Sparks; her début had been made possible by Susanna Maria Cibber's departure for Drury Lane, and probably by the fact that she and Barry were already lovers: 'what added to the performance, Romeo and Juliet were really in love, and well known to be so' (Wilkinson, 180). Her initial nervousness was accentuated by the aggressive presence of Mrs Cibber, who had previously made the part of Juliet her own, 'with an intent by the superior force of her own effrontery, to stare away the little degree of courage she had left' (Morgan, 5). However, the audience responded sympathetically to 'so fine a girl, in such distress' (ibid.) and she gradually gained confidence, going on to reprise the part on a number of occasions. She was thought by many to be the equal of Mrs Cibber, and by some to have surpassed her. Her natural poise and elegance were generally praised; she was possessed of a 'pleasing figure' and 'genteel accomplishments' (*Theatrical Biography*, 1.93), with a 'natural bloom' (Morgan, 6) that obviated the need for make-up, though *The Gray's Inn Journal* (20 October 1753) spoke for many in recognizing her need for further training in 'the management of her voice' and the attainment of 'a more simple elocution'. On 14 November she played opposite Barry again, as Belvedira in Thomas Otway's *Venice Preserv'd*, 'and in the mad scene did wonders from tuition, attention and strong understanding' (Wilkinson, 181). On 11 December she played the Countess of Rutland in *The Earl of Essex* by Henry Jones, and then on 22 January 1754 she took on the lead role in *Philoclea*, 'brought forward and wrote purposely to show her to advantage by McNamara Morgan', the play's author (Wilkinson, 181), who had earlier published a glowing eulogy of her talents as Juliet. For her first benefit night, on 18 March, she reprised her role as Juliet, a part with which she was always associated.

Nossiter now lived with Barry in Bow Street, but when her partner quarrelled over money with the Covent Garden impresario John Rich the couple decamped to act at the Smock Alley Theatre in Dublin, where Barry received £800 for the season and Nossiter £500. They returned to Covent Garden for the 1755–6 season; she made her first appearance as Monimia in Otway's *The Orphan* on 12 December, 'which she performed to a crowded audience' (Wilkinson, 220), and she played many roles opposite Barry, including Cordelia in *King Lear*, Lady Pliant in William Congreve's *The Double Dealer*, and Desdemona in *Othello*. She had a second benefit night on 29 March 1756. The initial praise for her début was now something of a distant memory, and she was less employed in the 1756–7 season, although she added a new part when she played Statira in Nathaniel Lee's *The Rival Queens*, after George Anne Bellamy, who was beginning to be preferred over her, broke her arm; she repeated the role for her benefit on 28 March 1757. She missed the next season completely, and when she returned to Covent Garden for the 1758–9 season (leaving Barry in Dublin to promote his new theatre in Crow Street, in which she was assigned an eighth share of the profits), she was replaced as Juliet by Mrs Bellamy. She reprised her Lady Pliant and again took a variety of roles, being last seen as Aurelia in *The Prophetess* by John Fletcher, on 18 April 1759. She died aged twenty-four at her Bedford Street address on 25 April 1759, of a broken heart according to Mrs Bellamy, after Barry had formed a new liaison in Dublin with Ann Dancer, a young widow and aspirant actress whom he later married. In fact, whatever the effect of Barry's desertion, she probably died of consumption, being 'naturally of a delicate constitution, which the fatigues of her profession made more so' (*Theatrical Biography*, 1.95). She had made a will on 8 August 1758 and it remained unaltered. 'By her death, however, she testified her connections with her Romeo were of the purest kind; as by her will she left him sole executor and legatee of her effects, which amounted in cash, clothes and jewels to upwards of £3,000' (*Letters*, 17). The money included her eighth share in the profits of the Crow Street theatre. She also left £50 to her brother, George Robert Nossiter, and her 'wearing apparell' to her maid, Mary Collins (Highfill, Burnim & Langhans, *BDA*).   JOHN BULL

Sources Highfill, Burnim & Langhans, *BDA* · M. Morgan, *A letter to Miss Nossiter occasioned by her first appearance on the stage, in which is contained remarks upon her manner of playing the character of Juliet, interspersed with some other theatrical observations* (1753) · *Letters which passed between Mr. West Digges, comedian, and Mrs. Sarah Ward, 1752–1759* (1833) · T. Wilkinson, *Memoirs of his own life*, 4 (1790) [incl. 'The mirror, or, actor's tablet'] · *The Gray's Inn Journal*, 53 (20 Oct 1753) · *Theatrical biography, or, Memoirs of the principal performers of the three Theatre Royals*, 2 vols. (1772) · *The theatrical examiner: an enquiry into the merits and demerits of the present English performers in general &c* (1757) · P. Hiffernan, *The tuner* (1754) · *The grand magazine of magazines*, 3 vols. (1758)
Likenesses W. Elliott, engraving, pubd 1753 (after R. Pyle) · A. Walker, engravings, pubd 1754 (as Juliet in *Romeo and Juliet*), Folger · R. Pyle, painting (as Juliet in *Romeo and Juliet*); formerly at Marina Henderson Gallery, Chelsea
Wealth at death over £3000: Highfill, Burnim & Langhans, *BDA*; *Letters which passed between Mr. West Digges, comedian, and Mrs. Sarah Ward, 1752–1759* (1833) · wearing apparel left to maid; £50 left to her brother

Nost, John (*d.* 1710), sculptor, was born in Mechelen, in the Low Countries, and is sometimes referred to as John Van Nost. His parentage and family are largely unknown, although he mentions a sister, Mary, and a cousin, John, in his will. Much of his training, life, and working practice remain obscure, but he is known to have been active in England before 1686, as Vertue described him as 'foreman' to the sculptor Arnold Quellin (Vertue, *Note books*, 4.35), who died in London in that year. Nost subsequently married his master's widow and sole heir, Frances (*d.* 1716), the daughter of the painter Jan Siberechts. His first recorded work was carried out between 1688 and 1691, when he carved five royal figures on horseback for the 'line of kings' at the Tower of London. Nost's first documented monument, to Sir Hugh Wyndham in Silton, Dorset, was set up in 1692, by which time Nost was clearly the head of a workshop. In 1695 he was paid £120 for stone statues of William III and Queen Mary for the royal exchange (destroyed). By 1701 he had attracted royal patronage and was employed at Hampton Court Palace in carving two marble chimney-pieces of very high quality. One, in purple and dove marble, has a central bust with two putti and two intertwined birds. The other contains one of Nost's finest works, a relief of a long-limbed Venus in her chariot, surrounded by a cascade of putti (*in situ*, Royal Collection).

From 1692 Nost was rated on a property in the Haymarket, from 1698 also on a property in Portugal Row, Hyde Park Corner, and between 1699 and 1710 on the Hyde Park Road, near the queen's mead-house. In 1697 he already commanded prices of £600 for a monument which was carved in London and shipped to Yorkshire. His patron on this occasion, Lady Noel, the widow of Edward Ingram, second Viscount Irvine, described him as 'one of the best hands in England' (Gilbert, 5). Nost's chief business, however, was the production of lead statuary for the gardens of country estates all over Britain. It is not known where or when he learned the art of lead figure making, but between 1688 and his death he appears as a supplier of statuary in the muniments of Chatsworth, Lowther Castle, Castle Howard, Rousham, Seaton Delaval, and Chirk Castle.

For his garden statues, Nost drew upon classical and Renaissance models. His workshop sold copies of the *Hercules Farnese* and the *Venus de Medici*, numerous fauns and satyrs, and copies after Giambologna. On one occasion he appears to have adapted details of Annibale Carraci's Farnese Palace ceiling for a series of fighting and reconciled lead *amorini*. These were made for Thomas Coke at Melbourne Hall, Derbyshire, who was a loyal customer of Nost's between 1699 and 1706. Nost charged Coke between £10 10s. for a pair of *amorini* to £90 for a *Sabine Rape* (which Coke considered too expensive). Nost was not just a copyist, however. His vase representing *The Four Seasons* (priv. coll.), which is over 8 feet high and richly decorated with busts, monkeys, and foliage, shows considerable skill and invention.

Nost's most influential work was for Hampton Court. His sundial supported by a statue of a *Blackamoor* proved a popular subject among subsequent statuaries, while the countless urns and putti which Nost supplied around 1700 must have boosted his reputation as a leading statuary. One of his last works is also one of his most famous. His monument to the duke and duchess of Buccleuch and Queensberry, at Durisdeer, Dumfries, shows a full-size statue of the duke mourning over the recumbent figure of the duchess (d. 1709), as four putti unfurl a commemorative scroll. The work, which Gunnis counted as among 'the most exciting and unexpected things' he had seen (Gunnis, 281), is also one of the best documented early British sculptures, as both a drawing (Bodl. Oxf.) and a preparatory model in wood and plaster (priv. coll.) survive.

Nost died, apparently childless, in 1710. His will, proved on 12 August 1710, left the bulk of his estate to his wife, Frances, and his sister, Mary; £50 was left to his cousin John Nost. A sale of his 'Marble and Leaden Figures, Busto's and Noble Vases, Marble Chimney Pieces, and Curious Marble Tables' was held on 17 April 1712, with the auctioneers boasting that 'this collection is the most Valuable that ever was Exposed to Sale in this Kingdom' (O'Connell, 805). Nost appears to have died a very wealthy man. When his widow died in 1716 she left over £1460, and the remaining 'marble goods and figures' to John Nost, her late husband's cousin. This John Nost (d. 1729) continued to run the workshop, and his son, John van *Nost the younger, made his career in Ireland. Nost's principal assistant, Andries Carpentière, subsequently became the most prominent lead sculpture manufacturer in England.

Vertue called Nost 'a master of reputation' (Vertue, *Note books*, 4.35), but despite his obvious importance and influence he still lacks a modern biographer. Until very recently he was confused with his cousin John, and was thought to have died in 1729. This has caused considerable confusion over the corpus of his work, and several monuments and garden statues have been inconclusively attributed to him. Nost was a competent monumental sculptor, but he is remembered chiefly as an influential manufacturer of lead garden statuary.   M. G. SULLIVAN

Sources Vertue, *Note books*, vols. 3–4 · J. Davis, *Antique garden ornament* (1991) · will, proved, 12 Aug 1710, LMA, archdeaconry of Middlesex, AM/PW 1710/89 · S. O'Connell, 'The Nosts: a revision of the family history', *Burlington Magazine*, 129 (1987), 802–6 [incl. TS of the Nost sale in 1712] · will, PRO, PROB 11/384, fol. 332 [Arnold Quellin] · will, PRO, PROB 11/555, sig. 234 [Frances Nost] · M. Whinney, *Sculpture in Britain, 1530 to 1830*, rev. J. Physick, 2nd edn (1988) · R. Gunnis, *Dictionary of British sculptors, 1660–1851* (1953); new edn (1968) · I. Roscoe, '"The statues of the sovereigns of England": sculpture for the second building, 1695–1831', *The Royal Exchange*, ed. A. Saunders (1997), 174–87 · A. Borg, 'Two studies in the history of the Tower armouries', *Archaeologia*, 15 (1975), 317–52 · H. M. Colvin and others, eds., *The history of the king's works*, 5 (1976) · G. Gilbert, 'A newly discovered monument by John Nost in Leeds', *Leeds Arts Calendar*, 50 (1962), 4–5 · F. Pearson, ed., *Virtue and vision: sculpture and Scotland, 1540–1990* (1991) [exhibition catalogue, NG Scot., 1991] · admin, May 1729, PRO, PROB 6/105, fol. 95 · rate-books, St Martin-in-the-Fields, City Westm. AC, F1176, F1241

Archives Castle Howard, archives, bills, and estimates · Chirk Castle, Denbighshire, archives, bills, and estimates · Hoare's Bank, bills and estimates, Ledger D.2 · priv. coll., bills and estimates · PRO Work, bills and estimates, 48/28, 48/30, 5/51, 5/52 · Rousham, Oxfordshire, archives, bills, and estimates · Seaton Delaval, Northumberland, archives, bills, and estimates · Stonyhurst College, Lancashire, archives, bills, and estimates · Temple Newsam Archives, bills and estimates · The City Cash Accounts, bills and estimates | E. Sussex RO, letter-book of the first Lord Ashburnham, bills and estimates, Ash 846 · Melbourne muniment room, letter to T. Coke, bills and estimates · Staffs. RO, bills and estimates, earl of Bradford MSS 18/4 · V&A NAL, James Sotheby archives, bills and estimates, 86zz, box V

Wealth at death specific bequests of £215, although Nost assumed that this amounted to less than two-thirds of one half of estate; chief beneficiary, widow Frances, left over £1460 in her will; she was also earlier the sole heir to her first husband, Arnold Quellin, also a successful sculptor: will, proved, 12 Aug 1710, LMA, archdeaconry of Middlesex, AM/PW 1710/89; will, PRO, PROB 11/555, sig. 234 [Frances Nost]

Nost, John van, the younger (d. 1780), sculptor, was born in Piccadilly, London, the son of John van Nost (d. 1729), also a sculptor, who was a cousin of the well-known Dutch sculptor John *Nost (d. 1710), who settled in London. John van Nost the younger, who had been apprenticed to Henry Scheemakers in 1726, arrived in Dublin around 1749 and quickly established a successful practice. Mrs Delany visited his studio in March 1752, and noted that he 'takes as strong a likeness as ever I saw taken in marble' (*Letters*, 275). From 1750 onwards van Nost served as an instructor in the modelling classes at the Dublin Society Schools and took on apprentices, including John Crawley and Patrick Cunningham. John O'Keeffe, who later became a successful actor and playwright, entered the School of Figure Drawing around 1753 and remembered that 'Van Nost, the celebrated statuary, often came amongst us' (O'Keeffe, 16). Van Nost's own sister is recorded as having won a prize at the Dublin Society Schools for a bust in clay of the prince of Wales in February 1754.

Among the first works van Nost produced in Dublin were a statue of George II, placed in an arched niche over the door of the Weaver's Hall in the Coombe, and busts of Thomas Prior and Samuel Madden for the Dublin Society. In 1752 he was asked to produce a monument to Thomas Prior (now in Christ Church Cathedral), and he was enlisted to design a monument to Dean Swift in Trinity College, Dublin, though that project was not carried out. Dr Bartholomew Mosse appointed van Nost to create a number of portrait busts and classical figures for display in the gardens of the Rotunda Hospital. This commission was not completed either, but the hospital did acquire in 1757 those sculptures which van Nost had finished. Among other important works are busts of Dean Delany, for Trinity College Dublin, and of Henry Boyle, speaker of the Irish House of Commons, for the farmers' club in Munster, as well as two sculptures for the gateway of Dublin Castle. Two statues by van Nost were erected in the city, one in Stephen's Green of George II (1758), and another, of General Blakeney, in Sackville Street (1759). In 1765 the earl of Northumberland commissioned van Nost to produce an idealized statue of King George III as a Roman general (NG Ire.) for the new exchange in Dublin. Van Nost also executed important works for locations in Cork, Longford, and King's county.

When van Nost's residence and studio in Aungier Street were auctioned in November 1759, Cunningham, his former student, was provided with sufficient funds by the Dublin Society to purchase 'such molds and models as are useful and necessary for carrying on his Designs in the business of a Statuary' (Turpin, *A School of Art*, 54). These may well have included busts in varnished plaster of Seneca, Aristotle, Galen, and Horace, which Mrs Delany says van Nost ordered for his library in 1752. By 1763 van Nost was living in the garden of the Rt Hon. Anthony Malone, on the east side of Stephen's Green, and in 1779 at 21 Mecklenburgh Street. In 1777 he went to London, where he was forced by poor health to stay for four years. On his return to Dublin he moved back to Mecklenburgh Street, where, according to the *Gentleman's Magazine* (50, 1780, 494), he died in 1780.

Van Nost, the only significant sculptor at work in Ireland in the mid-eighteenth century, prospered in the capital. Described by a committee of the corporation of Dublin in 1752 as 'the most knowing and skilfull statuary in this Kingdom' (Strickland, 480), he drew on a Netherlandish style for his figures but was also influenced by Italianate idealization, and he shared the English and Irish penchant for classicism.   BRENDAN ROONEY

Sources W. G. Strickland, *A dictionary of Irish artists*, 2 (1913) · J. Hill, *Irish public sculpture: a history* (Dublin, 1998) · R. Kennedy, *Dublin Castle art: the historical and contemporary collection* (Dublin, 1999) · J. Turpin, *A school of art in Dublin since the eighteenth century: a history of the National College of Art and Design* (Dublin, 1995) · A. Crookshank, *Irish sculpture from 1600 to the present day* (Dublin, 1984) · *Letters from Georgian Dublin: the correspondence of Mrs Delany, 1731–68*, ed. A. Day (1991) · P. Harbison, H. Potterton, and J. Sheehy, *Irish art and architecture from prehistory to the present* (1978) · A. Crookshank and D. Webb, *Paintings and sculptures in Trinity College, Dublin* (1990) · H. Potterton and M. Wynne, *National Gallery of Ireland: acquisitions, 1981–82* (Dublin, 1982) · J. Turpin, *John Hogan: Irish neoclassical sculptor in Rome, 1800–1858* (1982) · Redgrave, *Artists* · G. N. Wright, *An historical guide to the city of Dublin*, 2nd edn (1825) · W. M. Thackeray, *The Irish sketch book, 1842* (1985) · J. O'Keeffe, *Recollections of the life of John O'Keeffe, written by himself*, 2 vols. (1826) · *GM*, 1st ser., 50 (1780), 494

Notari, Angelo (1566–1663), composer, was born in Padua, Italy, on 14 January 1566 (according to his horoscope in BL, Sloane MS 1707). All that is known of his life in Italy is that he was a member of the Accademia degli Sprovisti of Venice (which had the nickname Il Negligente) and contributed a piece to Nicolo Legname's *Libro dei canzonette* (1608). Notari arrived in England some time before 1612, when he was listed as one of Prince Henry's musicians at the time of his death; from 1618 he was likewise in the service of Prince Charles.

Notari must have played an important part in introducing Italian music to England in the early years of the seventeenth century. His *Prime musiche nuove*, engraved by William Hole in London and dedicated to the earl of Somerset (dated 24 November 1613), contains examples of the various advanced styles current in Italy at the time, such as monody, strophic variation, canzonetta, and chamber duet, but not madrigal. The preface (in English) refers to the *trillo* as 'a kinde of sweetnes in your voice', which suggests tremolo or vibrato. Over and above his work as a composer, he was also an important copyist of Italian music by Monteverdi and others (BL, Add. MS 31440; parts of Christ Church, Oxford, MSS 878–880). Some of the anonymous pieces in these manuscripts may be by Notari himself; otherwise virtually nothing by him is known other than his published work.

Notari's name crops up in the state papers between 1621 and 1623 as a suspected spy for Gondomar, the Spanish ambassador. He was a known Catholic and sang at mass in the ambassador's chapel on Christmas day 1622. Following Charles's accession in 1625 he was named among the king's 'lutes and voices', and continued as such until 1639, when his name no longer appears on the list.

During the interregnum Notari may have travelled on the continent, but at the Restoration he was reappointed to his old position, assisted by Henry Purcell the elder, who eventually succeeded him. He died a few weeks short of his ninety-eighth birthday and was buried in St Martin-in-the-Fields on 26 December 1663.   IAN SPINK

Angelo Notari (1566–1663), by William Hole, pubd 1613

Sources A. Ashbee and D. Lasocki, eds., *A biographical dictionary of English court musicians, 1485–1714*, 2 (1998), 839–42 · I. Spink, 'Angelo Notari and his *Prime musiche nuove*', *Monthly Musical Record*, 87 (1957), 168–77 · P. J. Willetts, 'Autographs of Angelo Notari', *Music and Letters*, 50 (1969), 124–6
Likenesses W. Hole, engraving, pubd 1613, FM Cam. [*see illus.*]

Notary, Julian (*b. c.*1455, *d.* in or after 1523), printer and bookseller, came from Vannes (Morbihan), in Brittany, according to a record from the court of the official principal of the bishop of London which implies a birth date about 1455. We know almost nothing of his personal life beyond the limited information in his editions. Notary may have moved from Vannes to Paris or to Rouen to join the book trade, but the evidence is circumstantial. Although the bishop of London's record from 1510/11 indicates he had been in London for sixteen years, his first appearance is in 1496 as a printer of *De modis significandi* by Albertus Magnus. Printed in London at St Thomas the Apostle, the edition has no printer's name, though a device contains the initials I. N., I. B., and I. H. The first two are taken to be Julian Notary and John Barbier or Barbour; the third may be Jean Huvin, a stationer from Rouen. The edition's type is similar to those used by Wynkyn de Worde and Richard Pynson, with whom Notary clearly had close links. This is the first English edition of this book, though it had been printed in Venice in 1491. The same printer's device occurs in a *Horae ad usum Sarum*, issued in April 1497; but in 1498 Notary and Barbier alone (for the initials I. H. were cut out of the device) printed the Sarum *Missale*. Both texts were printed for de Worde in the same type as that of *De modis*, the latter at King Street, Westminster, now possibly Notary's home.

In January 1499 *Liber festivalis* and *Quattuor sermones* appeared in one volume though with two colophons. Notary was the sole printer, for in the old device all initials are excised and 'Iulianus Notarii' inserted within its lower circle. Both works had been printed many times already, especially by de Worde and Pynson. The edition, issued 'apud Westmonasterium', proves Notary had moved to Westminster, presumably to be close to de Worde. Despite their titles these two works are in English, as is Chaucer's poem *Mars and Venus* in a first edition about 1500. About that time Notary moved into the parish of St Clement Danes at Temple Bar, possibly in Pynson's former shop; de Worde moved to London in the same year.

For the first twenty years of the century we can usually identify at least one edition a year by Notary. His output consisted of religious, mainly liturgical, works such as the *Horae* and *Missale*; theological treatises such as *Parabolarum Alani* and *Liber Theodoli*, both with commentary; indulgences and other ephemera; and miscellaneous English works such as *Bevis of Hampton*, *St Alban's Chronicle*, and Hilton's *Scale of Perfection*. Although the last are in English, most of his editions are in Latin. Many had been printed previously by either de Worde or Pynson. Possibly *Mars and Venus* and other first editions were reprints of lost texts and as *Parabolarum Alani cum commento* had been printed by Pynson, *Theodolus cum commento*, published with it on 1 June 1505, may also have been issued earlier by

Pynson. Notary shows little originality in his choice of text: he generally printed from existing editions and was possibly invited to issue reprints by others. Nevertheless, he made a reasonable living and in the lay subsidy rolls of 1522/3 his goods are valued at £36 6s. 8d. He published about forty items. Several are noteworthy for their woodcuts and metal-engravings. Notary also worked as a binder, using a Tudor rose and shields with the cross of St George and the arms of the city of London as panel stamps.

At Temple Bar, Notary's house had the sign of Three Kings, and a little shop ('cellula', according to a title-page of 1510) at St Paul's Churchyard had the same sign. About 1515 he seems to have moved to St Paul's Churchyard beside the west door. Nothing is known of him after 1523.

H. R. TEDDER, *rev.* N. F. BLAKE

Sources H. R. Plomer, *Wynkyn de Worde and his contemporaries from the death of Caxton to 1535* (1925), 162–76 · E. G. Duff, *A century of the English book trade* (1905) · C. E. Welch, 'Julian Notary and Andrew Rowe: two contemporary records', *The Library*, 5th ser., 11 (1956), 277–8 · C. P. Christianson, 'Paternoster Row and the Tudor book-trade community', *The Library*, 6th ser., 11 (1989), 352–6 · E. Hodnett, *English woodcuts, 1480–1535* (1935)
Wealth at death goods valued at £36 6s. 8d. in 1522/3: lay subsidy rolls

Nothhelm [Nothelm] (*d.* 739), archbishop of Canterbury, was a priest of London and apparently not a monk. He was a friend of Albinus, abbot of St Peter's and St Paul's (later St Augustine's), Canterbury, who employed him to convey to Bede, both by letter and by word of mouth, information respecting the ecclesiastical history of Kent. Nothhelm visited Rome during the pontificate of Gregory II (*r.* 715–31) and, with his permission, searched the registers of the Roman see and copied several letters of Gregory the Great and other popes, which, by the advice of Albinus, he gave to Bede, that he might insert them in his *Historia ecclesiastica*. Part of Bede's reason for composing this work and for his collaboration with Nothhelm, it has been argued, was to prepare the ground for an independent northern ecclesiastical province with the co-operation of Canterbury.

Archbishop Tatwine having died in 734, Nothhelm was consecrated to the see of Canterbury in 735, the archbishopric of York being established about that time (and probably a little earlier than Nothhelm's consecration) by the gift of a pallium from Pope Gregory III to Ecgberht (*d.* 766). Nothhelm received his pallium from Gregory III in 736 and then consecrated Cuthbert (*d.* 760), who succeeded him at Canterbury, to the see of Hereford, Herewald to Sherborne, and Æthelfrith to Elmham. He received a letter from Boniface, then archbishop in Germany, asking for a copy of the letter containing the questions sent by Augustine of Canterbury to Gregory the Great and the pope's answers (*Responsiones*), together with Nothhelm's opinion on the case of a man's marriage with the widowed mother of his godson. Bede had included the text of Gregory's *Responsiones* in his *Historia ecclesiastica*. Suso Brechter considered this text a forgery and roundly accused Nothhelm and Archdeacon Gemmulus at Rome of the deed.

Paul Meyvaert effectively refuted this charge, though the case for Gregory's authorship, while strong, is not yet totally established.

In either 736 or 737 Nothhelm held a synod which was attended by nine bishops. In 737 a division was made between the Mercian and mid-Anglian bishoprics by the consecration of Hwita to Lichfield and Totta to Leicester. Nothhelm witnessed a charter of Eadberht, king of Kent, in 738. The works attributed to Nothhelm by Leland, Bale, and Tanner are merely suppositions. He sent thirty questions to Bede on the books of Kings, which Bede answered in his treatise *In regum librum XXX quaestiones*, addressed to Nothhelm. There is a ten-line verse eulogy on Nothhelm, of unknown origin, in a sixteenth-century manuscript in Lambeth Palace Library. Nothhelm died on 17 October 739 and was buried in the abbey church of St Peter and St Paul, Canterbury.

WILLIAM HUNT, *rev.* HENRY MAYR-HARTING

Sources Bede, *Hist. eccl.*, preface; 1.23 · *Venerabilis Baedae opera historica*, ed. C. Plummer, 2 (1896), 2–3 · A. W. Haddan and W. Stubbs, eds., *Councils and ecclesiastical documents relating to Great Britain and Ireland*, 3 vols. (1869–71) · Symeon of Durham, *Opera* · AS chart., S 27 · P. Meyvaert, 'Bede's text of the *Libellus responsionum* of Gregory the Great to Augustine of Canterbury', *England before the conquest: studies in primary sources presented to Dorothy Whitelock*, ed. P. Clemoes and K. Hughes (1971), 15–33 · S. Brechter, *Die Quellen zur Angelsachsenmission Gregors des Grossen* (1941) · W. Goffart, *The narrators of barbarian history* (1988) · Bede, 'In regum librum XXX quaestiones', ed. D. Hurst, in *Bedae venerabilis opera: pars 2, opera exegetica* (1962), 289–322 · H. Walther, ed., *Initia carminum ac versuum medii aevi posterioris Latinorum: alphabetiches Verseichnis der Verserfänge mittelateinischer Dichtungen*, 2nd edn (Göttingen, 1969), 13336 · [H. Wharton], ed., *Anglia sacra*, 2 (1691), 71 · John of Worcester, *Chron.*, s.a. 741

Nott, George Frederick (1767–1841), Church of England clergyman and literary editor, was the son of Samuel Nott (1739/40–1793), prebendary of Winchester, rector of Houghton, Hampshire, and vicar of Blandford, Dorset. His mother was Augusta (*d.* 1813), daughter of Pennell Hawkins, sergeant-surgeon to the king, and niece of Sir Caesar Hawkins (1711–1786). His uncle, the physician John Nott (1751–1825), was a classical scholar with an interest in sixteenth-century literature. George Nott inherited both his uncle's estate and his scholarly interests; the works of uncle and nephew have been sometimes confused.

Nott matriculated from Christ Church, Oxford, in October 1784, and graduated BA in 1788. He was a fellow of All Souls (from 1790 until 1814), and was ordained. He proceeded MA in 1792, BD in 1802, and DD in 1807. In 1801 he was a university proctor, and in 1802 preached the Bampton lectures, which were published in 1803 under the title of *Religious Enthusiasm*. The success of the lectures led to his appointment as sub-preceptor to Princess Charlotte and much clerical preferment. He became prebendary of Colworth in Chichester in 1802; perpetual curate of Stoke Canon, Devon, in 1807; vicar of Broadwindsor, Dorset, in 1808; prebendary of Winchester in 1810; rector of Harrietsham and Woodchurch in Kent (in exchange for Broadwindsor) in 1813; and prebendary of Salisbury in 1814. In

his parishes he repaired rectories and built new schoolhouses, but this enthusiasm for architecture later led to his (literal) downfall. As prebendary of Winchester he superintended repairs to the cathedral, and on 6 January 1817, while thus engaged, he fell a distance of some 30 feet, injuring his head. Apparently he never fully recovered from this accident, subsequently spending much time in Italy in a manner reminiscent of Dr Stanhope in *Barchester Towers*. Here he acquired many paintings from contemporary artists in Rome, and found himself in the midst of a minor scandal in Pisa. While visiting among the English community here, Mary Shelley heard a rumour that Nott had called her husband a scoundrel, which he denied; to show that she believed him, she attended his services once a month for three months, until she heard that Nott had denounced Shelley's atheism. Nott again denied the charge, but this did not stem the gossip.

Fluent in the language of his adopted country, Nott translated the Book of Common Prayer into Italian (1831) and published in Florence *Fortunatus siculus, ossia, L'advventuroso Ciciliano* (1832), with an Italian introduction and notes. His most significant work, however, had been published while he was still in England: it was an exhaustive edition of *The Works of Henry Howard, Earl of Surrey, and of Sir Thomas Wyatt, the Elder* (1815–16). Nott's edition of Wyatt's poetry was the first adequate edition, firmly based on the most significant sources: Richard Tottel's miscellany, *Songes and Sonnettes* (1557), and the Egerton and Devonshire manuscripts in the British Museum. (Equally, the biography of Wyatt, which he also included, was the first full-length account of Wyatt's life; it was not fully superseded until Kenneth Muir's *Life and Letters of Sir Thomas Wyatt* was published in 1963.) But despite amassing much material relating to the poems and their Italian sources, Nott failed to produce an authoritative text, often following Tottel's versions of Wyatt's poems rather than the poet's own text and presenting the poems in nineteenth-century English. Modern scholars also condemn Nott for adhering to the contemporary preference for the more classically based verse of Surrey, despite admiration for the simplicity and force of Wyatt's poetry. This preference, however, won Nott a more lasting editorial reputation: his edition of Surrey's poetry was not superseded until the 1920s, and his assessment of Surrey's significance in the development of English poetry has met with the qualified praise of the poet's most recent editor, Emrys Jones.

Earlier critics were less favourable: Edmond Bapst, in his *Deux gentilshommes: poètes à la cour de Henri VIII* (1891) condemned Nott's biography of Surrey, and in particular his adherence to the picturesque tradition that most of Surrey's poems were inspired by his passion for Lady Elizabeth Fitzgerald, the 'Fair Geraldine' (in fact, Surrey appears to have addressed only one sonnet to her, possibly when she was as young as nine years old).

Nott died at his house in the close, Winchester, on 25 October 1841, and was buried in the north transept of the cathedral. The sale of his library, comprising 12,500 volumes, and many prints and pictures, took place at Winchester in January 1842; his coins, gems, and bronzes were sold in April in London. Several Italian works, with manuscript notes by Nott, are in the British Library.

ROSEMARY MITCHELL

Sources GM, 2nd ser., 17 (1842), 106–7, 299 · Ward, Men of the reign · Allibone, Dict. · Foster, Alum. Oxon. · K. Muir, The life and letters of Sir Thomas Wyatt (1963), vii · The poems of Sir Thomas Wyatt, ed. A. K. Foxwell, 1 (1913), vi · E. M. W. Tillyard, The poetry of Sir Thomas Wyatt (1949), 55 · H. Howard [earl of Surrey], Poems, ed. E. Jones (1964), xxiii, xxx–xxxii · E. W. Sunstein, Mary Shelley: romance and reality (1989), 209
Archives U. Birm. L., corresp. and drawings

Nott, John (1751–1825), physician and classical scholar, was born in Worcester on Christmas eve 1751, the son of Samuel Nott. His father was of German origins and had held an appointment in George III's household. Nott studied surgery in Birmingham under Edmund Hector and in London under Sir Caesar Hawkins; he also studied in Paris. About 1775 he went to the continent with an invalid gentleman and returned to London two years later. In 1783 he travelled to China as surgeon on board an East India Company vessel. During his three years abroad he learned Persian, and he later demonstrated his proficiency in the language with a faithful translation into English entitled Select Odes from the Persian Poet Hafez (1787). His love of travel was not yet exhausted, for soon after returning to England he accompanied his brother and his family on a journey abroad for their health.

On his return in 1788 Nott was urged to graduate by Dr Richard Warren, the king's physician. This he duly did, although it is not known where, and on 8 October 1789 he became an extra-licentiate of the Royal College of Physicians. On Warren's recommendation he was appointed physician to Georgiana, duchess of Devonshire, and her sister, Lady Duncannon, on their tour to the continent. While in Italy he investigated the medical properties of thermal waters at Pisa and the springs at Asciano. He published his findings in 1792. He remained the duchess's physician until 1793, when he settled at the Hotwells in Bristol, where he continued to practise medicine. He published two further works, one on the Hotwells, and one on the local outbreak of influenza in 1803.

Nott was also an accomplished classical scholar. Having acquired a taste for classical poetry at an early age he made some translations from the Latin classics while at school. His most significant publications were his translations of his favourite authors, Petrarch, Horace, and Catullus, the first two of which appeared in 1777 and 1803 respectively. The publication of The poems of Caius Valerius Catullus, in English verse, with Latin text versified, and classical notes (2 vols., 1794) sealed his reputation as a gifted classicist and poet. Among his other classical works were a translation of Lucretius, and Sappho: after a Greek Romance (1802). He also contributed to the Gentleman's Magazine and other journals and published his own verses, including two juvenile works, Alonzo, or, The Youthful Solitaire (1772)

and Leonora: an Elegy on the Death of a Young Lady (1775); Leonora had been the subject of his youthful affections. Admired by some for the precision and neatness of his language, Nott's scholarship was dismissed by Charles Lamb and Algernon Swinburne as superficial and pedantic.

During his last eight years Nott suffered from hemiplegia, which confined him to his house. He none the less continued his studies and at his death had just finished a complete translation of Petrarch. He died, unmarried, in a boarding-house in Dowry Square, Clifton, on 23 July 1825 and was buried in the old burial-ground in Clifton. His nephew and heir, the Revd Dr George Frederick Nott, conducted the funeral service.

W. P. COURTNEY, rev. M. J. MERCER

Sources Munk, Roll · GM, 1st ser., 95/2 (1825), 565–6 · Allibone, Dict. · A. C. Swinburne, 'Charles Lamb and George Wither', Nineteenth Century, 17 (1885), 66–91 · Bristol Gazette (28 July 1825) · N&Q, 10 (1854), 27 · N&Q, 5th ser., 10 (1878), 204 · N&Q, 6th ser., 10 (1884), 267
Archives BL, letters to Philip Bliss, Add. MSS 34567–34568

Nott, Sir Thomas (1606–1681), royalist army officer, was born on 11 December 1606, the eldest son of Roger Nott (c.1581–1670/71), citizen and merchant tailor of All Hallows Staining, London. He entered Merchant Taylors' School, London, in 1618 and matriculated at Cambridge University in 1621 as a pensioner of Pembroke College. He graduated BA in 1625 and proceeded MA in 1628. In 1637 he married Elizabeth Thynne (bap. 1613, d. in or before 1661), daughter of Thomas Thynne of St Margaret's, Westminster. In the same year he bought the manors of Sagebury and Obden in the parish of Dodderhill, Worcestershire, from Sir Arthur Smythes and his son, and in 1640 acquired the remainder of the crown lease of Twickenham Park, Middlesex, from the countess of Home.

In 1639 Nott was knighted at Whitehall. The commissioners of array listed him among the gentlemen of Worcestershire who would supply horses for the king's service in 1642. He served in the royalist army during the first civil war, as a colonel or lieutenant-colonel. He was described as a lieutenant-colonel in the parliamentarian sources which mistakenly reported his death during the capture of Highworth, Wiltshire, in June 1645 by a detachment of the New Model Army. He may have been captured there, although that is uncertain. He had surrendered by December 1645, but could not pay his fine for delinquency because of debts. In 1649 the committee for compounding fined him £1257, one-sixth of the value of his estates. He was discharged from various assessments in 1650 on payment of £50.

Nott was prominent in the royalist uprising in Glamorgan in June 1647, although he had no strong interests in the county. He was a signatory of letters sent to Major-General Laugharne and responsible for raising an armed force at Cowbridge, which reached Llandaff before dispersing on the approach of Laugharne's troops. Nott and the other royalist leaders escaped. He may also have been involved in the second civil war in 1648. The council of state ordered that he should be disarmed following a royalist demonstration at Twickenham in 1649 which had been instigated by Lady Nott. Indeed, he asked for compensation for damage to his property there during the commotion.

In 1659 Nott sold Twickenham Park and bought a house in Richmond. At the Restoration he became gentleman-usher to the king and he was a gentleman of the privy chamber from 1670 until his death. He was one of the original fellows when the Royal Society was formed in 1663, but was expelled in 1675 for non-payment of his subscription. He made his will on 18 December 1681 and died soon after at St Margaret's, Westminster; he was buried at Richmond on 22 December. His will mentions his son Thomas (1638–1703) and grandson, also Thomas. Nott's second wife, Anne (c.1606–1694), whom he had married in 1661, and his children Roger, Edward, Susan, and Beatrice were his executors. Anne was buried near him on 17 November 1694.   STEPHEN PORTER

Sources DNB · J. R. Phillips, *Memoirs of the civil war in Wales and the marches, 1642–1649*, 2 (1874), 335–43 · will, PROB 11/369, fol. 7 · *Mercurius Civicus*, 110 (26 June–3 July 1645), 979 · *CSP dom.*, 1649–50, 290, 293 · M. A. E. Green, ed., *Calendar of the proceedings of the committee for compounding* … 1643–1660, 3, PRO (1891), 1544 · M. A. E. Green, ed., *Calendar of the proceedings of the committee for advance of money, 1642–1656*, 1, PRO (1888), 255 · *Diary of Henry Townshend of Elmley Lovett*, ed. J. W. Willis Bund, 2, Worcestershire Historical Society (1920), 77 · *VCH Worcestershire*, 3.64 · Venn, *Alum. Cant.*, 1.270 · Mrs E. P. Hart, ed., *Merchant Taylors' School register, 1561–1934*, 1 (1936) [Knott]

Likenesses R. White, line engraving, 1678, BM, NPG

Wealth at death see will, PRO, PROB 11/369, fol. 7

Nott, Sir William (1782–1845), army officer in the East India Company, was born on 20 January 1782 near Neath, Glamorgan, the second son of Charles Nott of Shobdon in Herefordshire and his wife, a Miss Bailey of Seething, near Loddon, in Norfolk. His family had for many generations been yeomen. At a school in Neath, where his father rented a farm, and afterwards at the grammar school at Cowbridge, Nott received an indifferent elementary education. In 1794 his father moved to the town of Carmarthen, became the proprietor of the Ivy Bush inn, and began business as a mail contractor. He also retained a large farm, on which he was assisted by his sons.

Early years in India In 1798 Nott enrolled in a volunteer corps in Carmarthen, and this led him to aspire to an army commission. A Bengal cadetship was obtained for him, and he embarked in 1800 for Calcutta in the East Indiaman *Kent*. After much hardship, as a result of the *Kent's* seizure by a French privateer and the transfer of the passengers to a small Arab vessel, Nott finally reached Calcutta. On 28 August 1800 he was appointed an ensign, and posted to the Bengal European regiment at Berhampore. He soon afterwards transferred to the 20th native infantry, and on 21 February 1801 he was promoted lieutenant.

In 1804 Nott commanded a detachment in the expedition under Captain Hayes, Bombay marine, against the peoples on the west coast of Sumatra. He distinguished himself in the capture of Moko. For alleged indiscipline Captain Robertson, who commanded the vessel in which

Sir William Nott (1782–1845), by Thomas Brigstocke, exh. RA 1845

Nott sailed, arrested and confined him. On reaching Calcutta, Nott demanded a court martial, at which he was honourably acquitted while Robertson was admonished.

On 5 October 1805 Nott married, at Calcutta, Letitia, second daughter of Henry Swinhoe, solicitor of the supreme court, Calcutta, and they had fourteen children, of whom only five survived him. He sent his sons to Eton College and Cambridge. His wife died in October 1838. On 1 March 1811 he was appointed superintendent of native pensions and paymaster of family pensions at Barrackpore. He was promoted captain-lieutenant on 15 June 1814 and captain on 16 December.

In December 1822 Nott visited England with his wife and daughters. He was promoted major in 1823 and regimental lieutenant-colonel on 2 October 1824. On 25 November 1825 he returned to Calcutta and took command of the 20th native infantry at Barrackpore. Although he had been so long in a semi-military post, he brought his regiment into such a state of efficiency that his services were required to do the same for other regiments. He commanded a succession of native infantry regiments and on 1 December 1829 was promoted colonel.

First Anglo-Afghan War, 1838–1842 At the outbreak of the First Anglo-Afghan War in 1838 Nott was transferred to the command of the 42nd native infantry, with a view to his commanding a brigade on active service. On 28 June 1838 he was promoted major-general, and in September was appointed a brigadier-general of the second class, to command the 2nd brigade, 1st division, of the army of the Indus. The following month his wife died suddenly at Delhi. Nott was overwhelmed with grief. He sent his family to England, and proceeded to the rendezvous at Karnal in a very depressed state.

After the arrival of the troops at Ferozepore, Nott was, on 4 December, appointed temporarily to command the division of Sir Willoughby Cotton, who had succeeded Sir Henry Fane in the command of the Bengal troops. The Bengal column moved on 12 December down the Sutlej towards the Indus, and from there by the Bolan Pass to Quetta. On 5 April 1839 Sir John Keane and the Bombay column joined the Bengal force at Quetta, and Keane took command of the army. Nott resumed his brigade command and, despite his protestations, was left with his brigade at Quetta in order, he believed, to allow queen's officers, although junior to himself as generals, to go on to Kabul. He was ordered to exercise general superintendence and military control in the province of Shal. The force at Quetta was gradually strengthened, and by the beginning of July 1839 Nott had with him four infantry regiments, some cavalry and horse artillery, and a company of European artillery, with engineers, sappers, and miners.

Nott was a blunt, brave, experienced officer, full of common sense, but quick-tempered and outspoken. He much resented the superiority accorded to royal officers over the company's and was quick to take offence. He wrote: 'A queen's officer, be he ever so talented, is totally unfit to command the Company's Army' (Stocqueler, 1.82).

On 15 October 1839 Nott was ordered to command the troops at Quetta and Kandahar. Under instructions from Keane he advanced with half his brigade to Kandahar, where he arrived on 13 November. In spring 1840 he sent out forces which defeated the Ghilzais. In July Nott left Captain Woodburn with a small force at Robat and himself returned to Kandahar with the main body. On the way he learned that Kalat was in rebellion. He strengthened the defences of Kandahar and Quetta, and on 9 September, as ordered, moved from Kandahar to Quetta, arriving on 25 October at Mastung. He then marched on Kalat; the enemy evacuated the fortress, and Nott entered it on 3 November 1840. Having placed Colonel Stacey in political charge at Kalat, Nott returned to Quetta, and on 18 November marched to Kandahar. He received the thanks of parliament and of the East India Company.

In early 1841 Nott's forces crushed an Afghan rebellion and forced the submission of the rebel leader Aktur Khan. On 28 June 1841 Nott was appointed to command the 2nd infantry brigade in Afghanistan. His forces defeated various rebels, and in early November he returned to Kandahar. On 8 November 1841, as ordered, he sent Maclaren's brigade back to India, but they had not gone far when news came of the uprising at Kabul. Nott recalled the brigade and, as ordered by Major-General Elphinstone, who

had succeeded Cotton in command in Afghanistan, sent it towards Kabul. Nott called in the scattered garrisons and prepared against any rising at Kandahar. Maclaren's brigade soon returned to Kandahar because of the weather.

Commander in Afghanistan On 13 January 1842 Nott was appointed commander of all troops in Lower Afghanistan and Sind, and of the political officers there. On 12 January 1842 Safter Jang, Atta Muhammad, and others advanced to near Kandahar. Nott moved out of the city and attacked their position on the right bank of the Arghandab, soon dispersing the enemy, who retreated with small loss.

On 31 January 1842 Nott heard of the murder of Macnaghten at Kabul. In February he was concerned for the safety of Kalat-i-Ghilzai and the citadel of Ghazni. The enemy had captured the city of Ghazni in December 1841 and driven the garrison into the citadel. On 21 February 1842 orders came to Kandahar from Elphinstone at Kabul that the troops at Kandahar and Kalat-i-Ghilzai were to return to India. Nott decided that, Elphinstone having written under coercion, the Kabul convention was not binding on him, and that he would remain where he was, pending orders from Calcutta. Sale, at Jalalabad, replied similarly. News of the fate of Elphinstone's army retreating from Kabul reached Nott immediately after, and he wrote to the government of India, urging the need to hold Jalalabad and Kandahar in order to advance later on Kabul and punish the murderers of Macnaghten. He stated that he would not himself move unless so ordered. Nott then expelled all Afghans from Kandahar. In the beginning of March, with the enemy, 12,000 strong, having approached Kandahar, Nott marched out on the 7th and dispersed them, his lack of cavalry alone saving the main body from destruction. But when Nott was some 30 miles from Kandahar a strong enemy force made a flank march to Kandahar; they were repulsed with great loss by the garrison, under Major Lane, on 11 March 1842.

Ghazni and its aftermath, 1842 On 15 March 1842 Colonel Palmer was compelled to make terms at Ghazni. Treachery followed: many of his force were killed and many sepoys enslaved, and he and some of the officers were eventually carried off as prisoners to Bamian. On 22 March Major-General Richard England arrived with reinforcements at Quetta. He moved from Quetta on the 28th, then, being repulsed at Haikalzai, returned to Quetta. Nott was deeply concerned for the loss of Ghazni and the repulse of General England. But, as he was without money to pay his troops, and lacked sufficient medicine and ammunition, he could not move. He ordered England to bring his force to Kandahar by the Khojak Pass, and he sent a force to the northern end of the pass to safeguard it. England joined him in Kandahar early in May. Lord Ellenborough, the new governor-general, who had arrived in February, at first favoured a policy of retreat. He appointed Pollock to the chief command in Afghanistan, and ordered him to relieve Sale at Jalalabad. At the same time he corresponded with Nott, whom he allowed to maintain his position.

While a large force had been dispatched by Nott to withdraw the garrison of Kalat-i-Ghilzai, Aktur Khan, the Durrani chief, assembled 3000 men and joined the force under Safter Jang and Atta Muhammad on the right bank of the Arghandab. Nott moved out with a part of his force, leaving General England to protect Kandahar. On 29 May he attacked and defeated the enemy, and drove them in confusion and with great loss across the Arghandab River.

On 22 July Nott received from Ellenborough orders to withdraw from Afghanistan, either by the Quetta route or round by Ghazni, Kabul, and Jalalabad. Nott decided to march with a small, compact, and well-tried force upon Ghazni and Kabul, and to send General England back to India by Quetta and Sukkur. General Pollock at once communicated with Nott, and it was arranged that they should meet at Kabul. On learning Nott's decision, Ellenborough supported the forward movement. He directed Nott to bring away from Ghazni the club and mace of Mahmud of Ghazni and the gates of the temple of Somnath.

By the end of July Nott had completed his preparations. He transferred the Sind command to General England, and saw him start with his column for India on 8 August. Nott then moved slowly away from Kandahar by short marches, as he desired to give General England a fair start while he was within reach. On 30 August, as Nott approached within 40 miles of Ghazni, Shams al-Din, the Afghan governor, met him at Karabagh with 12,000 men. After a short action Nott defeated and dispersed the enemy, darkness alone preventing the complete destruction of the enemy's infantry. Shams al-Din fled to Ghazni.

On 5 September Nott was before Ghazni, which the Afghans evacuated. Its walls, gates, and citadel were destroyed so far as the means and time available permitted. More than 300 sepoys, sold into slavery when Palmer capitulated in March, were recovered. Nott removed the gates of Somnath from the tomb of Sultan Mahmud, but the club and mace could not be found.

Nott continued his march towards Kabul, and as he approached Beni Badam and Maidan he found Shams al-Din, Sultan Jan, and other Afghan chiefs, with an army of 12,000 men, occupying a succession of strong mountain positions directly on his road. On 14 and 15 September Nott's troops dislodged them, and they dispersed. Pollock reached Kabul first, and Nott arrived on 17 September, camping a few miles from the city. The combined army remained at Kabul until 12 October, when it marched for India by way of Jalalabad. At Gandamak, Nott received a letter from Ellenborough acknowledging the splendid services of the army, praising Nott, and notifying his appointment from 30 November as resident at the court of Lucknow, with the title of envoy to the king of Oudh. On 23 December the army reached the Sutlej, over which a bridge of boats had been thrown, and Ellenborough and the commander-in-chief, accompanied by several Indian princes, received the troops with much ceremony and display, marred by incompetence: the triumphal arch caused the troops great mirth. Before leaving Ferozepore, Ellenborough presented Nott with a valuable sword in the name of the British government.

Praise, second marriage, and death Nott went to Lucknow to take up his new appointment, but soon after he was installed at the court of the king of Oudh he was summoned to Agra by Ellenborough to be invested with the GCB; the ceremony, in March 1843, was performed amid great splendour. On 20 February the thanks of both houses of parliament were voted to the generals and their armies for their operations in Afghanistan, and Nott was praised by Wellington and by Peel. Lord Ellenborough, writing to Wellington, opined that Nott was superior to all the other generals. Ellenborough was right. Despite his cantankerous nature Nott was by far the best general in the Anglo-Afghan War. He was also a protagonist of the sepoy, whom he compared favourably with the British soldier.

On 26 June 1843 Nott married, at Lucknow, Rosa Wilson, daughter of Captain Dore of the Buffs, 3rd foot. In October he had a recurrence of an illness contracted in Afghanistan, and in 1844 went on leave to the Cape of Good Hope and then to England, arriving in the summer of 1844. He received numerous invitations, but he was too ill even to go to Windsor. He lived in retirement at Carmarthen, where he had purchased an estate, Job's Well. The directors of the East India Company granted him an annuity of £1000 and the City of London bestowed upon him the freedom of the city. But Nott's heart disease rapidly worsened, and he died on 1 January 1845 at Carmarthen. He was buried on 6 January in the churchyard of St Peter's, beside his parents' grave. He was survived by his second wife.

Nott was a self-reliant man and, when the opportunity offered, a successful commander. He had a strong sense of duty, and was a strict disciplinarian. Nevertheless he was himself impatient of control, and freely criticized the conduct of his superiors, with whom he was apt to disagree. Reserved in manner, he was intimate with few.

R. H. Vetch, *rev.* James Lunt

Sources J. H. Stocqueler, *Memoirs and correspondence of Major-General Sir William Nott*, 2 vols. (1854) · *Hart's Army List* · J. W. Kaye, *History of the war in Afghanistan*, rev. edn, 3 vols. (1857–8) · Fortescue, *Brit. army*, vol. 12 · P. Macrory, *Signal catastrophe: the story of a disastrous retreat from Kabul, 1842* (1966) · J. A. Norris, *The First Afghan War, 1838–1842* (1967) · H. Havelock, *Narrative of the war in Afghanistan in 1838–39*, 2 vols. (1840) · H. M. Durand, *The First Afghan War and its causes* (1879) · W. Hough, *Narrative of the war in Afghanistan, 1838–9* (1841) · *The Afghan war, 1838–42: from the journal and correspondence of the late Major-General Augustus Abbott*, ed. C. R. Low (1879) · *GM*, 2nd ser., 23 (1845)

Archives BL, letters to Sir Henry Rawlinson, Add. MS 47662 · PRO, corresp. with Lord Ellenborough and relating to his memorial, 30/12

Likenesses T. Brigstocke, oils, exh. RA 1845, Oriental Club, London [*see illus.*] · E. Davis, bronze statue, 1851, Carmarthen · T. Brigstocke, portrait, Carmarthen Town Hall · B. Faulkner, portrait, Addiscombe Military College · B. R. Faulkner, oils, BL OIOC · J. D. Francis, oils, NMG Wales

Nottingham. For this title name *see* Ferrers, Robert de, first Earl Ferrers [earl of Nottingham] (*d.* 1139); Mowbray,

Thomas (II), second earl of Nottingham (1385–1405); Howard, Charles, second Baron Howard of Effingham and first earl of Nottingham (1536–1624); Finch, Heneage, first earl of Nottingham (1621–1682); Finch, Daniel, second earl of Nottingham and seventh earl of Winchilsea (1647–1730); Hatton, George William Finch-, tenth earl of Winchilsea and fifth earl of Nottingham (1791–1858).

Nottingham, William of (d. 1254), Franciscan friar, was the fourth minister provincial of the English province of the Friars Minor. Nothing is known of his family beyond the fact that he had a brother named Augustine, also a Franciscan, who served at the papal curia and became bishop of Laodicea. As a young friar William studied under Robert Grosseteste (d. 1253) at Oxford in the years before 1235. He acted as vicar to the English minister provincial Haymo of Faversham (d. 1244), but apart from that he had, according to Thomas Eccleston, held no other office in the order when he was chosen in 1240 to succeed Haymo as provincial. He followed the tradition established by his three predecessors in his zeal for maintaining a strict observance of the poverty enjoined by the rule of St Francis. At Shrewsbury he halted the construction of the walls of the friars' dormitory with stone, which had been donated by a benefactor, and ordered their replacement by mud. At the general chapter of Genoa in 1249, with the support of his English colleague Gregory de Bosellis and in the teeth of opposition from almost the whole chapter, he carried a proposal to suspend the relaxations to the rule permitted in 1245 by Innocent IV's privilege *Ordinem vestrum* and to return to the observance sanctioned by Gregory IX (r. 1227–41).

The major achievement of William's ministry was the creation of a scholastic organization for the English province. He energetically promoted biblical studies. The Franciscan schools at Oxford and Cambridge were used to provide theological education for lectors, who were sent to staff the friaries throughout the province and instruct their brethren. With the help and advice of Adam Marsh (d. 1259), the first English Franciscan to incept as a doctor of theology, he chose the ablest men and had them groomed to teach at the universities. To ensure a succession of teachers, he devised a system of assignation, by which each student friar at the university was assigned as future lector to a particular house, which was required to supply him with books and materials while he was at the schools. The success of this plan was hailed by Eccleston, who observed that by the end of William's tour of office 'there were no fewer than thirty lectors in the province holding solemn disputations' (*De adventu*, 50)—who had, in other words, qualified at the universities.

William was discharged from office in 1254 by the general chapter of Metz. Journeying thence to the pope as an emissary of the chapter, he halted at Genoa to nurse his companion who had been taken ill, and himself succumbed to plague in the summer of 1254. He was buried in Genoa. His English brethren, hearing of his release from office, but unaware of his death, convened a provincial chapter and re-elected him—an indication of the affection in which he was held. No literary remains of his have been identified except a sermon on obedience, preserved in Cambridge, Pembroke College, MS 265, fols. 192–6. He must be distinguished from another William of Nottingham, a distinguished theologian who was provincial of the English Franciscans from 1316 to 1330.

C. H. LAWRENCE

Sources *Fratris Thomae vulgo dicti de Eccleston tractatus de adventu Fratrum Minorum in Angliam*, ed. A. G. Little (1951) · 'Adae de Marisco epistolae', *Monumenta Franciscana*, ed. J. S. Brewer, 1, Rolls Series, 4 (1858), 77–489 · A. G. Little, *Studies in English Franciscan history* (1917) · A. G. Little, *Franciscan papers, lists, and documents* (1943) · B. Smalley, 'Which William of Nottingham?', *Mediaeval and Renaissance Studies*, 3 (1954), 200–38 · C. H. Lawrence, 'The letters of Adam Marsh and the Franciscan school at Oxford', *Journal of Ecclesiastical History*, 42 (1991), 218–38
Archives Pembroke Cam., MS 265, fols. 192–6

Notton, William (d. in or after 1365), justice, was probably one of the Nottons of Notton, Yorkshire, whose pedigree is partially given by Hunter (2.391). In William's time, however, the manor had already passed into the hands of the Darcys. In 1343 Notton received lands in Fishlake, Yorkshire, from John Wingfield, a grant which the king confirmed or extended in 1346, and in 1352 he was granted lands in Litlington, Cambridgeshire. He appears as a serjeant-at-law in the year-books (where his arguments are frequently noted) and rolls of the common bench from Michaelmas term 1342; he was appointed king's serjeant in 1345 and held this office until 1355. In that year he was made a justice of the king's bench, and when on circuit in this and the following year was directed to remove the sheriffs of Oxfordshire and Northumberland. In 1358, as one of those who had passed judgment upon Thomas Lisle, bishop of Ely (d. 1361), for knowingly harbouring a killer, Notton was cited to answer for his conduct at the papal court at Avignon; he neglected to appear and was excommunicated. This did not, however, interfere with his judicial promotion. In 1361 he was formally appointed chief justice of the justiciar's bench in Ireland. It has been suggested that this appointment never took effect, but Notton may still have gone to Ireland as one of the lords named to the council of Lionel, earl of Ulster (d. 1368), the king's son and lieutenant in Ireland. Since he appears once again in England by November of 1364, he could have accompanied Lionel on the latter's return to England in 1364–5.

Notton served regularly on commissions of the peace, commissions to enforce labour legislation after the plague, and commissions of oyer and terminer. Several of the last involved matters of some sensitivity, such as the breaking of the treasury and chaces of the queen (which broadened into an investigation of oppressions by her officials also), and the crimes committed within the verge of the household of the king's son Lionel, both in the summer of 1347. Another set of commissions in 1354–5 entailed issues of public order in urban settings, such as the investigation of conspiracies, resistance to the king's ministers, rescues of arrested men, and opprobrious talk in London.

Such work did not, of course, endear Notton to all. In 1358 several men were brought into court, charged with asserting they would gladly strike Notton and his fellow justice William Shareshull if they could, and in 1344, after especially vigorous and financially profitable oyer and terminer sessions conducted at Ipswich by Notton and Shareshull, some citizens killed a man who had 'busied himself about the king's business there before William de Shareshull and his fellows'. As soon as the justices had left, the townspeople, rich and poor alike, feasted the killers with delicacies and honoured them with gifts, 'as if God had come down from Heaven' (Sayles, 6.37). Then from the very steps of the hall of pleas they mockingly summoned the justices to appear before them, Notton's appearance being demanded under penalty of £40.

Both Notton and his wife, Isabel, were benefactors of the priories of Bretton, Yorkshire, and Royston, Hertfordshire, and granted to the latter the nearby manor of Cocken Hatch. Notton is last recorded in February 1365, and probably died at about that date. Copies of his seals are preserved in the British Museum.

A. F. POLLARD, rev. RICHARD W. KAEUPER

Sources Chancery records · G. O. Sayles, ed., Select cases in the court of king's bench, 7 vols., SeldS, 55, 57–8, 74, 76, 82, 88 (1936–71), vols. 3, 6–7 · M. C. B. Dawes, ed., Register of Edward, the Black Prince, 4 vols., PRO (1930–33) · H. G. Richardson and G. O. Sayles, The administration of Ireland, 1172–1377 (1963) · J. Hunter, South Yorkshire: the history and topography of the deanery of Doncaster, 2 vols. (1828–31) · Baker, Serjeants · R. Lascelles, ed., Liber munerum publicorum Hiberniae … or, The establishments of Ireland, later edn, 2 vols. in 7 pts (1852) · Rymer, Foedera · W. Dugdale, 'Chronica series', Chronica juridicialia, ed. and trans. E. Cooke (1685) · RotP · H. Playford and J. Caley, eds., Rotulorum originalium in curia scaccarii abbreviatio, 2 vols. (1805–10) · S. E. Thorne and J. H. Baker, eds., Readings and moots at the inns of court in the fifteenth century, 2, SeldS, 105 (1990) · CPR, 1361–4, 69, 140

Nouell, Ralph. See Ralph (d. in or after 1151).

Nourse, Edward (bap. **1701**, d. **1761**), surgeon, son of Edward Nourse (d. 1738), surgeon of Oxford, and Elizabeth Towersey (1680–1740), and grandson of Edward Nourse of St Michael Cornhill, London, was baptized at St Giles's, Oxford, on 27 June 1701. His younger brother John *Nourse became a bookseller. His father had practised in Oxford from 1686. He was apprenticed to John Dobyns, one of the assistant surgeons to St Bartholomew's Hospital, on 2 December 1717, and paid the sum of £161 5s. on apprenticeship. He was examined for his diploma at the Barber-Surgeons' Hall in Monkwell Street, London, on 10 December 1725, and received a diploma under the common seal of the company. Before this date the candidates had always entertained the court of examiners at supper, but on this occasion Nourse gave each examiner, and there were more than twelve, half a guinea to buy two pairs of gloves instead of the supper; this became the accepted method of payment. He was elected FRS in 1728. From 1729 he gave lectures in anatomy at his house in Aldersgate Street.

When Dobyns, his master, died, Nourse was, on 22 January 1731, elected assistant surgeon to St Bartholomew's Hospital, where he was on the staff with John Freke, and

afterwards with his own pupil, Percivall Pott. He was elected surgeon to the hospital on 29 March 1745, and went on to become senior surgeon. He was elected demonstrator of anatomy by the Company of Barber–Surgeons on 5 March 1731, and held office until 5 March 1734. On resigning he announced that he was 'designing to have no more lectures at my own house, I think it proper to advertise that I shall begin a Course of Anatomy, Chirurgical operations, and Bandages, on Monday 11 Nov. [1734] at St Bartholomew's Hospital' (Peachey, 35). He thus became the first surgeon to give lectures at the hospital. However, in March 1735 he was advertising lectures to be given in St Paul's Churchyard.

Nourse's only publication is a syllabus of his lectures, printed in 1729, and entitled Syllabus totam rem anatomicam complectens et praelectionibus aptatus annuatim habendis; huic accedit syllabus chirurgicus quo exhibentur operationes quarum modus peragendarum demonstrandus. In these lectures he began with the general structure of the body, then treated of the bones in detail, then of the great divisions of the body, then of arteries, veins, and lymphatic glands; next of the urinary and generative organs, then of the muscles, of the brain and sense organs, of the spinal cord, of the arm and leg, of the uterus and foetus, and concluded the course of twenty-three lectures by one De oeconomia animali. Nourse, who towards the end of his life lived in Red Lion Square, London, died on 13 May 1761.

NORMAN MOORE, rev. MICHAEL BEVAN

Sources minute books of St Bartholomew's Hospital, London · S. Young, The annals of the Barber–Surgeons of London: compiled from their records and other sources (1890) · Foster, Alum. Oxon. · G. C. Peachey, A memoir of William and John Hunter (1924) · V. C. Medici and J. L. Thornton, eds., The Royal Hospital of St Bartholomew, 1123–1973 (1974) · S. C. Lawrence, Charitable knowledge: hospital pupils and practitioners in eighteenth-century London (1996) · GM, 1st ser., 31 (1761), 284 · P. J. Wallis and R. V. Wallis, Eighteenth century medics, 2nd edn (1988)
Likenesses J. Highmore, oils, c.1750, RCS Eng. · portrait, repro. in Medici and Thornton, eds., Royal Hospital of St Bartholomew

Nourse, John (bap. **1705**, d. **1780**), bookseller, was baptized in Oxford on 8 July 1705, the fourth child of Edward Nourse (d. 1738), surgeon, and his wife, Elizabeth Towersey (1680–1740); his elder brother was Edward *Nourse, surgeon. Apparently educated in Oxford, John Nourse was apprenticed to the London bookseller John (I) Osborne on 6 August 1722, becoming free in October 1729. He may then have been associated with William Mears—one of the publishers of Daniel Defoe's Tour through the Whole Island of Great Britain and a dealer in plays and legal and botanical books—whose activities ceased in 1734. Nourse advertised the Hortus Elthamensis of J. J. Dillenius, the first Sherardian professor of botany at Oxford, in 1732 and from then on was a well-known London bookseller at the Lamb without Temple Bar, opposite Catherine Street on the Strand. He specialized in language books, contemporary foreign literature, and in scientific, particularly mathematical, books, becoming bookseller to the Society for the Encouragement of Learning and to the commissioners of longitude, and claiming the title of bookseller to the king from 1762 to 1780.

Nourse's London shop was a rendezvous for scientific discussions; here he sold not only his own publications, numbering in all well over four hundred editions, but also older works and recent foreign books. By 1742 he had a contractual arrangement with the important Hague bookseller Pierre Gosse and he visited Paris in 1765, where he was interviewed by the authorities on the state of the London trade. He also conducted a long exchange trade with the leading continental booksellers, the Luchtmans of Leiden, allowing them to supply works such as the Royal Society's *Philosophical Transactions* to places such as St Petersburg. The accounts for the latter trade survive at Universiteitsbibliotheek, Amsterdam. He was in touch both with important Enlightenment writers, such as Montesquieu and Voltaire, and with their publishers, and was thus able to reprint their works in England in French (while arranging simultaneously for an English translation), sometimes including passages those authors had not been able to publish abroad. His editions were so well known on the continent that his name was used by clandestine publishers there as a disguise, once even occurring in the form 'Toujours à Londres chez l'éternel Jean Nourse' (F. A. Chevrier, *L'Almanach des gens d'esprit*, 1762). His early anonymous reprint of Voltaire's *Candide* (1759) was probably made from a proof copy and it represents an earlier state of the text than that of the Geneva first edition. The 'Philosophical Books' that he advertised included works not only by such authors as Voltaire, but also minor foreign writers, in addition to the *Nautical Almanac* and lexicographical and grammar books; he also sold children's books, and mathematical and scientific works by writers such as Robert Dossie, William Emerson, John Harrison, Sir John Hills, Colin Maclaurin, and Thomas Simpson.

Nourse was therefore one of the great European booksellers of the Enlightenment; he made English publications available abroad and was a major source of Enlightenment works, both in the original and in translation, in England. He never married and he died in Kensington on 25 April 1780. His firm passed into the nominal care of his brother, Sir Charles Nourse (d. 1789), before being taken over by Nourse's assistant, Francis Wingrave, later succeeded by John Collingwood. The firm probably came to an end about 1824. The file of business letters received by Nourse, including letters from many well-known academic, literary, and scientific people of the period, was acquired by the autograph collector William Upcott, and letters addressed to Nourse are therefore to be found in many libraries. He is said to have been buried (on 2 May 1780) in the churchyard of St Giles's Church, Oxford.

GILES BARBER

Sources G. Barber, 'Voltaire and the "maudites éditions de Jean Nourse"', *Voltaire and his world: studies presented to W. H. Barber*, ed. R. J. Howells (1985), 151–69 · G. Barber, 'Book imports and exports in the eighteenth century', *Sale and distribution of books from 1700*, ed. R. Myers and M. Harris (1982), 77–105 · parish register (baptism), Oxford, St Giles, 8 July 1705 · parish register, Oxford, St Giles · parish register, Oxford, St Mary

Nourse, Timothy (c.1636–1699), agricultural and religious writer, was born at The Place, Newent, Gloucestershire, a younger son of Sir Walter Nourse (d. 1652). His mother may have been Sir Walter's first wife, Mary, daughter of Sir Edward Engeham of Gunston, Kent, who died in childbirth in 1636. However, it is also possible given the dates that he was the son of Sir Walter's second wife, also Mary (1609/10–1673), who died of an apoplexy during divine service: she stood up at the anthem, 'Lord hasten to my aid', and expired. The family monument at Newent (where, unusually, her cause of death is also recorded) describes Sir Walter and his second wife as 'most beloved parents'.

Nourse matriculated at University College, Oxford, on 28 March 1655, graduated BA on 19 February 1658, was elected a fellow of the college on 19 January 1659, and proceeded MA on 17 December 1660. As bursar of University College he exercised his office with exceptional efficiency. Having taken holy orders, he became a noted preacher; he was such an admirer and imitator of the preaching style of Dr Robert South that South himself was sometimes accused of poaching Nourse's style. Nourse took a very different path from the emerging latitudinarian outlook of the Calvinist South; already accused of consorting with Catholic clergy and hearing mass in Queen Catherine of Braganza's chapel at Somerset House, after the Test Act he converted to Roman Catholicism in 1672. Deprived of his fellowship on 5 January 1673, he retired to Southerns, his small country house and estate at Newent, which he later refaced and set within a new continental-inspired garden. He married Lucy (d. 1732), a fellow Catholic convert, daughter of Richard Harwood, prebendary of Gloucester; they had no children. She subsequently married Thomas Stokes and died on 11 January 1732.

A story is recorded that Nourse, taken ill while staying in London in October 1677, sent for Dr Simon Patrick, rector of St Paul's, Covent Garden, in order to receive communion in the protestant form, repenting of his conversion to Rome. Nourse regretted his actions when he recovered, returning to Catholicism. It was also said that Nourse 'suffered much' in the reactions to the Popish Plot of 1678, although no specific details are given. In Newent, meanwhile, Nourse retained his pew in the newly rebuilt Anglican parish church, over which there had been an acrimonious dispute during his absence overseas, travelling in France, Italy, and the Low Countries until 1681, and was at least an occasional conformist. He used Roman Catholic forms in writing his will. (No Catholics were recorded for Newent in the 1676 Compton census.)

In his religious writings Nourse was an advocate of natural religion and an apologist for a Catholic outlook, often using analogies and examples drawn from his travels to Rome and the Low Countries. *A discourse upon the nature and faculties of man, in several essays, with some considerations upon the occurrences of humane life* was published in London in 1686, with subsequent editions in 1689 and 1697; *A discourse of natural and reveal'd religion, in several essays, or, The light of nature a guide to divine truth* was published in 1691. An earlier book, mentioned by Thomas Hearne as having been written in answer to Daniel Whitby's *Discourse Concerning the Idolatry of the Church of Rome* (1674), does not seem to have been published. Nourse is particularly remembered by posterity for his posthumously published book *Campania foelix, or, A Discourse of the Benefits and Improvements of Husbandry*, a volume on agricultural improvement, garden design, the abuses of servants, alehouses, the poor law, and justices of the peace that drew directly from local and personal experience. Published in 1700 and republished in 1706 and 1708, it came to the attention of later eighteenth-century writers on agricultural improvement. With its emphasis on new crops, improvements in tillage, and especially on the importance of pastoral as opposed to arable husbandry, the book underscores current views of significant changes during that period in agrarian history.

Nourse died on 21 July 1699 at Newent, of a stroke—'hemiplegia quatriduana hydropi diutino' ('overcome in four days by a stroke having long suffered from dropsy') as is unusually and graphically described on his memorial tablet in the parish church. He was buried at Newent on 24 July. Thomas Hearne considered Nourse a man 'of great probity and eminent virtues', although Anthony Wood thought him 'conceited' and recounted stories to reinforce that opinion. Nourse bequeathed his fine coin collection of 532 separate pieces to the Bodleian Library (it has since been subsumed into the Ashmolean collection), and books were left to the library of University College, 'of which I was an unworthy member'. Bequests totalling £120 were made in Newent, Gloucester, and Worcester, establishing charities that embodied schemes for providing work and badging the poor—'a numerous party in a Commonwealth' he had called them—advanced in *Campania foelix* (Nourse, *Campania foelix*, 1700, 214). These charities still exist, albeit absorbed within general local funds.   DAVID SOUDEN

Sources T. Nourse, *A discourse upon the nature and faculties of man, in several essays, with some considerations upon the occurrences of humane life* (1686); 3rd edn (1697) · T. Nourse, *A discourse of natural and reveal'd religion, in several essays, or, The light of nature a guide to divine truth* (1691) [BL copy, 857.b.19, has MS corrections] · T. Nourse, *Campania foelix, or, A discourse of the benefits and improvements of husbandry … with some considerations upon, 1, justices of the peace, 2, inns and alehouses, 3, servants and labourers, 4, on the poor, to which are added two essays, 1, Of a country house, 2, Of the fuel of London* (1700) · T. Nourse, *Campania foelix*, 2nd edn (1706) · T. Nourse, [*Campania foelix*] *The mistery of husbandry discover'd, containing several new and advantageous ways of tillage, sowing, planting, manuring and improving of all sorts of meadows, pasture, cornland, woods, gardens, orchards*, 3rd edn, to which is added *The compleat collier* by J.C. (1708) · *DNB* · Foster, *Alum. Oxon.* · notes of W. Nourse's 'History of Newent', *c*.1715–1725, Glos. RO, D412/Z3 [transcript] · accounts of Timothy Nourse's charity, Newent, Glos. RO, P225a CH 1/9 · Newent charities, Glos. RO, D 1466 · parish register, Newent, 24 July 1699, Glos. RO, P225 IN 1/2 [burial] · will, 30 Nov 1698, Glos. RO, DR 1700/57 · R. Bigland, *Historical, monumental and genealogical collections, relative to the county of Gloucester*, ed. B. Frith, 3 (1997), 900 · archives, University College, Oxford, formerly Pyx LL.6, n.9–13 · Wood, *Ath. Oxon.*, new edn, vol. 4 · *The life and times of Anthony Wood*, ed. A. Clark, 1, OHS, 19 (1891) · *Remarks and collections of Thomas Hearne*, ed. C. E. Doble and others, 1, OHS, 2 (1885) · *Letters of Humphrey Prideaux … to John Ellis*, ed. E. M. Thompson, CS, new ser., 15 (1875) · *VCH Gloucestershire*, vol. 4 · H. G. Nicholls, *The Forest of Dean* (1866) · A. Kussmaul, *Servants in husbandry in early modern England* (1981) · private information (2004) [Dr K. Tomlinson, Newent] · R. A. Beddard, 'James II and the Catholic challenge', *Hist. U. Oxf.* 4: 17th-cent. Oxf., 907–54 · G. Reedy, *Robert South (1634–1716): an introduction to his life and sermons* (1992) · R. Atkyns, *The ancient and present state of Gloucestershire* (1712); repr. (1974) · A. Whiteman and M. Clapinson, eds., *The Compton census of 1676: a critical edition*, British Academy, Records of Social and Economic History, new ser., 10 (1986) · M. B. Rowlands, ed., *English Catholics of parish and town, 1558–1778*, Catholic RS, monograph ser., 5 (1999) · memorial, Newent parish church, Gloucestershire

Archives Glos. RO, collection of papers incl. antiquarian notes and records of charities founded

Novar. For this title name *see* Ferguson, Ronald Crauford Munro, Viscount Novar (1860–1934).

Nove [*formerly* Novakovsky], **Alexander** [Alec] (1915–1994), economist and historian, was born on 24 November 1915 in St Petersburg (then Petrograd), the only child of Russian Jewish parents. His father, Jacob Novakovsky (1875–1933), was a Social Democrat of Menshevik persuasion, his mother, Rachel Zorokhovich (1878–1947), a doctor who graduated from St Petersburg medical school in 1904, having gained admittance to the university in defiance both of parental disapproval and of obstacles placed in the paths of Jews.

Following the 1917 revolution Jacob Novakovsky was twice arrested and subsequently released by the Bolsheviks, and in 1922 was given the choice between long-term exile in Siberia or applying for an exit visa. He left Russia later that year and was employed in London by a Dutch firm trading with the Soviet Union. It took another six months before the seven-year-old Alec and his mother were given permission to join him in Belsize Park. Shortly after their arrival the family abbreviated their name, having discovered distant relatives in Manchester who had emigrated at the turn of the century and who had decided that Nove would be less of a mouthful for the British.

Alec Nove was educated at King Alfred School in north London and at the London School of Economics, where he graduated with a BSc (Econ) in 1936 and became a research officer for a trade union. On 26 August 1939, just before the outbreak of war, he married Joan Rainford (1916–1995), the daughter of Richard Rainford, a provision store manager. There were two sons of the marriage: David, who was a tax inspector, and Perry, who became a detective inspector.

Nove joined the Territorial Army early in 1939, and when war came served in the Royal Signals. He was among the last British soldiers to get back from France in 1940. Twice a ship on which he might have sailed was sunk. When half his unit was sent to Singapore, he happened to be in the other half. His sense of being fortunate to be alive was deepened by the knowledge of how unlikely his survival would have been had he, the son of a Jewish anticommunist, remained in Russia. His chances of outliving the successive onslaughts of Stalin and Hitler would have been slim indeed. He remained in the army until 1946, finishing as a major in intelligence. His marriage did not survive the war, and on 12 May 1951 he married a Scot from

Alexander Nove (1915–1994), by James L. Millar

Glasgow (Elizabeth) Irene Justine MacPherson (*b.* 1918), the daughter of Charles MacPherson, a groundsman. This second marriage lasted happily for over forty years and produced a son, Charles (*b.* 1960), who became a BBC presenter.

In 1947 Nove joined the civil service, working first at the Board of Trade on price control and export targets. In his spare time he pursued research on the Soviet Union, and submitted articles to *Soviet Studies*. During 1952–4 the Board of Trade allowed him to spend two years at the department of Soviet studies at the University of Glasgow, after which he returned to Whitehall, transferring in 1956 to the economic section of the Treasury and the joint intelligence bureau of the Ministry of Defence. It was as late as 1958 that he became a full-time scholar, beginning his academic career with the rank of reader at the London School of Economics. In 1963 he was given a chair of economics at Glasgow University and appointed director of the university's Institute of Soviet and East European Studies, a post which he held until 1982, though after formal retirement he remained at the institute as honorary senior research fellow. He was elected to a fellowship of the British Academy in 1978.

Nove won international recognition as an outstanding specialist on the Soviet Union and communist Europe and lived long enough to become a perceptive analyst of these countries' difficulties in moving to a market economy. A prolific writer and witty and engaging lecturer, he drew on his experiences from each stage of his life in his writing and teaching. His wartime career in the British army and post-war work as a civil servant in the Board of Trade

enhanced his understanding of Soviet hierarchical and bureaucratic organizations, as did his reading of the Russian literary journals, which often revealed more of the reality of Soviet social and economic life than publications in the social sciences.

Nove was among the first authors to show that behind the monolithic façade which the Soviet system presented to the outside world bureaucratic battles were fought. He noted how reliant was Gosplan (the state planning committee) on information supplied to it by the branch economic ministries, and he drew attention to the struggle for a greater share of resources among the latter. These were aspects of the Soviet system which the totalitarian paradigm overlooked. His first major book, *The Soviet Economy*, was published in 1961. It went through three editions and was then radically rewritten as *The Soviet Economic System* (1977; 2nd edn, 1980; 3rd edn, 1986). He was equally at home as a political economist and as an economic and social historian. His perceptive *Economic History of the USSR* (1969; 2nd edn, 1989; 3rd edn, 1992) won a deservedly high reputation.

Nove published eleven single-author books in his lifetime and two more were published posthumously in 1998: *Alec Nove on Economic Theory: Previously Unpublished Writings*, 1; and *Alec Nove on Communist and Postcommunist Countries: Previously Unpublished Writings*, 2 (both edited by Ian Thatcher). In addition to these there were two co-authored books, eight books of which he was editor and part-author, and several hundred scholarly articles and contributions to symposia. Yet the quality of the work was even more impressive than the quantity.

Nove had a remarkable ability to see what mattered and to make connections which others missed. Even his most scholarly work was not especially heavily footnoted. He read widely, but his work is outstanding more for its uncommon insights and intellectual clarity than for the detail of its documentation. He was one of a small minority of specialists on the USSR who, some years before Gorbachev came to power, took seriously the possibility of a reformer becoming Soviet leader. He was equally percipient in his last years. In the early 1990s, when there was a widespread assumption that 'reform' had triumphed in post-Soviet Russia, Nove (not by nature a prophet of doom) feared that a 'new Time of Troubles' lay ahead. His predictions in 1992 that the policies being pursued by Russian 'reformers' with the blessing of the International Monetary Fund and Western governments would lead to massive flight of capital and to minimal investment in the real economy were ignored, although they were based both on vast knowledge of Russia and on his practical experience in the Board of Trade, helping to administer the *gradual* dismantling of Britain's wartime controls. Nove was never in thrall to intellectual fashion, whether to Marxism in its heyday or to the neo-classical economics which was so pervasive during his last years. By the end of the century fashionable opinion on the Russian economy and society was, however, belatedly catching up with him.

Alec Nove had no religious belief; his good fortune while

others suffered misery, death, and destruction fortified, rather than undermined, his rejection of the idea of a benevolent deity. 'There but for the grace of God', he later wrote, 'but why should God have shown me grace? I was just lucky' (Brown and Cairncross, 629). Politically Nove was a convinced social democrat. He strongly favoured a limited number of publicly owned utilities including, especially, public transport. He never owned a car and adduced economic as well as social arguments against the closure of supposedly uneconomic railway lines. In his *Efficiency Criteria for Nationalised Industries* (1973) he was alarmed by the trend towards commercial principles of operation. If nationalized industries were to model themselves on the private sector, why had they been taken into public ownership in the first place? It came as no surprise to him that the eventual upshot of adopting commercial principles of pricing and profit-making was privatization.

Nove retained boundless energy, enthusiasm, and intellectual curiosity to the end. After spending a short time lecturing in his native St Petersburg, and travelling to Stockholm where he received an honorary degree, he suffered a heart attack while holidaying with his wife on the Norwegian fjords and died in Norway on 15 May 1994. His body was returned to Glasgow for cremation and his ashes were scattered by his family on the Isle of Coll.

ARCHIE BROWN

Sources A. Brown and A. Cairncross, 'Alec Nove', *PBA*, 94 (1997), 627–41 · *The Times* (19 May 1994) · B. Wallace and T. Dalyell, *The Independent* (20 May 1994) · m. certs.
Likenesses J. L. Millar, photograph, priv. coll. [*see illus.*] · photograph, repro. in Brown and Cairncross, 'Alec Nove', facing p. 627 · photograph, repro. in *The Times*
Wealth at death £259,911.44: confirmation, 21 Oct 1994, *CCI*

Novello, (Joseph) Alfred (1810–1896), music publisher, was born in London on 12 August 1810, the eldest son of Vincent *Novello (1781–1861), music publisher, arranger, and composer, and Mary Sabilla Novello, *née* Hehl (1789–1854). Apprenticed to the York music dealer, John Robinson, from 1824 to 1829, he commenced business in Frith Street, Soho, in 1830. Initially, he inherited the catalogue already established by his father and one of his most important early ventures was to complete publication of Vincent Novello's arrangement of Purcell's *Sacred Works* (1832). In 1836 he both secured the copyright to Mendelssohn's *St Paul* and launched the *Musical World*, perhaps England's first modern music periodical, actions which much enhanced his reputation. A fine bass singer, he performed in concerts and at provincial festivals and was a member of the Lincoln's Inn chapel choir. His *Concise Explanation of the Gregorian Note* (1842) was a useful contribution to the growing interest in plainsong.

Novello's reputation ultimately rests, however, on his work as a publisher of 'cheap' music. In 1842 he published Joseph Mainzer's sight-singing manual *Singing for the Million* and the weekly *Mainzer's Musical Times and Singing-Class Circular*. These were central texts of the mass singing-class movement, enthusiastically supported by those concerned with working-class morality in an age of political

(Joseph) **Alfred Novello** (1810–1896), by unknown engraver, pubd 1896

and industrial radicalism. He took over Mainzer's journal in 1844, including in its pages a musical supplement in the octavo format, adopted as the company standard from 1847. As the *Musical Times*, the journal eventually became a major periodical, especially for amateurs. These ventures propelled Novello's business toward mass production, a process encouraged by his growing awareness of the burgeoning amateur choral movement that he encountered on promotional tours in the provinces. In August 1846 he made the first of many price reductions, publishing the vocal score and keyboard accompaniment for *Messiah* for 6s. 6d.: previously, a *Messiah* piano score could cost up to 1 guinea. Further reductions followed and by 1859 a pocket edition of *Messiah* and other major oratorios was available for 1s. 4d., with shilling editions following from 1862.

Novello established his own printing company in 1847 and, following the example of William Clowes, he opted to use musical type rather than engraved prints. This method, although expensive, facilitated the extended print runs upon which his pricing policy depended. He was opposed in this by London printing unions and he utilized non-union labour in order to circumvent their objections. In the late 1840s and 1850s he campaigned vigorously against the 'taxes on knowledge' (duties on paper, advertisements, and other tax burdens), although the claims made by later writers associated with the Novello Company that he was 'largely' or 'solely' responsible for their eventual abolition, were hugely exaggerated.

After Novello announced his retirement in October 1856 the business gradually passed to Henry Littleton, a senior employee who became a partner in 1861 and sole proprietor in 1866. It has been suggested that Novello's appetite for business was largely fuelled by devotion to his mother and the desire to fulfil ambitions she held for him; her death in 1854 released him from any such obligations. Novello retired with his father and sisters Mary and Sabilla, first to Nice and then, in 1861, to Genoa. Although maintaining an editorial interest in the *Musical Times* until 1863, he devoted ever more time to gardening and the scientific and technological experimentation that had long interested him. He died in Genoa on 16 July 1896, leaving an estate of £63,386, money accrued not only from his publishing business but from well-considered investment in the railway and steel industries. Hagiographic literature of the late nineteenth century tended to portray Novello as the philanthropically inspired inventor of the Victorian choral tradition. Rather, he was an extremely astute businessman, albeit one guided by a strong sense of moral purpose, who recognized the strength of an existing market and nourished and expanded it with determination and skill.   DAVE RUSSELL

Sources M. Hurd, *Vincent Novello—and company* (1981) · [J. Bennett], *A short history of cheap music, as exemplified in the records of the house of Novello, Ewer & Co.* (1887) · *The Times* (18 July 1896) · *MT*, 37 (1896), 513–15 · *CGPLA Eng. & Wales* (1897)
Archives Granada Publishing, company archives · U. Leeds, Brotherton L., Novello–Cowden Clarke collection, letters and business material
Likenesses engraving, pubd 1896, NPG [*see illus.*] · photograph, repro. in P. Scholes, *Mirror of music*, 2 (1947), facing p. 756
Wealth at death £63,386 2s. 10d.: resworn probate, Jan 1897, *CGPLA Eng. & Wales*

Novello, Clara Anastasia [*married name* Countess Clara Anastasia Gigliucci] (1818–1908), singer, was born on 10 June 1818 at 240 Oxford Street, London, the fourth daughter of the music publisher Vincent *Novello (1781–1861) and his wife, Mary Sabilla Hehl (1789–1854). Clara revealed musical talent at an early age. Her first official music lessons were at York with John Robinson, organist of the Catholic chapel in the city, where her brother (Joseph) Alfred *Novello was already serving as an apprentice. On advice from François-Joseph Fétis, she was placed in the prestigious singing class of Alexandre Choron, at the Institution Royale de Musique Classique et Religieuse in Paris. During this period she also made the acquaintance of Rossini, who was impressed with the talents of the young soprano and frequently requested her to perform his music in later years.

With the political climate in France in upheaval, Clara Novello returned to England in 1830 and made her public début on 22 October 1832 at a benefit concert at the Theatre Royal, Windsor. By 1833 she had regular public engagements, notably at the Three Choirs festival (Worcester, 1833) and at the Philharmonic Society concerts. Other important performances from early in her career included those at Birmingham in 1837, of Mendelssohn's *St Paul* for the opening of the town hall, and, again for Mendelssohn, in Leipzig at the Gewandhaus concerts. There followed an extensive and successful tour of European cities, among them Berlin, Vienna, Dresden, and Weimar.

In 1838 Clara went to Milan to study operatic technique with the cavaliere de Micheroux; she made her Italian opera début in Padua on 6 July 1841 in Rossini's *Semiramide*. Rossini also selected her to perform in the Italian première of his *Stabat mater*. During her engagement in 1842 to sing in the Italian city of Fermo, she met Count Giovanni Baptista Gigliucci, whom she married in London on 22 November 1843.

Following the custom of the time, after her marriage Clara put aside her career to live with the count in Italy,

Clara Anastasia Novello (1818–1908), by Edward Petre Novello, 1833

where she raised a family and assisted her husband in the fight for Italian independence. The couple had four children: Giovanni (1844–1906), Porzia (1845–1938), Mario (1847–1937), and Valeria (1849–1945). During the uprisings of 1848, however, the count lost his property and Clara willingly returned to the stage and resumed her professional life. Although she continued to sing sacred works, in this second half of her career she focused more frequently than before on the opera repertory, especially when singing on the continent, and her performances included *Semiramide* and *Robert le diable*, as well as *Rigoletto* at La Scala.

Clara Novello's career in England, however, was based largely on her performances of oratorio, which continued its general popularity over opera. She appeared at large choral festivals, including, again, the Three Choirs festival and the reopening of the Crystal Palace in 1854. She also sang before Queen Victoria in 1852 and on various other occasions. Writing in her diary on 13 May 1852, Queen Victoria noted, 'Madame Clara Novello, a native artist, has a very powerful, fine and clear voice and sings extremely well.' In comparison with other British sopranos of her day, she maintained a strong following and a long-lasting popularity, and was especially loved for her performances of oratorio.

Although still popular, in 1860 Clara felt it time to close her career and withdraw from public performance; her final appearance was on 21 November 1860, at St James's Hall, London. The concert included selections from oratorio as well as opera and boasted an orchestra and choir of 250 performers. Clara and her husband retired to Rome and Fermo; Count Gigliucci died on 29 March 1893 and Clara died on 12 March 1908 at Rome.

Clara Novello's singing was considered agile, and contemporary accounts remarked on its fluidity and perfection. Writing to her brother Joseph Alfred Novello, Mendelssohn noted after the performance of *Messiah* in Leipzig in 1837, 'she possesses just those two qualities of which the public is particularly fond here, purity of intonation and a thoroughbred musical feeling' (Mackenzie-Grieve, 52).   VICTORIA L. COOPER

Sources A. Mackenzie-Grieve, *Clara Novello, 1818–1908* (1955) · M. Hurd, *Vincent Novello—and company* (1981) · L. Swinyard, *A century and a half in Soho: a short history of the firm of Novello, publishers and printers of music, 1811–1961* (1961) · *Clara Novello's reminiscences*, ed. V. Gigliucci (1910)
Archives U. Leeds, Brotherton L., letters to Sir John Trevelyan [microfilm]
Likenesses E. P. Novello, oils, 1833, NPG [*see illus.*] · Kriehuber, engraving (after Magnus), repro. in Mackenzie-Grieve, *Clara Novello* · E. Magnus, oils, repro. in Gigliucci, ed., *Clara Novello's reminiscences* · D. J. Pound, engraving (after photograph by Mayall), priv. coll. · prints, BM, Harvard TC, NPG

Novello, Ivor [*real name* David Ivor Davies] (1893–1951), composer, actor, and playwright, was born on 15 January 1893 at Llywn yr Eos (Nightingales' Grove), 95 Cowbridge Road, Cardiff, the only son of David Davies (1852?–1931), a rent collector for Cardiff council, and his wife, Clara Novello Davies (1861–1943), a singing teacher and choral conductor. His parents had married on 31 October 1883 at Salem Chapel in Cardiff, and the independently minded Clara had increasingly developed a reputation as a singing teacher and choral conductor. Six months after Ivor's birth she took her Welsh Ladies' Choir to the Colombian Exposition in Chicago; they won first prize in the women's choral competition and then embarked on a tour of America. Following a royal command performance at Osborne for Queen Victoria, the choir was given the royal appellation. It subsequently toured further, and in 1899 won prizes at the Paris Exhibition. Clara established a teaching practice in London at 13 George Street, Hanover Square, and also taught at her London home (143 Sutherland Avenue, Maida Vale), where Ivor became acquainted with leading performers of the day, including members of George Edwardes's Gaiety Girls and such friends of his mother as Dame Clara Butt, Adelina Patti, and Landon Ronald. After private education in Cardiff and Gloucester, where he studied harmony and counterpoint with the cathedral organist, Dr Herbert Brewer, he gained a scholarship to Magdalen College School, Oxford, where for three of his five years he was a solo treble in Magdalen College choir. He later attributed his fondness for the composers of the Romantic era, particularly Wagner, to a reaction against this exposure as a boy to early sacred choral music.

Early songwriting Visits to the Gaiety and Daly's theatres in London led the young man towards early vocal compositions: his waltz 'Spring of the Year' was featured on a programme given by his mother's choir at the Albert Hall,

Ivor Novello (1893–1951), by Paul Tanqueray, 1928

but it was only with 'The Little Damozel' (1910) that he attracted any attention. He spent some time in Cardiff teaching the piano, but moved permanently to London in 1913 and took a flat at 11 Aldwych, which became his London residence for the rest of his life. There he fell under the patronage of Sir Edward Marsh, who encouraged his composition and also facilitated his career through practical introductions. Davies began to use the name Ivor Novello professionally and formally changed his name by deed poll in 1927.

Novello did not escape entirely from the First World War: in 1914 he achieved one of his greatest songwriting successes with 'Till the boys come home' ('Keep the home fires burning'), to words by the American poet, Lena Guilbert Ford. It was not until June 1916 that he reported to Crystal Palace training depot as a probationary flight sub-lieutenant, but after crashing twice, and through the influence of Marsh, he was moved to the Air Ministry office in the Hotel Cecil. He continued his musical theatre writing and had his first major success with *Theodore & Co.* (Gaiety Theatre, 14 September 1916), a production by George Grossmith and Edward Laurillard that had a score written jointly by Novello and Jerome Kern. Novello then contributed to André Charlot's revue *See-Saw* (14 December 1916) and another production by Grossmith and Laurillard, the musical comedy *Arlette* (6 September 1917). In 1917 he was introduced through Marsh to the actor Robert (Bobbie) Andrews (1895–1976), and the two became lovers and lifelong companions. Further shows raised Novello's profile even further, with the musical comedies *Who's Hooper?* by Fred Thompson (13 September 1919; a joint score with Howard Talbot) and *The Golden Moth* by Thompson and P. G. Wodehouse (5 October 1921), and with his continuing association with Charlot through the revues *Tabs* (15 May 1918), *A to Z* (21 October 1921; including 'And her mother came too', with the lyricist Dion Titheradge), and *Puppets* (2 January 1924).

Silent film star Despite his inexperience, Novello was offered a silent-film role in *The Call of the Blood* (1920) by the French film director Louis Mercanton, who employed him as a romantic lead on the strength of a publicity photograph. Through this, over the next decade Novello embarked on a successful film career and was also prompted to develop his stage ability. His next film, *Miarka* (1920) was also for Mercanton, and in 1921 he appeared on stage in an amateur performance of E. G. E. Bulwer Lytton's 1850 play *Not as Bad as We Seem*. He made his professional stage début in a straight play as a Young Man in *Deburau* (Ambassadors Theatre, 1921), in which the role of Charles Deburau was played by Bobbie Andrews. Novello made his first English film, *Carnival*, in 1921, and his first film in America, *The White Rose* (1923), for D. W. Griffiths. Clara Novello Davies had also enjoyed a continuing reputation, and after the First World War she built up a teaching practice in New York, where her pupils included many of the singers from the shows of Florenz Ziegfeld and Charles Dillingham, among them Dorothy Dixon (at that time a dancer rather than a singer) and the leading soprano Mary Ellis, both of whom were later to star in Novello's London musical romances.

Novello's increasing prominence as a silent film star did not prevent his development of stage material, and in 1924 he produced and starred in the successful play *The Rat* (Prince of Wales's Theatre, 9 June 1924). Credited to the pseudonymous David L'Estrange, it was written by Novello with his friend the actress Constance Collier. Most importantly, the film of *The Rat* (1925) was a major success and led to a sequel, *The Triumph of the Rat*, in 1926; a further sequel, *Return of the Rat*, was produced in 1928. Novello starred in further films, notably in Alfred Hitchcock's *The Lodger* (1926), which Hitchcock credited as being the first film in his own style. A contract with the Gainsborough Film Company in 1927 led to his making *The Constant Nymph* in the Austrian Tyrol in the autumn of that year and in addition enabled him to purchase Munro Lodge, Littlewick Green, near Maidenhead. He renamed the property Redroofs, and it remained his main residence outside London for the rest of his life. In 1928 he appeared in the silent adaptation of Noël Coward's *The Vortex* and made his last silent film, *A South Sea Bubble*.

Novello returned to the musical stage with the revue *The House that Jack Built* (Adelphi Theatre, 8 November 1929), to which he contributed eight items to a score that also included music by Vivian Ellis, Arthur Schwartz, and Sydney Baynes. Although Novello had retained some musical theatre compositional presence with a few song contributions to shows, since *Puppets* he had been involved primarily with the straight theatre, acting in Ferenc Molnar's *Liliom* (Duke of York's Theatre, 23 December 1926) and

Noël Coward's *Sirocco* (Daly's, 24 November 1927) and producing his own play *Symphony in Two Flats* (New Theatre, 14 October 1929). In 1930 he went to New York for a short run of *Symphony in Two Flats* (Shubert Theater, 16 September 1930) and then a more successful production of his *The Truth Game* (Ethel Barrymore Theater, 27 December 1930), which brought him to the attention of Hollywood studios. With a contract from MGM as both a screen writer and an actor, he arrived in Hollywood in the summer of 1931 and initially began working on a screen adaptation of *The Truth Game*. His abilities were hardly utilized by the large studio system and he made only one minor film as an actor; the period has been better remembered for his work on the script for *Tarzan the Ape Man*, for which he reputedly originated the line that gave rise to the now mythical if inaccurate 'Me Tarzan. You Jane' (originally—with appropriate pointing—'Tarzan. Jane.'). His father died in October 1931 while Novello was in Hollywood, and—tired of his relatively insignificant role in the studio system—he returned to London.

Major musicals The 1930s for Novello were characterized by prolific work as an actor and playwright and by the beginning of a series of musical theatre works for which he is best remembered. He had written the play *I Lived With You* while in Hollywood, and it was produced in the West End at the Prince of Wales's Theatre in the spring of 1932. The following year saw great success, with simultaneous London productions of *Fresh Fields* (Criterion), *Proscenium* (Globe), and *Sunshine Sisters* (Queen's). Also in 1933 his *Flies in the Sun* employed Christopher Hassall (introduced to Novello by Marsh) as an understudy for a tour, and who was also to appear in *Murder in Mayfair* (5 September 1934). It was with Hassall as lyricist that Novello wrote his first musical romance for Drury Lane, *Glamorous Night* (2 May 1935), and its extravagant mix of theatrical effects and a pared-down operetta lyricism ensured its immediate popularity; Hassall was to contribute lyrics to nearly all of Novello's later musical stage shows. Novello played the romantic lead himself—something he continued to do in all but his last musical, *Gay's the Word*, in 1950—while his leading lady was Mary Ellis. With its combination of a Ruritanian princess and a television inventor, set pieces that included the sinking of an ocean liner, and a musical style that drew heavily on the operetta tradition of Franz Lehár and the Victorian ballad, it was a peculiarly British concoction. Despite its acclaim, *Glamorous Night* was closed in order to make way for the traditional Christmas pantomime; however, with the following year's *Careless Rapture* (Drury Lane, 11 September 1936) Novello sealed what has become an enduring association both with the theatre and with a style of musical theatre work that was uniquely his own. *Crest of the Wave* (Drury Lane, 1 September 1937) continued this style combining large-scale theatrical effects and well-placed lyrical numbers in an otherwise escapist plot. Its duet 'Why isn't it you' is a witty ironic revue number that signals Novello's background in revue, while with 'Rose of England' he made one of his most eloquent statements of a sincere patriotic feeling.

Clara Novello Davies had remained active in music, despite her supposed retirement in 1926, when she left New York to take up residence in her son's Aldwych flat. In her mid-seventies she was rehearsing her choir for a short tour abroad, and in 1937 she was an official representative of Wales along with her Royal Welsh Ladies' Choir at the Paris Exhibition; at their first concert on 16 October at the Palais du Bois she was presented with the médaille de mérite by the French government and the gold medal of the Renaissance Française. A somewhat injudicious tour to sing for international peace just before the outbreak of the Second World War—abruptly curtailed—effectively marked the end of a remarkable career, and her attentions were diverted by her son into the writing of her autobiography, *The Life I have Loved* (1940). She died peacefully on 1 March 1943.

In 1938 Novello played the title role in a limited engagement of *Henry V* at Drury Lane. He received complimentary notices for his performance, but this was only a brief excursion into more heavyweight drama, and in the same year his play *Comédienne* was produced. Based on the character of Mrs Patrick Campbell, the play is typical in Novello's use of a theatrical world for its setting—a device he employed in other plays, such as *Sunshine Girls*, and, with the inclusion of opera singers, in his musical romances. For someone whose life was so completely bound up in the theatre from an early age, surrounded by both performers and writers, it was inevitable that it would provide his primary source of reference and inspiration. *The Dancing Years* (Drury Lane, 23 March 1939) has become Novello's most lasting musical stage work, and among its wealth of melodies is his archetypal waltz song 'Waltz of my Heart'. Hugely successful, it was driven out of its home at Drury Lane with the onset of the Second World War and so toured the country for several years, finally returning to the West End at the Adelphi on 14 March 1942, to run until 8 July 1944. During this extensive run *Arc de Triomphe* (Phoenix, 9 November 1943), another showcase for Mary Ellis, was much less well received.

Imprisonment and final years On 24 March 1944, following the improper use of his car during wartime rationing, Novello was charged with unlawful conspiracy to commit offences against the motor vehicles (restriction of use) order 1942. The victim of duplicitous acts by a supposed fan and assistant, Dora Grace Constable, Novello was none the less deemed liable, and on 24 April 1944 at Bow Street court he was sentenced to eight weeks in prison. Constable was fined £50 with £25 costs. An appeal (16 May 1944) reduced the sentence from eight weeks to four, but his brief spell in Wormwood Scrubs, however ameliorated by his fame and the influence of his friends, severely shook him mentally and physically, with lasting effects. After a period of recovery at Redroofs he returned to *The Dancing Years* in June 1944 and received a rapturous ovation upon his first entrance.

Perchance to Dream opened at the Hippodrome (21 April 1945) and introduced another of Novello's most enduring numbers, the Victorian parlour ballad pastiche 'We'll gather lilacs'. Despite continually playing to full houses,

the London production was closed after 1000 performances and the company taken on tour to South Africa. Novello flew to South Africa via a short trip to New York, arriving in the second week of December to open the show at His Majesty's Theatre, Johannesburg, on 23 December 1947. He subsequently appeared at Cape Town for two weeks from 20 February 1948.

Novello's last major musical romance was *King's Rhapsody* (Palace, 15 September 1949), which used a plot that mirrored many elements of the abdication crisis. Apart from his own portrayal of Prince Nikki, the romance introduced Vanessa Lee as Princess Christiane; her 'Someday my heart will awake' was the last of the characteristic sweeping waltz songs that became a defining feature of Novello's output. On 16 February 1951 his last show, *Gay's the Word*, opened at the Saville. A musical comedy that took as its subject the contrasting styles of European operetta and post-war American musicals in the West End, it starred the comedienne Cicely Courtneidge and for the first time had no role for Novello; the lyricist was the young and acerbic Alan Melville, who had his roots in intimate revue, rather than the highly poetic Hassall. Novello was still playing in the hugely successful run of *King's Rhapsody* but had increasingly been feeling unwell. A Christmas holiday to his house on Jamaica, Wyndways at Montego Bay, failed to restore his health. He returned to London in February 1951, unwisely insisted on performing, and died of coronary thrombosis at his home at about 2.15 a.m. on 6 March 1951, shortly after completing his evening performance in *King's Rhapsody*. The committal was held at Golders Green crematorium at 1 p.m. on 12 March 1951, and his ashes were buried under a lilac tree. A memorial service at St Martin-in-the-Fields on 28 May 1951 was relayed outside on loudspeakers to a crowd of several thousands. His will included a substantial bequest to Bobbie Andrews and various legacies to theatrical charities; Redroofs was later sold at auction (the proceeds went to Andrews) and the property became a convalescent home for actors.

Novello was an extraordinary figure, combining high achievement in writing and performing, both on stage and in films; the guest books for his homes are a virtual compendium of the leading stars of the day, and regularly include the names of such figures as Gladys Cooper, Vivien Leigh, Douglas Fairbanks junior, and Noël Coward. The establishment of his matinée idol image in the 1920s, drawing on his elegant and strong profile, was a significant factor in retaining his appeal as a stage performer. His writing and performing brought a sense of genuine emotion to otherwise light and artificial material and made a virtue of them. Many of his plays and musical romances contain an acerbic and well-observed barbed wit, which Novello particularly indulged for his company stalwart and unofficial housekeeper, Olive Gilbert, in *Perchance to Dream*. High-quality artifice, escapism, and a sense of the exotic were at the heart of his approach to theatre. A scholarship in his memory was established at the Royal Academy of Dramatic Art, and in 1952 a bronze bust of Novello sculpted by Clemence Dane, and previously in the Aldwych flat, was unveiled in the rotunda of the Theatre Royal, Drury Lane. A commemorative panel was installed in the actors' church of St Paul's, Covent Garden, and in 1972 a memorial stone was unveiled in St Paul's Cathedral to mark the twenty-first anniversary of his death.   JOHN SNELSON

Sources MSS and source material, Samuel French Ltd, London, Ivor Novello archives [musical MSS, draft/working librettos and playscripts, printed music, and legal papers] · MSS and source material, Covent Garden Theatre Museum Archive, Blythe House, Ivor Novello archives [photo archives; visitors' books; cuttings] · S. Wilson, *Ivor* (1975) [incl. complete listings of works and films] · W. Macqueen-Pope, *Ivor: the story of an achievement* (1951) · J. Harding, *Ivor Novello* (1987) · C. N. Davies, *The life I have loved* (1940) · P. Noble, *Ivor Novello: man of the theatre* (1951) · C. Hassall, *Edward Marsh: patron of the arts* (1959) · R. Traubner, *Operetta: a theatrical history* (1983), 347–53 · I. Novello, 'My life has been so thrilling', *News of the World* (17–24 Sept 1943); (8–29 Oct 1943) · R. Rose, *Perchance to dream: the world of Ivor Novello* (1974) · CGPLA Eng. & Wales (1951) · *The Stage* (1 April 1976)

Archives Samuel French Ltd, London, musical MSS, draft/working librettos and playscripts, printed music, and legal papers · Theatre Museum, London, corresp. | BL, corresp. with League of Dramatists, Add. MS 63422 · NL Wales, corresp. with Sir Edward Marsh |FILM BFI NFTVA, performance footage · BFI NFTVA, 'The songwriters', BBC, 13 July 1978 |SOUND BL NSA, documentary recording · BL NSA, 'Glamorous nights: the Ivor Novello story' (parts 1–7), 1998, H10562/4, H10576/4, H10595/4, H10632/5, H10670/4, H10706/5, H10729/2 · BL NSA, performance recordings

Likenesses photographs, 1923–45, Hult. Arch. · P. Tanqueray, photographs, 1928–34, NPG [*see illus.*] · A. McBean, photograph, 1937, NPG · C. Beaton, photograph, NPG · C. Dane, bronze bust, Theatre Royal, London · Foulsham & Banfield, postcard, NPG · H. Leslie, silhouette, drawing, NPG; repro. in *Record Books*, vol. 4 · Sasha, postcard, NPG · photographs, Theatre Museum, London · sculpture, St Paul's Cathedral, London

Wealth at death £146,245 2s. 4d.: probate, 7 July 1951, CGPLA Eng. & Wales

Novello, Vincent

Novello, Vincent (1781–1861), music publisher, was born on 6 September 1781 in London at 240 Oxford Road. He was the son of an Italian father, Giuseppe Novello, of Piedmontese origins, who had emigrated to England in 1771, and an English mother, Joan Wins. Vincent was one of two surviving children, the other being his elder brother Francis (*b.* 1779).

Vincent Novello can be considered one of the leading contributors to the development of British musical life and education in the first half of the nineteenth century. His musical career began as a choirboy and organ student at the Sardinian embassy, Lincoln's Inn Fields, under the direction of the organist and composer Samuel Webbe senior. Novello exhibited skill and musicianship as an organist and at the age of sixteen became a professional, with his first appointment at the Catholic chapel of the Portuguese embassy, South Street, Grosvenor Square.

From his position as chief organist, Novello acquainted himself with a large body of the sacred repertory, much of it from earlier periods, which he, in turn, presented to the congregation. At the time, this music was rarely performed and available only in manuscript. In an effort to disseminate it more widely, in 1811 Novello published his

Vincent Novello (1781–1861), by Edward Petre Novello, early 1830s

first edition, entitled *Collection of Sacred Music as Performed at the Royal Portuguese Chapel in London*. He was soon publishing other edited collections, his market being primarily other professional organists and skilled amateurs. From these beginnings Novello established himself as a music publisher, paying special attention to the English eighteenth-century sacred repertory. For his editions he sought out music, whether from manuscripts of long-forgotten works or from earlier published versions, which would entertain yet educate his audience. His fund of musical sources was wide-reaching: he found new prospects in the music manuscript collections of the British Museum, the collections of churches and chapels, and the private libraries of colleagues. His interest in musical life and performance drew him to like-minded musicians, and he became a founding member of the Philharmonic Society (1813).

Among Novello's early editions were *Purcell's Sacred Music* (five vols., 1828–32) and *The Fitzwilliam Music* (1825), an edition of sacred music from the collection of the Fitzwilliam Museum, University of Cambridge. Many of Novello's publications contain informative introductory notes describing the benefits of the chosen typographical design and page layout; these prefaces suggest an editorial philosophy and indication of his intended market. Some editions, such as the collection of Haydn masses (orchestral accompaniment edition, 1828), contain a list at the beginning of the first violin part of required instruments for performance, to aid the leader and conductor. Further evidence of Novello's editorial style can be seen in a collection of 'workbooks' (located in the British Library and the

Royal College of Music) which he used to transcribe music from his manuscript sources. These oblong notebooks, filled with pages of music manuscript paper, appear to have been used in the 1820s and 1830s not only to copy out the pieces he wished to publish, but also occasionally to make the musical arrangements for his own editions. Novello's own distinctive handwriting can also be seen on some of the manuscripts he consulted at the British Museum while collecting new works.

By 1825 Novello was known for his accessible editions of the main repertory as well, particularly his collections of the sacred music of Haydn and Mozart (although a number of the works attributed to both composers have since proved to be spurious). He also began to publish more contemporary works, including pieces by Mendelssohn, who became a family friend, and Spohr, although these were limited primarily to the sacred repertory. The firm did not begin to publish contemporary music in a systematic way until the 1850s and 1860s.

On 17 August 1808 Novello married Mary Sabilla Hehl (1789–1854); they had eleven children. Three were to make names for themselves in English cultural life: (Joseph) Alfred *Novello (1810–1896) succeeded his father as head of the publishing house in 1829 and developed the firm to become one of the leading music publishers; Clara Anastasia *Novello (1818–1908) became a well-known oratorio and opera singer; and Mary Victoria [see Clarke, Mary Victoria Cowden (1809–1898)] married the author Charles Cowden Clarke and became a respected writer on literature, her works including *The Life and Labours of Vincent Novello* (1864). The family took an active part in musical and literary London life. Their circle included Charles Lamb, Leigh Hunt, Shelley, and Dickens.

A frequently reproduced portrait of Vincent Novello, an engraving by William Humphrys after an oil painting by Novello's son Edward Petre, shows him to be of stout build, set jaw, and determined demeanour. This trait later developed into outward indications of ill humour which might be attributed to depression. Suffering from ill health, in 1848 Mary Novello retired to Nice and her husband joined her the following year. Mary died of cholera on 25 July 1854; Vincent survived until 9 August 1861, when he also died at the Villa Quaglia. In 1863 a memorial window, showing St Cecilia, was placed in the north transept of Westminster Abbey; the window was destroyed during an air raid in 1941.

Vincent Novello not only established what became a major and influential publishing house; he also provided accessible editions of important yet neglected music to both entertain and educate the growing Victorian middle class.   Victoria L. Cooper

Sources [J. Bennett], *A short history of cheap music, as exemplified in the records of the house of Novello, Ewer & Co.* (1887) · L. Swinyard, *A century and a half in Soho: a short history of the firm of Novello, publishers and printers of music, 1811–1961* (1961) · M. Hurd, *Vincent Novello—and company* (1981) · V. Cooper, 'The Novello stockbook, 1858–1869: a chronology of publishing activity', *Notes*, 44 (1987), 240–51 · C. Humphries and W. C. Smith, *Music publishing in the British Isles,* *from the beginning until the middle of the nineteenth century: a dictionary of engravers, printers, publishers, and music sellers*, 2nd edn (1970) · N. Temperley, ed., *The lost chord: essays on Victorian music* (1989) · N. Temperley, ed., *Music in Britain: the romantic age, 1800–1914* (1981) · D. Russell, *Popular music in Britain, 1840–1941: a social history* (1987) · P. A. Scholes, *The mirror of music, 1844–1944: a century of musical life in Britain as reflected in the pages of the Musical Times*, 2 vols. (1947); repr. (1970)

Archives BL, Music MSS, Add. MSS 65382–65525, 69851–69864 · Royal College of Music, London · U. Leeds, Brotherton L., MSS · U. Mich., Clements L. | BL, letters to Leigh Hunt, Add. MSS 38108–38110, 38523–38524 · BL, corresp. with Samuel Wesley and others, papers relating to Academy of Vocal Music, etc., Add. MSS 11729–11732 · Bodl. Oxf., Deneke MSS · U. Leeds, Brotherton L., Cowden-Clarke MSS

Likenesses E. P. Novello, oils, c.1830–1833, NPG [see illus.] · E. P. Novello, group portrait, c.1831 (*The Novello family and their friends*) · etching, 1834 (after E. P. Novello), NPG · W. Humphreys, line engravings (after E. P. Novello), NPG · E. P. Novello, woodcut (after G. De Wilde), NPG

Novikov [*née* Kiréev], **Olga** (1840–1925), journalist and apologist for Russia, was born in Moscow on 29 April 1840. She was one of the five children of Aleksey Kiréev (d. 1849) and his wife, Aleksandra, *née* Alabyev. Her father was educated by W. E. Baxter, later a Liberal MP, and, though strongly Slavophile, he spoke English as his second language, as did her mother. In 1860 she married Ivan Novikov (d. 1890), a colonel, and later general, in the *état major*; they had one child, Aleksandr. The Novikovs continued to move in pan-Slavist circles and were friends of Rector Keyserling of Dorpat University and K. P. Pobedonostsev, later the procurator of the Holy Synod. Initially by correspondence, Olga established connections with C. P. Villiers, Lord Clarendon, A. W. Kinglake, and John Tyndall. She was a keen supporter of links between the Old Catholics and the Orthodox churches. She first visited England in 1868 and returned in 1873, on which occasion she met the prince of Wales, Gladstone, and Disraeli. She argued that there was no necessary antagonism between Britain and Russia in central Asia and that good sense could lead to an entente.

In July 1876 Olga Novikov's brother Aleksandr was the first Russian volunteer to be killed in Serbia, and she embarked on an anti-Turkish crusade, which was bitterly hostile to Disraeli's government. She came to Britain in 1876, just after agitation against the Bulgarian atrocities had begun in earnest, setting up in Claridge's Hotel and becoming a prominent public figure through her letters and articles justifying the Russian position: it was for her activities at this time that Disraeli called her 'the MP for Russia in England'. She was always a representative of Muscovite pan-Slavism, rather than official Russian policy. Although less influential than her notoriety at the time suggested, she was an unusual figure and, as a woman taking part in a political campaign on a foreign policy question together with the duke of Westminster and a former prime-minister, almost unique. Rumours that she was Gladstone's mistress—'an extremely accomplished whore' was R. B. D. Morier's description (Gladstone, *Diaries*, 9.lxxxix, note)—were wholly unfounded, as

Wealth at death £2806 5s. 7d.: probate, 6 June 1925, *CGPLA Eng. & Wales*

Olga Novikov (1840–1925), by unknown photographer, 1875

was the story that Gladstone escorted her to her hotel following the famous conference on the Eastern question on 7–8 December 1876. However, she supplied the anti-atrocitarian campaign with much information and was a convenient link with Russian opinion. She became a regular writer of articles on Anglo-Russian affairs in W. T. Stead's *Northern Echo* and *Pall Mall Gazette*, the *Fortnightly Review*, *Contemporary Review*, *Fraser's Magazine*, and other journals. She later crossed swords with Gladstone on Russia's record on liberty and on the pogroms of the 1880s. At the end of the century she defended the autocracy and later opposed the Duma. Olga Novikov had a considerable interest in spiritualism and played a part in introducing Helena Blatavsky to London life. She continued to visit Britain quite frequently and regarded the Anglo-Russian entente of 1907 as the fruit of her endeavours. During the First World War she wrote extensively for the *Westminster Gazette* and the *Asiatic Review*. Although she settled in London after 1917, living with one of her nieces, she was always something of a nomad, moving from personality to personality and collecting tokens of recognition. She died of pneumonia at 4 Brunswick Place, London, on 21 April 1925. H. C. G. MATTHEW

Sources W. T. Stead, *The M.P. for Russia*, 2 vols. (1909) · Gladstone, *Diaries* · H. Gladstone, *After thirty years* (1928) · *The Times* (22 April 1925) · *CGPLA Eng. & Wales* (1925) · H. C. G. Matthew, *Gladstone, 1875–1898* (1995)

Archives priv. coll. · University of Kansas, Kenneth Spencer Research Library, corresp. and papers | BL, corresp. with W. E. Gladstone, Add. MS 44268 · Bodl. Oxf., letters to F. W. Chesson · U. Edin. L., corresp. with Charles Sarolea

Likenesses photograph, 1875, repro. in Stead, *M.P. for Russia*, vol. 1 [*see illus.*] · photographs, priv. coll., Novikov MSS

Novosielski, Michael (*c.*1747–1795), scene painter and architect, although Polish in name, was born in Rome. When he arrived in England is not known, but by 1772 he was living in Golden Square, London. On 3 September 1776 he married the singer Regina Felicia Pasquali (*d.* 1820) at St Pancras Old Church. The Drury Lane account book in the Folger Shakespeare Library shows that he worked on at least two occasions for that theatre in 1777. But in 1781 he began his long scenic association with the King's Theatre in the Haymarket, where in 1783 he was made master painter. He worked with Gaetano Marinari, and with Cornelius Dixon, Thomas Luppino, and A. Thiselton as assistants.

Between 1781 and 1784 Novosielski prepared scenery and machinery for many operas and ballets at the King's Theatre. Jean-Georges Noverre was ballet master and had an exacting eye for scenic standards. It should be remembered that many individual scenes would be taken from stock and that Novosielski may have only contributed by adding occasional new scenes and supervising the refurbishment of existing ones. In this way, during his first season, 1780–81, he worked on the operas *Mitridate*, *Il barone di Torre Forte*, and *Piramo e Tisbe* and the ballets *Les caprices de Galathée*, *Médée et Jason*, and *La frascatana*. In 1781–2 he prepared scenes for the ballets *Les amants réunis*, *Le triomphe de l'amour conjugal*, and *Rinaldo and Armida* and the operas *Giuno Bruto*, *Apollen et les Muses*, and *Ifigenia in Aulide*. In 1782–3 he designed scenes for the ballets *Il ratto delle Sabine* and *Il riposo del campo* and the operas *Cimene*, *The amours of Alexander and Roxane*, and *La dame bienfaisante*.

In 1782 the King's Theatre underwent considerable rebuilding, planned by Novosielski. Confined to the original walls of 1705, he increased capacity by reducing stage depth and planning the auditorium on the lines of an Italian opera house: 'The stage and pit were rebuilt, and four tiers of boxes completely encircled the auditorium' (Nalbach, 28). However, 'Being confined to the original walls, Mr Novosielski had not the opportunity of giving it greater width; the form therefore remained extremely bad, and the stage and its appendages wretchedly confined and inconvenient' (Saunders, 80). In fact, Novosielski added some width to the auditorium by placing corridors and access to the boxes outside the walls of the original building.

During 1783–4, when Jean Dauberval was appointed ballet master and Auguste Vestris junior the principal dancer, Novosielski contributed to the ballets *The Pastimes of Terpsychore*, *The Slaves of Conquering Bacchus*, and *The Four Ages of Man* and the operas *Il trionfo d'Arianna* and *Le due gemelle*. During his final season in 1784–5 he designed scenes for the ballets *Le jugement de Paris* and *Il convitato di pietra* and the operas *Il curioso indiscreto* and *Artaserse*.

At the close of this season Novosielski's architectural interests led him to begin what was to be a secondary career as a property developer. In 1785 he took a lease on land to the south of Brompton Road in Kensington, where he built seventy-seven houses in three developments—

Michael's Place, Michael's Grove, and Brompton Crescent. He later built speculatively in Grosvenor Square and in Piccadilly. On his death he left a half-completed development (Fortfield Terrace) at Sidmouth, Devon.

Early in the 1783–4 season the management of William Taylor at the King's Theatre foundered, and while he was in gaol for debt Novosielski was appointed one of five trustees to whom Taylor's business interests were assigned. *The Case of the Opera-House Disputes, Fairly Stated* (1784) criticized the work of the trustees, charging Novosielski with sacking staff and misappropriating theatre income in order to invest in the Royal Circus. He was accused of taking a holiday in Italy, accompanied by his wife, and claiming expenses of £1500 from the opera fund for it as a recruiting trip for new singers. Novosielski was also charged with increasing his salary from £300 to £750 per annum and claiming expenses for coals, candles, and dinners at the theatre. It was claimed that his wife was paid £150 per annum for superintending the candles and that her father was paid £200 as 'superintendent of something, but what that something is, heaven only can tell'.

The theatre was destroyed by fire on 17 June 1789, and, notwithstanding these charges, Novosielski, assisted by his pupil William Capon, planned the rebuilding to permit enlargement of audience capacity by increasing the overall size by 30 feet in width and by 38 feet in length. The *London Chronicle* on 7 October 1790 reported:

> The span of the roof is 25 feet wider than that of Westminster Hall … The formation gives the idea of a lyre. The boxes consist of four complete tiers, besides an additional tier on each side. The whole, as they rise, are thrown back, by which means every person in the boxes will be visible from any part of the house. The boxes exceed in number those in any former theatre—sixty.

The theatre was 'hailed as an architectural marvel of a size and magnificence to rival Piermarini's La Scala in Milan' (Price, Milhous, and Hume, 562). The theatre opened on 26 March 1791 with Joseph Haydn 'presiding at the harpsichord' (Hogan, 1277). In spite of the speed and shoddiness of its construction, Novosielski's theatre lasted for over fifty years.

During 1794–5 Novosielski returned to the theatre and prepared scenery for the opera *L'amor contrastato*. He probably died on 8 April 1795 in Ramsgate, and his will was proved on 11 April. His executor was left £20 to undertake his duties and to dispose of 'sundry Household Estates … in the County of Middlesex'. From the estate, one-third was to go his 'dear wife Regina Felicia Novosielski' and the remaining two-thirds to his four children. His will does not name the children, but Regina's will, administered in 1820, names three of the four: Michael Peter, Mary Ann, and Ursula.

It is presumed that Novosielski's scene designs were destroyed in the 1789 theatre fire—hence, perhaps unfairly, his reputation relies upon his architectural work, where some evidence survives. But his age applauded his scenic work and very early in his career he was expected 'to rival soon in scene painting, even Loutherbourg himself'

(*General Advertiser*, 27 Feb 1781). His portrait by Angelica Kauffman, executed in 1791, shows him holding his 1789–90 plans for the rebuilding of the King's Theatre.

Christopher Baugh

Sources Highfill, Burnim & Langhans, *BDA* · D. Nalbach, *The King's Theatre, 1704–1867* (1972) · C. Price, J. Milhous, and R. D. Hume, *Italian opera in late eighteenth-century London*, 1: *The King's Theatre, Haymarket, 1778–1791* (1995) · G. Saunders, *A treatise on theatres* (1790) · C. B. Hogan, ed., *The London stage, 1660–1800*, pt 5: *1776–1800* (1968) · S. Rosenfeld and E. Croft-Murray, 'A checklist of scene painters working in Great Britain and Ireland in the 18th century [pt 2]', *Theatre Notebook*, 19 (1964–5), 49–64, esp. 51–2 · S. Rosenfeld, *Georgian scene painters and scene painting* (1981) · *IGI* · *New Grove*
Likenesses A. Kauffman, oils, 1791, NG Scot.
Wealth at death left executor £20 for a 'mourning ring'; mandate to dispose of 'sundry household estates … in the county of Middlesex'; third of proceeds to wife; two-thirds to his four children: will, 11 April 1795, Highfill, Burnim & Langhans, *BDA*

Nowell, Alexander (*c.*1516/17–1602), dean of St Paul's, was the second son of John Nowell (*d.* 1526), esquire, of Read Hall, Whalley, Lancashire, and his second wife, Elizabeth, daughter of Robert Kay of Rochdale; Laurence *Nowell [*see under* Nowell, Laurence (1530–*c.*1570)], dean of Lichfield, was his younger brother. The exact date of Alexander's birth is not known, and earlier writers have made different estimates, ranging from 1506 to 1511. Some guidance may be provided by the fact of his graduating BA in 1536. Since this usually occurred when a student was twenty or twenty-one, it might be surmised that Nowell was born about 1516. A portrait engraved after his death bears an inscription stating that he died aged ninety-five, which would support his biographer Ralph Churton in placing Nowell's birth in or around 1507. The most careful estimate, however, is perhaps that of A. D. K. Hayward in the *History of Parliament*, where the date 1516 or 1517 is based on Nowell's own recollection, made in old age, that he was thirteen when he went from school at Middleton, Lancashire, to Oxford, and that he spent most of the next thirteen years there before being appointed master of Westminster School in 1543.

Studies and early career Nowell's college at Oxford was Brasenose, where he is said to have shared rooms at one time with the martyrologist John Foxe, who later described him as 'a man earnestly bent on the true worshipping of God' (*HoP, Commons, 1509–58*, 3.28). He graduated BA in 1536 and was elected a fellow of the college in the same year, subsequently proceeding MA in 1540 and DTh in 1545. Having left Oxford for a while to study logic at Cambridge, he returned to Oxford to give public lectures on logic in 1541 or 1542. He also took holy orders.

In 1543 Nowell was appointed master of Westminster School. Here he introduced the study of Terence and read the Greek text of St Luke's gospel and the Acts of the Apostles with the older scholars. On 27 November 1551 he was appointed canon of the third prebend at Westminster, and according to Strype was soon recognized as a notable preacher. At almost exactly the same time he became involved in religious controversy following the death, on 2 November, of John Redman, the first master of Trinity

Alexander Nowell (c.1516/17–1602), by unknown artist

College, Cambridge. Redman had been a moderate reformer, of humanistic rather than evangelical sympathies. Nowell, who was with him shortly before his death, subsequently published a short account of what were said to be the dead man's final views on religious issues. He was attacked by the Catholic controversialist Thomas Dorman and others for having misrepresented Redman's opinions (which were not, indeed, easily summarized), but was supported in other quarters. No copy of his original work is known to survive, but there are extant copies of two of Nowell's later tracts refuting Dorman, published in 1565 and 1567 (STC, 18739–18742), as well as Dorman's counterblast, A Disproufe of M. Nowelles Reproufe, printed at Antwerp in 1565 (STC, 7601). Dorman and Nowell later also engaged in lively controversy over John Jewel's Apology of 1562, with both men publishing treatises attacking the other.

In the meantime Nowell was returned to the House of Commons in Queen Mary's first parliament (October 1553), as one of the two burgesses for (West) Looe, Cornwall. The borough belonged to the duchy of Cornwall, and it is likely that Nowell was the nominee of the duchy's staunchly protestant steward, John Russell, first earl of Bedford. However, he was not permitted to take his seat; his election was challenged, and a committee appointed to inquire into its validity decided that as a prebendary of Westminster with a seat in convocation, Nowell could not also sit in parliament. Order was therefore given that another burgess should be chosen in his place, but the result of that election is unknown. The episode was important in establishing the constitutional principle that members of convocation could not sit in the Commons.

Exile As a staunch protestant holding a prominent position, and trusted by Edward VI's government, which gave him a preaching licence in 1547, Nowell predictably went into exile under Mary. He was deprived of his prebend on 30 March 1554 but kept his post at Westminster School for another year before fleeing abroad. It is said that Bishop Bonner of London intended to arrest Nowell, but that Francis Bowyer, a merchant from a strongly protestant family who later became sheriff of London (and the nephew of Thomas Bowyer, whose widow would later become Nowell's first wife), assisted his escape. Izaak Walton refers to the same incident in The Compleat Angler, telling how Bonner, seeing Nowell catch fish in the Thames, resolved to catch Nowell instead.

Nowell went first to Strasbourg, but by October 1556 had joined the group of exiles in Frankfurt am Main. Serious disputes arose over the liturgy to be used, between those who favoured the Cranmerian prayer book, led by Richard Cox, future bishop of Ely, and radicals led by John Knox. Nowell tried to reconcile the two groups but subsequently sided with the Calvinist supporters of the 'new discipline', defending their position against the criticisms of Robert Horne, later bishop of Winchester. He continued to act as a peacemaker, however, and when at the time of Mary's death a group of exiles at Geneva sought to form a group that would press for further reform in England, Nowell and several of his Frankfurt associates retorted that 'We purpos to submit oure selves to such orders as shall be established by authoritie, beinge not of themselves wicked, so we would wishe you willingly to do the same' (Whittingham, 187–91).

Elizabethan appointments Following the accession of Elizabeth, Nowell returned to England and soon began to receive ecclesiastical preferment. He was listed by Sir William Cecil as a clergyman who merited promotion, in memoranda that indicate that he was being considered for a bishopric, but he was never raised to the episcopate; probably his religious views were thought too radical. On 23 December 1560 Nowell preached at the consecration of Edmund Grindal as bishop of London; the new bishop made him his chaplain, and on 1 January 1560 collated him to the archdeaconry of Middlesex. On 14 February he was also collated to the canonry of the sixth prebend in Canterbury Cathedral, and on 21 May the queen appointed him a prebendary of Westminster. Later that year Nowell and his brother Laurence, who had also been in exile under Mary, both received major appointments. Laurence became dean of Lichfield, while on 27 November Alexander was elected dean of St Paul's, London. He held this position for the rest of his life, but soon resigned his archdeaconry, to which a successor was appointed on 31 January 1561. He also gave up the rectory of Saltwood with Hythe, Kent, to which he had been collated in February 1560, but retained his prebends at Canterbury and Westminster until 1564. At St Paul's he held the prebend of Weldland (exchanged for Totenhall in 1588) as well as the deanery. He soon established himself as a leading preacher, often preaching both at Paul's Cross and at court. Following the fire of 4 June 1561 that devastated St Paul's he delivered a sermon before the lord mayor and aldermen, exhorting them to take immediate steps to repair the damage.

Nowell's advanced religious opinions, which may have deprived him of a see, became increasingly apparent in the 1560s. The organ of St Paul's played at his installation, but in the convocation of 1563 he was among the reformers who supported the abortive proposal to eliminate organs and 'curious singing' from church services, leaving only the psalms to be either sung in unison by the entire congregation or, if that proved impossible, simply recited. Nowell played an important part in this convocation. He was chosen to preach in Westminster Abbey on 12 January for the official opening of parliament, which met concurrently with convocation. As well as calling on the queen to marry, he argued that no one should be punished for private opinions, but that those who opposed reform and spread heresy should be 'cut off'. When convocation assembled the next day, Archbishop Parker proposed that Nowell be named prolocutor of its lower house. He was duly elected, and throughout the session served as a channel of communication between the two houses, often reporting the actions of the lower house to their episcopal superiors. There was a general consensus within convocation in favour of reform. Both houses did adopt the Thirty-Nine Articles of religion, based on the forty-two articles promulgated under Edward VI, as well as a second Book of Homilies, which included a lengthy attack on images. But neither the Book of Discipline which Nowell and others presented to the bishops, nor attempts to eradicate the use of vestments, could prevail against the opposition of the queen. Two years later, at the time of the vestiarian controversy, Nowell showed himself sympathetic to the radicals, making one of a group who tried to moderate Parker's demands for conformity.

Nowell and the catechism Nowell's greatest and most lasting contribution to the English church lay in his several versions of the catechism. Before convocation met in 1563 he had prepared the draft of a Latin catechism, called the 'Catechismus puerorum'. The radicals in the lower house knew of this, and in their pre-convocation 'general notes' they called for 'a catechism … to be set forth in Latin, which is already done by Mr. Dean of Paul's and wanteth only viewing' (Haugaard, 277). They hoped that it would be joined with the Thirty-Nine Articles and John Jewel's *Apology*, all three to be printed together in a single volume. The entire lower house subscribed to Nowell's catechism, and the bishops 'allowed' it with some revisions, an unusual action which permitted its use though without granting it the official status the lower clergy had desired. Nowell sent the text to Cecil, hoping that he would persuade the queen to sanction it, but she took no action. The catechism was not printed until 1570, when it appeared as *Catechismus, sive, Prima institutio disciplinaque pietatis Christianae* (STC, 18701), with Parker's approval but still

with no claim of official status. The canons of 1571, however, ordered all schoolmasters to use Nowell's catechism and no other, and to teach an English version made by Thomas Norton (*A catechism, or, First instruction of Christian religion*; STC, 18708), which had also been published in 1570.

Nowell's original or longer catechism ran to 176 quarto pages with an eight-page index, and was considered too long for use by most catechumens. A shorter version, the 'middle catechism', was published in English in 1572 (*A catechisme, or, Institution of Christian religion, to bee learned of all youth next after the little catechisme, appointed in the Booke of Common Prayer*; STC, 18730), and in Latin two years later (STC, 18712); a version in both Latin and Greek appeared in 1575 (STC, 18726), the Greek translation being the work of Nowell's nephew William Whitaker. Even this ran to nearly 100 pages; it was a condensation, not a simplification, of the larger work. A still smaller and somewhat more elementary version, the 'shorter catechism', was published in Latin in 1573 as *Catechismus parvus pueris primum Latine qui ediscatur, proponendus in scholis* (STC, 18711), followed by a Latin and Greek edition in 1574 (STC, 18711a). Nowell's various catechisms constituted both one of the doctrinal foundation documents of the Church of England—some bishops ordered that it be used in the parishes—and an important educational tool. The canons of 1604 required all schoolmasters to teach either the larger or shorter catechism, in either English or Latin, and it was used to teach both Latin and doctrine until well into the seventeenth century. The writers of later catechisms, men like John More and Eusebius Pagit, drew heavily on Nowell's work. By 1638 the several versions of his catechism had appeared in sixty-one editions, most of them in Latin; the middle catechism was the most popular, with forty editions.

Nowell's catechisms are drawn chiefly from John Calvin's Geneva catechism of 1541, which formed part of the 'new discipline' he had accepted at Frankfurt. Calvin's teachings are especially evident in Nowell's treatment of the sacraments, where the doctrine of the real presence is upheld. Like Calvin, Nowell sees the church as the society of the elect and makes a consequent distinction between the church visible and invisible. He also declares that elders in local congregations should establish a godly discipline by acting as censors of morals with powers of excommunication. But despite his debt to Geneva, Nowell also displays some characteristically English concerns, including the need for confirmation, the threat from idolatry, and the role of law, above all that represented by the Decalogue. The Bible, he maintains, contains all that is necessary for salvation, but the writings of the fathers and the decrees of church councils can still help in its explication. Nowell also emphasizes the universality of the Christian church, comparing it with the narrowness and exclusivity of Judaism. One of the first English theologians to associate the sacraments with grace, baptism and the Lord's supper both represent to him what he calls 'a secret and spiritual grace' (Green, 513). On the whole he either avoids or takes a moderate line on contentious issues; he defends the doctrine of predestination, but though he is clear that justification comes by faith in Christ alone, he also argues that good works are among the most important ways in which true faith makes itself known. But his comment on the fifth commandment, that offending the king is a more serious sin than offending one's parents, is uniquely his.

Role in public life Nowell's relations with Queen Elizabeth were equivocal. Her lack of enthusiasm about clerical marriage may have made her less than sympathetic towards him. It is said that Parker urged the queen to name Nowell provost of Eton College if she could accept a married minister in that post, but instead it went to the celibate William Day (who almost immediately married a daughter of William Barlow and eventually became bishop of Winchester). The issue of images twice caused Elizabeth to fall out with the dean. On 1 January 1562 Nowell placed a richly bound prayer book, lavishly illustrated with woodcuts, on the queen's cushion in St Paul's, imagining this to be an appropriate new year's gift. But Elizabeth immediately demanded its removal, telling the verger to bring back her old book, and at the end of the service she berated the dean for disregarding her proclamation against 'images, pictures, and Romish relics' (Strype, *Annals*, 1/1.408–10). Deeply discomfited, Nowell could only plead ignorance and good intentions. For his part Nowell disapproved of the crucifix which Elizabeth continued to keep in her private chapel, so strongly that he referred to the offensive image during a Lenten sermon at court in 1564. His strictures prompted the famous outburst: 'To your text, Mr Dean—leave that, we have heard enough of that' (Strype, *Parker*, 1.318–19). Shocked and dismayed, Nowell was unable to continue his sermon; Parker took him home and comforted him, and the dean subsequently wrote to Cecil defending his action.

Nowell probably learned tact from these bruising confrontations. Charged with unduly flattering Elizabeth in his court sermons, he replied that 'he had no other way to instruct the queen what she should be but by commending her' (Collinson, *Religion*, 27). He had a less stormy encounter with Elizabeth in 1585, when she directed Burghley to inform Archbishop Whitgift that she wished to appoint a layman, Daniel Rogers, as treasurer of St Paul's. Whitgift passed the order on to Nowell, and subsequently the chapter petitioned the queen not to make the appointment, as it was contrary to the statutes of their church, while Nowell asked Burghley to intercede. The matter was suitably resolved by the appointment on 1 February 1586 of Richard Bancroft, later bishop of London and archbishop of Canterbury. In 1588 Elizabeth granted Nowell the first vacant canonry at Windsor, to be held together with his existing preferments, but he only obtained his stall in April 1594.

Nowell was a celebrated preacher, who often took the pulpit both at court (where he gave the first in the Lenten series of sermons every year from 1561 to 1592) and at Paul's Cross, and also at funerals, delivering commemorative addresses for Roger Ascham, whose deathbed he had attended, in 1568, for Archbishop Edmund Grindal in

1583, and for Mildred, Lady Burghley, and Frances, countess of Sussex, both in 1589. In 1572 he and John Foxe visited Thomas Howard, fourth duke of Norfolk, in the Tower, and at Easter he gave the duke communion. Norfolk requested that Nowell be with him on the scaffold, and the dean duly attended his execution on 2 July. In the following year he ministered to a very different prisoner, when he tried to bring Ann Sanders, convicted of murdering her husband, to repentance. Following the defeat of the Spanish Armada he preached before the mayor and aldermen of London at Paul's Cross on 20 August 1588, and then in the cathedral on 8 September following when captured Spanish flags were displayed.

Ecclesiastical and educational activities Nowell was a lifelong friend of Edmund Grindal, and the links between them were strengthened between 1559 and 1570, when Grindal was bishop of London. The bishop clearly appreciated the dean's liturgical talents, and in 1563, when London was devastated by plague, engaged him to provide a homily responding to the crisis, 'concerning the justice of God'. Nowell was no less impressed by the qualities of his bishop, and in 1575, when Archbishop Matthew Parker was known to be dying, wrote to Burghley urging that Grindal, who was now at York, be appointed to succeed to the primacy: 'of all the clergy I think the archbishop of York to be a man of the greatest wisdom and ability to govern, and unto whom the other bishops with best contentation would submit themselves' (Collinson, *Grindal*, 221). When Grindal died he referred to Nowell as 'my faithful friend' and left him 'my ambling gelding, called Grey Olephant' (ibid., 281).

Nowell's effectiveness as dean during his long tenure is hard to assess. Although the fact that he himself held a prebend in St Paul's strengthened his position within the chapter of which he was the nominal head, the leading role in the cathedral's affairs was often taken not by the dean but by the bishop; it was Grindal who did most to implement repairs after the fire of 1561. Nowell may have been at least partly to blame that nothing was done to improve the condition of St Paul's and the conduct of its services, but when Bancroft held his primary visitation on 22 October 1598, one of the minor canons blamed what was amiss on the failure of successive bishops to act on their own findings—'thease disorders have been most of them complayned on at every Visitation, and yet continue in theyr oulde irregularitye' (Simpson, 277). All that can be said for certain, however, is that although Bancroft heard much in 1598 about the careless and irreverent behaviour of the minor canons and choristers, and about the dirt, noise, and smell encountered everywhere in the cathedral, no action was taken to remedy the situation, by Nowell or anyone else.

It cannot have benefited the administration of St Paul's that Dean Nowell was often employed elsewhere. In 1563 he was made a member of the ecclesiastical commission set up under the Elizabethan Act of Supremacy. In that capacity he signed the warrant of 11 December 1573 for the arrest of Thomas Cartwright, who had been advocating a presbyterian church system. He also took part in the trial of two Flemish Anabaptists, John Peters and Henry Turwert, both of whom were executed. In 1590 he helped examine the dean of Lincoln, Ralph Griffin, who had been charged with preaching false doctrine, and in the following year, with his chaplain Lancelot Andrewes, he visited John Udall, who was lying in prison under sentence of death for preaching against episcopacy and thereby spreading sedition. Nowell was subsequently prominent in the campaign that secured a pardon for Udall early in June 1592, though its beneficiary died soon afterwards.

On at least two occasions, in 1568 and 1580, Nowell returned to his native Lancashire, where he made determined efforts to persuade Catholic recusants to conform to the state church. His preaching was said to have been effective, and to have won many over. He also tried to further the work of preaching by others, and in 1576 drew Burghley's attention to the importance of Manchester collegiate church, with its large fellowship, 'in respect of the good instruction of the whole people of that country in their duties' (Haigh, 299). Nowell was also several times involved in efforts to convert his own half-brother John Towneley, the son of his mother's second marriage. A wealthy and influential man, and therefore particularly worth winning for protestantism, Towneley was imprisoned at York in 1573; on that occasion Nowell tried in vain to keep him out of prison, but fared better in 1574, following an appeal to the privy council. Towneley was soon back in prison, however, but in 1577 Nowell secured his release on bonds, and in the following year had the custody of his half-brother in London. Towneley still refused to conform, and Nowell's efforts to convert him, and also to keep him out of gaol, continued into the 1580s. In 1581 it was proposed that Nowell should write a reply to the tract *Rationes decem* by the Jesuit missionary Edmund Campion. That work was eventually undertaken by Nowell's nephew William Whitaker, but Nowell and William Day did hold a disputation with Campion, who was a prisoner in the Tower, later in the year. In 1583 the privy council designated Nowell as being fit to hold conferences with papists. He was also named to a commission to deal with abuses in printing, and in 1583 the privy council directed him to help raise funds to assist protestants in Geneva.

Perhaps because he had no descendants to whom he might bequeath his property, Nowell was a generous benefactor to several educational establishments. He and his brother Robert, a prosperous lawyer, re-endowed the grammar school at Middleton, 'where we were brought up in our youth' (Collinson, *Grindal*, 34). He stipulated that the school should be called Queen Elizabeth's School, and that it was to be governed by the principal and fellows of Brasenose College. He also provided for thirteen exhibitions at Brasenose, to be held by scholars from Middleton, or from the schools at Whalley and Burnley. Out of gratitude for his services to the college (which included damp-proofing the lower chambers by laying floorboards in 1572, at a cost of £40) he was chosen its principal in September 1595, a position he held in a purely honorary capacity until the end of the year. Nowell may also have been

a benefactor to St Paul's School (more likely the old cathedral establishment than John Colet's new foundation) and Emmanuel College, Cambridge. More certainly, he drafted statutes and curricula for several schools, including those at Brentwood, Colchester, Tonbridge, Burnley, and Bangor, and gave advice to Archbishop Parker concerning the founding of a school at Rochdale. In addition he conscientiously administered a fund for providing assistance to poor scholars established by Robert Nowell in his will of 1569. The beneficiaries included Thomas Bilson, Richard Hooker, and Richard Hakluyt, as well as many young men who never achieved fame.

Last years, death, and assessment In a letter to Burghley dated new year's day 1585 Nowell referred to his 'extreme age and much sickliness', and suggested that his deanery might soon become vacant (Strype, *Whitgift*, 1.443-8). Nevertheless he lived until 13 February 1602, and is said to have retained his faculties to the end. He was buried in St Mary's Chapel behind the high altar of St Paul's; a headless trunk may survive from his effigy, otherwise destroyed by the great fire. In appearance he was described as being a slight man with a thin pointed face, a delicate complexion, and bright eyes, and with a small beard and moustache. He had married twice. His first wife, Jane, daughter of Robert Mery of Northaw, Hertfordshire, and widow of Thomas Bowyer of London, died on 3 August 1579. He later married Elizabeth Hast of Wyndham, Sussex, widow successively of Lawrence Ball and of Thomas Blount of London, who died about 1612 and was buried at Mundham, near Chichester. There were no children of either marriage.

Nowell had made his will on 8 January 1591, and added codicils to it in 1597 and 1602 (PRO, PROB 11/99, fols. 86v–90r). In 1591 he showed himself mindful of his decanal position and responsibilities, directing that gowns and money should be given to every member of the cathedral establishment who attended his funeral, and leaving £20 'towards the Reparacions of the upper parte of Pawles Church which is above the greate stayres or steppes of stone'. He remembered several servants and disposed of a number of books; the library of Brasenose was to receive the strongly protestant church history of the Magdeburg centuriators, a Greek lexicon, and 'all the historie of Martirs written by Mr John Foxe, in two volumes of the best paper, and fayre bound'. His wife, 'in Token of the Love that I have continually borne, and doe beare unto her', was to be both residuary legatee and sole executor. The first codicil, dated 29 April 1597, was primarily concerned with the administration of a valuable wardship which Nowell and William Whitaker (now deceased) had obtained in 1586. Although writing of himself that 'I growe very weake and sicklye by extreme Age', Nowell still showed himself concerned with education, directing that from the money received from the estate during the heir's minority, £50 apiece was to be paid yearly to the universities of Oxford and Cambridge, with all but £5 from each sum being distributed among poor scholars there.

The second codicil, dated to the day before his death, contains bequests to Nowell's relations and servants, and 40s. 'to Claiton servant to Mr Claton the Apothecarie'.

Nowell's most enduring memorial consists of his highly influential catechism and the various schools and colleges he promoted and endowed. But he also left a strong impression as a representative ecclesiastical figure, a committed mainstream reformer much like his friend Grindal, and several writers acclaimed him as such in his own lifetime. When the opponents of Richard Hooker wanted to accuse him of attacking the Church of England, Nowell was cited as one of the authorities whose true doctrine was being undermined. This centrality was appreciated by Nowell's early nineteenth-century biographer Ralph Churton, who described his subject's life as 'one of the best mirrors to discern the true spirit and temper of the age and character of the Reformation' (Churton, viii). But he was also valued for his personal qualities. Nowell's contemporaries regarded him as meditative, wise in counsel and grave in carriage, and it is in keeping with their views that he should also have been remembered by Izaak Walton, to whom he was 'as dear a lover, and constant practiser of Angling, as any Age can produce' (Walton, 76).

STANFORD LEHMBERG

Sources W. P. Haugaard, *Elizabeth and the English Reformation* (1968) · I. M. Green, *The Christian's ABC: catechisms and catechizing in England, c. 1530–1740* (1996) · C. H. Garrett, *The Marian exiles: a study in the origins of Elizabethan puritanism* (1938); repr. (1966) · P. Collinson, *The Elizabethan puritan movement* (1967) · P. Collinson, *Archbishop Grindal, 1519–1583: the struggle for a reformed church* (1979) · H. H. Milman, *Annals of St Paul's Cathedral* (1868) · S. Lehmberg, *The reformation of cathedrals* (1988) · HoP, *Commons, 1509–58,* 3.28–9 · will, PRO, PROB 11/99, fols. 86v–90r · R. Churton, *Life of Nowell* · Wood, *Ath. Oxon.,* new edn, 1.716–19 · J. Strype, *Annals of the Reformation and establishment of religion … during Queen Elizabeth's happy reign,* new edn, 4 vols. (1824) · J. Strype, *Ecclesiastical memorials,* 3 vols. (1822) · J. Strype, *The life and acts of Matthew Parker* (1711) · J. Strype, *The history of the life and acts of the most reverend father in God Edmund Grindal,* new edn (1821) · J. Strype, *The life and acts of John Whitgift,* new edn, 3 vols. (1822) · *Fasti Angl., 1541–1857,* [St Paul's, London] · I. Walton, *The compleat angler, 1653–1676,* ed. J. Bevan (1983) · *Hist. U. Oxf.* 3: *Colleg. univ.* · J. Simon, *Education and society in Tudor England* (1966) · P. Lake, *Anglicans and puritans? Presbyterianism and English conformist thought from Whitgift to Hooker* (1988) · P. Lake and M. Questier, *The Antichrist's lewd hat* (2002) · C. Tyerman, *A history of Harrow School, 1324–1991* (2000) · P. E. McCullough, *Sermons at court: politics and religion in Elizabethan and Jacobean preaching* (1998) [incl. CD-ROM] · W. R. Matthews and W. M. Atkins, eds., *A history of St Paul's Cathedral* (1957) · P. Collinson, *The religion of protestants* (1982) · C. Haigh, *Reformation and resistance in Tudor Lancashire* (1975) · [W. Whittingham?], *A brief discourse of the troubles at Frankfort,* ed. E. Arber (1908) · W. S. Simpson, ed., *Registrum statutorum et consuetudinum ecclesiae cathedralis Sancti Pauli Londinensis* (1873) · *DNB*

Archives BL, Lansdowne MSS · CCC Cam., MSS · Chetham's Library, Manchester, sermon notes (MS)

Likenesses W. Hollar, etching (after monument in old St Paul's Cathedral, London), BM, NPG; repro. in W. Dugdale, *The history of St Paul's Cathedral in London* (1658) · Passe, line engraving, BM, NPG; repro. in H. Holland, *Heröologia* (1620) · oils, Brasenose College, Oxford [*see illus.*] · oils, Chetham's Library, Manchester · oils, second version, Bodl. Oxf.

Nowell, Increase (*bap.* **1593,** *d.* **1655**), colonial administrator, was baptized on 19 August 1593 at Sheldon, Warwickshire, the son of Alexander Nowell and his wife,

Sarah Smyth, grandson of Laurence *Nowell (*c.*1516–1576), dean of Lichfield [*see under* Nowell, Laurence (1530–*c.*1570)], and great-nephew of Alexander Nowell, dean of St Paul's. He may have been educated at Trinity College, Dublin. His marriage to Parnell Parker (1603–1687), daughter of Thomas Gray and Katherine Gray (*née* Myles), at Holy Trinity, Minories, London, on 8 July 1628 linked him to such transatlantic mercantile families as Graves, Tyng, and Coytmore. He was recommended as 'good counsel concerning buying a ship' in 1629 (Anderson, 2.1346). He was an original patentee of the Massachusetts Bay Company and assistant in 1629, annually re-elected until 1654. Emigrating in 1630, he was a founder of Charlestown and first ruling elder of the Boston–Charlestown church. In 1632 he helped to institute Charlestown's own church, but as a lay magistrate, military commissioner (1634), and colonial secretary (1636–50) he was advised to decline further ecclesiastical office. He was an active and efficient administrator, but did not engage in colonial commerce. His estate after his death, in Boston, on 1 November 1655 was valued at £592, mainly in land. In 1656 the general court, 'sensible of the low condition of the family', granted 2000 acres, and a further 3200 acre grant was sold before 1664 (Shurtleff, 4.1, 281–2; 5.2, 111).

The eldest surviving son of his three sons and two daughters, **Samuel Nowell** (1634–1688), was born in Charlestown on 12 November 1634, graduated from Harvard College in 1653, and was elected fellow and tutor in 1655–6 and college treasurer pro tem from 1683 to 1686. After 1676 he married Mary (*d.* 1693), daughter of William and Mary Alford and widow of Peter Butler and Hezekiah Usher. Though a student of divinity and a preacher, he never settled in the ministry. He was chaplain under General Josiah Winslow in King Philip's War (1675–6). At the 19 December 1675 Great Narragansett Swamp fight in Kingston, Rhode Island, he displayed remarkable bravery. Thereafter, he concentrated on lay affairs. Elected assistant in 1680, he led opposition to colonial concessions to the crown, and was described by Edmund Randolph as 'factious' (*Sibley's Harvard Graduates,* 1.336). He held office as colony treasurer from October 1685 until royal authority was imposed the following year. In 1687 he went to England on behalf of the old charter, which had been revoked, and died in London on 16 October 1688.

ROGER THOMPSON

Sources R. C. Anderson, ed., *The great migration begins: immigrants to New England, 1620–1633,* 2 (Boston, MA, 1995), 1342–6 · private information (2004) [J. E. Anderson] · T. B. Wyman, *Genealogies and estates of Charlestown* (1879), 710–12 · R. J. Crandall and R. J. Coffman, 'From emigrants to rulers', *New England Historical and Genealogical Register,* 131 (1977), 19, 130 · T. Hutchinson, *The history of the colony and province of Massachusetts-Bay,* ed. L. S. Mayo, 1 (1936), 16 · N. B. Shurtleff, ed., *Records of the governor and company of the Massachusetts Bay in New England,* 5 vols. in 6 (1853–4), vol. 4/1, pp. 281–2; vol. 5, p. 111 · *DNB* · C. K. Shipton, *Sibley's Harvard graduates: biographical sketches of graduates of Harvard University,* 17 vols. (1873–1975), vol. 1, pp. 335–7 · K. B. Murdock, *Increase Mather* (1925), 49, 120, 192, 206 · S. E. Morison, *The tercentennial history of Harvard College and University, 1636–1936,* 3–4: *Harvard College in the seventeenth century* (1936), 107, 346–7, 652–3 · M. G. Hall, *The last American puritan: the life of Increase Mather, 1639–1723* (1988), 189, 191, 204, 215–16, 218

Wealth at death £592: Anderson, *Great migration*, vol. 2, p. 1344

Nowell, John (1802–1867), weaver and bryologist, was born at Springs, near Todmorden, Yorkshire, the illegitimate son of William Midgley, smallholder and publican at Kebcote, and Miriam Nowell (*c.*1781–1852). He lived with his grandparents and, other than a short attendance at Sunday school, received no education until, aged twenty, he joined a grammar class held at Shore Chapel by the Baptist minister. As a young child he wound bobbins before beginning to weave when nine years old. After working as a hand-loom weaver until about 1829, he found employment as a twister-in at one of the Fielden Brothers' cotton mills. By this time Nowell was engaged in both botany and politics.

Nowell's interest in plants began with the herbs his grandmother used to prepare cattle medicines for his grandfather, a butcher and cow doctor. His enthusiasm was shared by his boyhood friend Abraham Stansfield and together they saved up to buy botanical books. By the early 1820s, Nowell was acquainted with the ardent botanist Edmund Holt, overseer of the Fielden Brothers' mill at Lumbutts, as well as his son (also Edmund Holt), who was deeply involved in radical politics. Nowell was probably one of Holt's 'young recruits who think they can take Botany by storm' (as Holt reported in a letter to Roberts Leyland on 11 July 1822). Like Holt's son, in 1831–2 Nowell was also a council member of the Todmorden Political Union, campaigning for the reform of parliament, along with the manufacturer John Fielden. In 1852, when Nowell and Stansfield founded the Todmorden Botanical Society, as vice-president and president respectively they encouraged the mixed-class membership that had been characteristic of the Political Union.

From 1825 Nowell paid particular attention to mosses and his skill at finding and distinguishing these plants gave him an international reputation. The bryologist Wilhelm Philip Schimper, who visited and botanized with Nowell in 1865, named the moss *Zygodon nowellii* and William Mitten named a genus of liverworts *Nowellia*. Nowell maintained a large correspondence and many of his discoveries were communicated to and reported by William Wilson. When work was slack, he was willing to act as collector for gentlemen botanists, often taking excursion trains to travel further afield. The botanist Benjamin Carrington considered Nowell's eyesight to be almost microscopic.

Nowell published *A Supplement to Baines' Flora of Yorkshire*, part 2, *The Mosses of the County* in 1854 and Stansfield and Nowell's *Flora of Todmorden* was published posthumously in 1911. He also prepared and published sets of moss specimens with the shoemaker Richard Buxton. Active at the pub meetings held by working-men botanists, after John Horsefield's death in 1854 Nowell often undertook to identify the mosses which had been collected by the participants. He was fondly recalled as an old man botanizing with younger enthusiasts and he bequeathed his herbarium to the Todmorden Botanical Society.

Nowell and his wife, Hannah, married young and raised six children. A daughter Mary died in 1856 aged twenty-two and his wife died on 10 April 1865. Although he continued to work at the mill until his death, failing health contributed to Nowell's increasing destitution, which was relieved only by a little help from the philanthropist Edward William Binney and some remuneration for light garden work from Stansfield. Nowell died from heart disease on 28 October 1867 at his home in White Hart Fold, Todmorden. His funeral, arranged by Stansfield, took place on 2 November at St Paul's Church, Cross Stone. The streets were packed with mourners and afterwards a hundred botanists and friends dined at the White Hart inn. A year later the Todmorden Botanical Society, having raised £90, set up a granite obelisk in St Mary's churchyard, Todmorden, commemorating how Nowell's 'unassuming manners, kind disposition, as well as his extensive knowledge of cryptogamic botany, endeared him to a wide circle of admiring friends'.

ANNE SECORD

Sources 'The late Mr John Nowell, the botanist', *Manchester Guardian* (5 Nov 1867) · A. Stansfield, 'Moss-gatherers: a Lancashire specimen', *Papers of the Manchester Literary Club*, 8 (1882), 205–18 · W. D. Foster, 'John Nowell of Todmorden, 1802–1867', *Bulletin of the British Bryological Society*, 35 (Jan 1980), 13–20 · L. Croft, *John Fielden's Todmorden* (1994) · A. Secord, 'Corresponding interests: artisans and gentlemen in nineteenth-century natural history', *British Journal for the History of Science*, 27 (1994), 383–408 · L. H. Grindon, *Manchester walks and wild-flowers: an introduction to the botany and rural beauty of the district* [1859], 128–9 · B. Carrington, draft memorial of Abraham Stansfield, Manchester Museum, botany department, B. Carrington MSS · W. B. Crump and C. Crossland, *The flora of the parish of Halifax* (1904), lx–lxi · W. J. Hooker, W. Borrer, and others, *Supplement to the English botany of the late Sir J. E. Smith and Mr. Sowerby*, 3 (1843), 2840 · W. J. Hooker, W. Borrer, and others, *Supplement to the English botany of the late Sir J. E. Smith and Mr. Sowerby*, 4 (1849), 2907 · R. Buxton, *A botanical guide to the flowering plants, ferns, mosses, and algae, found indigenous within sixteen miles of Manchester* (1849), x, xiv · J. Travis, *Round about Todmorden, its hills and dales* (1890), 3 · Roberts Leyland correspondence, Calderdale Central Library, Halifax
Archives Calderdale Central Library, Halifax, Roberts Leyland corresp. · NHM, William Wilson corresp. · Warrington Central Library, William Wilson corresp.
Likenesses West End Studio, Hebden Bridge, photograph, Liverpool Museum, botany department, A. A. Dallman MSS
Wealth at death herbarium to the Todmorden Botanical Society: Foster, 'John Nowell'

Nowell, Laurence (*c.*1516–1576). *See under* Nowell, Laurence (1530–*c.*1570).

Nowell, Laurence (1530–*c.*1570), antiquary, was the second son of Alexander Nowell of Read Hall, Whalley, Lancashire, and Grace, daughter of Rafe Catherall of Mitton in the same county. About 1540 his family moved to Woolden Manor, Eccles, near Manchester. By 1550 he had matriculated at Christ Church, Oxford, where in April he was elected to the second rank of philosophers, and by October had become lector in mathematics. He graduated BA in 1552, and his name appears in the buttery books as late as December 1554. While at Oxford, he apparently had a dispute with Francis Alford, also of Christ Church, that may have led him to depart for Paris in late 1553. After visiting Rouen, Antwerp, and Louvain, he returned to

Oxford but soon set out for Paris via Dieppe. He then journeyed to Geneva to become tutor of two of the sons of Sir James Harington of Exton, Rutland, and in 1557–8 went from Venice to Padua and Rome. Although these visits coincided with Queen Mary's reign, Nowell was neither a religious refugee nor an ordained churchman like his cousin and namesake the future dean of Lichfield.

Shortly after Queen Elizabeth's accession, Nowell returned home and represented Knaresborough, Yorkshire, in her first parliament that sat from 25 January until 8 May 1559. He may have owed his seat to the patronage of Sir Ambrose Cave, chancellor of the duchy of Lancaster. Before the session ended he went into Wiltshire, probably with William Lambarde. If so, it was his earliest known association with this friend who shared his scholarly interest in Old English. Nowell continued exploring the realm, visiting Kent, Chichester, the Isle of Wight, and Northampton. His travels were interrupted by an illness in late 1559, but in 1560 he visited his family in Lancashire and then sailed to Ireland. During his journeys, he kept a commonplace book (University of California at Los Angeles, special collections 170/529) in which he made notes principally from classical works. It was probably not until 1561 that he began to study Anglo-Saxon, which he learned by using as cribs the Latin equivalents of the Old English Bede, the Old English Orosius, the Anglo-Saxon laws, and Aelfric's *Grammar and Glossary*, all of which he was in part at least to transcribe or translate. By early 1563 at the latest he was residing at Sir William Cecil's house in the Strand, London, where he made a transcription (BL, Add. MS 43703) of several Anglo-Saxon texts, including the Old English Bede and the Anglo-Saxon Chronicle. He also owned what is now BL, Cotton MS Vitellius A.xv in the British Library, the collection of Anglo-Saxon writings sometimes known as the Nowell codex, which contains the only surviving text of *Beowulf*.

Thomas Randolph had recommended Nowell as a scholar and cartographer to Cecil, who by June 1563 appointed Nowell as the tutor of his ward and future son-in-law, Edward de Vere, seventeenth earl of Oxford. About that time, having requested employment as Cecil's map maker in a Latin letter, Nowell produced for him a pocket map of the British Isles (BL, Add. MS 62540) on which he sketched images of himself and of Cecil. His other maps, except for four lost after Lambarde presented them to Nowell's friend Adrian Stokes in 1574, are at the British Library (Cotton MS Domitian xviii).

On or about 25 March 1567, having named Lambarde as one of the executors of his last will and testament, Nowell departed for the continent in order to become more fluent in foreign languages and to pursue other studies. While at the University of Paris, he forwarded to Lambarde a transcript of the *Gesta Normannorum ducum* of William of Jumièges (University of Virginia, MS Hench 6435a, 4). His friend Daniel Rogers, whom he met in Paris at this time, addressed three poems to him (Hunt., MS HM 31188), one of them dated in July 1569. Nowell moved on to Venice and Padua and then enrolled at the University of Vienna. Next he travelled to Basel and was at Leipzig by August 1569.

The last record of his whereabouts is his October matriculation at the University of Freiburg im Breisgau. That same year his cousin Robert Nowell of Gray's Inn bequeathed to him a £5 annuity and some satin cloth. In 1571, having had no message from him for two years, his brothers Charles, John, and Thomas, and seven others petitioned the court of requests to declare Nowell dead and to order Lambarde to release their inheritances. Lambarde reluctantly granted their petition but retained the library Nowell had left in his custody, not only making full use of his manuscripts and books in his own writings but also sharing them with friends. Over the centuries this collection has been widely scattered, especially after the final dispersal of the Lambarde library in 1924.

Nowell's greatest legacy is the *Vocabularium Saxonicum*, used by generations of lexicographers in manuscript until it was printed as recently as 1952. Although he was familiar with more than half the extant corpus of Old English poetry, his major interest was texts with obvious historical or topographical content, particularly Anglo-Saxon laws. He made the first critical edition of Alfred's laws along with a modern English translation (BL, Henry Davis collection, MS 59 [M 30]), which was used by Lambarde for his *Archaionomia* (1568). He studied other early laws including the code known as Cnut I–II (Canterbury Cathedral, MS Lit. E 2). No complete inventory of his transcripts and manuscripts can be compiled since discoveries continue to be made. Some of the other most important ones can be found in the libraries of Canterbury Cathedral, Glasgow University, Lambeth Palace, Westminster Abbey, and the Bodleian, Oxford. Although he is best known for his pioneering work in Anglo-Saxon studies, his journeys abroad point to a deep interest in learning about the past that extended well beyond the history of England.

Until recently, Laurence Nowell the antiquary has been confused with **Laurence Nowell** (*c*.1516–1576), who became dean of Lichfield, and who had the same paternal grandparents. The latter Laurence Nowell was the third son of John Nowell (*d*. 1526) of Read Hall, Whalley, Lancashire, and his second wife, Elizabeth, daughter of Robert Kay of Rochdale. After entering Brasenose College, Oxford, in 1536, he migrated to Cambridge University to study logic, graduating BA in 1542. Oxford incorporated this BA and awarded him an MA in 1544. Two years later he became master of the grammar school at Sutton Coldfield, Warwickshire. In 1550 the town's corporation, as the school's patrons, charged him in chancery with neglect of duty, but he appealed to the privy council, which issued an order forbidding the warden and fellowship of Sutton to remove him from office. In November 1550 Nicholas Ridley, bishop of London, ordained him deacon. Upon Queen Mary's accession he took shelter with Sir John Perrot in Pembrokeshire and later joined his brother Alexander *Nowell on the continent, though it is not known where Laurence finally took refuge. In 1558, when he returned home, he was promoted archdeacon of Derby, and in 1560 dean of Lichfield. In the convocation of 1563 he voted with Alexander, now dean of St Paul's, to modify church ceremonies. That year he obtained the prebend of Ferring in

Chichester Cathedral and the rectories of Haughton and Drayton Basset in Staffordshire. In 1566 he received a prebend in York Minster, and in 1567 pleaded with Archbishop Matthew Parker on behalf of two nonconformists.

Nowell married Mary Glover, a widow with two sons, and between 1567 and 1574 they had four daughters and five sons, including his namesake heir who matriculated at Brasenose College in 1590. With Alexander, Laurence served as executor of their brother Robert's will in 1569. The next year, he denied the charge of Peter Morwent, a prebendary of Lichfield, that he had made seditious speeches against Queen Elizabeth and Robert Dudley, earl of Leicester. In 1575 he bought an estate in Sheldon and some lands in Coleshill, Warwickshire. In his will, dated 17 October 1576, he named Alexander and his half-brother John Towneley his overseers. He was dead by 22 November, when his successor as dean, George Boleyn, was installed. He was probably buried at Weston, Derbyshire.

RETHA M. WARNICKE

Sources C. T. Berkhout, 'Laurence Nowell (1530–ca. 1570)', *Literature and philology*, ed. H. Damico, D. Fennema, and K. Lenz (1998), vol. 2 of *Medieval scholarship: biographical studies on the formation of a discipline*, 3–17 [incl. bibliography and list of Nowell's MSS] · C. T. Berkhout, 'The pedigree of Laurence Nowell the antiquary', *English Language Notes*, 23/2 (1985), 15–26 · R. M. Warnicke, 'Note on a court of requests case of 1571', *English Language Notes*, 11 (1973–4), 250–56 · R. M. Warnicke, 'The Laurence Nowell manuscripts in the British Library', *British Library Journal*, 5 (1979), 201–2 · R. Flower, 'Laurence Nowell and the discovery of England in Tudor times', *PBA*, 21 (1935), 46–73 · A. B. Grosart, ed., *The Townley Hall manuscripts: the spending of the money of Robert Nowell of Reade Hall, Lancashire, brother of Dean Alexander Nowell, 1568–1580* (1877) · *Laurence Nowell's 'Vocabularium Saxonicum'*, ed. A. H. Marckwardt (1952) · HoP, *Commons, 1558–1603*, 3.149 · U. Cal., Los Angeles, Department of Special Collections, 170/529 · M. McKisack, *Medieval history in the Tudor age* (1971) · records of the court of requests, proceedings, PRO, REQ 2/45/13, fols. 1–2 · BL, Lansdowne MS 6 · R. Churton, *The life of Alexander Nowell, dean of St Paul's* (1809) · *CSP dom.*, 1547–80, 393 · CCC Cam., MS 113, no. 340 · prerogative court of Canterbury, wills, PRO, PROB 11/59 · G. Jack, *Beowulf: a student's guide* (1994), 1

Likenesses sketch, BL, Add. MS 62540

Nowell, Ralph. *See* Ralph (*d.* in or after 1151).

Nowell, Samuel (1634–1688). *See under* Nowell, Increase (*bap.* 1593, *d.* 1655).

Nowell, Thomas (1730?–1801), Church of England clergyman and religious controversialist, was the son of Cradock Nowell of Cardiff. He entered Oriel College, Oxford, in 1746, and the following year won the duke of Beaufort's exhibition. He graduated BA in 1750, became an exhibitioner on the foundation of Bishop Robinson in 1752, and proceeded MA in 1753. Oriel elected him a fellow the same year, and he served his college as junior treasurer (1755–7), senior treasurer (1757–8), and dean (1758–60 and 1763).

Around the age of thirty Nowell first revealed his taste for controversy. In 1759 Dr Benjamin Buckler had preached a flippant sermon at All Souls College, Oxford, entitled *Elisha's Visit to Gilgal, and his Healing the Pot of Pottage, Symbollically Explain'd*. Nowell anonymously wrote a rebuttal, *A Dissertation upon that Species of Writing called Humour, when Applied to Sacred Subjects* (1760). In it he argued that biblical topics deserved to be treated on all occasions with 'decency and seriousness' rather than humour and levity.

Nowell was public orator of Oxford University, 1760–76. Oriel nominated him junior proctor in 1761, and he worked for many years as secretary to the chancellor of the university. He became principal of St Mary Hall in 1764 and rapidly proceeded BD and DD in the same month as that appointment. Having become well established in Oxford society, in 1764 he married Sarah Munday (the daughter of Sir Thomas Munday, Oxford upholsterer). Their son Thomas died in childhood in 1768. He resigned his Oriel fellowship on his marriage. Lord North appointed him in 1771 to the regius professorship of modern history at Oxford, and he held this post, and also that of the principalship of St Mary Hall, until his death. Although he seemed to be an active public and private lecturer, he published no historical works.

Nowell's high-church piety and severity came into action in 1768, when Oxford expelled six Methodist students at St Edmund Hall for disreputable backgrounds and trades, illiteracy in Latin and Greek, holding methodistical doctrines of 'faith without works' and perfectionism, attending and preaching and praying at lay, plebeian conventicles, and showing irreverent disrespect to university authorities. Sir Richard Hill anonymously wrote *Pietas Oxoniensis* (1768) to criticize this expulsion. Nowell, with the help of the vice-chancellor's imprimatur and the Clarendon Press, defended the university's actions in *An Answer to a Pamphlet Entitled 'Pietas Oxoniensis' … in a Letter to the Author* (1768). In this work Nowell argued that the undergraduates' teaching amounted to the 'impeaching or depraving the doctrine of the Church of England, the book of common prayer … and discipline established in the church' (*Hist. U. Oxf.* 5: *18th-cent. Oxf.*, 463). Holding prayer meetings in private houses was contrary to the rules of the university, the canons of the church, and the statutes of the realm. Nowell's pamphlet was sufficiently popular to merit a second edition with large additions and a postscript, in 1769.

The resulting pamphlet war pitted Hill's partisans against Nowell and his defenders. Hill, in addition to his own reply to Nowell, had Augustus Toplady (first pseudonymously as Clerus), John Fellows (pseudonymously as Philanthropos), George Whitefield, and the scurrilous pseudonymous author No Methodist as allies. On the other hand, John Wesley refused to intervene because he approved of Nowell's interpretation that the seventeenth article did not teach Calvinist doctrine, and others, including the whiggish *Monthly Review*, supported the expulsion.

Nowell's next brush with controversy occurred in 1772, when he was chosen to preach before the House of Commons on 30 January, the annual national fast on the anniversary of the execution of Charles I. These 30 January sermons to parliament had in the past three decades generally tended to preach the value of unity and the danger of faction, whether royal or parliamentary. Instead, Nowell took a strongly high-church and partisan pro-court tone. His sermon compared the virtues of George III to those of the innocent, divinely appointed, and patriotic Moses and Charles I. He also implied that the current House of Commons in its oppositionism to George III was like Korah, who opposed Moses, or the 'factious' and 'turbulent' Long Parliament, which defied 'the royal martyr' Charles I. Furthermore, he declared the 'pretended grievances', remonstrances, and petitions of rights of the 'levelling' subjects of Moses, Charles, and George to have been no possible apology for rebellion by such 'enemies of the constitution', and advocated the power of religion (even if doctrinally false) to maintain men in obedience. A pro forma audience of the speaker and four other members of the house had sat in the cold January congregation, and these five reflexively voted without debate for thanks and orders to print on the following day.

It was only after the printed version of Nowell's sermon appeared that objections to the Commons imprimatur on its ultra-monarchist high-church arguments began. The first demurrals were raised on 21 February, when it became apparent that the house had inadvertently thanked and ordered to print material they now found objectionable. In the course of the debate Thomas Townshend threw the sermon three times on the table, declaring it ought to be burnt by the common hangman. The house agreed for the moment that it could not consistently censure something it had already thanked. It instead moved that in future, no thanks be given until the printed version of the sermon had been seen. Lord North reminded the house of the vote of thanks, and carried a motion for the order of the day.

The second debate about Nowell's sermon, on 25 February, began with a motion to expunge the vote of thanks from the votes of the house. After hearing the three most potentially offensive passages read aloud, the house expunged the entry of thanks without a division. Parliamentary repercussions were slight. Even Nowell's rural 'tory' supporters abandoned him. George III, after a conversation with Lord Denbigh, informed North that 'the Country Gentlemen were at first hurt that they were not supported in defending Dr. Noel, but that now they are appeased' (Donne, 1.91–3).

The sermon raised a great deal more interest 'out of doors'. Edward Gibbon noted on the first day of Commons debate about Nowell that the 'Sermon of Dr Knowell' had been paradoxically helped by the allegations that it contained 'arbitrary, Tory, High flown doctrines'. Gibbon wrote that Nowell's publisher was 'much obliged to the Right Honourable Tommy Townshend' for profits, since controversial sermons generally inspired more purchases than politically benign ones (*Letters of Edward Gibbon*, 309–10). It was also clear that the controversy had strong echoes of the earlier furore following Dr Sacheverell's sermon, 'more particularly since Nowell had originally preached the offending sermon in 1766 without provoking any comment whatsoever' (*Hist. U. Oxf.* 5: *18th-cent. Oxf.*, 169).

With his hopes of advancement in the church wrecked by mid-1772, Nowell spent many of the remaining years of his life either at St Mary Hall, or in his 'beautiful villa at Iffley', the Manor House, which overlooked a lock on the Isis 2 miles from Oxford. Johnson and Boswell dined with him at Iffley in 1784. Johnson, who had strongly approved of the expulsion of the six Oxford students, told Boswell, 'Sir, the Court will be very much to blame if Nowell is not promoted', an opinion that Boswell repeated to Nowell. Boswell later reflected in writing the *Life* that 'Dr. Nowell will ever have the honour which is due to a lofty friend of our monarchical constitution', since he was opposed only on account of 'turbulence and faction' (Boswell, *Life*, 4.296). Amid conversations about scandalous clergy and the coarse speech of MPs, the 'well entertained and happy' guests 'drank "Church and King" after dinner with true Tory cordiality' (Marshall, 50–52).

By 1800 the septuagenarian Nowell still read 'on certain days of every week during term, giving without interruption both public and private lectures, in person for the most part, and by substitution when his impaired health confines him at home' (*DNB*). He died at his lodgings in St Mary Hall on 23 September 1801. No edited volume of Nowell's sermons or writings was compiled after his death, as was common with other Georgian clergy. His more lasting legacy was in his benefactions to Oxford. He established a fund for rebuilding the western side of the quadrangle at the hall; some portion was rebuilt, and an additional storey was raised on the south side. Under Nowell's will certain shares held by him in the Oxford Canal navigation were used to found an exhibition at St Mary Hall.   J. J. CAUDLE

Sources Foster, *Alum. Oxon.* · *GM*, 1st ser., 42 (1772), 93 · *GM*, 1st ser., 71 (1801), 963 · *The correspondence of King George the Third with Lord North from 1768 to 1783*, ed. W. B. Donne, 1 (1867) · *Letters of Edward Gibbon*, ed. J. E. Norton, 3 vols. (1956) · Boswell, *Life* · E. Marshall, *An account of Iffley* (1874) · A. Wood, *The ancient and present state of … Oxford*, ed. J. Pechell (1773) · *Hist. U. Oxf.* 5: *18th-cent. Oxf.* · G. Rupp, *Religion in England, 1688–1791* (1986) · S. L. Ollard, *The six students of St Edmund Hall expelled from the University of Oxford in 1768* (1911) · [J. Hurdis], *A word or two in vindication of the University of Oxford and of Magdalen College in particular, from the posthumous aspersions of Mr Gibbon* (privately printed, Oxford, [1800]) · *DNB*
Likenesses oils, Oriel College, Oxford

Nowers [Nower, Noer], **Francis** (d. **1670**), heraldic painter, belonged to a family long established at Ashford and Pluckley in Kent. Nowers was employed for many years in the ordinary avocation of a heraldic painter, especially during the time of the Commonwealth. In 1660 he edited the fourth edition of John Guillim's *A Display of Heraldrie* before the restoration of Charles II, after which event a new edition was issued, omitting certain additions under the Commonwealth. In 1661 he provided heraldry for the lord mayor's show. Nowers resided in Bartholomew Lane, near the Exchange, in London; in 1670 a fire broke out there, in which Nowers, with two of his children and two servants, perished. Administration of his effects was granted on 15 August 1670 to his widow, Hester (d. 1700), daughter of Isaac Bargrave, dean of Canterbury. Francis Nowers was father of Beaupré Nowers (d. 1690), afterwards fellow of Christ's College, Cambridge.

L. H. CUST, *rev.* ANNETTE PEACH

Sources *DNB* · Venn, *Alum. Cant.* · E. Croft-Murray, *Decorative painting in England, 1537–1837*, 1 (1962), 234 · private information (2004) [A. D. Nowers]

Nowlan, James (1855–1924),

sports administrator, was born in Kilkenny. His working profession was as a cooper, but his main interest lay with the Irish cultural revival of the late nineteenth century. From the late 1870s he became a keen advocate of the Irish language movement and of traditional pastimes. As an alderman of Kilkenny and a supporter of radical nationalist politics, he rose quickly through the ranks of the Gaelic Athletic Association (GAA), which in its formative decades was an organization closely linked with the physical force nationalism of the Irish Republican Brotherhood. In 1896 he was elected chairman of the Kilkenny GAA county board, and was thus able to take his seat on the central council of the GAA. In 1899 he was elected vice-president of the association, a post he held for two years.

In 1901 Nowlan was elected GAA president, a post he held for twenty years, a record that remains unsurpassed. While president, he oversaw the reinvigoration of the GAA and its promotion to its position as the largest sporting organization within Ireland. There was a steady growth in the number of GAA clubs, the rules of hurling and Gaelic football were refined so that both games grew in popularity as a public spectacle, and the GAA's hitherto unstable finances were put on a sound footing. He also promoted the close linkage which developed between the GAA and Sinn Féin. In 1913 he encouraged all GAA members to join the Irish Volunteers so that they could 'learn to shoot straight'. In 1916, in the wake of the Easter rising, he was arrested and imprisoned by the British, who saw him as a leading voice within the forces of Irish nationalism. Throughout the remainder of that period Nowlan was regularly arrested because of his links with the nationalist movement. In October 1919 Nowlan was arrested in Cork and was found to be in possession of a revolver and cartridges. Despite his pleas that he needed the firearm to protect the GAA's gate takings he was sentenced to twenty-eight days in prison.

In 1921 Nowlan announced his official resignation from the post of GAA president. Although he was given the title of honorary president for life, his links to Sinn Féin and the Irish Republican Brotherhood placed him out of step with wider developments following the Anglo-Irish treaty in 1921. He died on 30 June 1924 at the Jervis Street Hospital, Dublin, from long-term illnesses that were exacerbated by his periods of imprisonment, and was buried on 2 July. He never married and, having no children, left his estate to Luke O'Toole, long-serving secretary of the GAA.

MIKE CRONIN

Sources M. de Búrca, *The G.A.A.: a history of the Gaelic Athletic Association* (1980) · W. F. Mandle, *The Gaelic Athletic Association and Irish nationalist politics, 1884–1924* (1987) · C. Lúthchleas Gael, *A century of service, 1884–1984* (1984) · *Irish Independent* (2 July 1924)
Archives Gaelic Athletic Association Archives, Croke Park, Dublin, Central Council Minutes
Likenesses photograph, repro. in de Búrca, *The G.A.A.*, following p. 120
Wealth at death £892 1s. 10d.: probate, 1 Dec 1924, *CGPLA Éire*

Noy [Noye], William (1577–1634),

lawyer and politician, was the son of Edward Noye of Carnanton, Mawgan in Pyder, Cornwall, and his wife, Jane Crabbe.

Early life Noy matriculated at Exeter College, Oxford, on 27 April 1593 but left the university without a degree. He was admitted a member of Lincoln's Inn on 24 October 1594 and was called to the bar in 1602. He was a bencher from 1618, a reader in autumn 1622, and treasurer in 1632. He was married and had three children—two sons, Edward (*d.* 1636) and Humphrey (1614–1679), and a daughter, Katherine—but nothing is known of his wife.

Noy's professional progress, if unspectacular, was perfectly respectable. After being called to the bar he laboured with modest success in private practice, building a loyal clientele and earning the reputation as a popular and skilled barrister on circuit. By 1614 he had attracted the attention of no less a figure than Sir Francis Bacon, then the attorney-general, who subsequently nominated him an official recorder for the courts of common law. Under Bacon's sponsorship he joined a committee of distinguished lawyers and judges to undertake a comprehensive review of English statute law. Their aim was to clarify and rationalize existing statutes as part of Bacon's broader programme of law reform. His work on that committee greatly enhanced his reputation as an authority on English law and widened significantly his range of contacts among important figures of the legal profession. It also prepared him to take a leading role in the House of Commons in subsequent parliamentary debates over legal matters.

Parliamentary politician Noy served as an MP for constituencies in his native Cornwall in every parliament up to the close of the 1620s. He represented Grampound in James I's first two parliaments (1604–11 and 1614), Helston in his third (1621), and Fowey in his fourth (1624). In 1625 he represented St Ives, and in 1628 was returned a second time from Helston. He lost little time making his mark as an MP. As early as 1610 he could be found addressing colleagues on significant and controversial matters—advocating, for instance, resistance to any crown-sponsored attempts to restrain parliamentary debate, or urging MPs to consult with constituents before agreeing to the final terms of the great contract. It was in the parliament of 1621, however, that he emerged as a leading figure, one of the 'chiefest pilots', in the House of Commons. He spoke frequently on a wide range of issues, served on numerous committees, and helped draft a variety of important bills, such as those for the regulation of monopolies and for the prohibition of trade in judicial offices. Indeed, he remained a dedicated advocate for law reform throughout the 1620s.

Noy's early reputation as an ideological opponent of the Stuart regime derived largely from the role he played in the singular controversies of the later 1620s. He served as a legal adviser to the Commons committee which drew up charges against the duke of Buckingham. He took a very hard line against the forced loan of 1626 and even acted as defence counsel for one of the 'five knights', Sir Walter Erle. In the 1628 parliament he responded to the growing concerns raised by the five knights' case about the crown's use of arbitrary arrest and imprisonment by advocating the passage of a habeas corpus act, which would have restated the law and imposed stricter guarantees for swift access to the writ. When that proposal was rejected by the Commons, he became an outspoken champion of the petition of right. He also took a firm stand in the early months of 1629 against the king's claim to levy tonnage and poundage without statutory authority, and indeed, had already served as defence counsel for the notorious firebrand Richard Chambers when he was prosecuted for failure to pay the levy.

However, it would be misleading to read into these positions a pattern of consistent or reflexive opposition to royal authority. Noy's response in these matters was almost always based on a careful, lawyerly reading of the specific issues, and often derived from a wish to create a compromise among the various political interests. He sought to mediate both the major conflicts of 1628–9, over the petition of right and tonnage and poundage, by proposing fundamentally conservative, declaratory legislation which simultaneously recognized the legitimate claims and needs of the crown while protecting the long-term legal interests of the subject. He was not a party-line politician—he refused, for instance, to support parliament's so-called protestant 'war policy' which advocated England's involvement in the defence of the Palatinate during the Thirty Years' War—and, for all of his opposition to particular crown initiatives, he was not by nature hostile to royal interests. Indeed, he maintained a healthy and positive relationship with the crown and cultivated numerous personal and professional connections at court. During the early 1620s he served as an adviser to Prince Charles, and in 1624 accepted the prince's nomination to the seat at Fowey. Three years later he assumed a prominent position on the government's commission on fees, and in the same year worked closely with the attorney-general and solicitor-general to arbitrate a trade dispute between the Muscovy Company and local merchants in the north. He was a close confidant and political client of the earl of Bridgewater (the duke of Buckingham's great defender in the parliament of 1626) and on at least one occasion served as legal counsel to Lord Willoughby, Charles I's future lord great chamberlain. Archbishop Laud became a friend and admirer as well.

Like many of his contemporaries, Noy travelled comfortably in a variety of professional and political circles and however strongly he may have felt about particular disagreements he was unwilling to allow temporary political differences to create permanent divisions. While he sometimes undoubtedly trimmed his sails to conform to majority opinion in the Commons and subsequently to assuage his colleagues in Charles I's government, he seems on the whole to have exercised remarkable independence of judgement, and was generally considered a man of integrity. His appointment in 1631 as attorney-

general to Charles I therefore seems somewhat less surprising than some of his contemporaries made it appear.

Attorney-general, 1631–1634 Noy's appointment seems to have left him curiously unimpressed. He is famously reported initially to have responded to the king's offer by asking about his wages and, rather gracelessly, by expressing concern about his potential loss of income. He then compounded the error by accepting the post without even offering the king customary thanks. If the slight was overlooked it was no doubt because Charles I sensed that he was getting in Noy precisely the kind of attorney-general he wanted: an extremely competent, learned, experienced lawyer whose legal advice would be sound, accurate, and dependable, and whose decisions, moreover, would never be compromised by extraneous political considerations. It has been argued that in terms of policy making Noy's appointment represented a departure—and a notable degradation of the office—since, unlike his great predecessors such as Coke, Bacon, or Egerton, he was not expected to act in a political capacity or to serve as a political adviser. He was a 'functionary' who was to provide legal advice (or advocacy) without regard to its political impact (Jones, 'Gamaliel', 217). To that extent he did indeed exemplify one of the principal failings of Charles I's government: its misguided belief that the law could be used to pursue government policies without long-term political consequences.

In the event Noy's three-year tenure as attorney-general was marked by controversy. He gained notoriety early on by seeming to direct much of his prosecutorial zeal toward puritans. In 1632 he took responsibility for prosecuting the crown's suit in the exchequer chamber against the feoffees for impropriations, a London-based organization whose efforts to buy up lay impropriations—with a view to guaranteeing better compensation for ministers, lecturers, and schoolmasters—had drawn the government's ire. Charles I and Archbishop Laud objected in principle to lay control over church appointments and were concerned—not without reason—that this group was misappropriating its funds to subsidize puritan lectureships. The attorney-general successfully moved the court to dissolve the organization and confiscate its assets.

Noy's first two criminal prosecutions likewise suggested an underlying antipathy toward puritans. They involved in turn Henry Sherfield and William Prynne—both, ironically, fellow benchers of Lincoln's Inn. Sherfield was cited in Star Chamber in February 1633 for smashing a stained-glass window in the parish church of St Edmund's, Salisbury. At first sight the transgression hardly seemed worthy of a crown prosecution, but in the event it involved more than a simple act of vandalism. Sherfield's fellow vestrymen had already decided to remove the window in question and replace it with clear glass, but they had been explicitly denied permission to do so by their bishop, John Davenant. Sherfield was fully aware of these circumstances and therefore appeared to have proceeded in open defiance of the ordinary. It was that, rather than his iconoclasm, which attracted the attention of the crown. Charles I and Archbishop Laud were determined to make an example of Sherfield. The king himself directed Noy to bring the case in Star Chamber—despite numerous highly placed pleas for clemency on Sherfield's behalf—and, once conviction had been secured and a fine imposed (£500), intervened again, personally drafting Sherfield's submission to ensure its maximum effect.

Noy's prosecution of Prynne in Star Chamber evolved in similar fashion. Prynne was charged with seditious libel in 1633 after the publication of *Histriomastix*, his famous attack on the contemporary theatre. The work was ostensibly condemned both for its implicit criticism of Queen Henrietta Maria (whose enjoyment of theatre and frequent participation in plays were well known) and for its broader, insinuating comparisons between contemporary English government and Nero's Rome. Noy's own views on the work are unclear. If Prynne is to be believed, Noy had found nothing worthy of condemnation in the book and had proceeded only under pressure from Archbishop Laud. However, that claim was made long after Noy's death, during the trial of Laud, when Prynne had every reason to shift blame toward the archbishop. It accords uncomfortably with Noy's diligent pursuit of the crown's complaint against Prynne and his reported enjoyment at witnessing Prynne's subsequent suffering in the stocks. Moreover, in May 1634, months after Prynne's condemnation and punishment, Noy threatened Star Chamber prosecution again, this time for a strikingly intemperate letter Prynne had allegedly written to Laud, denouncing the archbishop's participation in the earlier proceedings. This confrontation was particularly bitter and led the attorney-general to claim that Prynne was 'a man without Grace', and to suggest that Prynne should be denied pen and paper during the remainder of his confinement. This outburst may simply have reflected his impatience with the notoriously obstreperous Prynne, rather than, as was alleged, his long-standing antipathy toward puritans in general, but the effect was to solidify his reputation as an enemy of the godly. For his part, Prynne felt personally betrayed by the whole affair. Noy, he claimed 'was formerlye a friende in apparance but an inveterate enemy in trewthe' (Jones, 'Gamaliel', 206).

The infamy which subsequently attached to Noy's tenure as attorney-general really derived, however, from the role he played in creation of Charles I's so-called 'fiscal feudalism'—the attempt to revive ancient crown rights for financial exploitation. He came to be closely associated with three of these projects—forest fines, monopolies, and ship money—but in truth his involvement with each of them was rather limited. It was, in all probability, his idea to resurvey the boundaries of the royal forests in 1634 and he clearly envisioned extending them in order to impose lucrative fines on those who encroached on the resulting 'royal preserves'. But he died before the programme could be fully set in motion and the notorious abuses and extortionate fines which later came to define the programme were the work of other officials and projectors.

The same was really true of the notorious ship money. Noy certainly did the initial investigation into the possibility of levying ship money in 1634, and it seems clear that, drawing on well-established precedents, he certified to its legality. It was also his suggestion that the initial levy should be converted into a monetary rate and that the assessment should be spread more widely across all maritime counties (rather than being imposed as a service just on port towns, as had been the previous practice). It was his recommendation as well that assessment and collection should be placed in the hands of county sheriffs. In the event, neither recommendation was followed in the first instance, but both would come to be adopted in subsequent years and would become the source of considerable political discord. For that reason he came to be seen as responsible for the worst features of the levy, despite the fact that he died months before the first ship money writ was ever drawn.

Noy's association with monopolies was more direct. He had been an outspoken opponent of the whole concept of trade monopolies in the 1620s and had helped draft the one successful piece of restrictive legislation passed in 1624. As attorney-general, however, he found himself responsible for defending the interests of the monopolists themselves. The most glaring case involved the so-called 'Soapers of Westminster', a consortium of investors who incorporated in 1632 for the purposes of manufacturing and selling a new kind of soap. The company was not actually granted a monopoly for either the manufacture or sale of soap, but it was given the right to inspect and subsequently restrict the sale of soaps made by independent manufacturers which did not, in its view, meet its own standards—a right which it exercised repeatedly to restrict the trade of its competitors, thereby effectively achieving the same impact as a monopoly. The independent soapmakers of London protested repeatedly, but to no avail. Many of them therefore defied the terms of the crown's grant to the Westminster company and continued to manufacture and sell their soaps without benefit of the company's inspection. It fell to Noy, under orders from the privy council, to prosecute them in Star Chamber, which he did in November 1633. His success would earn him the condemnation of the Long Parliament in 1640.

Reputation Noy's health declined rapidly from mid-1634. He died on 9 August in the parish of New Brentford and was buried without service two days later in the chancel of the parish church. Predictably perhaps, his death provoked a wide range of responses. He was not, on the whole, a person who inspired deep affection. He lacked the social graces, and could be, by turns, sarcastic, abrasive, petulant, and surly. He had little capacity for the polite courtesies and deferential behaviour which typically defined life at the English court. All the same, it is clear that at least some of his colleagues held him in high regard. Archbishop Laud, for example, claimed to have lost a 'dear friend' and a true supporter of the Church of England, and Anthony Wood's posthumous assessment suggests that that there was a general respect for Noy's professionalism: 'His apprehension (as 'tis said) was quick and clear, his judgement was methodical and solid, his memory was strong, his curiosity deep and searching, his temper patient and cautious, all tempered with an honest bluntishness, far from court insinuation' (Wood, *Ath. Oxon.*, 1.595).

In other circles, of course, Noy's death was treated with relief or as a cause for sober reflection. Henry Burton appended an additional section about him to his book *A Divine Tragedie Lately Acted* (1636), a morality tale designed to demonstrate the wages of sin and the range of God's punishment for transgressors. Noy's seemingly early death was taken as a sign of divine retribution for his support of the Book of Sports, his toleration of sabbath breakers, and his general treatment of the godly—to say nothing of his complicity in Charles I's schemes of fiscal feudalism. Burton claimed that the stone from which he was alleged to have died could not be found after his death (thereby indicating the hand of God), that the cadaver was bloodless, and that the heart was shrivelled like an old leather purse (Jones, 'Gamaliel', 207). Shortly after his death Noy became the subject of a popular London stage farce called *A Projector Lately Dead*, in which he was dissected on stage, 'a hundred proclamations being found in his head, a bundle of moth-eaten records in his mouth and a barrel of soap in his belly'. When parliament finally met again in April 1640, Noy—conveniently dead—became the scapegoat for all of the grievances of the past decade, and was denounced by former colleagues and foes alike as the 'inventor' of the innovations of the personal rule.

Noy's fame and reputation have traditionally rested on his work as a so-called 'opposition' MP in the parliaments in the 1620s, or on his subsequent tenure as attorney-general or, more particularly perhaps, on the seeming political *volte face* which made the second career possible after the first. Along with his colleague Thomas Wentworth he became a symbol of Stuart political opportunism. Contemporary chroniclers denounced him as a turncoat who had abandoned his principles and his political bedfellows in order to advance his own professional career:

> He was for many years the stoutest champion for the subject's liberty, until King Charles entertained him to be his Attorney. No sooner did the King show him the line of advancement, but, quitting all his former inclinations, he wheeled about to the prerogative, and made amends with his future service, for all his former disobligements. (D. Lloyd, *State Worthies*, 1670, 892)

That assessment has varied little over the ensuing centuries. Thomas Carlyle colourfully described Noy as a 'morose, amorphous, cynical Law Pedant, an invincible living heap of learned rubbish: once a Patriot in Parliament, till they made him Attorney General and enlightened his eyes' (T. Carlyle, *Oliver Cromwell's Letters and Speeches*, 2 vols., 1845, 1.74–5) and S. R. Gardiner, while more sensitive to the nuances of Stuart politics, none the less dismissed Noy as 'a dry technical lawyer' with little appreciation of English constitutional law and even less political integrity. Since 'his brain was a mere storehouse of legal facts, it

may have seemed as easy to quote precedents on one side as on the other' (Gardiner, 7.221).

These characterizations, while containing some truth, are generally unfair because they fail adequately to reflect either Noy's genuine professionalism, or the complex and often contrary demands placed on a career politician in the early modern world. He had had a long and distinguished career and was held in high esteem as both an MP and a lawyer. If his subsequent work as attorney-general created enduring political controversy, his legal decisions always reflected an honest and intelligent reading of contemporary law. The scope of his learning was beyond dispute. He wrote or compiled a number of thoughtful and important works on the law, including *A Treatise on the Rights of the Crown* (1634), *A Treatise of the Principall Grounds and Maximes of the Lawes of this Kingdom* (1641), *The Compleat Lawyer* (1651), and at least one volume of contemporary law reports, all of which were published some time after his death, despite the political odium presumably associated with his name. Perhaps his greatest legacy was the learning he passed on to the subsequent generation of lawyers. Among his pupils were Sir Orlando Bridgman, Sir John Maynard, and most notably, Sir Matthew Hale.

JAMES S. HART JR

Sources DNB · J. Rushworth, *Historical collections*, 5 pts in 8 vols. (1659–1701) · W. Notestein, F. H. Relf, and H. Simpson, eds., *Commons debates, 1621*, 2–4 (1935) · W. Notestein and F. H. Relf, eds., *Commons debates for 1629* (1921) · H. Burton, *A divine tragedie lately acted* (1636) · *Diary of Thomas Burton*, ed. J. T. Rutt, 4 vols. (1828); repr. (1974), vol. 2, pp. 444–5 · Wood, *Ath. Oxon.*, 2nd edn · W. J. Jones, '"The Great Gamaliel of the law": Mr Attorney Noye', *Huntington Library Quarterly*, 40 (1976–7), 197–226 · W. J. Jones, *Politics and the bench* (1971) · K. Sharpe, *The personal rule of Charles I* (1992) · S. D. White, *Sir Edward Coke and the grievances of the Commonwealth* (Chapel Hill, 1979) · R. Zaller, *The parliament of 1621: a study in constitutional conflict* (1971) · S. R. Gardiner, *History of England from the accession of James I to the outbreak of the civil war*, 10 vols. (1883–4)

Archives Exeter College, Oxford, MS · Inner Temple, London, MS · Lincoln's Inn, London, MS | BL, Cotton MS, Additional MS · BL, Harley MS · BL, Lansdowne MS

Likenesses W. Faithorne the elder, line engraving, 1674, BM, NPG; repro. in W. Noy, *The compleat lawyer* (1674) · C. Johnson, oils, Exeter College, Oxford · line engraving (after C. Johnson), BM, NPG; repro. in, *The history of the grand rebellion*, 3 vols. (1713)

Wealth at death estates at Carnanton, Mawgan-in-Pyder, and Wartstow, Cornwall

Noyce, (Cuthbert) Wilfrid Francis (1917–1962), mountaineer and writer, was born at Simla, India, on 31 December 1917, the elder son in a family of two sons and a daughter of Sir Frank Noyce (1878–1948) of the Indian Civil Service and his wife, Enid Isabel, daughter of W. M. Kirkus, of Liverpool. He was educated at Charterhouse, where he became head of the school, and in 1936 he went to King's College, Cambridge, as a major scholar. He obtained first-class honours in the classical tripos (part 1, 1939) and in the preliminary examination for part 2 of the modern languages tripos (1940), before graduating BA in 1940 and MA in 1945. In 1939 he joined the Friends' Ambulance Unit, but in 1940 joined the Welsh Guards as a private. Commissioned in the King's Royal Rifle Corps in 1941, he spent the years 1942–6 in India, first as a captain in intelligence and

(Cuthbert) **Wilfrid Francis Noyce** (1917–1962), by Howard Coster, 1953

then as chief instructor at the aircrew mountain centre in Kashmir.

From 1946 until 1950 Noyce was an assistant master teaching modern languages at Malvern College. On 12 August 1950 he married Rosemary Campbell (*b.* 1925/6), daughter of Henry Campbell Davies, and there were two sons. Subsequently he taught for ten years at Charterhouse. In the latter period he served for some years on the Godalming borough council. He retired from teaching in 1961 in order to give more time to writing.

Already, at eighteen, Noyce was a fine rock climber, partly through the influence of a brilliant older companion, J. Menlove Edwards, with whom he climbed regularly between 1935 and 1937. He survived a serious accident on Scafell in 1937, when he fell 180 feet and was magnificently held by Edwards on a rope of which two of the three strands had parted. He was badly injured, especially about the face, and the completeness of his recovery was astonishing. In two early alpine seasons, 1937 (shortly before this accident) and 1938, climbing with either Armand Charlet or Hans Brantschen, both great guides, he made a series of major climbs in very fast times. During the war, when he was stationed in India, his exceptional stamina and capacity to acclimatize were demonstrated when he and Sherpa Angtharkay reached the top of Pauhunri in Sikkim (23,385 ft) fifteen days after leaving Darjeeling.

In 1946, climbing in a gale in the Lake District, Noyce was blown from his holds and broke a leg, and for some years he climbed to more ordinary standards. He was

nevertheless an obvious choice for the 1953 Everest expedition, and at a critical stage it was Noyce and Sherpa Annullu who opened the route to the south col. Ten days later Noyce reached the col again, without oxygen, in support of the successful summit climb. Subsequently he had several impressive seasons in the Alps and one (1961) in the High Atlas, but his major ventures were further afield. In 1957 he was turned back by bad weather just below the top of Machapuchare (22,997 ft), a difficult peak in western Nepal, and in 1960 he led an expedition to Trivor (25,370 ft) in the Karakoram, where Noyce himself was one of the pair that reached the summit. His main reason for joining the Pamirs expedition on which he died was his wish to promote friendship between British and Russian mountaineers.

Noyce was a cultivated, unassuming man with an almost diffident manner. Despite his outstanding achievements, his appreciation of mountains was largely aesthetic and his instincts scholarly and literary. In 1947 he wrote an unusual autobiography, *Mountains and Men*, the first of more than a dozen books. These included two volumes of poetry, *Michael Angelo: a Poem* (1953) and *Poems* (1960); some of the poems were written at 21,000 feet, on Everest. His main reputation was as a mountaineering author. He had a gift for conveying, vividly but with restraint and complete honesty, what mountain experiences were really like. This was skilfully demonstrated in *South Col* (1954), his personal story of Everest and easily his most successful book; but the same approach characterized his two later expedition books, *Climbing the Fish's Tail* (1958) and *To the Unknown Mountain* (1962). An earlier work, *Scholar Mountaineers* (1950), was a study of various historic figures who in different ways were both lovers of mountains and men of thought. He wrote one mountain novel, *The Gods are Angry* (1957). Latterly, he was moving away from purely mountain subjects; in *The Springs of Adventure* (1958) he explored the motives for engaging in any sort of hazardous activity, and in *They Survived* (1962) he made a case study of mankind's will to survive in desperate situations.

Noyce died in the USSR on 24 July 1962, when he and a companion fell, descending from the summit of Garmo Peak (*c.*21,500 ft) in the Pamirs. His wife survived him. His death cut short a literary career of notable achievement in a particular field, but one whose wider promise was not yet fulfilled.   A. D. M. Cox, *rev.*

Sources A. D. M. Cox, 'In memoriam: Cuthbert Wilfrid Frank Noyce, 1917–62', *Alpine Journal*, 67 (1962), 384–91 · *Annual Report of the Council* [King's College, Cambridge] (1963), 56–9 · private information (1981) · personal knowledge (1981) · *CGPLA Eng. & Wales* (1962)

Archives FILM BFI NFTVA, documentary footage

Likenesses H. Coster, photograph, 1953, NPG [*see illus.*]

Wealth at death £33,598 14s. 5d.: probate, 19 Oct 1962, *CGPLA Eng. & Wales*

Noyes, Alfred (1880–1958), poet, was born on 16 September 1880 in St Mark's Road, Wolverhampton, the son of Alfred Noyes, a grocer who later became a teacher, and his wife, Amelia Adams, *née* Rowley. He went to school in

Alfred Noyes (1880–1958), by Howard Coster, 1934

Aberystwyth, where he developed a lifelong enthusiasm for boats and the sea. His father, a devout Anglican, had been prevented by financial difficulties from going to university, but the young Noyes entered Exeter College, Oxford, in 1898. Here he gave much of his time to rowing, and this interest continued throughout his life.

Noyes was supposed to be studying for a degree in English under the aegis of Ernest de Selincourt. Instead of taking his final examinations, however, he travelled to London to fulfil an appointment with Grant Richards, a publisher who had become interested in Noyes's poems, and published them as *The Loom of Years* (1902). It can now be perceived that Noyes's poetry, essentially looking back to his great idol, Tennyson, appealed to a generation of elderly men who dominated the literary establishment of the time. A crucial admirer was R. C. Lehmann, editor of the *Daily News*, who introduced Noyes to H. W. Massingham of *The Nation* and J. A. Spender of the *Westminster Gazette*. These influential periodicals published many of the young writer's poems.

Noyes's most signal triumph came early, in the form of his poem 'The Highwayman', a characteristically atavistic subject. The subject occurred to him when he was twenty-four, living at Bagshot Heath. Noyes records that it was a blustery night that inspired the famous first section:

> The wind was a torrent of darkness among the gusty trees.
> The moon was a ghostly galleon tossed upon cloudy seas.
> The road was a ribbon of moonlight over the purple moor,
> And the highwayman came riding—

> Riding—riding—
> The highwayman came riding, up to the old inn-door.

Readers who do not consciously recall Noyes's name may none the less recognize this piece, as for half a century and more hardly a school anthology was complete without it. The poem was collected, with many in a similar vein, in such volumes as *Forty Singing Seamen* (1907), *Tales of the Mermaid Tavern* (1912), and successive volumes of *Collected Poems* (1910, 1913, 1920). These poems, compounded of books rather than perceptions, were equipped with stirring metres that could be fairly said to have put a spin on the familiar form of the ballad. This formula, resembling that enjoyed in Victorian verse collections, ensured that for a time Noyes was lauded as the true successor of Tennyson. Noyes himself was an explicit opponent of anything that he deemed to be contemporary realism. His book *Some Aspects of Modern Poetry* (1924) pillories various unnamed writers as 'destructive forces'.

For some time now, Noyes had been able to earn his living by writing verse. He supplemented this by giving lectures in the United States. He had strong connections with America through his wife, (Kate) Garnett Upham, *née* Daniels (1881/2–1926), whom he had married on 25 July 1907; she was the daughter of the American consul, Colonel Byron Gordon Daniels. The first of Noyes's tours was suggested in 1911 by Frederick A. Stokes, his American publisher, and arranged by an agency, William B. Feakins Inc. Noyes was invited in 1913 to give the Lowell lecture at Harvard; his chosen title was 'The sea in English literature'. His delivery was no doubt enhanced by a resonant voice, a sturdy physique, and a forehead of distinction emphasized by his increasing baldness. Out of this performance came (in 1914) an appointment as Murray professor of English literature at Princeton University. There he lectured twice a week for half of each college year. Among his auditors were Edmund Wilson and F. Scott Fitzgerald. He continued in this post until 1923. Necessarily, his tenure was interrupted by the First World War, and although he was rejected for military service on the grounds of poor eyesight, 1916 found him working for the Foreign Office in the news room, the precursor of the Ministry of Information. Here he got into trouble for writing a book about methods of trapping enemy submarines. The censure was lifted, however, when it was found that all the information supplied by Noyes was already in the public domain.

Noyes's first wife died suddenly in 1926, shortly after they had visited the monastery at Roncesvalles. Within the year, Noyes entered the Roman Catholic church, and on 27 September 1927 married Mary Angela Weld-Blundell, *née* Mayne (b. 1889/90), herself a member of an old Catholic family, and the widow of an officer killed in the war. They settled first in London, where Noyes had preserved his many literary acquaintances, and, from 1929, on the Isle of Wight. From 1926 to 1930 Noyes produced a three-volume history of science called *The Torch-Bearers*. More importantly, however, and one of the fruits of his conversion, was a biography of Voltaire (1936), which sought to exculpate that philosopher from charges of atheism.

During the Second World War, Noyes moved with his wife and their three young children to Canada and the United States, where he continued to give his lectures. His vision had continued to deteriorate, and a disastrous operation for glaucoma in the mid-1940s ensured that he would never read again. The Noyes family returned to the Isle of Wight in 1949, where Noyes managed to continue with his studies. As late as 1957 Noyes produced a book persuasively seeking to exonerate the Irish patriot Roger Casement from authorship of some homosexual diaries with which he had been smeared as part of the prosecution in a trial for treason. Noyes had been shown a typescript of these diaries during his time with the Foreign Office, and had at that time thought them genuine, but came to revise his opinion.

Alfred Noyes died at the Isle of Wight County Hospital in Ryde on 28 June 1958, aged seventy-seven; he was buried at Farringdon on the Isle of Wight. He had received honorary doctorates from Yale, Glasgow, Berkeley, and Syracuse, and in 1918 had been appointed CBE. Little of his work has held public attention, apart from 'The Highwayman', among other anthologized poems. One such poem, found in Philip Larkin's *Oxford Book of Twentieth-Century Verse*, genuinely deserves a place in the canon: 'Spring, and the Blind Children' uses failing eyesight as an allegory of the vain attempt on the part of humankind to understand the providence of God.   PHILIP HOBSBAUM

Sources DNB · A. Noyes, *Two worlds for memory* (1953) · *The Times* (30 June 1958) · W. Jerrold, *Alfred Noyes* (1930) · A. Noyes, *The accusing ghosts* (1957) · m. certs
Archives Hunt. L., corresp. · NL Scot., corresp. and literary MSS | BL, letters to E. H. Blakeney, Add. MS 63088 · Cumbria AS, Carlisle, letters to Lord Howard of Penrith · Dickens House Museum and Library, London, letters to A. W. Edwards · NL Scot., corresp. with *Blackwood's* and literary MSS · U. Leeds, Brotherton L., letters to Edmund Gosse; letters to Thomas Moult · Westm. DA, MSS related to controversy with ecclesiastical censors
Likenesses W. Tittle, lithograph, 1922, Frick Art Reference Library, New York · B. Partridge, chalk and pencil drawing, 1929, NPG · H. Coster, photographs, 1929–34, NPG [*see illus.*] · W. Stoneman, photograph, 1953, NPG · W. King, bronze relief, priv. coll.; copy, Newport Asylum for the Blind, Isle of Wight
Wealth at death £67,452 15s. 11d.: probate, 12 Nov 1958, CGPLA Eng. & Wales

Nsibirwa, Martin Luther (*c*.1885–1945), administrator in Buganda, was born probably in the county of Bugerere, on the eastern side of the kingdom of Buganda, subsequently the heartland of the British Uganda protectorate. He was the son of Kiwana, ceremonial clan head of Kirindi, who, like the other clan heads of Buganda, by the late nineteenth century had little real power. In his early youth Nsibirwa was sent to the royal capital at Mengo to serve in the enclosure of Sir Apolo Kagwa (1864–1927), *katikiro* (chief minister) of the Buganda government. There he received a basic education from Anglican missionaries, from whom he gained his forenames. He remained a committed Anglican for the rest of his life. He married and raised a family, of whom no details survive.

Nsibirwa's first official posting was as a clerk in the *lukiko*, the Buganda parliament. Successful there, he became a *gombolola* (sub-county chief) of Kagwe before being promoted to *saza* (county chief) of Bugerere and then of Singo. In 1928 he was appointed *omuwanika* (treasurer) of Buganda, the most junior of three ministerial posts. Six months later, in 1929, on the resignation of the *katikiro*, Nsibirwa himself was raised to chief minister, a position that he retained for twelve years. In 1937 he was made an MBE.

The colonial government considered Nsibirwa in 1945 (when he was described as 'about 60 years of age') to be 'a strong man … very active, loyal and pro-British' (PRO, CO 536/211–40080/1) but this loyalty provoked the hostility of some of his compatriots at a time of rising national sentiment. He was criticized for being autocratic and out of touch, and was accused of favouritism in his administrative duties. He was seen as representing 'the old school' in Buganda, following his former master, Apolo Kagwa, in the tradition of diligent and firm administration.

Nsibirwa was attacked most vehemently for flouting local custom when he agreed to the remarriage of the *namasole*, the widow of the late *kabaka* (king) Daudi Chwa (1896–1939), who was six months pregnant by a local schoolteacher. Long-established tradition prohibited her remarriage but Nsibirwa, a man of deep religious conviction and a vice-president of the Church Missionary Society, was determined to uphold Christian moral values. He openly supported the union and drove the couple to the wedding in his own car, much to local disgust. He became so isolated in his stand that in July 1941 he was forced to resign from office.

When a series of strikes and riots shook the colonial government in January 1945 Nsibirwa was considered the only man capable of restoring peace and order to Buganda. He was brought out of his enforced retirement and reinstated as *katikiro*. The colonial authorities used him to push through an unpopular land acquisition act widely suspected of being a sinister plot to allow European settlement. Such was the depth of resentment, against Nsibirwa personally and against the government that he represented, that the day after the bill was passed, on 5 September 1945, he was assassinated.

As was his daily custom, Nsibirwa was about to attend morning communion at the Anglican cathedral, Namirembe, Kampala, when he was shot dead on the cathedral steps. He was buried, in the cathedral grounds, the following day. The murder came to symbolize the political disenchantment of many in Buganda both with the Anglican church, when it threatened to displace local custom, and with the chiefs, when they appeared to be collaborating too closely with their British overlords. The *kabaka*, Mutesa II (1924–1969), claimed that Buganda had 'never known so dastardly an outrage' and that the name of his kingdom had been disgraced (*Uganda Herald*). According to the governor, Sir John Hall, for those who committed this 'foul murder of an old and defenceless man on the very threshold of God's House' there could be 'nothing but execration' (ibid.). The assassin, George William Senkatuka, was executed on 6 April 1946, and fourteen others were deported without trial for conspiracy in the crime. But the government's response failed to address the root causes of political and economic discontent. Instead it created new grievances and tensions that exploded in a further wave of riots in Buganda during April 1949. Nsibirwa's assassination exemplified the difficulties confronting Britain in post-war Buganda.

CAROLINE HOWELL

Sources *Uganda Herald* (12 Sept 1945) · D. E. Apter, *The political kingdom in Uganda: a study in bureaucratic nationalism*, rev. 3rd edn (1997) · Buganda affairs: relations with H. H. the kabaka, PRO, CO 536/211–40080/1 · Buganda affairs: death of the katikiro, PRO, CO 536/211–40080/14 · appeals to privy council: Senkatuka, PRO, CO 536/215–40321/3 · 'Note on the resignation of the katikiro of Buganda', 25 July 1941, PRO, CO 536/208–40080/9 · C. E. Stuart, letters, LPL, Lang papers, vol. 184 · A. M. Williams, annual letter, 1941, U. Birm. L., special collections department, Church Missionary Society archive, AF AL 1940–49 · 'Standing committee minutes', 9 Oct 1941, U. Birm. L., special collections department, Church Missionary Society archive, AF 35–49 G3 A7/3 · M. L. Pirouet, *Historical dictionary of Uganda* (1995) · *The Times* (2 Feb 1937)
Likenesses double portrait, photograph (with S. Kulubya), repro. in D. A. Low, *Buganda in modern history* (1971), facing p. 149

Nu, U (1907–1995), prime minister of Burma, was born on 25 May 1907 in Wakema, Myaungmya, Burma, the elder son of U San Htun, merchant, and his wife, Daw Saw Khin. His parents were prosperous traders, selling monks' robes from a drapery store in the Wakema bazaar. According to Burmese tradition, Saturday-born first children were supposed to be quarrelsome, and to induce quarrelsomeness between their parents. Hence he was given the name Nu (Gentle) and was nominally sold to his aunt Daw Gyi and her husband, U Shwe Gon, well-to-do landowners who lived with his parents. Like all Burmese names Nu's was attended by several honorific titles. He was known as Maung Nu as a youth and young man and as U Nu thereafter. He was given a special title of Thakin Nu, as were all the members of the Dobama Asi-ayone (Our Burma Association). It was usual for the members of associations to take a personal title from their membership but Nu never took on this modest claim to fame, although he was known by others as Thakin Nu for most of his adult life.

Nu was educated first at the Wakema Anglo-Vernacular Government School, but he left in 1920 following the school strike called in response to the promotion to university status of Rangoon College. He then attended the new national school in Wakema and, from 1922, Myoma national high school, Rangoon. He had a wayward adolescence, frequently embarrassing his parents by his excessive drinking, and contracting venereal disease from one of many encounters with prostitutes. At the age of eighteen he resolved to follow a Buddhist way of life, and gave up alcohol as a token of his commitment. In the same year, 1925, he entered the University of Rangoon. Graduating in 1929, he became superintendent of a national school at Pantanaw, of which the headmaster was U Thant, later to be secretary-general of the United Nations. In 1931 he eloped with and married Ma Mya Yi, daughter of U Aung Nyein, a wealthy rice miller and president of the

Pantanaw national school committee. Following his marriage (to which his parents-in-law became reconciled) Nu taught in Thongwa before returning in 1934 to Rangoon, where he worked for a Burmese-language newspaper and enrolled as a law student at the University of Rangoon.

In his second spell as a university student Nu was actively involved in the Rangoon University Students' Union, and became a close colleague of Aung San, editor of *Oway*, the students' paper. In 1936 Nu wrote an article in *Oway* which was highly critical of the university's British principal, D. J. Sloss, and for this he was expelled. For several weeks the university students went on strike. Nu was allowed to return, though he left the university without completing his course. The victory of Nu and the students' union marked a new impetus both in student affairs and in opposition to British rule. His subsequent activities in the Dobama Asi-ayone and as organizer of the Nagani (Red Dragon) book club, disseminating nationalist literature, led the government to imprison him in 1940, along with many of his closest colleagues. He was then released by the British authorities in a vain attempt to send him as an emissary to China's Kuomintang leaders.

This was the situation when the Japanese invaded Burma in December 1941. They set up a Burmese government with Ba Maw as leader. Nu initially remained outside the government, but in August 1943 he joined it as foreign minister, although, as he said himself, he was a 'Minister without a Ministry'. He made several visits overseas as a minister and lieutenant for Ba Maw. All this came to an end when the British expelled the Japanese in mid-1945. Nu used his new-found freedom to write a serious study of the effects of Japanese rule in Burma. This first appeared in the Burmese language but J. S. Furnivall, a retired Burma civil servant, assisted Nu in producing an English-language version of his study which eventually appeared under the title *Burma under the Japanese: Pictures and Portraits* (1954). The book was frank about the relationship between the Burmese and their Japanese masters.

When the war ended, Nu retired into private life: however, his move away from politics did not last long. In 1946 he was elected vice-president of the Anti-Fascist People's Freedom League (AFPFL), into which Aung San had brought most of the nationalist elements in Burma. In June 1947 Nu was elected to the nominally non-party role of speaker of the constituent assembly formed to draft a constitution, following the London agreement of January 1947 between Aung San and Clement Attlee. Although the returning British were in a strong position with their military forces, Aung San was able to rival their strength: the AFPFL had emerged as the strongest political movement in Burma, although Ba Maw tried to come forward with a rival organization, financed by the money he had amassed under the Japanese. On the fringe of both these leading organizations there were quasi-military elements only loosely controlled by the rival leaders. Certain of Ba Maw's lieutenants tried to enhance the power of their boss by building up his military power. This rivalry ended in July 1947 when Ba Maw's thugs burst into the secretariat (the political and administrative centre for Burma) and gunned down Aung San and his cabinet. Ba Maw hoped to cause chaos in Aung San's political machine. Fortunately for him, Nu was not present at the ill-fated cabinet meeting and in any case was too popular to be disposed of summarily. The governor, Sir Hubert Rance, was not prepared to see his new political reforms disposed of, and he sent for Nu to ask him to become prime minister. If Rance and Nu had not acted so quickly, there is no doubt that something like civil war would have consumed central Burma. As it was, their action pre-empted opposition.

Nu was able to take advantage of Aung San's charisma to push ahead with political reform. In September 1947 the new constitution was agreed, and in October, Nu signed the treaty of Burmese independence, in London, leading to independence on 4 January 1948 (a date set following Nu's consultations with astrologers). By then Nu had achieved useful administrative changes, although the army (Aung San's principal legacy) was out of control. For several months the rebellious soldiers were almost into the suburbs of Rangoon, but Nu, who had no experience of this kind of politics, was able to return most of the country to something like normal life. He followed Aung San's style by setting up five- and ten-year plans designed to bring about a more stable society. The first ten years of his administration were to be the most successful, and he was able to introduce some of his most cherished objectives.

The army leaders, notably the commander-in-chief General Ne Win, were jealous of Nu's success, and in September 1958 (following a split in the AFPFL and a deteriorating security situation) Nu was persuaded to relinquish power to a caretaker government led by Ne Win, which would restore stability and prepare the country for elections in 1960. However, the military junta followed much the same directions as Nu and his friends. They had promised to get away from the office and lead the country from the field: but this did not happen. Indeed, military rule brought in even more bureaucratic methods. By the time of the 1960 elections it was clear that military rule had little if anything to add to the regular methods of government—that is, a bureaucracy with a veneer of parliamentary control—and the people began to look back to the parliamentary period with nostalgia. Nu returned to power following the elections in February 1960, supported by some of his faithful allies and by a new face on the scene—Aung San Suu Kyi, daughter of Aung San. The army gave way to Nu with ill grace, and despite his renewed popularity he could not feel that he was altogether secure. In March 1962 he was again ousted by Ne Win and the army. Nu had attempted to change the government's policy towards the hill peoples: he endeavoured to bring their leaders back into government, thus challenging one of the main parts of the army's programme. He had also, shortly before the coup, announced a series of nationalization measures.

Following the March 1962 coup many of Nu's lieutenants were gaoled and in some cases executed. Nu himself was not treated so severely, though he was placed under house arrest. In 1967 he was permitted to leave Burma for health reasons. Until 1972 he lived in Thailand, from where he organized opposition to the military government in Burma; he then abandoned politics and went to live quietly in a Buddhist monastery in India. He returned from exile in 1980, at the invitation of Ne Win. He spent the following years translating Buddhist texts. Following the fall of Ne Win in 1988 he formed the Alliance for Peace and Democracy, and declared himself the legitimate prime minister. However, he failed to gain much popular support, and in September 1988 another military junta seized power. Nu was again placed under house arrest, until April 1992. After his release he campaigned on behalf of Aung San Suu Kyi, who he now realized was recognized as the leader of the pro-democracy movement in Burma.

Nu died in Rangoon on 14 February 1995. He was survived by three daughters and two sons, his wife having predeceased him. When U Thant had died, students at Rangoon University had demonstrated their fervent support for his work, causing the university to be closed once again. After Nu's death the army took precautions to avoid a similar demonstration and his funeral therefore was on a limited scale.

HUGH TINKER

Sources *The Times* (15 Feb 1995) · *The Independent* (20 Feb 1995) · U Nu, *U Nu, Saturday's son* (1975) · R. Butwell, *U Nu of Burma* (Stanford, CA, 1963) · H. Tinker, A. Griffin, and S. R. Ashton, eds., *Burma, the struggle for independence, 1944–1948: documents from official and private sources*, 2 vols. (1983–4) · H. R. Tinker, *The union of Burma: a study of the first years of independence*, 4th edn (1967)

Likenesses B. Hardy, photographs, 1949, Hult. Arch. · photograph, 1962, Hult. Arch. · photograph, repro. in *The Times* · photograph, repro. in *The Independent* · photographs, repro. in Tinker, Griffin, and Ashton, eds., *Burma* · photographs, repro. in U Nu, *U Nu, Saturday's son*, between pp. 192 and 193 · photographs, repro. in Butwell, *U Nu of Burma*

Nuce, Thomas (*c.*1545–1617), poet and translator, was probably the fourth son of Clement Newce of Much Hadham, Hertfordshire, citizen and mercer of London (*d.* 1579), and his wife, Mary, daughter of John Davy of Ely, Cambridgeshire. He was admitted fellow-commoner at Peterhouse, Cambridge, in 1559, graduating BA in 1562, whereupon he was elected fellow of Pembroke College (MA, 1565; senior treasurer, 1568; BTh, 1572). In 1563 he was appointed rector of Cley, Norfolk, the first of many church livings.

Nuce's 'Dialogus inter academiam, villam Cantab & reginam' is the first contribution from 'Aula Penbrokiana' in the manuscript compilation presented to Elizabeth I on her visit to the university in August 1564 (CUL, Add. MS 8915, fols. 121*r*–122*v*). Nuce contributed dedicatory verses, in Latin and English, to John Studley's translation of Seneca's *Agamemnon* (1566), defending his friend's literary inexperience against the 'nippyng wordes' of rancorous 'carpers'. Nuce's own undated translation, the *Ninth Tragedie of ... Seneca called Octavia*, was published in the same year, though perhaps composed somewhat earlier, since its dedication to the earl of Leicester describes the piece as the 'first fruits of my yong study'.

Appointed university preacher in November 1572, Nuce gave evidence in the case of an allegedly heretical sermon delivered that Christmas by the controversial churchman

John Browning. He was still in residence a year later, when he featured in the hectic, gossipy correspondence of Gabriel Harvey, one morning oversleeping ('the bel began to ring before M. Nuce began to rise out of his bed'; BL, Sloane MS 679, fol. 2v.), and on another occasion vainly dissuading Harvey from his academic quarrels ('M. Nuce willid me … not to kindle ani more coales'; ibid., fol. 2v). Nuce abandoned his bachelor life shortly afterwards, assuming in 1576 the rectorship of Beccles, Suffolk (a living he held until 1583) and at about the same time marrying his wife, Ann (d. 12 Jan 1614), before settling, as its vicar, at Gazeley, Suffolk, in August 1578. A series of further ecclesiastical benefices followed: the rectorships of Oxborough, Norfolk (1582–3), and Market Weston, Suffolk (1599), and a prebendal stall at Ely Cathedral in 1585 (in which year he resigned from the rectorship at Cley).

Meanwhile Nuce's *Octavia* had been reprinted in 1581 as part of Thomas Newton's deeply influential *Seneca his Tenne Tragedies*—the first collected works of any classical author to appear in English translation. Now considered neither Seneca's nor a tragedy—rather, 'the only extant Roman historical drama' (Share, xxix)—Nuce's *Octavia* stands out from the other nine in eschewing their laborious fourteeners (largely in favour of decasyllabic couplets); avoiding their occasional abridgements and interpolations; and appearing unrevised in Newton's collection, where its 'type … is larger and clearer than that of the other plays' (Spearing, 43).

Nuce died in Gazeley on 8 November 1617 and was buried in the chancel of Gazeley church beside his wife,

> who in a Number even,
> Five Sons brought him, Daughters Seven

(ten of the children had been baptized there between 1578 and 1595). It is tempting to suppose that Nuce composed the spirited epitaph upon his tomb, quoted above.

NICK DE SOMOGYI

Sources T. A. Walker, *A biographical register of Peterhouse men*, 2 (1930) • J. Venn, ed., *Grace book Δ* (1910) • E. M. Spearing, *The Elizabethan translations of Seneca's tragedies* (1912) • D. Share, ed., *Seneca in English* (1998) • *Calendar of the manuscripts of the most hon. the marquis of Salisbury*, 13, HMC, 9 (1915) • T. Warton, *The history of English poetry … a new edition*, 4 (1824) • W. C. Metcalfe, ed., *The visitations of Hertfordshire*, Harleian Society, 22 (1886) • VCH *Hertfordshire* • T. S. Eliot, 'Seneca in Elizabethan translation', *Selected essays* (1932) [orig. pubd as introduction to Seneca, *Tenne tragedies*, ed. T. Newton (1927)] • J. Bentham, *The history and antiquities of the conventual and cathedral church of Ely* (1771) • Tanner, *Bibl. Brit.-Hib.* • N. T. Pratt, *Seneca's drama* (1983) • private information (2004) [J. Ringrose, Pembroke College, Cambridge]

Archives BL, 'Gabrielis Harvei epistola &c', Sloane MS 679 • Coll. Arms, Hertfordshire visitations, 1572 (MS G.17.18); 1634 (MS C28³ 24) • Pembroke Cam., MS C E; MS C B; MS A A; MS M A • U. Cam., 'Orationes et carmina academiae Cantabr. ad Elizab. regina 1564', Add. MS 8915, fols. 121r–122v

Nuffield. For this title name *see* Morris, William Richard, Viscount Nuffield (1877–1963).

Nugent. For this title name *see* individual entries under Nugent; *see also* Grenville, George Nugent, second Baron Nugent of Carlanstown (1788–1850).

Nugent, Sir Charles Edmund (*bap.* 1759, *d.* 1844), naval officer, was baptized on 19 July 1759, an illegitimate son of Lieutenant-Colonel Edmund Nugent (1731–1771), army officer and politician. Charles Nugent entered the Royal Navy in 1771 and the next year was posted to the Mediterranean, serving in Sir Peter Parker's flagship, the *Trident*. In 1775 he was sent to American waters and served again in Parker's flagship, the *Bristol*, which was heavily engaged in the unsuccessful assault on Sullivan's Island, off Charles Town, on 28 June 1776, though Nugent was uninjured.

Nugent followed Parker back to Britain and remained there until 1778, when they went to the West Indies. Parker appointed him commander (though officially he had yet to receive his lieutenant's commission) which secured him his first mention in the navy list. In May 1779 he was made a captain. His main action here was his distinguished role in the little expedition in October 1779 which took the coastal fort of Omoa, and the rich prizes sheltering behind it. During the initial stages of the expedition Nugent's ship was surrounded by Spanish warships and he and his men taken prisoner. Preparations were made for their execution, but when another British ship appeared the Spaniards decamped and Nugent and his men broke out of gaol. Further reinforcements arrived and it was decided, after an unsuccessful foray to Roatan Island, to seize Omoa by storm. This was accomplished on 20 October and more than 3 million Spanish dollars were seized.

Nugent remained in the West Indies for the rest of the war, returning to Britain in 1782. A year later he became MP for Buckingham. He never addressed the house, however, and always voted with the government, except over the duke of Richmond's fortification scheme of 1788. On 2 July 1790 he married Deborah Charlotte Johnstone, *née* Dee, widow of George Johnstone, politician; they had one daughter.

With the outbreak of war in 1793 Nugent returned to sea, serving with Sir John Jervis in the West Indies and at the capture of Guadeloupe. He came back to Britain in May 1794 and early the next year was posted to command the *Caesar* in the channel. He was promoted rear-admiral in February 1797 and vice-admiral in 1801. He continued to serve at sea, spending time as captain of the fleet off Brittany in 1805, but by then he was noted as 'tired' and anxious for relief. He was accordingly placed on half pay, but became a full admiral in April 1808; in April 1833 he was made admiral of the fleet and in March 1834 he received the grand cross of the Royal Guelphic Order. Nugent died on 7 January 1844 at the house of George Bankes MP in Studland, Dorset. At his death he was senior admiral on the navy list.

J. K. LAUGHTON, *rev.* MICHAEL PARTRIDGE

Sources J. Ralfe, 'Charles Edmund Nugent', *The naval biography of Great Britain*, 2 (1828), 136–40 • *GM*, 2nd ser., 22 (1844), 89–90 • J. Marshall, *Royal naval biography*, 1/1 (1823), 94–9 • 'Biographical memoirs of Charles Edmund Nugent, vice-admiral of the blue squadron', *Naval Chronicle*, 10 (1803), 441–68 • PRO, naval service records, ADM 11/64 • D. Syrett, *The Royal Navy in American waters, 1775–1783* (1989), 36–8 • R. Gardiner, ed., *Navies and the American revolution* (1996), 42–

5, 98 • *Letters and papers of Charles, Lord Barham*, ed. J. K. Laughton, 3, Navy RS, 39 (1911) • J. Brooke, 'Nugent, Charles Edmund', HoP, *Commons, 1754–90*

Likenesses engraving, repro. in 'Biographical memoirs of Charles Edmund Nugent', facing p. 441

Nugent, Christopher, fifth Baron Delvin (1544–1602), nobleman, was the eldest son of Richard Nugent, fourth Baron Delvin (1522/3–1559), and Elizabeth Preston, daughter of Jenico, Viscount Gormanston. He succeeded to the title on the death of his father on 10 December 1559, and during his minority was the ward of Thomas Radcliffe, third earl of Sussex, chief governor of Ireland. He matriculated as a fellow-commoner of Clare College, Cambridge, on 12 May 1563, and was presented to Queen Elizabeth when she visited the university in 1564. On coming of age, about November 1565, he returned to Ireland with letters of commendation from the queen to the lord deputy, Sir Henry Sidney. Already a substantial landowner through inheritance in Westmeath, Delvin extended his propertied interests through a series of grants from the crown. As an undertaker in the plantation of Leix (Laois) and Offaly, he had obtained, on 3 February 1564, a grant of the castle and lands of Corbetstown in Offaly (King's county). He got leases of the abbeys of All Saints and Inchmore as well as the custody of Sleaught-William in the Annaly (co. Longford), and of the abbey of Fore and other lands in Westmeath. Secure in his landed position Delvin began his active service of the English administration in 1566, when he distinguished himself against the rebellious Shane O'Neill and was knighted at Drogheda by Sidney.

A hybrid culture Although proud of his English ancestry and heritage, Christopher Nugent was a person of the hybrid culture of the western marches of the pale. His family had patronized the Gaelic bardic clan of Ó Cobhthaigh, and he continued the tradition. Christopher's brother William was an accomplished poet in Irish as well as English. Probably while at Cambridge, Christopher had composed a primer of the Irish language for presentation to Queen Elizabeth. The lessons were based on direct speech rather than grammar, and contained Latin as well as Irish and English vocabulary and phrases. In his dedication of the book to Elizabeth he praised the queen's zeal for learning the language of 'your people' in Ireland and he pointed to the advantages of the use of Irish as a means of 'reformation' of the country in order to establish obedience, justice, and civility. His commitment to the advancement and welfare of his country was an abiding one.

The network of marriages of which Delvin was part also reflects the family's ethnically mixed world. Christopher married Mary, daughter of Gerald *Fitzgerald, eleventh earl of Kildare, and Mabel Browne, his English-born wife. Through this union Delvin was close to the heart of politics and society in the Englishry of Ireland. They had twelve children, six sons and six daughters, whose matrimonial alliances tied the Nugents to both the Gaelic and the English of Ireland. Their son Gerald married Mary O'Donnell, sister of Rory, first earl of Tyrconnell. Their daughter Mabel was married twice, on both occasions to leading Gaelic noblemen, Murrough O'Brien, Baron Inchiquin, and John Fitzpatrick of Upper Ossory. Mary, another daughter, married Anthony O'Dempsey, son of Viscount Clanmalier. The bond with the family of Fitzgerald of Kildare was cemented by a marriage between Elizabeth Nugent and Gerald Fitzgerald, the fourteenth earl of Kildare. Other alliances with the families of Cheevers of co. Meath and Aylmer of co. Kildare consolidated links with the gentry of the pale.

Resisting the Dublin government The first in a series of crises in Delvin's relations with the Dublin government occurred in 1574. In July of that year he refused, along with Lord Gormanston, to sign a proclamation of rebellion against the earl of Desmond. He gave as his reason for non-compliance the fact that the proclamation was directed to the council of Ireland, of which he was not a member. This explanation failed to satisfy both the Irish and English privy councillors, and Delvin and Gormanston, accused of 'undutiful dealings' and 'wilful partiality to an offender against her majesty' (*Calendar of Carew Manuscripts, 1515–74*, 490), were peremptorily ordered to submit. Fresh letters of explanation from Delvin and Gormanston in February 1575 were deemed to be insufficiently plausible and both were placed under restraint. They thereupon submitted and were restored to government favour.

While there may have been substance in the accusation of partiality towards the earl of Desmond, given his connection with the Geraldine party in Ireland, it is more likely that Delvin's recalcitrance was based on his perception of the oppressiveness of the Dublin government's dealings with the aristocracy of the pale. Controversy over the cess, an arbitrary system of taxation for the victualling of the army in Ireland, was mounting by 1574, and it was to embroil Delvin and other pale noblemen in another confrontation with the government in the later 1570s. By 1576 he had become a leader of the 'country cause' against the cess, rallying resistance to its payment and helping to prepare the arguments of a trio of delegates to the queen against the constitutionality of the imposition. In May 1577 Delvin, Lord Howth, Viscount Baltinglass, and others were confined in Dublin Castle for a number of weeks until they acknowledged the queen's prerogative in respect of extraordinary levies. In early 1578 Delvin appeared as spokesman for the gentlemen of the pale in proceedings before the court of the castle chamber in Dublin and was again imprisoned for his opposition to the cess. The issue was eventually resolved but only at the expense of a breakdown of trust between the Dublin administration and the older English community of Ireland.

This was clearly manifested when Viscount Baltinglass went into rebellion against the crown in July 1580, driven by religious and political disaffection. There is little doubt that Delvin, known for his recusancy, was implicated in the planning of the insurrection, but he fought shy of direct involvement. Nevertheless, in December 1580 he and the earl of Kildare were arrested and committed to Dublin

Castle on a charge of having abetted the rebellion in the pale. Despite numerous interrogations and notwithstanding an armed conspiracy forged by Delvin's brother, William Nugent, to free the captives, the charge was not substantiated. After eighteen months of imprisonment in Dublin, Delvin and Kildare were sent to England in the custody of Nicholas Bagenal. Further questioning in London carried out by Lord Chancellor Mildmay and Master of the Rolls Gerard failed to elicit proof of guilt, but Delvin was retained in England until 1585. While held there under easy restraint he cultivated the patronage of Lord Burghley, whose favour sustained him for most of the rest of his career.

Restored to Ireland In 1585 Delvin was allowed to return to Ireland to oversee the execution of the will of the earl of Kildare who had died that year. He managed with some difficulty to re-establish his proprietorship over his estates, aided by a renewal of the leases that he held from the crown. Apart from another trip to England in 1587–8, Delvin spent most of the rest of his life based at Clonyn in Westmeath. The insights distilled from his 'late troubles' were reflected in the 'Articles for the reformation of certain abuses in Ireland', which he drew up in the mid-1580s. He identified therein the ills of the country including the 'absolute authority' of the governor (Gilbert, 189), the partiality of the judges, the extortion of the countryside by the soldiery, and breaches of faith in respect of protection and safe passages on the part of the state. In order to remedy these abuses Delvin proposed that there should be accountability in the choice and conduct of the governor, that the consent of the local community should be forthcoming for taxation and all other measures, that a standing army of 1000 should be supplemented by the traditional rising out of the pale community, and that the dieting and payment of the soldiery should be tightly regulated. In sum, Delvin was advocating the upholding of the old constitution in which the nobility of the realm of Ireland were securely incorporated.

Returned to his native Westmeath in the late 1580s Delvin attempted to resume an orderly life, as he wrote to Burghley, avoiding discontented society, following the law in Dublin each term for the recovery of his lands, and serving the queen at the assizes in his own neighbourhood. The rest of his time he spent 'in books and building' (*CSP Ire.*, 1588–92, 420). A bitter feud with the Dillon family of co. Meath, however, overshadowed his life until 1594 and brought him into conflict with senior officials in Dublin, including Lord Deputy Fitzwilliam. The target of Delvin's hatred was Robert Dillon, chief justice of the common pleas, whom he blamed for the judicial murder in 1582 of his kinsman Nicholas *Nugent, Dillon's predecessor in office. In retribution for Dillon's vindictiveness and the frustrating of his suits for some of his lands, Delvin, with the assistance of Nicholas, Lord Howth, launched an implacable campaign to have Dillon convicted of treachery. Despite the accumulating of a huge amount of evidence and the calling of many witnesses,

Dillon was acquitted, whereupon Delvin charged Fitzwilliam with partiality.

The Nine Years' War As the disturbances caused by the Nine Years' War began to affect the northern midlands, Delvin emerged as a significant commander against the rebels. He was particularly active against insurgents among the O'Farrells and the O'Reillys, cutting off the heads of 246 people over four years, according to his own account. On a visit to England in 1597 he was ordered a grant of lands to the value of £100 per annum in the O'Farrells' and O'Reillys' territories of Longford and Cavan, but he never lived to make good the warrant. Hugh O'Neill, earl of Tyrone, achieved mounting military successes in the late 1590s and expanded his ambitions for a pan-insular war. Consequently it became extremely difficult for Delvin to maintain his defences in the northern and western pale, and in dispatches to Dublin in 1599 he complained repeatedly about his predicament in holding centres such as Athboy and Trim, and expressed fears about the safety of his wife and children at Clonyn. Delvin also referred to the hatred of O'Neill towards him, especially because he had maintained his loyalty to the crown in spite of his Roman Catholicism.

The pressure became unbearable in 1599–1600 as O'Neill's armies marched through his lands, and Delvin was forced to submit to the earl. From the perspective of officials in Dublin, however, this seemed to confirm long-standing doubts about Delvin's allegiance to the crown. There is no doubt that Delvin had been involved in intelligence gathering for the government about O'Neill's activities, sending an agent into the Tyrone camp and interpreting letters in Irish sent by O'Neill to his allies. However, those such as Secretary Fenton who believed that Delvin was engaged in conspiracy appeared to be vindicated by the events surrounding O'Neill's expedition to Kinsale in 1601. There were reports of contacts between O'Neill's chaplain, Peter Nangle, and the baron; O'Neill was said to have dined at Clonyn on his journey southwards; and O'Neill's brother Cormac wrote to Delvin from Kinsale.

Arrest and death Early in 1602 Delvin was arrested and lodged in Dublin Castle. It is evident that the government was preparing to put him on trial for treason as seven articles of indictment against him were drawn up by the Irish council. His wife, Mary, wrote despairingly to Robert Cecil, reminding him of his father Burghley's great favour in the past. Citing his 'pain and travail' in her majesty's service, Lady Delvin pleaded that her husband, now 'in his old age and decayed health' (Gilbert, 197), be permitted to stay in more commodious lodgings to receive medical treatment. She was prepared to travel to England to make his case before the court. Before the matter came to trial, however, Delvin died in Dublin Castle on 5 September 1602 (though by other accounts on 17 August or 1 October). He was buried at Castle Delvin in Westmeath on 5 October 1602, and was succeeded by his eldest son Richard *Nugent, created earl of Westmeath in 1621.

Christopher Nugent's case illustrates in a most acute

form the dilemma of an older English resident of Ireland, caught up in the two cultures. His political loyalty was to the English establishment there, recently enhanced by the upgrading of the island's status to kingdom. His confessional allegiance to Rome was increasingly expressed in the form of open recusancy but in no way did it entail a transfer of fealty to the Roman Catholic enemies of England. He was a fervent upholder of the medieval Anglo-Norman constitution which enshrined the corporate rights of the colonial community in church and state. The thrust of religious and political reforms in the Elizabethan period threatened to override these rights of consultation and representation which Delvin had at heart. While resisting the diplomatic inducement of O'Neill during his rebellion, Delvin's close links with Gaelic society rendered him open to suspicion of collusion with the arch-traitor, and his antagonists in the Dublin administration seized the opportunity to disgrace him.

COLM LENNON

Sources J. T. Gilbert, ed., *Account of facsimiles of the national manuscripts of Ireland* (1884) · J. S. Brewer and W. Bullen, eds., *Calendar of the Carew manuscripts*, 2: *1575–1588*, PRO (1868) · *CSP Ire.*, *1574–1603* · B. Iske, *The green cockatrice* (1978) · H. C. Walshe, 'The rebellion of William Nugent, 1581', *Religion, conflict, and coexistence in Ireland: essays presented to Monsignor Patrick J. Corish*, ed. R. V. Comerford and others (1990), 26–52 · J. Morrin, ed., *Calendar of the patent and close rolls of chancery in Ireland, of the reigns of Henry VIII, Edward VI, Mary, and Elizabeth*, 2 (1862) · J. S. Brewer and W. Bullen, eds., *Calendar of the Carew manuscripts*, 1: *1515–1574*, PRO (1867) · *DNB* · H. C. Walshe, 'Some responses to the protestant Reformation in sixteenth-century Meath', *Ríocht na Midhe*, 8 (1987), 97–109
Wealth at death considerable amount of land

Nugent, Christopher (*c.*1655–1731), Jacobite army officer, was the eldest son of Francis Nugent (*b. c.*1629) of Dardistown, co. Westmeath, and Bridget Dongan, sister of William Dongan (1630–1698), created earl of Limerick in 1685. He married his cousin, Bridget Barnewall, second daughter of Robert Barnewall, ninth Baron Trimleston or Trimlestown (*d.* 1687), and Margaret Dongan (*d.* 1678), his mother's sister. They had at least six children.

In 1686, with many other Catholics, Nugent was commissioned into the Irish army, serving in the cavalry as lieutenant in the duke of Ormond's regiment (1 March), and in 1687 transferring to the duke of Tyrconnell's regiment (26 March) in which he was promoted captain in the autumn. Also in 1687 he attended the imperial army's campaign against the Turks in Hungary. In 1689 he represented the borough of Fore in the Jacobite parliament. During the war of 1689–91 he was major in Tyrconnell's horse, until in January 1690 he transferred to the second troop of Horse Guards, of which he rose to be lieutenant-colonel.

After the capitulation of Limerick he elected to go to France, for which he was attainted, and arrived at Brest on 3 December 1691. He was given command of the two troops of Irish horse guards, and served in the army for the invasion of England in 1692 and afterwards in Flanders, where he was wounded at Landen in 1693. In 1694 he

served with the army of Germany, under the duc de Lorges, and in 1695 with the army of the Moselle. On 25 May 1695 he was appointed *mestre-de-camp de cavalerie*, and continued with the army of the Moselle in 1696–7. On the disbandment of the Irish horse guards on 27 February 1698, he was attached as a reformed *mestre-de-camp* to the new cavalry regiment of Sheldon. He joined the army of Italy in July 1701, fought under Villeroi at Chiari on 1 September, and under Vendôme at Luzzara on 15 August 1702. In the following year he served with the army of Germany, and at Speyer he suffered seven wounds while leading a spirited charge by Irish cavalry against their imperial counterparts, thereby helping to secure a French victory. He was created brigadier on 1 March 1705, and, on the retirement of Colonel Sheldon, succeeded to the command of the regiment on 16 January 1706. As the regiment of Nugent it fought under his command at Ramillies, Oudenarde, and Malplaquet. He was employed about Calais during the winter of 1711–12, and was present at the battle of Denain on 24 July 1712, and at the siege of Douai in September. The following year he was transferred to the army of Germany, and was present at the siege of Landau (June–August), at the defeat of General Vaubonne on 20 September, and at the capture of Freiburg im Breisgau in November. In 1714 he served with the army of the Lower Meuse.

He was a staunch Jacobite, and without permission he accompanied James III (James Francis Edward Stuart) to Scotland for the attempted insurrection of 1715. This led to a protest by the British ambassador in Paris, and he was deprived of his regiment, which, however, was conferred on his son, the comte de Nugent, who retained command until 1733. Although his active military career was over, on 13 September 1718 he was promoted *maréchal-de-camp* or major-general of horse. In 1720 he expressed the hope that his worsened circumstances would be relieved by a £2000 legacy from his uncle, the earl of Limerick, which he planned to collect in London. He died in France on 4 June 1731.

ROBERT DUNLOP, *rev.* HARMAN MURTAGH

Sources R. Hayes, *Biographical dictionary of Irishmen in France* (1949), 211–12 · J. C. O'Callaghan, *History of the Irish brigades in the service of France*, [new edn] (1870), 153–5 · J. Lodge, *The peerage of Ireland*, rev. M. Archdall, rev. edn, 1 (1789), 220 · J. C. R. Childs, *Nobles, gentlemen and the profession of arms in Restoration Britain, 1660–1688: a biographical dictionary of British army officers on foreign service* (1987), 66 · P. Fagan, ed., *Ireland in the Stuart papers*, 1: *1719–42* (1995) · *The manuscripts of the marquis of Ormonde*, [old ser.], 3 vols., HMC, 36 (1895–1909), vol. 1 · *CSP dom.*, *1686–7* · J. G. Simms, ed., 'Irish Jacobites: lists from Trinity College Dublin MS N.1.3', *Analecta Hibernica*, 22 (1960), 11–230 · Burke, *Peerage* · GEC, *Peerage* · IGI

Nugent, Christopher (1698–1775), physician, was born in Ireland, probably in co. Meath and, according to Sir Richard Murgrave, was 'a most bigoted Romanist bred at Douay in Flanders' (O'Brien, 38). After graduating MD in France, Nugent went into practice, first in the south of Ireland, and afterwards at Bath, where he had considerable success. Some time about 1750 Nugent treated Edmund Burke, who later in a verse addressed to Nugent wrote:

Tis now two Autumn's, since he chanc'd to find,
A youth of Body broke, infirm of mind ...
(Copeland, 1.117)

It was during his stay in Nugent's house that Burke is supposed to have met Nugent's daughter, Jane Mary (1734–1812), whom he married in 1757. Burke called his younger son Christopher, after his father-in-law.

Early in 1764 Nugent removed to London living first in Queen Anne Street, where his daughter and son-in-law lived with him for a while, and afterwards in Suffolk Street, the Strand. He was one of the nine original members of the Literary Club. Nugent was a regular attender, and was present when Boswell was admitted. In the imaginary college at St Andrews, discussed with Johnson, he was to be professor of physic. On 25 June 1765 he was admitted a licentiate of the Royal College of Physicians. In the same year he was elected FRS. His only medical publication was *An Essay on the Hydrophobia* published in 1753 and translated into French over a century later.

Nugent died at his house in Suffolk Street on 12 November 1775. In a letter to Jane Burke after her father's death Johnson wrote of

a friend whom I loved much, and whom you undoubtedly loved much more. His death has taken from us the benefit of his counsel, and the delight of his conversation, but it cannot without our own fault, deprive us of the influence of his virtues, or efface the pleasing remembrance of his Worth his integrity, and his piety.   (Copeland, 3.237)

Burke's attachment to his father-in-law may be gauged from remarks he made when Nugent had been ill four years earlier: 'I do assure you, real good men are scarce. A father, a friend, and physician in one would be an heavy loss to those who have other things to console them; guess how we must be affected with it' (Hoffman, 505).

NORMAN MOORE, rev. MICHAEL BEVAN

Sources Munk, *Roll* · *The correspondence of Edmund Burke*, ed. T. W. Copeland and others, 10 vols. (1958–78) · C. C. O'Brien, *The great melody: a thematic biography of Edmund Burke* (1992) · R. J. S. Hoffman, *Edmund Burke, land agent* (1956) · J. Boswell, *The life of Samuel Johnson*, ed. [E. Malone], 7th edn, 5 vols. (1811) · *The record of the Royal Society of London*, 4th edn (1940)
Likenesses G. P. Harding?, wash drawing, 1806 (after J. Barry, 1772), Wellcome L.

Nugent, Christopher Robert

Nugent, Christopher Robert (1852?–1926), banker, was probably born at Bruges, Belgium, one of six children and the eldest son of Robert Nugent and Emma, daughter of John Hunter. The family was of Irish descent and included among its forebears the statesman and political philosopher Edmund Burke, who in 1757 had married Jane Nugent, the daughter of his physician. When Christopher was six the children were orphaned and taken to England to be educated.

Nugent's City career began in 1870 when, at the age of eighteen, he joined the discount firm of Grigg & Co. Here he learned the business of dealing in bills of exchange that was to be his life's work. His exceptional ability quickly brought him to prominence and in 1879 he accepted an invitation to become deputy manager of the United Discount Corporation. In the following year he was

made manager and thus at the age of twenty-seven took control of a major joint-stock discount company.

United Discount was a 'reconstruction' of a discount company that had suffered in the crisis of 1866. In 1885 it merged with another 'reconstruction', the General Credit and Discount Company, to form the Union Discount Company of London Ltd, with Nugent as the first manager. Here he found full scope for his financial genius and during the thirty-seven years in which he guided the company's fortunes he established Union Discount as the leading house in the market. Such was his personal standing that in the early years the company was more usually referred to as 'Nugent's' (King, 261 n. 4).

Success in the discount business depended on the dealer's ability to assess correctly the quality of bills offered for discount and in this Nugent was an acknowledged master. It was said that he was able to 'sense good paper' (Cleaver and Cleaver, 58), though in reality his judgement was informed by a minute knowledge, tirelessly accumulated, of the names on bills. He corresponded regularly with bankers worldwide and supplemented the knowledge thus gained of local conditions by means of annual trips abroad. For all the seriousness of his approach to business and the strict code of conduct he required of his clerks, Nugent was nevertheless a popular figure in the market, noted for the 'geniality and infectious gaiety of disposition' that endeared him to a very wide circle of friends (*Banker's Magazine*, June 1926, 912).

It was inevitable that Nugent's views would be sought on important issues of the day. In 1910 he gave evidence to the national monetary commission in the USA (the Aldrich commission), and in 1918 he represented the market before the Treasury committee on bank amalgamations (the Colwyn committee) and the committee on currency and foreign exchanges after the war (the Cunliffe committee). More immediately, he played a prominent part in the affairs of the discount market. He was chairman of the London Discount Houses Committee, which from before the First World War met to discuss the setting of interest rates, and of the sub-committee established in 1914 to liaise with the Bank of England. He was also the first chairman of the London Discount Market Association, which replaced the committee in 1919.

Nugent, who was married and had a family, retired in 1922, on reaching the age of seventy. In retirement he maintained contact with the company through retention of his seat on the board, to which he had been elected in 1909. The rest of his time he divided between his houses in Pinner, where a road—Nugent's Park—was named after him, and at Totland Bay, Isle of Wight. He also continued to travel extensively abroad.

Nugent was taken ill while returning from a stay in Ceylon, and he developed pneumonia soon after reaching home. He died at 14 Berkeley Square, Mayfair, London, on 27 April 1926 and was widely mourned, not least by the older members of the market who remembered him as 'the last of the Victorians' (*The Times*, 28 April 1926).

GORDON FLETCHER

Sources G. Cleaver and P. Cleaver, *The Union Discount: a centenary album* (1985) · *Bankers' Magazine*, 114 (1922), 105, 241 · *Bankers' Magazine*, 121 (1926), 912–14 · *The Times* (25 April 1885) · *The Times* (28 April 1926) · *The Times* (1 May 1926) · *The Times* (4 May 1926) · *The Times* (30 June 1926) · *WWW* · R. S. Sayers, *The Bank of England, 1891–1944, 1* (1976), 237, 276 · T. E. Gregory, ed., *Select statutes, documents and reports relating to British banking, 1847–1928* (1929), vol. 2 of *Select statutes, documents and reports relating to British banking, 1832–1928*, ed. T. E. Gregory, pt 4 · H. Boylan, *A dictionary of Irish biography* (1978) · W. T. C. King, *History of the London discount market* (1936) · d. cert. · *CGPLA Eng. & Wales* (1926)
Archives Union plc, London
Wealth at death £51,986 10s. 1d.: probate, 23 June 1926, *CGPLA Eng. & Wales*

Nugent [*formerly* Fennings], **Sir George**, **first baronet** (1757–1849), army officer, born on 10 June 1757, was the illegitimate son of Lieutenant-Colonel the Hon. Edmund Nugent, 1st foot guards, who died unmarried in 1771. His mother's surname was probably Fennings, as it was with this name that he attended Charterhouse School as an oppidan (day boy), before proceeding to the Royal Military Academy, Woolwich. From here, as George Nugent, he was commissioned on 5 July 1773 as ensign in the 39th foot, with which he served at Gibraltar from February 1774 to March 1776. On 23 November 1775 he obtained a lieutenancy in the 7th Royal Fusiliers, which he joined in September 1777 at New York, serving in the expedition up the Hudson, and at the storming of forts Montgomery and Clinton the following month. He accompanied the regiment to Philadelphia, where he did duty with it until the evacuation of the city in June 1778. Meanwhile, on 28 April 1778, he had been promoted to captain in the 57th foot. He served with them in the Jerseys and Connecticut, obtaining a majority in the regiment on 3 May 1782. On 8 September 1783 he was promoted to the lieutenant-colonelcy in the 97th foot, and returned to England in November 1783. The regiment was disbanded before he joined it, and he was placed on half pay.

On 20 December 1787 Nugent became lieutenant-colonel of the 13th foot, stationed in Dublin, and was shortly afterwards appointed first aide-de-camp to the lord lieutenant of Ireland, his uncle, George Nugent-Temple-Grenville, later first marquess of Buckingham. Buckingham failed to obtain the colonelcy of a cavalry regiment for Nugent, although Pitt and William Grenville secured for him the lieutenant-colonelcy of the 4th dragoon guards (also in Ireland) on 16 June 1789. On 6 October 1790 he transferred to the Coldstream Guards, which was stationed in the London area. Nugent was MP for Buckingham from 1790 to 1802, and regularly attended the Commons until 1793, when he went with his regiment to the Netherlands, and was present at the sieges of Valenciennes and Dunkirk and the action at Lincelles. When the army went into winter quarters Nugent returned home and in three months, aided by the Buckingham family interest, raised at Buckingham and Aylesbury a regiment, the 85th, of which he was appointed colonel on 1 March 1794. In command of the Buckinghamshire Volunteers he proceeded to Ireland, and in September 1794 to Walcheren in the Netherlands, where he held the local

rank of brigadier-general. Joining the duke of York's army on the Waal, he was appointed to command a brigade; but Lord Cathcart having been appointed to command that part of the army, no officers of the rank of brigadier-general were allowed to serve with it, and Nugent returned to England.

In April 1795 Nugent was appointed brigadier-general on the staff in Ireland, promoted to major-general on 3 May 1796, and made captain and keeper of St Mawes Castle the same year. In Belfast on 15 or 16 November 1797 he married Maria Skinner (1770/71–1834) [*see* Nugent, Maria], daughter of Cortlandt *Skinner (1727–1799), lawyer and army officer. They had two sons and two daughters. During the 1798 rising he commanded the northern district of Ireland and served as adjutant-general in Ireland from July 1799 to March 1801; he represented Charleville, co. Cork, in the last Irish parliament. On 1 April 1801 he was appointed lieutenant-governor and commander-in-chief of Jamaica with the local rank of lieutenant-general, and was sworn in at Spanish Town on 3 August. He left Jamaica on 20 February 1806. His attempts to improve the defences and barrack accommodation there were frustrated by the parsimony of the assembly, and he was annoyed at being rewarded for his efforts with a baronetcy (28 November 1806) rather than being made a knight of the Bath, an honour which George III refused him on account of his illegitimacy. While in Jamaica he became a substantive lieutenant-general on 25 September 1803, and on 27 December 1805 colonel of the 62nd foot.

On 26 May 1806 he transferred to the colonelcy of the 6th foot, and on 21 August was appointed to command the western district. The same year he returned to the Commons as MP for Aylesbury, and held the seat until 1812. He moved to the Kent district in July 1809, resigning that command on 10 October.

In March 1811 Nugent was appointed commander-in-chief in India, and reached Calcutta on 14 January 1812. He was promoted general on 4 June 1813. On 4 October 1813 Lord Moira arrived in Calcutta as the new governor-general and commander-in-chief, relegating Nugent to the command of the Bengal presidency; as compensation he was invested with the KB, which had finally been awarded him on 1 February 1813. Nugent, however, came to resent his supersedence and resigned in October 1814; his hopes of becoming governor of the Cape of Good Hope instead were not realized. He was advanced to the grand cross of the Bath on 2 January 1815, was MP for Buckingham from 1818 to 1832, and was made an honorary doctor of civil law at Oxford in 1819. He lived the remainder of his life at Westhorpe House, Little Marlow, purchased in October 1809. He gave two religious paintings to the village church and made bequests to the local school and the poor. He was promoted to field marshal on 9 November 1846. He died, aged ninety-one, at Westhorpe House on 11 March 1849 and was buried at the church of St John the Baptist, Little Marlow.   PETER B. BOYDEN

Sources NAM, Nugent MSS, 1968-07-173 to 1968-07-183, 1968-07-370-18 to 1968-07-370-30 · D. R. Fisher, 'Nugent, George',

HoP, *Commons* · J. Philippart, ed., *The royal military calendar*, 3rd edn, 1 (1820) · *Lady Nugent's journal: Jamaica one hundred and thirty years ago*, ed. F. Cundall, 2nd edn (1934) · R. L. Arrowsmith, ed., *Charterhouse register, 1769–1872* (1974) · *VCH Buckinghamshire*, vol. 3 · G. Lipscomb, *The history and antiquities of the county of Buckingham*, 4 vols. (1831–47), vol. 3 · monthly returns, PRO, WO 17/2790–2792 · *DNB* · monumental inscription, St John the Baptist church, Little Marlow, Buckinghamshire

Archives BL, corresp. · NAM, corresp. and MSS · National Library of Jamaica, Kingston, corresp. and MSS relating to Jamaica | BL, letters to Lord Grenville, Add. MS 59004 · Bodl. RH, corresp. with Sir John Duckworth · Bucks. RLSS, corresp. with Fremantle family · CKS, corresp. with Lord Camden · Hunt. L., letters to Grenville family · NL Scot., corresp. with first earl of Minto · PRO NIre., corresp. with earl of Gosford · U. Nott. L., letters to Lord William Bentinck

Likenesses R. Woodman, stipple (after J. Downman, c.1811), NAM, NPG

Wealth at death £3499: PRO, estate duty register, IR 20/1846

Nugent, James (1822–1905), social reformer and Roman Catholic priest, was born on 3 March 1822 at Hunter Street, Liverpool, the eldest of nine children, three boys and six girls, of John Nugent, fruiterer, and his wife, Mary, *née* Rice (1803–1887). He was baptized a Catholic at St Nicholas's Church on 17 March. His father was a Catholic from co. Meath and his mother was a convert to Roman Catholicism. On the completion of his education at a private academy in Queen Square, Liverpool, from about 1827 to 1837, his father's ambition for him to be a merchant was overruled by his devout mother and the local priest who encouraged him to enter the priesthood.

Trained at St Cuthbert's College, Ushaw (1838–42), and the English College in Rome (1843–6), Nugent was ordained at his local church of St Nicholas's, Liverpool, on 30 August 1846. His first ministry was at St Alban's, Blackburn, and then at St Mary's, Wigan (March to December 1848). He then moved back to Liverpool, in the midst of a crisis of poverty and disease, where ten out of twenty-four priests had died, and where the Irish immigrants needed hope and a brighter future.

Nugent's whole life was given to the task. As an educationist he opened on 7 November 1850 a Catholic middle school for boys in Rodney Street, and by 31 October 1853 had opened the Catholic Institute, becoming its first director. He served the educational needs of both children and adults for the next ten years and set the tone which was to be followed by his successors.

Nugent felt the need to look after street children, whom he called nobody's children, his slogan being 'Save the child'. He set up shelters, training schools (one on the River Mersey), and residential homes. Later, he assisted a large number of the children to emigrate to the New World. He became the pioneer of children's emigration and travelled extensively in the USA on a mission which was encouraged by Archbishop Ireland, a fervent colonizer. Some of the schemes were total failures, such as the attempt of 1882 to settle poor families from Ireland on farms in Minnesota.

As the first Catholic chaplain at Walton gaol (appointed under the act of 1863) Nugent saw how drink made men and women criminals, and he established the Total Abstinence League of the Cross, a movement which spread to India, America, and Australia. He also saw the potential of the press, and in 1861 established a printing press that produced newspapers including the *Northern Press* (renamed the *Catholic Times* in 1872), which soon had a circulation of 73,000.

At the time Nugent retired in 1885 he was still extremely active, travelling extensively and overseeing the building of new churches such as St Joseph's, Blundelsands. Honours came his way: he was created a monsignor in 1892, was given a testimonial by Liverpool city council in 1897, and his portrait by Sir James Shannon, later based in the Walker Art Gallery, was painted. On a return journey from New York in 1903 he had a serious fall. His health declined and two years later a chill which he caught in Southport turned to pneumonia. He died at Harewood, Duke Street, Freshfield Road, Formby, on 27 June 1905 and was buried at Ford cemetery, Liverpool, on 30 June. Ten thousand mourners gathered for his funeral. A statue to his memory was unveiled on 8 December 1906 and placed in St John's Gardens, Liverpool. D. BEN REES

Sources J. Bennett, *Father Nugent of Liverpool* (1949) · B. O'Connell, 'The Irish nationalist party in Liverpool, 1873–1922', MA diss., U. Lpool, 1971 · P. T. Winskill, *Temperance standard bearers of the nineteenth century: a biographical and statistical temperance dictionary*, 2 vols. (1897–8) · P. J. Waller, *Democracy and sectarianism: a political and social history of Liverpool, 1868–1939* (1981) · R. Lawson, 'The Irish community in Liverpool in 1851', *Irish Geography*, 4/1 (1959) · D. Gwynn, *A hundred years of Catholic emancipation (1829–1929)* (1929) · S. C. Johnson, *A history of emigration: from the United Kingdom to North America, 1763–1912* (1913) · *CGPLA Eng. & Wales* (1905)

Likenesses J. J. Shannon, portrait, 1897, Walker Art Gallery, Liverpool · statue (unveiled 8 Dec 1906), St John's Gardens, Liverpool

Wealth at death £7630 18s. 5d.: probate, 5 Dec 1905, *CGPLA Eng. & Wales*

Nugent, John, fifth earl of Westmeath (1671/2–1754), army officer in foreign service, was born probably in Ireland, the third son of Christopher Nugent, Lord Delvin (d. before 1680), landowner, and Mary Butler (1640/41–1737). He was the grandson of Richard *Nugent, second earl of Westmeath, and the younger brother of Thomas *Nugent, fourth earl. He followed his brother into the service of James II and was present as cadet in the Horse Guards at the battle of the Boyne and at the siege of Limerick. In 1691 he withdrew, with the bulk of the Irish swordsmen, to France. He served as lieutenant to the *mestre de camp* of the King's regiment of Irish horse on the French coast and in Flanders until the peace of Ryswick in 1697. He was attached as reformed captain to Sheldon's regiment in February 1698 and he served in Italy at the battle of Chiari in 1701, at the defence of Cremona, and at the battle of Luzzara in 1702. He served with the army of Flanders in 1704, and, having on 5 April 1705 obtained his captain's commission, fought under the French standard at Ramillies in 1706, at Oudenarde in 1708, and at Malplaquet in 1709. He won favour at the Jacobite court and was appointed equerry of the stables to James III (James Francis Edward Stuart) and Mary of Modena in December 1707. On 7 January 1711 he married, at St Germain-en-Laye, Margaret Molza (d. 1776), daughter of Count Charles Molza and

Véronique Angelotti, who both served in the household of Mary of Modena.

In 1712 Nugent was present at the battle of Denain, and at the sieges of Douai and Quesnoy. He served with the German army in 1713 and with the army of the lower Meuse in 1714. He was promoted brevet major on 3 January 1720, and on 15 February 1721 was appointed *mestre de camp de cavalerie*. He served at the siege of Kehl in 1733, at the attack of the lines of Etlingen, at the siege of Philippsburg in 1734, and at the affair of Klausen in 1735. He became lieutenant-colonel of his regiment on 23 May 1736 and was promoted brigadier on 1 January 1740. During the War of the Austrian Succession he served in Westphalia under Maréchal de Maillebois in 1741, on the frontiers of Bohemia in 1742, and in lower Alsace under Maréchal de Noailles in 1743. He was made brevet *maréchal de camp* or major-general on 2 May 1744. He left the service in June 1748 and succeeded his brother Thomas as fifth earl of Westmeath in 1752; he died in retirement at Nivelles in Brabant on 3 July 1754. His wife survived him and died in France on 18 January 1776. Thomas, their third, but eldest surviving, son succeeded as sixth earl of Westmeath; he conformed to the established religion and became the first protestant peer in his family.

ROBERT DUNLOP, rev. D. M. BEAUMONT

Sources Pinard, *Chronologie historique-militaire*, 8 vols. (Paris, 1760–78), vol. 7, p. 208 · J. C. O'Callaghan, *History of the Irish brigades in the service of France*, [new edn] (1870), 500 · GEC, *Peerage*
Archives Archives Nationales, Paris, fonds guerre, Nugent and state Irish army in France · Bibliothèque Nationale, Paris, Nugent and state Irish army in France

Nugent, Lavalin [*name in religion* Francis] (**1569–1635**), Capuchin friar, was born in the second half of 1569, the second son of Sir Edward Nugent of Ballybranagh, near Mullingar in co. Westmeath, and Margaret O'Connor, a daughter of the prince of O'Connor Faly. He was younger brother to Robert (*d.* 1620) and elder brother to Andrew, who inherited the family estates. His family 'held the traditional political outlook of the Pale nobility' (Martin, *Friar Nugent*, 8), and his father was a blood relative of Christopher Nugent, Lord Delvin, who was suspected of treachery and whose brother William Nugent rebelled in 1581 but escaped capture and fled to France. Sir Edward Nugent decided to send Lavalin there in 1582, to the Scots and Irish college run by Jesuits at Pont-à-Mousson in Lorraine. The principal there, Dr Cheyne, was an associate of William Nugent. While still young Lavalin Nugent had showed 'a religious bent of mind' (ibid., 14), and at Rouen happened to see some Capuchins and expressed a desire to become one.

The college at Pont-à-Mousson had to close in 1588, and Nugent went to Louvain, where he had become a master of arts and lecturer on philosophy by 1590. The Capuchins had entered the Spanish Netherlands in the 1580s and had no Irish member. When he contacted them at Brussels in 1591 he arranged for his books to be kept at Louvain until he could take them to Ireland, revealing an intention to return there; one of the books indicated an interest in medieval mystics. He entered the order on the feast of St

Francis of Assisi, and was thenceforth also known as Francis of Ireland. Professed in 1591, he was ordained a deacon in 1594 and preached at Valenciennes and Mons, where he became a priest in June 1595, before being appointed guardian of the friary at Béthune in August. He became interested in the current mystical movement in the Netherlands, subsequently termed pre-quietism. As a result he was twice reported to Rome, in 1596 and 1598, but managed to have his orthodoxy tried not by the Capuchins but by the more impartial court of the Roman Inquisition, securing acquittal on 1 April 1599 and again on 16 August 1600.

Nugent became renowned for his preaching in French, Latin, and Italian. He trained Capuchin students, including Joseph de Paris, Richelieu's *éminence grise*. He taught theology in Paris (1604) and was elected a definitor or Capuchin adviser; by February 1606 he was back in Belgium, and became vicar then guardian at Lille (1606–9). There he contrived, despite difficulties, to set up a college for needy students of the humanities from Leinster. He was moved to Arras (1609) and then to Douai (1610), but a Capuchin mission to Ireland was always in his mind. Back in May 1608 he had obtained a papal decree establishing on paper such a mission to England, Scotland, and Ireland containing a clause granting dispensations from Capuchin regulations (such as the use of money and the wearing of the habit) that had been made an excuse to hinder the mission. He was helped in obtaining Irish candidates by his cousin Christopher Cusack, president of Irish colleges in the Netherlands.

However, Nugent's plans were interrupted when in August 1610 he was sent to make a Capuchin foundation on the lower Rhine. Cologne was the first site, and the early Capuchins there included several of his Irish recruits, but fraternal strife over supposed innovations drove him out of the Rhineland in April 1615. He was offered a new friary in the new town of Charleville in France as a base for the Irish mission, and from 1615 began sending Capuchins to Ireland. By November 1619 he had fifteen candidates at Charleville. He was then fifty years of age, and had been described in 1617 by an unimpressed William Trumbull, the English representative at Brussels, as a man of medium height, bald, fat, with reddish hair and a long forked beard; he was also crippled with arthritis.

Nugent was a disciplinarian, not always tactful, and even his community opposed him at first, but in 1623 he won the battle to receive Irish applicants directly at Charleville. He was appointed visitor to the Capuchins in Ireland in September 1623. To get a safe conduct he offered to assist James I's efforts to restore the Palatinate to his son-in-law Frederick. But he was no diplomat, and eventually left secretly for Ireland, which he reached by June 1624 and established a Capuchin base in the capital. The diocesan clergy, who saw in him a zealous, experienced Anglo-Irish cleric, asked him to take to Rome their report on the state of religion in Ireland that praised the Capuchins. There in the summer of 1625 he won independence for the friaries in Charleville and Dublin, which were placed directly under the minister-general and not the Belgian Capuchins. Being nominated for the archbishopric of Armagh, he was described by the papal nuncio at Brussels as 'a person of great zeal and goodness, but very attached to his own opinion' (Jennings, 137). He rejected the nomination in a controversial memorandum. He carried letters from Pope Urban VIII to the French court seeking reassurances for the Catholics of Ireland. He was in favour of an English–French connection for Ireland rather than a Spanish one.

In the late summer of 1629 Nugent travelled to Ireland again. Rumours of his being linked with Patrick Cahill's opposition to the religious orders in Ireland, with proselytizing among Trinity College students, and of his investing improperly money given by his cousins, the Plunketts, for Irish students made a bad impression at Rome and in Brussels, where he was in dispute with the Belgian Capuchins. He lost control of the Irish mission, but lived at Charleville bedridden for three years. There he wrote an apologia in two documents, 'Mementoes for the understanding of my several doings' and 'A declaration for deathe'. He died at Charleville on 18 May 1635, in his sixty-sixth year, and was buried in the church there, which was destroyed during the French Revolution. His account of a miracle by St Francis was printed.

IGNATIUS FENNESSY

Sources F. X. Martin, *Friar Nugent: a study of Francis Lavalin Nugent (1569–1635), agent of the Counter-Reformation* (1962) • F. X. Martin, 'An Irish Capuchin missionary in politics: Francis Nugent negotiates with James I, 1623–4', *Bulletin of the Irish Committee of Historical Sciences*, 90 (1960), 1–3 • F. X. Martin, 'A thwarted project: the Capuchin mission to England and Scotland in the seventeenth century, 1608–1660', *Miscellanea Melchor de Pobladura*, ed. I. Villapadierna, 2 (Rome, 1964), 211–41 • F. X. Martin and A. de Meijer, 'Sources for the history of the Irish Capuchins', *Collectanea Franciscana*, 26 (1956), 67–79 • M. a Tugio, ed., *Bullarium ordinis ff. minorum S. P. Francisci Capucinorum*, 7 vols. in 4 (Rome, 1740–52), vols. 4–5 • B. Jennings, ed., *Wadding papers, 1614–38*, IMC (1953) • H. van Hooglede, 'Un mouvement pseudo-mystique chez les premiers capucins belges', *Franciscana*, 7 (1927), 257–63 • H. van Hooglede, 'Les premiers capucins belges et la mystique', *Revue d'Ascétique et de Mystique*, 19 (1938), 245–94 • J. H. Sbaralea, *Supplementum … ad scriptores … S. Francisci*, 3 vols. (Rome, 1908–36), vol.1 • L. Bieler, 'Father Francis Nugent, founder of the Irish Capuchins', *Irish Book Lover*, 30 (1946–8), 98–9 • J. Brady, 'More about Lavalin Nugent', *Irish Book Lover*, 30 (1946–8), 100–02 • A. Dasseville, 'Francis Nugent', *Round Table of Franciscan Research*, 15 (1950), 103–17 • *Historia Capuccina … in Lucern*, ed. P. a Melchior, 2 vols. (1946), vol. 1 • H. C. Walshe, 'The rebellion of William Nugent, 1581', *Religion, conflict, and coexistence in Ireland: essays presented to Monsignor Patrick J. Corish*, ed. R. V. Comerford and others (1990), 26–52 • J. P. Mahaffy, *An epoch in Irish history: Trinity College, Dublin, its foundation and early fortunes, 1591–1660* (1903) • C. Cuthbert, *The Capuchins: a contribution to the history of the Counter-Reformation*, 2 vols. (1928) • Father Paschal, 'The Capuchins in Ireland', *Capuchin Annual* (1964), 371–5 • Father Angelus, *Pages from the story of the Irish Capuchins* (1915) • R. Hayes, *Biographical dictionary of Irishmen in France* (1949) • J. Lodge, *The peerage of Ireland*, 4 vols. (1754) • J. J. Silke, 'The Irish abroad, 1534–1691', *A new history of Ireland*, ed. T. W. Moody and others, 3: *Early modern Ireland, 1534–1691* (1976), 587–633

Archives Archives départementales de l'Aube, Troyes, France, Bibliothèque Municipale • Archivio Vaticano, Vatican City • Archivum Generale OFM Capuccinorum, Rome • Biblioteca Apostolica Vaticana, Vatican City • Franciscan Library, Killiney, co.

Dublin • Irish Capuchin Provincial Archives, Dublin • Sacra Congregazione di Propaganda Fide, Rome

Nugent, Lavall, Count Nugent in the nobility of the Austrian empire (1777–1862), army officer in the imperial service, was born at Ballinacor, co. Wicklow, Ireland, on 3 or 30 November 1777. Burke states that he was the elder son of John Nugent (d. 1781) of Bracklin, co. Westmeath, and afterwards of Ballinacor, and his wife, Jane (d. 1820), the daughter of Bryan McDonough, and that he went to Austria in 1789, having been adopted by an uncle, Oliver, Count Nugent (d. 1824), a colonel in the Austrian army. Austrian biographers describe him as the son (probably meaning adopted son) of Count Michael Antony Nugent (d. 1812), master of the ordnance and governor of Prague. All that appears certain about his early years is that on 1 November 1793 he was appointed a cadet in the Austrian engineer corps, with which he served as lieutenant and captain until the end of February 1799. He obtained his captaincy during the fighting round Mainz in April 1795, where he repeatedly distinguished himself by his coolness under fire. He served with distinction on the quartermaster-general's staff, to which he was transferred on 1 March 1799, and with which he was present at the siege of Turin (11–20 June), the investment of the castles of Serradella and Savona (August), and other operations in the Italian campaign of 1799 and in the Marengo campaign of 1800. He won the Maria Theresa cross, and was promoted major at Monte Croce, where the Austrians defeated the French on 10 April 1800.

Nugent obtained his lieutenant-colonelcy at Caldiero, near Verona, where the French, under Massena, were defeated on 29–30 October 1805. He was appointed commandant of the 61st infantry regiment in 1807, and was transferred to the general staff at the beginning of the campaign of 1809, through which he served. He was second plenipotentiary at the peace conference which preceded the marriage of Bonaparte with the Archduchess Maria Louisa, but refused to sign the proposed conditions. While on the unemployed list of general officers he appears to have visited England. In a letter to Lord Wellington dated 12 October 1812, Earl Bathurst, then secretary of state for war, stated that Nugent was at the time in London, having been sent from Sicily by Lord William Bentinck to represent his views in respect of a descent on Italy. Nugent had been in England on the same errand in the summer of 1811, and had been thought highly of by Marquess Wellesley, then foreign secretary. Bathurst believed that Nugent had been promised the rank of major-general in the British service by the prince regent and Wellesley. The difficulties were explained to him, and he did not press the execution of the engagement. On his way back to Sicily early in 1813 Nugent went to Spain to pay his respects to Wellington, having been provided with letters of introduction by the government. He preferred to wear British uniform, but this was without official significance: he did not wish to figure as an Austrian general. Lord Liverpool wrote that Nugent was 'a very intelligent man, but more attached to an Italian operation than I am' (*Supplementary Despatches*, 7.463). Wellington appears to have made Nugent, whose visit was most opportune, the bearer of his views to Vienna, and Liverpool wrote again that the British government 'are much pleased with your having done so' (ibid.).

On 1 July 1813 Nugent was again placed on the active list of the Austrian army. He appears to have originated the idea of bringing the Croats into the field and opening up the Adriatic with the aid of the British cruisers. On 27 July he wrote to Wellington from Prague, congratulating him on the victory at Vitoria, and stating that he was on the point of starting with 5000 light troops to raise the Croats. On 11 August 1813 Austria again declared war against France. Nugent began operations at Karlstadt, where he won back the troops of five districts to the Austrian standard. In a series of successful engagements he drove the French behind the Isongo and speedily effected a junction with generals Staremberg and Folseis. He besieged Trieste and blockaded the castle from 16 to 30 October 1813, when it surrendered. After landing with the aid of the British naval squadron and marines in November 1813 at Volturno, south of the Po and in the rear of the French army, he was joined by a small contingent of British troops from Lissa, consisting of two companies of the 35th foot, two guns, and some detachments of Corsicans and Calabrians in British pay. He fortified Comachio, fought actions at Ferrara, Forli, and Ravenna, and completed the blockade of Venice in December 1813. Early in 1814, having been reinforced, Nugent took the offensive, defeated the French in sanguinary engagements at Reggio, Parma, and Piacenza, and ended the campaign at Marengo in Piedmont, on receiving news of the general peace. The British contingent, the only British troops that had marched right across Italy, joined Lord William Bentinck at Genoa. Lord Castlereagh recommended that Murat's claims to the kingdom of Naples be submitted to Nugent. Nugent became lieutenant or lieutenant-general in the same year. In 1815 he was made an honorary KCB, but except in this capacity his name does not appear in any British army list as having held British military rank.

Nugent entered Florence at the head of a division of Marshal Bianchi's army on 15 April 1815; he invested Rome at the beginning of May, which led to the adhesion of the pontiff to the European alliance. He was afterwards ordered to Sicily to confer with Lord William Bentinck. He commanded an Austrian division in the south of France later in the year, when a British force held Marseilles. He commanded the Austrian troops in Naples in 1816, in which year he was made a prince in the papal nobility, and became colonel proprietor of the 30th infantry regiment. With the emperor's permission he commanded the Neapolitan army, with the rank of captain-general, from 1817 to 1820, but he was dismissed when King Ferdinand accepted the new constitution at the time of General Pepe's insurrection. In 1828 he was appointed to command a division at Venice and superintended the erection of the defences of Trieste and on the adjacent coast of Istria. In 1829 he was created a magnate of Hungary, a dignity conferring a hereditary seat in the upper house of the Hungarian diet. From 1830 to 1840 he was master of the ordnance, and commanded the troops in Lower Austria and the Tyrol; he attained the rank of full general in 1838. In 1841–2 he commanded in the Banat and adjoining districts, and from 1843 to 1848 again in Lower Austria.

At the time of the revolt in Lombardy in 1848 Nugent was appointed to command the reserve of the army in Italy, which he resigned on the ground of ill health, but immediately afterwards he organized a reserve corps, with which he moved on the right flank of the Austrians into Hungary, where the revolution broke out on 11 September. By his judicious arrangements he effected the capitulation of Essigg on 14 February 1849 and afterwards held Peterwaraden in check, so as to secure the navigation of the Danube and the imperial magazines on it. He organized a second reserve corps in Styria and marched with Prince Windischgratz's army against Comorn. With the raising of the siege of Comorn in July 1849, when the corps under his command was driven back towards Serbia, Nugent's services in the field came to a close. He became a field marshal in November 1849. His last service was at the age of eighty-two, when he was present as a volunteer on the field of Solferino on 24 June 1859.

Nugent married, in 1815, Jane, duchess of Riario Sforza, the only child and heir of Raphael, duke of Riario Sforza, and his wife, Beatrix, the third daughter and coheir of Francis Xavier, prince of Poland and Saxony, the second son of Augustus III, king of Poland, and Maria Josephine of Austria, the eldest daughter of Joseph I, emperor of Germany. They had, among other children, Albert, eventually prince and count, who was an Austrian staff officer at the capture of Acre in 1841.

Nugent, who held many foreign orders, died at Bosiljevo, near Karlstadt, Croatia, on 21 August 1862, in the words of the emperor: 'den ältesten, victor-probten und unermüdlichen Soldaten der k. k. Armee' ('the oldest, victory-proven and indefatigable soldier of the imperial army').　　　H. M. CHICHESTER, rev. ROGER T. STEARN

Sources Burke, *Peerage* (1862) · Burke, *Peerage* (1892) · Otto, Graf zu Stolberg-Wernigerode, ed., *Neue deutsche Biographie* (Berlin, 1953–) · Ward, *Men of the reign* · *Annual Register* (1813–16) · Boase, *Mod. Eng. biog.* · *Supplementary despatches (correspondence) and memoranda of Field Marshal Arthur, duke of Wellington*, ed. A. R. Wellesley, second duke of Wellington, 15 vols. (1858–72)

Nugent [*née* Skinner], **Maria, Lady Nugent** (1770/71–1834), diarist, was probably born in the American colony of New Jersey. She was the fifth of seven daughters in the family of twelve of Cortlandt *Skinner (1727–1799) and his wife, Elizabeth, *née* Kearny (1731–1810). Her father, advocate-general of New Jersey, remained a loyalist during the American War of Independence, and came to England with his family on the declaration of peace. In 1797 she married George *Nugent (1757–1849), an army officer and MP for Buckingham. In 1801 he was appointed lieutenant-governor and commander-in-chief of Jamaica, where he remained until 1806; rewarded with a baronetcy, he resumed his military and political career in England before being appointed in 1811 commander-in-chief in India. His wife, who accompanied him abroad, recorded her experiences in Jamaica and India in journals which were privately printed in 1839.

Maria Nugent was an attractive person, described by a contemporary in 1800 as 'very pretty … she has the smallest head that can be, very thin and little. She is an amazing dresser, never appears twice in the same gown' (Fremantle, 3.26). She sketched and wrote poetry, and, with her vivacity, sense of humour, religious feeling, and concern for individuals, was a perceptive observer of society wherever she went. However, her changing domestic circumstances and the differing British involvement in Jamaica and India were reflected in the tone of the two journals. The Nugents had no children when they arrived in Jamaica. Avoiding comment on political issues, her journal at first concentrates on Jamaican society and planter life. Slavery concerned her, not only in its effect on the black population, but also in the sexual exploitation by European men which it encouraged at all social levels. Turbulence and uprisings in the Caribbean among the slaves soon transformed her vision of them as essentially happy, childish creatures; in common with Jamaican planter society, she learned to distrust and fear the slaves, whom she came to perceive as dangerous, wild savages. The birth of a son in 1802, and a daughter within eleven months, provided a different focus of interest, and concern for their health encouraged her early return to England in 1805.

Two other surviving children were born in England, and the necessity of leaving her family behind on her departure for India in 1811—a son had been born just six weeks before—in many ways determined Maria Nugent's experience of the country. She was grief-stricken at the separation, constantly ill, and isolated in her misery. Her accustomed spirits only revived when she left Calcutta to accompany her husband on a year's tour (1812–13) of the areas round Delhi, recently settled by the British following the end of the Second Anglo-Maratha War. She gives a perceptive picture of British society and its relations with the Indian ruling classes at a period when British hegemony was not fully assured. In an as yet uncertain balance, many Indian rulers were courted as equals, and customs and habits were shared and exchanged. Nevertheless, the pattern of subsequent British social life was beginning to emerge, underpinned by British women who, though very few in number, were often present in even the remotest areas. The old-established cultures and religions of India provoked in Lady Nugent a different response from the planter society of Jamaica. While she deplored the beliefs of Hindus, she genuinely admired their piety, and accepted the limited possibility for conversion. Relations with Indian women were also of a different order; marriage or formal unions with Indians or Eurasians were common, and their offspring were accepted socially at an official level in a manner unthinkable in Jamaica. Yet, as in Jamaica, Lady Nugent was constantly concerned at young men's involvement in liaisons with non-Europeans, revealing her disquiet at racial mixing.

The private nature of the journals enabled Maria Nugent to explore such topics in a way that is enlightening for the later reader, and they are an invaluable record for historians. Her frankness about individuals and situations reveals much about British colonial society and attitudes. Equally, her record of her own feelings illustrates the reality of women's experience, particularly in India. In sketchy note form when she is depressed and ill, expansive when her interest is engaged, her writing reflects the intense pressures imposed by separation from family, loneliness, illness, and extreme heat. Sir George Nugent gave up his role as governor-general in 1814 and left India the following year. The family moved to Westhorpe House, Little Marlow, Buckinghamshire, where Lady Nugent spent the remainder of her life, involving herself in charitable work until her death there on 24 October 1834. She was buried on 1 November at Little Marlow parish church.   ROSEMARY CARGILL RAZA

Sources M. Nugent, *A journal from the year 1811 till the year 1815 including a voyage to and residence in India, with a tour of the north-western parts of the British possessions in that country, under the Bengal government*, 2 vols. (1839) · *Lady Nugent's journal: Jamaica one hundred years ago*, ed. F. Cundall (1907) · *Lady Nugent's journal of her residence in Jamaica from 1801 to 1805*, ed. P. Wright, new edn (1966) · *The Wynne diaries*, ed. A. Fremantle, 3 (1940) · Bucks. RLSS, D/FR/43/H

Likenesses J. Downman, pencil and wash drawing, 1806, BM · G. Adcock, engraving, repro. in Nugent, *Journal from the year 1811 till the year 1815* · J. Downman, group portrait, oils (with family), priv. coll. · portraits, repro. in Wright, ed., *Lady Nugent's journal of her residence in Jamaica*

Nugent, Nicholas (*d.* 1582), judge, was the fifth son of Sir Christopher Nugent and Marian or Marion, daughter of Nicholas St Lawrence, third Baron Howth. Having entered Lincoln's Inn in 1558, he was involved in 1560 in an altercation with two other students from Ireland, Robert Dillon and John Talbot, for which he was bound over to keep the peace. This animosity between Dillon and Nugent, grounded in personal and familial rivalry, was eventually to lead to Nugent's downfall.

Nugent's service to the crown in Ireland began when he was named as a commissioner for determining the title to certain lands on 19 November 1564. His appointment during pleasure to the office of chief solicitor to the crown on 5 December 1566 was in the place of Lucas Dillon (the cousin of Robert Dillon), recently created attorney-general. With the two Dillons and twenty-three other leading judges and lawyers from the pale, Nugent shared in the renewal of the royal lease of the Blackfriars or King's Inns near Dublin in January 1567. Although the lawyers' aspirations to establish a system of legal training there may have come to nothing, the influence of their profession on the reform programme of the early Elizabethan period was significant. Nugent, for example, served on a number of government commissions in the 1560s and 1570s for establishing the political and legal writ of the Tudor administration in Munster, Connaught, and the north midlands.

The advancement of Nugent's legal career was undoubtedly aided by his marriage to Ellen (*d.* 1615), daughter of Sir John Plunkett, chief justice of the queen's bench, and widow of Walter Marward, baron of Skreen, co. Meath.

The couple had at least one son, Richard [see below], and Nugent also took on the wardship of his stepdaughter, Jenet Marward. On 18 October 1570 he was created second baron of the exchequer, but his service on the bench was jeopardized by his growing involvement in the campaign of the leading landowners of the pale against cess, the government's policy of arbitrary taxation for the victualling of the army in Ireland. He was twice imprisoned in Dublin Castle in 1577 and 1578 for his recalcitrance, and was eventually deprived of his office by the lord deputy, Sir Henry Sidney. On Sidney's retirement he was appointed to the office of chief justice of common pleas on the recommendation of the lord chancellor, Sir William Gerard. While popular with many of the gentry of the pale, Nugent's appointment was bitterly resented by Robert Dillon, who had regarded the job as his entitlement.

With the support of higher officials in Dublin such as Sir Henry Wallop (who asserted that Gerard had received £100 as a bribe from Nugent), Dillon succeeded in overturning the appointment and securing his own elevation in 1581. Against the background of the Nugent conspiracy led by his nephew William *Nugent (d. 1625), who had married Nicholas's stepdaughter after a dramatic abduction, Nicholas was vulnerable to the charge of complicity, especially as he had been made responsible by the Irish privy council for William's younger son Christopher. In the course of his negotiations over the boy, Nugent had had dealings with one John Cusack of Ellistonrede, co. Meath. Cusack had played a conspicuous part in William Nugent's rebellion but turned state's evidence on the promise of a pardon. On Cusack's information Nicholas Nugent and Edward Cusack, son and heir of Sir Thomas Cusack, were committed to Dublin Castle on 28 January 1582.

They were tried before a special commission at Trim on 4 April. The only witness against Nugent was John Cusack, by whom he was charged with being privy to William Nugent's rebellion and with planning the assassination of Sir Robert and Sir Lucas Dillon. Nugent objected that the evidence of one witness—his personal enemy—was insufficient. His objection being overruled, Nugent denied the truth of Cusack's accusations, and he also denied some admissions he had apparently made earlier to Sir Lucas Dillon and Sir Geoffrey Fenton. The lord deputy, Arthur, Lord Grey of Wilton, who 'sate upon the benche to see justice more equally ministered' (CSP Ire., 1574–85, 364), addressed the jury before it retired. When it appeared that the jury was in favour of an acquittal, Sir Robert brought pressure on the members to find Nugent guilty of treason. Judgment followed, and on the eve of Easter (6 April 1582) Nugent was hanged, 'to which death he went resolutely and patiently, protesting that sith he was not found trewe, as he said he ought to have been, he had no longinge to live in infamy' (BL, Sloane MS 4793, fol. 132).

Nugent's conviction and execution, widely regarded as a travesty of justice, were engineered by his bitter rival, Sir Robert Dillon, with the connivance of senior figures in the Dublin administration. After his death his widow, Ellen, succeeded in obtaining a reversal of his attainder, despite the opposition of Wallop, and on 27 August 1584 the queen granted his estate to her for life. The heir to Nicholas and Ellen Nugent was **Richard Nugent** (b. 1564/5, d. in or after 1615). At the time of the Nugent conspiracy in 1581 (when he was sixteen), he was taken hostage by the Irish privy council as a surety for the delivery of his cousin, son of the leading insurgent, William Nugent. He was released on recognizances of £1000. He married Anne, daughter of Christopher Bath of Rathfeigh, co. Meath, and had at least one child, Christopher. In keeping with the literary traditions within the Nugent family, Richard was, like his first cousin William, an accomplished poet. He was apparently the author of *Rich. Nugent's Cynthia, containing direfull sonnets, madrigalls and passionate intercourses, describing his repudiate affections expressed in loves owne language*. The work was printed by Thomas Purfoot for Henry Tomes in London in 1604. Richard succeeded his mother to the Nugent estate on 9 November 1615 but the extent of his tenure is uncertain, as is the date of his death.   COLM LENNON

Sources 'A discourse touching the proceedings upon the triall and executing of Mr Nicholas Nugent, chief justice of the common pleas', c.1590, BL, Sloane MS 4793, fols. 127–40 • CSP Ire., 1574–85 • F. E. Ball, *The judges in Ireland, 1221–1921*, 2 vols. (1926) • B. Iske, *The green cockatrice* (1978) • 'Calendar of fiants, Henry VIII to Elizabeth', *Report of the Deputy Keeper of the Public Records in Ireland*, 7–22 (1875–90), appxs • J. S. Brewer and W. Bullen, eds., *Calendar of the Carew manuscripts*, 2: 1575–1588, PRO (1868) • H. C. Walshe, 'The rebellion of William Nugent, 1581', *Religion, conflict, and coexistence in Ireland: essays presented to Monsignor Patrick J. Corish*, ed. R. V. Comerford and others (1990), 26–52 • DNB • C. Kenny, *King's Inns and the kingdom of Ireland* (1992) • J. Lodge, *The peerage of Ireland*, rev. M. Archdall, rev. edn, 7 vols. (1789) • D. Cregan, 'Irish Catholic admissions to the English inns of court, 1558–1625', *Irish Jurist*, new ser., 5 (1970), 95–114 • [R. Nugent], *Rich. Nugents Cynthia* (1604) • valuation of traitors' lands in the pale, April 1582, SP 63/90/59, PRO
Wealth at death lands valued at £140 p.a.: valuation of traitors' lands in the pale, April 1582, PRO, SP 63/90/59

Nugent, Sir Oliver Stewart Wood (1860–1926), army officer, was born on 9 November 1860 at South Camp, Aldershot, Hampshire, the only surviving son of Major-General St George Mervyn Nugent (1825–1884) of Farren Connell, Mount Nugent, co. Cavan, Ireland, and his wife, Emily Frances (d. c.1920), daughter of the Rt Hon. Edward Litton of co. Tyrone. He was educated at Harrow School and in 1883 commissioned from the militia (the Royal Munster Fusiliers) into the King's Royal Rifle Corps (KRRC). From 1886 to 1895 he served in India; he campaigned on the north-west frontier in 1891–2 and again in 1895 with the Chitral relief column, earning the DSO. In 1897–8 he attended the staff college, where his fellow students included Douglas Haig, and on 7 February 1899 he married Catherine Percy (1875–1970), daughter of Thomas Lees, an English MP, with whom he had a son and two daughters. In October 1899, serving with the 1st KRRC, he was severely wounded at Talana Hill, one of the opening engagements of the Second South African War, and spent several months as a prisoner before being invalided home. In 1906–10 he commanded the 4th KRRC and from 1911–14, as a colonel, a territorial infantry brigade.

Early in 1914 Nugent returned to Ireland on half pay and

during the home rule crisis supported the Ulster Unionists, helping train the Cavan contingent of the Ulster Volunteer Force. Despite the widespread support which the Unionists enjoyed in the army's officer corps (evidenced by the Curragh incident), this was not in retrospect an episode with which he felt comfortable. However, the outbreak of war in August ended the immediate crisis in Ireland, and Nugent was recalled to organize the Hull defences. In May 1915 he took command of 41st brigade (14th division), a New Army formation which in late July suffered heavy losses near Ypres in a German assault using flame-throwers, their first use against the British. In September 1915 he was promoted to command the 36th (Ulster) division—in effect the pre-war Ulster Volunteer Force in khaki, following Carson's offer in September 1914 to place that force at the government's disposal—and took it to France the following month. Despite his protestant Ulster background, Nugent's relationship with the division's political supporters proved difficult. He was an Irish rather than an Ulster Unionist, and was not always in sympathy with the political and religious feelings of his fervently loyalist soldiers. Tensions were not eased by his quick temper (exacerbated by his South African wounds) and his inability to suffer fools, into which category he lumped on occasion both military superiors and political acquaintances.

It was somewhat ironic, then, that it was Nugent who commanded the division in its first and most famous battle, the attack on the Schwaben redoubt near Thiepval on 1 July 1916, the first day of the battle of the Somme, which made its military reputation and proved one of the defining experiences of the Ulster protestant/unionist tradition in the twentieth century. In an exceptional performance Nugent's highly motivated troops overran five lines of trenches, captured the redoubt, and penetrated the German main second position, an advance of almost 2 miles despite the failure of the divisions on their flanks, before being forced back in desperate fighting to the German front line. Their 5000 casualties devastated many Ulster communities and created a folk memory which remains powerful today. Nugent could do little to influence events once the attack had begun because of inadequate communications: his key contributions to the division's initial success were his comprehensive pre-battle training and his decision to push his leading waves into no man's land before zero hour, so enabling them to overrun the forward German positions before they could be manned.

After the battle the division faced a new threat. Irish recruiting, always proportionately lower than in Britain, had by 1916 fallen away further, and without Irish conscription, losses in Irish units could not be replaced. Nugent, a strong supporter of compulsory service, was openly scathing about the 'failure' of Irish politicians, unionist and nationalist, fully to support the war effort. This was resented in Ulster, which had provided a disproportionate number of Irish recruits in 1914–15, but Nugent was unrepentant, his ire intensified by the decision of the Ulster Unionist leadership—with whom his

relations had by now virtually broken down—to pursue a partitionist Irish settlement which excluded Cavan. It seemed that the Ulster division and other Irish formations would disappear through amalgamation or disbandment, but the decision was eventually taken for political reasons to reinforce them with drafts from Britain, and by early 1917 they were back up to strength.

In June 1917 Nugent commanded the division in the highly successful assault at Messines under Plumer, a general he greatly admired. By contrast their next battle, in August 1917 at Ypres in appalling conditions, was a costly and dispiriting failure for which Nugent never forgave Gough, the army commander. In November/December 1917 the division fought at Cambrai and in March 1918 only narrowly escaped annihilation during the German spring offensive; Nugent deserves credit for holding it together during some ferocious fighting. In May 1918 he was replaced, in line with the army's policy of bringing in younger commanders, and commanded the Meerut division in India until his retirement in 1920. Two years later he was knighted, an honour which was widely believed to have been delayed by Haig, with whom he did not get on. He died on 31 May 1926 at Farren Connell and was buried in Mount Nugent churchyard on 3 June.

Nugent was an energetic and capable soldier under whom the Ulster division won an enviable reputation. His dismissive attitude towards politicians was an obvious disadvantage when commanding so political a formation, while greater tact might have secured him further advancement professionally. But although demanding he cared deeply for his men and sought never to waste their lives, in so doing earning their respect and gratitude. In contrast to his military reputation as a disciplinarian, in his private life he was a devoted husband and father and a considerate landlord.

NICHOLAS PERRY

Sources C. Falls, *The history of the 36th (Ulster) division* (1922) • *The Times* (2 June 1926) • *Irish Times* (1 June 1926) • *Belfast News-Letter* (1 June 1926) • *The King's Royal Rifle Corps* (1927) • J. E. Edmonds, ed., *Military operations, France and Belgium, 1916*, 1, History of the Great War (1932) • J. E. Edmonds, ed., *Military operations, France and Belgium, 1917*, 2, History of the Great War (1948) • J. E. Edmonds, ed., *Military operations, France and Belgium, 1918*, 1–2, History of the Great War (1935–7) • W. Miles, ed., *Military operations: France and Belgium, 1917*, 3 (1948) • P. Orr, *The road to the Somme* (1987) • N. Perry, 'Politics and command: General Nugent, the Ulster division and relations with Ulster unionism, 1915–17', *Look to your front: British commission for military history* (1999), 105–20 • *WWW* • private information (2004) • b. cert.

Archives PRO NIre., Farren Connell MSS, corresp. and MSS | FILM IWM FVA, actuality footage

Likenesses W. Conor, oils, 1926?, Belfast City Council • photograph, repro. in Falls, *History of the 36th (Ulster) division*

Wealth at death £10,677 1s.: probate, 9 Oct 1926, *CGPLA Eng. & Wales*

Nugent, Richard, first Baron Delvin and baron of Delvin (d. **1475**), administrator, was the son of Sir William Nugent (d. c.1415), who was recognized in 1387–8 as hereditary baron of Delvin, Meath, and of Katherine, daughter of John Fitzjohn, baron of Delvin (fl. 1372), and heir of her brother, John, who died, after their father, in 1382. The dates of birth of Richard and his younger brother, William (*fl. c.*1430–1444), are uncertain, but the former, as his mother's heir, was sufficiently adult to be granted custody of some small properties in Meath in September 1406. He succeeded to the barony on his father's death and was knighted in 1425. He was twice seneschal (1420, 1423) for the then lord of the liberty of Meath, Edmund Mortimer, earl of March, and again at least once (1452/3) under March's successor, Richard, duke of York (*d.* 1460). He also served in Meath as a justice and keeper of the peace and at least three times (1425, 1428, 1430–31) as sheriff. Apparently the latter office became burdensome: the only parliament over which he presided as deputy lieutenant exempted Irish peers from future shrieval service in 1449.

Nugent first became deputy at a time of great tension in Dublin following the summons of the then lieutenant, James Butler, fourth earl of Ormond (*d.* 1452), to England to answer charges of treason. On 28 August 1444 the two men agreed detailed arrangements for Nugent to govern until Ormond's return or at least until 1 May 1445. However, controversial orders from the earl to remove the Irish exchequer and common bench to Drogheda could not be enforced, and on 22 January Nugent was ousted prematurely by the election of Ormond's leading opponent, Richard Talbot, archbishop of Dublin, as justiciar. In less difficult circumstances Nugent was deputy for Richard of York from late 1448 (*ante* 23 December) until York's first arrival in Ireland as lieutenant on 5 or 6 July 1449. On this occasion, besides holding parliament in Dublin, Nugent, with Ormond's assistance, intervened in defence of Louth in an Ó Raghallaigh succession dispute. A military campaign proved unsuccessful, but peace was restored by their negotiation of a truce.

As baron, Nugent attended Irish parliaments at least until 1468. His lengthy career has raised the possibility of there having been two successive lords Delvin of the same name (Gorman, 174), but this was not the case. He married Katherine, daughter of Thomas Drake (*fl.* 1388–1390?) of Carlanstown, Meath. Their eldest son, James (married *c.*1445), predeceased his father about 1450 or 1451 and on Nugent's death in 1475 his successor was James's son, Christopher, who gained livery of the barony that July. A patron of bardic poets, Nugent was lamented that year by a Gaelic annalist as 'an eminent leader' of 'charity and humanity' and 'knowledge of every science' (Hennessy and MacCarthy, 3.256–7).   ELIZABETH MATTHEW

Sources E. Tresham, ed., *Rotulorum patentium et clausorum cancellariae Hiberniae calendarium*, Irish Record Commission (1828) · Ferguson MSS, NA Ire. · E. A. E. Matthew, 'The governing of the Lancastrian lordship of Ireland in the time of James Butler, fourth earl of Ormond, c.1420–1452', PhD diss., U. Durham, 1994 · Nugent pedigrees, Genealogical Office, Dublin · H. F. Berry and J. F. Morrissey, eds., *Statute rolls of the parliament of Ireland*, 4 vols. (1907–39), vols. 2–4 · W. M. Hennessy and B. MacCarthy, eds., *Annals of Ulster, otherwise, annals of Senat*, 4 vols. (1887–1901), vol. 3 · R. Frame, ed. and trans., 'Commissions of the peace in Ireland, 1302–1461', *Analecta Hibernica*, 35 (1992), 1–43 · K. Simms, 'Bards and barons: the Anglo-Irish aristocracy and the native culture', *Medieval frontier societies*, ed. R. Bartlett and A. MacKay (1989), 177–97 · W. G. H. Quigley and E. F. D. Roberts, eds., *Registrum Iohannis Mey: the register of John Mey, archbishop of Armagh, 1443–1456* (1972) · V. Gorman, 'Richard, duke of York, and the development of an Irish faction', *Proceedings of the Royal Irish Academy*, 85C (1985), 169–79 · NL Ire., Ormond deeds, D 1718 · PRO · *AFM*, vol. 4 · J. Lodge, *The peerage of Ireland*, 1 (1754)

Archives NL Ire., Ormond deeds, D 1718

Nugent, Richard, third Baron Delvin (*d.* 1538), governor of Ireland, was the son and heir of Christopher Nugent, second Baron Delvin, and Anne Preston, daughter of Robert, first Viscount Gormanston. The title's origins are obscure, but the feudal barony of Delvin was later deemed to include a peerage, making Richard Nugent twelfth feudal baron of Delvin and third Lord Delvin. He was perhaps under age when his father died of plague in 1478, but he was among the lords of Ireland circularized by Richard III in September 1484. Perhaps first summoned to the Irish parliament in 1486, he attended the parliaments of 1491, 1493, and 1499 when he was fined 40s. for absence from the second session at Castledermot. In May 1488 he was pardoned with other pale magnates for his role in the Lambert Simnel conspiracy the previous year.

The location of Delvin's estates in the north-west marches of Meath, notably the small but strategically situated barony of Delvin, meant that he was a key figure in the defence of the Meath Englishry, and by the 1490s his military reputation was growing. On 25 June 1496, as English military activity in Ireland wound down in the aftermath of Poynings's expedition, Delvin was appointed chief captain of the king's forces, with a salary of £200 a year, pending Kildare's reappointment as governor. At the battle of Knockdoe in August 1504, he commanded the English cavalry stationed on the left flank of the main battle, and in the preliminary skirmishing he slew one of the Burkes with a casting spear. He apparently also served on the peace commission for Meath, and by 1522 he was a member of the king's council, although not normally a regular attender.

Despite his military prowess and political reliability, however, Delvin's meagre landed patrimony and localized *manraed* hampered his attempts to play more than a local role in the lordship's politics. He was one of the five or six most prominent Meath landowners, but despite recent acquisitions of marchland there, his exposed Westmeath estates yielded no more than £80 a year, with perhaps the same from lands in co. Louth, and £30 annually from scattered co. Dublin estates. Thus, after the king had chosen Delvin as acting governor of Ireland—in the absence of the earls of Kildare and Ormond, who were summoned to court in another attempt to reconcile their differences—he was soon in difficulties. In preparation for this new role, Delvin's landed influence in Westmeath was in September 1526 consolidated by a fifty-year lease for £10 annually of the manors of Belgard and Four, of which he had earlier had the custody and which were worth £44 a year. He had been absent from Ireland since June, presumably at court, but he assumed office in 1527, nominally as Kildare's deputy, superseding the earl's brother, Sir Thomas Fitzgerald. His relations with Kildare were so poor, however, that in 1524 the earl had been compelled to undertake not to stir up any war against him.

None the less, despite the weakness of his position, Delvin dealt high-handedly as governor with the Gaelic border chiefs. In retaliation for robberies on the Englishry—stirred up by Kildare's supporters 'in the hope he should the rather come home'—Delvin withheld the blackrents traditionally paid to O'Connor Faly and O'Neill, against the council's advice (*LP Henry VIII*, vol. 4, no. 3698). Consequently, 'this poor londe hathe taken great lostes and damagies this winter', according to Archbishop Inge and Chief Justice Bermingham in February 1528. Highlighting Delvin's inadequacies, they complained that 'the vice deputy is nat of power [i.e. lacks tenants] to defende the Englisshrie'. He extended the incidence of coign and livery, so that 'the poor people is ferr more chargid and oppressed by hym than they have been, thErll of Kildare being here'. Moreover, Delvin 'hathe no great londes of his owne' and without the parliamentary subsidy which had recently expired, the revenues barely sufficed to pay officers' salaries (*State Papers, Henry VIII*, 2.126).

Continuing raids by O'Connor Faly eventually led to a parley on 12 May 1528, by Sir William Darcy's border castle of Rathyn, where Delvin was kidnapped by the chief, his footmen slain, and his horsemen wounded or taken prisoner. O'Connor then refused to release the baron without a ransom and restoration of his blackrent. Lord Butler, who visited him at O'Connor's house on safe conduct, reported that Delvin was closely confined and only allowed to speak with him openly in Irish, so that their conversation could be understood. In the emergency Sir Thomas Fitzgerald was initially elected chief captain in Delvin's place, until the earl of Ossory's appointment as deputy in August. Yet by February 1529, when the deputy secured the council's agreement to peace with O'Connor and the restoration of his blackrent in return for Delvin's release, much of Meath had been wasted and destroyed by the chief.

After his release Delvin apparently withdrew from high politics. In November 1529 he agreed the marriage of his son and heir, Christopher, to Marian or Marion St Lawrence, Lord Howth's daughter, providing a jointure worth 20 marks annually in return for a dowry of 220 marks. Christopher died in 1531 but had nine children, presumably through an earlier marriage, including Richard, later fourth baron. Following the death of his first wife, Isabella Fitzgerald, Kildare's cousin, Delvin married Elizabeth St Lawrence (*d.* 1559), presumably Marion's sister, probably on 4 February 1531. In June 1534, however, another emergency following Thomas Fitzgerald's resignation and rebellion saw the veteran captain again elected governor by the council. He served unavailingly for eight weeks as the rebels consolidated their hold on the pale. Following the arrival of Lord Deputy Skeffington with the king's army in October, Delvin's local knowledge and military experience were more fruitfully employed in breaking down rebel resistance. Given command of one of the army garrisons, Delvin had by spring 1535 a general oversight of the defence of Meath. He participated in the final expedition to the borders of Offaly, signing the letter of 27 August to the king which described Thomas Fitzgerald's surrender, and later received 40 marks as the king's reward for his services.

Despite his advanced age Delvin remained remarkably active in the aftermath of the revolt, supervising the defence of Westmeath and participating in occasional expeditions. In May 1536, when he came up to parliament, Lord Deputy Grey refused Delvin and Lord Butler licence to repair to court because, after Ossory, they were 'the best and politic captains of the Englishry' (*State Papers, Henry VIII*, 2.317). Delvin distinguished himself in the deputy's hosting against O'Connor in June 1537, detaching O'Molloy, Mageoghegan, and O'Melaghlin, the chief's *uir-rioghtha* (vassal-chiefs) from him before conducting the army by an unusual route into Offaly, where the Dangan, O'Connor's strong new castle, was captured and razed. A similar hosting the following November was less successful, however, and tension developed between Grey and Delvin, resulting in a complete breach between them during a third hosting against O'Connor in February 1538. Against the advice of experienced marchers, Grey led the army into Offaly by a dangerous ford of the River Barrow, then in flood, ordering them to swim their horses across, whereupon some were lost. The baron, 'being an old man and an ancient captain', with other Meath lords refused to cross, at which Grey called them traitors and had them stripped of their horses, harness, and weapons, and left to shift for themselves in enemy country. This notorious incident later formed one of the more serious charges against Grey in 1540, but Delvin 'toke suche grief and fantasie of the said myshandelinges, and especiallie that the lorde deputie callid him traitor' that he never recovered (*State Papers, Henry VIII*, 3.37–8). He lingered until 28 February 1538, and was buried in the local church of Castletown Delvin. His grandson Richard, then aged fourteen, succeeded him as fourth baron; but of his surviving younger sons, Thomas had already emerged as a resourceful marcher during his father's lifetime, and William, executor of his father's will, was the last prior of Fore and rector of Trim and Ardnurgher. Delvin's widow, Elizabeth, lived until 1 March 1559.

Later Tudor barons of Delvin had a pronounced interest in the Gaelic language and culture, but it is unclear whether the third baron shared these, beyond speaking the language. He was certainly a familiar figure in the Gaelic world, respected as 'ridire cródha cogthach' ('a brave and warlike knight') who provided 'sgiath didin ocus cliath ghaeithe Ghall re Gaeidheluibh' ('a shield of shelter and a windbreak to the English against the Irish'; *Annals of Loch Cé*, 2.310–11). Among the Englishry, Delvin epitomized the traditional virtues of a border baron—a shrewd mind, a good captain, a loyal English subject with numerous retainers—at a time when these qualities were in short supply among the palesmen. Sir Anthony St Leger, reporting his death (eighteen days prematurely, as it transpired), described him as 'oon of the best marchers of this countre', adding that 'the kyngis highnes hath a grete losse of hym' (*State Papers, Henry VIII*, 2.546).

STEVEN G. ELLIS

Sources LP Henry VIII · State papers published under … Henry VIII, 11 vols. (1830–52) · M. C. Griffith, ed., *Calendar of inquisitions formerly in the office of the chief remembrancer of the exchequer*, IMC (1991) · G. Mac Niocaill, ed., *Crown surveys of lands, 1540–41, with the Kildare rental begun in 1518*, IMC (1992) · J. Gairdner, ed., *Letters and papers illustrative of the reigns of Richard III and Henry VII*, 2 vols., Rolls Series, 24 (1861–3) · CPR, 1485–94 · A. Conway and E. Curtis, *Henry VII's relations with Scotland and Ireland, 1485–1498* (1932) · N. B. White, ed., *Extents of Irish monastic possessions, 1540–41*, IMC (1943) · Burke, *Peerage* · GEC, *Peerage*, new edn, vol. 4 · S. G. Ellis, *Reform and revival: English government in Ireland, 1470–1534*, Royal Historical Society Studies in History, 47 (1986) · S. G. Ellis, *Ireland in the age of the Tudors* (1998) · B. Bradshaw, *The Irish constitutional revolution of the sixteenth century* (1979) · W. M. Hennessy, ed. and trans., *The annals of Loch Cé: a chronicle of Irish affairs from AD 1014 to AD 1590*, 2 vols., Rolls Series, 54 (1871), vol. 2
Archives NA Ire., Ferguson transcripts, Irish memoranda roll extracts · St Peter's College, Wexford, Hore transcripts, Irish memoranda roll extracts
Wealth at death approx. Ir£240 p.a.: Griffith, ed., *Calendar of inquisitions*; Mac Niocaill, ed., *Crown surveys of lands*

Nugent, Richard (*b*. 1564/5, *d*. in or after 1615). *See under* Nugent, Nicholas (*d*. 1582).

Nugent, Richard, first earl of Westmeath (1583–1642), nobleman, was the eldest of six sons of Christopher *Nugent, fifth Baron Delvin (1544–1602), and Lady Mary or Marie (*d*. 1610/11), daughter of Gerald *Fitzgerald, eleventh earl of Kildare, and succeeded to his father's title, aged nineteen, in October 1602. He was knighted at Dublin Castle on 29 December 1603, and in or before 1604 married Jane, daughter of Christopher Plunkett, Lord Killeen, and Genet Dillon. They had five sons, of whom the eldest, Christopher, was born in 1604, and two daughters.

Delvin was implicated in the conspiracy which was uncovered after the 'flight of the earls' in 1607, having promised Rory O'Donnell, earl of Tyrconnell, that he would help to seize Dublin Castle if Spanish military aid was forthcoming. The main reason for his plotting seems to have been that the government forced him to surrender title to certain lands in Longford. He was imprisoned in Dublin Castle in November 1607 but escaped and fled to co. Cavan. From there he wrote to Lord Deputy Chichester (himself accused of abetting the escape) asking pardon for his inchoate plotting and pleading youth and *naïveté* as an excuse. Unable to capture him, and fearful of the return of the earls of Tyrone and Tyrconnell with outside military assistance, Chichester promised him a pardon if he submitted. He did so in May 1608, and then went to court where his conduct was forgiven and he was granted lands in recompense for those he had surrendered by royal command.

Delvin again incurred the displeasure of the government in 1613. 'Unmindful of his majesty's great favour to him' (*Calendar of the Carew Manuscripts*, 1603–23, 275), he participated in Catholic protests against the creation of new boroughs to secure a protestant majority in the new parliament. In 1620 he was one of three Irish representatives who had some success in petitioning James I with, the latter noted approvingly, 'much modesty, humility and discretion' (*CSP Ire.*, 1614–25, 282) against new alehouse licensing arrangements. Evidently Delvin regained royal favour since he was created earl of Westmeath on 4 September 1621. His attempt, from December 1623 to April 1624, to mobilize opposition to a proposed plantation in Ossory aroused the hostility of Lord Deputy Falkland, who was particularly stung by Westmeath's prescient claim that this was a prelude to a larger plantation in Connaught. It is unlikely to be coincidence that informers now emerged to allege, variously, that Westmeath claimed to be king of Ireland, that he was in correspondence with Spain, and that he would be the next lord deputy. Embarrassed by the allegations, the earl was required to satisfy himself with 'private exercise of his conscience', not to 'set himself up hereafter in the conceit of the multitude' (ibid., 488) and to go to London to clear his name.

War with Spain in 1625, and later with France, and the threat of invasion created the apparent opportunity for Irish Catholics to extract concessions from the crown. Following the refusal of the government to entrust defence to local trained bands in 1626, Westmeath played a leading role in attempts to secure guarantees of religious toleration in return for subsidizing an expanded standing army. Arriving in London in March 1626, he and Sir John Bath presented Catholic grievances to Charles I. They secured what seemed to be significant concessions with the enumeration of 'matters of grace and bounty' including the promise to replace the oath of supremacy with an oath of allegiance as a qualification for formal inheritance of estates, office-holding, and the practice of law. The Catholic leadership as a whole, however, did not consider the concessions adequate, and in May 1627 Westmeath was sent again to England, where he persuaded Charles I to agree to discuss the wider ramifications of his policy with a full delegation. He took part in another delegation, in 1628, which secured additional concessions including, crucially, the promise to renounce crown titles to land of more than sixty years' standing. Ultimately, however, these latter 'graces' were withheld and a period of repression followed.

In 1632 Westmeath lobbied successfully to be chosen to go to England to present a statement of Catholic grievances to Wentworth, the newly appointed lord deputy. He was granted a royal audience and returned despite the efforts of the administration in Dublin to have him detained in London, citing as their reason that he was 'a vehement papist and of a popular carriage among the Irish … none of that religion appears in more eminency upon all occasions for the papists' (*CSP Ire.*, 1625–32, 689). Wentworth's subsequent denial of the promised 'graces' and the impotence of parliamentary opposition were among the longer-term factors which alienated the Old English and precipitated their involvement in the 1641 rising. It also marked the end of Westmeath's political activism.

Westmeath held back from personal involvement in the

rising despite the pleas of the Catholic lords of the pale that he raise 1000 men to reinforce their siege of Drogheda. While one of his sons armed many of the household servants and brought them to the siege with 'the said Earl's privity' (TCD, MS 820, fol. 65), that was the extent of Westmeath's involvement. In June 1642 Ormond, the commander of the king's army, rested his army for a few days at the earl's castle at Clonyn while marching reinforcements to relieve Athlone. While Ormond was there Westmeath pleaded unsuccessfully with him for the life of an elderly Catholic priest taken in a clash with insurgent troops. This expedition proved to be the high-water mark of the government's counter-attack and Westmeath's co-operation with Ormond now exposed him to revenge attacks. Shortly afterwards insurgent cavalry intercepted him while fleeing to the nearest government garrison at Trim, dragged him out of his coach, and shot him in the thigh. He died of his wounds and subsequent manhandling, apparently some time in the summer of 1642, and was probably buried at Clonyn. His will, dated 2 October 1640, was proved by his widow, Countess Jane, on 12 February 1643. Christopher Nugent, Lord Delvin, their eldest son and heir, having died in 1625, their grandson Richard *Nugent succeeded to the earldom.

PÁDRAIG LENIHAN

Sources CSP Ire., 1606–32 · GEC, Peerage · A. Clarke, The Old English in Ireland, 1625–1642 (1966), 36, 42, 73, 89, 188 · J. F. Ainsworth and E. MacLysagh, eds., 'Nugent papers', Analecta Hibernica, 20 (1958), 126–215 · J. T. Gilbert, ed., A contemporary history of affairs in Ireland from 1641 to 1652, 1 (1879), 18–20 · History of the Irish confederation and the war in Ireland … by Richard Bellings, ed. J. T. Gilbert, 1 (1882), 257–8 · deposition of Dame Jane, countess of Westmeath, TCD, MS 820 (co. Westmeath), fol. 9 · examination of William Parker, TCD, MS 820 (co. Westmeath), fols. 65–6 · V. Treadwell, Buckingham and Ireland, 1616–28: a study in Anglo-Irish politics (1998), 85, 110, 115–17, 240, 281, 283 · B. O'Ferrall and D. O'Connell, Commentarius Rinuccinianus de sedis apostolicae legatione ad foederatos Hiberniae Catholicos per annos 1645–1649, ed. J. Kavanagh, IMC, 1 (1932), 303–5 · F. X. Martin, Friar Nugent, 1569–1635 (1962), 265 · J. S. Brewer and W. Bullen, eds., Calendar of the Carew manuscripts, 5: 1603–1623, PRO (1871), 275
Wealth at death £3000 p.a. rental income: deposition of Dame Jane, countess of Westmeath; 24 Jan 1643, TCD, MS 820 (co. Westmeath), fol. 9

Nugent, Richard, second earl of Westmeath (1626–1684), army officer, was the only son of Christopher Nugent, styled Lord Delvin (c.1604–1625), and his wife, Lady Anne MacDonnell (d. before 1676), eldest daughter of Randal *MacDonnell, first earl of Antrim (d. 1636). On his father's death Richard Nugent became heir to his grandfather, also Richard *Nugent (1583–1642), first earl of Westmeath. In or before 1641 he married Mary (1623–1672), daughter of Sir Thomas Nugent of Moyrath.

In England at the time of his grandfather's death in 1642, Westmeath was detained at Beaumaris while seeking passage to Ireland. He was not permitted to proceed home until after the cessation of September 1643 between the confederate Catholics and the earl of Ormond, Charles I's representative in Ireland. In July 1645 he raised a regiment of infantry and a troop of horse to take part in the proposed confederate expeditionary force to Cheshire to assist Charles I. When the expedition was cancelled in the spring of 1646, the expeditionary regiments were incorporated into the confederate armies, with Westmeath being commissioned as a colonel in the Leinster army. In December 1646, at the confederate blockade of Dublin, he and Clanricarde acted as go-betweens for Ormond in the latter's attempt to detach the Leinster army from its allegiance to the confederate supreme council and foil the proposed attack on Dublin. The attack was abandoned, but Westmeath was subsequently reconciled to the confederates. He was present, on 7 August 1647, with most of his regiment at Dungan's Hill when the Leinster confederate army was destroyed by the parliamentarian commander Michael Jones. He was taken prisoner but subsequently exchanged for Viscount Montgomery. In 1648 he again sided with the Ormondist party against the papal nuncio, Rinuccini, and the clericalist party during the renewal of confederate internal conflict, heading the list of those recorded as taking the June 1648 oath to uphold the supreme council against Rinuccini's excommunication. In October 1648 he was appointed one of the commissioners to negotiate a peace treaty with Ormond, concluded the following January. Westmeath was appointed a field marshal by the supreme council in January 1649 and by 1650 had been given command of all forces in Leinster within the new pan-royalist alliance headed by Ormond. Following Ormond's departure for France in December 1650, Westmeath gave his support to Ormond's deputy, the earl of Clanricarde.

Westmeath's conduct of the war was the subject of criticism from the clericalist party. He was, claimed the author of the 'Aphorismical discovery', 'a man that never gathered an army into the field since he was appointed general, nor any party did stick unto himself that did act worth 6d.; rather worked all the means possible for faction, dispersion, rent, and division' (Gilbert, Contemporary history). He was blamed for not taking proper measures for the defence of Finnea, for not relieving Ballynacargy, co. Cavan, and for bringing about the surrender of his Leinster army to parliament on 12 May 1652, on conditions known as the articles of Kilkenny. That there may have been truth in the clericalist jibes is suggested by his subsequent petition to parliament that he be allowed to keep his estate, or a portion of it, because of his loyalty 'so different from all other Catholics of this Nation' and because 'he attended to the advancement & interests of England'. Although listed among those to be excluded from pardon for life and estate by the Act for the Settling of Ireland of August 1652, on 13 April 1653 he obtained an order to enjoy such parts of his estate as lay waste and undisposed of, and on 16 November the order was extended to the enjoyment of a full third of his estate. Having raised his regiment for the Spanish service as permitted by the articles of Kilkenny, he obtained a pass permitting him to transport himself and two servants, with travelling arms and necessaries, to and from Flanders, provided he gave notice of his arrival to the governor of the place where he should first land. He appears to have taken advantage of this permission. On the apprehension of fresh disturbances in the summer of 1659 he was, with other leading royalists, placed under arrest. He recovered his liberty and his estates at the Restoration, but seems to have taken no further interest in politics. In 1680 he rebuilt the chapel of Fore, to be a place of burial for himself and his posterity, and, dying in 1684, was interred there.

Besides two sons who died in infancy, Westmeath had four sons and five daughters. Christopher, Lord Delvin, his eldest son, married Mary, eldest daughter of Richard Butler of Kilcash, co. Tipperary, and, predeceasing his father, left Richard, third earl of Westmeath, who died in holy orders in 1714; Thomas *Nugent, fourth earl of Westmeath (1668/9–1752); and John *Nugent, fifth earl of Westmeath (1671/2–1754). The second earl's other children were Thomas *Nugent, created Baron Nugent of Riverstown (d. 1715); Joseph, a captain in the service of France; William, MP for County Westmeath in 1689, and killed at Cavan in 1690; Mary, who married Henry, second Viscount Kingsland; Anne, who married, first, Lucas, sixth Viscount Dillon, and, secondly, Sir William Talbot of Cartown, co. Meath; Alison, who married Henry Dowdall of Brownstown, co. Meath; Elizabeth, who died young; and Jane, who married Alexander MacDonell, called Macgregor of Dromersnaw, co. Leitrim. PÁDRAIG LENIHAN

Sources History of the Irish confederation and the war in Ireland … by Richard Bellings, ed. J. T. Gilbert, 7 vols. (1882–91), vol. 4, p. 357; vol. 5, p. 260; vol. 6, pp. 80, 262, 289; vol. 7, pp. 133, 241, 349 · B. O'Ferrall and D. O'Connell, Commentarius Rinuccinianus de sedis apostolicae legatione ad foederatos Hiberniae Catholicos per annos 1645–1649, ed. J. Kavanagh, IMC, 2 (1936), 431, 667, 675, 689; 3 (1939), 37, 364; 4 (1941), 264; 5 (1944), 23 · T. Carte, An history of the life of James, duke of Ormonde, 3 vols. (1735–6), vol. 1, pp. 590, 595; vol. 2, pp. 5, 60, 157 · J. Lodge, The peerage of Ireland, rev. M. Archdall, rev. edn, 1 (1789), 241–5 · J. F. Ainsworth and E. MacLysagh, eds., 'Nugent papers', Analecta Hibernica, 20 (1958), 126–215 · J. Hogan, ed., Letters and papers relating to the Irish rebellion between 1642–1646 (1936), 23 · deposition of Dame Jane, countess of Westmeath, TCD, MS 817 (co. Westmeath), 9 · W. Petty, 'Down survey parish maps of Westmeath: parishes of Killva', NL Ire., MS 725 · J. T. Gilbert, ed., A contemporary history of affairs in Ireland from 1641 to 1652, 1 (1879) · H. Piers, 'History of Westmeath', Collectanae de rebus Hibernicus, ed. C. Vallancey, 1 (1786), 62–4 [repr. 1981]

Nugent, Robert Craggs, Earl Nugent (1709–1788),

politician and poet, was born Robert Nugent, the only surviving son of Michael Nugent (d. 1739), landowner, of Carlanstown, co. Meath, and his wife, Mary, youngest daughter of Robert Barnewall, styled ninth Baron Trimleston of Ireland. Born into an old Roman Catholic gentry family he was educated at Fagan's academy in Dublin. As a young man he allegedly seduced his cousin Clare Nugent, who gave birth to an illegitimate son, Robert, in 1730. He fled to London that year to avoid marrying her and he always refused to recognize her child. When the latter subsequently became a debtor in the Fleet prison he published *The unnatural father, or, The persecuted son: a candid narrative of the most unparalleled sufferings of Robert Nugent jnr. by the means and procurement of his own father* (1755). Despite the embarrassment caused Nugent remained unmoved by the young man's plight.

Marriages, apostasy, and financial security Nugent became a tutor in the household of Justin Plunkett, fifth earl of Fingall, whose sister Lady Emilia (d. 1731) he married on 14

Robert Craggs Nugent, Earl Nugent (1709–1788), by Thomas Gainsborough, exh. Society of Artists 1761

July 1730. She was the second daughter of Peter Plunkett, fourth earl of Fingall, and Frances Hales. She died in childbed on 16 August 1731, survived by their son, Edmund (d. 1771). Shortly afterwards Nugent abandoned Roman Catholicism to enter the Church of England. He had always lamented that his family estate in 'the wildest part of Ireland' was 'great in bulk and small in revenue' (Jucker, 162) but even before he inherited it, on his father's death in 1739, he had greatly improved his finances through his second marriage, on 23 March 1737. His bride was the wealthy and twice widowed Anne (1697–1756), daughter and coheir of James *Craggs (bap. 1657, d. 1721), postmaster-general, and Elizabeth Richards (c.1662–1712), and sister and coheir of James *Craggs (1686–1721), secretary of state. Her only son, James (1715–1769), from her first marriage, to John Newsham (1673–1724) of Chadshunt, Warwickshire, unsurprisingly coveted the Craggs fortune and did everything in his power to prevent his mother's marriage to Nugent until she had settled £50,000 on him. Her second husband, John Knight (1686?–1733), had controlled one of the parliamentary seats at St Mawes, Cornwall, and owned a substantial estate at Gosfield, Essex, which he bequeathed to her following the death of their only son, John, in 1727. On his marriage to

Anne, Nugent assumed the additional name of Craggs but a match that gave him wealth, landed estate, and parliamentary influence was not a personal success. Once it was obvious that the marriage was destined to remain childless Nugent made no attempt to remain faithful to his less than attractive wife and acted the part of 'a man of consideration, fortune and fashion, living in the highest company of the metropolis' (*Memoirs of … Wraxall*, 1.94). He also maintained a house at 11 North Parade, Bath, and amused himself by forming an extensive park at Gosfield, which in later years won high praise from Arthur Young. Poetry provided a further outlet when Alexander Pope, who was already well known to Anne, befriended him. Nugent's *Ode to William Pulteney* (1739), which described his religious conversion from 'error's poison'd springs', achieved great fame throughout the eighteenth century. However, Thomas Gray strongly doubted whether it was actually Nugent's own composition and the suspicion grew that he had paid David Mallett to write it. An initially admiring Horace Walpole thus recorded waspishly: 'Nugent had lost the reputation of a great poet, by writing works of his own' (Walpole, *Memoirs of the Reign of George the Second*, 1.46).

In parliament By the late 1730s Nugent had become embroiled in politics. Anne had introduced him to Lord Chesterfield, who encouraged both his hostility to Sir Robert Walpole and his election as MP for St Mawes at the general election of 1741. Horace Walpole soon noted that he was talking 'a prodigious deal of nonsense in behalf of English liberty' (*Letters of Horace Walpole*, 1.151). Contemporary correspondence is full of references to his frequent, sometimes chaotic, but often witty speeches. Shortly after his re-election for St Mawes in 1747 he was appointed comptroller of the household to Frederick, prince of Wales, who borrowed money in return for promising Nugent high office in his projected administrations. However, Nugent exasperated Frederick by clashing with Egmont over a possible accommodation with Pelham's ministry. This readiness to negotiate facilitated Nugent's reconciliation with government shortly after Frederick's death on 20 March 1751. The following May he supported the Regency Bill and in June he successfully acted as an intermediary between Granville and Pelham, who both sought unsuccessfully to reward him with a lucrative office. Shortly afterwards he reintroduced a bill for the naturalization of foreign protestants, which he had first attempted in 1747. In Horace Walpole's characteristically partial appraisal of the occasion:

> The Irishman's style was floridly bombast; his impudence as great as if he had been honest … he affected unbounded good humour and it was unbounded but by much secret malice, which sometimes broke out in boisterous railing, oftener vented itself in still-born satires … Nugent's attachments were to Lord Granville; but all his flattery addressed to Mr. Pelham, whom he mimicked in candour, as he oftener resembled Lord Granville in ranting. (Walpole, *Memoirs of the Reign of George the Second*, 1.45–6)

Nugent also spoke in favour of the bill for the naturalization of the Jews in April 1753. However, he vigorously opposed the ministry over Hardwicke's marriage bill the next month, asking: 'Will you confine the great people to marry merely among one another and prevent them from getting a little wholesome blood which they so much want? Will you marry disease to distemper?' (*Buckinghamshire MSS*, 314).

As the general election of 1754 approached, Nugent's interest in questions concerning trade and navigation began to attract extra-parliamentary attention. In particular the Bristol merchants noted the sharp contrast between his championship of the out-ports and the silence of their existing representatives on such issues. They therefore invited him to contest the constituency. There was considerable prestige to be derived from sitting for the second city in the kingdom but Nugent demurred when the whigs requested a large contribution towards the likely costs of the election. With a safe borough of his own and a similar offer to stand at Liverpool he was able to drive a hard bargain. Before he consented the Bristol merchants agreed to indemnify him up to the sum of £10,000, while Newcastle's ministry appointed him a lord of the Treasury on 6 April 1754. After a hard contest Nugent was elected head of the poll, whereupon he vacated St Mawes, where he had returned himself as an insurance policy. For the next twenty years he was 'intrusted with the nomination to every place and employment in the disposal of government within the city of Bristol' (Tucker, 16) and was careful to promote local citizens, in contrast to previous practice. Throughout the 1754 parliament he remained one of Newcastle's most stalwart supporters. He reiterated his belief in the duke's fundamentally honourable nature so frequently that on 12 May 1756 a nauseated Horace Walpole recorded that Nugent 'added his usual panegyric on the honesty of the Duke of Newcastle' (Walpole, *Memoirs of the Reign of George the Second*, 2.193). Nugent remained at the Treasury until December 1759, in which month he was sworn of the privy council. In January 1760 he was promoted to the lucrative sinecure of joint vice-treasurer of Ireland.

A new marriage and new allegiances The late 1750s brought further changes to Nugent's personal life. He wasted little time when his unloved wife, Anne, died on 22 November 1756. On 2 January 1757 he carried off his third bride, the wealthy Elizabeth (1719/20–1792), widow of Augustus Berkeley, fourth earl of Berkeley, and daughter of Henry Drax (1693?–1755) of Ellerton Abbey, Yorkshire, and his wife, Elizabeth Ernle. Personal happiness, however, continued to elude him. Suspicion of his wife's alleged affairs led Nugent to disown Louisa, the second of their two daughters, and the couple ultimately lived apart for many years. Contemporaries were none the less so struck by Nugent's evident skill in marrying rich widows that Horace Walpole invented the word Nugentize to describe the phenomenon. Meanwhile the poet Richard Glover aptly recalled 'a jovial and voluptuous Irishman, who had left Popery for the Protestant religion, money, and widows' (Duppa, 47).

A financially inspired compromise ensured Nugent's unopposed return at Bristol in both 1761 and 1768. On the accession of George III he transferred his allegiance to

Bute and Grenville, taking with him a small connection of quasi-followers, consisting of his son Edmund and three relatives through marriage: James Colleton (1709?–1790), Thomas Drax (1721?–1789), and Edward Eliot (1727–1804). He soon found himself supporting contentious issues such as the cider excise and general warrants, while being lambasted as an unreliable, self-seeking time-server. As Lord George Sackville commented: 'Nobody can depend upon his attachment. His great aim is to keep his present employment, and upon the least appearance of minister-ial jumbles he is in violent agitation till he has found a safe harbour' (*Stopford-Sackville MSS*, 1.95). On the formation of the Rockingham administration in July 1765 Nugent reluctantly resigned to pre-empt his likely dismissal. George Grenville was delighted to learn that they retained 'the same sentiments … with regard to … public opinions' (*Additional Grenville Papers*, 313) and together they opposed the ministry's repeal of the Stamp and Cider Acts and Dowdeswell's new window tax. On 7 February 1766 Nugent castigated 'those who call law option, and attempt to disrupt the legislative authority of this country' ('Parlia-mentary diaries of Nathaniel Ryder', 290). Throughout his career Nugent strove to relieve Ireland of impediments to its trade. On 17 June 1766 he expressed his fear to Grenville that the American Duties Act would have an adverse effect, adding characteristically that this was 'the genuine production of the maiden and spotless Treasury. But I must not laugh; it hurts my bowels' (*Grenville Papers*, 3.249).

Yet only five months later Grenville suddenly found his friend's language 'so different' and his opinions 'so con-trary' (*Grenville Papers*, 3.382) that he could draw only one conclusion. Chatham had targeted Nugent as a former king's friend who might bolster his recently formed administration. On 4 December 1766 Nugent accordingly became first lord of trade, and on 19 January 1767 he was raised to the Irish peerage as Viscount Clare. On 27 Febru-ary he 'spoke with encomium of Lord Chatham' (Walpole, *Memoirs of the Reign of George the Third*, 2.299) in critical response to the manner in which the temporarily united opposition had just forced through a reduction in the land tax. Clare retained his post at the Board of Trade when Lord Hillsborough became American secretary in January 1768 but resigned it six months later, when he resumed that of joint vice-treasurer of Ireland. Thereafter he spoke on the government side on all the important questions of the period. In addition he occasionally addressed issues in a manner that revealed a surprisingly compassionate side to his nature. Thus on 2 March 1774 he intervened in a debate on a bill to prevent vexatious removals of the poor, in which he blamed the poor laws for the high number of executions in London. His Bristol seat was still generally thought to be safe in 1774, when he received influential support from the publication of Josiah Tucker's *Review of Lord Vis. Clare's Conduct as Representative of Bristol* (1774). However he withdrew his candidature at the close of the first day's poll. On 15 January 1775 his Bristol successor and political opponent, Edmund Burke, identified the key factor when he noted that any residual gratitude to Clare

was 'not for his American politics, but for his attention to the local interests and commercial welfare of this city' (*Correspondence*, 3.96). Burke subsequently disparaged 'the disciples of Lord Clare' as 'the worst sort of Tories, the Sunshine gentlemen of the last reign' (ibid., 207), and mockingly agreed when someone called 'the days of Lord Clare *Golden*; for to him (the member) they certainly were such' (ibid., 239).

Poetry and character Throughout these years Clare main-tained his interest in poetry. He eagerly sought the acquaintance of Oliver Goldsmith when the latter achieved distinction with *The Traveller* in 1764. Goldsmith subsequently visited him and a close friendship devel-oped. When Clare sent him a gift of venison from Gosfield Park the kindness of a jovial Irish peer was immortalized in the posthumously published *The Haunch of Venison, a Poetical Epistle to Lord Clare* (1776). Clare continued to com-pose poetry, including the anonymous *Faith* (1774). His *Verses to the Queen* (1775), sent to accompany a new year's gift of some Irish manufactures, was reciprocated by the anonymous *The Genius of Ireland, a New Year's Gift to Lord Clare* (1775). More substantial royal recognition followed on 21 July 1776, when he was promoted Earl Nugent in the Irish peerage. Nathaniel Wraxall, who was visiting Gos-field at the time, recorded his impressions of the new earl:

> Of an athletic frame and a vigorous constitution, 'though very advanced in years, he was exempt from any infirmity, possessing a stentorian voice, with great animal spirits and vast powers of conversation. He was a man of very considerable natural abilities, though not of a very cultivated mind … He spoke fluently, as well as with energy and force, was accounted an able debater, and possessed a species of eloquence altogether unembarrassed by any false modesty or timidity. (*Memoirs of … Wraxall*, 1.91)

In addition he remained possessed of 'a coarse and often licentious wit, which no place nor company prevented him from indulging, and the effect of which was aug-mented by an Irish accent that never forsook him' (ibid., 93).

Abandonment of party allegiance Following his judicious retreat from Bristol, Clare returned himself for St Mawes at the general elections of 1774 and, as Earl Nugent, those of 1780 and 1784. His emphatic opposition to the eco-nomic reform movement led Lord George Gordon to call him 'the old rat of the constitution' (Cobbett, *Parl. hist.*), to which he responded by observing that a rat 'always cau-tiously avoided gnawing through the sides of the vessel: it never made a hole which would endanger the ship' (ibid.). He continued to speak frequently on American affairs. On 23 January 1775 he 'ridiculed the opinion of those who said we had a right to tax America yet ought not to exer-cise it' (Almon, 1.108). In late 1777, following news of the surrender of Saratoga, he outlined the enormous issues he saw at stake:

> The contest now was not whether America should be dependent on the British Parliament, but whether Great Britain or America should be independent. Both could not be so, for such would be the power of that vast continent across the Atlantic that was her independence established this

island must expect to be made a dependent province. (ibid., 8.29–30)

Unlike some of his colleagues he was realistic and pragmatic enough to recognize a lost cause, even as early as 6 April 1780, and on 27 November 1781 he observed that 'it would be more advisable even to acknowledge their independency than to go on playing the same losing game against them' (Debrett, 5.41). News of the Yorktown disaster confirmed this conviction but he felt unable to vote against Lord North, with whom he resigned in March 1782.

Nugent's professed inclination was now to support measures, not men. Accordingly in 1783 he declined to be one of the sixteen founding knights of the Order of St Patrick and also refused Pitt's offer of 'an office of emolument' (*Rutland MSS*, 3.158). However, he seemed genuinely unable to grasp the deep antagonism between Pitt and Fox. On 29 January 1784 he praised both Pitt's ministry and Fox's abilities but reflected critically on 'the administration of a dictator' who had been 'the author of the East India bill' (Debrett, 13.22–4). On 20 February he urged a positive union between the two rivals. Recalling how Granville and Pelham had successfully resolved their differences over dinner and some fine wines, Nugent unrealistically offered his house for a similar purpose: 'They may even if they please get gloriously drunk. And I will answer for it, over the bottle their punctilios and distrust will vanish, while confidence will spring up where diffidence previously existed' (*Memoirs of … Wraxall*, 3.305). In June 1784, only three months into the new parliament, Nugent took the Chiltern Hundreds and retired from politics.

In his final years Nugent returned to the Roman Catholic faith. He died at the house of General O'Donnel in Rutland Square, Dublin, on 14 October 1788 and was buried at Gosfield on 26 October. The bulk of his personal property, worth over £200,000, and his interest at St Mawes went to his daughter Mary Elizabeth (d. 1812), who was created Baroness Nugent of Carlanstown in her own right on 26 December 1800. She had married George Grenville [see Grenville, George Nugent-Temple, first marquess of Buckingham (1753–1813)], by then marquess of Buckingham; he succeeded to the Nugent earldom, the real estate (which carried an annual rental of over £14,000), and took the name Nugent. PATRICK WOODLAND

Sources E. Cruickshanks, 'Nugent, Robert', HoP, *Commons, 1715–54* · J. Brooke, 'Nugent, Robert', HoP, *Commons, 1754–90* · C. Nugent, *Memoir of Robert, Earl Nugent* (1898) · J. Tucker, *A review of Lord Vis. Clare's conduct as representative of Bristol* (1774) · GEC, *Peerage* · Matthew Brickdale, parliamentary diary, 11 vols., 1770–74, Bristol University · J. Almon, ed., *The parliamentary register, or, History of the proceedings and debates of the House of Commons*, 17 vols. (1775–80) · Cobbett, *Parl. hist.*, 21.407–8 · J. Debrett, ed., *The parliamentary register, or, History of the proceedings and debates of the House of Commons*, 45 vols. (1781–96) · *The Grenville papers: being the correspondence of Richard Grenville … and … George Grenville*, ed. W. J. Smith, 4 vols. (1852–3) · *Additional Grenville papers, 1763–1765*, ed. J. R. G. Tomlinson (1962) · 'Parliamentary diaries of Nathaniel Ryder, 1764–7', ed. P. D. G. Thomas, *Camden miscellany, XXIII*, CS, 4th ser., 7 (1969) · H. Walpole, *Memoirs of the reign of King George the Second*, ed. Lord Holland [H. R. Fox], 2 vols. (1846) · *The historical and the posthumous memoirs of Sir Nathaniel William Wraxall, 1772–1784*, ed. H. B. Wheatley, 5 vols. (1884) · H. Walpole, *Memoirs of the reign of King George the Third*, ed. G. F. R. Barker, 4 vols. (1894) · *The correspondence of Edmund Burke*, 3, ed. G. H. Guttridge (1961), 2 · A. Newman, ed., 'Leicester House politics, 1750–60, from the papers of John, second earl of Egmont', *Camden miscellany, XXIII*, CS, 4th ser., 7 (1969), 85–228 · *The letters of Horace Walpole, fourth earl of Orford*, ed. P. Toynbee, 1 (1903) · P. D. G. Thomas, *British politics and the Stamp Act crisis: the first phase of the American revolution, 1763–1767* (1975) · L. B. Namier, *The structure of politics at the accession of George III*, 2nd edn (1957) · *The Jenkinson papers, 1760–1766*, ed. N. S. Jucker (1949) · *GM*, 1st ser., 58 (1788), 938 · 'Parliamentary memorials of James Harris', Hants. RO, Malmesbury papers · *The manuscripts of J. B. Fortescue*, 10 vols., HMC, 30 (1892–1927), vol. 1, pp. 358–60 · *The manuscripts of the earl of Carlisle*, HMC, 42 (1897), 183 · *The manuscripts of his grace the duke of Rutland*, 4 vols., HMC, 24 (1888–1905), vol. 3, p. 158 · *The manuscripts of the earl of Buckinghamshire, the earl of Lindsey … and James Round*, HMC, 38 (1895) · *Report on the manuscripts of Mrs Stopford-Sackville*, 1, HMC, 49 (1904) · R. Duppa [R. Glover], *Memoirs of a celebrated literary and political character, from … 1742 to … 1757* (1813) · P. Langford, *The first Rockingham administration, 1765–1766* (1973) · DNB

Archives Hunt. L., corresp. and papers | BL, letters to George Grenville, Add. MS 57813 · BL, corresp. with Charles Jenkinson, Add. MSS 38201–38208, 38304–38307, 38458, *passim* · BL, corresp. with Lord Liverpool, Add. MSS 38201–38208, 38304–38307, 38458 · BL, corresp. with duke of Newcastle and others, Add. MSS 32699–32968, *passim* · Port Eliot, Saltash, Eliot papers, letters to Edward Eliot

Likenesses T. Gainsborough, oils, 1760, Bristol Town Hall · T. Gainsborough, oils, exh. Society of Artists 1761, priv. coll.; on loan to Holburne Museum of Art, Bath [*see illus.*] · T. Gainsborough, oils, exh. Society of Artists 1765; formerly at Stowe, Buckinghamshire · J. Sayers, caricature, etching, pubd 1782, BM, NPG · line engraving, BM, NPG; repro. in *European Magazine* (1784)

Wealth at death £200,000 in personal property; £14,000 p.a. in real estate: DNB · small bequests; pensions for life for which £500 annuity set aside: will, PRO, PROB 11/1170, sig. 500

Nugent, Thomas, **first Baron Nugent of Riverston** (d. **1715**), judge, was the second son of Richard *Nugent, second earl of Westmeath (1626–1684), army officer, and his wife, Mary (1623–1672), daughter of Sir Thomas Nugent, bt, of Moyrath, Westmeath. Born into a prominent Old English family with a strong legal tradition, he was domiciled at Clonyn, Westmeath, when he entered the Inner Temple in 1669; he was admitted to King's Inns in Dublin on 21 November 1674 and practised as a barrister. In 1680 (probably in September) he married a member of another leading Old English family, Marianna (1662–1735), daughter of Henry Barnewall, second Viscount Barnewall of Kingsland. They had several daughters and two sons.

After the accession of James II, Nugent was one of a number of Catholic barristers to become king's counsel (12 September 1685). The second earl of Clarendon, who came to Ireland as viceroy in January 1686, treated him as a representative of the Roman Catholic interest. When Nugent was made a judge of the king's bench (23 April 1686), Clarendon wrote of his being 'a man of birth indeed … but no lawyer, and so will do harm upon the account of his learning' (*Correspondence*, 1.356). On taking his seat he was reported by Clarendon to have had a wrangle with another judge, Sir John Lyndon, about precedence, 'as brisk as if it had been between two women' (ibid.). In May 1686 he was appointed to the Irish privy council, and in October of the following year, with Tyrconnell now lord lieutenant, he was made chief justice of the king's bench. The court of king's bench under his tenure was regarded by William King and others as promoting the Catholic interest at the expense of protestants. He was alleged to have declared it treasonous to possess weapons without licence, when in fact a fine of £20 was the highest penalty prescribed by law. On another occasion he was said by William King to have declared the robbery of protestants to be necessary for the furtherance of James II's policy. Clarendon recorded some instances of what he saw as judicial partiality, though he admitted that Nugent had shown humanity in a particular case.

Early in 1688, with the king's approval, Tyrconnell sent Nugent to England with Chief Baron Rice carrying alternative draft bills for the modification of the Restoration land settlement. According to William King, they were met in London by a hostile mob who escorted them with potatoes fixed on sticks, amid cries of 'make room for the Irish ambassadors' (King, chap. 3, section 12, 2). They returned to Ireland in April with a draft bill of settlement. Preparations for an Irish parliament were soon under way, but events in England intervened and by August the calling of an Irish parliament had been indefinitely postponed.

Nugent's response to William of Orange's intervention in England was robust. In a charge to the Dublin grand jury he was said to have expressed a hope that William's followers would soon be 'hung up all over England' in 'bunches like a rope of onions' (Ingram, 43). Holding the assizes at Cork in March 1689 he ordered the protestant people of Bandon, who had declared for William III and attacked the Jacobite garrison on 22 February, to be indicted for high treason, but he was persuaded by General Justin MacCarthy into respecting Bandon's capitulation. After James II had landed at Kinsale on 12 March 1689 he consulted Nugent in the presence of both Avaux and Melfort.

With a parliament summoned for May, James signed a warrant on 3 April 1689 for a writ of summons to Nugent to sit in the House of Lords as Baron Nugent of Riverston, one of the rare occasions when a writ of summons created a hereditary peerage by express words. On 13 May, six days after the opening of parliament, Nugent introduced a bill for the repeal of the Restoration Acts of Settlement and Explanation, a far more sweeping measure than the draft bill he had brought back from London the previous year. He was generally active in the House of Lords, frequently presiding at committees. On 6 July, two weeks before parliament was prorogued, he was appointed a commissioner of the Irish Treasury (renewed 17 June 1690), and he continued to sit on the bench, taking the spring assizes in Connaught in 1690. He was at Limerick during or soon after William's abortive siege, and in September 1690 he was appointed to act as secretary for war when Sir Richard Nagle travelled to France with Tyrconnell for consultations. During Tyrconnell's absence Nugent was dismissed from office by Berwick acting under Sarsfield's influence, though he was soon restored by Tyrconnell on his return in January 1691. Regarded as a personal adherent of the Jacobite viceroy, he was accused by the anti-peace party of holding secret and treasonable communication with the Williamites. After Tyrconnell's death in August 1691 he seems to have played no significant part in the negotiations that led to the treaty of Limerick (3 October 1691), though he was covered by its terms, retained his estates, and was granted a licence to carry arms—all of which suggests that he was not regarded with particular animosity in post-war protestant Ireland, despite the antagonism he had aroused as a judge in the later 1680s.

With the war over, Nugent's public career was at an end. Although his barony was treated as invalid by the Williamite authorities, both he and his sons who succeeded him were referred to as Baron Nugent of Riverston. When he died in May 1715 he was succeeded by his elder son, Richard Hyacinth Nugent (d. 1738), who in turn was succeeded by his younger brother, William (d. 1756). The title was merged with the earldom of Westmeath in 1839.   RICHARD BAGWELL, rev. JAMES McGUIRE

Sources F. E. Ball, *The judges in Ireland, 1221–1921*, 2 vols. (1926); repr. (1993), vol. 1 · *The correspondence of Henry Hyde, earl of Clarendon, and of his brother Laurence Hyde, earl of Rochester*, ed. S. W. Singer, 2 vols. (1828) · [W. King], *The state of the protestants of Ireland under the late King James's government* (1691) · J. G. Simms, *Jacobite Ireland, 1685–91* (1969) · J. Dalrymple, *Memoirs of Great Britain and Ireland*, new edn, 3 vols. (1790) · J. Macpherson, ed., *Original papers, containing the secret history of Great Britain*, 1 (1775) · P. Wauchope, *Patrick Sarsfield and the Williamite war* (1992) · T. D. Ingram, *Two chapters of Irish history* (1888) · J. T. Gilbert, *A Jacobite narrative of the war in Ireland, 1688–91* (1892) · [C. O'Kelly], *Macariae excidium, or, The destruction of Cyprus*, ed. C. O'Callaghan (1850) · *CSP dom.*, 1687–9 · G. Bennett, *The history of Bandon* (1862) · GEC, *Peerage* · E. Keane, P. Beryl Phair, and T. U. Sadleir, eds., *King's Inns admission papers, 1607–1867*, IMC (1982) · F. A. Inderwick and R. A. Roberts, eds., *A calendar of the Inner Temple records*, 1–3 (1896–1901) · J. L. J. Hughes, ed., *Patentee officers in Ireland, 1173–1826, including high sheriffs, 1661–1684 and 1761–1816*, IMC (1960) · *Calendar of the Stuart papers belonging to his majesty the king, preserved at Windsor Castle*, 7 vols., HMC, 56 (1902–23), vol. 1
Likenesses P. Lely, portrait; formerly at Pallas, co. Galway

Nugent, Thomas, fourth earl of Westmeath (1668/9–1752), army officer, was the second son of Christopher Nugent, Lord Delvin (d. before 1680), the eldest son of Richard *Nugent, second earl of Westmeath (1626–1684), and of his wife, Mary (1640/41–1737), eldest daughter of Richard Butler of Kilcash, co. Tipperary, and niece of James Butler, first duke of Ormond. His elder brother, Richard Nugent (d. 1714), was a Capuchin friar in France, and on the death of his grandfather in 1684 Thomas succeeded to the extensive family estates centred on his residence at Clonyn, Delvin, co. Westmeath. From then on he was generally styled earl of Westmeath, taking his seat as such in the upper house of the 1689 Irish parliament, by royal dispensation as he was under age. In 1684, aged sixteen, he married Margaret (d. 1700), only daughter of Sir John Bellew, later Baron Bellew of Duleek. They had eleven children, of whom two sons and two daughters survived to adulthood.

Westmeath travelled abroad for a few years, returning to Ireland to enter the army, which was being expanded in the crisis preceding the Williamite wars. He served first as lieutenant-colonel of the earl of Tyrone's infantry regiment, and from the summer of 1689 as colonel of the infantry regiment raised by Colonel Francis Toole, which in 1690 he led at the battle of the Boyne and the first siege of Limerick. For the 1691 campaign he transferred to command of a cavalry regiment and fought at the battle of Aughrim. He steered a middle line between the defeatist and militant factions on the Jacobite side, approving the acquittal by court martial of Brigadier Henry Luttrell on a charge of corresponding with the enemy, but supporting the arrest of Brigadier Robert Clifford for failing to obstruct the passage of the Williamites across the Shannon. When the Jacobites asked for terms on 23 September, he hurried to Limerick from the nearby cavalry camp, dining with Ginkel while passing through the Williamite lines. Subsequently he was one of four Jacobite peers exchanged as hostages during the negotiations which led to the treaty of Limerick. He was attainted in both England and Ireland for his participation in the war, but in 1692 he was pardoned under the Limerick articles and recovered his estates. Thereafter, as a Roman Catholic, he was excluded from public life. In 1705 he sought a pass for himself and his son to travel to Holland in order to settle his son there for education.

Westmeath's eldest daughter, Mary (d. 1725), married Francis (Bermingham), Lord Athenry, and her son, Thomas, was created earl of Louth in 1759. His second daughter, Catherine (d. 1756), married Andrew Nugent of Dysart, co. Westmeath, and was the mother of Lavalin Nugent. Westmeath died, aged about eighty-three, on 30 June 1752. As he was predeceased by both his sons, Christopher, Lord Delvin (d. 1752), who was unmarried, and John (d. 1725), his title passed briefly to his brother, the soldier John *Nugent, and on his death to his son Thomas (1714–1792), who took his seat in the House of Lords, having conformed to the established church in order to avoid the adverse inheritance implications of the penal laws.

G. Le G. Norgate, rev. Harman Murtagh

Sources J. Lodge, *The peerage of Ireland*, rev. M. Archdall, rev. edn, 1 (1789), 241–8 · GEC, *Peerage* · J. D'Alton, *Illustrations, historical and genealogical, of King James's Irish army list (1689)*, 2nd edn, 2 vols. (1860–61), vol. 2, pp. 205, 469 · J. G. Simms, ed., 'Irish Jacobite: lists from Trinity College Dublin MS N.1.3', *Analecta Hibernica*, 22 (1960), 11–230 · D. Murtagh and H. Murtagh, 'The Irish Jacobite army, 1689–91', *Irish Sword*, 18 (1990–92), 32–48 · G. Story, *A continuation of the impartial history of the wars of Ireland* (1693), 229–30 · *Négociations de M. le Comte d'Avaux en Irlande, 1689–90*, ed. J. Hogan, 2 vols., IMC (1934–58) · S. Mulloy, ed., *Franco-Irish correspondence, December 1688 – February 1692*, IMC, 2–3 (1984) · *The journal of John Stevens ... 1689–1691*, ed. R. H. Murray (1912) · W. Harris, *The history of the life and reign of William-Henry* (1749) · *The manuscripts of his grace the duke of Portland*, 10 vols., HMC, 29 (1891–1931), vol. 4, p. 216
Wealth at death probably among the richest Irish Catholics; 17,500 acre family estate in 1876, probably little changed since 18th century

Nugent, Thomas (*c*.1700–1772), writer and traveller, was born in Ireland, and apparently graduated from Trinity College, Dublin, but spent most of his life in London. Comments in his works show him to have been a protestant, and an ardent supporter of the Hanoverian constitutional settlement. In 1765 he received from the University of Aberdeen the honorary degree of LLD, and in 1767 was made a fellow of the Society of Antiquaries. He has been confused with Johnson's friend and Edmund Burke's father-in-law, Dr Christopher Nugent (1698–1775), to whom he may have been related, and who is mentioned in Thomas Nugent's will.

Nugent was a prolific author and a skilful translator. He wrote so much that he thought it had taken its toll on his health. In his lifetime he was perhaps best known for his *New Pocket Dictionary of the French and English Languages* (1767), which went to at least twenty-eight editions. After his death, in Britain and more especially in Germany, he was best known for *The history of Vandalia: containing the ancient and present state of the country of Mecklenburg, its revolutions under the Venedi and the Saxons, with the succession and memorable actions of its sovereigns* (3 vols., 1766–73); *Travels through Germany, with a particular account of the courts of Mecklenburg: in a series of letters to a friend* (2 vols., 1768); and *The Grand Tour, or a Journey through the Netherlands, Germany, Italy, and France* (4 vols., 1749). *Travels through Germany* presents a mixture of history, topographical descriptions, quotations from other authors, and anecdotes about the trials of daily life. Above all he seeks to describe the 'customs and manners' of the people (p. 5). There are flashes of humour as when he, a doctor of law, remarks, 'As Hamburg is over-stocked with most commodities, so it is with lawyers' (p. 61). The work is in epistolary form, ostensibly unrevised for the press, but his standard disclaimer wears very thin, notably when his ship strikes a sandbank in the middle of the night as he is returning to England, and his immediate impulse is to recite an ode of Horace. *Travels through Germany* describes much that is entertaining from the author's own travels, while *The Grand Tour* is a guidebook in the much narrower sense of providing information on inns, road and boat connections, and sights to visit. It is a compilation of his own experience and that of others reproduced in duodecimo for ease of packing. He uses the format later popularized by Murray and the Blue Guides of taking in sights by means of a series of tours from the capital. Among Nugent's very numerous translations, mostly from French, his translation of Benvenuto Cellini's autobiography (2 vols., 1771) attracted considerable attention and ran through several editions.

Nugent made his will on 24 April 1772 and died in his rooms at Gray's Inn on 27 April 1772. His residuary legatee and sole executor was Mary Hooper, spinster, 'for her long and faithful service and attendance'. He appears to have been unmarried and childless. Elizabeth Baigent

Sources T. Nugent, *The grand tour*, 4 vols. (1749) · T. Nugent, *Travels through Germany*, 2 vols. (1768) · *GM*, 1st ser., 42 (1772), 247 · PRO, PROB 11/976, sig. 143 · W. B. S. Taylor, *History of the University of Dublin* (1845) · DNB
Likenesses stipple, BM

Nugent, William (1550–1625), insurgent, was born in Westmeath, probably at Clonin, the younger son of Richard Nugent, fourth Baron Delvin (1522/3–1559), and his wife, Elizabeth (d. in or before 1580), daughter of Jenico Preston, fifth Viscount Gormanston. His father was a member of the Irish council and William inherited from him a castle and land near Lough Sheelin. William's elder brother was Christopher *Nugent, fifth Baron Delvin (1544–1602), and he had a sister, Mary, who married Thomas Nugent of Moyrath. On the death of his father in 1559 William, with his brother Christopher, became a ward of the earl of Sussex. He may have received his early education at the hands of an Irish foster family, most likely the O'Coffeys, although it is possible that his guardian took him to England to be tutored. Nugent matriculated at Hart Hall, Oxford, in 1571, and although he does not appear to have taken a degree he was of literary inclination, composing poems in English and Irish; a handful of these may be found in manuscripts still extant. By 1573 he had returned to Ireland and in December that year he abducted and married Jane Marward (d. 1629), daughter of Walter Marward, Baron Skryne, who had died in 1564 leaving Jane as his sole heir. While still a minor, she had been betrothed to her mother's relative, Baron Dunsany, but her stepfather, Nicholas Nugent, second baron of the exchequer, was William's uncle and a marriage between William and Jane had earlier been proposed. They had three sons: Richard, Christopher, and James.

During the 1570s prominent figures in the English pale in Ireland mounted a campaign against the levy known as cess. William Nugent was one such campaigner and in May 1575 was, with his brother and others, placed under a form of house arrest. In July 1577 the campaigners made a series of submissions to the queen's government but the issue of cess did not die away and in August 1580 political grievance combined with religious fervour to trigger a rebellion within the pale. The leader was James Eustace, Viscount Baltinglass, with whom both Nugent and his brother, the baron, had had secret talks during the previous year. Baron Delvin ultimately declined to give open support to the viscount and it seems that William Nugent was, if anything, even less inclined to participate.

The sudden arrest of Delvin and his brother-in-law, the earl of Kildare, on 20 December 1580 brought a sharp reaction from Nugent, however. Warned that he himself was to be arrested, he eluded the sheriff's forces and escaped to his castle on Lough Sheelin. By Christmas day he had gathered some 200 men about him and sought aid from his Nugent uncles and the chiefs of Maguire and O'Neill. At this point his main objective appears to have been to secure the release of his brother but by March 1581 he had assembled 300 men in co. Meath and was regarded by the Dublin administration as being in open rebellion. He was regarded, by some supporters at least, as the pope's representative in Ireland and he does not appear to have discouraged that view.

Substantial support from the Gaelic chiefs was difficult to find but protection was extended to Nugent by Tuirleach Luineach, chief of the O'Neills of Tyrone, along with some military aid. In July 1581 Nugent invaded Longford with Sir Brian O'Rourke and later that summer he and a supporter, John Cusack of Ellistonread, co. Meath, met various young men of the English pale who seemed likely to join them. In September he allied with the O'Connors,

attacking properties of Adam Loftus, archbishop of Dublin. However, the prosecution of the rebels by government forces, in Leinster and elsewhere in Ireland, was bearing fruit, and by November many key rebels were dead or in hiding, tendering their submissions or, like Baltinglass, fleeing the country. In the pale the government had arrested several young men suspected of contact with Nugent and some had made confessions. Some women had also been questioned and detained, including Nugent's wife, Jane. By late November Nugent was, according to Secretary Fenton, 'left to a few horsemen and wandering from wood to wood … as an outlaw and robber' (PRO, SP 63/86/80). The same month saw a rash of executions, including those of about twenty young gentlemen of the pale. In January Nugent withdrew to Tyrone and from there departed in early 1582 to seek assistance from the Catholic powers of Europe. His erstwhile ally John Cusack of Ellistonread, meantime, had turned queen's evidence and made damaging allegations against Nugent's wife, the lord and lady Delvin, and others who had been arrested or suspected of rebel involvement. These allegations would ultimately lead to the execution of Nicholas Nugent, William's uncle and chief justice of the common pleas.

Nugent remained abroad until 1584 when he was with a small force of Scots which entered Ireland through the north. He attempted to garner support from Maguire and O'Rourke but after a clash between the Scots and the queen's forces in early December he submitted to Lord Deputy Perrot, who granted him a pardon. Nugent's wife had already been released from confinement and though the formal restoration of his confiscated properties was delayed until 1608, it is clear that he had use of them long before that date. Nugent and his brother Delvin believed that the Dillon family had, for personal reasons, actively induced John Cusack of Ellistonread to make accusations against their uncle the chief justice and during the 1590s they pursued Robert Dillon, who had succeeded to that office, on charges of corruption. In the end these efforts failed and Dillon was declared innocent.

Nugent died on 30 June 1625, probably at Kilcarn, co. Meath, without having ever again participated in rebellious action, and possessed of lands in counties Meath, Westmeath, and Dublin; his wife died in 1629. Records regarding their sons are sketchy and contradictory, and some inaccurate information has been published. As far as can be established their eldest son, Richard, who was a supporter of the Gaelic chiefs during the campaigns against the earl of Tyrone, may have died on a mission to Europe on their behalf in 1600. However, there is some evidence that he was alive in 1602, after which he disappears from the records. The second son, Christopher, born at the end of 1582, appears to have died childless, but there is conflict in the records as to the date of his death, and he may still have been alive in 1640. Their son James lived on until 1634; though he was twice married, records of any children are uncertain.

HELEN COBURN WALSHE

Sources state papers, Ireland, PRO, SP 63 · *CSP Ire.*, *1509–1625* · J. S. Brewer and W. Bullen, eds., *Calendar of the Carew manuscripts*, 6 vols., PRO (1867–73) · M. C. Griffith, ed., *Irish patent rolls of James I*, 1 vol. in 2 (1846–52) · 'Calendar of fiants, Henry VIII to Elizabeth', *Report of the Deputy Keeper of the Public Records in Ireland*, 7–22 (1875–90), appxs · *CSP for.*, *1547–89* · E. O'Tuathail, 'Nugentiana', *Eigse*, 2 (1940), 4–15 · G. Murphy, 'Poems of exile by Uilliam Nuinseann', *Eigse*, 4 (1948), 8–15 · J. F. Ainsworth and E. MacLysagh, eds., 'Nugent papers', *Analecta Hibernica*, 20 (1958), 126–215 · H. C. Walshe, 'The rebellion of William Nugent, 1581', *Religion, conflict, and coexistence in Ireland: essays presented to Monsignor Patrick J. Corish*, ed. R. V. Comerford and others (1990), 26–52 · Wood, *Ath. Oxon.*, new edn · J. Lodge, *The peerage of Ireland*, rev. M. Archdall, rev. edn, 1 (1789), 231 · J. Morrin, ed., *Calendar of the patent and close rolls of chancery in Ireland*, 3 vols. (1861–3) · [J. Hardiman], ed., *Inquisitionum in officio rotulorum cancellariae Hiberniae asservatarum repertorium*, 2 vols., Irish Record Commission (1826–9), vol. 1, nos. 18 and 80, Chas I; vol. 2, Meath, no. 57, Jas I · J. C. Erck, ed., *A repertory of the inrolments on the patent rolls of chancery, in Ireland* (1846)

Archives PRO, state papers Ireland, letters, 63 series

Wealth at death see PRO, state papers, Ireland, SP 63; 'Calendar of fiants', no. 3009; Griffith, ed., *Irish patent rolls of James I*, 114–15; Hardiman, ed., *Inquisitionum in officio*, 2, no. 57, Jas I

Nun of Watton

Nun of Watton (*b.* 1146x9), Gilbertine nun and figure of scandal, is known only from the account of the two miracles associated with her that was written by Ailred of Rievaulx (*d.* 1167) in the early 1160s. It survives in one manuscript, probably written in the late 1160s and now Cambridge, Corpus Christi College, MS 139, folios 149r–151v. The Nun was received when she was four years old into the Gilbertine priory of Watton, Yorkshire, at the request of Henry Murdac, archbishop of York from 1147 until 1153. Since Watton was founded about 1150, she was born between 1146 and 1149, probably towards the beginning of that period. Although her behaviour as a girl showed that she was unsuited for monastic life, she took the veil, presumably as a novice at the age of fifteen, and was called a nun in the *explicit* of the manuscript of Ailred's text. Watton was a double house and included lay brothers and lay sisters as well as nuns and canons. The Nun was attracted to one of 'the brothers to whom the care of external affairs is entrusted' (*Patrologia Latina*, 195.791), who was either a canon or lay brother, and they arranged to meet. When the affair was discovered and she was found to be pregnant, the Nun was imprisoned and the man fled and resumed a secular habit. He was captured at the order of Gilbert of Sempringham (*d.* 1189), however, and handed over to the nuns, who forced the Nun to cut off his male parts (*virus*) and placed them in her mouth. The man was then returned to the brothers and disappears from the story. The Nun was again imprisoned and prepared to give birth, but while she was sleeping the deceased Archbishop Henry appeared with two women who took the baby, leaving the Nun in a girlish 'not to say virginal state', and subsequently removed her fetters (*Patrologia Latina*, 195.795). These miracles absolved the Nun from guilt and reconciled her with the community. Nothing more is known of her. The Nun's deliverance is an early example of the miracle story belonging to the Mary legends, later known as 'The Abbess Delivered'. Ailred's account also sheds light on the early history of the Gilbertine order, especially the reception of children and the relative ease of contacts between male and female members, who were later (perhaps as a result of this episode) strictly segregated. GILES CONSTABLE

Sources Ailred of Rievaulx, 'De sanctimoniali de Watton', *Historiae Anglicanae scriptores X*, ed. R. Twysden (1652), 415–22 · G. Constable, 'Aelred of Rievaulx and the Nun of Watton: an episode in the early history of the Gilbertine order', *Medieval women*, ed. D. Baker, SCH, Subsidia, 1 (1978), 205–26 · R. Foreville, ed., *The book of St Gilbert*, ed. and trans. G. Keir, OMT (1987), liv–lv · S. Elkins, *Holy women of twelfth-century England* (1988), 106–11 · B. Golding, *Gilbert of Sempringham and the Gilbertine order, c.1130–c.1300* (1995), 33–8

Nunburnholme. For this title name *see* Wilson, Charles Henry, first Baron Nunburnholme (1833–1907).

Nuncomar. *See* Nandakumar, maharaja (1705?–1775).

Nunes

Nunes [Nuñez], **Hector** [*known as* Dr Hector] (1520–1591), physician and merchant, was born in Evora, Portugal. His family were among those Jews who had been forcibly baptized in 1497 by order of King Manuel I. He studied medicine at Coimbra University, taking a BA in 1540 and an MB in 1543. Because at this time the Portuguese Inquisition started to persecute the New Christians, he left Portugal. In 1549 he was living in London, in the parish of St Olave, Hart Street. In 1553 he was fined by the College of Physicians for practising medicine without a licence. In 1554 he was elected a fellow and in 1563 a censor of the college, with the responsibility for examining candidates and deciding which should be admitted and allowed to practise medicine. He had an uncle, Henrique Nunes, who was a merchant and physician living in Bristol from 1546 to 1554, to whom Nunes used to send the correct dates of the Jewish festivals.

Like his uncle, Nunes combined his medical practice with foreign trade. The London port book of 1566 shows him importing nineteen butts of sack from Cadiz. On 29 September in the same year he married Leonor (or Elinore) Freire of Antwerp, who also came from a Portuguese crypto-Jewish family. They lived in Mark Lane in the city of London. He figures frequently in the acts of the privy council as a trader with Portugal, where he is usually called 'Dr Hector'.

As well as trading as a merchant, Nunes had a court practice as a physician. He prescribed for Lord and Lady Burleigh. He must have rendered service to the government, possibly in connection with the treaty negotiations with Portugal of 1572, for in 1573 he was granted a fifteen-year monopoly of the importation of Spanish wool for making felts and felt hats, subject to paying double customs. In 1574 he was granted the lands of St Mary's Abbey in Ireland, formerly belonging to the earl of Desmond. This transaction was followed by a series of unsuccessful attempts to win a lawsuit against the earl with the backing of the privy council, but the earl had powerful friends in Ireland and Nunes did not. In 1575 his wool patent was reissued and extended to twenty years. He was endenizened as an English subject in 1579 and after that publicly conformed to the Church of England, while presumably practising Judaism in the privacy of his home. The statute concerning the burning of heretics (*De haeretico comburendo*) made it unsafe to do otherwise. Lawsuits in the admiralty and queen's bench courts show that he traded to Spain and Portugal, imported Brazilian sugar, and acted as a marine insurance broker. In 1582 his household included his wife, three clerks, and two black women. Nunes and his wife had no surviving children.

In 1583 Lord Henry Howard, then a state prisoner in the Fleet, wrote to the secretary of state, Sir Francis Walsingham, to ask permission to consult his old physician 'Dr Hector'. Walsingham employed Nunes as his intermediary from 1585 to 1586 in opening peace negotiations with Spain. This he did by corresponding with Dr António Castilho, who had been Portuguese ambassador in London in 1580. After these negotiations failed, Nunes kept Walsingham informed about the preparations of the Spanish armada in Lisbon. In 1588 Spaniards in London reported this back to Philip II. Nunes's brother-in-law and partner, Bernardo Luis Freire, was arrested and interrogated in Madrid.

Nunes died in Mark Lane, London, in September 1591 and was buried at his request in the churchyard of St Dunstan and All Saints, Stepney. The provisions of his will imply that he had modest means. In it Nunes describes Lord Burleigh as his 'verie good lorde' and mentions his friendship with Sir Thomas Heneage.

Nunes was a well-known figure in Elizabethan London, both as a physician and as a merchant. His trading connections with Spain and Portugal, his vulnerability as a refugee, and his loyalty made him valuable to the English government. Walsingham made good use of him both as a diplomatic intermediary and as a source of intelligence about the Spanish armada. EDGAR SAMUEL

Sources L. Wolf, 'Jews in Elizabethan England', *Transactions of the Jewish Historical Society of England*, 11 (1924–7), 1–91 • C. Roth, 'The case of Thomas Fernandes before the Lisbon Inquisition', *Miscellanies of the Jewish Historical Society of England*, 2 (1935), 32–56 • C. Meyers, 'Dr Hector Nunez: Elizabethan merchant', *Miscellanies of the Jewish Historical Society of England*, 13 (1981–2), 129–31 • C. Meyers, 'Debt in Elizabethan England: the adventures of Dr Hector Nunez, physician and merchant', *Jewish Historical Studies*, 34 (1994–6), 125–40 • G. Clark and A. M. Cooke, *A history of the Royal College of Physicians of London*, 3 vols. (1964–72) • C. Read, *Mr Secretary Walsingham and the policy of Queen Elizabeth*, 3 vols. (1925) • L. Stone, *An Elizabethan: Sir Horatio Palavicino* (1956) • L. Wolf, 'Jews in Tudor England', in L. Wolf, *Essays in Jewish history*, ed. C. Roth (1934), 71–90 • Historical MSS Commission report 9, Hatfield papers II and XIII • Historical MSS Commission report 77, De Lisle I • Historical MSS Commission report 72, Laing I • *CSP Spain, 1587–1603* • *CSP for., 1585–6* • R. E. G. Kirk and E. F. Kirk, eds., *Returns of aliens dwelling in the city and suburbs of London, from the reign of Henry VIII to that of James I*, 4 vols., Huguenot Society of London, 10 (1900–08) • B. Dietz, ed., *The port and trade of early Elizabethan London: documents*, London RS, 8 (1972) • *CPR* • will, PRO, PROB 11/78, sig. 66
Archives Archivo General, Simancas

Nunhouse, Isabel (*fl.* 1441–1442). *See under* Women in trade and industry in York (*act. c.*1300–*c.*1500).

Nunn family (*per. c.*1815–1847), hymn writers, were the children of John Nunn of Colchester. The eldest son, another **John Nunn** (1782–1861), was born in Colchester on 23 May 1782 and was educated at St John's College, Cambridge, from 1802, graduating BA in 1806. He married Elizabeth, daughter of William Tipton of Shrewsbury. After serving various curacies he became domestic chaplain to the earl of Galway (1849–53) and rector of Thorndon, Suffolk, in 1854, where he died on 15 April 1861; he was buried at Thorndon. Nunn was a friend and fellow curate of Patrick Brontë. In 1817 he published *Psalms and Hymns*, which was reprinted several times, the last edition appearing in 1861. It contained several hymns by Nunn himself, but these soon passed out of use. Nunn's sister, **Marianne Nunn** (1778–1847), born on 17 May 1778, also wrote hymns and is remembered for her adaptation of John Newton's hymn 'One there is above all others, O how he loves' to the Welsh tune 'Ar hyd y nos'. The original appeared in John Nunn's *Psalms and Hymns*; in various variant versions it remained popular as a children's hymn into the early twentieth century. Marianne Nunn died, unmarried, in 1847. Her younger brother, **William Nunn** (1786–1840), was born on 13 May 1786 and educated at St John's College, Cambridge, graduating BA in 1814 and MA in 1817. Ordained priest in 1814, he served as the incumbent of St Clement's Episcopalian Chapel in Manchester from 1818. He married Elizabeth, daughter of Philip Vaughan of Kidwelly, on 14 June 1819; they had at least two sons. William Nunn wrote several hymns, of which the most popular were 'O could we touch the sacred lyre' and 'The gospel comes, ordained of God'. Both appeared in his 1827 *Selection of Psalms and Hymns*. He died in Manchester on 9 March 1840, and was buried at All Saints' Church there.

ROSEMARY MITCHELL

Sources J. Julian, ed., *A dictionary of hymnology*, rev. edn (1907), 823–4 • Venn, *Alum. Cant.* • J. Miller, *Singers and songs of the church* (1869), 362 • R. Garrett Horder, *The hymn lover* (1899), 142 • E. R. Pitman, *Lady hymn-writers* (1892), 152–3 • *GM*, 2nd ser., 13 (1840), 664 • *GM*, 3rd ser., 10 (1861), 703 • *CGPLA Eng. & Wales* (1861) [John Nunn]
Wealth at death under £2000—John Nunn: probate, 28 May 1861, *CGPLA Eng. & Wales*

Nunn, Jean Josephine (1916–1982), civil servant, was born at Rixlade, Abbotsham, Devon, on 21 July 1916, the daughter of John Henry Nunn, a captain in the Royal Field Artillery, and his wife, Doris Josephine Gregory. Her father (by then a major) was killed when she was eighteen months old. She was educated at St Leonard's School, Ealing, at the Royal School for Officers' Daughters at Bath, and at Girton College, Cambridge (1934–7), where she read both parts of the history tripos.

In 1938 Nunn passed the examination for the administrative grade of the civil service and joined the Home Office. She soon made her mark. It was no novelty for the Home Office to have a woman in this grade, but there had been no one quite like this new entrant. After only three years she was appointed private secretary to the permanent under-secretary of state, and was then promoted to be an acting principal when only twenty-six. After a spell in the police division she won golden opinions as secretary to the royal commission on the press (1947–9). She then served with distinction as the principal private secretary to two home secretaries—James Chuter Ede and Sir David Maxwell-Fyfe. It was the first time that this key post had been held by a woman.

On promotion to assistant secretary Nunn headed, in turn, divisions concerned with civil defence, police, and—for some five years—criminal justice. In this last post she was concerned notably with capital cases and with preparing the 1957 Homicide Act. This act introduced the defence of diminished responsibility into English law and, in a provision destined to have only a short life, sought to distinguish between categories of capital and non-capital murder. She also readily responded to the desire of the incoming home secretary in 1957, R. A. Butler, to nurture interest in criminological research.

In 1961 Nunn was promoted to be an assistant under-secretary of state and was put in charge of the children's department. Her stay there was brief. In 1963 she moved to the Cabinet Office, and three years later was promoted to the post of deputy secretary there—the first woman to achieve such high rank in that demanding organization. As well as serving the cabinet and various cabinet committees, she took on much of the administrative work of running the Cabinet Office itself. Then, in 1970, when she seemed to be heading irresistibly towards the headship of one of the great departments of state, she was struck down by illness and had to leave the service to which she was so devoted.

Sensible, creative in her thinking, crystal-clear in her writing and in oral exposition, Nunn had over the years won the regard of ministers and officials alike. She had the characteristic of raising her eyebrows if she felt some doubt about the arguments put to her, and all who knew her thought it wise to pay regard to that signal. Her doubts were always worth listening to. Throughout there was a sharp wit and on occasion a sense almost of gaiety. Her wit once provided entertainment to a wider audience than usual when in 1946 the home secretary, Chuter Ede, read out to an enraptured House of Commons her highly entertaining account of a meeting in the Albert Hall where the members of the small fascist body which had organized the meeting had been heavily outnumbered by their communist opponents.

It might perhaps be said of Nunn that, in her understandable anxiety to demonstrate that a woman could do just as well as a man in finding solutions to problems, she did not find it easy to accept that occasionally the best course might be to do nothing. But she was indeed an outstanding public servant fully deserving of the high reputation she achieved across the service.

There was more to Nunn's life than a brilliant official career. She enjoyed social contacts; she was fond of acting, and was good at it; and after her mother died she travelled extensively. Throughout, her Christian faith never wavered. She was for some years a warden in her local church in Pimlico, and served on the London diocesan board for adult education. It was of some solace to her in the early days of retirement that in 1971 she was made an honorary fellow of her old college and was appointed CB. When she had been made CBE in 1966 she had been quietly told that the Bath was not open to women. But the rules were changed, and she was the first to benefit.

The illness which caused her to retire was cerebral arteriosclerosis. For twelve long years she was lovingly cared for by a friend, but her capacities slowly declined. Jean Nunn died at Oakhill House, Eady Close, Horsham, Sussex, on 24 November 1982.   ALLEN OF ABBEYDALE

Sources *The Times* (26 Nov 1982) · personal knowledge (2004) · private information (2004) · b. cert. · d. cert. · *Hansard 5C* (1946), 420.1260–4 · K. T. Butler and H. I. McMorran, eds., *Girton College register, 1869–1946* (1948) · *Girton Newsletter* (1983)

Wealth at death £145,627: probate, 2 March 1983, *CGPLA Eng. & Wales*

Nunn, John (1782–1861). *See under* Nunn family (*per. c.*1815–1847).

Nunn, Joshua Arthur (1853–1908), army veterinary surgeon, born on 10 May 1853 at Hill Castle, co. Wexford, Ireland, was the son of Edward W. Nunn JP DL. Nunn was educated at Wimbledon School, and he served in the Royal Monmouthshire engineer militia from 1871 to 1877. In 1874 he entered the Royal Veterinary College at Camden Town, London, and was admitted MRCVS on 4 January 1877. In the same year he obtained a certificate in cattle pathology from the Royal Agricultural Society. He was also gazetted veterinary surgeon on probation in the army veterinary service on 21 April 1877 and veterinary surgeon to the Royal Artillery on 24 April 1877, being the last officer to obtain a commission under the old regimental system.

Nunn proceeded to India in December 1877, and from September 1879 to August 1880 he took part in the Anglo-Afghan War as the veterinary officer in charge of transport on the Khyber line of communication. Later, accompanying the expeditionary column in the Laghman valley, he was in charge of the transport base hospital at Gandamak. For these services he was awarded the Afghan medal.

Nunn was employed on special duty from 1880 to 1885 as a civil servant under the Punjab government, first in the suppression of glanders under the Glanders and Farcy Act and, afterwards, in connection with the agricultural department of Punjab, as the veterinary inspector. In this capacity he travelled widely to collect all manner of information and statistics about cattle, including folklore and disease. This he embodied in a series of valuable reports: *Animal Diseases in Rohtak* (1882); *Diseases in Sialkote and Hazara* (1883); and *Diseases in the Montgomery and Shapur Districts* (1884–5). He also lectured to students at the Lahore Veterinary College. Before he left India in 1886, the government of the Punjab recognized his valuable services in a special minute.

After taking short courses in bacteriology at Cambridge and Paris, Nunn was ordered to South Africa in January 1887 to investigate 'horse sickness', thought to be due to anthrax; he proved that the disease was malarial in type. Engaging meanwhile in the campaign against the Zulu in 1888, he was at the surrender of the chief Somkali at St Lucia Lagoon.

Nunn returned to India on 11 December 1888, and was appointed inspecting veterinary officer of the Chittagong column during the Chin Lushai expedition of 1889. Nunn was mentioned in dispatches and was decorated with the

Distinguished Service Order on 12 December 1890, being the first member of the army veterinary service to receive this distinction. In 1890 he was appointed principal of the Punjab Veterinary College, where he worked for six years and laid the foundations of the local veterinary service. He was rewarded by becoming CIE in 1895. Nunn did much to advance the cause of veterinary science in India. Of untiring energy, he was personally popular with his associates.

Nunn was joint editor of the *Veterinary Journal* from 1893 to 1906, and also published *Report on South African Horse Sickness* (1888); *Notes on Stable Management in India* (1896); *Lectures on Saddlery and Harness* (1902); *Veterinary First Aid in Cases of Accident or Sudden Illness* (1903); *The Use of Molasses as a Feeding Material* (1903), which was translated from the French of Edouard Curot; *Diseases of the Mammary Gland of the Domestic Animals* (1904), also translated from the French of P. Leblanc; and *Veterinary Toxicology* (1907).

From December 1896 to August 1905 Nunn was in England, spending part of his time studying law, though in 1901 he also passed his examinations as a meat inspector. He was called to the bar at Lincoln's Inn in November 1899, and was later admitted as advocate of the bar of the supreme court of the Transvaal. Again in England, he was from 1901 to 1904 deputy director-general of the army veterinary department, and then was principal veterinary officer in South Africa, in 1904–5. He was transferred to India in June 1906 and there he filled a similar position. He was made a CB on 26 June 1906. In Bombay on 12 January 1907 he married Gertrude Ann, widow of W. Chamberlain and daughter of E. Kellner CIE. He remained in India, despite illness, until 23 January 1908, when he returned to England. He died by his own hand in the Warneford Hospital, Oxford, on 23 February 1908. He was survived by his wife.   D'A. POWER, *rev.* LINDA WARDEN

Sources *Veterinary Journal* (March 1908) · *Veterinary Record* (29 Feb 1908) · records, war office, 3/30 Nov 1962, Royal Army Veterinary Corps, Aldershot, WORC ENCL 2/26/DOCS/48 (DI(?)) · student entry book, 1873–82, Royal Veterinary College, London, p. 8 · F. Smith, *A history of the royal army veterinary corps, 1796–1919* (1927) · *Oxford Times* (29 Feb 1908), 3 · d. cert.
Likenesses portrait, repro. in *Veterinary Journal*, 105–6
Wealth at death £10,987 17s. 3d.: probate, 24 March 1908, CGPLA Eng. & Wales

Nunn, Marianne (1778–1847). *See under* Nunn family (*per.* c.1815–1847).

Nunn, Sir (Thomas) Percy (1870–1944), educationist, was born on 28 December 1870 in Bristol, the second son of Edward Smith Nunn (d. 1890) and his wife, Harriette (*née* Luff). Both his father and grandfather were schoolmasters, and in 1873 their proprietary school was transferred to Weston-super-Mare. There Nunn received his own education and began to teach. He subsequently studied at Bristol University College. His interests at this time included the writing and producing of school plays and the making of scientific instruments. In 1890, on the death of his father, Nunn decided against taking over responsibility for management of the school. In the same year he gained a London BSc degree; he took the degrees of

BA in 1895 and MA in 1902. In 1894 he married Eliza Alice (Ethel), daughter of Edmund John Hart, a carter. Their daughter, Elsa, also obtained a London MA, in 1929, and was principal of Fishponds Training College, Bristol (1930–54).

Nunn taught in schools in Halifax and London, where by 1903 he was senior science master at the William Ellis School. From March of that year he was engaged on a part-time basis by the London Day Training College (LDTC) to demonstrate methods of teaching mathematics and science. In 1905 he was appointed vice-principal there. In 1913 he was accorded the title of professor of education by the University of London, and in 1922 he succeeded John (later Sir John) Adams as principal at the LDTC. Nunn's personality and educational philosophy were to exercise a considerable influence over the LDTC and more widely. An early contribution to the nature of scientific knowledge was *The Aim and Achievements of Scientific Method: an Epistemological Essay* (1907), a study based on his London University doctoral thesis, presented in the same year. Publications of 1912–14 intended for classroom teachers included a co-authored *First Class Book of Chemistry* and two volumes on algebra. He also served as editor of Black's Elementary Science Series and in 1923 wrote a study entitled *Relativity and Gravitation*.

But the work for which Nunn became best known was *Education: its Data and First Principles*, written in the concluding years of the First World War and published in 1920. Its central thesis was 'that nothing good enters into the human world except in and through the free activities of individual men and women and that educational practice must be shaped to accord with that truth' (T. P. Nunn, *Education*, 1920, 5). This book went through three editions and more than twenty reprints, and was required reading for student teachers for some forty years.

Nunn presided over a number of important changes at the LDTC, including the establishment of a department for higher degrees and research and a colonial department (1927). He was knighted in 1930. Two years later the academic status and international role which Nunn had fostered were recognized by the transmutation of the LDTC into the London University Institute of Education. In spite of the talented team which Nunn collected around him, including Cyril Burt, Fred Clarke, H. R. Hamley, Susan Isaacs, and Marion Richardson, his authority and pre-eminence were unquestioned. As another colleague, P. Gurrey, wrote:

> Over this collection Nunn towered in every way: intellectual ability, force of character, and width of interest and knowledge. There was no doubt about our realisation of his supreme position as a thinker, organiser, mathematician and teacher. The legend of Nunn did not grow after he had left us: we saw it growing.   (A. S. Harrison and others, 46)

Nunn, however, was always accessible. His personal charm and whimsical humour were coupled with a great gift for explaining complex issues in simple and clear language. One of his former students, G. B. Jeffery, who in 1945 succeeded Clarke as director of the institute, recalled of Nunn that:

He never talked down to you. He put himself by your side ready to share your enthusiasms, taking it for granted that you would share his. You were learning and he was learning; you were learning together. The remarkable thing is that it was perfectly true. In teaching you, his vivid and adventurous mind was sure to see some new light and you shared the discovery together. (ibid., 14)

Nunn's interests were boundless. He had a great admiration for Plato and bought a Greek fount for his printing press so that he could produce Greek quotations and verses. He also took great delight in music, both classical and light, and penned parodies for LDTC concerts—from 'Phyllis was a Fair Maid' to 'Knocked 'em in Southampton Row'. Yet in spite of his commitment to all aspects of the life of the LDTC and institute, and of the university, he also played significant roles in the Aristotelian Society, the British Association, the British Psychological Society, the Mathematical Association, and the Training College Association. In his later years Nunn's prodigious workload began to take its toll and he suffered considerably from bronchitis and emphysema. He found increasing difficulty in breathing in foggy weather and in climbing stairs (the five-storey Southampton Row building had no lifts). In 1932 he spent most of an intended recuperation cruise in the ship's hospital, and on his return to London he was diagnosed as suffering from extreme exhaustion. In 1936 he retired to Funchal, Madeira, where he died on 12 December 1944; he was buried on 13 December at the British cemetery, Funchal.

Nunn was awarded honorary degrees by the universities of Liverpool, St Andrews, and Trinity College, Dublin. The status accorded to *Education* has been questioned by such academics as J. W. Tibble (*British Journal of Educational Studies*, 10, 1961, 58–75), and in *All Must Have Prizes* (1996) the journalist Melanie Phillips included Nunn—who wrote chapters in *Education* on the importance of 'Play' and 'Freedom in Education'—among those whom she accused of promoting 'cranky views' (Phillips, 203). Indeed Nunn himself, in company with many of his students, would probably have placed his lectures and writings in the field of teaching mathematics and science above his treatment of educational principles. But his commitment in *Education* to the roles of the individual and of individuality in education was of central importance in a world that was increasingly dominated by totalitarian regimes. His gravestone in the British cemetery at Funchal bears a fitting epitaph: 'Teacher, Philosopher, Mathematician. Revered by the Academic World, Mourned by his Disciples, Loved by his Friends'.   RICHARD ALDRICH

Sources J. W. Tibble, 'Sir Percy Nunn', *British Journal of Educational Studies*, 10 (1961–2), 58–75 • H. R. Hamley, 'Sir Percy Nunn', *British Journal of Educational Psychology*, 15 (Feb 1945), 1–4 • R. Aldrich, *The Institute of Education, 1902–2002: a centenary history* (2002) • A. S. Harrison and others, *Studies and impressions, 1902–1952* (1952) • C. W. Dixon, *The institute: a personal account of the history of the University of London Institute of Education, 1932–1972* (1986) • Institute of Education, *Jubilee lectures* (1952) • M. Phillips, *All must have prizes* (1996) • *CGPLA Eng. & Wales* (1945) • *DNB* • burial register, British cemetery, Funchal, Madeira, 13 Dec 1944

Archives JRL, letters to Samuel Alexander • U. Lond., Institute of Education, archives

Likenesses H. Lamb, oils, 1937, Institute of Education, London
Wealth at death £4318 7s. 1d.: probate, 2 June 1945, *CGPLA Eng. & Wales*

Nunn, Thomas Hancock (1859–1937), social reformer, was born on 14 March 1859 at 23 Euston Square, London, the fourth of the five children of John Nunn, wine merchant, and his wife, Sarah Hancock. He attended University College School and Christ's College, Cambridge (1880–84), where he took an honours degree in moral sciences and history. At Cambridge he met Canon Samuel Barnett, vicar of St Jude's, Whitechapel—a meeting which was to determine the course of his life.

Barnett was looking for socially conscious young men to join him in the fight against poverty in London's East End, and in 1885 Nunn became a founder resident of Toynbee Hall, the first of the university settlements, which was also to include Clement Attlee among its early members. Nunn lived and worked at Toynbee for the next ten years, until his marriage in 1894 to his cousin Katherine Hannah Bourne (*d.* 1933), although he continued to work there for a further four years even after the couple set up home in Hampstead. While at Toynbee Hall, Nunn became honorary secretary of the Stepney Charity Organization Society and a poor law guardian of Stepney Union, and this mix of public and voluntary sector interests was to be a recurrent theme of his working life and underpin his emerging philosophy of social welfare.

Canon Barnett was a firm believer in the importance of the voluntary principle: the view that people should be looked after first and foremost by friends and neighbours, and only as a last resort by the state if all other avenues had failed. However, unlike many others involved in charitable work at this time, he eschewed the notion of a separation of spheres between charity and state, advocating instead co-operation and partnership between the two agents of social policy. Through his work both locally and nationally he paved the way for a new approach to charity and social welfare which was to come together with the founding of the National Council of Social Service at the end of the First World War.

After Toynbee Hall, Nunn joined the Hampstead Charity Organization Society and in 1899 he laid the foundations for the Hampstead Council of Social Welfare, the first of a new wave of voluntary associations which were to seek closer ties with the poor law authorities. Over the next decade he was involved in setting up numerous voluntary associations, many related to his two main passions—public education and health. He became a manager of the Kilburn Group of Elementary Schools in 1902, and in the same year formed the Hampstead Health Society. In 1908 he founded the first clinic for schoolchildren and in 1913 the Hampstead Health Institute.

On the national stage Nunn's most influential work was as a member of the royal commission on the poor laws from 1906 to 1909. He was a signatory to the majority report and bitterly disagreed with Beatrice Webb, the author of the minority report, for her wholehearted rejection of the poor law. He wrote a memorandum which was published with the majority report, which spoke of the necessity 'to connect organically the statutory and the voluntary bodies' (*Thomas Hancock Nunn*), and called for the setting up of councils of social service across the country. In 1919 he was one of five promoters in the establishment of the National Council of Social Service. Much of the rest of his life was spent consolidating the pioneering work of his earlier years.

In April 1933 Nunn's wife died. In May 1934 he married Florence Kathleen Urwick, whom he had known for thirty-six years after having met her when she was a young volunteer at the Hampstead Charity Organization Society. Nunn's work at Toynbee and in Hampstead was all-consuming and left little time for relaxation. While at Cambridge he had enjoyed mountaineering, especially in Switzerland, and in later life he would enjoy walking on the downs near his bungalow retreat in Shoreham, Sussex. But perhaps his greatest passion was for poetry, and he wrote several (unpublished) works on Wordsworth, Browning, and Swinburne.

In November 1936 Nunn was awarded the freedom of the borough of Hampstead. He died at his Sussex home, Harbour St Mary, Shoreham, on 22 June 1937, being survived by his second wife. Hancock Nunn House in London—model apartments—commemorates his name.

JUSTIN DAVIS SMITH

Sources *Thomas Hancock Nunn: the life and work of a social reformer … by his friends* (1942) · *CGPLA Eng. & Wales* (1937) · **Likenesses** photograph, repro. in *Thomas Hancock Nunn* · **Wealth at death** £4717 1s. 3d.: resworn probate, 5 Oct 1937, *CGPLA Eng. & Wales*

Nunn, William (1786–1840). *See under* Nunn family (*per.* c.1815–1847).

Nunna (*fl.* 692–714?). *See under* South Saxons, kings of the (*act.* 477–772).

Nunneley, Thomas (1809–1870), surgeon, born at Market Harborough, Leicestershire, in March 1809, was the son of John Nunneley, a gentleman of property in Leicestershire, descended from a Shropshire family. He was educated privately, a spinal complaint necessitating a long course of treatment, and was apprenticed to a surgeon in Wellingborough, Northamptonshire. He afterwards became a student at Guy's Hospital, London, where he met and later became a close friend of Sir Astley Paston Cooper, and served as surgical dresser to Charles Aston Key. He was admitted a licentiate of the Society of Apothecaries on 12 July 1832, and became a member (1832) and one of the first honorary fellows (1843) of the Royal College of Surgeons of England. As soon as he had obtained his licence to practise, he travelled to Paris to increase his professional knowledge. On his return to England he applied unsuccessfully to be house surgeon to the Leeds General Infirmary, but as an opportunity for practice became available in that town, he settled there, and was soon afterwards appointed surgeon to the Eye and Ear Hospital, a post he successfully occupied for twenty years. In the Leeds school of medicine he lectured on anatomy and physiology, and later on surgery, until 1866. He was appointed surgeon to the Leeds General Infirmary in 1864. For three years he

was a member of the Leeds town council, and for many years was an active member of the Leeds Philosophical and Literary Society.

Nunneley was one of the earliest surgeons outside London to specialize in ophthalmic surgery, and was among the first to attempt excision of the tongue. He was clear, vigorous, and logical as a writer, at times holding opinions obstinately. His energy and excessive determination were exhibited during his final illness, in performing one operation, then going aside to vomit, but returning to perform another operation. He was a decisive professional witness in favour of William Palmer (1825–1856), who was convicted of poisoning J. P. Cook by strychnine in 1856, and against William Dove, who poisoned his wife with the same drug in the course of that same year.

Nunneley's chief work was *The Organs of Vision, their Anatomy and Physiology* (1858), which sold poorly after adverse criticism in professional journals, which appears to have been due to personal animosity. He also published works on erysipelas, anaesthetic agents, and the effects of hydrocyanic acid.

Nunneley continued to work until three weeks before his death from uraemia on 1 June 1870 in Leeds. He was buried at Woodhouse cemetery, Leeds. Nothing is known of his family life, except that he had a son, John Albert, also a surgeon.

D'A. POWER, *rev.* HUGH SERIES

Sources *BMJ* (11 June 1870), 614 · S. Hey, 'Brief report of the last illness of T. Nunneley, FRCS, and of the post-mortem examination', *BMJ* (11 June 1870), 598–9 · G. Burrows, *Proceedings of the Royal Medical and Chirurgical Society*, 6 (1867–71), 354–6 · *Medical Times and Gazette* (11 June 1870), 648–9 · *CGPLA Eng. & Wales* (1870) · private information (1894) · **Likenesses** photograph, repro. in *Photographs of eminent medical men*, 2 (1867), 33 · **Wealth at death** under £10,000: resworn probate, Oct 1874, *CGPLA Eng. & Wales* (1870)

Nur Begam. *See* Banu, Halime (1770–1853), *under* Indian visitors (*act. c.*1720–*c.*1810).

Nureyev, Rudolf Hametovich (1938–1993), dancer and choreographer, was born in Siberia in mid-March 1938, the youngest child (after three sisters) of Hamet Nuriakhmetovich Nureyev (1903–1966), a Red Army political officer, and his wife, Farida Agilivulevna (1905–1988). She was on a train to join him near Vladivostok and gave birth prematurely near Lake Baikal. Rudolf's birth was registered as 17 March but was eventually found to be probably three days earlier. Nureyev's kin were Tartars, of peasant stock in the Bashkir republic, but his father, seizing opportunities brought by the Bolshevik Revolution, advanced to the rank of army major. Rudolf, only three when Germany invaded Russia, had no memories of his father earlier than Hamet's return from military service five years later. That explains the distance between father and son, made worse because he had fixed on what Nureyev senior thought the unmanly career of dancing.

Introduction to ballet From earliest days Nureyev loved music; at seven he saw ballet for the first time. Evacuated from Moscow, the family shared a wooden house in Ufa, the Bashkir capital. Food was scarce, winters long and

Rudolf Hametovich Nureyev (1938–1993), by Sir Cecil Beaton

agonizingly cold. Everyone suffered, but the Nureyevs were poorer than some. Boiled potatoes were their main food, and Nureyev started school barefoot and wearing one of his sisters' overcoats. The town, however, did have an opera house with good standards. On new year's eve 1945 Farida Nureyeva smuggled her children in to see the patriotic ballet *Song of the Cranes* starring the Leningrad-trained Bashkir ballerina Zaituna Nazretdinova. At once Nureyev wanted to be a dancer. After folk dances at school and with the Pioneers, he was recommended to a ballet teacher, Anna Udeltsova, who eighteen months later passed him on to another, Elena Vaitovich. Both told him about dancers they had seen (including Pavlova and the Diaghilev company), and taught him that there was more to dancing than technique. Seeing his potential, they urged that he ought to study in Leningrad's academy, considered the best in the world.

That seemed impossible, especially when Nureyev's father forbade his dancing classes because they were affecting his school results and therefore his prospects in a 'suitable' career. But his mother turned a blind eye when he sneaked off to lessons under pretence of other activities. At fifteen he began serving as an extra at the opera house, gaining some income and classes with the ballet company. He progressed to dancing in the corps, and got himself on a ten-day tour to Moscow by taking over, impromptu, a folk-dance solo from an injured dancer. This was the first example of an astonishing memory for dances he had only seen, which later facilitated many of his productions.

Leningrad and the Kirov In Moscow, Nureyev auditioned for the Bolshoi ballet school, and was accepted; Ufa also offered him a full contract. He decided, however, to persevere in trying for Leningrad: reputed to be the best school,

and residential, which helped living costs. So he spent his earnings on a ticket taking him to Leningrad. There he was accepted with the comment 'you'll become either a brilliant dancer or a total failure—and most likely a failure'. At seventeen he was raw, without skills already acquired by contemporaries who had entered the academy seven years earlier, but he took this as a challenge to gain knowledge and control without losing the spontaneity and individuality of his natural talent. For three years he drove himself hard, practising between classes the steps he found most difficult, determined to overtake the others. Yet he notoriously defied rules he thought silly; for instance, watching attentively every performance he could at the Kirov Theatre, even though absence from the dormitory incurred punishment. He also, being put in the sixth grade, begged for transfer to the eighth (out of nine), afraid he might be called to military service before completing the course. This increased his reputation for being difficult, but when his wish was granted it brought him under an exceptional teacher, Alexander Pushkin.

Once convinced of his determination, Pushkin helped Nureyev greatly, even taking him into his own home, and coached him into the top grade. Nureyev spent two years there and on graduation danced with such fervour and brilliance that both the Kirov and Bolshoi ballets offered him a soloist contract. Unsurprisingly he chose the former, and made his début partnering their ballerina Natalia Dudinskaya in one of her famous roles, *Laurentia*. Demanding both virtuosity and strong drama, the ballet brought him great success. Shortly afterwards he injured an ankle but soon got back on stage despite a doctor saying he would never dance again. Thereafter, however, throughout his career he had pain and ankle problems that would have deterred anyone less resolute.

During three years with the Kirov, Nureyev danced another fifteen roles (including the major classic leads) and partnered all the ballerinas. Although not tall, he had a powerful presence and his face with its Asiatic bone structure was expressive. A fan club developed, watching his every performance, drawn by the passion of his dancing and the personal reading he gave each ballet. He even redesigned some costumes, and argued with rehearsal directors, sometimes walking out of the studio to practise alone.

The leap to freedom Nureyev's reputation for misbehaviour and his achievement grew simultaneously (he came top in an international competition in Vienna), so when the Kirov went to Paris in 1961 for its first foreign tour, he could hardly be left behind but was closely watched. Still unconforming, when buses took the company to its hotel each night, he went out with French dancers and other locals. One or two colleagues did likewise, but it was Nureyev who caused most alarm to the tour's political managers. Consequently, when everyone arrived at the airport to travel for performances in London, he was given a ticket to Moscow and told he was needed for a gala. Nureyev was sure this really meant relegation and never again being allowed abroad. Deciding to seek asylum in the West, he managed to get word to friends who came to see him off. They found that he must approach French police; he did this and was granted permission to stay in France. All later travel had to be done on temporary documents until eventually he was given Austrian citizenship. Soviet officials disparaged the 'defector', and in his absence Nureyev was sentenced to seven years' imprisonment; not until 1987 was he permitted to visit his elderly sick mother.

Following his spectacular success with the Kirov, the Grand Ballet du Marquis de Cuévas engaged him, but he stayed only a few months, violently disliking their *Sleeping Beauty* production, although he admired their ballerina Rosella Hightower, and worked with her on his first choreography, the *pas de deux* from the *Nutcracker*. He next found that Erik Bruhn (1928–1986) was about to dance in Copenhagen; Nureyev, on the strength of an amateur film, admired Bruhn more than any other male dancer. So he went to Copenhagen, where the two men fell in love, their close feelings continuing, despite quarrels and separations, until Bruhn's death. Both of them perfectionists, they did their daily class together and Nureyev began assimilating Western style to add to what he had learned in the Soviet Union. Bruhn's attitude to his roles confirmed Nureyev's belief that men should be allowed to dance as expressively as women. This later led each of them to add a soft, andante solo to *Swan Lake*, introducing a new gentle style of male dancing later taken up by other choreographers.

From Copenhagen, Nureyev was invited to make his London début at Margot *Fonteyn's annual gala for the Royal Academy of Dancing. He danced *Black Swan* with Hightower and a solo, *Poème tragique*, made for him by Frederick Ashton. The Royal Ballet asked him to dance *Giselle* with Fonteyn the next season, also other classics with the guest ballerinas Sonia Arova and Yvette Chauviré. Meanwhile, Nureyev danced with Bruhn, Arova, and Hightower in Cannes and Paris, performing pieces created or staged by the two men, and he made his New York début on television (substituting for the injured Bruhn), then on stage with Ruth Page's Chicago Opera Ballet.

Margot Fonteyn and the Royal Ballet Thus was laid the groundwork for Nureyev's international career: a lasting link with the Royal Ballet, frequent appearances elsewhere, activities as producer and choreographer, and above all his partnership with Fonteyn. Both of them danced with many other partners who almost always looked better in consequence, but they were most proud of what they achieved together. He at twenty-three gave her at forty-two a new burst of energy; she helped him settle down. They learned much from each other and danced at their very best together. He greatly wanted to show Leningrad what they had achieved (unfortunately, when he was eventually allowed there, she had retired and he was past his best). They remained lifelong close friends, and when Fonteyn was dying of cancer Nureyev paid her medical bills.

The Royal Ballet became Nureyev's base until the 1970s, when new directors began to squeeze him and Fonteyn out. Through the years, however, he danced with dozens of companies, eager for new roles and new styles. For Paul Taylor, whose choreography he greatly admired, and Martha Graham he appeared without fee. A notably quick learner, he amassed an unusually large and varied repertory. Besides the old classics in many different versions, he took well over 100 roles by more than forty choreographers. About two-fifths of these were created specially for him by a diverse array of talents including Rudi van Dantzig, Flemming Flindt, Graham, and Kenneth MacMillan. The new-made part that best brought out his gifts was Ashton's Armand, full of poetry and passion with Fonteyn's Marguérite. But the emotion he found in Maurice Béjart's Wayfarer, his insouciant humour in *Jazz Calendar* (Ashton) and *Le bourgeois gentilhomme* (Balanchine), the knotty complexity he brought to Glen Tetley's *Laborintus*, or his sheer flamboyance in Roland Petit's *Paradise Lost* all left strong memories. To the standard repertory he brought character and illumination, even where dance was primary: *Apollo*, Hans van Manen's *Four Schumann Pieces*, or Jerome Robbins's *Dances at a Gathering*. Naturally this was even more true in narrative roles, such as Colas in *La fille mal gardée*, *The Prodigal Son*, Des Grieux in *Manon*, John Neumeier's Don Juan, or the title part in Valery Panov's *The Idiot*. He especially liked reinterpreting parts made for his great predecessor Nijinsky, and made rare sense of the delicate sexual allure of *Le spectre de la rose*.

Nureyev was one of the first ballet dancers to perform with contemporary dance companies, being particularly successful in capturing the character and weight of the Revivalist in Graham's *Appalachian Spring* and the slippery smoothness of dances Murray Louis made for him. Yet many thought him so incomparable in the classics that they regretted the time he devoted to contemporary dance. The immense airborne thrust of his *Bayadère* solos, his utter commitment in *Giselle*, ardour and melancholy in *Swan Lake*, vivacity and fun in *Don Quixote* gave strength to this argument, and above all *The Sleeping Beauty*, where the intelligence of his acting and perfection of his dancing were unmatched. In some other roles the improvement in male dancing started by his example has sometimes allowed others to vie with his former easy supremacy, but in the *Beauty* his execution, phrasing, and finish were unique.

When Nureyev first danced the Royal Ballet's *Giselle* and *Swan Lake*, many people complained about his additions and alterations to the choreography, but Ashton and de Valois strongly defended him. Questioning received versions of the classics soon led him to make his own productions. He began with existing choreography unfamiliar in the West, notably the Shades scene from *La bayadère*, but in 1964, aged twenty-six and inexperienced as a choreographer, he put on two major works within a few months: a much revised version of Petipa's *Raymonda* for the Royal Ballet and a completely new *Swan Lake* at the Vienna State Opera. These were the first of six old ballets he mounted, always in more than one staging for various companies, allowing him to develop and improve his ideas. All had positive virtues and outlived him in performance, with *La bayadère* remaining the closest to its source, *Don Quixote* the most successful reanimation of its original, and *The Nutcracker* the best completely new interpretation. On a similarly large scale are his two Prokofiev ballets, a highly dramatic *Romeo and Juliet* faithful to Shakespeare (and Shakespeare's sources) and a *Cinderella* reinterpreted in terms of Hollywood. There were also several original one-act ballets, outstanding among them the Byronic heroics of *Manfred* and the cool characterizations of *The Tempest*. Unsurprisingly his productions contained good roles for the leading dancers, but remarkably he taught himself, through studying Petipa's ballets, to make interesting, often very demanding, dances for the ensemble too: something rare in latter-day choreographers. Nureyev's productions always owed much to his general culture: widely read, assiduous in attending films, plays, and galleries at any spare moment, loving to play music alone or with friends, and applying his prodigious memory to the detail of everything he saw or heard.

Paris When the Royal Ballet needed a new director in 1977, Nureyev's name was considered, but rejected because he insisted that he would continue dancing. However, in 1983 he was offered and accepted the position of ballet director at the Paris Opéra, which he held for six years, surrounding himself with first-rate ballet staff able to sustain and later continue his policies. Chief among these was widening the repertory, through his own productions and by bringing in an immense variety of ballets by leading choreographers and also by aspirants whose talent seemed real. He wanted the dancers, like himself, to experience many styles: from the great classics (not previously well represented in Paris) and revivals or reconstructions of historic French works, to the best ballets of modern times and many creations. He stimulated the dancers, besides, by giving early opportunities to newcomers from the excellent attached school (which also benefited under him from new premises, while the company similarly gained new rehearsal studios). More performances and increased touring were other benefits. The dancers found working with him made their work exciting and fulfilling, and he was famed for being always ready to help any dancer who asked him. A proclivity for temper tantrums was notorious too, but usually with good reason and not for long. He spoke several languages fluently, with a strong accent, and could curse violently in all of them.

On top of his dance activities, Nureyev made time to act in two films, *Valentino* (1977) and *Exposed* (1983): neither of them very good, though he upheld his roles well, explaining that he found little difficulty in a non-dancing role because much of ballet involves acting. Similarly, on leaving Paris he toured North America in the musical *The King and I*. But dancing was always his main concern and he took every opportunity to perform, appearing every night on long tours or during extended London seasons (these also gave opportunities to major companies he invited from America, Australia, Canada, Italy, Japan, and Switzerland). Additionally, he invented—initially for a Broadway run, and later often elsewhere—a new format, 'Nureyev and friends', to give programmes of works with small, specially assembled casts. When his stamina

declined with age, he used this format to present himself in roles needing drama or plasticity while others took the technically more demanding parts. He also moved on to different roles in longer ballets: the old toymaker Dr Coppelius, or parts made specially for his maturity in *The Overcoat* and *Death in Venice*. The very last new role he took, not long before his death, was the mimed part of Carabosse in a new Berlin production of his *Sleeping Beauty*.

Final years Before that Nureyev had already branched out in another sphere, as an orchestral conductor. Some of his many musician friends had suggested this, knowing of his devotion to music, and he took serious coaching for it. He successfully gave concerts with a Viennese orchestra and conducted a gala performance of *Romeo and Juliet* at the Metropolitan Opera House, New York. Conducting seemed to offer a fresh career, and in addition he had plans for creating several further ballets, but declining health prevented this. Within a year or so of becoming director in Paris, he had been diagnosed HIV-positive. Because AIDS often develops slowly, it was believed then that only a few of those with the virus would develop the disease, but that proved false. Nureyev's determination enabled him to continue working for a decade, and later he was given such experimental treatment as was available. With time, however, he weakened, and his final production for the Paris Opéra was completed only with painful difficulty, helped by colleagues he trusted. This staging of *La bayadère* (it had long been his wish to mount it) proved one of his most successful ballets, but photographs of him at the première revealed to the world how ill he had become. Even then he hoped to go on working, but his strength went. Nureyev died on 6 January 1993 in Paris, and was buried at the cemetery of Ste Geneviève-des-Bois, Essonne. A memorial tribute in words and music was held in London, at the Royal Opera House, Covent Garden, on 25 April 1993.

His legs, as Nureyev once put it, had made him a rich man. He enjoyed having several homes on both sides of the Atlantic, with collections of paintings, other art objects, and musical instruments he liked playing. The collections were later sold at auction. After making provision for his two surviving sisters and their families, he left everything to two foundations for benefiting ballet, helping young dancers, and promoting dancers' health (the Rudolf Nureyev Foundation and the Rudolf Nureyev Dance Foundation). Even in death he made the world of dance richer and stronger for his life.

In performances of a uniquely wide repertory night after night all over the world with charisma and dedication Nureyev reached a wider audience than any rival. Millions more saw him in films and on television. The dramatic circumstances of Nureyev's 'leap to freedom' put him on the front pages of the world's newspapers, but his determination kept him there, using that fame to develop in his own way.   JOHN PERCIVAL

Sources J. Percival, 'Biographie', www.nureyev.org/biographie. php [Rudolf Nureyev Foundation], 15 May 2002 · J. Percival, *Nureyev: aspects of the dancer* (1976) · *Nureyev: his spectacular early years: an*

autobiography, ed. A. Bland (1993) · D. Solway, *Nureyev: his life* (1998) · A. Bland, *The Nureyev image* (1976)

Archives Rudolf Nureyev Foundation, Paris · Rudolf Nureyev Foundation, New York | GL, corresp. with publishers | FILM NYPL, Nureyev Film and Video Collection

Likenesses photographs, 1962–77, Hult. Arch. · C. Beaton, photograph, Sothebys, Cecil Beaton Archive [*see illus.*] · photographs, Rudolf Nureyev Foundation, New York · photographs, Rudolf Nureyev Foundation, Paris

Nuri al-Said (1888–1958), army officer and prime minister of Iraq, was born in December 1888 in Baghdad, the only son (there were also four daughters) of Said Taha (*d.* 1904), a minor official in Baghdad's Ottoman government, and his wife, Fatima. The family lived modestly in the northern part of the city, with fellow Arabs (rather than Turks) as neighbours. As a Sunni Muslim he was instructed in the Koran before attending infant school. Aged eight he entered Baghdad's military school, and when not quite fifteen he transferred to Istanbul Military Academy for a further three years of training. After receiving a commission in September 1906 he was assigned to a mounted infantry unit based in Baghdad.

The unit's work collecting taxes on livestock from nomads provided Lieutenant Nuri with practical soldiering skills and fostered in him a lifelong empathy for tribal life. About 1909 he married Naaima, daughter of Mustafa al-Askari, and a son, Sabah, was born in December 1910. Earlier in 1910 Nuri had returned to Istanbul for advanced staff college training. While there he witnessed the internal political struggles of the disintegrating Ottoman empire and became involved with secessionist groups advocating Arab autonomy. He fought loyally for the Turks during the Balkan wars (1912–13) but subsequently became disillusioned with the chauvinism of the Turkish government and so joined an illegal military society called al-Ahad ('the covenant') to work for complete Arab independence.

In April 1914 Nuri fled to Basrah to avoid arrest and joined with prominent Mesopotamian dissidents. He was ill in hospital when the British seized the town in November, shortly after the outbreak of war against Turkey, and spent a year in India as a prisoner of war. In December 1915, however, the British released him to assist in planning the 'Arab revolt' against Turkish rule. He joined Sharif Hussein, the Hashemite leader of the revolt, in Jiddah in July 1916 with 700 Arab volunteers. His brief was to turn the men into an effective fighting force. He did so—distinctively clad in khaki tunic and a loosely tied *kufiyah* round his head—with infectious energy, establishing himself as a highly valued chief of staff to Emir Feisal, the military leader of the revolt. Helped by T. E. Lawrence, Nuri deployed hit-and-run sabotage tactics with great success, earning a DSO for his part in the military operations. Vivid accounts of his actions later featured in Lawrence's *Seven Pillars of Wisdom*: 'Most men talked faster under fire, and added a betraying ease and joviality. Nuri grew calmer' (Lawrence, 532). The relaxed atmosphere among his officers—card games and drinking into the night—made him and his clique agreeable company to British officers.

When Damascus was captured in October 1918 it was Nuri who rode into the city and established a pro-Hussein governor. He was promoted general and remained as Feisal's chief of staff, accompanying him to the Paris peace conference in 1919 (at Britain's specific request). In the following year he attended the San Remo conference, which dissected the Middle East along British and French imperial lines, with France acquiring the Syrian mandate. His Baghdadi connections were subsequently instrumental in mediating Feisal's candidacy for the prospective kingdom of Iraq. The kingmaker Gertrude Bell wrote that the moment she saw Nuri, who arrived in Baghdad in October, she 'realised that we had before us a strong and supple force which we must either use or engage in difficult combat' (Gallman, 12). He was duly appointed chief of staff in the Ministry of Defence, headed by his brother-in-law Jafar al-Askari, and he used his new post to tour the country, pressing Feisal's claims. The enthronement of Feisal on 23 August 1921 was thus a day of great personal fulfilment.

For the next nine years Nuri developed Iraq's armed forces, first as chief of staff and later as minister of defence. His priorities were mechanization (replacing camels and mules) and the creation of an air force, the latter aimed at ending Iraq's reliance on the RAF for internal policing. The first Iraqi officers attended Cranwell in 1928, followed later by Nuri's son (who also earned an engineering degree from Cambridge University and went on to run Iraq's railways). In June 1926 Nuri visited Turkey to sign a treaty resolving the Mosul frontier dispute. The reception from his old enemies—including Mustafa Kemal, his senior in the Ottoman army—was pleasingly cordial.

Nuri became Iraq's prime minister for the first time in March 1930. His administration's most significant achievement was a defence treaty with Britain in June, clearing the way for Iraq's entry into the League of Nations in October 1932, which terminated the British mandate. Iraqi independence was compromised, however, by Britain's retention of two air bases, Shaybah and Habbaniyyah. A generation of Iraqi nationalists grew up hating both the treaty and Nuri's collusive relationship with the British imperialists.

The next decade was dominated by political instability. Nuri's first administration lasted until October 1931, but his relatively humble background counted against him—Iraqi politics being dominated by large landowners and tribal sheikhs. He preferred office in the defence and foreign ministries; he accompanied Feisal during his state visit to London in June 1933 and was at his deathbed in September. In October 1936 he and his family fled to Egypt (on board an RAF aeroplane) after his brother-in-law Jafar was assassinated. A ten-month spell on a Nile houseboat permitted some rest, plus a chance to think about wider Arab issues such as the future of Palestine. In December 1938 he formed his second ministry with an agenda to make parliament a better mouthpiece for the people.

However, the approaching conflict in Europe further unsettled Iraqi politics, obliging Nuri to strengthen the state rather than pursue electoral reform. He reaffirmed the Anglo-Iraqi alliance a day after Britain declared war on Germany (4 September 1939), added the interior ministry to his responsibilities, and introduced draconian security measures. When cabinet splits forced his resignation as premier in March 1940, he recommended Rashid Ali as his successor and assumed responsibility for the foreign ministry, where he attempted to work with Haj Amin al-Husayni, the *mufti* of Jerusalem. Nuri's pro-British credentials remained intact only because al-Husayni ignored the approach. Meanwhile Rashid Ali became increasingly associated with pro-German elements in Iraq's army, which staged an anti-British coup in April 1941. Nuri and the regent escaped to Amman, where they stayed as the guests of Emir Abdullah, the Hashemite ruler of Transjordan, until British tanks reinstalled them in Iraq in October. Firmly suppressing any opposition, Nuri stayed in power until June 1944.

Meanwhile, Nuri tried to check the rise of Egyptian regional dominance with a succession of Arab unity projects. His 'Fertile Crescent Plan', published as *Arab independence and unity* (1943), entailed combining Syria, Lebanon, Palestine, and Transjordan to create a 'Greater Syria', which would easily subsume the Jews of Palestine, so allaying the danger of a Jewish majority ever emerging in an Arab state. However, the other governments of the region dismissed Nuri as a schemer on behalf of the Hashemites and instead settled (in March 1945) on a loose intergovernmental organization—the Arab League—whose headquarters, significantly, was in Cairo.

The events of the Second World War made Nuri the unrivalled strongman of Iraq's ruling élite. A slightly built man with expressive, dark-lined eyes and pock-marked cheeks, he was always neatly dressed (mostly in Western-style suits). His mode of business seemed secretive and somewhat irregular to foreign diplomats. Meetings were usually one-on-one, and notes were not taken. The conversation would be animated, with ideas coming rapidly and illogically (as he fiddled with his prayer beads). After the business was completed, he would relax and, with friends, display a mischievous but kindly humour. A revolver was always near at hand. He lived simply and did not use office for personal gain. His weakness was for the ceremonial aspects of public life, especially military displays, justified as a means of promoting the prestige of his country.

The main problem for Nuri after 1945 was his reliance on Britain—and vice versa. While he was of a generation that had gained and consolidated power with British backing, younger, Westernized Iraqis felt excluded from the political process. The Nuri-dominated ruling élite and British imperialism were therefore identified as the twin enemies of progress. British diplomats realized that the 'old gang' had an increasingly fragile control over Iraqi society, but their dilemma was between staying with Nuri as a stabilizing element or encouraging reform. With mounting problems elsewhere in the Middle East, Britain decided to stick with its principal collaborator, even though he was not interested in reform or Western-style democracy. The Iraqis, he believed, needed a strict but benevolent patriarch.

Nuri's attempt to replace the defence treaty of 1930 with a less imperialistic arrangement—the treaty of Portsmouth (January 1948)—failed to satisfy Iraqi nationalists and it was abandoned after violent protests. The first Arab–Israeli war in 1948 prompted a period of martial law at home, while the Iraqi army did little beyond occupying defensive positions on the West Bank. Nuri cleverly linked Zionism with communism to prevent his domestic opponents from exploiting the Palestine question, with its anti-imperialist overtones, as a tool for rallying opposition to the regime.

The rise of Nasser in Egypt after July 1952 exacerbated the Egyptian–Iraqi struggle for leadership of the Arab world. Nasser's achievement in negotiating the evacuation of the Suez base in 1954 increased pressure on Nuri to alter Iraq's defence relationship with Britain. Nuri responded in January 1955 by tying Iraq to the Turkey–Pakistan defence accord, thereby creating the Baghdad pact (which Britain joined in April 1955 as a means of veiling its military access to Iraq). Nasser denounced the new organization with an intensity that surprised and infuriated Nuri.

When news of Egypt's nationalization of the Suez Canal Company broke on 26 July 1956, Nuri and Feisal II were having dinner with Anthony Eden during a state visit to Britain. They all agreed that Nasser had to be deposed. Yet the method used—the Anglo-French-Israeli aggression of 29 October to 5 November—brought severe rioting to Iraq's cities, placing Nuri (who was not told about Britain's collusion with Israel) and the Hashemite monarchy in mortal danger. The closing of schools and universities along with the rounding up of trouble-makers eventually restored calm. 'The house of the master is secure,' he boasted in December (Abdul-Salaam Yousif, 182). But Iraq's oil industry remained badly affected by Syria's sabotage of the pipelines running over its soil. The loss of revenues slowed Iraq's long-term development programmes, which were Nuri's paternalistic alternative to social and political reform. Moreover, Nasser was emboldened as the champion of third-world anti-colonialism.

Nuri's next major challenge occurred in February 1958 when Nasser announced the formation of the United Arab Republic, uniting Syria and Egypt. Iraq responded a few days later by forming the Arab Union, a federation of the two Hashemite dynasties, which came into effect in May with Nuri as its first (and only) prime minister. Although he was unenthusiastic about the union (Jordan would be an economic drain), his loyalty to the Hashemites remained steadfast. His attention became fixed on Kuwait, long considered an integral part of Iraq but about which he had done nothing in case he upset Britain (which 'protected' the Arab sheikhdoms along the Persian Gulf). While pushing for Kuwait's accession to the Arab Union, he ignored the incipient rebellion at home.

On 14 July a small band of middle-ranking army officers seized power. Encouraged by the new regime, mobs took to the streets and hunted down leading figures from the old order. Feisal II was brutally murdered that same day. Nuri went into hiding at a friend's house in Baghdad, as official radio broadcasts announced a reward for his capture. His wife was in London, but his son was found and killed. The next morning, while disguised as an Arab woman, Nuri was recognized by soldiers on a street close to the American embassy in Baghdad and was shot dead. He was buried that same day in a cemetery near the North Gate, Baghdad, but shortly afterwards 'revolutionaries' dug up the body, stripped it naked, and dragged it through the streets of Baghdad. A car then drove backwards and forwards over it before it was finally strung up and set ablaze.

Nuri's political life coincided with Iraq's existence as a British mandate and quasi-colonial state. Besides heading fourteen governments, he served in other key ministries, and for the brief periods when he was out of office his influence at the palace was usually decisive. But it was his connections to the last days of Ottoman rule and his association with British imperialism that resulted in his downfall. To Nasser's generation (the Arabs who reached their thirties about the time of the Palestine débâcle of 1948), Nuri was—and always would be—Britain's stooge in the Middle East. Insufficiently attuned to modern Arab thinking, Nuri failed to prevent Iraq's army (his own child) from seizing power, à la Nasser. The policy of paying the armed forces well but keeping them 'short of oats' was an insufficient barrier against the powerful pan-Arab political currents in the wake of the Suez crisis. Ironically, Nuri personally authorized the issuance of extra ammunition to the two brigades that led the uprising, thinking that Brigadier Abdul Karim Qasim and his accomplice Colonel Abdul Salam Arif were loyal commanders. (Qasim ruled Iraq until his deposition and murder in 1963.) Britain, for its part, relied too much on Nuri, often trusting his assessments of Iraqi politics over their own observations. The rise and fall of British influence in Iraq was thus irrevocably entwined with that of Nuri.

MICHAEL T. THORNHILL

Sources Lord Birdwood, Nuri as-Said: a study in Arab leadership (1959) · W. R. Louis, The British empire in the Middle East, 1945–1951 (1984) · W. J. Gallman, Iraq under General Nuri: my recollections of Nuri al-Said, 1954-1958 (1963) · G. de Gaury, Three kings in Baghdad, 1921–1958 (1961) · S. Falle, My lucky life (1996) · D. Fromkin, A peace to end all peace (1989) · C. Tripp, 'Iraq and the 1948 war: mirror of Iraq's disorder', The war for Palestine, ed. E. L. Rogan and A. Shlaim (2001) · M. J. Cohen and M. Kolinsky, eds., Demise of the British empire in the Middle East (1998) · Abdul-Salaam Yousif, 'The struggle for cultural hegemony during the Iraqi revolution', The Iraqi revolution of 1958, ed. R. A. Fernea and W. R. Louis (1991) · M. Elliot, 'Independent Iraq': the monarchy and British influence, 1941–1958 (1996) · C. Tripp, A history of Iraq (2000) · T. E. Lawrence, Seven pillars of wisdom (1962)
Archives Jesus College, Oxford, T. E. Lawrence corresp. and papers · U. Newcastle, Robinson L., Gertrude Bell collection
Likenesses photographs, repro. in Birdwood, Nuri al-Said · photographs, repro. in Gallman, Iraq under General Nuri · photographs, St Ant. Oxf. · photographs, IWM

Nurse, Malcolm Ivan Meredith [known as George Padmore] **(1902–1959)**, anti-colonial political activist and author, was born in Arouca district, Tacarigua, Trinidad, the only son of James Hubert Alfonso Nurse, a schoolmaster and agronomist, and Antigua-born Anna Symister. His exact date of birth remains unconfirmed: baptismal

records at Tacarigua's Anglican church apparently give 28 July 1902; but he himself, and family members, gave contradictory accounts, and the relevant public records for Arouca have apparently not survived. He was very much a product of the island's then newly emerging black middle class. His was both a bookish and a politically formative upbringing—James Nurse was an outspoken advocate of racial justice, and owned what may have been Trinidad's most extensive private library.

Nurse's family moved to the Trinidadian capital, Port of Spain, in his infancy. There he attended St Mary's College of the Immaculate Conception and the Pamphylian high school. On graduation, he took employment as a junior reporter on the local Weekly Guardian. The work bored him, he clashed with editor E. J. Partridge (an English expatriate whom Nurse thought a racist) and was eventually dismissed. On 10 September 1924 he married a near neighbour, Julia Semper. A daughter, Blyden, was born in June 1925. By then Nurse had already left for the United States in pursuit of his deferred dream of higher education. He registered at Fisk University in Nashville, Tennessee, initially to study medicine but soon shifting to a law course. At Fisk he edited the student newspaper and became an active campus politician and orator.

Nurse did not complete his Fisk degree—apparently in part because, as a locally prominent black activist, he attracted the attentions of the Ku Klux Klan—but moved to New York, enrolling initially at New York University, then in September 1927 at Howard University in Washington, DC, like Fisk a historically black campus. That summer he also joined the Communist Party of the USA. It was widespread practice at the time for communist activists to adopt alternative names, and although registered at Howard under his real name, in his political capacity he began to be known as George Padmore. The surname was that of a cousin and the first name that of his father-in-law. His wife, Julia, now joined him, leaving the infant Blyden in the care of grandparents.

Padmore rapidly emerged as one of the most prominent black communists in the USA, publishing and travelling under the party's auspices and, in late 1929, going to Moscow to be appointed head of the 'Negro Bureau' of the Red International of Labour Unions. Julia did not accompany him; she and their daughter seem thereafter to have played a very little role in his life. The Negro Bureau mutated into the International Trade Union Committee of Negro Workers (ITUC-NW), still with Padmore in charge, in early 1930. Over the following few years Padmore was peripatetic (spending time in Hamburg, Vienna, London, and Paris, as well as Moscow), prolific (writing at least five pamphlets for the ITUC-NW and numerous articles for the communist press, as well as the influential short book Life and Struggles of Negro Toilers in 1931 and several contributions to the even more widely noted Negro Anthology, edited by Nancy Cunard in 1934) and, within the confines of an increasingly Stalinized Communist International, powerful. By 1933-4, however, following Hitler's accession to power, the USSR was seeking rapprochement with the western European powers. As part of this move, the

ITUC-NW was disbanded in August 1933—though it was soon to be revived under more pliable leadership than Padmore's—and he resigned from the communist movement. Thereafter he was to be a stubbornly independent figure on the anti-colonialist left.

After his break with the communists and a period living in Paris, Padmore moved to London in 1935. He became part of a circle of mainly West Indian and west African political activists in Britain, including his Trinidadian childhood friend the polymathic author and critic C. L. R. James. Later, various young African nationalists, as students or temporary residents in London, were to join the circle: perhaps most importantly Ghana's future ruler, Kwame Nkrumah. Padmore's role as ideological mentor to such figures forms probably his major claim to historical significance. A series of small but, at least indirectly, very influential organizations emerged from Padmore's group: the International African Friends of Abyssinia, the International African Service Bureau, and the Pan-African Federation. The October 1945 Manchester congress, arranged by the last-named body, was widely seen as the crucial 'coming of age' for post-war African nationalist politics.

Padmore also worked closely with the Independent Labour Party, at the time quite separate from Clement Attlee's Labour Party, and far more strongly committed to colonial independence than were either the latter or the British Communist Party. Padmore was apparently never formally a member of the Independent Labour Party, and rejected suggestions that he should stand for parliament on its behalf, but contributed prolifically to its publications and was a major influence on its colonial policies. In 1937 Padmore met and began to live with Dorothy Pizer (d. 1964). Dorothy, the largely self-educated daughter of an impoverished north London Jewish family, was to give essential research and secretarial help in all Padmore's subsequent political and literary projects. Although their relationship was often stormy, she remained his companion to the end of his life.

Padmore produced a stream of polemical, anti-colonial books from their successive and usually penurious London homes: from *How Britain Rules Africa* in 1936 to *The Gold Coast Revolution* in 1953. The latter was a largely uncritical celebration of the colony's emergence towards independent statehood, under the leadership of Padmore's friend and protégé Nkrumah. At the end of 1957 Padmore himself moved to the new state, becoming Nkrumah's personal adviser on African affairs. The fact that the post was in the prime minister's private office rather than being at cabinet level (as Padmore had apparently expected), however, indicated his position as an outsider to Ghanaian politics. Many members of the new government viewed him with suspicion and conspired to marginalize him: as a West Indian interloper, as an excessively close confidant of Nkrumah, as a supposedly doctrinaire socialist, and increasingly as an unwelcome critic of their own financial corruption.

Padmore's last book was his most wide-ranging and influential. *Pan-Africanism or Communism?* (1956), as the title suggests, urged the need for Africans to unite against Soviet as well as Western 'neocolonial' threats. Despite this, Padmore remained committed to the belief that Africa's best hope lay in Soviet-style state development plans.

Padmore's health had long been uncertain, even before the move to Ghana, and in September 1959 he returned to London for treatment. He died in University College Hospital on 23 September, from cancer of the liver. After a funeral service at Golders Green crematorium, Padmore's ashes were flown to Ghana and interred there in a state ceremony, at Christiansborg Castle, Accra, on 4 October.

The long-term significance of Padmore's work remains hard to interpret. The causes of colonial, and especially African, political independence for which he and his associates agitated were doubtless destined for rapid success in any case, and his activities were only a very small part of the complex of causes pressing towards that result. As to the influence of his ideas in post-independence African states, this was very limited—as the disillusionment he experienced in Ghana suggests. While Padmore was by no means the tragic, even pathetic figure of Peter Abrahams's thinly disguised fictional portrait as 'Thomas Lanwood' in *A Wreath for Udomo* (1956), his long-term hopes that political decolonization would entail African renaissance and global socialist revolution were largely to be disappointed.   STEPHEN HOWE

Sources J. R. Hooker, *Black revolutionary* (1967) · *The C. L. R. James reader*, ed. A. Grimshaw (1992) · C. L. R. James, 'George Padmore: black Marxist revolutionary', in C. L. R. James, *At the rendezvous of victory* (1984), 251–63 · P. Fryer, *Staying power: the history of black people in Britain* (1984) · J. G. La Guerre, *The social and political thought of the colonial intelligentsia* (1982) · private information (2004) [M. Sherwood] · H. Adi and M. Sherwood, *The 1945 Manchester pan-African congress revisited* (1995) · J. A. Langley, *Pan-Africanism and nationalism in west Africa, 1900–1945: a study in ideology and social classes* (1973)
Likenesses photographs, repro. in Hooker, *Black revolutionary*
Wealth at death no substantial personal wealth

Nurse, Rebecca (*d.* 1692). *See under* Salem witches and their accusers (*act.* 1692).

Nursey, Perry (*bap.* 1771, *d.* 1840), landscape painter, was baptized at Stonham Aspal, Suffolk, on 25 June 1771, the second son of John Nursey, a surgeon apothecary, and his wife, Catherine Fairfax (*c.*1742–1827).

Nursey followed his father's profession as a surgeon, having probably been his apprentice. He entered a practice at Woodbridge in 1794, perhaps not long after which he became surgeon to the workhouse at Melton, close by. In 1795 he eloped to Scotland with Anne Simpson (*c.*1776–1844), the heir to an estate at Little Bealings, between Ipswich and Woodbridge, and a ward in chancery, and there they married. He gave addresses in London in 1799 and 1801, though he was almost certainly living at Little Bealings by the end of 1799. There, at The Grove, he 'laid out the grounds in the best style of ornamental planting' (Page, 43). In 1814 he published an *Essay on Picturesque Gardening, Planting, and Rural Improvements*, in which he related the man-made scene to paintings by seventeenth-century masters of classical landscape, such as Claude. He was credited by J. C. Loudon with having discerned, in or before 1816, a variety of the black poplar (*Populus nigra viridis*).

In 1832 Nursey was referred to as an architect and landscape gardener. He had sold The Grove in 1826–7 and moved to Foxhall nearby, where he built himself a house; he was living there in 1831. He altered the exterior of Theberton Hall between 1830 and 1834, probably having done the same to The Grove for its new owner. In 1832 he was occupying a friend's house, Foxburrow Hill (now Foxboro Hall), outside Melton. Designated an architect, of Melton, he was declared bankrupt on 31 December 1833; there had already, in 1822, been a passing suggestion of financial insecurity. A forced auction of his art collection was held at Foxburrow on 10–11 April 1834. Advertisements for it in the *Ipswich Journal* offered some 350 prints after old masters, gathered with some emphasis on the seventeenth century and on landscape; 100 prints after Thomas Gainsborough; 43 drawings by David Wilkie; 25 pictures with attributions—probably unreliable—to seventeenth-century Dutch and Flemish painters; finally, 150 paintings and sketches by himself, cried up as 'vivid and faithful transcripts' of local scenery (*Ipswich Journal*, 7, 26 March 1834).

According to Dawson Turner, Nursey had an 'enthusiastic love for the art [of painting], that I have seldom, if ever, known exceeded' (Turner, 87). It is, indeed, as an amateur landscape painter that he is still faintly remembered. Much of his work was done in oils, generally on a modest scale; he painted out of doors, and his subjects were frequently topographical. He appears to have had some instruction, probably when young, from Alexander Nasmyth, for whose manner of landscape painting his own sometimes came to be mistaken. None of his work can now be securely identified. Nothing by him is recorded as in a public collection, but several works remain known through reproductive prints. He exhibited some landscapes at the Royal Academy in 1799 and 1801, and another in 1830 with the Norwich Society of Artists, with whom he also exhibited a portrait. At the British Institution in 1815 he exhibited a large picture of an episode in the Peninsular War, based on a drawing by a witness. In London, W. P. Frith derided his landscapes for having a greenness beyond old-masterly sanction. His admirers were, rather, among his country neighbours. The poet Edward Fitzgerald, a poor judge of pictures, owned a number of his works and was indulgently content to find in them a 'genuine feeling of Nature' (*Letters*, 1.213). Another literary friend and admirer in the district, again no judge, was Bernard Barton. Conferring more credit on Nursey, although not necessarily as a painter, is a reference to him in a letter by John Constable, written from London in 1814 to the elder John Dunthorne. Although concerned with one of his own pictures, Constable's words imply that both he and his correspondent knew Nursey, and that he heeded his opinion. There is no record of their further association, but pictures by Nursey have passed occasionally (and optimistically) as by Constable. A glimpse of Nursey's responsiveness to older masters of landscape is allowed by Thomas Green, who noted in 1821 that he 'looked with ecstasy at my Hobbema' (*GM*, 456).

Nursey's particular relationship was not, however, with any landscapist but with Wilkie, whom he came to know by 1814, possibly through the piano maker William Stodart. In the warmer months of 1816, 1818, 1822, and 1823 Wilkie made short visits to The Grove, where he and Nursey painted. Nursey enjoyed Wilkie's technical experience, also learning through making copies of his pictures. Wilkie, himself diffident about painting landscape, was with little doubt spurred on in the endeavour by Nursey's enthusiasm for it. As well as the drawings by Wilkie already mentioned, Nursey collected prints after his pictures and found local buyers for them. Their easy friendship was shared by their families, and was strengthened by an attachment formed between Nursey's eldest son, Robert, and Wilkie's sister Helen. Robert died in 1824 while staying with Wilkie. In 1825 Wilkie left for three years on the continent, and soon afterwards the Nurseys moved from Little Bealings. These events appear to have dissolved the relationship. Wilkie has left an expressive drawing of Nursey, made in 1823 and now in the Ashmolean Museum, Oxford.

The impression left of Nursey in the country is of a convivial man, esteemed in his neighbourhood, churchgoing and attentive to the poor. He left Suffolk for London after 1834, perhaps after 1837, and died at his home, 3 Broadley Terrace, Marylebone, on 12 January 1840.

Famously, Nursey proclaimed his commitment to art by naming five of his ten children after painters. His youngest son, Claude Lorraine Richard Wilson (1816–1873), taught in schools of art at Leeds, Bradford, Belfast, and Norwich, and was said to have been one of Wilkie's assistants. Nursey's second son, also Perry (1799–1867), became a clergyman, a poet, and a painter of landscapes which are sometimes confused with his father's.

HAMISH MILES

Sources *East Anglian Miscellany* (1943), p. 39, no. 11,068; (1944), p. 1, no. 11,072, p. 19, no. 11,148; (1946), p. 27, no. 11,483, p. 32, no. 11,502; (1954), p. 3, no. 12,645, p. 4, no. 12,650 · 'Wilkie's letters to Perry Nursey', *The Academy* (28 Sept 1878), 323–4, 345–6 · David Wilkie, MS letters to Nursey (9 May 1814; 18 Oct 1816; 30 Jan, 17 Oct 1818; 6 Jan, 24 Sept 1823; Helen Wilkie, MS letter to Nursey (7 March 1826), Thomas Wilkie, MS letter to Nursey (21 Oct 1827), BL, Add. MS 29991, fols. 8–9, 12–13, 14, 16–17, 38–9, 48–9, 53–4, 55 · D. Wilkie, letters to A. Raimbach, Hunt. L., MSS 1051, 1061 [2 July 1818; 29 June 1822] · advertisements, *Ipswich Journal* (March 1834) · Graves, *RA exhibitors* · Graves, *Brit. Inst.* · M. Rajnai, *The Norwich Society of Artists, 1805–1833: a dictionary of contributors and their work* (1976) · Colvin, *Archs.* · A. Page, *Topographical and genealogical history of ... Suffolk* (1847) · J. C. Loudon, *Arboretum ... Britannicum*, 2nd edn, 3 (1844) · W. P. Frith, *Further reminiscences* (1888) · *John Constable's correspondence*, ed. R. B. Beckett, 1 (1962–75); Suffolk RS, 4 (1962) · D. Turner, *Outlines in lithography* (1840) · sale catalogue (1852) [Turner sale; Christies, 14 May 1852] · *The letters of Edward FitzGerald*, ed. A. M. Terhune and A. B. Terhune, 1–3 (1980) · *Selections from the poems and letters of Bernard Barton*, ed. L. Barton (1849) · T. Green, 'Diary of a lover of literature', *GM*, 2nd ser., 18 (1842), 456 · A. N. L. Munby, ed., *Sale catalogues of libraries of eminent persons*, 1 (1971) · A. N. L. Munby, ed., *Sale catalogues of libraries of eminent persons*, 9, ed.

R. Park (1974) · I. Fleming-Williams and L. Parris, *The discovery of Constable* (1984)
Likenesses D. Wilkie, drawing, 1823, AM Oxf.

Nussey, Helen Georgiana (1875–1965), welfare worker, was born on 27 November 1875 at 4 Montague Villas, Richmond, London, the daughter of Antony Foxcroft Nussey, solicitor, and his wife, Mary Anne, *née* Charrington. She was the last surviving granddaughter, on her father's side, of John Nussey (d. 1862), apothecary to the royal household. Educated at Cheltenham Ladies' College, she became the first almoner at Westminster Hospital in London, where she worked for seven years.

In 1914, in her late thirties, Miss Nussey was appointed by the London county council (LCC) as one of two principal assistant organizers of the school care service, which underwent a massive expansion just before the First World War. The care service had been set up in 1907, following pioneering work by Margaret Frere, to ensure that poor school children in London were sufficiently fed, clothed, and shod to benefit from their schooling. The service was centred on care committees attached to elementary schools, which were staffed by women voluntary workers who provided pupils with welfare help such as school dinners and medical inspections. In order to do this work they visited pupils' homes and in this way they acted 'as the link between the child, its school and its home' (*The Times*, 27 July 1932). Their work was co-ordinated by professional women like Miss Nussey, who were employed by the LCC. She was allocated to the education department, while her counterpart, Miss K. Lewis, was allocated as principal assistant organizer to the public health department; they both worked under Theodora Morton, the first principal organizer of the care service. In 1930, when Miss Morton retired, Miss Nussey was herself appointed principal organizer. She had complete faith in the value of the care committees to London's children and she successfully resisted plans developed by the LCC in 1932–3 to merge the care service with the school attendance service.

Under Miss Nussey's leadership the care service flourished: by 1939 there was a care committee in every elementary school in London and about 5000 volunteers, despite a reduction nationwide in the ranks of leisured women available for public work. These volunteers came from affluent homes and had no direct experience of a working-class family's struggle from day to day. Despite this difference in background, the fact that they were carrying out their work without pay was seen by many parents as a testament to their genuine concern. The number of salaried staff had grown to 158 by 1939.

By 1930 there had been many improvements in the life of the poor children of London and barefoot urchins had virtually disappeared from the streets. The care service therefore diversified and the care committees became increasingly involved in activities like aftercare, which helped young people to prepare for life after school. School-leaving conferences were organized, which brought together the schoolchild and parent, the head teacher, an official of the Board of Trade, the vicar, and a care committee worker. Nussey urged care committee workers to ensure that no children leaving school at fourteen were ignorant of the possibilities available for employment, further education, and social recreation. She also encouraged the setting up of spectacle clubs, which collected the necessary pennies every week for the purchase of spectacles and sought to break down the opposition of schoolchildren to the wearing of spectacles (*The Times*, 27 July 1932). When war began in 1939 she took a key role in the evacuation of children from London to the safety of the countryside.

Miss Nussey retired from the LCC in 1940, when she was appointed OBE for her work for the children of London. She worked as a volunteer for the London Council of Social Service and she also continued her interest in gardens, which had led in 1909 to the publication, with Olive J. Cockerell, of *A French garden in England: a record of the successes and failures of a first year of intensive culture*. She helped to organize the London Gardens Society, of which she had been made honorary organizer in 1939, a year which also saw the publication of *London Gardens of the Past* (reissued in 1948). This book contains a picture of a garden on an LCC housing estate, with the caption, 'Like children, those [gardens] that have needed the most care are often the best loved.' Miss Nussey also wrote *Miniature Alpine Gardens* (1949).

Helen Nussey died in Beckenham Hospital, Kent, on 5 February 1965. She belonged to one of the first generations of professional social workers, whose growing importance contributed to the gradual disappearance of women voluntary workers. On the one hand, she firmly defended the role of the volunteer and argued that a partnership between the voluntary sector and the state was fundamental to the success of the school care service. But at the same time social workers like herself gradually took over the areas of activity that had previously been the domain of women volunteers. When the school care service of London eventually merged in 1970 with the school attendance service to form an education welfare service for the capital, the role of the volunteer had become almost entirely redundant.

SUSAN WILLIAMS and TENDAYI BLOOM

Sources A. S. Williams, P. Ivin, and C. Morse, *The children of London: attendance and welfare at school, 1870–1990* (2001) · *The Times* (10 Feb 1965) · *The Times* (27 July 1932) · *London County Council Gazette* (3 Aug 1914) · b. cert. · d. cert.
Wealth at death £20,644: probate, 23 April 1965, *CGPLA Eng. & Wales*

Nutaaq (d. 1577). *See under* American Indians in England (*act. c.*1500–1609).

Nuthall, Betty May (1911–1983), tennis player, was born at Sutherland House, Kingston, Surrey, on 23 May 1911, the daughter of Stuart Nuthall, a club proprietor, and his wife, Mary Madge James. Her parents were both keen tennis players and taught her to regard the game 'as one of the most important … as well as *the* jolliest, in the world'. Coached by her father, she was 'never allowed to knock a ball about just for the sake of doing so', but had always to improve (Nuthall, 13–14). The intensive training produced results: she developed into a 'fine aggressive player' and won the British junior singles championships three times in succession (*The Times*, 10 Nov 1983). She became a familiar figure in British tennis from the age of nine, and spectators queued early for her Wimbledon début in 1927, when she defeated the German Cilly Aussem. She went on to beat the reigning American champion, Anna (Molla) Mallory, before losing to Helen Jacobs in the quarter-finals. In 1927 she also became, at sixteen, the joint youngest finalist in the history of the US ladies' singles championship, when she was beaten 6–1, 6–4 by Helen Wills Moody. For this match she served underarm, as she was then accustomed to do, but she soon afterwards made the change to overarm. She also reached the final of the ladies' doubles at Forest Hill that year, and became the youngest player to represent Britain in the Wightman cup, when she defeated Helen Jacobs in her first match. In all she made eight Wightman cup appearances between 1927 and 1939.

When she was still only seventeen, Nuthall went into print with a textbook for the beginner, *Learning Lawn Tennis* (1928), to which her mother wrote a preface. But she proved unable to sustain the remarkable momentum built up in 1927. Her only major title in the next two years was the mixed doubles at the US championships in 1929. As a result she was bypassed for the Wightman cup team in 1930. She marked her omission by becoming the first British player to win the US ladies' singles championship, defeating the top seed, Anna McCune Harper, in the final 6–1, 6–4. Nuthall also won the ladies' doubles title with Sarah Palfrey. She enjoyed another remarkable year abroad in 1931, when she won the ladies' doubles and the mixed doubles at both the American and French championships. She also reached the final of the ladies' singles in France. The defence of her US singles title at Forest Hill ended in a semi-final defeat by her Wightman cup teammate and occasional doubles partner Eileen Bennett Whitingstall.

In 1932 Nuthall retained the mixed doubles at the French championship, with Fred Perry, and the following year she secured her third and final ladies' doubles title in the US championship. In 1933 she also reached the semi-final of the ladies' singles at Forest Hill, impressing onlookers by pushing Helen Wills Moody to three sets, 2–6, 6–3, 6–2. In five of the seven years during which she was at her peak (1927–33) Nuthall was ranked in the world's top ten.

Nuthall was a good tactical player, equipped with 'aggressive forcing strokes' and an especially powerful forehand (*The Times*, 10 Nov 1983). She played at speed and hit hard, with good judgement of line and length. Ultimately, though, she lacked the strategic awareness of opponents' strengths and weaknesses that is the mark of enduring champions. Despite her success abroad, in particular at Forest Hill, Nuthall never advanced to the final stages at Wimbledon. There was special disappointment in 1931, when she was defeated in straight sets in the quarter-final by Helen Jacobs. Nuthall later married Franklin C. Shoemaker and made her home in the United States. She died in New York on 8 November 1983.

MARK POTTLE

Sources *The Times* (20 April 1939) · *The Times* (10 Nov 1983) · b. cert. · J. Huntington-Whiteley, ed., *The book of British sporting heroes* (1998) [exhibition catalogue, NPG, 16 Oct 1998 – 24 Jan 1999] · 'International Tennis Hall of Fame', www.tennisfame.com · O. Davidson and C. M. Jones, *Great women tennis players* (1971) · A. D. C. Macaulay and J. Smyth, *Behind the scenes at Wimbledon* (1965) · *Wimbledon who's who and tennis celebrities* (1934) · B. Nuthall, *Learning lawn tennis* (1928)
Likenesses photograph, 1932, repro. in Huntington-Whiteley, *Book of British sporting heroes* · photographs, repro. in Nuthall, *Learning lawn tennis* · photographs, Hult. Arch.

Nuthall, Thomas (*d.* 1775), lawyer and public official, was probably born in Norfolk, but nothing else is known of his background or parentage, or where he trained as a solicitor. His Norfolk background may have helped him win his first official post from Sir Robert Walpole's ministry, as registrar of warrants in the Excise Office (1740). In 1749 he became receiver-general for hackney coaches. Nuthall also transacted legal business for at least two Norfolk politicians: Charles, third Viscount Townshend, and the elder Horace Walpole, the diplomat, as well as for Charles Yorke. In 1751 Nuthall was engaged by the younger Horace Walpole to provide legal support for his scheme to detach the heiress Margaret Nicoll from her guardians, with the intention that she should marry George Walpole, third earl of Orford. The younger Horace became convinced that Nuthall was working against the family interest, to Nuthall's frustration, and the marriage plan collapsed in acrimony.

A more successful relationship developed between Nuthall and William Pitt. Nuthall drew up Pitt's marriage settlement in 1754. By 1762 he was negotiating on behalf of Pitt with Thomas Pelham-Holles, duke of Newcastle, over the terms by which they might collaborate in bringing down the ministry of John Stuart, third earl of Bute. Nuthall received a series of appointments which he attributed to Pitt, his 'great benefactor and patron' (*Correspondence of William Pitt*, 2.325n.). These included the position of solicitor to the East India Company. On the retirement of Philip Carteret Webb in July 1765 he was appointed solicitor to the Treasury, an appointment through which Charles Watson-Wentworth, second marquess of Rockingham, hoped to win Pitt's support for his ministry. Nuthall characterized himself as a loyal follower of Pitt, writing that he would resign his offices if he were called upon to 'do anything that I can even surmise to be repugnant to your generous and constitutional principles' (ibid.).

Nuthall's moment came in February 1766 when Rockingham used him as an intermediary in an attempt to bring Pitt into the ministry. The period of negotiation, when much government business was on hold, has been called the 'Nuthall interlude' (Sherrard, 206). Nuthall expressed his relief when the negotiations were done, agreeing with Pitt that 'ambassadorship is a troublesome trade' (*Correspondence of William Pitt*, 2.401). He seems to

Thomas Nuthall (*d.* 1775), by Nathaniel Dance

will was drawn up on 14 January 1774 Nuthall's wife was Jane, *née* Spencer, from Hadley, near Epsom, Surrey. He also had two illegitimate sons, Thomas, aged four in 1774, who was at school at Chigwell in Essex, and John, with his nurse in Chelsea.

Nuthall seems to have been in partnership with a solicitor called John Skirrow at Lincoln's Inn in 1766; he later nominated Skirrow one of his executors. Nuthall's death was unexpected. Returning to London from Bath on 7 March 1775, his coach was attacked by a highwayman on Hounslow Heath, Middlesex. The attacker left when Nuthall returned fire. On reaching an inn at Hounslow, Nuthall wrote a description of the man for Sir John Fielding, but 'had scarcely closed his letter when he suddenly expired' (*Correspondence of William Pitt*, 2.166n.).

Nuthall's death exposed further irregularities in his conduct. Following a complaint by the deputy Treasury solicitor, Thomas Francis, the Treasury prevented administration being granted to Nuthall's executors. Francis successfully proved that he was owed £2002 15*s*. in unpaid expenses and a further £3282 18*s*. in unpaid fees, as Nuthall had deferred finalizing his accounts since his second year in office. The Treasury appointed Francis and William Masterman as trustees with the task of realizing Nuthall's debt from his effects; by February 1776 they had raised £2239 16*s*. 6*d*. Horace Walpole, never one to forget a grudge, wrote in 1775 that Nuthall 'had embezzled £19,000' (Walpole, *Corr.*, 41.311).

Nuthall did not share the antiquarian interest in legal precedents that made his predecessor at the Treasury, Webb, a highly regarded government servant. His use was as a political man of business, who maintained excellent relations with Pitt for a number of years, but events proved that his skills, when tested, were limited.

MATTHEW KILBURN

Sources *Correspondence of William Pitt, earl of Chatham*, ed. W. S. Taylor and J. H. Pringle, 4 vols. (1838–40) • O. A. Sherrard, *Lord Chatham and America* (1958) • P. Langford, *The first Rockingham administration, 1765–1766* (1973) • B. Tunstall, *William Pitt, earl of Chatham* (1938) • *The Grenville papers: being the correspondence of Richard Grenville … and … George Grenville*, ed. W. J. Smith, 4 vols. (1852–3) • will, PRO, PROB 11/1006, sig. 111 • PRO, T1/512/174–175 • PRO, T1/515/235–236 • PRO, T1/524/221–222 • corresp. with Pitt, PRO, 30/70/1/26, 30/70/1/29 • Walpole, *Corr.* • Add. MS 35637, BL, fols. 17, 27, 47
Archives PRO, corresp. as treasury solicitor, PRO T • PRO, letters to Lord Chatham and Lady Chatham, PRO 30/8 • PRO, corresp. with Pitt, PRO 30/70/1/26–30/70/1/29
Likenesses F. Hayman, oils, *c*.1748, Tate collection • T. Gainsborough, oils, 1771 • F. Hayman, stipple, pubd 1825 (after W. Derby), BM, NPG • N. Dance, oils, Tate collection [*see illus.*] • F. Hayman, double portrait, oils (with Hambeldon Custance), Upton House, Warwickshire • etching, NPG
Wealth at death over £2239 16*s*. 6*d*.: PRO, T1/524/221–222; will, PRO, PROB 11/1006, sig. 111

have avoided political intrigue after that date, corresponding with Pitt over the scheme he had devised as ranger of Enfield Chase for conserving its oak trees for the construction of naval vessels. Pitt commended his plan, but the scheme failed to survive Nuthall's death, and the chase was divided and disafforested by act of parliament in 1777.

In August 1767 Nuthall drew up the power of attorney through which Pitt's wife, Hester, could direct her husband's financial affairs. Nuthall's good relationship with Pitt (from 1766 earl of Chatham) was seriously damaged in 1772, when he revealed to Chatham that he had mismanaged the mortgage agreement that had enabled Chatham to buy an estate at Hayes in Kent from Thomas Walpole. The purchase had been financed by a loan from Chatham's brother-in-law, Richard Grenville-Temple, second Earl Temple. Temple assessed Nuthall as 'that facetious man of business in so many departments … whose fellow is not easily to be met with' (Smith, 4.545) and listed further examples of incompetence, including Nuthall's failure to have Chatham's marriage settlement witnessed.

On 24 November 1757 Nuthall had married at St Helen, Bishopsgate, London, Susan, widow of Hameldon Custance, and she may have been the mother of his son, Robert, mentioned in Nuthall's will. However, by the time the

Nutt, Alfred Trübner (1856–1910), publisher and Celtic scholar, was born in London on 22 November 1856, the eldest and only surviving son of David Nutt (*d.* 1863), a foreign bookseller and publisher, and his wife, Ellen, daughter of Robert Carter and granddaughter of William Miller, publisher, of Albemarle Street, London, predecessor of John (II) Murray. His second name commemorated his father's partnership with Nicholas Trübner. He was educated first at University College School, London, and afterwards at Collège de Vitry-le-François in the Marne département, France, until 1873. Having served three years' business apprenticeship in Leipzig, Berlin, and Paris, in 1878 he took his place as head of his father's firm which, founded in 1829 at 58 Fleet Street, London, was moved in 1848 to 270–271 Strand. The business, which had been mainly confined to foreign bookselling, soon benefited by young Nutt's energy and enterprise, especially in the publishing department, which he mainly devoted to folklore and antiquities. Among his chief publications were the collection of unedited Scottish Gaelic texts known as *Waifs and Strays of Celtic Tradition*, the Northern Library of Old Norse texts, the Tudor Library of rare sixteenth-century works, the Tudor translations (in sixteenth-century prose), the Grimm Library, the Bibliothèque de Carabas, a critical edition of *Don Quixote* in Spanish, Nutt's Juvenile Library, the works of W. E. Henley, and the collection of English, Celtic, and Indian fairy tales. He also produced a number of excellent school books. The business was carried on in London at 57–59 Long Acre, 'At the sign of the Phoenix', from 1890 to 1912, when it was removed to Grape Street, New Oxford Street.

Nutt was not only an astute businessman, but was also a lifelong student of folklore and of the Celtic languages, and displayed scholarship and power of original research in both fields. His name was 'definitely associated with the plea for the insular, Celtic, and popular *provenance* of the Arthurian cycle' (*Folk-Lore*, 513). Nutt founded the *Folk-Lore Journal* (afterwards *Folk-Lore*), was one of the earliest members of the Folk-Lore Society (1879), and was elected president in 1897 and 1898. Besides presidential addresses he contributed many valuable articles to the society's journal, the *Folk-Lore Record*, and in 1892 he edited a volume of *Transactions* of the International Folk-Lore Congress (1891). In 1886 he helped to establish the English Goethe Society and he was one of the founders of the movement which led in 1898 to the formation of the Irish Texts Society. His most important literary productions included 'Studies on the legend of the holy grail, with special reference to the hypothesis of its Celtic origin' (*Folk-Lore Record*, 23, 1888), and two essays on the Irish vision of the afterlife and the Celtic doctrine of rebirth, appended to *The Voyage of Bran, Son of Febal, to the Land of the Living* (Grimm Library, vols. 4 and 6, 1895–7). He also wrote numerous studies of the *Mabinogion*, the holy grail and of Celtic and Gaelic literature, and produced an annotated edition of Matthew Arnold's *Study of Celtic Literature* (1910).

On 21 May 1910, while on holiday at Melun on the Seine, Nutt drowned trying to save his invalid son, who had fallen into the river. His wife, Mrs M. L. Nutt, who had been his secretary for several years, succeeded him as head of the firm. Two sons survived him.

H. R. TEDDER, rev. SAYONI BASU

Sources E. Clodd, *Folk-Lore* (30 Sept 1910) · *The Times* (24 May 1910) · *Athenaeum and Publisher's Circular* (28 May 1910) · *The Bookseller* (27 May 1910) · J. Wood, 'Folklore studies at the Celtic dawn: the rôle of Alfred Nutt as publisher and scholar', *Folklore*, 110 (1999), 3–12 · WWW
Archives King's Cam., letters to Oscar Browning · UCL, letters to Karl Pearson
Likenesses lithograph, repro. in Clodd, *Folk-lore*

Nutt [*formerly* Carr], **Elizabeth** (*b.* in or before **1666**, *d.* **1746**), printer and bookseller, is of uncertain origins. At the time of her marriage to the printer John Nutt (*d.* 1716) on 29 December 1692 she was named Elizabeth Carr. Her first known entry into the world of print was as a mercury (newspaper and pamphlet wholesaler and retailer). Much later, in a petition of 1728, she described herself as 'an Antient Woman near Seventy years of Age', and claimed that 'it ha[d] been her business for about Forty years to sell News Papers and Pamphlets at the Royal Exchange' (PRO, SP 36/9, pt 2, fol. 249), which suggests that she had embarked on this enterprise in the late 1680s, or shortly before her marriage to Nutt. She was almost certainly the person referred to by John Dunton in 1705 as one of 'the honest (mercurial) women, Mrs. Baldwin, Mrs. Nutt, Mrs. Curtis [etc.]' (J. Dunton, *The Life and Errors of J. D.*, 236). The family resided in the Savoy, off the Strand, throughout Elizabeth's marriage and widowhood, except for a brief period, from about 1698 to 1705, when they lived in the parish of St Martin Ludgate. Between 1693 and about 1711 Elizabeth Nutt had thirteen children.

About 1705 John Nutt set up shop in the Savoy and a few years later he acquired the assignment of a lucrative patent for printing law books. Nutt died in 1716 and Elizabeth Nutt's imprint ('Eliz. Nutt' or 'E. Nutt at the Savoy') began appearing on books that same year. In 1722 she brought in her second son, Richard *Nutt, on the law book patent and over the next two decades they produced many of the standard legal treatises and reports of the day. In the early 1720s Elizabeth Nutt also entered into a loose bookselling arrangement with another mercury and bookseller, Anne Dodd, that was to last until the former's death more than twenty years later. Over 130 titles bearing their joint imprint (generally 'printed for A. Dodd, E. Nutt [et al.]', indicating that they were the distributors or booksellers) are still extant; most are cheap nonfiction of a bawdy, sensationalist, and occasionally feminist nature, with a good many forays into religious and political controversy.

During the period of Robert Walpole's ascendancy Elizabeth Nutt and members of her family were often arrested and imprisoned for selling Jacobite, tory, or radical whig pamphlets and newspapers, the latter including the *London Evening-Post* (which Elizabeth Nutt's son Richard printed), *The Craftsman*, and *Mist's Weekly Journal*. By at least the early 1730s Elizabeth had come to own a number of pamphlet and newspaper shops or stalls around the Royal Exchange, which her daughters, Alice and Catherine Nutt, helped her to manage, and the large scale of Nutt's operations meant that she helped to expose a wide audience to the ideas of the radical opposition. Elizabeth Nutt was active as a printer until 1741 and as a bookseller and, presumably, newspaper distributor, until she died five years later, by this time over eighty years of age. She was buried on 14 November 1746 in the queen's chapel of St John the Baptist in the Savoy.

MARGARET R. HUNT

Sources M. Harris, 'The London newspaper press, c. 1725–1746', PhD diss., U. Lond., 1973 · M. Hunt, 'Hawkers, bawlers and mercuries: women and the London press in the early Enlightenment', *Women and the Enlightenment*, ed. M. Hunt, M. Jacob, P. Mack, and R. Perry (1984), 41–68 · T. Hunt, 'Elizabeth Nutt: an eighteenth-century London publisher', *Antiquarian Book Monthly*, 23 (1996), 20–24 · P. McDowell, *The women of Grub Street: press, politics and gender in the London literary marketplace, 1678–1730* (1998) · will, PRO, PROB 10/2018 · PRO, State papers domestic, SP 36/8, pt 2, fols. 152–3, 155, 157, 161, 165, 169 · PRO, State papers domestic, SP 36/9, pt 2, fol. 249 · PRO, State papers domestic, SP 36/13, fols. 110, 114–17, 123, 127, 131, 160 · PRO, State papers domestic, SP 36/50, pt 2, fol. 282 · PRO, State papers domestic, SP 44/82 [18 July 1729, 26 Jan 1731, 30 Jan 1731, 24 April 1732, 22 April 1740, 2 April 1744] · parish register, queen's chapel of St John the Baptist in the Savoy, London, 29 Dec 1692 [marriage] · parish register, queen's chapel of St John the Baptist in the Savoy, London, 14 Nov 1746 [burial] · IGI

Nutt, Joseph (*bap.* 1700, *d.* 1775), surveyor of highways, son of Robert Nutt and his wife, Sarah, *née* Cooper, was born in Hinckley, Leicestershire, and was baptized there on 2 October 1700. He was educated at the free grammar school, Hinckley, and was subsequently apprenticed to John Parr, a local apothecary. He went on to study in London hospitals before returning to Hinckley, where he became successful and popular, frequently treating the poor for nothing. Having been elected as a surveyor of highways for Hinckley parish, he introduced a system of periodically flooding the roads, producing a firm, substantial, and smooth surface for the considerable local traffic generated by the nearby coal mines. The regular flooding also benefited adjacent farmland.

Nutt's procedure was resisted; there were efforts to eject him from office, and he was subjected to ridicule, but the success of his methods ensured considerable local support. His opinion as a land valuer was also highly regarded locally. John Dyer, the poet, was a friend of Nutt, and celebrated his useful talents in his poem 'The Fleece' (1757).

Nutt married Susannah Goode (1714–1799) on 25 December 1774. He died at Hinckley on 16 October 1775, and was buried in the churchyard. By his will he left six oak trees to provide, within forty years of his death, the fabric for a new market place for Hinckley, with a school and town hall above it.

CHARLOTTE FELL-SMITH, *rev.* RALPH HARRINGTON

Sources J. Nichols, *The history and antiquities of the county of Leicester*, 4 vols. (1795–1815); facs. edn (1971) · *Collections towards the history and antiquities of the town and county of Leicester* (1790), pt 50 [7/3] of *Bibliotheca topographica Britannica*, ed. J. Nichols (1780–1800)

Nutt, Richard (1693/4?–1780), printer and publisher, was the second eldest of the thirteen children of John Nutt (1667–1716) and Elizabeth *Nutt, *née* Carr (d. 1746), who both worked as printers and publishers in London. The date of his birth is based on the stated but unconfirmed age of eighty-six at his death (*GM*, 50.155). He may have been born in Ireland, as his father was one of the workmen sent over by the king's printer, Edward Jones, in the Savoy, during his attempt to obtain the further grant as king's printer in Ireland. The first imprints to carry John Nutt's name appeared in London in 1698 and perhaps mark his first independent work after his return. Richard may have been apprenticed at the premises 'near Stationers' Hall' where his father followed an active career as printer and publisher of pamphlets for the trade, although Richard Nutt was not made free of the Stationers' Company until 1725. By this time he was working in partnership with his mother who owned and ran a printing office in the Savoy. Their names appeared jointly on the imprints of law books from 1722 and reflect the interest in the law patent which Elizabeth Nutt had inherited from her husband at his death in 1716. Initially she assigned a moiety to the bookseller Robert Gosling and at some later stage a one-third interest was transferred to her son Richard.

Nutt's career as a printer took a sharp upward turn in 1724 when, on 6 February, he married Elizabeth (*bap.* 1704), the twenty-year-old daughter of Hugh Meere, printer in the Old Bailey, and his wife, Cassandra (*née* Grover). Hugh Meere had died in April 1723 and the printing office had been taken over by Cassandra who also became a partner in a family type founding business. Cassandra died in August 1725 and left her estate in equal shares to Elizabeth and Richard Nutt and to her son Thomas (*b.* 1708). Nutt probably obtained his freedom in order to legitimize his position within the City as part-owner and manager of the Old Bailey printing office. It is possible that he moved at this time or later into his father's old premises, as although both he and his associate John Meres were described in 1754 as printers in the Old Bailey, they were located in different parishes—St Martin Ludgate and St Sepulchre respectively. This may indicate that two related printing offices were at work in the street. In taking over the business in 1725 Nutt obtained a valuable interest in a range of publications including the *Historical Register* and the popular *Daily Post*. He also became a member of a partnership which included his colleague in the law patent Robert Gosling, who had acted as one of Cassandra Meere's executors. The Water Lane type foundry, inherited jointly by the daughters of Thomas Grover (*d.* 1712), came into the *de facto* possession of Richard Nutt, and, although an attempt was apparently made in the late 1720s to dispose of it, the foundry remained an adjunct to Nutt's printing office into the 1750s. Nutt apparently gave up the 'mercury' trade of newspaper selling which had been run by Cassandra Meere. It is possible that he transferred it to his mother and sisters, who were involved in what was known as 'the morning business' at the Royal Exchange for at least twenty years. At the Old Bailey printing office he continued to extend the interest in serial production which must have benefited from his easy access to new type. As well as inheriting an interest in the *Historical Register* and the *Daily Post* from the Meeres he was probably a founder of and shareholder in one of the most successful tri-weekly papers of the eighteenth century, the *London*

Evening-Post. He also printed the weekly *Universal Spectator* from its establishment in 1728.

The newspapers printed by Nutt tended to have an opposition flavour, and the *London Evening-Post* in particular was characterized by its virulent attacks on the government. During the excise crisis (1733), and again during the general election of 1754, its distribution through the Post Office was officially banned. The prosecutions for seditious libel launched against it under the Walpole administration led Nutt to have his name replaced on all the newspaper imprints, initially by his journeyman Samuel Neville and later (1737) by John Meres, apparently a relative by marriage who shared his political views. This did not prevent his mother and sisters and probably his wife from being taken up for publishing his papers on several occasions. His personal commitment to opposition politics was indicated in 1736 when for the first time he stood successfully in the tory interest for the common council for the ward of Farringdon Without. His willingness to challenge established authority can also be identified in his commercial relationships. During winter 1741, in association with the prominent bookseller Thomas Osborne, he launched a campaign within the Stationers' Company to extend the influence of printers and others within the organization. His family was well represented among the underprivileged freemen as in May 1740 his brother Benjamin, and his sisters Alice, Catherine, and Sarah, were admitted simultaneously by patrimony under the sponsorship of their mother Elizabeth. After a period of struggle the challenge failed and Richard Nutt's position in the company may have been damaged. It may also have marked a stage in his withdrawal from direct involvement in the printing trade. He had bound his son Richard as apprentice in 1742 but he was never freed and he may have died or taken up another trade. Richard senior's mother died in 1746 (aged about eighty) as did his brother, the printer Benjamin Nutt (their wills were proved on the same day).

The final act opened in 1754 when, at the age of sixty, Nutt, with John Meres, was taken up for printing an allegedly seditious letter in the *London Evening-Post*. Official doubts about legal action led to a delay, but in July 1755 the case against Nutt came on at the Guildhall. The only printed account of the proceedings seems to have appeared in the *Gentleman's Magazine* (25, 1755); surprisingly, none of the London newspapers reported the case. Nutt was evidently found guilty and sentenced later in the year to two years' imprisonment in the king's bench. He was also ordered to pay a fine of £500 with sureties and to stand in the pillory at Charing Cross for an hour. Whether this severe sentence was carried out is uncertain. At all events, this seems to mark the end of Nutt's career as a printer. His name and the Old Bailey address continued to appear on a few recurrent imprints to 1760 and it is possible that John Meres had taken over part or all of the business well before this. The foundry, which had come into the absolute possession of Nutt by inheritance, was sold in September 1758 to the founder John James. Nutt died in Bartlett's Buildings, Holborn, London, on 11 February 1780

and the land tax assessments indicate that he was succeeded in the house by 'Miss Nutt'. Was this one of his elderly sisters who looked after him during his long retirement? It is hard to get a sense of Nutt's social relationships. He was caught up in a series of family lawsuits during the 1730s, but this seems to have been an almost inevitable part of middling, commercial life and there are no other indications of his personal status within his close-knit community. He does not appear to have left a will.

MICHAEL HARRIS

Sources M. Harris, *London newspapers in the age of Walpole* (1987) · Michael Treadwell, unpublished notes, Trent University, Ontario · wills, PRO, PROB 11 [John, Elizabeth, and Benjamin Nutt] · court of chancery, Meres *v.* Nutt, 1735, PRO, C11/772/14 · D. F. McKenzie, ed., *Stationers' Company apprentices*, 3 vols. (1961–78), vols. 2–3 · H. R. Plomer and others, *A dictionary of the printers and booksellers who were at work in England, Scotland, and Ireland from 1668 to 1725* (1922) · H. R. Plomer and others, *A dictionary of the printers and booksellers who were at work in England, Scotland, and Ireland from 1726 to 1775* (1932) · *London Evening Post*, BL, Burney collection of newspapers, 1727– · manuscripts, land tax assessments by parish, GL · *IGI* · C. Blagden, *The Stationers' Company: a history, 1403–1959* (1960) · E. Deacon, *The family of Meres* (Bridgeport, Conn., 1891) · *GM*, 1st ser., 50 (1780)

Nuttall, Enos (1842–1916), archbishop of the West Indies, was born at Clitheroe on 26 January 1842, the eldest son of James Nuttall, farmer and builder, of Coates, St Mary-le-Gill, Yorkshire, and his first wife, Alice, daughter of William and Martha Armistead of Aynhams, in the same parish. His education was such as his mother and the parish school could give him, but he developed powers of self-tuition, and being placed by his father in charge of a farm, gave his leisure to learning. James Nuttall was a Wesleyan, and Enos became at seventeen a local preacher of some power. Anxious for mission work abroad, he applied to the Revd George Osborn, secretary of the Wesleyan Missionary Society, was accepted, and, after a period of training under the Revd Andrew Kessen, was posted by the society to Jamaica, for which he sailed on 2 December 1862, in his twenty-first year, to work as a layman.

While his brother Ezra (1850–1915) won distinction in South Africa as a Methodist minister, Enos offered himself in Jamaica for the ministry of the Church of England. He was ordained deacon on 18 February 1866 in the cathedral at Spanish Town, and priest on 8 April in the parish church, Kingston, where fifty years later (23 February 1916) his last sermon was addressed to a departing war contingent. He was appointed 'island curate' of St George's, Kingston, with a stipend derived from the government, and technically he retained the post until his death. In December 1869 notice was given that state endowment (saving some life interests) would cease at the end of that year, and Nuttall, young as he was, took a leading part in the reorganization of the disestablished Church of England in Jamaica, helping to draft its canons and to settle its financial system, and engaging in public controversy with the governor, Sir John Peter Grant. He was made secretary of synod in 1870 and of the diocesan board of finance in 1874. Archbishop Tait recognized his work by giving him in 1879 the Lambeth degree of BD.

In 1880, on the resignation of Bishop George William Tozer, the synod chose Nuttall as bishop of Jamaica, and he was consecrated by Tait in St Paul's Cathedral on 28 October. From 1881 to 1891 he was also responsible for the supervision of the diocese of British Honduras, while his efforts among the West Indians working on the Panama Canal caused that district to be transferred temporarily in 1885 to the diocese of Jamaica. In 1883 the first meeting of the provincial synod of the West Indies was held in Jamaica, five bishops attending, and Nuttall was mainly responsible for drafting its canons and constitutions. He was elected primate of the West Indies in 1893 and in 1897, in consequence of a resolution of the West Indian bishops passed (30 July) during the Lambeth conference, he assumed the title of archbishop of the West Indies.

On 14 January 1907 Jamaica suffered a destructive earthquake. At the time the archbishop was attending a meeting of the West India Agricultural Conference; his coolness averted a panic, and his immediate organization and guidance of all the measures for relief and reconstruction were beyond praise. Throughout his fifty-four years in Jamaica he was intimately concerned in the daily welfare of the islanders—education, nursing, housing, agriculture—and was in constant consultation with the Colonial Office at home.

Nuttall married in 1867 Elizabeth Duggan, daughter of the Revd Philip Chapman, a Wesleyan minister, with whom he had two sons and three daughters. In his later years, in spite of frequent visits to England, his health failed, though he continued to work. He died at Bishop's Lodge, Kingston, on 31 May 1916, and was buried in the churchyard of St Andrew, Halfway Tree, in Jamaica.

E. H. PEARCE, rev. H. C. G. MATTHEW

Sources The Times (3 June 1916) · F. Cundall, Life of Enos Nuttall (1922) · J. B. Ellis, The diocese of Jamaica (1913) · Jamaican Diocesan Gazette (July 1924) · H. L. Clarke, Constitutional church government (1924) · personal knowledge (1927)
Archives National Library of Jamaica, Kingston, papers | LPL, corresp. with Archbishop Benson · LPL, corresp. with A. C. Tait and related papers
Likenesses J. Russell & Sons, photograph, NPG · oils; at Bishop's Lodge, St Andrews, Kingston, Jamaica, in 1917 · photograph, NPG
Wealth at death £301 16s. 1d.: probate, 1917, Jamaica

Nuttall, George Henry Falkiner (1862–1937), bacteriologist, was born in San Francisco, California, on 5 July 1862, the second son of Robert Kennedy Nuttall MD, from Tittour, co. Wicklow, and his wife, Magdalena, daughter of John Parrott of San Francisco. In 1865 the family returned to Europe, and the children were educated in England, France, Germany, and Switzerland. With his cosmopolitan upbringing Nuttall could speak several languages, which helped him greatly in his work and travels. He returned to America in 1878 and entered the University of California, where he proceeded MD in 1884. He went to Germany in 1886 and stayed for four years, studying mainly botany and zoology, subjects that led to an interest in parasitology, which became the main scientific interest of his life. In 1891 he returned to America as assistant to W. H. Welch, professor of pathology at Johns Hopkins University, Baltimore, but went back to Germany in 1892 to work on hygiene at Göttingen and Berlin. In 1895 he married Paula (d. 1922), daughter of Kammerherr Hans von Oertzen-Kittendorf of Mecklenburg; they had two sons and a daughter.

In 1899 Nuttall gave a course of lectures on bacteriology at Cambridge, and a year later he was appointed university lecturer in bacteriology and preventive medicine. In 1901 he founded the Journal of Hygiene which he edited up to the time of his death, and in 1908 Parasitology, which he edited until 1933. In his editorial work he displayed the same thoroughness as in his research. He considered part of an editor's duties to be educational and was prepared to spend time in correcting and improving papers and advising young and inexperienced colleagues. As an editor he exerted great influence on associates all over the world, and his journals became models upon which the publications of several scientific societies were based.

In 1906 Nuttall was elected the first Quick professor of biology at Cambridge and a fellow of Magdalene College, with the duty of studying 'protozoa, especially such as cause disease'. In 1919 he appealed for funds to build an institute for parasitological research. This led to the erection of the Molteno Institute for Research in Parasitology (later known as the Molteno Institute of Biology and Parasitology), which was formally opened in 1921. In 1920 the words 'study of parasitology' were substituted for 'study of protozoa' in the regulations concerning the duties of the Quick professor.

By this time, Nuttall's scientific work had covered a very wide field; in addition to several books, he had published papers on bacteriology, serology, hygiene, tropical medicine, and parasitology. Among his contributions to science was his discovery in 1888 that defibrinated blood possesses a strong bactericidal property against anthrax bacilli, and that this property disappears on heating the blood to 55 °C. This work was the foundation for the study of humoral immunity and was the forerunner of great discoveries such as that of anti-toxic immunity. In 1892 he studied with Welch the anaerobic gas-forming microorganism, later known as Clostridium welchii, the importance of which as a pathogenic agent was not fully appreciated until the war of 1914–18. With H. Thierfelder (1895–7) he also carried out the first successful experiments on life under aseptic conditions.

In 1897 Nuttall turned his attention to the part played by arthropods in the spread of disease, a subject to which he devoted the later period of his life. In 1901 he showed that the disappearance of malaria from England was not due to the extinction of the mosquito genus Anopheles, which still prevailed in all formerly malarious districts. In the same year he became interested in the precipitin reaction, and in 1904 he published his monograph Blood Immunity and Blood Relationship, which demonstrated a distinct similarity in chemical structure of the blood in animals which are related phylogenetically. Nuttall then began his investigations into diseases transmitted to animals by ticks. Using infected ticks (Haemophysalis leachi) from South

Africa, he succeeded in infecting dogs with piroplasmosis, a disease unknown in England. One result of this investigation, which had great economic importance, was the discovery of the curative property of trypan blue for piroplasmosis in dogs, cattle, and sheep. This study was followed by an extensive investigation with Cecil Warburton and Louis Edward Robinson of the anatomy, biology, life history, and systematics of ticks, which occupied Nuttall during the remaining years of his life.

Nuttall resigned the Quick professorship in 1931 and became emeritus professor of biology. He died suddenly at the Craven Hotel in London on 16 December 1937 on the eve of a dinner in his honour to be given by sixty colleagues on his retirement from his editorship of the *Journal of Hygiene*. He was cremated on 21 December 1937 at Golders Green.

Nuttall was of distinguished appearance, had great charm, was an excellent raconteur, and was at ease in whatever company he found himself. He was elected FRS in 1904, received honorary degrees from several universities, and was elected corresponding member of many scientific societies.

G. S. GRAHAM-SMITH, rev. MARY E. GIBSON

Sources G. S. Graham-Smith, 'George Henry Falkiner Nuttall (5 July 1862–16 December 1937)', *Journal of Hygiene*, 38 (1938), 129–39 · G. S. G.-S. and D. K., 'George Henry Falkiner Nuttall, 1862–1937', *Parasitology*, 30 (1938), 403–18 · G. S. G.-S., 'Obituary notice of deceased member: George Henry Falkiner Nuttall, 1862–1937', *Journal of Pathology and Bacteriology*, 46 (1938), 389–94 · G. S. Graham-Smith and D. Keilin, *Obits. FRS*, 2 (1936–8), 493–9 · *BMJ* (25 Dec 1937), 1308–9 · *The Times* (18 Dec 1937) · *The Times* (22 Dec 1937) **Archives** RS | London School of Hygiene and Tropical Medicine, Ross archives **Likenesses** photograph, 1901 · W. Stoneman, photograph, 1917, NPG · photographs, 1920, NPG · P. A. de Laszlo, pencil drawing, 1935, Magd. Cam. · photograph, c.1935, repro. in Graham-Smith, 'Obituary notice of deceased member' · Ramsey & Muspratt, photograph, 1936 · P. A. de Laszlo, oils (presented in 1932); formerly in family possession, 1949 · photographs, repro. in Graham-Smith, 'George Henry Falkiner Nuttall', pl. 2, 7 **Wealth at death** £26,169 11s. 3d.: probate, 6 April 1938, *CGPLA Eng. & Wales*

Nuttall, Josiah (1770–1849), naturalist, was baptized at Heywood, Lancashire, the son of John Nuttall, a handloom weaver. Early in life he became a collector of birds, a close observer of nature, and in time an expert taxidermist. For some years he worked in the museum of the antiquary William Bullock (b. c.1780, d. after 1827) of Liverpool, and subsequently at the Royal Institution in the same town.

When Nuttall had raised sufficient means, he purchased property in his native village, where he retired with a good collection of British and foreign birds. Here he turned his attention to literary pursuits, and in 1845 published an epic poem entitled *Belshazzar, a wild rhapsody and incoherent remonstrance, abruptly written on seeing Haydon's celebrated picture of Belshazzar's feast*, a work as curious in itself as in its title. He died unmarried at Heywood on 6 September 1849.   C. W. SUTTON, rev. YOLANDA FOOTE

Sources *Manchester Guardian* (15 Sept 1849) · *IGI*

Nuttall, Thomas (1786–1859), botanist, was born on 5 January 1786 at Long Preston, near Settle, Yorkshire, the first of three children of James Nuttall (d. 1798) and his wife, Margaret (1759–1841), daughter of Richard Hardacre and Agnes, *née* Taylor. He was educated at the local village school, leaving when fourteen years old to begin a seven-year apprenticeship under his uncle Jonas Nuttall, printer, in Liverpool. About this time he became interested in natural history and undertook excursions to investigate the botany and geology of the Craven district, west Yorkshire. In 1807 he moved to London, but the following year sailed for Philadelphia where he soon became devoted to the study of American natural history, especially botany, partly through his early association with Benjamin Smith Barton.

In the spring of 1811 Nuttall joined the expedition of John Jacob Astor's Pacific Fur Company, travelling up the Missouri River for 1500 miles and plant collecting in hostile Indian territory. The results of this trip resulted in Nuttall's pioneering American flora, *The Genera of North American Plants, and a Catalogue of the Species, to the Year 1817* (1818). In the autumn of 1811 he sailed for England, not returning to Philadelphia until 1815. From 1818 to 1820 he botanized along the Arkansas River. In 1822 he was appointed curator of the botanical garden at Cambridge, Massachusetts, and lecturer in natural history at Harvard University. However, in 1834 he left Harvard to join Nathaniel Jarvis Wyeth's second expedition to Oregon, and subsequently collected plants along the Californian coast and in Hawaii before returning to Boston, via Cape Horn, in September 1836. From his return until 1841 he lived mainly at Philadelphia.

In early 1842 Nuttall returned to England, where, apart from a short trip to Philadelphia in 1847–8, he lived at his family estate, Nutgrove, Sutton, near St Helens, Lancashire. Here he devoted himself largely to horticulture. From 1856 his health declined; he suffered from rheumatism and acute gastritis, but died at Nutgrove Hall, apparently from chronic bronchitis, on 10 September 1859. Nuttall never married and was always reticent about his private life.

Nuttall became a fellow of the Linnean Society, London, in 1813, and in 1817 was elected to both the Academy of Natural Sciences and the American Philosophical Society. He remains 'the preeminent figure in the discovery of the flora of the American West' (Thomas), but he also made important contributions to zoology, geology, ornithology, and ecology. His more important published works include a three-volume appendix to a new edition of F. A. Michaux's *The North American Sylva* (1842–9). He also published some twenty-eight papers, including three on geology, mainly in the *Journal of the Academy of Natural Sciences of Philadelphia* and the *Transactions of the American Philosophical Society*.   ANDREW GROUT

Sources J. E. Graustein, *Thomas Nuttall, naturalist: explorations in America, 1808–1841* (1967) · F. A. Stafleu and R. S. Cowan, *Taxonomic*

literature: a selective guide, 2nd edn, 3, Regnum Vegetabile, 105 (1981), 781–7 · P. D. Thomas, 'Nuttall, Thomas', DSB · Catalogue of scientific papers, Royal Society, 4 (1870)

Archives Harvard U., Gray Herbarium, papers | RBG Kew, Bentham MSS; Hooker MSS

Likenesses J. Thomson, stipple, pubd 1825 (after drawing by W. Derby, 1824), BM, NPG; repro. in Graustein, Thomas Nuttall · S. Austin, life mask, c.1832, Harvard U., Gray Herbarium; repro. in Graustein, Thomas Nuttall · J. T. Booth, ink, Harvard U., Gray Herbarium; repro. in Graustein, Thomas Nuttall · etching, NPG

Wealth at death under £300: probate, 7 July 1860, CGPLA Eng. & Wales

Nuttall, Thomas (1828–1890), army officer, born in London on 7 October 1828, was son of George R. Nuttall MD, one of the physicians of the Westminster Dispensary. His mother was daughter of Mr Mansfield of Midmar Castle, Aberdeenshire. He was sent to a private school at Aberdeen, but his character is said to have been formed chiefly by his mother, a good and clever woman. He sailed for India as an infantry cadet on 2 August 1845, and was posted as ensign in the 29th Bombay native infantry from that date. He became lieutenant in the regiment on 26 June 1847 and captain on 23 November 1856. From December 1851 to November 1856 he was adjutant of his regiment. As captain of the regimental light company, he was detached with the light battalion of the army in the Persian expedition of 1857. He returned to Bombay in May that year, and in August rejoined his regiment at Belgaum.

During the Indian mutiny and after, from 9 November 1857 to 25 March 1861, Nuttall was detached on special police duty against disaffected Bhils and Kolis in the Nasik districts. He organized and disciplined a corps of one of the most war-like peoples of the Deccan, the Kolis of the Western Ghats, which did excellent service and was engaged in many skirmishes. The assistant collector at Nasik reported that the dispersion of the Bhil rebels and the prompt suppression of the Peint rebellion were entirely due to Nuttall's exertions, and for two years he and his men endured much hardship and privation. He five times received the commendation of government.

From June 1860 to August 1865 Nuttall was police superintendent successively at Kaira, Sholapur, and Kaladgi, having in the meantime been transferred to the Bombay staff corps (June 1865). He received the brevet of major in the same year. In September 1865 he went on sick leave to England, and returned to India in April 1867, when he resumed his police duties at Kaladgi, and in October was appointed second in command of the Land Transport Corps in the Abyssinian expedition, with which he did good service at Koumeylee; he was mentioned in dispatches and promoted brevet lieutenant-colonel. From August 1868 to February 1871 he served with the 25th Bombay native infantry, and from April 1871 to April 1876 with the 22nd Bombay native infantry as second in command and then as commanding officer, during a portion of which time (from 8 May to 30 October 1871) he was in temporary command of the Neemuch brigade. He became lieutenant-colonel on 2 August 1871 and brevet colonel on

3 December 1873. On 5 April 1876 he became acting commandant, and on 25 January 1877 commandant, of the Sind frontier force, with headquarters at Jacobabad.

On 20 November 1878 Nuttall was appointed brigadier-general in the Afghan expeditionary force, and commanded his brigade in the Pishin valley and at the occupation of Kandahar. After the departure of Sir Michael Biddulph and Lieutenant-General Sir Donald Stewart he commanded the brigade of all arms left for the occupation of Kandahar. After the 2nd division of the army was broken up he commanded a brigade left at Vitakri until 17 May, when it also was broken up, and he returned to his post on the Upper Sind frontier. When the Anglo-Afghan War entered its second phase Nuttall was appointed brigadier-general of the cavalry brigade formed at Kandahar in May 1880, and commanded it in the action at Girishk, on the Helmand, on 14 July 1880, in the cavalry affair of the 23rd, and in the disastrous battle of Maiwand on 27 July, after which he was criticized for his handling of his brigade. He was in the sortie of 16 August from Kandahar (mentioned in dispatches), commanded the east face of the city during the defence (mentioned in dispatches), and took part in the battle of Kandahar and pursuit of the Afghan army on 1 September 1880. He became a major-general in 1885 and lieutenant-general in 1887.

Nuttall was a popular, active, and energetic officer. Although not an outstanding cavalry leader he was one of the best riders and swordsmen in the Indian army, a frequent competitor at, as well as patron of, contests in skill at arms, and a renowned shikari with hogspear and rifle. He married, at Camberwell, London, on 7 February 1867, Caroline Latimer Elliot, daughter of Dr Elliot of Denmark Hill, and they had a son. Nuttall died at Newton Farm, Wardhouse, Insch, Aberdeenshire, on 30 August 1890.

H. M. CHICHESTER, rev. JAMES FALKNER

Sources Indian Army List · A. Forbes, The Afghan wars, 1839–42 and 1878–80 (1892) · Hart's Army List · P. Cadell, History of the Bombay army (1938) · B. Robson, The road to Kabul: the Second Afghan War, 1878–1881 (1986) · CGPLA Eng. & Wales (1890)

Wealth at death £1718 14s. 7d.: probate, 6 Nov 1890, CGPLA Eng. & Wales

Nuttall, William (d. 1840), topographer, son of John Nuttall, master fuller, was born at Rochdale, Lancashire. He kept a school in that town for many years and lived opposite St James's Church, Whitworth Road. He married three times, the last time unhappily. His first wife was Mary, daughter of William Dutton of Morton Wood, Shropshire. They had two daughters.

Nuttall wrote Le voyageur, or, The Genuine History of Charles Manley (1806) and Rochdale, a Fragment, with Notes, Intended as an Introduction to the History of Rochdale, which was published in 1810. It is in doggerel verse, and is curious as the first attempt at a history of the town. In his opening address to George Gordon, Lord Byron, baron of Rochdale, he claimed to have 'nothing in view but the Welfare of my Fellow Townsmen, and a desire to render myself useful to Mankind'. The manuscript of his intended history of Rochdale was utilized by Edward Baines in his History of

Lancashire, but Baines made no acknowledgement of this in his preface.

About 1828 Nuttall moved to Oldham but, overcome by poverty, he committed suicide in 1840. He was buried in Oldham churchyard.

C. W. SUTTON, *rev.* JOANNE POTIER

Sources H. Fishwick, *The Lancashire library* (1875), 266–7 · W. Robertson, *Rochdale past and present: a history and guide* (1875), 315

Nuttall, William (1835–1905), promoter of the co-operative movement, was born in Manchester in December 1835, the son of Charles Nuttall, who was a cotton weaver, and Mary, *née* Ratcliffe. He was baptized on 27 March 1836, and grew up in Manchester, Saddleworth, and Oldham. He married Ann Newton on 25 September 1862 in Prestwich; they had six children.

Apprenticed as a shoemaker, Nuttall worked in that trade at Greenacres Hill, Oldham. In the early 1860s, however, he became interested in the co-operative movement, becoming secretary of the Greenacres Hill Co-operative Society in 1862. From 1863 to 1865 he was the first paid permanent secretary of the Oldham Equitable Co-operative Society. He then became an accountant for the North of England Co-operative Wholesale Society (later the CWS). He was a member of the latter's general committee on two occasions (1865–6 and 1876–7) and its cashier for two years (1868–70). When the Central Co-operative Board was organized in 1870, Nuttall became its secretary. Nuttall was a friend and supporter of George Jacob Holyoake (1817–1906), who was one of the chief propagandists for secularism and the co-operative movement. In 1871 Holyoake's publication, *The Reasoner*, promoting his interest in secularism, was being issued on an irregular basis. Nuttall headed a publishing committee that attempted to support and publish *The Reasoner* on a regular monthly schedule.

Nuttall travelled throughout Britain in the 1870s, in both an official and a private capacity to promote the co-operative movement speaking at many local and regional meetings. He attended and actively participated in all the co-operative congresses down to 1883. Nuttall founded the Co-operative Printing Society and was also one of the founders of the *Co-operative News* and an early editor and contributor to its columns. He edited the CWS *Annual* for 1883 and prepared the 1884 edition.

Nuttall became one of the principal figures in the formation of limited liability cotton-spinning companies in the Oldham district, the so-called 'working-class limiteds' (*DLB*); and by 1875 he was involved with at least twelve such businesses. Down to 1883 he was also promoting similar companies in coal mining, iron production, and paper manufacturing. Yet Nuttall invested much of his own money in such ventures, primarily in the Manchester area, and he lost heavily. This was undoubtedly one of the reasons why he decided to leave England. Before he left he was presented with testimonials by activists in Manchester, London, and Newcastle, reflecting his contribution to the co-operative movement.

In December 1883 Nuttall emigrated with his wife and five of his children to Australia, settling in Melbourne, where he worked as cashier and secretary for the Equitable Co-operative Society. He was not particularly successful in promoting co-operation in the Melbourne region, and he and his wife returned to Manchester about 1900. However, he was unable to regain his former prominent position in the movement. He attended meetings, including the co-operative congresses of 1901–4, and visited friends and fellow co-operators but was no longer a major influence. He died of heart disease at his home, 21 Brookfield Road, Crumpsall, Manchester, on 26 October 1905; he was survived by his wife. His funeral at Manchester southern cemetery on 30 October was attended by only a few members of the movement.

According to contemporaries, Nuttall had a forceful, independent personality, and he was often blunt and opinionated. One observer noted that his 'restlessness' kept him moving to new challenges and jobs (*Oldham Co-operative Record* 4, 1898, 110). According to Holyoake he had 'the genius of figures' (p. 85) and he made important contributions to the early development of the co-operative movement in Britain. C. A. WATSON

Sources censuses for 1841–71 · m. cert. · d. cert. · 'Death of Mr William Nuttall', *Co-operative News* (4 Nov 1905), 1341–2 · 'Mr William Nuttall', *Oldham Co-operative Record*, 4 (1898), 109–10 · 'Death of Mr William Nuttall', *Oldham Co-operative Record*, 7 (Nov 1905), 270 · J. Saville and R. E. Tyson, 'Nuttall, William', *DLB*, vol. 1 · W. Nuttall, 'Melbourne and its district', *Co-operative Wholesale Society Annual* (1888), 194–236 · G. J. Holyoake, *Self-help by the people: the history of co-operation in Rochdale*, 2 (1878), 85 · W. Nuttall, 'The Reasoner publishing committee', *The Reasoner*, 892 (Jan 1871), 13–14 · C. Walters, *History of the Oldham Equitable Co-operative Society from 1850 to 1900* (1900), 31–49 · D. A. Farnie, 'The English cotton industry, 1850–1896', MA diss., University of Manchester, 1953, 259–60 · R. E. Tyson, 'The Sun Mill Company Limited: a study in democratic investment, 1858–1959', MA diss., University of Manchester, 1962, 220–21

Nutter, Alice (*d.* 1612). *See under* Pendle witches (*act.* 1612).

Nutter, William (1759?–1802), engraver and draughtsman, is said to have been a pupil of John Raphael Smith and may have worked on stipples published under Smith's name in the 1780s. His name appears on a few prints published by Smith after 1785, including Smith's own design *The Moralist* (1787). He went on to engrave many good dotted plates after contemporary artists, twelve of them for the printseller Emanuel Matthias Diemar or his widow. *The Benevolent Cottager* (1788) after Francis Wheatley, *Sunday Morning, a Cottage Family Going to Church* (1795) after William Redmore Bigg, and *Rosebud, or, The Judgment of Paris* (1796) after Richard Westall, are typical enough of his better plates. *The Destruction of the Bastille* (1792) after Henry Singleton and *The Burial of General Fraser* (1794) after John Graham were unusually large and ambitious historical subjects. Nutter was a prolific engraver of the leading miniaturist Samuel Shelley, including those prepared for *The Cabinet of Genius* (1787), a collection of poems each adorned with an original design by Shelley. Much of Nutter's other output consisted of portraits, but he exhibited some allegorical designs at the Royal Academy in 1782 and 1783. He died, unmarried, at his residence in Somers Town, London, on 14 March 1802 and was buried in the dissenters' ground of Whitefield's Tabernacle, Tottenham Court Road. In his will he left £50 in trust for 'the charity called the Sick Mans Friend at Whitefields Chapel' (fol. 420v) besides other small gifts to his professional colleagues.

TIMOTHY CLAYTON and ANITA MCCONNELL

Sources Redgrave, *Artists* · M. Huber and C. G. Martini, *Manuel des curieux et des amateurs de l'art*, 9 (Zürich, 1808), 361–2 · *GM*, 1st ser., 72 (1802), 286 · E. B. Chancellor, *London's old Latin quarter* (1930) · T. Dodd, 'History of English engravers', BL, Add. MS 33403, fols. 144–5 · will, PRO, PROB 11/1371, sig. 219 · M. Webster, *Francis Wheatley* (1970) · E. D'Oench, *Copper into gold: prints by John Raphael Smith, 1751–1812* (1999) · *A catalogue of all the valuable copper plates … being the entire stock of Mrs Diemar, printseller and publisher* (1799) [sale catalogue, Christies, 1 June 1799]

Nutting, Sir (Harold) Anthony, third baronet (1920–1999), politician and author, was born on 11 January 1920 at the Shrewsbury Nursing Institution, Quarry House, Atcham, Shropshire, the third and youngest son (there were no daughters) of Sir Harold Stansmore Nutting, second baronet (1882–1972), landowner and army officer, and his wife, Enid Hester Nina (d. 1961), an accomplished violinist and daughter of Francis Berry Homan-Mulock of Bellair, King's county, Ireland. Nutting's paternal grandfather, Sir John Gardiner Nutting (1852–1918), had 'amassed a fortune out of bottled beer and Irish railways' (*Daily Telegraph*, 25 Feb 1999), and was made a baronet in 1903. Sir Harold Nutting, the second baronet, was aide-de-camp to the governor-general of Australia from 1911 to 1913, a captain in the 17th lancers during the First World War (being wounded), and at various times master of the North Shropshire, Megnell, and Quorn hunts. The family owned large estates at Quenby Hall, Leicestershire, and Achentoul, Kinbrace, Sutherland. Both Nutting's elder brothers died on active service in the Second World War, and he succeeded to the baronetage on his father's death in 1972.

Nutting was educated at Eton College and Trinity College, Cambridge, where he read agriculture but did not take a degree. Shortly before the outbreak of the Second World War he enlisted as a trooper in the Leicestershire yeomanry, but was invalided out of the army with asthma early in 1940. He entered the Foreign Office in February that year, serving in the embassies in Paris, Madrid, and Rome, and in 1942 was briefly private secretary to Anthony Eden, the foreign secretary, with whom he formed a close friendship. On 6 August 1941 he married Gillian Leonora Strutt (b. 1918), daughter of Edward Joliffe Strutt. They had two sons, John Grenfell (b. 1942) and David Anthony (b. 1944), and a daughter, Zara Nina (b. 1947).

In the general election of 1945 Nutting was elected Conservative MP for the Melton division of Leicestershire. It was in the Conservative Party at large that he first made his mark, as chairman of the Young Conservatives (1946), and then chairman of the National Union in 1950, when he presided over the party's annual conference at the age of only thirty. When his party returned to power in October 1951, Churchill appointed him joint parliamentary under-secretary of state for foreign affairs, again under Eden. His intelligence, eloquence, integrity, and lean good looks soon made him a popular figure in parliament. In October 1954 he was promoted minister of state and privy councillor, and negotiated with Colonel Nasser the withdrawal of British troops from the canal zone. His next role was to lead, with notable success, the British delegation to the United Nations and the UN Disarmament Commission.

Soon after Nutting's return from New York in 1956, when Nasser nationalized the Suez Canal, he was in no doubt that firm action must be taken to restore it to some form of international control. He strongly supported the efforts of Selwyn Lloyd, the foreign secretary under Anthony Eden, now prime minister, to devise a formula acceptable to Egypt and the users of the canal, but Eden distrusted these negotiations, and was persuaded by the French to join them in a secret plot to invade Egypt in collusion with the Israelis.

Nutting, who was privy to the inner secrets of the government, was horrified by the duplicity involved. He considered it 'a sordid manoeuvre … morally indefensible and politically suicidal', which necessitated concealing Britain's true intentions from its allies and parliament (Nutting, 14 and 96). He foresaw that because it originated in deceit it would end in failure. On 31 October he wrote Eden a letter of resignation, saying that he found it impossible to defend the policy in public. His letter was published in *The Times* on 5 November 1956, the day before British and French paratroops landed at Port Said. He then resigned his seat in parliament because his constituents disowned him publicly, but he refrained from making the customary resignation speech in the House of Commons, since to reveal details of the collusion plot might result in the fall of the government at a moment of acute national crisis.

Nutting's reticence did him no good. Eden never spoke to him again. Selwyn Lloyd passed off the incident with a light laugh, calling it 'Much Ado about Nutting' (*The Independent*). Harold Macmillan, who told him that his silence would one day be rewarded by leadership of the party, gave him but half a line in his memoirs. Although Nutting was proved right in all his forebodings, the Conservative Party regarded his resignation as spiteful, and when, eleven years later, he at last revealed the secrets of Suez in *No End of a Lesson* (1967), he was threatened with prosecution for breaking the privy councillor's oath.

After the Suez episode Nutting retired from public life, dividing his time between London and his inherited estate in Scotland. His first marriage having ended in divorce in 1959, on 27 May 1961 he married a beautiful model, Anne Gunning Parker (b. 1929), daughter of Arnold Barthrop Parker, of Cuckfield, Sussex. Following her death in 1990 he married, on 11 April 1991, Margarita Sanchez Butterwick (b. 1934), daughter of Carlos Sanchez, of Havana, Cuba.

Nutting became a prolific author, with a clear, taut style,

mainly of books connected with his political past, such as *Disarmament* (1959), *The Arabs* (1964), and biographies of Lawrence of Arabia (1961), Gordon of Khartoum (1966), and Nasser (1972). He was a good companion, a witty man, hospitable to friends in London and Scotland. If, in his later years, he sometimes succumbed to melancholy, it was perhaps because he found it disheartening that he had been denied any credit for those three weeks in 1956 when he stood by his political and moral principles at the cost of a career which seemed destined for the highest offices of state. He died at the Brompton Hospital, London, of a heart attack on 23 February 1999, and was cremated at West London crematorium on 4 March. He was survived by his third wife and the three children of his first marriage, the eldest of whom, John, succeeded him as fourth baronet. NIGEL NICOLSON

Sources A. Nutting, *No end of a lesson: the story of Suez* (1967) • A. Eden, *Full circle* (1960) • S. Lloyd, *Suez, 1956* (1978) • R. R. James, *Anthony Eden* (1986) • E. Shuckburgh, *Descent to Suez: diaries, 1951–6* (1986) • K. Kyle, *Suez* (1991) • *The Times* (25 Feb 1999) • *Daily Telegraph* (25 Feb 1999) • *The Guardian* (26 Feb 1999) • *The Independent* (3 March 1999) • Burke, *Peerage* • WWW • b. cert. • m. cert. • personal knowledge [2004] • private information (2004) [John Nutting, son; J. Profumo]
Archives priv. coll., corresp.
Likenesses photograph, 1951, repro. in *Daily Telegraph* • S. Pavlenko, oils, *c*.1980, Achentoul, Highland • photograph, 1996, repro. in *The Times* • photograph, repro. in *The Guardian* • photograph, repro. in *The Independent*
Wealth at death £2,758,764—gross; £2,728,412—net: probate, 7 June 1999, *CGPLA Eng. & Wales*

Nutting, Joseph (1660–1722), engraver, was born in 1660, though nothing is known of his parents. He served as an apprentice to John Savage about 1680 before setting up in business as a printmaker and printseller in Fleet Street, at the Gold and Blue Fans, near Salisbury Court. His output consisted mainly of portraits of near-contemporaries, such as Sir Edmund Berry Godfrey and John Locke, although one of his best prints is of Nicholas Monk, bishop of Hereford (d. 1661), and another shows Charles I with a group of his most prominent supporters (1706). Since Nutting worked extensively for the book trade, it is not surprising that many portraits by him were used as frontispieces, including those of Thomas Greenhill (*The Art of Embalming*, 1705), Sir Bartholomew Shower (*The Reports of Sir Bartholomew Shower of Cases Adjudg'd in the Court of King's Bench*, 1708), and Dr Henry Sacheverell (*The Tryal of D*r *Henry Sacheverell before the House of Peers*, 1710). He also engraved other subjects, among them topographical plates for John Slezer's *Theatrum Scotiae* (1693, 1710), an unusually large three-sheet *New Prospect of the North Side of the City of London, with New Bedlam and Moore Fields* (*c*.1690), and a book of penmanship (untraced). According to Vertue, Nutting was still working in London in 1713. He died in 1722. RICHARD SHARP

Sources J. Strutt, *A biographical dictionary, containing an historical account of all the engravers, from the earliest period of the art of engraving to the present time*, 2 vols. (1785–6) • *Engraved Brit. ports.* • Bryan, *Painters* (1873) • Thieme & Becker, *Allgemeines Lexikon* • *DNB* • A. Griffiths

and R. A. Gerard, *The print in Stuart Britain, 1603–1689* (1998) [exhibition catalogue, BM, 8 May – 20 Sept 1998] • Redgrave, *Artists* • Vertue, *Note books*

Nye, Sir Archibald Edward (1895–1967), army officer, was born in Ship Street barracks, Dublin, on 23 April 1895, the youngest but one in the family of three sons and three daughters of Charles Edward Nye (d. 1930) and his Irish wife, Mary Sexton. His father was a regimental sergeant-major in the Oxfordshire and Buckinghamshire light infantry. Having been an outstanding scholar at the Duke of York's royal military school, Dover, he was preparing to become an army schoolmaster when war began in August 1914. He volunteered for combatant duty and, serving as a non-commissioned officer in France, was selected in 1915 for a commission in the Leinster regiment. Twice wounded in action, and awarded the MC for gallantry thereafter, he was granted a regular commission in 1922 in the Royal Warwickshire regiment, given the demise of the Leinsters, a southern Irish regiment. Lacking any private means, Nye never drank, and helped to pay his mess bills by winning games of billiards. In the military doldrums of the 1920s Nye's quick, keen mind drew him to the staff. In 1924–5 he attended the Staff College, Camberley. He soon acquired a high reputation, brevet, and accelerated promotion through exchange of regiments. While holding demanding appointments he managed simultaneously to qualify as a barrister at the Inner Temple in 1932.

Recognized as a potential general officer, Nye was returned to regimental duty to command the 2nd battalion, Royal Warwickshire regiment in 1937, earned at once a recommendation for higher command, and was appointed to raise the Nowshera brigade in India in 1939. Nye married (Una Sheila) Colleen, daughter of General Sir Harry Hugh Sidney Knox, during that year, and they had one daughter. Colleen also had two children from her previous marriage to Colonel N. D. Stevenson.

War once again changed Nye's plans. He was recalled to London a few months after leaving for India, and was soon later promoted major-general as director of staff duties in the War Office, the branch concerned with organization and co-ordination. During the crises of 1940 his enterprise, moral courage, and mastery of complex politico-military policy impressed Winston Churchill; when Sir John G. Dill was removed as chief of the imperial general staff in 1941, Nye was one of three possible successors in his mind. But seniority and experience in high command weighed in this selection. Sir Alan Brooke was chosen; Nye was promoted lieutenant-general and vice-chief. Fortunately the two men complemented and had absolute confidence in each other. They carried a formidable workload for four years until victory in 1945. Nye accompanied Brooke on many of his important journeys during the war. At its end Brooke wished to make Nye adjutant-general, but another option was offered: governor of Madras. Retiring as CB (1942), KBE (1944), and KCB (1946) Nye returned to India in 1946.

Nye's support for independence there inspired Jawaharlal Nehru to ask him to stay in post when imperial government ended. Further, his firmness and wisdom in the ensuing political, racial, and caste turbulence prompted the Indian government to suggest his appointment as United Kingdom high commissioner at Delhi when he completed his extension in Madras in 1948. In this second post he developed successfully the new and friendly relationship between the British and Indian governments, enhancing it by skilful diplomacy during the opening and greater part of the Korean War.

Nye departed from India in 1952 with the honours GCIE (1946) and GCSI (1947), and was appointed high commissioner to Canada. In his four years in Ottawa his most notable success was the extension of British–Canadian trade; perhaps his most difficult political task was the representation of British policy on the Suez Canal. Retiring in 1956, Nye left many official and personal friends in Canada. He had received the freedom of the capital city, academic honours from Bishop's, McGill, Toronto, and McMaster universities, and had been appointed GCMG by his own government in 1951. For some years he held several directorships in commercial companies, but in 1962 he returned temporarily to government service as chairman of a committee to consider reorganizing the War Office. The work of this body—the Nye committee—influenced profoundly the reshaping of the army's headquarters for the rest of the century.

Nye made an important contribution to the high political and military policies of his country, and often played a crucial part in their execution over more than twenty years. His reputation is, happily, unsullied by any manifestation of jealousy, bitterness, or disregard towards those with whom he served. It is remarkable that he caught the attention of three prime ministers—Churchill, Attlee, and Nehru—each of whom wanted to place him in a significant position. Nye died in London on 13 November 1967.   ANTHONY FARRAR-HOCKLEY, *rev.*

Sources *The Times* (15 Nov 1967) · *WWW* · private information (1981) · *CGPLA Eng. & Wales* (1968) · d. cert. [Edward Charles Nye]
Archives King's Lond., Liddell Hart C., corresp. with Sir B. H. Liddell Hart · Nuffield Oxf., corresp. with Lord Cherwell | FILM BFI NFTVA, news footage · IWM FVA, news footage
Likenesses W. Dring, pastel drawing, 1942, IWM · H. Lamb, oils, 1942, IWM
Wealth at death £38,559: probate, 15 Jan 1968, *CGPLA Eng. & Wales*

Nye, John (*bap.* 1620, *d.* 1686?), Church of England clergyman and religious writer, was baptized on 26 March 1620 at Cobham, Surrey, where his father, Henry Nye (*bap.* 1588, *d.* 1643) was vicar; his mother's name was probably Lettice. Within a few months of John's birth Henry Nye moved to Clapham, Sussex, where he continued as rector until his death in August or September 1643. John matriculated from Magdalen Hall, Oxford, on 12 December 1634, aged fourteen, and graduated BA on 26 May 1638. He was back in Clapham when late in 1641 or early in 1642 he signed the protestation issued by the House of Commons. On 4 January 1647 he was 'approved on his former examination' (Mitchell and Struthers, 318) by the Westminster assembly, of which his uncle Philip *Nye (*d.* 1672) was a

prominent member, presumably preparatory to serving the latter in his ministry at Acton, Middlesex, a position he was certainly holding by 1650. By the summer of 1647 he married Elizabeth (*d.* 1654), the second daughter of another leading figure in the assembly, Stephen *Marshall (1594/5?–1655); their son Stephen *Nye was born in 1647 or early in 1648 and a second son, John, in 1650 or early 1651.

By mid-1654 Nye was minister of Cottenham, Cambridgeshire; his wife was buried there on 2 August. That year he was appointed assistant to the county's commission of triers and ejectors and he became an active member of the voluntary association of ministers in the county. On 25 June 1656 at nearby Willingham he married Elizabeth, sister of the rector of the parish, Nathaniel Bradshaw (*d.* 1690), who was a fellow member of the commission.

At the Restoration the sequestered rector of Cottenham, John Manby, was reinstated. Nye was ordained priest at Chichester on 25 June 1661 and the same day presented to the vicarage of Great Chishill, Cambridgeshire. Unlike his uncle, who was an Independent, and his brother-in-law Bradshaw, who was ejected, Nye subscribed to the Act of Uniformity in 1662, signing on 22 July as a chaplain of the Savoy, London. On 27 August he became rector of Quendon, acquiring an additional Essex living at Rickling in 1674; his son John, who was ordained deacon in London in May 1670 and priest at Peterborough in May 1676, served as his curate. It was from Quendon that on 25 October 1675 he signed the preface to *A Display of Divine Heraldry Vindicating the Foundation of the Christian Religion* (1678). Although he assured the 'Christian Reader' that Jesus's miracles 'infallibly prove him to be the Christ of God, though we could not shew by what Ancestors he descended from Abraham and David' (sig. A2), the work was a discussion of the differing genealogies of Jesus given in the gospels of Matthew and Luke which concluded that they 'are as a Golden key to open the truth of the Story, without which it is impossible to read the Scriptures with true understanding' (pp. 51–2). In contrast to his son Stephen later, he rejected the Socinian viewpoint and asserted both the divine and the human nature of Christ. Nye made his will on 8 November 1681, and probably died in 1686; the will was proved on 25 August that year. He was survived by his second wife, whom he made executor, by his son Stephen, and by three daughters, Elizabeth, Joanna, and Catherine; he left landed property in Cambridgeshire and Essex.

Nye has sometimes been confused with his first cousin **John Nye** (*bap.* 1630, *d.* 1672), second surviving of five sons of Philip Nye and his wife, Judith Kiddington (*d.* 1680?). This John Nye was baptized on 30 November 1630 at St Dionis Backchurch, London, where his father was then lecturer. On 3 July 1650 he was admitted a pensioner at Emmanuel College, Cambridge, but he subsequently migrated to Oxford, where he matriculated from Magdalen College on 23 February 1654 and graduated BA the same day. By June that year he was acting as a clerk to the commission of triers and ejectors, of which his father was a prominent member. When one of the clergymen examined by the commission, Anthony Sadler, aired objections to his treatment in a pamphlet entitled *Inquisitio Anglicana*, it was almost certainly Nye who published anonymously a systematic defence of the commissioners' proceedings, *Mr Sadler Re-Examined, or, His Disguise Discovered* (1654). 'The Approvers', he asserted, 'do the utmost in them lies to keep mens souls from being starved by the remainder of this Episcopall generation' (p. 13). He claimed to be 'now in no relation to them' (p. 1) and indeed on 10 February 1655 Nye was admitted to the Middle Temple, but he seems to have continued as clerk until the Restoration: in 1662 he was ordered to hand over the triers' papers to the archbishop of Canterbury. On 14 April 1664 he married at Stoke Newington, Middlesex, Anne Chumley or Cholmley, with whom he had two sons, John and Cholmley. He died in 1672, and was buried on 14 October at St Michael Cornhill, London, just seventeen days after his father had been interred there.

VIVIENNE LARMINIE and TIM WALES

Sources W. H. Challen, 'Nye family of Sussex and elsewhere', *N&Q*, new ser., 206 (1961), 284–8 • Foster, *Alum. Oxon.* • Venn, *Alum. Cant.* • *Calamy rev.*, 369–70 • *IGI* [parish registers, Willingham, Cambridgeshire, and Cobham, Surrey] • will, PRO, PROB 11/384, sig. 109, fol. 148r–v • A. F. Mitchell and J. Struthers, eds., *Minutes of the sessions of the Westminster assembly of divines* (1874), 318 • 'Minutes of the Cambridge classis', *Minutes of the Bury presbyterian classis, 1647–1657*, ed. W. A. Shaw, 2 vols., Chetham Society, new ser., 36, 41 (1896–8), vol. 2, pp. 189–204 • C. Evans, 'Dame Grace Knatchbull and her family connexions', *N&Q*, new ser., 205 (1960), 226–7 • M. Spufford, *Contrasting communities: English villagers in the sixteenth and seventeenth centuries* (1975), 275, 317 • J. L. Chester, ed., *The reiester booke of Saynte De'nis Backchurch parishe … begynnynge … 1538*, Harleian Society, register section, 3 (1878), 102 • H. A. C. Sturgess, ed., *Register of admissions to the Honourable Society of the Middle Temple, from the fifteenth century to the year 1944*, 1 (1949), 155

Wealth at death left landed property in Cambridgeshire and Essex

Nye, John (*bap.* 1630, *d.* 1672). *See under* Nye, John (*bap.* 1620, *d.* 1686?).

Nye, Nathaniel (*bap.* 1624), mathematician and master gunner, was baptized at St Martin's, Birmingham, on 18 April 1624, the son of Allen Nye. A list of governors of King Edward VI's School, Birmingham, for 1638 includes an Allen Nye, who may have been Nathaniel's father. Nathaniel Nye wrote *A New Almanacke and Prognostication* for 1642; *A Prognostication* and *A New Almanacke and Prognostication* for 1643, calculated for 'the fair and populous Town of Birmicham', in which he describes himself as 'Mathematitian, Practitioner of Astronomy'; and two almanacs for 1645.

Against the background of Birmingham's arms trades in the civil war, Nye developed an interest in gunnery. In 1643 he tested a Birmingham cannon, and he described an experiment with a saker which he carried out in the Deritend area of the town in March 1645. Following the parliamentarian capture of Evesham in May 1645 Nye held the post of master gunner to the garrison there, and he directed the artillery at the siege of Worcester, from May to July 1646. He then served with the parliamentarian garrison of the city, for he was described as 'Master Gunner of the City of Worcester' on the title page of his book, *The Art of Gunnery*, published in 1647. Nye's avowed intention in writing the book was to restore the reputation of gunners, which had suffered through the appointment of men because of their connections rather than their ability. Arguing that it was as easy to fire a piece of ordnance as a musket, he provided a detailed practical guide to the preparation and employment of artillery, stressing the importance of arithmetic and geometry. The book's second section, with a separate title page, is entitled 'A treatise of artificiall fire-works for warre and recreation', and includes information on treatments for gunpowder burns. While pointing out that the book was written from his own experiences, he also acknowledged his debt to earlier writers on the use of artillery and preparation of fireworks: William Bourne, John Bate, John Babington, Robert Norton, Niccolò Tartaglia, and Thomas Malthus. The works on arithmetic to which he refers the reader include those by Robert Recorde and Marcus Jordanus.

Nye also had a practical interest in cartography, and recommended that a gunner should have a map of the environs of his garrison that marked all prominent features within range of the defences. He had copies of such plans for Worcester and Coventry, although they are not included in the book. While he does not state that they were prepared by him, that is implied.

Despite his service with the parliamentarian forces, Nye dedicated *The Art of Gunnery* to the prominent royalist and member of the king's household Montague Bertie, second earl of Lindsey. In the dedication he mentions 'the particular service I ever did owe and beare to your Lordship and Noble Family', although the nature of the connection is unknown. Further editions appeared in 1648 and 1670. The frontispiece is a portrait of Nye by Wenceslaus Hollar, drawn in 1644. Nothing is known of Nye's life after 1647.

STEPHEN PORTER

Sources PRO, SP 28/138/16, 17 • *N&Q*, 6th ser., 12 (1885), 384 • *N&Q*, 8th ser., 7 (1895), 102 • *VCH Warwickshire*, vol. 7 • *The records of King Edward's School, Birmingham*, 6, ed. J. Izon, Dugdale Society, 30 (1974), 15

Likenesses W. Hollar, etching, 1644, BM, NPG; repro. in N. Nye, *The art of gunnery* (1647), frontispiece

Nye, Philip (*bap.* 1595, *d.* 1672), Independent minister, was born in Sussex and baptized on 19 January 1595, the ninth of eleven children of John Nye (*d.* 1626) of Hayes, Slinfold, Sussex, and his wife, Dorothy West (*d.* 1622). Like his elder brother, Henry Nye (1589–1645), vicar of Cobham, Sussex, from 1615 to 1620 and rector of Clapham, Sussex, from 1620, Nye entered Brasenose College, Oxford, matriculating on 28 June 1616. He transferred to Magdalen Hall, where he was placed under 'a puritanical tutor' (Wood, *Ath. Oxon.*, 3.963) and earned the reputation of 'a very hard student' (*Nonconformist's Memorial*, 1.96). He graduated BA on 24 April 1619 and proceeded MA on 9 May 1622. He apparently began to preach in 1620. On 20 May 1624 he married Judith Keddington (*d.* 1680?); they had at least five sons and two daughters. In 1627 he became curate of All Hallows Staining, and in 1630 was lecturer at St Michael Cornhill, both in London.

Overseas activities and early Independency In 1632 Nye was one of those who tried to persuade John Cotton, then in hiding in London, to conform but by August 1633 Nye himself was suspect as a nonconformist and it was rumoured that he would go with John Davenport to New England. He seems, however, to have remained in England: daughters were baptized at Hackney in March 1635 and June 1636, and in London he was associated with puritan colonizing ventures and through them forged early connections with influential dissidents. Already in 1632 he had links with Providence Island and in the same year was one of those to whom the earl of Warwick, as president of the Council for New England, granted joint tenancy of lands along the Connecticut River; over five years sales of cattle there netted £161 15s. for Nye.

Some potential colonizers were disturbed by reports from Massachusetts Bay of the 'blurring of civil and religious jurisdictions', a theme to which Nye and other Independents frequently returned (K. O. Kupperman, *Providence Island, 1630–1641*, 1993, 326). The Connecticut River patentees prepared to act, and in the summer of 1635 Nye was a confidential intermediary and financial agent for the projected settlement, ensuring, as he said, that the younger John Winthrop, its governor, would enjoy 'all the advantages the busines will afford for your comfortable and creditfull going on in this project' (*Winthrop Papers*, 3.201). In September Nye reported on 'Gentlemen of the North' who were 'in a way of selling off their estates with the greatest expedicion' (ibid., 3.211), and in November 1636 he represented other gentlemen who, in the interests of God and profit, were prepared to supply clothing to the colony at a reasonable rate in return for a monopoly of the trade. He was thus already engaged as a trusted agent whose skills in management and negotiation served both God and Mammon.

Nye's interest in New England survived the outbreak of civil war. In 1645 he and other Independents wrote to the general court in Boston deploring its persecution of Anabaptists. They pointed out that they themselves benefited from toleration 'from them whose established lawes and orders about the worship of god we Dissent from' and that persecution by beneficiaries of such liberty would only encourage those who favoured 'such severityes' to employ them against the Independents (*Winthrop Papers*, 5.24).

Between 1636 and 1639 Nye and Thomas Goodwin published in London six of the works of Richard Sibbes, but by 1639 Nye was in the Netherlands, where he remained until 1640 as one of three ministers of an Independent church in Arnhem. Its prosperous congregation included some of the 'Gentlemen of the North' from Yorkshire, and three of its members had been fellow Connecticut patentees with Nye. John Archer was 'pastor' and Goodwin and Nye 'teachers', an arrangement later espoused by Nye for Independent congregations in England. Indeed, the Arnhem church was to become a model for later Independents. Only the truly godly—so judged after thorough scrutiny—were admitted, and the church provided an exemplary case of dispute resolution to which Nye and

the Independent cadre in the Westminster assembly later reverted in their *Apologeticall Narration*. Nye's role in settling a conflict in the English church in Rotterdam demonstrated, they believed, that disputes within individual congregations could be resolved by the mediation of peer congregations without reference to an authoritative external body. His record was less pacific in his own church, where his censure of one member led to a long-running dispute and charges of 'pride [and] want of charity' (Edwards, 36).

By 1640 Nye, already in middle age, held fully formed views on church government and church–state relations, and was committed to a church organization of non-parochial gathered churches rather than one of parochial congregationalism. When the times began to change in England most of the Arnhem congregation dispersed homewards, where Independents were for the first time confronted by the complex problem of the relation between gathered churches and a national parochial church system. Nye went first to Hull where his influence alarmed the orthodox and led to the formation of a small Independent church in May 1643. An unfriendly witness declared that after his return Nye 'lived a great part of his time … in Noblemen's families' (Edwards, 217) where he cultivated useful connections. By April 1642 the earl of Manchester, Warwick's son-in-law, had presented him to the living of Kimbolton, Huntingdonshire; in that month Nye was chosen as one of the county's two representatives to the Westminster assembly.

Religious politics in London, 1643–1659 Henceforth Nye's career centred on London and national religious politics. Until then he had preached little there, but according to Thomas Edwards he had 'acted the State-parasite and played the polititian the more, … dealing in private, under hand, and hand to hand with some men of note' (Edwards, 217). He quickly emerged as a powerful Independent leader. In 1643 he and the eminent presbyterian Stephen Marshall accompanied the parliamentary commissioners to Edinburgh to negotiate Scottish entry into the war; there he praised the solemn league and covenant as 'warranted by both human and divine story' (Wood, *Ath. Oxon.*, 3.963). Nevertheless he recognized English reservations, and in a letter to the Westminster assembly he and Marshall claimed the agreement had been drawn up with such 'warinesse … there might be no bogling at it' (*A Letter from Mr. Marshall, and Mr. Nye*, 1643, 2). On his return to London he presented the draft agreement to parliament on 25 September 1643. His speech before the reading of the covenant, together with Alexander Henderson's on the same occasion, was printed by order of parliament as *The Covenant with a Narrative of the Proceedings and Solemn Manner of Taking it* (London, 1643) and *Two Speeches Delivered before the Subscribing of the Covenant* (Edinburgh, 1643).

Although he strongly supported the solemn league and covenant, Nye stopped short of advocacy of a presbyterian system; instead his tone was moderate and he deplored the bitterness of debates over church government. Independents were alarmed, but he exerted his influence to abort their petition of protest. The royalists acknowledged his standing in late 1643 when they vainly attempted to lure him and Goodwin to their side with offers of toleration, preferment, and a royal chaplaincy for Nye. Nye, however, renewed his advocacy of the covenant with an exhortation read in the House of Commons on 9 February 1644, now emphasizing the 'righteousnesse' of the Scots and the dangers from 'Popish and Prelatick Projectors' (*An Exhortation to the Taking of the Solemne League and Covenant*, 1644, 6).

In the Westminster assembly, Nye was a leader of the small band of Independent clergy whose disproportionate influence enabled them to obstruct the presbyterian programme and, Edmund Calamy complained, buy time for their party to gain ground in the army and parliament (*Nonconformist's Memorial*, 1.9). In November 1643 London ministers petitioned the Westminster assembly against gathered churches, a breach of the agreement reached in 1641 that religious differences between allies would not be publicly aired. With the other leading 'Dissenting Brethren' (Goodwin, Sidrach Simpson, Jeremiah Burroughes, and William Bridge, all returned émigrés) Nye published *An Apologeticall Narration*. They made much of the moral authority bestowed by exile and stressed their clerical respectability in order to dissociate themselves from Brownists. They emphasized their Englishness, distinguishing themselves from churches abroad, including that of Scotland, and argued against rigidity and making 'present judgement and practice a binding law … for the future' (Goodwin and others, 10). Doctrine had been settled by 'the good old Non-conformists' (ibid., 4); instead they concentrated on their programme for church government, advocating autonomous, gathered congregations exempt from any external 'Presbyteriall' authority to excommunicate either churches or individuals. To the dismay of the Scots they accepted civil authority over the church, and in 1644 Nye argued in the Westminster assembly for 'the inconsistency of a presbytery with a civil state' (Tolmie, 96). Although his speech to parliament on his return from Scotland in 1643 was reprinted in January 1646 as *The Excellency and Lawfulnesse of the Solemne League*, his Independent credentials remained untarnished, perhaps in part because of the work's moderate tone. In 1644 Nye and Goodwin in a preface to John Cotton's *The Keyes of the Kingdom of Heaven* defended the Independent '*Middle-Way* … between … *Brownisme*, and the Presbyteriall-government' ('To the reader', Cotton), and defended the autonomy of the individual church. They also struggled to delineate the respective powers of pastors, elders, and brethren of the gathered church.

Nye wrote the preface to the Westminster assembly's *Directory for the Publique Worship of God* and he preached, albeit infrequently (six times between 1643 and 1653), before parliament. He also preached a Sunday morning and a weekly lecture at St Margaret's, Westminster, and gave a termly lecture in Westminster Abbey. In 1643 parliament installed him in the rectory of Acton, Middlesex, on the ejection of the incumbent, Dr Daniel Featley. In 1646 Nye was a member of the committee for sending ministers into the northern parts of the kingdom, and in December 1647 he and Stephen Marshall accompanied the commissioners to the king on the Isle of Wight. He was also one of the 'pestilent *Firebrands of Sedition*' dispatched to calm the restive army in the winter of 1647–8 (*Mercurius Elenticus*, 12–19 Jan 1648, 59).

At the debate in the general council of the army at Whitehall on 14 December 1648, on whether the power of the civil magistrate derived from God and could be exercised in matters of religion, Nye was allied with Henry Ireton against the radicals. He allowed extensive powers to the magistrate, for authority to act in a commonwealth did 'nott in the least lie in the Ministeriall power butt in the Legislative power'. These powers were 'conveyed to him by the people'; hence 'the thinges of our God' that were 'of publique good and publique concernment' were legitimate areas for magisterial action (*Clarke Papers*, 2.118–19). If the magistrate lacked a positive right to determine and enforce true religion, he none the less had negative powers to act against false religion.

Nye protested in 1648 against a personal treaty with the king. Although he was said to object to Pride's Purge and the king's execution, Cromwell employed Nye in 1649 to negotiate with the London presbyterians and to try to persuade secluded members to return to parliament. He joined with presbyterians in 1651 in their vain intervention on behalf of Christopher Love, and again in 1652 in opposing Fifth Monarchist attacks on tithes and a national church. With John Owen and others he presented the *Humble Proposal* for a religious settlement to the Rump and later the Barebones parliaments. Their approach, favouring toleration for those who accepted the 'fundamentals' of Christianity, met with Cromwell's approval, and Nye's career prospered under his regime. He was a member of the commissions appointed in 1654 to 'try' candidates for livings and to eject the undesirable. Anthony Sadler's record of his own failed candidature, *Inquisitio Anglicana* (1654), reveals Nye's cross-examination as hectoring and inquisitorial, an impression not refuted by the defence published anonymously by Nye's son John *Nye [see under Nye, John], who served as his clerk. In 1655, against the wishes of the parishioners, Cromwell gave the living of St Bartholomew by the Exchange to Nye and his gathered church. The parishioners complained that they were now excluded, for both pulpit and pews had been taken over by 'strainge congregacons' (Shaw, 2.133). They withheld their tithes and the rancorous dispute continued until the Restoration.

Nye was prominent in the Savoy conference of 1658 and was one of the leaders who drafted its *Declaration of the Faith and Order* of English congregational churches (1659). He participated in efforts to reconcile Independents and presbyterians but was prepared to make few compromises. Richard Baxter recognized his 'very great power' with the Independents but Nye rebuffed efforts to achieve agreement 'between the Honest and Moderate' of both parties, remaining elusive and ultimately intransigent (*Calendar*, 1.298–9). He objected that Baxter's criterion for admission to church membership—'a credible profession of faith & holinesse'—failed to meet the need for 'deeper discoverie', and he rejected any association based on a covenant regarding church practice, 'for hee said ... hee was borne free & why should hee come under bonds?' (ibid., 1.306). Owen's 'Pride, & Mr. Philip Nye's Policie', said Baxter, 'increased the flame, & kept open our wounds' (G. Nuttall, 'The MS of *Reliquiae Baxterianae*', *Journal of Ecclesiastical History*, 6, 1995, 78).

Restoration Independency and the civil magistrate At the Restoration, Nye was initially excluded from clemency because he 'had acted so highly ... against the king, and had been instrumental in bringing all things into confusion' (Wood, *Ath. Oxon.*, 3.964). In the end his life was spared on condition that he never again hold civil or ecclesiastical office. In May 1660 he signed an address to Charles II, and in the same year he published *Beames of Former Light* (1660) in which, although he argued against using the threat of ejection to enforce conformity, he still acknowledged the magistrate's powers in religion. He later fruitlessly urged Baxter to join him in 'owning' the king's proposed declaration of indulgence. He remained, however, an object of mistrust and he was accused of corruption and abuse of power as a trier. In 1662, in his only personal statement, he defended himself in a brief pamphlet entitled *The Case of Philip Nye, Minister, Humbly Tendered to the Consideration of the Parliament* and appealed for sympathy: he had been a preacher for forty years, was now infirm and dependent on voluntary contributions, and had a wife and three children (all in fact now adult) to provide for.

In 1662 Nye published *The Lawfulness of the Oath of Supremacy*, which argued for the king's power in ecclesiastical affairs and reiterated his earlier views on the legitimate powers of the civil magistrate to protect 'a gospel-Ministry' and regulate the practice of religion (*Lawfulness*, 1683, 25). The work revealed both caution in the face of restored monarchy and the alarm induced in an orderly and authoritarian cleric by interregnum radicalism and 'unseemly' religious proceedings (*Beames*, 4). He denied coercive power to the clergy but allowed it to the civil power. Outward conformity, he now said, was a means to 'restrain our inbred corruption' and while it could not save it could 'work preparatively to Conversion'. Christ's presence in men's souls was made manifest in their outward behaviour: politeness, civility, and 'Civil Relations' had become signs of godliness (*Lawfulness*, 25–8).

Posthumously published works apparently dating from this period of Nye's 'unhappy leisure' similarly accommodated the Independent position to changed political circumstances. He argued that church members might legitimately hear the sermons of ministers of the established church and, in a work diplomatically dedicated to James II by Nye's son Henry in 1687, he asserted the king's right to dispense with penal laws in religion. He was also reported to have written 'a compleat history of the old Puritan Dissenters' which burned in the fire of London in 1666 (*Nonconformist's Memorial*, 1.97). Nye returned to London after the fire. In 1669 he was a lecturer in the Hackney combination, and in April 1672 he was licensed to preach in an Independent church in which he served as 'doctor' and John Loder as pastor. He died at Brompton in September 1672 and was buried on 27 September at St Michael Cornhill.

Nye and his contemporaries In an age of vivid clerical personalities Nye's remains elusive. The works published in his lifetime were largely co-operative and programmatic; those few of his sermons that found their way into print had a specific political purpose. His long-standing partnerships, notably with Goodwin and Marshall—whose daughter married his nephew John *Nye (bap. 1620, d. 1686?)—and his rapid emergence as an influential figure in religious politics indicate force of intellect and personality as well as political skill, yet the absence of affectionate or admiring tributes is notable. Instead assessments ranged from wary to hostile. Baxter thought Nye able but deplored the exclusive rigour of his Christianity, noting that at Acton he admitted so few to the communion that this 'rigour made the People think hardly of [him]' (*Reliquiae Baxterianae*, ed. M. Sylvester, 1696, 3.46). Calamy praised Nye's thorough knowledge of 'the Disciplinarian controversy', and Nye had the reputation 'of a man of uncommon depth, who was seldom or never outreached, but ... was of too warm a spirit' (*Nonconformist's Memorial*, 1.96–7).

Nye's enemies said that he grew rich through greed and corruption. Wood claimed that parliament gave him £500 after his expedition to the king at Carisbrooke Castle, and a living worth £400 per annum. He certainly had 4s. a day for expenses as a member of the Westminster assembly, and £120 per annum for his lectureships at St Margaret's, Westminster, and the abbey. There were presumably other similar payments, and when bishops' lands were sold in 1651 Nye bought land in Yorkshire and, with a partner, a manor in Somerset for £722. On the other hand, he paid rent for the house assigned to him in Westminster; some grants were contingent on raising money from designated sources (sometimes problematic); and his income from lecturing appears to have been significantly less than that of a star preacher such as Marshall.

Nye was 'a great politician' (D. Neal, *The History of the Puritans*, 5 vols., 1822, 4.416) who was disliked for his 'policie and subtility' (Edwards, 242); he was one of the 'two politic pulpit-drivers of Independency' (*Clarke Papers*, 2.75n.a). He was clearly a skilled political manager whose belief in the legitimate power of the civil magistrate facilitated flexibility in changed secular circumstances, while at the same time he remained intransigent in those religious matters that absorbed his attention, namely the government and organization of gathered churches. He was a libertarian in his demands for the unfettered autonomy of each church, but he was not a democrat. Authority in the church lay in the elders, a few 'select persons' (never women, excluded from power by 'Statute-law' of Christ'), and in particular in the minister who alone had 'a Ministeriall Doctrinall authority' over all its members 'to instruct, rebuke, [and] exhort with all authority' (Cotton). These views, joined with Nye's determination, religious inflexibility, and exclusiveness, help to explain the quarrels that marked his career and the reservations of more moderate and ecumenical colleagues. His surviving legacy was not in England but, through the influence of the *Declaration of Faith* of the Savoy conference, in the congregational churches of New England.   BARBARA DONAGAN

Sources Wood, *Ath. Oxon.*, new edn · *Calamy rev.* · *The nonconformist's memorial … originally written by … Edmund Calamy*, ed. S. Palmer, [3rd edn], 3 vols. (1802–3) · T. Goodwin and others, *An apologeticall narration* (1643) · *Calendar of the correspondence of Richard Baxter*, ed. N. H. Keeble and G. F. Nuttall, 2 vols. (1991) · Foster, *Alum. Oxon.* · W. A. Shaw, *A history of the English church during the civil wars and under the Commonwealth, 1640–1660*, 2 vols. (1900) · T. Edwards, *Antapologia* (1644) · *The Winthrop papers*, ed. W. C. Ford and others, 3–5 (1943–7) · J. Cotton, *The keyes of the kingdom of heaven* (1644) · *The Clarke papers*, ed. C. H. Firth, [new edn], 2 vols. in 1 (1992) · M. Tolmie, *The triumph of the saints: the separate churches of London, 1616–1649* (1977) · K. L. Sprunger, *Dutch puritanism: a history of English and Scottish churches of the Netherlands in the sixteenth and seventeenth centuries* (1982) · A. E. Trout, 'Nonconformity in Hull', *Trans. Congregational Historical Society*, 9 (1924–6), 29–43 · B. M. Gardiner, ed., 'A secret negociation with Charles the First, 1643–4', *Camden miscellany, VIII*, CS, new ser., 31 (1883), 1–37 · Greaves & Zaller, *BDBR* · *DNB* · W. H. Challen, 'Nye family of Sussex and elsewhere', *N&Q*, 206 (1961), 284–8 · administration, Jan 1681, PRO, PROB 6/56, fol.1
Archives LPL, records of the Triers

Nye, Stephen (1647/8–1719), Church of England clergyman and religious controversialist, was the elder son of John *Nye (*bap.* 1620, *d.* 1686?), Church of England clergyman, and his first wife, Elizabeth Marshall (*d.* 1654). Nye's parentage linked him to leading puritan figures of the 1640s: his father's uncle was Philip Nye (whom the father was assisting at Acton, Middlesex, about the time of Stephen's birth), and his mother's father, Stephen Marshall. Ironically, John Nye was the author of an anti-Socinian tract.

Nye went to school in Cambridge before being admitted sizar at Magdalene College, Cambridge, on 11 March 1662, aged fourteen. After graduating BA in 1666, he was ordained deacon by the bishop of London in March 1667 and ordained priest by the bishop of Ely on 24 December 1671. On 25 March 1679 he became rector of Little Hormead, Hertfordshire, a poor living with a population of about 100 inhabitants. Here he spent the rest of his life, and here on 15 February 1690 he baptized his only child with his wife, Mary (*d.* 1713/14). Nye regularly read the service, preached 'once every Lord's day', and had 'an opportunity very seldom lacking of supplying some neighbouring cure' (*DNB*). It is clear from his will that he possessed a library of books, of which he undoubtedly made good use.

Nye early counted the businessman and philanthropist Thomas Firmin a close friend, and influenced his theological stance in the trinitarian controversy prompted by Sherlock's *Vindication of the Doctrine of the Trinity* (1690). He wrote a number of tracts which were published at Firmin's expense. A ready and erudite writer, he adopted a Sabellian attitude, regarding the persons of the Trinity as several modes of the one God. At the same time he stoutly defended his right to adhere to the Church of England. Publishing anonymously, as was then necessary to avoid legal punishment and social discrimination, he was the first writer to employ the term 'unitarian' in the English

language. This was in his *Brief History of the Unitarians, called also Socinians, in Four Letters to a Friend* (1687). The friend was Firmin, and an appended letter was by Henry Hedworth, layman and pamphleteer and follower of John Biddle (Bidle). Biddle had published the *Racovian Catechism* (in Latin) in 1652, a work based upon the writings of the Italian reformer Faustus Socinus, who denied both the deity and the pre-existence of Christ.

The so-called *Unitarian Tracts* (from 1694 onwards), to which Nye (and possibly also John Locke) contributed, were published and bound into at least five collections. Nye's *Considerations on the Explications of the Doctrine of the Trinity* (1694), addressed to Hedworth, and his *Institutions Considering the Holy Trinity* (1703), which the author considered his most mature work, were widely circulated. Nye was also the author of *Some Thoughts upon Dr Sherlock's Vindication of the Doctrine of the Holy Trinity* (1696), using phrases and quotations from Socinian scholars. In this tract he wrote, characteristically:

> I am neither a Papist nor a Lutheran, a Calvinist nor a Socinian … I am a Christian. I side only with Truth … and take shelter in the bosom of that Catholic Church which stands independently of anything under the name of a Party. (p. 18)

Nye's intention throughout was to define the doctrine of the Trinity in a way acceptable to the growing number of Anglican clergymen who found themselves unable to accept a doctrine capable of a tritheistic interpretation. Like John Locke, he believed in the truth and reasonableness of Christianity and not in metaphysical dogma. The writers of the tracts invariably used the term 'unitarian' in an inclusive sense, covering Sebellians, Arians, unitarianism, and Socinians, though the last of these names was regularly employed by the orthodox as a term of reproach and abuse. Nye is notable for propounding the principle common to unitarians and the Dutch and Irish remonstrants, that consciences ought to be free in matters of faith.

In 1712 Nye drew up a manuscript account of the glebe and tithes of Little Hormead, about which there had been disputes. His health declined, and he died on 6 January 1719. He was buried at Little Hormead four days later. In his will he remembered not only his family but his 'trusty friends and neighbours' and showed his concern for 'the poor'. His wife, Mary, predeceased him by five years.

H. J. McLACHLAN

Sources *DNB* · R. Wallace, *Anti-trinitarian biography*, 3 vols. (1850), vol. 1 · H. McLachlan, *The story of a nonconformist library* (1923), 53–87 · H. J. McLachlan, *Socinianism in seventeenth-century England* (1951) · E. Wilbur, *A history of Unitarianism in Transylvania, England, and America* (1952) · M. Watts, *The dissenters: from the Reformation to the French Revolution* (1978) · will, PRO, PROB 11/567, sig. 13, fols. 101*v*–102*r*

Nyerere, Julius Kambarage (1922–1999), president of Tanzania, was born on 13 April 1922 in Butiama, Tanganyika, one of twenty-six children of Chief Nyerere Burita, one of a number of chiefs in the small Zanaki tribe in western Tanganyika. He was educated at a local native authority primary school and at Tabora Boys' Secondary

Julius Kambarage Nyerere (1922–1999), by unknown photographer, 1960

School. At the age of twenty he was baptized a Roman Catholic and assumed his Christian name, Julius. His Roman Catholic faith continued to be important to him spiritually throughout his life.

Education and early political career After studying education at Makerere University College in Kampala, Uganda, Nyerere taught for three years (1946–9) at St Mary's School, Tabora. He then proceeded on a scholarship to Edinburgh University (1949–52), where he took a degree in history, philosophy, and economics, becoming the second Tanganyikan African to receive a degree from a university outside Africa. While in Edinburgh he joined the local Fabian Society, but also took a close interest in Scottish nationalism. When Kwame Nkrumah, leader of the nationalist movement in the Gold Coast, was released from prison and elected chief minister, Nyerere 'saw the Gold Coast students changing physically … They no longer looked like the rest of us. They carried themselves differently, stood up straighter, held their heads higher and looked like proud, independent people' (*The Scotsman*, 15 Oct 1999). On returning to Tanganyika he married, in April 1953, Maria Magige. They had five sons and two daughters.

Nyerere initially accepted a teaching post at a leading Catholic secondary school near Dar es Salaam. He had by that time developed a wide range of intellectual interests which ensured that he remained a reader of serious literature all his life. He was also a keen scholar of the language and literature of Swahili. Later, as a source of relaxation, he translated two of Shakespeare's plays, *Julius Caesar* and *The Merchant of Venice*, into Swahili verse. However, circumstances denied him a life of teaching and scholarship. From his earliest adult days he saw colonial rule as an offensive denial of African equality. In 1953 he became president of the African Association in Dar es Salaam, and in 1954 he resigned his teaching post and was elected the first president of the newly formed Tanganyika African National Union (TANU).

Within a year, TANU had a membership of 250,000, and could claim support throughout Tanganyika. In 1955 Nyerere presented the TANU programme to the United Nations Trusteeship Council, returning the following year. He advocated non-violence, but warned of widespread civil disobedience if TANU was ignored. 'I am a troublemaker because I believe in human rights strongly enough to be one', he declared (*Daily Telegraph*, 15 Oct 1999). In July 1957 he was appointed a member of the legislative council by the governor, Sir Edward Twining, but he resisted attempts to co-opt him and in December resigned in protest at government policies. From then on Tanganyika's advance to independence was remarkably swift. Nyerere was elected a member of the legislative council in 1958, and led his party in negotiations with Twining and his successor, Sir Richard Turnbull, resulting in elections under a new constitution in August 1960, in which TANU won seventy of the seventy-one elected seats, fifty-eight of them uncontested. Nyerere immediately became chief minister. After only thirteen months of responsible government, on 9 December 1961, Tanganyika became independent, with Nyerere its first prime minister. He became president of Tanganyika following the declaration of a republic in 1962, and president of Tanzania after the union of Tanganyika and Zanzibar in 1964.

President of Tanzania Nyerere was a slight and slim man of simple tastes and unassuming manners. Once elected president, he quickly decided against living in the grand Government House, the residence of the colonial governor, and instead built for himself a pleasant unostentatious beach house which remained his Dar es Salaam home throughout his life. His integrity, personal warmth, intelligence, and his commitment to the welfare of his people won for him the steadfast and lifelong loyalty and affection of almost all who worked with him, including such Asian and European colleagues as cabinet ministers Amir Jamal and al-Noor Kassam, his attorney-general, Roland Brown, and his personal assistant and trusted confidante for some forty years, Joan Wicken. In contrast to the titles often assumed by leaders of newly independent countries, Nyerere was universally and affectionately referred to as Mwalimu (Teacher).

Nyerere was one of the first African leaders to support the liberation struggle in southern Africa: he spoke in London in 1959 at the launch of the Boycott Movement, renamed the Anti-Apartheid Movement the following year. He remained one of the liberation struggle's most resolute allies, assisting its organizations, aiding its operations, and sheltering its leaders. This commitment to African self-rule brought him into conflict in the mid-1960s with both Britain and the United States, whom he pressed for much stronger initiatives in regard to oppression in southern Africa than they were willing to contemplate. He was particularly critical of Harold Wilson's handling of the Rhodesian problem.

Within Tanzania, Nyerere was centrally preoccupied with pursuing four domestic objectives: the development of the Tanzanian economy; securing national control of the direction of Tanzania's economic development; creating political institutions that would sustain the extraordinary sense of common purpose which in the early years united Tanzanians under his leadership and that of TANU; and building a just society in Tanzania, free of severe inequalities in income. He shared the first of these, the economic development of his country, with most other leaders of the newly independent colonial territories. Although he greatly valued the ethical values and close communal character of traditional African societies, he never romanticized the life of the African farmer who, with family, lived off the subsistence crops which she, as was so often the case, grew. He disapproved of the acquisitive individualism that exposure to the wealth of the developed world had begun to generate, but he did not wish Africans to be denied the undoubted advances in their welfare that greater wealth could bring. Indeed one of the reasons for the emphasis which in the mid-1970s he placed on moving the rural population from their scattered holdings into villages was that African peasants would then be much more accessible to agricultural extension workers, rural dispensaries, primary schools, and other agents of development.

Nyerere's second central concern—that Tanzania should not surrender control of the direction of its economic development—reflected not only nationalist aspirations but also a profound sense that integration into the international economic system would bring few advantages to the poorest countries if they could not manage that integration skilfully and selectively. This concern remained important to Nyerere throughout his life.

Nyerere's originality emerged in particular in his efforts to address his third and fourth preoccupations. He recognized from the start how shallow and unsubstantial were the roots of the Westminster model of constitutional government which the British had hurriedly transplanted in their final years in Tanganyika. By 1965 he was ready to replace it with a hybrid constitutional order, the democratic one-party state. This democratic one-party state was not a subterfuge either for oligarchic rule or for an ideological vanguard party on the Leninist model. It was a highly original effort carefully crafted to provide meaningful popular elections, greater answerability of the political leadership, and genuine political participation by ordinary Tanzanians, while protecting Tanzania from the divisive ethnic, regional, and religious factionalism which could easily destroy its fragile unity and which a fully open competition between rival parties might generate.

Nyerere was always steadfastly opposed to TANU becoming a closed party, ruled by an ideological élite. His belief in human equality, his recognition of the ease with which élites that are not answerable to the people become both corrupt and authoritarian, and the value he attached to the participation of ordinary citizens in the nation's political processes ensured that the genuine democratic elements in the Tanzanian one-party democracy were retained and rule by a self-appointed ideological vanguard was avoided. The democratic one-party state was never

without flaws and contradictions, and Nyerere was much criticized for his use of the Preventive Detention Act to silence his opponents. Nevertheless, for over twenty years the one-party system provided a largely unchallenged framework within which Tanzanians ordered their public affairs, enjoyed continuous and stable civilian rule, and engaged in the public discussion of party and government policies more freely than was permitted in most African states at that time. Then under Nyerere's close guidance the Tanzanian constitution was peacefully amended to permit competitive multi-party elections.

It is more difficult to appraise Nyerere's pursuit of the fourth of his central objectives, the building of a just society free from severe income differentials. He knew that Tanzania would be poor for a very long time and that the building of a just society would become vastly more difficult if severe class differences became entrenched. One of his most insistent and recurrent themes was that the members of the new African élite had to remain intimately integrated within Tanzanian society and willing to advance in material well-being together with, rather than vastly ahead of, ordinary Tanzanians. As early as 1962 he warned of the grave danger that Tanzania might be 'swamped by the temptation of personal gain or the abuse of power by those in authority' (J. Nyerere, *Ujamaa: the Basis of African Socialism*, 1962, 11). However, in the first years of independence he was unable to block significant salary increases and attractive perquisites of office for both party and government senior officials. He then observed that the members of this new bourgeoisie began to seek additional ways to augment their income. Moreover, he questioned the pattern of development that was occurring in the rural areas. He feared that the cultivation of cash crops on single farm holdings would undermine communal values and would lead to rural class stratification and the creation of a landless rural proletariat.

The major socialist initiatives taken in 1967 and shortly thereafter reflected Nyerere's conviction that, unless these trends were swiftly reversed, Tanzania would soon have sacrificed any chance of creating modern equivalents to its traditional communal and egalitarian values. The socialist measures which he introduced were breathtaking in range and scope. He sought to place Tanzania immediately and irrevocably on the road to a genuinely socialist society. The banks, the foreign-owned plantations, and important parts of the limited industrial sector were nationalized; an attempt was made to regulate a wide range of private economic activities; a stringent leadership code was introduced to contain corruption and to block private economic activities by senior politicians and officials; there was an extensive expropriation of household properties that were not occupied by their owners; there was a reform of the educational system designed to ensure that young Tanzanians would embrace the values and acquire the skills appropriate to a national society of equals; TANU took on the task of inducing peasants to farm collectively; and very large numbers of peasants were moved, sometimes forcibly, from their rural holdings to newly created villages.

The creation of effective democratic controls and a robust public ethic, and the pursuit of development strategies that would equitably share throughout the whole of Tanzanian society the material benefits of economic growth, were not as straightforward as Nyerere initially hoped. On the contrary, it soon became clear that many of his socialist initiatives were not appropriate instruments for the development of a very poor country, especially not all at once and in a country whose public service was already overextended. They caused a severe economic slowdown and a good deal of administrative chaos. So much so, indeed, that by the early 1980s Nyerere and his colleagues came to recognize that many of these initiatives had hindered the accomplishment of their objectives, and they accepted and facilitated a 180 degree change in the direction of Tanzania's economic policies.

Retirement In 1985 Nyerere handed over power to his vice-president, Ali Hassan Mwinyi, though he remained chairman of the Chama Cha Mapinduzi (Revolutionary Party) for another five years. He returned to his home village of Butiama, and 'eased gradually into the role of benign elder statesman' (*Daily Telegraph*, 15 Oct 1999). In his last years he devoted much time to two major international issues, the search for justice and reconciliation in Burundi, and the strengthening of the South Centre, an organization striving to be the seed of a southern parallel to the Organization for Economic Co-operation and Development. He died at St Thomas's Hospital, London, on 14 October 1999, of leukaemia, and was survived by his wife, Maria, and their seven children. He was buried in Butiama following a state funeral in Dar es Salaam on 21 October, attended by numerous heads of government from Africa and further afield. CRANFORD PRATT

Sources C. Pratt, *The critical phase in Tanzania, 1945–1968: Nyerere and the emergence of a socialist strategy* (1976) · C. Pratt, 'Julius Nyerere: the ethical foundation of his legacy', *Round Table*, 355 (July 2000), 365–7 · M. Bates, 'Tanganyika', *African one party states*, ed. G. Carter (1962), 395–483 · L. Cliffe, *One party democracy* (1967) · L. Cliffe and J. Saul, eds., *Socialism in Tanzania*, 2 vols. (1972–3) · B. C. Nindi, 'Compulsion in the implementation of Ujamaa', *Capitalism, socialism and the development crisis in Tanzania*, ed. N. O'Neiland and K. Mustafa (1990), 62–8 · J. Boesen, K. J. Havnevik, J. Koponen, and R. Odgaard, eds., *Tanzania: crisis and struggle for survival* (1981) · R. Yeager, *Tanzania: an African experiment*, 2nd edn (1989) · J. C. Scott, *Seeing like a state* (1998) · Lady Listowel, *The making of Tanganyika* (1963) · B. Mwansasu and C. Pratt, *Towards socialism in Tanzania* (1979) · *The Times* (15 Oct 1999) · *The Guardian* (15 Oct 1999) · *Daily Telegraph* (15 Oct 1999) · *The Independent* (15 Oct 1999) · *The Scotsman* (15 Oct 1999) · WWW · *International who's who* · personal knowledge (2004)

Archives National Archives of Tanzania, Dar-es-Salaam · University of Dar-es-Salaam Library, Tanzania

Likenesses photograph, 1960, Hult. Arch. [*see illus.*] · photograph, 1967, repro. in *Daily Telegraph* · photograph, 1983, repro. in *The Times* · J. Bown, photograph, repro. in *The Guardian* · photograph, repro. in *The Independent* · photograph, repro. in *The Scotsman*

Nyholm, Sir Ronald Sydney (1917–1971), chemist, was born at Broken Hill, New South Wales, on 29 January 1917, the fourth of six children of Eric Edward Nyholm (1878–1932), a railway guard, and his wife, Gertrude Mary Woods, of Marryatsville, South Australia. His paternal grandfather, Erik Nyholm (1850–1887), had emigrated to Australia from Finland in 1873. Following education at the local high school, where his interest in chemistry was aroused, he entered the University of Sydney in 1934. Here, under the influence of the philosopher J. Anderson, Nyholm became a freethinker in religion while he pursued a training in chemistry under C. E. Fawsitt, T. Iredale, and G. J. Burrows, the last inspiring Nyholm's lifetime interest in co-ordination compounds.

After graduating in 1938 with first-class honours, Nyholm joined the Ever Ready Battery Company in Sydney as a research chemist. In 1940 he was appointed a lecturer at Sydney Technical College, where he began to collaborate with F. P. J. Dwyer (1910–1962) on the co-ordination compounds of rhodium, using tertiary arsine ligands. In 1947, having published more than twenty papers in Australian chemical journals, he sailed from Sydney to join C. K. Ingold at University College, London, in the department of chemistry. Nyholm was first an Imperial Chemical Industries fellow, but was appointed to a lectureship in 1950. He gained a London PhD in 1950 and DSc in 1953 (he had received a Sydney MSc in 1942). He left London in 1951 to become an associate professor in inorganic chemistry in the University of New South Wales the following year. In 1955, at Ingold's insistence, he returned to a chair of inorganic chemistry at University College, a post which he occupied with distinction until his death. From 1963 he was head of the department of chemistry.

Nyholm was a cricket devotee, with precise recall of scorecards and events, especially from the era of Donald Bradman. He was himself a competent and spirited performer on the field. In 1948 he married Maureen, daughter of Norman Richard Richardson, merchant, of Sydney. They had one son and two daughters.

Nyholm's contributions to inorganic chemistry were in the stabilization of new or unusual valence states, in stereochemistry, and in magnetochemistry. With Francis Dwyer he prepared the first properly characterized complex of the metal rhodium in its quadrivalent state and later made complexes of trivalent nickel and of quadrivalent nickel and iron. In his inaugural address at University College in 1956, entitled 'The renaissance of inorganic chemistry' (*Journal of Chemical Education*, 34, 1957, 166–9), he spoke of inorganic chemistry growing from 'a collection of largely unconnected facts' into 'the integrated study of the formation, composition, structure and reactions of the chemical elements and their compounds, excepting most of those of carbon'. In his work on stereochemistry, especially with Professor Ronald Gillespie, he aimed to systematize understanding of the spatial arrangement of inorganic molecules. This work was a lasting advance and greatly clarified the teaching of the subject, in which he excelled. His studies of the complexes of the transition metals, particularly nickel and iron, were notable for his use of physical methods, especially magnetic susceptibility, in investigating molecular structure and bond types.

New thinking in the 1950s and 1960s about chemical education in schools and universities roused Nyholm's enthusiasm. He was the first chairman of the Nuffield Foundation's chemistry consultative committee in 1962, and oversaw the creation of the Nuffield O level chemistry materials. His sympathy with schoolteachers, personal warmth, and ability to convince formed a powerful combination and were especially evident in the series of annual summer schools for teachers that he established at University College in 1957. The Association for Science Education made him president in 1967. The establishment of a new British journal, *Education in Chemistry*, in 1964 owed much to his persuasive skills.

Nyholm was a member of the chemistry committee of the Department of Scientific and Industrial Research in 1961–4, its chairman in 1964–7, and a member of the Science Research Council from 1967 to 1971. The British Museum elected him a trustee in 1968. He was Corday-Morgan medallist (1950), Tilden lecturer (1960), and Liversidge lecturer (1967)—all of the Chemical Society—and its president in 1968–70. In that office he saw to completion the amalgamation, long in the making, of the Chemical Society, Faraday Society, Royal Institute of Chemistry, and the Society for Analytical Chemistry. He was elected FRS in 1958, and the next year a corresponding member of the Finnish Chemical Society, which gave him much pleasure. The Italian Chemical Society (1968) and the University of Bologna (1969) bestowed honours on him. He held honorary doctorates of the University of East Anglia (1968), the City University (1968), and the University of New South Wales (1969). He was knighted in 1967. He died in a motor-car accident on the outskirts of Cambridge on 4 December 1971.

Nyholm's success as a teacher and in both scientific research and public science reflected high qualities of personality coupled with technical flair. His Australian irreverence cut through pomposity, deviousness, and flannel, and but for his early death he would undoubtedly have become Britain's leading scientific statesman. In his address at Nyholm's memorial service Lord Annan, provost of University College, described him as 'a life enhancer' and went on to say: 'Wherever he was, he raised the temperature. But he raised it not with pugnacious self-assertiveness but with bonhomie, good sense, and enthusiasm' (Maccoll, 341). D. P. CRAIG, *rev.* W. H. BROCK

Sources D. P. Craig, *Memoirs FRS*, 18 (1972), 445–75 · A. Maccoll, *Chemistry in Britain*, 8 (1972), 3.341 · *The Times* (6 Dec 1971), 17g · *The Times* (7 Dec 1971), 16g · *The Times* (15 Dec 1971), 17g · W. H. Brock, *Fontana history of chemistry* (1992), chap. 15 · WWW
Archives UCL, chemistry department MSS
Likenesses W. Birch, photograph, RS; repro. in Craig, *Memoirs FRS*, 445
Wealth at death £3659: probate, 7 April 1972, *CGPLA Eng. & Wales*

Nyndge, Alexander (*fl.* 1574), demoniac, was the son of William Nyndge, a gentleman of Herringswell, Suffolk. William was the wealthiest inhabitant of Herringswell, according to the subsidy assessment of 1568. What fame Alexander Nyndge has he owes to his brother, Edward, who not only directed the exorcism of Alexander but published an account of it. Edward, who was about thirty years old at the time of his brother's possession, had graduated MA from Christ's College, Cambridge, and was subsequently a fellow of Gonville and Caius College.

His education probably explains Edward's commanding role in his brother's exorcism, despite the presence of his parents and the town curate. On 20 January 1574, about 7 p.m., Alexander had a seizure. Edward was immediately convinced that this seizure was the work of an evil spirit. Edward addressed the spirit, telling him that he was a master of arts of Cambridge and ordering him by the death and passion of Christ to state why he was troubling Alexander. Getting no response, Edward had neighbours brought in and led them in prayer. Edward once again commanded the spirit, in the name of Jesus, to speak. A voice, deeper than Alexander's usual voice, issued from Edward's brother and said that he came for Alexander's soul. The people present began to pray to God and the Virgin Mary, whereupon Edward sharply rebuked them, declaring that such prayers 'offend God'. In obedience to Edward's instructions pieces of paper with biblical verses written on them were laid on Alexander's body and the windows were left open. Alexander's convulsions ceased about 11 p.m., and Edward declared that the demon was cast out of his brother. But in the next nine hours, Alexander had two fits. Finally, Edward instructed the town curate to read from the Bible while the bystanders prayed. This time the exorcism was successful, though in a second edition of his account of his brother's possession, published in 1615, Edward stated that Alexander was tormented by demons for a further six months, until 23 July. Nothing further is known of either Alexander or Edward Nyndge.

The exorcism of Alexander Nyndge contained a mixture of folkloric elements (the placing of biblical verses on Alexander's body) and the characteristics of later puritan exorcisms (the reliance on group prayer to expel the demon). And Edward Nyndge, with his instant diagnosis of possession, his control of his brother's exorcism, and his concern to see that it did not involve practices which would 'offend God', was a precursor of such later puritan exorcists as John Foxe and John Darrell.

THOMAS S. FREEMAN

Sources E. Nyndge, *A booke declaring the fearfull vexasion of one Alexander Nyndge* [1574] · E. Nyndge, *A true and fearefull vexation of one Alexander Nyndge* (1615)

Nyren, John (1764–1837), cricket historian, son of Richard *Nyren (1734–1797) [see under Hambledon cricket club] and his wife, Frances Pennycud (*c.*1740–*c.*1830), of Slindon, in Sussex, was born at Hambledon, Hampshire, on 15 December 1764. The Nyrens bore the Sussex name variously known as Nieren or Niering—the latter being the name borne by John's grandfather. Research in the 1990s challenged the accepted view that they were of Jacobite origin and kinsmen of the Nairnes who supported the Jacobite risings in 1715. There remains, nevertheless, the testimony of John Nyren's granddaughter Mary Nyren, who recalled being told that her grandfather had compared watch-chain seals with William, Lord Nairne, towards the end of his life and found the crests on them were identical

(Lucas, 99). Richard Nyren, whom his son later called 'a thorough-bred old English yeoman', had learned his cricket from his uncle Richard Newland at Slindon. He moved to Hambledon, where he became 'the chosen General of all the matches' acting as secretary to the cricket club and playing an intermediary role between its aristocratic patrons and the players themselves. As a player, he scored 98 for Hambledon against Surrey in 1775 and 70 against England in 1776 but he is known chiefly for his stewardship of the club's affairs and his role as landlord of the Bat and Ball inn at Hambledon.

John Nyren was educated by a Jesuit who taught him a little Latin, 'but I was a better hand at the fiddle'. He interested himself in cricket at an early age, 'being since 1778 a sort of farmer's pony to my native club of Hambledon'. He was a left-handed batsman who played a few times for Hambledon in the club's last years in the 1780s. In 1799 he joined the newly formed Homerton club, then second in importance only to the slightly older Marylebone Cricket Club. For the one against the other at Lord's in 1801 he made 49. He played for England from 1802 to 1805 and appeared for the Gentlemen in 1806 in the first ever match against the Players. Cricket was for him a 'recreation, not an occupation'. His last match of importance was for Lord Frederick Beauclerk's eleven at Lord's in 1817 against a team raised by William Ward. It was to Ward that Nyren later dedicated the book on which his reputation rests. This was *The Young Cricketer's Tutor and the Cricketers of my Time* 'by John Nyren: the whole collected and edited by Charles Cowden Clarke' (1833).

By the time of the book's publication Nyren—'still a sort of youth at seventy, hale and vigorous and with a merry twinkle of his eye'—was living in London. He had become part of a cultural and social circle that included Leigh Hunt (who wrote those words in 1834), Charles Lamb, the organist, composer, and publisher Vincent Novello, and Novello's son-in-law the Shakespearian scholar Charles Cowden Clarke. While he played the violin and talked music with Novello, Nyren chatted on cricket to Clarke and out of their conversations emerged the book. The first part is severely functional and didactic but the second sees the old Hambledon club and its great players through the rose-coloured spectacles of nostalgia at a distance of some forty years. Nyren evokes their way of life as much as their cricket, and provides what John Arlott called one of 'the few peasant portraits in the language'.

There are Tom Walker and his brother Harry—'never sure came two such unadulterated rustics into a civilized community'; John Small who charmed 'a vicious bull' with his fiddle; George Lear, the longstop, 'as sure of the ball as if he had been a sandbank'; Tom Suetor, 'the manliest and most graceful of hitters' and the sweetest of tenors; David Harris, the bowler, whom 'Phidias would have taken as a model'; Lamborn, the shepherd, 'a plain-spoken bumpkin' whose off-breaks were too good for the duke of Dorset; and William Beldham (Silver Billy), the only Hambledon player to survive into the photographic age.

These men have passed into the folklore of cricket history yet intriguing questions remain about their biographer. Talented as he undoubtedly was as a musician, it seems doubtful that he could have aspired to such flights of fancy as a writer. He readily conceded Clarke's editorship and his friend must have had the wit and wisdom to capture the romantic enthusiasm of the spoken word. Mrs Cowden Clarke in her autobiography, *My Long Life* (1896), recalled 'the chuckling pride' with which Nyren told his tale to her husband. The book won instant praise from the reviewers, including Hunt in the *London Journal* and John Mitford in the *Gentleman's Magazine*. It ran to eleven editions in twenty-five years. Over a hundred years later Arlott wrote that it was 'one of the very few books ever written on any game which [could] stand squarely upon its merits outside the literature of sport'.

John Nyren left Hambledon on his marriage in 1791 to Cleopha Copp (b. 1775), a 'wealthy' sixteen-year-old girl of German parentage. They settled in Portsea, Hampshire, before moving to Bromley in Kent and then to Battersea. He was a calico printer on a large scale until his premises were burnt down. During the years of his literary and musical friendships he lived in Cheyne Walk, Chelsea. In 1824 at Lord's he met the sixth Lord Nairne (whose attainted title George IV had restored), which is how the two men came to compare watch-chains.

Some seventy years after Nyren's death the essayist E. V. Lucas became acquainted with his granddaughter, who set down her memories for him. Nyren had 'an instinctive admiration of everything good and tasteful, both in nature and art'. He was a good enough composer to have three of his pieces published by Novello, including an *Ave verum*, and he had been for thirteen years choirmaster at St Mary Moorfields, where Novello himself was organist.

Nyren's wife predeceased him. They had three daughters, one of whom—Mary A. Nyren (1796–1844)—became superior lady abbess of the English convent at Bruges. Nyren died at Bromley, Kent, on 30 June 1837, and was buried in Bromley churchyard.

John Nyren (*fl.* 1827–1830), an officer in HM customs and author of *Tables of the Duties, Bounties, and Drawbacks of Customs* (1827; 4th edn, 1830), was a first cousin of the cricket historian. The two were confused in the catalogue of the British Museum Library.   GERALD M. D. HOWAT

Sources [A. Haygarth], *Frederick Lillywhite's cricket scores and biographies*, 1 (1862) · F. S. Ashley-Cooper, *Hambledon cricket chronicle, 1772–1796* (1924) · J. Goulstone, *Hambledon: the men and the myths* (2001) · D. Underdown, *Start of play* (2000) · E. V. Lucas, *The Hambledon men* (1907) · J. Arlott, ed., *From Hambledon to Lord's* (1948) · J. Mitford, *GM*, 1st ser., 103/2 (1833), 41–6, 235–40 · J. Mitford, 'John Nyren', *GM*, 2nd ser., 8 (1837), 213 · E. V. Lucas, *English leaves* (1933) · L. Hunt, *Leigh Hunt's London Journal* (21 May 1834) · *DNB*

Likenesses British School, oils, c.1805, MCC Pavilion, Lord's, London · F. Grehan, drawing, 1844 (after drawing by E. Novello), repro. in Lucas, *Hambledon men*

Nyren, John (*fl.* 1827–1830). *See under* Nyren, John (1764–1837).

Nyren, Richard (1734–1797). *See under* Hambledon cricket club (*act.* c.1750–c.1796).

Nyth-brân, Guto. *See* Morgan, Griffith (1700–1737).

Oakeley, Sir Charles, first baronet (1751–1826), administrator in India, second son of William Oakeley (*d*. 1803), rector of Forton, Staffordshire, and his wife, Christian (*d*. 1790), daughter of Sir Patrick Strachan, was born at the rectory, Forton, on 27 February 1751. After attending Shrewsbury School, he obtained, through his father's friend, Lady Clive, a nomination to a writership on the East India Company's Madras establishment. He was appointed in October 1766, and arrived in Madras on 6 June 1767. For five or six years he was assistant to the secretary to the civil department; in January 1773 he was promoted to succeed Mr Goodlad in the secretaryship; and in May 1777 he was given the corresponding post in the military and political department, combined with the offices of judge advocate-general and translator. That year, on 19 October, he married Helena (*d*. 1839), only daughter of Robert Beatson of Kilrie, Fife, a woman of great energy and artistic talent. Oakeley's superiors noted his diligence, but he was compelled to resign in November 1780 because of ill health.

In the summer of 1781, when Lord Macartney, the governor of Madras, had succeeded in obtaining from the nawab of Arcot an assignment of his revenues to defray the expenses of the war in the Carnatic, a committee, called the committee of assigned revenue, was appointed to superintend the collection of the revenues. Of this committee Oakeley was made president. He began his duties in January 1782. In spite of the hostility of the nawab's servants and subjects, and of the great extent of Haidar Ali's conquests in the territories of the nawab, the board succeeded in raising the Arcot contribution to the war fund from 1¼ *pagodas* to nearly 44 *pagodas*. Most of this was used to feed the company's army, but a considerable surplus was handed over to the nawab on the conclusion of the war in March 1784. For these services the committee was publicly thanked by the governor-general and the council of Bengal; and even Burke, in his speech 'on the Nabob of Arcot's debts' spoke of its services in high terms.

Oakeley's achievements in Arcot led to his appointment in April 1786 by Sir Archibald Campbell to the presidency of the new board of revenue of Madras. Family affairs, however, compelled him to resign early in 1788, and in February 1789 he sailed for Europe on board the *Manship*. Although he had been twenty-two years in India, he still lacked seniority in membership in the council, so had little expectation of promotion. Pitt and Dundas, however, to whom Campbell had recommended him, pressed him to return, and, the court of directors having in 1789 placed on record its high appreciation of his services, he was in April 1790 appointed to succeed General Medows as governor of Madras, and was also gazetted a baronet on 5 June. It was expected that Medows would be transferred to the governorship of Bengal, and Oakeley was accordingly sworn in as governor. But when the news arrived of the outbreak of fresh hostilities with Tipu Sultan, Medows's transfer was postponed, and Oakeley was placed second in

Sir Charles Oakeley, first baronet (1751–1826), by John Smart, 1786

council at Madras. He arrived in Madras on 15 October 1790 and, finding General Medows in the field, assumed, in his absence, charge of the civil administration of Madras, a task made doubly difficult by the great and constant needs of the army, and the extreme financial embarrassment of the company's Madras exchequer. As this was largely due to lack of public confidence in the government, Oakeley, instead of borrowing from Bengal or Europe, proceeded to improve the administration of Madras. He retrenched expenses, enforced a more efficient collection of revenue, and exacted a subsidy of 10 lakhs (Rs 1 million) per annum from the raja of Travancore, on the grounds that the company was defending him against Tipu. But perhaps the measure which most tended to restore public credit was the resumption of cash payments for all army and public obligations, which had previously been made only in the case of the most pressing debts. The only exception which he made was in the case of his own official salary, which remained unpaid until the close of the war, though he had meantime to borrow money at 12 per cent for his own private expenses.

These measures were taken only just in time. On 26 May 1791 Lord Cornwallis, the governor-general, had come south to take charge of the army, but was forced to retire from Seringapatam, destroying his battering train for lack of transport. Heavy requisitions were consequently made on the Madras government for draught cattle, stores, and funds. Fortunately, Oakeley's reforms had enabled the presidency revenue to meet a large portion of the expenses of the war: Cornwallis's needs were promptly and amply met. Oakeley poured into the field of operations money, grain, and cattle. Cornwallis recognized the value of this assistance, and the Bengal presidency benefited greatly by the ability of Madras to bear so large a part of the burden. On the conclusion of the war in March 1792 General Medows left Madras, and Oakeley entered on the full authority of governor. Cornwallis did not, in fact, have a very high opinion of Oakeley's ability to carry out needed reforms in Madras, but he concluded that at least he was the best of the company's servants (*Correspondence of … Cornwallis*, 2.170).

Oakeley first attacked the question of the company's debt. Accordingly, when the news reached India, in June 1793, of the outbreak of war with France, a fully equipped army was promptly dispatched against Pondicherry, and 5 lakhs of *pagodas* (about Rs 1,750,000) remitted to Bengal without damaging the government's credit. The Pondicherry expedition was planned and directed by the Madras government, and had in fact been undertaken on Oakeley's own responsibility some weeks in advance of instructions from Britain, and as soon as the news of the outbreak of war arrived overland. It was successfully completed by the fall of Pondicherry in August 1793. On 7 September 1794 Oakeley handed over the government to Lord Hobart. He returned to England, where he received, on 5 August 1795, the thanks of the court of directors for his eminent services. Not the least of these was his revenue work, which, however painful its immediate impact on the peasants, laid the foundation for a modern system of government in the Madras region.

Always much attached to the region in which he had spent his early years, Oakeley settled at The Abbey, Shrewsbury, near his father, who was now rector of Holy Cross, Shrewsbury, and lived there until in 1810 he moved to the bishop's palace, Lichfield. A seat in parliament had been offered him by Sir William Pulteney during his visit to England in 1789, but the offer was declined. Shortly after his final return he was informally sounded as to his willingness to be considered for the governor-generalship; this he also declined. He corresponded with Dundas on Indian affairs from time to time, but for the most part occupied himself with classical studies and with the education of his sons. At the time of the expected invasion by Napoleon Bonaparte, Oakeley commanded a volunteer regiment of foot raised in Shrewsbury.

Although he had served the East India Company in Madras at a time when it was a byword for corruption and oppression, people who knew him after his return to England spoke of his 'fervent and unaffected piety' and his generosity in support of local charitable institutions (*GM*, 371). Having been acquainted with the educational work in Madras of Dr Andrew Bell, he assisted in the establishment of the National Society's schools on Bell's system in Shrewsbury and Lichfield. He died at his home, the bishop's palace, Lichfield, on 7 September 1826, and was buried privately at Forton. There is a monument to his memory by Chantrey in Lichfield Cathedral.

The Oakeleys had eleven children, ten of whom survived him, including his sons Sir Herbert *Oakeley and Frederick *Oakeley; a third son, Henry, became a judge of the supreme court, Calcutta, and predeceased his father by a few months, dying on 2 May 1826.

J. A. HAMILTON, rev. AINSLIE T. EMBREE

Sources C. C. Prinsep, *Record of services of the Honourable East India Company's civil servants in the Madras presidency from 1741 to 1858* (1885) • BL OIOC, board of control MSS [minutes] • *The private correspondence of Lord Macartney, governor of Madras*, ed. C. Collin Davies, CS, 3rd ser., 77 (1950) • *GM*, 1st ser., 96/2 (1826), 371 • *Correspondence of Charles, first Marquis Cornwallis*, ed. C. Ross, 3 vols. (1859) • *Some account of the services of Sir Charles Oakeley, bart. in India … drawn up by himself*, ed. H. Oakeley (1836) • E. Lodge, *The peerage and baronetage of the British empire*, [new edn] (1881) • IGI

Archives BL OIOC, corresp. relating to India, home misc. series • BL OIOC, letter-book, MS Eur. D 746 | BL, Macartney MSS, Add. MSS 22415–22464 • Bodl. Oxf., Macartney MSS, MSS Eng. hist. c. 66–117 and b. 173–186

Likenesses J. Smart, miniature, 1786; Christies, 27 March 1984, lot 290 [*see illus.*] • Chantrey, monument, Lichfield Cathedral, Staffordshire • S. W. Reynolds, mezzotint (after T. Barber), BM, NPG

Oakeley, Frederick (1802–1880), Roman Catholic convert, priest, and author, was born on 5 September 1802, at the Abbey House, Shrewsbury, the eleventh and youngest child of Sir Charles *Oakeley, first baronet (1751–1826), former governor of Madras, and his wife, Helena (d. 1839), only daughter of Robert Beatson. His elder brother, Sir Herbert *Oakeley, third baronet, later became a Church of England clergyman. In 1806 he broke the thigh bone in his right leg, which left him with a pronounced limp for the rest of his life, and ill health continued throughout his childhood. Apart from a short period as a day scholar at the grammar school in Lichfield in 1814, he was educated by his parents at home until he was sent to a private tutor, Charles Sumner, later bishop of Winchester, in 1817. In June 1820 Oakeley matriculated from Christ Church, Oxford, gaining a second class degree in *literae humaniores* in 1824. After graduation he decided to stay at Oxford and study for a college fellowship. He won the chancellor's Latin and English essay prizes in 1825 and 1827 respectively, and the Ellerton theological prize also in 1827.

He was elected as chaplain fellow of Balliol in March 1827. He was ordained deacon by the bishop of London at the Chapel Royal, Whitehall, and priest one week later, by his former tutor Charles Sumner, now bishop of Llandaff. In 1830 he became tutor and catechetical lecturer at Balliol, and in 1832 a prebendary of Lichfield Cathedral. Among his students at Balliol was Archibald Campbell Tait, for whom he retained a lifelong friendship. In 1831 he was select preacher at Oxford, and in 1835 one of the public examiners to the university. In 1837, on the recommendation of Edward Pusey, Bishop C. J. Blomfield of London appointed him preacher for the University of Oxford at the Chapel Royal, Whitehall. On this appointment Oakeley resigned his tutorship, but retained his fellowship and his prebendal stall at Lichfield until he joined the Roman Catholic church in 1845. He was a friend of John Henry Newman through their membership of a small dining club which met in the years 1829–33, but Oakeley's period of evangelicalism from about 1830 to 1835 ensured that he played no role in the earliest days of the Oxford Movement. His growing attraction to the movement was due partly to his friendship with William George Ward, a fellow of Balliol from 1834, and partly to the influence of Froude's *Remains*, published in 1838. Oakeley and Ward became firm friends and almost inseparable companions during their remaining years in the Church of England. Oakeley's Whitehall sermons were published in 1839 and prefaced by a long essay in which he declared his commitment to the principles of the Oxford Movement. In July 1839 he was licensed as minister of Margaret Chapel, the predecessor of All Saints, Margaret Street, and moved to London.

During his six years at Margaret Street (1839–45) Oakeley transformed an undistinguished little chapel into a centre of musical and liturgical excellence. Among his congregation were Edward Bellasis, Alexander Beresford-Hope, and William Ewart Gladstone. After his arrival at Margaret Street, the Oxford Movement took on the appearance of two movements—one at Oxford concerned with doctrine, and the other at London concerned with ceremonial—and Oakeley's great strength was as a competent and acknowledged authority on liturgy. Writing more than fifty years later, R. W. Church (371) remembered Oakeley as

the first to realize the capacities of the Anglican ritual for impressive devotional use, and his services are still remembered by some as having realized for them in a way never since surpassed, the secrets and consolations of the worship of the Church.

Oakeley had a love of music, inherited from his mother, and formed a choir. Samuel Wilberforce visited the chapel in 1844 and was critical of everything except the Gregorian chanting, which he found 'quite marvellously beautiful' (A. R. Ashwell and R. G. Wilberforce, *Life of Samuel Wilberforce*, 1880, 1.237). In 1843 Oakeley published a preface on antiphonal chanting to Richard Redhead's *Laudes diurnae*, and his English translation of 'Adeste fideles' ('O come, all ye faithful') in 1841 guaranteed him an abiding place in English hymnology.

After the publication of Tract 90 in 1841, Oakeley became the most prominent member of an unofficial 'Romeward' section of the Oxford Movement, a new and younger generation that caused much embarrassment to Newman. In the same year he published a controversial article on Bishop Jewel in the *British Critic*. The article was heavily critical of the English sixteenth-century protestant reformers and prompted William Palmer to write the first history of the Oxford Movement. The year 1845 was a turning point in Oakeley's life. The publication of Ward's *Ideal of a Christian Church* in 1844 fuelled increasing agitation against the Romeward movement. In response Oakeley published a tract in which he asserted a claim 'to hold, as distinct from teaching, all Roman doctrine'. He was cited before the court of arches by the bishop of London and, although he resigned his licence before the trial began, he was suspended on 30 June 1845 from all clerical duty in the province of Canterbury until he had 'retracted his errors'.

In September 1845 Oakeley joined Newman's community at Littlemore and, on 29 October, he was received into the Roman Catholic church in the little chapel at St Clement's over Magdalen Bridge, Oxford, three weeks after Newman. On 1 November he was confirmed, with Newman, at Oscott, and was a seminarian at St Edmund's College, near Ware, from January 1846 to August 1848. In the summer of 1848 he joined the staff of St George's Cathedral, Southwark. On 22 January 1850 he was made missionary rector of St John's Church, Duncan Terrace, Islington; the church had opened in 1843 and was still heavily in debt. He remained there, increasingly lame and with failing eyesight until his death, ministering to a large Irish congregation who affectionately called him 'our Father O'Kelly'. He received no preferment beyond being created a canon of the diocese of Westminster in 1852. R. W. Church went to see him and regretted this fact:

The Romans made nothing of him, but sent him up to Islington to live poorly in a poor house with two Irish colleagues, with just a print or two and a few books remaining of the Oxford wreck, which was the overthrow of his old idea of life. (B. A. Smith, *Dean Church: the Anglican Response to Newman*, 1958, 225)

He continued to publish many works on aspects of liturgy and devotion, notably *The Ceremonies of the Mass* (1855), a standard work at Rome, where it was translated into Italian by Lorenzo Santarelli. He was elected a member of the Roman Academy of Letters in 1868. He remained in touch with Newman, Ward, and the other converts of 1845 until the end of his life, and from the mid-1850s he renewed his links with Tait, warmly congratulating him on his appointment as bishop of London in 1856 and archbishop of Canterbury in 1868. The two men remained fond of each other, despite their divergence, and Oakeley could sometimes be persuaded to dine quietly with his former pupil at Fulham and Lambeth palaces. In 1872 he was invited to dine at high table in Balliol College, and was touched by Tait's speech, in which the archbishop said how much he owed to his former tutor.

Oakeley died at 39 Duncan Terrace, Islington, on 29 January 1880, and was buried at Kensal Green cemetery. To his contemporaries he was a memorable figure. Newman, in his *Apologia*, was impressed by his literary ability and classical cast of mind, while R. W. Church recalled his patience, kindness, and gentle humour. Others left more vivid portraits: Thomas Mozley (2.5) remembered him

limping about the streets of London … a misshapen fabric of bare bones upon which hung some very shabby canonicals. Yet his eye was bright, and his voice, though sorrowful, was kind, and he was always glad to meet an old friend.

E. Bourne (p. 361) remembered him as being

short in stature and halting in gait, with a rough shock head and features deeply lined. … His first word arrested the attention, and the fascination increased with every sentence that he uttered. His sincerity was so evident … his reasoning so lucid and his choice of language so exquisite—that when his sharp metallic voice ceased to be heard … all remained clearly fixed upon the mind for future meditation.

PETER GALLOWAY

Sources P. J. Galloway, 'Frederick Oakeley: the career of a Tractarian', PhD diss., U. Lond., 1987 · P. J. Galloway, *A passionate humility: Frederick Oakeley and the Oxford movement* (1999) · E. Bellasis, *Memorials of Mr Serjeant Bellasis*, 2nd edn (1895) · E. Bourne, 'Old Margaret Street Chapel', *Merry England*, 4 (1884–5), 357–63 · L. M. Quiller-Couch, ed., *Reminiscences of Oxford by Oxford men, 1559–1850*, OHS, 22 (1892) · T. Mozley, *Reminiscences, chiefly of Oriel College and the Oxford Movement*, 2 vols. (1882) · E. M. Oakeley, *Frederick Oakeley and some sidelights on the Oxford movement* (1922) · F. Oakeley, *Historical notes on* the Tractarian movement (1865) • F. Oakeley, Personal reminiscences of the "Oxford Movement" (1855) • R. W. Church, The Oxford Movement: twelve years, 1833–1845 (1891) • W. Benham and R. T. Davidson, Life of Archibald Campbell Tait, 2 vols. (1891) • Correspondence on church and religion of William Ewart Gladstone, ed. D. C. Lathbury, 2 vols. (1910)

Archives Balliol Oxf., commonplace book; MS autobiography | Birmingham Oratory, letters to J. H. Newman • BL, corresp. with W. E. Gladstone, Add. MSS 44356–44786 • Bodl. Oxf., corresp. with H. E. Manning • Bodl. Oxf., letters to Samuel Wilberforce • LPL, corresp. with A. C. Tait • Pusey Oxf., letters to E. B. Pusey • Westm. DA, letters to W. R. Cawthorne, N. P. S. Wiseman, etc.

Likenesses engraving, repro. in Bourne, 'Old Margaret Street Chapel', facing p. 357

Wealth at death under £300: probate, 13 Feb 1880, CGPLA Eng. & Wales

Oakeley, Sir Herbert, third baronet (1791–1845), Church of England clergyman, third son of Sir Charles *Oakeley, first baronet (1751–1826), and his wife, Helena, née Beatson (d. 1839), was born at Madras, where his father was governor, on 10 February 1791. Frederick *Oakeley, the Tractarian and convert to Rome, was his younger brother. His parents took him to England in 1794, and, after some years at Westminster School, he entered Christ Church, Oxford. In 1810 he took a first class in literae humaniores; he graduated BA on 23 February 1811 and obtained a senior studentship. At the installation of Lord Grenville as chancellor on 6 July in the same year he recited, in the Sheldonian Theatre, with excellent effect, a congratulatory ode of his own composition. He proceeded MA on 4 November 1813. Having been ordained, he became in 1814 domestic chaplain to William Howley, then bishop of London, to whom he owed his subsequent preferment, and lived with the bishop for twelve years, until his marriage. He was presented by Bishop Howley to the vicarage of Ealing in 1822, and to the prebendal stall of Wenlock's Barn in St Paul's Cathedral. On 5 June 1826 Oakeley was married at St Margaret's Church, Westminster, to Atholl Keturah Murray (1801–1844), daughter of the Revd Lord Charles Murray Aynsley, and niece of John, fourth duke of Atholl, and then took up his residence at Ealing. By the death without male issue of his elder brother, Charles, who had held the baronetcy only three years, he succeeded in 1830 to the title.

In 1834 Howley, now archbishop of Canterbury, presented Oakeley to the valuable rectory of Bocking in Essex, a living held by Lady Oakeley's father in her childhood. The living then carried with it the right of jurisdiction, under the title of dean and as commissary of the archbishop of Canterbury, over the Essex and Suffolk parishes, which were extra-diocesan and constituted the archbishop's peculiar. This jurisdiction was abolished shortly after Sir Herbert's death. Both at Ealing and at Bocking, Oakeley was one of the first to carry out what became a general system of parochial organization, the innovations including district visitors, weekday services, and Sunday schools. Bocking contained many nonconformists, with whom Oakeley became engaged in lively disputes about church rates; none the less, he was held in general esteem. In 1841 he succeeded Archdeacon Lyall as archdeacon of Colchester, and when the bishopric of Gibraltar was founded in 1842, it was offered to him and

declined. Oakeley was unusually reticent in print, for his time, but in 1836 he edited his father's memoirs; he also had privately printed a number of his poems. On 26 January 1844 Oakeley's wife died, and he was so much affected by her loss that he died also in London on 27 March 1845. He left three daughters and four sons, of whom the eldest, Charles William, succeeded to the title and the second, Sir Herbert Stanley *Oakeley (1830–1903), became professor of music in the University of Edinburgh.

J. A. HAMILTON, rev. H. C. G. MATTHEW

Sources Mrs F. Drummond, Notes of the life of Herbert Oakeley (1892) • Foster, Alum. Oxon.

Archives BL, corresp. with Sir Robert Peel, Add. MSS 40355–40489

Oakeley, Sir Herbert Stanley (1830–1903), composer and organist, was born on 22 July 1830 at the vicarage, Ealing, the second son of the Revd Sir Herbert *Oakeley, third baronet (1791–1845), and his wife, Atholl Keturah Murray (1801–1844), the daughter of Lord Charles Murray Aynsley (whose father was John, third duke of Atholl) and his wife, Alicia. Educated at Rugby School (1843–6) and at Christ Church, Oxford, he graduated BA in 1853 and proceeded MA in 1856. A talented keyboard player, he took lessons in harmony at Oxford from Stephen Elvey, organist of New College. Though his intention had been to take holy orders in the Church of England, music came to occupy him more and more. Visits to Canterbury, Durham, Norwich, and Winchester confirmed in him a love for cathedral music. His circumstances enabled him to travel widely: he studied the piano with Ignaz Moscheles and Louis Plaidy (Leipzig, 1855) and organ with Johann Schneider (Dresden, 1863), and met leading musicians including Liszt and Meyerbeer. As music critic of the Manchester Guardian from 1858 to 1868 he wrote on musical events at home and abroad.

In 1865, to the surprise of many in the musical world, Oakeley was appointed Reid professor of the theory of music at the University of Edinburgh in succession to John Donaldson. A carriage accident in the Swiss Alps in June 1872 left his right leg permanently impaired, although he continued to give organ recitals and conduct. He was knighted on 17 August 1876, following the unveiling of the Albert memorial in Charlotte Square, Edinburgh, at which he directed the music: Queen Victoria observed that 'Professor Oakeley … is a wonderful musician, and plays beautifully on the organ' (Victoria, 327). On 19 September 1881 she conferred on him the title of 'Composer of Music to Her Majesty in Scotland'. His first music degree was a doctorate from the archbishop of Canterbury (1871). Later he received honorary degrees from many universities; other honours included membership of the Accademia Filarmonica of Bologna (1888) and the Accademia di Santa Cecilia of Rome (1892).

Oakeley directed the resources of the Reid chair towards 'the promulgation of musical art' in Scotland. An excellent organist with a flair for improvisation, he gave 200 recitals between 1866 and 1891 on the fine organ by William Hill & Sons (1861, rebuilt 1869) in his classroom. Under his administration the Reid memorial concerts

Sir Herbert Stanley Oakeley (1830–1903), by William Hole, pubd 1884

graduate in that subject' (Oakley, 23–4), and he argued the case for musical degrees before the Scottish universities commissioners in 1877 and 1890; but the syllabus eventually introduced in 1894 was Niecks's, not his. Ill health and increasing deafness, coupled with the impending institution of music degrees and Sir Charles Hallé's decision to withdraw from the Reid concerts, precipitated Oakeley's early retirement from his professorship in 1891. During his last years he lived in Dover, but continued to travel. He died at 53 Grand Parade, Eastbourne, on 26 October 1903 and was buried at Eastbourne parish church.

As a composer Oakeley won respect as 'an earnest and conscientious artist' (*Musical Times*, 17, 1875–6, 206). But apart from hymn tunes such as 'Abends' and 'Dominica', his compositions, like much Victorian music, made no impact on the twentieth century. His best work is perhaps to be found in his songs: he wrote to the music critic Joseph Bennett (23 February 1887) that he hoped he had earned 'a place as a representative composer of this kind of music' (U. Edin. L., MS Dk.7.38⁵). Other pieces loyally marked occasions such as the duke of Edinburgh's marriage (*Edinburgh Festal March*, Liverpool festival, 1874) and Queen Victoria's golden jubilee (*A Jubilee Lyric*, Cheltenham festival, 1887). After retiring he devoted his energies particularly to writing anthems, such as *The Glory of Lebanon* for the 800th anniversary of Winchester Cathedral (1893). Among his prized possessions was the autograph of Bach's prelude and fugue BWV 544 for organ.

CHRISTOPHER D. S. FIELD

Sources E. M. Oakeley, *The life of Sir Herbert Stanley Oakeley* (1904) • W. B. Hole, *Quasi cursores: portraits of the high officers and professors of the University of Edinburgh at its tercentenary festival* (1884) • M. Shirlaw, 'The faculty of music', *History of the University of Edinburgh, 1883–1933*, ed. A. L. Turner (1933), 284–303 • Queen Victoria, *More leaves from the journal of a life in the highlands, from 1862 to 1882* (1884) • G. Grove, 'Reid concerts', Grove, *Dict. mus.* • H. S. Oakley, 'University music societies', Grove, *Dict. mus.* • W. H. Husle, 'Oakley', Grove, *Dict. mus.* • 'Royal commission to inquire into the universities of Scotland', *Parl. papers* (1878), vol. 32, C. 1935; vol. 33, C. 1935-I; vol. 34, C. 1935-II; vol. 35, C. 1935-III • H. Oakeley, letters to Joseph Bennett, 1877–90, U. Edin. L., MS Dk.7.38⁵ • J. S. Blackie, *The Scotsman* (24 March 1876) [letter] • J. S. Blackie, *The Scotsman* (22 March 1877) [letter] • *MT*, 12 (1865–7), 181 • *MT*, 12 (1865–7), 447–8 • *MT*, 13 (1867–9), 326–7 • *MT*, 17 (1875–6), 206 • *MT*, 31 (1890), 267–8 • *MT*, 32 (1891), 83 • J. D. Brown, *Biographical dictionary of musicians: with a bibliography of English writings on music* (1886) • *WW* • *The Scotsman* (28 Oct 1903) • *MT*, 44 (1903), 800 • H. S. Oakley, *Two inaugural addresses on music* (1897) • *CGPLA Eng. & Wales* (1903) • W. P. Anderson, *Silences that speak* (1931)

Archives BL, letters to F. G. Edwards, W. B. Squire, and others, Add. MSS 39680, 41574; Egerton MS 3095 • NL Scot., letters to J. S. Blackie, William Blackwood • Reid Music Library, Edinburgh, corresp. from E. M. Oakley's letter-book, diplomas, Reid concert programmes • U. Edin. L., letters to Joseph Bennett • U. St Andr., letter to Sir James Donaldson

Likenesses C. K. Robertson, oils, 1884, U. Edin. • W. Hole, etching, NPG; repro. in Hole, *Quasi cursores*, 95 [*see illus.*] • photograph, NPG • photographs, repro. in Oakeley, *Life of Sir Herbert Stanley Oakeley* • photographs, Reid Music Library, Edinburgh

Wealth at death £2058 19s. 10d.: probate, 24 Dec 1903, *CGPLA Eng. & Wales*

were transformed into artistic events of high quality, at which many major works received their first performances in Scotland. In 1867–8 August Manns was engaged to conduct; from 1869 to 1891 the concert became the centrepiece of a Reid festival given by Charles Hallé and his orchestra. Soloists included Clara Schumann, Alfredo Piatti, Therese Tietjens, and George Henschel; a piece by Oakeley was usually included in the programme. Another innovation was the founding of Edinburgh University Musical Society. From 1871 Oakeley conducted annual concerts of its male students' chorus and a semi-professional orchestra. He also encouraged the formation of similar societies at Aberdeen, St Andrews, and Glasgow. When in 1876–7 John Stuart Blackie attacked him in *The Scotsman* for neglecting Scottish song he responded with his *National Melodies*, dedicated to the university musical societies of Scotland. The *Scottish Students' Song Book* (1891) owed much to his enthusiasm, and includes his songs for Edinburgh ('Alma mater', 1884) and St Andrews ('Carmen saeculare', 1890).

Oakeley's efforts to develop music as an academic subject at Edinburgh made less headway. Classes were held (including from 1884 one for women) and certificates awarded, but comparatively few students enrolled. In his inaugural lecture (1866) Oakeley looked forward to the time when students might matriculate 'for the especial purpose of obtaining aid in cultivating music, and to

Oakeley, Hilda Diana (1867–1950), educationist and author, was born in Durham on 12 October 1867, the third of the five children of Sir (Henry) Evelyn Oakeley (1833–1915), HM inspector of schools, and his wife, Caroline Howley Turner (*d.* 1925), daughter of William Hallows Belli of the Bengal civil service. She had an elder brother, who died in childhood, and four sisters. The Oakeleys, a Shropshire gentry family, had long-standing connections with India, as did the more cosmopolitan Bellis: Hilda's paternal great-grandfather Sir Charles Oakeley was governor of Madras and a maternal great-grandfather, John Belli, was secretary to Warren Hastings. Her father, a younger son without private means, was a Cambridge mathematics graduate, briefly a fellow of Jesus College and also briefly employed in the Indian Civil Service. His wife's delicate health brought them back to England and he became instead in 1864 one of the first government inspectors of schools, responsible at first for the British Wesleyan and non-denominational schools in the north of England. The family lived in Durham, moving to Manchester in 1878 when Evelyn Oakeley was promoted to chief inspector and to London when he became chief inspector of training colleges in 1885.

Hilda recalled a happy and stimulating childhood in a liberal Anglican family with academic connections (among them her uncle, the composer Professor Sir Herbert Stanley *Oakeley). The sisters had visiting tutors in Durham but formative influences came from the family circle: a father who loved reading aloud, a mother with a keen amateur interest in history and anthropology, the society of the learned canons of Durham and friends who visited, such as the writer F. W. H. Myers. Her abiding concern with the spiritual life, despite a painful loss of faith in later years, she attributed to this childhood environment. In Manchester, Hilda, always a studious child, attended Ellerslie Ladies' College, a well-run private school which prepared her for higher local examinations. She did not take up her father's offer to send her to Newnham Hall, Cambridge, preferring to live in London, where Christian socialism and the settlement movement were firing the idealism of the young, and to study independently in preparation for a literary career. She worked in a laundry-girls' club in Fulham while following an ambitious reading programme in philosophy and psychology. After attending Bernard Bosanquet's university extension lectures she was awarded a prize for an essay on 'Aristotle and modern democracy'. The examiners' view that she should 'go through the mill of Oxford' finally persuaded her to go to university (Oakeley, *My Adventures*, 54).

In 1894, aged twenty-seven, Hilda Oakeley went up to Somerville College. She had no Greek but followed advice that classical Greats provided 'the best education'. Taught by the leading scholars of the time, she emerged in 1898 with a first—a rare achievement for a woman. At Somerville she encountered a distinguished generation of students, including Eleanor Rathbone (who became a close friend), Edith Deverell, and Margery Fry. 'Very clever and if she *ever* was frivolous she would be quite delightful' was their verdict on her (Jones, 45). Although still extremely shy, she found an appreciative audience in their select college discussion group, the 'Associated Prigs'. Issues both

practical and philosophical figured in their Sunday evening talks and Hilda was among the many products of an Oxford Idealist training to leave university with a vocation for practical as well as intellectual work. She taught briefly in working-class adult education at Morley College, London, and was offered a studentship at the London School of Economics. Instead she accepted in 1899 the post of head of Canada's first residential women's college, the newly founded Royal Victoria College at McGill University.

In Montreal, Miss Oakeley found academic recognition and opportunities as both scholar and administrator. She became an MA of McGill (her Oxford MA dates from 1920 when its degrees were first opened to women) and, as lecturer in philosophy, the first woman member of its faculty of arts. In 1900 she was the first woman to deliver McGill's annual university lecture, a well-received address on 'History and progress', distilled from her studies for Greats. As a public figure in Montreal she was remembered not only as an intellectual but also as a leader of the movement to provide children with playgrounds. She set out to form Victoria College on the model of Somerville, which for her had realized Newman's ideal of a university where the student breathes 'a pure and clear atmosphere of thought' (Oakeley, *My Adventures*, 68–9). There, as in later posts, her title of 'warden' echoed the name by which Somervillians had known their principal, Agnes Maitland. But Miss Oakeley happily fell in with the more relaxed conventions of Canada on relations between the sexes and dealt sensitively with critics of the English idea of the women's college. She appreciated the stimulus of intellectual life at McGill, where colleagues included Ernest Rutherford and A. E. Taylor, and spent a summer studying psychology at the co-educational University of Chicago. She also visited the American women's colleges and Jane Addams's settlement, Hull House.

Intending to spend more time on philosophy, Hilda Oakeley returned to the UK in 1905. For two frustrating years she was university lecturer in philosophy, tutor to women students, and warden of Ashburne Hall at Manchester University. Students 'loved and admired her' as a 'darling woman of great perception', with 'her quiet voice and brilliant mind … her sweet nature and gracious presence' (Judd, 55). But opportunities for lecturing turned out to be limited and an irksome chaperonage system still survived. Her parents lived in London and in 1907 she moved back there as lecturer in philosophy and vice-principal at the women's department of King's College in Kensington. She remained in London for the rest of her life and was a prominent figure in academic circles, especially the Aristotelian Society and the newly founded British Federation of University Women (of which she was a vice-president from 1909 until her death).

King's College for Women (KCW) was incorporated in 1910 and Hilda Oakeley became its warden. She had a vision of KCW, in the event frustrated, as a new kind of women's college: non-residential but with distinctive traditions of its own, catering especially for Kensington residents, whether they were degree students or women bent on self-culture rather than qualifications, and offering an unusually wide range of subjects, including art, music, divinity and, from 1908, the first university courses in household science. Among the promoters and benefactors of household science were conservatives who saw it as providing a form of higher education especially suited to women. It was accordingly much criticized by women dons and feminists. Miss Oakeley found herself at odds with women whose aims and values she shared. Prepared by her contacts with the American home-economics tradition, she defended KCW with conviction. Household science offered not just a university training for domestic science teachers but also (the prospect that inspired her as a scholar and progressive educationist) a starting-point for a new applied science of the home and a new form of education for social workers. As she conceived it, this new discipline would draw on ethics and psychology as well as the natural sciences and provide a 'liberal education' within the context of a multi-disciplinary college.

All hope of shaping household science on those lines was lost in 1913, when the Haldane report on London University recommended, in the interests of rationalizing teaching provision, that KCW should cease to exist as an independent college. In 1914 the household science department in Kensington became King's College of Household and Social Science (later Queen Elizabeth College) and all other departments moved to King's College on the Strand. Hilda Oakeley did her best to fight these recommendations, then, acknowledging defeat, to implement them smoothly. In 1915 she resigned as warden, though retaining a part-time lecturership in philosophy at King's.

During the war Hilda Oakeley threw herself into social work as resident warden (1915–21) of the Passmore Edwards (later Mary Ward) Settlement. There she discovered an unexpected talent for running boys' clubs and built on the work of the settlement's founder, Mrs Humphry Ward, who had pioneered the education of invalid children and 'play-centres'. A new wartime venture was the development of training facilities for teachers of continuation classes for school leavers. Always concerned as a philosopher with the individual's relation to the state, and a critic of both *laissez-faire* and doctrinaire collectivism, Hilda Oakeley saw settlement work as an illustration of the value of voluntary associations in experimenting with new forms of social and educational provision.

In 1921 she left the settlement to live with her mother in Earls Court. As university reader in philosophy (1921–31) she now became a full-time academic. She was acting head of the philosophy department at King's College from 1925 to 1930 and head in 1931, and twice chaired the University of London's board of studies in philosophy (1923–6 and 1929–31). In 1928 she was awarded the London degree of DLitt. A prolific contributor to philosophical journals, she was also a gifted teacher, lecturing to popular audiences and non-specialists as well as to honours students and graduates. Before her retirement she published three books: a well-reviewed volume of collected essays, *History*

and Progress (1923); a reader on *Greek Ethical Thought* (1925; repr. 1950); and *A Study in the Philosophy of Personality* (1928). Later books—*History and the Self* (1934), *The False State* (1937), and *Should Nations Survive?* (1942)—develop themes that reflect her critical appreciation of the Idealist tradition. It had failed those who looked to it for philosophical defence against loss of faith, and it had fostered illusions about the conditions of human progress and the benign influence of the state. Yet she remained within that tradition, unfashionable as it became, and tried to adapt it by borrowing from Sir Alfred Lyall's (equally unfashionable) writings on Hindu philosophy, where she found support for her belief in the value of 'creative personality'. Respected in her lifetime as a reflective if sometimes obscure thinker, she was president of the Aristotelian Society in 1940–41. She died at her home in Westminster, 22 Tufton Court, on 7 October 1950.

Hilda Oakeley's memoirs, *My Adventures in Education* (1939), give an intimate account of the work for which she is chiefly remembered. They also reveal her aesthetic sense (natural beauty and the visual arts delighted her and she published a volume of poems, *A Philosopher's Rhyme and other Stray Verses* in 1937) and a political awareness that was, however, rarely expressed in activism. Walking with Edwardian suffrage processions she recalled as 'something of an ordeal' (Oakeley, 76–7). She acknowledged an 'extreme constitutional dislike of controversy and friction' (ibid., 146) and was conscious that it had handicapped her in professional life, the more so as her ideas often challenged current orthodoxies. As a philosopher she retained a certain detachment from political and feminist movements (witness her admiration for such prominent anti-suffragists as Lyall and Mary Ward). Historians have differed in their interpretation of her role in the home science movement (Dyhouse, 45–8; Blakestad, 102–3, 118, 121–3). But there is no doubt that the demise of KCW, which she continued to regret, deprived women's higher education of an innovative and liberal administrator.   JANET HOWARTH

Sources H. D. Oakeley, *My adventures in education* (1939) · H. D. Oakeley, 'King's College for Women', in F. J. C. Hearnshaw, *The centenary history of King's College, London, 1828–1928* (1929), appx A · *The Times* (28 Oct 1950) [first edn only; typescript in King's Lond. archive] · Burke, *Peerage* · *WWW* · E. H. Jones, *Margery Fry: the essential amateur* (1966) · M. D. Stocks, *Eleanor Rathbone: a biography* (1949) · D. Judd, *Alison Uttley: the life of a country child* (1986) · N. L. Blakestad, 'King's College of Household and Social Science and the household science movement in English higher education, c.1908–1939', DPhil diss., U. Oxf., 1994 · C. Dyhouse, *No distinction of sex? Women in British universities, 1870–1939* (1995) · H. J. Morgan, ed., *The Canadian men and women of the time*, 2nd edn (1912) · [J. E. G. Montgomery], review of *History and progress, and other essays and addresses*, *TLS* (8 Feb 1923), 84 · [G. O. Wood], 'The metaphysical self', *TLS* (8 Nov 1928), 830 [review of *A study in the philosophy of personality*] · [H. M. Stannard], 'Personality and history', *TLS* (13 Sept 1934), 612 · 'Other new books', *TLS* (22 Jan 1938), 63 [incl. review of *The false state*] · [G. West], 'Masses and man', *TLS* (23 May 1942), 254 · N. Marsh, *The history of Queen Elizabeth College* (1986) · *CGPLA Eng. & Wales* (1950)

Archives King's Lond. | Somerville College, Oxford, Margery Fry MSS

Wealth at death £10,872 6s. 0d.: probate, 22 March 1951, CGPLA Eng. & Wales

Oakes, Sir Henry, second baronet (1756–1827). *See under* Oakes, Sir Hildebrand, first baronet (1754–1822).

Oakes, Sir Hildebrand, first baronet (1754–1822), army officer, was born on 19 January 1754 at Exeter, Devon, the eldest son of Lieutenant-Colonel Hildebrand Oakes (1733–1797), late of the 33rd foot, and his wife, Sarah (d. 1775), the daughter of Henry Cornelison of Braxted Lodge, Essex. He was made ensign in the 33rd foot (later the Duke of Wellington's regiment) on 23 December 1767 and promoted lieutenant in April 1771. In December 1775 he accompanied his regiment to America, where he served under Lord Cornwallis. He was present at the attack on Charlestown in June 1776, was promoted captain on 8 August following, and served throughout the American War of Independence until the peace. He returned to England in May 1784.

In May 1786 Oakes was aide-de camp to Major-General Bruce on the staff in Ireland. On 18 November 1790 he was promoted brevet major, then on 13 September 1791 major in the 66th foot. In February 1792 he took temporary command of his regiment at St Vincent in the West Indies, whence he embarked with it to Gibraltar. On the arrival of a new lieutenant-colonel in February 1794 he returned to England, becoming a brevet lieutenant-colonel on 1 March. Oakes served as aide-de-camp to Sir Charles Stuart in Corsica in April, became deputy quartermaster-general there in May, and was promoted quartermaster-general of the army in the Mediterranean in June 1794. Although on 12 November 1795 he was made lieutenant-colonel of the 66th foot, he was transferred to the 26th ten days later; at the same time he retained his staff position in Corsica until June 1796. On 3 December 1796 he became quartermaster-general to Stuart's forces in Portugal, and on 1 January 1798 was made brevet colonel. He was promoted brigadier during the capture of Minorca.

Oakes joined Sir Ralph Abercromby's army in the Mediterranean in August 1800, serving with distinction in the Egyptian campaign of 1801 as second in command of the reserve under Sir John Moore. On 21 March he was wounded at the battle of Alexandria. For this service he was included in the votes of thanks from parliament. Between October 1802 and August 1804 he was brigadier-general at Malta, and on 10 November 1804 he became lieutenant-governor and commandant at Portsmouth. Promoted major-general on 1 January 1805, in June Oakes was appointed a commissioner of military inquiry, whose reports appeared in the parliamentary papers (*Parl. papers*, 1806–7, 2). On 11 July 1806 he was appointed major-general on the staff and quartermaster-general to the army in the Mediterranean. After returning home from Sicily with the troops under Moore in December 1807 he was given command of the Malta garrison in March 1808 and received the local rank of lieutenant-general on 30 April 1810. In

May 1810 Oakes accepted the civil and military commissionership of the island, but he did so reluctantly, telling Hudson Lowe, 'I shall not be sorry when the appointment passes into other hands' (Gregory, 319). Nevertheless he held the post until ill health forced him to relinquish it to Sir Thomas Maitland in October 1813, when he returned home. He became a lieutenant-general on 4 June 1811 and a baronet in recognition of his service on 2 November 1813. The outbreak of plague in Malta, which killed 5000 people, occurred during Oakes's government in 1813.

In January 1814 Oakes was appointed lieutenant-general of the ordnance, a post he retained until his death, and in May 1820 he was made GCB. His other appointments included colonel of the 1st garrison battalion (23 November 1803) and colonel of the 3rd West India (24 April 1806). On the death of Sir Thomas Moore he succeeded to the colonelcy of the 52nd light infantry on 25 January 1809. He was a member of the consolidated board of general officers, and one of the commissioners of the Chelsea Hospital and the Royal Military College. He died, unmarried, at Hereford Street, Mayfair, London, on 9 September 1822, and was succeeded by his younger brother Henry Oakes.

Sir Henry Oakes, second baronet (1756–1827), army officer in the East India Company, was born at Exeter on 11 July 1756. He received an India cadetship on 8 February 1775 and was appointed a second lieutenant in the Bombay army on 18 May 1775. Thereafter he saw extensive service in India, serving in Gujarat in 1775–6, in the Poona expedition of 1778, and at the sieges of Tellicherry, Onore, Mangalore, and Bednur in 1780–81. He was adjutant-general of General Mathew's force, which on 28 April 1783 surrendered at Bednur, where he was taken prisoner by Tipu Sultan of Mysore. After his release in 1784 the Madras government made him captain-commandant of a sepoy battalion on 10 June 1784. Following its disbandment, Oakes commanded the grenadiers of the 2nd Bombay European regiment, and in September 1788 was transferred to the 12th Bombay native infantry. In 1790 he served with this regiment, first as quartermaster-general and later as commissary of supplies. He was present at the sieges of Cannanore and Seringapatam in 1791, at Cotapore in Malabar, and later in Palghautcherry with troops under Major John Cuppage in October 1791. In October 1792 he became deputy adjutant-general of the Bombay army, and on 9 December 1792 he married Dorothea (d. 1837), the daughter of General George Bowles of Mount Prospect, co. Cork, Ireland; they had four sons and two daughters. In 1796 he received the title of adjutant-general, having attained the rank of major on 6 May 1795 and lieutenant-colonel on 8 January 1796.

Oakes returned home on sick leave in 1798, but went again to India in 1802 and became colonel of the 7th Bombay native infantry. Once more ill health forced him to go back to England, but he was in India again in 1807, as military auditor-general at Bombay. However, he was soon obliged to return home. On 25 July 1810 he became major-general and on 4 June 1814 lieutenant-general. In his last years his ill health led increasingly to bouts of insanity, and on 1 November 1827 he killed himself with a pistol in the stable of his home at Mitcham, Surrey. His widow died on 24 May 1837.   CHRISTOPHER DOORNE

Sources J. Philippart, ed., *The royal military calendar*, 3rd edn, 2 (1820) · J. Philippart, *East India military calendar*, 2 (1824) · *GM*, 1st ser., 92/2 (1822), 373; 97/2 (1827), 560–61 · Burke, *Peerage* · D. Gregory, *Malta, Britain and the European powers, 1793–1815* (1996) · *DNB*
Archives NL Scot., letters and accounts | BL, corresp. with H. Lowe, Add. MSS 20107–20190, *passim* · Bodl. Oxf., letters to the Bruce family · U. Nott. L., letters to Lord Bentinck
Likenesses P. J. de Loutherbourg, group portrait, oils, 1802, Scot. NPG · W. Nicholls, stipple, 1813, BM, NPG; repro. in *Military Chronicle* (1813) · portrait, repro. in Gregory, *Malta, Britain and the European powers*, p. 175

Oakes, John Wright (1820–1887), landscape painter, was born on 9 July 1820 at Sproston House, near Middlewich, Cheshire. He was educated in Liverpool and studied art under John Bishop at the Liverpool Mechanics' Institute. He was then apprenticed to a house decorator and followed this trade until about 1846, when he turned full-time to painting. At about the same time, or shortly afterwards, he married. His wife had a successful corset-making business, and it may have been her wealth, rather than a growing reputation, that enabled him to relinquish his trade.

Oakes's earliest works were fruit pieces. He first exhibited at the Liverpool Academy in 1839 with *Fruit*, priced at 5 guineas. About 1843 he began painting landscapes, making studies among the sand dunes and beaches of the Wallasey peninsula. An early work was entitled *Sketch on the Lancashire Coast*. Oakes began modestly but developed 'a brilliant, almost unerring, sense of composition, a fine perception of light, atmosphere, and colour and the poetry of nature' (Bryan, *Painters*, 4.31). Many of his landscapes were dark and heavy in colour, but these characteristics were less evident in his larger and finer canvasses. As he progressed he made less use of heavy impasto and bitumen, artifices common in his earlier works. His favourite locations were in Scotland, Ireland, Devon, and particularly Wales, where he painted many pictures of mountain, moorland, and coastal scenery. A few pictures of Swiss subjects, painted during a foreign tour, were much less successful than the studies of countryside that he knew well, such as north Wales and Anglesey.

In 1846 Oakes exhibited ten landscapes of local or Welsh subjects at Liverpool Academy, of which he was elected an associate the following year. He became a full member in 1850 and served as its honorary secretary from 1853 to 1855. A man of 'practical sagacity' (Bryan, *Painters*, 4.30), he was described as 'probably the best secretary that the Academy ever had' (Marillier, 183). The practice of pricing pictures in the academy catalogue was introduced during his regime. In 1855 he moved to London and afterwards seldom exhibited in Liverpool. The Walker Art Gallery possesses one of his landscapes, *A North Devon Glen*, depicting a group of cattle in a shady pool lit by an autumn sun.

In 1847 Oakes sent *Nant Frangcon, Carnarvonshire* to the British Institution; it was his first work to be exhibited in London. It was followed in 1848, at the Royal Academy, by *On the River Greta, Keswick*. Thereafter he was represented at the Royal Academy almost every year until his death, exhibiting a total of ninety works there. He also sent twenty-eight pictures to the British Institution, eleven to Suffolk Street, and over twenty-four to galleries elsewhere in London. Oakes painted in watercolours as well as oils, and in 1874 he was elected an associate of the Institute of Painters in Water Colours. He resigned in 1875, doubtless prompted by ambition to be elected an associate of the Royal Academy. He was elected ARA the following year, but was never elected a full academician. Among his best works were *The Bass Rock in Calm* (1867), 'a fine sunset picture' (Marillier, 187); *Moreton Mill* (1869), a sea piece with fishing boats on a transparent green sea; and *The Reaper's Rest* (1886), a large canvas depicting swallows circling over a pool of water, against a background of cornfields and trees.

Oakes was 'of sturdy appearance, more like a sea-captain than a painter, much marked by small-pox' (Bryan, *Painters*, 4.31). Serious and retiring by nature, he habitually wore an elegant frock coat and black satin waistcoat. He was unusual in that he did not allow people to watch him paint, although he did sketch with other artists, notably his close friend John Bishop. From 1881 Oakes suffered chronic ill health due to asthma, which greatly interfered with his art. He nevertheless continued to paint, and in 1883 he was elected an honorary member of the Royal Scottish Academy. Oakes died at his residence, Leam House, 34 Addison Road, Kensington, on 8 July 1887, and was buried in Brompton cemetery. He left a daughter, Emily. There was a sale of his remaining pictures at Christies on 10 March 1888, which realized almost £4000. His painting *The Warren* was exhibited posthumously at the Royal Academy that year.   MARK POTTLE

Sources H. C. Marillier, *The Liverpool school of painters* (1904) · Mallalieu, *Watercolour artists* · *The Times* (13 July 1887) · *Art Journal*, 7 (1887), 287 · E. Morris and E. Roberts, *The Liverpool Academy and other exhibitions of contemporary art in Liverpool, 1774–1867* (1998) · Bryan, *Painters* (1903–5) · exhibition catalogues of the RA, British Institution, Society of British Artists, and Liverpool Academy, 1839–88 · d. cert.
Likenesses wood-engraving (after photograph), NPG; repro. in *ILN* (13 May 1876) · woodcut, NPG
Wealth at death £3881 16s.: probate, 5 Aug 1887, CGPLA Eng. & Wales

Oakes, Thomas (1644–1719). *See under* Oakes, Urian (*c*.1631–1681).

Oakes, Urian (*c*.1631–1681), ejected minister and college head, was born in England, possibly in or near London, the son of Edward Oakes (*c*.1604–1689), yeoman and Massachusetts Bay Colony representative, and his wife, Jane (*d*. after 1691). The English origins of the Oakes family are obscure; the family does not emerge from the shadows until 1640, when Edward and Jane arrived in Cambridge, Massachusetts, with at least two children including Urian, then about nine years old. Edward Oakes quickly became a community leader; he served Cambridge as a selectman beginning in 1642 and as a representative to the colony's general court from 1659. During King Philip's War he was an officer in the Massachusetts militia.

After local preparation Oakes entered Harvard College in 1645. He graduated four years later and became a tutor at the college while he read for the ministry. He received his master's degree in 1652. Like many of his Harvard contemporaries, Oakes believed that his best opportunities for a good settlement lay in England. He returned home in 1654 and served briefly as a private chaplain before settling in the parish of Titchfield, Hampshire, in 1656. This sojourn lasted until 1662, when he fell victim to the Act of Uniformity, was deprived of his living, and forbidden to preach. Oakes briefly became the master of the grammar school in Southwick, Hampshire, where he ministered to a nonconformist congregation with Richard Symmonds, the ejected curate there. Oakes must have married during his early years in Titchfield, because his eldest son, also Urian, was born in or about 1657. Two other children were born in England, a son, Edward, and a daughter, Hannah. Tradition holds that Oakes's wife was Ruth, the daughter of the theologian William Ames, but there is no evidence to support this conclusion, and his wife's identity is uncertain. She was dead by 1669.

Jonathan Mitchell, the minister to the church in Cambridge, Massachusetts, died in 1668, and in the ensuing months Oakes was invited to return as Mitchell's successor. He travelled to Cambridge during the summer of 1671 and was installed as the church's pastor the following November 8. From his new pulpit he expressed the fear, common among New England's puritan clergy in the 1670s, that the region was suffering severely from spiritual and moral decay. In his four published sermons he warned New Englanders that their lapses of faith and conduct jeopardized both their individual prospects for salvation and their community's special relationship with God, who had made them, they believed, his chosen people in succession to the tribes of Israel. As a minister of one of the six original towns of the colony, Oakes automatically assumed a seat on one of Harvard College's two governing bodies, the board of overseers; in 1672 he was also elected to the other, the corporation, which oversaw the institution's daily affairs. Oakes promptly resigned from the corporation when he lost confidence in President Leonard Hoar, whose stern administration alienated most of the undergraduates. Hoar in turn resigned the presidency in 1675 when it became apparent that he could not regain the respect of the students.

Widely respected as New England's most capable Latinist and the minister of one of the region's most visible churches, Oakes was an obvious candidate to succeed to Harvard's presidency. Reluctant to give up his church, however, and aware of rumours that he had intentionally undermined Hoar through his resignation from the corporation, Urian accepted the position only on an acting basis while the college's governors attempted to make a permanent appointment. When several candidates refused the office, Urian finally acceded in 1680, making it a condition that he would retain his pulpit.

As president Oakes oversaw a small institution. Only thirty-one students graduated during his presidency, although this number included several of the colony's future leaders, notably Cotton Mather. The second Harvard Hall (1678), the college's major edifice until it was destroyed by fire in 1764, was completed during Oakes's tenure. Surviving addresses in Latin (in which he punned on his short stature) and a printed elegy in English confirm his reputation as an eloquent orator as well as the most capable poet of his era in New England. Oakes died of a fever at Cambridge on 25 July 1681, and was buried there.

Thomas Oakes (1644–1719), politician in America, brother of Urian Oakes, was born in Cambridge, Massachusetts, on 18 June 1644. He graduated from Harvard with the class of 1662, then trained as a physician. One of the colony's most prominent doctors, he also became active in government. In 1689 Boston elected him to the Massachusetts house of representatives, which chose him as speaker. Between 1690 and 1692, he was part of a mission to the royal court to secure a new charter for the Massachusetts Bay Colony. Upon his return from London, Oakes fell foul of Governor Joseph Dudley, who repeatedly nullified his election to the governor's council. Oakes died in Wellfleet, Massachusetts, on 15 July 1719. His wife, Martha (c.1649–1719), had died the previous April.

CONRAD EDICK WRIGHT

Sources S. E. Morison, *The tercentennial history of Harvard College and University, 1636–1936*, 3–4: *Harvard College in the seventeenth century* (1936) · C. K. Shipton, *Sibley's Harvard graduates: biographical sketches of graduates of Harvard University*, 17 vols. (1873–1975), vol. 1, pp. 173–85 · J. Savage, *A genealogical dictionary of the first settlers of New England*, 4 vols. (1860–62), vol. 3, pp. 302–3 · J. Quincy, *The history of Harvard University* (1840) · C. Mather, *Magnalia Christi Americana*, 7 bks in 1 vol. (1702) · L. R. Paige, ed., *History of Cambridge, Massachusetts, 1630–1877* (1877) · J. A. Schutz, *Legislators of the Massachusetts general court, 1691–1780* (1997) · J. A. L. Lemay, 'Jonson and Milton: two influences on Oakes's "Elegie"', *New England Quarterly*, 38 (1965), 90–92 · W. J. Scheick, 'Standing in the gap: Urian Oakes's elegy on Thomas Shepard', *Early American Literature*, 9 (1975), 301–6 · L. M. Kaiser, ed., 'The unpublished *Oratorio secunda* of Urian Oakes, Harvard, 1675', *Humanistica Lovaniensia*, 21 (1972), 385–412 · S. E. Morison, ed., 'Urian Oakes's salutory oration, commencement, 1677', *Publications of the Colonial Society of Massachusetts*, 31 (1935), 405–36 · L. M. Kaiser, ed., 'The *Oratorio quinta* of Urian Oakes, Harvard, 1678', *Humanistica Lovaniensia*, 19 (1970), 485–508 · *Calamy rev.*, 370

Archives Harvard U., MSS

Oakeshott, Michael Joseph (1901–1990), philosopher, was born on 11 December 1901 at Chelsfield, Kent, the second of the three sons (there were no daughters) of Joseph Francis Oakeshott of Harpenden, Hertfordshire, a Fabian civil servant who had played a part in founding the London School of Economics (LSE), and his wife, Frances Maude Hellicar. Oakeshott was educated at St George's School, Harpenden, a progressive co-educational school, and left moving accounts of the excitements a boy of scholarly disposition might enjoy as he came into contact with his classical inheritance. He went to Gonville and Caius College, Cambridge, in 1920, and after a year in Germany in 1923–4 following graduation (he was placed in the second division of the first class in both parts—1922 and 1923—of the history tripos), and a short period as a schoolmaster at Lytham St Anne's grammar school in

Michael Joseph Oakeshott (1901–1990), by Paul Gopal-Chowdhury, 1985

Lancashire, became a history fellow of the college in 1925.

Oakeshott's early interests were in religion and historiography. Both led him on to philosophy and generated *Experience and its Modes* (1933), in which he distinguished the different forms of human activity. R. G. Collingwood admired particularly its treatment of history, but the reception of the book was cool. The 1000 copies printed took over thirty years to sell out. In 1936 Oakeshott collaborated with Guy Griffith on *A Guide to the Classics, or, How to Pick the Derby Winner*, an analysis of horse-racing, the second edition of which was called *How to Pick the Winner* (1947). In 1939 he published *The Social and Political Doctrines of Contemporary Europe*, an anthology of political writings with commentary.

During the Second World War, Oakeshott enlisted as a gunner and rose to be a captain in Phantom, a special unit whose dangerous work it was to report on the effect of artillery fire from close to the front. In 1945 he returned to Cambridge and wrote his famous introduction (1946) to Hobbes's *Leviathan* (1651). He edited the *Cambridge Journal* from 1947 until its demise in 1954 and contributed actively to making it a centre of intellectual resistance to the ideas of social engineering, collectivism, and state planning dominant at that period. His love of freedom was so radical that his conservatism had anarchic tendencies. Most of the essays later reprinted in *Rationalism in Politics* (1962) first appeared in the journal. In 1949 he went to Nuffield College, Oxford, as an official fellow, and in 1951 he was appointed to the chair of political science at the LSE.

The contrast between the public profile and enthusiastic socialism of Harold Laski, his predecessor, and Oakeshott's sceptical conservatism made the LSE appointment a dramatic one, and his famous inaugural lecture, *Political Education* (1951), made an appropriate splash. During his years at the LSE he lived in a small flat in Covent Garden. He administered the government department at the school with unostentatious efficiency, sending a stream of elegant handwritten notes to his colleagues, and was a familiar figure in the common room. He

avoided committees when he could, but none the less played his part, and his unmistakable prose in, for example, describing the duties of a tutor, was to pass unscathed through several revisions of the BSc (Econ.) degree.

In 1961 the University of London established the one-year master's degree, and although Oakeshott thought it an absurd idea, he set up an option within it on the history of political thought, which led to a distinguished seminar he ran with several colleagues. It drew scholars from all over the world, and he continued to attend until his late seventies. The work he did for this seminar, continually revised, appeared in *On History* (1983).

Oakeshott retired from the LSE in 1969 and eventually moved to Acton, near Langton Matravers in Dorset. Two cottages near a stone quarry had been knocked together, and he lined the walls with bookcases. Typically, he made something stylish out of the second-hand materials around him. He lived there until he died in 1990, though he often went to London to stay with his friends William and Shirley Letwin, or travelled to Hull or Durham, where favourite pupils were established in departments. He did venture to Harvard University, and to Colorado College in Colorado Springs, a favourite place which elicited 'A place of learning', later republished among other essays on education in *The Voice of Liberal Learning* (1989), edited by Timothy Fuller. More commonly, he travelled to France.

Oakeshott was slight of build and elegant in his dress without being ostentatious. Many of his clothes, like the furniture of his cottage in Dorset, were picked up second-hand. In everything he did he was stylish without being precious. His voice was light, but carried remarkably well. No one could better him at making some sense out of the most opaque academic paper; he was a matchless discussant. The real passion of his life, however, was to understand the uniquely human. Philosophy he took to be the search for the postulates of human activities. As exclusively concerned to understand rather than control the world, it was a pure, almost morbid, preoccupation. In *Experience and its Modes*, the most insidious of errors was found to be irrelevance—applying to one mode of activity the criteria appropriate to another. In his masterpiece *On Human Conduct* (1975), on which he had been working for years at the LSE but which came out after he had retired, the idea that experience is composed of a few discrete modes (practice, history, science, poetry) was loosened and replaced by 'conditional platforms of understanding', from which the enquirer casts his net to see what may be caught by any particular set of ideas.

Oakeshott argued that a modern state is best understood in terms of a distinction between two sorts of human association, which he called 'civil' and 'enterprise'. Characteristically, the first of the three essays in the book delineates what it is to enquire philosophically about human conduct, the second postulates the purely ideal forms of civil and enterprise association, and only in the third, long, historical essay does Oakeshott engage with the historical literature on the modern state, of which he had undoubtedly the most profound understanding of anyone in his generation. He has often been described as a 'conservative philosopher', but he regarded this expression as a solecism, for philosophers should not be partisans. Nevertheless he did eloquently characterize a conservative disposition: it corresponded to his own character.

Oakeshott was married three times. In 1927 he married Joyce Margaret, daughter of Guy Fricker, electrical engineer, of Harpenden; they had one son, Simon. The marriage was dissolved in 1938 and in the same year he married Katherine Alice Burton (d. 1964), daughter of Charles Frederick Burton, of Neuilly-sur-Seine, France. The couple had no children and their marriage was dissolved in 1951. In 1965 he married Christel Schneider, who had been brought up in Nuremberg, the daughter of Johann Schneider, bookkeeper and later dairy worker. They had no children.

Oakeshott refused public honours and honorary doctorates from several universities, but he did accept honorary doctorates from Colorado, Durham, and Hull. In 1966 he became a fellow of the British Academy. He died at his home, Victoria Cottage, in Acton, Dorset, on 18 December 1990.   KENNETH MINOGUE, rev.

Sources N. Johnson, 'Michael Joseph Oakeshott, 1901–1990', PBA, 84 (1994), 403–24 · J. Norman, ed., The achievement of Michael Oakeshott (1993) · The Times (22 Dec 1990) · The Independent (22 Dec 1990) · personal knowledge (1996) · CGPLA Eng. & Wales (1991)
Archives BLPES, corresp. and papers | CUL, corresp. with Sir Herbert Butterfield
Likenesses P. Gopal-Chowdhury, portrait, 1985, Gon. & Caius Cam. [see illus.]
Wealth at death £191,084: probate, 5 Feb 1991, CGPLA Eng. & Wales

Oakeshott, Sir Walter Fraser (1903–1987), schoolmaster and college head, was born on 11 November 1903 in South Africa, the second of two sons among the four children of Walter Oakeshott, medical practitioner, of Lydenburg, Transvaal, and his wife, Kathleen Fraser. After Dr Oakeshott's early death his wife brought the family home to England. Walter went to Tonbridge School, Kent, where he became head boy, leaving with an exhibition to Balliol College, Oxford, in 1922. He achieved first classes in classical honour moderations (1924) and literae humaniores (1926).

Oakeshott became an assistant master at Tooting Bec School, London, whence in 1927 he proceeded to Merchant Taylors' School. In 1931, after a year spent working for the Kent county education committee, he was appointed an assistant master at Winchester College, where he remained until 1938. Two events of his time there were important for him. The first was his discovery in 1934, among the manuscripts in the fellows' library, of the unique manuscript of Morte d'Arthur by Sir Thomas Malory. (His own full account of the find is given in Essays on Malory, edited by J. A. W. Bennett, 1963.) The second was the invitation to serve with the inquiry into unemployment sponsored by the Pilgrim Trust, for which he was given a year's leave of absence from the school (1936–7).

He took a major part in writing up the findings of the inquiry, in William Temple's Men without Work (1938).

In 1939 Oakeshott became high-master of St Paul's School, in London. On the outbreak of war he had to supervise the evacuation of the school to Crowthorne, Berkshire; the evacuation, and St Paul's adaptation to new surroundings and unfamiliar routines, were a triumph for his charismatic leadership. Soon after he had brought the school back to London in 1945 he was appointed headmaster of Winchester College, a post which he held from 1946 to 1954. Apart from one dire confrontation at the very end of his time, when his request to a housemaster to resign was challenged and upheld by only a majority on the governing body, this was a period of successful stewardship in a highly individual style. Although capable in administration he had no great taste for it, and where he shone was as a teacher and inspirer of the young, especially of those whom he stirred to share his own keen appreciation of artistic beauty. His personal rapport with boys of all ages and tastes left a very strong impression, fondly recalled by Wykehamists who were in the school during his time.

In 1954 Oakeshott was elected rector of Lincoln College, Oxford, where he presided for the next eighteen years. His was a period of remarkable expansion for the college, during which its tutorial fellowship more than doubled and its student accommodation greatly increased. In 1962–4 he was vice-chancellor of Oxford, and during his term a commission of inquiry into Oxford University (1964–6) was initiated, under the chairmanship of Lord Franks.

Both at Winchester and at Oxford, Oakeshott took a keen interest in buildings and restoration. At Winchester he was instrumental in the recovery of surviving panels of the college chapel's original medieval stained glass, dispersed in the nineteenth century, and their refitting in the windows of Thurbern's chantry. At Lincoln he was the moving spirit in the acquisition by the college of the redundant church of All Saints, for conversion into the college library. In Oxford he played a leading part in the restoration work made possible by the Oxford historic buildings appeal, in particular in the restoration of the stonework, sculptures, and interior of the Sheldonian Theatre.

Oakeshott dedicated the interstices of his busy life to scholarship, where his interests were many-sided. He wrote on Renaissance cosmography and early exploration (Founded upon the Seas, 1942, and several learned articles). His purchase and subsequent identification of a notebook belonging to Sir Walter Ralegh, written when he was collecting materials for The History of the World (1614), prompted research into the court culture of Elizabethan England and into Ralegh's poetry (The Queen and the Poet, 1962). His most abiding interest was in medieval art history, and his two studies of the Winchester Bible (The Artists of the Winchester Bible, 1945, and The Two Winchester Bibles, 1981) were authoritative and influential, especially the former, a pioneering work identifying the hands and styles of the painters who worked on the Bible and the influences which shaped their work. Among his other books were *Mosaics of Rome* (1967) and *Sigena Wall Paintings* (1972).

Oakeshott held honorary doctorates of the universities of St Andrews and East Anglia, and was an honorary fellow of both Balliol (1974) and Lincoln (1972). He was elected a fellow of the British Academy in 1971 and was knighted in 1980. He was master of the Skinners' Company (1960–61), a long-serving trustee of the Pilgrim Trust, and president of the Bibliographical Society (1966–8).

Oakeshott was a tall man, of gracious bearing, with a high forehead, eyebrows which fluttered in animation, and a characteristically beaming smile. His manner was gentle and courteous; he had an instinctive personal modesty, a delightfully whimsical wit, and a gift for friendship. In teaching, research, and life he strove continually for what he believed could inspire and elevate. He married in 1928 Noël Rose, daughter of Robert Oswald Moon, consultant physician. They had twin sons and two daughters, and the family was a close and affectionate one. His wife predeceased him in 1976, and he was buried beside her after he died, on 13 October 1987, at his home, the Old School House, Eynsham, Oxfordshire. M. H. KEEN, rev.

Sources J. Jones and S. Viney, eds., *The Balliol College register, 1930–1980*, 5th edn (privately printed, Oxford, 1983?) · F. R. Salter, *St Paul's School, 1909–1959* (1959) · *Lincoln College record, 1986–7* (1987) · *The Trusty Servant* (Dec 1987) [Winchester old boys' periodical] · J. Alexander and M. Keen, 'Walter Fraser Oakeshott, 1903–1987', *PBA*, 84 (1994), 421–44 · J. C. Dancy, *Walter Oakeshott: a diversity of gifts* (1995) · *The Times* (14 Oct 1987) · *The Times* (7 Dec 1987) · *The Independent* (15 Oct 1987) · *The Independent* (27 Oct 1987) · personal knowledge (1996) · private information (1996) · *CGPLA Eng. & Wales* (1988)
Archives BL, corresp. with Sir Sydney Cockerell, Add. MS 52742
Likenesses H. Oakeshott, sketch (in old age), repro. in W. F. Oakeshott, *The word of the spirit* · portrait, Winchester College · portrait, Lincoln College, Oxford
Wealth at death £26,908: probate, 11 Feb 1988, *CGPLA Eng. & Wales*

Oakley, Edward (*d.* in or before **1765**), architect, was first recorded in 1721 as an unsuccessful applicant for the post of clerk of works at the church of St Martin-in-the-Fields, London. This was presumably after his return from a period of 'civil service' abroad, where, he claimed, he had 'long contemplated a famous Republick', most likely in Venice (E. Oakley, *The Magazine of Architecture, Perspective, and Sculpture*, 1730, pt 2, preface).

Organized freemasonry occupied much of Oakley's time from 1724 to about 1731. He was one of the founders of the lodge of the Nag's Head and Star in Carmarthen, south Wales, in 1724 or 1725 and its senior warden in 1726. But the centre of his masonic activity was the lodge at the Three Compasses (or Carpenters' Arms) in Silver Street, London, of which he was senior warden in 1725 and later master. The speech he delivered to this lodge on 31 December 1728 was one of the earliest to define the qualifications and duties of members of the fraternity, laying stress on the dissemination of architectural knowledge through lectures and books. It gained considerable authority among a widespread audience of operatives in the building trades by its publication in Benjamin Cole's popular,

pocket-size edition of *The Ancient Constitutions of the Free and Accepted Masons* (1728–9).

Oakley practised what he preached: in 1730 he published *The Magazine of Architecture, Perspective, and Sculpture*, containing 'the most material Precepts from our best Authors … reduced … to the Easiest Practice'. For the benefit of craftsmen who could not afford this impressive folio he issued a second edition between October 1732 and May 1733 in sixteen fortnightly instalments costing 12*d.* each. His final contribution, *Every man a compleat builder, or, Easy rules and proportions for drawing and working the several parts of architecture*, published in 1766, was a reissue of W. Robinson's *Proportional Architecture* (1733) to which he added practical material lifted without acknowledgement from other authors.

As a builder in his own right, Oakley is not memorable. Though he advertised his services as a surveyor, measurer, designer, draughtsman, and manager of buildings, he did not make a name for himself in any of these fields. He competed unsuccessfully for the design of Westminster Bridge in 1735 and submitted the same indifferent designs in 1756 for Blackfriars Bridge with the same negative result. An engraving of the latter scheme was published in William Maitland's *History of London* (1756). The greenhouses and hothouses at Chelsea Physic Garden are the only buildings known to have been executed to his designs, of which he published an engraving by Benjamin Cole. They were begun in 1732 and finished in 1734. Oakley probably died in 1765; he was described as 'the late Edward Oakley' in a publisher's advertisement dated 20 November 1765 for his last book, *Every Man a Compleat Builder* (1766). EILEEN HARRIS

Sources Colvin, *Archs.* · E. Harris and N. Savage, *British architectural books and writers, 1556–1785* (1990), 333–4 · D. Knoop, G. P. Jones, and D. Hamer, eds., *Early masonic pamphlets* (1945), 5–7, 210–14 · J. T. Thorp, *Ars Quatuor Coronatorum*, 27 (1914), 145–7

Oakley, John (1834–1890), dean of Manchester, son of John Oakley, estate and land agent, of Blackheath, Kent, was born at Frindsbury, near Rochester, Kent, on 28 October 1834. He was educated at Rochester Cathedral school, and afterwards at Hereford grammar school. He entered Brasenose College, Oxford, as an exhibitioner in 1852 and graduated BA in 1857 (MA, 1859). He was an ebullient president of the Oxford Union for the Michaelmas term of 1856, during which he was sent down for non-attendance at college chapel. His father intended him for the profession of civil engineer, and for a short time he worked in an engineer's office at Chatham, but his own leanings were towards the church.

In 1858 he was ordained deacon, and had his first curacy at St Luke's, Berwick Street, Soho, London. After ordination to the priesthood in 1859 he served as curate at St James's, Piccadilly, while acting as secretary to the London diocesan board of education and as a promoter of the London Lay Helpers' Association. On 21 January 1861 he married Clara, daughter of Joseph Phelps of Madeira; they had a large family.

In 1867 Oakley was appointed vicar of the slum parish of St Saviour, Hoxton, London, where he remained until 1881 and proved a zealous and popular pastor. He was a committed high-churchman, but his ritualism aroused no opposition. A follower of Frederick Denison Maurice, his views on political and social questions were essentially liberal and he had genuine sympathy with working people and with the cause of the trade unions. He served as chairman of several conferences of trade union members and other parties. His popular touch earned him the compliment of a costermonger who dubbed him 'the poor bloke's parson'.

In 1881 Oakley accepted the offer of the deanery of Carlisle from W. E. Gladstone, one of whose sons was curate at Hoxton. Before leaving London, Oakley received an address and testimonial from a large number of clergy and laity. He remained at Carlisle for only two years, but this was long enough to make his mark as an innovator who sat light to the dignity of his office and eschewed gaiters. In November 1883 he was appointed dean of Manchester at a time of considerable difficulty, on account of legal disputes between the cathedral chapter and the Manchester rectors, and the prosecution and imprisonment of the ritualist S. F. Green, whose cause Oakley defended in opposition to Bishop James Fraser. In Manchester, as in London and Carlisle, movements that aimed to improve the condition of the working classes won his wholehearted support, even if this meant conflict with the more conservative members of his flock. Oakley cultivated ecumenical relations with the free churches and with Roman Catholics, took a keen interest in local education, and was a frequent contributor on church matters to the *Manchester Guardian*. His articles for that newspaper, signed Vicesimus, include a memoir (14 November 1883) of his friend H. N. Oxenham (1829–1888). Besides many separate sermons and papers, he published *The Christian Aspect and Application of the Decalogue* (1865) and 'The Conscience Clause': its History, Terms, Effect and Principle (1866).

Oakley's commanding figure, approachable manner, and fine countenance impressed all who met him. His health, however, was undermined by the strain of incessant activity, and he died, aged only fifty-five, at Deganwy, near Llandudno, on 10 June 1890. He was buried at Chislehurst, Kent, and a stained glass window was erected by public subscription to his memory in the south aisle of Manchester Cathedral.

C. W. SUTTON, rev. G. MARTIN MURPHY

Sources *The Guardian* (18 June 1890), 973 · *Manchester Guardian* (16 June 1890) · H. A. Morrah, *The Oxford Union, 1823–1923* (1923), 154–62 · M. Hennell, *The deans and canons of Manchester Cathedral, 1840–1948* [1988] · O. Chadwick, *The Victorian church*, 2nd edn, 2 (1972), 392 · 'The Very Rev. John Oakley DD, dean of Manchester', *Health Journal*, 5 (1887–8), 11–13

Archives BL, corresp. with W. E. Gladstone, Add. MSS 44412–44502 · LPL, letters to A. C. Tait

Likenesses photograph, c.1887, repro. in 'The Very Rev. John Oakley DD', 11–13 · R. T., wood-engraving (after photograph by Russell & Sons), NPG; repro. in *ILN* (21 June 1890)

Wealth at death £3755 16s. 3d.: administration with will, 28 July 1890, CGPLA Eng. & Wales

Oakley, Sir John Hubert (1867–1946), surveyor, was born at 65 Gloucester Place, Kensington, London, on 11 October 1867, the eldest son of Christopher Percival Oakley, surveyor, of Chislehurst, and his wife, Kate, daughter of Charles Kingsford, of Lewisham Hill, Kent. He was a nephew of John Oakley, dean of Manchester, and the grandson of John Oakley, surveyor, a founder in 1868 of the Surveyors' Institution, later the Royal Institution of Chartered Surveyors. Educated at Uppingham School, Oakley entered the Royal Agricultural College, Cirencester, in 1885, where he excelled as a student and athlete. A tall man of powerful physique, at rugby football he was captain of the college fifteen, capped for Gloucestershire, and tried for England.

Having passed out of Cirencester with honours at Christmas 1887, Oakley joined the family firm of Daniel Smith, Son and Oakley (later Daniel Smith, Oakley and Garrard), surveyors, land agents, and auctioneers, of London, which had been founded in 1780. He remained with them all his life, first as an articled pupil, from 1892 as partner, and from 1898 senior partner. Oakley married on 11 November 1891 at St James's Church, Croydon, Ida (b. 1869/70), only daughter of Daniel Watney, surveyor, of Brittleware, Croydon; they had one daughter, Margery Ruth.

A modest and kindly man, Oakley was held in respect and affection throughout his profession. His experience, founded upon an early training in agriculture, ranged over the whole field, urban and rural, of successful general practice. His reputation as a surveyor and valuer of real property was considerable; and his professional knowledge was reinforced with good judgement. His services as an arbitrator were in frequent demand; he once had to make what amounted to a valuation of the whole city of Hong Kong in order to resolve differences between two government departments. On another occasion he was appointed by the London county council and the landowners concerned to assess the betterment rate, then one of the first of its kind, to be levied upon lands benefited by, but surplus to, the Kingsway improvement scheme between Aldwych and Holborn. He followed his father as land agent for the St Germans estates at Blackheath and was responsible for their development.

Oakley served on the council of the Surveyors' Institution for twelve years and remained a member until his death. Like his father and father-in-law before him, and his brother-in-law after him, he became president of the institution, holding office in 1918. In the institution's *Transactions* for 1918–19 he reviewed its history and work (vol. 51, no. 642, 1–38) as it celebrated its golden jubilee. In 1925 he was elected president of the College of Estate Management, founded in 1919 as a centre of education for surveying and allied professions.

Oakley was a member of the royal commission on the universities of Oxford and Cambridge (1919–21); the committee on crown and government lands (1921–2); the royal commission on compensation for suffering and damage caused by enemy action (1922–4); the River Ouse drainage commission (1925–6); the Irish grants committee (1926–30); and the advisory committee on crown lands (1933–9). He was knighted in 1919 and appointed GBE in 1928. A member of the Conservative Club, he gave his interests as fishing and shooting.

Oakley died on 5 December 1946 at Welbeck Palace Hotel, Welbeck Street, London. His widow survived him.

H. G. TYRRELL-EVANS, *rev.* ELIZABETH BAIGENT

Sources *The Times* (7 Dec 1946) · *WWW* · *Debrett's Peerage* (1924) · *Journal of the Royal Institution of Chartered Surveyors* (Jan 1947) · *CGPLA Eng. & Wales* (1947) · private information (1959) · personal knowledge (1959) · b. cert. · m. cert. · d. cert.
Likenesses R. G. Eves, oils, Royal Institution of Chartered Surveyors, London
Wealth at death £32,281 15s. 3d.: probate, 25 June 1947, *CGPLA Eng. & Wales*

Oakley, Kenneth Page (1911–1981), anthropologist, was born on 7 April 1911 at Amersham, Buckinghamshire, the only child of Tom Page Oakley, schoolmaster and later headmaster of Dr Challoner's Grammar School, Amersham, and his wife, Dorothy Louise Thomas. He was educated at Challoner's Grammar School, University College School in Hampstead, London, and University College, London, where in 1933 he graduated BSc in geology (with anthropology as a subsidiary subject), gaining first-class honours and the Rosa Morison memorial medal. He then began PhD research at London University, successfully completing his thesis on Silurian pearl-bearing Bryozoa (Polyzoa) in 1938. That his research took five years to complete was due to his appointment in 1934 to a post with the geological survey and a year later to an assistant keepership in geology (palaeontology) at the Natural History Museum. Here he spent the rest of his working life, with the exception of secondment for war service back to the geological survey to work on water supply and mineral resources in Britain. In 1941 Oakley married (Edith) Margaret (*d.* 1987), daughter of Edgar Charles Martin, adjutant to the assistant comptroller at the Patent Office; she was a psychiatric social worker. They had two sons.

In 1955 the museum created a sub-department of anthropology within its department of palaeontology, and Oakley became its head, holding the title deputy keeper (anthropology) from 1959 to 1969, when the relentless progress of multiple sclerosis forced his premature retirement. Though he suffered much pain for the rest of his life, and was eventually confined to a wheelchair, his mental powers and his appetite for anthropological research remained strong and he continued to study and to publish his work right to the end.

While it is correct to describe Oakley as an anthropologist, this somewhat masks the breadth of his further expertise in geology, archaeology, and other disciplines within Quaternary studies. In the 1930s he did work of lasting importance on the palaeolithic and Pleistocene successions of the Thames valley, and was secretary and an influential member of the research committee set up in 1937 by the Royal Anthropological Institute to superintend work at Barnfield Pit, Swanscombe, Kent, following discovery of the famous Swanscombe skull fragments. Early hominid fossils fascinated Oakley, and his principal research throughout his career concerned them in one way or another. Soon after the war he began work with

Kenneth Page Oakley (1911–1981), by Walter Stoneman, 1957

various colleagues on methods of dating bone, notably by analysis of its fluorine content. An early result was his demonstration (with M. F. Ashley Montagu) that a supposedly Middle Pleistocene human skeleton from Galley Hill, Swanscombe, was in fact much younger than the gravels in which it was found. The fluorine method was also a starting point for his important contribution, working with C. R. Hoskins, J. S. Weiner, W. E. Le Gros Clark, and others, to the exposure of the Piltdown skull hoax, a revelation which caught the public's imagination in the mid-1950s and has held it ever since.

Oakley later became involved with radio-carbon dating of hominid remains, and for many years was widely consulted on problems concerning the age and status of hominid fossils all over the world. He travelled extensively to study material and attend conferences. He also became deeply interested in the mental capacities and cultural attainments of our early ancestors, for example when they first made tools or used fire, and in evidence for their collecting decorative curiosities such as fossil shells. His popular handbook *Man the Tool-Maker*, first published in 1949, went to six editions and a Japanese translation. His *Frameworks for Dating Fossil Man* (1964 and two later editions) combined his palaeoanthropological and archaeological interests into something approaching a textbook of early prehistory, which delighted many students. With B. G. Campbell and T. I. Molleson he produced the three-part *Catalogue of Fossil Hominids* (1967, 1971, 1975), a scholarly and invaluable reference work. Oakley's many dozen journal articles, spread over forty-five years, are distinguished by their clarity and readability, regardless of subject. His lectures were equally clear and always well received, and he was a stimulating and incisive contributor at conference discussion sessions.

Many academic honours marked Oakley's career, including the Wollaston Fund award (1941), the Henry Stopes memorial medal of the Geologists' Association (1952), fellowship of the Society of Antiquaries (1953), a London University DSc (1955), election as a fellow of the British Academy (1957), a fellowship of University College, London (1958), presidency of the Anthropological Section of the British Association for the Advancement of Science (1961), and the Prestwich medal of the Geological Society of London (1963).

Particularly during the last ten years of his life, Oakley fought a gallant and uncomplaining battle against his illness, sometimes seeming to take a scientist's dispassionate interest in its progress. He spent his final years living at Oxford, where friends from all over the world flocked to visit him and bring him news, a striking tribute to the esteem and affection in which he was held. He retained his interest in art (having been, like his father, an accomplished amateur painter) and in listening to music, and he never lost his charm of manner or his quiet sense of humour. He died on 2 November 1981 at Oxford, having worked up to the final weeks on publications which appeared posthumously. DEREK A. ROE

Sources *The Times* (5 Nov 1981) · F. W. Shotton, 'Kenneth Page Oakley, 1911–1981', *PBA*, 68 (1982), 617–26 · J. S. Weiner, *The Piltdown forgery* (1955), 26–53 · *CGPLA Eng. & Wales* (1982) · personal knowledge (2004) · private information (1990) [colleagues, esp. T. I. Molleson, BM, Natural History]
Archives NHM, corresp. and notebooks | Bodl. Oxf., letters to O. G. S. Crawford · NHM, corresp. with W. R. Dawson
Likenesses D. Farson, photographs, 1953, Hult. Arch.; repro. in *Nature's back room boys* (1953) · W. Stoneman, photograph, 1957, NPG [*see illus.*] · photograph, repro. in *The Times*
Wealth at death £79,805: probate, 23 March 1982, *CGPLA Eng. & Wales*

Oakley, Octavius (1800–1867), watercolour painter, was born in Bermondsey, London, on 27 April 1800, the eighth child of a wealthy London wool merchant. Intended for a medical career, he was sent to the school of Dr Nicholas at Ealing, but when his father's business collapsed after the price of wool fell in 1815 he was placed instead with a cloth manufacturer near Leeds. He had shown in any case a marked distaste for medicine, and he displayed no greater liking for the wool trade, his real interest being art. Of 'somewhat elegant appearance, and comparatively slight in physique, the "fine London chap"' struggled to gain acceptance in his new surroundings (Roget, 2.269) and found solace in making pencil sketches of his acquaintances. As his skill increased he began to charge for his work, and when the sitters became numerous he set up as a professional artist. He later learned to work in watercolour, developing 'a vigorous and bold style of painting, amounting sometimes almost to coarseness' (*Art Journal*).

Oakley's portraits of Yorkshire farmers gained wide repute, and when he moved to Derby, about 1825, he soon found aristocratic patrons. At Chatsworth, where he was invited to stay, he painted the duke of Devonshire and many of his distinguished guests. He also executed a watercolour portrait of Sir George Sitwell of Renishaw, great-grandfather of Sir Osbert Sitwell, who reproduced it in his memoir *Left Hand, Right Hand* (1945): 'finely drawn and composed ... it shows Oakley as a worthy successor to Henry Edridge' (Hardie, 98). Between 1826 and 1832 Oakley exhibited seventeen portraits at the Royal Academy, including those of Lord Melbourne (1829) and the duke of Rutland (1831). In addition he painted landscapes and rustic figures, singly and in groups, and for a number of years he abandoned the position of a fashionable portrait painter to concentrate on Gipsy subjects, earning him the nickname Gipsy Oakley.

Before the move to Derby, Oakley had married Maria Moseley, with whom he had three daughters, the last born about 1832. Maria Oakley's premature death meant the breakup of the family home, and Oakley spent a brief time in London in 1836 before settling in a villa in Holly Walk, Leamington, from where he continued his Gipsy studies. He later married again, his second wife being Mary Ann Oakley (d. 1900). In or about 1841 he was persuaded by artist friends to move to London, and shortly afterwards, on 4 February 1842, he was elected an associate of the Society of Painters in Water Colours; he became a full member on 10 June 1844. Oakley's 'clean, smooth and highly finished drawings' (Hardie, 268) became a familiar sight at Pall Mall East, where he exhibited 210 studies of rustic figures and landscapes, some of which were executed during visits to Guernsey and Sark in the Channel Islands. In the late 1840s he went with Paul Naftel to north Wales, where they sat at the feet of David Cox. In London he painted Italian organ boys, and he also resumed his portraiture, sending thirteen works to the Royal Academy between 1842 and 1860. Among them was *Mrs Octavius Oakley* (1860). He died at his home, 7 Chepstow Villas, Bayswater, on 1 March 1867, survived by his widow, and was buried in Highgate cemetery. His remaining works were sold at Christies on 11 and 12 March 1869. Examples of Oakley's works are held in the British Museum and Victoria and Albert Museum, London; Blackburn Art Gallery; Grundy Art Gallery, Liverpool; and Newport Art Gallery.

Each of Oakley's three daughters was a painter. The eldest, Agnes Oakley (1829–1866), who was active from about 1854, painted flowers and still life and exhibited five watercolours at Suffolk Street, including *Study of Roses* and *Ptarmigan and Grey Men*. Maria Louisa Oakley, Mrs Mark Anthony Bourdin (1830–1929), painted flowers and fruit and exhibited five watercolours at Suffolk Street, among them *Study in a Garden* and *Study of Camellias*. The youngest, Isabel Oakley [see Naftel, Isabel, under Naftel, Paul Jacob], who was baptized in Derby on 20 July 1832, painted portraits, genre, landscapes, and flowers, and married the watercolour painter Paul Jacob Naftel (1817–1891).

R. E. GRAVES, *rev.* MARK POTTLE

Sources J. L. Roget, *A history of the 'Old Water-Colour' Society*, 2 vols. (1891) · Bryan, *Painters* (1903–5) · Wood, *Vic. painters*, 2nd edn ·

M. Hardie, *Watercolour painting in Britain*, 3: *The Victorian period* (1968) • *DNB* • Redgrave, *Artists*, 2nd edn • Mallalieu, *Watercolour artists* • *Art Journal*, 29 (1867), 115 • B. Stewart and M. Cutten, *The dictionary of portrait painters in Britain up to 1920* (1997) • H. M. Cundall, *A history of British watercolour painting* (1929) • S. W. Fisher, *A dictionary of watercolour painters, 1750–1900* (1972) • *The exhibition of the Royal Academy (1826–60)* [exhibition catalogues] • exhibition catalogues, Society of Painters in Water-Colours, 1842–67 • *CGPLA Eng. & Wales* (1867)

Wealth at death under £3000: probate, 15 April 1867, *CGPLA Eng. & Wales*

Oakman, John (c.1748–1793), engraver and writer of songs and novels, was born at Hendon, Middlesex. He received a grammar-school education and was apprenticed to the map engraver Emanuel Bowen. He left before completing his indenture, having proved troublesome to his master; furthermore, he seduced Bowen's daughter, whom he married when he came of age. Oakman next opened a shop in the Haymarket with Darley and Harry Howard in order to sell their caricatures and humorous prints; he supplemented his income by writing bawdy novels, for which he also cut plates. *The Life and Adventures of Benjamin Brass* (1765), based in part on Oakman's own early career, was rapidly followed by others of the kind. *The Adventures of William Williams, an African Prince* emerged from his getting to know Williams in Liverpool gaol (for undefined misdeeds); the book enjoyed some contemporary success, especially among the Quakers, for its attack on the institution of slavery.

Equally prolific and more successful as a songwriter, Oakman was credited with many of the pieces sung at Vauxhall Gardens and Bermondsey Spa, and with others of a moral character for children; in addition he published collections of fables. Having travelled on foot throughout England and Wales, he had a fund of droll stories to relate about his experiences. His poverty was relieved from time to time by Christopher Anstey, author of *The Bath Guide*, by Anstey's father, and by a Mr Hughes for whom he wrote burlettas. Oakman's dislike of the settled life prevented his living in the comfort his songwriting might have afforded him. He died in October 1793 at the house of his sister, who kept a butcher's shop in one of the several King streets in Westminster, and was buried at Holy Trinity Minories. ANITA McCONNELL

Sources H. Lemoine, 'Letter and memoir of John Oakman', *GM*, 1st ser., 63 (1793), 1080–81 • Redgrave, *Artists*

Oaksey. For this title name *see* Lawrence, Geoffrey, third Baron Trevethin and first Baron Oaksey (1880–1971).

Oasland [Osland], **Henry** (*bap.* 1625, *d.* 1703), clergyman and ejected minister, was born at Lower Snead Farm, Rock, near Bewdley, in Worcestershire, the second son of 'Edward Osland and Elizabeth his wife', and he was baptized in Rock church on 22 May 1625. His father, a substantial yeoman, owned Lower Snead Farm. Henry was educated at Bewdley grammar school and at Trinity College, Cambridge, where he was greatly influenced by the master, Thomas Hill. Oasland had a conversion experience while attending the sermons of Samuel Hammond, fellow of Magdalene College, Cambridge. After conversion Oasland, as his manuscript autobiography records, felt contrition for the time he had spent in his youth in dancing, archery, and stage plays. He was admitted a sizar at Trinity College, Cambridge, on 27 April 1646, and graduated BA in 1650 and MA in 1653.

On new year's day 1650 Oasland attended the famous disputation on infant baptism between Richard Baxter and the anti-paedobaptist John Tombes, held in Bewdley Chapel. For a brief period Oasland officiated at Sheriffhales in Shropshire, in the absence of the incumbent, and later in 1650, having refused the post twice already, he accepted the position of curate at Bewdley Chapel, where he remained until his ejection in 1662. He was ordained in 1651 at St Bartholomew by the Exchange in London.

There can be no doubt that the dominant influence on Henry Oasland during his Bewdley ministry was Richard Baxter, the minister in nearby Kidderminster. After the inception of the Worcestershire Association of ministers in 1652 Oasland was one of Baxter's chief supporters and helpers. Baxter thought him 'the most lively, fervent, moving Preacher in all the County' (*Reliquiae Baxterianae*, 3.91). In 1653 Oasland was able to alert Baxter to the need to write about the contribution that magistrates could make to clerical discipline, a topic that Baxter discussed at length in the years 1656–9.

Oasland's letters to Baxter, together with other evidence, reveal the problems that he faced in Bewdley: the interference of John Boraston, rector of Ribbesford (his ecclesiastical superior) and the attitude of the Bewdley Baptists, to whom he wrote two letters in 1652 urging them to recognize his authority. He wanted to institute church discipline and pastoral oversight on the pattern of what Baxter was doing in Kidderminster, but felt that his opportunities at Bewdley were severely limited, though he does seem to have achieved a considerable measure of success. At one point he wanted to form a 'private' church out of his congregation, an idea that Baxter opposed—successfully, it seems (*Correspondence of Richard Baxter* 1.121). Calamy says that Oasland catechized the children of Bewdley on Thursdays, and if he was late in coming from Baxter's lecture, they would go and meet him and bring him to the town 'in a sort of triumphant manner' (Calamy, *Continuation*, 2.886).

On 24 July 1660 Oasland married Mary Bradley, *née* Henzey (*d.* 1706), at Old Swinford church. A widow, she was the daughter of the Stourbridge glass maker Joshua Henzey. In November 1661 Oasland was arrested because of his alleged involvement in the so-called Packington plot, an alleged presbyterian rising. He remained a prisoner until April 1662. On Bartholomew day, 24 August, he preached his farewell sermon. After his ejection he lived both in Stourbridge and in Bewdley. He continued, says Baxter, 'Preaching up and down privately where he can have opportunity, with Zeal and Diligence' (*Reliquiae Baxterianae*, 3.91), and Calamy recorded that 'He has often preach'd to a numerous Congregation of Nailors and Colliers, &c., in a Place surrounded by a Mud-wall, and he stood under a Tree' (Calamy, *Continuation*, 2.890). He preached in most of the midland counties.

The sufferings of the nonconformists at this period led Oasland, like many others, to become impatient of the non-separating nonconformity favoured by Richard Baxter. In 1670 the differences between the two friends widened into an at least temporary breach, in which Oasland wrote to a friend about Baxter, 'No man hath so lost himself', and Baxter wrote to Oasland accusing him of 'servility and people-pleasing' (*Correspondence of Richard Baxter* 2.92, 93). Under the declaration of indulgence of 1672 Oasland's houses at Bewdley and Oaken in Codsall, Staffordshire, were licensed for presbyterian worship. The declaration was withdrawn in 1673, but the situation of nonconformists was eventually to improve after the passing of the Act of Toleration in 1689. Oasland continued preaching until about a fortnight before his death, at Wordsley, Kingswinford, in Staffordshire, on 19 October 1703. When he was buried in Kingswinford church, no fewer than twelve funeral sermons were preached for him.

Henry Oasland died intestate, but there is an inventory of his goods (totalling nearly £38), taken on 1 November 1703, at the record office in Lichfield. In the parlour chamber are 'some old books', valued at £5 6s. 8d. The most interesting item is 'the decedent's Interest in the Coal Works', worth £18 12s. 6d. The 'Coal Works' in question were probably at Wordsley in Kingswinford, where Oasland was living at the time of his death. Henry Oasland has perhaps two main claims to our attention. He was a key member of the Worcestershire Association of ministers in the 1650s, and he was, after 1662, a nonconformist preacher in the heroic mould. In addition, his spiritual autobiography (which deserves to be far better known) offers a remarkable insight into the mentality of a seventeenth-century puritan. C. D. GILBERT

Sources Oasland's spiritual autobiography [reprinted *Bewdley Parish Magazine* (March 1878)] · *Reliquiae Baxterianae, or, Mr Richard Baxter's narrative of the most memorable passages of his life and times*, ed. M. Sylvester, 1 vol. in 3 pts (1696) · *Calendar of the correspondence of Richard Baxter*, ed. N. H. Keeble and G. F. Nuttall, 2 vols. (1991) · *Calamy rev.* · E. Calamy, *A continuation of the account of the ministers … who were ejected and silenced after the Restoration in 1660*, 2 vols. (1727), vol. 2, pp. 886–93 · J. R. Burton, *A history of Bewdley* (1883) · D. R. Guttery, *From broad glass to cut crystal* (1956) · A. Yarranton, *A full discovery of the first presbyterian sham-plot* (1681) · G. F. Nuttall, 'The Worcestershire Association: its membership', *Journal of Ecclesiastical History*, 1 (1950), 197–206 · R. D. Thompson, *Rock* (1981) · parish register, Rock and Heightington, 22 May 1625 [baptism] · parish register, Old Swinford, Worcestershire, 24 July 1660 [marriage] · W. M. Lamont, *Richard Baxter and the millennium: protestant imperialism and the English revolution* (1979) · H. Oasland, *The dead pastor yet speaketh* (1662) · D. Gilbert, 'Richard Baxter and Henry Oasland', *Baxter Notes and Studies*, 7/3 (1999), 2–13 · inventory of Henry Oasland, 1703, Lichfield Joint RO

Archives BL, letters to the Bewdley Baptists, sent to Edward Harley, Harley MS 6866 [copies] · DWL, Baxter letters

Wealth at death £37 18s. 9d.: 1 Nov 1703, inventory, Lichfield Joint RO

Oastler, Richard (1789–1861), factory reformer, was born on 20 December 1789 in St Peter's Square, Leeds, the eighth and last child of Robert Oastler (1748–1820), a local

Richard Oastler (1789–1861), by James Posselwhite (after B. Garside)

linen merchant, and his wife, Sarah Scurr (d. 1828). Of his mother's family little is known save that they were devout and respected middle-class folk who had been established in Leeds for many years. The Oastlers were yeoman farmers and freeholders of the parish of Kirby Wiske in the North Riding of Yorkshire. Robert Oastler had lived in Kirby Wiske until the age of sixteen, when his youthful embrace of Methodism led to an estrangement from his father. Disinherited, Robert went to the nearby market town of Thirsk, where he was raised by an uncle who shared his evangelical fervour. A chance acquaintance with John Wesley in 1766 'ripened into a more than common friendship' (Driver, 5), and by the time Richard was born in 1789, his father was a well-known leader of the local Methodist community. On the occasion of his last visit to Yorkshire in 1790, Wesley is said to have blessed young Richard Oastler in his arms. True or not, Oastler's entire upbringing reflected the spirit of that blessing, 'for from the moment of his birth he was breathing the air of deepest piety' (ibid., 13).

From the age of nine Oastler attended the Moravian boarding-school at Fulneck, near Leeds, where his tutor, Henry Steinhauer, left a deep impression on him as a man of real religious feeling. On quitting Fulneck aged seventeen, Oastler meant to become a barrister, but his father had prohibitive scruples about the law, and after a failed effort as an architect's apprentice in Wakefield, Oastler settled down as a commission agent, a sort of middleman, that is, between the wholesale houses of Leeds and the small retailers in the towns and villages of the West Riding. Before long he ranked among the principal merchants in Leeds, 'respected for his sterling integrity and honour and considered as one whose superior talents for business would shortly raise him to affluence and distinction' (Bull). In 1816 Oastler married Mary Tatham (1793–1845), the daughter of a wealthy Wesleyan lace manufacturer in Nottingham. They had two children, Sarah and Robert, both of whom died in infancy in 1819.

The circumstances of Oastler's life changed abruptly in 1820. His business failed and in February that year he was declared bankrupt. After his father's death in July 1820 he was appointed to succeed him as steward to Thomas Thornhill, the absentee squire of Fixby, near Huddersfield. Up to now, everything about Oastler's life—his Methodism, his commercial acumen, his political progressivism—had reflected his urban and middle-class upbringing. The assured social order of the landed estate was completely new to him, but he took to it at once, abjuring his radical Wesleyanism in favour of tory Anglicanism. Indeed, in Thornhill's absence Oastler became quite the squire *manqué*. He revived old manorial customs such as rent day and harvest fair. He rode the fields, got to know the tenants, and carefully disbursed alms among the cottagers. Community, family, and custom became his social ideals, as his awareness of the continuities of history deepened and his prejudices against trade and industry hardened. Of his essential nostalgia there can be no doubt. But nostalgia can generate social protest as much as social complacency, as Oastler's contemporaries were shortly to discover.

As it happened, Oastler had for some time been a prominent abolitionist, a well-known supporter of William Wilberforce's crusade against slavery in the colonies. Yet he was wholly ignorant, he later claimed, of the cruelties routinely practised in English textile mills when he rode over to Bradford in September 1830 to visit his friend John Wood. As the celebrated legend of 'Oastler's awakening' would have it, Wood told Oastler about the appalling conditions in the Bradford mills, and Oastler, aghast and unbelieving, at once (29 September 1830) dashed off the letter to the *Leeds Mercury* on 'Yorkshire slavery' that started the factory movement. The facts were probably less dramatic. Oastler's father had long been acquainted with the conditions of labour in the mills. Oastler himself had already joined with Michael Sadler in various sorts of philanthropic work among unemployed operatives in Leeds. And across the Pennines, in Lancashire, the factory movement was already well under way. Still, there is no discounting the dramatic effect of Oastler's intervention. For the first time a prominent local citizen of impeccably abolitionist credentials had asserted that:

> thousands of our fellow creatures and fellow subjects, both male and female, the miserable inhabitants of a *Yorkshire town* … are this very moment existing in a state of slavery *more horrid* than are the victims of that hellish system—'*colonial slavery*'. (Cole, 85)

The effect of these words, coming as they did at a time when, as Samuel Kydd remembered, 'England was moved from centre to circumference with appeals on behalf of the liberation of West Indian slaves' (Kydd, 1.108–9), was to turn factory reform into a compelling national issue.

In February 1831, largely in response to the factory furore that Oastler had provoked, John Cam Hobhouse, the radical MP for Westminster, announced a bill providing for an eleven-and-a-half-hour day for all textile workers under the age of eighteen. In Glasgow and Halifax woollen masters at once organized a campaign of resistance, and Hobhouse, fearful of losing his bill altogether, agreed to confine its provisions to cotton mills. Oastler was outraged, and in a manifesto significantly addressed 'to the Working Classes of the West Riding', he urged workers to take the issue of factory reform into their own hands. Within weeks scores of short time committees had sprung up across Yorkshire, closely patterned on the Wesleyan 'class meetings' and ambitiously pledged to a universal ten-hour day. June 1831 saw the sealing of the famous Fixby Hall compact, whereby Oastler and the workers of Huddersfield agreed to work together, without regard to party or sect, toward the ten-hour day. More than the effective beginning of the factory movement, the Fixby compact marked the birth of the idea of tory democracy. Still an unrepentant tory whose motto was 'The Altar, the Throne, and the Cottage', Oastler nevertheless now came forward as insurgent and rebel, the quintessential tory radical.

With the defection of Hobhouse, parliamentary leadership of the factory movement fell to Michael Sadler, an old friend of Oastler's and one who shared his radically paternalist disposition. Sadler at once introduced a Ten Hours Bill into the still unreformed parliament, only to see it shunted into a select committee of inquiry. Oastler testified at length before Sadler's committee, and in April 1832 he took the chief part in organizing the 'pilgrimage to York', the first of many outdoor marches and meetings that he was to dominate by force of his imposing stature—he was over 6 feet tall—and a voice 'stentorian in its power and yet flexible, with a flow of language rapid and abundant' (T. A. Trollope, *What I Remember*, 1887, 2.13). In outdoor demagoguery, in fact, Oastler now discovered his true calling. An essentially unsophisticated man, broad-shouldered, fresh-complexioned, abounding in joviality and health, and animated by an unequivocal moral code, he had, his biographer says, an oratorical power amounting 'almost to genius' (Driver, 127). It was this, more than anything, that earned him the sobriquet of the Factory King.

The factory movement suffered a serious set-back in December 1832, when, despite Oastler's best efforts on his behalf, Michael Sadler lost his seat at the general election following the passage of the Reform Bill. Sponsorship of Sadler's bill fell to Lord Ashley, later the seventh earl of Shaftesbury. The new whig government, meanwhile, anxious to appease the factory reformers without alienating manufacturers, appointed a royal commission of inquiry into the factory question. Oastler, furious at what he regarded as needless temporizing, at once organized a boycott of the commission's proceedings. Undaunted, the commissioners compiled a report that essentially confirmed Sadler's and Ashley's assertions, and in July 1833 the government carried a bill that, while it left the question of adult labour untouched, provided a twelve-hour day for workers between thirteen and eighteen years of age, and an eight-hour day for those under thirteen.

The period following the passage of Althorp's Act (as it came to be known) was one of confusion and disarray for the factory movement, as textile workers throughout the north were drawn into Robert Owen's elaborate schemes for the establishment of a 'new moral world'. In late 1833 John Fielden, the radical MP for Oldham, joined with Owen in organizing a general strike for eight hours, but Oastler stood aside from this effort. Paternalist that he was, he abhorred strikes and trade unions as much as he did the chimera of universal suffrage, and thus it was with grimly mixed satisfaction that he watched the collapse, in 1834, of Owen's grandiosely conceived Grand National Consolidated Trades Union. His own attention, meanwhile, had been distracted by the (to his mind) awful spectre of the new poor law. In his view, outdoor relief to the needy was a solemn obligation enjoined by God and tradition on the local community. To see that obligation abdicated in favour of 'the workhouse test' was more than he could bear, and when the time came, when the poor law commissioners in London attempted to impose their deterrent logic on the north, he would show to what lengths of turbulent defiance tory radicalism could extend.

Meanwhile, the government's attempt, in 1835, to repeal one of the provisions of Althorp's Act had dramatically revived the factory movement and restored Oastler to the popular attention he craved. At a meeting organized by the Blackburn short time committee in September 1836, he taxed the magistrates with their refusal to enforce the Factory Acts and threatened to show the factory children how to apply their grandmothers' old knitting-needles to the spindles 'in a way which will teach these law-defying millowner magistrates to have respect even to "Oastler's law"' (Driver, 327). Not surprisingly, this incitement to sabotage raised a great outcry, and Oastler found himself under the constant surveillance of the Home Office. Up to now, he had generally had his employer's support in his public commitments, but after the publication of *The Law or the Needle* (1836), relations between the two men were increasingly strained. When Oastler's campaign against the new poor law proved equally incendiary, Thornhill dismissed him from his position as steward (28 May 1838) and initiated legal proceedings against him for recovery of debts accumulated during his stewardship at Fixby. Pretext though they were, the debts were real and, unable to pay them, Oastler was committed to the Fleet prison for three and a half years on 9 December 1840.

From his prison cell Oastler edited a weekly newspaper, the *Fleet Papers*, in which he mixed accounts of his personal troubles with attacks on the whigs and the new poor law. But 'the pen was not Oastler's natural weapon' (Cole,

102); for all its energy the *Fleet Papers* exerted little influence. In 1842 his friends and admirers started an 'Oastler liberation fund' that amounted to £2500 by the end of 1843. The balance of his debts secured by Fielden, Oastler was freed in February 1844. Though lately eclipsed by Chartism, the factory movement was then at its height, but Oastler, ill and depressed, had little more to do with it. After his wife died in 1845 he retired to Guildford, in Surrey, on a small income provided by his friends. From 1851 to 1855 he edited a magazine, *The Home*, 'addressed primarily to working-class families and consecrated to disseminating the message of Christian Tory Democracy' (Driver, 513). His last years passed quietly, and he died in obscurity, of a heart attack, at Harrogate, Yorkshire, on 22 August 1861. He was buried (probably on 24 August) at St Stephen's Church, Kirkstall, near Leeds, and is remembered not as a thinker, nor as a writer, but as 'the embodiment of a folk-dream which had an especial cogency in the days of transition to an industrial economy' (ibid., 128–9). Homestead and hall, church and cottage, craftsmanship and harmony of function: these were the things that possessed his imagination, and in their name, paradoxically enough, Richard Oastler for ten turbulent years trod the edges of revolution.

STEWART A. WEAVER

Sources C. H. Driver, *Tory radical: the life of Richard Oastler* (1946) · G. D. H. Cole, 'Richard Oastler', *Chartist portraits* (1941), 80–105 · G. S. Bull, 'Lecture on the career and character of Richard Oastler', *Leeds Intelligencer* (7 Feb 1863) · DNB · A. Kydd [S. H. G. Kydd], *The history of the factory movement, from the year 1802 to the enactment of the Ten Hours' Bill in 1847*, 2 vols. (1857) · S. A. Weaver, *John Fielden and the politics of popular radicalism, 1832–1847* (1987) · d. cert.

Archives BL, corresp. and papers, Add. MS 41748 · Col. U., papers · LUL, Goldsmith's Library of Economic Literature | BLPES, letters to Thomas Allsop, etc., coll. misc. 525–6 · JRL, letters to John Fielden

Likenesses W. Barnard, mezzotint, 1832 (after T. H. Illidge), NPG · E. Morton, lithograph, 1838 (after portrait by W. P. Frith), NPG · G. E. Madeley, lithograph, 1840, repro. in *Fleet Papers*, 1 (1841), frontispiece · lithograph, 1840, NPG · photograph, c.1860, repro. in *Bradford Antiquary* (Oct 1911) · J. B. Phillips, bronze statue, 1866, Rawson Square, Bradford · B. Garside, oils, Huddersfield Public Library · B. Garside, stipple and line engraving (after J. Posselwhite), NPG · J. Posselwhite, stipple and line engraving (after B. Garside), NPG [*see illus.*]

Oates, Francis (1840–1875), traveller and naturalist, the second of three sons of Edward Oates of Meanwoodside, near Leeds, Yorkshire, and Susan, daughter of Edward Grace of Burley, in the same county, was born at Meanwoodside on 6 April 1840. He matriculated from Christ Church, Oxford, on 9 February 1861, but took no degree, owing to bad health. For some years from 1864 he was an invalid. In 1871 he travelled in North and Central America, where he made a collection of birds and insects. On his return in 1872 he was elected a fellow of the Royal Geographical Society. On 5 March 1873, accompanied by his brother W. E. Oates, he sailed from Southampton for Natal hoping to make a journey to the Zambezi and, if possible, to some of the unexplored country to the north to study the geography and zoology. He left Pietermaritzburg on 16 May 1873 and spent some time in the Matabele (Ndebele) country north of the Limpopo River. Three attempts to proceed were frustrated by the weather and the opposition of the local people. Finally, starting on 3 November 1874, he arrived on the banks of the Zambezi on 31 December, and made large collections of specimens of natural history. He was one of the first outsiders to see the Victoria Falls in full flood; but no entries are found in his journal after his arrival there. The unhealthy season came on, and Oates contracted a fever. After an illness of twelve days, he died when near the Makalaka kraal, about 80 miles north of the Tati River, on 5 February 1875, and was buried the following morning. Dr. A Bradshaw, who happened to be in the neighbourhood, attended him, and saw to the safety of his collections. Oates's journals were edited and published by his brother Charles George Oates in 1881, under the title of *Matabele Land and the Victoria Falls*. A second, enlarged, edition (1889) has appendices by experts on the natural history collections which proved of more value than the text itself.

G. C. BOASE, *rev.* ELIZABETH BAIGENT

Sources *Journal of the Royal Geographical Society*, 45 (1875), clii · C. G. Oates, 'Memoir', in *Matabele Land and the Victoria Falls …: from the letters and journals of the late Frank Oates*, ed. C. G. Oates, 2nd edn (1889), xix–xlii · *The Times* (26 May 1875) · J. Foster, ed., *Pedigrees of the county families of Yorkshire*, 3 vols. (1874)
Likenesses portrait, repro. in Oates, 'Memoir'

Oates, Lawrence Edward Grace (1880–1912), Antarctic explorer, was born on 17 March 1880 at Putney, London, one of the four children, and the elder son, of William Edward Oates (1841–1896), gentleman, of Gestingthorpe Hall, Essex, and his wife, Caroline Anne, *née* Buckton, of Meanwood, Leeds. He spent two years at Eton College but was withdrawn with ill health and was afterwards educated privately. In 1898 he was gazetted to the 3rd West Yorkshire (militia) regiment and in April 1900 he was commissioned into the regular army, and posted to the 6th (Inniskilling) dragoons. He served with distinction in the Second South African War and was severely wounded in the thigh on 6 March 1901. He was mentioned in dispatches and invalided home, but returned to his unit before the end of the year and was promoted lieutenant on 2 February 1902. He afterwards served with his regiment in Ireland, Egypt (where he became captain and adjutant in 1906), and India.

Oates was devoted to hunting and steeplechasing and was happiest when working with horses, but he was also a keen yachtsman and had a thirst for adventure. When army life in India began to pall he applied to join Captain Robert Falcon Scott's second Antarctic expedition and in March 1910 learned that he had been accepted. He had offered to contribute £1000 to expedition funds but it was for his expertise with horses that he was taken on, and he was put in charge of the nineteen ponies that were vital to the south pole attempt.

Nearly 6 feet tall with a strong frame, Oates was an independent-minded character with little time for ceremony or pretence. He arrived at the expedition ship *Terra Nova* in London in the spring of 1910 wearing an old raincoat and was scrutinized by the crew who, according to

Lawrence Edward Grace Oates (1880–1912), by Herbert George Ponting, *c.*1911 [right, with Cecil H. Meares, at the blubber stove]

the Irishman Tom Crean, 'never for a moment thought he was an officer, for they were usually so smart. We made up our minds he was a farmer.' Crean added: 'but oh! he was a gentleman, quite a gentleman, and always a gentleman!' (Gregor, 34). As the only cavalry officer on an expedition staffed primarily by naval men, Oates won respect by his hard work and he grew to be more popular with the seamen than perhaps any other officer. Such was his contribution to the *Terra Nova* that he was kept on the ship for the voyage south, instead of being sent to oversee the purchase of the expedition ponies in Siberia.

In retrospect this was a grave mistake, and when Oates first saw the animals, at Lyttelton, New Zealand, he was dismayed at the selections made. Scott, however, was inclined to think that he was too pessimistic and there was considerable tension between them as a result. News that a Norwegian expedition was also bound for the south pole sharpened Oates's misgivings about the British undertaking and of Roald Amundsen he wrote: 'If he gets to the Pole first we shall come home with our tails between our legs and no mistake … I myself think these Norskies are a very tough lot' (Limb and Cordingley, 123). Rather ominously he noted that they had 200 dogs: the British expedition had 32.

Once ashore at Cape Evans, Oates urged that the ponies be worked hard in preparation for the polar journey, but Scott would not allocate the necessary manpower. The animals struggled during the depot-laying expedition across the great ice barrier (now the Ross Ice Shelf) during

January and February 1911, and Oates spent the polar winter striving to build up their strength. Known on the expedition as 'Titus', or 'the Soldier', he was conservative in outlook and naturally taciturn. He affected a dislike of foreigners, an indifference to society in general and women in particular (he was unmarried), and preferred long periods in the relative isolation of the stables to life in the cramped expedition hut. But for all his austerity and reserve he was well liked, with 'a fund of dry humour, and a store of anecdote from which gems would drop at the most unexpected moments' (Ponting, 161). His care of the ponies was universally admired. More than most he suffered from the perpetual darkness and he wrote to his mother, to whom he was extremely close, that he had no intention of remaining for a second winter if it could be avoided.

As the southern journey approached, Oates's frustration with Scott reached its pitch. The failure of the expedition's two experimental motor sledges put extra pressure on the ailing ponies and in a letter to his mother on 24 October 1911, Oates complained: 'it is perfectly wretched starting off with a lot of cripples … I dislike Scott intensely and would chuck the whole thing if it was not that we are a British expedition and must beat those Norwegians' (Limb and Cordingley, 169). But he later added: 'please remember that when a man is having a hard time he says hard things about other people which he would regret afterwards' (ibid., 173).

After the main polar party set out across the ice barrier on 1 November, Scott began to appreciate better the true extent of the ponies' failings and of Oates's achievement in bringing them so far. The animals performed their task of transporting loads across the barrier and when the last was shot, at the foot of the Beardmore Glacier on 9 December, a load was lifted from Oates's shoulders. On new year's eve, sitting in Scott's tent high on the polar plateau, he unusually took the lead in the conversation and talked openly for hours about his home and horses and life in the army. One of those present, Lieutenant Edward Evans, later recalled:

At length Captain Scott reached out and affectionately seized him in the way that was itself so characteristic of our leader, and said, 'You funny old thing, you have quite come out of your shell, Soldier. Do you know, we have all sat here talking for nearly four hours?' (Evans, 'Captain Oates', 626)

On 3 January 1912 Scott announced a five-man team for the pole. Along with Dr Edward Adrian Wilson, Lieutenant Henry Robertson Bowers, Petty Officer Edgar Evans, and Scott himself, it included Oates, who was selected for his strength and toughness. Scott must also have felt that he deserved the honour because of his work with the ponies, and as a representative of the army. In a letter to his mother, to be taken back with the last returning party, Oates was restrained in his reaction to the news, but wrote emotionally about his longing for his home and family. Dr Edward Atkinson, leader of the team that had turned back on 21 December, thought that by then Oates did not want to go on. His feet were wet and cold and he was troubled by his old war wound, and gave the impression of someone

'who knew he was done—his face showed him to be and the way he went along' (Limb and Cordingley, 194). On 15 January, about 30 miles from the pole, Oates wrote that he 'felt very depressed and homesick' (Huntford, 512). Scott's team reached the pole on 18 January 1912 and Oates was ungrudging in his respect for the Norwegians who had beaten them there (on 14 December 1911): they seemed to have had, he noted, 'a comfortable trip with their dog teams, very different from our wretched man-hauling' (Limb and Cordingley, 196).

The return journey was from the outset a struggle for survival, and after the death of Edgar Evans on 17 February 1912 Oates was the principal cause for concern. From 26 February to 2 March the minimum temperatures dipped below $-30\ °F$ every day, and on the latter date Oates revealed to Dr Edward Wilson his badly frostbitten feet. By 5 March they were in a 'wretched condition' and although he never complained, he had become, in Scott's words, 'a terrible hindrance' to the others (Scott, *Diaries*, vol. 2, 5 and 6 March 1912). On 10 March, Oates asked Wilson if he 'had a chance', to which Wilson replied that he did not know, and Scott recorded: 'In point of fact he has none' (ibid., 10 March 1912). In fighting for his own life Oates risked jeopardizing the survival of his companions and Scott wrote on 11 March: 'he is a brave fine fellow and understands the situation, but he practically asked for advice—nothing could be said but to urge him to march as long as he could' (ibid., 11 March 1912). Scott, however, compelled Wilson to give to each man thirty opium tablets from the medicine case, 'the means of ending our troubles' (ibid.). They were not used. At lunch on 15 March Oates proposed that the others should leave him behind in his sleeping-bag, but they persuaded him to go on. He woke next morning, 16 March 1912, and according to Scott:

It was blowing a blizzard; he said I am just going outside and may be some time. He went out into the blizzard and we have not seen him since … We knew that poor Oates was walking to his death but though we tried to dissuade him we knew it was the act of a brave man and an English gentleman. (ibid., 16/17 March 1912)

His thoughts were of his regiment and, lastly, his mother: 'he did not—would not give up hope till the very end' (ibid.).

Oates's three companions made only about 18 miles before their final camp at 79°50′ S on 19 March, where they died about ten days later. Their tent was found by the relief expedition led by Edward Atkinson on 12 November 1912 and a cairn was built over it, commemorating also Evans and Oates. Scott's diary revealed what had happened to the polar party and the relief expedition travelled two days south in a vain search for Oates's body. As near as they could judge to the site of his death they built a memorial cairn. At the burial service on 12 November Scott's moving account of Oates's death was read aloud and from this point onwards the legend of his heroism spread. His parting words became familiar to successive generations of his countrymen and his noble deed an inspiration. R. C. K. Ensor, in his *England, 1870–1914* (1936), saw the praise reaped by Oates in Edwardian England as indicating the shifting moral emphasis of the time (p. 553), and in 1961 the lord chancellor, Viscount Kilmuir, arguing in a debate on the Suicide Bill for a more sympathetic approach, noted that Captain Oates 'commands the respect and admiration of us all' (*Hansard 5L*, 2 March 1961, col. 247).

In a less romantic age Oates's tragic end has become key evidence in the historical inquiry conducted into Scott's leadership of the expedition, and his death has been portrayed not as an act of heroic self-sacrifice so much as of suicide brought on by unbearable pain. But it is the original interpretation that endures, encapsulated in the inscription left by the relief expedition at his memorial cairn:

> Hereabouts died a very gallant gentleman, Captain L. E. G. Oates of the Inniskilling Dragoons. In March, 1912, returning from the Pole, he walked willingly to his death in a blizzard, to try and save his comrades, beset by hardships. (Evans, *South with Scott*, 254)

The Oates Coast (69°30′ S, 159°00′ E) and the Oates Piedmont Glacier (76°25′ S, 162°35′ E) in Antarctica are named after him. MARK POTTLE

Sources S. Limb and P. Cordingley, *Captain Oates: soldier and explorer*, rev. edn (1995) · *DNB* · R. F. Scott, *Scott's last expedition: the journals* (1951) · R. F. Scott, *The diaries of Captain Robert Scott: a record of the second Antarctic expedition, 1910–1912*, 6 vols. (1968), vol. 2 · H. G. R. King, ed., *Edward Wilson: diary of the 'Terra Nova' expedition to the Antarctic, 1910–1912* (1972) · A. Cherry-Garrard, *The worst journey in the world: Antarctic, 1910–1913* (1951) · E. R. G. R. Evans, *South with Scott* (1921); repr. (1962) · E. R. G. R. Evans, 'Captain Oates: my recollections of a gallant comrade', *Strand Magazine* (Dec 1913), 615–26 · H. G. Ponting, *The great white south* (1921) · J. Debenham Back, ed., *The quiet land: the diaries of Frank Debenham* (1992) · G. Seaver, 'Birdie' *Bowers of the Antarctic* (1938) · G. Hattersley-Smith, ed., *The Norwegian with Scott: Tryggve Gran's Antarctic diary, 1910–1913* (1984) · S. Solomon, *The coldest March: Scott's fatal Antarctic expedition* (2001) · G. C. Gregor, *Swansea's Antarctic explorer: Edgar Evans, 1876–1912* (1995) · S. Wheeler, *Cherry: a life of Apsley Cherry-Garrard* (2001) · R. Huntford, *Scott and Amundsen* (1993) · W. Young, 'On the debunking of Captain Scott', *Encounter*, 54/5 (May 1980), 8–19 · F. Spufford, *I may be some time: ice and the English imagination* (1996) · E. Huxley, *Scott of the Antarctic* (1977) · Burke, *Gen. GB* (1914) [Oates of Gestingthorpe Hall] · private information (2004) [Scott Polar RI]
Archives Gilbert White Museum, Selborne, Hampshire, Oates Memorial Library, corresp. and papers · Scott Polar RI, letters, mainly to his mother
Likenesses J. Weston & Son, photographs, c.1900, Scott Polar RI · photographs, c.1907–1908, Scott Polar RI · F. Debenham, photograph, c.1911 (in Antarctic), Scott Polar RI · H. G. Ponting, photograph, c.1911, NPG [see illus.] · H. G. Ponting, photographs, c.1911–1912, Scott Polar RI · photographs, 1912, repro. in Limb and Cordingley, *Captain Oates* · J. N. Holroyd, oils, c.1951–1952 (after photograph), Scott Polar RI · Lady Scott, bronze medallion, Eton · A. G. Walker, bronzed plaster statues (with R. F. Scott and E. A. Wilson), Scott Polar RI · oils, Gestingthorpe Hall, Essex · portrait, repro. in Limb and Cordingley, *Captain Oates*
Wealth at death £28,828 5s. 7d.: probate, 2 Jan 1914, *CGPLA Eng. & Wales*

Oates, Samuel (*bap.* 1614, *d.* 1683), General Baptist preacher and Leveller, was baptized at St Saviour's Church, Norwich, on 26 September 1614, the son of Titus Oates, a Church of England clergyman, and his wife, Anne. He is not to be confused with a namesake, the son of

another Norfolk clergyman, born at Marsham in 1610. Nothing is known of Oates's youth, and we have only his own claim, reported by John Drew, that during the early 1640s he received 'a direct and lawful call from a church in Norfolke to a pastorall charge there' (Drew, 11). In 1647 hostile witnesses described him variously as a weaver and a button maker.

Oates was probably rebaptized by Thomas Lamb, the soapboiler, perhaps on the latter's visit to Norwich in early 1642. Oates's fame spread quickly: on 14 December 1643, at Westminster, John Lightfoot referred to him as a 'notorious anabaptist about Norwich' (*Whole Works*, 13.81). Oates continued there for some months, but visited London in early 1645, preaching at Lamb's church in Bell Alley. He seems to have joined that congregation soon after, and in September set off with Lamb on a missionary tour, giving sermons at Guildford and Portsmouth. This apprenticeship served, he struck out on his own in a career of itinerant evangelism which caused acute anxiety to the authorities in several counties.

In Essex, the following spring, it was noted that Oates 'hath been sowing his Tares, Bookmong, and wild Oates in these parts these five weeks without any controll, hath seduced hundreds, and dipped many in Bocking River'; he was 'a lusty young fellow' who 'traded chiefly with young women and young maids, dipping many of them, though all is fish that comes to his net, and this he did with all boldnesse, and without all controul for a matter of two months' (Edwards, 2.147–8). This lurid picture probably owed much to the imaginations of the presbyterian ministers who painted it. But at the Essex quarter sessions at Chelmsford, in March 1646, Oates was certainly charged with unlawful assembly at Braintree and Bocking, in breach of the peace and in contempt of authority. Imprisoned for a time in Colchester gaol, he was reported to have been visited by large numbers of friends from London, some in coaches. In April he was acquitted of having caused the death of a young woman by immersing her in a river. At Terling he debated with John Stalham, who also recalled a sermon by Oates 'at the corner of a corn field in our town' (Stalham, preface). On 29 June he disputed for several hours with Ralph Josselin, vicar of Earls Colne, and the following morning commenced three days of exercises at Chelmsford. Essex magistrates seem not to have succeeded in stopping his activities, but the following year Oates turned his attention elsewhere.

In March 1647 Oates appeared in Rutland, where the parish ministers urged the authorities to act against him. But here, as in Essex, it was impossible to mobilize the machinery of the law when the political and military will to punitive action was wanting. Oates continued to win a following, partly on the basis of agitation around the issue of tithes; lay preachers thought it proper to 'live of the gospel', and he seems to have achieved success in this by passing his own hat among the audiences. By early December 1647 nineteen parish ministers of Rutland were complaining to parliament that he continued touring 'from town to town preaching and rebaptising very many and drawing a concourse of people after him'. To

Oates, they attributed much doctrinal deviancy, including the belief that Christ had died for all men and that the soul died with the body. And his meetings became more openly political: it was reported that the preacher had 'lately been a great dispenser and promoter' of 'that seditious paper Called the *Agreement of the People*, bringing or sending it to diverse places through the country, which he hath by himself or his agents brought or sent to several towns in the countie' (Betteridge, 207–9). One of these agents was probably Robert Everard, an agent of Cromwell's regiment, who had published the agreement in November and was soon after active among the Baptists of nearby Leicestershire.

This turbulence evidently provoked the central authorities to act: on 11 December the House of Lords ordered that Oates be arrested and brought before them, but on the 31st they found it necessary to issue a second order, admitting that he had escaped, and instructing the sheriffs of Lincolnshire, Rutland, Leicestershire, and Northamptonshire to return him to London, should they succeed in apprehending him. Neither this, nor a further order of 22 January 1648, had much practical consequence. Rearrested in Rutland, Oates was bound to appear before the judges of assize; he did not attend, but was acquitted anyway on a technicality. In May 1648 the Lords received further news. Oates remained active in Rutland, unrepentant and highly politicized, having uttered 'most sedicious and treasonable speeches against monarchy itself': in another outraged petition the county ministers pleaded for 'the dissolving of the schismatical and mutinous meetings of his deluded followers' (Betteridge, 210–11). But Oates continued on his way. At Barrow-on-Soar, Leicestershire, he had a hostile encounter with George Fox; it was probably about this time that an excursion to Lincolnshire provoked the pamphlet against him by John Drew, rector of Barrowby. And at Oakham, Rutland, some time during the first half of 1649, Oates's wife, Lucy (*d.* in or after 1697), a midwife from Hastings, gave birth to a baby boy, to whom they gave the name Titus [*see* Oates, Titus (1649–1705)].

On 30 October 1649 Oates disputed in public with William Sheffield, rector of Ibstock, at Leicester Castle. Here the proponent of anti-paedobaptism was said to have been reduced to silence, but this victory (if such it was) was not enough for the magistrates. For his speeches Oates was the following day incarcerated in the castle's dungeon, together with his associate, Ralph London. Soon, however, he was freed, and by February 1650 was commissioned chaplain to Colonel Pride's regiment, possibly through the influence of another General Baptist, John Mason, who had been made lieutenant-colonel about August 1648; this was one of the regiments which invaded Scotland in July 1650 and pursued the Scottish forces to Worcester the following year.

Like other political radicals, Oates opposed the trend in General Baptist churches towards the receiving of members with the laying on of hands (though he was later accused of inconsistency), and some time in 1653, being in the county, he intervened at the request of a Lincolnshire church who opposed their pastor's adoption of it. About May 1653 Oates was in London, disputing with John Spittlehouse, an open-membership Calvinistic Baptist who also espoused this practice. Perhaps a little later, Cromwell received a letter concerning the dissolution of the Rump and the new assembly on behalf of the congregation at the Stone Chapel, St Paul's, led by Edmund Chillenden. This was signed by Oates and other men, chiefly military figures.

Oates was again chaplain of Pride's regiment when it returned to Scotland in April 1654; his service may have been continuous from 1650. On 2 December he wrote from Aberdeen to Corporal Parkinson of Whalley's regiment

> in great heaviness to think how we made the hearts of the righteous sade … by our not answering there expectations; for we have promised to make them a free people, and that they should have free and sucksessive parlements, but parforme neither

and enclosed a summary of a letter already sent to sympathizers in several regiments, urging them to meet at the Green Dragon in Edinburgh on 1 January (Nickolls, 132). Papers found on Oates indicate his deep disquiet with the powers vested in Cromwell as lord protector. Perhaps, he wondered, the new regime might be better than it appeared; he struggled to suppress his fears, in the hope that some authoritative representative of the new order would allay his anxieties. These musings did not amount to any well-worked plan, but on 16 January 1655, as Monck reported, Oates was arrested. He was expecting trouble, complaining bitterly against the 'cry that is unjustly on me'. There was 'not word of sedition' in the letter circularized to soldiers: 'we intended nothing but was consonant to the ground and end of our warres, and the honest declarations we have made, and concluded in fine to offer our service in this matter in an humble petition to the Protector' (MS Rawl. A.34, fols. 49–50).

The context, however, was one in which several high army officers in Scotland were planning a coup involving the enforced installation of Robert Overton as commander. Overton seems not to have been a party to the conspiracy, and it is also possible that Oates was merely an auxiliary, to whom the military plans were not confided. Still, he was courtmartialled, cashiered, imprisoned, and shortly afterwards taken to London. Here he was granted a reprieve, and perhaps the satisfaction he had sought, for on 31 March, Monck reported that 'yesternight Oates was with his highness, who gave him only a sharp reproof for his folly, upon promise of his faithful deportment for the future' (Firth, *Clarke Papers*, 3.31).

Very little is known about Oates after the Restoration. The government suspected him of involvement in the Yorkshire plot in 1663, but this is unlikely. On 29 June 1667, following a brief stay at Merchant Taylors' School, Titus Oates was admitted to Caius College, Cambridge; the following year his father abandoned the Baptists and was instituted to the rectory of Hastings. In 1673 he resigned and returned to London, rejoining his old denomination. In 1682 he visited Henry Danvers and may have been on the fringes of groups that were plotting against the government. He died on 6 February 1683, leaving his widow and sons Titus, Samuel, and Constant.

STEPHEN WRIGHT

Sources *The Clarke papers*, ed. C. H. Firth, 4 vols., CS, new ser., 49, 54, 61–2 (1891–1901) · T. Edwards, *Gangraena, or, A catalogue and discovery of many of the errours, heresies, blasphemies and pernicious practices of the sectaries of this time*, 3 vols. in 1 (1646) · A. Betteridge, 'Early Baptists in Leicestershire and Rutland [pts 1 and 3]', *Baptist Quarterly*, 25 (1973–4), 204–11, 354–78 · *Original letters and papers of state addressed to Oliver Cromwell … found among the political collections of Mr John Milton*, ed. J. Nickolls (1743) · C. H. Firth, ed., *Scotland and the protectorate: letters and papers relating to the military government of Scotland from January 1654 to June 1659*, Scottish History Society, 31 (1899), 238, 241, 248, 251, 252 · letter to Robert Jeffes, 15 Nov 1653, Bodl. Oxf., MS Rawl. A. 8, fol. 127 · copy of papers found on Oates at Leith, *c.*Jan 1655, Bodl. Oxf., MS Rawl. A. 34, fols. 49–50 · J. Drew, *A serious address to Samuel Oates* (1649) · *The diary of Ralph Josselin, 1616–1683*, ed. A. MacFarlane, British Academy, Records of Social and Economic History, new ser., 3 (1976) · *The journal of George Fox*, rev. edn, ed. J. L. Nickalls (1952) · J. Stalham, *Vindiciae redemptionis in the Fanning … Samuel Oates* (1647) [E384(10)] · *Records of the borough of Leicester*, 4: *1603–1688*, ed. H. Stocks (1923) [Hall papers XII 551] · E. B. Underhill, ed., *Records of the Churches of Christ, gathered at Fenstanton, Warboys, and Hexham, 1644–1720*, Hanserd Knollys Society (1854) · D. Witard, *Bibles in barrels: a history of Essex Baptists* (1962) · J. Venn and S. C. Venn, *Admissions to Gonville and Caius College … March 1558–9 to Jan 1678–9* (1887) · R. L. Greaves, *Secrets of the kingdom: British radicals from the Popish Plot to the revolution of 1688–89* (1992) · W. T. Whitley, 'An early recruit from the clergy', *Baptist Quarterly*, 2 (1924–5), 330–32 · *The whole works of the Rev. John Lightfoot*, ed. J. R. Pitman, 13 vols. (1822–5), vol. 13 · Greaves & Zaller, *BDBR*, vol. 2, 271–2

Archives Bodl. Oxf., MS Rawl. A

Oates, Titus (1649–1705), informer, was born at Oakham, Rutland, a younger son of Samuel *Oates (*bap.* 1614, *d.* 1683), Baptist preacher, and his wife, Lucy (*d.* in or after 1697), a midwife from Hastings. His father, son of a Church of England clergyman in Norfolk, was a radical preacher in several counties, including Rutland, in the 1640s and chaplain to Colonel Pride's regiment in the 1650s. At the time of the Restoration in 1660 the family was living in Hastings and decided to rejoin the Church of England, Titus and his brother Constant being baptized at All Saints' Church, Hastings, on 20 November 1660. Titus also had an elder brother, Samuel, and two sisters, Hannah and Anne.

Early life Domestic violence and his father's dislike of him marred Oates's early life. He was later described as a dull, unlovable child who suffered from convulsions, a runny nose, and a tendency to dribble. In 1664 he attended Merchant Taylors' School in London as a free scholar under the tuition of William Smith, whom he later accused of playing a part in the Popish Plot. Smith found Oates a dullard and, discovering that Oates had cheated him of his tuition fees, subsequently expelled him. In 1665 he attended a school at Seddlescombe, some 6 miles from Hastings, and in June 1667 he went up to Gonville and Caius College, Cambridge, where he gained a further reputation for stupidity, homosexuality, and a 'Canting Fanatical way' (Elliot, 1–2). Oates transferred to St John's College in 1669, but fared no better. He left Cambridge

Titus Oates (1649–1705), by Robert White, 1679

without a degree in 1669, but having become skilled in mendacity.

Oates falsely claimed to hold a BA degree and in due course the bishop of London licensed him to preach. Oates took holy orders at Ely in May 1670 and was made vicar at Bobbing in Kent in March 1673. His coarse temper and odd lifestyle soon caused divisions with the parishioners and he was dismissed from the living, returning to Hastings, where he became curate to his father, who had obtained the living at All Saints' about 1666. At Easter 1675 Oates accused the local schoolmaster, William Parker, of sodomy with one of his pupils. Oates wanted Parker's post but the accusation was false and resulted in Oates being bound over to appear at the next sessions on a charge of perjury. He fled to London and sought refuge as a naval chaplain in 1675 on the ship *Adventure* bound for Tangier. It was during his visit to Tangier, Oates later claimed, that he heard the first rumours of the Popish Plot that was to make his name. However, on his return to England in 1676 Oates was expelled from the navy for homosexual practices and went to London. There he took up with his father, who had left his living in the wake of the Parker affair. In August 1676 his former tutor William Smith met Oates in the company of a Catholic actor named Matthew Medburne. Shortly afterwards Oates was arrested and returned to Hastings to await his trial for perjury, but he escaped again and went back to London, where he renewed his acquaintance with Medburne and other members of a Catholic club in Fuller's Rents. Through this acquaintance, in 1676 Oates managed to obtain the post of chaplain to the protestants in the household of a Catholic nobleman, Henry Howard, earl of Norwich and future sixth duke of Norfolk. Although much admired for his theatrical preaching, he soon lost his position. In spite of his protestant upbringing, on 3 March 1677 Oates was received into the Roman Catholic church by Father Berry, alias Hutchinson, an apparently mentally unbalanced priest.

Oates and the Catholics There is little doubt that Oates's conversion to Roman Catholicism was insincere. He later wrote:

> I myself was lulled asleep, by the allurements of the Popish Syrenes, and the bewitching sorceries of the Man of sin ... But as Joseph was sold to AEgypt for the Preservation of his Brethren, so was I laid aside, by the permission of Divine providence, for the safety both of my King and country. (T.O., 1)

In reality he was probably motivated by the poverty in which he found himself, a craving for acceptance, and the potential for blackmail. Oates claimed that he soon became a prominent courier for the Jesuit order, but his conversion did little for his career and he remained unemployed. It was at this time that he was also introduced, via his father, to Dr Israel Tonge, an eccentric former clergyman and fervent anti-papist obsessed with the Jesuit menace and the author of several treatises on the subject. Oates proved ecumenical enough to sponge money from protestant as well as Catholic clergy, and willingly offered to co-author pamphlets with Tonge against the Catholics. In the role of a poverty stricken convert Oates also took to begging from the Catholic priests at Somerset House and repaid their kindness with theft: he stole some of the host, which he afterwards boasted that he used as wafers to seal his letters. In April 1677 Oates had his first good stroke of fortune in a meeting with Father Richard Strange, the provincial of the Jesuits in England, who arranged for him to attend the English Jesuit College at Valladolid in Spain. The reasons for this assistance are unclear. J. P. Kenyon speculated that Strange was also homosexual and consequently felt obliged to help Oates, but it may be that Oates, an accomplished liar, convinced Strange of his worth. By this stage in his career Oates had created a past for himself in which he was the former recipient of a rich benefice of the Church of England but had given it all up for the Church of Rome. Under the alias of Titus Ambrose or Ambrosius, Oates arrived in Bilbao in May 1677 and at the English College at Valladolid in June, where he was received by Father Manuel de Calatayud, who later noted:

> I admitted him, very much against the grain though it was ... Little more than a month went by, and he was in so much of a hurry to begin his mischief that I was obliged to expel him from the College. He was a curse. What I went through and suffered from that man, God alone knows. (Williams, 49)

While at Valladolid Oates met William *Bedloe, his future partner in the plot. It is possible that he had known Bedloe during his time in the earl of Norwich's household. In Spain the pair were reacquainted before Bedloe stole some money from Oates and absconded for other adventures. The idea that they concocted most of the evidence of the Popish Plot at this point is unlikely, but their acquaintance was to be renewed in London in 1678.

Oates soon returned to England, claiming to have received a doctorate from the University of Salamanca. At the height of his fame he was ridiculed as the Salamanca doctor, but out of vanity he retained the spurious doctorate until the end of his life.

Oates resumed his begging lifestyle until Father Strange decided once more to indulge his odd client and arranged for him to attend the Catholic seminary at St Omer in December 1677. Oates, travelling under the name of Samson Lucy, swiftly revealed both his ignorance and unsuitability for the school; the institution found great difficulty in accommodating the 28-year-old tobacco chewing, foulmouthed, and coarse tempered Oates. He was disliked by most of the students, one of whom 'broke a pan about his head for recreation' (*State trials*, 10.1110).

While at St Omer, Oates begged to be admitted to the Jesuit order and to keep him quiet was briefly sent to another Jesuit seminary, where he caused so much trouble that he was sent straight back to St Omer. His private investigations also allowed him to learn much (and invent the rest) about the order's councils in England; although his later claim that he was trusted to carry their correspondence is highly unlikely. He also claimed that he attended a significant Jesuit 'consult' in London in April but in reality he was at St Omer until June 1678, when he was in fact expelled from the seminary by the new English Jesuit provincial, Father Thomas Harcourt, alias Whitebread. In July 1678 a desperate Oates returned to London and promptly renewed his acquaintance with Israel Tonge. It was once suspected by many historians that Tonge was the prime mover of the Popish Plot evidence that followed and indeed that it was Tonge who prompted Oates. In fact Oates, the stronger character, had his own bitter need for vengeance against those who he now believed had continually slighted him and Tonge became merely a sounding board for his own crude prejudices.

Initially Oates sought only to regale Tonge with tales of his own desperate struggles with the papists and even flattered the older man into believing that Tonge was a target for Jesuit vengeance due to his writings against the Catholics. Tonge asked him to write it all down and Oates, eager to have an audience, did so. In forty-three articles or depositions Oates revealed for the first time the nature of the so-called Popish Plot. He claimed to have been informed at various times by rather garrulous, or plainly stupid, Roman Catholics of plans to murder Charles II and his brother James, duke of York (unless as a Catholic the latter agreed to the plot), by bullet or poison. A number of attempts had already been made to kill the king by wouldbe assassins John Grove and Thomas Pickering, whose silver bullets were continually foiled by poor guns and failing flints. Large sums of money were also to be made available for the scheme. He also had tales of potential Scottish, English, and Irish rebellions, and a Europe-wide conspiracy guaranteed to alarm any rabid anti-Catholic. He backed up his accusations with much, apparently concrete, detail about the secret comings and goings of both himself and his Catholic friends. Oates was also to claim that he had seen numerous letters detailing the plot and yet, as the duke of York later pointed out, he 'kept not so much as one for a proof' (Clarke, 1.522). Most of Oates's revelations stemmed from either his vivid imagination, with a distinct twist of bitterness against his former Catholic friends, or from the previously published accounts of real or imagined plots from the 1660s with their tales of gathering rebel armies, secret commissions, and planned assassinations. By far the most significant aspect of the revelations was Oates's tale of a secret conclave of the Jesuits held at the White Horse tavern in London on 24 April 1678, at which he claimed to have been present and where matters of treason were discussed.

At Tonge's request Oates gave him a copy of the articles and on 11 August 1678 he also furtively left another copy under the wainscot at the home of Sir Richard Barker, Tonge's former landlord and another rabid anti-papist. At this point Oates may also have attempted to sell his tale to the Jesuits in the hope of making money out of them, but he was rebuffed. Tonge was now anxious to reveal all to Charles II directly and involved his friend Christopher Kirkby, who was acquainted with the king, in the scheme. Kirkby approached Charles in St James's Park on the morning of 13 August 1678 with revelations of a popish plot. Charles promptly passed the information to his first minister, the earl of Danby, who interrogated both Kirkby and Tonge and appears to have guessed immediately that a shrewder mind than either of theirs was responsible for the information. Danby sought to discover this person's name but Tonge, believing that Danby was not taking the plot seriously was reluctant to reveal Oates as his informant. Ever full of 'projects and notions' Tonge subsequently attempted to seek other ways of bringing the plot to the notice of the public (Burnet's History, 2.156). Tonge then unsuccessfully tried to embroil Sir Joseph Williamson in the affair before being advised by some 'honourable friends' to bring Oates before the Westminster magistrate Sir Edmund Berry *Godfrey to have his evidence legally sworn (I. Tonge, 'Journal of the plot, 1678', in Greene, 35). On 6 September 1678 Godfrey reluctantly took the Oates depositions, but seems to have guessed the false nature of the evidence. Then on 28–9 September 1678 first Tonge, and then Oates, came before the privy council for investigation. Oates seized the opportunity to reveal still more of the fabricated plot, having by this time expanded his accusations to eighty-one articles. Despite the presence, and the shrewd questioning, of Charles II, Oates's lies convinced the privy council, especially when he revealed that the duchess of York's secretary Edward Coleman had handled money for the plot and had also been in correspondence with Father la Chaise, Louis XIV's confessor. Oates had, in Coleman, unluckily for the latter, hit upon one of the more likely figures for a serious Catholic plot. In accusing Coleman he may have been prompted by leading questions from Danby, or he may have heard independently

something of the secretary's activities, for Coleman was a prominent Catholic eager to see the re-establishment of his church in England. Oates sought to please his audience with ever more audacious revelations, which were also, however, increasingly complex and inconsistent. The duke of York later noted with some dismay that Oates was always allowed the 'liberty … of contradicting at pleasure what he had sworne before' (Clarke, 1.521), while Sir Henry Coventry, who saw Oates give his evidence, noted that 'If he [Oates] be a liar, he is the greatest and adroitest I ever saw, and yet it is a stupendous thing to think what vast concerns are like to depend upon the evidence of one young man who hath twice changed his religion' (Ormonde MSS, new ser., 4.207). In spite of any doubts the privy council may have had they soon sent Oates speeding 'hither and thither, accompanied by soldiers, and enjoying complete power to imprison those he chose … his greatest pleasure was to be feared by everyone and to harm as many as possible' (Walner, 1.202). The Jesuit fathers William Ireland and John Fenwick were arrested. Thomas Pickering, a Benedictine lay brother, and John Grove were also caught up in Oates's net. The Jesuit William Harcourt, who was ill, was left in his lodgings with a guard at the door. Oates was given lodgings in Whitehall and an initial pension of £40 per month. The seizure of Coleman's papers appeared to confirm some of Oates's tale and, although he did not even recognize Coleman when he appeared before the council, he grew bolder. Further apparent confirmation of the reality of the plot followed with the mysterious death of Edmund Godfrey in October 1678 and the actions of the House of Commons, when, in the same month, they tried to take over the investigation of the plot and turned it into a real crisis.

Oates and the Popish Plot trials Oates was summoned before the House of Commons in October 1678 and subsequently made further appearances. He impressed the house with the apparent solidity of his stories and his confident delivery. A mixture of boldness and bluster he always tried to mix some elements of the truth, however tenuous and convoluted, into his statements and when in doubt would construct yet another lie. With his flexible memory new revelations from Oates could never be ruled out and he increasingly struck out against those who had antagonized him in the past. In case such men were thought too insignificant to organize any plot he also added the names of the so-called five Popish lords as the main conspirators: Bellasis, Petre, Powis, Stafford, and Arundel. As a result he received the thanks of parliament for his pains in discovering the plot. The duke of York noted that Oates 'did not positively accuse any Lord, till he had been before the Commons, and that he saw how they relished it; nor did he till then, give them their different implyements, which how fit they were for, all the world might judge' (Clarke, 1.521). In any event such matters convinced an audience already primed to believe such tales through decades of anti-Catholic propaganda. Serious investigations into the plot soon revealed the obvious contradictions in Oates's tales, and many later commentators challenged Oates to 'Tell us how all this heterogeneous Medley can be reconciled to common sense ... all those hidden incongruities, Absurdities, Amusements, and Contradictions, that have composed your Testimony, in which you have over and over again been buffoon'd' (*Eikon brotoloigou, or, The Picture of Titus Oates DD Drawn to the Life in a Letter to Himself*, 1697, 16). His apparent openness about having been a sinner, moreover, and his claim that he had repented, as well as his continued, though unwarranted, use of clerical dress, gave him dignity. Oates depicted himself as a man who had seen the light and braved many dangers to save the nation. His initial grasp of very complex and detailed evidence was also impressive. Indeed, so complex did the story become that it was soon necessary to print collated versions to give the public at least some understanding of the threats involved.

The arrival of William Bedloe on the scene in November 1678, eager to add his own evidence about the plot, meant that Oates had to adjust his story somewhat, but this rivalry did not prevent him joining Bedloe in an attempt to implicate the queen in the plot that same month. This was going too far for some in the government and for a short while Oates was confined to his lodgings and his papers seized. Oates had a tense relationship with other important informers. Bedloe, for a time, somewhat stole his glory, although Tonge and Kirkby were swiftly ignored, while Miles Prance was merely described as a 'blockhead' (W. Smith, *Contrivances of the fanatical Conspirators in Carrying on their Treasons under the Umbrage of the Popish Plot, Laid Open*, 1685, 25). The trial of Edward Coleman on 27 November 1678 saw Oates make his first attempt as a chief witness in a legal setting. This first trial set a precedent for the others in that during the course of the proceedings flimsy evidence was accepted as certain fact. Oates remained vague on the details, and apparently made up his story as he went along, weaving in new material with the old. In the trials of Grove, Pickering, and Ireland on 17 December 1678, Oates's evidence was on more stable ground, as many of those involved could not deny knowing him and printed versions of his story were now available for him to use as a crib.

Although Oates was given helpful judges and many other prompts his perjuries often became obvious in court. Evidence was given to show that he was in St Omer in April 1678 and therefore could not have attended any secret Jesuit consult in London on 24 April, let alone have seen Father Ireland there, as he claimed. Oates often sought refuge in stories of poor light, or his failing eyesight, or his selective memory, thus enabling him to claim blithely that he did not recognize people. If this failed then he turned to headaches and became unwell. The inherent problems with Oates's evidence were ignored by a legal system all too obviously keen to convict these men and they were executed on 3 February 1679. In April 1679 Oates's sixty-eight-page version of the plot was officially published by order of the House of Lords. He appeared as a witness in more trials in June, including that of the Catholic lawyer, Richard Langhorne. All of the accused were convicted and executed. In the trial of the queen's physician, Sir George Wakeman, in July 1679, however, he overreached himself in his evidence and the judge, Lord Chief Justice Scroggs, disparaged him. Both Oates and Bedloe attempted revenge by presenting articles implicating Scroggs in the plot to the privy council in January 1680 but failed utterly when Scroggs ably defended himself. At Viscount Stafford's trial on 30 November in the same year Oates resorted to stating that he needed to give his evidence 'to his own method and be uninterrupted', however, 'he spoke positively ... with many shrewd circumstances, nor could any cross-questions discompose him' (*Ormonde MSS*, new ser., 5, 1908, 513).

The collapse of the plot Oates at the height of his career had been responsible in one way or another for the deaths of some thirty-five men. By 1681 however the tide had begun to turn against him and he lost several cases of libel against those who attacked his opinions or person. One hostile contemporary gave a description of him at this time suggesting a most repulsive appearance:

> [his] off leg behind is somewhat shorter than the other ... his face a Rainbow colour, and the rest of his body black: Two slouching ears ... His mouth is in the middle of his face, exactly between the upper part of his forehead and the lower part of his chin; He hath a short neck ... a thin Chin, and somewhat sharp. (*A Hue and Cry*)

By 1682 Oates's pension had been reduced and he was forced to take refuge in the City. With the plot in collapse by 1683 many of the informers now suffered the consequences of their actions. William Bedloe had died in 1680, as had Israel Tonge, but others were available for punishment. Titus Oates was finally arrested at the Amsterdam coffee house on 10 May 1684 on a charge of *scandalum magnatum* after a suit by the duke of York, whom Oates had called a traitor. Fined £100,000 after refusing to plead Oates was placed in the Compter in default of payment and was later moved to the king's bench prison. In October and December 1684 he was presented on charges of perjury. The trial was delayed by the death of Charles II on 6 February 1685 but finally took place on 8–9 May 1685. His 'behaviour during the trial was very confident: many hott words pass'd between the chief justice [Jeffries] and him' (Luttrell, 1.342). Oates was convicted on two counts: that he had falsely sworn on 8–12 August 1678 to a 'consult' of Jesuits at the White Horse tavern and that he had also falsely sworn to the presence of William Ireland in London on the same dates. A week later he was sentenced. He was to be imprisoned for life, divested of his canonical garb for ever and brought to Westminster Hall with a paper on his head with the inscription: 'Titus Oates convicted upon full evidence of two horrid perjuries' (ibid., 343). He was also placed in the pillory in Palace Yard, Westminster, on 19 May and was roundly pelted with eggs and other rubbish. This part of the sentence was to be repeated five times every year of his life in different parts of London. As part of the first round of his punishment, on 20 May Oates was led at the cart's tail and whipped from Aldgate to Newgate 'with hideous bellowings, and [he] swooned several times with the greatness of the anguish' (L. Echard, *History of England*, 3 vols., 3rd edn, 1720, vol. 3, p. 1054). On 22 May he was whipped again from Newgate to Tyburn. Oates later claimed that he had 'suffer'd some thousands of stripes' (W. H. Hart, 'Petitions of Dr Titus Oates', *N&Q*, 2nd ser., 2, 1856, 282). He had survived this torture only through the care of his surgeon and in spite of further cruelties by his gaolers who, while he was still weak, got into his cell and pulled the bandages from his back. He had also been placed in 'the Hole or Dungeon of the sd prison' (ibid.) loaded down with irons, despite his gout, and had apparently become subject to convulsions. Oates was lodged in the king's bench and remained there for three years. Rumours of his death were given out in 1688, but in fact the revolution of that year temporarily revived his fortunes.

Last years After the flight of James II and the revolution Oates was released from prison in December 1688. He then sought succour from several 'Noblemen and Gentlemen, Citizens and others … for his support and maintenance' (W. H. Hart, 'Petitions of Dr Titus Oates', *N&Q*, 2nd ser., 2, 1856, 282). He also sought reinstatement as the idol of the public and saviour of the nation. He stated his grievances in various petitions to the House of Lords but, impatient at delays, he also petitioned the Commons. He then fell foul of the House of Lords for breach of privilege and was soon back in gaol. On 30 May 1689 he once more came before the Lords but refused, out of conscience he said, to give up his claim to hold the degree of doctor of divinity from Salamanca and was sent back to the king's bench prison. His case made little progress, becoming caught up in the post-revolution rivalry between the houses. His obstreperous and unpleasant character also hindered his cause, and when eventually released in August 1689 he remained a convicted perjurer. Despite this William III ordered £40 a month to be paid to Oates out of secret service funds, which sum Oates was said to have thought rather mean spirited. This pension lasted from 1689 to 1692 and was then retrenched.

In these later years Oates moved into a house in Axe Yard, Westminster, and sought to promote himself mainly through writing pamphlets retelling the story of the plot. He took care to condemn both Charles II, now safely dead, as a papist, and James II. He also stressed his own courage as a martyr in the face of adversity. His new bogey was a Franco-Jacobite plot and he took to associating with whigs such as Aaron Smith, John Arnold, John Tutchin, and also the former government agent, William Fuller. Fuller, no novice at spying, lodged with Oates and under his tutelage claimed knowledge of a Jacobite plot, but was later discredited. Oates seems to have acted as mentor to a number of zealous anti-Catholic individuals who frequently met at his house.

As a result of his involvement with Fuller, and his furious anti-Jacobite writings, Oates's pension was cut and to save his finances he married Rebecca (*b.* 1669/70, *d.* in or after 1705), daughter of John Weld, a wealthy London draper, on 17 August 1693 at St Mary Magdalen, Old Fish Street, amid much satirical comment and in spite of the strong rumours that Oates was homosexual. One of the

milder satires against him claimed that he married only because he had been 'touched in [his] conscience for some juvenile gambols that shall be nameless … and made a vow to sow his wild oats, and not hide the talent which God had plentifully given him in an Italian napkin' (Brown, 2–3). Rebecca was a 'young gentlewoman in the citty, worth 2000 *l*' (Luttrell, 3.165). The couple had one child, baptized Rebecca on 3 October 1700. According to rumour Oates also had an illegitimate son by another woman in the king's bench prison in 1688.

Although in September 1693 Oates's new wife was received at court and kissed the queen's hand, he allegedly ran through his wife's fortune in less than six months and in May 1694 claimed that he had few clothes left to wear and 'not one shilling to buy my poor wife and family bread. I am in debt 508 *l*, and must the latter end of this month go to prison and there starve' (*Downshire MSS*, 1.661). He received a gift of £100 in July 1694, but by December 1697 he was once more claiming poverty and that 'He had a poor aged mother to maintain, and his wife and family will be turn'd out of doors, and [he would] perish in Prison' (W. H. Hart, 'Petitions of Dr Titus Oates', *N&Q*, 2nd ser., 2, 1856, 282). He asked for a payment of his arrears and received a restoration of his pension to £300 per annum and £1000 to pay his debts.

In June 1696 Oates had decided to alter his religion once more and return to the Baptist church of his father. Lengthy negotiations with elders of the congregation which met in Virginia Street finally led to his admission into the church in summer 1698, with the generous concession that he could continue to wear his Church of England clerical robes. He took to preaching before his brethren and, with his morbid tales of Catholic abominations, proved popular. Unfortunately he fell out with the congregation in October 1699 over arrangements for the funeral of Hester Parker, a rich widow. Mrs Parker had heartily disliked Oates and consequently he was not invited to the funeral nor asked to preach the funeral sermon. On the day of the sermon, however, Oates prevented it from taking place by suddenly occupying the pulpit and preaching on an entirely unrelated topic, while the congregation's bewilderment turned to anger. This farcical situation, so typical of Oates, was compounded when he encouraged Mrs Parker's husband to contest her will, which had left most of her estate to two members of the congregation. Eventually he caused so much trouble that he was expelled from the sect in November 1701. Trouble continued to dog Oates's later career. In June 1702, while visiting the court of requests, he was confronted by the printer Eleanor James, who had been affronted at hearing him criticize the Church of England, and making 'scandalous and reflecting Expressions' about Charles II and God, while wearing his usual canonical robes ('An account of the proceedings against Dr Titus Oates', *Scarce and Valuable Tracts … Lord Somers*, 4.420–22). Oates, whose violence was never far below the surface, lost his temper and struck her with his cane. He was indicted at the Westminster quarter sessions on 2 July 1702. Claiming poverty he was fined 6 marks and dismissed, but 'not without a severe check for acting so irreverently and unbecoming his profession' (ibid.). After this incident little is known about Oates's final years. He appears to have died in obscurity, largely unnoticed by most commentators, at Axe Yard on 13 July 1705. His widow was granted administration of his estate on 16 August 1705.

Conclusion Oates remains an unusual figure in British history and there are a number of explanations for both his personality and career. Early writers were repelled as much by his homosexuality as by his personality. Moreover, his unusual appearance and his abrasive manner meant that he could scarcely be ignored. With his limp, red face, bull neck, nasal drawl, and harsh and brassy voice he proved a raucous and difficult personality. Roger North noted that Oates's 'common conversation was larded with lewd oaths, Blasphemy, saucy atheistical, and in every way offensive discourse' (R. North, *Examen, or, An Enquiry into the Credit and Merits of Pretended Complete History*, 1740, 224). Oates's actions have usually been explained as a psychotic's revenge but, given the hostility and rejection which he encountered almost constantly, could equally well be seen as, in part at least, a desire for acceptance and respectability. Oates remained a fantasist: a man who saw himself in the role of the saviour of the nation, fighting demon popes and Jesuits. In his writings he often depicted himself as a man of action, daring to say or do what others would not. He was the secret hero who, despite his outward appearance, managed to infiltrate a most dangerous conspiracy. For a time Oates succeeded beyond his dreams and was genuinely honoured as the saviour of the nation, but the sordid reality of his life in which there were no great secrets to uncover, only back alley meetings, stealing, begging, and poverty, vice, fear, and hatred, and above all failure, soon caught up with him.

ALAN MARSHALL

Sources *The life of Titus Oats from his cradle to his first pilloring for infamous perjury* (1685) · *The memoires of Titus Oates, written for publick satisfaction* (1685) · T. Brown, *The Salamanca wedding, or, A true account of a swearing doctor's marriage with a Muggletonian woman in Bread Street* (1693) · *Strange and wonderful news from Southwark, declaring how a sham doctor got two aldermen students of the same university with child* (1684) · *A true narrative of the tryal of Titus Oates for perjury at the kings-bench barr … on Friday the 8th of May 1685* (1685) · *The character of an ignoramus doctor* (1681) · J. Lane [E. Dakers], *Titus Oates* (1949) · N. Luttrell, *A brief historical relation of state affairs from September 1678 to April 1714*, 6 vols. (1857) · A. Elliot, *A modest vindication of Titus Oates, the Salamanca doctor from perjury* (1682) · T. O. [T. Oates], *Sound advice to Roman Catholicks … to which is added a word to the people called Quakers* (1689) · M. E. Williams, *St Alban's College, Valladolid* (1986) · *State trials*, vols. 7–10 · *A hue and cry after Dr T. O.* (1681) · *The life of James the Second, king of England*, ed. J. S. Clarke, 2 vols. (1816) · Burnet's *History of my own time*, ed. O. Airy, new edn, 2 vols. (1897–1900) · A. G. Greene, ed., *Diaries of the Popish Plot* (New York, 1977) · J. Warner, *The history of English persecution of Catholics and the presbyterian plot*, ed. T. A. Birrell, trans. J. Bligh, 2 vols., Catholic RS, 47–8 (1953) · *DNB* · J. Kenyon, *The Popish Plot* (1972) · probate, City Westm. AC, Act book (1705), fol. 29 · G. J. Armytage, ed., *Allegations for marriage licences issued by the vicar-general of the archbishop of Canterbury, July 1687 to June 1694*, Harleian Society, 31 (1890) · *Report on the manuscripts of the marquis of Downshire*, 6 vols. in 7, HMC, 75 (1924–95) · *Calendar of the manuscripts of the marquess of Ormonde*, new ser., 8 vols., HMC, 36 (1902–20) · *A collection of scarce and valuable tracts … Lord Somers*, 4 (1750) · *IGI*

Archives E. Sussex RO, MSS relating to imprisonment · Leics. RO, MS books relating to plot · Surrey HC, account of examination by House of Commons | Arundel Castle, corresp. with Charles Howard · Hastings Museum and Art Gallery, petitions to the king · HLRO, MSS relating to appeal for pardon to House of Lords · PRO, privy council registers, PC 2/55–59 · PRO, Charles II, SP 29

Likenesses R. White, line engraving, 1679, BM, NPG; repro. in *A poem upon Mr Tytus Oates* (1679) [*see illus.*] · line engraving, pubd 1685, BM · woodcut, pubd 1685, BM; repro. in *The doctor degraded, or, The reward of deceit* (1685) · G. Bower, medal, BM · L. Crosse, miniature, Buccleuch estates, Selkirk, Scotland · R. Tompson, mezzotint (after T. Hawker), BM, NPG · medal, BM · mezzotint, NPG · pen-and-ink drawing, NPG

Oatley, Sir Charles William (1904–1996), electrical engineer, was born on 14 February 1904 at 5 Badcox, Frome, Somerset, the only child of William Oatley (1860–1944), baker, and his wife, Ada Mary Dorrington (*d.* 1911), schoolteacher. His father was intensely interested in scientific matters, and passed his enthusiasm on to his son. Coincidentally, 1904 was the year mains electrical power was brought to Frome, and William Oatley installed it in his bakery immediately it became available. Thus the young Oatley was surrounded by electrically powered machinery almost from birth, and his natural scientific bent was nurtured from the earliest years. After attending the local council school he went to Bedford Modern School, in 1916, as a boarder, becoming head boy and captain of the swimming and rugby fives teams. From Bedford Modern he won two exhibitions to St John's College, Cambridge, entering in 1922. There he read for the natural sciences tripos, taking a first in part one and a second in part two (physics). In his second year he obtained a half-blue for swimming, and in his final year he captained the university swimming team. His supervisor at St John's was Edward Appleton, who first aroused his interest in electronics. He also became acquainted with John Cockcroft, who was then at St John's reading mathematics. These two men were to have a profound influence on Oatley's life and career.

In 1925, on Appleton's advice, Oatley joined Radio Accessories, a small company in Willesden manufacturing radio valves. There he gained valuable experience of manufacturing techniques and, as the only graduate in the company, was called upon to tackle a wide variety of physical problems. After two years, however, he was invited to return to academic life by Appleton, who had moved to the physics department at King's College, London. The next twelve years at King's were spent largely teaching and examining, but he produced a number of papers on a variety of research topics, and, with the publication in 1932 of his Methuen monograph, *Wireless Receivers*, he became an acknowledged expert in the field. These years were, as he acknowledged in his writings, among the happiest of his life. He married Dorothy Enid West, the daughter of his science master at Bedford Modern, on 31 July 1930, and their sons John and Michael were born in 1932 and 1935 respectively.

In the summer of 1939 Oatley received a letter from Cockcroft, acting on behalf of the Air Ministry, inviting him to join a small party of university physicists to spend a few weeks learning about scientific developments which would be important in the event of war. Members of Cockcroft's party were assembled at Bawdsey Manor, where much of the initial work on radar (then known as radiolocation or radio direction finding: RDF) was carried out. Cockcroft later recalled the occasion:

> I arranged hurriedly with Watson-Watt to go to Rye instead, for Bawdsey was evacuated on 1st September. I had with me Oatley, Kempton, Shire, Latham, Ashmead and Dunworth; a very good party. We sat in the sun at Rye and taking the sacred handbook of Chain Home (CH) to pieces, learnt our RDF chapter by chapter from it.   (Cockcroft, 3)

Soon afterwards, Oatley joined the newly formed air defence experimental establishment at Christchurch, Hampshire, where in the early years of the war he built up a highly successful group to undertake precision measurements on valves and components supplied by industry and components designed in the establishment. In 1943 he became deputy to Cockcroft, who had earlier been appointed chief superintendent of the establishment. When Cockcroft moved to Canada in 1944 to undertake nuclear work, Oatley was appointed acting superintendent. He was appointed OBE in 1956 in recognition of his outstanding contributions to the development of radar.

Immediately after the war Oatley was offered a fellowship at Trinity College, Cambridge, and a lectureship in the engineering department, which was then under the dynamic leadership of John Fleetwood Baker. With Baker's encouragement, Oatley revolutionized the teaching of electrical subjects in the department, particularly electronics, which culminated in his election to the chair of electrical engineering in 1960 (which he held until his retirement in 1971), and the introduction of the electrical sciences tripos in 1963.

Oatley's greatest achievement came with the development at Cambridge of the scanning electron microscope (SEM). His interest in the instrument was first aroused when he learned of pre-war work by Manfred von Ardenne in Germany. This had produced inconclusive results, but with his wartime experience Oatley perceived that new techniques and methods were available which could be applied to the scanning concept. His first research student commenced in 1948 and a working instrument was produced by 1951. This incorporated a novel configuration of the electron optical image-forming elements, producing startlingly realistic images of surfaces, capable of interpretation even by the uninitiated. These early results convinced Oatley that the SEM would become an important laboratory tool; however, this was far from being the consensus among microscopists. The new instrument was met with indifference and even, in some quarters, ridicule. Undeterred, Oatley took on more research students and ploughed more resources into the project. Over the following decade new instruments with improved performance were constructed, and new fields of application explored. After many setbacks and disappointments, his persistence was finally rewarded in 1965 with the launch of the world's first series production SEM:

the Stereoscan, manufactured by the Cambridge Instrument Company. His book on the subject, *The Scanning Electron Microscope*, was published in 1972.

Many honours followed from this success, chief among which were Oatley's election to the Royal Society in 1969, and receipt of its royal medal (1969) and Mullard award (1973), and in 1970 the award of the Faraday medal of the Institution of Electrical Engineers. He was knighted in 1974. In 1976 he became a founder member of what was to become the Royal Academy of Engineering. His colleagues and research students held him in great esteem. Over 100 of them attended a one-day seminar held in his honour at Churchill College on the occasion of his ninetieth birthday. He died at his home, 16 Porson Road, Cambridge, on 11 March 1996. He was survived by his wife and two sons.   K. C. A. SMITH

Sources K. C. A. Smith, *Memoirs FRS*, 44 (1998), 331–47 · C. W. Oatley, 'My work in radar, 1939–45', CAC Cam. · J. D. Cockcroft, 'Memories of radar research', *IEE Proceedings*, A132 (1985), 327–39 · *The Independent* (21 March 1996) · *The Times* (1 April 1996) · *WWW* · personal knowledge (2004) · private information (2004)
Archives CAC Cam., corresp. and papers; papers relating to wartime work on radar
Likenesses Hughes-Hallett, portrait, University Engineering Department, Cambridge · photograph, repro. in *The Independent* · photographs, repro. in Smith, *Memoirs FRS*
Wealth at death £133,509: probate, 17 Sept 1996, *CGPLA Eng. & Wales*

Oats, Francis (1848–1918), mining engineer and authority on diamonds, was born on 24 October 1848 at South Torfrey Farm, Golant, near Fowey, Cornwall, the elder child of Francis Oats (1796–1874), farmer, and his wife, Marion, *née* Rundle (*b.* 1810). About 1854 his family moved to St Just. As a working miner he attended the classes of the Mining Association of Cornwall and Devon and was top of his class in 1866, when he obtained a first-class pass in mineralogy and passes in mining and chemistry, becoming a pupil–teacher in 1867. Poverty prevented him from accepting the free place offered to him at the Royal School of Mines.

In 1870 Captain Frank Oats—as he was commonly called—became an underground superintendent at Botallack mine, St Just, and in 1874 he was sent by the Griqualand West government to the Kimberley diamond fields in South Africa as provincial engineer and inspector. Also in 1874, on 17 August, he married Elizabeth Ann (*b.* 1855), daughter of John Olds, a butcher, at St Just parish church. They had four children—three sons and a daughter—born between 1880 and 1888. Oats was back at Botallack in 1876 but returned to Kimberley in 1877 as engineer to the Kimberley Mining Company and manager of the Victoria Diamond Mines Company. Here he stressed the technical arguments in favour of consolidating the diamond producers' interests as a director of the Victoria Company. That concern was taken over by De Beers Consolidated Mines in 1887, when Oats joined its board; he was chairman from 1906 to 1918. From 1889 he was a member of the De Beers diamond sales committee, and from 1898 to 1908 he represented Namaqualand in the Cape parliament. Being the best-qualified director on the De Beers board, he undertook work for the company in Mashonaland, Nama Land, and south-west Africa, prospecting for diamonds, and elsewhere in South Africa for other minerals. He visited British Guiana and Brazil in 1901 to inspect diamond mines, and in 1907 he went to France and exposed as fraudulent the claim by Henri Lemoine that he had made artificial diamonds. Besides directorships in numerous South African companies, some not connected with mining, he was a director of Levant Mine, St Just (1889–1918), and director and later chairman of Basset Mines, Illogan (1896–1918), spending half of each year in Cornwall and half in South Africa.

Frank Oats died at his daughter's house at 1 Bird Street, Port Elizabeth, Cape Province, South Africa, on 1 September 1918. His *Times* obituary described him as a very able Cornishman, ambitious, somewhat pugnacious, and masterful, but a born captain of industry .

JUSTIN BROOKE

Sources private information (2004) [D. Claire Leith, granddaughter and archivist of Francis Oats] · *Cornishman and Cornish Telegraph* (4 Sept 1918) · Boase & Courtney, *Bibl. Corn.*, 1.406/2; 3.1295/1 · *Mining Journal* (23 June 1866) · *Mining Journal* (12 Dec 1874) · *Mining Journal* (4 Feb 1888) · *Mining Journal* (7 Sept 1918) · *Mining World* (21 Oct 1876) · *Mining World* (7 Sept 1918) · *Mining World* (6 Dec 1919) · *The Times* (9 Sept 1918) · *DSAB* · C. Newbury, *The diamond ring: business, politics and precious stones in South Africa, 1867–1947* (1989) · private information (2004) [A. Barrett, archivist, ICL] · m. cert. · *CGPLA Eng. & Wales* (1919) · parish register, Golant, St Sampson, 24 Oct. 1848 [birth] · parish register, Golant, St Sampson, 25 Dec 1848 [baptism]
Archives priv. coll.
Likenesses portrait, De Beers Consolidated Mines Ltd, Kimberley
Wealth at death £73,771 7s. 4d.: probate, 25 Nov 1919, *CGPLA Eng. & Wales*

O'Beirne, Thomas Lewis (1749–1823), Church of Ireland bishop of Meath, was born a Roman Catholic in Farnagh, co. Longford, the son of Lewis O'Beirne, farmer, of Longford, and Margaret O'Meagher of Cloona, co. Tipperary. As several generations of his family had been educated abroad, and his grand-uncle, Thomas O'Beirne, was bishop of the Catholic diocese of Ardagh (1739–47), it can be assumed that the O'Beirnes were reasonably circumstanced. Following his early education at Ardagh diocesan school, in 1763 Thomas was sent to the Collège des Lombards in Paris, where he performed well academically. Many Irish students at the college, his brother Denis included, became Catholic priests. It is not clear if this was Thomas's intention, but, after his return home to recuperate from illness in 1768, a chance meeting with John Hinchcliffe, the Church of England bishop of Peterborough, set O'Beirne on the journey that was to result in his making his recantation, taking orders, and entering Trinity College, Cambridge, as a ten-year man in 1773. He received a BD degree in 1783.

O'Beirne's first benefice was the college living of Grendon, Northamptonshire, which he held for two years until he was appointed chaplain in the fleet under Lord Howe in 1776. This brought him to America, where he preached a striking discourse at St Paul's, New York, the only church

Thomas Lewis O'Beirne (1749–1823), by Andrew Dunn, 1808

which was preserved from the flames during the calamitous fire of September 1776. On his return to England, O'Beirne vindicated the brothers Howe against criticism of their conduct in the tract *A Candid and Impartial Narrative of the Transactions of the Fleet under Lord Howe* (1779) by impugning the accuracy of the information they were given. Lord Howe was instrumental in securing him the crown living of West Deeping in Lincolnshire in 1779, but his introduction to Lord Fitzwilliam and other Rockingham whigs led him to write in 1780 for the periodical *The Englishman*, and to contribute to a daily newspaper a series of articles critical of Lord North, the first six of which were reprinted as a pamphlet. Having proved himself as a controversialist, O'Beirne produced three further pamphlets anonymously in quick succession—*A Short History of the Last Session of Parliament* (1780), *Considerations on the Late Disturbances, by a Consistent Whig* (1780), and *Considerations on the Principles of Naval Discipline and Courts-Martial, in which the Doctrines of the House of Commons and the Conduct of the Courts-Martial on Admiral Keppel and Sir Hugh Palliser are Compared* (1781). For the theatre he adapted from the French play *Le Dissipateur*, by Destouches, a comedy entitled *The Generous Impostor*, which ran for seven nights at Drury Lane in November 1780. O'Beirne assisted the duchess of Devonshire in translating and adapting for the English stage two dramas from the French, but they met with no success. He was also the author of an ode to Lord Northampton, and of some minor contributions to the *Rolliad*, most of which, he reflected later, were 'deservedly consigned to oblivion' (*Public Characters*, 159).

Having proved his value to the whigs, in 1782 O'Beirne

attended the duke of Portland, the viceroy of Ireland, as chaplain and private secretary. While in Ireland he secured a promise of 'the living of Longford' (*Correspondence of Edmund Burke*, 5.29) on the demise of its incumbent. He had to wait nine years; in the meantime Edmund Burke's intercession ensured the restoration of the stipend he had received from Earl Fitzwilliam prior to his Irish appointment. This guaranteed that O'Beirne remained active in whig circles, and he became Portland's private secretary once again in 1783 when that statesman became the first lord of the Treasury. This time Portland ensured that O'Beirne was looked after: on his last day in office the duke gave him the valuable livings of Whittingham and Stanfordham. These enabled O'Beirne to provide for himself and for his wife, Jane, the only surviving child of Francis Stuart, brother of the eighth earl of Moray. They married on 17 November 1783, and had one son and two daughters.

Out of power, O'Beirne played an important part in the whigs' efforts to force William Pitt from office by galvanizing opposition to the prime minister's scheme for a commercial union with Ireland in 1785. He wrote *A Reply to the Late Treasury Pamphlet Entitled 'The Proposed System of Trade with Ireland Explained'* (1785), and was responsible for liaising with and supplying the Irish opposition with ideas and materials. Health problems during the winter of 1785 obliged him to spend some time on the continent, but this did not prove efficacious and he returned to Longford, resigned his English livings, and, on their becoming vacant in 1791, took up the rich benefices of Templemichael, which he had been promised in 1782, and Mohill. He spent the next three years ministering in the parish in which he was born and in which his brother Denis was the Catholic parish priest. His ambition was the episcopal bench, and the way was cleared when he became first chaplain and private secretary to Earl Fitzwilliam upon his appointment as viceroy in 1794. Shortly afterwards O'Beirne was rewarded by the bishopric of Ossory, to which he was consecrated at Christ Church, Dublin, on 1 February 1795.

O'Beirne's hope that 'a change of disposition towards them in the government' (O'Beirne to Portland, August 1794, Portland MSS) would induce propertied Catholics to align themselves with the crown was negated by the recall of Fitzwilliam. This so depressed him that he vowed 'to devote himself to the duties' (O'Beirne to Fitzwilliam, 30 March 1796, Fitzwilliam MSS) of his diocese, and to this end he convened meetings of his clergy to debate theological issues. There was no escaping politics, however, and as Ireland became more disorderly, O'Beirne's disenchantment with the Irish whigs grew. He felt at the time that Grattan had pressed the question of Catholic emancipation with too much vigour in 1794–5; by the spring of 1797 he freely attributed Catholic disaffection to Grattan's advocacy of policies which O'Beirne deemed to be more appropriate to a United Irishman than to a whig, and he sundered his connections with the Irish whigs.

O'Beirne's growing conservatism, which facilitated his translation from Ossory to the more lucrative diocese of Meath in December 1798, was also manifest in his advocacy of the inclusion of protestants on the board of the Catholic seminary at Maynooth and, when an act of union was being agitated, in his proposal that the Church of Ireland and the Church of England should also be unified. His contention that this would render the Church of Ireland 'unassailable to our adversaries' reflected his intensifying perception that his church was a 'persecuted church' (O'Beirne to D. Ryder, first earl of Harrowby, 12 Nov 1816, Harrowby MSS). He contrived to defend its position in a number of controversial tracts—*A Letter to Dr Troy* (1805), *A Letter from an Irish Dignitary … on the Subject of Tithes* (1807), *A Letter to Canning on his Proposed Motion on Catholic Emancipation* (1812), and *A Letter to the Earl of Fingal* (1813)—but he made a greater impact as a pastor. Between his appointment as bishop of Meath and his death in February 1823, fifty-seven churches and seventy-two glebe houses were built, and he produced three volumes of collected sermons (1799, 1813, and 1821). By appointing to vacant benefices on the ground of merit, enforcing personal residence, reviving the office of rural dean, and insisting upon the stricter examination of candidates for ordination, O'Beirne left the church in the diocese considerably stronger than he found it. He died at Lee House, Ardbraccan, Navan, on 17 February 1823, and was buried in the local churchyard, in the same vault as Bishop Pococke.　　　　　　　　　　　　　　　JAMES KELLY

Sources Fitzwilliam papers, Sheff. Arch., Wentworth Woodhouse muniments · *Public characters*, 10 vols. (1799–1809), vol. 1, pp. 147–59 · J. J. MacNamee, *History of the diocese of Ardagh* (1954) · J. Almon, *Biographical, literary and political anecdotes of several of the most eminent persons of the present age*, 3 vols. (1797) · *The correspondence of Edmund Burke*, ed. T. W. Copeland and others, 10 vols. (1958–78) · Windham MSS, BL, Add. MS 37877 · A. P. W. Malcomson, ed., *Eighteenth century Irish official papers in Great Britain*, 2 vols. (1973–90) · J. Kelly, *Prelude to Union: Anglo-Irish politics in the 1780s* (1992) · *Memoirs and correspondence of Viscount Castlereagh, second marquess of Londonderry*, ed. C. Vane, marquess of Londonderry, 12 vols. (1848–53) · A. Cogan, *The diocese of Meath: ancient and modern*, 3 vols. (1862–70) · U. Nott. L., Portland MSS · PRO NIre., Harrowby MSS · *DNB*
Archives Beds. & Luton ARS, letters to William Stuart, DDWY/994–995 · BL, letters to third Lord Hardwicke, Add. MSS 35689–35765 · BL, corresp. with Robert Peel, Add. MSS 40225–40346 · BL, Windham MSS, Add. MS 37877 · PRO NIre., corresp. with Castlereagh, D3030 · Sheff. Arch., corresp. with Edmund Burke; corresp. with Earl Fitzwilliam · U. Nott. L., Portland MSS
Likenesses A. Dunn, watercolour on ivory, 1808, NG Ire. [*see illus.*] · engraving, NL Ire.; repro. in *Ireland's Mirror* (Jan 1805)

Oberon, Merle [*real name* Estelle Merle O'Brien Thompson] (**1911–1979**), actress, was born in Bombay, India, on 19 February 1911; she was baptized on 16 March at Emmanuel Church, Gorpori, Bombay, the daughter of Arthur Thompson, a British-born railway engineer, and his Ceylonese wife, Constance (BL OIOC, N/3/105, fol. 27). Oberon's dark beauty, her inheritance from her mother, was an embarrassment in her search for a successful career in films in colour-conscious America. For many years her mother travelled and lived with Oberon, but was always referred to as her maid.

After probably being educated in India, Oberon surfaced

Merle Oberon (1911–1979), by Bassano, 1937

in London at the age of seventeen, under the name of Queenie O'Brien, working as a café hostess, and as an extra in British films. She graduated to playing small parts under the name of Estelle Thompson, although this aspect of her career is again open to question as she later admitted having invented several credits, 'to make myself appear more interesting' (Shipman, 425). During this period, she was spotted by the film director Alexander Korda, who added further touches to her grooming as a film star, including the name by which she is known.

In the early 1930s, after playing a variety of small roles, including a harem girl in the Crazy Gang's *Alf's Button* (1930) and several temptresses and 'other women', a type of role she found it hard to escape in her early career, she graduated to playing leading roles in British films. A significant moment was when Alexander Korda cast her as Anne Boleyn in *The Private Life of Henry VIII*, starring Charles Laughton, in 1933. Literary figures also became an area of casting for which her beauty, poise, and unforced photogenic attraction seemed to suit her. She had a compelling presence on the screen but brought no idiosyncratic features, which made her a malleable persona which a strong director could fashion as he wished. She was taken to Hollywood by Korda, who sold part of her contract to Sam Goldwyn. Throughout the 1930s she commuted between London and Hollywood, from success to success. She was nominated for an Academy award for her role as Kitty Vane in *Dark Angel* (1935), a melodrama, in which, for once, she played the central role in a love triangle; the story cast her as the fiancée of a blinded war

hero who tries to persuade her to marry his best friend without her discovering his condition.

As well as in Hollywood films with largely contemporary settings, Oberon continued during the 1930s to appear in British period films, often with literary settings. After *Anne Boleyn* she appeared as Antonia, supporting Douglas Fairbanks senior as an ageing philanderer, in *The Private Life of Don Juan* (1934) and as Marguerite Balcony, supporting Leslie Howard, in *The Scarlet Pimpernel* (1935). In 1937 she starred in Korda's most ambitious project, a film version of *I, Claudius*, with Charles Laughton in the leading role. During the filming Oberon was involved in a near fatal car crash, which miraculously left her beauty intact, but which led to the film's being cancelled. After some mediocre films, in Britain and Hollywood, she returned to major projects as Cathy, partnered by Laurence Olivier, in *Wuthering Heights* (1939). In this she looked beautiful and posed romantically, but never reached the emotional complexity of the character. Her performances always displayed a sense of style and polish, which led to her being cast in more historical roles or period melodramas. She appeared, and narrowly escaped being a victim of Jack the Ripper, in *The Lodger* (1944), in which she had to dance the cancan twice, or, as one critic commented, the 'can't-can't' (Shipman, 426). She appeared as Georges Sand in *A Song to Remember* (1945), a film which well deserves to be remembered as the worst biographical film ever; the dialogue included the line 'Chopin, I want you to meet Franz Liszt'. She played the Empress Josephine in *Desirée* (1954) and Sigmund Romberg's lyric writer Dorothy Donnelly in *Deep in my Heart* (1954). Along with these were a string of comedies and lachrymose romances that are best forgotten, some of which never rose above B-feature distribution. She continued to be a star, but rarely in star vehicles. Late in her career she had several roles in which her beauty, poise, and age combined to make her suitable to play fading stars and aristocrats. In two of these films her performance significantly raised inferior material to a superior level: *The Oscar* (1965), and *Hotel* (1966).

On 3 June 1939 Oberon married Alexander *Korda (1893–1956), divorcing him in 1945 to marry Lucien Ballard, a film cameraman. That marriage ended in divorce in 1949. Her third husband, from 1957, was Bruno Pagliai, a wealthy industrialist, with whom she lived in Mexico, largely suppressing her film career to live as a wealthy socialite. When the marriage ended in divorce in 1973 it left Oberon a rich woman. She had no children of her own, but adopted two children, Bruno junior and Francesca, during her marriage to Bruno Pagliai.

Throughout her film career Oberon worked with prestigious directors (including Korda, Ernst Lubitsch, René Clair, Jules Duvivier, King Vidor, and William Wyler), though not necessarily in their best pictures. The leading men who played opposite her included Gary Cooper, Charles Laughton, Douglas Fairbanks senior, Leslie Howard, Laurence Olivier, George Sanders, and Marlon Brando. Academy awards eluded her, but her dark beauty and svelte appearance added distinction and star quality to the films in which she appeared. In this, she complemented the more outstanding talent of the actors who played opposite her, and provided a fitting and enhancing setting for the display of their talents. There was a smouldering energy beneath her poised appearance which threatened to break loose from all control; it never did, but it attracted and sustained the cinema audience's attention. In 1973, the year of her divorce from Bruno Pagliai, she made a comeback in *Interval*, in which she starred and was also the producer. The film followed the story of a young man, played by Robert Wolders, who falls in love with an ageing star, played by Oberon. Ironically, she later married Wolders in 1975. From then on, she retired from films and she and Wolders entertained high society lavishly. Oberon died of a stroke, aged sixty-eight, in Los Angeles, on 23 November 1979. She was survived by Wolders. CLIVE BARKER

Sources *International dictionary of films and filmmakers*, 3rd edn, 3: *Actors and actresses*, ed. A. L. Unterberger (1997) · D. Shipman, *The great movie stars: the golden years*, rev. edn (1979) · *The Times* (26 Nov 1979) · J. Law, ed., *Cassell companion to cinema* (1997) · D. Thomson, *A biographical dictionary of film*, 3rd edn (1994) · E. Katz, ed., *The Macmillan international film encyclopaedia*, 2nd edn (1994)
Archives FILM BFI NFTVA, documentary footage · BFI NFTVA, performance footage | SOUND BL NSA, documentary recordings · BL NSA, performance recordings
Likenesses photographs, 1932–66, Hult. Arch. · Bassano, photograph, 1937, NPG [*see illus.*]

Obolensky, Alexander [Aleksandr] (1916–1940), rugby player, was born in Petrograd on 17 February 1916, the first son of Prince Sergey Obolensky, captain in the imperial horse guards, and his wife, Lubov Aleksandrovna Naryshkina. His family escaped from Russia in 1919, travelling from Riga on the *Princess Margaret*. He was educated at Trent College and in 1934 entered Brasenose College, Oxford, where he took a fourth in philosophy, politics, and economics in 1938.

Obolensky's talent for rugby was first recognized at Trent College, where he scored forty-nine tries in one season. At Oxford he won blues in 1935 and 1937, but missed the 1936 game against Cambridge University owing to injury. He won four England caps in 1936 and played club rugby for Rosslyn Park from 1936.

Obolensky's fame, far greater and more enduring than that of many players with much longer international careers, rests firmly on a single match. His international début, against New Zealand at Twickenham on 2 January 1936, is remembered as 'Obolensky's match' (Morgan and Nicholson, 217) for his two tries in a 13–0 victory: England's first ever win over New Zealand and its last until 1973. His second try, when he ran at an angle from his position on the right wing to score near the opposite corner, was called by his team-mate Peter Cranmer 'the most talked-about of my generation' (Cranmer, 10). Obolensky was still to be naturalized as a British citizen, a process completed a few weeks later. This led to an icy pre-match conversation with the prince of Wales (later Edward VIII), who asked him what qualified him to play for England. Obolensky replied: 'I am a student at Oxford University …

Alexander Obolensky (1916–1940), by Bassano, 1935

sir' (ibid.). After taking British nationality he requested no longer to be known as 'prince'.

The rest of Obolensky's international career was, by comparison, an anticlimax. He received hardly a pass in three more matches in 1936 and, in spite of scoring seventeen tries—believed to be a record for senior rugby—against Brazil at Niterói on a tour of South America in August 1936, was not selected in subsequent seasons. He remained a favourite with crowds at Rosslyn Park, who encouraged team-mates to 'give it to Obo' (Alston).

The enduring image of Obolensky as 'a romantic figure capable of doing almost incredible things' (*Daily Telegraph*, 1 April 1940) rests in part on his exotic background, but also on the pace and unorthodoxy demonstrated by his famous try at Twickenham. E. H. D. Sewell wrote that 'for a right wing to touch down several yards wide of the left-hand post was just one of those things that were not done' (Sewell, 232). Wilfred Wooller, who played against him for Cambridge, described Obolensky as 'a strongly built wing, with a low centre of gravity, [who] could move with breath-taking speed down the touchline' (Arlott, Wooller, and Edelston, 131). He was exceptionally fast—timed at 10.6 sec. for the 100 yards—and a pioneer in the use of lightweight boots. While not renowned as a defender, he saved a draw for Oxford in the 1935 varsity match with a tackle on the opposite wing. The Welsh international Vivian Jenkins called him 'a real White Russian Parisian type who loved to celebrate—truly one of the lads' (Frost, 79). He was reported to prepare for matches by consuming a dozen oysters. A more serious side was reflected in his contribution to the book *Be Still and Know: Oxford in Search of God* (ed. K. Briant and G. Joseph, 1936) and his disagreement with the Oxford Union's vote not to 'Fight for King and Country'.

Commissioned in the Royal Air Force Volunteer Reserve in May 1938, Obolensky was called up on the outbreak of war in 1939. He died when his plane crashed at Martlesham, Suffolk, on 29 March 1940. The first England rugby international to die in the Second World War, he was buried in Ipswich cemetery on 2 April 1940. He was unmarried. HUW RICHARDS

Sources E. H. D. Sewell, *Rugger: the man's game*, 3rd edn, rev. O. L. Owen (1950) · P. Cranmer, 'Obolensky's try', *Touchdown and other moves in the game*, ed. G. Nicholson (1970) · D. Frost, *The Bowring story of the varsity match* (1988) · J. Arlott, W. Wooller, and M. Edelston, *Wickets, tries and goals* (1949) · R. Alston, ed., *One hundred years: a history of Rosslyn Park football club, 1879–1979* (1979) · A. R. McWhirter and A. Noble, *Centenary history of Oxford University Rugby Football Club* (1969) · *The Isis* [Oxford] (22 Jan 1936) · *Daily Telegraph* (30 March–2 April 1940) · www.trentcollege.nott.sch.uk [web page] · W. J. Morgan and G. Nicholson, *Report on rugby* (1958)

Archives Rugby Football Union Library and Archive, Twickenham, papers | FILM BFI NFTVA, sports footage

Likenesses Bassano, photograph, 1935 [*see illus.*] · photographs, Rugby Football Union Library, Twickenham, Obolensky papers

O'Braein, Tighearnach. *See* Ua Bráin, Tigernach (d. 1088).

Ó Briain [O'Brien], **Brian Ruadh** (d. 1277), king of Thomond, was the son of Conchobhar *Ó Briain and his wife, Mór, a member of the Mac Con Mara family. He succeeded his father as king in 1268, without opposition according to the *Caithréim Thoirdhealbhaigh* ('The triumphs of Toirdelbach'), a work written in the mid-fourteenth century to support the claims of the descendants of Brian's brother Tadg against those of Brian. Thomond was at that time in a highly disturbed state, and in 1270 the situation worsened when Ó Briain began to attack the nearby English settlements just north of the Shannon, around Clare and Bunratty. In 1270 he captured Castle Clare. It is notable that at the same time, further north, Aedh Ó Conchobair was making significant progress against the de Burghs in Connacht. The English made four attempts over the next few years to settle the country, taking hostages from Brian Ó Briain, but the situation was obviously unstable and the need for a strong central English authority was apparent. On 26 January 1276 Thomas de Clare, brother of the earl of Gloucester and a close friend of Edward I, was granted the whole of Thomond. He was also close to the Fitzgeralds, being married to the daughter of Maurice fitz Maurice Fitzgerald (d. 1286).

In 1275 Sioda mac Neill mac Conmara, who had proclaimed Brian Ruadh Ó Briain king, rose against him in the interests of Brian's nephew Toirdelbach. Their forces expelled Brian from his stronghold at Clonroad and he was forced to flee across the Shannon with his son Donnchad and others who were loyal to him. Needing an ally, he turned to Thomas de Clare. By this act he brought the rivalry between the Fitzgeralds and the de Burghs into play: it was only a short time before Toirdelbach allied himself with the de Burghs of Connacht. Ó Briain appears

to have offered a significant amount of land to Clare for his help: 'all lands between Limerick and Athsolus' according to the *Caithréim* (Mac Craith, 2.6). Meeting at Limerick, the allied forces successfully took Clonroad, although Toirdelbach was absent at the time. Gathering more support, Brian continued his advance towards Quin (in what is now Clare). The opponents eventually met at Moygressan in 1277, where the allied forces were defeated by Toirdelbach after a long battle. In some disorder, the opposing forces retreated to the new Clare stronghold of Bunratty.

What happened next is unclear. According to the *Caithréim*, Clare's wife was furious at the death of her brother Patrick at Moygressan, and demanded the execution of Brian Ó Briain. Since her father, Maurice fitz Maurice, was also present, Clare acquiesced and executed Brian on 11 May. The *Caithréim* says that he was killed on a gibbet. The story that he was drawn between horses is unlikely: it first emerges in the later Ó Néill Remonstrance to Pope John XXII, but would almost certainly have been used by the author of the *Caithréim*, had he known of it, because his chief purpose was to show the perfidy of the Clares and the folly of Brian Ruadh. The more reliable annals of Inisfallen do not give this version, but do suggest that the execution took place with the complicity of some of Brian's own captains.

Although the sons of Brian Ó Briain, led by his heir, Donnchad, took their revenge by attacking the Clares at Quin the next year, they could not do without Clare support for long. The alliance was soon renewed and the civil war continued against Toirdelbach. In 1281 a settlement was made between the two factions but conflict soon flared up again and continued off and on until 1317, when Brian's descendant triumphed. The war had a serious long-term effect on the powers of the region, both Gaelic and English, but the real losers in the long run were the Clares, whose power was undermined by the de Burghs to such an extent that when the dispute was finally settled, the Uí Briain were able to expel both families from Thomond. MARCUS B. S. FLAVIN

Sources S. Mac Airt, ed. and trans., *The annals of Inisfallen* (1951) · W. M. Hennessy, ed. and trans., *The annals of Loch Cé: a chronicle of Irish affairs from AD 1014 to AD 1590*, 2 vols., Rolls Series, 54 (1871) · A. M. Freeman, ed. and trans., *Annála Connacht / The annals of Connacht* (1944); repr. (1970) · W. M. Hennessy and B. MacCarthy, eds., *Annals of Ulster, otherwise, annals of Senat*, 4 vols. (1887–1901) · S. Mac Ruaidhrí Mac Craith, *Caithréim Thoirdhealbhaigh / The triumphs of Turlough*, ed. S. H. O'Grady, 2 vols., ITS, 26–7 (1929) · T. W. Moody and others, eds., *A new history of Ireland*, 2: *Medieval Ireland, 1169–1534* (1987) · A. Nic Ghiollamhaith, 'Dynastic warfare and historical writing in north Munster, 1276–1350', *Cambridge Medieval Celtic Studies*, 2 (1981), 73–89 · A. Nic Ghiollamhaith, 'The Uí Briain and the king of England, 1248–1276', *Dal gCais*, 7 (1984), 94–9 · A. Nic Ghiollamhaith, 'Kings and vassals in later medieval Ireland', *Colony and frontier in medieval Ireland: essays presented to J. F. Lydon*, ed. T. Barry and others (1995), 201–16 · R. Frame, *Ireland and Britain, 1170–1450* (1998) · G. H. Orpen, *Ireland under the Normans*, 4 vols. (1911–20) · A. J. Otway-Ruthven, *A history of medieval Ireland* (1968)

Ó Briain, Conchobhar [Conor O'Brien] (d. 1268), king of Thomond, succeeded his father, Donnchad Cairprech *Ó

Briain, in 1242. The early years of his reign were dominated by a series of royal grants which threatened to move a great deal of the Uí Briain lands, already essentially limited to modern co. Clare, into Anglo-Norman hands. Pleas to Henry III had little effect (Ireland had been granted to Henry's son Edward in 1254), and in 1257 a wave of invasions into Thomond threatened to overwhelm Conchobhar. He and his more militant son Tadg seem to have held firm against these, and the following year Conchobhar raided into Galway and destroyed manors of the English Fitzgerald family, while Tadg went to a meeting at Cáeluisce with Brian Ó Néill, recorded in the annals and, in rather more detail, in the *Caithréim Thoirdhealbhaigh* ('The triumphs of Toirdelbach'). This was written in the mid-fourteenth century, to promote the history of the descendants of Tadg over those of his brother Brian, and to vilify the treacherous Clares, Brian's erstwhile allies. The *Caithréim* relates that the meeting fell apart when Tadg's gift of a hundred horses to Ó Néill (a traditional claim to supremacy, and thus, in this context, to the high-kingship) was returned with two hundred more.

In 1259 Tadg died, an event described by the annals as 'good news to the foreigners' (annals of Inisfallen, s.a. 1260, *recte* 1259). According to the *Caithréim*, Conchobhar Ó Briain fell into a deep depression and no longer appeared in public, as a result of which his subjects ceased paying their royal dues. This story, however, may stem from the *Caithréim's* concern to promote Tadg's importance: certainly Conchobhar had a notable success against the Fitzgeralds when they invaded in 1260, though in 1261 he seems to have made his peace. He attempted to reassert his authority in the context of intensified rivalries between the great Anglo-Irish lords, particularly between the de Burghs and the Fitzgeralds. These may have been exacerbated by the absence of central control during the barons' war in England. After the seizure of the justiciar by Maurice fitz Maurice Fitzgerald (*d.* 1286) and Maurice Fitzgerald (*d.* 1268) in December 1264, Ireland descended into civil war, and the Gaelic lords must have seen their opportunity. Conchobhar Ó Briain mustered his forces and raided across the Shannon for tribute, bringing it back to a newly constructed stronghold at Clonroad.

Soon after, in 1268, Ó Briain raided northwards once more. This time, though, he was attacked by Diarmait, son of Muirchertach Ó Briain, at Belaclugga, and he and many of his family and followers were killed, on 22 May 1268 according to the annals of Inisfallen. The *Caithréim* account ascribes the attack to 'Conor *carrach* Ó Lochlainn', but the annals seem clear that the only Ó Lochlainn mentioned, Dublochlann Ó Lochlainn, was on Conchobhar's side and that Diarmait, whose death soon after they record with an air of satisfaction, was the attacker. The body was taken to the monastery of East Burren or Corcomrua and buried there, where an effigy survives.

With his wife Mór, a member of the Mac Con Mara family, Conchobhar Ó Briain had three known sons, Tadg, Seonin, and Brian Ruadh *Ó Briain, of whom only Brian survived to succeed. His daughter and her son with Ruaidri Ó Grada were killed alongside Conchobhar and Seonin

at Belaclugga. Tadg's son Toirdelbach survived however, and the struggle between his family and that of Brian Ruadh for the leadership of the Uí Briain was to dominate Thomond for many years.   MARCUS B. S. FLAVIN

Sources S. Mac Airt, ed. and trans., *The annals of Inisfallen* (1951) · W. M. Hennessy, ed. and trans., *The annals of Loch Cé: a chronicle of Irish affairs from AD 1014 to AD 1590*, 2 vols., Rolls Series, 54 (1871) · A. M. Freeman, ed. and trans., *Annála Connacht / The annals of Connacht* (1944); repr. (1970) · W. M. Hennessy and B. MacCarthy, eds., *Annals of Ulster, otherwise, annals of Senat*, 4 vols. (1887–1901) · S. Mac Ruaidhrí Mac Craith, *Caithréim Thoirdhealbhaigh / The triumphs of Turlough*, ed. S. H. O'Grady, 2 vols., ITS, 26–7 (1929) · T. W. Moody and others, eds., *A new history of Ireland*, 2: *Medieval Ireland, 1169–1534* (1987) · A. Nic Ghiollamhaith, 'Dynastic warfare and historical writing in north Munster, 1276–1350', *Cambridge Medieval Celtic Studies*, 2 (1981), 73–89 · A. Nic Ghiollamhaith, 'The Uí Briain and the king of England, 1248–1276', *Dal gCais*, 7 (1984), 94–9 · A. Nic Ghiollamhaith, 'Kings and vassals in later medieval Ireland', *Colony and frontier in medieval Ireland: essays presented to J. F. Lydon*, ed. T. Barry and others (1995), 201–16 · R. Frame, *Ireland and Britain, 1170–1450* (1998), chaps. 3, 4 · G. H. Orpen, *Ireland under the Normans*, 4 vols. (1911–20) · A. J. Otway-Ruthven, *A history of medieval Ireland* (1968)
Likenesses tomb effigy, abbey of Corcomrua, Ireland

Ó Briain, Donnchad [Donogh O'Brien] (1425–1460), bishop of Killaloe, was mistakenly identified as Terence or Toirdhelbhach Ó Briain by James Ware (*d.* 1666) and others. The second son of Toirdhelbhach Ó Briain, king of Thomond from 1446 to 1459, he owed his clerical promotion to his family connections. Before his provision to Killaloe on 26 July 1443, Ó Briain held parishes and prebends in Killaloe and Kilfenora without having been admitted to any holy order. In a petition to Pope Eugenius IV, the future bishop admitted that:

> in his youth he took part in battles and conflicts in which many were wounded and some killed, but neither wounded nor killed any one with his own hand; that less than two years ago, while playing on horseback a game of those parts in which the players throw sticks at one another's backs, his stick accidentally struck in the eye of one of the players, who looked round, and blinded him. (*CEPR letters*, 9.331)

Given such an inauspicious beginning to a clerical career, it is not altogether surprising that he was accused of accepting a gift of two horses in return for appointing a priest to a vicarage. He was killed by a cousin at Ennis in 1460, no doubt in consequence of his involvement in family intrigues, and was probably buried in his cathedral at Killaloe.   C. A. EMPEY

Sources *CEPR letters*, vol. 8 · A. Gwynn and D. F. Gleeson, *A history of the diocese of Killaloe* (1962) · *AFM*

Ó Briain, Donnchad Cairprech [Donogh Cairbrech O'Brien] (*d.* 1242), king of Thomond, was one of three surviving sons of Domnall Mór *Ua Briain, king of Thomond (*d.* 1194). It is not certain when Donnchad became king, but he appears to have emerged as the leading member of his turbulent family when King John knighted him in 1210. Longevity was not a notable feature of leadership in the Gaelic world, yet Donnchad successfully held his ground for more than thirty years in the face of internal strife and the wiles of his Irish and Norman foes. This was no mean achievement in circumstances where the Normans were triumphant everywhere along his borders.

Ó Briain's early years were preoccupied with the struggles for the succession. His brother Muirchertach appears to have succeeded to the kingship in 1194, but almost immediately there was fraternal strife. A third brother, Conchobhar, emerged as the initial victor by capturing Donnchad in 1196, allying himself with the Normans in the following year, and seizing the kingship from Muirchertach in 1198. His triumph was short-lived, for in 1202 he was killed by his deposed brother's followers. Trouble broke out afresh in 1207, when Muirchertach, who had attacked Norman castles in northern Tipperary, was betrayed by Donnchad to the English of Limerick. He remained in captivity until his release in 1210.

Political ascendancy was reinforced by royal favour. King John knighted Ó Briain at Waterford in 1210, and thereafter appears to have regarded him as a tenant-in-chief, holding land for an annual rent of 60 marks. He immediately awarded him the custody of William de Burgh's strategic castle of Carrigogunnell, near Limerick, possibly because Ó Briain was married to William's daughter. It also suggests that John intended to use Ó Briain to counter the ambitions of the Norman lords in north Munster. Nevertheless, he stopped short of recognizing him as king of Thomond: royal writs addressed to Donnchad during John's reign conspicuously avoided the title. Nor was Ó Briain granted exclusive lordship of Thomond. The king retained three cantreds in Corcu Baiscinn and the cantred of Tradree, which he granted to the justiciar, John de Gray, who in turn granted them to Reginald of Finegal and Thomas fitz Adam. Muirchertach Ó Briain seems to have been regarded in royal sources as a tenant-in-chief also, holding territory in Thomond by annual rent.

Donnchad Ó Briain was careful to avoid direct conflict with either the crown or the great Norman lords. Only once did he incur royal disfavour, when in 1234 he made fine for having sided with William (II) Marshal. For this lapse he paid heavily when Thomond was ravaged by the justiciar in the following year. He allied himself with the Normans in raids on the Mac Carthaigh kingdom of Desmond in 1201, 1206, and 1214, while in 1225 and 1230 he was similarly involved in invasions of Connacht. His father had been no friend of the Mac Carthaighs, so the outlines of traditional rivalries are discernible behind such alliances. Much the same is probably true of Ó Briain's interventions in Connacht in support of the sons of Cathal Croibhdhearg Ó Conchobhair, whose wife, Mór (d. 1217/18) was Donnchad's sister. It was no doubt on the basis of his prosecution of traditional rivalries that Ó Briain earned the approval of the chronicler in the annals of Inisfallen on his death in 1242: 'there was not during his time a better Munsterman, or one more affable, or of greater retinue, or better provided with victuals than he'. According to Sir James Ware (d. 1666), Donnchad was buried in the Dominican convent, Limerick.

Ó Briain was predeceased by his wife, Sadh (d. 1240), daughter of Ó Cennétig. An earlier marriage to an unnamed daughter of William de Burgh is attested only by a comparatively late Gaelic source. His son Conchobhar *Ó Briain (d. 1268) succeeded him as king of Thomond. His remaining sons, Muirchertach and Tairdelbhach, died in 1242. His daughter Sadb, wife of Sefraid Ó Donnchada, was killed in 1253.   C. A. EMPEY

Sources A. M. Freeman, ed. and trans., *Annála Connacht / The annals of Connacht* (1944); repr. (1970) · S. Mac Airt, ed. and trans., *The annals of Inisfallen* (1951) · S. Ó hInnse, ed. and trans., *Miscellaneous Irish annals, AD 1114–1437* (1947) · W. M. Hennessy, ed. and trans., *The annals of Loch Cé: a chronicle of Irish affairs from AD 1014 to AD 1590*, 1, Rolls Series, 54 (1871) · AFM · D. Murphy, ed., *The annals of Clonmacnoise*, trans. C. Mageoghagan (1896); facs. edn (1993) · H. S. Sweetman and G. F. Handcock, eds., *Calendar of documents relating to Ireland*, 5 vols., PRO (1875–86), vol. 1 · *Close rolls of the reign of Henry III*, 14 vols., PRO (1902–38) · C. A. Empey, 'The settlement of the kingdom of Limerick', *England and Ireland in the later middle ages: essays in honour of Jocelyn Otway-Ruthven*, ed. J. Lydon (1981) · A. Gwynn and D. F. Gleeson, *A history of the diocese of Killaloe* (1962) · J. Ware, *De Hibernia et antiquitatibus ejus, disquisitiones* (1654)

O'Brian [*formerly* Russ], **(Richard) Patrick** (1914–2000), novelist, was born on 12 December 1914 at his parents' house, Walden, in Chalfont St Peter, Buckinghamshire, the son of Charles Russ (1877–1955), venereologist, and his wife, Jessie Naylor Goddard (1878–1918). His grandfather Carl (later Charles) Russ, a furrier from near Leipzig, had emigrated to Britain in 1862. After establishing himself in business in London he had died in 1893 with a shop on New Bond Street, a villa in St John's Wood, and a fortune of £40,000. His eldest son, Charles, took up medicine. His spendthrift habits and researches into the use of electricity to cure venereal disease bled his share of the inheritance, and he was declared bankrupt in 1925. Patrick Russ's youth was overshadowed by the declining fortunes of his increasingly aloof father as the family moved from rustic Buckinghamshire to the suburbs of north-west London. The family was briefly split up on the death of Patrick's mother when he was three, but was reunited when Charles Russ remarried in 1922, and Patrick Russ evidently felt considerable affection for his stepmother.

Patrick Russ Russ is known to have attended Marylebone grammar school, London, and in 1926–7 the Old Grammar School at Lewes, Sussex, where his father briefly lived. However, his formal schooling was seriously disrupted by the recurrent respiratory complaints which dogged him throughout his childhood. He compensated by voracious, endless reading: most notably his stepmother's collection of eighteenth- and early nineteenth-century literature and the stories of Rudyard Kipling. He also early displayed a fascination with natural history. At fifteen he wrote his first book, *Caesar: the Life Story of a Panda Leopard*, which was published in 1930. In a foreword Russ's father expressed the belief that 'the author's immaturity of literary style and method—which are quite unspoiled by any senior pen—may also contribute to its favourable reception' (p. v). Other animal stories followed, published in magazines, in boys' annuals published by Oxford University Press, and in a collection, *Beasts Royal* (1934). The range of his stories broadened over the years, and in 1938 he expanded several into a picaresque novel set in India, *Hussein: an Entertainment*. Favourable reviews marked Russ out as a promising writer.

In 1934 Russ failed a course to become a pilot officer in the RAF. On 27 February 1936 Russ married (Sarah) Elizabeth Jones (*b.* 1910/11) at the Chelsea register office. A son, Richard Francis Tudor Russ, was born on 2 February 1937. The marriage was evidently unhappy, the couple incompatible in temperament and intellectual interests and chronically short of money. During the summer of 1937 Russ took work as a travel representative in Switzerland for the Workers' Travel Association, claiming to some he met then that he was Irish. The marriage was further strained when their daughter, Jane Elizabeth Campaspe Tudor Russ, was born on 8 February 1939 with spina bifida. The family moved from Chelsea to a cottage in Suffolk where Russ could write and hunt and scavenge for firewood to support his family. In the summer of 1940 he abandoned them and returned to London, his eldest brother and his wife taking over their care.

Russ drove an ambulance during the blitz, and met a fellow driver, Mary (1915/16–1998), the daughter of Howard and Mary Wicksteed and estranged wife of Dimitry Mihailovich, Count Tolstoy Miloslavsky, a barrister—according to members of the Russ family, when French speakers were called to a free French army billet which had been struck by a bomb. After the blitz they were both recruited into the political warfare executive, a propaganda and intelligence unit where they worked in the French section. Jane Russ died from the complications of spina bifida in the spring of 1942. Mary's divorce became official in November of that year. Russ's followed on 25 June 1945, and on 4 July 1945 they were married. The marriage proved very happy, and Mary's perceptive scrutiny of his manuscripts was much valued by her husband. He dedicated many of his books to her.

Patrick O'Brian   With the war's end Russ suppressed his past. On 20 July 1945 he changed his name by deed poll to Richard Patrick O'Brian. The surname had been adopted in Australia by his elder brother Michael, who had died in a bombing raid over Dortmund in 1943. Patrick O'Brian claimed to be an Irishman: the brief biography attached to the American edition of one of his books in 1955, for instance, stated that 'O'Brian was born in the west of Ireland and educated in England' (King, 182). His contact with his Russ siblings became limited to occasional letters and visits. O'Brian maintained relations with his son Richard, who stayed with him during summer holidays in the late 1940s and early 1950s and lived with him for a time in 1948–9. However, a permanent breach between father and son occurred in the spring of 1964, when the latter chose to revert to the name of Russ upon his marriage.

North Wales and the south of France   In 1945 the O'Brians moved to Cwm Croesor in north-west Merioneth, where he hunted, fished, helped out on a neighbouring farm, and later recalled: 'dear people, splendid mountains, but a terrible climate' (O'Brian, 'Black, married & choleric', 17). In 1949 they moved to Collioure, a small village on the

south-west coast of France with a reputation for attracting artists and writers, a place where life was initially as frugal but the climate more hospitable, and where in time O'Brian built a home among the vineyards away from the town centre.

In 1947 O'Brian published an anthology of seventeenth- and eighteenth-century travel writing, *A Book of Voyages*. From his years in Wales came a volume of short stories, *The Last Pool* (1950). Several of his stories were published by *Harper's Bazaar* in the USA, and in 1955 he published another collection, *The Walker and Other Stories* (published the following year in Britain with a slightly different selection as *Lying in the Sun and Other Stories*). As a novelist O'Brian produced in the 1950s intense works exploring adult themes and lighter works for a younger readership. In 1952 he published *Three Bear Witness* (called in its American edition and its reissue of 1994 *Testimonies*), a novel about a love triangle set in the Welsh mountains. It received particularly favourable reviews in America, where it was praised for its matching of style and feeling. *The Frozen Flame* (in the United States entitled *The Catalans*) appeared in 1953, taking as its theme love and the inability to love. Following these two difficult and intense novels, he later recalled that he had turned—'for fun' and 'by way of a holiday'—to writing a book for young adults, *The Golden Ocean* (O'Brian, 'Black, married & choleric', 18), which told with humour and a strong sense of period the story of Commodore Anson's voyage to the Pacific in 1740–44 as seen through the eyes of an Irish midshipman, Peter Palofox. Although apparently written earlier it was not published until 1956, after another novel for young readers, *The Road to Samarcand* (1955). *The Unknown Shore* (1959) was a sequel of sorts; it told of the fate of another ship in Anson's fleet, which was wrecked on the shore of Patagonia. The central relationship of the book was the chalk-and-cheese friendship between the midshipman, Jack Byron, and the eccentric surgeon's mate Tobias Barrow. In 1962 O'Brian published *Richard Temple*, another novel for adults which explored the plight of the artist in society.

Aubrey and Maturin   For much of the 1960s O'Brian was a much respected translator of French books, largely non-fiction. He published nineteen translations between 1961 and 1969, including most notably the works of Simone de Beauvoir from 1966 onwards. O'Brian's career was transformed when in 1967 he was approached by the American publishing house of J. B. Lippincott, which had read *The Golden Ocean*, to write a naval adventure for an adult readership set during the Napoleonic wars. C. S. Forester, the creator of Captain Horatio Hornblower, had died in the previous year, and it was hoped that O'Brian would write a series to rival Forester's. Although his manuscript was rejected by his intended English publisher it was enthusiastically taken up by another, Collins, and the novel, *Master and Commander*, was published at the end of 1969.

It turned out to be the first in a series of twenty novels which O'Brian published during the next thirty years, relating the adventures of the naval captain Jack Aubrey and his friend the surgeon, spy, and polymath Stephen

Maturin. A thorough researcher, O'Brian knew the eighteenth and early nineteenth centuries intimately, and consulted contemporary logbooks, memoirs, official letters, and publications. Throughout the series O'Brian often appropriated particular historical incidents for his heroes. For the naval narrative of *Master and Commander*, for instance, he borrowed the exploits of Lord Thomas Cochrane in the sloop *Speedy* in the western Mediterranean in 1800–01; this was the first of several occasions when he used episodes from the life of that brilliant but vain and mercurial Scottish frigate captain and radical politician. However, as O'Brian later recalled, 'I did not borrow Lord Cochrane himself because I meant Jack Aubrey to be essentially English and, in fact, a much more agreeable person, one based on many Englishmen of the better sort I have known, particularly sailors' (O'Brian, 'Just a phase').

At the heart of the books was the exploration of the friendship between the bluff, generous-spirited Aubrey and the secretive Maturin—half Irish, half Catalan, illegitimate, learned but short on the niceties of social convention, an outsider whose voice throughout the series often provided the commentary on human relationships. The books also contrasted the microcosm of the ship and its formal hierarchy with the unpredictability of the sea and of events. In his taste for humour and the picaresque, O'Brian looked back more to Captain Marryatt, the founder of the naval genre, than to Forester. As early admirers such as his editor at Collins, Richard Ollard, and the leading historical novelist Mary Renault appreciated, O'Brian managed to place his subjects in a convincing world which went far beyond getting the details of shipboard life and naval tactics right. Music, natural history, astronomy, poetry, folklore, food, the codes of honour and politeness—all were drawn on to create the culture in which Aubrey and Maturin negotiated questions of friendship, love, ageing, and responsibility as much as fought the war against Napoleon, and in a prose style sensitive to the terminology and rhythms of the language of the period.

The Aubrey–Maturin novels did not absorb all O'Brian's energies, especially in their early years. He continued to publish translations (nine between 1970 and 1978 and a further three between 1982 and 1990), including more works by de Beauvoir and, in 1970, a translation of *Papillon*, the memoirs of the French convict Henri Charrière, a bestseller whose royalties helped support O'Brian's own writing. In 1973 he published a collection of short stories, *The Chian Wine*, which included revised versions of many of his earlier stories. Moreover, in that year he was commissioned to write a biography of Pablo Picasso, published three years later. Picasso had visited Collioure for two summers, and O'Brian knew several of the painter's friends; the study also drew on O'Brian's love of Catalonia. According to O'Brian, returning to his naval tales in the late 1970s, it was 'borne in upon me that this is the right kind of writing for a man of my sort' (O'Brian, 'Black, married & choleric', 21). In 1987 he published a biography of the eighteenth-century naturalist Sir Joseph Banks.

For many years sales of the Aubrey–Maturin series in Britain were steady but were far from entering the bestseller category. O'Brian received mostly positive reviews, but the shadow of Forester (to whom he was frequently compared by critics, albeit usually in his favour) at once helped provide O'Brian with a following while tending to limit his appeal beyond the niche of naval yarns. Nevertheless sales in Britain were cumulatively impressive as the books went through successive reprints over the decades, reaching 2.1 million copies sold in paperback by the end of 1999. In the USA, where reviews were less sympathetic, sales were so poor that after three books the series was dropped by Lippincott; a second publisher fared no better, and after the fifth book no more were published in America for almost a decade.

Acclaim In the USA, O'Brian's fans with publishing connections urged editors to look again at the author. W. W. Norton picked up the series, beginning with the twelfth book, *The Letter of Marque*, in 1990. In the following year an essay on the front page of the *New York Times Book Review* hailed O'Brian as one of the great unknown writers of his generation and the Aubrey–Maturin novels as 'the best historical novels ever written'. With this boost and astute marketing sales rose rapidly. His success in the American market encouraged something of a critical rediscovery in Britain, where from the early 1990s enhanced literary esteem and a broadened readership was translated into more tangible recognition. In 1991 he became a fellow of the Royal Society of Literature. Three years later the British Library brought out a critical bibliography of his work, an unprecedented honour for a living author. In 1995 O'Brian was appointed Commander of the British Empire. The following year Max Hastings, the editor of the *Evening Standard*, and his literary editor, A. N. Wilson, organized a banquet in the Painted Hall of the Royal Naval College at Greenwich to honour O'Brian. The author and guests—who included politicians, civil servants, fellow writers, artists, naval officers, and other admirers—were served a menu which could have been set before Jack Aubrey: pea soup, salt beef, potatoes, and suet pudding.

O'Brian himself professed himself bemused by his late recognition, commenting that 'the books now praised are exactly the same as those which were scorned. The merit or lack of merit has not altered.' He concluded that it could well be a 'matter of phase':

> Cezanne and Van Gogh said little to most of their contemporaries; our grandfathers could have bought an El Greco for a hundred guineas or less; and my early Encyclopaedia Britannica does not even mention Monteverdi. They were out of phase: the phases, ruled by who knows what laws, now coincide. (O'Brian, 'Just a phase')

Certainly some of O'Brian's prominent supporters evidently welcomed the traditional literary virtues that they found in his novels. The Conservative politician William Waldegrave, for instance, praised the cosmopolitanism and depth of research of O'Brian's writing and compared him to Sir Walter Scott, Rudyard Kipling, Charles Reade, and John Buchan, writers

[who] embarrass much of our current literary establishment because of the clarity of their vision and the sharpness of their contempt for those who denigrate the values which they themselves do not doubt. This is perhaps why O'Brian's first acclaim came in the USA not here, and why his fame in Britain, where self-doubt has reached epidemic status amongst our elites, spreads like wildfire by word of mouth helped only by a few brave souls who have always had the independence to welcome excellence, in whatever shape. (Waldegrave, 12)

Hastings considered that O'Brian 'possesses the literary grace so often lacking in younger British novelists', elsewhere finding in his writings 'a pervasive serenity, a generosity towards human frailty' (King, 357, 384).

O'Brian's life before 1945 remained hidden, and he was reluctant to provide personal details about himself, regarding 'privacy as a jewel' (O'Brian, 'Black, married & choleric', 15). It remained generally accepted that he was Irish by birth. The British Library bibliography listed none of the Richard Patrick Russ books from the 1930s. In the same volume O'Brian himself in an autobiographical sketch confirmed the impression of his upbringing. He briefly touched on his childhood, recording the loss of his mother, his affection for his stepmother, and his endless reading. But his suburban London upbringing was translated to Ireland and to a rather more elevated social status. Sent to live 'with more or less willing relative relatives in Connemara and County Clare' he had a governess, 'dear Miss O'Mara, and some tutors whom I shall always remember with gratitude'. 'I may observe', he added, 'that although I spent long periods in England, liking the people very much, it was Ireland and France that educated and formed me, in so far as I was educated and formed' (O'Brian, 'Black, married & choleric', 16).

However, with O'Brian's late literary and commercial recognition came curiosity about the life of this very private man, the dedicated writer whose cultural codes seemed to belong to the world of which he was writing, devoted to his library of books of the period, his vineyard, and the flora and fauna around him. In the autumn of 1998 the BBC produced a documentary which hinted at inconsistencies in O'Brian's account of himself, while the *Daily Telegraph* broke the story that Patrick O'Brian, Irishman, was indeed Patrick Russ, Londoner. An American journalist and admirer, Dean King, was already researching for a biography that appeared a few months after O'Brian's death. 'News of the pending biography caused Patrick a distress so deep that it all but destroyed the pleasure he derived from his belated acclaim and the social and financial success it brought him', his stepson recorded (Tolstoy, 13). In 1999 O'Brian acknowledged his pre-war writings when he wrote forewords to editions of *Caesar* and *Hussein* published by the British Library.

O'Brian's wife, Mary, died in hospital in Perpignan in March 1998. He had been awarded an honorary doctorate of letters by Trinity College, Dublin, in 1997, and in the winter of 1998–9 stayed in rooms in the college where he worked on his last book. *Blue at the Mizzen*, in which Aubrey at last achieved his much longed-for promotion to flag rank, appeared in November 1999. O'Brian died on 2 January 2000 at the Fitzwilliam Hotel, Stephens Green, Dublin. He was buried nine days later beside his wife in Collioure.   TIM WALES and BILL PESCHEL

Sources D. King, *Patrick O'Brian: a life revealed* (2000) · R. Snow, 'An author I'd walk the plank for', *New York Times Book Review* (6 Jan 1991) · *Washington Post* (2 Aug 1992) · b. cert. · m. certs. · divorce cert. · deed poll name change cert. · d. cert. · A. E. Cunningham, ed., *Patrick O'Brian: critical appreciations and a bibliography* (1994) · P. O'Brian, 'Black, married & choleric', *Patrick O'Brian: critical appreciations and a bibliography*, ed. A. E. Cunningham (1994), 15–21 · P. O'Brian, 'Just a phase I'm going through', www.wwnorton.com/pob/vol4i.htm [*Patrick O'Brian Newsletter*, 4/1 (March 1995)], 20 Nov 2002 · A. E. Cunningham, 'A bibliography of the writings of Patrick O'Brian', *Patrick O'Brian: critical appreciations and a bibliography*, ed. A. E. Cunningham (1994) · W. Waldegrave, introduction, *Patrick O'Brian: critical appreciations and a bibliography*, ed. A. E. Cunningham (1994) · 'A word from Patrick O'Brian', www.wwnorton.com/pob/vol2i.htm#author [*Patrick O'Brian Newsletter*, 2/1 (March 1993)], 20 Nov 2002 · A. Hamilton, 'Fastsellers, 2000', *The Guardian* (6 Jan 2000) · N. Tolstoy, 'Wait for my version', *Literary Review* (Aug 2000), 12–13
Archives Indiana University, Bloomington, Lilly Library
Likenesses S. Pyke, 'c' type colour print, 1996, NPG

O'Brien [*née* Ball], **Anna Maria** (1785–1871), philanthropist, was born at 5 Werburgh Street, Dublin, the second of five children of John Ball (1728–1804), silk merchant, and his second wife, Mable Clare Bennett (d. 1831). Like many wealthy Irish Catholic girls she was educated at the Bar Convent, York, England (1800–03). On 12 November 1805 Anna Maria Ball married John O'Brien, a Dublin businessman, to whom she brought a dowry of £5000. The couple remained childless, although they adopted the three children of Anna Maria's half-brother, John Ball, after his death in 1812. Mrs O'Brien also engaged in philanthropic activities, directed primarily at rescuing young girls: in 1809, with some other women, she opened a house of refuge in Ash Street, Dublin.

In 1807 Cecilia Ball, Anna Maria's sister, entered the Ursuline convent in Cork as a novice, and Mrs O'Brien and her sister Frances *Ball (1794–1861), who was to form the Congregation of Loreto Sisters in 1821, accompanied her on the journey. While in Cork, Mrs O'Brien met Mary Aikenhead (1787–1858), whom she invited to come to Dublin. Aikenhead arrived there the following year, and the two engaged in charitable work in the city. The Revd Daniel Murray (1768–1852) was a regular visitor to the O'Brien house and a close friend of Mrs O'Brien, who attended mass every day in his private oratory in Dublin. In 1809 Murray became archbishop, and coadjutor to the see of Dublin. He was keen to establish a religious congregation of nuns in the city to engage in charitable work and O'Brien introduced him to Aikenhead as a possible founder of such an enterprise: a friendship developed between Murray and Aikenhead, which led to the foundation of the Sisters of Charity in 1815.

Mrs O'Brien became intimately connected with the new religious congregation. Not only did she provide funding for a number of its enterprises but she also engaged in philanthropic work with the community. The Ash Street house of refuge was put in the Sisters' care, and when the nuns engaged in prison visitation, she accompanied them. When the Sisters of Charity thought of establishing a hospital in Dublin, Mrs O'Brien and her husband travelled to Paris with three nuns sent to train there in 1833. When the Sisters took over the Kings Inns Street primary schools, she was, most unusually, appointed their manager; she was also credited with supporting a large number of orphanages in Dublin city in the early years of the nineteenth century.

Mrs O'Brien suffered from senility in the last two years of her life and died on 28 March 1871, at her home, 5 Mountjoy Square, Dublin. She was part of a community of wealthy Catholic women who, working closely with powerful clerics, played a key role in developing religious communities of nuns during the early nineteenth century, as well as a network of lay Catholic philanthropy which worked closely with convent communities.

MARIA LUDDY

Sources B. B. Butler and K. Butler, 'Mrs John O'Brien: her life, her work, her friends', *Dublin Historical Record*, 33/4 (1979–80), 141–56 • S. A. [S. Atkinson], *Mary Aikenhead: her life, her work and her friends* (1879) • D. Forristal, *The first Loreto sister, Mother Teresa Ball, 1794–1861* (1994) • M. Luddy, *Women and philanthropy in nineteenth-century Ireland* (1995)
Archives Sisters of Charity Generalate, Dublin
Likenesses N. J. Crowley, portrait, c.1844, Sisters of Charity Generalate, Milltown, Dublin • photograph, repro. in Atkinson, *Mary Aikenhead*, 267

O'Brien, Barnabas, sixth earl of Thomond (1590/91–1657), nobleman, was the second son of Donough *O'Brien, fourth earl of Thomond (d. 1624), and his second wife, Lady Elizabeth (d. 1618), fourth daughter of Gerald *Fitzgerald, eleventh earl of Kildare. His elder brother, Henry, fifth earl of Thomond, who succeeded to the earldom on his father's death in 1624, was a strenuous adherent of the government in Ireland and was warmly commended by Strafford for his loyalty. He died without male issue in 1639. Barnabas O'Brien matriculated from Brasenose College, Oxford, on 20 February 1605, aged fourteen, and entered Lincoln's Inn in 1613. On 17 July 1615, at Easton Neston, Northamptonshire, he married Mary (bap. 1592, d. 1675), youngest daughter of Sir George Fermor and widow of James, Lord Crichton of Sanquhar. At some point he purchased the manor of Great Billing, Northamptonshire, and was resident in the county for a time, being appointed a JP. He entered the Irish parliament in 1613 as a member for Coleraine. In 1634 he was returned as an MP for County Clare but, being compelled to go to England for a time, a writ was issued for a fresh election and he was, it seems, succeeded by his uncle Daniel O'Brien, later Viscount Clare. He was also returned for Carlow borough and for Ennis.

In 1639 O'Brien succeeded his brother as sixth earl, and was made governor of co. Clare on 21 November the same year, the governorship to merge with that of Munster after his death. A protestant, he was appointed to the Irish privy council. Following the outbreak of the 1641 rising, he presided over a county meeting which resulted in plans to raise troops and obtain arms against the insurgents. His lenient stance as governor 'perhaps as much the result of

want of authority as of personal inclination', however, saw the rising spread to Clare and by January 1642 the county had declared for the insurgents (Clarke, 194–5). Residing quietly in his principal stronghold, Bunratty Castle, he sheltered local protestants and English. In spite of the support given to the confederacy by his kinsmen he did not sign the oath of association and remained in frequent communication with Ormond, the lord lieutenant. The confederate leadership planned, unsuccessfully, to gain control of his person and castle through his kinsmen, principally his uncle Sir Daniel O'Brien. In 1644 their supreme council forbade his tenants to pay their rents to him, or his agents to collect them, and announced their intention to set his lands. On 3 May 1645 Charles I created him marquess of Billing under the privy seal, but the patent never passed the great seal.

In March 1646 Thomond admitted to Bunratty troops sent by the English parliamentarians (though he later claimed he was not aware in advance of their coming), in spite of the earl of Glamorgan's remonstrances and appeals to his loyalty. He went to live in England and, petitioning parliament, claimed always to have opposed the rebellion and to have sustained considerable losses through seizure of his lands, and through expenditure on troops early in the war and after the arrival of the parliamentarian garrison. His petition for recompense was at least partially granted, and he apparently gave no cause for suspicion to the Commonwealth or protectorate regimes. He died in November 1657 and was buried on 15 November, in Great Billing. In his will, dated 1 July 1657, he complained of his impoverishment, and left some bequests to Great Billing, 'which would have been greater had my losses and sufferings in Ireland been less' (Royal Irish Academy, MS 3.A.40, fol. 161). The will was proved in England on 6 February, and in Ireland on 28 April 1658. He left one son, Henry (1621–1691), his successor, and one daughter, Penelope, who married Henry Mordaunt, second earl of Peterborough. The seventh earl matriculated from Exeter College, Oxford, on 19 August 1636, aged fifteen. He was governor of co. Clare in 1661–70 and again from 1679, and died at Billing on 2 May 1691.

A. F. POLLARD, rev. BERNADETTE CUNNINGHAM

Sources GEC, *Peerage*, new edn, 12/1.705–9 • R. Lascelles, ed., *Liber munerum publicorum Hiberniae ... or, The establishments of Ireland*, later edn, 2 vols. in 7 pts (1852), vol. 1, pt 2, p. 185 • J. Lodge, *The peerage of Ireland*, rev. M. Archdall, rev. edn, 7 vols. (1789) • F. Peck, ed., *Desiderata curiosa*, 2 (1735), 193–4, 322 • J. T. Gilbert, ed., *A contemporary history of affairs in Ireland from 1641 to 1652*, 1 (1879), 105–6 • P. Dwyer, *The diocese of Killaloe: from the Reformation to the close of the eighteenth century* (1878), 196, 206, 220, 267 • T. Carte, *An history of the life of James, duke of Ormonde*, 3 vols. (1735–6); new edn, pubd as *The life of James, duke of Ormond*, 6 vols. (1851) • J. Morrin, ed., *Calendar of the patent and close rolls of chancery in Ireland, of the reign of Charles I* (1863) • Foster, *Alum. Oxon.* • G. Baker, *The history and antiquities of the county of Northampton*, 1 (1822–30), 20–21 • CSP dom., 1645–7, 243, 429 • CSP Ire., 1633–60 • H. Kearney, *Strafford in Ireland, 1633–1641: a study in absolutism* (1959) • A. Clarke, *The Old English in Ireland, 1625–1642* (1966) • J. Hogan, ed., *Letters and papers relating to the Irish rebellion between 1642–46* (1936) • *History of the Irish confederation and the war in Ireland ... by Richard Bellings*, ed. J. T. Gilbert, 7 vols. (1882–91) • V. Treadwell, *Buckingham and Ireland, 1616–28: a study in Anglo-Irish politics* (1998)

Archives Petworth House, West Sussex, archives, Thomond collection
Likenesses C. Johnson, oils, 1643, Petworth House, West Sussex
Wealth at death impoverished: will, Royal Irish Acad., MS 3.A.40, p. 161

O'Brien, Brian Ruadh. *See* Ó Briain, Brian Ruadh (*d.* 1277).

O'Brien, Charles, styled fifth Viscount Clare (1670–1706), Jacobite army officer, was born at Carrigaholt, Ireland, a younger son of Daniel *O'Brien, styled third Viscount Clare (*c.*1630–1690), and Philadelphia (*bap.* 1644, *d.* in or after 1699), daughter of Francis Lennard, fourteenth Baron Dacre. Nothing is known of his early years or education. The O'Brien family were Roman Catholics and strong supporters of the Stuart cause, for which David had fought at the battle of the Boyne (1690) and had thereafter had his title forfeited. After the revolution of 1688 Charles commanded a regiment of foot in James II's army in Ireland, one of several regiments raised by his father on behalf of the deposed king in 1689 and 1690. Taking command of a cavalry regiment in 1691, he served at the second siege of Limerick.

Having joined James II in France in 1692, O'Brien first served as a captain in the king's *gardes du corps*, and was subsequently attached to the queen of England's regiment of *dragons-à-pied*, of which he became the colonel on the death of Francis O'Carroll at the battle of Marsaglia in Italy on 4 October 1693. His elder brother, Daniel, the fourth viscount, was mortally wounded on the same occasion, and Charles succeeded to the title. On 8 April 1696 he became colonel of the Clare regiment, so named in honour of his family, and he served at the siege of Valenza in Lombardy and on the Meuse during the campaigns of 1696 and 1697. On 9 January 1697 at St Germain-en-Laye he married Charlotte (*d.* in or after 1714), eldest daughter of Henry Buckeley, master of the household to Charles II and James II, and Sophia Stuart. His support of the Jacobites led to his being attainted before 1699.

When the War of the Spanish Succession broke out Clare joined the army of Germany, was promoted brigadier-general on 2 April 1703, and took a distinguished part in the rout of the imperialists at the battle of Hochstadt on 20 September 1703. Early in 1704 he was promoted major-general and commanded the Irish regiments of Clare, Lee, and Dorrington at the battle of Blenheim, cutting his way out of the village of Oberklau, and escaping with his three regiments, in admirable order, to the Rhine. Appointed *maréchal-de-camp* on 26 October 1704, Clare joined the army of the Moselle in Flanders. He was wounded at Ramillies eighteen months later and died at Brussels on 23 May 1706. Following his burial in the city's Irish monastery a monument to his memory was erected by his widow in the church of the Holy Cross at Louvain. She married on 19 July 1712 at St Germain-en-Laye Count Daniel *O'Mahony, who died two years later, leaving her a widow once more. Clare was survived by a daughter, Laura, who married the comte de Breteuil, and a son, Charles *O'Brien, styled sixth Viscount Clare, and later styled ninth earl of Thomond, who succeeded him in the title. The command of the Clare regiment devolved

upon its lieutenant-colonel, a kinsman of the Clare family, Murrough O'Brien, but 6000 livres p.a. were set apart by order of Louis XIV, out of the emoluments of the position, for the maintenance of the young viscount.

THOMAS SECCOMBE, *rev.* P. J. C. ELLIOT-WRIGHT

Sources J. C. O'Callaghan, *History of the Irish brigades in the service of France*, [new edn] (1870), 38–46 · GEC, *Peerage* · R. Hayes, *Biographical dictionary of Irishmen in France* (1949), 31 · B. Burke, *A genealogical history of the dormant, abeyant, forfeited and extinct peerages of the British empire*, new edn (1883), 407 · Mrs M. J. O'Connell, *The last colonel of the Irish brigade*, 1 (1892), 149, 176, 179, 181, 187

O'Brien, Charles, styled ninth earl of Thomond (1699–1761), army officer in the French service, was born at St Germain-en-Laye and baptized there on 17 March 1699, the eldest son of Charles *O'Brien, styled fifth Viscount Clare (1670–1706), outlawed in Ireland for his role in the Williamite wars, and his wife, Charlotte, eldest daughter of Henry Bulkeley, master of the household to James II. In 1703, as a child, Charles was commissioned captain and attached to the Franco-Irish regiment commanded by his father, to whose title he succeeded in 1706. He was a page at the French court. His active military career commenced in Spain in 1719 with the duke of Berwick, whose second wife was his mother's sister. He was present at the sieges of Fuenterrabiá, San Sebastian, Urgel, and Roses. In August 1720 he was appointed to command the regiment of Clare, remaining its colonel proprietor throughout the rest of his life. He visited his kinsman, the eighth earl of Thomond, in England on several occasions and was presented to George I. He might have had his father's attainder reversed to become Thomond's heir, save for his refusal to conform to the established church. He did, however, inherit £20,000 on Thomond's death in 1741, styling himself thereafter as ninth earl of Thomond. He continued to maintain an exact and up-to-date knowledge of his family's former estate in Ireland, which he cherished hopes of recovering. Although he retained formal relations with James III (James Francis Edward Stuart), the Pretender, he took little active part in Jacobite politics, concentrating instead on his career in the French army. In 1733 he served under Berwick on the Rhine. He was promoted brevet brigadier of infantry in 1734, and at the siege of Philippsburg the same year he was grazed on the shoulder by the cannon shot that killed Berwick. He was advanced to brevet *maréchal de camp* in 1738 and was appointed inspector-general of infantry in 1741. He was posted to Bohemia the same year, displaying much resolution and bravery in the unsuccessful defence of Linz in 1742. After his release from captivity, Clare transferred to the army of the Rhine and fought at Dettingen in 1743. In the following year he was promoted lieutenant-general and transferred to Flanders, where he took part in several sieges. The Irish brigade under his command played a notable part in the French victories at Fontenoy (1745), Rocoux (1746), and Laffeldt (1747).

In 1745 a plan to send Clare to England to second the efforts of Prince Charles Edward Stuart in Scotland was frustrated by British naval superiority. He was made a chevalier of the order of the Holy Ghost in 1747 and was appointed governor of Neuf-Brisach in 1756. In recognition of his distinguished military record Clare was created a marshal of France on 24 February 1757. In November 1757 he was appointed to command the troops on the Mediterranean coast and made commander-in-chief of Languedoc. A year later he was accorded the honour of *entrée* to the king of France's bedchamber. In 1759 he featured prominently in French plans for an invasion of the British Isles, but the defeat of the French fleet forced the abandonment of this project. He was described as 'a gay flattering audacious Frenchman [who] was thought an Adonis by a set of ladies' (GEC, *Peerage*, 3.254). Clare married late in life, on 10 March 1755, Marie Genvieve Louise (1737–1763), daughter of François (Gauthier), marquis de Chiffreville, Normandy. His own means were 'very unconsiderable' (Fagan, 2.186), and his wife brought him a substantial fortune, which in time was expected to increase by inheritance. They had two children: Charles, seventh Viscount Clare (1761–1774), who died unmarried, and Antoinette Charlotte Marie Septimanie (*b.* 1758), who married the duc de Choiseul-Praslin. Clare died of a fever at Montpellier on 9 September 1761.

HARMAN MURTAGH

Sources J. C. O'Callaghan, *History of the Irish brigades in the service of France*, [new edn] (1870), 42–4 · GEC, *Peerage*, new edn, 3.253–4 · J. Lodge, *The peerage of Ireland*, rev. M. Archdall, rev. edn, 2 (1789), 34 · R. Hayes, *Biographical dictionary of Irishmen in France* (1949), 32–3 · T. W. Moody and others, eds., *A new history of Ireland*, 4: *Eighteenth-century Ireland, 1691–1800* (1986) · F. McLynn, *The Jacobites* (1988) · P. Fagan, ed., *Ireland in the Stuart papers*, 2: 1743–65 (1995), 86, 138, 186, 206, 227
Archives NL Ire., papers

O'Brien, Charles. *See* Byrne, Charles (1761–1783).

O'Brien, Charlotte Grace (1845–1909), author and social reformer, born on 23 November 1845 at Cahirmoyle, co. Limerick, was the younger daughter in a family of five sons and two daughters of William Smith *O'Brien (1803–1864), Irish nationalist, and his wife, Lucy Caroline (*d.* 1861), eldest daughter of Joseph Gabbett, of High Park, co. Limerick. She was educated at St Columba's College, Rathfarnham, near Dublin, and privately. Smith O'Brien had been transported to Van Diemen's Land after the 1848 rebellion, and on his release in 1854, his daughter joined him in Brussels, and stayed there until he was allowed to return to Cahirmoyle in 1856. After her mother's death in 1861 she and her father moved to Killiney, near Dublin, and she lived with him until his death at Bangor, Wales, in 1864. From 1864 she lived at Cahirmoyle with her brother Edward, a widower, caring for his children, until his remarriage in 1880. She then went to live at Foynes, co. Limerick, and there devoted herself to writing.

Charlotte O'Brien was a committed nationalist, supported the Land League, and opposed the 1881 Coercion Act. She contributed articles and letters to the *Nineteenth Century* and the *Pall Mall Gazette*, attacking the government's Irish policies, in 1880 and 1881.

One particular interest, however, increasingly occupied her time. The disastrous harvest in Ireland in 1879, combined with Irish political unrest led to a sharp rise in the number of emigrants to America. At Queenstown, co. Cork, the port of embarkation, women emigrants suffered greatly from overcrowded lodgings and from robbery. Charlotte O'Brien's article in the *Pall Mall Gazette* (6 May 1881) led to an investigation of the White Star Line by the Board of Trade, and the enforcement of the law on lodging-houses. In 1881 she founded a boarding-house at Queenstown to receive and protect women about to emigrate. In order to improve the steamship accommodation for women emigrants, and to study their prospects, she made several steerage passages to America. In New York she founded another boarding-house for women.

When she retired in 1886 Charlotte O'Brien returned to Ardanoir, Foynes, on the bank of the Shannon, to write and to study plant life; she contributed articles on the flora of the Shannon district to the *Irish Naturalist*. In 1887 she converted to Roman Catholicism. She died on 3 June 1909 at her home, Ardanoir, Foynes, and was buried at Knockpatrick.

O'Brien's contributions to *The Nation* and to *United Ireland* were vigorous and direct. As well as writing for the periodical press, she wrote fiction, drama, and poetry. Her novel *Light and Shade* (1878) was based on the recollections of the Fenian leaders whom she knew, and deals with events in the 1867 rising. In *Lyrics* (1886) she wrote nationalist ballads and poems describing emigrant life. She wrote a series of sonnets in praise of W. E. Gladstone, collected by Stephen Gwyn (1909), and corresponded with him. Works by Charlotte O'Brien have been incorrectly attributed to Charlotte Grace O'Brien.

W. B. OWEN, *rev.* MARIE-LOUISE LEGG

Sources *The Times* (26 June 1909) · D. J. O'Donoghue, *The poets of Ireland: a biographical and bibliographical dictionary* (1912) · J. Sutherland, *The Longman companion to Victorian fiction* (1988) · D. J. Hickey and J. E. Doherty, *A dictionary of Irish history* (1980); pbk edn (1987) · *Charlotte Grace O'Brien: selections from her writings and correspondence*, ed. S. L. Gwynn (1909) · Gladstone, *Diaries* · CGPLA Eng. & Wales (1909) · CGPLA Ire. · *The Times* (5 June 1909)
Archives TCD, corresp. regarding her death
Wealth at death £631 19*s.* 3*d.*—in England: Irish probate sealed in England, 9 Oct 1909, CGPLA Eng. & Wales · £3808 9*s.* 4*d.*: probate, 21 Aug 1909, CGPLA Ire.

O'Brien, Christopher Michael (1861–1935), physician and skin specialist, was born on Christmas day 1861 at St Ruth's, Milltown, co. Roscommon, the tenth of the thirteen children of Bartholomew O'Brien (1813–1889), farmer and poor-law guardian, and his wife, Kathleen Mary Hevehan. The O'Briens had long been established as prosperous farmers, millers, and merchants in and near Athlone and according to tradition the family house was named St Ruth's because James II's commander-in-chief, the marquis de St Ruth, stayed there before the battle of Aughrim on 12 July 1691.

O'Brien was educated locally before going to Trinity College, Dublin, where he studied medicine, graduating MB in 1887. He subsequently qualified for licences to practise from the Rotunda Hospital (in midwifery), the Royal College of Surgeons in Ireland, and the Royal College of Physicians of Ireland. O'Brien decided to specialize in the study of cancer and skin diseases, studying in Paris at the Curie

Radium Laboratory, in Copenhagen under N. Finsen, and in Berlin under W. C. Röntgen. Subsequently he wrote a thesis on leprosy for the degree of MD of the University of Durham, which was accepted in 1900. At a time when London had no fewer than five such specialist hospitals, it became obvious to O'Brien that a specialized institution for the treatment of diseases of the skin was needed in Dublin. He announced his plans for the establishment of a hospital for cancer and diseases of the skin in 1899 and his venture quickly received the support of the Dublin medical establishment. The hospital was founded under the name of the City Hospital for Treatment of Diseases of the Skin and Cancer (later St Anne's Hospital). O'Brien obtained a small quantity of pure radium bromide from the Curies and erected two Finsen-light lamps and an X-ray machine in his new hospital, which was little more than a two-room clinic at 10 Beresford Place. Despite the demand for treatment the hospital was dogged with financial problems, largely due to poor patients being treated gratis, until a house in Holles Street was offered by Sir Andrew Horne.

In addition to his hospital work O'Brien wrote many papers on cancer and skin diseases. However, his most important influence was through his teaching, especially in organizing courses of postgraduate lectures in Dublin. He was an honorary member of the Dermatological Society of France, a member of the dermatological section, Royal Society of Medicine, fellow of the Medical Society, London, and a fellow of the Royal Academy of Medicine, Ireland.

During the Easter rising of 1916 O'Brien gave aid to those in distress from both sides. He went to the aid of injured volunteers at the battle of Mount Street Bridge, later contradicting propaganda by General Maxwell that the volunteers had broken the rules of war. During the disturbances O'Brien also gave shelter in his house at 29 Merrion Square to a friend from his undergraduate days who was serving in the army and had been caught out in the streets. Like many Irishmen his attitude changed quickly over the next few years and during the troubles the same house in Merrion Square sheltered 'boys on the run'. One of those who was in the General Post Office during the 1916 rising, Dr Jim Ryan, was later appointed to the staff of O'Brien's hospital and became a close friend. When minister for agriculture in the 1930s Ryan obtained extra export licences for the cattle O'Brien produced on a 200 acre farm he had purchased at Kilmessan, co. Meath.

O'Brien's hospital flourished during the 1910s and early 1920s, acquiring two more houses in Holles Street. A daily communicant, O'Brien was happy to see increasing Roman Catholic involvement in the management of a hospital he had made a point to advertise in 1902 as being open to all creeds. Since 1919 three sisters of the Order of Charity of St Vincent de Paul had been joint matrons of the hospital and in 1921, on the death of Sir Charles Cameron, the Roman Catholic archbishop of Dublin was invited to become patron. In 1926 the life governors voted to transfer the hospital to the ownership of the Order of Charity. At the same time the hospital was moved from its premises in Holles Street to Northbrook Road. The following year O'Brien retired, aged sixty-six. By the 1920s O'Brien had made a substantial fortune through his private practice and lived very comfortably at his houses at 29 Merrion Square, Dublin, and Oldbawn, near Bray, co. Wicklow.

O'Brien was a swimming enthusiast and was president of the Half Moon bathing club from 1906 to 1932. Another holder of that office described O'Brien's regular habit of having his chauffeur bring him to the Pidgeon House from where he would walk the 2 miles to the Battery to bathe in the sea. When finished he would dry himself by running back to his car.

O'Brien married Mary Teresa (Minnie) Rooney, daughter of Daniel Rooney, wine merchant, on 5 June 1900. She was active in the life of O'Brien's hospital, being one of the honorary life governors and president of the ladies' committee, which organized fund-raising events and the annual flag day. They had three sons, Barra (who became an Irish High Court judge), Turlough, and Esmonde, all of whom piously bore the additional Christian name of Mary.

O'Brien died at 97 Lower Leeson Street, Dublin, on 5 August 1935.   MIHAIL DAFYDD EVANS

Sources M. Browne, ed., *St Anne's Hospital founded 1899: city hospital for diseases of skin and cancer* (Dublin, [1973]) · Royal College of Physicians of Ireland, Kirkpatrick MSS · *Down through the years: St Anne's Hospital, 1926–1976* (1979) · *Thom's Irish who's who* (1923) · *Irish Independent* (6 Aug 1935), 10 · m. cert. · d. cert.
Archives Royal College of Physicians of Ireland, Dublin, Kirkpatrick MSS
Likenesses L. Whelan, oils, 1932, St Anne's Hospital, Dublin, Ireland
Wealth at death £6814 2s. 4d.: probate, 22 Nov 1935, CGPLA Éire

O'Brien, Conor, lord of Thomond (*d.* **1539**), chieftain, was the eldest of eight children of Turlough Donn O'Brien (*d.* 1528), lord of Thomond, and Raghnailt, daughter of John MacNamara, chief of Clancullen. His father was O'Brien chief of Thomond. Conor acceded to the chieftaincy of one of Ireland's largest and most powerful Gaelic clans upon his father's death. An ambitious and truculent chief, Turlough had extended O'Brien influence east of the Shannon—beyond the traditional boundaries of Thomond—into Limerick and Tipperary, exacting 'blackrents' from the former and threatening Butler influence in the latter. O'Brien's bridge, a physical manifestation of Turlough's ambition, was constructed in 1506 to facilitate the movement of troops and supplies over the Shannon. Efforts made by Thomas Butler, seventh earl of Ormond, and Gerald Fitzgerald, eighth earl of Kildare, in 1499 and 1510 respectively, to arrest O'Brien expansion were largely unsuccessful; it was hoped that Conor would prove a more tractable chief whose ambition would be confined to Thomond.

Conor's accession to the O'Brien chieftaincy had been assured for over a decade. He emerged as a client of Gerald Fitzgerald, ninth earl of Kildare, in 1515. In return, he received gifts of horses and by the early 1520s was resident in Kildare's lands at Castlecurry, co. Kildare, where he threatened his Butler neighbours. The nomination of his brother Murrough *O'Brien (d. 1551) as tanist—following the vacancy left by the death of another brother, Donough, in 1531—obviated any immediate internal rivalry while his marriages strengthened his hand in both Connaught and Munster. He married first Annabella (d. c.1520), youngest daughter of Ulick Burke of Clanricarde and Egelina, daughter of Hugh Courtenay, with whom he had an only son, Donough. He then married Ellice, daughter of Maurice Fitzgerald, ninth earl of Desmond, and Ellen, daughter of Maurice Roche, Viscount Roche of Fermoy, with whom he had five sons, Donald, Turlough, Teig, Murrough, and Mortagh. Conor was in a secure and commanding position.

By 1528 the lordship of Thomond had become polarized between feuding Geraldine and Butler interests. O'Brien's marital ties to Desmond and continued affiliation with Kildare placed him firmly within the former camp. His eldest son, Donough, sensing that his stepbrothers' interests would be pursued ahead of his own, sought allies in unlikely quarters: he married Helen, daughter of Piers Butler, earl of Ossory, in 1533. The O'Briens were divided by the rebellion in 1534 of Thomas Fitzgerald, tenth earl of Kildare; Conor supported him while Donough supported Ossory.

O'Brien brushed aside resistance from Donough and his Butler allies, ravaging Butler lands as the rebellion gathered momentum. In July, O'Brien petitioned Charles V for military assistance claiming that his family was of Spanish descent and that they had 'never ceased to oppose the pride of the English' (LP Henry VIII, 7, no. 999). He offered to submit to the emperor's authority and place some 15,000 men at his disposal. Foreign aid, however, was not forthcoming and the arrival of a relief army under Sir William Skeffington, the lord deputy, dashed any hopes of a Geraldine victory. Kildare sought refuge in Thomond, Connaught, and contemplated sailing to Spain to solicit aid from Charles. Recognizing the futility and the potential repercussions of such a gesture, O'Brien counselled against the voyage; Kildare surrendered in August 1535. O'Brien wrote, in English, to Henry VIII in October begging his forgiveness for harbouring the earl and offered to serve the king's representative in Ireland. O'Brien's power and autonomy survived the immediate aftermath of the rebellion intact.

Lord Leonard Grey, the new lord deputy, guided by Donough, Conor's son, marched to the Shannon in August 1536 and destroyed O'Brien's bridge. The expedition, however, was egregiously under-funded and the soldiers refused to cross the Shannon. Grey returned to Dublin having done little to limit O'Brien's power. O'Brien adopted an increasingly defiant posture by refusing to surrender either the young Fitzgerald heir, who received succour in Thomond for six months, or the treasure entrusted to him by Kildare before his surrender. The Irish privy council reported to Sir Thomas Cromwell, principal secretary, that O'Brien 'thinketh it not to be his duty to recognise the King's Majesty, neither yet to abide any indifferent or reasonable order upon any wrong by him done to the King and his subjects' (Brewer and Bullen, no.

88). O'Brien could afford such insouciance so long as his clan remained united behind his leadership and the government refused to expend its limited resources on a major military campaign. Grey made another expedition to the Shannon in June 1538 destroying a rebuilt bridge, but managed only to secure from O'Brien a year-long truce. O'Brien died in December 1539. Murrough, his tanist, was elected chief. Conor was the last independent O'Brien chief before the introduction of the surrender and regrant initiative that saw his successors created earls of Thomond following their submission to the king.

CHRISTOPHER MAGINN

Sources State papers published under ... Henry VIII, 11 vols. (1830–52) • LP Henry VIII • AFM • G. Mac Niocaill, ed., Crown surveys of lands, 1540–41, with the Kildare rental begun in 1518, IMC (1992) • J. S. Brewer and W. Bullen, eds., Calendar of the Carew manuscripts, 6 vols., PRO (1867–73) • J. O'Donoghue, Historical memoirs of the O'Briens with notes, appendix, and a genealogical table of their branches (1860) • I. O'Brien, O'Brien of Thomond: the O'Briens in Irish history, 1500–1865 (1986) • J. Lodge, The peerage of Ireland, rev. M. Archdall, rev. edn, 7 vols. (1789) • DNB

O'Brien, Conor, third earl of Thomond (c.1535–1581), landowner and rebel, was the eldest son of Donough O'Brien, second earl of Thomond (c.1515–1553), and Helen, youngest daughter of Piers Butler, eighth earl of Ormond. He was the first O'Brien to inherit the earldom since Sir Anthony St Leger, the lord deputy, engineered a compromise in 1543 whereby Donough O'Brien succeeded his uncle Murrough *O'Brien, first earl of Thomond, as second earl. The first earl's title of baron of Inchiquin was vested in his male descendants. Donough O'Brien's stepbrother Donnell O'Brien, however, gained little from the compromise and murdered him in April 1553 following the former's successful bid to have the earldom permanently vested in his male descendants. Conor O'Brien was thus challenged by his uncle Donnell O'Brien who was recognized by many clansmen to have succeeded by the Gaelic custom of tanistry—a development that the 1543 compromise had aimed to avoid. The more experienced Donnell O'Brien, supported by his brothers Tadhg and Donough O'Brien, quickly gained the upper hand among the divided O'Briens. The government, which could not be seen to allow Gaelic custom to overrule English law, interceded on Conor O'Brien's behalf in the summer of 1558, when Thomas Radcliffe, third earl of Sussex, lord deputy, forcibly installed him as third earl of Thomond. Yet Thomond's position was dangerously reliant on English support.

Tadhg and Donough O'Brien, supported by Gerald Fitzgerald, fourteenth earl of Desmond, assembled a force and defeated Thomond and his ally, Richard Burke, second earl of Clanricarde, at Cnoc Fuarchoilli (Spancel Hill), near Ennis. The attempted coup was thwarted, however, after Sir William Fitzwilliam, lord justice, intervened. This allowed Thomond a brief respite during which he could consolidate his position; but despite earning praise from the government for accompanying Fitzwilliam on an expedition against Shane O'Neill in August 1561 he failed to win unilateral support among the O'Briens. His marriages, moreover, failed to secure any powerful allies. He married first Ellen (d. 1560), daughter of Donald MacCarthy More and widow of James Fitzgerald, thirteenth earl of Desmond, whose claim to Desmond lands only aggravated relations with the Geraldines. They had no children. He later married Úna (d. 1589), daughter of Turlough Mac I Brien Arra, with whom he had three sons and three daughters; his eldest son, Donough *O'Brien (d. 1624), the young baron of Ibrackan, was raised at court. In 1562 Tadhg and Donnell O'Brien mounted another challenge to Thomond's leadership. They received support from Desmond, while the earl again turned to the government. English ordnance lent to Thomond ensured his survival, but it was clear that the threat posed by his half-uncles had to be addressed.

In September 1564 Thomond and the crown offered Donnell O'Brien a truce on generous terms that amounted to virtual joint rule of Thomond. O'Brien was not satisfied because he was not given recognition or a peerage and resumed hostilities in the spring of 1565. Thomond outfought him with English ordnance.

O'Brien surrendered his claim to the lordship of Thomond in April 1565 settling for possession of Corcomroe. Thomond was still not secure. The government, moreover, had become sceptical of his abilities: visiting Munster in 1566 Sir Henry Sidney, lord deputy, noted the utter desolation of Thomond, and in 1567 blamed the earl's 'lack of discretion and insufficiency to govern' for co. Limerick's desolation (PRO, SP 63/20/66). Thomond became alienated and receptive to overtures from James Fitzmaurice who rebelled in June 1569.

Sir Edmund Fitton was concurrently appointed president of Connaught and set about erecting Thomond into the county of Clare and annexing it to Connaught. This, coupled with his appointment of Tadhg O'Brien as sheriff of co. Clare, pushed Thomond into a desperate attempt to restore his authority. In February 1570 he drove Fitton out of Ennis and arrested Tadhg and Donnell O'Brien, and William Martin, the provost-marshal. He quickly linked his actions to those of Thomas Howard, fourth duke of Norfolk, and the northern earls, proclaiming 'he woulde do nothinge with the lord deputie nor lord president but as the Duke of Norfolk would say' (PRO, SP 63/30/15). His rebellion was short-lived as his kinsman and former ally Thomas *Butler, tenth earl of Ormond, was immediately dispatched to bring order to Thomond. He fled to France in June after failing to secure the restoration of his possessions and was subsequently proclaimed a rebel.

In Paris, Thomond became acquainted with Sir Henry Norris, the English ambassador. He hoped that Norris would intercede with Elizabeth I for his pardon. Norris, however, approached the situation with caution, closely watching Thomond's behaviour while keeping the queen fully abreast of his actions. Though Thomond wrote to Elizabeth begging for clemency and claimed that he arrived in France 'without ani intention to practise with the French', it became clear to Norris that he was willing to practise with anyone who suggested intrigue (PRO, SP 63/30/72). Norris noted 'he is tractable enough and rather apt to follow perilous counsel than to be a deviser therof' (CSP for., no. 1110). Elizabeth would not grant his pardon, but realized that he posed a more serious threat while in France and, through Norris, implored him to return to Ireland. He reluctantly departed following promises that his grievances would receive a favourable hearing upon his return.

Thomond returned to Ireland in December and was pardoned by Sidney after publicly confessing his treason. The following April he surrendered his lands to the queen and obtained leave to travel to court to solicit their restoration. He received a warrant for the restoration in June 1573, but was prevented from travelling to court due to his own precarious position in Thomond. In 1572 Thomond hanged three poets in his territory. Though an isolated incident it earned him the enmity of the Gaelic learned classes who vilified him in verse:

> The earl of the Í Bhriain, an enemy of the schools, is the most dangerous of monsters; he is a monster whom no man should trust; he is instructed in petty stratagems.   (Ó Cuív, 132)

Thomond's enemies among the O'Briens, moreover, had not melted away and the two factions clashed at Ard na gCabog, in Thomond, in 1573. The fighting continued intermittently until April 1576 when Sidney was once again forced to intervene. Despite the earl's favourable disposition toward the government, the lord deputy had to acknowledge Donnell O'Brien's superior position and ability. He insisted that Thomond surrender his authority to O'Brien who was made sheriff of co. Clare. Spent from years of feuding and in no position to challenge O'Brien militarily, Thomond sought an audience with Elizabeth to press his claims and those of his son. He repaired to England in autumn 1577 and in October a warrant for a new patent was issued upholding the terms of his former patent. His son's succession assured, he remained on good terms with the government despite the introduction of composition during his absence. He died in January 1581 and was buried in the abbey of Ennis, co. Clare. He was succeeded by Ibrackan. In a life marked by contradiction and struggle Thomond failed to exert control over his kinsmen and was uncomfortable with his transition from Gaelic chief to English landlord. Yet his ultimate acceptance of English sovereignty allowed his son, later president of Munster, to acquiesce more fully in English rule. The four masters note that he was:

> the first man of the descendants of Cormac Cas who had sat in his father's place over that portion of Munster possessed by the descendants of Lughaidh Meann, a junior branch [of his family], who had wrested the government of his principality from the hands of his seniors, according to the laws, regulations, and ordinances of the sovereign of England.   (AFM, s.a. 1580)

CHRISTOPHER MAGINN

Sources state papers, Ireland, Elizabeth, PRO, SP 63 · AFM · J. S. Brewer and W. Bullen, eds., *Calendar of the Carew manuscripts*, 6 vols., PRO (1867–73) · *The Irish fiants of the Tudor sovereigns*, 4 vols. (1994) · J. Morrin, ed., *Calendar of the patent and close rolls of chancery in Ireland, of the reigns of Henry VIII, Edward VI, Mary, and Elizabeth*, 2 (1862) · CSP for., 1569–71 · J. O'Donoghue, *Historical memoirs of the O'Briens with notes, appendix, and a genealogical table of their branches*

(1860) • I. O'Brien, *O'Brien of Thomond: the O'Briens in Irish history, 1500–1865* (1986) • B. Ó Cuív, 'The earl of Thomond and the poets', *Celtica*, 12 (1977), 125–45 • *DNB* • C. Brady, *The chief governors: the rise and fall of reform government in Tudor Ireland, 1536–1588* (1994), 98–9, 109, 179, 182–5, 266 • S. G. Ellis, *Ireland in the age of the Tudors* (1998), 8, 178, 257, 270, 274, 276–7, 280, 286, 298–9, 301, 323, 379 • *Journal of the Royal Society of Antiquaries of Ireland*, 10 (1868–9) [pedigree of the earls of Desmond]

Archives LPL, names of all castles in Thomond; offers of agreement proposed to earl of Thomond, MS 611 • NL Ire., inspeximus of Queen's letters of pardon for earl of Thomond, D.2769

O'Brien, Cornelius (1843–1906), Roman Catholic archbishop of Halifax (Nova Scotia), born near New Glasgow, Prince Edward Island, on 4 May 1843, was seventh of the nine children of Terence O'Brien of Munster and his wife, Catherine O'Driscoll of Cork. After school he was briefly employed, but at nineteen entered St Dunstan's College, Charlottetown, to study for the priesthood. In 1864 he passed to the College of the Propaganda in Rome, and concluded his seven years' course in 1871 by winning the prize for general excellence in the whole college. While he was in Rome, Garibaldi attacked the city, the Vatican Council was held, and the temporal power of the pope fell. O'Brien, who had literary ambition and a taste for verse, founded on these stirring events a historical novel which he published later under the title *After Weary Years* (1886).

On his return to Canada, O'Brien was appointed a professor in St Dunstan's College and rector of the cathedral of Charlottetown, but failing health led to his transfer in 1874 to the country parish of Indian River. There he devoted his leisure to writing, publishing *The Philosophy of the Bible Vindicated* (1876), *Early Stages of Christianity in England* (1880), and *Mater admirabilis* (1882). He later wrote *St Agnes* (1887), *Aminta* (1890), and a life of Edmund Burke (1753–1820), first bishop of Halifax (1894). He twice revisited Rome, and in 1882, on the death of Archbishop Hannan, was appointed his successor in the see of Halifax. O'Brien administered the diocese with great energy, building churches and schools, founding religious and benevolent institutions, and taking an active part in public affairs whenever he considered the good of the community demanded it. His hope of seeing a Catholic university in Halifax was not realized, but he established a French college for the Acadians at Church Point, and founded a collegiate school, St Mary's College, in Halifax, which was to be the germ of the future university. He died suddenly in Halifax on 9 March 1906, and was buried in the cemetery of the Holy Cross, Halifax, Nova Scotia.

O'Brien, who was elected president of the Royal Society of Canada in 1896, was a representative Irish-Canadian prelate, combining force of character with depth of sentiment and winning the esteem of his protestant fellow subjects while insisting on what he believed to be the rights of the Roman Catholic minority. Advocating home rule for Ireland, he was at the same time a staunch imperialist and a strong Canadian.

D. R. KEYS, *rev.* H. C. G. MATTHEW

Sources K. Hughes, *Archbishop O'Brien: man and churchman* (1906) • *The Globe* [Toronto] (10 March 1906) • *Proceedings and Transactions of the Royal Society of Canada*, 2nd ser., 12 (1906), vi–vii

Cornelius O'Brien (1843–1906), by unknown photographer, 1903

Likenesses photograph, 1903, repro. in Hughes, *Archbishop O'Brien*, frontispeice [*see illus.*] • oils, 1912, archbishop's palace, Halifax, Nova Scotia, Canada • portrait, repro. in Hughes, *Archbishop O'Brien*

O'Brien, Daniel, first Viscount Clare (1577?–1663), politician and soldier, was the third and youngest son of Conor *O'Brien, third earl of Thomond (c.1535–1581), and his second wife, Úna (Owyne; d. 1589), daughter of Turlough Mac I Brien Arra of co. Tipperary. Unlike his protestant brother Donough *O'Brien and his nephews, Henry and Barnabas *O'Brien, he remained a staunch Catholic throughout his life. During the Nine Years' War he fought for the crown. In 1598 he defended his brother Donough's estates in co. Clare from rebels under the command of the earl of Tyrone but was forced to surrender Ibrickan Castle in 1599. He was wounded during the assault, and the insurgents took him prisoner, but released him a week later. On the return of his brother Donough from England, O'Brien fought alongside him for the remainder of the war and in July 1604 received a knighthood and lands for his loyalty; henceforth he was known for most of his adult life as Sir Daniel O'Brien of Moyarta and Carrigholt. In 1600 he married Lady Catherine, third daughter of Gerald Fitzgerald, sixteenth earl of Desmond; they had four sons and seven daughters.

In 1613 O'Brien sat as MP for County Clare and became involved in the furore over the election of the speaker of the House of Commons, allegedly holding the Catholic candidate, Sir John Everard, in the chair. Summoned to England to answer for his conduct, he escaped with a reprimand (perhaps due to the influence of Donough, who had been dispatched to court as an agent for the government). In 1634 he was re-elected MP for County Clare in place of his nephew Barnabas who had gone to England, but clashed with Lord Deputy Wentworth in parliament over the proposed plantation of Connaught. Increasingly the Anglicizing and tenurial policies of the earls of Thomond aroused O'Brien's ire and he complained that the fourth earl had forcibly acquired lands from McNamarras prior to 1624, 'being then Lord President of Munster and so powerful that [none] could or dare oppose him in any his actions', and that the fifth earl was 'so powerful, so wealthy and allied and befriended with all the gent[lemen] Freeholders in the several countries of this kingdom as your supplicant [O'Brien] may not expect any indifference of trial to be had by course of common law' (petition of February 1637, Thomond papers, Petworth House Archives, W. Sussex RO).

O'Brien was an active confederate during the 1640s, and regularly sat in the general assemblies. He took part in the siege of Ballyally Castle, co. Clare, but in 1645 his nephew Barnabas pre-empted his attempt to seize Bunratty Castle by surrendering it to forces loyal to parliament. His own castle of Carrigholt, co. Clare, fell to the Cromwellians on 7 November 1651. Despite this he appears to have reached an accommodation with the Cromwellian army and was one of twenty-six major Catholic landowners to secure an exemption from the Act for the Settling of Ireland (1652), perhaps thanks to the marriages of two of his sons to prominent protestant families. The influence enjoyed by his grandson Daniel *O'Brien at the exiled royalist court ensured that O'Brien was named in Charles II's 'gracious declaration' (30 November 1660), and raised to the peerage as Baron Moyarta and Viscount Clare in 1662 (patent of 11 July). He died the following year. His heir, Donough, predeceased him, and Conor (c.1605–c.1670), his second son, succeeded to the viscountcy. Like his father Conor had been an active confederate, representing County Clare on the supreme council. He married his third cousin, Honora, daughter of Daniel O'Brien of Dough, and had seven daughters and one son, Daniel. Thanks to the latter's royalist contacts, the Act of Settlement (1662) and the Act for Explanation (1665) restored the family to their pre-war estates and to a house in Limerick. An extant lease of 1667 suggests that the second viscount was an 'improving' landlord, requiring his tenants to enclose an acre of land with a stone wall, to build a stone house, and to plough any land 'after the English manner' (Ainsworth, 365).

JANE OHLMEYER

Sources D. O'Brien, *History of the O'Briens* (1949) • I. O'Brien, *O'Brien of Thomond: the O'Briens in Irish history, 1500–1865* (1986) • J. Ainsworth, ed., *Inchiquin manuscripts*, Irish Manuscripts Commission (1961) • *CSP Ire.*, 1625–47 • G. Radcliffe, *The earl of Strafforde's letters and dispatches, with an essay towards his life*, ed. W. Knowler, 2 vols. (1739) • *History of the Irish confederation and the war in Ireland … by Richard Bellings*, ed. J. T. Gilbert, 7 vols. (1882–91) • J. T. Gilbert, ed., *A contemporary history of affairs in Ireland from 1641 to 1652*, 3 vols. (1879–80) • M. Hickson, ed., *Ireland in the seventeenth century*, 2 vols. (1884) • *DNB* • J. Lodge, *The peerage of Ireland*, rev. M. Archdall, rev. edn, 7 vols. (1789) • GEC, *Peerage*
Archives PRO, state papers, Ireland • W. Sussex RO, Petworth House archives, Thomond papers
Likenesses portrait, Dromoland Castle, co. Clare; repro. in O'Brien, *History*

O'Brien, Daniel, styled third Viscount Clare (c.1630–1690), army officer, was the only son among eight children of Conor O'Brien, later second Viscount Clare (c.1605–c.1670), and his wife, Honora (d. in or after 1701), daughter of Daniel O'Brien of Dough, co. Clare. Nothing is known of his education or early life, except that during the interregnum he served for a time in the Spanish army. He also attended the exiled Charles II, with whom he possessed sufficient influence at the Restoration to secure a peerage for his paternal grandfather, Sir Daniel O'Brien, third son of the second earl of Thomond, together with the restoration of his immense estate in co. Clare.

O'Brien succeeded to both title and estate upon the death of his father. His principal residence was Carrigaholt Castle on the Shannon estuary, where he strove to become 'the greatest breeder of horses in the king's dominions' (O'Brien, 182). He married in or before 1670 Philadelphia (*bap.* 1644, *d.* in or after 1699), daughter of Francis *Lennard, fourteenth Baron Dacre (1619–1662). Two sons were born of the marriage: Daniel O'Brien, styled fourth Viscount Clare (c.1669–1693), and Charles *O'Brien, styled fifth Viscount Clare (1670–1706).

The marriage of Clare's brother-in-law Thomas Lennard, fifteenth Lord Dacre and later earl of Sussex, to a bastard daughter of Charles II probably helped to influence his appointment in 1674 as colonel of a new Irish regiment in the Anglo-Dutch brigade. The following year he was accused of spying for the French and lost his command. As a Francophile and a Roman Catholic, he was disliked by the duke of Ormond, who viewed with scepticism his claim, during the Titus Oates terror, that he was a protestant who was active in hunting priests. He took the deception too far in 1681 when he organized a petition in Ireland to condemn Charles II's prorogation of the whig-dominated English parliament during the exclusion crisis. This provoked the king to order his removal from the Irish bench as a justice of the peace and from his command of a militia troop. He remained out of favour for the remainder of Charles's reign.

In 1689, when James II attempted to recover his lost thrones with Irish Catholic support, Clare was made an Irish privy councillor and lord lieutenant of co. Clare. In the same year he attended the Irish parliament, as did his elder son, Daniel, who represented County Clare in the Commons. Clare made a notable contribution to the enlargement of the Irish army, raising a dragoon regiment, mounted from the resources of his horse farm, and two infantry regiments commanded by his sons. He initially commanded the regiments in Cork, but his harsh treatment of the local merchants displeased James, and he was replaced in February 1690. In July he commanded his regiment on the right of the Jacobite position at the battle of the Boyne. It was alleged that his dragoons were the first to flee the scene, but later they redeemed their reputation by helping to escort the French artillery to safety. However, the setbacks of the campaign increased Clare's disillusionment with the Jacobite leadership, and in August 1690 he wrote to Louvois, who held him in some regard, begging Louis XIV to take over Ireland and win it back from William. Despite this he was a member of the military council appointed to advise the duke of Berwick, who became commander of the Irish army in September 1690.

Clare died on 19 or 21 November 1690, probably at Carrigaholt Castle. Having been outlawed with his sons for high treason, his estate of 30,000 acres in Clare was confiscated after the war. His son and successor, Daniel, styled fourth Viscount Clare, was wounded in action with his regiment at the battle of Marsaglia, and died at Pignerol in 1693. He in turn was succeeded by his younger brother, Charles.   HARMAN MURTAGH

Sources GEC, *Peerage*, new edn, 3.251–3; 4.13–14 · J. Lodge, *The peerage of Ireland*, rev. M. Archdall, rev. edn, 2 (1789), 32–4 · J. C. R. Childs, *Nobles, gentlemen and the profession of arms in Restoration Britain, 1660–1688: a biographical dictionary of British army officers on foreign service* (1987), 17 · S. Mulloy, ed., *Franco-Irish correspondence, December 1688 – February 1692*, IMC, 1 (1983), esp. nos. 271, 669, 677, 925, 1031, 1952, 1966–7, 1992 · J. C. O'Callaghan, *History of the Irish brigades in the service of France*, [new edn] (1870), 38–46 · D. Murtagh and H. Murtagh, 'The Irish Jacobite army, 1689–91', *Irish Sword*, 18 (1990–92), 32–48 · J. G. Simms, *The Williamite confiscation in Ireland, 1690–1703* (1956), 178 · W. King, *The state of the protestants of Ireland under the late King James's government* (1730), appx, pp. 60, 65, 91–2 · I. O'Brien, *O'Brien of Thomond: the O'Briens in Irish history, 1500–1865* (1986), 85, 95–7, 100, 106–9, 112–16, 126, 179–82, 194

O'Brien, Donal. *See* Ua Briain, Domnall Mór (*d.* 1194).

O'Brien, Donat Henchy (1785–1857), naval officer, second son of Michael O'Brien of Ennistimon, co. Clare, was born in Ireland in March 1785 into a family claiming descent from one of the ancient kings of Ireland. He entered the navy in 1796, on the *Overyssel* (64 guns), in which, despite his youth, he was employed on boat service. In 1799 he was put in command of a hoy laden with stone, to be sunk at the entrance of Goree harbour so as to block in three enemy line-of-battle ships. In a sudden squall the hoy sank in the wrong place at the wrong time, and O'Brien and his men were with difficulty rescued. He passed his examination in February 1803, and a year later was master's mate of the frigate *Hussar* when she was wrecked on the Île de Sein on 8 February 1804. O'Brien was sent as a prisoner of war to Verdun, where he remained for three years before trying to escape. Two of his attempts failed, owing to severe hardship from cold, wet, and hunger; a third attempt proved successful, and in November 1808 he, with two companions, reached Trieste, and finally boarded the *Amphion*, from which he was sent to Malta. There he joined the *Ocean* (98 guns), flagship of Lord Collingwood. The latter promoted him, on 29 March 1809, lieutenant of the *Warrior* (74 guns), in which he served at the capture of the Ionian Islands. In March 1810 he was appointed to the *Amphion*, and was still in her in the action off Lissa, in the Adriatic, on 13 March 1811, when a British frigate squadron under Captain William Hoste defeated a larger Franco-Venetian force. In November 1811 he followed Hoste to the *Bacchante* (38 guns) and, after repeatedly distinguishing himself in the arduous and dashing service of the frigates and their boats, was promoted commander on 22 January 1813. In 1814 O'Brien published *The narrative of Captain O'Brien, R.N., containing an account of his shipwreck, captivity, and escape from France.*

From 1818 to 1821 O'Brien commanded the *Slaney* (20 guns), on the South American station, which then included the west coast. On 5 March 1821 he was promoted captain, though the news did not reach him for some months. In October he was relieved in the *Slaney*, and returned to England. He married, on 28 June 1825, Hannah, youngest daughter of John Walmsley of Castle Mere in Lancashire; they had seven children. In 1839 he published, in two volumes, *My Adventures during the Late War*. In conjunction, to some extent, with the similar narratives by Edward Boys and Henry Ashworth, it formed the basis for part of Marryat's *Peter Simple*.

O'Brien had no further service after 1821, but was promoted rear-admiral on the reserved list on 8 March 1852. He died at Yew House, Hoddesdon, Hertfordshire, on 13 May 1857. A memorial window was placed in Broxbourne church.   J. K. LAUGHTON, *rev.* ANDREW LAMBERT

Sources T. Pocock, *Remember Nelson: the life of Captain Sir William Hoste* (1977) · O'Byrne, *Naval biog. dict.* · GM, 3rd ser., 3 (1857), 742 · J. Marshall, *Royal naval biography*, suppl. 4 (1830), 231–87 · Boase, *Mod. Eng. biog.*

Likenesses J. R. Brown, stipple (after J. Pelham), BM; repro. in D. H. O'Brien, *My adventures during the late war* (1839) · portrait, repro. in Pocock, *Remember Nelson*, 96

O'Brien, Donough. *See* Mac Briain, Donnchad (*d.* 1064).

O'Brien, Donough, fourth earl of Thomond (*d.* 1624), nobleman, was the eldest son of Conor *O'Brien, third earl of Thomond (*d.* 1581), and his second wife, Úna (*d.* 1589), daughter of Turlough Mac I Brien Arra of Arra, co. Tipperary. He was educated at Elizabeth's court and was described as 'as truly English as if he had been born in Middlesex' (*CSP Ire.*, 1600, 111). He was still at the court in 1577 when he was mentioned in a new patent granted to his father (7 October) as baron of Ibrickan in Clare. Shired by Sir Henry Sidney in 1565, the county was then added to the province of Connaught. Due to Donough O'Brien's persistence in seeking the county's removal from Connaught jurisdiction it was assigned to Munster in 1602. O'Brien succeeded his father as fourth earl of Thomond in 1581 and returned to Ireland the following year. By 1585 new arrangements for the government of the province, known as the composition of Connaught, were introduced. These involved the introduction of rent payments instead of dues and services, and abolished the names, styles, and titles of native Irish authorities. Thomond was declared overlord of the main portion of his lordship but did not secure a palatine jurisdiction like that held by the earls of Ormond or Desmond, though it was said that 'he lookith for like libertyes in *Toomond*' (Collins, 1.226). Rather, two large areas were put under the control of collateral branches of the O'Briens. Early suspicions of his loyalty on his return to Ireland may have stemmed from these divisions of patrimonial lands. However, he proved that his loyalty was in no doubt, shrewdly calculating that he had more to gain as an earl with an English-style title than as the Gaelic O'Brien. Accordingly he was assiduous in his attendance on the lord deputy, Sir John Perrot, in

1584, and in April 1585 he attended the parliament in Dublin. He keenly promoted English reforms and subdued rival O'Briens, and was appointed to the Connaught council in 1588.

Thomond played a prominent part as a staunch ally of the crown during the war against Hugh O'Neill, earl of Tyrone. In July 1595 he commanded a large force to the Erne fords and succeeded in penetrating the territory of Tyrone's ally Red Hugh O'Donnell in modern Donegal, but had to withdraw the following month. In September 1596 the then lord deputy Sir William Russell sent him to aid in the defence of Newry with five companies of foot soldiers and 145 horse. In 1597 he accompanied Russell and commanded in the campaigns of Russell's successor, Thomas, Lord Burgh, mainly on the borders of Ulster at the Blackwater Fort. For most of 1598 he was back in London during a year in which O'Neill's victories encouraged insurrection throughout Ireland. On 6 December he was given a royal warrant to command the forces of Munster, but under the jurisdiction of Sir Thomas Norris, lord president of the province.

In Clare, Thomond's brother Tadhg or Teige O'Brien of Dromore had been accused of seeking aid for the O'Neill cause from the king of Spain. He was imprisoned in Limerick and released on protesting his loyalty, but joined Red Hugh O'Donnell when, in 1599, he reinvested north Connaught and again invaded Clare. O'Donnell captured most of the castles, ravaged the countryside, and took prisoner Thomond's other, youngest, brother Daniel *O'Brien, who was defending the territory in his absence. On his return from England, Thomond spent three months in Kilkenny with his kinsman the earl of Ormond collecting forces and ordnance from Limerick to recover his possessions and avenge his brother's capture. That summer he laid siege to such castles as resisted. Dunbeg, defending the Bay of Dunmore, surrendered to him instantly but he had the entire garrison hanged in couples on trees. During the remainder of the year he accompanied the new chief governor, the second earl of Essex, on his Munster progress, was appointed governor of co. Clare on 15 August, and made a member of the Munster council on 22 September. He vigorously assisted Sir George Carew, president of Munster, in the prosecution of the war throughout 1600. In April, while in a parley with Owen McRory O'More which ended in a mêlée, he and Carew narrowly escaped capture and though Thomond received a pike wound in the back, he managed to save Carew's life. He was also in the thick of the action against Florence MacCarthy Reagh (confirmed as the MacCarthy More by Hugh O'Neill), helping to bring him to submission in May 1600. In June he was in Clare repulsing further O'Donnell raids. He entertained the new lord deputy, Mountjoy, at Bunratty Castle, which he was later to refortify and glaze. In February 1601 he held an assize in Limerick at which sixteen men were hanged. Again he went to England to pursue his causes, especially to get his patrimonial lands transferred into Munster. Fynes Moryson, Mountjoy's secretary, thought Thomond much preferred attendance at court to action in the field, a comment perhaps occasioned by the usual delays in England in getting reinforcements to Ireland.

At length Thomond set off from Bristol with 1000 foot and 100 horse and, though some of his ships were blown off course, made a landing at Castlehaven on 11 November 1601. He proceeded to encamp on the west side of Kinsale on Ballincubby Hill to prevent a junction between the besieged Spaniards and O'Donnell, and took a prominent part in the ensuing siege and battle. After the Spanish surrender he proceeded to mop up pockets of resistance in the Bantry Bay area. The siege of Dunboy (11–18 June), which had been fortified by Donal O'Sullivan Beare and was resolutely held by its constable, Richard MacGeoghegan, was his last great military action. On its final capitulation on 18 June 1602 he hanged fifty-eight of the survivors.

Once again Thomond sailed for England and in recognition of his 'forward services' his demand for the transfer of Clare was granted, despite the opposition of the lord deputy and the Irish council. He returned to Ireland in early October 1602 and, as a further reward, the queen ordered his name be placed next to those of the lord deputy and the lord chief justice in commissions of oyer and terminer and gaol delivery. In September 1603 his governorship of co. Clare was confirmed and he was appointed to the Irish privy council. On 30 July 1604 he was appointed constable of Carlow, and subsequently given a grant of that manor. In the 1613 parliament he strongly supported the protestant party in opposition to the recusants in the disputes over the election of the speaker to the Irish House of Commons, although he had previously blocked the attempt of the administration to exclude certain Catholic Munster peers from parliament. On 6 May 1615 he became lord president of Munster. He proved an energetic lord president, moved the presidency headquarters to Limerick, and acquired former plantation lands in co. Limerick. He became one of the sureties for Florence MacCarthy Reagh, who, since his surrender in 1600, had been in the Tower, where he wrote on the antiquities and prehistory of Ireland and dedicated these studies to Thomond.

Thomond was married twice, first to Eveleen or Ellen (d. 1583), daughter of Maurice Roche, Viscount Fermoy. By his second marriage, to Lady Elizabeth (d. 1618), fourth daughter of Gerard Fitzgerald, eleventh earl of Kildare, he had two sons, Henry, fifth earl (d. 1639), and Barnabas or Barnaby *O'Brien, sixth earl of Thomond (1590/91–1657). Tadhg O'Brien survived until at least 20 January 1642, while Daniel O'Brien, later first Viscount Clare, became a leading confederate. Elizabeth, countess of Thomond, died on 12 January 1618 and her husband on 5 September 1624. He was buried in St Mary's Cathedral, Limerick, where a fine monument with a marble incised inscription was erected to his memory by his son Henry; it was destroyed in 1642, and re-erected by Henry, the seventh earl, in 1678. In a letter of 27 September 1600 George Carey, Lord Hunsdon, had written:

> If the rest of the Irish nobility had followed the example of my noble friend the Earl of Thomond her Majesty's expenses

and losses had never been as they are and will be. His services hath proceeded out of a true nobleness of mind and from no great encouragement received from hence. (Brewer and Bullen, 3.450)

J. J. N. McGurk

Sources DNB · J. S. Brewer and W. Bullen, eds., *Calendar of the Carew manuscripts*, PRO, 1–4 (1867–70) · J. Morrin, ed., *Calendar of the patent and close rolls of chancery in Ireland for the reigns of Henry VIII, Edward VI, Mary, and Elizabeth*, 2 vols. (1861–2) · J. O'Donoghue, *Historical memoir of the O'Briens* (1860) · M. Lenihan, *Limerick: its history and antiquities* (1866) [facs. 1991] · T. Stafford, *Pacata Hibernia*, ed. S. O'Grady, 2 vols. (1896) · *The Irish fiants of the Tudor sovereigns*, 4 vols. (1994) · T. W. Moody and others, eds., *A new history of Ireland*, 10 vols. (1976–96), vols. 3, 9 · B. Ó Dálaigh, 'History of an O'Brien stronghold: Clonroad, c.1210–1626', *North Munster Antiquarian Journal*, 29 (1987), 16–31 · B. Ó Dálaigh, 'A comparative study of the wills of the first and fourth earls of Thomond', *North Munster Antiquarian Journal*, 34 (1992), 48–63 · H. Sydney and others, *Letters and memorials of state*, ed. A. Collins, 2 vols. (1746) · D. Kennedy, 'The presidency of Munster', MA diss., National University of Ireland (University College, Cork), 1974 · D. O'Brien, *History of the O'Briens* (1949) · T. J. Westropp, 'The principal ancient castle of the county Limerick', *Journal of the Royal Society of Antiquaries of Ireland*, 37 (1907), 153–64 · T. J. Westropp, 'Promontory forts in the "Irrus", county Clare', *Journal of the Royal Society of Antiquaries of Ireland*, 38 (1908), 28–47 · R. Bagwell, *Ireland under the Tudors*, 3 (1890); repr. (1963) · V. Treadwell, 'Sir John Perrot and the Irish parliament of 1585–6', *Proceedings of the Royal Irish Academy*, 85C (1985), 259–308 · *AFM*, vols. 5–6

Archives Petworth House, West Sussex, Thomond collection | BL, pedigrees of the O'Briens, Egerton MS 101 · Chatsworth House, Derbyshire, letters to first earl of Cork · Glos. RO, letters to Lord Berkeley and Lady Berkeley

Likenesses portrait, Dromoland Castle, co. Clare; repro. in O'Brien, *History*, facing p. 72 · recumbent stone effigies (on his tomb tand hat of his second wife, Elizabeth), St Mary's Cathedral, Limerick

Wealth at death earldom of Thomond: transcript of will, Petworth House, West Sussex, archives, 1600, in Ó Dálaigh, 'Comparative study' · by 1626 Clonroad leased at £20 p.a. for 120 acres: NL Ire., microfilm P4769; Petworth House, West Sussex, archives

O'Brien, Edward (1808–1840), author, third son of the nine children of Sir Edward O'Brien, fourth baronet (1773–1837), of Dromoland, co. Clare, and his wife, Charlotte (d. 1856), daughter of William Smith of Cahirmoyle, co. Limerick, was born at Dromoland on 6 December 1808. Through his father, the MP for Ennis and County Clare, he could claim descent from Brian Boru and the kings of Thomond. His elder brother was William Smith *O'Brien, the Irish rebel leader, while a younger sister, Harriet *Monsell, became the founder of the Anglican community of St John Baptist at Clewer. After education at Bewdley, Worcestershire, he entered Trinity College, Cambridge, on 1 February 1825 and there read law, graduating BA in 1829 and MA in 1832. He was a friend and contemporary at Cambridge of Richard Monckton Milnes and, like his brother William before him, was elected to membership of the Apostles. Having been admitted to the Inner Temple on 30 January 1828, he entered King's Inn, Dublin, the following year and was called to the Irish bar in 1832.

As a young man O'Brien underwent a religious crisis, on which he corresponded with Richard Whately, Robert

Southey, and R. C. Trench, but having recovered his Christian faith dedicated himself to charitable work and founded a night refuge in Dublin for the destitute poor. His one literary work, *The lawyer: his character and rule of holy life, after the manner of George Herbert's country parson*, published posthumously in 1842, was an idealized depiction, in the archaic language of Herbert and Hooker, of the Christian lawyer's 'high and holy calling'. On 15 August 1839 O'Brien married Louisa Susan, daughter of James Massy-Dawson MP, of Ballynacourty, co. Tipperary. He died of a sudden fever on 19 May 1840 at Whitkirk vicarage, Yorkshire, the home of his brother-in-law, the Revd A. Martineau, leaving his widow in what a contemporary obituarist termed 'a peculiarly interesting and delicate situation'. She bore a son three months after his death. His friend Aubrey de Vere contributed an introduction to *The Lawyer* and in his later *Recollections* paid tribute to the author's 'benevolence and candour'.

G. Martin Murphy

Sources Venn, *Alum. Cant.* · E. Keane, P. Beryl Phair, and T. U. Sadleir, eds., *King's Inns admission papers, 1607–1867*, IMC (1982) · A. de Vere, *Recollections* (1897), 82–6 · G. R. Weir [G. R. O'Brien], *These my friends and forebears: the O'Briens of Dromoland* (1991) · Burke, *Peerage* · P. Allen, *The Cambridge Apostles: the early years* (1978), 223

Archives NL Ire., Inchiquin MSS

O'Brien, Harriet. *See* Monsell, Harriet (1811–1883).

O'Brien, Henry (1808–1835), antiquary, was born in co. Kerry. His parentage is unknown. He was educated at Trinity College, Dublin, where he graduated BA in 1831. In 1832 he wrote a dissertation on 'The round towers of Ireland' for the prize offered by the Royal Irish Academy. Although he did not win the prize, he was awarded a small gratuity. In 1833 he published a translation of a work by Estengo Villanueva's, under the title *Phoenician Ireland*, but his introduction and notes were ridiculed as fanciful by a reviewer in the *Gentleman's Magazine*. In 1834 he published *The round towers of Ireland, or, The mysteries of freemasonry, of Sabaism, and of Budhism for the first time unveiled*. The object of this work (which was an expanded version of his prize essay) was to show that the round towers were Buddhistic remains. The book was condemned as wild and extravagant in the *Gentleman's Magazine* and by George Petrie, a fellow Irish antiquary. Thomas Moore wrote a hostile review in the *Edinburgh Review*, and, in response O'Brien accused Moore of appropriating his discoveries in his *History of Ireland*. F. S. Mahony, known as Father Prout, a warm friend and admirer of O'Brien's, came to his defence in *The Reliques of Father Prout* (1836).

Enthusiastic and self-deluding, O'Brien spoke of compiling a dictionary of Celtic, a subject of which he knew nothing. He also announced that he was writing a book on the pyramids of Egypt but it was never published. He died on 28 June 1835 in the house of a friend, at The Hermitage, Hanwell, Middlesex. He was buried in Hanwell churchyard. A fanciful sketch by Daniel Maclise of O'Brien lying on his deathbed appeared in Prout's *Reliques*.

W. W. Wroth, *rev.* Marie-Louise Legg

Sources *The journal of Thomas Moore*, ed. W. S. Dowden, 4 (1987) · A. M. Brady and B. Cleeve, eds., *A biographical dictionary of Irish writers*, rev. edn (1985), 178 · *GM*, 2nd ser., 1 (1834) · *GM*, 2nd ser., 2 (1834) · F. S. Mahony, *The reliques of Father Prout*, rev. edn (1860)

Likenesses engraving, *c*.1835–1839, repro. in Mahony, *Reliques of Father Prout*, 162 · D. Maclise, lithograph, BM, NPG; repro. in *Fraser's Magazine* (1835) · D. Maclise, pencil study, V&A

O'Brien, Ignatius John, Baron Shandon (1857–1930), lord chancellor of Ireland, was born in Cork on 31 July 1857, the ninth child and youngest son of Mark Joseph O'Brien, merchant, and his wife, Jane, daughter of William Dunne, of Cork. He was educated at the Vincentian school, Cork, and then privately; at the age of sixteen he entered the Catholic University of Ireland, Dublin, an institution which had no power to award recognized degrees. He left after only two years, because of financial difficulties at home, and had to earn his own living immediately. He worked first as junior reporter on *Saunders' Newsletter*, a Dublin Conservative daily newspaper, and then for *Freeman's Journal*, while studying for the bar in his free time.

O'Brien was called to the bar in 1881, but he continued to have to support himself through his freelance journalism and was very slow to build up a practice. In his first year at the bar he made only 6 guineas and in his second only 29; in his third year he began to acquire a small practice on the Munster circuit. Despairing of any real success, he was about to emigrate to New South Wales when he unexpectedly won public acclaim. In 1887 the parish priest of Youghal, Canon Keller, had been questioned in the bankruptcy court as a witness to the financial circumstances of some of his parishioners. Since the priest had acquired his knowledge in his capacity as confessor, and so was bound to silence according to Catholic canon law, he refused to give evidence, and was sent to prison for unsatisfactory answering. T. M. Healy, supported by the Land League, suggested that O'Brien should bring a motion of habeas corpus to secure Canon Keller's release. Although unsuccessful in the court of Queen's Bench, O'Brien secured an order of release from the Court of Appeal, and became a popular Irish Catholic hero, which helped him to build up a good practice. On 11 February 1886 O'Brien had married Anne (*d*. 1929), daughter of John Talbot Scallan, a well-known Dublin solicitor. O'Brien soon gave up circuit business and devoted himself to cases in Chancery and bankruptcy; before long he was a leading authority in bankruptcy law, and in 1899 he finally took silk.

Once his career was launched, O'Brien's professional success was from 1906 ensured by the steady rise of the Liberal Party, which reflected his own political preferences. Since there were very few eminent Liberals in the Irish bar, he helped his party at elections, though he did not stand as a candidate himself. In 1907 he became a bencher of King's Inns, and in 1910 he was promoted to the position of serjeant-at-law. In 1911 he was appointed solicitor-general for Ireland and in 1912 he became attorney-general and was admitted a privy councillor for Ireland. In 1913 the offices of lord chancellor and of lord chief justice of Ireland became vacant at the same time,

and as attorney-general O'Brien sought for and obtained the chancellorship.

The same political climate which enabled O'Brien to rise in his profession also made his tenure of office rather insecure at times, as Conservative English politicians attempted to oust him from office. When the first coalition government was formed in 1915 he was on the verge of being superseded in favour of the unionist James Henry Mussen Campbell, a former solicitor-general and attorney-general for Ireland, but the government feared American and Irish nationalist opinion too much to appoint such a staunch and uncompromising unionist as Campbell. In the end, an outcry was averted and O'Brien kept his position. On 15 January 1916 he was created a baronet, and in 1917, when his rival Sir James Campbell was made lord chief justice, his position seemed safe. However, in 1918 Conservative opinion again seemed to be in the ascendant and O'Brien was dismissed as lord chancellor in favour of Campbell, being offered consolation in the form of a peerage in July 1918. He accepted, choosing the title of Baron Shandon after the church bells described in the poem 'The Shandon Bells' by Father Prout (Francis Sylvester Mahony). Horrified and exasperated by the violence perpetrated and justified by Sinn Féin, who had raided his own house, he left Ireland for good; he sold his Irish property at Ardtona, near Dublin, and went to live at St Lawrence on the Isle of Wight. He also kept a house at 12 Newton Court, Church Street, Kensington, London. He was called to the English bar by the Middle Temple in 1923.

Initially sceptical about the House of Lords, Lord Shandon found the peers unexpectedly agreeable and even became reconciled to the hereditary system. He took an active part in negotiations and debate over the abortive Government of Ireland Act (1920), but afterwards became less voluble, speaking only on questions which directly affected Ireland, or on matters in which he had legal expertise. His last speech was delivered in 1927, on the Law of Libel Amendment Bill, which he opposed. He died at his London home on 10 September 1930; since he had no children, the peerage became extinct on his death.

Unlikely to be remembered as a truly great advocate, judge, or statesman, Shandon worked hard all his life and will be remembered as a competent judge. During the troubled times when he was in office, he exercised a moderating influence over the political activists of his day. His wish was for home rule in Ireland without severing completely the imperial tie with Britain. However, his views were overborne by those of his more vociferous political opponents.   T. C. K. MOORE, *rev.* SINÉAD AGNEW

Sources L. G. Pine, *The new extinct peerage, 1884–1971: containing extinct, abeyant, dormant, and suspended peerages with genealogies and arms* (1972), 249 · F. E. Ball, *The judges in Ireland, 1221–1921*, 2 (1926), 322, 327, 383 · F. C. Burnard, ed., *The Catholic who's who and yearbook* (1920), 250 · H. A. C. Sturgess, ed., *Register of admissions to the Honourable Society of the Middle Temple, from the fifteenth century to the year 1944*, 3 (1949), 874 · *The Times* (12 Sept 1930) · *Thom's Irish who's who* (1923)

Likenesses W. Stoneman, photograph, 1918, NPG

Wealth at death £452 2*s*. 3*d*.: probate, 17 Jan 1931, *CGPLA NIre.* · £13,948 7*s*. 3*d*.: probate, 23 Oct 1930, *CGPLA Eng. & Wales*

O'Brien, James. *See* O'Bryen, James, third marquess of Thomond (1769–1855).

O'Brien, James [*pseud.* Bronterre O'Brien] (1804–1864), Chartist, was born at Granard, co. Longford, Ireland, in early February 1804, the second son of Daniel O'Brien and his wife, Mary Kearney. His father, who was a wine and spirit merchant and a tobacco manufacturer in co. Longford, failed in business during O'Brien's childhood, and died soon after. O'Brien was educated at the local parochial school and then at Edgeworthstown School, which had been promoted by Richard Lovell Edgeworth. He then went to Trinity College, Dublin, where he graduated BA in 1829. He entered the King's Inns, Dublin, and then went to London, where he was admitted as a law student at Gray's Inn in March 1830. In London he met Henry Hunt and William Cobbett.

In 1831 Henry Hetherington started up and edited the *Poor Man's Guardian*, but O'Brien became its effective editor and also contributed to Hetherington's *Poor Man's Conservative*. He signed his articles Bronterre, and from this moment called himself James Bronterre O'Brien. At first O'Brien adopted many of William Cobbett's views on the national debt and the currency, but soon he began to develop his own ideas. He read widely in the literature of the French Revolution, and visited France on three occasions in 1837–8. In 1836 his translated edition of Buonarotti's *History of Babeuf's Conspiracy* was published and in 1838 the first volume of his eulogistic *Life of Robespierre* appeared. By this time O'Brien's own opinions were insurrectionary and socialistic. In 1837 he began *Bronterre's National Reformer*, which soon failed, and in 1838 *The Operative*, which ended publication in July 1839. He had, meanwhile, married in the mid-1830s (the name of his wife is not known); he had four children.

From the beginning of the Chartist movement O'Brien was one of its most prominent figures. He was a member of the original London Working Man's Association, and was a delegate to the Chartist meeting in Palace Yard (17 September 1838) which opened the campaign in London. In 1838 he joined Feargus O'Connor at the *Northern Star*, and toured the country as a 'missionary' lecturer. Although regarded as a physical-force advocate, O'Brien was careful not to overstep the limits of the law. As he put it in the draft of the Chartist convention's address (8 May 1839), 'it was his intention to tell the people to arm without saying so in so many words'. He represented the Chartists of Manchester at the Chartist convention in the spring of 1839, and opposed the plan for a general strike.

As a result of the Newport rising of November 1839 a number of trials for sedition took place in the spring of 1840. O'Brien acted in his own defence and was acquitted at Newcastle in February on a charge of conspiracy, but was found guilty at Liverpool in April of seditious speaking. He was sentenced to eighteen months' imprisonment. Towards the end of his sentence O'Brien and Feargus O'Connor both began to communicate with the press, and carried on a controversy with one another as to the best policy for Chartists to pursue at the general election

James O'Brien [Bronterre O'Brien] (1804–1864), by unknown engraver

of 1841. O'Connor advocated an active alliance with the Conservatives, while O'Brien opposed this. Although still in prison O'Brien stood as a Chartist candidate at Newcastle upon Tyne in the general election.

Released in September 1841, O'Brien continued the series of bitter personal quarrels with O'Connor, whom he later called the Dictator. O'Connor in turn nicknamed him the Starved Viper. O'Brien resumed his journalistic career, using various editorships to put forward his views on currency reform and continue his attack on O'Connor. He edited the *British Statesman* between June and December 1842, and in 1845 became editor of the *National Reformer*. During the Chartist campaign against the Anti-Corn Law League, O'Brien argued that free trade would lower prices, and so increase the proportion of the national wealth that landlords and owners of stock were able to appropriate. In the *National Reformer* he advocated 'symbolic money' and 'banks of credit accessible to all classes' (Gammage, 280). He opposed O'Connor's land scheme, and joined in with the moderate reform programme of the National Complete Suffrage Union.

O'Brien was one of the delegates at the Chartist convention which met on 4 April 1848. He spoke strongly against physical force. However, on 9 April he withdrew from the convention on the grounds that the convention was likely to 'go too fast' (Plummer, 191) and collide with the government. After the failure of the Chartist petition in 1848, O'Brien worked with G. W. M. Reynolds on *Reynolds' Political Instructor* and *Reynolds' Weekly News*. In October 1849 he used the former journal to launch his National Reform

League, which advocated nationalization of the land and the monetary system. During the 1850s O'Brien lived on his lecturing at the Eclectic Institute in Denmark Street, Soho, but never gave up the hope of more regular journalistic employment. His own weekly paper, the *Power of the Pence*, ran for five months during the winter and early spring of 1848–9, and during the following decade he hoped for work on papers as diverse as those of Reynolds, the Cobdenite *Morning Star*, and *The Empire*. O'Brien also remained politically active during the 1850s. He wrote several pamphlets—on Lord Palmerston, Lord Overstone, Napoleon Bonaparte, and Robespierre. He was a member of the Stop-the-War-League during the Crimean War, travelled to Tiverton in April 1857 with the intention of contesting Lord Palmerston's seat (he later withdrew), and in May 1858 established the National Political Union, which reiterated the call for the Charter. O'Brien's later years were beset with poverty and alcohol-related illness. On several occasions his books were seized for debt. In February 1862 Charles Bradlaugh lectured for the 'Bronterre O'Brien testimonial fund'.

O'Brien died at his home in Pentonville, London, on 23 December 1864. His wife survived him. In 1885 several of his followers published a series of his newspaper articles in book form, under the title of *The Rise, Progress, and Phases of Human Slavery*. As Graham Wallas noted, O'Brien was one of the few Chartists whose radicalism was the product of an original mind. Posterity has treated him unkindly. His alcoholism and embittered personal relationships leave the impression of a rancorous and impracticable politician. But he was one of the few non-Utopian socialists in England. He developed a vision of an alternative society which was based on a definitive programme of nationalization of the land and of the monetary system. He was also probably the only Chartist who had any conception of popular insurrection and the means by which the labouring classes might appropriate power through a temporary dictatorship. For all his failings and idiosyncrasies O'Brien was a powerful character. He gained a large personal following among the artisans of Soho, who, in the aftermath of his death, became involved in both the Reform League and the First International.

MILES TAYLOR

Sources R. G. Gammage, *The history of the Chartist movement, from its commencement down to the present time* (1854) • A. Plummer, *Bronterre: a political biography of Bronterre O'Brien, 1804–1864* (1971) • W. H. Maehl, 'O'Brien, James [Bronterre]', *BDMBR*, vol. 2 • S. Shipley, *Club life and socialism in mid-Victorian London* [1971] • M. Taylor, *The decline of British radicalism, 1847–1860* (1995) • *DNB*
Archives BL, corresp. • BLPES, letters to Thomas Allsop • Labour History Archive and Study Centre, Manchester, letters to Mr Mathews with accounts of fund for widow
Likenesses portrait, repro. in Plummer, *Bronterre*, frontispiece • stipple, NPG [*see illus.*]

O'Brien, James Francis Xavier (1828–1905), Irish nationalist, born in Dungarvan, co. Waterford, Ireland, on 16 October 1828, was the son of Timothy O'Brien (*d.* 1853), a merchant there, who owned some vessels which traded between England, Ireland, and south Wales. His mother,

James Francis Xavier O'Brien (1828–1905), by Sir Benjamin Stone, 1898

Catherine, also belonged to an O'Brien family. James Francis Xavier was the sixth of their ten children. When Father Mathew, the total abstinence missionary, visited Dungarvan, O'Brien, then aged eight, took the pledge, which he kept until he was twenty-one. He was educated successively at private schools in Dungarvan and at St John's College, Waterford, where he was a student from autumn 1848 to summer 1849. On leaving he became involved in the secret revolutionary movement directed by James Fintan Lalor and others, which culminated in the abortive attack on the police barracks of Cappoquin in September 1849. A warrant was issued for O'Brien's arrest, but he escaped to Wales in one of his father's vessels.

On his return to Ireland O'Brien engaged, at first at Lismore and then at Clonmel, in the purchase of grain for the export business carried on by his father and family. After his father's death in 1853 he gave up this occupation in order to study medicine. In 1854 he gained a scholarship at the Queen's College, Galway, but left in 1855 to accompany a political friend, John O'Leary, to Paris, where he continued his medical studies. He attended lectures at the École de Médecine, and visited the hospitals of La Pitié, La Charité, and Hôtel Dieu. Among the acquaintances he formed in Paris were those of the artist James MacNeill Whistler and the Young Irelanders John Martin and Kevin Izod O'Doherty. Ill health led him to break off his medical studies. After returning to Ireland in 1856 he sailed for New Orleans, with the intention of seeking a new experience by taking part in William Walker's expedition to Nicaragua. Through the influence of Pierre Soule, then attorney-general for the state of Louisiana, O'Brien joined Walker's staff. He sailed with the expedition to San Juan and up that river to Fort San Carlos, but Walker made terms without fighting. On returning to New Orleans, O'Brien became a book keeper there and enjoyed considerable success in business. In 1859 he married Mary Louisa, née Cullimore (d. 1866), the widow of another emigrant, Patrick O'Brien. They had a son. On the outbreak of the American Civil War in 1861 O'Brien signed up as assistant surgeon in a volunteer militia regiment for the defence of New Orleans, but saw no action.

Late in 1862 O'Brien returned to Ireland, and joined the Irish Republican Brotherhood (IRB), or Fenian organization, in Cork. He also contributed many letters to the Fenian newspaper the *Irish People*. He deemed the rising in 1867 to be premature, but on the night of 3 March 1867 he loyally joined his comrades at the rendezvous on Prayer Hill outside Cork, and led an attack upon the Ballynockan police barracks, which surrendered. The party seized the arms there, and marched on towards Bottle Hill, but scattered on the approach of a body of infantry. O'Brien was arrested near Kilmallock, and taken to Limerick gaol. He was subsequently taken to Cork county gaol, and in May tried for high treason. He was convicted, and was sentenced to be hanged, drawn, and quartered. The sentence was commuted to penal servitude for life. O'Brien was the last person to be sentenced to the barbarous punishment provided by the old law of treason. From Mountjoy prison, Dublin, he was soon taken with some twenty-nine other political prisoners, chained together in gangs on a gunboat, to Holyhead and then Millbank, where he was kept in solitary confinement for fourteen months. Next he was removed to Portland with others, chained in sets of six. In Portland he worked at stone-dressing. He was finally released on 4 March 1869 in the first batch of Fenian prisoners granted amnesty by Gladstone's newly formed cabinet. On visiting Waterford, and subsequently Cork, he received popular ovations.

He found that the leadership of the IRB had been reorganized in 1868 along representative lines under a supreme council. He made a major contribution towards the consolidation of this change by conveying that he knew the still-imprisoned Fenian notables to be opposed to the continuation of the old ascendancy of James Stephens. O'Brien and James O'Connor (another amnestied prisoner) seem to have assumed charge of the revival of the IRB and to have controlled the emergence of a new supreme council in the summer of 1869. O'Brien then or soon afterwards became president of the supreme council. It was he who proposed the significant innovation which saw Fenian resources being directed to having the imprisoned colleague Jeremiah O'Donovan Rossa elected MP for Tipperary in November 1869. By 1874, however, O'Brien had left the leadership of the IRB, although he continued to associate with some of his old colleagues, including Charles J. Kickham, a successor of his as president of the supreme council.

Before his arrest O'Brien had worked with Cleary & Co., a wholesale tea and wine business at Cork. He was re-employed on his release, and was soon appointed a traveller for the firm, a post which facilitated his Fenian business. From 1873 he was accountant with the Cork Gas Company. In 1882 he moved to Dublin as senior partner in the tea and wine business of W. H. O'Sullivan. In 1870 he had married Mary Teresa O'Malley, with whom he had three daughters and two sons.

Meanwhile, O'Brien was gradually drawn into the parliamentary home-rule movement under Parnell's leadership. He was nationalist MP for South Mayo from 1885 to 1895 and for Cork City from 1895 until his death. In the schism of 1891 he opposed Parnell. O'Brien's expertise in business and accountancy was turned to good use for party purposes. From 1886 he was *de facto*, and then formally, a treasurer of the Irish Parliamentary Party. From 1888 (in which year he moved to London with his family) he was treasurer and (from 1890) secretary of the Irish National League of Great Britain. In 1900 he became general secretary of the United Irish League of Great Britain, an office which he held for life. He died at his home, 39 Gauden Road, Clapham, on 28 May 1905, and was buried on 1 June in Glasnevin cemetery, Dublin.

R. B. O'BRIEN, rev. R. V. COMERFORD

Sources P. Nolan, 'J. F. X. O'Brien, M.P. (1828–1905)', MA diss., University College, Cork, 1971 · J. O'Leary, *Recollections of Fenians and Fenianism* (1896) · private information (1912)
Archives NL Ire., corresp. and papers, incl. draft autobiography | NL Ire., William O'Brien MSS · NL Ire., Harrington MSS · TCD, corresp. with John Dillon · University College, Cork, William O'Brien MSS
Likenesses B. Stone, photograph, 1898, NPG [*see illus.*] · Connolly, portrait; formerly in family possession, 1912 · photograph, NA Ire., Fenian papers

O'Brien, James Thomas (1792–1874), Church of Ireland bishop of Ossory, Ferns, and Leighlin, born at New Ross, co. Wexford, on 27 September 1792, was the son of Michael Burke O'Brien (d. 1826), a corporation officer with the title of deputy sovereign of New Ross, and Dorothy, daughter of Thomas Kough. His father, who came originally from co. Clare, was descended, although he himself became a protestant, from a Roman Catholic branch of the O'Brien family, which had been deprived of its property by the penal laws. James was educated at the endowed school at New Ross, which was supported by the corporation, and entered Trinity College, Dublin, as a pensioner in November 1810. A portion of the cost of his education was defrayed by the borough of New Ross; in September 1826 he refunded the amount—£116—and was voted the freedom of the borough and a gold box. O'Brien obtained a scholarship at Trinity College in 1813 and graduated BA with gold medal in 1815. He was especially distinguished in mathematics, and in 1820 obtained a fellowship; having taken holy orders, he was created DD in 1831. He was one of the six Dublin University preachers from 1828 to 1842, and became Archbishop King's lecturer in 1833, when the divinity school in the university was thoroughly reorganized.

O'Brien maintained strongly evangelical views throughout his life. He was well read in the works of the reformers and their opponents, and in those of Bishop Butler and the deists. His university sermons of 1829 and 1830 on the Reformation doctrine of justification by faith became, when published in 1833, a standard work. He lectured on 'The evidences of religion, with a special reference to sceptical and infidel attempts to invalidate them, and the Socinian controversy'. In 1836 he married Ellen (*d.* 1906), second daughter of Edward *Pennefather, lord chief justice of Ireland. They had eight sons and five daughters. O'Brien resigned his fellowship in the same year, and became vicar of Clonderhorka, Raphoe, but moved in 1837 to the vicarage of Arboe, co. Tyrone, which he held until 1841. On 9 November 1841 he was nominated dean of Cork, and instituted on 5 January 1842. On 9 March in the same year he was made bishop of the united dioceses of Ossory, Ferns, and Leighlin.

O'Brien was a daily worshipper in his cathedral. He seldom preached or spoke except at the meetings of the Church Education Society (of which he was an active champion); the society was the Church of Ireland's response to the national schools, of which he was correspondingly critical. Naturally opposed to the Oxford Movement, he did what he could to stem its advance in sermons and writings between 1840 and 1850, singling out Newman for especial disparagement. In 1850 appeared his *Tractarianism: its Present State, and the Only Safeguard Against it*. Tract 90 he described as 'shifting, evasive, and disingenuous' (Carroll, 16). To the disestablishment of the Irish church O'Brien opposed a well-sustained resistance, and Archbishop Trench of Dublin acknowledged the value of his advice in the course of the struggle. When disestablishment came, O'Brien helped to reorganize the church, and cautioned his evangelical friends in their efforts to revise the prayer book in accordance with their own principles—for instance, where infant baptism was concerned—fearing 'lest, in raising bulwarks against ritualism and popery, the Church itself should be narrowed' (Warren, 21).

O'Brien's chief work, *An Attempt to Explain the Doctrine of Justification by Faith Only, in Ten Sermons* (1833), ran to five editions. His primary and second charges, 1842 and 1845, published in London, and directed in great part against Tractarianism, each went to several editions. In 1833 he attacked Edward Irving's views in *Two Sermons Relating to the Human Nature of our Blessed Lord*, which were re-published in 1873 with a *Plea from the Bible and the Bible Alone for the Doctrine of Baptismal Regeneration*. His charge of 1848 (published in 1850) discussed, *inter alia*, the alliance between church and state.

O'Brien died at 49 Thurloe Square, London, on 12 December 1874, and was buried in the churchyard of St Canice's Cathedral, Kilkenny, on 19 December. His successor, Dr Robert Gregg, in his primary charge praised O'Brien's 'unvarying consistency, calm judgement, and chastened self-restraint'.

G. C. BOASE, rev. KENNETH MILNE

Sources J. B. Leslie, *Ossory clergy and parishes* (1933) · H. Cotton, *Fasti ecclesiae Hibernicae*, 6 vols. (1845–78) · W. G. Carroll, *A memoir of the Right Rev. J. T. O'Brien* (1875) · R. B. McDowell, *The Church of Ireland, 1869–1969* (1975) · R. R. Warren, ed., *Speeches delivered in the general convention of the Church of Ireland* (1870) · D. Bowen, *The protestant crusade in Ireland, 1800–70* (1978) · W. A. Phillips, ed., *History of the Church of Ireland*, 3 vols. (1933–4) · *Irish Times* (17 Dec 1874) · *Irish Ecclesiastical Gazette* (23 Dec 1874)

Archives U. Hull, Brynmor Jones L., corresp., literary MSS, and papers | LPL, letters to Charles Golightly

Likenesses Hennah & Kent, photograph, Representative Church Body Library, Dublin, MS 223/7 · portrait, bishop's palace, Kilkenny

Wealth at death under £30,000: probate, 4 Feb 1875, *CGPLA Ire.*

O'Brien, John (1701–1769), Roman Catholic bishop of Cloyne and Ross and lexicographer, was born in Ballyvoddy, near Glanworth, co. Cork, the son of Thomas O'Brien, a farmer, and his wife, Eleanor McEniry. His parents, both of good descent, were well connected both at home and on the continent. By 1720 he had already left for France to study for the priesthood, principally at the Irish College in Toulouse, where he was permitted to hear confessions in April 1727, evidence of his recent ordination. At the University of Toulouse he graduated bachelor of divinity in 1733, being already a doctor of both civil and canon law. From 1733 to 1737 he travelled widely in France and Spain as tutor to the sons of several aristocratic Irish expatriates, namely Simon Connock, governor in the Spanish service; Thomas Fitzgerald, the Spanish ambassador in London; and Arthur Dillon, lieutenant-general in the Irish brigade.

On O'Brien's return to Ireland in 1738, his first employment was as parish priest of Castlelyons and Rathcormack, co. Cork. These parishes belonged to Cloyne, a diocese then subject to the bishop of Cork. Very soon he was also named archdeacon and vicar-general. He was to reside at Castlelyons, close to the still thriving centre of Gaelic literature Carraig na bFear, for most of his life.

By papal brief dated 10 January 1748, O'Brien became bishop of Cloyne and Ross, two areas physically separated by the diocese of Cork. To repair church structure and discipline undermined by penal laws over the preceding fifty years, he published in 1756 an elaborate set of diocesan statutes entitled *Monita pastoralia et statuta ecclesiastica*. Their aim was to foster a well-trained and zealous body of priests whose first duty would be to preach and catechize. The statutes also sought to improve the behaviour of the laity with regard both to their religious duties and to some aspects of their social behaviour: superstitions, faction-fighting even at funerals, and meetings by night at holy wells. Clandestine marriages were severely condemned. A second and shorter work, *Vindiciae quarundum consuetudinum*, published with the *Monita*, was sent to Rome as a spirited defence of Irish bishops, accused of non-residence and neglect of their duties, against their hidden slanderers.

O'Brien's work of diocesan renewal was hampered for twenty years by the unhelpful interference of James Butler, the coadjutor-bishop of Cashel from 1750 and archbishop from 1757; sometimes he was delated to the civil authorities by unworthy priests whom he had tried to discipline. He also had to grapple with problems arising from the activities of the Whiteboys, a secret and supposedly Catholic network of agrarian terrorists. To counteract the

Whiteboys he issued a stern pastoral letter to his clergy in 1762. To improve clerical education he established bursaries in 1764 at the Irish colleges of Paris and Louvain. Despite his reputation as a disciplinarian, he retained the loyalty of his priests. During the years 1765 and 1766 he personally conducted a general mission for his two dioceses, spending four months in the field each autumn with a band of confessors. Ireland had seldom seen missions of this kind before, nor would it often see them again.

O'Brien wrote a treatise on the history of Munster, thought to have been that published by Charles Vallancey under his own name in the fourth volume of his *Collectanea* in 1774. With the help of a scholar named Ó Conaire he also compiled the manuscript generally known as the 'Dublin annals of Inisfallen'. His great work, however, was as general editor of an Irish dictionary, *Focalóir Gaoidhilge–Sax-Bhéarla, or, An Irish–English Dictionary*, compiled by other scholars under his supervision before 1762, and eventually printed at Paris in 1768. This too was intended to help the church, for O'Brien believed that the preservation of the faith in Ireland depended essentially on the preservation of the native language. Inspired by the works of Edward Lluyd and Conor O'Begly, he drew on earlier compilations but omitted several thousand words then in use. His dictionary contains valuable historical and genealogical information and useful definitions, but is marred by fanciful etymologies and a lack of grammatical detail.

Partly because of ill health and partly to escape the powerful Nagle family, protectors of a dissolute priest accused of using the confessional to seduce female tenants of the Nagles, O'Brien left Ireland for ever in the summer of 1767. Having first made his way to Paris to oversee the printing of his dictionary in 1768, he died on 13 March 1769 at Lyons, where he was buried in the church of St Martin d'Ainay.   HUGH FENNING

Sources DNB · J. Coombes, *A bishop of the penal times: the life and times of John O'Brien, bishop of Cloyne and Ross, 1701–1769* (1981) · P. Fagan, ed., *Ireland in the Stuart papers*, 2 vols. (1995) · B. Ó Conchúir, *Scríobhaithe Chorcaí, 1700–1850* (1982) · S. Ó Cearnaigh, 'The Irish–English dictionary of Bishop John O'Brien', *Linenhall Review*, 10/1 (1993), 15–17

O'Brien, Katherine [Kate] (1897–1974), writer, was born at Boru House, Limerick, on 3 December 1897 into a wealthy Catholic middle-class family, the fourth daughter and sixth of nine children of Thomas O'Brien (1850/51–1916) of Boru House, a very successful horse breeder and celebrated rider, and his wife, Catherine, *née* Thornhill (1863/4–1903). When her mother died from cancer in 1903 Kate was placed as a boarder in the Laurel Hill convent in Limerick, at the age of five and a half. She was a pupil here until 1916, with the French nuns of the order of the Faithful Companions of Jesus. Here she became habituated to good food, good manners, and the French language. Her father died in June 1916, and in the financial dearth after his death it was thought that Kate would need to earn her own living immediately, but with the help of a scholarship she became a student at University College, Dublin, where she read English and French.

Kate O'Brien's first job was in the foreign languages department of the *Manchester Guardian*, then under the editorship of C. P. Scott. When the paper discontinued its page on foreign papers, she moved to London and taught for six months at St Mary's Convent in Hampstead. After a marriage proposal about which she felt uncertain she then went to Spain, a country she loved for the rest of her life, spending a year as a governess in Bilbao. She then returned to Hampstead where she married the Dutch journalist Gustaaf Johannes Renier on 17 May 1923, but the marriage foundered after less than a year. She was at that stage a woman of striking good looks, blue-eyed and black-haired, and though in later years she became bulky and heavy featured, she was always an impressive presence.

Kate O'Brien had a wide range of contacts with educated and professional women, and was comfortable in the strongly lesbian circle of the staff of Lady Rhondda's *Time and Tide* at about this period. She kept up her old friendships from University College, Dublin, and it was as a result of a bet with one of them, Veronica Turleigh, by then a successful actress in London, that she wrote her first play, *Distinguished Villa*, produced in London in May 1926. It was a resounding success and made an instant reputation for its author. Her work as a journalist and reviewer increased as a result, and she was commissioned to write a novel by Heinemann. On the strength of the advance she moved to Ashford in Kent, an area that attracted her throughout her life.

Kate O'Brien took some time over this novel—*Without my Cloak* did not appear until 1931. Like all her novels it treats of the Irish middle class, and the position of women in it. Many of her women characters prize the rewards of a satisfying profession over the rewards of marriage and motherhood. In comparison with Irish novels of the time she wrote freely of women's sexuality. Naturally her work was anathema to the Irish Censorship Board. In 1936 her novel *Mary Lavelle* was banned for its description of sex outside marriage and again *Land of Spices* in 1941 for openly mentioning male homosexuality. *Mary Lavelle* had also contained a well-drawn and sympathetic portrayal of a lesbian spinster. But it is more for her critical portrayal of Irish Catholic society than for her inclusive range of sexuality in her characters that she was shunned in Ireland.

Perhaps for the same reason Kate O'Brien was successful in England; *Without my Cloak* had won the James Tait Black memorial prize and the Hawthornden. In her person as well as in her writing Kate O'Brien was a revelation to the English common reader who was for long accustomed to think of Ireland as a society composed entirely of a lower order. She became well known, too, through her reviewing work for *The Spectator*, and through a travelogue in 1937, *Farewell Spain*, so critical of Franco that she was barred from the country until 1957. In 1946 she had a great success, financial and critical, with the Spanish historical novel *That Lady*. After a trip to America in 1949, with a relaxation of control in Ireland and with comfortable finances she was able to return to Ireland, at first to Dublin, but soon to Roundstone in Connemara, where she had a house until 1960. In 1958 she published what is for modern readers perhaps her most absorbing novel, *As Music and Splendour*. Again on the theme of Irish convent girls achieving a professional life, it is a richly detailed study of opera singers at work in Italy, well balanced and quite remarkable for its open description of a calm and adult love between two women, in a company of friends in emotional turmoil.

Kate O'Brien returned to Kent in 1960 and lived at Boughton; she went into a productive and financial decline, writing reviews and journalism, but depressed through the lack of inspiration. She made her will on 14 January 1961, naming as her executor her friend Mary O'Neill, a painter and illustrator who had been one of her pupils at St Mary's, Hampstead. She prohibited the publication of any letters to or from her. She died in the Kent and Canterbury Hospital, Canterbury, on 13 August 1974. Although a lapsed Catholic for many years she received the last rites, and was buried in the public cemetery beside the church of Our Lady of Mount Carmel in Faversham.

GIFFORD LEWIS

Sources DNB · L. Reynolds, *Kate O'Brien: a literary portrait* (1987) · E. Walshe, ed., *Ordinary people dancing: essays on Kate O'Brien* (1993) · personal information (2004) [D. O'Brien, L. Reynolds] · *The Times* (14 Aug 1974)
Archives priv. coll.
Likenesses Sasha, photographs, 1926, Hult. Arch. · H. Coster, photograph, 1934, priv. coll. · M. O'Neill, portrait, c.1935, priv. coll. · M. O'Neill, oils, 1936, NPG · J. Sleator, oils on linen, c.1950, Limerick City Gallery of Art · H. Coster, photographs, NPG
Wealth at death £10,572: further administration with will, 10 April 1975, *CGPLA Eng. & Wales* · £1034: probate, 29 Jan 1975, *CGPLA Eng. & Wales*

O'Brien, Leslie Kenneth, Baron O'Brien of Lothbury (1908–1995), banker, was born on 8 February 1908 in Dulwich, London, the son of Charles John Grimes O'Brien (1878–1949) and his wife, Caroline, née Abbott (1879–1969). His father's family came originally from Killaloe in co. Clare, Ireland, but settled in England in the early nineteenth century. O'Brien was educated at Wandsworth School, London, from about 1918 to 1926, and joined the Bank of England as a clerk in 1927. During the next twenty-four years he rose steadily in the bank's hierarchy as his innate abilities were recognized in what was already a hierarchy of merit, at least until the glass ceiling which separated court and the governor from the mundane professionals. Of significance for the future, he served early on as secretary to the governor, Montagu Norman, after the twin crises of the second Labour government's fall in 1931 and the subsequent National Government's abandonment of the gold standard in 1932. While not privy to the highest-level negotiations, O'Brien learned something of crisis atmospheres and the intricacies where high politics and banking interacted to produce harsh burdens for central bankers confronted with politicians playing by very different rules.

After his marriage to Isabelle Gertrude (1908–1987), daughter of Francis Pickett, on 2 April 1932, O'Brien moved to Worcester Park, Surrey, where their only child, Michael, was born. Promotion followed rapidly, giving O'Brien a senior post in the overseas department and a widening acquaintance with European, dominion, and United States central bank officials. During and after the Second World War it was of great value for him not only to know and understand the intricacies of exchange control, but to see the heavy problems of the sterling area and the outstanding sterling balances (which had financed much of Britain's early war effort), through the eyes of Australian, Canadian, or Indian bank governors and, even more important, those of the American federal reserve. Dedicated to the institution all his life, full of insight and innovation, but undramatic and virtually apolitical, O'Brien (who, with his family, settled comfortably in Wimbledon from 1942) appeared to be one of the Bank of England's leading technicians—a quality recognized when he was appointed deputy chief cashier in 1951. With Sir Kenneth Peppiatt, his senior, and then as chief cashier himself after 1954, he matured techniques for using bank rate as an instrument of monetary management for the first time since Britain had left the gold standard twenty years earlier.

From 1954 until 1962 the note issue bore O'Brien's name, and he was fortunate in that the rules which evolved—or were relearnt—appeared to work in the barely inflationary 1950s. O'Brien became an executive director in 1962 and then deputy governor in 1964. For a man with a relatively humble background, the glass ceiling still appeared impervious, as it had done for other professionals in the long era of Norman and his patrician successors, lords Cobbold and Cromer. But whereas Cobbold had set out in tandem with government and dominion central bankers to ensure Britain's post-war financial stability, Cromer's outspokenness and independent-mindedness estranged Harold Wilson, prime minister from 1964. Wilson required a man who would not set the bank's view against the government's when it came to defining the national interest—in this case the uneasy relationship of sterling to the dollar at a time when the Labour government not only had to borrow but was under strong American pressure to support the war in Vietnam in return for any support of sterling.

No one doubted O'Brien's intellectual ability and experience, but few actually knew much about the man or about the lessons he had unobtrusively drawn from experience over the previous thirty crisis-ridden years. Appointed governor in 1966 in a striking display of the meritocratic flavour of the 1960s Wilson government, O'Brien displayed the ability but none of the docility predicted by Treasury officials. He had seen how Norman had shaped the bank to the state's requirements long before nationalization, in preparation for war in the late 1930s, and as a loyal official O'Brien had fully accepted its subordinate position thereafter. But though he deplored both Cromer's methods and his *de haut en bas* attitude, he shared his predecessor's mistrust of the way that Keynes's prescriptions were already being misused as a permanent cure-all, with the inevitable risk of inflation. Accepting, as he always did, decisions once they had been made, O'Brien robustly argued the bank's case for a stable monetary policy so long as discussions with the chancellor continued.

After the July 1966 crisis and through the devaluation débâcle in 1967 (against which he struggled hard but without effect) O'Brien addressed four principal policy areas: first how to stabilize sterling, now that it was merely a volatile adjunct to the dollar system; second, how to manage the economy at a time of rapidly rising inflation, created at least partly (in his view) by excessive increases in public spending; third, how to renew the flow of investment to domestic industry; and, finally, how to modernize the City of London's financial institutions before their markets were lost to American banks, and later to Japanese and European contenders. O'Brien was perhaps the first post-war governor with the capacity to answer each of these problems, but the late 1960s were a bad time to argue the virtues of monetary and fiscal prudence.

The sterling balances were indeed stabilized (in the short term), thanks partly to O'Brien's skilful diplomacy at Basel in 1968. With Harold Lever, Wilson's financial emissary, he also helped to avert a second devaluation in March the same year by negotiating with the American authorities. Soon afterwards, and under a new chancellor, Roy Jenkins, the bank's *Quarterly Bulletin* was able to take a more explicit line about O'Brien's desire for a permanent but flexible monetary policy, and for a bank rate more influenced by market demand. But the chosen means, 'competition and credit control' (CCC), as evolved by O'Brien and his team, were disputed by the Treasury precisely because of this element of market demand from industry, which would have diminished governmental influence. Revived by Anthony Barber in 1971, CCC emerged in a different form at a uniquely unsuitable time. After the reintroduction of bank rate as minimum lending rate (MLR) in the 1972 crisis, it was suspended on Treasury demand.

O'Brien had transferred his admiration for Roy Jenkins to Heath (who confirmed his second term of office in 1970) mainly because he believed that EEC entry would induce Britain's long-delayed industrial transformation; but that did not survive Iain McLeod's premature death, which left Anthony Barber, the new chancellor, in thrall to a prime minister who set aims, notably curbing unemployment, above monetary discipline. O'Brien agreed with Heath that industrial managers had failed to take advantage of the new credit regime, but disagreed with him on how to deal with the malignant combination of high wage-inflation and speculative property lending which in 1973 produced a 25.6 per cent increase in money supply accompanied by a real interest rate of 1.2 per cent. Like Cromer, O'Brien had to confront the prime minister and chancellor to ask them to raise MLR in mid-1972. They refused, fearing the effect on the cost of living and subsequent trade-union wage demands. All O'Brien could do, informally and with Treasury officials' assent, was to manipulate the Treasury bill rate sufficiently to push the rate to 9 per cent in June. The governor's special deposits scheme, which he evolved later in 1972, might have helped to check the boom, but that too was denied him. Finally

implemented by his successor Gordon Richardson as the so-called 'corset', it may, paradoxically, have intensified the final post-oil-shock collapse.

O'Brien was no more successful in freeing the retail banks from government controls on lending, in order to compete on a more equal level with the American institutions and the secondary or fringe banks, which enjoyed a laxer supervision by the Board of Trade. His long policy of encouraging industry to seek medium-term loans and consequently to innovate and make structural adjustments rather than to rely on overdraft finance was, like CCC in its latter form, overtaken by the sustained crisis faced by Edward Heath's government in June 1972, when sterling was floated. O'Brien regarded this with extreme distaste, believing that fixed rates were the basis of sound monetary discipline, but he was not called back from holiday to advise, nor was he included in the discussions which preceded Heath's Industry Act of 1972.

O'Brien's contribution to his fourth policy problem, that of reforming the City's financial institutions, drew strength from work done earlier—from Anthony Crosland's inquiry into banking profits, and from his establishment of the Mergers and Takeover Panel. Committed to the principle of self-regulation, O'Brien made sure that the bank modernized itself and its services with more transparent presentation of its accounts. Among his reforms, the Institutional Investors' Working Party had some effect on the flows and quality of investment. In the bank's domestic aspect O'Brien's skills as a negotiator and broker of opinion accentuated sound existing trends, but the forces of inertia in the City remained almost as powerful at the time of O'Brien's retirement as they had been in 1966.

As governor of the Bank of England, O'Brien became a protagonist in a dual struggle between an increasingly global set of financial realities and the domestic British defence of an eroding, post-war, welfare-state economy; and between the bank community, guarding the currency and the nation's long-term financial stability, and the political parties and elected governments whose top priority remained high employment. In so far as 1969–72 saw a determined government defence of the post-war settlement, O'Brien was denied the influence that Richardson later possessed, once the focus of monetary policy changed. His own marker can be found in a definitive speech, delivered in October 1977 to the Belgian Royal Society, in which he clearly linked central bank independence to effective control of money supply and the curbing of inflation.

Angered by the policies of the Heath government, but too loyal to the state either to protest publicly or resign, O'Brien retired in February 1973 on his sixty-fifth birthday, only half way through his second term of office. He was created Baron O'Brien of Lothbury on his retirement (having been knighted GBE in 1967 and appointed a privy councillor in 1970). In retirement he served as a director of Prudential Assurance, Unilever, the Rank Organization, and various other companies, and he also served on the boards of the National Theatre and the Royal Opera House development appeal. He kept up late in his life an enthusiasm for tennis as well as music and the theatre. His first wife, Isabelle, having died in 1987, he married, on 6 January 1989, Marjorie Violet Taylor, *née* Ball (*b.* 1923), with whom he moved to Oxted, Surrey. He died at the East Surrey Hospital, Redhill, on 24 November 1995, following a stroke. A lifelong Anglican, his ashes were buried in the graveyard of St Peter's Church, Tandridge, Surrey, on 1 December. He was survived by his second wife, Marjorie, and the son of his first marriage, Michael.

KEITH MIDDLEMAS

Sources *The Times* (25 Nov 1995) · *The Independent* (27 Nov 1995) · K. Middlemas, *Power, competition and the state*, 2 (1990) · *WWW, 1991–5* · private information (2004) [Michael O'Brien] · personal knowledge (2004)
Archives Bank of England Archive, London · priv. coll. | SOUND BL NSA, National Life Story Collection, 'City lives', C409/003/01–03
Likenesses E. Halliday, oils, 1973, priv. coll. · D. Poole, oils, *c.*1974, priv. coll. · photograph, repro. in *The Independent* · photograph, repro. in *The Times*
Wealth at death £187,112: probate, 25 March 1996, *CGPLA Eng. & Wales*

O'Brien, **Sir Lucius Henry**, third baronet (1733–1795), politician, was born on 2 September 1733, in Dromoland, co. Clare, Ireland, a member of a younger branch of the O'Briens, earls of Thomond and of Inchiquin. He was the eldest son of Sir Edward O'Brien, second baronet (*d.* 1765), of Dromoland, politician, who represented County Clare in the Irish House of Commons for thirty years, and his wife, Mary, daughter of Hugh Hickman of Fenloe. He matriculated at Trinity College, Dublin, on 9 July 1748, graduated BA in the spring of 1752, and, after entering the Middle Temple on 18 September 1753, was called to the Irish bar on 17 November 1758. He married, on 26 May 1768, Anne (*d. c.*1798), daughter of Robert *French (1716–1779), the prominent patriot MP of Monivae, co. Galway, and his wife, Nicola Acheson (*d.* 1762). They had six daughters and five sons.

O'Brien entered parliament in 1763 as member for Ennis borough and in the same year announced his arrival with a long speech in a debate over tithes, in which he described the condition of the country, which was subsequently quoted by Lecky in his *History of England*. He became friends with Charles Lucas, the patriot MP, and soon became a prominent member of the parliamentary opposition. According to Barrington:

> By means of a rational understanding and very extensive and accurate commercial information he acquired a considerable degree of public reputation, though his language was bad—his address miserable and his figure and action unmeaning and whimsical—yet, as his matter was generally good, his reasoning sound, and his conduct frequently spirited and independent, he was attended to with respect, and in return always conveyed considerable information. (Barrington, 1.213–14)

In 1765 O'Brien succeeded his father as third baronet; in March of the following year he was placed at the head of a committee to prepare and introduce a bill making the judges' offices tenable *quamdiu se bene gesserint*, and not as previously in Ireland during the king's pleasure. The bill

was passed, being a popular opposition measure, but did not receive the assent of the English privy council until 1782. In 1768 O'Brien contested his father's seat, County Clare, at the cost of £2000; he was elected, and represented the county until 1776, when he was returned for Ennis. When, however, Hugh Dillon Massy, one of the members for County Clare, was unseated O'Brien was returned in his stead and chose to sit for the county.

O'Brien busied himself with endeavours to remove the restrictions on trade between England and Ireland, and made frequent speeches on the subject in parliament in opposition to the government; but his speeches lacked lucidity, and his audience was said to be seldom the wiser for them. He visited England in 1778–9 in pursuance of the same object. In the same year he reported to the lord lieutenant on the state of co. Clare, and was one of the first to urge the arming of the militia to meet the expected invasion of Ireland. Following the lead of Charlemont, he headed the volunteer movement in co. Clare, though somewhat reluctantly given the weakness of protestant numbers in the county, and took an active part in the agitation for Irish legislative independence. In 1780 he led the opposition to the government in the matter of the import duties between Portugal and Ireland, and in 1782 he supported Grattan's motion for an address to the king in favour of legislative independence. He was never a fully devoted member of Grattan's patriots and instead concentrated his energies on economic improvement both on his debt-ridden estate and in the surrounding counties through the medium of internal navigation. Like Robert French, his patriotism was much more of the economic than the constitutional kind, which made him a potential government supporter and also a rather old-fashioned kind of country gentleman when in opposition.

Perhaps because of limited advocacy of the popular cause, O'Brien was defeated at County Clare in 1783 by a leading county volunteer; he was, however, returned for a purchased seat in Tuam, which he represented until 1790. In 1787 he was sworn of the privy council and appointed clerk of the crown and hanaper in the high court of chancery. He was regarded as a supporter, if a somewhat unreliable one, of the government. He took a prominent part in the debates on Pitt's proposals for removing the restrictions on Irish trade, and also on the regency question of 1788, and in both cases took the patriot side. In 1790 he was returned for Ennis, and he represented it until his death. In 1791 he moved a resolution for the more satisfactory trying of election petitions, and his last recorded speech in parliament was made in March of the same year on the subject of India trade. Arthur Young acknowledged his indebtedness to O'Brien, at whose house he stayed, and who was indefatigable in procuring materials for Young's *Tour in Ireland*. O'Brien died on 15 January 1795 at Dromoland, where he was buried. He was succeeded by his eldest son, Edward O'Brien, fourth baronet (1773–1837), who was the father of William Smith O'Brien (1803–1864), Irish nationalist, and Edward O'Brien (1808–1840), author.

A. F. POLLARD, *rev.* EOIN MAGENNIS

Sources W. E. H. Lecky, *A history of England in the eighteenth century*, 8 vols. (1879–90), vol. 4, p. 326 · J. Barrington, *Historic memoirs of Ireland* (1846) · *The manuscripts and correspondence of James, first earl of Charlemont*, 2 vols., HMC, 28 (1891–4) · GEC, *Peerage* · Burtchaell & Sadleir, *Alum. Dubl.* · Burke, *Peerage* · NL Ire., Inchiquin MSS
Archives c/o PRO NIre., co. Clare MS, history of the Irish parliament · NL Ire., corresp. and MSS | NL Ire., French MSS · PRO NIre., Emly MSS
Wealth at death see NL Ire., Inchiquin MSS

O'Brien, Matthew (1814–1855), mathematician, was born at Ennis, co. Clare, Ireland, the son of Matthew O'Brien MD. He was first educated at Dublin where he attended Trinity College from 1830 to 1834, and then entered Gonville and Caius College, Cambridge, in 1834, graduating as third wrangler in 1838. He was elected a fellow of Caius in 1840 but resigned in the following year. At Caius he overlapped with two other notable mathematicians, George Green and Robert Murphy.

O'Brien was professor of mathematics and natural philosophy at King's College, London, from 1844 to 1854, serving also as lecturer in practical astronomy at the Royal Military Academy, Woolwich, from 1849 to 1854, and as professor of mathematics at Woolwich, from 1854 to 1855. He wrote four books and sixteen papers. His texts *An Elementary Treatise on the Differential Calculus* (1842) and *A Treatise on Plane Coordinate Geometry* (1844) are good examples of expository writing of their time. The calculus text uses limits to define the basic concepts and to prove the necessary theorems. His papers mainly concerned astronomy and mathematical physics.

The most interesting aspect of O'Brien's work is the development of the algebraic properties of vectors. Hamilton's work on quaternions inspired many contemporaries to produce a similar theory for three-dimensional vectors. Most of these were unsuccessful because their authors tried to include both multiplication and division of vectors into their systems. O'Brien avoided this trap (in two papers published in 1849 in the *Transactions of the Cambridge Philosophical Society*), distinguishing clearly the vector and scalar products and eschewing the division of vectors. Further, he introduced notations for the two products and one corresponding to the Laplacian operator $i\Delta$. He applied his vector algebra in an effective manner to solve problems in mechanics and geometry. His work, which in some measure anticipated that of Gibbs in the 1880s, had little influence on contemporaries.

Nothing is known of O'Brien's personal and family life. He died at Petit Ménage, Jersey, on 22 August 1855.

G. C. SMITH

Sources G. C. Smith, 'M. O'Brien and vectorial mathematics', *Historia Mathematica*, 9 (1982), 172–90 · *DNB* · Venn, *Alum. Cant.*
Likenesses T. C. Wageman, watercolour drawing, Trinity Cam.

O'Brien, Murrough, first earl of Thomond (d. 1551), chieftain and rebel, was the third son of Turlough Donn O'Brien (d. 1528), lord of Thomond, and Raghnailt, daughter of John MacNamara, chief of Clancullen. In 1531 Murrough became tanist to his older brother Conor *O'Brien, the O'Brien chief, filling the vacancy left by the death of his brother Donough. Murrough lived in Inchiquin, co.

Clare, from 1531. He controlled the strategically important lands near the Shannon, including O'Brien's bridge. The bridge—constructed by his father in 1506 to facilitate the movement of goods and supplies across the Shannon—was a symbol of O'Brien strength and its destruction the objective of repeated government expeditions. In the summer of 1538 Lord Leonard Grey, the lord deputy, secured a year-long truce with Conor who subsequently aided the deputy in an invasion of Murrough's country and presided over the bridge's destruction. Conor's independent negotiations with Grey coupled with his belated attempt to divert the succession to his sons with his second wife, Ellice, daughter of Maurice Fitzgerald, ninth earl of Desmond, alienated Murrough and many clansmen. Conor died in 1539 and Murrough succeeded by custom of tanistry.

Grey's aggressive behaviour and his suspected complicity with Conor pushed Murrough O'Brien into confederacy with Con Bacach O'Neill and Manus O'Donnell, whose nominal aim was the restoration of Thomas Fitzgerald, tenth earl of Kildare. O'Brien's entry broadened the Geraldine league's support outside Ulster. This rare mustering of Gaelic strength was a worrying development for the government and demanded immediate action. Grey was consequently summoned to court in April. He was replaced by Sir Anthony St Leger who, shortly after his arrival in July, embarked on a markedly more conciliatory initiative to defuse the confederacy. O'Brien proved receptive and met St Leger at Limerick in early 1541.

St Leger spoke plainly to O'Brien, offering him peace and future stability in exchange for his acknowledgement of Henry VIII's laws and sovereignty. He insisted, moreover, that O'Brien's authority be confined to west of the Shannon and assured him that failure to comply would result in war. The submission of other nobles and chieftains left O'Brien with little choice; he asked for time to consider, however, and retired to Thomond in Munster. In November he wrote directly to Henry professing his loyalty and requested a pardon. He also expressed an interest in personally submitting to the king whom he desired to see 'above all creatures on yerthe lyvinge, now in myne old days; whiche sight I dowbt not but shall prolonge my lyff' (*State Papers, Henry VIII*, 3.345). Yet O'Brien failed to include his decision regarding the limitation of his authority. In February 1542 he attended the lord deputy in Limerick and finally agreed to the limitation of his authority to west of the Shannon. Though St Leger described O'Brien as 'a very sobre man, and very like to contynewe Your Majesties trewe subjecte', he recognized that O'Neill's submission two months earlier had exercised a profound effect upon his decision (ibid., 3.363).

The application for a peerage—the next stage of submission in St Leger's policy of surrender and regrant—presented several problems. O'Brien was married to Eleanor, daughter of Sir Thomas Fitzgerald, knight of Glyn, with whom he had four sons and three daughters. He had succeeded by tanistry and under English law his legitimate male descendants would inherit his peerage. This, however, would deny Donough O'Brien—Conor's eldest son and ally to the crown—any possibility of succession. To avoid a succession dispute upon O'Brien's death St Leger devised a far-sighted solution: O'Brien would be created earl of Thomond and Baron Inchiquin for life with the latter title reverting to his eldest son, Dermod; his nephew Donough would concurrently be created baron of Ibrackan until Murrough's death when he would become earl of Thomond. The king accepted the unorthodox solution but warned that 'the heire of thErle of Thomond, from hensforth, must abide his tyme to be admitted as a member of our Parlyment, till his father or parent shalbe decessed' (*State Papers, Henry VIII*, 3.395). O'Brien, accompanied by Ulick Burke and Donough, repaired to England—their expenses covered by Ir£100 loaned by St Leger—where they were on 1 July 1543 created earl of Thomond, earl of Clanricarde, and Baron Ibrackan respectively. Their acceptance of English titles, however, was not wholly welcomed:

> Banbha's Síol mBriain under Murrough's chieftaincy are covenanted to the King of England; they have turned their backs on their ancestral inheritance—it is a pitiful surrender. (Ó Cuív, 272)

Thomond maintained the peace for the duration of the 1540s, functioning as an extension of the government in Munster, which was seldom touched by the Tudor regime. In the late 1540s he settled disputes among the O'Carrolls and Burkes on behalf of the lord deputy and lent his protection to several towns in Munster. In reward he received all the suppressed religious houses in Thomond, property near Dublin, and, in August 1543, a place on the Irish privy council. He remained a close supporter of St Leger's regime. He died, probably at Inchiquin, some time between 26 June and 28 October 1551.

Despite his compliance with Tudor rule, the annals recorded that Thomond was a brave and wealthy man. His nephew Donough succeeded as earl of Thomond while his son Dermod succeeded as Lord Inchiquin; but despite St Leger's ingenious statecraft the factions arising from Conor O'Brien's two marriages reared their head when in 1553 the second earl died following an attack launched by his stepbrothers. Murrough O'Brien's ostensibly successful transformation from Gaelic chief to English earl was not universally accepted and the next generation inherited the divisive legacy of surrender and regrant.

CHRISTOPHER MAGINN

Sources *State papers published under … Henry VIII*, 11 vols. (1830–52) · *LP Henry VIII* · *AFM* · J. Morrin, ed., *Calendar of the patent and close rolls of chancery in Ireland, of the reigns of Henry VIII, Edward VI, Mary, and Elizabeth*, 1 (1861) · J. S. Brewer and W. Bullen, eds., *Calendar of the Carew manuscripts*, 6 vols., PRO (1867–73) · *The Irish fiants of the Tudor sovereigns*, 4 vols. (1994) · Burke, *Peerage* · B. Ó Cuív, ed., 'A sixteenth century political poem', 15 (1973–4), 261–76 · J. O'Donoghue, *Historical memoirs of the O'Briens with notes, appendix, and a genealogical table of their branches* (1860) · I. O'Brien, *O'Brien of Thomond: the O'Briens in Irish history, 1500–1865* (1986) · *DNB*
Archives U. Oxf., letters patent making Murrough O'Brien first earl of Thomond, MS Talbot b.11/18
Wealth at death see will, 1551, NL Ire., D.7232

O'Brien, Murrough, first earl of Inchiquin (*c*.1614–1674), nobleman and army officer, was the eldest son of Dermod

Murrough O'Brien, first earl of Inchiquin (*c*.1614–1674), by John Michael Wright, *c*.1660–70

O'Brien, fifth Baron Inchiquin (1594–1624), and his wife, Ellen, eldest daughter of Sir Edmond Fitzgerald of Cloyne.

Ancestry, wardship, and marriage Murrough O'Brien's ancestry was distinguished on both sides. The O'Briens claimed descent from the earliest kings of Ireland, and the family name was derived from the eleventh-century king Brian Boru, who died at the battle of Clontarf in 1014. On his mother's side Inchiquin was from Anglo-Norman stock, and was a descendant of the earls of Desmond. The patrimonial estates were concentrated in counties Clare and Limerick—traditional strongholds of the O'Briens of Thomond and the Fitzgeralds of Desmond, respectively—but the accidents of heredity had greatly reduced their value to the young baron. His grandfather Murrough, the fourth baron, had succeeded as a minor, and on his death at Erne in July 1597 (fighting for Elizabeth I) left a two-year-old heir; the fifth baron had died aged thirty, and Murrough came to the title at about the age of ten, in 1624. This succession of minors inevitably created a series of wardships, as well as the removal of jointure lands by surviving dowagers; both helped to weaken the family estate—a situation which afflicted many other Gaelic and Old English families at this time, most notably the earls of Kildare.

Like his contemporary George Fitzgerald, sixteenth earl of Kildare, Inchiquin soon found himself subject to government policies which encouraged the acquisition of Catholic wardships by eminent protestant settlers, who were to bring up the young nobles in the new faith and as loyal vassals of the crown. At first Inchiquin's wardship was held by an Old English protestant, Patrick Fitzmaurice, baron of Kerry and Lixnaw, but in February 1632 Charles I gave the estate to the president of Munster, Sir

William St Leger. As well as continuing his protestant upbringing, St Leger seems to have intended a programme of investment in Inchiquin's estates, reclaiming mortgages and securing titles in much the same way as Richard Boyle, first earl of Cork, tried to strengthen the earls of Kildare and Barrymore in the same period. As with Cork, the keystone of St Leger's plan was the marriage of the native lord with his own daughter, Elizabeth (d. 1685), and the wedding took place in October 1635—nine months before the king gave Inchiquin livery of his lands on 23 June 1636. The birth of a son and heir in winter 1637–8 was important not only to the St Legers but also to the protestant community in Munster. The child, named William after his grandfather, was christened at the St Leger seat of Doneraile in January 1638, and his godparents were Sir William St Leger and the earl of Cork, as well as Cork's daughter, Alice, countess of Barrymore.

A later writer referred to Inchiquin as 'the ingrafted, inoculated and artificial scion taken from that venerable old stock' (*Egmont MSS*, 1.191), and there is no doubt that his relationship with St Leger was very close indeed. It may have been at St Leger's behest that Inchiquin went abroad (presumably in early 1638) to gain military experience with the Spanish forces in Italy. Inchiquin had returned to Ireland by the beginning of 1640, taking his seat in the Irish House of Lords in the parliament which met in March of that year. On 2 April, in a further sign of St Leger's trust, Inchiquin was made vice-president of Munster. This promotion may have contributed to the decline in relations between the president and the earl of Cork, which had started in the late 1630s. Cork was concerned at St Leger's increasing influence in the province, and his suspicions were further aroused by reports that the president 'tides too much with the Irish' (NL Ire., MS 12813/579)—possibly a reference to the growing importance of Inchiquin in the Munster council. This importance, and the tensions which it created, grew markedly with the outbreak of the Irish rising in October 1641.

Munster and the Irish rising to 1644 As president of Munster, St Leger had command of the protestant forces there, but he could do little without the co-operation of the earl of Cork, the wealthiest and most influential landowner in the province. At first the two men agreed to bury their differences, and Inchiquin soon came to the fore as one of the few protestant officers with previous military experience. In April 1642, for example, he led a counter-attack against the Catholic forces under Donough MacCarthy, Viscount Muskerry, who were besieging Cork, forcing them to withdraw from the area. In July 1642 St Leger died after a short illness, but he had already passed orders giving the management of the province to a council of war dominated by his allies, including Inchiquin. With St Leger's death, Inchiquin tried to stage a coup against Cork and his sons, but the ploy was foiled by the lords justices in Dublin, who instead opted to give joint control of civilian affairs to Inchiquin and Cork's son-in-law, David Fitz-David Barry, earl of Barrymore. Inchiquin remained commander of the government forces in Munster. Despite continuing tensions, this arrangement seems to have

worked, and Inchiquin's victory over Richard Butler, Lord Mountgarret, at the battle of Liscarrol in September 1642 was achieved with the full support of the Boyle family. The victory had divisive results, however. Barrymore was mortally wounded, and when he died civilian power became concentrated in Inchiquin's hands. Furthermore, after lobbying by Inchiquin's agents in England, on 29 September parliament promoted Inchiquin to be captain-general of Munster. In response the Boyles went on the offensive, with Cork accusing the vice-president of colluding with the confederate Catholics, insinuating that he was 'unnecessarily cordial to his popish cousins in the Irish camp' (D. Townsend, *The Life and Letters of the Great Earl of Cork*, 1904, 413). In November 1642 Cork's sons Richard and Roger Boyle, Lord Dungarvan and Lord Broghill, were sent to London in an attempt to discredit Inchiquin, and in the hope of having one of the Boyles appointed to the vacant presidency of Munster. Their failure to achieve either goal may have been the result of lobbying by Inchiquin's main ally in parliament, William Jephson, whose own 'cousins' at Westminster included John Pym and Arthur Goodwin.

The factionalism in Munster in 1642–3 was not the only factor weakening the protestant position there. With the onset of the civil war in England, the willingness of the king or parliament to provide men, money, and supplies for Ireland was greatly reduced. As Inchiquin told the earl of Ormond in December 1642, the English were 'so involved in their own danger that a word of Ireland will not be heard' (Bodl. Oxf., MS Carte 4, fol. 83r). In the next nine months the crisis deepened, and Inchiquin, with other commanders, was forced to take Ormond's lead and sign a cessation of arms with the confederates in September 1643. Apart from relieving the immediate pressures of supply, the cessation was designed to release troops to reinforce the king's armies in England, and over the next few months Inchiquin sent five regiments across the Irish Sea. As a result, Inchiquin was indicted in November 1643 for treason by the English parliament. In recompense he hoped that the king would confirm his position in Munster by making him lord president, and in January 1644 he travelled to the royal court at Oxford to claim his reward. Arriving there on 10 February he discovered that the king had already promised the presidency to an outsider: Jerome Weston, second earl of Portland. Worse still, there were rumours that Lord Dungarvan (now second earl of Cork) was negotiating to buy the office from Portland. Although Portland eventually refused to sell the presidency, the damage had been done. As one commentator told Ormond on 19 February, 'Lord Inchiquin is returning as full of anger as his buttons will endure' (Bodl. Oxf., MS Carte 9, fol. 243). In his absence, Inchiquin's reputation at Oxford received another blow, with allegations by the confederate agents (including Viscount Muskerry) that he was already 'rather for the Parliament than the king's cause' (Bodl. Oxf., MS Carte 11, fol. 214). This climate of distrust was exacerbated by local tensions in Munster, where the protestants felt increasingly under pressure from the confederates, who refused to abide by the terms of the cessation of arms. The flashpoint came in July, when news broke of a conspiracy by the Irish to seize Cork and the other protestant towns. Inchiquin responded by expelling all Catholics from the towns, and, fearing reprisals, put his forces on a war footing. With his confidence in the king and his policies already diminished, there seemed only one chance for the Munster protestants; and on 17 July 1644 Inchiquin and his officers wrote to parliament announcing their rejection of the cessation, and their abandonment of the king's cause.

Parliament's lord president of Munster, 1644–1648 If Inchiquin thought the defection to parliament would solve his immediate military problems, he was very much mistaken. With the English civil war still raging, there were few resources available for Munster, and every shipload had to be wrung out of the parliamentarian authorities with intensive lobbying. In one respect Inchiquin got what he wanted from Westminster—in January 1645 he was appointed parliament's lord president of Munster—but even that promotion lacked the royal authority needed to command the loyalty of the province. In the three years after the defection, from summer 1644 until summer 1647, Inchiquin could only play a defensive role in the Irish war; and it was only the incompetence of the confederates which prevented the Munster enclave from being overrun. These local tensions provided the ground base for the factionalism which soon re-emerged among the Munster protestants, and which once again focused on Inchiquin's feud with the Boyle family. The leadership of the Boyle interest in Munster had shifted in 1644, with Roger, Lord Broghill, taking over from his brother, Richard, second earl of Cork, who remained in England. Indeed, Broghill rejected his brother's royalism, and joined Inchiquin's defection to parliament in July 1644. This amity with Inchiquin did not last, however, and by the end of the year serious disagreements had again emerged between the two factions.

The causes of hatred between the two men were various. First, Inchiquin's relations with the Irish and with the royalists at Dublin were far more equivocal than Broghill's. By September 1644 Inchiquin, starved of funds by parliament, had started to explore *ad hoc* cessations with the local confederates, and in the winter made a deal with Viscount Muskerry, which lasted until spring 1645. He was even in contact with James Touchet, third earl of Castlehaven, during the latter's campaign against the Munster protestants in the next few months. Equally, although publicly rejecting the king, Inchiquin continued to correspond with his lord lieutenant, the marquess of Ormond. In June 1645 Inchiquin employed his brother-in-law, Dean Michael Boyle, to travel to Dublin to negotiate with Ormond, and told the bishop of Cloyne that he was willing to contemplate joining a final peace settlement between the royalists and the confederates. Broghill, who trusted that parliament could be persuaded to fund the Irish war, rejected any peace initiatives with the confederates, and condemned Ormond for his dealings with them. The seizure of letters in July 1645, revealing royalist hopes

that Inchiquin could be persuaded to rejoin the king, hardened Broghill's hostility towards the president.

The second cause of disagreement between the two was religion. While Broghill and his friends were convinced of the need for the solemn league and covenant to be taken by the Munster soldiers, Inchiquin was less enthusiastic, not least because the royalists treated subscription to it as proof of disloyalty. In a list of Irish protestants who had taken the covenant (drawn up in April 1645) Inchiquin is conspicuous by his absence (Bodl. Oxf., MS Carte 14, fol. 425). While Broghill was becoming increasingly hardline in his attitudes, Inchiquin remained attached to the Church of Ireland. He protected the clergy within the Munster garrisons, and protested to Cloyne in 1645 that his attachment to parliament was merely pragmatic:

> I do profess that I do earnestly desire the continuance of the same government in the church that we have hitherto had, yet I doubt there is no possibility to enjoy the liberty of our religion of this kingdom, but by adhering to those who as yet pretend to pull down episcopacy, which in that cause I could much rather tolerate. (Bodl. Oxf., MS Carte 63, fol. 341*v*)

A third cause of tension between Inchiquin and Broghill was the increasing convergence of Irish and English politics. The emergence in England of two 'parties' during 1644 and 1645—known as the 'presbyterians' and 'Independents'—encouraged the existing factions within the Irish protestant community to align themselves with one side or the other. Inchiquin, in part reacting to Broghill's connections with the Independents, grew closer to the presbyterians. Inchiquin's friends at Westminster included Irish presbyterians such as William Jephson, Sir Robert King, and Sir Philip Perceval; and he, with Ormond, became a key player in attempts by the English presbyterian leadership to promote a 'British' solution to Ireland, involving Irish royalists and the Ulster Scots as well as English troops loyal to parliament. The appointment of a Star Chamber committee of Irish affairs in July 1645, created and dominated by William Jephson, Sir John Clotworthy, and their allies, at last promised to take Munster seriously, and through the winter there were efforts to raise men and send money to Inchiquin's beleaguered garrisons. Yet the presbyterian ascendancy was short-lived, and the Independents soon came to control Irish affairs. The appointment of the Independent peer Philip Sidney, Viscount Lisle, as parliament's lord lieutenant in April 1646 widened the rift between Inchiquin and Broghill. Lisle challenged Ormond's authority, and his policies were from the start hostile to Inchiquin. The new Irish committee soon fell into Independent hands; plans were advanced to give Broghill an independent command in Munster; and a concerted propaganda campaign undermined the president's authority and questioned his allegiance. Inchiquin went to London to defend his position, but to no avail. In February 1647 Lisle crossed to Munster and took control of the province from his deputy, in a move condemned by Inchiquin as having 'the semblance rather of a conquest than of relief' (*Egmont MSS*, 1.367–8). In matters of policy Lisle deferred to Broghill, who, as Inchiquin bemoaned, was now 'commanding all things at his pleasure, so as my lord lieutenant puts the execution of my place in effect into his hands' (*Egmont MSS*, 1.380). Inchiquin's officers were replaced, his troops dispersed, and his advice ignored. It was only as a result of factional changes in England, and the seizure of power by the presbyterians in the new year of 1647, that Inchiquin's position began to improve. Lisle's year-long commission was not renewed and in April, Inchiquin, assisted by soldiers still loyal to him, forced the former lieutenant and his entourage to return to England.

The departure of Lisle left Inchiquin in charge of Munster, but it did not bring his troubles to an end. Broghill, assisted by his brother-in-law Sir Arthur Loftus, with the encouragement of Sir John Temple and other Irish Independents, spent much of the summer trying to blacken Inchiquin's name. A mark of their success was Inchiquin's inclusion in the articles presented against the eleven members in June, saying that the presbyterians had deliberately suppressed charges of high treason against the president. Inchiquin was accused of harbouring papists, of allowing mass to be said publicly, and of plotting to join the confederates. He was also attacked for his ethnic background. Ignoring his claims that his Irishness was 'my misfortune, not my fault' (*Egmont MSS*, 1.377), his enemies repeatedly linked ethnicity with disloyalty, characterizing Inchiquin as 'an Irish general' and one of the 'natural Irish', and thus not to be trusted ('A letter from Lieutenant Colonel Knight in the province of Munster', 22 July 1647, BL, E.399(23), pp. 4, 12).

Inchiquin's position in summer 1647 was further undermined by the departure of Ormond, who had surrendered Dublin to parliament under articles signed in June, and left Ireland in July; and by the dramatic failure of the presbyterians to stage a coup at Westminster—an attempt which, in early August, brought the Independents back to power in the wake of the New Model Army's march on London. Irish affairs at Westminster were again under the control of Broghill and his Independent friends, and the prospects for Inchiquin looked bleak. His response was to go on the offensive. If he could not defeat his critics in London he could strengthen his position in Munster, and this he proceeded to do, launching a major campaign into counties Waterford and Tipperary. During summer 1647 he had captured Dungarvan and Cappoquin, and by September was marching north-east, probably intending a strike against the confederate capital at Kilkenny. Lack of artillery meant that the advance came to a halt before Clonmel by the end of the month, but *en route* Inchiquin had taken the Rock of Cashel, where his troops massacred the defenders and desecrated the cathedral. In this bold campaign Inchiquin seems to have had two intentions: to create *Lebensraum* for his soldiers, securing control over a wider area in an effort to make them independent of outside resources; and to demonstrate to parliament and to the Irish protestants that he was still committed to their cause. For the Irish, however, his main intention seemed to be to shed blood and commit sacrilege. In the eyes of the ordinary people he became infamous as Murchadh na dTóiteán, or Murrough of the Burnings; and to the clergy

he was 'the most hateful enemy of the Catholic religion' (Murphy, 'Inchiquin's changes of religion', 62). Alarmed by Inchiquin's victories, the confederate council ordered their Munster commander, Theobald Taaffe, Viscount Taaffe, to advance on the Munster ports. Inchiquin met him at Knocknanuss, near Mallow in co. Cork, on 13 November. With a smaller force he attacked the confederate army and routed it, killing 4000 men.

Despite Inchiquin's military successes, he was increasingly marginalized by the English parliamentarians during winter 1647–8. This was caused by a general lack of interest in Irish affairs at Westminster once Dublin had been secured in July 1647, compounded by the influence over the dominant Independent faction enjoyed by Inchiquin's enemies, including Lord Broghill. The immediate effect was a reduction in the amount of money and supplies allowed to the president. In January 1648 Inchiquin complained to Speaker Lenthall that he could not control enough territory to feed his existing forces, and asked for support from England or, failing that, permission to send some of his English troops home and to make conditions with the confederates 'for the rest of the wretched English who cannot remove hence with their families, but must submit to a worse than Egyptian or Turkish servitude' (*Portland MSS*, 1.443–4). Such appeals grew stronger over the next few months—as did Inchiquin's alarm at events in England, where the Independents and the army seemed intent on forcing radical changes to the government and religion. These two factors pushed Inchiquin into signing a truce with the confederate forces in Munster, agreed in April and ratified in May 1648.

Royalist general, 1648–1650 In signing the truce Inchiquin had rejected parliament and returned to his allegiance to the king; yet in doing so his focus was not on high politics, but on the practicalities of keeping his army together. His first move was to purge the officer corps. This was designed to bring the Munster army firmly under his control, and thus emphasize its importance as the most experienced—and most successful—protestant army in Ireland. The purge also gave him high-profile hostages, including Sir William Fenton, Colonel Edmund Temple, and Lieutenant-Colonel Robert Phayre, who could be used as a possible bargaining tool with parliament—a point made all the more important by the presence of Inchiquin's own son and heir, William *O'Brien, Lord O'Brien, in prison in London. Beyond this it is uncertain how far Inchiquin planned to go. Although there were fears that he planned an amphibious assault on Cornwall in support of the English insurgents, and rumours that he was in league with the confederates and the Scots, there is little evidence that Inchiquin could afford the luxury of thinking in 'British' terms in the summer of 1648. At this stage the most pressing need was to secure his truce with the confederates and to gain much-needed supplies for his men, many of whom 'have died of hunger, after they had a while lived upon cats and dogs as many do now' (*Ormonde MSS*, 6.550).

While Inchiquin was concentrating on his immediate

problems in Munster, his truce was having dramatic consequences at Kilkenny. The agreement, ratified by the supreme council on 20 May 1648, finally destroyed the uneasy relationship between the papal nuncio, Cardinal Rinuccini, and the Old English. A week later, the nuncio declared his opposition to the cessation and threatened to excommunicate anyone subscribing to it. With that, he fled to the Ulster forces of Owen Roe O'Neill, currently occupying western Leinster. The split ensured that any future peace treaty would not involve a large part of the Catholic forces in Ireland, and would thereby prevent an army being sent to aid Charles I in the other kingdoms. Inchiquin, from a purely local standpoint, greeted the breakdown of the confederate alliance not as a disaster, but as an opportunity. On 15 July he wrote to the parliamentarian commander Michael Jones at Dublin, urging him to make his own truce, and to join the king. In turn Jones invited Inchiquin to return to parliament. Inchiquin soon recovered from the rebuff. Armed with a new commission as lord president of Munster (sent from the prince of Wales on 2 July), he prepared for a new royalist offensive, and urged Ormond to return from the continent. Ormond's arrival at Cork, on 2 October, provided Inchiquin with much-needed supplies, and allowed a combined campaign with the Catholic forces under Ulick de Burgh, earl of Clanricarde, against O'Neill's men in Leinster.

But Inchiquin's renewed optimism was soon dented by news of a mutiny within the Munster garrisons. This was not so much a protest about pay and conditions as a reflection of deep-seated concerns among the officers that Inchiquin was to strike a deal with the Catholics which would threaten their religion. The leaders of the mutiny soon made contact with Jones and even O'Neill, and parliament sent agents to try to stir up discontent, including Inchiquin's former hostage Edmund Temple. The mutiny was put down with little trouble, but its effects were important. First, it cast doubt on Inchiquin's value as an ally to the confederates, and, according to Ormond, set back the peace negotiations by a precious few weeks. It also reduced the ability of the royalists to plan a concerted campaign across the three kingdoms, despite Inchiquin's hope that the presbyterians in England might be persuaded to rebel once more. Worse still, Ormond was forced to ask the prince of Wales to withdraw his fleet to the Munster coast, to prevent further trouble. The level of discontent is revealed by Inchiquin's insistence that the Church of Ireland clergy sign a declaration of loyalty (on 5 January 1649), and promise not to preach against the royalist cause. Inchiquin remained nervous even after the execution of the king, which had forced agreement in Ireland (under the second Ormond peace) and demanded a vigorous response. In February 1649 he feared the growing tensions between protestants and Catholics in Munster and was advised by the confederates once again to purge his army. There were also concerns about the level of supplies allowed to Inchiquin's men, and in March 1649—nearly a year after his defection to the king—the

president was still complaining of the sufferings of his men, and the urgency of relief.

Inchiquin still enjoyed great authority over his army, but only when he commanded in person. The joint offensive of March 1649, which saw Inchiquin in league with Clanricarde, Taaffe, and Castlehaven in a successful bid to push O'Neill out of Leinster, was followed by a drive through the midlands, capturing Queen's county on 16 May, and forcing the garrisons at Trim and Dundalk to capitulate. On 4 July, Inchiquin captured Drogheda by siege and, leaving a force to garrison the town, his army rejoined Ormond, encamped before Dublin. Victory seemed assured as long as Inchiquin was present, and his field army lived up to expectations. But the new campaign had taken Inchiquin away from the Munster garrisons for five months, and there were fears of a new mutiny, compounded by rumours that Oliver Cromwell intended to target Munster first. On 27 July, Inchiquin was ordered to take two cavalry regiments south, and when Michael Jones confronted Ormond at Rathmines on 2 August, the lord lieutenant lacked his ablest commander. Inchiquin's men fought well during the battle, but in the aftermath of defeat they deserted to parliament in droves. Inchiquin, now at Cork, managed to hold his garrisons for a few months more, but with the English army's advance south he began to lose control. Cromwellian agents had been in Munster since the summer, and on 16 October, Inchiquin had imprisoned Colonel Richard Townsend, Colonel William Warden, and Colonel John Giffard, fearing that they were in contact with Lord Broghill and other enemies with local influence. On 26 October there were reports that Inchiquin had been barred by his own troops from entering Cork, Youghal, Dungarvan, and Bandon. By 14 November the towns had agreed articles with Cromwell, and received English garrisons, rejoicing at 'the happy uniting of all of us, with those of your army; which God hath been pleased in a wonderful manner to bring to pass' (BL, Add. MS 25287, fol. 41). The agreement allowed for two foot regiments and a double regiment of horse to be raised from the Munster forces to fight alongside Cromwell's troops. Inchiquin's enemy Lord Broghill, who had joined Cromwell just before the invasion, persuaded Bandon and Kinsale to reject Inchiquin and, as a sign of his victory, requisitioned the president's house in Cork for use as his private residence.

With the surrender of the Munster ports, Inchiquin was left with little territory and few troops. In the new year of 1650 he gathered the remnants of his army—perhaps 2000 men—at Kilmallock in co. Limerick, and began raiding the English quarters in co. Cork. When Cromwell marched north against the confederate armies he had to leave Broghill with a strong force to keep Inchiquin in check. In March 1650 Inchiquin was caught near Mallow by cavalry under Broghill and Henry Cromwell, and routed. It was perhaps appropriate that the final annihilation of Inchiquin's army should be at the hands of his old adversary—and so close to the site of his own great victory at Knocknanuss. After the battle at Mallow, Inchiquin retreated into Connaught, eventually joining Ormond.

Without an army, the two were at a disadvantage when negotiating with the increasingly hostile Catholic commanders, who offended Inchiquin in August by accusing him of betraying Munster to Cromwell. The refusal to give Inchiquin another command, and the appointment of Emer MacMahon, Catholic bishop of Clogher, as O'Neill's successor in the north, were further signs that there was little room for protestant royalists in Ireland. In a bid to create still more division within the royalist camp, Cromwell offered safe-conduct passes to both Ormond and Inchiquin, but they were refused, and Inchiquin followed the lord lieutenant into exile in France in December 1650.

Exile, conversion, and captivity, 1651–1663 During the 1650s Inchiquin remained on the continent, in an exile which was only in part self-imposed. Unlike many other former Irish royalists (notably the second earl of Cork, who returned to Munster in 1651), Inchiquin had been condemned as a traitor by parliament in April 1649 and excepted from pardon in August 1652, and there was no prospect of regaining his estates or retaining his position as president of Munster. Not that life in France was entirely comfortable: immediately on his arrival Inchiquin was faced with accusations, levelled by Sir Lewis Dyve, that he had acted dishonourably in Munster. These had been quashed as early as in May 1651, but it was not until April 1652—and then only with Ormond's intervention—that Inchiquin received letters from the king attesting to his loyalty. In the meantime Inchiquin spent most of his time at Caen, where other protestants, including Ormond, had settled. It was probably Ormond's influence which secured Inchiquin a place on the king's council in May 1652, and his ally, Sir Edward Hyde, considered Inchiquin as 'a gallant gentleman, of good parts and great industry, and a temper fit to struggle with the affairs on all sides we are to contend with'. The appointment was against the wishes of the Catholics at court, mindful of Inchiquin's part in the sack of Cashel and other atrocities, and as Hyde added, 'I believe neither the queen, Lord Jermyn nor Lord Wilmot are much pleased with it' (*Clarendon State Papers*, 3.67). The Irish exiles, and especially the priests, also opposed Inchiquin, using their influence to block his appointment to a senior military command in France in 1653, on the ground that he was 'a murderer of priests, friars and such like' (Thurloe, 1.562). Inchiquin was given command of one or two French regiments at this time, but Mazarin had to wait before offering him a more important post. Despite Catholic hostility, Inchiquin attended the royal council in 1653–4, and, after a warrant signed by the king on 4 May 1654, on 21 October he was created Baron O'Brien of Burren and earl of Inchiquin.

The grant of an earldom was the high point of Inchiquin's favour at the hands of Charles II. From 1654 onwards, however, he became increasingly distanced from those with influence around the king. There were two reasons for this. First, in autumn 1654 Inchiquin returned to a military career, serving in Catalonia as governor of the areas controlled by France, and encouraging

Irish soldiers to defect from the Spanish to the French service. His duties took him away from Paris for long periods (1654–5, 1656–7, and 1657–8), and may have allowed his enemies to slander him unchecked. The second reason for Inchiquin's loss of influence at court was confessional. On his return to Paris in summer 1657, Inchiquin declared his conversion to the Church of Rome. The trigger for this may have been a period of acute illness, and his decision came as a complete surprise, not least to his wife, who was a convinced protestant. There followed a period of deep tension within the family. The English ambassador, William Lockhart, writing in July 1657, said the countess and her son Lord O'Brien 'have been so persecuted by her husband and the Roman Catholics' (Thurloe, 6.385) that he felt obliged to offer her a pass to travel to England. This is substantiated by Sir Edward Nicholas, who commented: 'I am very sorry for the Earl of Inchiquin's care to make his sons as himself papists, but it is no marvel to hear that a zealous presbyter proves a bigot in popery' (letter of 19/29 June 1657, BL, Sir Richard Browne papers, uncatalogued). There followed a period of high drama, when Inchiquin, with the queen mother's support, abducted his younger son, Charles O'Brien, from Lockhart's house, where he had taken refuge. By December the French court had forced him to return the boy and threatened to banish the father from the realm. Soon afterwards the countess fled to England with her children, and for a brief period Lord O'Brien even returned to Ireland, before rejoining his father on the continent at the end of the year. Although Lord O'Brien remained a protestant, Charles and the youngest son, John, had reportedly 'turned Catholic' by 1659 (*Egmont MSS*, 1.603). Inchiquin's conversion not only alienated his wife, it also lost him the support of men like Ormond and Hyde, who remained attached to the established church. By September 1658 Inchiquin complained that Ormond was treating him with 'contempt' and 'distrust' (*Clarendon State Papers*, 3.414). In consolation, his conversion had made him more acceptable to the Catholics around the queen mother, but their influence was at a low ebb. From 1658, therefore, Inchiquin found himself increasingly isolated at court, and his hopes of being included in royalist plans to invade England had little chance of being realized. In 1659 Inchiquin corresponded with the countess of Dysart and other royalists in England, with Hyde in Holland, and with James, duke of York, but his letters show that he was no longer included in the innermost counsels of the exiled king.

Frustrated by his lack of progress at court, Inchiquin during 1659 again looked for military employment in foreign service. The peace negotiations between France and Spain effectively removed him from the governorship of the disputed province of Catalonia, and he was forced to look further afield. By July 1659 he had been offered command of a Portuguese army, and in September he decided to accept, although he promised to return if the king needed his help in an invasion of England. Arriving at La Rochelle at the end of October, he took ship for Portugal but was captured by an Algerian corsair off the Spanish coast after a battle in which Lord O'Brien lost an eye. Inchiquin remained in prison during the Restoration, and was released only with the intervention of Charles II's council in summer 1660. His son remained in Algiers until November, when the king finally agreed to pay the ransom. The whole episode seems to have confirmed Inchiquin in his devotion to Catholicism, and gave him further cause to atone for his past sins. During his captivity he wrote to two priests, confessing to one that 'no punishment is severe enough for such a persecutor of the church as I have been' (Murphy, 'Inchiquin's changes of religion', 63). After the Restoration, Inchiquin was firm in his new faith, and was not tempted to reconvert to the established church, although he still had hopes of political preferment. Instead, he became high steward in the household of the queen mother, and used his influence to curry favour with the king, who agreed to restore him to his estates in Ireland, and compensated him for his military arrears before 1649 and for his sufferings since then. In 1662–3 Inchiquin accepted a position as commander of English troops sent to Portugal. This second Portuguese expedition was nearly as disastrous as the first. The Portuguese accused him of treachery (by agreeing to defect, with his troops, to Spanish service) and his brother, Christopher O'Brien, was imprisoned. Inchiquin protested that, although the Spaniards had approached him, he had refused to treat with them, and had advised the English government to withdraw altogether. By May 1663, with Inchiquin back in Limerick, Charles II relieved him of the command, leaving the earl to petition Secretary Bennet for yet another letter from the king stating his confidence in him. This may have been the last straw for Charles II. In later years Inchiquin continued to receive royal favour, but he was never again employed in an official capacity.

Last years: Munster, 1663–1674 From 1663 Inchiquin lived in Munster in a state of semi-retirement, rebuilding his estates in counties Clare and Limerick, and preferring as a residence Rostellan Castle near Cork city. He remained an important member of the Catholic community in Munster, and signed the remonstrance to the king from the Irish Catholic nobles and gentry protesting their loyalty in 1666. In his will, written in 1673, he left money for the friars at Ennis, co. Clare, presumably for masses to be said for his soul. Yet during the last years of his life Inchiquin made every effort to reintegrate himself and his family into the old protestant community he had rejected so dramatically at his conversion a few years before. Central to this was his successful attempt to make friends with his former enemy, Lord Broghill, now earl of Orrery. Orrery, who had finally achieved the presidency of Munster (for which Inchiquin, as a Catholic, was disqualified) in 1660, was now the most powerful man in the province, and, despite their earlier enmity, in 1665 a match was arranged between his daughter, Margaret Boyle, and Inchiquin's heir, William, Lord O'Brien. The initiative seems to have come from Inchiquin, but Orrery saw the merit of the plan. Like St Leger thirty years earlier, Orrery recognized the significance of the ancient O'Brien clan, and valued their influence over the native Irish in the region. He also

had no objection to Lord O'Brien, who remained a protestant despite his father's conversion, and he may have shared the proselytizing ambitions of his father, the first earl of Cork. The late 1660s and early 1670s thus saw the Boyles and the O'Briens again working together, but this time without the underlying rivalry, ethnic tension, and religious animosity which had done so much to hamper the protestant cause in the 1640s. In 1667 Orrery used his position to restore Inchiquin to possession of Rostellan, which had been seized by those who claimed a legal right themselves. In 1669, when Orrery was faced with impeachment proceedings in England, this incident was used against him; but in his defence he was able not only to defend his own actions, but also Inchiquin's honour. In 1672, when he got wind of a presbyterian plot against the Irish government, Inchiquin sent his servant 50 miles to where Orrery was staying, to warn him of it. In 1679, just before his death, Orrery further cemented relations between the two houses with the marriage of his younger son, Henry, with Inchiquin's youngest daughter, Mary O'Brien.

This amicable relationship with Orrery was not matched by a reconciliation between Inchiquin and his wife, who remained bitterly opposed to his Catholicism. A measure of their unhappiness can be seen in their choice of burial places. Inchiquin, who died on 9 September 1674, had asked to be buried in Limerick Cathedral, probably intending to join his ancestors in the O'Brien tomb there; his countess chose to be buried with the St Legers, in the church which her father had built at Doneraile. Their separation in death is poignant testimony to the failure of this particular attempt to mix Catholic oil with protestant water. It also highlights the personal, political, and confessional tensions which dogged Inchiquin throughout his eventful life.

PATRICK LITTLE

Sources P. Little, 'The political career of Roger Boyle, Lord Broghill, 1636-60', PhD diss., U. Lond., 2000 · J. A. Murphy, 'The expulsion of the Irish from Cork in 1644', *Journal of the Cork Historical and Archaeological Society*, 69 (1964), 123-31 · J. A. Murphy, 'Inchiquin's changes of religion', *Journal of the Cork Historical and Archaeological Society*, 72 (1967) · J. A. Murphy, 'The sack of Cashel, 1647', *Journal of the Cork Historical and Archaeological Society*, 70 (1965), 55-62 · J. Ainsworth, *The Inchiquin manuscripts*, Irish Manuscripts Commission (1961) · *Report on the manuscripts of the earl of Egmont*, 2 vols. in 3, HMC, 63 (1905-9) · *Calendar of the manuscripts of the marquess of Ormonde*, new ser., 8 vols., HMC, 36 (1902-20) · *The manuscripts of the marquis of Ormonde*, [old ser.], 3 vols., HMC, 36 (1895-1909) · *The manuscripts of his grace the duke of Portland*, 10 vols., HMC, 29 (1891-1931) · *CSP Ire.*, 1633-70 · *CSP dom.*, 1644-75 · Chatsworth House, Derbyshire, Lismore MSS, 17-30 · *Clarendon state papers*, 3 vols. (1757) · Thurloe, *State papers* · BL, Egmont MSS, esp. Add. MSS 46929-46931 · BL, Browne papers [uncatalogued] · Bodl. Oxf., MSS Carte 3-30, 67 · Bodl. Oxf., Clarendon MSS · *Calendar of the Clarendon state papers preserved in the Bodleian Library*, ed. O. Ogle and others, 5 vols. (1869-1970) · J. Lodge, *The peerage of Ireland*, rev. M. Archdall, rev. edn, 7 vols. (1789) · GEC, *Peerage* · F. P. Verney and N. M. Verney, *Memoirs of the Verney family during the seventeenth century*, 2 vols. (1907) · A. B. Grosart, ed., *Lismore papers*, 10 vols., 2 series (1886-8) · J. S. Wheeler, *Cromwell in Ireland* (1999)

Archives BL, corresp. and papers, Add. MSS 46924-46948 · Dromoland Castle, co. Clare, MSS · NL Ire., corresp. | Bodl. Oxf., Carte MSS · Bodl. Oxf., Clarendon MSS · Chatsworth House, Derbyshire, letters to Boyle family

Likenesses J. M. Wright, oils, c.1660–1670, Man. City Gall. [*see illus.*] · A. Simon, gold and silver medal, BM

O'Brien, Murtagh. *See* Ua Briain, Muirchertach (c.1050–1119).

O'Brien, Patrick. *See* Cotter, Patrick (1760/61–1806).

O'Brien, Paul (1762/3–1820), Irish-language scholar and teacher, was born in the district of Breakey in co. Meath, near its border with co. Cavan; the names of his father and mother have not been preserved. In the late eighteenth century this district was a stronghold of Irish language and culture, with a number of poets—Paul O'Brien's great-grandmother had been a sister of the greatest of them, Turlough *Carolan (1670–1738)—and a strong scribal tradition. It was therefore very natural that he should develop an interest in the Celtic languages and cultures. Precise dates are lacking, but it appears that, after being educated at local classical schools, in the early 1780s he travelled in Gaelic-speaking Scotland and to the Isle of Man. After his return to Ireland he went to Paris to study for the priesthood, presumably in the Irish College there. This must have been about 1790, for it is recorded that he had to flee home after a very short stay, as almost all the Irish seminaries were closed by the French Revolution at the end of 1792 and the beginning of 1793.

In Ireland, St Patrick's College, Maynooth, opened as a Roman Catholic seminary in 1795, but for many years it was quite unable to provide as many places as had been lost in Europe, much less absorb those individuals who had been displaced. The college authorities naturally preferred younger students, and O'Brien, already mature in years, had to wait until 1801 before being accepted. Shortly afterwards, however, he began to be noted as a person who could impart a practical knowledge of the Irish language to those students for whom it was necessary in their ministry. In 1804 he was ordained priest and appointed professor of Irish. What was expected from his course was modest; his greatest problem was the scarcity of printed books, for the native tradition of Irish learning was still of necessity a manuscript one. He had to rely on two works printed in Paris, Hugh McCurtin's *English–Irish Dictionary and Grammar* (1732) and Andrew Donlevy's bilingual *Catechism* (1742). Copies of these were scarce, and this prompted him to write his own *Practical Grammar of the Irish Language*. This was delivered in 1806 to Hugh Fitzpatrick, who was already styling himself 'publisher to the Roman Catholic College of Maynooth'. It had to wait for three years, appearing only in 1809, because Fitzpatrick was busy printing theological works for the college. The aim of the grammar, O'Brien himself said, was entirely practical, to help his students. It was heavily censured by John O'Donovan in the lengthy introduction to his own *Grammar*, published in 1845, as the worst he had met. This judgement is over-severe, but his comments on O'Brien's poetry as 'jungling rhyme' are well directed, though by this time traditional Irish poetry had in general degenerated.

In the early nineteenth century efforts were made to modernize Irish literary culture specifically through printed editions of texts. O'Brien was active in a number of societies with this aim—the short-lived Gaelic Society (1807) and Iberno-Celtic Society (1818), and the still-thriving Royal Irish Academy (1785). He did not live to complete a projected dictionary, dying at the college on 13 April 1820 at the age of fifty-seven. He was buried in the college cemetery. Regrettably, his books and manuscripts were auctioned and dispersed. He left fleeting but real impressions of a lively personality and a gifted teacher. In 1822, two years after his death, one of his pupils, John McEncroe, published a substantial reworking of Donlevy's *Catechism*, and another, Donal O'Sullivan, a translation of the *Imitation of Christ*. It was to be near the end of the century before Maynooth got another professor of Irish as capable as Paul O'Brien.   PATRICK J. CORISH

Sources names of the collegians of the Royal College of St Patrick, St Patrick's College, Maynooth, B4/10/2, liber matriculationum, 1 · St Patrick's College, Maynooth, Conwell letters · Down and Connor diocesan archives, Belfast, McMullan letters · 'Papers relating to the Royal College of St Patrick, Maynooth', *Parl. papers* (1808), 9.371, no. 152 · 'Commissioners of Irish education inquiry: eighth report', *Parl. papers* (1826–7), 8.378, no. 509 · *Transactions of the Gaelic Society of Ireland*, 1 (1808) · 'A biographical sketch of the Rev. Paul O'Brian, professor of the Irish language at Maynooth', *Irish Magazine* (Jan 1810), 30–32 · J. Warburton, J. Whitelaw, and R. Walsh, *History of the city of Dublin*, 2 vols. (1818), 929, 933 · E. O'Reilly, *A chronological account of … four hundred Irish writers … down to … 1750, with a descriptive catalogue of … their works* (1820) · C. Anderson, *Historical sketches of the native Irish and their descendants*, 2nd edn (1830) · J. O'Donovan, *A grammar of the Irish language* (1845), lxi–lxii · P. Mulvaney, 'Some notices of the baronies of Kells', *Ríocht na Midhe*, 4/75, 20–22 · P. J. Corish, *Maynooth College, 1795–1995* (1995), esp. 75, 474–5 · *DNB* · tombstone, St Patrick's College, Maynooth, cemetery

Archives Down and Connor diocesan archives, Belfast, McMullan letters · St Patrick's College, Maynooth, Conwell letters

Likenesses portrait, c.1860, St Patrick's College, Maynooth

O'Brien, Peter, Baron O'Brien (1842–1914), judge, was born on 29 June 1842 at Carnelly House, Ballynalacken, co. Clare, the fifth son of John O'Brien JP (1794–1855), of Ballynalacken, MP for Limerick from 1841 to 1852, and his wife, Ellen (d. 1866), daughter of Jeremiah Murphy, of Hyde Park, co. Cork. Brought up a Catholic and educated at Clongowes Wood School, he entered Trinity College, Dublin, on 5 November 1858; he graduated BA in 1865 and MA in 1874. He entered the Middle Temple in London on 9 June 1862 and was called to the Irish bar at King's Inns, Dublin, in 1865. He devilled for Christopher Palles (later chief baron) and acted as registrar for his uncle, Mr Justice James O'Brien. He failed to be elected as a whig for County Clare in 1879 and became queen's counsel in 1880. On 8 August 1867 he married Annie Clarke, daughter of Robert Hare Clarke JP, of Bansha, co. Tipperary, and they had two daughters and one son.

Ireland was in a state of political upheaval after the failure of home rule, and O'Brien took silk at a time when judges were under police protection, prosecutors ran the risk of intimidation, the country was subject to insurrection and violence, and the Land League conspiracy was at its height. Retained by the crown in all important cases, O'Brien was rapidly promoted to the position of serjeant

(1884), solicitor-general (1887), and attorney-general (1888). His attorney-generalship was notable for his administration of Arthur Balfour's Crimes Act, passed in an attempt to restore national order. O'Brien was aided by Edward Carson and Stephen Ronan in his efforts. Where possible, every prosecution was apparently tested microscopically on appeal. Public order was eventually restored and in 1889 O'Brien was appointed lord chief justice. He remained in the post for twenty-four years, enjoying a reputation for an urbane sense of humour. He won the confidence of juries by his rectitude and leniency. He was popular with the bar and the public alike. He was also hospitable, often entertaining at his residence in Donnybrook, co. Dublin, and hunting with friends and colleagues.

O'Brien retired in 1913, having been created a baronet on 28 September 1891; he was raised to the peerage as Baron O'Brien of Kilfenora on 16 June 1900. He lived at 41 Merrion Square East, Dublin, and at Airfield, Donnybrook, co. Dublin, where he died on 7 September 1914, survived by his wife; their son had died young, and so the peerage became extinct with his death. A Roman Catholic, he was known to most not as Lord O'Brien but informally, as Peter. SINÉAD AGNEW

Sources L. G. Pine, *The new extinct peerage, 1884–1971: containing extinct, abeyant, dormant, and suspended peerages with genealogies and arms* (1972), 209 · J. S. Crone, *A concise dictionary of Irish biography*, rev. edn (1937), 175 · F. E. Ball, *The judges in Ireland, 1221–1921*, 2 (1926), 317, 320, 328, 378 · Burtchaell & Sadleir, *Alum. Dubl.* · P. O'Brien, *The reminiscences of the Right Hon. Lord O'Brien* (1916), 1, 5, 16, 171–2 · A. T. C. Pratt, ed., *People of the period: being a collection of the biographies of upwards of six thousand living celebrities*, 2 (1897), 224 · *Men and women of the time* (1899), 811 · F. C. Burnard, ed., *The Catholic who's who and yearbook* (1920), 252 · H. A. C. Sturgess, ed., *Register of admissions to the Honourable Society of the Middle Temple, from the fifteenth century to the year 1944*, 2 (1949), 535
Likenesses photograph (after portrait), repro. in O'Brien, *Reminiscences*, flyleaf
Wealth at death £5134 10s. 0d.: Irish probate sealed in England, 15 Oct 1914, CGPLA Eng. & Wales · £29,231 3s. 1d.: probate, 30 Sept 1914, CGPLA Ire.

O'Brien, Richard Barry (1847–1918), Irish nationalist, journalist, and author, was born in Kilrush, co. Clare, Ireland, on 7 March 1847, the youngest child of Patrick Barry O'Brien. As a boy he witnessed a local priest saying mass on the seashore from a home-made mobile church below the high-water mark as a landlord had refused to provide a site for the purpose. He went to St Laurence O'Toole's Preparatory School, Dublin, at the age of sixteen, and subsequently entered the Catholic University, Dublin. He sided with those students who sympathized with physical-force nationalism (as distinct from those who supported the constitutionalism of Alexander Martin Sullivan) and took part in pro-Fenian demonstrations, though he does not appear to have joined the Irish Republican Brotherhood. Later he developed more moderate views as a result of reading John Bright's speeches on Irish questions, which made him realize that there were Englishmen who wished to do justice to Ireland. O'Brien always admired Bright, despite that statesman's opposition to home rule, and published a biography of him in 1910 which describes their occasional contacts.

In 1869 O'Brien went to London to study for the English bar. He was present all day in the gallery of the House of Commons in 1869 at the conclusion of the debate on Gladstone's legislation for the disestablishment of the Church of Ireland, and was nearly expelled for cheering. He was called to the Irish bar in 1874 and the English bar in 1875, but never built up an extensive practice; he was primarily a journalist. He joined the Home Government Association in 1871, and was employed as political secretary by the prominent lawyer Patrick MacMahon (MP for New Ross until his death in 1879). His work for MacMahon introduced him to high-level political and legal circles. It was at this time that he made the acquaintance of the future lord chief justice, Lord Russell of Killowen. Their long friendship and political association led to O'Brien's choice as Russell's official biographer. *Lord Russell of Killowen* (1901), based on extensive conversations with its subject, remains the principal source for the judge's life. In 1877 O'Brien married Kathleen Mary Teevan, whose father was a doctor in West Kensington. They had five sons and two daughters.

O'Brien first came to prominence with the publication of *The Irish Land Question and English Public Opinion* (1879), a history of nineteenth-century parliamentary debate on the matter which challenged the view that the question had been settled by the 1870 Land Act. The book attracted considerable attention, since it coincided with the appearance of the Land League in Ireland. In 1880 O'Brien produced a fuller treatment of the subject, *A Parliamentary History of the Irish Land Question*, which was welcomed by Gladstone and Bright as a contribution to the debate surrounding proposals for new land legislation. Over the next decade he produced several other books compiled from parliamentary papers and other official sources on British handling of Irish problems under the Union, notably *Fifty Years of Concessions to Ireland, 1831–1881* (2 vols., 1881–3) and *Irish Wrongs and English Remedies* (1885). These books were presented as reference works and written in a dry, impersonal tone eschewing the emotionalism of much nationalist literature. They aimed at distilling from official sources a history of Irish Catholic and nationalist grievances on such matters as education and land in order to convince British readers that the Union parliament had shown itself incapable of governing Ireland through ignorance of Irish conditions and inability to appeal to Irish national sentiment, whereas if the Irish were given responsibility for their own affairs they would be reconciled to Britain. (*Irish Wrongs* was first published in 1885 as a series of articles; it was instigated by an emissary of Gladstone in preparation for the public announcement of his conversion to home rule.) The books were useful to subsequent historians, but have been largely superseded by researchers drawing on a wider range of sources and moving away from his administrative and political perspective. *The Home Ruler's Manual* (1887) summarizes his work for use by pro-home-rule controversialists. In 1889 he published *The Life of Thomas Drummond* (under-secretary for Ireland, 1835–40, in the Melbourne administration), whose struggles with Ascendancy forces are implicitly presented as prefiguring the Gladstonian attempt to do justice to Ireland.

O'Brien supported Parnell in the split of the Home Rule Party in 1890–91 because he saw him as the only leader of sufficient stature available to the party. He was asked to stand as Parnellite candidate in the North Kilkenny by-election but withdrew, since a parliamentary career would have interfered with his livelihood as a journalist. In 1899 O'Brien published Parnell's official biography; his work excludes discussion of its subject's private life and has been superseded by the availability of further source material, but remains valuable for its use of interviews and personal recollections.

O'Brien worked as sub-editor on *The Speaker*, founded in 1890 as the Gladstonian weekly rival to *The Spectator*, and served as acting editor in the period leading up to its acquisition by younger 'new Liberals' in 1899. He also served as auditor to the National Bank of Ireland, and was a director from 1911 to 1918.

In 1893 O'Brien was a founder of the Irish Literary Society of London, and as chairman (1893–1905) was on friendly terms with many leading figures in the Irish literary revival, including W. B. Yeats and Lady Gregory. (O'Brien, a devout Catholic, withdrew his children from acting in the première of Yeats's play *The Hour Glass* because their characters uttered anti-religious sentiments.) He was also president of the society from 1905 to 1911.

O'Brien remained close to John Redmond, Parnell's successor (Redmond contributed forewords to some of O'Brien's later books and O'Brien edited a 1910 selection of Redmond's speeches), but for financial and political reasons never became an MP. (Although an Irish party supporter he had 'advanced nationalist' sympathies and many separatist friends; he edited the autobiography of Wolfe Tone in 1893. He may also have been seen as too conciliatory towards Liberal Unionists; in the 1890s he told Horace Plunkett that he might become the nation's leader if he would accept home rule.) After 1901 he published several small historical and polemical works, such as *A Hundred Years of Irish History* (1902), *England's Claim to Ireland* (1905), and *Fontenoy* (1907), which commemorates the erection of a memorial to the Irish brigade on the battlefield. *Dublin Castle and the Irish People* (1909), a useful reference work in the style of the 1880s, studies the Irish administration from a nationalist perspective, emphasizing its inefficiency and political bias.

Like Redmond, O'Brien supported the allies in the First World War, and three of his sons served in the British army. His last literary work was as editor of an account of the experiences of the nuns of the ancient Irish convent in Ypres during the German invasion of Belgium. He died at 100 Sinclair Road, West Kensington Park, London, on 17 March 1918, after a short illness; he was survived by his wife. After a funeral service in Westminster Cathedral his body was taken to Dublin for burial in Glasnevin cemetery.

O'Brien belonged to the corps of London Irish journalists and professionals who provided the Irish party and its support organizations with many of their personnel. He played an important role in providing Liberal and nationalist publicists with arguments for home rule, but is now remembered only as a biographer.   PATRICK MAUME

Sources *Freeman's Journal* [Dublin] (19 March 1918) · *Irish Independent* (19 March 1918) · *WWW* · *Lady Gregory's diaries, 1892–1902*, ed. J. Pethica (1996) · S. E. Koss, *Sir John Brunner: radical plutocrat, 1842–1919* (1970) · A. Milligan, 'Barry O'Brien: a man from Clare', *New Ireland* (30 March 1978), 336–7
Archives NL Ire., Redmond MSS
Likenesses photograph, repro. in *Freeman's Journal*
Wealth at death £3285 19s. 5d.: administration, 25 May 1918, *CGPLA Eng. & Wales*

O'Brien [*née* Raffalovich], **Sophie** (1860–1960), author and Irish nationalist, born on 16 January 1860 in Odessa, was the only daughter of Hermann Raffalovich (*d.* 1893), a wealthy Russian Jewish banker to the tsar, and his wife, Marie (*d.* 1921). Sophie spent most of her first thirty years in Paris, where her family lived in exile at 10 avenue du Trocadéro. Hers was a cultured family: her mother was renowned for her salon; her elder brother, Arthur, was a well-known economist; and her younger brother, André, to whom Sophie was particularly close, was a poet and lifelong friend of fellow poet John Gray, with whom he shared his life in Edinburgh. Sophie was well-read and intelligent: among her copious works were books on Lord Shaftesbury and John Bright, and a translation of John Morley's biography of Richard Cobden; after her marriage to the Irish nationalist William *O'Brien (1852–1928) on 11 June 1890 she published eight books reflecting on her life, marriage, and friends in Ireland, of which the most important were *Golden Memories* (1929–30) and *My Irish Friends* (1937). She also wrote numerous articles, mainly for journals such as the *Irish Monthly* and the *Catholic Bulletin*, and was responsible for a series, 'Chats with women', for the woman's page of her husband's paper, the *Cork Free Press*.

Both Sophie Raffalovich and her mother supported Irish nationalism and the land war of the 1880s. Sophie and O'Brien were brought together by the translation she and her mother were making of O'Brien's first novel, *When we were Boys* (1890). Sophie O'Brien was not a beauty, and was a determined, self-effacing woman, content to act in the background as an essential support to O'Brien in his political life, devoting herself to helping and looking after him, acting as his secretary, and using her substantial wealth to help finance his Irish nationalist ventures. They had no children, but their relationship was a happy and affectionate one, a real companionate marriage. She had not sought marriage as a 'natural outlet', and had shunned society life. Her social conscience from an early age had encouraged her to help those in need, and this was a pronounced feature of her work in Westport, co. Mayo, where the O'Briens lived for the first twenty years of their marriage, and also in Mallow, co. Cork, where they lived for the next two decades. Before her marriage she converted from Judaism to the Roman Catholic church, in which she had been interested since the age of ten. She became very committed to her new church, and many of her close friends were nuns; the Catholic influence was pronounced in her writings, especially on the image of women. She believed that women should receive higher education and follow careers (albeit within accepted female occupations such as teaching), but she was not a supporter of women's rights, and, contrary to her husband's views, never agreed with female suffrage, refusing to vote when women were enfranchised.

After her husband's death in 1928 Sophie O'Brien remained in Ireland for four years before returning to France to live with two close friends, the Guilmart sisters, in Eplessier, near Amiens. The German occupation of France in the Second World War forced her to seek safety in the Pyrenees; from 1949 she lived in Neuilly-St Front (near Soissons) until her death in Paris in early January 1960, a week before her hundredth birthday. She was buried at Neuilly-St Front, the Irish ambassador attending the funeral. She had spent the last decades of her life in poverty, her fortune having been lost through the impact of two world wars and her generosity to Ireland. In her final years, however, she was granted a small pension by the Irish government as recognition of her contribution to Ireland's development.　　　　　SALLY WARWICK-HALLER

Sources NL Ire., MSS 4213–4217 · NL Ire., MS 14218 · *Golden memories: the love letters and the prison letters of William O'Brien*, ed. S. O'Brien, 2 vols. (1929) · E. O'Mahony, 'A tribute to a great woman', *Sunday Review* (17 Jan 1960), 9 · *Irish Independent* (9 Jan 1960) · *Irish Independent* (13 Jan 1960) · S. Warwick-Haller, *William O'Brien and the Irish land war* (1990), 144–7 · *Cork Free Press* (8 June 1912) · *Cork Free Press* (15 June 1912) · *Cork Free Press* (22 June 1912) · *Cork Free Press* (29 June 1912) · *Cork Free Press* (20 July 1912) · *Cork Free Press* (16 Aug 1913) · S. O'Brien, *My Irish friends* (1937) · S. O'Brien, *Around Broom Lane* (1931) · S. O'Brien, *In Mallow* (1920) · S. O'Brien, *Under Croagh Patrick* (1904)
Archives NL Ire. | NL Ire., Michael MacDonagh MSS · TCD, Anne Deane MSS · University College, Cork, William O'Brien MSS
Likenesses photographs, repro. in O'Brien, ed., *Golden memories* · photographs, repro. in M. Macdonagh, *The life of William O'Brien* (1928)
Wealth at death died in poverty

O'Brien, Terence [*name in religion* Albert] (1600–1651), Roman Catholic bishop of Emly, was born at Tuogh in Limerick (Emly diocese). His Old Irish family were descended from the ancient house of Thomond and held almost 1600 acres in the Limerick city area. With eleven siblings, O'Brien was initially educated by his pious mother and an aged priest who resided with his family. He was then placed under the care of his uncle, Maurice O'Brien, prior of the Limerick Dominicans, before joining the order in 1622 and receiving Albert as his religious name. His religious formation continued at the Dominican convent of St Peter Martyr in Toledo, where he spent eight years from 1622. He then returned to Ireland as an ordained priest and was successively prior of the Dominican convents at Lorrha (Tipperary) and Limerick city.

By 1643 O'Brien was provincial of the Irish Dominicans and was one of two representatives of the province at the general Dominican chapter held in Rome in 1644. He was a prominent force at the chapter, displaying his commitment to reform of the Irish Dominicans through the revival of the order's ancient schools in Dublin, Limerick, Cashel, Athenry, and Coleraine. His enthusiasm did not go unnoticed, and he was appointed judge of controversies over conventual boundaries for Munster and was awarded an MA in theology at what became the Gregorian University in Rome. He returned to Ireland via Lisbon in order to visit the two Irish Dominican institutions there. A report that he had been appointed bishop of Emly recalled him to Ireland, but this preferment was delayed by the death of Pope Urban VIII in July 1644.

At this time O'Brien became involved in the politics of the confederation, immediately displaying the political and religious allegiances which he would maintain until his death in 1651. As Dominican provincial, he signed the protest against the peace with Ormond in February 1646 on the grounds that it did not offer sufficient guarantees to Catholicism, and like many other Old Irish thus aligned himself with the papal party of the nuncio, Rinuccini. No doubt influenced by this support, Rinuccini twice recommended O'Brien for the episcopate as an individual of 'prudence and sagacity, who have been in Italy, and is so expert in the management of church revenues that happy results might be expected from his care' (O'Reilly, 235).

O'Brien was appointed bishop of Emly on 11 March 1647 and consecrated in Kilkenny eight months later. Closely involved in confederate politics, he resided in or near Kilkenny in 1648, and was one of five bishops who recommended Thaddeus (Tadhg) O'Clery to Rome for the bishopric of Derry in May of that year. He may also have held a diocesan synod at this time. Yet his attention was primarily directed towards the negotiations between the confederation and the royalists, and his stance was consistently influenced by papal policy. In August 1648 he was among the bishops who signed the declaration against Inchiquin's truce, pronouncing its ratification as a 'deadly sin against the law of God and of his church' (Gilbert, 6.279). Supported by O'Brien, Rinuccini subsequently issued ecclesiastical censures, declaring excommunication against those who supported the truce. Still adhering to the nuncio, O'Brien then travelled to Galway to join him, but found that Rinuccini had sailed to the continent. As the war in Ireland entered its final phase, O'Brien then attended the meeting of bishops at Clonmacnoise in December 1649. Faced with the arrival of Cromwell in Ireland, the bishops, although deeply divided, succeeded in agreeing a call for loyalty to Ormond. O'Brien's disquiet with this position became clear in his subscription to the declaration of Jamestown just eight months later, which released the people from their duty of obedience to Ormond and excommunicated all those who persisted in following him. He was also involved in the desperate plan to offer the title of protector royal to the duke of Lorraine in return for military aid against Cromwell, although the negotiations never came to fruition.

The situation was now acute, not least in O'Brien's own diocese of Emly, which was controlled by the English army. The bishop spent the remainder of his life in Limerick city, which was under siege by Ireton's forces during the summer of 1651. O'Brien worked intensively during this period to buoy up the spirit of the Limerick citizens, urging stubborn resistance to the besieging army. His refusal of the terms of surrender offered by Ireton meant that when the city capitulated (29 October 1651) he was among the twenty-two citizens excluded by name from protection of life and property. Reputedly, O'Brien refused a bribe of £40,000 and a safe passage from Limerick, though this appears to be part of the hagiographic tradition which emerged following his death. Having been discovered in the city hospital, where he was administering to the sick, O'Brien was executed in Limerick on 31 October 1651 and his head exposed on St John's Gate in the city. He was finally buried, some years later, in or near the old Dominican priory of Limerick. Subsequent hagiography has stressed O'Brien's place within Irish martyrology and nationalism on the basis of his staunch support for Catholicism against the royalist and parliamentary forces, upon his care of the plague-ridden of Limerick during the 1651 siege, and upon his manner of death and the miraculous preservation of his hair and flesh for several years. Certainly his active tenures as prior and then bishop reveal O'Brien as a man of initiative, stringent in his demands upon himself and others, acting on behalf of Catholics and acutely aware of the political and religious issues at stake during the civil wars.

ALISON FORRESTAL

Sources P. Moran, *Historical sketch of the persecutions suffered by the Catholics of Ireland under the rule of Cromwell and the puritans*, 3rd edn (1884) · P. F. Moran, ed., *Spicilegium Ossoriense*, 3 vols. (1874–84) · M. O'Reilly, ed., *Memorials of those who suffered for the Catholic faith in Ireland* (1868) · C. P. Meehan, *The rise and fall of the Irish Franciscan monasteries and memoirs of the Irish hierarchy in the seventeenth century*, 5th edn (1877) · P. J. Corish, 'Ormond, Rinuccini, and the confederates, 1645–9', *A new history of Ireland*, ed. T. W. Moody and others, 3: *Early modern Ireland, 1534–1691* (1976), 317–35 · P. J. Corish, 'The Cromwellian conquest, 1649–53', *A new history of Ireland*, ed. T. W. Moody and others, 3: *Early modern Ireland, 1534–1691* (1976), 336–52 · A. Valkenburg, *Two Dominican martyrs of Ireland* (1992) · *DNB* · D. De Burgo, *Hibernica Dominica* (1762) · *History of the Irish confederation and the war in Ireland … by Richard Bellings*, ed. J. T. Gilbert, 7 vols. (1882–91) · M. Lenihan, *Limerick: its history and antiquities* (1866)

O'Brien, Turlough. *See* Ua Briain, Toirdelbach (1009–1086).

O'Brien, William, second earl of Inchiquin (*c*.1640–1692), colonial governor, was the son of the soldier Murrough *O'Brien, known as Murchadh na dTóiteán ('Murrough of the Burnings'), first earl of Inchiquin (*c*.1614–1674), and his wife, Elizabeth (d. 1685), daughter of Sir William St Leger, president of Munster. Brought up in London at the house of Sir Philip Percival, his father's friend, he was a companion to his guardian's son, afterwards Sir John Percival. In 1648 he was briefly confined in the Tower of London following his father's change of allegiance to the royalists and seizure of Lord Broghill's children as hostages. In 1658 Henry Cromwell reported that O'Brien had come to him in Ireland without pass or permission.

O'Brien's early manhood was spent with his father in the service of France, especially in Catalonia. In February 1660 he accompanied his father on his way to Lisbon with a French force intended to assist the Portuguese against Spain. Near Lisbon, their vessel was boarded by an Algerian corsair. In the fight that ensued he lost an eye by a shot, and with his father was brought prisoner to Algiers. At the request of Lady Inchiquin the English council of state sought their release. The earl at once returned to England, but his son remained a hostage until the following year when he was freed on payment of a hefty ransom. O'Brien married first, in December 1665, Lady Margaret (d. 1683), third daughter of Roger Boyle, first earl of Orrery, who bore him four children: William (1666–1719), his successor, Henry (d. in infancy), James (d. 1693), and Margaret. His wife was a lady-in-waiting to Mary of Orange at The Hague in 1680, but died in December 1683 and was buried in London. His second wife was Elizabeth (1651–1718), widow of the third Baron Herbert of Cherbury and a daughter and coheir of George Bryges, sixth Baron Chandos, but there were no children of this marriage.

O'Brien was appointed a member of the Irish privy council in 1671. In 1674 he was appointed governor and vice-admiral of Tangier and became colonel of the 2nd Tangier regiment of foot. However, in the clashes with the Moors he displayed little military capability, and in 1675 he was responsible for rashly committing part of the garrison to a cattle raid which cost 150 casualties. Thereafter he was frequently absent in England. In 1680, having failed to prevent the outer fortifications of Tangier from being overrun, he was recalled under something of a cloud, but mollified Charles II with a gift of a pair of ostriches. In 1674, on the death of his father, he succeeded to the earldom of Inchiquin and inherited an immense estate of 60,000 acres in Munster. This included the family home of Rostellan Castle overlooking Cork harbour, where he resided after his return from Tangier. Although his estate was valued at £2500 per annum, he appears to have been in considerable debt, and unsuccessfully attempted to push his eldest son into marriage with the daughter of a wealthy London merchant who was prepared to pay a large dowry.

Inchiquin was omitted from the Irish privy council after the accession of James II in 1685. At the revolution of 1688 he took the side of William and Mary, and early in 1689, with his Boyle relatives, played a leading role in the armed resistance of the Munster protestants to Tyrconnell's Jacobite regime in Ireland. General Justin MacCarthy suppressed the Munster Williamites, but allowed Inchiquin to leave Cork for England with a considerable sum of money. This was against King James's wishes, but MacCarthy may have been influenced by the fact that his father, Lord Muskerry, and Inchiquin's father had been old comrades in arms. Soon afterwards Inchiquin and his eldest son were among the several thousand protestants attainted by James II's Irish parliament. In London he offered his services to William, and in September 1689 he was appointed governor and vice-admiral of Jamaica, where, accompanied by his wife and younger son, he landed on 31 May 1690. His salary was £2000 per annum.

The nineteen months of Inchiquin's personal rule that followed were beset by difficulties, which he struggled to overcome. He re-established the law courts which had not functioned for two years and suppressed a revolt by 500 slaves on one of the inland plantations. Concerned that Jamaica would be prey to French attack, he asked for warships from England and in the meantime fitted out five sloops and a captured vessel to counter growing French strength on neighbouring Hispaniola. The treasury was empty, and he was soon at loggerheads with the 'turbulent and pernicious advisers' who formed the executive council (*CSP col.*, 13.295). In August 1691 he angrily dissolved the island's assembly after a six-week session, following clashes over what he claimed were its attempts to undermine his authority and deprive him of revenue. His proposal for a land tax was rejected, and he refused to countenance a tax on the lucrative slave trade which the assembly put forward as an alternative. It was afterwards alleged that Inchiquin benefited personally from the trade, amassing as much as £15,000 during his time in Jamaica. His health deteriorated, and he sought leave to return to England. But on 16 January 1692, 'after a long indisposition through fever and ague which ended in a flux', he died at Santiago de la Vega, Jamaica, where he was buried the same day in the parish church (ibid., 597).

W. W. WEBB, *rev.* HARMAN MURTAGH

Sources GEC, *Peerage*, new edn · J. Lodge, *The peerage of Ireland*, rev. M. Archdall, rev. edn, 2 (1789), 57 · I. O'Brien, *O'Brien of Thomond: the O'Briens in Irish history, 1500–1865* (1986) · J. Childs, *The army of Charles II* (1976), 119, 142–5, 147–8, 151 · *CSP col.*, 13.142–3, 146, 151, 161, 184–5, 204, 249–50, 295, 315–17, 348–9, 522–4, 593–5, 597, 624–5 · C. Dalton, ed., *English army lists and commission registers, 1661–1714*, 1 (1892), 181; 3 (1896), 13, 17 · *CSP dom.*, 1689–90, 329, 412, 539, 541 · D. C. Boulger, *The battle of the Boyne* (1896), 84
Likenesses oils, Dromoland Castle, co. Clare
Wealth at death inherited estate of *c*.60,000 acres in Munster, yielding £2530 p.a. in 1690; said to have amassed £15,000 in Jamaica in 1689–91: O'Brien, *O'Brien of Thomond*, 96, 237; *CSP col., America and West Indies*, 1689–92, 625

O'Brien, William (1738?–1815), actor and playwright, the son of a fencing master, was related to the O'Briens, viscounts Clare, who, having lost their fortunes supporting the Stuart cause, joined the Irish brigade in France. He was apparently 'bred' to the fencing profession but abandoned it for the stage. While performing in Dublin the handsome young actor was recruited by David Garrick to replace Henry Woodward, and on 3 October 1758 he made his début at Drury Lane, as Captain Brazen in Farquhar's *The Recruiting Officer*. For the next six seasons he played 'what Garrick could never reach, coxcombs and men of fashion' (Walpole, 38.524).

Coached by Garrick, O'Brien quickly became a favourite with London audiences, noted for his easy, natural style and charming, polished manners. It was claimed that 'in the drawing of his sword he threw all other performers at a wonderful distance, by his swiftness, grace, and superiour elegance' (Genest, 4.537). Between 1758 and 1764 he played comic parts, specializing in 'harlequin' and fine gentlemen. He created the original roles of Felix in

John Hill's *The Rout*, Young Clackit in Garrick's *The Guardian*, Lovel in James Townley's *High Life below Stairs*, Edgar in John Hawkesworth's *Edgar and Emmeline*, Belmour in William Whitehead's *The School for Lovers*, and Colonel Tamper in the elder George Colman's *The Deuce is in Him*. His Mercutio was considered second only to that of Woodward. On 19 October 1763 his Sir Andrew Aguecheek was so comical that one of the sentinels flanking the stage laughed until he fell over, to the unbridled merriment of the house.

On 5 April 1764 O'Brien appeared as Fribble in Garrick's *Miss in her Teens* in what was to be his last performance. Two nights later, on Saturday 7 April 1764, he was unavailable to play his assigned part of Lovel in *High Life below Stairs*, having that morning married by stratagem at St Paul's Church, Covent Garden, without the knowledge or consent of her family, Lady Susanna Sarah Louisa Fox-Strangways (1743–1827), the daughter of Stephen Fox-Strangways, first earl of Ilchester, and Elizabeth, the daughter of Thomas Strangways Horner. Lady Susan Strangways, as she was known, was the niece of Henry Fox, later first Lord Holland, and a cousin of Charles James Fox, who had a youthful romantic attachment to her. W. M. Thackeray appears to have based the character of Hagan, the Irish actor who marries Lady Maria Esmond in *The Virginians*, on O'Brien. Following his marriage, O'Brien withdrew from the stage.

Mr and Lady Susan O'Brien, as they were known, having alienated Lord Ilchester through their impetuous marriage, sailed for America in September 1764, and endured a voluntary exile first in New York, where they were aided financially by Lord Holland and Lady Ilchester, and later in Philadelphia and Quebec. A colonial post under the New York governor, Sir Henry Moore, was secured for O'Brien, and in May 1768 he was made secretary and provost-master-general of Bermuda. The couple returned to England in 1770. Soon after, O'Brien was dismissed from a post under the Ordnance because they refused to return to America.

O'Brien launched a career as a playwright with *Cross Purposes* (1772), a farce based on J. de La Font's *Les trois frères rivaux* (1713), and *The Duel* (1772), a comedy adapted from M. J. Sedaine's *Le philosophe sans le savoir* (1765). *Cross Purposes*, an afterpiece in two acts with realistic, conversational dialogue, was 'acted with great applause' at Covent Garden (Davies, 2.245) on Saturday 5 December 1772. Three nights later, on 8 December 1772, while *Cross Purposes* again played at Covent Garden, *The Duel*, as mainpiece, opened at Drury Lane. 'The parties engaged in this *Duel*, not giving the audience *satisfaction*, were put under an *arrest*' (Oulton, 1.9). The play was hissed during the second act and subsequently withdrawn, though some said that it was 'unjustly condemned' (Genest, 5.343) and 'deserved a much better fate than it met with' (Davies, 2.245). *Cross Purposes*, however, remained a popular afterpiece for half a century.

O'Brien wrote no more for the stage, but a satirical, sometimes bawdy work known as the *Lusorium* (*O'Brien's Lusorium*, 1782; *The Lusorium*, 2nd edn, 1783; *O'Brien's*

Lusorium, 3rd edn, 1796) and a pamphlet postscript (*The End of the Lusorium*, 1798) have been attributed to him. It is far more probable that they are by the 'C. [Charles?] O'Brien' whose name appears in the imprint of the second edition. 'C. O'Brien', printer, stationer, book and music seller, may also have been a minor actor and singer at Sadler's Wells in the 1790s.

After studying unsuccessfully for the law between 1781 and 1783, William O'Brien returned with his wife to Stinsford House, an estate owned by the Strangways family near Dorchester, Dorset, and in later life he attempted to 'sink the player, and to bury in oblivion those years of his life which are the most worth being remembered' (Genest, 4.537). He formed a close friendship with his neighbour William Morton Pitt jun. MP. O'Brien was made commissioner for the island of St Domingo and then granted, through the influence of the earl of Ilchester, with whom over the years the O'Briens had been reconciled, the post of receiver-general of taxes for Dorset, which he held until his death, on 2 September 1815, at Stinsford House. He was buried at Stinsford church on 9 September. O'Brien left his estate to his wife, Lady Susan, his 'faithful and inseparable companion' (Hutchins, 2.567), who died aged eighty-three in 1827. They apparently had no children. O'Brien was eulogized in the *Gentleman's Magazine* as 'a model of the polished gentleman to those who have attempted the same line of character' and the 'most perfect representative of the Man of Fashion that had ever been seen on the stage' (*GM*, 1st ser., 85, 1815, 285). PAGE LIFE

Sources *The life and letters of Lady Sarah Lennox*, ed. M. E. A. Dawson, countess of Ilchester and Lord Stavordale, 2nd edn (1902) · Walpole, *Corr.* · Genest, *Eng. stage* · *Annual Register* (1815) · *GM*, 1st ser., 85/2 (1815), 285 · J. Hutchins, *The history and antiquities of the county of Dorset*, 3rd edn, ed. W. Shipp and J. W. Hodson, 2 (1863), 567, 663 · D. E. Baker, *Biographia dramatica, or, A companion to the playhouse*, rev. I. Reed, new edn, rev. S. Jones, 3 vols. in 4 (1812) · T. Davies, *Memoirs of the life of David Garrick*, 3rd edn, 2 vols. (1781) · Highfill, Burnim & Langhans, *BDA* · Earl of Ilchester [G. S. Holland Fox-Strangways], *Henry Fox, first Lord Holland, his family and relations*, 2 vols. (1920) · J. Doran and R. W. Lowe, 'Their majesties' servants': annals of the English stage, rev. edn, 3 vols. (1888) · Mr Dibdin [C. Dibdin], *A complete history of the English stage*, 5 vols. (privately printed, London, [1800]) · A. Graydon, *Memoirs of a life, chiefly passed in Philadelphia* (1811) · W. C. Oulton, *The history of the theatres of London*, 2 vols. (1796) · Allibone, *Dict.* · *The poetical works of Charles Churchill*, ed. D. Grant (1956) · C. Churchill, *The Rosciad and The Apology*, ed. R. W. Lowe (1891) · [Marshall], *Catalogue of five hundred celebrated authors of Great Britain, now living* (1788) · *Critical Review*, 34 (1772), 471 · *Critical Review*, 35 (1773), 71 · *Critical Review*, 55 (1783), 76–7 · T. Gilliland, *The dramatic mirror, containing the history of the stage from the earliest period, to the present time*, 2 vols. (1808) · S. Halkett and J. Laing, *Dictionary of anonymous and pseudonymous English literature*, ed. J. Kennedy and others, new edn, 9 vols. (1926–62) · *Correspondence of Emily, duchess of Leinster (1731–1814)*, ed. B. Fitzgerald, 3 vols., IMC (1949–57) · Princess Marie Liechtenstein, *Holland House*, 3rd edn, 2 vols. in 1 (1875) · I. Maxted, *The London book trades, 1775–1800: a preliminary checklist of members* (1977) · A. Nicoll, *A history of English drama, 1660–1900*, 6 vols. (1952–9) · *N&Q*, 8th ser., 4 (1893), 448, 495–6 · *N&Q*, 8th ser., 5 (1894), 72–3, 152, 219 · D. J. O'Donoghue, *The poets of Ireland: a biographical and bibliographical dictionary* (1912); repr. (1970) · W. C. Russell, *Representative actors* [1888] · R. Ryan, *Biographica Hibernica: a biographical dictionary of the worthies of Ireland* (1819–21) · W. Van Lennep and others, eds., *The London stage, 1660–1800*, 5 pts in 11 vols. (1960–68) · [J. Watkins and F. Shoberl], *A biographical dictionary of the living authors of Great Britain and Ireland* (1816) · Watt, *Bibl. Brit.*

Archives BL, family correspondence, journals, and MSS, Add. MSS 51342, 51352–51362, 51374 | priv. coll., Lady Susan O'Brien, letters to her niece Lady Elizabeth Fox-Strangways

Likenesses F. Cotes, pastels, 1763, priv. coll. · W. J. Ward, group portrait, mezzotint (after painting, *Garrick in the green room* by W. Hogarth?), BM · J. Watson, mezzotint (after pastel drawing by F. Cotes), BM, NPG · process block of photograph (after painting by J. Reynolds?), BM

Wealth at death well off but far from rich; most money invested at 3 per cent; estate to wife: Highfill, Burnim & Langhans, *BDA*

O'Brien, William

O'Brien, William (1852–1928), journalist and Irish nationalist, was born in Mallow, co. Cork, on 2 October 1852. He was the second son of James O'Brien, a solicitor's clerk, and his wife, Kate, daughter of James Nagle, a local shopkeeper. On his mother's side he was descended from an old and distinguished local family, of which Edmund Burke's mother had been a member, although that family no longer enjoyed either the status or prosperity it once had. O'Brien received his secondary education at the local Anglican school, Cloyne Diocesan College, and was brought up in an environment generally noted for its religious tolerance. From an early age he appears to have greatly valued this climate, and to have attached great importance to the need for such tolerance in Irish national life.

Early journalism and political ideas In 1868 financial misfortune caused O'Brien's family to move to Cork, where he began to write, in the hope that this might earn him an income. At Queen's College, Cork—an institution indicted by the Catholic hierarchy as a 'godless college'— he studied law, one of the few courses not discountenanced by the church. The death of his father in 1869, and the illness of his elder brother and younger brother and sister, meant that he had to turn his attention at an early age to the financial support of his mother and siblings, and thus he never graduated. However, he retained a lifelong attachment to the institution which, later in his life, was to become University College, Cork, and it is there that one of the finest portraits of him hangs and the major part of his private papers is deposited. The habit of prolific writing, which was to remain with him for the rest of his life, began early, and by 1869 it had earned him a job as a reporter on the Cork *Daily Herald*. This established him in what was to be his primary career, and it was as a journalist that he first attracted attention as a public figure.

As with so many of his contemporaries in the nationalist movement, O'Brien's political ideas were largely shaped by two influences, the Fenian movement and the plight of the Irish tenant farmers. Although he was himself too young to be a participant in the abortive rebellion of 1867, his elder brother did take part and O'Brien shared much of the excitement of those around him. Afterwards he became actively involved himself in the Fenian brotherhood, but resigned in the mid-1870s because of what he later described as 'the gloom of inevitable failure and horrible punishment inseparable from any attempt at separation by force of arms' and 'the miserable mire of recrimination in which beaten movements in Ireland …

William O'Brien (1852–1928), by Sir William Orpen, 1905

the 1880s, O'Brien made a major contribution to the consolidation under Parnell of a confident and aggressive nationalist political culture, encompassing the aspirations of widely diverse elements of nationalist Ireland.

O'Brien was first elected to parliament in 1883, at a by-election for the seat of Mallow, where he secured a significant victory, a product both of his own local standing and of the new political power of Parnellism. This was to mark the beginning of a long and significant parliamentary career, though one characterized throughout by a strong disinclination for the parliamentary role as distinct from political activity in Ireland itself. He foreshadowed this at his Mallow victory with the declaration that 'to be a member of the English Parliament is to me a matter of repugnance rather than of joy' (Warwick-Haller, 63). Despite this, he was a member of the House of Commons almost continuously until the general election of 1918, there being only three periods of absence: in 1886–7, between 1895 and 1900, and for eight months in 1904. As a member he added considerable colour to the house, often providing highly theatrical representations of occurrences in Ireland. During one of his imprisonments, when his refusal to wear prison clothes resulted in his being left without clothing, a Blarney tweed suit was smuggled into him; he later wore this much publicized apparel for his parliamentary confrontation with his incarcerator, Arthur Balfour. Apart from Mallow (1883–5), he was also member for Tyrone South (1886), North East Cork (1887–92), and Cork City (1892–5 and 1901–18).

Marriage and the split in the Irish party, 1890–1891 The year 1890 marked a major turning point in O'Brien's personal and political life. On 11 June of that year he married Sophie Raffalovich [see O'Brien, Sophie (1860–1960)], the daughter of a Russian Jewish banker, Hermann Raffalovich, domiciled in Paris. His wife brought to the marriage very considerable wealth, which was to enable O'Brien thereafter to act more independently in politics and to back his judgement with the necessary financial resources, to the point even of being able to establish his own newspapers. He also received from his wife very substantial moral and emotional support for his political pursuits; the correspondence between them attests to her deep commitment to his public life. In addition, their marriage began what was for O'Brien to be a deep and abiding love of France and interest in its affairs and politics. Their wedding had another less auspicious significance: it was the last occasion on which virtually the whole of the Irish Parliamentary Party was gathered together before its disruption by the O'Shea divorce case.

The ensuing split in the party and the death of Parnell in 1891 were to affect O'Brien with particular force. Together with his leading colleagues he was now to be thrust into primary responsibility for the party's affairs, but unlike most of them he found peculiar difficulty in reconciling himself to either side of the chasm which had opened over the issue of Parnell's continued leadership. Remaining personally and emotionally loyal to Parnell, he none

are sure to end' (O'Brien, *Evening Memories*, 443–4). His attention as a journalist had, in any case, turned to the sufferings of tenant farmers, especially the poorest and most miserable of them. In particular, over Christmas 1877, O'Brien—now on the staff of the *Freeman's Journal*—toured the Buckley estate in the Galtee Mountains, where the impoverished tenants were threatened with eviction. The articles he wrote describing their conditions were subsequently published in pamphlet form under the title *Christmas on the Galtees* (1878). It is here that O'Brien first revealed his belief that parliamentary reform, the secret ballot, and the new power of press and public opinion had opened up the prospect of pursuing Irish issues through constitutional and open political activity. In this he was, with so many, responding to the hope that the new home-rule movement associated with Isaac Butt might marshall Irish opinion around a linking of political and agrarian reform.

Editor of *United Ireland* and MP It was the dominance of Charles Stewart Parnell that raised O'Brien to the first rank of Irish nationalist politicians of the new generation. Parnell, recognizing his exceptional talent as a writer and journalist, appointed him in 1881 to be the editor of the new weekly Land League newspaper *United Ireland*. While imprisoned in Kilmainham gaol with the other nationalist leaders between October 1881 and April 1882, O'Brien drafted the famous 'No rent' manifesto which escalated the conflict between the Land League and Gladstone's government. Through his editorship of *United Ireland* during the less took the view that Parnell's actions were insupportable politically. Having failed in negotiations at Boulogne to persuade Parnell to withdraw from the leadership, he returned to the United Kingdom, where he and John Dillon gave themselves up to the prison sentence for conspiracy which they had been evading in the United States and in France, and in the relative calm of Galway gaol he began to consider his political future. Unlike Dillon, he thought they should remain aloof from any alignment, preserving themselves as a 'dispassionate tribunal' (O'Brien, *Olive Branch*, 54) to which other nationalists might turn as the fratricidal strife receded. However, he subordinated his judgement to that of Dillon, who saw the weight of political strength on the anti-Parnellite side, rather than risk an open split with one with whom he was so closely identified personally and politically.

Politics after Parnell O'Brien was never comfortable in the anti-Parnellite party. He worked hard in the negotiations leading to the 1893 Home Rule Bill, but with its defeat in the House of Lords and with Gladstone's retirement he was face to face with what he saw as the irrelevance of the party, both at Westminster and in Ireland. On the one hand, he thought that it was now essential for Irish nationalism to re-establish its independence of the Liberal Party, but he was also hostile to the solely parliamentary strategy which was being pursued. His own views had been shaped by the 'new departure' in the 1870s, when the combination of Fenian, agrarian, and parliamentary elements had given a new vitality to nationalist action. Whereas Parnell had appeared to think that the extra-constitutional dimension of the movement could be allowed to fall into abeyance once his immediate objectives had been secured, O'Brien saw such agitational politics as a necessary means both of preserving the attachment of more extreme nationalists to constitutionalism and of maximizing pressure on British parties at Westminster. For this reason, in 1886 he and others had launched the Plan of Campaign in the face of opposition from Parnell. In the mid-1890s he saw the necessity of a similar mobilization, but resistance now came from the leaders of all the nationalist factions.

In 1895 O'Brien gained his freedom from a political involvement that he found increasingly intolerable. Threatened with bankruptcy on account of debts incurred politically and for which he was being held personally responsible, he seized the excuse this gave him to withdraw from parliament. He and his wife settled, for the first period of relative domesticity since their marriage, at Mallow Cottage, beautifully located between Croagh Patrick and Clew Bay, near Westport, co. Mayo, where he also established connections with the tenant farmers of that area and began to articulate their political aspirations. From these origins he established a new agrarian and political organization, the United Irish League, founded in January 1898. Exploiting the centenary of the United Irishmen's rebellion, as well as agrarian discontent and disenchantment with the factionalism of national politics, this new body proved extremely popular and had, by 1900, extended its network of branches over most of the country. While O'Brien's objective was the achievement of national unity through organized popular opinion, the effect of the league's success was to stimulate a largely defensive reunion by the discredited parliamentary factions. This unity, achieved in January 1900, was a disappointment to O'Brien, for it prevented the league from using its control of selection of candidates to remove from the parliamentary party its less effective members, most of whom were re-elected in the general election of 1900. Recognizing the impossibility of openly opposing reunion, O'Brien hoped that the vitality and relative autonomy of the United Irish League would serve as a stimulant to a more active and imaginative political strategy.

Irish politics after 1900 With the reunion of the Irish Parliamentary Party and the dominance of the United Irish League as the national organization, O'Brien became the most influential figure within the nationalist movement, although not formally its leader. His initial strategy was to intensify agitation for completion of land purchase by the tenant farmers, pressuring the government to use powers of compulsory purchase to buy out the landlords. Instead, the major effect of the agitation was an initiative by moderate landlords for a conference of landlords and tenants to reach a settlement by agreement. As a result of its success, and the consequent Wyndham Land Act of 1903, O'Brien guided the official nationalist movement into endorsement of a new policy of conciliation, designed to remove the sharp polarization between the erstwhile landlord and tenant classes and to allow for a broadening of the basis of nationalism. To O'Brien this was the logical outcome of the abolition of landlordism. He also saw in this new approach, which he labelled 'Conference, Conciliation, Consent', the potential to bridge some of the divisions along religious and ethnic lines which had been so marked an attribute of Irish politics since 1886. He already foresaw that, unless this could be done, nationalist objectives would be frustrated, and he lived to see the realization of his worst fears in the partition of Ireland. For many of his colleagues, however, the adoption of a conciliatory approach to the 'hereditary enemy' involved too sharp a deviation from the political and cultural habits of a lifetime, and—led by John Dillon, Michael Davitt, and Thomas Sexton—a campaign was launched against that policy. Faced with the failure of the party's leader, John Redmond, to discipline the opponents of the new policy, O'Brien resigned in November 1903 from his positions of leadership in the movement, hoping thereby to shock the party and public opinion into realizing the need for adherence to policy. The effect of his action, however, was to secure for his opponents control of the party and its organization and effectively to exclude him thereafter from influence within the movement which he had played the principal part in reconstructing.

From 1903 to 1916 O'Brien's contribution to Irish political life took three forms. First, he assumed the role of principal critic of the strategy being pursued by his former colleagues, warning against the increasingly sectarian basis of nationalist action, condemning the refusal to reciprocate the co-operative attitude of more moderate members of the landlord class, and predicting the resurgence of revolutionary nationalism. Secondly, despite initial inclinations to withdraw from active political life, he became the parliamentary leader of a small group of dissident nationalists, known from 1909 onwards as the All-for-Ireland League, which had its principal basis of support in the anti-sectarianism of county Cork. While never holding more than ten seats in the House of Commons, this group was able to keep alive a broader concept of nationalism and deny to the party of John Redmond a universality of representation to which it thought itself entitled. Thirdly, during these years O'Brien applied himself to writing both general literary works and autobiographical and other accounts of the events in which he had been a participant. His robust and colourful language, together with the distinctiveness of his point of view on political events, made his works popular in Ireland. While out of accord with the dominant political strategy of the Irish party, they stand the test of time extremely well, embodying a view of Irish politics more able than the established historiography to accommodate events since his death. All told, his publications comprise: two novels, evocative in their own way of the periods in which they were set and both written during terms of imprisonment; about ten substantial literary, autobiographical or historical volumes; approximately ten pamphlets, some of them embodying his speeches; and more than twenty articles in contemporary journals. His editorship, proprietorship, and sponsorship of newspapers must also be added to this body of writing: *United Ireland* in the 1880s; the *Irish People* from 1899 to 1909; the *Cork Accent* in 1910; and the *Cork Free Press* from 1910 to 1916.

Retirement, death, and assessment In 1918 O'Brien finally withdrew himself and his small party from active political life, believing that Sinn Féin had earned the right to represent the nationalist interest. Many of his own supporters in the All-for-Ireland League had already transferred their allegiance to the revolutionary movement, and by the time of the Irish Free State election of 1927 O'Brien had publicly committed himself to the republican side, more on account of his opposition to partition than for support of republicanism.

To O'Brien the unity of Ireland was to be preserved at all costs. His alienation after 1903 from many of his lifelong friends and colleagues was attributable to his belief that by their attachment to older habits of conflict they would stereotype sectarian divisions and make the ideals of national autonomy and unity impossible of achievement. 'Any price for a United Ireland, but partition never' (MacDonagh, 224) was his view, and he would have preferred the indefinite deferral of national independence to one based on the establishment of two confessional states. It was a perspective to which subsequent events have given more substance than most of his contemporaries were prepared to acknowledge.

O'Brien died suddenly of heart failure on 25 February 1928 at the Belgravia Hotel, Grosvenor Gardens, Victoria, while on a visit to London with his wife. A requiem mass at Westminster Cathedral, where he had often worshipped while in London as a member of parliament, preceded the return of his body to Ireland, for burial in the churchyard at Mallow. His wife later returned to live in Paris, where she lived into the 1950s. They had no children. Both O'Brien's parents, and his three siblings, had all died before he was thirty.   PHILIP BULL

Sources M. MacDonagh, *The life of William O'Brien* (1928) · S. Warwick-Haller, *William O'Brien and the Irish land war* (1990) · W. O'Brien, *Christmas on the Galtees* (1878) · W. O'Brien, *Recollections* (1905) · W. O'Brien, *Evening memories* (1920) · P. J. Bull, 'The United Irish League and the reunion of the Irish parliamentary party, 1898–1900', *Irish Historical Studies*, 26 (1988–9), 51–78 · P. J. Bull, 'The significance of the nationalist response to the Irish Land Act of 1903', *Irish Historical Studies*, 28 (1992–3), 283–305 · *The Times* (27 Feb 1928) · *Irish Times* (27 Feb 1928) · *Irish Independent* (27 Feb 1928) · *DNB* · *Dod's Parliamentary Companion* (1883–1918) · W. O'Brien, *An olive branch in Ireland and its history* (1910)
Archives NL Ire., corresp. and literary papers · University College, Cork, corresp., literary MSS, notebooks | BL, corresp. with Macmillans, Add. MS 55242 · Bodl. Oxf., corresp. with H. H. Asquith · NL Ire., MacDonagh MSS · PRO NIre., corresp. with Sir Edward Carson · TCD, corresp. with John Dillon
Likenesses H. Holiday, pencil drawing, 1888, NG Ire. · A. J. Thaddeus, portrait, 1890, University College, Cork · W. Orpen, chalk drawing, 1905, Crawford Art Gallery, Cork [*see illus.*] · W. Orpen, oils, 1905, Hugh Lane Gallery of Modern Art, Dublin · B. Stone, photographs, 1908, NPG · S. P. Hall, pencil drawings, NG Ire. · W. Orpen, chalk drawing, NG Ire. · F. Pegram, pencil drawing, NPG; repro. in *The Pictorial World* (16 May 1889) · C. P. Renouard, group portrait, charcoal drawing (with other Nationalist MPs), NG Ire. · Spy [L. Ward], caricature, watercolour study, NPG; repro. in *VF* (15 May 1907)
Wealth at death £212 13s. 11d.: probate, 17 March 1928, *CGPLA Eng. & Wales* · £440 3s. 9d.: probate, 24 April 1928, *CGPLA Éire*

O'Brien, William (1881–1968), labour leader in Ireland, was born on 23 January 1881 at Ballygurteen, Clonakilty, co. Cork, Ireland, the youngest of four children of a member of the Royal Irish Constabulary. The family moved to Carrick-on-Suir, co. Tipperary, in 1888 and, upon the retirement of the father, to Dublin in 1896. O'Brien trained as a tailor and practised that trade in the north Dublin workhouse until 1919.

At the age of eighteen O'Brien began a lifetime commitment to socialism when he joined James Connolly's tiny Irish Socialist Republican Party. He also began a similar involvement in the trade union movement when he became a member of the tailors' union, immediately becoming active in its affairs. A publicly aloof, austere bachelor, he was an honest, efficient, and demanding organizer and administrator. His club foot earned him the nickname Hoofy. Although almost all his energy went into the trade union movement, it would not be accurate to call him a syndicalist as he always was an advocate of labour electoral participation.

O'Brien was one of the original proponents of the organization of unskilled general workers. In 1908 he supported the leadership of James Larkin in the formation of the Irish Transport and General Workers' Union. He also was largely responsible for facilitating the return of James

Connolly from the United States to Ireland in 1910. The next year he successfully proposed that the Dublin Trades Council establish a local labour party. He became president of the council in 1911. The same year he was elected to the executive of the Irish Trade Union Congress, in which position he became a strong advocate of expanded labour activity. He was a long-standing leader in the body, serving as its president in 1913, 1918, 1925, and 1941. With the apparent advent of home rule, the congress voted in 1912 to form a national labour party in Ireland.

In the great labour conflict in Dublin of 1913 O'Brien played a characteristically effective role in providing organizational support. With the departure of James Larkin for the United States the next year, James Connolly became the Transport Union's acting general secretary, with O'Brien providing advice and support. After the outbreak of the First World War, O'Brien joined Connolly in aligning with adamant nationalists who were prepared to use violence to achieve Irish self-government. Although he was not a member of Connolly's Irish Citizen Army, he worked closely with him in preparing for the 1916 rebellion. He was not a participant in the rising, but was imprisoned for three months, thus associating further with the leaders of the independence movement.

Upon his release O'Brien became involved in the revival of the Transport Union, of which he became a member at the beginning of 1917. He soon became a leader of a group who successfully fought for control of the union, with another faction, led by P. T. Daly, claiming the mantle of James Larkin. On the basis of wartime prosperity and nationalist enthusiasm as well as effective union recruitment, the Transport Union rapidly expanded, particularly in areas outside Dublin; it was to remain the largest union in the country. O'Brien quickly rose in the union leadership, being elected treasurer in 1918 and acting general secretary the next year.

When the threat of conscription in Ireland loomed in mid-1918, O'Brien was a leader in the one-day general strike that helped to defeat it. At the end of 1918, as the war drew to a close and a general election appeared imminent, O'Brien was the key labour leader in negotiations with the newly dominant Sinn Féin concerning the selection of parliamentary candidates. In the event, rather than cause a fissure in the trade union movement, the Irish Labour Party decided not to contest the December 1918 election.

When the victorious Sinn Féin formed a revolutionary government, O'Brien joined Thomas Johnson in writing the 'democratic programme' which was accepted by the Dáil Éireann as a statement of social and economic objectives. Throughout the ensuing Anglo-Irish conflict, the Transport Union continued its expansion, while remaining an unofficial but effective bulwark of support for both the political and the military activities of the Dáil government, in which O'Brien had a reputation as a reliable and indomitable ally. Now an alderman in the Dublin corporation, he was arrested in 1920 and was released after a prolonged hunger strike. Always preoccupied with the need

for stable administration, he opposed revolutionary action by the union.

When the Anglo-Irish agreement of December 1921 divided both Sinn Féin and the Irish public, O'Brien, Johnson, and other labour leaders, while accepting the 'treaty', worked tirelessly to prevent civil war. In the June 1922 election O'Brien won a seat in the Irish national assembly. Although he was a Dáil candidate seven times in the period 1922–38 and was elected three times, his parliamentary career was brief, owing to short-lived sessions of the Dáil.

By 1923 O'Brien and the Transport Union were faced with crisis. Economic recession and the ravages of civil war had reduced union membership. Then James Larkin returned from America and sought to oust the new leadership. The resulting conflict was Ireland's version of the clash between revolutionary socialism and moderate Labour political and union activity. In an extended legal battle, O'Brien and his colleagues retained control of the union and Larkin established a rival union. Two-thirds of the Dublin members aligned with the Workers' Union of Ireland, while most of the members outside Dublin remained with the Transport Union. The Larkin controversy also hurt the development of the Labour Party.

After the party separated from the congress in 1930, O'Brien was a leading member of the party executive throughout the 1930s. During the Second World War there was a renewal of Labour radicalism in Dublin, and in 1941 James Larkin returned to the party, where he soon became a popular figure. Determined to stop the spread of 'communism' as well as to thwart Larkin, O'Brien and his allies split the Labour Party, forming the National Labour Party in 1944. The next year the Transport Union, in support of Irish-based unions and the head of Larkin's union, left the trade union congress to form a rival body.

This was the position of the Irish labour movement when O'Brien reached his union's mandatory retirement age in 1946. He remained as an adviser to the union and contributed to its periodical. He also joined with Desmond Ryan in editing the papers of the Fenian John Devoy and the works of James Connolly. In the late 1960s he tape-recorded his memoirs, though going little beyond 1923, and these were published, with valuable appendices, in 1969. His massive collection of papers, leaflets, and reports was donated to the National Library of Ireland. He died at a convalescent home at Bray, co. Wicklow, on 30 October 1968, and was buried at Glasnevin cemetery, Dublin, on 3 November 1968.   ARTHUR MITCHELL

Sources *Forth the banners go: reminiscences of William O'Brien*, ed. E. MacLysaght (1969) · William O'Brien papers, NL Ire. · A. Mitchell, 'William O'Brien, 1881–1968, and the Irish labour movement', *Studies: an Irish Quarterly Review*, 60 (1971), 311–31 · A. Mitchell, *Labour in Irish politics, 1890–1930* (1974) · D. R. O'Connor Lysaght, 'The rake's progress of a syndicalist: the political career of William O'Brien, Irish labour leader', *Saothar: Journal of Irish Labour History Society*, 9 (1983), 48–62 · H. Boylan, *A dictionary of Irish biography* (1978) · C. O'Shannon, *Liberty* (Nov 1968) · *Irish Times* (31 Oct 1968) · *Irish Times* (2 Nov 1968) · F. Robbins, *Irish Independent* (2 Nov 1968) · *The Leader* [Dublin] (31 Jan 1953) · D. J. Hickey and J. E. Doherty, *A dictionary of Irish history* (1980), 415–16

Archives NL Ire., papers | Irish Labour History Society, Dublin, archives · NL Ire., Thomas Kennedy MSS · NL Ire., Thomas Johnson MSS
Likenesses Walshe, double portrait, photograph, 1922 (with J. O'Farrell), Hult. Arch. · A. Devereux, repro. in O'Brien, *Forth the banners go*, frontispiece · S. O'Brien, chalk sketch, Irish Labour History Society

O'Brien, William Smith (1803–1864), Irish nationalist, was born on 17 October 1803 at Dromoland Castle, near Newmarket-on-Fergus, co. Clare, the second son of Sir Edward O'Brien, fourth baronet (1773–1837), and his wife, Charlotte (1781–1856), elder daughter of William Smith of Cahirmoyle (or Cahermoyle). The author Edward *O'Brien was a younger brother. William was descended from the medieval Irish high king Brian Bóruma. In the eighteenth century the Dromoland O'Briens, a junior branch of the family, had played a leading role in the all-protestant Irish parliament and voted to end many of the penal laws against the Catholic majority. Sir Edward O'Brien opposed the 1800 Act of Union with Great Britain, but ultimately accepted it as a *fait accompli* and attended parliament at Westminster. William's maternal grandfather, an attorney providing loans to the O'Briens and other gentry, accumulated a large estate based on Cahirmoyle in co. Limerick. The decision of his parents to allocate to William his mother's property resulted in the addition of Smith to his name, though he normally signed himself William S. O'Brien.

O'Brien attended a preparatory school in Kent, and later accompanied his elder brother, Lucius (later thirteenth Baron Inchiquin), to Harrow School in 1813. In his later teens he studied at a private educational establishment run by a Mr Scott at Great Harborough, before following Lucius to Trinity College, Cambridge, in 1821. He graduated in 1826 and was admitted to Lincoln's Inn in 1827. In 1828 Sir Edward nominated William for the pocket borough of Ennis. He joined his brother Lucius, sitting for County Clare. William, a more enthusiastic member than Lucius, made his maiden speech on 3 June 1828, supporting paper currency. Acceding to the wishes of his liberal tory father, O'Brien voted regularly with the Wellington ministry, but only after it had passed Catholic emancipation.

First steps in politics Irish politics were transformed when Daniel O'Connell won the 1828 County Clare by-election, defeating the senior member for County Clare, Vesey Fitzgerald, who was supported by the Dromoland O'Briens. O'Connell, disqualified as a Catholic, successfully encouraged the Catholic tenants to defy their landlords at the polls. In parliament on 3 July 1828, William supported Catholic claims and revealed his membership of O'Connell's Catholic Association, but deplored O'Connell's threat to the legitimate political interests of local co. Clare landlords. A careless statement that all Clare gentry had opposed O'Connell, re-elected after Catholic emancipation in 1829, led to a duel on 30 July 1829 with Thomas Steele, a minor Clare landholder who passionately supported O'Connell.

At the general election of 1830, Sir Edward O'Brien

William Smith O'Brien (1803–1864), by Stephen Smith the elder

forced, against opposition, the re-election of William for the borough of Ennis, subsequently conceded to the O'Briens' ally Vesey Fitzgerald in the election of 1831. Meanwhile O'Brien fought a second duel with W. R. Mahon on behalf of his brother Lucius, accused of fabricating evidence against a political rival (*Limerick Evening Post and Clare Standard*, 22 March 1831). Campaigning for his father, who tried to regain the seat of County Clare, O'Brien missed a vital division on the whig government's new Reform Bill, but he voted with the reformers on 19 April 1831. His Irish Poor Law Bill of 8 February 1831, supported by a pamphlet, *Plan for the Relief of the Poor in Ireland* (1831) was dropped. He was a founder member of Edward Gibbon Wakefield's National Colonisation Society and defended the East India Company's monopoly in a strongly imperialistic pamphlet, *Considerations Relative to the Renewal of the East-India Company's Charter* (1830). On 2 June 1840 he expounded Wakefield's views at length in the House of Commons, but the former's position on India had by then changed.

Out of parliament after 1831, O'Brien turned down an invitation to stand for the reformed borough of Ennis; he was about to leave co. Clare for co. Limerick. Having paid off his mistress, Mary Anne Wilton, with whom he appears to have had two children, on 19 September 1832 he married Lucy Caroline Gabbett (1811–1861), eldest daughter of William Gabbett of High Park, co. Limerick, a former mayor of the city and an alderman until his death in 1864. The couple lived initially in Limerick City, where O'Brien achieved prominence campaigning for emigration, education, and port development. They then settled at Cahirmoyle with 5000 acres, where O'Brien, after joining O'Connell's Anti-Tory Association, was nominated by the Limerick Liberal Club. With its help he unseated a sitting member in the general election of 1835 and became an independent whig MP for County Limerick. He retained his seat easily in 1837; a tory petition, associated with the so-called 'Spottiswoode conspiracy', against Catholic clerical dictation on O'Brien's behalf was dropped. Normally voting with Melbourne's whig government, O'Brien continued to distance himself from O'Connell, despite the latter's support in the 1837 election. They differed on the need for an Irish poor law, O'Brien's desire to replace tithes to the minority Church of Ireland with payments to all churches, O'Brien's Registration of Voters' Bill, and O'Brien's opposition to repeal of the corn laws. O'Brien co-operated with Thomas Wyse on extensive non-denominational education reform.

O'Connell's partisans nearly forced O'Brien out of parliament in 1839, when the latter voted against Melbourne's bill to suspend the Jamaica assembly. Melbourne's government, co-operating with O'Connell on Irish reform, resigned in favour of Sir Robert Peel's tories. When a Limerick Liberal meeting demanded their errant member's resignation, O'Brien convened a public meeting which supported his continuation as MP. The 'bedchamber crisis' returned the whigs to office, which they retained until they lost the 1841 election. While many Irish MPs supporting O'Connell were defeated, O'Brien was re-elected unopposed for County Limerick.

The Repeal Association Although O'Brien had established his independence of O'Connell, he now moved closer to his rival. In 1843 O'Connell held a series of 'monster' meetings throughout Ireland to demand repeal of the union. O'Brien resigned as JP on finding that others lost their commissions for attending O'Connell's gatherings. In June, O'Brien delivered a powerful speech, published by the Repeal Association, in which he indicted British rule in Ireland and urged religious equality, industrial development, and an extension of the franchise for Ireland. He foreshadowed an imminent mass conversion to repeal. In October 1843 O'Brien formally joined the association after O'Connell and his lieutenants had been charged with sedition.

With O'Connell's blessing, O'Brien acted as *de facto* leader of the Repeal Association during the former's trial and imprisonment until his conviction was overturned by the Lords in September 1844. Controlling the weekly Repeal Association meetings and establishing a parliamentary committee, which published a number of well-researched reports, O'Brien worked closely with a group of younger men led by Thomas Davis and associated with the influential *Nation* newspaper, edited by Charles Gavan Duffy.

Tension between 'Old' and 'Young' Ireland developed in early 1845, when Peel legislated for three Irish non-denominational university colleges. O'Brien and the Young Irelanders endorsed the principle, but O'Connell and his son John, supporting Catholic Archbishop John MacHale, were strongly opposed. Although O'Brien eventually voted against the bill when safeguards for Catholics were omitted, the Young Irelanders were now widely denounced as secularists.

In 1846 O'Brien was strongly backed by the Young Irelanders when incarcerated for twenty-five days by the House of Commons for refusing to serve on a Scottish railway committee, irrelevant to Ireland. Together they opposed O'Connell's overtures to Lord John Russell's new whig government. When the Young Irelander Thomas Meagher was silenced at the Repeal Association in August 1846 for attacking O'Connell's 'peace provisions', which renounced the use of violence in all places and at all times, O'Brien initiated a split by walking out.

The Young Irelanders reverted to newspaper propaganda, and O'Brien led by addressing his fellow landlords on 'Reproductive employment'. Here O'Brien, exculpating his class from major responsibility for the great potato famine (1845–9), demanded investment in Irish railways, colonization schemes, and useful works such as docks, piers, and canals. Local landlords, he claimed, were bankrupted by poor rates expended on futile relief schemes. In parliament O'Brien proved a relentless critic of Russell's *laissez-faire* famine administration which distributed quotations from Adam Smith instead of food.

After negotiations with O'Connell broke down in late 1846, O'Brien became the reluctant *de facto* leader of the Young Irelanders' Irish Confederation, established in January 1847. The death of O'Connell in May 1847 increased the bitterness between the Repeal Association, now controlled by John O'Connell, and the confederation, accused of hastening the demise of the 'Liberator'. Leading a delegation to win over Orangemen in Belfast, O'Brien found his meetings disrupted by furious Catholics venerating O'Connell. At the general election of 1847 the Young Irelanders made little impact. Reluctant to stand again, O'Brien, in his absence, was narrowly re-elected for County Limerick.

The road to rebellion While famine deepened, the Irish Confederation split in January 1848. John Mitchel, demanding a rate strike, refused to accept the ten resolutions for constitutional action drawn up by O'Brien with the support of Gavan Duffy. The French revolution of February 1848 brought temporary unity as O'Brien and Duffy made a volte-face in favour of physical force. After a mass demonstration in Dublin on 21 March 1848, when O'Brien demanded arms and a national guard, he and others were indicted for sedition. Awaiting trial, in late March, O'Brien led a delegation to France, but was rebuffed by Lamartine's provisional government. Addressing a furious House of Commons on 10 April, O'Brien denied seeking military aid from France, but admitted advising the Irish to arm and welcomed aid from the Chartists.

Stoned on 29 April in Limerick by a mob incensed at Mitchel's attacks on O'Connell, O'Brien recuperated at Cahirmoyle, and visited Dublin in bandages for his trial on 15 May. Like Meagher, he was discharged when his jury disagreed. On Mitchel's transportation for treason-felony on 27 May, O'Brien opposed an uprising in his favour. Instead, O'Brien promoted the union of the repealers and confederates in a new Irish League. Though not a member of the Dublin caucus planning rebellion in the autumn, or the elected executive of the clubs springing up to support the revolutionary movement, O'Brien welcomed the new

Irish League with the question 'when will Ireland strike?' (*The Nation*, 17 June 1848). Unfortunately, his claim that the new organization embodied all the objects of the confederation encouraged John O'Connell and other repealers to hold back when the league met on 11 July.

O'Brien's hope for self-government through a show of force rather than insurrection was indicated by his leisurely tour of southern organizations in July 1848. At Cork he suggested that teaching men co-operation in bodies was more useful than instruction in military drill. O'Brien claimed to have been 'very cautious in the language used' (Davis, *William Smith O'Brien: Ireland–1848–Tasmania*, 21) at a meeting of the new Irish League in Dublin.

The whig government arrested several leading Young Irelanders, including Duffy, and on 22 July suspended habeas corpus. In Wexford, O'Brien, advised of a warrant for his arrest, recognized three choices: accept arrest, escape, or initiate rebellion. Honour required the third, though he later believed the first more appropriate. The enthusiasm of towns such as Enniscorthy, Kilkenny, and especially Carrick-on-Suir was not translated into active assistance. Attempting to gather support in the co. Tipperary villages of Ballingarry, Mullinahone, and Killenaule, O'Brien was followed by several thousand potential defenders, who dropped away when he refused to commandeer provisions and the Catholic priests advised against him. A minor success was achieved at Killenaule by forcing a troop of hussars to pass, one by one, through a barricade. At a council of war at the Boulah Commons on 28 July, O'Brien told his lieutenants to disperse. Later it was suggested that there was a move to depose, or even assassinate, O'Brien. His most revolutionary action was to threaten the owners of the Boulah coal mines with dispossession if they did not raise the wages of the miners and lower their prices.

On 29 July 1848 a party of forty-seven armed police, challenged by O'Brien's depleted force, barricaded themselves inside Widow McCormack's house at Farrenrory, near Ballingarry, taking her children as hostages. O'Brien was nearly killed in a parley with the police to secure the children when stone-throwing by his supporters evoked volleys of fire, killing two men. The rebel army disintegrated and O'Brien was obliged to escape on horseback when relief arrived for the police. Though pockets of resistance continued for some weeks in other areas, the rebellion was effectively over. The leaders were either arrested or forced to flee overseas. After being harboured for several days, O'Brien was arrested on 7 August at Thurles railway station, attempting to return home.

At Clonmel court house in October 1848 O'Brien and his three colleagues Thomas Meagher, Patrick O'Donohoe, and Terence MacManus were sentenced to death for high treason. An aura of martyrdom enveloped the bungled rebellion. For the next eight months the convicted leaders lived in relative comfort, mostly in Richmond prison. Public opinion precluded execution. O'Brien's appeal through a writ of error was rejected and he was formally expelled from the House of Commons. Hopes for an early pardon were dashed when the government, by special legislation, against the wishes of the prisoners, commuted the sentence to transportation for life to Van Diemen's Land.

O'Brien in exile The journey of O'Brien and his three colleagues on the naval sloop *Swift* from Dublin to Van Diemen's Land, via the Cape of Good Hope, lasted from 9 July to 31 October 1849. O'Brien, unlike his companions, and three other Young Irelanders—John Mitchel, Kevin O'Doherty, and John Martin—initially refused to give his parole for a ticket-of-leave. As a result he was restricted to small cottages at the convict probation station at Île Maria from November 1849 to August 1850, and the penal station of Port Arthur from August to November 1850. After two months' close confinement and isolation at Île Maria, with very limited space for exercise, O'Brien's health deteriorated. Publicity on O'Brien's treatment fuelled a movement for his release, not only in the United Kingdom but also in the United States and Canada. Until an unsuccessful escape attempt in August 1850, he was allowed to take walks under supervision. In this period O'Brien was well treated by the superintendent, Samuel Lapham, and formed an embarrassing attachment to the latter's thirteen-year-old daughter Susan (later Susan Wood, an author). He read voraciously and kept a journal, later published as *'To Solitude Consigned': the Tasmanian Journal of William Smith O'Brien* (1995). At Port Arthur, O'Brien was restricted to a small garden for exercise. He finally took his ticket-of-leave, urged by a petition to him from friends in Hobart. He also hoped to help Lapham, sacked for lenience towards him, and pay off debts incurred by the escape attempt. From November 1850 to February 1851, and from January 1852 to March 1854, O'Brien lived comfortably at Elwin's Hotel, New Norfolk. He entertained friends and Young Ireland colleagues, including John Mitchel, and made numerous house visits to local settlers, especially the Irish landowner and prominent local politician Captain Michael Fenton (1789–1874), subsequently speaker of the Tasmanian house of assembly. From February to December 1851 O'Brien raised money by tutoring the sons of an Irish settler, Dr Henry Brock, at Red Rock, near Avoca.

O'Brien was living at Richmond when conditional pardons, forbidding domicile in the United Kingdom, arrived for himself, John Martin, and Kevin O'Doherty, the other four Young Irelanders having escaped. Having left Tasmania on 6 July 1854 after dinners in his honour, O'Brien attended receptions in Melbourne and Geelong before proceeding to Brussels, via Madras and Egypt. In Brussels he published his two-volume *Principles of Government, or, Meditations in Exile*, in which he gave a favourable account of transportation as a punishment and showed little of the Irish rebel and much of the Wakefield imperialist. He included a model constitution for a self-governing Tasmania, originally published anonymously in a local paper, the *Launceston Examiner* (31 August 1853).

While touring Greece with his eldest son, Edward, in May 1856, O'Brien learned of his unconditional pardon, assisted by a petition signed by MPs of all parties. He returned to Ireland on 6 July 1856 amid great rejoicing. He had travelled extensively through France, Italy, and Switzerland during his European exile.

Return to Ireland Back in Ireland, O'Brien was offered nominations for Tipperary and other seats but rejected them as he required time with his family and considered attendance at Westminster futile. He preferred to educate by press and pamphlet, never renouncing his 1848 principles, but insisting that physical force was impossible while England remained at peace. In 1862 he unsuccessfully challenged Sir Robert Peel the younger, then Irish chief secretary, to a duel for sneering at his behaviour at Ballingarry (*The Nation*, 1 March 1862). Though he participated in the funeral service of his lieutenant Terence MacManus in 1861, O'Brien gave no countenance to the secret, revolutionary Fenians who deliberately exploited the occasion. Instead, O'Brien fulfilled his duties as a landlord, chaired the Newcastle West poor-law guardians, encouraged industrial development and the arts, and wrote many articles for *The Nation*, then edited by A. M. Sullivan. His fame as an elder statesman and a martyr for Ireland ensured respect for his opinions and demonstrations in his favour as he moved about the country.

Foreign affairs attracted much of O'Brien's attention. He denounced British repression during the Indian mutiny (1857), but was unsympathetic towards the Italian Risorgimento, and supported the papal temporal power. France under Napoleon III incurred his suspicions, and O'Brien debated with his fellow exile John Martin, who appeared to believe that war between France and England would help Ireland. O'Brien published the controversy in a pamphlet which effectively expressed his political philosophy, *Correspondence between John Martin and William Smith O'Brien, Relative to a French Invasion* (1861).

Most significant were O'Brien's views on America after a three-month tour of 7000 miles in the United States and Canada in early 1859. He encountered an enthusiastic response, not only from Irish Americans, but also from the leading politicians. Received by President James Buchanan, he met Lincoln's future secretary of state William Seward and future Confederate politicians, such as Alexander Stephens. He continued to deplore slavery in principle, though he was satisfied with what he saw in practice. In Canada he advised the French and Irish to work together. O'Brien expounded his experience in speeches in Dublin, later published as a pamphlet, *Lectures on America* (1860). After the outbreak of the American Civil War in 1861 O'Brien attempted to mediate between Seward, who politely rebuffed his suggestions for a cease-fire, and southern politicians. Though he disapproved of secession, O'Brien believed that, once a *fait accompli*, it could not be put down by force. The Irish should not be involved. He differed from his colleagues John Mitchel, an ardent partisan of the South, and Thomas Meagher, who commanded an Irish brigade for the North.

Last years O'Brien's comfortable existence was destroyed on 13 June 1861 by the death of his wife, Lucy. In 1848, to avoid the confiscation of his property after conviction for treason, he had placed it in trust with his brother Lucius

and friend Woronzow Greig. A bitter dispute arose when they were unable to allow O'Brien control after Lucy's death. A compromise accepted in Chancery conferred Cahirmoyle on O'Brien's son Edward William (1837–1909), who agreed to pay his father the considerable annuity of £2000. Still furious with the trustees, O'Brien sadly resigned his responsibilities in Limerick and took up residence in Killiney, near Dublin, but spent much of his time in European travel. In late 1861 he visited Hungary and saw in action Ferenz Déak, working for the restoration of the ancient constitution denied by Austria. O'Brien approved heartily of Déak's passive resistance, which achieved success in 1867. In 1863 O'Brien visited Poland and gave an address, in aid of Polish exiles, on the country's repression by Russia; this was published as another pamphlet, *Lecture on Poland* (1863).

At the Penrhyn Arms at Bangor in Wales, on 18 June 1864, O'Brien died of a heart attack apparently brought on by a liver complaint. Though the family endeavoured to prevent a popular demonstration at the funeral, vast crowds followed the coffin as it was borne through Dublin for transport by rail to Cahirmoyle. The funeral and interment in the family mausoleum at Rathronan churchyard, co. Limerick, took place on 24 June, with O'Brien's brothers-in-law the Revds J. and R. Gabbett, reading the service. In 1870 a statue of William Smith O'Brien by Thomas Farrell in Caravazzi marble was unveiled by John Martin. It now stands close to that of Daniel O'Connell in O'Connell Street, Dublin.

O'Brien in perspective O'Brien was 5 feet 11 inches tall, an athletic figure, running to corpulence in later years. Of dark complexion, his hair was dark brown and his eyes grey. He had a very light Irish accent. A keen linguist, he had broad literary and historical interests. Though speaking only English and French fluently, O'Brien could 'understand with more or less facility' Latin, Greek (ancient and modern), Italian, German, Spanish, and the Gaelic of his ancestors, which he worked hard to acquire. In the right company he could be very sociable, and he was far from humourless. Although he was no rhetorician, O'Brien's speeches, logical and informative, were often enthusiastically received. He was proud of his prose, but not his poetry, of which he wrote a great deal. His writings show a sometimes vulnerable personality. O'Brien was no saint; apart from his Île Maria dalliance, he had a mistress before marriage. His wife, Lucy, though otherwise devoted, had no sympathy with his politics. For his part, O'Brien showed some insensitivity by lecturing Lucy on her dislike of frequent pregnancies and lack of preparation for childbirth. Of their five sons and two daughters, only Robert Donough (1844–1917) and Charlotte Grace *O'Brien (1845–1909) were publicly identified as Irish nationalists. As a father, Smith O'Brien, sometimes patriarchal, was relaxed towards ceremony and dress, and encouraged intelligence and the acquisition of marketable skills by his daughters. He allowed his daughter Lucy Josephine (1840–1907) to study classical languages like her brothers. Married to the Revd John Gwynn, subsequently regius professor of divinity at the University of Dublin, Lucy became the ancestor of a line of eminent scholars.

Frankly admitting that pride was a serious failing, O'Brien declared: 'I should be a prouder man than I now am if I had been born the son of a chimney sweep, and had subsequently raised myself to distinction by my talents or by my public service' (*The Nation*, 27 Sept 1862). He balanced pride with sympathy towards Vandiemonian convicts, whom he saw as victims of their poverty-stricken environments. He opposed feudal behaviour such as the uncovering of peasants before gentry.

O'Brien's stubbornness, sincerity, and courage were universally acknowledged. He disclaimed originality, and acknowledged his adaptation of the ideas of others. Conservative in his basic thought, he was nevertheless prepared to modify opinions when convinced by argument. American democracy persuaded him to rethink some of his principles. As a liberal protestant, he was without sectarian prejudice. Supporting the common education of Catholics and protestants, he conceded public funds to Catholics if they insisted on separate institutions.

O'Brien has often been regarded as a noble, if wooden, idealist. He was in fact a pragmatist who, adapting to the O'Connellite revolution in Ireland, turned it to his advantage and restored the national reputation of his family. A scholar and a critic rather than a man of action, O'Brien in his politics paradoxically combined a devotion to Ireland's self-government and cultural identity with a consistent belief in the British empire. He sympathized with indigenous peoples, especially black South Africans and Australian Aborigines, but denied that they could legitimately exclude European emigrants from their under-utilized territories. His final political position, endorsing Déak's passive resistance in Hungary, anticipated Arthur Griffith's 'Hungarian policy' and the Sinn Féin movement after 1905. RICHARD P. DAVIS

Sources NL Ire., William Smith O'Brien MSS · *The Nation* (1843–64) · NL Ire., Inchiquin MSS · *'To solitude consigned': the Tasmanian journal of William Smith O'Brien*, ed. R. Davis and others (1995) · *Hansard 2* (1828–30) · *Hansard 3* (1830–31); (1835–48) · *Public Register, or, Freeman's Journal* (1803–64) · D. Gwynn, *Young Ireland and 1848* (1949) · D. Gwynn, *O'Connell, Davis and the Colleges Bill* (1948) · R. Davis, *William Smith O'Brien: Ireland—1848—Tasmania* (1989) · R. Davis, *The Young Ireland movement* (1987) · G. R. Weir [G. R. O'Brien], *These my friends and forebears: the O'Briens of Dromoland* (1991) · *Charlotte Grace O'Brien: selections from her writings and correspondence*, ed. S. L. Gwynn (1909) · C. G. Duffy, *Young Ireland: a fragment of Irish history, 1840–1845*, rev. edn, 2 vols. (1896) · C. G. Duffy, *Four years of Irish history, 1845–1849: a sequel to 'Young Ireland'* (1883) · B. Touhill, *William Smith O'Brien and his Irish revolutionary companions in penal exile* (1981) · W. Dillon, *Life of John Mitchel*, 2 vols. (1888) · J. Mitchel, *Jail journal, or, Five years in British prisons* [1860–76] · P. A. Smith, *Heart of exile* (1986) · J. G. Hodges, *Report on the trial of William Smith O'Brien for high treason* (1849) · R. Davis, 'William Smith O'Brien as an imperialist', *Irish-Australian studies*, ed. R. Pelan (1994), 228–42 · Venn, *Alum. Cant.* · H. Weir, 'William O'Brien's secret family', *The Other Clare*, 20 (April 1996), 55–6

Archives NL Ire., corresp. and papers, incl. diaries · priv. coll. · Royal Irish Acad. · TCD, corresp. and family papers · TCD, collected papers relating to Irish history and literature; letters | NL Ire., Davis MSS · NL Ire., Duffy MSS · NL Ire., Inchiquin MSS · TCD, Dillon MSS

Likenesses J. P. Haverty, group portrait, lithograph with watercolour, pubd 1845 (after his earlier drawing *The monster meeting of the 20th September 1843, at Clifden in the Irish highlands*), NG Ire. · J. Hayes, double portrait, watercolour drawing, 1848 (with Thomas Francis Meagher), President's Residence, Dublin · T. Farrell, statue, 1870, O'Connell Street, Dublin · J. Doyle, caricatures, drawings, BM · Gluckman, daguerreotype, NL Aus. · G. F. Mulvaney, pencil drawing, NG Ire. · H. O'Neill, lithograph (after daguerreotype), BM · S. Smith the elder, oils, NG Ire. [*see illus.*] · double portrait, photograph (with Thomas Meagher), priv. coll. · group portrait, chromolithograph (*The illustrious sons of Ireland*), NPG · portraits, NL Ire. · portraits, repro. in Davis, *William Smith O'Brien*

Wealth at death under £7000: probate, 16 Aug 1864, *CGPLA Ire.*

O'Brolchain, Flaibhertach. *See* Ua Brolcháin, Flaithbertach (*d.* 1175).

Ó Bruadair, Dáibhí (*c.*1625–1698?), poet, has left little documentary evidence of his life apart from his poems. Even these have very little concrete information and so much of what can be said about him is speculation, however plausible. The surname Ó Bruadair may be an amalgamation of the Gaelic Ua/Ó (=grandson of) and the Norse Brodir and it occurs in several places in Ireland, especially in Munster and south-east Leinster. The surname is Anglicized as Bruder and Broderick. Dáibhí was associated with both co. Cork and co. Limerick and the suggestion that he was born and brought up in the former is very likely. Some of his poems refer to the Barrys of Timoleague as being his early friends and patrons. His literary early connections are also with co. Cork. Although he did not belong to one of the hereditary families of learning he had obviously received training in one of the poetic schools which were in a state of great decline in the first half of the seventeenth century, probably the school of the Ó Dálaigh poetic clan at Blarney. His date of birth can be speculated by working back from the earliest of his poems that can be dated which is about 1648, suggesting that he may have been born about 1625 or even slightly earlier. His family seem to have been moderately well off as he often makes comparisons between the conditions of his early life and later hardships. There is no record of when he transferred to co. Limerick but it must have been in the 1650s or early 1660s when he looked for and received patronage from the well-to-do families of that territory, the Roches, Bourkes, and Fitzgeralds.

As mentioned above Ó Bruadair did not belong to one of the hereditary families of traditional learning and before this period of decline this would have shut him out for ever from becoming a master of what he called the 'séada rúin' or mysterious treasures of traditional Irish lore. However one of the features of the decline was that those, like him, who were interested and able, took the place of the traditional families and acted as preservers and transmitters of that lore. They read and wrote Irish, making important copies of the few manuscripts there were, and taught others to do likewise. Some, like Dáibhí, were inspired to add their own compositions to this work of preservation. Dáibhí is known to have written manuscripts, making at least one copy of Geoffrey Keating's

'History of Ireland' and a copy of another historical compilation of the well-known O'Mulconry family of hereditary historians. Unfortunately there are only fragments of his scribal work still extant.

Ó Bruadair also copied his own poems and Seán Stack, a scribe who copied them from Dáibhí's hand, reports that the poet himself annotated them in English, although Stack was unwilling to 'stain his own book with English'. We have some proof of Ó Bruadair's knowledge of and competence in English. One of his patrons and a friend, Sir John Fitzgerald of Clenlish, co. Limerick, was implicated in the Popish Plot and Dáibhí wrote a poem in Irish accompanied by a letter in English to Lord Chief Justice John Keating in 1682 thanking him for the fact that Fitzgerald and others had been acquitted. The letter not only shows him to be interested in affairs of political importance, it also contains some direct information about himself which is worth quoting:

> The Author of the Inclosed Poem is a man not concerned at all in the Weighty Affairs of this World, yet see'th an can smile or frown on things as well as any other fool. He is a great Lover and admirer of honest men, and as great a hater of the adverse party. He holdeth his abode in the proximity of a quiet Company, the Dead, being banished the Society of the living for want of means to rent so much as a House and Garden amongst them. He lives like a Sexton without Salary, in the Corner of a Churchyard, in a Cottage (thanks be to God) as well contented with his stock, which is only a little Dog, a Cat, and a Cock, as the Prince of Parma with all his Principalities. (*Poems*, ed. MacErlean, 1.xxxiii–xxxiv)

Although Ó Bruadair above indicates his satisfaction with his lowly estate a poem composed, according to its title in 1674, 'Mairg nár chrean re maitheas saoghalta' ('Alas the person who did not save worldly wealth'), on the occasion of his fall from a comfortable position, also gives us personal information about him. The title declares him to be stricken with poverty ('i ndíth costais') and tells us that his friends did not come to his aid. In it he contrasts his former condition when he had money to spend and was acceptable to all and sundry as both poet and wit with his present penury and isolation. Having lost his means of wealth, probably his entitlement to sufficient land, he has become an outcast and 'a horseman on foot'. Servants will no longer serve him drink and food and he must engage in manual labour with a spade which causes his knuckles to swell and gives him pains in his joints. The complaint is made even more effective as Ó Bruadair sees his suffering in contrast with the honour due to a poet and scholar in the Gaelic tradition. For example, a poet who was forced to travel on foot would be a disgrace not only to himself but also to all those who could be considered his potential patrons. This poem also mentions a wife and family but it is not known who the wife was nor how many children he had.

Ó Bruadair's poetry spans almost the whole of the second half of the seventeenth century. This alone makes it of great importance. Altogether about seventy items exist which can be confidently ascribed to him and most of these have been published, with copious notes and literal, but sometimes untrustworthy, translations, in the three-volume edition by John C. MacErlean, (1910–17). These poems cover not only the demise of poetry and learning but also comprise a sharp and invaluable commentary on the politics and events of Irish history from Cromwell to the penal laws. His poetry clearly portrays each of the most important events and the major personalities with realistic changes of mood as the fortunes of the native Irish ebbed and flowed. It is notable that as his own fortunes changed for the worse his poetry became more eloquent and passionate. There is no direct evidence that he had read the political poetry in English of the period, like that of Abraham Cowley, or Samuel Butler's *Hudibras*, or the *Poems on the Affairs of State*, but the flavour of his work is very similar to all of these. He combines this sharp political commentary with a metrical and verbal virtuosity that has seldom been equalled in Irish. Some of his poems were translated into English by the Irish writer James Stephens, who described Ó Bruadair's poetry as 'an unending rebellious bawl which would be the most desolating utterance ever made by man, if it were not also the most gleeful'. A more recent, and equally free, verse translation of a selection of the poems was published by Michael Hartnett, an Irish poet hailing from the border region between Limerick and co. Kerry that was Ó Bruadair's home in the second part of his life.

Like much else about Ó Bruadair's life the date of his death is uncertain. He is known to have followed the careers of the 'Wild Geese', military exiles who went to the continent after the treaty of Limerick, especially Patrick Sarsfield and his friend and patron Sir John Fitzgerald, the fortunes of both of whom he celebrated in poems. His last datable poem was composed in 1693 and most scholars believe he died about five years later in 1698. There is a tradition that he lived for a number of years longer.

ALAN HARRISON

Sources *Duanaire Dháibhidh Uí Bhruadair* / *The poems of David Ó Bruadair*, ed. J. C. MacErlean, 3 vols., ITS, 11, 13, 18 (1910–17) · G. Murphy, 'David Ó Bruadair', *Irish Ecclesiastical Record*, 5th ser., 78 (1952), 340–57 · P. de Brún, 'Tuireamh laidne ar Dháibhí Ó Bruadair', *Éigse*, 12 (1967–8), 327–30 · B. Ó Cuív, 'Literature in Irish', *A new history of Ireland*, ed. T. W. Moody and others, 3: *Early modern Ireland, 1534–1691* (1976), 509–45 · S. H. O'Grady, ed., *Catalogue of Irish manuscripts in the British Museum*, 1 (1926) · S. H. O'Grady, ed., *Catalogue of Irish manuscripts in the British Museum*, 2, ed. R. Flower (1926) · P. de Brún, B. Ó Buachalla, and T. Ó Concheanainn, eds., *Nua-dhuanaire*, 1 (1971)

O'Bryan [*formerly* Bryant], **William** (1778–1868), founder of the Bible Christians (Bryanites), was born on 6 February 1778 at Gunwen Farm, Luxulyan, Cornwall, the second son (and third of four children) of William Bryant (1733–1796) and his wife, Thomasine, *née* Lawry, prosperous church Methodist farmers and tinners. The family claimed—probably mistakenly—descent from one of Oliver Cromwell's Irish officers who had settled in Cornwall, a tradition which William junior cherished to such an extent that by about 1810 he had assumed the name O'Bryan.

Bryant was educated at four local schools and then apprenticed to a St Austell draper, returning to Gunwen after the death of his father in 1796. Having undergone conversion experiences in May 1789 and November 1795, he had become a Wesleyan local preacher by 1803, the year in which he married, on 9 July, Catherine Cowlin (1781–1860). In 1808, following a crisis caused by the death of his infant son, Bryant commenced work as a freelance evangelist in mid-Cornwall, forming several societies around Newquay. He had aspirations to enter the Wesleyan ministry but was turned down by the Cornwall district meeting in 1810 on account of his family responsibilities. This set-back reinforced his natural tendency to defy authority. He preached in disregard of the circuit plan and even proposed that the ministry be supported by voluntary contributions; and in November 1810 he was expelled by the Wesleyans, ironically at Gunwen Chapel, which he himself had built on land he had donated. He then engaged in independent evangelism on the western edge of Bodmin Moor, creating a group of societies which were absorbed into the Bodmin and Liskeard circuits in 1814 when O'Bryan was reconciled with the Wesleyans. His irregular evangelistic activities in the Stratton mission on the Cornwall–Devon border from January 1815 soon led to further friction and a second expulsion, and on 1 October 1815 he established an autonomous circuit at Week St Mary, the creation of the first (Arminian) Bible Christian society following eight days later at Lake Farm, Shebbear.

O'Bryan dominated the Bible Christian Connexion during its early years, seeing its membership grow from 237 in 1816 to 8054 in 1827 and spread beyond Devon and Cornwall. Its theology and polity were avowedly Methodist, although its use of women preachers was more distinctive. O'Bryan occupied the movement's key offices, including those of general superintendent (1819–26), president of conference (1819–27), book steward (1819–23), connexional editor (1822–8), and secretary of the general missionary committee (1821–2, 1825–6, 1828–9). He was also the author of its principal foundation documents, such as *The Rules of Society* (1818), and the official hymnbook (1824), as well as the first editor of, and regular contributor to, the *Arminian Magazine*. However, from 1824 there was increasing resistance to his autocratic rule, and disputes over his control of preachers and chapels and his casual approach to connexional and personal finances came to a head in 1828, when he relinquished the conference chair. After losing a further power struggle in 1829, O'Bryan separated with two itinerants and several hundred members, who reassumed the name of Arminian Bible Christians.

On 4 September 1831 O'Bryan and most of his family sailed from Liverpool to emigrate to America; here he settled initially at Bethany, Connecticut, where two of his daughters kept a girls' school, and formed a Methodist circuit. For most of his American years, though, he was resident in New York and its vicinity, continuing to expound the gospel there and even undertaking preaching tours to Ohio and Canada, but never enjoying the scale of evangelistic success he had achieved in England. In 1835 most of those who had seceded in 1829 rejoined the Bible Christians, a condition of the reunion being that O'Bryan relinquished his copyright in the hymnbook and all other claims on the connexion in exchange for £85 and an annuity of £20. He visited England six times between 1834 and 1861, mainly to see relations and to renew old acquaintances in Devon and Cornwall, and latterly even preaching in Bible Christian chapels. He died at Brooklyn, New York, on 8 January 1868, and was buried in Greenwood cemetery, Brooklyn. William and Catherine O'Bryan had seven children, two sons and five daughters, one of whom, Mary [see Thorne, Mary (1807–1883)], married Samuel Thorne, another prominent Bible Christian, and became a celebrated preacher in her own right.   CLIVE D. FIELD

Sources [W. O'Bryan], 'The rise and progress of the connexion of people called Arminian Bible Christians', *Arminian Magazine*, 2–6 (1823–7) • W. O'Bryan, *A narrative of travels in the United States of America* (1836) • S. L. Thorne, *William O'Bryan, founder of the Bible Christians*, 2nd edn (1888) • G. J. Stevenson, *Methodist worthies: characteristic sketches of Methodist preachers of the several denominations*, 6 (1886), 861–7 • O. A. Beckerlegge, 'The rule of William O'Bryan', *Proceedings of the Wesley Historical Society*, 33 (1961–2), 30–35 • L. H. Court, 'William O'Bryan: the man and his book', *United Methodist Magazine*, 8 (1915), 333–7 • T. Shaw, 'The Stratton mission (1811–18) and Bible Christian origins', *Proceedings of the Wesley Historical Society*, 30 (1955–6), 120–26 • T. Shaw, *The Bible Christians, 1815–1907* [1965] • M. J. L. Wickes, *The west country preachers: a new history of the Bible Christian church, 1815–1907* (1987) • F. W. Bourne, *The Bible Christians: their origin and history (1815–1900)* (1905) • [J. Thorne, R. Kinsman, J. H. Prior, and M. Robins], *A jubilee memorial of incidents in the rise and progress of the Bible Christian Connexion* (1865) • S. L. Thorne, *Obedience to the call of god: a funeral sermon on the death of W. O'Bryan* [1868]
Archives Cornwall RO, family corresp. • JRL, Methodist Archives and Research Centre, diaries • JRL, family corresp.

O'Bryen, Dennis (1755–1832), playwright and political pamphleteer, was born in Ireland. He became a surgeon but relinquished the profession and settled in London. The work that first brought him notoriety was the ironical *Defence of the earl of Shelburne from the reproaches of his numerous enemies, in a letter to Sir George Saville, bart., to which is added a postscript addressed to the earl of Stair* (1782; 2nd edn, 1783). Contrary to O'Bryen's title, the work was in fact a mock-defence and it provoked replies from William Petty, first marquess of Lansdowne. On 5 July 1783 O'Bryen's comedy *A Friend in Need is a Friend Indeed* was performed at the Haymarket and thereafter eight times at the theatre. The play, which in some respects resembles Oliver Goldsmith's *Good-Natured Man*, received some unfavourable reviews and was never printed but it did give rise to a newspaper controversy between the author and the theatre manager George Colman the elder, who wrote the epilogue. During the early 1780s O'Bryen published two papers called *The Reasoner* which subsequently appeared in several compilations, the first being attributed by the compiler to Lord Erskine, the second to Sheridan. Other works by O'Bryen include: *A gleam of comfort to this distracted empire, demonstrating the fairness and reasonableness of national confidence in the present ministry*—meaning the ministry of Pitt (1784); *A View of the Commercial Treaty with France* (1786); *Lines Written at Twickenham* (1788), followed in the same year by the anonymously published *The prospect before us, being a series of papers upon the great question which now agitates the public mind*, which was reproduced under the title *The Regency Question* with a new preface, in consequence of the return of the king's insanity in 1810. In 1796 he published *Utrum horum? The Government or the Country?* which rapidly passed through three editions.

O'Bryen's political writings reflect his activism as a supporter of the Fox administration and his key role as Fox's 'public relations adviser' (Reid). On 11 February 1790 O'Bryen and others arranged a meeting to assuage the breach between Burke and Sheridan; the outcome was that it was agreed not to discuss the subject of the French Revolution in the House of Commons. It appears that in 1799 O'Bryen and Sheridan may have had dealings with Arthur O'Connor who was involved in a conspiracy to overthrow English rule in Ireland. It has been suggested that during O'Connor's trial O'Bryen and Sheridan instigated a fracas in the courtroom with the intention of aiding O'Connor's escape. The ensuing mêlée did not achieve this objective and in April 1799 O'Bryen and others stood trial on the charge of inciting a riot. The event was described by the attorney-general as 'one of the most heinous … in the history of our Law': O'Bryen was found not guilty but his fellow accused both received sentences (O'Toole).

O'Bryen was an intimate of Sheridan although he took issue with his suitability to follow Fox as MP for Westminster and succeeded in winning 'Mr. Fox from his purpose' at the end of June 1802 (Fox to O'Bryen, BL, Add. MS 47566, fol. 67). On the change of ministry in 1806 he succeeded to the lucrative sinecure of deputy paymaster-general and he was appointed to the patent office of marshal of the Admiralty at the Cape of Good Hope, worth, it was said £4000 per annum. During the same year O'Bryen secured a £400 loan for Sheridan and in 1816 wrote in emotive terms to the *Morning Post* calling for assistance for Sheridan. O'Bryen died at Margate on 13 August 1832 having resided at 21 Craven Street, Strand, London. His manuscripts and correspondence were sold after his death at auction by Mr Evans.   GAIL BAYLIS

Sources F. O'Toole, *A traitor's kiss: the life of Richard Brinsley Sheridan* (1997) · L. M. Brown and I. R. Christie, eds., *Bibliography of British history, 1789–1851* (1977) · L. Reid, *Charles James Fox: a man for the people* (1969) · *The letters of Richard Brinsley Sheridan*, ed. C. Price, 3 vols. (1966) · C. B. Hogan, ed., *The London stage, 1660–1800*, pt 5: *1776–1800* (1968) · *Literary Gazette* (6 Dec 1834), 820–21 · *GM*, 2nd ser., 3 (1835), 48 · *GM*, 1st ser., 102/2 (1832), 188 · *DNB* · C. J. Fox to O'Bryen, BL, Add. MS 47566, fol. 67
Archives BL, corresp. with C. J. Fox, Add. MS 12099, fols. 16–17 · BL, corresp. with C. J. Fox, Add. MS 47566, fols. 134–5 · BL, corresp. with Lord Holland and Lady Holland, Add. MS 51592 · NRA Scotland, priv. coll., corresp. with William Adam

O'Bryen, Edward (*b.* in or before **1753**, *d.* **1808**), naval officer, details of whose parents and upbringing are unknown, served for nearly five years in the *Aeolus* (36 guns) in the Mediterranean, and for more than three years in the East Indies, in the *Prudent* (64 guns). He passed his examination on 9 August 1775, being then, according to his certificate, more than twenty-one. He was promoted lieutenant on 11 April 1778 and commanded the galley *Ferret*, part of Admiral Lord Howe's fleet in the encounter with d'Estaing at the battle of 11 August off Narragansett

Bay. On 13 November he became a lieutenant in the *Ostrich* (16 guns) and six months later, 2 June 1779, he became second lieutenant in the *Ambuscade* (36 guns), attached to the Channel Fleet. On 1 March 1781 he was appointed first lieutenant to the *Actaeon* (44 guns), serving on the Jamaica station, and on 17 March 1783 he was promoted commander of the sloop *Jamaica* (16 guns). He was promoted to post rank on 14 June and on 6 August assumed command of the *Resistance* (44 guns) which he brought home and paid off in 1784.

During the peace O'Bryen was unemployed and it was not until 1 April 1795 that he was appointed captain of the *Southampton* (32 guns), before moving in June to command the *Windsor Castle* (90 guns), Rear-Admiral Robert Man's flagship, under Admiral William Hotham. The French put into Cadiz and were watched there by Man until 29 July 1796, when he left to rejoin Admiral John Jervis at San Fiorenzo. But Man neglected to bring essential stores from Gibraltar and Jervis sent him back there to remedy this. As Man returned he was sighted by a Spanish squadron and chased into Gibraltar. He called a council of his captains who decided to return to England. This 'extraordinary decision' (Laird Clowes, 4.287) reduced the Mediterranean Fleet by one third and left Jervis in a highly vulnerable position. When Man arrived home in the *Windsor Castle* he was censured, ordered to strike his flag, and not employed afloat again.

O'Bryen's association with this decision and the danger in which it placed Britain may explain why he was unemployed until 20 February 1797 when he was appointed to the *Nassau* (64 guns). He took command on 28 April 1797 when the *Nassau* was flying the flag of Vice-Admiral Richard Onslow at Yarmouth and formed part of the North Sea Fleet under Admiral Adam Duncan. Her crew, whose pay was nineteen months in arrears, were already mutinous and an attempt by O'Bryen to punish the insolent behaviour of one man by dismissing him from the ship was thwarted by the crew's resistance. The situation steadily deteriorated. The Nore mutineers sent delegates urging the North Sea Fleet to join them and on 26 May, when the *Nassau* was ordered to sail to join Duncan, she refused. Two days later the crew determined to hang the boatswain and a seaman for opposing them. When O'Bryen's arguments had no effect, he 'hove his hanger overboard and said if they were going to hang an officer he should be the first or heave himself overboard' (Lloyd, 289), but the crew would not allow this and the arguments continued until O'Bryen 'left them distracted' (ibid.) and seemed intent on suicide. When the *Nassau* ultimately followed other mutinous ships to Sheerness on 31 May, O'Bryen left her and though invited by the crew to return he refused to do so until the red flag had been hauled down. O'Bryen returned to the ship on 14 June 'on which the ship's company discovered the strongest inclination of regard and affection' (ibid., 295).

Onslow had shifted his flag to the *Adamant* (50 guns) after 26 May and on 25 July transferred to the *Monarch* (74 guns). O'Bryen, who had been appointed his flag captain on 4 July, took a distinguished part in the battle of Camperdown on 11 October 1797. Leading the larboard division, the *Monarch* approached the Dutch line and when O'Bryen reported he could see no gap to pass through Onslow replied 'the *Monarch* will make a passage' (R. D. Franks, 'Admiral Sir Richard Onslow', *Mariner's Mirror*, 67, 1981, 335), and insisted no shot be fired until the Dutch vice-admiral was separated from the vessel astern of him. The *Monarch* passed between the Dutch ships *Jupiter* and *Haarlem*, firing into each and then concentrating on Rear-Admiral Reyntjes's *Jupiter*. The Dutch frigate *Monnikendam* gallantly but vainly threw herself between the two only to receive the full blast of *Monarch's* second broadside. Onslow's concentration brought nine British ships against five Dutch, four of which surrendered within the next hour. The *Monarch's* casualties, 36 killed, 100 wounded, her hull riddled with shot, are evidence that she bore the brunt of heavy fighting. O'Bryen himself refuted a later insinuation, made to George III, that Onslow was lucky to have him as his captain (Stirling, 1.55). But O'Bryen must have been very busy in the months following the battle, when Onslow took command of the North Sea Fleet, until Duncan rejoined in August 1798. The *Monarch* returned to Yarmouth for repairs but was in the North Sea again in early October meeting heavy gales before being relieved in December.

O'Bryen does not appear to have been employed between 1798 and the end of the war. He is said to have commanded the *Kent* (74 guns) in the Mediterranean between 1801 and 1803, but was invalided in May of that year. He had no further service, retiring to his house at Cattisfield, Hampshire. He was married to Mary Alsop of London, who died some time in the spring of 1807, at Cattisfield, after a lingering illness, leaving a daughter, Mary. In April 1808 O'Bryen married Mrs Martha Charlotte Bradby of Cattisfield; they had no children, but an earlier liaison had left an illegitimate son, John Cavendish, to whom O'Bryen left 20 guineas in his will.

Although O'Bryen was employed during the war with the American colonies, his slow promotion and unemployment between 1783 and 1795 illustrates a lack of influential patronage. However, his reputation as a brave and professional officer finally brought appointment, though on a station, the North Sea, not noted for prize money. The mutiny on the *Nassau* was the result of long-standing grievances and the crew expressed their respect and affection for him. But to be associated with failure or mutiny, however blameless, was to have a black mark against one's name, no less significant for being invisible. Thereafter ill health prevented the possibility of a more exciting career in the Napoleonic wars. Promoted rear admiral of the blue on 9 November 1805 and of the white on 28 April 1808, O'Bryen died on 18 December 1808 at Cattisfield. He was survived by his second wife.   P. K. CRIMMIN

Sources DNB · *Naval Chronicle*, 17 (1807), 352 · *Naval Chronicle*, 19 (1808), 352 · *Naval Chronicle*, 21 (1809), 88 · C. Lloyd, 'New light on the mutiny on the Nore', *Mariner's Mirror*, 46 (1960), 286–95 · *Pages and portraits from the past: being the private papers of Sir William Hotham*, ed. A. M. W. Stirling, 2 vols. (1919) · W. L. Clowes, *The Royal Navy: a history from the earliest times to the present*, 7 vols. (1897–1903), vols. 3–4 · will, PRO, PROB 11/1493/129 · PRO, ADM 6/21, 22, 25, 26, 27, 28 · D. Syrett and R. L. DiNardo, *The commissioned sea officers of the Royal Navy, 1660–1815*, rev. edn, Occasional Publications of the Navy RS, 1 (1994) · D. Lyon, *The sailing navy list: all the ships of the Royal Navy, built, purchased and captured, 1688–1860* (1993)

Likenesses G. Noble and J. Parker, group portrait, line engraving, pubd 1803 (after J. Smart; *Commemorating of 11th Oct 1797*), BM, NPG · W. and J. Skelton, line engraving, pubd 1809 (after J. Smart), BM

Wealth at death house and contents at Cattisfield, near Fareham, Hampshire; farm at Titchfield; approx. £3000 invested in 3 per cent consols: will, PRO, PROB 11/1493/129

O'Bryen [O'Brien], **James, third marquess of Thomond** (1769–1855), naval officer, was second son of Edward O'Bryen (*d.* March 1801), army captain, and his wife, Mary Carrick. His uncle, Murrough O'Bryen, was first marquess of Thomond. As a captain's servant, O'Bryen entered the navy on 17 April 1783 on the *Hebe*, stationed in the channel. From 1786 to 1789 he was a midshipman in the frigates *Pegasus* and *Andromeda*, both commanded by the duke of Clarence, under whom he also served with the Channel Fleet in the *Valiant* in 1790. Promoted lieutenant on 19 November 1790, O'Bryen joined, in succession, on the home station, the *London* (98 guns), the *Artois* (38 guns), and the *Brunswick* (74 guns). In the last he was present at Cornwallis's retreat from a greatly superior French force off Brest on 16 and 17 June 1795. On 5 December 1796 he was promoted to command the sloop *Childers*.

O'Bryen married, on 25 November 1800, Eliza Bridgman (*d.* 14 Feb 1802), second daughter of James Willyams of Carnanton, Cornwall. From 1800 to 1804 he commanded the *Emerald* (36 guns), on the West Indian station, where, on 24 June 1803, he captured the *Enfant Prodigue*, a French schooner of 16 guns, and in the spring of 1804 distinguished himself in forwarding the supplies at the capture of Surinam, as well as by defeating a projected enemy expedition against Antigua. In 1806, while in the West Indies, he married Jane Horsford (*d.* 8 Sept 1843), daughter of Thomas Ottley, and widow of Valentine Horne Horsford, of Antigua. In February 1808 his uncle, the marquess, died and his brother, William, succeeded to the title. O'Bryen was advanced to the same precedency as if his father had succeeded to the marquessate of Thomond, and he was henceforth known as Lord James O'Bryen. From September 1813 until November 1815 he served in the channel in the *Warspite* (74 guns). He became rear-admiral in 1825.

On the accession of William IV, O'Bryen was made a lord of the bedchamber, and was made GCH on 13 May 1831. He was made vice-admiral in 1837 and succeeded his brother, William O'Bryen, on 21 August 1846, as the third marquess of Thomond in the Irish peerage. In January 1847, at Bath, he married Anne Fane (*d.* 22 Oct 1874), daughter of William Flint, sister of Sir Charles William Flint, and widow of Rear-Admiral Fane. He became a full admiral on 13 May 1847, and an admiral of the red in 1853. He died at his home near Bath on 3 July 1855, and was buried in the catacombs of St Saviour's Church, Walcot, Bath, on 10 July. O'Bryen left no children, so the marquessate of Thomond became extinct; of his subsidiary titles the earldom of Inchiquin became extinct but the barony of Inchiquin devolved to a male heir.

G. C. BOASE, *rev.* ANDREW LAMBERT

Sources D. Syrett and R. L. DiNardo, *The commissioned sea officers of the Royal Navy, 1660–1815*, rev. edn, Occasional Publications of the Navy RS, 1 (1994) • O'Byrne, *Naval biog. dict.* [see 'Thomond'] • *GM*, 2nd ser., 44 (1855), 193 • GEC, *Peerage*
Archives NL Ire.
Wealth at death under £50,000: GEC, *Peerage*

Observator, the. *See* Parker, Henry (1604–1652).

O'Byrne, Fiach MacHugh (*c.*1544–1597), chieftain, was probably born at Ballinacor in co. Wicklow, the first child of Hugh MacShane O'Byrne (*c.*1525–1579), chief of the Gabhal Raghnaill branch of the O'Byrne clan, and his first wife, Sadhbh (*c.*1530–*c.*1600), daughter of Phélim Buidhe MacLorcan O'Byrne. Fiach was heir both to his father's inaccessible lands centring on Glenmalure in the Wicklow Mountains and to the precarious political situation that had grown out of the treaty signed by his grandfather Shane Oge MacRedmund in 1542. The treaty saw the multi-branched O'Byrne clan unilaterally surrender its lands to the crown only to have them regranted under English law and custom. It became clear, however, that the senior O'Byrnes of Crioch Branach, occupying the more fertile lowlands east of the Gabhal Raghnaill, were unduly favoured under the terms of the treaty, while the junior branches, particularly the Gabhal Raghnaill, were marginalized. Moreover, Tudor rule at the local level had by the 1560s become intrusive and high-handed, providing a visible focal point for Gaelic anger. Thus Fiach inherited an increasingly acrimonious relationship both with the senior O'Byrnes and with the Tudor administration: his father commenced hostilities in both directions in order to establish the status denied to the Gabhal Raghnaill by the 1542 treaty.

Hugh MacShane's legacy Fiach's early years were spent close to his father, whose reputation as a resourceful chief or 'wily' upstart had been growing. Fiach first appears in January 1563 when he was pardoned alongside his father for attempting to procure his neighbours' support in a rebellion against Lord Deputy Sussex; it was rumoured that Sussex planned to kill them in their beds at Christmas. The later 1560s saw similar pardons granted to Fiach as his father employed the dual strategy of acting aggressively toward the crown—by capturing government officials, or by harbouring Irish rebels or exacting black rents—and then securing a pardon for his actions. It was during this extension of Gabhal Raghnaill power, about 1565, that Fiach married Sadhbh (*c.*1550–*c.*1581), daughter of a leading member of the Kavanaghs. His sister Margaret married Rory Oge O'More, leader of the expropriated O'More clan. These carefully planned marriages at once strengthened Hugh MacShane's hand and increased the frequency of co-ordinated Gaelic attacks against the crown.

In April 1572 Fiach and his brother-in-law Brian MacCahir Kavanagh were implicated in the murder of Robert Browne, an influential south co. Wexford landlord. The incident's severity was greatly aggravated because Browne had married the daughter of Nicholas White, seneschal of Wexford. Worse still, White, who was at court when the murder occurred, attracted the queen's personal interest in the matter. Elizabeth demanded justice and in July, Francis Agard, seneschal of O'Byrne's country, attacked the Gabhal Raghnaill, killing Fiach's brother who had allegedly been present at the murder. There is no evidence that Fiach had any involvement in Browne's murder other than his association with the Kavanaghs. Nevertheless he offered to apprehend the murderers. The compromise, however, was undermined as the vengeful White attacked the Gabhal Raghnaill, pushing them and their Gaelic allies into open rebellion. The revolt was suppressed by February 1573, but only following a concerted effort by seneschals White and Agard who, in the end, agreed to pardon both Fiach and his father. The affair established Fiach's reputation as a principal Gaelic leader in Leinster who reputedly commanded 200 kerne.

Fiach gradually eclipsed his father's influence. He pursued a more aggressive strategy toward his neighbours. The ageing Hugh MacShane, however, continued as the Gabhal Raghnaill chief, carrying out negotiations with government representatives while his son 'independently' committed depredations against them. In December 1575 Lord Deputy Henry Sidney, following a progress from Dublin to Waterford which was incessantly hampered by Fiach, wrote of the Janus-faced O'Byrnes, 'the father was with me without protection, but the son lyveth aloof' (PRO, SP 63/59/17). In 1578 Thomas Masterson, then seneschal of Wexford, invited Fiach to a conference where the latter's capture or murder was intended. But following the massacre at Mullaghmast, Fiach approached the meeting with ample circumspection and soon received intelligence that alerted him to Masterson's ploy. He launched a successful counter-attack that might have resulted in the capture and ransom of Masterson himself. The government, however, continued an aggressive campaign. Rory Oge and many of his followers were killed and Hugh MacShane and Fiach MacHugh eventually surrendered in September–October 1578. Fiach submitted at Christ Church where he recognized the new seneschal of the O'Byrnes, Sir Henry Harrington, as his 'captain'. Following this, Fiach and his father travelled to Castledermot, co. Kildare, where they submitted to Lord Justice Sir William Drury. These dual roles, as dangerous rebel and obedient client, played masterfully by Fiach and Hugh MacShane, were now ended.

An autonomous chieftaincy bordering Dublin Fiach succeeded as chief of the Gabhal Raghnaill following his father's death in late 1579. The government now dealt with the Gabhal Raghnaill quite separately from the increasingly Anglicized senior O'Byrnes. Thus upon his accession Fiach had, in a way, achieved the distinction his father sought so desperately: he became the focus for Gaelic resistance in Leinster. Accordingly, in November

1579 the earl of Desmond—in a desperate effort to extend his Munster rebellion to Leinster—dispatched a letter to Fiach urging his support. Fiach did not throw in his lot with Desmond; instead he waited for more favourable circumstances to arise. This occurred rather unexpectedly when James Eustace, third Viscount Baltinglass, a landed Leinster gentleman imbued with Counter-Reformation Catholicism, tapped into Gaelic Leinster's disaffection with aggressive governmental policies and pledged to overthrow the queen in the pope's name. Fiach's religious devotion is difficult to gauge, but he at least paid lip-service to the zealous Baltinglass. By summer 1580 Fiach had allied himself with a leading member of the Crioch Branach O'Byrnes and some neighbouring O'Tooles and Kavanaghs. Fiach, belying his principal motivation, ravaged Wexford, thus taking revenge on seneschal Masterson who had in April murdered members of the Kavanagh clan. Thus a confluence of interests embodied by Fiach and Baltinglass brought a certain unity to Gaelic elements in Leinster while concurrently breathing life into Desmond's faltering rebellion. Yet Baltinglass failed to garner the active support of the pale gentry and the rebellion in Leinster lost momentum.

The deputy elect, Arthur, Lord Grey of Wilton, eager to suppress the rebellion, impetuously pursued the rebels into the fastness of the Wicklow Mountains. With a large but inexperienced retinue, Grey was defeated at Glenmalure on 25 August 1580. English losses were not heavy but a disproportionate number of officers had fallen. The victory was total and instilled confidence in the rebels. Fiach had trebled his strength of a decade earlier, now commanding some 600 kerne. A comparison with the estimated forty kerne available to his great-grandfather less than a century earlier illustrates his startling rise. In the months following, Fiach and his allies burnt Wicklow and attacked several lowland targets, including a settlement within 6 miles of Dublin. Their hopes were quickly dashed, however: Grey received further reinforcements and slaughtered Desmond's foreign aid in November. Militarily the rebels were no match for an amply supplied Grey who by May 1581 had placed garrisons near Fiach's power base at Castlekevin and Kilcommon. Moreover, certain of the senior O'Byrnes fought for the crown, in one instance killing four of Fiach's best men, and they perhaps facilitated Grey's burning of Ballinacor in April. Following Baltinglass's flight to the continent Fiach came to terms with the government, being pardoned in September after unsuccessfully attempting to secure religious freedom and a pardon for Desmond. Fiach's considerable military capacity, though diminished, was not destroyed and he remained an unpredictable and largely autonomous presence near the centre of English power in Ireland.

In the following years Fiach, watched closely by a suspicious government, kept the peace. In 1584 he renewed his submission to Lord Deputy Perrot and helped Harrington punish thieves who resided within his lands. Fiach posed few problems so long as his sovereignty was respected. By this time he had married a second time, to Rose (c.1558–c.1600), daughter of Fiach O'Toole of Castlekevin. His four known legitimate children, however, were all born to him by Sadhbh. Fiach was the most powerful and prominent member of the O'Byrne clan following the death in 1580 of Dunlang MacEdmund, the last recognized chief of Crioch Branach. Thus it was Fiach whom the government summoned to attend parliament in April 1585 (although he did not sit), and who appeared before the deputy in English apparel in early 1586. Nevertheless Fiach, seated so near to Dublin, remained for successive English officials a glaring example of the failure of Tudor policy. In May 1587 Perrot petitioned the queen for:

> suche small allowance as heretofore I have requested in that behalf, I truste within one 6 or 8 weekes, to have his hedd or drive him into the sea and settle that parte that it shalbe no more a galle to Leynester. (PRO, SP 63/129/64)

But the campaign against Fiach did not materialize, and it later emerged that Perrot had explored the more inexpensive strategy of having him assassinated. His every move, real or exaggerated, aroused suspicion in Dublin. Ultimately, this led to his downfall.

Even at peace Fiach was a conduit for disaffected elements in Leinster. He harboured known felons—most notably his son-in-law Walter Reagh Fitzgerald—and in 1591 his proximity to Dublin facilitated the escape of both his own pledges and the future O'Donnell chief Hugh Roe. He also intrigued with Spain, although the chances of 5000 Spanish troops appearing in Glenmalure were slender; it was Fiach's virtual independence and penchant to harbour rebels that were an embarrassing reality for the government. Yet the largely independent Gaelic dimension of Fiach's refuge must not be underestimated. Following the Anglicization of the Crioch Branach O'Byrnes and their abandonment of Gaelic chiefly succession, Fiach represented the bulwark of Gaelic culture in the district. This, combined with the autonomy enjoyed in Glenmalure in the face of English cultural and administrative encroachment, allowed for a flowering of Gaelic culture, manifested in poetry and song. Gaelic poets travelled from far and wide to receive the patronage of the last powerful Gaelic chief in Leinster: 'Baile na Corra ár gcuan sealga, seanróimh oinigh Innsi Néill; beag an t-iongnadh buadh gá bhuidhnibh, d'iolradh na sluagh suilbhir séimh' (TCD, MS 1288, fol. 107b: 'Ballinacor is our resort for the chase, ancient sanctuary of Innis-Neill's generosity; such is the multitude of its blithe and accomplished companies that 'tis small wonder though its denizens bear away the palm').

The inflow of expropriated clansmen and dissident English into such an environment undoubtedly politicized the situation; and in March 1594 Fiach's sons, along with the felon Walter Reagh, burnt to death Sir Pierce Fitzgerald, sheriff of Kildare, and his family at Ardree. In a gesture reminiscent of his father, Fiach disclaimed their actions and later—following the arrival of the new deputy, Sir William Russell—offered submission in return for confirmation of his lands by letters patent. It was, however, too late as Fitzgerald's murder, coupled with an outbreak of hostilities in Ulster, at last forced the government to address the reality of Fiach's autonomy.

Fiach's slow destruction and the failure of Tudor policy Russell, careful to avoid a repeat of the 1580 débâcle, attacked an unsuspecting Ballinacor in January 1595. Fiach narrowly escaped, but the subsequent garrisoning of Ballinacor limited his manoeuvrability. The senior O'Byrnes supported the deputy, and Fiach's former ally, Hugh Duff O'Byrne, emerged, with government support, as Fiach's internal rival. Russell was determined to crush Fiach so that he might fully devote his energies to the worsening situation in Ulster. Fiach, however, repeatedly eluded capture despite Russell's sustained investment of time, money, and men in the Wicklow Mountains. The capture and execution of Walter Reagh in April 1595 failed to induce Fiach to surrender; but following the capture of his wife, Rose, Fiach surrendered his eldest son Turlough as a pledge for her release and presented himself before the deputy in November. Yet Fiach was not imprisoned (though Turlough was executed), and he successfully petitioned for a full pardon and the restoration of Ballinacor. He was considered a spent force, too old and weak to resume hostilities, and the government was eager to turn its attention towards Ulster.

The agreed pardon, however, did not materialize and the aged Fiach threatened the government through depredations committed by his surviving sons and by negotiations with O'Neill. Communication between Fiach and the Ulster chiefs was by the mid-1590s well established and may have dated back to Baltinglass's rebellion. O'Neill doubtless exploited Fiach's proximity to Dublin, believing him capable of diverting large numbers of government troops away from the Ulster theatre. Fiach, for his part, used the threat of an alliance with O'Neill as a bargaining chip. In truth, co-ordinated military action and the dispatch of thousands of Ulster troops to Glenmalure were no more real than a Spanish landing there. Nevertheless, government preoccupation with Ulster facilitated Fiach's recapture of Ballinacor in September 1596. Russell was enraged and launched the first of several expeditions against Fiach, but once again achieved little save the desolation of much of the district. In January 1597 O'Neill criticized Fiach's persecution, stating that he had been included in a truce concluded between himself and Sir John Norris. Russell, however, disregarded O'Neill's protests and continued the hunt for Fiach. By this point Fiach was militarily broken, Russell frequently entering his country and returning unscathed. This dominance allowed Russell to gain valuable intelligence that revealed Fiach's movements. Thus on Sunday 8 May 1597 Russell's men, doubtless acting on such intelligence, descended upon a virtually unguarded Fiach, probably at a place called Farranerin, and killed him. A sergeant to Captain Lee beheaded him and brought his head to Russell, which, along with his quartered body, was displayed at Dublin Castle. The four masters noted succinctly: 'Fiacha mac

Aodha mic Seaain o Ghleand Mhaoilugra do thuitim iar ttarraing ceilcce da combrathair fair ar furáileamh ard iustír na hereann Sir Uilliam Russel isin ceaid mí do shamhradh na bliadhna so' ('Fiagh, son of Hugh, son of John from Glenmalure, was slain in the first month of summer in this year, having been treacherously betrayed by his relative at the bidding of the chief justiciary of Ireland, Sir William Russell'; *AFM*, *sub anno* 1597).

Russell reported that the inhabitants of the district rejoiced at the death of their oppressor. Such sentiment, however, was not universal and may represent Russell's own eagerness to secure a propaganda victory. Captain Sir Edward Stanley, worried about the repercussions of Fiach's death, noted 'the people heare ther hearts be so hardened towards us that fewe of them rejoyseth at any good ceruice don' (PRO, SP 63/199/30). The prolonged campaign against Fiach did not bring the district under English control and his sons and followers allied themselves even more closely to O'Neill. In May 1599 Fiach's son and heir Phélim routed a force under Sir Henry Harrington between Ballinacor and Rathdrum, but received a full pardon in 1601, retaining certain Gabhal Raghnaill lands under English law. Thereafter Phélim, accepting the reality of the English conquest, adopted a more co-operative relationship with the government and sought to achieve recognition of his landed claims through English courts. The days of militant Gaelic resistance to English expansion in O'Byrne country ended with the death of Fiach, the failure of Tyrone's rebellion, and the completion of the Tudor conquest.

Contemporary English chroniclers and later English historians ignored the significance of O'Byrne's career, depicting him as a savage thief, mindlessly raiding both his English and Irish neighbours from his mountain refuge. Ironically the preponderance of Irish nationalist historians, bent on correcting such perceived ethnocentrism, similarly ignored Fiach, perhaps regarding him more as an outlaw than a patriot. They concentrated instead on powerful, 'legitimate' chiefs geographically further removed from English influence. Only recently, coinciding with the four hundredth anniversary of Fiach's death, have historians begun to re-examine his career. Drawing on a meticulously researched, but largely forgotten, history of Fiach and the O'Byrnes written by Liam Price in the 1930s, a clearer picture of this remarkable figure is emerging, offering a window into a Gaelic culture coping not only with military encroachment, but also with cultural and religious Anglicization emanating from the adjacent pale.   CHRISTOPHER MAGINN

Sources PRO, SP 63 (Elizabeth) · TCD, MS 1288 · J. S. Brewer and W. Bullen, eds., *Calendar of the Carew manuscripts*, 6 vols., PRO (1867–73) · CSP Ire., 1509–73 · S. Mac Airt, ed., *Leabhar Branach* (Dublin, 1944) · AFM · *The Irish fiants of the Tudor sovereigns*, 4 vols. (1994) · S. H. O'Grady, ed., *Catalogue of Irish manuscripts in the British Museum*, 1 (1926) · T. Ó Laidhin, ed., *Sidney state papers, 1565–70*, IMC (1962) · C. MacNeill, ed., 'The Perrot papers', *Analecta Hibernica*, 12 (1943), 3–65 · [J. Hardiman], ed., *Inquisitionum in officio rotulorum cancellariae Hiberniae asservatarum repertorium*, 2 vols., Irish Record Commission (1826–9) · *Calendar of the Irish patent rolls of James I* (before 1830);

facs. edn as *Irish patent rolls of James I* (1966) • M. A. S. Hume, ed., *Calendar of letters and state papers relating to English affairs, preserved principally in the archives of Simancas*, 4 vols., PRO (1892–9) • W. M. Hennessy, ed. and trans., *The annals of Loch Cé: a chronicle of Irish affairs from AD 1014 to AD 1590*, 2 vols., Rolls Series, 54 (1871) • E. Spenser, *A view of the present state of Ireland*, ed. W. L. Renwick (1970) • L. Price, 'Notes on Feagh McHugh O'Byrne', *Journal of the Kildare Archaeological Society*, 60 (1930), 134–75 • C. O'Brien, ed., *Feagh McHugh O'Byrne, the Wicklow firebrand*, Rathdrum Historical Society (1998) • L. Price, 'The Byrnes' country in county Wicklow in the sixteenth century', *Journal of the Royal Society of Antiquaries of Ireland*, 7th ser., 3 (1933), 224–42

Archives TCD, 'An Leabhar Branach' or 'Book of the O'Byrnes', MS 1288

O'Byrne, William Richard (1823–1896), naval biographer, was elder son of Robert O'Byrne, of Cabinteely, near Dublin, and his wife, Martha Trougher, daughter of Joseph Clarke of Norwich. His brother, Robert Henry O'Byrne, was the author of the *Representative History of Great Britain and Ireland* (1848). He was educated at University College School, London (1838–9).

O'Byrne was scarcely out of his teens and 'a civilian, previously unconnected with the Service' (O'Byrne, v), when he had the idea of compiling and publishing a record of the service of every living naval officer of the executive branch. Permitted access to Admiralty records, he worked at this for six years, publishing the first parts in 1845, and completed the volume of 1400 closely printed pages, on nearly 5000 officers, in 1849. The labour was great for the Admiralty records, his major source, were in a semi-chaotic state. He had extensive correspondence with his subjects, but he seems to have checked their statements against official documents in all cases. The *Naval Biographical Dictionary* is a work of almost unparalleled accuracy—a fact which Sir John Laughton had many occasions to test and to prove during the compilation of the *Dictionary of National Biography*. A factual compilation, the dictionary is an invaluable reference work. It was not, however, a financial success for the author. An edition of 2000 was sold at 42s. a copy; but out of the proceeds £100 was all that O'Byrne received for six years' labour and expenses. The Admiralty awarded him £100, and Sir Francis Thornhill Baring (Lord Northbrook) appointed him its librarian; but Baring left office shortly afterwards and his successor, the duke of Northumberland, refused to confirm the appointment. A testimonial from naval officers was started, and, at a meeting at the Royal United Service Institution, O'Byrne was presented with a piece of plate and a purse of £400. In 1857 he was specially elected a member of the Athenaeum.

O'Byrne married, in 1851, Emily, eldest daughter of John Trougher Handy of Malmesbury, Wiltshire; they had one daughter. Mrs O'Byrne predeceased her husband. From about 1856 to 1880, O'Byrne was a navy agent in London with his brother, Robert (barrister, Lincoln's Inn), as O'Byrne Brothers. In 1859 he began a second edition of the dictionary, updated and containing data on officers of the civil branches of the service. This—which was not as accurate as the first edition—did not pay, and was not carried beyond the letter G, with the less regret on O'Byrne's

part, as at about that time, on the death of his cousin Georgiana O'Byrne, he succeeded to the Cabinteely estate in co. Wicklow, which had been in the family for many generations, though probably not the fifty-four that was claimed. In 1872–3 he was high sheriff of Wicklow, and was Liberal MP for the county from 1874 to 1880. He favoured denominational education, further amendment of the Land Act in Ireland, and Irish home rule.

O'Byrne's property was heavily mortgaged, and on the depreciation of Irish land he was unable to pay the interest. The mortgagees foreclosed, and he was left practically destitute. Years of privation and struggle followed. In 1884 he was awarded £100 from the royal bounty, and tried to get the Admiralty to appoint him officially, at a regular salary, to prepare a new edition of his dictionary. The Admiralty refused to do this, or to help to further the project, as—with their improved records system—the work would be useless to them, while the fact that it would not pay a publisher to take it up seemed to show that the public did not want it. During his later years O'Byrne's health broke down, and he was mainly dependent on his daughter. In summer 1896 he was granted £125 from the royal bounty, but it was too late. He died at 258 Fulham Road, South Kensington, London, on 7 July 1896. His *Biographical Dictionary* was reprinted in 1986 and remains a standard work of reference.

J. K. LAUGHTON, rev. ANDREW LAMBERT

Sources BL, O'Byrne MSS, Add. MSS 38039–38054 • *The Times* (16 July 1896) • private information (*c.*1901) • O'Byrne, *Naval biog. dict.* • *WWBMP*, vol. 1 • Kelly, *Handbk* (1879) • Boase, *Mod. Eng. biog.*

Archives BL, collections relating to naval biographical dictionary, Add. MSS 38039–38054 | BL, corresp. with Lord Dundonald, Add. MS 26652

O'Cahan, Sir Donnell Ballagh [Domhnall Ballach Ó Catháin] (*d.* 1626?), chieftain, himself illiterate, was fostered in the household of Turlough Luineach O'Neill, and was the eldest son of Rory O'Cahan, being chosen (*doirdnead*, 'was ordained'; *AFM*, s.a. 1598), after the latter's death on 14 April 1598, to succeed as lord of O'Cahan's country, which took in much of the modern co. Londonderry, in Ulster. His principal castle and demesne lands were near Limavady. The military might of O'Cahan was estimated variously, with figures of 140 horse and 400 foot being sometimes exceeded. O'Cahan was O'Neill's principal *uriaght*, or vassal, and had a special role in the O'Neill inauguration ceremony.

Donnell O'Cahan succeeded during the Nine Years' War, in which he participated, and was to be the last O'Cahan lord in the Gaelic order. His role in the war was mainly a local one, and after Sir Henry Docwra was placed at Derry in 1600, he made a number of incursions into O'Cahan's country and took Enagh Castle in June 1601. In June 1602 O'Cahan sought negotiations with Sir Arthur Chichester, then bringing military pressure on him from Carrickfergus, and on 27 July Docwra procured his submission and consequent desertion of the O'Neill cause, itself weakened by the earlier Spanish failure at Kinsale. By its terms, approved by Lord Deputy Mountjoy, he should receive title under the crown to much of the lordship, but surrender significant parts, principally a substantial area opposite Derry, the castle at Coleraine, an area at Dungiven, and certain fishing rights. He received a grant of the custody of the restored land, but not an outright patent, on 20 October following, and, on 21 October, a pardon to himself, his then wife, Rosa, a daughter of Hugh O'Neill (formerly married to Hugh Roe O'Donnell), his family, chaplain, and other followers, and the inhabitants of O'Cahan's country. Thereafter he supported the English side with his forces.

However, in the pacification of Ulster after 1603 (Mountjoy's final strategy), O'Neill was restored as earl of Tyrone, with the lands granted to him to include O'Cahan country. O'Cahan, still wanting independent ownership, felt betrayed by Docwra, the local commander, and by Mountjoy, who had now secured his recall. In addition, his relations soon deteriorated with O'Neill, who sought O'Cahan's full compliance. On 17 February 1607 O'Cahan reached an agreement with Tyrone whereby he should hold in freehold under him, but claim no other right or title, paying an annual rent of 200 cows, the easterly lands 'from the mountain [Slieve Gullion] to the Bann' to be held by the earl as assurance for its payment, and with O'Neill to arbitrate any disputes between O'Cahan and 'his gentlemen and followers' (*CSP Ire., 1606–8*, 110–11). However, on 4 March George Montgomery, the recently appointed bishop of Derry, whose primary aim was to secure title to the extensive termon lands as temporalities for the Church of Ireland, reported to Dublin that O'Cahan, desiring not to be in 'thrall if he might be free', still sought separate title under the crown, provided his country were not divided like Monaghan, 'of which he had some fear' (ibid., 125). The 'settlement' of Monaghan in 1591 had abolished MacMahon lordly power there by diffusing ownership among the heads of competing branches, and the Dublin government under Sir Arthur Chichester, wishing to extend its rule over the larger northern lords and reduce their power, had revived that settlement there in 1606.

In May 1607 O'Cahan, encouraged by Montgomery, initiated a suit against Tyrone before the lord deputy and council. He claimed longstanding ancestral possession of O'Cahan's country, insisting that the O'Cahan obligation to the O'Neills had been essentially that of military service—with 100 horse and 300 foot—together with an annual tribute of twenty-one cows, and requested a separate patent of the entire area. Tyrone answered with an assertion that there was no such thing as O'Cahan's country, insisting that the O'Cahans had always been O'Neill tenants at sufferance, and, requesting a new patent to himself, appealed in like terms to the king. At hearing, the case became acrimonious with Tyrone snatching and tearing up a document of O'Cahan's, and a temporizing order was made, to be subject to royal instructions on the matter: O'Cahan should hold two-thirds and the earl one-third, namely the Maghery region in the south-east. O'Cahan was also knighted in Dublin on 28 June 1607.

However, since both sought recourse to the king, so now London was plied with recommendations for a thoroughgoing settlement of landownership conducive to more effective rule and revenue raising. Montgomery, concerned for the security of himself and others at the remote outpost at Derry, recommended favour to O'Cahan, but also that he should be separated from O'Neill, as O'Doherty had been from O'Donnell, and retain to himself a substantial scope of land sufficient to be a baron, with more to be granted to the English military men who had stayed on since the war. The attorney-general, Sir John Davies, visualized a radical outcome which would reduce the landownership of both O'Cahan and O'Neill in tandem. Relying on the act of attainder of Shane O'Neill in 1569, he argued that present titles could be questioned, and ownership not only be dispersed among lesser Irish figures but, crucially, a body of new English proprietors be introduced also. Were this opportunity not taken, and O'Neill in particular not reduced to the 'moderate condition of other lords in Ireland and in England at this day', then there would be 'no commonwealth in Ulster' (*CSP Ire., 1606–8*, 212–13). In July the king decided that both should go to England in the autumn for a final determination in his presence, with Davies in attendance. The flight of the earls in September 1607 put paid to such potentialities and left O'Cahan in uncertainty. In the atmosphere of mutual suspicion and fear of conspiracy that followed, he kept distant from those placed in authority locally, and was absent when Davies, in preparation for plantation, brought about Tyrone's indictment at Strabane at the end of the year. On the view of London that he might 'shake the rod' (ibid., 399), Chichester had him arrested and brought to Dublin in February 1608. It was not surprising, he thought, that O'Cahan and others were inconstant and wavering because their priests assured them that the earls would return to renew warfare, and in March he was advised not to release him 'considering the corner he dwells in' (ibid., 434).

After delays due to other business, O'Doherty's rising and vacillation, O'Cahan was indicted on six charges of treason, some deriving from evidence from ambitious relatives, including one that he had both intended to accompany O'Neill in flight and to join with him if he returned with foreign forces. When the parallel case against Niall Garbh O'Donnell, begun in June 1609, looked unlikely to secure a conviction, that against O'Cahan was deferred pending further instructions from London, and on 31 July a royal warrant was issued for both to be sent to England. He was dispatched, with the charges against him, at the end of October and placed in the Tower of London. From there, in 1610, he presented petitions against his confinement, denying complicity with O'Neill, and, in an impoverished state, tried in 1613 to raise income from cattle dispersed among now unresponsive followers, but did not gain his release. His incarceration eliminated a potential focus of opposition to plantation, and ensured that in the distinctive co. Londonderry plantation that followed from 1610, the Irish were restored to less land than in the other Ulster planted counties.

O'Cahan's marriage to O'Neill's daughter fell victim to

their dispute. His first wife, probably, was Mary, daughter of Sir Hugh MacManus O'Donnell, Lord of Tirconnell; she subsequently married Sir Teig O'Rourke. His second wife (even possibly his first liaison), and the mother of his sons, was Honora, herself an O'Cahan by birth. Donnell reverted to her after his third, and political, marriage to Rosa O'Neill broke down, and thus it was Honora who was referred to as O'Cahan's wife by the English privy council in September 1613. Honora was in London in 1613, and she and their sons, Rory and Donnell, were allocated land in freehold under the Londoners in 1611. Rory took part in an abortive plot in 1615, with the aim, it was alleged, of overthrowing the plantation in its infancy by burning some of the new settlements while saving a number of its leading figures as hostages for the release of his father and other Ulster prisoners, and was executed after conviction at the Derry assizes on 31 July 1615. Sir Donnell died in the Tower, probably in August 1626, and appears to have been buried there on 11 August.   R. J. HUNTER

Sources AFM · H. Docwra, 'A narration of the services done by the army imployed to Lough-Foyle', *Miscellany of the Celtic Society*, ed. J. O'Donovan (1849), 233–86 · *CSP Ire., 1600–14* · T. H. Mullin and J. E. Mullan, *The Ulster clans* (1984) · T. W. Moody, *The Londonderry plantation, 1609–41* (1939) · J. S. Brewer and W. Bullen, eds., *Calendar of the Carew manuscripts*, 4–5, PRO (1870–71) · P. Walsh, *The will and family of Hugh O'Neill, earl of Tyrone* (1930), 36–8 ff. · F. Moryson, *An itinerary containing his ten yeeres travell through the twelve dominions*, 3 (1908) · *APC, 1613–17* · R. Gillespie, *Conspiracy: Ulster plots and plotters in 1615* (1987) · LPL, Carew MSS, 626, p. 271; 635, fols. 31, 33, 77 · register of the chapel of St Peter ad Vincula, 1550–1821, burials, Tower of London, 8
Wealth at death everything confiscated for plantation: Moody, *Londonderry plantation*

Ó Caiside, Tomás [Thomas O'Cassidy] (*fl. c.*1734), Irish-language poet, was born and raised at Leacht an Driseacháin, about 5 miles north-east of Castlerea, co. Roscommon. He was, however, a member of a well-known literary family from co. Fermanagh. He became an Augustinian friar, and although he does not name the establishment, it seems likely that it was the friary at Ballyhaunis, relatively near his home. An illicit romance seems to have ended that period in his life. He then spent a number of years travelling through every corner of Ireland. It appears that he was kidnapped and taken abroad where he was 'sold' to an officer of the French army. The War of the Polish Succession broke out following the death of King Augustus in February 1733. Ó Caiside in his *eachtra* ('adventure') 'An Caisideach Bán' relates some of his exploits during this war, being present when Kehl was taken on 28 October and again at the fall of Philippsburg, in July 1734. The *eachtra* is a loosely structured, autobiographical prose narrative interspersed with verse, describing his adventures as a soldier, a wandering preacher, and entertainer. It has echoes of the cumulative verbosity of medieval Gaelic romance and a share of its burlesque humour, but also possesses a refreshing vernacular tone, together with an earthy Dionysian irascibility.

Ó Caiside deserted the French army after the fall of Philippsburg and was persuaded by a Prussian officer named Fischer, to join that side. There is speculation that he was a member of the élite Potsdam guards, the three brigades who acted as a personal bodyguard to Friedrich Wilhelm I, the Prussian king. He subsequently returned to Ireland, spending some time in England on the way. In Ireland the president of the Augustinian order reinstated him. Ó Caiside stayed at the abbey in Naas, co. Kildare, but found his fellow friars disagreeable. Consequently he did not remain long. According to his own account, he spent the rest of his life as a wandering minstrel and preacher, performing tricks at fairs, also occasionally conducting weddings. The two poems for which he is best known, 'An Caisideach Bán' and 'Máire Bhéal Átha Amhnais', are still current in oral tradition. Both songs are sorrowful meditations on the theme of the ill-starred love affair that caused his original departure from the religious life. The former still enjoys great popularity in the Irish-speaking regions of co. Galway, and also, though less so, in co. Donegal. Despite the rhetorical flourishes, the depiction of an eighteenth-century press-ganged soldier's precarious and sometimes brutal existence has a certain ring of truth. It is imaginable that Ó Caiside might have recited some of the prose or verse passages to attract audiences for his performances at the various gatherings he frequented. The *eachtra* is also informative on why he became a popular figure in the oral folk tradition of Connaught. It is found in Royal Irish Academy manuscript 23. o 35, copied from the author's own hand by his contemporary Brian Ó Fearghail, who freely admits that he carried out some emendations.   LILLIS Ó LAOIRE

Sources M. Nic Philibín, *Na Caisidigh agus a gcuid Filíochta* (1938)
Archives BM, Egerton MS 178, article 15 · Royal Irish Acad., MS 23. o 35 · Royal Irish Acad., E IVI

O'Callaghan, Edmund Bailey (1800–1880), journalist and historian, the youngest of the six children of Owen O'Callaghan, merchant, was born in Mallow, co. Cork, about 1 March 1800, and was educated in his home town. About 1820 he went to Paris to study medicine and remained there for two years. In 1823 he emigrated to Canada, where in 1826 he obtained the post of apothecary at the Montreal General Hospital. Licensed to practise medicine in 1827, he was the surgeon at the Quebec emigrants' hospital from 1828 to 1829. At the same time he was actively involved in several societies for the relief and welfare of Irish immigrants. In 1830 he married Charlotte Augustina Crampe, an Irishwoman. She died in 1835, having borne one son who did not survive infancy.

O'Callaghan soon became a spokesman and champion of the Irish community in Canada. In 1833 he moved to Montreal, where he became a close associate of Louis-Joseph Papineau, the leader of the nationalist Patriote Party, and in 1834 was appointed editor of *The Vindicator*, the party organ, in which he attacked the colonial government and sought to rally Irish support for the French Canadian cause. He was elected in the same year to the Canadian assembly as the member for Yamaska. His calls for agitation and civil disobedience contributed to the heightening of the political tension in the autumn of 1837, when his editorial offices were sacked by loyalists. When the revolutionary party met at Richelieu River in October to determine their final course of action, although O'Callaghan supported Papineau in condemning the resort to arms, he took the field with the rebels, and was in the action at St Denis on 23 November 1837. On the failure of the rising he fled with Papineau to the United States.

O'Callaghan found such a congenial home in New York state that, when his companions returned to Canada under amnesty, he remained in Albany, where he practised as a doctor from 1839 to 1847. On 9 May 1841 he married Ellen Hawe, of Albany; there was one son of the marriage, who died in infancy. He continued his journalistic activity, and while researching some articles on anti-rent agitation for the *Northern Light* became interested in the original Dutch land grants and other documents relating to the early history of New Amsterdam, which lay neglected in the office of the secretary of state. He learned Dutch in order to pursue his researches more widely, and in 1846 published the first volume of his *History of New Netherland, or, New York under the Dutch*, a work which marked a new epoch in American historiography. In 1848 he gave up medicine to become the archivist of the state of New York, and to edit the transcripts of documents copied from archives in The Hague and elsewhere by J. R. Brodhead. A selection of these was published in his four-volume *Documentary History of the State of New York* (1849–51). The full translated collection was subsequently published as *Documents Relative to the Colonial History of the State of New York*, (11 vols., 1853–61). In these the French source material on the border dispute between New France and New York was made available for the first time. Earlier, in 1847, he had published a seminal paper which first drew attention to the importance of the Jesuit *Relations* as sources for North American history.

In 1870 O'Callaghan was persuaded by Mayor Abraham Oakey Hall to move to New York in order to edit the minute books of the city council, but the fall from power of his political patrons in the Tweed Ring scandal halted publication of the series in 1872. The fifteen manuscript volumes of the work have survived in the archives of the New York Historical Society. After 1877 he was, owing to an accident, confined to his house, 651 Lexington Avenue, New York, where he died on 29 May 1880. He was buried on 2 June in Calvary cemetery, New York. His library, containing a unique collection of Jesuit *Relations*, was sold on 4 December 1882 by Bangs & Co. of New York for $12,098.

O'Callaghan was particularly gratified by the honorary degree of MD awarded to him in 1845 by the University of St Louis; it was his only medical qualification. A man of deep Catholic faith, he retained to the end of his life a strong sense of loyalty to his Irish homeland. The final harnessing of his energies to archival research resulted in work which put the early colonial history of North America on a solid foundation.   G. MARTIN MURPHY

Sources J. Verney, *O'Callaghan: the making and unmaking of a rebel* (1994) · J. Monet, 'O'Callaghan, Edmund Bailey', *DCB*, vol. 10 · A. E. Peterson, 'O'Callaghan, Edmund', *DAB* · F. S. Guy, *Edmund Bailey O'Callaghan: a study in American historiography* (1934) · B. Quaritch, ed., *Contributions towards a dictionary of English book-collectors*, 13 (1899)

Archives L. Cong. · NA Canada · New York Historical Society

O'Callaghan, Sir Francis Langford (1839–1909), civil engineer, was born on 22 July 1839, the second son of James O'Callaghan JP, of Drisheen, co. Cork, and his wife, Agnes, daughter of the Revd Francis Langford. He was educated at private schools and at Queen's College, Cork. From 1859 to 1862 he received training in applied engineering while employed under Henry Conybeare on railway construction in Ireland and south Wales. Success in a competition for a position in the public works department of India led to his appointment as a probationary assistant engineer on 13 June 1862.

By promotion, often temporary well before the confirmed advance, O'Callaghan rose through the various grades of the department: he achieved the permanent positions of executive engineer fourth class in April 1866 (first class, March 1871), superintending engineer third class in January 1880 (first class, March 1886), and chief engineer third class in April 1889. In May 1889 he was promoted to chief engineer first class and appointed consulting engineer to the government of India for state railways. In August 1892 he became secretary to the government of India, public works department. Posted from 1862 to 1870 to the Northern road and related bridge works (Kanhan Bridge, 1866), in the Central Provinces, O'Callaghan began his association with the state railways when he joined the Nagpur and Raipur railway survey in February 1871. A posting to the Wardha valley railway works (1872) followed, then a furlough, during which time he married, on 22 September 1875 Anna Maria Mary (d. 1911), second daughter of Lieutenant-Colonel Henry Clarinbold Powell of Banlahan, co. Cork. From 1877 to 1879 he was chief engineer of the Tirhut state railway. He next served with great success as engineer-in-chief for a number of demanding railway projects, surveys, and constructions on India's north-west frontier: the Rawalpindi–Peshawar section of the Punjab Northern (1879–83); Sind–Sagar surveys (1884–5); the Bolan line through the Bolan Pass to Quetta (1885–6); the Khwaja–Amran (1887); and the Sind–Pishin railway (1887–9). Repeatedly commended by government he was made CIE (1883) for his work on the Attock Bridge over the Indus and CSI (1888) for the line through the Bolan Pass.

O'Callaghan's technical skills were complemented by his popularity, tact, and sound judgement. He retired from India service in 1894 and returned to England where the Colonial Office appointed him in September 1895 to the demanding position of managing member of the Uganda Railway committee, a position he held until the committee was dissolved on 30 September 1903 and for which he was made KCMG in 1902. During the often controversial construction of that line O'Callaghan had to respond to criticism, to provide testimony to parliamentary investigations, and to make trips of inquiry to east Africa. He also served as a company director of the Burma Railway and the Egyptian Delta Light Railways.

Elected an associate of the Institution of Civil Engineers on 12 January 1869 and a full member on 23 April 1872 O'Callaghan was also a fellow of the Royal Geographical Society. He published in 1865 an adaptation of *Bidder's*

Earthwork Tables for use in India. O'Callaghan died suddenly at Redbraes, London Road, Guildford, on 14 November 1909. He was Anglican by faith, and his funeral and burial took place a few days later at Holy Trinity Church, Guildford. He was briefly survived both by his wife and their only son, Captain Francis Reginald Powell O'Callaghan RE (1880–1910).   IAN J. KERR

Sources *PICE*, 179 (1909–10), 364–5 · *The Times* (15 Nov 1909) · Government of India, public works department, *History of services of the officers of the engineer, accounts and state revenue establishments*, 2 vols. (1893) · *India Office List* (1895) · *The Times* (18 Nov 1909) · 'The Attock bridge', *Engineering* (28 Nov 1884); (12 Dec 1884); (26 Dec 1884) · M. F. Hill, *Permanent way: the story of the Kenya and Uganda Railway*, 2nd edn (1961) · P. S. A. Berridge, *Couplings to the Khyber: the story of the North Western Railway* (1969) · d. cert. · *CGPLA Eng. & Wales* (1909)
Wealth at death £14,275 9s. 9d.: probate, 8 Dec 1909, *CGPLA Eng. & Wales*

O'Callaghan, John Cornelius (1805–1883), journalist and historian, was born at Dublin, the son of John O'Callaghan, one of the first Catholics allowed to practise law in Ireland after the partial relaxation of the penal laws in 1793. He was educated at the Jesuit school of Clongowes Wood, co. Kildare, and afterwards at a private school at Blanchardstown, near Dublin. He was called to the Irish bar in 1829 but, preferring to pursue a literary career, did not practise. From 1831 to 1833 he contributed to *The Comet*, a weekly newspaper published in Dublin by the influential Comet Club. This paper, to which Daniel O'Connell also contributed, advocated the disestablishment of the Church of England in Ireland. When *The Comet* ceased publication, O'Callaghan wrote for the *Irish Monthly Magazine*. His pieces in these two journals, along with other writings, were collected and published as *The Green Book, or, Gleanings from the Writing Desk of a Literary Agitator* (1840). When the Dublin *Nation* was started in 1842 as the organ of the Young Ireland party, O'Callaghan joined the staff and he became an important contributor. The first number of the paper contained, under the pen name Gracchus, his poem 'The Exterminator's Song', subsequently republished in *The Spirit of the Nation* (1845), a collection of the poetry of the Young Irelanders.

O'Callaghan was best known as a historical writer and editor. In 1846 he published in Dublin for the Irish Archaeological Society an annotated edition of *Macariae excidium, or, The Destruction of Cyprus*. This was a history, using disguised names, of the Williamite war of 1688–91, written in 1692 by Colonel Charles O'Kelly, an officer in James II's army. O'Callaghan's masterpiece, *History of the Irish brigades in the service of France, from the revolution in Great Britain and Ireland under James II to the revolution in France under Louis XVI*, was the result of over twenty-five years' research. It was published in Glasgow in 1870, after O'Callaghan failed to interest a Dublin publisher. Superseding an earlier work by Matthew O'Conor, this carefully researched if prolix study became a standard source. O'Callaghan also wrote *The Irish in the English Army and Navy* (1843). As a writer he was verbose and addicted to an ornate style modelled upon the French Romantic historians whom he admired. But he was also an accurate,

John Cornelius O'Callaghan (1805–1883), by Henry O'Neill, 1874

objective, fair, and thorough scholar, who painstakingly verified and critically evaluated his sources.

O'Callaghan was keenly interested in Irish politics. He was a member of Daniel O'Connell's Loyal National Repeal Association, for which he designed a membership card in 1843. At one of O'Connell's 'monster meetings' in 1840 at Tara Hill, the crowning-place of ancient Irish kings, O'Callaghan and the sculptor John Hogan placed a laurel crown on the head of the 'Liberator'. Although attracted to the more radical Young Ireland party, O'Callaghan remained an admirer of O'Connell, who had aided his historical research.

O'Callaghan died at his home, 15 Belvidere Place, Dublin, on 23 April 1883. Sir Charles Gavan Duffy, a colleague in Young Ireland, described him as tall, strong, and loud-voiced.   D. M. CREGIER

Sources *Freeman's Journal* [Dublin] (25 April 1883) · P. J. Hally, introduction, in J. C. O'Callaghan, *History of the Irish brigades in the service of France* (1969), v–viii · *Freeman's Journal* [Dublin] (5 Feb 1892) · B. McKenna, *Irish literature, 1800–1875: a guide to information sources* (1978) · *DNB* · Boase, *Mod. Eng. biog.* · *CGPLA Ire.* (1883)
Likenesses H. O'Neill, oils, 1874, NG Ire. [*see illus.*]
Wealth at death £2344 0s. 9d.: probate, 9 June 1883, *CGPLA Ire.*

O'Callaghan, Sir Robert William (1777–1840), army officer, second son of Cornelius O'Callaghan, first Baron Lismore (1741–1797), and Frances (1757–1827), second daughter of Mr Speaker Ponsonby, was born in October 1777. He was descended from one of the few indigenous families in the Irish peerage. He was appointed ensign in the 128th regiment on 29 November 1794, and was transferred as lieutenant to the 30th light dragoons on 6 December 1794; he became captain on 31 January 1795. He was transferred to the 22nd light dragoons on 19 April

1796, was appointed major to the 40th regiment on 17 February 1803, and became lieutenant-colonel in the 39th regiment on 16 July 1803. In March 1805 he embarked in command of the 1st battalion of the 39th regiment, which had been selected to form part of the expedition destined for the Mediterranean under Lieutenant-General Sir James Craig, and subsequently went from Malta to Naples with the flank companies. When they returned to Malta in February 1806 he remained in Sicily, and at the battle of Maida (4 July 1806) he commanded a grenadier battalion, receiving after the victory a gold medal. At the end of August 1811 he went with the 1st battalion of the 39th from Sicily to join the army in the Peninsula, and attained the brevet rank of colonel. At the battle of Vitoria (21 June 1813) he was in temporary command of the brigade, and his gallant conduct was praised in Wellington's dispatches. He also commanded the brigade during the actions in the Pyrenees in July 1813, and was at the passage of the Nivelle and the Nive. His conduct at Garris (15 February 1814) was mentioned in dispatches. He was present at the victory of Orthez (27 February 1814), and received a gold cross with two clasps for Maida, Vitoria, Pyrenees, Nivelle, Nive, and Orthez.

O'Callaghan was promoted major-general on 4 June 1814, and was made a KCB on 2 January 1815. He was appointed to the staff of the army in Flanders on 25 June 1815 and to the staff of the army in France on 22 April 1818, and commanded the troops in Scotland from 15 June 1825 to 22 July 1830. He was gazetted colonel of the 97th regiment on 7 September 1829, and was promoted lieutenant-general on 22 July 1830. He was appointed to command the army at Madras on 4 October 1830, and was made colonel of the 39th on 4 March 1833. In the spring of 1835, on the departure of Lord William Bentinck for England, he held for some months command of the troops in India, and was in command at Madras until October 1836. O'Callaghan was made GCB on 19 July 1838. He died, unmarried, in London on 9 June 1840.

B. H. SOULSBY, *rev.* JAMES FALKNER

Sources Army List · Hart's Army List · R. Cannon, ed., *Historical record of the thirty-ninth, or the Dorsetshire regiment of foot* (1853) · C. T. Atkinson, *The Dorsetshire regiment*, 1 (1947) · GEC, *Peerage*
Likenesses H. Edridge, pencil drawing, c.1820, Holker Hall Collection; copy, priv. coll.

Ó Caoimh, Eoghan (1656–1726), poet and scribe, was one of three sons of Caomh Ó Caoimh. His mother's name is not known, nor is his place of birth.

Eoghan recorded in Limerick MS O (pp. 268–9) that he married Eilíonóir de Nógla in 1681, that they had seven children, that Eilíonóir died in 1707, and that his eldest son, Art, had recently, on 18 July 1709, sailed from Cork for France. Art was to train for the priesthood. A later note (p. 302) plaintively records that Art had died thirty days after his arrival.

Eoghan valued his descent from the once important Ó Caoimh family of Glenville, a parish 10 miles north-east of Cork, bordering on the diocese of Cloyne. He described his paternal lineage in Cork MS M62 (p. 347); his headstone more succinctly affirms that he was 'of the family of

Gleanphriahane'—Gleann an Phréacháin, now Glenville. John O'Daly consequently supposed that Eoghan was born in Glenville, but his lineage shows, and Eoghan specifically asserts, that his descent parted from the direct Glenville line with his great-great-grandfather Art Óg Ó Caoimh. After more than a century of war and upheaval, it seems improbable that Eoghan's immediate family still resided in Glenville. During his productive period as a scribe from 1679 to 1710, Eoghan resided mainly in the east of co. Kerry, near Brosna, close to the co. Limerick border, south of Abbeyfeale: he was evicted from a farmholding there in 1692, and his wife was buried in Brosna. It may have been his native place.

Eoghan's descent ensured that he was welcome among the élite of the Irish-speaking community in mid-Cork: he received patronage from Eoin Baiste Mac Sleighne, bishop of Cork, Cloyne, and Ross from 1693 until his deportation in 1702; Uilliam Mac Cairteáin (1668–1724), from Whitechurch in the same area, was godfather to his son Art; he knew Diarmaid Mac Cárthaigh (d. 1705) of Blarney, and composed an elegy on his death. His descent also enhanced his eligibility for clerical appointment in the diocese of Cloyne.

After 1710, Eoghan prepared for entry to the priesthood. He was ordained in 1717, and was later appointed parish priest of Doneraile in the north of co. Cork, in the diocese of Cloyne.

Of Ó Caoimh's scribal work, there are extant: ten full manuscripts, four produced in co-operation with Art, and three to which he made small contributions. Their present locations are: Catholic bishop of Limerick's house (O), University College, Cork (C62, C168), Maynooth (C88), National Library of Ireland (G17, G114, G312), National Library of Wales (413D), Royal Irish Academy (23 E 17, 23 E 23, 23 G 2, 23 H 14, 23 I 7, 23 M 25–34, 24 L 6), Stonyhurst College (A II 20, 2), Trinity College, Dublin (H.5.4). They contain genealogies, prose texts, and verse. The writings of Séathrún Céitinn are well represented: there are six copies of his history 'Forus Feasa ar Éirinn', and the earliest extant copy of his poem 'Óm sgeol ar ardmhagh Fáil' ('From my tidings of the great land of Fál'). The whole corpus is a valuable source for scholarship. About thirty of Eoghan's own verse compositions are extant in manuscript copies, eleven in autograph. Not all have appeared in print. His popular piece 'Ar treascradh in Eachroim' ('All who fell at Aughrim'), which was prompted by his eviction in 1692, was first printed in *The Nation* (15 May 1858); O'Grady printed the full text; and Ó Donnchadha included it in the uncompleted sequence which he published in *Gadelica*. Subsequently, Ó Cuív published his commendation of a friend, and Ó Murchadha published his ode to the bishop who ordained him.

Eoghan is a fine example of the scholar-scribes who struggled in adversity to maintain the native Irish tradition of literature and learning. His work was admired by contemporaries and by later scribes. For the latter there was also the fascination of his remarkable life: the relatively early death of his wife, the loss of a cherished son, and his late ordination to become a respected priest in penal times.

Eoghan Ó Caoimh died on 5 April 1726 in Doneraile and was buried nearby at Old Court.

MÁIRTÍN Ó MURCHÚ

Sources B. Ó Conchúir, *Scríobhaithe Chorcaí, 1700–1850* ['Cork scribes, 1700–1850'] (1982), 33–6 · T. Ó Donnchadha (al. Torna), 'An tAthair Eoghan Ó Caoimh: a bheatha agus a shaothar' ['Father Eoghan Ó Caoimh: his life and work'], *Gadelica*, 1 (1912–13), 3–9, 101–11, 163–70, 251–9 · S. H. O'Grady, *Catalogue of manuscripts in the British Library [Museum]* (1926), 1.527–8 · M. Ó Murchadha, 'Dán le hEón Ó Caoimh' ['A poem by Eoghan Ó Caoimh'], *Éigse*, 10 (1961–3), 19–25 · P. Ó Riain, 'Dán ar Shéafraidh Ó Donnchadha an Ghleanna' ['A poem on Séafraidh Ó Donnchadha of Glenflesk'], *Éigse*, 12 (1967–8), 123–32 · B. Ó Cuív, 'Eón Ó Caoimh do chan' ['Eoghan Ó Caoimh cecinit'], *Éigse*, 9 (1961–3), 262 · J. O'Daly, *Poets and poetry of Munster* (1849), 38–9

Ó Caollaidhe, Maolseachlain. *See* Queally, Malachy (1586–1645).

O'Caran, Gilbert. *See* Ua Caráin, Gilla in Choimded (*d.* 1180?).

O'Carroll, Ferganainm (*d.* 1541). *See under* O'Carroll, Mulroney (*c.*1470–1532).

O'Carroll, Maolsuthain. *See* Ua Cerbaill, Máel Suthain (*d.* 1010).

O'Carroll, Margaret. *See* Ní Chearbhaill, Mairgréag (*d.* 1451).

O'Carroll, Mulroney [*called* Mulroney the Great] (*c.*1470–1532), chieftain, was the son of John O'Carroll (*d.* 1491). Mulroney was the last secure ruler of his dynasty, descended from the ancient kings of northern Éile in what was to become the King's county and the borderlands of northern Tipperary. The family lands of the descendants of the early eleventh-century Cearbhall (Carroll), in a crucial region of the midlands straddling the road between Dublin and Limerick, had been settled by the English in the early thirteenth century and regained by Teige O'Carroll about 1320. The grandson and namesake of Mulroney the Bearded (*d.* 1443), Mulroney succeeded his uncle William as chieftain about 1491, in which year he and his stepgrandmother Bibiana O'Dempsey founded a monastery at Roscrea.

'The most esteemed captain of the land' and commanding substantial levies, Mulroney fought at Knockdoe in 1504 with Connaught lords against his powerful neighbour Gerald Fitzgerald, eighth earl of Kildare and lord deputy. In 1513 Kildare besieged Mulroney's strongest fortress, Leap Castle—a massive keep which defied his attempt—and was fatally shot while bringing reinforcements. In 1516 the ninth earl took the castle and 'demolished it on its guards' despite Mulroney's use of artillery lent by his cousin Sir Piers Butler, claimant to the earldom of Ormond, his other principal neighbour. In 1520 Kildare authorized Mulroney to embarrass his successor as lord deputy, the earl of Surrey, by stirring up war in the midlands; his activities were duly investigated by the authorities.

Mulroney's prestige enabled him to marry his daughter Grace to Ulick Bourke, later earl of Clanricarde, coercing him when he had second thoughts at the ceremony. Mulroney died at Leap in 1532, a bitter succession dispute between his son and brothers ensuing. His skill lay in maintaining a balancing act among his powerful neighbours, a situation which greater royal interest and the rigours of English law denied to his successors.

Ferganainm O'Carroll (*d.* 1541), chieftain, was the illegitimate but favourite son of Mulroney the Great and a daughter of the Wicklow chieftain McMurrough Kavanagh. Married to a daughter of Gerald *Fitzgerald, ninth earl of Kildare, and an English hostage in 1520, Ferganainm became Mulroney's effective deputy, and at Pentecost 1525 was required to give evidence of his father's dealings with the earl of Ormond. When Mulroney died in 1532 Ferganainm relied on Kildare to enforce his claims against his uncles Donough and Owny, and the earl was seriously wounded besieging Birr Castle. Kildare took Donough's castles for Ferganainm in 1534, thus securing his position, and in return in 1535 Ferganainm was a leading supporter of his rebel brother-in-law Thomas *Fitzgerald, tenth earl of Kildare—'the traitor's right eye' according to Ormond. On their defeat Donough deposed Ferganainm, but while Donough was dying in June 1538 Ferganainm prevailed upon Lord Deputy Leonard Grey, a Kildare connection, to appoint him as successor.

Grey retook Birr and expelled Donough's sons; Ferganainm soon murdered the eldest, William Moyle. Marrying his sister More to James *Fitzgerald, thirteenth earl of Desmond, he formally rented Éile from the crown from 1539 but his close links to Grey led to complaints to Cromwell that the deputy relied on ex-rebels. In November 1540 these links were cited as part of Grey's indictment for treason. Government action against Ferganainm was anticipated by Donough's son Thady, who in early summer 1541 infiltrated Clonlisk Castle and killed Ferganainm and twelve servants. Though he was blind and ailing, Ferganainm's resistance was recorded as heroic by the annalists.

Tadhg O'Carroll, baron of Ely (*d.* 1553), chieftain, was the eldest son of Ferganainm O'Carroll and his Fitzgerald wife. He married Gille or Egidia Butler. On Ferganainm's assassination in 1541 by his cousin Thady, four rival contenders to be 'captain of Éile' approached the Irish privy council. On 2 July the council selected Tadhg and his cousin Calvach; Tadhg's sponsor was his brother-in-law Lord Clanricarde. Tadhg visited London in June 1542 to seek the status of tenant-in-chief and crown protection, assisted by his uncle James, earl of Desmond. He was received by Henry VIII, but his legal status was still undetermined when the government began to settle Offaly from 1547, and in 1548 he fought against an invasion by Edmund Fahy, 'captain of the King's kerne', and Sir Francis Bryan. He restored his evacuated castles when they withdrew, and in devastating reprisal 'burned Nenagh upon the Red Captain [Fahy]'. Calvach, in government custody, was released to counter him but proved equally unreliable: Lord Deputy Bellingham upbraided

Tadhg for not obeying his summons and for writing to him in Gaelic.

The authorities decided to come to terms, and after Tadhg's submission to Sir William Brabazon he was knighted in 1551 or 1552, receiving the coveted status of 'Lord Baron of Ely'. As a royal vassal he was protected as long as the government trusted him, but under English law primogeniture determined succession and the beneficiary might not have the necessary local backing. This turned out to be the case when Tadhg was murdered in Éile in summer 1553 by Calvach, who dispossessed his sons. The barony lapsed, but Tadhg's legal precaution of tying his family's power to English landholding was vindicated by their subsequent harassment by the Butlers.

Sir William O'Carroll (*d.* 1581), chieftain, Ferganainm's second son, married Sabine Fitzpatrick (*d.* 1583); he may also have had children with More Delahyde or Delahunt. He avenged Tadhg's murder on their cousin Calvach in 1554 and regained Éile. Calling himself Lord O'Carroll but not officially recognized, he gave refuge to his dispossessed neighbour O'Connor Faly in 1557 and had to flee Lord Deputy Sussex's forces. He drove out Sussex's garrisons when he retired to Dublin, but was evicted again the following year. His supplanter could not secure his claim without English garrisons, and Sussex's successors preferred to secure William's loyalty. Seeking the peerage, O'Carroll was knighted by Sidney on 10 March 1567. Sidney passed on his request to the queen, who replied 'We do well like that O'Carroll (whom ye do much commend) be made a baron as his brother was'.

The grant was never made, probably thanks to Thomas, tenth earl of Ormond, who sought to incorporate Éile in co. Tipperary and launched attacks while Sir William was in London in 1568 to encourage retaliation. Returning empty-handed, O'Carroll allied with Ormond's hostile neighbour Fitzpatrick of Ossory but had enough influence in Dublin to escape punishment for his raids. In 1578 he formally secured a crown grant of his lands as tenant-in-chief for £100 rent p.a. but not the peerage. Cousin to the rebel Desmond, his lands were ravaged by Lord Deputy Grey in 1580 and in 1581 he was detained in Dublin. On his homeward journey he was murdered by some O'Connors, possibly with the collusion of his son John, who succeeded. The independence of Éile, pressed by Ormond's legal manoeuvres and raids, ended with the murder of Sir William's illegitimate son Charles in 1600, during the Nine Years' War; the territory was planted in 1619.

TIMOTHY VENNING

Sources AFM · J. S. Brewer and W. Bullen, eds., *Calendar of the Carew manuscripts*, 1: 1515–1574, PRO (1867) · *CSP Ire.*, 1509–85 · *State papers published under … Henry VIII*, 11 vols. (1830–52), 1520, 1542, 1546 · J. Morrin, ed., *Calendar of the patent and close rolls of chancery in Ireland for the reigns of Henry VIII, Edward VI, Mary, and Elizabeth*, 2 vols. (1861–2) · GEC, *Peerage* · earl of Kildare, *The earls of Kildare and their ancestors, 1057–1773* (1857) · *The Irish fiants of the Tudor sovereigns*, 4 vols. (1994), Edward VI, nos. 1018, 1146; Elizabeth I, nos. 274, 974, 3399 · J. T. Gilbert, ed., *Facsimiles of national manuscripts of Ireland*, 4 vols. in 5 (1874–84) · Bodl. Oxf., MS Carte 58 · *Report on the manuscripts of Lord De L'Isle and Dudley*, 1–2, HMC, 77 (1925–33) · W. A. Shaw, *The knights of England*, 2 (1906) · genealogical databank, Carroll Institute of Irish History

Wealth at death held chieftainship manors and rents (mainly in kind) of Eile, Offaly, incl. at least two major stone castles: AFM

O'Carroll, Tadhg, baron of Ely (*d.* 1553). *See under* O'Carroll, Mulroney (*c.*1470–1532).

O'Carroll, Sir William (*d.* 1581). *See under* O'Carroll, Mulroney (*c.*1470–1532).

O'Casey, Eileen Kathleen (1900–1995). *See under* O'Casey, Sean (1880–1964).

O'Casey, Sean (1880–1964), playwright and writer, born on 30 March 1880 at 85 Upper Dorset Street, Dublin, was baptized John Casey on 28 July, the youngest of the five children surviving into adulthood of Michael Casey (*c.*1836–1886), a clerk for the Irish Church Mission, and his wife, Susan, *née* Archer (1836/7–1918). The facts surrounding John Casey's childhood are vague, a situation not helped by the playwright's tendency to memorial mythologizing in his later years. Clearly the family lived in relative poverty after the father's death, the quality of their actual homes deteriorating with each of several shifts of residence; but they appear not to have known the abject indigence prevalent in many a Dublin tenement. Susan Casey, daughter of an auctioneer, strove to preserve a semblance of protestant gentility; her writer son, as his socialist sympathies grew, tended to stress a solidarity with the working-class values and lifestyle of their Catholic neighbours.

The onset of trachoma in his childhood greatly affected Casey's sight for the rest of his life; initially, it seriously affected his ability to undergo a sustained education, though his sister Isabella, a trained schoolmistress, did secure him a modicum of traditional schooling. Though he was largely self-taught, his reading was avid, open-minded, and wide-ranging. Equally varied with adulthood were his growing allegiances to cultural and political organizations. When he joined the Drumcondra branch of the Gaelic League in 1906, with the intention of learning the Irish language, he Gaelicized his name to Sean O'Cathasaigh; for their *Journal* he wrote his first stories. From 1907 he was a member of the St Laurence O'Toole Club and he was founder member and secretary of the St Laurence O'Toole Pipers Band. He joined Jim Larkin's Irish Transport and General Workers' Union in 1911, and was secretary first of the Women and Children's Relief Fund during the Dublin lock-out strike of 1913 and later of the union's most militant wing, the Irish Citizen Army (ICA). Although he resigned this position in 1914, when the ICA backed Patrick Pearse's revolutionary stance and severely criticized the Easter rising of 1916, he was to publish *The Story of the Irish Citizen Army* in 1919. After his sacking from the Great Northern Railway in 1911, what earned income he had over this period came from casual labour. He appears not to have begun playwriting until *c.*1916 when the Abbey Theatre rejected *Profit and Loss*, but by then certain abiding values had become fixed: a fervent championing of social equality and as fervent a hatred of all processes or institutions that he saw as entrapping the

Sean O'Casey (1880–1964), by Augustus John, 1926

human spirit, inciting enmity or aggression, or provoking death. These values were to inform all his future writing, together with an exuberant joy in language and a highly attuned ear for the niceties of Dublin speech and its idiosyncratic rhythms and phrasing.

By 1920, when he began regularly submitting plays to the Abbey Theatre, O'Cathasaigh had re-Anglicized his name to Sean O'Casey. The Abbey directors rejected his next four submissions (*The Harvest Festival*, *The Frost in the Flower*, *The Seamless Coat of Kathleen*, and *The Crimson in the Tri-Colour*) but the fifth, *The Shadow of a Gunman*, was accepted for staging in April 1923. It established the form that his next two major plays would follow, investigating the impact of events sparked by national political unrest (the black and tan raids in this instance) on the lives of impoverished tenement families. O'Casey's was what Brecht would term an epic drama by virtue of its exploration of the relationship between the processes of political history and the apparent vagaries of everyday contingencies in working-class life. The action of *Juno and the Paycock* (staged March 1924) is situated during the civil war, while *The Plough and the Stars* (staged February 1926) is set at the time of the Easter rising. In all three plays the violence of the public world sets at hazard the attempts by the characters within their domestic sphere to sustain an indomitable spirit; and this juxtaposition creates the unique tone of O'Casey's drama which is skilfully pitched between the comic and the tragic, the one never quite asserting pre-eminence over the other as the action unfolds. What impresses is the rapidity with which O'Casey mastered stagecraft, learning to deploy stage space, properties, and settings to enhance and develop his themes in ways which owe little to the Irish dramatic tradition which preceded him. He evolved too a wholly new depiction of working-class heroism, focused especially on his female characters who resiliently refuse to succumb to circumstance, whatever social adversities confront them.

It was wholly fitting that W. B. Yeats should describe O'Casey as a genius when defending *The Plough and the Stars* against nationalist rioters at its fourth performance: O'Casey's innovations in dramaturgy in the six years since he had first offered a play to the Abbey were remarkable, as was reflected in the award of the Hawthornden Prize for *Juno* in 1926. But that questing innovatory impulse was steadily to take O'Casey further away from the Abbey in ensuing years. The visit to London to receive the Hawthornden introduced him to George Bernard Shaw and Augustus John, who painted his portrait in May 1926, and to West End managements who could offer greater financial recompense for his work than the Abbey could hope to equal. There too he met his future wife, Eileen Carey.

Eileen Carey was the stage name of the singer–actress Eileen Kathleen Reynolds [**Eileen Kathleen O'Casey** (1900–1995)], daughter of Edward Reynolds, of Athlone, Westmeath, and Kathleen Carey (*d.* 1962), from Belmullet, co. Mayo. She was born in Dublin on 27 December 1900, when the family returned from Johannesburg with the outbreak of the Second South African War. She was chiefly educated as an orphan at an Ursuline convent school in Brentwood, Essex, after her father was institutionalized on account of his increasing mental instability, forcing her mother, a fiercely indomitable woman, to work for their security. After various forms of employment, Eileen Reynolds began her theatrical career in London in the chorus of the D'Oyly Carte Opera Company (1923) and then worked increasingly in musical comedy (*The First Kiss* in 1924, *Love's Prisoner* and *Rose Marie* in 1925) before attempting to find employment in America. She and O'Casey met on her return, after a performance of the London production of *Juno and the Paycock*. In 1926, though contracted as understudy, she took over the role of Nora Clitheroe for the initial performances of the first English staging of *The Plough and the Stars* (a part she believed O'Casey was instrumental in her getting). Later she was directed by Barry Jackson as Minnie Powell in *The Shadow of a Gunman* at the Royal Court. The couple were married at the church of All Souls and the Redeemer, Chelsea, on 23 September 1927.

Despite a protracted holiday in Ireland by way of honeymoon, the couple appear never to have considered settling in Dublin; by January 1928 they had found a home at 19 Woronzow Road, St John's Wood, where their son Breon was born the following April. However, what confirmed O'Casey's decision to begin a lifelong exile in England was the Abbey's rejection that same April of *The Silver Tassie*. The Abbey arguably did not possess the resources to stage the play in the monumental manner which it clearly demanded, but Yeats couched his refusal in aesthetic terms (chiefly that the First World War was not a subject for drama) which O'Casey found insulting and absurd.

O'Casey took issue and, not for the last time in his career, went public with the debate, clearly relishing a new-found gift for vituperation. (James Agate, Noël Coward, Kingsley Martin, Malcolm Muggeridge, George Orwell, and the archbishop of Dublin were all to suffer O'Casey's attack.) The play was eventually staged by C. B. Cochran at the Apollo Theatre, London, in October 1929 with a setting for the scene in the trenches by Augustus John. It was that second act (not the three remaining acts set in Dublin) with its daring mixture of ritualism, doggerel, the choric and scenographic techniques of German expressionism, and quotation from the Authorized Version of the Bible which indicated the path that O'Casey's imagination was now to follow.

Within the Gates (staged February 1934) and *The Star Turns Red* (staged by the Unity Theatre in March, 1940) are modern morality plays, their didacticism offset as in many expressionist dramas by a brilliant deployment of stylized scenic effects and passages of powerful choral chanting. They are very much of their time, especially *The Star Turns Red* with its confrontation of fascist and communist forces; but both contain passages of sexual lyricism and of wry knockabout comedy, which are not to be found in the German prototype of this genre of play. These passages together with the scenic experimentalism foreshadow the wholly unique style of theatre that O'Casey was to invent for his last plays. The thirties were a difficult period. Eileen's theatrical engagements were sporadic (notable appearances were in the chorus for Noël Coward's *Bitter Sweet*, Rutland Boughton's *The Immortal Hour* in a revival by Barry Jackson, Reinhardt's staging of *The Miracle*, and A. P. Herbert's *Mother of Pearl*). The family moved to Chalfont St Giles and then back to Battersea, before settling by 1938 at Tingrith, a house in Totnes, Devon, to enable the children to attend Dartington School. (A second son, Niall, was born on 15 January 1935 and a daughter, Shivaun, on 28 September 1939.) The family moved again in 1954 to Villa Rosa Flats, 40 Trumlands Road, St Marychurch, Torquay. Eileen O'Casey gave up her stage career to devote herself to creating the right working environment for her husband. The banning in Ireland of *Windfalls* (a collection of stories, poems, and short plays published in 1934) initiated a series of such acts of censorship there; but compensation for this and the loss of London theatre contacts came with O'Casey's visit to New York in September that year for the American staging of *Within the Gates*, when he established friendships with critics George Jean Nathan and Brooks Atkinson and the playwright Eugene O'Neill.

Later there came creative compensation of a different kind. If shaping plays was a slower process for O'Casey at this time, the chance writing in 1931 of a personal sketch, 'A child is born', initiated a project which steadily grew into six volumes of autobiography by 1954: *I Knock at the Door* (published 1939), *Pictures in the Hallway* (1942), *Drums under the Windows* (1945), *Inishfallen, Fare thee Well* (1949), *Rose and Crown* (1952), and *Sunset and Evening Star* (1954). It was a prodigious achievement, casting a cold satirical eye on Irish and English cultural and political life, as O'Casey recorded the development of his sensibility through private triumphs and adversities in a richly rhetorical prose.

The fifteen years following from the staging at Dublin's Olympia Theatre in March 1943 of *Red Roses for Me* were prolific: *Purple Dust* opened at the Liverpool Playhouse in October 1945; *Oak Leaves and Lavender* in Hammersmith in May 1947; *Cock-a-Doodle Dandy* in Newcastle in 1949; *The Bishop's Bonfire* in Dublin in 1955; and *The Drums of Father Ned* was commissioned by the Dublin International Theatre Festival for 1958 but was withdrawn after clerical opposition (the première was in Lafayette, Indiana, the following year). In all these plays the didactic impulse is still strong in the recurrent contrasting of fiercely anticlerical satire with images of wild Dionysian liberation; intimations of pantomime and melodrama are present, but transformed by a personal vision that blends song, dance, vaudeville routines, magic, ecstatic drumming, knockabout farce, and stylized violence into a theatricality that is rich and enriching because fuelled continually by an urgent sense of the need to be wholly open to life's possibilities. An awareness of the dangers of repression within society brings to these plays a dark, threatening tone: the moments of transcendence are hard won and so without sentiment or whimsy. Earlier generations of English reviewers found the lack of stylistic unity irritating, because devoid of art; continental and American directors thought otherwise. It became a critical commonplace to infer that with exile from Ireland, O'Casey lost his prime inspiration; but a compassionate awareness of contemporary Ireland is deeply woven into the fabric of these plays (with the one exception of *Oak Leaves and Lavender*), showing the depth of O'Casey's detestation of de Valera's insular policies, of familism, and the bigotry they both encouraged. These late plays make profound demands in terms of ensemble playing and require highly versatile performers: being about the imagination, they ask for a vibrant and daring imagination in the staging. So too does the group of one-act plays O'Casey published in 1961 (*Behind the Green Curtains*, *Figuro in the Night*, and *The Moon Shines on Kylenamoe*), the year in which, politely but on strong socialist grounds, he refused a doctorate from Trinity College, Dublin. His prodigal genius also saw into print volumes of theatre criticism and stories: *The Flying Wasp* (1937) which was expanded into *The Green Crow* (1956) and *Under a Coloured Cap* (1963); *Blasts* appeared posthumously in 1967.

There seemed scant sign of failing creative powers, though O'Casey's health had been deteriorating since 1956 when he underwent two operations and suffered the death of his younger son from leukaemia. He died in Torbay Clinic, St Luke's Road, Torquay, on 18 September 1964 after sustaining a heart attack. His body was cremated four days later in Torquay, but his ashes were scattered in the gardens at Golders Green crematorium, Middlesex, on 3 October.

In later years the O'Caseys had enjoyed the friendship of Sean's publisher Harold Macmillan, often staying at his home. After the death of their respective spouses, Macmillan and Eileen (now living in Holland Park) sustained their friendship. How platonic their relationship remained has been a subject of some debate. At the invitation of Macmillans, Eileen O'Casey wrote a biographical memoir of her husband, published as *Sean* in 1971, and an autobiography, *Eileen*, in 1976. She died of natural causes on 9 April 1995 and was cremated at Golders Green.

RICHARD ALLEN CAVE

Sources *The Times* (21 Sept 1964) · *The Times* (11 April 1995) [obit. for Eileen O'Casey] · D. Krause, *Sean O'Casey: the man and his work* (1960) · D. Krause, *Sean O'Casey and his world* (1976) · M. B. Marguiles, *The early life of Sean O'Casey* (1970) · H. Kosok, *O'Casey the dramatist* (1985) · R. Ayling and M. Durkin, *Sean O'Casey: a bibliography* (1978) · private information (2004) · E. O'Casey, *Eileen* (1976)
Archives NL Ire., corresp., literary MSS, and papers · NYPL, corresp., MSS · Ransom HRC, transcript of *The silver tassie* and related letters | BL, letters to George Bernard Shaw, Add. MS 50543 · Harvard U., Houghton L., corresp. with Horace Reynolds · LUL, letters to Peter Newmark · NL Ire., letters to Jack Daly · NL Ire., letters to Peter Newmark · NL Ire., letters to Lennox Robinson · PRO NIre., letters to Lady Londonderry · U. Newcastle, Robinson L., letters to Percy Trower · U. Reading L., corresp. with Nancy Astor | FILM NBC film for TV made by Robert Ginna and Ejon Mili, 1953 | SOUND BL NSA
Likenesses photographs, *c*.1925–1959, Hult. Arch. · A. John, oils, 1926, NG Ire. [*see illus.*] · P. Evans, pen-and-ink drawing, *c*.1926–1930, NPG · A. John, oils, 1927, Metropolitan Museum of Art, New York · H. Kernoff, pastel drawing, 1930, NG Ire. · Elliott & Fry, photographs, 1934, NPG · W. Suschitzky, photograph, 1955, NPG · P. Tuohy, pencil drawing, Hugh Lane Municipal Gallery of Modern Art, Dublin
Wealth at death £1702: probate, 17 Nov 1964, *CGPLA Eng. & Wales*

O'Cassidy, Thomas. See Ó Caiside, Tomás (*fl. c*.1734).

Ó Catháin, Domhnall Ballach. See O'Cahan, Sir Donnell Ballagh (*d*. 1626?).

Occam, Nicholas of. See Ockham, Nicholas (*d. c*.1320).

Occam, William. See Ockham, William (*c*.1287–1347).

Occom, Samson (1723–1792), leader of the Mohegan Indians and Presbyterian clergyman, was born in a Mohegan village near New London, Connecticut, in 1723, the son of Joshua Ockham and Sarah Samson, both Mohegans. At seventeen he was converted to Christianity by James Davenport, an apostle of the early American religious great awakening. The Pious Mohegan, as Occom came to be known, embraced Christianity as a strategy for American Indian survival. He was appointed to the Mohegan council by the sachem Ben Uncas II on 1 July 1742. On 6 December 1743 Occom enrolled in Eleazar Wheelock's Preparatory School in Lebanon, Connecticut, aided by a stipend from the Church of England's Society for the Propagation of the Gospel in Foreign Parts (SPG). In the course of five years he obtained a rudimentary education in English and theology. Poor health prevented Occom from transferring to Yale College, but his remarkable progress as a scholar motivated Wheelock to establish Moor's

Samson Occom (1723–1792), by Jonathan Spilsbury, pubd 1768 (after Mason Chamberlin)

Indian Charity School in 1754, a special institution to train Indian missionaries.

Late in 1749 Occom was employed as schoolmaster by the Montauk of Long Island, also serving as their minister, scribe, and legal adviser until 1761. In 1751 he married Mary Fowler, a Montauk (*b*. 1730), who outlived him and with whom he had eleven children. Occom was ordained by the Long Island presbytery at Easthampton on 30 August 1759. Between 1761 and 1763 Occom journeyed three times to the Oneida in New York, but his missionary endeavours there were upset by the pan-American rising against the British, the Pontiac War, which erupted in 1763. At the close of 1764 the SPG hired him as a minister to the Mohegan and other Christian Indian communities in Connecticut. He was also taken into service by the newly established Connecticut Board of Correspondents of the Scotch Society.

Following his return to Mohegan in 1764, Occom became embroiled in a long-standing land dispute between a Mohegan faction and the Connecticut assembly, known as the Mason controversy. In sympathizing with the Mohegan faction demanding restitution, Occom incurred the disapproval of his superiors, who threatened to revoke his licence. On 12 March 1765 he wrote a letter of apology to the commissioners for his 'imprudent, rash, and offensive Conduct', but his relation with the SPG was strained thereafter (Blodgett, 79–80; Love, 127; Richardson, 28–9).

Late in 1765 Occom accompanied the Revd Nathaniel Whitaker on a fund-raising tour to Great Britain. They set sail from Boston on 23 December 1765 and landed at Brixham in Tor Bay on 3 February 1766. From there they proceeded to the Revd George Whitefield's residence in London. Occom delivered over 300 sermons throughout England, Scotland, and Ireland, before departing again in the spring of 1768. He was patronized by numerous British dignitaries, developing a lifelong friendship with Selina Hastings, countess of Huntingdon, and John Thornton. The erudite Mohegan preacher collected nearly £12,000 for Wheelock's school. Most of the donations, however, were used to establish Dartmouth College, which was granted a royal charter in 1769.

Occom's occupational prospects dimmed after his return to New England. The SPG refused to re-employ him, and his relationship with Wheelock also deteriorated when he accused the cleric of misappropriating the moneys he had generated for the express purpose of educating Indians. This charge proved well grounded as Dartmouth soon evolved into an élitist institution for white students. Although Occom received some financial support from the Society in Scotland for the Propagation of Christian Knowledge, his subsequent activities were beset with privation.

Some time in 1773 Occom developed the plan to found Brothertown, an independent community of Christian Indians in Oneida territory in New York. With the assistance of two relatives, Joseph Johnson (1752–1776), a Mohegan, and David Fowler (1735–1807), a Montauk, Occom enlisted participants from among the Mohegan, Mashantucket, Stonington, Farmington, Charleston, Niantic, and Montauk. The project was postponed temporarily because of the outbreak of the American War of Independence. Occom and his family finally emigrated to Brothertown in the spring of 1789. He taught and ministered at Brothertown and the neighbouring Christian Indian community of New Stockbridge until his death, in New Stockbridge, on 14 July 1792. He was probably buried near Utica.

Occom's major work is *A Sermon Preached at the Execution of Moses Paul* (1772), which went through at least nineteen editions by the turn of the century. Several hymns contained in his *Choice Collection of Hymns and Spiritual Songs* (1774) are believed to be original. Occom also produced a brief ethnography entitled 'An account of the Montauk Indians, on Long Island' (1809).

The descendants of the New England Christian Indians still honour Occom as an elder who helped them survive through difficult times. On the recommendation of the Montauk Historical Society, Samson Occom day was celebrated in June 1970. The Brothertown Indian Nation, which at the start of the twenty-first century was seeking federal recognition in Wisconsin, regards him as its founding father.   BERND C. PEYER

Sources W. D. Love, *Samson Occom and the Christian Indians of New England* (1899) · H. Blodgett, *Samson Occom: the biography of an Indian preacher* (1935) · L. B. Richardson, ed., *An Indian preacher in England* (1933) · B. C. Peyer, *The tutor'd mind: Indian missionary-writers in antebellum America* (1997), 54–116 · M. Szasz, 'Samson Occom: Mohegan as spiritual intermediary', *Between Indian and White worlds: the cultural broker*, ed. M. Szasz (1994), 61–78 · D. D. Nelson, '"I speak like a

fool but I am constrained": Samson Occom's short narrative and economies of the racial self', *Early Native American writing: new critical essays*, ed. H. Jaskoski (1996), 42–65 · H. E. Wyss, '"One head, one heart, and one blood": Christian community and native identity at Brothertown', *Writing Indians: literacy, Christianity and native community in early America* (2000), 123–53

Archives Connecticut Historical Society, Hartford, papers · Dartmouth College, Hanover, New Hampshire, typescript diaries | Dartmouth College, Hanover, New Hampshire, E. Wheelock MSS
Likenesses N. Simbert, oils, *c.*1751–1756, Bowdoin College Museum of Art, Brunswick, Maine · J. Spilsbury, mezzotint, pubd 1768 (after portrait by M. Chamberlin), BM, NPG [*see illus.*] · M. Chamberlin, oils · A. Tenney, portrait (after mezzotint by J. Spilsbury, 1768) · portraits, Dartmouth College, Hanover, New Hampshire, Baker Library, Special Collection

Ó Ceallaigh [O'Kelly, Kelly], **Ralph** (*d.* 1361), archbishop of Cashel, was born at Drogheda, Louth, his parents, according to Bale, being David Ó Buge, the Carmelite theologian and canonist, and the wife of William Kellei, a Drogheda merchant. He was educated in the Carmelite house at Kildare, where he joined the order, and he later studied canon law at Rome and Avignon. He was procurator-general of his order from 1327 to 1333 and again from 1339 to 1344, having been removed in 1333 for disagreeing with John XXII's views on the beatific vision. On 7 February 1344 he was appointed to the see of Leighlin by Clement VI in the belief that it was vacant. As bishop he procured benefices in Ireland for his kinsmen and acted as suffragan in the diocese of York, but his provision was ineffective as his predecessor was still alive.

On 9 January 1346 Ó Ceallaigh was advanced to the archbishopric of Cashel and, on his way back to Ireland, acted briefly as suffragan in the diocese of Winchester. In 1347 he opposed the levying of a subsidy granted at a great council held at Kilkenny in the previous year, on the grounds that the bishops had not consented to it. He and three suffragans met at Tipperary and decreed that all beneficed clergy contributing to the subsidy should be *ipso facto* deprived of their benefices, and be incapable of holding any preferment within the province, and that lay tenants of church lands who contributed should be *ipso facto* excommunicated, and their children to the third generation likewise disqualified from holding benefices. The archbishop and his suffragans openly excommunicated several persons, including William Epworth, archdeacon of Cork and chief collector of the subsidy in Munster. In answer to charges brought against him in the justiciar's court, the archbishop pleaded that Magna Carta guaranteed the freedom of the church and provided for the excommunication of those who infringed the liberties granted in it. He and the bishop of Lismore were found guilty but the outcome of the case is not known. However, he afterwards co-operated with the secular authorities, being appointed to array men in Tipperary to suppress the rebellion of Ó Ceinnéidigh in 1355. In 1359 he attended a great council held at Waterford and consented to a subsidy in aid of the war against Art Mac Murchadha.

In 1353 Ó Ceallaigh was involved in a vehement dispute with Roger Cradock, bishop of Waterford. Two Irishmen found guilty before the bishop of heresy, or possibly of insulting the Virgin Mary, had been burnt by his order, without any licence from the archbishop. The dispute culminated in Ó Ceallaigh's attacking Cradock in his lodgings in Waterford, grievously wounding him and his companions, and robbing him of his goods.

Ó Ceallaigh visited Avignon in 1358, possibly in connection with the attacks on the mendicant orders by Richard Fitzralph, archbishop of Armagh. He died at Cashel on 20 November 1361 and was buried in his cathedral there. He was the author of a volume of 'familiar letters' and a work on canon law, and of other works whose names are not known.   B. H. BLACKER, *rev.* PHILOMENA CONNOLLY

Sources P. O'Dwyer, *The Irish Carmelites (of the Ancient Observance)* (1988) • Bale, *Cat.*, 1.243–4 • NL Ire., Harris MSS, vol. 2, MS 2 • E. Tresham, ed., *Rotulorum patentium et clausorum cancellariae Hiberniae calendarium*, Irish Record Commission (1828) • W. H. Bliss, ed., *Calendar of entries in the papal registers relating to Great Britain and Ireland: petitions to the pope* (1896) • *CEPR letters* • D. F. Gleeson, 'A fourteenth century Clare heresy trial', *Irish Ecclesiastical Record*, 5th ser., 89 (1958), 36–42 • D. F. Gleeson, ed., 'The annals of Nenagh', *Analecta Hibernica*, 12 (1943), 155–64 • *Chancery records* • S. F. Hockey, ed., *The register of William Edington, bishop of Winchester, 1346–1366*, 1, Hampshire RS, 7 (1986) • J. A. Watt, *The church and the two nations in medieval Ireland* (1970)

Ó Ceallaigh, Seán Tomás. *See* O'Kelly, Seán Thomas (1882–1966).

Ó Cearbhalláin, Toirdhealbhach. *See* Carolan, Turlough (1670–1738).

Ó Cearnaigh, Seán. *See* Kearney, John (*b. c.*1545, *d.* after 1572).

Ochiltree. For this title name *see* Stewart, Andrew, second Lord Ochiltree (1521?–1594?).

Ochiltree, Michael (*d.* 1445×7), bishop of Dunblane, is of unknown origins. Described in 1429 as the son of a married man (a priest in another account) and an unmarried woman, he may have come from the barony of Ochiltree in the sheriffdom of Ayr. He was dean of Dunblane by 25 November 1420 and was provided to the see of Sodor in 1422, although this was never made effective. In 1424 he is recorded as the king's almoner-general, raising the possibility that he had taken service with James I before the latter's return to Scotland in that year. He had also obtained the degree of bachelor of canon law and held a tenement in Perth, a prebend and vicarage in the diocese of Dunkeld, and by 1427 a church in the diocese of Glasgow. On 22 June 1429 Ochiltree was provided to the see of Dunblane, made vacant by the death of William Stephenson, having been granted a dispensation for his illegitimate birth; he was consecrated between 4 July 1430 and 12 April 1431. On 24 January 1430 he was one of the commissioners appointed to negotiate a truce with England.

Although not the premier ecclesiastic in Scotland, it was Ochiltree who crowned the young James II at Holyrood on 25 March 1437 following the assassination of James I, possibly because his loyalty to the late king and to the queen was unquestioned at a time of political turmoil. He was involved in negotiating the terms of the 'Appoyntement' of 4 September 1439, which laid down the conditions for the keeping of the young James II during his minority, and

it was through the queen's patronage that Ochiltree obtained a royal charter consolidating the lands of his bishopric into a regality in 1442. On 16 August 1443 he was one of the prelates before whom Alexander Livingston purged himself of the killing of Sir Malcolm Fleming. Eighteen months later, on 5 February 1445, Ochiltree and the queen sought the arbitration of James Kennedy, bishop of St Andrews, in a suit concerning patronage. Ochiltree was present in the parliament held on 28 June 1445, but may have died shortly afterwards, as he does not appear again in the records and his successor, Robert Lauder, had been provided to the see of Dunblane by 27 October 1447.   C. A. MCGLADDERY

Sources J. Dowden, *The bishops of Scotland … prior to the Reformation*, ed. J. M. Thomson (1912), 206 • *CEPR letters*, vols. 7–8 • J. M. Thomson and others, eds., *Registrum magni sigilli regum Scotorum / The register of the great seal of Scotland*, 11 vols. (1882–1914), vol. 2 • *APS*, 1424–1567 • *CDS*, vol. 4 • W. B. D. D. Turnbull, ed., *Extracta e variis cronicis Scocie*, Abbotsford Club, 23 (1842)

Ochino, Bernardino (*c.*1487–1564/5), Capuchin friar and evangelical reformer, was, according to his later writings, born in Siena about 1487, the son of a barber, Domenico Tommasini. He is said to have taken his name from the district of Oca ('the goose').

Capuchin preacher Few details are recorded of Ochino's early life, but he probably entered the Franciscan Observant order about 1503. The seventeenth-century Capuchin historian Zaccaria Boverio asserts that Ochino later studied medicine at Perugia, where he became a friend of the future Pope Clement VII, but this claim cannot be verified. During the early 1520s, however, Ochino played a prominent role in the negotiations which resulted in the division of the Tuscan province of the Franciscan Observants (1523); he subsequently assumed the leadership of the newly formed province of Siena. At this stage Ochino was closely allied with the order's controversial general, Paolo Pisotti, whom he represented on several missions to the provincial chapter of Venice in 1531–2. Following Pisotti's removal from office in 1533, many of his former associates left the Franciscan Observants for the breakaway Capuchin order. Ochino was perhaps the best-known of the defectors, becoming a Capuchin some time in early 1534.

Ochino quickly emerged as a leading figure within the new order, partly on the strength of his links with Vittoria Colonna, one of the early Capuchins' most important patrons. At a chapter-general in November 1535 he was elected the order's first definitor, and on 3 June 1538 he succeeded Bernardino d'Asti as general (a position in which he was confirmed three years later). During the second half of the 1530s Ochino presided over the consolidation of the Capuchins' position in Italy, but his achievements in this regard were overshadowed by his growing reputation as a preacher. Between 1534 and 1542, his itinerary took in Naples, Perugia, Venice, Florence, Lucca, Siena, Ferrara, Bologna, and Palermo; there is evidence that city magistrates competed fiercely for his services. The impact of Ochino's oratory on listeners was by all accounts dramatic. His preaching in Naples during Lent

1536 prompted one observer, Gregorio Rosso, to remark that it was enough to make the stones weep.

It was during this first visit to Naples that Ochino became associated with the Spanish evangelical Juan de Valdés and his followers. Although Ochino may first have encountered evangelical ideas some years earlier, via contacts with the Augustinian preachers Agostino Mainardi and Giulio da Milano, he seems to have been particularly attracted by Valdés's syncretic approach, which combined a crypto-protestant understanding of justification with a spiritualism rooted in Franciscan tradition. Valdés, for his part, seized on Ochino's preaching as an opportunity to communicate his ideas to a wider public. The papal protonotary Pietro Carnesecchi later testified that when he was in Naples Ochino used to receive notes from Valdés on the evenings before he was due to preach, outlining the theme for the next day's sermon.

The break with Catholicism The timing of Ochino's break with Catholic orthodoxy is difficult to establish with any precision. He himself later claimed that by the time of his defection to the Capuchins he had already renounced the papacy. Unfortunately, while in Italy Ochino published relatively few works against which that statement can be measured. Of the hundreds of sermons that he preached during the late 1530s and early 1540s, for example, only fifteen survive. These were published in two main collections: the *Prediche nove*, a series of sermons dating from Easter 1539 and first printed in Venice in March 1541; and the collection known as the *Prediche lucchesi*, also published in 1541, of which a single copy survives in the British Library. Ochino may also be the author of an anonymous *Dialogo dil maestro e discepolo*, published in Asti in 1540, and of a short text included in the Spanish manuscript version of Valdés's *110 Divine Considerations*. However, his best-known work of the period is a collection of dialogues, the *Dialogi sette*, first published by the Venetian printer Zoppino in 1540 (although some of the dialogues date back to 1536). The title page of the *Dialogi sette* features a woodcut illustration of Ochino, bearded and in the habit of his order, praying before a crucifix. Although neither the sermons nor the dialogues are overtly heterodox, both are characterized by an emphasis on the crucified Christ at the expense of other traditional devotions, and appear to teach a mild doctrine of justification by faith. When considering these writings, one must also bear in mind Ochino's later claim that, while in Italy, he had been forced to preach Christ 'masked', revealing the true extent of his differences with Rome only to a trusted few. There is independent evidence of Ochino's secret proselytizing activity in the testimony of the Anabaptist Pietro Manelfi, who reported that Ochino had supplied him with copies of works by Luther and Melanchthon.

In that context it is hardly surprising that doubts about Ochino's orthodoxy began to be voiced; at Easter 1539 he was forced to defend himself publicly against the allegation that he had denied the existence of purgatory. These charges gained new credibility when, while preaching in Venice during Lent 1542, Ochino condemned the continuing imprisonment of his fellow evangelical Giulio da Milano, who had been forced to make a public abjuration of heresy only a few months before. Ochino's comments were communicated to the curia, and in July he received a summons from Paul III to appear at Rome. At first he appeared intent on obeying, but in Florence he encountered Pietro Martire Vermigli, who persuaded him of the need for a decisive break with the Roman church. After discarding his clerical habit and informing Vittoria Colonna of his intentions (22 August), Ochino fled across the Alps to the safety of Morbegno in the Valtellina. From there he proceeded via Zürich to Geneva, where he arrived towards the end of September 1542.

In Geneva Ochino was licensed to preach to the city's small Italian-speaking community, first at the chapel of the cardinal of Ostia in St Pierre and then at the church of St Gervais. In 1543 he married an exile from Lucca (she died in 1563, but her name is unknown), with whom he had at least six children. The eldest, Aurelia, who was born in Geneva, later married the Lucchese merchant Lorenzo Venturini. Ochino's very public apostasy had made him a target of Catholic polemicists, and during his first year in Geneva he was forced to issue a series of public defences of his actions (*Responsio ad Marcum Brixiensem*, *Responsio ad Mutium Justinopolitanum*, *Epistola alli Signori di Balìa della città di Siena*, all 1543). Between October 1542 and August 1545 he also published seven short volumes of sermons in Italian; a short but trenchant attack on the papacy, the *Imagine di Antechristo*; and a commentary on Romans (*Espositione sopra la epistola di San Paolo alli Romani*). Like the other vernacular works published in the early years of his exile, all were clearly intended for an Italian readership. Most of the sermons, which set out Ochino's by now fully protestant understanding of faith, justification, and predestination, were later republished by Michael Isengrin in Basel as a two-volume edition of *Prediche*.

Germany and England In August 1545 Ochino left Geneva, perhaps in search of a more lucrative posting; there is no evidence to suggest that his decision was prompted by doctrinal or personal differences with Calvin, who in April 1543 had declared himself perfectly satisfied of Ochino's orthodoxy. After short stays in Basel and Strasbourg, Ochino was offered a preaching position by the city council of Augsburg, with an annual stipend of 200 gulden (December 1545). Here he published a second major commentary, the *Espositione sopra la epistola di Paolo a i Galati*, and a number of shorter devotional works, which appeared only in German (*Ain Gesprech der flaischlichen Vernunfft*; *Ain christliches schönes und tröstliches Bett*; *Von der Hoffnung aines Christlichen gemüts*). In Augsburg Ochino also had contacts with local followers of the radical reformer Kaspar Schwenckfeld, who were attracted by the spiritualist aspects of his theology. However, his stay in the city was short-lived: in January 1547 Augsburg was besieged by the army of Charles V, who demanded, among other things, that Ochino be surrendered into imperial custody. Accompanied by another Italian exile, Francesco Stancaro, he fled to Basel, where he was received at the home of the printer Johannes Oporinus. The Spanish evangelical Francisco de Enzinas (Dryander) attempted to obtain a position for Ochino in Zürich, but these plans were superseded by an invitation from Thomas Cranmer to assist with the reformation of the English church. A similar offer was extended to Ochino's compatriot Vermigli, who accompanied him to London in November–December 1547.

Ochino's activities in England are not particularly well documented. At first he lodged with Cranmer at Lambeth Palace, and in February 1548 the imperial ambassador François Van der Delft reported that he had begun preaching to London's Italian community. On 9 May that year he was appointed a prebendary of Canterbury, with an annual salary of 40 marks, although he remained resident in London. Shortly afterwards he secured Cranmer's backing for a plan to invite Wolfgang Musculus, another victim of the defeat of the Schmalkaldic League, to join the growing band of foreign theologians in England (the invitation was eventually declined). Ochino also cultivated links with the household of Princess Elizabeth; her manuscript translation into Latin of one of his Genevan sermons is held at the Bodleian Library. Ochino was one of several foreign theologians commissioned by Cranmer to write against the western rebellion in summer 1549. In the resulting 'Dialogus regis et populi', preserved among Cranmer's papers at Corpus Christi College, Cambridge, he evinces a certain amount of sympathy for the rebels' socio-economic grievances, but condemns their resistance to the reform of worship (MS 340, 97–108). Four editions of Ochino's sermons in English were also published during Edward VI's reign, in translations by Richard Argentine and Anne Cooke, later Lady Bacon. Better known is his *Tragoedie, or, Dialogue of the Uniuste Usurped Primacie of the Bishop of Rome*, which appeared in two variant editions, published before and after the fall of Protector Somerset in October 1549. This semi-dramatic work, which survives only in the English translation by Cranmer's chaplain John Ponet, attempts over the course of nine scenes to expose the doctrine of papal supremacy as a satanic strategy for the undermining of Christ's church, now thankfully restored to its pristine state in England by the reforms of the young Josiah (that is, Edward VI) and his father. In its structure and subject matter, the *Tragoedie* closely resembles the *Pammachius* of Thomas Kirchmeyer, which had been translated into English by Ochino's friend John Bale.

Return to Switzerland Following Mary's restoration of Catholicism, Ochino, like his compatriot Vermigli, was obliged to return to the continent. Passing through Geneva in October 1553, he is reported to have condemned the execution of Michael Servetus, 'quae res eum reddidit invisum' (S. Castellio, *Contra libellum Calvini*, 1612, sig. A6r). Once again, Ochino took up temporary residence in Basel, where a third volume of his *Prediche* had appeared around 1550. This was now followed by the *Apologi* (1544), a collection of anecdotes satirizing Catholic doctrine and devotional practices, and the fourth volume of the *Prediche*. In June 1555 Ochino accepted an invitation from the Zürich council to take up a position as minister to the community of evangelical exiles from Locarno that had settled in the

city. While in Zürich he published some of his most important theological works: the *Syncerae et verae doctrinae de coena domini defensio* (1556), a defence of the Swiss reformed doctrine of the eucharist against the Lutheran Joachim Westphal; the *Dialogo del purgatorio* (1556), in which a protestant 'Theodidatto' successfully rebuts arguments for the existence of purgatory proposed by representatives of five different Catholic religious orders; *Il catechismo* (1561), written for the use of the Locarnese church; the *Disputa intorno alla presenza del corpo di Giesu Christo nel sacramento* (1561), a collection of sermons aimed mainly against the mass; a fifth volume of *Prediche* (1562); and the *Laberinti del libero o ver servo arbitrio* (1560), which tackled the thorny question of predestination. Of interest are Ochino's continuing links with English reformers such as John Jewel and Thomas Sampson; when the newly enthroned Elizabeth I enraged her bishops by insisting on retaining a crucifix in her private chapel, Sampson urged Ochino to use his influence with the queen to persuade her to remove the offending object. Ochino subsequently dedicated his *Laberinti* to Elizabeth, fondly recalling their earlier association.

Although Ochino initially enjoyed good relations with Zürich's senior minister, Heinrich Bullinger (who had recommended his appointment), his later works suggest a growing disquiet with the theological drift of the Zürich church, and an interest in the ideas of dissident thinkers such as Sebastian Castellio and Lelio Sozzini. The *Laberinti* and *Disputa*, in which Ochino followed Castellio in proposing that controversial questions (such as the relationship between divine predestination and the human will, and the mode of Christ's presence in the eucharist) be treated as adiaphora, caused some disquiet in orthodox reformed circles, but it was the unauthorized publication, in spring 1563, of Ochino's *Dialogi XXX* that brought matters to a head. The *Dialogi*, which were translated into Latin by Castellio, contained devastating criticisms of the reformed understanding of justification, the atonement, and the sacraments (mitigated only to the extent that they were voiced by Ochino's fictional antagonists). Some passages in dialogue 19 indicate that Ochino was familiar with Lelio Sozzini's antitrinitarian commentary on the prologue to John's gospel. However, it was dialogue 21, on polygamy, that gave most grounds for offence. When it was brought to Bullinger's attention by a group of Zürich merchants, he felt that he had no choice but to recommend to the city council that Ochino be dismissed (22 November 1563).

Death and influence After being refused sanctuary in Basel and Mulhouse, Ochino spent the winter in Nuremberg, where he penned his final work, the autograph of which is held at the British Library (Add. MS 28568). In this *Dialogo della prudenza humana* he denounced the inhumanity of the Zürich theologians and magistrates, reiterating (this time openly) the criticisms of the reformed churches contained in the *Dialogi XXX*. In spring 1564 he left Nuremberg for Poland, where he was welcomed by members of the minor (antitrinitarian) church in Cracow. However, in August, the Polish king Sigismund II issued the edict of

Parczów, expelling non-Catholic foreigners from the realm. Forced into exile once more, Ochino found a haven with the Anabaptist community headed by Niccolò Paruta at Slavkov (Austerlitz) in Moravia. It was there, while preparing to take up an invitation to preach in Transylvania, that he is believed to have died in late 1564 or early 1565.

In the century and a half following his death Ochino assumed an honoured place in antitrinitarian historiography, as one of the founding fathers of Socinianism. He was less favourably treated by his former colleagues in the mainstream reformed churches, for whom his 'betrayal' represented an acute embarrassment. Josias Simler, in *De aeterno Dei filio* (1568), and Girolamo Zanchi, in *De tribus Elohim* (1572) denounced his views on the Trinity, while Theodore Beza published a refutation of the dialogue on polygamy (*Tractatio de polygamia*, 1568). During the 1650s Ochino's works enjoyed something of a revival in England; *A Dialogue of Polygamy, Rendered into English by a Person of Quality* was published in London in 1657, and it has been suggested that Milton drew on the *Dialogi XXX* for his views on the Trinity and marriage. Ochino later attracted interest from Pierre Bayle and from the eighteenth-century German antiquarian Johann Georg Schelhorn, who published a manuscript, now lost, of the *Dialogo della prudenza humana*. Twentieth-century scholarship is divided over the extent of Ochino's differences with reformed orthodoxy—exaggerated, perhaps, in the light of his expulsion from Zürich—but his career remains emblematic of the difficulties that many Italian evangelicals of the early modern period experienced in exile.

MARK TAPLIN

Sources R. Bainton, *Bernardino Ochino, esule e riformatore senese del Cinquecento, 1487–1563* (1940) · K. Benrath, *Bernardino Ochino von Siena, ein Beitrag zur Geschichte der Reformation*, 2nd edn (1892) · B. Nicolini, *Studi cinquecenteschi I: ideali e passioni nell'Italia religiosa* (1968) · B. Nicolini, *Studi cinquecenteschi II: aspetti della vita religiosa, politica e letteraria* (1974) · B. Ochino, *I 'Dialogi sette' e altri scritti del tempo della fuga*, ed. U. Rozzo (1985) · D. Cantimori, *Eretici italiani del Cinquecento e altri scritti*, ed. A. Prosperi (Turin, 1992) · U. Rozzo, 'Nuovi contributi su Bernardino Ochino', *Bollettino della Società di Studi Valdesi*, 146 (1979), 51–83 · G. Fragnito, 'Gli spirituali e la fuga di Bernardino Ochino', *Rivista Storica Italiana*, 84 (1972), 777–813 · E. Campi, *Michelangelo e Vittoria Colonna: un dialogo artistico-teologico ispirato da Bernardino Ochino, e altri saggi di storia della Riforma* (Turin, 1994) · E. Campi, '"Conciliazione de dispareri": Bernardino Ochino e la seconda disputa sacramentale', *Das Reformierte Erbe: Festschrift für Gottfried F. Locher*, ed. H. Oberman and others, 2 vols. (1992–3), 1.77–92 · P. McNair and J. Tedeschi, 'New light on Ochino', *Bibliothèque d'Humanisme et Renaissance*, 35 (1973), 289–301 · M. Taplin, 'The Italian reformers and the Zürich church, c.1540–1620', PhD diss., U. St Andr., 1999 · E. Hassinger, 'Exkurs über die Theologie Bernardino Ochino's vornehmlich in seiner Spätzeit', *Studien zu Jacobus Acontius* (1934), 97–109 · G. G. Williams, 'The theology of Bernardino Ochino', PhD diss., University of Tübingen, 1959 · B. Nicolini, 'Il pensiero di Bernardino Ochino', *Atti della Reale Accademia Pontaniana di Scienze Morali e Politiche*, 95 (1938), 171–268 · G. L. Betti, 'Bernardino Ochino francescano osservante', *Bollettino Senese di Storia Patria*, 98 (1991), 102–8 · P. McNair, 'Bernardino Ochino in Inghilterra', *Rivista Storica Italiana*, 103 (1991), 231–42 · P. McNair, 'Ochino's apology: three gods or three wives?', *History*, new ser., 60 (1975), 353–73 · BL, Add. MS 28568 · C. Madonia, 'Bernardino Ochino e il radicalismo religioso europeo', *Bollettino Senese di Storia Patria*, 98 (1991), 109–29 · U. Mazzone, 'Ochino, Bernardino', *Theologische Realenzyklopädie*, ed. G. Krause, G. Müller,

and S. Schwertner, 25 (Berlin, 1992), 1–6 · B. Ochino, *Seven dialogues*, ed. R. Belladonna (1988) · R. Belladonna, 'Bernardino Ochino's fourth dialogue ("Dialogo del ladrone in croce") and Ubertino da Casale's "Arbor vitae": adaptation and ambiguity', *Bibliothèque d'Humanisme et Renaissance*, 48 (1985), 125–45 · M. Taplin, 'Bernardino Ochino and the Zürich polygamy controversy of 1563', MLitt diss., U. St Andr., 1995 · U. Rozzo, 'Antonio da Pinerolo e Bernardino Ochino', *Rivista di Storia e Letteratura Religiosa*, 19 (1982), 341–64 · E. Campi, 'Bernardino Ochino's Christology and 'Mariology' in his writings of the Italian period (1538–42)', *Protestant history and identity in sixteenth-century Europe*, ed. B. Gordon, 2 vols. (1996), 1.108–22 · P. Simoncelli, 'In margine a una edizione di scritti ochiniani', *Critica Storica*, 22 (1985), 439–48 · P. McNair, 'Ochino on sedition: an Italian dialogue of the sixteenth century', *Italian Studies*, 15 (1960), 36–49 · V. Gabrieli, 'Bernardino Ochino, "Sermo di Christo": un inedito di Elisabetta Tudor', *La Cultura*, 21 (1983), 151–74 · J. G. Schelhorn, *Ergötzlichkeiten aus der Kirchenhistorie und Literatur*, 3 vols. (1764) · A. Rotondò, *Studi e ricerche di storia ereticale italiana del Cinquecento* (1974) · *Correspondance de Théodore de Bèze*, ed. H. Aubert, [24 vols.] (Geneva, 1960–) · L. Sozzini, *Opere*, ed. A. Rotondò (1986) · *Epistolae Tigurinae de rebus potissimum ad ecclesiae Anglicanae Reformationem pertinentibus conscriptae 1531–1558* (1848) · H. Robinson, ed. and trans., *The Zurich letters, comprising the correspondence of several English bishops and others with some of the Helvetian reformers, during the early part of the reign of Queen Elizabeth*, 2 vols., Parker Society, 7–8 (1842–5) · *DNB* · F. Meyer, *Die evangelische Gemeinde in Locarno, ihre Auswanderung und ihre weitern Schicksale: Ein Beitrag zur Geschichte der Schweiz im sechzehnten Jahrhundert*, 2 vols. (1836) · D. Bertrand-Barraud, *Les idées philosophiques de Bernardin Ochin de Sienne* (1924) · V. Marchetti, *Gruppi ereticali senesi del Cinquecento* (1975) · D. Cantimori, *Italiani a Basilea e a Zurigo nel Cinquecento* (1947) · Cuthbert of Brighton, *The Capuchins: a contribution to the history of the Counter-Reformation*, 2 vols. (1928) · F. Buisson, *Sébastien Castellion: sa vie et son oeuvre: étude sur les origines du Protestantisme libéral français*, 2 vols. (1892) · D. Caccamo, *Eretici italiani in Moravia, Polonia, Transilvania (1558–1611): studi e documenti* (1970) · L. Hein, *Italienische Protestanten und ihr Einfluss auf die Reformation in Polen während der beiden Jahrzehnte vor dem Sandomirer Konsens (1570)* (Leiden, 1974) · C. Ginzberg, ed., *I costituti di don Pietro Manelfi* (1970) · G. H. Williams, *The radical reformation*, 3rd edn (1992) · M. Firpo, *Tra Alumbrados e 'Spirituali': studi su Juan de Valdés e il Valdesianesimo nella crisi religiosa del '500 italiano* (1990) · L. A. Wood, *The form and origin of Milton's antitrinitarian conception* (1911) · P. McNair, ed., *Patterns of perfection: seven sermons preached in patria by Bernardino Ochino, 1487–1564* (1999)

Archives BL, Add. MS 28568 · CCC Cam., MS 340, 97–108 · Staatsarchiv, Zürich, E II 367

Likenesses woodcut, 1540, repro. in Ochino, *I 'Dialogi sette'* · engraving, 1600–99, repro. in Ochino, *I 'Dialogi sette'* · portrait, repro. in Ochino, *I 'Dialogi sette'*

Ochs, Johann Rudolph (1673–1749/50). *See under* Ochs, John Ralph (1704–1788).

Ochs, John Ralph (1704–1788), medallist, was the son of **Johann Rudolph Ochs** (1673–1749/50), gem-engraver and sealcutter, from Bern, Switzerland. Johann Rudolph Ochs the elder worked for a time at the Royal Mint as assistant. Füssli (p. 474) described him as being 'appreciated as one of the great modern artists'. Johann Rudolph Ochs went back to Switzerland for a period, but returned to Britain in 1719 where he died in 1749 or 1750.

Probably taught by his father, John Ralph Ochs was employed at the mint between c.1727 and 1787. He was promoted to become third assistant engraver in 1757. He was still third engraver in 1768 when he was paid an annual salary of £80. As second engraver at the mint in 1779 Ochs was offered the position of first engraver after

Richard Yeo's death that year. He declined owing to his advanced years and by 1786 he was incapable of working at all. In 1787 he retired at the age of eighty-three, having worked at the mint for more than fifty years. Hocking attributes the maundy money of George III (1763–86) to Ochs. Although he would, as chief engraver, have been entitled to an annual pension of £200, his position as assistant engraver would have paid him only £80 yearly. Lewis Pingo, the then chief engraver, proposed to give Ochs a higher pension in acknowledgement of his long working life at the mint, officially permitting him an annual pension of £120 and 6 guineas.

On Ochs's death in 1788 his widow, Frances, was appointed office sweeper at the mint. Challis considers her salary of £10 yearly to have been generous, since she was elderly and infirm and not able to perform her official duties. As the widow of a mint engraver she continued to receive a pension until her death in 1806.

W. W. WROTH, rev. LORNA COLBERG GOLDSMITH

Sources C. E. Challis, ed., *A new history of the royal mint* (1992) • W. J. Hocking, *Catalogue of the coins, tokens, medals, dies, and seals in the museum of the royal mint*, 2 vols. (1906–10) • L. Forrer, ed., *Biographical dictionary of medallists*, 8 vols. (1902–30) • R. Ruding, *Annals of the coinage of Great Britain and its dependencies*, 3rd edn, 1 (1840) • J. R. Füssli and H. H. Füssli, *Allgemeines Künstlerlexikon*, [rev. edn], 2 vols. (Zürich, 1779–1824), 474 • A. Seubert, *Allgemeines Künstler-Lexikon*, 2nd edn (Stuttgart, 1879), 3.2 • Thieme & Becker, *Allgemeines Lexikon*

Archives PRO, Mint 1/13 • PRO, Mint 1/14 • PRO, Mint 4/21 • PRO, T1/466/156 • PRO, T1/374/35

Wealth at death approx. £150 (at time of writing will); wife to inherit all, or if predeceased him, Charles Wyatt and wife of Prescott Street, Goodman's Fields, Middlesex, to receive £10 each and easy chair; Thomas Dalrymple (lived with Ochs) to receive £10 and liquor case; C. Johnson, Swann Street, to receive 5 guineas, and to invest £100 and give interest to C. Wyatt the younger until he is twenty-five (or his brother John if CW died): will, PRO, PROB 11/1169, sig. 408

Ochterlony, Sir David, first baronet (1758–1825), army officer in the East India Company, was born on 12 February 1758 in Boston, Massachusetts. He was the eldest of three sons of David Ochterlony (*d.* 1765), merchant sea captain of Scottish ancestry, and his American-born wife, Katherine (*d.* 1783), daughter of Andrew Tyler and his wife, Miriam. Although his father died insolvent in St Vincent in August 1765, the young David continued to live in the family property in Salem Street, Boston, and attended the Boston public Latin school. In 1770 his mother brought her three sons to England, where, on 7 March 1770, she married Isaac *Heard, whom she may have met during his voyages to America in the 1750s. Heard arranged the settlement of the late David Ochterlony's debts and used his influence as Lancaster herald to send his stepson David to India in 1777 as a cadet.

Early military career, 1778–1808 Ochterlony was commissioned on 7 February 1778 as ensign in the 31st Bengal native infantry, and was promoted to lieutenant later the same year. In 1781, while with the 24th native infantry, Ochterlony joined Colonel Thomas Deane Pearse's force, which marched 1100 miles from Bengal to Madras to reinforce Lieutenant-General Sir Eyre Coote's army engaged in war against the ruler of Mysore, Haidar Ali,

Sir David Ochterlony, first baronet (1758–1825), by Henry Hoppner Meyer, pubd 1816 (after Arthur William Devis)

and his French allies under Bussy. At Cuddalore on 25 June 1783 the 24th regiment, alone and in fierce hand-to-hand fighting, threw back a determined French attack. In the thick of the battle Ochterlony was wounded and taken prisoner. Following the death of Haidar Ali and the ratification of a treaty with his son Tipu Sultan (21 February 1784), the prisoners were released. Pearse and his troops marched back to Bengal, arriving in Calcutta on 15 January 1785. Ochterlony was appointed deputy judge-advocate-general with a Bengal army division in Dinapore. He served as a staff officer for the next eighteen years, being promoted captain on 7 January 1796 and major on 21 April 1800. Following the death of Ochterlony's mother on 30 August 1783, Isaac Heard remarried. In 1784 he became Garter principal king of arms, an influential appointment which he was to hold for thirty-eight years. Having no children of his own from either marriage, Heard derived from David Ochterlony 'all the satisfaction of a father, and experienced the warm attachment of a son' (Heard's obituary). They exchanged frequent correspondence and David Ochterlony wrote openly to Heard as his 'dear and most honoured friend and father', frankly disclosing his 'anti-matrimonial habits' (19 Jan 1817, Ochterlony MSS, priv. coll.).

In 1803, on the outbreak of war with the Marathas, the commander-in-chief, Lord Lake, brought Ochterlony back on active service. As a lieutenant-colonel (18 March 1803) in command of the 2nd battalion 12th Bengal native infantry, Ochterlony showed such skilful leadership at the capture of the forts of Sasni, Bijaigarh, and Kachawa in the doab that Lake appointed him deputy adjutant-general of his forces. He was with Lake at the battles of Koil (19 August 1803) and Aligarh (4 September 1803), and the capture of Delhi (11 September 1803), which wrested the Mughal emperor, Shah Alam, and his court from Maratha influence. While Lake and his army moved on, Ochterlony was left at Delhi as provisional resident with responsibility for the protection of the city and fortress of Delhi and its environs, and for ensuring the safety of Shah Alam. He organized the repair of 7 miles of crumbling city walls and the fortification of strong defensive parapets, calling in Lieutenant-Colonel Burn from Saharanpur to take command of all the troops available, about 2500 men with eleven guns. Together they held off Holkar, a Maratha chief, and his army of 18,000 men and 160 guns for nine days until relieved. A general order of the commander-in-chief dated 24 October 1804 commended Burn and expressed the highest approbation of Ochterlony's wise and timely precautions, energy, and decision.

The value of Ochterlony's service was recognized by his permanent appointment as resident at Delhi. His gallantry and courtly manners so earned Shah Alam's admiration that he was given the Mughal title of Nasir ud-Daula (defender of the state), and the town of Nasirabad was named after him. Like many of his British contemporaries in India, Ochterlony was very comfortable in Mughal–Hindustani culture but, contrary to legend, probably no more so than was customary for British officers who served for long periods at Indian courts. In what was to become the pattern of Ochterlony's career this period of success and recognition was followed by unwelcome news. In April 1806 a peremptory letter conveyed the governor-general's instruction to hand over the residency to a civil servant successor, Archibald Seton. Despite the protests of Lord Lake and Shah Alam, Ochterlony was assigned the command of the fortress and station of Allahabad, half-way between Calcutta and Delhi. As some compensation, no reduction was made in his emoluments as resident.

Middle years, 1808–1814 Growing anxiety in London about possible French invasion of India via the north-west frontier revived Ochterlony's career on active service. On the instruction of the governor-general, Lord Minto, Charles Theophilus Metcalfe left Delhi on 28 July 1808 to seek the collaboration of the raja of Lahore, in a defensive pact. Ranjit Singh, a rising power in the Punjab, saw the British as an obstacle to the further spread of his influence in the Jumna–Sutlej Doab. The governor-general in council decided that Ranjit Singh's action in launching a third trans-Sutlej expedition on 25 September 1808 was a threat to the security of British possessions south of the Sutlej. Metcalfe was therefore instructed on 31 October 1808 to extend British protection to the Sikh chiefs south of the Sutlej; to require the raja of Lahore to withdraw his army across the river; and to establish a military post near the Punjab frontier. Ochterlony, who had met and befriended Metcalfe during Lake's campaign in 1803, was summoned from Allahabad to lead a military detachment to the Sutlej in support of Metcalfe. Ochterlony set out from Delhi on 27 January 1809, followed by a strong force under Major-General St Leger. En route for Ludhiana he halted his

detachment for five days, at the request of Ranjit Singh, while a headstrong Sikh commander was persuaded to cross the Sutlej. Unfortunately this brought a charge of insubordination from the commander-in-chief. Neil Benjamin Edmonstone, the governor-general's secretary, used his persuasive skills to defuse the incident, and with Metcalfe's strong support Ochterlony retained his command at Ludhiana. A treaty of perpetual friendship between the British and the raja of Lahore, concluded on 25 October 1809, put an end to Ranjit Singh's trans-Sutlej incursions. The importance of Ludhiana as a listening post was marked in 1810 by its upgrading to a political agency. At the same time Ochterlony was appointed agent to the governor-general and military commander there. He was promoted colonel on 1 January 1812. His immediate concern was the presence of Kaji Amar Singh Thapa's Nepalese army close to the northern borders of the lowland states protected by the British. Having been defeated by Ranjit Singh at Kangra in 1809 and forced to recross the Sutlej, the kaji had decided to secure the Nepalese hold on the thirty Cis-Sutlej Hill states with a network of defensive fortifications. Incidents which had occurred sporadically since 1806 along the imprecisely defined southern border of Nepalese territory brought a general state of tension. By 1813, when Lord Moira (later marquess of Hastings) became governor-general and commander-in-chief, there was already a prospect of war between Britain and Nepal. An incident at Butwal on 29 May 1814, in which a chief police officer and eighteen policemen were killed by the Nepalese, provided the provocation.

War with Nepal and after, 1814–1822 Hastings, a general in his own right, planned for four divisions to invade Nepalese territory simultaneously. He appointed Ochterlony to command the third field division at Ludhiana with the rank of major-general. Ochterlony's orders were to destroy Kaji Amar Singh Thapa's army and to annihilate Gurkha influence and authority between the Jumna and the Sutlej. Hastings regarded these as 'objects of primary interest' (*Papers Respecting the Nepaul War*, 702). Having toured the border territory in 1813 and gathered intelligence about Nepalese forces and their tactical skills and stockaded defences, Ochterlony was aware that he was faced with an entirely different species of warfare in steep and difficult mountainous country. He was also aware that to fulfil his orders he needed troops highly trained and experienced in mountain warfare, and that no such soldiers existed in the Bengal army. Ochterlony set out from Rupar, moving via Palasi (the capital of Hindur) towards Nalagarh. He took with him a formidable array of artillery, and resolved to spend whatever time was necessary surveying the terrain and, helped by the raja of Hindur's labour force, constructing roads for his guns. Breaches made by 6 pounder guns and the threat of heavier battering guns caused the garrison of Nalagarh Fort and of nearby Taragarh to surrender. Ochterlony took care to reassure the ninety-five prisoners of their personal safety and of 'everything which would reconcile them to their captors' (ibid., 453). Hastings left it to Ochterlony's discretion to offer service to enemy troops, subject to his ratification. On 24 January 1815 Ochterlony signed and sealed a memorandum of four propositions offered by Jeykishen, a Brahman provincial governor of Kumaon, to the effect that every man who joined the British from the Nepalese army with his musket would receive Rs 10 and be retained in the British service on the Nepalese rates of pay. Larger monetary rewards would be paid to Nepalese officers. Ochterlony informed Hastings of these arrangements in early April 1815, by which time he had in his camp a body of 324 men 'in whose fidelity he felt the most perfect confidence' (BL OIOC, H/653, 136). Ochterlony's proposal to form them into a 'Nusseree Pulteen' (Nasiri battalion, so named after his Mughal title) received Hastings's enthusiastic approval.

In the meantime, Ochterlony had made steady and methodical progress capturing, sometimes with great difficulty, the forts across the precipitous ranges of the Cis-Sutlej hills. He drove each garrison to Malaun Fort, where, from intercepted letters, he knew that Kaji Amar Singh Thapa had elected to make his principal stand. Encamped at the foot of the Malaun hills, Ochterlony sent his troops, including the Nasiris, by night to occupy two undefended hilltops. From there, with feint attacks to mislead the kaji, he closed on a prominence overlooking Malaun Fort, beating off sustained and heroic counter-attacks with his field artillery. Under threat of Ochterlony's battering guns the kaji was forced to honourable surrender. Hostilities were brought to an end by a convention between Kaji Amar Singh Thapa and Ochterlony dated 15 May 1815. Clause 5 of this convention stated that Nepalese troops were at liberty to enter service with the British if they so wished and provided that the British chose to accept them. With the surrender of Malaun, Jaithak, and all other forts in the Jumna–Sutlej Doab, 4700 Nepalese soldiers joined the British. Of these perhaps 1500 were Gurkhas, the remainder being almost all Kumaonis and Garhwalis. Kaji Amar Singh Thapa and his son Ranjor Singh Thapa were given full military honours and were allowed to return to Nepal with their families and belongings. Ochterlony was appointed KCB and created a baronet. A grateful court of directors of the East India Company granted him an annual pension of £1000.

When the Nepalese government refused to ratify a treaty signed at Sagauli on 2 December 1815, a second campaign became necessary and Ochterlony was given overall command of an army of 33,000 men and 100 guns. With little more than two months of the campaigning season in which to fulfil Hastings's objectives in the east, Ochterlony lost no time. Having quickly gathered his ordnance and pioneer companies, he deployed two brigades to left and right, and led the other two through dense forests of sal trees to the precipitous and heavily fortified hills of the Churia Ghati range. Finding his way blocked at the Bichraltar Pass, Ochterlony led a brigade up a very steep and narrow ravine, leaving his pioneers to construct a passage for unladen elephants and for manhandling guns.

The sudden appearance of the British beyond the Bichraltar defences caused the Nepalese defenders to fall back on the main Nepalese position at Makwanpur. Having assembled two brigades and his heavy ordnance near Makwanpur, Ochterlony sent a strong force to occupy an abandoned hill position on the Makwanpur range. This he defended successfully with reinforcements and artillery against waves of Nepalese counter-attacks. The arrival of the other two brigades, the capture of Makwanpur Fort, and the consequent threat to the Katmandu valley persuaded the Nepalese government to ratify the treaty of Sagauli without further delay, thereby bringing the war to an end on 5 March 1816. Ochterlony's triumph was recognized by his promotion to GCB, by addresses in both houses of parliament, and by the augmentation of his coat of arms with the word Nipal. Hastings gave Ochterlony the privilege of forming the recruits from the Nepalese army into four battalions. The 1st and 2nd Nasiri and the Sirmur battalions were stationed in key forts in the Cis-Sutlej hills. The Kumaon battalion was based at Almora, near the Kumaon border with Nepal.

Hastings now led an army of 120,000 with 300 guns to subdue the Maratha chiefs and associated roving Pindari hordes which had been laying waste British territory in central India. Ochterlony was given the important task of commanding a division protecting Delhi and supporting operations in Rajputana. His reputation and tactical skills persuaded Amir Khan, a Maratha chief who had ravaged Jaipur and neighbouring territory, to ratify a treaty. With his army disarmed and disbanded, Amir Khan became a peaceful ally of the British. In March 1818 Hastings appointed Ochterlony resident in Rajputana and commissioner-general to the Rajput states, with command of British troops. In December 1818 he was appointed resident at Delhi, and in 1822 he became resident of Malwa and Rajputana, basing his headquarters at Neemuch.

Later career and reputation, 1822–1825 Despite this recognition, Ochterlony's life from 1822 was full of sadness. With his health deteriorating he bade farewell to his grandson, Charles Metcalfe Ochterlony, aged four, who sailed for Scotland on 16 January 1822. On 11 August 1822 Ochterlony's only son, Roderick Peregrine Ochterlony, who had been his Persian interpreter from 1809 to 1815, died. In the same year Ochterlony received news of the death on 29 April 1822 of his beloved stepfather and confidant, Sir Isaac Heard. In 1823 Lord Hastings, with whom Ochterlony had the greatest rapport, was succeeded as governor-general, after a brief interim period, by Lord Amherst. With neither political nor military standing, Amherst had doubts about his own competence. By December 1823 Ochterlony's health had so seriously declined that he sought a less demanding post. The government in Calcutta, determined that he should retire completely, soon seized an opportunity. Early in 1824 Ochterlony complied with an earnest request by Baldeo Singh, raja of Bharatpur, to invest his infant son as his heir apparent. A year later, when Baldeo Singh died, his nephew Durjan Singh seized power. Ochterlony, long convinced of the need for swift and decisive action at times of unrest in India, issued a proclamation calling on the people to support their rightful ruler, and prepared to march on Bharatpur. Amherst, fearful of repeating Lake's disastrous failure to take Bharatpur in 1805, ordered Ochterlony to cancel his proclamation and to halt his troops. Deeply hurt by this treatment, Ochterlony felt himself 'abandoned and dishonoured' (Kaye, 2.137). He resigned his appointment and, having moved to Meerut for a change of air, died late on 14 July 1825. He was buried at St John's Church there on the next day. With Metcalfe's persuasion, the governor-general in council passed a resolution on 16 September 1825 which vindicated Ochterlony's action at Bharatpur. Metcalfe was present when a large army under Lord Combermere stormed and took Bharatpur fortress on 3 January 1826. Ochterlony's Nasiris and the Sirmur battalion were in the forefront of the assault. At a public meeting on 26 September 1825 Metcalfe had paid tribute to his great friend Ochterlony: 'Never, perhaps, was there another so universally admired as a public man, at the same time so generally and fervently beloved' (ibid., 132).

Ochterlony never married, but is known to have had at least six children, a son and five daughters, with two or more Indian women. The tradition that Ochterlony took the evening air in Delhi with thirteen wives on thirteen elephants probably owes much to folklore. His two youngest daughters were born of Mahruttun, entitled Mubarak al-Nisa ('Blessed among women') and often called Begum Ochterlony. Ochterlony, 'who was uniformly spoken of as a kind, honourable and worthy man' (Heber, 2.19), showed care and affection for his family. His three elder daughters having married comfortably to East India Company officials, he provided funds in trust for his two youngest daughters. For his grandson, Charles Metcalfe Ochterlony, to whom the remainder of Ochterlony's baronetcy passed by second patent in 1823, he arranged guardians and the purchase of land and heritable estates in Scotland. In his will he left his estate and effects in India to Begum Ochterlony and thence to his two youngest daughters. Ochterlony paid no heed to acquiring a great fortune, but lived on his army and diplomatic emoluments.

A. P. COLEMAN

Sources DNB · A. P. Coleman, *A special corps: the beginnings of Gorkha service with the British* (1999) · V. C. P. Hodson, *List of officers of the Bengal army, 1758–1834*, 4 vols. (1927–47) · *Papers respecting the Nepaul war* (1824), 1453, 702 · A. R. Wagner, 'An eighteenth century king of arms collection of American pedigrees', *New England Historical and Genealogical Register*, 95 (1941), 25 · J. W. Kaye, *The life and correspondence of Charles, Lord Metcalfe*, 2 vols. (1854), 2.132, 137 · R. Heber, *Narrative of a journey through the upper provinces of India*, [new edn], 2 vols. (1844) · priv. coll., Ochterlony MSS · BL OIOC, Home misc., 653, 136 · A. Fisher, *Christian tombs and monuments, North West Province and Oudh, Meerut district* (1896), 7, no. 15, BL OIOC · *The path of glory: being the memoirs of the extraordinary military career of John Shipp*, ed. C. J. Stranks (1969), 106–7 · will, 26 July 1824, and codicils, 14 Nov 1824, 28 Feb 1825
Archives BL OIOC, corresp. relating to India · priv. coll., family papers | BL OIOC, letters to W. Pitt Amherst, MS Eur. F 140 ·

Mount Stuart Trust, Isle of Bute, letters to Lord Hastings · NRA, priv. coll., letters to W. Fraser
Likenesses A. W. Devis, oils, 1816, Scot. NPG; repro. in Coleman, *Special corps* · H. H. Meyer, mezzotint, pubd 1816 (after A. W. Devis), BM, NPG [*see illus.*] · S. Alam, group portrait, oils, c.1820 (*A darbar at Delhi*), BL OIOC · gouache drawing, c.1820, Gov. Art Coll. · miniature, c.1820, NPG · H. H. Meyer, mezzotint, Scot. NPG · R. R. Reinagle, oils, Oriental Club, London · group portrait, watercolour (*Durbar at Delhi of Akbar II*), BL OIOC · oils, West Museum, The Castle, Edinburgh · oils, Broadwindsor, West Dorset · oils, Oriental Club, London · print, repro. in W. K. Watkins, *The Ochterloney family of Scotland and Boston in New England* (privately printed, Boston, USA, 1902) · print, Royal Military Academy, Sandhurst, Indian Army Room

Ockham, Nicholas (d. c.1320), Franciscan friar, theologian, and philosopher, was born in Ockham in Surrey. The course of his career suggests that he was born in the early 1240s. After joining the Franciscan order he was sent to Paris for his first theological studies, between 1270 and 1274, most likely attending the lectures of Roger Marston. He was subsequently closely linked to the so-called neo-Augustinians, adherents of the intellectual tradition of Alexander of Hales and Bonaventure, of whom Marston was one. It is probable that Ockham was a bachelor of the Bible at Oxford in 1278 and 1279 and a bachelor of the *Sentences* from 1280 to 1282. Finally he became the eighteenth regent master of the Franciscan school at Oxford, probably between 1286 and 1288. Almost nothing is known of his later life, but it has been argued that he died about 1320.

Scholarly research in the late twentieth century has produced ten manuscript copies of Nicholas Ockham's commentary on the *Sentences*. Questions, or parts thereof, from books 1–4 have been edited in various books and journals. Fifteen *quaestiones disputatae* belonging to Nicholas are to be found divided between codex 158 and codex 196 of the municipal library of Assisi. Among these disputed questions is the 'Question on the plurality of forms'. This dispute, attributed to William Ockham by a number of early historians, is in fact the response of Nicholas to Thomas Sutton's 'Treatise against the plurality of forms'. Some of the other disputed questions fall naturally into groups, such as the four questions that are united in the edition entitled *Quaestiones disputatae 'De dilectione Dei'* (1981).

S. F. BROWN

Sources C. S. Alarcón, 'Nicolás de Ockham OFM († c. 1320). Vida y obras', *Antonianum*, 53 (1978), 493–573 · Nicolai de Ockham, *Quaestiones disputatae 'De dilectione Dei'*, ed. C. S. Alarcón, Spicilegium Bonaventurianum, 21 (1981), 3*–106* · R. Schönberger and B. Kible, *Repertorium edierter Texte des Mittelalters* (Berlin, 1994), n. 15930 · A. G. Little and F. Pelster, *Oxford theology and theologians*, OHS, 96 (1934), 88–9, 124–6 · V. Doucet, 'Nicholas d'Occam', *Archivum Franciscanum Historicum*, 47 (1954), 146–8

Ockham, William (c.1287–1347), philosopher, theologian, and political theorist, later known as the Venerable Inceptor, was born at Ockham, north-east of Guildford in Surrey.

Early life and writings Ockham entered the Franciscan order before the age of fourteen, and probably received his philosophical education at the Franciscan convent in London, which was the school for the London custody, one of seven divisions of the English province of the order. It was in London, at Southwark, that he was ordained subdeacon in 1306 by Robert Winchelsey, archbishop of Canterbury. If Ockham ever studied at Paris, for which there is no positive evidence, it would have been about 1310, as part of the quota of students in theology that each province was permitted to send to Paris for advanced training in theology, before either being appointed as a lector at a local convent, or being chosen to proceed to a theological degree at a university. Whether his initial theological education was solely in England or partially at Paris, he was eventually sent to Oxford, and in 1317–19 lectured on the *Sentences* of Peter Lombard as bachelor of theology at Greyfriars. The *Reportatio* of books 2–4 of his *Sentences* commentary dates to this period. While at Oxford, in June 1318, he was granted a licence by the bishop of Lincoln to hear confessions. According to the Oxford curriculum, Ockham would have given his bachelor's lectures on the Bible after completing those on the *Sentences*. This would place his biblical lectures as bachelor in the academic year 1319–20, although nothing has remained from that scholastic activity.

Between 1321 and 1324 Ockham was active in one of the order's schools as a lecturer in logic and natural philosophy, awaiting his opportunity to proceed to the doctorate at Oxford, or possibly Paris. These were the most productive years of an active life of writing. He revised his questions on the first book of the *Sentences*, which became known as his *Ordinatio*. He lectured on Aristotle's logic, producing his *Expositio aurea* and his *Expositio super libros elenchorum*. He wrote his *Expositio in libros physicorum* on Aristotle's *Physics*. He engaged in quodlibetic disputations, the results of which form the first five series of disputations in his *Quodlibeta septem*. He wrote a massive, revisionary, textbook in logic known as *Summa logicae*. And he may well have begun one or both of his treatises on the eucharist (*De quantitate* and *De corpore Christi*, the first or both of which became known as *De sacramento altaris*). These works were written in the same convent in which Walter Chatton was a lecturer in theology, and where Adam Wodeham was both a student in Chatton's classroom and an assistant (*socius*) to Ockham. Both Chatton's *Reportatio* on the *Sentences* (1321–3), and his *Lectura* on book 1 of the same work (1323–4), reveal a textual interdependence with Ockham's *Quodlibeta* and *Expositio in libros physicorum* that could only have resulted from close proximity in time and space. The location of this intense activity was probably the London convent, as Gedeon Gál has argued, although the Oxford convent cannot be excluded.

Ockham's positions on the status of universal concepts, his belief that only substances and qualities were real entities, and the implications of these views for the doctrine of the eucharist had already been criticized by Walter Chatton by 1322. These discussions led Ockham to modify his view on universals, as well as to intensify his attack on the view that quantity, relation, place, time, and motion were real entities, apart from absolute substances and their qualities.

Charges of heresy Ockham's ideas soon attracted attention outside the schools as well. At a provincial chapter of his order, apparently at Cambridge in 1323, he was called upon to explain his views on thirteen propositions derived from his teaching on the Aristotelian categories, especially the category of 'relation'. While the annual provincial chapter for the English Franciscan province was normally held between mid-August and early September, and in 1323 was held at Bristol, the chapter at which Ockham responded may have been called specifically for that purpose and could, according to the calendar then in use, have occurred as late as March 1324. No action against Ockham is known to have resulted, but this internal inquiry may have led to the lodging of a complaint against his teaching at the papal court.

Late in the spring of 1324 Ockham was apparently summoned to Avignon to have his writings, specifically his lectures on the *Sentences*, examined for heretical or erroneous teaching. It may be that his title, inceptor, meant that he was about to become regent master, probably at Oxford, in the following autumn term had he not been summoned to Avignon on charges of false teaching. However, the title inceptor was applied by the Franciscan William Woodford to three other Franciscan theologians, William Ware, Robert Cowton, and Walter Chatton, who had all, like Ockham, entered the order before the age of fourteen, but of whom only one (Chatton) is known to have become a regent master in theology.

In the summer of 1324 Ockham crossed the channel, travelled to Provence (perhaps pausing briefly at the Franciscan convent at Paris on the way), and took up residence at the Avignon convent. There he came into association with several important Italian Franciscans: Francisco da Marchia, a Scotistic theologian and doctor of Paris; Bonagratia da Bergamo, procurator-general of the order; and Michele da Cesena, the minister-general of the order. The evaluation of the text of Ockham's *Sentences* commentary, which he had brought with him to Avignon, was initially entrusted to John Lutterell, former chancellor of Oxford, who had arrived in Avignon the year before. Whether Lutterell's opposition to Ockham dated back to their time together at Oxford, or began at Avignon, is not known. Lutterell extracted fifty-six philosophical and theological statements from Ockham's work of before May 1325 that he felt were erroneous or heretical. Subsequently a commission was appointed to inspect Ockham's work in light of Lutterell's list. Those serving on the commission, in addition to Lutterell, were the Dominicans Raimond Béguin, Dominique Grenier, Durand de St Pourçain, and two Augustinian friars, the theologians Gregorio da Lucca and Jean Paignote. All of them were Paris doctors of theology and, with the exception of Paignote, were prelates or bishops-elect.

This commission removed from consideration most of Ockham's statements on the ontological status of such categories as relation, time, motion, place, and quantity unless they were directly part of a theological proposition. The commission compiled a list of fifty-one propositions by 1326, which was subsequently altered and reduced to a list of forty-nine. In addition, the Cistercian bishop of Pamiers, Jacques Fournier (later Pope Benedict XII), who was also a doctor of theology from Paris, with considerable experience in rooting out heresy in his diocese, wrote a critical evaluation of Ockham's teaching based on these lists. In the end no formal condemnation took place, possibly because some of the positions on which Ockham was being accused of erroneous teaching had defenders, both on the commission and within the larger scholastic theological community, especially among Scotists.

Opponent of the papacy Although in no way a restriction on the ability of the commission to proceed, the situation was altered in 1328 when Ockham and several fellow Franciscans, specifically Michele da Cesena and Bonagratia da Bergamo, arrived at the conclusion that the position taken by Pope John XXII on the issue of the poverty of Christ and the apostles was heretical. Expecting no justice from a heretical pope, they fled Avignon for the Mediterranean port of Aigues-Mortes during the night of 26 May 1328. There they took sail for Genoa and Pisa, where they joined the entourage of Emperor Ludwig of Bavaria, the leading political opponent of the pope. Ockham and his companions were excommunicated, and John XXII eagerly but unsuccessfully sought their arrest and return to Avignon. Ockham remained with the imperial court when it returned from Italy to Munich, and he resided at the Franciscan convent in Munich for the remaining two decades of his life, never to return to England.

The flight to Italy and Germany was not only a geographical relocation for Ockham; it marked a radical shift in his intellectual preoccupations. From then on Ockham concerned himself with the question of a heretical pope, the issues on which he based that view of John XXII, and the implications of those ideas for church polity. Among the many books and treatises on political theory that he produced in this period, the two most important were his *Opus nonaginta dierum*, written, as the title states, in ninety days, and his *Dialogus*. In these works Ockham attacked John XXII's condemnation of the Franciscan doctrine of evangelical poverty as expressed in the papal constitutions *Ad conditorem canonum* (8 December 1322), *Cum inter nonullos* (12 November 1323), *Quia quorundam* (10 November 1324), and *Quia vir reprobus* (16 November 1329). In the climate of the imperial court and the Franciscan convent at Munich, fed by the views of Michele da Cesena and Marsiglio da Padua, the state and future of the church took precedence over other interests for Ockham. His earlier plan to write a commentary on Aristotle's *Metaphysics*, which had been on his agenda before leaving England, was dropped. While his philosophical and theological views continued to be debated at Oxford and Paris in the 1330s and 1340s, Ockham himself was silent on those subjects after 1328.

When Michele da Cesena died in 1342, Ockham took possession of the seal of the Franciscan order, although he was not the order's minister-general in exile. Without recanting his position on papal heresy or on any other issue, Ockham died at Munich on 10 April 1347, two years before the black death struck that city, where he was buried. The seal was restored to the order by Ockham's assistant (*socius*), also named William (de Anglia), at the general chapter at Verona in June 1348, and the petition of the latter for reconciliation with the papacy was granted on 8 June 1349.

Ockham's writings and their reception Ockham left behind him a sizeable body of writings. In the area of theology these include a revised edition of his commentary on the first book of the *Sentences* (his *Ordinatio*), a *reportatio* of his commentary on books 2–4 of the *Sentences*, his seven *Quodlibeta* composed in England and Avignon, his questions on the eucharist, and various disputed questions. While all of these works contain material important to philosophy, they are essentially works in theology. Ockham's major writings in logic and natural philosophy are his *Summa logicae*, his commentaries on the logic of Porphyry and Aristotle, commentaries and questions on Aristotle's *Physics*, and his treatise on God's predestination and foreknowledge of future contingents. All these works have now been critically edited, a task only completed in 1988.

Critical editions of Ockham's equally important works in political thought have been only partially realized. These include his *Opus nonaginta dierum*, his letter to the general chapter of the Franciscan order meeting at Assisi in 1334, his treatises against John XXII and Benedict XII, and his eight questions on the power of the pope (*Octo quaestiones de potestate papae*). His single most important work on the relation of church and state, his *Dialogus de potestate imperiali et papali*, except for certain sections that have been edited, is available only in the defective edition of Melchior Goldast published in 1614. A critical edition based on the manuscripts was in progress in 1998.

Ockham's intellectual armoury Ockham's contributions to medieval thought lie in two areas, his philosophical and theological writings on the one hand, composed between 1317 and 1326, and his political writings on the other, composed after 1328. Since these coincide with two distinct periods in his life, they will be discussed in that order.

In approaching Ockham's philosophical thought, it is important to keep in mind that it was the product of someone who was a theologian. His earliest philosophical views are contained in his lectures on the *Sentences*, which were a product of an academic requirement of the theological programme. Moreover, all his commentaries on Aristotle, as well as his *Summa logicae*, were written after he had lectured on the *Sentences*, and they were intended to be of use to those preparing for or practising theology, as he makes clear in his introduction to his *Summa logicae*. Ockham was never a 'pure' philosopher, but rather one who used philosophical ideas as tools for theological enquiry. On the other hand, Ockham's theology, as was true for others of his and previous generations at Oxford and Paris, was heavily dependent on the tools of philosophical enquiry and analysis, and, in his case, on semantic theory.

Somewhat over-confidently, Ockham assumed that

proper philosophical and linguistic tools were capable of helping to solve certain types of theological and exegetical questions, and that one of the problems with the theology of the previous generation, particularly that of Henri de Ghent and John Duns Scotus, despite the many differences in the thought of those two individuals, was that their philosophical tools and approaches were inadequate for the task, or misled them. Thus Ockham shared many of Scotus's theological positions, such as his views on grace and justification, much of his sacramental theology, and his ethical theories, and he even reformulated some of Scotus's philosophical views, such as intuitive cognition. But he disapproved of Scotus's tendency to reify abstract nouns into existent entities, and to distinguish, within one and the same thing (*res*), non-identical features or entities (*formalitates*) that had ontological status (a formal distinction *ex parte rei*) in between a real distinction and a mental distinction. For Ockham a formal distinction applied only to the distinction of persons in the Godhead, and should not be applied to the created order, or even to the divine attributes.

The principles of Ockham's thought Ockham employed a number of fundamental principles that shaped his approach to many problems in philosophy and theology. Each of these had a history in earlier thinkers, but their combination in Ockham gives a distinctive character to his thought. The first of these is his belief in the total transcendence of God, and, correspondingly, the complete contingency of the created order in all its aspects. Duns Scotus believed that the term 'being' had a meaning that was applicable both to God and creatures, and that this 'univocity' of being allowed theologians to make statements about God based on a concept of being that was derived from the created order. Ockham, by contrast, broke with the Platonic idea of the universe as a 'great chain of being', in which God and creation were linked together ontologically. For Ockham, only God was absolutely necessary; everything else, including the physical, metaphysical, and moral orders, was contingent and unnecessary.

A second, related, principle already established in thirteenth-century theology, is the distinction between God's power considered from the standpoint of simple capacity (*potentia absoluta*), and that same power considered from the standpoint of divine volition and divine decrees (*potentia ordinata*). Ockham uses that distinction to identify and explore the non-necessary character of causal relationships and states of affairs in the orders of nature and salvation. Any entities that are individually distinct, such as fire and the combustion of a flammable substance, or acts done in a state of grace and God's acceptance of those actions as meritorious of eternal life, can be separated in such a way that one could exist without the other. As biblical miracles attest, God can produce or conserve directly any effect normally produced through secondary causality without the presence of that cause, just as he can produce or conserve a cause without its normal effects. God's power, considered simply or absolutely, extends to anything that does not involve a direct contradiction. Yet God does not act arbitrarily. God has bound himself to uphold and work within the natural and spiritual orders he established. The reliability and predictability of the laws of nature, which Ockham affirms, are the result of the reliability of God's promises to sustain the system he created. Their reliability is not grounded in the inherent, necessary, and eternal nature of things. In this regard Ockham is continuing the attack on the Greek philosophical view of the necessary character of natural relationships that began with the Parisian articles of 1270 and 1277.

Ockham's belief that the laws of nature and grace were established by God and contingent on his will permits him to substitute a system of contractual efficacy in place of a system of inherent virtues or natures—a third guiding principle in his thought. Ockham's notion of ascribed value, again inherited from thirteenth-century thinkers, which he applies to natural forces as well as sacramental efficacy, is another dimension to his attack on the Greek understanding of the nature of the universe and causal relationships.

A fourth principle is Ockham's belief that the fundamental realities in the external world are individual substances and their qualities: as the world is composed of individually existing things, it is not individuation that requires explanation, but similarity and universality.

The final principle, frequently referred to as 'Ockham's razor', is the principle of economy, or parsimony: plurality ought not to be posited without necessity ('pluralitas sine necessitate non est ponenda'—the often cited phrase 'entia non sunt multiplicenda praeter necessitatem' is only an approximation to what Ockham actually wrote). This is not a principle of nature, since Ockham is convinced that God, for his own reasons, does many things in a more elaborate way that could have been done in a shorter or simpler way. The principle of economy is a hermeneutical principle, through which Ockham rejects assumptions and explanations in the argumentation of others that he feels are unnecessary.

The implications of nominalism Since the fifteenth century Ockham's name has been linked with nominalism, which became an important current of thought in the universities of Europe in the fifteenth and early sixteenth centuries. By 'nominalism' is usually meant a theory on the status of universal concepts and how they come to be known. As stated above, Ockham believed that the external world was composed of individual substances and qualities. Even a mental concept is universal only in the sense that it can be predicated of many individuals in external reality. Ockham did not believe that the similarity observed in individuals belonging to the same species was a creation of the mind superimposed on external reality, but was an accurate perception that individuals of the same species had similar qualities. For example, each individual human being is described as a rational animal. Yet the language through which that truth is affirmed, when expressed collectively, speaks of sharing a common nature, or having something in common.

Such expressions for Ockham are true in the sense that they are a linguistic shorthand for a multitude of statements about individuals, but they are false if what is meant is that things actually share one common nature or have a nature in common. To be a citizen of a country does not mean that individuals share citizenship as an entity that inheres in them or is divided among them. For Ockham there are no common natures that exist apart from individuals or that inhere in individuals. Socrates is a rational animal, as is Plato. But they do not share rationality as a common nature or possession that makes them rational. The problem for Ockham was that these linguistic expressions were often mistaken for ontological realities. General terms such as 'rationality' are convenient ways of talking collectively about characteristics that individuals have individually. Similarly, propositions containing general terms are simplified equivalents of a collection of propositions containing singular terms.

It is difficult to know whether Ockham's belief in the primacy of the individual and the ontological status of universals shaped his logic and natural philosophy, or whether his understanding of the relation of language and external reality led to his view of universal concepts. Ockham was opposed to any logic that assigned ontological status to parts of speech, linguistic expressions, or abstract nouns. The only realities for Ockham were substances and qualities, and the other Aristotelian categories, such as quantity, relation, place, motion, and time, were simply ways of describing substances and qualities, not separate entities in themselves.

Ockham's interpretation of the Aristotelian categories led to a distinctive natural philosophy that set it apart from most previous interpretations, and from the common opinion of his day. Most contemporaries accepted the view that motion, time, place, space, relation, and quantity were things that existed separately from individual things that existed in time and space. For them the sequential flow of time would exist even if there were no things (and thus no events) to 'take place'. Similarly, the concept of motion had ontological status apart from things in motion, just as relation existed apart from things that were related. In fact, to talk about things 'in motion' or 'related' seemed to presuppose the existence of such things as 'motion' and 'relation' separate from real individuals. For Ockham, however, statements about things in time or in motion were again linguistic shorthand for a multitude of statements arranged sequentially. Similarly, the category of quantity was not an entity separate from things, but another way of saying that individual things were extended in space. It should be noted, however, that Ockham was opposed to atomism. He believed in the infinite divisibility of temporal and spatial continua.

Ockham's epistemology In the area of epistemology Ockham developed Duns Scotus's theory of intuitive cognition into a self-sufficient epistemology based on direct sense experience. In place of a multi-stage process, by which an essentially passive mind extracted and abstracted knowledge from sense images or 'species' that were thought to emanate from an object, Ockham gave primacy to the immediate intuitive (that is, sensory, especially visual) knowledge of individual things. Both sensible and intelligible species or images, which had formed the basis for much of thirteenth-century epistemology, were dismissed by Ockham as unnecessary elements in explaining knowledge by sense experience. While Ockham's contemporaries and successors accepted the idea of intuitive cognition, most retained species as part of the explanation of the process of knowing. Similarly, most were critical of Ockham's redefinition of intuitive cognition as that sense experience that informed human beings of the existence or non-existence of an object. For others, information about what was not present was part of reflection, and was derived from abstractive cognition.

On the grounds that individual things are separate entities, and that God can preserve an effect without its normal cause or a cause without its normal effect, as biblical miracles attested, Ockham argues that one can have an intuitive cognition of something that is non-existent or no longer in existence. Despite the false witness of sense experience in this instance, Ockham's belief in certitude led him to espouse the position that the mind would be able to judge that the object was not in fact present.

The influence of Duns Scotus Much of Ockham's theology was derived from the Franciscan tradition, and from the writings of Duns Scotus in particular. God is not a debtor to man, or obliged in any absolute way to uphold or conform to the created orders of nature and grace. God remains free and exists outside time. Yet God has bound himself to uphold the created order, and to act within a system and according to rules that are of his own design. In the physical world this contingent, covenantal (as distinct from necessary) arrangement works through secondary causality. In the order of grace and salvation it works through ascribed value, that is, sacraments produce their proper effects not because of powers inherent in them, but because of the system God has ordained through which, when properly administered, grace is received. Only the eucharist, as the body and blood of Christ, has inherent virtue. Ockham also accepted Scotus's view that the presence of the habit of grace in the soul does not require God to grant the reward of eternal life. Absolutely speaking, God remains free to reject those in a state of grace and to reward those not in a state of grace. God has bound himself, however, to reward with eternal life only those who possess the habit of grace. This Scotistic doctrine of divine acceptation (*acceptatio divina*) remained an important yet controversial element in Ockhamist theology throughout the late middle ages.

Ockham's political thought The last area of Ockham's thought to be examined is his political theory, which occupied his attention during the last two decades of his life. Ockham's conviction that Pope John XXII had erred both in his condemnation of the Franciscan position on apostolic poverty (that Christ and the apostles owned nothing), and in his belief that the souls of the blessed did not enjoy the vision of the divine essence until the last judgement, led Ockham to re-examine a number of fundamental issues regarding temporal and political power. One of these was a penetrating analysis of the concepts of lordship (*dominium*), ownership, and use, through which Ockham defended the Franciscan position of a natural right of use that did not entail legal ownership. Another was the effect on the structure of the church and ecclesiastical authority of the possibility—for Ockham a reality—of the pope's falling into heresy. This led Ockham to revive and refine conciliar theories that had been worked out in canon law in the thirteenth century.

Ockham's political philosophy has often been associated with that of Marsiglio da Padua as expounded in the latter's *Defensor pacis* in 1324. Both were writing in the same period and were attached to the court of Ludwig of Bavaria, both were concerned with the relationship of church and state, and both were critical of the papacy. Ockham, however, was far more conservative than Jean de Paris or Marsiglio da Padua regarding the power and autonomy of secular government, and on the role that king or emperor might play in the governmental structure of the church. For Ockham the papacy was an institution founded by Christ, and the pope possessed a doctrinal and administrative authority in the church that exceeded that of the episcopate, priesthood, or doctors of theology. Monarchy, be it secular or papal, was the ideal form of government for Ockham. Yet it was scriptural truth that ultimately mattered on issues of doctrine. The question was over the appropriate authority for interpreting scripture and deciding what was doctrinal error, and also what mechanisms of redress existed in cases where the single monarchical authority proved inadequate for the task or had fallen into error.

In the case of a pope who had erred into heresy, correction came through the doctrinal authority of the church as a whole. This might take the form of a general council which, in the absence of any other governmental authority, could be summoned by king or emperor. General councils, however, were not infallible. While God would not allow the church as a whole to fall into error, the interpretation and defence of true doctrine was not vested in any one person or group within the church. The only institution that came close to infallibility for Ockham, despite John XXII, was the papacy.

In contrast to Marsiglio da Padua, Ockham defended a two-power political structure in which coercive temporal jurisdiction was vested in the secular monarch while spiritual jurisdiction was vested in the pope. The one did not have supreme or preferential authority over the other. Although Ockham and other political theorists of his age have often been criticized for discussing politics in the abstract—what should be, rather than dealing with things as they are—Ockham's two-power political world, and his reluctance to accord to any one institution or individual total sovereignty in society or doctrine, may have been more truly reflective of the real world in which he lived.

Ockham's influence and reputation Well before Ockham's death in 1347 his thought and reputation had attracted followers and produced vocal critics—the former sometimes invoking his name for positions he did not maintain and the latter sometimes accusing him of holding or implying views he apparently did not intend. His name, alongside that of Scotus and a handful of others, remained at the centre of scholastic debate at Oxford until the late fourteenth century, although Ockhamism never became a dominant school of thought in fourteenth-century England, as was once thought. By the 1330s at Paris an as yet unidentified group of Ockhamists in the arts faculty emerged, espousing positions in logic and natural philosophy that were influenced by Ockham's writings but were not faithful reflections of his thought. The prohibitions on Ockham's writings, and the attempt in the faculty of arts to condemn members and ideas belonging to the Ockhamist sect, coincided with a papal suspension of university privileges and a demand for reform, which may have aided the anti-Ockhamist masters of arts in mobilizing opinion against writings and ideas linked to a major critic of the pope.

The attempt to suppress Ockhamist ideas at Paris appears to have been only partially successful, since Ockham's natural philosophy had several defenders at Paris in the faculty of theology during the 1340s, and the statutes and oaths concerning his teaching were removed from registers of the arts faculty and nations in the 1350s. Ockham's ideas continued to be discussed at Paris as a legitimate part of contemporary scholastic thought until the end of that century, and were especially influential on the philosophy, theology, and political thought of Pierre d'Ailly. Although opposition to Ockham increased in the fifteenth century as a result of the rise of Albertism and the reawakening of Thomism and Platonic thought, he was recognized as a major authority by those who called themselves nominalists and adhered to the *via moderna*.

Thus although Ockham's thought remained controversial in the later middle ages, especially in the fields of epistemology, the doctrine of justification, and sacramental theology, he also continued into the sixteenth century to be regarded as a major theologian and philosopher. Theologians active on the eve of the Reformation, such as the Scot John Mair at Paris, and Gabriel Biel in Germany, counted themselves as Ockhamists. And although Martin Luther came to be particularly critical of Ockham's theology, he nevertheless acknowledged an indebtedness to Ockham, especially as transmitted through Biel.

As philosophical and theological currents changed in the course of the sixteenth century, Ockham and late medieval nominalism declined in importance. But with the revival of interest in late medieval thought that took place in the second half of the twentieth century, Ockham has re-emerged as one of the major figures of scholastic thought, generally ranked on the level of Thomas Aquinas and John Duns Scotus. And from the standpoint of the philosophy of the 1980s and 1990s, Ockham's interest in terminist logic, linguistic theory, and semiotics has placed him in the forefront of those medieval thinkers used as sources in contemporary philosophical discussion.

W. J. COURTENAY

Sources W. Ockham, *Opera philosophica et theologica*, 17 vols. (St Bonaventure, NY, 1974–88) · W. Ockham, *Philosophical writings*, trans. P. Boehner (1957); rev. S. F. Brown (1990) · W. Ockham, *Predestination, God's foreknowledge, and future contingents*, trans. M. M. Adams and N. Kretzmann (New York, 1969) · W. Ockham, *Quodlibetical questions*, trans. A. J. Freddoso, 2 vols. (1990) · *Ockham's theory of terms: part 1 of Summa logicae*, trans. M. J. Loux (Notre Dame, 1974) · *Ockham's theory of propositions: part 2 of Summa logicae*, trans. A. J. Freddoso and H. Schuurman (Notre Dame, 1980) · [W. Ockham], *Opera politica*, ed. H. S. Offler and others, 4 vols. (1940–96) · [W. Ockham], *A letter to the Friars Minor and other writings*, ed. A. S. McGrade and J. Kilcullen (1995) · W. Ockham, *A short discourse on tyrannical government*, ed. A. S. McGrade and J. Kilcullen (1992) · J. P. Beckmann, ed., *Ockham-Bibliographie, 1900–1990* (Hamburg, 1992) · Emden, *Oxf.*, 2.138-7 · M. Adams, *William Ockham*, 2 vols. (Notre Dame, 1987) · L. Baudry, *Guillaume d'Occam: sa vie, ses oeuvres, ses idées sociales et politiques* (Paris, 1950) · P. Boehner, *Collected articles on Ockham*, ed. E. M. Buytaert (1958) · S. F. Brown, 'Walter Chatton's *Lectures* and William of Ockham's *Quaestiones in libros physicorum Aristotelis*', *Essays honoring Allan B. Wolter*, ed. W. A. Frank and G. J. Etzkorn (1985), 81–115 · W. J. Courtenay, 'Ockham, Chatton, and the London studium: observations on recent changes in Ockham's biography', in W. Vossenkuhl and R. Schönberger, *Die Gegenwart Ockhams* (Weinheim, 1990), 327–37 · G. J. Etzkorn, 'Codex Merton 284: evidence of Ockham's early influence in Oxford', *From Ockham to Wyclif*, ed. A. Hudson and M. Wilks (1987), 31–42 · G. Etzkorn, 'Ockham at a provincial chapter: 1323, a prelude to Avignon', *Archivum Franciscanum Historicum*, 83 (1990), 557–67 · G. Gál, 'William of Ockham died "impenitent" in April 1347', *Franciscan Studies*, 42 (1982), 90–95 · E. Hochstetter, *Studien zur Metaphysik und Erkenntnislehre Wilhelms von Ockham* (Berlin, 1927) · E. F. Jacob, 'Ockham as a political thinker', *Essays in the conciliar epoch* (1943), 85–105 · J. Koch, 'Neue Aktenstücke zu dem gegen Wilhelm Ockham in Avignon geführten Prozess', *Recherches de Théologie Ancienne et Médiévale*, 7 (1935), 350–80; 8 (1936), 79–93, 168–197; repr. in J. Koch, *Kleine Schriften* (1973), vol. 2, pp. 275–365 · G. Leff, *William of Ockham: the metamorphosis of scholastic discourse* (1975) · A. S. McGrade, *The political thought of William of Ockham* (1974) · J. Miethke, *Ockhams Weg zur Sozialphilosophie* (Berlin, 1969) · J. Miethke, 'Ockham-Perspektiven oder Engführung in eine falsche Richtung? Eine Polemik gegen eine neuere Publikation zu Ockhams Biographie', *Mittelalterliches Jahrbuch*, 29 (1994) · E. A. Moody, *The logic of William of Ockham* (1935) · A. Pelzer, 'Les 51 articles de Guillaume Occam censurés, en Avignon, en 1326', *Revue d'Histoire Ecclésiastique*, 18 (1922), 240–70; repr. in A. Pelzer, *Études d'histoire littéraire sur la scolastique médiévale* (Louvain, 1964), 508–19 · K. Tachau, *Vision and certitude in the age of Ockham* (Leiden, 1988) · B. Tierney, *Collected essays: church law and constitutional thought* (1979) · B. Tierney, *Ockham, the conciliar theory, and the canonists* (Philadelphia, 1971)

Ockley, Simon (*bap.* 1679, *d.* 1720), orientalist, was baptized at Topsham, near Exeter, on 17 February 1679, the son of Thomas Okely of Great Ellingham, Norfolk, and his wife, Thomazin. Although he came of a gentleman's family, he struggled against poverty throughout his career, sometimes aided by patrons. The first of these, Sir Algernon Potts of Mannington in Norfolk, befriended him as a boy, and perhaps obtained his admission as a sizar to Queens' College, Cambridge, in February 1694. He took his BA in 1698, and already showed considerable linguistic talent. Perhaps in 1700, he was appointed to a Hebrew lectureship worth £10 annually. On 15 April 1696 he married Martha Austin (*d.* 1728) at Knapwell in Cambridgeshire; six children were born to them between May 1702 and December 1708.

Ockley took deacon's orders before he was twenty, and

by 1701 was curate of Swavesey, near St Ives in Cambridgeshire, probably on the recommendation of Simon Patrick, bishop of Ely. In 1705 he was ordained priest, and was presented by Jesus College, Cambridge, to the living of Swavesey, worth £80 annually. He never received any further ecclesiastical preferment. He was admitted BD at Cambridge in 1710, and in the same year was appointed chaplain to Robert Harley, who in 1711 became earl of Oxford and lord high treasurer of England. Ockley was clearly out of his depth in high society, and in 1714 apologized at length to his patron for some obscure indiscretion in company, and defended himself against the imputation of 'sottishness'. He had indeed a propensity to get into scrapes. In September 1710 Ockley obliged William Whiston with the partial translation of an Arabic version of the Didascalia (a fourth-century Christian work, the major part of a collection of ecclesiastical rules and customs, the apostolic constitutions, ascribed to the apostles). Whiston, as well as being Sir Isaac Newton's successor as Lucasian professor of mathematics, was devoted to the restoration of primitive Christianity, and regarded the Didascalia as an essential support to his cause. Ockley soon realized that he was straying into dangerous company. Whiston, as a result of his theological opinions, was deprived of his chair, and banished from the university in October 1710. A sermon by Ockley (published in 1711) was probably aimed at Whiston, and an exculpatory letter written by him was printed by the author of a controversial pamphlet in 1712.

Ockley's scholarly interests soon turned from Hebrew to Arabic, and more specifically to the early history of Islam. This shift was probably due to his acquaintance with Humphrey Prideaux, dean of Norwich, who published in 1697 a widely read biography of the Prophet, tendentiously entitled *The True Nature of Imposture Display'd in the Life of Mahomet*. Ockley's move into wider fields was marked by his first publication, *Introductio ad linguas orientales*, printed at his own expense in 1706, and dedicated to Simon Patrick. In the preface to this work Ockley, like earlier advocates of the study of oriental languages, recommends them primarily as essential to the theologian. He resumed this theme in his inaugural lecture as Sir Thomas Adams's professor of Arabic, published in 1712.

Two other publications appeared in these years. In 1707 Ockley published a *History of the Present Jews throughout the World*, translated from an Italian work by Leon Modena, a Venetian rabbi. Of greater significance was his translation of an Arabic fictitious work by Ibn Tufayl, a twelfth-century physician in Muslim Spain. The story of Hayy ibn Yaqzan describes the life of a solitary child growing up in a state of nature on a desert island, and his gradual acquirement of the practical skills and intellectual qualities of humanity, culminating in his attainment of a natural religion. Later contact with a believer in revelation showed that both faiths were fundamentally the same. This theme was congenial to some thinkers of the seventeenth and eighteenth centuries. The younger Edward Pococke, a son of the first Laudian professor of Arabic at Oxford, published the Arabic text with a Latin translation in 1671, under the title *Philosophus autodidactus*. From this Latin, an English translation was made in 1674 by a Scottish Quaker, George Keith, through whom it influenced the Quaker theology of the period. Another English translation was made in 1686 by George Ashwell, an Anglican controversialist. Ockley's translation was intended as a counter-blast against such unorthodox views. He introduced his *Improvement of Human Reason Exhibited in the Life of Hai Ebn Yokdhan* (1708) with an apologia stating that he was unwilling to undertake the translation as there were already two, by Ashwell and:

> by the Quaker, who imagin'd that there was something in it that favoured their Enthusiastick Notions. However, taking it for granted, that both these Translations were not made out of the Original Arabick, but out of the Latin; I did not question but they had mistaken the Sense of the Author in many places. ... I at last ventur'd to translate it a-new. (Arberry, 23)

Not only did Ockley translate it, he also added an appendix:

> Lest otherwise, that Book, by me design'd for the Innocent, and not altogether unprofitable Diversion of the Reader, might accidentally prove a means of leading some into Error, who are not capable of judging aright; and of confirming others in their Mistakes, who ... have the Misfortune to be led out of the way.   (ibid.)

At the time the Bodleian Library was incomparably the richest storehouse of oriental manuscripts in the country, and it was therefore to Oxford that Ockley went to pursue his research into Arab history. There he caught the eye of the antiquarian Thomas Hearne, who stigmatized him as 'somewhat crazed' (T. Hearne, *Remarks and Collections of Thomas Hearne*, ed. C. E. Doble, 1889, 3.286), but noted his indefatigable industry and high reputation as an Arabist. Hearne mentions Ockley's two short visits to Oxford, in August 1701 and again in the spring of 1706, when he was incorporated MA on 15 April and stayed until 17 May. The reading he accomplished in these two visits, each of six weeks, provided him with the materials for the volume which he published in 1708 under the title *The Conquest of Syria, Persia, and Aegypt by the Saracens*, which dealt with Islamic history under the first three caliphs (632–56). In his preface he explained his reason for not commencing with the life of the Prophet: 'but that is already written by the Reverend and Learned Dr. Prideaux, now Dean of Norwich'. Evidently Ockley, although now far more erudite than Prideaux, did not wish to compete with the popular work of his former patron. However, in the introduction to his second volume, published ten years later, he hints at its limitations as being 'sufficient to give a general *Idea* of the Man and his Pretensions, and admirably accomodated to his [Prideaux's] principal Design of shewing the Nature of an Imposture' (Ockley, *History*, 2.xxxv). Ockley's work on his first volume was, he believed, facilitated by his discovery of a manuscript purporting to be an account of the conquest of Syria by al-Waqidi (*d.* 823), whom, he says, 'I have here endeavour'd to make speak English' (Ockley, *Conquest*, xix). Unfortunately for Ockley, later research has shown that this source on which he so much relied was written in the time of the crusades.

In 1711 Ockley was appointed, probably through Harley's sponsorship, to the Sir Thomas Adams chair of Arabic, in which he succeeded John Luke (professor from 1685 to 1702) and Charles Wright (from 1702 to 1710), two academic nonentities. The one memorial of Luke's scholarship is indeed his erroneous assurance to Ockley concerning the great chronicler al-Tabari, that 'he had never met with him in the *East*, and that he was to be despaired of in Arabick' (Ockley, *History*, 2.xxxiii). Ockley had hoped to succeed Luke as professor, and his disappointment seems to have led to an estrangement from the fellows of Queens' College, as a result of which he lost preferment to a living in their gift. When he at last obtained the chair, his annual income was increased by £40. The post probably entailed little teaching in view of the decay of Arabic studies in eighteenth-century universities.

In 1713 Ockley published an *Account of South-West Barbary*, allegedly based on the report of a Christian slave. Described by Arberry as 'a pot-boiler' (Arberry, 36), this book contains in an appendix Ockley's translation of two letters from the ruler of Morocco. Perhaps in consequence of this display of his competence in Arabic, Ockley was briefly employed by the government in 1714 to translate correspondence from the same ruler, Mawlay Isma'il (1672–1727), with whom England had commercial relations. Two of his translations, now in the Public Record Office, have been identified (Kararah, 82; Arberry, 36–8). However, Harley's fall from power in July 1714 lost Ockley his most influential patron, and he had no further employment under government.

Ten years after the publication of *The Conquest of Syria*, Ockley produced a continuation entitled *The History of the Saracens* (1718). Again he visited Oxford, this time for a stay of five months. He drew upon a fairly wide range of sources, and identified a fragment of the chronicle of al-Tabari, of which Luke had despaired. He also made extensive use of Bartholomé d'Herbelot's *Bibliothèque orientale*, which had appeared in 1697, and which gave him access to Persian materials. Ockley speaks regretfully of his frequent attempts to perfect himself 'in that easy and delicate language', and of his ignorance of Turkish (Ockley, *History*, 2.xxxii). This second volume continues the account of early Islamic history from the fourth caliph, Ali, to the Umayyad 'Abd al-Malik (656–705). This point of termination, roughly half-way through the Umayyad caliphate, is by no means obvious or natural, but may well be explained by the growing difficulties of Ockley's daily life. The two volumes were republished in 1757 under the common title of *The History of the Saracens*, for the benefit of Ockley's daughter Anne. An anonymous 'Life of Mahomet', there prefixed to Ockley's own work, is ascribed by Arberry on internal evidence to his successor as Sir Thomas Adams's professor, Leonard Chappelow (Arberry, 29).

Ockley's two volumes marked an important stage in the development of Arabic and Islamic studies. Earlier scholars had written in Latin for an international academic readership, but Ockley wrote in English for the instruction of his fellow countrymen, who not being, he says, 'sufficiently acquainted with that Nation, have entertain'd too mean an Opinion of them, looking upon them as meer Barbarians, which mistaken Notion of theirs, has hinder'd all further Enquiry concerning them' (Ockley, *Conquest*, xi). In the introduction to his second volume he gives some of the comments made on its predecessor:

> that it was the strangest Story they ever heard since they were born! They never met with such Folks in their Lives as these *Arabians*! That they never heard of this Account before, which certainly they must have done of course if any body else had! A Reverend Dignitary asked me, If when I wrote that Book I had not lately been reading the History of *Oliver Cromwell*! (Ockley, *History*, 2.xv)

Ockley's second volume is directly linked with the last of his patrons, Thomas Freke of Hannington Hall in Wiltshire. 'You', he says, 'were pleased first to invite me to that Work; and the Publick will be indebted to You, at least, that it was done so soon, if not that it was ever done at all' (Ockley, dedication to 'Sentences of Ali', in *History*, vol. 2). Freke had, it appears, in the first place invited Ockley to translate a collection of Arabic proverbs ascribed to the Caliph Ali. Collections so entitled formed a standard part of the pabulum for Arabic students of the period, but Ockley's translation was a selection made from a Bodleian manuscript. Freke paid the expenses of Ockley's stay in Oxford when he was preparing to write his second volume. When and how Ockley became acquainted with Freke is not clear, although Kararah says that he 'took great interest in oriental and especially Arabic studies' (Kararah, 85).

When *The History of the Saracens* came out, Ockley was held prisoner in Cambridge Castle for a debt of £200. His friends organized a collection on his behalf, to which Harley contributed £20, and Freke promised £40 by instalments 'if when your affairs are finally settled at Cambridge you will go to Oxford and translate all the sentences of Ali into English' (Arberry, 45). Ockley never fulfilled this last commission of his patron. He was released from gaol in the summer of 1718, and returned to Swavesey. He died there on 9 August 1720, and was buried in Swavesey the next day, leaving his family in destitution. His widow was also buried at Swavesey, on 2 August 1728.

Ockley's work, undertaken with such difficulty in adverse circumstances, has long been superseded. Yet his lasting influence was not limited to the small circle of contemporary orientalists, to whom his books were in the first place addressed. He had a part in the formation of a greater historian of a later generation, Edward Gibbon, who wrote: 'Simon Ockley, an original in every sense, first opened my eyes; and I was led from one book to another, till I had ranged around the whole circle of Oriental history' (E. Gibbon, *Autobiography, World's Classics*, n.d., 32).

P. M. HOLT

Sources DNB · A. Kararah, 'Simon Ockley: his contribution to Arabic studies and influence on Western thought', PhD diss., U. Cam., 1955 · A. J. Arberry, 'The pioneer', *Oriental essays: portraits of seven scholars* (1960), 11–47 · S. Ockley, *The conquest of Syria, Persia, and Aegypt by the Saracens* (1708) · S. Ockley, *The history of the Saracens*, 2 (1757) · parish register, Topsham, 17 Feb 1679, Devon RO [baptism] · parish register, Swavesey, Cambs. AS, 10 Aug 1720 [burial] **Archives** BL, corresp., Add. MSS 15911, 23204 · CUL, corresp. and MSS

Ocland, Christopher (*d.* in or after **1590**), writer, was a native of Buckinghamshire, though his parentage is unknown. When St Saviour's Grammar School in Southwark obtained its charter in 1562, Ocland became its first headmaster, and held the position for seven years. In 1571, when St Olave's Grammar School, located near by in the same borough, was founded, he was the first man to present himself for election to become its master, arriving with letters from Robert Horne, the bishop of Winchester, and William Fleetwood, the recorder of London. He was offered the post but, informed that there would be a fortnight's delay before he could enter on it, he refused 'and went on his way being angrie, and set the matter lighte' (Carrington, 27–9, 46; Ellis, 65). About 1574 Ocland became the first headmaster of Richard Pate's grammar school at Cheltenham; it is not known precisely when or why he left the post (Bell, 25).

Ocland's principal work, *Anglorum proelia* ('The Battles of the English'), a lengthy poem of almost 3500 Latin hexameters dealing with English military history from Edward III to Mary Tudor, was published at his own expense in 1580. Such a broad sweep of time means that detail is often lacking, but Ocland's clear Latin and lucid narrative style suggest that the book was written with a pedagogical intention. Apart from set speeches there is a minimum of literary embellishment, and the tone of Ocland's poem has been criticized as too little varied. He writes with enthusiasm, though, and with reverence for victorious monarchs: at Crécy, Edward III and his son the Black Prince embody English prowess in battle:

> Fulminat ense pater Princeps Edvardus, & eius
> Filius impubes; illoque Britannica virtus
> Quanta sit eluxit bello, quo millia caesa
> Triginta aut plus eo, campique cruore madebant.
> ('King Edward blazes with his sword, as does his youthful son; British valour shone out to its full extent in that battle, in which thirty thousand or more were killed, and the fields were sodden with gore.' Sig. F2r)

Eirēnarchia, sive, Elizabetha (1582) brought Ocland's versification of history up to date. The verse is in much the same vein as before, but the volume has interest as a historical poem dealing with recent events and for its treatment of contemporary figures—it contains a brief, laudatory catalogue of the leading men of the day. This poem also contains more literary touches, in particular Anne Boleyn's dream prophesying the future of the Tudor dynasty and the triumph of protestantism (sig. B4v).

The quality of Ocland's verse and his patriotic treatment of England's martial glory received commendation at court (APC, 13.389). When *Anglorum proelia* was reissued in 1582 with *Eirēnarchia* (and, in some editions, Alexander Neville's Latin poem on Kett's rebellion), it was prefixed by letters, signed by members of the privy council and the ecclesiastical high commission, commanding that the book should be taught in every grammar and free school within the kingdom. While it is unclear how far this injunction was carried out (see Baldwin, 1.112; Clarke, 11), the book's influence can be traced in literary and historical works in Latin and the vernacular. The second edition of Raphael Holinshed's *Chronicles* (1587), for example, draws freely from it, and Joshua Barnes, composing his Anglo-Latin epic on Edward III, the *Franciad*, a century later, cites Ocland on several occasions. *Anglorum proelia* is also alluded to in the satires of Bishop Joseph Hall (bk 4, satire 3), and was acclaimed by William Webbe (Webbe, 30). *Eirēnarchia* and *Anglorum proelia* were popular enough at the time they were published to be rendered into English: *The Valiant Actes and Victorious Battails of the English Nation* and *Elizabeth Queene* were both translated by John Sharrock and emerged in 1585. In addition, *Eirēnarchia* was still sufficiently well known in 1680 for its relation of Anne Boleyn's vision—selected for its anti-Catholic sentiment—to be translated anonymously as *The Pope's Farewell, or, Queen Ann's Dream*.

Ocland's narration of Elizabeth's reign in Latin verse continues in the final instalment of his series of historical poems, *Elizabetheis* (1589), much of which is devoted to the events of the Armada year. His only other published work was *The Fountaine and Welspring of All Variance, Sedition, and Deadlie Hate* (1589). This is a turgid tract of exegesis in English prose, which demonstrates that the descriptions of Babylon in the book of Revelation signify Rome, and that sundry other passages from the same source indicate that the day of judgement is nigh. It has been conjectured that Ocland contributed to *Certaine Notes Set Forth in Foure and Three Parts to be Song*, printed by John Day in 1560 (reprinted 1565), but this was in fact the composer Robert Okeland (*fl.* 1532–1555) (*New Grove*, 1980, 13.523).

Poverty blighted Ocland's later career. In September 1589 he was penniless, residing at the sign of the George in Whitechapel, Middlesex, and on 13 October 1590 he wrote to Lord Burghley, begging for relief in his distress (Ellis, 70–74). He humbly desired that her majesty might give him a prebend or benefice—suggesting that he was in holy orders—and claimed that his literary labours had gone unrewarded. In the same letter he mentioned that a certain serjeant of London had a *capias utlagatum* out for him over a debt that he owed. Anne, his wife, had been paralysed for upwards of three years, he wrote, and her malady worsened daily on account of the indigence of her children. He concluded: 'I teach schole at Grenewych, where my labor wyll not fynde me bread and drynck' (*DNB*). The letter also alludes to a new work in four books that Ocland had been working on, concerning the baseness of Catholicism and the persecution of protestants; it was never published.

Christopher Ocland's is a sizeable *œuvre* that should not be overlooked. He was one of a number of schoolmaster Latin authors of the sixteenth century, but his importance stems from the high regard in which his historical verse was held, and for its long-lasting influence.

ROSS KENNEDY

Sources R. C. Carrington, *Two schools: a history of the St. Olave's and St. Saviour's grammar school foundation* (1971) · J. W. Binns, *Intellectual culture in Elizabethan and Jacobean England: the Latin writings of the age* (1990), 30 · L. Bradner, *Musae Anglicanae: a history of Anglo-Latin poetry, 1500–1925* (1940); repr. (1966), 37 · PRO, PROB 615, fol. 9r · H. Ellis, ed., *Original letters of eminent literary men of the sixteenth, seventeenth, and eighteenth centuries*, CS, 23 (1843) · M. L. Clarke, *Classical education in Britain, 1500–1900* (1959) · T. W. Baldwin, *William Shakespere's small Latine and lesse Greeke* (1944) · W. Webbe, *A discourse of English poetrie*, ed. E. Arber (1870) · *DNB* · A. E. Bell, *Tudor foundation* (1974)

Oclatinius Adventus, Marcus (*fl.* 205–218). *See under* Roman officials (act. AD 43–410).

Ó Cléirigh, Cú Choigcríche [Cucogry O'Clery] (*fl.* 1624–1664), scholar and scribe, was the son of Diarmuid Ó Cléirigh, in turn the son of An Cosnamhach Ó Cléirigh. There has been considerable confusion between this Cú Choigcríche and a supposed son of Lughaidh Ó Cléirigh (author of *Beatha Aodha Ruaidh*, the life of Aodh Ruadh Ó Domhnaill) bearing the same name. Attempts to disentangle the two seem to lead to the conclusion that all, or virtually all, of the work ascribed to the son of Lughaidh was actually written by the son of Diarmuid. Indeed, the existence of the supposed 'son of Lughaidh' may be in doubt and it has been suggested that the son of Diarmuid may have been wrongly affiliated to Lughaidh in a nineteenth-century pedigree. (The matter is contentious and still awaits resolution.) Lughaidh Ó Cléirigh, in turn, had a brother named Cú Choigcríche (son of Mac Con) who left behind a number of poems. There seems to be no way of knowing whether the 'Coochogery O'Clery' who held land in the parish of Killybegs Lower in 1632 is to be identified with any of the aforementioned bearers of the name of Cú Choigcríche Ó Cléirigh.

Cú Choigcríche, son of Diarmuid, is associated above all with the great work of scholarship which culminated in the production of the 'Annals of the kingdom of Ireland' (popularly known as the annals of the four masters), compiled between 1632 and 1636. He is named among the compilers as one of the principal assistants to his kinsman, the scholar and Franciscan lay brother Míchél Ó Cléirigh. Even before Míchél Ó Cléirigh's return to Ireland in 1626, Cú Choigcríche was involved in that great enterprise. As early as 1624 he had been engaged by the Franciscans of Donegal, in their place of refuge along the River Drowes, to arrange the martyrologies of Aonghus and Ó Gormáin in the style of the Roman martyrology. He is mentioned in relation to the 'Seanchas ríogh Éreann accus genealuighi na Naomh nÉreannach', penned in Athlone in 1630 and concerned with the lives and pedigrees of the kings and saints of Ireland, and the revised version of the traditional accounts of successive settlement of Ireland, the *Leabhar gabhála Éireann* ('Book of invasions') written in Lisgoole, near Enniskillen, in October 1631. In August 1633 'in the convent of Donegal' (on the banks of the River Drowes) he testified to the reliability of Brother Míchél's copy of the martyrology of Ó Gormáin. Some years after Míchél Ó Cléirigh's return to Louvain (July 1637) Cú Choigcríche Ó Cléirigh and his fellow worker, Fear Feasa Ó Maoil Chonaire, appeared in August 1641 before a general chapter of the Franciscan order in Multyfarnham, co. Westmeath, and defended their work against the rather petty strictures of the young Franciscan Tuileagna Ó Maoil Chonaire.

One Cú Choigcríche Ó Cléirigh composed poems about 1655 for Toirdhealbhach mac Cathbhairr and Calbhach Rua Ó Domhnaill, and Cú Choigcríche, son of Diarmuid, is known to have composed a poem in 1662 on the death of Máire, sister of Aodh Ruadh Ó Domhnaill. Manuscript works ascribed to Cú Choigcríche Ó Cléirigh, son of Lughaidh, but which may possibly be the work of the son of Diarmuid, consist of a copy of the 'topographical poems' of Seaán Ó Dubhagáin and Giolla na Naomh Ó hUidhrín; the unique manuscript copy of Lughaidh Ó Cléirigh's life of Aodh Ruadh; a copy of the four masters' recension of *Leabhar gabhála Éireann*, the O'Clery book of genealogies; an important collection of verse and prose preserved in the National Library of Ireland (NL Ire., MS G 131); and manuscripts 2542–2543 in the Bibliothèque Royale, Brussels.

Towards the end of his life Cú Choigcríche Ó Cléirigh was living in west Mayo, where, at Corr na hEilte (Gortnaheltia, parish of Addergoole), near Burrishoole, he penned his will in or about the year 1664. Now largely indecipherable and prefixed to his book of genealogies, his will recorded his intention to leave his possessions to his sons Diarmuid and Seán and directed that he be buried in Burrishoole friary, co. Mayo. There is no indication of the date of his death, but it probably occurred some time in the 1660s. NOLLAIG Ó MURAÍLE

Sources A. B. Clery, 'Sean O Clery of Dublin (1778–1846)', *Irish Book Lover*, 30 (1946–8), 124–8 • M. Dillon, C. Mooney, and P. de Brún, eds., *Catalogue of Irish manuscripts in the Franciscan Library, Killiney* (1969) • B. Jennings, *Michael O Cleirigh, chief of the four masters, and his associates* (1936) • E. O'Curry, *Lectures on the manuscript materials of ancient Irish history* (1861), 178–80, 560–9 • S. Pender, ed., 'The O'Clery book of genealogies', *Analecta Hibernica*, 18 (1951), 1–195 • P. Walsh, *Genealogiae regum et sanctorum Hiberniae, by the four masters* (1918) • P. Walsh, 'The four masters', *Irish Book Lover*, 22 (1934), 128–31 • P. Breathnach, 'What we know of Cuchoigriche O Cleirigh', *Irish Book Lover*, 23 (1935), 60–66 • P. Walsh, *The Ó Cléirigh family of Tír Conaill* (1938) • P. Walsh, 'A link with Tadhg Dall O hUiginn', *Irish men of learning*, ed. C. O Lochlainn (1947), 74–9 • L. Ó Cléirigh, *The life of Aodh Ruadh Ó Domhnaill*, ed. P. Walsh and C. Ó Lochlainn, 2, ITS, 45 (1957), 1–16 • S. P. Ó Mórdha, 'Seán Ó Cléirigh from Drung and his manuscripts', *Heart of Breifne*, 3/1 (1986), 105–12 • *DNB*
Archives Royal Irish Acad., MSS • Royal Library of Belgium, Brussels, MSS • TCD, MSS
Wealth at death books, horse, foal: will, 8 Feb 1664, Pender, 'The O'Clery book', xvii–xviii

Ó Cléirigh [O'Clery], **Lughaidh** (*fl.* 1603–1616), Gaelic poet and historian, was one of five sons of Maccon Ó Cléirigh (*d.* 1595), *ollamh* (court poet) to the O'Donnells of Tír Conaill (co. Donegal). His mother is not known. The Ó Cléirighs were one of the last great learned families of Gaelic Ireland, the Tír Conaill branch having served the O'Donnells for over two centuries. The Ó Cléirigh genealogies appear in a seventeenth-century manuscript in which Lughaidh and his brothers are the last generation of the Tír Conaill branch to be included.

Little is known of Lughaidh's life, other than that he was involved as a juror and commissioner in the land surveys in Donegal, leading up to the Ulster plantation. He is best known for his biography of Hugh Roe O'Donnell, which served as a source for the annals of the four masters. This undated biography covers O'Donnell's life from 1587 until his death in 1602. While it contains much detail not found in other sources, there are many errors, resulting from Lughaidh's desire to exaggerate O'Donnell's involvement with Hugh O'Neill in the Irish uprisings.

Lughaidh also participated in the contention of the bards, which took place probably between 1616 and 1624. The contention began as a poetic dispute between Tadhg Mac Bruaideadha (Brody, Brodin, Mac Dire) and Lughaidh, composing in support of the south and north of Ireland respectively, with other poets soon joining in. The purpose of the contention is unclear, but may have been a sympathetic effort to promote a Gaelic culture that was fast disappearing under English rule, a fact that was not lost on the poets themselves, as witnessed by the often wistful tone of their compositions. In all, thirty poems were composed, four by Lughaidh.

The date of Lughaidh's death is not known. Unlike that of his father and brother Duibhgeann, Lughaidh's death is not recorded in the *Annals*, suggesting that he was still alive in 1616, the terminal date of the *Annals*. This is confirmed by the fact that the contention of the bards probably did not begin until 1616, and continued for a number of years. It has been suggested that Lughaidh had died by 1632 (*DNB*), but this is based on an assumption that he was the father of Cucoigriche Ó Cléirigh, and that the latter had inherited Lughaidh's land by that date. However, the idea that Cucoigriche was Lughaidh's son is based on a letter written in 1842 by John O'Clery to John O'Donovan, in which O'Clery presented himself as the direct descendant of Lughaidh. In his letter O'Clery cited a will written by 'Cucoigri', dated 1664, naming the testator's brother as 'Cairbre'. O'Clery identified both as the sons of Lughaidh, which O'Donovan accepted (O'Donovan, *Genealogies*, 395). However, it is not clear that the will is that of Cucoigriche Ó Cléirigh, and there is no corroborating evidence to support the suggestion that he was Lughaidh's son.

O'Clery's letter also added to confusion over the author of the biography of O'Donnell. As one of the sources for the *Annals*, Lughaidh's work is identified in the *Annals'* 'Testimonium' merely as the book of Lughaidh Ó Cléirigh, covering 1586 to 1602 (O'Donovan, *Annals*, 1.xii). This vague description eventually led scholars to believe that the biography was composed by Cucoigriche Ó Cléirigh, identified as one of the four masters, and in whose hand it appears to be. O'Clery supported this idea in his letter. O'Donovan, who published the *Annals* in 1851, realized that Lughaidh had composed annals, which were used as a source by the four masters, but did not recognize these as the biography of Hugh O'Donnell, and in his edition he repeatedly referred to the 'Life of O'Donnell' as the work of Cucoigriche. Shortly afterwards, Eugene O'Curry correctly identified the 'book of Lughaidh O'Clerigh' as the biography of O'Donnell, believing Cucoigriche to have been the scribe, not the author (O'Curry, 22).

Opinions about the style of Lughaidh's biography have also changed. Its language is archaic, apparently so even in its own day, as the four masters frequently used its facts but changed its style for their *Annals*. This stiffness may have appealed to Victorian sentiments, as it was described in 1894 as being written in 'literary but not pedantic Irish, … free from the archaic and sometimes stilted diction found in parts of the "Annals of the four masters"' (*DNB*). However, by the twentieth century, attitudes had changed (Hyde, 564), and more recently its style has been referred to variously as 'affected' (Foster, 38), 'disappointing' (Moody and others, 516), and 'repulsive' (Pender, 19).

ELIZABETH SCHOALES

Sources L. Ó Cléirigh, *The life of Aodh Ruadh Ó Domhnaill*, ed. P. Walsh and C. Ó Lochlainn, 1, ITS, 42 (1948) • L. Ó Cléirigh, *The life of Aodh Ruadh Ó Domhnaill*, ed. P. Walsh and C. Ó Lochlainn, 2, ITS, 45 (1957) • L. McKenna, ed., *Iomarbag na bfilead: the contention of the bards*, ITS, 20, 21 (1918) • P. Walsh, *The Ó Cléirigh family of Tír Conaill* (1938) • 'The O'Clery book of genealogies', ed. S. Pender, *Analecta Hibernica*, 18 (1951), 1–195 • J. Leerssen, *The contention of the bards and its place in Irish political and literary history*, ITS, subsidiary ser., 2 (1994) • *AFM* • J. O'Donovan, ed. and trans., *The genealogies, tribes, and customs of Hy-Fiachrach, commonly called O'Dowda's country*, Irish Archaeological Society, 2 (1844) • E. O'Curry, *Lectures on the manuscript materials of ancient Irish history* (1861) • *DNB* • 'Ulster plantation papers, 1608–13', *Analecta Hibernica*, 8 (1938), 179–297, esp. 195–297 • T. W. Moody and others, eds., *A new history of Ireland*, 3: *Early modern Ireland, 1534–1691* (1976) • R. Foster, *Modern Ireland, 1600–1972* (1988) • D. Hyde, *A literary history of Ireland, from earliest times to the present day* (1901)

Ó Cléirigh, Míchél [Michael O'Clery] (*b.* in or after **1590**?, *d.* **1643**?), scribe and chronicler, was born at Kilbarron, near Ballyshannon in south co. Donegal, the youngest of four sons of Donnchadh, a grandson of Tuathal Ó Cléirigh (*d.* 1512), and a member of a hereditary learned family; his mother was Onóra Ultach. Given Tadhg as his baptismal name, he was known as Tadhg an tSléibhe ('Tadhg of the mountain') until, on entering religious life, he adopted the name Míchél (Michael). Of two elder brothers, Uilliam and Conaire, very little is known, except that the latter was a scribe who collaborated for a time in Míchél's greatest scholarly project. A third, Maolmhuire, born in 1588 or 1589, entered the Irish College at Salamanca in 1610 and became a Franciscan in 1616 in the Irish College of St Anthony at Louvain in the Spanish Netherlands; ordained a priest in 1619, he took the name Bernairdín, and by the 1630s was guardian of the Franciscan convent of Donegal, with which Míchél was also associated. Tadhg himself seems to have received a thorough grounding in traditional Irish learning, probably in one of the few remaining Gaelic schools—he indicates, for example, that he was taught by one Baothghalach Ruadh Mac Aodhagáin, whose precise identity is uncertain but who may have conducted a school at Ballymacegan in north co. Tipperary. Tadhg followed his older brother to the continent, and it has been suggested that he served for a time as a soldier. He may be identical to the Don Tadeo Cleri to whom the Spanish authorities in July 1621 granted 2 crowns monthly on account of 'the persecution and loss of estate he had suffered for the Catholic cause in Ireland' (Breatnach, 13). He joined the Franciscan order as a lay brother some time before March 1623. Never ordained priest, he was known as An Bráthair Bocht Míchél ('the poor Brother Michael').

Ó Cléirigh was based at Louvain, where plans were already well advanced to gather for publication all available material on the lives of the early Irish saints. Directing this project was another Donegal man, Father Hugh Ward, who was supported and advised by his friend and colleague Father Patrick Fleming. It was they who in 1624 conceived the idea of 'sending Brother Clery to Ireland' (Breatnach, 11) to collect relevant source material in Irish or Latin and transmit it back to Louvain. In the summer of 1626, on Ward's election as guardian of St Anthony's, Brother Míchél returned to his homeland. During his period of just over a decade at home, his principal base of operations was the so-called 'Franciscan convent of Donegal'—which had been forced by intermittent persecution to relocate to a 'place of refuge' on the banks of the small River Drowes that marks the border between counties Donegal and Leitrim (and, therefore, between the provinces of Ulster and Connaught). Details of Brother Míchél's activities and travels on his return to Ireland emerge from the numerous colophons, giving dates and places of writing, which he inserted into many of his works.

It would appear that Ó Cléirigh spent much of his first year in Ireland in the convent 'at Drowes' (otherwise known as the convent of Donegal). The earliest datable piece transcribed by him was penned on 28 March 1627. By the late summer of 1627 (and possibly earlier) he had set out—probably on horseback—on the first of several journeys throughout Ireland. This took him to Dublin and its vicinity in August. In Drogheda he copied material—including, it would seem, the early ninth-century martyrology of Tallaght—from ten detached leaves of the twelfth-century Book of Leinster. These leaves, probably found in the library of the Church of Ireland primate, Archbishop James Ussher, soon afterwards passed, via the convent of Donegal, to Louvain, but there is no information on Ó Cléirigh's presumed role in the transfer.

Brother Míchél moved on to the friary of Kildare, where in October he transcribed material from the main body of the Book of Leinster. Some time later he returned to his base at Drowes. There, between January and late June 1628, he copied several texts, presumably from manuscripts he had collected, borrowed, or hastily transcribed during his journey through Leinster. His citation in May 1628 of one of the sources he used, *Lebor na hUidre*—the earliest surviving collection of early Irish prose texts—is the first extant reference to that celebrated manuscript (dating from about 1100) since the year 1470. An important text whose transcription Ó Cléirigh completed in this year was the so-called short recension of the martyrology of Donegal, on which work had begun as early as 1624, two years before he returned to Ireland.

Back in Dublin by mid-July 1628 Brother Míchél transcribed several saints' lives. In co. Wicklow he copied a metrical account of St Coemgen (Kevin) of Glendalough and in mid-September, in co. Carlow, he copied a prose life of the same saint. He reached Cashel by early October and apparently remained in the south for more than a year: a letter to Hugh Ward in Louvain in January 1629 tells of 'your Brother Clery' having been sent to Ormond 'to write there for a time' and reports that he had 'made a collection of more than three or four hundred lives' (Breatnach, 19). During his Munster sojourn he visited the school of history and law conducted by Flann Mac Aodhagáin at Ballymacegan, co. Tipperary. In February he was doing transcription work in the convent of the friars of Athlone, at Killinure, co. Westmeath, and in March, in the Franciscan house at Multyfarnham, co. Westmeath, he copied the twelfth-century propaganda tract *Cogadh Gaedhel re Gallaibh*. In late spring he appears to have moved south again, to Clonmel and Wexford, where he copied further saints' lives, and on to Timoleague in west Cork, where, in mid-June, he copied from the great codex, the Book of Mac Carrthaig Riabach, now known as the Book of Lismore. Later in June and early July he copied numerous texts in Cork city and then moved north, via counties Limerick and Clare (where he picked up some further items), reaching co. Galway by early October. There he consulted at least part of the great Book of Duniry, now known as the *Leabhar Breac*.

By mid-November 1629 Brother Míchél was finally back at Drowes and there, during the winter, he penned some two dozen lives of saints and other texts—many of them, no doubt, fair copies of works previously borrowed or hastily transcribed. In April he completed the final revised version of the great compilation *Félire na naomh nÉrennach* (the longer recension of the martyrology of Donegal).

Nothing is known of Ó Cléirigh's activity from mid-April to early October 1630. Then, for a month, he and three assistants—Fearfeasa Ó Maolchonaire from co. Roscommon, Cú Choigcríche Ó Cléirigh from co. Donegal, and Cú Choigcríche Ó Duibhgeannáin from co. Leitrim—worked at Killinure, near Athlone, compiling, under the patronage of a local gentleman, Toirdhealbhach Mac Cochláin, the genealogical work *Seanchas Ríogh Éreann accus Genealuighi na naomh nÉreannach* (also known as *Réim Ríoghraidhe na hÉireann agus Seanchas a naomh* and by the Latin title *Genealogiae regum et sanctorum Hiberniae*). On completion it received the approbation of a local scholar, Conall Mag Eochagáin. By late December Brother Míchél was back at Drowes and early in 1631 he penned extracts from the ninth-century martyrology of Óengus.

From late October to late December 1631 Brother Míchél, along with four assistants—the three mentioned above and a Fermanagh scholar, Giolla Pádraig Ó Luinín—were working at Lisgoole, co. Fermanagh. Under the patronage of Briain Ruadh Mag Uidhir (Maguire), Baron of Enniskillen, they compiled a new recension of the medieval work of Irish pseudo-prehistory *Leabhar gabhála Éireann* ('The book of conquest of Ireland'). This marked a new departure, with Ó Cléirigh beginning also to collect and transcribe secular material.

Some time in 1632 work on assembling the largest of all sets of Irish annals commenced at Drowes, under the patronage of Fearghal Ó Gadhra, MP for co. Sligo. It resulted, over the next four years, in the compilation for which Ó Cléirigh is principally remembered, the enormous collection known as *Annála Ríoghachta Éireann* ('Annals of the kingdom of Ireland') but more popularly known, in reference to Brother Míchél and his assistants, as the annals of the four masters. (The four in question were himself and the three principal assistants already named as working on the *Réim Ríoghraidhe* and *Leabhar gabhála*, but two others also helped: Muiris mac Torna Uí Mhaolchonaire, for a month, and Brother Míchél's elder brother Conaire, for a slightly longer period.) The first portion of the work (to the year 1208) was completed before the close of 1632. Brother Míchél appears not to have left Drowes throughout this year—except for a possible brief visit to Ballymacegan, where, on 31 August, Flann Mac Aodhagáin signed a short approbation for the *Réim Ríoghraidhe*.

In August 1633 Ó Cléirigh copied the twelfth-century martyrology *Féilire Uí Ghormáin* at Drowes, but he probably spent most of this and the following year, 1634, assembling further materials for the annals. In summer 1634, however, he returned to co. Clare to collect more hagiographical material. While much of the next year, 1635, was devoted to compiling most of the second part of the annals (from 1208 down to the early seventeenth century), Brother Míchél took time in May to copy a saint's life at Drowes and in November to copy (for a second time) the bulky volume *Cogadh Gaedhel re Gallaibh*. In April 1636, also at Drowes, he penned a copy of the lengthy hagiographical poem *Naoimhshenchus naomh Innsi Fáil*. By the middle of August 1636 his and his team's epic labours on the annals were completed.

In autumn 1636, having obtained the signatures of his Franciscan confrères in the convent of Donegal for the annals (of which two manuscript copies had been penned), Ó Cléirigh set off to seek approbations for his various works from scholars and ecclesiastical authorities. On his way south, in late October, he visited the Poor Clare sisters at Bethlehem, co. Westmeath, where he copied an Irish translation of part of the 'Rule of St Clare'. In November Flann Mac Aodhagáin in Tipperary, Conchubhar Mac Bruaideadha in co. Clare, Archbishop Malachy O'Queely in Galway city, and Bishop Boethius MacEgan of Elphin, elsewhere in co. Galway, all provided glowing testimonials for *Genealogiae regum et sanctorum Hiberniae*, *Félire na naomh nÉrennach*, and the 'Annals'. Early 1637 saw Ó Cléirigh in Leinster, where Bishop Ross Mac Geoghegan of Kildare in January and Archbishop Thomas Fleming of Dublin in February also approved his writings.

Early in 1637 Brother Míchél may have returned briefly to co. Clare, where Conchubhar Mac Bruaideadha had just died, and he may also have returned to Drowes one last time before, in July, making his way to Carrickfergus, co. Antrim, where—it is presumed—he took ship for the continent.

Just prior to his departure, Ó Cléirigh's great annalistic compilation was fiercely criticized by a fellow Franciscan, Tuileagna Ó Maolchonaire, who sought—on rather petty grounds—to prevent its publication and have the approbations withdrawn. Brother Míchél made a reply, now lost, and the matter may have been discussed at a Franciscan chapter in Munster in 1638. In August 1641 Tuileagna and two of the compilers, Cú Choigcríche Ó

Cléirigh and Fearfeasa Ó Maolchonaire, appeared at a provincial chapter at Multyfarnham. A committee that considered the charges decided against the accuser, but as late as 1646 Tuileagna was still persisting in his arguments with Fearfeasa. The fact that most of Ó Cléirigh's voluminous collections did not appear in print until the nineteenth, or even the twentieth, century—and a good deal still remains unpublished—was not, however, due to Tuileagna's objections but rather to the poverty and other difficulties, including illness and death, that dogged the Louvain project. And his confrère's criticisms may not have been the greatest risk run by Brother Míchél: a contemporary remarked that it was 'no small miracle that Tadhg Ó Cléire was not hanged in Ireland, since everyone knew of his journeyings, and that he failed in nothing that he set out to do—gathering everything into his granary' (Ó Maonaigh, 203).

Míchél Ó Cléirigh returned to Louvain some two years after Hugh Ward's untimely death, and work on the saints' lives was now being directed by the Inishowen man Father John Colgan, later responsible for the 'four masters' appellation. The only other thing known of Ó Cléirigh is that in autumn 1643 was published the only work of his to appear in print during his lifetime, a glossary entitled *Foclóir nó sanasán nua*. After that, all is silence. It is thought that the humble, hard-working lay brother Míchél Ó Cléirigh died in Louvain, at St Anthony's College, before the close of 1643, but even this is uncertain, as is the location of his grave. There is surely a great irony in the fact that this greatest recorder of the lives of holy men and others in the whole history of Ireland should himself have left such sparse biographical detail. His lasting monument, that for which he deserves to be remembered, is his voluminous manuscript writings, scattered between Ireland and Belgium, notably in the Bibliothèque Royale in Brussels. In the words of one leading authority, 'This humble Brother, who hid himself so completely while accomplishing so much … has written his name large across the history of his country, and has left it engraved indelibly on the hearts of his countrymen' (Jennings, 174).

NOLLAIG Ó MURAÍLE

Sources P. A. Breatnach, 'An Irish Bollandus: Fr Hugh Ward and the Louvain hagiographical enterprise', *Éigse*, 31 (1999), 1–30 • B. Jennings, *Michael O Cleirigh, chief of the four masters, and his associates* (1936) • J. F. Kenney, *The sources for the early history of Ireland* (1929), 39–43 • T. Ó Cléirigh, *Aodh Mac Aingil agus an Scoil Nua-Ghaeilge i Lobháin* (Dublin, 1935); 2nd edn, ed. T. de Bhaldraithe (Dublin, 1985) • E. O'Curry, *Lectures on the manuscript materials of ancient Irish history* (1861), 142–78 • N. Ó Muraíle, 'The autograph manuscripts of the Annals of the Four Masters', *Celtica*, 19 (1987), 77–95 • P. Walsh, *The Ó Cléirigh family of Tír Conaill* (1938) • P. Walsh, *Genealogiae regum et sanctorum Hiberniae, by the four masters* (1918) • P. Walsh, 'Travels of an Irish scholar', *Catholic Bulletin*, 27 (1937), 123–32 • P. Walsh, 'The work of a winter', *Catholic Bulletin*, 28 (1938), 226–34 • P. Walsh, *The four masters and their work* (1944) • *DNB* • M. Dillon, C. Mooney, and P. de Brún, eds., *Catalogue of Irish manuscripts in the Franciscan Library, Killiney* (1969) • C. Ó Maonaigh, 'Franciscan Library MS A30.4', *Irish Book Lover*, 27 (1940–41), 202–4

Archives Franciscan Library, Killiney, co. Dublin • Royal Irish Acad. • Royal Library of Belgium, Brussels, MSS • TCD

O'Clery, Cucogry. *See* Ó Cléirigh, Cú Choigcríche (*fl.* 1624–1664).

O'Clery, Lughaidh. *See* Ó Cléirigh, Lughaidh (*fl.* 1603–1616).

O'Clery, Michael. *See* Ó Cléirigh, Míchél (*b.* in or after 1590?, *d.* 1643?).

Ó Cobhthaigh family (*per.* 1415–1586), Gaelic poets, were hereditary poets settled during the fifteenth and sixteenth centuries in the barony of Rathconrath, Westmeath. Their work was frequently cited by other poets. Members of the family wrote works which survive or are mentioned in chronicles.

An Clasach Ó Cobhthaigh (*d.* 1415) was a famous poet and man of learning. Maeleachlainn Ó Cobhthaigh (*d.* 1429), son of An Clasach, was killed by Edmond Dalton, who had conquered his district. **Domhnall Ó Cobhthaigh** (*d.* 1446), another son of An Clasach, was killed, with his two sons, on the island called Cróinis in Lough Ennell, Westmeath, by Art Ó Maelsheachlainn and the sons of Fiacha MacGeoghegan. Domhnall was famous as a soldier as well as a poet. One of his poems, of 168 verses, is extant: 'Aire riot a mhic Mhurchadha' ('Be cautious, oh son of Murchadh!'). It urges the Leinstermen to resist the English.

Aedh Ó Cobhthaigh (*d.* 1452), described by O'Clery as a learned poet, kept a house of hospitality. He died of the plague at Fertullagh, Westmeath. Thomas Ó Cobhthaigh (*d.* 1474) and Murchadh 'the lame' Ó Cobhthaigh (*d.* 1478) are both mentioned in the chronicles as ollavs (professors of poetry). **Tadhg Ó Cobhthaigh** (*fl.* 1554), son of another Aedh, wrote a poem of sixty-eight verses in praise of the cross, beginning 'Crann seoil na cruinne an chroch naomhtha' ('The holy cross is the mast of the world'), and 100 verses on the death of Brian O'Connor Failghe; both are extant. He was probably also the author of the poem in praise of Manus, son of Black Hugh O'Donnell, beginning 'Cia re ccuirfinn séd suirghe' ('Who sends gifts of courtship'). It contains twenty stanzas, for each of which O'Donnell gave the poet a mare.

Uaithne Ó Cobhthaigh (*d.* 1556), son of William, was murdered, with his wife, at Ballinlig, Westmeath, in 1556. He wrote a poem of 156 verses in praise of James, earl of Desmond, beginning 'Mó ná iarla ainm Shémais' ('Greater than an earl is the name of James'), and a theological poem of 160 verses, beginning 'Fada an cuimhne so ar chóir nDé' ('Long be this remembrance on the justice of God'). **Diarmait Ó Cobhthaigh** (*fl.* 1584) wrote a lament of 150 verses for Uaithne which begins 'Dá néll orchra ós iath Uisnigh' ('Two clouds of woe over the land of Uisneach'). He also wrote five theological poems: 'Díon cloinne a n-écc a n-athar' ('Safeguard of children in the death of their father'), a poem of 160 verses; 'Fiú a bheatha bás tighearna' ('The cost of life the death of a lord'), of 156 verses; 'Mairg as aidhne a n-aghaidh breithimh' ('Alas! pleader is facing the judge'), of 148 verses; 'Mairg nach taithigh go teagh ríogh' ('Alas! that I did not go to the king's house'), of 156 verses; and 'Deacair aidhneas earca ríogh' ('A powerful argument the tributes of a king'), of 160 verses. Copies of all these are extant, and some are in the collection of the Royal Irish Academy.

Muircheartach Ó Cobhthaigh (*fl.* 1586) wrote a poem on salvation, of 140 verses, beginning 'Dlighidh liaigh leigheas a charaid' ('The right of a physician is the cure of his friend'); one of 148 verses on the death of Garrett Nugent, baron of Delvin, beginning 'Mairg is dáileamh don digh bhróin' ('Alas! that sorrow is attendant on drink'); another, on Christopher Nugent, fourteenth Baron Delvin, of 184 verses, beginning 'Geall re hiarlacht ainm barún' ('The name baron is the promise of an earldom'); and one of 124 verses on William Nugent, beginning 'Do ghní clú áit oighreachda' ('Place of inheritance gives reputation').

Donnchadh Ó Cobhthaigh (*fl.* 1584) wrote a composition of three Irish verses on penitence, beginning 'Acht mar uisge d'éis a leata' ('Just as water, after it has frozen'), as a translation of three elegiac couplets, three hexameters, and three pentameters in Latin, beginning 'Lympha coacta gelu' ('Liquid, condensed by cold'), which he entered into a blank half-column of Oxford, Bodleian Library, MS Rawlinson B 505, a collection of Irish saints' lives (fol. 89vb).   NORMAN MOORE, *rev.* DÁIBHÍ Ó CRÓINÍN

Sources AFM, vols. 3–4 · 'Calendar of fiants, Henry VIII to Elizabeth', *Report of the Deputy Keeper of the Public Records in Ireland*, 7–22 (1875–90), appxs · Nugent poem-book, NL Ire., Gaelic MS G992 · B. Ó Cuív, *The Irish bardic duanaire* (1973) · D. Ó Cróinín, 'A poet in a penitential mood', *Celtica*, 16 (1984), 169–74

Ó Cobhthaigh, Aedh (*d.* **1452**). *See under* Ó Cobhthaigh family (*per.* 1415–1586).

Ó Cobhthaigh, An Clasach (*d.* 1415). *See under* Ó Cobhthaigh family (*per.* 1415–1586).

Ó Cobhthaigh, Diarmait (*fl.* **1584**). *See under* Ó Cobhthaigh family (*per.* 1415–1586).

Ó Cobhthaigh, Domhnall (*d.* 1446). *See under* Ó Cobhthaigh family (*per.* 1415–1586).

Ó Cobhthaigh, Donnchadh (*fl.* **1584**). *See under* Ó Cobhthaigh family (*per.* 1415–1586).

Ó Cobhthaigh, Muircheartach (*fl.* **1586**). *See under* Ó Cobhthaigh family (*per.* 1415–1586).

Ó Cobhthaigh, Tadhg (*fl.* **1554**). *See under* Ó Cobhthaigh family (*per.* 1415–1586).

Ó Cobhthaigh, Uaithne (*d.* **1556**). *See under* Ó Cobhthaigh family (*per.* 1415–1586).

O'Coigly [O'Coigley], **James** (1761–1798), Irish nationalist and Roman Catholic priest, was born in August 1761 at Castleraw, Kilmore, co. Armagh, the second son of James Coigley, farmer, and Louisa, *née* Donnelly. His maternal ancestors, the O'Donnellys of co. Tyrone, were a landed Jacobite family who suffered grievous losses at the battle of the Boyne (July 1690). His father's family had also been heavily engaged in the Williamite wars, but afterwards recovered their economic stability and were engaged in farming and weaving in the 1760s. James O'Coigly was

educated in Dundalk's grammar school, co. Louth, and ordained in the Roman Catholic church in January 1785. He travelled in June of that year to Paris for further studies at the Collège des Lombards, where his leadership talents were displayed at the head of a student body agitating for better conditions. Although reputedly involved in the storming of the Bastille in July 1789 with fellow Irish student James Blackwell, the anti-clerical character of the French Revolution obliged him to flee to Ireland from Dieppe in October. On returning to Armagh, O'Coigly found himself in the middle of worsening civil strife between the Ulster Presbyterian Peep o' Day Boys and the Catholic defenders. He is believed to have written the anonymous pamphlet *An Impartial Account of the Late Disturbances in the County of Armagh* which was published in Dublin in 1792.

During the early 1790s, while based in a Louth parish and chaplain to Dundalk prison, O'Coigly became deeply engaged in radical politics and an influential supporter of the defenders. He was probably a leading member of the group and was also associated with the United Irishmen. In 1791–3 he was one of several activists who attempted to harness the paramilitary manpower of the defenders to the more sophisticated revolutionary politics of the United Irishmen. He visited Randalstown, Dungiven, Newtownlimavady, Magilligan, Maghera, and other Ulster centres during this time and liaised with radical Belfast Presbyterians who formed the backbone of the United Irishmen in the north. O'Coigly allegedly introduced Dublin radical James Napper Tandy to the Louth defenders, a meeting which obliged Napper Tandy to flee to Philadelphia. More certain is that O'Coigly's cousin led the defenders at the battle of the Diamond in September 1795 which presaged the formation of the Orange order. Other close family members were prominent in Armagh, co. Tyrone, and Louth defenderism, and the homes of his father and brother were singled out for attack by loyalists.

O'Coigly's stature in the United Irishmen rose in 1796 owing to arrests, the society's incorporation of the defender movement, and the emergence of the Lord Edward Fitzgerald clique to which he was attached. In June 1797 O'Coigly travelled to Manchester and London to help arrange co-operation between French-backed English, Scottish, and Irish revolutionaries. Having conferred with Colonel Edward Despard and Thomas Evans of the London Corresponding Society, he went from Hamburg to Paris with fellow United Irish delegate the Revd Arthur McMahon, where they fell in with Tandy's circle. On reporting to Valentine Lawless and other London contacts in December 1797 and to Fitzgerald in Dublin in January 1798, O'Coigly prepared to return to France in company with Arthur O'Connor, John Binns, John Allen, and John O'Leary.

The party were arrested on 28 February 1798 at Margate when seeking passage to France and high treason proceedings commenced. O'Coigly completed a defiant pamphlet when in Maidstone gaol on 30 April and contemptuously ate an orange when his trial began on 21 May. O'Coigly, variously referred to as Coigly, O'Coigley, and

Quigley, was the most incriminated of all the defendants owing to documents recovered on his person. He was convicted of high treason and hanged at Pennenden Heath, near Maidstone, Kent, on 7 June 1798. In July 1900 Coigly was commemorated by a window in the Roman Catholic church of St Francis of Assisi in Maidstone.

RUÁN O'DONNELL

Sources D. Carroll, *Unusual suspects: twelve radical clergymen* (1998) · *Life of the Rev. James Coigly*, ed. V. Derry (1798) · M. Elliott, *Partners in revolution: the United Irishmen and France* (1982) · B. Macevoy, 'Father James Quigley', *Seanchas Ardmhacha*, 5 (1969–70) · R. O'Muiri, 'Father James Coigly', *Protestant, Catholic and Dissenter*, ed. L. Swords (1997), 118–64

Ó Comhraidhe [Ó Comhraí], **Eoghan**. *See* O'Curry, Eugene (1794–1862).

Ó Conaill, Peadar. *See* O'Connell, Peter (1754/5–1826).

Ó Conchobhair, Cathal [Cathal O'Connor, Cathal Croibhdhearg] (1152–1224), king of Connacht, was a son of Toirdelbach Mór *Ua Conchobair (d. 1156), king of Connacht and high-king of Ireland. The third to rule Connacht after the Anglo-Normans arrived in Ireland, Cathal Croibhdhearg could not restore the high-kingship, but he secured a place for his kingdom within a wider world by obtaining rights and recognition from both the English crown and the papacy. He was honoured in several contemporary bardic poems and in the most majestic obituary eulogy in the Irish annals.

According to his obituary, Cathal Croibhdhearg was born at Ballinchalla on Lough Mask, Mayo, and was three and a half years old when his father died. This places his birth in November 1152. Three of the many women with whom Toirdelbach had at least seventeen sons have been named as Cathal's mother. However, neither 'the daughter of MacDiarmata' (erroneously said to be also the mother of Cathal's much older brother Ruaidrí *Ua Conchobair), nor Derbforgaill, daughter of Domnall Mac Lochlainn (who died in 1151), is a convincing candidate; and the tradition that his mother was Gearrogingen hUí Mugroin, a concubine, is supported by an interpolation in the fifteenth-century Leabhar Donn. However, much of the traditional story—his exile as an agricultural labourer in Leinster as well as the witchcraft that caused his birthmark—appears to be a fanciful construct. Ruaidrí succeeded Toirdelbach and was himself succeeded in 1183 by his son Conchobhar Maonmhaighe, while Cathal was fostered by Tadhg Ua Concheanáinn of the Uí Diarmada, one of the Síol Mhuireadhaigh chiefs who traditionally attended the king of Connacht's inauguration and formed his inner circle. It is noteworthy that Conchobhar Maonmhaighe was assassinated in 1189 by some of his own officials at the instigation of a rival, probably a brother, called Conchobhar of the Uí Diarmada. His son Cathal Carrach avenged his death, but it was Cathal Croibhdhearg who won the kingship.

A poet patronized by Cathal Croibhdhearg Ó Conchobhair has given a striking, if somewhat idealized, image of him: 'He casts off the flower of his raiment while playing chess, he throws back his sleek soft hair with his long-fingered smooth red hand' (Greene and Kelly, 260). Clustering locks and tapering hands are standard bardic images, but the poets seem trustworthy when they say that Cathal's birthmark covered his left hand (which accounts for his epithet) and that he wore 'A crimson tunic like a red berry, a scarlet mantle decked with great ornaments, and a fine shirt like white chalk' (ibid.). Other items mentioned are his buskin with ornamental ribbing, his glove, and the ring on his left hand. Ó Conchobair married Mór (d. 1217/18), daughter of Domnall Mór Ua Briain, king of Thomond. Two of their sons became kings of Connacht, Aodh (r. 1224–8) and Feidhlimidh (r. 1230–31 and 1233–65); their daughter Lasairfhiona (d. 1282) married Domhnall Mór Ó Domhnaill, king of Tír Conaill. Other children were Taghd (d. 1205), Toirdhealbhach (d. 1214, a hostage with the Anglo-Normans), Sadhbh (d. 1266), and the mysterious Ruaidrí, who called Feidhlimidh his brother and Felix Ó Ruadhain, archbishop of Tuam, his uncle in a charter of c.1230.

Ó Conchobhair initially maintained his predecessor's hostile policy towards the Anglo-Normans, the treaty of Windsor (made on Ruaidrí's submission to Henry II in 1175) having expired with Conchobhar Maonmhaighe's accession in 1183. After surviving a violent storm on Lough Ree in 1190 that claimed thirty-six of his men as his ship sank and fleet scattered, Cathal Croibhdhearg tried to revive the high-kingship by promoting himself as a national saviour, 'a beautiful salmon with red rounded fins' who would deal with the Anglo-Normans, described as 'blue shoals of coarse fish, ugly shapes' (Ó Cuív, *Ériu*, 171). However, he found little demand for his services. He did send forces to aid the kings of Tír Conaill, Ulaid, and Desmond in 1195–6, but they were not used against the Anglo-Normans.

In 1195, apparently after Count John had granted Connacht to William de Burgh, Ó Conchobhair burned castles in Tipperary where de Burgh had settlements. However, the same year he also revealed an understanding of Anglo-Norman society—probably acquired from Anglo-Norman mercenaries employed in Connacht—and a flair for diplomacy. Exploiting the jealousy caused by the grant, he made peace with Walter de Lacy and John de Courcy at Athlone. He also seems to have made a feudal grant of the cantred of Maonmhagh to Gilbert de Angulo, who provided him with military service. However, his attacks on Anglo-Norman settlements along and beyond the Shannon in 1199–1200 were very much in the Irish cattle-raid tradition.

A series of military disasters made Ó Conchobhair seek long-term tenure under the English crown. He was routed leading off livestock in Westmeath and lost control of his kingdom in 1200 when de Burgh invaded it in support of Cathal Carrach. After he returned from northern Ireland in 1201 with Irish allies who deserted him, Cathal Carrach defeated his Anglo-Norman allies and he was imprisoned in Meath as security for wages. He did overthrow his rival in 1202 by making a (short-lived) alliance with de Burgh, and he was probably behind the massacre of de Burgh's troops in Connacht later that year. However, he offered no resistance to de Burgh's attacks in 1203. It was King John who stopped the conquest: he wanted a royal castle built at Athlone on the Shannon first. In 1205, during negotiations between the two kings, Cathal Croibhdhearg demanded that he hold one-third of Connacht in fee of the crown as a barony, and the remainder for tribute. By 1207 John had given him a charter.

Ó Conchobhair tried to bridge the gap between Irish succession and Anglo-Norman primogeniture by making his son Aodh a co-ruler and calling him his heir. However, he offended King John in 1210 when, after assisting him against the Lacys, he arrived without Aodh, fearing for his safety when John offered to give Aodh his own charter. John seized hostages and had Athlone Castle built; but Cathal, after a serious illness, made amends with a fine and military service and spent Christmas with the justiciar, John de Gray. On 13 September 1215 John made grants of Connacht in fee both to Ó Conchobhair and to de Burgh's heir, Richard, warning Cathal that tenure depended on loyal service and assuring him that disseisin required the judgment of the king's court. When de Burgh tried to obtain seisin during Henry III's minority, Ó Conchobhair appealed to his uncle Hubert, justiciar of England; but when Walter de Lacy built Athleague Castle on the Shannon in 1221, Cathal knocked it down, allowing the garrison to leave first. However, despite this and a similar attack by the Connachtmen in 1223, Ó Conchobhair continued to receive royal protection, perhaps because the Lacy expansion into Bréifne was unsanctioned. In 1224 the justiciar of Ireland vouched for his loyalty and supported his request that Aodh be given his own charter for Connacht as well as Bréifne lands taken by the rebellious William de Lacy. The regency could not make permanent grants, but it granted Aodh the Bréifne lands during pleasure.

The papacy recognized Ó Conchobhair's royal rights even though it approved of English lordship over Ireland. In 1200–01 Innocent III confirmed, and warned him not to abuse, his prerogative to assent to ecclesiastical elections within his kingdom; he also answered his questions regarding sanctuary so authoritatively that his reply became *Decretals*, 3.49.6. However, Cathal's relationship with Felix Ó Ruadhain, elected archbishop of Tuam with the help of the papal legate in 1202, seems to have fluctuated. In 1213 Felix, whose diocesan reforms were controversial, was maintained by the justiciar during a period of exile; and in 1216 the pope seemed to rebuke Ó Conchobhair when he told him to help the archbishop to implement the decrees of the Lateran Council, suppress hereditary succession, and allow free elections. Whether Cathal was behind Felix's imprisonment on his return from Rome is unclear, but in 1220–21 Pope Honorius III granted Cathal and Aodh protection for themselves and their kingdom. His obituaries say that it was in Cathal's time that tithes were first levied in Ireland.

Cathal Croibhdhearg Ó Conchobhair died on 27 May 1224. He was buried at the Cistercian house he had founded at Abbeyknockmoy, Galway, in 1190. The annals of Clonmacnoise say he died in Briole, Roscommon, but the other annals say that he died in the habit of a monk at Abbeyknockmoy. His other foundations were the Benedictine convent of Kilcreevanty (*c*.1200)—which later became the chief Arroasian convent in Connacht—and the Augustinian abbey of Ballintubber, Mayo (1216), a church that is still in use. The poets imply that Rathcroghan, in Roscommon, the traditional royal stronghold, was his chief seat. In the annals of Connacht's magnificent obituary eulogy, Ó Conchobhair is portrayed as fierce and feared, yet generous, peace-loving, pious, and pure, a model Celtic-Christian king with a reign of plenty. However, Cathal and his circle were more cosmopolitan than this characterization might suggest. It is significant that two bardic poems were written for him from abroad, one possibly from Scotland, where two of the poets he patronized sometimes resided, the other from near Monte Gargano, Italy, on the return portion of these two poets' pilgrimage to the Holy Land. One of them also visited the Roman curia. Ó Conchobhair seems to have had a highly developed, continental concept of royal prerogative. It is detectable in his relations with the papacy, in the growth of royal justice, and even, possibly, in the adoption of royal trappings not customarily used by Irish kings. The crowned head on a nave pier in Abbeyknockmoy—with its fleurs-de-lis rising above the delicately wrought circlet and branching curled locks that seem to embody bardic ideals—is thought to have been carved *c*.1224, perhaps as a tribute to his benefactions. After Cathal's death, Aodh used the theocratic title *Dei gratia rex Connactie*, while Feidhlimidh's effigy in the Dominican friary of Roscommon has a crown and sceptre with fleurs-de-lis. However, the story in the *Histoire des ducs de Normandie* that Cathal graciously accepted King John's gift of a great warhorse in 1210, but removed the saddle before mounting it, cautions against exaggerating his acculturation. The use of a chancellor in Connacht predates his reign, but his administrative system was largely a homegrown product of the twelfth century that enabled the king of Connacht to become a more autocratic ruler. His reign was one of stability—except for the years 1200–03—despite difficulties with a few sub-kings and rivals.

Cathal Croibhdhearg Ó Conchobhair's death was a turning point. A widespread rebellion against Aodh in 1225 was suppressed with Anglo-Norman assistance but it revived Anglo-Norman interest in what now seemed a weak Connacht. After the conquest in 1235–6, Feidhlimidh held five cantreds (one-sixth of Connacht) of Henry III during pleasure, later less. Cathal's line through Aodh continued, but split into two rival branches, Ó Conchobhair Donn and Ó Conchobhair Ruadh, in 1384. The former has survived to the present, but the title 'king of Connacht' was not used after 1474.

'A Vision of Connaught in the Thirteenth Century' by the poet James Clarence Mangan (1803–49) tells of the times of 'Cáhal Mór of the Wine-red Hand'.

HELEN PERROS (WALTON)

Sources A. M. Freeman, ed. and trans., *Annála Connacht / The annals of Connacht* (1944); repr. (1970) · D. Murphy, ed., *The annals of Clonmacnoise*, trans. C. Mageoghagan (1896); facs. edn (1993) · J. F.

Lydon, 'Lordship and crown: Llywelyn of Wales and O'Connor of Connacht', *The British Isles, 1100–1500*, ed. R. R. Davies (1988), 48–63 · H. Perros, 'Crossing the Shannon frontier: Connacht and the Anglo-Normans, 1170–1224', *Colony and frontier in medieval Ireland: essays presented to J. F. Lydon*, ed. T. Barry and others (1995), 117–38 · A. Gwynn and R. N. Hadcock, *Medieval religious houses: Ireland* (1970) · R. Stalley, *The Cistercian monasteries of Ireland* (1987) · P. J. Dunning, 'Pope Innocent III and the Irish kings', *Journal of Ecclesiastical History*, 8 (1957), 17–32 · J. A. Watt, *The church in medieval Ireland* (1972) · K. Simms, 'Frontiers in the Irish church—regional and cultural', *Colony and frontier in medieval Ireland: essays presented to J. F. Lydon*, ed. T. Barry and others (1995), 177–200 · D. Greene and F. Kelly, eds., *Irish bardic poetry: texts and translations together with an introductory lecture by Osborn Bergin* (1970) · E. C. Quiggin, 'A poem by Gilbride MacNamee in praise of Cathal O'Conor', *Miscellany presented to Kuno Meyer*, ed. O. Bergin and C. Marstrander (1912) · B. Ó Cuív, 'A poem for Cathal Croibhdhearg Ó Conchubhair', *Éigse*, 13 (1969–70), 195–202 · B. Ó Cuív, 'An Irish poet at the Roman curia', *Celtica*, 14 (1981), 6–7 · B. Ó Cuív, 'A poem composed for Cathal Croibhdearg Ó Conchubhair', *Ériu*, 34 (1983), 157–74 · G. Murphy, 'Two Irish poems written from the Mediterranean in the thirteenth century', *Éigse*, 7 (1953–5), 71–9 · F. Michel, ed., *Histoire des ducs de Normandie et des rois d'Angleterre* (Paris, 1840) · *Leabhar Donn*, Royal Irish Acad., MS no. 1233, 23/Q/10, fol. 14r, col. b · E. Friedberg and A. Richter, eds., *Corpus iuris canonici*, 2nd edn, 2 vols. (Leipzig, 1879–81); repr. (Graz, 1959) [standard edn of medieval canon law, incl. 13th-century *Decretals*] · M. P. Sheehy, ed., *Pontificia Hibernica: medieval papal chancery documents concerning Ireland, 640–1261*, 2 vols. (1962–5) · S. Duffy, 'King John's expedition to Ireland, AD 1210: the evidence reconsidered', *Irish Historical Studies*, 30 (1996–7), 1–21 **Archives** PRO, treasury of receipt, letters to Henry III, MISC. 54/11/2,16 · PRO, royal letters, letter to Hubert de Burgh, justiciar of England, no. 790

Daniel O'Connell (1775–1847), by George Mulvany

O'Connell, Daniel [known as the Liberator] (**1775–1847**), Irish nationalist leader, was born on 6 August 1775 near Carhen, Cahirciveen, co. Kerry, the eldest of the ten children of Morgan O'Connell (1739–1809) and his wife, Catherine O'Mullane (1752–1817).

Background and early life The O'Connell family inhabited a series of overlapping cultures. They were Roman Catholics in a society in which a small minority of adherents of the protestant state church monopolized political privilege. The O'Connells in their turn enjoyed the privilege and prestige of landholding, which was emblematic of claims to an ancient Gaelic lineage. But their status was scarcely aristocratic: Derrynane House, the residence of Maurice O'Connell (1728–1825), alias Hunting Cap, O'Connell's uncle and the head of the family, was a sturdy pile that fell short of Georgian grandeur. And it was status bolstered rather than tarnished by trade: O'Connell's father was a farmer, merchant, and retailer as well as landowner and middleman; proximity to a remote, indented coastline had facilitated generations of profitable smuggling. France loomed large not only in commerce but as a land of opportunity where Catholicism was not a barrier to office-holding and a talented Irishman (or Corsican) with claims to a lineage at home could be admitted to privileges from which the vast majority of French subjects were excluded on the basis of birth. Another of the young O'Connell's uncles, also Daniel, was lieutenant-general in the service of Louis XVI and, from 1783, a count of France. The nephew of the count passed his earliest years in a herdsman's mud cabin, being fostered out to a retainer until he was four. In the foster family he was immersed in the Irish language, the dominant vernacular of the countryside that had already been replaced by English in his parents' house.

Within a year or two of his return to Carhen, O'Connell's young life took a significant turn when he was sent to Derrynane to become informal heir to the childless Hunting Cap, and so to the effective headship of the extended family. Private instruction at Derrynane was followed in 1790–91 by a period in a one-teacher Catholic boarding-school near Cork. In August 1791 O'Connell and his brother Maurice arrived in Liège in the Austrian Netherlands, sent by Hunting Cap to have their education finished in the ambience of an English Catholic college. Unable to gain entry in Liège, they spent six weeks in Louvain before being admitted to the English College in St Omer, where they remained from October 1791 to August 1792, when they transferred to the English College at Douai. So O'Connell lived through the last disjointed months of an *ancien régime* institution while the revolution gathered pace all around: the battle of Jemappes on 6 November 1792, which opened the way for French armies to enter the Austrian Netherlands, was fought within earshot of Douai. Meanwhile foreigners and those identified with the old order were streaming out of France. Belatedly, on 21 January 1793, the date of the execution of Louis XVI, the O'Connells joined the rush to cross the channel.

Law studies and intellectual formation The flight from Douai to London had major symbolic significance. Henceforth for the O'Connells and others like them opportunity would lie not in continental Europe but in the realm of George III. In 1792 the entry of Catholics to the Irish bar had been legislated for, and by the end of 1793 O'Connell was set on a legal career. He was enrolled at Lincoln's Inn from January 1794 to early 1796, following which he spent a term at Gray's Inn. While the inns monitored attendance at dinners, acquisition of legal knowledge was a matter for the aspiring lawyer himself. It was a responsibility that O'Connell undertook with determination through avid reading of the corpus of legal authorities from Blackstone down. Thus was founded the sound knowledge of the law on which so much of his future success was to be based.

Legal texts apart, O'Connell at this time read voraciously, taking in the established classics—Shakespeare, Gibbon, Voltaire—and also the radical literature of the age. Exposed to works such as Paine's *Age of Reason* and Godwin's *Political Justice*, and emboldened by acquaintance with individual devotees of the new thinking, O'Connell by the age of twenty had become a democratic radical. He kept at this time a diary that witnesses to a loss of conventional Christian faith and an intellectual conversion to deism. When in adult life he became a public figure devout Catholicism was integral to his persona, but the London-based radicalism of the mid-1790s was to remain part of his make-up. Typically of the young romantic, he not only committed his innermost thoughts to paper for a number of years, but planned to write a novel of high adventure.

Intent on making his career in Ireland, O'Connell arrived in Dublin in May 1796 and immediately entered the King's Inns, where he completed his legal apprenticeship over the following two years. In a time of high political tension he was drawn to the radical world view of the burgeoning Society of United Irishmen and at the same time was repelled by the prospect of a violent revolution that would overthrow the social system on which his present and prospective status depended. His experience in France had undoubtedly coloured his view of revolution. In the panic following the attempted French landing at Bantry in December 1796 O'Connell enlisted with the lawyers' artillery, a volunteer corps dedicated to upholding the status quo. This had no apparent implications for his radical views and he may have formally joined the United Irishmen in 1797. He certainly talked radical politics with some abandon, although he clearly was never close to the conspiratorial core. A few days after his call to the bar in May 1798, rebellion broke out in Wexford and spread quickly to other parts of the east and midlands. With the courts suspended, the new barrister made his way to co. Kerry. A bout of serious illness extended his stay and he was not back in Dublin until November 1798.

O'Connell's career as a practising barrister began in 1799, when he set out on the Munster circuit as junior counsel. He proved to have an extraordinary capacity for the toil of producing quotidian legal documents and on circuit he displayed an instinctive talent for the theatre of forensic confrontation. He became in a relatively short number of years one of the most sought-after of barristers in the country, and eventually took special cases at venues outside the Munster circuit. It was as Counsellor O'Connell that he first acquired fame and admiration among the populace, and that was how a great many of his plebeian followers continued to refer to him even when from the late 1820s others preferred to salute him as the Liberator.

Marriage, family, and fortunes In the autumn of 1800 O'Connell met and fell in love with Mary O'Connell (1778–1836) of Tralee, the daughter of a deceased third cousin, impoverished and without dowry. They entered into a pledge of engagement but kept the arrangement secret from all except a few friends. Hunting Cap was already planning a suitably profitable match for his heir apparent; an undowered marriage would threaten everything that the uncle had striven to secure for the extended family and in particular for O'Connell. While never wavering in his devotion to Mary, O'Connell was very slow to face the expected wrath of his family. They married at O'Connell's Dublin lodgings on 24 July 1802, after which Mary returned to Tralee. The relationship continued on a furtive basis until Mary's pregnancy forced disclosure. The family in general took the blow sufficiently well for Mary to be admitted to the parental home at Carhen following the birth of a son, Maurice, on 27 July 1803. Co-existence with her in-laws was not without its difficulties, but Mary had no home of her own until in November 1805 O'Connell set up house in Dublin at 1 Westland Row. By then another son, Morgan *O'Connell (1804–1885), had been born and a daughter, Ellen (1805–1883), was about to arrive. Of eight further children, four would survive infancy: Catherine, called Kate (1807–1891); Elizabeth Mary, called Betsy (1810–1893); John *O'Connell (1810–1858); and Daniel (1816–1897).

O'Connell's relationship with his wife is marvellously documented in the more than 600 surviving letters they exchanged during their frequent periods of separation, not least when he was on circuit or, in later years, attending parliament at Westminster. They reveal ongoing struggles about domestic matters, always resolved amicably in the end, and his sharing with her of all the achievements and frustrations of his public life. As the record of a loving relationship that lost none of its freshness over a period of more than thirty years, they constitute a remarkable archive.

O'Connell retained the headship of the extended family for which he had been destined, but his decision to marry improvidently altered the character of that position. Both the sorely aggrieved Hunting Cap and O'Connell's father changed their testamentary arrangements to his disadvantage, and to the benefit of his brothers. However, he would still inherit Derrynane and other properties from the uncle, while the inheritance from his father, which fell to him in 1809, included a lease of extensive portions of the Kerry estate of Trinity College, Dublin. As landlord and middleman his rent roll would run to thousands of pounds per annum.

Hunting Cap lived long enough to enjoy seeing his protégé achieve a near heroic public stature, but this did not encompass the financial competence for which the mentor had laboured. Perhaps because the tyranny of the uncle had destroyed his sense of responsibility in this respect, O'Connell never managed his financial affairs successfully. His income from his practice exceeded £1000 per annum by 1806 and moved upwards dramatically thereafter. But neither earned income, nor rents, nor even the national tribute that he was to receive from 1829 onwards, however compounded, could meet his outgoings. The acquisition in 1809 of 30 Merrion Square as a family residence was an extravagance, but O'Connell's basic financial problem was not caused by ostentatious living. He never made realistic cash flow projections, and out of vanity and kindness he was all too ready to lend and spend or to act as guarantor for loans, especially when caught up in the trammels of local society in his beloved co. Kerry. At the same time he borrowed recklessly and shamelessly from the rich and the plain, thinking only of immediate needs and never of the longer term. As a landlord he allowed customary outlays and clientilist practices to get in the way of efficient management of his estates. It is certain that his financial problems predate, and therefore cannot be blamed on, the absorption of his time by national politics.

A serious reduction in rental income in the early 1820s occasioned by agricultural depression led O'Connell to send his wife and family in May 1822 to reside in France (at Pau and later at Tours). He visited them in September 1822 and again in October 1823, when he took them to see Paris. Soon the household was relocated to Southampton. This was meant as a staging post for a return to Dublin, which came to pass in May 1824 and was now represented in its turn as an economizing measure. O'Connell came into possession of Derrynane in 1825 following Hunting Cap's death. Soon his wife and family were installed there for half the year. To facilitate this supposedly expense-saving measure, O'Connell embarked on substantial and very expensive extension and refurbishment.

Entering political life It was as a boy in Derrynane in the 1780s that O'Connell became a student of politics and first cast himself as a political actor. The stage was that of the Irish parliament, independent after a fashion from 1782 and illuminated by the heroic-seeming Henry Grattan. When in 1799 and 1800 the proposed union threatened abolition of the Irish parliament, O'Connell was implacably opposed and utilized a rhetoric of independence newly coined in the 1790s. He was unmoved by the argument of prominent Catholics, including Hunting Cap, that union offered them and their co-religionists an escape from the dominance of the Irish protestant ascendancy. He did not at this time see himself as a Catholic but as a deist, and like the United Irishmen he was happy to proclaim that religious differentiation had no future as a factor in Irish politics. While he soon abandoned that conceit, opposition to the union was to remain one of the most consistent planks in his political platform. Even more central was his opposition to any resort to physical force as a means of undoing the union or remedying any of Ireland's problems. His own brush with the French Revolution, the vested interests of a lawyer and landowner, and sheer political pragmatism all supported such an outlook. Godwin's *Political Justice* (1793) provided his ideological conviction about the futility of violence. With the passage of time he developed a detestation of bloodshed, based on humane and religious considerations. From the start he had a horror of social unrest and all his political work has to be assessed in the knowledge that avoiding or preventing social revolution was always uppermost in his mind. His uninhibited use for rhetorical purposes of past Irish military conflicts (with the exception of 1798) and his enthusiasm for the South American wars of national liberation in the 1810s and 1820s, and for the Belgian revolution of 1830, show the limits of his pacifism. In 1803, during the scare caused by Robert Emmet's abortive rising, O'Connell joined the Kerry yeomanry, as he had rallied to the crown forces in the panic of 1797. But he was to be bitterly disappointed by the news of Waterloo. O'Connell carried forward into the post-revolutionary era (which in Ireland had begun by 1800) a congeries of radical attitudes that mark him as a quintessential liberal: these included dislike of state involvement with religion, detestation of slavery, resentment of unearned privilege, and commitment to the principles of freedom of conscience, freedom of association, freedom of contract, and the sanctity of property rights. Between 1828 and 1831 he had an exchange of ideas with Jeremy Bentham in which he made clear his attachment to the views of the apostle of utilitarianism.

For most middle-class Irish Catholics of O'Connell's own and earlier generations their civil disadvantage was a historical misfortune to be ameliorated as opportunity offered. For O'Connell, the product of the 1790s, it was also an affront to a universal principle and an intolerable barrier to himself as an individual. The initiation of the union on 1 January 1801 was not accompanied or followed by the abolition of Catholic disabilities. When the veteran campaigners for Catholic emancipation reassembled on 16 November 1804 as the Catholic Committee, they were joined by O'Connell, who made a sufficient impact to have himself appointed to the standing committee. Addressing the meeting, he explicitly cited the barriers to the progress of his own career posed by the existing state of the law, which effectively excluded Roman Catholics from parliament, all the high offices of state, and numerous positions of advantage including the inner bar.

Joining a campaign for Catholic rights amounted to acceptance by O'Connell that the transcending of religious division had been a mirage. Separating his religious affiliation from his career was not an available option. He was thus publicly renewing his identification with a religion to whose tenets he did not then subscribe. It was to be another four or five years before he began to resolve the anomaly by resuming the practices of Catholicism, such as regular mass attendance and prayers, lenten fast, and abstinence from meat on Fridays. A freemason from 1799, he subsequently abandoned the brotherhood in obedience to papal pronouncement. In his later life he was notable for a piety more intense than anything that mere political expediency might have produced.

O'Connell brought to the campaign for Catholic emancipation a sense of anger and impatience not shared by the older and partially aristocratic membership of the Catholic Committee. After the latest initiative had collapsed with the defeat of a relief bill at Westminster in May 1805, O'Connell's authority was strengthened as one of the few prominent Catholics who had discerned the false promise of the union. Between 1805 and 1808 his advocacy of a belligerent policy as against the moderation of the older members won him effective leadership but not total dominance of the Catholic Committee. The policy of continued petitioning forwarded by O'Connell resulted in May 1808 in another predictable parliamentary rebuff, but it also occasioned a compromise proposal by Irish whig MPs, which they believed to have episcopal support and under which the abolition of those legal disabilities affecting Catholics would be balanced by the concession to the government of a veto over Catholic episcopal appointments in Ireland. O'Connell took the lead in voicing opposition to this and, by vigorously stirring up lay Catholic opinion through the newspapers, he was mainly responsible for inducing the bishops to assemble in September 1808, when they repudiated the veto offer in which a number of them had been complicit.

The next stimulus to agitation of the case for emancipation came in late 1810 with the prospect of a regency. Again the lead in formulating a petition was taken by O'Connell and again his hard line provoked the fears of moderates. His attempts to co-ordinate agitation on a countrywide basis provoked the civil authorities into efforts to restrict the operations of the Catholic Committee. There ensued a game of legalistic chess of a kind at which O'Connell excelled: even if he lost advantage he gained enormously in the admiration of supporters for his ability to challenge the government on its own ground. A typical ploy was the disbanding of the Catholic Committee at the end of 1811 and its replacement by the Catholic Board.

When a new cabinet opposed to concessions for Catholics was formed in June 1812, the Catholic Board adopted a resolution intimating that the prince regent's judgement was controlled by the 'witchery' of his mistress, Lady Hertford. When shortly afterwards the Commons resolved to deal with the Catholic issue in the next session, O'Connell propelled the board into an intransigent 'all or nothing' stance. The Relief Bill that followed in May 1813 predictably offered less than 'all' and was the occasion for another outpouring of Catholic resentment orchestrated by O'Connell and culminating again in an episcopal declaration that could be seen as following his dictation. In the event the bill did not proceed, but a significant element withdrew from the board in protest against O'Connell's intransigence. If he had been acting, instinctively or otherwise, to oust rivals for leadership by adopting an emotionally appealing line of policy he had

certainly succeeded handsomely, even if it was at the expense of alienating a significant group of lay Catholic campaigners. But it must be recognized also that his stance on the veto question in these years was consistent with the radical attitudes to church–state relations that he had acquired in the 1790s. He had certainly pushed the bishops into a far more radical stance than they would have otherwise adopted. When in February 1814 a formal Vatican judgment warmly approved the principle of the veto, O'Connell set his well-practised tactics in motion and within months the bishops effectively repudiated the Roman position. In January 1815, in anticipation of a well-signalled papal rescript, O'Connell pushed his defiance of Roman compromise on the veto to new limits. When, in May 1815, Rome pronounced the acceptability of a veto, with the full authority of Pope Pius VII, the Irish Catholic bishops once again repudiated the possibility.

Dublin Castle watched O'Connell anxiously. With the appointment of the youthful Robert Peel as chief secretary for Ireland in 1812, a gigantic antagonism was initiated. Peel systematically utilized the legal system to silence those newspapers that were the most effective vehicles of O'Connell's propaganda and in June 1814 he found a pretext to suppress the Catholic Board. O'Connell's impact on public life owed not a little to the brilliance, scurrility, and vehemence of his verbal and written assaults on opponents. The new chief secretary he instantly and woundingly derided as 'Orange Peel'. Defending John Magee, editor of the *Dublin Evening Post*, in court in July 1813 he subjected the attorney-general, William Saurin, to humiliating personal abuse. Throughout his career O'Connell's robust and inspired oratory, whether in court or on the public platform, was a potent factor in his popular standing.

The bitterly personal conflict with the establishment led to O'Connell's participation in two affairs of honour in 1815. John D'Esterre was a merchant who chose to take insult at a remark of O'Connell's concerning Dublin corporation. On 1 February 1815 they faced one another with pistols at Bishop's Court, co. Kildare. D'Esterre was fatally wounded, an outcome that further enhanced O'Connell's heroic stature. He was subsequently affected by remorse at having killed a man and left a family bereft. That did not prevent him from being drawn into another affair later in 1815. This time his adversary was the chief secretary, who was deemed to have impugned O'Connell's honour with a remark in the Commons. In the event Peel travelled to the agreed venue—Ostend—while the authorities in London intercepted O'Connell on his way there. When another duel seemed imminent in 1817 face was saved on both sides when O'Connell made the distinction between political and personal criticism. In later years O'Connell repudiated duelling and condemned it as an affront to reason and religion. The fact that he was no longer prepared to offer the opportunity of exacting satisfaction in the time-honoured fashion to those whom he continued to insult came to be seen as further evidence of his want of gentlemanly qualities.

In 1815 and the years immediately following the conditions for agitation were unfavourable. Having tried various other tactical devices, O'Connell in 1818 began to adopt an apparently more flexible line on the veto issue and to make friendly overtures to the aristocratic Catholic leaders and also to the whigs. On this basis he appeared to have achieved a working arrangement with Henry Grattan before the latter died in June 1820. But when in 1821, in an initiative beyond O'Connell's influence, the Commons was passing a bill for Catholic relief with provision for a veto, he endeavoured to stir up popular opposition to the measure. The intransigent anti-Catholic majority in the Lords came to O'Connell's aid by defeating the bill in April 1821.

On the occasion of the visit to Ireland of George IV in August 1821 O'Connell joined with tories and Orangemen in extending a most loyal welcome. The affirmation of unswerving loyalty to the crown was one of the few fixed points of his political strategy; professing common cause with the Orangemen was a tactic employed only on occasion. When, at O'Connell's suggestion, the lord lieutenant, Lord Wellesley, prohibited an Orange march in Dublin on 4 November 1822 fierce protests ensued, culminating in the pelting of the lord lieutenant's box at the Theatre Royal with missiles. O'Connell joined ostentatiously in the consequent public meeting of notables of various persuasions to express disgust at the insult, and he was a member of the delegation deputed by the meeting to wait on the lord lieutenant with expressions of regret.

The Catholic Association In May 1823 O'Connell was a barrister of twenty-five years' standing and of universally acknowledged brilliance and capacity. Yet on the basis of his religious affiliation he was denied advancement beyond the lowest rung of the profession. That was the month in which he took the lead in founding a new Catholic Association. In preparation he had mended fences with Thomas Wyse and other notable Catholics previously alienated by his intransigent line on the veto. At O'Connell's insistence the new body had a stated objective much wider than the simple 'relief' or emancipation which would allow a small minority of Catholics like himself to proceed to inner bar, bench, or parliament: it was to address all the concerns of the Roman Catholic collectivity. This signalled the start of a mobilization of the populace for constitutional political ends which had little precedent anywhere, was contrary to the instincts of contemporary Liberals, and was to make O'Connell a historical figure of European significance. For some years he had been promoting aggregate meetings in provincial centres as weapons in his struggle with the vetoists, especially in the Munster towns which he himself visited on circuit. The Catholic Association was intended to provide for structured country-wide agitation. It was also intended to draw in the lower socio-economic classes. At a public meeting in Dublin on 15 June 1813 he had advocated, or at least predicted, popular mobilization; he now set about achieving this by introducing associate membership of the Catholic Association at 1*d*. per month. Thus was instituted the 'Catholic rent'. A phenomenal organizational

effort by O'Connell, making astute use of the Catholic parish structure, raised about £20,000 by early 1825.

The impact of this mobilization on political opinion was evident when O'Connell led a delegation to London in February 1825. Whig and Catholic notables swarmed around him: on 6 March he was entertained to dinner with thirteen peers of the realm by the twelfth duke of Norfolk. In another form of compliment the government was busily putting through the Unlawful Societies (Ireland) Act (6 Geo. IV c. 4), clearly intended to curb both the Catholic Association and the Orange order. More encouragingly, O'Connell was consulted by Sir Francis Burdett about his private member's bill proposing to grant Catholic emancipation. This was carried in the Commons but defeated in the Lords in May 1825. The upper house had merely postponed O'Connell's victory, ensuring that its impact on the political system would be all the more traumatic. O'Connell had consented to the inclusion in Burdett's measure of state payment of the Catholic clergy, and the suppression of the 40*s*. freehold franchise in Irish counties. In compromising thus on his previous position of principle he left himself open to criticism from radical voices in Ireland, but he dealt easily with the opposition, and his return to Ireland in May 1825 was a triumph. He quickly set about reorganizing the Catholic Association on a basis that evaded the strictures of the recent act.

The systematic mobilization achieved by O'Connell in 1824–5 was the basis for a momentous development in the general elections of 1826: in co. Waterford and a number of other constituencies Catholic 40*s*. freeholders were put under irresistible pressure to vote for candidates declaring support for Catholic emancipation, even when this meant defying the established expectation that their landlords could command their votes. What was 'democratizing' about this was not so much independent action by 40*s*. freeholders—a small group, mainly consisting of farmers of some substance—but that their votes were influenced by the opinion of the unenfranchised masses. When, in the wake of the 1826 elections, the chagrined landlords called in the arrears of rent owed by 40*s*. freeholders who had defied them at the polls, O'Connell accepted the responsibility of the Catholic Association for these victims of its policy, and used this as a pretext for another round of fund-raising—and another round of mobilization.

The influence gained by O'Connell's mobilization of Catholic power in Ireland was demonstrated when he proceeded to give direction to various Irish county members during the months of manoeuvring at Westminster that preceded the emergence of Canning as prime minister in April 1827. Soon he was trying with limited success to influence the government's appointments to the Irish administration in Dublin Castle. O'Connell raised by a few notches the pressure he was now exerting on the political system at the very top by a resumption of campaigning. In the most impressive exercise to date meetings were held in about 1600 parishes on Sunday 13 January 1828. At least 1 million participants adopted the same precirculated resolutions. O'Connell's determination to maintain pressure was strengthened by the appointment of the duke of Wellington as prime minister (and his old antagonist Peel as home secretary) later in January: between whigs and tories O'Connell was instinctively partisan, and he went along with a resolution of the Catholic Association that henceforth every candidate supporting the government would be opposed at Irish elections. Vesey Fitzgerald, member for County Clare, was appointed to the new government as president of the Board of Trade and so had to seek re-election. Fitzgerald was a long-standing advocate of the Catholic cause and was so highly regarded among all classes in co. Clare that no local notable could be found to oppose him. In order to preserve the credibility of the Catholic Association's strictures O'Connell himself was prevailed upon to stand as a candidate, although as a Catholic he could not as the law stood take his seat if elected. The marshalling of the electorate from all corners of co. Clare to the poll in Ennis in the early days of July 1828 was a masterpiece of electoral logistics accompanied by an unprecedented carnival of popular politics. O'Connell was declared elected on 5 July with a vote of 2057 to 982. His subsequent journey from Ennis to Dublin was reminiscent of the homecoming of a victorious Roman general. 'They must crush us or conciliate us. There is no going on as we are'. So O'Connell declared to the Catholic Association on 10 July. It was now the task of the victor of Waterloo to persuade the king and numerous members of his own party that the Catholics would have to be conciliated.

There ensued a period of high political tension during which O'Connell had to keep his organization on the boil while preventing it from spilling over. Word of the agreement of George IV and his ministers to concede emancipation was reported in early February 1829 and on 6 February O'Connell left for London. When the Roman Catholic Relief Bill was published a month later, he was overjoyed that emancipation was not to be tied to any veto over ecclesiastical appointments or any scheme of state payment for the priesthood. The exclusion of the monarchy and a handful of high offices besides showed that pragmatism rather than principle was at work, but that caused him little distress. A few sops to disappointed prejudice in the form of restrictions on religious orders and on the use of ecclesiastical titles he dismissed (correctly) as unenforceable. Less easy to dismiss was the blow to O'Connell's interests contained in the Irish Parliamentary Election Bill, designed to accompany the relief measure onto the statute book. This raised the threshold for the county franchise from 40s. to £10, thereby disenfranchising the bulk of his electoral battalions. He quickly accepted that his protests against this coup were futile and set about making the most of the achievement of Catholic emancipation, which received the royal assent on 13 April 1829. However, when O'Connell presented himself to the clerk of the House of Commons on 15 May, he was tendered the old oath of supremacy obnoxious to Roman Catholics, to which he declined to subscribe: the act applied only to those elected after its passage. On 18 May he was permitted to argue his case for immediate admission from the bar of the house. In the subsequent debate his election for County Clare was voided and a by-election called, with many hoping that the new, greatly reduced electorate would be less amenable to his influence. In the event he was returned unopposed for County Clare on 30 July 1829 and eventually took his seat on 4 February 1830.

In parliament On entering parliament O'Connell largely, though not entirely, abandoned his legal career. Fittingly, just a few months before he had given the most famous of those forensic performances that would have assured him of folk-hero status even if he had never entered politics. This was at the Doneraile conspiracy trial before a special commission in Cork in October 1829, where popular amazement at his feats on behalf of the defence was enhanced by the fact that he was summoned to act while on vacation in Derrynane after the first batch of defendants had been convicted, and that he rushed the 90 miles to Cork in a celebrated overnight ride, dismounting outside the court house as the trial of the next batch began. Over the following days he jousted verbally with the prosecution team and reduced the crown witnesses to pathetic incoherence, with acquittals and commuted sentences as the outcome. In folk memory it became the Counsellor's finest hour.

It was not only that the demands of parliament left O'Connell with less time for the courts: emancipation did not immediately secure for him the professional opening that his accomplishments merited. The first group of Catholics was called to the inner bar in October 1829 as the Relief Act allowed, but O'Connell was not included. Whatever the indignity of continuing as a junior counsel, he could not have abandoned his legal income without having an alternative. In March 1829 an O'Connell testimonial fund was established, which enabled a grateful nation to display its appreciation by contributing up to £30,000. Henceforth he was the beneficiary of an annual tribute estimated to have averaged about £12,000. This arrangement owed everything to Patrick Vincent Fitzpatrick, O'Connell's financial manager from 1830, who brought some order to the still insoluble problem of finance. The tribute was spent indiscriminately on O'Connell's political business and on his private needs, now more insatiable than ever. Setting up his family was a major drain. It has been estimated that he spent up to £20,000 on marriage settlements alone. In 1834 he founded the national bank: eight years later he was forced to resign from the position of governor because of an overdraft exceeding £30,000. Another venture into business, the purchase of a small Dublin brewery, proved similarly unsuccessful.

The extraordinary talents and skills that had served him so well in the courts and in Irish politics enabled O'Connell to become from the start an outstanding parliamentary performer. If none could deny his capacity, many mistrusted and despised him. He had forced his way in by invoking the power of the masses and he was dependent for his income on public subscriptions. The harshness of his vituperation against opponents and his wounding invective made matters worse. Disraeli, he opined, was surely descended from the impenitent thief of Calvary. If in the eyes of some of his fellow MPs he would always be an outcast, he had himself partly to blame. Some of the antagonism he encountered, such as that evinced by *The Times*, was so virulent and enduring that parallels would be difficult to find.

The matters on which O'Connell campaigned during his parliamentary career were general liberal or radical issues, reforms specific to Ireland, and repeal of the Act of Union. The excitement caused by the recent revolutions in France and Belgium prompted him to raise the flag of repeal at a series of public meetings in Munster in October 1830. However, with the advent of a whig government in November 1830 reform beckoned. Within a matter of months O'Connell had put repeal out of sight and was supporting the government's push for parliamentary reform. It was, however, an alliance marked by suspicion and uncertainty. O'Connell had even been arrested in January 1831 on a trumped-up conspiracy charge. By October 1831 he had been admitted to the inner bar and had secured the promise of a job for a son-in-law. The imminent 'reform' of the Irish administration intimated at the same time amounted to a redirection of spoils, but O'Connell himself had not pursued various possibilities for personal advancement that had been held out to him. In and out of parliament O'Connell identified with those seeking more thoroughgoing reform than the act of 1832 provided for. The corresponding Irish legislation (2 & 3 Will. IV c. 88) was particularly unadventurous, despite O'Connell's efforts to have it improved. Even as reform was being legislated, O'Connell was preparing to resume his agitation for repeal.

O'Connell had fought the general election of May 1831 solely in the interest of reform: 'Reform and Negro emancipation' was his slogan, and he used his influence to assist the return of supporters of reform in a series of constituencies. At the general election of December 1832 his plan was to give his approval only to candidates declaring for repeal and signing a pledge to promote it if elected. By this device he formed a group of thirty-nine MPs, a prototype of the modern political party. While he had taken a strong anti-whig line on the hustings, he used his newfound strength not to oppose the whig government but to increase his bargaining power. A move by the government to trim the ecclesiastical establishment in Ireland delighted O'Connell both as an Irish Catholic and as a radical, although he denounced its final form in the Church Temporalities Act as inadequate. When, early in 1833, the government introduced the Suppression of Disturbances (Ireland) Bill, which incorporated some very stringent measures, O'Connell and the more reliable of his followers mounted a stiff opposition, exploiting the procedures of parliament to force substantial amendments from the government. However, with the government in danger of losing its majority on other issues in the early summer of 1833, O'Connell and his followers rallied to its support in the voting lobbies.

O'Connell had pioneered the independent Irish party, an institution that was to reappear in various forms later in the century. One of his problems in 1833 was that the raising in parliament of the party's ostensible *raison d'être*, repeal, would simply produce an overwhelming rebuff, with inevitably demoralizing effects on his support in Ireland. Feargus O'Connor, repeal MP for Cork, caused considerable trouble for O'Connell by encouraging activists at home to demand that the repeal issue be raised. It was with difficulty that O'Connell held off the pressure in 1833 and eventually he did so only by agreeing to move in 1834. He presented a brave face when putting forward a motion, on 22 April 1834, for a select committee to inquire into the effects of the Act of Union. He was humiliated but not surprised when this was defeated by 523 votes to 38.

Consolation was soon at hand as the attrition of the government's support in the Commons placed O'Connell and his followers in a pivotal position, so that by early summer the placating of O'Connell was a prime issue for the cabinet. When Grey was replaced by Melbourne as prime minister in July 1834, O'Connell could claim to have influenced a change greatly to his liking. Over the following months he was encouraged to convey his likes and dislikes in the matter of Dublin Castle appointments to the whig inner circle. At the general election of January 1835 his platform was anti-toryism, and his weight was thrown behind whigs of every type where they were not in competition with his fellow repealers. He could claim subsequently to be the leader, at least informally, of a party of sixty and in the then fissiparous state of party allegiance this was enough to give him something akin to the balance of power in the Commons. Confirmation of his status came when he was invited to join an exploratory meeting of Liberal MPs on 18 February. The outcome of this and other contacts was an unwritten and unacknowledged understanding—the so-called 'Lichfield House compact'—under which all talk of repeal was put in abeyance, Melbourne's new government was assured of O'Connell's support when needed, and O'Connell's views would be heeded in the matter of Irish appointments and Irish legislation.

The new administration entering in Dublin Castle represented a dream come true for O'Connell, even if nothing came of suggestions that he himself might be installed as holder of an appropriate office. Roman Catholic law officers (some soon to be judges) were appointed for the first time since the reign of James II. The protestant appointees all had Liberal credentials, thus ousting what O'Connell saw as an Orange ascendancy clique. Most significantly, the new regime was alive with the mission of bringing good government to Ireland, a mission epitomized by Thomas Drummond, under-secretary from 1835 to 1840. At county level the appointment of Liberals, Catholic and protestant, as sheriffs and resident magistrates followed. A nominee for the office of sheriff of co. Kerry was blocked at O'Connell's behest because he was obnoxious to the O'Connell family: Hunting Cap could scarcely have dreamed of such a reversal of fortunes. O'Connell relations shared in the redirected spoils of office but not to such an extent as to offend against the standards of the age.

From 1828 onwards O'Connell had identified with popular radical and reform movements in Britain. In September 1835 his new relationship with the government provided an apposite context for a series of mass meetings in northern England and Scotland. Reform of the House of Lords was his theme, reflecting his frustration with the capacity of the upper house to prevent change. He had experienced this with the rejection of two Irish bills—on tithes and municipal reform—that he had triumphantly seen through the Commons. Favourable legislation was to prove the most difficult part of the Lichfield House compact to secure. Elaborate attempts to obtain measures on tithes and municipal government failed again in 1836. As the year ended, a deal about Irish measures was agreed between whigs and tories (whom the Lords would follow) that involved considerable compromise on O'Connell's part. Little enough progress had been made when the death of William IV occasioned a dissolution. At the consequent general election O'Connell's loose combination of assorted repealers, whigs, and Liberals gained a few extra seats in Ireland, but the results in Britain reduced the government's strength in the Commons. When the government responded to its new situation by definitively rejecting most planks of the British reformers' platform, O'Connell nevertheless remained loyal and so lost the sympathy of the radicals. The same disillusionment contributed to the emergence of a Dublin artisan movement which seriously challenged O'Connell's authority in late 1837 and which he crushed in January 1838, but only by calling on his substantial reserves of authority.

On 21 February 1838 O'Connell and his sons were introduced to Queen Victoria at a levee in St James's Palace. It was an honour that he appreciated. Ostentatious expressions of loyalty to the young queen had been part of his stock-in-trade since her accession, and would continue to be. In legislative terms 1838 produced a Poor Relief Act of great moment (which O'Connell had the luxury of opposing because it was supported by both sides of the house) and a Tithe Act which was emasculated by the Lords. Tithes were an aspect of the establishment that upset Roman Catholic opinion generally much more than it did O'Connell, partly because they constituted a species of property.

No surviving example of privilege in Ireland offended O'Connell more than the unreformed municipal corporations. Their abolition in 1840 placed city and town governments in the hands of elected councils, and provided O'Connell with the only opportunity in his career to hold an official executive office. A brilliantly organized campaign secured nearly 80 per cent of the seats on the new Dublin city council for his followers, and in November 1841 he became the first lord mayor of Dublin under the new dispensation, and the first Roman Catholic holder of the title since 1688. During the one-year term he proved himself to be an efficient administrator and he greatly enjoyed the pomp and public pageantry of the office.

The disadvantage of O'Connell's connection with the government from 1835 was that it precluded him from agitation in Ireland and thereby threatened his influence in the country. As early as August 1838 he had attempted to get up an agitation compatible with support of the government in the form of the Precursor Society of Ireland. This was replaced in September 1839 by the Reform Registration Association. It was only because he had become convinced that the days of the government were numbered that O'Connell in August 1840 founded an organization devoted unequivocally to repeal, the Loyal National Repeal Association. At the general election of 1841 O'Connell and his adherents ran as repealers, for the first time since 1832, but co-operated with Liberals and anyone else opposing the tories. The final figure of eighteen repeal MPs (compared with thirty-nine in 1832) was an index of how the years of co-operation with government had blunted the appetite for repeal. It was O'Connell's last general election. He had represented County Clare (1829–30), County Waterford (1830–31), County Kerry (1831–2), Dublin City (1832–5), Kilkenny City (1836–7), and Dublin City again (1837–41). In 1841 he lost his Dublin City seat to the Conservatives but was returned for both Meath and Cork counties and chose to sit for the latter.

The repeal campaign With the tories returning to power, the years of influence at Westminster and Dublin Castle were over. O'Connell was ready with his response: a great campaign for repeal. The initial popular reaction was lukewarm. Having completed his term as lord mayor of Dublin, he turned his attention to the orchestration of a mass mobilization. By means of emissaries, correspondence, and the newspaper press the parochial structures of the Repeal Association were established throughout the land. The money began to flow and public demonstrations, ostensibly to petition for repeal, were organized. As 1843 progressed these meetings took on massive proportions and became elaborate set-piece triumphal processions for O'Connell. He addressed more than thirty such meetings, invariably delivering a lengthy address and playing with all his accumulated expertise on the emotions of the crowd, or as much of the crowd as could hear him: nobody can say with certainty how many attended these meetings but it certainly ran into hundreds of thousands on various occasions. Another of the great events of the year was a formal debate over three days in Dublin corporation, at which O'Connell himself spoke for four hours.

The stated objective of the repeal campaign was the re-establishment of the Irish parliament so that Ireland would once again be ruled by its 'queen, lords and commons'. It would be naïve to think that O'Connell was committed to a very specific formula. It might also be questioned whether his actual objective was to win repeal or to put himself in a position to bargain for something else: certainly flexibility was an enduring feature of his political outlook. The government had responded to the repeal campaign with caution before moving on 7 October to suppress the final 'monster' meeting of 1843 arranged to be held on the following day at Clontarf, near Dublin. Showing impressive logistical ability, O'Connell and his staff succeeded in turning back the long columns of supporters already converging on Dublin. This determination to stay within the law was poorly rewarded when, a few days later, O'Connell, his son John, and a number of other prominent repealers were arrested on a charge of conspiracy. After a three-week trial they were convicted on 10 February 1844. The sentence, handed down on 30 May, was for a fine of £2000 and one year of imprisonment. During the interval between trial and sentencing O'Connell had been to England, where he received a standing ovation from the opposition as he entered the Commons chamber. He was honoured with banquets and public demonstrations in London, Birmingham, Wolverhampton, and Liverpool.

The incarceration of O'Connell and his comrades in Dublin's Richmond gaol was a mild form of detention: he occupied a suite in the governor's house and was allowed visitors as and when he pleased. The sentences were quashed by the House of Lords on 4 September 1844 on the grounds of unsatisfactory procedures in the formation of the jury. The journey from prison to the house on Merrion Square was an occasion for another of those triumphal processions that were such a marked feature of his public life and of the political culture which he had so largely formed.

Meanwhile Peel had been endeavouring to sap some of the foundations of the repeal movement. During 1844 Dublin Castle took to conferring appointments on Roman Catholics not identified with O'Connell's movement. Legislation for a commission of charitable bequests allowed the Catholic church to secure in law its corporate property at the price of formal public participation in a government initiative. The dramatic improvement in the funding of Maynooth College in 1845 amounted to an endowment of the Roman Catholic church in Ireland, and significantly constrained the ability of the bishops to participate in any further repeal campaign. Legislation, again in 1845, to establish a series of new university colleges was calculated to appeal to middle-class interests, but the provision that they be non-denominational was contentious for church people of all persuasions. O'Connell chose to denounce the proposed institutions as the 'godless' colleges; this secured his support with the section of the Roman Catholic hierarchy most useful for the purposes of political agitation. It also provoked a conflict at the very heart of his own organization.

The challenge of Young Ireland *The Nation*, launched in October 1842, was a weekly newspaper that had contributed immensely to the popularity of the repeal campaign. However, its editorial line and content, especially as formulated by Thomas Davis, were redolent of the romantic nationalism of European contemporaries and introduced an idealistic element quite alien to O'Connell's essentially pragmatic ideology. The proprietors, the leading contributors, and their close associates, who had almost all been born or grown up after Waterloo, were well read, well educated, and mainly middle-class, and came to be known collectively as Young Ireland. They included protestants (including Davis) in numbers greatly out of proportion to their representation in the repeal movement generally.

From the time of O'Connell's imprisonment *The Nation* became the focus of an independent and increasingly critical pole of influence.

While O'Connell always maintained that his vision of Ireland was one where the state would guarantee the fullest freedom to all religions, in practice his repeal campaign was replete with Catholic overtones, not least in the role of the priests as key organizers throughout the provinces. These overtones offended Davis and already in the autumn of 1844 he and O'Connell had exchanged written recriminations centred on intimations of 'bigotry'. Davis saw the rejection of the non-denominational colleges by O'Connell and others as an instance of Catholic bigotry and developed an argument for the superiority, from a national viewpoint, of 'mixed education'. When the subject came up for discussion at a public meeting of the Repeal Association on 26 May 1845 a dramatic confrontation ensued, with O'Connell brutally decrying the right of *The Nation* to speak for the Roman Catholic people of Ireland and asserting that he and 'Old Ireland' would stand by one another. In the past truculent performances like this had put down opposition.

After a short attendance at the Commons in the summer of 1845 O'Connell set in train a revival of the repeal organization and in September and October meetings in the style, and approximating to the scale, of 1843 were held at four well-scattered venues. The feasibility of such demonstrations disappeared quite suddenly with the destruction of a large proportion of the potato crop that became evident from mid-September onwards. O'Connell's assessment of the problem was gloomy from the beginning and he was one of the principal movers of the Mansion House committee established in Dublin in October 1845 to promote relief measures.

Soon the political situation seemed to brighten with the prospect of a return to power by the whigs. O'Connell spent most of the first half of 1846 at Westminster, preparing the ground for a renewal of his former alliance. Meanwhile *The Nation* conducted an editorial barrage against this very prospect, in the name of a more principled nationalism, and O'Connell felt obliged to reassert his authority over the repeal movement. He chose the issue of physical force for his challenge: various Young Irelanders had been led by the logic of their romantic nationalism to imagine the theoretical prospect of a resort to arms to vindicate Irish national claims. At a general meeting of the Repeal Association on 13 July he proposed and had accepted—over a few helpless protests from the Young Irelanders—a motion repudiating not only any resort to physical force but any theoretical case for it under any circumstances. Within a few weeks the Young Irelanders had withdrawn from the association, not because they had any plans to employ violence but because they refused to accept any longer the authority of the domineering old leader.

Meanwhile O'Connell was busily dealing with the new government of Lord John Russell to secure a share of the spoils of office for his assorted following of whigs, Liberals, Catholics, repealers, neighbours, acquaintances, and his son Morgan. He advocated the need to extend Castle patronage to Roman Catholic tradesmen, and not only to the professional middle classes. But gradualist, co-operative, clientilist politics was no answer to a mounting socio-economic catastrophe: the potato crop of 1846 had failed totally and with the consequent sharp rise in food prices affected both countryside and town. O'Connell took measures intended to provide for the needs of the tenants on his own estate and canvassed plans for meetings and co-ordinated action on the part of his fellow proprietors through the land. He asked Russell to provide money for public works, which would give employment, and the government responded by voting £450,000 for this on 17 August 1846. But even when forthcoming, the government's efforts were hopelessly mismanaged and many of those affected by the crisis who had the opportunity to respond in political terms blamed the government and recoiled from the whig alliance. In order to prevent the defection of a large section of the Loyal National Repeal Association O'Connell had to agree in December to consider proposals for a reconciliation with the Young Irelanders.

The collapse On his annual, and last, sojourn in Derrynane in the autumn of 1846 O'Connell saw at first hand the desperate plight of the rural poor. He also saw the imminent collapse of much of the world he had inhabited for over seventy years. It was grimly appropriate, if entirely coincidental, that the same vacation witnessed the sudden collapse of his own physical strength. The deterioration of his voice and vigour was noticed by all when he returned to Dublin. O'Connell had been troubled by a tendency to corpulence throughout much of his life and had responded by taking regular walking exercise; in prison in 1844 he covered 3 miles daily on the yard. On his annual autumn vacations in Derrynane he followed his pack of beagles on foot over miles of challenging mountain terrain. His decline was caused not by any inevitable collapse of his remarkably robust constitution, but by an accidental brain infection. A late twentieth-century medical assessment, published as an appendix to a volume of biography, is decisive in ascribing the infection to the surgical treatment for piles he received in London in 1845 (O. Mac-Donagh, *The Emancipist: Daniel O'Connell, 1830–47*, 1989, 338–9).

Back in Dublin in late 1846 O'Connell realized that his days were numbered. He reviewed his last will and made other final arrangements before leaving for London at the end of January 1847. Here he had strength for one final dramatic political act when on 8 February, trembling and barely audible, he addressed the Commons on the subject of the famine in Ireland. As his last appearance on the political stage it was entirely apposite. Gaining access to Westminster and achieving influence in its counsels had been his great achievement. His language, as always, suited his assessment of the particular circumstances: no cajoling now, nor rancour, but a sober statement of the plight of his country. He predicted with accuracy the likely loss of population and acknowledged that only parliament could halt the disaster. But he could not say how:

parliament, he said, was bound to find a means. Within weeks parliament had passed legislation to provide for the public soup kitchens at which by summer 1847 up to 3 million people were being fed. Parliament and government could have done much better, but even their best would not have been enough. There can be few more tragic figures in modern history than the dying Daniel O'Connell who watched in early 1847 as his long decades of gargantuan political effort and achievement were turned to dust and ashes by a natural catastrophe.

O'Connell's chaplain, Father John Miley, arrived from Dublin in mid-February and contributed to the decision that O'Connell should travel to Rome. His desperate physicians were recommending a sunny climate. Though deeply committed to papal authority in religious matters, O'Connell disapproved of the secular government of the papacy. The accession of the initially liberal Pius IX in 1846 was an apparent vindication of O'Connell's religious politics. After a few weeks of rest and preparation at Hastings, O'Connell set out for Rome on 22 March 1847, accompanied by Miley, his son Daniel, and a servant. They went by steamboat from Folkestone to Boulogne and thence by rail to Paris. O'Connell was visited in his hotel by the archbishop of Paris and by a delegation of liberal Catholic notables, with the comte de Montalembert at its head. He could barely respond to their compliments. From Paris to Marseilles the journey was by road: with an eleven-day break at Lyons it took five weeks. From Marseilles they took a boat to Genoa, where they arrived on 5 May. Throughout the journey crowds had turned out to admire the famous O'Connell but he scarcely noticed them. There were occasional bouts of raving, but when lucid he was in deep gloom. He had a fixation about the danger of being buried alive. But predominant was concern for his spiritual salvation. He insisted that Miley, the agent of final absolution, should not leave his sight.

In his rooms at the Hotel Feder in Genoa, O'Connell's mental and physical condition worsened. By 8 May he had ceased to take food. After days of great turmoil peace of mind and body descended on 13 May, and on Saturday 15 May at 9.35 p.m. O'Connell died, fortified with the last rites of his church. In accordance with his wishes his embalmed heart was sent to Rome, where his passing was marked with all possible liturgical solemnity. His body was similarly received when it arrived in Dublin. Interment was in Glasnevin cemetery on 5 August 1847, first in a temporary grave, and from 1869 in the vault of a specially designed memorial dominated by a replica round tower 165 feet high. In due course the major street of Dublin was named O'Connell Street, with his large-scale statue and plinth, by J. H. Foley, the most prominent monument in the Irish capital.

Reputation Apart from one of the non-dominant strains of Irish Catholic nationalism, O'Connell has not been the chosen prophet of any political grouping since the collapse of the repeal movement within a few years of his death. It might be said that he gave too many hostages to fortune, or that a character with so many facets is difficult to turn into an icon. Young Irelanders, such as John

Mitchel and Charles Gavan Duffy, have spread far and wide an awareness of the deficiencies of his political strategies and tactics. W. E. H. Lecky, mindful of how O'Connell's efforts had, however unintentionally, exacerbated the polarization of Irish politics, wondered if on balance his career had been a blessing or a curse for Ireland. What nobody has seriously challenged is the largeness of his place in modern Irish history. Victorious nationalists of a later generation did not rename Dublin's main thoroughfare for any of their own leaders or heroes but for O'Connell. Indeed it might be said that neither partisan nor professional historians have adequately addressed the question of how much O'Connell created and how much he borrowed. Independently of scholars or politicians, O'Connell became in his lifetime and afterwards a folk hero. Historians aware of the historical record of a faithful husband and devout family man were puzzled by his reputation for fathering numerous bastards throughout the land (priggishly drawn down by W. B. Yeats for his own purposes) until experts pointed out that this is a standard feature of the depiction of the folk champion and has no necessary relation to historical facts. Similarly, tales of his prowess in the courts, in parliament, and in contests of various kinds abound in the folklore collections.

While in popular esteem O'Connell is the quintessential Irish national champion, his international significance is underestimated. He was a key figure in the emergence of European democracy and no Irish person before or since has commanded so much attention on the continent as he did in his lifetime. Similarly forgotten to a large extent is his role as an advocate of the rights of those civilly disadvantaged such as Jews, black slaves, and Australian Aborigines. Universalist and nationalist, champion of the weak and truculent bully, man of principle and shameless opportunist, O'Connell remains, like Napoleon or Gladstone, one of those figures with whom historians will never even imagine that they have finished.

R. V. COMERFORD

Sources *The correspondence of Daniel O'Connell*, ed. M. R. O'Connell, 8 vols., IMC (1972–80) · O. MacDonagh, *O'Connell: the life of Daniel O'Connell, 1775–1847* (1991) · M. MacDonagh, *The life of Daniel O'Connell* (1903) · A. Houston, *Daniel O'Connell: his early life and journal, 1795 to 1802* (1906) · F. O'Ferrall, *Daniel O'Connell* (1981) · D. McCartney, ed., *The world of Daniel O'Connell* (1980) · K. B. Mowlam and M. R. O'Connell, eds., *Daniel O'Connell: portrait of a radical* (1984) · A. D. Macintyre, *The Liberator: Daniel O'Connell and the Irish party, 1830–1847* (1965) · W. J. O'M. Daunt, *Personal recollections of the late Daniel O'Connell, M.P.*, 2 vols. (1848)
Archives BL, corresp. and papers, Add. MSS 62712–62715 · Boston PL, papers · National University of Ireland, papers · NL Ire., corresp. and papers · NL Ire., family corresp. · NL Ire., fee book · NRA, priv. coll., family corresp. · Royal Irish Acad., journal · University College, Dublin, corresp. and papers | BL, Peel papers · NL Ire., W. S. O'Brien papers · NRA, priv. coll., corresp. with Maurice Fitzgerald · PRO NIre., corresp. with first marquess of Anglesey, D619 · TCD, corresp. with Lord Donoughmore
Likenesses J. Gubbins, oils, 1817–18, Derrynane House, co. Kerry · J. P. Haverty, group portrait, oils, 1828 (with his contemporaries, the Clare election), NG Ire. · J. P. Dantan, sculpture, 1834 (group with William Cobbett), Musée Carnavelet, Paris · G. Hayter, oils, 1834, NPG · B. Mulrenin, miniature, 1836, NPG · D. Wilkie, oils, 1838, Royal Bank of Scotland, London · J. E. Jones, marble bust, 1843, NG Ire. · oils, 1846–7, St Patrick's College, Maynooth · oils, 1846–7, priv. coll.; repro. in O'Connell, ed., *Correspondence*, vol. 1, p. 23 · Count D'Orsay, bronze sculpture, 1847, NG Ire. · J. Comerford, miniature, NG Ire. · J. Doyle, drawings, BM · J. H. Foley, bronze statue, O'Connell Street, Dublin · J. P. Haverty, oils, Reform Club, London · B. R. Haydon, group portrait, oils (*The Anti-Slavery Society Convention, 1840*), NPG · G. Hayter, group portrait, oils (*The House of Commons, 1833*), NPG · J. Hogan, marble statue, City Hall, Dublin · W. Holl, stipple (after T. Carrick), BM, NPG · Irish school, wax death mask, NG Ire. · D. Maclise, watercolour drawing, V&A · G. Mulvany, oils, NG Ire. [*see illus.*] · Paul Pry [W. Heath], group portrait, coloured etching (*Keeping the child quiet*; with others), V&A · medals, National Museum of Ireland, Dublin · plaster death mask, St Patrick's College, Maynooth · prints, BM, NPG

O'Connell, Daniel Charles, Count O'Connell in the French nobility (1745–1833), army officer in the French service, the youngest surviving son of Daniel O'Connell (*c.*1701–1770), landowner, and Maire O'Donoghue (*c.*1708–1795) of Derrynane, co. Kerry, was born in Derrynane on 21 May 1745, though August 1747 was the date cited during much of his lifetime. There is no specific information, but the fact that as a teenager he could read and write fluently and was conversant with French, English, and Latin indicates that he received some formal education. His career of choice was soldiering and his evident intention when he set off for Europe in 1760 was to join the imperial Austrian army. However, a chance encounter in Flanders resulted in his entering the French service as a boy cadet in the royal Swedish regiment. Promoted within a few months to the rank of sub-lieutenant, he was sufficiently confident of his future by 1764 to dismiss a suggestion from his brother Maurice that he should join the Spanish service as 'imprudent' on the grounds that it would oblige him 'to relinquish a sure establishment for an uncertainty' (*Last Colonel*, 1.83). Having seen action in the German theatre during the later phases of the Seven Years' War, O'Connell augmented his military knowledge in the winter of 1765–6 in the prestigious military academy at Strasbourg, following which he was promoted above 'elder officers' (ibid., 1.99) to the rank of first lieutenant. This helped him to endure the seven uneventful years he spent with the royal Swedish in Alsace and his continuing dependence on financial support from home. His promotion to the rank of sous-aide-major in 1768 and, following his decision to join Lord Clare's Irish brigade in 1769, to that of aide-major represented progress, and he was posted in the early 1770s to the French East Indies. His failure to secure a regimental majority in 1773 led him to lament the lack of 'encouragement for merit and ability' (ibid., 1.174) in the French army, and his 'expectations' (ibid., 1.184) were dealt a further set-back when Clare's Irish brigade was dissolved in 1775. Made a second captain, he devoted his free time to study. His prospects in the French service seemed slim when his insightful observations on military discipline attracted official notice and resulted in his elevation to the brevet rank of colonel, and the award of the cross of St Louis and a small pension. This did not relieve him from financial dependence upon his brother, but it helped him in 1776 'to decline offers seemingly very advantageous made me by the emissary of the

American congress' (ibid., 1.199). He was encouraged to reach this decision by his strong sense of loyalty to France, 'where I early found an asylum when refused one at home' (ibid., 1.207). He demonstrated his 'inviolable fidelity' (ibid., 1.207) to the French king when, following the outbreak of war with Great Britain in 1778, he rejoined the royal Swedish as a lieutenant-colonel and performed heroically during the capture of Minorca and the siege of Gibraltar in 1781–2. This was O'Connell's finest fighting hour, and it resulted in his promotion to the rank of colonel-commandant and the bestowal upon him of the distinction of the title count.

Having finally attained a measure of financial security, a noble rank that gave him an entrée to the highest levels of French society, and a military rank that ensured him a regimental command, O'Connell seemed set fair. His preference was for active military service. He was prepared, he informed his brother in 1785, 'cheerfully [to] spill the last drop' of his blood (*Last Colonel*, 2.40) for Louis XVI but instead he was given the task of revising the military code. This was not complete when the country was plunged into revolution in the summer of 1789. The outbreak of the French Revolution was 'extreamly disadvantageous' to O'Connell and others like him who 'held … favours from [the] Court' (ibid., 2.89). In the short term his loyalty to France enabled him to bear the loss of his pension and to ignore the invitations of aristocratic acquaintances to conspire against the revolution. His promotion to major-general in the summer of 1791 seemed to suggest he might even profit by it, when his dislike of 'the changes that have taken place' and 'the state of military anarchy' he observed (ibid., 2.95) meant he would have preferred to have declined the honour. Under threat of arrest, he fled France in the summer of 1792 and joined the royalist army in Germany as a private, but by November he was in London. He managed to protect his French property from confiscation by providing a false alibi to the effect that he was in Ireland while he sized up his options. He determined to continue the struggle against the revolution, and a proposal he submitted to William Pitt in 1794 became the basis of a plan to establish an Irish brigade in the service of George III. O'Connell was appointed colonel of the 4th regiment of the proposed brigade, but administrative difficulties, some of which derived from opposition to the recruitment of Catholics in Ireland, meant that his intentions that the brigade would fight against the French were not realized.

At the French chapel in King Street, Covent Garden, London, in 1796 O'Connell married Martha Gourand, countess of Bellevue (*d.* 1807), despite the objections of his brother, and with this his life entered a quieter phase. He and his wife and stepchildren returned to France after the peace of Amiens, where the combination of his military income and his wife's wealth enabled him to live well. By 1813 he maintained that 'retirement, ease and study' were his 'sole enjoyments' (*Correspondence*, 1.369), but his appointment as lieutenant-general in the army of France on the restoration of the Bourbons indicated that he was not entirely without consequence. He was not to soldier again, and he devoted his time thereafter to the care and advancement of his family. Having determined in 1801 to 'transfer … his ambition' (ibid., 1.52) to his nephew, Daniel *O'Connell (1775–1847), then an emerging lawyer, he proved remarkably supportive financially of his fiscally profligate namesake. He was not always comfortable with his nephew's political tactics, but his belief in the 'justice and policy of Catholic Emancipation' (ibid., 1.369) and his manifest pleasure at Daniel O'Connell's rising 'reputation' (ibid., 2.408) ensured they remained on warm terms. His loyalty to the main branch of the Bourbons prevented him from taking an oath of allegiance to Louis-Philippe in 1830 and, though he became a naturalized Frenchman in 1831, he was deprived of his military pension. He lived thereafter at the Château Bellevue at Madon, near Blois, where he died on 9 July 1833. He was buried in the village cemetery at Condé, near Madon.   JAMES KELLY

Sources Mrs M. J. O'Connell, *The last colonel of the Irish brigade*, 2 vols. (1892); repr. in 1 vol. (1977) · J. C. O'Callaghan, *History of the Irish brigades in the service of France*, [new edn] (1870) · L. Swords, *The green cockade: the Irish in the French Revolution, 1789–1815* (1989) · O. MacDonagh, *O'Connell: the life of Daniel O'Connell, 1775–1847* (1991) · Burke, *Gen. Ire.* (1976) · *DNB* · *The correspondence of Daniel O'Connell*, ed. M. R. O'Connell, 8 vols., IMC (1972–80) · M. F. Cusack, *Life and times of the liberator* (1872)

Archives priv. coll., O'Connell (Fitz-Simon) MSS, family MSS [microfilm in NL Ire.]

Likenesses P. Guerin, oils, *c*.1815, Dublin, collection of the Office of Public Works

O'Connell, Daniel Joseph Kelly (1896–1982), astronomer, was born at 143 Clifton Road, Rugby, Warwickshire, on 25 July 1896, one of the three children of an Irishman, Daniel O'Connell, an Inland Revenue officer, and his wife, Rosa Susannah Helena, formerly Kelly. Following the deaths of both his parents, at the age of twelve he was sent to Ireland and was educated at Clongowes Wood College. When he was seventeen he joined the Irish province of the Jesuit order and attended University College, Dublin, gaining the degree of MSc in mathematics in 1920. The long years of training for the priesthood included three years at the Jesuit house in Valkenburg in the Netherlands and three years teaching at Riverview College, near Sydney, Australia. He was ordained in Dublin in 1928.

In 1931 O'Connell was sent to continue his scientific studies at Harvard University, where he joined Harlow Shapley's vibrant school of astronomy and astrophysics. There he began the researches on variable stars and in particular on eclipsing binaries, which were to remain his main astronomical interest throughout his life. O'Connell was exceptionally happy at Harvard, but his indifferent health caused his superiors to send him back in 1933 to the better climate of Australia. Under the influence of the geophysicist Father W. O'Leary SJ at the observatory which was attached to Riverview College O'Connell turned his hand to seismology, and got on so well in this field that he was put in charge of Riverview Observatory on O'Leary's death in 1938. All the while he continued diligently with his own researches on variable stars using the observatory's modest photographic cameras, for which he was awarded the degree of DSc by the National University of Ireland in 1949.

O'Connell's active years in Australia ended in 1952, when Pope Pius XII appointed him director of the Vatican observatory. The appointment came at an auspicious time for O'Connell, since it coincided with the Rome assembly of the International Astronomical Union and gave him an opportunity to meet many of the world's astronomers on what was now his home ground. Being an excellent linguist as well as a man of warm personality, he built up and retained a wide circle of devoted astronomical friends.

At the observatory, the 'Specola Vaticana', situated on the upper floors of the pope's summer residence at Castel Gandolfo, O'Connell found a well-equipped institution with some first-class instruments. In 1957 he added a fine Schmidt telescope, which he installed in the beautiful Barberini Gardens, and which was used by his young Jesuit assistants principally for objective prism spectroscopy.

O'Connell's scientific concerns were closely bound up with his *ex officio* membership of the Pontifical Academy of Sciences, where he consorted with scientists of many fields of learning and could work for an improvement in the often misunderstood relations between the Roman Catholic church and the scientific community. As a member of the academy—of which he was president from 1968 to 1972—O'Connell organized two conferences devoted to astronomical problems, the proceedings of which (edited by him), *Stellar Populations* (1957) and *Nuclei of Galaxies* (1970), became classics of astronomical literature. In a different vein, O'Connell published *The Green Flash* (1958), a scientific account with colour photographs of that elusive phenomenon as observed from the roof of the observatory at Castel Gandolfo before the encroachment of smog from the city of Rome.

Living in the papal palace from 1952 until his retirement in 1970, O'Connell was on close personal terms with three popes—Pius XII, John XXIII, and Paul VI. When the first man landed on the moon on 20 July 1969, Paul VI, escorted by O'Connell, followed the event on television from the dome of the Schmidt telescope and transmitted live from there his greetings and blessing to the astronauts. Pope John Paul II visited O'Connell during his last illness at Jesuit House, the headquarters of the Society of Jesus, at Borgo di Santo Spirito, Rome, where he died on 14 October 1982.   HERMANN A. BRÜCK

Sources G. V. Coyne and M. F. McCarthy, *Quarterly Journal of the Royal Astronomical Society*, 24 (1983), 363–4 • S. Maffeo, *In the service of nine popes: 100 years of the Vatican observatory*, trans. G. V. Coyne (Vatican City, 1991), 95–104, 142–3, 175–8, 184–7 [It. orig., *Nove papi, una missione* (1991)] • J. Begley, 'Fr Daniel O'Connell S.J. (1896–1982)', *Jesuit Life Newsletter, Australian Province* (summer 1996), 42–6 • R. Haynes and others, *Explorers of the southern sky: a history of Australian astronomy* (1996), 126, 172 • b. cert.

Archives Castel Gandolfo, Vatican observatory archives
Likenesses photograph, *c.*1952, Vatican Observatory, Castel Gandolfo; repro. in Maffeo, *In the service* • photograph, repro. in Haynes and others, *Explorers*

O'Connell, John (1810–1858), politician, third son of Daniel *O'Connell (1775–1847) and his wife, Mary (1778–1836), was born in Dublin on 24 December 1810. His elder brother was Morgan *O'Connell. He attended Clongowes Wood College, Trinity College, Dublin, and the King's Inns. Called to the bar in 1837, he had little opportunity to practise. Of Daniel O'Connell's sons he was the one most interested in politics, in which he was already active at the age of thirteen. He was returned to parliament for Youghal on 15 December 1832, as a supporter of his father's campaign for repeal of the Act of Union. In 1835 he was re-elected, in spite of an unsuccessful petition against his return, and he went on to hold the seat until 1837. He was returned unopposed for Athlone on 4 August 1837; on 3 July 1841 he succeeded Joseph Hume in the representation of Kilkenny without a contest, and in August 1847 he was returned both for Kilkenny and for Limerick, and elected to sit for the latter constituency. On 28 March 1838 he had married Elizabeth, daughter of Dr James Ryan of Bray, co. Wicklow. They had eight children.

During the early part of his career O'Connell took a very active part as his father's lieutenant in the repeal agitation. He prepared reports for the repeal association: 'Poor-Law Remedies' and 'Commercial Injustices to Ireland', both in 1843, and 'Fiscal Relations of the United Kingdom and Ireland' in 1844; also in the same year his *An Argument for Ireland* was separately published; it reached a second edition in 1847. He also wrote for *The Nation* his *Repeal Dictionary*, which was separately published in 1845. He was tried alongside his father in 1844, and shared his imprisonment in Richmond gaol, where he organized private theatricals and conducted a weekly paper for his fellow prisoners. He rode in his father's triumphal car when the prisoners were released on the success of their appeal to the House of Lords. During his father's frequent absences he was the effective head of the repeal association in Ireland. In this capacity he strenuously opposed the Young Ireland party, and incurred its bitter enmity. To the succession to his father's 'uncrowned kingship' he asserted almost dynastic claims. The Young Ireland party, willing to defer to the age and genius of the father, revolted against such pretensions on the part of his youthful and less able son. A bitter struggle ensued, but on his father's final departure from Ireland, O'Connell succeeded to the control, and, on the father's death in May 1847, to the titular leadership, of the association. The election of thirty-five MPs in August 1847 was a considerable achievement for the repealers. But the government's dismissal of repeal in April 1848 and the spread of revolution in Europe swung political opinion in Ireland away from O'Connell and towards the Young Irelanders. In 1849, with the revolutionary excitement over, O'Connell endeavoured to revive the repeal association, but in vain. With the Irish Catholic whigs taking up popular causes, he found himself on the opposite side, supporting the government.

When a tenant-right agitation began to gain ground in 1850 O'Connell used his influence against it; and he gave great offence during the excitement produced by the Ecclesiastical Titles Bill by voting with the government on the motion which led to the temporary fall of Russell's ministry in February 1851. The corporation of Limerick passed a resolution of censure on their member, and in August 1851 he accepted the Chiltern Hundreds to create a vacancy for the earl of Arundel, who in consequence of the secession of his father, the duke of Norfolk, from the Roman Catholic faith had resigned the family borough of Arundel on 16 July. On 21 December 1853 O'Connell re-entered parliament as member for Clonmel; but his position in the House of Commons was now one of insignificance. In February 1857 he quitted public life, on appointment to the clerkship of the Crown and Hanaper Office, Ireland; and on 24 May 1858 he died suddenly at his house in Tivoli Terrace, Gowran Hill, Kingstown, near Dublin, where he had lived for some years. He was buried in Glasnevin cemetery on 28 May, following a funeral that was reputedly the largest in Dublin since that of his father. Following his death a public testimonial raised £5000 in support of his family.

O'Connell published a *Life and Speeches* of his father (1846; 2nd edn, 1854) and *Recollections and Experiences* of his own parliamentary career (1846). Before and after his death O'Connell provided Young Irelanders and other opponents of his father with an easy target for criticism and even ridicule, and his reputation has suffered accordingly. Attempting as he was to follow in the footsteps of a giant, his chances of making a favourable impact on the world were limited.

J. A. HAMILTON, rev. R. V. COMERFORD

Sources M. R. O'Connell, 'O'Connell and his family', *The world of Daniel O'Connell*, ed. D. McCartney (1980), 19–29 · *The correspondence of Daniel O'Connell*, ed. M. R. O'Connell, 2–3, IMC (1973–4) · C. G. Duffy, *Four years of Irish history, 1845–1849: a sequel to 'Young Ireland'* (1883) · C. G. Duffy, *The league of north and south, 1850–54* (1886) · O. MacDonagh, *O'Connell: the life of Daniel O'Connell, 1775–1847* (1991) · A. J. Webb, *A compendium of Irish biography* (1878) · *CGPLA Ire.* (1858)

Archives NL Ire., MSS

Likenesses W. J. Linton, group portrait, woodcut, 1844 (*The state trial portraits, 1844*; after H. Anelay), BM · J. Gubbins?, oils, Derrymans House, co. Kerry

Wealth at death £450: administration, 24 July 1858, *CGPLA Ire.*

O'Connell, Sir Maurice Charles (1812–1879), soldier, administrator, and politician in Australia, was born on 13 January 1812 at the military barracks in what became Wynyard Square, Sydney. He was the eldest son of Sir Maurice Charles Philip *O'Connell (1768–1848), lieutenant-governor of New South Wales, and his wife, Mary Putland (1782/3–1864), daughter of former governor William Bligh. In 1814 the family were transferred with his father's regiment to Ceylon, where Maurice lived until the age of seven, when he was sent for his education to Britain. He attended Dr Pinkney's School at East Sheen, Surrey, then Edinburgh high school, followed by studies in Dublin, then at the Collège Charlemagne in Paris. At the age of sixteen he joined the 73rd regiment, and later described himself as 'zealously devoted' (McDonald, 116) to the military profession. He served with his regiment in Gibraltar, Malta, and Jersey, and was made lieutenant in January 1834. On 23 July 1835 O'Connell married Eliza Emiline (1813–1903), daughter of Colonel Philip Le Geyt of the 63rd regiment. They had no children.

In September 1835 O'Connell left for Spain as part of the British Legion, to fight in the First Carlist War, leading a regiment of volunteers he had raised in Ireland. During two years in Spain he rose to the rank of brigadier-general in the legion, and received three Spanish decorations. On returning to Britain he was reappointed a lieutenant in the 51st regiment, and in June 1838 purchased the commission of captain in the 28th regiment. Soon afterwards, he travelled to serve with his regiment in New South Wales in the company of his father, who had been appointed to the command of all military forces in the colony, and to whom he became assistant military secretary. In 1842, when his regiment was transferred to India, O'Connell chose to remain in New South Wales, before selling his commission two years later and becoming established as a horse breeder and pastoralist.

O'Connell then took an interest in the politics of the colony, and in 1843 stood for a place in the newly created New South Wales legislative council. Although closely aligned with the 'exclusives' of the town (*Brisbane Courier*, 24 March 1879, 3) and being a 'rather conservative' candidate (Shaw, 216), he also received significant support from the Irish population—a result, it seems, of his family's connection with the Irish nationalist leader Daniel O'Connell, a cousin of his father. Rioting during the election by his sympathizers, including '500 supporters dressed in green' (McDonald, 118) who declared he 'was standing for the Roman Catholic church and freedom for Ireland' (Shaw, 216), was said to have lost him much support among other voters. He was defeated easily, but in August 1845 was elected to the council to represent the Port Phillip (later Victoria) district, an event that 'greatly gratified' the governor, George Gipps, as O'Connell had defeated a leading spokesman of the squatter opposition to the government (Shaw, 350).

O'Connell remained in the council for three years, before being appointed crown lands commissioner for the Burnett pastoral district, then in the far north of the colonized area of Australia. In 1854 he was appointed official resident in the development of Port Curtis as a government post. The establishment of this post has been called 'one of Sydney's most devious acts of self-interest' (Fitzgerald, 109), as it clearly had the aim of fostering a township (to be known as Gladstone) as a capital for the soon to be formed colony of Queensland. It was feared in New South Wales that the likely southern location of the new capital, at Brisbane, would mean that the northern parts of the older colony would look to it rather than to Sydney.

Excessive expenditure, with little return in terms of development, was incurred to achieve this aim, and for this O'Connell received the blame when the political atmosphere in New South Wales altered. Henry Parkes succeeded in having a select committee of inquiry into the post of resident established in August 1855. The committee criticized not only the apparent waste of government funds but also O'Connell's capabilities. Particularly condemned were his 'capriciousness and want of consideration' in dealing with those under him, and the fact that his inordinate 'love of power' affected his ability to encourage the district's development (McDonald, 97). The position of government resident was abolished, and O'Connell returned to the post of lands commissioner. He was briefly reinstated as resident in response to a gold rush in the area in 1858, but again relieved of the post when Queensland was established in late 1859.

O'Connell resented the offer to return again to relatively junior positions and began a long campaign to receive compensation for the abolition of his post and the financial sacrifices he claimed his time at Port Curtis entailed. A later historian has suggested that his appointment to the Queensland legislative council in May 1860 was probably made 'for diplomatic reasons' (McDonald, 119). He was a minister without portfolio for three months in the Herbert government before being offered the presidency of the council in August 1860. As president, he acted in the place of the governor of the colony on four occasions, in gaps between viceregal appointments, and in 1868 was knighted.

O'Connell was embroiled in controversy on two occasions during his time as president. As acting governor in 1871 he was accused of accepting a bribe for agreeing to dissolve parliament. The resultant debate brought into the open his parlous financial state, and he was forced to admit that unpaid debts owing to the Bank of Queensland on his pastoral properties meant that the bank's official liquidator was about to take action against him. In 1875 his family connections to Daniel O'Connell again led to political difficulties. He attended a function commemorating the centenary of the nationalist leader's birth. During the ceremonies a toast to the health of the pope preceded the loyal toast to the queen. This caused a degree of outrage, and O'Connell was forced quickly and clearly to restate his loyalty to the monarch.

Most remembered of O'Connell was his tendency to appear 'hot of temper, sometimes inconsistent, inordinately proud' (McDonald, 88). Politically, he was 'very conservative … described as a high Tory' (*Brisbane Courier*, 24 March 1879, 3). He was provincial grandmaster of the freemasons of the Irish constitution, colonel of the Queensland volunteer brigade, and president of the Australasian Association and the Queensland turf club.

O'Connell remained president of the council until he died of throat cancer, while staying at Parliament House in Brisbane during renovations to his own home, on 23 March 1879. He was buried at Toowong cemetery, Brisbane, on 25 March.   MARC BRODIE

Sources *Brisbane Courier* (24 March 1879) · *Brisbane Courier* (26 March 1879) · H. J. Gibbney, 'O'Connell, Sir Maurice Charles', *AusDB*, vol. 5 · L. McDonald, *Gladstone: city that waited* (Gladstone, 1988) · *Gipps–La Trobe correspondence, 1839–1846*, ed. A. G. L. Shaw (1989) · R. Fitzgerald, *From the dreaming to 1915: a history of Queensland* (1982) · J. H. Heaton, *Australian dictionary of dates and men of the time* (1879) · F. Johns, *An Australian biographical dictionary* (1934) · P. Mennell, *The dictionary of Australasian biography* (1892) · *DNB*
Archives Mitchell L., NSW, corresp. and papers · Mitchell L., NSW, corresp. and papers [microfilm]
Likenesses portrait, 1845, Mitchell L., NSW; repro. in McDonald, *Gladstone* · photograph, 1869, repro. in McDonald, *Gladstone*

Wealth at death 'in straitened circumstances': *DNB*

O'Connell, Sir Maurice Charles Philip (1768–1848), army officer and colonial administrator in Australia, was born in co. Kerry, Ireland, the son of Charles Philip O'Connell. Tall, strapping, and penniless, the son of a younger son, he was dependent on the bounty of his kinsman, Count Daniel O'Connell, of the Irish brigade. With this support he studied for two or three years in Paris for the Roman Catholic priesthood, but in 1785 his father arranged his entry to a military school, and in 1792 he became a captain in the French émigré forces serving on the French frontier under the duke of Brunswick.

When the Irish brigade was taken into British pay O'Connell was appointed captain in Daniel O'Connell's 4th regiment of the Irish brigade, from 1 October 1794, and served with it in the West Indies until it was broken up and he was put on half pay. On 12 May 1800 he obtained a company in the 1st West India regiment with which he served in Surinam, Grenada, and Dominica. In January 1805 he was promoted brevet major and transferred to the 5th regiment. He saw much action in the West Indies, and particularly distinguished himself at Roseau in Dominica in February 1805 when it was unsuccessfully attacked by greatly superior French forces. In October 1806 he was transferred to the 73rd regiment, of which he became lieutenant-colonel on 4 May 1809.

In December 1809 the 1st battalion of the 73rd, with O'Connell in command, arrived in Port Jackson with the new governor of New South Wales, Lachlan Macquarie. O'Connell was commissioned lieutenant-governor in January 1810 and on 8 May, soon after his first arrival in Sydney, he married Mary Putland (1782/3–1864), daughter and lifelong defender of the deposed governor William Bligh and widow of Lieutenant John Putland. He was appointed a trustee of the Female Orphan Institution, steward of the racecourse, and president of the Philanthropic Society. But by August 1813 Macquarie was urging the removal of O'Connell and the 73rd regiment from the colony.

In April 1814 O'Connell sailed for Ceylon with the regiment, which he commanded during the war in Kandy in 1815. He failed to obtain appointment to Van Diemen's Land as lieutenant-governor and retired on half pay on the return home of his troops. In 1819 he was promoted colonel, and in July 1830 major-general. He was knighted and made a KCH in 1834, became a lieutenant-general on 9 November 1841, and was appointed colonel of the 80th foot in 1844.

O'Connell returned to Sydney in 1838 having been appointed to command the forces in New South Wales. On his arrival he was appointed to the executive and legislative councils. In 1843–4 he was a nominated member of the partly elected legislative council. When Governor Gipps departed in July 1846, O'Connell administered the government until the arrival of Sir Charles Fitzroy the next month. He was succeeded as commander of the forces in New South Wales by Major-General Wynyard in 1847. Thenceforth, he remained in the colony but took no part in public affairs. He died at Darlinghurst, Sydney, on 25 May 1848 and was buried at St James's Church, Sydney. His widow lived in Paris for some years and then in London, where she died in 1864. There were two sons and one daughter. The elder son was the well-known Australian statesman Sir Maurice Charles *O'Connell.

H. M. CHICHESTER, *rev.* JOHN EDDY

Sources *AusDB* · [F. Watson], ed., *Historical records of Australia* (1914–25) · R. Cannon, ed., *Historical record of the seventy-third regiment* (1851) · J. D. Ritchie, *Lachlan Macquarie* (1986) · M. Austin, *The army in Australia, 1840–50* (1979) · Mrs M. J. O'Connell, *The last colonel of the Irish brigade*, 2 vols. (1892) · *Army List* · *GM*, 2nd ser., 30 (1848), 543

Archives Mitchell L., NSW, corresp. and papers

O'Connell, Morgan (1804–1885), soldier and politician, second son of Daniel *O'Connell (1775–1847) and his wife, Mary (1778–1836), was born in Tralee, co. Kerry, on 31 October 1804. Together with his elder brother, Maurice, he was a student at the Jesuit Clongowes Wood College from early 1815 but did not apply himself to his studies. In 1819 General John Devereux was in Dublin to enlist military aid for the revolution in South America. He succeeded in embodying the Irish South American legion, and O'Connell was one of the officers who purchased a commission in it. The second contingent of the legion reached the Spanish main in June 1820, with O'Connell in the position of aide-de-camp to Devereux. At Barranquilla in late August 1820 he obtained an introduction to Simón Bolívar, to whom he presented a letter of greeting and support from his father, dated 17 April 1820. Following a series of mishaps O'Connell arrived home safely in early 1822, still aged only seventeen. Apprenticeship to an attorney and cadetships in the French and British forces having been considered and rejected by the family, O'Connell set out on a career in the Austrian army. He served with them in northern Italy and in Hungary before returning to Ireland in 1830.

On 19 December 1832 O'Connell entered parliament for County Meath as a supporter of his father's policy of repeal of the union, and continued to represent that constituency until January 1840, when he was appointed assistant registrar of deeds for Ireland. Soon after, he married, on 23 July 1840, Kate Mary, youngest daughter of Michael Balfe of South Park, co. Roscommon. They had no children. In 1846, following representations by his father, he was appointed registrar of deeds, a position he held until his retirement in 1869. During his parliamentary career he fought a duel with William, second Baron Alvanley, a lieutenant-colonel in the army, at Chalk Farm on 4 May 1835. A challenge had been sent by Alvanley to O'Connell's father, who, in accordance with a vow he had made after killing a man in a similar affair of honour, declined the meeting. Morgan thereupon took up the challenge: two shots each were exchanged, but neither party was hurt. Afterwards, in December 1835, O'Connell declined to meet a challenge from Benjamin Disraeli, in consequence of an attack made on Disraeli by Morgan's father.

Morgan O'Connell died at his home, 12 St Stephen's Green, Dublin, on 20 January 1885, and was buried in Glasnevin cemetery on 23 January.

G. C. BOASE, *rev.* R. V. COMERFORD

Sources M. R. O'Connell, 'O'Connell and his family', *The world of Daniel O'Connell*, ed. D. McCartney (1980), 19–29 · *The correspondence of Daniel O'Connell*, ed. M. R. O'Connell, 2–4, IMC (1973–7) · *Freeman's Journal* [Dublin] (21 Jan 1885), 5 · *Freeman's Journal* [Dublin] (24 Jan 1885), 5 · R. Blake, *Disraeli* (1966), 125–6 · *The Greville memoirs*, ed. H. Reeve, pt 1, vol. 1 (1874), 256–7 · *The Times* (5 May 1835), 4 · *The Times* (31 Dec 1835), 5 · *The Times* (22–4 Jan 1885) · Burke, *Gen. GB* (1894) · *CGPLA Ire.* (1885) · O. MacDonagh, *O'Connell: the life of Daniel O'Connell, 1775–1847* (1991)

Archives NL Ire. · University College, Dublin

Likenesses J. P. Haverty, group portrait, lithograph with watercolour, pubd 1845 (after his earlier drawing *The monster meeting of the 20th September 1843, at Clifden in the Irish highlands*), NG Ire. · J. Doyle, caricature, chalk drawing, BM · J. Gubbins, oils, Derrynane House, co. Kerry

Wealth at death £2034 2s. 6d.: probate, 13 March 1885, *CGPLA Ire.* · nil in England: Irish probate sealed in England, 7 May 1885, *CGPLA Eng. & Wales*

O'Connell, Moritz [Murty], **Baron O'Connell in the nobility of the Holy Roman empire** (1738–1830), army officer in the Austrian service, was born in Ireland; he was christened Murty (*recte* Muircheartach), but this name was subsequently changed to Moritz. The son of Maurice O'Connell of Tarmon, co. Kerry, and his wife, Mary O'Sullivan Beare, sister of Murty Oge O'Sullivan Beare; he was the grandson of John O'Connell, captain in the king's guard, who had fought at Limerick, Londonderry, Aughrim, and the Boyne. In spring 1761 Murty O'Connell travelled to the continent with his cousin and lifelong friend Daniel Charles O'Connell. A family ballad written at the time lamented the fact that Catholics were forced to leave Ireland to forward their careers; it urged: 'to the land of the lily [France] bear the shamrock of our isle, may they bloom above the blood stained rose [England]' (O'Connell, 1.69). However, it was to be Daniel's nephew, also Daniel O'Connell, who finally gained Catholic emancipation for Ireland.

Both men served in the last two campaigns of the Seven Years' War, Moritz O'Connell as an Austrian officer in Marshal Daune's regiment of horse and his cousin as an officer in the French infantry regiment. O'Connell, who was known as Moritz in Austria, attracted the notice of Empress Maria Theresa while he was serving as a sentry in one of her palaces, and received the gift of a watch. He was soon transferred from his military duties to the imperial chamberlain's department. He held the office of imperial chamberlain for fifty-nine years under the emperors Joseph, Leopold, and Francis, and by 1806 he had been created a baron and had attained the rank of general. He married and had one daughter. O'Connell died in Vienna early in 1830, aged ninety-one, and left his property to his relative Geoffrey O'Connell of Cork.

H. M. CHICHESTER, *rev.* ROSEMARY RICHEY

Sources Mrs M. J. O'Connell, *The last colonel of the Irish brigade*, 2 vols. (1892) · *Annual Register* (1831), 254–5 · IGI

O'Connell, Peter [Peadar Ó Conaill] (**1754/5–1826**), Irish scholar and lexicographer, was born at Carne, now Money Point, about 5 miles east of Kilrush in co. Clare, in an Irish-speaking district. Nothing is known of his parents (he had a brother, Patrick) or his early education. A 'tall, gaunt, swarthy man, large-limbed and black-haired, dark-eyed, and strongly built' (Wall, 102), Peter O'Connell was a hedge-school master and scholar–scribe. Typically some of his extant manuscripts contain later verse, Ossianic tales, and devotional matter. Atypically he probably possessed more printed books than other scribes, and was more acquainted with contemporary scholarship. His interests evolved towards genealogy and, more notably, towards lexicography. He possessed Edward Lhuyd's *Archaeologica Britannica* and James MacPherson's *Temora*, and knew William Shaw's *Galic and English Dictionary* (1780).

These books may have influenced O'Connell's remarkable decision in 1785, as he began work on an Irish–English dictionary, to travel in Ireland, the Scottish highlands, and Wales, and to spend time on studying records in Dublin and at the house of Charles O'Conor at Belanagare, co. Roscommon. He returned to co. Clare in 1800. In 1812 O'Connell accepted accommodation from Dr Simon O'Reardon of Limerick to work solely on the dictionary. He was assisted by Malachi O'Curry (Maoilsheachlainn Ó Comhraidhe), brother of the Irish scholar Eugene O'Curry (Eoghan Ó Comhraidhe) who knew O'Connell well. He remained in Limerick until 1819 when O'Reardon died. According to Séamus Ó Casaide it was most likely Dr O'Reardon's death, and not some disagreement between them, that led to O'Connell's departure and to the abandonment of preparations for the publication of his Irish dictionary. Thereafter O'Connell was obliged to return to Carne and resided for the rest of his life in his brother's house. He died aged seventy-one on 24 February 1826 and was buried at Burrane, near Killimer, Kilrush, co. Clare.

After his death O'Connell's dictionary was acquired by James Hardiman, who 'had it transcribed for the press' by John O'Donovan (Hardiman, Egerton MS 83). In 1832 Hardiman sold his manuscripts to the British Museum (the autograph of the dictionary is now Egerton MS 83 and O'Donovan's two-volume transcript is Egerton MSS 84 and 85). It was never published, but was, nevertheless, O'Connell's greatest achievement. It does not distinguish the parts of speech, and citations are far too sporadic, but it is a comprehensive delineation of the Irish lexicon. Its definitions are authoritative, and Standish Hayes O'Grady was delighted to find in it proof that native scholarship, independently of German 'keltologues', understood the early infixed pronouns. It has been consulted with profit by later lexicographers and editors. O'Connell led the way for the generation which made the Irish-language heritage accessible to wider scholarship. For one of the greatest of that generation, Eugene O'Curry, he was 'the justly celebrated Irish scholar'.   MÁIRTÍN Ó MURCHÚ

Sources T. O'Rahilly and others, *Catalogue of Irish manuscripts in the Royal Irish Academy*, 30 vols. (Dublin, 1926–70) · S. H. O'Grady, R. Flower, and M. Dillon, *Catalogue of Irish manuscripts in the British Museum*, 3 vols. (1926–53) · P. Ó Fiannachta and P. Walsh, *Lámhscríbhinní Gaeilge Choláiste Phádraig Má Nuad*, [8 pts] (1943–73), vols. 2–8 [MSS C 74(c) C 25(d), C 99] · J. Hardiman, prefatory notes, BL, Egerton MS 83; 84 · E. O'Curry, notes, BL, Egerton MS 83; Maynooth MS C 38(k) · T. Wall, 'Teige Mac Mahon and Peter O'Connell: seanchaí and scholar in co. Clare', *Béaloideas*, 30/1962 (1964), 89–104 · S. Ó Casaide, 'Peadar Ó Conaill's literary patron', *Irish Booklover*, 16 (1928), 119 · D. F. Gleeson, 'Peter O'Connell: scholar and scribe, 1755–1826', *Studies*, 23 (1944), 342–8

Archives BL, Irish glossaries, Add. MS 28257, fol. 2b; Add. MS 28258 · Royal Irish Acad., genealogies, 23 H 22 · Royal Irish Acad., glossary to *Caithréim Thoirdhealbhaigh*, 23 G 18 · Royal Irish Acad., lexicographical notes, 23 L 21 · Royal Irish Acad., Ossianic and miscellaneous matter, 23 C 30 | NL Ire.

Wealth at death books and MSS; insignificant monetary value; one lot sold for £7: Wall, 'Teige Mac Mahon', 97

O'Connolly, Owen (*d.* 1649), plot discloser and parliamentarian army officer, was born in co. Monaghan; his parents' names are unknown. He was brought up a puritan in the household of Sir Hugh Clotworthy and was the servant of the latter's son, Sir John Clotworthy; by 1641 he was living on Clotworthy lands at Moneymore, co. Londonderry. By then he was also married to an Englishwoman, with a son, Arthur (who was mentally handicapped), and a daughter, Martha, who later married Hugh Rowley (whose mother Letitia was a daughter of Sir Hugh Clotworthy).

O'Connolly was cousin, foster-brother, and friend to Colonel Hugh *Mac Mahon, the 1641 conspirator. On 22 October 1641 O'Connolly made one statement on the disclosure of the plot, and a more extensive statement some time later. O'Connolly's account of the 1641 plot has inconsistencies and shortcomings; he may have been more involved than he subsequently cared to admit, and may have concocted the account to explain his knowledge of the plot. In O'Connolly's version the plot was characterized by widespread involvement of Catholic gentry and nobility, and included a plan for a general massacre of protestants. Such allegations were highly influential, for it was in this form that the Dublin and London governments first heard of the plot. According to O'Connolly, about April 1641, while in Dublin, Mac Mahon spoke to O'Connolly about an intended Irish combination against the English. O'Connolly urged him to forswear this plot, and reveal it to the lords justices. On 18 October the colonel wrote to his cousin, asking him to meet him at his house in Monaghan, but when O'Connolly arrived the conspirator had left, and O'Connolly proceeded to Dublin on 22 October, arriving about 6 p.m. at Mac Mahon's lodging. The pair then went to Connor, Lord Maguire's lodging; there Mac Mahon disclosed to O'Connolly the plot to take Dublin Castle on the morrow, and to attack the English throughout the country. O'Connolly again sought to dissuade him, and advised him to reveal the plot to the authorities. Later that evening, pretending to relieve himself (they had been drinking), O'Connolly slipped away from Mac Mahon's party, and arrived at Lord Justice Sir William Parsons's home after nine o'clock, to disclose what he had just heard.

Parsons was at first reluctant to believe the report of this unknown, lowly, and inebriated informant; however, he gave order for the castle guard to be strengthened, and for the mayor and sheriffs to have strong watches set; Mac Mahon and Maguire were among those captured. On 25 October O'Connolly wrote to Mac Mahon, saying he disclosed the plot 'out of conscience to God, and loyalty to his majesty, and pity to the many innocent souls that would have been cut off' (Gilbert, 1.786). Hearing of O'Connolly's disclosure, Colonel Owen Roe O'Neill was furious, saying he wondered 'how or where that villain should live, for if he were in Ireland, sure they would pull him in pieces there; and if he lived in England there were footmen and other Irishmen enough to kill him' (ibid., 1.398).

On 25 October the lords justices sent O'Connolly with a letter to the lord lieutenant of Ireland, the earl of Leicester, in London. On 1 November the English parliament made him an award of £500, together with a pension of £200 p.a.; on 3 November John Pym presented O'Connolly's sworn examination to the parliament. By December parliament had recommended the Irishman for a military command (Oliver Cromwell promoted his petition), and in 1642 he was an officer in Sir John Clotworthy's foot regiment. Throughout he adhered to the parliamentarian side. In November 1643 the English parliament sent O'Connolly to introduce and promote the solemn league and covenant among the British commanders in Ulster. In February 1646, with the rank of lieutenant-colonel, he received a commission to command Clotworthy's regiment in Ulster. As a military officer O'Connolly became a ruling elder, and was often a member of the presbytery. In December 1646 the parliamentary commissioners at Belfast sent him as emissary to the Scottish parliament. In spring 1647 O'Connolly was one of the agents representing the Irish parliamentarian regiments; while in England, he was placed in charge of a regiment destined for Ireland, but in July 1647 this regiment was disbanded by order of parliament.

By the autumn of 1648 a charge was being levelled against O'Connolly, and it was being investigated by Colonel George Monck, then commander-in-chief in Ulster. The case may have referred to an allegation that O'Connolly had killed an officer's brother in a duel in 1648. In March 1649 O'Connolly went to London, and a committee of the council of state was appointed to examine his case. In April Monck was ordered to proceed with O'Connolly's trial, as there was great need of the Ulsterman's service. O'Connolly presented a report on the besieged Dublin garrison from Colonel Michael Jones to the English parliament in July. The London authorities expressed confidence in O'Connolly, continuing payments to him, and Cromwell wrote to parliament on his behalf.

In the autumn of 1649 O'Connolly was shot in a skirmish with soldiers of Colonel John Hamilton's regiment at Dunadry, co. Antrim. He died of his wounds at Connor, co. Antrim, and was buried at Antrim.

BRIAN MAC CUARTA

Sources J. T. Gilbert, ed., *A contemporary history of affairs in Ireland from 1641 to 1652*, 1 (1879), 353–9, 398, 786 · A. Clarke, *The Old English in Ireland, 1625–42* (Dublin, 1966); repr. (2000), 161 · [E. Hogan], *The history of the warr of Ireland from 1641 to 1653* (1873) · P. Adair, *A true narrative of the rise and progress of the Presbyterian church in Ireland (1623–1670)*, ed. W. D. Killen (1866), 84, 176–7 · *CSP Ire.*, 1633–47, 437, 559–62; 1647–50, 755–6; 1660–62, 456–7; 1663–5, 59 · *CSP dom.*, 1648–9, 317; 1649–50, 27, 42, 62, 77, 242 · C. H. Firth and G. Davies, *The regimental history of Cromwell's army*, 2 vols. (1940), vol. 1, pp. 350–51; vol. 2, pp. 652–4 · G. Hill, ed., *The Montgomery manuscripts, 1603–1706* (1869), 172–3, 326 · *The writings and speeches of Oliver Cromwell*, ed. W. C. Abbott and C. D. Crane, 4 vols. (1937–47), vol. 1, pp.147–8; vol. 2, p. 98 · *Report on the manuscripts of the earl of Egmont*, 2 vols. in 3, HMC, 63 (1905–9), vol. 1, pp. 356, 365 [letters of John Davies to Sir Philip Perceval, [Feb] 1647] · *JHC*, 6 (1648–51), 268 · M. Perceval-Maxwell, *The outbreak of the Irish rebellion of 1641* (1994), 210–11

O'Connor. *See also* Ó Conchobhair, O'Conor, Ua Conchobair.

O'Connor, Aedh. *See* Ua Conchobair, Áed (d. 1067).

O'Connor [*formerly* Conner; *later* Condorcet-O'Connor], **Arthur** (1763–1852), Irish nationalist and political theorist, was born on 4 July 1763 at Connerville, near Bandon in co. Cork, the second youngest of nine children, four daughters and five sons, of Roger Conner (d. 1798), MP, and Anne Longfield (d. 1782), daughter of Robert Longfield MP and sister of Richard Longfield, made Viscount Longueville in 1800. Arthur and his brother Roger Conner [*see* O'Connor, Roger] changed their surname to O'Connor in the 1780s. Arthur's upbringing and education were typical of the prosperous Munster Anglican gentry and he was steeped in their attitudes, including their notorious anti-Catholicism. His early schooling was at Bandon and at Mr Browne's school, Castlelyons, and he entered Trinity College, Dublin, as a pensioner in 1779. He delayed his legal education at the inns of court owing to his grief at his mother's death but was called to the Irish bar in 1788, though he never practised. His father broke up the family estate after his wife's death and Arthur's portion allowed him to buy his own property and build a house, Fort Arthur, in the vicinity of Kinsale. Through his uncle's political influence he was MP for Philipstown from 1790 and was appointed high sheriff of Cork for 1791.

O'Connor's intellectual and cultural interests differentiated him from his class. He was an early and passionate enthusiast for Adam Smith's political economy. He renounced anti-Catholicism through his discovery, or perhaps invention, of his own descent from the O'Connors of co. Kerry, a Gaelic noble family. This motivated his connection with Charles O'Conor of Belangare and an interest in Irish antiquity. A visit to France in 1784 had convinced him that there the monarchy could not survive and he confirmed his enthusiasm for the French Revolution, despite an acquaintance with Edmund Burke, in a return journey in 1792, when he first met Lafayette. Yet these views did not prevent his uncle, Richard Longfield, from proposing to William Pitt in 1792 that O'Connor be given office in the Irish administration as part of the package of measures to encourage independent support for the ministry in the Irish House of Commons.

The outbreak of war with France in 1793, for which, in common with much of the opposition, O'Connor blamed Pitt, strained his commitment to establishment politics.

Arthur O'Connor (1763–1852), by John Godefroy (after François Pascal Simon, Baron Gérard, c.1804)

He finally broke with them after the débâcle of the Fitzwilliam viceroyalty. The debate on the Catholic Emancipation Bill in 1795 gave him a platform from which to announce his support of emancipation, manhood suffrage, and the full agenda of political reform, and from which to hint at separatism and the possibility of revolution:

> France must have lost her senses if she hesitates as to what part she must take: it is not an eighty-fourth department you will have moulded to her wishes; it is not simply *La Vendée* you will have kindled in the bosom of your country.
> ('Arthur O'Connor's speech on the Catholic question, in the House of Commons, on the 4th of May 1795', *The Beauties of the Press*, 1800, 597)

This speech catapulted him to prominence in radical politics in England as much as in Ireland. He made lasting political friendships with Richard Brinsley Sheridan and Sir Francis Burdett as well as gaining entry to the Devonshire circle. His connections among the Foxites, including Charles James Fox himself, Lord Moira, and Sheridan, were his character witnesses when he was tried for treason at Margate in May 1798.

O'Connor's politics would have made him a radical in England, but the political conditions in Ireland made a principled but pacific opposition to the government almost impossible. As political options polarized, few members of the establishment chose republicanism over protestant ascendancy; O'Connor and his friend Lord Edward Fitzgerald were the two most prominent members of the religious and political establishment to do so. In 1796 O'Connor joined the United Irishmen and travelled in company with Fitzgerald in May and June through Hamburg and Basel to Angers to negotiate a French invasion in support of an Irish rising. Building on Wolfe Tone's impressive diplomatic work, O'Connor and General Hoche agreed to French military support for an independent Irish republic. The result was the abortive landing at Bantry Bay in December 1796.

O'Connor played little part in the planning for the 1798 rebellion. Though he represented Ulster on the United Irish Directory he could play little part in its deliberations. He was jailed from February to August 1797 and then arrested in England while trying to travel to France in April 1798 and so was either incarcerated or abroad for most of this period. His major contribution was as the most sophisticated political thinker in the movement. He developed his ideas in the pages of his Dublin newspaper *The Press* and in his most important pamphlet, *The State of Ireland* (1798). His project was to reinterpret Irish social and political development in the context of general European trends. Working from the Scottish social theorists, especially Smith, he argued for an ideal of the nation as a productive community organized through an equality of political and civil rights. His work blended French universalist ideas of politics with British patterns of commercial development to create a commercial republicanism. O'Connor thought that the defects of the British constitutional order were most spectacularly evident in Ireland, but not confined to it. His eventual goal was to transform the British Isles into a comity of sister republics. The alternative, he argued, was state oppression punctuated by outbreaks of sectarian *jacquerie*. O'Connor was by no means the only United Irishman who thought in terms of universal political principles and in an international context, but his work made the most original use of those principles in the complexity of the Irish situation.

After the failure of the 1798 rebellion O'Connor was confined in Fort St George, along with twenty other prisoners, where previous disagreements between O'Connor and Thomas Addis Emmett over political tactics degenerated into personal antipathy. O'Connor had a domineering personality and an ironic disposition; Benjamin Constant wrote of him that 'he has something of the French defect of joking about his own opinion' (B. Constant, *Journaux intimes*, ed. A. Roulin and C. Roth, 1952, 189), and this made him a difficult partner in adversity. His personal fortunes did improve after his release to France on the peace of Amiens in 1802. Napoleon gave him the rank of *général de division* in 1804, though without any command. He became part of the *idéologue* circle and in 1807 married the writer Eliza Condorcet (1791–1867), the daughter of Sophie de Grouchy and Marie-Jean-Antoine-Nicolas de Caritat, marquis de Condorcet. His last publication was to be the definitive edition of Condorcet's works and he took the name Condorcet-O'Connor as the family title. In 1808 he and his wife bought the former château of Mirabeau père at Le Bignon in the department of the Loiret. He took French nationality in 1818.

Condorcet-O'Connor's later life was difficult. His three sons predeceased him and his relationship with his brother Roger collapsed over disputes about Roger's use of the power of attorney he had been given over Arthur's Irish property. This put a barrier between Arthur and Roger's son, Feargus O'Connor, leader of the Chartists. Furthermore, his reputation in Ireland suffered an eclipse. To the Irish public, Lord Longueville's judgement that 'of all bad men he is the worst' was too epigrammatic to resist. Though he initially made friendly contact with Daniel O'Connell during his visit to Ireland in 1834, he later condemned him as a tool of the Jesuits. Much of his later work, including his *Monopoly, the Cause of All Evil* (1849), relapsed into rampant anti-Catholicism and he has not been included in the pantheon of national heroes. He died at Le Bignon on 25 April 1852, and was buried there in the park.   JAMES LIVESEY

Sources Le Bignon, Loiret, France, O'Connor MSS · NA Ire., Rebellion MSS, 620/15/3 · R. R. Madden, *The United Irishmen: their lives and times*, 2nd edn, 2nd ser. (1858) · W. J. McNeven, *Pieces of Irish history* (1807) · M. Elliott, *Partners in revolution: the United Irishmen and France* (1982) · N. J. Curtin, *The United Irishmen: popular politics in Ulster and Dublin, 1791–1798* (1994) · *The letters of Richard Brinsley Sheridan*, ed. C. Price, 3 vols. (1966) · F. MacDermot, 'Arthur O'Connor', *Irish Historical Studies*, 15 (1966–7), 48–69
Archives Le Bignon, Loiret, France | NA Ire., Rebellion MSS, 620/15/3
Likenesses Irish school, line and stipple engraving, pubd 1797, NG Ire. · W. Ward, mezzotint, pubd 1798 (after J. D. Herbert), NG Ire. · F. Gérard, oils, 1804?, Le Bignon, Loiret, France · J. Godefroy, line and stipple engraving, pubd after 1804, NG Ire. · Isambey, engraving, 1807? · J. Gillray, caricatures · J. Godefroy, stipple (after F. Gérard, *c.*1804), NPG [*see illus.*] · Irish school, stipple (after J. D. Herbert), NG Ire.; repro. in *Irish Magazine* (1809) · group portrait, coloured lithograph (*The United Irish patriots of 1798*), NPG · oils, Le Bignon, Loiret, France

O'Connor, Brian [Bernard] (*d.* after **1559**), chieftain and rebel, was probably born in Dangan in co. Offaly, the eldest son of Cahir O'Connor (*d.* 1511), chieftain, and his first wife. Cahir was chieftain of the O'Connor Faly sept or clan from 1474 to 1511. The O'Connors emerged as the dominant midland sept in the mid-fifteenth century under the leadership of Cahir's grandfather Calvagh More O'Connor (*fl.* 1425–1458). Cahir lacked Calvagh's authority and junior O'Connor branches re-emerged as challengers for the lordship. Such discord within the sept attracted the predatory attentions of Gerald Fitzgerald, eighth earl of Kildare, who sought to establish Geraldine dominance over the midlands. He had Cahir assassinated in 1511, ousted the ruling O'Connors, and established a client regime under the MacTadhgs (Brian O'Connor's cousins). However, Offaly's minor septs still supported Cahir's family and Brian rose to power during the confinement in England of Gerald Fitzgerald, ninth earl of Kildare (1487–1534), from 1519 to 1523. After a brief succession struggle, the details of which are unknown, Brian was accepted by his sept as the O'Connor Faly by mid-1520.

Brian dealt with the prospect of a MacTadhg restoration by supporting Geraldine interests, calculating that Kildare would accept his accession in return for O'Connor backing. In 1520–21 Brian assisted pro-Geraldine attacks on the pale. His strategy worked, and after Kildare's restoration in 1523 he formally became the earl's client, with Con Bacach O'Neill acting as *sláinte* or guarantor. Brian's

marriage to Mary (*d.* in or after 1596), eldest daughter of Kildare and his second wife, Elizabeth, before 1526, strengthened the alliance further. The couple had nine sons, including Cathal O'Connor [*see below*], and two daughters. Brian was closely identified with Geraldine interests from the 1520s and was Kildare's chief ally during the 1525 campaign against Mulroney O'Carroll. During Kildare's second detention in England (1526–30), Brian, acting on the earl's secret instructions, played the key role in demonstrating that the Irish lordship could not be governed without Geraldine co-operation. Throughout 1527–8 he ravaged the pale, famously shoeing his horse at Tara, co. Meath, and even captured the vice-deputy, Richard Nugent, third Baron Delvin, on 12 May 1528. It worked. Kildare was allowed to return to Ireland in 1530 in order to suppress 'confederacies that … Ochonour had made with divers great Hirishemen' (*State Papers, Henry VIII*, 2.127–8). He displayed his gratitude by bestowing gifts of horses and armour upon Brian. In addition Kildare persuaded the Irish privy council to resume payment of Brian's blackrent (cancelled in 1528) and to pardon his offences in November 1530.

Brian's influence was at its zenith, secure from challengers within his lordship and the dominant lord in the midlands. However, his relationship with Kildare tied his fortunes inextricably with those of the Geraldines and this explains why, even as the Kildare revolt of 1534–5 collapsed, Brian remained loyal to the last. By mid-1535 only Brian's support allowed his brother-in-law Thomas *Fitzgerald, tenth earl of Kildare (1513–1537), to continue in rebellion. This persuaded the government to maintain Brian's brother and tanist Cahir Roe O'Connor (*d.* 1548), who had long sought to be lord, against the rebels. His defection proved decisive, and in August 1535 Kildare and Brian submitted.

Despite his prominent role in the rebellion Brian escaped lightly: after humbly submitting and undertaking to live as a dutiful subject, he was fined 800 cattle. Thereafter, the government, preoccupied with reordering the pale, withdrew support for Cahir Roe, allowing Brian to restore his authority within Offaly. Cahir Roe was expelled from Offaly in 1536. This flagrant repudiation of his submission, coupled with his failure to pay his fine, persuaded the new lord deputy, Leonard Grey, Viscount Graney, to punish Brian. Therefore in May 1537 Graney, guided by Brian's former prisoner Delvin, invaded Offaly. He captured Brian's strongholds of Brackland and Dangan, and placed them, along with 'the governaunce of the countrie', in Cahir Roe's hands (*State Papers, Henry VIII*, 2.442–5). Brian, who fled before the lord deputy, remained at large, dividing his time in exile between Offaly, Tipperary, and Leix. Although Graney believed Brian was 'more lyker a begger then he that ever was a captyn or ruler of a contre', and celebrated his reduced circumstances—'goyng from on [one] to another of hys olde frynds to have mete and drynke'—Brian retained support among Offaly's lesser septs (ibid., 2.474–5). With their backing, and that of Ferganainm O'Carroll, the O'Dunne family, and the O'Meagher family, Brian regained the lordship in

November 1537. Recognizing that Cahir Roe was unable to uphold his authority without substantial government assistance, and despite his earlier description of Brian as 'as ranke a traitour alwey to the King [Henry VIII] as can be divised', Graney accepted the political reality and thereafter sought to use Brian's regional influence to stabilize the midlands (ibid., 2.437–9).

At his formal submission before the Irish privy council Brian renounced his blackrents, promised to pay rent to the king, and petitioned to be elevated to the peerage as baron of Offaly, with confirmation of title to his lands. For some time afterwards he remained quiet, but following Graney's fall he once more ravaged the pale in April and May 1540. Brian's duplicity had long exasperated the king, but, conscious of Brian's continuing influence among the midland septs, the new lord deputy, Sir Anthony St Leger, convinced the king to pardon him. In 1541 St Leger persuaded Brian to formally renew his submission and to accept government arbitration of his dispute with Cahir Roe. During the remainder of his first term of office St Leger overlooked Brian's minor indiscretions in the midlands, while Brian paid his rents and refrained from disturbing the pale. This accommodation—which saw St Leger propose Brian's elevation to the peerage and grant him a house and lands in Dublin for his better maintenance while in attendance on the government—prompted the lord deputy's Irish opponents to sardonically describe Brian as 'your lordshipes old frende'.

However, when Brian attacked the pale in 1546, during St Leger's absence in England, he finally exhausted the government's patience. Upon his return in mid-1547 St Leger devastated Offaly twice, without engaging Brian in battle or receiving his submission. Although Brian escaped to Connaught, where he remained until early 1548, St Leger's punitive campaigns greatly eroded his support within Offaly, and upon his return he discovered 'that, through terror, no one dared to give [him] food or protection'. Although Brian continued in opposition until the following winter, 'having been abandoned by the Irish', he was forced to seek government support to regain his former authority (*AFM*, s.a. 1547). To this purpose he submitted in November 1548. He was arrested and transferred to the Marshalsea prison in London, where he remained until 1554, although he was pardoned in February 1549. A programme of plantation was instituted in the midlands in his absence. Against this background his sons Donagh (d. 1558) and Rory sought control of Offaly, but other O'Connor Faly kin-groups contested their claim and the lordship descended into anarchy.

Although Brian escaped from London in early 1552, he was recaptured as he tried to cross the border with Scotland, and promptly returned to prison. His release was granted by Mary I after the intercession of his daughter Margaret, who 'went to England, relying on the number of her friends and relatives there, and her knowledge of the English language' (*AFM*, s.a. 1553). The reality was that St Leger, anxious to settle Offaly, hoped Brian's restoration might end the disruptive succession struggle. On securing Rory as a pledge, the government permitted Brian to return to Ireland with Gerald Fitzgerald, eleventh earl of Kildare. However, Brian's influence was spent and when it became apparent that Rory's incarceration was undermining Donagh's position, St Leger swiftly arranged another exchange of hostages: Rory was released and Brian returned to Dublin Castle, where he died some time after 1559. He was survived by sons, among whom Donagh, Rory, Cormac (*fl.* 1550–1573), and Calvagh (d. 1564) were the most prominent, and daughters.

Cathal [Charles] **O'Connor** [*known as* Don Carlos] (1540–1596), spy and rebel, was sent to Scotland when still a child and accompanied Henri Cleutin, seigneur d'Oysel, the French ambassador, to France in 1560. He petitioned Sir Francis Throckmorton for his restoration and was advised, in order to prove his loyalty to Elizabeth I, to join the household of Mary, queen of Scots, as a spy. He was rewarded with the restoration of lands in Offaly in 1563, including Castle Brackland, but joined the rebellion of James fitz Maurice Fitzgerald and Gerald fitz James Fitzgerald, fourteenth earl of Desmond. He murdered Captain Henry Mackworth in 1582 and was forced to leave Ireland, first for Scotland, then for Spain. Cathal served Alessandro Farnese, duke of Parma, in the Netherlands but returned to Spain after the defeat of the Spanish Armada. He was known as Don Carlos, which caused unfortunate cases of mistaken identity because people thought that he was Philip II's only son with his first wife, and was granted an annual pension of 360 crowns. He continued to interest himself in Irish affairs, corresponding with Hugh O'Neill, second earl of Tyrone, and mediating for him with Philip. In November 1596 Cathal, along with his mother, wife, and children, joined the new armada planned for Ireland at Lisbon, and drowned when the ship carrying them was wrecked on the way there.

DAVID FINNEGAN

Sources *State papers published under … Henry VIII*, 11 vols. (1830–52) · *AFM* · F. Fitzsimons, 'The lordship of O'Connor Faly, 1520–70', *Offaly: history and society*, ed. W. Nolan (Dublin, 1998) · state papers Ireland, Henry VIII, PRO, SP 60 · *The Irish fiants of the Tudor sovereigns*, 4 vols. (1994) · *DNB* · *Report on the manuscripts of Lord De L'Isle and Dudley*, 6 vols., HMC, 77 (1925–66)

O'Connor, Calvach, Don [Calvach O'Connor] (1584–1655), clan leader, was the eldest son of Hugh O'Connor Don (d. 1632) and his wife, Mary, daughter of Brian O'Rourke, lord of Breifne (co. Leitrim). The term don (*recte* donn, or brown) was used to distinguish this branch of the sept from the collateral O'Connor Roe (*recte* rua, or red) branch. In 1610 Hugh O'Connor Don executed a deed dividing his extensive territory, known as the Maghery (*Irish, machaire*, plain) in North Roscommon between his sons Calvach and Hugh Oge. The division did not, however, receive royal sanction and was therefore delayed. Some time before 1616 Calvach married Mary, daughter of Sir Theobald Burke, or Tibbot na Long (*Irish, long*, ship). O'Connor was apparently elected member of parliament for co. Roscommon for the 1613 parliament but the presiding officer called a second vote after most of O'Connor's voters had left the premises. With O'Connor's supporters allegedly prevented from returning by soldiers posted at the door, a candidate representing the New English interest was then elected. A government commission subsequently found that no impropriety had taken place. The finding was unsurprising in view of the government's determined, and successful, efforts to secure overall New English control of the Irish parliament. On Hugh O'Connor Don's death in 1632 his lands were finally divided between Calvach and his younger brother Hugh Oge. Calvach acquired the castle and demesne of Ballintober, co. Roscommon.

Following the outbreak of the 1641 rising, Calvach O'Connor was present, on Christmas eve, at an attack on the abbey of Roscommon as the 'reputed general of Roscommon' (deposition of John Ridge, TCD, MS 830, fol. 4) under the overall command of Con O'Rourke of Leitrim. O'Connor received some popular acclamation as 'King of Connacht' (deposition of Elizabeth Holliwell, TCD, MS 830, fol. 35)—a faint echo of the former prominence of the O'Connor Don lineage. Others, however, assumed a more prominent role. Con O'Rourke led the insurgent attack on Castle Coote, a strong government outpost south of Ballintober on the Galway border. In the course of this operation Hugh *O'Connor Don, eldest son of Calvach, was taken prisoner in March/April 1642 when Charles Coote surprised the besiegers' camp at Creggs. Calvach O'Connor was one of those subscribing in January 1642 to an appeal to the earl of Clanricarde to assume leadership of the Connaught forces. However, his brother Hugh and Lucas Dillon took the leading role in these negotiations.

According to Edmund Borlase, O'Connor remained inactive in the months following his son's capture 'though the tacit votes of that province did seem to own him as their king' (Borlase, 81). However, in July 1642 'he began to awake' (ibid.) and mobilized an army of about 2000 men at Ballintober. On the approach of government forces from Athlone a body of Irish pikemen attacked without waiting for support from their musketeers. The pikemen were driven back by superior firepower and the disordered formation routed by a cavalry charge and pursued back to Ballintober.

O'Connor did not play a prominent part in the military or political affairs of the confederate Catholic regime established in 1642. He was elected a member of the general assembly of the confederates on three occasions during the 1640s. He was one of the individuals exempted by name from pardon by the Cromwellians in 1652. He died in 1655, leaving two sons, Hugh and Charles. His widow, as a person (notionally) transplanted to Connaught, secured 700 acres out of a total estate of about 6000 acres.   PÁDRAIG LENIHAN

Sources C. O. O'Conor Don, *The O'Conors of Connaught: an historical memoir* (1891), 222–42 · C. O. O'Conor Don, *O'Connors of the county Roscommon* (1862) · [E. Borlase], *The history of the execrable Irish rebellion* (1652), 49, 81 · *History of the Irish confederation and the war in Ireland … by Richard Bellings*, ed. J. T. Gilbert, 1 (1882), 94–5 · deposition of John Ridge, TCD, MS 830, fol. 6 · deposition of Elizabeth Holliwell, TCD, MS 830, fols. 35–6 · P. O'Connor, *The royal O'Connors of Connaught* (1997) · TCD, MS 840, fol. 129 · M. Ó Siochrú, *Confederate Ireland, 1642–1649: a constitutional and political analysis* (1999), 258 ·

U. Burke, *Memoirs and letters of the marquis of Clanricarde and earl of St Albans* (1757), 67 · F. Grose, *The antiquities of Ireland* (1794), 83–4 · Burke, *Gen. Ire.* (1976), 900–01

O'Connor, Cathal. See Cathal mac Conchobair (*d.* 1010); Ó Conchobhair, Cathal (1152–1224).

O'Connor, Cathal (1540–1596). *See under* O'Connor, Brian (*d.* after 1559).

O'Connor, Charles Yelverton (1843–1902), civil engineer, the youngest son of John O'Connor (*d.* 1863), a landowner, of Gravelmount, Castletown, co. Meath, and (Mary) Elizabeth O'Keefe (*d.* 1863), the granddaughter of George Yelverton of Belle Isle, Tipperary, and great-niece of Barry Yelverton, first Lord Avonmore, was born at Gravelmount on 11 January 1843. In 1850 the family moved to Waterford, where Charles was later educated at the endowed school; at the age of seventeen, he was articled to John Chaloner Smith, a railway engineer. After experience of railway work in Ireland, in 1865 he emigrated to New Zealand, where he was employed by the Canterbury provincial government as an assistant engineer on the construction of the coach road from Christchurch to the Hokitika goldfields on the west coast. He was gradually promoted, and in 1870 was appointed engineer for the western part of the province. On 5 March 1874 he married Susan Laetitia, the daughter of William Ness, a Scottish-born architect then living in New Zealand. Later that year, when provincial governments were abolished, O'Connor worked for the national New Zealand government as district engineer for the combined Westland and Nelson districts. In 1880 he was elected to the London Institution of Civil Engineers. From then until 1883 he was inspecting engineer for the whole of the South Island; from 1883 to 1890 he was under-secretary for public works for New Zealand; and in 1890 he was made marine engineer for the colony.

In April 1891 O'Connor was appointed engineer-in-chief and general manager of railways in the colony of Western Australia at a salary of £1200, but after effecting striking improvements and extensions to the railway system he resigned the latter post in December 1896, in order that he might devote all his time to engineering work. The discovery of the Coolgardie goldfield in 1892 led to an extraordinary and rapid development of Western Australia, in which O'Connor, as engineer-in-chief, played a part second only to that of the premier, Sir John Forrest. In eleven years he undertook two important projects, namely Fremantle harbour and the Coolgardie water supply, besides a large number of roads, bridges, harbours, and jetties. He was also responsible for all new railway work, for which he had a lifelong passion. Under his leadership major lines were built from Perth to the southwest and northern regions of Western Australia and to its eastern goldfields.

The Fremantle harbour works, carried out from 1892 to 1902, at a cost of £1,459,000, provided a safe harbour for the largest ocean steamships at all states of the tide and in all weathers. It was formed by constructing north and south moles, and an inner harbour with wharves and jetties was established by dredging the mouth of the Swan River. The Coolgardie water scheme, carried out between 1898 and 1903 at a cost of £2,660,000, supplied water to the principal goldfields of the colony. The source was the Helena River, on which, about 23 miles from Perth, a reservoir was constructed whence 5 million gallons of water could be pumped daily to Coolgardie, a distance of 328 miles. This bold plan, without precedent anywhere in the world at that time, was supported by Premier Forrest and approved by a panel of British experts, but many colonists were sceptical. O'Connor's use of an untried electric caulking machine to join the pipes drew particular fire in the local press. After Forrest left Perth for federal politics in 1901 O'Connor was particularly isolated and received little public backing from a weak and unstable government. By March 1902 tests had convinced him that the scheme would work. But the strain had affected his mental balance. On 10 March 1902, ten months before Forrest turned on the water, he rode his horse into the water near Robb's Jetty, Fremantle, and shot himself. He was buried at Fremantle cemetery on 12 March. He was survived by his wife and seven of their eight children, one of whom, Kathleen (Kate), later become a distinguished artist.

O'Connor was a tall and athletic man who enjoyed riding and often swam. The courtly manners of the Irish gentry which he had acquired in his youth were unusual in Perth, but despite a degree of reserve he was generally liked. Only his willingness and ability to work very long hours enabled him to cope with the demands of his job. His professional achievements earned him respect from his engineering peers in Britain as well as in New Zealand and Australia. He was created CMG in 1897.

W. F. SPEAR, *rev.* B. K. DE GARIS

Sources M. Tauman, *The chief, C. Y. O'Connor, 1843–1902* (1978) · M. Harris, 'O'Connor, Charles Yelverton', *AusDB*, vol. 11 · R. Erickson, ed., *Dictionary of Western Australians, 1829–1914*, 5 vols. (1979–86), vol. 5 · F. K. Crowley, *Australia's western third* (1960) · A. Hasluck, *C. Y. O'Connor* (1965) · C. H. Rason, *History of the Coolgardie water scheme*, 3rd edn (1903) · P. R. May, ed., *Miners and militants: politics in West land, 1865–1918* (1975)
Archives Battye Library of West Australian History, Perth
Likenesses P. Porcelli, bronze statue, 1911, Fremantle, Australia · P. Porcelli, bust, Mundaring Weir, near Perth, Western Australia

O'Connor, Feargus Edward (1796?–1855), Chartist leader, son of Roger *O'Connor (1762–1834) and his second wife, Wilhelmina Bowen, of Connorville in the parish of Kinneigh, co. Cork, was born at Connorville, probably on 18 July 1796. Arthur O'Connor was his uncle.

Family, education, and early political activity Feargus had three brothers and three sisters as well as a half-brother and half-sister from his father's earlier marriage. He came from a family of wealthy protestant landowners, although both his father and uncle changed their surnames from Conner to O'Connor and became United Irishmen. Feargus first attended school in London after his father's exile from Ireland in 1801 and was subsequently educated at several schools near Dublin. He probably went to Trinity College, Dublin, but did not take a

Feargus Edward O'Connor (1796?–1855), by William Wolfe Alais, 1840

degree. He lived on his father's Dangan Castle estate, co. Meath, where Roger O'Connor was allowed to return in 1803 and where as a young man Feargus pursued a keen interest in horse-racing. Around 1819 he was admitted to the King's Inns, Dublin, and in 1826 joined Gray's Inn, London; in 1830 he was admitted to the Irish bar, but he practised law only briefly. Around 1820 Feargus inherited the estate of Fort Robert, co. Cork, from his uncle Robert Conner. O'Connor was a reforming landlord and later claimed that he took part in Whiteboy activity. In 1822 he published his first political tract, *A State of Ireland*, in which he denounced corruption in local government. O'Connor did not participate in the movement for Catholic emancipation, but during the reform agitation of 1831–2 came forward as an advocate of Irish rights and democratic political reform. At this time his extraordinary talents as a public speaker first became evident.

After the passing of the Reform Bill, O'Connor stormed the country organizing the registration of the new electorate. In the general election of December 1832 he was returned as a repealer at the head of the poll for co. Cork. As a member of Daniel O'Connell's repeal party, O'Connor was an outspoken critic of the whig government's policies in both Ireland and England. He soon allied himself with London's popular radicals and was involved in various radical campaigns, including those for press freedom and the return of the transported Dorchester labourers. In summer 1833 O'Connor clashed with O'Connell over the

'Liberator's' refusal to move a motion for the repeal of the union. O'Connell's faith in *laissez-faire* political economy and hostility towards trade unionism further alienated O'Connor. He fully detailed his differences with O'Connell in his *Series of Letters … to Daniel O'Connell*, published in October 1836. O'Connor was re-elected for co. Cork in 1835, but was unseated in June 1835 owing to his lack of the necessary freehold property qualification. The same month he offered himself as a radical candidate for the seat at Oldham vacated by William Cobbett's death, and although he withdrew early on the first day's polling, his thirty-two votes were enough to secure victory for the tory candidate over Cobbett's son. O'Connor now embarked on a career primarily as a leader of English popular radicalism, although he continued to bring Irish issues to the fore.

The groundwork of Chartism and the *Northern Star* As an independent agitator O'Connor did more than any single leader to lay the groundwork for Chartism. Having founded the Marylebone Radical Association in September 1835, he toured the industrial north as its missionary in 1835 and 1836, establishing radical associations and campaigning for universal male suffrage, repeal of the newspaper stamp, abolition of the new poor law, and shorter factory hours. In November 1836 he became an honorary member of the London Working Men's Association (LWMA), and in March 1838 he supported the formation of the London Democratic Association, an ultra-radical rival to the LWMA. However, O'Connor increasingly turned his attention to the industrial districts of England and Scotland. Most significantly, in 1837 he established the *Northern Star*, a weekly newspaper published at Leeds. Within four weeks of the paper's first number (18 November 1837) the paper was returning a profit and within a year it was the most widely circulated provincial paper in the land. The *Northern Star* became, in effect, Chartism's official journal, publishing not only O'Connor's weekly letter addressed to the 'unshaved chins, blistered hands, and fustian jackets', but a wide range of local Chartist news. In the columns of O'Connor's paper adherents became aware of the movement's national scope. The establishment of the *Star* coincided with the height of the anti-poor law agitation in which O'Connor joined Richard Oastler and the Revd J. R. Stephens at large rallies characterized by violent rhetoric. O'Connor's influence was crucial during the spring of 1838 in committing the forces of northern working-class radicalism to the Birmingham Political Union's national petition, the People's Charter drawn up by the LWMA, and plans for a national convention. He attended nearly all the 'monster' demonstrations from the late summer through the winter of 1838 that elected delegates to the convention. He assumed the role of national leader, co-ordinating and unifying the agitation. But O'Connor's close identification with the lawless tone of northern radicalism, his presence at torchlight meetings, and his refusal to dissociate himself from Stephens and from recommendations

for popular arming, alarmed moderate leaders in Birmingham, London, and Scotland. O'Connor openly confronted his critics in their own districts, where he won overwhelming approval from the local rank and file.

Chartism and gaol At the Chartist convention which assembled on 4 February 1839, O'Connor was from the beginning the chief figure, declaring the body to be 'the only constituted authority representing the people of this country' (*Charter*, 24 Feb 1839, 76). The convention faltered over the question of what to do once parliament rejected the petition. O'Connor continually pressed the convention to take decisive action in conformity with his own strategy for attaining the Charter through intimidation and the mere threat of violent conflict. In July 1839, however, after the convention had committed the movement to a 'national holiday', O'Connor's opposition was crucial in reversing this decision on the grounds that Chartists were unprepared for a showdown with government authorities and in substituting a token three-day strike. O'Connor probably knew something of the secret plans afoot for armed insurrection in autumn 1839, although he left for Ireland on 5 October and did not return to England until 2 November. He was not involved in the preparations for the Newport rising on 4 November and warned Chartists against clandestine associations.

On 17 March 1840 O'Connor was found guilty at York assizes of seditious libel for speeches—his own and those of others—published in the *Northern Star*, and on 11 May he was sentenced to eighteen months' imprisonment in York Castle. From prison he continued to write for the *Northern Star*. Despite his relatively good treatment in prison, he fully exploited the popular image of the patriot martyr. In July 1840 the National Charter Association (NCA), Chartism's most important national association, was established. O'Connor strove to make it the party of all Chartists. He first joined the NCA executive in September 1843 as treasurer and was re-elected annually until 1851. On 30 August 1841 O'Connor was released from prison. Ever the populist showman, he emerged wearing a suit of working man's fustian to signal his allegiance to the people.

Until after 1848 O'Connor had no real rivals for the loyalty and active support of Chartism's rank and file, who regarded his leadership as crucial to maintaining national unity. During the early 1840s, however, O'Connor clashed with various radical leaders over Chartism's direction. In spring 1841 he condemned 'Church Chartism, Teetotal Chartism, Knowledge Chartism, and Household Suffrage Chartism' (*Northern Star*, 3 April 1841, 1), based on his fears that such tendencies could lead to sectarianism or compromise the movement. More serious was the split over the Complete Suffrage Union (CSU), a middle-class initiative launched by the Birmingham Liberal Joseph Sturge and aimed at uniting middle-class and working-class reformers. During 1842 various leaders, including William Lovett and James Bronterre O'Brien, welcomed the CSU. While O'Connor anticipated winning the 'industrious portion' of the middle class (principally shopkeepers) to Chartism, he viewed the complete suffrage move as an attempt to undermine his own leadership and Chartism's independence as a working-class movement. O'Connor again faced trial on 1 March 1843 at Lancaster, along with fifty-eight others, on charges of seditious conspiracy arising from the Chartist strikes that swept the industrial districts of the north and midlands in August 1842. O'Connor supported these strikes, although he held factory owners belonging to the Anti-Corn Law League responsible for their instigation. Convicted on one count, that of endeavouring to excite disaffection by unlawfully encouraging a stoppage of labour, O'Connor was never brought up for sentencing owing to a procedural error.

O'Connor, the Chartist land movement, and the Commons As Chartism waned during the years 1843–7, O'Connor kept the suffrage demand to the fore, although he encouraged causes he deemed complementary. He supported Lord Ashley's factory bill, backed O'Connell's final push for repeal of the Act of Union, and rallied support for trade unionism. He opposed the Anti-Corn Law League, and in August 1844 he engaged Richard Cobden in public debate at Northampton. Increasingly, however, O'Connor stressed the importance of working people's alienation from the land. As early as 1841 he declared: 'Lock-up the land to-morrow, and I would not give you two pence for the Charter the next day' (*Northern Star*, 24 July 1841, 1). In 1843 an NCA conference at Birmingham approved his proposal for establishing Chartist land communities, although it was not until April 1845 that the Chartist Co-operative Land Society was established. His scheme was to buy agricultural estates, divide them into smallholdings, and let the holdings by ballot. O'Connor elaborated his agrarian vision in his book *A Practical Work on the Management of Small Farms*, published in 1843, in the *Northern Star*, and in *The Labourer* (4 vols., 1847–8), a monthly journal that he co-edited with Ernest Jones. The land plan is best understood in terms of long-standing popular radical interest in and ideas on the land and notions of collective self-reliance. After 1845 much of O'Connor's energy was absorbed by the land plan, raising money, trying to register the company as a friendly society, buying land, and supervising the building of cottages. On May Day 1847 settlers moved into O'Connorville, an estate near Watford, the first of five Chartist settlements (Charterville at Minster Lovell, near Oxford, survives largely intact). At the general election of July 1847 O'Connor was returned at Nottingham, becoming Chartism's first and only MP.

The final phase of Chartism In 1848, inspired in part by the revolution in France and bolstered by co-operation with Irish nationalists, Chartism again mobilized large numbers with O'Connor at its head. A third national petition was organized and a convention sat to co-ordinate Chartist strategy. O'Connor presided at the great Kennington Common demonstration on 10 April 1848 and managed to persuade the people to abandon the proposed procession to the House of Commons to present the petition, thus avoiding a violent confrontation with government troops, police, and a large middle-class force enrolled as special constables. That evening O'Connor presented the national petition to the Commons, claiming that it contained 5,706,000 signatures. O'Connor was greatly embarrassed when the committee on petitions reported that the total came to 1,975,496, a figure that included many bogus signatures. In summer 1848 a select committee of the House of Commons reported that the land company was illegal, although O'Connor was found to have sunk £3400 of his own money in the company. In fact, the company's legal problems arose directly from the refusal of parliament and the law courts to allow for a popularly owned and controlled association of small-holders. After 1848 Chartism went into sharp decline, although O'Connor remained a prominent leader, offering radical redirection without sanctioning socialism.

Decline, death, and reputation Some time in 1851 O'Connor suffered the onset of serious mental illness, perhaps the final stage of syphilis. There is no indication that he was possessed of anything but fully sound mind before this. On his return from a visit to the United States in 1852, he struck two fellow members in the Commons, and was arrested and confined in the Palace of Westminster. In June 1852 he was admitted to Dr Harrington Tuke's asylum at Chiswick, where he remained until just before his death. O'Connor died on 30 August 1855 at his sister Harriet's home, 18 Albert Terrace, Notting Hill, London. Fifty thousand persons were reported to have attended his funeral on 10 September at Kensal Green. O'Connor never married, although in the 1830s it was rumoured that he and Louisa Nisbett, a celebrated actress, were lovers. He fathered several illegitimate children. Through much of his Chartist career he lived in Hammersmith, having leased his Irish estate; he died a poor man. His claim that he exhausted his personal wealth in the cause of radicalism is probably true.

Physically imposing, possessed of enormous energy and gentlemanly bearing, O'Connor fitted the popular image of the gentleman orator. Although he wrote profusely for the *Northern Star* and other Chartist journals and published over twenty political tracts, O'Connor was an activist rather than a theoretician. The early histories of Chartism portrayed him as vainglorious and irresponsible, a rabble-rouser who wrecked the work of Lovett and a small band of enlightened artisans. Recent studies, however, stress O'Connor's efforts to impart national unity, organizational coherence, and direction to a diverse political movement and recognize his extraordinary ascendancy over almost all sections of the movement as well as the degree to which he was held accountable to his followers.

JAMES EPSTEIN

Sources D. Read and E. Glasgow, *Feargus O'Connor: Irishman and chartist* (1961) · J. Epstein, *The lion of freedom: Feargus O'Connor and the chartist movement, 1832–1842* (1982) · F. O'Connor, 'Life and adventures of Feargus O'Connor', *National Instructor* (1850) · D. Thompson, *The Chartists: popular politics in the industrial revolution* (1984) · J. F. C. Harrison and D. Thompson, *Bibliography of the chartist movement, 1837–1976* (1978) · J. Belchem, '1848: Feargus O'Connor and the collapse of the mass platform', *The Chartist experience: studies in working-class radicalism and culture, 1830–60*, ed. J. Epstein and D. Thompson (1982), 269–310 · T. M. Wheeler, *A brief memoir of the*

late Feargus O'Connor (1855) • D. J. V. Jones, *Chartism and the chartists* (1975) • W. J. O'Neill Daunt, *A life spent for Ireland: being selections from the journals of the late W. J. O'Neill Daunt* (1896) • W. J. O'Neill Daunt, *Eighty-five years of Irish history, 1800–1885*, 2 vols. (1886) • T. Cooper, *The life of Thomas Cooper, written by himself*, [new edn] (1872) • R. G. Gammage, *History of the Chartist movement, 1837–1854*, new edn (1894); repr. with introduction by J. Saville (1969)
Archives BLPES, Allsop collection, letters to Thomas Allsop • York Castle Museum, letters to Sergeant Talfourd
Likenesses W. W. Alais, watercolour, 1840, NG Ire. [*see illus.*] • J. Doyle, caricature, pencil drawing, 1848, BM • J. B. Robinson, stone statue, 1859, Nottingham arboretum • W. Read, stipple, NPG • four portraits, Manch House, Ballineen, co. Cork • portrait, Mechanics' Institute, Nottingham • portrait, repro. in *The labourer* (1847), frontispiece • portrait, repro. in *ILN*, 12 (1848), 243 • stipple and line engraving, NPG
Wealth at death died a poor man; bequested all to nephew: O'Neill Daunt, *Life spent for Ireland*

O'Connor, Frank. *See* O'Donovan, Michael Francis Xavier (1903–1966).

O'Connor, Hugh, Don (1617–1669), soldier, was the eldest son of Calvach *O'Connor Don (1584–1655) and his wife, Mary, daughter of Sir Theobald Bourke, or Tibbot *na long* (of the ships). He in turn married Isabella Bourke. The name Don (from *donn*, 'brown') was used to distinguish this, the senior, branch of the sept from the O'Connor Roe (*rua*, 'red') branch. At the outbreak of the 1641 rising Calvach assumed leadership of the Catholic insurgents in north Connaught with specific responsibility for co. Roscommon. As early as Christmas eve 1641 Hugh was present at an attack on the abbey of Roscommon as a colonel in the insurgent army, along with other detachments from Leitrim and Longford. According to the historian Edmund Borlase he was captured in January 1642 while besieging Castle Coote, a strong government outpost south of Ballintober on the Galway border. In fact, he was captured there later, in March/April 1642, most likely while making an unsuccessful cattle raid. His capture caused the insurgents to suspend hostilities until July 1642: '[Calvach] O'Conner Dun of Ballintobber, ever since his son was taken, till now had acted nothing, though the tacit votes of the province did seem to own him as their king' (Borlase, 81). Calvach O'Connor then mustered an army of more than 2000 infantry near Ballintober but the force was routed in a pre-emptive strike by government forces from Athlone.

Hugh O'Connor was imprisoned at Castle Coote before being brought to Dublin in February 1643 for questioning. At his interrogation he justified the rising by the Roscommon gentry on the grounds that it was 'the King's pleasure that the said gentry should take up arms for that the Puritan Parliament of England would otherwise destroy them' (examination of Hugh O'Connor, 1643). He defended himself against accusations of having murdered Hugh Connaghan, a footman of Major Ormsby of Boyle, on the grounds that it was a justifiable act of war because Connaghan was intercepted bringing a message to Castle Coote. He was subsequently released, most likely after the cessation of September 1643. He retained the rank of colonel but did not serve with either of the two Connaught regiments which joined Castlehaven's Ulster

expedition of 1644, in the 1645 expedition to recover Sligo, or in the 1646 campaign which finally secured all of co. Roscommon for the confederate Catholics. In July 1652 he was one of the royalist officers who concluded articles of surrender with the Cromwellians. A condition of the articles was that he could recruit his followers for the Spanish service. By June 1653 he had raised 200 soldiers but, while preparing to embark, he was again questioned about the alleged murder of Connaghan. On this occasion he offered the primary defence of alibi rather than justification, claiming that he was absent in Mayo when his father condemned Connaghan to death for, allegedly, having deserted from the insurgent army. He was acquitted and ultimately followed the exiled Charles II to France where he served as a captain in the duke of Gloucester's regiment.

After the Restoration in 1660 he applied for the restoration of his estate of about 6000 acres but died in 1669 before the claim was decided. In 1683 his son Hugh *óg* recovered 1100 acres of the original estate. There are faint echoes of the former prominence of the O'Connor Don lineage in popular acclamation of Calvach as 'King of Connacht' (deposition of Elizabeth Holliwell), at the time of the rising. In the event, neither Calvach nor Hugh O'Connor lived up to popular expectations and the 'Old English' Bourkes, Dillons, and Taaffes assumed the leadership of the Catholic cause in Connaught.   PÁDRAIG LENIHAN

Sources C. O. O'Conor Don, *The O'Conors of Connaught: an historical memoir* (1891), 242–8 • examination of Hugh O'Connor, 11 Feb 1643, TCD, MS 830, fol. 9; 17 June 1653, MS 830, fols. 57–8 • deposition of Major Roger Ormsby, TCD, MS 830, fols. 53–5 • [E. Borlase], *The history of the execrable Irish rebellion* (1680), 49, 81 • *History of the Irish confederation and the war in Ireland … by Richard Bellings*, ed. J. T. Gilbert, 1 (1882), 94–5 • deposition of John Ridge, TCD, MS 830, fol. 6 • deposition of Elizabeth Holliwell, TCD, MS 830, fols. 35–6 • P. O'Connor, *The royal O'Connors of Connaught* (1997)

O'Connor, James (1836–1910), journalist and politician, was born on 10 February 1836 in the Glen of Imaal, co. Wicklow, to Patrick O'Connor, a farmer, and Anne, *née* Kearney, of Donard in the same county. Following education at a local national school, he entered a commercial career and then was an early member of the Irish Republican Brotherhood (Fenians). When its organ, the *Irish People*, was established in 1863 with John O'Leary as editor, he joined the staff, working mainly as a bookkeeper though he seems to have had a limited aptitude for business. Along with other members of the newspaper when it was suppressed, O'Connor was arrested on 15 September 1865, convicted, and sentenced to ten years' imprisonment. His incarceration was mainly in Millbank and Portland prisons and he was released in 1869 along with Charles Kickham, who later lived with O'Connor's family from November 1879 until his death on 22 August 1882. After his release O'Connor joined the staff of Richard Pigott's Fenian newspapers, becoming chief writer on *The Irishman* and editor of *The Shamrock*. Meanwhile he resumed work in the Irish Republican Brotherhood: a younger brother, John, was the long-time secretary of the supreme council and in 1870 James was an envoy to the

Clan na Gael in the United States. He also attended the meeting at the Bilton Hotel in Dublin on 19 May 1870 at which the modern home rule movement was founded.

Initially O'Connor opposed the so-called 'new departure' (1879) which linked Fenianism and Charles Stewart Parnell, but like many of his compatriots he drifted towards support of the land war (1879–82), joining the Land League. When Pigott's newspapers were sold to a consortium headed by Parnell in mid-1881, he moved to the successor newspaper, *United Ireland*, as sub-editor. In December 1881 he was detained without trial under the Protection of Person and Property Act (1881) in Kilmainham gaol with Parnell and other leaders of the agrarian agitation, and he was released with them in mid-1882. He remained on *United Ireland* until December 1890, when he supported the anti-Parnellites and was ejected from his position. When rival journals were established in March 1891, O'Connor was appointed editor of the *Weekly National Press*. At the general election of 1892 he successfully stood as an anti-Parnellite for Wicklow County West, and he retained the seat (which was contested in 1895, 1900, and 1910) until his death at Kingstown, co. Dublin, on 12 March 1910.

O'Connor's first wife, Molly, with four of their children, died on 30 June 1890 from eating poisonous mussels at Monkstown, co. Dublin. He was survived by his second wife (*née* McBride) and their daughter. After a funeral mass at St Michael's Roman Catholic Church, Kingstown, he was buried in Glasnevin cemetery alongside his first wife (14 March). A public monument was erected over their graves.   ALAN O'DAY

Sources W. O'Brien and D. Ryan, eds., *Devoy's post bag, 1871–1928*, 2 vols. (1948–53) · J. Denieffe, *A personal narrative of the Irish Revolutionary Brotherhood* (New York, 1906); facs. edn (Shannon, 1969) · J. O'Leary, *Recollections of Fenians and Fenianism* (1896) · M. F. Ryan, *Fenian memories*, ed. T. F. O'Sullivan (1945) · J. O'Donovan Rossa, *Rossa's recollections, 1838–1898* (New York, 1898) · M. Bourke and J. O'Leary, *A study in Irish separatism* (1967) · R. V. Comerford, *Charles J. Kickham: a study in Irish nationalism and literature* (1979) · R. V. Comerford, *The Fenians in context: Irish politics and society, 1848–82* (1985) · R. Pigott, *Personal recollections of an Irish national journalist* (1882); repr. (Cork, 1979) · A. M. Sullivan, *New Ireland*, [new edn] (1877) · T. W. Moody, *Davitt and Irish revolution* (1982) · *United Ireland* (5 July 1890) · *The Nation* (5 July 1890) · *Freeman's Journal* [Dublin] (14 March 1910) · *Irish Times* (14 March 1910) · *DNB*
Archives HLRO, letters to David Lloyd George · NL Scot., John Devoy MSS · NL Scot., J. F. X. O'Brien MSS · NL Scot., John Redmond MSS · TCD, corresp. with Thomas Bodmin · TCD, John Dillon MSS
Likenesses B. Stone, photographs, NPG

O'Connor, James Arthur (1792–1841), artist, was born at 15 St Aston's Quay, Dublin. His father, William O'Connor (*d. c.*1807), was a printseller and engraver, and is likely to have trained him in his profession. O'Connor did not pursue a career in that field himself, however, but quickly took to landscape painting, in which he may have received some direction from the Irish painter William Sadler (*c.*1782–1839). He first exhibited in 1809, at the Dublin Society and the Society of Artists of Ireland. About 1812, he made the acquaintance of two young landscape painters, George Petrie and Francis Danby, and in 1813 these three friends made an expedition to London, where

possibly all, and certainly Petrie, were presented to Benjamin West. Petrie soon left London for home, and a short time afterwards, O'Connor and Danby, having run out of money, followed his example, arriving on foot at Bristol, where Danby decided to stay, while O'Connor continued on to Dublin to care for his sisters, now orphaned. He exhibited regularly in Dublin and received some important commissions, including a series of sixteen paintings for the second marquess of Sligo and Lord Clanricarde. In 1818 O'Connor was also directly involved in the organization of the 'Exhibition of the artists of Ireland'. During this period he married a woman called Anastatia Agnes. Despite his heightened profile and receipt of a premium of 25 guineas from the Royal Irish Institute, O'Connor returned to London in 1822, sensing that it would afford him greater opportunities. His name appears in the catalogue of the Royal Academy for the first time that year, and on sixteen subsequent occasions, up to 1840. He also exhibited with the Society of British Artists, of which he was elected a member. His contributions were always landscapes. In May 1826 he proceeded to Brussels in the company of a dealer, and remained until the following year. While there he is reputed to have painted several successful pictures, but the expedition proved unfortunate as he was swindled out of a sum of money, possibly by the dealer himself. He continued to exhibit at the British Institution, the Society of British Artists, and the Royal Academy, and visited Ireland in 1830 (and possibly in 1828). In September 1832 O'Connor and his wife went to Paris, where he continued painting, with some success, until the following May. They planned to visit Italy, but decided on the advice and offers of lucrative introductions of a stranger, who also proved to be a swindler, to travel instead to the region of the Saar and Moselle in Germany. O'Connor was so delighted with the landscape that he abandoned his Italian tour altogether and stayed there for six months, travelling extensively and painting throughout. He and Anastatia arrived back in London on 1 November 1833.

Over the next six years, O'Connor showed his work at the principal London exhibitions, but otherwise enjoyed at best moderate success. In 1839 his health began to decline, and his incapacitation led to considerable pecuniary difficulties, from which he was partly extricated by the generosity of Sir Charles Coote, who commissioned a picture and paid for it in advance. O'Connor was deeply appreciative of Coote's beneficence, and may have returned to Ireland before his death to paint a picture for him. He exhibited at the Royal Hibernian Academy for just the second time in 1840. O'Connor died at his home, 6 Marlborough Street, College Street, Brompton, on 7 January 1841, leaving his wife in financial straits. About fifty of his landscapes were sold at Christies on 12 February 1842, but none realized much money. According to his obituarist, O'Connor was 'a spirit of exceeding mildness; manly, ardent, unobtrusive, and sincere; generous in proclaiming contemporary merit, and unskilled and reluctant to put forth his own' (*Dublin Monthly Magazine*, April 1842).

Though O'Connor was committed almost exclusively to

landscape, there is considerable variety in his work which ranged from topographical pictures such as *View of Westport with Croagh Patrick* (1818; Westport House, co. Mayo), and *Westport House* (*c*.1818; priv. coll.), to picturesque rural scenes which demonstrate his knowledge of and debt to the work of Claude such as *Landscape with Mill* (1821; priv. coll.); *A River Scene, Co. Wicklow* (1828; priv. coll.), and the romantic landscapes of *Thunderstorm, the Frightened Wagoner* (1832) and *The Poachers* (1835) (both National Gallery of Ireland, Dublin), all of which he executed with great facility and application.

RICHARD GARNETT, *rev.* BRENDAN ROONEY

Sources J. Hutchinson, *James Arthur O'Connor* (1985) [exhibition catalogue, NG Ire., Nov–Dec 1985] · A. Crookshank and the Knight of Glin [D. Fitzgerald], *The painters of Ireland, c.1660–1920* (1978), 211–14 · T. Bodkin, *Four Irish landscape painters* (1920) · W. G. Strickland, *A dictionary of Irish artists*, 2 (1913), 179–82 · J. Hutchinson, 'The Romantic landscapes of James Arthur O'Connor', *Irish Arts Review*, 2/4 (1985), 50–55 · 'M', 'Memoirs of native artists, no. VII: James O'Connor', *Dublin Monthly Magazine* (April 1842), 255–66 · P. Harbison, H. Potterton, and J. Sheehy, *Irish art and architecture from prehistory to the present* (1978)
Archives NRA, priv. coll., corresp.
Likenesses J. A. O'Connor, self-portrait, miniature, repro. in Strickland, *A dictionary of Irish artists*, 2.183 · J. A. O'Connor, self-portrait, oils, priv. coll. · J. A. O'Connor, self-portrait, oils (after himself), priv. coll. · J. A. O'Connor, self-portraits, oils, repro. in Hutchinson, ed., *James Arthur O'Connor*
Wealth at death £200: administration, 1841

O'Connor, John (1824–1887), lawyer and politician in Canada, was born on 21 January 1824 in Boston, Massachusetts, the son of John and Mary O'Connor, who had emigrated thence from co. Kerry, Ireland, in 1823. In 1828 they moved to the Roman Catholic settlement of Maidstone township, Essex county, Upper Canada. Unable to work on his parents' farm after an accident in which he lost his left leg, O'Connor began in 1848 to study law, first in Sandwich (Windsor) and then in Toronto. In April 1849 he married Mary Barrett; they had nine children. He was admitted to the bar of Upper Canada in 1854 and worked first in Windsor and then, from 1863 to 1865, in Toronto. He was very active in local politics in Essex in the 1860s, and represented the county in the legislative assembly in 1863 and again from 1867 to 1874. The only Irish Roman Catholic member at a time when Ontario's Irish Catholics were becoming an important political force, he had some success in forging a Catholic–Conservative alliance. From 1872 to 1873 he served in the government of Sir John A. Macdonald as president of the privy council, minister of inland revenue, and finally postmaster-general, but he was defeated in Essex in the federal election of 1874.

O'Connor left Windsor to establish a legal practice in Ottawa, where he was again active in Irish Catholic affairs. He was found a safe seat in 1878 and was returned to parliament as the member for Russell and held a number of minor cabinet offices between 1878 and 1881. By this time illness prevented his regular attendance at cabinet meetings and debates and his cultivating his constituents. He pestered Macdonald for help, not least because he was in financial need. Macdonald dismissed him from his cabinet but was finally persuaded to appoint him judge of the court of queen's bench for Ontario on 11 September 1884, in which office he proved 'an embarrassment to both the government and the bench' (Swainson). While he was regarded by the legal profession as incompetent through illness and lack of practice, O'Connor saw himself as underpaid and generally ill-used. His action against the government for extra payment for legal work was being heard when he died at Cobourg, Ontario, on 3 November 1887. Swainson considers that his successes were won not because of his personal abilities or merits, but because he was the only person able to represent the Ontario Irish Catholics when their support mattered to the Conservative Party.

ELIZABETH BAIGENT

Sources D. Swainson, 'O'Connor, John', *DCB*, vol. 11 · G. M. Rose, *A cyclopædia of Canadian biography* (1888) · M. J. Galvin, 'Catholic-protestant relations in Ontario, 1864–1875', MA diss., University of Toronto, 1962
Archives NA Canada · Public Archives of Ontario, Toronto

O'Connor, John (1830–1889), scene-painter and topographical painter, was born on 12 August 1830 in co. Londonderry, the third son of Francis O'Connor and his wife, Rose Cunningham; both his parents worked in the theatrical business. He was educated at the Church Educational Society's school in Dublin. Orphaned by 1842, he supported himself and his grandfather, Francis O'Connor, up to the latter's death in 1845. His mother's brother was lessee of the Belfast and Liverpool theatres and O'Connor assisted with scene painting and acted as call-boy at the Dublin theatre. In 1845 he joined a travelling group of actors as scene-painter but, to make a better living, he returned to Dublin and made silhouettes with the pantograph. In 1844 he painted scenery for Sir E. Tierney and in 1847 for the earl of Bective. On 2 April 1848 he arrived in London, having brought introductions to scene-painters, and afterwards worked at the Drury Lane Theatre. In October he became one of the scene-painters at the Haymarket Theatre, where John Baldwin Buckstone was manager and playwright between 1853 and 1878; he was principal scene-painter here from 1863 to 1878.

O'Connor returned to Ireland in the summer of 1849 to paint scenes for the moving diorama of the visit of Queen Victoria to that country. The diorama was shown by Philip Phillips in 1850 at the Chinese Gallery at Hyde Park Corner, London, where O'Connor lived for over a year until the exhibition closed. In 1864 he painted the scenery for the Shakespeare tercentenary performances at Stratford upon Avon; he also designed tableaux vivants held at Cromwell House and elsewhere, including Shakespearian scenes (1874), *The Tale of Troy* (1883), *The Dream of Fair Women* (1884), the *Masque of Painters* (1886), and the *Masque of Flowers* (1887). At Cambridge, as a member of the Cambridge Amateur Dramatic Club, he painted scenery for productions of Greek dramas, including *Ajax* (1882), *The Birds* (1883), *The Eumenides* (1886), and *Oedipus tyrannus* (1887). He also produced scenery for private theatrical performances and had many patrons in London society. By the 1870s he had gained the reputation of being a most talented scene-painter, with few equals as a master of architectural design, and an admirable colourist. In 1878 he resigned from his post at the Haymarket Theatre in order to concentrate on conventional painting, though he later painted act-drops for Sadler's Wells Theatre and St James's Theatre and the 'Minuet' act-drop for the Haymarket Theatre.

From 1853 to 1888 O'Connor exhibited oils and watercolours of architectural subjects at the Society of British Artists (twenty-six works), the British Institution (six works), and the New Watercolour Society (twelve works). He showed at the Royal Academy for the first time in 1857 and thereafter in most years, especially in the 1870s and 1880s, up to 1888. In 1855 he made the first of many visits to the continent, where he made studies for future pictures. He later travelled to France, Germany, Italy, Spain, and Algeria, and the majority of his exhibited works were of continental, mainly architectural, subjects. From 1855 to 1858 he was drawing-master at the London and South-Western Literary and Scientific Institution. During the Franco-Prussian War he was in Sedan; he published a first-hand description, 'Three days in Sedan', in *The Dark Blue* in July 1871. During the Prussian occupation of Paris, he visited that city several times with the son of the duke of Sutherland, Lord Ronald Gower, a sculptor; in 1872 he took a studio with Gower at 47 Leicester Square, in the house formerly occupied by Sir Joshua Reynolds. In 1874 O'Connor was commissioned by the first duke of Westminster to decorate rooms at Eaton Hall with three large oil paintings (only two were apparently completed), and eight smaller views of Cliveden, Trentham, and Dunrobin for the first duchess's sitting-room (unrecorded in inventories in the 1920s, and untraced). Probably through his contacts with the Westminster and Sutherland families, he was commissioned to paint watercolours for Queen Victoria, *The Marriage Procession of Princess Louise, 1871* and *Queen Victoria Driving out of Buckingham Palace with the Duke and Duchess of Edinburgh, 1874* (both Royal Collection). He was among the artists who contributed to the decoration of Lawrence Alma-Tadema's house in St John's Wood, London. In 1878 he built a house and studio at 28 Abercorn Place, St John's Wood, where he lived until his health failed; in 1888 he went to live at Yateley, Hampshire. He became an associate of the Royal Hibernian Academy in 1883 and a member of the Royal Institute of Painters in Watercolour in 1887. O'Connor was married twice and had two sons from each marriage. He travelled to India to see the two younger ones, but soon after his return he died of paralysis on 23 May 1889 at his home, Heath Croft, in Yateley; he was buried in Finchley cemetery, Middlesex. Lord Ronald Gower wrote that 'he was not only a good artist, but a thoroughly good fellow, which is a much scarcer quality than the former' (Gower, 92).　　　　DELIA MILLAR

Sources DNB · Bénézit, *Dict.*, 3rd edn · Mallalieu, *Watercolour artists* · Wood, *Vic. painters*, 2nd edn · Graves, *RA exhibitors* · Graves, *Brit. Inst.* · R. S. Gower, *Old diaries, 1881–1901* (1902) · J. O'Connor, 'Three days in Sedan', *The Dark Blue*, 1 (July 1871), 556–67 · R. de Cordova, 'The panels in Sir Lawrence Alma-Tadema's hall', *The Strand*, 24 (1902), 615

Likenesses wood-engraving (after photograph by A. Bassano), BM; repro. in *ILN* (8 June 1889)

Wealth at death £1358 15s. 6d.: probate, 3 July 1889, *CGPLA Eng. & Wales*

O'Connor, Luke Smythe (1806–1873), army officer, born in Dublin on 15 April 1806, was appointed ensign in the 1st West India regiment on 27 April 1827, becoming lieutenant on 22 March 1831, captain on 17 January 1834, brevet major on 9 November 1846, major on 1 January 1847, brevet lieutenant-colonel on 3 February 1853, brevet colonel on 28 November 1854, regimental lieutenant-colonel on 21 September 1855, and major-general on 24 April 1866. All his regimental commissions were in the 1st West India, of which he was adjutant in 1833–4. When it was decided, in 1843, that the garrisons on the African west coast should be supplied by the West India regiments instead of by the 3rd West India alone, as previously, O'Connor was detached from Barbados to Sierra Leone with two companies of his regiment. In 1848, as major, O'Connor was sent from his regiment in Jamaica to British Honduras, where there were disturbances with the Yucatan.

In September 1852 O'Connor was appointed governor of the Gambia, and was invested with the command of all the troops in west Africa. On his advice the headquarters were removed from Sierra Leone to Cape Coast Castle. He commanded detachments of the three West India regiments, black pensioners, Gambia militia, and seamen and marines against the Muslim rebels of Combos, stormed their stronghold of Sabajee on 1 June 1853, and acquired by treaty a considerable tract of territory, for which he received official praise from the government. On 16 July 1853 he attacked and repulsed a numerous force of Muslims under Omar Hadjee, the 'Black Prophet', during which action, out of 240 British, 29 were killed and 53 wounded. O'Connor was wounded with two shots through the right arm and one in the left shoulder, but remained in action. He subsequently commanded the combined British and French forces against the Muslim rebels of Upper and Lower Combos. After four hours' fighting in the pass of Boccow Kooka on 4 August 1855, he stormed the rebel stockade and routed the enemy, who lost some 500 men. He received the reward for distinguished service in 1855 and the CB on 4 February 1856.

O'Connor was brigadier-general commanding the troops in Jamaica during the 1865 rebellion, and was thanked for his prompt and efficient measures by Governor Eyre, the legislative council and house of assembly, and by the magistrate and inhabitants of Kingston. He was president of the legislative council and senior member of the privy council of Jamaica in January 1867; he administered the government during the absence of Sir John Peter Grant and retired shortly afterwards.

O'Connor married Anne Mitchell in 1856; she survived him. He died of dropsy and atrophy at 7 Räcknitzstrasse, Dresden, Saxony, on 24 March 1873.

　　　　H. M. CHICHESTER, *rev.* JAMES FALKNER

Sources *Army List* · *Hart's Army List* · *Colonial Office List* · A. B. Ellis, *History of the first West India regiment* (1885) · *CGPLA Eng. & Wales* (1873)

Wealth at death under £600: probate, 24 June 1873, *CGPLA Eng. & Wales*

O'Connor, Sir Richard Nugent (1889–1981), army officer, was born at Srinagar, Kashmir, India, on 21 August 1889, the only child of Maurice Nugent O'Connor, a major in the Royal Irish Fusiliers, and his wife, Lilian, daughter of Sir John Morris of Killundine, Argyll. After attending Wellington College (1903–7) O'Connor entered the Royal Military College, Sandhurst, in 1908, and was commissioned into the Scottish Rifles (Cameronians) in 1909. As signal officer of 22nd brigade in the 7th division, he fought in the first battle of Ypres in 1914, the battles of Neuve Chapelle and Loos in 1915, gaining an MC, and the battle of the Somme in 1916. Having been awarded a DSO when brigade-major of 185th brigade in the 62nd division, he was promoted in June 1917 lieutenant-colonel to command the 2nd battalion of the Honourable Artillery Company, which took part in the third battle of Ypres (Passchendaele). At the end of that year his battalion was transferred to the Italian front, where, in October 1918, O'Connor was awarded a bar to his DSO for the capture of the island of Papadopoli.

After the war O'Connor returned to the 2nd battalion of the Cameronians as adjutant before attending the Staff College at Camberley in 1920. Over the next fifteen years he held a number of staff appointments, twice returning to duty with his regiment. In 1927–8 he returned to the Staff College as an instructor at the same time as B. L. Montgomery, and among his students were three future field marshals, H. R. L. G. Alexander, A. F. Harding, and G. W. R. Templer. In 1935 he attended the Imperial Defence College and was then posted to succeed Auchinleck in command of the Peshawar brigade on the north-west frontier of India. On 21 December 1935 he married a divorcée, Jean Marina True Phelps (1897/8–1959), daughter of Brigadier-General Walter Ross. They had no children, but the son of Jean O'Connor's previous marriage took his stepfather's surname by deed poll in 1944.

In 1938 O'Connor was promoted major-general and appointed to command the 7th division, dealing with Arab insurgents in Palestine, the post bringing with it that of military governor of Jerusalem. He was there when the Second World War broke out in September 1939. When Italy entered the war and threatened Egypt from Libya in June 1940, O'Connor was promoted lieutenant-general to command the western desert force in Egypt, which consisted of only the weak 7th armoured division and one infantry brigade. With these 10,000 men, O'Connor faced the potential threat of Marshal Graziani's 215,000 Italian troops in Libya. In September 80,000 of them, in General Berti's Tenth Army, advanced cautiously 50 miles into Egypt. In great secrecy General Sir Archibald Wavell ordered O'Connor to plan an operation to eliminate Berti's force. O'Connor's attack at Sidi Barrani, launched on 9 December 1940, was brilliantly successful. To O'Connor's dismay, Wavell insisted on switching his only infantry division, the 4th Indian, to the Sudan to deal with the Italians in Abyssinia, prejudicing O'Connor's exploitation of his victory. Wavell agreed that this could be extended at least as far as Tobruk, providing the 6th Australian division to replace the Indians. The garrisons of

Bardia and Tobruk were, in quick succession, surrounded, attacked, and forced to surrender, the rest of General Berti's army withdrawing to Benghazi.

By then, the end of January 1941, the war cabinet in London had decided to transfer Wavell's effort to Greece; but, when O'Connor received reports of Italian withdrawal from Benghazi towards Tripolitania, he sought and obtained authority to try to cut them off by a direct move across the desert to the Gulf of Sirte, although the force he could deliver and maintain there would be exiguous and far inferior to that still available to the Italians. A much reduced 7th armoured division succeeded in intercepting the Italian withdrawal at Beda Fomm on 6 February, 25,000 Italians surrendering with 100 guns and an equal number of tanks. In two months O'Connor's force had advanced 350 miles, capturing 130,000 prisoners, nearly 400 tanks and 845 guns at a cost to itself of 500 killed, 1,373 wounded, and 55 missing. It was a famous victory, on which O'Connor's reputation was to rest.

O'Connor then returned to Cairo to command British troops in Egypt, being replaced by Sir Henry Maitland Wilson and later by Sir Philip Neame who faced the Germans under Rommel. When the latter's attack in March 1941 threw Neame's force into confusion, Wavell sent O'Connor up from Cairo, intending that he should replace Neame, but O'Connor persuaded Wavell to leave Neame in command with himself as adviser. In the withdrawal from Benghazi both were captured and sent to Italy, where O'Connor made two attempts to escape from his prison camp. After Italy surrendered in September 1943, an Italian general let him out, and, with the help of partisans, he reached Eighth Army's lines a few days before Christmas and returned to Britain.

In January 1944 O'Connor assumed command of the 8th corps, which landed in Normandy at the end of June. There it was involved in major battles intended to achieve a break-out, known as operations Epsom and Goodwood. The corps was then switched to the western end of Second Army's sector, and, from 28 July to 4 August, drove a deep wedge south to Vire, as the Americans broke out into Brittany.

O'Connor was given only a subsidiary role in the fighting which followed the liberation of Belgium, and was disappointed when he was transferred to India, first to eastern command and then north-west army, neither involving any responsibility for operations. He was promoted general in April 1945 and returned to Britain in 1946 to join the army council as adjutant-general; but he resigned in 1947 rather than agree to an army council decision to reduce the numbers returning from the Far East for demobilization, owing to a shortage of shipping. On retirement he lived at Kincardie House, Rosemarkie, north of Inverness, and played a full part in Scottish public life, being lord lieutenant of Ross and Cromarty from 1954 to 1964, in which year he was lord high commissioner of the general assembly of the Church of Scotland. His wife died in 1959, and on 2 April 1963 he married (Muriel) Dorothy Vernon (1900/01–1988), widow of Brigadier Hugh Russell, and daughter of Walter Summers, a Dublin barrister. He was appointed CB (1940), KCB (1941), GCB (1947), and KT (1971). He became an honorary DCL (St Andrews, 1947), was a member of the Légion d'honneur, and held the Croix de Guerre with palm. In 1978 the O'Connors moved from Rosemarkie to Flat 3, 28 Lennox Gardens, London, SW1, where O'Connor died on 17 June 1981.

MICHAEL CARVER

Sources J. Baynes, *The forgotten victor* (1989) · I. S. O. Playfair, *The Mediterranean and the Middle East*, 1–2 (1954–6) · B. Pitt, *The crucible of war* (1980) · M. Hastings, *Overlord* (1984) · King's Lond., O'Connor MSS · private information (2004) · personal knowledge (2004) · m. certs. · *CGPLA Eng. & Wales* (1981) · *WW*
Archives King's Lond., Liddell Hart C., papers · NAM, Desert War diary | King's Lond., Liddell Hart C., corresp. with Sir B. H. Liddell Hart · priv. coll., MSS relating to his appointment as commissioner for Imperial War Graves Commission | FILM BFI NFTVA, news footage · IWM FVA, actuality footage | SOUND IWM SA, 'World at war', Thames TV, 1972, 2919 · IWM SA, 'British commander of Peshawar bridge in India, 1936–1938, military governor in Jerusalem, 1938–1939', IWM, 1974, 12 · IWM SA, oral history interview
Likenesses group photograph, 1946, Hult. Arch. · photograph, 1948, Hult. Arch. · J. Aris, oils, 1950–59, IWM
Wealth at death £93,351: probate, 27 Nov 1981, *CGPLA Eng. & Wales*

O'Connor, Roderic. *See* Ua Conchobair, Ruaidrí (*d.* 1118).

O'Connor [*formerly* Conner, Connor], **Roger** (1762–1834), Irish nationalist, born at Connorville, co. Cork, was the son of Roger Conner (*d.* 1798) of Connorville, MP for Bandonbridge, co. Cork, and Anne (*d.* 1782), daughter of Robert Longfield MP, and sister of Richard Longfield, first Viscount Longueville. The Connor or, more correctly, Conner family was descended from a rich London merchant, and its claims to ancient Irish descent were totally spurious. Arthur *O'Connor, the leading United Irishman, was Roger's younger brother and they were the only two of the nine children in the family to change their name to O'Connor. Roger entered Trinity College, Dublin, in 1777, and was called to the English bar in 1784.

O'Connor's early bias was in favour of the old tory regime; as a young man he entered the Muskerry yeomanry, and helped to hunt down 'Whiteboys'. He soon, however, changed his views and, with his brother Arthur, joined the United Irishmen, in which he displayed some gifts for organization; he was involved in setting up the short-lived radical newspaper *The Harp of Eirinn*. In 1797 a warrant left Dublin Castle for his arrest, at the instance of his own brother Robert, who was an inveterate enemy of his two errant brothers. He was imprisoned at Cork, was tried and acquitted. On his liberation in April 1798 he went to London, with the intention, as he said, of 'residing there and avoiding any interference in politics'; but his brother Arthur had just been arrested at Margate, and the Home Office again decided on imprisoning Roger. He was sent from place to place in the custody of king's messengers, and on 2 June 1798 was finally committed to Newgate in Dublin.

In April 1799, with his fellow prisoners T. A. Emmet, Chambers, his brother Arthur, and others, O'Connor was moved to Fort George in Scotland. In the same year he managed to publish *Letters to the People of Great Britain.*

After some years' imprisonment, during which his health suffered, he obtained an early release. While the brothers were in prison, the family home at Connorville had been looted by government forces who had lived there at free quarters during the rebellion, but Roger's claim for damages (£681 8*s.* 8*d.*, including £10 15*s.* for grapes and other fruit) was disallowed. He renewed the claim in 1811, though this time the sum in question had grown to £2190: once again he failed to get compensation. In the meantime, he had rented Dangan Castle, Trim, co. Meath: this house burnt down shortly after he had taken out insurance for £5000 on it. As a result of Arthur's exile in France, Roger had been given by him full power of attorney to deal with his Irish property, but after an early remittance of £500 nothing further was sent. By the time that Arthur realized that he was being swindled, some, if not most, of the property had gone. At the end of the Napoleonic wars, and still unable to travel to Ireland himself, Arthur sent his wife, Eliza, daughter of the marquis de Condorcet, to confront Roger, but he proved adept at suppressing documentary evidence and she was forced to return empty-handed to France. Eventually a decree against Roger was obtained in the courts, but this had little value. In a sensational development, he was arrested at Trim in 1817 for having headed a band of his retainers in robbing the Galway coach. The son of O'Connor's agent later asserted that this raid was made by O'Connor not for money, but in quest of a packet of love letters written by his friend Sir Francis Burdett, which were likely to be used in evidence against Burdett at the suit of a peer who suspected him of criminal intimacy with his wife. Sir Francis Burdett hurried to Ireland as a witness on O'Connor's behalf at his trial at Trim, and Roger was acquitted.

In 1822 O'Connor published *The chronicles of Eri, being the history of the Gael, Sciot Iber, or Irish people: translated from the original manuscripts in the Phoenician dialect of the Scythian language*. The book is mainly, if not entirely, the fruit of O'Connor's imagination. Roger's portrait is prefixed with the description, 'O'Connor Cier-rige, head of his race, and O'Connor, chief of the prostrated people of this Nation. *Soumis, pas vaincus.*' O'Connor is described as a man of fascinating manners and conversation, and he certainly made an impression on Sir Francis Burdett, but R. R. Madden, the biographer of the United Irishmen, considered that his wits were always more or less disordered. Throughout his life he professed himself to be a sceptic in religion, and declared that Voltaire was his god. He married, first, in 1784, Louisa Ann, daughter of Colonel Strachan; and second, in 1788, Wilhelmina, daughter of Nicholas Bowen of Bowenscourt. Feargus *O'Connor, the Chartist, was a son of the second marriage. O'Connor died at his home, Knockenmore Cottage, Kilcrea, co. Cork, on 27 January 1834, and was buried in Kilcrea Abbey.

W. J. FITZPATRICK, rev. THOMAS BARTLETT

Sources F. MacDermot, 'Arthur O'Connor', *Irish Historical Studies*, 15 (1966–7), 48–69 · *Correspondence of Charles, first Marquis Cornwallis*, ed. C. Ross, 3 vols. (1859), vol. 2 · M. Elliott, *Partners in revolution: the United Irishmen and France* (1982) · *Dublin and London Magazine* (1828), 30 · private information (1894) · R. R. Madden, *The United Irishmen:*

their lives and times, 3rd ser., 7 vols. (1842–6) · *GM*, 2nd ser., 1 (1834), 342
Archives NL Ire., letters to W. J. Fitzpatrick on O'Connor
Likenesses A. Wiell, mezzotint, 1822, NPG · portrait, repro. in R. O'Connor, *The chronicles of Eri* (1822)

O'Connor, Rory. *See* Ua Conchobair, Ruaidrí (*c*.1116–1198).

O'Connor, Thomas Power (1848–1929), journalist and politician, was born at Athlone on 5 October 1848, the eldest son of Thomas O'Connor, a shopkeeper, and his wife, Theresa Power. He was educated at the College of the Immaculate Conception, Athlone, and in 1863 he entered Queen's College, Galway, where he took his BA degree in 1866 (he was awarded an MA by the college in 1873). After an attempt to enter the civil service, in 1867 he began as a reporter on the staff of *Saunders's Newsletter*, a Conservative Dublin daily paper. In 1870 he went to London, and at the outbreak of the Franco–Prussian War his command of French and German led to his appointment as a sub-editor on the *Daily Telegraph*. Here he remained only briefly, moving on to the London office of the *New York Herald*, only to be dismissed after eighteen months. He became a freelance journalist, working in the press gallery of the House of Commons. The hardships of these years were said to have made him an extreme radical, and he took part in debates in working men's clubs, becoming vice-president of the Lambeth Radical Association in 1880.

During 1876 O'Connor's first book, a life of Disraeli, appeared anonymously in serial numbers. It was so unsparing an attack on the prime minister that it attracted considerable notice; when it was published under his name in 1879, its success provided a spur to his entry into politics. Initially O'Connor wanted to stand as a British radical but he was persuaded by Parnell to stand as a home-rule candidate for the borough of Galway, which he won in 1880. He became one of the most voluble and pertinacious speakers among the Parnellites who opposed the Liberal government. In 1885 he stood for the Scotland division of Liverpool, and wrote an address from the Irish party to the nationalist voters in Great Britain, urging them to defeat the Liberals by supporting the Conservative candidates; at the general election of 1886, when Gladstone had adopted home rule, he wrote another address to the same electors, exhorting them in even more moving terms to vote Liberal.

Throughout his long life O'Connor combined journalism with politics and was better known, perhaps, as a journalist than as a politician. John Morley, editor of the *Pall Mall Gazette* from 1880, engaged him to write a nightly sketch of the proceedings in parliament, and thought him unrivalled in depicting the personalities of the party fight of that day, and its dramatic episodes. In 1888 O'Connor founded the *Star*, an evening journal noted both for its radicalism and for its inauguration of the 'new' journalism. Differences arose between him and the proprietor, and O'Connor was bought out reportedly for £15,000, subject to the condition that he should not start another evening paper in London for three years. In 1891 he brought out the *Sunday Sun*, subsequently called the *Weekly Sun*. In 1893, when he was able to start another evening paper, he

Thomas Power O'Connor (1848–1929), by James Russell & Sons

founded the *Sun*, but it was less successful. His next venture, in 1902, *T. P.'s Weekly* (he was known familiarly as T. P.), a penny literary paper, was extremely popular. He started other weekly papers, such as *M.A.P.* (Mainly about People) and *P.T.O.* (Please Turn Over), both devoted chiefly to gossip, and experimented with a monthly called *T.P.'s Magazine*. Of his books the more important are *The Parnell Movement* (1886) and *Memoirs of an Old Parliamentarian* (1929).

As a journalist O'Connor was not a publicist, writing few leading articles of weight and influence on public affairs. He was content rather to be an observer of life and its chronicler in an easy style, full of reminiscences and anecdotes. Nor as a parliamentarian did he ever aspire to leadership. As the voice of the Irish in Britain, his role was as mediator and ambassador for the cause of Irish nationalism. President of the Irish National League of Great Britain from 1883 to 1918, he played an important role in making links between Ireland and the Irish in Britain. He promoted Irish home rule policies in France, and raised funds for the Irish Parliamentary Party in America.

In 1917 O'Connor became the first president of the British Board of Film Censors, nominated by the film trade, but independent of trade control or influence. O'Connor's signature on the censors' certificate that preceded the presentation of every film thus became familiar to millions. He was successful in ensuring that disputes between the Home Office, local authorities, and the board were eased, and the board's decisions were accepted as final. He was made a member of the privy council in 1924 by the first Labour government. He was also for many years 'father' of the House of Commons by right of the longest unbroken period of service. O'Connor loved the Commons for its history, its customs, and its sociabilities, and wrote innumerable articles about its more prominent members, their fortunes and fates.

O'Connor married, in 1885, Elizabeth Howard, *née* Paschal, the daughter of a judge of the supreme court in Arkansas, USA; they had no children, and she died in 1931 (her son from her first marriage, Francis Howard, was the father of Brian Howard, the dilettante). O'Connor died on 18 November 1929, and was buried in the Roman Catholic cemetery, Kensal Green.

M. MACDONAGH, *rev.* MARIE-LOUISE LEGG

Sources L. W. Brady, *T. P. O'Connor and the Liverpool Irish* (1983) · T. P. O'Connor, *Memoirs of an old parliamentarian*, 2 vols. (1929) · H. Fyfe, *T. P. O'Connor* (1934) · *The Times* (18 Nov 1929) · *The Times* (19 Nov 1929) · E. O'Connor, *I, myself* (1910) · J. C. Robertson, *The British Board of Film Censors: film censorship in Britain, 1896–1950* (1985)

Archives HLRO, letters to David Lloyd George · JRL, *Guardian* MSS, letters to C. P. Scott · Lpool RO, corresp. with seventeenth earl of Derby · TCD, corresp. with John Dillon

Likenesses J. F. Bacon, oils, exh. RA 1904, Walker Art Gallery, Liverpool · H. Furniss, caricature, pen-and-ink sketch, NPG · S. P. Hall, pencil sketch, NPG · J. Lavery, oils, NG Ire. · E. H. Mills, photograph on postcard, NPG · A. P. F. Ritchie, print on cigarette card, NPG · J. Russell & Sons, photograph, NPG [*see illus.*] · Spy [L. Ward], caricature, watercolour study, NPG; repro. in *VF* (25 Feb 1888) · B. Stone, photographs, NPG · bronze bust, Fleet Street, London

Wealth at death £1248 15s. 3d.: probate, 31 July 1930, *CGPLA Eng. & Wales*

O'Conor, Charles (1710–1791), antiquary and religious propagandist, was born on 1 January 1710 at Kilmactranny, co. Sligo, Ireland, the eldest son of Denis O'Conor (d. 1750), farmer, and Mary O'Rourke (d. 1760?), daughter of Tiernan O'Rourke, a colonel in the French army who was killed in the battle of Luzara in 1702. Both his paternal grandfather and great-uncle had fought on the Jacobite side in 1688–90. As a result, the family estate at Belanagare, co. Roscommon, was confiscated, but for technical reasons a significant portion of it was restored in 1703, although the family did not return to live there until the 1720s. The O'Conors of Belanagare were a prime example of the last remnants of the native Irish landowning nobility, particularly since they were descended from the last nominal high-king of Ireland, Ruaidhrí O Conchobhair (Rory O'Conor). They continued the Gaelic tradition of artistic and scholarly patronage, and hence in the 1720s the young Charles received instruction from Dominic O Duigenan, one of a family of hereditary historians, under whose direction he first began to copy Gaelic manuscripts. His uncle, Thaddeus O'Rourke, Catholic bishop of Killala, was unable to move freely about the country in this period of strict state control of the clergy. He was thus free to supervise the education of his nephew, so that in addition to traditional Gaelic learning O'Conor attained proficiency in standard classical subjects, for which purpose he was also sent to the Skelton Academy in Dublin for a period. In addition he was taught music by Turlough O'Carolan, the famous harper, who availed of the O'Conors' patronage.

Charles O'Conor (1710–1791), by Maguire

On 8 December 1731 O'Conor married Catherine Fagan (d. 1741), daughter of John Fagan, and settled on a farm in co. Roscommon. They had four children before Catherine's death in 1741. In 1750, on the death of his father, O'Conor took possession of the family estate at Belanagare. He was concerned to build up the estate and reported later in life that partly through land reclamation he had amassed somewhere between 700 and 800 acres of farming land. As a gentleman farmer he began to collect Gaelic manuscripts and to make copies and extracts of others. Among his collection was an original edition of the first part of the *Annála ríoghachta Éireann* by Mícheál O Cléirigh and his assistants. Increasingly, he was asked by non-Gaelic-speaking historians to make extracts and translations from manuscripts in his possession. He was thus an important link in a tradition of scribal activity dating back to medieval times.

In 1748 O'Conor's most famous antiquarian work, *Dissertations on the Antient History of Ireland*, first appeared anonymously in separate numbers; it was later published in book form in 1753. This series of essays on the pre-colonial period of Irish history was in the tradition of earlier works by Geoffrey Keating and Hugh MacCurtin, among others, which defended the early Irish against the charge of barbarism made by many, mainly English, writers. O'Conor aimed to show the 'indelible signatures of the Use of Govt and Letters in Ireland' long before the arrival of Christianity in the sixth century. Although he consulted the medieval Gaelic annals in his possession, his depiction of pre-colonial Ireland was mainly shaped by his political concerns, in particular the iniquities of the penal laws in force against Catholics in his own time. Thus he claimed that early Christian Ireland was a haven of religious toleration and 'true Liberty', where none was punished who 'submitted to the Laws of the Land' and where conversion was achieved by persuasion, 'the only Manner in which it can be conducted' (C. O'Conor, *Dissertations on the Antient History of Ireland*, 86–7). Reflecting his immersion in Enlightenment writing on progress, he argued that early Irish history was the story of the gradual triumph of liberty and virtue over faction and tyranny (ibid., x).

A second edition of the book was published in 1766, but 'antient' was removed from the title and the text was amended in places quite significantly, to the extent that it should be treated as a separate work. Its central theme was unaltered, but the breathless writing style of the first edition was jettisoned in favour of a more polished one. More important, many of the changes involved the removal of passages which could be considered impolitic, such as one on the role of the Gaelic poets in stirring up rebellion after the Anglo-Norman conquest. The 1766 edition, which appeared under O'Conor's name, omitted the entire chapter on the colonial era and substituted for it an essay disputing the authenticity of James Macpherson's Ossian poems.

In 1760 O'Conor gave over the main house and the management of the estate to his eldest son, Denis, and built a smaller house in the grounds which he called his 'hermitage'. For the last three decades of his life he divided his time between the hermitage and Dublin, where most of his friends and interests were. Together with his friend the historian John Curry and Thomas Wyse he founded the Catholic Committee in 1760 to represent Catholic interests and to press for the relaxation of the penal laws. O'Conor wrote anonymously a number of pamphlets in support of the Catholic cause, including *A Counter Appeal to the People of Ireland* (1749) and *The Case of the Roman Catholics of Ireland* (1755). Adopting an English protestant identity in most of these, he argued that the laws had a catastrophic economic effect by discouraging Catholic industry as well as investment. He also maintained that Irish Catholics were loyal subjects, and together with Curry and others he formulated addresses and petitions designed to show this. He was much involved in the drawing up of a test oath for Catholics, which was the basis of a Test Act passed in 1774.

Following the publication of the second edition of the *Dissertations* O'Conor was acknowledged as the foremost Irish antiquary and had entry to some of the wealthiest and most influential protestant as well as Catholic circles at a time when the protestant élite was becoming interested in the Gaelic past. Thus he socialized with George Faulkner, the prominent Dublin printer, and with William Burton (later Burton Conyngham), teller of the exchequer and enthusiast for Gaelic antiquities. Thomas Leland, the librarian at Trinity College, Dublin, invited him to consult the library's great holdings of Gaelic manuscripts in 1766. He was invited to become a member of three protestant-sponsored learned societies concerned with antiquities, the short-lived select committee for antiquities of the Dublin Society (1772–4), the Hibernian Antiquarian Society (1778–83), and the Royal Irish Academy, which was founded in 1785. O'Conor's success in straddling these two worlds can be seen in a letter to his son of February 1779, in which he recounted attending a dinner party at William Burton's house where the topic was Irish antiquities, followed a few days later by his attendance at a meeting of the Catholic Committee. Yet in spite of this success O'Conor, as a Catholic, was vulnerable in very immediate ways to the penal laws against which he campaigned. In 1777 his youngest brother, Hugh, conformed to the Church of Ireland and sued for possession of the family property under laws relating to Catholic property. The case dragged on for eight years and was finally settled out of court, but Charles wasted much time and expense on it. At one point, just weeks after dining with William Burton, O'Conor was put under house arrest for his attorney's failure to comply with court requirements.

O'Conor continued his antiquarian researches and writings well into his seventies, publishing, for example, three articles in Charles Vallancey's journal, *Collectanea de Rebus Hibernicis*, between 1782 and 1784. He was too feeble to make progress on his larger project, a history of Ireland from the earliest times up to the Restoration, which remained unpublished. He lived long enough to see many of the penal laws dismantled and in 1785 noted with satisfaction that 'no man is now forbid[den] the benefits of our Civil Constitution' (*Letters of Charles O'Conor of Belanagare*, ed. C. C. Ward and R. E. Ward, 2.227). All his work had tended towards that object and for this reason his antiquarian writings, though having a certain significance in the history of scholarship, are immeasurably more important for giving a profound insight into Irish Catholic political concerns in the eighteenth century.

O'Conor died at Belanagare on 1 July 1791. His grandson Charles *O'Conor (1764–1828), Roman Catholic priest, wrote a life of him, the first volume of which was published in 1796 but quickly suppressed because of its polemical and inaccurate account.

CLARE O'HALLORAN

Sources *The letters of Charles O'Conor of Belanagare*, ed. C. C. Ward and R. E. Ward, 2 vols. (1980) · *Letters of Charles O'Conor of Belanagare: a Catholic voice in eighteenth-century Ireland*, ed. R. E. Ward, J. F. Wrynn, and C. C. Ward (1988) · C. D. A. Leighton, *Catholicism in a protestant kingdom: a study of the Irish ancien régime* (1994) · *DNB* · A. J. Webb, *A compendium of Irish biography* (1878)
Archives Clonalis House, Castlerea, Roscommon, MSS · Royal Irish Acad., MSS | BL, Egerton MSS · BL, letters to Thomas O'Gorman, Add. MS 21121 · BL, Stowe MSS · Dublin City Library, Dublin, Gilbert MSS
Likenesses Maguire, engraving, AM Oxf., Hope collection [*see illus.*] · Maguire, stipple, NPG · B. Mulrain, watercolour drawing (after portrait), NG Ire. · engraving (aged seventy-nine), repro. in *Memoirs of the life and writings of Charles O'Conor of Belanagare* [1796]

O'Conor, Charles (1764–1828), Roman Catholic priest and scholar, was born on 15 March 1764 at Belanagare, co. Roscommon, the second of the six sons of Denis O'Conor (1732–1804), landowner, and his wife, Catherine Browne, daughter of Martin Browne of Cloonfad, co. Roscommon.

His grandfather Charles *O'Conor (1710–1791) of Belanagare was a greatly esteemed scholar and collector of Irish manuscripts. In 1760 he had handed over Belanagare to his son Denis, and during his grandson's childhood he lived nearby at the Hermitage. The grandson was intended for the church and in 1779 he was sent to the Irish College in Rome, where he was ordained and received a doctorate in divinity, before returning to Ireland in 1789. While in Rome he developed his scholarly tastes by working on the Vatican manuscripts and was commissioned to search out Irish manuscripts in Italy for the Royal Irish Academy. Presentation to the parish of Kilkeevan (Castlerea) lay with O'Conor Don, the head of his family, and in 1792 O'Conor was installed as parish priest there. He initiated the building of the first Roman Catholic chapel in the town of Castlerea. In 1796 he published the first volume of a life of his grandfather, *Memoirs of the Life and Writings of the Late Charles O'Conor*. It was an outspoken work, as well as a confused and inaccurate one, and he quickly suppressed it.

In 1788 the marquess of Buckingham, when he was lord lieutenant of Ireland, had promised O'Conor's grandfather a pension if he would give his manuscripts to the Royal Irish Academy. He wrote to his friend Charles Vallancey that he would bequeath them to the academy, but they passed to his second son, another Charles. However, O'Conor got his grandfather's books and papers. Buckingham did not forget the Irish manuscripts and in 1798 persuaded the family to give them to him, but against O'Conor's wishes. Eventually he too was persuaded, but so that he could continue his scholarly work on them it was arranged that he would accompany the manuscripts to Stowe in the guise of chaplain to the marchioness, Mary Elizabeth Buckingham. Initially his bishop gave him eighteen months' leave of absence from his parish and this was later extended, but by 1803 the bishop was referring to O'Conor as 'the late incumbent'.

Life at Stowe was an escape for O'Conor from the grinding poverty of his flock at Castlerea and at least for a time moving among the great had its attractions. Besides this, O'Conor seems to have been very much attached to the Buckinghams. Several times the possibility of an Irish bishopric loomed—Achonry twice (in 1803 and again in 1808) and Elphin (in 1810)—but despite vigorous pressing by his family he disapproved of the methods of appointment and seems to have preferred the luxurious and scholarly life he led at Stowe. When the marchioness died in 1812 he lost his chapel, which returned to being a dressing-room, but by then he was well installed as librarian. The first marquess had built up a very large collection of important manuscripts and Sir John Soane was employed to remodel the library room into a magnificent gothick chamber.

Residence at Stowe not only gave O'Conor access to his grandfather's Irish manuscripts but also made it relatively easy for him to use those in the British Museum and the Bodleian. His work *Rerum Hibernicarum scriptores veteres* appeared in four volumes between 1814 and 1826. The first volume was devoted to a general survey of early Irish manuscripts, the others to the first edition in a Latin translation of the main Irish annals. O'Conor's scholarship was not equal to the task and by the later nineteenth century these volumes were no longer consulted, their value becoming historiographical. But for the first half of the nineteenth century their importance was considerable as the only gateway to early Irish history. The first volume, which revealed the existence of the early Irish manuscripts, included the first facsimile of the Book of Durrow and initiated the controversy, which raged through most of the twentieth century, as to which manuscripts are Irish and which Anglo-Saxon. In 1818 O'Conor published a catalogue of the manuscript collection at Stowe in two volumes: *Bibliotheca MS. Stowensis*. The manuscripts were sold to the fourth earl of Ashburnham in 1849. The fifth earl in turn sold them to the government in 1883, when they were divided: the Irish element went to the Royal Irish Academy, finally fulfilling the elder Charles O'Conor's promise of 1788, and the rest to the British Museum.

Because the O'Conors were one of the few Irish Roman Catholic landed families to survive the seventeenth-century confiscations, they were expected to, and did, take an active part in the effort to achieve Catholic emancipation. O'Conor's grandfather was a prolific pamphleteer in the cause and even his father, Denis, who had no taste for politics, played his part; his older brother Owen, who succeeded to the headship of the family and the title O'Conor Don, was also very active. In O'Conor's time the subject of greatest controversy was whether the government could be allowed a veto in the appointment of bishops. In 1810, just at the time when his family had begun a serious campaign to have O'Conor appointed bishop of Elphin, he published the first of a series of seven letters in which he took a different line on this matter from his family, the bishops, and most of the Irish Roman Catholic laity, by decrying papal influence in appointments. The pamphlets entitled *Columbanus ad Hibernos*, some of book size, appeared successively between 1810 and 1816. Only the first was anonymous; later he did not hesitate to subscribe himself 'Rev. C. O'Conor D.D.'. The pamphlets involve lengthy disquisitions on Irish history, particularly in relation to the 1641 rebellion, where he took the side of Ormond and Clanricarde against Rinuccini, the papal nuncio. Such was the stir he created that John Douglass, vicar-general of the London district, his immediate ecclesiastical superior in England, withdrew his priestly faculties. And when he arrived in Ireland, to see about his publications and to work in Trinity College Library, John Troy, the archbishop of Dublin, did likewise. He appealed to the pope and eventually the interdict was lifted.

O'Conor remained at Stowe for the rest of his active life, but when, in 1827, senility set in, he was moved to a Dublin asylum and finally to his old home at Belanagare, where he died on 29 July 1828. He was buried with his ancestors at Ballintubber Abbey, co. Roscommon.

WILLIAM O'SULLIVAN

Sources C. O. O'Conor Don, *The O'Conors of Connaught: an historical memoir* (1891) · *Letters of Charles O'Conor of Belanagare: a Catholic voice in eighteenth-century Ireland*, ed. R. E. Ward, J. F. Wrynn, and C. C. Ward (1988) · G. W. Dunleavy and J. E. Dunleavy, *The O'Conor papers: a descriptive catalogue … of the materials at Clonalis House* (1977) · G. Costigan, 'The tragedy of Charles O'Conor: an episode in Anglo-Irish relations', *American Historical Review*, 49 (1943–4), 32–54 · *DNB* · *Buckinghamshire*, Pevsner (1960)
Archives BL, extracts from Vatican MSS, Stowe MS 1054 · Clonalis House, Castlerea, co. Roscommon, corresp. and papers, notebooks · Hunt. L., corresp. and papers | BL, letters to George Faulkner, additions to O'Brien's Irish–English dictionary, Egerton MSS 87, 201 · BL, letters to Thomas Grenville, Add. MSS 41857–41859 · Bucks. RLSS, MS catalogue of the Stowe library · Royal Irish Acad., MSS · TCD, corresp. with W. C. Mason · TCD, letters to J. C. Walker · Westm. DA, corresp. with bishops Douglass and Poynter
Likenesses Nugent, lithograph, BM · portrait (in middle age), Clonalis House, Castlerea, co. Roscommon

O'Conor, Charles Owen [*known as* O'Conor Don] (1838–1906), landlord in Ireland and politician, was born on 7 May 1838 in Dublin. He was the eldest son of Denis O'Conor of Belanagare and Clonallis, co. Roscommon, and Mary, *née* Blake, daughter of Major Blake of Towerhill, co. Mayo. The O'Conors were among Ireland's most ancient and renowned Catholic families. Charles's father, MP for co. Roscommon from 1831 to 1847, died when he was a child, leaving him large estates in Roscommon and Sligo.

O'Conor was educated at the Benedictine public school St Gregory's College, Downside, near Bath, and in 1855 entered London University, but did not take a degree. He was married twice: first, on 21 April 1868, to Georgina Mary (*d.* 1872), the third daughter of Thomas A. Perry of Warwickshire; they had four sons. Seven years after Georgina's death he married Ellen, the third daughter of John S. More O'Ferrall, of Granite Hall, Kingstown, and Lisard, Edgeworthstown, co. Longford. Coming from a Catholic landed family, O'Conor was destined to play a significant role in political life. He was made her majesty's lieutenant and *custos rotulorum* of co. Roscommon in 1858; and at the parliamentary by-election on 26 March 1860 he was returned unopposed as a Liberal for that county, which he represented until his defeat in the general election of 1880. Although not particularly skilled as a debater, he enjoyed considerable influence in the House of Commons because of his mastery of detail. He took particular interest in education, land tenure, prisons, workshop conditions, Irish Sunday closing, state purchase of Ireland's railways, grand jury reform, the taxation of Ireland, and Catholic issues generally. During his lifetime he wrote pamphlets on Irish taxation, land tenure, and education. His immense local status and close connections with the Catholic ecclesiastical hierarchy made him a valuable channel of communication between Westminster politicians and Catholic clergy.

O'Conor stood unopposed for re-election as a Liberal in the general elections of 1865 and 1868. In the early 1870s he flirted with the home-rule movement, attending and speaking at the national conference held in Dublin in November 1873 which founded the Home Rule League. During the proceedings he expressed reservations about the precise formulation of home rule, but nevertheless stood as a home-ruler at the general election of 1874 and was once again returned unopposed; his younger brother Denis O'Conor was elected without a contest for Sligo in the home-rule interest at the same election. Although O'Conor declined to join the newly formed Home Rule Party, he gave it independent support. During the debate on home rule in June 1874 he expressed reservations about its application to Ireland and in subsequent years opposed the party on various questions. During these years he advocated the extension of the 'Ulster custom', giving tenants the right to sell their 'interest' in their holdings, to the rest of Ireland. He played a significant part in negotiations leading to the Irish Intermediate Education Act in 1878 and was involved in the discussions of the University Act of the following year. His interest in education and contribution to the Royal University, where he was a member of senate for many years, led to the conferment of an honorary LLD in 1892. Although standing as a home-ruler at the general election of 1880, he was one of those old-style MPs displaced by a follower of Charles Stewart Parnell. O'Conor made one further attempt to re-enter the House of Commons, contesting Wexford borough against W. H. K. Redmond, brother of the Irish nationalist John Redmond, at the by-election on 27 July 1883, when he was defeated decisively.

O'Conor's chief political role was as a member of numerous committees and commissions and in local administration. He served on the penal servitude commission (1862), the factories and workshops commission (1875), the registration of deeds commission (1878), the land law commission (1880), the reformatories and industrial schools commission (1882), and the royal commission on the financial relations between Great Britain and Ireland (1894). On the death of H. C. E. Childers in 1896 he became chairman of this last body, a post he held at the time it reported. His involvement in local administration was also extensive. He was a magistrate, deputy lord lieutenant of Roscommon from 1888 until his death, and was elected to the Roscommon county council following its creation under the Local Government Act of 1898. He was also a member of the intermediate education board and of the executive committee of the Irish landowners' convention.

O'Conor also took a strong interest in Irish history and language. He was for many years president of the Antiquarian Society of Ireland, president of the Royal Irish Academy, and president of the Irish Language Society. In 1881 he was sworn of the Irish privy council. He secured the introduction of the Irish language into the curriculum of the intermediate education board, while his interest in antiquarianism resulted in the publication in 1891 of a history of the O'Conors of Connaught. O'Conor died at his home, Clonallis, Castlerea, co. Roscommon, on 30 June 1906, leaving an estate valued at £33,272 4s. 4d., of which £6937 13s. 4d. was in England. On 5 July he was buried in the new cemetery, Castlerea.

G. Le G. Norgate, *rev.* Alan O'Day

Sources *The Times* (2 July 1906) · *The Times* (5 July 1906) · *The Times* (21 Sept 1906) · H. Boylan, *A dictionary of Irish biography*, 2nd edn

(1988) • *WWBMP* • D. Thornley, *Isaac Butt and home rule* (1964) • *Dod's Parliamentary Companion* • E. R. Norman, *The Catholic church and Ireland in the age of rebellion, 1859–1873* (1965) • A. M. Sullivan, *New Ireland*, [new edn] (1882) • E. Larkin, *The consolidation of the Roman Catholic church in Ireland, 1860–1870* (1987) • E. Larkin, *The Roman Catholic church and the home rule movement in Ireland, 1870–1874* (1990) • E. Larkin, *The Roman Catholic church and the emergence of the modern Irish political system, 1874–1878* (1996) • K. T. Hoppen, *Elections, politics, and society in Ireland, 1832–1885* (1984) • E. Malcolm, *'Ireland sober, Ireland free': drink and temperance in nineteenth-century Ireland* (1986) • M. MacDonagh, *The home rule movement* (1920)
Archives Clonalis House, Castlerea, Roscommon, corresp., diaries, and papers | Dublin Diocesan Archives, Cullen MSS
Wealth at death £33,272 4*s.* 4*d.*: probate, 5 Sept 1906, *CGPLA Ire.* • £6937 13*s.* 4*d.*: Irish probate sealed in London, 18 Sept 1906, *CGPLA Eng. & Wales*

O'Conor, Matthew (1773–1844), historian, the sixth son of Denis O'Conor (1732–1804) of Belanagare and Catherine, daughter of Martin Browne of Cloonfad, co. Roscommon, was born in co. Roscommon on 18 September 1773. Like his brother Charles *O'Conor (1764–1828), he was intended for the priesthood, and studied in the English College at Rome, but unlike Charles, who duly entered the church, Matthew O'Conor adopted the legal profession and became eminent therein. He supplemented his practice at the bar by studying and writing upon subjects in connection with Irish history and there is some evidence that he always hankered after a military career. He married Priscilla Forbes in 1804 and they had five children: Denis (1808–1872), of Mount Druid, who was sheriff of his county in 1836; Arthur (*d.* 1870), of the Palace, Elphin; Matthew, of Mount Allen; and two daughters, about whom nothing is known.

O'Conor was the author of *The history of the Irish Catholics from the settlement in 1691, with a view of the state of Ireland from the invasion of Henry II to the revolution* (Dublin, 1813). This work, which was polemical in tone, was based upon some valuable documents in the possession of the writer's grandfather Charles *O'Conor of Belanagare, an antiquary and an early activist on behalf of Irish Catholics.

The posthumously published *Military history of the Irish nation; comprising memoirs of the Irish brigade in the service of France, with an appendix of official papers relative to the brigade from the archives at Paris* (Dublin, 1845) was part of a larger work contemplated by O'Conor. It goes down only to 1738, and, as a consequence of not being revised by the author, contains errors. But the work is based upon genuine research and on material presented to O'Conor by Colonel Montmorency Morres. It was a valuable contribution to military history, and was critically commended at the time, but was soon superseded by *Irish Brigades in the Service of France* (1851), by John Cornelius O'Callaghan, and by later works. O'Conor died on 8 May 1844, probably at his seat, Mount Druid, co. Roscommon.

THOMAS SECCOMBE, *rev.* THOMAS BARTLETT

Sources C. O. O'Conor Don, *The O'Conors of Connaught: an historical memoir* (1891) • *Dublin University Magazine*, 25 (1845), 593–608 • Burke, *Gen. Ire.* (1958) • *GM*, 2nd ser., 24 (1845), 271 • A. J. Webb, *A compendium of Irish biography* (1878) • Allibone, *Dict.*
Archives Hunt. L., letters to his brother

O'Conor, Sir Nicholas Roderick (1843–1908), diplomatist, born at Dundermott, Ballymoe, co. Roscommon, on 3 July 1843, was the youngest of three sons of Patrick A. C. O'Conor, of Dundermott, and his wife, Jane, second daughter of Christopher Ffrench, of Frenchlawn, co. Roscommon. He was educated at Stonyhurst College, and afterwards at Munich under J. J. I. von Döllinger, and entered the diplomatic service in 1866. After some months of employment in the Foreign Office he was appointed attaché at Berlin, where he attained in 1870 the rank of third secretary. After service at Washington and Madrid he returned to Washington to be second secretary in 1874, and was transferred in 1875 to Brazil, where he was employed on special duty in the province of Rio Grande do Sul in November 1876. In October 1877 he was moved to Paris, where he had the advantage of serving for six years under Lord Lyons.

In December 1883 O'Conor was appointed secretary of legation at Peking (Beijing), and on the death of the minister, Sir Harry Parkes, in March 1885, he assumed charge of the legation for a period of fifteen months. He found himself almost immediately involved in somewhat awkward discussions with the Chinese and Korean governments with regard to the temporary occupation of Port Hamilton, a harbour formed by three islands at the entrance to the Gulf of Pecheli (Beizhili), of which the British admiral had taken possession as a coaling station, following the deterioration of Anglo-Russian relations over Afghanistan. The question was eventually settled, after the alarms about war with Russia had disappeared, by the withdrawal of the British occupation, the Chinese guaranteeing that no part of Korean territory, including Port Hamilton, would be occupied by any foreign power.

The annexation of Upper Burma to the British Indian empire, proclaimed by Lord Dufferin in 1886, gave rise to an equally embarrassing issue. The Chinese government viewed the annexation with great jealousy. The Burmese shared a frontier with China and with the Chinese vassal state of Tibet. China claimed indeterminate and rather obsolete rights of suzerainty over the Burmese, recognized by a decennial Burmese mission to China. After a tedious negotiation O'Conor succeeded in concluding an agreement on 24 July 1886, making provision for the delimitation of the frontier by a joint commission, for a future convention to settle the conditions of frontier trade, and agreeing to the continuance of the decennial Burmese mission, in return for a waiver of any right of interference with British authority and rule. Although this agreement was only the preliminary to a series of negotiations, it paved the way for a friendly solution. On its conclusion O'Conor, who had been made CMG in February 1886, was created CB.

After a brief tenure of the post of secretary of legation at Washington, in January 1887 O'Conor succeeded Frank Lascelles as agent and consul-general in Bulgaria. The principality was at the time in a critical situation. Prince Alexander, whose nerve had been shaken by his abduction, having failed to obtain the tsar's approval of his

Sir Nicholas Roderick O'Conor (1843–1908), by James Russell & Sons, pubd 1896

resumption of power, had abdicated in September 1886, and the government was left in the hands of three regents, of whom the principal was the former prime minister, Stambulov. For the next few months, in the face of manoeuvres on the part of Russia to prolong the interregnum or procure the selection of a nominee who would be a mere vassal of Russia, vigorous attempts were made by the regency to obtain a candidate of greater independence. On 7 July 1887 Prince Ferdinand of Saxe-Coburg and Gotha was elected, and Stambulov again became prime minister. O'Conor, who united great shrewdness with a blunt directness of speech which, although not generally regarded as a diplomatic trait, had the effect of inspiring confidence, exercised a steadying influence on the energetic premier. Excellent relations were maintained between them in the course of five years' residence. Among other results was the conclusion in 1889 of a provisional commercial agreement between Great Britain and Bulgaria.

In April 1892 O'Conor was again appointed to Peking, this time in the position of envoy to the emperor of China and to the king of Korea. A notable change in the etiquette towards foreign representatives was made by the court in his reception at Peking; he was formally received with the staff of the legation at the principal entrance by the court officials and conducted to a personal audience with the emperor in the Cheng Kuan Tien (Zhengguandian) Palace. In July 1894 the disputes between China and Japan over the introduction of reforms in the administration of Korea led to open war between the two countries, and

O'Conor's responsibilities were heavy. The Chinese forces were routed by land and sea, and in April 1895 the veteran statesman Li Hung-chang (Li Hongzhang) concluded the treaty of Shimonoseki, by which China made substantial concessions to Japan, including the peninsula of Liaotung (Liaodong). O'Conor handled this and subsequent negotiations about Port Arthur in 1895 with considerable skill and was made KCB in May 1895.

In October 1895 O'Conor left China to become ambassador at St Petersburg. The following year he attended the coronation of Tsar Nicholas II. He received the grand cross of St Michael and St George and was sworn of the privy council in the same year. He was as popular at St Petersburg as at his previous posts, but towards the close of his residence British relations with Russia were seriously complicated by the course taken by the Russian government in obtaining from China a lease of Port Arthur and the Liaotung peninsula. The discussions, which at one time became somewhat acute, were carried on by O'Conor with his usual tact; but a dispute arose between him and Count Muravyov, the Russian minister for foreign affairs, as to an assurance which the latter had given but subsequently withdrawn that Port Arthur, as well as Talienwan (Dalianwan), should be completely open to international commerce. This incident, and the manner in which Count Muravyov endeavoured to explain it, made it on the whole fortunate that in July 1898 there was an opportunity for O'Conor to be transferred to Constantinople. He had been promoted GCB in 1897.

The last ten years of O'Conor's life, which were passed in Constantinople, were very laborious. He worked under great difficulties for the policy of administrative reform, which was strenuously pressed whenever possible by the British government. He succeeded, however, in winning to a considerable extent the personal goodwill and confidence of the sultan and of the ministers with whom he had to deal, and by persistent efforts cleared a large number of long outstanding claims and subordinate questions which had been a permanent burden to his predecessors. Among the more important questions which he succeeded in bringing to a settlement were those of the Turco-Egyptian boundary in the Sinai peninsula, and of the British frontier in the hinterland of Aden.

O'Conor had married, on 13 April 1887, Minna, eldest daughter of James Robert Hope-*Scott and his second wife, Lady Alexandrina Howard. They had three daughters. O'Conor had succeeded in May 1877 to his brother Patrick's estate of Dundermott, but was never able to live there. His health had never been strong since his residence in China, and in 1904 he returned to Britain for advice, and underwent a serious operation. The strain of work on his return to Turkey was too much for him, and he died at his post in the British embassy, Constantinople, on 19 March 1908. He was buried with every mark of affection and respect in the cemetery at Haydar Pasha, where a monument erected by his widow bears with the date the inscription 'Nicolaus Rodericus O'Conor, Britanniæ Regis apud Ottomanorum Imperatorem Legatus, pie obiit'. It was at that time unusual for a Roman Catholic Irishman to be appointed ambassador. O'Conor showed a safe pair of hands in several complex negotiations.

T. H. SANDERSON, *rev.* H. C. G. MATTHEW

Sources *The Times* (20 March 1908) · *FO List* (1908) · G. P. Gooch and H. Temperley, eds., *British documents on the origins of the war, 1898–1914*, 11 vols. in 13 (1926–38) · R. P. Churchill, *The Anglo-Russian convention of 1907* (1939)
Archives CAC Cam., corresp., diaries, and papers | CUL, corresp. with Lord Hardinge · NL Scot., corresp. with Lord Rosebery · Trinity Cam., letters to Sir Henry Babington Smith
Likenesses J. Russell & Sons, photograph, pubd 1896, NPG [*see illus.*] · Spy [L. Ward], caricature, mechanical reproduction, NPG; repro. in *VF* (1 May 1907)
Wealth at death £44,277 13s. 6d.—in England: Irish probate sealed in England, 16 June 1908, *CGPLA Eng. & Wales*

O'Conor, Roderic Anthony Mary Joseph (1860–1940), artist, was born on 17 October 1860 at Milton, co. Roscommon, Ireland. He was the second child and first son of Roderick Joseph O'Conor JP (*d.* 1893), a wealthy landowner who was to become high sheriff of Roscommon in 1863, and Eleanor Mary Browne. He was to be followed by one other brother and four sisters. O'Conor was directly descended from one of the most noble families of Ireland, which had ruled Connaught in the middle ages. He was sent to the Roman Catholic school of St Lawrence's, Ampleforth, in Yorkshire (1873–8), and following his matriculation returned to Dublin, where in 1881 he registered at the Metropolitan School of Art. He there won the Cowper prize for drawing the antique, and after a period at the Royal Hibernian Academy, where he won bronze medals for drawing, he returned to the Metropolitan in 1882 for a further year, before following his friend Nathaniel Hill and other Irish students to study at the Académie Royale des Beaux-Arts in Antwerp. After a year there he returned to Dublin before leaving in 1886 to enrol in C. E. A. Duran's atelier in Paris. He continued to receive an allowance from his father, and began to exhibit at the Salon; *Portrait of Paul Vogelius* was accepted in 1888, and *Spinning Wheel* the following year. These were probably painted in a solid academic Flemish influenced style, as were some surviving works of the same time.

O'Conor never left France again except for short periods. Working at Grez-sur-Loing he adopted an impressionist technique in paintings such as *Autumn Landscape* of 1886 (oil on canvas; priv. coll.), and is held to be the earliest artist from the British Isles to do so. In 1889 he started exhibiting with the Salon des Indépendants, and in 1891 went to Pont Aven in Brittany. There Gauguin's friend Emile Bernard first showed him the work of Vincent Van Gogh, whose approach influenced him strongly: *Breton Peasant Woman Knitting* (oil on board, 1893; priv. coll.) is a striking example of his new approach, with its intense complementary colours painted in stripes of heavy impasto. He became a close friend of Armand Séguin, Cuno Amiet, Władysław Ślewiński, Paul Sérusier, and the Englishman John Forbes-Robertson, and was to maintain prolonged contact with this Pont Aven group of artists centred around Paul Gauguin. Gauguin himself dedicated a monotype, *L'angélus* (1894), to him. O'Conor was present at the celebrated incident when Gauguin's ankle was broken in a fight with some sailors at Concarneau in 1894, and at this time Gauguin hoped that he would accompany him on his return to Tahiti. O'Conor ceased to paint in thick swirling strokes after his contact with Gauguin, but his handling of paint was not closely influenced by the French artist; it was always energetic, using varied techniques from applying it thickly with a palette knife to thinly staining the canvas, and his use of colour remained vivid. He executed some forty etchings, and a little sculpture. He bought several paintings by Gauguin, a great many prints, and a woodcarving. Between 1903 and 1910 O'Conor sold most of the Roscommon estates (his father had died in 1893) and grew wealthy over the years from investments, but sold little of his work. In 1904, after periods living at Pont Aven, at Rochefort-en-Terre, and at Fontainebleau, he moved to Paris, where he lived for the next twenty-nine years. He exhibited regularly at the Salon d'Automne, until 1935, twice serving on the jury, once when joint vice-president. He preferred not to have a dealer. He loved literature, and his studio was frequented in Paris by many writers including the young Clive Bell, Arnold Bennett, and Somerset Maugham (whom he disliked), and his work was noticed with approval in the press by French critics of distinction such as Charles Morice, Alfred Jarry, and Guillaume Apollinaire. At this time the English painter Matthew Smith became a devoted follower, and Roger Fry, Duncan Grant, and Vanessa Bell owed much to his friendship. In 1910 he visited Italy for the first time, and in 1912, Spain. In 1916 Henriette (Renée) Honta (1894–1955) became his model, mistress, and pupil—she was to become a successful painter in her own right. Although O'Conor had had many liaisons with women, he always lived alone, and continued to do so until he married Renée in 1933. He then bought a large bourgeois house (in her name) at Neuil-sur-Layon, and in the following year they settled there together. He continued to work until he died at home on 18 March 1940 of a stroke and a heart attack with oedema. He was buried in the cemetery at Neuil.

O'Conor was a tall, erect man, with combed-back hair, a long, tapering, severe-looking face, and a long nose. A routine French police description described him as having blue eyes and a full mouth. For years he wore a moustache, and in later life had spectacles. His *Self Portrait* of 1903 (oil; National Gallery of Ireland, Dublin) shows his dark complexion. He was very fond, as a young man, of outdoor pursuits such as cycling and hunting. He also enjoyed playing the violin.

The French state bought *Le pot chinois* (oil, 1927; Musée d'Orsay, Paris) in the year it was painted. His *Still-Life with Bottles* (oil, 1892) is in the Tate collection as well as four other works; *The Farm at Lezaver, Finistère* (oil, 1894) is in the National Gallery of Ireland. These and other examples of his work (in the Museum of Modern Art, New York, the Scottish National Gallery of Modern Art, Edinburgh, and elsewhere) were acquired from Roland, Browse, and Delbanco, who bought some sixty pictures at the 1956 sale in Paris of the contents of his studio, following the death of his widow. Until then O'Conor, by now almost unknown in Britain, had also been largely forgotten in France, and so it is to that London gallery that the beginning of his recognition as one of the most important artists of his time is due. ALAN WINDSOR

Sources J. Benington, *Roderic O'Conor: a biography and catalogue* (1992) · R. Johnston, *Roderic O'Conor, 1860–1940* (1985) [exhibition catalogue, London, Belfast, Dublin, and Manchester, 12 Sept 1985 – 10 May 1986] · *Gauguin* (1989) [exhibition catalogue, Galéries Nationales du Grand Palais, Paris] · H. Roland, *Behind the façade* (1991) · L. Browse, *Duchess of Cork Street* (1999)
Likenesses R. O'Conor, self-portrait, oils, 1903, NG Ire.

O'Conor [O'Connor], **William Anderson** (1820–1887), Church of England clergyman and author, was born in Cork. His family came from Roscommon, and spelt their surname O'Connor. After attending school in Cork for a short period he was dogged by ill health, which kept him at home for several years. Eventually, at nearly thirty years of age, he went to Trinity College, Dublin, with the intention of entering the ministry. His course there was, however, interrupted by his father's financial difficulties, and he resumed his studies by entering St Aidan's Theological College, Birkenhead, Cheshire, where he was appointed Latin lecturer. He did not finally graduate until 1864. After his ordination in 1853 he became curate first of St Nicholas's Church, Liverpool, and then, in 1854, of St Thomas's, Liverpool. From 1855 to 1858 he had sole charge of the church of St Michael and St Olave, Chester, and in 1858 he was appointed rector of St Simon and St Jude, Granby Row, Manchester, a very poor city parish, where he worked for the rest of his life. On 3 March 1859 he married Charlotte Boydell (*b.* 1829), daughter of Isaac Temple. They had no children.

Several years after O'Conor settled in Manchester his eloquence and originality as a preacher began to attract attention. He worked hard as a parish priest but found his surroundings uncongenial and discouraging. He was said to find much relief in literary pursuits and in the society of men of literary tastes, among whom he shone as a witty and versatile conversationalist and writer. He became a frequent contributor to the *Proceedings* of the Manchester Statistical Society and the Manchester Literary Club, and the many papers which he read to the latter were said to have been marked by originality, subtlety, and humour. As well as writing on literary subjects he published a number of sermons, biblical commentaries, and a *History of the Irish People* (2 vols., 1882), which was arguably not so much a history as an indictment against English rule in Ireland. Originally a pamphlet, the work was revised and reprinted in 1886–7. He became involved in fashionable societies such as the Dramatic Reform Association and the Manchester Art Museum Committee. He also acted as a poor-law guardian for a time.

In 1885 O'Conor went to Italy, in the hope that this would be beneficial to his health; while there he became chaplain of an Anglican church in Rome. After his return to England he was soon absorbed in work, but before long became ill again. He then went to Torquay, where he died

on 22 March 1887 and where he was buried; his wife survived him. At the time of his death he was in straitened circumstances, his estate amounting to less than £250.

O'Conor was a tall, slim man, his features pale and ascetic-looking. A good likeness of him was printed in Peter Okell's paper in the *Manchester Quarterly* (January 1891). C. W. SUTTON, *rev.* DAVID HUDDLESTON

Sources *N&Q*, 7th ser., 7 (1889), 68, 174 · *W. A. O'Conor's essays in literature and ethics*, ed. W. E. A. Axon (1889) · P. Okell, 'The Rev. W. A. O'Conor, B.A.: his life and work', *Manchester Quarterly*, 10 (Jan 1891), 1–26 · Boase, *Mod. Eng. biog.* · m. cert. · d. cert.
Likenesses portrait, repro. in Okell, 'The Rev. W. A. O'Conor, B.A.', 10, facing p. 1
Wealth at death £238 8*s.* 5*d.*: administration, 7 May 1887, *CGPLA Eng. & Wales*

Ó Criomhthain, Tomás Dhónaill [Tomás Ó Crohan] (*bap.* 1855, *d.* 1937), writer, was born on the Great Blasket Island, co. Kerry, Ireland, and baptized there on 29 April 1855, the youngest of the eight children of Dónal Mac Criomhthain (*bap.* 1808) and Cáit Ní Shé, who were married on 26 January 1837. The Great Blasket Island (An Blascaod Mór)—a narrow island about 5 kilometres long and 1 kilometre wide—is the largest of the seven islands in the Blasket archipelago and lies off the south-west coast of Ireland in co. Kerry. At the east of the island and closest to the mainland lie the remains of the island village where Tomás Ó Criomhthain was born and lived out his life. The Irish-speaking island community never exceeded 200 inhabitants, and the community depended for its livelihood on the sea.

Tomás Ó Criomhthain attended the Roman Catholic national primary school on Great Blasket Island from 1864, when the school was first opened, to some time in 1876, when he may have served as a 'monitor' for a short period. The standard of teaching was generally poor and the entire curriculum was in English, a language which was not generally understood by the island community. Although the islanders were predominantly Roman Catholic, a number of them were adherents to the Church of Ireland and there had been a Church of Ireland missionary school on the island between 1839 and 1863 where the language of instruction was Irish. With the revival of the language movement within Ireland and the Anglo-Irish literary movement, for a time the Blasket Islands became a centre for those wishing to study the Irish language. John Millington Synge came to the Great Blasket in 1905, and his account of island life, *In West Kerry* (1907), generated further interest. The first prominent scholar visitor was Carl Marstrander of the University of Oslo, who came to the island in 1907 and befriended Tomás Ó Criomhthain, who in turn became his mentor in Irish and island lore. Marstrander recommended the island to Robin Flower of the British Museum, who was completing a catalogue of the museum's extensive collection of medieval manuscripts in the Irish language. Flower first came to the island in 1910 and remained a constant visitor until his death. He became a close friend of Ó Criomhthain and worked with him in his collection of island material, much of which was narrative recording of Tomás Ó

Criomhthain's own accounts of island life. Flower's book on the island culture, *The Western Island* (1944), opened the Great Blasket to a wider audience when the material was given as a series of lectures at the Lowell Institute in Boston, Massachusetts, in 1935.

Notwithstanding the scholars' attention which Ó Criomhthain enjoyed, he had set himself to write and began in the first instance from 1908 with accounts of island life for Irish language periodicals. How a fisherman from the Blasket Islands became literate in his own language at a time when reading and writing in the Irish language were not widespread remains intriguing. Certainly the scholar visitors brought Irish language literacy skills to the island, but Tomás Ó Criomhthain was able to read the visitors' texts with them. Ó Criomhthain in his own accounts tells of his learning to read and write Irish from schoolchildren on the mainland when he was stormbound as an adult. The origins of his literacy in Irish are more likely to derive from the legacy of the protestant missionary school on the island. It was not, however, the visiting scholars who played the vital role in persuading Tomás Ó Criomhthain to write his insider's view of island life. Brian Ó Ceallaigh from Killarney (also known as Bryan Albert Kelly) came to the island in 1917 and established a supportive and intellectual friendship with Ó Criomhthain; the two discussed literature and writers in other cultures. Ó Ceallaigh introduced Tomás Ó Criomhthain to the works of Maksim Gorky, Pierre Loti, and Boccaccio in translation. Ó Ceallaigh persuaded Ó Criomhthain to write his island journal *Allagar na hInise* and autobiography *An tOileánach*; these texts were written on sheaves of foolscap provided by Ó Ceallaigh and were sent to him by post. Ó Ceallaigh tried to have the texts published but finally deposited them with an Irish language scholar, author, and publisher, Pádraig Ó Siochfhradha, who edited them for publication. Ó Criomhthain's two books *Allagar na hInise* (1928) (published in translation by T. Enright as *Island Cross Talk*, 1986) and *An tOileánach* (1929) (published in translation by R. Flower as *The Islandman*, 1937) mark a unique chapter in the canon of Irish literature. As both were written from within the island culture, Ó Criomhthain's voyage was into uncharted seas; there were no exemplars for his work in the then emerging and tentative literary movement in modern Irish.

Allagar na hInise (*Island Cross Talk*) is essentially a book of sketches written by Ó Criomhthain between 1918 and 1923. The book is constructed for the most part into sequences, which contain conversations and events which engaged the writer. What emerges is a powerful series of images constructed around his neighbours on the island and his mobilization of their characters and speech habits. Taken together the portraiture is a very vivid series of notes on the community which hang together well as a portfolio of everyday island life. *An tOileánach* (*The Islandman*), written between 1923 and 1928, is an autobiography ranging from the nineteenth-century childhood memories of Tomás Ó Criomhthain to the second decade of the twentieth century. The time frame is frequently set from events which had an impact on the

island community. What he achieves in his camera sweep is an insider's view made accessible to the outsider: an inscape. The style is taut, but within its compass the writer copes with personal matters such as his first love for a girl from the neighbouring island of Inis Icíleáin, and of his hard life after marriage to another woman, Máire Ní Chatháin (*bap.* 1859), on 5 February 1878. His account of island life is perhaps best summarized by his stated and rather stern aim in writing the book in the ultimate chapter:

> I have written minutely of much that we did, for it was my wish that somewhere there should be a memorial of it all, and I have done my best to set down the character of the people around me so that some record of us might live after us, for the like of us will never be again. (trans. R. Flower)

Tomás Ó Criomhthain died on 7 March 1937 on the Great Blasket Island, and was buried on the mainland at Dún Chaoin in the churchyard of Baile An Teampaill facing across to the Blasket Islands. His descendants carried on his literary legacy. He was followed as a writer by his son Seán, his grandson Pádraig Ua Maoileoin (*b.* 1913), and his great-nephew Muiris Ó Súilleabháin (1904–1950).

MUIRIS DIARMUID MAC CONGHAIL

Sources T. D. Ó Criomhthain, *An tOileánach*, ed. S. Ó Coileáin (2002) · 'An tOileánach', NL Ire., MS G1020 · 'Allagar na hInise', NL Ire., MS G1022 · Dingle Public Library, Dingle, Kerry, Tomás Ó Criomhthain Memorial Collection · R. Flower, *The western island, or, The Great Blasket* (1944) · S. Ó Duilearga, *Seanchas Ón Oileán Tiar* (1956) · M. Mac Conghail, *The Blaskets: a Kerry island library* (1987) · parish register, Kerry, Ballyferriter, 29 April 1855 [baptism] · parish register, Kerry, Ballyferriter, 9 Feb 1859 [baptism, wife] · parish register, Kerry, Ballyferriter, 5 Feb 1878 [marriage]
Archives Dingle Public Library, Kerry, Ireland · NL Ire., MSS G 1020 and 1022 · University College, Dublin
Likenesses photographs, University College, Dublin, department of Irish folklore, National University

Ó Crohan, Tomás. *See* Ó Criomhthain, Tomás Dhónaill (*bap.* 1855, *d.* 1937).

Octa (*fl.* 512?). *See under* Kent, kings of (*act. c.*450–*c.*590).

Octavians (*act.* 1596–1598), financial administrators, were eight reformers prominent in the government and politics of Scotland under James VI. On 9 January 1596 they were appointed as joint commissioners of a new permanent exchequer, with full powers over the collection and disbursement of royal revenues. Their appointment was for life and the king was to appoint no further members to the commission without their agreement; nor could he spend money without their prior approval.

The Octavians, in the order in which their commission named them, were: Alexander *Seton (1556–1622), commendator of Pluscarden, later first earl of Dunfermline; Walter *Stewart (*d.* 1617), commendator of Blantyre, later first Lord Blantyre; David *Carnegie of Colluthie (*d.* 1598), later laird of Kinnaird; John *Lindsay of Menmuir (1552–1598), later laird of Balcarres; James *Elphinstone of Invernochty (1557–1612), later laird of Barnton and first Lord Balmerino; Thomas *Hamilton of Drumcairn (1563–1637), later Lord Binning, earl of Melrose and first earl of Haddington; John *Skene of Curriehill (*c.*1540–1617); and Peter *Young of Seton (1544–1628).

The nucleus of the group had been formed in 1593, when six of the future Octavians (Elphinstone, Hamilton, Lindsay, Seton, Stewart, and Young) were appointed to constitute the queen's financial council. On 1 January 1596 Queen Anne presented her husband with a large purse of gold as a new year's gift, symbolizing her council's financial efficiency and legitimizing the promotion of its members. In February the English ambassador reported that four new councillors—Elphinstone, Hamilton, Lindsay, and Seton—had been promoted. But the group's identity, and the name of Octavians, was soon universally established. A later contemporary account added Stewart to the group's active members, implicitly characterizing the others as passive. However, these perceptions focused on those who were most prominent as politicians, and the Octavians were not simply politicians. Part of their team's strength lay in its diverse membership, with each person making a distinctive contribution. Together they had social status and connections, political acumen, legal training, and financial expertise.

The three Octavians regarded as passive illustrate the point. Skene was a hard-working bureaucrat, whose assiduous researches into the government records in his care seem to have been behind some of the Octavians' attempts to reassert royal rights. Carnegie's particular area of expertise was finance—he had long experience as an auditor of exchequer and of other financial commissions, and had personally speculated in government debts. Young's skills were in humanist learning and diplomacy. Three Octavians—Elphinstone, Seton, and Lindsay—were younger sons of peers, and two were closely connected to the king personally: Young had been the king's tutor (along with George Buchanan) between 1569 and 1580, while Stewart had been one of the four youths whom he educated alongside the royal pupil. Young had since acted periodically as an ambassador and held the honorific post of royal almoner, and Stewart had become a gentleman of the king's chamber. All the members of the group except Stewart had university degrees; his lack of one presumably reflects his attachment to the court since his youth.

All but two Octavians were judges in the court of session, which required legal expertise and usually significant formal training; the two exceptions, Carnegie and Young, also had some legal expertise. All were privy councillors, though they had not necessarily attended council meetings regularly. Two were already officers of state: Seton had been lord president of the court of session since 1593 and Skene had been clerk register since 1594. Stewart had been keeper of the privy seal, a lesser office, since 1582. All officers of state had lately been overshadowed by the chancellor, John Maitland of Thirlestane, but Maitland's death in September 1595, and James's decision to leave his office vacant, left a political gap which the Octavians moved astutely to fill. The team had no leader, though there was some initial jockeying for position between the two members of highest status, Seton and Stewart. Seton wanted to be president of the council, whereas Stewart wanted the keepership of the great seal.

Each felt that such promotion would make them the recognized leader of the team. However, neither obtained his wish, and they evidently recognized the advantage of co-operation.

The Octavians' sweeping powers attracted immediate attention, and critics denounced their effectiveness in cutting expenditure seen as necessary to the king's status. Their initial intention was merely to supervise and control the royal officials responsible for revenue administration. Soon the Octavians changed from supervising to take most financial and other offices for themselves. This may have increased their efficiency but it tarnished their disinterested public image. They pursued various policies in increasing revenue. They reformed the customs administration, and introduced wholly new customs on imports in May 1597. They put much effort into reviving the ancient dues from the crown lands. They helped to put a larger-than-ever direct tax through parliament in November, though much of their work at restoring the land revenues was perceived as being an attractive alternative to direct taxation. Finally, they stepped up the crown's hitherto nominal claim to highland revenues: having sent a military expedition to the highlands in 1596 they asserted sweeping powers over the chiefs in 1598, which stored up much future trouble. One policy to which they did not stoop, debasement of the coinage, was resumed with a vengeance after their removal. However, it was their efforts to reduce expenditure that attracted most hostility—cuts in household fees and in pensions to the nobility, which hit the pockets of the well-connected.

The Octavians' regime was diluted on 30 November 1596, when eight nobles and two other administrators were appointed to assist them, apparently to deflect criticism. This seems to have made little practical difference. A more serious challenge came the next month, as the Octavians were caught up in the struggle of the radical leaders of the church against the political influence of certain Roman Catholic nobles. Four of the Octavians—Elphinstone, Hamilton, Lindsay, and Seton—were believed to be closet Catholics (Elphinstone and Seton indeed were). The uprising in Edinburgh (17–19 December) collapsed for lack of noble support, but in the aftermath the Octavians were forced to resign, on 7 January 1597.

However, ten days later the Octavians were reappointed to a new exchequer commission, further enlarged to twenty-two members of whom they themselves formed the core (most of the others were unlikely to act regularly). Their powers were as before, except that they now held office during royal pleasure rather than for life. The commission could not act without Stewart, who now held the two key offices of comptroller and treasurer. This arrangement worked at first, but Stewart's offices ran him into debt and he soon sought to resign. In October he entered negotiations with Thomas *Foulis, a goldsmith and financier who had extended large credit to the king and who had managed several branches of the revenue before the Octavians' advent. The result, on 29 December 1597, was a new commission of exchequer with a similar membership to the previous one, but with Foulis and his two deputies added, and with a proviso that Foulis's authority was necessary to all expenditure. With the addition of a private agreement between Stewart and Foulis, the latter now had full effective control over the royal revenue.

Foulis's imposing-looking regime soon came crashing down. One Octavian, Lindsay, engineered its destruction with the king's connivance, by a contrived failure to meet royal obligations to Foulis. This indicates division in the Octavian ranks, since Stewart seems to have been sincerely committed to Foulis and Hamilton had recently married Foulis's sister. On 17 January 1598 Foulis's scheme collapsed and the king charged Stewart to resume his office of treasurer, signalling that there was no longer any immediate intention of repaying the large royal debt to Foulis. This, effectively a royal bankruptcy, was one of the main legacies of the Octavian period.

After this the Octavians retained a collective identity for five more months, as a political faction opposed to the gentlemen of the chamber. The end came on 29 June 1598, when the permanent exchequer, the Octavians' power base, was abolished by a convention of estates. This signalled an end to policies of restraint in royal generosity to the nobility, evidently as a quid pro quo for the convention's other main measure, the Act anent Feuding by which the nobles agreed to submit blood feuds to royal justice. The Octavians' demise thus brought some benefit to James, who had long sought such an act, though his finances went from bad to worse until 1603.

The Octavians themselves went their separate ways after 1598. Two (Carnegie and Lindsay) died in that year. For the survivors, especially Elphinstone, Hamilton, and Seton, membership of the group had launched their careers while not tying them to any continuing group loyalty. In 1611 Hamilton and Seton were among the members of a new eight-man financial commission, immediately dubbed the New Octavians. The Octavians placed financial reform, or at least the idea of it, on the agenda for a generation of Scottish politicians.   JULIAN GOODARE

Sources A. L. Murray, 'Sir John Skene and the exchequer, 1594–1612', *Stair Society Miscellany*, 1 (1971) • J. Goodare, 'Thomas Foulis and the Scottish fiscal crisis of the 1590s', *Crises, revolutions and self-sustained growth: essays on fiscal history, 1130–1830*, ed. W. M. Ormrod and others (Stamford, 1999) • J. H. Burton and D. Masson, eds., *The register of the privy council of Scotland*, 1st ser., 14 vols. (1877–98), 1545–1625 • *CSP Scot.*, 1547–1603 • *APS*, 1593–1625 • *Scots peerage* • D. Johnstone, 'History of Scotland', 1655, NL Scot., Adv. MS 35.4.2 • 'A historical discourse on Scotland, 1031–1600', BL, Add. MS 35844 • *Memoirs of his own life by Sir James Melville of Halhill*, ed. T. Thomson, Bannatyne Club, 18 (1827) • J. M. Thomson and others, eds., *Registrum magni sigilli regum Scotorum / The register of the great seal of Scotland*, 11 vols. (1882–1914), vols. 5–6 • R. Zulager, 'A study of the middle-rank administrators in the government of King James VI of Scotland, 1580–1603', PhD diss., U. Aberdeen, 1991 • D. Moysie, *Memoirs of the affairs of Scotland, 1577–1603*, ed. J. Dennistoun, Bannatyne Club, 39 (1830)

Ó Cuileannáin, Eóin. *See* O'Cullenan, John (1584/5–1656?).

Ó Cuinn, Diarmaid. *See* O'Quinn, Jeremiah (*d.* 1657).

O'Cullane [O'Cuiléin, Collins], **John** (1754–1816), poet, was born in co. Cork. He belonged to a family whose original territory was Ui Conaill Gabra, now the baronies of Upper and Lower Connello, co. Limerick. Many of them continued to live in the district in the nineteenth century, but the chief family of the clan was driven from their original estate and settled near Timoleague, co. Cork, where the family was finally dispossessed by the Boyles, earls of Cork. Several of the O'Cullanes were buried in the Franciscan priory of Timoleague. John O'Cullane's parents had a small farm, gave him a good education, and hoped that he would become a priest. He, however, preferred to be a schoolmaster, married, and had several children. His school was at Myross in Carbery.

Two of O'Cullane's poems have been printed and translated—'An buachaill bán' ('The Fair-Haired Boy'), written in 1782, published in 1860 by John O'Daly, and 'Machtnadh an duin e dhoilghiosaidh' ('Meditation of the Sorrowful Person') which is printed in Irish (Hardiman, 2.234), and paraphrased in verse by Thomas Furlong and by Sir Samuel Ferguson. He also translated into Irish Campbell's 'Exile of Erin'. Many of his poems remained in manuscript, however, as did part of a history of Ireland that he had compiled, and part of an English–Irish dictionary. John O'Cullane died at Skibbereen, co. Cork, in 1816.

NORMAN MOORE, *rev.* M. CLARE LOUGHLIN-CHOW

Sources J. Hardiman, ed., *Irish minstrelsy, or, Bardic remains of Ireland*, 2 (1831), 234–5, 401–11 • J. O'Dely, ed., *The poets and poetry of Munster*, trans. G. Sigerson, 2nd ser. (1860) • S. M. O'Donovan, *The topographical poems of John O'Dubhagain and Giolla na naomh O'Huidhrin* (1862) • S. Lewis, *A topographical dictionary of Ireland*, 2nd edn, 2 vols. (1850) • A. J. Webb, *A compendium of Irish biography* (1878)

O'Cullen [Culin], **Patrick** (*d.* 1534), bishop of Clogher, came from a family of physicians of Clogher diocese, possibly a branch of the O'Cullen sept of *erenaghs* in Clogher. Patrick was an Augustinian friar who, before February 1517, had become the prior of the Augustinian house of St John without Newgate, Dublin. By that time he held a doctorate in theology. He was reputed to be talented in history and in writing poetry.

On 11 February 1517 O'Cullen was provided to the see of Clogher by Leo X. He was also elected bishop by Clogher's dean and chapter. Clogher is an extensive diocese which encompasses much of southern Ulster. However, in 1517 the revenues of its ordinary were reckoned to be worth only 50 ducats (£11–12) and O'Cullen was allowed to retain his priorship *in commendam* until 1531 to ensure him a reasonable income.

Clogher Cathedral enjoyed a very modest liturgical regimen before O'Cullen's arrival, with mass being celebrated on Sundays only, with one set of vestments, one chalice, a wooden cross, and a bell. The new bishop set about reforming his diocese with energy. Already by 1522 there were five chasubles available for cathedral services, an indication of an improvement in its liturgical provision. In 1528 Bishop O'Cullen composed a Latin office in praise of St Macartan, the patron saint of the diocese, which is still sung on his feast day in Monaghan Cathedral. Furthermore, O'Cullen worked with his archdeacon, Rory O'Cassidy, an eminent historian in his day, to reform the diocesan archives. The result of their efforts is the register of Clogher. That manuscript was lost in the second half of the seventeenth century but Kenneth Nicholls has reconstructed much of the register from extracts transcribed before its disappearance. The register is one of the most important historical sources for the church in late medieval Ireland, though it has yet to be studied systematically. It preserves a miscellany of material, including many documents pertaining to the see, lands, and revenues of Clogher from the course of the later middle ages; a catalogue of the bishops of Clogher; some church courts' *acta*; records of some synodal legislation; a couple of legends relating to St Patrick and St Tigernach; and Bishop O'Cullen's office of St Macartan.

O'Cullen's episcopate in Clogher was interrupted in 1527 as a consequence of a hard-fought succession dispute among the ruling Maguires of Fermanagh. He secured a papal dispensation to reside outside his diocese temporarily, conceivably in his priory at Dublin. Yet he had returned to Clogher before the close of 1528 and resumed his ministry in the diocese. O'Cullen died at Clogher in the spring of 1534 and was buried inside St Macartan's Cathedral, Clogher.   HENRY A. JEFFERIES

Sources *The whole works of Sir James Ware concerning Ireland*, ed. and trans. W. Harris, rev. edn, 1 (1764) · W. M. Brady, *The episcopal succession in England, Scotland, and Ireland, AD 1400 to 1875*, 1 (1876) · K. W. Nicholls, 'The register of Clogher', *Clogher Record*, 7 (1971–2), 361–431 · W. M. Hennessy and B. MacCarthy, eds., *Annals of Ulster, otherwise, annals of Senat*, 4 vols. (1887–1901), vol. 3 · A. Gwynn, *The medieval province of Armagh, 1470–1545* (1946) · M. J. Haren, 'A description of Clogher Cathedral in the early sixteenth century', *Clogher Record*, 12 (1985), 48–54

O'Cullenan, Gelasius (*c.*1554–1580). *See under* O'Cullenan, John (1584/5–1656?).

O'Cullenan, John [Eóin Ó Cuileannáin] (1584/5–1656?), Roman Catholic bishop of Raphoe, was born at Mullaghnashee, Ballyshannon, co. Donegal, the seventh and youngest son of Donncha Ballach Ó Cuileannáin, gentleman, and his wife, Iníon Dubh Ní Dhuíbhir. The O'Cullenans, of royal Munster descent, were prominent followers of the O'Donnells of Tír Conaill, and Niall, Donncha's brother, and Cormac, his son, fought in Red Hugh's campaigns. Donncha's wife was presumably related to Émann Dubh Ó Duíbhir, abbot of Assaroe. John O'Cullenan had at least one sister, mother of Father Philip Clery, reputedly martyred in 1642. The Cistercian abbey of Assaroe adjoined Mullaghnashee, and John had four Cistercian brothers, three at least, including Gelasius [*see below*], being abbots.

Despite the disparity in their ages, John O'Cullenan's eldest brother was **Gelasius** [Glaisne] **O'Cullenan** (*c.*1554–1580), Cistercian monk. Born at Mullaghnashee, he became a Cistercian monk, probably at nearby Abbey Assaroe, a daughter-house of Boyle Abbey, co. Roscommon, Latinizing his name to Gelasius, and was ordained priest. He studied at Louvain and Paris, becoming DTh of the Sorbonne. While in Paris he was appointed titular abbot of Boyle (still functioning although suppressed), and went there about 1579, apparently by way of Rome. Setting vigorously about restoring monastic life and ministering to the neighbouring population, he received practical help from a local personage, possibly MacDermot of Moylurg. He went to Dublin and secured from the privy council sanction for permission, previously given, for a limited monastic revival at Boyle. But John Garvey, dean of Christ Church, Dublin, fearful of the damage done to the Reformation cause in Connaught and Ulster by the zeal of Gelasius, persuaded his fellow councillors to have him and his companion Eóin O'Mulkern, the Premonstratensian abbot of Lough Cé monastery, near Boyle, arrested. Offers of high office in the established church were made in vain to both. They were then cruelly tortured and afterwards tried, probably by martial law, for treason, in that they rejected the queen's ecclesiastical authority as expressed in the 1560 Acts of Supremacy and Uniformity. Found guilty, they were hanged and, it seems, then beheaded at the public place of execution outside Dublin city, on 21 November 1580. The Cistercian historians Henríquez and Hartry claim that their steadfast demeanour brought 500 bystanders back to the practice of Catholicism. Gelasius's place of burial is unknown. The reputation as martyrs (*fama martyrii*) of the two was constant from the beginning.

John O'Cullenan was fostered by Sir Hugh O'Donnell and then studied humanities at home for four years, going on at the age of twenty to the Irish College, Salamanca. He read theology at Louvain, Paris, Rome, and Rheims, where he became DTh. Tutor to the earl of Tyrconnell in Brussels, he was made vicar apostolic (1621), and then in 1625 (consecrated 1626) bishop, of his native diocese of Raphoe. Arrested in 1628 in an invasion scare, he was in 1636 gaoled for three months in Dublin Castle by an actively protestant administration. Imprisonment and penury took their toll on his health. Yet the bishops had made some progress in reorganizing Catholicism, and he as vice-primate, with extensive faculties of absolving and dispensing, was busy. While his chiefly rank merited him eulogy in seven poems in *deíbhidhe* metre by the Tír Conaill bards, he himself was aware of the pastoral value of the contemporary literary activity—historical, ascetical, and apologetic—in Irish.

Taken captive again in 1642 O'Cullenan narrowly escaped the fate of the seventy-two insurgents accompanying him, who were slaughtered by the protestant Lagan forces in north-west Ulster, only to endure the rigours of a Londonderry dungeon for four years. He refused to conform to the established church and was eventually released, arriving in Kilkenny in April 1647. He supported Rinuccini's condemnation of the Ormond peace of 1646 and the cessation with Lord Inchiquin of 1648. One of the three bishops who followed the nuncio to Galway, he endured the months of siege of that city by the marquess of Clanricarde. At Ormond's instance he treated with Owen Roe O'Neill at Ballykelly in August 1649, but no agreement was reached. At this time the bishops, he among them, sought Catholic unity in defence of faith and king. Then in September 1650 he was chief of the committee of four bishops who at Jamestown made public the excommunication of all who supported Ormond, the viceroy.

Driven to take refuge on Inishbofin, O'Cullenan and Bishop Lynch of Clonfert were exiled by the parliamentarians in 1653, and reached Brussels in April. With the divisions among Irish Catholics caused by Rinuccini's censures still persisting, O'Cullenan was now among those who called for a general absolution. Pope Alexander VII, however, demanded prior repentance and gave to O'Cullenan and three other named bishops sole power to absolve. The pope's brief (2 August 1655) was published in Belgium, prefixed by a passionate appeal to all who had opposed the censures to seek absolution. While this appeal, O'Ferrall thought, was the work of Dr Walter Enos, it appeared over the names of O'Cullenan (the only bishop of the four resident in Belgium) and his three colleagues. It may be taken as his curtain speech in the fateful Irish drama in which he had played a part. A list of Irish bishops in 1656 does not include his name, which suggests that he probably died earlier that year. He is buried in the chapel of the Blessed Virgin, in the church of Sts Michael and Gudule, Brussels.   JOHN J. SILKE

Sources B. O'Ferrall and D. O'Connell, *Commentarius Rinuccinianus de sedis apostolicae legatione ad foederatos Hiberniae Catholicos per annos 1645–1649*, ed. J. Kavanagh, 6 vols., IMC (1932–49) · P. F. Moran, ed., *Spicilegium Ossoriense*, 3 vols. (1874–84) · J. McErlean, 'Eóin Ó Cuileannáin, bishop of Raphoe, 1625–61', *Archivium Hibernicum*, 1 (1912), 77–121 · B. Jennings, ed., *Wadding papers, 1614–38*, IMC (1953) · E. Maguire, *A history of the diocese of Raphoe*, 2 vols. (1920), 1.132–46 · P. Ó Gallachair, 'Tirconaill in 1641', *Father John Colgan*, ed. T. O'Donnell (1959), 70–100 · P. J. Corish, *The origins of Catholic nationalism* (1968), vol. 3/8 of *A history of Irish Catholicism* · *Cause of … Richard Creagh … and companions*, 2 vols. (Diocese of Dublin, 1998), 1.303–62 · C. Ó Conbhuidhe, *Studies in Irish Cistercian history* (1998) · C. Henríquez, *Fasciculus sanctorum ordinis Cisterciensis* (1623) · M. Hartry, *Triumphalia chronologica*, ed. D. Murphy (1891) · D. Murphy, *Our martyrs* (1896) · D. J. O'Doherty, 'Students of the Irish College, Salamanca (1595–1619) [pt 1]', *Archivium Hibernicum*, 2 (1913), 1–36 · W. M. Brady, *The episcopal succession in England, Scotland, and Ireland, AD 1400 to 1875*, 3 vols. (1876–7) · P. O'Sullivan-Beare, *Historiae Catholicae Iberniae compendium*, ed. M. Kelly (1850) · *Father Luke Wadding: commemorative volume*, ed. Franciscan Fathers dún Mhuire, Killiney (1957) · C. P. Meehan, *The rise and fall of the Irish Franciscan monasteries and memoirs of the Irish hierarchy in the seventeenth century*, 5th edn (1877)

Archives Archivio Vaticano, Vatican City, Nunziatura di Fiandra · Franciscan Library, Killiney, co. Dublin · Sacra Congregazione di Propaganda Fide, Rome, Acta, Scritture originale riferite nelle congregazioni generali (SOCG)

Wealth at death practically penniless: Archivio Vaticano, Vatican City, Nunziatura di Fiandra, vols. 37 (1653), 38 (1654), 39 (1655), and 142 (1655)

O'Curry, Eugene [Eoghan Ó Comhraidhe, Eoghan Ó Comhraí] (1794–1862), Irish scholar, was born on 20 November 1794 at Dunaha, near Carrigaholt, co. Clare, Ireland, the third son of Eoghan Ó Comhraí (Eugene O'Curry), a farmer, and his wife, Cáit Uí Chomhraidhe (Catherine O'Curry), Ní Mhadagáin (Madigan) of Dunaha.

O'Curry's father had spent some time as a wandering pedlar, and had acquired a deep interest in Irish folklore and music; the fact that he possessed a number of Irish manuscripts suggests that he was literate. There is no record of O'Curry's having received a formal education, but it seems likely that his father taught him to read and write, and the Irish scholar Peter O'Connell (Peadar Ó Conaill), who compiled an unpublished Irish–English dictionary with the help of O'Curry's brother Malachy (Maoilsheachlainn), used to visit the house.

O'Curry worked on his father's farm, and was also a schoolmaster for a time. At the age of about thirty-three he got a post in the lunatic asylum at Limerick. He spent seven years in this employment, and married Anne Broughton of Broadford, co. Limerick, on 3 October 1824. It is clear that he was an enthusiastic supporter of Catholic emancipation at this period, and he wrote a poem congratulating Daniel O'Connell on his election to parliament in 1828. A year later he sent an address and historical poem to the Royal Irish Academy, which is preserved (MS 23 H 30, 91–5).

O'Curry gradually established a reputation as an authority on Irish language and history, and a letter written to him by John O'Donovan in 1834 contains a request for information on the survival in Limerick of traditions relating to Muircheartach Ó Briain, king of Thomond. O'Donovan had been employed since 1830 on the topographical and historical section of the Irish Ordnance Survey, and recommended that O'Curry be appointed to the staff, though he expressed anxiety that the heavy work and travel might prove too much of a burden. He was appointed in 1835, and in fact did little travelling on behalf of the survey, remaining for the most part in Dublin. In January 1840 O'Donovan married Mary Anne, Mrs O'Curry's sister.

The work of this section of the Ordnance Survey was stopped in 1842, though O'Donovan continued to be paid until his death as adviser on the forms of the place names used in the maps. Between 1842 and 1844 O'Curry was mainly employed in cataloguing the Irish manuscripts in the possession of the Royal Irish Academy. After this work was completed, he supported himself by transcribing manuscripts. For example, in 1848 he transcribed the Book of the O'Conor Don for the Royal Irish Academy for a fee of £100. In 1849 he was likewise paid £100 for cataloguing the Irish manuscripts in the British Museum. It was he who transcribed the Irish manuscripts which O'Donovan edited in seven volumes between 1848 and 1851 as *The Annals of the Kingdom of Ireland by the Four Masters*.

The 1850s saw an improvement in O'Curry's financial situation, as well as increased recognition by other scholars. In 1851 he was elected a member of the Royal Irish Academy, in spite of O'Donovan's fears that his strongly expressed Catholic views might prevent some of the protestant members from voting in his favour. He contributed editions of Irish texts to a number of important publications. Thus he was responsible for the translation of the *Rule of Columkille* in William Reeves's edition of *Primate Colton's Visitation of the Diocese of Derry*, published in 1850. He also provided the text and translation of the Irish poems in Reeves's 'Description of the Codex Maelbrighte' in the *Proceedings of the Royal Irish Academy* of 1851. The songs in the first volume of George Petrie's *Collection of the Ancient Music of Ireland*, published in 1855, were mostly edited or dictated by him. He also helped Petrie with the preparation of the second volume: in September 1857 he accompanied O'Donovan, Petrie, and some members of the British Association to the Aran Islands, where they recorded the words and tunes of local songs. Reeves's 1857 edition of *Adamnan's Life of Columba* includes four poems relating to the saint which were edited and translated by O'Curry.

As well as contributing to the publications of other scholars, O'Curry also published under his own name. Worthy of mention are his edition of the poem 'Ogum i llia uas lecht' in the *Transactions of the Ossianic Society* for the year 1853, and of *Cath Mhuighe Léana* ('The Battle of Magh Léana'), which was published by the Celtic Society in 1855. A number of Irish poems were edited by him in the *Proceedings of the Royal Irish Academy*.

In 1854 the Catholic university was set up in Dublin by John Henry Newman, and in May of the same year O'Curry was appointed to the professorship of archaeology and Irish history. In 1855–6 he delivered a series of lectures—which Newman regularly attended—on the 'Manuscript materials of ancient Irish history'. This outstanding and still valuable work was published at the expense of the university in 1861. A later series of lectures, entitled 'On the manners and customs of the ancient Irish', was post-humously published by W. K. Sullivan in 1873. In 1858 he published a translation of 'The Sick-Bed of Cuchulainn and the Only Jealousy of Eimer' in *Atlantis*, the journal of the Catholic university.

The transcription, editing, and translation of the Irish legal manuscripts was a massive undertaking, involving many scholars. In 1851 Dr James Henthorne Todd and Dr Charles Graves asked O'Curry to transcribe and translate a law text entitled *Leabhar aicle* from a manuscript in the library of Trinity College, Dublin. They were so impressed with the result that they submitted in February 1852 a proposal to the government for the publication of all known law texts. O'Curry was sent to catalogue and collate the legal manuscripts in the British Museum and in the Bodleian Library. The first meeting of the commission for publishing the ancient laws and institutes was held in December 1852. Graves was chosen as secretary, and O'Donovan as editor. Not surprisingly, O'Curry was unhappy with this arrangement, and refused to work as a subordinate to O'Donovan. This disagreement was resolved by appointing both as co-editors, but it soured the hitherto cordial relations between the two men. None the less, the work of transcription proceeded at a fair pace, and was finished by October 1855. O'Curry's transcription comprised 2906 pages and that of O'Donovan 2491 pages. Problems relating to editorial policy further bedevilled the project. O'Curry had hoped that the brilliant Irish scholar Whitley Stokes might be persuaded to help. However, Stokes felt that his own legal knowledge was inadequate for taking

on the task. In 1859 the commissioners appointed the lawyer William Neilson Hancock as co-editor, and in 1861 they agreed that he and O'Donovan should start editing the *Senchas már* texts without O'Curry. The idea seems to have been that O'Curry should continue to work on *Leabhar aicle*. O'Curry refused, and urged that the principle of editorial co-responsibility should be retained. The death of O'Donovan on 10 December 1861 administered a severe blow to the project. Basic disagreements between Hancock and O'Curry persisted, and were still unresolved when O'Curry died of a heart attack, at his home, 2 Portland Street, Dublin, on 30 July 1862, leaving behind two sons and two daughters, whose mother had died earlier. He was buried three days later at Glasnevin cemetery, Dublin.

The Ancient Laws and Institutes of Ireland was published between 1865 and 1901; many of the work's flaws can be attributed to the premature deaths of O'Donovan and O'Curry, who were largely responsible for establishing sound Irish scholarship. O'Curry's industry and profound learning have ensured him a prominent place in the history of Irish studies. FERGUS KELLY

Sources E. O'Curry, *Lectures on the manuscript materials of ancient Irish history* (1861) · E. O'Curry, *On the manners and customs of the ancient Irish*, ed. W. K. Sullivan, 3 vols. (1873) · É. de hÓir, *Seán Ó Donnabháin agus Eoghan Ó Comhraí* (1962) · P. Ó Fiannachta, ed., *Eoghan Ó Comhraí: saol agus saothar* (1995) · *Síoladóirí: Eoghan Ó Comhraidhe agus Seán Ó Donnabháin*, Bráthair Críostamhail (Baile Átha Cliath, 1947) · P. MacSweeney, *A group of nation-builders: O'Donovan, O'Curry, Petrie* (1913) · M. Tierney, 'Eugene O'Curry and the Irish tradition', *Studies: an Irish Quarterly Review*, 51 (1962), 449–62 · M. Herity, 'Eugene O'Curry's early life: details from an unpublished letter', *North Munster Antiquarian Journal*, 10 (1966–7), 143–7 · T. Lee, 'Eugene O'Curry', *Limerick Field Club Journal*, 1/1 (1897–1900), 26–31 · T. Lee, 'Eugene O'Curry', *Limerick Field Club Journal*, 1/3 (1897–1900), 1–11 · T. Lee, 'Eugene O'Curry', *Limerick Field Club Journal*, 2 (1903), 177–89 · S. Atkinson, 'Eugene O'Curry', *Irish Monthly Magazine*, 2 (1874), 191–210 · CGPLA Ire. (1862)

Archives BL, catalogue of the Irish MSS in the British Museum, Add. MS 43376 · Royal Irish Acad., ordnance survey letters | Royal Irish Acad., Brehon law commission MSS

Likenesses F. W. Burton, pencil, 1857, NG Ire. · B. Mulrenin, portrait, repro. in de hÓir, *Seán Ó Donnabháin agus Eoghan Ó Comhraí*, facing p. 2 · photograph, repro. in Bráthair Críostamhail, *Síoladóirí*, frontispiece

Wealth at death under £1000: administration, 26 Aug 1862, CGPLA Eng. & Wales

Oda [St Oda, Odo] (*d.* 958), archbishop of Canterbury, was the son of a Dane who arrived in England in the army that invaded in 865, led, according to one version of the Anglo-Saxon Chronicle, by Ubbe and Ivarr. Oda's father had apparently settled in East Anglia, where his son later held lands.

Family background and early advancement Oda's family produced a number of prominent churchmen in this period. His nephew *Oswald was later archbishop of York, and the latter's kinsmen, Oscytel, archbishop of York between 958 or 959 and 971, and Thurcytel, abbot of Bedford (and perhaps of Crowland), may also have been kinsmen of Oda. In his *Vita sancti Oswaldi* (written probably between 997 and 1002), Byrhtferth of Ramsey relates that, despite his father's paganism and discouragement, Oda attended church services and joined the household of a pious Anglo-Saxon aristocrat, Æthelhelm, where he was educated by a 'religious man' (Raine, 1.404). He remained with Æthelhelm and was ordained priest, accompanying him on a pilgrimage to Rome, during which Oda miraculously healed his patron's illness. Byrhtferth's statement that, on his return, Oda was appointed bishop of Wilton by 'the king', Æthelhelm's brother, is muddled: no chronologically plausible English king is known to have had a brother of that name. Byrhtferth's account is probably to be preferred to that of the early twelfth-century *Gesta pontificum* of William of Malmesbury (d. 1142), largely followed in some manuscripts of John of Worcester's *Chronicle*, in which Oda fought under Edward the Elder, joined the clergy, became bishop of Wilton, and then archbishop of Canterbury at Æthelstan's instigation. In reality, Oda doubtless did owe his appointment as bishop of Ramsbury (not Wilton) to King Æthelstan (r. 924–39), but it was Æthelstan's brother King Edmund (r. 939–46) who subsequently promoted him to the archbishopric of Canterbury in 941, one of a number of ecclesiastics who exerted great influence in Edmund's reign.

Oda first appears in contemporary sources in 928, witnessing royal charters as bishop of Ramsbury. His attestations show that he continued to attend royal councils for the next thirty years. Little is known of his career under Æthelstan. Writing at the end of the tenth century, Richer of Rheims reports that Oda acted as a diplomat for the king in the negotiations with Hugh the Great, duke of the Franks, aimed at restoring Æthelstan's nephew, Louis IV d'Outremer, to the West Frankish throne in 936, but this statement lacks contemporary authority. It is equally uncertain whether Oda accompanied Æthelstan on the 'Brunanburh' campaign, though Eadmer, in his life of Oda (*Vita sancti Odonis*, composed between 1093 and 1125), relates that he miraculously repaired the king's sword at that battle. In 940, in concert with Wulfstan, archbishop of York, he acted as peacemaker between Edmund and Olaf Guthfrithson at Leicester.

Participation in government As archbishop under King Edmund, Oda maintained his close alliance with royal authority: in his pastoral letter to his bishops, for instance, he urged them to obey the royal will. He is probably the Archbishop Otto who is recorded in the life of Catroe escorting that saint to a channel port at King Edmund's behest. Oda's collaboration with Edmund produced a burst of legislation; curiously, indeed, all Oda's legislative activity took place in Edmund's reign. This material—Edmund's first law code (1 Edmund), Oda's pastoral letter, and his so-called 'chapters' or 'constitutions'—can be dated no more closely than to the period between his elevation to Canterbury in 941 and Edmund's death in May 946. Edmund's first law code was promulgated at an Easter synod held at London and deals entirely with religious matters, requiring the payment of church taxation, including the tithe, and imposing celibacy on the clergy. These interests are shared by the document christened *Constitutiones Odonis* in the seventeenth century, but perhaps more appropriately to be termed his

'Chapters', which makes considerable, though selective, use of the decrees of the papal legates of 786, and also draws on the *Collectio canonum Hibernensis*. It omits such eighth-century concerns as the banning of pagan ritual, consisting as much of moral exhortation as of legislation, with sections on the duties of kings, bishops, priests, and monks. It encourages almsgiving and, like 1 Edmund, forbids the violation of nuns and enforces payment of the tithe. Oda's address to his suffragans survives only in fragments recorded by William of Malmesbury in his *Gesta pontificum*. In addition to urging obedience to the king, it issues, in florid Latin, a reminder to the bishops of their pastoral responsibilities. During his archiepiscopate the East Anglian see was reorganized, with the creation of a new bishopric at North Elmham. The profession of faith of its first incumbent, Eadulf, is the only one to have survived from Oda's time (indeed, from the entire tenth century), perhaps indicating that Oda had a particular reason for recording and preserving it. His personal involvement would reflect his pastoral interests, as well as, perhaps, his family roots in the Danelaw.

Little can be said of Oda's activity in the reign of Eadred (r. 946–55) except that he very probably crowned the king and, as his charter attestations show, continued to attend the royal court. He was, however, a beneficiary of Eadred's will, by which he acquired 200 mancuses of gold, and was to hold 400 pounds of silver at Christ Church for the relief of the peoples of Kent, Surrey, Sussex, and Berkshire in times of emergency. The accession of Eadwig (r. 955–9) saw a palace revolution in which a number of Eadred's preferred advisers fell from favour. The earliest life of Dunstan, written c.1000 by an author known only as B, relates that Oda urged that Eadwig be induced to return to his coronation feast after he had left it to consort with a noblewoman and her daughter. This episode presumably reflects tensions which became apparent in 957 or 958 when Oda separated the king from his wife, Ælfgifu, on grounds of consanguinity. Byrhtferth's claim that Oda rode to the king's mistress's estate, seized her, and forced her expulsion from the country is unlikely, not least since Ælfgifu was certainly Eadwig's wife and not just his mistress. It is possible that in separating the king from his wife in 958 Oda was prompted by his support for the claims of Eadwig's younger brother Edgar, who, for reasons which are unclear, became king of the English north of the Thames in 957. The attestations of Eadwig's charters show a hiatus in Oda's attendance at court in 957 that may have been caused by his conflict with the king. Alternatively, given that he died in the following year, he may simply have been ill. Certainly, his absence did not prevent Eadwig from granting Oda 40 hides of land at Ely in 957.

Associations with reform Oda was one of a group of monasticizing bishops, including Cenwald of Worcester and Ælfheah of Winchester, whose attitudes and activities presaged widespread ecclesiastical reform in the next generation. He himself is reported by Byrhtferth to have taken the cowl at the monastery of St Benoît-sur-Loire at Fleury, where St Benedict's relics were preserved, though it is not known at what point in his career this occurred. It was to Fleury that he sent his nephew Oswald, whose earlier education he had undertaken, to learn what was believed to be the superior monastic practice of that house. While Oda thus set Oswald on the path to becoming one of the triumvirate of leading reformers, his role in the careers of the other two, Dunstan and Æthelwold, is less clear. One of Dunstan's early eleventh-century biographers, Adelard, relates that Dunstan was consecrated bishop of Worcester by Oda who inadvertently called him 'archbishop of Canterbury', thereby predicting the saint's future promotion. Oda's presence here, however, may simply be an assumption, or a convenient insertion, on Adelard's part.

One characteristic of reforming monasticism on the continent was its devotion to the cult of saints. As with Æthelwold and Oswald, there is evidence for Oda's interest in saints, and especially in their relics. When the minster church at Ripon, founded in the 660s by St Wilfrid, was burnt down during Eadred's northern campaign (usually dated 948), Oda had the saint's relics seized and brought to Canterbury, along with Ripon's copy of Stephen of Ripon's life of Wilfrid. He enshrined the relics in a splendid new reliquary at Christ Church, and in honour of this translation commissioned Frithegod, a member of his *familia*, to write a verse version of the saint's life, the *Breviloquium vitae Wilfridi*. Its prose preface, which, though in Oda's name, was probably drafted by Frithegod, defends what amounted to a relic theft by accusing the Northumbrian clergy of neglecting the saint's remains. According to Eadmer, Oda also acquired for Canterbury relics of the Frankish saint Ouen, whom a later source attests was the subject of another life by Frithegod.

Oda's association with Fleury, evident also from an acrostic poem addressed to Dunstan by Abbo of Fleury, was not his only continental connection. He is also listed as bishop of Ramsbury in the confraternity book of the alpine monastery of St Gallen, and as archbishop of Canterbury in that of nearby Pfäfers. Both entries may have been the fruits of trips to Rome, in the case of Pfäfers perhaps to collect his pallium. It is possible, on the other hand, that his appearance in the St Gallen confraternity book is linked with that of Bishop Cenwald of Worcester, who visited the monastery in 929. However, journeys to the continent by English prelates were not unusual, and Oda may have been abroad at other times and on other business. For similar reasons, it is difficult to attach his sojourns at Fleury, either for his profession as a monk or afterwards, to events like the possible diplomatic trip of 936.

At Canterbury, Oda had Christ Church renovated, reroofing the cathedral and raising its walls by 20 feet. Although two charters, one purporting to restore many estates to the cathedral, the other granting land at Twickenham, are transparent forgeries, more reliable evidence shows that Oda was able to enlarge Canterbury's landed estate. A genuine charter of Eadred of 949 (its authority has sometimes been mistakenly challenged), which may even be in the hand of Dunstan himself, granted Reculver

Minster to the cathedral. A charter fabricated in the mid-tenth century, which purported to be a seventh-century grant of land in Sussex to Wilfrid, may well be connected with the reception of that saint's cult at Canterbury; at any rate, it seems to have succeeded in gaining for the cathedral a large tract of land on the south coast. A charter recording the terms of a lease of Christ Church's lands at Ickham, Kent, to the Kentish thegn Æthelweard is witnessed by the archbishop and his community, giving valuable evidence for the latter's composition at the time. The Canterbury clergy were clearly differentiated from monks by being ranked in the various clerical grades. They may also have worn better clothing and retained some private, though inalienable, property during their lifetimes. Nevertheless, it is likely that Oda encouraged members of the community to follow his example and take monastic vows.

Death and memorials Oda died on 2 June 958 and was buried in Christ Church, immediately to the south of the principal altar on the chord of the east apse, probably the first archbishop of Canterbury to be interred within the cathedral. In his life of Dunstan, Osbern (d. 1094) says that Oda's monument was 'in the shape of a pyramid' (Stubbs, 109). This can be interpreted as meaning either a triangular-sectioned stone coffin lid, echoing some Roman sarcophagi, or a tall, slender, tapering pillar, like the shaft of a stone cross. During the twelfth-century rebuildings of the cathedral, the relics of Oda and Wilfrid were temporarily put in the former resting-places of Dunstan and Ælfheah, before both were installed in the corona, or 'chancel', of the Trinity Chapel, Oda's shrine standing on the south side. Eadmer reports that Oda had acquired the epithet 'the Good' during his lifetime, and that it was still current in his own day; he also states that Dunstan, after he became archbishop in 959, was in the habit of genuflecting as he passed Oda's tomb. Lack of contemporary testimony for the cult suggests, however, that Dunstan failed to capitalize on Oda's reputation for holiness. The first evidence for Oda's cult appears in Byrhtferth's life of Oswald, which contains a lengthy account of Oda's life and recounts four miracles. Eadmer wrote the first free-standing life of Oda, drawing on the reports in B's life of Dunstan and Byrhtferth's life of Oswald, slightly embellishing them and adding only two new episodes about the saint's life, probably derived from Canterbury tradition. Although Byrhtferth reports the hostility to Oda of his successor Ælfsige—which is why, he says, the latter died in the Alps in 959 on his way to collect his pallium—this may simply reflect the author's antipathy to Ælfsige, who was never identified with the reformist tendency in the English church. Oda's feast day is given on 2 June in the early thirteenth-century calendar of Christ Church, Canterbury; some later calendars give 29 May or 4 July.

CATHERINE CUBITT and MARIOS COSTAMBEYS

Sources [Byrhtferth of Ramsey], 'Vita sancti Oswaldi auctore anonymo', *The historians of the church of York and its archbishops*, ed. J. Raine, 1, Rolls Series, 71 (1879), 399–475 · *ASC*, s.a. 958 (recte 957); s.a. 961 [text D; text F] · 'Historia regum', Symeon of Durham,

Opera, vol. 2 · AS chart., S 230, 546, 1506 · S. Keynes, *An atlas of attestations in Anglo-Saxon charters, c.670–1066* (privately printed, Cambridge, 1993) · D. Whitelock, M. Brett, and C. N. L. Brooke, eds., *Councils and synods with other documents relating to the English church, 871–1204*, 1 (1981), 67–74 · Eadmer, *Vita Sancti Odonis*, PL 133.931–4 · M. Lapidge and M. Winterbottom, eds. and trans., *The early lives of St Dunstan*, OMT (2000) · W. Stubbs, ed., *Memorials of St Dunstan, archbishop of Canterbury*, Rolls Series, 63 (1874), 410 · *English historical documents*, 1, ed. D. Whitelock (1955), no. 107 · A. J. Robertson, ed., *The laws of the kings of England from Edmund to Henry I* (1925) · *Willelmi Malmesbiriensis monachi de gestis pontificum Anglorum libri quinque*, ed. N. E. S. A. Hamilton, Rolls Series, 52 (1870), 23–4 · *Frithegodi monachi breviloquium vitae beati Wilfredi et Wulfstani*, ed. A. Campbell (Zurich, 1950), 1–62 · A. O. Anderson, ed. and trans., *Early sources of Scottish history, AD 500 to 1286*, 1 (1922), 431–43 · Richer of Saint-Rémy, *Histoire de France, 888–995*, ed. and trans. R. Latouche, 2 vols. (Paris, 1930–37) · S. E. Kelly, ed., *Charters of Selsey*, Anglo-Saxon Charters, 6 (1998) · John of Worcester, *Chron.*, vol. 2 · F. Wormald, ed., *English Benedictine kalendars after AD 1100*, 2, HBS, 81 (1946), 139–46 · M. Lapidge, *Anglo-Latin literature* (1996) · S. Keynes, 'King Athelstan's books', *Learning and literature in Anglo-Saxon England: studies presented to Peter Clemoes on the occasion of his sixty-fifth birthday*, ed. M. Lapidge and H. Gneuss (1985), 143–201 · J. Armitage Robinson, 'Oda, archbishop of Canterbury', *St Oswald and the church of Worcester*, British Academy Supplemental Papers, 5 (1919), 38–51 · N. Brooks, *The early history of the church of Canterbury: Christ Church from 597 to 1066* (1984) · M. Lapidge, 'A Frankish scholar in tenth-century England: Frithegod of Canterbury / Fredegaud of Brioude', *Anglo-Saxon England*, 17 (1988), 45–65 · G. Schoebe, ed., 'The chapters of Archbishop Oda', *BIHR*, 35 (1962), 75–83 · D. N. Dumville, 'Learning and the church in the England of King Edmund I, 939–46', *Wessex and England from Alfred to Edgar* (1992), 173–84 · A. T. Thacker, 'Cults at Canterbury: relics and reform under Dunstan and his successors', *St Dunstan: his life, times, and cult*, ed. N. Ramsay, M. Sparks, and T. Tatton-Brown (1992), 221–45

Ó Dálaigh [Ua Dálaig, O'Daly] **family** (*per. c.*1100–*c.*1620), poets, apparently originated as local chieftains of Corcu Roíde (roughly the barony of Corkaree, Westmeath). Five eminent *ollamhain* ('master poets') of the surname are recorded during the twelfth century, the first of whom, Cú Chonnacht Ua Dálaig, described in the annals of Tigernach as 'the best poet in Ireland' died in 1139 as an old man in religious retirement at the ecclesiastical settlement of Clonard. Mael Ísa Ua Dálaig (*d.* 1185), whom the annals of Loch Cé call the 'master-poet of Ireland and Scotland, and high chieftain of Corcu Roíde', also died in old age at Clonard. Two others, Ragnall (*d.* 1161), and Gilla na Trinóiti (*d.* 1165), are described as master poets for the kingdom of Desmond, or south Munster, indicating that they were court poets to the Mac Carthaig kings there. The family acquired in the course of this century an extraordinarily high reputation, being among the earliest practitioners of the newly regulated art of *dán díreach* ('strict composition'), though no extant texts attributed to its members predate the early thirteenth century.

A number of fresh and elegant compositions ascribed to **Muireadhach Ó Dálaigh** (*fl.* 1213) of Lissadill, Sligo, date from this period. The two best-known (Bergin, nos. 20, 22) are: first, his address to the young Richard de Burgh (*d.* 1243), *Créd agaibh aoidhigh a gcéin?* ('Whence comes it that ye have guests from afar?') in which he styles himself Ó Dálaigh Midhe, and petitions the Anglo-Norman lord for refuge from the anger of Domhnall Ó Domhnaill, king of Tír Conaill (*r.* 1208–41), whose servant he has killed in a quarrel; and, second, his lament for his dead wife, Maol Mheadha—*M'anam do sgar riomsa araoir* ('My soul parted from me last night'), mourning her as his first love, who during twenty years of marriage had borne him eleven children. The account of his life in the annals is a semi-legendary composition of a later century. It relates that he went to Scotland after his exile by Ó Domhnaill, and he has been claimed as the ancestor of the distinguished Scottish poetic family of MacMhuireadhaigh. Fifteenth-century Irish genealogies (Royal Irish Academy, MS 1233, fol. 36r–v) assert that Muireadhach of Lissadill was brother to the celebrated **Donnchadh Mór Ó Dálaigh** (*d.* 1244), 'a master of poetry who never has been excelled and never will be', according to the annals of Connacht, where it is also stated that he was buried in the Cistercian monastery of Boyle; another version of his obit says that he kept a guest house, or hostel for travellers, a charity commonly offered by Irish scholars at the top of their profession. Such was his reputation as a religious poet that many folk hymns and ballads of the seventeenth and eighteenth centuries have been fathered on him, but a group of poems preserved in the fourteenth-century Book of Uí Mhaine (McKenna, *Dán Dé*) are probably genuine compositions of Donnchadh Mór. They are long and austere, and do not translate well, but the Irish text corruscates with redundance of rhyme, since like all true bardic poetry it was intended for public recitation. In *Gabham deachmhaidh ar ndána* Donnchadh Mór pledges to address a tithe of all his professional eulogies to God, and ends with a prayer that those learning or reciting his poem may receive heaven as their reward. Very few of his secular poems survive, the most striking being his lament for the death of his son Aonghus, *Ar iasacht fhuaras Aonghus* ('I obtained Aonghus on loan'; MacCionaith, *Dioghluim Dána*, no. 69). Another possible example is a eulogy for the three sons of Mac Giollamhuire (a chief in north Down): *Cuaine ríoghna rug Éadaoin* ('Éadaoin bore a queen's litter [of whelps]'; Book of the Dean of Lismore, p. 75; NL Ire., MS 992, fol. 37), which ends with an envoi to Aodh, son of Aodh Ó Néill, who may be the king Aodh Méith *Ó Néill (*d.* 1230).

Some poems from late thirteenth- and early fourteenth-century Connacht are ascribed to Mac Cearbhaill Bhuidhe ('Son of Yellow-Haired Cearbhall'), perhaps for a time the title of the head of a particular line in the Ó Dálaigh family. Cearbhall Buidhe Ó Dálaigh himself died in 1245. His son Tadhg, court poet to Aodh son of Feidhlim Ó Conchobhair, king of Connacht, died in 1274, the same year as his patron. Another Mac Cearbhaill Bhuidhe, court poet to Aodh, son of Eoghan Ó Conchobhair, king of Connacht (*r.* 1296–1309), composed one, perhaps both, of two poems in honour of the king's palace (MacCionaith, no. 119; Quiggin, 333–52), the first variously ascribed to Cúchonnacht son of Cearbhall Buidhe, Aonghus son of Cearbhall Buidhe, or Aonghus son of Tadhg son of Cearbhall Buidhe, and the second attributed to Aonghus Ruadh Ó Dálaigh, or Aonghus son of Cearbhall Ruadh (Red-Haired Cearbhall) Ó Dálaigh. The other Mac Cearbhaill Bhuidhe poems are also of a high quality, but most remain unpublished.

Genealogies indicate that the line of Ó Dálaigh Breif-neach, who composed poems for the Ó Raighilligh chief-tains in the late medieval and early modern period, des-cended from this section of the family.

In the mid-fourteenth century the main line of Ó Dálaigh Midhe (Ó Dálaigh of Meath) divided, when its head, **Aonghus Ruadh Ó Dálaigh** (*d.* 1350), son of Donnchadh son of Aonghus son of Donnchadh Mór, quar-relled with a local chief in co. Westmeath, Ruaidhrí Ó Maolmhuaidh (*d.* 1383). In a poem to the latter, *Ceangal do shíoth riom a Ruaidhri* (McKenna, 'Irish bardic poems', 317–25), Aonghus Ruadh threatened that if the quarrel were not resolved, he would reside with the more prominent Ó Briain chieftains of Thomond, in modern co. Clare. The existence in 1415 of a line of Ó Dálaigh of Corcumroe, Clare, headed by Fearghal (*d.* 1420), son of Tadhg son of Aonghus Ruadh, suggests that this threat was fulfilled.

However, from the fourteenth century onwards the poetic gifts of the Meath, Breifne, and Corcumroe lines of the family were outshone by the Munster branches of Ó Dálaigh Fionn (Ó Dálaigh the Fair) and Ó Dálaigh Cair-breach (Ó Dálaigh of Carbery, barony, in west Cork). This trend began with the career of **Gofraidh Ó Dálaigh Fionn** (*d.* 1387), styled by the annals of Ulster *Ollam Erenn re dán* ('chief master of Ireland in the art of poetry'). Edu-cated by the Mac Craith poets of Thomond, he soon outdid his teachers, much to their disgust, as the poem *Mairg chaitheas dlús re dalta* ('Woe to him who favours a pupil'; MacCionaith, no. 104) suggests. Gofraidh's earliest patron was Conchobhar Ó Briain (*d.* 1328), but he also addressed chiefs of Tír Conaill and Uí Mhaine, besides Mac Carthaigh Mór, Mac Carthaigh Cairbreach, and their sub-chieftains, and was court poet to the first, second, and third earls of Desmond. His association with the third earl, Gerald the Rhymer (Gerald fitz Maurice Fitzgerald, *d.* 1398), began during the latter's childhood and may have influenced the earl's subsequent development as an amateur poet in the Irish language. In some famous verses to the child Gerald and his father Maurice, the first earl, Gofraidh states: 'In the foreigners' poems we promise that the Irish shall be driven from Ireland, in the Irishmen's poems we promise that the foreigners shall be routed across the sea' (MacCionaith, no. 67). Religious poems and verse tracts on the composition of poetry are also attributed to him.

By the sixteenth century a branch of the Ó Dálaigh fam-ily had settled at Pallis, Wexford. One member was Aong-hus son of Doighre Ó Dálaigh (*fl.* 1598), poet to the Gabhal Raghnallach, or clan Ranelagh O'Byrnes. From this branch also came the semi-legendary lover of the seven-teenth century, Cearbhall na mBan (Cearbhall of the Women). However most prominent at this time was the Munsterman **Aonghus Ó Dálaigh Fionn** (*d.* 1601x9), son of Amhlaoibh Ó Dálaigh Fionn and author of a lament for Domhnall Mac Carthaigh, earl of Clancare (*d.* 1596): *Soraidh led chéile a Chaisil* ('Farewell to thy Husband, O Cashel!'; Book of O'Conor Don, Royal Irish Academy, MS 2, fol. 363a), and one for the latter's son Tadhg, baron of Val-encia (*d.* 1587/8): *A theachtaire thig ó'n bhFrainnc* ('Messenger who comes from France'; Royal Irish Academy, MS 490, p.

151). After the earl's death Ó Dálaigh Fionn appears to have concentrated on religious compositions, becoming nick-named Aonghus na Diadhachta (Aonghus of the Divinity). He ran a poetic school at his residence in Duhallow, under the patronage of the local chief, Domhnall Ó Caoimh, who died in the same year as his eminent protégé. A con-temporary, Aonghus Ruadh, or Aonghus na nAor (Aong-hus of the Satires) Ó Dálaigh (*d.* 1617) lived on the penin-sula of Muntervary in West Carbery, and composed a libel-lous poem, 'The tribes of Ireland'. From the same period, Lochlainn (*fl.* 1596–1620) son of Tadhg Óg Ó Dálaigh, prob-ably of the Ó Dálaigh Breifneach branch, is a transitional figure, who composed genre poetry as well as eulogies for patrons, including a lament for the collapse of Gaelic soci-ety in the wake of the plantations, *C'áit ar ghabhadar Gaoidhil?* ('Where have the Gaels gone?'), which mentions the new generation's indifference to his family's historic profession.   KATHARINE SIMMS

Sources *The tribes of Ireland: a satire by Aenghus O'Daly … together with an historical account of the family of O'Daly*, ed. J. O'Donovan (1852) • O. Bergin, *Irish bardic poetry*, ed. D. Greene and F. Kelly (1970) • L. MacCionaith [L. McKenna], *Dioghluim Dána* (1938) [repr. 1969] • L. McKenna, ed., *Dán Dé* (1922) • L. McKenna, 'Some Irish bardic poems', *Studies*, 37 (1948), 317–25 • E. C. Quiggin, 'O'Connor's house at Cloonfree', *Essays and studies presented to Wil-liam Ridgeway*, ed. E. C. Quiggin (1913), 333–52 • C. McGrath, 'Ó Dálaigh Fionn cct.', *Éigse*, 5 (1946), 185–95 • T. F. O'Rahilly, 'Irish poets, historians and judges in English documents, 1538–1615', *Proceedings of the Royal Irish Academy*, 36C (1922), 86–120 • W. Gillies, 'A poem on the downfall of the Gaoidhil', *Éigse*, 13 (1970), 203–10 • J. E. Doan, 'The poetic tradition of Cearbhall Ó Dálaigh', *Éigse*, 18 (1980), 1–24 • B. Ó Cuív, 'Eachtra Mhuireadhaigh Í Dhálaigh', *Studia Hibernica*, 1 (1961), 56–69 • S. Ó hInnse, ed., *Miscellaneous Irish annals, AD 1114–1437* (1947); repr. (1993) • W. M. Hennessy and B. MacCarthy, eds., *Annals of Ulster, otherwise, annals of Senat*, 4 vols. (1887–1901) • A. M. Freeman, ed. and trans., *Annála Connacht / The annals of Con-nacht* (1944) • W. M. Hennessy, ed. and trans., *The annals of Loch Cé: a chronicle of Irish affairs from AD 1014 to AD 1590*, 2 vols., Rolls Series, 54 (1871); repr. (1939) • *AFM*, 2nd edn • S. Mac Airt, ed. and trans., *The annals of Inisfallen* (1951) • W. Stokes, ed., 'The annals of Tigernach [8 pts]', *Revue Celtique*, 16 (1895), 374–419; 17 (1896), 6–33, 119–263, 337–420; 18 (1897), 9–59, 150–97, 267–303, 374–91; pubd sep. (1993) • S. Pender, ed., 'The O'Clery book of genealogies', *Analecta Hibernica*, 18 (1951), 1–195

Ó Dálaigh, Aonghus, Fionn (*d.* 1601x9). *See under* Ó Dálaigh family (*per.* c.1100–c.1620).

Ó Dálaigh, Aonghus [Aengus O'Daly; *called* Aonghus na n-Aor, an Bard Ruadh] (*d.* **1617**), poet, was the author of *Muintir fhiodhnacha na mionn*, a long series of satirical quat-rains on numerous Gaelic clerical and noble families. Although at least three well-known poets called Aonghus Ó Dálaigh flourished *c.*1600, oral tradition locates the sat-irist as having lived on the Muntervary peninsula between Dunmanus Bay and Bantry Bay, co. Cork. This was the home of Ó Dálaigh Cairbreach, head of a cadet branch of the poetic dynasty of *Ó Dálaigh. In 1852 substantial remains of the Ó Dálaigh Cairbreach school were still pointed out in the townland of Drumnea, parish of Kilcro-hane, whereas tradition identified a smaller ruin in the townland of Corra, once part of a larger townland of Bally-roon, as the house of the Bard Ruadh. On these grounds

Edward O'Reilly identified the Bard Ruadh with the Aonghus Ó Dálaigh of 'Ballyorroone', recorded in an inquisition at Old Castle in Cork (18 September 1624) as having died on 16 December 1617 (possibly in Ballyroon), leaving a legitimate son, Aonghus Óg Ó Dálaigh.

T. F. O'Rahilly argued that 'Eneas keaghe O Daly of Moyntervarye' mentioned in a fiant of 31 August 1590 was also a reference to the Bard Ruadh, though the adjective 'keaghe', *caoch*, 'squinting' or 'one-eyed' is not otherwise associated with the satirist. More convincingly, O'Rahilly cited a co. Cork reference in the patent rolls of James I (p. 32a) to 'Eneas Odaly otherwise Odaly of Cahir, yeoman' in 1604. The townland of Caher adjoins the modern townland of Ballyroon on the Muntervary peninsula, and the wording indicates that Aonghus became head of his kindred.

The number of families lampooned in the only composition to be firmly associated with this author is too great to be explained by personal animus. O'Reilly retailed a theory that these scurrilous verses, in loose *óglachas* metres, were commissioned by 'the agents of the Earl of Essex and Sir George Carew' (O'Reilly, clxxvii), but this is difficult to believe, since the verses actually eulogize rather than satirize the arch-rebel Ó Domhnaill and Mac Cana of north Armagh, and it is noteworthy that the rebellious Mág Uidhir chiefs of Fermanagh are passed over, while 'the English Maguire', Sir Conchobhar Ruadh, is savagely attacked. Ó Dálaigh's remark that should he satirize the Ó Domhnaill dynasty of Donegal, 'the race of Adam would not be a shelter to me' (O'Donovan, 55), suggests the years 1599–1600 as the date of composition, when Ó Domhnaill's troops were ravaging Munster. Like the hasty eulogy to Ó Domhnaill composed by Maoilín Óg Mac Bruaideadha, Ó Dálaigh's lampoons could have been composed for the practical purpose of earning protection against the Ulster army, by ridiculing families in various parts of Ireland who had offended Ó Domhnaill by failing to support his uprising. However, as O'Donovan points out, the manuscripts containing the satires are late and full of variations, and as the style of versification is so crude, additional verses against particular families could have been added in the course of transmission.

KATHARINE SIMMS

Sources *The tribes of Ireland: a satire by Aenghus O'Daly … together with an historical account of the family of O'Daly*, ed. J. O'Donovan (1852); repr. (Cork, 1976) • E. O'Reilly, *A chronological account of nearly four hundred Irish writers … with a descriptive catalogue of their works* (1820); repr. with introduction by G. S. Mac Eoin (1970), 176–7 • T. F. O'Rahilly, 'Irish poets, historians and judges in English historical documents, 1538–1615', *Proceedings of the Royal Irish Academy*, 36C (1921–4), 86–120, esp. 99 • *The Irish fiants of the Tudor sovereigns*, 4 vols. (1994) [incl. new introduction by K. Nicholls and preface by T. G. Ó Canann] • *Calendar of the Irish patent rolls of James I* (before 1830); facs. edn as *Irish patent rolls of James I* (1966) [incl. foreword by M. C. Griffith]
Wealth at death three carrucates of land, at 10s. p.a.: O'Reilly, *Irish writers*

Ó Dálaigh, Aonghus Ruadh (d. 1350). *See under* Ó Dálaigh family (*per. c.*1100–*c.*1620).

Ó Dálaigh, Donnchadh Mór (d. 1244). *See under* Ó Dálaigh family (*per. c.*1100–*c.*1620).

Ó Dálaigh, Gofraidh, Fionn (d. 1387). *See under* Ó Dálaigh family (*per. c.*1100–*c.*1620).

Ó Dálaigh, Muireadhach (*fl.* 1213). *See under* Ó Dálaigh family (*per. c.*1100–*c.*1620).

O'Daly, Aengus. *See* Ó Dálaigh, Aonghus (d. 1617).

O'Daly, Daniel Dominic (1595–1662), Dominican friar and diplomat, was born at Kilsarkan, near Castleisland, co. Kerry, into the Kerry branch of the bardic family of Ó Dálaigh. He entered the Dominican order at Lugo in Galicia, Spain, and studied at Bordeaux, Burgos, and Salamanca during 1622–3. As early as 1625 the nobility of co. Kerry wanted him as bishop of Ardfert. After a stay in Ireland he went to the Low Countries where the Irish Dominicans had been present since about 1613. By the early 1620s a Dominican house had been established in Louvain of which O'Daly was the superior in 1626. Worsening relations between Spain and England interrupted the flow of funds from Ireland, endangering the college's financial security, and in 1627 O'Daly was given permission to travel to Madrid to organize support for the college and to transact business for the province. By 1628 he had left Louvain to take up residence in Madrid.

Once in Spain O'Daly became involved in efforts to found an Irish Dominican convent in Lisbon in Spanish-ruled Portugal. The aim was to provide priests for the Irish church, which, in the relative peace of the 1610s, was undergoing significant administrative and organizational reform. These reforms were inspired by the Council of Trent but, given the impoverished, war-weary condition of the Irish Catholic population, outside assistance was necessary to kick-start and sustain the reform process. Given the Spanish commitment to Catholicism and Habsburg domination, it is understandable why Spain and Spanish-ruled Portugal acted like magnets for Irish Catholic exiles in the early seventeenth century and from as early as 1615 a Dominican college in Lisbon had been mooted. Hugh O'Neill, the former earl of Tyrone, had supported the venture and a Portuguese nobleman, Garcias de Norohna, had actually donated a site. Pius V's 1615 brief, *In apostolicae dignitatis culmine*, addressed to the papal collector of Portugal, approved the foundation. However, the proposal lacked the approval of both the Spanish crown and the local Portuguese authorities. By 1623 Philip IV's support had been enlisted but the Portuguese proved more difficult to convince. They had prohibited new religious foundations and questing on the grounds that Lisbon could ill afford to support another religious establishment. Further, they resented the Spanish-backed Irish and feared that they might prevail on Madrid to use the navy against the Dutch.

It was into this difficult situation that O'Daly stepped on arrival in Lisbon in 1629. Armed with letters of commendation from Philip IV he mounted a successful charm campaign and won the support of a number of Portuguese high-ranking families and religious figures. Realizing that the question of an Irish Dominican college in Lisbon had become a test case for diplomatic relations between Lisbon, Madrid, and Rome, O'Daly cleverly manoeuvred initially for a mere hospice to house Dominican students prior to their embarking for Ireland. Permission for this was eventually granted late in 1629, and gave O'Daly the toehold he desired. He secured the patronage of Luis de Castro do Rio, lord of Barbacena, grand alcayde of Covilhã, and his wife, Catarina Telles de Meneses, who granted the Dominican community more commodious accommodation. This gradually metamorphosed into a convent of which O'Daly was appointed first rector by the Dominican master general Nicholas Ridolfi in 1634. In its early years the college was involved in serious legal wrangles with the heirs of Andreza de Vargas de Saraina, a benefactor.

O'Daly next applied his diplomatic talents to the establishment of a convent of Irish Dominican nuns in Lisbon, partly to provide for exiled Irish noblewomen. In March 1639 Philip IV assented to a foundation and in November a community took possession of its cloister in the suburbs of Lisbon, under the title *Bom Sucesso*. In order to secure the king's support O'Daly had undertaken to recruit soldiers for the Spanish army, a venture that had already taken him to Ireland on at least two visits in 1636–7. In pursuit of the same end he travelled to England, where he briefly lodged in prison, an exploit which greatly enhanced his reputation in Lisbon. He appears to have been in contact with Henrietta Maria, wife of Charles I, at this time, probably on papal business.

O'Daly kept a close eye on the rapidly evolving political situation in Portugal. When a *coup d'état* occurred in 1640 and the house of Braganza, in the person of João IV, was restored, O'Daly calmly switched allegiance from Madrid to the Portuguese throne and transfiliated his college to the Portuguese province of the Dominicans. He became an adviser to the new queen regent, Luisa de Gusmão, who generously endowed the Dominican foundations. In 1644 the Dominican general chapter in Rome recognized O'Daly's achievement by bestowing on him the title *magister sacrae theologiae* (doctor of theology) and shortly afterwards he was nominated confessor to Queen Luisa. The combination of her patronage and his own natural flair propelled O'Daly into an important diplomatic career in the service of Braganza at the Stuart, Bourbon, and papal courts. He already had considerable foreign experience. Thanks to his sojourn in the Low Countries in the 1620s he had valuable contacts there. Negotiations at the Madrid court in 1633 to secure the royal viaticum for Irish Dominicans returning home had further raised his profile. So too had his successful efforts to found the two Dominican convents in Lisbon. Indeed, through all these activities O'Daly posed not only as the representative of Irish Dominican interests but also as a spokesman for Irish interests generally. Given these qualifications and the Portuguese monarchy's need of experienced envoys to help it gain diplomatic recognition abroad, O'Daly was nominated envoy to Charles I about 1642. The beleaguered Stuart requested that O'Daly go to Ireland with a view to uniting the various royalist factions into an effective opposition to the parliamentarians. O'Daly made this proposed Irish mission conditional on royal concessions regarding civil and religious liberties for Irish Catholics. As these were not forthcoming O'Daly withdrew from the negotiations, thereby missing the opportunity to become involved in the constitutional experiment of the confederation of Kilkenny in the 1640s. An indication of what his line on Irish affairs might have been may be gleaned from a letter he wrote in 1650 to the lord lieutenant of Ireland, James Butler, the earl of Ormond, in which he declared himself for an independent kingdom of Ireland. In 1655 O'Daly published at Lisbon his *Initium, incrementum et exitus familiae Geraldinorum Desmoniae*, an account of the earls of Desmond and the religious persecutions following their demise, which contains significant hagiographical material.

O'Daly's activities sought to draw Irish political and religious life into the mainstream of European Catholic concerns. He envisaged a Catholic restoration for Ireland and its integration into the European family of Catholic nations. Habsburg enmity with England, and Spain's commitment to the Catholic reform made it easier for him to pursue his mission. His negotiations with the Spanish crown to secure the viaticum for returning Irish priests was part of this overall scheme and ensured a sympathy among Spanish-educated Irish priests for Spanish diplomatic aims. This goes some way to explain the Dublin government's nervousness concerning Irish connections with Spain. Once he had transferred his allegiance to the house of Braganza, however, O'Daly's room for manoeuvre on behalf of his native country was more limited but he compensated by rendering admirable service to his new patrons.

Throughout the 1640s and 1650s O'Daly's view of Irish politics was informed by his diplomatic activity on behalf of Portugal, a small country struggling to find a sustainable place on the European political stage. In 1649 he travelled to Ireland to raise troops for the Portuguese crown. Portuguese diplomats like O'Daly recognized that freedom from Spanish domination depended on the French and the English; however, Portuguese negotiations with these powers troubled the papal court, then under Spanish influence. Indeed, at this time João IV had difficulty in obtaining papal confirmation of episcopal nominations in Portuguese territories. In 1650 O'Daly was in Rome to attend the general chapter of the Dominican order and to act as agent for Charles II. He took the opportunity to represent João IV's position to the pope; however, the problem of episcopal nomination was settled only in 1656, by which time O'Daly was Portuguese ambassador to France. Rumours that Portugal was contemplating an alliance with France, Sweden, and England concerned the pope. The French, for their part, mistrusted O'Daly as they suspected that João IV was actually in league with Spain and they refused to negotiate a new treaty with Lisbon. Meanwhile the 1654 treaty with Oliver Cromwell poisoned relations with Madrid and the situation was defused only by the death of the Portuguese king in late 1656.

As councillor of the regent, Queen Luisa, O'Daly maintained the traditional Portuguese diplomatic policy of courting England and France in order to thwart Madrid even at the risk of alienating Rome. He continued to promote the Quadruple Alliance with France, Sweden, and England, on behalf of the new king, Alfonso VI. Negotiations with the Commonwealth were successfully pursued and O'Daly was clear-sighted enough to realize that England's continued support was necessary if Portugal was to avoid Spanish and French domination. Portuguese diplomats managed to keep this scheme afloat without alienating Charles II, and following Charles's Restoration in 1660 an Anglo-Portuguese treaty was signed. It included a royal marriage between Charles II and Catherine, second daughter of João IV. Thus Portugal edged its way back onto the European political stage without alienating France, falling under Spanish influence, or completely disaffecting Rome—an achievement due in no small part to O'Daly's diplomatic talents.

O'Daly refused nominations to the sees of Goa and Braga. However, in 1662 he accepted nomination as bishop of Coimbra, but died in Lisbon on 30 June as bishop-elect and president of the state council of Portugal. He was buried in the Dominican college where his monument is preserved.   THOMAS O'CONNOR

Sources T. S. Flynn, *The Irish Dominicans, 1536–1641* (1993) · B. Curtin, 'Dominic O'Daly: an Irish diplomat', *Studia Hibernica*, 5 (1965), 98–112 · B. MacCurtain, 'An Irish agent of the Counter-Reformation', *Irish Historical Studies*, 15 (1966–7), 391–406 · M. B. Curtin, 'Daniel O'Daly, 1595–1662', MA diss., University College Dublin, 1958 · B. Jennings, ed., *Wadding papers, 1614–38*, IMC (1953) · H. V. Livermore, *A history of Portugal* (1947), 299–303

Odda [Odo, Odda of Deerhurst, Æthelwine], **earl** (*d.* 1056), magnate, is said to have been a kinsman of Edward the Confessor. It has been suggested that he was the son of *Ælfhere of Mercia (*d.* 983); a more likely ancestor is *Æthelweard (*d.* 998?), chronicler, ealdorman of the western shires, and a descendant of King Æthelred I of the West Saxons, since Odda was earl of the same region in 1051–2 and was, moreover, a benefactor of Pershore Abbey, whose refoundation is attributed to Æthelweard by William of Malmesbury. He may be the Odda *minister* who attests charters late in the reign of Æthelred the Unready (the earliest is *AS chart.*, S 931, dated 1013) and throughout the reigns of Cnut (*d.* 1035) and Harthacnut (*d.* 1042); he is certainly the Odda who attests charters of Edward the Confessor, as *minister* or *nobilis*, between 1042 and 1050, often in conjunction with Beorhtric, son of Ælfgar, lord of Tewkesbury, Gloucestershire (and another possible descendant of Ealdorman Æthelweard) and Ordgar, patron of Tavistock Abbey, Devon, another kinsman of the king. In the 1030s and 1040s Odda, sometimes with his brother Ælfric, attests charters of Lyfing, bishop of Worcester, and Ælfwold, bishop of Sherborne (S 1393–4, 1396–7, 1406, 1474).

Odda's estates included the manor of Deerhurst, Gloucestershire, assessed at 119 hides in Domesday Book, where stood an early minster church, of which he was patron. He also held Longdon, Worcestershire, assessed at 30 hides. Land at Mathon, Herefordshire, assessed at 5 hides, was held by two of his thegns, Ælfweard of Longdon and Merewine; in 1051–2 the former attested, in his lord's company, a charter of Ealdred, bishop of Worcester, as one of 'the leading thegns in Worcestershire' (*AS chart.*, S 1409). Any land of Odda's brother Ælfric is now untraceable, but their sister Edith held 9 hides at Upleadon, Herefordshire. Although his full estate cannot be reconstructed, Odda was clearly one of the most extensive landholders among King Edward's thegns.

When Earl Godwine was banished in 1051, Odda was given the western shires, part of Godwine's former earldom. In 1052 he and Earl Ralph were appointed to command the fleet at Sandwich 'in order that they might keep watch for Earl Godwine' (*ASC*, s.a. 1052, texts C, D), but they were unable to prevent his successful return. On Godwine's reinstatement, Odda lost the western shires, but received another earldom in compensation. Presumably this was Worcestershire, for he attests charters of Ealdred, bishop of Worcester, as earl (*dux*) in the early 1050s (*AS chart.*, S 1407–9). John of Worcester (who gives Odda's alternative name of Æthelwine) describes him in fulsome terms as 'the lover of churches, succourer of the poor, defender of widows and orphans, helper of the oppressed, guardian of virgins' (John of Worcester, *Chron.*, 2.580–81), an elaboration of the Anglo-Saxon Chronicle's eulogy: 'he was a good man and pure and very noble' (*ASC*, s.a. 1056, text D). Odda was remembered as the restorer of Pershore Abbey, which had experienced hard times since its refoundation in the reign of King Edgar. Its lands had been seized (allegedly) by Ælfhere of Mercia and in 1002 all its records were lost in a disastrous fire; the only surviving early charter is a grant of Æthelred II, giving Mathon to Leofwine, earl of Worcestershire, in 1014 (*AS chart.*, S 932); presumably Odda restored it to Pershore. The abbey was functioning by the 1020s, for Brihtheah, bishop of Worcester (1033–8), had previously been abbot of Pershore.

Odda's brother Ælfric died at Deerhurst on 22 December 1053, and in his memory Odda built the church now known as 'Odda's Chapel', consecrated in honour of the Holy Trinity by Ealdred, bishop of Worcester, on 12 April 1056. On 31 August 1056 Odda died and was buried, with his brother, at Pershore, having earlier received the monastic habit from Ealdred. He left no heirs and his lands passed to his kinsman the king, who gave Odda's secular estate at Deerhurst to the abbey of St Denis in Paris, leaving the minster church of St Mary with only 50 of the original 119 hides. Pershore suffered even worse spoliation, for two-thirds of its 300 hides were abstracted and bestowed upon the king's own foundation at Westminster.   ANN WILLIAMS

Sources A. Williams, *Land, power and politics: the family and career of Odda of Deerhurst* (privately printed, Deerhurst, 1997) · *ASC*, s.a. 1051–2 [text E]; s.a. 1053, 1056 [text D] · John of Worcester, *Chron.* · *Willelmi Malmesbiriensis monachi de gestis regum Anglorum*, ed. W. Stubbs, 2 vols., Rolls Series (1887–9) · *Willelmi Malmesbiriensis monachi de gestis pontificum Anglorum libri quinque*, ed. N. E. S. A. Hamilton, Rolls Series, 52 (1870) · *AS chart.*, S 931b, 932–4, 951, 953–4, 962–3, 969–71, 975, 994, 998–9, 1001–3, 1005–8, 1010–12, 1017, 1019, 1021, 1044, 1391–4, 1396–7, 1406–9, 1474 · A. Farley, ed., *Domesday*

Book, 2 vols. (1783), 1.174v, 175v, 180v, 184v, 186, 186v • C. S. Taylor, 'Deerhurst, Pershore and Westminster', *Transactions of the Bristol and Gloucestershire Archaeological Society*, 25 (1902), 230–50 • P. Wormald, *How do we know so much about Anglo-Saxon Deerhurst?* (1993) • A. Williams, 'An introduction to the Worcestershire Domesday', *The Worcestershire Domesday*, ed. A. Williams and R. W. H. Erskine (1988), 1–31 • A. Williams, 'An introduction to the Gloucestershire Domesday', *The Gloucestershire Domesday*, ed. A. Williams and R. W. H. Erskine (1989) • S. Keynes, *An atlas of attestations in Anglo-Saxon charters, c.670–1066* (privately printed, Cambridge, 1993)
Wealth at death held extensive estates in west of England

Odell, Noel Ewart (1890–1987), geologist and mountaineer, was born on 25 December 1890 in St Lawrence, Isle of Wight, the third child in the family of two sons and three daughters of the Revd Robert William Odell, rector of St Lawrence, and his wife, Mary Margaret, daughter of James Bell Ewart, timber merchant, of Dundas, Ontario, Canada. He was educated at Brighton College and at the Royal School of Mines at Imperial College, London, where he studied geology and gained the ARSM. During the First World War he was commissioned as a lieutenant in 1915 in the Royal Engineers. Wounded three times, he returned to civilian life in 1919, having, in 1917, married Gwladys Mona (*d.* 1977), daughter of Robert Jones, rector of Gyffin, north Wales. They had one son.

Odell embarked on a career in the petroleum and mining industries, first as a geologist with the Anglo-Persian Oil Company (1922–5) and then as a consultant in Canada (1927–30). In his late thirties he transferred to academic geology, first as a lecturer in geology and tutor at Harvard University (1928–30), then as a research student and lecturer at Cambridge, where he stayed on as a fellow commoner and supervisor of studies at Clare College (1931–40). His research for the degree of PhD, awarded in 1940, investigated the geology, glaciology, and geomorphology of north-east Greenland and northern Labrador. In 1940–42 he served as a major in the Bengal Sappers and Miners.

After the Second World War he took up various appointments at universities in Canada, New Zealand, and Pakistan. He lectured at McGill and was visiting professor at the University of British Columbia (1948–9). He was also professor of geology at the University of Otago (1950–56) and at Peshawar University (1960–62). On finally retiring he returned to Clare and in 1983, at the age of ninety-two, was made an honorary fellow, an event which much pleased him.

Although Odell published several important papers on the geology of the Himalayas, and other mountain regions, and was a fellow or member of numerous geological, geographical, glaciological, and Arctic institutions, he probably never aspired to be in the front rank of academic research. It was in mountaineering that he made his name, and managed with singular success to combine the career of a geologist with the pleasures of mountaineering. Odell made his first discovery of the hills of the Lake District at the age of thirteen and soon acquired wide climbing experience in Britain and the Alps. Many an aspiring rock climber has cut his teeth on Odell's severe tennis shoe climb on the uncompromisingly smooth slabs of Cwm Idwal in north Wales (1919). He

participated in the Oxford University Spitsbergen expedition (1921) and led the Merton College Arctic expedition (1923).

Odell was picked for the Everest expedition of 1924 and was the last man to see George Mallory and Andrew Irvine before they disappeared in their attempt to scale the final slopes of the world's highest mountain. Odell was in close support. In a period of four days he climbed mostly without oxygen, first alone to 25,000 feet to look for them, and then twice alone beyond Camp 6 to over 27,000 feet and back. On returning home he was invited to a private audience by George V. Odell was undoubtedly most widely known for his account of the last sighting of Mallory and Irvine which contributed to the enduring mystery of whether they ever reached the summit of Everest. The sensational discovery of Mallory's body by a special research expedition on 1 May 1999 on the slopes where he had fallen at 26,770 ft has renewed speculation but still not solved the mystery.

There followed several visits for geological research, mountaineering, and exploration in the Canadian Rockies (1927–47) and with American friends to north Labrador (1931), north-east Greenland (1933), and the St Elias Mountains in Yukon and Alaska (1949 and 1977). While at Harvard he inspired a generation of undergraduates to climb steep ice and to organize expeditions to the greater ranges of the world. An ice route he pioneered in the White Mountains bears his name, Odell Gully, and two mountains, a lake, and a glacier are also named after him.

Odell's greatest mountaineering achievement was the first ascent of Nanda Devi (25,695 feet) in 1936, with an Anglo–American party. H. W. Tilman and Odell reached the summit, which for fourteen years remained the highest peak climbed. Two years later he again joined Tilman in the 1938 attempt on Everest, but deep powder snow made the last 1500 feet impossible to climb. Odell continued to defy the normal limitations of old age. In 1984, at the age of ninety-three, he strode across the glacier to attend the seventy-fifth anniversary of the Britannia hut in the Alps, and recalled that as a young climber he had also been present at its opening. He was a founder member of the Himalayan Club and an honorary member of the Alpine Club and of kindred clubs in North America, Canada, South Africa, New Zealand, Switzerland, and Norway. He received the Livingstone gold medal (1944) of the Royal Scottish Geographical Society and, unusually, a star in the constellation Lyra was named after him (*International Star Register*, 1925). He became a familiar figure at the Alpine Club and the Royal Geographical Society, retaining in old age his earnest enthusiasm and the tall, spare figure and purposeful gait which had carried him to record heights on the earth's surface. His genial nature and patriarchal figure earned him the nickname Noah, which he relished. Odell died suddenly on 21 February 1987 at his home, 5 Dean Court, Holbrook Road, Cambridge, and his body was donated to medical science at the Cambridge anatomy department.

GEORGE BAND, *rev.*

Sources *The Times* (24 Feb 1987) · P. Lloyd, 'In memoriam: Noel Ewart Odell, 1890–1987', *Alpine Journal*, 93 (1988–9), 309–11 · personal knowledge (1996) · *CGPLA Eng. & Wales* (1987) · J. Hemmleb, L. A. Johnson, and E. R. Simonson, *Ghosts of Everest* (1999) · private information [Peter E. Odell, grandson]
Archives Scott Polar RI, journal during the Oxford University expedition to Spitzbergen and the Merton Arctic expedition | Alpine Club, London, archives | FILM Alpine Club, London, Everest 1924 film
Wealth at death £44,810: probate, 26 March 1987, *CGPLA Eng. & Wales*

Odell, Thomas (1691–1749), playwright, was the son of a substantial Buckinghamshire landowner. About the age of twenty-three he went to London, where through the interest of Lord Wharton he secured a pension from the government. But the death of Wharton in 1715 'and some other accidents' left his fortunes 'somewhat impaired' (Mottley, 270) and Odell was thrown back on his own resources.

Odell turned to the theatre for a profession, and on 19 January 1721 his first play, *The Chimera: a Farce*, was performed at the Theatre Royal, Lincoln's Inn Fields, and ran for three nights. He was later to write other dramatic pieces, but his major venture was the building of a new theatre in Goodman's Fields. There were only three theatres in London at this time, and so the building of a fourth represented a significant expansion, occasioned by an increase in the popularity of the stage resulting from the success in 1728 of John Gay's *The Beggar's Opera* and Sir John Vanbrugh's *The Provok'd Husband*. The new theatre opened in 1729, the first production being George Farquhar's *The Recruiting Officer* on 31 October. This speculation proved a success; the new company achieved an impressive 185 performances in this first season, mostly of contemporary comedy, and Odell 'got not less than one hundred pounds a week by this undertaking' (Baker, xxxiv).

But opposition to the new playhouse had started before its opening, with application to the justices 'to prohibit the theatre' (Avery, xxi). Soon after the opening Arthur Bedford, a lifelong opponent of the stage, preached a sermon at St Botolph, Aldgate, against the newly erected playhouse, warning that the 'apprentices and journeymen of a leading part of the city would be led into dissipation' (*Thespian Dictionary*). As a result on 28 April 1730 a petition was sent to the king from 'the Lord Mayor and Court of Aldermen of the City [of] London addressing his Majesty to suppress it' (Mottley, 270). Odell was forced to close the theatre temporarily, but he reopened it on 16 September 1730. The second season saw less opposition, but Odell sold the theatre in 1732 to Henry Giffard, an actor in his company who had arrived from Ireland in 1730, the final performance under Odell being on 23 May. The impending sale was a subject of rumour long before this date; a playbill for *A Bold Stroke for a Wife* dated 4 June 1731 has the following footnote:

> NB The article in the Daily Advertiser of Wednesday last (June 2) which mentions Mr Odell's intending to decline concerning himself any longer with the management of Goodmans Fields playhouse, is a false and scandalous libel, for which the printer &c of the paper will be prosecuted with the utmost severity by me. Tho. Odell.   (Genest, *Eng. stage*, 3.320)

The truth seems to be that Odell did not have the acumen and determination to succeed as a theatre manager. Giffard, on the other hand, did, and under his management the theatre prospered, and was soon replaced:

> Mr Odell, from not understanding the management of a company (as indeed how should any one, that is not, in some way, brought up in that knowledge?) soon left it to Giffard that did; who in the year 1733 caused to be built an intire, new, beautiful convenient Theatre.   (Chetwood, 169)

The new theatre was in Ayliffe Street, and it was in this new theatre that Garrick was to give the first performance of his London career in 1741.

In 1738 Odell began a new career. William Chetwyn was sworn in as licenser of the stage in February, and Odell was appointed deputy 'that he [Chetwyn] might not be too much fatigued with reading half a dozen plays in the course of a twelvemonth' (Genest, *Eng. stage*, 3.522). Odell was to hold this position for the rest of his life. Odell was the author of a number of other dramatic works: *The Smugglers: a Farce* (1729), *The Prodigal, or, Recruits for the Queen of Hungary* (1744), *The Patron: a Ballad-Opera* (1729), as well as several poetical pieces.

At the end of his life Odell was living in somewhat impecunious conditions, and at his death was engaged on an account of his experiences and acquaintances. He had not made a great success in the theatre as either a manager or an author: 'It does not seem that he possessed the ambition peculiar to author-managers, having produced no piece at his own theatre' (*Thespian Dictionary*). But he was remembered as

> a great observator of everything curious in the conversation of his acquaintance; and his own conversation was a living chronicle of the remarkable intrigues, adventures, sayings, stories, writings etc of many of the Quality, Poets and other Authors, Players, Booksellers …   (Oldys, 161)

Odell died of 'gout in his stomach' (ibid.) on 24 May 1749, at his house in Chapel Street, Westminster, and was buried at the Chapel Street churchyard. He was married, but nothing is known of his wife.   WILLIAM R. JONES

Sources DNB · D. E. Baker, *Biographia dramatica, or, A companion to the playhouse*, rev. I. Reed, new edn, rev. S. Jones, 3 vols. in 4 (1812) · Genest, *Eng. stage*, vol. 3 · W. Oldys, 'Choice notes', *N&Q*, 2nd ser., 11 (1861), 161 · E. L. Avery, ed., *The London stage, 1660–1800*, pt 2: 1700–1729 (1960) · *The thespian dictionary, or, Dramatic biography of the eighteenth century* (1802) · [J. Mottley], *A compleat list of all the English dramatic poets*, pubd with T. Whincop, *Scanderbeg* (1747) · W. R. Chetwood, *A general history of the stage, from its origin in Greece to the present time* (1749)

O'Dempsey, Dermot. *See* Ua Diummusaig, Diarmait (d. 1193).

O'Devany, Conor (c.1535–1612), Roman Catholic bishop of Down and Connor, was born about 1535, inferred from the general agreement that he was nearly eighty at the time of his death. The names of his father and mother have not been preserved, but their social position can be established. They were the *erenagh* family of the parish of Raphoe in co. Donegal, the *erenagh* being a layman who farmed church lands by hereditary right. Inquisitions taken in 1609 in preparation for the plantation of Ulster found the lands of 'Tollohedeveny' to be church lands. These were Tulach Ó Dhuibheanaigh (O'Devany's Hill), today shortened to Tully, and it may be presumed that Conor was born there. Before he was twenty years old O'Devany entered the Observant Franciscan friary in the town of Donegal, the Observants being a particularly effective force in a society based on kin groups, a kind of society that sometimes did not fit well into the framework of the territorial parish. Though nothing is known in detail of his personal ministry, his training in the Observant friary of Donegal would have given it a dedicated character.

The papal excommunication of Elizabeth I in 1570 quickly polarized the religious situation in Ireland. O'Devany followed many other Irish clerics to Rome, where he was nominated bishop of Down and Connor on 27 April 1582. With two other Irish bishops he was consecrated on 13 May in the church of Santa Maria dell'Anima. He then returned to his diocese, situated in Gaelic Ulster in the extreme north-east of Ireland. The only detail of his episcopate preserved concerns a synod attended by him and six other bishops in 1587. It had been called to promulgate the decrees of the Council of Trent in the northern ecclesiastical province of Armagh. The grip of the government was tightening only slowly in Gaelic Ulster, but pressure was stepped up because of the threat from the Spanish Armada. Bishop O'Devany was captured. He escaped, but was recaptured, and was imprisoned in Dublin Castle. In a petition for his release in November 1590 he said he had been imprisoned by Lord Deputy Perrot, and therefore before 30 June 1588, when Perrot's successor was sworn in. O'Devany's petition was granted almost immediately. He gave a carefully worded undertaking admitting that he had committed 'divers faults worthy of condign punishment' in 'matters of religion', but promised to be of good behaviour in this respect for the future. But when he returned to his diocese in Ulster he found growing resentment at government pressure. In 1593 a number of bishops joined in an appeal for help to Philip II of Spain. It is not known if Conor O'Devany was one of them, or even how many they were.

In 1594 resentment became revolt. Under the cautious leadership of Hugh O'Neill the war lasted for nine years. The leading family in O'Devany's diocese was a collateral O'Neill branch, which took part in the war, but with some reluctance because of having to take orders from Hugh O'Neill and his family. Against this background there is a small piece of direct evidence to suggest that Bishop O'Devany was not deeply involved in war or politics. It is a report to Rome on Irish ecclesiastical affairs, unsigned and undated, but drawn up about 1600 by Peter Lombard, Hugh O'Neill's agent in Rome. He dismissed Conor O'Devany as 'a good man indeed, but too guileless [simplicior] to be of any great assistance' (Archivio Segreto Vaticano, fondo Borghese, III, 124C, fol. 78).

O'Neill was forced to surrender on 30 March 1603. In 1607 most of the Gaelic chiefs of Ulster left Ireland ('the flight of the earls'), and this resulted in the confiscation and plantation of their lands. To secure a parliamentary majority for the crown, new boroughs were then freely created in the planted areas, and intimidatory pressure on the Old English was stepped up. By this time Conor O'Devany was again in prison. Events in his native Ulster had steadily deprived him of protectors, and he was in fact a fugitive when he was captured in the early summer of 1611 and lodged in Dublin Castle. As part of the preparation for parliament the privy council in London suggested to Sir Arthur Chichester in a letter dated 20 August 1611 that it would be well if 'some titular bishops could be punished in an exemplary manner' provided it could be made clear that they were not being punished for their religious activities (CSP Ire., 1611–14, 96). This implied a trial for treason. There were only two Roman Catholic bishops in Ireland, and O'Devany, a native of Gaelic Ulster, was actually in captivity. He was indicted for treason by a grand jury in January 1612, together with Patrick O'Loughran, one of a number of priests in prison, picked out because he had been personal chaplain to Hugh O'Neill.

They stood trial at the court of king's bench in Dublin on 28 January 1612. No official account of the trial has survived, but there are many accounts from Roman Catholic sources, some deriving directly from eyewitnesses. They agree substantially with one another, and with the known format of trials for treason at the time. In such trials the government took every precaution to secure a favourable verdict. O'Devany pleaded that he was on trial because he was a bishop; that he had confined himself to his ecclesiastical functions during the war; and that in any case there had been a general amnesty. But he and O'Loughran were found guilty and sentenced to be executed as traitors on 1 February.

Again, there are many accounts of the executions, including one from a protestant, Barnaby Rich. The prisoners were drawn on hurdles from the castle to the place of execution, a little hillock about a mile distant on the opposite bank of the Liffey. They were accompanied by large and growing crowds, which must have numbered at least several thousand by the time the gallows was reached. There was no doubt of the sentiments of these crowds, and from time to time they became threatening. When the bishop and the priest had been executed with all the bloody ritual of traitors' deaths there was an unstoppable scramble for relics of those already regarded as martyrs for their religion. O'Devany's head was apparently recovered. The next day the dismembered corpses were buried on the spot. The following night they were exhumed and buried in a city churchyard. Which one it was remained a secret.

The government plan to intimidate the Old English Roman Catholics by executing a bishop went badly wrong. On 6 February, Chichester wrote to Cecil lamenting that the bishop and priest 'being lately executed here for treason merely, are notwithstanding … thought martyrs and adored for saints' (PRO, SP 63/232/8). As a later authority put it succinctly, 'O'Devany's death was an event of unexpected importance in the development of the counter-reformation in Ireland' (Clarke, 209). It stiffened resolve among the Old English electorate. Conor O'Devany and Patrick O'Loughran continued to be venerated as martyrs and on 27 September 1992 they were formally declared blessed by Pope John Paul II.

O'Devany was the compiler of an 'index martyrialis', which he sent to the Jesuit superior Christopher Holywood shortly before his execution. The 'index' included the names and dates of death of all the bishops and priests who had been martyred since 1585. Though it has not survived, the names were included by David Rothe in his *Analecta*. PATRICK J. CORISH

Sources *The analecta of David Rothe, bishop of Ossory*, ed. P. F. Moran (1884) · P. O'Sullivan-Beare, *Historiae Catholicae Iberniae compendium*, ed. M. Kelly (1850) · R. Bolton, *A justice of peace for Ireland* (1638) · M. O'Reilly, ed., *Memorials of those who suffered for the Catholic faith in Ireland* (1868) · J. O'Laverty, *An historical account of the diocese of Down and Connor*, 5 (1895) · D. Murphy, *Our martyrs* (1896) · state papers Ireland, PRO, SP 63, esp. SP63/166/59 (i), petition for release, 1590 · *CSP Ire.*, *1611–14* · *AFM* · Archivio Vaticano, Vatican City, Fondo Borghese · A. Clarke, 'Pacification, plantation, and the Catholic question, 1603–23', *A new history of Ireland*, ed. T. W. Moody and others, 3: *Early modern Ireland, 1534–1691* (1976), 187–232

Odger, George (1813–1877), shoemaker and trade unionist, was born in Roborough, south Devon, the son of John Odger, a Cornish miner. After attending the village school, he became a shoemaker at an early age, tramping about the country before settling in London, where he became active in the Ladies' West End Shoemakers' Society. A first-class craftsman, he was the only significant labour leader of his generation to practise his trade throughout his life: his death certificate described him as 'Ladies Boot Maker and Public Orator' (d. cert., 4 March 1877). Odger, who rose to prominence in delegate meetings of London trades to support building workers in the 1859 strike and lock-out, helped to initiate the London Trades Council, succeeding George Howell as secretary in 1862 and serving in that capacity until 1872.

With the London Trades Council as his organizational base, Odger, who never held office in his trade union, promoted the cause of parliamentary suffrage through the Manhood Suffrage and Vote by Ballot Association, of which he became the chairman in 1862. Odger was instrumental in persuading the labour newspaper *The Bee-Hive* to reverse its pro-Confederate position in the American Civil War and spoke at a meeting held at St James's Hall on 26 March 1863 in support of the Unionist cause. He was also involved in the popular welcome to Garibaldi and in meetings to express sympathy with the Polish revolt in 1863. His fraternal address to French workers in December 1863, following a French deputation over the Polish question, was a precursor of the International Working Men's Association, established in September 1864; Odger became president and subsequently chairman of its council. His influence within the First International, like that of other British workers, proved transitory, and he resigned in June 1871 in protest against the promulgation of Karl Marx's socialist interpretation of the Paris Commune.

An opponent of George Potter's management of *The Bee-*

George Odger (1813–1877), by W. H. Midwinter

Hive, Odger transformed the *Workman's Advocate* (later *Commonwealth*) into the organ of the International and of the Reform League. Serving as editor of *Commonwealth* in 1866–7, he voiced support for manhood suffrage, land redistribution, reduction of hours of work, and legal protection of trade unions. He was employed as a paid lecturer for the Reform League in 1866 and an election organizer in 1868, canvassing on behalf of the Liberal Party in Devon and Cornwall. In 1867 Odger became a member of the Conference of Amalgamated Trades formed by the junta of amalgamated union leaders to articulate the case for legalization, and was a member of the parliamentary committee of the Trades Union Congress in 1871 and in 1873–4.

On five occasions Odger contested parliamentary seats, but his candidacy was invariably blocked by the official Liberals. In Chelsea (1868) he was obliged to withdraw when an arbitration committee decided in favour of another Liberal candidate. In Stafford (1869), despite local support, he withdrew after coming third in a test ballot, and in Bristol (1870) he retired rather than split the Liberal vote. In Southwark (1870) Odger went to the poll, losing to the Conservative by only 304 votes after Sir Sidney Waterlow declined to withdraw. Four years later Odger, opposed again by both Liberals and Conservatives, came third in the Southwark contest.

During the early 1870s Odger flirted with republicanism and endorsed the Land and Labour League's advocacy of land nationalism. More radical than contemporaries like

George Howell and Robert Applegarth, he was never a socialist or a revolutionary, believing that working-class advance could be achieved only by legitimate political and industrial means. A brilliant orator, effective in parliamentary deputations, he was a popular leader but lacked the capacity for sustained administrative tasks.

Odger died from congestion of the lungs on 4 March 1877, survived by his wife, two sons, and a daughter. His funeral on 10 March followed a procession of London workers to Brompton cemetery, where eulogies were delivered by Professor E. S. Beesly and Henry Fawcett MP.

F. M. Leventhal

Sources D. R. Moberg, 'George Odger and the English working-class movement, 1860–1877', PhD diss., U. Lond., 1954 · S. J. Webb and B. P. Webb, *The history of trade unionism, 1666–1920* (1920) · F. M. Leventhal, *Respectable radical: George Howell and Victorian working class politics* (1971) · R. Harrison, *Before the socialists: studies in labour and politics, 1861–1881* (1965) · H. Collins and C. Abramsky, *Karl Marx and the British labour movement* (1965) · W. H. G. Armytage, 'George Odger: a founder of the British labour movement', *University of Toronto Quarterly*, 18 (1948), 68–75 · *The Times* (5 March 1877) · *The Times* (12 March 1877) · R. J. Hinton, *English radical leaders* (1875) · d. cert.

Likenesses Faustin, chromolithograph caricature, NPG · W. H. Midwinter, photograph, NPG [*see illus.*]

Odhran [St Odhran, Odran, Óran] (*supp. d. c.*563), holy man and self-sacrifice, lends his name (Óran and Odran are alternative Gaelic forms) to a chapel and a graveyard on the island of Iona. The oldest extant version of his story, which resembles one told of St Finnbarr in the thirteenth-century revision of the Latin life of that saint, appears in a Middle Irish homily of the mid-twelfth century. According to this source, Odhran was one of the original companions of Columba. On their arrival on Iona from Ireland *c.*563, Columba said to his company: 'Someone among you should go down into the soil of the island to consecrate it.' Odhran readily volunteered and Columba told him: 'No one will be granted his request at my own grave, unless he first seek it of you' (Herbert, 261). At this, Odhran promptly died. The graveyard on Iona, still called Reilig Odrain ('the grave of Odhran') in modern times, is likely, therefore, to have been so called already in the mid-twelfth century. The cult of Odhran, which the homily places on a par with that of Columba in terms of its attractiveness to pilgrims, can be traced back much further. In his life of Columba (completed *c.*697), Adomnán relates the story of Báetán, a contemporary of Columba, which he says was told to him by the monk Máel Odrain, whose name means 'devotee of Odhran'. Since, according to his own report, Máel Odrain was alive and adult very shortly after Báetán's death, his name indicates that Odhran was commemorated in the circle of Iona within a generation of the date of his death given in the twelfth-century story.

The tale of Odhran's death had survived with few changes when Manus O'Donnell assembled his early Modern Irish life of Columba (*Betha Coluim Cille*) in 1532. By 1698, however, oral tradition, as recorded by William Sacheverell, told the story in order to explain the name of St Oran's Chapel, a twelfth-century structure which still

stands some 100 yards south-west of the present abbey on Iona. Moreover, it was then said that Columba had dreamed that a famine could be ended only if a man were buried alive; that Odhran was so buried, upright, with the promise that his grave would be opened again after twenty-four hours; and that, when he was dug up, the still-living Odhran described the other world with such precision that Columba could trust him no longer in the land of the living and ordered him to be buried again. Eighteenth- and nineteenth-century writers give lines in Gaelic, clearly derived from oral tradition, said to report Odhran's blasphemous utterances on his emergence from his tomb: 'There is no wonder in death, and hell is not as it is reported'; and the response of the shocked Columba: 'Dust, dust over Odhran's eye, that he may speak no more' (Adomnán, 362).

Marios Costambeys

Sources Adomnán of Iona, *Life of St Columba*, ed. and trans. R. Sharpe (1995) · M. Herbert, *Iona, Kells, and Derry: the history and hagiography of the monastic familia of Columba* (1988)

Odingsells, Gabriel (1690?–1734), playwright, was probably born in the parish of St Dionis Backchurch, London, the third child of Gabriel Odingsells (*bap.* 1653) and Mary Love (1660?–1690). He was admitted to Pembroke College, Oxford, matriculating on 23 April 1707, but left without taking a degree. He took residence in London, with the aim of making a living as a dramatic writer. His first piece, *The Bath Unmask'd*, was first performed at Lincoln's Inn Fields on 27 February 1725 and ran for a week. The play, which has characters with such names as Sir Captious Whiffle and Pander, was described as 'an indifferent comedy—he meant by the title to imply that he had described the humours of Bath' (Genest, *Eng. stage*, 3.168).

At the end of the same year, on 8 December, a second dramatic piece by Odingsells, *The Capricious Lovers*, was first performed at Lincoln's Inn Fields. It contains Mock-Youth, a colonel who is 'twice frightened by the ghost of a lawyer who had forged a will in his favour'. Genest comments:

> this is a poor comedy by Odingsells, there is however a considerable degree of humour in the character of Mrs Mince-Mode, who (as the author expresses it) grows sick at the sight of a man, and refines upon the significancy of phrases till she resolves common conversation into obscenity. (Genest, *Eng. stage*, 3.178)

Odingsells's final work, *The Bays' Opera*, was produced at Drury Lane for three nights from 30 March 1730. It concerns the threat to Tragedo, the lawful heir to the empire of wit, by a usurper, one Cantato. The work is prefaced by an essay 'concerning that way of writing' (Mottley, 271). Genest's verdict was that it was 'very dull—the design is much better than the execution' (Genest, *Eng. stage*, 3.258).

Odingsells became mentally unstable, and took his own life by hanging on 10 February 1734 at his house in Thatched Court, Westminster. A publication appeared posthumously in 1742: *Monumental inscriptions, or, A curious collection of near five hundred of the most remarkable epitaphs … collected by the late ingenious Gabriel Odinsells* [*sic*].

William R. Jones

Sources D. E. Baker, *Biographia dramatica, or, A companion to the playhouse*, rev. I. Reed, new edn, rev. S. Jones, 3 vols. in 4 (1812) · Genest, *Eng. stage*, vol. 3 · Foster, *Alum. Oxon.* · *IGI* · *DNB* · [J. Mottley], *A compleat list of all the English dramatic poets*, pubd with T. Whincop, *Scanderbeg* (1747) · J. L. Chester, ed., *The reiester booke of Saynte De'nis Backchurch parishe … begynnynge … 1538*, Harleian Society, register section, 3 (1878)

Odington [*name in religion* Evesham], **Walter** (*fl. c.*1280–1301), Benedictine monk and scholar, was also known as Walter Evesham and as Walter de Otyngton, monk of Evesham, and has in the past had his identity masked by sixteenth-century bibliographers, who attributed important treatises on music and science to separate writers bearing some variants of these names. Thus Leland ascribed the scientific works to an Odendunus active around 1280, and the musical treatise to a Gualterius de Evesham, whom Bale described as working about 1240. Only with the reintegration of these two figures into one has a more accurate assessment of his work become possible.

Odington was probably born at Oddington in Oxfordshire and became a monk of the Benedictine abbey of Evesham near Worcester, for which he produced a *Kalendarium* beginning with the year 1301. In 1298 he was named in the distinguished company of the abbots of Malmesbury, Tewkesbury, and Pershore as a member of a committee for the administration of Gloucester College, the Benedictine college at Oxford for monks of the Canterbury province. In 1463 William Worcester noted on a manuscript of a *Declaratio motus octavae spherae* that it was the work of 'Master Walter Evesham who made his deliberations at Oxford about 1316' (Bodl. Oxf., MS Laud misc. 674, fol. 75*r*). On this basis Odington has been misidentified with a Walter Evesham who was a fellow of Merton College documented between *c.*1331 and 1346. (He was also confused with Walter of Eynsham, an unsuccessful candidate for the see of Canterbury in 1228.) A fellowship of Merton and membership of a religious order were mutually exclusive, and if Odington did indeed work at Oxford it would presumably have been at Gloucester College. John North has questioned Worcester's note, arguing for the accuracy of Leland's estimate that Odington flourished *c.*1280, thus placing his birth around 1260 or earlier. The date of the *Kalendarium* and the placement of Odington's musical treatise about 1300 extend the period of his activity into the fourteenth century.

Surviving works ascribed to 'Frater Walterus de Evesham' consist of an alchemical treatise, the *Ycocedron* (so called from its division into twenty—*eikosi*—chapters), extant entire or in part in five manuscript sources (Bodl. Oxf., MS Digby 119; ed. P. D. Thomas); the *Summa de speculatione musicae*, in three manuscripts (Cambridge, Corpus Christi College, MS 410; ed. F. Hammond); a *Tractatus de multiplicatione specierum in visu*; an *Ars metrica*; a compilation of the fifth book of Euclid; and the almanac for Evesham (all CUL, MS Ii.1.13). The *Declaratio motus octavae spherae* occurs in two manuscript sources of which MS Laud misc. 674 in the Bodleian Library (ed. J. D. North) contains Worcester's note. John of Ashenden, writing in

1347, ascribes to Odington another work, a treatise on the age of the world: 'Odynton monachus de Evesham in suo tractatu de etate mundi' (Oxford, Oriel College, MS 23). Leland ascribes to Odendunus a *Kalendarium*, a treatise on planetary motions, and a treatise *de mutatione aeris*. Tanner, two centuries after Leland, reunites the two Odingtons and lists among his works the *Summa* (which he knew at first hand), *Ycocedron*, *Declaratio*, *De aetate mundi*, and planetary tables. (Thorndike's assignment of Richard Wallingford's *Exafrenon* and an *Ars completa* to Odington has been dismissed by North.)

Odington's importance, like the story of his life, has been as much obscured as it has been clarified by historians. The manuscript tradition of his works suggests that his scientific writings—notably the *Ycocedron* on the fascinating subject of alchemy—were of greatest interest to his contemporaries. North points out that the *Ycocedron* suggests the possibility of quantitative measurement of certain virtues, such as heat and dryness, and that Odington employs the concept of intension and remission of qualities, a terminology which he also applied to musical pitch. However, the first of Odington's treatises to be published in a modern edition was not the *Ycocedron* but the treatise on music, the *Summa* (Coussemaker, *L'Art harmonique*, 1865); but the importance of this work has been distorted by inaccurate dating and inappropriate scholarly claims.

Owing to Bale's separation of the scientific writer from the author of the musical treatise, which he dated more than half a century before its probable composition, the *Summa* appeared a prodigy to later scholars. Charles Burney—that rich source of slightly inaccurate information—in 1776 accepted the dating of *c.*1240, and was followed by Fétis, Coussemaker, and Eitner. The *Summa* was also seized upon by Hugo Riemann, who employed its misdating in order to claim the treatise as the source of two 'progressive' and 'English' tendencies, the theoretical recognition of duple metre and the acceptance of the third as a consonance. The first is a misreading, but Odington did raise the question of employing intervals of the third and sixth as musical consonances, which was admitted in practice in fourteenth-century music, although such intervals lacked the theoretical justification of the simple mathematical proportions demonstrated by the octave (2:1), fifth (3:2), and fourth (4:3).

Far from being an isolated monument, as Burney claimed, the *Summa de speculatione musicae* fits into the context of Odington's other work as one element in a corpus of treatises encompassing the mathematical arts: arithmetic, geometry, music, and astronomy. The encyclopaedic character of Odington's musical treatise resembles the apparently little-known work of Jerome of Moravia, dated between 1272 and 1304, and the *Speculum musicae* of Jacques de Liège (*c.*1330). The first four of the six books comprising the *Summa* are theoretical in nature. Book I deals with arithmetic, Book II with music as number related to sound. Book III demonstrates these proportions in a discussion of musical instruments on a theoretical rather than a practical level. Book IV treats poetic metres as examples of the same proportional relationships. Book V is a tonary, a handbook of ecclesiastical chant, and Book VI comprises a treatise on writing metred polyphonic music or discant. Most of Odington's sources are conventional ones: Boethius's *De arithmetica* and *De musica* for Books I–II, the *De musica* and a number of anonymous treatises for Book III, Isidore of Seville's *Etymologiarum* for Book IV, the Sarum *Tonale* for Book V, and the works of Jean Garland (*c.*1240) and Jerome of Moravia for Book VI. However, Odington also cites lesser-known writers such as Fulgentius and Avicenna, and the division of knowledge which he ascribes to Adelard of Bath follows one attributed to Garland by Jerome.

In his description of musical forms and genres, Odington was the only musical theorist to describe the rondellus, a three-voice piece based on a technique of canonic voice exchange, which was 'known as typically and rather quaintly English as early as *c.*1225' (Sanders, 'Rondellus', 171) and disappeared after 1300. This genre forms an important part of the musical fragments connected with Worcester Cathedral—only 15 miles from Evesham Abbey—between *c.*1270 and *c.*1290.

FREDERICK HAMMOND

Sources Bale, *Cat.* · Burney, *Hist. mus.* · E. de Coussemaker, *L'art harmonique aux XIIe et XIIIe siècles* (Paris, 1865) · R. Eitner, *Biographisch-bibliographisches Quellen-Lexikon*, 10 vols. (1900–04) · F.-J. Fétis, *Biographie universelle des musiciens, et bibliographie générale de la musique*, 2nd edn, 8 vols. (Paris, 1860–65); repr. (1875–83); suppl. A. Pougin, ed., 2 vols. (1878–80) · *Walteri Odington: Summa de speculatione musicae*, ed. F. Hammond, Corpus Scriptorum de Musica, 14 (1970) · *Commentarii de scriptoribus Britannicis, auctore Joanne Lelando*, ed. A. Hall, 2 vols. (1709) · J. D. North, 'Cosmology and the age of the world', *Stars, minds and fate: essays in ancient and medieval cosmology* (1989), 91–115 · *Richard of Wallingford: an edition of his writings*, ed. and trans. J. D. North, 3 vols. (1976) [Lat. orig., with parallel Eng. trans.] · H. Riemann, *Geschichte der Musiktheorie im IX–XIX Jahrhundert* (1898) · H. Riemann, *A history of music theory*, trans. Raymond Haggh (1962) · E. Sanders, 'Binary rhythm and alternative third mode in the 13th and 14th centuries', *Journal of the American Musicological Society*, 15 (1962), 249–91 · E. Sanders, 'Rondellus', *New Grove* · Tanner, *Bibl. Brit.-Hib.* · P. D. Thomas, 'David Ragor's transcription of Walter of Odington's *Icocedron*', *Wichita State University Bulletin* [University Studies], no. 76 (1968) · L. Thorndike, *A history of magic and experimental science*, 8 vols. (1923–58), vols. 1–4

Archives Bodl. Oxf., MS Digby 119 · Bodl. Oxf., MS Laud misc. 674 · CCC Cam., MS 410 · CUL, MS Ii.1.13

Odling, William (1829–1921), chemist, was born on 5 September 1829 in Southwark, the elder child and only son of George Odling (1795–1872), medical practitioner, and his wife, Mary Ann Watson (1800–1884). Destined for his father's career he studied at Guy's Hospital where, in 1850, he became demonstrator in chemistry. He became MB (1851) and FRCP (1859). He was appointed lecturer at St Bartholomew's Hospital in 1863, succeeded Michael Faraday as Fullerian professor of chemistry at the Royal Institution five years later, and in 1872 became Waynflete professor of chemistry at Oxford (where he became a fellow of Worcester College), retiring in 1912. In 1872 he married Elizabeth Mary (d. 1919), daughter of Alfred *Smee, surgeon and metallurgist. They had three sons.

Odling's contributions to chemistry were in two main directions: medical and theoretical. As the first medical officer of health for Lambeth he gained direct experience of cholera and other water-borne diseases. For drinking purposes, he concluded that well water, with possibilities of immediate pollution, was less desirable than river water, with its natural processes for purification. He served for many years as examiner for the London water supply and held strong views on sewage purification.

It was not long before purely chemical interests supplanted those of medicine. In 1885 Odling translated the *Méthode de chimie* (1854) of Auguste Laurent, proponent of the French 'type theory' of chemical constitution. His commitment to this view was reinforced and directed by a year spent in Paris as a student of C. F. Gerhardt, another leader in the field. In its opposition to structural formulae, and in its reform of atomic weights later continued by Stanislao Cannizzaro, the type theory found a ready British exponent in Odling. His lectures and writings played a considerable part in shaping fundamental chemical theory, and in several respects laid the foundations for the theory of valency, as defined by Edward Frankland and August Kekulé. Ironically his most famous expression of the type theory, in a formula for bleaching powder, was later found to be wrong. He gave the correct formula for ozone (1861).

Odling's prowess as a lecturer at the Royal Institution was maintained at Oxford where, however, he regarded it as 'not etiquette' to enter the chemical laboratory, having assistants to teach students and doing little experimental research himself. Among his publications were *A Course of Practical Chemistry* (1854), *A Manual of Chemistry, Descriptive and Theoretical* (1861), and *Outlines of Chemistry* (1870). In 1859 Odling became FRS. He served on the Chemical Society's council for sixty-five years, having terms as secretary (1856–69), vice-president (1869–73), and president (1873–5). He was president of the Institute of Chemistry from 1883 to 1888. His interest in literature, art, and drama found expression in his collection of engravings and his membership of the Garrick Club and the Athenaeum.

On retiring from the professorship in 1912 Odling commenced another book, called *The Technic of Versification* (1916). Dedicated to his wife, it was written in his favourite style, eschewing principal verbs, and containing a fine anthology of English poetry. Odling died at his home, 15 Norham Gardens, Oxford, on 17 February 1921, after being knocked down by a cyclist. COLIN A. RUSSELL, rev.

Sources H. B. D., *PRS*, 100A (1921–2), i–vii · J. E. Marsh, *JCS*, 119 (1921), 553–64 · W. H. Brock, 'Odling, William', *DSB*, vol. 10

Archives Open University, Milton Keynes, Edward Frankland archive [microfilm] · Oxf. U. Mus. NH, letters to Sir E. B. Poulton · Royal Society of Chemistry, London, Royal Institute of Chemistry archive

Likenesses photograph, repro. in Marsh, *JCS* · photographs, Royal Society of Chemistry

Wealth at death £47,587 18s. 7d.: probate, 6 June 1921, *CGPLA Eng. & Wales*

Odlum, Doris Maude (1890–1985), psychiatrist, born on 26 June 1890 in Folkestone, Kent, was the only child of Walter Edward Odlum (1862–1922), an accountant, and his wife, Maude (1860–1942), *née* Gough; both her parents were hoteliers. She was educated at Talbot Heath high school, Bournemouth, from about 1899 to 1909, and at St Hilda's Hall, Oxford, from which she graduated in 1912 with a third in classics. On graduation she spent some time lecturing for the Workers' Education Association in the midlands and north of England. She was also active in the campaign for women's suffrage where she retained her belief in non-violence. In 1914 Doris Odlum moved to London where she joined the Women's Volunteer Reserve Corps, working one evening a week in the canteen at the Woolwich arsenal. In 1914 she received her BA from London University, and in 1915 her diploma in education.

Although Odlum had initially intended to teach, an interest in medicine, which stemmed partly from a childhood contact with Helen Boyle, aroused her interest in some psychological aspects of medicine. As a result, in 1915 she entered the London School of Medicine for Women, part of the Royal Free Hospital of Medicine, to train as a doctor. Her medical education was interrupted by her work as commander of a forage guard in the New Forest between 1917 and 1919. In 1919 she was one of the first seven to receive an MA from Oxford University, and in 1920 she started her clinical work in London at St Mary's, Paddington, when it first opened its doors to women. She graduated LRCP and MRCS in 1924, and began work with Helen Boyle at the Lady Chichester Hospital for Women with Nervous Diseases in Hove where her interest in psychiatry grew. The Lady Chichester Hospital was one of the few hospitals to provide consultancy positions for women.

In 1926 Odlum became honorary consultant at the Lady Chichester Hospital and assistant medical officer at Camberwell House, London. She also began work part time at the Maudsley Hospital. In 1927 she gained her diploma in psychological medicine, and in 1928, with Dr Streatham, co-founded the psychiatric department at Boscombe Hospital, near Bournemouth. In the same year she inaugurated the psychiatric medicine department and also a child guidance clinic at the Royal Victoria Hospital, and between 1928 and 1948 she was honorary physician for psychiatry at the Royal Victoria and West Hampshire Hospital as well as consultant physician at the Lady Chichester Hospital.

Odlum became particularly interested in the early psychiatric problems of children, almost certainly an interest which grew from her work at the Lady Chichester Hospital, one of the first hospitals to work with the early psychological problems of children, and concentrated much of her efforts into this field. This interest is reflected in most of her publications, and she clearly believed that early treatment and a stable background were effective in preventing mental illness in children.

In 1929 Odlum was elected vice-president of the Medical Woman's International Association, and in 1937 she joined the psychological medicine group of the British Medical Association (BMA) as a founder member. In the same year she was made honorary consultant psychiatrist to the West End Hospital for Nervous Diseases, London,

and helped form the psychiatric department at the Elizabeth Garrett Anderson Hospital. She was also co-opted on to the London county council as a member of the mental health committee and was invited to stand for parliament.

Between 1943 and 1946 Odlum was chairman of the psychological medicine group of the BMA, in 1946 became vice-president of the National Association for Mental Health for England and Wales, and between 1946 and 1950 was vice-president of the National Medical Women's Association. In 1948 she was elected chairman of the psychological medicine committee of the BMA—the only woman member. Between 1948 and 1951 she was a member of the World Federation of Mental Health, between 1950 and 1952 president of the British Medical Women's Association, and from 1950 to 1954 vice-president of the International Medical Women's Association. From 1953 to 1956 she was president of the European League for Mental Hygiene. She retired as senior physician of psychological medicine to the Elizabeth Garrett Anderson Hospital in 1955.

Odlum's interests, apart from psychiatric medicine, were varied although almost entirely with a focus on children. She was a member of the Home Office committee on adoption law in 1954, and in 1956 was a member of the Magistrates Association, producing a report on cruelty to and neglect of children. She also played an active part in the development of social work, occupational therapy, and child guidance. She had an interest in eugenics, and between 1931 and 1957 was a member of the Eugenics Education Society, a pressure group whose main purpose was to promulgate eugenic concepts within society, including the voluntary sterilization of 'mental defectives'. Odlum had a great interest in the Samaritans' organization, becoming honorary consultant in psychiatry to them in 1961. In the same year she helped with the founding of the Bournemouth Samaritans and was a member of their committee on suicide which campaigned to legalize suicide. She was made life president of the Samaritans in 1973.

After her retirement Odlum continued her work in psychiatry, being made a fellow of the BMA in 1958, and in 1971 was made a foundation fellow of the Royal College of Psychiatrists. In 1980 St Hilda's College, Oxford, awarded her an honorary fellowship. She continued lecturing, contributing at conferences, and broadcasting on the radio. In 1961 she endowed a Doris Odlum prize at the BMA for research work in psychiatry.

Among Odlum's publications were: 'Women and war' in *Medical Opinions on War* (1939?), *You and your Children: BBC Talks by a Woman Medical Psychologist* (1946), 'Modern trends in public life', *Modern Treatment Year Book* (1949), *Psychology, the Nurse and the Patient* (1952), *Journey through Adolescence* (1957), *The Mind of your Child* (1960), *Psychology Problems and Pastoral Care* (1964), *Puber puberteit* (1965), *The Male Predicament* (1975), and *Adolescence* (1978). She shared her personal life primarily with women, spending the last thirty-seven years of her life with the artist Zoe Jarret. Odlum's leisure interests were tennis, swimming, painting, travelling, golf, and rowing. In 1916 she had stroked the first women's eight race ever rowed and in 1919 she was reserve in the British National Fencing Championships.

Odlum died in Bournemouth on 14 October 1985 of a heart attack. She was buried at the church of Transfiguration, Canford Cliffs, Bournemouth, a week later.

EMMA MILLIKEN

Sources L. M. Hellstedt, *Women physicians of the world: biographies of medical pioneers* (1978) · *BMJ* (9 Nov 1985), 1356 · *Bournemouth Evening Echo* (17 Oct 1985) · *WW* (1985) · *Medical Directory* · *Medical Register* · private information (2004) · *CGPLA Eng. & Wales* (1986) · *WWW* · Royal Free Hospital, London, archives

Archives E. Sussex RO · Royal Free Hospital, London · Wellcome L.

Wealth at death £177,717: probate, 17 Jan 1986, *CGPLA Eng. & Wales*

Odo. *See* Oda (*d.* 958); Odda, earl (*d.* 1056).

Odo, earl of Kent (*d.* 1097), bishop of Bayeux and magnate, was the son of Herluin de Conteville (*d. c.*1066), a Norman magnate of vicomte status who held lands around Grestain to the south of the Seine estuary, and of Herleva (*fl. c.*1010–*c.*1055), the former concubine of Robert (II), duke of Normandy (*d.* 1035). He was thus the half-brother of *William the Conqueror.

Origins and family Herluin and Herleva are known to have produced one further son, *Robert (*d.* 1095), who was appointed count of Mortain in the late 1050s, and two daughters, Adelaide, who married in succession Enguerrand, count of Ponthieu, Lambert of Lens, and Odo, count of Champagne, and Muriel, who married the Norman magnate Eudo, vicomte of the Cotentin. Two other half-brothers, Ralph and John, sons of Herluin's second marriage, are known, both relatively minor figures who held some lands in Normandy. In all probability there was also at least one other sister, or half-sister, who married the southern Norman magnate William de La Ferté-Macé, but whose name is unknown. Odo had one son, John of Bayeux, who was one of Henry I's chaplains; his mother's name has not been recorded. The date of Odo's birth is uncertain because the earliest sources, Orderic Vitalis and William of Malmesbury, both writing in the twelfth century, disagree as to whether Herleva was married to Herluin before or after Duke Robert's death. It is also unclear which of Odo and Robert, count of Mortain, was the senior; Robert's succession to Herluin's lands may well indicate that he was the elder. On balance, a birth date in the early 1030s fits the evidence best. Odo was certainly well below thirty, the canonically required age for promotion to a bishopric, when he became bishop of Bayeux at a date between his predecessor's death, some time after attending the Council of Rheims in October 1049, and 23 April 1050. Little is known about his education; William of Poitiers implies that he was educated in the ducal household.

Early career and invasion of England Odo's appointment to Bayeux on the say-so of his half-brother William was a typical promotion for a close male kinsman of a Norman duke. Politically it was an aspect of William's consolidation of his rule in western Normandy after his victory at

Odo, earl of Kent (*d.* 1097), embroidery (Bayeux Tapestry) [seated, third from right]

the battle of Val-ès-Dunes in 1047. Although Odo's importance in Normandy before 1066 is indicated by his prominence among the attestations to ducal charters, this period of his life is a relatively obscure one. It is primarily his status in England and Normandy after the conquest and his accomplishments at Bayeux on the basis of foundations laid before 1066 which show how active and important he must already have become.

Odo was prominent in the crucial discussions which preceded the invasion of England. According to an early twelfth-century ship list, he supplied one hundred ships to the invasion fleet. His role in the battle of Hastings is known mainly from the Bayeux tapestry, of which Odo was beyond any reasonable doubt the patron and on which his importance has probably been inflated. He and Count Robert are portrayed in council with William immediately before the battle, with Odo speaking animatedly to an attentive duke, as if laying out the battle plan. During the battle he appears in a quasi-military role, arrayed in a haubergon (but without the full protection afforded by a hauberk), carrying a mace-like instrument and rallying troops at a strategically significant moment in the battle. This portrayal is not necessarily in conflict with William of Poitiers's statement that Odo was not personally responsible for the shedding of blood at Hastings, but it does suggest that his opinion that Odo and Geoffrey, bishop of Coutances, were there to help with their prayers was less than the truth.

Earl and regent, 1067–1082/3 Along with William fitz Osbern, Odo acted as William I's deputy in England after the newly crowned king had returned to Normandy in February 1067. He was created earl of Kent soon after 1066, and his initial responsibilities involved him in supervising the defence and subjugation of the south-eastern part of the kingdom. The months until William's return to England in December were principally occupied in building castles, overcoming English revolts, and, specifically, moving towards Dover when the castle there was attacked by William's former ally, Eustace, count of Boulogne. The treatment of Odo's conduct during this period in the main literary sources raises immediately the problem of interpreting his role in the history of the Norman conquest of England. The Anglo-Saxon Chronicle, in key respects echoed by Orderic Vitalis (who wrote in the 1120s), tells of oppression and illegality. William of Poitiers (whose panegyric of William the Conqueror was completed before 1077), in contrast, praises Odo's activities and remarks that the English will in due course come to appreciate him. The perspectives from which each author approached his subject are of course crucial. The dichotomy is fundamental to interpreting Odo's career in England (see below).

The period between 1066 and his arrest and imprisonment by William in late 1082 or early 1083 is the apogee of Odo's career. A range of literary sources concur that he ruled England when William was in Normandy. Domesday Book shows that he had become the wealthiest English landholder after the king, with estates scattered throughout twenty-two counties in the south and east of the kingdom. His chief residences appear to have been at Dover, Rochester, Deddington in Oxfordshire, and Snettisham in Norfolk. His charter attestations show that his itinerary was that of a cross-channel magnate, present at such great events as Queen Mathilda's coronation at Whitsun 1068 and the settlement of the primacy dispute at Windsor at Whitsun 1072; and that he was usually at the great crown-wearings and assemblies which were a feature of the Conqueror's rule on both sides of the channel, as well as at ecclesiastical councils of the Norman church. He was one of the royal generals in eastern England during the 1075 revolt of the three earls; and in the autumn of 1080 he led an army which devastated Northumbria to avenge the murder in the previous year of Walcher, bishop of Durham. In 1074 the king gave the large estate of Le Plessis-Grimoult to Odo's cathedral; and on 14 July 1077, Odo's new cathedral church was consecrated in the presence of the king and many Norman notables. Odo is addressed in his capacity of earl in most of the surviving royal writs concerned with Kent; and he exchanged and granted lands to the major churches of the shire, notably the abbey of St Augustine's, Canterbury.

The nature of Odo's role in England between 1066 and 1082/3 has posed problems for historians. Although clearly identified in contemporary sources as having been regent when the king was in Normandy, Odo was himself often in Normandy with William. Also, there were others, notably Archbishop Lanfranc, who clearly acted in England as William's deputy. Lanfranc in particular appears as the first addressee in numerous royal writs in a way

which Odo does not and was manifestly playing the central co-ordinating role during the 1075 revolt. The most plausible interpretation of the evidence of the literary sources is that Odo alone could act with the equivalent of royal authority when William was not in England; this interpretation is seemingly confirmed by Domesday Book's insistence that only Odo's seal had the same status as the king's and by its frequent references to, and acceptance of, property disputes settled on Odo's authority. There would probably have been periods of time, most notably from late 1077 to early 1080 when William was dealing with the warfare provoked by his eldest son, Robert Curthose, when Odo was *de jure* presiding over the settlement of conquered England.

The way in which Odo exercised his responsibilities attracted strong criticism; Orderic Vitalis, for example, places him in the category of the *tyranni*, rulers who disregard equity and law. Surviving accounts of land pleas convey an ambivalent impression. A Rochester text shows him going to considerable lengths to restore an estate to the church and to demonstrate that English witnesses had perjured themselves because of threats made by a Norman sheriff. The Evesham chronicle describes his role in an inquiry into the abbey's lands held at Four-Shire Stone, Warwickshire, as that of a ravening wolf; it should, however, be noted that even in this case some of the lands which Odo appropriated to himself were not the abbey's, but had been granted to Abbot Æthelwig (d. 1078) on a temporary basis. These charges of unfairness and oppression need to be set in the context of other evidence for Odo's conduct. Domesday Book certainly shows that Odo and his tenants in some places acted aggressively to expand their lands. In 1072 he and his tenants in Kent were involved in the great land plea held at Penenden Heath near Maidstone, at which they were adjudged to have illegally taken over a considerable number of estates belonging to the archbishop and monks of Christ Church, Canterbury. Even though much of the litigation had its origins in pre-1066 tenurial disputes, and taking into account that all the surviving testimony was written by Odo's opponents, the protracted disputes which followed the Penenden plea undoubtedly reinforced a general impression of acquisitiveness and overweening power. The overall charge of oppression cannot in the end be gainsaid. But there is plenty of evidence to show that Odo's rule in England was neither entirely arbitrary nor entirely self-seeking. And there is also no doubt that after the Norman conquest Odo was given responsibility for a situation of great tenurial and political complexity.

Bishop of Bayeux and the Bayeux tapestry While there is good evidence to indicate that the new cathedral church at Bayeux had been begun by Odo's predecessor, the architecture of the building's surviving eleventh-century parts suggests that most of the construction took place in Odo's time. Two Bayeux charters dating from 1092 and 1093 provide the earliest extensive evidence of the personnel of the cathedral chapter, mentioning nine chapter dignitaries and thirty canons. As a measure of the extent of the chapter's evolution, these figures need to be set against the twelve dignitaries and forty-nine canons of the fully-fledged thirteenth-century Bayeux chapter. It was once thought that Odo formally instituted at Bayeux the 'four-square' chapter typical of several English medieval cathedrals; that idea must now be abandoned in favour of an evolutionary and conceptually derivative view of the chapter's development. It remains certain that English developments were influenced through the activities of Odo's protégés. Odo also founded the abbey of St Vigor outside Bayeux at an unknown date before 1082, intending it to be the burial church for himself and future bishops of Bayeux; he was able to attract the distinguished scholar Robert de Tombelaine to be its first abbot. A considerable body of charter evidence shows Odo making grants of limited exemption from episcopal authority to abbeys within his diocese, accumulating property for his church and protecting his clergy. Despite his many absences, Odo was undoubtedly a successful and committed bishop of Bayeux. Comparison with the parallel contemporary developments in other Norman bishoprics demonstrates, however, that he operated on a much grander and more lavish scale than his colleagues; sculpture surviving from the cathedral, for example, indicates a monumentality, ambition, and stylistic range of reference of a quite remarkable kind.

The most famous product of Odo's artistic and intellectual patronage is the unique Bayeux tapestry. Almost certainly produced in England, this complex and brilliant embroidery is the most spectacular illustration of a wide-ranging patronage whose ramifications were felt not only throughout Normandy and England, but in many regions of France north of the Loire. Odo's patronage supported scholars for study at Liège and elsewhere, nurtured poets writing at Bayeux and throughout northern France, and assisted the development of Bayeux as an intellectual centre. Nine of Odo's protégés obtained bishoprics in either England or Normandy and four became abbots. Although their personal qualities varied, and some, such as Samson, bishop of Worcester (d. 1112), or the notorious Ranulf Flambard (d. 1128), were certainly excessively worldly, the likes of Thomas (I), archbishop of York (d. 1100), William de Rots, abbot of Fécamp (d. 1107), and William of St Calais, bishop of Durham (d. 1096), were churchmen of either high personal and moral character or exceptional administrative competence. Odo's patronage also extended to include some of the most significant poets of the time, such as Marbod of Rennes and Hildebert de Lavardin, and controversial theologians, such as the grammarian Roscelin of Compiègne. The intellectual tone of Odo's Bayeux, to judge principally from the works of the poet Serlo of Bayeux, tended to the conservative, praising the virtues of the secular clergy and critical of fashionable Benedictine monasticism and many of the ideas being advanced by the Gregorian reformers.

Imprisonment Either late in the year 1082, or early in 1083, Odo was seized by the king and, after a trial, was imprisoned. Although the earliest source for this event, the Anglo-Saxon Chronicle, places it in 1082, the statement by Orderic Vitalis that Odo was in prison for four years would probably place the arrest in early 1083; Odo's attestation of a charter at Downton, Wiltshire, in the autumn of 1082 and William's return to Normandy by Easter 1083 provide the chronological limits. The chronicle offers no explanation of the arrest. While the next earliest source, Guibert of Nogent, writing c.1108, suggests that Odo was planning to seize the English kingdom after William's death, the opinion that Odo was preparing an expedition to Rome to become pope after Gregory VII (r. 1073–85), which appears with different embellishments in Orderic, William of Malmesbury's Gesta regum, and the so-called Hyde chronicle, is generally preferred. This story has no echoes in papal sources. Orderic's dramatic account of the trial stresses that Odo was diverting warriors from England for an expedition overseas and that William was disturbed by his oppressive and arrogant rule in England; he also suggests that William himself had to seize Odo because the magnates assembled at court feared him so much. Odo remained in prison at Rouen until released by the dying king in September 1087; Orderic suggests that only the supplications of the magnates present, led by Count Robert, weakened William's resolve to keep Odo in prison for ever.

Rebellion, crusade, and death After attending the Conqueror's funeral at Caen in September 1087, Odo crossed to England and regained his lands and his earldom. He attended the Christmas court of the new king of England, *William Rufus, but by April 1088 at the latest he was in arms at the head of an extensive coalition of many of the most powerful magnates of the conquest generation, which was seeking to overthrow the Conqueror's death-bed division of Normandy and England between *Robert Curthose and William Rufus in Robert's favour. While superficially imposing, the conspiracy failed because Rufus and his allies were able to defeat their opponents before they could unite their forces, and because Robert Curthose failed to land in England. Odo himself was besieged in his brother Count Robert's castle at Pevensey and then at Rochester. After Rochester's capitulation, Odo was exiled from England for ever. Back in Normandy, he participated in Robert Curthose's campaigns in Maine and southern Normandy in late 1088 and was with Robert when he sought assistance from the French king in 1089. He also took personal responsibility for the imprisonment in 1088 of the youngest of the Conqueror's sons, the future Henry I, whose activities in western Normandy threatened to destabilize the duchy. He continued as far as possible to intrigue against William Rufus. Orderic portrays Odo as Robert Curthose's chief counsellor during these years, but comments that the wayward duke did not always follow his advice.

Odo also set about regaining estates lost to his cathedral during his imprisonment and restoring the monastic community of St Vigor, which had been plundered by the Conqueror and had disbanded. His intellectual and clerical patronage also revived. It is clear, however, that Odo was unable to restore fully his church's possessions or to do much to prevent the disintegration of Robert's rule in Normandy. In 1095 he was among the Norman bishops who attended the Council of Clermont at which Pope Urban II preached the first crusade. In the months that followed he made arrangements for the re-established monastery of St Vigor to become a priory of the strict abbey of St Bénigne of Dijon, before departing for the crusade with Duke Robert's army. The army wintered with their fellow Normans in southern Italy and around Christmas Odo crossed to Sicily to visit the Norman ruler of the island, Roger the Great Count. He died on 6 January 1097 and was buried in the cathedral at Palermo. His last illness, of which nothing is known, must have been a short one.

Assessment   Orderic Vitalis's verdict on Odo that, although excessively worldly, he was none the less a curious mixture of virtues and vices, and that he did a lot of good, remains a just one. He was regarded at Bayeux as a good bishop and his activities in England, while undoubtedly at times oppressive and tyrannical, have sometimes been too severely censured because overmuch attention has been given to the testimony of those who suffered at his hands. He was undeniably the most colourful and flamboyant of the Norman conquerors of England, a forceful character whose energy contributed mightily to the success of the conquest. On the other hand his restlessness and turbulence led to quarrels with the Conqueror, Archbishop Lanfranc, and William Rufus and must have contributed significantly to destabilizing Norman rule in England and Normandy. A prince-bishop on a grand scale, his generosity and patronage shaped the careers of many laymen and clergy who played significant roles in the Norman achievement and in the society of the eleventh-century medieval West. The Bayeux tapestry survives as brilliant testimony to the many strands of a remarkable career.   DAVID BATES

Sources Ordericus Vitalis, *Eccl. hist.* · A. Farley, ed., *Domesday Book*, 2 vols. (1783) · D. Bates, 'The character and career of Bishop Odo of Bayeux, 1049/50–1097', *Speculum*, 50 (1975), 1–20 · D. Bates, 'The land pleas of William I's reign: Penenden Heath revisited', *BIHR*, 51 (1978), 1–19 · D. Bates, 'The origins of the justiciarship', *Anglo-Norman Studies*, 4 (1981), 1–12, 167–71 · D. Bates, 'Le patronage clérical et intellectual de l'évêque Odon de Bayeux, 1049/50–1097', in S. Lemagnen, *Chapitres et cathédrales en Normandie* [Bayeux 1996] (1997), 104–5 · *The Gesta Guillelmi of William of Poitiers*, ed. and trans. R. H. C. Davis and M. Chibnall, OMT (1998) · D. M. Wilson, ed., *The Bayeux tapestry* (1985) · V. Bourrienne, ed., *Antiquus cartularius ecclesie Baiocensis* (*Livre Noir*), 2 vols., Société de l'Histoire de Normandie (1902–3)
Likenesses embroidery (Bayeux Tapestry), Bayeux, France [*see illus.*]

Odo of Canterbury. *See* Canterbury, Odo of (*d.* 1200).

Odo of Cheriton. *See* Cheriton, Odo of (1180s–1246).

Ó Dochartaigh, Cathaoir. *See* O'Doherty, Sir Cahir (1587–1608).

O'Doherty, Sir Cahir [Cathaoir Ó Dochartaigh] (**1587–1608**), chieftain, was born in Aileach Mor on the Inishowen peninsula, co. Donegal, the eldest legitimate son of Sir John (Seán Óg) O'Doherty (*d.* 1601), lord of Inishowen. Although Sir John had striven to assure the English authorities of his loyalty, he fled from his territory with his family and possessions in 1600 to the lands of Hugh Roe O'Donnell (Aodh Rua Ó Domhnaill) and died on 27 January 1601, a traitor in the eyes of the authorities. But in accordance with native Irish law, the inheritance of his title and estates fell to Felim Oge O'Doherty, Cahir's uncle, who was inaugurated by Hugh O'Donnell in order to ensure that Inishowen remained under his control. The exclusion of Cahir from the lordship on account of his youth gave offence to Aodh Buidhe McDavitt and Felim Riabhach MacDavitt (Mac Dáibhéid), who belonged to a sept of the O'Dohertys, and with whom Cahir had been fostered from childhood. Aodh Buidhe promised to Lord Deputy Mountjoy to submit himself to Queen Elizabeth and renounce allegiance to Hugh O'Neill and O'Donnell if Cahir's right to succession were acknowledged. After some persuasion by the MacDavitts, Cahir was confirmed as successor by the lord deputy and privy council in Ireland to ensure peace and stability in an area of strategic importance. He was removed from O'Donnell's territory, and returned with his family and possessions to Inishowen, where he was taken under the tutelage of Sir Henry Dowcra in Derry, who styled him the Ó Dochartaigh and educated him as an English gentleman. Dowcra even suggested in a letter written in September 1601 to the privy council that Cahir be taken to England and educated there, but it was not acted upon.

Cahir O'Doherty became a fine soldier, and was knighted for bravery by Mountjoy at Augher, near Clogher, in co. Tyrone in 1602. In the following year he visited the court of James I in London, where he claimed his father's title and lands, which were in due course restored to him. On his return to Ireland, in 1604 he married Mary (*d.* in or after 1609), daughter of Christopher Preston, fourth Viscount Gormanstown, was made a JP, and became an alderman of the city of Derry. When he came of age in 1605, he was established as lord of Inishowen. He stood out from his fellow clansmen by virtue of his great stature, red hair, and English dress.

In the summer of 1606 Dowcra retired from the governorship of Derry because of a disagreement with Lord Deputy Chichester and gave it to George Paulet, who was generally unpopular and disliked. The loss of the support of Dowcra curtailed O'Doherty's power. Early in November 1607 O'Doherty went on certain manoeuvres which aroused Paulet's suspicions and he reported to the lord deputy that O'Doherty was preparing a revolt. O'Doherty denied this and signed a document to that effect in the presence of two sureties before the lord deputy in Dublin Castle on 2 December 1607. This document, with his signature, survives.

In 1608 O'Doherty was appointed to a commission to rule the territory of co. Tyrone, and acted as foreman of the jury that indicted the earls of Tyrone and Tyrconnell, O'Neill and O'Donnell, of treason after their flight from Ireland in 1607 with their families and followers. This led to the confiscation of their lands and became known as the 'flight of the earls'. Although O'Doherty did not follow them in flight, in the hope of something better arising from the new situation, he was ultimately driven into open rebellion. In April 1608 he was charged with treason, stripped of his lordship, and verbally and physically abused by Paulet, 'so that he would rather have suffered death than live to brook such insult and dishonor, or defer or delay to take revenge for it' (O'Donovan, s.a. 1608). He planned to take the fort of Culmore, which he succeeded in capturing through the unwilling assistance of the wife of Captain Harte, constable of the fort, whom he had imprisoned after inviting the couple to dine at his residence at Inishowen. He and Felim Riabhach later marched on Derry, which was sacked and burnt—an attack in which Paulet was one of the first victims. The garrison was put to the sword, but the unarmed men were spared. Following this O'Doherty attacked Lifford, but was tracked down and killed by a shot in the head from the English forces under Sir Francis Rushe at Kilmacrenan in co. Donegal on 5 July 1608. His body was quartered and his head removed and sent to Dublin, and stuck on a spike above the main gate for public exhibition. Felim Riabhach was later tried for treason at Derry, convicted, and executed. Niall Garbh O'Donnell, who had ambitions of becoming the new earl of Tyrone and who had at least tacitly sided with O'Doherty, was arrested and accused of taking part in the insurrection, and sent to the Tower, where he remained for the rest of his life. O'Doherty's widow was held under arrest in Dublin but was later released and in 1609 given a pension of £40 per annum out of the rents of Inishowen by Chichester. Cahir O'Doherty had an only daughter from his marriage and his younger brothers, John (Eoghan) and Rory (Ruairi), were still in fosterage at the time of his rebellion. Rory joined the 'wild geese' and died in service in Belgium; John married Eliza, daughter of Patrick O'Cahan of Derry, and died in 1638.

The revolt had lasted only eleven weeks, but its results for Cahir O'Doherty's allies were catastrophic: the Mac-Davitts were rendered powerless and the entire barony of Inishowen was confiscated and later granted to Chichester in May 1609. The flight of the earls and the suppression of O'Doherty's brief rebellion paved the way for the plantation of Ulster between 1609 and 1613, which had certainly been the chief objective of James I's government in Ireland. Ironically, O'Doherty had at the end sought a place at court in an attempt to exert some influence over the colonial government in Dublin, and an order was received for his restoration to his former lordship on the day that his rebellion broke out.   AIDAN BREEN

Sources *CSP Ire.*, 1600–01, 189–94, 218, 339, 363; 1603–6, 78, 316–18, 320, 406; 1608–10 · *Calendar of the Irish patent rolls of James I* (before 1830); facs. edn as *Irish patent rolls of James I* (1966), 3.459 · AFM, 6.2236–7, 2358–65 · H. Dowcra, *A narration of the services done by the army employed to Lough Foyle under the leading of me, Sir Henry Dowcra, knight*, ed. J. O'Donovan (1849) · J. Perrot, *The chronicle of Ireland, 1584–1608*, ed. H. Wood, IMC (1933), 185–60 · L. Ó Cléirigh, *Beatha Aodha Ruaidh Uí Dhomhnaill*, trans. D. Murphy (1895) · B. Bonner, *That audacious traitor* (1975), 111–98 · P. S. Robinson, *The plantation of Ulster* (1994) · F. Gillespie, 'The Gaelic families of Donegal', *Donegal history and society: interdisciplinary essays on the history of an Irish county*, ed. W. Nolan, L. Ronayne, and M. Dunlevy (1995), 759–838

O'Doherty, Kevin Izod (1823–1905), politician and physician, was born in Gloucester Street, Dublin, on 7 September 1823, the son of William Izod O'Doherty, solicitor, and his wife, Anne, *née* McEvoy, and was baptized at the Roman Catholic church of St Andrew. He was educated at Dr Wall's school, Hume Street, Dublin, and began medical training, first at the medical school, Cecilia Street, Dublin, from November 1842 until April 1843. He was an assistant in St Mark's Ophthalmic Hospital for diseases of the eyes and ears (December 1845 – July 1847), and a clinical practising assistant in the Meath Hospital, Dublin (October 1847 – May 1848). His subsequent life fell into four phases: Young Ireland and transportation to Australia; qualification, medical practice, and Queensland politics from the mid-1850s to 1885; a brief incursion into Ireland's political arena in the mid-1880s; and a relatively obscure resumption of private life in Brisbane after 1888.

In May 1843 O'Doherty became associated with the Young Ireland movement and contributed to its newspaper, *The Nation*, then under the stewardship of Charles Gavan Duffy; he was also a founder of the students' and polytechnic clubs, which opposed the policies of Daniel O'Connell. When John Mitchel seceded from *The Nation* and advocated revolution, O'Doherty, who although essentially a moderate had been radicalized by the experience of treating patients suffering from famine diseases, followed him to support the confederation and contributed to Mitchel's new journal, the *United Irishman*. When this was suppressed, O'Doherty co-founded a successor newspaper, *The Tribune*, which first appeared on 10 June 1848. Five weeks later the paper was seized and O'Doherty along with several colleagues was arrested on 8 or 9 July and charged with treason-felony. After three trials an all-protestant jury found him guilty on 3 October 1849 and O'Doherty was given the extended sentence of transportation for ten years to Van Diemen's Land. He arrived in Hobart Town on 31 October 1849.

Like other transported political prisoners, O'Doherty enjoyed comparative freedom: he was granted a ticket-of-leave and allowed to settle in the Oatlands district, where he continued his medical studies. In November 1850 O'Doherty was given permission to transfer to Hobart, where he worked with a local physician and became manager of the dispensary. During this period he regularly met his fellow exiles. One meeting discovered in December 1850 led to confinement for three weeks in January 1851 in a prison colony where he was obliged to 'split shingles' alongside ordinary criminals. From August 1851 to September 1853 O'Doherty was acting surgeon at St Mary's Hospital, Hobart, and then in autumn that year he moved to Huon River, though he proved unable to develop a successful medical practice there.

In March 1855 it was announced that O'Doherty would be given a conditional pardon, which forbade residence in the United Kingdom. Before departing for Europe he and P. J. Smyth travelled to the Australian gold fields. In 1855 he went to Paris, where he studied surgery for a year at the Pitie hospital and then anatomy for a further six months. In 1855 he made a surreptitious trip to London to marry (on 23 August) the nationalist poet Mary Anne Kelly [see O'Doherty, Mary Anne (1830–1910)], 'Eva of *The Nation*', to whom he had become engaged in spring 1848, before his conviction. They went through another marriage ceremony in Paris on 30 November, to avoid the detection of his violation of the terms of his conditional pardon. Kelly had declined O'Doherty's offer to release her from the engagement following his sentence. He received a pardon the following year and returned to Ireland, where he became a fellow of the Royal College of Surgeons and Physicians of Ireland in June 1857. O'Doherty practised in Dublin until emigrating in 1860 first to New South Wales, then to Ipswich, Queensland, for three years before settling in 1865 in Brisbane, where he became a leading physician. He was an early president of the Queensland Medical Society and carried out extensive honorary work at Catholic hospitals. Between 1867 and 1873 he was a member for Brisbane in the legislative assembly of Queensland, where he was responsible in 1872 for the first Health Act. From May 1877 to 1885 he was a member of the Queensland legislative council, where he sponsored the bill to stop the recruitment of Kanakas. In November 1882 he was made surgeon-major of the Queensland volunteer force. He remained active in Irish affairs: he established the Queensland Hibernian Society in 1871 and was president of the Irish Australian Convention in 1883.

On returning to Ireland in 1885 O'Doherty received a rapturous reception and was granted the freedom of Dublin. At the request of Charles Stewart Parnell he stood as nationalist parliamentary candidate for North Meath at the general election in 1885 and was returned unopposed on 27 November but did not stand again at the general election in July 1886.

Having been unable to establish a successful medical practice, O'Doherty returned to Brisbane in 1888 but failed to recover his position. In 1892 he was appointed surgeon to the central board of health and also was supervisor of the quarantine station, posts which brought him £250 per annum. He suffered from advancing blindness during his final years, which were marred by straitened financial circumstances, and following his death on 15 July 1905 at his home in Torwood, Brisbane, his widow was supported by a fund raised for her relief. Of his eight children, only one daughter survived him. O'Doherty and his wife (who died on 21 May 1910) were interred in the Woowong cemetery, where a monument provided by the Queensland Irish Association stands over their graves.

ALAN O'DAY

Sources B. M. Touhill, *William Smith O'Brien and his Irish revolutionary companions in penal exile* (1981) · T. J. Kiernan, *The Irish exiles in Australia* (1954) · *AusDB*, vol. 5 · R. Davis, *The Young Ireland movement* (1987) · R. Davis, *Revolutionary imperialist: William Smith O'Brien* (1998) · J. Mitchel, *Jail journal … with a continuation of the journal in New York and Paris* (1913) · H. Boylan, *A dictionary of Irish biography*, 3rd edn (1998) · C. G. Duffy, *Young Ireland*, rev. edn, 2 (1896) · A. M. Sullivan, *New Ireland* (1877) · B. O'Cathaoir, *John Blake Dillon* (1990) · T. F. O'Sullivan, *The Young Irelanders*, 2nd edn (1945) · T. De Vere White, *The road of excess* (1946) · D. J. Hickey and J. E. Doherty, *A dictionary of Irish history* (1980) · K. B. Nowlan, *The politics of repeal* (1965) · R. Patrick and H. Patrick, *Exiles undaunted: the Irish rebels Kevin and Eva O'Doherty* (1989)
Archives Mitchell L., NSW, MSS [microfilm] · NL Aus., MSS [microfilm] · State Library of Queensland, South Brisbane, John Oxley Library, MSS [microfilm] | NL Ire., John Devoy MSS · NL

Ire., Thomas F. Meagher MSS · NL Ire., W. Smith O'Brien MSS · NL Ire., P. J. Smyth MSS
Likenesses portrait, repro. in Touhill, *William Smith O'Brien*, p. 6

O'Doherty [*née* Kelly], **Mary Anne** [*called* Eva of *The Nation*] (**1830–1910**), poet, was born on 15 February 1830 at Headford, co. Galway, the daughter of Edward Kelly, a country gentleman, and his wife, Mary O'Flaherty. One of seven children, she spent her childhood at Headford. She was educated by governesses, one of whom encouraged her literary talents, which she soon turned to nationalist ends, perhaps influenced by her cousin John Blake Dillon and her uncle Martin O'Flaherty, who were both Young Irelanders.

After her poem 'The Leprechaun' appeared in the Young Ireland newspaper *The Nation* on 28 December 1844 under the signature Fionnuala, she began writing passionate nationalist verses under the signature Eva for *The Nation* and then for John Mitchel's *United Irishman* and the *Irish Felon* and the *Irish Tribune*. Her most famous poems were 'Down Britannia' and 'The Men in Jail for Ireland'. In 1848, during a visit to her uncle, a Dublin solicitor active on behalf of imprisoned Young Irelanders, she met Kevin Izod *O'Doherty (1823–1905), a young medical student imprisoned for his nationalist political activities. They became engaged before O'Doherty was convicted and sentenced to transportation to Van Diemen's Land in 1849. Her promise to wait for him, his clandestine return to Ireland after he was partially pardoned in 1854, and their subsequent marriage became the stuff of romantic nationalist legend. John Mitchel celebrated the love of his fellow exile O'Doherty for Eva, as she had become known, 'a dark-eyed lady, a fair and gentle lady, with hair like blackest midnight; and in the tangle of those silken tresses she has bound my poor friend's soul' (J. Mitchel, *Jail Journal*, 254).

Kevin O'Doherty and Mary Anne Kelly were married in London on 23 August 1855 and again in Paris on 30 November 1855 so that his presence in London, which violated the conditions of his partial pardon, would not be known. O'Doherty completed his medical studies in Paris and, after he received a full pardon in 1856, in Dublin, where the first of their eight children was born in May 1856. In 1859 they emigrated to Australia, where Kevin O'Doherty practised medicine, first in Sydney and eventually in Brisbane. Mary Anne devoted her energies to raising her young family, but her correspondence revealed her continuing literary aspirations. After the birth of her fourth child in 1860, she published forty poems in the *Sydney Freemen's Journal*, many of which expressed an exile's longing for Ireland and a continued commitment to social justice for the poor and oppressed.

Mary Anne O'Doherty and her husband were active in church and political circles with fellow emigrants from Ireland. She wrote verse in commemoration of the Daniel O'Connell centenary in 1875 and the Thomas Moore centenary in 1879. *Poems by Eva of 'The Nation'*, published in San Francisco in 1877, represented the full range of her poetic output: fervent nationalist verse, passionate love poetry, and melancholy musings on life and death. Passionate, popular, and effective political propaganda, her conventional themes and mediocre verses are now only of historical interest.

Eva's poetry and her romantic courtship and marriage earned her a place in Irish national legend which has overlooked the tragic aspects of her life. After an initially successful medical career, her husband's Irish nationalism and support for the Land League adversely affected his medical practice. Three of their children died in infancy, and of the five who lived to be adults only their daughter Gertrude survived her parents. Between 1890 and 1900 four sons died, and Kevin O'Doherty went blind. He died on 15 July 1905. In 1909 a testimonial in Australia and the publication of a collection of her poems in Dublin raised some money for the impoverished Eva, who died of influenza in Brisbane the following year on 21 May 1910. She was buried in Brisbane, beside her husband.

MARY HELEN THUENTE

Sources R. Patrick and H. Patrick, *Exiles undaunted: the Irish rebels Kevin and Eva O'Doherty* (1989) · P. J. Dillon, 'Eva of The Nation', *Capuchin Annual* (1933), 261–6 · *Poems by Eva of 'The Nation'*, ed. [S. McManus] (1909) [introduction and preface] · 'Irish literary celebrities 5, Mary Izod O'Doherty', *The Nation* [Dublin] (8 Dec 1888), 3 · B. Anton, 'Women of The Nation', *History Ireland* (1993), 34–7 · *DNB*
Archives priv. coll. | PRO NIre., letters to John Martin

O'Doherty, William James (1835–1868), sculptor, was born in Dublin. Of his parents or early education, nothing is known. From 1848 to 1853 he studied in the Government School of Design attached to the Royal Dublin Society, with the intention of becoming a painter, but, on the advice of Constantine Panormo, at that time one of the assistant masters, he turned his attention to modelling. He won several prizes for this, including a bronze medal in 1853 for *Night*, after Bertel Thorvaldsen, and *Boy and Bird*—both shown at the great Industrial Exhibition in Dublin in 1853. On the death of Panormo in 1852, he studied under his successor in the school of design, Joseph R. Kirk, until 1854, when, at the suggestion of the sculptor John Edward Jones, he went to London.

O'Doherty's first appearance at the Royal Academy was in 1857, when he exhibited, under the name of Dogherty, a plaster model of *Gondoline*, a subject taken from the poems of Henry Kirke White, and which he afterwards executed in marble for the banker R. C. L. Bevan. In 1860 he sent to the Royal Academy the model of the marble statue of *Erin*, executed for the marquess of Downshire; an engraving of it by T. W. Knight appeared in the *Art Journal* of 1861. Both in 1860 and in 1861, when he sent to the British Institution *One of the Surrey Volunteers*, his works appeared under the name of Doherty; but in 1862 he appears to have reverted to O'Doherty. His subsequent works included *Alethe*, a marble statuette executed for Bevan and exhibited at the Royal Academy in 1862, and some portrait busts exhibited in 1863 and 1864. He went to Rome in 1864 to pursue his studies and to execute a commission for the marquess of Downshire, the subject of which was to be 'the martyr'. O'Doherty never married

and his last years are obscure. His early death in February 1868, at La Charité Hospital in Berlin while on a visit to that city, ended a brief career of much promise.

R. E. GRAVES, *rev.* JOHN TURPIN

Sources W. G. Strickland, *A dictionary of Irish artists*, 2 (1913), 184–5 · *Art Journal*, 23 (1861), 252 · *Art Journal*, 30 (1868), 73 · Graves, *RA exhibitors* · Graves, *Brit. Inst.*

Ó Doirnín, Peadar [Peter O'Doirnin] (*d.* 1769), poet, may have been born in Cashel, co. Tipperary, although almost nothing is known for certain about his biographical details. Some of his poems suggest, however, that he may have spent some time in that vicinity. What is certain is that he lived the greater part of his life in south Armagh and north Louth, part of an Irish-speaking area which also encompassed parts of counties Meath, Cavan, Monaghan, and Down. The region formed a linguistic unit in the eighteenth and nineteenth centuries, and was a centre of intense literary activity in the Gaelic tradition of manuscript copying and poetic composition. It was here that many of the late new romances, including some in the Ulster cycle, were composed. Ó Doirnín himself is thought to be 'author' of the last recension of *Táin bó Cuailgne* compiled in the region in the early eighteenth century.

Ó Doirnín's life and work have been the cause of much conjecture and not a little embroidery. In the mid-nineteenth century Nicholas Kearney (Nioclás Ó Cearnaigh) passed off a number of his own compositions as Ó Doirnín's work and altered his biography to suit his own ideas and prejudices, rendering the facts of Ó Doirnín's life difficult, if not impossible, to ascertain (Kearney's 'Memoir' is published in full in S. de Rís, *Peadar Ó Doirnín*, 1969). Kearney's poems are easily recognized by their style, redolent of the period's romantic nationalism and quite distinct from the voice of the 'Independent man', Ó Doirnín's only extant poem in English, in which he outlines his philosophy clearly:

> For kings or their guards I care not a straw
> No colour at all shall make me stand
> To Dukes or to Lords or to Ladys at ball
> I never will crawl with a cap in my hand.
> (Ó Buachalla, *Peadar Ó Doirnín*, 12)

This attitude is readily discernible in much of his other work in Irish, particularly in 'Gearán Uí Dhoirnín' and 'Mianta Uí Dhoirnín'. Significantly, when most of his fellow poets in the region regarded the Catholic clergy as allies, his is a dissenting voice, satirizing one of them for his avarice in the mixed prose and verse *crosántacht*, 'An Cléireach Bán', thought to be about a certain Father Toirealach Ó Cuinne of Creggan (An Creagán), co. Armagh. He also satirized Muiris Ó Gormáin, one of the foremost scribes of the area, lampooning Ó Gormáin's poor command of English in an imagined conversation between Ó Gormáin and a young girl he met on the road to Drogheda. Ó Doirnín did not continually lament for the glories of past days but wished for material ease and comfort in his present circumstances, something for which he would have readily exchanged his learning. He also celebrates the benefits and pleasures of whiskey drinking.

In his love songs, which form the greater part of his work, and which fall within the conventions of *amour courtois*, Ó Doirnín was not above satirizing himself, sometimes portraying himself as an ardent, but sexually impotent, and consequently unsuccessful, wooer of women. In others, it is because of his lack of means that he is rejected. The picture that emerges from the work is of a significant talent, a man with a love of sensual pleasure, aware of the constraints placed upon him by the dominant, exclusionary, sectarian, Anglophone culture of the period. Ó Doirnín died at Nurney (An Urnaí), co. Louth, early in April 1769. He was buried near the north-east wall of the churchyard at An Urnaí. His mellifluous love song 'Úrchnoc Chéin Mhic Cáinte' was set again to music by Peadar Ó Dubhda in 1907, and remains popular, particularly in Ulster. For the commemoration of his death in 1969, Seán Ó Riada set his 'Mná na hÉireann' to a new air which has been notably recorded by the English pop singer Kate Bush, among others. LILLIS Ó LAOIRE

Sources A. Ui Laoi and others, *Seoda sean-nóis as Tír Chonaill / Traditional Irish singing from Donegal* (1996) [CD-ROM] • S. de Rís, *Peadar Ó Doirnín* (1969) • A. Heusaff, *Filí agus cléir san ochtú haois déag* (1992) • B. Ó Buachalla, 'Peadar Ó Doirnín agus Lucht Scríte a Bheatha', *Studia Hibernica*, 5 (1965), 123–54 • P. Ó Doirnín, *Amhráin*, ed. B. Ó Buachalla (1969) • J. O'Daly, *Poets and poetry of Munster* (1849) • *Art Mac Cumhaigh: dánta*, ed. T. Ó Fiaich (Baile Átha Cliath, 1973) • D. Ó hÓgáin, *An file, staidéar ar osnádúrthacht na filíochta sa traidisiún Gaelach* (Dublin, 1982) • D. Ó Súilleabháin, *Scéal an Oireachtais, 1827–1924* (Dublin, 1984) • *DNB* • S. Watson, 'Coimhlint an dá chultúr: Gaeil agus Gaill i bhFilíocht Chúige Uladh san Ochtú hAois Déag', *Eighteenth-Century Ireland*, 3 (1988), 85–104

Ó Domhnaill, Aodh Bailldearg. *See* O'Donnell, Hugh Balldearg (*c.*1650–1703/4).

O'Domhnaill, Daniel. *See* O'Donnell, Daniel (1666–1735).

Ó Domhnaill, Gofraidh [Godfrey O'Donnell] (*d.* 1258), king of Tír Conaill, was one of five recorded sons of Domhnall Mór Ó Domhnaill (*d.* 1241), king of Tír Conaill (which comprised most of the modern co. Donegal) and overlord of territories in Fermanagh, Monaghan and northern Sligo; he was grandson to Éigneachán Ó Domhnaill (*d. c.*1208), first of this dynasty to achieve local kingship. A bardic poem by Giolla Brighde Mac Con Midhe names Gofraidh's chief residence as Inis Saimhéar (Fish Island) at the mouth of the River Erne. It contains this significant remark, 'Gofraidh would be similar to Domhnall Mór if the foreigners did not hold sway' (Williams, 61). In the thirteenth century a renewed westward expansion by the Anglo-Normans in Ireland saw Maurice Fitzgerald (*d.* 1257) become lord of Sligo, with a speculative grant of the kingdom of Tír Conaill itself to hold in fee from the earl of Ulster. Fitzgerald's first raids northwards came before the death of Domhnall Mór and continued through the reign of Gofraidh's (presumably elder) brother Maoilsheachlainn Ó Domhnaill, culminating in the latter's defeat and death at the battle of Ballyshannon in 1247. Kingship of Tír Conaill was then awarded by the victorious Fitzgerald to Ruaidhrí Ó Canannáin, member of an earlier ruling dynasty of the area, also backed by Brian Ó Néill, the powerful king of neighbouring Tír Eoghain, whose western borders had been threatened by Ó Domhnaill expansion.

Gofraidh Ó Domhnaill recovered his inheritance by persuading Maurice Fitzgerald to invade Tír Conaill yet again in 1248, banish Ruaidhrí Ó Canannáin, and install Gofraidh as his vassal-king. When Ruaidhrí Ó Canannáin subsequently re-entered the country with a force from Tír Eoghain, Ó Domhnaill killed him, and another claimant, Niall Ó Canannáin, was killed by Maurice Fitzgerald in 1250. Once rid of his rivals, Gofraidh Ó Domhnaill proved anything but submissive. According to the annals of the four masters, supported by the contemporary poem mentioned above, he plundered the Anglo-Norman lordship of Sligo in 1249, raided and defeated Brian Ó Néill in 1252, and forced submissions from Fermanagh and Bréifne (the modern co. Leitrim) in 1256. As a result of Ó Domhnaill's constant warfare, Mag Éine (that part of modern co. Donegal lying south of the River Erne) was annexed to the kingdom of Tír Conaill, though remaining part of Clogher diocese. In 1257 Maurice Fitzgerald died, and Ó Domhnaill promptly brought an expedition to raze his castle of Belleek and invade the Anglo-Norman lordship of Sligo, burning the town itself and killing many of the settlers. A pursuing army of colonists was heavily defeated at Credran, near Drumcliff in Sligo, though Ó Domhnaill himself received a mortal wound there. The four masters, using a literary source, state that Gofraidh was wounded in single combat with Maurice Fitzgerald himself, lingered on his sickbed for another year at Lough Beagh (near Glenveagh Castle, Donegal), and led the troops of Tír Conaill to a last victory against Brian Ó Néill in 1258, while lying on his bier. After the battle, they say, the bier was carried back to Conwal, where Gofraidh died. A late medieval genealogical source states more plausibly that Credran was fought against the sons of Maurice Fitzgerald, that Gofraidh died in Lough Beagh a year later, and that Ó Néill invaded as Gofraidh's people were carrying their king on his bier, but was repulsed. KATHARINE SIMMS

Sources *AFM*, 3.326–67 • N. J. A. Williams, ed., *The poems of Giolla Brighde Mac Con Midhe* (1980), 54–63 • P. Walsh, ed., *Beatha Aodha Ruaidh*, 2 vols. (1957), 2.158–9 • G. H. Orpen, *Ireland under the Normans*, 4 vols. (1911–20), vol. 3, pp. 272–3 • G. MacNiocaill, ed., *The Red Book of the earls of Kildare* (1964), 113–15 • K. W. Nicholls, 'The register of Clogher', *Clogher Record*, 7 (1971–2), 361–431, esp. 392 • W. M. Hennessy and B. MacCarthy, eds., *Annals of Ulster, otherwise, annals of Senat*, 4 vols. (1887–1901), vol. 2, pp. 308–25 • A. M. Freeman, ed. and trans., *Annála Connacht / The annals of Connacht* (1944); repr. (1970), 90–127 • W. M. Hennessy, ed. and trans., *The annals of Loch Cé: a chronicle of Irish affairs from AD 1014 to AD 1590*, 1, Rolls Series, 54 (1871), 376–427 • S. Ó hInnse, ed. and trans., *Miscellaneous Irish annals, AD 1114–1437* (1947), 124–9

Ó Domhnaill, Maghnus. *See* O'Donnell, Manus, lord of Tyrconnell (*d.* 1563).

Ó Domhnaill, Ruaidhrí. *See* O'Donnell, Rury, styled first earl of Tyrconnell (1574/5–1608).

Ó Domhnaill, Uilliam. *See* Daniel, William (*c.*1575–1628).

Ó'Dónaill, Aodh. *See* O'Donnell, Hugh, lord of Tyrconnell (1572–1602).

O'Donel, James Louis (1737–1811), vicar apostolic of Newfoundland, was born at Knocklofty, co. Tipperary, the son of a local farmer, Michael O'Donel, and his wife, Ann Crosby. He and his older brother Michael began their schooling under a private tutor, followed by classical studies in Limerick. At the age of eighteen he entered the Franciscan order and left Ireland for theological studies in St Isidore's College, Rome, an institution run by the Franciscans of the Irish province. After ordination in Rome, he taught theology and philosophy in Prague at Immaculate Conception College, an Irish Franciscan seminary, for several years. He returned to Waterford in 1767 in order to take up duties as guardian of the Franciscan house there. In 1779 he was elected provincial of the order in Ireland, and remained in office until the end of his term in 1782.

In 1783 the governor of Newfoundland, John Campbell, permitted the construction of a Roman Catholic chapel in St John's, and a group of local Catholic merchants made application to Bishop William Egan of Waterford for O'Donel's services. Bishop Egan corresponded with Bishop James Talbot, the vicar apostolic of the London district and the official responsible for any Catholic mission work in Newfoundland. Bishop Talbot wrote to Rome, asking that O'Donel be made prefect apostolic of Newfoundland, which would place the territory directly under O'Donel's jurisdiction and make him answerable directly to the Holy See.

Shortly after O'Donel arrived in St John's on 4 July 1784, he received news that he had been made prefect apostolic. He was the first officially recognized Roman Catholic priest in the area. He subsequently encountered some difficulties in asserting his authority over two priests, first with Patrick Lonergan, a Dominican whose conduct created some tension with the civil authorities, and later with Patrick Power, a Franciscan who worked in Placentia without proper ecclesiastical permission and who attempted to discredit O'Donel. O'Donel excommunicated both Lonergan and Power, although it took some time and much correspondence between St John's, the Irish bishops, and the head of the Roman Congregatio de Propaganda Fide, before Power eventually departed the island.

O'Donel also faced opposition from the two governors who succeeded Campbell. One of Governor John Elliot's captains was Prince William Henry, later William IV (1830–37), who arrived in Newfoundland in 1786. While stationed there the prince revoked some privileges granted Catholics in Placentia in the summer of 1786 and later publicly insulted O'Donel, throwing an iron file at the priest in a fit of rage. Two years later Captain Edward Pellew, surrogate for Placentia, passed on some defamatory information about O'Donel, given him by Power, to Governor Elliot, who considered restricting the presence of priests on the island. Elliot backed down only after hearing O'Donel out. Governor Mark Milbanke, Elliot's successor, accused O'Donel of encouraging fishermen to remain resident in Newfoundland over the winter, and refused permission to Thomas Anthony Ewer, one of O'Donel's assistants, to construct a chapel at Ferryland.

After O'Donel made some protestations to Milbanke, the governor threatened further restrictions. The arrival in 1791 of Chief Justice John Reeves, who was more favourably disposed to a Catholic presence on the island, put an end to the proposed restrictions.

Despite these tensions and difficulties, O'Donel's mission prospered. On 5 January 1796, at the request of some prominent laypeople, O'Donel was made vicar apostolic of Newfoundland, and on 21 September was consecrated at Quebec as titular bishop of Thyatira. In 1801 he published a body of diocesan statutes and divided the diocese into missions, he himself, owing to the shortage of clergy, being obliged to act as a mission priest. He used his influence to check disaffection to the government among the predominately Irish Roman Catholics, advocating obedience and co-operation with the civil authorities during a period shortly after the Irish rising and the French Revolution, when tensions between Irish and English residents on the island would have been high. O'Donel's constant discouragement of violence among the Catholics of the colony helped to prevent wide-scale popular involvement during the planned mutiny of some soldiers in the Royal Newfoundland fencible regiment in 1800. As a token of thanks for his service to the colony, a number of prominent members of the community and Governor Sir Erasmus Gower asked for and secured a British government pension of £50 per annum for Bishop O'Donel.

O'Donel's missionary exertions wore out his health, and, having suffered a stroke, he wrote to the pope requesting a coadjutor bishop on 15 July 1804. His successor, Patrick Lambert, arrived in St John's in August 1806, and O'Donel resigned on 1 January 1807, remaining on the island until July of that year. He was fêted by the prominent members of the St John's community and given a silver urn in appreciation.

O'Donel spent his last years at Waterford, where he died on 1 April 1811, having suffered serious burns in a house fire a few days before. He was buried in St Mary's Church, Irishtown, Clonmel, in co. Tipperary.

G. LE G. NORGATE, *rev.* G. TRUDEL

Sources R. J. Lahey, *James Louis O'Donel in Newfoundland*, Newfoundland Historical Society (1984) · C. Mooney, 'Irish Franciscan provincials', *Archivum Franciscanum Historicum*, 56 (1963), 1–11 · A. Faulkner, *Liber Dublinensis: chapter documents of the Irish Franciscans* (1978) · *GM*, 1st ser., 81/1 (1811), 497 · 'O'Donel, James Louis', *DCB*, vol. 5
Archives Archives of the Roman Catholic Archdiocese of St John's, Newfoundland, inventory series 100

Ó Donnabháin, Seán. *See* O'Donovan, John (1806–1861).

O'Donnel, James Louis. *See* O'Donel, James Louis (1737–1811).

O'Donnell, Calvagh, lord of Tyrconnell (*d.* 1566), chief, was the eldest son of Manus *O'Donnell (*d.* 1563), lord of Tyrconnell, and his first wife, Siobhán (*d.* in or after 1549), daughter of O'Reilly, chief of East Breifne. Calvagh first appears in the historical record in the early 1540s, when he is noted as supporting his father in his military campaigns in north Connaught and Ulster. In 1541 and 1542

Calvagh travelled to Dublin to endorse Manus's agreement with Sir Anthony St Leger, lord deputy, and in 1544 he brought military assistance from Dublin to Tyrconnell. By 1547, however, Calvagh was clearly trying to usurp his father's leadership in Tyrconnell and to prevent his brother Sir Hugh MacManus O'Donnell (d. 1592) from seizing control in the lordship.

Manus inflicted a military defeat on Calvagh and his ally, the O'Cahan, in 1548, and in the following year Sir Edward Bellingham, lord deputy, attempted to arbitrate between father and son. Both were summoned to Dublin, and Calvagh undertook to 'follow his father in all things lawful, and keep the King's peace towards his father and the whole country' (*Calendar of the Carew Manuscripts, 1515–1574*, 221). In return, Calvagh was confirmed in possession of Lifford Castle, co. Donegal. Attempts were also made to resolve the conflict between Calvagh and his brother Hugh which seemed to have its origins in territorial control of the area around Lifford in east Tyrconnell.

Despite the 1549 agreement and another arbitration attempt by St Leger, again lord deputy, in 1552, the power struggle within Tyrconnell continued. In 1555 Calvagh bolstered his position with an agreement with Archibald Campbell, fourth earl of Argyll, through which he acquired the assistance of significant numbers of Scottish mercenary soldiers, or redshanks, and the use of a ramming gun for breaking castle walls, the famous 'gonna cam' or 'crooked gun' (*AFM*, 5.1555). Strengthened by this military reinforcement, Calvagh imprisoned his father and seized control in Tyrconnell. Manus never resumed the position of lord.

Throughout the sixteenth century the O'Donnell lordship was riven with dynastic and family feuding, and Calvagh's conflicts with his father and brother were not unlike those which Manus had had with his own father and brothers in the early decades of the century. The feuding among the O'Donnells undermined the family's control in Tyrconnell and made it possible for Shane O'Neill to extend his ascendancy over the western part of Ulster. O'Neill also fuelled the dynastic struggle among the O'Donnells through his support for Manus's brother.

In 1557 O'Neill raided Tyrconnell with a large army. Calvagh reportedly sought military advice from his imprisoned father, and through a surprise nocturnal attack on the invader's camp he won a temporary victory over O'Neill's forces at Balleighan on Lough Swilly, co. Donegal. Calvagh's position was also bolstered by the plan of Thomas Radcliffe, third earl of Sussex, the new lord deputy, to form an alliance of Ulster chiefs against O'Neill. Among Sussex's proposals was the creation of Calvagh as earl of Tyrconnell and the granting of tenure of his lands on the English model in order to enhance his status as leader of the anti-O'Neill forces in Ulster. In 1560 Calvagh, with Sussex's approval, strengthened his links with the Campbells through his marriage to Katherine (d. 1588), daughter of Hector Mòr MacLean of Duart and his wife, and widow of Argyll. In his marriage agreement, which was partly a renewal of the 1555 arrangement, Calvagh gained access to 500 redshanks. In return, he agreed to pay

annually to Archibald Campbell, fifth earl of Argyll, £66 13s. 8d., the collection of which may have, in the long term, eroded his political support in Tyrconnell. Calvagh's daughter by a previous marriage to Seaén O'Neill (d. before 1560), Mary, was O'Neill's wife. O'Neill mistreated her as a consequence of his defeat by Calvagh and she died in 1561. Katherine had received an excellent education and was described as 'very sober, wise and no less subtle, being not unlearned in the Latin tongue, speaketh good French, and as is said some little Italian' (PRO, SP 63/3/84). It is likely that the mother of Conn O'Donnell (d. 1583) was Calvagh's first wife, rather than Katherine. Conn was the father of Sir Niall Garbh *O'Donnell (1568/9–1626?).

On 14 May 1561 O'Neill fatally weakened Sussex's Ulster confederacy by seizing Calvagh and his wife and imprisoning them at Tyrone. The couple were taken from the monastery of Kildonnell in co. Donegal. Sir William Fitzwilliam, lord justice, suspected Katherine of complicity in the seizure. However, Calvagh was in no doubt that O'Neill was assisted by his own kinsmen, particularly Hugh. During his imprisonment he claimed that he was subject to degrading treatment. An iron collar was placed around his neck which was fastened by a short chain to bolts on his ankles so that he could neither stretch his legs nor stand up straight. In the meantime, O'Neill was strengthening his control over the leaderless Tyrconnell. He devastated the countryside—killing, by Calvagh's estimate, almost 4500 people, which must have represented a sizeable percentage of the total population in the lordship. O'Neill also garrisoned several castles and recognized Hugh as lord of Tyrconnell. When Sussex led a military campaign into Tyrone to avenge Calvagh's capture, the latter was moved into the inner recesses of the region to prevent the lord deputy rescuing him. In early 1564 O'Neill agreed to release Calvagh on payment of a ransom and the promise that Lifford Castle would be delivered to him. Katherine was not released at the same time, allegedly because O'Neill hoped to secure a ransom from the MacLeans for her. She was reported to have been chained by day to the arm of a small boy and released only at night when O'Neill was present. She may have subsequently married O'Neill with the support of her family. She had several children with him and was with him when he was killed.

On Calvagh's release he refused to abide by the terms of his ransom. In response O'Neill imprisoned Conn and threatened to cut his leg off if he did not get Lifford. Calvagh in the meantime travelled to Dublin to ask for military assistance against O'Neill. The Dublin administration under Sir Nicholas Arnold, lord justice, was unwilling to take any action which might provoke O'Neill's hostility and refused a licence to Calvagh to travel to London. In his report to the privy council Sir Thomas Cusack, lord chancellor, suggested that Calvagh had little support in Tyrconnell and downplayed his criticisms of O'Neill. Defying the instructions of the Irish privy council, Calvagh went to London where he submitted his grievances to Elizabeth I. His account of his treatment at the hands of O'Neill and the continuing reports of the latter's military victories in

Ulster convinced the queen that O'Neill could not be dealt with through the conciliatory policy advocated by the Irish privy council. She wrote to Arnold that she was not without sympathy for Calvagh's position and ordered him to pay him some maintenance. Nevertheless, Calvagh was not returned immediately to Dublin and remained in London until 1566.

In 1565 Sir Henry Sidney was appointed lord deputy and formulated a plan to consolidate crown support among the lesser chiefs of Ulster and north Connaught which included the restoration of Calvagh to the lordship of Tyrconnell. Calvagh travelled back to Ireland with Sidney and in September 1566 he accompanied the lord deputy on his two-month journey through Ulster. Sidney formally returned Calvagh to the castles in Tyrconnell which had been seized by O'Neill. On 20 October, at Ballyshannon, co. Donegal, in an indenture with Sidney, Calvagh thanked the queen for his restoration, pledged his loyalty to her, and undertook to assist the lord deputy in his military campaigns against O'Neill. He also agreed to support Elizabeth if she 'should hereafter be pleased to change the usages or institutions of his country, and to reduce it to civil order and obedience to her laws like the English parts of this realm' (*Calendar of the Carew Manuscripts, 1515–1574*, 374). Sidney also made separate indentures with Calvagh's brother Hugh and his uncle Hugh Dubh O'Donnell, although the question of the O'Donnell succession was left undecided. In the event, Calvagh had little time to test the strength of his family's loyalty or that of Sidney. On 26 October 1566, as he was riding to Derry to assist the English captain Edward Randolph, he fell dead from his horse, having suffered either a fit or a heart attack. He was buried in Donegal Abbey. Calvagh was praised by Gaelic annalists for his bravery, steadfastness, and kindness. He was succeeded by his brother Hugh. MARY O'DOWD

Sources *Á bhfuil aguinn dár chum Tadhg Dall Ó Huiginn, 1550–1591: idir mholadh agus marbhnadh aoir agus ábhacht iomarbháigh agus iomchasaoid*, ed. E. Knott, 2, ITS, 23 (1926), 36 • PRO, SP 63/3, nos. 84, 85; SP 63/7, nos. 19, 21, 22; SP 63/11, nos. 1, 3, 9, 10, 96, 99, 110; SP 63/17, no. 13 • *CSP Ire., 1509–73* • AFM, vol. 5 • *CSP Scot., 1547–69* • J. S. Brewer and W. Bullen, eds., *Calendar of the Carew manuscripts*, 6 vols., PRO (1867–73) • J. MacKechnie, 'Treaty between Argyll and O'Donnell', *Scottish Gaelic Studies*, 7/1 (1951), 94–102 • C. Brady, *Shane O'Neill* (Dundalk, 1996) • G. A. Hayes-McCoy, *Scots mercenary forces in Ireland (1565–1603): an account of their service* (1937) • T. B. Lyons, 'Shane O'Neill: a biography', MA diss., University College Dublin, 1947 • DNB

O'Donnell [O'Domhnaill], **Daniel** (1666–1735), army officer in the French service, was born in Ireland, the son of Terence O'Donnell and Johanna O'Donnell, who both were from co. Donegal and belonged to the family of O'Donnell or O'Domhnaill chiefs in Tyrconnell. He was appointed a captain of foot in James II's army on 7 December 1688 and in 1689 was acting colonel. After the treaty of Limerick in 1691 he entered the French service but could obtain only the rank of captain in the marine regiment of the Irish brigade, commanded by Lord Henry FitzJames, grand prior of England, a natural son of James II, and

brother of the duke of Berwick. O'Donnell, whose commission was dated 4 February 1692, served with this regiment, known as the 'régiment de la marina', on the coast of Normandy during the projected invasion of England, which was averted by the French defeat in 1692 at La Hogue, and afterwards in Germany in the campaigns of 1693–5. His regiment was reformed in 1698, and his commission as captain redated 27 April 1698. He served in Germany in 1701, and afterwards in five campaigns in Italy, where he was present at Luzzara, Borgoforte, Nago, Arco, Vercelli, Ivrea, Verrua, Chivasso, and Cassano; he was lieutenant-colonel of the regiment at the siege and battle of Turin.

Transferred to the Low Countries in 1707, O'Donnell fought against Marlborough at Oudenarde in 1708, succeeded Nicholas FitzGerald as colonel of a regiment on 7 August 1708, and commanded the regiment of O'Donnell of the Irish brigade in the campaigns of 1709–12, including the battle of Malplaquet and the defence of the lines of Arleux, Denain, Douai, Bouchain, and Quesnoy. He then served under Marshal Villars in Germany, at the sieges of Landau and Freiberg, and at the forcing of General Vaubonne's entrenchments, which led to the peace of Rastadt between Germany and France in March 1714. In accordance with an order of 6 February 1715, the regiment of O'Donnell was reformed, one half being transferred to Colonel Francis Lee's regiment, the other half to that of Major-General Murrough O'Brien, to which O'Donnell was attached as a 'reformed' or supplementary colonel. He became a brigadier-general on 1 February 1719, and retired to St Germain-en-Laye, where he died, without any surviving children, on 7 July 1735.

A jewelled casket containing a Latin psalter said to have been written by the hand of St Columba belonged to O'Donnell, and was regarded by him, in accordance with its traditional history, as a talisman of victory if carried into battle. It was presented to the Royal Irish Academy in the nineteenth century.

H. M. CHICHESTER, *rev.* D. M. BEAUMONT

Sources J. P. Ainsworth, 'Report on the O'Donnell papers', NL Ire., list 306 • J. C. O'Callaghan, *History of the Irish brigades in the service of France*, [new edn] (1870) • J. D'Alton, *Illustrations, historical and genealogical, of King James's Irish army list (1689)*, 2nd edn, 2 vols. (1860–61)
Archives Archivo Historico Nacional Caballeros de Calatrava, Madrid • Bibliothèque Nationale, Paris, fonds français dossiers bleus

O'Donnell, Frank Hugh [*formerly* Francis Hugh MacDonald] (1846–1916), writer and controversialist, was born in an army barracks in Devonport, Devon, on 9 October 1846, the elder son of Sergeant Bernard MacDonald and his wife, Mary, *née* Kain, daughter of William Kain or O'Cahan of Ballybane, co. Galway. His younger brother was Charles James MacDonald, later O'Donnell (1849–1934). He was educated at the Erasmus School, Galway, St Ignatius College, Galway, and Queen's College, Galway, graduating MA in 1868 with gold medals in English literature, history, and political economy. MacDonald probably assumed the name by which he was known as an expression of his belief that he was a direct descendant of Roderick O'Donnell, last earl of Tyrconnell. Frank Hugh O'Donnell had a brief career as a journalist on the *Morning Post* (he shared a bed with T. P. O'Connor in his early days in London), and was elected MP (nationalist) for Galway in 1874, but unseated on petition, becoming MP for Dungarvan, co. Waterford, in 1877, holding the seat until 1885, when his constituency disappeared during redistribution. A controversial figure in parliament, he was 'silenced' in June 1880 by Gladstone and was known as Crank Hugh O'Donnell. O'Donnell, who had hoped to lead the Irish party and who claimed to have invented the policy of obstruction, opposed the Land League and abandoned orthodox politics in 1885. *O'Donnell* v. *Walter*—his unsuccessful action against *The Times* in 1888, when he had sought £50,000 in damages for libel—resulted in the parliamentary special commission into Parnellism and crime in 1888–9 and the exposure of the Pigott forgeries. O'Donnell was hostile to Parnell and remained aggressively anti-Parnellite. O'Donnell's *A History of the Irish Parliamentary Party* (2 vols., 1910) is biased and untrustworthy, grossly inflating his own role; however it contains vivid characterization of— *inter alia*—Michael Davitt and John O'Leary.

O'Donnell was initiated into the Irish Republican Brotherhood by Dr Mark Ryan, the London Fenian leader, and subsequently moved to the Irish National Alliance. O'Donnell's Fenian career was as chequered as his parliamentary career had been. In 1897 he embarrassed his colleagues by pseudonymously running a series of articles in *United Ireland* purporting to be from a revolutionary organization called 'Fuath na Gall' (hatred of the stranger). In 1898 he issued, under an Irish National Alliance signature, a pamphlet attacking Michael Davitt as a renegade and British agent. Maud Gonne and W. B. Yeats had this pamphlet repudiated. O'Donnell's retaliation came with the first performance of Yeats's *The Countess Cathleen* in May 1899. O'Donnell issued another pamphlet, *Souls for Gold!*, viciously attacking the play as anti-Catholic and anti-Irish, guaranteeing a controversial reception. In *The Stage-Irishman of the neo-Celtic Drama* (1904) O'Donnell returned to the attack, describing Yeats's plays as the 'wedding of Madame Blavatsky and Finn MacCumhail' (p. 9).

O'Donnell's source of income remains unclear, although he was a prolific freelance journalist. He probably worked as an agent for a number of powers—Maud Gonne thought him a spy for Britain and W. B. Yeats thought him an Austrian agent—and he lived for various periods in France, Austria, and Germany. During 1900 when O'Donnell, like other Irish nationalists, was pro-Boer, he promised to mobilize British working-class opposition to the war, via the National Democratic League, if a large enough sum of money were paid to him by the Transvaal government. He also claimed to have prevented 50,000 Irishmen from enlisting in the English army. O'Donnell succeeded in obtaining the considerable sum of £4500 from the Transvaal government for pro-Boer activities—there is no evidence that the whole sum was passed on to Irish organizations. Despite his eccentricity

and dishonesty, O'Donnell was not expelled from the Irish National Alliance, even when, in April 1900, he circulated letters naming Irishmen whom Maud Gonne had enlisted for the Boer cause. He finally alienated himself from nationalists by publishing *At the Sign of the Harp and the Guillotine*, a pamphlet which attacked Wolfe Tone and the other 1798 leaders for destroying the Irish parliament. The *United Irishman* disowned him in June 1900 and later referred to him as 'Chevalier of the Order of Ananias and Sappira … High Shepherd of the Golden Fleecers and Grand Master of the Knights of the Black Mail' (21 Sept 1901, 3). Mark Ryan's judgement was that O'Donnell had 'no fixed political convictions' (Ryan, 62–3).

O'Donnell became vehemently anti-clerical, while still professing himself a good Catholic. He wrote books and pamphlets attacking the political power of the Irish Catholic clergy, including *The Ruin of Education in Ireland* (1902) and *Paraguay on Shannon: the Price of a Political Priesthood* (1908). He became an advocate for secular mixed education—reversing the stance of his *Mixed Education in Ireland: Confessions of a Queen's Collegian* (1870)—but his coarse rhetoric was probably counter-productive.

To T. P. O'Connor, the young O'Donnell had seemed like 'a figure from Balzac: one of the self-confident adventurers, like Lucien de Rubempré' and he regretted 'the miserable downfall in which his career ended' (O'Connor, 1.68, 70). W. B. Yeats was to characterize O'Donnell as a 'mad rogue' and as 'half genius, half sewer-rat', recalling this distinguished-looking man transforming himself into a 'half-drunken Country Councillor shaking his fist in an opponent's face' (*Collected Letters*, 2, 80, 712, 710).

Most of O'Donnell's life was spent out of Ireland and he settled in London, dying there unmarried on 2 November 1916. He was buried in Glasnevin cemetery, Dublin. Despite his facility as a writer and speaker and a life dedicated to political activity, O'Donnell remains a marginal figure in Irish history.

DEIRDRE TOOMEY

Sources F. H. O'Donnell, *The stage-Irishman of the neo-Celtic drama* (1904) • *United Irishman* (21 Sept 1901) • M. F. Ryan, *Fenian memories*, ed. T. F. O'Sullivan (1945) • T. P. O'Connor, *Memoirs of an old parliamentarian*, 2 vols. (1929) • *The collected letters of W. B. Yeats*, 2, ed. W. Gould, J. Kelly, and D. Toomey (1997) • b. cert. • d. cert.
Archives NYPL, corresp. with John Quinn • priv. coll., corresp. with John Quinn
Likenesses photograph, 1898, Sligo County Library • H. A. Kernoff, pastel drawing, NG Ire. • caricature, repro. in *Punch* (15 Nov 1884) • photograph, repro. in F. H. O'Donnell, *A history of the Irish parliamentary party* (1910)
Wealth at death £690 1s. 8d.: administration, 8 May 1917, *CGPLA Eng. & Wales*

O'Donnell, Hugh [Aodh Ó'Dónaill; *known as* Red Hugh, Hugh Roe, Aodh Rua], **lord of Tyrconnell** (1572–1602), chieftain and rebel, was born on or about 20 October 1572, the eldest son of Sir Hugh O'Donnell, lord of Tyrconnell (*b.* in or before 1535, *d.* 1600), Irish chieftain, and his second wife, Fionnuala, called Iníon Dhubh (Dark Girl; *d.* 1611?), daughter of James MacDonnell of the Isles. His grandfather was Manus *O'Donnell, lord of Tyrconnell, and his uncle was Calvagh *O'Donnell, lord of Tyrconnell. Among his many siblings were his half-sister Siobhan (*d.* 1591), who in 1574 married Hugh *O'Neill, third baron of Dungannon and second earl of Tyrone; his elder sister Nuala, who married Niall Garbh *O'Donnell; and his brother Rury *O'Donnell, first earl of Tyrconnell. Hugh Roe was fostered in various chiefly households and his foray into O'Rourke country at the age of twelve was an exploit precocious enough to be recorded by the annalist of Loch Cé.

Early career, 1585–1593 Tyrconnell was at this time under threat from both increasing governmental pressure and fierce internal rivalry. This rivalry, begun in the 1540s between Calvagh and Hugh, sons of Manus O'Donnell, and maintained by their respective families, allowed the government (which favoured Calvagh and then his son Conn) in 1543 and again in 1566 in effect to partition the lordship. Thereafter the rich lands of Cinéal Moain, extending along the west bank of the Foyle and the Finn, with Lifford and Finn castles, were in contention between the two houses. Sir John Perrot, governor of Ireland, suspected Sir Hugh O'Donnell's loyalty and moved to reduce his power. He shired Tyrconnell in 1585, rejected Sir Hugh's claim to lordship over Sligo, and gave four of his castles to Hugh, son of Dean O'Gallagher, reputed to be Calvagh O'Donnell's illegitimate son, who disputed Sir Hugh's right to the lordship of Tyrconnell. In 1587, after Sir Hugh had failed to give sufficient demonstrations of his loyalty, Perrot sent a ship to Tyrconnell, with the design, apparently sanctioned by Elizabeth I, of kidnapping Sir Hugh, his wife, and Hugh Roe. At Rathmullan the *Mathew* secured Hugh Roe and some companions, who by late September 1587 were in close confinement in Dublin Castle, probably in one of the gate towers. To add to Tyrconnell's woes, at the end of 1588 the new lord deputy Sir William Fitzwilliam appointed Donal, Hugh Roe's half-brother, as sheriff of Tyrconnell. At the same time both the MacSweeneys of Banagh and the O'Boyles were locked in internecine strife. Tyrone, calling Hugh Roe his son-in-law, pleaded with Sir Francis Walsingham and Lord Leicester that only this youth could restore peace to Tyrconnell. The 'match' between Hugh Roe and Tyrone's daughter was still spoken of as late as 1595, but apparently he never married. Sir Hugh brought thirty Spanish armada survivors to Dublin, but Perrot, then on the privy council, blocked Hugh Roe's release. In January 1591 he attempted escape; recaptured, he was put in irons and incarcerated in the Record Tower. In a second attempt, on 5 January 1592, assisted by Tyrone's outlay of largesse, he escaped to Wicklow, where eventually Fiach MacHugh O'Byrne and Felim O'Toole came to his rescue. He suffered grievously from exposure in the mountains, his companion in flight Art O'Neill, son of Shane O'Neill, perishing there. The resourceful Turlough Buí O'Hagan, Tyrone's confidential servant, conducted him to the north and, helped on his way by Sir Edward Moore, Tyrone, and Hugh Maguire, he came at last to the safety of Ballyshannon Castle. During his incarceration his indomitable mother arranged the murder of two of his rivals, Hugh O'Gallagher (*d.* 1588) and her stepson, Donal the sheriff. Donal, however, was replaced by Captain Willis who, with his undisciplined soldiery, oppressed all south-west Tyrconnell.

Hugh Roe was ill for over a year and the surgeon had to amputate his two big toes, but in February 1592 he expelled Willis. At Kilmacrenan on 24 April Sir Hugh stepped down and Hugh Roe was elected and inaugurated O'Donnell. The redoubtable Hugh MacHugh Dubh, the tanist, had the superior claim, but Hugh Roe was not to be denied. Dunlop in the *Dictionary of National Biography* echoes Fitzwilliam's belief that Hugh Roe's 'party were filled with joy' at the realization of a prophecy of succession by Hugh O'Donnell to his father Hugh, but this lacks verification. He formally, though with little sincerity, submitted to the queen in August at Dundalk, thus securing the capitulation of his domestic enemies, Hugh MacHugh and Niall Garbh. Sir John O'Doherty he imprisoned. Before the end of 1592 he was master of Tyrconnell, to which, according to Ó Clérigh, he restored tranquillity. His attacks on Turlough Luineach O'Neill at Strabane in 1592 and 1593 were meant to strengthen his ally Tyrone's position in the O'Neill clan.

These were O'Donnell's first steps in his design of a national struggle, to be supported by Spain, against England. In all Ireland, only Ulster at this time maintained any real independence of the crown. Even within Ulster, Cavan and Monaghan had seen the introduction of English tenure and primogeniture, while the groundwork for this had been laid in Tyrconnell and Fermanagh. It seemed inevitable that the jurisdiction of O'Donnell, Maguire, and even Tyrone would be supplanted by that of crown sheriffs (of whom the odious Willis was typical) and Irish law and custom would yield to crown law. The northern bishops, led by Primate Magauran and Archbishop O'Hely of Tuam, had already sounded out Philip II and in 1592 confederated with the new O'Donnell, his cousin Hugh Maguire of Fermanagh, Brian O'Rourke, and some of the Mayo Burkes to form a Catholic league. O'Donnell was a realist, not a dreamer, and planned to extend the league beyond Ulster and northern Connaught into Leinster and Munster, so as to include Fiach Mac Hugh O'Byrne and the exiled claimants to the Baltinglass, Offaly, and Desmond titles. In April 1593 the two archbishops and O'Donnell put it to Philip that Spanish aid to Ireland would be an effective counter to England's support of the rebel Dutch. Philip, however, was noncommittal.

War against the English, 1593–1601 Urged on by O'Donnell, Maguire was the first to revolt in 1593. Suffering a reverse at Tulsk (where Primate Magauran was killed), he went on to raid Monaghan and had the aid of O'Donnell and O'Rourke in investing Enniskillen in 1594. By 1595 Tyrone was also openly committed to the league and took a leading role in the Nine Years' War. The declared demands of the confederates were liberty of conscience, withdrawal of sheriffs and garrisons outside Newry and Carrickfergus, and full pardon. O'Donnell, Tyrone, and Maguire maintained a war of attrition against the English while they perfected their military machine, sought alliance from elsewhere in Ireland and especially from Munster, and awaited Spanish aid. They defended Ulster along a line from the River Erne to Lough Neagh, O'Donnell maintaining the defence of the western side. From Tyrconnell there were two passages into Connaught, one over the Erne by Ballyshannon, the other by Enniskillen between the lakes. O'Donnell held Ballyshannon, the 'key of the province' of Ulster (*CSP Ire.*, *1596-7*, 333-4), and in 1595 Maguire recovered Enniskillen. Ulick Burke killed George Bingham, governor of Sligo, who had sacked the Carmelite monastery at Rathmullan and plundered Tory Island, and delivered Sligo Castle to O'Donnell, who levelled it and other castles in north Connaught. From Enniskillen and Ballyshannon he now controlled north Connaught. From 1595 he and his lightly armed, mobile forces made repeated forays into Connaught, weakening English power there. He set up Tibbot Burke as Mac William and in this same year assisted Tyrone to hold the Blackwater line.

Protracted negotiations begun in autumn 1595 led to pardons for Tyrone and O'Donnell in 1596. Meanwhile, however, these leaders were entertaining missions from Philip II and offering the crown of Ireland to Archduke Albert. O'Donnell laid in provisions for the expected Spanish expedition, but Padilla's fleet was destroyed by October gales off Viana. In July 1597, while Lord Deputy Burgh marched against Tyrone, Sir Conyers Clifford attacked Ballyshannon. O'Donnell, by continuous sorties with horse and foot, made the governor's position untenable and demonstrated that here was a leader who had advanced far beyond the traditional hit-and-run methods of Irish warfare. Clifford, learning of Burgh's repulse by Tyrone at the Blackwater and of the approach of Irish reinforcements, abandoned the attack. O'Donnell harried him as he crossed the Erne and in a hot pursuit for 15 miles killed many of his men.

O'Donnell's success in Connaught, was such that at the battle at Yellow Ford on 14 August 1598, when he commanded the left wing, he had 1000 Connaught men among his troops. The Irish here won a famous victory. Then, while Tyrone went on the offensive in Leinster and Munster, in order to keep the way open should the anticipated Spanish army land in the south, O'Donnell with the same purpose led a great army into Connaught, again set up his Mac William, seized Ballymote Castle, raided Clanricarde and even Thomond's county of Clare, and took immense booty. By this time the confederates sought free and open profession of 'the Catholic, Apostolic and Roman religion' (Maxwell, 182–3), confirmation to Tyrone, O'Donnell, and Desmond of all the lands and privileges enjoyed by their predecessors for 200 years past, and that all officers of state (apart from the viceroy) and churchmen should be Irish. But Clifford, urged on by the earl of Essex, made a determined land and sea attack on Sligo. O'Donnell dispatched a force of 400 men to defend the castle from Tibbot na Long's naval attack, another of 200 horse to keep O'Connor Sligo in Collooney Castle, and himself ambushed Clifford at Bellaghboy Pass in the Curlew Hills. On 5 August 1599 the governor's army was repulsed with great loss, Clifford himself being among the dead, a notable victory over an experienced leader in command of veterans. O'Connor Sligo surrendered Collooney Castle to O'Donnell, who had both repulsed

attacks on himself and made any assault on Tyrone's defensive line from the Blackwater to Armagh and even to Monaghan much more hazardous. In June 1600 he drove as far south as Loop Head and in Moylurg turned Clanricarde back from another attempt on Sligo.

The new Spanish king, Philip III, sent envoys and some arms to Tyrconnell in 1599 and again in 1600. But in O'Donnell's absence in Connaught, Sir Henry Docwra landed an army at Lough Foyle in May 1600. O'Donnell at first discounted the threat, but Docwra won over Sir Art O'Neill, Turlough Luineach's son, and, more importantly, Niall Garbh, who meant to displace Hugh as O'Donnell, and it was he who ensured Docwra's success. Over the following year Docwra seized Rathmullan Carmelite friary while Niall Garbh gained Lifford and Donegal Franciscan friary. In fighting against Niall Garbh the valiant Manus, younger brother of O'Donnell, received a mortal wound.

In October 1601 O'Donnell, informed that the Spanish had landed at last in far-away Kinsale, but with too small a force to take the offensive (both O'Donnell and Tyrone had strongly advised that so small a force, 4000 men, should come at least as far north as Limerick), abandoned his siege of Donegal, and assembled his forces for a demanding winter march to the south. It was a desperate throw, for it left Ballyshannon open to English conquest. He left Ballymote on 2 November and exactly a month later eluded Sir George Carew in his memorable night march of 32 Irish miles over frozen Slieve Felim, 'the greatest march with carriage', acknowledged Carew, 'that hath been heard of' (Silke, 'Red Hugh', 12). By 2 December he had arrived in Bandon, gathering southern reinforcements as he went. A few days later Tyrone joined him. They had transported their armies and carriage by winter over or through fifty swollen rivers and besieged Lord Deputy Mountjoy as he invested Kinsale.

Defeat, exile, and death, 1601–1602 Stout Spanish resistance and the news of the Irish arrival made Mountjoy give up his intention of an assault in force. Meanwhile General Zubiaur landed at Castlehaven with some reinforcements, gaining also Baltimore and Bantry harbours. The west Munster lords, MacCarthys, O'Driscolls, and O'Sullivan Beare, declared for Spain. Mountjoy drew his investment tighter, but of his 11,500 foot and 900 horse, many died of exposure. The Irish armies numbered perhaps 6000 infantry and 800 horse, while the Spanish commander Águila claimed only 2500 effective fighters. Tyrone planned, if reinforced by Zubiaur's men, to force a breakthrough to Águila; Zubiaur, however, sent only 200 Spaniards, although the O'Sullivans brought 1200 Irish. Águila encouraged the Irish to rendezvous with him for a joint attack. Tyrone, realizing that the Irish, despite his and O'Donnell's notable successes, would be at a disadvantage in attacking the entrenched English, preferred to harry Mountjoy and let disease and famine do their work on the latter's army, but O'Donnell's voice for attack prevailed, and so the Irish moved up to Belgooly. At the sight of them Mountjoy exclaimed, 'This kingdom is lost today' (Archivo General de Simancas, guerra antigua 3144). Early on 24 December, while it was still dark, the Irish set out, Captain

Tyrrell with his Meath and Leinster men leading the van, Tyrone the main force, and O'Donnell with his Tyrconnell and Connaught men in the rear. Águila planned to join them between Thomond's camp and the west fort but things went disastrously wrong as old rivalries re-emerged. 'Their chiefs were at variance, each of them contending that he himself should go foremost' (AFM, 6.2283). The battalions marched out shoulder to shoulder instead of in order. In the dark they lost contact and went astray. Tyrrell did not find the agreed position, and Águila stayed in the town. At dawn Tyrone, observing this, withdrew. Mountjoy, seeing his opportunity, launched a cavalry charge against Tyrone; it was repulsed, but a second broke his army. Águila, although he heard musketry fire, refused to lead out his men. Tyrrell came up but was made to retreat. O'Donnell's men, even further off, at sight of the two other battalions being routed ignored his exhortations to turn and fight, and fled. A pursuit of Tyrone accounted for between 500 and 1000 casualties in the main battle. A volley at the end made Don Juan stir but, realizing that it signalled an English victory, he quickly retreated. O'Donnell succeeded, but too late, in rallying his men on a hill 8 miles away.

O'Donnell, urging Tyrone and his brother Rury, to whom he entrusted his own command, to remain encamped, then sailed from Castlehaven to seek Spanish reinforcements. But Tyrone went home, suffering many more losses on the way, although Rury then brought his army safely to Connaught. O'Donnell was welcomed to Corunna by Governor Caracena and Philip III ordered the immediate dispatch of a relief squadron to be sent to Castlehaven, Baltimore, and Berehaven, to be followed up by a fresh army, 6000 strong. News of Águila's surrender, however, and the return from Kinsale on 26 and 27 February 1602 of twenty Spanish companies halted the preparations. These returning soldiers blamed O'Donnell for the rout and the king resolved to give him 50,000 ducats and send him back to Ireland. Then, however, opinion against him hardened; permission for him to leave was refused and he remained a virtual prisoner in Corunna.

At last in August, O'Donnell was allowed to leave Corunna for the court at Valladolid. Reaching Simancas Castle, he took to his bed and after seventeen days' illness died on 30 August 1602. He probably was not poisoned by one James Blake of Galway, as was once thought. According to Donagh Mooney, a soldier turned friar who knew O'Donnell well, he succumbed to grief and the rigours of the Castilian climate. Among those present at his bedside were Florence Conry, his confessor; Matthew Tully, his secretary; and Dr John Nynan. In his will, drawn up shortly before his death, he named Rury heir to all his 'estates, lands, lordships, and vassals' (Silke, 'The last will', 58) and asked that Philip III should apportion any help equally between Tyrone and Rury and hold them and their heirs in equal regard. He was buried in the Franciscan convent of Valladolid. When this was later secularized, his body was disinterred and its present location is unknown.

Mooney left a pen-portrait characterizing O'Donnell as a prince and leader:

He was above middle height, strong, handsome, well-built and of pleasing appearance. His voice was musical. In action he was quick and decisive. He loved justice and was stern with evildoers. He was resolute, faithful to his word and steadfast in time of trial. Maintaining a rigorous military discipline, he led by example in battle. To all he was courteous and affable. He was not married. He was gracious, without pretension. (Mooney, 116)

Mooney went on to speak of O'Donnell's zeal for the restoration of the Catholic faith, his anxiety for a worthy clergy, and his contempt for the world. He had often heard him say that if the war ended favourably he would become a Franciscan. However, this description is perhaps not wholly derived from life because Mooney was drawing here from work by Polydore Vergil.

O'Donnell spent ten years fighting to maintain what he claimed as his by right of inauguration, maintained a firm alliance with Tyrone, carried the war to the rest of Ireland, drew in the Spaniards, and made the conflict one of national, international, and religious significance. Then, with the balance poised, submerged rivalries within the alliance resurfaced, his luck ran out, and the way was open for completion of the English conquest of Ireland.

JOHN J. SILKE

Sources L. Ó Clérigh, *Beatha Aodha Ruaidh Uí Dhomhnaill*, ed. and trans. D. Murphy (1893) · L. Ó Cléirigh, *The life of Aodh Ruadh Ó Domhnaill*, ed. P. Walsh and C. Ó Lochlainn, 2 vols., ITS, 42, 45 (1948–57) · *AFM*, 5–6 · *CSP Ire.*, 1574–1603 · J. S. Brewer and W. Bullen, eds., *Calendar of the Carew manuscripts*, PRO, 1–4 (1867–70) · *fondos* Estado and Guerra y Marina, Archivo General de Simancas · P. O'Sullivan Beare, *Historiae Catholicae Iberniae compendium* (1621); later edn, ed. M. Kelly (1850) · H. Docwra, 'Narration of the services done by the army ymployed to Lough-Foyle', in J. O'Donovan, *Miscellany of the Celtic Society* (1849), 231–325 · J. J. Silke, 'Red Hugh O'Donnell, 1572–1601', *Donegal Annual*, 5 (1961), 1–19 · J. J. Silke, 'The Irish appeal of 1593 to Spain', *Irish Ecclesiastical Record*, 5th ser., 92 (1959), 279–90, 362–71 · J. J. Silke, *Kinsale: the Spanish intervention in Ireland at the end of the Elizabethan wars* (1970); paperback edn (2000) · S. Ó Domhnaill, 'History of Tír Conaill in the sixteenth century', MA diss., University College Dublin, 1946 · R. Bagwell, *Ireland under the Tudors*, 3 (1890) · D. Mooney, 'De provincia Hiberniae S. Francisci', ed. B. Jennings, *Analecta Hibernica*, 6 (1934), 12–138 · F. Moryson, *An history of Ireland … 1599–1603*, 2 vols. (1735) · H. Morgan, *Tyrone's rebellion: the outbreak of the Nine Years' War in Tudor Ireland*, Royal Historical Society Studies in History, 67 (1993) · J. J. Silke, ed. and trans., 'The last will of Red Hugh O'Donnell', *Studia Hibernica*, 24 (1984–8), 51–60 · C. Maxwell, *Irish history from contemporary sources, 1509–1610* (1923) · *DNB* · G. Hill, *Plantation in Ulster* (1877)
Archives Archivo General, Simancas, *fondos* Estado, some of his letters addressed to Philip II, Philip III, and others, 185, 188, 839, 840, 2604 · Archivo General, Simancas, *fondos* Guerra Antigua, some of his letters addressed to Philip II, Philip III, and others, 587, 3144
Wealth at death bequeathed all 'estates, lands, lordships and vassals' to brother: will, 28 Aug 1602, Archivo Historico Provincial y Universitario, Valladolid, Protocollos 1501, fols. 106*r* (329*r*)–108*r* (331*r*)

O'Donnell, Hugh Albert, styled second earl of Tyrconnell (1606–1642). *See under* O'Donnell, Rury, styled first earl of Tyrconnell (1574/5–1608).

O'Donnell, Hugh Balldearg [Aodh Bailldearg Ó Domhnaill] (*c.*1650–1703/4), army officer, was born in co. Donegal, Ireland, the son of John (Seán) O'Donnell (*d.* 1655), an Irish officer in the Spanish service, and Catherine

O'Rourke. His grandfather was Hugh O'Donnell of Ramelton, grandson of Calvagh, who died the head of the O'Donnells in 1566. The chieftaincy passed in Elizabeth's time to a younger branch in the person of Rory O'Donnell, who was granted the earldom of Tyrconnell, and the evidence would appear to suggest that Hugh Albert, the last titular earl, who died childless in 1642, made Hugh Balldearg his testamentary heir, thus restoring the headship of the clan to the elder line. It is suggested that Balldearg inherited the O'Donnell family papers and that although he was not a descendant of the first earl he was descended from the brothers of Sir Niall Garbh O'Donnell. The name Balldearg, which means 'red spot', is derived from a personal peculiarity found in several members of the family.

Nothing is known of O'Donnell's early life, but by the early 1670s he lived in and owned property in Spain. There he was known as Count O'Donnell and earl of Tyrconnell, though he had no legitimate claim to the titles, and commanded an Irish regiment of horse in the Spanish army with the rank of colonel. In 1689 he was refused leave to go to Ireland, where he wished to serve James II, and in the process recover his Irish title and estates. Instead, he went secretly to Lisbon, where he published a manifesto, and put himself in contact with the French ambassador.

O'Donnell eventually reached Cork in July 1690, four days after the battle of the Boyne, and visited the fugitive king on board ship at Kinsale harbour. After James recommended him to Richard Talbot, the then earl of Tyrconnell, O'Donnell was given a commission to raise 3000–4000 men. By the magic of his name, and with the help of an old prophecy that Ireland should be saved by an O'Donnell with a red spot, he raised fourteen regiments in the north, and sent a memorandum to the French ambassador to the effect that he could easily raise 30,000 if arms and ammunition were provided. According to the earl of Melfort 'the very friars and some of the bishops had taken arms to follow him' (O'Kelly, 469). But despite granting commissions to members of the leading Old Irish families in Ulster and Connaught the regiments under O'Donnell's command were never completely taken into service. Jealousies between the Old English Catholics and Old Irish were rife, as personified in the dispute between Tyrconnell and O'Donnell which prevented the latter from taking an active part in the 1691 campaign. Moreover, Fumeron, the intendant with the French troops and faithful servant of Louis XIV, looked upon Balldearg as a doubtful ally.

Disillusioned with the treatment meted out to him and by the losses at Athlone, Aughrim, and Galway, by mid-1691 O'Donnell had proposed to the Williamite General Godert van Ginckell that he would serve in the Williamite army on condition that he would be granted the earldom of Tyrconnell and £2000 for his expenses. These negotiations were later published, much to O'Donnell's distress, in an August edition of the *London Gazette*. By September, after some further feints, he openly joined the Williamites before Sligo with 1000 men. Although Ginckell remained suspicious of Balldearg, he certainly contributed to the fall of the town. On 7 October

the two met once again and terms were arranged, but few of O'Donnell's men followed him. A pension of £500 a year was settled on him for life, but an intention to employ him in Ireland was abandoned in deference to the protestant interest.

O'Donnell's appearance at Kensington Palace in London in December 1691 created enormous interest and it was reported that 'he is still respected by the Irish, and has the manners and character of a Spaniard, and he will return to Spain if he can' (Mulloy, 2, no. 1751). In 1693, after recovering from a long illness, he left England for the Spanish Netherlands before moving to Piedmont, where he was given command of a regiment of foot. Balldearg and his regiment were in Catalonia by 1695, but saw little military action. With the peace of Ryswick in 1697 he moved to the Spanish court, was made a major-general in the Spanish army, and was sent to serve in Flanders. His place of death is unknown but it is believed that O'Donnell died in 1703 or 1704.

Irish writers generally have dealt hardly with O'Donnell's memory, but John O'Donovan wrote in his defence in 1860, and modern writers are more favourable towards him. It is now acknowledged that he was consistent in his loyalties—to his Roman Catholic faith and to Spain.   RICHARD BAGWELL, *rev.* SHEILA MULLOY

Sources J. O'Donovan, 'The O'Donnells in exile', *Duffy's Hibernian Magazine*, 1 (1860), 50–57, 106–13 · AFM, 2nd edn, 6.2377–420 · C. O'Kelly, *Macariae excidium, or, The destruction of Cyprus*, ed. J. C. O'Callaghan (1850) · S. Mulloy, ed., *Franco-Irish correspondence, December 1688 – February 1692*, 3 vols., IMC (1983–4) · *Négociations de M. le Comte d'Avaux en Irlande, 1689–90*, ed. J. Hogan, 2 vols., IMC (1934–58) · *Fourth report*, HMC, 3 (1874) · J. C. T. MacDonagh, 'Heirs to the chieftaincy and earldom of Tirconaill', *Donegal Annual, Journal of the County Donegal Historical Society*, 4/1 (1958), 22–34 · P. Melvin, 'Balldearg O'Donnell abroad and the French design in Catalonia, 1688–97', *Irish Sword*, 12 (1975–6), 42–54, 116–30 · R. Ó Cochláin, 'Na Dálaigh (The O'Donnells of Tirconaill)', *Journal of the County Donegal Historical Society*, 1/4 (1950), 263–81 · J. G. Simms, *Jacobite Ireland, 1685–91* (1969) · J. G. Simms, 'Sligo in the Jacobite war', *Irish Sword*, 7 (1965), 124–35 · J. T. Gilbert, ed., *A Jacobite narrative of the war in Ireland, 1688–1691* (1892) · *LondG* (1689–93) · G. Story, *A continuation of the impartial history of the wars of Ireland* (1693) · *The life of James the Second, king of England*, ed. J. S. Clarke, 2 (1816) · W. King, *The state of the protestants of Ireland under the late King James's government* (1730), appx 8, 59 · E. O'Donnell, *The Irish abroad* (1915), 260

O'Donnell, John Francis (1837–1874), journalist and poet, was born in Limerick City, the son of a shopkeeper. He was educated by the Christian Brothers. He then learned shorthand, and when he was seventeen joined the *Munster News*, Limerick, as a reporter. At the same time he began to contribute verse to *The Nation*, for which he continued to write prose and poetry until his death. After two years on the *Munster News*, O'Donnell was appointed sub-editor on the *Tipperary Examiner*, published in Clonmel. He also contributed to the *Kilkenny Journal*. In 1860 he went to London, to work for the *Universal News*, a weekly Roman Catholic and Irish nationalist paper. He also contributed verse to *Chambers's Journal* and *All the Year Round*. He was married and had four children, but the name of his wife is not known.

In 1862 O'Donnell returned to Dublin to join *The Nation*,

then edited by A. M. Sullivan; at the same time O'Donnell edited *Duffy's Hibernian Magazine*. In 1864, however, he returned to London to edit the *Universal News*, and in 1865 became sub-editor of *The Tablet*, where he remained until 1868.

It is not known whether O'Donnell was a Fenian, but he was one of their ablest propagandists in the press. From 1863 he wrote articles and contributed nationalist poetry to James Stephens's *Irish People* until it was suppressed in 1865. He also wrote for Richard Pigott's *The Irishman* and *The Shamrock* magazine. In all these papers he used the pseudonyms Caviare and Monkton West. In September 1873, through the Irish chancellor Lord O'Hagan, O'Donnell obtained an appointment in the London office of the agent-general of New Zealand. He died, after a brief illness, on 7 May 1874, in London, and was buried at Kensal Green cemetery. O'Donnell published three collections of prose and poetry in his lifetime, and the Southwark Irish Literary Society published a posthumous edition of his poems in 1891.

MICHAEL MACDONAGH, *rev.* MARIE-LOUISE LEGG

Sources D. J. O'Donoghue, *The poets of Ireland: a biographical and bibliographical dictionary*, [rev. edn] (1901) · *The Nation* (9 May 1874) · *The Nation* (13 May 1874) · *Limerick Reporter and Tipperary Vindicator* (12 May 1874) · D. J. Hickey and J. E. Doherty, *A dictionary of Irish history* (1980); pbk edn (1987)

Likenesses portrait, repro. in M. McDonagh, *Irish graves in England* (1888)

O'Donnell, Manus [Maghnus Ó Domhnaill], **lord of Tyrconnell** (*d.* 1563), chieftain, the eldest of fourteen sons of Sir Hugh O'Donnell, lord of Tyrconnell (*d.* 1537), and his first wife, a daughter of O'Boyle of Boylagh. Manus is known to have had four wives: Siobhán, daughter of O'Reilly, chief of East Breifne (married later to Maguire, lord of Fermanagh), and mother of Calvagh *O'Donnell, lord of Tyrconnell; Joan (*d.* 1535), sister of Conn Bacach O'Neill and mother of Sir Hugh, lord of Tyrconnell; Margaret (*d.* 1544), daughter of Angus Macdonald of the Isles, from whom he had separated by 1538; and Eleanor, sister of Gerald *Fitzgerald, ninth earl of Kildare, and widow of Donal MacCarthy Reagh of Carbery, whom he married about June 1538. That he was also married to a daughter of Maguire is most improbable. Besides Calvagh and Hugh, Manus had at least six other sons: Niall Garbh, Donough, Rory, Caffar, Manus Óg, and another Manus, and seven daughters: Rose, Sheila, Evelyn, Mary, Fionnghuala (wife of Sir Cú Chonnacht Maguire and mother of Sir Hugh, killed in 1600), Grace, and Joan.

Manus's grandfather (who was chieftain between 1461 and 1503) and father had broken O'Neill supremacy in the north of Ireland, and had established effective control over lower or northern Connaught. The lordship of Tyrconnell (or Tír Conaill; later co. Donegal), controlling the coast from Broadhaven to Lough Foyle, exchanged fish for wine, salt, iron, and munitions. Breton and Spanish traders knew Manus in his day as 'king of fish'. In his father's absence abroad (1510–12) Manus defended Tyrconnell against O'Neill. Father and son then campaigned vigorously in both Connaught and Tír Eoghain (Tyrone), and

in 1514 O'Neill formally acknowledged O'Donnell's rights to the tributes of Cinéal Moain (the modern barony of Raphoe), Inishowen, and Fermanagh. Conn Bacach, the new O'Neill, renewed the fighting, and Manus built a frontier castle at Lifford in 1527. The castle had its refinements, as the poet Tadhg Dall Ó Huiginn tells us; and Manus gathered here a number of scholars, who in 1532 completed *Betha Colaim chille*, a life of the great Cenél Conaill saint, Columba. It was a document for the times, a rich fusion of classical hagiography and folklore. Manus himself was a poet, composing syllabic verses, now tender, now satirical, but the claim that he composed the life 'out of his own mouth' may suggest no more than that he had the work read to him as it proceeded, and with his poet's ear gave approval or criticism.

His brother Hugh Boy was now challenging Manus for the succession, and the divisions within Tyrconnell allowed O'Connor Sligo in 1533 to win back Sligo Castle, held by O'Donnell since 1516. This weakened O'Donnell domination of the west. Sir Hugh, unable to call on the help of these two sons for a foray on Connaught, found it best in 1535 to surrender to the king half the tributes of lower Connaught and half the cocket of Sligo. But his threat to attack O'Neill was sufficient to deter the brothers-in-law Manus and Conn Bacach (whose wife was sister to the ninth earl of Kildare) from going to the aid of Silken Thomas.

Death took Sir Hugh in 1537, and Manus was inaugurated O'Donnell. He now made attacks on Connaught and in 1538 won back Sligo Castle. The same year he assumed the leadership of the Geraldine league, about June marrying Eleanor Fitzgerald, the guardian of her nephew Gerald. The alliance of Irish and Anglo-Irish lords feared for their autonomy and were urged on by 'the friers and preestes of all the Yrishtree, not oneley of Odownelles country' (*State Papers, Henry VIII*, 3.141, n. 1), preaching a religious war. The resentment provoked by Henry VIII's reforms that had been one of the factors motivating the earlier Kildare rebellion was now grown greater. Manus sent out pleas to the papacy, the empire, France, and James V, and in 1539 O'Neill and he ravaged the pale and made a symbolic appearance at Tara. Though mauled by Grey in Monaghan on their way home, the allies were back again in the pale in 1540. But Eleanor, now distrustful of Manus, carried Gerald off to France; and in 1541 Manus, splendidly dressed for the occasion, submitted at Cavan to the politic St Leger, accepting Henry's sovereignty and supremacy, at least on paper. His reward for accepting the status of tenant-in-chief under the crown was to receive in absolute ownership the territory of Tyrconnell (certain rights *vis-à-vis* MacWilliam Burke also being accorded to him). This was the conciliatory policy of 'surrender and regrant'. Grateful for his bringing in O'Neill, the administration in 1543 accepted his overlordship of Inishowen, to the disappointment of O'Neill, now earl of Tyrone.

Manus had nominally lost his absolute independence. But now, in place of usufruct of certain lands, Tyrconnell was his in absolute ownership, to be transmitted to his son by law of primogeniture. He might also claim the protection of the crown. There now began a period of diplomatic chess between Manus and the government. O'Donnell listened to overtures from France, England's enemy, and in 1545 secured ratification of his rights over Inishowen. But he yielded up the episcopal revenues he had seized on the death in 1543 of the papal bishop of Raphoe, facilitating continuation of the Roman succession with the appointment of Art O'Gallagher as bishop in 1547. The government, on the other hand, favoured Manus's rebellious son Calvagh, to whom Bellingham in 1549 awarded Lifford Castle, with extensive adjoining lands. Manus was allowed Castle Finn, but his brother Conn, as tanist, was also given a large estate. Manus again turned to France, but after the peace between Henri II and Warwick (March 1550) could only write to disclaim practice of treason. He was now elderly and ailing, and Calvagh made him captive in 1555. Hugh had gone over to Shane O'Neill, and would not help. But when Shane attacked Tyrconnell in 1557, Calvagh turned to his father, by whose advice he was able to drive Shane off. Then in 1561 Shane, O'Neill since 1559, kidnapped Calvagh.

With Tyrconnell leaderless and at a low ebb, Manus died 'in his own fortress of Lifford', say the four masters, on 9 February 1563, and was interred at the Franciscan friary founded by his grandparents in Donegal. The erosion of the independence of the Gaelic lords had begun before his day, and England, with its increase in armed might, was able to take advantage of the weaknesses of the Gaelic system, its competition for power, and its feuding between states. He had, however, done something to adumbrate a national programme for future Irish leaders, which would have religion for a cement and which would seek to exploit an English weakness, susceptibility to attack from the continent through its back door, Ireland. If unable to restrain the rebels within his own family, he had established the rule of Tyrconnell in his own line, and all its remaining lords would be his descendants. And his support of Bishop Art O'Gallagher was of consequence in ensuring that the Reformation would make no progress in his territory during the sixteenth century. He was *ilcherdach* ('many-skilled'), say the four masters: man of action and diplomat, with a taste for finer things, including literature. An older contemporary of Manus might have said that he possessed *virtù*.   JOHN J. SILKE

Sources *AFM*, vols. 5–6 · A. M. Freeman, ed. and trans., *Annála Connacht / The annals of Connacht* (1944); repr. (1970) · W. M. Hennessy, ed. and trans., *The annals of Loch Cé: a chronicle of Irish affairs from AD 1014 to AD 1590*, 2 vols., Rolls Series, 54 (1871), vol. 2 · S. Pender, ed., 'The O'Clery book of genealogies', *Analecta Hibernica*, 18 (1951), 1–195 · *Betha Colaim Chille: life of Columcille compiled by Manus O'Donnell in 1532*, ed. and trans. A. O'Kelleher and G. Schoepperle (1918) · T. D. Ó Huiginn, *Bardic poems*, ed. E. Knott, 2 pts (1922–6) · T. F. O'Rahilly, ed., *Dánta grádha … 1350–1750* (1926), nos. 49–53 · T. F. O'Rahilly, ed., *Dánfhocail* (1921) · J. S. Brewer and W. Bullen, eds., *Calendar of the Carew manuscripts*, 1: *1515–1574*, PRO (1867) · *State papers published under … Henry VIII*, 11 vols. (1830–52), vols. 1–3 · *LP Henry VIII*, vols. 8–21 · S. Ó Domhnaill, 'History of Tír Conaill in the sixteenth century', MA diss., University College Dublin, 1946 · A. Gwynn, *The medieval province of Armagh, 1470–1545* (1946) · J. J. Silke, 'Raphoe and the Reformation', *Donegal: history and society*, ed. W. Nolan (1995), 267–82 · P. Wilson, *The beginnings of modern Ireland*, another edn (1914) · B. Bradshaw, 'Manus "the magnificent": O'Donell as Renaissance prince', *Studies … presented to R. D. Edwards*, ed. A. Cosgrove and D. McCartney (1979), 15–37 · J. G. Simms, 'Manus O'Donnell, 21st lord of Tír Conaill', *Donegal Annual*, 5 (1962), 115–21 · M. Carney, ed., 'Agreement between Ó Domhnaill and Tadhg Ó Conchobhair concerning Sligo Castle, 23 June 1539', *Irish Historical Studies*, 3 (1942–3), 282–96 · P. A. Breathnach, 'In praise of Maghnus Ó Domhnaill', *Celtica*, 16 (1984), 63–72 · R. Sharpe, 'Maghnus Ó Domhnaill's source for Adomnán's *Vita s. Columbae* and other *vitae*', *Celtica*, 21 (1990), 604–7 · J. Szövérffy, 'Manus O'Donnell and Irish folk tradition', *Éigse*, 8 (1955–7), 108–32 · L. Ó Clérigh, *Beatha Aodha Ruaidh Uí Dhomhnaill*, ed. P. Walsh, pt 2 (1957), 21–2, 212–13 · P. Walsh, ed., 'O'Donnell genealogies', *Analecta Hibernica*, 8 (1938), 373–418 · *DNB* · P. Walsh, *Irish men of learning*, ed. C. O Lochlainn (1947), 160–78 **Archives** Royal Irish Acad., copy of agreement between Manus and O'Connor, Sligo, MS 998, 23 F 21, fol. 17 **Wealth at death** see *Carew manuscripts*, 205–7; *AFM*, 220–22

O'Donnell, Lady Mary Stuart (*b.* 1607?, *d.* in or after **1639**), noblewoman, was the daughter of Rury *O'Donnell, first earl of Tyrconnell (1574/5–1608), and his wife, Lady Brigid Fitzgerald (*c.*1589–1682), only daughter of Henry Fitzgerald, twelfth earl of Kildare, and Frances, daughter of Charles Howard, first earl of Nottingham. In September 1607 her father, disappointed with the numerous exclusions to his patent as earl, fled Ireland for the continent with his infant son, Hugh Albert *O'Donnell (1606–1642) [*see under* O'Donnell, Rury], and Hugh O'Neill, earl of Tyrone. At the time of this flight, Tyrconnell's wife was at her family's Maynooth estate waiting to give birth. Although the earl intended Brigid to follow him abroad, she found herself in a disturbing predicament, forsaken by her husband and caught up in the political wake stirred by his actions. Guiding her through this crisis was her mother, the dowager countess of Kildare. She counselled her daughter to dissociate herself from her exiled husband, by denying foreknowledge of his 'unfortunate journey' and repudiating her husband's 'ungrateful behavior' in 'so wicked an enterprise as to rebel against his prince' (*CSP Ire.*, *1600–08*, 296–7, B. O'Donnell to lord deputy, September 1607; *Salisbury MSS*, 9.482, B. O'Donnell to lord deputy, 1607).

After her disavowal, Brigid went to England to defend herself, and in London gave birth to Mary, probably in late 1607. Brigid, at an opportune moment, took the infant and pleaded her case before the king. James I was moved by her desperate condition and her 'sweet' and 'well favoured' appearance. He confessed that he could not understand how her husband 'left so fair a face behind' (Nichols, 2.157). The king granted her a pension of £200 from the revenues of her husband's escheated estates and the baby was placed under royal protection. Henceforth, the child was known as Mary Stuart O'Donnell.

Mary returned while still an infant with her mother to Ireland, where she was raised as a Catholic on the Maynooth estate. In 1619, two years after Brigid remarried, Mary was sent to England to live with her maternal grandmother. (Her stepfather was Nicholas Barnewall, first Viscount Kingsland.) Within a few years, the strong-willed adolescent estranged her benefactors and family with disputes over her annuities, her Irish Catholic associations, and her marital status. She was a desirable heiress and both the Howard family and her grandmother believed that a protestant husband would resolve many of Mary's difficulties. But in 1626 she became involved in a plot that freed two young native Irish hostages from the Tower. Summoned to testify before the royal council, Mary, disguised as a young man, escaped to the continent and made her way to the Spanish Netherlands. In Brussels she met for the first time her brother, Hugh Albert O'Donnell, titular second earl of Tyrconnell. Through his influence she was well received at the infanta's court and was recommended by the Roman Catholic archbishop of Tuam, Florence Conry, and Guido di Bagno, the papal nuncio, to Cardinal Barberini, the papal secretary of state. Before their dispatches were forwarded, Pope Urban VIII sent his blessings: 'You, our daughter, have given to the world proof of … what strength and courage are imparted by the true faith.' Praising her 'heroic' nature and her resistance to the allurements of court, the menaces of the English king, and the 'horrors of an alliance with a Protestant', Urban celebrated her defiance and welcomed her tenderly into the bosom of the Roman church (Urban VIII to M. S. O'Donnell, 13 Feb 1627, Barberini Latini MS 6207, fol. 7r–v; MacGeoghan, 545).

These good feelings were spent when Mary refused to be used as a marital tool to heal the tensions between the O'Donnell and O'Neill factions. Florence Conry secured her a dowry and the support of the infanta for a marriage to John O'Neill, third earl of Tyrone. Anticipating a serious estrangement if she rejected this match, Mary took matters into her own hands. In the spring of 1627 she made a desperate appeal to Lord Conway, the English secretary of state. She explained away her London flight on her 'smallness of means and the fear of losing her reputation'. Mary also suggested she might 'draw her brother into the King's service' with the right royal guarantees (O'Donnell to Conway, c.March 1627, CSP Ire., 1625–32, 108). The futility of her appeal exposed the hopelessness of her position. She was in love with a poor Irish captain, Dudley (Dualtach) O'Gallagher, (d. c.1635), and, true to her own legacy, in 1631 the pregnant Mary fled to Italy with her companion. About this time the young couple married, and while living in Genoa, Mary gave birth to a boy. With Rome unwilling to support their 'worthy daughter' the young couple survived on a meagre subsidy from the infanta. As for her brother, Tyrconnell complained that a woman posing as his sister was defaming him and his house. Mary and her husband ultimately found refuge in Austria where Dudley perished in the imperial service about 1635. The widowed Mary made her way back to Rome and was last heard of in 1639.

Mary Stuart O'Donnell was a shadowy romantic figure whose notoriety was regularly noted in the dispatches and reports of gossipy field agents. Her father, Rury O'Donnell, died in Rome in July 1608 and his brother Caffar died there about a week later. This left Mary's brother Hugh Albert to claim the title of titular earl of Tyrconnell. He commanded an Irish regiment in the Spanish Netherlands with the title of colonel and died in the service of Spain in August 1642. Mary's mother, Brigid, eventually became Viscountess Kingsland from her second marriage, and had five sons and four daughters with her new husband. Widowed in 1663, she lived until 1682, the oldest surviving person associated with the 1607 'flight of the earls'.

JERROLD I. CASWAY

Sources APC, 1625–6 · Barberini Latini MSS, NL Ire. [microfilm] · CSP Ire., 1606–32 · J. Casway, 'Mary Stuart O'Donnell', Donegal Annual, 39 (1987), 28–38 · B. Jennings, 'The career of Hugh, son of Rory O'Donnell, earl of Tyrconnell in the Low Countries, 1607–1642', Studies: an Irish Quarterly Review, 30 (1941), 219–34 · B. Jennings, ed., 'Documents of the Irish Franciscan college at Prague', Archivium Hibernicum, 9 (1942), 173–294, esp. 275–80 · B. Jennings, ed., 'Miscellaneous documents, 1588–1715 [pt 1]', Archivium Hibernicum, 12 (1946), 70–200, esp. 136–8 · B. Jennings, ed., Wadding papers, 1614–38, IMC (1953) · B. Jennings, ed., Wild geese in Spanish Flanders, 1582–1700, IMC (1964) · J. MacGeoghan, History of Ireland (1845) · C. P. Meehan, The fate and fortunes of Hugh O'Neill, earl of Tyrone, and Rory O'Donel, earl of Tyrconnel, 3rd edn (1886) · B. de Meester, ed., Correspondance du nonce Giovanni-Francesco Guidi di Bagno (1621–1627), 2 vols. (Brussels, 1938) · J. Nichols, The progresses, processions, and magnificent festivities of King James I, his royal consort, family and court, 2 (1828) · Calendar of the manuscripts of the most hon. the marquis of Salisbury, 9, HMC, 9 (1902)
Wealth at death small subsidy from infanta

O'Donnell [Ó Domhnaill], **Sir Niall Garbh** (1568/9–1626?), magnate and soldier, was the eldest son of Conn O'Donnell (d. 1583) and his wife, Rose, daughter of Shane (Seán) O'Neill, and grandson of Calvagh *O'Donnell, lord of Tyrconnell. Conn, who appears to have been married previously, had eight sons and at least two daughters. In 1567 the then lord deputy, Sir Henry Sidney, had delivered Lifford and Finn fortresses to Conn, and Niall was probably born in Finn Castle. By his marriage to Nuala (Fionnghuala), sister of Red Hugh O'Donnell, Niall had at least two children, Neachtan and Manus (killed at Benburb in 1646), but his wife deserted him in 1600. In 1602 he was reported to be contemplating marriage with the dead Hugh Maguire's sister, the widow of Sir Arthur O'Neill. Whether or not they married, he seems to have had more than the two children. Niall was three years older than Red Hugh, his father's first cousin and his own foster-brother and brother-in-law. But rivalry between their two houses went back to the 1540s, when the English government had in effect partitioned Tyrconnell. The English favoured Calvagh's branch, represented now by Niall.

Red Hugh having in 1592 established himself as lord of Tyrconnell and taken over Lifford, from which to challenge O'Neill (Turlough Luineach) at Strabane, made both Niall and Hugh mac Hugh Dubh of Ramelton, 'sinnsear sleachta Dálaig' ('the senior O'Donnell'), submit. Niall, although his ambitions were thwarted and he had lost Lifford, served Red Hugh faithfully in the war, up to 1600. O'Donnell sent him to Hugh Maguire's aid in 1592; thereafter he saw much service in Connaught and presumably shared in the victory of the Curlews (the poet who after 1632 wrote his elegy extols his valour shown in Connaught and in Ulster). But on 3 October 1600 he with his three brothers, Hugh Boy, Donal, and Conn Og, went over to the English at Lough Foyle. Sir Henry Docwra, the English commander in north-west Ulster, had offered him and his heirs the lordship of Tyrconnell, and his grant was enrolled on 18 March 1601. The lord deputy, Mountjoy, knighted him. Fearing Red Hugh's wrath, he joined Docwra before his further demands for the traditional O'Donnell overlordship of Inishowen and of Sligo were met.

The timing of Niall's defection, in wartime and with the English enemy established on the Foyle, leaves him open to the charge of treason. The disgusted Nuala promptly left him; she went into exile in 1607, died in or after 1617, and was buried in Louvain. Niall kept Docwra victualled and gained for him Lifford (8 October 1600), which, it is thought, Red Hugh had put under his charge. The nastier side of his nature was revealed when he and his men in a drunken fury upon an old grudge murdered Neachtan O'Donnell, Niall's own uncle and a man of great authority with O'Donnell. On 24 October Red Hugh's brothers, Rury and Manus, engaged him and his men. Manus was fatally wounded and Niall narrowly escaped death at Rury's hand. He took Donegal Franciscan friary (31 July 1601) as a base for attacking Ballyshannon Castle, which for Mountjoy was the key to bridling O'Donnell as the Blackwater fort bridled Tyrone. However, O'Donnell attacked Niall, who lost his brother Conn Og and 300 men. He retreated to Magherabeg friary but at the end of October Red Hugh, informed of the Spanish landing at Kinsale, broke the siege to go south. Niall won over MacSweeney Banagh, whose keep commanded Killybegs harbour, and while Ballyshannon fell to the English (25 March 1602), he also secured Castlederg. The historian John Lynch blamed Niall for allowing Docwra's soldiers to kill the aged bishop of Derry, Redmond O'Gallagher. In August, Niall provisioned Mountjoy at Augher, with cattle seized in co. Tyrone and in Breifne O'Rourke. He also destroyed Enniskillen and garrisoned the monasteries of Devenish and Lisgoole.

Docwra, while acknowledging Niall's ambitious and refractory nature, pleaded with Mountjoy to honour his promises to one who had proved indispensable to the success of the Foyle operation. But Mountjoy thought Rury O'Donnell the man to keep Tyrconnell at peace. The outraged Niall seized Rury's cattle and had himself inaugurated O'Donnell (1603). (The four masters, knowing Rury to be tanist, do not acknowledge the inauguration's validity.) He then came to Derry, where he was arrested, but he broke free with the cattle, 7000 head, which Docwra by prompt action recovered. Still Niall accompanied Mountjoy to London, where Tyrconnell was divided. Rury was made earl, with grant of the major part of the county, but with reservation of Ballyshannon (which, Docwra complained, had been won by himself) and 1000 acres adjoining to Sir Henry Folliott. Niall was apportioned the lands along the Finn that he had held in the time of Sir Hugh O'Donnell. English army officers received grants, which included ecclesiastical lands, while the crown reserved to itself the right to build forts. All this left three people

much dissatisfied: the earl of Tyrconnell, Niall Garbh, and Docwra.

By 1604 Niall had so strengthened his hand that the earl was forced to retreat to the pale. At Strabane in 1605 Lord Deputy Chichester gave judgment in the disputes between Tyrconnell and Niall and between the latter and Tyrone (over the lands to the south of Lifford, Cinéal Moain or Moentacht): he awarded 43 quarters of land in Glenfin and the Moentacht to Niall, made Tyrconnell recognize his sub-chiefs as freeholders, and reserved Lifford (although it had not been excepted from Tyrconnell's patent) to the crown. Niall continued in dispute with Tyrconnell and in August 1606 deposed that the earl and Cuconnacht Maguire were planning to seize the northern garrisons. Chichester in December bound Tyrconnell and Niall in recognizances to accept his own decisions in their disputes. Sufficient amity prevailed for Niall to serve under Tyrconnell at the siege of Doe Castle in March 1607, Niall being severely wounded.

By 1608 Chichester was ready to double Niall's grant in Glenfin and Moentacht but now Niall was accused, even by his two brothers, of instigating Sir Cahir O'Doherty's rebellion. Tyrconnell's mother, Iníon Dubh, included the brothers with Niall's son Neachtan among the plotters. Niall's complicity was, however, probably limited. Neachtan, a student first of St John's College, Oxford, and then of Trinity College, Dublin, had been taken hostage by Chichester for his father's good behaviour. Then, straight after the revolt, Niall sought a patent for both Tyrconnell and Inishowen, promising to bring in O'Doherty's head. The rebellion over, on 14 June Niall and his brothers were arrested, as was Sir Donal Ballagh O'Kane, all charged with complicity in the insurrection. They were brought to Dublin in the *Tramontana*, the pinnace that had brought Niall to Holyhead with Mountjoy. Marshal Wingfield had given Niall protection and a jury failed to convict him. Despite that, Niall, Neachtan, and O'Kane were sent to the Tower of London. Niall died there, aged fifty-seven, probably in 1626; Neachtan is said to have died in the Tower, although there is no trace of him after 1623. In the plantation his lands were sequestrated, but it appears that a request made by him in 1613 that the rents he claimed be devoted to the support of his surviving sister and the maintenance of his children at school, and a similar request from O'Kane, were honoured by Chichester. Brave if overbearing, Niall had striven by every means to secure Tyrconnell with all its chieftains' ancestral rights and lived to regret joining the English camp. Through his son Manus he was ancestor of the O'Donnells of Newport, co. Mayo, the Leitrim line stemming from his brother Hugh Boy and the Austrian and Spanish lines from his other brother Conn Og.   JOHN J. SILKE

Sources H. Docwra, 'Narration', *Miscellany of the Celtic Society*, ed. J. O'Donovan (1849), 231–326 • L. Ó Clérigh, *Beatha Aodha Ruaidh Uí Dhomhnaill*, ed. P. Walsh, 2 vols. (1948–57) • *AFM*, 2nd edn • *CSP Ire.*, 1600–08 • R. J. Hunter, 'The end of O'Donnell power', *Donegal: history and society*, ed. W. Nolan (1995), 229–66 • S. Ó Domhnaill, 'Sir Niall Garbh O'Donnell and the rebellion of Sir Cahir O'Doherty', *Irish Historical Studies*, 3 (1942–3), 34–8 • C. Falls, 'Neill Garve: English ally and victim', *Irish Sword*, 1 (1949), 2–7 · P. Walsh, 'Elegy on Niall Garbh Ó Domhnaill', *Gleanings from Irish manuscripts*, 2nd edn, with additions (1933), 27–52 · P. O'Sullivan-Beare, *Historiae Catholicae Iberniae compendium*, ed. M. Kelly (1850) · G. Hill, *An historical account of the plantation in Ulster … 1608–20*; repr., introd. J. G. Barry (1970), 62–3, 234–7 · 'Ulster plantation papers, 1608–13', *Analecta Hibernica*, 8 (1938), 179–297 · J. Morrin, ed., *Calendar of the patent and close rolls of chancery in Ireland for the reigns of Henry VIII, Edward VI, Mary, and Elizabeth*, 2 vols. (1861–2)

O'Donnell, Patrick [Pádraic Ua Domhnaill] (1856–1927), cardinal, was born on 28 November 1856 at Kilraine, near Glenties, co. Donegal, the second son of nine children of Daniel O'Donnell, tenant farmer, and Mary Breslin, of Gortlosk, co. Donegal. He was educated at the local national school and the high school at Letterkenny. He was nominated for a place at the Pontificio Collegio Irlandese, Rome, but was sent instead in 1873 to the faculty of arts and science in the Catholic University, Dublin. In 1875 he entered St Patrick's College, Maynooth, and in 1879 became a student of the Dunboyne Establishment. In 1880 he was ordained and was appointed to a chair in theology. During his time at Maynooth he contributed a number of articles to the *Irish Ecclesiastical Record*. In 1884 he was appointed prefect of the Dunboyne Establishment. In 1888, at the unusually young age of thirty-two, he was appointed to the see of Raphoe, comprising most of co. Donegal.

Patrick O'Donnell (1856–1927), by unknown photographer

As bishop of Raphoe, O'Donnell was energetic in both religious and secular affairs. During his episcopate the ancient cathedral chapter was re-established by Pope Leo XIII in 1901 and St Eunan (St Adomnán) was declared joint patron saint of the diocese with St Columba. The cathedral was opened in 1901, and new schools and churches were built. On 28 April 1922 he was installed as coadjutor, with the title archbishop of Attalia, to Cardinal Michael Logue, whom he succeeded as primate in November 1924. In December 1925 he was created cardinal and took the title Santa Maria Della Pace. On his return to Ireland from Rome he was greeted by President Cosgrave, two government ministers, a guard of honour of fifty men, and a pipe band. As he travelled north to Armagh he was welcomed by groups ranging from the Gaelic League and Knights of Columbanus to the Royal Ulster Rifles. He attended the International Eucharistic Congress in Chicago in 1926 and received a warm welcome from Irish Americans. His final religious event of major significance was a plenary synod of the Irish hierarchy at Maynooth in August 1927.

As bishop of Raphoe—a diocese frequently afflicted by famine—O'Donnell took a keen interest in the plight of the small farmer. He was a member of the congested districts board from its establishment in 1896 to its dissolution in 1923, and a member of the royal commission on congested districts in 1906. He also promoted the revival of the cloth-making industry in Donegal.

O'Donnell took a keen interest in national politics and was actively involved in the Irish parliamentary party. He retained the confidence of both sides when the party split following the death of Parnell and he helped promote reunion. He presided at the Irish Race Convention in January 1896, and was the only bishop present. O'Donnell supported the United Irish League, which was to become the constituency organization of the Irish parliamentary party, but had some difficulty in leading his clergy to support it. He was responsible for the removal of the hierarchy's ban on the Ancient Order of Hibernians in 1904 and this organization was to form an important part of the party's political machine in the north-east. O'Donnell was appointed a trustee of the reunited party and was to prove a valuable adviser to leader John Redmond until 1918. Between 1917 and 1918 he was one of four episcopal representatives in the Irish Convention which deliberated on an Irish settlement. There he argued strongly in favour of fiscal autonomy. He rejected a compromise suggested by Redmond and led the nationalists in the convention when Redmond withdrew. Before the post-war election of 1918 he suggested that all Irish party members withdraw from the election, a suggestion John Dillon rejected. After the eclipse of the party in the 1918 election O'Donnell maintained a close friendship with leading party members Dillon and Joe Devlin.

While O'Donnell always considered partition lamentable, he realized at an early stage that some form of exclusion of the north-east from home rule might be inevitable and warned against any form of autonomy which might have detrimental effects on Catholic education. Strictly constitutional in the methods he espoused, O'Donnell kept his distance from Sinn Féin during the struggle for independence, unlike some of his episcopal colleagues. His statements increasingly dealt with human rights issues rather than party politics. During the civil war he tried in vain to prevent the execution of Erskine Childers, who had helped him during the Irish Convention of 1917–18. In 1924 he appealed for the release of political prisoners both north and south. The following year he spoke of the obligation of both governments to protect the rights of minorities. When the boundaries of the Northern Irish state had been settled, he urged Catholics to use legitimate means to further their objectives and expressed hope in the goodwill of unionists.

A fluent Irish speaker, O'Donnell sought in many ways to promote the language. As bishop he issued pastoral letters in Irish as well as English. He expounded on his views on the language question in the preface he wrote for the autobiography of another language enthusiast, An tAthair Peadar Ua Laoghaire. In Letterkenny, O'Donnell clashed with the Gaelic League when their fund-raising for an Irish college for teachers conflicted with his campaign for St Eunan's Cathedral. O'Donnell established his own Irish college for teachers and his own Irish-language organization, the Crann Eithne. Nevertheless, the rift was not permanent and in 1926 he supported a Gaelic League proposal for a separate Irish-language organization in Northern Ireland. He frequently spoke at Feis Thír Chonaill in promotion of the language.

O'Donnell was involved in a variety of educational initiatives during his life. He was rector of the Catholic University, a member of the governing body of the Catholic school of medicine, and member of the governing body of the National University of Ireland, which awarded him an honorary doctorate in law in 1915. In 1918 he represented the bishops on the vice-regal committee of inquiry into primary education (the Killanin committee). As primate his relations with Lord Londonderry, the first minister of education in Northern Ireland, were cordial. Together they resolved the impasse reached in relation to the provision of teacher training for Catholic males by sending them to St Mary's College, Hammersmith. He made suggestions to the Northern Ireland ministry of education on the teaching of Irish to young children, and expressed his concerns about school buildings to both Belfast and Dublin governments.

O'Donnell was generally recognized as handsome, with a charming manner. He was frequently described as 'of princely bearing' and was a skilled orator. He was a fine swimmer and a keen walker. His enduring fault, however, was his notoriously bad handwriting, which unfortunately rendered his copious writings on political issues a trial for his contemporaries and for later researchers. He died at his summer residence at Carlingford, co. Louth, on 22 October 1927. The immediate cause of death was an embolism, but he had also been suffering from pneumonia and had developed pleurisy. He was buried in St Patrick's cemetery, Armagh, on the 28th. During his lifetime he was known to respect the views of his political opponents and was seen by many protestants as a force for reconciliation. O'Donnell had been impressed at the healing of old political divisions he witnessed during his visit to the United States in 1926 and hoped for similar reconciliation

in Ireland. On the day of his death the bells of both Catholic and protestant cathedrals in Armagh tolled for him. After his death the *Belfast News-Letter* described him as 'an honourable opponent'.

MARY N. HARRIS

Sources D. W. Miller, *Church, state and nation in Ireland, 1898–1921* (1973) · M. Harris, *The Catholic church and the foundation of the Northern Irish state* (1993) · F. S. L. Lyons, *John Dillon: a biography* (1968) · J. Healy, *Maynooth College: its centenary history* (1895) · *Irish Times* (24 Oct 1927) · *Cork Examiner* (24 Oct 1927) · *Irish Catholic Directory* (1928) · *Catholic Bulletin*, 15/12 (1925) · *Catholic Bulletin*, 17/11 (1927) · P. Ó Laoghaire, *Mo Sgéal Féin* (1915) · P. Mac Aonghusa, *Ar son na Gaeilge: Conradh na Gaeilge, 1893–1993* (Baile Átha Cliath, 1993) · *Irish Independent* (24 Oct 1927) · *Belfast News-Letter* (24 Oct 1927) · *CGPLA Ire.* (1928)

Archives Armagh Roman Catholic Diocesan Archives, episcopal corresp. and papers | Dublin Archdiocesan Archives, Dublin, Walsh MSS · NL Ire., Redmond MSS · Plunkett Foundation, Long Hanborough, Oxfordshire, corresp. with Sir Horace Plunkett · TCD, corresp. with John Dillon

Likenesses photograph, repro. in *Northern Whig* (24 Oct 1927) · photographs, repro. in E. Phoenix, *Northern nationalism: nationalist politics and the Catholic minority in Northern Ireland, 1890–1914* (1994) [see illus.] · photographs, repro. in *Catholic Bulletin*, 17/11

Wealth at death £408—in England: probate, sealed London, 23 July 1928, *CGPLA Eng. & Wales* · £4057 17s. 1d.: probate, 16 March 1928, *CGPLA Éire*

O'Donnell, Peadar (1893–1986), Irish nationalist and writer, was born on 22 February 1893 in Meenmore, near Dungloe, co. Donegal, the fifth of the nine children of James O'Donnell, a kiln worker, migrant labourer, and musician, and Brigid Rogers. Educated at national school in Meenmore and St Patrick's Teacher Training College, Drumcondra, co. Dublin (1911–13), he taught on the Inishfree and Aranmore islands off co. Donegal. He became interested in the island labourers who migrated annually to Scotland and, while observing their conditions there, he was introduced to socialist ideas. In 1918 he left teaching to work as an organizer for the Irish Transport and General Workers' Union.

In 1920 O'Donnell joined the 2nd brigade of the IRA's 1st northern division in co. Donegal. By the end of the War of Independence in June 1921 he was in command of the brigade. An opponent of the Anglo-Irish treaty, he was captured by the free state government in June 1922 following its assault on the republican-held Four Courts in Dublin. He was incarcerated in Mountjoy gaol where he was close to Liam Mellows, whose posthumous 'Notes from Mountjoy' greatly influenced republican socialism. Before his escape from internment in March 1924 he was elected to the Dáil as a republican deputy for Donegal in August 1923.

On 25 June 1924 O'Donnell married Lile O'Donnell, the daughter of a wealthy Mayo landlord. A member of both the IRA executive and the army council, he was a prominent post-civil war IRA leader. Under his successful editorship (1926–31) the IRA newspaper, *An Phoblacht*, espoused radical socialist views. He was the most influential intellectual among the left of the IRA, which was then attempting to shift the organization from its traditional militarism to socialist agitation. He was active in myriad radical and often unpopular organizations in this period, including revolutionary workers' groups (1930) and Saor Éire (1931), an unsuccessful republican socialist initiative. Most notably, he was a leading organizer of a popular campaign against the payment of land annuities in rural Ireland, which contributed towards Fianna Fáil's electoral victory in 1932.

O'Donnell was central among the left republicans who split from the IRA in 1934 to establish Republican Congress, which aimed to unite workers and labourers in a radical united front; but, hampered by internal dissensions, and falling between the militaristic republicanism of the IRA and the more pragmatic republicanism of Fianna Fáil, congress failed to attract support. During the Spanish Civil War he was a prominent supporter of the republican government, visiting Spain twice and organizing pro-republican meetings in Ireland.

As well as politics, O'Donnell devoted considerable time to writing. His first novel, *Storm*, was published in 1926, followed by *Islanders* (1927), *Adrigoole* (1929), *The Knife* (1930), *On the Edge of the Stream* (1934), *The Big Windows* (1955), and *Proud Island* (1975). The themes of his often didactic literary works—social conflict, rural poverty, and sectarianism in Ulster—reflected the preoccupations of his political life. He published three autobiographical works, *The Gates Flew Open* (1932), *Salud! An Irishman in Spain* (1937), and *There will be Another Day* (1963). In 1940 he assisted Sean O'Faolain to found *The Bell*, an innovative literary and political monthly. He replaced O'Faolain as editor from 1946 until *The Bell's* demise in 1954.

O'Donnell remained committed to the problems of rural migrants. In the late 1930s he liaised between migrant labourers and the British and Irish governments. He worked as an emigration welfare officer with the department of industry and commerce (1940–43) and was a member of the government commission on emigration and other population problems (1948–54). In the final decades of his life he remained involved in political activism. He opposed US intervention in Vietnam during the 1960s and subsequently campaigned against South African apartheid, nuclear weapons, US foreign policy, and Ireland's entry into the European Economic Community. He died in Dublin on 13 May 1986.   FEARGHAL MCGARRY

Sources M. McInerney, *Peadar O'Donnell, Irish social rebel* (1974) · R. English, *Radicals and the republic* (1994) · T. P. Coogan, *The IRA*, 4th edn (1995) · G. Freyer, *Peadar O'Donnell* (1973) · H. Patterson, *The politics of illusion* (1997) · P. O'Donnell, *Monkeys in the superstructure* (1986)
Archives SOUND BL NSA, documentary recording
Likenesses photograph, repro. in O'Donnell, *Monkeys in the superstructure*, cover · photograph, repro. in S. Cronin, *Frank Ryan: the search for the Republic* (1980)
Wealth at death £13,554: probate, 22 May 1987, *CGPLA Éire*

O'Donnell, Rury [Rory; Ruaidhrí Ó Domhnaill], **styled first earl of Tyrconnell** (1574/5–1608), magnate and soldier, was the second son of Sir Hugh O'Donnell (*b.* in or before 1535, *d.* 1600), lord of Tyrconnell, and his second wife, Fionnuala, called Iníon Dhubh (Dark Girl; *d.* 1611?), daughter of James MacDonnell of the Isles and his wife, Agnes Campbell. The sons of Sir Hugh and Fionnuala

were, in order of birth, Red Hugh (Hugh Roe) *O'Donnell (1572–1602), lord of Tyrconnell, Rury, Manus, and Caffar. Rury was tanist to Red Hugh from at least 1597 and it may be presumed that he was fostered in a friendly household, receiving an education and training appropriate to his status as the son of a chieftain.

The Nine Years' War During the campaign, Rury was in action in Connaught and then at Lough Foyle against Sir Henry Docwra and his own cousin and brother-in-law, Niall Garbh O'Donnell. He and Manus fought as cavalrymen, with lance, short sword, and target. Near Derry, Manus was fatally wounded (24 October 1600), while Niall Garbh narrowly escaped death at Rury's hands. The latter and two companion horsemen next dispatched six English foot and a sergeant. The action moved to Lifford, where Rury was wounded. The death of Manus hastened that of his father, which occurred on 27 November. In the spring of 1601 Rury failed to recapture Doe Castle, which Red Hugh, the new O'Donnell, secured in July. The sources give no account of Rury's part in such actions as that against Sir Conyers Clifford, president of Connaught, in the Curlews. He went south to Cork on the great march in 1601, but again the authorities are silent on what part he played at Kinsale. It is not impossible that he played a more prominent part in the war than Ó Clérigh's *Life of Hugh Roe* and, deriving from that, the account by the four masters give him credit for.

After Kinsale, Red Hugh O'Donnell committed his command to Rury, urging him and Hugh O'Neill to remain in the south pending his return. However, they took their separate ways homewards, Rury bringing his forces into the safety of lower Connaught, where O'Donnell on his way to Kinsale had left O'Gallagher in charge of his cattle. Rury made headquarters at Ballymote Castle, apparently awaiting his brother's return with Spanish reinforcements. In any case the way home was closed to him, with Ballyshannon and Donegal in enemy hands. In the summer of 1602 he successfully evaded a pincer attack on him by government armies and in August O'Connor Sligo and he repulsed Lambert at the Curlews. The death of O'Donnell in Simancas (30 August) made it easier for Rury to accept terms from Lord Deputy Mountjoy, to whom he and O'Connor Sligo submitted at Athlone on 14 December. Rury claimed that O'Donnell had kept him in irons for arranging with Governor Clifford to serve Queen Elizabeth. Perhaps: but Clifford was dead, and Red Hugh O'Donnell had shown confidence in Rury after Kinsale, so possibly Rury, with his army intact, was making the best of what was not a bad hand. Niall Garbh, now abandoned by a Mountjoy anxious for peace, seized Rury's herds and had himself proclaimed O'Donnell, but had to yield to Docwra.

Earl of Tyrconnell and the O'Donnell–Geraldine alliance In the 1603 peace arrangements, Rury O'Donnell was, in Christchurch, Dublin, created earl of Tyrconnell, with remainder to Caffar, and knighted by Lord Deputy Carey on 29 September; he was granted a patent for his lands on 10 February 1604. Cúcoigcríche Ó Clérigh celebrated the new era with a praise-poem: *Rug cabhair air Chonallchaibh.* But Eóghan Ruadh Mac an Bhaird, reflecting a conviction now current that the old order was over, was fearful: 'do mealladh mac Uí Dhomhnoill' ('O'Donnell's son has been beguiled'; O. Bergin, *Irish Bardic Poetry*, 1970, 127). Yet Tyrconnell was now a good match, and the old O'Donnell–Geraldine alliance was renewed when about 1604 he married Lady Brigid Fitzgerald (*c.*1589–1682), only daughter of Henry, twelfth earl of Kildare. Brigid's mother was Frances, daughter of Charles Howard, earl of Nottingham, lord high admiral and one of the Spanish party among the king's councillors. Hugh Albert O'Donnell, born about October 1606, was the only son of this marriage, Mary Stuart *O'Donnell being born about a year later. Some authorities give an eldest child, Elizabeth, probably illegitimate, who became first wife of Luke Plunkett, first earl of Fingall.

Villamediana, Spanish resident in London, suspected Nottingham's hand behind Tyrconnell's visit to him late in 1604. The earls of Tyrone and Tyrconnell had already sounded the ambassador on a possible renewal of the war with Spanish help. Philip III's council of state, which, with the ink on the peace of London scarcely dry, had no wish to offend England, supported Villamediana's cool response. The conclusion arrived at by some modern writers of a plot between the earls and Spain is untenable. Nor did the payment by Spain in 1607 of a subvention to the earls constitute a conspiracy. 'Feeding another's dog' ('dar pan a perro ajeno') is how Gondomar, who disliked it, termed this commonplace practice (P. Aguado Bleye, *Manual de historia de España*, t. 2: *Reyes Católicos—Casa de Austria*, 8th edn, Madrid, 1959, 718).

A hollow patent Tyrconnell's patent made him tenant-in-chief of co. Donegal in as ample a manner as any of his ancestors had enjoyed Tyrconnell, with remainder to Caffar, but excluded from the patent were: overlordship of Inishowen (granted to Sir Cahir O'Doherty) and of co. Sligo; Derry (which received an urban charter in July 1604), with the Foyle fishings; the land, at least 12,900 acres, and castles of the Finn valley (allotted to Niall Garbh); and the castle and town of Ballyshannon, with which also went the Erne fishery and a (conservatively) estimated 1000 acres adjoining. A network of government strongholds controlled the Swilly and the way into co. Tyrone and Connaught. Valuable lands, both demesne and mensal, were wrested from Tyrconnell, and the government commissioners apportioned freeholds throughout the county. In 1605 he was forced to acknowledge (contrary to the chief's ancient rights, lately confirmed) that the three MacSweeneys and O'Boyle held independently of him. Servitors availed of one device or another—general grants or declaration of both monastic lands and fishings as royal property—to enrich themselves at Tyrconnell's expense. Thus Sir Henry Folliott, already holding Ballyshannon and its fisheries, acquired extensive further lands and fisheries in Tirhugh. At the other end of Donegal, Sir Ralph Bingley came by the Rathmullan and Kilmacrenan abbey lands, together with Inch

Island and the Swilly fishings. Donegal again and co. Tyrone had sheriffs by 1603, and Donegal saw its first assize sittings in that year. Richard Bingley received the grant of the customs of Derry and Ballyshannon ports. Such severe restrictions on his patent made Tyrconnell's appointment as lord lieutenant of the county in 1605 quite hollow. Finally James I's bishop of Derry, Raphoe, and Clogher, George Montgomery, was working to appropriate, again contrary to ancient law, the ownership of all church and monastic lands.

Ralph Bingley, at the considerable price of £1600, Tyrconnell later asserted, sold him the Kilmacrenan lands, 29,000 acres, with some smaller lots. But Bingley's tenant remained on the Kilmacrenan holding, paying no rent. The recovery of Doe Castle in 1607 was also at the cost of Tyrconnell, as lord lieutenant, while Chichester put Bingley into the fortress, making Tyrconnell grant him a lease. Tyrconnell was now left with just two castles, Donegal and nearby Lough Eske. In April 1607 King Philip made a sum of 8000 ducats available in equal shares to Tyrone and Tyrconnell. But there was no promise of an annuity, and Tyrconnell's share (about £1250 in contemporary terms) would go only in part to cover debts he had incurred when forced to mortgage a considerable portion of his land to Dublin merchants. Chichester himself estimated that his debts left Tyrconnell no better revenue than £300 a year.

The flight of the earls On 4 September 1607 a shipload of about ninety people, including the earls of Tyrconnell and Tyrone and Cuconnacht Maguire, sailed from Rathmullan, on the Swilly, bound for Spain. Tyrconnell and Maguire (apportioned only part of co. Fermanagh) were both disappointed men and planned, it seems clear, to abandon Ireland. Tyrone in vain advised Tyrconnell first to seek royal leave. About mid-May 1607 Maguire left for the Netherlands. There Father Florence Conry informed him that James I would certainly arrest Tyrone should he go to London to press his claim that he held ownership in fee of O'Kane's country, and that Tyrconnell would be taken in Ireland. While these arrests were more possible than probable, Maguire, probably in August, sent urgent warning to the earls and the archdukes were concerned enough to finance his hire of a ship. When he arrived unexpectedly, Tyrconnell and even Tyrone were ready to go, hoping it seems to return with an army (of which Henry O'Neill's regiment would be the backbone) or else of securing through Spanish intercession reversal by James of the Anglicizing and protestantizing policies his Irish ministers now followed in Ulster. Tyrconnell took with him his son Hugh, less than a year old, in his haste leaving his pregnant countess behind in Kildare. His sister, Nuala, who had left her husband, Niall Garbh, when he deserted to the English, and Caffar and his wife, Rose, sailed also. Equinoctial gales drove the ship to land, not in Spain, but at Quilleboeuf, in the mouth of the Seine.

The 'flight of the earls' caught the Dublin administration unawares. Lord Howth had, at tedious length and without impressing Salisbury or Chichester overmuch, given information of a conspiracy involving Tyrconnell, Maguire, Lord Delvin and others. Later Delvin would report that Tyrconnell had plotted with him to seize Dublin Castle, a confession that would test credulity by implicating Tyrone and Philip as well. The argument that the 'mandates' episode, whereby named individuals were required to attend worship in the established church, had caused certain Old English to consider their loyalty and engage in serious plotting with the northern leaders is implausible.

In an extended period of leisure at Louvain over the Christmas of 1607, Tyrone and Tyrconnell set down justification for their flight in separate documents. To James they stressed the high-handed actions of his Irish ministers, Tyrone emphasizing fear for his life, Tyrconnell the pressure put upon him to abandon his religion. But, as Bagwell noted, Tyrconnell had temporal grievances that were real: rights and prerogatives unacknowledged; lands and fisheries allotted away; impoverishment; and seizure of his cattle and horses by the garrisons, whose soldiers were guilty of continuous outrages, all without redress. To Philip, on the other hand, they spoke of an Irish Catholic 'league' formed by them and ready for action at Spain's command. They had, they said, negotiated with most of the Catholic nobles and gentry (alternatively it was with the towns) heretofore loyal to Elizabeth but now disillusioned by enforcement of the recusancy laws. These newfound allies would immediately on receiving some aid from Philip join the earls in a fresh uprising. There had been no occasion to inform Philip of this plan (which is very short on specifics) until then. These plots were no more substantial, as Philip and his first minister Lerma could see, than the alleged confederacies of the mid-sixteenth century, which had failed to interest Philip II or his astute ambassador in London, Quadra. Since then the two Hughs, O'Neill and O'Donnell, had won the support of Philip II, engaged as he was after 1580 in a Catholic crusade, and then of the pervervid Philip III. But now the latter and especially Lerma had been brought to recognize that the protestant powers were firmly established.

Philip then refused the party including Tyrconnell entry into Spain and they had to repair to the hospitality of the papal court. Reaching Rome on 9/19 April 1608, they were met at the Milvian Bridge by Archbishop Lombard of Armagh, who would now advocate peace rather than war with James. By this time Tyrconnell had been attainted, and thereafter his honours were forfeited. The pope showed them every honour, but the O'Donnell brothers very soon became victims of the Italian climate, Tyrconnell dying at the age of thirty-three in Rome, probably on 18/28 July (though his gravestone—presumably erroneously—gives a date two days later), and Caffar on 26 August/5 September. They were laid to rest in one grave in San Pietro in Montorio on the Janiculum. The four brothers, all so full of promise, Manus, Red Hugh, Rury, and Caffar, were gone, each cut off in his prime. So abruptly and tragically ended the O'Donnell lordship of Tyrconnell which had lasted for 400 years and which had had behind that another eight centuries of rule by the Cenél Conaill, the dynasty which had also given ten high-

kings to Tara. Now Donegal and Ulster would experience change of gravest consequence.

Tyrconnell's only son, **Hugh Albert O'Donnell**, styled second earl of Tyrconnell (1606–1642), army officer in the Austrian service, was born in Kildare Castle about October 1606. The blood of the earls of Tyrconnell, Kildare, Nottingham, and Argyll ran in his veins, but O'Donnell was his proudest title. Left behind at Louvain when in 1608 his father departed for Rome, he succeeded as titular earl of Tyrconnell at his father's death. In 1611 his aunt Nuala came from Rome, but her efforts to persuade James I to restore Hugh to his estates were in vain. Archduke Albert of Austria was sponsor at his confirmation, and he added Albert to his name. At the archducal court from 1613, he enrolled at Louvain University in 1621 and in May 1625 was made knight of Alcántara. The following November he was commissioned captain of a cavalry company and he was on garrison duty in Sichem between 1627 and 1630. He fought during the costly campaign in which Frederick Henry of Orange won Bois-le-Duc, was at the entry into Bruges, and in 1632 helped to repel the Dutch there; alongside John O'Neill, conde de Tiron, he also sought to keep control of episcopal appointments by Rome in Ulster and Connaught, with limited success.

In 1626 Philip IV toyed with a project to launch another invasion of Ireland and set up Tyrconnell and John O'Neill, titular earl of Tyrone, as joint leaders of a Catholic republic. Conry, now archbishop, proposed a match between Tyrconnell's sister, Mary Stuart, and Tyrone, something the unconventional Mary did not favour. Finally, Philip decided against expanding the Anglo-Spanish war, cancelled the invasion, and concluded a new treaty with England (1630).

The O'Donnell–O'Neill jealousy was maintained to the end. But Tyrconnell was at last (1632) given his own infantry regiment and proceeded to recruit fifteen companies of Irish. In that year he married Anne Marguerite de Heynin, a kinswoman of the last duke of Guise. They had no children. In 1638 he was ordered with his regiment to Spain and perished when the French set his ship on fire, apparently in August 1642. Tyrconnell consistently maintained his claims to the title O'Donnell, to lordship over lower Connaught and Sligo, and to the earldom of Tyrconnell. He was said to be a polished courtier and an excellent and brave soldier, but without the ripe judgement of John O'Neill. With him the final curtain falls on the long drama of the O'Donnells as princes of Tyrconnell.

JOHN J. SILKE

Sources C. P. Meehan, *The fate and fortunes of Hugh O'Neill, earl of Tyrone, and Rory O'Donel, earl of Tyrconnel*, 3rd edn (1886) · AFM, 2nd edn · H. Docwra, 'A narration of the services done by the army ymployed to Lough-Foyle', ed. J. O'Donovan, *Miscellany of the Celtic Society* (1849), 231–325 · T. Ó Cianáin, *The flight of the earls*, ed. P. Walsh (1916) · CSP Ire., 1603–8 · J. C. Erck, ed., *Calendar of the patent and close rolls of chancery in Ireland, commencing with the reign of James I*, 1 (1846) · *Calendar of the Irish patent rolls of James I* (before 1830); facs. edn as *Irish patent rolls of James I* (1966) · F. Moryson, *An history of Ireland from the year 1599 to 1603*, 2 vols. (1735) · R. J. Hunter, 'The end of O'Donnell power', *Donegal: history and society*, ed. W. Nolan (1995), 229–66 · J. Mc Cavitt, 'The flight of the earls, 1607', *Irish Historical*

Studies, 29 (1994–5), 159–73 • B. Jennings, 'The career of Hugh, son of Rory O'Donnell, earl of Tyrconnell in the Low Countries, 1607–42', *Studies: an Irish quarterly review*, 30 (1941), 219–34 • B. Jennings, ed., *Wadding papers, 1614–38* (1953) • J. S. Brewer and W. Bullen, eds., *Calendar of the Carew manuscripts*, 2: *1575–1588*, PRO (1868) • G. Hill, *An historical account of the plantation in Ulster at the commencement of the seventeenth century, 1608–1620* (1877) • J. Casway, 'Mary Stuart O'Donnell', *Donegal Annual*, 39 (1987), 28–38

O'Donoghue, Daniel [*called* the O'Donoghue of the Glens] (1833–1889), politician, was the only son of Charles James O'Donoghue (1806–1833) and his wife, Jane Frances O'Connell, who was widowed in the year of her son's birth and subsequently married John McCarthy O'Leary. The O'Donoghues belonged to a congeries of interconnected families of Gaelic lineage (including also O'Connells, McCarthys, and McGillacuddys), who retained possession of lands in co. Kerry and west Cork into the nineteenth century. Daniel's mother was the niece of Daniel O'Connell, the Liberator. The designation of the head of the family by definite article and surname was a translation of Gaelic usage. Young Daniel inherited the title and lands in the first year of his life, and was educated by the Jesuits at Stonyhurst College in Lancashire between 1844 and 1847. On reaching his majority the O'Donoghue (as he was called) was generous, if not downright profligate, in his dealings with tenants and others. On 10 February 1858 he married Marie Sophie (*d.* 1891), daughter and heir of John Ennis of Ballinahowen Court, co. Westmeath. Six sons were born to them between 1859 and 1875.

The O'Donoghue arrived on the Irish political scene in the mid-1850s as a youthful swashbuckler. He sided with the independent oppositionists such as George Henry Moore MP, against the Catholic-Liberals who followed the policy of co-operation with the whigs. The O'Donoghue was returned as MP for co. Tipperary in March 1857 following an epic by-election contest with a Catholic whig. With Moore out of parliament from 1857, the O'Donoghue's role was enhanced. Over the years that followed he was prominent in almost every public manifestation of popular nationalist sentiment. Behind the scenes he was one of a group of about a dozen notables who from early 1858 discussed among themselves the launching of an organization to renew campaigning for national independence. In December 1860 the O'Donoghue publicly advocated a policy of abstention from Westminster, thus presaging a move to set himself up as leader of a nationalist movement. In May 1861 he travelled to Boulogne to meet John Mitchel and won the latter's endorsement for a programme combining constitutional and non-constitutional campaigns. However, the Fenian leader, James Stephens, would co-operate only on his own terms. From 1861 to 1864 Stephens used his secret organization to obstruct the O'Donoghue's attempts at launching a public movement. The O'Donoghue eventually abandoned his nationalist project in 1865–6, embracing instead the emerging alliance between majority Irish opinion and the Liberals which came to be embodied by Gladstone. In 1865 he transferred to the borough of Tralee—a less expensive constituency than Tipperary—and

represented it until its abolition in 1885. Although he described himself in the 1880 election as a home-ruler, he in fact remained aloof from both the Buttite and Parnellite movements. He died on 7 October 1889 at his home, Ballinahowen Court, co. Westmeath, after a brief illness. He was buried in the family vault at Muckross Abbey, Killarney, on 10 October 1889. A grandson, Geoffrey O'Donoghue, was prominent among the members of the Connaught Rangers in the Punjab who mutinied in June 1920 in sympathy with Sinn Féin.

R. V. COMERFORD

Sources Burke, *Gen. Ire.* (1976) • Burke, *Gen. Ire.* • R. V. Comerford, *The Fenians in context: Irish politics and society, 1848–82* (1985) • *Freeman's Journal* [Dublin] (8 Oct 1889) • *Freeman's Journal* [Dublin] (10 Oct 1889) • *Freeman's Journal* [Dublin] (11 Oct 1889) • student records, Stonyhurst College, Lancashire
Archives BL, corresp. with W. E. Gladstone, Add. MSS 44412–44495, *passim* • NL Ire., William Smith O'Brien MSS; Alexander Martin Sullivan MSS
Likenesses Spy [L. Ward], pencil and watercolour drawing, 1880, NG Ire. • L. M. Ward, oils, 1880, NG Ire.

O'Donovan, Edmund (1844–1883), journalist, was born at Dublin on 13 September 1844, son of Dr John *O'Donovan (1806–1861) and his wife, Mary Anne Broughton, and received his early education at a Jesuit day school, St Francis Xavier's College. Thence he went to the Royal College of Science at St Stephen's Green, Dublin. Subsequently he studied medicine at Trinity College, Dublin, where he gained prizes for chemistry, but never graduated. During his course he held the appointments of clerk to the registrar and assistant librarian. Having also shown great taste for heraldry, he was appointed aide to Sir Bernard Burke, Ulster king of arms, and carried a banner at the installation of the duke of Connaught as knight of St Patrick. According to Justin McCarthy, when a young man O'Donovan was engaged in the Fenian movement, and after its failure turned to journalism, an occupation favoured by middle-class Irishmen.

In 1866 O'Donovan began his newspaper career by occasionally contributing to the *Irish Times* and other Dublin papers. Between then and 1870 he made several journeys to France and America, and in the latter continued his medical studies, attending courses at the Bellevue Hospital Medical College, New York. After the Franco-Prussian War broke out in 1870, O'Donovan's adventurous spirit led him to join the foreign legion, after Sedan. He took part in the battles round Orléans, and was wounded and made prisoner. Interned at Straubing in Bavaria, he sent to several Dublin and London papers accounts of his experiences. When the Carlist rising took place in 1873 he went to Spain, and many letters from him were published in *The Times* and *The Hour*. In the summer of 1876, when Bosnia and Herzegovina rose against the Turks, he went to the scene as *Daily News* correspondent. In 1877 he went as its correspondent to Asia Minor, where he remained during the Russo-Turkish War (1877–8).

In 1879 O'Donovan, still in search of adventure, undertook, again as *Daily News* correspondent, his celebrated journey to Merv in Turkestan—a daring, difficult, and hazardous feat, with which his name became associated. From the Russian advanced posts on the south-eastern shores of the Caspian Sea he travelled through Khorasan, and eventually, with great difficulty and at considerable risk, accompanied only by two native servants, he reached Merv. He was at first suspected by the Turkomans of being an agent of the Russians, who were then threatening an advance on Merv. For several months he consequently remained in Merv in a sort of honourable captivity, in danger of death any day, and with no prospect of release.

According to his own account, O'Donovan helped mount artillery, and was made one of the ruling triumvirate. He managed to send into Persia a message, which was thence telegraphed to John Robinson, the manager of the *Daily News*. In this dispatch O'Donovan explained his position, and appealed to his friend: 'For God's sake get me out of this'. Robinson applied to the Foreign Office and to the Russian ambassador in London, and immediate steps were taken to effect O'Donovan's release. However, by his own efforts, combining courage with diplomacy, he extricated himself from his perilous position. On returning to London 'the man of Merv' was a celebrity, and he read a paper to the Royal Geographical Society. In 1882 he published a book on his adventures, *The Merv oasis: travels and adventures east of the Caspian during the years 1879, 1880, and 1881* (2 vols.).

O'Donovan was an eccentric, nomadic 'incurable Bohemian' who likened himself while living in London to 'a Red Indian in patent leather boots' (*Fifty Years of Fleet Street*, 178). His London rooms were 'a cross between a laboratory and an arsenal' (O'Shea, 15). He enjoyed playing practical jokes, firing pistol blanks out of his windows, smoking a water pipe, and reciting from Thomas Moore's *Lalla Rookh*. From the window of his Bloomsbury lodgings he shot the hat off a dozing cabman with his airgun, after which his landlady told him to leave: 'this is not a private madhouse' (ibid., 17). He moved to an Irish hotel in Holborn where his ways were understood.

In 1883 O'Donovan went to the Sudan as *Daily News* correspondent, and accompanied the army of William *Hicks Pasha, which marched on al-ʿUbayd to suppress the Mahdists in the Sudan. He wrote in a letter that 'to die out here, with a lance-head as big as a shovel through me, will meet my views better than the slow, gradual sinking into the grave' (*Fifty Years of Fleet Street*, 178–9). On 3 November 1883 the army was ambushed at Kashgil, near al-ʿUbayd, and on that and the two following days was annihilated. No information was received of O'Donovan's fate, but there can be no doubt that he died with the other Europeans. Probate of his will, however, was not granted until 1891, as there was a lingering hope that he would reappear. A tall, handsome man, 'slender, black, thin-visaged, and straight in the nose' (O'Shea, 8), O'Donovan was kindly, genial, generous, and popular, as restless and adventurous as he was brave. His attainments were broad rather than deep. He was a good linguist, speaking French, German, Spanish, and Jagatai Tartar. He knew something of medicine and botany, and was a fair draughtsman and a

good surveyor. He was an intrepid traveller who achieved much, though apparently also a flamboyant poseur in the quasi-Byronic tradition of Victorian exotic adventuring.

W. W. KNOLLYS, *rev.* ROGER T. STEARN

Sources *The war correspondence of the 'Daily News', 1877–8* (1878) · E. O'Donovan, *The Merv oasis: travels and adventures east of the Caspian during the years 1879, 1880, and 1881*, 2 vols. (1882) · private information (1893) · *Fifty years of Fleet Street: being the life and recollections of Sir John R. Robinson*, ed. F. M. Thomas (1904) · J. A. O'Shea, *Roundabout recollections*, 1 (1892) · J. McCarthy, *Reminiscences*, 2 (1899) · F. L. Bullard, *Famous war correspondents* (1914) · *GM*, 3rd ser., 13 (1862) · Boase, *Mod. Eng. biog.* · J. J. Matthews, *Reporting the wars* (1957) · R. Furneaux, *News of war* (1964) · J. Symons, *England's pride: the story of the Gordon relief expedition* (1965) · R. F. Foster, *Paddy and Mr Punch: connections in Irish and English history* (1993)
Likenesses stipple, NPG · wood-engraving (after photograph), NPG; repro. in *ILN* (27 Jan 1883)

O'Donovan, Gerald [*formerly* Jeremiah Donovan] (1871–1942), Roman Catholic priest and writer, was born on 15 July 1871 in Newry Street, Kilkeel, co. Down, Ireland, the youngest of six children of Jeremiah Donovan, pier builder in the board of works, and Margaret Regan. O'Donovan attended national schools in Cork, Galway, and Sligo, and secondary school at Ardnaree College (then the seminary for Killala diocese). After training in St Patrick's College, Maynooth (1889–95), Father O'Donovan became administrator of the Loughrea parish, co. Galway (1896–1904), where he was the model of an engaged priest. He founded a branch of the Total Abstinence Society in a disused military barracks and set about the reinvigoration of town life. His enthusiasm for the Gaelic League, Irish Cooperative Association, and National Literary Society made him a national figure, the plain-speaking patriot priest. Both in articles and lectures, O'Donovan laid blame for the condition of Ireland—poor, English-speaking, and spiritless—partly on the clergy themselves.

Given his head in the decoration of St Brendan's Cathedral in Loughrea, O'Donovan chose in 1901 to employ Irish artists such as Sarah Purser, John Hughes, and the Yeats sisters, some of whom were not themselves Catholic. St Brendan's, heavily financed by O'Donovan's close friend the landlord and playwright Edward Martyn, is a museum of *fin de siècle nouveau*-Celtic decoration and the most notable cathedral of its period in Ireland.

In 1903 a new bishop was installed in Loughrea, Thomas O'Dea, a Maynooth priest who had once disciplined O'Donovan for reading books deemed unbecoming for a seminarian to read. Bishop O'Dea tightened the reins once again; rather than submit, O'Donovan left Loughrea in October 1904. Of the hundreds of townspeople who gathered along the road to the railway station, some knelt to be blessed by the troubled, departing priest, who would never bless another.

Armed with letters of introduction from Ascendancy literary friends, Lady Gregory, W. B. Yeats, and George Moore (who drew on O'Donovan's dilemma for his novel *The Lake*, 1905), O'Donovan tried to continue his life as a writer-priest in London, but as a priest he had difficulty finding employment. In May 1908, bankrupt and 'out of sorts', by his own choice he unfrocked himself. His reformist impulses found a footing at Toynbee Hall in London's East End, where be became sub-warden in March 1910. Months later, while on summer holiday in Donegal, O'Donovan, 5 feet 9 inches tall, a balding, broad-shouldered man of thirty-nine (whose blue eyes under a heavy dark brow looked, H. G. Wells said, like two gun barrels from behind a hedge), met the tall Florence Emily Beryl Verschoyle (1886–1968), the twenty-four-year-old daughter of an Irish protestant colonel. They were married in the White-chapel register office on 15 October 1910. The couple moved out of Toynbee Hall in June 1911, before the birth of their first child, Brigid, in December. Two more children followed, Dermod (*b.* 1913) and Mary (*b.* 1918).

In O'Donovan's first and most famous novel, the semi-autobiographical *Father Ralph* (1913), the hero, Ralph O'Brien, is the single child of a Catholic Ascendancy family in Dublin with a big house in the country; his mother dedicates him to God and the priesthood while he is yet in the womb. Ralph's life is a sequence of excruciating disillusionments with the church but not with religion. The worst comes when Ralph is sent to serve under Father Tom Molloy, a cunning and lustful bully in league with the local gombeen man, a combination of shopkeeper, publican, usurer, middleman, and politician. They conspire to destroy every effort for the improvement of town life, including Father Ralph's Temperance Society. Working with the bishop (who has already extracted the title to the O'Brien estate from Ralph's widowed mother), Father Molloy drives Father Ralph out of town and the priesthood. Ralph takes off the clerical collar, and, puzzled, must learn once again how to tie a cravat.

The novel is remarkable for its varied gallery of priests, depicted alone and with one another. To judge from the indignation expressed in *The Tablet* ('a grotesque libell!'), and the delight in papers such as the *Northern Whig* ('so accurate and so convincing'), O'Donovan succeeded in settling scores with the hierarchy at the cost of giving hostages to unionists.

After the publication of his first novel O'Donovan used the forename Gerald instead of Jeremiah. His subsequent novels tend to repeat elements of *Father Ralph*—the maleficent Father Molloy, for instance, turns up regularly under new names. The subject of *Waiting* (1914) is the difficulties undergone by an idealistic young schoolteacher who wishes to marry a protestant girl after the 1907 *Ne temere* decree which severely restricted mixed marriages.

By 1914 Gerald O'Donovan was a patriotic Englishman with a perfect accent (only the 'o' in words like 'cook' gave him trouble). Commissioned as first lieutenant in 1915, he became head of the Italian section of the Ministry of Information in 1918. There his secretary was the novelist Rose Macaulay [*see* Macaulay, Dame (Emilie) Rose (1881–1958)]; the two soon fell in love.

After the war, O'Donovan published *How They Did It* (1920), an exposé of wartime corruption; *Conquest* (1920), made up of dinner table conversations, and illustrating the conversion of its hero to Sinn Féin; *Vocations* (1921), about Irish postulants without true vocations; and,

finally, *The Holy Tree* (1922), a poetical story of a love triangle in Irish peasant idiom, dedicated to Rose Macaulay. O'Donovan's secret, intimate relationship with Macaulay continued without breaking up his marriage. In 1939 the two were motoring in the Lake District towards Hadrian's Wall, when Macaulay drove into another vehicle. O'Donovan suffered a head injury, then a stroke. It was cancer that ended his life three years later on 26 July 1942 at his home, Church Lane Cottage, in Albury, Surrey; he was attended by his wife and two surviving children, Brigid and Dermod. He was buried three days later at Albury after an Anglican service.

ADRIAN FRAZIER and JOHN F. RYAN

Sources J. F. Ryan, 'Gerald O'Donovan: priest, novelist, and Irish revivalist', *Journal of the Galway Archaeological and Historical Society*, 48 (1996), 1–47 · C. B. Smith, *Rose Macaulay* (1972) · J. Emery, *A writer's life* (1991) · J. F. Ryan, preface, in G. O'Donovan, *Father Ralph*, [new edn] (1993) [repr. 1993] · B. O'Donovan, 'Locusts food', [*sic*], unpublished memoir, John F. Ryan collection · 'Father O'Donovan's departure', *Western News* (15–22 Oct 1904) · *George Moore in transition: letters to T. Fisher Unwin and Lena Milman, 1894–1910*, ed. H. E. Gerber (1968) · J. O'Donovan, 'The churches and the child', *Independent Review* (Feb 1905), 78–89 · H. Plunkett, diary, Plunkett House, Oxford · 'A notable Irish novel', *Northern Whig* (17 May 1913) · 'Father Ralph', *The Tablet* (31 May 1913) · [P. Tomlinson], *TLS* (15 Aug 1942), 403
Archives priv. coll., papers | NYPL, John Quinn collection · University of Illinois, Urbana-Champaign, H. G. Wells collection · University of Washington, Seattle, Joseph M. Hone collection | SOUND Radio Telefís Eireann
Likenesses photograph, 1918, repro. in Ryan, 'Gerald O'Donovan'; priv. coll. · D. O'Brien, oils, repro. in Ryan, 'Gerald O'Donovan'; priv. coll. · photograph, repro. in *Irish Homestead* (Jan 1900) · photograph, repro. in Ryan, 'Gerald O'Donovan'; priv. coll.
Wealth at death approx. £800: will, Principal Registry of the Family Division, London · £31,128 7*s.*: probate, 2 Dec 1942, *CGPLA Eng. & Wales*

O'Donovan, John [Seán Ó Donnabháin] (1806–1861), Gaelic Irish scholar, the third son and seventh child (of nine) of Edmond Donovan and Eleanor Hoberlin, was born in Atateemore townland, Kilcolumb parish, south co. Kilkenny, on 25 July 1806. He was descended from one Edmond O'Donovan of Bawnlahan, in south-west co. Cork, who had settled in Gaulstown, co. Kilkenny, married the daughter of the last chief of a local Norman family, the Gall Burkes, and died in battle in 1643. John O'Donovan's father died in July 1817. In the previous year the family had been forced by a rent increase to move to a farm at Ballyrowragh, near Atateemore.

John was educated at a local 'hedge school' and, from 1821, at a private school (Hunt's academy) in nearby Waterford. In 1822 he opened an evening school at Redgap, in his home parish. He spent a good deal of time at this period with a much travelled uncle, Patrick O'Donovan, who possessed a wealth of folklore and other learning. In 1823 his eldest brother, Michael, went to Dublin in search of employment and John soon followed him. There he attended a 'Latin school' (perhaps Dr Doyle's classical academy on Ussher's Island) from late 1823 to 1827. After leaving school, he considered entering Maynooth College as a clerical student, but instead he obtained employment as a scribe from the historian and commissioner of the public records, James Hardiman. He copied Peter O'Connell's Irish dictionary and other Irish manuscripts for Hardiman, but his employment may have been part-time, for in 1828 he transcribed an Irish manuscript, under the supervision of the elderly scholar Edward O'Reilly, for a patron, Myles John O'Reilly of the Heath House, Maryborough, and he also worked as a schoolteacher. When, early in 1830, he became seriously ill, he was invited to stay at the Heath House; as he recuperated he read voraciously and did some light scribal work. While there, he learned of the death of Edward O'Reilly, who had served as a topographical expert to the newly established Ordnance Survey of Ireland. O'Donovan, who two years earlier had given some Irish lessons to the superintendent of the survey, Lieutenant Thomas Aiskew Larcom, applied for and obtained the vacant post. He joined the survey as 'Orthographer and Etymologist' on 28 September 1830. Before the end of 1831, O'Donovan made the acquaintance of the scholar and artist George Petrie who would soon be put in charge of the survey's topographical department. That year Petrie had purchased one of the autograph manuscripts of the annals of the four masters, and very soon O'Donovan was working both on it and on a copy of Dubhaltach Mac Fhirbhisigh's great seventeenth-century collection of Irish genealogies. This was to result, more than a decade later, in two of the magnificent editions for which O'Donovan is justly celebrated, his *Hy-Fiachrach* in 1844 and his monumental *Annals of the Kingdom of Ireland* in 1848–51. In 1832 Petrie established the *Dublin Penny Journal* and O'Donovan soon contributed the first of some twenty articles by him which were to appear there over the next eleven months.

O'Donovan resigned from the Ordnance Survey in January 1833 but returned seven months later with a substantial increase in pay. The precise circumstances of the incident are unclear but, on his return, O'Donovan was soon the leading member of Petrie's new topographical department, on which a total of some twenty people served over the next eight years. Early in 1834 O'Donovan embarked on his arduous but invaluable series of fieldwork tours throughout the length and breadth of Ireland to study tens of thousands of place names on behalf of the Ordnance Survey. Covering the country, often on foot, over the next seven years, O'Donovan—with the assistance of a few colleagues, notably O'Conor, O'Curry, and O'Keeffe—sent back to headquarters in Dublin a voluminous and most valuable stream of letters (the celebrated 'Ordnance Survey letters'); these dealt with various aspects not alone of the toponymy, but also of the history and antiquities of twenty-nine of the thirty-two counties on the very eve of the great famine. O'Donovan was also closely involved in the production of the only volume to be published of the ill-fated *Ordnance Survey Memoir* (1837). Although the topographical department was disbanded rather suddenly by the British government at the end of 1842, O'Donovan was retained by the Ordnance Survey as a part-time adviser on onomastic matters until the time of his death.

On 18 January 1840 John O'Donovan married in Dublin Mary Anne Broughton, a sister-in-law to his colleague in the survey Eugene O'Curry; soon they had a young family to support. When in 1840 the Revd James Henthorn Todd, assistant librarian in Trinity College, Dublin, established the Irish Archaeological Society (IAS), O'Donovan became the first and most prolific contributor to its publications. (He had already worked part-time for Todd since 1836, cataloguing the Irish manuscripts in press H in Trinity College Library.) Almost every year from 1841 to 1846 saw the appearance of an IAS volume meticulously edited and painstakingly annotated by O'Donovan: in 1841 *The Circuit of Ireland ... a Poem Written in 942*; in 1842 *The Banquet of Dun na n-Gedh and the Battle of Magh Rath*; in 1843 *The Tribes and Customs of Hy-Many*; in 1844 *The Genealogies, Tribes and Customs of Hy-Fiachrach*; and in 1846 more than half the material in the *Miscellany of the Irish Archaeological Society*. Another learned society, the Celtic Society, issued its first publication in 1847, an edition by O'Donovan of the 'Book of rights'. The society's *Miscellany*, dated 1849 but not published until 1851, contained five items running to a total of more than 460 pages, all edited by O'Donovan. His most exemplary work to date was his encyclopaedic *Hy-Fiachrach* (1844), but this was soon to be dwarfed by his greatest achievement, his remarkable edition—including text, translation, and notes—of the annals of the four masters (1848–51; 2nd edn, 1856). Meanwhile, in 1845, he had published the first serviceable *Grammar of the Irish Language*, prepared at the urging of J. H. Todd for the use of the recently established St Columba's College. The only other book of his to appear during his lifetime was *Annals of Ireland: Three Fragments ... by Dubhaltach Mac Firbisig*, published in 1860 by the Irish Archaeological and Celtic Society. The same society issued two further works of his posthumously: *The Topographical Poems of John O'Dubhagain and Giolla na Naomh O'Huidhrin* (1862) and *The Martyrology of Donegal* (1864). In addition to these books, O'Donovan published numerous articles, including seven pieces on the 'Origin and meaning of Irish family names' in the *Irish Penny Journal* (1841), a dozen or so articles on various topics in the *Journal of the Kilkenny Archaeological Society* (later the *Journal of the Royal Society of Antiquaries of Ireland*) between 1850 and 1860, eleven in the *Ulster Journal of Archaeology* (1857–61), and seven in *Duffy's Hibernian Magazine* (1860–61). Moreover, he generously assisted other authors, notably Todd, Hardiman, and Reeves, in preparing editions of various texts and contributed detailed footnotes to the second volume of the Revd Matthew Kelly's edition of John Lynch's *Cambrensis eversus* (1849). Among the works on which he laboured but which were brought to completion by others were: *Sanas Cormaic: Cormac's Glossary* (from AD *c.*900), published by Whitley Stokes (Calcutta, 1868); Edward O'Reilly's *Irish Dictionary, with Supplement by O'Donovan* (1864); and *The O'Conors of Connaught: an Historical Memoir*, edited by Charles Owen O'Conor Don (1891).

O'Donovan in 1849 was appointed to the chair of Celtic languages in the newly established Queen's College, Belfast, having previously been offered a lectureship in the same subject at Cork College. Having no students in Belfast, he fulfilled his obligations by delivering six public lectures each year. He and his family continued to live in

Dublin. His acceptance of a post at Queen's College brought him into disfavour with the Catholic hierarchy, including Archbishop John MacHale of Tuam with whom he had been quite friendly. As a result, it was his brother-in-law Eugene O'Curry rather than he who was appointed in 1853 to the chair of Irish archaeology and history in John Henry Newman's new Catholic University in Dublin. Most of the final decade of O'Donovan's life was occupied with work for the Brehon law commission, which had been established in 1852 to prepare for publication the Ancient Laws of Ireland. However, the difficulties and frustrations encountered by him and his fellow worker O'Curry in relation to the Brehon law commission led to unhappiness and dissension between the two. Then, in early November 1861 O'Donovan caught a severe cold; this developed into rheumatic fever which caused his untimely death, at his home, 36 Upper Buckingham Street, Dublin, on 10 December 1861. His impressive funeral—attended by such eminent personages as Sir Thomas Larcom, under-secretary for Ireland (O'Donovan's former superior in the Ordnance Survey), the president of Maynooth College, and several Church of Ireland clergymen—took place from his house on 13 December to the O'Connell Circle in Glasnevin cemetery, where his grave is marked by a stone memorial. The dimensions of the funeral and the location of the grave reflected the widespread recognition of O'Donovan as the greatest Irish scholar of the nineteenth century; already, as early as 1833, George Petrie had declared him 'the most able and judicious Irish scholar and topographer Ireland has produced for the last century' ('The abbey of Inch, county of Down', *Dublin Penny Journal*, 8 June 1833, 396). The passage of a century and a half has done little to dim scholarly admiration for the pioneering and enduring work of the little scholar (5 feet 2 inches in height) from south Kilkenny.

O'Donovan was survived by his wife, Mary Anne, who died in 1893, and by six of their nine sons, aged from nineteen down to five years. Four of the sons later became involved with the Fenian Brotherhood; the most celebrated of these, Edmund *O'Donovan (1844–1883), went on to have a particularly colourful career which included a period in the French Foreign Legion, assignments as a 'war correspondent' (a novel designation) in Spain and Bosnia, a daring journey to the Merv oasis on the borders of Afghanistan in central Asia, and a fatal final assignment to the Sudan in 1883 to cover the revolt of the Mahdi.

NOLLAIG Ó MURAÍLE

Sources É. de hÓir, *Seán Ó Donnabháin agus Eoghan Ó Comhraí* (1962) • P. Boyne, *John O'Donovan, 1806–1861* (1987) • A. Ó Maolfabhail, 'An tSuirbhéireacht Ordanáis agus logainmneacha na hÉireann, 1824–34', *Proceedings of the Royal Irish Academy*, 89C (1989), 37–66 • A. Ó Maolfabhail, 'Éadbhard Ó Raghallaigh, Seán Ó Donnabháin agus an tSuirbhéireacht Ordanáis, 1830–4', *Proceedings of the Royal Irish Academy*, 91C (1991), 73–103 • C. Swift, 'John O'Donovan and the framing of early medieval Ireland in the nineteenth century', *Bullán: An Irish Studies Journal*, 1/1 (1994), 91–103 • N. Ó. Muraíle, *The celebrated antiquary: Dubhaltach Mac Fhirbhisigh (c. 1600–1671)* (1996); repr. (2002), 318–30 • N. Ó Muraíle, 'Seán Ó Donnabháin, "An Cúigiú Máistir"', *Scoláirí Gaeilge XXVII: Léachtaí Cholm Cille*, ed. R. Ó hUiginn (1997), 11–82

Archives NL Ire., corresp. • NRA, priv. coll., letters • TCD, letters • University College, Dublin, corresp. | Bodl. Oxf., corresp. with Sir Thomas Phillipps • NL Ire., letters to James O'Donovan • NL Ire., letters to W.S. O'Brien; letters to George Petrie; letters to Jeremiah O'Donovan Rossa; letters to J. H. Todd; corresp. with Sir William Wilde and Douglas MacCarthy Glas • PRO NIre., Wyndham-Quinn MSS • Royal Irish Acad., letters to James Graves; letters to John Hardiman; letters relating to ordnance survey; corresp. with M. J. O'Reilly • St Patrick's College, Maynooth, letters relating to ordnance survey • University of Limerick Library, corresp. with George Petrie and Lord Dunraven

Likenesses C. Grey, oils, 1838, NG Ire. • B. Mulrennan, portrait, 1856, NG Ire.

Wealth at death under £570: administration with will, 1 April 1862, *CGPLA Ire.*

O'Donovan, Michael Francis Xavier [*pseud.* Frank O'Connor] (**1903–1966**), writer, was born on 17 September 1903 above a shop on Douglas Street, Cork, the only child of Michael (Mick) O'Donovan (1869–1942), soldier and labourer, and his wife, Mary Theresa, *née* O'Connor (1865–1952), a domestic worker and shopkeeper. Mary O'Connor was born in Cork. She became an orphan at an early age when her father was killed in a brewery accident and her mother sent to an asylum. Mick O'Donovan was born in Donnybrook but grew up in the Barrack Stream area of Cork. An unskilled labourer, he joined the Munster fusiliers at nineteen and was serving in South Africa at the time of O'Donovan's birth. During the First World War he re-enlisted. Michael O'Donovan's childhood and adolescence were marked by poverty. His mother was loving and reliable, but his father drank to excess, behaved violently toward his wife, and after being discharged from the fusiliers, was chronically unemployed.

In Cork, O'Donovan's education began at Strawberry Hill School, near Blarney Lane, and continued at the St Patrick's national school near St Luke's Crossing. He was a precocious reader. In one autobiography, *An Only Child* (1961), he describes himself as 'a mother's boy' who was physically frail and shy but emotionally intense. He suffered periodically from ailments of the stomach and lungs throughout his life.

One of O'Donovan's teachers at St Patrick's, Daniel Corkery, influenced the young man enormously, introducing him to the study of Irish language and culture. Because of chronic illness, O'Donovan withdrew from St Patrick's for several months and did not return after he recovered. However, he remained in contact with Corkery, who later encouraged his interest in Irish republicanism and supported his budding literary aspirations. He continued his formal education, which ended when he was fourteen, at the Monastery of Our Lady's Mount under the tutelage of the Christian brothers.

After the Easter rising in 1916, O'Donovan became involved in republican political groups. In 1918 he enlisted in the 1st brigade of the Irish Republican Army, serving as a courier and helping to write and distribute pamphlets. In that year he met Sean O'Faolain, who also belonged to the 1st brigade. Like O'Donovan, O'Faolain became a well-known writer; the two men were lifelong friends.

Michael Francis Xavier O'Donovan (1903–1966), by Alfred A. Knopf

In 1922 civil war broke out between supporters and opponents of the treaty with Britain establishing an Irish free state. O'Donovan was among the opponents. Carrying political documents, he was arrested by 'free state' soldiers in February 1923. Had he also been carrying a gun, he would have been subject to execution. He was held first in the women's gaol in the town of Sunday's Well but was soon transferred to an internment camp in Gormanstown, outside Dublin. He was released late in December 1923 a few months before a general amnesty was declared. Although O'Donovan remained a supporter of Irish independence from Britain, his internment caused him to doubt the efficacy and leadership of the Irish Republican Army and to become less idealistic about politics.

Because of his participation in the 1st brigade, O'Donovan had difficulty finding work after his release from the Gormanstown camp. Eventually his former teacher Daniel Corkery arranged for him to be trained as a librarian. A librarians' conference was the occasion of his first trip outside Ireland and to London (spring 1924). Between 1924 and 1927 he served effectively as a librarian in Sligo, Wicklow, and Dublin. He also used the new vocation to continue his education, reading voraciously, and he began seriously to write verse and translate Irish poetry. He did not officially retire from the library service until 1938.

While serving as a librarian in Wicklow and Dublin, O'Donovan became friends with George Russell, who—

under the pseudonym AE—edited the *Irish Statesman* and published poetry and essays. Russell mentored O'Donovan, introducing him to William Butler Yeats in 1926 and publishing many of O'Donovan's early poems and translations in the *Statesman*, including a translation of 'Suibne Geilt Aspires', the first work to appear under the pseudonym Frank O'Connor (14 March 1925). Thereafter, Michael O'Donovan published under the name—and consequently became known as—Frank O'Connor. Throughout the late 1920s and early 1930s O'Connor was among the regular guests at literary gatherings in the homes of Russell and Yeats, and he became increasingly involved in Irish theatre as actor, writer, producer, and director. In 1928, for example, he acted in and produced plays by Chekhov and Ibsen for the Cork Drama League.

The year 1929 proved crucial in O'Connor's life. He met James Joyce in Paris, and the short story 'Guests of the Nation' was accepted for publication by the *Atlantic Monthly*, an important American magazine. From O'Connor's perspective, the meeting with Joyce was anticlimactic; none the less, it symbolized a link between Ireland's two most accomplished writers of modern short stories. 'Guests of the Nation' remains one of O'Connor's best-known and most widely reprinted stories. Its appearance in the *Atlantic Monthly* enabled O'Connor to attract the interest of book publishers in Great Britain.

O'Connor's first collection of stories, *Guests of the Nation*, was published in 1931 by Macmillan, which also published his first novel, *The Saint and Mary Kate* (1932). Yeats's Cuala Press published *The Wild Bird's Nest*, a collection of Irish poems translated by O'Connor, in 1932.

In 1935 O'Connor joined the board of directors of the Abbey Theatre, the Irish 'national' theatre Yeats had helped to establish. During the next several years O'Connor produced, wrote, and directed numerous plays for the Abbey, often collaborating with Hugh Hunt. Although he helped to broaden the range of the theatre's offerings, he had to struggle against rigid censorship, and he became embroiled in several disagreements with other members of the board, from which he was forced to resign in 1939. O'Connor believed that many Irish intellectuals, including his former mentor Daniel Corkery, were defining 'Irish culture' in ways that were too insular, nationalistic, and religiously narrow. While working with the Abbey Theatre, he continued to publish poetry, translations, and essays, but he also began to focus more on writing and publishing stories, some of which he read for BBC broadcasts.

On 11 February 1939, in Chester, England, O'Connor married Evelyn Bowen Speaight following her divorce from Robert Speaight. Their son, Myles O'Donovan, was born on 18 July 1939. A daughter, Liadain, was born on 27 November 1940. The family moved to Dublin in 1941. A liaison between O'Connor and Joan Knape resulted in the birth of a son, Oliver, in 1945.

Between 1940 and 1945 O'Connor continued to publish short stories, served as poetry editor of the literary journal *The Bell*, wrote opinion pieces (under the pseudonym Ben Mayo) in the *Sunday Independent* newspaper, developed an interest in Irish architecture, and became increasingly critical of Irish politics and censorship. His only other published novel, *Dutch Interior*, appeared in 1940. In 1945 the influential American magazine the *New Yorker* began publishing O'Connor's short stories; over the next sixteen years it would publish almost fifty of them.

In 1951 O'Connor left Ireland for the United States, where he taught first at Northwestern University, then at Harvard University. Having divorced his first wife, Evelyn, in 1952, he married an American woman, Harriet Rich, in 1953. That same year saw the publication of *The Stories of Frank O'Connor*, which attracted widespread critical praise. Between 1954 and his death, O'Connor divided his time between Ireland and the United States. While teaching at Stanford University in Palo Alto, California, he suffered a stroke in 1961; thereafter his health remained fragile. He died on 10 March 1966 in Dublin and was buried two days later at Dean's Grange.

In *The Lonely Voice: a Study of the Short Story* (1963), O'Connor describes modern short fiction as a form that depicts the lives of ordinary people at moments of crisis, and he argues that writers of fiction should pay attention to the 'submerged population' in their cultures, meaning persons and groups that are disaffected, disenfranchised, or oppressed. 'That submerged population changes in character from writer to writer, from generation to generation. It may be Gogol's officials, Turgenev's serfs, Maupassant's prostitutes, Chekhov's doctors and teachers, Sherwood Anderson's provincials, always dreaming of escape' (O'Connor, *Lonely Voice*, 18).

O'Connor's own short fiction, which he revised exhaustively before publication, often concerns the lives of Irish men and women who are variously 'submerged' socially, politically, or psychologically. It is also known for its linguistic subtlety and sense of structure. His achievement in the genre is at least equal to that of James Joyce, Katherine Mansfield, D. H. Lawrence, Ernest Hemingway, Sherwood Anderson, Langston Hughes, Eudora Welty, to name but a few major writers associated with the modern short story in English and roughly contemporary to O'Connor. 'What he longed for', observes critic Richard Ellmann:

> was candor, not circumlocution, cards on the table rather than held close to the chest. For this reason and others, he could not approve of [James] Joyce, feeling that when artistic method had become so dominating life was lost …. In him the struggle to express was always involved with a sense of exhilaration, whether he was writing or talking. (Ellmann, xiii)

HANS OSTROM

Sources J. Matthews, *Voices: a life of Frank O'Connor* (1983) · R. Ellmann, 'Introduction', in F. O'Connor, *Collected stories* (1981) · F. O'Connor, *The lonely voice: a study of the short story* (1963) · R. C. Evans and R. Harp, eds., *Frank O'Connor: new perspectives* (1998) · F. O'Connor, *An only child* (1961) · F. O'Connor, *My father's son* (1968) · M. Steinmann, ed., *A Frank O'Connor reader* (1994) · *Twentieth Century Literature* ['Frank O'Connor Issue'], 36/Fall (1990), 237–380 · *CGPLA Éire* (1967)
Archives Boston University, Mugar Memorial Library, corresp., literary MSS, and papers · Cork Public Museum, Ireland · Harvard U., Pusey Library, material incl. teaching material · NRA, corresp. and literary papers · TCD, corresp. and literary papers · University of Florida, Miami, papers · University of Toronto | University of Tulsa, Oklahoma, Richard Ellmann papers |FILM BFI NFTVA, 'Adventures in Translation', January 1962 BBC broadcast · Scottish Home Service Archive, 'Only Child', 11 Oct 1959, Scottish Home Service, BBC |SOUND BBC Radio Archives · 'Frank O'Connor Reads', long playing record, Caedmon Records, TC 1036
Likenesses S. Murphy, bronze bust, 1957, NG Ire. · E. Erwitt, photograph, repro. in Matthews, *Voices* · A. A. Knopf, photograph, priv. coll. [*see illus.*] · ten photographs, repro. in Matthews, *Voices*, following p. 226
Wealth at death £601: probate, 12 Jan 1967, *CGPLA Éire*

O'Dowde, Thomas (*d.* 1665), physician, trained as an apothecary. The only account of his life, published by his daughter, Mary *Trye, says that he had been born into a 'generous' family in Ireland, but that his father's death and mother's remarriage, together with the troubles in that country in the 1640s, caused him to lose his inheritance. He therefore entered the service of Charles I not long before the king's execution, and thereafter became an agent for the royalist cause, moving from place to place, being imprisoned several times (sometimes with his wife), and even (it was claimed) being examined by Cromwell himself on threat of death. Banished from England, he secretly returned to Nottingham and was taken prisoner shortly before Cromwell's death, but he escaped again to join the king, returning to England upon the Restoration. During this time he also began to practise medicine full time to support himself and his family. Following the Restoration, Charles II 'was pleased to give [him] a kinde aspect, from a consideration of some notable Cures' he performed.

In O'Dowde's earliest known publication, a broadside licensed by the royal censor, Roger L'Estrange, on 28 April 1664 and titled *The Poor Man's Physician*, he proudly signed himself 'one of the Grooms of the Chamber to his Sacred Majesty King Charles the Second'. He gave his address as a 'laboratory' located 'against St Clements Church in the Strand', meaning that he had established a chemical practice on the well-travelled road between the City of London and Westminster. The pamphlet promised that he could do great things that could not be matched by the Galenists, including curing the plague in a mere six hours. It also included a list of people cured by O'Dowde, all of whom were well-born royalists from the area around the north and east of Chester, who now had important places at court, particularly in the circle of the duke of York. Since O'Dowde also mentioned in his broadside that he had practised in Derbyshire for four and a half years, and since his daughter related that he spent time in Nottingham, it would seem that O'Dowde had acquired these patients while he practised in the region of the southern Pennines during his period as a royalist agent.

In early 1665, in the midst of defensive struggles by the London College of Physicians to maintain its authority, O'Dowde led an attempt to obtain a royal charter for a rival medical organization in London. He published a 100-page pamphlet, *The Poor Man's Physician, or, The True Art of Medicine … the Third Edition*, announcing in its dedication to Gilbert Sheldon, archbishop of Canterbury, the formation of a society of chemical physicians. According to this dedication, the pamphlet was published 'in obedience to your Lordships, and their Lordships the Earl of Clarendon, Lord High Chancellor of England, and his Grace the Duke of Buckingham's Commands'. O'Dowde's little book for the most part advertised cures he had performed, but its preface strongly condemned the Galenists, and its conclusion contained two petitions: the first, for incorporation, was addressed to the king by the thirty-five men who made up the potential membership of the society; the second, in support of the chemists, was signed by thirty-eight noblemen and gentlemen. The signatories of O'Dowde's membership petition varied in their orientation towards medicine and in their political affiliations, with the exception that they all pursued medical chemistry as an aspect of the 'new philosophy'. Interest in the new philosophy also seems to have been strong among the courtiers who signed O'Dowde's petition of support: eleven of the thirty-eight signatories had already become fellows of the Royal Society. The list was headed by the archbishop of Canterbury, followed by the duke of Buckingham, eleven earls, the bishop of London, a viscount, and twenty-three gentlemen. A large number of the gentlemen were associated with the duke of York's household.

O'Dowde's petitions to create a society of chemical physicians were considered by the king and the privy council during an audience at either the end of March or the beginning of April 1665. But O'Dowde met with his first rebuff at this meeting. Unfortunately, the English state papers contain no references to the interview. The chemists, and particularly O'Dowde, seem to have met with great difficulties, since former chemical associates of O'Dowde's tried to distance themselves from him almost immediately. According to the later testimony of one of the chemists, George Thomson, one or more members of the College of Physicians sent out a spy to gather information on some of the chemists in order to show that they were quacks and politically suspect. Thomson also declared that one 'Mr. Galen' presented the complaints of the physicians to the privy council; perhaps he was the same person who had earlier told the king that O'Dowde was a quack. The version of the meeting written by the College of Physicians' chemist, William Johnson, indeed says that O'Dowde and his confederates were accused of quackery, and political subversion. It is clear at least that O'Dowde was found to be illiterate (that is, without a knowledge of Latin), and that he was also charged with causing harm to some of his patients. George Thomson believed that the admission of 'mock chemists' into the society had damaged the reputation of all the members. The light in which O'Dowde's practice and proposal were placed may have caused several of the better chemical practitioners who had signed O'Dowde's membership petition to withdraw at least some of their support from the scheme, leaving, according to Thomson, only the 'illiterate' ones to support O'Dowde.

The great plague of London, however, made its first signs visible almost at the very moment O'Dowde was proposing the society. Although the king and his council soon consulted the College of Physicians regarding what measures to take in the face of this grave public emergency, many chemists began to berate the physicians for deserting their stations while they themselves stayed on. Soon O'Dowde, together with others, published an advertisement for chemical medicines claiming that these medicines were prepared during the plague 'in pursuance of his Majesties Command'. One month later O'Dowde published yet another broadside publicizing the Society of Chemical Physicians' response to 'His Majesties Commands by the Lord Ashley' to send one of its members to help relieve the plague in Southampton (a particularly sensitive spot, given its military importance during the war with the Dutch): they nominated and sent Edward Bolnest. Despite his sure cures for the disease, however, O'Dowde and his wife perished of plague in mid-August 1665. It was rumoured at the time that O'Dowde and some others had died as the result of performing an autopsy on a plague victim. Because Mary Trye makes no claim to this kind of martyrdom for her father, however, we can assume that her father had nothing to do with the plague anatomy in fact carried out by George Thomson.

HAROLD J. COOK

Sources H. J. Cook, 'The Society of Chemical Physicians, the new philosophy, and the Restoration court', *Bulletin of the History of Medicine*, 61 (1987), 61–77 · P. M. Rattansi, 'The Helmontian–Galenist controversy in Restoration England', *Ambix*, 12 (1964), 1–23 · H. Thomas, 'The Society of Chymical Physitians: an echo of the great plague of London, 1665', *Science, medicine and history*, ed. E. A. Underwood, 2 (1953), 56–71 · C. Webster, 'English medical reformers of the puritan revolution: a background to the "Society of Chymical Physitians"', *Ambix*, 14 (1967), 16–41 · T. O'Dowde, 'The poor mans physician: the true art of medicine as it is prepared and administered for the healing of all diseases incident to mankind', 1664, Harvard U., Houghton L., Bute broadsides, No. A158 · T. O'Dowde, *The poor man's physician, or, The true art of medicine … the third edition* (1665) · M. Trye, *Medicatrix, or, The woman-physician* (1675) · 'Two letters concerning the cure of plague', July 1665, Harvard U., Houghton L., Bute broadsides · N. Hodges, *Vindiciæ medicinæ et medicorum* (1666) · G. Thomson, *Galeno-Pale, or, A chymical trial of the Galenists* (1665) · G. Thomson, *Loimotomia, or, The pest anatomized* (1666) · G. Thomson, *'Plano-Pnigmos', or, A gag of Johnson* (1665) · W. Johnson, *'Agurto-Mastix', or, Some brief animadversions upon two late treatises* (1666) · H. Ellis, ed., *Original letters illustrative of English history*, 2nd ser., 4 (1827), 35–8 [J. Tillison to Dr. Sancroft, 14 Sept 1665]

Ó Dubhagáin, Seán Mór [John the Great O'Dugan] (d. 1372), historian and poet, was the most distinguished in a line of hereditary historians to the Ó Ceallaigh chiefs of Uí Mhaine, in eastern Galway. According to a tradition preserved in the seventeenth-century Registry of Clonmacnoise, the head of the Ó Dubhagáin family held estates from the Uí Mhaine at Ballinruane and Ballydugan, Galway, in return for keeping a true record of all grants made to the church of Clonmacnoise. Seán Mór himself was scribe of an early portion of the Book of Uí Mhaine (or *Hy Many*, in BL, Egerton MS 90, fols. 20–24) and author of a number of historical poems, the most famous of which, *Triallam timcheall na Fódla*, minutely details the ruling families of Ulster, Connacht, and Leinster, naming their hereditary jurisdictions, but totally ignores the Anglo-Norman invasion and subsequent colonization of large portions of the country. The poem is incomplete, as his original intention was to discuss the whole island of Ireland, and this may have been one of Ó Dubhagáin's latest works. Other poems by him deal with the history and genealogy of the Ó Ceallaigh chiefs, eulogize his contemporary, Muircheartach Ó Maolmhuaidh, while reciting the genealogies of the Cineál Fiachach of Westmeath, give the succession of the provincial kings of Cashel as far as Domnall Mór Ua Briain (d. 1194), and expound a method for establishing the date of movable feasts in the church's year.

Ó Dubhagáin was apparently practising his profession for some time before 1339, a year which saw the earliest datable works by his pupil, Ádhamh Ó Cianáin (d. 1373), a Fermanagh historian and prolific scribe. Ó Cianáin's book of prose genealogies, dating c.1344-5, is described in a colophon as having been copied (in whole or in part) 'from the book of his great tutor, that is, Seoan Ó Dubagán' (Bannerman, 143-5). This evidence for Seán's activity in the first half of the fourteenth century indicates that he was already *ollamh* ('court poet' or 'historian') of Uí Mhaine when the chieftain William Ó Ceallaigh issued a general invitation to the bardic classes of all Ireland to attend a Christmas feast at his residence in 1351, perhaps under Ó Dubhagáin's influence, since it was the first time the host to such a gathering had not been a member of the learned classes himself. About 1365 Ó Dubhagáin retired 'from the delights of the world' to spend his declining years at the priory of St John the Baptist (Crutched Friars) at Rindown, Roscommon. On his death in 1372 he was described in the annals as *ardsheanchaidh na hÉireann* ('chief historian of Ireland').   KATHARINE SIMMS

Sources J. Bannerman, 'Senchus Fer n-Alban [pt 1]', *Celtica*, 7 (1966), 143-5 · J. Carney, ed., *Topographical poems by Seaán Mór Ó Duthagáin and Giolla-na-Naomh Ó hUidhrín* (1943), vii-xi · F. Henry and G. Marsh-Micheli, 'Manuscripts and illuminations, 1169-1603', *A new history of Ireland*, ed. T. W. Moody and others, 2: *Medieval Ireland, 1169-1534* (1987), 792-3; repr. with corrections (1993) · A. Gwynn and R. N. Hadcock, *Medieval religious houses: Ireland* (1970), 215-16 · A. M. Freeman, ed. and trans., *Annála Connacht / The annals of Connacht* (1944); repr. (1970), 306, 340 · W. M. Hennessy and B. MacCarthy, eds., *Annals of Ulster, otherwise, annals of Senat*, 4 vols. (1887-1901), vol. 2, pp. 546-7 · E. Knott, 'Filidh Éireann go hAointeach', *Ériu*, 5 (1911), 50-69 · D. Murphy, ed., *The annals of Clonmacnoise*, trans. C. Mageoghagan (1896); facs. edn (1993), 298 · T. Ó Donnchadha, ed., *An Leabhar Muimhneach* (1940), 412-25 · M. E. Dobbs, 'Cenel Fiachach m Néill', *Zeitschrift für Celtische Philologie*, 21 (1938-9), 1-23

Archives BL, Egerton MS 90, fols. 20-24

O'Duffy, Eimar Ultan (1893-1935), writer and political economist, was born on 29 September 1893 at 26 Gardiner Place, Dublin, the elder son of Kevin Emmet O'Duffy, a prominent dentist, and his wife, Pauline, *née* Campbell. His grandfather John O'Duffy had been the founder (with others) of the Dublin Dental Hospital, while his father would become dentist-in-ordinary to the lord lieutenant of Ireland, which gave the family entry to Dublin Castle society. His grandfather's house was on fashionable Rutland Square (now Parnell Square), and Eimar too was reared in a large Georgian mansion, 85 Harcourt Street.

Eimar Ultan O'Duffy (1893-1935), by Lafayette, 1926

The scenes of childhood in his novel *The Wasted Island* (1920) reflect in detail the atmosphere of this period of his life.

Eimar was sent in 1903 to the Jesuit school Stonyhurst College, Lancashire, where many upper-class Irish Catholics sent their sons to be educated and to acquire better accents. He went on to University College, Dublin, in preference to an English university, matriculating in summer 1911. There he studied for the bachelor in dental surgery degree.

O'Duffy joined the Irish Republican Brotherhood (IRB) and was active in the Irish Volunteers as an adjutant with the 2nd battalion. He was also director of supply and communications for the Dublin brigade. His slight British accent was resented by some. He wrote 'A military causerie' for the republican movement's weekly paper, the *National Volunteer*, from 6 October 1914.

With the outbreak of the First World War in August 1914 O'Duffy's father threatened to disown both sons if they did not join up. The younger, Kevin Emmet O'Duffy, was commissioned in September 1914 but Eimar refused to join the British army and was expelled from the family home. From now until 1920 he lived in lodgings in the Rathmines area.

At college O'Duffy was known for his light satirical topical verse and for his contributions to the Literary and Historical Society, the college debating forum, where he won a silver medal for debating in 1915-16. He had his early plays—*The Walls of Athens*, *The Phoenix on the Roof*, and

Bricriu's Feast—produced by Edward Martyn's Irish Theatre but another play, *If I Were You*, was refused by the Abbey. His interview with the widow of the late exiled Fenian O'Donovan Rossa appeared in the *Irish Volunteer* (7 August 1915).

O'Duffy's association with Bulmer Hobson and J. J. O'Connell, when the Irish Volunteers split, led to his involvement in trying to prevent the Easter rising of 1916. He was one of Professor Eoin MacNeill's messengers in the hectic days before the rising began, being sent up to Belfast by Bulmer Hobson to ensure that the volunteers there would obey the orders of MacNeill, and not those of Pearse and the inner core of IRB members who plotted the rising. During Easter week O'Duffy remained in hiding from the authorities in Belfast. He returned to find Dublin in public and private turmoil. During the rising his grandfather John O'Duffy, then eighty-one, was shot while walking in Moore Street, and died of his wounds in Jervis Street Hospital. O'Duffy's younger brother, by then promoted to lieutenant with the 7th Royal Munster Fusiliers, had been killed at Suvla Bay on 6 August 1915, the first day of the landings during the Gallipoli campaign. These deaths led to a reconciliation with his father, but Eimar was not allowed to wear his volunteer uniform at home in Harcourt Street.

O'Duffy qualified as a dentist in spring 1917 (with second-class honours) and became a member of the British Dental Association. At first he practised with his father in Harcourt Street, then set up on his own at 8 Fitzwilliam Street in 1919. He gave up his practice before August 1920 to devote himself to his writing.

For a period O'Duffy worked as a teacher at Father Sweetman's famous school, Mount St Benedict's, near Gorey, though by 1920 he thought of himself as an author rather than as a dentist or teacher. He published *A Lay of the Liffey and other Verses* in 1918 and edited *A College Chorus*—'a collection of Humorous Verses by the students of University College'—in 1919. By October 1919 he had completed a largely autobiographical novel about the years leading up to 1916, which was printed in Dublin late in 1919. It was published in February 1920 as *The Wasted Island*. Dedicated to O'Duffy's mother, the novel deals with the emotional and political development of a young Irishman much like himself. Woven into his account of political developments was his contempt for many aspects of the Irish literary movement, its lack of ambition, its amateurism, and contentment to do things on a small scale. The events of the rising left O'Duffy embittered at what he saw as the futile gesture of 'schemers'. The *Irish Book Lover* noted in its review that 'the author denounces the falsehood and treachery towards their comrades, of the extremists who rushed into the rebellion. Here, as elsewhere, he is remarkably outspoken, but the whole tone of the books is marked by clear and independent thinking' (*Irish Book Lover*, 11/8, March 1920, 82).

On 16 August 1920 O'Duffy, then living at 4 Williams Park, Rathmines, married Cathleen Patricia (b. 1891/2), daughter of John Cruise O'Brien, a solicitor; they had two children. Further novels followed. *Printer's Errors: a Comedy of Dublin Manners* (1920) satirized many of his associates in the small theatrical world of the city; *The Lion and the Fox* (1921) was a historical novel; and *Miss Rudd and Some Lovers* (1923) was a comic novel set in a Rathgar boarding-house during the troubles. These books made him little money, however.

O'Duffy supported the Anglo-Irish treaty (December 1921) from a Liberal point of view and as a result he was employed for a period during 1922 in the new department of external affairs, then headed by Desmond Fitzgerald. In winter 1922–3 he edited with Bulmer Hobson and P. S. O'Hegarty seven issues of the *Irish Review*, in which he printed his own review of Joyce's *Ulysses* (9 December 1922). It was one of the few commentaries on the novel to appear in the Irish press.

O'Duffy was actively disliked by many. Asked on one occasion to take the chair at the Literary and Historical Society at University College, Dublin, he was barracked by the students and had to withdraw. Justice Cahir Davitt, a college contemporary, recalled that those on the left disliked him because of the positions he had taken up as an editor of the *Review*, while the nationalists shunned him because of his role in 1916 and for his opinions in *The Wasted Island*.

O'Duffy's short sharp manner was due in large part to the ulcer which he developed as a young man. Yet to Cahir Davitt he was 'a quiet little man whom I knew only as an ex-schoolmaster who had published some poems, one of them worthy of more notice than it has received'.

The O'Duffys were living in Daffodil Cottage, Orwell Road, Rathgar, when in late 1924 O'Duffy lost his job in external affairs. That autumn, early in October, a few weeks after the birth of their daughter, they left Ireland and moved to Paris, where O'Duffy had taken a post on the night staff of the European edition of the *Chicago Tribune*. They lived in an apartment in the rue Byron, in the 8th *arrondissement*, behind the Étoile. In summer 1926 O'Duffy obtained a post in the Liberal publications department (then at 41 Parliament Street, London). The family lived first at 82 Woodland Gardens, Muswell Hill, and then at 25 Leaside Avenue, Fortis Green, a short distance away.

After three years in preparation, the first of O'Duffy's Cuanduine trilogy, his satire on modern Ireland, was published in 1926. *King Goshawk and the Birds* was a critical success and immediately reprinted. In 1927 a short play, *Romulus and Remus*, was published under his pen-name Oliver Sidgwick in a volume entitled *Short Plays for Small Stages*, produced by the Liberal publications department. The second volume of the Cuanduine trilogy, *The Spacious Adventures of the Man in the Street*, appeared in 1928, while a revised version of *The Wasted Island* was published in 1929.

Between summer 1929 and autumn 1931 O'Duffy turned from literature to journalism. He was a publicity agent to the Lloyd George Liberals (1931–5) for a period, but not in any way that brought him personally to the public attention. Indeed his support of the group made him redundant at the Liberal publications office. A political pamphlet poem, *National Christmas*, was published in a limited edition of a hundred signed copies at Christmas 1931 by Blue Moon Books. Yet he was popular among the Irish colony in London and wide journalistic connections as he 'wrote in a sparkling style on the most abstruse problems of economics and finance' (*Irish Times*).

It was while working out his satires that O'Duffy developed his ideas of financial reform and he became absorbed with the money theories of the social credit apostle Major C. H. Douglas. Social credit appealed to O'Duffy and many others between the wars as providing an escape from the morass of depression and poverty without resort to nationalization or socialism. In his enthusiasm O'Duffy published a series of books on financial and social reform: *Life and Money* in 1932, *Machinery: Captor or Liberator?*, *The Procrustean Fallacy*, and *The Leisure State*, all in 1932. He was a founder member of both the Leisure Society and the Prosperity League. In 1934 he made a very successful lecture tour of various towns in Norway at the invitation of a Norwegian businessmen's group interested in social credit.

At the end of 1931 the O'Duffys moved out of London to 65 Kings Road, Byfleet, near Cobham, in Surrey. At this time O'Duffy acted as a reader for various publishers and he also published a series of detective thrillers: *The Bird Cage* (1932), *The Secret Enemy* (1933), and *Head of a Girl* (1935). These did not do much to retrieve a literary reputation already in decline. He was also working on a musical comedy in three acts which was to be called 'Let's be Modern'. The last of the Cuanduine trilogy, *Asses in Clover*, was published in 1933. He finished what was to be his final novel, the thriller *Head of a Girl*, at Byfleet in October 1934.

O'Duffy had been eking out a living as a freelance journalist, but the reunification of the Liberal Party brought him back to the Liberal publications office at the end of 1934. The family then moved to 64 Portland Avenue, New Malden, Surrey.

Brian O'Duffy recalled that his father was 'quite short, probably 5′6″ or so […] nearly all our male friends were noticeably taller than he was. He was slim and lightly built' (private information). He had delicate features and wore glasses.

While writing his later books O'Duffy was in almost continual pain. Following an operation on a perforated duodenal ulcer, he died a few days later on 21 March 1935 at St Anthony's Hospital, Cheam, Surrey. Though his health had obviously been failing, his sudden death 'was a loss almost as unexpected as it was widely lamented' (*New English Weekly*). His remains were interred in the cemetery at Morden, Surrey. He was survived by his wife.

Though it had been announced for publication in 1934, an autobiographical book, 'The portrait gallery', which contained some unflattering remarks about friends and relatives, was withdrawn by his own wish and the materials later destroyed. After his death O'Duffy's books went quickly out of print and interest in him did not revive until the 1960s. O'Duffy's was an uneven career. Dying in his early forties, O'Duffy had hardly fulfilled his promise, and even his admirers have to admit that his reputation rests precariously on the trilogy of Cuanduine satires, on his plays, and most of all on *The Wasted Island*, which though flawed was one of the most moving recreations of developments in Ireland during the years between 1900 and 1916. To his political friends in the social credit movement Eimar O'Duffy had been 'a highly valued and spirited colleague' (private information); and despite his faults and his early death, he survives as one of the most significant Irish writers of the later years of the Irish literary revival.   PETER COSTELLO

Sources private information (2004) · b. cert. · m. cert. · d. cert. · *CGPLA Eng. & Wales* (1935) · *Irish Times* (22 March 1935) · *New English Weekly*, 6/24 (28 March 1935), 489 · *WWW*, 1929–40 · R. Hogan, *Eimar O'Duffy* (1972) · R. Hogan, ed., *Journal of Irish Literature*, 7 (1978) [special O'Duffy issue]
Archives National State Archives, Brussels, corresp. and literary papers · NL Ire., papers | BL, corresp. with Macmillans, Add. MS 55013 · TCD, corresp. with A. C. Garrad and papers
Likenesses Lafayette, photograph, 1926, NPG [*see illus.*]
Wealth at death £149 18s. 9d.: probate, 11 May 1935, *CGPLA Eng. & Wales*

O'Duffy, Eoin (1890–1944), Irish revolutionary and politician, was born on 28 January 1890 in Cargaghdoo, near Castleblayney, co. Monaghan, the fifth son and youngest of the seven children of Owen Duffy (c.1837–1915), farmer, and his wife, Bridget Fealy (c.1854–1902). O'Duffy was educated at Laggan national school and Laragh national school in Monaghan. In 1910 he was appointed a clerk (later assistant surveyor) in the Monaghan county surveyor's office. O'Duffy was a prominent figure in the Gaelic Athletic Association (GAA), a fertile breeding ground for nationalist revolutionaries, holding various offices between 1912 and 1921 including secretary of the Monaghan county board, secretary of the Ulster council and GAA central council member. He held the honorary position of Ulster council treasurer and was an influential figure on the GAA central council between 1921 and 1934.

In 1917 O'Duffy joined Sinn Féin, which was rapidly reviving in the wake of the 1916 Easter rising, and was subsequently appointed secretary of the north Monaghan *comhairle ceantair* (constituency organization). In mid-1917 O'Duffy joined the Irish Volunteers (later known as the IRA) in Clones, where he resided, and began organizing the IRA throughout Monaghan. Late in 1917 Michael Collins, who was largely responsible for O'Duffy's rapid rise in the nationalist movement, enrolled him into the influential Irish Republican Brotherhood (IRB). O'Duffy later succeeded Collins as IRB supreme council treasurer in 1921. The Monaghan IRA became a well-organized force and O'Duffy gained a reputation for his organizational ability. He was elected commandant of the Monaghan brigade (August 1918), appointed commandant of the 2nd Northern division (March 1921), and appointed the IRA's director of organization in June 1921, shortly before the end of the War of Independence. He was briefly imprisoned in September 1918 and again in April 1920, following a successful attack on the Royal Irish Constabulary barracks in Ballytrain, co. Monaghan. In July 1921 he was appointed IRA liaison officer for Ulster and gained notoriety for his 'Give them lead' speech, threatening IRA reprisals for sectarian attacks on Belfast Catholics.

Eoin O'Duffy (1890–1944), by unknown photographer, 1934

O'Duffy was appointed IRA deputy chief of staff in August 1921 and succeeded Richard Mulcahy as chief of staff, holding the office from January to July 1922. Despite his extreme nationalism and irredentist views on Ulster, O'Duffy strongly supported Michael Collins's advocacy of the Anglo-Irish treaty and was influential in winning northern IRA support for the Irish Free State. As a Sinn Féin deputy for Monaghan (1921–2) O'Duffy supported the treaty in the Dáil and he was prominent in the negotiations to prevent an IRA split in the first half of 1922. In July 1922, following the outbreak of the Irish Civil War, O'Duffy was assigned control of the new national army's south-western command and, with Richard Mulcahy and Michael Collins, was a member of the provisional government's war council.

In September 1922, following a mutiny among the recently established Garda Síochána (police), O'Duffy was appointed garda commissioner. Under the direction of Kevin O'Higgins, the minister for home affairs, O'Duffy's initial years as commissioner were successful. He instilled discipline into the police and secured their acceptance as an unarmed and respected force amid a civil war. His insistence that the gardaí reflect a nationalist and Catholic ethos through involvement in such activities as Gaelic sports and religious pilgrimages ensured that the new force was not seen as another Royal Irish Constabulary. While garda commissioner, O'Duffy played a leading role in promoting sports, serving as president of the Irish Amateur Handball Association, president of the National Athletic and Cycling Association, and president of the Irish Olympic Council. He was an influential defender of the GAA's nationalist ethos, particularly its ban on members playing or attending designated foreign games such as soccer and rugby. In 1932 he led a successful Irish Olympic team to Los Angeles, where two gold medals were won.

Following a mutiny in the national army and the resignation of the minister of defence and senior army command, O'Duffy was appointed general officer commanding and inspector-general of the national army in March 1924, and held the post until February 1925. In sole command of both the army and police, he oversaw the retrenchment of the national army during an unstable period but encountered greater difficulties with policing. From the mid-1920s, as the previously non-political gardaí took over the army's role of suppressing the anti-treaty IRA, O'Duffy advocated increasingly repressive methods. As his volatile temperament became evident in the latter part of the decade, O'Duffy's role as commissioner came under increasing scrutiny. Although an exceptional organizer and motivator, he was rash, egotistical, and disinclined to remain within constitutional limits in his coercion of the IRA. On several occasions serious tensions arose with the Cumann na nGaedheal government and O'Duffy came close to dismissal in 1926 when he refused to dismiss several guards for assaulting IRA prisoners. However, the IRA's assassination in 1927 of the minister for justice, Kevin O'Higgins, resulted in authoritarian legislation of the type demanded by O'Duffy. In 1931 the constitution was amended to allow the police draconian powers to crack down on what government and church leaders feared was a conspiracy against the state by an alliance of republicans and communists. The 'red scare' proved unsuccessful and the republican party, Fianna Fáil, was elected in 1932 despite its links with the IRA. The transition of government proved peaceful although O'Duffy was rumoured to have urged a *coup d'état* to prevent De Valera from assuming power. O'Duffy's hold on his position as police commissioner was inevitably tenuous, given his role in the repression of republicans since 1922, and he was dismissed in February 1933.

O'Duffy's dismissal, and his refusal of an offer of equally paid employment in a less sensitive position, evoked much public sympathy. Supporters of the previous regime regarded it as the beginning of a campaign to discriminate against supporters of the treaty and secure Fianna Fáil's control over the state. In July 1933 O'Duffy was offered the leadership of the Army Comrades Association (the Blueshirts), a pro-treaty organization of national army veterans which shared many characteristics with European fascist movements. He renamed the organization the National Guard and steered it in a more right-wing and aggressive direction. In August 1933 O'Duffy announced a march on Dublin—which some feared might emulate Mussolini's march on Rome—causing De Valera to ban the march and the Blueshirt organization. Fearing domination by Fianna Fáil, the main opposition parties (Cumann na nGaedheal and the Centre Party) sought to unify political opposition against De Valera by merging with the Blueshirts. Despite his low opinion of politicians and parliamentary democracy, O'Duffy was asked to become the first president of Fine Gael. Throughout late 1933 and early 1934 the government unsuccessfully attempted to prosecute O'Duffy and suppress the

Blueshirts. However, tensions began to surface between O'Duffy and Fine Gael's more constitutional politicians over such issues as O'Duffy's support for violent opposition to the payment of land annuities, his belligerent rhetoric on Northern Ireland and his admiration for fascism. He resigned as president of Fine Gael in acrimonious circumstances in September 1934.

O'Duffy's attempts to retain the loyalty of the Blueshirts failed when the movement split and rapidly declined. In 1935 he adopted an openly fascist stance, forging contacts with European fascist movements and establishing in June of that year the unsuccessful National Corporate Party which advocated a corporatist state based on Mussolini's model. In the summer of 1936 O'Duffy declared his support for General Franco's nationalists in the Spanish Civil War, a cause which evoked much sympathy from Irish Catholics, and began organizing an Irish brigade to fight in Spain. O'Duffy's 700-strong force proved militarily incompetent and was ordered to leave Spain by Franco within months. This further political failure fatally undermined his credibility and he declined into relative obscurity.

In 1942 O'Duffy regained the presidency of the National Athletic and Cycling Association and campaigned unsuccessfully for a national sports stadium. Although in failing health, O'Duffy was seen by both fascist sympathizers and Irish military intelligence as a potential quisling during the Second World War. He was a leader of the tiny pro-Nazi People's National Party and had some contact with German spies. His proposal for the formation of a green legion to fight for Germany on the Russian front in 1943 met with little enthusiasm. A heavy drinker and smoker, O'Duffy developed heart disease in 1939 and died, unmarried, at 4 Upper Pembroke Road, Dublin, on 30 November 1944. He was granted a state funeral by the taoiseach, Éamon De Valera, and buried on 2 December 1944 in Glasnevin cemetery, as he requested, close to the grave of Michael Collins. Although remembered primarily for his disastrous political career, particularly his leadership of the Blueshirts and Irish brigade, O'Duffy's achievements in the early history of the Irish state, through his roles in the IRA, national army, and Garda Síochána, were considerable. He was also an influential figure in the Irish Free State's cultural nationalist movement, notably the Gaelic sports and Irish language revivals.

FEARGHAL MCGARRY

Sources L. Walsh, 'General O'Duffy: his life and battles', unpublished MS, NL Ire. • C. Brady, *Guardians of the peace* (1974) • F. McGarry, *Irish politics and the Spanish civil war* (1999) • J. M. Regan, *The Irish counter-revolution, 1921–1936* (1999) • *Irish Press* (1 Dec 1944) • *Irish Independent* (1 Dec 1944)
Archives NL Ire., MSS, incl. diaries written while in prison and in Spain | NA Ire., Department of Justice records • University College, Dublin, Ernest Blythe MSS; Richard Mulcahy MSS | FILM BFI NFTVA, news footage
Likenesses oils, c.1933, Monaghan County Museum • photograph, 1934, Hult. Arch. [see illus.] • photographs, Monaghan County Museum
Wealth at death £9377 6s. 9d.: probate, 26 Feb 1945, CGPLA Éire

O'Dunne, Gillernew. *See* Ua Duinn, Gilla na Náemh (1102/3–1160).

O'Dwyer, Edward Thomas (1842–1917), Roman Catholic bishop of Limerick, was born at Holycross, co. Tipperary, in January 1842, to John Keating-O'Dwyer, an excise officer and member of a Tipperary Catholic gentry family, and his wife, *née* Quinlivan, of Limerick. A few years later the family moved to Limerick, where O'Dwyer received his primary and secondary education at the Christian Brothers' school (c.1848–c.1860). In 1860 he entered St Patrick's, the national seminary at Maynooth, co. Kildare. He was ordained a priest in Limerick in 1867. He ministered on a temporary basis at Rathkeale, Cappagh, Bruff, and St Patrick's, Limerick, and served briefly as president of the Limerick diocesan seminary before being appointed a curate in the parish of Adare in 1870. In 1872 he was transferred to the curacy of Newcastle West, and in 1874 to that of Shanagolden. Shortly thereafter he was appointed curate of St Michael's parish in Limerick city. Upon the death of Bishop George Butler in 1886 he was the choice of a majority of the parish priests of the diocese to succeed to the see, and he was consecrated bishop of Limerick on 29 June.

In the 1870s O'Dwyer had supported the conservative home-rule movement led by Isaac Butt, MP for Limerick city. His sentiments were sincerely nationalist, but he was troubled by the tactics by which the younger generation of nationalist leaders, especially Charles Stewart Parnell and John Dillon, forced Butt from leadership of the parliamentary party in 1879. As the party allied itself with the land agitation, O'Dwyer's landed gentry background (which was quite unusual for an Irish priest) no doubt contributed to his growing alienation from the party even though he was also committed to land reform. When Rome issued the 1888 rescript against boycotting and the Plan of Campaign, O'Dwyer very publicly denounced the efforts of party leaders to minimize the extent to which Catholics were bound by it. In this way he frustrated the wishes of the great majority of his episcopal colleagues, who preferred to put as much distance as possible between the Irish hierarchy and the highly unpopular papal rescript.

During the period of Parnell's ascendancy in Irish politics such actions gained O'Dwyer the reputation of being a 'castle bishop', which was still remembered three decades later at the end of his career when he startled the country by publicly identifying himself with Sinn Féin. To understand this apparent volte-face one must attend to his role within the episcopal body. During the year or so prior to his succession to the see of Limerick the hierarchy had reached a fairly explicit compact with Parnell's Irish Parliamentary Party by which the bishops agreed to support the party and its home rule agenda while the party agreed to defend the church's educational interests in the political arena. O'Dwyer never trusted this arrangement.

He had hardly become a member of the hierarchy when he was in conflict with his fellow bishops over his acceptance of an appointment by the Conservative government to one of the seats on the senate of the Royal University. By thus compromising the hierarchy's effort to establish the precedent that the two seats they had been promised on the senate would be filled by their own nominees, O'Dwyer demonstrated his willingness to defy the spirit of the rules and conventions which the hierarchy had developed over the preceding generation to enhance its collective authority. His behaviour also reflected his expectation that Catholic educational claims would be best met by the Conservatives.

O'Dwyer's deep suspicion of secularist designs on the part of the Liberals placed him permanently at odds with the Irish party, for whom alliance with the Liberal Party was a *sine qua non* after 1886. This alienation was compounded after 1900 by his long-standing antagonism towards John Dillon, who played a very visible role in the leadership of the reunited Irish party. As the Conservative administration of 1895–1905 was drawing to a close he did make some tentative gestures of reconciliation with the party under John Redmond's chairmanship. In December 1906, however, he published an intemperate attack on the party for its actions on the English Education Bill without stopping to learn that Redmond had carefully concerted his tactics with the archbishop of Westminster.

During these years O'Dwyer was increasingly drawn into sympathy with the younger generation of cultural nationalists, whom he saw as unsullied by contact with English secularism. Redmond may have increased his alienation from the party by declining in 1915 to accede to O'Dwyer's request to pressure the government to honour the pope's recent peace proposals. Although most bishops who responded publicly to the 1916 Easter rising deplored it, O'Dwyer permitted the publication of a letter to General Maxwell in which he pointedly refused to discipline two priests implicated in the rebel cause. During the following year he explicitly supported the Sinn Féin opposition to the parliamentary party. While the political foundations of this decision were discernible in a long series of public denunciations of the party during his career, the theological basis for his support of a movement which contemplated revolutionary violence was less evident to contemporaries. It is now known, however, that during the last year of his life, in his correspondence with Michael Fogarty, bishop of Killaloe, O'Dwyer set out a new theological position on the right of revolution substantially in advance of received Catholic thinking on the subject. He died at the palace, Corbally, Limerick, on 19 August 1917, and was interred on the 22nd in St John's Cathedral, Limerick. His place as the most advanced nationalist in the Irish ecclesiastical hierarchy was soon to be overshadowed by Bishop Fogarty.

DAVID W. MILLER

Sources D. W. Miller, *Church, state and nation in Ireland, 1898–1921* (1973) · E. P. O'Callaghan, 'Bishop Edward Thomas O'Dwyer and the course of Irish politics, 1870–1917', MA diss., University College, Galway, 1976 · E. Larkin, *The Roman Catholic church and the Plan of Campaign in Ireland, 1886–1888* (1978) · E. Larkin, *The Roman Catholic church in Ireland and the fall of Parnell, 1888–1891* (1979) · J. Begley, *The diocese of Limerick from 1691 to the present time* (1938) · *Freeman's Journal* [Dublin] (20 Aug 1917) · *Freeman's Journal* [Dublin] (23 Aug 1917)

Archives Dublin Roman Catholic archdiocese, archives, letters | TCD, letters to W. J. M. Starkie · U. St Andr. L., corresp. with Wilfred Ward

Likenesses photograph, repro. in Begley, *Diocese of Limerick from 1691 to the present time*, frontispiece

O'Dwyer, Sir Michael Francis (1864–1940), administrator in India, was the sixth son in the family of fourteen children of John O'Dwyer, a landowner of Barronstown, co. Tipperary; he was born on 28 April 1864. His mother was Margaret, daughter of Patrick Quirk, of Toom, co. Tipperary. He was educated at St Stanislaus College, Tullamore, and passed the open competition for the Indian Civil Service in 1882 and the final examination in 1884. The intervening two years of probation he spent at Balliol College, Oxford, where in a third year he obtained a first class in jurisprudence. Joining the service in India in 1885 he was first posted to Shahpur in the Punjab. He enjoyed the initiative and authority that administrators had traditionally wielded in the Punjab, and rose rapidly in the service. He greatly distinguished himself in land revenue settlement work, and was made director of land records and agriculture in the Punjab (1896); the next year he was placed in charge of the settlements of the Alwar and Bharatpur states. He was a fine rider and sportsman; he was also highly skilled in the vernacular. On 21 November 1896 he married Una Eunice (1872–1956), daughter of Antoine Bord of Castres, France. They had one son and one daughter.

After a long furlough which he spent largely on examination leave in Russia, passing for an interpretership, O'Dwyer was selected by Lord Curzon for a prominent part in the organization of the new North-West Frontier Province and its separation from the Punjab: he was revenue commissioner from 1901 to 1908. From 1908 to 1909 he was acting resident in Hyderabad, and agent to the governor-general in central India from 1910 to 1912. In December 1912, while Lord Hardinge of Penshurst was viceroy, he was appointed to be lieutenant-governor of the Punjab, a post which he held until May 1919.

O'Dwyer's sympathies were with rural India. He was of the paternalist school, believing that Britain's role in India was to bring security and material prosperity, not to encourage the development of politics or democratic institutions. He built good relations with the traditional leaders of Punjab society but alienated the urban groups, especially the educated classes, with his outspoken views. In his pugnacious book, *India as I Knew it, 1885–1925* (1925), O'Dwyer explains how the threat of terrorism in the strategically vital Punjab province preoccupied him during his administration. He believed in the importance of nipping such movements in the bud and taking early action to stop the spread of political agitation to the Punjab. The firm measures he took against the revolutionary Ghadr (revolt) movement among Sikh emigrants returning from North America and the Far East averted a very dangerous situation in the early months of the First World War. O'Dwyer was single-minded, dynamic, and skilful in organizing the Punjab for the war effort. The Punjab provided 360,000 recruits, more than half the number provided by the whole of India during the war. By the end of the war one male Punjabi in every twenty-eight had been mobilized. His services were recognized by his appointment as GCIE in 1917; he had been created KCSI in 1913.

Much to O'Dwyer's annoyance, nationalist politicians did not cease their activities for the duration of the war and, indeed, wartime conditions—the demands of recruitment, price inflation, increased government intervention in the economy, and concern about the progress and outcome of the war—alienated many Indians from the government, and won support for a growing home rule movement.

Like many administrators O'Dwyer believed that 'extremist' nationalist politics and terrorism were interconnected. He had been successful in persuading the government of India to bring in a special Defence of India Act in 1915 to give greater powers to deal with terrorism. However, that act would come to an end with the war, and there was concern that terrorism, especially in Bengal and the Punjab, would resurface. Following a report by Mr Justice Rowlatt, an emergency bill was passed into law as the Anarchical and Revolutionary Crimes Act in March 1919. This measure was very unpopular and led directly to Gandhi's first nationwide *satyagraha* (non-violent resistance) in protest. Despite Gandhi's wishes, the movement resulted in violence in some parts of India, the worst taking place in the Punjab where O'Dwyer took strong measures to counteract it. In some areas the situation became critical, and there was a fear of widespread rebellion against British rule. At Amritsar on 13 April, Brigadier-General Reginald *Dyer ordered his troops to fire on a very large crowd assembled in a walled area known as the Jallianwalla Bagh. More than 300 people were killed and more than 1000 wounded, according to British estimates, but Dyer did not wait to treat the wounded or to count his victims. It is likely that the casualties were considerably higher. O'Dwyer was not alone among British officials in initially giving his support to Dyer, based on the rather limited information he received on the circumstances. However, he staked his reputation in the coming months and years by backing Dyer, even when fuller information about the scale of the killings, and the fact that Dyer had used the shooting to create a 'moral and widespread' effect among the people of the Punjab, became available.

O'Dwyer was himself in the thick of the action in Lahore: it was his decision to expel two Indian political leaders, Kitchlew and Satyapal, from Amritsar that triggered the violence. He clearly believed that firm action had averted a widespread rebellion in north India, which might have been supported by an Afghan invasion. His decision to implement martial law in some parts of the Punjab was controversial, and some of the punishments meted out by the military were excessive and designed to humiliate communities rather than to punish individuals. O'Dwyer argued that he could not be held responsible for what took place under martial law, as the government of India had refused his request to maintain control

of martial law administration, apart from the purely military operations. In the circumstances, he had used his influence where appropriate to control any excesses. There can, however, be no doubt that O'Dwyer was responsible for the orders given for an aeroplane to restore order in and around the town of Gujranwala. In the bombing and machine-gunning that ensued at least a dozen people were killed, including children. These appalling events coincided with O'Dwyer's intended retirement, which was now delayed until May 1919. He left the Punjab still popular among the traditional élites, but vilified by the rising political classes, whose views O'Dwyer had completely failed to understand or even consider. Ironically, his actions proved to be one of the most significant factors in the rapid rise of mass nationalism in India under Gandhi's leadership.

The controversy over events in the Punjab in 1919 continued for several years. The Hunter committee which inquired into the causes and handling of the disturbances was highly critical of Reginald Dyer, whose military career was now ended. The committee was divided along racial lines on the broader question of whether the situation in the Punjab justified the implementation of martial law. The secretary of state for India, Edwin *Montagu, was highly critical of O'Dwyer's methods, and had to be constrained by his colleagues from expressing his views publicly. O'Dwyer himself felt that the Hunter committee had neither been representative in its personnel nor fair in its conclusions; he believed that Dyer had been condemned without a proper army hearing. His chance to justify his viewpoint came in 1922 when Sir Sankaran Nair published a book entitled *Gandhi and Anarchy* which O'Dwyer believed libelled him. The majority of the jury in the ensuing trial before Lord Justice McCardie found in O'Dwyer's favour, and damages of £500 were awarded.

O'Dwyer served on the Esher committee on the administration of the army in India (1919–20). He often wrote letters to *The Times* on Indian affairs in which he argued the case for continued British control in India, and was dismayed by the failure to tackle the Gandhian non-co-operation movement more firmly. He had opposed the Montagu–Chelmsford constitutional reforms of 1919 while he was lieutenant-governor of the Punjab, and continued to do so in his retirement. He was an important contributor to 'die-hard' opposition to both the 1919 and the 1935 reforms, and continued to state his opinions with frankness and courage. In the end he paid with his life, for on 13 March 1940 at a meeting of the Royal Central Asian Society at the Caxton Hall in London he was shot at close range by Udham Singh, believed to have been an eyewitness to the Amritsar massacre more than twenty years earlier. O'Dwyer's injuries were fatal and he died in the Caxton Hall. Udham Singh was tried, convicted, and hanged for the offence. O'Dwyer was survived by his wife, who had been made DBE in 1919, and their children.

PHILIP WOODS

Sources M. F. O'Dwyer, *India as I knew it, 1885–1925* (1925) · P. G. Robb, *The government of India and reform: policies towards politics and the constitution, 1916–1921* (1976) · A. Draper, *Amritsar: the massacre*

that ended the raj (1981) · R. Perkins, *The Amritsar legacy: Golden Temple to Caxton Hall, the story of a killing* (1989) · *The Times* (14 March 1940) · *The Times* (15 March 1940) · 'Report of the committee to investigate the disturbances in the Punjab, etc.', *Parl. papers* (1920), 14.1001, Cmd 681 · Burke, *Peerage* (1924) · *WWW, 1951–60*
Archives BL OIOC, Chelmsford MSS · BL OIOC, Thompson MSS · Bodl. Oxf., corresp. with Sir Aurel Stein · CUL, corresp. with Lord Hardinge
Likenesses W. Stoneman, photograph, 1920, NPG
Wealth at death £32,393 16s. 6d.: resworn probate, 14 May 1940, *CGPLA Eng. & Wales*

Oengus (d. 834). *See under* Picts, kings of the (*act. c.*300–*c.*900).

Oengus [Angus] **mac Forgusso** [Onuist son of Uurguist] (d. **761**), king of Picts, was also called Angus; both names are Celtic and have Pictish equivalents, Onuist and U(u)r-guist. The name of his father, Forgus, however, is unrelated to the later name form Fergus. Since Oengus's brother, who succeeded him, is called king of Fortriu in 763, it may be supposed that Oengus also was primarily king of that Pictish province [*see* Picts, kings of the]. In 724 the king Nechtan, Derile's son, had received *clericatus* (probably 'the monastic habit') and relinquished the kingship, perhaps unwillingly. There then followed five years of conflict. The first contestants for the kingship are named simply as Drust and Alpin, possibly Nechtan's nephews. In 728 Oengus, Forgus's son, now heard of for the first time, intervened. After a series of battles in which Drust was killed and Alpin driven out, Nechtan was apparently reinstated for some months of 729. But the end result was that Oengus became overking. His reign, however, was reckoned from 731, if the 'thirty years' of the king-lists is to be believed. Nechtan died in 732.

In 731 comes the first mention of hostility between Oengus and a Talorg, son of Congus. The names suggest that Talorg's father was of royal Dál Riatan descent and his mother Pictish. He was engaged in battle, and routed, by a son of Oengus named Brude (or Bridei). It seems that Talorg possessed, or obtained soon after 731, support from Dúngal, Selvach's son, the head of the Lorne family of Dál Riata, who had held and then lost the overkingship of the Dál Riata [*see* Dál Riata, kings of]. In 733 Dúngal dragged Brude out of sanctuary in Tory Island, and in the next year Oengus took his revenge. A fortress of Dúngal's was destroyed and he fled, wounded, to Ireland, 'to be out of the power of Oengus' (Anderson, *Early Sources*, 1.232). In the same year Talorg was handed over to the Picts by his own 'brother', possibly the Alpin (by then part-king of the Dál Riata) who had once held the Pictish kingship. The Picts put Talorg to death by drowning. It is to be supposed that Oengus's son Brude had been set at liberty.

In this year 734 also a Talorgan, son of Drostan, was captured near the Lorne fortress of Dunollie. He too was drowned, by order of Oengus, five years later, when he is described as king of Atholl. Nothing more is known about him, unless he was the Talorg, son of Drostan, who had been imprisoned by Oengus's predecessor Nechtan in 713.

In 736 Oengus led a major attack on Dál Riatan territory. He himself took the great fortress of Dunadd, burnt an

unidentified 'Creic', and captured Dúngal and his brother. A Dál Riatan army led by Dúngal's cousin Muredach was routed by Oengus's brother Talorgan, probably at Ederline near Loch Awe, in a district called Calathros. Rock-carvings at Dunadd, it has been suggested, may be evidence of a formal take-over by Oengus. There is no other evidence of him as an acknowledged king of Dál Riata. An annal entry of his 'smiting of Dalriada' (Anderson, *Kings and Kingship*, 186) as late as 741 suggests that he may not have gained immediate control of the whole country in 736.

Of the latter part of Oengus's reign little is known (the Iona annal source dries up about 740). In 750 a battle was fought between Picts and Britons at a place which Skene identified as Mugdock, a few miles east of Dumbarton, the Britons' chief fortress. Among the many Pictish dead was Oengus's brother Talorgan. In the same year an annalist in Ireland wrote of the 'ebbing of the sovereignty of Oengus' (Anderson, *Early Sources*, 1.240), perhaps referring to the Picts' recent defeat, but more directly to beginnings of Dál Riatan resurgence. In 756 Oengus joined Eadberht, king of Northumbria, in a successful expedition against Dumbarton.

Oengus died in 761. His son Brude had died in 736. A later Pictish king, Talorgen, son of Oengus, was possibly another son. A continuator of Bede's history says of Oengus that 'as a slaughtering tyrant he carried on his reign's beginning with bloody crime even to the end' (Anderson, *Scottish Annals*, 57). It is not possible to tell whether the Northumbrian writer had a special reason for this judgement, apart from what is known of Oengus's undoubtedly forceful career.

MARJORIE O. ANDERSON

Sources *Ann. Ulster* · A. O. Anderson, ed. and trans., *Early sources of Scottish history, AD 500 to 1286*, 2 vols. (1922); repr. with corrections (1990) · M. O. Anderson, *Kings and kingship in early Scotland*, rev. edn (1980), 248, 263, 266, 273, 280, 287 · Bede, *Hist. eccl.*, 577 · T. F. O'Rahilly, *Early Irish history and mythology* (1946), 368 · W. J. Watson, *The history of the Celtic place-names of Scotland* (1926), 105 · W. F. Skene, *Celtic Scotland: a history of ancient Alban*, 2nd edn, 1 (1886), 295 · A. O. Anderson, ed., *Scottish annals from English chroniclers, AD 500 to 1286* (1908) · I. Henderson, *The Picts* (1987)

Óengus of Tallaght [St Óengus, Óengus the Culdee] (*fl. c.*830), bishop and writer, was the son of Óengoba, but was more commonly known as the grandson of Oíblén who, according to a late pedigree, belonged to the Dál nAraidi, who controlled a territory corresponding to the north of modern co. Down and much of co. Antrim. Little that can be trusted is known of Óengus's career. In the late preface to the martyrology attributed to him, he is said to have been raised at Cluain Eidnech (now Clonenagh in the barony of Maryborough West, Laois), where he is also supposed to have been buried. However, this is not supported by the internal evidence of the martyrology, which, for example, relegates the feast of St Fintan, patron of Cluain Eidnech, to second place in the list for his day. What is clear from the martyrology is that Óengus was a cleric—he uses *pauperán* and *deidblén*, both meaning 'pauper' (that is, cleric), to describe himself. He belonged to the community of St Máel Ruain at Tallaght, a few miles south of the modern city of Dublin. To this coincidence is owed his possibly bogus title of Céile Dé, or Culdee, which has been commonly assigned to him since the seventeenth century. As a centre of the ascetic reform of the late eighth and early ninth century, Tallaght was closely associated with the new emphasis on the role of the *céile Dé* (literally, 'God's client').

The office more properly Óengus's, however, appears to have been that of bishop. He is so described, for instance, in an addition to the list of saints commemorated on 11 March in the martyrology of Tallaght, a work composed at about the same time and in the same place as his. Therefore, he would have occupied a very important position, with primary responsibility for many liturgical functions, not only within his own monastery, but also possibly within the whole group of reformed churches associated with Tallaght. Many of these were new foundations and Óengus seems to have been directly involved in at least two of them, both named Dísert Óengusa ('Óengus's Hermitage') after him; one is in what is now co. Limerick, the other in Laois.

As a bishop, with primary responsibility for liturgical matters, and as a reformer, Óengus would have been well qualified to undertake the composition of a martyrology. The text attributed to him, the martyrology (or *Féilire*) of Óengus, survives in some ten manuscripts, the earliest of which, the Leabhar Breac ('Speckled book'), now MS 23 P 16 (or 1230) in the Royal Irish Academy, dates to the early fifteenth century. Previously thought to have been composed between 797 and 808, the martyrology has recently been redated to between 828 and 833. It remains, however, the earliest extant vernacular metrical martyrology, consisting of 365 quatrains in strict metre preceded by a prologue of 340 lines and followed by an epilogue of 566 lines. A prose preface was added to the text at a later stage, together with extensive notes and glosses.

When composing his martyrology, Óengus used as his only source the martyrology of Tallaght, a shortened version of the Hieronymian martyrology with extensive added lists of Irish saints for each day of the year. This survives incompletely in three manuscripts, the earliest of which, the Book of Leinster, now Dublin, Trinity College, MS 1339, was begun about 1151. Based on an exemplar which has been shown to have reached Ireland from Northumbria, passing on the way from Lindisfarne to Iona, this text can be dated to about the same time as that attributed to Óengus.

There are cogent grounds for believing that Óengus may also have been the author or compiler of his source, the martyrology of Tallaght. A priori, it is extremely unlikely that anyone else would have been as experienced as he in these matters in the monastery of Tallaght at this time. Also, the assumption that he had recently compiled the much more substantial text of his one and only source would make greater sense of the claim in the epilogue to his metrical work that he had used several other named sources including 'the antigraph of Jerome, the martyrology of Eusebius' and 'Ireland's host of books' (*Félire Óengusso Céli Dé*, ll. 137–41). And, most importantly, having 'reckoned their feasts' he went on in his epilogue (ibid., ll. 229ff.) to number the troops of his saints, referring by name in the process to several figures excluded from his own martyrology but included in the martyrology of Tallaght. Cases in point are Noah, Isaiah, Abraham, Honoratus, and Benedict.

If, as is suggested here, Óengus was the author not only of the metrical martyrology called after him but also of its source, the martyrology of Tallaght, then he has the distinction of standing at the very beginning of the extant Irish martyrological tradition. The influence of his texts can be seen at work in all later martyrologies belonging in this tradition, which ended with the compilation of the martyrology of Donegal by Mícheál Ó Cléirigh in 1630. Few if any early medieval Irish authors can have been more influential than Óengus over a period of almost exactly eight hundred years.   PÁDRAIG Ó RIAIN

Sources *Félire Óengusso Céli Dé / The martyrology of Oengus the Culdee*, ed. and trans. W. Stokes, HBS, 29 (1905) · R. I. Best and H. J. Lawlor, eds., *The martyrology of Tallaght*, HBS, 68 (1931) · P. Ó Riain, 'The Tallaght martyrologies redated', *Cambridge Medieval Celtic Studies*, 20 (1990), 21–38 · P. Ó Riain, *Anglo-Saxon Ireland: the evidence of the martyrology of Tallaght* (1993) · J. Hennig, 'Studies in the Latin texts of the *Martyrology of Tallaght*, of *Féilire Oengusso*, and of *Féilire húi Gormain*', *Proceedings of the Royal Irish Academy*, 69C (1970), 45–112 · J. Hennig, 'The notes on non-Irish saints in the manuscripts of *Féilire Oengusso*', *Proceedings of the Royal Irish Academy*, 75C (1975), 119–59
Archives BL, Egerton MSS · Bodl. Oxf., MSS Laud · Bodl. Oxf., MSS Rawl. · Franciscan Library, Killiney · Royal Irish Acad., MS 23 P 16 · Royal Library of Belgium, Brussels

Oertling, Ludwig (1818–1893), maker of scientific instruments, was born in Schwerin in the grand duchy of Mecklenburg-Schwerin on 18 August 1818, one of thirteen children and the eldest child of Johann Oertling's second marriage. Mecklenburg, which lies between Berlin and the Baltic Sea, suffered during the Napoleonic wars against Prussia and Russia, and both Ludwig and his elder half-brother Johann August Daniel (1803–1866) emigrated. Johann was apprenticed to Karl Philip Heinrich Pistor (1778–1847), a notable instrument maker in Berlin, where he later set up his own successful instrument making business under the name August Oertling. Ludwig travelled to Paris and then to London with other German nationals, about the time of Queen Victoria's marriage in 1840 to her cousin Albert, duke of Saxe-Coburg and Gotha.

Oertling married Caroline Rowlatt (d. 1893) at St Bride's, Fleet Street, in the City of London on 1 January 1846; there were two children, Henry Rowlatt Augustus (1848–1921) and Amelia Charlotte Mary (1852–1941). In 1847 Oertling was running his own scientific instrument making business at Jewin Street in the City, but by the time Henry was born the family had moved to 13 Store Street, Bloomsbury. By 1851 Oertling was already employing five workmen.

August Oertling's son Friedrich Leopold (*b.* 1831) joined Ludwig Oertling as his apprentice and in 1861 the latter went into partnership with Edward Wilds Ladd (1800–1879) at premises in Bishopsgate and Moorgate Street in the City. Ladd had previously worked for Robert Brettel Bate, and his expertise enabled the firm to expand into the production of hydrometers for the excise. By the time Henry was old enough to join the firm, Ladd had retired and Oertling had moved to large purpose-built premises in Turnmill Street, Clerkenwell, where the firm remained until after the First World War.

Oertling manufactured standards of weight and measure for a variety of commercial and industrial needs; he also developed, built, and maintained chemical, assay, and bullion balances noted for their high degree of accuracy and sensitivity, a tradition that was maintained throughout the 150 years of the firm's existence. Oertling gradually replaced the traditional steel knives and planes in balances by polished agate, and devised ever more effective arrestment systems. These ensured that the beam and pans were always lowered gently and smoothly into position so that the knives on which they turned aligned accurately on the planes and kept wear to a minimum. He produced balances to a wide range of designs to meet the needs of customers. These included private individuals with a keen interest in science like John Bennett Lawes, founder of the Rothamsted Experimental Station in Hertfordshire; laboratory suppliers such as Griffin & Co. and Jackson and Townsend; and science-based firms such as the pharmacists Allen and Hanbury and the platinum manufacturers Johnson Matthey. A rapid expansion in scientific education in the second half of the nineteenth century brought a demand for research and student balances from, among others, the Royal College of Chemistry in London, Owens College (later to become Manchester University), Trinity College, Dublin, and Harvard College (later the University), Cambridge, Massachusetts. He supplied large financial institutions, including the Royal Mint and the Bank of England, and many mints and assay offices around the world including Ottawa, San Francisco, Melbourne, and Madras. Oertling balances were ordered by the warden of the standards, H. W. Chisholm, for the comparison and verification of standard weights by the standards commission. He also supplied scales and weights and measures to inspectors of weights and measures as parliamentary legislation worked to improve standards of commercial weighing throughout the kingdom and from mill to market place.

In 1873 Oertling travelled to St Petersburg to discuss with the chemist D. I. Mendeleyev (1834–1907) the design of his new balance, and in 1886 he made a balance for J. H. Poynting, with which Poynting determined the mean density of the earth in 1891. George Hogarth Makins, assayer to the Bank of England, came to Oertling with his ideas, from which evolved a whole family of assay balances with delicate skeleton beams. By 1893 the finest was accurate to 0.005 mg; they came into use by assay offices around the world. For the banks he designed an improved machine which would weigh individual gold coins and rapidly sort those too light or too heavy into separate containers, and bullion balances for weighing the gold bars.

Sir William Ramsay (1852–1916) and Lord Rayleigh (1842–1919) used his balances but the majority of sales went to more humble customers such as Lionel John Beale of Long Acre, surgeon and medical officer of health for St Martin-in-the-Fields, who bought a simple balance costing £3 in 1847 for the dispensary serving his patients who lived in the back streets of Seven Dials and Covent Garden.

Instruments of such quality made by a skilled and stable workforce attracted attention at international exhibitions and Oertling received the highest awards on each occasion that he exhibited: at London in 1851, 1862, and 1885, and in Paris in 1855. His daughter said of him that he was a most lovable man and as good as he was clever. He died of heart disease at his home, Mecklenburg House, Kingston Road, New Malden, Surrey, on 2 September 1893 and was buried five days later in Norbiton cemetery, Kingston upon Thames.

P. D. BUCHANAN

Sources private information (2004) · *CGPLA Eng. & Wales* (1893) · d. cert. · parish register (marriage), St Bride's, Fleet Street, 1 Jan 1846 · *The Times* (5 Sept 1893)
Archives Birm. CL, papers in Avery collection · National Museum of Scotland, Edinburgh, collection of balances · Sci. Mus., collection of balances · Sci. Mus., medals presented to the firm, 1851 exhibition, etc. (on loan)
Likenesses J. A. A. Berrie, portrait, 1930?–1939 (after photograph), GEC/Avery Ltd, Soho Foundry, Smethwick, Warley, Avery Museum of Weighing Apparatus
Wealth at death £16,496 15s. 9d.: probate, 13 Oct 1893, *CGPLA Eng. & Wales*

O'Faoláin, Seán (1900–1991), writer, was born John Francis Whelan on 27 February 1900 at 16 Half Moon Street, Cork, the youngest of the three sons of Denis Whelan (1861–1928), a constable in the Royal Irish Constabulary, and his wife, Bridget, *née* Murphy (d. 1944), who ran a boarding-house. In the revised version of his autobiography, *Vive moi!* (1993), O'Faoláin described his parents as 'of that class of ambitious poor folk who refuse to accept their poverty and all the natural and easy compensations of poverty' (O'Faoláin, 49). They were equally ambitious for their children. 'Rise in the world!' was the regular maxim of his mother, while his father instilled in his offspring a respect for Britain and the crown. Given such a background, it was not surprising that John and his father felt a sense of betrayal when Pádraig Pearse and his compatriots engineered the Easter rising in Dublin in 1916. The loyalty of the Whelans was to the army fighting in Flanders and France, but when the British executed fifteen leaders of the insurrection, along with Roger Casement, the teenager's fidelity to the British cause soon flagged.

In 1912, following primary education at the Lancasterian national school, Cork, John entered the Presentation Brothers' secondary school, where he was influenced by his Irish teacher Padraig Ó Dómhnaill. While there he became a fluent Irish speaker, and by 1918, when he entered University College, Cork, to study English, Irish, and Italian, he had adopted the Gaelic form of his name, Seán O'Faoláin, and pledged himself to the cause of Irish nationalism. O'Faoláin's routine studies were enlivened by the renewal of his boyhood friendship with the future short-story writer Michael O'Donovan (Frank O'Connor) and by the encouragement of his teacher, the Gaelic enthusiast Daniel Corkery. The latter, in particular, cultivated his interest in Irish politics, but O'Faoláin subsequently repudiated Corkery's overt 'Irish-Ireland' stance. In the same year that he entered university, O'Faoláin became involved in the republican movement and in 1920 joined the Irish Volunteers (later the Irish Republican Army). Later, during the civil war that followed the Anglo-Irish treaty of 1921, he tried his hand at bomb making, meanwhile earning a meagre living as a commercial traveller for educational books. In 1923 he was appointed director of propaganda for the first southern division of the IRA, based in Dublin. He became disillusioned, however, when he realized that the irregulars lacked the practical skills to create the revolutionary Ireland of their dreams.

In 1924, after returning to University College to do an MA in Irish (an MA in English and a higher diploma in education followed in 1926), O'Faoláin became a teacher at the Christian Brothers' school, Ennis, co. Clare. In 1926, sponsored by George Russell (A. E.), he went on a Commonwealth fellowship to Harvard University, Cambridge, Massachusetts, where he was joined by Eileen Gould (1900–1988), his first girlfriend, whom he had met, aged eighteen, while studying Irish at a summer school in the West Cork Gaeltacht. On 3 June 1928 the pair were married at the Cathedral of the Holy Cross, Boston, Massachusetts. Eileen, a schoolteacher, shared her husband's interest in creative writing and became a writer of children's stories. In autumn 1929, after O'Faoláin had spent spells as a lecturer at Harvard, Princeton University, and Boston College, and after a brief summer stay in Ireland, the couple moved into a flat in Richmond, Surrey, as O'Faoláin had obtained a post as senior lecturer in English language and literature at St Mary's Teachers' Training College, Strawberry Hill, Twickenham, Horace Walpole's former home. There were two children of the marriage: Julia, later herself a noted writer, born in 1932, and Stephen, born in 1938. Although devoted to Eileen until her death in 1988, O'Faoláin had an inherent inability to resist the lure of beautiful, intelligent women which drew him into three intimate relationships: with the Anglo-Irish novelist Honor Tracy (1913–1987), an assistant on The Bell; with the writer Elizabeth Bowen (1899–1973), which lasted from 1937 to 1939; and with the American socialite Alene ('Kick') Erlanger (1895–1969).

O'Faoláin and his family remained in England until 1933, when they realized their dream of returning to Ireland, renting a house in co. Wicklow. O'Faoláin was now determined to make his living as a writer. He had written his first stories when in America and had sent one to Richard Garnett, reader for Jonathan Cape. On reading it Garnett encouraged O'Faoláin to write enough to make up a book. The result was Midsummer Night Madness and Other Stories (1932), a collection drawing on the initial romance with, and subsequent divorce from, national revolutionary activity. The volume was banned by the Irish Censorship Board, but O'Faoláin persevered, and the 1930s and 1940s saw the publication of a succession of historical

biographies, including those of Eamon De Valera (1933, 1939), Constance, Countess Markevicz (1939), Daniel O'Connell (1938), and Hugh O'Neill (1942). The three historical novels A Nest of Simple Folk (1933), its title an intentional contrast with Turgenev's A Nest of the Gentry; Bird Alone (1936), dealing with Parnellism and the theme of a betrayed leader; and Come Back to Erin (1940), took the form of a family saga, spanning the period from the Fenian uprising of 1867 to the Anglo-Irish War of 1919–21 and the years that followed. The theme was the brave individual torn between the revolutionary ambitions of his youth and the more moderate viewpoint of established Irish (later Anglo-Irish) society.

In 1940 O'Faoláin became the founding editor of The Bell, a literary magazine that served as a forum for those whose sympathies did not necessarily lie with orthodox Irish Catholic nationalism. O'Faoláin's editorship ended in 1946, when he left Ireland again, this time for Italy. While there, he was intrigued to find the same moral duality as in Ireland, with its mixture of corruption and petit bourgeois respectability. O'Faoláin now gradually distanced himself from Irish social issues and concentrated increasingly on the short story, the genre for which he is best remembered today. After Midsummer Night Madness came There's a Birdie in the Cage (1935) and A Born Genius (1936). His best collection, however, is generally held to be The Man who Invented Sin and Other Stories (1948), its title story dealing with sexual repression and social conformity. This was followed, among others, by I Remember! I Remember! (1961), The Heat of the Sun: Stories and Tales (1966), and The Talking Trees (1970). O'Faoláin's stories range in style from the lilting 'Irishry' of his younger days to the assured moral tone of later volumes. Taken overall, they reveal a true human perspective on Ireland and chart O'Faoláin's own transition from idealistic nationalism to a more critical and disillusioned engagement with cultural conditions. The Collected Stories appeared as three volumes (1980–82).

The themes of many of the stories in later volumes were often European, so that when O'Faoláin was elected the first recipient of an Allied Irish Bank award by the Irish Academy of Arts in 1975, he was referred to by the actor Michael MacLiammoir as a 'European writer' (Andrews, 233). O'Faoláin himself, in an interview late in life, said that he preferred to be regarded as an Irishman writing in English, rather than an Irish writer. In a ninetieth birthday tribute in the Irish Times, Maurice Harmon described O'Faoláin's life as having two halves: for the first forty-five years as 'the leading intellectual of his generation', and for the remaining forty-five years as 'the cosmopolitan Irishman', whose work was 'the expression of a sophisticated sensibility' (ibid.).

In 'Seán at eighty', a profile written by Julia O'Faoláin for Fathers: Reflections by Daughters (1983), O'Faoláin described himself as 'a bit of a loner … Loneliness—being alone—is important to me. I have to be able to close the door—sometimes for no reason, just to rest. Sometimes to start articulating my feelings through the medium of other, imaginary people'. The protagonist of his novel And Again? (1979) proves life to be worth living by doing so a second time, beginning at sixty-five and 'younging' back to infancy. Tall, slim, and carefully groomed, with a benign, bespectacled face, O'Faoláin hardly matched the traditional concept of an Irish writer, and his appearance gave no hint of the high self-discipline and great deliberation with which he wrote, aiming at a daily total of 500 words. At the same time there were those who were intimidated by what they took as a certain aloofness.

The Italian government honoured O'Faoláin with the star of Solidarity, but he remained unhonoured in his native Ireland until 1986, when he was the first writer since Samuel Beckett to be elected to the position of *Saoi* ('senior') by the *Aos Dána* ('men of art'), the name adopted by the Irish Arts Council (of which he had been a director for two years from 1957) for an affiliation of retired artists. O'Faoláin also received the freedom of Cork. He declined to attend either ceremony. On 20 April 1991, following a decline in health that ended in memory loss and mental confusion, Seán O'Faoláin, inveterate traveller, keen gardener, voracious reader, died of pneumonia in Aclare House, a nursing home in Dún Laoghaire, donating his body to Trinity College, Dublin, as Eileen had done before him.   ADRIAN ROOM

Sources M. Harmon, *Sean O'Faolain: a life* (1994) · S. O'Faoláin, *Vive moi! An autobiography*, ed. J. O'Faoláin (1993) · M. Harmon, *Sean O'Faolain: a critical introduction* (1984) · R. Welch, ed., *The Oxford companion to Irish literature* (1996) · S. J. Connolly, ed., *The Oxford companion to Irish history* (1998) · D. Andrews, ed., *The annual obituary, 1991* (1992) · N. Watson, ed., *Reference guide to short fiction* (1994) · M. Amt, *A critical study of Sean O'Faolain's life and work* (2001) · *Daily Telegraph* (22 April 1991)
Archives TCD · U. Cal., Berkeley, Bancroft Library |FILM BFI NFTVA |SOUND BBC Sound Archives · Radio Telefis Eireann Sound Archives
Likenesses S. O'Sullivan, oils, 1963, repro. in Harmon, *Sean O'Faolain* · G. Graham, photograph, 1972 · M. Moloney, photograph, 1990 · portraits, repro. in Harmon, *Sean O'Faolain*

O'Farrelly, Feardorcha (d. 1746), Irish-language poet, was born in Mullagh, co. Cavan, Ireland, the son of John O'Farrelly, son of Feidlimidh O'Farrelly. The family were 'erenachs', hereditary stewards of church lands. One member of this family had been abbot of Drumlane, co. Cavan, in 1025, and another, canon of Drumlane in 1484. John O'Farrelly wrote 'Seanchas an dá Bhreifne' ('The history of the two Brefnys'), which is said to have been largely burnt by Feardorcha's mother: this incident became the subject of one of his poems.

O'Farrelly was intended for the priesthood, but was rejected because of some sacrilegious act of another family member in 1641; instead he became a farmer in co. Cavan. He was the friend of many writers and artists who flourished in that district in the early eighteenth century, including Cathair MacCabe and Torlogh O'Carolan the harper. He was often the guest of the Mortimers of Cloghwallybeg and their family, who were the chief landowners in the area.

O'Farrelly's poems include one in praise of William Peppard of Kingscourt: a copy of it made in 1827 by Peter Galligan is in Cambridge University Library. O'Farrelly's work also includes such poems as 'Beir beannacht uaim sios go

baile na ccraobh' ('A blessing from me on Ballynacree'), 'Suibhal me cuig coige na Fodla' ('I walk the five provinces of Ireland'), and 'Bhidh me lá deas' ('I was one fine day'). O'Farrelly died, probably in co. Cavan, but certainly in Ireland, in 1746.   JULIA GASPER

Sources H. Boylan, ed., *The dictionary of Irish biography* (1978); 3rd edn (1998) · M. Farrelly, 'Farrelly surname history', *Irish Roots Magazine*, 3 (1998), 8–9; repr. online: www.local.ie/content/27479.shtml [web page] · *DNB*

O'Ferrall, Richard More (1797–1880), politician and colonial governor, probably born in Dublin, was the eldest son of Ambrose O'Ferrall (1752–1835) of Balyna, co. Kildare, and his first wife, Anne, daughter of John Bagot. Unlike his brother John Lewis More, later commissioner of police (d. 1881), he declined, as a conscientious Catholic, to enter the protestant university in Dublin. From an early age he joined in the struggle in Ireland for civil and religious liberty as a member of the Catholic Association, and long corresponded with James Warren Doyle, the bishop of Kildare. After the Catholic Relief Bill passed, he became in 1830 member of parliament for co. Kildare, which he represented from 1830 to 1847 and again from 1859 to 1865. He also sat for a short time from April 1851 to July 1852 for co. Longford, in which his family held property. O'Ferrall did not take the repeal pledge, but remained on good terms with Daniel O'Connell. He became associated with the faction of the whig party led by the third Earl Grey and Charles Wood in the 1830s and 1840s.

In 1835, under the Melbourne administration, O'Ferrall became a lord of the Treasury; in 1839 he became secretary to the Admiralty, and in July 1841 secretary to the Treasury. In March 1846 he warned Lord John Russell not to attempt to return to the style of government of Lord Normanby (1835–9) in Ireland, and urged remedial measures to promote the 'regeneration' of Ireland. He married, on 28 September 1839, the Hon. Matilda (d. 1882), second daughter of Thomas Anthony, third Viscount Southwell. They had a son and a daughter.

On 1 October 1847 O'Ferrall severed his connection with Kildare to assume the governorship of Malta. On 22 November 1847 he was sworn of the Irish privy council. He resigned the governorship of Malta in 1851, on the ground that he declined to serve under Lord John Russell, the prime minister, who in that year carried into law the Ecclesiastical Titles Bill, attempting to outlaw creation of a Catholic hierarchy in England. In 1851–2 O'Ferrall voted mostly with the 'Irish brigade'.

O'Ferrall died at Kingstown, near Dublin, at the age of eighty-three, on 27 October 1880. He had been a magistrate, grand juror, and deputy lieutenant for co. Kildare, and at his death was the oldest member of the Irish privy council.   W. J. FITZPATRICK, *rev.* PETER GRAY

Sources *WWBMP* · O. MacDonagh, *The emancipist: Daniel O'Connell, 1830–47* (1989) · J. H. Whyte, *The Irish independent party, 1850–9* (1958) · *Annual Register* (1880) · *The Times* (30 Oct 1880) · *Freeman's Journal* [Dublin] (28 Oct 1880)
Archives National Archives of Malta, corresp. as governor of Malta | PRO, Russell MSS · Staffs. RO, letters to E. J. Littleton · U. Durham L., archives and special collections, letters to Henry George and copies of letters from same

Offa (*fl.* 709). *See under* East Saxons, kings of the (*act.* late 6th cent.–*c.*820).

Offa (*d.* 796), king of the Mercians, rose to power during the brief period of civil war which followed the murder of King *Æthelbald in 757. Offa was the son of Thingfrith, the son of Eanwulf; and Eanwulf was first cousin to Æthelbald: both the great Mercian kings of the eighth century were direct descendants of Eowa, brother and perhaps co-ruler of the celebrated seventh-century King Penda.

Origins Several records in the Worcester archive associate Offa and his grandfather Eanwulf with the kingdom of the Hwicce and in particular with the minster at Bredon in modern Worcestershire, which was supposedly founded by Eanwulf in 716 or 717 (*AS chart.*, S 55, 116, 117, 146, 147). As they stand these documents would seem to be forgeries, but collectively they may preserve a valid tradition. It has been suggested that Eanwulf may have had some family connection with the royal dynasty of the Hwicce, perhaps through marriage, though there is no direct evidence. One of the suspect Worcester charters has an intriguing subscription of Offa, who confidently attests as 'noble youth [*puer indolis*, perhaps equivalent to atheling] in the province of the Hwicce, not yet having received from God the kingdom of the Mercians' (*AS chart.*, S 55). This is evidently retrospective, but does reveal at least a very early tradition that Offa grew up among the Hwicce. Since he went on to reign for almost forty years, he is likely to have been a young man in 757. He was probably named from Offa, king of Angeln, one of the legendary ancestors of the Mercian royal dynasty. His heroic descent is emphasized in a collection of royal genealogies which would appear to have been compiled during his reign (although probably in Northumbria rather than Mercia).

Domination over southern England Offa became ruler in Mercia in 757 after driving out a certain Beornred, who had taken over the kingdom in the aftermath of Æthelbald's death. The ascendancy over southern England which Æthelbald had enjoyed in the last decades of his reign is likely to have been dissipated or at least reduced by the period of civil war in Mercia. But Offa contrived by military prowess and political astuteness to equal and then exceed his predecessor's power and reputation. By the end of his reign he was the dominant ruler in England and a force to be reckoned with on the European stage, treated as a (near) equal by Charlemagne. His ambitions were huge, and he struggled hard to establish a long-lasting dynasty; but the early death of his son and successor brought ultimate, posthumous failure.

In Offa's hands the old patterns of Anglo-Saxon overlordship began to change. Earlier kings who had dominated southern England, including Æthelbald, seem to have been for the most part content to exercise their authority in an indirect fashion, interfering relatively lightly in the internal affairs of subordinate kingdoms.

Offa (*d.* 796), coin

During the 770s Offa began to operate on a different level, which involved removing (or at least demoting) local kings and absorbing their territories into a Mercian empire. The first to have experienced this new policy were the South Saxons, then ruled by a multiplicity of minor kings. Offa conquered the people of the Hastings area in 771 and the kings of the South Saxons seem rapidly to have capitulated. A charter issued by Offa in 772 was witnessed by four South Saxons, at least three of whom had formerly ruled as kings in Sussex: they are now called *dux* or ealdorman, which indicates that they had been demoted below royal status (*AS chart.*, S 108). From now on their role was to govern Sussex in Offa's name, as his appointees. Something similar seems to have happened in the kingdom of the Hwicce, in the west midlands, long dominated by Mercia. In 757 the Hwicce were ruled by three brothers, members of the established local dynasty. Charters show them operating only with Offa's permission and licence: they are called *regulus* ('kinglet') or even *subregulus* ('sub-kinglet'), and by 777 one of them is referred to as *dux*. After *c.*780 there is no sign of an independent local dynasty of the Hwicce: the territory is ruled directly by Offa. About the other midland and Middle Anglian tribes whose territories collectively made up the kingdom of Greater Mercia, almost nothing is known; but it seems likely that any other surviving native dynasties were treated by Offa like the Hwiccean rulers. Offa seems to have been set on ambitiously extending the territory which he ruled directly, eschewing reliance on sub-kings with some pretence to royal dignity.

The kingdoms of Sussex and the Hwicce were relatively small fry, but the wealthy kingdom of Kent was another matter. Offa took advantage of the turmoil which followed the death of King Æthelberht II in 762, and by 764 he was in a position to dispose directly of an estate in Kent, with merely the meek consent of a local ruler (*AS chart.*, S 105). The situation seems to have changed in 776, when the Mercians and men of Kent met in battle at Otford in West Kent. The notice of the clash in the Anglo-Saxon Chronicle frustratingly fails to mention the outcome. Later medieval historians assumed that Offa had triumphed, and produced circumstantial accounts of his victory; modern historians generally side with the view that this may have been a Mercian defeat, followed by a brief period of Kentish independence under King Ecgberht II. The circumstances leading up to the battle will never be known, but the fact that the clash took place in the west of Kent does suggest that Offa's forces were invading the kingdom, perhaps with the aim of ousting local rulers and imposing direct Mercian rule. This was certainly the ultimate result of Offa's pressure on Kent. The last known charter issued by a Kentish king in his own right is dated 784 (*AS chart.*, S 38; the date may not be reliable); after this there is no trace of any local rulers, and Offa was in sole charge by 785. Thereafter Kent was entirely subject to Mercia until it was conquered by Ecgberht of Wessex in the ninth century, apart from a brief period of revolt which broke out on Offa's death. The leader of the revolt was 'King' Eadberht Præn, a former priest who may have been a member of the native dynasty. He is probably the man of the same name who was given protection by Charlemagne, along with other exiles who feared death at Offa's hands.

It is difficult to make any confident pronouncements about Offa's relations with the other kingdoms of southern England. About the East Saxons there is little information: they still had their own kings in the ninth century, which would seem to show that Offa did not treat their territory as he did Kent, Sussex, and the west midlands (although it is possible that there was a hiatus and a restoration after Offa's death). The one concrete detail about the large and obscure kingdom of East Anglia is that in 794 Offa had the East Anglian king Æthelberht beheaded, apparently while he was attending the Mercian court. Hagiographical sources connected with Æthelberht (who was later venerated as a martyr) lay the blame on Offa's wife, *Cynethryth (*fl. c.*770–798), but it seems likely that Offa had political reasons for ordering the execution. A little light is thrown on East Anglian affairs by the activities of the kingdom's moneyers in the second half of the eighth century: some struck coins for Offa, some for the local kings Beonna, Æthelberht, and Eadwald. At the least this shows that Offa exercised some kind of influence over East Anglia.

Debate has raged over whether Offa was able to claim any degree of overlordship over the relatively powerful kingdom of Wessex. King Cynewulf (r. 757–86) seems to have operated fairly independently, although Offa was able to use his superior military muscle to seize control of disputed territory in the upper Thames valley (*ASC*, s.a. 779; *AS chart.*, S 1258). Cynewulf's successor, *Beorhtric (or Brihtric), may have been more vulnerable. He married Offa's daughter Eadburh and co-operated with him in the expulsion of Ecgberht, the future West Saxon king, in 789; whether this operation most benefited Beorhtric or Offa it is difficult to say. Some hint of subservience is betrayed in the three surviving charters of Beorhtric, where the royal styles are curiously humble and tentative (*AS chart.*, S 267–9); in one instance he is 'king of this province', which contrasts noticeably with the forthright title 'King of the [West] Saxons' usually applied to his predecessors and successors. It seems very likely that Offa dominated his son-in-law.

In 792 Offa married another daughter, Ælfflæd, to the Northumbrian king *Æthelred I [*see under* Oswulf]. Æthelred had had a tempestuous reign (and was to be murdered in 796) and the alliance may have been arranged in order to ensure Offa's support; it seems unlikely that the Mercian would not have made capital from the situation. Northumbria had been politically unstable for decades, and there is a possibility that Offa may have interfered on earlier occasions. Whether he did harbour ambitions to be recognized as the pre-eminent overlord of northern England as well as the south is incapable of proof. Some significance has been seen in the fact that in a small number of Offa's diplomas he is styled *rex Anglorum*, 'king of the English'; in one, from 774, he is even *rex totius Anglorum patriae*, 'king of the whole fatherland of the English' (*AS chart.*, S 111). It is a problem that none of the charters with this extravagant style survives in its contemporary state; all of them are later copies, and many of them are suspicious or downright fraudulent. In surviving contemporary documents, Offa is invariably simply *rex Merciorum*, 'king of the Mercians'. So perhaps the identification of Offa as *rex Anglorum* owes more to his great reputation among later generations than to his own ambitions. Nevertheless, the more impressive royal style does occur in diplomas from several archives, and there is clearly a possibility that it was used by Offa in certain circumstances. It is interesting to note that Offa would seem to have owned a manuscript of Bede's *Historia ecclesiastica gentis Anglorum*; he may have been inspired by the careers of the Northumbrian kings Eadwine, Oswald, and Oswiu, who had authority over both north and south, to aspire to a more considerable status over all the English kingdoms.

Offa's Dyke Offa owes much of his posthumous fame to a single monument: Offa's Dyke, a military earthwork on a huge scale, originally running from the north coast of Wales to the mouth of the Wye. No doubt the dyke was intended to counter insurgent raids from the Welsh, and it may also have played a part in the devastating onslaughts which Offa is known to have inflicted on the Welsh kingdoms in 778 and 784. Its military function is still much debated, and it is possible that its importance lay as much in its symbolic value as a demonstration of Offa's power: perhaps it is no coincidence that one of the remembered achievements of his heroic namesake, Offa of Angeln, was to have established a boundary between his own people and their neighbours. Huge resources of labour and capital must have been needed to complete Offa's Dyke, as well as sophisticated organization. Evidence about eighth-century royal administration is for the most part lacking. Offa's agents must have been able to make use of great quantities of tribute from conquered and subordinate kingdoms, and there is reason to think that the king's revenues were extended by the confiscation of estates previously controlled by ousted kings. In addition, Offa could make use of a system of military obligations set up in Mercia by his predecessor Æthelbald, according to which landowners were supposed to make provision for building and repairing bridges and fortifications, and to participate in military activity or arrange for substitutes to stand in for them. Some manipulation of these obligations may have helped build the dyke. Offa is known to have extended these military conditions to Kent in 792 (*AS chart.*, S 134), and probably did the same in other subordinate kingdoms. Controlling resources of this kind would have enabled him to counter the threat of viking raiders, who were already appearing on the coasts at the end of his reign; at the same time they would have reinforced his military presence in subjugated kingdoms. It is unclear whether Offa's rule of the conquered provinces also involved the imposition of other Mercian laws. King Alfred refers to a law code of Offa as one of the sources for his own legal compilation. This has not survived, and modern scholars disagree on its nature; possibly it was merely Offa's endorsement of a body of ecclesiastical legislation, rather than a full secular code.

Relations with Charlemagne Offa also seems to have exercised a level of control over the ports of southern England, which would have been the main conduits of luxury and overseas trade. The great emporium at London had been a Mercian monopoly since the earlier eighth century, and the important trading settlements in Kent fell into his hands in the 780s. His domination over English trade was such that he could use a total embargo on foreign merchants as a political tool. About 790 Alcuin referred in a letter to a dispute between the Frankish king Charlemagne and Offa which had led both kings to prohibit the passage of merchant ships. Possibly this is the same episode referred to in a ninth-century Frankish source, according to which the quarrel arose from failed marriage negotiations. A match was being arranged between Offa's daughter and Charlemagne's son; but Offa complicated matters by demanding a reciprocal match between his son, Ecgfrith [*see below*], and one of Charlemagne's daughters. There would have been serious questions of status involved here: by attempting to make the alliances exactly equal, the Mercian king was probably intent on ensuring that he stood on an equal footing with Charlemagne, and was not left open to pressure by the presence of a hostage daughter in the other's court. In a spectacular tantrum, Charlemagne barred all English merchants from his realm; Offa responded in kind. Relations had been patched up by 796, by which time the two kings were in correspondence on commercial matters. In response to a letter of Offa (which has not survived), Charlemagne wrote with guarantees for the safety and privileges of English merchants and pilgrims in his realm. He promised to make sure that Offa received some mysterious 'black stones' which he had requested, and in return asked that Offa do something about the length of the cloaks being sent from England.

The commercial links between the two kingdoms are underlined by an increase in the weight of Offa's penny coinage in the 790s, which brought it into line with coins issued by Charlemagne.

Last years and death The last decade of Offa's reign was triumphant. In 787 he manoeuvred to ensure the succession of his son, **Ecgfrith** (d. 796), by having the young man consecrated king. It is impossible to discover exactly what this involved, and whether it reflected a formal royal anointing or a less significant blessing, but it does seem very likely that Offa found inspiration in Charlemagne's arrangements to have his sons consecrated by the pope in 781. By associating Ecgfrith with himself in the kingship, Offa was asserting his legitimacy and paving the way for an undisputed succession. (He also seems to have used more reprehensible methods, for Alcuin mutters sadly about the blood which he shed to secure the kingdom for his son.) The other significant event of 787 was the division of the Canterbury diocese to create a second archbishopric in southern England, with the archbishop's seat at Lichfield, in the heartland of Mercia. This needed papal permission, and is probably to be connected with a fact-finding papal embassy sent from Rome to England in the previous year. There were good practical reasons for dividing the ancient southern diocese, which was one of the largest in Europe. But there may also have been a personal motive, for Offa is said to have been on very bad terms with the current archbishop of Canterbury, Jænberht. The synod in 787 called to authorize the elevation of Lichfield was contentious, but Offa had his way, and obtained the services of a compliant archbishop in his own territory. Modern historians have been tempted to link this episode with Ecgfrith's consecration, and to see Jænberht's humiliation as the consequence of his refusal to co-operate with Offa's plans for his son. A connection has also been made with a letter of Pope Hadrian to Charlemagne (undated, but written between 784 and 791), which shows that the pope had been unsettled by rumours that Offa was conspiring with the Frankish king to oust him and replace him with a Frankish candidate; it has been suggested that these reports were spread by Jænberht's party, with a view to discrediting Offa. Clearly there was considerable diplomatic activity between Rome and England at this time, although it is unclear whether the most important bone of contention was the consecration of Ecgfrith or the division of the Canterbury diocese (which could be seen as a legitimate reform). The sources for the episode are deeply hostile to Offa and ascribe his actions to personal antagonisms; yet he must have had a serious practical case for persuading the pope to agree to the elevation of Lichfield into an archbishopric.

Offa's wife, Queen Cynethryth, enjoyed an exalted status; her husband had coins struck in her name, and she witnessed his land charters on a regular basis from *c.*770. The marriage probably did not take place much before this date, since their children do not seem to have reached marriageable age until the late 780s and 790s. Ecgfrith is the only known son, but there were at least three daughters: *Eadburh, who married Beorhtric of Wessex; Ælfflæd, who married Æthelred of Northumbria; and Æthelburh, an abbess who corresponded with Alcuin. The identification of Æthelburh with a namesake who was abbess of Fladbury Minster, in what is now Worcestershire, seems to be incorrect. During his career Offa founded many religious houses and gained control over others through conquest and other means. From Pope Hadrian he acquired a privilege guaranteeing the rights of his wife and offspring over these minsters. Cynethryth became abbess of Cookham when she was widowed, and controlled at least one other minster; Æthelburh was no doubt abbess of another family house.

Offa died on 29 July 796, and Ecgfrith inherited the kingdom (the first time that a son had succeeded his father in Mercia for many generations). But he was dead before the end of the year and the kingship passed to Cenwulf, a very distant relative; it may be that Offa had made away with all nearer claimants. It was later claimed at St Albans Abbey that plans for Offa's burial there were thwarted by Ecgfrith, and that he was actually laid to rest in a chapel near Bedford on the River Ouse, his body later being lost. The minster at St Albans was reputedly founded and endowed by Offa after he miraculously discovered the remains of the eponymous Romano-British martyr, an episode which naturally provoked considerable interest in the Mercian king's career among later historiographers at the abbey. One of the products generated from this was *Vita duorum Offarum*, probably written by Matthew Paris *c.*1250, which enthusiastically invents parallels between the life of the Mercian king and that of his heroic namesake. Matthew and other St Albans historians who wrote on Offa, notably Roger of Wendover, may have had access to a tract on Offa which may have included some genuine details about his life and his relations with St Albans; but it is tedious and ultimately unrewarding to attempt to extract any worthwhile information from the essentially legendary material presented in the thirteenth-century sources. Offa's actual burial place is unknown.

S. E. KELLY

Sources ASC, s.a. 757, 776, 779, 787, 789, 794, 796 · Symeon of Durham, *Opera*, vol. 2 · *AS chart.*, S 34–8, 55–63, 104–47, 267–9, 1258 · *English historical documents*, 1, ed. D. Whitelock (1955), nos. 19, 191, 195–8, 202, 204–5 · W. Levison, *England and the continent in the eighth century* (1946) · H. Loyn and J. Percival, *The reign of Charlemagne* (1975), 132–4 · P. Wormald, 'In search of Offa's lawcode', *People and places in northern Europe, 500–1600: essays in honour of Peter Hayes Sawyer*, ed. I. Wood and N. Lund (1991), 25–45 · P. Grierson and M. Blackburn, *Medieval European coinage: with a catalogue of the coins in the Fitzwilliam Museum, Cambridge*, 1: *The early middle ages (5th–10th centuries)* (1986), 276–82, nos. 1124–35 · C. E. Blunt, 'The coinage of Offa', *Anglo-Saxon coins: studies presented to F. M. Stenton*, ed. R. H. M. Dolley (1961), 39–62 · K. Sisam, 'Anglo-Saxon royal genealogies', *PBA*, 39 (1953), 287–348 · D. N. Dumville, 'The Anglian collection of royal genealogies and regnal lists', *Anglo-Saxon England*, 5 (1976), 23–50 · R. Vaughan, *Matthew Paris*, Cambridge Studies in Medieval Life and Thought, new ser., 6 (1958), 41–8, 89–90, 189–94 · C. Fox, *Offa's Dyke* (1955) · F. Noble, *Offa's Dyke reviewed*, ed. M. Gelling (1983) · F. M. Stenton, 'The supremacy of the Mercian kings', *Preparatory to 'Anglo-Saxon England': being the collected papers of Frank Merry Stenton*, ed. D. M. Stenton (1970), 48–66 · F. M. Stenton, *Anglo-Saxon England*,

3rd edn (1971), 206–25 · S. Bassett, 'In search of the origins of Anglo-Saxon kingdoms', *The origins of Anglo-Saxon kingdoms*, ed. S. Bassett (1989), 3–27 · P. Sims-Williams, *Religion and literature in western England, 600–800* (1990), 36–9, 152–66, 182–3 · N. Brooks, *The early history of the church of Canterbury: Christ Church from 597 to 1066* (1984), 111–27 · P. Wormald, 'Bede, the "Bretwaldas" and the origins of the "gens Anglorum"', *Ideal and reality in Frankish and Anglo-Saxon society*, ed. P. Wormald, D. Bullough, and R. Collins (1983), 99–129 · N. Brooks, 'The development of military obligations in eighth- and ninth-century England', *England before the conquest: studies in primary sources presented to Dorothy Whitelock*, ed. P. Clemoes and K. Hughes (1971), 69–84 · J. M. Wallace-Hadrill, *Early Germanic kingship in England and on the continent* (1971), 98–123 · J. M. Wallace-Hadrill, *Early medieval history* (1975), 155–80
Likenesses coin, BM [*see illus.*]

Offaly. For this title name *see* Digby, Lettice, Lady Digby and *suo jure* Baroness Offaly (*c.*1580–1658); Fitzgerald, Thomas, tenth earl of Kildare [*known as* Lord Offaly] (1513–1537).

Offley, Sir Thomas (*c.*1505–1582), mayor of London, born at Stafford, was the eldest son of William Offley, a native of Staffordshire who became sheriff of Chester in 1517; his mother's maiden name was Cradock. Sent to London at the age of twelve, Offley studied under William Lily, the first master of St Paul's School, and sang in the choir there. He was apprenticed to Lily's friend John Nichols, a merchant taylor and merchant of the staple at Calais; and in due course Offley married Nichols's daughter and heir, Joan (*d.* 1578). Offley rose through the ranks to become master of the Merchant Taylors' Company in 1547 and a prosperous wool exporter. In 1549 he served as alderman of Portstoken ward and translated to Aldgate on 22 May 1550; in 1553 he was sheriff of London, and in 1556 became lord mayor.

Taking his oath as mayor on 28 October 1556, Offley went by water to Westminster, accompanied by other community leaders and the bachelors from his company. Queen Mary knighted him at Greenwich on 7 February 1557 along with William Chester, alderman. Clode posits that while some of Offley's fellow guildsmen 'suffered under evil times', Offley 'carried laws into effect'; however, Offley's civic service during the reign of Mary I did not prevent him from being 'an advocate of the new learning' (Clode, 2.144; 1.150). Offley's mayoralty introduced the institution of night-bellmen, but is better remembered for the 'burning fevers' that killed seven aldermen within two months. During Offley's year of tenure Philip II of Spain came to Greenwich to visit his wife, the queen, and the royal couple rode through London. On 23 March 1557 Offley met them at the Tower wharf and escorted them through the city amid great fanfare and pomp. That same year he attended the memorial for the king of Denmark on 28 August as the city's chief mourner.

Following his varied civic office-holding, Offley was mayor of the staple in 1560, 1564–5, and 1569. He helped draw up a new book of ordinances for the staplers in 1565. He was also a charter member of the Muscovy Company and, by the first years of Elizabeth I's reign, was among the wealthiest men in London. None the less, there is little extant evidence of his business activities. He obtained former chantry property in Wolverhampton by a grant from

Philip Bold in 1556, and in 1578 was still bringing '800 tod of wool by water to Chard'.

Offley lived in Lime Street, then in the parish of St Dionis Backchurch. While an alderman for Lime Street he successfully asserted the ward's rights over the church and grounds of St Augustine on the Wall in a dispute with Aldgate ward. He defended the interests of the Merchant Taylors' Company before a parliamentary committee in a confrontation with the Clothworkers' Company in 1566 over jurisdictional questions. His association with the Merchant Taylors' continued long after his death, as ten members of his family joined the guild between 1551 and 1628, including his sons Thomas, Henry, and Richard. He was godfather to Alderman John White's son Thomas, baptized at St Bartholomew by the Exchange on 3 February 1561.

Offley's wife, Joan, predeceased him, together with three of their sons, including the first-born, Hugh; only one, Henry (b. c.1536), survived Offley. Izaak Walton dedicated his *Compleat Angler* to Offley's grandson Sir John Offley of Madeley. Offley died in London on 29 August 1582 (Stow says 1580) and was buried at his testamentary instruction in the church of St Andrew Undershaft near the tomb of his wife. He made many magnanimous bequests in his will, dated 5 August 1580; half of his estate, plus £200 deducted from the other half, was given in charity to be administered by his executors. Among his donations were gifts to the poor of St Andrew Undershaft, to the sick in London hospitals, to destitute prisoners incarcerated throughout London, and to impoverished students at Oxford and Cambridge. Despite his munificence, Offley is remembered for the simplicity of his private tastes in a popular rhyme:

> Offley three dishes had of daily rost,
> an egg, an apple, and (the third) a toast.
> (*Diary of Henry Machyn*, 353)

ELIZABETH LANE FURDELL

Sources DNB · will, PRO, PROB 11/64, sig. 39 · *The diary of Henry Machyn, citizen and merchant-taylor of London, from AD 1550 to AD 1563*, ed. J. G. Nichols, CS, 42 (1848); repr. (1968) · C. M. Clode, *The early history of the Guild of Merchant Taylors of the fraternity of St John the Baptist, London*, 2 vols. (1888) · J. Stow, *The survey of London* (1912) [with introduction by H. B. Wheatley] · R. Grafton, *A chronicle at large* (1569) · A. B. Beaven, ed., *The aldermen of the City of London, temp. Henry III–[1912]*, 2 vols. (1908–13) · T. S. Willan, *The Muscovy merchants of 1555* (1953) · G. D. Ramsay, *The City of London in international politics at the accession of Elizabeth Tudor* (1975) · R. Cooke, *Visitation of London, 1568*, ed. H. Stanford London and S. W. Rawlins, [new edn], 2 vols. in one, Harleian Society, 109–10 (1963) · *CPR, 1555–7* · C. Jamison, G. R. Batho, and E. G. W. Bill, eds., *A calendar of the Shrewsbury and Talbot papers in the Lambeth Palace Library and the College of Arms*, 1, HMC, JP 6 (1966)

Wealth at death no value given: will, PRO, PROB 11/64, sig. 39

Offor, George (1787–1864), literary editor and book collector, was the son of George Offor. He started in business as a bookseller at 2 Postern Row, Tower Hill, London, from which he retired with a competency. By the advice of his friend J. S. C. S. Frey, he learned Hebrew, and afterwards studied Greek and Latin. His knowledge of sixteenth- and seventeenth-century English literature, especially of theology, became very extensive, and he assembled a very large collection of early printed English Bibles, psalters, and testaments. In religion a Baptist, Offor was an enthusiastic admirer of John Bunyan, and gathered together a unique collection of Bunyan's scattered writings and of early editions of *The Pilgrim's Progress*. An interest in William Tyndale took him to Brussels in search of details of his martyrdom. During the revolution of 1830, while near Vilvoord, Offor was taken prisoner by a detachment of Dutch troops and was briefly detained in the prison built on the ruins of the castle at Vilvoord where Tyndale had been confined. Offor, who was a justice of the peace, was married to Sarah Ann and had at least two sons, George and Charles. He died at his home, Grove House, Grove Street, South Hackney, on 4 August 1864, and was buried in Abney Park cemetery.

Offor's biographical work on Bunyan, which drew on much new material he had found in the State Paper Office, was marred by a cumbrous style and bitter polemical spirit, and has long been superseded. His bibliography of Bunyan, prefixed to a three-volume collected edition of Bunyan's *Works* (1853), remained useful until replaced by F. M. Harrison's *Bibliography* (1932). Offor's 1853 edition continued for even longer—with all its faults—to be the sole collection of Bunyan's writings. It was from 1976 replaced by the Oxford edition, whose general editor, Roger Sharrock, justly commented on Offor's work as containing 'an amount of painstaking if amateur bibliographical information, and a verbose and often melodramatic evangelical commentary'. His other Bunyan publications included a careful reprint (1848) of the first edition of *The Pilgrim's Progress* with notes of all subsequent authorial adjustments.

Offor's library, with nearly 4000 literary items and including more than 500 Bunyan rarities, was destined for sale at Sothebys over eleven days from 27 June 1865 onwards, but much was lost in a fire at the auction rooms on 29 June. About a thousand volumes salvaged from the blaze were sold by Puttick and Simpson the following year. Many of the surviving Bunyan items came into the possession of Sir Leicester Harmsworth (sale, Sothebys, February 1947); the Offor family's portion of the remainder was presented in 1964 by his grandson Richard (1882–1964), sometime librarian of the University of Leeds, to the Elstow Moot Hall, in the village of Bunyan's birth, and is now in the charge of the Bedford Central Library.

Offor compiled an introductory Hebrew reader (1812) and produced a revised edition of the Hebrew psalter (1820). A reprint of Tyndale's 1526 New Testament, with an introductory memoir (1836), was more substantial. He edited several other protestant reprints and projected a reprint of Coverdale's Bible. His collections towards a history of the English Bible between 1525 and 1679 are in the British Library (Add. MSS 26670–26674). The British Library also holds many printed volumes bearing Offor's copious annotations.

GORDON GOODWIN, *rev.* ALAN BELL

Sources GM, 3rd ser., 17 (1864), 396, 528 · *The Athenaeum* (24 June 1865), 831 · *The Athenaeum* (3 April 1886), 449 · N&Q, 3rd ser., 6

(1864), 150, 485 • *N&Q*, 3rd ser., 8 (1865), 20, 85, 160 • *The miscellaneous works of John Bunyan*, ed. R. Sharrock and others, 13 vols. (1976–94), vol. 1 • F. M. Harrison, *A bibliography of the works of John Bunyan* (1932) • *CGPLA Eng. & Wales* (1864)
Archives BL, collections for history of the English Bible and extracts from religious tracts, Add. MSS 26670–26674 | Elstow Moot Hall, Bedfordshire, books from Offor's collection
Likenesses T. Gilks, woodcut, BM, NPG
Wealth at death under £6000: probate, 2 Nov 1864, *CGPLA Eng. & Wales*

Offord, Andrew (b. c.1305, d. in or before 1358), diplomat, was the younger brother of John *Offord (c.1290–1349). The family may have come from Offord in Huntingdonshire. He was educated at Oxford, being styled *magister* by 1325, and DCL in 1340. His legal acumen was recognized by Bishop Hempnall, who appointed him joint vicar-general, and later chancellor, in the diocese of Worcester. A career clerk, Offord was supported by income from benefices which included, successively, canonries of Salisbury, St Paul's in London, and York. The king granted him the subdeanery of York in 1348, but this was revoked a year later, when he received dispensation to hold the provostship of Wells, together with the archdeaconry of Middlesex, a canonry of Beverley, and the benefice of Over in the Ely diocese.

With his brother's promotion to be chancellor of England in 1345, Offord became a chancery clerk. In the following year he was appointed a member of the king's council. He had already embarked on a diplomatic career with a commission on 20 May 1343 to treat with the French ambassadors before Pope Clement VI. Abroad for most of June, he returned with a virulent letter from the pope denouncing royal councillors for infringement of ecclesiastical liberties, an allusion to Edward III's attempts to inhibit papal provisions, particularly of aliens, to English benefices. Returning to the curia, with his brother John, he reported in November to the council on the unsuccessful negotiations with France, before being reappointed as an envoy in April 1344. On 1 July 1345 Offord was made a member of the regency council of Lionel of Antwerp, the king's second son, while Edward III was in the Low Countries (3–26 July). During that year he was also engaged on a further mission to the curia in Avignon, and on another to the north, then plagued by Scottish raids. Later that year, and in the spring of 1346, he was in Spain as proctor of Joan of the Tower, for her marriage contract with Pedro, the infante of Castile. He was subsequently in Flanders for consultation with two cardinals sent by the pope to negotiate between the English and French kings, and attended Edward III during his visit to France in 1346–7.

In March 1348 Offord was one of those appointed to accompany Joan of the Tower on her journey to Castile, while between 23 March and 17 April 1349 he was negotiating with the French at Calais. He was there again in May, but returned to England in time to be present at the death of his brother, the chancellor, at Tottenham Court, on 20 May 1349. The next day he delivered the great seal to the

king at Woodstock. Between August 1349 and the early months of 1353 Offord was mainly abroad treating with French and Spanish envoys, with the count of Flanders, and with the duke of Bavaria. On 4 August 1353 he was appointed one of three keepers of the great seal and in the parliaments of 1354–5 was a trier of petitions. Further embassies to France followed, and by 18 November 1358 he had died at Avignon. ROY MARTIN HAINES

Sources Hemenhale, *Worcester register* • Special Collections, Ministers' Accounts, PRO, SC 6/740/13 • Exchequer, King's Remembrancer, Accounts Various, PRO, E 101 • Exchequer, *Pipe rolls*, PRO, E 372 • *Fasti Angl., 1300–1541*, [Salisbury; St. Paul's, London; York; Bath and Wells] • Emden, *Oxf.*, vol. 2 • Tout, *Admin. hist.*, vols. 3, 5–6 • *Adae Murimuth continuatio chronicarum. Robertus de Avesbury de gestis mirabilibus regis Edwardi tertii*, ed. E. M. Thompson, Rolls Series, 93 (1889) • Rymer, *Foedera*, 3rd edn, vols. 2/2–3/1 • Chancery records • W. H. Bliss, ed., *Calendar of entries in the papal registers relating to Great Britain and Ireland: petitions to the pope* (1896) • R. M. Haines, *The administration of the diocese of Worcester in the first half of the fourteenth century* (1965), 10, 104, 125, 126, 135, 324, 329

Offord, John (c.1290–1349), diplomat and administrator, was a brother of Andrew *Offord (b. c.1305, d. in or before 1358) and possibly a kinsman of the John Offord who died in 1375. Presumably born in Offord in Huntingdonshire, where in 1332 he was to have custody of lands pending the majority of the heir, he was a bachelor fellow of Merton College, Oxford, in 1313, and fellow in 1315. He had probably vacated his fellowship by 1322 by when he was MA. Subsequently he studied law, perhaps at Cambridge if, as seems likely, he is identifiable as the man recorded in the register of Bishop John Salmon of Norwich. He was BCL by 1327 and DCL by 1331.

Offord is termed king's clerk in 1328, but between 1332 and 1336 he appears intermittently as dean of the court of arches. In common with other well-qualified lawyers he soon found employment in diplomatic service. Appointed on 5 November 1334 to renew the truce with France, he continued to serve on various missions during 1337–8, and in October 1338, following the breakdown of negotiations, he accompanied Edward III to the Low Countries. From there he was sent to the curia in Avignon, where he was resident proctor for a year from May 1339, and where with William Bateman, dean of Lincoln, and John Thoresby he presented the king's case against Archbishop John Stratford, using arguments anticipating those of the *libellus famosus* of the following year. He was also entrusted with securing dispensation for the marriage of Hugh Despenser, son of Edward II's favourite, with Elizabeth Montagu—for the quieting of former quarrels between their families. In 1341 he was engaged in missions both to the French court and to Edward's allies or prospective allies, the dukes of Brabant and Gueldres, the marquess of Juliers, and the count of Hainault, while in 1342 he negotiated with the French ambassadors at Aunteyn near Tournai, and in April to May was appointed principal commissioner for negotiating a truce. He returned to France in June at the request of the papal envoy.

Between October 1342 and March 1343 Offord was with

the king during the latter's indecisive intervention in Brittany and was involved in negotiating the truce of Malestroit (19 January 1343). At the Easter parliament of 1343 the king ordered the annulment of the articles of 1341 against Stratford, and directed Offord to bring the documents into the chamber for destruction. In August he and his brother Andrew were members of an embassy to Avignon. This was to negotiate a final peace with the French envoys, subject to the 'private arbitration' of Pope Clement VI—who hoped to unite the French and English in a crusade—and to renew the long-standing request for a dispensation permitting marriage between the prince of Wales and Margaret, daughter of the duke of Brabant. At the beginning of October 1344 Offord's letters incorporating the pope's proposals were discussed at a secret royal council. In the event little was achieved. The claim of Edward III to the French throne doomed the peace negotiations from the start, the pope's reluctance blocked the dispensation, and the continental alliance against France rapidly disintegrated. Offord was the last of the disappointed English envoys to leave. Two years later he was engaged with William Edington and John Stratford in raising loans for Edward's expedition to the continent.

Although especially respected as a diplomat, Offord also held high office at home, acting as keeper of the privy seal from 4 June 1342 until after 29 September 1344. While with the king in Brittany during 1342–3 he was entrusted with the great seal, which thus for the first time since 1340 returned to clerical hands. He was appointed chancellor on 26 October 1345, an office he held until his death in 1349, and with Edington, the treasurer, he shared responsibility for government during Edward's absence in France in 1346–7. As might be anticipated, a man so constantly engaged in royal business benefited from royal patronage and papal provision. Offord's first benefice was Deepdale rectory in Norfolk, to which he was admitted as a 'clerk' on 21 April 1316. In 1327 he was provided to a canonry of St Paul's with expectation of a prebend, and secured that of Totenhall by exchange in 1330, at which time he was also canon and prebendary of St Chad's, Shrewsbury. He was collated to a canonry of Lincoln with Liddington prebend in 1331, and the king granted him the long-disputed Leighton Buzzard prebend in 1342, though he failed to gain possession. He likewise failed to secure the archdeaconry of Chester in 1330, but was archdeacon of Ely between 1335 and 1344. Royal nomination to the deanery of York in 1343 proved unsuccessful owing to a papal provision, but in the following year he was himself provided to the deanery of Lincoln, notwithstanding his canonries and prebends of York, Lincoln, London, Wells, Salisbury, and Hereford. On the vacancy at Canterbury following John Stratford's death on 23 August 1348, the chapter of Christchurch elected Thomas Bradwardine, but Offord was provided to the see at the king's wish by bulls dated 24 September 1348—four days before the election. The temporalities were restored on 14 December 1348 but before he could be consecrated he died, on 20 May 1349 at Tottenham, probably of the plague. The Rochester chronicler William Dene described him as being by then a weak and paralytic man, who had uselessly borrowed a great sum of money only to die and leave his creditors impoverished, and who was buried secretly in his cathedral church.
ROY MARTIN HAINES

Sources Historia Roffensis, BL, MS Cotton Faustina B.V · *Adae Murimuth continuatio chronicarum. Robertus de Avesbury de gestis mirabilibus regis Edwardi tertii*, ed. E. M. Thompson, Rolls Series, 93 (1889) · Rymer, *Foedera* · *Chancery records* · Tout, *Admin. hist.*, vols. 3–6 · E. Déprez, 'La conférence d'Avignon (1344)', *Essays in mediaeval history presented to T. F. Tout*, ed. A. G. Little and F. M. Powicke (1925), 301–20 · H. S. Lucas, *The Low Countries and the Hundred Years' War, 1326–1347* (1929) · R. M. Haines, *Archbishop John Stratford: political revolutionary and champion of the liberties of the English church*, Pontifical Institute of Medieval Studies: Texts and Studies, 76 (1986) · R. M. Haines, *Ecclesia Anglicana: studies in the English church of the later middle ages* (1989) · Emden, *Oxf.*, vol. 2 · *Fasti Angl., 1300–1541*, [Lincoln; Hereford; Salisbury; Mon. cath (SP); St. Paul's, London; York; Bath and Wells; Coventry; Introduction]

Offwood, Stephen (*b.* 1564, *d.* in or after 1635), separatist writer and publisher, was baptized on 29 October 1564 in Thornham Magna, Suffolk, the elder son and second of three surviving children of Thomas Offwood the younger, yeoman farmer, and his wife, Anne. By 1586 he had become active in Suffolk puritan circles, attending fortnightly conventicles held by Simon Harleston, a former Marian exile, and, after Harleston's death in 1591, moving towards more radical separatist positions. On 11 January 1590 Offwood married Francis Coleman; they had at least three children—two sons, who died in infancy, and a daughter, Susanna.

In 1602 legal troubles stemming from Offwood's separation and the illness of one of his children caused him to seek refuge in Amsterdam, where he became a successful merchant and innkeeper. There he joined the 'Ancient' separatist congregation of Francis Johnson and remained a member until 1610, when it split into two parts—one led by Johnson and the other by Henry Ainsworth. Offwood sided with the Ainsworthians until 1617, when he was excommunicated for quarrelling with Thomas Stafford, another church member, who was seeking to marry Susanna.

Although his family remained Ainsworthians, Offwood subsequently joined the Dutch Reformed church, and there he stayed until 18 April 1629, when he moved to the English Reformed church of Amsterdam—a congregation affiliated with the Dutch Reformed church, pastored by John Paget, and composed of a combination of former separatists and puritans. Offwood quickly became a leader of the ex-separatist faction. This group's views increasingly tended towards the emerging congregationalist conception of church polity, whereas Paget and the rest remained strongly attached to the Reformed position. In the conflicts that followed, Offwood and his party tried and failed to get Thomas Hooker and later John Davenport named co-pastor of the church. By 1635 these failures, together with his acquaintance with congregationalist thinkers and his own Bible study, apparently led Offwood to reject the Reformed church and embrace congregationalism.

Offwood's publishing projects reflected his political and

religious interests. He translated, reprinted, or edited works, adding prefaces and postscripts of his own, which he signed simply S. O. In conjunction with English printers in Amsterdam, he mostly reprinted anti-Catholic and anti-Spanish books during the 1620s. These included *An Oration or Speech … unto the … Princes of Christendom*, to which he attached a partially translated work of his own entitled *An Adioynder* (1624); *A Relation of Sundry Particular Wicked Plots … of the Spaniards* (1624); and *A Second Part of Spanish Practises* (1624). In the 1630s his attention shifted to religious topics. He published *The Originall of Popish Idolatrie* in 1630, and he brought out another work of his own, *An Advertisement to Ihon Delecluse, and Henry May the Elder*, in 1632. This latter work denounced the Amsterdam separatists for their exclusiveness and intolerance. In 1633 he acted as publisher for *A Fresh Suit Against Human Ceremonies in Gods Worship*, by William Ames, and another work entitled *The Opinion … Concerning Bowing at the Name, or Naming, of Jesus*. His final effort was the publishing in 1635 of *Four Sermons*, by John Forbes.

Offwood's religious activism gave him a widespread reputation as a leading layman in Amsterdam's English religious community, and he was widely suspected of playing a key role in the production of many other nonconformist religious tracts. He may have done so, but conclusive evidence for this wider publishing role is lacking. The date and place of his death are unknown.

MICHAEL E. MOODY

Sources parish records, Thornham Magna, Suffolk RO, Ipswich · will, Norfolk RO, Norwich consistory court wills, 101 Bunne · S. Ofwod [S. Offwood], *An advertisement to Jhon Delecluse and Henry May the elder* [1632] · consistory register of the English Reformed church, Gemeente Archief, Amsterdam · M. E. Moody, 'Trials and travels of a nonconformist layman: the spiritual odyssey of Stephen Offwood (1564–c.1635)', *Church History*, 51 (1982), 157–71

O'Fihely, Maurice. *See* Ó Fithcheallaigh, Muiris (*d*. 1513).

Ó Fithcheallaigh, Domhnall (*fl*. 1505). *See under* Ó Fithcheallaigh, Muiris (*d*. 1513).

Ó Fithcheallaigh, Muiris [Maurice O'Fihely, Mauritius de Portu] (*d*. 1513), theologian and archbishop of Tuam, was a native of Cork (either Clonfert or Baltimore), and became a conventual Franciscan friar about 1475. He subsequently studied at Oxford. The chapter at Cremona named him regent of studies at the Franciscan school in Milan in 1488. He became regent master of theology at Padua in 1491, and continued to lecture publicly on Scotistic theology there until at least 1505. He took part in the deposition of the minister-general, Ægidius Delphinus, in the first general chapter of the conventuals, held at Rome in 1506. On 26 June in the same year he was provided to the archbishopric of Tuam by Pope Julius II, who consecrated him in Rome. He continued to reside in Italy, and was present at the Fifth Lateran Council in 1512, signing the acts of the first two sessions. At length he departed for Ireland, but died at Galway on 25 May 1513, and was buried at the Franciscan friary there.

Ó Fithcheallaigh is chiefly known as the editor of many of the works of Duns Scotus. He edited, with omissions, chapter headings, expansions, and explanatory notes, the following treatises attributed to the Doctor Subtilis: *De primo principio*; *Theoremata*; *Expositio in XII libros Metaphysicorum*; *Quaestiones in Metaphysicam Aristotelis*; *Commentarium in libros I et II sententiarum*; *De formalitatibus*; and *Collationes*. These were published between 1497 and 1517. Although his additions to Scotus's own words make his editions at times problematic, his explanatory notes are often very helpful, since Scotus himself is frequently unclear. Ó Fithcheallaigh was not only an editor, but also an expositor, critic, and author. Among his expositions, published between 1497 and 1519, are *Annotationes in quaestiones metaphysicales Scoti*; *Expositio in quaestiones metaphysicales Scoti*; and *Expositio quaestionum Doctoris Subtilis in quinque universalia Porphyrii* (or *Expositio in quaestiones dialecticas J. Duns Scoti*). He wrote a short treatise entitled *Enchyridion fidei* (or *De rerum contingentia et divina predestinatione*), dedicated to Gerald Fitzgerald, eighth earl of Kildare (*d*. 1513), which was published at Venice in 1505. He also produced, while lecturing at Padua, a version in hexameters of the four books of the *Sentences*, called *Compendium veritatum* (Venice, 1505). Extending himself beyond the works of Scotus, Ó Fithcheallaigh also edited the *Expositio in Metaphysicam* of Antonius Andreae, and began an edition of the works of François de Meyronnes (finally published in 1520). The *Distinctiones ordine alphabetico* sometimes attributed to him were the work of a Friar Maurice of the thirteenth century.

A relative, **Domhnall Ó Fithcheallaigh** (*fl*. 1505), was the author of some annals in Gaelic, dedicated to Florence O'Mahony. These 'Irish Annals' were seen in manuscript by Sir James Ware in London in 1626, but are now lost.

S. F. BROWN

Sources G. Brotto and G. Zonta, *La facultà teologica dell'Università di Padova* (1922), 183–5 · P. Conlan, *Franciscan Ireland* (1988), 23–5 · J. Duns Scotus, *Opera omnia*, ed. L. Wadding and others, new edn, 1 (1891), 51 · A. G. Little, *The Grey friars in Oxford*, OHS, 20 (1892), 267–8 · E. Longpré, 'Maurice du Port (O'Fihely)', *Dictionnaire de théologie catholique*, ed. A. Vacant and others (Paris, 1903–72) · L. Wadding, *Annales minorum*, ed. J. M. Fonseca and others, 3rd edn, 6 (1931), 135, 151–2; 15 (1933), 312, 360, 422, 502 · L. Wadding, *Scriptores ordinis minorum* (1650); repr. (1967), 256–7 · *DNB*

Likenesses portrait, Irish Franciscan School of Theology, Rome, Italy, College of St Isidore; possible copy, Irish Institute for European Affairs, Pater Damianplein, Leuven, Belgium

O'Flaherty, Liam (1896–1984), novelist and short-story writer, was born on 28 August 1896 at Gort na gCapall on Inishmore, the largest of the Aran Islands, the second son of Michael O'Flaherty (*b*. 1846), farmer and fisherman, and Margaret Ganly (*b*. 1856?). His father was a nationalist who had been active in the Land League and his mother was descended from Plymouth Brethren who had moved from co. Antrim early in the century to build lighthouses. The boy grew up speaking English and Irish, and wrote short stories in both languages. His last published work was *Dúil* (1953), a collection of stories in the Irish language.

O'Flaherty received his early education at Oatquarter national school, close to the family cottage, but in the autumn of 1908, through the influence of a visiting priest, Thomas Naughton of the Holy Ghost order, he was sent to

Rockwell College in co. Tipperary to complete his secondary education. Naughton's hope was that this bright Aran Island youth would study for the priesthood with a view to working as a missionary priest in Africa. He did well at school, but when the time came for him to assume the clerical soutane, appropriate dress for a priestly novice, he flatly refused to do so and went home to Inishmore. Father Naughton then arranged for him to enter the order's college at Blackrock, near Dublin, in September 1913. He won an entrance scholarship in classics to University College, Dublin, but in reaction to the strict Thomism of his university lecturers began to read the writings of Karl Marx and other works of social revolution. Claiming that he was tired of waiting for revolution to break out in Ireland, he withdrew from the university and on 1 February 1916 enlisted in the Irish Guards. He signed on as William Ganly, choosing to use his mother's maiden name for what his family might regard as a surprising decision to renege on his Irish nationalist background by joining the British army. After training at Caterham barracks, he went with his regiment to France. His experiences at the front informed one of his poorest fictional works, *The Return of the Brute*, the grossly realistic semi-documentary which he published in 1929. In September 1917, while working with a transport unit between the canal at Boesinghe and the front, he was wounded in the head by an exploding shell and suffered severe shell-shock. Diagnosed as suffering from melancholia acuta, he was invalided out of the army on 7 May 1918, received a small pension, and was placed in his father's care. In the autobiographical *Shame the Devil* (1934) he wrote, 'You have to go through life with that shell bursting in your head', and for the rest of his life he suffered periodic bouts of depression as a result of his war injuries.

There followed a period of wandering worldwide. This took O'Flaherty as an ordinary seaman to South America in 1920. He subsequently visited Greece, Turkey, Canada, and the United States and took such work as he could find—sometimes in factories, at other times as a lumberjack. When he gradually tired of all this restless travelling, he returned to Ireland. In the savage civil war which followed the signing of the treaty and the establishment of the Irish Free State, he fought on the unsuccessful republican side. In January 1922 he enacted his own eccentric mini-revolution when, with a handful of unemployed dockers, he seized the Rotunda building at the northern end of Dublin's O'Connell Street and raised a red flag over it. He gave himself the title of 'Chairman of the Council of the Unemployed' but after three days he abandoned this rather absurd effort at social rebellion and fled to Cork. From there he went to London and began trying to write. After numerous rejections he embarked on his first serious effort at a novel about his native island, *Thy Neighbour's Wife* (1923). This was accepted by Jonathan Cape on the recommendation of their reader Edward Garnett, who became for a time O'Flaherty's friend and literary mentor. Garnett's wife, Constance, a celebrated translator of numerous Russian classics, was also to exert considerable influence on O'Flaherty, many of whose tormented, guilt-ridden characters owe a debt to such Russian predecessors as Dostoyevsky's Raskolnikov. The decade and a half from 1922 to 1937 proved O'Flaherty's most prolific period and saw the publication of more than a dozen novels and four collections of short stories. On 8 March 1926 he married Margaret Louise Curtis, *née* Barrington (1895/6–1982), a fellow writer. They had one daughter.

Broadly speaking, O'Flaherty's novels, with the exception of the historical trilogy *Famine* (1937), *Land* (1946), and *Insurrection* (1950), choose as setting either his native Inishmore or the Dublin which provided his main urban experience. Both the Aran and Dublin novels show him as a caustic, indeed corrosive, critic of the social pressures which shaped early twentieth-century Ireland and, in particular, the new Ireland which emerged with the founding of the Irish Free State. His principal target was the Catholic church, whose clerics figure prominently as villains in his fiction, and he excoriated them memorably in the satirical *A Tourist's Guide to Ireland* (1929).

In his novels O'Flaherty generally discarded the disciplines of style in favour of energy and passion. 'In order to be a work of genius', he once wrote, 'a novel must offer something more than a perfect style … It must be a relentless picture of life' (*Irish Statesman*, 7 March 1925). Accordingly, his fictional protagonists tend to be powerful figures mired in violence. His *œuvre* offers an impressive gallery of such types: Gypo Nolan in his greatest popular success, *The Informer* (1925); Fergus O'Connor in *The Black Soul* (1924); the eponymous heroes of *Mr Gilhooley* (1926) and *Skerrett* (1932); Ramon Moore in *The House of Gold* (1929). His second novel, *The Black Soul* (1924), was inspired largely by the author's own experience of depression and near despair after his war injuries. In this novel Fergus O'Connor flees to 'Inverara' where he eventually finds solace in the arms of the wife of an islandman. The pair finally elope to the mainland after a climactic cliff-top adventure in which O'Connor saves the life of the cuckolded husband. O'Flaherty had hoped for a great success with this intensely personal novel and was disappointed by the lukewarm critical response. He reacted by abandoning the intensity and Lawrentian sensuality of *The Black Soul* and embarked instead on his first thriller, which ironically proved his greatest popular success. *The Informer* (1925) is the story of Gypo Nolan, a stupid giant who betrays a comrade and is hunted to his death as an informer. The novel, filmed for the first time in 1929 and again by John Ford in 1935 with Victor MacLaglen in the title role, was the work by which most people knew O'Flaherty. While the murky Dublin first depicted in this contrived thriller continued to provide an appropriately Dostoyevskyan locale for morbid novels—such as *Mr Gilhooley* (1926), *The Assassin* (1928), and *The Puritan* (1932)—O'Flaherty located his more convincing fictions in the Aran Islands, where he was in every sense more at home. *Skerrett* (1932), based on a real-life story of conflict between the island's schoolteacher and an arrogantly authoritarian priest, in which Skerrett is subjected to a Lear-like process of suffering and utter frustration, is one of O'Flaherty's most considerable achievements. Only in *Famine* (1937), the first novel of his historical trilogy, did O'Flaherty again find a theme huge and horrible enough to sustain his intense sense of human suffering. This memorable study of the anguish of the Irish people in the great famine of 1845–8 is focused on the destruction of the Kilmartin family by hunger and disease. In Mary Kilmartin the author achieved his finest portrait of female heroism and endurance. Regrettably, the other two novels of the trilogy, *Land* (1946) and *Insurrection* (1950), failed to match the opening volume. *Insurrection*, a sentimental and melodramatic version of the Easter rising of 1916, was O'Flaherty's last novel. Critics have speculated on the reasons for his creative decline, but no definitive biography which might throw light on this problem has yet appeared.

In sharp contrast to the violent complexity of the novels, O'Flaherty's short stories, now seen by critics as his most enduring legacy, were often models of forceful brevity. Many are vivid, minutely observed sketches of the world of nature, in which he manifests a remarkable empathy with animals, birds, and even fish. Other stories depict the harsh world of his native island. Some of the stories adopt an anti-romantic, even satirical, stance. Young love is given its *congé* in 'The Touch', where two lovers are parted when the girl is given in marriage to a suitor selected by her mean-spirited father. In 'The Fairy Goose', which, according to O'Flaherty's celebrated contemporary Frank O'Connor (in *The Lonely Voice*), contains in its few pages the 'whole history of religion', superstition and rustic intolerance are portrayed with bleakly comic vigour. In his finest stories O'Flaherty achieves a marvellous detachment which contrasts sharply with his very evident personal involvement in the tormented lives of the protagonists of his novels. Where the violence of the novels suggests (in the words of his friend Sean O'Faolain in 'Don Quixote O'Flaherty', *London Mercury*, 37, 1937, 170–75), 'the scream of a safety valve', the short stories generally present the author as a wisely detached observer of nature and of man in nature. George Russell (AE) summed up this contrast by saying, 'When O'Flaherty thinks, he's a goose, when he feels, he's a genius' (F. O'Connor, *The Lonely Voice*, 38).

In addition to his novels and short stories O'Flaherty published two idiosyncratic autobiographies: *Two Years* (1930) and *Shame the Devil* (1934). In 1930 he visited Russia, and the following year published an account of his trip entitled *I Went to Russia*. While scriptwriting in Hollywood in 1934, he met a young divorcée, Kitty Harding Tailer (*d.* 1990), who remained his companion for the rest of his life. O'Flaherty's marriage ended in separation in 1936. He spent the Second World War in America with Kitty, sometimes working in Hollywood, and visiting Arizona, Florida, and Connecticut. In 1952 he rented an apartment in Dublin at 9 Wilton Court. This was one of the first apartment blocks in Dublin and was O'Flaherty's home for the rest of his life. His letters, many to Kitty Tailer, offer a painfully revealing glimpse of his life during this period when his creative powers declined and he suffered from protracted writer's block. He embarked on a novel, *The Gamblers*, to which he occasionally refers in his letters, but it

remained unfinished and exists now only as a 40,000 word typescript. He was seen at occasional public events in Dublin and still visited Europe from time to time until his health began to fail. In the 1970s Wolfhound Press began to reissue some of his novels which had long been out of print. University College, Galway, awarded him an honorary degree in 1974. He made a final visit to his native island in the summer of 1980. He died in St Vincent's Hospital, Elm Park, Dublin, on 7 September 1984. The funeral service at the university church on St Stephen's Green on 10 September was followed by cremation at Glasnevin cemetery. JOHN CRONIN

Sources P. Sheeran, *The novels of Liam O'Flaherty* (Dublin, 1976) · J. N. Zneimer, *The literary vision of Liam O'Flaherty* (New York, 1970) · P. Costello, *Liam O'Flaherty's Ireland* (Dublin, 1996) · J. H. O'Brien, *Liam O'Flaherty* (Lewisburg, 1973) · P. A. Doyle, *Liam O'Flaherty* (New York, 1971) · A. A. Kelly, *Liam O'Flaherty the storyteller* (New York, 1976) · *The letters of Liam O'Flaherty*, ed. A. A. Kelly (Dublin, 1996) · R. Hogan and others, eds., *The Macmillan dictionary of Irish literature* (1980)
Archives McMaster University, Hamilton, Ontario, corresp., literary MSS, and papers · NL Ire., corresp. and literary MSS
Likenesses A. Stones, bronze cast of head, 1984, NG Ire.; repro. in Costello, *Liam O'Flaherty's Ireland*, 114 · A. Stones, maquette (in youth), repro. in Costello, *Liam O'Flaherty's Ireland*, dedication page
Wealth at death £45,799: probate, 1985, *CGPLA Éire*

O'Flaherty, Roderic [Roger; Ruaidhrí Óg Ó Flaithbheartaigh] (1627×30–1716×18), historiographer, was probably born at Moycullen Castle on the western shore of Lough Corrib, co. Galway, the only son among the five children of Aodh mac Ruaidhrígh (*d.* 1631), chief of one of the principal O'Flaherty septs, and Elizabeth Darcy (*d.* 1636), an offspring of one of the 'tribes' of Galway. When his mother died he was made a ward of the crown. Despite a good deal of (frequently confused) speculation on the subject, virtually nothing is known of his early years and education. Given his later friendship with them, however, it seems likely that O'Flaherty had close contact with Archdeacon John Lynch and Dubhaltach Mac Fhirbhisigh before those scholars left Galway as the city succumbed to the Cromwellian onslaught in the early 1650s.

O'Flaherty married a daughter of Colonel Murchadh na dTuagh O'Flaherty in 1652 and in the following year obtained a decree—on the grounds of 'innocency'—from the Athlone and Loughrea commissioners of delinquency of 'a considerable portion' of his hereditary estate, but the heavy contributions levied by the Cromwellian regime virtually nullified this partial reversal of the confiscation of his lands. Although in 1677 he obtained by legal proceedings a further small part of the estate of which he had been dispossessed (a mere 500 acres of poor land), he became increasingly impoverished throughout the remainder of his long life.

In September 1665 O'Flaherty wrote the learned 'Letter on the chronology of Irish history' to the exiled John Lynch; his place of writing, 'Armorica Galviensi', indicates that he was already residing in Cois Fhairrge—perhaps at Park, near Spiddal, where he was to end his days. The letter, which was published twenty years later, suggests that he and Lynch had been engaged in a lengthy correspondence on the subject of Irish chronology. The next extant item of his to which a definite date can be assigned was written in 1682; in this, a brief communication to one Robert Downing, he rebuts allegations by Dr Edmund Borlase about the number of protestant settlers said to have been massacred at the outbreak of the Ulster rising of 1641. One of O'Flaherty's most celebrated works is his 'Description of Iar Connacht', written early in 1684 when William Molyneux of Dublin was collecting materials relating to Ireland for a work entitled 'The English atlas' being planned (though not ultimately effected) by the London bookseller Moses Pitt. In the event O'Flaherty's 'Description' did not appear in print until James Hardiman issued an annotated edition in 1846.

The year 1685 saw the publication of O'Flaherty's *magnum opus*, a substantial book in Latin entitled *Ogygia, seu, Rerum Hibernicarum chronologia*, on which the author had clearly been working since the 1660s at least. Characterized as 'a learned treatise, compiled from manuscript sources … a substantial and significant book … patently the work of a learned man' and 'the first scholarly presentation of Irish history to the English public', the work was dedicated to James, duke of York, who by the time the book appeared had succeeded to the throne as James II. Its publication drew a sharp retort from the Scottish controversialist Sir George Mackenzie and to this O'Flaherty penned a reply (in English); entitled *Ogygia Vindicated Against the Objections of Sir George Mackenzie*, this work did not appear in print until 1775. Another work, entitled 'Ogygia Christiana: annals of the Christian ages to the dissolution of the Irish monarchy', survived in manuscript into the nineteenth century but is now lost. O'Flaherty saw one other work of his in print during his lifetime. This was a Latin poem celebrating the birth in June 1688 of James II's son, later known as the Pretender.

O'Flaherty's contribution to William Molyneux's abortive project led to a lasting friendship, and a lengthy correspondence, between the two. Shortly after Molyneux's untimely death in 1698, O'Flaherty came into contact with the Welsh antiquary and collector of manuscripts Edward Lhuyd. Some thirty letters written by O'Flaherty to Lhuyd between 1702 and 1708 still survive. Lhuyd, in correspondence with others, alludes to the Irish scholar's impoverished state; already, in 1696–7, he had spent time in Galway gaol, presumably for an undischarged debt. O'Flaherty refers poignantly to his situation as 'a banished man within the bounds of my native soil; a spectator of others enriched by my birth-right'. A celebrated description of him by Samuel Molyneux (son of his old friend William), who visited him in 1709, states that he:

> lives very old, in a miserable condition at Park … his ill-fortune has stripped him of [his old Irish manuscripts] as well as his other goods, so that he has nothing now left but some few pieces of his own writing, and a few old rummish books of history, printed. (A. Smith, 'A journey to Connaught—April, 1709', *Miscellany of the Irish Archaeological Society*, 1846, 171)

O'Flaherty also left extensive, and often valuable, annotation in several Irish manuscripts which passed through his hands. Among the most notable of these are Dubhaltach Mac Fhirbhisigh's autograph copy of the Chronicum Scotorum, and one of the autograph volumes of the annals of the four masters (TCD).

In his declining years O'Flaherty was embarrassed by the activities of his son-in-law Edward Tyrrell, who gained notoriety as a priest-hunter and was executed in 1713 on a charge of bigamy. A tradition that his son, Michael, 'was a fool' seems at odds with the fact that the latter engaged in a lengthy and ultimately successful lawsuit to recover some of his ancestral lands from Richard Martin, esquire, who had retained them following the proceedings of 1677 in which O'Flaherty had some of his estate restored. The younger O'Flaherty's 'plaint' of February 1717, as part of the lawsuit, refers to himself as being the son and heir of 'Roger Flaherty, late of Parke'—which seems to suggest that his father was dead by that date. On the other hand, Walter Harris, writing in 1746, declared that O'Flaherty died on 8 April 1718, in his eighty-ninth year.

Roderic O'Flaherty features prominently in local west Galway folklore down to modern times. While some of the tales relating to him are rather far-fetched, one that was recorded more than a century and a half ago may contain more than a grain of truth. This is to the effect that his son, Michael, buried the venerable scholar under the floor of his own house at Park, as a means of strengthening his hold on the ancestral estate.   NOLLAIG Ó MURAÍLE

Sources N. Ó Muraíle, 'Aspects of the intellectual life of seventeenth century Galway', *Galway history and society: interdisciplinary essays on the history of an Irish county*, ed. G. Moran and R. Gillespie (1996), 149–211, esp. 182–96, nn. 206–319 · *DNB* **Archives** Bodl. Oxf., letters to Edward Lhuyd · Royal Irish Acad., MSS

Ó Flaithbheartaigh, Ruaidhrí Óg. *See* O'Flaherty, Roderic (1627×30–1716×18).

O'Flanagan, Michael (1876–1942), Roman Catholic priest and politician, was born on 13 August 1876 at Kilkeevan, Cloonfower, near Castlerea, co. Roscommon, the son of Edward Flanagan (*fl.* 1840–1900), farmer, and his wife, Mary Crawley (1843–1925). He was educated at the diocesan college at Summerhill, Sligo, and at Maynooth, where, by 1900, the year of his ordination, he had been awarded primary degrees in philosophy, theology, and canon law. He taught at Summerhill until 1912, becoming deeply involved in the Irish language revival movement. As curate in Cliffoney, co. Sligo, he became a champion of radical social and political change, advocating land reform and Irish independence and opposing conscription. In October 1915, following his proposal that cattle ranches should be divided among farmers willing to engage in tillage, he was transferred to Cootehall, near Boyle, co. Roscommon. There, as a result of complaints by police agents and southern unionists that O'Flanagan had made a speech disloyal to the crown, his bishop, Dr Bernard Coyne, ordered him not to attend any meeting outside his parish without episcopal sanction.

On 20 June 1916 O'Flanagan offended many nationalists

when, in a letter to the *Freeman's Journal*, he supported Lloyd George's proposal that the twenty-six southern counties should have immediate home rule, with the six north-eastern counties excluded. From 1917 on he played an increasingly important role in nationalist politics. His successful campaign in support of the Sinn Féin candidate, Count Plunkett, in the North Roscommon by-election in February 1917 demonstrated his considerable skills as a platform orator, organizer, and inspirational force. At the October 1917 convention of the new 'republican' Sinn Féin, he and Arthur Griffith were elected joint vice-presidents. In May 1918, after he addressed public meetings in co. Cavan on behalf of Arthur Griffith, without the permission of the local parish priests, his priestly faculties were withdrawn by his bishop, though they were restored in 1919 when he was appointed to a curacy at Roscommon town.

Along with Harry Boland and others O'Flanagan prepared the Sinn Féin election manifesto in 1918, and campaigned throughout the country on behalf of Sinn Féin candidates. He was involved in the proceedings of the first Dáil in 1919, and in 1920 drew up a revolutionary plan for land distribution. His approaches to Lloyd George in December 1920 and January 1921 without the authority of the Dáil or cabinet caused considerable disquiet at the highest levels of the national movement in Ireland; his intervention was widely believed to have diminished Lloyd George's interest in negotiating an Irish settlement.

O'Flanagan vigorously opposed the Anglo-Irish treaty of December 1921. He raised considerable sums of money in Australia and the USA for the anti-treaty cause from 1922 to 1924. His extreme anti-episcopal pronouncements during the 1925 by-election campaigns troubled even members of his own party and led to his second suspension from the priestly ministry. When de Valera founded Fianna Fáil, a constitutional party which soon acknowledged the *de facto* legitimacy of the Free State parliament, he took the great majority of Sinn Féin supporters with him, leaving O'Flanagan and a dwindling number of republican purists to preach the gospel of an independent republic of Ireland. O'Flanagan continued to maintain a radical stance on social issues, canvassing the merits of Bolshevism in the republican journal *An Phoblacht*, and sharing a platform with the communist trade unionist James Larkin. From 1924 until 1932 he combined his political activity with his preparation of a fifty-volume edition of the letters of John O'Donovan, the nineteenth-century antiquary.

In October 1933 O'Flanagan was elected president of Sinn Féin. In 1932, at the request of the new Fianna Fáil government, he had begun to compile a series of county histories for use in schools. This was interpreted by some of his enemies within Sinn Féin as a recognition of the authority of the government of the Free State. O'Flanagan survived their challenge until January 1936, when he was expelled from Sinn Féin following his participation in a radio programme. He became a passionate advocate of the republican cause in the Spanish Civil War, which he regarded as a class struggle rather than a religious one.

In 1939 O'Flanagan's attempts to have his priestly faculties restored were finally successful, mainly through the efforts of the papal nuncio, Archbishop Paschal Robinson. He ended his career as chaplain to a convent and to a private hospital in Dublin. He died of cancer at 7 Mount Street Crescent, Dublin, on 7 August 1942, and was buried at Glasnevin cemetery, Dublin, three days later.

PATRICK MURRAY

Sources D. Carroll, *They have fooled you again: Michael O'Flanagan (1876–1942), priest, republican, social critic* (1993) · D. Greaves, *Father Michael O'Flanagan, republican priest* [1956] · B. P. Murphy, *Patrick Pearse and the lost republican ideal* (1991) · University College, Dublin, de Valera MSS · *CGPLA Éire* (1942)
Archives NL Ire., MS memoir
Wealth at death £4567 9s. 4d.: probate, 3 Sept 1942, *CGPLA Éire*

Oftfor (d. c.699), bishop of Worcester, was a pupil of Abbess Hild of Whitby (d. 680), and studied the Bible in her monasteries at Whitby and Hartlepool. 'Being anxious to reach still greater heights', he proceeded to Canterbury to study with the learned Theodore of Tarsus (archbishop from 669 to 690), before going on to Rome, 'which in those days was considered to be an act of great merit'—as Bede adds, perhaps revealing a later scepticism (Bede, *Hist. eccl.*, 4.23). Oftfor's name, which means 'the much travelled', was no doubt a nickname alluding to these journeys. On his return to England he went to the kingdom of the Hwicce, which was then ruled by Osric (*fl.* 674–679), and spent a long period preaching there. As Bosel, the first bishop of the Hwicce (whose see was at Worcester), became incapacitated by ill health, Oftfor was consecrated in his place by St Wilfrid, bishop of the Middle Angles from 691 or 692 until 702 or 703, at the command of Æthelred, king of the Mercians, soon after the death of Archbishop Theodore in 690. Oftfor was not the first of Hild's pupils to be appointed to the see, for another one, Tatfrith, had been appointed before Bosel but died before his consecration. This was perhaps about 675, when the Bath foundation charter refers to Osric's establishment of the see (in pursuit of the Synod of Hertford, 672 or 673) yet notably lacks the attestation of a bishop of Worcester. Tatfrith's replacement may have been delayed and Bosel may not have become bishop until 679, the traditional date for the foundation of the see. Perhaps Oftfor had originally come to Osric's kingdom at Theodore's instigation and as a substitute for his confrère Tatfrith; but, if so, there is no clue as to why he was initially passed over in favour of Bosel.

Charters show that Oftfor was involved in the rapid growth of monasticism in his diocese. For example, in 693 or later he witnessed a grant of land to an Abbess Cuthswith to establish a monastery at 'Peni[n]tanham' (probably Inkberrow); and according to another charter Æthelred of the Mercians granted Fladbury to Oftfor to re-establish monastic life there, 'for the forgiveness of my sins and those of my late wife Osthryth (d. 697)' (*AS chart.*, S 76). Possibly Fladbury (perhaps 'Flæde's monastery') takes its name from Osthryth's sister Ælfflæd (d. c.714), who received her education from Hild at Whitby, and could perhaps have moved south with her sister, before returning to Whitby in the 680s. The statement of John Bale (d. 1563) that Oftfor wrote homilies (cited in *DNB*) is probably merely an inference from Bede's account of Oftfor as a scholar and preacher. He has left no known literary remains, but he is possibly the link that explains why certain details about Gregory the Great in the Whitby life of that saint recur in the writings of Bishop Werferth of Worcester and of John of Worcester. Moreover, it may well have been Oftfor who brought the fifth-century Italian manuscript of Jerome (Würzburg, Universitätsbibliothek, MS M.p.th.q.2), which bears the *ex libris* of the above mentioned Abbess Cuthswith, from Rome to Worcester. Oftfor's 692 obit in John of Worcester's chronicle is not to be preferred to the evidence of the Fladbury charter cited above (*AS chart.*, S 76) that Oftfor was still alive in 697. Evesham sources, admittedly unreliable, suggest that his successor Ecgwine was already in place in 699; hence the 'c.699' obit above. PATRICK SIMS-WILLIAMS

Sources Bede, *Hist. eccl.*, 4.23 • P. Sims-Williams, *Religion and literature in western England, 600–800* (1990) • P. Sims-Williams, *Britain and early Christian Europe: studies in early medieval history and culture* (1995) • *AS chart.*, S 51, 53, 76, 77

Ó Gallchoir, Séamus. *See* Gallagher, James (c.1690–1751).

Ogborne, David (d. **1800/01**), artist, was married and settled before 1740 at Chelmsford, Essex, where he is described in the parish register as a 'painter' or 'limner'. With his first wife, Ruth, he had four sons and three daughters. His only surviving son, John *Ogborne (1755–1837), was an engraver. Ogborne gained a certain reputation by his portraits of local provincial monsters, such as a winged fish caught at Battle Bridge, and a calf with six legs produced at Great Baddow; but he also painted a portrait of Edward Bright, a grocer of Maldon, Essex, who weighed 43½ stone, and died on 10 November 1750, aged twenty-nine. This portrait was engraved by James MacArdell and published on 1 January 1750. Another of his portraits was of Thomas Wood, the miller of Billericay.

Ogborne is better known as the painter of *An exact perspective view of Dunmow, late the priory in the county of Essex, with a representation of the ceremony and procession in that manor, on Thursday the 20 June 1751*, engraved by C. Mosley and published in January 1752. It represents the town's flitch of bacon ceremony, and shows in the foreground a portrait, more or less caricatured, of the then vicar of Dunmow. Another well-known Essex print by Ogborne is *A perspective view of the county town of Chelmsford in Essex, with the judges procession on the day of entrance attended by the high sheriff and his officers*, engraved by T. Ryland and published on 2 August 1762.

Ogborne also wrote some poetry and plays; however, only one play was ever published, locally, *The Merry Midnight's Mistake, or, Comfortable Conclusion: a New Comedy* (1765). The prologue and epilogue were written by George Saville Carey, and the piece was produced, with indifferent success, by a company of ladies and gentlemen at the Saracen's Head inn, Chelmsford. Ogborne died at Chelmsford, and was buried in the churchyard there on 6 January 1801. CHARLOTTE FELL-SMITH, *rev.* J. DESMARAIS

Sources *Essex Review*, 8 (July 1899) • D. E. Baker, *Biographia dramatica, or, A companion to the playhouse*, rev. I. Reed, new edn, rev. S. Jones, 1 (1812), 547; 3 (1812), 37 • *Albert Magazine and Home Counties Miscellany* [Chelmsford] (Dec 1865), 78 • C. E. Russell and J. C. Smith, *English mezzotint portraits*, 2 vols. (1926) • Chelmsford parish register • T. Gilliland, *The dramatic mirror, containing the history of the stage from the earliest period, to the present time*, 2 vols. (1808) • Watt, *Bibl. Brit.* • Bénézit, *Dict.*, 4th edn • *GM*, 1st ser., 71 (1801), 189 • Thieme & Becker, *Allgemeines Lexikon* • *Checklist of British artists in the Witt Library*, Courtauld Institute, Witt Library (1991)

Ogborne [*née* Jackson], **Elizabeth** (**1763/4–1853**), antiquary, was the daughter of Sir John *Eliot, first baronet (1736–1786), of Peebles, physician to the prince of Wales, and Jane Jackson, a tea dealer in Tottenham Court Road Terrace, London. She was almost certainly illegitimate, and seems to have lived with her mother until her marriage, about 1790, to John *Ogborne (1755–1837). Ogborne, an artist and engraver, was the fourth and only surviving son of David *Ogborne, a painter. The couple had one son, John Fauntleroy (1793–1813), and lived at 58 Great Portland Street, London, where they housed Euphemia Boswell, the eccentric daughter of Johnson's biographer.

After their son died in 1813, the Ogbornes attempted to assuage their grief by pursuing an interest in the history of Essex, John Ogborne's native county. Elizabeth prepared the first volume of a county history, while her husband contributed engravings to illustrate it. The antiquary Thomas Leman offered much assistance, and contributed a short account of Essex antiquities to the volume; Joseph Strutt is also believed to have helped the Ogbornes. The first volume of *The History of Essex* was apparently published in 1817 (although the date of 1814 appears on the title-page), and contained descriptions of parishes in the hundreds of Becontree, Waltham, and Ongar, and the liberty of Havering. Beautifully illustrated, and written in a simple and informative style, it later won the approval of the *Gentleman's Magazine*, where it was described as 'creditable to both the artist and the author' (*GM*, 220). However, the lack of public response and the straitened means of the Ogbornes (they became pensioners of the National Benevolent Institution in later years) prevented the publication of any further volumes.

Elizabeth Ogborne died on 22 December 1853 at 58 Great Portland Street. She was described by Edward A. Fitch as a little woman, old-fashioned in her style of dress and 'very precise and particular'. He dwelt on her 'very high and proud spirit' (Fitch, 140), her love of display, and her obvious learning. This last quality was displayed in her papers, which met with a sad fate after her death, when they fell into the hands of her servant, the wife of a marine-store dealer. Many of them had already been used as waste paper before the remainder were purchased by a passing antiquary, E. J. Sage. They contained unpublished material on Rochford and other Essex hundreds, including many extracts from the works of earlier Essex historians and the Harleian and other manuscripts.

ROSEMARY MITCHELL

Sources E. A. Fitch, 'Historians of Essex, VII—Elizabeth Ogborne', *Essex Review*, 8 (1899), 129–44 · *GM*, 2nd ser., 41 (1854), 220 · H. W. King, 'The Morant and Astle MSS and other historical and topographical collections relating to Essex', *Transactions of the Essex Archaeological Society*, 2 (1863), 147–54, esp. 153–4 · *N&Q*, 9 (1854), 322
Archives Essex RO, Chelmsford, drafts and notes for *The History of Essex* (unfinished); papers relating to publication of *The History of Essex*
Likenesses J. Strutt, pencil and colour drawing, repro. in Fitch, 'Historians of Essex', facing p. 129

Ogborne, John (1755–1837), engraver, was born on 22 July 1755, and baptized at Chelmsford, Essex, on 6 August, the fourth of seven children but the only surviving son of David *Ogborne (*d.* 1800/01), an artist, and his first wife, Ruth Howe. He was apprenticed to William Wynne Ryland and was later one of the stipple engravers who worked for him. He may himself have taught his sister Mary Ogborne (*b.* 1764), who was an equally capable stipple-engraver and produced plates after William Redmore Bigg and William Hamilton for John Raphael Smith and John Thane.

One of John Ogborne's earliest employers was John Thane, for whom he engraved a number of stipples during the 1780s as well as contributing portraits to his *British autography: a collection of facsimiles of the handwriting of royal and illustrious personages, with their authentic portraits* (1788–93). After Thane's death in 1818 Ogborne engraved a portrait of him by Bigg (1819) which was added to later editions of *British Autography*. He did similar work for other printsellers, such as Thomas Macklin and James Birchall. Ogborne also worked for Messrs Boydell, engraving a fine plate of *Mrs Jordan in the Character of the Country Girl* (1788) after Romney, three plates after Richard Westall, and four large plates for the *Shakspeare Gallery*. Two of his prints reproduced paintings by Josiah Boydell (1794, 1795) and proved, through no fault of Ogborne's, to be two of the worst in the series. The other two, after Robert Smirke (1791, 1801), were much better.

Ogborne's marriage to Elizabeth Jackson (1763/4–1853) [*see* Ogborne, Elizabeth] probably took place around 1790 at the dissenting Tottenham Court Road Chapel. They resided at her house, 58 Great Portland Street, Westminster, from where Osborne published a few of his own prints, including *Rural Misfortune* (1793), after Bigg.

Their son, John Fauntleroy Ogborne (1793–1813), was a student at Middlesex Hospital and had already qualified in surgery and dressing in 1813 when he died in May from blood poisoning contracted during a dissection. After his death Elizabeth began work on her history of Essex, to which Ogborne contributed drawings and engravings.

In 1828 Ogborne exhibited a picture at the British Institution and in 1837 another at the British Artists in Suffolk Street, but he died in November that year, a pensioner of the National Benevolent Institution, and was buried at Tottenham Court Road burial-ground on 13 November.

TIMOTHY CLAYTON and ANITA McCONNELL

Sources E. A. Fitch, 'Historians of Essex, VII—Elizabeth Ogborne', *Essex Review*, 8 (1899), 129–44 · Farington, *Diary*, 1.199, 258–9; 3.867 · T. Clayton, *The English print, 1688–1802* (1997) · E. D'Oench, *Copper into gold: prints by John Raphael Smith, 1751–1812*

(1999) · S. C. Hutchison, 'The Royal Academy Schools, 1768–1830', *Walpole Society*, 38 (1960–62), 123–91

Ogden, Charles Kay (1889–1957), psychologist, was born on 1 June 1889 at Rossall School, Fleetwood, Lancashire, the elder son of a housemaster, Charles Burdett Ogden (*d.* 1923), and his wife, Fanny Hart. He was educated at a preparatory school in Buxton by his uncle, Thomas Jones Ogden, and then at Rossall. He was a good athlete, with school colours for fives, until a serious attack of rheumatic fever when he was sixteen. Turning to intensive study he won a scholarship to Magdalene College, Cambridge, where he obtained a first class in part one of the classical tripos in 1910 and played billiards for the university. During 1913 he visited schools and universities in Italy, Germany, Switzerland, and India, investigating methods of language teaching. On his return in 1914 he published, with R. H. Best, *The Problem of the Continuation School*, and also translated Dr Georg Kerschensteiner's *Grundfragen der Schulorganisation* as *The Schools and the Nation* (1914).

In 1912 Ogden founded the weekly *Cambridge Magazine* which, selling at 1 *d.*, was astonishingly successful. In 1916 he converted it into an organ of international opinion and comment on politics and the war, digesting and translating from 200 periodicals weekly for a regular survey of the foreign press, which in 1917 and 1918 filled more than half of each issue. The circulation rapidly rose to more than 20,000. Poems by Siegfried Sassoon and John Masefield, and contributions from Hardy, Shaw, Bennett, and other well-known authors were other unusual features of this university magazine. Throughout this period Ogden was also very busy as president of the Heretics Society, which he had founded in 1911 together with H. F. Jolowicz, P. Sargant Florence, and F. P. Ramsey. The Heretics too became a publishing outlet and papers read before the society by Jane Harrison, Shaw, Chesterton, F. M. Cornford, and G. M. Trevelyan were published between 1911 and 1914.

During a discussion with I. A. Richards on 11 November 1918 Ogden outlined a work to correlate his earlier linguistic studies with his wartime experience of 'the power of Word-Magic' and the part played by language in contemporary thought. Ogden converted the *Cambridge Magazine* into a quarterly in which he and Richards published a series of articles as a first draft of the book which appeared in 1923 as *The Meaning of Meaning*. This empirical approach to theoretical confusion about language, setting forth principles for the understanding of the function of language, rapidly became one of the important books of the decade. Chapter 7, a study of the linguistic factor in aesthetics, appeared separately in expanded form under the title *The Foundations of Aesthetics* in 1922 as the joint work of Ogden, I. A. Richards, and the artist James Wood.

After the demise of the *Cambridge Magazine* in 1922 Ogden took over the editorship of the international psychological journal *Psyche*, which he had helped to found in 1920, as a vehicle for publishing research in international language problems and continuing the work of the post-war *Cambridge Magazine*. He also accepted the planning and editing of two major series: 'The history of civilisation' and 'The international library of psychology, philosophy and scientific method'. The latter series produced 100 volumes in its first decade, many of them stimulated and initiated by Ogden. With the help of F. P. Ramsey he translated for this series the *Logisch-philosophische Abhandlung* of Ludwig Wittgenstein, whom he introduced to English readers by a translation of the *Tractatus logico-philosophicus* as early as 1922.

Throughout this busy period Ogden's linguistic researches gathered pace and momentum. From his earlier studies of the writings of Horne Tooke and Bishop Wilkins he moved to the neglected contributions to linguistics of Jeremy Bentham. Ogden's earliest publications on Bentham and those containing the germ of his idea for Basic English appear side by side in the issues of *Psyche* between 1928 and 1930. The latter progress from speculation on the simplification of Basic and discussion of universal language to Basic English, so called for the first time in 1929. Basic English was conceived as:

> an auxiliary international language comprising 850 words arranged in a system in which everything may be said for all the purposes of everyday existence. Its distinctive features are the selection of words so that they cover the field, the restriction of the vocabulary, and the elimination of verbs except for the sixteen verb-forms which deal with the fundamental operations ('put', 'take', 'get', etc.) and their replacement by the names of operations and directions ('go in', 'put in', etc.).

Ogden established the Orthological Institute in 1927, revised and published the Basic vocabulary for copyright purposes in 1929, and in rapid succession published the first four essential books: *Basic English* (1930), *The Basic Vocabulary* (1930), *Debabelization* (1931), and *The Basic Words* (1932). He edited editions of Bentham's *Theory of Legislation* (1931) and *Theory of Fictions* (1932), and published his Bentham centenary lecture, entitled *Jeremy Bentham, 1832–2032* (1932).

Basic English developed rapidly, setting up agencies in thirty countries, and at the outbreak of war in 1939 Ogden had produced, in *Psyche*, Psyche Monographs, Psyche Miniatures, and other series, some 200 titles in print in or about Basic English. In 1943 Winston Churchill set up a cabinet committee on Basic English and made a statement to the House of Commons on its report on 9 March 1944. He outlined the steps which the government would take to develop Basic English as an auxiliary international and administrative language through the British Council, the BBC, and other bodies. A Basic English version of this statement and of the Atlantic charter, side by side with the original texts, was published as a white paper (*Parl. papers*, 1943–4, 8, Cmd 6511) later in the month. Thereafter Ogden, as he tersely recorded in *Who's Who*, was 'bedevilled by officials, 1944–6'. He was requested to assign his copyright to the crown, which he did in June 1946, and was compensated by £23,000, a sum selected because it was the compensation paid to Bentham for his expenditure on the Panopticon or reformed prison. The Basic English Foundation was established with a grant from the Ministry of Education in 1947.

Throughout his life Ogden, who never married, was a voracious collector of books, amassing complete housefuls of thousands of volumes. In 1953 University College, London, bought his manuscripts, incunabula, early printed books, and his collection on Bentham and Brougham, which included almost 60,000 letters to Lord Brougham. The 100,000 books he left when he died in a London clinic, at 20 Devonshire Place, on 20 March 1957 were bought by the University of California at Los Angeles.

Though Ogden was never able to reassemble the worldwide network of Basic English teaching agencies that had flourished before the Second World War, the sound principles and obvious pedagogical advantages of Basic have continued to attract teachers and users around the globe. The Basic English Association in Tokyo, for example, boasts thousands of members, and the Caterpillar Corporation produces all the manuals for the heavy-duty equipment which it manufactures in a standard system adapted from Basic English.

J. W. Scott, *rev.* W. Terrence Gordon

Sources W. T. Gordon, *C. K. Ogden: a bio-bibliographic study* (1990) · I. A. Richards, 'Some recollections of C. K. Ogden', *Encounter*, 9/3 (1957), 10–12 · private information (1971) · personal knowledge (1971) · *CGPLA Eng. & Wales* (1957)
Archives BBC WAC · CUL, corresp. and MSS · Magd. Cam. · McMaster University, Hamilton, Ontario, MSS and corresp. · PRO · U. Cal., Los Angeles, MSS · U. Reading · UCL, corresp. file · UCL, MSS | Bodl. Oxf., letters to O. G. S. Crawford · McMaster University, Hamilton, Ontario, corresp. with Bertrand Russell · U. Sussex, letters to J. G. Crowther · UCL, corresp. with William Francis Jackson Knight · UCL, MSS relating to legal affairs and the Basic English Foundation
Likenesses J. Wood, oils, priv. coll.
Wealth at death £15,792 16s. 10d.: probate, 10 April 1957, *CGPLA Eng. & Wales*

Ogden, James (1718–1802), poet and author, was born in Manchester, and while his parentage remains to be discovered, it is known that he was one of at least three children and the cousin of the well-known author the Revd Samuel Ogden. His childhood and personal life remain equally obscure, though it can be determined that he fathered at least one son, William Ogden (1753–1822). It seems that the Ogden family had a close connection with the local cotton industry in the Manchester district and thus James found early employment as a fustian shearer, before travelling as a young man to Europe where he visited France and Germany, spent a year in the Netherlands at either The Hague or Leiden, and witnessed the battle of Dettingen on 23 June 1743.

On his return to England, Ogden soon took up a post as master of a school in connection with the Manchester collegiate church, and it was probably about this time that he secured the patronage of the first Lord Ducie. Ogden was not a physically imposing man, later described by William E. A. Axon as 'rather under the middle height, with spare but sinewy frame, a thin face, ruddy complexion, and large aquiline nose' (Ogden, *Manchester*, xv), but he had a 'cheerful disposition, and natural urbanity, [which] endeared him to a large circle of acquaintance' (*Manchester Gazette*). He maintained well-defined and strong opinions on diverse subjects: he was an advocate of the abolition of the slave trade, held a peculiar dislike for what he called the 'modern game' of cricket (Ogden, *Archery*, 55), and had a passion for archery which saw him distinguished as an officer in a Manchester archery society.

By 1772 Ogden had returned to his former trade as a fustian shearer, continuing well into the 1790s in this line of employment, but it was his literary pursuits which over the years brought him fame. The *Manchester Gazette*, in an obituary notice, stated that he was 'a person well known in the literary world', and although the *Manchester Directory* designates him as a poet for the first time in 1797, Ogden's first publications appeared some thirty-five years earlier with *An Epistle on Poetical Composition* (1762), a poem entitled *On the Crucifixion and Resurrection* (1762) which was an orthodox comment on Jesus Christ published specifically for release on Good Friday, and *The British Lion Rous'd, or, Acts of the British Worthies, a Poem in Nine Books* (1762) which was published by subsidy of 600 subscribers and is indicative of the kind of recognition Ogden's literary talents received. As a poet Ogden was more consistently productive than prolific in the years to follow, with his writings presenting fairly standard, albeit poetically elegant, observations on the subjects he discussed. In 1774 he produced *A Poem, on the Museum, at Alkrington, Belonging to Ashton Lever*, followed some years later by *The Revolution, an Epic Poem* (1790) which presents William III as a hero and is devoted to the third Lord Ducie, nephew of Ogden's former patron; *Archery: a Poem* (1793), a composite volume praising the sport of archery as well as a concluding piece, in recognition of his subscribers' interests, on agricultural pursuits; and *Emanuel, or, Paradise Regained: an Epic Poem* (1797). Ogden's two most interesting and important poetical compositions appeared some twelve years apart, the first being *Poem, Moral, Philosophical and Religious, in which is Considered the Nature of Man* (1788), which was published anonymously. Arguably his finest poem, this work encompasses by way of subject the grand moral scheme of providing all the women of Manchester and its districts with good husbands, this to be achieved by a reform in domestic economy; Ogden also advocates a gradual abolition of the slave trade. His other significant work was also his last: *Sans Culotte and Jacobine, an Hudibrastic Poem* (1800). This is a staunchly conservative piece of writing which rejects calls for political reform, particularly universal suffrage and annual parliaments, on the grounds that such reforms would promote corruption and bribery in the world of politics. Ogden also argues that political changes would ultimately destroy the industrial spirit of the British nation by diverting the attention of the people away from work towards politics. For these reasons Ogden goes on to oppose the whig calls for Manchester to be represented in parliament. The author further confirms his conservatism in a prefixed song dedicated to the volunteer forces which defended church and state during the 1790s against radical enthusiasts. Ironically the work was published by Ogden's son William who later distinguished himself as an ardent radical reformer.

Ogden's efforts as a writer of prose were less voluminous, but no less significant, with *A Description of Manchester*, originally published anonymously in 1783 and reprinted in 1887 as *Manchester a Hundred Years Ago* with an introduction by William E. A. Axon, and *A concise narrative of all the actions, in which the British forces were engaged, during the present war, on the continent of Europe* (1797). Ogden resided for many years at 27 Wood Street, with his son living in later years at 26 Wood Street, until his death in Manchester, on 13 August 1802, at the age of eighty-four. While it is understood that he was buried in the grounds of the Manchester collegiate church, the location of his grave remains to be discovered.   MICHAEL T. DAVIS

Sources [J. Ogden], *Manchester a hundred years ago: being a reprint of a description of Manchester by a native of the town*, ed. W. E. A. Axon (1887) · DNB · *Cowdroy's Manchester Gazette and Weekly Advertiser* (21 Aug 1802) · *Manchester Directory* (1772–1800) · J. Ogden, *Archery: a poem* (1793)
Likenesses caricature, repro. in J. Ogden, *Emanuel, or, Paradise regained: an epic poem* (1797)

Ogden, Jonathan Robert (1806–1882), composer, son of Robert Ogden (d. 1816), merchant, was born at Leeds on 13 June 1806 and was educated there, partly under Joseph Hutton, minister of Mill Hill Unitarian Chapel. He became a Unitarian, though his parents were members of the Church of England. For a short time he was placed in the office of Thomas Bolton, a sometime partner of his father's, at Liverpool, but he had no taste for mercantile life, and showed an early talent for music. When very young he played the cello at a concert, but his instrument was the piano. To forward his musical education, his mother (whose maiden name was Glover) moved to London. Here Ogden became a pupil of Ignaz Moscheles, and later of August Kollman. He studied for a year at Paris under Johann Peter Pixis, and for three years at Munich under Joseph Hartmann Stuntz; in 1827 he visited Vienna. In 1834 he married Thomas Bolton's daughter, Frances, after which he settled in the Lake District at Lakefield, Sawrey, near Hawkshead, where he lived the life of a country gentleman.

James Martineau, when compiling his *Hymns for the Christian Church and Home* (1840), invited Ogden to supply tunes of unusual metre. The result was Ogden's *Holy Songs and Musical Prayers* (1842). A feature of the volume that evoked criticism was the adaptation as hymn tunes of pieces by Beethoven and others. From the seventh and much enlarged edition (1872) the adaptations were omitted. The style of Ogden's original music was not ecclesiastical, nor were his compositions well adapted for ordinary congregational use, but their spirit was rightly indicated in the title of the volume.

Ogden died at Lakefield on 26 March 1882, and was buried in Hawkshead churchyard. He was survived by his wife and a granddaughter.

ALEXANDER GORDON, rev. K. D. REYNOLDS

Sources *The Inquirer* (1 April 1882), 207 · W. Thornley, *The Inquirer* (22 April 1882) [memoir] · *CGPLA Eng. & Wales* (1882)
Wealth at death £29,186 10s. 11d.: probate, 20 April 1882, *CGPLA Eng. & Wales*

Ogden, Peter Skene (1789/90–1854), fur trader and explorer in North America, was baptized on 12 February 1790 at the cathedral of the Holy Trinity, Quebec. He was the youngest of the six children of Judge Isaac Ogden (1740–1824) and his second wife, Sarah, *née* Hanson. In 1794 the family moved to Montreal, centre of the Canadian fur trade, and in 1809 the young Ogden joined the North West Company. This was a period of fierce competition in the fur trade between the North West Company and the London-based Hudson's Bay Company, and Ogden soon earned an unenviable reputation for violence. When in 1821 the two companies agreed to a coalition, Ogden was specifically excluded from future employment; the ban was lifted when the Hudson's Bay Company realized that he would be a dangerous rival. In 1815 or 1816 he married an unknown Cree Indian woman with whom he had at least one child; when this marriage dissolved in 1818, he married Julia Rivet, a Spokan Indian, in a second 'country marriage', which lasted until 1854. Seven children of this marriage survived him. In 1823 he was appointed chief trader with orders to lead a trapping expedition into the Snake River country.

On Ogden's six Snake country expeditions between 1824 and 1830 his combative temperament was given full rein. The region extended south of the Columbia River from the continental divide to the Pacific coast, and was one of natural hazards, unpredictable Indians, and rival American traders. Accompanied by 'brigades' of men and horses, he travelled across present-day Oregon and Idaho, and much of California, Nevada, Utah, and Wyoming. He discovered the Humboldt River and sighted Great Salt Lake; on his last expedition in 1830 he may have reached the Lower Colorado River and the Gulf of California. He did much to determine the geography of a region with confusing watersheds and drainage areas, at a time when existing maps showed mysterious westward-flowing rivers and inland seas.

For the Hudson's Bay Company exploration took second place to trapping. In 1818 the British and American governments had agreed that until a permanent boundary was established the region should be open to nationals of both countries, and company policy was to trap it bare. It was, in effect, a 'scorched-earth' policy to keep the Americans at bay. Ogden proved the ideal man for this task, and under him the Snake country yielded 100 per cent profits. They were profits made at a cost, for even by the tough standards of the fur trade the hardships of the region were exceptional. Men and horses fell sick, were killed by Indian attack, froze in winter, and suffered from heat, lack of water, and fever in the summer. Either to explore or to trap furs was difficult across such terrain; to combine the two as Ogden did was an impressive achievement.

The rest of Ogden's long career was less remarkable. Promoted chief factor in 1834, he supervised the company's operations in northern British Columbia before returning to Fort Vancouver on the Columbia in 1845. Under the Oregon treaty (1846) this territory became American, and although in 1847 Ogden earned widespread respect when he negotiated the release of forty-seven American settlers taken hostage by Indians after the Whitman massacre, his last years were frustrating ones. Settlers and prospectors replaced fur traders, and in August 1854, in ill health, Ogden left the Columbia for Oregon City, where he died of a brain disease on 27 September 1854 at the age of sixty-four, and was buried.

GLYNDWR WILLIAMS

Sources G. C. Cline, *Peter Skene Ogden and the Hudson's Bay Company* (1974) • *Peter Skene Ogden's Snake country journals, 1824–25 and 1825–26*, ed. E. E. Rich and A. M. Johnson (1950) • *Peter Skene Ogden's Snake country journal, 1826–27*, ed. K. G. Davies and A. M. Johnson (1961) • *Peter Skene Ogden's Snake country journals, 1827–28 and 1828–29*, ed. G. Williams (1971) • P. S. Ogden, 'Peter Skene Ogden's notes on Western Caledonia', ed. W. N. Sage, *British Columbia Historical Quarterly*, 1 (1937), 45–56 • [P. S. Ogden (?)], *Traits of American-Indian life and character, by a fur trader* (1853) • A. Binns, *Peter Skene Ogden: fur trader* (1967)
Archives Provincial Archives of Manitoba, Winnipeg, Hudson's Bay Company archives
Likenesses daguerreotype, *c*.1822, Oregon Historical Society, Portland • H. J. Warre, pencil sketch, 1845, NA Canada • portrait, 1850–54, Oregon Historical Society, Portland • J. M. Stanley, portrait, Archives of British Columbia, Victoria, Canada
Wealth at death 5320 acres of land on the Columbia; cash; Bank of Montreal stock; Puget's Sound agricultural stock: Cline, *Peter Skene Ogden*, chap. 10

Ogden, Samuel (1627/8–1697), ejected minister and schoolmaster, was born at Fowleach, Oldham, the son of John Ogden, a yeoman, and attended school for three years at nearby Littleborough. He was admitted at Christ's College, Cambridge, on 4 May 1648, aged twenty, under the supervision of Samuel Ball, fellow of Christ's College from 1644 to 1651. Ogden graduated BA in 1651 and on 6 January the following year married Hester (or Esther) Barnett, sister of Josiah Barnett, curate of Over Darwen, Lancashire, who had been educated under John Ball of Whitmore, Staffordshire, the father of Samuel Ogden's tutor. William Bagshawe, the Apostle of the Peak, who became friends with Ogden after meeting him at a lecture at Saddleworth, praised Hester, 'who being the Daughter of a good old Nonconformist, when in a single State, shone as a Star of the first Magnitude, among Matrons near Ouldam' (Bagshaw, 98).

Also in 1651 Ogden was instituted as curate of Buxton, a chapelry attached to the church of Bakewell, Derbyshire, at the meagre stipend of £8 per annum. On 17 September 1652 the committee for plundered ministers ordered that tithes of Great and Little Huckley in the parish of Hope, worth £10, 'sequestered from Rowland Eyre, papist and delinquent and the tithe corn and hay of Buxton and Blackwell in the said county, sequestered from the Earl of Newcastle delinquent, impropriator thereof … amounting in the whole to the yearly sum of £32 13 4d' should 'be from henceforth continued and paid unto Mr Samuel Ogden, minister of the said chapel' (Calamy, *Abridgement*, 2.190). This area came within the jurisdiction of the Wirksworth classis. Having presented testimonials as to his fitness for the ministry and having preached before the classis at Brassington on 15 September 1653, Ogden was ordained at Wirksworth on 27 September by Robert Porter, Thomas Shelmerdine, Martin Topham, Edward

Pole, John Oldfield, Samuel Moore, and Thomas Miles. The following year he was presented by John Manners, eighth earl of Rutland, to the chapelry of Fairfield, but it appears there was resistance, for it proved necessary for Ogden to travel to London, and to present his claim to the commissioners for approbation, who granted their consent on 23 October 1654. In May 1658 Ogden settled at Mackworth, Derbyshire, acting as vicar and schoolmaster there.

Ogden was hostile to restoring the Book of Common Prayer. He 'thought the idolising the Common Prayer, and placing all Religion in it, was a provocation to the good spirit of God' (Calamy, *Abridgement*, 2.196). After his ejection in 1662 he continued to make entries in the parish register for some months. His successor was instituted on 9 June 1663, but Ogden continued to teach at Mackworth until in 1666 he was compelled by the Five Mile Act to move his operations first to Yorkshire and then to Marton, near Derby. In 1669 'Mr Ogden late of Marton by Derby' was reported to be preaching at Little Ireton 'every Lord's day at the house of Colonel [Thomas] Saunders' where '200, 300, 400 at a time' were said to congregate (Turner, 1.49). On 8 May 1672 he was licensed as a presbyterian preacher for this house. Throughout this period Ogden seems to have been able to continue teaching, possibly in his own house. Rachel Ogden, one of three daughters known to have survived their father, married Zachary Merrill, who acted for many years as the usher of his school and kept a notebook detailing his methods. Ogden's evident success eventually provoked the master of the free school at Derby to a law suit. When the court of arches found against him in 1685, Ogden was forced to desist from teaching at Marton. From 1686, through the patronage of Sir John Gell and, according to Bagshawe, with the collusion of 'Persons Dignified in the Church', he became master of the free school at Wirksworth (Bagshaw, 98). In 1689 he took the oaths under the Toleration Act at Derby quarter sessions and his house at Wirksworth was certified as a meeting-place.

Ogden was by no means a narrow, stereotypical puritan. He was knowledgeable about anatomy, medicine, and botany:

> and took delight in algebra, trigonometry, and the several parts of mathematics. He was acquainted with some of the greatest men of the age in that science and taught his scholars … to charm them into a love of those studies … And he was used to observe that very few good mathematicians were lewd and scandalous. He was a great lover of music, both vocal and instrumental. He was also well versed in Natural Philosophy, and very ready in the Cartesian scheme … He took great delight in poetry, and especially in Latin verse, and did so even to his old age.   (Calamy, *Abridgement*, 2.193)

In 1697, as Calamy explains, 'being of a melancholy disposition, and apt to be incumbered with troublesome fears about dying, it pleased God he was on a Lord's day seized with a palsy, as he was in the pulpit' (ibid., 197). He died a few weeks later, on 25 May 1697, and was buried in the church at Wirksworth two days later. Bagshawe, who also observed the melancholy with which 'this Dear Brother was more than touched', remembered his friend as 'a burning as well as shining light', 'one of another (and choicer) Spirit than many in the Ministry are' (Bagshaw, 97).   STEPHEN WRIGHT

Sources E. Calamy, ed., *An abridgement of Mr. Baxter's history of his life and times, with an account of the ministers, &c., who were ejected after the Restauration of King Charles II*, 2nd edn, 2 vols. (1713) · *Calamy rev.* · J. C. Cox, ed., *Minute book of the Wirksworth classis, 1651–58* (1880) · J. Peile, *Biographical register of Christ's College, 1505–1905, and of the earlier foundation, God's House, 1448–1505*, ed. [J. A. Venn], 1 (1910) · Venn, *Alum. Cant.* · E. Calamy, *A continuation of the account of the ministers … who were ejected and silenced after the Restoration in 1660*, 2 vols. (1727) · A. Gordon, ed., *Freedom after ejection: a review (1690–1692) of presbyterian and congregational nonconformity in England and Wales* (1917) · G. L. Turner, ed., *Original records of early nonconformity under persecution and indulgence*, 3 vols. (1911–14) · W. Bagshaw, *De spiritualibus Pecci* (1702), 96–8 · *IGI*
Archives Bodl. Oxf., sermons

Ogden, Samuel (1716–1778), Church of England clergyman, was born on 28 July 1716 at Manchester, the only son of Thomas Ogden (1690/91–1766), a dyer of Manchester, who died aged seventy-five, leaving a widow, who lived to be eighty-five. He was educated at the Manchester Free Grammar School, then admitted briefly at King's College, Cambridge, as a sizar in March 1733 before entering St John's College in August 1736. From there he graduated BA in 1737, MA in 1741, BD in 1748, and DD in 1753. He was elected a fellow of St John's on 24 March 1740, being the senior fellow from 1758 to 1768. Ogden was 'an excellent classical scholar, a scientific divine, and a proficient in the Oriental languages' (*DNB*).

Ogden was ordained priest by the bishop of Lincoln in November 1741. He moved to Yorkshire, where he was appointed curate of Coley, Halifax, in 1745, and of Elland two years later. He also acted as master of the Heath grammar school, Halifax, from 1744 until 1753. The Cambridge antiquary William Cole considered him a born schoolmaster and regretted that he left the profession, but Cole's description of the way in which he would return to his old school in Manchester 'and terrify the boys by his strict and severe examination' (Hughes, 1.ii) casts doubt on his pedagogical abilities.

In 1753 Ogden returned to Cambridge, having been appointed vicar of the round church of the Holy Sepulchre there. It was here that he made his name as a preacher, his congregations consisting chiefly of members of the university. His return to Cambridge was also marked by his taking the degree of DD, performing disputations with John Green, afterwards bishop of Lincoln, as his opponent. Green's patron, the duke of Newcastle (chancellor of the university), was so impressed by Ogden's performance that in 1754 he conferred on him the vicarage of Damerham in Wiltshire—a post he held until 1766. However, despite Newcastle's favour, Ogden was denied further advancement from him because he proved not to be a '*producable* man; for he was singularly uncouth in his manner, and spoke his mind very freely upon all occasions' (Gunning, 1.237). His university connections nevertheless secured him a number of preferments: in 1764 he was appointed to the Woodwardian professorship of geology and in 1766 he was presented to the

Samuel Ogden (1716–1778), by G. Scott, pubd 1793 (after C. Sharp, after Frans van der Mijn)

through 'the contemplation of the works of nature', and, in the language of physico-theology, argued that: 'Articles of faith are established … upon as good grounds as systems of physics' (Hughes, 1.126–7). He also expressed his distaste for 'enthusiasm' by contending that religion 'is seen to best advantage when adorned with moderation' (ibid., 2.19).

In appearance Ogden was 'a stout and very athletic man' (Whitaker, 388) and he was evidently a good trencherman, since one of his few remembered remarks is that a goose was a silly bird, being too much for one and not enough for two. For all his personal idiosyncrasies he was generally respected. Gilbert Wakefield, for example, considered him 'a good scholar, a liberal-minded Christian, and an honest man' (Hughes, 1.v). He died following a fit on 23 March 1778 and was buried on the south side of the communion table at the church of the Holy Sepulchre, Cambridge, where a table was raised to his memory. Ogden left his Arabic books to William Craven, master of St John's College, who, through Ogden's influence, had been appointed to the professorship of Arabic.

JOHN GASCOIGNE

Sources S. Hallifax, ed., *Sermons of Samuel Ogden to which is prefixed an account of the author's life, together with a vindication of his writings against some late objections*, 4th edn, 2 vols. (1788) · H. Gunning, *Reminiscences of the university, town, and county of Cambridge, from the year 1780*, 2 vols. (1854) · T. Baker, *History of the college of St John the Evangelist, Cambridge*, ed. J. E. B. Mayor, 1 (1869), 305; 2 (1869), 1079 · *Boswell's Life of Johnson*, ed. G. B. Hill, 6 vols. (1887) · T. Hughes, ed., *Sermons by the Rev. S. Ogden … with some account of his life*, 2 vols. (1832) · T. Whitaker, *Loidis and Elmete, or, An attempt to illustrate the districts described in those works by Bede* (1816) · Nichols, *Lit. anecdotes*, 1.566 · Venn, *Alum. Cant.* · *DNB* · *GM*, 1st ser., 48 (1778), 142 **Likenesses** F. van der Mijn, portrait · G. Scott, stipple (after C. Sharp, after F. van der Mijn), BM, NPG; repro. in *The biographical mirrour* (1793) [see illus.] · oils, St John Cam.

college living of Lawford in Essex. The former post he accepted without any knowledge of the field—a situation he did little to change during his tenure of office, which lasted until his death. Ogden's hopes of becoming master of his college were conclusively dashed at the elections of both 1765 and 1775; he gained a mere three votes on the latter occasion. However, in 1766 he obtained the rectory of Stansfield in Suffolk, a post in the gift of the lord chancellor.

Though known for his rusticity of manner in most social situations, in the pulpit he was considered 'remarkably striking', commanding 'the attention of all who heard him' (Hallifax, 1.ix–x). Indeed, his rather singular mannerisms appear to have enhanced his abilities as a preacher. For he had 'a sallow complexion, stern expression of countenance, and very vivid black eyes', and a deep and solemn tone of voice that helped to capture the attention of his audience (Whitaker, 388). In their printed form, too, Ogden's sermons were widely admired by his contemporaries, including George III and Bishop Hurd, who urged that they be put into the hands of the young princes. Boswell, who admired their 'subtility of reasoning' (*DNB*), persuaded Dr Johnson to read them and was heartened that Johnson 'praised my favourite preacher, his elegant language, and remarkable acuteness' (*Boswell's Life of Johnson*, 5.350). Johnson also considered that 'he fought infidels with their own weapons' (ibid., 5.351). There is nothing exceptional in the theology embodied in the sermons with its familiar eighteenth-century appeal to the authority both of the scriptures and of reason. Ogden urged, for example, the way in which one could come to a knowledge of the Creator even without revelation,

Ogden, William (*fl. c.*1790), bookmaker, is a figure whose life is obscure, but is nevertheless credited as the 'father of bookmaking' ('Bookmaking then and now', 78).

For centuries horse-racing involved the matching of two horses by owners who wished to bet against each other. These contests were often foregone conclusions and were sterile for betting purposes. Consequently by the late 1750s sweepstakes had come into vogue. Such races included more horses and so had a variety of outcomes. The increased number of owners involved in a contest meant that there was a selection of odds against their horses winning. This meant that a clever owner could bet in a more sophisticated fashion. He could cover himself against the loss of his horse and the prize money by backing other runners to win.

This system of hedging bets was adopted enthusiastically and it attracted professional betters who were called 'blacklegs'. With the owners they gathered at Hyde Park Corner at Tattersall's, where there was a subscription room for patrons 'to transact their Turf financial business' and to make bets well before a particular contest was run (Fairfax-Blakeborough, 7). At the racecourses betters gathered at a betting chair, as Thomas Rowlandson showed in a drawing in 1789. Their aim was 'to get round' in their transactions, to make sure that they did not lose whatever the result. These bets were laid on a one-to-one basis and no person stood up to take bets from all comers.

It is believed that Ogden 'made his appearance about 1790 or thereabouts' (Hodgson, 2). Strictly speaking, he was not a bookmaker in the modern sense. He was a practitioner of 'betting one with the field', favouring a single horse in a race and offering one price for the rest of the runners collectively. Unlike a bookie he did not offer individual odds for each horse, but in contrast to other betters he was prepared to lay bets on all the runners. Ogden was nevertheless one of a number of men who were the architects of the final stage in the development of professional betting into bookmaking, as sweepstake racing became dominant in the early nineteenth century. Nothing is known about his death, but he was reputed to be 'the only betting man who was ever admitted to the club at Newmarket' (The Druid, 46–7).   CARL CHINN

Sources The Druid [H. H. Dixon], *The post and the paddock: with recollections of George IV, Sam Chiffney, and other turf celebrities* (1856) • H. Hodgson, 'Bookmakers and betting', *Sporting Chronicle, 1871–1971: centenary supplement* (1971) • 'Bookmaking then and now', *Banyan* [National Association of Bookmakers] (25 April 1936), 78–9 • C. Chinn, *Better betting with a decent feller: bookmakers, betting and the British working class, 1750–1990* (1991) • J. Fairfax-Blakeborough, 'Origin and evolution of "Tattersall's Ring"', *Banyan* [National Association of Bookmakers] (Sept 1951), 7–9 • *Memoirs of the late Thomas Holcroft*, ed. W. Hazlitt, new edn (1852) • 'Epsom races', *ILN* (1 June 1850) • L. H. Curzon [J. G. Bertram], *A mirror of the turf* (1892)

Ogdon, John Andrew Howard (1937–1989), pianist and composer, was born on 27 January 1937 in Mansfield Woodhouse, Nottinghamshire, the youngest in the family of three sons and two daughters of Howard Ogdon, teacher, who wrote about music, and his wife, Dorothy Mutton, a former secretary, who also encouraged her children's musicianship by ensuring that they learned the piano from an early age. John began piano lessons when he was four years old. His gifts were such that at the age of eight he went to the Royal Manchester (later the Royal Northern) College of Music as a pupil of Iso Elinson. After attending Manchester grammar school, he returned in his mid-teens to the college, where he found a gifted group of contemporaries—Alexander Goehr, Harrison Birtwistle, Peter Maxwell Davies, and Elgar Howarth—who were later known as the 'Manchester School'. Ogdon took piano with Elinson, Claude Biggs, and Gordon Green, and composition with Richard Hall.

Ogdon's superlative sight-reading gifts and his phenomenal musical memory enabled him to tackle the most difficult scores virtually at sight, but his technical mastery was allied to a deep intellectual grasp, which soon marked him out as a re-creative musician of extraordinary range and depth. When he was still a child, his father had suffered a schizophrenic breakdown; it may well have been that this experience chastened Ogdon's own development: musically he was prodigiously gifted, and physically he was (so described by Goehr) 'a big, clumsy, untidy, roly-poly boy'. His character was shy and reserved, his speech quietly withdrawn; only at the piano, it seemed,

John Andrew Howard Ogdon (1937–1989), by Godfrey Argent, 1970

did his personality publicly flower, when he was overwhelming.

As a student Ogdon entered the Belgian Queen Elisabeth competition in 1956 but was unsuccessful. On graduating soon afterwards (with distinction in every subject), he gave Brahms's D minor concerto, conducted by Sir John Barbirolli, which prompted his Hallé Orchestra début at the age of twenty. Postgraduate work with Denis Matthews in London and Egon Petri (a pupil of Ferruccio Busoni) in Basel led, in 1958, to his playing Busoni's vast piano concerto from memory, conducted by John Pritchard, in Liverpool. The Busoni performance was much praised and on 8 August 1959, at less than forty-eight hours' notice, Ogdon made his Promenade Concert début in Franz Liszt's E♭ concerto, after coming second in the Liverpool international piano competition, and a month before his Wigmore Hall début in London.

In July 1960 Ogdon married Brenda Mary, daughter of John Gregory Lucas, civil servant; they had a son and a daughter. Ogdon and his wife made a notable two-piano team. In December, Ogdon began his record career with a Busoni–Liszt album for EMI. Although he later recorded for other labels, his main recorded legacy is with EMI. In January 1961 he took first prize in the Liszt competition, and he achieved world fame as joint winner (with Vladimir Ashkenazy) of the first prize at the Tchaikovsky competition in Moscow in 1962.

One of the most sought-after artists of his day, Ogdon travelled widely, notably to the USA and Russia, where he was adored. Unlike other virtuosi, he championed new and unusual music, including concertos written for him by Alun Hoddinott (with whom he founded the Cardiff music festival in 1967), Robert Simpson, and Gerard Schurmann, alongside standard repertory. He also found time to compose, among other music, a piano concerto, a symphony, solo piano works, and two string quartets. His immense energy ensured a full engagement book, yet his chain-smoking and excessive drinking, his unkempt appearance, and a tendency to overwork meant that the strains thus placed upon him took their toll.

In 1973 Ogdon began to exhibit symptoms of an alarming personality change. This previously gentle man became prone to degenerative mental and physical violence, eventually attacking his wife with such ferocity that she was hospitalized: he attempted suicide on numerous occasions. His condition at first eluded diagnosis, his treatment ranging from drugs and electric shock to psychotherapy. Some of his earlier treatment was experimental; he seemed to suffer from paranoid schizophrenic psychosis. Ogdon spent eighteen months in the Royal Maudsley Hospital in London; by 1977 he had improved enough to take his first teaching post, at Indiana University in Bloomington, where he stayed until 1980. Under care, he resumed concert-giving, which he had never really abandoned: an American doctor who had observed him for a year concluded that he was not schizophrenic but manic depressive and prescribed lithium, claiming Ogdon was an obsessive genius living a vital inner life against which the 'real' world could appear remote.

The treatment was a success and, although never 'cured', Ogdon was able gradually to resume his career. His history meant that his condition was watched constantly; his earlier instability led to his affairs being taken over by the court of protection. Symptomatic of a new confidence was his recital in 1988 of the legendary three-and-a-half-hour solo piano work *Opus clavicembalisticum* by Kaikhosru Sorabji, which he also recorded. Ogdon was a fellow of the Royal Manchester College of Music (1962) and the Royal Academy of Music (1974), and an honorary fellow of the Royal Northern College of Music (1986). He was also a recipient of the Harriet Cohen international award (1960). His publications included contributory chapters to *Franz Liszt: the Man and his Music* (ed. A. Walker, 1976) and *Keyboard Music* (ed. D. Matthews, 1972).

In late July 1989 Ogdon complained of feeling unwell. He saw a new doctor, who asked if he had been diagnosed as diabetic and who arranged for him to be examined by several specialists some days later. But his condition worsened, and his wife found him unconscious on the morning of 31 July, the day of his first specialist visit. Rushed to Charing Cross Hospital in London, he was found to be in a diabetic coma. He had, moreover, contracted bronchial pneumonia, from which he died in hospital early the following day, 1 August 1989.

ROBERT MATTHEW-WALKER, *rev.*

Sources B. Lucas Ogdon and M. Kerr, *Virtuoso* (1981) • *The Independent* (3–18 Aug 1989) • *The Times* (2 Aug 1989) • *CGPLA Eng. & Wales* (1989) • personal knowledge (1996) • private information (1996)

Archives Royal Northern College of Music, Manchester
Likenesses double portrait, photograph, 1962 (with D. Matthews), Hult. Arch. • group portrait, photograph, 1962, Hult. Arch. • photographs, 1962, Hult. Arch. • G. Argent, photograph, 1970, NPG [*see illus.*]
Wealth at death £565,100: probate, 6 Oct 1989, *CGPLA Eng. & Wales*

Ogg, Sir William Gammie (1891–1979), soil scientist and farmer, was born on 2 November 1891 at Craigbank Farm, Cults, Peterculter, Aberdeenshire, the only child of James Ogg and his wife, Janet Gammie, whose families had farmed in Aberdeenshire for generations. After Ogg's father died within a few months of his birth, his widowed mother and her sister continued the running of Craigbank Farm. Ogg was educated at Robert Gordon's College, Aberdeen, and at the University of Aberdeen, where he was awarded the degrees of MA, BSc (Agr.), and BSc in 1912, 1913, and 1914 respectively.

After graduating, Ogg was appointed a research assistant in soil science in the agricultural chemistry department of Aberdeen University by Professor James Hendrick, but was almost immediately recruited for war service in explosives factories, at Oldbury and at Greetland, Yorkshire. At the end of the war, he accepted a research fellowship from the board of agriculture for Scotland which enabled him in 1919–20 to travel to the United States and Canada, where he became interested in soil classification and the techniques of soil survey propounded by the Russian scientist Glinka. He returned briefly to Aberdeen to work on a survey of Scottish soils in 1920, but soon moved to Cambridge where he spent four years as a postgraduate student at Christ's College. During this time, in 1922, he married Helen, younger daughter of Henry Hilbert, of Halifax. They had a son and a daughter.

Ogg returned to Scotland in 1924, to an appointment as government advisory officer in soils based at the Edinburgh and East of Scotland College of Agriculture. He was awarded his Cambridge PhD in 1925, for research on pectins. In 1930 he was offered the post of founding director of the newly established Macaulay Institute for Soil Research at Craigiebuckler, Aberdeen, and immediately set about recruiting promising young research staff and shaping the scientific programme of the institute. The soil analysis and interpretation services of the North of Scotland College were transferred there, and research on soil fertility, soil survey, pedology, mineralogy, organic soils, soil acidity, and the reclamation of peat moorland was quickly set in train. In 1935 Ogg established a spectrochemistry department, believing spectrographic methods for analysing soils and plants would greatly improve the scientist's knowledge of the chemical properties and composition of these materials, and also aid in advisory work on fertilizing and manuring. The Macaulay Institute soon achieved, and continued to enjoy, an international reputation for its analytical facilities and its research on trace elements and the molecular structure of soil minerals.

When Sir E. John Russell retired as director of the prestigious Rothamsted Experimental Station in 1943, Ogg was invited to succeed him. He accepted but remained honorary director of the Macaulay until 1945, whereupon he became a member of its council of management and remained so until his death. He arrived at Rothamsted at a time when British agriculture was struggling to come to terms with the upheavals of the war years and the attendant food shortages. During Ogg's directorship (1943–58) the number of staff increased from 140 to 471 and three new departments—biochemistry, nematology, and pedology—were formed. In 1946 the headquarters of the soil survey of England and Wales were transferred to Rothamsted and Ogg served as chairman of the Agricultural Research Council's soil survey research board from 1950 to 1965. His other responsibilities included those of director of Woburn Experimental Station and consultant director of the Imperial Bureau of Soil Science (subsequently the Commonwealth Bureau of Soils). He served as president of the Society of Chemical Industry for two years (1953–5) and participated in many overseas visits and tours as a lecturer.

In 1925 Ogg was elected to the Royal Society of Edinburgh and became one of its senior fellows. He was knighted for his services to agriculture in 1949 and awarded an honorary LLD by the University of Aberdeen in 1951. He received many other honours and awards during his career. He was chairman of the governors of the North of Scotland College of Agriculture from 1958 to 1968 and in 1975 was elected one of the first honorary fellows of the Macaulay Institute.

Following his retirement in 1958, Ogg returned to Scotland where he farmed in partnership with his son, Douglas, at Arnhall, near Edzell, Angus. Ogg was regarded by contemporaries as a self-reliant man, of strong character, who was not only a perceptive judge of people but also a scientist and administrator with a sound sense of practicalities. He died at Arnhall on 25 September 1979, after a fall in the garden of his home.   R. E. WHITE, *rev.*

Sources R. L. Mitchell, *Year Book of the Royal Society of Edinburgh* (1980), 67–71 · *Chemistry and Industry*, 18/7 (18 July 1953), 706 [biography] · *Profile 39* (Macaulay Institute for Soil Research) · *Reports of Rothamsted Experimental Station* · private information (1986)

Ogilby, John (1600–1676), publisher and geographer, was born on 17 November 1600 at 'Kellemeane', near Dundee, Forfarshire. Nothing is known either of his parents or of his early education, and even the date of his birth is known only from later statements by John Aubrey and Elias Ashmole. Aubrey noted that Ogilby was from 'a gentleman's family and bred to his grammar' (*Brief Lives*, 2.99). It is probable that his father was admitted to the Merchant Taylors' Company in London in 1606 and that Ogilby himself was likewise admitted, on 6 July 1629. Aubrey tells us that the young Ogilby paid his father's debts with money secured from a lottery managed by the Virginia Company in March 1612, and that about 1619 he was apprenticed to John Draper, a London dancing-master. It is possible to see several phases to Ogilby's varied career: dancing-master, courtier, and theatre owner between about 1620 and 1641; poet and translator from 1649; and,

John Ogilby (1600–1676), by William Faithorne the elder, pubd 1654 (after Sir Peter Lely)

from about 1669, compiler of geographical works and atlases, culminating in his *Britannia* (1675).

Ogilby is thought to have danced in Jonson's masque *The Gypsies Metamorphosed* in 1621, and it may have been then that he injured himself and became lame thereafter. The details of his life in the later 1620s are uncertain, though he may have soldiered. It is known that in Somerset he taught dancing to Ralph Hopton's sisters (*c.*1632–3). He moved to Ireland in the summer of 1633, under the patronage of Viscount Wentworth, later earl of Strafford, to become master of the revels. Ogilby was responsible for the opening in 1637 of Ireland's first theatre, the New Theatre in Dublin's Werburgh Street, and for the development of the theatre's company. This ceased with the Irish rising in 1641. After service to the earl of Ormond, Ogilby returned to England about 1644, first to Bristol, then, about 1645, to Cambridge, and by 1648 to London. He married Christian (Katherine) Hunsdon on 14 March 1650, in St Peter-le-Poer parish: she was the widow of one Thomas Hunsdon, merchant taylor, of Blackfriars, London. William Morgan, the son of her married daughter Elizabeth, was later to become involved with John Ogilby in mapping and publishing projects.

In 1649 Ogilby published his first translation, of Virgil. This was followed in 1651 by Aesop's *Fables* and further translations of Virgil in 1654 and 1658. His translations, particularly the 1654 folio, were magnificent productions:

his style was direct and he paid great attention to paper quality, clear type, and the illustrations. Later translations—of Homer's *Iliad* (1660) and *Odyssey* (1665), of Aesop's *Fables* and *Aesopics* (in 1665 and 1668, respectively), and of Virgil in 1666—are splendid examples of seventeenth-century printing and of the patronage networks through which men like Ogilby promoted both themselves and polite learning. This was not, then, just an individual or a particularly British enterprise. Ogilby drew upon the translations of Virgil by the Spanish Jesuit de la Cerda and others, like Nicholas Caussin. In such ways, classical learning, book production, and patronage promoted élite authority and the learned publics of seventeenth-century Europe. Ogilby was involved in the illustration and production of a two-volume edition of the Bible, which, like his *Iliad*, he dedicated to Charles II. Ogilby's support from and for royalty is most clearly evident in *The Entertainment of his Most Excellent Majestie Charles II* (1661), which he both wrote and printed, a commemoration of the new king's coronation. Drawing upon earlier traditions of triumphal royal processions, Ogilby used the capital's streets as a theatrical stage for the promotion of civic virtue, royal authority, and future prosperity.

From 1661 Ogilby petitioned the king in order to safeguard publication rights and, in particular, to ensure a monopoly on his successful *Entertainment*. In March that year he was reconfirmed as master of the revels in Ireland, and he probably secured his title of master of the king's imprimeries (king's printer) in the same year. About July 1662 he moved to Ireland again to establish a theatre in Dublin, and he may have met Robert Boyle at this time. By late 1665 or early 1666 he was again settled in London. After the great fire of 1666 (in which he lost much of his own stock) he was appointed one of the city's assistant surveyors, a position that brought him into contact with Robert Hooke and Christopher Wren. He published his *Embassy to China* in 1669, and it was at this time that he conceived of a series of atlases to cover the whole world, to be funded through lotteries, subscription plans, and advertisements. The first, *Africa*, appeared in 1670. Others followed soon after: *Atlas Japannensis* (1670), *America* (1671), *Atlas Chinensis* (1671), and *Asia* (1673). These were not the fruits of Ogilby's own work but rather well-produced compilations of extant translations and others' accounts, a common practice at that time. His and others' work in this sense thus both reflected and directed growing public interest in distant places and foreign peoples.

Ogilby secured the additional title of his majesty's cosmographer early in 1671. It is clear that he again drew upon the support of the king and other patrons in the production and publication of *Britannia … an illustration of the kingdom of England and dominion of Wales: by a geographical and historical description of the principal roads thereof* (1675), the work for which he became best known. Chiefly a road atlas, it was securely based on contemporary and collaborative research. It was followed by *Mr Ogilby's tables of his measur'd roads … with other remarks … to which is added, A true account of the markets and fairs, &c. collected in his survey* (1676). In *Britannia* Ogilby drew out 2519 miles of road in the form

of 100 strip maps, a technique that was widely imitated throughout the following century. Measuring distances by waywiser (his 'great wheel'), he made allowance for roads that ascended hills yet had to be depicted in two dimensions on paper, and his surveys helped to standardize the mile at 1760 yards throughout the kingdom. *Britannia* marked the first major advance in cartography in England since the Tudor period, though it did echo earlier traditions. It was republished in 1698, 1719, and 1720, and on subsequent occasions up to modern times.

Ogilby died in London on 4 September 1676, and was buried the next day at St Bride's, Fleet Street. His work was continued by William Morgan. Although Ogilby's translations in particular were decried by eighteenth-century critics, his reputation as a translator and printer was high during his lifetime, and *Britannia* has secured him enduring importance in British cartographic history.

CHARLES W. J. WITHERS

Sources K. van Eerde, *John Ogilby and the taste of his times* (1976) · J. Ogilby, *Africa* (1670), preface · *Brief lives, chiefly of contemporaries, set down by John Aubrey, between the years 1669 and 1696*, ed. A. Clark, 2 (1898), 98–105 · J. Aubrey, *Letters by eminent men and lives of eminent men* (1813), 3.466–70 · parish register (marriage), London, St Peter-le-Poer, 14 March 1650

Archives Bodl. Oxf., Aubrey MSS

Likenesses W. Faithorne the elder, line engraving (after P. Lely), BM, NPG; repro. in J. Ogilby, *Works* (1654) [*see illus.*] · R. Gaywood, etching, BM, NPG; repro. in J. Ogilby, *The fables of Aesop*, 3rd edn (1673) · attrib. P. Lely, oils, Bodl. Oxf.; repro. in J. Ogilby, trans., *The works of Publius Virgilius Maro* (1654) · P. Lombart, line engraving (after P. Lely), BM, NPG · W. Marshall, line engraving, BM, NPG; repro. in J. Ogilby, trans., *The works of Publius Virgilius Maro* (1649)

Ogilvie. *See also* Ogilvy.

Ogilvie, Charles Atmore (1793–1873), Church of England clergyman, son of John Ogilvie of Whitehaven, Cumberland (*d.* 25 April 1839 at Duloe, Cornwall), and his wife, Catharine Curwen of the Isle of Man, was born at Whitehaven on 20 November 1793. He matriculated from Balliol College, Oxford, on 27 November 1811; after taking a first class in 1815, he won the chancellor's prize for the English essay in 1817. He graduated BA in 1815, MA in 1818, and BD and DD in 1842. In 1816 he was elected a fellow of his college, and was ordained. He was tutor from 1819 to 1830, bursar in 1822, and senior dean in 1842. He was appointed a university examiner in 1823 and 1824, and examiner in the classical school in 1825. He greatly assisted Richard Jenkyns, the master of Balliol, in improving the tone and discipline of the college. Ogilvie is reputed to have been the major influence in the introduction of the open scholarship system on which Balliol's later academic reputation rested (Jones, 187). Ogilvie saw himself as 'an attached and zealous member of the Church of England' (ibid., 181). Though at the end of the 1820s he was looked on as a leader of the high-church party in Oxford, he gave little active support to the Oxford Movement. He was a select preacher before the university in 1825, 1832, and 1844, and was Bampton lecturer in 1836, the lectures being published as *The Divine Glory Manifested* (1836).

Ogilvie held some clerical preferments while still fellow and tutor of Balliol. He was rector of Wickford, Essex, from 4 January 1822 to 1833; rector of Abbotsley, Huntingdonshire, from 30 August 1822 to 1839; and vicar of Duloe from 20 October 1833 to 1840. The rectory and vicarage of Ross, Herefordshire, conferred on him on 6 December 1839, he held until his death (together, from 1849, with his Oxford canonry). For a time he acted as domestic and examining chaplain to Archbishop William Howley. He resigned his fellowship in 1834, having ceased to teach in 1830. On 18 April 1838 he married Mary Ann Gurnell (*d*. 2 Oct 1875), daughter of Major Armstrong; they had two daughters.

On the foundation of a chair of pastoral theology in the university, Ogilvie became the first regius professor on 23 April 1842, and as professor he succeeded in 1849 to a canonry at Christ Church. His selection reflected the concern of Peel's government that the post should not go to a whig or to one of the many then embroiled in clerical dispute. He actively supported tory candidates in elections for the university burgess-ship. Through life Ogilvie maintained a close friendship with M. J. Routh, president of Magdalen College, with whom he corresponded on literary subjects from 1847 to 1854. He was also friendly with Joseph Blanco White and was a quite regular correspondent of Hannah More. Ogilvie published little beyond his Bampton lectures: a sermon (1836), two pamphlets on subscription (1845 and 1863), and an essay, *On the union of classical and mathematical studies*, (*Oxford English prize essays*, vol. 3, 1836). While lecturing on 15 February 1873 he was seized with paralysis, and he died in his house at Christ Church, Oxford, two days later. He was buried in the Latin chapel in Christ Church Cathedral.

G. C. BOASE, *rev.* H. C. G. MATTHEW

Sources *Guardian* (19 Feb 1873) · Boase, *Mod. Eng. biog.* · J. M. Chapman, *Reminiscences of three Oxford worthies* (1875) · J. Jones, *Balliol College: a history, 1263–1939* (1988) · J. W. Burgon, *Lives of twelve good men*, [new edn], 2 vols. (1888–9) · L. M. Quiller-Couch, ed., *Reminiscences of Oxford by Oxford men, 1559–1850*, OHS, 22 (1892) · W. R. Ward, *Victorian Oxford* (1965)
Archives Bodl. Oxf., corresp. and papers
Wealth at death under £8000: probate, 21 March 1873, *CGPLA Eng. & Wales*

Ogilvie, Emilia Mary. *See* Fitzgerald, Emilia Mary (1731–1814).

Ogilvie, Sir Frederick Wolff (1893–1949), economist and college head, was born at Valparaiso, Chile, on 7 February 1893, the youngest son of William Maxwell Ogilvie, an engineer, and his wife, Mary Ann Wolff. The Ogilvies were Scots from Dundee. Ogilvie was educated at Clifton College and at Balliol College, Oxford, where he had a quiet university career, taking a first in classical moderations in 1913. His reading for *literae humaniores* was interrupted by the outbreak of the First World War and within two days he was in the forces as a second lieutenant, 4th Bedfordshire regiment. He quickly found himself in France. In April 1915 he was seriously wounded at Hill 60, and lost his left arm; he remained in the army, however, until the end of the war, and was demobilized in 1919 with the rank of captain.

Ogilvie returned at once to Balliol and in the autumn of

Sir Frederick Wolff Ogilvie (1893–1949), by unknown photographer, 1939

the same year became lecturer in economics at Trinity College, Oxford, being elected to a fellowship in 1920. Ogilvie married in 1922 Mary Helen (1900–1990), eldest daughter of Alexander Beith Macaulay, professor of apologetics and systematic theology at Trinity College, Glasgow; they had three sons. In 1926 he was appointed to the chair of political economy in Edinburgh.

The interest in the study of economics which Ogilvie had shown from his early undergraduate days was due partly to a growing social sense, and in Oxford and Edinburgh he was a sympathetic teacher of the subject. At all times his quality as a teacher and friend of the young was enriched by his knowledge of music and his unrestrained enjoyment of the outdoor life. He was also invited to act as guide and mentor in economic matters to a group of younger, and later most distinguished, Conservative members of parliament. During these years his main interests within his subject proved to be the tourist industry of Great Britain and the economic problems of Scotland. His only book, *The Tourist Movement*, was published in 1933, and he later contributed on the subject to the new edition of *Chambers's Encyclopaedia*. He was a member of the Edinburgh chamber of commerce and of trade boards, and also concerned himself with adult education and juvenile employment in Scotland.

In the autumn of 1934 Ogilvie left Edinburgh for Belfast, where he became president and vice-chancellor of the Queen's University. There he remained for four years, and left his mark in his own way. The university found in him a strength, integrity, and courtesy rarely combined in one person. He believed strongly in the value to a university of a wide social and cultural life, and he used his great personal charm and the persuasive impact of his own inner enjoyment of learning and the arts to very good purpose. He might well have been one of the great vice-chancellors, but in the summer of 1938 he was drawn away from the academic world to become the second director-general of the British Broadcasting Corporation in succession to Sir John Reith, who had guided its growth from the beginning and whose masterful single-mindedness had largely made it what it was.

In his memoirs Reith praised Ogilvie's personal charm, but added, 'I was quite sure he was not the man for the BBC' (Briggs, 2.637). Such indeed proved to be the case, the historian of the BBC describing Ogilvie's tenure of office as 'short, stormy and in some ways calamitous' (ibid.). The most insistent problems of Broadcasting House in wartime were organizational and administrative. The corporation emerged from the war in most remarkable esteem for its unremitting care for truth and for human sympathy throughout a remorseless struggle. But in order to play its part at all, triumphs of technical and administrative adjustment had to be achieved almost daily. This was not Ogilvie's sphere. Indeed, R. C. Norman, chairman of the BBC at the time of Ogilvie's appointment, later admitted that he had every quality 'except that of being able to manage a large organization, the one quality which was indispensable' (ibid., 2.638). Early in 1942 Ogilvie resigned. Though uncomplaining, he must have been deeply disappointed; but he secured notable personal success in performing special war duties for the British Council between 1943 and 1945.

At this time Ogilvie thought seriously of taking up editorial work in the national press, but in 1944 he became principal of Jesus College, Oxford. He was now fifty-one, and he had fewer than five more years to live; but in that short time he showed, as in Belfast, his great gifts for educational work in a university. His wide cultural contacts and his record of public service enabled him to give much to the college. By quietly infusing his own enjoyments and convictions into its way of life he made it a more friendly community, more enlightened, and more civilized. In 1948 he was grievously stricken by the death of his eldest son, James William Ogilvie, in a climbing accident on the Matterhorn, but he was a remarkable principal in the humane tradition.

In person Ogilvie was tall and fair, with grey eyes. His expression was serious and thoughtful, but a smile was never far away, for he was easily moved by friendship and his sense of humour was readily aroused. He was knighted in 1942 and died in London on 10 June 1949. Lady Ogilvie became in 1953 the principal of St Anne's College, Oxford. Their son Robert Maxwell Ogilvie became a fellow of Balliol in 1957.   C. R. Morris, *rev.*

Sources *The Times* (11 June 1949) · *WWW* · I. McIntyre, *The expense of glory: a life of John Reith* (1993) · A. Briggs, *The history of broadcasting in the United Kingdom*, 1–4 (1961–79) · I. Elliott, ed., *The Balliol College register, 1833–1933*, 2nd edn (privately printed, Oxford, 1934) ·

CGPLA Eng. & Wales (1949) · personal knowledge (1959) · private information (1959)

Archives BL, letters to Albert Monsbridge, Add. MS 65261 · U. Edin. L., corresp. with Charles Sarolea

Likenesses D. Foggie, pencil drawing, 1932, Scot. NPG · W. Stoneman, photograph, 1938, NPG · photograph, 1939, BBC Picture Archives, London [*see illus.*]

Wealth at death £10,546 10*s.* 2*d.*: confirmation, sealed in London, 24 Aug 1949; confirmation, Scotland, 1949

Ogilvie, Sir George, of Barras, first baronet (*fl.* 1634–1679), royalist army officer, was descended from the Ogilvies of Balnagarno, Forfarshire, and was the son of William Ogilvie of Lumgair, Kincardineshire, and Katherine, niece of Alexander Strachan of Thornton. In 1634, by a contract dated 31 January, he married Elizabeth, daughter of the Hon. Sir John Douglas of Barras, Forfarshire, fourth son of William, earl of Angus, and purchased Barras from his wife's brother.

Having in early life served in the German wars, Ogilvie was in 1651 appointed by William Keith, sixth Earl Marischal, with the title of lieutenant-governor, to hold the earl's castle of Dunnottar against the forces of Cromwell. Special importance attached to the trust committed to him from the fact that the regalia of Scotland had been placed in the castle, but for the supply of armaments and provisions he was almost wholly dependent on his own exertions. On 31 August 1651 the committee of estates addressed an order to Alexander Lindsay, first earl of Balcarres, authorizing him to receive the regalia from Ogilvie, whom they directed to deliver them up to Balcarres; but Ogilvie declined to do so on the ground that Balcarres was not properly authorized to relieve him of the responsibility, which had been imposed on him by parliament. He, however, declared his readiness to deliver them up if relieved of responsibility, or his readiness to defend his charge to the last if properly supplied with men, provisions, and ammunition. The castle was summoned by Cromwell's troops to surrender on 8 and 22 November, but Ogilvie expressed his determination to hold out. While the castle was closely besieged, the regalia were, at the instance of Margaret Erskine, dowager Countess Marischal, delivered by Lady Ogilvie to Mrs Grainger, the wife of the minister of Kinneff, who concealed them about her person, and, passing the lines of the besiegers without suspicion, took them to the church of Kinneff, where they were placed below the floor. Although Ogilvie had received a warrant from the Earl Marischal (a prisoner of war in London) empowering him to deliver up the castle to Major-General Deane, he maintained a firm attitude until he obtained terms as favourable as it was possible to grant. On 1 February 1652 he sent a letter to the king asking for speedy supplies of ammunition and provisions. These were not granted him, but on 12 April the king sent him a message approving of his fidelity, urging him to hold out until winter, and permitting him either to ship the regalia in a vessel sent to transfer them to Holland, or to retain them should he think the removal would dishearten the garrison. The castle was surrendered on 24 May to Colonel Thomas Morgan, who had received the siege guns needed to reduce the fortress. The conditions were that the garrison should march out with the usual honours, and be permitted to pass to their homes unmolested. The favourable terms were granted in the hope of obtaining possession of the regalia; but as Ogilvie failed to deliver them up, he and Lady Ogilvie were detained prisoners in a room of the castle until 10 January 1653, only obtaining their liberty when all hope of recovering the regalia was dissipated by a false but circumstantial report that they had been carried abroad. Ogilvie was also required to find caution in £2000 sterling.

The regalia remained in concealment at Kinneff until the Restoration, when they were delivered up by Ogilvie to Charles II. For his services in connection with their preservation, he was by letters patent on 5 March or 5 July 1662 created a baronet of Nova Scotia, and on 3 March 1666 received a new charter of the lands of Barras, which was ratified by parliament on 22 August 1670 and on 17 August 1679. In 1667 he was named a commissioner of supply for Kincardineshire, and in 1670 a commissioner of excise for the county. There is no record of the date of his death. He was buried at Kinneff, where there is a monument to him and his wife. He had a son, Sir William Ogilvie, who in 1701 published a pamphlet setting forth the special services of his father as preserver of the regalia, in contrast to those rendered by the Earl Marischal, the title being *A true account of the preservation of the regalia of Scotland*. The pamphlet, which was reprinted in the Somers Tracts, gave rise, at the instance of William Keith, second earl of Kintore, to an action before the privy council, which, on 8 July 1702, passed an act for burning the book at the cross of Edinburgh, and fined Sir William Ogilvie's son David, one of the defenders, £1200 Scots. The baronetcy became extinct with the death (*c.*1840) of Sir William Ogilvie, the eighth baronet.

T. F. HENDERSON, *rev.* EDWARD M. FURGOL

Sources GEC, *Baronetage*, 3.333 · F. D. Dow, *Cromwellian Scotland, 1651–1660* (1979) · *Reg. PCS*, 3rd ser. · *Calendar of the Clarendon state papers preserved in the Bodleian Library*, ed. O. Ogle and others, 5 vols. (1869–1970) · D. G. Barron, ed., *In defence of the regalia, 1651–2* (1910) · B. Whitelocke, *Memorials of English affairs*, new edn, 4 vols. (1853) · *APS*, 1661–86

Ogilvie, George (*d.* 1785). *See under* Mirror Club (*act.* 1776–1787).

Ogilvie, James (1760–1820), scholar, who claimed connection with the Ogilvys, earls of Findlater, was born in Aberdeen, and was educated there. He may be the James Ogilvie who graduated at King's College, Aberdeen, in 1790. He emigrated to the United States, where he ran a school, first in Milton, Virginia, and then in Richmond. He left the impression of being 'a man of singular endowments', gifted with 'the power of rousing the mind from its torpor and lending it wings' (*Southern Literary Messenger*, 14). He closed the school in 1809 and retired to a remote Kentucky cabin, where he wrote lectures, rebutting the theories of Godwin, and depending to some extent for his living on financial help from former pupils. He lectured with success throughout Virginia and the Atlantic states and was employed as a lecturer at the South Carolina College in 1815. He returned to Scotland to claim the lapsed earldom

of Findlater as a relative of James Ogilvy, the last earl of Findlater and Seafield of the Ogilvy line, who had died at Dresden in 1811. His claim, however, was not entertained. Constitutionally sensitive and excitable, and worn out with narcotics, he was believed to have committed suicide in Aberdeen on 18 September 1820.

Ogilvie's *Philosophical Essays* appeared at Philadelphia in 1816. The book is summarily discussed in *Blackwood's Magazine* (18, 18xx, 198), and it is criticized at length by E. T. Channing in the *North American Review* (4, 18xx).

T. W. BAYNE, *rev.* K. D. REYNOLDS

Sources *Who's who in American history* · Irving, *Scots.* · J. Ogilvie, 'Autobiographical sketch', *Philosophical essays* (1816) · "one of his pupils" ("H. of Richmond"), 'Recollections of James Ogilvie, earl of Findlater', *Southern Literary Messenger*, 14 (1848), 534–7 · private information (1894)

Ogilvie, John [St John Ogilvie] (1578/9–1615), Jesuit, the eldest son of Walter Ogilvie of Drum (and later perhaps of Milton), was born in Strathisla, Banffshire. Brought up a Calvinist, he matriculated in August 1592 at the protestant University of Helmstedt in northern Germany. In 1596, having become a Catholic, he entered the Scots College of Douai, at that time at Louvain. In June 1598 he was sent to the Scottish Benedictine abbey at Regensburg but by the end of the year was a student at the Jesuit college in Olomouc.

In November 1599, aged twenty, he entered the noviciate of the Jesuit Austrian-Bohemian province at Brno and two years later, on 26 December 1601, made his vows. The next nine years were spent in study and work in various places in the province. After three years of philosophy at Graz he taught for two years or more at Vienna. There followed an additional year of apologetics to prepare him for controversy, then for two years he studied theology at Olomouc, during which time he was in charge of a students' sodality, that is, a devotional confraternity. In August 1610 he was sent by the Jesuit-general to Paris, where he was ordained priest, and went on to Rouen to teach for three years.

At that time the general wished to resume missionary work in Scotland, though it was a particularly difficult and dangerous time for Catholicism, with John Spottiswood, archbishop of Glasgow, energetically supporting the Erastianism of James VI and I. Ogilvie volunteered and finally in 1613 received orders to go to Scotland. He landed at Leith in November 1613, in the guise of John Watson, horse dealer. We know very little of his movements, except that he went up to the north-east for a time, then returned south to Edinburgh. There followed a mysterious episode. About the end of February 1614 he went to London and was for a time at the royal court. Towards the end of March he travelled to Paris. His superior, James Gordon, was displeased and sent him back with orders not to return without permission, but the general was more sympathetic and commended his zeal. Though the purpose of his journey to France is not known it is most significant that he travelled from London to France and back with a safe conduct. The king surely knew Ogilvie and the plan he had in mind.

Back in Scotland in June, Ogilvie resumed his work of administering the sacraments to Catholics, reconciling those who had lapsed, and making new converts. He was active in Edinburgh, Glasgow, and Renfrewshire. It was secret and dangerous work, for at any time he could be betrayed, which is what happened. On 4 October 1614 he was captured while walking in a Glasgow street. Two narratives of his imprisonment were printed: the authorities' *True Relation*, their account of his examinations and execution, and his own description of his sufferings and his dealings with various interrogators. The latter, written in Latin, was continued by his Scottish associates and later published as *Relatio incarcerationis*. Further details were added by the later testimonies of his associates. Despite their very different purpose and slant the accounts agree on the main events.

On 5 October, the day after his capture, Ogilvie was examined by a group headed by Spottiswood, and their report was sent to the king. Ogilvie refused to answer on oath anything that would incriminate himself or others or would imply acceptance of the king's authority to put questions on spiritual matters. After two months' confinement in Glasgow he was taken to Edinburgh and on 12 December was examined before five lords commissioners appointed by the king. Again he refused to divulge where or with whom he had stayed, and for the same reasons. So, as the king had given leave for him to be tortured, he was kept awake for (according to his own narrative) eight days and nine nights until he was not far from death. How much he divulged in this condition is not clear. After only one day's respite the examination was resumed, then he was taken back to Glasgow by Spottiswood, arriving on Christmas eve.

Ogilvie's narrative was apparently written during this second period in Glasgow. It is a fresh and lively account though also diffuse and circumstantial, with details of ill treatment as well as of questioning on matters of religion, to which he replied with spirit. Not surprisingly it has many difficulties and ambiguities but clearly the treatment he received was inconsistent, perhaps deliberately so. At times his feet were bound to a massive iron bar, yet with Spottiswood he visited a neighbour's gardens and house. Spottiswood spoke to him in public in friendly fashion, yet increased the rigours of his imprisonment. He was denied pen and paper, yet he was able to write letters and his lengthy narrative.

On 18 January 1615 he was formally questioned on five points concerning the king's power and the pope's jurisdiction. These were drawn up by the king, and the five men conducting the inquiry were appointed by the king. In fact, apart from the initial investigation immediately after Ogilvie's capture, the legal proceedings did not follow the ordinary course of law but were put in place by the king personally. James had been controverting on these matters with Jesuit theologians and during the examination works by Bellarmine and Suarez lay on the table. The five questions did not concern the king's authority alone but whether the pope's authority was superior.

To the first two questions Ogilvie answered clearly that the pope could judge the king, had power over him in spiritual matters, and could excommunicate him. The next three questions were whether the pope could depose the king, whether it was lawful to kill the king so deposed, and whether the pope could release subjects from their allegiance to the king. To each of these Ogilvie refused to reply, as the king had no authority to judge such matters. At his first examination, however, Ogilvie had declared that he detested the assassination of kings and had condemned the Gunpowder Plot.

Ogilvie's final trial was fixed for 28 February. He was told beforehand (and at the trial itself this was stated explicitly) that he was not accused of saying mass or converting anyone to Catholicism or for matters of conscience, but for declining the king's authority. The proceedings were formal, with four judges, assisted by a group of notables headed by Spottiswood, and a jury of fifteen men of some standing. Ogilvie refused to change his previous answers, and was found guilty and condemned to be hanged. Three hours later he was taken to a gallows erected nearby and executed. There are various accounts of incidents on the scaffold which must have given much publicity to the Jesuit's fate. He was buried that day outside the city.

A number of those who had sheltered Ogilvie were condemned to death but the sentences were commuted to exile. Indeed Ogilvie was the only Catholic in Scotland ever to be judicially sentenced and executed for his religion. Even James Moffat, a Scots Jesuit who was captured one month after Ogilvie, was tried by ordinary process of law and exiled, as was Patrick Anderson only six years later, though they shared Ogilvie's views on papal and royal authority. The strong suspicion remains that there was something personal between Ogilvie and the king. Ogilvie at his final trial declared that he and Father William Crichton, a Scots Jesuit who had consistently supported James's succession to the English throne, had done more for James abroad than any of his accusers. He was surely referring to his mission to France in the spring of 1614. James knew him and knew his purpose.

Ogilvie's posthumous renown spread quickly on the continent. The *Relatio incarcerationis* was published in eight places and he featured increasingly in the printed literature of Europe. Initial steps for his beatification were taken by an examination in 1628 at Würzburg of two of his associates in Glasgow, both of them now monks in the Scots monastery there, and in 1629 at Rome of an Edinburgh associate. Nothing more was done until in the nineteenth century the publication of Scottish historical sources led to his rediscovery and so to the production of Catholic devotional literature featuring him. In December 1929 he was beatified and in October 1976 formally canonized.

MARK DILWORTH

Sources W.E. Brown, *John Ogilvie* (1925) • C. Carrell and G. Boardman, eds., *St. John Ogilvie S.J., 1579–1615* (1979) • W. J. Anderson, '"A Jesuit that calls himself Ogilvy"', *Innes Review*, 15 (1964), 56–65 • M. Dilworth, 'Three documents relating to St John Ogilvie', *Innes*

Review, 34 (1983), 51–65 • J. Schmidl, *Historia Societatis Jesu Provinciae Bohemiae*, 2 (1749), 200–01, 561, 578–9, 790–96 • *Reg. PCS*, 1st ser., vol. 10 • H. Chadwick, 'An important letter on Blessed John Ogilvie', *Innes Review*, 15 (1964), 182–3
Archives Archivum Romanum Societatis Iesu, Rome, letters
Likenesses M. K., line engraving, NPG • portrait, repro. in Brown, *John Ogilvie*, facing p. 250 • portrait, parish church, St Gilles, Pecquincourt, Nord, France; repro. in Brown, *John Ogilvie*, frontispiece
Wealth at death goods confiscated after capture

Ogilvie, John (1732–1813), Church of Scotland minister and poet, was born on either 18 or 28 November 1732 in Aberdeen, and was baptized on 7 December at his father's church, St Nicholas's, in the town. He was the eldest of six children of James Ogilvie (1695–1776), minister, and his wife, Elizabeth Strachan (*d.* 1778). He graduated from Marischal College, Aberdeen, in 1750, and after a period studying, probably in Edinburgh, was licensed as a minister in the Church of Scotland on 16 July 1755. He was ordained to the parish of Lumphanan, south Aberdeenshire, on 15 March 1759, but was translated to the neighbouring parish of Midmar, 15 miles west of Aberdeen, on 27 March 1760. He remained as minister there for fifty-three years and was noted as a kindly, mild-mannered pastor 'with all the simplicity of a child' (*Scots Magazine*). He married, on 22 January 1771, Margaret (Peggy) Reid (1751/2–1804), daughter of Patrick Reid, minister of Clatt, Aberdeenshire; they had eleven children. He had an early literary friendship with James Beattie; David Dalrymple, Lord Hailes, advised on and corrected some of his works. He travelled to London several times, and is unfairly remembered principally as the butt of Samuel Johnson's remark, at a dinner party in 1763, that 'the noblest prospect that a Scotchman ever sees, is the high road that leads him to England' (Boswell, *Life*, 1.425). Ogilvie recorded that, contrary to Boswell's account, he had been a diffident young guest, who only ventured on a gentle defence of some aspects of Scotland in reply to a prolonged disparagement by Johnson who, he discovered, had never yet been there (*Edinburgh Magazine*, 355).

Ogilvie was a prolific and varied writer in poetry and prose. His earliest published poems, including *The Day of Judgment* (published 1753), were written before the age of seventeen. Other early verse included odes and elegies, but his poems became progressively longer and more ambitious, supported with long erudite prefaces and footnotes. *Providence* (1764) is a blank verse theodicy, justifying God's plan in the natural order, the lateness of the Christian revelation, and the apparent injustices of human life. Later he turned to epic subjects and style with *Rona* (1777), a tragedy set on a Hebridean island, *The Fane of the Druids* (1787–9), a partly mythical early history of Scotland, inspired by druid remains in his parish, and finally *Britannia, a National Epic Poem* (1801). This massive work, preceded by a dissertation justifying the use of epic machinery of angels and demons, described in over 15,000 lines of blank verse the legendary founding of Britain by a descendant of Aeneas of Troy. It had a distinguished list of

John Ogilvie (1732–1813), by James Heath, pubd 1801 (after A. Robertson)

subscribers, headed by the prince of Wales, but the *Monthly Review* feared that 'few persons will be able to accomplish a progress through the whole'. In his eighth decade he was still energetically contributing to *The Poetical Register*, and published anonymously a poem, *Human Life* (1806): the sections on 'Infancy' and 'Childhood' are attractively and accurately observed. His last published poem was an elegy written in his seventy-ninth year.

Ogilvie wrote on the theory of aesthetics, most notably in *Philosophical Observations on the Nature, Character and Various Species of Composition* (1774), which has some originality in its exploration of the psychology of literary composition, and the interaction between the faculties of reason and imagination. He also published sermons, both in a collected volume (1766) and individually, and *An Inquiry into the Causes of the Infidelity and Scepticism of the Times* (1783), exploring the social psychology of religious disbelief.

Ogilvie's works, whose sales were small, show great erudition in the ancient classics, but refer surprisingly little to his literary contemporaries. Although he was praised by John Langhorne, William Duff, and Thomas Blacklock, a fair contemporary judgement was that his undoubted talents had been spread on too many and too varied works to make any lasting impact. According to the entry in Joseph Robertson's *Lives of the Scottish Poets* (1822), Ogilvie was 'an able man, lost', whose 'intellectual wealth and industry were wasted in huge and unhappy speculations' (Robertson, 3.136). He was awarded a DD from Marischal College in 1766, was appointed to the committee for the revision of the translations and paraphrases used in the

Church of Scotland in 1775, and in 1789 was elected a fellow of the Royal Society of Edinburgh. He died at Aberdeen on 17 November 1813.   ROGER J. ROBINSON

Sources *Fasti Scot.*, new edn · *Scots Magazine and Edinburgh Literary Miscellany*, 76 (1814), 79 · J. R. Irvine, 'Gerard, Beattie, and Ogilvie: the evolution of the "new" rhetoric at Aberdeen', PhD diss., University of Iowa, 1974 · U. Edin. L., MSS La. II. 588, 595 · NL Scot., Newhailes MSS · NL Scot., MS 3813, fols. 37–8 · John Murray, London, archives · U. Aberdeen, MS 30/1/1,2 · W. Walker, *The bards of Bon-Accord, 1375–1860* (1887) · Boswell, *Life* · *Edinburgh Magazine, or, Literary Miscellany*, 14 (1791), 355–7 [letter from Ogilvie to the editor] · [J. Robertson], *Lives of Scottish poets*, 3 vols. (1821–2) · R. H. Carnie, 'A biographical and critical study of the life and writings of Sir David Dalrymple, Lord Hailes', PhD diss., U. St Andr., 1954 · *Monthly Review*, new ser., 37 (1802), 359–64 · G. Chalmers, 'The history of the poetry and music of Scotland, from the earliest times to the nineteenth century', U. Edin. L., MS La. III. 521.3 · Nichols, *Illustrations*, vol. 4 · W. Duff, *An essay on original genius* (1767) · J. Langhorne, *Genius and valour: a Scotch pastoral* (1763) · T. Blacklock, *Poems, together with an essay on the education of the blind* (1793) · bap. reg. Scot.
Archives NL Scot., Newhailes MSS · NL Scot., MS 3813, fols. 37–8 · U. Edin. L., letters to *Poetical Register*, MSS La. II. 588, 595
Likenesses J. Heath, stipple (after A. Robertson), BM, NPG; repro. in J. Ogilvie, *Britannia, a national epic poem* (1801), frontispiece [*see illus.*]

Ogilvie, John [*pseud.* Iota] (**1797–1867**), lexicographer, born on 17 April 1797 in the parish of Marnoch, Banffshire, was the son of William Ogilvie, crofter, and his wife, Ann Leslie, daughter of a farmer in a neighbouring parish. He received some elementary education at home, and attended the parish school for two quarters. Ogilvie then worked as a ploughman until he was twenty-one. In 1818, following an accident, one of his legs had to be amputated above the knee. Afterwards he taught successively in two subscription schools in the Banffshire parishes of Fordyce and Gamrie. At the same time, by intensive study and with the help of a neighbouring schoolmaster, he prepared for university, and in October 1824 entered Marischal College, Aberdeen. Having added to his income by private tuition he graduated MA on 14 April 1828. He remained in Aberdeen as a private tutor until 13 May 1831, when he was appointed mathematical master in Gordon's Hospital, an important educational establishment in the city. On 15 November 1842 Ogilvie married Susan Smart (*d.* 1853), daughter of a farmer near Stonehaven, Kincardineshire. Marischal College conferred on him the honorary degree of LLD on 15 January 1848. He retained his mastership until July 1859.

To the short-lived *Aberdeen Magazine* (1831–2) Ogilvie contributed, under the signature Iota, ten spirited and amusing imitations of Horace in the Scottish dialect. In 1836 he worked on Blackie & Son's annotated edition of Thomas Stackhouse's *History of the Bible*. Messrs Blackie engaged him in 1838 to revise and enlarge Webster's *English Dictionary*, the result being *The Imperial Dictionary, English, Technical, and Scientific*, issued in parts from 1847 onwards, and published complete in 1850, with a supplement in 1855. In 1863 Ogilvie issued an abridgement of the dictionary under the title *Comprehensive English Dictionary, Explanatory, Pronouncing, and Etymological*, with the pronunciation supplied by Richard Cull. In 1865 appeared the *Students' English Dictionary, Etymological, Pronouncing, and Explanatory*, in which etymology and definitions received special attention. Two features of all three dictionaries were their attention to science and technology and their engravings, the *Imperial* claiming to be the first after Bailey's to use pictorial illustrations. A modern evaluation regards it as 'a hugely competent work, very well-suited to its times, and one which enjoyed much success in subsequent editions. It marks the flowering of the encyclopaedic dictionary in Britain' (*International Encyclopedia of Lexicography*). Ogilvie's last work was a condensation of the *Students' English Dictionary* for use in schools (1867). An unfinished revision of *The Imperial Dictionary* was issued in 1882–3 by Charles Annandale.

In his later years Ogilvie suffered a partial loss of sight, and after his retirement was almost blind. He died of typhoid fever at Aberdeen on 21 November 1867. His wife predeceased him on 20 May 1853, leaving two daughters and a son.   T. W. BAYNE, *rev.* JOHN D. HAIGH

Sources W. Walker, *The bards of Bon-Accord, 1375–1860* (1887), 613–16 · *An international encyclopedia of lexicography*, 2 (1990), 1960 · J. Green, *Chasing the sun: dictionary-makers and the dictionaries they made* (1996), 361

Ogilvie, Patrick (**1606–1674**), army officer in the Swedish service, was born in Scotland, the son of Colonel William Ogilvie, a younger brother of Sir Patrick Ogilvie of Inchmartin, and either his wife, Elizabeth Langlands, or Barbara Kinnaird. Not much is known of Ogilvie's early life, until he entered Swedish military service as an ensign in 1624 in the regiment of James Spens, the son of the Stuart ambassador in Stockholm, Sir James Spens. From 1632 he served as a major in the conscripted infantry regiment from the Åbo region, and after ten years' service he was promoted lieutenant-colonel. He continued with this regiment until he became its colonel in 1657.

Although Ogilvie married three times, the dates of the marriages and whether he had children remain unclear. His first wife, a Scotswoman, was the daughter of James Scott and Margareta Gibson. His second wife was a Swedish noblewoman, Catharina Mannersköld, as was his third wife, Helena Sass.

Ogilvie undertook an active role in civic life in Sweden, and made donations to the poor in July 1640. He was keen to be integrated further into Swedish society and so produced two documents in order to initiate the ennoblement process in Sweden. The first was signed in 1640 by his fellow Scottish officers James Lumsden, David Leslie, William Borthwick, Hans Ramsay, and William Weiners. The second document was witnessed in 1642 by Baron Patrick Ruthven, Baron Vilhelm Spens, Ludvig Leslie, James Hamilton, Hugo Mowatt, and Patrik Morus. The two documents claimed that Ogilvie was of Scottish noble descent on both maternal and paternal sides. As a result he was introduced to the Swedish house of nobility in 1642; he received donations of land from Queen Kristina in 1648. The following year Ogilvie provided the Riksdåd (the Swedish parliament) with a further document from Perth dated 1647.

Ogilvie was a colourful character, as the records of the

Riksråd (Swedish state council) reveal. In 1650 they discussed punishing Ogilvie for having attacked a burgess in Stockholm. He had already been pardoned by Queen Kristina for unlawfully firing a weapon on her birthday. Despite these misdemeanours Ogilvie remained in royal favour and obtained the rights to two further properties in 1651. The land he held included Selkis and Voltis in Kumo parish, Årlak in Virmo parish, Otrova by Narva and Reguleva in Koporie region in Ingermanland, Vurda in Jama region, and Teivaala in Birkkala parish in Finland. Ogilvie did not confine himself to military duties, but entered the Swedish diplomatic service, and conveyed correspondence between the Russian General Nashchokin and the Swedish military commander Magnus de la Gardie in 1656. Sweden was at war with Poland at the time and Russian support was vital to Swedish success. The following year he moved from the Åbo to the Viborg region infantry, and soon took on the position of governor. He also served in Riga in 1657 informing the Swedish government of shortages in manpower, provisions, and ammunition there. In 1660 he was again a governor, this time in the Kexholm region. After that nothing is known of him until his death in 1674.   A. N. L. GROSJEAN

Sources G. Elgenstierna, *Den introducerade svenska adelns ättartavlor med tillägg och rättelser*, 9 vols. (1925–36), vol. 5 · *Anglica*, Riksarkivet, Stockholm, vol. 4, fol. 22 · *Svenska sändebuds till utländska hof och deras sändebud till Sverige*, 1841, Riksarkivet, Stockholm · katalog öfver sköldebref, 1841, Riddarhusarkivet, Stockholm, Sweden · military muster rolls, Krigsarkivet, Stockholm, 1635/1; 1636/14; 1638/15; 1639/10; 1640/9; 1641/11; 1642/9; 1645/17; 1647/11, 14; 1649/7; 1650/6; 1651/4, 6; 1652/6, 1654/4–5; 1655/4; 1658/6; 1659/7; 1660/9; 1661/9; 1666/6 · N. A. Kullberg, S. Bergh, and P. Sondén, eds., *Svenska riksrådets protokoll*, 18 vols. (Stockholm, 1878–1959) · S. Bergh and B. Taube, eds., *Sveriges ridderskaps och adels riksdagsprotokoll*, 17 vols. (1871), *passim* · J. M. Thomson and others, eds., *Registrum magni sigilli regum Scotorum / The register of the great seal of Scotland*, 11 vols. (1882–1914), vol. 9, p. 369 · *Reg. PCS*, 2nd ser., 7.205 · *Scots peerage* · T. A. Fischer [E. L. Fischer], *The Scots in Sweden* (1907)

Ogilvie, William (*d.* 1635), abbot of Würzburg, was probably from north-east Scotland, for he used the arms of the Ogilvies of Deskford, Banffshire. Nothing is known of his parentage or early life, but the description 'senex' on his tombstone suggests he was probably born no later than 1575. Converted to Catholicism, he entered the Scots Benedictine monastery at Würzburg, Germany, probably in 1598, at which time the mutual relationship of the three Scots monasteries in Regensburg, Würzburg, and Erfurt was not defined. Ogilvie, elected abbot of Erfurt in the winter of 1611–12, was administrator of Regensburg the following winter and in 1613 returned to Würzburg.

On 22 January 1615 Ogilvie was elected abbot of Würzburg. From the start he was subject only to the bishop. His firm and efficient rule led to growth in numbers and prestige, helped greatly by the recent discovery of the grave of St Macarius, its reputedly saintly founder, whose relics became the focus of growing devotion and visits by pilgrims. Prestige was also increased by associates of the Jesuit martyr John Ogilvie entering as novices. The arrival in particular of John Mayne (Silvanus in religion) led to plans for the Scots monks to undertake mission work in Scotland. When Mayne procrastinated William Ogilvie was, in 1629, put in charge of the enterprise by Rome.

Ogilvie began his abbacy with six resident monks. By 1625 there were twelve and he built a residential block and a gatehouse. Four young monks matriculated at Würzburg University, then in 1628 Ogilvie was elected its rector magnificus. The bishop made him judge in an ecclesiastical court and in 1627–8 appointed him administrator of Schwarzach Abbey nearby.

The Thirty Years' War was raging and Swedish protestant forces came to Würzburg in October 1631. This was Ogilvie's finest hour. As the notables fled he remained and was the town's delegate to treat with the Swedes. Exactly three years later he played a notable part in the recapture of the town. Both during and after the Swedish occupation he was an official for regulating church affairs. Within a year, however, on 17 September 1635, he died.

The wars caused enormous destruction in south Germany. The Scots monks were scattered; Ogilvie's achievements were largely destroyed. It was, however, his monastic recruits, notably Alexander Baillie, who administered all three abbeys after the débâcle and helped to rebuild their fortunes. Würzburg monks continued to work in Scotland. Ogilvie, the greatest of the Würzburg abbots, was described on his tombstone in the abbey church as 'de Franconia bene meritus' ('deserving of Franconia's gratitude').   MARK DILWORTH

Sources M. Dilworth, *The Scots in Franconia* (1974) · T. A. Fischer, *The Scots in Germany* (1902) · M. Dilworth, 'Two necrologies of Scottish Benedictine abbeys in Germany', *Innes Review*, 9 (1958), 173–203

Ogilvie, William (1736–1819), classical scholar and advocate of common property in land, was the only son of James Ogilvie, landowner and farmer, of Pittensear, in Moray, and his wife, Marjory Steuart, of Tannachy. His parents died when he was quite young, leaving him in charge of the estate and with the care of his four sisters. It is likely that he attended the nearby Elgin grammar school before entering King's College, Aberdeen, as third bursar of his year, in 1755. Having graduated MA in 1759 he was schoolmaster at Cullen, Banffshire, for a year. He attended Glasgow University for the winter session of 1760–61 and Edinburgh University for the winter session of 1761–2. Through the influence of his relative Lord Deskford (later earl of Seafield) he was appointed an assistant professor of philosophy in King's College, Aberdeen, on 25 November 1761, on the assurance that he would move into the first vacancy of a regent's place that occurred. He began teaching in November 1762, as an all-round professor of philosophy, and became a full regent in 1764. He was appointed professor of humanity in 1765, by an exchange of offices, and continued in that role until 1817, when failing health necessitated the appointment of an assistant.

Ogilvie enthralled his students with the outstanding quality of his translations of classical writers, especially Virgil and Horace, although these were never published. His scholarship extended to natural history and the fine arts and he was a keen antiquary, medallist, and numismatist. He collected specimens for a museum of natural history in King's College as well as a group of rare prints, mainly portraits. D. C. Macdonald was strongly convinced that Ogilvie visited the continent at some stage, possibly as travelling tutor and companion to Alexander Gordon, fourth duke of Gordon, but the latter's grand tour coincided with the commencement of Ogilvie's teaching duties and he is known to have taken another tutor.

In 1781 Ogilvie published anonymously *An Essay on the Right of Property in Land*. In it he asserted the birthright of every citizen to an equal share of property in land and outlined means by which this could be progressively achieved. He considered land values as having three parts, the original, the improved, and the improvable values; the first and third of these belonged to the community and only the second to the landholder. He argued from experience and wrote in the context of having inherited property, though he had sold the estate of Pittensear to the earl of Fife in 1772, while retaining the mansion house. In 1773 he purchased the property of Oldfold and Stonegavel, just outside Aberdeen, for £1500. With the aid of a £2000 loan from the duke of Gordon extensive improvements to the property were carried out before it was sold, in 1808, for £4000.

Ogilvie's clarity of thought, freedom from preconceptions, and disinterested motives inevitably brought him into conflict with colleagues in King's College. In 1783 he was perturbed at the sale of college ground that might have been used as a botanic garden. He was conscious of the college's other dubious practices, including the misappropriation of bursary funds, and found himself in a minority in opposing private interest pursued to the detriment of the college. These established party lines not surprisingly held good in 1786, when he revived the issue of union between King's College and Marischal College. Given two universities within a mile of one another the eventual fusion of the colleges seemed only a matter of time. However, in spite of the positive attitude of Marischal College and Ogilvie's wholehearted sponsorship, self-interest prevailed at King's College and the union proposals were rejected. Ogilvie had at least won the argument with his lucid and ironic advocacy, and collected much support from outside the college as well as that of the rector, Sir William Forbes, before the latter was deposed.

In 1793 Ogilvie received the honorary degree of STD from Columbia College, New York. Pryse Lockhart Gordon, a former student, visited the already gout-crippled Ogilvie in 1800, bearing Greek and Roman coins and fragments from Pompeii. He recalled:

> It was delightful to see how the eyes of the old antiquary sparkled (or rather squinted), when I laid before him these treasures as a *ricordanza*, and the pleasure with which he examined them. I was much surprised to find in our conversation the minute acquaintance which he had of every work of art in Italy, the correctness of his taste and wonderful memory. (Gordon, 24)

While Ogilvie's agrarian views were never likely to find powerful friends in their day, his *Essay* became a point of reference for subsequent advocates of land reform. His unquestioned benevolence and personal sincerity meant that his radicalism provoked a less hostile reaction than might otherwise have been the case. Having been a lifelong bachelor of reclusive habits, Ogilvie died at Aberdeen on 14 February 1819, recognized as 'one of the most accomplished scholars of the age' (*The Times*, 23 Feb 1819), and was buried in the south transept of St Machar's Cathedral, Aberdeen.   LIONEL ALEXANDER RITCHIE

Sources D. C. Macdonald, *Birthright in land* (1891) · *The Times* (23 Feb 1819) · P. L. Gordon, *Personal memoirs, or, Reminiscences of men and manners at home and abroad*, 1 (1830), 23–5 · *Memoirs of the life of the Right Honourable Sir James Mackintosh*, ed. R. J. Mackintosh, 2 vols. (1835), vol. 1, p. 17 · F. Douglas, *A general description of the east coast of Scotland* (1782), 198–9 · D. Sage, *Memorabilia domestica* (1889), 317–18 · W. R. Humphries, *William Ogilvie and the projected union of the colleges, 1786–1787* (1940) · P. J. Anderson, ed., *Officers and graduates of University and King's College, Aberdeen, MVD–MDCCCLX*, New Spalding Club, 11 (1893), 49, 63 · Nichols, *Illustrations*, 4.837–8 · *Scottish Notes and Queries*, 3 (1889–90), 3–5 · DNB
Likenesses engraving, repro. in Macdonald, *Birthright in land*, frontispiece

Ogilvy. *See also* Ogilvie.

Ogilvy, Alexander, of Inverquharity (*d.* 1446), landowner, was the eldest son of John Ogilvy of Inverquharity, son of Sir Walter Ogilvy of Auchterhouse (*fl. c.*1368–1392), hereditary sheriff of Forfar. It was in this part of north-east Scotland that lands, office, and family connections made the Ogilvys influential. Ogilvy's uncle Sir Walter Ogilvy of Lintrathen served James I as master of the king's household and treasurer, and his cousin Marjory, daughter of Alexander Ogilvy of Auchterhouse, sheriff of Forfar, married David Lindsay, third earl of Crawford. Ogilvy's son, another Alexander, served as a hostage for the ransom of James I from 1427 until 1432, when he is described as the son of the sheriff of Forfar.

On 28 May 1442 Ogilvy was himself present at the sheriff court held at Inverbervie in the sheriffdom of Kincardine, and on 1 August that year he witnessed an agreement between two powerful north-east magnates, Alexander Seton, Lord Gordon, and Robert, Lord Keith, the marischal, at Cluny, in the sheriffdom of Aberdeen. Ogilvy's only recorded appearance as a witness to a royal charter was on 7 September 1444, when he was with the king at Dalkeith, but it is clear from the exchequer accounts for 1445 that he held the offices of bailie of Panmure and keeper of Methven Castle, further evidence of the importance of the extended Ogilvy family as royal agents in the Forfar region.

In 1445, according to the Auchinleck chronicle, the Ogilvys took part in a raid mounted against the Fife possessions of James Kennedy, bishop of St Andrews, for which Kennedy excommunicated the perpetrators. The chronicler ties this in with a dispute which arose in the following year concerning Ogilvy's designs upon the justiciarship of the abbey of Arbroath, contested between himself and Alexander Lindsay, master of Crawford. The abbey deposed Lindsay in favour of Ogilvy, but the former was unwilling to relinquish his position without a fight. Battle was joined at Arbroath, the Auchinleck chronicle reports, late on Sunday 23 January 1446, and resulted in the death of David, third earl of Crawford, who had tried to mediate. Ogilvy, severely wounded, was said by one chronicle source (probably following a local tradition in Angus) to have been taken to Crawford's castle of Finavon, where Ogilvy's cousin Marjory, distraught at hearing of the death of her husband, smothered him to death.

C. A. McGLADDERY

Sources J. M. Thomson and others, eds., *Registrum magni sigilli regum Scotorum / The register of the great seal of Scotland*, 11 vols. (1882–1914), vol. 2 · T. Thomson, ed., *The Auchinleck chronicle* (privately printed, Edinburgh, 1819); repr. (1877) · G. Burnett and others, eds., *The exchequer rolls of Scotland*, 5 (1882) · W. B. D. D. Turnbull, ed., *Extracta e variis cronicis Scocie*, Abbotsford Club, 23 (1842) · A. I. Dunlop, *The life and times of James Kennedy, bishop of St Andrews*, St Andrews University Publications, 46 (1950)

Ogilvy, Sir Alexander, first baronet, Lord Forglen (*d.* **1727**), judge, was the second son of George Ogilvy, second Lord Banff, and his wife, Agnes, only daughter of Alexander Falconer, first Lord Halkerton. In 1685 Ogilvy was accused by Sir Alexander Forbes of Tolquhoun of having taken from Forbes's house a silver mazer, or cup, and sued for its value, but it transpired that Forbes had forgotten that he had earlier taken the mazer to a goldsmith for repair. Forbes was subsequently fined 20,000 merks for this defamation of Ogilvy's character, half as a penalty, which was subsequently remitted, and half as compensation to Ogilvy, which he was obliged to pay.

Although there is no record of his legal training, Ogilvy was described as an advocate when he was appointed deputy keeper of the signet on 22 February 1699. In the same year he was appointed warden of the Royal Mint. On 4 June 1701 he was created a baronet, and he sat in the Scottish parliament as commissioner for the burgh of Banff in 1702 and in 1703–7. In 1703 he and Lord Belhaven were ordered into custody for having quarrelled and come to blows in the parliament house in the presence of the lord high commissioner. On 30 June, having admitted their offence, they were to be freed, but had to await the king's pleasure; Lord Belhaven was fined £5000 for having struck Ogilvy, the additional order that he should ask pardon on his knees having been dispensed with. Ogilvy was appointed to the council of trade in 1705, and in 1706 was a commissioner for the Union, which he warmly supported in parliament.

On 23 July 1706 Ogilvy was appointed a lord of session, with the title Lord Forglen, and later that year he was made a privy councillor. With his first wife, Mary (*b.* 1663), eldest daughter of Sir John Allardice of Allardice, Kincardineshire, he had four sons and four daughters. There were no children from his second marriage, to Mary (1656–1748), daughter of David *Leslie, first Lord Newark, and widow of Sir Francis Kinloch of Gilmerton. He died on 3 March 1727, and was succeeded in the baronetcy by his grandson Alexander Ogilvie.

T. F. HENDERSON, *rev.* ANITA McCONNELL

Sources M. D. Young, ed., *The parliaments of Scotland: burgh and shire commissioners*, 2 (1993), 551 · G. Brunton and D. Haig, *An historical account of the senators of the college of justice, from its institution in MDXXXII* (1832), 482–4 · R. Douglas, *The peerage of Scotland*, 2nd edn, ed. J. P. Wood, 1 (1813), 193–4; 2 (1813), 306 · J. Lauder, ed., *The decisions of the lords of council and session*, 2 vols. (1759–61)

Ogilvy, David, styled sixth earl of Airlie (**1725–1803**), Jacobite army officer, was the eldest son of John Ogilvy, styled fifth earl of Airlie (1699–1761), and Margaret (*d.* 1767), eldest daughter and heir of David Ogilvy of Cluny, Aberdeenshire. He was born in Scotland on 16 February 1725, and educated in Perth and afterwards perhaps at King's College, Aberdeen, and at Edinburgh University. A scion of a family whose Stuart loyalism is commemorated in the song 'The Bonnie Hoose o Airlie', he was commissioned as Jacobite lord lieutenant of Angus (Forfarshire) before the beginning of the 1745 rising, and promised his services to Prince Charles Edward at Perth in September. Ogilvy joined the Jacobite army with a battalion of Angus men on 3 October 1745, going off thereafter to raise the excise there. He was accompanied by his wife, the 'strikingly beautiful' Margaret [**Margaret Ogilvy**, Lady Ogilvy (**1724–1757**)], daughter of Sir James Johnstone, baronet, of Westerhall, Lanarkshire, and niece of Patrick Murray, Lord Elibank; they had a son, David, who did not assume the title, and two daughters. Not only did Lady Ogilvy share in the hardships of the army in Scotland, she also took an active part in the campaign, 'standing upon the Cross of Cupar in Angus with a drawn sword in her hand' on one occasion (Seton and Arnot, 3.238–9). The anti-Jacobite tract *The Female Rebels* (1747) described her as an exemplar of the 'unwomanly' qualities of female Jacobitism, exchanging 'delicacy of sentiment, mercy, tenderness, and compassion, the peculiar ornaments of the fair sex' for the immoral and wanton activities of the 'wild transports of lawless ambition, the lust of power, cruelty, revenge' (Mackenzie, 247). Ogilvy's Forfarshire regiment (which later included a second battalion raised under Sir James Kinloch when Ogilvy was in England) is the best-attested of all the Jacobite units, since a detailed regimental order book survives (printed in volume one of the Spalding Club *Miscellany* in 1841). Its maximum strength was about 800, and it is instructive to note that the names of many ordinary lowland small-town tradesmen and merchants appear on its muster roll. Chosen as one of the prince's council of war and privy council, Ogilvy was among the majority who expressed reservations concerning Charles's conduct during the rising, being also (with Elcho and Lord George Murray) highly critical of the prince's Irish advisers. Despite the composition of his own regiment, he was also disappointed at the lack of greater lowland support. Irritated by being allotted what he deemed the 'dirty work' of command of the baggage train after the fall of Carlisle (McLynn, *Jacobite Army*, 46), he threatened to resign his commission. At Derby he was among the foremost of those arguing for a retreat at the council of war.

On the army's return to Scotland, during which some of his soldiers had been sacrificed in the garrison at Carlisle,

Ogilvy's regiment was involved in the ill-fated siege of Stirling. At Falkirk both battalions stood at the centre of the Jacobite second line; Lady Ogilvy herself insisted on being up with the reserve. At the battle of Culloden, ordered back from the right flank into the reserve, they were, at the end of the battle, the only intact regiment who had taken part: even so, in the confusion Ogilvy was reported dead after the battle. Facing about several times as they withdrew in formation, by keeping Lieutenant-General Henry Hawley's cavalry in check the Forfarshires saved much of the right wing of the Jacobite army. Many retreated intact back to Angus, where units of Ogilvy's regiment seem to have caused trouble to the government for some time. After the battle, Ogilvy skulked in his own country before escaping via Bergen, in Norway (where he was briefly confined in May 1746), and Sweden to France, Lady Ogilvy meanwhile being taken prisoner by Cumberland in Inverness. In June she was sent to Edinburgh, but contrived to make her escape in November, joining her husband in France, where she died in 1757.

Once he arrived in exile, Ogilvy was seen as 'inclined … to make a figure in France', as Lochiel put it (McLynn, *Jacobites*, 129). This he did, gaining command of Ogilvy's regiment in 1748 and eventually rising to lieutenant-general in Louis XV's service. Ogilvy's regiment was mentioned for possible use in subsequent Jacobite attempts: it was the place where 'most of the refugees from the [Jacobite] army … seeking further military service found a haven' (Gibson, 166). In exile, he continued to write to his family under pseudonyms drawn from their locality, such as Eskside, Elyth (or Alyth), and Lintrathen (the original title was Lord Ogilvy of Alith and Lintrathen). Following his father's death in July 1761 he became titular sixth earl of Airlie. Nine years later he married his second wife, Anne (d. 1798), daughter of James Stewart of Blairhill, Perthshire; they had no children.

In 1778 Ogilvy was pardoned by George III and returned to Scotland, where his pardon was confirmed by parliament in 1783. He was the recipient of a French pension, which Napoleon offered to continue on his coming to power: Ogilvy declined. He died at Cortachy on 3 March 1803. He was among 'the most handsome of the Jacobite commanders' (McLynn, *Jacobite Army*, 19) and, as a near contemporary put it, 'a nobleman of the old school, kind and indulgent to his menials and dependents, of the most correct manners, full of courtesy, integrity, and honour' (Douglas, 1.35–6). On the death, without issue, of his son, David Ogilvy, Walter Ogilvy of Clova laid claim to the title of earl of Airlie before the House of Lords, but failed to elicit from them any decision. Walter's son David was, however, continued in the title by act of parliament on 26 May 1826.   MURRAY G. H. PITTOCK

Sources DNB · J. Stuart, ed., *The miscellany of the Spalding Club*, 1, Spalding Club, 3 (1841) · summary description of Airlie muniments, NA Scot., GD 16 · GEC, *Peerage* · F. J. McLynn, *The Jacobite army in England, 1745: the final campaign* (1983) · F. J. McLynn, *Charles Edward Stuart: a tragedy in many acts* (1988) · R. Douglas, *The peerage of Scotland*, 2nd edn, ed. J. P. Wood, 2 vols. (1813) · NL Scot., MS 17523 · J. H. Burton and D. Laing, eds., *Jacobite correspondence of the Atholl family* (1840) · B. G. Seton and J. G. Arnot, eds., *The prisoners of the '45*, Scottish History Society, 3rd ser., 13–15 (1928–9) · K. Tomasson and F. Buist, *Battles of the '45* (1962) · A. Livingstone, C. W. H. Aikman, and B. S. Hart, eds., *Muster roll of Prince Charles Edward Stuart's army, 1745–46* (1984) · A. Mackintosh, *The muster roll of Forfarshire* (1914) · F. McLynn, *The Jacobites* (1985) · J. S. Gibson, *Lochiel of the '45* (1994) · M. Moor and W. Ross, *The 'Forty-Five* (1995) · A. M. Mackenzie, *Scottish pageant* (1950) · M. G. H. Pittock, *Jacobitism* (1998) · D. Dobson, *Jacobites of the '15* (1993)
Archives NA Scot., corresp., personal accounts; corresp. and papers relating to Le Regiment Ogilvy · NL Scot., MSS | U. Aberdeen L., Macbean collection · U. Edin. L., letters to Lady Ogilvy
Likenesses C. Alexander, oils, 1750–59, Airlie Castle, Tayside · D. Martin, oils (after A. Ramsay), Airlie Castle, Tayside · oils (after A. Ramsay), Airlie Castle, Tayside

Ogilvy, David Mackenzie (1911–1999), advertising executive, was born in West Horsley, Surrey, on 23 June 1911, the fifth and last child and younger son of Francis John Longley Ogilvy (1866–1943), stockbroker, who had gained a first in classics and a rugby blue at Cambridge, and his wife, Dorothy Fairfield. His mother's niece was Cicily Fairfield (the author Rebecca West). Although his lineage and connections were socially respectable, David Ogilvy gave a lifelong impression that he would have liked them to have been grander; he ostentatiously brushed aside any suggestion of kinship to the earls of Airlie. His sense of self-doubt and insecurity, which often expressed itself in boastfulness, sprang partly from sibling and adult depreciation of him as the youngest child, and in part from an early realization that he could never match the academic and other accomplishments of his father and brother, Francis (1903–1964). In 1915, following the outbreak of the First World War, his father was ruined financially, doubtless being hammered on the stock exchange. The family thereafter had to get by in reduced circumstances. He gained a scholarship to his father's school, Fettes College, of which a great-uncle, John Inglis, Lord Glencorse, had been an influential trustee, and he entered Christ Church, Oxford, as a scholar in 1929. However, he went down two years later, having failed both college and university examinations.

That débâcle was probably due to a recognition that for him it had to be first class or nothing; as was his decision to become a kitchen hand in the Hotel Majestic, Paris, working ten hours a day for six days a week, under an autocratic head chef. He later claimed that the high standard of food preparation under extreme pressure instilled in him a sorely needed physical and mental discipline, so that running a hotel kitchen and an advertising agency could be said to require strikingly similar gifts. A year later, in 1932, he took the job of salesman for Aga stoves in Scotland, his initial coup being a sale to Glenalmond School. Having found a client in Andrew Joseph McDonald, the Roman Catholic archbishop of St Andrews and Edinburgh, he gained a lucrative *entrée* into all the convents of the diocese.

In 1935 Ogilvy composed *The Theory and Practice of Selling the Aga Cooker*, a handbook for the company's salesmen.

This unpublished Aga saga wittily and acutely demonstrated his early interest in statistics (only 10,000 Aga owners in 12 million British households), lists (selling points and likely objections to overcome), and the psychology of doorstepping a client (choosing the most favourable time of day, carefully studying the householder's circumstances). His brother, Francis, after high Cambridge honours, had joined the London advertising agency Mather and Crowther. Having put David through an apprenticeship, in 1938 he dispatched him to study the advertising market in the United States.

David took effortlessly to the American lifestyle, a year later marrying Melinda Street, from Virginia, and resigning to join as an opinion pollster George H. Gallup's Audience Research Institute at Princeton, New Jersey. The latter—but not the former—he characterized as the luckiest break of his life, as it furnished him with immeasurably useful knowledge about the techniques of marketing research, as well as about what made United States citizens really tick.

These skills proved their worth when in 1942 Ogilvy was invited to join William Stephenson, as a kind of supersleuth, in the office of British Security Co-ordination in New York. He organized polls to gauge the current state of American opinion about Britain, which threw up ideas on ways to improve transatlantic relations; from 1944 to 1945 he was second secretary in the British embassy. His pollstering helped the allied war effort far more than the acts of derring-do which he was later to recount. From 1946 onwards he lived with his wife and young son as a farmer in Lancaster county, Pennsylvania, close to the Amish community; its way of life deeply impressed him, even though as the offspring of dedicated freethinkers he had no time for dogmatic religion. As he lacked basic farming and mechanical skills, the venture did not prove a success.

By 1948 Francis Ogilvy and Robert Bevan, of the rival agency S. H. Benson Ltd, were recognized as among the most brilliant advertising figures in Britain. Aware of the need to break into the American market, they jointly arranged for David to set up a New York agency, entitled (from 1952 onwards) Ogilvy Benson and Mather. With capital of no more than $6000 and a staff of two, never having written a single advertisement, David Ogilvy brought to his new assignment both determination and, for an Englishman, a rare familiarity with the country's ways. The late 1940s happened to be precisely the time when the American advertising scene appeared to be ripe for a shake-up. The United States economy was forging ahead at such a pace as to make sellers complacent about publicity. In consequence, those in the know deplored the general lack of creativity among the industry's practitioners. Advertisers chose to offer safe and uninspired copy rather than striving after originality and distinctiveness. Ogilvy and his American contemporary William Bernbach were credited with being the pioneers of that revolution.

Ogilvy's advertising strategy began with the fundamental notion: 'The consumer is not a moron. She is your wife. Try not to insult her intelligence' (*Blood, Brains and Beer*, 94). In 1950 he had two major clients, Guinness and Wedgwood. Then two years later he made his name with a sequence of advertisements for a shirtmaking firm, using a man with an eyepatch, Baron Wrangell, who for nineteen years advertised Hathaway shirts; he accompanied that striking image with five paragraphs of detailed copy.

In 1953 Schweppes of Britain entered the soft-drinks market in North America. Schweppes' overseas director, Commander Edward Whitehead, of memorable ginger-bearded appearance, was persuaded by Ogilvy to pose for the advertisements. Sales thereafter rocketed; Whitehead became the second most widely recognized Englishman in the United States, after Winston Churchill. Whitehead appeared regularly until 1971, when Ogilvy lost the agency. By contrast, in 1954 Ogilvy publicized Puerto Rico as an attraction for tourists and inward investors alike.

In 1957 Ogilvy was offered the Rolls-Royce account: after four days of virtually non-stop toil he produced twenty-six different slogans. The one chosen became the most celebrated of all automobile advertisements, 'At 60 miles an hour the loudest noise in this new Rolls-Royce comes from the electric clock', but once again he set out the car's bull points at length below this heading. Although he claimed to abhor humour in his advertising, with typical effrontery he portrayed an anonymous diplomat who sent his son to Groton on what he allegedly saved by driving a modest Austin car. (The headmaster being unamused, Ogilvy had to withdraw his own son from that most exclusive of schools.) Nor could he resist the punning slogan, 'I'm head over heels in Dove', a brand of soap.

The New York agency soon built up a client list that was the envy of Madison Avenue, including Shell, Royal Dutch, KLM, Gillette, and Morgan Guaranty. Ogilvy reserved his most intensive efforts, and achieved his most noteworthy successes, for companies which yielded his agency the least income; he preferred to leave the giants, with the largest advertising budgets, to subordinates, while still closely supervising their work. He spent each day in his office, meeting people, and undertook most of his composing at home. His practice there, often battling through the night, was thoroughly to research into the product before him. He then pared his findings and ideas down to the characteristic that best summed up that product, thereby making it into not just a brand but a byword.

Ogilvy's first marriage did not survive this workaholism, exacerbated by a very public spat with Rosser Reeves, chairman of the rival Ted Bates agency, who in the early days had been his mentor and then brother-in-law. In 1955 Ogilvy was divorced from Melinda Street, and two years later he married Anne Finch Cabot, of Boston. Tallish, slim, and affecting a scholar's stoop, personable, with dark blond hair, pale skin, and black-rimmed glasses, he presented himself as a *milord anglais*, clad in British tweeds, striped shirts, and red braces. He flattered interlocutors by dropping Americanisms into his conversation. He added a touch of the unexpected by mixing socially, not with fellow moguls of his profession, but with celebrities of all kinds. The greatest and the good were not immune to his charisma; he paid the former first lady, Eleanor Roosevelt, $35,000 to make a television commercial for Good Luck margarine, then unaware that viewers remembered the celebrity while forgetting the product. His *Confessions of an Advertising Man* (1963), which sold 400,000 copies in its first five years, made him the only advertising figure whose reputation went far beyond that rather inward-looking industry. An autobiography, *Blood, Brains and Beer* (1978), gave him an opportunity for name-dropping on a grand scale.

In the early 1960s Ogilvy felt himself to be an extinct volcano; by then he wrote little copy and was losing interest in the business of advertising. Meanwhile, his New York agency had outstripped in size Mather and Crowther in London. After Francis Ogilvy died prematurely in 1964, the two agencies merged to become Ogilvy and Mather International Inc., with fees and commission income equivalent to £8.6 million and profit after tax to nearly £540,000. A public share issue of 1966 made him a rich man, but left the combine vulnerable to the vagaries of international stock markets. He asserted that he was unable to read a balance sheet or work a computer, while matters of finance and organization patently bored him. Aware that an advertising agency's only creative capital was its people, he nurtured his employees, but seldom gave them praise.

Ogilvy took on a number of good causes. A director of the New York Philharmonic Orchestra from 1957 to 1967, he raised funds for the Lincoln Center in New York. He was appointed CBE in 1967, and a year later was elected chairman of the United Negro College Fund. In 1973 he retired as chairman of Ogilvy and Mather International, and moved to France, where he had bought a 60-bedroom château at Touffou, near Poitiers; that year he married his third wife, Herta Lans. In 1975 he was appointed to the executive council of the World Wildlife Fund, and two years later to the American Advertising Hall of Fame. As a non-executive director, he travelled extensively for the company in between gardening, oversaw some of its advertising, and worked on the guiding principles of his métier, set out in his most celebrated work, *Ogilvy on Advertising* (1983).

In 1989 the company, which had acquired S. H. Benson in 1971, was bought by the British company WPP plc, for £450 million. Ogilvy in disgust branded the purchaser, Martin Sorrell, as 'an odious little jerk' (*The Times*, 22 July 1999). Sorrell craftily cultivated this irascible septuagenarian and, much to the surprise and dismay of Ogilvy's friends, appointed him non-executive chairman at a suitably elevated salary. In 1992 Sorrell, having to refinance the loans he had raised for that purchase, was compelled by his bankers to sack Ogilvy, who demanded (and got) the title of emeritus president, with six-figure emoluments.

During the final year of his life Ogilvy suffered from Parkinson's disease, and he died at Touffou on 21 July 1999. He was survived by his wife, and by his only son. His chief regret was that he had not been awarded a knighthood. Although he had reached the advanced age at which the British authorities are wont to honour their most far-flung expatriates, he was clearly judged to have contributed too little to the land of his birth. David Ogilvy's reputation was nevertheless secure as perhaps the most creative advertising entrepreneur of the twentieth century.

T. A. B. CORLEY

Sources D. Ogilvy, *Confessions of an advertising man* (1963); (1987) · D. Ogilvy, *Blood, brains and beer* (1978) · D. Ogilvy, *Ogilvy on advertising* (1983) · J. Raphaelson, *The unpublished David Ogilvy* (1988) · S. R. Fox, *The mirror makers* (1984) · S. Pigott, *OBM, a celebration* (1975) · S. Klaus, 'Is Ogilvy a genius?', *Fortune* (1965) · *The Guardian* (22 July 1999) · *New York Times* (22 July 1999) · *Daily Telegraph* (22 July 1999) · *The Independent* (22 July 1999) · *The Times* (22–3 July 1999) · *The Scotsman* (23 July 1999) · *Financial Times* (23 July 1999) · *WW* (1999) · *International who's who* (1998–9) · D. A. Simmons, *Schweppes: the first 200 years* (1983) · H. Montgomery Hyde, *The quiet Canadian* (1962) · F. Meynell, *My lives* (1971) · M. Barnes, *Ad: an inside view of advertising* (1973) · M. Mayer, *Madison Avenue, USA* (1958)
Archives L. Cong. | History of Advertising Trust, Norwich, WPP plc archives
Likenesses photograph, *c.*1960, repro. in Ogilvy, *Ogilvy on advertising* · photograph, *c.*1970, repro. in *The Times* · photograph, *c.*1970, repro. in *The Guardian* · photograph, *c.*1970, repro. in *Daily Telegraph*

Ogilvy, Sir George, of Barras. *See* Ogilvie, Sir George, of Barras, first baronet (*fl.* 1634–1679).

Ogilvy, George, **first Lord Banff** (*d.* 1663), royalist army officer, was the eldest son of Walter Ogilvy of Dunlugas and Banff (*d.* 1627/8) and Helen Urquhart, daughter of Walter Urquhart of Cromarty. Ogilvy married Margaret Irvine, daughter of Alexander Irvine of Drum, in or before 1611, and they had one daughter. After her death he married Janet Sutherland, daughter of William Sutherland of Duffus, and they had at least four children—one son (George, second Lord Banff) and three daughters. In July 1629 Janet submitted a complaint to the privy council alleging that her husband had treated her and two of their children with cruelty, seeking to starve her to death and leaving her for dead after beating her. After hearing the parties and witness the council absolved Ogilvy.

Ogilvy was created a baronet on 30 July 1627, having been knighted previously, and played an active role in local affairs. In the turbulent feuding of north-east Scotland he killed his cousin James Ogilvy in 1628, and made assythment (compensation) to the family of his victim. He supported James Crichton of Frendraught in his feud with the Gordons of Rothiemay, but was not prosecuted for his involvement in the killing of William Gordon of Rothiemay in 1630 as he had had a commission to arrest him. He was appointed a JP for Banffshire in 1634, and sheriff in 1636. In the first bishops' war of 1639 Ogilvy took the leading role in persuading local royalists to resist the covenanters. When the marquess of Huntly and other leaders prevaricated or submitted he 'stoutly stood out the king's man' (Spalding, 2.163). He inspired the successful attack, led by him and Sir John Gordon of Haddo, on covenanting forces at the 'trot of Turriff' on 13 May, and entered Aberdeen two days later. However, on 22 May the royalist forces withdrew, and reached an agreement with the covenanters to lay down their arms. On 30 May Ogilvy sailed from Macduff, intending to join Charles I in England, but, after meeting with a ship bringing Lord Aboyne and others north to resume resistance, he landed with them in Aberdeen. However, their position was unsustainable, as the earl of Montrose had marched strong covenanting forces northwards, and again the royalists were forced into submission, but Ogilvy refused to swear to the national covenant and about September joined the king in England. He remained in England during the second bishops' war of 1640, during which the covenanters took their revenge for his conduct in 1639 by destroying his houses and confiscating his revenues. Charles I is said to have provided partial compensation for his losses by a gift in 1642 of 10,000 merks Scots in gold. Ogilvy was with the king on the latter's visit to Edinburgh late in 1641. He remained in Scotland when the king left, but again visited him in England in 1642, being created Lord Banff on 31 August. He took no active part in the royalist risings of Huntly and Montrose in 1644, but his lack of commitment to the covenanting cause none the less brought action against him, including a fine, though by March 1647 he was sufficiently rehabilitated to be appointed a member of the committee of war for Banffshire.

In 1648 Banff supported the engagement alliance of royalists and moderate covenanters. After taking his seat in parliament (for the first time) on 2 March 1648, he was appointed a colonel and a member of the Banffshire committee of war. He appears to have played no active military role (though his son fought in the engagers' army), but his support for the engagement was sufficient to arouse the wrath of the church. After the defeat of the engagers his case was considered for nearly a year by church courts before his declarations of repentance and of adherence to the solemn league and covenant were accepted by the presbytery of Fordyce in April 1651. After the Cromwellian conquest of Scotland, Banff's royalism (or perhaps rather that of his son, who had fought at the battle of Worcester in September 1651) brought renewed persecution. A fine of £1000 sterling was imposed on him in 1654, though this was soon reduced by two-thirds and he was appointed a JP in 1656. Restoration of monarchy in 1660 brought new troubles, for he was summoned by the privy council for the slaughter of John Gordon. Banff took his seat in parliament again on 18 June 1663, but he died on 11 August.

Lord Banff's role in stirring the royalists of north-east Scotland into military opposition to the covenanters in 1639 was notable, earning from enemies the judgement that he was 'a rash and profane man' (R. Baillie, *Letters and Journals*, 3 vols., 1841–2, 2.204). He seems to have quickly repented this rashness, for after the destruction of his houses that it brought about he was, as James Gordon commented, 'never more cordiall [whole-hearted] in the King's service' and 'never did engadge any mor' (J. Gordon, 2.263–4), advancing age and financial difficulties doubtless helping to restrain him from action.

DAVID STEVENSON

Sources DNB · *Scots peerage*, 2.15–18 · GEC, *Peerage* · J. Spalding, *Memorialls of the trubles in Scotland and in England, AD 1624 – AD 1645*, ed. J. Stuart, 2 vols., Spalding Club, [21, 23] (1850–51) · J. Gordon,

History of Scots affairs from 1637–1641, ed. J. Robertson and G. Grub, 3 vols., Spalding Club, 1, 3, 5 (1841) · R. Gordon and G. Gordon, *A genealogical history of the earldom of Sutherland … with a continuation to the year 1651* (1813) · *Reg. PCS*, 1st ser. · *Reg. PCS*, 2nd ser. · *Reg. PCS*, 3rd ser. · W. Cramond, ed., *The annals of Banff*, 2 vols., New Spalding Club, 8, 10 (1891–3) · C. H. Firth, ed., *Scotland and the protectorate: letters and papers relating to the military government of Scotland from January 1654 to June 1659*, Scottish History Society, 31 (1899)

Ogilvy, James, fifth Lord Ogilvy of Airlie (1540/41–1606), nobleman, was the eldest son of James Ogilvy, master of Ogilvy (*c.*1520–1547), and his wife, Katherine *Campbell (*d.* 1578), daughter of Sir John *Campbell [*see under* Campbell family, of Cawdor] and Muriel Calder of Cawdor. His father having died at the battle of Pinkie on 10 September 1547, he succeeded his grandfather, James, fourth Lord Ogilvy of Airlie, some time before 13 July 1548. His mother married the ninth earl of Crawford in 1549 and in 1558 he himself married Jean Forbes (1541–*c.*1610), eldest daughter of William, seventh Lord Forbes, and his wife, Elizabeth, daughter of Sir William Keith. They had eight sons: James, sixth Lord Ogilvy of Airlie; Sir John of Craig; David of Pitmuies; William, a pensioner of Kirriemuir and Newtyle; Archibald, who probably died young; Patrick of Muirton; Francis of Newgrange; and George of Friock; as well as a daughter, Margaret, who wed first George Keith, fifth Earl Marischal, and then, after his death, Alexander Strachan of Thornton.

A powerful figure in Forfarshire, Lord Ogilvy joined the lords of congregation at Perth in June 1559 and was one of the Scottish commissioners who brokered the treaty of Berwick on 27 February 1560. The decision taken by Alexander Ogilvy of Deskford and Findlater in 1545 to disinherit his son in favour of his wife's relation Sir John Gordon, third son of the fourth earl of Huntly, caused great division between the Ogilvys and Gordons, which had reached its peak by the time Queen Mary returned to Scotland in August 1561. On 10 September 1562 Gordon of Deskford attacked Lord Ogilvy outside the Aberdeen tolbooth, severely wounding his right arm. Ogilvy joined the crown forces brought north to bring Deskford to heel and when the Gordons opposed these at Corrichie on 28 October they were routed, Deskford being taken prisoner and executed. Ogilvy received a commission with neighbouring lords in September 1563 to remove the MacGregors from their lands. When the earl of Moray and the duke of Chatelherault rebelled in 1565, Ogilvy supported the crown. He attended the dinner given by Lord Bothwell in the Ainslie tavern in April 1567 and signed the bond supporting the earl's marriage to the queen, but subsequently joined the confederacy of nobles who gathered at Stirling in June determined to safeguard the infant prince and separate Mary from Bothwell. He was not present at Carberry on the 15th, however, and cannot have approved of the subsequent forced abdication and imprisonment of the queen.

When Mary escaped from Lochleven Castle on 2 May 1568 Ogilvy signed the Hamilton bond and rode north to muster forces, but was unable to reach the queen's army before its precipitate defeat at Langside on the 13th. Lord Ogilvy, who was able to carry most of the Ogilvy lairds, including Inverkeilor and Balgro, into the queen's party, assembled with other Marian supporters at Largs at the end of July. Though he signed a bond in April 1569 acknowledging Moray's authority as regent, he wrote to Mary the following month confirming his allegiance. He attended the Perth convention in July, voting against the queen's divorce from Bothwell. In December, Ogilvy and his wife were ordered to desist from oppressing John Stirling of Easter Brakie. The following August, Ogilvy acted in concert with the earl of Crawford and Sir James Balfour of Pittendreich in proclaiming the queen at Brechin and Forfar. However, the earl of Morton's sudden descent on Forfarshire forced him to retreat to Aberdeen and, leaving his wife as commissioner of his estates, he took ship for France in October. He returned to Airlie in 1572, but was shortly after arrested and warded in Linlithgow Palace. In May 1576 he was transferred to Glasgow and in February 1577, through the solicitation of various noblemen, to St Andrews. On his way to Fife he halted in Edinburgh to speak with Morton, who surprisingly expressed his respect for the queen. He was finally released on 14 March 1578, when James VI first asserted his personal authority, and at the Stirling convention was briefly admitted to the privy council; but when Morton recovered control of government Ogilvy retired to Bolshan Castle. He attended the October 1579 parliament which extended the pacification of Perth to many former Marians but unexpectedly forfeited the Hamiltons.

Morton fell irrevocably from power at the end of 1580 and Ogilvy gave his support to the new government of the duke of Lennox. The kirk had voiced suspicions as to his Catholic leanings, and to dispel these doubts he subscribed the negative confession in January 1581. He joined the privy council in March and sat on the assize which condemned Morton for Darnley's murder in June. The Ruthven raid of August 1582 brought down Lennox and for its duration removed Ogilvy from participation in government. In 1585 he was called before the council to answer for reiving the property of Patrick Wood of Bonnyton. He was also closely associated with the Catholic conspiracies of King James's early reign and was known to shelter Jesuit missionaries in his houses, while his son Sir John of Craig was vigorously pursued by the government for much of his life for his persistent support of the Jesuit missions. Ogilvy nevertheless continued to enjoy royal favour, and in June 1596 was appointed with the bishop of Dunkeld as an ambassador to attend the coronation of Christian IV of Denmark, returning in September with rich rewards.

Between 1557 and 1560 Lord Ogilvy had purchased the lands of Forter from the abbot of Coupar Angus, displacing the MacKerrows to install his own kinsmen on the lands and building Forter Castle to control the passes. This expansion north into Glenisla brought the Ogilvys into conflict with Campbells settled on the old abbey lands and with the earls of Atholl who disputed the lordship. Ogilvy had acquired a feu of the lands and castle of Farnell from the sixth earl of Argyll and bishop of Brechin in 1574, but failed to meet payment, and when the young seventh earl

raised an action to recover the same in July 1590 relations between the families worsened, reaching a bloody conclusion when the master of Ogilvy and his brothers murdered four Campbells in Glenisla on 18 August 1591. The Campbells retaliated days later, bringing down over 3000 men in a brutal raid on Ogilvy lands, killing indiscriminately and forcing Lord Ogilvy and his family to flee Forter Castle. Argyll was ordered to withdraw his clansmen, but the Campbells remained on the hills, to raid Glenisla and Glen Cova again in September. Later in the month Lord Ogilvy and the earl of Crawford captured and summarily executed at Perth two MacGregors who had participated in the raids, infuriating Argyll and Atholl, whose protection the MacGregors claimed. Lord Ogilvy was unsuccessful in seeking redress for the raids before the council, the king choosing to reconcile the affair through arbitration. In February 1599 Ogilvy was summoned with the sixth earl of Atholl to appear before council to resolve their feud, but both men proved reluctant to compear, the master appearing for his father on 19 April, while Atholl sent no representation.

In the later years of his life Ogilvy, who enjoyed good relations with his nephew Crawford, sought to avoid a resurgence of his family's old feud with the Lindsays, but was unable to restrain his sons. In March 1600 the master and some of his brothers attacked Alexander Lindsay, Lord Spynie, on the road between Kinblethmont and Gardyne, wounding his head and killing Patrick, son of William Rynd of Carse. All parties were required to find caution and Lord Ogilvy was ordered to ward himself in Arbroath. None the less his son David was fatally stabbed by David Lindsay, an illegitimate son of the earl of Crawford, as he made his way to his lodgings in Edinburgh's Canongate on 13 July 1602, while the master continued to pursue his feud with Spynie, blowing off the gate of Kinblethmont Castle to sack it during a night raid on 30 January 1603. Lord Ogilvy died at Farnell Castle in October 1606 and was buried with Catholic rites in the aisle of Kinnell church.

JOHN SIMMONS

Sources *Reg. PCS*, 1st ser., vols. 1–7 · *CSP Scot.*, 1547–1603 · NA Scot., Airlie muniments, GD16 · W. Wilson, *The house of Airlie* (1924) · GEC, *Peerage*, 1.71 · *Scots peerage*, 1.118–22 · R. Pitcairn, ed., *Ancient criminal trials in Scotland*, 7 pts in 3, Bannatyne Club, 42 (1833) · *The works of John Knox*, ed. D. Laing, 6 vols., Wodrow Society, 12 (1846–64) · E. J. Cowan, 'The Angus Campbells and the origin of the Campbell–Ogilvie feud', *Journal of School of Scottish Studies*, 25 (1981), 25–38 · M. Livingstone, D. Hay Fleming, and others, eds., *Registrum secreti sigilli regum Scotorum / The register of the privy seal of Scotland*, 5–8 (1957–82) · J. M. Thomson and others, eds., *Registrum magni sigilli regum Scotorum / The register of the great seal of Scotland*, 11 vols. (1882–1914), vols. 4–6 · G. Donaldson, *All the queen's men* (1983) · will, NA Scot., CC 8/8/43, fols. 107v–111v

Wealth at death see will, NA Scot., CC 8/8/43, fols. 107v–111v

Ogilvy, James, first earl of Airlie (1586–1666), nobleman, was the eldest son of James Ogilvy, sixth Lord Ogilvy of Airlie (c.1565–c.1617x19), and his first wife, Lady Jean (d. 1612), daughter of William *Ruthven, first earl of Gowrie. He succeeded his father on the latter's death, after 12 October 1617. He married (contract dated 22 November 1610) Lady Isobel or Isabella (1596–1682), second daughter of

Thomas *Hamilton, first earl of Haddington. In 1631 he was one of the commissioners appointed to inquire into the burning of Frendraught Castle, as part of a Gordon–Crichton feud. A committed royalist, he was created earl of Airlie and Lord Ogilvy of Alyth and Lintrathen by a royal patent dated at York on 2 April 1639.

In 1640 Airlie went to England to avoid having to take the covenant, leaving his eldest son, James *Ogilvy, Lord Ogilvy, in charge of his estates. The covenanting earl of Argyll marched to Airlie Castle with 5000 men and demanded its surrender. When Lord Ogilvy refused, and prudently departed, Argyll burned both the castle and the other principal Airlie seat at Forter, Forfarshire. A contemporary commented that 'they have not left him in all his lands a cock to crow day' (*CSP dom.*, 1640, 53) and the episode later inspired the well-known Scottish ballad 'The Bonnie Hoose o'Airlie'. Returning to Scotland, Airlie sat in the covenanting parliament of 1643, but the following year he and his three sons joined the marquess of Montrose's royalist army. As a result he suffered forfeiture of life, titles, and estates by parliament on 11 February 1645. On 15 August he led the first charge at the battle of Kilsyth and routed the covenanters. He was present at Montrose's subsequent defeat at Philiphaugh (13 September) where James, Lord Ogilvy, was captured; the latter only escaped death when his sister managed to smuggle him out of prison. Airlie's second son, Thomas, had been killed on the royalist side at the battle of Inverlochy (2 February 1645).

Airlie was exempted from the general pardon of 11 February 1646 and was excommunicated by the Church of Scotland on 27 July 1646. Not until 17 March 1647 was his forfeiture finally rescinded, thanks to the intervention of John, first earl of Middleton, who had been authorized to pacify northern Scotland. His participation was expected in the 'start' in October 1650, a failed attempt to free Charles II from covenanter tutelage by rallying royalist support. Thereafter he appears to have taken no more part in public affairs, living quietly with his wife. By 1664 he was complaining that he could not 'get anywhares abroad [outside] for my age and infirmitie, I being thre scoir and eighteen yeirs' (*Scots peerage*, 1.124). He died on 21 February 1666. HENRY PATON, *rev.* ROSALIND K. MARSHALL

Sources Airlie muniments, NA Scot., GD16 · J. Spalding, *Memorialls of the trubles in Scotland and in England, AD 1624 – AD 1645*, ed. J. Stuart, 2 vols., Spalding Club, [21, 23] (1850–51) · *Scots peerage*, 1.123–4 · R. Douglas, *The peerage of Scotland*, 2nd edn, ed. J. P. Wood, 1 (1813), 2 · S. R. Gardiner, *History of the Commonwealth and protectorate, 1649–1660*, 3rd edn, 4 vols. (1901) · GEC, *Peerage* · P. Donald, *An uncounselled king: Charles I and the Scottish troubles, 1637–1641* (1990)
Archives NA Scot., Airlie muniments, corresp. and papers, GD16
Likenesses oils, Airlie Castle, Tayside Region; black and white negatives, Scot. NPG

Ogilvy, James, first earl of Findlater (*d.* 1652), nobleman, was the son of Walter Ogilvy of Findlater (*d.* 1623/4), created Lord Ogilvy of Deskford in 1615, and Mary, daughter of William Douglas, earl of Morton. He married, by a contract dated 13 February 1610, Elizabeth, daughter of Andrew *Leslie, fifth earl of Rothes, and widow of David Wemyss. After her death he married Marion (*d.* 1661),

daughter of William Cunningham, eighth earl of Glencairn.

On succeeding his father, Ogilvy concerned himself mainly in local Banffshire affairs, becoming a justice of the peace there in 1634. He was admitted to the Scottish privy council on 22 June 1637 and was created earl of Findlater on 20 February 1638 (infuriating the head of his kin, Lord Ogilvy of Airlie, who was not made an earl until a year later). In the early stages of the revolt of the covenanters he was inclined to support Charles I, but in March 1639, 'being a man of a peaceable temper, and one who was knowne to have no stomacke for warre' (Gordon, 2.213), he mediated between the royalist marquess of Huntly and the earl of Montrose, who led covenanting forces in the north-east of Scotland. 'Shortly afterwards [Findlater] fell in to the Covenant' (Gordon, 2.213), but he showed no inclination to involve himself in politics (though he took his seat in parliament in 1641, 1645–6, and 1648). In 1644–5 he served intermittently against the marquess of Montrose (who was now leading a royalist rising), perhaps mainly to protect his own estates, but, being involved in the defeat of the covenanters at Auldearn (9 May 1645), he withdrew from the contest. In the war against the Cromwellian invasion in 1651 he was active in raising supplies in the north-east for the Scottish army. He died in 1652 in his house at Cullen.

DAVID STEVENSON

Sources GEC, *Peerage* · *Scots peerage* · *APS*, 1643–60 · J. Gordon, *History of Scots affairs from 1637–1641*, ed. J. Robertson and G. Grub, 3 vols., Spalding Club, 1, 3, 5 (1841) · E. M. Furgol, *A regimental history of the covenanting armies, 1639–1651* (1990)

Ogilvy, James, second earl of Airlie (1611–1704), royalist army officer, was born about Christmas 1611 at Airlie Castle, Forfarshire. He was the eldest of the three sons of James *Ogilvy, master of Ogilvy, later seventh Lord Ogilvy of Airlie and first earl of Airlie (1586–1666), and his wife, Lady Isabella (1596–1682), second daughter of Thomas Hamilton, first earl of Haddington. He was tutored by William Robertson, at home from an early age and then from 1626 to 1630 at the University of St Andrews, where (Robertson assured the young nobleman's father) young Ogilvy took delight in the study of geometry. At St Andrews, Ogilvy associated with his friend and cousin, James Graham, earl of Montrose. Ogilvy courted Magdalene, the youngest daughter of David, Lord Carnegie. According to tradition, as Ogilvy was on his way to propose to her he was thrown from his horse while fording a river. Regarding the ducking as an unfavourable omen, he proceeded no further. The core of truth to the story is Magdalene's rejection of Ogilvy and her later marriage to Montrose. Ogilvy shortly afterwards, and while still at St Andrews, married Helen (*d.* 1664), daughter of Sir George *Ogilvy, later first Lord Banff: the marriage contract was dated 20–25 March 1629. Together they had at least seven children, two sons and five daughters. Following the coronation of Charles I in Edinburgh in 1633 Ogilvy travelled abroad for two years. In France he attended the school of 'Monsieur Anglo at Paris' where he learned swordsmanship, dancing, and riding; in Italy he met Montrose again.

Ogilvy was no friend to hardline presbyterianism, and indeed there is evidence of his Catholicism, though later he was clearly a member of the Church of Scotland, albeit of strongly episcopalian sympathies. He was an ardent royalist in the bishops' wars (1638–40) along with his father, who was created earl of Airlie by Charles I for his services in 1639 (henceforward Ogilvy was known as Lord Ogilvy until he succeeded to the earldom). In the autumn of 1639 Ogilvy defended Airlie Castle against Montrose, who had been ordered to take and raze it. Instead, after a token struggle, and as part of Montrose's increasing distancing of himself from the covenanter cause, the castle was surrendered and a small garrison put in, while Ogilvy was permitted to escape. Montrose was sharply challenged by Argyll for this. The July following, Argyll's punitive campaign of fire and sword against the highland royalists brought him to the castle. Taking revenge on Montrose and Ogilvy, Argyll seized Airlie Castle, evicting Ogilvy's heavily pregnant wife and her children, and burnt the place down. Later balladry recorded that he did not 'leave a stan'in' stane in Airly' (Wilson, 1.215). Ogilvy, who had left the castle upon Argyll's approach to warn his mother and raise more troops, was to remind Charles II that:

> The House off Airlie was caste downe and the House of Forthar burned in the year of God 1640, having refused to covenant and joyn in armes with them. Also att tyme my wyff being big with chyld was necessitatt to flie from hir house, and having only two chyldren thay were carried awa prisoners and kepit in Dundee, the eldest of thame nott being much above thrie or foure yeirs off age. (Wilson, 2.21)

With a warrant out for his arrest, Ogilvy fled to England. In October 1641, after returning to Scotland with Montrose, Ogilvy was involved in the 'incident', the conspiracy which had been approved by the king to arrest, and possibly assassinate, Argyll and the marquess of Hamilton. Ogilvy continued a close companion of Montrose, acting as his aide-de-camp. In February 1643 he accompanied Montrose to Charles I's court at Oxford to concert measures for waging war against the covenanters and then accompanied him to north-east Scotland where he sought to co-ordinate support for a rising. Refusing to obey the order of the Scottish parliament to appear before them and give security for keeping the peace, he was declared a rebel and specially exempted from pardon in August 1643. In April 1644 Ogilvy rode with Montrose in his brief invasion of south-west Scotland, and following its failure crossed the border again in disguise to scout out royalist prospects. However, when Montrose went north to begin his string of victories Ogilvy was not with his kinsman: carrying dispatches from Montrose to the king at Oxford, he had been captured by parliamentarian troops near Preston in Lancashire in August. He was handed over to the Scots and taken prisoner to Edinburgh, where he remained a prisoner in the Tolbooth for more than a year. He underwent frequent examination because he refused to accept the authority of the high court of justice to try him and demanded to be tried by his peers and to be tried as a prisoner of war rather than a rebel. He was frequently

visited by his mother, sister, and wife, who in August 1645 petitioned for his removal from the then plague-infested town, and obtained an order for his removal to the Bass Rock.

Before this change of prisons could be effected, however, Montrose inflicted a severe defeat on the covenanters at Kilsyth (15 August 1645), which placed most of Scotland at his disposal, and sent orders to Edinburgh for the release of Lord Ogilvy and other prisoners, which were at once obeyed. Rejoining Montrose, Ogilvy resumed active service, and was present at the battle of Philiphaugh (13 September 1645). There he was captured again when the royalist army was routed. On 16 January 1646 he stood trial for treason at St Andrews and was condemned to death. The day appointed for his decapitation was 20 January. On the evening before, however, his elder sister changed clothes with him in his prison in the castle of St Andrews, and he escaped; £1000 sterling was offered for his capture dead or alive, but the reward was ineffectual. In the following July, as part of the peace terms negotiated with Montrose's followers, Ogilvy secured a pardon from General John Middleton, which the Scottish parliament was obliged to confirm. He also gave satisfaction to the kirk, and was released from excommunication.

In May 1649 Ogilvy took part in the royalist rising in the north of Sir Thomas Mackenzie of Pluscarden. He was excommunicated again in July. In 1650 he was involved in planning another rising, though he laid down his arms in October when instructed to by Charles II following the failure of his attempted coup against his new covenanter allies. Instead in December he was appointed colonel of a cavalry regiment, a position he was able to take up once he had submitted to the kirk on 9 February 1651. After the defeat of the Scottish forces by George Monck's English army in Scotland, Ogilvy was captured, along with the members of the committees of estates, near Alyth in Forfarshire, on 28 August 1651. He was sent a prisoner from Dundee to Tynemouth Castle, and on to the Tower of London. A year later he was released on condition that he would not leave London without permission; but on a general order he was soon recommitted to the Tower. He remained a prisoner until January 1657, with the exception of three months' leave granted in July 1655 for the purpose of visiting Scotland. In a petition to Cromwell in 1656 he stated that he was seized by a party of horse under General Monck while peaceably residing at his mansion-house in Scotland and protested that he had never taken an active part against the Commonwealth. He was released in 1657 on finding security in £20,000.

At the Restoration, Ogilvy's attempts to redeem his losses by grants from the king met with little success: a pension of £500 a year was only erratically paid. He succeeded as second earl of Airlie on the death of his father in February 1666. He is frequently mentioned in the parliamentary proceedings of the reigns of Charles II and James VII. He also served actively in defence of the Restoration episcopalian settlement. In the spring of 1665 he commanded a troop of horse under the commander-in-chief in Scotland, Thomas Dalyell, taking part in November in the defeat of the covenanter rising at Rullion Green. In 1667 he was in command of a force stationed at Perth to keep watch against Dutch incursions and to keep in check the presbyterians of Fife.

Airlie's first wife, Helen Ogilvy, died in early July 1664. His second marriage was to Mary (*d.* 1707), daughter of Sir John Grant of Freuchie and widow of Lewis Gordon, third marquess of Huntly. Their courtship was prolonged initially by the opposition of his mother and Mary's son and then by the difficulties in obtaining the sanction of the Church of Scotland for Airlie to marry a woman who, as a convert to Catholicism, stood excommunicate. Their marriage contract was dated 31 October 1668 but it was only in June 1669 that the banns were publicly read and the marriage performed privately. In 1678 Dalyell was appointed commander of one of three cavalry troops raised for the renewed repression of the covenanters. Airlie spent the following years in these policing duties, stationed at different times in Renfrewshire, Ayr, and Galloway. In June 1679 his troop was in Glasgow to repel the attack of the covenanters fresh from their victory at Drumclog. By 1680 Dalyell was complaining of the absenteeism of his lieutenant (and of half Airlie's troop) and Airlie was superseded in command. The elderly earl successfully protested against this, but refused to serve again under Dalyell. Under James VII, with John Graham of Claverhouse as commander-in-chief in Scotland, Airlie was again offered a command, patrolling the Ayrshire coast with a regiment of dragoons. He was active in the retribution which followed Argyll's abortive rising in 1685, laying claim to the forfeited estate of George Melville, earl of Melville.

By the summer of 1687 Airlie's loyalty to the crown was being severely tested by the policies of the Catholic James and, forced to choose between his monarch and his episcopal kirk, Airlie resigned his commission. At the revolution of 1688 he declared for William and Mary and in March 1689 he signed the act declaring the legality of the meeting of the estates of parliament. Thereafter his great age, and perhaps his disillusion when a presbyterian church settlement was rapidly imposed, made him withdraw. He was fined £1200 Scots for not attending the meeting of parliament in 1693. In 1698 and 1700 his attendance was excused on account of his age and infirmities and his fines remitted. He died, aged ninety-two, at his lodgings in Banff on 16 February 1704. He was survived by his second wife and was succeeded by his second but eldest surviving son, David (*d.* 1717).

HENRY PATON, *rev.* JAMES S. WHEELER

Sources D. Wilson, *The house of Airlie*, 2 vols. (1924) · *CSP dom.*, 1639–63 · *APS*, 1641–1700 · G. Wishart, *The history of the king's majesties affairs in Scotland under the conduct of the most honorable marquis of Montrose*, 2nd edn (1652) · J. Buchan, *Montrose* (1931) · C. V. Wedgwood, *Montrose* (1952) · E. J. Cowan, *Montrose: for covenant and king* (1977) · M. Linklater and C. Hesketh, *Bonnie Dundee: John Graham of Claverhouse* (1992) · D. Stevenson, *The Scottish revolution, 1637–1644* (1973) · F. D. Dow, *Cromwellian Scotland, 1651–1660* (1979) · S. R. Gardiner, *History of the great civil war, 1642–1649*, new edn, 4 vols. (1901–5) · S. R., *The history of the Commonwealth and republic*, 4 vols. (1903) ·

K. Brown, 'Courtiers and cavaliers: service, Anglicisation and loyalty among the royalist nobility', *The Scottish national covenant in its British context*, ed. J. Morrill (1990), 155–94 · *Scots peerage* · GEC, *Peerage*
Archives NA Scot., corresp. and papers | BL, letters to Lord Lauderdale and Charles II, Add. MSS 23124–23137, 23242–23247
Likenesses attrib. W. Dobson, oils, Airlie Castle, Tayside region

Ogilvy, James, fourth earl of Findlater and first earl of Seafield (1663–1730), politician, was born on 11 July 1663, the second son of the five children of James Ogilvy, third earl of Findlater (*d.* 1711), and Lady Anna Seton (*c.*1632–1687), eldest daughter of Hugh *Montgomery, seventh earl of Eglinton. He was educated under the guidance of a private tutor, Patrick Innes, and in May 1675 he proceeded to Marischal College, Aberdeen, where he studied for three years. After a brief stay in the Netherlands in 1683, he settled down to his legal studies and was admitted to the bar as an advocate on 16 January 1685. In 1687 he married Anne (1671/2–1708), daughter of Sir William Dunbar.

Ogilvy's political and parliamentary career began when he was elected to represent the burgh of Cullen, Banffshire, in the 1689 convention of estates, and he also represented Cullen in the parliament of 1689–95. Ogilvy initially played a dubious role in the convention. On 16 March he subscribed the act which stated that the convention was a free and lawful meeting of the estates, but he was also one of the five members who voted against the 'forfaulture' of James VII. George Lockhart of Carnwath in his memoirs observed that Ogilvy was 'much taken notice of by reason of a speech he made against the forfeiting of King James' (*'Scotland's Ruine'*, 18). Yet Ogilvy appears to have fallen into line with the dominant faction very quickly, and on 5 April he was nominated to the committee of the convention instructed to oversee the election of magistrates for a new town council for Edinburgh, to be held in St Giles's on 10 April. Furthermore, on 13 April he was named as a member of the committee to consider the political condition and state of the councils and magistrates in the burghs of the kingdom as a whole. Ogilvy's speedy rehabilitation with the dominant faction was reflected in his appointment to the three-man committee of 12 April which was ordered to consider a proclamation in which no one would be allowed to speak or write against the government. On 23 April Ogilvy was also appointed as one of the commissioners to treat for a union of the kingdoms with England. He was also politically active in the parliamentary session of 15 April to 22 July 1690. On 27 July he was appointed to a committee to consider overtures given by the viscount of Tarbat in open parliament, and on 1 July he was added to the committees for the act concerning lease making, fines and forfeitures, and prohibiting the import of brandy and rum. Likewise, on 18 July he was appointed to the commission for plantation of kirks.

In 1693 Ogilvy was knighted and appointed as sheriff of Banffshire as well as solicitor-general of Scotland, a position which, according to Lockhart of Carnwath, was due to the patronage of William, third duke of Hamilton. He

James Ogilvy, fourth earl of Findlater and first earl of Seafield (1663–1730), by Sir Godfrey Kneller, 1704

took the oath of allegiance and the assurance in parliament on 18 April 1693, and he was a member of the committee for security of the kingdom in the 1695 session of parliament. He supported the parliamentary report into the Glencoe massacre, but, pragmatic as ever, he informed William Carstares, the king's chaplain and close adviser in Scottish affairs, that he had 'acted a moderate part in all this' and he was prepared to be ordered by King William 'as to the method of serving him as is my duty' (*State papers*, 258). As solicitor-general he had visited London on more than one occasion and made a favourable impression on the king. In the aftermath of the 1695 parliament Ogilvy was appointed as joint secretary of state with John, earl of Tullibardine, following the dismissal of James Johnston.

Ogilvy attended the 1696 parliament in the capacity of a lesser officer of state, and Sir John Hamilton took his place as the elected member of parliament for Cullen. On 24 June 1698 he was created Viscount Seafield and Lord Ogilvy of Cullen, and was appointed as the president of the 1698 session of parliament which met on 16 July. Sir James Murray of Philiphaugh noted that Seafield presided 'very extraordinary well, both readily, boldly, and impartially' (*State papers*, 383). Seafield managed the session to defend the king's interest, a difficult task given the controversy concerning the Darien crisis. He was one of the 108 members on 26 January 1700 who voted for a parliamentary address to the king concerning Caledonia, as opposed to a formal act. Seafield appears to have been opposed to the Darien scheme from the start, and Lockhart of Carnwath argued that Seafield was 'visibly against

the interest of his country, and trimmed and tricked so shamefully in the affair of Darien that he thereby, from being generally well-beloved, drew upon himself the hatred of all who wished well to that glorious undertaking' ('*Scotland's Ruine*', 18–19). His hostility to the scheme aroused the anger of the Edinburgh mob, and in June 1700 his Edinburgh lodgings were attacked after news reached the city of Campbell of Finnab's victory over the Spaniards at Darien in a small-scale skirmish. Ogilvy was appointed lord high commissioner to the general assembly of the Church of Scotland in 1700, and on 24 June 1701 he was created earl of Seafield, viscount of Reidhaven, and Lord Ogilvy of Deskford and Cullen.

Seafield retained the office of secretary of state, and, following the death of King William in 1702, a new warrant for a patent and commission was issued on 12 May by which he was appointed joint secretary, along with James, duke of Queensberry, with an annual pension of £1000 sterling. Seafield therefore retained his political influence after Queen Anne's accession, and in 1702 he was appointed as one of the members of the ill-fated commission to treat for union with England. On 1 November of that year he was appointed lord high chancellor of Scotland and lord high commissioner to the general assembly which met in Edinburgh on 10 March 1703. He was present in the 1703 and 1704 sessions of parliament in the capacity of lord chancellor, and on 8 August 1704 he was appointed as one of the commissioners of supply for Banffshire. Later that year he was ousted from the chancellorship by John, second marquess of Tweeddale, but on 17 October he was appointed as joint secretary of state (with John, earl of Roxburghe) once more, and on 9 March 1705 he was reappointed as lord chancellor, following Tweeddale's dismissal.

In March 1706 Seafield was appointed to the second commission to treat for a union with England, the commission which negotiated the treaty of union with English commissioners. Seafield played an important role as lord chancellor and adherent of the court faction in managing the treaty through the parliament of Scotland in the final session of its existence. In his speech to the parliament on the opening day of the session on 3 October 1706, Seafield informed the house that:

> it must be of great Advantage to have this whole Island Unite under one Government, and Conjoyned entirely in Interest and Affection, having Equality of all Rights and Privileges, with a free Communication and Intercourse of Trade, which must certainly Establish our Security, Augment our Strength, and Increase our Trade and Riches.

The pragmatic nature of Seafield's character was reflected in his belief that 'We can never Expect a more favourable Juncture for Compleating this Union, than at present, when her Majesty has not only Recommended it, but Declared, That she will Esteem it the greatest Glory of Her Reign, to have it perfected' (*APS*, 1702–7, 11.98–9). Lockhart's memoirs indicate that Seafield was fully aware of the role played by the Scottish treasurer, David Boyle, earl of Glasgow, in the distribution of £20,000 sterling for payment of arrears of salary in the winter of 1706, which would later lead to the view that Scottish members of parliament had been bribed. Seafield received £490 sterling of this money. In one of the most famous events in Scottish history, Seafield signed the Act of Union in the capacity of chancellor of Scotland, and, in face of the assembled Scottish parliament, handed it back to the clerk, exclaiming 'now there's ane end of an old song' ('Scotland's Ruine', 204).

Seafield was chosen as one of the sixteen peers to represent Scotland in the new parliament of Great Britain, and he was continuously re-elected until 1727. He was sworn of the English privy council in 1707, and was also appointed as lord chief baron of the exchequer in the same year. His services in securing the Union in Scotland were recognized in 1708 with a pension of £3000 sterling per annum. Following the death of his father in 1711, he took the additional title of earl of Findlater. Nevertheless, his disillusionment with the progress of the Union came to the fore in 1713, when he introduced a bill for its repeal. His main grievance focused on the application of the malt tax to Scotland, but he also cited the abolition of the Scottish privy council, the extension of English treason legislation to Scotland, and the bar on Scottish peers' being peers of Great Britain. His motion was defeated by only four votes, a telling indication of the state of the Union at that particular time. In November 1713 he was reappointed lord chancellor, and he became keeper of the great seal of Scotland shortly afterwards. Seafield died on 15 August 1730 at Cullen, where he was buried. He left a historical legacy as one of the key Scotsmen in the securing of the Union of 1707.   JOHN R. YOUNG

Sources DNB · APS, 1689–1707 · Seafield correspondence from 1685–1708, ed. J. Grant, Scottish History Society (1912) · Lord Seafield's letters, 1702–1707, ed. P. H. Brown, Scottish History Society (1935) · 'Scotland's ruine': Lockhart of Carnwath's memoirs of the union, ed. D. Szechi, Association of Scottish Literary Studies, 25 (1995) · State papers and letters addressed to William Carstares, ed. J. M'Cormick (1774) · G. H. Rose, A selection from the papers of the earls of Marchmont, 3 vols. (1831) · M. D. Young, ed., The parliaments of Scotland: burgh and shire commissioners, 2 vols. (1992–3) · P. W. J. Riley, King William and the Scottish politicians (1979) · P. W. J. Riley, The Union of England and Scotland (1978) · Scots peerage
Archives NA Scot., corresp. and papers · NRA Scotland, priv. coll., letters relating to politics · U. Edin. L., corresp., papers, and memoranda | BL, corresp. with earl of Nottingham, Add. MS 29588 · BL, letters to Lord Godolphin, Add. MS 34180 · Hunt. L., letters to earl of Loudon · NA Scot., corresp. with earl of Mar; letters to Lords Leven and Melville; letters to duke of Montrose · NL Scot., corresp. with first and second marquesses of Tweeddale
Likenesses J. B. de Medina, oils, 1695, Scot. NPG · G. Kneller, oils, 1704, Royal College of Surgeons, Edinburgh [see illus.] · J. B. de Medina, portrait, Royal College of Surgeons, Edinburgh · oils, Hopetoun House, Lothian Region, Scotland

Ogilvy, James, sixth earl of Findlater and third earl of Seafield (c.1714–1770), agriculturist, was the only son in the family of one son and two daughters of James, fifth earl of Findlater and second earl of Seafield (c.1689–1764), and his first wife, Lady Elizabeth Hay, second daughter of Thomas, seventh earl of Kinnoull. Before succeeding his father in 1764 he was known as Lord Deskford, and while travelling abroad he made the acquaintance of Horace

Walpole, who, in a letter to General Conway on 23 April 1740, wrote of him, 'There are few young people have so good an understanding', but who also referred to his 'solemn Scotchery' as not a 'little formidable' (Letters, 1.46). On 9 June 1749 Ogilvy married Lady Mary (1720–1795), second daughter of John *Murray, first duke of Atholl. They had two sons, one of whom died in 1763. The other, James, who died in 1811, was the last earl of the Ogilvy line.

Ogilvy became interested in encouraging industry and agriculture early in his career. In 1752 he opened a large bleachfield in the parish of Deskford, and he started a factory in Cullen for the manufacture of linen and damask. From 1754 to 1761 he was one of the commissioners of customs for Scotland, and in 1765 he was appointed one of the lords of police. He was also a trustee for the improvement of fisheries and manufactures, and for the management of the annexed estates in Scotland. By his example and encouragement he did much to promote advanced methods of agriculture in Banffshire. He introduced turnip husbandry, and granted long leases to his tenants on condition that within a certain period they should enclose their lands and adopt certain improved methods of cropping. To prevent damage to young plantations on his estate, he agreed to give certain of his tenants, on the termination of their leases, every third tree, or its value in money.

Ogilvy died at Cullen House, Banff, on 3 November 1770.   T. F. HENDERSON, rev. ANNE PIMLOTT BAKER

Sources Burke, Peerage · The letters of Horace Walpole, earl of Orford, ed. P. Cunningham, 9 vols. (1857–9) · The new statistical account of Scotland, 15 vols. (1845) · W. Cramond, ed., The annals of Banff, 2 vols., New Spalding Club, 8, 10 (1891–3) · GEC, Peerage
Archives NA Scot., corresp. and papers | BL, corresp. with duke of Newcastle, etc., Add. MSS 32736–32992 · NA Scot., letters to Lord Kames · NA Scot., letters to Sir Andrew Mitchell

Ogilvy, John [known as Pourie Ogilvy] (fl. 1587–1601), adventurer, was the son of Gilbert Ogilvy of Pourie (d. 1601). His sister, Anne Ogilvy, married on 30 November 1587 Sir Thomas Erskine, a gentleman of the bedchamber of James VI and later earl of Kellie.

Scattered details about Pourie Ogilvy's life point to a career in espionage from the late 1580s. For example, when Thomas Phelippes, an informant of the earl of Essex in Flanders, encountered Ogilvy in 1595 he advised the earl to question Archibald Douglas, a diplomat of James VI in London, who had 'won' Ogilvy 'to be a spy for Sr. Fr. Walsingham' in Scotland, so that he had sent letters in cipher, for which 'he got a good store of coin from Mr. Secretary' (Salisbury MSS, 6.512). After Walsingham's death in 1590 Ogilvy occasionally reported to Douglas; in a letter to Douglas written on 8 January 1593, Ogilvy gave special attention to Angus, Huntly, and Erroll (ibid., 4.279). In the revelations of the 'Spanish blanks' in December 1593—the blank sheets alleged to incriminate the three earls and others in clandestine negotiations with the king of Spain—Ogilvy was identified as the original messenger to bring 'the Scotch king's instructions to Spain' (ibid., 4.216), but he escaped arrest by leaving the paper with George Kerr, who was charged with treason. However, Ogilvy's chances for advancement were ended on 30 September 1594, when he was proclaimed 'traitor' and 'trafficking papist' by order of the Scottish privy council.

Undaunted by this loss of status Ogilvy went to Flanders in June 1595 as a self-appointed deputy of 'the Catholics of Scotland', who, according to Phelippes, told English Catholic exiles that 'the king of Scots is well inclined, and if he may see men in the field he will venture all to be free' (*Salisbury MSS*, 6.512–13). Later, he claimed to be 'speaking on behalf of his king' to Esteban de Ibarra, secretary of state and war, in offering certain Scottish fortresses to Spanish control if troops were sent to support King James (Stafford, 150–52). He had also elevated himself to the title of baron, although the standard authorities on the peerage have no evidence for a barony of Pourie. He arrived in Rome in December 1595 to see the papal secretary of state, Cardinal Aldobrandini, and the Spanish ambassador, the duke of Sessa, whom he visited privately at night. He revealed that James was hoping for financial aid 'to protect himself from rebel vassals' as well as support for his claim to the English throne. He said he carried a sealed document declaring James's intention to become a Catholic, and prepared a list of 'Considerations' showing James's benign treatment of Catholics. Aldobrandini gave no commitment and Sessa commented in his long report that Ogilvy seemed 'cunning', while Ibarra had thought him 'full of inventions' (Archivo General de Simancas, estado 967, 30 Jan 1596). Sessa also quoted the critical doubts of John Cecil, an English priest and secret informant for Robert Cecil (*CSP dom.*, *1595–7*, 144–6), but gave Ogilvy and John Cecil funds to go to Spain.

Upon arrival at the court in May, John Cecil informed Juan de Idiáquez, secretary of the council of state, that Ogilvy 'claims to come on behalf of his king', and as a baron 'is anxious to be treated with deference' (Archivo General de Simancas, estado 967, 15 May 1596). In a review of his papers, dated 15 June, Ogilvy recalled most of what he had told Sessa earlier in Rome, but on Ibarra's motion the council advised that confirmation of Ogilvy's credentials be secured from James VI and that he remain in Barcelona.

Meanwhile, an unexpected revelation outside Spain damaged Ogilvy's remaining hopes of returning to the service of King James. Word spread that copies of the letters of Sessa relating Ogilvy's activities had been seized by a French ship and, after they reached the courts of London and Edinburgh, had created a furore. When Bowes, the English ambassador, protested to James about Ogilvy's 'practices in Spain', the king denied 'any participation in them' (*CSP Scot. ser.*, 1589–1603, 717–18), so that Ogilvy's claim to 'speak in behalf of his king' appeared more dubious. A detailed list of objections, submitted by John Cecil on 1 December 1595, led to Ogilvy's confinement for over two years, because it confirmed the suspicions of the Spanish council. In the summer of 1598 his brother-in-law, Sir Thomas Erskine, pleaded for his release, but rather than return to Scotland, Ogilvy went to Madrid to petition the council in December 1598 for a 'salary' of 100

escudos (about £25) a month, on his claim of leaving Scotland 'because of his faith' and suffering imprisonment and 'many trials'. The council refused the salary, but 'to get him out of here more quickly' gave him alms (Archivo General de Simancas, estado 2763, 12 Jan 1599). Even then Henry Neville heard in Paris that Ogilvy stayed in Madrid on his so-called 'important business' (*CSP dom.*, *1598–1601*, 221) before returning to Scotland. Later in 1600, the keeper of Brancepeth Castle related that 'by secret direction of the Privy Council, [he] apprehended a Scottish laird called Ogilby that came from the court above, kept him safe for 40 days and sent up [to London] his letters and papers' (*Salisbury MSS*, 10.204).

In the same year, in a deal similar to the one he had made earlier with Walsingham, Ogilvy sent reports from Scotland to Robert Cecil as 'John Gibsone' and was paid for them (*CSP Scot. ser.*, 1589–1603, 791). Even then, when he tried to enter England again in January 1601, he was arrested and placed in the custody of Robert Carey, the warden of the Middle March, until Cecil ordered that he be sent back northward, with the comment: 'of the man I have heard as evil as I have heard of any' (*Salisbury MSS*, 11.22). After this Ogilvy tried to make peace with King James, begging that 'your M. will use my poor wife and bairns according to your wonted clemency' and insisting that he 'never had or used' any commission from the king overseas and that he sought only 'justice and pity' (ibid., 11.559). On 4 July 1601 Ogilvy lamented to Cecil that peace with James was 'upon rigorous conditions which he cannot afford' (*CSP Scot. ser.*, 1589–1603, 799), but was told not to enter England again, since the queen did not countenance those subjects of James VI 'to whom he declares publicly his offence' (*Salisbury MSS*, 11.290). On the death of his father, Ogilvy inherited his lands, but, still under the ban of the privy council, he had to leave for the continent, where his subsequent adventures have yet to be traced.

A. J. LOOMIE

Sources sección de estado, Archivo General de Simancas, 176, 967, 2763 · T. G. Law, ed., 'Documents illustrating Catholic policy in the reign of James VI', *Miscellany … I*, Scottish History Society, 15 (1893), 3–70 · H. G. Stafford, *James VI of Scotland and the throne of England* (1940) · *CSP Scot. ser.*, *1509–1603* · *Calendar of the manuscripts of the most hon. the marquis of Salisbury*, 4, HMC, 9 (1892); 6 (1895); 10–11 (1904–6) · *CSP dom.*, *1595–1601* · F. Shearman, 'The Spanish blanks', *Innes Review*, 3 (1952), 81–103
Archives PRO, state papers domestic · PRO, calendar state papers, Scotland

Ogilvy [*née* Gore], **Mabell Frances Elizabeth**, **countess of Airlie** (1866–1956), courtier and literary editor, was born in Charles Street, London, on 10 March 1866, the eldest of the four children of Arthur Gore (1839–1901), who was at that time Lord Sudley and who succeeded as fifth earl of Arran in 1884, and his first wife, Edith Elizabeth Henrietta Jocelyn (*c.*1844–1871), daughter of Robert, Viscount Jocelyn. Her mother died when she was four, and she was brought up by her dour widowed grandmother, Frances, Lady Jocelyn, who was the daughter of Lady Palmerston and a lady of the bedchamber to Queen Victoria. Visits to the duchess of Teck at White Lodge in Richmond Park,

Mabell Frances Elizabeth Ogilvy, countess of Airlie (1866–1956), by John Singer Sargent, 1923

where Mabell met the duchess's daughter, Princess May (the future Queen Mary), were among the few events that lifted the enforced gloom of the children's childhood. Mabell and her two sisters received a restricted education from governesses.

On 19 January 1886 Lady Mabell Gore married an active army officer, David William Stanley Ogilvy, sixth or twelfth earl of Airlie (1856–1900)—the number is confused because of an eighteenth-century attainder—at St George's, Hanover Square. Despite being in love, she found it difficult to adapt to the submissive role required of young wives, and to cope with her six pregnancies, which produced three daughters and then three sons. Neither domesticated nor maternal by nature, Lady Airlie enjoyed army life, and her relationship with her husband deepened as she involved herself in his world. He went to South Africa with his regiment on the outbreak of the Second South African War, and on 11 June 1900 he was killed in action at Diamond Hill, Transvaal. Lady Airlie threw herself into managing Cortachy, the Airlie estate in Forfarshire, on behalf of her six-year-old son. In 1902 her old friend the princess of Wales (as Princess May had become) offered her the position of lady-in-waiting, and, after some hesitation, she accepted.

Thus began a fifty-year association between the two women. Lady Airlie offered a perceptive analysis of the relationships between Queen Mary, George V, and their children in her memoirs, and supported the queen through both world wars, the king's death, and the abdication of Edward VIII. She watched three generations of the royal family from close quarters, and encouraged the engagement of the future George VI to Lady Elizabeth Bowes-Lyon, whom she had known from their childhoods. In 1953 Elizabeth II recognized her long service by investing her with the GCVO. Lady Airlie was valued at court for her wisdom and her lively conversation. She became more attractive in maturity and enjoyed the company and conversation of men, but she did not remarry, maintaining that only her firm conviction that she would be reunited with her husband after death enabled her to enjoy life without him.

Away from court Mabell Ogilvy's priority was her family. Her working day began at four each morning, but she was always available to her children, whom she encouraged to be active and independent. She supported the Red Cross, and served for many years on the board of Queen Alexandra's Imperial Military Nursing Service. The First World War cut a swathe through her family: a son-in-law was killed in action in 1915, then her youngest son in 1917, and her third daughter was killed while exercising army horses in 1918.

When her eldest son married in 1917, Lady Airlie moved from Cortachy Castle to Airlie Castle, near Kirriemuir, where she began to edit family letters for publication. *In Whig Society, 1775–1818* (1921) and *Lady Palmerston and her Times* (1922) were based on the papers of her great-grandmother, and *With the Guards We Shall Go* (1933) followed a great-uncle through the Crimean War. Her volumes remain a fascinating source, although her editing skills, unsurprisingly, do not meet exacting modern scholarly standards. In later life she wrote *The Red Cross in Angus* (1950) and began work on her memoirs, but did not complete them. They were discovered after her death by Jennifer Ellis, who edited them for publication as *Thatched with Gold* (1962).

Famously outspoken, Mabell Ogilvy defied fashion: 'With her striking appearance, with masses of white hair piled up, usually beneath a large picture hat, she could easily have been the subject of a portrait by Gainsborough, and she rarely deserted that old and elaborate fashion' (*The Times*). But she adapted gracefully to a changing world. As early as the 1890s she had written a pamphlet advocating improvements in women's education and employment, and, when asked in the 1930s if the admission of a working-class woman to the Queen Alexandra nurses would lower the prestige of the service, her response was characteristically blunt: 'stuff and nonsense' (Airlie, 193). All forms of suffering moved her, and in her late eighties she was still looking for ways to help disabled former servicemen. The death of Queen Mary in 1953 was a blow, and in 1955 heavy taxation, the rising cost of living, and shortage of servants forced her to leave Airlie Castle. Declining to impose on her children, she clung to her independence, taking up residence at 129 Bayswater Road, Paddington. Even this reverse did not break her effervescent spirit, and on her ninetieth birthday her daughter found her dancing a jig. Lady Airlie died there a few weeks later, on 7 April 1956. The Airlie family maintained and extended the close relationship with the royal family established by Mabell Ogilvy: her eldest son served as Elizabeth II's lord chamberlain, while his second son, Angus, married Princess Alexandra, daughter of the duke of Kent.

CHARLOTTE ZEEPVAT

Sources Mabell, countess of Airlie, *Thatched with gold*, ed. J. Ellis (1962) • *The Times* (9 April 1956) • Burke, *Peerage* (1967) • GEC, *Peerage* • E. Longford, *Elizabeth R: a biography* (1983) • P. Ziegler, *King Edward VIII: the official biography* (1990)
Archives BL, corresp., Add. MSS 52418–52419 • NA Scot., corresp. and MSS | Herts. ALS, letters to Lady Desborough, etc. • NL Ire., letters to Alice Stopford Green
Likenesses J. S. Sargent, drawing, 1923, priv. coll. [*see illus.*] • P. A. de Laszlo, oils, 1930–1939?, Dundee Corporation Art Galleries and Museums Department • photographs, Royal Arch. • portraits, repro. in Mabell, *Thatched with gold*
Wealth at death £8549 0s. 5d. in England: probate, 7 Aug 1956, *CGPLA Eng. & Wales*

Ogilvy, Margaret, Lady Ogilvy (1724–1757). *See under* Ogilvy, David, styled sixth earl of Airlie (1725–1803).

Ogilvy, Marion (d. 1575), landowner and mistress of Cardinal David Beaton, was the youngest known daughter of James, first Lord Ogilvy of Airlie (d. 1504), and his fourth wife, Janet Lyle (d. in or before 1525). Her father had made only partial provision for her before his death, a marriage contract (1503) by which the heir of Gordon of Midmar would marry her elder sister Janet or, on her death, Marion. Janet appears to have died young but the contract was not implemented. Marion was unmarried when in 1525 she wound up the affairs of her late mother at Airlie. It was probably about then that she became the mistress of David *Beaton (1494?–1546), abbot of Arbroath and future cardinal-archbishop of St Andrews. Their association lasted until Beaton's death in 1546. Their circumstances, which differed little in outward appearance from marriage, offended those who wanted serious reform of the church, and who deplored the double standard by which prelates punished those who advocated the marriage of the clergy yet lived in open concubinage in violation of the rule of clerical celibacy.

In the 1520s and 1530s Marion Ogilvy built up considerable property, leased from the abbey, in and around Arbroath. As an unmarried woman she had the right to appear in the law courts in her own name in defence of her property rights, which she did frequently, on both her own behalf and that of her family. Her home at this period was at Ethie, the abbot's castle north of Arbroath. After Beaton succeeded his uncle James as archbishop of St Andrews (1539) she and her sons were granted lands on the archbishopric estates in Angus (Forfarshire). In 1543 the cardinal acquired a secular property, the barony of North Melgund near Brechin, for his family, settling the property on Marion for her lifetime and on their eldest son, David, after her. Melgund Castle, which he built, or rebuilt, bore his and Marion's coat of arms on the tower like those of a landed magnate and his wife. Having to manage her own affairs, Marion used a seal and also learned to write. Following Beaton's assassination on 29

May 1546—according to Knox's *History* (the only contemporary narrative to comment on their relationship) Marion spent the cardinal's last night with him in the castle of St Andrews—attacks were made on her houses by Lord Gray, Sir Robert Carnegie of Kinnaird, and others. In this vulnerable situation Marion married William Douglas (of no known designation) in the summer of 1547, after 15 May, but he had died by 18 September that year, and she never remarried. She relinquished Ethie to the Carnegies, having recovered her legal papers stolen by them, and lived at Melgund until her death.

David Beaton's eight recorded children were all the sons and daughters of Marion Ogilvy. George, mentioned only in letters of legitimation in 1531, may have died young. The oldest surviving son, David (d. 1592), was destined for an ecclesiastical career and studied in Paris in the 1540s and 1550s. With the acquisition of Melgund, however, he served in the French king's Scots guard and later as a master of the household to James VI. He married first Margaret, daughter of Lord Lindsay (c.1557), and, after they were divorced, Lucretia Beaton of Creich (1576). James (d. 1560), who also studied in France, became a canon of Glasgow and was incorporated in Glasgow University. John, last mentioned in 1559, may have gone to France. Alexander (d. c.1612), who also studied in France and held the archdeaconry of Lothian, married Margaret Annand; the cardinal's line continued with their descendants. When her sons were abroad Marion acted as their factor and sent them money through the Italian banker Timothy Cagnoli, who did business in Scotland. The eldest daughter, Margaret, was married to David Lindsay, master (later tenth earl), of Crawford, in April 1546, with considerable magnificence, a few weeks before her father's murder. When their marriage broke up in the early 1570s Margaret went to live with her mother at Melgund; divorce proceedings were in progress when the earl died in 1573. Elizabeth (1527–c.1573) married Alexander Lindsay of Vayne. Agnes, who lived into the early seventeenth century, married first James Ochterlonie of Kellie, second George Gordon of Gight, and third Sir Patrick Gordon of Auchindoun.

Several members of Marion Ogilvy's family, including David of Melgund, were prosecuted as Catholic recusants. On Queen Mary's escape from Lochleven Castle in May 1568 a letter from Lord Ogilvy rallying her Angus supporters was sent out from Melgund. Marion died at Melgund Castle between 22 and 30 June 1575, making her sons David and Alexander her executors. She left estate of over £3000 Scots, including £1000 in ready money. She asked to be buried in the Ogilvy aisle of Kinnell church. Less than two weeks after her death members of the family granted letters of slains, formal remission in return for assythment (compensation for the loss of a blood relative), to the cardinal's surviving assassin, John Leslie of Parkhill. Her family held Melgund for only two more generations.

MARGARET H. B. SANDERSON

Sources acts of the lords of council and session, NA Scot., CS 6 • register of acts and decreets, NA Scot., CS 7 • Edinburgh commissary court records, register of testaments, NA Scot., CC8/8/3, fol. 260 • NA Scot., GD 16 • NA Scot., GD 45 • *Scots peerage*, 1.114–15 •

Charles, eleventh marquis of Huntly, earl of Aboyne, ed., *The records of Aboyne MCCXXX–MDCLXXXI*, New Spalding Club, 13 (1894) · *John Knox's History of the Reformation in Scotland*, ed. W. C. Dickinson, 1 (1949) · R. K. Hannay, ed., *Rentale Sancti Andree, 1538–1546*, Scottish History Society, 2nd ser., 4 (1913) · M. H. B. Sanderson, *Cardinal of Scotland: David Beaton, c.1494–1546* (1986) · M. H. B. Sanderson, *Cardinal of Scotland: David Beaton, c.1494–1546*, rev. edn (2000) · M. H. B. Sanderson, *Mary Stewart's people: life in Mary Stewart's Scotland* (1987)

Archives NA Scot., Airlie muniments, records of the Ogilvy family

Wealth at death £3000 Scots: Edinburgh commissary court records, register of testaments, NA Scot., CC8/8/3, fol. 260

Ogilvy [Ogilvie], **Sir Patrick, of Boyne, Lord Boyne** (*d*. in or after **1705**), judge, was the eldest of three sons and three daughters of Sir Walter Ogilvie (*c*.1621–1666/7), sixth laird of Boyne, Banffshire, and his wife, Elizabeth, daughter of Sir Patrick Ogilvie of Inchmartin. In 1660 his father settled the barony and thanedom of Boyne on him. Ogilvy's first marriage, to Anna, eldest daughter of James, laird of Grant, produced a son, James (*b*. 1667). James became an active Jacobite who in 1707 fled to France, where he settled. Anna died in April 1667, and about 1679 Ogilvy married Anna, daughter of Douglas of Wittingham and widow of Patrick Barclay of Towie; a son, Archibald, was born in 1680.

On the death of his father Ogilvy had inherited a large estate, extending from Portsoy to Banff, with its principal seat at Boyne Castle. He developed the harbour of Portsoy, and the nearby marble quarries which produced a stone which was popular in Britain and was also exported. His long study of the law, coupled to influence, marked him out for political advancement and he represented Banff in the Scottish parliament of 1669–74 and thereafter for some twenty-four years, until 1693 when his seat was declared vacant because he had not signed the assurance. On 14 October 1681 he was named a judge of the court of session, with the title Lord Boyne, and at the same time received the honour of knighthood. In addition he undertook military duties, both as a volunteer and in the regular forces, holding commissions in various militia regiments.

Boyne ran into opposition when in 1684 he was recorded as having purchased a suit of English cloth, which incensed local manufacturers at Newmills who lodged a particular complaint against Andrew Irving, the Edinburgh merchant who had sold him the imported garments. An outspoken Jacobite, Boyne was one of those who in 1681 signed a declaration that it was unlawful to take up arms against the king. In January 1686 he received a pension from James II, for what reason it is not clear, but as he had in 1677 received a royal protection against paying annual rents on his mortgages, he was possibly already falling into financial difficulties and as a good Jacobite was considered worthy of support.

Boyne's third marriage, in December 1682, was to Lady Anne, youngest daughter of Hugh Montgomerie, seventh earl of Eglinton, and widow of Sir Andrew Ramsay, bt. She seems to have been the cause of a public dispute in March 1686 between Boyne and the younger Campbell of Calder,

by which time there was a rift between the couple and Anne was pregnant with a child whose paternity was disputed. Boyne was returning from court when Campbell confronted him in the High Street, Edinburgh, spat in his face, called him a rascal and a villain, and offered to strike him, saying that if Lord Boyne had been carrying a sword he would have run him through. The court of session committed Campbell to prison in the Tolbooth, and laid the matter before the king, who directed that Campbell should ask pardon of the king and the court, and, on his knees, of Lord Boyne, which he did on 14 September, gaining his release. Anne had departed by the time that the child was born in November 1686. It is not known if she was ever reconciled with her husband, nor what became of the child.

On the accession of Queen Anne, Boyne was sent as an emissary of the Jacobites to propose to her, 'the design of bringing the Pretender to succeed to the crown upon a bargain that she should hold it during her life', and that on his return 'he gave the party full assurance that she had accepted it' (*Bishop Burnet's History*, 5.455). He was mentioned in 1705 in the duke of Perth's instructions as one of those who had distinguished themselves by their loyalty to the exiled Stuart cause since the revolution of 1688. The date and circumstances of his death are not known.

T. F. HENDERSON, *rev.* ANITA MCCONNELL

Sources *Correspondence of Colonel N. Hooke*, ed. W. D. Macray, 2 vols., Roxburghe Club, 92, 95 (1870–71) · A. Tayler and H. Tayler, *The Ogilvies of Boyne* (1933) · *Bishop Burnet's History*, 5.455 · M. D. Young, ed., *The parliaments of Scotland: burgh and shire commissioners*, 2 (1993)

Ogilvy, Sir Walter, of Lintrathen (*c*.1380–1438), administrator and landowner, was the second son of Sir Walter Ogilvy of Auchterhouse (*fl. c*.1368–1392). His mother is said to have been Isabella, daughter and heir of Sir Malcolm Ramsay of Auchterhouse. From about 1400 the younger Walter built up his landed patrimony, *c*.1414 obtaining from Archibald Douglas, fourth earl of Douglas (*d*. 1424), a grant of the barony of Lintrathen, Angus, whence his style. His lands lay in Angus, Kincardineshire, Berwickshire, and Perthshire. He is also occasionally styled of Carcary or of Bolshan, both in Angus. In 1431 he received a licence from James I to erect his tower of Airlie, Angus, in the form of a castle.

Ogilvy was knighted at the coronation of James I on 21 May 1424, after the latter's return from captivity in England. By November 1424 he was styled king's treasurer, a post introduced by James I. The treasurer and the comptroller, another new office, exercised the financial powers formerly held by the chamberlain, but the division of responsibilities before the 1460s is unclear. In the 1420s, at least, it seems that both the new officials dealt with the finances of the royal household, although eventually the treasurer was concerned in the main with feudal casualties. Until late 1432 Ogilvy was almost always present as a witness when crown charters were granted. From July 1430 he is normally styled master of the king's household, a post he had yielded by August 1432. While Ogilvy seldom thereafter witnessed crown charters, he had not fallen from favour, as in November 1432 he and others had an (apparently unused) English safe conduct for a year to go as Scots ambassadors to the Council of Basel. In March 1436 he accompanied James I's daughter Margaret on her journey to France to marry the dauphin, the future Louis XI. (Also in March 1436 another unimpeachable source has a Sir Walter Ogilvy present at Florence promising Pope Eugenius IV and his cardinals to attempt to persuade James I to repeal legislation against ecclesiastical liberty. Ogilvy of Lintrathen cannot have carried out both missions, but the identity of the other Sir Walter Ogilvy is uncertain.)

After the murder of James I in 1437 Ogilvy was briefly treasurer again and may have resumed a career at court, but he died in late 1438; he is said to have been buried in Kinnell kirk. In 1427 and 1432 he founded chaplainries in Auchterhouse parish church. He and his first wife, Isabel (d. in or before 1405), whose surname was possibly Durward, had two sons. Sir John, the elder, married Margaret, countess of Moray, widow probably of Thomas Dunbar, third earl of Moray, and their eldest son, James, was created Lord Ogilvy of Airlie in 1491. Sir Walter married second Isabel (fl. 1405–1440), daughter of Sir John Glen of Inchmartin and Margaret Erskine. They had five sons and two daughters, one of whom, Isabel, married first Patrick Lyon, first Lord Glamis, and second Gilbert, first Lord Kennedy. Sir Walter's widow survived him and married Robert Cunningham of Auchenbowie (d. c.1466).

ALAN R. BORTHWICK

Sources NA Scot., Airlie muniments · J. M. Thomson and others, eds., *Registrum magni sigilli regum Scotorum / The register of the great seal of Scotland*, 11 vols. (1882–1914), vol. 2 · CDS, vol. 4 · G. Burnett and others, eds., *The exchequer rolls of Scotland*, 23 vols. (1878–1908), esp. vols. 4–5 · various collections of manuscript estate and other papers in archive offices and in private hands in Scotland and England · [J. Haldenston], *Copiale prioratus Sanctiandree: the letter-book of James Haldenstone, prior of St Andrews, 1418–1443*, ed. J. H. Baxter, St Andrews University Publications, 31 (1930) · W. Bower, *Scotichronicon*, ed. D. E. R. Watt and others, new edn, 9 vols. (1987–98), vol. 8 · W. Wilson, *The house of Airlie* (1924) · Register House charters, NA Scot., RH6/300A

Archives priv. coll. | NA Scot., Airlie muniments

O'Glacan, Nial [Nellanus Glacanus] (*fl.* 1602–1655), physician, was born in co. Donegal, Ireland. He may have gained the rudiments of a professional education—familiarity with the aphorisms of Hippocrates, and acquaintance with some of Galen's works—from one or other of the hereditary medical families, probably the MacDuinntsleibhes who served the O'Donnells, continuing his studies in continental schools. He evidently left Ireland at an early age, for he attended the exiled Hugh O'Donnell (d. 1602) in Spain.

Nellanus Glacanus, as he was known abroad, practised in Salamanca in 1621 and in the following year at Valencia. In the late 1620s, with commendable courage, he was treating plague in towns in the neighbourhood of Clermont and Toulouse, wearing the strange garb devised to give protection—a long red or black leather gown,

gauntlets, leather mask with glass-protected openings for the eyes, and a long beak filled with fumigants to cover the nose. O'Glacan was encouraged in his work by the bishop of Cahors, and in 1628, when the epidemic spread to Toulouse, he was appointed physician to its *xenodochium pestiferorum*. He published *Tractatus de peste, seu, Bevis, facilis, & experta methodus curandi pestem*, a small volume containing 274 pages, printed by Raymond Colomerius, the university printer, in May 1629, and dedicated to Giles de Masuyer, vicomte d'Ambrières. For many years O'Glacan remained in Toulouse; he was appointed physician to the king, and became professor of medicine in the university.

For one reason or another O'Glacan removed to Bologna in 1646, and possibly it was at about this time that he visited Rome. In collaboration with the bishop of Ferns and Sir Nicholas Plunkett he edited a series of poems in Latin in praise of the pope, *Regni Hiberniae ad sanctissimum Innocentium X pont. max. Pyramides encomiasticae* (1648). The preface is by O'Glacan, who mentions as his friends in Italy Francis O'Molloy, the author of 'Lucerna fidelium', Peter Talbot, Gerard O'Fearail, and John O'Fahy. The professor of eloquence at Lucca, Peter von Adrian Brocke, wrote a poem in praise of O'Glacan himself, the opening lines of which are quoted in Cameron's *History of the Royal College of Surgeons in Ireland* (p. 7) and by Fleetwood in *The History of Medicine in Ireland* (p. 49).

O'Glacan's quarto two-volume *Cursus medicus*, containing thirteen books in three parts (1, *Physiologica*; 2, *Pathologica*; and 3, *Semeiotica*), was published in 1655. An orthodox account of medicine, it is based firmly on Galen's teachings, making no attempt to foster new ideas. Commendatory verses are prefixed, and among those of part two are some by Gregory Fallon, a Connaughtman, who was at Bologna, and by another fellow countryman, the Revd Philip Roche SJ. Fallon says that O'Glacan is in Italy what Fuchsius was in Germany. Part one has two curious prefaces, one *lectori benevolo*, the other *lectori malevolo*.

These books are now great rarities, the availability of the *Cursus* in Great Britain confined to the British Library. Samuel Simms, who possessed a copy of the *Tractatus de peste*, regarded it as the more attractive, and was impressed by the personal observations scattered through the text, indicative of an extensive knowledge of the dreaded disease. O'Glacan provides a detailed account of the malady's clinical features, paying special attention to examination of the pulse and the urine, and indicating those signs which he regarded as indicating a putridity of the humours. He supplies notes of three post-mortem examinations, drawing attention to petechial haemorrhages on the pleural membrane, and to splenomegaly. As in other acute diseases the prognosis is dubious. In the preface O'Glacan speaks of the fame of Ireland for learning in ancient times, and refers to the achievements of the Irish physicians.

No personal details of the life of Nial O'Glacan have survived. According to Kenneth Dewhurst he died in Bologna 'around the middle of the century' (Dewhurst, xxxiv), but whether he lived to see the publication of the *Cursus* is not stated. Presuming he saw his book through the press, he must have exceeded the biblical span.   J. B. LYONS

Sources S. Simms, 'Nial O'Glacan of Donegal', *Ulster Medical Journal*, 4 (1935), 186–9 · J. F. Fleetwood, *The history of medicine in Ireland*, 2nd edn (1983) · C. A. Cameron, *History of the Royal College of Surgeons in Ireland*, 2nd edn (1916) · K. Dewhurst, ed., *Richard Lower's Vindicatio: a defence of the experimental method* (1983)

Oglander, Sir John (1585–1655), diarist, eldest son of Sir William Oglander (1554–1609) of Nunwell, near Brading, Isle of Wight, and West Dean, Sussex, and his first wife, Ann, daughter of Anthony Dillington of Knighton, Isle of Wight, was born on 12 May 1585 at Nunwell. His family, which was of Norman origin, had been settled there since the conquest. Pride in his ancestry is a notable feature of his 'Advice to his descendants' and the journal, which gives a vivid picture of his life. Having attended Winchester College, he matriculated from Balliol College, Oxford, on 8 July 1603, and spent three years there without taking a degree. In 1604 he also entered the Middle Temple, but he was not called to the bar. On 4 August 1606 he married Frances (1590–1644), fifth daughter of Sir George *More (1553–1632) of Loseley, Surrey. In the course of a very happy marriage they had four sons and three daughters. Following the death of his father on 17 March 1609, Oglander succeeded to the family estates, and was placed on the commission of the peace.

On 22 December 1615 Oglander was knighted by James I at Royston. In 1620 he was appointed deputy governor of Portsmouth, but he sold the office three years later, having discovered that it entailed a heavy outlay on entertainment. He accepted in 1624 the post of deputy governor of the Isle of Wight, a post which, being close to home, did not also demand neglect of his estates. He sat for Yarmouth, Isle of Wight, in the parliaments of 1625, 1626, and 1628–9, and partook of the general concern about the threat to freemen's liberties posed by money-raising expedients emanating from the privy council over those years, although he was personally charmed by the king during the latter's visit to the island in 1628. He grew to dislike London and its temptations, preferring life on the island, with its simple pleasures of riding and playing bowls on the downs. He made concerted attempts to improve his estates, planting scores of trees and fruit bushes, but by the early 1630s had concluded that an energetic farming policy was insufficient by itself to maintain his income at a level appropriate to his social status: a gentleman needed public office or a career as a lawyer to raise and maintain his family. He was commissioner of oyer and terminer for Hampshire in 1635, and sheriff of the same county from 1637 to 1639. During his shrievalty he displayed great zeal and activity in the collection of ship money.

On the outbreak of the civil war Oglander adhered to the king, and was superseded in the deputy governorship of the Isle of Wight by Colonel Carne. In June 1643 he was arrested and sent to London on suspicion of delinquency, having refused parliament's commission as governor of the island. Detained pending the investigation of the charges against him by the House of Commons, he was discharged after eight weeks, but was sent for again the following September and placed under arrest in January 1644, remaining close prisoner until procuring his release on condition that he remain within the lines of communication. He was discharged on 12 April 1645. A contribution of £500 was levied upon his estate, although he appears to have paid no more than £115 of it. He was among those who waited on Charles I to express their loyalty on 15 November 1647, the day after the king's arrival at Carisbrooke Castle. Those assembled were given to believe that the king had fled Hampton Court out of fear for his life, and he assured them that he looked forward to reaching a settlement with his parliament of England. By this time Oglander's experience of civil war and of what he considered the arbitrary rule of the island by a county committee composed of social upstarts had merely increased his bitterness and resolve. After the meeting he advised the king's servant Colonel William Legge that the only security against an invasion of the island by those 'Levellers' who wished the king dead was to have a boat in readiness to convey him to the mainland. A few days later, the king came to Nunwell. Oglander did not reveal the subject of their discussions, but prayed that 'God [would] send him happily hence … to regain his crown as his predecessor King John did here' (*Royalist's Notebook*, 116). As long as the king remained on the island Oglander visited him regularly until the governor, Colonel Robert Hammond, warned him that two of those about the king, Robert Preston, the keeper of the robes, and Captain Anthony Mildmay, were informing against those who resorted to their sovereign—'which (being in the fire before) made me forbear, though much against my will' (ibid., 120). However, Oglander was on hand to hear the king's speech of farewell, made at the departure from the island of the parliamentary commissioners for the treaty of Newport on 27 November 1648.

Oglander continued to keep his journal for a while after the king's death, noting his displeasure at what he considered the foolish marriage of his daughter Bridget in October 1649, and the visit he received from the duke of Gloucester at his coming to the island with his sister, the Princess Elizabeth, in 1650. He was again arrested and taken to London in January 1651 on suspicion of treasonable designs, and was released early in the following February, on again giving security to remain within the lines of communication. He died at Nunwell on 28 November 1655, and was buried in the family vault in Brading church. The recumbent effigy in full armour which he had commissioned makes an intriguing contrast with his pen-portrait of a 'somewhat corpulent, man of middle stature, with a white beard and somewhat big mustachios, riding in black or some sad-coloured clothes … on a handsome middling black stone-horse, his hair grey and his complexion very sanguine' (quoted in Heal and Holmes, 20). His wife, Frances, had died on 12 June 1644 and their much-loved eldest son, George, had died at Caen in Normandy. A diminished estate descended to the second son, William (1611–1670), who represented Newport in the Restoration parliament and was created baronet in 1665.

J. M. RIGG, *rev.* SEAN KELSEY

Sources M. A. E. Green, ed., *Calendar of the proceedings of the committee for advance of money, 1642–1656,* 3, PRO (1888), 444 · *The Oglander memoirs: extracts from the MSS of Sir J. Oglander, kt. of Nunwell, Isle of Wight* (1888) · *A royalist's notebook: the commonplace book of Sir John Oglander,* ed. F. Bamford (1936) · will, PRO, PROB 11/252, sig. 12, fols. 91r–92r · F. Heal and C. Holmes, *The gentry in England and Wales, 1500–1700* (1994) · M. W. Helms, O. Watson, and B. D. Hemming, 'Oglander, William', HoP, *Commons, 1660–90*
Archives Isle of Wight RO, Newport, diaries, corresp., and papers · Isle of Wight RO, Newport, photostatic copy of diary, also incl. accounts, recipes, etc. · U. Southampton L., MS notes relating to history of Isle of Wight [transcript]
Likenesses C. Johnson, oils, Nunwell House, Isle of Wight; repro. in *Royalist's notebook,* ed. Bamford, frontispiece · funeral effigy, Brading church, Isle of Wight
Wealth at death apart from real estate in Isle of Wight and Sussex, to which no value is assigned, will devised bequest of £200 to son: will, PRO, PROB 11/252, sig. 12, fols. 91r–92r

Ogle, Sir Chaloner (1680/81–1750), naval officer, was the son of John Ogle (1649/50–1740), a Newcastle barrister, and Mary Braithwaite (d. 1744). He entered the navy on 28 July 1697 as a volunteer per order, or king's letter-boy, on the *Yarmouth* with Captain Cleveland. He afterwards served in the *Restoration* and the *Worcester* before passing his lieutenant's examination on 11 March 1702 aged twenty-one.

On 29 April 1702 Ogle was promoted third lieutenant of the *Royal Oak*, and on 28 May he became second lieutenant on the *Anglesea*. In the West Indies he was given command of the captured sloop *St Antonio*, before moving on 21 April 1705 to the *Deal Castle*. After returning to England in December 1705 Ogle stayed with the *Deal Castle*, in which he was captured off Ostend on 3 July 1706 by three French ships. A court martial on 19 October acquitted Ogle of all blame. On 26 June 1707 he was appointed to command the *Queenborough*, and on 20 May 1708 he was posted to the frigate *Tartar*; he remained in her for the duration of the War of the Spanish Succession. In 1716 he commanded the *Plymouth* in the Baltic under Sir John Norris, and in 1717 the *Worcester* under Sir George Byng.

On 11 March 1719 he was appointed to the *Swallow* (60 guns). After convoying the trade to Newfoundland, thence to the Mediterranean, and so home, Ogle was ordered, on 31 January 1721, to the coast of Africa. On the passage he met the *Weymouth*. Both ships' companies were badly ravaged by sickness. On 20 September, Ogle wrote from Prince's Island that they had buried men and had still 100 sick. At Cape Coast Castle in November he received intelligence of two pirates plundering on the coast. At Ouidah he learned that they had lately captured ten sail, one of which they had burnt, with a full cargo of African slaves on board, the owners of the ship having refused to pay ransom. On 5 February 1722 he found them at anchor under Cape Lopez. One of the ships, a captured French vessel of 32 guns, commanded by a pirate named Skyrm, slipped her cable in chase, mistaking the *Swallow* for a

Sir Chaloner Ogle (1680/81–1750), by unknown artist, *c.*1718

merchantman. When they had run out of earshot the *Swallow* tacked towards the pirate, and, after a sharp action, captured her. Ogle then returned to Cape Lopez under a French ensign. The second pirate ship, the *Royal Fortune*, commanded by Bartholomew Roberts, waited for her, eager for the expected prize. The *Swallow* then hoisted the English flag and engaged the pirate ship. Roberts defended himself with obstinate bravery, but when he was killed his crew surrendered. The total number of prisoners was 262, including 75 African slaves, who were sold. Of the rest, 19 died before the trial at Cape Coast Castle, 77 were acquitted, 52 were hanged, 20 were sentenced to death and then sent to the mines, and the remainder were sent to prison in England.

Ogle's conduct received much praise, and on his return to England in April 1723 he was knighted. He also received, as a special gift from the crown, the pirates' ships and effects less the payment of £1940 head-money to his officers and men. Despite contrary claims from his officers and crew Ogle appears to have argued successfully that he should be the recipient of the remaining prize money, totalling more than £3000, which he regarded as a personal gift to support his new title.

On 2 April 1729 Ogle was appointed to the *Burford*, one of the fleet gathered at Spithead under the command of Sir Charles Wager. On 19 May 1731 he took charge of the *Edinburgh* in the fleet, also under Wager, which went to the Mediterranean. He was sent out to Jamaica as commander-in-chief in June 1732 and did not return to England until August 1735. Ogle was twice married. After the death of his first wife, Henrietta Issacson (1678–1737), he married on 30 October 1737 Jane Isabella (d. 1761), about whom further details are unknown; they do not appear to have had any children.

In June 1739 Ogle was appointed to the *Augusta*; on his promotion to rear-admiral of the blue (11 July), he hoisted his flag in her and, with strong reinforcements, joined Nicholas Haddock in the Mediterranean. His stay there was short, and by the following summer he was third in command of the fleet under Sir John Norris. On 10 September 1740 Ogle was ordered to escort an expeditionary army of over 8000, under the command of Lord Cathcart, to the West Indies. The objective was to attack the Spanish possessions in the Caribbean, but tension with France caused the ministry to send over thirty warships with Ogle to reinforce Vice-Admiral Edward Vernon's small squadron at Port Royal, Jamaica. Their combined fleet, numbering thirty sail of the line and some 10,000 British and American soldiers, constituted by far the largest force that had ever been assembled in the Caribbean. The attack on Cartagena in March and April was, however, a disastrous failure; other operations attempted against Cuba in the summer proved equally unsuccessful. Tension mounted within the command of the expedition, which showed itself in a violent quarrel between Ogle and Edward Trelawney, governor of Jamaica, after a council of war on 22 July 1742. On 3 September, Ogle was charged before the chief justice of Jamaica with assaulting Trelawney. The jury decided that Ogle had been guilty and there the matter ended, the governor requesting that no judgment should be given.

On 18 October 1742 Vernon sailed for England, leaving Ogle in command. The fleet was too much reduced to allow any operations against the coasts of the enemy, who themselves had no force at sea; Ogle's work was therefore restricted to protecting the British and scourging the Spanish trade. Only one incident stands out in this period. George Frye, a lieutenant in the marines, was charged and found guilty of disobedience and disrespect in March 1744. The court martial, of which Ogle was president, sentenced him to be cashiered, rendered incapable of holding a commission in the king's service, and imprisoned for fifteen years. The last part of the sentence was afterwards pronounced illegal, and Frye obtained a verdict of false imprisonment against Ogle and several other members of the court martial. Ogle was sentenced to pay £800 damages, which appears eventually to have been paid for him by the crown.

On 9 August 1743 Ogle was promoted vice-admiral of the blue. He was advanced to vice-admiral of the white on 7 December 1743 and on 19 June 1744 to admiral of the blue. He returned to England in the summer of 1745, and on 11 September was made commander-in-chief in the Thames, Medway, and Nore. In that month Ogle presided at the courts martial which tried sundry lieutenants and captains on a charge of misconduct in the action off Toulon on 11 February 1744. On 15 July 1747 he was promoted admiral of the white and on 1 July 1749 admiral and

commander-in-chief, entitled to fly the union flag. He died in London on 11 April 1750 and was buried at Twickenham.

J. K. LAUGHTON, *rev.* RICHARD HARDING

Sources J. Charnock, ed., *Biographia navalis*, 6 vols. (1794–8) · *GM*, 1st ser., 20 (1750), 188 · captains' letters 'd', PRO, ADM 1/2241–2 · Ogle, PRO, ADM 50/27 [(5 June 1732 – 21 Aug 1735)] · Admiral's journals, 29 Sept 1740–5 June 1745, PRO, ADM 50/18 · commission and warrant books, PRO, ADM 6/4–16 · admiral's reports: Ogle, PRO, SP 42/89 · Vernon, PRO, SP 42/90–92 · state papers admiralty, PRO, SP 42/30, fols. 365–8 · will, PRO, PROB 11/778/124 · *A true and genuine copy of the trial of Sir Chaloner Ogle* (1743) · M. H. Dodds, ed., *A history of Northumberland*, 12 (1926), 503

Archives NMM, corresp. and papers · PRO

Likenesses oils, *c.*1718, NMM [*see illus.*] · J. Bernigeroth, line engraving (after C. Zincke), BM · T. Hudson, oils, Bowes Museum, Barnard Castle; on loan to St Mary's College, U. Durham · Van Werdlen, mezzotint (after J. Hansson), BM · medal, BM

Ogle, Sir Charles, second baronet (1775–1858), naval officer, was born on 24 May 1775 at Worthy Park House, Martyr's Worthy, Hampshire. He was the eldest son of Admiral Sir Chaloner Ogle, first baronet (1727–1816), and his wife, Hester, daughter of John Thomas, bishop of Winchester, and was the great-nephew of Sir Chaloner Ogle. He attended Hyde Abbey School, Winchester, and entered the navy in 1787 on board the *Adventure*, with Captain John Nicholson Inglefield. After uneventful service in different ships on the coast of Africa and home stations, he was made lieutenant on the *Woolwich*, in the West Indies, on 15 November 1793. In January 1794 he was moved into the *Boyne*, flagship of Sir John Jervis (later first earl of St Vincent), and in May he was appointed acting captain of the *Assurance*. On 21 May 1794 he was confirmed as commander of the sloop *Avenger*, from which he was moved to the *Petrel*, and on 11 January 1796, in the Mediterranean, was posted by Jervis to the *Minerve*. During the following years, despite St Vincent's concern at his lack of steadiness, he commanded the frigates *Meleager*, *Greyhound*, and *Égyptienne*, for the most part in the Mediterranean, coming home in early 1802. On 22 April he married Charlotte Margaret (d. 1814), daughter of General Sir Thomas Gage, brother of Admiral Sir William Gage; they had two daughters and a son, Chaloner, who succeeded to the baronetcy.

In 1805 Ogle commanded the frigate *Unité*, and in 1806 was appointed to the yacht *Princess Augusta*, which he commanded until August 1815, when he took command of the *Ramillies* in the channel. In November 1815 he commanded the *Malta* at Plymouth, and in 1816 the *Rivoli* at Portsmouth. On the death of his father, on 27 August 1816, he succeeded to the baronetcy, and a considerable fortune. This financial security may well explain his limited post-war service. He was promoted rear-admiral on 12 August 1819. On 4 September 1820 he married Letitia (d. 1832), daughter of Sir William Burroughs, bt; they had one son, William, who succeeded as fifth baronet. From 1827 to 1830 Ogle was commander-in-chief in North America, and he became vice-admiral on 22 July 1830. He married, on 10 April 1834, Mary Anne Dalton (d. February 1842), daughter of George Cary of Tor Abbey, Devon, already twice a widow. They had no children. He became admiral on 23 November 1841, and was commander-in-chief at Portsmouth from 1845 to 1848. He was promoted admiral of the fleet on 8 December 1857. He died at Tunbridge Wells on 16 June 1858 and was buried at Ponteland church, Northumberland.

Ogle's two commands were well handled and successful; he was a man of some ability and, through his brother-in-law Gage, close to the tory party. He was a solid professional sea officer who made a significant contribution to naval charities, both in financial support and administrative effort.   J. K. LAUGHTON, *rev.* ANDREW LAMBERT

Sources P. Moore, *Sir Charles Ogle: a worthy admiral* (1988) · *Private papers of George, second Earl Spencer*, ed. J. S. Corbett and H. W. Richmond, 2, Navy RS, 48 (1924) · *Dod's Peerage* (1858) · O'Byrne, *Naval biog. dict.* · *CGPLA Eng. & Wales* (1858)
Archives NMM, corresp. and papers; letter-book | BL, letters to Sir Charles Napier, Add. MSS 40042–40043
Likenesses bronze medallion, NPG · portrait, repro. in Moore, *Sir Charles Ogle*
Wealth at death under £120,000: probate, 5 Oct 1858, *CGPLA Eng. & Wales*

Ogle, Charles Chaloner (1851–1878), journalist, fourth son of John Ogle of St Clare, near Ightham, Sevenoaks, Kent, was born on 16 April 1851, and educated, with other pupils, under his father at St Clare. He matriculated at London University in June 1869, and then devoted himself to the study of architecture, becoming a pupil of Frederick William Roper of 9 Adam Street, Adelphi, London. He was a contributor to *The Builder*, and in 1872 he both obtained a certificate for excellence in architectural construction and was admitted an associate of the Royal Institute of British Architects. Soon afterwards he visited Rome, and in August 1875 went for some months to Athens, where he worked in the office of Herr Ziller, the royal architect. While he was thus engaged, *The Times* accepted his offer to be their special correspondent in the 1878 war between Turkey and Montenegro and the insurgent Balkan provinces, and he accompanied the Turkish force against the Montenegrins. Ogle's reports from Montenegro and Herzegovina, from Greece, from Crete, and from Thessaly were full of picturesque details, with a kindly humour. While residing at Volo, on the Gulf of Thessaly, Ogle learned on 28 March 1878 that an engagement was imminent between the Turkish troops and the insurgents occupying Mount Pelion and the town of Macrynitza. He at once went unarmed to the scene of action. The battle took place and was prolonged to the following day; Ogle, unable to obtain a horse to return to Volo, slept at Katochori on 29 and 30 March. On 1 April his headless body was found lying in a ravine, and was identified by a scar on the wrist and a bloodstained telegram in his pocket book addressed to *The Times*. The body was taken on board HMS *Wizard*, and conveyed to Piraeus, Athens, where it was accorded a public funeral on 10 April. It was believed that Ogle's murder was an act of revenge ordered by Amouss Aga, the Turkish commander, because Ogle had criticized him for pillaging a village. To disguise the murder, a report was circulated that Ogle was aiding the insurgents. In a parliamentary paper issued on 18 June, Ogle was blamed for imprudence in venturing among the belligerents without necessity, and his death was attributed to a wound received while retreating with the insurgents after the second battle of Macrynitza; the correctness of these statements was strenuously denied by his friends.   G. C. BOASE, *rev.* ROGER T. STEARN

Sources E. Streit, *Mémoire concernant les détails du meurtre commis contre la personne de Charles Ogle* (1878) · *The Times* (2 April 1878) · *The Times* (10 April 1878) · *The Times* (11 April 1878) · *The Times* (25 April 1878) · *The Times* (19 June 1878) · *The Graphic* (20 April 1878), 401 · *ILN* (13 April 1878) · Boase, *Mod. Eng. biog.* · D. Dakin, *The unification of Greece, 1770–1923* (1972)
Likenesses wood-engraving (after photograph by P. Moraites of Athens), NPG; repro. in *ILN*

Ogle, George (*bap.* 1704, *d.* 1746), translator, was the second of six children of the attorney-at-law Samuel Ogle of Bowsden (1658–1718), MP for Berwick and commissioner of the revenue for Ireland, and his second wife, Ursula (1678–1725), who inherited Irish estates and other wealth both from her parents (Sir Robert Markham of Sedgebroke, and Mary, daughter of Sir Thomas Widdrington of Sherburn Grange) and from her first husband, Lord Altham Annesley of co. Cork (*d.* 1699). From his father's first marriage to Elizabeth (*d.* 1697), widow of Thomas Dawson of Newcastle, Ogle also had a half-sister. At least two of his brothers pursued military careers, Robert in Ireland and Samuel *Ogle in North America.

Although Ogle's father attended university at Edinburgh, and his son at Dublin, Ogle apparently learned from tutors the classical languages underlying his best-known writings: a dozen Horatian imitations, individually published from 1735 to 1739, that tend more toward jocularity than workaday translation. *Satire*, ii.5, becomes, for example, *Of Legacy Hunting … Dialogue between Sir Walter Raleigh and Merlin the Prophet* (1737). Another representative poem, dedicated to Ogle's elder brother Samuel while he was governor of Maryland, imitates Horace's *Epistle*, i.11, with jokes about the shortage of culture and taste in Annapolis (*The Eleventh Epistle*, 1738).

Ogle primarily resided and published in London. In 1735 he married Frances (1711–1750), the daughter and coheir of Sir Thomas (sometimes referred to as Frederick) Twysden of East Peckham. As landholder in Ireland, he might be the George Ogle who in 1737 served as MP for Bannow and high sheriff for co. Wexford. His father died in Dublin; and his son, George *Ogle (1742–1814), would long serve as MP for Wexford. Besides the son Ogle and his wife had two older daughters, Frances and Catherina-Isabella.

Nine years before his marriage to the heiress, Ogle had 'addrest to a young lady' *The Liffy* (1726), based on Ovid. Next he published imitations of Anacreon, Sappho, and other Greek poets in James Sterling's *Loves of Hero and Leander* (1728), which is dedicated to the 'ingenious young gentleman' Ogle. His publications may have influenced Alexander Pope's adaptations of Horace and Thomas Moore's of Anacreon (P. Dixon, 'Pope, George Ogle, and Horace', *N&Q*, 204, 1959, 396–7; *Journal of Thomas Moore*, ed. W. S. Dowden, 6 vols., 1983–91, 2.768). Besides working independently, Ogle composed an epilogue for Henry

Brooke's *Gustavus Vasa* (1739), which was banned in London but staged in Dublin (*Prologues and Epilogues of the Eighteenth Century*, ed. P. Danchin, 6 vols. to date, 1990–, 5.60–61). He collaborated also with Elijah Fenton and Edward Ward, to translate the sixteenth-century Latin *Basia* (*Kisses*) of Janus Secundus (1731), and with engraver Claude de Bosc for *Antiquities Explained* (1737; 2nd edn, *Gemmae antiquae caelatae*, 1741). This tome reproduces fifty carvings, for each of which Ogle quotes passages in Greek and Latin, provides his own and others' translations, and interweaves commentary that often justifies the figures' nudity. His final publication mocks a vain woman grown old and ugly (*GM*, 15, 1745, 48). In 1926 Ogle's reputation for mild erotica caused his name to become erroneously but persistently attached to an essay by Bernard Mandeville (*A Modest Defense of Publick Stews*, 1724, ed. R. Cook, 1973).

Ogle pursued mild erotica within his own vernacular tradition as well as in Graeco-Roman art and literature. In 1739 he published *Gualtherus and Griselda*, amalgamating the versions of Boccaccio, Petrarch, and Chaucer. He then assembled *Canterbury Tales of Chaucer, Modernis'd by Several Hands* (3 vols., 1741). Besides his own *Clerk's Tale* he supplied a modernization of Edmund Spenser's continuation of the *Squire's Tale* (as *Cambuscan*, concluded in 1785 by Joseph Sterling), and he adapted the *General Prologue* by Thomas Betterton (a pseudonym for Alexander Pope). Ogle also modernized links between tales.

Perhaps Ogle intended to supply modernized links and tales for the rest of Chaucer's work, but he died on 20 October 1746. To his heirs he left homes in the country (Hendon, Middlesex) and in the city (on Audley Street, his parish church being St George's at Hanover Square). He also left lands in Kent, Sussex, and Ireland; many possessions including furniture, plate, jewels, and a coach; and thousands of pounds. Most went to his wife, daughters, and trustees; to young George he bequeathed his books and bookcases.   BETSY BOWDEN

Sources DNB · H. A. Ogle, *Ogle and Bothal* (1902), 210–20 · D. F. Foxon, ed., *English verse, 1701–1750: a catalogue of separately printed poems with notes on contemporary collected editions*, 2 vols. (1975) · PRO, PROB 11/752 [will of George Ogle], sig. 18 · B. Bowden, ed., *Eighteenth-century modernizations from the 'Canterbury tales'* (1991), 80–118 · *The family of Twysden and Twisden: their history and archives from an original by Sir John Ramskill Twisden*, ed. C. H. Dudley Ward (1939), 293–4 · GEC, *Peerage*, new edn, 1.114–15 · PRO, PROB 11/575 [will of Samuel Ogle], sig. 161 · *National union catalog, pre-1956 imprints*, Library of Congress · BL cat. · D. J. O'Donoghue, *The poets of Ireland: a biographical dictionary with bibliographical particulars*, 1 vol. in 3 pts (1892–3)
Wealth at death substantial: will, PRO, PROB 11/752, sig. 18

Ogle, George (1742–1814), politician, was born on 14 October 1742, the only son of George *Ogle (*bap.* 1704, *d.* 1746), littérateur and MP, and Frances Twysden (1711–1750), coheir of Sir Thomas Twysden, fourth baronet, of Roydon Hall, Kent. His father died when he was four, and Ogle was entrusted to the care of a Church of Ireland vicar proximate to the family estate of Bellevue, Enniscorthy. Educated at Kilkenny School, he entered Trinity College, Dublin, in December 1759 but did not graduate. Following in his

George Ogle (1742–1814), by unknown engraver, pubd 1777

father's footsteps, Ogle's initial enthusiasm was for literature, and he achieved a measure of fame as a poet and the author of a number of well-known songs, of which 'Banna's Banks' and 'Molly Asthore' are the best known. The latter was written in praise of Mary Moore of Tinrahan, co. Wexford, whose sister Elizabeth (*d. c.*1798) became Ogle's wife. Ogle declined to publish his own creations, though he often visited Lady Miller's poetical assemblies at Bath and contributed to the volume *Poetical Amusements at a Villa near Bath* published by the lady's admirers in 1775.

Ogle's parliamentary career commenced with his election 'by his own interest' (Bodkin, 219) to the House of Commons to represent the county of Wexford in 1769. His 'great antipathy' (ibid.) to the then lord lieutenant, Lord Townshend, prompted him to vote with the opposition upon taking his seat. He continued to conduct himself thus during the lord lieutenancy of Earl Harcourt, leading Dublin Castle to conclude that he was a firm and committed member of the parliamentary opposition. Ogle denied this: 'The evil spirit of opposition never possessed me' (Black, 200), he informed the House of Commons in 1777. Rather, he was guided in his political actions by principle; his reputation as 'a respectable sensible man' (Bodkin, 219) and as 'one of the most popular characters of the kingdom' (Falkland, 24) derived first and foremost from the realization that he was 'a very independent man'

(Johnston, *Great Britain and Ireland*, 350). Ogle defined his role as that of 'guardian ... of ... publick liberty', based upon his conclusion that 'the glorious principles of virtue and publick liberty' that made the British constitution uniquely valuable had been 'restored' in 1688 following 'the tyrant reigns of the Tudor and Stuart families' (Black, 385). This combined with his commitment to 'stand forth [as] the Champion of this country' (ibid., 200) to ensure he kept a wary eye on the Irish administration and, following the outbreak of war in the American colonies—which he forecast 'would end in ruin' (ibid., 428)—to single out the embargo imposed on Ireland's freedom to trade. He maintained that the embargo was not just contrary to Ireland's commercial interest, it harmed the empire because 'the constitution and the commerce are the two pillars of the empire' (ibid., 385). His determined opposition led him personally to spend £440 on 200 barrels of beef and a further £200 plus on fees and other expenses in testing the effectiveness of the embargo in 1777. This won him public applause that might not otherwise have been forthcoming since he was not in the first rank of House of Commons orators. The bulk of his many contributions during the late 1770s, when he was at his most active, were of the nature of short, pointed, and frequently unvarnished interjections that, given the esteem in which he was held by his fellow MPs, were 'always heard with attention and deference' (Falkland, 25–6).

Ogle's dissatisfaction with the government of Britain and Ireland during the late 1770s and early 1780s, which stemmed from his reverence for the constitution, ensured that he was an active supporter of the patriots' efforts to win free trade and legislative independence. His willingness to support them in the division lobbies and his membership of the patriot club known as the Monks of St Patrick caused many to conclude that he was a mainstream patriot, whereas he was an independent country gentleman of strong whig views first and foremost. This was manifest in 1778 when he spearheaded the opposition to the proposal to dilute the laws against Catholics. The security of 'the constitution ... the Protestant interest ... landed property ... and the church and state in Ireland' (Cavendish diary, 10.2) was endangered, he insisted, by the proposal to allow Catholics to own property on the same terms as protestants. He could not prevent a generous measure of Catholic relief reaching the statute book, but his insistence that Catholics should not be allowed to acquire influence incompatible with the security of a protestant constitution ensured that they were not allowed to purchase land in fee simple. Ogle was not opposed, as he pointed out, to Catholic relief *per se*. He was prepared, he observed in 1782, when the matter at issue was the freedom to be allowed the Catholic church, 'to give the Papists every indulgence consistent with the safety of the established church' (*Parliamentary Register*, 1.200), but he drew a clear and immovable line at changing the constitution in church and state.

Ogle's determination to maintain the existing protestant constitution inviolate was consistent with his whig political principles. So too was his gravitation towards the

Irish administration during the lord lieutenancy of the duke of Portland, a whig. Ogle was drawn to co-operate with the administration by his conclusion that 'simple repeal' represented 'sufficient relinquishment' (*Parliamentary Register*, 1.415) of Westminster's disputed claim to possess the authority to make law for Ireland, but he also had financial reasons for doing so. Having engaged in 'prodigal spending' (Bodkin, 219) over two decades as a result of which he 'consumed a very large estate', he was in 'extreme distress' (Johnston, 195) financially by the early 1780s. At the same time his role in discrediting the Reform Convention held in Dublin in 1783 vividly demonstrated his potential to the administration. This paved the way for his admission to the Irish privy council in 1783, and for his appointment in 1784 as registrar of deeds, which was worth £1700 from the mid-1780s. As the register of deeds was a patent office, Ogle was not bound to vote with the Irish administration. None the less, his vote was forthcoming with sufficient regularity to ensure his inclusion on lists of Castle supporters from the mid-1780s. At the same time he demonstrated that he was not lobby fodder by taking an independent stand on parliamentary reform in 1784, the commercial propositions in 1785, and the regency in 1788–9. The issue that most agitated him was the security of what, in 1786, he termed 'the Protestant ascendancy', and while he helped successfully to galvanize resistance to a suggestion to commute the tithes paid to the Church of Ireland at that moment, his die-hard resistance in 1792 and 1793 to Catholic enfranchisement on the grounds that it would 'overturn ... the Protestant ascendancy in every town in the kingdom' (*Parliamentary Register*, 12.127) failed. As a result, he concluded that a legislative union was in the best interests of Irish protestants. He also promised 'never again [to] set my foot within' (ibid., 13.346) the Irish parliament, and while he returned to oppose Catholic emancipation in 1795 and to condemn parliamentary reform and emancipation respectively as the harbinger of 'a *republic* and a *separation* from Great Britain' in 1797 (ibid., 17.334), his appointment as governor of co. Wexford in 1796 did cause him to concentrate his energies on combating insurrection. He did not stand for re-election in 1797, but his growing reputation as neo-conservative champion resulted in his successful nomination to represent Dublin city in a by-election in July 1798.

In his capacity as MP for Dublin city Ogle articulated the dissatisfaction of neo-conservatives everywhere with Lord Cornwallis's leniency towards the defeated rebels of 1798. He reflected their wishes by voting against the Act of Union, though he had previously indicated his support so long as it was 'proposed on Protestant principles' (PRO NIre., Stanhope (Pitt) papers, T 3401/4/2). Once the Union was enacted, he had little difficulty accepting it and he was re-elected on a strong protestant platform to represent Dublin city in the imperial parliament in 1801. He did not retain his seat in 1802, but his nomination to serve as grand master of the Orange order in 1801 gave him a focus in later life. He died at his family seat, Bellevue, on 10 August 1814, some sixteen years after his wife, and was buried in the churchyard at Ballycarney, co. Wexford. He had no children and his property passed to his nephew George Ogle Moore, MP for Dublin from 1826 to 1830.

JAMES KELLY

Sources J. Porter, P. Byrne, and W. Porter, eds., *The parliamentary register, or, History of the proceedings and debates of the House of Commons of Ireland, 1781–1797*, 17 vols. (1784–1801) · *An edition of the Cavendish Irish parliamentary diary, 1776–1778*, ed. A. R. Black, 3 vols. (Delavan, WI, 1984–5) · *DNB* · E. M. Johnston, 'Members of the Irish parliament, 1784–7', *Proceedings of the Royal Irish Academy*, 71C (1971), 139–246 · G. O. Sayles, ed., 'Contemporary sketches of the members of the Irish parliament in 1782', *Proceedings of the Royal Irish Academy*, 56C (1953–4), 227–86 · Falkland [J. R. Scott], *A review of the principal characters of the Irish House of Commons* (1789), 24–6 · Burtchaell & Sadleir, *Alum. Dubl.* · M. Bodkin, ed., 'Notes on the Irish parliament in 1773', *Proceedings of the Royal Irish Academy*, 48C (1942–3), 145–232, esp. 219 · W. Hunt, ed., *The Irish parliament, 1775* (1907) · HoP, *Commons, 1790–1820*, 4.687 · E. M. Johnston, *Great Britain and Ireland, 1760–1800* (1963), 350 · H. Cavendish, parliamentary diary, L. Cong., vol. 10 · PRO NIre., Stanhope (Pitt) MSS, T 3401/4/2 · R. E. Burns, 'The Catholic Relief Act in Ireland, 1778', *Church History*, 32 (1963), 181–207 · J. Kelly, 'Conservative protestant political thought in late eighteenth-century Ireland', *Political ideas in eighteenth-century Ireland*, ed. S. J. Connolly (Dublin, 2000) · Burke, *Peerage* · J. Kelly, *Prelude to Union: Anglo-Irish politics in the 1780s* (1992)

Likenesses J. Smyth, marble statue, St Patrick's Cathedral, Dublin · F. Wheatley, group portrait, oils (*The Irish House of Commons 1780*), Leeds City Art Gallery · line engraving, BM, NPG · line engraving, NG Ire.; repro. in *Hibernian Magazine* (Dec 1777) [*see illus.*]

Ogle, James Adey (1792–1857), physician, was born on 22 October 1792 in Great Russell Street, London, the son of Richard Ogle, a general practitioner, and his wife, Hannah, formerly Adey. In 1808 he was sent to Eton College, of which Dr Joseph Goodall was then provost. He matriculated on 13 April 1810 as a commoner of Trinity College, Oxford, obtained a scholarship in 1812, and graduated BA in 1813 with a first class in mathematics and physics. Adopting his father's profession he commenced his medical studies at William Hunter's school of medicine in Great Windmill Street, London. On the proclamation of peace in 1814 he travelled to the continent, and in the course of that and some succeeding years he visited many of the leading medical schools of France, Italy, and Germany. He also passed (as was then customary) some winter sessions in Edinburgh, studying under professors Gregory, Duncan, Hamilton, Gordon, Home, and Jamieson. Through his Eton and Oxford connections he gained access to the city's intellectual circles. On returning to London he pursued his medical studies there as a pupil at the Middlesex Hospital, and subsequently at St Bartholomew's Hospital, and graduated at Oxford MA and BM in 1816 and 1817 respectively. In the latter year he also obtained a university licence to practise medicine.

Upon settling in Oxford, Ogle set up in practice. Although this thrived, his possession of independent means allowed him to lead a comparatively leisurely professional life and to indulge his love both of literature and of social activities. In 1819 he married Sarah, younger daughter of Jeston Homfray of Broadwaters, near Kidderminster. She died in 1835, leaving four sons and five

James Adey Ogle (1792–1857), by William Foxley Norris, 1838

daughters, one of whom became the wife of James Bowling Mozley, and another the wife of Manuel John Johnson. The third son, Dr William Ogle, became superintendent of statistics in the registrar-general's office.

In 1820 Ogle graduated DM and was appointed mathematical tutor of his old college, Trinity. One of his pupils was John Henry Newman, with whom he maintained a close friendship in later life, though he was not himself a Roman Catholic. Ogle was elected FRCP in 1822. In 1824 he became physician to both the Radcliffe Infirmary, where he was unanimously chosen in succession to Robert Bourne, and the Warneford Lunatic Asylum at Oxford. He was appointed Aldrich professor of medicine in the university in 1824, public examiner in mathematics in 1825, and Aldrich clinical professor of medicine in 1830. Ogle's professional duties were very light since he had few pupils. He gave occasional lectures at his home in St Giles. In 1835 he worked with Drs Kidd and Daubeny to improve the teaching of natural sciences and to revise the university statutes regulating medical degrees, which resulted in the introduction of a public examination for the degree of BM.

Ogle also revived practical instruction at the Radcliffe Infirmary. Between 1837 and 1840 he organized a course of clinical lectures, and by 1840 had a lecture room equipped. Between 1833 and 1840 he had some thirty-seven pupils, but only three were members of the university, and this fragile aspiration for a school of medicine was soon eclipsed. Between 1840 and 1854 there were only fourteen candidates for the BM degree. Ogle wrote nothing on medicine; during the 1854–5 cholera epidemic he compiled notes and statistics on the disease but did not write them up. During the outbreak he opposed the accommodation of cholera patients in the Radcliffe Infirmary, mainly on account of the cost. His only publication, *A letter to the Reverend the Warden of Wadham College, on the system of education pursued at Oxford; with suggestions for remodelling the examination statutes*, appeared in 1841. The pamphlet was noteworthy in containing the first suggestion of a school of natural science at Oxford; this was afterwards established by a statute proposed in 1851 on behalf of the reformers by Sir H. W. Acland. Yet Ogle was hostile to research, asserting in the pamphlet that 'the prosecution of Truth forms no part of our duties' (J. A. Ogle, *A letter to the Reverend the Warden of Wadham College*, 1841, 9). Ogle also anticipated another change, by his proposal that 'candidates for admission to the university should have their attainments tested *in limine* [at the outset]' by an examination which became known as 'responsions'.

Ogle was elected FRS in 1826. His professional success was marked by his delivery of the Harveian oration in 1844, and by his appointment as regius professor of medicine at Oxford by Lord John Russell in 1851, in succession to Dr John Kidd. He held the latter post in conjunction with the clinical and Aldrichian professorships and with the Tomline readership in anatomy. Ogle was president of the Provincial Medical Association at its meeting at Oxford in 1852, and was examiner in the new school of natural science in 1854–5.

Ogle died of apoplexy after an illness of thirty hours, at the vicarage, Old Shoreham, Sussex, the residence of his son-in-law James Bowling Mozley, on 25 September 1857; he was buried on 2 October in St Sepulchre's cemetery at Jericho in Oxford. He left 6000 guineas to his eldest son James, and £3000 to each of his other children.

Kindly and good-natured, Ogle was 'a man of liberal views and great depth and sincerity of feeling' (*Jackson's Oxford Journal*, 56). His house at Oxford was the rendezvous of a wide circle of friends. In appearance Ogle was 'handsome' and 'clean shaven … with an attractive expression' (Gibson, 113). By nature cautious, he was inclined to adhere to the older traditions of his profession, from the active practice of which he withdrew in his later years, though attending old friends and giving gratuitous advice to the poor. Nevertheless, he did not oppose modern developments of scientific study at the infirmary and in the university, which were the subject of keen controversy at the time.

W. A. GREENHILL and E. H. MARSHALL, *rev.* P. W. J. BARTRIP

Sources *Jackson's Oxford Journal* (3 Oct 1857), 5b · *Medical Times and Gazette* (10 Oct 1857), 385 · *The Lancet* (3 Oct 1857), 381 · A. G. Gibson, *The Radcliffe Infirmary* (1926) · H. Rolleston, 'The personalities of the Oxford medical school, from 1700–1880', *Annals of Medical History*, new ser., 8 (1936), 277–87 · d. cert. · Munk, *Roll*, 3.245 · *BMJ* (1857), 831 · *London and Provincial Medical Directory* (1858) · *Provincial Medical Directory* (1847) · *The historical register of the University of Oxford … to the end of Trinity term 1900* (1900) · A. Robb-Smith, 'Medical education', *Hist. U. Oxf.* 6: *19th-cent. Oxf.*, 563–82 · R. Fox, 'The University Museum and Oxford science, 1850–1880', *Hist. U. Oxf.* 6: *19th-cent. Oxf.*, 641–91
Likenesses W. F. Norris, portrait, 1838, Trinity College, Oxford [*see illus.*] · S. Lane, portrait, repro. in *Medical Circular* (28 July 1852)
Wealth at death approx. £28,000: *CGPLA Eng. & Wales*

Ogle, Sir John (*bap.* 1569, *d.* 1640), army officer, was baptized at Pinchbeck, Lincolnshire, on 28 February 1569, the fifth son of Thomas Ogle (*d.* 1574) of Pinchbeck and his wife, Jane (*d.* 1574), daughter of Adelard Welby of Gedney, Lincolnshire. Nothing is known of John Ogle's early life and he seems to have chosen a military career early on. He went to the Netherlands in 1591, where he joined the company of Sir Francis Vere, sergeant-major-general of the English forces aiding the Dutch republic, whose faithful follower he became. Much of what we know of Vere's campaigns comes from his *Commentaries*, but the original seventeenth-century editor included substantial chunks of material specially written by Ogle to flesh out Vere's manuscript.

In 1598 most of the English army under Vere was transferred into Dutch pay—becoming mercenaries in modern terms. On 30 June 1600 the English contingent of the Dutch army played a vital role in the great battle of Nieuwpoort. Ogle rescued his general when Vere was unhorsed ('his blood remained on my clothes'), helped to rally the retreating English infantry, and was in the forefront of their counter-attack, which helped to win a famous victory (Vere, 162). The following year Vere and his troops defended Ostend against the celebrated Spanish siege, which lasted until 1604: the city became known as 'the new Troy'.

By 1601 Ogle was Vere's lieutenant-colonel (a rank he acquired at some point after Nieuwpoort) and invaluable assistant. In early 1602 Ogle and Sir Charles Fairfax acted as hostages in the Spanish camp during 'capitulation' negotiations—actually aimed at gaining time. When reinforcements arrived and the talks were abandoned both men could well have been executed by the Spanish, as Vere knew from the start: 'What shall I do for my Lieutenant Colonel?' was his refrain and he was ready to pay Ogle's ransom 'five times over' (Vere, 195). But both hostages were released in time to do their part in repulsing a major Spanish assault. Ogle had already lost his left eye to 'a small shot' earlier in the siege (*Salisbury MSS*, 11.293); ever after he wore a black eye patch.

By this time it was obvious that Queen Elizabeth could not last long. The Dutch authorities saw a chance to integrate the English troops fully into the national army. Ambitious English officers intrigued against Sir Francis Vere hoping to win favour with the Dutch, but Ogle took his own steps against them. He personally thrashed the lieutenant of Callisthenes Brooke, who had attracted the general's ire, and incited his men to attack John Ridgeway, who frequently complained about Sir Francis. In the end, however, Vere resigned his command in 1604. He was replaced by his younger brother, Sir Horace, and the older Vere's departure proved a great opportunity for Ogle, who had been knighted on a visit home to England on 10

December 1603. Having distinguished himself in the capture of Sluys in the summer of 1604, he was made full colonel in the Dutch army in 1605. However, he was bitter against his fellow colonel Sir Edward Cecil who had agitated against Sir Francis Vere and there was considerable tension among English officers even after the twelve years' truce began in 1609, suspending the war with Spain.

In 1610 the first Arminian troubles broke out. It is a measure of the trust placed in Ogle that he was chosen as governor of Utrecht, where there had been a revolt. Sir John was, Horace Vere suggested, to 'administer verry dire' (Trim, 347). Ogle initially thought he could 'assure the loyalty of the citizens without need of a garrison at all' ('s'asseure si bien de la loyaulte des bourgeois … qu'il ne sera pas besoing de garnison en tout'; Rijksarchief Zuid-Holland, Den Haag, Archief van Johan van Oldenbarnevelt 1318), but though he soon wanted more troops, ultimately he was successful in conciliating the townsmen. Moving his family in straight away was a clever gesture of trust, while it must have helped that Ogle had married a Dutchwoman: Elizabeth, daughter of Cornelius de Vries of Dordrecht. They had four sons and eight daughters, one of whom died young, and two of whom, born in Utrecht, were named after the city: Utricia and Trajectina. The states of Utrecht even voted Utricia a life annuity of £20, which indicates Ogle's ability to win them over.

In this period Ogle led his regiment in Prince Maurice of Nassau's campaign in Cleves-Jülich in 1614, but otherwise remained in Utrecht. He kept Sir Thomas (later first baron) Fairfax updated with news from the continent, exchanging gloomy forecasts about future threats from the Habsburgs and indignant protests about a Spanish marriage for Prince Charles. When Fairfax's son William joined the Dutch army his father put him in Ogle's care. Ogle also kept in touch with potential patrons in England. He corresponded with Buckingham, promising to 'do his best' to procure a place in the states army for Buckingham's client Sir John Manwood (Bodl. Oxf., MS Add. D. 110, no. 276): in 1627, eight years later, Ogle's eldest daughter, Livinia, married Manwood, by then chief justice of common pleas.

Meanwhile Maurice of Nassau, stadholder and captain-general (and the man who had got rid of Francis Vere), had come into direct conflict with the advocate of Holland (and unofficial chief minister of the republic), Johan van Oldenbarnevelt, partly over Arminianism, which he had come loosely to support. In 1618 matters came to a head: Oldenbarnevelt was arrested (to be executed the following year). Ogle chose chaplains who were strongly orthodox Calvinists, but Oldenbarnevelt was his patron, so the Englishman must have felt torn. In the end he did not support Oldenbarnevelt in a proposed strike against Maurice—but neither did he act decisively against his benefactor. Consequently he was replaced in Utrecht by Horace Vere and, in 1619 or early 1620, went home. Ogle seems never to have returned to the Netherlands, but he did maintain a correspondence with his circle of Dutch friends, including important figures such as Constantijn Huygens. (The correspondence of his eldest son, Sir John Ogle the younger, with Huygens, preserved in Leiden University Library, is probably a continuation of his father's.)

Fortunately Ogle's good contacts in Jacobean England served him well. His time in the Netherlands had been profitable and he invested in the Virginia Company. He appears in both the second (May 1609) and third (March 1612) charters as one of the company's promoters and in 1623 was elected to its council. In the latter year he was appointed to a commission to inspect all England's coastal fortifications, from Land's End to the Thames estuary. Expert in siege warfare, he was well qualified, of course, but the links with Buckingham must have helped, and in the following year he was made a member of a new council of war, charged with considering whether England could intervene in the Thirty Years' War. It involved working with Sir Edward Cecil (now Viscount Wimbledon); unsurprisingly Ogle preferred to concentrate on his work as inspector of fortifications. In 1625, however, this caused him to be in Plymouth when troops were gathering for an expedition to Cadiz—commanded by Wimbledon! Ogle was obliged to take on responsibility for the ill-disciplined and inadequately supplied conscripts, a task he undertook reluctantly.

There were domestic matters to consider. In May 1622 Ogle obtained a grant of denization to his wife and children; but a draft bill of 1626 to naturalize all twelve never became law. His eldest brother, Sir Richard, hopelessly in debt, died insolvent in the Fleet prison in 1627. John bought from Richard their father's manor of Pinchbeck, and though he seems to have lived mostly in London, he also purchased other lands in Lincolnshire and maintained an interest in his home county and in Yorkshire. He personally invested £1100 in a venture promoted by the great Dutch fen-drainer Cornelius Vermuyden to drain Hatfield Chase in Yorkshire and Lincolnshire. Like so many plans of this type, it was opposed by those whose livelihood depended on their common rights in the fen, who in 1634 appealed for the venturers (including Ogle) to be imprisoned.

The financial problems caused by the project were probably the impetus for Ogle's return to the military sphere and that same year he obtained a captaincy in the Irish army from Lord Deputy Wentworth. His purpose was avowedly 'rather to mend his fortunes than to require his attendance' (DNB) but the 'thorough' Wentworth was unimpressed. By 1638 Sir John was owed £1464 11s. in back pay for himself and his company and had to solicit the king's letters for 'the speedy payment' of the arrears (CSP dom., 1637–8, 427).

Sir John Ogle died in 1640. He was buried in Westminster Abbey on 17 March, and on 15 July his will of 6 December 1628 was proved. In it he left £500 each to his younger sons, and £50 apiece to his five unmarried daughters (Livinia had married in 1627), leaving additionally to Elizabeth and Utricia, the two eldest, lands in Lincolnshire. His wife, Elizabeth, was appointed sole executrix, but with the aid of five overseers—three English and two

Dutch. In death, as in life, Ogle was a nexus between England and the Netherlands.

If he never achieved the success or status of fellow soldiers like Horace Vere and Edward Cecil, John Ogle certainly had a varied career and interesting life, and showed a breadth of interests common to English military men of his time. By turns professional soldier, duellist, administrator, colonizer, patron of godly ministers, engineer, country squire, and speculator, Ogle was, if not a Renaissance man, very much a gentleman of his time.

D. J. B. TRIM

Sources A. R. Maddison, ed., *Lincolnshire pedigrees*, 2, Harleian Society, 51 (1903) · C. H. Firth, 'Introduction', in F. Vere and others, *Commentaries of Sir Francis Vere, Stuart tracts, 1603–1693* (1964), 83–210 · will, PRO, PROB 11/183, sig. 105, fols. 407v–408v · *Report on the manuscripts of Lord De L'Isle and Dudley*, 6 vols., HMC, 77 (1925–66), vols. 2–3 · *Calendar of the manuscripts of the most hon. the marquis of Salisbury*, 24 vols., HMC, 9 (1883–1976), vols. 11–18 · Rijksarchief Zuid-Holland, The Hague, Archief van Johan van Oldenbarnevelt, 1318 · Fortescue state papers, 1617–20, Bodl. Oxf., MS Add. D 110, nos. 215, 276 · D. J. B. Trim, 'Sir Horace Vere in Holland and the Rhineland, 1610–1612', *Historical Research*, 72 (1999), 334–51 · J. I. Israel, *The Dutch republic: its rise, greatness and fall* (1995), chaps. 18–20 · H. Peacham, *A most true relation of the affaires of Cleve and Gulick* (1615) · *CSP dom.*, 1611–18; 1637–8 · Handschriften, Koninklijke Bibliotheek, 129.A.26, 135.F.30 · Nationaal Archief, The Hague, Archief van de Staten-Generaal, 8043–44, 12504 · Nationaal Archief, The Hague, Archief van de Raad van State, 24, 28, 1226, 1232 · Nationaal Archief, The Hague, Collectie Aanwinsten, 879 · Nationaal Archief, The Hague, Generaliteit Rekenkamer, 1232 · *Fourth report*, HMC, 3 (1874) · *The manuscripts of the marquess of Abergavenny, Lord Braye*, G. F. Luttrell, HMC, 15 (1887) · Universiteitsbibliotheek Leiden, Bibliotheek Dousa [department of Western MSS], MS Hug. 37/'John Ogle' · M. Wolffe, *Gentry leaders in peace and war* (1997)
Archives Hatfield House, Hertfordshire, letters and papers · Sheff. Arch., accounts of military campaigns in Low Countries and of earl of Essex's naval actions against Spain | Bodl. Oxf., Fortescue papers · Bodl. Oxf., Rawl. MSS · Koninklijke Bibliotheek, The Hague, collectie Blyenburgh, handschriften · Rijksarchief Zuid-Holland, The Hague, Archief van Johan van Oldenbarnevelt, 1318
Likenesses W. Faithorne, line engraving, BM, NPG; repro. in W. Dillingham, ed., *The commentaries of Sir Francis Vere* (1657)
Wealth at death £1875; plus lands (incl. manors at Pinchbeck and Spalding, Croyland, Lincolnshire): will, PRO, PROB 11/183 sig. 105

Ogle, John (*c*.1652/3–*c*.1692), wit and gambler, was born the youngest son of a gentleman at Ashburton in Devon, although one early nineteenth-century chapbook states Northampton. He was educated at Exeter, where he was trained in the arts of gentlemanly comportment, and he excelled at those equestrian displays of chivalry known to contemporaries as 'riding the great horse'. His father died when he was young, and he inherited nearly £200 per annum upon coming of age, although he quickly dissipated his estate. Immediately afterwards he made his way to London, and gained quick recognition in élite circles through surviving two duels with well-known gentlemen. Ogle's ability to manage quarrels with other gentlemen 'with discretion as well as courage' soon became public knowledge in London society (Lucas, 184). He gained thereby instant access to the court of Charles II as a noted 'man of spirit', and was soon known as Jack Ogle or Mad

Ogle. His sister also found her way into court society, perhaps as maid of honour to the duchess of York, but most notably as the duke of York's mistress. Her influence helped Ogle obtain a saddle in the 1st troop of Horse Guards under the colonelcy of the duke of Monmouth, and later a position in the life guard of James II.

His extravagancies kept Ogle constantly short of funds to maintain his horse and equipage, but his pranks and humour kept him in favour. He lived in Waterman's Lane, Whitefriars, the area of back alleys notorious to contemporaries as Alsatia. He apparently lost through his wagers on cock-fighting the sums he won at the gaming tables of London's beau monde, and eventually Ogle took to drinking excessive quantities of alcoholic spirits, which is said to have hastened his death at the age of thirty-nine, about 1692.

Ogle was buried in the churchyard of Henley upon Thames in Oxfordshire, but his name long retained currency as a symbol of eccentric profligacy and was often paired with that of John Wilmot, earl of Rochester. The memory of Ogle thus played a part in the eighteenth-century imagination of the reign of Charles II as an age of merry libertinism. Richard Steele reports on tavern talk in Queen Anne's reign in which

> the greatest wit of our company next myself, frequented in his youth the ordinaries about Charing Cross, and pretends to have been intimate with Jack Ogle … If any modern wit be mentioned, or any town frolic spoken of, he shakes his head at the dulness of the present age, and tells a story of Jack Ogle. (*The Tatler*, no. 132, 11 Feb 1710; Bond, 2.267)

Cheap print jest books such as the *Frolicks of Lord Mohun* and the *Fancies of King Charles and his Concubines* were associated with Ogle's name and his biography was included in Theophilus Lucas's *Memoirs of … Famous Gamesters*, as well as Granger's *Biographical History* and the *Eccentric Magazine*. His portrait was painted and subsequently engraved and collected by connoisseurs of English portraiture.

BRIAN COWAN

Sources *A supplement to the works of the most celebrated minor poets* (1750) · E. Evans, *Catalogue of a collection of engraved portraits*, 1 [1836], 254, no. 7831 · J. Granger, *A biographical history of England, from Egbert the Great to the revolution*, 3rd edn, 4 (1779), 199–200 · *Joaks upon joaks, or, No joak like a true joak: being the diverting humours of Mr John Ogle, or life guard-man* [n.d., 1720?]; see also later edns [n.d., 1770–1790?] · *Joaks upon joaks, or, No joak like a true joak: being the diverting humours of Mr John Ogle … the merry pranks of Lord Mohun … with Rochester's dream … together with the diverting fancies and frolicks of Charles II* [n.d., 1775?] · T. Lucas, *Memoirs of the lives, intrigues, and comical adventures of the most famous gamesters and celebrated sharpers in the reigns of Charles II, James II, William III and Queen Anne* (1714), 183–92 · Pepys, *Diary*, 9.468 · *Pills to purge melancholy, or, The merry exploits of Mr. Ogle … together with the witty, ingenious frolics of the earl of Rochester* (1780?) · *Rochester's joaks, containing, the merry pranks of Lord Rochester, Lord Moon, the earls of Warwick, and Pembroke, Ben Johnson, and Ogle the life-guardsman: with the diverting frolicks and fancies of King Charles and his concubines* [n.d., 1775?] · D. F. Bond, ed., *The Tatler*, 3 vols. (1987), vol. 2, p. 267 · *The diverting humours of John Ogle* (1805?) · H. Lemoine and J. Caulfield, *The eccentric magazine, or, Lives and portraits of remarkable persons*, 1 (1812), 192–6
Likenesses line engravings, BM, NPG · print, repro. in *Eccentric magazine*, vol. 1

Ogle, John William (1824–1905), physician, born at Leeds, Yorkshire, on 30 July 1824, was the only child of Samuel Ogle (*b.* 1797), a businessman, and Sarah Rathmell. His father, who was first cousin to Admiral Thomas Ogle and second cousin to James Adey Ogle (1792–1857), regius professor of medicine at Oxford, was a member of an old Staffordshire and Shropshire family which originally came from Northumberland. John was educated at Wakefield School, from which he moved in March 1844 to Trinity College, Oxford, where he graduated BA in 1847, and developed sympathy with the Tractarian movement. Ogle entered the medical school in Kinnerton Street attached to St George's Hospital, London, and became in 1850 a licentiate and in 1855 a fellow of the Royal College of Physicians. At Oxford he proceeded MA and MB in 1851 and MD in 1857.

On 31 May 1854 Ogle married Elizabeth, daughter of Albert Smith of Ecclesall, near Sheffield, whose family subsequently took the name of Blakelock. They had five sons and one daughter. The eldest son, John, became a barrister. Another son, Cyril, became a physician at St George's Hospital, while a third entered the church.

At St George's Hospital, Ogle worked at morbid anatomy, and was for years curator of the museum, along with Henry Grey, after whose death in 1861 Ogle became lecturer on pathology. In 1857 he was elected assistant physician, and in 1866 he became full physician; however, he resigned in 1876 owing to depression. When he recovered from this, soon after overcoming an attack of enteric fever, he returned to active practice, but not to his work at St George's Hospital, where instead he became consulting physician in 1877. Ogle spent the whole of his professional life in London, also running a successful private practice there from premises in the fashionable and prosperous locations of Upper Brook Street and, subsequently, Cavendish Square.

Apart from his posts at St George's, Ogle held numerous hospital and other positions. He was censor (1873, 1874, and 1884) and vice-president (1886) of the Royal College of Physicians, associate fellow of the College of Physicians of Philadelphia, vice-president of the Pathological Society, vice-president and fellow of the Royal Medical and Chirurgical Society, corresponding member of the Edinburgh Medical and Chirurgical Society, corresponding member of the New York Society of Neurology and Electrology and of the New York Neurological Society, fellow of the Society of Antiquaries, and fellow of the Royal Geographical Society. He was elected FSA on 7 March 1878. Ogle's hospital appointments included honorary posts at St James's Dispensary, St Leonard's Hospital, Sudbury, East Grinstead General Dispensary, Belgrave Hospital for Children, and the School for the Indigent Blind. In addition he was an examiner in medicine at the universities of Oxford and Cambridge. Ogle's main interest, though, lay in nervous diseases. In a lecture on aphasia, or inability to translate thoughts into words, he made some interesting historical references to the cases of Dr Johnson and Dean Swift. Always a strong churchman, he was on friendly terms with W. E. Gladstone, Cardinal Newman, who was a patient, Richard Church, Henry Liddon, Frederick Temple, and Edward Benson.

Ogle was active in medical literature, publishing several books including *On the Relief of Excessive and Dangerous Tympanites by Puncture of the Abdomen* (1888). But it was in the medical press that he made his greatest mark as a writer. Together with Timothy Holmes he founded the *St George's Hospital Reports* (1866–79), and he edited seven out of the ten volumes. He was also editor of the *British and Foreign Medico-Chirurgical Review*. He contributed very widely to medical periodicals and to the proceedings of learned societies, making 160 contributions to the *Transactions of the Pathological Society of London* alone. He delivered the Royal College of Physicians' Croonian lectures in 1869 and its Harveian oration for 1880. The oration, which was published, including in summary form in the *British Medical Journal*, contained a vigorous rebuttal of those critical of the state of medical education in Oxford University. This in turn elicited strong criticism in the form of an open letter signed by many distinguished figures including Joseph Lister.

After some years of increasing paralytic weakness, dating from 1899, Ogle died at St Michael's vicarage, Highgate, where he had been living for some time with his clergyman son, on 8 August 1905. He was buried later in the month at Shelfanger, near Diss in Norfolk.

H. D. ROLLESTON, *rev.* P. W. J. BARTRIP

Sources *The Lancet* (19 Aug 1905), 564–5 · *BMJ* (19 Aug 1905), 417 · Munk, *Roll* · Foster, *Alum. Oxon.* · census returns, 1881 · J. Ogle, 'Harveian oration', *BMJ* (31 July 1880), 159 · *BMJ* (14 Aug 1880), 276–8 · *Medical Directory* (1880) · H. B. Sutton, 'Some letters from Cardinal Newman to Dr J. W. Ogle', *Medical History*, 15 (1971), 88–91 · *The Times* (10 Aug 1905)

Archives RCP Lond., corresp. and papers · Wellcome L., notes and papers relating to castration | Bodl. Oxf., letters to second earl of Lovelace

Likenesses photograph, repro. in *The Lancet*

Wealth at death £30,701 19s. 1d.: probate, 14 Sept 1905, CGPLA Eng. & Wales

Ogle, Owen [**Ewyn**], **second Baron Ogle** (*c.*1440–1486), landowner, was probably born in Northumberland, the eldest surviving son of Robert (VI)*Ogle, first Baron Ogle (*c.*1406–1469), and his wife, Isabel (*d.* 1478), daughter of Sir Alexander Kirkby of Kirkby Ireleth, Lancashire. His elder brother, Sir Robert (VII) Ogle, was apparently dead by 20 October 1465, when Owen was associated with his father in making a grant of land at Great Tossan. By 26 May 1467 he had married Eleanor, daughter of Sir William Hilton, who brought him lands in Cumberland. Owen Ogle was said to be aged thirty at his father's death late in 1469, but whereas the first Lord Ogle had been prominent in the establishment of the Yorkist regime in Northumberland, his successor played little part in either local or national affairs. A chancery error continued to include Robert, Lord Ogle, in commissions of the peace for Northumberland between 1471 and 1485; it is unlikely that Owen served in this capacity as his father's heir. On 14 February 1473 Owen Ogle was granted a general pardon for offences committed before 30 September 1471, and all debts and accounts due to the king before 29 September 1469. The latter portion of the pardon was probably issued in respect of sums owed by his father. Between 1471 and 1474, as Ewyn, Lord Ogle, he was one of a number of lay and ecclesiastical notables who set their seals to a certificate concerning the Delaval inheritance, but elsewhere he was still being styled esquire in 1480, though in his first summons to parliament—issued as late as 15 November 1482—he is named as Owen Ogle of Ogle, knight.

Although a disability of some kind cannot be ruled out, the likeliest cause of Owen Ogle's inactivity is poverty. Not until 1484 was he licensed to enter the possessions of his father and mother. The latter died in 1478, having made a will bequeathing her Lancashire inheritance to her daughter Isabella, and to the latter's husband and children, and making no mention of her son at all. The fact that the lands disposed of in 1484 were specifically said to have been those of both his parents may indicate that they had been covered by a joint settlement of some sort; that the licence was accompanied by a pardon, 'upon al contemptes etc don upon the same' (*Harleian MS 433*, 1.190), suggests that Lord Ogle had chafed at being kept out of his inheritance, and may even have taken possession of it in the course of a dispute. None the less, in 1485 he conveyed Ogle Castle to feoffees, with the result that it does not appear among the Northumberland estates listed in his inquisition post mortem. These, eighteen manors or fractions of manors, were valued at only £111 13s. per annum, and even allowing for undervaluation and for the absence of Ogle (valued at £20 in 1492), they represent an exceptionally low income for a baron. The fact that Owen Ogle had apparently been knighted by 1482, and was summoned to parliament in that year, may have resulted from involvement in the Anglo-Scottish hostilities that broke out in 1480. The English commander was Richard, duke of Gloucester, and in 1485 Ogle was one of the northern barons and gentry said by *The Ballad of Bosworth Field* to have fought for Richard, now Richard III, at Bosworth. If he did indeed fight against the future Henry VII, Ogle cannot be shown to have suffered in consequence, and in any case he died soon afterwards, on 1 September 1486. He was succeeded by his son Ralph Ogle. A heraldic visitation also names a second son, Robert (VIII), and a daughter, Joan, who married Robert Clavering. Owen's widow, Eleanor, who was still alive in 1515, remarried twice; her later husbands were George Percy and Henry Raynfforth. RICHARD K. ROSE

Sources Chancery records · A. M. Oliver, ed., *Northumberland and Durham deeds from the Dodsworth MSS in Bodley's Library, Oxford*, Newcastle upon Tyne Records Committee, 7 (1929) · J. W. Clay, *The extinct and dormant peerages of the northern counties of England* (1913), 153 · *CIPM, Henry VII*, 1, no. 157; 3, nos. 9, 14 · *A history of Northumberland*, Northumberland County History Committee, 15 vols. (1893–1940), vol. 9, p. 151, n. 5 · J. Hodgson, *A history of Northumberland*, 3 pts in 7 vols. (1820–58), pt 2, vol. 1, pp. 384–92 · *Harleian MS 433*, ed. R. E. Horrox and P. W. Hammond, 1 (1979), 190 · M. J. Bennett, *The battle of Bosworth* (1985), 95, 171
Wealth at death £111 13s. p.a.: *CIPM*, 3, no. 14 · £20, value of principal estate

Ogle, Robert (II) (*c*.1305–1362), soldier, was head of a Northumberland family that had held Ogle in the barony of Whalton since the mid-twelfth century. Because for seven generations the eldest son was named Robert there are difficulties attributing exploits to the correct individual. Robert Ogle or his father, Robert (I) (*b. c*.1280), acted as messenger for stocking Mitford Castle in August 1318. Similarly one or other was pardoned in 1329 by Edward III for acts committed in the late rebellion (of Henry, earl of Lancaster). Robert the son married first Isabel Fernielaw, after whose death he married in 1331 Joan Heppale, whose father settled on them half the manor of Hepple and other land in mid-Coquetdale. In 1335 he was a commissioner of array both in Northumberland and in the regalian liberty of Hexhamshire, where he was bailiff. This was revoked in May in respect of Newcastle, where the community had agreed with the king to serve at sea against the Scots. Meanwhile Robert was amassing land throughout the county. In May 1341 Edward III granted him as 'king's yeoman' licence to crenellate his house at Ogle, with free warren in all his demesnes. The same year he was one of the commissioners to assess and levy the ninth in Northumberland. Whether he was responsible for an assault on the army of David II, king of Scots, that was laying siege to Newcastle in November 1341, has been doubted. In May 1344 he was commissioned to array the men of Northumberland against the Scots, renewed in April 1345.

It may have been this Robert Ogle, or more likely his son with Isabel Fernielaw, Robert (III), who participated in the defence of Cumberland in 1345 with the bishop of Carlisle and Sir Thomas Lucy, and served as seneschal of Annandale for William de Bohun, earl of Northampton and constable of Lochmaben. It was the elder Robert who was thanked by Edward III for his part in the battle of Nevilles Cross on 17 October 1346 and commissioned to bring down to the Tower of London Scottish prisoners captured there. These included the earl of Fife, Henry Rameseye, and Thomas Boyd, whom he was reputed to have captured personally. Conjointly with Robert Bertram, father-in-law to his son, he was also to deliver John Douglas, brother to the earl. (There is a tradition that after the battle the captive King David was taken to Ogle's castle at Ogle by John Coupland, who then refused to surrender his prisoner until favourable financial terms were offered.) On 10 December 1346 Robert Ogle senior was ordered to attend a council at Westminster to consider business concerning the state of England and war in Scotland.

In 1355 he was in charge of Berwick, under Lord Greystoke, where his son, Robert (III), was killed in the attack whereby the Scots captured the town but not the castle. Robert (III) had married Elena, the heir of Robert Bertram of Bothal, when his father settled half the manor of Hurworth-on-Tees on him and his wife. Robert (II) died on 16 June 1362, and his widow was given dower in Thursby in Cumberland. She and her second husband, John Phillipot, secured custody of the heir, Robert (IV), grandson of Robert (II). This Robert married the youngest coheir of Sir Alan Heton of Chillingham, and was a conservator of the truce between England and Scotland in 1386; his chantry chapel and tomb in Hexham Priory still survive. He settled on his second son, John, the Bertram barony of Bothal, being his grandmother's inheritance. This was disputed by the elder brother, Robert (V), who, after their father's death in 1409, laid siege to Bothal Castle with 200 armed men and archers and captured it. John petitioned in parliament for restitution and recovered possession. The barony remained in his family until a failure of male heirs in the 1470s, when it reverted to the senior line.

C. M. FRASER

Sources W. P. Hedley, *Northumberland families*, 2, Society of Antiquaries of Newcastle upon Tyne, Record Series (1970), 143–5 · GEC, *Peerage*, new edn, 10.24–6 · H. A. Ogle, *Ogle and Bothal* (1902), 36–41 · *RotP*, 3.629–30, appx. 80, 70 · *A history of Northumberland*, Northumberland County History Committee, 15 vols. (1893–1940), vol. 11, pp. 218–19 · G. Ridpath, *The border-history of England and Scotland*, ed. P. Ridpath (1776), 338–9 and notes · C. J. Neville, *Violence, custom and law: the Anglo-Scottish borderlands in the later middle ages* (1998)

Ogle, Robert (VI), **first Baron Ogle** (*c*.1406–1469), soldier and administrator, was the son of Sir Robert (V) Ogle of Ogle (*c*.1380–1436) and Matilda (*b. c*.1380, *d.* after 1451), daughter of Sir Thomas Grey of Heaton. Through this match he was nephew of the Sir Thomas Grey who married Alice Neville and was executed at Southampton for his part in the plot to murder Henry V, and first cousin to Thomas Grey, who married Isabel, daughter of Richard, earl of Cambridge. His father had been constable of Norham Castle, Northumberland, and sheriff of Norhamshire, 1403–36, a member of parliament for Northumberland in 1416, 1419–20, 1421, and 1425, and sheriff of Northumberland in 1416. He was also constable of Wark Castle in 1419, and warden of Roxburgh Castle in 1424. He died in August 1436. Robert Ogle married Isabel (*d.* 1478), daughter and heir of Sir Alexander Kirkby of Kirkby Ireleth in Lancashire, and had three sons, Robert, Thomas, and Owen *Ogle, and a daughter, Isabel.

Ogle was appointed with his father as a commissioner of truce in 1434, and in 1435 was styled as captain of Berwick, when he was captured in a skirmish by the Scots. He was ransomed for 750 marks and promised indemnification from a Scottish ship seized at Newcastle, but this proved to have been already sold, and he was still trying to get compensation in 1442. He succeeded his father as constable of Norham and sheriff of Norhamshire, and was on numerous commissions for conserving truces with Scotland and arraying the forces of Northumberland against the Scots. He served as sheriff of Northumberland in 1437–8, and was also a member of parliament in 1435 and 1442. In 1438 he was appointed captain of Roxburgh Castle and given charge of the east march of Scotland until a warden was appointed. He occurs in 1452 as bailiff and lieutenant of Tyndale. Three years later he supported the Yorkists when they took up arms, and brought 600 men from the marches to the first battle of St Albans, probably in the train of Richard Neville, earl of Warwick, being a retainer of his father, the earl of Salisbury, at a fee of £20. He was one of the commissioners appointed by the victors to raise money for the defence of Calais. Shortly after Towton (28 March 1461) he and Sir John Conyers were reported to be besieging Henry VI at Carham.

For his services, being the principal Northumbrian gentleman to support the Yorkist cause, Edward IV on 26 July 1461 summoned Ogle to his first parliament as Baron Ogle, and invested him (8 August) with the offices of steward and constable of the castles of Alnwick, Warkworth, and Prudhoe, and with other lordships forfeited by the earl of Northumberland. He was also appointed warden-general of the east marches, an office previously held by the earl. In October 1462 Ogle distinguished himself in the dash upon Holy Island, which resulted in the capture of all the French leaders who had come over with Margaret of Anjou, except de Brézé, and during the operations against the Northumbrian strongholds in the winter Ogle assisted John Neville, Lord Montagu, in the siege of Bamburgh, which surrendered on Christmas eve. Betrayed to the Lancastrians again in the following year, the castle was finally reduced in June 1464, and entrusted to Ogle as constable for life. Just a year later he was commissioned with Montagu, now earl of Northumberland, and others, to negotiate for peace with Scotland, and for a marriage between James III and an English subject. In compensation for the loss of custody of the Percy estates with their transfer to Montagu, he received in April 1465 a grant in fee tail of the lordship of Redesdale and castle of Harbottle in central Northumberland, forfeited by Sir William Tailboys of Kyme in Lincolnshire, who was executed after the battle of Hexham in 1464. To these were added other forfeited lands in Northumberland. Lord Ogle's consistent loyalty to the Nevilles and the house of York may be explained by the fact that William Bertram, the cousin whose inheritance of Bothal Ogle's father had disputed, had been retained since 1440 by Henry Percy, second earl of Northumberland. Ogle died on 1 November 1469.

C. M. FRASER

Sources W. P. Hedley, *Northumberland families*, 2, Society of Antiquaries of Newcastle upon Tyne, Record Series (1970), 146–8 · GEC, *Peerage* · H. A. Ogle, *Ogle and Bothal* (1902), 45–9 · A. J. Pollard, 'The northern retainers of Richard Nevill, earl of Salisbury', *Northern History*, 11 (1976), 52–69, esp. 57–68 · A. J. Pollard, *North-eastern England during the Wars of the Roses: lay society, war and politics, 1450–1500* (1990), 270, 285, 288, 298 · J. M. W. Bean, *The estates of the Percy family, 1416–1537* (1958), 92 · C. J. Neville, *Violence, custom and law: the Anglo-Scottish border lands in the later middle ages* (1998)

Ogle, Samuel (1702/3–1752), colonial governor, was born in Northumberland, the eldest son of Samuel Ogle (1658–1718), MP for Berwick, and his second wife, Ursula (1678–1725), daughter of Sir Robert Markham of Sedgebroke and his wife, Mary, and widow of Lord Altham Annesley of co. Cork. Among his brothers was the translator George *Ogle (*bap.* 1704, *d.* 1746). Little is known of Ogle's early life, but he probably spent part of his childhood in Ireland, where his father was commissioner for the revenue. He was serving as a cavalry captain when Charles Calvert, fifth Baron Baltimore and proprietor of Maryland, chose him as governor of Maryland on 3 September 1731. Ogle eventually served on three separate occasions in that capacity.

On his arrival in Annapolis, Maryland, on 2 December 1731, Ogle faced a restless colony. There was controversy over proprietary fees, the collection of quitrents on land, and the paper currency question. Exacerbating these issues was the fragile state of the economy, the result primarily of the overproduction of inferior tobacco. When Ogle had been in office for only a year, he was supplanted by the proprietor himself in December 1732. During the next six months Lord Baltimore instigated policies that were essentially to endure until the American War of Independence. After a spell as president of the colony's council, Ogle was again appointed as governor in June 1733. His principal task was to implement the new policies, often in the face of strong opposition from 'country party' members of the lower house of the colony's assembly. Although the economy improved in the late 1730s and the paper currency emission aided financial transactions, discontent over taxes and fees persisted. When Ogle asked the lower house for a continuation of the arms levy, for example, the delegates requested the appointment of an agent to represent them in London. The resulting stalemate forced Ogle to prorogue the assembly.

This failure resulted in Ogle's replacement by Thomas Bladen, Baltimore's own brother-in-law, in August 1742. Bladen, however, was even less successful in dealing with the lower house than Ogle had been, and Ogle succeeded him as governor in March 1747. His third term was his most successful. The assembly not only passed an acceptable bill for the purchase of arms, but also agreed measures for the inspection of tobacco and the limitation of officers' fees. The restrictions on fees removed a major source of discord, while the Tobacco Inspection Act was undoubtedly the most significant piece of legislation passed during Ogle's entire governorship. The salvation of the colony's economy, it allowed the export of only high-quality tobacco that had passed muster at provincial inspection houses.

In July 1741 Ogle married Anne (1723–1817), the daughter of his friend Benjamin Tasker (c.1690–1768). Raised in Maryland, she brought a dowry of £1500 sterling. The couple had five children, only three of whom survived infancy. Their son Benjamin Ogle (1749–1809) was governor of Maryland from 1798 to 1801. During Bladen's governorship the Ogles lived in London on Savile Row, Westminster. While in England, Samuel asked his father-in-law to build a house on land that Ogle had originally bought from him in 1737. The resulting mansion, Belair, was located in Prince George's county and survives today as a fine example of Georgian architecture. At his estate Ogle indulged in the planter class's favourite pastimes. He took an active interest in horse breeding, even importing stock from England. He also enjoyed racing and helped establish the Maryland Jockey Club.

Ogle died on 3 May 1752, probably in Annapolis, after an illness of several months. He was buried in St Anne's churchyard in Annapolis. At his death he was one of the wealthiest men in the colony. Incomplete inventories of his personal estate totalled £2553 11s. 4d., including fifty slaves and twenty horses. In addition Ogle owned bank stock in England worth approximately £5000. His landed property encompassed 2539 acres in Prince George's and Anne Arundel counties, two lots in Annapolis, and his Savile Row house in England. An obituary in the Annapolis *Maryland Gazette* (7 May 1752) highlighted his 'benevolent Disposition', 'Good Sense', and desire 'to promote the Public Good'.

KEITH MASON

Sources E. C. Papenfuse and others, eds., *A biographical dictionary of the Maryland legislature, 1635–1789*, 2 vols. (1979–85) · J. W. McWilliams, 'Ogle, Samuel', *ANB* · N. D. Mereness, 'Ogle, Samuel', *DAB* · D. C. Skaggs, *Roots of Maryland democracy, 1753–1776* (1973) · A. C. Land, *Colonial Maryland: a history* (1981) · S. Baltz, *The chronicle of Belair* (1976) · E. G. Bowie, *Across the years in Prince George's county* (1947) · A. C. Land, *The Dulanys of Maryland: a biographical study of Daniel Dulany, the elder (1685–1753) and Daniel Dulany, the younger (1722–1797)* (Baltimore, MD, 1955) · J. T. Scharf, *History of Maryland from the earliest period to the present day*, 3 vols. (1879) · W. H. Browne and others, eds., *Archives of Maryland* (1883–) · A. Pedley, *The manuscript collections of the Maryland Historical Society* (1968) · R. J. Cox and L. E. Sullivan, eds., *Guide to the research collections of the Maryland Historical Society* (1981)

Wealth at death £2553 11s. 4d.; plus est. £5000 of bank stock in England; 2539 acres of land in Prince George's and Anne Arundel counties, Maryland; two lots in Annapolis, and house in Savile Row, London: Papenfuse and others, eds., *A biographical dictionary*, 2.619

Oglethorpe, James Edward (1696–1785), army officer and founder of the colony of Georgia, was born in London on 22 December 1696, the third and youngest surviving son of Sir Theophilus *Oglethorpe (1650–1702), politician and army officer, and his wife, Eleanor, *née* Wall (1662–1732), and was baptized the following day at St Martin-in-the-Fields. The strong Jacobite sympathies of his parents, but especially of his mother, would cast a shadow over his career well into his middle age.

Early career, 1707–1730 In 1707, following a long-established family tradition of military service, James Edward, or 'Jemmy' as he was known at home, enlisted in Queen Anne's 1st regiment of foot guards and in 1713 was commissioned as a lieutenant. The following year he matriculated from Corpus Christi College, Oxford. In 1715, possibly on his own initiative or perhaps acting on the advice of his mother, who did not wish her son to be jeopardized by her overt support for the Pretender, Oglethorpe resigned his army commission and left England for France. Upon his arrival in Paris he enrolled as a student in the academy of Lompres. One of his fellow students, James Francis Edward Keith, like Oglethorpe from a family with staunch Jacobite connections, became a lifelong friend and ally. War between the Austrian empire and the Turks offered Oglethorpe and Keith an opportunity to experience active military service, and in 1716 they enlisted as volunteers in the imperial army commanded by Prince Eugene of Savoy. By the time Belgrade surrendered in 1717 Oglethorpe, who had distinguished himself at the battle of Petrovaradin (1716) and the siege of Timisora (1716), had been promoted by Prince Eugene to the rank of lieutenant-colonel. In 1718 he saw further action in Sicily. He could have remained in the imperial army but in 1719 chose instead to return to England.

Oglethorpe's hopes of a commission in the British army

James Edward Oglethorpe (1696–1785), by Thomas Burford, pubd c.1743–5

were quickly dashed. Neither Prince Eugene's strong recommendation nor Oglethorpe's distinguished military record could compensate for the taint of Jacobitism that attached to his family's name. In June 1719, with his military career seemingly at an end, he returned briefly to Corpus Christi College. Little is known about his time there, and he left without taking his degree.

In 1722 Oglethorpe's life took a new and unanticipated turn when he returned from Europe to manage the affairs of his expatriate brother Theophilus Oglethorpe (*bap.* 1684, *d. c.*1737). Like his father and brother Lewis before him, Theophilus had sat as the MP for Haslemere in Surrey. The Oglethorpe family assumed that James, in his turn, would occupy the seat, and such was their influence in the constituency that he was returned with a minimum of opposition. He held the seat until 1754.

The first few years of Oglethorpe's parliamentary career were largely unexceptional, but in 1728 an event occurred which quickly catapulted him into a position of national prominence. Robert Castell, a good friend of Oglethorpe's, fell into debt and was incarcerated in the notorious Fleet prison. Because he was so penurious that he could not afford to bribe the guards into giving him better living conditions, he contracted smallpox and died. Castell's death, and the unmitigated squalor of the Fleet and the other gaols in which debtors were imprisoned, horrified Oglethorpe and spurred him to action. In 1729 he persuaded the House of Commons to appoint a committee, to be chaired by him, which would prepare a detailed report on the conditions in English prisons.

The Georgia project, 1730–1742 Oglethorpe quickly developed a close understanding, and an excellent working relationship, with one of his colleagues on the gaols committee, Sir John Perceval, later first earl of Egmont. By 1730 Oglethorpe had formulated a far more ambitious scheme than that of prison reform. Perceval, who proved to be most receptive to his plan, was one of the first people to whom Oglethorpe revealed his proposal to establish a new American colony.

In some ways Oglethorpe's proposal was very traditional. Ever since the sixteenth century, a central strand in élite English thinking about colonization had been that colonies offered England the opportunity to rid itself of the unemployed and the unemployable—those who were both a drain on, and a potential social and moral threat to, society as a whole. The abundant resources of the New World would provide such people with every opportunity to improve themselves materially and, through their work, with the prospect of moral and social redemption. This was the essence of the plan Oglethorpe mooted to Perceval in 1730, a plan he believed would receive the enthusiastic backing of politicians and churchmen, as well as those merchants and manufacturers who stood to benefit from the commercial opportunities presented by a new colony.

In 1730 Oglethorpe had not finalized the exact location of his proposed colony, but, as his plan began to take shape, he realized the practical advantages of selecting a site in the region to the south of the Savannah River. Spain, with its heavily fortified presence in northern Florida, presented a serious threat to South Carolina's burgeoning rice economy. Oglethorpe reasoned that South Carolina's, and thereby England's, interests could be served by establishing a military buffer in these disputed borderlands. The House of Commons, he anticipated, would willingly support a colony which not only served this purpose but would also do so comparatively cheaply. The settlers of this new colony would function as soldier-farmers. They would be South Carolina's first line of defence. Between 1730 and 1732 Oglethorpe, ably assisted by Perceval, embarked on an ambitious campaign to promote his scheme. Oglethorpe was responsible for the earliest literary contribution to that campaign, an unpublished piece entitled 'Some accounts of the design of the trustees for establishing colonys in America'. This detailed analysis of the rationale for the founding of a new colony, and the precise form it would take, seems to have been written between late 1730 and the spring of 1731. Benjamin Martyn, later appointed to serve as the Georgia trustees' secretary, drew heavily on Oglethorpe's work for his *Some Account of the Designs of the Trustees for Establishing the Colony of Georgia in America* (1732) and *Reasons for Establishing the Colony of Georgia in America* (1733). As part of the continuing effort to secure support for Georgia, Oglethorpe wrote *A New and Accurate Account of the Provinces of South-Carolina and Georgia*, which was published in London in 1733. By June 1732 Oglethorpe and Perceval were ready to implement their plan. They, together with some of the parliamentarians, churchmen, and merchants subsequently known as the trustees, who were actively prepared to support their scheme, successfully petitioned the crown for a charter which authorized them to found their colony in the region between the Savannah and Altamaha rivers. In October 1732 Oglethorpe accompanied the first embarkation of settlers to Georgia, and for the next decade he played a decisive and highly controversial role in virtually every aspect of life in the colony. The paternalistic, if not authoritarian, attitude he displayed towards the early settlers, and his refusal to brook any criticism, produced mixed results. On the one hand his firmness, combined with his seemingly unflagging energy, was instrumental in securing the colony's survival during the initial years of settlement. At the same time his often inappropriate choice of men to serve as local officials, and his uncritical loyalty to them, stirred up a great deal of discontent.

By the mid-1730s the trustees, and Oglethorpe in particular, were being blamed by a growing number of colonists, and their allies in South Carolina, for a policy which they believed was stunting Georgia's economic development and thereby thwarting their own economic aspirations: the prohibition of black slavery. Oglethorpe and his colleagues on the Georgia board had not begun their venture with a view to excluding slavery, but Oglethorpe soon became convinced that their intentions for the colony were incompatible with chattel slavery. His uncompromising opposition to slavery was based more on pragmatism than it was on ideological objections to that institution.

Having seen South Carolina's slave system at first hand Oglethorpe was quickly persuaded that slavery would jeopardize Georgia's role as a military buffer. Enslaved Africans, he surmised, would not hesitate to do all in their power to assist the Spaniards if by that means they could secure their own liberation. Georgia, moreover, had not been founded with a view to replicating, and thereby competing with, South Carolina's rice economy. The subtropical commodities, the silk and the wine, which the trustees insisted would form the backbone of Georgia's economy, were not seen as necessitating the employment of enslaved workers. Finally, Oglethorpe was utterly convinced that the use of slaves would have a highly detrimental effect on the manners and morality of Georgia's white inhabitants. For all of these reasons he urged the other trustees to press for parliamentary legislation outlawing slavery in Georgia. In 1735 the House of Commons enacted the law sought by the Georgia board.

During the late 1730s the prohibition of slavery generated an increasingly bitter debate. The pro-slavery group of Georgia settlers and their South Carolinian backers managed to secure potentially powerful support in the House of Commons. While Oglethorpe remained in Georgia, effectively ensuring the continuation of the ban, Perceval marshalled the trustees' defences in London. Oglethorpe's victory over the Spaniards at the battle of Bloody Marsh (1742), together with his return to England in the following year, marked the beginning of the end of the prohibition. By 1747 the trustees had all but conceded defeat in their campaign to exclude slavery from Georgia, and three years later they reluctantly agreed to ask parliament to repeal the legislation of 1735.

Military life, 1736–1758 Oglethorpe may have made errors in his political judgements and in his civil administration of Georgia, but his military contribution was of the very highest order and significance. It was he who was mainly responsible for ensuring that Georgia successfully filled its designated military function. The trustees had always known that Spain would not take kindly to this English intrusion into the southern borderlands, and in 1736 a Spanish invasion seemed imminent. Oglethorpe cleverly bluffed the Spaniards into overestimating his firepower and, for the time being, postponed an assault which might have dislodged the English. Oglethorpe had bought the time he needed to build up Georgia's defences, and he returned to England to try to impress upon the House of Commons the urgency of providing troops to serve under his command in America. Parliament proved unwilling to supply regular soldiers, but authorized Oglethorpe to raise a volunteer regiment. In September 1738 he and his force of 600 men landed in Georgia. The war that Oglethorpe anticipated did not come for another year.

In the autumn of 1739 Britain declared war on Spain, and Oglethorpe was ordered to do all he could to harry the Spanish forces based in the Florida port of St Augustine. In May 1740 he hatched what proved to be an overly ambitious plan to take St Augustine. Within a month he was forced to concede defeat. The lack of wholehearted support from South Carolina, sickness in his army, and desertions left him with no realistic alternative but to withdraw the remnants of his forces back to the comparative safety of Georgia.

Two years later Oglethorpe found himself on the defensive when the Spaniards launched an all-out attack on Georgia. In what was to be a defining point in Anglo-Spanish relations in the southern borderlands, he repelled the Spanish forces at the battle of Bloody Marsh. His stunning victory meant that for the foreseeable future Georgia, and thereby South Carolina, were secure against the possibility of Spanish invasion. In 1743, in acknowledgement of his military achievements in America, Oglethorpe was formally accorded the rank of brigadier-general. He returned to England in 1743 to try to persuade the Pelham ministry to continue funding Georgia. He had left the colony with every intention of returning, but events conspired to ensure that he would spend the rest of his life in Europe.

On 15 September 1745, at the age of nearly forty-nine, and after a comparatively short courtship, Oglethorpe married the 31-year-old Elizabeth Wright (d. 1787), the only surviving daughter and wealthy heiress of Sir Nathan Wright. Whatever her other attractions, Elizabeth's wealth replenished Oglethorpe's much depleted purse. The newly-weds settled at Elizabeth's family home, Cranham Hall in Essex, where they lived more than comfortably on the £1500 per annum she brought to the marriage.

The couple had no children. If marriage detained Oglethorpe in England, then so did the Jacobite rebellion of 1745, an event which once more raised questions about the political loyalties of the Oglethorpe family. Oglethorpe, at the head of the troops he had raised for the defence of Georgia, was ordered to join General Wade at Hull. He and his regiment were afterwards transferred to the command of the duke of Cumberland, then in hot pursuit of the retreating Jacobite forces.

In December 1745 the duke of Cumberland alleged that Oglethorpe had been tardy in his harassment of the rebels and, without any firm evidence to support his charges, implied that this was because of his sympathy for the Jacobite cause. Oglethorpe, who at no point in his life had expressed any overt support for the Stuarts, was court-martialled. Although he was acquitted, his military career in both England and America had been effectively ended. After 1745 he ceased to play an active role in Georgia affairs. For the next nine years he remained MP for Haslemere, but lost his seat in 1754. In 1755 he sought to reactivate his Georgia regiment for service in America, but his application to the ministry was turned down.

Oglethorpe's keen desire to resume his military career, which may have reflected the boredom of his life as a country gentleman and the loss of his parliamentary seat, was satisfied, but in continental Europe rather than in America. He ended his military career as he had begun it: serving alongside his friend James Keith. By 1755 Keith had attained the rank of field marshal in Frederick the Great's army. Oglethorpe was with Keith when he died at the battle of Hochkirk (1758).

Retirement, 1758–1785 By now in his mid-sixties, Oglethorpe returned to England in 1760 and lived there for the remainder of his long life. He seems to have divided his time between Cranham and London. While he no longer took any active role in public life, he did become something of a celebrity in London society. His long and varied career, and his apparently jaunty personality, secured for him a wide circle of friends and associates, including Samuel Johnson, James Boswell, and Hannah More. Oglethorpe had been one of the 'warmest patrons' of Johnson's *London* (1738), and at one point Johnson intimated that he wished to write a biography of Oglethorpe, but the volume never materialized. Both Boswell and Johnson appear to have thought highly of a man who was said to have an 'uncommon vivacity' and 'variety of knowledge' which made his conversation both stimulating and sometimes 'desultory' (Boswell, 92, 756). Oglethorpe, who had enjoyed excellent health throughout his life, died of natural causes at Cranham on 1 July 1785, and was buried in the parish church there.   BETTY WOOD

Sources L. F. Church, *Oglethorpe: a study of philanthropy in England and Georgia* (1932) · A. A. Ettinger, *James Edward Oglethorpe: imperial idealist* (1936) · P. Spalding, *Oglethorpe in America* (1977) · P. Spalding, 'James Edward Oglethorpe's quest for an American Zion', *Forty years of diversity: essays on colonial Georgia*, ed. H. H. Jackson and P. Spalding (1984) · P. Spalding and H. H. Jackson, eds., *Oglethorpe in perspective: Georgia's founder after two hundred years* (1989) · J. C.

Inscoe, ed., *James Edward Oglethorpe: new perspectives on his life and legacy* (1997) · R. R. Sedgwick, 'Oglethorpe, James Edward', HoP, *Commons* · J. Boswell, *Life of Johnson*, ed. R. W. Chapman, rev. J. D. Fleeman, new edn (1970); repr. with introduction by P. Rogers (1980)

Archives American Antiquarian Society, Worcester, Massachusetts, papers relating to his American estates · Duke U., Perkins L., letters and papers · Georgia Department of Archives and History, Atlanta, Georgia, papers · Glos. RO, corresp. | CUL, letters to Sir Robert Walpole · Yale U., Beinecke L., corresp. with James Boswell

Likenesses portrait, *c*.1719, Oglethorpe University, Atlanta, Georgia · W. Hogarth, group portrait, oils, *c*.1729 (*The comitty of the House of Commons*), NPG · group portrait, oils, 1734 (after W. Verelst, *The Georgia Council*), Rhode Memorial, Atlanta, Georgia · W. Verelst, *c*.1734–1746, Henry Francis du Pont Winterthur Museum, Delaware · T. Burford, mezzotint, pubd *c*.1743–1745, BM [*see illus.*] · S. F. Ravenet, engraving, *c*.1757, repro. in T. Smollet, *A complete history of England*, 4 vols. (1757–8) · S. Ireland, etching, pubd 1785, BM, NPG · S. Ireland, sketch, 1785, Oglethorpe University, Atlanta, Georgia · R. W. Habersham, portrait, 1885, Georgia Historical Society, Savannah · attrib. J. Dassien, medal, BM · R. W. Habersham, portrait (copy?; after portrait of Oglethorpe as aide-de-camp to Prince Eugene, 1718), Solomon's Lodge No. 1 F & A.M., Savannah, Georgia · portrait, Oglethorpe University, Atlanta, Georgia

Oglethorpe, Owen (1502/3–1559), bishop of Carlisle, was the third son of George Oglethorpe of Newton Kyme, near Tadcaster, Yorkshire. In 1551 he was said to be forty-eight. Educated at Magdalen College, Oxford, Oglethorpe for most of his life was connected to the college and involved with academic and ecclesiastical politics. Already a fellow in 1524, he graduated BA in 1525 and MA in 1529, when he became a lecturer in logic. Lecturer in moral philosophy in 1534, he proceeded BTh and DTh in February and July 1536 respectively. In the same February began his long presidency of his college. In 1531 he was master of disputations, and in 1533–4 both keeper of the Winton Chest and junior proctor. In 1542 he became canon and prebendary of King Henry VIII College, holding the post until its dissolution in 1545, and still being in receipt of the pension at Pole's investigation in 1556. Vice-chancellor elect in 1551, his university career was now under a cloud because of his religious conservatism, and he was compelled to resign his presidency in September 1552, resuming it under Mary in October 1553, and finally vacating it in April 1555 to become registrar of the Order of the Garter in May 1555.

Oglethorpe's tenure of benefices followed a pattern familiar to such senior ecclesiastics. Priested in June 1531, a month later he was presented to the college living of Sele, Sussex, which he vacated by September 1536, and in 1534 to Bolton Percy, Yorkshire. He became a canon of Lincoln, with the prebend of Lafford, in 1536, only vacating on his elevation to Carlisle in 1556. He obtained the rectory of Newington, Oxfordshire, in 1537, which he vacated by 1557, and that of East Bridgford, Nottinghamshire, in 1538, in which year he had a dispensation to hold a second benefice. Canon and prebendary of St George's, Windsor (1540–4), he was canon also of Ripon and prebendary first of Nunwick (1541–4) and thereafter of Monkton. At the same period he gained other Yorkshire benefices: his native Newton Kyme in February 1541, and Romaldkirk in October 1541, obtaining in 1557 a dispensation to hold the latter *in commendam* with his bishopric. His rectory of St

Olave's, Southwark (October 1544), was however vacated on his elevation to Carlisle. Not surprisingly 1544 saw dispensations, citing him as king's chaplain, to hold a third and fourth benefice. He hoped for the archdeaconry of the East Riding on the death of Thomas Magnus in 1550, but college politics prevented his obtaining it. Finally he became dean of St George's, Windsor, in February 1554, which he vacated by November 1556, and bishop of Carlisle, to which he was consecrated on 15 August 1556.

Oglethorpe's career was beset by religious change. Under Henry VIII he suffered the loss of a canonry during the uncertainties over Cardinal College, although he had been one of the seventeen commissioners of 1540 to answer the 'Seventeen Questions' on the sacraments. His doctrinal position being well known, his conservatism was apt to cause him problems during Edward's reign. Tentative contacts with reformers did not save him from dissension in his college, where a radical minority sought to obtain a more sympathetic president. In November 1548 the president and fellows of Magdalen wrote to Somerset, defending themselves against the accusations of some reforming fellows that Oglethorpe had dissuaded them from accomplishing redress of religion, just as he had done at King Henry VIII College. Oglethorpe protested that he was protecting the college as he was bound by oath and statute to do, against changes for which he had no dispensation. He promised obedience to the protector, knowing that he would order nothing that was ungodly, and assured Somerset that the order of communion, not high mass, was in use at Magdalen, and that he had not expelled any dissentient fellow or scholar. This rather spineless conservatism seems characteristic of the man, and won him no friends. By September 1550 others were deliberately undermining him, suggesting then that someone of 'sincerer piety' (*CSP dom.*, 1547–53) should be chosen for ecclesiastical preferment, and in 1551 that Oglethorpe was in desperate need of the fellows' support if he were not to lose his presidency, and that he would forgo a major benefice (the archdeaconry) for the sake of the college. The writer thought his motivation not love but lucre, and believed the college to be split two to one in Oglethorpe's favour.

By 1552 Oglethorpe had given up the struggle: Cecil's notebook records him as content to surrender his house to the king's visitation in July, and in August an indenture of the terms on which he handed over to his successor preceded his departure. In the circumstances it is surprising to find Oglethorpe in correspondence with Bullinger, and mentioned in reformers' correspondence. A fulsome introductory letter of 1548 was followed by a reference in a letter of 1550 to Rudolph Gwalter to 'your friend Oglethorpe' (Robinson, *Original Letters*) being in prison for superstition, and about to lose his presidency. In the same year he is joined with Peter Martyr in affectionate salutations to Bullinger, and in 1552 there is word of Dr Oglethorpe, vice-chancellor, anxiously expecting a letter from Bullinger. Foxe likewise records Oglethorpe in 1552 as having recanted his former ignorance at the preaching of Peter Martyr. His next mention of Oglethorpe, however, is

as a disputant with the Oxford martyrs, dwelling in detail on the largely grammatical argument with Cranmer over whether the body of Christ was figuratively or literally present in the bread. Oglethorpe's promotions by Mary, in the light of such expressed theological views, are not surprising.

In July 1556 a licence was granted to the dean and chapter of Carlisle to elect a successor to Robert Aldridge; in October a grant of the temporalities was made to Owen Oglethorpe, dean of St George's, Windsor. But it was not until January 1558 that he was in full possession, as a result of papal provision to the see. The Marian gift of the advowson and collation to the four prebendal stalls in his cathedral, and, on 14 November 1558, of various Cumberland advowsons, not all within his diocese, should have put him in a position to act as a Catholic reforming bishop of Carlisle. The queen's death ended that hope, and Oglethorpe's episcopacy was effectively over before it ever truly began. In the absence of diocesan records for the period, only fragments remain to illustrate his work. Correspondence over a will shows him in the temporizing strain associated with his Oxford career, but at least resident in his diocese. The weak and shuffling reply which the bishop gave when questioned about the sale of plate at St George's, Windsor, seems typical. Likewise his consecration of a chapelry on his way south to Elizabeth's coronation simply shows a diocesan carrying out his regular duties. His pastoral role is unquantifiable.

The focal point of Oglethorpe's episcopal career was not his diocese, but his celebration of the Christmas eucharist, and participation in the coronation, of Elizabeth I. On Christmas day the queen walked out in displeasure at his elevation of the Host at the mass. The balance of probabilities is against his celebrating the mass at the coronation. That he should have been the officiating bishop at her coronation was largely accidental. With the see of Canterbury vacant, and York and his aged deputy at Durham infirm, Oglethorpe was the only remaining bishop of the northern province. There was perhaps some difficulty in finding any bishop not so closely connected to the previous regime as to be tarnished by it. The coronation robes had to be borrowed from Bonner of London, a great point being made of there being the full regalia, and all done in due order: 'universum apparatum pontificium quo uti solent Episcopi in huiusmodi magnificis illustrissimorum regum inaugurationibus' ('all the pontifical apparel which bishops are accustomed to wear at such occasions, the magnificent coronations of the most illustrious of kings'; *APC*, 1558–70, 42). Elizabeth was conscious of the service done her. When, in 1598, she wanted to flatter another bishop of Carlisle, she told him that she had been determined to appoint a worthy man to the see, for the sake of him who set the crown on her head (*VCH Cumberland*, 2.60).

Though he must have been aware of the confessional commitment of the new queen, Oglethorpe seems to have been content to be obedient. Faced with inevitable deprivation, like other Catholic bishops he behaved with dignity, regularly attending sessions of the Lords in March to

April 1559 and voting against the Uniformity Bill. He was assessed for a fine of £250 in May 1559, and deprived of Carlisle in June, losing also his *commendam* of Romaldkirk, which went to his eventual successor in August.

Uncertain of his future, and the validity of any plans made in a more favourable regime, Oglethorpe drew up his will on 10 November 1559, principally concerned to secure the foundation of a grammar school and almshouse at Tadcaster, Yorkshire. Several elements are of interest. The introductory formula claims, like any committed protestant, that he trusts to be saved by the merits of his saviour Jesus Christ. Numerous personal bequests, some very generous, are made; his friend Cuthbert Scott, the late bishop of Chester and one of the supervisors of the will, was to have a valuable cup and 'the ringe with thre diamonde on my finger'. Ample provision was made for the establishment and endowment of his school. What he hoped to be called Christ's Hospital, for twelve old people and as many scholars, is described in considerable architectural detail, with £500 allocated for its construction. Lands and tenements to the annual value of £40 were to be purchased for its upkeep, and a generous salary of 20 marks allotted to the schoolmaster. Even the quality of its intended occupants is specified. Numerous Oglethorpes were bound in the sum of £1000 to see the work completed (PRO, PROB 11/43, fols. 221–3). Tadcaster grammar school survived until 1968, and its successor preserved, at the close of the twentieth century, the proud memory of its founding bishop. A typical medieval prelate, conservative, primarily an academic, Oglethorpe died suddenly on 31 December 1559 after some months of virtual house arrest in London, and was buried on 6 January 1560 at St Dunstan-in-the-West. MARGARET CLARK

Sources Emden, *Oxf.*, 4.423–4 · *CSP dom.*, rev. edn, 1547–58 · H. Robinson, ed. and trans., *Original letters relative to the English Reformation*, 1 vol. in 2, Parker Society, [26] (1846–7) · *CPR, 1554–60* · PRO, PROB 11/43, fols. 221–3 · *VCH Cumberland*, vol. 2 · *The acts and monuments of John Foxe*, ed. S. R. Cattley, 8 vols. (1837–41), vol. 6 · W. P. Haugaard, 'The coronation of Elizabeth I', *Journal of Ecclesiastical History*, 19 (1968), 161–70 · C. M. L. Bouch, *Prelates and people of the lake counties: a history of the diocese of Carlisle, 1133–1933* (1948) · D. S. Chambers, ed., *Faculty office registers, 1534–1549* (1966) · Cumbria AS, Kendal, Fleming papers, WD/Ry/HMC no. 9 · *APC, 1558–70*

Wealth at death over £500 in cash; estates worth at least £40 p.a.: PRO, PROB 11/43, fols. 221–3

Oglethorpe, Sir Theophilus (1650–1702), army officer, was born at Oglethorpe Hall, Bramham, Yorkshire, and baptized on 14 September 1650 at Bramham, the son of Sutton Oglethorpe (*b.* 1612) and Frances, widow of Mark Pickering, daughter of John Matthew, and granddaughter of Tobie Matthew, archbishop of York. He came from an ancient Yorkshire family which had occupied the estate of Oglethorpe in the parish of Bramham since before the Norman conquest. His father was a royalist colonel during the first civil war, and governor of Beverston Castle, near Bristol, in 1644. For participation in the second civil war he was arrested in 1651 and fined £20,000, obliging the sale in 1653 of the heavily mortgaged Oglethorpe estate to

Henry Fairfax of Bolton Priory. Sutton Oglethorpe married in 1635. He and his wife had two sons; the elder, Sutton (1637–1727), a student at Gray's Inn in 1657 and MA (Oxon), 28 September 1663, became a page to Charles II, master of the royal stud, and in 1684 collector of the customs at Carlisle.

Theophilus Oglethorpe entered the military profession and trained in the French army from 1668, probably in Sir George Hamilton's English *gens d'armes*. He was a captain in Sir Henry Jones's regiment of light horse in the French army from 1672 until 1 February 1675, when he transferred into the duke of Monmouth's Royal English regiment, likewise in the service of Louis XIV. He returned to England in 1678 and was commissioned major of the Royal Dragoons on 19 February. On 10 July 1678 he was additionally appointed brigadier and lieutenant of the duke of York's troop of the life guard. Major Oglethorpe, at the head of his troop of the Royal Dragoons, led the van of Monmouth's small army against the Scottish covenanters at Crookham (14 September 1678) and Bothwell Bridge (22 June 1679). His modest exploits were rewarded by elevation, on 31 August, to guidon and major of the duke of York's troop of the life guard; and then to lieutenant and lieutenant-colonel on 1 November 1680, by which time he had relinquished his commission in the Royal Dragoons. In 1680 he married Eleanor Wall (1662–1732), daughter of Richard Wall of Rathkennan, co. Tipperary, a Roman Catholic and head laundress to Charles II, earning £2000 p.a. Eleanor, or Ellen, was a forceful, determined woman who had considerable political acumen, which she was to employ on behalf of the Jacobites.

Oglethorpe was a rake and a thug. He killed John Richardson in a duel in 1681 (he is known to have accepted at least two other challenges), was involved in the murder of Thomas Thynne by Count Königsmarck in 1681, and possibly involved with the Rye House plotters (1683). The best that can be said of his behaviour during the exclusion crisis was that he emerged finally on the winning side. Oglethorpe was returned as MP for Morpeth in 1685, probably on the interest of his friend Edward Howard, second earl of Carlisle, who had served as the cornet in Hamilton's *gens d'armes*. During Monmouth's rebellion in 1685 Oglethorpe commanded fifty troopers from the Life Guards to scout ahead of the earl of Feversham's royal army. Oglethorpe's men successfully charged the rebels at Keynsham, near Bristol, on 25 June 1685 and forced them to retire towards Phillips-Norton. However, during his night march to attack Feversham on Sedgemoor (4–5 July 1685) Monmouth slipped past Oglethorpe's carelessly positioned patrols. Nevertheless, Oglethorpe's men arrived on the battlefield in time to harass Monmouth's defeated army. Two days later he was promoted to full colonel and knighted for bringing news of the victory to James II. Further advancement, to colonel of the Holland regiment of foot (3rd foot, the Buffs), followed on 23 October. He also became a royal equerry, and in 1688 purchased the estate of Westbroke, near Godalming, Surrey. Promoted to brigadier-general on 11 November 1688, he brought news to James II in Salisbury of the military desertions to William of Orange at Warminster. Resisting blandishments to remain in the army, Oglethorpe was deprived of his commissions on 31 December 1688 and retired to Westbroke to dabble in Jacobite intrigue. First arrested and temporarily detained in 1689, a repetition in 1692 caused him to withdraw to France, where he remained until James II was prevailed upon to dismiss all protestants from St Germain-en-Laye. Disillusioned, he sailed to England and took the oaths to William III in 1698. Politically rehabilitated, he was returned as MP for Haslemere at the general elections in 1698 and February 1701. He died on 10 April 1702 and was buried at St James's, Piccadilly.

Oglethorpe and Eleanor had five sons and three daughters. Their eldest son, Lewis (1681–1704), succeeded his father as MP for Haslemere and also became a professional soldier. An equerry to Queen Anne, he was appointed aide-de-camp to Marlborough in April 1704 but was shot in the leg during the assault on the Schellenberg and died shortly afterwards. The second son, Theophilus (*bap.* 1684, *d. c.*1737), succeeded his brother as MP for Haslemere and became aide-de-camp to the duke of Ormond before retiring to the Jacobite court at St Germain-en-Laye. James, the third son, was born in 1689, while the fourth, Sutton, died aged seven weeks in 1693. General James Edward *Oglethorpe (1696–1785), founder of the colony of Georgia, was the fifth son. The eldest daughter, Anne (1683–1756), lived at St Germain-en-Laye and, allegedly, was the mistress of James III (James Francis Edward Stuart), the Pretender. Eleanor (1684–1775), the second daughter, was an active Jacobite. The third daughter, Louisa Mary, usually Molly (*b.* 1693), married the marquis de Bersompierre in 1733 before moving to the court of Spain.　　JOHN CHILDS

Sources G. Hampson, 'Oglethorpe, Theophilus', HoP, *Commons, 1660–90* · J. Childs, *The army of Charles II* (1976) · C. Dalton, ed., *English army lists and commission registers, 1661–1714*, 6 vols. (1892–1904) · A. A. Ettinger, *James Edward Oglethorpe* (1936) · *The manuscripts of his grace the duke of Buccleuch and Queensberry … preserved at Drumlanrig Castle*, 2 vols., HMC, 44 (1897–1903) · *CSP dom.*, 1685 · *Report on the manuscripts of Mrs Stopford-Sackville*, 2 vols., HMC, 49 (1904–10) · P. R. Newman, *Royalist officers in England and Wales, 1642–1660: a biographical dictionary* (1981) · J. Washbourn, ed., *Bibliotheca Gloucestrensis*, 2 vols. (privately printed, Gloucester, 1823–5) · DNB

O'Gorman, Marianus. *See* Ua Gormáin, Máel Muire (*d.* 1181?).

O'Gorman, Mervyn Joseph Pius (1871–1958), electrical and aircraft engineer, was born in Ireland on 19 December 1871, the son of Edmund A. O'Gorman of Harrogate, Yorkshire. After attending Downside School he read classics and science at University College, Dublin, before proceeding, in 1891, to the City and Guilds Central Institution, London, to study electrical engineering. In February 1893 he was put up by W. E. Ayrton as a student member of the Institution of Electrical Engineers (IEE). Having obtained the City and Guilds diploma in 1894, as the IEE was to learn, 'amongst the first in his year', he was appointed assistant engineer at the Fowler, Waring Cables Company, which supplied the telegraph, telephone, and power

industries. He was at once sent abroad to take charge of the company's cable network in Ostend and then to superintend long-distance telephone cabling from Grenoble, as well as to conduct other company business across the channel. In England he assisted with the laying of 3000 volt systems in Salford, Leicester, and Taunton and took part in high tension experiments to test celluloid as an insulator. Rewarded for all this industry and enterprise by appointment as chief engineer, he reorganized the layout of the company's factory near London before, in 1895, being sent to start a cable factory in Paris and to superintend it for a year before the French Poste took it over. He then, aged twenty-five, became Fowler Waring's general manager. In 1897 he married Florence Catherine, younger daughter of Arthur Rasch. The following year, when Fowler Waring became part of Western Electric, O'Gorman, together with E. H. Cozens-Hardy, started an engineering consultancy at 66 Victoria Street, London; they were guaranteed consultancy work from his former employers and retained for two years by W. T. Glover to advise on paper insulation in telephone cables, and so had an assured send-off.

Silvanus P. Thompson had recommended O'Gorman's associate membership of the IEE in March 1895 and J. W. Swan was one of his sponsors when he was recommended for membership in December 1898. In 1901 he presented a complex 75-page paper to the institution on insulation of cables, which one of the audience described as 'very difficult and heavy to digest'; but he remained well liked and served on the IEE council from 1906 to 1909. By 1906 he had also worked his way up from associate (1903) to member of the Institution of Mechanical Engineers, an added distinction for the consultancy of O'Gorman and Cozens-Hardy. The partnership was brought to an end, however, in October 1908 when Cozens-Hardy left London for St Helens to take his brother-in-law's place on the board of Pilkingtons, Britain's leading glass business.

The aeroplane was then about to become an effective military machine. R. B. Haldane, secretary of state for war, keen to see it developed for military purposes, saw in O'Gorman the person who would bring the necessary scientific rigour, management discipline, and enthusiasm to achieve this end. He was appointed superintendent of the government's balloon factory at Farnborough, reporting direct to the master-general of the ordnance at the War Office in order to overcome opposition from the military traditionalists. O'Gorman brought new life to what was to become known as the Army Aircraft Establishment and, later still, the Royal Aircraft Establishment. He appointed P. M. Green chief engineer; he in turn recruited Geoffrey De Havilland who had recently produced an aeroplane of his own design, bought by Farnborough for £400.

O'Gorman was an advocate of flying from the outset and served on the committee which led to the creation of the Royal Flying Corps in May 1912. In that year he was also signatory to a report on European aeronautics. In 1913 he was appointed CB. By the outbreak of war four squadrons were ready to fly to a base in Amiens, most of them designed, if not built, at Farnborough. Demand grew incessantly and O'Gorman was able to expand his team with graduate engineers such as B. M. Jones and scientists such as Frederick Lindemann. Large-scale losses of a particular type of plane designed there, however, led to a judicial inquiry and, in 1916, to O'Gorman's departure, which Percy Walker, in *Early Aviation at Farnborough*, went so far as to describe as 'political chicanery'. However, there was no question of O'Gorman's leaving in disgrace. As lieutenant-colonel in the Royal Flying Corps, he remained, from 1916 to 1919, consulting engineer to the director-general of military aeronautics.

Although Colonel O'Gorman, as he liked to be known for the rest of his life, served as chairman of the Royal Aeronautical Society in 1921–2, he never again returned to active management in the industry. His links were sedentary, as, for instance, chairman of the accident investigation and civil air transport committee of the Air Ministry and, in 1931, chairman of the League of Nations subcommittee on the rating of aeronautical engines. From the 1920s his main concern was road transport and road safety. He had written *O'Gorman's Motoring Pocket Book* (1904, 1907) and had added the Institution of Civil Engineers in 1916 to his bag of prestigious memberships, and took part in the discussions when road transport matters were being examined. He was actively involved in the Royal Automobile Club, becoming its vice-chairman, 1928–31, and its vice-president in 1952.

In 1926 O'Gorman's curiosity was aroused by the rate of traffic flow on the Portsmouth Road. He wrote an article for *The Times* in the following year, sending the technical algebra of his calculations to the ministry. In the 1930s he went to Germany to see the first stretches of the autobahns, paying particular attention to their access roads. He took the view in 1943, rather confusingly (he was getting old), that, while railways remained the backbone of Britain's transport system, roads provided 'the circulation of its lifeblood'. More sharply focused perhaps was his conclusion that 'general impressions on traffic are commonly proved wrong when the facts are examined'. He urged the more careful, precise use of terms: 'traffic safety', for instance, not 'road safety', because roads would be quite safe without traffic. A most versatile engineer, very active physically in his earlier years, he is also remembered for his skill as an artist, for his lacquer work, and for his ability to inspire loyalty in others. O'Gorman died at his home, 21 Embankment Gardens, Chelsea, on 16 March 1958, having bequeathed £2000 to his first centre of support, the Institution of Electrical Engineers.

THEO BARKER

Sources P. B. Walker, *Early aviation at Farnborough: the history of the Royal Aircraft Establishment*, 2 vols. (1971–4) · D. Edgerton, *England and the aeroplane: an essay on a militant and technological nation* (1991) · d. cert. · T. C. Barker, *Pilkington Brothers and the glass industry* (1960) · *WW* · C. F. Atkinson, 'Flying Corps', *Encyclopaedia Britannica*, 12th edn (1922) · *The Times* (17 March 1958) · *The Times* (10 April 1958) · *Chartered Mechanical Engineer*, 5 (1958), 503 · *The Times* (19–28 March 1958)

Archives Inst. EE

Wealth at death £163,224 14s.: probate, 12 May 1958, *CGPLA Eng. & Wales*

O'Gorman, Thomas [*known as* Chevalier O'Gorman] (1732–1809), army officer in the French service and antiquary, was born on 16 September 1732 at Castletown, co. Clare, Ireland, the son of Matthew O'Gorman or MacGorman (1705–1740) and Margaret O'Loughlin, daughter of Donogh O'Loughlin of Castletown and his wife, Coelia. The family, although dispossessed of its property, belonged to the Irish Catholic gentry and was sufficiently well connected for Charles O'Brien, sixth Viscount Clare, commander of one of the Hiberno-French regiments, to assist O'Gorman's entry about 1750 to the Irish College in Paris, where he attended the university medical school and in due course qualified as a physician. He was commissioned into the army. Little is known of his military career, but he served in the Franco-Irish regiment of Rothe, later Walsh. He achieved the rank of captain and was made a chevalier of the military order of St Louis.

In appearance O'Gorman was strikingly handsome and immensely tall, exceeding 6 feet 5 inches in height. In 1757 he married Marguerite Françoise Victoire D'Éon de Beaumont (1724–1788), daughter of the deceased Louis D'Éon de Beaumont (*d*. 1749) of Tonnerre, a member of the lesser Burgundian nobility who had held several public offices, and his wife, Françoise de Charenton. O'Gorman and his wife had three sons, all of whom served in the French army or navy. His brother-in-law was the Chevalier D'Éon de Beaumont (1728–1810), the celebrated transvestite French diplomat. In 1763 D'Éon reacted sharply to an attempt by O'Gorman to interfere in his affairs and spurned his advice. However, in 1776, in London, O'Gorman offered to fight a duel on D'Éon's behalf. D'Éon, in his will, claimed that he was owed 60,000 livres by O'Gorman, which he bequeathed to O'Gorman's sons.

Marguerite O'Gorman's dowry was a valuable winegrowing property in Burgundy, from which O'Gorman profited sufficiently to become a figure at court and maintain a costly establishment at Paris, where he moved in the best society. He was generous to his relatives and to Irish students in Paris. He was a native speaker of Irish and developed an interest in Irish antiquarian lore, especially genealogy. His wine business brought him regularly to Ireland, where his customers included noblemen such as the earl of Inchiquin. He took advantage of these visits to collect and copy manuscripts and to transcribe tombstone inscriptions, especially in co. Clare, co. Limerick, and co. Tipperary. O'Gorman came to be regarded as a 'perfect master of all matters relating to Irish pedigrees', and his work won acceptance from the authorities in France and Spain, where there was a ready market for Irish genealogical material among expatriates (Hayes, 'A forgotten Irish antiquary', 593–4). Genealogy handsomely supplemented his income: he charged up to £1000 for the preparation of a pedigree. His clients included such notable figures as Lord Clare and later his widow, and his fellow countrymen who fought in foreign service, General Count Alexander O'Reilly, General Daniel O'Connell, and others. There is no doubt that he did much useful work in this area, and the bulk of the extensive O'Gorman manuscripts in the Royal Irish Academy and the National Library of Ireland consists of genealogical correspondence, transcriptions, and notes.

In 1772 O'Gorman was present at a meeting of the antiquarian committee of the Dublin Society, at which he was commissioned to request a copy of the Book of Lecan from the superiors of the Irish College in Paris and their assistance in an enquiry into the antiquities of Ireland. The result was the establishment of a similar committee in Paris. Both bodies ceased to exist after a short time, but the contacts established may have helped lay the ground for the presentation of the Book of Lecan to the Royal Irish Academy in 1787. O'Gorman has been credited with securing the donation, but in fact he played no role in the final negotiations. He did, however, acquire the Book of Ballymote in Ireland, which in 1785 he presented to the Royal Irish Academy, of which he was made an honorary member. In 1787 he unsuccessfully sought the position of consul-general of France in Dublin.

An ardent royalist, O'Gorman was ruined financially by the French Revolution, which led to the confiscation of his estate in Burgundy and ended the market for his genealogical research. His wife, from whom he was estranged for many years, died in 1788, and in 1792 he married in Dublin, Mary Cuffe (*née* Ryan), the widow of Denny Baker Cuffe of Cuffesboro' in Queen's county. He took up permanent residence in Ireland from 1793. His sons also left France and entered the English service, two of them securing commissions in the 18th Royal Irish regiment. O'Gorman was soon heavily in debt and suffered harassment from his importunate creditors. To his embarrassment he was obliged to turn to friends and relations for support, and he wrote pitiful letters to various public figures for financial assistance to relieve his distress. To add to his troubles, the Irish government regarded him as a security risk, and he was temporarily imprisoned in the panic that followed the French expedition to Bantry Bay in 1796. Despite his misfortunes, he continued to pursue his antiquarian interests and retained his zeal for the discovery and presentation of manuscripts in the Irish language. Towards the end of his life he retired to his native co. Clare, settling at Drumellihy, near his childhood home, where he died on 18 November 1809. He was buried in the neighbouring churchyard of Kilmacduane.

HARMAN MURTAGH

Sources R. Hayes, 'A forgotten Irish antiquary: Chevalier Thomas O'Gorman, 1732–1809', *Studies: an Irish Quarterly Review*, 30 (1941), 587–96 · R. Hayes, *Biographical dictionary of Irishmen in France* (1949), 231–2 · E. MacLysaght, 'O'Gorman papers', *Analecta Hibernica*, 15 (1944), 382–4 · R. J. Hayes, ed., *Manuscript sources for the history of Irish civilisation*, 11 vols. (1965) · J. B. Telfer, *The strange career of the Chevalier D'Éon de Beaumont, minister plenipotentiary from France to Great Britain in 1763* (1885) · E. A. Vizetelly, *The true story of the Chevalier D'Éon* (1895) · *Journal of the North Munster Archaeological Society*, 4 (1919), 211 · 'Caithréim Thoirdhealbhaigh, and miscellaneous other items', Royal Irish Acad., MS 23.F.14 · S. O'Cassaide, 'Chevalier O'Gorman', *Irish Booklover*, 22 (1934), 66–7 · R. Atkinson, introduction, *The book of Ballymote: a collection of pieces (prose and verse) in the Irish language*, facs. edn (1887), 2 · Marquis MacSwiney of Mashanaglass, 'Notes on the history of the Book of Lecan', *Proceedings of the Royal Irish Academy*, 38C (1928–9), 31–50, esp. 49

Archives JRL, MSS · NL Ire., MSS · Royal Irish Acad., MSS

O'Grady, Sir James (1866–1934), trade unionist and politician, was born on 6 May 1866 in Bristol, the son of John O'Grady, a labourer, and his wife, Margaret. After an elementary education at St Mary's Roman Catholic School, he began work at the age of ten in a mineral water factory, the first of a series of menial occupations which ended when, at the age of fifteen, he obtained an apprenticeship in a cabinet-maker's workshop. Although this led to O'Grady's joining the ranks of the skilled workers, in his early twenties he had to travel around the country to find work, returning to Bristol after three years. In 1887 he nevertheless married Louisa James (*d.* 1929); they had two sons and seven daughters.

In Bristol, O'Grady was caught up in the twin movements of socialism and trade unionism, and he soon became known there as a vigorous speaker and effective organizer. For two years he sat on the city council. His reputation soon extended beyond his own union, the cabinet-makers', and in 1898 when the Trades Union Congress gathered in Bristol for its annual meeting he occupied the presidential chair. In an address that concluded with a quotation from 'The Day is Coming' by William Morris, he put the case for the trade unions' own political organization, independent of existing parties, and for a stronger industrial federation. Soon after he moved to London to become his union's full-time organizer. He was delegated to attend the 1903 conference of the Labour Representation Committee (LRC) and, in the following year, with the union's promise of financial support, became LRC candidate for Leeds East; numerous Irish voters there were expected to support him in a constituency covered by the electoral pact negotiated by Herbert Gladstone and Ramsay MacDonald. In the general election of 1906 he defeated the sitting Unionist in a straight fight. O'Grady represented Leeds East from 1906 to 1918, and was then MP for Leeds South East from 1918 to 1924.

At Westminster, O'Grady's membership of the Independent Labour Party (as well as his earlier association with the Social Democratic Federation) placed him on Labour's socialist wing. He was one of the few Labour MPs to have read the writings of Marx and Engels, though O'Grady told W. T. Stead that it was in the work of Thomas Carlyle that he found his solace and inspiration. As Labour's only Roman Catholic MP, in a party with a large nonconformist presence, he was also untypical. He frequently spoke in a range of debates, including those on foreign affairs. In common with several other Labour MPs he combined parliamentary duties with those of trade union officialdom. He remained the national organizer of the furnishing trades' association until 1912, and was active in the General Federation of Trade Unions, the management committee of which he chaired from 1912 to 1918. In this latter year he was appointed secretary of the newly formed National Federation of General Workers.

Sir James O'Grady (1866–1934), by Arthur Simpson, in or before 1910

In 1914 O'Grady supported the declaration of war and subsequently did much to promote the war efforts of the government. He visited the front in 1915 and went to Russia in April 1917 as a member of a Labour delegation that encouraged the Kerensky government to continue the war; as captain on the general list from 1918, he spoke on recruiting platforms, including those in Ireland, to where conscription was not extended. Though a vice-president of the ultra-patriotic British Workers' League he did not go the way of such figures as George Barnes and G. H. Roberts who had moved out of the Labour Party by the time of the general election of December 1918. His constituency was by then, because of redistribution, Leeds South East; his pro-war activities were rewarded when he was returned unopposed.

On the formation of the first Labour government in January 1924 there was some speculation that O'Grady might be sent to Moscow as British ambassador. He had maintained his wartime interest in Russia, notably by representing the British government in Copenhagen in November 1919 to negotiate an exchange of prisoners of war with Litvinoff, by campaigning for the end of military attempts to oust the Bolshevik regime, and by assisting in famine relief in 1921–2 as a representative of the International Federation of Trade Unions. However, he was instead made a KCMG and posted, in October 1924, to Tasmania as governor, for a tour of duty that was to last six years. In 1931 he was appointed as governor and commander-in-chief of the Falkland Islands. This posting was curtailed after about two years when he fell ill with blood poisoning and returned to England for treatment.

His health continued to be poor and he died in a London nursing home at 2 Nightingale Lane, Clapham Common, on 10 December 1934.   D. E. MARTIN

Sources *The Times* (11 Dec 1934) · H. A. Clegg, A. Fox, and A. F. Thompson, *A history of British trade unions since 1889*, 1 (1964) · K. D. Brown, ed., *The first labour party, 1906–1914* (1985) · A. Prochaska, *History of the General Federation of Trade Unions, 1899–1980* (1982) · W. T. Stead, 'The labour party and the books that helped to make it', *Review of Reviews*, 33 (1906), 568–82 · S. V. Bracher, *The Herald book of labour members* (1923) · S. R. Graubard, *British labour and the Russian revolution, 1917–1924* (1956) · WWBMP · d. cert.

Likenesses A. Simpson, photograph, in or before 1910, PRO [*see illus.*] · photographs, repro. in *Reformers' Year Book* (1907) · photographs, repro. in Bracher, *Herald book of labour members*

Wealth at death £9228 10s. 3d.: probate, 4 March 1935, CGPLA Eng. & Wales

O'Grady, Standish, first Viscount Guillamore (1766–1840), judge, was born in Limerick on 20 January 1766, the eldest son of Darby O'Grady (*d.* 1804), high sheriff, of Mount Prospect, Limerick, and his wife, Mary (*d.* 1809), daughter of James Smyth, also of co. Limerick. He matriculated at Trinity College, Dublin, on 8 November 1780, and graduated BA in 1784. He was admitted as a student at Middle Temple, London, on 19 April 1783, and at King's Inns, Dublin, was in 1787 called to the bar, and joined the Munster circuit. He quickly attained a considerable practice. In 1790 he married Katharine Waller (*d.* 1853), with whom he had seven sons and five daughters. On 28 May 1803, after the murder of Lord Kilwarden, O'Grady became attorney-general, and he was one of the prosecuting counsel at the trial of Robert Emmet. In 1805 he was made lord chief baron, in succession to Barry Yelverton, Lord Avonmore. He was considered to be a sound judge by his contemporaries, and David Richard Pigot, chief baron of the Irish exchequer, called him 'the ablest man whose mind I ever saw at work'. He was renowned for his wit and praised for his advocacy and knowledge of procedure. On his retirement from the bench in 1831 he was created Viscount Guillamore of Cahir and Baron O'Grady of Rockbarton, co. Limerick (28 January 1831). A paralytic stroke in the same year affected his speech and the movement of his hands. He then retired from his house in Baggot Street, Dublin, to his seat at Rockbarton, co. Limerick, and over the next nine years his health steadily declined. He died at Rockbarton on 21 April 1840 and was buried at Aney, co. Limerick.

His eldest son, **Standish O'Grady**, second Viscount Guillamore (1792–1848), army officer, was born on 26 December 1792. He was educated at Westminster School and at Trinity College, Dublin, where he matriculated on 4 July 1809. He did not take a degree but entered the army, in March 1811; he became lieutenant in 1812, captain in 1815, major in 1825, lieutenant-colonel in 1829, and colonel in 1842. It was as lieutenant that he served in the 7th hussars at the battle of Waterloo, where his skills as a commander gained him respect. He led his regiment in a charge against the French: the charge was successful, though many losses were suffered, and he was made captain. On 16 October 1828 he married the Hon. Gertrude Jane Paget (1805–1871), the eldest daughter of the Hon. Berkeley

Paget. They had several children, including Standish, third viscount (1832–1860); Paget Standish, fourth viscount (1838–1877); Hardress Standish, fifth viscount (1841–1918); and Frederick Standish, sixth viscount (1847–1927). The second viscount died at Rockbarton, co. Limerick, on 22 July 1848 and was buried at Aney, nearby. Some of his letters were published in *Waterloo Letters* (1891), edited by H. T. Siborne.   D. J. O'DONOGHUE, rev. SINÉAD AGNEW

Sources L. G. Pine, *The new extinct peerage, 1884–1971: containing extinct, abeyant, dormant, and suspended peerages with genealogies and arms* (1972), 139 · F. E. Ball, *The judges in Ireland, 1221–1921*, 2 (1926), 233, 244, 255–6, 260, 265, 271, 298–9, 336 · J. Wills and F. Wills, *The Irish nation: its history and its biography*, 3 (1875), 691–3 · Burtchaell & Sadleir, *Alum. Dubl.* · J. S. Crone, *A concise dictionary of Irish biography*, rev. edn (1937), 187 · J. R. O'Flanagan, *The Irish bar*, 2nd edn (1879), 190–94 · J. Foster, *The peerage, baronetage, and knightage of the British empire for 1882*, 1 [1882], 318 · J. R. O'Flanagan, *The Munster circuit: tales, trials and traditions* (1880), 232–7 · C. J. Smyth, *Chronicle of the law officers of Ireland* (1839), 145, 170 · J. Hutchinson, ed., *A catalogue of notable Middle Templars: with brief biographical notices* (1902), 178 · J. Barrington, *Personal sketches of his own times*, rev. T. Young, 3rd edn, 1 (1869), 269 · C. M. O'Keeffe, *Life and times of Daniel O'Connell, with sketches of some of his contemporaries* (1864), 183 · D. O. Madden, *Ireland and its rulers since 1829*, 3 vols. (1843), 1.126 · H. T. Siborne, ed., *Waterloo letters* (1891), 130–36

Archives BL, letters to third Lord Hardwicke, reports, and opinions, etc., Add. MSS 35742–35763

Likenesses group portrait, etching with watercolour, pubd 1811 (*A view of the Four Courts, Dublin*), NG Ire.

Wealth at death left £10,000 p.a. to eldest son for life; £400 p.a. to younger sons; £1000 p.a. to widow; also several legacies: O'Flanagan, *Munster circuit*, 236–7

O'Grady, Standish, second Viscount Guillamore (1792–1848). *See under* O'Grady, Standish, first Viscount Guillamore (1766–1840).

O'Grady, Standish James (1846–1928), journalist and historian, was born at Castletown, Berehaven, co. Cork, on 13 September 1846, the son of Thomas O'Grady, a Church of Ireland clergyman and small landowner, and Susanna Doe, who inherited property in her own right. He was one of a family of eleven children, and he was brought up in an atmosphere of evangelical piety and classical culture. He was educated at Tipperary grammar school, and entered Trinity College, Dublin, in 1864; he graduated in 1868. He won a classical scholarship and the university silver medal in ethics and psychology, and the philosophical society's medal for essay writing; he was also a noted sportsman. He was intended for the church, and studied for his vocation for two years, but then chose the law instead. He was called to the bar in 1872 and went on the Munster circuit.

It was now that O'Grady began to write, for the Conservative *Dublin Daily Express* (which connection he maintained until 1898) and the *Gentleman's Magazine* (1873–5). In 1875 he published his first book, *Scintilla Shelleiana*, under the pseudonym Arthur Clive, investigating Shelley's attitude towards religion. But his career as an influential writer began on a wet day in the west of Ireland, when, in his own words, he was twenty-four years of age (in fact, he was almost certainly twenty-seven or twenty-eight). He described in 1899 how, because of the 'stupid educational

Standish James O'Grady (1846–1928), by John Butler Yeats, 1904

system of the country', he knew nothing of Irish history and legend. But in a country house on a rainy day he browsed in the library and chanced upon Sylvester O'Halloran's *History of Ireland* (1774), 'the finest history of Ireland into which I have ever looked'. He asked himself how it was that 'all this interesting history of my own country' was 'never brought before my notice by any one' (Boyd, 3). This chance encounter sent him to the Royal Irish Academy, where he read similar works; and his reading of the Cú Chulainn epic inspired him to write, and publish at his own expense in 1878 and 1880, his *History of Ireland: Heroic Period*.

This work was, as O'Grady himself confessed, one of imagination. He knew no Irish, and did not try to learn it until 1899, and then with little success. He misspelt the name of his hero (using the form 'Cu Culain') and never bothered correcting his mistake; as late as 1933 this misspelling was repeated on the English title-page of a translation of *The Coming of Cuculain*, published by the Gaelic League. But the importance of the *History* lay in its impact upon leading figures of the Irish literary revival, including W. B. Yeats, T. W. Rolleston, and George Russell (AE). O'Grady's belief that Ireland had a continuous 'race history', and that this was centred in the imagination, the 'legends' which nations 'make for themselves ... that dim twilight region, where day meets night' (Brown, 525), appealed to Yeats, who included no fewer than six of O'Grady's books in a list of the 'thirty best Irish books' in 1895. Yeats declared that it was after reading O'Grady that 'I turned my back on foreign themes, decided that the race was more important than the individual, and began my "Wanderings of Oisin"' (*Collected Letters*, 502).

O'Grady was torn between his imaginative history and a more scientific approach to writing about the past. In 1881 he published his *History of Ireland: Critical and Philosophical*, which was an attempt to write a more 'scientific' history in a plain style. But he continued to defend his view that, while 'imagination' was the cause of many errors, yet 'nine tenths' of the errors of history arose from its being generally written by men 'destitute of imagination' and thus tied to 'conventional opinions'. O'Grady now developed an interest in Tudor Ireland, and published various works, including *Red Hugh's Captivity* (1889) and *The Bog of Stars* (1893), which was the second volume in the New Irish Library, a venture launched by Yeats and Sir Charles Gavan Duffy. But O'Grady's writings were inseparable from his political ideas, which he expounded in his *The Crisis in Ireland* (1882). O'Grady was a Conservative in politics, and he acted as honorary secretary to a landlords' meeting in Dublin in December 1881, when the landlords were embroiled in their conflict with the Land League and the followers of Charles Stewart Parnell.

O'Grady saw the landlords as essential to the welfare and stability of Ireland. In Tudor times the Anglo-Irish lords had looked to the crown 'as the lawful centre of order and authority and the fountain of honour'. Chieftains remained 'virtually kings, each man governing his own people'. Now he called on the landlords to reassert their authority, and control the 'wild, tameless democracy', 'tameless but tameable', 'in its heart desiring to be tamed'. He feared the consequences if the 'lowest and most dependent class' became sovereign, for it would produce leaders as 'the boiler sends up scum' (Boyd, 165–8). O'Grady drew lessons from Lord Randolph Churchill's brand of tory democracy, and in 1886 in his *Toryism and the Tory Democracy* he set out the principles which he maintained throughout his life: the landlords of Ireland must give a firm lead, rally their tenants, and reverse their decline into degradation. Landlords must stay on their estates, hire labour, and build up loyal retainers who would both love and fear their masters.

This feudal relationship was the only hope for the landlord class. O'Grady saw the opportunity for this class to revive its fortunes in the controversy over the report of the Childers commission which, in 1894, admitted that Ireland had been overtaxed to the sum of £250 million. This united nationalists and unionists in a common condemnation of the great abuse, and O'Grady, in his *All Ireland* (1898), urged the setting up of an Irish convention in Dublin, comprising all Irish opinions, and especially the Ulster protestants, which would convey legislative proposals to the Irish MPs in Westminster. This convention would be led by the landlords, now back in their rightful place. When nothing came of this scheme, O'Grady left Dublin and devoted his energies to the purchase and editing of a provincial Irish newspaper, the Kilkenny *Weekly Moderator*, a decision which was less eccentric than it seemed, for it was O'Grady's intention to spread his gospel

in rural Ireland, and his Christmas number for 1898 contained contributions from Yeats, George Russell, Lady Gregory, and T. W. Rolleston. A series of libel suits cost him his newspaper but, indefatigable as ever, in 1900 he founded the *All Ireland Review*, which the nationalist MP William O'Brien described as a 'one man show', but which had a circle of subscribers ranging from landlords like Lord Dufferin to the Fenian John O'Leary.

This publishing venture was typical of the intellectual mood in Ireland in the early years of the new century, when Irish people of various political persuasions were exploring the possibility of reconciliation between nationalist and unionist. But O'Grady's mood was by now deeply altered. In 'The great enchantment', a series of editorials in the *All Ireland Review*, he contemplated the inevitable fall of the landlord class. He linked this to his studies of the heroic period: in time of crisis, a mental and spiritual debility fell over Ireland, the consequence, apparently, of some past guilt. And now the Irish gentry were 'rotting from the land in the most dismal farce-tragedy of all time, without one brave deed, without one brave word' (Boyd, 180). He ceased editing the *All Ireland Review* when his health broke down in 1906.

O'Grady's political stock was not yet exhausted. Now he developed his political thought to encompass a concern for the poor and unemployed. In the *All Ireland Review* he wrote about the problems of the urban poor and the badly paid clerks who worked in Dublin. In the *Irish Review* (April 1912) he urged the 'governing classes' to set themselves to the task of 'getting our unemployed, under-fed multitudes out from these seething centres of want and discontent, out into the sane and wholesome country, and there setting them, in the first instance, to the cultivation of the good earth'. He wrote for A. R. Orage's *New Age*, advocating the construction of little labour colonies, but there was an echo of his earlier beliefs in his assertion that these should be headed by enlightened aristocrats.

By now O'Grady's journalistic and historical career was all but over. He was awarded a civil-list pension, which helped his financial position. O'Grady enjoyed a tranquil family life. He had married Margaret, the daughter of the Revd William Fisher, and they had three sons. In 1918 he left Ireland for health reasons, settling first in France, then in the south of England, and then in Northamptonshire, where his eldest son was vicar. He lived here for some years until his son was moved on, and then went to live on the Isle of Wight. He died outside the Home of Rest at Lake on the Isle of Wight, on 18 May 1928.

O'Grady had a Cork accent, and was of medium height; his portrait, by John B. Yeats, reveals a more introspective person than his bubbling enthusiasm would suggest. His works were not widely read in his day, but his role in inspiring the Irish literary revival is secure. Although he wrote about pagan Ireland, his rather apocalyptic vision was inspired by his deeply rooted evangelical protestant background, and he combined this with a scepticism and a great anxiety about the future of Ireland, and of England too, under the coming rule of the 'mob-men'. His creation of his hero Cú Chulainn as the figure embodying the truly

Irish spirit certainly inspired the 1916 conservative revolutionary Patrick Pearse, and it is not inappropriate that Yeats included O'Grady as one of his 'beautiful lofty things', recollecting O'Grady's drunken speech at a public dinner prophesying an uprising. He has been described as an Irish Carlyle, but he lacked the intellectual powers and cutting edge of Carlyle. Lady Gregory dubbed him a 'Fenian Unionist', which is acceptable provided it is acknowledged that his Fenianism consisted in a strong Irish patriotism, and a desire to defend Irish gentry rights even against England, rather than any inclination towards separatism. O'Grady defended the union; but his writings gained him the admiration of nationalists such as P. S. O'Hegarty (a member of Sinn Féin) and Daniel Corkery (who held the Anglo-Irish literary revivalists in contempt). It can be said of O'Grady (unlike most prominent Irishmen in his troubled times) that he had no enemies.

D. GEORGE BOYCE

Sources H. A. O'Grady, *Standish O'Grady* (1929) • P. L. Marcus, *Standish O'Grady* (1970) • E. Boyd, *Standish O'Grady: selected essays and passages* [1918] • V. Mercier, *Modern Irish literature: sources and founders* (1994) • *The collected letters of W. B. Yeats*, 1, ed. J. Kelly and E. Domville (1986) • T. Brown, ed., 'Cultural nationalism, 1880–1930', *The Field Day anthology of Irish writing*, ed. S. Deane, A. Carpenter, and J. Williams, 2 (1991), 516–26 • A. Clarke, 'Standish James O'Grady', *Dublin Magazine*, 68 (1947), 36–40 • d. cert.
Archives NL Ire., corresp. and literary papers
Likenesses J. B. Yeats, oils, 1904, NG Ire. [*see illus.*]

Ogston, Sir Alexander (1844–1929), surgeon and bacteriologist, was born at Ogston's Court, 84 Broad Street, Aberdeen, on 19 April 1844, the elder son of Francis *Ogston (*bap.* 1803, *d.* 1887), physician, and his wife, Amelia Cadenhead (*d.* 1852). After attending Archibald Storrie's school and the public school, Aberdeen, Ogston attended Marischal College, Aberdeen (1859–65), where he graduated MB CM in 1865 and MD in 1866. During the winter of 1863–4 he took the winter course at the University of Vienna; he then attended the summer session in Berlin, which was followed finally by two months in Paris. He became fluent in French and German and made friends with a number of continental physicians. After qualifying Ogston made another European visit before returning to Aberdeen, where he entered general practice. Between 1865 and 1873 Ogston was assistant to his father, who by this time was professor of medical jurisprudence at Aberdeen University. On 25 September 1867 Ogston married Mary Jane, daughter of James Hargrave of Stoke Newington, London; they had two sons and two daughters; following her death, he married on 1 August 1877 Isabella Margaret (*b.* 1847/8), daughter of James Matthews, architect; they had four sons and four daughters.

From 1868 to 1872 Ogston was joint medical officer of health for Aberdeen, and in 1872 he was given charge of the city's smallpox isolation hospital. After being appointed ophthalmic surgeon to Aberdeen Royal Infirmary in 1868 he became junior surgeon (1870) and acting surgeon (1874); he was senior surgeon from 1880 until his resignation in 1898, when he became consulting surgeon. At Aberdeen University he was lecturer in practical ophthalmology (1869) and examiner in medicine (1873–6). Following the retirement of Professor William Pirrie in 1882 Ogston became regius professor of surgery, a post he was to hold for twenty-seven years.

An early convert to Lister's methods, in 1880–81 Ogston, using a technique devised by H. H. R. Koch, examined for bacteria in more than 100 abscesses. After obtaining samples of pus from some ninety of his patients and examining them microscopically and by staining he concluded that of two main types of cell frequently present in cultures, one always accompanies suppuration and is normally absent in 'cold' cultures. A comprehensive study over two years confirmed that the properties of the *Staphylococcus* isolated from or tested in cultures of a variety of small mammals were independent of species, justifying the conclusion that *Staphylococcus* is a specific organism. After Ogston's death William Bulloch acknowledged 'his pioneer bacteriological work on inflammation and suppuration', and noted that 'It is not generally recognized that many of the current doctrines of infection and metastatic generalisation of bacteria really emanated from him' (*The Lancet*, 309).

A tall, commanding figure, Ogston was a slow, deliberate lecturer who never used an unnecessary word or repeated himself. He particularly enjoyed making sly digs at those he considered as being 'armchair theorists'. As a surgeon Ogston was a meticulous planner who clung to the use of the antiseptic spray 'so that before the operation was far advanced the well of the theatre was shrouded in a mist' (*BMJ*, 326). Early in his career Ogston had been interested in bone surgery and the operation he devised for genu valgum was practised widely until it was replaced by William Macewen's method. Ogston published widely in medical journals between 1868 and 1902.

Ogston also took a keen interest in military surgery. In 1885 he set out for Egypt to take part in the war of 1884–5. After service on the hospital ship *Ganges* he joined the first bearer company and worked with the wounded at Hasheen and Suakin. He was awarded the Egyptian campaign medal and the khedive's bronze star. After his return home Ogston in 1887 took advantage of being vice-president of the surgical section of the British Medical Association to deliver a thorough criticism of the conditions faced in Egypt by the British forces, especially the deficiencies in medical care. His criticisms so offended some sections of the medical establishment that he was not allowed access to the theatre of war in South Africa in 1899–1900, forcing him to appeal directly to Queen Victoria to intercede on his behalf. During his seven months in South Africa, Ogston was cold-shouldered by some of the medical authorities but was well treated by the military. However, his recommendations made after the Egyptian campaign were yet to have any significant effects.

On his return Ogston was appointed a member of the committee to consider the future organization of the army medical corps. During the First World War he acted as operating surgeon to the Southall Auxiliary Military Hospital, during the winter of 1914–15, before being given charge of a hospital detachment at Belgrade. In 1916 he became operating surgeon to the first British ambulance unit in Italy and worked with the second Italian army. He was awarded the Cavalier order of the Crown of Italy in 1920. His *Reminiscences of Three Campaigns* was published in 1919.

Ogston was appointed surgeon-in-ordinary in Scotland to Queen Victoria, Edward VII, and George V. He was created LLD by Glasgow University (1901) and Aberdeen University (1910), and became KCVO in 1912. Ogston died at his home, 252 Union Street, Aberdeen, in the early hours of 1 February 1929. He was survived by two sons and five daughters.   ALEXANDER G. OGSTON

Sources W. H. Ogston, ed., *Alexander Ogston, KCVO* (1943) · A. Ogston, *Reminiscences of three campaigns* [1919] · A. Macdonald and G. Smith, eds., *The staphylococci: the Alexander Ogston centennial conference* [Aberdeen 1980] (1981) · P. F. Jones, 'Two nineteenth-century surgeons', *BMJ* (19–26 Dec 1992), 1546–8 · P. F. Jones, 'Visiting Lister and his Scottish friends', *Journal of Medical Biography*, 4 (1996), 36–44 · *BMJ* (16 Feb 1929), 325–7 · *The Lancet* (9 Feb 1929), 309–10 · m. certs. · d. cert.
Archives Wellcome L., casebooks
Likenesses R. M. Morgan Ltd, photograph, Wellcome L.; repro. in *BMJ* (16 Feb 1929) · photograph, Wellcome L.
Wealth at death £40,278 11s. 5d.: confirmation, 1929

Ogston, Francis (*bap.* 1803, *d.* 1887), expert in forensic medicine, baptized in Aberdeen on 23 July 1803, was the third son of Alexander Ogston, the founder of a large soap factory in Aberdeen, and his wife, Helen Milne. He was educated at the grammar school and at Marischal College, Aberdeen, completing his medical course at Edinburgh University, where he graduated MD in 1824. Subsequently he travelled and studied on the continent. Having settled at Aberdeen, he soon acquired a large practice. In 1827 he began to teach chemistry privately.

In 1831 Ogston was appointed Aberdeen city police surgeon and began his long association with the city and university of Aberdeen. In 1839 he was appointed the first lecturer on medical jurisprudence at Marischal College. The appointment, coming in the wake of proposed reforms to university syllabuses, echoed the foundation of a regius chair of medical jurisprudence and public health at the University of Glasgow in 1839. The Aberdeen lectureship was elevated to a chair of medical jurisprudence and medical logic in 1857. The chair was endowed by Dr Alexander Henderson of Caskieburn, who stipulated that two-fifths of the course should be devoted to medical logic and that Ogston should be the chair's first incumbent. In an age when medical testimony was often suspect, Henderson's objective was to equip Aberdeen medical graduates with sound principles of reasoning when giving evidence in court. On 17 June 1841 Ogston married Amelia Cadenhead (*d.* 1852), daughter of Alexander Cadenhead, procurator fiscal for Aberdeen. They had at least two sons and a daughter. Ogston's brother-in-law, George Cadenhead, became procurator fiscal on his father's death in 1854 and remained in post until 1886 on his appointment as Aberdeen county procurator fiscal.

In 1860, when Marischal College was united to King's College to form the University of Aberdeen, under the Universities (Scotland) Act 1858, Ogston's appointment was maintained, and he continued to occupy the chair of medical jurisprudence until his retirement in 1883. Ogston frequently gave evidence in the judiciary courts and the lucidity of his medical reports drew praise even from the formidable Lord Deas. Ogston's lectures, *Lectures on Medical Jurisprudence*, edited by his son Frank, were published in 1878. The lectures drew heavily on continental and English writers but contained clear examples of Scottish procedures and local case histories. An example of Ogston's grim humour is evident in his repetition of Marie Devergie's instructions on exhumation: 1. Never to proceed to the operation fasting, and to be sure first to take a dram.

In 1862 Aberdeen appointed Ogston as its first medical officer of health under the terms of the 1862 Aberdeen Police Act. He remained MOH for Aberdeen until 1881. Ogston continued the established practice of Scottish medical dynasties and employed his two sons Alexander and Frank as assistants in both his university and city appointments. Alexander *Ogston went on to become professor of surgery at Aberdeen, and Frank, after failing to succeed his father in 1883, became professor of public health and forensic medicine at Otago University, New Zealand. Thus, in Aberdeen, the offices of police surgeon, professor of forensic medicine, crown witness, medical officer of health, and procurator fiscal were bound together by close familial ties for half a century.

Ogston was chosen dean of the faculty of medicine in Aberdeen, and was twice representative of the senatus at the university court. In 1883 he retired from the chair of medical jurisprudence. Two years afterwards the university conferred on him the honorary degree of LLD. He died suddenly at his home, 13 Albyn Terrace, Aberdeen, on 25 September 1887.   A. H. MILLAR, *rev.* BRENDA M. WHITE

Sources *Aberdeen Journal* (26 Sept 1887) · *The Lancet* (8 Oct 1887), 739–40 · *BMJ* (8 Oct 1887), 748 · E. H. B. Rodger, *Aberdeen doctors at home and abroad* (1893) · P. J. A. [P. J. Anderson], ed., *Aurora borealis academica: Aberdeen University appreciations, 1860–1889* (1899) · W. D. Simpson, ed., *The fusion of 1860: a record of the centenary celebrations and a history of the University of Aberdeen, 1860–1960* (1963) · *In Memoriam: an Obituary of Aberdeen and Vicinity* (1900) · J. A. Henderson, ed., *History of the Society of Advocates in Aberdeen* (1912) · M. A. Crowther and B. White, *On soul and conscience: the medical expert and crime* (1988) · C. Pennington, *The modernisation of medical teaching at Aberdeen in the nineteenth century* (1994) · J. D. Comrie, *History of Scottish medicine to 1860* (1927) · W. A. Knight, *Some nineteenth century Scotsmen* (1903); repr. (1908) · parish register (baptism), Aberdeen, 23 July 1803 · m. cert. · d. cert. · *CCI* (1887)
Wealth at death £5692 5s. 4d.: confirmation, 30 Nov 1887, *CCI*

O'Hagan, Henry Osborne (1853–1930), company promoter, was born on 18 March 1853 at Blackburn, Lancashire, one of at least two sons of Henry O'Hagan, a civil engineer of Ulster origins, who had married at Chatham in 1846 Emily, daughter of Charles Buchanan, bootmaker. He was educated at Rochester grammar school and privately at Streatham. At the age of fifteen Osborne O'Hagan (as he was usually known) began his City career as a clerk at a weekly salary of 10s. in a firm promoting private acts of parliament for railways and other public works. In

1874, when just twenty-one, he was prosecuted with J. S. Muir on a charge of obtaining £30,000 by false pretences by attempting to sell a colliery in Cumberland for £90,000 when the asking price was £60,000. He claimed that there were other intermediaries in the deal, to whom £30,000 was to be paid. *The Times* reported on 9 June: 'The Foreman of the Jury, addressing the Bench, said they could not say the prisoners were not guilty. The Recorder said there was no evidence to prove their guilt, the jury had no option but to acquit them.'

Afterwards O'Hagan became a company promoter specializing in tramways, collieries, and breweries. He does not seem to have gulled investors flagrantly: he converted mainly worthwhile concerns into public companies and tried to ensure a capital structure which would not wreck the prospects of each business by imposing a burden of long-term indebtedness on profits. His reputation for shrewd even-handedness was such that he was employed as an arbitrator in financial disputes involving such major figures as Weetman Pearson (later Lord Cowdray). For his part in the flotation of International Tea Stores in 1895 for H. E. Kearley, later Viscount Devonport, he typically received commission of £40,000.

In 1882 O'Hagan founded the City of London Contract Corporation, which was henceforth the main vehicle for his promotions. Although O'Hagan was chairman, most of the company's shares were held by discerning ordinary investors, as the company paid annual dividends varying from 15 to 60 per cent. Having become interested in various American businesses, particularly railroads, stockyards, cold storage, and meat wholesaling, O'Hagan formed the London and Chicago Contract Corporation in 1890. A convivial man, with a taste for music and theatricals of the cheerier sort, in 1889 he took a shareholding in Ronaschers, which controlled a Viennese hotel, restaurant, café, ballroom, and concert hall. This was one of many of his investments which suffered during the First World War.

O'Hagan's most important contribution to financial history was his popularization of underwriting for home industrial issues. This meant that he and his corporation acted as an issuing house in the public flotation of companies. Adapting the system prevalent in the foreign loan market since the 1860s, the capital to be underwritten in each promotion was put out by O'Hagan on a commission basis to brokers. As a result, the vendor was safeguarded from losses if the public failed to take up the issue of shares. With the removal of this risk for the vendor, many companies were encouraged to seek capital from the investing public. O'Hagan's system was important because until 1900 legislation precluded companies from issuing shares at a discount or paying commission to anyone taking up their shares.

In 1900 O'Hagan attempted what was to be a final master stroke before retirement, the amalgamation of all Britain's cement companies. By mischance the flotation of Associated Portland Cement Manufacturers coincided with a market crash on receiving the news of the Boxer uprising in China. As a result, £2.2 million of the shares

were not subscribed, and O'Hagan himself claimed to have been left responsible for £1.25 million. He took five months to cover this amount: friends took £400,000 of debentures and preference shares and he took £840,000 in ordinary shares. Although he had hitherto usually refused the distraction of outside directorships, he became vice-chairman of Associated Portland Cement and a managing director of British Portland Cement. These companies took most of his attention for twenty years, but he severed his links after vainly opposing a bold post-war expansion.

O'Hagan married in 1878 Elizabeth, daughter of John Philpot Jones, architect. He had one son, Henry Osborne O'Hagan (1882–1938), and an adopted daughter, Gladys; but his liking for the company of actresses, and interest in rescuing prostitutes, suggest a loud and restless bonhomie little suited to domestic happiness. It can be presumed that in later years he was estranged from his wife. For many years O'Hagan kept apartments at The Albany, and a villa, 'Riverhome', near Hampton Court, where he stored his collection of ancient coins, snuff boxes, and medals. Until 1919 he was president of the Thames Angling Preservation Society. He retired in 1924 to a villa at Roquebrune Cap Martin on the French riviera, where he indulged his taste for yachting. John Lane published two volumes of O'Hagan's memoirs entitled *Leaves from my Life* in 1929. They were written from memory, and may contain inaccuracies, but they constitute a rich, vivid source on a crucial epoch of British financial history: his feel for people and events was astute, even when self-serving. O'Hagan died suddenly after a long illness on 3 May 1930 at his French villa, Casa del Mare, Roquebrune Cap Martin, Alpes Maritimes.

Osborne O'Hagan was an energetic, domineering, obese, vainglorious man who enjoyed his luxuries and was a hearty trencherman. He was a wily and tenacious litigant, and could be an implacable enemy, but there are many signs of sly good nature in his memoirs. He was full of little jokes, often premeditated, to jolly along his business dealings, and had few illusions about his fellow men.

RICHARD DAVENPORT-HINES

Sources H. O. O'Hagan, *Leaves from my life*, 2 vols. (1929) · *The Times* (1 May 1874), 11 [law report] · *The Times* (9 June 1874), 13 [law report] · *The Times* (8 May 1930) · D. T. A. Kynaston and R. P. T. Davenport-Hines, 'O'Hagan, Henry Osborne', *DBB* · b. cert. · *CGPLA Eng. & Wales* (1930) · d. cert.
Likenesses photograph, repro. in Kynaston and Davenport-Hines, 'O'Hagan, Henry Osborne'
Wealth at death £243,571 19s. 10d.: probate, 31 July 1930, *CGPLA Eng. & Wales*

O'Hagan, John (1822–1890), judge, was born on 19 March 1822, at Newry, co. Down, the second son of John Arthur O'Hagan of Newry, and his wife, of whom little is known. After attending the Belfast Seminary he entered Trinity College, Dublin, on 3 July 1837; he graduated BA in 1842 and MA in 1865. He was called to the Irish bar by King's Inns, Dublin, in Trinity term, 1842, and joined the Munster circuit. An active member of the Young Ireland party, he was one of the counsel for Sir Charles Gavan Duffy on his trial for complicity in the rebellion of 1848. He also contributed to *The Nation*, both in prose and verse, his poems under the pseudonyms or initials Slíab Cuillinn, Carolina Wilhelmina Amelia, O., or J. O'H. They are collected in *The Spirit of the Nation* (1874). On 2 December 1865 O'Hagan married his cousin, the Hon. Frances Mary O'Hagan, daughter of Thomas O'Hagan, lord chancellor of Ireland.

O'Hagan was appointed commissioner of the board of national education in 1861, took silk on 8 February 1865, and was admitted a bencher of King's Inns in 1878. On 31 May 1881 he was made third serjeant, and under the Land Law (Ireland) Act of 1881 he was appointed judicial commissioner with the rank of justice of the High Court. He resided at 22 Upper Fitzwilliam Street, Dublin, and at Glenaveena, Howth, co. Dublin, where he died on 12 November 1890. He was survived by his wife.

O'Hagan was considered by his contemporaries to be a competent lawyer and was respected for his integrity and chivalrous courtesy. He was a prolific writer, and his patriotic songs were popular among nationalists of the time. Charles Gavan Duffy referred to him as 'the safest in council, the most moderate in opinion, [and] the most considerate in temper' (Duffy, *Young Ireland*, 1896, 1.133).

J. M. RIGG, *rev.* SINÉAD AGNEW

Sources D. J. O'Donoghue, *The poets of Ireland: a biographical and bibliographical dictionary* (1912), 355 · Boase, *Mod. Eng. biog.* · J. S. Crone, *A concise dictionary of Irish biography*, rev. edn (1937), 187 · Burtchaell & Sadleir, *Alum. Dubl.* · J. Foster, *The peerage, baronetage, and knightage of the British empire for 1882*, 1 [1882], 512 · Allibone, *Dict.* · *Irish Law Times and Solicitors' Journal* (15 Nov 1890), 587 · *Annual Register* (1844), 304 · *Thom's directory* (1871), 1088, 1096 · J. Haydn, *The book of dignities: containing rolls of the official personages of the British empire* (1851) · C. G. Duffy, *Young Ireland: a fragment of Irish history, 1840–1845*, rev. edn, 1 (1896), 133; 2 (1896), 210, 214 · C. G. Duffy, *Young Ireland: a fragment of Irish history, 1840–1845*, rev. edn (1884), 107–8 · C. G. Duffy, *Young Ireland, 2: Four years of Irish history, 1845–1849* (1887), 266, 271 · *CGPLA Ire.* (1891)
Archives CUL, letters to Lord Acton · NL Ire., letters to Lord Emly
Likenesses photographs, 1850–66, repro. in Duffy, *Young Ireland*, 1.133
Wealth at death £13,220 1s. 11d.: administration, 14 Jan 1891, *CGPLA Ire.*

O'Hagan, Thomas, first Baron O'Hagan (1812–1885), judge, was born in Belfast on 29 May 1812, the only son of Edward O'Hagan, a Catholic trader, and his wife, Mary, daughter of Captain Thomas Bell. His early education was at the Belfast Academical Institution, where he was at the time the only Catholic pupil. A keen interest in public speaking led to his early prominence in the school's debating society. In 1831 he was admitted as a student of the King's Inns, Dublin, and three years later he became a student of Gray's Inn in London, as a pupil of Thomas Chitty. O'Hagan was called to the Irish bar in 1836, the year of his marriage (on 1 February) to Mary, daughter of Charles Hamilton *Teeling of Belfast [*see under* Teeling, Bartholomew]. They were to have one son (who died in infancy) and five daughters.

Early legal career O'Hagan's early career at the bar was spent on the north-east circuit, principally as a criminal

Thomas O'Hagan, first Baron O'Hagan (1812–1885), by George Richmond, 1879

defence counsel. He combined legal practice with journalism, editing the *Newry Examiner*, a paper which supported Daniel O'Connell, from 1836 until 1840, when O'Hagan moved to Dublin. His association with O'Connell assisted his rise to prominence at the bar. O'Hagan's successful defence of Charles Gavan Duffy (then editor of the *Belfast Vindicator*) in a seditious libel case in 1842 enhanced his reputation as one of the leading barristers of his generation. Promotion in the profession followed. In 1847 O'Hagan became assistant barrister (or county court judge) for co. Longford, and two years later he became a QC. He became assistant barrister for co. Dublin in 1857. O'Hagan was appointed as third serjeant and elected a bencher of King's Inns in 1859.

O'Hagan's identification with his co-religionists is evident from a number of controversial cases where he appeared as counsel. In 1845 he was junior counsel in an appeal to the visitorial court of appeal of Trinity College, Dublin. The case concerned Denis Caulfied Heron, a Catholic student, who appealed against a decision of the provost and fellows of Trinity College which had refused him admission to a scholarship on the grounds that the scholarships were not tenable by Catholics. At the trial on 7 December 1855 of Father Petcherine, a redemptorist monk of Russian birth, on a charge of profanity for burning a copy of the Authorized Version of the scriptures, O'Hagan's address to the jury secured an acquittal. Outside the courts, O'Hagan helped to organize opposition to the Ecclesiastical Titles Bill and to proposed legislation on convents in 1852.

Political and religious beliefs In politics O'Hagan was strongly influenced by O'Connell, whom he described in 1875 in a centenary address as 'my great political benefactor, my deliverer and my friend'. However, O'Hagan did not support the repeal of the Act of Union. Instead he was prepared to work within the Union to bring about fair and just laws which he believed would give Catholics greater rights and might lead ultimately to acceptance of English law. As a founder member of the Dublin Statistical Society in 1847, which became the Statistical and Social Inquiry Society of Ireland in 1855, O'Hagan pioneered the study of statistical and economic science in Ireland. His later belief—that Ireland's social and economic problems could be remedied through legislation—was in keeping with the philosophy of the statistical movement. He collaborated with the leading Irish economist and statistician William Neilson Hancock in making law reform a major objective of the statistical movement in Ireland.

In 1858 O'Hagan was appointed a member of the board of national education for Ireland, for which he was criticized by Cardinal Cullen. Palmerston made him solicitor-general for Ireland in 1861, and a year later he became attorney-general for Ireland, which also brought him into conflict with the traditional and ultra-conservative side of Catholic nationalist opinion. He rejected the view that 'a Catholic Irishman, faithful to his Church and true to his country, is to ostracise himself and decline a position of dignity and power which he may have won by honest effort and fair capacity' (O'Hagan, 324–5). For a short period, from May 1863 to January 1865, he sat as a Liberal MP for Tralee. O'Hagan had little private means and his search for a safe seat at first proved difficult. He had been unsuccessful at Kinsale, largely because he could not provide the necessary financial patronage to secure local support, but at Tralee Daniel O'Connell's son retired to make way for him. His career as an elected politician was short-lived. In January 1865 he was appointed to the bench as a judge of the court of common pleas in succession to Nicholas Ball. According to *The Times*, O'Hagan commanded widespread support as a fair-minded judge.

Irish lord chancellor On the formation of Gladstone's first ministry in December 1868, O'Hagan became lord chancellor of Ireland, the first Catholic to hold the office since 1688. He was the first person to benefit from an act of parliament passed in 1867 (30 & 31 Vict. c. 75), by which the office of lord chancellor had been opened to all persons without regard to their religious beliefs. On 14 June 1870 O'Hagan was raised to the peerage as Baron O'Hagan of Tullahogue in co. Tyrone and took his seat in the Lords on 21 June 1870. Following the death of his first wife in October 1868, O'Hagan married on 2 August 1871 Alice Mary (*d.* 1921), daughter and coheir of Colonel Charles Towneley (*d.* 1870) of Towneley, Lancashire, a Catholic landowner and Liberal MP for Sligo in 1848 and 1852–3, through whom he acquired 5200 acres in Lancashire and Yorkshire.

O'Hagan was aware of the semi-political nature of the office of lord chancellor and aware, too, that his position as Irish lord chancellor was a political gesture to secure Irish Catholic support for Gladstone's ministry. O'Hagan was known to have support from the Catholic bishops. F. E. Ball, in the second volume of his *Judges in Ireland, 1221–1921* (1926), noted that the appointment was 'prompted by O'Hagan's representing more than any other Roman Catholic on the Bench national ideals'. Throughout Gladstone's first ministry O'Hagan played a prominent role, though he had occasion to complain that he was not initially consulted by Gladstone or the then Irish chief secretary, Chichester Fortescue (Lord Carlingford), over the contents of the 1870 Land Bill. The reform of the Irish jury system was identified as one of the major areas for legislation. Jury packing and an unfair jury-selection process were identified as shortcomings in the existing jury legislation. In 1871 O'Hagan introduced a Jury Bill, subsequently enacted as the Juries Act (Ireland) 1871, which lowered the property qualification for jurors (replacing the freehold qualification) and endeavoured to prevent jury packing by replacing the sheriff's discretion over jury selection with a system of alphabetical selection by rotation. This 1871 act was the first attempt to broaden the jury qualification to allow Catholics to sit on the jury in both civil and criminal cases. O'Hagan also introduced reforms in the law of lunacy and in the system of juvenile justice during the period of Gladstone's first ministry.

In 1869 O'Hagan had become president of the Dublin Statistical Society. Many of the papers read at the society's meetings, which were strongly influenced by the utilitarian ideas of Bentham and his followers, identified areas of the law that required reform. O'Hagan believed in codification as an overriding philosophy for law reformers. In the case of Ireland he believed that codification would allow easier comparison and perhaps assimilation of the law in England and Ireland. He also had the vision to imagine both England and Ireland linked to a codified system of law throughout Europe. This European perspective is a recurrent theme of O'Hagan's opening address at the Belfast meeting of the Social Science Association in 1867, entitled 'The study of jurisprudence—Roman, English and Celtic'.

Judicial office O'Hagan's decisions in the Irish court of chancery are reported in the *Irish Reports* (*Equity*), volumes 4–8. O'Hagan's work as a common-law advocate was not regarded by his fellow judges as the best qualification for work as a chancery judge, and his lasting legacy is not to be found in his contribution to judicial precedent. In his first period of office as lord chancellor he was embroiled in an embarrassing series of public and acrimonious controversies with his colleague in the chancery appeal court, Lord Justice Christian. Christian disliked the Land Act of 1870, which O'Hagan had supported. In a leading case on interpretation of tenant rights under the new act, *Re the Marquis of Waterford's Estates* (1871), Christian made strong objection to O'Hagan's judgment about the nature of the legal rights of tenants and attacked the act as 'shocking to all our ideas of property law'. In the case of *Mulholland* v. *Killen* (1874), Christian was highly critical of O'Hagan's 1871 Juries Act and of the class of new jurors enfranchised by the legislation. Christian was also critical of O'Hagan for allegedly not spending sufficient time on his judicial functions.

O'Hagan responded to Christian's attacks with characteristic dignity, his reputation for tact and good humour and his fair-minded and honest intention remaining intact. This underlines what appears from reading his letters and speeches: O'Hagan's genial nature and general optimistic view of the world. Perhaps naively, this optimism may have left O'Hagan unwilling or unable to come to terms with his disappointments; his jury reforms in the 1870s required constant amendment, his passion for law reform through codification of Irish law remained unfulfilled, and the land legislation of 1870 required fundamental change in the 1880s.

Later public activities In February 1874 O'Hagan resigned with the rest of Gladstone's ministry. During the following six years out of office, O'Hagan continued to take an active interest in public life. He supported reform of the Irish education system. He was one of the original members of the intermediate education board established in 1878 and later became its first vice-chairman. On the foundation of the Royal University of Ireland in 1880, O'Hagan was one of the university senators. In 1878 he delivered the Thomas Moore centenary address in Dublin, and in 1880 he made an address to Cardinal Newman at Edgbaston, Birmingham, on behalf of a deputation from the Catholics of Ireland. In 1881 he delivered the presidential address at the opening of the Social Science Congress in Dublin.

In May 1880, on the return of Gladstone to office, O'Hagan again became lord chancellor of Ireland and strongly supported another land bill in the House of Lords. Ill health forced him to resign in November 1881. O'Hagan was elected an honorary bencher of Gray's Inn in 1883 and he continued to attend the judicial sittings of the House of Lords after his retirement from the lord chancellorship. O'Hagan suffered a stroke on Christmas day 1884 and died on 1 February 1885 at his London home, Hereford House, Park Street. He was buried at Glasnevin cemetery, Dublin, on 6 February. He and his second wife, who survived him, had two sons and two daughters; his elder son, a protestant, who succeeded him as second baron, was killed on active service in the Second South African War.

O'Hagan's speeches and papers were published in *Occasional Papers and Addresses* (1884) and in *Selected Speeches and Arguments of Lord O'Hagan* (1885), edited by George Teeling. The published collections contain all of O'Hagan's major speeches, including the O'Connell centenary address published (though not delivered) by O'Hagan in Dublin in 1875. The statue of O'Hagan by Thomas Farrell, erected in 1887 in the Four Courts in Dublin, was destroyed along with the rest of the building in 1922.

JOHN F. MCELDOWNEY

Sources D. Hogan, '"Arrows too sharply pointed": the relations of Lord Justice Christian and Lord O'Hagan, 1868–74', *The common law tradition: essays in Irish legal history*, ed. J. F. McEldowney and P. O'Higgins (1990), 66–84 • J. McEldowney, 'Lord O'Hagan, 1812–1885', *Irish Jurist*, new ser., 14 (1979), 360–77 • J. McEldowney, 'William Neilson Hancock, 1820–1888', *Irish Jurist*, new ser., 20 (1985), 378–402 • J. F. McEldowney and P. O'Higgins, eds., *The common law tradition: essays in Irish legal history* (1990) • R. D. C. Black, *The Statistical and Social Inquiry Society of Ireland centenary volume, 1847–1947* (1947) • T. O'Hagan, *Occasional papers and addresses* (1884) • R. H. I. Palgrave, ed., *Dictionary of political economy*, [3rd edn], ed. H. Higgs, 3 vols. (1923–6) • C. Dewey, 'Celtic agrarian legislation and the Celtic revival: historicist implications of Gladstone's Irish and Scottish Land Acts, 1870–1886', *Past and Present*, 64 (1974), 30–70 • *Correspondence of Daniel O'Connell, the liberator*, ed. W. J. Fitzpatrick, 2 vols. (1888) • F. E. Ball, *The judges in Ireland, 1221–1921*, 2 (1926) • *The Times* (2 Feb 1885) • Burke, *Peerage* • *Freeman's Journal* [Dublin] (2 Feb 1885)

Archives PRO NIre., corresp. and papers | BL, corresp. with W. E. Gladstone, Add. MSS 44403–44783 • BL, Spencer MSS • Bodl. Oxf., corresp. with Lord Kimberley • Chatsworth House, Derbyshire, Devonshire MSS • CUL, letters to Lord Acton • NL Ire., Sir William Teeling MSS • Althorp, Northamptonshire, Spencer MSS

Likenesses G. Richmond, chalk drawing, 1879, NG Ire. [*see illus.*] • T. Farrell, statue, *c.*1888, Four Courts, Dublin • W. & D. Downey, carte-de-visite, NPG • G. Richmond, oils, priv. coll. • J. H. Walker, oils, King's Inns, Dublin • J. Watkins, bust, National Museum of Ireland, Dublin • J. Watkins, carte-de-visite, NPG • bust, Royal Courts of Justice, Belfast, Northern Ireland, Bar Library • portrait, repro. in O. J. Burke, *Lord chancellors of Ireland* (1879) • portrait, repro. in *Pump Court*, 2 (1884), 126 • portrait, repro. in *ILN*, 54 (1869), 385, 446 • portrait, repro. in *The Period* (2 July 1870), 91 • portrait, repro. in *Illustrated Times* (4 Feb 1865), 68 • wood-engraving, NPG; repro. in *ILN* (1 April 1865), 296

Wealth at death £25,776 1*s.* 6*d.* in England: Irish probate sealed in England, 19 May 1885, *CGPLA Eng. & Wales* • £53,013 19*s.* 2*d.*: probate, 10 April 1885, *CGPLA Ire.*

O'Haingli, Donatus. *See* Ua hAingliu, Donngus (*d.* 1095).

O'Haingli, Samuel. *See* Ua hAingliu, Samuel (*d.* 1121), *under* Ua hAingliu, Donngus (*d.* 1095).

O'Halloran, Sir Joseph (1763–1843), army officer in the East India Company, youngest son of the surgeon and antiquary Sylvester *O'Halloran (1728–1807) and his wife, Mary, *née* Casey (*d.* 1782), was born in co. Limerick on 13 August 1763. He was appointed midshipman on the East India Company's sloop of war *Swallow* on 22 February 1781, and in July obtained an infantry cadetship; he was made ensign in the Bengal army on 9 May 1782 and lieutenant on 6 January 1785. He married in 1790 Frances (1773–1835), daughter of Colonel Nicholas Bayly MP, of Redhill, Surrey, of the 1st foot guards, brother of the first earl of Uxbridge, and they had a large family. Their second son was Thomas Shuldham *O'Halloran (1797–1870).

On 7 January 1796 O'Halloran became captain, and from June 1796 to October 1802 was adjutant and quartermaster at Midnapore, and was attached to the public works department. On the abolition of his office he rejoined his unit, the 18th Bengal native infantry. In September 1803 he accompanied a force which crossed the Jumna to subjugate Bundelkhand, and on 12 October defeated a force of 15,000 Marathas at Kopsah. His gallantry at the sieges of Bursaar and Jeswarree in January 1804 led to his appointment to supervise the operations of an irregular force of 2000 men, under Sheikh Kurub Ali, in the interior of Bundelkhand. On 15 May he attacked and defeated, after a determined resistance, Raja Ram and 10,000 Bundelas entrenched among the rocks and hills of Mahaba. On 1 July he commanded two brigades of irregulars in another attack on Raja Ram and a force of 16,000 Bundelas and

Nagas on the fortified hills of Thana and Purswarree. Subsequently he served at the siege of Saitpur, and in December attacked and stormed several other towns and forts. In January 1805 he captured the forts of Niagacre and Dowra, in Pinwarree. His services were noticed by the Marquess Wellesley.

On 1 November 1805 O'Halloran was appointed commissary of supplies by Lord Lake. On the breaking up of the army on 1 June 1806 he rejoined his regiment, and on 25 April 1808 attained the rank of major. He commanded the attack on the strongly fortified hill of Rogoulee, in Bundelkhand, on 22 January 1809. Colonel Martindell, who commanded in Bundelkhand, made O'Halloran his military secretary, and his conduct at the head of the 1st battalion 18th native infantry at the siege of the fortress of Ajaigarh was specially noticed. He became lieutenant-colonel on 4 June 1814, served in the campaigns against the Nepalese in 1815 and 1816, in the first campaign covering the district of Tirhut, in the second at the siege of Harriharpur, and afterwards commanded his battalion in Cuttack during the disturbances there. For his services he was made CB. In August 1818 he was sent to join the 1st battalion 20th native infantry in the Straits Settlements, and on arrival there was appointed commandant of the 25th Bengal native infantry. In January 1825 he was appointed brigadier at Barrackpore. Before leaving he received the thanks of the government of the Straits Settlements, and the unusual honour of an eleven-gun embarkation salute. In December 1828 he became brigadier-general, and was appointed to the Saugor division. He became colonel of a regiment on 4 June 1829. With the expiration of his five years' period of staff service, on 23 December 1833, ended his active military career of fifty-three years, during which he had never taken any leave to Europe.

O'Halloran landed in England in May 1834. In February 1835 he was knighted by William IV, who observed that the distinction was well earned by his long meritorious and gallant services, and by his consecration of his eight sons to the service of his country. O'Halloran became major-general on 10 January 1837. He was made KCB in 1837, and GCB in 1841. He became a member of the Royal Asiatic Society of Great Britain and Ireland in 1836, an honorary member of the Royal Irish Academy in 1838, and received the freedom of his native city (Limerick) on 25 February 1838. He died at his residence, 42 Connaught Square, Hyde Park, London, on 3 November 1843, from the effects of a street accident in which the neck of his thighbone was fractured. He was buried in the catacombs at Kensal Green cemetery, Middlesex, immediately beneath the chapel. A memorial tablet was placed in the wall of the south cloister.

O'Halloran's sixth son, **William Littlejohn O'Halloran** (1806–1885), army officer, born at Berhampore, India, on 5 May 1806, went to England in 1811. On 11 January 1824 he was commissioned ensign in the 14th foot, which he joined at Meerut. He served with it at the siege and storm of Bharatpur in 1825–6, obtaining his lieutenancy in action. In April 1827 he exchanged into the 38th regiment, and served on the staff of his father at Saugor,

central India. He married in December 1831 Eliza Minton, daughter of John Montague Smyth. O'Halloran was employed on recruiting service in Belfast from 1832 to 1834. In 1834 he embarked for Sydney with a detachment of the 50th. From there he sailed for Calcutta, rejoined the 38th at Chinsura in 1835, and accompanied it to England in 1836. He obtained his company by purchase on 29 December 1837, and retired from the army in April 1840.

O'Halloran then embarked for South Australia, landed at Glenelg on 11 August 1840, and purchased a property near Adelaide. In August 1841 he was appointed a justice of the peace, in March 1843 a member of the board of audit, in June 1843 private secretary to Governor Grey and clerk of the councils, and in January 1851 auditor-general of South Australia. In 1866 he acted as chairman of a commission into the administration of the Northern Territory. On 22 January 1868 he retired, after serving the colonial government for upwards of twenty-four years. He died at Adelaide, South Australia, on 15 July 1885. He left two daughters and three sons, the eldest of whom, Joseph Sylvester O'Halloran CMG, became secretary to the Royal Colonial Institute in 1884.

H. M. CHICHESTER, rev. ROGER T. STEARN

Sources B. Burke, *A genealogical and heraldic history of the colonial gentry*, 1 (1891) • *East-India Register and Army List* • *Services of Sir Joseph O'Halloran* (pamphlet, published by Marshall, 21 Edgware Road, c.1844) • T. A. Heathcote, *The military in British India: the development of British land forces in south Asia, 1600–1947* (1995) • P. Spear, *The Oxford history of modern India* (1965)

O'Halloran, Sylvester (1728–1807), surgeon and antiquary, was born on 31 December 1728 at Caherdavin, co. Clare, Ireland, the third son of Michael O'Halloran, a substantial farmer, and Mary McDonnell. He attended a school in Limerick run by the Revd Robert Cashin and was taught Irish by the Jacobite poet Seán Clárach MacDomhnaill, a distant relative. At the age of sixteen or seventeen he went abroad to study surgery, one of the few professions open to Roman Catholics in Ireland at the time. In London he studied the methods of Joseph Hillmer and Chevalier Taylor, both noted eye surgeons. He was in Paris in 1747–8, during which time he attended the lectures of Antoine Ferrein. Tradition has it that he also studied in Leiden.

In 1749 O'Halloran returned to Limerick and set up practice. He married Mary Casey (d. 1782) of Ballycasey, co. Limerick, in 1752 and had five children, of whom Joseph *O'Halloran became a major-general with the East India Company. Sylvester O'Halloran was one of the founders of the County Limerick Infirmary which opened in 1761. His first medical work, published in 1750, *A Treatise on the Glaucoma, or Cataract*, showed his familiarity with the French literature of eye surgery, and suggested a modification of the current method of cataract treatment. *A New Method of Amputation* (1763) and *A Complete Treatise on Gangrene and Sphacelus* (1765), published immediately after the Seven Years' War, were directed particularly at the surgical problems posed by injuries sustained in battle, the former proposing a more efficient method of leg amputation. In an appendix to the latter work O'Halloran advocated the licensing of surgeons by public examination and the setting up of a teaching and examining body, and this may have played a part in the foundation of the Royal College of Surgeons in Ireland in 1784, of which he was elected an honorary member (equivalent to a later fellowship) in 1786. Despite this he felt he had been denied proper recognition by his fellow surgeons in Ireland, believing this neglect to be deliberate and due to his religion.

O'Halloran was unusually outspoken in his condemnation of the penal laws then in force against Roman Catholics and of what he felt was the hostile stereotyping of them as barbarous. All his medical writings adverted to these concerns, including *A New Treatise on External Injuries of the Head* (1793), in which he explained that the large number of head injuries that were presented to him had much to do with Irish hot temper, but that this national characteristic had been exacerbated by state oppression. By this stage O'Halloran had given up the thought of state preferment for his surgical works, but, naïvely, still had hopes that Edmund Burke could procure a civil pension for him in recognition of his antiquarian writing, which began as a pastime but came to have more importance for him in the 1770s and 1780s when the Catholic question was a crucial issue of debate in Ireland.

O'Halloran's first venture into antiquarianism was an article in the *Dublin Magazine* in January 1763 on the subject of James Macpherson's Ossian poems, in which he endeavoured to show that the poems were based on material that was originally Irish rather than Scottish. Privately he admired the poems and the heroic Gaelic world which Macpherson had presented in them. All of his own antiquarian works were concerned primarily with the military and heroic aspects of early Gaelic society. In *An Introduction to the Study of the History and Antiquities of Ireland* (1772) he argued that all the most distinctive laws, manners, and customs of Europe had originated among the Irish Celts, including the medieval concepts of knighthood and chivalry which had been spread by them throughout the continent. His *General History of Ireland* (1778) presented pre-colonial Ireland as a golden age of military valour and scholarly learning which was destroyed by the Anglo-Norman invasion. This was a reprise on a well-established theme in Irish historiography, but what set O'Halloran apart was his propensity for making direct links between the past and the contemporary political situation of the native population, and also the highly romantic colouring of his narrative. This latter was to make him an important influence on later nineteenth-century writers such as Standish O'Grady.

O'Halloran was made a member of the Royal Irish Academy in 1786 and contributed papers on medical and antiquarian matters to its *Transactions*. A portrait of him was published in *Dublin Quarterly Journal of Medical Science*, 6 (1848). He died in his home at Merchants' Quay, Limerick, on 11 August 1807 and was buried in the family vault at Kileely cemetery, Limerick. CLARE O'HALLORAN

Sources J. B. Lyons, 'Sylvester O'Halloran, 1728–1807', *Eighteenth Century Ireland*, 4 (1989), 65–74 · J. B. Lyons, 'Sylvester O'Halloran (1728–1807)', *Irish Journal of Medical Science*, 449–50 (1963), 217–32, 279–88 · J. B. Lyons, ed., 'The letters of Sylvester O'Halloran', *North Munster Antiquarian Journal*, 8 (1958–61), 168–81; 9 (1962–5), 25–50 · W. Wilde, 'Illustrious physicians and surgeons of Ireland, no. VI: Silvester O'Halloran M.R.I.A.', *Dublin Quarterly Journal of Medical Science*, 6 (1848), 223–50
Archives Bodl. Oxf., letters to Lord Macartney · NL Ire., letters to Charles O'Conor · Royal Irish Acad., Stowe MSS, letters to Charles O'Conor · Sheffield Central Library, Fitzwilliam collection, letters to Edmund Burke
Likenesses Irish school, stipple, pubd 1847 (after eighteenth-century Irish school portrait), NG Ire. · engraving (after miniature), repro. in Wilde, 'Illustrious Physicians and Surgeons of Ireland'

O'Halloran, Thomas Shuldham (1797–1870), army officer and police chief in Australia, was born on 25 October 1797 at Berhampore, India, the second son of Major-General Sir Joseph *O'Halloran (1763–1843) and his wife, Frances (1773–1835), the daughter of Colonel Nicholas Bayly and the niece of the first earl of Uxbridge. He followed in the strong military traditions of his family by becoming a cadet at the Royal Military College at Marlow, Buckinghamshire, in 1808. In 1813 he joined the 17th regiment in India as an ensign and took part in the Anglo-Nepal War (1814–16). He became a lieutenant in 1817.

On 1 August 1821 O'Halloran married Anne (*c*.1801–1823), the daughter of James Goss, of Dawlish, Devon. They had two children before she died two years later, in Calcutta, whence O'Halloran had gone to join the 44th regiment; the following year he was with them at Chittagong as paymaster, quartermaster, and interpreter. He served in the First Anglo-Burmese War, and became a captain in the 99th regiment in April 1827. Subsequently he exchanged into the 56th and then the 6th regiment, and served as an aide-de-camp to his father in Saugor, central India.

O'Halloran went on to the half-pay list and returned to England in 1834, where on 10 July he married Jane, the eldest daughter of James Waring. They had three sons and one daughter. In 1837 he returned to full pay as a captain in the 97th regiment, and commanded a force sent to quell a riot in Yorkshire. He finally sold his commission the following year and sailed with his family to take up residence on a series of land selections (later O'Halloran Hill) south of Adelaide, South Australia. Soon afterwards, with concern rising as to the lawlessness of the colony, the governor, George Gawler, sought to make use of O'Halloran's experience (particularly that of suppressing disorder in Yorkshire) and appointed him to the board of commissioners of the new South Australian police force. When in 1840 the governor formed a voluntary militia as a further measure to keep the peace, the 'dashing officer' O'Halloran (Ross) was made its major-commandant.

With the dismissal in May 1840 of the police commissioner, O'Halloran was appointed to the vacant position. In July of that year survivors of a shipwreck near Adelaide were killed by Aborigines, and he was ordered to lead an expedition to capture those responsible. This was, if possible, to be carried out without bloodshed. But, Gawler wrote, 'if in the execution of it, you are really compelled to abandon temperate measures, and to resort to those of extreme force against the whole tribe, you will not be held blamable' (Tolmer, 180). Two Aborigines were hanged and others were shot while escaping from O'Halloran's party. This was the first 'officially sanctioned punitive expedition' against the Aborigines in South Australia (Clyne, 51), setting a precedent for many in the years to come. Much of O'Halloran's time as police commissioner was taken up in organizing expeditions against Aboriginal 'crime', such as the traditional lighting of fires in grassland and the pilfering of animals and minor supplies. As noted by the historian of the South Australian police, regarding how O'Halloran undertook this duty, his 'judgement was heavily influenced by his military background … He might attempt to disguise or temper his martial belligerency in dealing with this frustrating problem, but he could not always hide it' (ibid., 55).

O'Halloran reorganized the police force along more efficient lines, but in 1843 he was asked, as part of an economy drive by the new governor, George Grey, to add the role of police magistrate to his duties. He resigned. Soon afterwards he was appointed by Grey to the legislative council. In 1846 he 'stalked out' (Whitelock, 70) of the council with a number of others in opposition to the imposition of mineral royalties. In 1857 he was elected to the first council formed after the granting of responsible government, heading the votes in a list of twenty-seven candidates. He resigned in 1863. After a lifetime of duty, carried out in his 'direct, forthright and uncomplicated' way (Ross), O'Halloran died, at his home in O'Halloran Hill, on 16 August 1870. He was buried at Christ Church, O'Halloran Hill.   MARC BRODIE

Sources R. Clyne, *Colonial blue: a history of the South Australian police force, 1836–1916* (1987) · A. Tolmer, *Reminiscences of an adventurous and chequered career at home and at the Antipodes* (1882) · D. B. Ross, 'O'Halloran, Thomas Shuldham', *AusDB*, vol. 2 · *IGI* · D. Whitelock, *Adelaide, 1836–1976: a history of difference* (1977) · H. Coxon, J. Playford, and R. Reid, *Biographical register of the South Australian parliament, 1857–1957* (1985) · *DNB*
Archives Mitchell L., NSW, Brown MSS; South Australian MSS
Likenesses G. H. Gye, bulletin drawings, Mitchell L., NSW · G. H. Gye, caricature, Mitchell L., NSW · photograph, repro. in Clyne, *Colonial blue*, 48 · portrait, repro. in *St Peter's College Magazine* (May 1922)

O'Halloran, William Littlejohn (1806–1885). *See under* O'Halloran, Sir Joseph (1763–1843).

O'Hanlon, John [*pseud.* Lageniensis] (**1821–1905**), Roman Catholic priest and hagiographer, was born in Stradbally, Queen's county, on 30 April 1821, the son of Edward and Honor Hanlon of Stradbally, who wanted him to become a priest. He went to a private primary school in Stradbally and then, aged thirteen, to an endowed school at Ballyroan. In 1840 he went to the ecclesiastical college at Carlow, staying there until May 1842, when he emigrated with some relatives to Quebec, Canada; in August he moved to Missouri in the United States. In 1847 he was ordained by Peter Richard Kenrick, archbishop of St Louis, and he spent the next few years as a missionary priest to Irish communities in Missouri. He later published *Life and Scenery in Missouri* (1890), an account of his experiences in

America. In September 1853 he returned to Ireland because of ill health. From 1854 to 1859 he was assistant chaplain of the South Dublin Union, and from 1854 to 1880 curate of St Michael's and St John's, Dublin. In May 1880 he became parish priest of St Mary's, Sandymount, co. Dublin, where he remained until his death. In 1886 he was made a canon and in 1891 he returned briefly to the USA for the golden jubilee of Archbishop Kenrick.

O'Hanlon dedicated himself to Irish ecclesiastical history, and especially to research into the lives of the Irish saints. In 1856 he was elected a member of the Kilkenny Archaeological Society, and he was also a member of the Royal Irish Academy. While still a curate he visited nearly all the important libraries of England and southern Europe in order to pursue his research and in 1856 he began to collect material for his great work, *The Lives of the Irish Saints*. The first volume appeared in 1875, and nine further volumes and part of a tenth were published before his death. He was also a prolific contributor to Irish reviews and newspapers, and his published works include *Abridgment of the History of Ireland from its Final Subjection to the Present Time* (1849), *The Irish Emigrant's Guide to the United States* (1851), *The Life of St Laurence O'Toole, Archbishop of Dublin* (1857), *The Life of St Malachy O'Morgair, Bishop of Down and Connor, Archbishop of Armagh* (1859), *The Life of St Dympna, Virgin Martyr* (1863), *Catechism of Irish History from the Earliest Events to the Death of O'Connell* (1864), *The Life of St Grellan, Patron of the O'Kellys* (1881), and *Irish-American History of the United States* (1902). Under the pseudonym Lageniensis he also published verse, including *Legend Lays of Ireland* (1870), *Irish Folk-Lore: Traditions and Superstitions of the Country, with Numerous Tales* (1870), *The Buried Lady: a Legend of Kilronan* (1877), and *The Poetical Works of Lageniensis* (1893). He edited Monck Mason's *Essay on the Antiquity and Constitution of Parliaments of Ireland* (1891) and Molyneux's *Case of Ireland … Stated* (1893). O'Hanlon died at 3 Leahy's Terrace, Sandymount, co. Dublin, on 15 May 1905, and was buried at Glasnevin cemetery, Dublin, on 17 May.

D. J. O'DONOGHUE, rev. DAVID HUDDLESTON

Sources D. J. O'Donoghue, *The poets of Ireland: a biographical dictionary with biographical particulars*, 1 vol. in 3 pts (1892–3), 188 · *Freeman's Journal* [Dublin] (16 May 1905), 1, 5 · *New Catholic encyclopedia*, 18 vols. (1967–89), vol. 10, p. 660 · personal knowledge (1912) · *BL cat.* · private information (1912) · *CGPLA Ire.* (1905)
Archives St Patrick's College, Maynooth
Wealth at death £535 4s.: probate, 23 Sept 1905, *CGPLA Eng. & Wales*

O'Hanlon, Redmond (*c.*1640–1681), outlaw, was born near Poyntzpass, co. Armagh, the son of Laughlin O'Hanlon. This is the account given in a contemporary pamphlet *The Life and Death of … Redmon O'Hanlon*. Claims that O'Hanlon served in the armies of the confederate Catholics, fled to France in 1653, and there served with distinction in the army of Louis XIV, would make him much older; however these appear only in the late nineteenth and early twentieth centuries and are not supported by any contemporary record. The same, contemporary, pamphlet's report that O'Hanlon attended an English school, along with Sir Francis Brewster's description of him after his death as 'a scholar and a man of parts' (Carte, 4.617), suggest that his family had some social standing, but no further details are available.

O'Hanlon, once again according to the account in *The Life and Death*, began his career as a servant of Sir George Acheson of Markethill, co. Armagh. Having been caught trying to sell a stolen horse he fled the area, finding employment as servant to a 'fanatic teacher', who subsequently made him clerk of his congregation. About 1660 O'Hanlon returned to Armagh where he was first a poll tax collector, then a farmer of the hearth tax. Unable to meet his liabilities in the latter position, and having run through the marriage portion brought him by his first wife, who died young, he turned to crime, in alliance with a kinsman, Laughlin O'Hanlon, whose sister he took as his second wife. On 14 December 1674 both men were proclaimed as outlaws, the first reference to O'Hanlon's activities in official records.

Contemporary and later accounts suggest that O'Hanlon commanded a band of outlaws based in the area of Slieve Gullion, from where they raided the counties of Armagh, Monaghan, and Down, and collected tribute in exchange for their protection. A second proclamation, in 1676, offering a reward for his capture, confirms his continued career as an outlaw. But it is only in 1678–9 that his name begins to appear in official correspondence as a major threat. In October 1678 he was singled out, under the nickname Count O'Hanlon, as the leading tory (bandit) in Ulster (*Ormonde MSS*, new ser., 4.213). Sir George Rawdon, on 31 May 1679, reported that he was still alive but 'has had many scapes lately very narrowly and was wounded' (*CSP dom.*, 1679–80, 161). His notoriety further increased when, on 9 September 1679, men identified as his followers killed Henry St John, owner of an estate near Tandragee and great-nephew of Sir Oliver St John, lord deputy of Ireland, 1616–22.

London newsheets in the first three months of 1680 report intensive searches for O'Hanlon. Intelligence passed to the government in October of that year alleged that he planned to join sixteen outlaws from Londonderry and co. Tyrone on a raid into co. Longford, wearing grey coats lined with red which they could reverse in order to pass for soldiers. The following month O'Hanlon, through the Annesley family of Castlewellan, made overtures for a surrender on terms. However, these were rejected by the Irish privy council, apparently overruling the lord lieutenant, Ormond. Meanwhile O'Hanlon had come to the notice of proponents of the Popish Plot. Henry Jones, bishop of Meath, Mrs Annesley's father, suggested that he might give evidence regarding plans for a French invasion. Sworn informations from two Irish witnesses later alleged that Shaftesbury and his accomplice William Hetherington had tried to have O'Hanlon and others brought to England to incriminate Ormond and members of the Irish council. Earlier, in 1678–9, there had been obscure intrigues involving another figure in the plot, Edmund Murphy, parish priest of Killevey, co. Armagh, who presented himself in a pamphlet as having opposed

O'Hanlon's depredations, although other evidence suggests that he himself had links with local tories.

On 4 March 1681 Ormond gave William Lucas of Down a commission granting full power to act against O'Hanlon. Lucas made contact with O'Hanlon's foster brother, Art O'Hanlon, who on the afternoon of 25 April shot Redmond O'Hanlon as he slept in a cabin near Eight Mile Bridge, co. Down. An account of the killing published soon after reported that a companion, acting on the dying man's instructions, removed his head to prevent it being captured and exhibited. However, it was subsequently found and placed on a spike over the entrance to Downpatrick gaol. His body was displayed at Newry, co. Down.

Memories of O'Hanlon's career were preserved in John Cosgrave's *A Genuine History of the Lives and Actions of the Most Notorious Irish Highwaymen, Tories and Rapparees*, first published some time before 1747 and many times reprinted. He was later the subject of a novel by William Carleton (1862), as well as of other works of fiction and popular history. Modern historians remain divided on how far his career, like that of other 'tories' of the Restoration era, should be seen as a rearguard action by the dispossessed Catholic élite against the new order created by the Cromwellian confiscations, or as an example of the banditry endemic on the periphery of early modern states. The O'Hanlons had at one time been an important Gaelic lineage in south Armagh, and the nickname Count O'Hanlon, used in contemporary as well as later references, may indicate that in this case O'Hanlon did in fact assume the persona of a dispossessed aristocrat. S. J. CONNOLLY

Sources T. W. Moody, 'Redmond O'Hanlon', *Proceedings of the Belfast Natural, Historical and Philosophical Society*, 1st ser., 1 (1937), 17–33 · *The life and death of the incomparable and indefatigable tory Redmond O'Hanlon, commonly called Count Hanlyn* (1682) · *CSP dom.*, 1673–82 · *Calendar of the manuscripts of the marquess of Ormonde*, new ser., 8 vols., HMC, 36 (1902–20), vols. 4–5 · T. Carte, *An history of the life of James, duke of Ormonde*, 3 vols. (1735–6); new edn, pubd as *The life of James, duke of Ormond*, 6 vols. (1851), vol. 4 · R. Q. Duffy, 'Redmond O'Hanlon and the outlaws of Ulster', *History Today*, 32/8 (1982), 9–13

O'hAogain, Eoghan. *See* McEgan, Owen (*d.* 1603).

O'Hara, Abel. *See* Banim, John (1798–1842).

O'Hara, Barnes. *See* Banim, Michael (1796–1874), *under* Banim, John (1798–1842).

O'Hara, Charles, first Baron Tyrawley (*d.* 1724), army officer, was probably from Leyny, co. Sligo. A henchman and client of the Butlers, dukes of Ormond, O'Hara attended James Butler, later second duke, probably as riding master, during his travels to France in 1675. In 1678 he was a captain in the Duke of York's Foot, but on 15 December 1679, his company having been disbanded, he was commissioned lieutenant of Henry Cornwall's company in Ossory's regiment in the Anglo-Dutch brigade. Having received a captaincy in the 1st foot (Grenadier) guards on 9 April 1686, he disposed of his Dutch commission to John Lister in May and returned to England. He negotiated the revolution of 1688 without personal mishap and, favoured as a former Dutch officer, was promoted lieutenant-colonel of the 1st foot guards on 16 March 1689, simultaneously receiving a brevet as colonel of infantry. Knighted on 27 August 1689, he fought in Flanders under William III and was promoted brigadier-general on 20 December 1695. On 12 November 1696, while in garrison in Ghent, he was appointed colonel of the Royal Fusiliers (7th foot) and subsequently entrusted with conducting many of the demobilizations between 1697 and 1699.

O'Hara was raised to the rank of major-general on 9 March 1702 and appointed one of the three officers of this rank to accompany the duke of Ormond's expedition to Cadiz in 1703 as part of the War of the Spanish Succession. He exercised a quiet influence over the duke, a reflection of their earlier master–pupil relationship. The advice of this calm, modest, competent soldier was normally sound—he 'does not want sense' (*Marlborough–Godolphin Correspondence*, 3.1520). Lacking independent means and reliant upon military pay and emoluments, he succumbed to temptation after the capture of Puerto Santa Maria and both permitted, and benefited from, widespread looting and pillage. Although O'Hara distinguished himself at the capture of Vigo and the destruction of the Spanish treasure fleet, he and Lieutenant-General Sir Henry Belasyse were arrested and court-martialled on their return to England. On the advice of the duke of Marlborough, the episode was played down, resulting in the acquittal of O'Hara. On 1 January 1704 he was promoted lieutenant-general. Recommended for a senior command in Spain in 1705, it was not until the following year that he assumed the duties of second-in-command to the earl of Galway, although his position was uncertain and disputed by the plethora of general officers attending Galway and the earl of Peterborough. In late July 1706 he commanded a detachment that prevented a French attempt to surprise the allies at Guadalajara. For this and other notable services during the 1706 campaign he was raised to an Irish barony, taking his title from Tyrawley in co. Mayo. At a council of war on 15 January 1707 held in Valencia, he strongly supported Galway and Stanhope in advocating an offensive against Madrid with undivided forces. The three generals put their arguments in writing and sent them to England. At the battle of Almanza (14 April 1707) he commanded the left of the allied army. His initial advance pushed back the French right before being held and repulsed; he then successfully withstood the French counter-attack. Although wounded, he led his forces back to Tortosa. He returned to England in September 1707 and unsuccessfully petitioned for £1000 compensation for his lost equipage. Having taken his seat in the Irish House of Lords on 25 May 1710, he was sworn of the Irish privy council, and resworn by George I in 1714.

In January 1711 the tories in the House of Lords initiated an investigation into the perceived mismanagement of the campaign of 1707 in Spain in order to cement their new alliance with the earl of Peterborough. Galway and Tyrawley were summoned to account for their actions, concentrating especially on the council of war of 15 January 1707. Both successfully argued that they had been obeying orders from the secretary of state, the earl of Sunderland. When pressed further, Tyrawley said that he had fought with the sword, not the pen. He had not carried ink with him and he had not kept a register and could therefore only recall generalities not details. Indeed, there was nothing in the official papers implicating him in anything other than the decision to launch the offensive against Madrid. A resolution declared that he was one of those responsible for the decision to advance on Madrid and for the conduct of the battle of Almanza. Galway and Tyrawley petitioned for time to produce answers and they were supported by two protests from the whig peers; no further action was taken.

Having resigned his colonelcy to his son on 15 November 1714, Tyrawley was appointed commander-in-chief in Ireland, remaining in office until 1721. He was sometime governor of Kilmainham Hospital. Before 1682 he had married Frances, daughter of Gervase Rouse of Rous Lench, Worcestershire, who died on 10 November 1733 and was buried in St Mary's, Dublin. They had at least two children, including a son, James *O'Hara, second baron, general and diplomatist, and a daughter, Mary, who died in 1759. Tyrawley died in Dublin on 8 or 9 June 1724 and was buried on 11 June in the chancel vault of St Mary's, Dublin.   JOHN CHILDS

Sources BL, Add. MS 23642 · BL, Add. MS 41819 · BL, Add. MS 17918 · BL, Add. MS 9755 · C. Dalton, ed., *English army lists and commission registers, 1661–1714*, 6 vols. (1892–1904) · A. D. Francis, *The First Peninsular War, 1702–1713* (1975) · *Calendar of the manuscripts of the marquess of Ormonde*, new ser., 8 vols., HMC, 36 (1902–20) · *CSP dom., 1702–3* · *The Marlborough–Godolphin correspondence*, ed. H. L. Snyder, 3 vols. (1975) · *The manuscripts of the House of Lords*, new ser., 12 vols. (1900–77) · GEC, *Peerage*

Archives BL, Add. MSS 23627–23642 · NL Ire., corresp.

O'Hara, Charles (*c*.1740–1802), army officer and colonial governor, was the illegitimate son of James *O'Hara, Baron Kilmaine and second Baron Tyrawley (1681/2–1773). He attended Westminster School, and was appointed ensign in Colonel Edward Wolfe's regiment, later the 8th foot, on 20 April 1751 and cornet in the 3rd dragoons on 23 December 1752. In January 1756 he became lieutenant and captain in the Coldstream Guards, of which his father was colonel. He served in Germany as aide-de-camp to John Manners, marquess of Granby, after Minden, then, with the brevet rank of lieutenant-colonel, was quartermaster-general in the short 1762 Portuguese campaign under Lord Tyrawley. In July 1766 he was appointed commandant at Goree in the new British territory of Senegambia and of the African corps, a unit largely of army convicts, pardoned on condition of service in Africa. He retained his position in the guards, however, and became captain and lieutenant-colonel in 1769 and brevet colonel in August 1777.

O'Hara served in the American War of Independence from October 1780, with the guards brigade of detachments from the three regiments. He was critical of the 'Temporising—moderation & delay' that 'have governed our councils', and he denounced British efforts to defeat the Americans as 'feeble' (September 1778, Hull University Library, Hotham papers, DDHO 4/18). His recommendation was for 'Fire & Sword' to 'Ruin & desolate the remotest corners' of the most rebellious provinces, so that 'every Man Experiences in himself, & dearest connections, the Rude & mercyless hand of war' (ibid.). This was hardly novel; many of his frustrated colleagues were urging the same course. But O'Hara's conviction that a destructive war was the only option was based on a different logic from that of most of the 'fire and sword' school. He was convinced that no dependence could be placed on the loyalists, and was very critical of 'the New Mode adopted of pursuing the War in this Country by Arming American against American' (West Suffolk RO, Grafton papers, Ac 423/189). No American could be trusted, in O'Hara's view, and he recommended a war of desolation not so much to terrorize the rebellious colonists into submission as to weaken the new United States for the foreseeable future (ibid., Ac 423/190).

O'Hara served in the southern campaigns under Lord Cornwallis. He was wounded at the battle of Guilford court house on 15 March 1781, and was with Cornwallis's army which surrendered at Yorktown, Virginia, on 19 October 1781. O'Hara, as Cornwallis's second in command, had to take the lead in the surrender ceremony, handing his sword to Washington's second in command, Benjamin Lincoln (a scene depicted in John Trumbull's painting of Yorktown). O'Hara remained a prisoner until 9 February 1782, when he was exchanged. He had in the mean time been promoted major-general (October 1781). In April 1782 he was appointed colonel of the 22nd foot, and the following month he took reinforcements from New York to Jamaica.

After serving as commanding officer at Gibraltar from 1787 to 1789, O'Hara became lieutenant-governor in 1792. In April 1791 he was transferred to the colonelcy of the 74th highlanders, then more lucrative than that of the 22nd. In October 1793 he was promoted lieutenant-general and given command of the British forces operating before Toulon. When the French attacked Fort Mulgrave on 23 November he was wounded and captured, and he remained a prisoner in the Luxembourg, Paris, until August 1795, when he was exchanged. Shortly afterwards he was appointed governor of Gibraltar. He became known as 'Old Cock of the Rock', and was described in his later years by Thomas Hamilton in his military novel *Cyril Thornton* (1827). O'Hara became a full general in January 1798, and in his last years was 'very rich' (*GM*).

O'Hara never married, though he was engaged in 1795–6 to Miss Mary *Berry (1763–1852), author, whom he had met at Rome in 1784. He had two children each with two mistresses at Gibraltar, and he left his mistresses and children £70,000 in trust in his will. He left his plate and some other property, valued in all at over £7000 (much more than he left his brother) to his black servant, Moyse.

After a six-month illness and suffering much from complications caused by his old wounds, O'Hara died at Gibraltar on 21 February 1802.   STEPHEN CONWAY

Sources DNB · GM, 1st ser., 72 (1802), 278 · *Old Westminsters*, vol. 2 · Walpole, *Corr.* · *Extracts of the journals and correspondence of Miss Berry*, ed. M. T. Lewis, 2nd edn, 3 vols. (1865–6) · U. Hull, Brynmor Jones L., Hotham MSS, DDHO · Suffolk RO, Bury St Edmunds, Grafton papers · Cornwallis papers, PRO · GEC, *Peerage*
Archives BL, corresp. with Lord Loudoun, Add. MSS 44067–44082 · BL, letters to Lord Nelson, Add. MSS 34906–34914, *passim* · BL, letters to his father, Lord Tyrawley, Add. MS 23635 · NL Scot., corresp. with Sir Thomas Graham · PRO, corresp. relating to defences at Gibraltar, PRO 30/11
Wealth at death over £79,000: GM, 1.278

O'Hara, James, second Baron Tyrawley and Baron Kilmaine (1681/2–1773), army officer and diplomat, was the only son of Charles *O'Hara, first Baron Tyrawley (d. 1724), and his wife, Frances (d. 1733), daughter of Gervase Rouse of Rous Lench, Worcestershire. O'Hara was commissioned on 15 March 1703 a lieutenant in his father's regiment, the Royal Fusiliers, and a captain on 24 March 1705. He fought at the siege of Barcelona in 1706 and was wounded at Almanza in 1707, and again at Malplaquet in 1709, when he served as an aide-de-camp to Marlborough. He succeeded to the colonelcy of his father's regiment on 29 January 1713 and then served with the regiment in Minorca until the end of the reign. O'Hara was named an aide-de-camp to George I in 1717 (continuing to hold office under George II until 1743), and in 1718–19 in the Mediterranean. His regiment was stationed in Ireland from 1719 to 1727.

O'Hara was created Baron Kilmaine in the Irish peerage on 8 February 1722, and took his seat in the Irish House of Lords on 29 August 1723. He succeeded his father on 8 June 1724 and on 25 June was sworn of the Irish privy council. In November 1724 he married Mary (b. in or after 1696, d. 1769), daughter of William Stewart, second Viscount Mountjoy. They had no children, though Tyrawley's extra-marital relationships produced several offspring. His attempt in 1727 to obtain the duke of Bridgewater's interest in a parliamentary borough, presumably Brackley, ended in a polite rebuff. Debts in Ireland led him to seek a diplomatic posting and on 11 February 1728 he was named envoy-extraordinary to Portugal. His long stay there ensured a close relationship with King João V and it was reported that he 'was almost naturalized amongst them, trusted and beloved there' (Walpole, *Corr.*, 22.48). He finally left Lisbon on 18 July 1741 and on his return was reported to have 'brought three wives and fourteen children' back with him (ibid., 18.104). His estates, too, were in better shape, aided by the £800 p.a. he gained after the death of his mother.

Meanwhile Tyrawley had become successively brigadier-general (1735), major-general (1739), and lieutenant-general (1743), as well as changing his regiment from the Royal Fusiliers to the 7th foot in 1739, the first of a rapid series of changes which finally saw him settle on his eighth regiment, the Coldstream Guards, in 1755. While in Dublin in 1741 he declined an American command, and he spent 1742–3 in England agitating for honours or employment before being appointed ambassador-extraordinary and -plenipotentiary to Russia on 17 December 1743. He left St Petersburg on 8 March 1745, and was available to serve under General George Wade during the forty-five.

In 1747, after approaching the duke of Newcastle, Tyrawley was named governor of Minorca, and at the end of the year, on 17 December, he was elected a fellow of the Royal Society. Unfortunately he was, as he put it, 'interdicted' from taking up his colonial post. This was still a grievance for Tyrawley in 1750, and no doubt explains his appointment in March 1752 as minister-plenipotentiary to Portugal, a post which he took up with alacrity in April before returning in July. Tyrawley was still an absentee governor when Minorca was besieged by the French. On 2 June 1756 he embarked from Portsmouth as the new governor of Gibraltar with orders to proceed via Gibraltar to pick up reinforcements with which to relieve Minorca, but it fell before his arrival.

Tyrawley spent his time at Gibraltar in strengthening the fortifications and complaining about the lack of supplies and his own under-employment. He was eventually allowed to return home on 16 April 1757. He presided over the court martial of Sir John Mordaunt on 14 December 1757. His conduct as governor of Gibraltar was the subject of a parliamentary attack by Lord George Sackville, particularly his expenditure on defensive fortifications. Tyrawley defended himself at the bar of the Commons on 13 April 1758 and virtually browbeat his accusers, so that he escaped censure. Tyrawley was also critical of the decision to make Charles Spencer, third duke of Marlborough, general of foot in 1758, though he received some recompense in 1759 when he was named governor of Portsmouth. Nor was Tyrawley averse to repaying Sackville, being outspoken in his criticism of Sackville's conduct at the battle of Minden in 1759. Tyrawley was named general on 7 March 1761. He was appointed commander-in-chief in Portugal in February 1762, but came home somewhat disenchanted in July 1762 claiming that the Portuguese only wanted British subsidies. He was sworn of the privy council on 17 November 1762, and made field marshal on 10 June 1763.

Tyrawley was offered the governorship of Minorca in 1766 in exchange for Portsmouth, Sackville remarking that 'his Lordship not being an accommodating genius, refused the change, though for his advantage' (*Stopford-Sackville MSS*, 1.110). This confirms Walpole's sketch of Tyrawley: 'he had a great deal of humour and occasional good breeding, but not to the prejudice of his natural temper, which was imperiously blunt, haughty and contemptuous, with an undaunted portion of spirit' (Walpole, *Memoirs of George II*, 3.14). Tyrawley's wife died on 5 February 1769, and Tyrawley himself was clearly ailing when he sent a message to Hester Pitt, countess of Chatham, which referred to his being 'so blind as to be forced to employ another hand to write, so deaf as not to hear half the nonsense said near him, and so simple of understanding, as

not to be able to conceal his own' (*Correspondence of William Pitt*, 4.208).

Tyrawley died on 14 July 1773 at Twickenham, aged ninety-one. He was buried on 24 July at the chapel of Chelsea Hospital, where he was governor. His will referred to money owed him by Sir Arthur Gore, bt, for the purchase of lands in co. Mayo and co. Sligo. He left his estate to his two 'natural' daughters, Anne and Jemima, 'both now living with me', and appointed as executors his son Charles *O'Hara and James Meyricke of Westminster. At least two other natural sons, Francis and James, predeceased him; another illegitimate daughter, apparently, was the actress George Anne *Bellamy (1731?–1788).

STUART HANDLEY

Sources GEC, *Peerage* · D. B. Horn, ed., *British diplomatic representatives, 1689–1789*, CS, 3rd ser., 46 (1932), 98, 100, 114 · N. B. Leslie, *The succession of colonels of the British army from 1660 to the present day* (1974) · C. Dalton, ed., *George the First's army, 1714–1727*, 2 (1912), 25–32 · Walpole, *Corr.* · will, PRO, PROB 11/990, sig. 313 · Newcastle papers, BL, Add. MSS 32697–32895 · *Report on the manuscripts of his grace the duke of Buccleuch and Queensberry … preserved at Montagu House*, 3 vols. in 4, HMC, 45 (1899–1926), vol. 1. pp. 377–88 · R. Whitworth, *William Augustus, duke of Cumberland: a life* (1992), 59, 175 · *Correspondence of William Pitt, earl of Chatham*, ed. W. S. Taylor and J. H. Pringle, 4 vols. (1838–40) · *Report on the manuscripts of Mrs Stopford-Sackville*, 1, HMC, 49 (1904), 110 · *An eighteenth-century secretary at war: the papers of William Viscount Barrington*, ed. T. Hayter (1988), 286–7, 395

Archives Alnwick Castle, Northumberland, copies of papers as envoy to Portugal · BL, diplomatic papers, corresp., Add. MSS 23627–23642, Add. MS 44068 · NL Ire., corresp. and papers | BL, letters to Lord Barrington, Add. MS 40760 · BL, corresp. with duke of Newcastle and others, Add. MSS 32697–33056, *passim* · NRA, priv. coll., letters to first Earl Waldegrave · PRO, letters to first earl of Chatham, PRO 30/8 · U. Nott. L., letters to Henry Pelham

Likenesses attrib. J. Verelst, double portrait, oils, 1712 (with second duke of Montagu), NPG

O'Hara, Kane (1711/12–1782), playwright, was born at Templehouse in Connaught, the son of Kean O'Hara, a squire and member of an ancient Sligo family. Young O'Hara received his early schooling from the Revd William Jackson at Mount Temple and entered Trinity College, Dublin, on 3 March 1728, aged sixteen, receiving his BA in spring 1732 and his MA in summer 1735. O'Hara is listed in university records as a pensioner, that is, a person of moderate income.

O'Hara's first professional play was *Midas, an English Burletta*, which had its première production at the Crow Street Theatre, Dublin, on 22 January 1762. *Midas* was a clever, chauvinistic response to the success of a touring Italian troupe, the D'Amici family, which had brought a lively production of an Italian burletta to the Smock Alley Theatre on 19 December 1761. The Italian burletta, a slight comic opera already modish on the continent, captivated Dubliners with its simple domestic plot and brisk galante music.

Lord Mornington, Garrett Colley Wellesley, father of the future duke of Wellington and then professor of music at Trinity College, urged O'Hara to respond to the Italian performers. O'Hara revised his slight mock pastoral *Midas*, which had been privately performed for William Brownlow MP at Lough Neagh, near Lurgan, co. Armagh, in April 1760. The Irish playwright John O'Keeffe recalled that, as a young boy, he was present at O'Hara's house in King Street, Stephen's Green, one morning when the three gentlemen, O'Hara, Lord Mornington, and Brownlow were settling the music for *Midas* (O'Keeffe, 1.53). O'Hara transformed his play into an eclectic *Midas*, incorporating the deities and the recitative aria musical pattern of Italian *opera seria* and the comic domestic plot and lively music of the Italian burletta, subtitling his play 'an English burletta'. *Midas* delighted Dubliners and was brought to London's Covent Garden with only minor revisions. Performed as a mainpiece on 22 February 1764, it was soon revised to a two-act afterpiece and was performed over 200 times by 1800; it was generally believed to be superior to all subsequent English burlettas. O'Hara's creation of the burletta was significant because it bridged the gap musically between the early-century ballad opera and the later, technically sophisticated, comic opera.

O'Hara's second burletta, *The Golden Pippin*, was initially rejected by the lord chamberlain because of satirical references to members of the royal family, but, after excision of contemporary allusions, it enjoyed substantial popularity at Covent Garden. O'Hara's next two burlettas, *April Day* (1777, Haymarket), and *Tom Thumb* (1780, Covent Garden), abandoned the use of mythological figures but preserved the musical style of the burletta. O'Hara's *The Two Misers: a Musical Farce* (1775, Covent Garden), an adaptation of M. de Falbaire's *Les deux avares*, enjoyed only moderate success.

A serious amateur musician, in 1757 O'Hara had founded, with Lord Mornington, the Dublin Academy of Music and served as one of its officers, meeting at the Fishamble Street Music Hall on Wednesday evenings to prepare concerts for charitable causes. O'Hara also wrote musical compositions of different types; the National Library of Ireland holds manuscript copies of five of his works: 'Fussalia' (1756), a musical masque; 'Isaac' (1767), an oratorio; 'Cupid's Triumph' (1768), a serenata; 'Orlando' (1772); and 'Tom Thumb the Great' (1774), a puppet show opera (MSS 9248, 9251, 9252, 9258, 9259).

In 1774 O'Hara established Mr Punch's Patagonian Theatre in a house in Abbey Street, Dublin, where the Irish tenor, Michael Kelly, as a young boy, sang the role of Daphne in *Midas*, 'instructed by the author himself' (Kelly, 19). The proceeds from all performances were given to charity. The Patagonian Theatre moved to Exeter Change, London, in October 1776, where it successfully presented puppet show performances of ballad operas, burlesques, and burlettas for five years.

O'Hara was a popular figure, respected in Dublin society as a successful playwright, skilful amateur musician, popular composer, and accomplished painter. Tall and lean, with slightly stooped shoulders, he was called by his friends 'St Patrick's Steeple' and was considered 'a very necessary man in every party for amusement' (Molloy, 2, 153). Though he lost his eyesight in 1778, O'Hara retained an avid interest in theatre. John O'Keeffe, who recalled dining with him in 1781, noted his exquisite manners and described him as 'a first-rate wit' (O'Keeffe, 1.53). O'Hara died in Dublin on 17 June 1782. PHYLLIS T. DIRCKS

Sources J. O'Keeffe, *Recollections of the life of John O'Keeffe, written by himself*, 2 vols. (1826) · P. T. Dircks, 'The Dublin manuscripts of Kane O'Hara', *N&Q*, 215 (1970), 99–100 · P. T. Dircks, *The eighteenth-century English burletta* (1999) · K. O'Hara, *Two burlettas of Kane O'Hara: Midas and The golden pippin*, ed. P. T. Dircks (1987) · R. Hitchcock, *An historical view of the Irish stage from the earliest period down to the close of the season 1788*, 2 vols. (1788–94) · M. Kelly, *Reminiscences*, 2 vols. (1826) · Burtchaell & Sadleir, *Alum. Dubl.* · W. J. Lawrence, 'Early Irish ballad opera and comic opera', *Musical Quarterly*, 8 (1922), 397–412, esp. 407 · A. Loewenberg, *Annals of opera, 1597–1940*, 2nd edn, 2 vols. (1955) · G. Speaight, *The history of the English puppet theatre*, 2nd edn (1990) · J. F. Molloy, *The romance of the Irish stage*, 2 vols. (1897) · B. Victor, *The history of the theatres of London and Dublin*, 3 vols. (1761–71)

Likenesses E. Dorrell, etching, pubd 1802, BM, NG Ire. · portrait, Annaghmore, co. Sligo

O'Hartegan, Mathew (1600–1666), Jesuit and diplomat, was born in St John's parish, Limerick. He went abroad to study, as no opportunities for study were permitted to Catholics in Ireland. It is likely that Bordeaux was his destination, and he seems to have had in mind to prepare himself for the priesthood or a secular career. When he entered the Society of Jesus at Bordeaux on 8 January 1626 he had already studied jurisprudence for four years, in addition to philosophy, and had graduated master of arts. After his noviceship in the order he was sent for a short period to teach at the Jesuit college, Agen, and then, in 1630, commenced his theological studies at Bordeaux. He was ordained priest in 1633, and at the end of his theology course was appointed professor of philosophy at Pau.

Two years later O'Hartegan was transferred to take charge of temporal administration in the college of La Rochelle. After a year there, at the end of 1637, he was sent back to Ireland in response to an appeal for men from the superior of the Irish mission, Father Robert Nugent. In September 1640 Nugent appointed him one of three chaplains to the king's army which had been raised to fight in Scotland. Nine months later, at Waterford, on the instruction of the Jesuit general Muzio Vitelleschi, he was advanced to the profession of the society's fourth vow, the special vow of obedience to the pope. On 24 April 1642 Nugent informed Vitelleschi that, following the outbreak of conflict in Ireland, the Catholic leadership was pressing him to send two of his men, one to France and one to Belgium, to seek aid from Catholic princes. Reluctantly, and only because of the exceptional circumstances, the general agreed. As one of the two Jesuit agents, O'Hartegan travelled to France in May 1642.

On 23 July 1643 the supreme council of the confederate Catholics formally appointed O'Hartegan and Geoffrey Baron, nephew of Luke Wadding OFM, agents to the French court. From May 1642 to January 1645 O'Hartegan worked with distinction as official representative of the Irish Confederation in Paris. Aid was obtained, and he gained the esteem of Cardinal Grimaldi, apostolic nuncio to France; of the queen regent, Anne of Austria; of Queen Henrietta Maria; and of high French officials of state. Then, late in 1644, there appeared alleged dispatches of O'Hartegan's, full of self-esteem and containing damaging remarks attributed to the queen as well as comments critical of members of the confederation and other key figures. These undermined his standing with the confederation, which called for his return home in March 1645, and with the queen. Her majesty, however, having met him, it seems, soon restored him to favour, which, together with other evidence, indicates that the letters were seen as having been deliberately forged to discredit him and his cause. This was further borne out by his continued high standing with successive Jesuit generals. He remained in Paris until April 1646, when he informed the general that he had completed his business there. He was appointed to Bordeaux to lecture in philosophy.

Before taking up that appointment, O'Hartegan travelled to Ireland and was present at Owen Roe O'Neill's victory at the battle of Benburb on 5 June 1646. From there he brought the captured standards to Limerick, where he presented them to the papal nuncio Rinuccini at a special celebratory religious service in St Mary's Cathedral. Subsequently, at Bordeaux, he helped prepare the Jesuit Mercure Verdier, about to be sent on an extraordinary visitation of the Irish mission. His assistance is the likely explanation of Verdier's remarkable grasp of the tangled Irish political–religious situation. O'Hartegan taught philosophy at Bordeaux during 1646–8, at Pau in 1648–50, and at Agen in 1657–60. His short time in each place raises questions about his success as a lecturer. He was actively involved in disagreements with Jansenists during these years. He also represented his Jesuit province of Aquitaine on business matters at Paris, and for a short while was a superior at Bayonne. In 1660 he was assigned to the *grand collège* of Poitiers, where he worked until his death there on 2 May 1666, aged sixty-six. He was buried at Poitiers.

THOMAS J. MORRISSEY

Sources Irish Jesuit Archives, Dublin, esp. MacErlean transcripts · T. J. Morrissey, 'The strange letters of Mathew O'Hartegan, S. J., 1644–45', *Irish Theological Quarterly*, 37 (1970), 159–72 · *History of the Irish confederation and the war in Ireland … by Richard Bellings*, ed. J. T. Gilbert, 7 vols. (1882–91), vol. 4 · B. O'Ferrall and D. O'Connell, *Commentarius Rinuccinianus de sedis apostolicae legatione ad foederatos Hiberniae Catholicos per annos 1645–1649*, ed. J. Kavanagh, IMC, 1 (1932), 496, 680–82, 703; 4 (1941), 127 · G. Aiazzi, *The embassy in Ireland of Monsignor G. B. Rinuccini*, trans. A. Hutton (1873) · R. Bagwell, *Ireland under the Stuarts*, 2 (1909) · E. Ludlow, *Memoirs of E. Ludlow*, 3rd edn (1751), 438, 450–51, 483

O'Healy [O'Hely], **Patrick** (*d.* 1579), Roman Catholic bishop of Mayo and martyr, may have been from Dromahair, co. Leitrim, or have been a member of the friary there. Having already taken his vows as a Franciscan, he arrived in Rome from Ireland in 1562, where he impressed the minister-general of the Observant Franciscans with his piety and intelligence. O'Healy was sent to Spain, where he studied grammar for two years at the friary of St Francis in Molina de Aragon, philosophy for four years in the friary in San

Clemente, and theology in the University of Alcalá. He became fluent in Catalan and was described as a good preacher.

About 1574–5, O'Healy became associated with a circle of exiled Irish who were urging Spanish military intervention in Ireland. He arrived in Rome on 16 June 1575, with letters of accreditation from Philip II and began canvassing support for James fitz Maurice Fitzgerald, a charismatic adventurer who wanted to lead a papal-sponsored crusade to Ireland. Frequently in contact with the Spanish papal ambassador, O'Healy spoke with Pope Gregory XIII about the persecution suffered by Irish Catholics. During his stay in Rome, he made enough of an impression to be consecrated as bishop of Mayo on 4 July 1576. In late 1576 he left for Madrid to bring the pope's invasion plan before Philip. Preparations gradually came to fruition, and on 18 November 1577 he set sail with Fitzgerald for Ireland as part of a small invasion force. However, severe storms caused them to put to harbour at Corunna in Galicia. There, the Breton captain and his crew refused to honour their contract by proceeding and were imprisoned, but on 5 January 1578 they escaped and made off with the ship.

Fitzgerald followed the crew to Brittany, while O'Healy journeyed to Paris, where on 7 April he secured a royal warrant for restitution of the stolen goods. At this point, O'Healy appears to have lost interest in Fitzgerald's crusade and did not play any part in the latter's renewed efforts to head an invasion of Ireland. O'Healy remained in Paris for about nine months, living in the Franciscan friary and engaging in academic disputations. In early 1579 he left Paris for Brittany, from where he took ship for Ireland.

O'Healy and his travelling companion, Conn O'Rourke, a friar and the son of an Irish chieftain, landed at Smerwick, co. Kerry, shortly before Fitzgerald's forces landed at the same harbour on 18 June 1579. O'Healy and O'Rourke hastened to the seat of Gerald fitz James Fitzgerald, fourteenth earl of Desmond, at Askeaton, co. Limerick, probably to encourage him to rebel. Desmond was absent, but his wife entertained them for three days. The earl's relationship with the government was tense at best and the actions of fitz Maurice Fitzgerald, his cousin, placed him in a very dangerous position. Either on her own initiative or at her husband's behest, the countess of Desmond sent a messenger to the mayor of Limerick informing him of O'Healy's presence. On leaving Askeaton, O'Healy and O'Rourke headed north towards Limerick, probably on their way to Connaught, but the forewarned authorities captured them *en route*.

O'Healy and O'Rourke were imprisoned in Limerick and tried under martial law by the lord president of Munster, Sir William Drury. O'Healy was tortured in an unsuccessful attempt to gain details of fitz Maurice Fitzgerald's plans. As part of this process, spikes were driven through his hands, severing his fingers. Drury then offered O'Healy the peaceful possession of his see, if he would renounce his faith, but he refused. Sentenced to death, O'Healy and O'Rourke were hanged about 13 August 1579 outside Kilmallock, co. Limerick. A woodcut of the hanging bodies was made and appears in Richard Verstegan's *Theatrum crudelitatum haereticorum nostri temporis* (1587). The bodies were left hanging for a week, before John fitz Edmund Fitzgerald of Desmond arranged for their burial on 27 August at Clonmel, co. Tipperary. In 1647 the bodies were transferred to the Franciscan house at Askeaton. O'Healy was the first Catholic bishop to be executed in Ireland since the advent of the Reformation and he quickly became the subject of a number of martyrologies. He was beatified in 1992. TERRY CLAVIN

Sources B. Millett, 'The beautiful martyrs of Ireland: Be. Patrick O'Hely, OFM, Be. Conn O'Rourke, OFM', *Irish Theological Quarterly*, 64 (1999), 67–78 · state papers, Elizabeth I, PRO, SP 63/69/5 · M. V. Ronan, *The Reformation in Ireland under Elizabeth, 1558–1580* (1930), 568–71 · W. M. Hennessy, ed. and trans., *The annals of Loch Cé: a chronicle of Irish affairs from AD 1014 to AD 1590*, 2 vols., Rolls Series, 54 (1871), 427, 429 · *CSP Ire.*, 1574–85, 133 · M. V. Ronan, *The Irish martyrs of the penal laws* (1935), 27–9 · D. Murphy, *Our martyrs* (1896)
Likenesses woodcut, repro. in R. Verstegan, *Theatrum crudelitatum haereticorum nostri temporis* (Antwerp, 1587), 81

Ó hÉanna, Muirgheas [Matthew O'Heney] (*d.* 1206), archbishop of Cashel and papal legate for Ireland, was a monk of the Cistercian abbey of Holy Cross, Tipperary. He became archbishop of Cashel before 1186, when, according to Gerald of Wales, he was present at the provincial synod summoned by Archbishop John Cumin to meet in Dublin during Lent; and Gerald attributes to him the famous remark regarding the propensity of the English race for making martyrs. About 1190 Ó hÉanna wrote two letters to Pope Clement III enquiring about points of canon law and it was this pontiff or his successor Celestine III who appointed the archbishop papal legate for Ireland in 1191–2. The annals of Inisfallen reported that the new legate held a great synod in Dublin in 1192 and Dublin ecclesiastical records testify to the presence in Dublin that year of the legate and other prominent Irish churchmen. During this period Ó hÉanna negotiated a settlement between the archbishop of Dublin and the Cistercian monks of St Mary's Abbey. He was in England *c.*1192–3 when John, lord of Ireland, granted a charter in his favour at Ludgershall, Wiltshire. In 1195 he is mentioned as one of the prelates who brought the body of Hugh de Lacy, first lord of Meath, to the abbey of Bective in Meath for re-interment.

Although Ó hÉanna's appointment as papal legate lapsed in 1198, he is described as legate by the annals of Inisfallen when in 1201 he acted as peace broker in Munster between the local Irish and William de Burgh. He incurred the displeasure of Pope Innocent III both for his refusal to consecrate a new bishop for Ardfert and for his involvement in the dispute between Archbishop John Cumin of Dublin and King John. Ó hÉanna apparently administered the Dublin spiritualities while Cumin was in exile. These offences resulted in his suspension by Innocent III's new legate in Ireland, Cardinal John of Salerno. It was reported to the pope in 1202 that because of his advanced age Ó hÉanna could not come to seek the pope's absolution in person. It is not known when the suspension

was lifted but by 1205 he was functioning again as archbishop. He died in Holy Cross Abbey in 1206 and was buried there. His obit in the annals of Ireland states that he was an able and religious man, the founder of many churches and religious beyond his fellow countrymen.

MARGARET MURPHY

Sources A. Gwynn, *The Irish church in the eleventh and twelfth centuries*, ed. G. O'Brien (1992) · A. Gwynn, 'Papal legates in Ireland during the twelfth century', *Irish Ecclesiastical Record*, 5th ser., 63 (1944), 361–70 · Gerald of Wales, *The history and topography of Ireland*, trans. J. J. O'Meara, rev. edn (1982) · M. P. Sheehy, ed., *Pontificia Hibernica: medieval papal chancery documents concerning Ireland, 640–1261*, 2 vols. (1962–5) · J. T. Gilbert, ed., *Chartularies of St Mary's Abbey, Dublin: with the register of its house at Dunbrody and annals of Ireland*, 2 vols., Rolls Series, 80 (1884–6) · K. W. Nicholls, 'A charter of John "lord of Ireland" in favour of Matthew Ua Hénni, archbishop of Cashel', *Peritia*, 2 (1983), 267–76 · S. Mac Airt, ed. and trans., *The annals of Inisfallen* (1951)

O'Hearn, Francis (1747–1801), Roman Catholic priest and author, was born in Derry in the parish of Modeligo, co. Waterford. He had at least two brothers, Thomas and Timothy, both of whom were ordained priests. He received his early education from an uncle, William Brown, parish priest of Clashmore, and at a very early age was sent to the Irish Pastoral College, Louvain.

In 1776 O'Hearn was nominated professor of syntax at Holy Trinity College, Louvain, and between 1781 and 1793 he was professor of rhetoric. In 1787 he published *Compositio rhetoribus*. His unpublished *Tractatus rhetoricae* is preserved in the Bibliothèque Royale Albert Ier, Brussels. During university vacations he appears to have travelled widely in Europe and mastered a number of languages. His prowess in Flemish was remarkable and he played a role in the cultural and political revival of the language. In 1785 he had been elected dean of the Flemish nation of the university. He was canon of St Peter's, Louvain, and of Bruges Cathedral. In 1791 he was considered by the nuncio in Liège as a candidate for the bishopric of Waterford. In 1793 he became professor of Christian eloquence and in the same year was rector of the Irish Pastoral College in succession to his fellow countryman John Kent.

When unrest engulfed the Austrian Netherlands during the Brabant Revolution (1789–90) O'Hearn was initially associated with Jean François Vonck, leader of the democrats, who were influenced by Enlightenment and French revolutionary thought. He quickly changed his allegiance to the more conservative Henri Van der Noot. He formed part of a Flemish embassy to Berlin. Later he travelled to the German lands. Just before his return to Ireland his nephew Francis O'Hearn was executed in Waterford for his part in the Irish rising of 1798. Bishop Thomas Hussey appointed him parish priest of St Patrick's, Waterford, in 1799. He died in Waterford on 22 October 1801 and was buried in the precincts of the city's Catholic cathedral.

THOMAS O'CONNOR

Sources *Journal of the Waterford and South-East of Ireland Archaeological Society*, 1 (1894), 236–8 · *Journal of the Waterford and South-East of Ireland Archaeological Society*, 5 (1899), 53–4 · *Journal of the Waterford and South-East of Ireland Archaeological Society*, 11 (1908), 43–4 ·

P. Power, *Waterford and Lismore: a compendious history of the united dioceses* (1937) · E. Van Even, *De Ierlander Francis O'Hearn die in Belgie de Vlaamsche dischtkunst beoefande* (1889) · B. Jennings and C. Giblin, eds., *Louvain papers, 1606–1827*, IMC (1968) · C. Giblin, *Irish exiles in Catholic Europe* (1971), vol. 4/3 of *A history of Irish Catholicism* · monument (burial), Waterford City Cathedral · *DNB* · *Waterford Mirror and Munster Packet* (26 Oct 1801) · parish registers, Waterford · university registers, Louvain

Archives Royal Library of Belgium, Brussels, Burgundian Library, MSS

O'Hely, Patrick. *See* O'Healy, Patrick (*d.* 1579).

Ó hEodhasa [O'Hussey], **Eochaidh** (*c.*1560–1612), Gaelic poet, from Ballyhose (Baile í Eodhasa), Fermanagh, was the son of Maoileachlainn Óg Ó hEodhasa, a known poet who was head of his name. According to his own evidence Ó hEodhasa trained as a poet at schools in the north (Leath Chuinn) and in Munster (Thomond). His father was probably his principal teacher. His training in Munster took place during the chieftainship of Hugh Maguire, as transpires in the poem 'Atám i gcás idir dhá chomhairle' (Mac Cionnaith, no. 70) (reliably attributed). This shows him in two minds whether to break off his studies in Thomond to return to Hugh Maguire's household. But his appointment to the Maguires seems to date from the lifetime of Hugh's father Cú Chonnacht, who is addressed in what purports to be the first poem of Ó hEodhasa's tenure as *ollamh* (or court poet), 'Anois molfam Mág Uidhir' (Greene). He was to be *ollamh* to successive Maguire (Mág Uidhir) chieftains. A special relationship with Hugh Maguire was forged prior to his succession to the chieftainship. The poem 'Connradh do cheanglas re hAodh' (Breatnach, 'Covenant') composed during Cú Chonnacht's lifetime, records how Ó hEodhasa came to undertake to append a quatrain in Hugh's honour to all his compositions, and the praise poem 'Bíodh aire ag Ultaibh ar Aodh' (Mac Cionnaith, no. 75) is also earlier than 1589. Among his numerous later poems for Hugh Maguire are the inaugural ode 'Suirgheach sin, a Éire ógh' (O'Grady, 476–8), the poem asserting his rights as office-holder to Maguire, 'Mór an t-ainm ollamh flatha' (ibid., 474–5), and the elegy 'Fada re hurchóid Éire' (ibid., 460).

English documents show Ó hEodhasa to have resided at Ballyhose (on Castlehume Lough, Lower Lough Erne, barony of Magheraboy) in the period from 1585 to 1591. A series of pardons was granted to him at this location, the earliest in 1585–6 during the chieftainship of Cú Chonnacht Maguire (*d.* 1589), who is also mentioned (*Fiants of Elizabeth*, no. 4810), and thereafter in 1591 as a 'freeholder' (ibid., no. 5602), and again in 1591–2 along with Hugh Maguire and others (ibid., no. 5716). He subsequently moved to lands located at Currin (near Ballinamallard, barony of Tirkennedy, close to the border with Lurg barony), as can be learned from the composition 'T'aire riomsa, a rí ó nUidhir' (Bergin, no. 33) addressed to Hugh Maguire in which the poet expresses dissatisfaction with the holding granted to him in virtue of his status as Maguire's *ollamh*. In 1610–11 he was allotted a plantation grant of 210 acres at Clanawley barony (adjoining

Magheraboy to the south), a fact suggesting an accommodation with the new order, which is borne out by a reference in his obituary to the esteem he enjoyed among the English.

Hugh's successor in the chieftainship, his half-brother Cú Chonnacht Óg, also patronized Ó hEodhasa who addresses him in several formal poems including 'Fada léigthear Eamhain i n-aontomha' (unpublished) which marks his inauguration, and the artistic eulogy 'Do féachadh fulang Ghaoidheal' (unpublished). Ó hEodhasa's compositions to patrons other than the Maguires comprise approximately half of the surviving total of fifty attributed to him (half of which have been published) and fall into two more or less equal groups, namely those dating from the years before Hugh Maguire's death, and those composed thereafter. The former category includes addresses to such notables as Aodh Ruadh Ó Domhnaill ('Díol fuatha flaitheas Éireann', O'Grady, 461) and Toirrdhealbhach Luineach Ó Néill ('An sluagh sidhe so i nEamhain', Ó Donnchadha). Also eulogized by him in this period were members of the O'Doherty, Mac Sweeney, and O'Rourke families in Ulster, members of the Burke, MacDermot, and O Conor families in Connaught, and, in Leinster, various of the O'Byrnes, whose family 'duanaire' contains five poems by Ó hEodhasa (Mac Airt). Among noteworthy poems composed in the period after 1600 'Mór theasda dh'obair Óivid' (Breatnach, 'Metamorphosis') celebrates the accession of James I (1603), while, in striking contrast, 'Beag mhaireas do mhacraidh Gaoidheal' (ibid., 471–2) addressed to Mac Mahon of Oriel, apparently after the flight of the earls in 1607, is marked by a deeply felt gloom concerning the Irish cause.

Eochaidh Ó hEodhasa was an outstanding eulogist whose gift surpassed that of either of his two most illustrious contemporaries, Fearghal Óg Mac an Bhaird and Tadhg Dall Ó hUiginn. His verse shows consistent compositional perfection, originality of expression and imagery (see for example the dazzlingly ornate address to Maguire's wounded hand, 'Slán fád lot, a lámh Aodha', unpublished), and a conscious versatility in the choice of apologues. Seriousness, grace, and intensity are characteristic qualities present in a number of personal poems such as his address to Hugh Maguire when absent on a campaign in Munster, 'Fuar leam an adhaighse d'Aodh' (Bergin, no. 29) and 'Fada óm intinn a hamharc' (Ó Maolagáin), composed for a similarly absent Cú Chonnacht Maguire. A keen awareness of his traditional rights and personal dignity shows in the poem 'Mór an t-ainm ollamh flatha' as also in 'Beir oirbhire uaim go hAodh' (unpublished) which reproves his patron for unwarranted public criticism of a poem. On the other hand good-natured self-deprecatory humour is evident in several informal compositions addressed to unspecified persons, as also in 'Ionmholta malairt bhisigh' (Bergin, no. 30), a poem in loose metre in which the merits of freer verse forms are extolled.

Ó hEodhasa died on 9 June 1612, and the record of his death (in Walsh) describes him as 'a notable archprofessor in poetry and learning and in the clear intellect of Irish art, a good hosteller and keeper of a guest house generally, and a renowned man amongst the Irish and the English' (editor's translation).

PÁDRAIG A. BREATNACH

Sources *Report of the Deputy Keeper of the Public Records in Ireland*, 15–16 (1883–4), appxs [calendar of fiants, Elizabeth] · P. Walsh, 'Short annals of Fir Manach', *Irish chiefs and leaders* (1960), 58 · C. McGrath, 'Í Eódhosa', *Clogher Record*, 2/1 (1957), 1–19 · P. A. Breatnach, 'The chief's poet', *PRIA*, 83/C (1983), 37–79 · J. Carney, *The Irish bardic poet* (Dublin, 1967) · P. Ó Maolagáin, 'Eochaidh Ó hEodhusa file Fhear Manach', *St Macarten's Seminary centenary souvenir*, 165–70 · P. A. Breatnach, 'A covenant between Eochaidh Ó hEodhusa and Aodh Mág Uidhir', *Éigse*, 27 (1993), 59–66 · P. A. Breatnach, 'Metamorphosis 1603: dán le hEochaidh Ó hEódhusa', *Éigse*, 17 (1977–8), 169–80 · O. Bergin, *Irish bardic poetry*, ed. D. Greene and F. Kelly (Dublin, 1970) · S. H. O'Grady, ed., *Catalogue of Irish manuscripts in the British Museum*, 1 (1926), 448–81 · S. Mac Airt, *Leabhar Branach* (1944) · L. Mac Cionnaith, *Dioghluim dána* (1939) · D. Greene, *Duanaire Mhéig Uidhir* (1972), no. 23 · T. Ó Donnchadha, *Leabhar Cloinne Aodha Buidhe* (1931), no. 8

Ó hEodhasa [O'Hussey], **Giolla Brighde** [*name in religion* Bonaventura] (*c*.1570–1614), Franciscan friar and poet, was born in the diocese of Clogher, perhaps in co. Fermanagh (although there is a tradition that he came from near Bundoran, co. Donegal). He was a member of a celebrated hereditary learned family whose best-known member was the poet Eochaidh (*d*. 1612). It is not known how closely Giolla Brighde and Eochaidh were related to one another. Giolla Brighde is first recorded, as an apprentice poet, about the time Aodh Ruadh Ó Domhnaill (Hugh Roe O'Donnell) was inaugurated as chieftain of Tír Conaill in the middle of 1592, when he composed an ode to the young chief. This work was apparently ignored by its recipient and does not seem to be extant, but shortly afterwards the young poet composed another poem, of eleven quatrains, 'A-tám ionchóra re hAodh' ('I can defend myself to Aodh'); this is preserved in the poem book known as *The Book of O'Donnell's Daughter*. Some time later (but prior to 1600), Giolla Brighde left Ireland for the continent, his leaving his country and friends occasioning two moving poems, 'Slán agaibh a fhir chumtha' ('Fare you well, my friend') and 'Truagh an t-amharc-sa, a Éire!' ('This is a sorrowful sight, O Ireland').

Ó hEodhasa next appears at Douai on 19 September 1605. He had taken a master's degree and was now seeking permission to go to Louvain to pursue his theological studies, rather than to Salamanca or Valladolid, where he had been asked to go. When the Irish Franciscan college of St Anthony was established at Louvain in 1607 he became one of the first members of staff, having entered the Franciscan order in November of that year and taken as his name in religion Bonaventura. He was ordained in April 1609 and lectured in philosophy and later in theology at Louvain. He had been guardian of St Anthony's for up to two years prior to his untimely death there in 1614.

Ó hEodhasa is especially celebrated in the history of Irish literature as the author of the first Catholic book in Irish to appear in print. This was *An teagasg críosdaidhe*, a catechism which was first issued from the press of Jacobus Mesius in Antwerp in 1611. A second edition, printed on

the Irish press at Louvain (which Bonaventura was instrumental in obtaining some months before his death), was published some time prior to 1619 (most probably in 1614 or 1615). A third edition was issued in Rome in 1707. The work is partly in verse, but mainly in prose. (The date of the first edition is somewhat disputed: some writers mention 1608 as the year in which it first appeared, but this seems unlikely.) The catechism became an exemplar for later works in the same genre. Apparently printed along with, or shortly after, the second (Louvain) edition of *An teagasg críosdaidhe* was a separate booklet of twenty-nine pages containing three poems by Bonaventura: 'Truagh liomsa, a chompáin, do chor' ('I pity your plight, my friend', ninety quatrains, addressed to a close friend 'who fell into heresy'), 'Gabh aithreachas uaim' ('Accept repentance from me'; twenty-one quatrains, and 'Truagh cor chloinne hÁdhaimh' ('Pitiable the condition of the children of Adam'; seventeen quatrains, translated from the Latin of St Bernard). Five further poems by Ó hEodhasa are extant (or possibly six, as in one instance the ascription is uncertain); these include a long catechetical poem which is to be found interspersed through the prose text of *An teagasg críosdaidhe*.

A treatise in Latin by Ó hEodhasa on Irish grammar, *Rudimenta grammaticae Hibernicae*, attempted for the first time to classify Irish nouns by declension, in imitation of the Latin model. This work, which did not appear in print for more than three and a half centuries after the author's death, was mainly intended for fellow Franciscans and other members of the clergy who would have some competence in reading Latin. Bonaventura shows clearly that, apart from his knowledge of Latin (and of some Greek and Hebrew), he was extremely well versed in the teachings of the traditional Irish grammarians. The examples he adduces, including isolated quatrains and sometimes longer passages of Irish classical poetry, are of particular interest.

Ó hEodhasa died of smallpox at Louvain on 15 November 1614, and was buried at St Anthony's College. His fellow scholar and Franciscan Aodh Mac Aingil (Hugh MacCawell) states that Ó hEodhasa had planned, had he not been cut off so prematurely, to write many other works which would be of benefit, both spiritual and temporal, to the nation. The future Roman Catholic archbishop of Armagh thus sums up his confrère's significance: 'There has not been for a long time a man so expert and eminent as Bonaventura in learning, in Gaelic and in piety' (Ó Cléirigh, 27).

NOLLAIG Ó MURAÍLE

Sources *DNB* · B. Jennings, *Michael O Cleirigh, chief of the four masters, and his associates* (1936) · P. Mac Aogáin, *Graiméir Ghaeilge na mBráthar Mionúr* (1968) · C. Mhág Craith, ed., *Dán na mBráthar Mionúr*, 2 vols. (1967–80) · C. McGrath, 'Three poems by Bonabhentúra Ó h-Eódhasa', *Éigse*, 4 (1943–4), 175–96 · C. McGrath, 'Í Eodhosa', *Clogher Record*, 1 (1953–7), 1–19 · F. Mac Raghnaill, 'Teagasc Críostaí Uí Eoghasa', *Galvia*, 8 (1961), 21–6 · F. Mac Raghnaill, *An teagasg críosdaidhe: Bonabhentura Ó hEodhasa a chum* (1976) · T. Ó Cléirigh, *Aodh Mac Aingil agus an Scoil Nua-Ghaeilge i Lobháin* (Dublin, 1935); 2nd edn, ed. T. de Bhaldraithe (Dublin, 1985) · L. Ó Cléirigh, *The life of Aodh Ruadh Ó Domhnaill*, ed. P. Walsh and C. Ó Lochlainn, 2, ITS, 45 (1957), 98–103, 113 · R. Welch, ed., *The Oxford* *companion to Irish literature* (1996) • A. Mac Aingil, *Scáthán Shacramuinte na hAithridhe*, ed. C. Ó Maonaigh (1952)

O'Higgin, Bernard (*d.* 1563), Roman Catholic bishop of Elphin, is of obscure origins; nothing certain is known of his family or background, though F. X. Martin, his biographer, suggested that he may have come from Leyney, now a barony in co. Sligo. About 1517 O'Higgin became a member of a community of Augustinian friars who were observant, 'a reform movement which seemed irresistible' in Ireland immediately prior to the Tudor reformations (Martin, 'Confusion abounding', 49).

O'Higgin first entered the historical record in April 1542 when he met the prior-general of the Augustinian friars in Florence to discuss with him the crises facing the order, and the Roman Catholic church, in Ireland. The last vicar provincial of the Irish Augustinians, Richard Nangle, had subscribed to Henry VIII's royal supremacy and become the first Church of Ireland bishop of Clonfert in 1537. In 1539–40 the English crown had suppressed the houses of the Augustinian friars in Ireland, with the exception of seven houses in Connaught.

On 5 May 1542 O'Higgin was provided as the Roman Catholic bishop of Elphin in western Ireland. He was consecrated on 7 September 1542, apparently at Rome. In the same month the prior-general of the Augustinians issued O'Higgin with a commission, appointing him as the vicar provincial or vicar-general of the Augustinian friars in Ireland for a period of six months only. In that time he was to summon a chapter of the Irish Augustinians and oversee the election of a new vicar provincial.

O'Higgin returned to Ireland and achieved a great deal in restoring order and in raising the morale of the depleted Augustinian communities in Ireland. His achievement won him very favourable comment from a later prior-general. However, O'Higgin failed to take possession of the see of Elphin. Manus O'Donnell, the powerful lord of Tyrconnell, had subscribed to the royal supremacy in order to have Henry VIII appoint his chaplain, Conach O'Shiel, as the bishop of Elphin in 1541. O'Higgin, by contrast, had no aristocratic support and the dean and chapter of Elphin were not well disposed towards him either because he was an outsider. Having completed his work in reorganizing the Augustinian friars O'Higgin returned to mainland Europe, probably in 1544.

It is not known how long O'Higgin stayed in exile, or where. However, with the death of Bishop O'Shiel in 1551 he tried again to take possession of Elphin. He was at Rome in November 1552 and secured letters from the Augustinian prior-general exhorting all Augustinian houses on his route to Ireland to receive and treat him kindly. The prior-general authorized O'Higgin to summon another chapter of the Irish Augustinians to elect a new vicar-general and appoint priors to the houses who would restore discipline, promote charity, and set the example of religious perfection. O'Higgin was unable to convene a chapter, however, and conditions among the Irish Augustinians remained unsatisfactory. He also met with failure in trying to establish himself as the bishop of Elphin. After O'Shiel's death Edward VI had appointed Roland Burke, who was already the bishop of Clonfert, to Elphin *in commendam*. Bishop Burke was the brother of the powerful earl of Clanricarde and O'Higgin could not take charge of the diocese against the will of so powerful a magnate, even with official backing from Queen Mary. He left Ireland once more, probably in 1554, and travelled to Lisbon and thence to Spain, where he spent three years in a number of Augustinian friaries.

David Wolfe, the Jesuit and papal nuncio to Ireland, wrote on 12 October 1561 that O'Higgin 'was a good and religious man in himself, but he was not acceptable to the people' (Moran, 85). Possibly at Wolfe's suggestion O'Higgin resigned that year as bishop of Elphin in favour of a local Dominican friar, Andrew O'Crean, who enjoyed considerable support in the diocese.

O'Higgin passed the last five years of his life in the Augustinian house at Villaviciosa in Portugal. He impressed the Spanish and Portuguese Augustinians with whom he lived as 'a very holy and deeply religious man, who was always praying. He was very unaffected and charitable' (Martin, 'Confusion abounding', 70). He died in the latter half of 1563 at Villaviciosa and was buried there in the friars' choir.
　　　　　　　　　　　　　　　　　HENRY A. JEFFERIES

Sources F. X. Martin, 'Confusion abounding: Bernard O'Higgin, O.S.A., bishop of Elphin, 1542–1561', *Studies in Irish history presented to R. Dudley Edwards*, ed. A. Cosgrave and D. McCartney (1979), 38–84 • F. X. Martin, 'The Irish Augustinian reform movement in the fifteenth century', *Medieval studies presented to Aubrey Gwynn*, ed. J. A. Watt, J. B. Morrall, and F. X. Martin (1961), 230–64 • F. X. Martin and A. de Meijer, eds., 'Irish material in the Augustinian general archives, Rome, 1354–1624', *Archivium Hibernicum*, 19 (1956), 61–134, 141–6 • P. F. Moran, *History of the Catholic archbishops of Dublin since the Reformation* (1864)

O'Higgins, Ambrosio [*formerly* Ambrose Higgins], **marquess of Osorno in the Spanish nobility** (*c.*1721–1801), army officer and colonial administrator in the Spanish service, was born Ambrose Higgins at Ballynary, co. Sligo, one of several children of Charles Higgins and his wife, Margaret, daughter of William O'Higgins and his wife, Winifred. In a pedigree supplied by the obliging Ulster king of arms in 1788 he was certified as being of noble ancestry but this seems incorrect. The details of his early life are obscure. At some stage, possibly in his youth, the family seems to have moved to Summerhill in co. Meath. Though his parents' circumstances appear to have been comparatively humble they were sufficient to pay for his education, which, to judge from his career, must have been to a good standard, especially in mathematics. Possibly he trained as a surveyor or draughtsman. He was reported late in life to have said that he served for a time in the English army but this seems unlikely as his background was Irish and, he claimed, pro-Jacobite. The traditional account that he was educated for the priesthood in Spain seems to be contradicted by his own statement that he went to Spain in 1751 to work in Cadiz for the Irish merchant firm of Butler. On its behalf he undertook a commercial journey to South America in 1756, taking the opportunity to visit his younger brother William, a former clerical student then living in Paraguay with his wife and two children.

In 1761 Higgins became a naturalized Spanish citizen and was commissioned as an engineer–draughtsman with the rank of lieutenant in the Spanish corps of military engineers. His appointment was assisted by John Garland, a Hispano-Irish engineer officer whom he accompanied to Chile in 1764, when Garland was appointed military governor of Valdivia. While crossing the Andes Higgins conceived the idea of improving the route from Mendoza to Santiago by constructing a chain of brick-built shelters. He directed this work so efficiently that by 1766 an all-year postal service was operating between the Atlantic coast and Chile, whereas previously communications had been impossible in winter. He returned to Spain, and in 1768 wrote a *Description of the Realm of Chile*, a well-informed memorandum with recommendations on a wide range of topics including agriculture, commerce, administration, and relations with the Indian population.

On his return to Chile Don Ambrosio, as he was known, was promoted steadily, becoming captain of dragoons in 1770, captain of cavalry in 1771, lieutenant-colonel and commander of cavalry in 1773, colonel in 1777, brigadier-general in 1783, commandant-general in 1780, major-general in 1789, and lieutenant-general in 1794. In the 1770s he successfully commanded troops against the Llanos and Pehuenches Indians of La Araucanía. He founded the fort of San Carlos and displayed considerable valour and leadership skills in a campaign during which he was twice wounded. His fair treatment of the Indians after their defeat ensured the future peace of the region. In 1778 he was appointed delegate-general of the forces in Chile. While *intendant* of Concepción he entertained with great courtesy the French circumnavigator Galaup de la Pérouse.

In 1787 Higgins was made governor and captain-general of Chile, and received a triumphant welcome in Santiago. He proved a vigorous and capable administrator, building roads and coastal fortifications, and founding or re-founding towns such as Los Andes, Osorno, and San Ambrosio de Ballenar, which he named after his birthplace. He improved the sanitation and water supply of Santiago and constructed dykes and jetties along the Río Maípo to preserve the city from flooding. He introduced reforms to taxation and public administration. He abolished the cruel *encomienda* system, whereby landowners kept Indian labourers in conditions close to slavery, and pushed forward reforms in the church to benefit the poor. His 1793 settlement with the Indians at the congress of La Laja laid the foundation for assimilation between colonists and natives. By about 1788 he had adopted O'Higgins as his name. In 1795 he was created baron of Ballenary and appointed viceroy of Peru, becoming marquess of Osorno in 1796. In Peru he continued to build roads and improved the coastal fortifications at Callao and Pisco, following the outbreak of war with England. Early in his viceroyalty he befriended his fellow countryman John Mackenna (1771–1814), who thus commenced a distinguished career under his auspices.

O'Higgins never married but a liaison with Maria-Isabel Riquelme de la Barra (1759–1839), the eighteen-year-old daughter of a respectable Creole family, resulted in the birth of a son, Bernardo (1778–1846). Maria-Isabel married in 1780 Felix Rodriguez y Riquelme. O'Higgins paid for his son's education in England and left him property in his will but otherwise their relationship was not close. Several of his nephews also served in the Spanish army, of whom Demetrius and Thomas O'Higgins, sons of his brother Thomas, joined him in South America and were beneficiaries under his will.

Aged about eighty, O'Higgins died suddenly at Lima, after a short illness, on 19 March 1801 and was interred in the church of San Pedro in Lima. Though stern and serious in character he was nicknamed 'the Shrimp' on account of his high complexion. His son, Bernardo, subsequently commanded the patriot army in the Chilean War of Independence, became president of the congress, and is regarded as the emancipator of his country.

HARMAN MURTAGH

Sources B. de Breffny, 'Ambrose O'Higgins: an enquiry into his origins and ancestry', *Irish Ancestor*, 2/2 (1970), 81–9 · J. Mehegan, *O'Higgins of Chile: a brief sketch of his life and times* (1913), 15–34 · J. G. Wilson and J. Fiske, eds., *Appletons' cyclopaedia of American biography*, 4 (1888), 566–7 · H. Boylan, *A dictionary of Irish biography* (1978)
Likenesses portrait, 1795, University of Chile, Santiago; repro. in de Breffny, 'Ambrose O'Higgins' · portrait, University of Chile, Santiago; repro. in de Breffny, 'Ambrose O'Higgins'
Wealth at death substantial; left estates to his son and nephews

O'Higgins, Kevin Christopher (1892–1927), politician and social reformer, was born on 7 June 1892 in the Dispensary House, Stradbally, Queen's county, fourth son and fourth of the sixteen children of Thomas Francis Higgins (*d.* 1923), medical officer for the Athy union and county coroner, and his wife, Anne or Annie (*d.* 1953), daughter of Timothy Daniel Sullivan (poet, patriot, MP, and lord mayor of Dublin), and sister of the wife of Timothy Michael Healy KC, first governor-general of the Irish Free State. His brothers included the medical officer, army officer, and politician in Ireland Thomas *O'Higgins (1889–1953). The family home soon became Woodlands, near Stradbally, and that is where Kevin O'Higgins grew up, attending the local convent school, then the Christian Brothers' school, Maryborough, Clongowes Wood College, and St Mary's College, Knockbeg, Carlow. With a view to entering the priesthood he then attended St Patrick's College, Maynooth, but had to move to Carlow seminary, in 1911, for breaking the non-smoking rules. Being further unwilling to accept the restricted seminary lifestyle, he abandoned notions of a vocation. He was briefly apprenticed to Maurice Healy, a Cork solicitor and brother of Timothy, while at the same time resuming his BA studies, in legal and political sciences—this time at University College, Dublin. Uninspired by his subject and increasingly distracted by his practical political activities, he obtained only a pass BA in 1915 and a similar LLB in 1919.

Already O'Higgins had committed himself to the cause of nationalist separatism by joining the Irish Volunteers in 1915, becoming captain of the Stradbally company, Carlow brigade, in 1917, and being imprisoned for five months in 1918 in Mountjoy gaol and Belfast internment camp. In the general election of December 1918 he was elected Sinn Féin MP for Queen's county. Efficient and forceful, he soon gained recognition in Dáil Éireann as it asserted itself as an alternative government at a time also of increasing armed resistance to London rule. He became assistant minister for local government in January 1919, and raised the republican loan in his constituency (a remarkable £10,000). When his minister, W. T. Cosgrave, was arrested in 1920, he became substitute minister, an appointment confirmed by the Dáil that June. In the May 1921 general election he was returned for the Laois–Offaly constituency unopposed, and that August he was again appointed assistant minister for local government.

When peace negotiations were arranged for October 1921 between British and Irish representatives, O'Higgins declined the position of secretary to the Irish delegation in order to marry Bridget Mary (1898–1961), schoolteacher daughter of Andrew Cole, of Drumlish, co. Longford. He approved the settlement, however, and was one of the ablest speakers in its favour in the Dáil, arguing that 'it represents such a broad measure of liberty for the Irish people and it acknowledges such a large proportion of its rights, you are not entitled to reject it without being able to show them [the plain people of Ireland] that you have a reasonable prospect of achieving more' (Dáil Éireann, 45). In January 1922 he became minister for economic affairs in Arthur Griffith's first Free State government and he held a similar position in the provisional government chaired by Michael Collins. In the election of that year he was returned, the second of four deputies, for the same Laois–Offaly constituency, and after the tragic deaths of both Arthur Griffith and Michael Collins that August, he became minister for home affairs and vice-president of the executive council. The home affairs ministry was changed to the ministry of justice in 1924, and to that responsibility he added external affairs in the summer of 1927. After transferring to co. Dublin for the election of 1923 he had headed the poll, on behalf of Cumann na nGaedheal, and this he repeated in the June elections of 1927. He had grown in these few years to be the outstanding political figure of his day, the main prop of the government and its principal international spokesman.

It was to O'Higgins that the task fell of steering through the founding constitution of the state, modified, unacceptably to some, from its original form by the requirements of the 1921 treaty, but still a humane, liberal, and democratic document. He regretted only that those who retained reservations about it would not join in the democratic struggle to build upon it to reach the goal sought by all. His description of the early provisional governments as 'eight young men in the City Hall standing amidst the ruins of one administration, with the foundations of another not yet laid, and with wild men screaming through the keyhole' (White, 84) remains a vivid example of his style. After years of civil strife, and physical and passive resistance to the institutions of the British state, it fell now to him to restore the rule of law and rebuild the state along national lines. For his work he is recognized as the father of the unarmed Garda Siochana,

the new national police force established in 1922. It was he who most prominently epitomized the determination of the government during the civil war of 1922–23, at the cost of the life of his father, murdered in retaliation on 11 February 1923. And it was O'Higgins, too, who took the lead in confronting and confounding those mutinous elements in the swollen state army as the government sought to return it to peacetime numbers in 1924. At the Imperial Conference of 1926, perhaps the most significant of such meetings, he had contributed vitally to the debates which were to complete the transformation of an empire of domination into a Commonwealth of partners.

It is as a reformer of the powerful Irish drink trade, with three Liquor Acts to his credit, and as a visionary for an Ireland reunited by consent, that O'Higgins will also be remembered. Strong, intelligent, of the most rigorous integrity, he strove to banish the evils that had blighted his country and to make of his countrymen proud upholders of the best in the Irish tradition. Shy and private, with a perhaps misleadingly tough exterior, he had a self-deprecating humour that expressed itself even at the most trying of moments. When asked by a British captor how he would like five or six bullets in his head, he is said to have replied that he would not particularly mind the last four or five (Foxall, 2 June 1963); even at the end, when close to death, when those around tried to offer encouragement, he had whispered 'There is no hope. I should be dead by now, only I have always been a bit of a diehard' (Belfast News-Letter).

O'Higgins had by then endured many hardships. Despite his good marriage, he had belatedly encountered and fallen in love with Hazel, Lady Lavery, wife of the distinguished painter, to whom he could only regret in his many letters that he had met her too late. He retained the joy in the birth and vitality of his two daughters, Maeve (b. June 1923) and Una (b. January 1927); but in between, his son, Finbarr Gerald, born in November 1924, had lived only twelve days. His hope for his girls was that they would grow up in an Ireland 'where all the creases in Irish life will have been ironed out. … Taxation will be halved, unemployment abolished, and Irish-speaking Orangemen will be boasting about Henry Joy McCracken in a Dublin Parliament' (Irish Times, 11 July 1927). That he was cut down in his prime, with so little time given to seek such ends, is one explanation for their slow progress. His death, however, was followed by a stringent Public Safety Act and an Electoral Amendment Act that finally forced the main opposition party, Fianna Fáil, to enter Dáil Éireann rather than risk political oblivion, and this did much to secure the democratic political institutions that were the object of his political life.

O'Higgins was assassinated on his way to attend mass at Booterstown, near Dublin, on 10 July 1927. His murder on a Sunday morning, just back from projecting his state's interests at a League of Nations naval conference in Geneva, and having considerably dismissed his escort for the short walk to mass, caused particular revulsion. As he lay dying, he forgave his killers, believing that no more blood should be shed in a country that had lost too many of its sons. (He had perforce signed the death warrant of his own best man, Rory O'Connor, during the civil war.) His death should have been instantaneous, but his strong will helped keep him alive for several hours as, having been carried back to his house, he put his affairs in order and took his leave of family and friends. The following day his remains were removed from his dwelling, Dunamase House, Cross Avenue, Booterstown, to the Mansion House, Dublin, where thousands filed past his coffin, which lay in state until 8 p.m. on Tuesday 12th. His funeral took place in the morning of 13 July after a requiem mass at St Andrew's Church, Westland Row. It was a sad and sombre day of national mourning, a state occasion attended by all leading Irish figures and by foreign and Commonwealth representatives, amid tributes from around the world. The funeral cortège stretched for over 3 miles along thronged and silent streets, with ten lorry-loads of flowers behind the family wreaths. O'Higgins was buried in the north-west corner of Glasnevin cemetery, in the division known as St Brigid's, in the same grave as his infant son.

DAVID HARKNESS

Sources T. de V. White, *Kevin O'Higgins* (1948) · *Irish Times* (11–15 July 1927) · *Irish Times* (18 July 1927) · S. McCoole, *Hazel: a life of Lady Lavery, 1880–1935* (1996) · *DNB* · *Tuairisg oifigiúil* (*official report*) *for periods 16th August, 1921,… to 8th June, 1922, Dáil Éireann* [1922] · R. Foxall, *Sunday Express* (26 May 1963) · R. Foxall, *Sunday Express* (2 June 1963) · B. M. Walker, *Parliamentary election results in Ireland, 1918–92* (1992) · private information (2004) [Una O'Higgins-O'Malley] · *Belfast News-Letter* (11 July 1927) · *Irish News and Belfast Morning News* (11 July 1927) · *The Times* (11 July 1927) · D. W. Harkness, *The restless dominion* (1969) · J. L. Garvin, 'Tribute', *The Observer* (17 July 1927)

Archives FILM BFI NFTVA, news footage

Likenesses group portrait, photograph, 1919 (with Sinn Fein leaders), Hult. Arch. · J. Lavery, oils, 1921, Hugh Lane Gallery of Modern Art, Dublin · Keogh, double portrait, photograph, 1922 (with M. Collins), Hult. Arch. · Walshe, group portrait, photograph, 1922 (with Cosgrave's cabinet), Hult. Arch. · double portrait, photograph, 1922 (with M. Collins), Hult. Arch. · photograph, 1922, Hult. Arch. · Walshe, photograph, 1923, Hult. Arch. · O. Sheppard, marble bust, 1932, NG Ire. · double portrait, photograph, 1933 (with E. O'Duffy), Hult. Arch. · L. Whelan, portrait, Leinster House, Dublin

Wealth at death £1526 18s. 11d.: administration, 1927, Ireland

O'Higgins [*formerly* Higgins], **Thomas Francis** (1889–1953), medical officer, army officer, and politician in Ireland, was born on 20 November 1889 in Stradbally, Queen's county (later co. Laois), Ireland, the second son of the sixteen children of Thomas Francis Higgins (*d.* 1923), surgeon and farmer, and his wife, Annie Sullivan (*d.* 1953), daughter of T. D. Sullivan, editor of *The Nation* and Irish Parliamentary Party MP. T. F. O'Higgins (he adopted the prefix in his youth) was born into a wealthy and influential Catholic nationalist family. He was a nephew of T. M. Healy, the first governor-general of the Irish Free State, and brother of Kevin *O'Higgins (1892–1927), vice-president of the executive council of the Irish Free State. Educated at the Christian Brothers' school, Portlaoise, and Clongowes Wood College, O'Higgins studied medicine at Trinity College, Dublin, and the Royal College of Surgeons in Ireland, qualifying as a doctor in November 1914. In

November 1915 he married Agnes McCarthy, with whom he had four sons and one daughter including Michael, a Fine Gael TD, and T. F., a Fine Gael cabinet minister and chief justice. He was appointed medical officer to Fontstown Dispensary, co. Kildare, in 1915 and was medical officer for Portlaoise between 1919 and 1922. (He subsequently served as medical officer for co. Meath until 1951.) O'Higgins joined the Irish Volunteers in 1913 and was active in Sinn Féin and the IRA during the War of Independence. He was arrested and imprisoned in Mountjoy prison in 1919. In the following year he was interned in the Curragh and was later transferred to Ballykinlar internment camp in northern Ireland; there he remained until the end of the War of Independence. His family were prominent supporters of the Anglo-Irish treaty, and when the Irish civil war began in 1922 he enlisted in the national army medical corps with the rank of captain. His father, Thomas Higgins, was killed by anti-treaty IRA in February 1923. In 1924 O'Higgins was appointed director of the Army Medical Services with the rank of colonel. He was a keen horseman and helped establish the army school of equitation.

The IRA's assassination in 1927 of his brother Kevin, the most influential member of the Cumann na nGaedheal government, influenced O'Higgins's decision to enter public life. He resigned from the army and won a by-election in North Dublin City for Cumann na nGaedheal in March 1929. In 1932 he was elected a Dáil deputy for Laois-Offaly which he represented until 1948. O'Higgins was a prominent supporter of the Army Comrades Association (the Blueshirts), a pro-treaty veterans' organization founded in response to the election of the republican Fianna Fáil government in 1932, and replaced Austin Brennan as its president in August 1932. Under his leadership the organization became increasingly politicized, adopting a blue shirt uniform and defending Cumann na nGaedheal public meetings from attack by republicans.

In 1933 O'Higgins was replaced as leader of the Blueshirts by Eoin O'Duffy. He retained a figurehead role as honorary president but disapproved of O'Duffy's radicalism and helped marginalize O'Duffy after the latter's appointment as president of Fine Gael (a new party comprising the Centre Party, Blueshirts, and Cumann na nGaedheal). In 1935, following O'Duffy's resignation, O'Higgins was elected vice-president of Fine Gael. In the following year he was appointed director-general of the Blueshirts but principally with the aim of winding down the discredited organization. He was a member of the all-party council of defence during the Second World War. Following W. T. Cosgrave's resignation in 1943 O'Higgins temporarily took over as leader of the parliamentary opposition. In 1948 O'Higgins, by then deputy leader of Fine Gael, contested the Cork City constituency and, along with two of his sons, Michael and T. F., was elected to the Dáil. O'Higgins served as minister for defence (1948–50) and of industry and commerce (1950–51) in the coalition government of 1948–51. He was known as a hard-working politician with a trenchant oratorical style and outspoken views.

O'Higgins died of lung disease and tuberculosis at his home in Woodbine Road, Blackrock, co. Dublin, on 1 November 1953 following a period of ill health. He was buried in Glasnevin cemetery on 3 November 1953. He was survived by his wife.   FEARGHAL McGARRY

Sources *Irish Press* (2 Nov 1953) · *Irish Independent* (2 Nov 1953) · T. de Vere White, *Kevin O'Higgins* (1966) · T. F. O'Higgins, *A double life* (1996) · J. M. Regan, *The Irish counter-revolution, 1921–1936* (1999) · M. Cronin, *The Blueshirts and Irish politics* (1997) · private information (2004) [T. F. O'Higgins] · b. cert. · d. cert.
Wealth at death Ir£3308: probate, NA Ire.

Ohthere [Óttarr] (*fl.* **871–899**), explorer, was a Norwegian chieftain who in the reign of Alfred the Great paid a visit to the royal court in Wessex and supplied some information about Scandinavia. This was included in the late ninth-century Old English translation of Orosius's 'History against the pagans', and provides the only source of knowledge about Ohthere. His account includes descriptions of three voyages and of Ohthere's way of living.

King Alfred is described as Ohthere's 'lord'. This probably reflects the fact that the king was protector of all visitors and guests at his court, whether their visit was brief or a long one. Ohthere told his hosts that he lived furthest to the north of all Northmen. This must have been in Hålogaland somewhere near modern Tromsø, Norway. The traditional boundary between the areas of *búmenn* (permanent settlers) and those of the nomadic Sami people is the Malangen Fjord; viking-age settlements have been excavated on islands just north of Malangen.

Ohthere supported himself by agriculture. He ploughed a little land with horses and kept cattle, sheep, and pigs, but only a score of each. His chief wealth was in reindeer, of which he had 600, and in the tribute which the Finnas (Sami) paid him. This consisted in skins of beasts, the feathers of birds, whalebone, and ship's ropes made from whale-hide and sealskin. He also hunted walrus; the ivory from their teeth was highly valued, and Ohthere brought some to Alfred. Tribute taken from the Samians was an important part of the economic basis of the chieftains of Hålogaland until the high middle ages, when this source of income was taken over by Swedish and Finnish tax collectors. Ohthere reports that he had to compete for it with the Cwenas, a Finnish tribe or group that sometimes raided the Norwegians.

One of Ohthere's journeys took him round the North Cape and along today's Lapmark, vast areas inhabited only by Finnas, and round the Kola peninsula, home of the Terfinnas (probably another Sami people), into the White Sea. Here he reached the permanently settled areas of the Biarmians, a Finnish people, but did not venture into them for lack of a peace agreement. His main reason for undertaking this journey, apart from exploring the land, was to hunt walruses; a party of six men had been able to kill sixty walruses in two days, he claimed. The scholars at Alfred's court seem to have been particularly interested to learn whether, when Ohthere changed direction, he did so because the land was turning, or because the sea was

penetrating the land. This would have helped them to establish whether Ohthere had been travelling along the utmost edge of the world, or was merely entering another inland sea like the Baltic, said to penetrate the land.

Another part of the account describes the journey from Ohthere's home to the port of 'Sciringesheal' in southern Norway. This has been identified as Kaupang near Larvik, an important market in viking-age Norway. This journey could, under adverse conditions, take as much as a month. Reference is made in the account to the location of Ireland and Britain, though not for any purpose of practical navigation. From Sciringesheal Ohthere continued his journey to Hedeby in the south of Jutland, which was reached in five days. He said that for the three days he had 'Denmark' to port and the open sea to starboard. Then for two days he had Jutland and 'Sillende' (south Jutland) and many islands to starboard; his interviewer commented that the Angles lived in those parts before they came to 'this land' (England). And on the port side he had those islands which belong to 'Denmark'. This distinction between Jutland and 'Sillende' and many islands on one side, and 'Denmark' and the islands belonging to it on the other, is matched in the introductory description of Europe beyond the Danube and the Rhine by a distinction between south Danes in 'Sillende' and Jutland, and north Danes in 'Denmark', Zealand, with adjacent islands and the south-western coastlands of modern Sweden.

       NIELS LUND

Sources *The Old English Orosius*, ed. J. Bately, EETS, supplementary ser., 6 (1980) · *Two voyagers at the court of King Alfred: the ventures of Ohthere and Wulfstan*, ed. N. Lund, trans. C. E. Fell (1984) · M. Korhammer, 'Viking seafaring and the meaning of Ohthere's *ambyrne* wind', *Problems of Old English lexicography: studies in memory of Angus Cameron*, ed. A. Bammesberger (1985), 171–3 · E. Roesdahl, *Hvalrostand, elfenben og nordboerne i Grønland* (Odense, 1995)

Ó hUiginn family (*per. c.*1300–*c.*1600), Gaelic poets, were notable as a learned bardic family in Connaught for several centuries. The origin of the surname Ó hUiginn is obscure, but it is a noteworthy fact that forenames of Norse origin (such as Iomhar, Maghnus) occur in several of the medieval generations in the genealogy of this family. Therefore, since no native forename Uige(a)nn (genitive Uiginn) has otherwise been attested, it is generally assumed that the surname has been based on a forename which was a borrowing of Norse *vikingr* 'viking'. In the sixteenth century the surname Ó hUiginn was to be found widely distributed in the midlands and west of the Shannon. The genealogy given in the seventeenth-century compilation now generally referred to as the *O Clery Book of Genealogies* was clearly for the Connaught branch of the family, apparently the only one which distinguished itself in the bardic profession. The principal patrons of this learned family over a period of almost 400 years were O'Conor-Sligo in Sligo (barony of Carbury), McWilliam Burke in Mayo, O'Hara in Sligo (barony of Leyny), O'Rourke in Leitrim, and O'Donnell in Donegal.

Tadhg Mór Ó hUiginn (d. 1315) could have been the son of Giolla Coluim Ó hUiginn. He was tutor to Maghnus (d.

1293), grandson of Ruaidhrí Ó Conchobhair, king of Connaught. Only two of his poetic compositions seem to be extant, the first is his poem on the warlike upbringing of this prince, *Gach éan mar a adhbha* ('Every bird has its nest'), and follows the general pattern of this theme but introduces a pleasant variation by comparing Maghnus and his steed to famous warriors and steeds recorded in Irish history and literature, such as Cú Chulainn and his Liath Macha, or Tadhg an Eich Gil ('Tadhg of the White Steed') Ó Conchobhair (*d.* 1030). Like all others of his profession he was clearly well versed in medieval Irish literature. In another remarkable poem, *sui generis* in Irish bardic verse, *Slán fat fholcadh | a Fhionnghuala réidh roicheolchar* ('In defiance of your bathing, O gentle music-loving Finola'), Tadhg describes the beauty of Fionnghuala, daughter of the same Maghnus. He employs the conceit that her whole form is in evidence as she washes her hair. This description undoubtedly was inspired by a scene from the Irish otherworld, namely that found in the tale *Tochmarc Étaíne* ('The wooing of Étaín'), which describes the unearthly beauty of the fairy maiden *Étaín* (Éadaoin) as she is loosening her hair to wash it.

Tadhg Óg Ó hUiginn (*d.* 1448) was a great-grandson of Tadhg Mór (*d.* 1315). His most renowned composition is an elegy on his elder brother and teacher, Fearghal Ruadh, *Anocht sgaoilid na scola* ('To-night the schools disperse'), written at the time of the seasonal closing of the schools in early summer. Fearghal Ruadh's death has been a disastrous loss to the profession of poetry:

> Gan mharthain do mhac Áine,
> rug don éigse a hamháille;
> mar théid clár a taoibh thunna,
> do sgaoil fál na foghluma.
>
> ('That Áine's son lives not has robbed poetry of its gaiety; as a plank falls out of the side of a cask, the wall of learning has collapsed.')

Here, by the bardic device called *dúnadh* ('closure'), the word *sgaoil* in the final line echoes part of the first line, thus associating the tragedy of the death of Fearghal Ruadh with the empty schools.

Tadhg Óg gained wide recognition throughout the Gaelic world in Ireland and Scotland, as is shown by the large number of his influential patrons. These included Ó Néill (in Tyrone), Ó Domhnaill, Ó Conchobhair Cairbreach (a family later called O'Conor-Sligo), Ó Ceallaigh of Uí Mhaine (O'Kelly of Hy-Many in co. Galway and co. Roscommon), Ó Conchobhair Chiarraighe (co. Kerry), Ó Cearbhaill of Éile (O'Carroll in co. Offaly and Tipperary), Mág Uidhir (in Fermanagh), Mac Domhnaill of Íle (Islay in Scotland), and Mac Diarmada (McDermott of Moylurg in Roscommon). It is impossible, however, to outline the events of Tadhg Óg's full life from any internal evidence in his poems, for the business of the bardic poets was not to record their own achievements but rather those of their patrons. In *Déanaidh comhaonta, a chlann Éibhir* ('Be ye united, O children of Éibhear') the poet, by a type of dramatic figure common in bardic poetry, urges Ó Cearbhaill to seize the ancient royal seat of Cashel, unite all the men of Munster and their kinsmen, the Luighne of Lower Connaught, and drive the *Goill* ('foreigners' / English) out of Ireland.

On the other hand, like many others of his profession, Tadhg Óg availed himself of the patronage of the descendants of several of the Anglo-Norman conquerors of Ireland, such as the earl of Ormond (Butler), Mac Uilliam Uachtair (the de Burghs of Clanricarde in east Galway), and Mac Uilliam Íochtair (in co. Mayo). Many other themes employed by the poet are commonplace in bardic verse and only a few of his poems are susceptible of exact dating. One of these is an elegy on Tadhg Ó Ceallaigh of Uí Mhaine who died in 1410, *Anois do tuigfidhe Tadhg* ('Now might Tadhg be understood'). Tadhg Óg's compositions were held in high esteem, and samples from his poems are frequently cited as illustrations in the grammatical and syntactical tracts employed in the schools. His many religious poems have largely been preserved in an anthology which has survived in the composite volume known as the Yellow Book of Lecan. This anthology has been published by Lambert McKenna under the title *Dán Dé*.

Tadhg Óg, 'chief teacher of the poets of Ireland and Scotland' (as he is described in the annals), died in 1448 at Cill Chonnla (Kilconla), Dunmore, co. Galway, and was buried in the monastery of Áth Leathan (Ballylahan), Templemore, Gallen, co. Mayo.

Maol Seachlainn na nUirsgéal ('of the allegories') Ó hUiginn (*fl.* 1400x50), was in the possession of lands at Mag Inghine an Scáil (unidentified) in Cairbre (Carbury), co. Sligo, and had a turbulent relationship with his lord and patron, Brian (mac Domhnaill) Ó Conchobhair, lord of Cairbre. He addressed several poems to Ó Conchobhair and one to Mág Aonghusa (Magennis) of Uíbh Eachach (Iveagh, co. Down).

Pilip Bocht Ó hUiginn (*d.* 1487), a member of the Franciscan order (hence *bocht*, 'poor'), was one of the chief exponents of Irish religious bardic poetry. His death is recorded in the annals of Ulster at 1487: 'Pilib bocht mac Cuinn Chrosaigh Uí Uiginn dhég in bhliadhainsi, idhón, Bráthair Minúr de Observancia, nech is mó7 is ferr duanaire diadhachta san aimsir dheigheanaigh' ('Philip the Poor, son of Conn the Pock-marked Ua hUiginn, namely a friar minor of observance, one who was the most copious and the best devotional poet of later times').

Domhnall mac Briain Ó hUiginn (*d.* 1502), as recorded in the annals, died in 1502 on his return from pilgrimage to Santiago de Compostela. Only one poem ascribed to him survives, *Misde nach éadmhar Éire* ('So much the worse that Ireland is not jealous'). It relates that 'Drong do Ghaoidhealaibh ghuirt Breagh ... do fhás ó mhacaibh Míleadh' ('a band of the Gaels from the field of Bregia [Ireland] which is descended from the sons of Míl') settled and prospered in Scotland; hence Ireland's right to be jealous.

Tadhg Dall Ó hUiginn (1550–1591) is the best known of the bardic poets of the classical modern Irish period, mainly by virtue of the edition and translations of his poems by Eleanor Knott. He was the son of Mathgham-hain Ó hUiginn and his birthplace was probably in Luighne (barony of Leyny). According to a statement in a poem addressed by him to Aodh Ó Domhnaill (Hugh O'Donnell), *Molfaid Conallaigh clann Táil* ('The race of Conall will praise the descendants of Tál'), he was fostered in Tír Conaill and it is presumed that he was educated at a bardic school there.

Among Tadhg Dall's more important poems are: an address to Conn Ó Domhnaill, *Tógaíbh eadrad is Éire* ('Raise the veil from Ireland'), urging him to make Ireland his spouse; *Iomdha sochar ag síol Néill* ('Many privileges have the descendants of Niall'), addressed to Toirdhealbhach Luineach Ó Néill (*an ghéag abhla d'fhiodh Teamhrach*; 'the apple-branch of the wood of Tara'); *Nodlaig do chuamar don Chraoibh* ('At Christmas we went to the Creeve') to the same patron, celebrating a Christmas banquet given by Ó Néill to the poets of Ireland; three poems to Cú Chonnacht Mág Uidhir (Maguire), *Daoine saora síol gColla* ('Free people are the descendants of Colla'), *Teallach féile Fir Mhanach* ('Fermanagh is the hearthstone of hospitality'), and *Mairg fhéagas ar Inis Ceithleann* ('Alas for him who looks on Enniskillen'); and *Pardhas Fódla Fir Mhanach* ('Fermanagh is the paradise of Ireland') in praise of Brian Mág Uidhir.

Tadhg Dall met with a tragic end: members of a local branch of the Uí Eadhra (the O'Haras) of Luighne, whom he had satirized, attacked him at his home in Cúil re Coill (now the townland of Coolrecuill) and cut his tongue out. The record of the poet's death is cited by Knott as follows:

> In an Exchequer Inquisition taken at Ballymote, Co. Sligo, January 12, 1593, it was testified that Thadeus, alias Teage Dall O Higinn, late of Cowlrecoyll, in the aforesaid county, *generosus*, died at Cowlrecoyll on the last day of March, 1591, and that Thadeus oge mc Teage O Higgen, at the time of his father's death nine years of age, and unmarried, was his legitimate son and nearest heir.   (Knott, 1.xv)

This Thadeus, **Tadhg Óg Ó hUiginn** (*b.* 1581/2), wrote an important tract on Irish grammar and prosody.

Maol Muire Ó hUiginn (*d.* *c.*1591), a brother of Tadhg Dall, was archbishop of Tuam and a trained poet. From Rome he addressed the poem *A fhir théid go Fiadh bhFuinidh* ('O man who goes to the western land') as an exile's greeting to Ireland through the person of a fellow countryman returning home. He died in Antwerp about 1591.

Mathghamhain Ó hUiginn (*fl.* 1584), Tadhg Dall's father, probably composed many poems, but only six are extant: three of these are included in the Poem Book of the Dillons (Royal Irish Academy, MS A.v.2) and one is found in the Book of the O'Byrnes.

Domhnall Óg mac Aodha Ó hUiginn (*fl.* *c.*1600) enjoyed the patronage of the lord of Luighne, Cian Ó hEadhra (*d.* 1612), and of his son and successor, Tadhg Buidhe (*d.* 1616). His extant poems to these chieftains have been preserved in a vellum manuscript (the Book of O'Hara, National Library of Ireland, Dublin). He addressed a poem to Fiachaidh (mac Aodha) Ó Broin (betrayed to the English in 1597), describing him as the prophesied one who is destined to rid Ireland of the foreigners.

Cormac mac an Ghiolla Choluim Ó hUiginn (*fl.*

1590), composed a long elegy on O'Conor-Sligo, Donnchadh (mac Cathail Óig) Ó Conchobhair.

Maol Muire (mac Eoghain) Ó hUiginn's known work is believed to consist of three poems addressed to An Calbhach Ruadh Ó Domhnaill about the middle of the seventeenth century, which have survived in a Poem Book of the O'Donnells compiled for Aodh Ó Domhnaill (of co. Mayo) in the early eighteenth century; one poem in the Poem Book of the Dillons compiled for seventeenth-century members of the family of Viscount Dillon of Costello-Gallen, co. Mayo, whose seat was at Lough Glynn, co. Roscommon; a poem in praise of Oilill Ó hEadhra of Luighne; and one in praise of Uilliam son of Uaithne Ó Maoil Mhuaidh of Fir Cheall (co. Offaly), of a family well known for their patronage of Irish learning.

Tomás Ó hUiginn (*fl.* mid-17th cent.) was probably a native of co. Sligo. He addressed poems to members of the Méig Uidhir of Fir Mhanach and to Oilill Ó hEadhra. He probably was also the author of *Féach féin an obair-si, a Aodh* ('See for thyself these doings, O Hugh'), an allegorical poem cast in the form of an address by a woman to her husband, Aodh Ó Ruairc, seeking his protection from a would-be suitor, Tomás Mac Coisdealbha (Costello). This artistic poem is, however, as James Carney has explained, merely a sustained metaphor to be understood as an appeal to Ó Ruairc by his 'spouse' (the poet) against a rival patron.

Ruaidhrí (mac Cairbre) Ó hUiginn of the branch seated at Tearmann Balla (Balla), Clanmorris, co. Mayo, compiled, in 1680, Leabhar Cloinne Aodha Buidhe, the Poem Book of the Uí Néill of Clann Aodha Buidhe (Clandeboy, co. Antrim). He lived at Gort an Chairn (Gortagharn), Drummaul, co. Antrim.

Sources E. Knott, ed., *The bardic poems of Tadhg Dall Ó hUiginn* (1550–1591), 1–2 (1922–6) • P. A. Breatnach, *The bardic poems of Tadhg Dall Ó Huiginn: a new introduction* (1996) • L. McKenna, *Dán Dé* [1923] • L. McKenna, *Philip Bocht Ó Huiginn* (1931) • L. McKenna, *Dioghluim Dána* (1938) • L. McKenna, *Aithdioghluim Dána*, 1–2 (1939–40) • L. McKenna, ed., *The 'Book of O'Hara': Leabhar I Eadhra* (1951) • S. H. O'Grady, *Catalogue of Irish manuscripts in the British Library*, 1 (1926), repr. 1992, 94 • S. H. O'Grady, ed., *Catalogue of Irish manuscripts in the British Museum*, 2, ed. R. Flower (1926) • T. O'Rahilly and others, *Catalogue of Irish manuscripts in the Royal Irish Academy*, 30 vols. (Dublin, 1926–70) • S. Mac Airt, *Leabhar Branach: the book of the O'Byrnes* (1944) • E. Mac Cárthaigh, ed., 'Three poems by Maol Muire Ó hUiginn to An Calbhach Ruadh Ó Domhnaill', *Ériu*, 48 (1997), 59–82 • T. Ó Cléirigh, 'A poem book of the O'Donnells', *Éigse*, 1 (1939–40), 51–61, 130–42 • J. Carney, 'Thomas Costello and O'Rourke's wife', *Celtica*, 1 (1950), 280–84

Ó hUiginn, Cormac, mac an Ghiolla Choluim (*fl.* 1590). *See under* Ó hUiginn family (*per.* *c.*1300–*c.*1600).

Ó hUiginn, Domhnall mac Briain (*d.* 1502). *See under* Ó hUiginn family (*per.* *c.*1300–*c.*1600).

Ó hUiginn, Domhnall Óg mac Aodha (*fl.* *c.*1600). *See under* Ó hUiginn family (*per.* *c.*1300–*c.*1600).

Ó hUiginn, Maol Muire (*d.* *c.*1591). *See under* Ó hUiginn family (*per.* *c.*1300–*c.*1600).

Ó hUiginn, Mathghamhain (*fl.* 1584). *See under* Ó hUiginn family (*per.* *c.*1300–*c.*1600).

Ó hUiginn, Tadhg Dall (1550–1591). *See under* Ó hUiginn family (*per. c.*1300–*c.*1600).

Ó hUiginn, Tadhg Mór (*d.* 1315). *See under* Ó hUiginn family (*per. c.*1300–*c.*1600).

Ó hUiginn, Tadhg Óg (*d.* 1448). *See under* Ó hUiginn family (*per. c.*1300–*c.*1600).

Ó hUiginn, Tadhg Óg (*b.* 1581/2). *See under* Ó hUiginn family (*per. c.*1300–*c.*1600).

O'Hurley, Dermot (*c.*1530–1584), Roman Catholic archbishop of Cashel and martyr, the son of William O'Hurley, gentleman, and his wife, Honora O'Brien, was born near Emly, co. Tipperary. At a later date, following his father's acquisition of the estate, he moved to Lickadoon Castle, co. Limerick. Some time before 1551, destined for a learned profession, he was sent to study at Louvain, where he took his master of arts degree at the Collège du Lis, and in 1559 he was appointed professor of philosophy there. In all he spent about fifteen years at Louvain, pursuing legal studies with great success, becoming a doctor of civil and canon law and dean of the college of St Ivo. About 1574, on the recommendation of Cardinal Guise, he left to take up a position at Rheims, where he remained for four years. According to Stanihurst, some time before 1577 he wrote a Latin treatise, *In Aristotelis Physica*, which secured his reputation as a 'commendable philosopher'. By 1580 he was in Rome. A Latin poem composed there in his honour in 1581 mentions that he taught law in the city; presumably he did so as a professor at the Sapienza. He was also connected with the Roman Inquisition, probably, it has been suggested, as a legal expert to whom problems were submitted.

Once in Rome, O'Hurley's career changed forever. Apparently at the request of Cardinal Como he was encouraged to involve himself in the planning of papal policy for Ireland. While serving in this capacity he sometimes acted as an interpreter between Como and the representatives of rebel Irish lords who appeared in Rome seeking aid. He was almost certainly the author of a report written for Como in 1580 outlining the conditions under which Catholics toiled in Ireland and providing a list of Irish clergy on the continent who could be called upon to return home to forward the papal interest. Curiously, the wider and implicitly political importance of this report has been somewhat ignored by Catholic historians. It offered a markedly positive vision of the prospect of the papacy succeeding in securing the allegiance of Ireland's predominantly Catholic population in the face of only a small force of English heretics. In so doing, it and other reports modelled on it helped to persuade the pope, Gregory XIII, to commit men and money to a combined Italian / Spanish landing in the south of Ireland in support of the rebellion of Gerald Fitzgerald, fourteenth earl of Desmond, an enterprise that was doomed to failure and ended with the slaughter at Smerwick, co. Kerry, of all those involved. Given these circumstances, it is difficult to accept without reservation the opinion of some scholars

that O'Hurley may have had nothing to do with Irish Catholic plots against English protestant power. This is no mere quibble, as his eventual beatification at the end of the twentieth century rested on the supposition that he was a purely religious martyr, his career untainted by involvement in political affairs.

After 1580, the invasion débâcle notwithstanding, the papacy continued to pursue an aggressive policy towards English rule in Ireland, and it was towards this end that O'Hurley was promoted to the vacant archbishopric of Cashel in 1581. That he was a layman—'scholaris Limericensis'—was no barrier to his advancement: extant documents in Rome show that he was admitted to the clerical state, given the four minor orders, and advanced to subdiaconate, diaconate, and priesthood within just sixteen days, between 29 July and 13 August 1581, the pope issuing a special papal brief in his favour. O'Hurley received his tonsure and orders from the Marian bishop of St Asaph, Thomas Goldwell, and during the papal consistory of 11 September 1581 he was proposed for Cashel by the archbishop of Sens, a close associate of Pope Gregory who was unofficially supervising Irish ecclesiastical affairs at this time.

The pope's eagerness to appoint him to Cashel is explained by O'Hurley's family background. The O'Hurleys were a well connected clerical dynasty in Munster. More particularly, Dermot's father had been a servant of the earls of Desmond, acting about 1540 as steward of Glenogra, a Desmond manor, and other sources reveal that William Oge O'Hurley of 'Lyckadowne', Dermot's half-brother, was likewise a Desmond associate at the time of the Desmond revolt. In 1581, with the rebellion still alive, there was no one in Rome better suited to represent the papal cause in Munster. Early the following year the pope entrusted him with a letter to Desmond, in which the earl and his allies were encouraged to continue their resistance to the heretical rule of Elizabeth; the archbishop of Sens, as 'Protector of Ireland', also gave him letters for Desmond.

O'Hurley left Rome to take possession of his diocese in the summer of 1582, proceeding via Rheims, where he stayed with the rector of the university, William Allen, and where in August he contracted a severe illness. He made a slow recovery, and it was not until August 1583 that he resumed his homeward journey. Having boarded a Drogheda ship at Le Croisic in Brittany, he put ashore on the east coast of Ireland later that month, disembarking at Holmpatrick, a small harbour at Skerries, co. Dublin. The Ireland to which he returned bore no resemblance to the country he had imagined while abroad. Far from being on the brink of overthrowing English rule, it lay covered by a blanket of government repression, the last embers of Catholic rebellion for the moment all but extinguished, with the main rebel, Desmond, holed up in the mountains of Munster in fear of his life. O'Hurley was soon a fugitive too. Shortly before his arrival the government had been forewarned of his coming. It set its spies to work, so that after an abortive journey towards Waterford he was forced to abandon temporarily his plans for reaching Desmond. When next he left Dublin, O'Hurley turned north instead of south in order to evade his pursuers. Even so he was nearly captured in Drogheda, and for refuge he had to turn to those he could not fully trust, the Catholic nobility of the pale who had remained loyal to the English crown throughout the recent unrest. Having stayed with 'some others of good account within the Pale', he made his way to Slane Castle, co. Louth, where, at the behest of Catherine, Lady Slane, he was hidden for a time in a secret chamber in the castle. While there he ventured into Cavan to meet local priests, but when he returned to Slane he had an uncomfortable encounter with another guest, Sir Robert Dillon, the chief justice of the queen's bench, and he was soon on the run again. Suspecting his arrest was imminent he decided to set out for Munster without delay, and he departed Slane in the company of Piers Butler, the bastard son of Desmond's chief tormentor, the queen's general in Munster, Thomas Butler, tenth earl of Ormond. By September he had arrived at Carrick-on-Suir Castle, co. Tipperary, Ormond's home, where through Piers Butler's introduction he had a face-to-face meeting with the earl.

The protestant overlord of a Catholic territory, Ormond was anxious not to arouse sympathy for O'Hurley by moving against him; moreover, he was probably curious to discover if the archbishop could be convinced to encourage Desmond to surrender. For his own part, O'Hurley hoped to persuade Ormond to spare Desmond's life. With so little common ground between them O'Hurley and Ormond could only agree that the archbishop could have the benefit of the earl's protection so long as he remained within the boundaries of his diocese, where the earl could have him watched. In the ensuing days O'Hurley paid a pilgrimage to Holy Cross Abbey, where he may have held mass: a government captain reported on 15 September that 'pilgrims from all parts' were repairing to the abbey, seemingly aware of the arrival there of the new papal archbishop. By 20 September he was back under Ormond's roof in Carrick, where such was his confidence in the earl's powers of protection that he decided to try to arrive at an arrangement with his ecclesiastical rival Miler Magrath, the Church of Ireland archbishop of Cashel, so that the two might share the same diocese without friction. To further this objective he wrote Magrath a brief letter, signing it Dermitius Hurrileus, his only known autograph letter. As a record of an age of religious conflict it is a curious artefact, full of pleasant platitudes from one foe to another, but it also reveals something of O'Hurley's political sense. Addressing Magrath as 'Most Reverend Lord', he promised to be a good neighbour—'I desire to plant and foster friendship and peace'—and he offered his rival an important concession, being prepared not to dispute Magrath's claim to the title of archbishop: 'For myself I am content with the academic title [Dr O'Hurley] or to be called by my own name' (Bodl. Oxf., MS Carte 55, fol. 546). Behind this apparent moderation, however, lay a more uncompromising message. With Ormond as his protector O'Hurley felt he was beyond the reach of Magrath and the state authorities. He hoped Magrath would appreciate

that it might be better to reach a mutually advantageous arrangement rather than become embroiled in a potentially damaging tussle for position.

The writing of this letter is O'Hurley's last recorded act as a free man. Shortly afterwards Ormond bowed to the request of his kinsman, Lord Slane, who had come down to Carrick to request that O'Hurley be handed over into his custody to be taken to Dublin. The circumstances behind this episode have never been adequately explained. According to a Catholic account of his life composed early in the seventeenth century, O'Hurley acquiesced in his own arrest, hastening to Dublin to appear before the Irish council so that he could defend Slane against allegations of conspiracy and convince the government 'that he himself had come to Ireland with a true ecclesiastical spirit and [only] to preach the faith' (*Analecta of David Rothe*, 429–31). If true, it proved a fatal miscalculation. The same source records that Slane had him put in chains, and on reaching Kilkenny, the main overnight stop on the journey to Dublin, he was locked up in the public gaol. Once in the capital he was imprisoned in Dublin Castle.

For the Dublin government, headed by the lords justices, Adam Loftus, archbishop of Dublin, and Sir Henry Wallop, O'Hurley's arrest and incarceration had as many drawbacks as benefits. Ideally they wished to see him transferred to the Tower of London, lest his continued presence in Dublin spark unrest. Their anxiety to wash their hands of him was all the greater as the decision had been taken at Whitehall before December 1583 to put him to torture, in order 'to gain his knowledge of all foreign practices against her majesty's state' (O'Reilly, 70–73). On 10 December they tried to effect his removal to London by claiming—untruthfully—that there were no instruments of torture in Dublin. After further prevarication, and acting on the advice of Secretary Walsingham, in March 1584 they issued a commission to Sir Edward Waterhouse and Sir Geoffrey Fenton to proceed against O'Hurley, and he was mercilessly tortured in Dublin Castle dungeon, among other things having his feet toasted against a fire while encased in tin boots. On 7 March they reported the outcome. Despite an offer of pardon should he confess all, he denied any involvement in political intrigue, utterly refusing to reveal the details of his mission or to implicate others. To his abusers his defiance was proof of his guilt, demonstrating 'with what bad mind he came to Ireland instructed from Rome to poison the hearts of the people with disobedience' (Brady, *State Papers*, 74–6).

The following day the lords justices again became agitated about O'Hurley's presence in their care on discovering that on the eve of his torture he had written a letter to Ormond, his 'patron and favourer', and another since, to a kinsman living in Dublin. Both letters were seized—they no longer exist—but Loftus and Wallop were concerned that he may have succeeded in smuggling others out, especially to Ormond, whom they feared greatly because of his influence with the queen. Accordingly they determined to do away with O'Hurley as quickly as possible, and Walsingham's approval was sought to have him executed by martial law, thus avoiding the thorny problem of putting his case before a Dublin jury. Although favouring this course of action, Walsingham could not readily accede to their request without first seeking the queen's opinion, for by this time the use of martial law in Ireland was under review, a matter of mounting controversy. Elizabeth I for her part gave a typically evasive response, in April sending instructions through an intermediary that if the desired verdict could be secured by ordinary course of law, O'Hurley should be put on trial; only if not should he be executed by martial law. Still the lords justices prevaricated, but eventually, on 20 June 1584, as a new lord deputy was due to arrive to take up office, and before the earl of Ormond landed in Dublin following a visit to court, O'Hurley was hanged under royal warrant. Far from being killed as an example to others, as Loftus and Wallop had once advocated, his execution was carried out quietly, occurring early in the morning at Hoggen's Green, a stretch of open ground outside the city walls. It was entirely counter-productive, generating more sympathy for him in his native country in death than he had ever enjoyed in life. He was at once hailed as a martyr by the citizens of Dublin, who rescued his remains for burial, and among women of the city a cult formed to venerate his memory. On the continent the enemies of Elizabeth I exploited to the full the propaganda potential of his violent death. In 1587 a woodcut illustration of his torture and execution appeared in a book printed in Antwerp, and subsequently more exaggerated accounts of his sufferings were published, so that in time his name became synonymous across Europe with the harsh plight of Ireland's Catholics.

In the 1970s O'Hurley's case as the principal Irish martyr of the sixteenth century was revived by the Dublin Diocesan Commission on Causes, and his beatification took place in Rome on 27 September 1992.

DAVID EDWARDS

Sources B. Millett, 'The ordination of Dermot O'Hurley, 1581', *Collectanea Hibernica*, 25 (1983), 12–21 · W. Hayes, 'Dermot O'Hurley's last visit to Tipperary', *Tipperary Historical Journal* (1992), 163–72 · W. M. Brady, *State papers concerning the Irish church* (1868) · *The analecta of David Rothe, bishop of Ossory*, ed. P. F. Moran (1884) · J. Hagan, ed., 'Miscellanea Vaticano-Hibernica', *Archivium Hibernicum*, 5 (1916), 74–185, esp. 158–63 · *The letters and memorials of William, Cardinal Allen (1532–1594)*, ed. T. F. Knox (1882), vol. 2 of *Records of the English Catholics under the penal laws (1878–82)* · A. Theiner, *Annales ecclesiastici* (1856) · Bodl. Oxf., MSS Carte · NA Ire., Betham MSS · *Cause for the beatification and canonisation of the servants of God, 1579–1651*, Congregation for the Causes of Saints, Rome (1988) · R. Verstegan, *Theatrum crudelitatum haereticorum nostri temporis* (1587) · M. O'Reilly, ed., *Memorials of those who suffered for the Catholic faith in Ireland* (1868) · P. F. Moran, ed., *Spicilegium Ossoriense*, 3 vols. (1874–84) · W. M. Brady, *The episcopal succession in England, Scotland, and Ireland, AD 1400 to 1875*, 3 vols. (1876–7) · D. Edwards, 'Beyond reform: martial law and the Tudor reconquest of Ireland', *History Ireland*, 5 (summer 1997), 16–21 · D. Edwards, 'The Ormond lordship in county Kilkenny, 1515–1642', PhD diss., TCD, 1998 · J. Begley, *The diocese of Limerick in the sixteenth and seventeenth centuries* (1927) · E. Hogan, *Distinguished Irishmen of the sixteenth century* (1894) · D. Forristal, *Seventeen martyrs* (1990) · Irish Jesuit Archives, MacErlean MSS · R. D. Edwards, *Church and state in Tudor Ireland*

(1935) · J. J. Silke, 'The Irish abroad, 1534–1691', *A new history of Ireland*, ed. T. W. Moody and others, 3: *Early modern Ireland, 1534–1691* (1976), 587–633 · P. F. Moran, *History of the Catholic archbishops of Dublin since the Reformation* (1864)

Likenesses woodcut, repro. in Verstegan, *Theatrum crudelitatum haereticorum nostri temporis*, 80

O'Hussey, Eochaidh. *See* Ó hEodhasa, Eochaidh (c.1560–1612).

O'Hussey, Giolla Brighde. *See* Ó hEodhasa, Giolla Brighde (c.1570–1614).

Oilly, Robert (II) d' (*d.* 1142), baron, was the eldest son of Nigel d'Oilly, brother and heir of the Domesday Book tenant Robert (I) d'Oilly (*d.* c.1093), and his wife, Agnes. Robert succeeded his father during the reign of Henry I. His Oxfordshire barony of Hook Norton had consisted of more than two dozen manors in 1066; Robert was later reported to have held thirty-three and a half knights' fees from Henry I. Along with his lands, most of them in Oxfordshire, he inherited the royal constableship of Oxford Castle, which he held in partnership with John de St John (*d.* 1150).

Robert d'Oilly's ties to Henry I were strengthened when about 1126 he married Edith, daughter of Forne, with whom the king had had a son known as Robert fitz Roy. By 1129 Robert and Edith had two sons: Henry d'Oilly, who later married Matilda de Bohun, and Gilbert. Edith, one of their daughters, married Wigan of Wallingford, a nephew of Brian fitz Count. Robert fitz Roy remained in close contact with his stepfather and half-brothers. In 1129 d'Oilly founded Osney Priory (later an abbey) for Augustinian canons, outside Oxford. He and his wife were also benefactors of the Benedictines at Godstow and Eynsham, the Augustinians at St Frideswide's in Oxford, the Cistercians at Thame, the templars, and the hospitallers.

After Henry I's death in 1135 Robert d'Oilly continued to hold Oxford Castle, operating as *ciuitatis Oxenefordiae sub rege praeceptor* ('ruler of the city of Oxford under the king'), but when King Stephen was captured by the forces of the Empress Matilda at Lincoln in February 1141, d'Oilly switched his allegiance to Henry I's daughter. He was with her troops at Winchester later that year, and after the rout there in September the empress fled north to his headquarters at Oxford. During most of 1142, while she conducted her business from Oxford, d'Oilly was in frequent attendance at her court, and even brought his brother Fulk, who otherwise remained loyal to Stephen, to witness one of Matilda's charters to Osney. Then, near the beginning of September 1142, Robert d'Oilly died; he was buried at Eynsham Abbey. Fifteen days after his death Stephen took the city of Oxford and laid siege to the castle. In December the empress escaped across the frozen Thames. Although Fulk d'Oilly remained with Stephen after his brother's death, Robert's son and heir, Henry, stayed with the Angevins until Henry II became king in 1154. The constableship of Oxford Castle went to Stephen's men in the meantime, but by 1155 Henry d'Oilly had succeeded to it, as well as to his father's barony.

EMILIE AMT

Sources *Ann. mon.*, vol. 4 · *Reg. RAN*, vol. 3 · K. R. Potter and R. H. C. Davis, eds., *Gesta Stephani*, OMT (1976) · H. E. Salter, ed., *Cartulary of Oseney Abbey*, 6 vols., OHS, 89–91, 97–8, 101 (1929–36) · H. E. Salter, ed., *Eynsham cartulary*, 2 vols., OHS, 49, 51 (1907–8) · *The Thame cartulary*, ed. H. E. Salter (1947–8) · H. Hall, ed., *The Red Book of the Exchequer*, 3 vols., Rolls Series, 99 (1896)

Oisín [Ossian] (*supp. fl.* **3rd–5th cent.**), legendary hero, was the son of Fionn mac Cumhaill in the Fenian or Ossianic cycle of tales and lays that belongs to the Gaelic literary and oral traditions of Ireland and Scotland. He was assigned a floruit in the third century AD by medieval Irish scholars whose chronology of events connected with the pseudo-historical *Fianna* (warrior or hunter bands) of Fionn mac Cumhaill was commonly accepted until the end of the nineteenth century. The name Oisín (earlier Osséne or Ossíne) is a diminutive formed from the noun *os* ('deer') and a verse source in the Book of Leinster, a twelfth-century manuscript, states that his mother, Blaí Derg, conceived him when she was in the shape of a hind. References to such a conception are also found in later Irish literary and oral sources, as well as in Scottish Gaelic oral tradition.

Although Oisín features in material dating from approximately the eighth century, it was not until the twelfth century that he appeared in his main role in Fenian literature, that of an aged survivor and eyewitness of the deeds of the *Fianna*. According to the oldest version of *Acallam na Senórach* ('The colloquy of the old men'), dating from about 1200, Oisín and Caílte, another member of the *Fianna*, survived the defeat and destruction of the *Fianna* and lived until the introduction of Christianity to Ireland by Patrick some 150 years afterwards. Both of them met Patrick and regaled him and other ecclesiastical and temporal dignitaries with anecdotes, in prose and verse, about the exploits of Fionn and his warriors and their association with various places in Ireland. Caílte is given a more prominent role than Oisín in the earliest version of *Acallam na Senórach*, but in the later version, and in many of the Fenian lays composed from the thirteenth century on, Oisín is cast as the main narrator and repository of traditional lore regarding the *Fianna* and the antiquities of Ireland.

The early literary tradition fails to explain Oisín's remarkable longevity. Oral tradition on the other hand declares that he spent the time between the destruction of the *Fianna* and the advent of Patrick in the mythical Land of Youth (*Tír na hÓige* or *Tír na nÓg*). According to some versions of this legend his deer-mother enticed him thither, but the most popular version of the story has it that he was brought to this happy otherworld by a supernatural lover. He remained there until an overwhelming desire to visit his father and former colleagues in arms compelled him to leave the Land of Youth and return to Ireland. By accidentally touching the soil of Ireland he became old and blind and after his meeting with Patrick he functions as a link between the pagan Fenian past and the Christian present. The eighteenth-century 'Laoidh Oisín ar Thír na nÓg' ('Oisín's lay about the Land of the Young'), attributed by some to the Clare poet and author Michael Comyn,

names the woman who brings Oisín to Tír na nÓg as Niamh Chinn Óir. This late literary version of Oisín's otherworld journey has, since its translation and appearance in print in 1859, appealed to a wide audience. William Butler Yeats utilized it in his long narrative poem 'The Wandering of Oisin', first published in 1889.

Another important literary development associated with the name of Oisín occurred in the eighteenth century with the publication by James *Macpherson of *Fingal: an Ancient Epic Poem* (1762) and *Temora* (1763), works allegedly translated from epic poems which Macpherson claimed had been composed by a blind third-century Caledonian poet called Ossian, a name based on the vernacular Scottish Gaelic form Oisean. The term Ossianic, used as an alternative appellation of the Fenian cycle, derives from Macpherson's Ossian. Samuel *Johnson denounced Macpherson's works on Ossian as fraudulent and a celebrated literary quarrel ensued (for which see their articles). An important result of the controversy surrounding these publications was the awakening of scholarly interest in Fenian literature in general. MAIRTIN O BRIAIN

Sources K. Meyer, ed. and trans., *Fianaigecht: being a collection of hitherto unedited Irish poems and tales* (1910) · W. Stokes, ed., *Acallamh na Senórach*, Irische Texte, 4 (1900) · N. Ní Shéaghdha, ed., *Agallamh na Seanórach*, 3 vols. (1942–5) · E. MacNéill and G. Murphy, eds. and trans., *Duanaire Finn / The book of the lays of Fionn*, 1–2, ITS, 7, 28 (1908–33) · B. O'Looney, ed., 'Tír na n-Óg: the Land of Youth', *Transactions of the Ossianic Society*, 4 (1859), 227–79 [incl. edn of 'Laoidh Oisín ar Thír na nÓg'] · J. F. Campbell, *Leabhar na Feinne* (1872) · G. Murphy, ed. and trans., *Duanaire Finn*, 3, ITS, 43 (1953) · G. Murphy, *The Ossianic lore and romantic tales of medieval Ireland* (1955) · D. Ó hÓgáin, *Fionn mac Cumhaill: images of the Gaelic hero* (1988) · M. Ó Briain, 'Some material on Oisín in the Land of Youth', *Sages, saints and storytellers: Celtic studies in honour of Professor James Carney*, ed. D. Ó Corráin, L. Breatnach, and K. McCone (1989), 181–99 · M. Ó Briain, 'Oisín's biography: conception and birth', *Text und Zeittiefe*, ed. H. L. C. Tristram, ScriptOralia, 58 (1994), 455–86 · D. S. Thomson, *The Gaelic sources of Macpherson's 'Ossian'* (1952) · H. Gaskill, ed., *Ossian revisited* (1991)

O'Kane, Eachmarcach (1720–1790), harpist, was born at Drogheda in 1720. He was of a northern family, and was taught to play the harp by Cornelius Lyons, harper to the earl of Antrim. Described as a very tall, strong, and athletic man, O'Kane's famed spirit of adventure sent him to Rome, where he played for the exiled Charles Edward Stuart, the Young Pretender. After visiting France he went on to Madrid, where a great number of Irish gentlemen living at the court praised him to the king. However, O'Kane achieved notoriety for his drunken and uproarious habits, and lost favour in the Spanish court. From Madrid he apparently walked to Bilbao, carrying his harp on his back. He did not seem to spend much time in Ireland, instead touring around Scotland, where he played mainly in Blair Atholl, Dunkeld, and the lowlands and isles. In 1775 Sir Alexander MacDonald in Skye gave him a silver harp key, long in the family, and originally left by another Irish harper, Ruaidhri Dall O'Cathain, or O'Kane. Boswell, in his *Tour to the Hebrides*, recounts the tale that O'Kane begged to have the harp key on the basis of his being a namesake of its donor, and that the MacDonald family agreed, being unaware of its true value. Arthur O'Neill, in his famous memoirs, describes how O'Kane sold the key and drank the money, leaving the MacDonalds to rue their loss. Of his musical ability, a contemporary (a Mr Dunn) states that 'he was … able (though blind) to play with accuracy and great effect the fine treble and bass parts of many of Corelli's correntos in concert with other music'; this may have taken place at the series of concerts which Castrucci (Corelli's last pupil) organized in Dublin. O'Kane apparently died in 1790.

NORMAN MOORE, *rev.* MARK HUMPHREYS

Sources E. Bunting, *The ancient music of Ireland* (1840) • J. Boswell, *The journal of a tour of the Hebrides with Samuel Johnson* (1785) • C. M. Fox, *Annals of the Irish harpers* (1911)

Oke, George Colwell (1821–1874), legal writer, was born on 8 February 1821 at St Columb Major, Cornwall, the son of William Jane Oke (*d.* 1859) of Truro. After education at Truro he started out as a solicitor's accountant, but by 1848 was acting as assistant clerk to the Newmarket bench of justices. In 1855 he became assistant clerk to the lord mayor of London, and in 1864 succeeded to the chief clerkship. Oke's knowledge of criminal law and of its practical application brought him a high reputation. It was impressively demonstrated in several celebrated fraud cases at the Mansion House, including those arising out of the Overend Gurney financial crash of 1866.

Oke's learning reached a wider audience through a series of practice books on legal subjects of particular importance to magistrates, such as licensing and the game laws. One, *The Friendly Societies' Manual* (1855), had to be withdrawn as infringing the copyright of another work, but several others, such as *The Law of Turnpike Roads*, proved highly successful. However, it was the complementary *Oke's Magisterial Synopsis* and *Oke's Magisterial Formulist*, first published in 1848 and 1850 and running into fourteen and seventeen editions respectively, which proved the most enduring, with the last edition of the *Formulist* being published as late as 1968. In 1862 he addressed the Social Science Congress, advocating 'a uniform and comprehensive code of magisterial procedure' and deprecating any extension of stipendary magistrates.

Oke was twice married: first to Eliza Neile Hawkins (*d.* 1868), and second on 20 April 1870 to Georgina Percy, stepdaughter of G. M. Harvey, of Upper Norwood. He lived in Peckham, first at 7 Devonshire Terrace, and then at Rosedale, St Mary's Road. On 6 January 1874 he was taken ill at work and died at home three days later on 9 January. He was buried on 15 January in Nunhead cemetery. He was survived by his second wife and children.

GORDON GOODWIN, *rev.* PATRICK POLDEN

Sources *The Times* (10 Jan 1874) • *Law Times* (17 Jan 1874), 207 • *Law Journal* (17 Jan 1874), 38 • *ILN* (24 Jan 1874), 80 • Boase, *Mod. Eng. biog.* • G. C. Boase, *Collectanea Cornubiensia: a collection of biographical and topographical notes relating to the county of Cornwall* (1890) • Holdsworth, *Eng. law*, vol. 15 • M. Williams, *Leaves of a life*, 2 vols. (1890) • *London Directory* • *The Graphic* (7 Feb 1874), 124, 131

Likenesses portrait, repro. in *The Graphic*, 131 • sketch, repro. in *ILN*

Wealth at death under £4000: probate, 3 Feb 1874, *CGPLA Eng. & Wales*

O'Kearney, Barnaby (1567–1640), Jesuit, was born in Cashel, co. Tipperary, on 29 September 1567, the son of Patrick Kearney and Elizabeth, *née* Convey. He studied humanities in Ireland, and then philosophy under the Jesuits at Douai. He graduated MA in 1588, and later took a doctorate. He entered the Jesuits at Tournai on 5 October 1589, and from 1591 to 1595 taught humanities successively at the Jesuit colleges at St Omer, Antwerp, and Lille. He completed his ecclesiastical studies at Louvain, and was ordained priest in 1598. While awaiting permission to return to Ireland, then experiencing the Nine Years' War, he resumed teaching at Bruges and Douai and made his tertianship, or year of prayer and retreat work, at Tournai, 1601–2. In late spring 1603 he returned to Ireland accompanied by his nephew, Walter Wale, also a Jesuit.

O'Kearney worked on the Irish mission for nearly forty years. On their arrival he and Wale sent a letter to the Jesuit general recording their adventures on the journey from the Spanish Netherlands to Dublin. At this time, following the death of Elizabeth, there was an expectation that King James would grant liberty of conscience in Ireland. Churches were reconsecrated and the Catholic religion was practised openly for a while. On 9 January 1605 Christopher Holywood, superior of the Irish Jesuit mission, reported to the general that Wale and O'Kearney were 'for the last two months with a sick man, whose conversion will redound to the great advantage of the church' (Hogan, *Distinguished Irishmen*, 420). The sick man was the earl of Ormond, whose conversion Holywood mentioned on 16 June. On that date Holywood also mentioned that he had sent O'Kearney to assist the vicar-general of Kildare. Thereafter O'Kearney is mentioned as working in co. Meath, Kilkenny, and throughout Munster, where his brother David had been archbishop of Cashel since 1603. At first O'Kearney worked openly, drawing great crowds by his sermons. He had marked successes as a healer of divisions between people, at converting noted robbers and pillagers, and in gaining restitution for injuries committed. In 1606, however, persecution began to reappear. Thereafter O'Kearney and his fellow missioners had to act with great circumspection. In more remote areas, however, his preaching still drew large crowds. He preached fluently in Irish as well as English. Persecution became more intense in Munster in 1617, and the Jesuit house at Cashel, which often served as his base, was raided, pictures and statues were destroyed, and the chapel turned into a stable. The missioners in these and subsequent years often were obliged to sleep in the open fields or in old ruins. Nevertheless, O'Kearney was a busy correspondent and also wrote an unpublished account of the death of the tenth earl of Ormond. He published two volumes of sermons, one at Lyons in 1622 on the priesthood and death, and another at Paris in 1633 on the liturgy of the passion. He died at Cashel on 20 August 1640.

THOMAS J. MORRISSEY

Sources Archives of the Irish province of the Society of Jesus, Dublin • E. Hogan, ed., *Ibernia Ignatiana, seu, Ibernorum Societatis Jesu patrum monumenta* (1880), 116–17, 135–41, 162–3, 171–2, 187–90, 216–

19 · E. Hogan, *Distinguished Irishmen of the sixteenth century* (1894), 177, 411, 423–4, 431–4, 456, 459, 462, 465, 477–85

O'Keefe, Eoghan. *See* Ó Caoimh, Eoghan (1656–1726).

O'Keeffe, Adelaide (1776–*c*.1855), poet and novelist, was born at Eustace Street, Dublin, on 5 November 1776, the only daughter and third child of Irish parents, the dramatist and actor John *O'Keeffe (1747–1833) and Mary Heaphy (1757–1813), actress. Her younger brother Gerald died in infancy. Her childhood was traumatic: her parents had a troubled marriage and her mother was often absent. Adelaide was put out to a nurse until she was five. After the marriage ended her mother was denied access to the children by Adelaide's father. In 1781 John O'Keeffe moved to London as an operatic composer and playwright for the Haymarket, Covent Garden, and Drury Lane theatres. Adelaide and her elder brother John Tottenham followed in 1782 to attend school in London but were shortly afterwards sent to France to avoid what were considered by John O'Keeffe to be the unwanted attentions of his wife. While her brother John enjoyed a 'superior and expensive education' in Paris, at Westminster School, and Exeter College, Oxford (O'Keeffe, xviii), Adelaide suffered the 'horror' of convent schooling until 1788 and subsequently assisted her then blind father in his compositions. She cared for her father until he died.

Adelaide O'Keeffe embarked on her own career in the early 1790s with the composition of a novel, *Llewellin* (1799), a fictionalization of the life of Piers Gaveston's son as narrated to Chaucer. In 1798 she wrote *Patriarchal Times, or, The Land of Canaan*, a fictional reworking of chapters from Genesis, but she was unable to find a publisher for it until 1811. It proved to be critically and commercially successful. But it was her poems published in Ann and Jane Taylor's *Original Poems for Infant Minds* (1804) which established her reputation and remain, to the detriment of her novels, her best-known work. Following this success, she continued to write verses for children which were witty and cautionary in equal measure, publishing *Original Poems Calculated to Improve the Mind of Youth* (1808), *National Characters Exhibited in 40 Geographical Poems* (1808), and *Poems for Young Children* (1849). She also continued to write novels: *Zenobia, Queen of Palmyra* (1814), the three-volume epistolary *Dudley* (1819), and *The Broken Sword: a Tale* (1854), a story of parental separation.

After her father gave up the stage in 1798, it seems that O'Keeffe was financially responsible for the household despite her modest income (she later called for authors to be rewarded by annual grants, and wrote to the publishers Harvey and Darton concerning her underpayment for her contributions to *Original Poems*: see *N&Q*, 7th ser., 3.361–2). O'Keeffe lived for most of her life with her father in London and then moved with him in 1815 to Chichester, where she worked as a governess; in 1830 they moved to Southampton where John O'Keeffe died. Devoted to her father from early childhood, she published a tribute to him in the *New Monthly Magazine* (1833) and a memoir in *O'Keeffe's Legacy to his Daughter* (1834). She died unmarried, probably in Southampton, about 1855. Her last known address was 3 Spring-Place Hill, Southampton, and her final work was *The Broken Sword, or, A Soldier's Honour*, with an introduction by the author dated Southampton, January 1854.   CLARE L. TAYLOR

Sources A. O'Keeffe, 'Memoir', in J. O'Keeffe, *O'Keeffe's legacy to his daughter* (1834) · J. Shattock, *The Oxford guide to British women writers* (1993) · Blain, Clements & Grundy, *Feminist comp.* · *N&Q*, 7th ser., 3 (1887), 361–2
Archives BL, letters to Royal Literary Fund, loan 96

O'Keeffe, John (1747–1833), playwright, was born on 24 June 1747 in Abbey Street, Dublin. Little is known of his parents but the O'Keeffes of Fermoy and his mother's family, the O'Connors of Wexford, had lost their landed property through their devotion to the Stuart cause.

O'Keeffe was educated at the school of Father Austin, a learned Jesuit. From an early age he studied art under Robert West at the Royal Academy, Dublin, with his brother Daniel (1740–1787), who became a professional artist. His formal education ended when he paid an extended visit to an aunt in London from August 1762. There he earned pocket money by painting and developed his interest in the theatre, seeing Garrick act at Drury Lane.

O'Keeffe returned to Dublin in 1764 and soon became an actor in the Smock Alley theatre company under Henry Mossop. On 14 January 1767 Mossop staged his afterpiece *The She Gallant*, which had some success in London when revised as *The Positive Man* (1782). During the next ten years O'Keeffe worked as an actor in Dublin, Cork, and Limerick, with some appearances in Belfast, Derry, Kilkenny, and Waterford. His one-act musical pastoral *Colin's Welcome* was premièred at Belfast in 1770, and he compiled and adapted the pantomimes *Harlequin in Waterford* (1767), *Harlequin in Derry* (1770), and *The Giant's Causeway* (1770). When in Kilkenny in 1770 O'Keeffe advertised a subscription series of drawings of local views. He enjoyed a reputation for 'gaiety, wit, and cheerfulness' (A. O'Keeffe, xxi), and acted Gratiano to Macklin's Shylock. He played Tony Lumpkin in Dublin performances of Goldsmith's *She Stoops to Conquer* and wrote the farces *Tony Lumpkin's Ramble thro' Cork* (1773) and *Tony Lumpkin in Town* (1774).

On 1 October 1774 O'Keeffe married Mary Heaphy (1757–1813), whose father, Tottenham Heaphy, managed the Cork and Limerick theatres. Mary was protestant, so there were both Catholic and protestant marriage ceremonies. They had three children: John Tottenham (1775–1804), Adelaide *O'Keeffe (1776–*c*.1855), and Gerald, who died in infancy.

For his Cork benefit in 1777 O'Keeffe produced David Garrick's *A Christmas Tale* with special effects, including 'the Giant in the Fiery Lake 20 feet high' (Clark, 107). That December John and Mary O'Keeffe travelled to London, where he sent a revised version of *Tony Lumpkin in Town* to George Colman, manager of the Haymarket summer theatre. It received six performances in 1778, and five the following summer. Mary O'Keeffe made some appearances on the London stage and John acted at Portsmouth in summer 1778, but in March 1779 they returned to Ireland. O'Keeffe quickly wrote an afterpiece, *The Son-in-Law*, and sent it to Colman. With music composed and arranged by

Samuel Arnold, it was O'Keeffe's first real success, with sixteen performances in summer 1779. The role of the ridiculous castrato, Signor Arionelli, was designed for the bass Charles Bannister, who was known to delight his friends with falsetto imitations of Italian singers. O'Keeffe's ability to write rewarding parts for actors was to play a large part in his success. Colman visited Dublin in winter 1779–80, bought the copyright of *The Son-in-Law* for £40, and asked for another play. O'Keeffe sent his musical afterpiece *The Dead Alive* and Colman staged it in June 1781, the month in which O'Keeffe left Ireland for London, never to return.

In the mid 1770s O'Keeffe had suffered from violent inflammation of his eyelids and tried remedies which made the condition worse. His eyesight steadily deteriorated, his career as an actor was threatened and he grew less extrovert. He and Mary acted at Crow Street, Dublin, in 1780–81, and at this time his wife apparently became involved with the actor George Graham. According to the *Catalogue of Five Hundred Celebrated Authors*, O'Keeffe 'demolished his wife's nose in a fit of jealousy' and departed for London. Mary lived with Graham as his wife for many years and they acted together in the English provinces and Scotland. O'Keeffe arranged for his children to come to England and made himself solely responsible for their upbringing and education. Adelaide wrote that her father was 'never heard to mention the name of his *wife*' and that after the death of his brother Daniel in 1787 'the reserve of his character became confirmed and habitual' (A. O'Keeffe, xvi, xxi). O'Keeffe's very successful afterpiece *The Agreeable Surprise*, with music by Arnold, was the last work he was able to write without an amanuensis. It was praised by Hazlitt who called O'Keeffe 'our English Molière' (*Complete Works*, 5.319). The *Public Advertiser* (6 September 1781) reported that the whole audience was 'in one continued Fit of Laughter' and particularly praised the comic actor and singer John Edwin, who played Lingo, the former schoolmaster who courts the ignorant dairymaid Cowslip with the song 'Amo, amas, I love a lass'.

Thomas Harris, the Covent Garden manager, then commissioned a full-length piece, for which O'Keeffe received 600 guineas, £120 of which he gave to Arnold for the music. *The Banditti*, a forerunner of romantic opera, failed on its first night (28 November 1781), but was an immediate success the following November when revised as *The Castle of Andalusia*. The strong cast included the contralto Margaret Kennedy in the breeches role of Don Alphonso, Giovanna Sestini in the tailor-made broken English role of Lorenza, and Edwin as Pedrillo. 25 November 1782 saw O'Keeffe's first Covent Garden pantomime, *Lord Mayor's Day*, a splendid spectacle with over 200 supernumeraries in the final procession and with music arranged and composed by William Shield. Meanwhile his *Harlequin Teague*, with music by Arnold, had been performed as the Haymarket summer pantomime, with a solo duet for Charles Bannister as a man with two heads. In summer 1783 O'Keeffe's first five-act comedy for London, *The Young Quaker*, was a success at the Haymarket; it continued to be performed well into the nineteenth century. He also provided lyrics for *Gretna Green*, a farce with 'Italian, French, Irish, Scotch, Welch, and English MUSIC' (*Public Advertiser*, 28 Aug 1783). Every year for the rest of the decade O'Keeffe had new works performed at both Covent Garden and the Haymarket, with music composed by Shield and Arnold respectively.

For the Haymarket O'Keeffe provided the afterpieces *Peeping Tom of Coventry* (1784), which remained popular for many years, and *A Beggar on Horseback* (1785). Another successful farce, *The Prisoner at Large* (1788), was dedicated to John Edwin, whose death in October 1790 was a serious blow to O'Keeffe, as was the mental decline of Colman after a stroke in 1785. The Haymarket management was gradually assumed by George Colman the younger, who was himself a skilful writer of comic afterpieces. O'Keeffe wrote for Harris at Covent Garden until the end of his career, producing two more successful full-length musical works, *Fontainbleau* (1784) and *The Highland Reel* (1788). His afterpiece *The Poor Soldier* (1783), adapted from his unsuccessful *The Shamrock*, was set in the Irish countryside and starred Margaret Kennedy as the soldier Patrick. The music incorporated some 'fine Irish airs of Carolan' (J. O'Keeffe, *Recollections*, 1.70), which O'Keeffe selected and sang to Shield. With forty performances in its first season, it remained popular well into the next century in Britain and the USA. A sequel, *Love in a Camp, or, Patrick in Prussia*, also did well. *The Farmer* (1787), which O'Keeffe adapted from his rejected play *The Plague of Riches*, was another success and included the song 'A Flaxen-Headed Cow-Boy', with Shield's delightful flute obbligato for the whistling boy, and a patter song for Edwin as the stay-maker Jemmy Jumps.

O'Keeffe's ability to rewrite failures into successes was remarkable, particularly in view of his near blindness. He provided words for the Covent Garden pantomimes *Friar Bacon* (1783, altered to *Harlequin Rambler* after sixteen performances), *Omai* (1785), *Aladin* (1788), and *Merry Sherwood* (1795). In spring 1791 he had two non-musical successes, the afterpiece *Modern Antiques* and the five-act comedy *Wild Oats*. The latter, 'calculated throughout to call forth the broad laugh and the tear of sensibility, alternately' (Baker, 3.410), has proved the longest lasting of his stage works. There were some Covent Garden flops, however. *The Blacksmith of Antwerp* (1785), *The Man-Milliner* (1787), and *Tantara-rara* (1788) folded very quickly, while *The Toy* (1789) and its revision *The Lie of the Day* (1796) had only limited success. At the Haymarket *The Siege of Curzola* failed as both a mainpiece and an afterpiece and *The Basket-Maker* (1790) received only five performances. O'Keeffe turned out pieces to celebrate special occasions, notably *The Birth-Day* (1783) for the twenty-first birthday of the prince of Wales and *Britain's Brave Tars!!* for the naval victories of 1797. There were also benefit pieces, *The Maid's the Mistress* for Sestini (1783), *The Pharo Table* for William Lewis (1789), *The Little Hunchback* for John Quick (1789), and *St George's Day* for Isabella Mattocks (1789). *The Czar*, premièred at Mrs Billington's benefit (1790), was revised as *The Fugitive* in the following season.

After the success of *Wild Oats* O'Keeffe produced nothing for two years. In summer 1791 he took a six-week holiday with his children in West Lulworth on the Dorset coast and he later drew on this for his popular three-act Haymarket comedy, *The London Hermit, or, Rambles in Dorsetshire* (1793). The tenor Michael Kelly, who had appeared with him in Dublin in the late 1770s when O'Keeffe was 'a fine, sprightly, animated young man', dined with him in 1793 and found him 'broken down, and almost blind; but still full of pleasantry and anecdote' (Kelly, 2.37). His only other new Haymarket offering was the unsuccessful afterpiece *The Magic Banner* (1796). Covent Garden had been enlarged to seat over 3000 in 1792 and the enormous auditorium and increasingly refined tastes of the audience militated against O'Keeffe. However, the musical mainpiece *Sprigs of Laurel* (1793) survived for five seasons and its revised version, *The Rival Soldiers*, proved remarkably popular in the USA in the early nineteenth century. The comedies *The World in a Village* (1793) and *Life's Vagaries* (1795) and the musical farce *The Irish Mimic, or, Blunders in Brighton* (1795) did quite well. O'Keeffe's last collaboration with Shield, *The Lad of the Hills* (1796), had little success, even when revised in two-act form as *The Wicklow Mountains*, and the comedy *The Doldrum* (1796) received only eight performances. *Olympus in an Uproar*, his reworking of Kane O'Hara's burletta *The Golden Pippin* with music by William Reeve, had thirteen performances in 1796. *Le grenadier* (1789) and *Jenny's Whim* (1794) failed to reach public performance because of censorship problems, and the same fate overtook his only piece for Drury Lane, *She's Eloped*, rehearsed with Mrs Jordan in May 1798.

O'Keeffe hoped to provide for his future by publishing his four-volume *Dramatic Works* by subscription in 1798, under the patronage of the prince of Wales. Harris permitted the inclusion of the works for which Covent Garden owned the copyright, but Colman the younger, who had inherited his father's debts with his theatre, withheld five works that he considered too valuable for general release. Financial returns were disappointing and in June 1800 Covent Garden staged a benefit for O'Keeffe, who was led on by William Lewis to give his specially written address to the audience. In 1803 Harris agreed to make O'Keeffe an annual payment in return for his remaining copyrights and unpublished plays. O'Keeffe received a £100 annual Treasury pension in 1808 and, when Harris's annuity ended in 1825, he was granted a royal pension of £100 a year. He had spent lavishly on the education of his son, who took orders and whose death in Jamaica in 1804 was a devastating blow. Adelaide O'Keeffe acted as her father's amanuensis from 1788 and was his companion in his old age. It was to her that he dictated his *Recollections* (1826), when they were living in Chichester.

John O'Keeffe's last few years were spent in Bedford Cottage, Southampton, where he died on 4 February 1833. According to his daughter he took pleasure in their country walks and in verse composition to within a few weeks of his death. He was buried on 11 February at All Saints, Southampton. O'Keeffe worked always in popular genres and so has received scant acclaim from literary critics, but

he 'gladdened the hearts of his auditors between twenty and thirty years and "sent them laughing to their beds"' (Baker, 1.551).   OLIVE BALDWIN and THELMA WILSON

Sources J. O'Keeffe, *Recollections of the life of John O'Keeffe, written by himself*, 2 vols. (1826) · A. O'Keeffe, ed., *O'Keeffe's legacy to his daughter* (1834) · J. O'Keeffe, *The dramatic works of John O'Keeffe, esq.* (1798) · J. O'Keeffe, *The plays of John O'Keeffe*, ed. F. M. Link (1981) · C. B. Hogan, ed., *The London stage, 1660–1800*, pt 5: *1776–1800* (1968) · W. S. Clark, *The Irish stage in the county towns, 1720–1800* (1965) · 'Biographical sketch of John O'Keeffe, esq.', *Monthly Mirror*, 4 (1797), 323–8; 5 (1798), 13–16, 70–72 · D. E. Baker, *Biographia dramatica, or, A companion to the playhouse*, rev. I. Reed, new edn, rev. S. Jones, 3 vols. in 4 (1812) · *The thespian dictionary, or, Dramatic biography of the eighteenth century* (1802) · *Public Advertiser* (6 Sept 1781) · *Public Advertiser* (28 Aug 1783) · M. Kelly, *Reminiscences*, 2 (1826) · *Catalogue of five hundred celebrated authors of Great Britain, now living* (1788) · 'An Account of John O'Keeffe, esq.', *European Magazine*, 14 (1788), 5–6 · *The complete works of William Hazlitt*, ed. P. P. Howe, 5 (1930) · R. Fiske, *English theatre music in the eighteenth century* (1973) · T. J. Walsh, *Opera in Dublin, 1705–1797* (1973) · S. L. Porter, *With an air debonair: musical theatre in America, 1785–1815* (1991) · *GM*, 1st ser., 103/1 (1833), 375–7

Archives Princeton University Library, New Jersey, papers

Likenesses D. O'Keeffe, watercolour miniature on ivory, 1776, NG Ire. · T. Lawranson, oils, 1786, NPG · S. Freeman, print, 1805 (after T. Lawranson), Harvard U. · J. Bennett, print (after A. O'K [Adelaide O'Keeffe]), repro. in O'Keeffe, ed., *O'Keeffe's legacy* · Blackberd, print (after T. Lawranson), repro. in T. Bellamy, *Bellamy's Picturesque Magazine* (1793) · T. Bragg, print (after T. Lawranson), repro. in O'Keeffe, *Recollections* · J. Corner, print (after T. Lawranson), repro. in *European Magazine* (1788) · print (after T. Lawranson), Harvard U.

O'Keeffe, Robert (1814–1881), Roman Catholic priest, was born on 11 April 1814 in Green Street, Callan, co. Kilkenny, the posthumous son of Robert O'Keeffe, grocer and ironmonger, and his wife, Eleanor Fennelly. He was educated at Callan, at St Kieran's College, Kilkenny (1831–4), and at St Patrick's College, Maynooth, co. Kildare (1834–40), where he was admitted to postgraduate studies in the Dunboyne Establishment. In 1840 he was ordained priest and appointed to St Kieran's College, where he was teacher and administrator until 1849. From 1849 to 1860 he served as curate at Ballyragget, co. Kilkenny, and in the latter year became parish priest of Rathdowney, Queen's county, and one of the vicars forane of the diocese. In January 1863 he became parish priest of his native Callan.

O'Keeffe mobilized opinion and resources in Callan in support of a number of projects including the devotional and charitable Society of St Vincent de Paul, but mainly in the field of education. The Christian Brothers opened their doors to the schoolgoing boys of Callan in September 1868 in substantial new premises provided through the voluntary effort and subscriptions of townspeople under O'Keeffe's direction. Pupils flocked to the brothers, leaving only a handful on the rolls in the boys' national school, of which O'Keeffe was *ex officio* manager. He was soon busily revitalizing the national school to compete with the Christian Brothers, and it reopened in January 1869 as Callan Academy. It had a board of management, a former model school headmaster as principal, and a wide range of subjects, and was affiliated to the Department of Science and Art, South Kensington. His promotion of the academy brought O'Keeffe into bitter conflict with his curates and the bishop, Edward Walsh. His offence was that by advancing an alternative to the conventional model of governance and curriculum in Irish Catholic schools he had broken ranks on one of the most contentious issues in the contemporary church–state conflict.

Between 1869 and 1875 O'Keeffe fought a series of civil actions for libel against the curates and Bishop Walsh, and eventually against Cardinal Cullen, who in 1871 had been given plenary papal authority to address the Callan problem. O'Keeffe was successful in most of these cases, but ultimately he was routed. For contravening the canonical prohibition against a cleric taking a fellow cleric before a civil court, he was first suspended and then, in November 1871, removed from office. He refused to yield up his parish church, which was thereupon placed under interdict by Cullen. Already the townspeople were bitterly divided between opponents and supporters of O'Keeffe, and riots and affrays were to be a feature of life in Callan for a number of years. On foot of the bishop's certification that he was no longer parish priest, O'Keeffe was removed by the relevant government bodies from his positions as school manager and workhouse chaplain. He appealed to British opinion and initially received substantial financial support; his case was raised in both houses of parliament during 1872. The title of his book *Ultramontanism v. Civil and Religious Liberty* (1874) signified an appeal to liberal and protestant sensibilities. By late 1875, however, it was clear that neither government nor parliament, courts, or British liberal opinion would prevent the deployment of canon law in Ireland against one who had freely submitted to it.

Comprehensively defeated and in dire financial straits, O'Keeffe held out until 1879, when he signed an unqualified apology and was granted a small pension. Thereafter he lived quietly with relatives near Thomastown, co. Kilkenny, until his death on 1 February 1881. His funeral mass in Thomastown was attended by a large number of priests and he was buried in his family's grave in Newtown cemetery, co. Kilkenny. The dramatic events in Callan with which he is identified have inspired two works of fiction: Francis MacManus, *The Greatest of these* (1943), and Thomas Kilroy, *The Big Chapel* (1971). R. V. COMERFORD

Sources P. Hogan, 'The Callan schism', *Old Kilkenny Review*, 3/4 (1987), 339–57 · St Kieran's College, Kilkenny, Carrigan MSS · P. J. Walsh, *William J. Walsh, archbishop of Dublin* (1928) · E. R. Norman, *The Catholic church and Ireland in the age of rebellion, 1859–1873* (1965) · P. J. Hamell, *Maynooth: students and ordinations index, 1795–1895* (1982) · H. C. Kirkpatrick, *Report of the action for libel brought by Rev. Robert O'Keefe, P.P., against his eminence, Cardinal Cullen* (1874) · Gladstone, *Diaries*
Archives BL, Gladstone MSS · St Kieran's College, Kilkenny, Carrigan MSS
Likenesses photograph, repro. in Hogan, 'The Callan schism'

O'Kelly, Charles (1621–1695), army officer and historian, was the eldest son of John O'Kelly (d. 1674), eighth lord of the manor of Screen, co. Galway, and Isma, a daughter of Sir William Hill. He was born at Screen, but educated at St Omer in the Spanish Netherlands. There 'he went thro' the Course of his Studies with Great Reputation, and

became well versed in the Knowledge of most of the European Languages, such as Greek, Latin, Italian, Spanish, French, English and Irish' (*General History of Ireland*). He returned to Ireland in 1642 after the outbreak of civil war and served with his father on the royalist side by commanding a troop of horse in Ormond's army. After the triumph of the English parliamentarians he sailed to Spain with 2000 Irish soldiers to serve the exiled Charles II. He later joined the king in France, but was forced to return to Spain following Cromwell's treaty with the French in 1657. He travelled to England at the Restoration in 1660, 'highly esteemed for his Learning, Loyalty and great services both at home and abroad' (ibid.) and his father was able to reclaim the family lands in Galway. O'Kelly succeeded his father as lord of Screen in 1674. He married Margaret O'Kelly (*fl.* 1650), a daughter of Teigue O'Kelly of Gallagh, co. Galway.

On the outbreak of civil war in 1689 O'Kelly, at the age of sixty-eight, volunteered for service in King James's Irish army. Although he neither raised nor commanded a regiment, he was given the rank of colonel and served in a staff capacity. After being forced to abandon Sligo in August 1689, Patrick Sarsfield pulled his forces back to Roscommon where he left O'Kelly in command while he travelled to Dublin to report. Seeing that the enemy had not pursued Sarsfield from Sligo, O'Kelly took it upon himself to march back to Boyle and establish himself there. At daybreak on 20 September 1689 he was attacked by Thomas Lloyd's Enniskillen troops, who routed his men at what became known as 'the break of the Boyle'. O'Kelly was forced to flee, leaving behind him all his baggage and his portmanteau of private papers. Nevertheless, the Enniskilliners' success was short-lived as in the next month O'Kelly marched back with Sarsfield and helped to command the force that recaptured Sligo.

In 1690 O'Kelly was appointed high sheriff of co. Roscommon, where it would seem he remained until September 1691. After the battle of Aughrim (12 July 1691) and the surrender of Galway (28 July), the Irish troops in Roscommon and Sligo were isolated from the main army at Limerick. On the road to Sligo he met, by chance, Baldearg O'Donnell, who commanded a private army of Ulster Gaels. O'Donnell had entered into negotiations with the Williamites, and O'Kelly attempted to persuade him to remain faithful to the Jacobite cause. Nevertheless, O'Donnell and his men changed sides and reinforced the Williamite troops in Roscommon, who then marched on Sligo in early September. On their way they forced O'Kelly to surrender a castle outside Boyle. The terms of surrender allowed him to march to Limerick, which he reached before the siege began. On 14 September 1691 O'Kelly warned Sarsfield that Brigadier Robert Clifford, who commanded the Jacobite troops on the co. Clare bank of the Shannon where a Williamite crossing was anticipated, was not to be trusted. He urged him either to send a trusted officer or come himself to command. His advice was not taken and that night the enemy built a pontoon bridge across the river and at dawn established themselves on the Clare bank. Nine days later a ceasefire was agreed, after which Sarsfield wanted him to assist in negotiating the terms of a treaty. Nevertheless, he took no part, perhaps because his uncompromising views were thought unhelpful.

O'Kelly's family estates were secured by his being included under the terms of the treaty of Limerick (3 October 1691), after which he retired to Screen. In the following year he wrote the curiously entitled *Macariae excidium, or, The Destruction of Cyprus containing the last war & conquest of that kingdom written originally in Syriak by Philotas Phyloxypres, translated into Latin by Gratianus Ragallus P.R. and now made into English by C:ô K: anno domini: 1692*. The work remained obscure until the nineteenth century, when it was published three times. There are early manuscript copies in the British Library and Trinity College, Dublin. All the named participants and places are disguised by classical names: Ireland is referred to as Cyprus, and England as Cilicia. James II, William III, St Ruth, and Tyrconnell are given the names Amasis, Theodore, Phyrrus, and Coridon. Sarsfield is given that of the Spartan general Lysander. *Macariae excidium* is primarily a political rather than a military account of the war in Ireland of 1689–91. 'The loss of Cyprus cannot be justly imputed to the Cowardice or Infidelity of the Natives, but rather the wrong Politicks of a weak Prince' (O'Kelly, *Macariae*, 6). The work is particularly hostile to Tyrconnell, whom O'Kelly accused of betraying the Irish cause to the English, and although the portrayal of Sarsfield is generally favourable, he did not escape O'Kelly's criticism for administrative incompetence and for negotiating with the enemy. He was highly critical of the treaty of Limerick. It would, he wrote, take someone else to write a history of the treaty as it would require 'Ink mixed with the Writer's Teares; and the Fountain of my weak Eyes hath been drained up already by the too frequent Remembrance of the Slaughter at Acra [Aughrim], and the sad Separation at Paphos [Limerick]' (ibid., 159).

O'Kelly wrote another account of the war, as well as an account of the war that followed the 1641 rebellion, in his 'Mémoires du Colonel Charles O'Kelly de Skryne, sur les guerres d'Irlande de 1641 et suivans, et de 1689 et suivans'. This document was preserved by the O'Kelly–Farrell family in France, but was lost at the time of the French Revolution. He again used the device of disguising the names and, as the key to the names referred to in the 'Mémoires' survived, it would appear that the account of the 1689 war contained more detail than is to be found in *Macariae excidium*.

O'Kelly died at Screen aged seventy-four. 'He was a person of great abilities, piety, and universal knowledge, and was justly esteemed one of the wisest as well as the most accomplished men of the age' (*General History of Ireland*). His only son, Captain Dennis O'Kelly, served at Aughrim and succeeded to the lands at Screen. He married a daughter of Lord Bellew, but became 'attached to low intrigues and dissipation' (O'Kelly, *Macariae*, xviii). He was predeceased by his three children, and his wife fled to France to get away from him. He died in 1740, leaving his lands to his uncle John O'Kelly. PIERS WAUCHOPE

Sources *The general history of Ireland collected by the learned Jeoffry Keating*, ed. D. O'Connor (1723), appx, 10 · T. C. Croker, ed., *Narratives illustrative of the contests in Ireland in 1641 and 1690*, CS, 14 (1840) · J. O'Donovan, ed. and trans., *The tribes and customs of Hy-Many, commonly called O'Kelly's country*, Irish Archaeological Society (1843) · C. O'Kelly, *Macariae excidium, or, The destruction of Cyprus*, ed. J. C. O'Callaghan (1850) · J. D'Alton, *Illustrations, historical and genealogical, of King James's Irish army list (1689)*, 2nd edn, 2 vols. (1860–61) · C. O'Kelly, *The Jacobite war in Ireland*, ed. G. N. Plunkett and E. Hogan (1894) · *An exact account of the royal army with particulars of a great defeat … near Boyle* (1689)

Wealth at death owned the manor of Screen, co. Galway

O'Kelly, Dennis (*c*.1728–1787), racehorse owner, was born in Ireland of 'humble' parents, and had no formal education. After arriving in London about 1748, aged twenty, he became first a chair carrier, and then kept the scores at the billiard table and tennis court. However, he soon met Charlotte Hayes (*d*. 1787), a noted courtesan whom he later married. She financed his gambling speculations, the success of which provided him with capital. His major break occurred when he paid 650 guineas for a part-share in Eclipse, a horse that had never run a race. The purchase paid off, Eclipse rapidly demonstrating that it was the best horse of the day by winning its first race, the Queen's Plate at Winchester, with such style that O'Kelly was able to collect on a famous bet that he had made—he had wagered that Eclipse would be at least 240 yards ahead of the rest of the field; everyone was amazed at such a feat, and this prompted O'Kelly to pay a further 1100 guineas to become the animal's sole owner.

O'Kelly's earnings from Eclipse were undermined by three factors: the most valuable races at Newmarket were confined to horses belonging to the Jockey Club, an élite body which refused to admit O'Kelly; Eclipse's reputation meant that it was difficult to arrange matches elsewhere, for few owners would back their horses against him; and Eclipse was 'an indifferent foal getter', thus limiting its value as a stud (*Sporting Magazine*, 6, 1795, 119). Despite this, O'Kelly rejected an offer of 11,000 guineas for the horse. O'Kelly's primary goal was fame rather than money, and he much preferred racing his horses to selling them. Much of his behaviour was probably motivated by a resentment of his treatment by aristocrats, particularly his exclusion from membership of clubs patronized by the higher orders. In addition, he alleged that he had been sold 'half-bred' mares with false signatures testifying to their pedigree. These factors go some way towards explaining his regular denunciations of aristocrats as 'black-legs'.

Betting, on both horses and cards, allied to the profits from his breeding stud, made O'Kelly a very rich man, though one who was regarded as 'a disreputable adventurer' (Black, 150). Money enabled him to gain some admittance to society, notably his purchase of commissions in the Middlesex militia, in which he eventually attained the rank of colonel. He also bought a country house at Clay Hill, Epsom, and subsequently the famous estate of Cannons, near Edgware, formerly the house of the duke of Chandos.

O'Kelly was described as having 'a bear-like figure, dark

and saturnine visage, with the accompaniment of his rough striped coat and old round hat'. Although his looks resembled a ruffian, he was very 'peaceable' and had 'the manners of a gentleman, and the attractive quaintness of the humorist' (*Sporting Magazine* 6, 1795, 98–100). Contradictions permeated his nature. His kindness towards his servants made them 'look at him more as a friend than a master' (*Sporting Magazine*, 2, 1793, 335) and he retained jockeys on an annual basis, permitting them to ride for other owners providing they did not ride against him. However, he displayed immense meanness in almost all of his business transactions, and jockeys invariably struggled to be paid. Similarly, although he was a heavy gambler and had no interest in religion, he refused to permit play at his own table. Indeed, he inserted a clause in his will specifically punishing his heir should he gamble.

O'Kelly died childless at his house in Piccadilly Grove, London, on 28 December 1787 and was interred in a vault at Whitechapel. While he left his widow well provided for, including the bequest of a famous parrot that he had bought for 50 guineas, which was able to whistle the 104th psalm, the bulk of his estate went to his nephew, Andrew Dennis O'Kelly, who had been educated in England and France. Despite his uncle's stipulations Andrew embraced horse-racing, and was so successful as both owner and jockey that he became a member of the Jockey Club. He was regarded with respect both by contemporaries and by posterity—something Dennis O'Kelly never achieved.

ADRIAN N. HARVEY

Sources *A genuine memoir of Dennis O'Kelly* (1787) · *GM*, 1st ser., 57 (1787), 1196–7 · *Sporting Magazine*, 2 (1793), 331–6 · *Sporting Magazine*, 6 (1795), 19–20, 222 · *Sporting Magazine*, 44 (1814), 98–100 · R. Black, *The Jockey Club and its founders* (1891) · C. Chinn, *Better betting with a decent feller: bookmakers, betting and the British working class, 1750–1990* (1991), 37–8
Likenesses R. St G. Mansergh, etching, pubd 1773 (*The eclipse macarony*), NPG
Wealth at death very wealthy: *GM*, 1196

O'Kelly, Joseph (1832–1883), geologist, was born in Dublin on 31 October 1832, the second son of Matthias Joseph O'Kelly, and his wife, Margaret Shannon. His father was noted for a love of natural history, especially of conchology, and for his activity in the cause of Catholic emancipation. Joseph O'Kelly entered Trinity College, Dublin, in 1848, took his BA in 1852, his diploma in engineering in 1853, and his MA in 1860.

In 1852 O'Kelly joined the Geological Society of Dublin (after 1864 the Royal Geological Society of Ireland) and he served frequently on its council. He briefly was employed in the valuation office under Richard John Griffith, but on 13 November 1854 he became an assistant geologist with the geological survey of Ireland under Joseph Beete Jukes. He was promoted to senior geologist on 1 April 1863. O'Kelly mapped chiefly in west Cork, in co. Kerry, in the Limerick volcanic beds, and in the southern Irish midlands. His name is on twenty-three sheets of the one-inch geological map of Ireland and he contributed extensively to the accompanying memoirs. While mapping the Slieveardagh coalfield during the winter of 1858–9 atrocious

weather and foul accommodation left him with bronchial problems which eventually terminated his field career. In 1863 he was granted six months' sick leave so that he might pass the winter in Malaga.

In October 1866 O'Kelly permanently quitted the field to become secretary in the survey's Dublin office. There his services were of great value, not only because of his extensive knowledge of Irish geology, but also because his honesty and genial disposition helped to cool tempers within a survey where strong personal animosities existed.

O'Kelly married, in 1870, Miss Dorothea Smyth; they had a family of five sons and four daughters. He died of acute bronchitis on 13 April 1883 at his home, 72 Eccles Street, Dublin. His contributions to the literature of geology, practically restricted to the memoirs published by the survey, indicate his powers and his thoroughness as a geological observer. He was elected a member of the Royal Irish Academy on 8 January 1866.

GORDON L. HERRIES DAVIES

Sources *Geological Magazine*, new ser., 2nd decade, 10 (1883), 288 · G. L. Herries Davies, *North from the Hook: 150 years of the Geological Survey of Ireland* (1995) · private information (1894)
Archives Geological Survey of Ireland, Dublin
Likenesses group photograph, *c.*1860, repro. in Davies, *North from the Hook*
Wealth at death £1057 19s. 11d.: probate, 3 Aug 1883, *CGPLA Ire.*

O'Kelly, Patrick [called Bard O'Kelly] (1754–*c.*1835), poet, was born in Loughrea, co. Galway. O'Kelly gradually built up a local reputation as a poet in Ireland before publishing his first volume, *Killarney: a Poem*, in 1791. Thereafter, his fame rapidly spread and his subsequent volumes were issued by subscription. Admirers, many of whose eulogistic verses found a place in O'Kelly's own volumes, included the future King George IV of England, who, having ordered fifty copies of O'Kelly's second volume, met the poet at Phoenix Park in Dublin, while visiting Ireland. O'Kelly was also later to meet Sir Walter Scott at Limerick in 1825.

Despite having such famous admirers, O'Kelly could not live by subscription alone, and spent much of his life travelling throughout south-west Ireland selling his books. In July 1808, while visiting Doneraile, co. Cork, O'Kelly's watch and chain were, unfortunately, stolen. The mishap, however, led indirectly to his most popular verse, the 'Doneraile Litany', a string of curses in poetic form on the town and its people. O'Kelly made further poetic capital out of the locale, writing a sequel, 'The Palinode', which revoked all the previous curses, when Lady Doneraile herself, on reading the 'Litany', was inspired to replace his property. A less profitable relationship was that of O'Kelly's fellow poet Michael McCarthy, whose popular 'Lacas delectabilis' (1816) was, according to O'Kelly, plagiarized from a poem he had earlier written. O'Kelly's other works are equally comic in nature, and include a so-called 'ethicographical survey of the Western parts of Ireland'.

O'Kelly died about 1835, and his clever, but often plagiarizing, works, although frequently anthologized, largely fell into disrepute. At the turn of the twentieth century, for example, the esteemed Irish critic D. J. O'Donoghue, although in admiration of O'Kelly's 'extraordinary character', nevertheless characterized his verse as being, without exception, 'of a very pedestrian order' (*DNB*). O'Kelly should not be confused with another Patrick O'Kelly of his era, who published *A General History of the Rebellion of 1798* (1842), and translated works by Abbé McGeoghegan and W. D. O'Kelly.   JASON EDWARDS

Sources D. J. O'Donoghue, *The poets of Ireland: a biographical dictionary with bibliographical particulars*, 1 vol. in 3 pts (1892–3), 192 · T. C. Croker, ed., *The popular songs of Ireland* (1839) · *Watty Cox's Irish Magazine* (Sept 1810) · J. G. Lockhart, *Memoirs of the life of Sir Walter Scott*, [new edn] (1845), 562 · *DNB*

O'Kelly, Ralph. *See* Ó Ceallaigh, Ralph (*d.* 1361).

O'Kelly, Seán Thomas [Seán Tomás Ó Ceallaigh] (1882–1966), president of Éire (Ireland), was born at 4 Lower Wellingon Street, Dublin, on 25 August 1882, the eldest son of Samuel O'Kelly and his wife, Catherine, *née* O'Dea (*d.* 1923), originally from co. Clare. His family soon moved to Berkeley Road, where his father established a boot making business. He was educated at the convent of the Sisters of Holy Faith, Mountjoy Street, the Christian Brothers' schools at St Mary's Place, and, briefly, at the O'Connell Schools, North Richmond Street. On leaving school in 1898, he became a junior assistant in the National Library, and remained in that post until 1902.

During this time O'Kelly joined the Ard Craobh branch of the Gaelic League, and was taught Irish there by Sinead O'Flanagan, the future wife of Eamon de Valera. In 1902 he joined the Archbishop McHale branch of the league, and eventually became secretary and president of that branch. O'Kelly also attended meetings of the Celtic Literary Society, where he met Arthur Griffith and William Rooney, and this contact led him to make contributions to the *United Irishman*. O'Kelly joined the Irish Republican Brotherhood (IRB) in 1902, enrolling in the Bartholomew Teeling Club, which had about twenty members. He was a dedicated member and travelled to Wexford, Sligo, and Galway swearing in new members. He also helped to set up the Confederate Literary and Debating Society to further recruitment to the IRB. In 1903 he was named as business manager of *An Claidheamh Soluis*, the weekly journal of the Gaelic League, and Patrick Pearse was appointed editor. O'Kelly's task was to secure advertisements for the paper and to promote its sales.

O'Kelly joined Sinn Féin at its inception in 1905, and he was fortunate to be chosen by lot to represent the Inns Quay branch of the party in the municipal council election of 1906. He was elected to the Dublin corporation, and served on it in various capacities until 1932. He acted on committees for the waterworks, finance, and technical education. In 1908 he went to Rome, as part of a delegation from Dublin corporation, and was chosen to read the official address, in Irish, to Pope Pius X. At the same time he was advancing his position within the Sinn Féin. He served on the Sinn Féin Co-operative Savings Bank, and in 1906 he was elected to the national executive. From 1907 to 1909 he was honorary secretary. All of these activities

adversely affected O'Kelly's performance as manager of *An Claidheamh Soluis*. Pearse, while praising O'Kelly's other works, complained that he was not managing *An Claidheamh Soluis* properly. Other difficulties were also apparent, and both men resigned from their positions in 1909.

This set-back did not harm O'Kelly's career prospects. In the same year, 1909, he was elected to the executive of the Gaelic League, a position he held until 1915. He was also appointed secretary of the Sinn Féin Printing and Publishing Company in 1909, and subsequently worked with Griffith in publishing *Sinn Féin*, *Scissors and Paste* and *Nationality*.

O'Kelly enrolled in the Irish Volunteers when they were founded on 25 November 1913, and in September 1914 he attended a meeting of the IRB and the Irish Citizen Army, which was held with the intention of securing a common front between the two groups. O'Kelly was appointed secretary of the Irish Neutrality League, an open organization for the group, but it was quickly suppressed. Acting for the IRB he went to the United States in March 1915 and made contact with John Devoy, Judge Cohalan, and Joe McGarrity. He informed them of plans for an insurrection, and was given a donation of $5000, which he delivered to Eoin MacNeill in May 1915. In August 1915 O'Kelly was appointed secretary of the Gaelic League at the Dundalk Ard Fheis, in a move by the IRB to gain control of the organization. Douglas Hyde remarked in his memoir that this appointment was political, although he accepted that O'Kelly was 'a very nice little gentlemanly man' (University College, Dublin, folklore department).

When the Easter rising started on 24 April 1916 O'Kelly was instructed to act as a staff captain under the command of Pearse in the General Post Office. Following the surrender O'Kelly was arrested and held in Richmond barracks, Dublin. He was then deported, and spent some time in custody at Wandsworth, Woking, Fron-goch, and Reading gaols, before he was released, just before Christmas day 1916, as part of a general amnesty. He was deported again in February 1917, and remained in England until June 1917. On his return to Ireland he participated in the negotiations that culminated in the creation of the new republican Sinn Féin at the end of October 1917, and he was elected to the executive of the party. He did not, however, resume activity in the IRB. In the following year, on 1 April, he married Mary Kate (*d.* 1934), a lecturer in French at University College, Dublin, second daughter of John Ryan, farmer, of Tomcoole, co. Wexford, and sister of Dr James Ryan (1891–1970), a participant in the Easter rising.

O'Kelly played an influential role in the Sinn Féin election victory of December 1918, himself winning the contest for College Green, Dublin. He was subsequently appointed to act as chairman of a committee to plan a new assembly, and to be a member of a foreign affairs committee. He played a crucial role in preparing for the first meeting of Dáil Éireann on 21 January 1919, and in formulating the proclamations, especially the democratic programme, that were made on that day. He was appointed speaker (chairman) of the Dáil on 22 January, and was re-elected to that position in April 1919, although, since February, he had been acting as the Irish republican envoy in Paris. His brief was to present the case for Irish independence to the peace conference in Paris. The mission, while unsuccessful in its main aim, did much to enhance the Irish cause.

O'Kelly spent some time in Rome from February 1920, and significantly advanced the standing of nationalist Ireland. With the help of Monsignor Hagan, rector of the Irish College, and Father Curran, he drafted memoranda on Ireland's case for recognition, one of which he presented personally to Pope Benedict XV on 12 April. The beatification of Oliver Plunket in May, thanks to O'Kelly's influence, was not only a religious celebration, but also an affirmation of Irish nationalist values. O'Kelly also met Mussolini in June 1920, and engaged in plans to import arms into Ireland, which ultimately proved abortive.

In August 1920 O'Kelly returned to Paris as envoy, being confirmed in his position by the second Dáil in 1921. Although he voted against the Anglo-Irish treaty on 7 January 1922 he retained his post as envoy under the new administration of Griffith. He opened the Irish Race Congress in Paris on 23 January on behalf of Gavan Duffy, the new minister for foreign affairs, but he was criticized for supporting de Valera rather than the representatives of the provisional government. Matters came to a head on 26 January, when O'Kelly and Harry Boland appealed to representatives to the coming Sinn Féin Ard Fheis to support the existing republic. They were both dismissed as a result. O'Kelly received notification of his dismissal on 20 February, but he remained in Paris until 24 March.

In the election on 16 June 1922 O'Kelly retained his seat for mid-Dublin. When the attack on the Four Courts and the civil war began on 28 June, O'Kelly reported back for armed duty, and was in the Granville Hotel immediately prior to the shooting of Cathal Brugha on 5 July. He was arrested on 28 July, after letters were found in his possession which linked himself, de Valera, and Harry Boland in a plan to bring guns into Ireland from America. Boland was shot in controversial circumstances within twenty-four hours, and O'Kelly remained in prison until the end of the civil war in April 1923.

While in prison O'Kelly was appointed to the council of state of the second Dáil government, which had been restored by de Valera on 25 October 1922. He was elected for Dublin North as the republican candidate in August 1923 but, like all other anti-treaty candidates, he did not take his seat. However, O'Kelly played a significant role in the illegal second Dáil administration, and acted as its chairman from December 1923 until his appointment as its envoy to America in 1924. When de Valera broke with Sinn Féin in 1926 O'Kelly played a crucial role in winning over a majority of the American Association for the Recognition of the Irish Republic to the side of de Valera and of Fianna Fáil. He also took initiatives among Irish-Americans which strengthened de Valera's claim to the Dáil Éireann funds in opposition both to the Free State and other republicans.

On his return to Ireland in 1926 O'Kelly played a significant role in building up the Fianna Fáil. He was appointed a vice-president of the party, and in March 1927 he became editor of The Nation. Following the June election of 1927, in which Fianna Fáil won forty-five seats, O'Kelly, acting as spokesman for the party, declared that the oath would be taken as an 'empty formula', like the signing of a visitors' book. When Fianna Fáil became the government in March 1932 O'Kelly was appointed vice-president of the executive council and minister of local government and public health. His main achievement as minister was the supervision of a house building programme which produced some 12,000 houses a year. He also represented the government at the Ottawa Commonwealth conference of 1932, and at the League of Nations in 1933. His first wife died in 1934, and in August 1936 he married her sister, Phyllis, an analytical chemist, who was to survive him (dying on 19 November 1983). There were no children of either marriage.

O'Kelly fully identified with the broader thrust of de Valera's policy, and after the new constitution of 1937, his official position became that of tánaiste. In September 1939 he became minister of finance in a cabinet reshuffle, and during the war he served on the committees of internal security and of economic planning. Following the retirement of Douglas Hyde, the first president of Ireland, in 1945, O'Kelly was nominated by Fianna Fáil to contest the June election for the presidency. He won the election with 565,156 votes on the second count, and was re-elected unopposed in 1952, remaining in office as president until 1959.

Following the act which made Ireland a republic in 1949 O'Kelly used his enhanced position of undisputed head of state to visit other countries, notably the United States, to represent the Republic of Ireland. He received many honours during his lifetime, of which the papal award of the grand cross of the order of St Gregory the Great (1933) reflected the close relationship between himself and the Roman Catholic church on a personal and diplomatic level.

O'Kelly retired to Roundwood, in co. Wicklow, in 1959, and lived quietly there until his death at Dublin Nursing Home, Roundwood, co. Wicklow, on 23 November 1966. He was buried at Glasnevin, Dublin. His obituary fittingly recorded that, as president, he 'had as fully transcended the political sphere as his natural dignity overcame his diminutive stature' (Irish Times, 24 Nov 1966). Stories about his size were legend, and the cry of 'cut the grass so that we can see him' was often affectionately heard as he met visiting teams before soccer internationals. However, the wearing of morning suit and top hat, which he had come to love as envoy in Paris, became his hallmark, and did much to enhance his standing.   BRIAN P. MURPHY

Sources NL Ire., O'Kelly MSS, 27672–27734 · S. T. Ó Ceallaigh, *Seán T*, ed. P. Ó Conluain and P. Ó Fiannachta, 2 vols. (1972) [in Irish] · *Documents on Irish foreign policy, 1919–1922* (1998), vol. 1 of *Documents on Irish foreign policy* · B. P. Murphy, *John Chartres: mystery man of the treaty* (1995) · D. Macardle, *The Irish republic* (1937) · A. Mitchell, *Revolutionary government in Ireland: Dáil Éireann, 1919–1922* (1995) ·

R. D. Edwards, *Patrick Pearse: the triumph of failure* (1977) · B. P. Murphy, *Patrick Pearse and the lost republican ideal* (1991) · R. Davis, *Arthur Griffith and non-violent Sinn Fein* (1974) · T. P. Coogan, *De Valera: long fellow, long shadow* (1993) · D. Keogh, *Twentieth century Ireland: nation and state* (1994) · J. J. Lee, *Ireland 1912–1985, politics and society* (1989) · *Irish Times* (24 Nov 1966)

Archives NL Ire., addresses and papers · NL Ire., MSS 27672–27734, 8385, 8469, 10192 | NL Ire., Eamon Kent MSS, 8838 · NL Ire., Art O'Brien MSS, 8461 · PRO, Home Office, 144/1458/316095 · University College, Dublin, De Valera MSS | FILM BFI NFTVA, current affairs footage · BFI NFTVA, 'Dublin: farewell to a statesman', 1 Dec 1966 · BFI NFTVA, news footage **Likenesses** photograph, 1933, Hult. Arch. · group portrait, photograph, 1938, Hult. Arch. · S. O'Sullivan, charcoal drawing, 1949, NG Ire. · L. Whelan, portrait, Aras an Uachtarain, Phoenix Park, Dublin

Okely, Francis (1719–1794), Moravian minister and translator of mystical writings, was born at Bedford on 27 March 1719, the first child of Francis Okely (*d. c.*1733), wig maker, and Ann (1691–1766), the daughter of John Battison. His mother came from a respectable Northamptonshire family, but his father died in a debtors' prison. His mother subsequently became a milliner and shopkeeper in Bedford. As a young man Okely made a small but significant contribution to the evangelical awakening, but his inner life was troubled, and he soon revealed the lack of consistency characteristic of his middle years.

Okely's evangelicalism first made itself felt in 1736 when, on leaving Charterhouse School, London, he awoke similar sentiments in his mother. At St John's College, Cambridge, where he graduated in 1739, he formed a small religious society. Ann Okely became a central figure around which the Moravian community at Bedford developed, and Okely and his student friends were also to be drawn into the Moravian church. In his own case, his brother John was a crucial influence. This, however, was not before Okely was rebaptized in 1740 at Blunham, near Bedford, and became a Baptist minister. Expelled from the Baptists two years later, Okely is said to have told his followers that he had 'now found the people of God' in the Moravians (Welch, 210). Extended visits to Moravian centres in Germany followed; he was received into the church in 1743 and ordained in January 1747. In the same month he proposed to Elizabeth Collins (1725–1801), and they subsequently married on 3 February 1747 at Herrnhaag, Germany.

Okely returned to England during 1747 and laboured as a minister mainly at Bedford and Bristol. While he was minister at Dukinfield (1755–6), near Manchester, the poet John Byrom became an influential acquaintance. In May 1755 Elizabeth Okely was ordained deaconess of the Moravian church at Bethelsdorf, Germany. In 1757 an inner crisis caused Okely to 'retreat' to Bedford. 'I cannot preach because I have not faith', he explained to John Wesley a year later, after a brief foray with him to Ireland (*Letters of … John Wesley*, 4.34). Two interviews with William Law in 1760, however, led to intensive study of his works and those by Jakob Boehme (1575–1623), the Lutheran theosophist. This marked a new beginning, and Okely retained the greatest respect for these two mystics.

Two attempts by Okely to find 'useful' employment failed. He was refused Anglican ordination in 1763, which meant that the offer by Lord Dartmouth of the curacy of Olney, Buckinghamshire, was closed, and, later, a post at the countess of Huntingdon's college was also denied him. His conduct in seeking a living in other churches dismayed the tolerant Moravians, but he had run out of options and needed to provide for his family's education. Okely emerged from this crisis in 1767 as an untypical Moravian and he moved to Northampton, where he cared for a small society and assisted in the development of others nearby. Three years later he led ceremonies, endorsed by the presence of Moravian dignitaries and a large crowd, that opened the chapel in the town.

A fervent advocate of the spiritual way and of unity among Christians, Okely's extempore preaching attracted a select following. William Bull and John Ryland (1753–1825) were among the dissenting ministers in the neighbourhood with whom he established a warm relationship. Okely was a bibliophile and master of German; at Northampton, where he spent the rest of his life, he applied the fruits of his 'long and dear-bought experience' to writing edifying works and making extracts in manuscript from authors he deemed 'truly spiritual' (Okely, *Memoirs of … Jacob Behmen* [Boehme], 4.vi). His translations from the writings of Boehme and John Englebrecht (1599–1642) of Brunswick are among his most substantial publications. His fondness for mystics extended to Tauler, the fourteenth-century Dominican, whose *Evangelical Conversion* he translated, and to St John of the Cross (1542–1591), whose life he described as 'amazing light in the Midst of Popish Darkness' (F. Okely to W. Bull, 26 Nov 1782, Bull MS 3097, 65).

Okely's constant wish to assist others towards finding faith was realized when the young William Carey, later the pioneer of Baptist missions overseas, read his versification from Law's writings in *Seasonally Alarming and … Exhilarating Truths* (1774). His *Dawnings of the Everlasting Gospel-Light* (1775), a collection of letters written in the early 1740s, gives a useful insight into what Okely and other young Englishmen then found particularly appealing in Moravian evangelicalism.

In early May 1794 Okely preached at Bedford for the last time. He was seized with a paralytic stroke and died there on 9 May. He was buried on 15 May at the Moravian burial-ground in Bedford. His widow survived him until her death on 29 December 1801. Of their children, their second son, William (1762–1830), a physician at Northampton, later became a Moravian minister. William's grandson, William Sebastian Okely, was the first Cambridge MA who was not a member of the established church (Venn, *Alum. Cant.*).   JOHN C. S. MASON

Sources J. D. Walsh, 'The Cambridge Methodists', *Christian spirituality: essays in honour of Gordon Rupp*, ed. P. Brooks (1975), 249–83, 251ff · E. Welch, ed., *The Bedford Moravian church in the eighteenth century*, Bedfordshire Historical RS, 68 (1989), 210 · G. Smith, *The life of William Carey* (1885), 11 · private information (2004) [C. J. Podmore] · F. Okely, preface, in A. von Frankenberg and C. Weissner, *Memoirs of the life, death, burial, and wonderful writings, of Jacob Behmen … with an introductory preface of the translator*, ed. and trans. F. Okely

(1780) · F. Okely, 'Preface', *A faithful narrative of God's gracious dealings with Hiel* (1781) [preface confirms Okely's date of birth] · The Old Meeting Baptist Church, Blunham, church book, 1724–1891, U. Lond., Institute of Historical Research, BC402 · 'Moravian marriages', *Moravian History Magazine*, 14 (1998), 18 · *The letters of the Rev. John Wesley*, ed. J. Telford, 4 (1931), 34 · Moravian register, St Peter's at Bedford, 1 March 1742/1743–1 July 1837, Family Records Centre, London, RG4 306 · will, PRO, PROB 11/1250, sig. 517 · *The private journal and literary remains of John Byrom*, ed. R. Parkinson, 2 vols. in 4 pts, Chetham Society, 32, 34, 40, 44 (1854–7), 2.629, 642–8 · LPL, Bull MSS, MSS 3097, 3974 · Beds. & Luton ARS, Moravian MSS [reference MO] · Venn, *Alum. Cant.*, 2/4 · *DNB* · Herrnhut, Germany, Moravian Archives

Archives Beds. & Luton ARS · Moravian Church House, London, archives of the Moravian Church

Likenesses portrait, St Luke's Church, Bedford; repro. in Welch, ed., *Bedford Moravian Church*

Wealth at death see will, PRO, PROB 11/1250, sig. 517

Okeover [Oker], **John** (*bap.* 1595?, *d.* 1663?), organist and composer, was probably the John Oker baptized at St Michael's, Worcester, on 7 October 1595, son of John Oker (*d.* 1620), a local builder, and his wife, Anne. Treasurer's accounts at Worcester Cathedral for 1611 refer to a John Oker as a senior chorister (a treble), though accounts for immediately following years relegate him to the bottom of the ranks, presumably owing to the breaking of his treble voice. Such a state of affairs would be entirely commensurate with a boy born about 1595, and the Worcester treble may well be synonymous with the St Michael's John Oker. If so, he would have received his musical instruction from Thomas Tomkins, organist and master of the choristers at Worcester from 1597. Recent researches into property records in Gloucester and Wells spanning the period 1627–1660 have raised the distinct possibility that there were two (or even three) related composers named John Okeover, the first of whom would have died at Wells about 1640 (Scrase); if this is true the Gloucester Okeover may have been that composer's son.

When his father died on 3 January 1620, Okeover—then aged twenty-five—did not inherit his business, which was bequeathed jointly to the widow and an elder brother, Samuel, a fact that perhaps suggests that by this date John had moved elsewhere to pursue a career in music. This may be confirmed by a carving of 1616 in the wall of the organ loft at Winchester College, which notes that 'M IO. OKER', or John Oker, was organist, and an entry in the papers of William, second Lord Petre, of Ingatestone Hall, Essex, which describes music books 'all of which were placed in the charge of John Oker June 1616 with a chest of vialls' (Essex RO, MS D/DP.E.2/8). If these refer to the composer, then he had already gained valuable experience prior to taking up the position of vicar-choral and organist at Wells Cathedral (in succession to Richard Browne) on 16 February 1620.

In 1625 Okeover was made master of the choristers at Wells, thereafter performing occasional duties as receiver, senior, and escheator. His relationship with the dean and chapter later deteriorated owing to differences of opinion regarding the precise application of the Book of Common Prayer in choral services. According to

Anthony Wood, Okeover graduated BMus from New College, Oxford, on 5 July 1633. By about this time he appears to have married Elizabeth, daughter of John Beaumont, a member of a well-known family in Wells, who left legacies to his daughter and to Okeover in his will of 5 March 1634. From the mid-1630s he evidently developed links with Gloucester Cathedral, where he became organist and master of the choristers in 1640.

Following the Restoration, Okeover returned to Wells. The account books there contain no references to him after 1663, in which year he probably died. His surviving compositions include a handful of anthems (of which only one is complete) and nineteen pieces for viols in three and five parts. The geographical spread of the manuscript sources of his compositions suggests that Okeover's reputation was local rather than national, though he was nevertheless a competent practitioner of his craft.

JOHN IRVING

Sources W. K. Ford, 'The life and works of John Okeover (or Oker)', *Proceedings of the Royal Musical Association*, 84 (1957–8), 71–80 · P. J. Willetts, 'Music from the circle of Anthony Wood at Oxford', *British Museum Quarterly*, 24 (1961), 71–5 · G. Dodd, *Thematic index of music for viols* (1980–) · J. Morehen, 'The Gloucester Cathedral bassus part-book MS93', *Music and Letters*, 62 (1981), 189–96 · E. H. Meyer, *Early English chamber music* (1982) · Wood, *Ath. Oxon.: Fasti* (1815), 386, 468 · J. Bennett, 'John Oker/Okeover', *Chelys*, 16 (1987), 3–11 · A. J. Scrase, *Notes and Queries for Somerset and Dorset* [forthcoming]

Okes, Richard (1797–1888), college head, was the son of Thomas Verney Okes, a surgeon in extensive practice at Cambridge. Of his twenty children, Richard was the nineteenth, and was born at Cambridge on 25 December 1797. Richard Porson, the Greek scholar, was a visitor at the house, and took a kindly interest in young Richard. Educated on the foundation at Eton College, where he was contemporary with William Mackworth Praed, Edward Stanley (later Lord Derby, the premier), E. B. Pusey, and Shelley (who was some years his senior), he proceeded in 1817 to a scholarship at King's College, Cambridge. He was Browne's medallist in 1819 and 1820, graduating BA in 1822, MA in 1825, and DD in 1848. He was a fellow of King's from 1820 to 1826, when he married Mary Elizabeth, daughter of the late Thomas Sibthorpe of Guildford. They had a daughter, Julia Mary Anna.

Okes had been ordained in 1822 and was appointed assistant master at Eton in 1823, and lower master in 1838. During the years of his mastership, and afterwards at Cambridge, he was a conspicuous figure in the school and college world, and innumerable anecdotes grew up round his marked and vivid personality. Many generations of Etonians carried away a lively recollection of his dry and caustic wit, his shrewd remarks, his slow and deliberate speech, his inimitable Latin quotations, drawn chiefly from familiar sources, such as Horace or the Eton Latin grammar, and his curious punctiliousness about minutiae of school discipline, usages, and phraseology. He was a successful tutor, having at times as many as ninety pupils, and impressed his colleagues, as well as the boys, with a strong sense of his painstaking accuracy. During the latter part of Dr Keate's headmastership he took much interest in the improvement of geographical studies by the introduction of the *Compendium of Ancient and Modern Geography* (1831) by Aron Arrowsmith the younger, to which he contributed most of the illustrative notes.

On his election to the provostship of King's College in 1850, one of Okes's first acts (1 May 1851) was to abandon the privilege which entitled members of King's College to take the BA degree without examination. The wisdom of this reform was proved by the success of King's men in the tripos lists. This important innovation, however, marked the limit of his reforming zeal. Although his provostship coincided with the introduction of great changes in the university and his college, Okes was a conservative in principle and feeling and could not always agree with reforms such as the opening of King's to men from schools other than Eton; he nevertheless took part loyally in the introduction and conduct of such changes and presided over the college with much dignity and kindliness for thirty-eight years. The year following his appointment as provost he filled the office of vice-chancellor, but after the expiration of his year of office he could never again be induced to serve. He was the editor of a new series of *Musae Etonenses* for 1796–1833 (2 vols., 1859–69), which he enriched with sketches of the authors written in Latin, full of felicitous and witty phrases. The heraldic window in the school museum at Eton was his gift in conjunction with Dr E. C. Hawtrey. He was chairman of the Cambridge Waterworks Company from 1858 to 1887, and was a JP for the borough of Cambridge. He died at The Lodge, King's College, Cambridge, on 25 November 1888, and was buried in King's College chapel. His wife predeceased him.

J. J. HORNBY, rev. M. C. CURTHOYS

Sources Boase, *Mod. Eng. biog.* • Venn, *Alum. Cant.* • L. P. Wilkinson, *A history of King's* (1980) • C. N. L. Brooke, *A history of the University of Cambridge*, 4: 1870–1990, ed. C. N. L. Brooke and others (1993) • private information (1894) • *GM*, 1st ser., 96/2 (1826), 172
Archives CUL, letters to George Stokes • Herefs. RO, letters to John Arkwright • King's AC Cam., letters to Henry Bradshaw • King's AC Cam., letters to Oscar Browning • NRA, priv. coll., corresp. with S. H. Walpole
Likenesses H. von Harkomer, oils, 1881, King's Cam.
Wealth at death £14,378 8s.: probate, 22 Dec 1888, *CGPLA Eng. & Wales*

Okey, John (bap. 1606, d. 1662), parliamentarian soldier and regicide, was the sixth child and second son of William Okey of St Giles-in-the-Fields, London, and his wife, Margaret Wetherley. The Okey family owned property in London and possessed a coat of arms. John was baptized on 24 August 1606 at St Giles-in-the-Fields, and he married Susanna Pearson in the same church on 21 January 1630. By 1640 he was the proprietor of a ships' chandler's business near the Tower of London and, according to the republican writer Edmund Ludlow, was a citizen of London. The Oxford antiquarian Anthony Wood, who suggested he was employed as a humble drayman and stoker before the civil war, almost certainly underestimated his social origins. After the death of his first wife Okey married in 1658 Mary (1629–1697), the widow of John Blackwell. Okey possessed a radical religious outlook, and worshipped as both a Baptist and a Congregationalist.

At the start of the civil war Okey enlisted in the earl of Essex's parliamentarian army and served first as a quartermaster and then as a captain of horse. He was later a major in Hesilrige's regiment and in April 1643 he took part in the defence of Lichfield. On the formation of the New Model Army in 1645 he was appointed colonel of a regiment of dragoons formerly commanded by John Lilburne. Later that year he fought at the battle of Naseby, where he saved the day for John Butler's cavalry regiment, which was in danger of being routed by Prince Rupert's cavalry. In a communication written after the battle he declared that the parliamentarians 'should magnifie the name of our God that did remember a poore handfull of dispised men, whom they had thought to have swallowed up before them' (Tibbutt, 11). Later in 1645 he fought at Burroughbridge and Bath in Somerset and at the siege of Bristol, where he was captured by the royalist garrison but released after the city's surrender. He was later present at the siege of Exeter.

During the upsurge of political activism in the New Model Army following its victory in the first civil war, Okey's regiment was not one of the conspicuous centres of radicalism. While it did elect agitators in June 1647 it declined to appoint 'new agents' a few months later and in December a number of the troops presented a loyal address to the commander of the army, Thomas Fairfax. During the second civil war in 1648 Okey and his regiment served in south Wales and took part in the battle of St Fagans and the siege of Pembroke Castle. At the end of that year he entered London with Thomas Fairfax. Okey was named one of the commissioners for Charles I's trial; subsequently he attended most of the court's sittings and signed the king's death warrant [see also Regicides]. He was one of the army officers charged with overseeing the arrangements for the subsequent execution.

In the spring of 1649 Okey and his regiment were among the soldiers loyal to the high command who pursued the mutinying Leveller troops through the Thames valley before defeating them at Burford in Oxfordshire. Okey was subsequently awarded an honorary MA degree by Oxford University for his part in their suppression. The same year he attempted to remove from his regiment one of his captains, Francis Freeman, whom he believed upheld Ranter beliefs and whom he accused of singing bawdy songs. Freeman's men backed their captain and the matter was eventually brought before Cromwell, who prevailed upon Freeman to resign his commission. Freeman subsequently outlined his version of events in the pamphlet *Light Vanquishing Darkness*.

Okey travelled to Scotland in 1650 and remained in service there under first Cromwell and later Monck until the end of 1651. In August 1651 he arrested several Scottish commissioners who were raising forces near Glasgow and he subsequently took part in the siege of Stirling, the storming of Dundee, and the occupation of Aberdeen. He returned to England in late 1651 or early 1652 and in February 1652 presented a petition to parliament calling for a number of religious reforms, including measures to propagate the gospel and reform the parochial ministry.

The following August he was one of the officers who presented to the Rump Parliament the army petition which called upon it to proceed quickly with a range of constitutional and legal reforms. When Cromwell forcibly expelled the Rump in April 1653 Okey's regiment subscribed to the army *Remonstrance* supporting the action, but Okey himself was critical of the methods used by the lord general and from that point on he became increasingly suspicious of him. At the end of 1653 he firmly opposed the 'Instrument of government' which established the protectorate, and throughout the remainder of the 1650s he displayed a consistent republican outlook, resisting all efforts to impose a more conservative, monarchical constitution upon the country.

Okey returned to Scotland in the spring of 1654 and subsequently accompanied Monck on his sweep through the highlands the following summer. In September 1654 he was returned to the first protectorate parliament as MP for Linlithgow, Queens Ferry, Perth, Culross, and Stirling. He refused, however, to take the engagement to the 'Instrument of government' which was imposed upon the members by Cromwell a few days after the opening of parliament, and as a consequence was prevented from sitting. He began instead to attend secret meetings of those opposed to the instrument, and in October 1654 he helped to draw up *The Humble Petition of Several Colonels of the Army*, a document which was highly critical of Cromwell and the protectorate and called for the summoning of a free parliament. For this breach of army discipline he was arrested in November 1654, tried by court martial, and condemned to death. His sentence, however, was commuted by Cromwell, and he was instead cashiered from the army.

Okey retired to Bedfordshire, where he had acquired substantial crown property during the early 1650s, including the honour of Ampthill, the manor of Millbrook, Brogborough Park and Lodge, and lands at Leighton Buzzard. He also owned a share of Newmarket House, Cambridgeshire. The combined value of the properties was about £8000. As the Long Parliament had settled upon him lands in Scotland worth £300 per annum, he was by now a wealthy man. He also owned a residence known as Barbers Barn at Hackney in Middlesex, as well as the lease of a number of tenements in Old Street, London, belonging to St Bartholomew's Hospital, of which he was a governor. He lived both at Hackney and at Brogborough Round House in Bedfordshire during the 1650s, and was active as a JP in both Bedfordshire and Middlesex, and as an ejector of scandalous ministers in the former county. He was also probably involved in the establishment of John Bunyan's Baptist church in Bedford in 1653.

In July 1656 Okey was summoned before the council and questioned about his attendance at secret meetings in London called by the government's Fifth Monarchist and republican opponents. He was released with a warning and the following month was decisively defeated in the poll in Somerset for the second protectorate parliament. In early 1657 he strongly opposed parliament's plan to make Cromwell king and signed *The Humble and Serious Testimony of Many Hundreds of Godly People in the County of Bedford*, a petition against the move organized by the Bedfordshire gathered churches. During 1657 he attended a number of the republican meetings convened by John Wildman at The Nonsuch inn in Bow Street, London, and in April of that year was again arrested and held for several days after the government discovered that Thomas Venner and his Fifth Monarchist followers were planning an armed insurrection.

Following the death of Oliver Cromwell in 1658 Okey was elected to Richard Cromwell's parliament for Bedfordshire. After Richard Cromwell's resignation and the fall of the protectorate, the republican members of the returned Rump reappointed him to the command of a regiment. At the end of 1659 he supported the Rump in its quarrel with Lambert and Fleetwood, but his new regiment refused to follow him against them and he was subsequently dismissed from his post by the council of army officers. He remained opposed to the army leadership and in early December was involved in a failed attempt to seize control of the Tower of London, after which he took refuge with the fleet. When the Rump was recalled for a second time later that month, Okey once more recovered his commission and on 26 December he was appointed one of the seven parliamentarian commissioners responsible for the running of the army. The following day he attempted forcibly to prevent the readmission of the secluded members to parliament, an action for which he and several other officers were subsequently charged with assault. In February 1660 Monck again dismissed him from the army, handing his regiment over to Colonel Rossiter. The following month a scurrilous ballad, *Colonel Okie's Lamentation, or, A Rumper Cashiered*, was published and circulated in London. Fearing that Monck intended to bring about the return of the Stuarts, Okey settled his differences with Lambert and joined him in his attempted *coup d'état*. He was with Lambert when he was captured at Daventry but managed to escape himself.

At the Restoration Okey fled to Germany with Sir John Barkstead. In 1661, however, he travelled to the Netherlands where, along with Barkstead and Miles Corbet, he was arrested by the English ambassador, Sir George Downing, and sent back to England. Downing's action was widely regarded as treacherous, as he was a former associate of Okey and had acted as a chaplain to his dragoons. Following a brief trial Okey was executed on 19 April 1662. Three of his letters from prison and his scaffold speech and prayers were published that year in *The Speeches, Discourses and Prayers of Colonel John Barkstead, Colonel John Okey and Mr Miles Corbet*. He died professing his belief in the rightness of his actions and his commitment to Congregationalism, and declared that he was confident that

> that cause which we first took up the sword for, which was for righteousness and for justice and for the advancement of a godly magistracy and a godly ministry (however some men turned [it] about for their own ends), shall yet revive again. (*Speeches, Discourses and Prayers*)

On the grounds that Okey had shown remorse for his

involvement in the death of Charles I, and had advised those attending his own execution to submit peaceably to the Stuarts, Charles II initially agreed that Okey's mutilated corpse could be returned to his widow, Mary, for burial. The funeral was to have taken place at St Dunstan and All Saints, Stepney, but when the government learned that a large crowd was expected to attend, it changed its mind and Okey was interred instead within the Tower of London.   CHRISTOPHER DURSTON

Sources H. G. Tibbutt, *Colonel John Okey, 1606–1662*, Bedfordshire Historical RS, 35 (1955) · C. H. Firth and G. Davies, *The regimental history of Cromwell's army*, 2 vols. (1940) · *Memoirs of Edmund Ludlow*, ed. C. H. Firth, 2 vols. (1888) · F. Freeman, *Light vanquishing darkness* (1650) · T. Saunders, J. Okey, and M. Allured, *To his highness the lord protector … the humble petition of several colonels of the army* (1654) [Thomason tract 669.f.19(21)] · *The speeches, discourses and prayers of Colonel John Barkstead, Colonel John Okey and Mr Miles Corbet* (1662) · *DNB* · I. Gentles, 'The debentures market and military purchases of crown land, 1649–1660', PhD diss., U. Lond., 1969 · certificates of sale of crown land, PRO, E121/1/1/37, E121/1/4/56 · chancery close rolls, PRO, C 54/3962/30–31; 54/3691/30; 54/3933/9
Likenesses Claussin, etching, pubd 1812 (after unknown artist), BM, NPG · P. Stent, engraving · line engraving, BM · line engraving, NPG
Wealth at death estate confiscated for treason

Okey, Samuel (*b.* **1741**?, *d.* in or after **1780**), mezzotint engraver and printseller, was the son of Samuel Okey (*fl.* 1721–1756), printseller, and his wife, probably called Mary Atterbury. He may have been the Samuel Okey baptized at St Stephen, Coleman Street, London, on 17 April 1741. Samuel Okey senior appraised the court of orphans inventory of Thomas Bowles in 1721 and in the years about 1750 published a number of prints from his shop at the back of St Dunstan's Church in Fleet Street. In competitions held by the Society for the Encouragement of Arts, Manufactures, and Commerce Samuel Okey junior won an 8 guinea prize for a mezzotint head in 1765 and a 5 guinea prize in 1767. He exhibited mezzotints with the Society of Artists in 1767 and 1768 and published a portrait of the actor William Powell in 1770. In that year he also engraved and published *Sweets of Liberty* after John Collett. F. G. Stephens described this large mezzotint as a satire on Wilkesite opposition to supposed court tyranny, but the verses clearly celebrate Wilkes and liberty, and the publication suggests that Okey's sympathies lay with the radicals. It was sold from the address of Charles Reak in Butchers' Row, Temple Bar. Soon after, Okey and Reak both emigrated to Newport, Rhode Island, where they set up shop as stationers and printsellers on the Parade and published a number of prints, the earliest of which is dated October 1773. Okey's portrait of Samuel Adams (1775), leader of the radical party at Boston, was engraved with verses that imply strongly that the publishers were not loyalists. By 1780 both had vanished without trace.
                                    TIMOTHY CLAYTON

Sources J. C. Smith, *British mezzotinto portraits*, 3 (1880), 950–54 · G. C. Groce and D. H. Wallace, *The New York Historical Society's dictionary of artists in America, 1564–1860* (1957) · T. Clayton, *The English print, 1688–1802* (1997) · Graves, *Soc. Artists* · F. G. Stephens and M. D. George, eds., *Catalogue of prints and drawings in the British Museum, division 1: political and personal satires*, 11 vols. in 12 (1870–1954) ·

Engraved Brit. ports. · *A register of the premiums and bounties given by the society instituted at London for the encouragement of arts, manufactures, and commerce from the original institution in the year 1754, to the year 1776 inclusive* (1778) · IGI

Okey, Thomas (1852–1935), basket-maker and Italian scholar, was born on 30 September 1852 at 16 Quaker Street, Spitalfields, London, one of eight children of Thomas Okey, a basket-maker, and his wife, Maria, *née* Biggs. After elementary school in Bethnal Green, he too was apprenticed at thirteen as a basket-maker, a trade he followed for over thirty years. A passionate reader, he was largely self-taught, studying French, German, and Italian over breakfast before going to work at 6 a.m., and attending evening classes afterwards. He later attended classes at Toynbee Hall, and from 1888 onwards, on his own initiative, organized educational trips to Italy for East End adult learners. In 1896 he ceased basket-making and became a full-time adult education teacher, principally at Toynbee Hall (from 1892 to 1901). On 8 June 1901 he married Amy Louisa Rye of Chiswick, a widow a year older than him; she was the daughter of Joseph Haslam, a silk mercer. There were no children from the marriage.

Okey's initial publications were translations: Mazzini's *Essays* (1894), a clear hint of his convictions, and in the same year *The Little Flowers of St Francis of Assisi*, which eventually ran to over a dozen editions. A translation of Dante's *Purgatorio* for Temple Classics (1899) was followed by an English edition of the same author's *Vita nuova* and lyric poetry (1906). His first major original work, *Italy Today* (1901 and 1909), was written in collaboration with the influential Risorgimento historian Bolton King. Benedetto Croce later chose it as the first work to be translated and published by the new Laterza publishing house, and in Italy it is still quoted in political debate about the southern question. Further collaboration with Bolton King appeared in volume 12 of the Cambridge Modern History (1910). Sole-authored books on Venice, *Venice and its Story* (1903), *The Story of Venice* (1905), *The Old Venetian Palaces and Old Venetian Folk* (1907), alternated with books of French interest, *Paris and its Story* (1904), *The Story of Paris* (1906), and *The Story of Avignon* (1911). Basket-making was not abandoned, however, for in 1912 Okey wrote *An Introduction to the Art of Basket-Making*, which is still in print and recommended by enthusiasts, even over the internet. He also compiled the entry on the craft for the eleventh edition of *Encyclopaedia Britannica*. During the First World War Okey was employed at the Foreign Office, where his knowledge of French and Italian was useful.

At sixty-seven, and recently widowed, Okey was surprised to be called to the Serena chair of Italian at Cambridge in 1919, as the first incumbent, despite his complete lack of formal qualifications. He fitted in easily, however, helped by welcoming and sympathetic colleagues. Elected a fellow of Gonville and Caius College in 1920, he acquired a reputation as a fine lecturer, placing a special, almost reverent, emphasis in his teaching on the works of Dante. In 1922, the same year as the march on Rome, he represented Cambridge University at the anniversary of the founding of the University of Padua, and there received an honorary doctorate, the only academic accolade to accompany his recognition as an honorary freeman in the Worshipful Company of Basket-Makers. His Mazzinian convictions, however, made him increasingly uneasy at the rise of fascism. He retired from the Serena chair in 1928 for reasons of advanced age and failing health (after a stroke he complained eloquently in a private letter of 'aphasia in five languages'), and returned once more to basket-making, publishing his short autobiography, *A Basketful of Memories*, in 1930. In the year before he died he made a final pair of waste-paper baskets for friends at Jesus College, comparing them cruelly with handiwork much earlier in his career (a pre-war basket had constituted a special illustration for the *Encyclopaedia Britannica*). Along with a photograph of an octogenarian Okey engaged in his craft, one of these late baskets passed in 1981 into the hands of a subsequent chair-holder, Professor Patrick Boyde, almost as the insignia of office. Okey died on 4 May 1935 at his home, Barnwood, Brasted, Sevenoaks, Kent, of a cerebral thrombosis. His reputation today rests largely on his work as a timely popularizer of Italian culture and his main significance lies in his belonging to that transitional generation which, from an insecure academic base, saw to the establishment of Italian studies as a coherent discipline in British universities.

JONATHAN USHER

Sources *The Caian*, 43/3 (1935), 94–101 · T. Okey, *A basketful of memories: an autobiographical sketch* (1930) · U. Limentani, 'The Cambridge chair of Italian', *Britain and Italy from Romanticism to modernism*, ed. M. L. McLaughlin (2000), 154–77 · b. cert. · m. cert. · d. cert. · CGPLA *Eng. & Wales* (1935)
Archives BL, corresp. with S. Cockerell, Add. MS 52742
Wealth at death £18,780 13*s*. 10*d*.: probate, 1 July 1935, CGPLA *Eng. & Wales*

Okham, John (*d.* 1327/8), administrator, is of unknown origins. He is first recorded in 1296, as a clerk in the king's wardrobe, where much of his career was to be spent, and of which by June 1308 he had been promoted to be cofferer. He held that office until July 1309, and again from February 1311 to September 1314. Okham appears to have aroused considerable distrust, for the second set of ordinances of 1311 demanded that he be dismissed. However, the demand was ignored by Edward II; Okham attended the king when he withdrew to Yorkshire at the end of that year, and apparently accompanied him to France in 1313. Only in 1314, after Edward's position had been weakened by defeat at Bannockburn, was Okham obliged to leave the royal household. But once the king began to recover lost ground Okham returned to office; on 18 June 1317 he was appointed a baron of the exchequer, and was subsequently exempted by name from attempts to reduce the number of barons. He was paid as a baron until Easter 1320. He was not disgraced, for having been summoned to parliaments as a royal councillor in 1318 and 1320 he was summoned again in the same capacity in 1321 and 1322.

In January 1324 Okham was called upon to account for wardrobe receipts from the beginning of the reign, a move in the current programme of exchequer reform, and not a sign of animosity towards him—in 1325 he was

given custody of the deanship of St Martin's-le-Grand, London, where he was already a canon. There is no evidence that he became a priest, however, although he had been ordained acolyte in 1309. By then he had been presented by the king to West Horsley church, Hampshire, to which he added Broad Chalk, Wiltshire, in 1312 and Nether Wallop, Hampshire, in 1314. His wealth, whether derived from office or from his livings, enabled him to make some substantial loans, suggesting that the mistrust felt for him by the ordainers may have been due to suspicions of corruption, as well as of undue influence with the king.

Following the deposition of Edward II the new regime made further efforts to scrutinize earlier wardrobe receipts, which in 1327 led to Okham's being ordered to attend in the exchequer and answer for money that had passed through his hands. He was to die in debt to the king, but no evidence appears to have been found that he had been guilty of embezzlement. Okham was probably still alive on 20 July 1327, but had died by 27 October 1328, leaving goods and chattels valued at £114 18*s*. They may have included the book (a work on the art of *dictamen*, or epistolary composition) that in 1311 he lent to a colleague in the wardrobe, specifying that it was to be returned within a week and paid for with a goose; if held for longer, interest was to be payable not in money but in geese, at the rate of one per week.

HENRY SUMMERSON

Sources *Chancery records* · [R. E. Latham], ed., *Calendar of memoranda rolls (exchequer)* …: *Michaelmas 1326 – Michaelmas 1327*, PRO (1968) · F. Palgrave, ed., *The parliamentary writs and writs of military summons*, 2/3 (1834) · Tout, *Admin. hist.*, vols. 2, 6 · Sainty, *Judges* · *Registrum Simonis de Gandavo, diocesis Saresbiriensis, AD 1297–1315*, ed. C. T. Flower and M. C. B. Dawes, 2 vols., CYS, 40–41 (1934) · *The registers of Roger Martival, bishop of Salisbury, 1315–1330*, ed. K. Edwards, C. R. Elrington, S. Reynolds, and D. M. Owen, 4 vols. in 5 pts, CYS, 55, 57–8, 68 (1959–75) · *Rotuli parliamentorum Anglie hactenus inediti, MCCLXXIX–MCCCLXXIII*, CS, 3rd ser., 51 (1935) · M. Buck, *Politics, finance and the church in the reign of Edward II: Walter Stapeldon, treasurer of England*, Cambridge Studies in Medieval Life and Thought, 3rd ser., 19 (1983) · T. F. Tout, *The place of the reign of Edward II in English history: based upon the Ford lectures delivered in the University of Oxford in 1913*, rev. H. Johnstone, 2nd edn (1936) · *Registrum Henrici Woodlock, diocesis wintoniensis, AD 1305–1316*, ed. A. W. Goodman, 2 vols., CYS, 43–4 (1940–41) · *Calendar of the fine rolls*, PRO, 4 (1913), 107, 121
Wealth at death £114 18*s*. 0*d*.—value of goods and chattels: *Calendar of the fine rolls*, 121

Oking, Robert (*d.* in or before **1559**), Church of England clergyman, is first recorded in 1521 as vicar of Hardwick, Cambridgeshire. He studied at Jesus College, Cambridge, where he proceeded BCL in 1524–5. He seems to have transferred to Trinity Hall, since a letter of 1538 refers to him as of the 'bringing up' of Stephen Gardiner, who became master there in 1525. In the latter year he became rector of St Nicholas, Feltwell, Norfolk. Commissary of the university in 1529, he became DCL in 1534. In the latter year he was appointed commissary to John Capon (or Salcot), bishop of Bangor. Almost at once he was caught up in a power struggle between William Glyn of Glynllifon and Sir Richard Bulkeley, which in 1535 resulted in his being accused by the diocesan registrar of authorizing the sale of indulgences. Bulkeley wrote to Thomas Cromwell on Oking's behalf, saying that he had heard nothing but good of him, and that he 'spoke as much at all times in the annulling of the bishop of Rome's authority as any man I know in these parts' (Williams, 66). This testimony notwithstanding, Oking remained a marked man, and at Christmas 1536, according to Bulkeley, he was in danger of being murdered in Bangor Cathedral as he held his consistory there.

In May and June 1539 Oking attended Cromwell's vicegerential synod which debated what would become the Act of Six Articles. He himself at first supported the evangelical opposition, but eventually voted with the conservative majority. Shortly afterwards Bishop Salcot, who had tried unavailingly to obtain preferment for Oking in 1538, took his commissary with him when he was translated to Salisbury in July. In July 1543 he took part in the trial at Windsor of the composer John Marbeck and other suspected heretics. By 16 January 1544 he had been presented to the prebend of Ratfyn, on 20 July 1546 he was installed as archdeacon of Salisbury, and on 23 August 1547 he was admitted a canon residentiary. In the latter year's convocation Oking was among those appointed to draw up a statute regulating the payment of tithes in cities and towns; he was also in the minority that opposed the legalization of clerical marriage. When Thomas Hancock preached against superstition in St Thomas's, Salisbury, Oking and Edmund Steward, chancellor of Winchester, walked out of the church and were reproved by the preacher.

In spite of his conservatism on marriage and other issues, Oking himself married when it became lawful for him to do so. Consequently he was deprived of his Salisbury benefices in 1554, resigning his house in the cathedral close on 26 May. But his wife may have died, or he may have separated from her, for on 11 October 1556 Oking was presented to the prebend of Highleigh in Chichester Cathedral, a living that carried with it the mastership of the grammar school. He also became rector of Fishbourne. He had probably died by 5 May 1559, when a new rector was presented, and certainly by 23 December.

W. A. J. ARCHBOLD, rev. ANDREW A. CHIBI

Sources G. Williams, Wales and the Reformation (1997) · LP Henry VIII, vols. 8–9 · D. MacCulloch, Thomas Cranmer: a life (1996) · J. Strype, Ecclesiastical memorials, 3 vols. (1822) · The acts and monuments of John Foxe, ed. J. Pratt, [new edn], 8 vols. in 16 (1853–70) · J. Strype, Memorials of the most reverend father in God Thomas Cranmer, 2 vols. (1848) · Venn, Alum. Cant., 1/3.277 · Cooper, Ath. Cantab., vol. 1 · R. W. Dixon, History of the Church of England, 6 vols. (1878–1902) · Fasti Angl., 1541–1857, [Chichester] · Fasti Angl., 1541–1857, [Salisbury]
Archives PRO, SP 1/92 · PRO, SP 1/116

Óláf (d. 1153). See under Godred Crovan (d. 1095).

Olaf [Olaf the Black, Olaf Godredsson] (1173/4–1238), king of Man and the Isles, was the son of *Godred Olafsson [see under Godred Crovan], king of Man and the Isles (d. 1187) and Fingola, daughter of Mac Lochlainn and granddaughter of Muirchertach *Mac Lochlainn, 'king of Ireland' (d. 1166). He was also known as Olaf the Black and Olaf

Godredsson. Godred died on 10 November 1187, leaving three sons, Ragnvald, Olaf, and Ivar. Since Ragnvald had been born out of wedlock, Godred had instructed that his legitimate son Olaf should succeed. But Olaf was only about thirteen years old, and rather than accept a minor as king the Manxmen summoned Ragnvald to the throne in 1188. Olaf was given the island of Lewis for his maintenance, but he became dissatisfied with this poor island and journeyed to Man to seek augmentation of his portion. Ragnvald, however, had Olaf arrested, and then had him imprisoned by William the Lion, king of Scots. There he remained for seven years, until just before his death in 1214 William ordered the release of all his prisoners. Olaf then returned briefly to Man, before setting out on pilgrimage to the shrine of Santiago de Compostela in Spain. On his return he was reconciled to Ragnvald, who married Olaf to Lauon, his own wife's sister. He granted Olaf possession of Lewis as before, and Olaf resumed residence there.

Olaf cannot have been any more content than previously, and probably looked to Norway for support. At an unspecified date Ragnvald, bishop of the Isles since 1217, summoned a clerical assembly and annulled the marriage of Olaf and Lauon as being within prohibited degrees of relationship. Afterwards Olaf married Christina, daughter of Farquhar *Mactaggart, earl of Ross [see under Ross family]. King Ragnvald's wife is said to have taken offence, and to have sent a letter under her husband's seal to her son Godred in Skye, instructing him to arrest and kill Olaf. In 1223 Godred collected an army and attacked Lewis, but Olaf escaped and fled to his father-in-law, the earl of Ross. Olaf and the earl swore alliance and set out to take revenge. Learning that Godred and a few followers were on 'St Columba's Isle', apparently near Skye, they surrounded and attacked them. Godred was taken, blinded, and castrated, allegedly without Olaf's consent.

Ragnvald had long been feeling the pressure of Olaf's opposition. In 1218–19 he was mending fences with Henry III of England, travelling to England to do homage and to make amends for excesses of his men in England and Ireland. Then in November 1220, Henry III ordered his justiciar of Ireland to assist Ragnvald in the defence of his kingdom. At this time the chieftains of the Hebrides were revolting against Norwegian rule, and in the spring of 1224 it was rumoured at the Scottish court that Norwegian intervention was imminent. But Olaf remained loyal to Norway and his successes that summer removed the necessity for such intervention. He took hostages from all the chieftains and, arriving at Ronaldsway with thirty-two ships, confronted Ragnvald once more. Upon negotiations it was agreed that Ragnvald should retain Man, the title of king, and a part of the Isles, while Olaf should have the remainder.

Ragnvald now turned for help to Alan, lord of Galloway, the constable of Scotland. In 1225 Ragnvald and Alan mounted an expedition to Skye and Lewis to recover what had been ceded to Olaf. However the Manxmen refused to fight against either Olaf or the people of the Isles, and the expedition returned without achieving anything. Some time afterwards Ragnvald extorted 100 marks from his subjects on pretext of visiting the English king. But with this money he visited Alan of Galloway and contracted a marriage alliance between his daughter and Alan's illegitimate son Thomas. Almost certainly Thomas was intended to succeed as king of Man. The Manxmen revolted against this prospect, and summoned Olaf from the Isles to become king. Thus in 1226 Olaf finally recovered his inheritance and reigned in peace for two years.

Forced to recognize the weakness of Ragnvald's position, Henry III attempted to broker a peace in 1228. Olaf wrote to Henry, giving details of his case against Ragnvald and requesting Henry to use his influence with the king of Scots to put a stop to raids by Alan of Galloway. In April a safe conduct was granted Olaf to go to England to make peace with Ragnvald. But that same year, while Olaf was on expedition to the Isles, Ragnvald, supported by Alan of Galloway and his brother, Thomas, earl of Atholl, devastated the south of Man. Alan returned to Galloway, but he left officials on the island to collect tribute. On his return, Olaf put these officials to flight; but during the winter Ragnvald mounted a further attack. He destroyed Olaf's fleet anchored off St Patrick's Isle, toured the island, and stayed at Ronaldsway for about forty days. During that time he collected support from the south of the island while Olaf mustered his forces in the northern part. On 14 February 1229 the two sides clashed at Tynwald and Ragnvald was killed.

But Alan of Galloway still threatened Man. In the spring of 1230 Olaf arrived at the court of King Haakon IV Haakonsson of Norway to seek help, just as the Norwegians were preparing to launch an expedition to pacify the Hebrides. The fleet was intended to install Ospak Asmundsson—notwithstanding his Scandinavian name a descendant of Somerled of Argyll (d. 1164)—as client king of the Hebrides. Godred Don, a son of King Ragnvald, was one of Ospak's lieutenants. Despite this Olaf agreed to accompany them. They set off, first to Orkney, where they collected reinforcements, and then to Skye, Islay Sound, and Bute. There Ospak was fatally wounded while capturing Rothesay Castle from the Scots. On the approach of Alan's fleet of 200 ships the Norwegians withdrew. Ospak died, and Olaf, taking command of the Norwegian fleet, brought it to Man. There Olaf agreed to partition the kingdom with Godred Don, Olaf retaining Man, while Godred Don received the Hebrides. The following spring the Norwegians departed, having restored their influence in the region. Godred Don was killed while travelling to Lewis and Olaf once more resumed control over the whole kingdom.

In the summer of 1235 Olaf journeyed to the English court to confer with Henry III. The fruit of this negotiation was revival of an arrangement which had already existed between Ragnvald and the English. In return for homage and for the service of guarding at his own cost the Irish Sea coasts of England and Ireland, Olaf was to receive an annual fee from Ireland of 40 marks, 100 crannocks of wheat, and five tuns of wine. But Olaf remained primarily

the client of Norway, and when in 1236 he was commanded to attend the Norwegian court, the English king granted him protection for his possessions. It was a prolonged visit, for in April 1237 he had not yet returned.

Olaf died on 21 May 1237 on St Patrick's Isle and was buried in St Mary's Abbey, Rushen. He was succeeded in his kingdom by his three sons in turn, Harald (1237–48), Ragnvald (1249), and Magnus (1254–65). COLM MCNAMEE

Sources G. Broderick and B. Stowell, eds., *The chronicle of the kings of Mann and the Isles* (1973), 24–34 · G. W. Dasent, trans., 'The saga of Hacon', *Icelandic sagas and other historical documents*, 4, Rolls Series, 88 (1894), 150–54 · Rymer, *Foedera*, new edn, 1.105–231 · *CDS*, 1.151, 182; 5.136 · *CPR*, 1216–25, 133, 150, 204; 1225–32, 184; 1232–47, 100, 112, 147, 178 · *CClR*, 1234–7, 356–7 · T. D. Hardy, ed., *Rotuli litterarum clausarum*, RC, 1 (1833), 439 · K. J. Stringer, 'Periphery and core in thirteenth-century Scotland: Alan, son of Roland, lord of Galloway and constable of Scotland', *Medieval Scotland: crown, lordship and community: essays presented to G. W. S. Barrow*, ed. A. Grant and K. J. Stringer (1993), 82–113 · W. Bower, *Scotichronicon*, ed. D. E. R. Watt and others, new edn, 9 vols. (1987–98), vol. 5, p. 149 · A. A. M. Duncan and A. Brown, 'Argyll and the Isles in the early middle ages', *Proceedings of the Society of Antiquaries of Scotland*, 90 (1956–7), 199–202 · J. R. Oliver, ed., *Monumenta de Insula Manniae, or, A collection of national documents relating to the Isle of Man*, 2, Manx Society, 7 (1861), 2.42 · R. A. McDonald, *The kingdom of the Isles: Scotland's western seaboard, c.1000–c.1336* (1997)

Óláf Guthfrithson [Óláfr Guðrøðarson] (d. 941), king of Dublin and of Northumbria, was the son of *Guthfrith (d. 934) [see under Sihtric Cáech], a grandson of Ívarr. *Ragnall Guthfrithson was his brother. From his father, who died as king of Dublin, having also been briefly king of Northumbria, Óláf had inherited interests in both Ireland and Britain; the latter would lead to his defeat at the battle of 'Brunanburh' (937) by the English king Æthelstan. Óláf first appears in the Irish chronicles in 933, when he sailed a fleet into Strangford Lough and plundered Armagh on 10 November. He then joined with the king of Ulaid, Matudán mac Áeda, to raid as far as Slíab Beagh and Muchnoe (Monaghan). There the allies were confronted by Muirchertach mac Néill, and in the ensuing battle Óláf was defeated with the loss of several hundreds of men. Upon the death of his father, Guthfrith, in 934 Óláf assumed the kingship of the men of Dublin. The following year he attacked his northern neighbours Síl nÁeda Sláine, during which he destroyed their fortress at Lagore (Meath) and plundered the cave of Knowth. Óláf then turned his attention westwards and began his campaigns to bring the midlands under his control. The army of Dublin raided the important monastery of Clonmacnoise in 936, and Óláf quartered his troops there for two nights. In revenge the high-king Donnchad mac Flainn burned Dublin. The next year, 937, on 1 August, Óláf attacked Lough Ree, which had been a base for the vikings of Limerick since 931. Óláf ensured its demise when he destroyed the boats after capturing the rival captain and his troops.

Óláf's Irish campaigns were interrupted when he led his troops to Britain. His personal sense of grievance against the English king Æthelstan, who had expelled his father from Northumbria, in addition to his desire to take the province himself, led him to fight Æthelstan at the battle of 'Brunanburh'. Óláf was joined in that battle by the

Scots and by the Britons of Strathclyde. This unexpected alliance had been promoted by the Celts themselves, and a Welsh poem *Armes Prydein* ('Prophecy of Britain') is a call to arms for an alliance of the Welsh, vikings, and Gaels against Æthelstan. The ensuing battle is best known through the Old English poem preserved in the Anglo-Saxon Chronicle and through semi-legendary accounts such as that in *Egils saga*; it was a murderous and hotly contested fight, but in the end Óláf and his allies were defeated. Óláf fled back to Dublin 'in ships with nailed sides' as noted in the Old English poem. His defeat at 'Brunanburh' gave courage to his Irish foes, and in 938 territory controlled by Dublin, as far as the River Greece, was attacked by the high-king Donnchad mac Flainn and Muirchertach mac Néill. The vikings who attacked Ailech and briefly held Muirchertach in 939 might have been Óláf and his troops, seeking revenge. Óláf raided the monastery of Kilcullen in 939, and soon afterwards left Dublin. While one chronicle claims that his departure was due to divine intervention, the real reason was an invitation from the men of Northumbria who, after the death of Æthelstan, invited Óláf to return to Britain as their king. He had little time to enjoy this prize for in 941, after raiding St Baldred's Church at Tyninghame, he died. Little can be said of his personal life. In later medieval records his wife is called Alfgith, daughter of Orm, but he is also said to have been the son-in-law of the Scottish king Constantine II, his ally at 'Brunanburh'. His children might have included the Maccus, son of Óláf, who killed the Norwegian prince and king of Northumbria Erik Bloodaxe in 954, and the Guthfrith, son of Óláf, who died in 961.

BENJAMIN T. HUDSON

Sources Ann. Ulster · ASC, s.a. 937, 941–2 [texts A, D, E] · AFM · Symeon of Durham, *Opera* · E. Hogan, *Onomasticon Goedelicum* (1910) · W. M. Hennessy, ed. and trans., *Chronicum Scotorum: a chronicle of Irish affairs*, Rolls Series, 46 (1866) · S. Nordal, ed., *Egils saga Skallagrímsson* (Reykjavik, 1933) · Taliesin, *Armes Prydein / The prophecy of Britain*, ed. I. Williams, trans. R. Bromwich (1972) · Paris, *Chron*.

Óláf Sihtricson [Óláfr Sigtryggsson, Amlaíb Cúarán] (*c*.926–981), king of Dublin and of Northumbria, was the son of *Sihtric Cáech (*d*. 927) and, although her name and origin is uncertain, one record claims that his mother was named Orgiue (perhaps Eadgifu) and that she was the daughter of the Anglo-Saxon king Edward the Elder. Óláf's career at the height of the viking age would be, for a time, triumphant before ending ultimately in failure, but his legend grew after his death, reaching an apogee as the model for Havelok the Dane. His father, Sihtric, had ruled as king of Northumbria since 921, after a reign as king of Dublin; in January 926, the West Saxon king *Æthelstan gave to him his sister in marriage. After Sihtric's sudden death in 927, and the annexation of Northumbria by Æthelstan, it is assumed that Óláf, who may have been born at York, was removed from Britain to Ireland.

In 941 Óláf was accepted as king by the Northumbrians, and he led a raid on Tamworth in 943, where he was victorious. Edmund, the Anglo-Saxon king who had ceded Northumbria to Óláf's predecessor, did not allow this challenge to go unanswered. He besieged Óláf, together with Archbishop Wulfstan of York, in Leicester; the pair were able to avoid capture when they fled the town under the cover of darkness. A desire to forestall attacks from the south, and to have his kingship recognized, may have played some small part in Óláf's decision to convert to Christianity in that same year; his sponsor was Edmund. This period of cordial relations did not long endure, and in the following year Edmund invaded Northumbria. Óláf and another noble named Ragnall Guthfrithson were driven from the province. Óláf then retired to Ireland, and was made king of Dublin, in the place of a Blacair Guthfrithson. He promptly allied with a claimant to the Irish high-kingship named Congalach mac Máel Mithig of the Uí Néill dynasty of Síl nÁeda Sláine. In 945 they attacked an invading army that belonged to Congalach's rival, another Uí Néill prince named Ruaidrí ua Canannáin of Cenél Conaill, in the territory of Conailli (Louth); Óláf and Congalach were victorious. During the temporary lull in the hostilities in 946, and without regard for his newly declared beliefs, Óláf raided churches in Meath and Westmeath as well as along the River Shannon, culminating with the sack of the great monastery of Clonmacnoise. This period of leisure came to an end in 947, when Ruaidrí ua Canannáin personally led an army against Congalach and Óláf, in revenge for the defeat of his army two years earlier. In a battle fought at Slane, Congalach and Óláf were routed, with an immense slaughter of the men of Dublin. The defeat may have encouraged Óláf's rivals, for in 948 the Blacair whom he had forced to abdicate Dublin three years earlier was in control of Dublin. Blacair attacked Congalach, but was defeated with 1600 men killed or captured.

Events now turned in Óláf's favour. During his absence from Northumbria a member of the Norse royal house, Erik Bloodaxe, had established himself in Northumbria in opposition to the West Saxons; Erik was forced to abdicate, temporarily as it transpired, and in 949 Óláf was invited to return by the Northumbrians. This second reign was no less fraught than the first, for Óláf had to face two invasions from powerful foes. The first, in 949, was led by Máel Coluim I, king of Scots, as far as the River Tees in what was a great victory for the Scots. The second invasion was in 951 and the attacking force was a coalition of the Scots, Anglo-Saxons, and Britons of Strathclyde; this time, however, Óláf was victorious. The real threat came from rivals, and in 952 Erik Bloodaxe returned to Northumbria. Óláf was deposed in favour of Erik, who reigned for two years until he was slain in Westmorland by a Maccus son of Óláf, who could have been a son of Óláf Sihtricson, or of his predecessor, Óláf Guthfrithson, or of another Óláf altogether.

Óláf returned to Dublin, where he spent the rest of his career. There was a new order in Ireland, for his old foe Ruaidrí ua Canannáin had been slain in 950, and his ally Congalach was now the undisputed high-king. This alliance, however, was fated for an unhappy end, and by 956 Congalach's success as high-king had begun to alarm Leinster and Dublin. Óláf plotted with the men of Leinster to lure Congalach to a spot known only as 'Tech Guigenn' located somewhere near the River Liffey, where he was slain in the company of his retinue. After this Óláf was determined not to become a subject of the powerful Uí Néill princes, so the next quarter century was devoted largely to conflict with the various branches of that dynasty, and there is also some evidence that suggests the expansion of his lordship into those lands. In 960 a dynast of Clann Cholmáin named Carlus son of Conn, a descendant of the early tenth-century high-king Flann Sinna was slain at Dublin. In 967 Óláf and Cerball mac Lorcáin, a prince of Leinster, raided Brega, in revenge for which Domnall ua Néill of Cenél nEógain, Congalach's successor in the high-kingship, led an army to Dublin where he unsuccessfully besieged the fortress for several months. Domnall was a special threat to Óláf because he, unlike his contemporaries among the Irish, relied on his fleet in his campaigns. In the face of this threat Óláf resurrected his alliance with Síl nÁeda Sláine, this time with Congalach's son Domnall. In 970 Óláf and Domnall attacked the high-king at Kilmona (Westmeath), where the allies won a celebrated victory. Although Domnall ua Néill escaped with his life, several of his allies did not, including the kings of Ulaid and Airgialla, together with several other lesser princes. Óláf also had an ally in Murchad mac Finn, king of Leinster, whose daughter Gormflaith he married; in 970 they plundered Kells, and defeated the southern Uí Néill at Ardmulchan, Meath.

Óláf was not without concerns. In 964 he had been defeated by the men of Osraige at Innistiogue (Kilkenny). A new enemy appeared in 975 in the person of Máel Sechnaill II Mór of Clann Cholmáin, who was to succeed Domnall ua Néill as high-king in 980, when he attacked Dublin and, although he could not breach the fortress, savaged the town's sacred grove known as Caill Tomair ('Thor's Wood'). A more worrisome attack had come in 962 when **Sihtric Cam** [Sigtryggr Cam] (*fl.* 962), warrior, raided Dublin's territory. Sihtric's ships landed to the north of Dublin and raided from the sea to Uí Colgáin (near Lusk). Óláf led a force against him, but in the ensuing fray he was struck by an arrow through the leg (perhaps the origin of his epithet, which means 'the Crooked'). His injury notwithstanding, Óláf drove Sihtric back to his ships and out of his territory.

These relatively minor mishaps made little impression on Óláf, who apparently feared neither human nor divine foes. He already had offended an important element of Irish society—the church—with raids on religious houses in the neighbourhood of Dublin, such as attacks on Kildare in 964 and a second in 967, when Abbot Muiredach mac Fáeláin was slain. After 975 he began to war on two fronts. In 976 a Dublin force captured Augaire mac Tuathal, king of Leinster. The following year Óláf ordered the slaying of Muirchertach, the son of the high-king Domnall ua Néill, and Congalach, the son of his former ally Domnall mac Congalach. Augaire's freedom must have been secured in the meantime, for in 978 he was defeated and slain by Óláf at the battle of Belan (Kildare). Belan was a significant victory for Óláf, for the list of the

notable slain includes princes throughout the province, and was matched in 979 with the capture of the provincial king of Leinster, Domnall Clóen, who remained in captivity until the following year. This was a personal vendetta, for Domnall had slain Óláf's father-in-law, Murchad mac Finn, in 972, in circumstances of treachery.

By 980 Óláf could be considered one of the most powerful princes in Ireland. By the standards of the day he was an old man, well past his half-century, and his sons began to play a more active role. The continuing rise to power of Máel Sechnaill was troubling and the decision was made to take the fight to him, with the Dublin troops to be led by Óláf's son Ragnall. Also in that force were troops from the kingdom of the Isles, and the men of Leinster, whose presence was probably compelled by the holding of their king as hostage at Dublin. Battle was joined at the ceremonial site of Tara; neither side emerged unscathed, but it went the worse for the invaders. Ragnall and the law speaker of Dublin were both slain, alongside a multitude of others, including princes of Leinster. Máel Sechnaill followed the fleeing troops back to the fortress of Dublin. After a siege of three days the stronghold capitulated and agreed to terms. The price was steep. The lands of the southern Uí Néill dynasties were freed from the payment of tribute, all the Irish hostages (including Domnall Clóen) were released in addition to the payment of 2000 head of cattle, jewels, and treasures. In the aftermath of this disaster Óláf abdicated in favour of his son Glúniairn, who was Máel Sechnaill's half-brother, and, seeking comfort in religion, he retired to the monastery of St Columba on Iona, where he died in 981.

A summary of political events needs to be complemented with recognition of Óláf as a patron of commerce and the arts. Dublin thrived during his reign, and was becoming one of the main trading towns of northwestern Europe. Óláf's sobriquet *cúarán* ('shoe') refers to the production of footwear at Dublin, evidence for which survives in the shoe pieces uncovered during excavations at Wood Quay. Óláf is also the first viking leader in Ireland for whom there is an indication of a court culture. He was a patron of the Icelandic poet Thorgils Grouse-poet and the Irish poet Cináed ua hArtacáin, who composed verses on the legendary history of the Hill of Skreen. His love of poetry and song may have inspired the legend of Óláf as a poet. William of Malmesbury claims that Óláf was present at the battle of 'Brunanburh' (fought in 937), when he disguised himself as an itinerant poet, or skald, in order to spy out the battle order of the English. Unfortunately for a good story, there is little indication that Óláf was even present at that battle.

Equally important was the fame and longevity of Óláf's dynasty. Although his family lost control of Dublin during the eleventh century, they ruled in the kingdom of the Isles for several centuries; in the seventeenth century the merchants of Dublin claimed to be his descendants. The names of two of Óláf's wives have survived. One was Dúnlaith, the daughter of the famous Uí Néill prince, Muirchertach of the Leather Cloaks; their son was the Glúniairn who succeeded his father and reigned until his murder in 989. The other known wife of Óláf was Gormflaith, daughter of Murchad mac Finn, the provincial king of Leinster; their son was *Sihtric (Sigtryggr Óláfsson), who succeeded his half-brother Glúniairn and died in 1042. Other sons of Óláf included: Ragnall, who was slain at the battle of Tara in 980; Harald, who was slain at the battle of Glenn Máma in 999; Dubgall, who was slain at the battle of Clontarf in 1014; and possibly another son named Sihtric who is claimed to have raided Kells in 970. Óláf also had three daughters whose names have been preserved: Radnailt, who was the mother of Muirchertach ua Congalaich of Síl nÁeda Sláine; Máel Muire, who was the wife of Máel Sechnaill II Mór and died in 1021; and Gytha, who married first an Anglo-Saxon noble and then, after being widowed, married the Norwegian king Olaf Tryggvason.   BENJAMIN T. HUDSON

Sources J. Earle, ed., *Two of the Saxon chronicles parallel with supplementary extracts from the others*, rev. C. Plummer, 2 vols. (1892–9) · *ASC*, s.a. 941–4, 949, 952 [texts A, D, E] · R. Vaughan, ed., 'The chronicle attributed to John of Wallingford', *Camden miscellany, XXI*, CS, 3rd ser., 90 (1958) · *Ann. Ulster* · M. C. Dobbs, ed. and trans., 'The Ban-shenchus [3 pts]', *Revue Celtique*, 47 (1930), 283–339; 48 (1931), 163–234; 49 (1932), 437–89 · J. H. Todd, ed. and trans., *Cogadh Gaedhel re Gallaibh / The war of the Gaedhil with the Gaill*, Rolls Series, 48 (1867) · M. A. O'Brien, ed., *Corpus genealogiarum Hiberniae* (Dublin, 1962) · E. Hogan, *Onomasticon Goedelicum* (1910) · *AFM* · W. Stokes, ed., 'The annals of Tigernach [pt 2]', *Revue Celtique*, 17 (1896), 6–33 · F. M. Stenton, *Anglo-Saxon England*, 2nd edn (1947) · Bodl. Oxf., MS Rawl. B. 488

Óláf the White [Óláfr inn Hvíti] (*fl.* 853–871), viking leader, was active in Ireland and northern Britain during the ninth century. His career is given in the Old Norse *Landnámabók*, which claims that his father was named Ingiald, and that his wife was Aud the Deepminded, the daughter of Ketil Flat-Nefr (Ketill Flatnose), who ruled in the Hebrides. Their son was named Thorstein, and his daughter Groa was the ancestor of the earls of Orkney. The career of Óláf the White corresponds with that of the Olaf 'son of the king of Lochland' (Norway) (*d.* 875), also known as Óláf, king of Dublin (*c.*853–871), whose activities are recorded in the Irish chronicles; many scholars consider them to be the same individual. They were active at the same time, in the same place, and were recognized as the leaders of the vikings in Ireland.

Óláf of Dublin carved out an empire in Ireland and northern Britain, and was the overlord of the vikings in those lands. He first appeared in Ireland in the mid-ninth century, when he took lordship over the vikings and collected taxes from the Irish. In 857 he and his brother Ívarr led an expedition to Munster and defeated a Caittel Find and his army of vikings and renegade Irish. The brothers made an alliance with Cerball mac Dúnlainge, the lord of Ossory, in 859 and raided Meath. In 860 Óláf was allied with the future high-king *Áed Findliath mac Néill in a confrontation with the high-king Máel Sechnaill mac Máele Ruanaid who had made a show of force at Armagh. The next year the allies raided Máel Sechnaill's lands in Meath. By this time Áed's daughter was Óláf's wife. This alliance ended with the accession of Áed to the high-kingship, and in 863 Óláf, together with his brothers Ívarr

and Auisl, made a new alliance with Lorcán mac Cathail, the lord of Clann Cholmáin, and plundered Brega. In the course of their campaign they searched four famous caves: 'Achadh Aldai' (possibly to be identified with Newgrange), Knowth, Dowth, and Drogheda. This alliance had ended when, at the monastery of Clonard in 864, Óláf drowned Conchobar mac Donnchada of Clann Cholmáin. Óláf moved into Britain in 866 when he and his brother Auisl raided central Scotland with a force drawn from the vikings of Ireland and Britain in a campaign that lasted from 1 January to St Patrick's day. Áed Findliath took advantage of Óláf's absence to lead a sweeping campaign against the vikings in the north of Ireland, destroying their fortresses from Donegal to Antrim. More disasters followed in the next year when a fortress at Clondalkin, called Dún Amhlaim ('Óláf's fort'), was destroyed by the Irish. The same year Óláf's brother Auisl was slain. One record states that he was killed by the men of Munster, when he and Óláf were attacking the monastery of Lismore, although another story claims that Auisl wanted Óláf's wife, the daughter of Cináed mac Conaing of Brega, and Óláf killed him in a jealous rage. Óláf raided the monastery of Armagh in 869, when reputedly a thousand persons were either captured or killed by the vikings. The following year Óláf and Ívarr returned to Britain and raided until 871, when they returned to Dublin. In that year Óláf departed from Ireland and returned to Scandinavia, leaving behind a son named Oistín, who was slain in 875.

Although the Norse sagas claim that Óláf the White was slain in Ireland, the Scottish chronicle claims that Óláf of Dublin was in Scotland when he was slain in battle by Constantine I, king of Scots, about the year 875. The two accounts are not exclusive, for there is no indication that at this date the Norse were aware of distinctions between the Gaelic-speaking communities in Ireland and Britain.   BENJAMIN T. HUDSON

Sources J. Benediktsson, *Landnámabók*, 1 (1968) · *Ann. Ulster* · J. N. Radner, ed., *Fragmentary annals of Ireland* (1978) · J. H. Todd, ed. and trans., *Cogadh Gaedhel re Gallaibh / The war of the Gaedhil with the Gaill*, Rolls Series, 48 (1867) · B. T. Hudson, *Kings of Celtic Scotland* (1994) · E. Hogan, *Onomasticon Goedelicum* (1910) · W. M. Hennessy, ed. and trans., *Chronicum Scotorum: a chronicle of Irish affairs*, Rolls Series, 46 (1866) · *AFM* · B. Hudson, *Prophecy of Bérchan* (1996) · B. T. Hudson, 'The Scottish chronicle', *SHR*, 77 (1998), 129–61

Óláf [Óláfr] **Tryggvason** (*d.* 999), king of Norway, first appears in 994 when in the company of Swein Forkbeard (*d.* 1014) he failed to conquer London and afterwards raided Essex, Kent, Sussex, and Hampshire. His first appearance in England has often been dated to 991 and he has been made a participant in the famous battle of Maldon in that year. This story is, however, based on an entry in the A text of the Anglo-Saxon Chronicle, which conflates information relating to both 991 and 994. Óláf had probably joined Swein on his expedition of 994 because Swein exercised the traditional Danish overlordship of Norway. While the army was wintering in Southampton, however, Æthelred II (*d.* 1016) persuaded Óláf to enter his service. A treaty, known as II Æthelred, was set up to regulate the relationship between the English and the Norwegians while they were in England. The deal also involved Óláf's baptism at Andover and an agreement that Óláf would return to Norway and never return to England with hostile intentions. Æthelred no doubt meant to make mischief between Óláf and Swein, since stirring up problems for Swein in Scandinavia would help keep him away from England.

In later Norwegian historiography Haraldr inn Hárfagri (Harald Finehair; d. c.930) was regarded as the founder of Norway, which was called his *allod* (his personal estate). Legitimacy therefore required descent from him. Óláf is duly presented as a great-grandson of Harald but the account of his childhood and youth given by the Icelanders Oddr Snorrason (c.1200) and Snorri Sturluson (1179–1241), based on Oddr, is conventional hagiography showing that ideas about his origin were very dim indeed. The story is that Óláf's father, Tryggvi Óláfsson, was killed before Óláf was born. His mother then fled to Sweden, and, having been separated from her, Óláf first spent six years as a slave in Estonia and later came to the court of King Vladimir (d. 1008) at Kiev. At the age of eighteen he left, intending to return to Norway but only reaching Poland where he married a princess and governed half the kingdom for three years. He then left the Baltic and went raiding in western Europe, finally marrying the sister of Óláf Sihtricson (d. 981), king of Dublin. In reality Óláf must have been a chieftain of some standing in Norway when he accompanied Swein to England. His descent from Harald is a postulate made in the twelfth century when the myth of Harald Finehair was constructed.

On his return to Norway Óláf based himself in Trøndelag and secured recognition as king after the murder of Hákon, earl (*jarl*) of Hlathir. He extended his influence to all coastal Norway, partly through alliances with leading magnates like Erling Skjalgsson, who was married to Óláf's sister. Óláf is credited with a determined effort to evangelize Norway by the sword, although the eleventh-century chronicler Adam of Bremen described him as a pagan wizard. Efforts to organize the government of Norway and the appointment of *lendmen* as his local representatives are also ascribed to him, but the basis for this is very slender and the role accorded him in the Christianization of Iceland is pure myth. The only tangible evidence of his government is a few coins struck in his name. On these the moneyer's name is Godwine, but this Anglo-Saxon moneyer did not work for Óláf any more than he did for Swein Forkbeard or Olof Skötkonung, king of Sweden, on whose coins his name also appears: the three kings simply imitated the same Anglo-Saxon coin type.

Whatever its character Óláf's rule was too brief to leave permanent traces. He was killed fighting against Swein Forkbeard and Olof Skötkonung at the battle of Svold in 999 (a more probable date than the traditional 1000). According to legend he jumped into the sea from his ship, the *Long Serpent*, when the battle was lost, in order not to fall into the hands of his enemies. Danish overlordship over Norway was re-established until challenged by King Óláf Haraldsson (d. 1029). Niels Lund

Sources Oddr Snorrason Munk, *Saga Óláfs kunungs Tryggvasonar*, ed. F. Jónsson (1932) · Snorri Sturluson, *Heimskringla: Nòregs konunga sogur*, ed. F. Jónsson, 4 vols. (1893–1901) · S. Bagge, 'Helgen, helt og statsbygger—Olav Tryggvason i norsk historieskrivning gjennem 700 år', *Kongsmenn og krossmenn: Festskrift til Grethe Authén Blom*, ed. S. Supphellen (1992), 21–38 · C. Krag, 'Norge som odel i Harald Hårfrages ætt. Et møte med en gjenganger', *Historisk Tidsskrift*, 68 (1989), 288–302 · C. Krag, *Ynglingatal og Ynglingesaga: en studie i historiske kilder* (Oslo, 1991) [incl. Eng. summary] · N. Lund, 'The Danish perspective', *The battle of Maldon, AD 991*, ed. D. Scragg (1991), 114–42 · N. Lund, 'Scandinavia, c. 700–1066', *The new Cambridge medieval history*, 2, ed. R. McKitterick (1995), 202–27

Olcán (*fl.* 5th cent.). *See under* Ulster, saints of (*act.* c.400–c.650).

Old, John (d. 1557), translator and religious controversialist, was possibly a son of John Olde of Sheriffhales in Shropshire. His early biography is shrouded in obscurity: the date and place of his birth are unknown and little information concerning his formal education has survived. That he was a graduate is undoubted: his contemporaries, and later the historian John Strype, describe Old as a doctor of theology, though none of them gives any indication as to which university he attended.

The earliest known event of Old's life shows him already closely associated with persons who favoured reform of the English church in a protestant direction. In 1543 he was living in Staffordshire, and between July and December of that year granted shelter to the protestant reformers Thomas Becon and Robert Wisdom after their recantations in London on 8 July. Old had known Becon for a long time, and the two men obviously shared the same religious outlook. Becon describes Old as a man 'ancient in true godliness and Christian life', and implies that Old, like Wisdom and himself, was a member of a persecuted community analogous to the early church saints: 'He was to us, as Jason was to Paul and Silas' (Becon, 422). It seems probable that Old, whom Strype calls 'a teacher of youth as well as a teacher of the gospel', ran a school at this time, and with the help of Becon tutored the sons of the local gentry (Strype, *Ecclesiastical Memorials*, 2/1.47). About 1545, 'impelled by urgent' but undisclosed causes, he left Staffordshire and travelled with Becon into Warwickshire, settling at Coventry (Becon, 424). Once again he invited Becon to share his home, an arrangement that must have brought him into contact with the circle of protestants that Becon is known to have met in the county. This group included Old's friend of many years Hugh Latimer, who had originally converted him from Roman Catholicism to the protestant faith. Latimer stayed regularly at Baxterly Hall, the Warwickshire house of John Glover, where he was visited by Becon and almost certainly by John Old. John Glover's brother Robert was one of the attendants of Lord Ferrers of Chartley, and may possibly have recommended Old to his employer. Certainly by 1546 Old was chaplain to Lord Ferrers, in which capacity on 10 July he was examined at Westminster by the privy council on suspicion of sacramentarianism. After an abject recantation he professed himself 'unfeynedly to receyve the kinges majestes doctrine' and after promising good behaviour he was released (*APC, 1542–7*, 479).

Old's fortunes improved after the establishment of a protestant regime on the accession of Edward VI. In early May 1547 a royal visitation of the church was ordered, and Old was appointed registrar to the team of commissioners who were to visit the dioceses of Peterborough, Lincoln, Oxford, and Coventry and Lichfield. Alongside his duties as registrar he was one of the visitation's preachers, evangelizing on behalf of those protestant reforms that the visitation had been designed to promote. During the same year he took part in the translation of the first volume of the *Paraphrases* of Erasmus upon the New Testament (published on 31 January 1548) which by order of royal injunctions of 31 July 1547 were to be placed in every parish church in England. Old subsequently accepted a commission from his friend the printer Edward Whitchurch to translate Erasmus's *Paraphrases* upon seven of St Paul's New Testament epistles. This arduous task, which constituted almost all of a second volume, was completed by mid-1549 and published on 19 August 1549. While executing this commission Old probably lived and worked in Whitchurch's printing shop at Fleet Street in London. On 22 March 1549 he was presented to the vicarage of Cubbington in Warwickshire by the crown. His appointment was due to a recommendation made on his behalf by Hugh Latimer to the duchess of Somerset. In his preface to the second volume of the *Paraphrases*, Old admits his debt, both to his 'singular friend' Hugh Latimer, and to the duchess, to whom he dedicated the work on 15 July 1549. Further ecclesiastical preferments soon followed: on 19 August 1551 Old was granted the prebend of Dernford in Lichfield Cathedral, and on 4 October 1552 he was made a prebendary of the cathedral church at Hereford.

The accession of the Roman Catholic Queen Mary in 1553 removed the need for caution from those who had always resented Old's appointments and his religion. Clergy who had conformed under the previous regime became openly hostile, threatening him with a prosecution for heresy. At Cubbington the 'malicious force and rage of some unthankful people' (Old, sig. E7r), presumably unappreciative Catholic parishioners, contributed to Old's decision to quit his vicarage and ultimately to leave England. He fled abroad probably shortly before 19 November 1554, when he was deprived of his prebend at Lichfield and his living at Cubbington. He later admitted that his departure had been made 'somewhat before extreme trouble came' (ibid., E7v), and imputed his precipitancy to doubts about his own constancy in the face of persecution.

Old probably settled for a time at Emden in East Friesland, and became a citizen there on 6 May 1556. Between 1555 and 1557 he devoted his energies to the propaganda campaign waged by the exile community in Emden against the Catholic regime in England. To this end Old used his considerable skills as an author and a translator to produce works of protestant polemic which were printed in Emden and secretly distributed back in England. *The Acquital or Purgation of the most Catholyke Prince Edward the VI*, Old's first original work, was published at Emden on 7 November 1555. It was followed five months later by his *A Confession of the Moost Auncient ... Catholike Olde Belefe* of April 1556. The aim of both these tracts was to strengthen the commitment of the English to Edward VI's protestant religious settlement, and to prevent their apostasy to Roman Catholicism. The same purpose was served by his translation of Rudolph Gualter's sermons upon Antichrist, a violently anti-papal work that was published the same year. Old also edited for publication at Emden documents written by his persecuted co-religionists in England. The speed with which these works were published after their composition suggests that Old was still in contact with protestants in England who must have smuggled the manuscripts out to him. These included Nicholas Ridley's account of his prison 'conferences' with Hugh Latimer, and possibly Thomas Cranmer's letters to Queen Mary and Drs Martin and Scory; both these works were published in 1556.

Old left Emden and finally settled at Frankfurt-am-Main in Germany with his wife (her name is unknown). His name appears on the city tax lists for 15 January 1557, which record that he had no property. As a member of the English stranger church in Frankfurt during 1557 he became involved in the dispute concerning church government between the minister, Robert Horne, and the greater part of his congregation. Old sided with the majority, and in April 1557 signed the reformed scheme of discipline, whereupon Horne and his deacon, Richard Chambers, left Frankfurt, taking the church alms with them. By 10 June Old was living with his wife in the house of Edward Oldsworth, another member of the English congregation in the city, while on 30 June he was one of those to whom Chambers addressed a letter justifying his 'administration of the church funds' (Garrett, 241). Old died at Frankfurt on 15 September 1557.

C. BRADSHAW

Sources T. Becon, 'The jewel of joy', *The catechism of Thomas Becon ... with other pieces written by him in the reign of King Edward the sixth*, ed. J. Ayre, 3, Parker Society, 17 (1844), 411–76 • I. O. [J. Old], *A confession of the moost auncient and true christe catholike olde belefe* (1556) • W. W. Old, 'Memorials of Dr John Old the Reformer', *TRHS*, 2 (1873), 199–211 • C. H. Garrett, *The Marian exiles: a study in the origins of Elizabethan puritanism* (1938); repr. (1966) • A. Pettegree, *Marian protestantism: six studies* (1996) • [W. Whittingham?], *A brief discourse of the troubles at Frankfort*, ed. E. Arber (1908) • *APC, 1542–7* • J. Strype, *Ecclesiastical memorials*, 3 vols. (1822), vol. 2 • J. Strype, *Memorials of the most reverend father in God Thomas Cranmer*, new edn, 2 vols. (1840), vol. 1 • *The seconde tome or volume of the paraphrase of Erasmus upon the Newe Testament*, trans. M. Coverdale and J. Old (1549) • J. Fines, *A biographical register of early English protestants and others opposed to the Roman Catholic Church 1525–1558* (1981) • R. Demaus, *Hugh Latimer* (1908) • Bale, *Cat.*

Archives BL, MSS concerning ecclesiastical appointments, Cotton MS Julius B.ix, fol. 87

Oldcastle, Hugh (d. 1543), schoolmaster and author, of a text on double entry accounting, was the third and youngest son of Richard Oldcastle (d. 1520), a shearman carrying on his trade in the city of London, and his wife, Joan (Johane). The date of Hugh's birth is unknown but he was alive in 1510 when he is mentioned in his father's will written that year. Richard Oldcastle bequeathed to Hugh property at Almeley in Herefordshire which formerly belonged to Sir John Oldcastle, an ancestor of the family. Hugh Oldcastle was involved in legal actions relating to the property, suggesting, as does his own failure to make a will, that he was unable to take possession of it. He died intestate early in 1543 in Hart Street (off Mark Lane) in the parish of St Olave, Hart Street, next to the Tower of London, where he had been a teacher of arithmetic and bookkeeping. Administration of his estate was granted to his widow, Anice, on 28 February 1543.

Oldcastle's widow arranged the publication in book form by John Gough on 14 August 1543 of the manuscript from which Oldcastle may have taught bookkeeping; the title was *Here ensueth a profitable treatyce called the instrument or boke to learne to knowe the good order of the kepying of the famouse reconying, called in Latyn dare et habere, and in Englyshe debitor and creditor.* No copy of the book is extant (the last certain reference is in a sale catalogue of 1799) but a revised edition was published in 1588 by John Mellis, a schoolmaster and teacher of arithmetic of St Olave Southwark. Mellis retitled the book *A briefe instruction and maner how to keepe bookes of accompts after the order of debitor and creditor.* He did not state the title of his original but, unusually for that period, wrote in his preface that he was 'but the renuer and reviver of an auncient old copie … collected, published, made and set forth by one Hugh Oldcastle Scholemaster', adding that he had 'bewtified and enlarged' Oldcastle's text. Although Mellis does not acknowledge it, he also borrowed from the works on bookkeeping of James Peele, father of George Peele the poet, and of John Weddington. Yamey argues that Mellis's work is 'not to be treated as an even approximately faithful reproduction of the Oldcastle text' (Yamey, 216). Mellis added an illustrative set of account books.

Oldcastle's book owed much to the first printed exposition on double entry by Luca Pacioli, *Particularis de computis et scripturis,* which formed part of his *Summa di arithmetica geometria proportioni et proportionalità* published in Venice in 1494. The extent to which Oldcastle's work is a translation of Pacioli is a matter on which historians of accounting have disagreed. It has been argued that both are based on a source which existed only in manuscript form and perhaps in Latin rather than Italian but no such manuscript has been discovered. Oldcastle occasionally mistranslates from the Italian (confusing, for example, *cassa* and *casa*) and shows a preference for Latin terms (*dare & habere, capsa, lucrum et damnum*) rather than their Italian equivalents.

Oldcastle may be responsible for the adoption of the word 'ledger' to describe the principal double entry book of account rather than 'great book' as in other European languages. His importance in the history of accounting is as the first expositor in English of double entry, the main technique of modern accounting. Neither he nor his 'reviver' Mellis was an innovator. Both were plagiarized in part by John Carpenter in his *A most excellent instruction* (1632). **R. H. Parker**

Sources P. Sutherland [R. R. Coomber and C. Gordon], 'Hugh Oldcastle and the *Profitable treatyce* of 1543', *The Accountant* (23 March 1940), 334–6 · R. R. Coomber, 'Hugh Oldcastle and John Mellis', *Accounting Research,* 7 (1956), 201–16; repr. in *Studies in the history of accounting,* ed. A. C. Littleton and B. S. Yamey (1956), 206–14 · P. K. [P. Kats], 'Hugh Oldcastle and John Mellis', *The Accountant* (27 March 1926), 483–7; (1 May 1926), 641–8 · B. S. Yamey, 'Oldcastle, Peele and Mellis: a case of plagiarism in the sixteenth century', *Accounting and Business Research,* 9 (1979), 209–16 · commissary court of London, administrations, GL, MS 9168/9 [act book], fols. 270, 272

Oldcastle, John, Baron Cobham (*d.* 1417), soldier, heretic, and rebel, came from a Herefordshire family that emerged in the fourteenth century.

Family background and early connections with heresy Oldcastle's great-grandfather Peter is the earliest recorded member of his family, and his grandfather, another John, represented the shire in parliament in 1368 and 1372. His father, Richard, was more obscure, but cannot have been insignificant, for he was the first of the family to be knighted, probably, although only conjecturally, after service in the French wars. It is not known when he died, but possibly it was when Oldcastle was still young. During his youth Oldcastle's most prominent relative was his uncle Thomas, the sheriff of Herefordshire in 1386 and 1391. He was a trusted royal servant, for in 1393 the king ordered him to act against anyone interfering with the trial of the Welsh Lollard layman Walter Brut. Thomas also served Bishop John Trefnant of Hereford (*d.* 1404), and in 1394 was involved in arbitration concerning the bishop's right to the chase of Malvern. He was alive in 1397, but died early in the fifteenth century, when his widow, Alice, married a former knight of John of Gaunt, duke of Lancaster. Thomas's will was strongly orthodox, endowing masses for his soul and those of members of his family. John Oldcastle's date of birth is unknown; unreliable estimates of it range from around 1360 to 1378. The earliest record of him was in 1397, when he received letters of protection to go to Ireland with the earl of March. As he was then described as 'esquire', a birth date in the mid-1370s seems probable. In Easter term 1400 he appeared as plaintiff in a suit in the court of common pleas concerning the advowson of the parish church of Almeley, the village that was the centre of his family's power. The plea was adjourned, but no record of a settlement survives. He had been knighted by the autumn of the same year, when he served with Henry IV's army in Scotland.

Although it cannot be proved, Oldcastle may have been attracted to heresy when still young, as the area in which he grew up had seen manifestations of religious radicalism during these years. Sir John Clanvow (*d.* 1391), the author of the pious tract *The Two Ways* (in which he identified himself with the despised Lollards), had estates at Hergest, Herefordshire, and Michaelchurch-on-Arrow, Radnorshire, both within a few miles of Almeley, and Walter Brut's more limited lands lay close to Hereford. Even more significant is that when Bishop Trefnant attempted to cite the fugitive Lollard evangelist William Swinderby before his court, two parish rectors to whom the citation was directed were those of Almeley and Whitney-on-Wye, which lay between Almeley and Michaelchurch. Swinderby had allegedly preached at Whitney on 1 August 1390 and Oldcastle, then perhaps in his mid-teens, may have been influenced by him. Possibly Clanvow, who was still alive in 1390, may have protected Swinderby, before his own departure for the East on a crusade during which he died. There is considerable evidence of heretical activity in the Welsh marches—the Lollard priest Richard Wyche came from the diocese of Hereford, William Thorp is associated with Shrewsbury (the place of origin of Sir Roger Acton, who was executed after Oldcastle's rising), and Richard Colfox is described as 'of Cheshire' in a pardon granted after the same rebellion. Connections existed between the Clanvow family and Oldcastle, which may have drawn him into association with the survivors of the Lollard knights whom the chroniclers identified in Richard II's time. In 1404 Oldcastle was named (with Colfox) as an executor of Sir Lewis Clifford, and two overseers of the will were Sir Thomas Clanvow (Sir John's heir and probably his nephew) and Sir John Cheyne (d. 1414), another knight with known Lollard sympathies. (Although Clifford was originally a Devonian, he secured the castle of Ewyas Harold in Herefordshire from the family of his second wife, Eleanor de la Warr. Cheyne was probably the youngest of the Lollard knights identified, belatedly, by the St Albans chronicler Thomas Walsingham.) Oldcastle, therefore, was already associated with religious radicalism by 1404, although as yet not necessarily very actively.

Secular advances Glyn Dŵr's rising brought Oldcastle into prominence as a military leader on several occasions. In September 1403 he was appointed to receive into the king's grace any rebels who surrendered in various south Wales lordships, and in 1404 he and John ap Harry, another prominent local man, who, despite his evident Welsh origin, served three times as parliamentary knight of the shire, were described as captains of the castle of Hay. They remained close associates throughout the Welsh wars, and as custodians of certain Mortimer lands, in the king's hands because of the earl of March's minority. In 1404 he was also commissioned to investigate reports of the provision of food from the shire to the Welsh rebels, and in 1405 he and other royal servants conducted similar investigations in both Herefordshire and Gloucestershire. He also gave non-military service, as knight of the shire in the first parliament of 1404, receiving payment of his expenses for seventy-five days, as a collector of the subsidy in 1404, as a Herefordshire commissioner of the peace in 1404, 1405, and 1406, and as sheriff in 1406–7. During his year as sheriff, however, he was not always present in the shire for he received a pardon for the escape of a prisoner from his custody, on the grounds that he was absent as keeper of Carmarthen Castle. In September 1407 he was at the surrender of Aberystwyth to the royal forces, and was clearly recognized as a man of some importance, as his name was mentioned among the knights present by the St Albans chronicler. His services attracted rewards, including the grant of a wardship in Wales in November 1408.

Some time before June 1408 Oldcastle's second marriage transformed him from a Herefordshire knight with predominantly local interests into one of the greater men of the realm. With his first wife, Katherine ferch Richard ab Ieuan, he had three daughters and two sons, John, who died in 1420, and Henry, who eventually recovered the family estates and played an active part in the shire community from the late 1420s until his death about 1460. (Some writers have suggested that these were half-brothers, but they probably were children of the same marriage.) His second wife, Joan (d. 1434), was of higher social standing, the granddaughter and sole heir of John Cobham, third Baron Cobham, who had died in January 1408. She had already been widowed three times, and had one surviving daughter, with her second husband, Sir Reginald Braybrooke. How far she herself was responsible for choosing Oldcastle as her fourth husband is unknown, but although widows could often be independent in their choice of later partners, it is unlikely that she would have chosen Oldcastle if he had not been a rising man, who could assist in managing her extensive estates, and who would be acceptable to the society within which she moved. Possibly Richard, Lord Grey of Codnor (d. 1419), whose estates bordered on the Cobham lands in Kent, and under whom Oldcastle had served in Ireland, Scotland, and Wales, might have provided a link between her and her new partner. The Cobham properties were widespread, in Norfolk, Wiltshire, Northamptonshire, Kent—where Cooling Castle was a major stronghold—and London. One of Oldcastle's actions as Lord Cobham, which reflects his marital influence, came in February 1410, when he reached an agreement to marry his stepdaughter to Thomas Broke, the son of a Somerset knight of the same name. Although Broke and his father were never accused of heresy, their wills are couched in similar tones to those of some Lollard suspects. Possibly similar religious sensibilities led Oldcastle and the elder Broke to become associates.

His marriage extended Oldcastle's area of service to Kent; in both 1409 and 1411 he was appointed to commissions *de walliis et fossatis* on the Thames. He was also summoned individually to every parliament from 1410 until he was accused of heresy in 1413, probably *iure uxoris*, although he may have been called as a trusted royal servant who had effective control over substantial estates. Certainly in the writs of summons he is described merely as 'John Oldcastle, chivaler' rather than as Lord Cobham. (It is perhaps significant that after his death, his wife's fifth husband was not similarly summoned.) In October 1409 he participated in a tournament at Lille, with two other Englishmen against three Frenchmen. This reflects his new social status, and the recognition of his military capacity is further demonstrated by his being part of the small force that was sent to France in 1411 under the leadership of the earls of Warwick and Arundel to aid the duke of Burgundy. His involvement in this expedition may have been at the wish of the prince of Wales, then dominant in the council, under whom Oldcastle had served in the Welsh wars.

Growing involvement with Lollardy By this time, however, Oldcastle's interest in heresy is documented for the first time since 1404. Possibly as a member of the upper house he may have promoted various anti-clerical measures in the parliament of 1410 and thereby drawn hostile attention to himself. Certainly, in that April, Archbishop Thomas Arundel (d. 1414) instituted inquiries into the suspect preaching of a chaplain called John, who was living in Oldcastle's house and had been preaching heresy in various Kentish churches, including Cooling. The archbishop laid the churches under interdict and cited the chaplain for trial, although he went into hiding. The interdict was relaxed out of respect for Lady Cobham, possibly on account of her daughter's marriage to Thomas Broke. The interdict may have been simply a warning shot, but it may not have been coincidental that the anti-clerical measures were dropped. But although Oldcastle may have shown more caution publicly, he continued to favour Lollardy, and may even have been recognized as a leader of the sect (if it can be so called). Possibly his baronial rank gave him additional standing, even ahead of his acquaintance Sir John Cheyne, the last Lollard knight of the older generation.

This prominence was reflected in two letters written to Bohemia on 8 September 1410, one by the Lollard priest Richard Wyche to Jan Hus, the other by Oldcastle to one of Hus's lay patrons, Woksa of Waldstein. Although Oldcastle's letter was dated from Cooling and Wyche's from London, the dating makes it clear that they were accomplices. The length of their acquaintanceship is unknown, for although Wyche himself came from the diocese of Hereford, no evidence survives of earlier contact with Oldcastle. This letter was not isolated; Oldcastle remained in touch with the Bohemians, indeed in 1411 writing to King Wenceslas himself, mentioning that he had been in touch with Hus. Although the English ecclesiastical authorities must by now have suspected him of unorthodoxy, he avoided heresy proceedings until after Henry V's accession. Even after these had already begun, a royal warrant of 20 July 1413 to him for the payment of 400 marks, in settlement of a debt, suggests that he could have hoped to benefit from royal patronage from Henry, who, according to the St Albans chronicler, was personally friendly to him.

Trial and rebellion Probably the new king's undoubted orthodoxy gave Archbishop Arundel the confidence to act against heresy. When convocation met in March 1413, shortly before Henry IV's death, action was taken against a chaplain, John Lay, who claimed to have celebrated mass in Oldcastle's presence. During the summer evidence was accumulated against Oldcastle, and the seizure of various heretical tracts belonging to him enabled the archbishop to challenge him on his beliefs, and to do so in front of the king. He was the first influential layman to be publicly accused of heresy, although the church authorities almost certainly knew that various knights, often with court connections, had extended patronage to Lollard clergy, whose views they presumably accepted. Possibly Arundel had been watching Oldcastle, whom he might have suspected,

justifiably, of being the most prominent heretical layman in the country, and was hoping, by attacking him, to deal a serious blow to all religious dissent. Oldcastle's social prominence, and his friendship with the king, compelled Arundel to move carefully. The proceedings were protracted, and marked by both royal intervention and a futile attempt by Oldcastle to avoid facing the court by returning to Cooling Castle and barricading himself in there. After he was brought to trial, the archbishop proceeded cautiously, trying to elicit a clear statement of his beliefs (something that Oldcastle for a long time tried to avoid giving). But when Oldcastle was challenged on the question of papal authority, he broke out into a tirade against the church, denouncing the pope as the head of Antichrist, the prelates as his members, and friars as his tail. Arundel, in the end, had no option but to condemn him, although one need not distrust the official record that suggests he was more concerned with trying to bring Oldcastle back to the fold of the church than with condemning him. Equally clearly, he was faced with a man whose sincerity in his beliefs was unquestioned, and who, in the last resort, would not avoid the issues. After the trial, an account of it, based on the archbishop's register, was circulated to the country because the events are recorded in both the St Albans chronicle and the *Fasciculi zizaniorum*. By publicizing Oldcastle's beliefs the archbishop was clearly determined to make an example of him, presumably hoping that this might remove the Lollard threat to the church.

After the heresy trials of Henry IV's reign, condemned offenders were sent to early execution, but Oldcastle's social standing and his relationship with the king gave him another chance. He was reprieved, and sent to the Tower of London for forty days, to be given an opportunity to recant. But he was not securely held, and escaped on 19 October, with the assistance of some London allies. His precise movements are unknown, but he established contacts with various Lollard communities, and attempted to mount an armed revolt with the aim of taking the king captive. It was an ill-considered enterprise, nor is it clear what he might have done if he had succeeded in seizing Henry and his brothers. The revolt was more a desperate attempt at revenge than a calculated plan to overthrow the existing order in church and state. It did reveal, however, that Oldcastle as leader commanded substantial loyalty, as well as something of the extent of heretical activity throughout the realm, for although there were only a few hundred active rebels (far from the 20,000 suggested by royal propaganda and reproduced by the St Albans chronicler), their geographical origins were widespread, extending from Bristol in the west through the midlands to Essex.

The authorities, however, penetrated the plot before it came to fruition; indeed, rewards were given on 5 January to two men for disclosing it to the king. When the rebels converged on London on the night of 9–10 January, they walked into a trap and were rounded up. Over forty were executed, and seven were also burnt. Oldcastle himself escaped from the rendezvous at St Giles's Fields, just outside London, but thereafter was a man on the run. Hardly surprisingly, he was excluded from the general pardon to the rebels on 28 March, along with ten of his closest supporters, but later he might still have come to terms with the king, who issued a general pardon in December. A further pardon to him is recorded a year later, in December 1415. His failure to emerge from hiding to claim this probably reflects his religious convictions; however willing the king might have been to forgive his treason, Henry could not guarantee immunity from renewed ecclesiastical measures against heresy, and Oldcastle presumably felt that it was safer to lie low. As late as January 1417 the proclamation of a reward for taking him affirmed that he was refusing to sue for pardon, but was persevering in his nefarious intention of destroying the church and the king. His lands were forfeited and remained in royal hands for many years. A further effect of his rebellion was to blacken the whole reputation of Lollardy by associating it with treason.

Last years and execution Oldcastle was not captured until 1417, but his movements in these years are virtually unknown, as he was constantly on the move, trying to keep ahead of his pursuers. Various sources, both chronicle and documentary, mention alleged sightings of him, but few are reliable. Probably his main hiding places were in the midlands and the Welsh marches, and the most likely genuine traces of him are those that led to action against individuals alleged to have sheltered him, such as John Prest, vicar of Chesterton in Warwickshire, later pardoned for entertaining him on 5 August 1415, and a chaplain of Piddington in north Oxfordshire, executed for sheltering him in October 1416. He was reported at different times to have been at Malvern, or between Shrewsbury and Oswestry, but although his name is associated with various outbreaks of heretical activity, his presence cannot be proved. Equally unverifiable, although not impossible, are accusations of conspiracy with the pseudo-Richard II and the Scots, and with the earl of Cambridge, and there may be more substance in alleged contacts with the Welsh rebels. He certainly had contacts in Wales; his secretary, Thomas Payn, came from Glamorgan.

Only in 1417 did the authorities obtain a clear lead. In July Oldcastle was in Northamptonshire, later going west to his own lands in Hereford, where he lay low from August to mid-October. He then went north, where he met Gruffudd ab Owain, a son of Owain Glyn Dŵr. He was eventually taken, after a struggle, on the lands of Edward Charlton, Lord Powys (d. 1421), by Ieuan and Gruffudd, two sons of Sir Gruffudd Vaughan, in November. The news of his capture reached Westminster by 1 December, and he was brought there, where parliament was in session. When charged with treason before it on 14 December Oldcastle retorted by preaching the mercy of God and saying that he should be left to it. Attempts to silence him may have brought forth a retort that his true king, Richard II, was alive in Scotland, although this is reported only by Walsingham and not in the official record. Walsingham also suggests that he claimed that he would rise on the third day, but this story is otherwise unattested. He was already a condemned heretic and outlaw, so there was nothing to prevent his immediate execution and burning, and the sentence was carried out the same day.

Influence and afterlife Oldcastle's support was limited, and the suppression of his revolt easy. Various possible supporters had been rounded up after the failure at St Giles's Fields and there may have been further arrests during later Lollard scares. Oldcastle's wife, Lady Cobham, was also imprisoned and was only released from the Tower on 17 December, three days after her husband's death. Her treatment suggests, however, that she herself was not suspected of treason or heresy, for her son-in-law, Sir Thomas Broke, and a Kentish esquire, Richard Cliderow, who had married a daughter of Oldcastle, were granted some of her property in London to hold to her use as early as October 1414. Broke himself was in custody for a time, but clearly was not regarded as a rebel, although his own religious predilections may have been sympathetic to an evangelical style of piety. Nor were Oldcastle's sons apparently suspected of involvement in their father's treason; the elder, John, was granted lands inherited from his maternal grandmother in June 1417, before his father's capture and death.

Oldcastle's posthumous history also merits comment. Contemporary political verses denounced him, and although he was regarded as a manly knight he was also seen as a man who would overturn the temporal as well as the spiritual order. (Writers suggested that a knight should concern himself with war rather than with matters of religion.) He was not particularly remembered by the Lollards immediately after his death; the only early description of him as a martyr was by William Emayn of Bristol in 1429. But his fame survived (though how is not known), for references to him reappear in early Reformation propaganda; in 1531 *A Boke of Thorpe or of John Oldcastelle* was condemned by Bishop John Stokesley of London (d. 1539). This recorded the sufferings of famous Lollards, and was clearly intended to inspire their followers. In the 1540s John Bale produced an improved version of the narrative of Oldcastle's trial, describing him as a 'valyaunt captayne'. Indeed, Bale attempted to set up Oldcastle in place of Becket as a hero for emulation in the new world of the Reformation. He also provided the material on which John Foxe drew for his *Acts and Monuments*, the so-called book of martyrs, the master-work of English protestant historiography in which Sir John features significantly. The contrary hostile tradition, depicting Oldcastle as a malign companion of Henry V's youth, culminated in his being presented in that role in William Shakespeare's two *Henry IV* plays (1597). The perceived insult to a previous holder of his title led to protests by the tenth Baron Cobham, which in turn caused Oldcastle's name to be replaced by that of Falstaff (itself adapted from that of the fifteenth-century soldier Sir John *Fastolf). Protestant opinion must also have favoured the change, which in 2 *Henry IV* resulted in the epilogue's being extended to include a formal disclaimer, 'for Oldcastle died a martyr, and this is not the man'.

JOHN A. F. THOMSON

Sources Chancery records · T. Walsingham, *The St Albans chronicle, 1406–1420*, ed. V. H. Galbraith (1937) · [T. Netter], *Fasciculi zizaniorum magistri Johannis Wyclif cum tritico*, ed. W. W. Shirley, Rolls Series, 5 (1858) · D. Wilkins, ed., *Concilia Magnae Britanniae et Hiberniae*, 3 (1737) · F. Taylor and J. S. Roskell, eds. and trans., *Gesta Henrici quinti / The deeds of Henry the Fifth*, OMT (1975) · W. T. Waugh, 'Sir John Oldcastle', *EngHR*, 20 (1905), 434–56, 637–58 · K. B. McFarlane, *John Wycliffe and the beginnings of English nonconformity* (1952) · K. B. McFarlane, *Lancastrian kings and Lollard knights* (1972) · J. A. F. Thomson, *The later Lollards, 1414–1520* (1965) · W. W. Capes, ed., *The register of John Trefnant*, 1 (1914) · HoP, *Commons* · GEC, *Peerage*

Oldcoates [Ulecot], **Sir Philip of** (*d.* 1220), soldier and administrator, took his name from Oldcoates in Nottinghamshire. The only son of Gerard of Styrrup (*d.* in or before 1200) and of Matilda daughter of Ingeram, he is first recorded in 1194, when, as a knight of the honour of Tickhill, he suffered forfeiture of his lands, evidently for aiding the rebellion of Count John of Mortain (since 1189 lord of Tickhill) against his brother Richard I. When John came to the throne five years later, he rewarded Philip with interests in Northumberland. Philip then married Johanna, daughter of Robert de Meinil, on payment to John of £100 and a war-horse. With Hubert de Burgh, Oldcoates defended the castle of Chinon against the French in 1204–5. When the castle fell, Philip was captured, and the king paid 200 marks (£133 6s. 4d.) towards his ransom. Philip's northern involvement increased, as John put men of his own *familia* into local administration. In 1209 he was made joint custodian of the vacant bishopric of Durham. To counter the baronial rebellion, John made him sheriff of Northumberland in August 1212. He captured Eustace de Vescy's castle at Alnwick, and supplied men for the garrisoning of royal castles. In 1215–16 he defended the north-east against the barons' ally, Alexander II, king of Scots. When John died in October 1216, Oldcoates was holding the lands of the rebels Eustace de Vescy and Roger Bertram, the lands of the bishopric of Durham, and the royal castles of Bamburgh and Newcastle.

The policy of the government during the minority of Henry III was to restore their former lands to rebels who submitted, and to recover for the crown all revenues, lands, and castles in the hands of officials. Oldcoates was one of the more persistent in hanging on to the fruits of office until he was given a more secure reward. In November 1217 the regent William (I) Marshal granted Philip the farms of Newcastle, Bamburgh, and Corbridge until the king came of age, and promised eventual grants of lands worth £300 a year; but this was not enough to induce him to restore the castle and lands of Mitford to Roger Bertram, or to surrender custody of the lands of Eustace de Vescy. Despite further grants in 1218 and 1219, repeated calls for Mitford and the Vescy lands fell on deaf ears. In the early summer of 1219 Philip was with difficulty persuaded to attend a great council at Gloucester, where he probably agreed to surrender the Vescy lands and compensate the recipient, the earl of Salisbury. But although the government threatened Oldcoates with excommunication in December 1219 and February 1220, it was not until Hubert de Burgh dismissed him from his shrievalty on 18 June 1220 that he gave up Mitford Castle.

Meanwhile Oldcoates was chief justice on eyre for the north-western circuit (Westmorland, Cumberland, and Lancashire) from November 1218 to January 1219. Awkward he might be, but his local knowledge was indispensable.

In the summer of 1220 Hubert de Burgh planned to send Philip of Oldcoates to Poitou as seneschal: it would provide worthy occupation for a troublesome official. Moreover, Philip had fought in the Loire valley and might have the grit to resist Hugues de Lusignan's threat to this part of the dwindling Angevin empire. Philip did not want to go: as he explained in a passionate letter to the legate Pandulf, he would leave his interests a prey to his northern enemies, and he feared that he would not be given the resources to defend Poitou honourably. Hubert de Burgh reaffirmed the promise to provide him with land worth £300, and reinstated him in his position as sheriff of Northumberland and constable of Bamburgh and Newcastle, while Pandulf loaned money to the government from which 500 marks were paid to Oldcoates for Poitou. On 16 September 1220 de Burgh provided ships for his journey; but by 2 November the government learned that Philip had died at Étampes in northern France.

Philip of Oldcoates died without legitimate offspring, and his five sisters shared his lands.   JOHN M. TODD

Sources J. C. Holt, *The northerners: a study in the reign of King John* (1961) · D. A. Carpenter, *The minority of Henry III* (1990) · R. T. Timson, ed., *The cartulary of Blyth Priory*, HMC, JP 17 (1973) · D. Crook, *Records of the general eyre*, Public Record Office Handbooks, 20 (1982), 73 · Chancery records · Pipe rolls · Ann. mon., 3.64–5

Oldcorne, Edward (1561–1606), Jesuit, was born in York, son of John Oldcorne, a bricklayer, and his wife, Elizabeth. He abandoned medical studies and went to the continent to study for the Roman Catholic priesthood. He arrived at the English College, then situated in Rheims, on 12 August 1581. On 23 February 1582 he was sent to the English College in Rome and was ordained priest in the Lateran on 23 August 1587. On 15 August 1588 he and John Gerard entered the Society of Jesus. Dispatched almost immediately for England, they arrived in Rheims on 21 September and departed for England via Eu on the 26th. Surveillance at English ports increased because of the Armada so the two paused at Eu to decide on their next move. They left Eu in late October or early November and landed in East Anglia in late November. Oldcorne set off immediately for London to establish contact with Henry Garnet, superior of the English Jesuits.

In early spring 1589 Oldcorne accompanied Garnet on a missionary tour of the midlands and remained in Warwickshire upon Garnet's return to London. By spring of either 1589 or 1590 (the sources are unclear), he was residing at Hindlip House near Worcester, seat of the ancient Catholic family of Habington. There he remained, labouring zealously as a missioner, making many converts, and placing many clergy with recusant families. One of the most important was the reconciliation of Dorothy Habington, according to Thomas Lister SJ, 'a very obstinate and perverse heretic' who did all she could 'to keep, or rather to drive away Catholic priests from the house' because she blamed them for her brother Edward's destruction in the Babington plot. With her assistance Hindlip House became 'the most famous house in England for entertainment of priests'. Oldcorne was a popular preacher and Lister testified that he had 'seen oftentimes more people come from his sermons than from the service of the Protestant minister on Sundays from the parish church' (Foley, 4.214–15). Of his activity John Gerard said: 'he founded and governed nearly all the domestic churches in those parts' (ibid., 4.212).

Humphrey Littleton, imprisoned on a charge of harbouring some of the conspirators after the discovery of the Gunpowder Plot, sought to save his own life by informing the privy council that Oldcorne was at Hindlip and that Garnet most likely would also be found there. The search began on 20 January 1606: Nicholas Owen and Ralph Ashley were discovered on the 23rd, and Garnet and Oldcorne on the 27th. Oldcorne was incarcerated first in the Gatehouse and later in the Tower, where he was tortured. He persistently denied all knowledge of the plot. Sent from the Tower to Worcester on 21 March, he was arraigned at the Lenten assizes on three charges: that he had invited Garnet, a denounced traitor, to hide at Hindlip; that he had asked the assistance of fellow Jesuit Robert Jones in Herefordshire in concealing two conspirators, consequently making himself an accomplice; and that he had considered the plot a good action. Oldcorne was found guilty of high treason, and on 7 April 1606 he was drawn on a hurdle to Red Hill, near Worcester, and there hanged, disembowelled, and quartered. His body was destroyed. Littleton, who suffered at the same time, publicly asked pardon of God for having wrongfully accused Oldcorne of the conspiracy. Oldcorne was beatified on 15 December 1929.

THOMPSON COOPER, rev. THOMAS M. MCCOOG

Sources T. M. McCoog, *English and Welsh Jesuits, 1555–1650*, 2 vols., Catholic RS, 74–5 (1994–5) · T. M. McCoog, ed., *Monumenta Angliae*, 1–2 (1992) · H. Foley, ed., *Records of the English province of the Society of Jesus*, 7 vols. in 8 (1875–83) · G. Anstruther, *The seminary priests*, 1 (1969) · T. F. Knox and others, eds., *The first and second diaries of the English College, Douay* (1878) · W. Kelly, ed., *Liber ruber venerabilis collegii Anglorum de urbe*, 1, Catholic RS, 37 (1940) · J. Morris, *The life of Father John Gerard of the Society of Jesus*, 3rd edn (1881) · *John Gerard: the autobiography of an Elizabethan*, trans. P. Caraman, 2nd edn (1956) · P. Caraman, *Henry Garnet, 1555–1606, and the Gunpowder Plot* (1964) · *The condition of Catholics under James I: Father Gerard's narrative of the Gunpowder Plot*, ed. J. Morris (1871) · M. Hodgetts, *Secret hiding-places* (1989)
Archives Archives of the British Province of the Society of Jesus, Stonyhurst College, Lancashire, MSS · Archivum Romanum Societatis Iesu, Rome, MSS
Likenesses G. Bouttats, line engraving, NPG · C. Weld, pencil drawing (after portrait formerly in the Gesù in Rome), Stonyhurst College, Lancashire; repro. in Foley, ed., *Records*, vols. 4 and 7 · engraving, repro. in C. Hazart, *Kerckelycke historie van de gheheele werelt*, 3: *vervattende de historien van Nederlandt ende Enghelandt* (Antwerp, 1669) · line engraving, BM, NPG

Oldenborch, Niclaes van. *See* Mierdman, Steven (*c.*1510x12–1559).

Oldenburg, Henry [Heinrich] (*c.*1619–1677), scientific correspondent and secretary of the Royal Society, was born in

Henry Oldenburg (*c.*1619–1677), by Jan van Cleef, 1668

the free city of Bremen, Germany, one of two children of Heinrich Oldenburg (*d.* 1634), a teacher at the Bremen *Paedegogium* and later a professor at Dorpat University. His ancestors, originally from Münster, had been Calvinist teachers since the mid-sixteenth century. Oldenburg's grandfather, also Heinrich, had repaired the buildings of the vicaria of St Liborius at the protestant cathedral, in return for which he, his son, and his grandson inherited an annual income of 100 reichsthaler, which was paid only fitfully and precariously.

Developing years Oldenburg began his education at the *Paedegogium* where his father taught, and transferred in May 1633 to the *Gymnasium illustre* for a thorough grounding in religion, classical languages, the liberal arts, and theology; he received the degree of master of theology on 2 November 1639 for a thesis on relations between church and state. In May 1641 he left Bremen for the Netherlands with letters of introduction to various scholars. (He was perhaps influenced by the fact that his sister was about to marry Heinrich Koch, a relation of Johannes Koch, or Coccejus, professor of theology at Leiden.) Oldenburg settled briefly in Utrecht, which possessed a lively university where Cartesianism was taught. However, he found Utrecht expensive and began in August to look for employment 'instructing either the son of a nobleman or the son of some honest merchant' (*Correspondence*, 1.3–6). For the next twelve years he travelled on the continent and in England as tutor to a succession of young men, mostly English, with both royalist and parliamentary connections, as indicated by surviving drafts of letters in his commonplace book. His aim was not only to earn his living but to learn about relations between church and state and to see the world. In all of this he was clearly very successful, becoming fluent in the languages of the countries he visited. He met many Englishmen living abroad, notably John Dury and John Pell, with both of whom he later had connections.

In the later spring of 1653 Oldenburg visited Bremen, probably to try to secure the title to his vicaria. The city was suffering from the effects of the First Anglo-Dutch War, which put at risk its all-important merchant fleet, and the senate was about to appoint an envoy to England to negotiate recognition of Bremen's neutrality. Oldenburg secured the post on 30 June 1653. He arrived in England in late July and began negotiations promptly, though inconclusively, as he told the Bremen senate; in any case the war ceased in the next spring. Soon afterwards the senate asked him to beg Cromwell to intercede between the Swedes and the city: Oldenburg found Cromwell favourably disposed and a strong letter was written to Sweden, but with little result. However, the mission proved very profitable to Oldenburg himself, not in money but in a growing acquaintance with English politicians and scholars, particularly with Milton, who admitted him into his personal circle, which included Lady Katherine Ranelagh and her young brother Robert Boyle. All seem to have found Oldenburg an attractive man, and Milton wrote approvingly that he had 'learnt to speak our language more accurately and fluently than any other foreigner I have ever known' (*Correspondence*, 1.34). During most of 1654 and 1655 Oldenburg lived in Kent with the Honywood family, to one of whom he had acted as tutor; he kept in touch with many former charges while looking for another post. This search ended with his appointment in 1656 to supervise Richard Jones (1641–1712), son of Viscount and Lady Ranelagh, first at Oxford and then abroad.

The rise to prominence In resuming his career as tutor Oldenburg sacrificed his independence but cemented his relations with Robert Boyle, his lifelong patron; developed a keen interest in natural philosophy; and learned how to elicit information from new acquaintances and how to maintain a scientific correspondence. When he went to Oxford with Jones for some reason he 'entred [sic] as a Student', as Anthony Wood put it (*Athenae Oxoniensis*, 1721, 2.114), under the designation of 'nobilis Saxo'—a curious act of self-aggrandizement, for though he could fairly call himself a Saxon he was never a noble. He supervised his pupil while at the same time educating himself in natural philosophy by frequenting on terms of equality the circle centred around John Wilkins, whom he had already met in London. This circle included Boyle, John Wallis, Seth Ward, Dr Jonathan Goddard, Thomas Willis, Christopher Wren, Richard Lower, and Robert Hooke, who was then assistant to, successively, Willis and Boyle—all men who, as Oldenburg told a Dutch friend, 'are followers of nature itself and truth' (*Correspondence*, 1.89–92). He quickly absorbed their spirit and appreciated their activities, and was able to understand their achievements.

Boyle admitted Oldenburg to his confidence, allowing him to copy out some drafts of essays that were not to be published for some years.

In May 1657 Oldenburg and Jones left for what became a three-year sojourn on the continent. They settled in Saumur, which they chose for its protestantism and its educational establishments. Thence Oldenburg wrote to Milton about theological controversies, to Boyle about chemistry and the natural philosophers he met, and to Hartlib about practical matters. The next spring he and Jones undertook a five-month tour of Germany: they visited courts and universities, meeting physicians, alchemists, mechanicians, the nobility, and minor royalty with equal interest and aplomb, Oldenburg having obviously mastered the art of extracting information from all whom he met. They were welcomed everywhere and Oldenburg reported carefully to Boyle and Hartlib what they would wish to learn about natural philosophy and mechanics. They spent the winter in the south of France, again meeting natural philosophers in academies and universities and being welcomed warmly.

In 1659 Oldenburg and Jones travelled via La Rochelle to Paris; they arrived in March and stayed for over a year. Here life duplicated that of the previous winter. Oldenburg saw that his pupil received instruction in the polite arts and in varied intellectual activities. Academies had proliferated in Paris in the early seventeenth century and Oldenburg soon sought out those devoted to natural philosophy, especially the famous Montmor Academy, in whose animated discussions and scientific debates he participated fully. His descriptions sent to Boyle and his friends in the south of France are vivid accounts of the intellectual life of Paris at this time. During this period he matured as a virtuoso and mastered the art of scientific communication. He frequented libraries and reported on their contents, beginning the familiarity with publications that was later to enable him to act as a book agent.

In May 1660 Oldenburg and Jones were summoned home, and arrived in time for Charles II's triumphant entry into London. Although both religion and acquaintances had inclined Oldenburg to parliamentarian government, like most of his friends (except Milton) he fully accepted the Restoration government. But he now had no settled employment and it is not obvious how he lived. Presumably he worked for Boyle, who was always his patron and for whom he was soon acting as translator. On 28 November 1660 the organizational meeting of what was to become the Royal Society of London was held, and Oldenburg's name was on the list of potential members. He was soon formally elected, and he played an active role.

In the summer of 1661 Oldenburg took a month's continental trip. He went briefly to Bremen and then to Holland, where he visited friends in Amsterdam and Leiden; in the latter city he saw relatives and met and conversed with Spinoza, after which he went to The Hague to renew acquaintance with Christiaan Huygens, whom he had already met in London. An important result was a well-known correspondence with Spinoza, with whom Oldenburg discussed theology and natural philosophy, in the latter field with the assistance of Boyle whose approach to the subject he adopted and fully supported. (The correspondence was first published in Spinoza's *Opera posthuma*, 1677.) Oldenburg continued to act as purveyor of news to Boyle, as he was to do throughout his life. He became 'publisher' (acting as intermediary between author and printer) of many of Boyle's books, as signed prefaces show, and translator of many into Latin for the continental market. Boyle paid him at agreed rates, which was a source of income for his lifetime.

In July 1662 the Royal Society came officially into existence and acquired a formal structure with the granting of a royal charter. Oldenburg was named as a member of council and one of the two secretaries, and the structure was reinforced the next spring with the grant of a second charter. The charters specifically gave permission for the society (through the secretaries) to correspond freely at home and abroad, while newly enacted statutes specified that a secretary must attend all meetings, take minutes, attend to correspondence, and maintain the society's 'books' (its records). Oldenburg was to be the only active secretary: immensely hard-working and a brilliant correspondent, he was soon to symbolize the much admired Royal Society in the eyes of learned foreigners. Because he was so conscientious the bulk of his correspondence survives, showing its range and scope (both large) and revealing much about the state of natural philosophy of the time in England. Like Pepys, Oldenburg was a skilful administrator, holding the society together and helping to make it work: going to meetings whose content he helped to organize and supply; conferring regularly with his working colleagues, often in coffee houses, between meetings; proposing foreign fellows; and directing the amanuensis who acted as his copying clerk. All this was without pay, and he began to think of making money by purveying news, a plan that was brought into being a few years later.

On 22 October 1663 Oldenburg married Dorothy West (c.1623–1665), 'aged about 40 and a mayden of her owne Disposing' as the marriage licence states, declaring himself to be 'aged about 43 yeares'. Nothing is known about the bride except that her trustees were two baronets and she possessed a dowry of £400. The couple set up house in Pall Mall, very near Lady Ranelagh (but not in the lodgings that Oldenburg had used previously). They soon acquired a family in the shape of John Dury's daughter, Dora Katherina (1654–1677), officially a ward of the London church of Austin Friars. As the child possessed property, presumably Oldenburg's income then increased. His wife died at the beginning of February 1665 and thereupon he very properly requested the elders of the church to make other arrangements for Dora Katherina Dury, and this seems to have been done. Although he then received the remainder of his wife's dowry it soon vanished in necessary expenses.

Oldenburg now decided to bring his plans for a news sheet to fruition. In the spring of 1665 he instituted his *Philosophical Transactions*, which was intended to incorporate news derived partly from his correspondence and partly from the activities of the Royal Society, with, soon, reviews of scientific books. It is the oldest continuous scientific journal: though the *Journal des Sçavans* preceded it by a few weeks, this was primarily a book-reviewing journal, and not predominantly devoted to natural philosophy. The *Philosophical Transactions*, as his private venture, brought Oldenburg fame but never much income (seldom as much as £40 a year). So great was the demand abroad that four volumes by different translators appeared in Latin (1666–9), a partial French edition was made for the use of the Académie Royale des Sciences, and an Italian edition was published in 1729. Publication was disrupted by the outbreak of plague in London—the court and much of the society dispersed, while Oldenburg stayed in the city, dealing with public and private business, his only precaution being to smoke a pipe of tobacco every evening.

In 1666, when life returned to normal in London as the plague diminished, the Royal Society's meetings resumed and Oldenburg's life also went on as before. He had now acquired financial support from Sir Joseph Williamson of the state paper office, who, with the outbreak of the Second Anglo-Dutch War (February 1665), was anxious to acquire knowledge of French and Dutch public opinion and, as a loyal fellow of the Royal Society, to assist its hard-working secretary. The arrangement was that Oldenburg should have a postal address, Mr or Monsr Grubendol, which ensured that all letters so addressed went direct to Williamson's office; Williamson then paid the postage and had the unopened letters delivered by hand to Oldenburg. The latter copied out any political or military news and gossip and sent this to Williamson.

Besides saving the cost of postage, this work, together with the translation of intercepted letters in Germanic languages, earned Oldenburg some unspecified but useful income. It was, however, the cause of personal misfortune: on 20 June 1667, a fortnight after the public disaster of a Dutch raid on the Medway and Chatham, Oldenburg was closely imprisoned in the Tower of London by order of Lord Arlington, secretary of state and thus Williamson's superior. He was accused of 'dangerous desseins and practices' (*Correspondence*, 3.448) or, as Pepys noted in his diary (24 June 1667), of 'writing news to a Virtuoso in France'. He repeatedly expressed his innocence and insisted that it was patriotism alone that led him to regret that the war had gone so badly from 'oversights and omissions some where' (*Correspondence*, 3.448). Arlington was much blamed for the failure of his intelligence service to forewarn the English navy of Dutch plans, and, perhaps genuinely ignorant of the arrangements with Williamson, seems to have used Oldenburg as a scapegoat, not releasing him until 26 August 1667.

The years of achievement Bravely Oldenburg returned to his usual duties, finding that almost all his acquaintances and correspondents responded as usual, the sole exception being his neighbour Dr Thomas Sydenham. His correspondence soon even increased in volume, diversity, and importance; he was described in 1668 by Glanvill as 'render[ing] himself a great Benefactor of Mankind by his affectionate care, and indefatigable diligence and endeavours in maintaining Philosophical Intelligence, and promoting Philosophy' (Glanvill, 103). For the last ten years of his life Oldenburg's unremitting correspondence kept him fully occupied, except for the need to earn a decent income. Unfortunately the *Philosophical Transactions* never sold as well as he had hoped; he had to give away many copies, and the printers were exigent. In 1668 he began a campaign to secure a salary from the Royal Society in view of his many duties, and appealed to Boyle and others. That year the society voted him a gift only of £50, but the next year relented and voted an annual salary of £40.

Oldenburg continued to supply news to Williamson and to publish and translate for Boyle, particularly in 1670 and 1671. He also began publishing for others, notably the Italian comparative anatomist and microscopist Malpighi, from whose letters he compiled books. He translated and published works by François Bernier and A. Piganius (1671), and attached Steno's *Prodromus* to Boyle's *Essays of Effluviums* (1673). He continued to hope for patronage and in 1676 Williamson secured him a place as licensor of books on history; sadly he proved too conscientious for the post and resigned it after three months, partly because of complaints against him, more because of the work involved.

The increased need for income arose from Oldenburg's second marriage, at the age of about fifty, to Dora Katherina Dury, in August 1668. According to the marriage licence she was aged sixteen, but her father's friend John Pell declared she was only fourteen years and three months. In any case, she married with her father's consent. By the marriage Oldenburg secured the income of his wife's property, two farms (Battens and Wansunt) near Dartford Heath, Bexley, Kent, said to bring in £60 a year, where family holidays were to be spent regularly. Children followed—Sophia (*b.* 1672) and Rupert (1675–1724).

A portrait by Jan van Cleef in the Royal Society, dated 1668 and said since at least 1804 to be of Oldenburg, shows a vigorous man with dark and wavy hair to his shoulders and a small moustache, in dark clothes and bands (he must have been in minor orders), with the habitual frown of a conscientious and short-sighted man. Brought up in the Calvinist faith and deeply pious, with a devout personal religion and a keen interest in millenarianism, he was no bigot; he publicly conformed to the Test Act of 1673, which demanded a firm Anglicanism, as he did again in 1677 in order to apply for naturalization (which was granted on 6 April).

During all the upheavals of his private life, Oldenburg continued to work for the good of the Royal Society and of natural philosophy. By now he had perfected his techniques: he had learned how to encourage talent (as his support and promotion of such men as Malpighi, Flamsteed, Leeuwenhoek, Leibniz, De Graaf, Martin Lister, and others show). Equally significant was his ability to persuade men reluctant to publish to permit him to insert their papers in his *Philosophical Transactions* and to continue to do so even when this provoked controversy. The most important example is undoubtedly that of Newton. From 1671 to 1677 he painstakingly coaxed the at first little-known Lucasian professor to submit his papers on optics to the Royal Society, then to permit their publication in his journal, and finally to respond to criticisms by those who could not accept his conclusions or repeat his experiments. It was a triumph of diplomatic skill of the greatest benefit to the world of natural philosophy. Just as important was Oldenburg's treatment of those few examples of his mathematical skill that Newton reluctantly released to him, culminating in the energetic exchanges with Leibniz in 1676–7. This involved Oldenburg in the tedious and difficult copying out of many pages of complex mathematical text, which indicates incidentally that he could follow advanced mathematics and perhaps even understand it.

From 1668 Oldenburg was Huygens's principal correspondent in England, giving him news of the Royal Society's affairs (Huygens had been a fellow since 1663), serving as an intermediary on mathematical subjects between him and Sluse of Liège, as on optical subjects between him and Newton. Oldenburg and Huygens had become good friends, so much so that in 1675 the latter offered any possible English patent for his newly invented spring-regulated watch either to the society or to Oldenburg. Brouncker, as president, resigned the potential advantages to Oldenburg, who promptly drafted a petition for a patent (which was never granted). Hooke, who claimed that he had long since invented the application of springs to regulate watches (but had never made one) was furious, and with his usual fertile ingenuity designed such a watch for which he now claimed a patent, insisting that Oldenburg had 'betrayed' him by telling Huygens of it—which was not the case (and Hooke's idea had appeared in print in any case). Twelve years of friendly association of two colleagues were forgotten and Hooke denounced Oldenburg bitterly, becoming more vindictive after the Royal Society's council supported his rival; he was to pursue his enmity even after Oldenburg's death. It was a bitter and troublesome episode. Historians have often accepted Hooke's view that Oldenburg was at fault, but it is difficult to see why—most of his colleagues and correspondents found him open, friendly, accommodating, tactful, and fair.

Oldenburg seems to have been generally healthy, with no more episodes of illness than normal. According to Hooke's diary he was seriously ill on 3 September 1677 'with ague'; two days later he was dead, 'being stricken speechless and senseless'. His death probably occurred at home in Pall Mall, London, though he was buried at St Mary the Virgin, Bexley, on 7 September. His young widow died on 17 September and was buried the next day in London. MARIE BOAS HALL

Sources *The correspondence of Henry Oldenburg*, ed. and trans. A. R. Hall and M. B. Hall, 13 vols. (1965–86) · A. R. Hall and M. B. Hall, 'Additions and corrections to *The correspondence of Henry Oldenburg*', *Notes and Records of the Royal Society*, 44 (1990), 143–50 · M. B. Hall,

Henry Oldenburg: shaping the Royal Society (2002) · T. Birch, *The history of the Royal Society of London*, 4 vols. (1756–7), vols. 1–3 · F. Althaus, 'Oldenburg', *Beilage zur Allgemeinen Zeitung*, 212 (2 Aug 1889), 1–3 [see also nos. 229–33] · A. R. Hall and M. B. Hall, 'Some hitherto unknown facts about the private career of Henry Oldenburg', *Notes and Records of the Royal Society*, 18 (1963), 94–103 · A. R. Hall and M. B. Hall, 'Further notes on Henry Oldenburg', *Notes and Records of the Royal Society*, 23 (1968), 33–42 · *The diary of Robert Hooke … 1672–1680*, ed. H. W. Robinson and W. Adams (1935) · E. Hasted, *The history and topographical survey of the county of Kent*, 1 (1778), 40, 165 · G. H. Turnbull, *Hartlib, Dury and Comenius: gleanings from Hartlib's papers* (1947) · J. Glanvill, *Plus ultra* (1668), 103 · Pepys, *Diary* · parish register (burial), 7 Sept 1677, Bexley, St Mary the Virgin · marriage licences

Archives Bibliothèque Nationale, Paris, letters · BL, corresp. and papers, Add. MSS 4255–4476, *passim* · BL, corresp. and papers relating to double-bottomed ships · Bodl. Oxf. · Bremen Archives, early letters, W.9.b.1.6 · Paris Observatoire, letters · PRO · RS, commonplace book, MS M1 | Bodl. Oxf., letters to Martin Lister · Christ Church Oxf., Evelyn MSS, Petty MSS, letters (Bowood House) · CUL, corresp. with Sir Isaac Newton · Kongelige Bibliotek, Copenhagen, Boll Brevs U⁴ no. 730 · Mass. Hist. Soc., Winthrop MSS, letters and MSS · Paris Observatoire, Hevelius corresp. · RS, letters to Robert Boyle · University of Bologna Library, Malpighi archives, MS 2085 · University of Sheffield, letetrs to Samuel Hartlib

Likenesses J. van Cleef, oils, 1668, RS [*see illus.*]

Wealth at death contemporaries said either £60 or £40 p.a.; *c*.200 acres (second wife's estate)

Oldfield, Anne (1683–1730), actress, was the daughter of Anne Oldfield and her husband, whose name may have been James; she was born perhaps in Pall Mall. Her grandfather had made a good living at the George tavern on Pall Mall, and left several properties to her father. According to the anonymous *Authentick Memoirs*, her father mortgaged these to buy a post in the Horse Guards, but he died young, leaving Anne and her mother in the care of her uncle George, a hosier in St James's Street. George 'put her to School, where she soon took her Learning with admirable Proficiency' (*Authentick Memoirs*, 7). Anne and her mother then sheltered with her aunt Mrs Voss, at the Mitre tavern, St James. It was here, according to Egerton's biography of Oldfield, collected from several hands, that Anne was discovered by George Farquhar. The story runs that 'he heard Miss Nanny reading a Play behind the Bar, with so proper Emphasis, and such agreeable Turns suitable to each character, that he swore the Girl was cut out for the Stage' (*BDA*), and on Farquhar's recommendation John Rich took her into the Drury Lane company in 1699 at 15*s*. a week. She does not appear to have been given many roles during her first season: only Candiope in Dryden's *Secret Love* and Sylvia in John Oldmixon's *The Grove*. Cibber charts her slow rise through the company from:

> the Year 1699, Mrs. *Oldfield* was first taken into the House, where she remain'd about a Twelve month almost a Mute and unheeded, 'till Sir *John Vanbrugh*, who first recommended her, gave her the Part of *Alinda* in the *Pilgrim* revis'd.

However, *The Pilgrim* (by John Fletcher, revised by Vanbrugh) was performed on 6 July 1700 for Mrs Oldfield's sole benefit, which implies she was considered more highly than Cibber's account of her coming 'but slowly forward 'till the Year 1703' would suggest. In the 1700 season Oldfield performed two prologues, including one

Anne Oldfield (1683–1730), by Edward Fisher (after Jonathan Richardson)

to the first play from Susannah Centlivre, *The Perjured Husband*. This was the beginning of a long collaboration between the two women. Oldfield also played Lucilia in Catharine Trotter's *Love at a Loss* and the prim, virtuous Ann of Brittanie in Trotter's *The Unhappy Penitent*. The following season she developed new roles, including Lady Sharlot, the shy younger sister in Richard Steele's *The Funeral*, Cimene in Bevil Higgins's *The Generous Conqueror*, and witty, bantering Jacinta in Vanbrugh's *The False Friend*, for which she also delivered the epilogue. Accounts for the period imply she was earning around £70 for the season, less than Elizabeth Barry and Anne Bracegirdle at the other house, but considerably more than Mary Porter and Mrs Willis. The selection of roles and her salary suggest that Oldfield established herself more rapidly within the company than Cibber remembers.

About 1703 Oldfield began a long-term liaison with Arthur Mainwaring (1668–1712), MP for Preston and an auditor for the imprests. He was a friend of Owen Swiny at the Haymarket, and was to support Anne's career and write several epilogues for her. 1703 was also the year that there was further opportunity for Oldfield to become a leading player. Susanna Verbruggen's illness and eventual death in childbirth meant Oldfield took on some of her roles, including Leonora in John Crowne's *Sir Courtly Nice*. Cibber gives a self-mocking account of rehearsals where:

> she could scarce prevail with me to rehearse with her the Scenes she was chiefly concern'd with in with Sir *Courtly*, which I then acted. However, we ran them over with a mutual Inadvertancy of one another. I seem'd careless … she

mutter'd out her Words in a sort of mifty manner at my low Opinion of her.   (BDA)

However, Cibber had to revise his opinion when he saw her perform, and she even inspired him to complete his *The Careless Husband*, which he had put to one side with the loss of Mrs Verbruggen. Anne's improved position in the company is suggested by the verbal contract she negotiated with John Rich in March 1704, which was to run for five years at 50s. a week. Under this arrangement she took on many new parts; in 1703 these had included Victoria in Steele's *The Lying Lover* and Queen Mary in *The Albion Queens*, by John Banks. The following season Oldfield guaranteed the success of Cibber's *The Careless Husband* with her portrayal of Lady Betty Modish, a character written for her and partially drawn, Cibber confessed, from 'sentiments … originally her own, or only dress'd with a little more care that when they negligently fell from her lively Humour' (ibid.). She also brought her comic talent to Biddy Tipkin in Steele's *The Tender Husband* and Mariana in Peter Motteux's *Farewell Folly*. By 1705–6 Oldfield was often performing opposite Robert Wilks in such leading parts as Lady Reveller in Centlivre's *The Basset Table*, Arabella in Thomas Baker's *Hampstead Heath*, and Silvia in Farquhar's *The Recruiting Officer*. When the companies reorganized in 1706 and Oldfield moved to Swiny's management at the Haymarket, she was receiving 13s. 4d. 'every day a Play shall be acted by the Company' (Lafler, 37). This move allowed Oldfield to take up many new roles, such as Elvira in Dryden's *The Spanish Fryar*, Florimel in his *Marriage à la mode*, Mrs Sullen in Farquhar's *The Stratagem*, Imoinda in Southerne's *Oroonoko*, Lady Lurewell in Farquhar's *The Constant Couple*, and Narcissa in Cibber's *Love's Last Shift*. However, the combination of companies also brought her into conflict with Anne Bracegirdle, who had been playing these kinds of part at the other house. Egerton tells a story of a contest between the two in the title role of Betterton's *The Amorous Widow*, in which the town judged Oldfield the winner. Whether this contest actually took place or not, when Oldfield's benefit was set for 25 February 1707, before that of Mrs Bracegirdle, the latter left the stage in disgust.

Anne Oldfield moved regularly during the next few seasons, each time bettering her terms of employment. In January 1708 a united company for spoken drama was established at Drury Lane, and the Queen's Theatre, Haymarket, was reserved for music. Oldfield moved with the company and tried to enforce an agreement for a salary of 4 guineas per week 'and a Benefit-Play every year paying, only, out the Receipt Fourty-Pounds' (PRO, LC 7/3 fol. 104). Rich attempted to slice more than the stipulated £40 house charge, pointing out that no actress was receiving more than 50s. per week, and it is not clear how the dispute was settled. However, in April 1709 Oldfield returned to the Haymarket and entered an agreement with Swiny for thirteen years at an annual salary of £200 and a February benefit, as well as being free each summer. Zachary Baggs, Rich's treasurer, published the company accounts to rebuff accusations of underpaying actors, and alleged

that Mrs Oldfield had been better off at Drury Lane, estimating her annual income at £252 6s. 7d. Finally, in 1711 Oldfield moved back to Drury Lane as a managing partner and sharer with the triumvirate of actor–managers Cibber, Wilks, and Thomas Doggett. However, Doggett objected to a female sharer, and instead she was offered an assured £200 each year and a charge-free benefit. This rose to 300 guineas a year, and her benefit, according to Cibber's estimate, brought her twice that. This made Oldfield one of the highest paid performers in the company, although the figures are provided by Cibber in his memoirs, and might be suspected of being glossed.

Anne Oldfield was to remain at Drury Lane for the remainder of her career, where she continued to expand her range of comic heroines and ladies of quality, such as Violante in Centlivre's *The Wonder*, as well as adding many more serious roles to her repertoire, among them Andromache in Ambrose Philips's *The Distrest Mother*, Arpasia in Nicholas Rowe's *Tamerlane*, Cleopatra in Dryden's *All for Love*, Indamora in his *Aureng-Zebe*, and the title roles in Rowe's *Jane Shore* and *Lady Jane Gray*. She appears to have been a confirmed whig, as was her partner, Mainwaring, although after his death her loyalty was questioned. Mainwaring died in November 1712, leaving her and their son, Arthur, the majority of his estate, with only £1000 for his sister. The tory *Examiner* railed against this 'Whig-Honesty' to 'a *Celebrated Actress*, who is too much admired upon the Stage to have any Enquiry made into her Conduct behind the Curtain' (Lafler, 106). But the whig *Flying-Post* came to her defence, vowing, 'I do not believe she is gone off [the whig cause]; so far from it, that I am credibly informed she has refused great Sums, because she insists upon her Lover's voting on our Side' (Egerton, 35). Oldfield's whiggish credentials were to be firmly established through her performance of the self-sacrificing Marcia in Joseph Addison's hit of 1713, *Cato*. The play gathered cross-party support for its nationalist sentiment, and often Oldfield and Booth would have to pause in their performances to allow the applause to die down. Fairly soon after Mainwaring's demise Anne began an affair with Charles Churchill (c.1678–1745), a nephew (though illegitimate) of the first duke of Marlborough, and moved in his circle as if she were his wife. By him she had another son, Charles, who married Lady Catherine Walpole, the statesman's illegitimate daughter. Although Oldfield never left the stage, these alliances clearly left her financially secure, as her sale of £1500 of South Sea stock in 1723 indicates.

One of Oldfield's greatest triumphs in the later years was her playing of Lady Townly in Vanbrugh's *The Provoked Husband* in January 1728. Cibber, who had completed the play, was delighted at her performance, made her a gift of 50 guineas, and raved about her acting in the preface to the printed work. He had considerably revised his first impression of her and now found her:

of a lively Aspect and a Command in her Mien, that like the principal Figure in the Finest Paintings, first seizes, and longest delights the Eye of the Spectator. Her Voice was Sweet, strong, piercing, and melodious: her Pronunciation voluble, distinct, and musical; and her Emphasis always placed where the Spirit of the Sense, in her Periods, only demanded it.

Her benefit, which was the first in the 1729 season, apparently made her £500, and she was given by 'several Persons of Quality, &c. five, ten and twenty Guineas each'. This was on top of her salary of 12 guineas a week. Mrs Oldfield was so renowned by 1729 that, on Richard Steele's death, a paper quipped that she 'hath obtained a reversionary grant of the Patent of Master of the Theatre-Royal in Drury-lane, granted by his Majesty King George the 1st' (Lafler, 157). Her final stage appearance was as Lady Brute in Vanbrugh's *The Provoked Wife* on 28 April 1730. During her final illness she was loyally nursed by Margaret Saunders, whose acting career she had sponsored. Oldfield died at her home, 59 Grosvenor Street, London, on 23 October 1730, and her body was carried to Westminster Abbey, where she was buried on 27 October. Her will revealed the same financial acumen that had characterized all her affairs. She left the Grosvenor Street house she had had built to Charles Churchill and ordered her holdings converted into cash. Arthur Mainwaring was to have the interest on £5000, and the capital sum when he was thirty. Oldfield left her mother 10 guineas and a £60 annuity, Margaret Saunders had a £10 annuity, and her aunt Jane Gourlaw the same. The remainder of the estate was divided, with one-third going to Charles Churchill and two-thirds to Arthur. Her share in the patent at Drury Lane passed back to Cibber, Wilks, and Booth. The sale of her effects, which were all 'in the most elegant and Fashionable manner', including books in French and English, lasted five days. Her popularity is confirmed by the two biographies which were rushed out within the year, the short, anonymous *Authentick Memoirs*, and Edmund Curll's longer biography written under the pseudonym William Egerton. The memoirs were printed with engravings taken from the many portraits painted of her, most significantly those by Godfrey Kneller and J. Richardson.   J. MILLING

Sources Highfill, Burnim & Langhans, *BDA* · J. Lafler, *The celebrated Mrs Oldfield* (1989) · C. Cibber, *An apology for the life of Mr. Colley Cibber* (1740) · W. Egerton [E. Curll], *Faithful memoirs of the life, amours and performance of … Anne Oldfield* (1731) · *Authentick memoirs of the life of the celebrated actress, Mrs Anne Oldfield* (1730) · T. Betterton, [W. Oldys and others], *The history of the English stage* (1741) · R. Gore-Brown, *Gay was the pit: the life and times of Anne Oldfield, actress, 1683–1730* (1957)
Likenesses E. Fisher, mezzotint (after J. Richardson), BM, NPG [*see illus.*] · attrib. G. Kneller, oils (presented in 1836), Garr. Club · attrib. J. Richardson, oils, Garr. Club · J. Richardson, portrait, Petworth House, Sussex · J. Simon, mezzotint (after J. Richardson), BM, NPG · A. de Wolfe Gibbs, miniature on ivory, Harvard TC · oils, Garr. Club · oils, NPG
Wealth at death under £15,000: extracts of will in Highfill, Burnim & Langhans, *BDA*

Oldfield, Henry George (*fl. c.*1785–1805), antiquary and topographical artist, was the son of John Oldfield (*d.* 1788), bricklayer and parish clerk of Wingham, Kent; nothing more is known of his background or early life. He was practising as an architect from premises in Scotland Yard, London, in the 1780s, and became architect to Princess Amelia (1710–1786), daughter of George II, who lived at Gunnersbury Park and was ranger of Richmond Park; no documents survive of the work that he carried out for her. His only known work is the rebuilding of the parish church of St Mary in Chatham, Kent, following a fire in 1786. A special vestry committee appointed him to survey the church in February of that year, and in July accepted his estimate of £7000 for the reconstruction, which was completed in 1788.

Oldfield exhibited architectural designs at the Royal Academy, London, in 1787 and 1788 and at the Society of Artists in 1790. He had a keen interest in antiquities and topography and wrote a guide to St Giles's, Camberwell, about 1785. He was co-author, with Richard Randall Dyson (*b.* 1770), of *The History and Antiquities of the Parish of Tottenham High Cross*, which was published in 1790. Among the subscribers was the antiquary Richard Gough, who subscribed for five copies. A second edition was published in 1792; Oldfield's name was omitted from the title-page, which has led to the incorrect assumption that he had died by this date. In 1791 he wrote *Anecdotes of Archery, Ancient and Modern*, which he dedicated to the first marchioness of Salisbury. In January 1793 he was known to be living at Finchley Common, Middlesex, having left Scotland Yard about 1790.

In the 1790s and early 1800s Oldfield made a living by selling his coloured topographical sketches of Hertfordshire. 1500 or more of these, bound in nine volumes, are in Hertfordshire Record Office (Herts. ALS); fewer than ten are dated, and only one bears his signature. He sold his drawings for 4*s.* each plus expenses, but his sketch of the nave ceiling of St Albans Abbey cost 6 guineas at auction, or 5 guineas by private sale. His sketches of churches are accompanied by descriptions copied from Sir Henry Chauncy's *The Historical Antiquities of Hertfordshire* (1700). The coloured sketches of buildings generally are simple but those of monuments, achievements, and coats of arms are of superior draughtsmanship and colouring. Oldfield's sketches initially were attributed by J. E. Cussans to John Pridmore (1760–1836), village schoolmaster at Tewin, Hertfordshire, for Pridmore had made copies for Earl Cowper. H. C. Andrews successfully demonstrated that the drawings were by Oldfield and that their original owner was John Meyrick (1753–1805), of Parsons Green, Fulham, who had commissioned Oldfield to record Hertfordshire's antiquities. Meyrick wrote to Oldfield a few months before his own death, on 7 January 1805; Oldfield's drawings were bought by Baron Dimsdale of Essendon, at the auction of Meyrick's library on 21 April 1806.

Oldfield appears to have depended also on the patronage of Richard Gough and Thomas Baskerfield. In a letter to Gough of 2 May 1799 he wrote that he had been arrested for debt and imprisoned in Hertford gaol for the last two months. As he 'was wholly out of employ' he offered to make copies of his drawings for Gough; some of his drawings are in the Gough collection in the Bodleian Library, Oxford, and in Baskerfield's grangerized copies of

Chauncy's and Nathanael Salmon's histories of Hertfordshire in the British Library. Nothing is known of what became of Oldfield after he completed his Hertfordshire drawings, or of when and where he died.

JOHN LEIGH CORFIELD

Sources H. C. Andrews, 'Henry George Oldfield and the Dimsdale collection of Herts drawings', *Transactions of E. Herts Archaeological Society*, 11 (1942), 212–24 · W. Minet, 'Aspenden church, 1793', *Transactions of E. Herts Archaeological Society*, 7 (1927), 323–34 · parish records, special vestry minutes, 1786, St Mary's, Chatham, Kent · Graves, *Soc. Artists* · Graves, *RA exhibitors* · *DNB* · H. Chauncy, *The historical antiquities of Hertfordshire*, 2 (1700); repr. (1975) · *GM*, 1st ser., 58 (1788), 271; 63 (1793), 19 · parish register, Wingham, Kent, 20 March 1788 [burial: J. Oldfield, father] · J. Summerson, *The vision of J. M. Gandy: heavenly mansions and other essays on architecture* (1963) · J. E. Cussans, *A history of Hertfordshire*, 2 (1784–1878); 3 (1879–81)
Archives BL, Thomas Baskerfield MSS · Bodl. Oxf., Gough MSS · Herts. ALS, Clutterbuck MSS

Oldfield, John (1626/7–1682), clergyman and ejected minister, was born near Chesterfield, Derbyshire. He was educated at the grammar school at Dronfield, Derbyshire, and though of no university, was justly reputed an able scholar. In 1647 he obtained the vicarage of Crich, Derbyshire, but left two years later, with the approval of the assembly of divines, to become rector of Carsington in the same county. He regularly attended the Wirksworth classis from December 1651 until its last recorded session in November 1658, serving as moderator fifteen times. Leading Derbyshire presbyterians, such as Robert Porter, Thomas Shelmerdine, and the Hieron brothers, John and Samuel, highly esteemed Oldfield, and invited him to preach before them on several occasions, including the first ordination held by the classis in January 1652. They approved his sermon of July 1655 as 'seasonable and orthodox', and, in January 1656, appointed him to deliver a lecture against Socinian errors (Cox, *Minute Book*, 186). Oldfield married Porter's sister, Ann; their eldest son was born on 1 November 1654, their youngest about 1673. Despite Calamy's claim that Oldfield won the affection of a peculiarly 'ticklish and capricious' flock, the fact that he had to request the assistance of lay elders from outside Carsington suggests his own parishioners were either unwilling or unfit to serve in that capacity (Calamy, *Abridgement*, 2.172). Nevertheless, he declined a more lucrative offer of the perpetual curacy of Tamworth to remain with his people. Oldfield's nonconformity cost him his living in 1662. Following his ejection he settled at Alfreton, Derbyshire, where, though occasionally attending public worship, he preached in conventicles. In 1672 he took out a licence to preach in the house of John Spateman at Road Nook, as well as in his own house and at Derby.

Between 1663 and 1671 Oldfield published three works. His 'Stumbling at the Sufferings of the Godly', printed in *England's Remembrancer* (1663), a collection of farewell sermons by ejected ministers, reveals his sense of having been abandoned at the Restoration. He expected the profane multitude to hail the ejections as well-deserved retribution, above all for the presbyterians' obnoxious attempts to restrict access to the sacrament. But it stung to hear even the godly whisper about their pastor as 'an ignorant, scrupulous, or obstinate fool'. Though it looked indeed as if God had 'spit in our faces', Oldfield reminded his hearers (and himself) that Christians were called to a life of suffering; besides, he added with more gusto, providence would eventually vindicate the godly ministers (Oldfield, 'Stumbling', 245, 241). He also defended his reluctance to submit to reordination and his refusal to accept ceremonies he deemed not only unedifying, but positively forbidden in scripture. A particularly full account of Oldfield's objections to conformity survives because, in addition to this sermon, Calamy printed lengthy extracts from his private deliberations drawn up in the agonizing months prior to August 1662.

As befitted one who 'knew well the inside of Religion', Oldfield's two later books grappled with the problem of formalism, or the tendency to rest in outward performances, devoid of grace (Porter, 51). In 1666 he published *The First, Last, or the Formal Hypocrite Further from Salvation … than the Prophane Sinner*. In his treatise on prayer, *The Generation of Seekers* (1671), he positioned himself in the tradition of Jacobean puritanism, recalling the practical works of John Brinsley the elder, Robert Bolton, and Daniel Dyke. He hoped his exposition of the Lord's prayer would 'help to improve that which … is turned at this day into a piece of formality, by so frequent repetition in public' (Oldfield, *Generation*, epistle).

Oldfield died in Alfreton on 5 June 1682, aged fifty-five, and was buried in Alfreton church, where there is a brass plate to his memory. With his wife, Ann Porter, he had four sons who became clergymen. The eldest son, John (*b*. 1654), received presbyterian ordination in September 1681, but afterwards conformed. The others adhered to their father's principles: the presbyterian minister and nonconformist tutor Joshua *Oldfield (1656–1729); Nathaniel (*d*. 1696), who was minister at Maid Lane, Southwark; and Samuel, who was pastor at Woolwich, Kent, and from 1719 at Ramsbury, Wiltshire.

Oldfield's reflections as he faced his crisis in the summer of 1662 were to echo into the eighteenth and nineteenth centuries. They were drawn on in the 1770s by the unitarian Theophilus Lindsey when he found that his beliefs meant that he could no longer in conscience retain his Anglican living, and Lindsey's writings are quoted by Elizabeth Gaskell in *North and South*. Facing the same hard choice between conscience and retaining one's living, the Revd Hale takes inspiration from the 'soliloquy' of John Oldfield, 'a clergyman in a country parish, like myself … His trials are over, he fought the good fight':

When thou canst no longer continue in thy work without dishonour to God, discredit to religion, foregoing thy integrity, wounding conscience, spoiling thy peace, and hazarding the loss of thy salvation; in a word, when the conditions upon which thou must continue (if thou wilt continue) in thy employments are sinful, and unwarranted by the word of God, thou mayest, yea, thou must believe that God will turn thy very silence, suspension, deprivation, and laying aside, to His glory, and the advancement of the Gospel's interest.　(E. Gaskell, *North and South*, 1855, chap. 4)

JIM BENEDICT

Sources E. Calamy, ed., *An abridgement of Mr. Baxter's history of his life and times, with an account of the ministers, &c., who were ejected after the Restauration of King Charles II*, 2nd edn, 2 vols. (1713), vol. 2, pp. 172–8 · R. Porter, *The life of Mr John Hieron, with the characters and memorials of ten other worthy ministers of Jesus Christ* (1691), 51–2 · J. C. Cox, ed., *Minute book of the Wirksworth classis, 1651–58* (1880), 150–220 · E. Calamy, *A continuation of the account of the ministers … who were ejected and silenced after the Restoration in 1660*, 2 vols. (1727), vol. 2, p. 233 · *Calamy rev.*, 373 · W. Wilson, *The history and antiquities of the dissenting churches and meeting houses in London, Westminster and Southwark*, 4 vols. (1808–14), vol. 4, p. 157 · J. C. Cox, *Notes on the churches of Derbyshire*, 1: *The hundred of Scarsdale* (1875), 8; 2: *The hundreds of the High Peak and Wirksworth* (1877), 562 · J. Hunter, *Familiae minorum gentium*, ed. J. W. Clay, 3, Harleian Society, 39 (1895), 1052, 1058 · I. Murray, ed., *Sermons of the great ejection* (1962), 150–72 · *Walker rev.*, 106 [William Thorpe] · J. Oldfield, 'Stumbling at the sufferings of the godly', *England's remembrancer: being a collection of farewel-sermons* (1663) · J. Oldfield, *The generation of seekers* (1671)

Archives Derbys. RO, family MSS of the Oldfield family of Ownslow farm, Carsington, Derbyshire, D4925

Oldfield, Sir John (1789–1863), army officer, only son of John Nicholls Oldfield, lieutenant in the Royal Marines, who served with distinction on the staff of the army and with the 63rd regiment in the Anglo-American War, and of Elizabeth, only daughter of Lieutenant Hammond RN, was born at Portsmouth on 29 May 1789. He was descended from Sir Anthony Oldfield, created a baronet in 1660, and he claimed to be the fifth baronet, but the proof was incomplete. A re-creation was deemed to be necessary, the cost of which Oldfield declined to incur, and the matter was dropped. His father retired from the service about the date of Oldfield's birth, and purchased a small estate at Westbourne, Sussex, dying in 1793.

In 1799 Oldfield's uncle, Major Thomas *Oldfield, Royal Marines, was killed at Acre. His distinguished conduct led to offers from Lord St Vincent, Lord Nelson, and Sir Sidney Smith to provide for John Oldfield in the navy, while Earl Spencer offered a commission in the Royal Marines, and the Marquess Cornwallis a nomination for the Royal Military Academy at Woolwich. The latter was accepted. When Oldfield was old enough to go to Woolwich, he was only 4 feet 6 inches high, and a dispensing order had to be obtained from the master-general of the ordnance to allow his admission to the Royal Military Academy, the minimum standard being then 4 feet 9 inches. The junior cadets at that time went first to Great Marlow, Buckinghamshire, where he joined, on 23 August 1803, and was afterwards transferred to Woolwich. When George III inspected the cadets on 29 May 1805, Oldfield was one of the senior cadets. The king was struck with his diminutive stature, asked his name and age, and spoke warmly to the young man of his uncle's services at Acre.

Oldfield joined the trigonometrical survey at Bodmin in Cornwall in September 1805, and was commissioned as second lieutenant in the Royal Engineers on 2 April 1806, stationed initially in Portsmouth. He was promoted lieutenant on 1 July. The following summer he was sent to Halifax, Nova Scotia, and after two years' service in North America he returned to England, being stationed in September 1809 at Dorchester. He was promoted second captain on 1 May 1811.

From Dorchester, Oldfield went to Fort George in Scotland, and remained there until he embarked for the Netherlands in 1814. He landed at Hellevoetsluis on 28 March, and entered Antwerp with Sir Thomas Graham on 5 May. He was promoted captain on 26 January 1815. He was at Brussels on 7 April 1815, when news was received of Napoleon's escape from Elba, and at once he sent his family back to England. Oldfield was sent to Ypres to construct new defence works, and was entrusted with the inundation of the surrounding area, a difficult and unpopular operation. He shortly after joined the army of the duke of Wellington as brigade major of the Royal Engineers. He made a sketch plan of the field of Waterloo for the use of the duke, and took part in the battle of Waterloo and the subsequent occupation of Paris. In April 1819, in consequence of a reduction in the corps of Royal Engineers, he was placed on half pay, and passed his time chiefly at Westbourne.

In October 1823 Oldfield was sent on a special commission to the West Indies. He returned in 1824, and was quartered for some years in Ireland. On 23 July 1830 he was promoted brevet major and belatedly made a KH for his services in 1815. In September he was appointed commanding royal engineer (CRE) in Newfoundland. On 19 November 1831 he was promoted lieutenant-colonel, and in October 1835 returned to England to be appointed to the command of the Royal Engineers at Jersey. In March 1839 he was sent to Canada as CRE and colonel on the staff; he was there during the French Canadian uprising and rendered valuable service. On 9 November 1841 he was promoted colonel in the army and appointed aide-de-camp to the queen. He returned from Canada in the spring of 1843, and was appointed CRE in the western district. He was promoted regimental colonel on 9 November 1846 and was appointed to command the Royal Engineers in Ireland in 1848. On 20 June 1854 he was promoted major-general and went to live at Westbourne, becoming lieutenant-general on 10 May 1859. He was made a colonel-commandant of the corps of Royal Engineers on 25 October 1859, and was promoted general on 3 April 1862.

Oldfield was married three times. First, on 12 March 1810, at Dorchester, he married Mary, daughter of Christopher Ardens of Dorchester, Dorset; they had seven children, and Mary died at Le Mans, France, on 6 July 1820. On 8 July 1822, at Cheltenham, he married Alicia, daughter of the Revd T. Hume, rector of Arden; they had eight children and Alicia died at Plymouth on 5 February 1840. On 12 March 1849, at Plymouth, he married Cordelia Anne, daughter of the Revd D. Yonge; she survived him. Oldfield died at his home, Oldfield Lawn, Westbourne, Sussex, on 2 August 1863, and was buried at Westbourne.

Oldfield's eldest son, John Rawdon, was a colonel in the Bengal Engineers; Anthony, a captain in the Royal Artillery, was killed at Sevastopol; Rudolphus, a captain, RN, and aide-de-camp to the queen, died on 6 February 1877; Richard became colonel-commandant, Royal Artillery (1900), and a general officer.

R. H. VETCH, *rev.* JAMES FALKNER

Sources *Army List* · *Hart's Army List* · Boase, *Mod. Eng. biog.* · *CGPLA Eng. & Wales* (1863)
Wealth at death under £4000: probate, 29 Sept 1863, *CGPLA Eng. & Wales*

Oldfield, Joshua (1656–1729), Presbyterian minister, was born at Carsington, Derbyshire, on 2 December 1656, the second son of John *Oldfield (1626/7–1682) and his wife, Ann, daughter of William Porter, a musician of Nottingham. His father was the rector of Carsington until he was ejected from the living in 1662, after which he continued to preach at presbyterian conventicles. Joshua received his early education from his father, and the family lived in the area of Alfreton, Derbyshire. In the 1670s he studied at Magdalene College, Cambridge, which he entered as a sizar in February 1674, and also at Lincoln College, Oxford, and Christ's College, Cambridge. He did not take a degree, however, as he refused to subscribe to the articles of the church. Oldfield followed his father into the ministry as a presbyterian, for which he prepared at John Shuttlewood's academy at Sulby, Northamptonshire. He became private chaplain to Sir John Gell at Hopton Hall, Derbyshire, and later tutor to the son of Paul Foley who subsequently became speaker of the House of Commons. It was during this period that he received tempting offers to conform but always turned them down.

In the 1680s Oldfield was for a short time chaplain to Lady Susan Lort in Pembrokeshire, and gained experience in the ministry in both Dublin and at Fetter Lane, London. He became the first minister of a presbyterian congregation at Tooting, Surrey, in 1686 and was ordained at Mansfield, Nottinghamshire, on 18 March 1687. Early in 1691 he became minister of the congregation at Oxford, where he renewed his friendship with Edmund Calamy, whom he had met at Tooting. Calamy says of Oldfield at Oxford that 'he was in his prime … With him I daily conversed … [and] fell into the utmost freedom with him, and have reason to be thankful for it' (Calamy, *Life*, 1.224). He adds that Oldfield took great pains with his work although he had little encouragement. He was shy and not free in conversations with university students and his small congregation, but his profile increased in the city following the part he played in a public discussion on infant baptism.

In 1694 Oldfield became copastor with William Tong of the presbyterian meeting at Coventry. There he quickly formed an academy for training students for the ministry with the assistance of Tong. This brought him into wider prominence, with the result that in October 1697 he was arraigned before the ecclesiastical court for teaching young men without a licence from the bishop. He resisted the action which was then moved to Lichfield, where the cause was listed as teaching with no licence, not subscribing to the whole Book of Common Prayer and all the Thirty-Nine Articles, and contrary to the 77th canon. Oldfield demanded a hearing in the public courts before the king's bench in London, where in due course the action was dropped, 'Not without intimation from his Majesty (upon his having the state of the case laid before him) that he was not pleased with such Prosecutions' (Calamy, *Abridgement*, 1.553).

Joshua Oldfield (1656–1729), by unknown artist

Oldfield left Coventry in 1699 to succeed Thomas Kentish as minister at Globe Alley meeting, Maid Lane, Southwark, a post previously held by his brother Nathaniel (his other brothers John and Samuel were also ministers). He took his academy with him, and carried it forward first in Southwark and later at Hoxton Square, London. The teaching he provided at Hoxton in association with William Lorimer, John Spademan, and later Jean Cappel was recognized as among the best available to dissenters at the time. 'He allowed his pupils the greatest freedom of access and conversation, and yet kept up a just authority and esteem among them' (Harris, 40).

It was in the early years of the eighteenth century that Oldfield became more widely known, and established contacts with both John Locke and Isaac Newton:

> He was naturally very thoughtful and of great penetration. Sometimes he forgot to eat and was unaffected by noise around him. He was not always so happy in expression, and conveying his sense to others … He was a man of staid passion, and great meekness and calmness of temper … He was of no party, but that of God against the Devil and of all serious Christians; and had great charity and moderation to those who differed from him.　(Harris, 39)

Oldfield was considered as a minister who avoided extremes in religious controversy, but who was at the same time a strong supporter of civil and religious liberty. The University of Edinburgh recognized his learning and position among the dissenters by awarding him a DD in 1709.

Oldfield's published output was meagre for a man of his abilities, and consisted mainly of sermons and a work on the Trinity published in 1721. His congregation dwindled until it was revived with the appointment of Obediah Hughes as his copastor from 1721. Oldfield is mainly known for being the chairman of the Salters' Hall debates on subscription to the Westminster confession in 1719, perhaps the defining event for dissenters in the first half of the eighteenth century. His eirenical approach to religious matters meant that he was probably the best man for this difficult task although he could not prevent the split taking place between those who insisted on subscription to a Trinitarian creed and those who took their stand on the sufficiency of scripture. While orthodox in theology he voted for the non-subscribers probably on the basis that the need to affirm religious liberty and freedom was paramount. Some saw him as partly responsible for the split, as a decision he made as chairman of the conference was its immediate cause.

Oldfield was one of the first trustees of the various foundations made under the will of his close associate Dr Daniel Williams, and in 1723 he was appointed one of the original distributors of government money under the English *regium donum* to poor ministers and their widows. He may have been the presbyterian minister who married Catherine Massey at Ashbourne, Derbyshire, on 29 July 1707; there is no record of any children. He died at his home in Redcross Street, Southwark, on 8 November 1729 while still the minister at Southwark, and was buried in the same month in Bunhill Fields burial-ground.

ALAN RUSTON

Sources W. Harris, *The love of Christ's appearance* (1730) · A. Gordon, ed., *Freedom after ejection: a review (1690–1692) of presbyterian and congregational nonconformity in England and Wales* (1917), 322 · W. Wilson, *The history and antiquities of the dissenting churches and meeting houses in London, Westminster and Southwark*, 4 vols. (1808–14), vol. 4, pp. 160–66 · Venn, *Alum. Cant.*, 1/3 · C. Surman, index of dissenting ministers, DWL, card O.76 · E. Calamy, ed., *An abridgement of Mr. Baxter's history of his life and times, with an account of the ministers, &c., who were ejected after the Restoration of King Charles II*, 2nd edn, 2 vols. (1713), vol. 1, pp. 551–3 · J. Waddington, *Surrey Congregational History* (1866), 105, 312 · D. Bogue and J. Bennett, *History of dissenters, from the revolution in 1688, to … 1808*, 2nd edn, 2 (1833), 214–15 · E. Calamy, *An historical account of my own life, with some reflections on the times I have lived in, 1671–1731*, ed. J. T. Rutt, 1 (1829), 223–4, 264–6 · *Calamy rev.*, 373, 395 · A. W. Light, *Bunhill Fields: written in honour and to the memory of the many saints of God whose bodies rest in this old London cemetery*, 1 (1913), 184–6 · DNB · IGI · E. E. Cleal, *Congregationalism in Surrey* (1908), 209 · M. Watts, *The dissenters: from the Reformation to the French Revolution* (1985)
Likenesses engraving, repro. in Wilson, *History and antiquities of dissenting churches*, facing p. 160 · oils, DWL [see illus.]

Oldfield, Josiah (1863–1953), lawyer, physician, and writer on health, was born at Ryton, Shropshire, on 28 February 1863, the son of a provision dealer, David Oldfield, and his wife, Margaret, *née* Bates. He attended Newport grammar school, and then went to Oxford to read theology, matriculating with a non-collegiate affiliation on 15 April 1882. He graduated BA in 1885. He then trained as a barrister at Lincoln's Inn (BCL 1888) and practised on the Oxford circuit. He was married with at least one daughter, Josie.

Some time during his stay at Oxford, Oldfield became a vegetarian and turned towards medicine, which became a second career. He took his medical diploma at St Bartholomew's Hospital, and subsequently founded the Humanitarian Hospital of St Francis, of which he was for some years chairman and senior physician. He was also warden and senior physician to the Lady Margaret Fruitarian Hospital at Sittingbourne. The Fruitarians were members of an Order of the Golden Age, with headquarters at Barcombe Hall, Paignton, in Devon. They were dietary reformers who abstained from all foods obtained by the cruel infliction of pain, and who lived mainly on gathered, preferably uncooked, fruits, vegetables, nuts, and grains. Oldfield became a prolific popular health author for the vegetarian and humanitarian cause, publishing on average a book every two years between 1892 and 1953. His first two books, *The Cost of Living* (1892) and *The Ideal Diet in Relation to Real Life* (1892), were both published by the Vegetarian Society, as were *The Influenza* (1892), *Tuberculosis, or, Flesh-Eating a Cause of Consumption* (1897, 2nd edn), and other dietary tracts on indigestion, rheumatism, and appendicitis. The Ideal Publishing Union issued Oldfield's *The Evils of Butchery* (1895), *A Groaning Creation* (1895), *The Voice of Nature, or, What Man should Eat* (1898), and also *The Claims of Common Life, or, The Scientific Relations of Humans and non-Humans* (1898), a book which discussed the ethics of killing animals, and the social responsibility of science—'science increases the rights of animals by deepening the rights of man' (p. 71).

Oldfield addressed the rights of man when he founded the Society for the Abolition of Capital Punishment in 1901, with an accompanying book; he also took a study tour of India that year, looking at political grievances. He remained active in legal reform circles, publishing *Hanging for Murder* (1908), and becoming chairman of the Romilly Society in 1910. He was admitted to the Jamaican bar in 1920, and became a fellow of the Royal Society of Medicine in 1920. During the First World War Oldfield raised and commanded a casualty clearing station and was mentioned in dispatches; he was invalided out with the rank of lieutenant-colonel.

Between 1905 and 1935 he published a steady stream of successful commercial books on natural diet cookery and aspects of what was then becoming known as naturopathy—such as *The Best Sixpenny Cookery* (1916), *The Raisin Cure* (1923), *The Dry Diet Cure* (1925), *Fasting for Health and Life* (1924), *Deep Breathing and Breathing Exercises* (1928), *Eat and be Happy* (1929), and *The Beauty Aspect of Health and Living* (1935). He was still writing prolifically in his eighties, with his series comprising *Mystery of Marriage* (1949), *Mystery of Birth* (1949), and *Mystery of Death* (1951), and a Fruitarian longevity tract, *The Crown of Grapes: Eat Right and Live Long* (1952). By this time he was living in Fruitarian retreat at Margaret Manor, Doddington, near Faversham, Kent, listing his recreations in *Who's Who* as tree planting and Fruitarian lecturing. The Fruitarians published his final volumes of letters and a valedictory *Popular Guide to Fruitarian Diet and Cookery* in 1952. Oldfield died at Doddington on 2 February 1953.

VIRGINIA SMITH

Sources WWW · J. Oldfield, *The claims of common life, or, The scientific relations of humans and non-humans* (1898) · b. cert. · d. cert. · Foster, *Alum. Oxon.* · *CGPLA Eng. & Wales* (1953)
Wealth at death £33,200 6s. 3d.: administration with will, 22 May 1953, *CGPLA Eng. & Wales*

Oldfield, Sir Maurice (1915–1981), intelligence officer, was born on 16 November 1915 in the village of Over Haddon, near Bakewell, Derbyshire, the eldest of eleven children of Joseph Oldfield, tenant farmer, and his wife, Ada Annie Dicken. He was educated at Lady Manners School in Bakewell, where he learned to play the organ and began his lifelong devotion to the Anglican church. In 1934 he won a scholarship to Manchester University and specialized in medieval history. After the award of the Thomas Brown memorial prize, in 1938 he graduated with first class honours in history and was elected to a fellowship. The war upset his plans for an academic career.

After joining the intelligence corps, Oldfield's service was spent mostly at the Cairo headquarters of SIME (security intelligence Middle East) where his talent was spotted by Brigadier Douglas Roberts. Oldfield finished the war as a lieutenant-colonel with an MBE (1946). When Roberts joined the Secret Intelligence Service (SIS), whose head was traditionally known as 'C', at the end of 1946 as head of counter-intelligence, Oldfield became his deputy from 1947 (until 1949). There followed two postings to Singapore from 1950 to 1952 and from 1956 to 1958, first as deputy and later as head of SIS's regional headquarters covering south-east Asia and the Far East. It was here that he established himself as a flyer. In 1956 he was appointed CBE. Throughout his life he never lost interest in the family farm and kept up his organ playing and regular attendance in church, both at home and abroad.

Following a short spell in London from 1958 to 1959, Oldfield was selected for the key post of SIS representative in Washington, where he remained for the next four years, with the main task of cultivating good relations with the Central Intelligence Agency (CIA). In 1964 he was appointed CMG. His close ties with James Angleton, the head of the CIA's counter-intelligence branch, were reinforced by their shared interest in medieval history. But Angleton also persuaded Oldfield to swallow the outpourings of the KGB defector, Anatoly Golitsyn, who was claiming, *inter permulta alia*, that the Sino-Soviet conflict and President Tito of Yugoslavia's breach with Moscow were clear cases of Soviet disinformation. Soon after leaving Washington, Oldfield withdrew his belief in most of Golitsyn's fairy stories. If, however, he confessed his errors when on his knees, there was, understandably, no overt explanation of how someone of his calibre had been led up the garden path.

On his return to London, Oldfield became director of counter-intelligence and in 1965 C's deputy. He therefore had reason to feel aggrieved when he was passed over in 1968 in favour of Sir John Rennie from the Foreign and Commonwealth Office, whom he later succeeded as C in 1973. This made Oldfield the first member of the post-war intake to reach the top post. Under his leadership, SIS benefited from the good relations he cultivated with both Conservative and Labour ministers at home and from its improved standing with friendly foreign intelligence services with which he kept in personal touch. Oldfield was appointed KCMG in 1975 and GCMG on his retirement in 1978: the only C so far to have received this award. He was also the first to cultivate chosen journalists at meetings in the Athenaeum. This led to the smile on his pudgy face behind horn-rimmed glasses appearing in the press.

All Souls made Oldfield a visiting fellow in 1978, where he began a study of Captain Sir Mansfield Cumming, the first C, but soon lost interest in it through lack of material. He therefore welcomed Margaret Thatcher's proposal in October 1979 to appoint him co-ordinator of security intelligence in Northern Ireland. In Belfast he did his best to improve relations between the chief constable and the new general officer commanding, but the strains of office soon told on him. It was not only incipient cancer, but also alleged evidence on his unprofessional contacts that caused his return to London in June 1980. Subsequent interrogation resulted in the withdrawal of his positive vetting certificate, after he confessed he had lied to cover up his homosexuality. There is, however, no evidence that his private life had prejudiced the security of his work at any stage in his career. He died, unmarried, in London on 11 March 1981. NIGEL CLIVE, *rev.*

Sources *The Times* (12 March 1981) · R. Deacon, *'C': a biography of Sir Maurice Oldfield* (1984) · personal knowledge (1990) · private information (1990) · WWW · *CGPLA Eng. & Wales* (1981)
Wealth at death £113,300: probate, 15 April 1981, *CGPLA Eng. & Wales*

Oldfield, Thomas (1756–1799), marine officer, was born at Stone, Staffordshire, on 21 June 1756, the third son of Humphrey Oldfield (d. c.1775), also an officer in the Royal Marines; his mother was Elizabeth, daughter of Major-General Nicholls, of the East India Company.

Oldfield accompanied his father to America in the autumn of 1774, or in the following spring, and served as a volunteer with the marine battalion at Bunker Hill on 17 June 1775. In this action he was twice wounded, and his wrist permanently injured. Shortly afterwards, his father died and Oldfield accepted a commission in a provincial loyalist corps—possibly the mounted legion led by Lieutenant-Colonel Banastre Tarleton. In 1776 he took up a commission in the Royal Marines which was intended for his brother, but which had been made out in his name by mistake. He was promoted to first lieutenant on 16 April 1778, but at the siege of Charles Town, South Carolina, in 1780, he served with the 63rd regiment. Noticed for his intelligence and gallantry, he was placed on the staff of the quartermaster-general's department, and as deputy assistant quartermaster-general he was attached to the headquarters of Lord Cornwallis and to Lord Rawdon who both repeatedly testified to his zeal, gallantry, and ability. He was taken prisoner with Lord Cornwallis at the capitulation of Yorktown.

After the war Oldfield returned to England, and while quartered at Portsmouth, purchased a small place in the parish of Westbourne, which he named Oldfield Lawn. It was presumably at this time that he married, and started a family; details of his wife are not known.

In 1788 Oldfield went to the West Indies, but returned in very poor health. He was promoted captain in 1793 and returned to the West Indies in the *Sceptre* (64 guns, Captain Dacres). In 1794 Oldfield commanded the Royal Marines landed from the squadron to co-operate with the army on the island of Santo Domingo. He reputedly distinguished himself on every possible occasion. In storming one of the enemy's works at San Nicolas Mole he was the first to enter it, and with his own hand struck the enemy's colours. He returned to England in the autumn of 1795, again in precarious health.

In 1796 Oldfield was employed on the recruiting service at Manchester and Warrington. The following year he embarked on board the *Theseus* (74 guns), and sailed to join the squadron under the orders of the earl of St Vincent off Cadiz. Upon the *Theseus*'s reaching her destination she became the flagship of Rear-Admiral Horatio Nelson, then serving under St Vincent. Oldfield was wounded on the night of 5 July 1797 during the bombardment of the Spanish fleet in Cadiz, while in a boat with Nelson. His wound could not have been too serious, however, for he quickly recovered and on the night of 24 July was able to lead the marines in Nelson's brave but disastrous attack on Santa Cruz, Tenerife. In attempting to land, his boat was swamped, but he swam ashore, and on landing injured himself. Oldfield looked back on these events as the hardest actions he had fought.

In 1798 the *Theseus* was detached to join Nelson, who had shifted his flag to the *Vanguard* and gone in pursuit of the French squadron up the Mediterranean. Oldfield related in a private letter how, after the disappointment of not finding the French fleet at Alexandria, the *Zealous* made the signal at midday on 1 August that it was in Abu Qir Bay. At 3.30 p.m. the French fleet was plainly seen, and an hour later Nelson ordered the *Theseus* to go ahead of him. Oldfield in the *Theseus* was alongside the *Guerrier* at a quarter to seven and having poured in a broadside which carried away the latter's main and mizen masts, she passed on to the *Spartiole* and anchored abreast of her, Nelson anchoring on the other side ten minutes later. After the action, Oldfield (the senior Royal Marines officer in Nelson's fleet) was sent with his marines to the *Tonnant*, to guard upwards of 600 prisoners.

Oldfield was promoted major on 7 October 1798, and the *Theseus* spent some time at Gibraltar and Lisbon repairing damage sustained in the battle of the Nile. Then, with Oldfield on board, she was sent to join the blockade of the French army in Alexandria, and arrived there on 2 February 1799. On 8 March she sailed for Acre under Sir Sidney Smith's orders to organize the defences of that town against Bonaparte's advancing army, arriving on 12 March and being joined by Smith himself in the *Tigre* three days later. For two months British seamen and marines from the two ships, along with the Turkish defenders, were besieged in the town by 15,000 French troops. But Oldfield did not live to see the siege lifted on 20 May. At daybreak on 7 April a party of the defenders with Oldfield leading the centre of three columns sallied out from the walls to attack and destroy a mine which was being dug by the French to weaken their defences. Oldfield's column advanced to the entrance of the mine and according to General Berthier, chief of staff of the French army in Egypt, attacked like heroes. Oldfield was one of the first to be cut down. Both sides tried to recover his body, a French grenadier succeeding, reputedly by hooking a halberd into Oldfield's side and dragging him off, only to discover that he was still alive. Oldfield died shortly afterwards, and was buried with full military honours by the French, in recognition of his bravery. A tablet to his memory was later erected in the garrison chapel, Portsmouth. Sir Sidney Smith praised Oldfield's courage in his official dispatch; and Napoleon, on his way to exile on St Helena, is said to have spoken of Oldfield's gallantry to the marine officers on board the *Northumberland*.

RANDOLPH COCK

Sources W. L. Clowes, *The Royal Navy: a history from the earliest times to the present*, 7 vols. (1897–1903); repr. (1996–7), vol. 4 · T. Pocock, *A thirst for glory: the life of Admiral Sir Sidney Smith* (1996) · IGI · DNB

Oldfield, Thomas Hinton Burley (1755–1822), political reformer and historian, was born in Derbyshire. The identity of his parents remains undiscovered and very few details of his personal life are known, except that he fathered several children, two of whom became merchants in Baltimore. Having earned a living practising law, Oldfield is referred to in the *Gentleman's Magazine* as 'an attorney of great celebrity' (*GM*, 566), although his name is unknown to the law list. As a lawyer, Oldfield was actively engaged in politics as an election agent for candidates, a duty which encompassed the important responsibility of organizing and managing local campaigns. From 1777 Oldfield maintained a close association with various groups for parliamentary reform, including the Society for Constitutional Information, earning a reputation as a zealous pioneer of parliamentary reform. His connection with these societies ensured his familiarity with many reformers of the day, but it was, according to his obituary, his 'cheerful temper' (*Monthly Magazine*, 178) which particularly endeared him to friends like Sir George Saville, John Jebb, Christopher Wyvill, Granville Sharp, Major John Cartwright, and John Horne Tooke.

As an author Oldfield found another vent for his political beliefs, and was quite productive and influential in this pursuit despite the somewhat disparaging reference to him, by one contemporary, as 'an obscure writer on the Boroughs' (Mathias, 30). He was the author of an undated and untraceable *History of Wainfleet and Candleshoe*; his first extant book chronicled *An Entire and Complete History, Political and Personal, of the Boroughs of Great Britain* (3 vols., 1792), and was followed by a *History of the Original Constitution of Parliaments* (1797). Oldfield continued to expound the ideas of electoral reform through such historical treatises as a *History of the House of Commons* (4 vols., 1812), *The Representative History of Great Britain and Ireland* (6 vols., 1816), and *A Key to the House of Commons* (1820). Oldfield did not publish any further works before his death on 25 July 1822 at the age of sixty-seven. The cause of death and place of burial remain unknown, and the *Gentleman's Magazine* and *Monthly Magazine* present conflicting accounts of the place where Oldfield passed away, with the former suggesting he died in Exeter on his way to the Cornwall assize and the latter stating that he expired at his apartments in Skinner Street, London.   MICHAEL T. DAVIS

Sources GM, 1st ser., 92/2 (1822), 566 · *Monthly Magazine*, 54 (1822), 178 · T. J. Mathias, *The pursuits of literature: a satirical poem in four dialogues*, 8th edn (1798) · [J. Watkins and F. Shoberl], *A biographical dictionary of the living authors of Great Britain and Ireland* (1816) · Allibone, *Dict.* · R. Robson, *The attorney in eighteenth-century England* (1959) · F. O'Gorman, *Voters, patrons, and parties: the unreformed electoral system of Hanoverian England, 1734–1832* (1989) · *EdinR*, 26 (1816), 338–83

Archives N. Yorks. CRO, corresp. with Christopher Wyvill

Oldhall, Sir William (d. 1460), soldier and speaker of the House of Commons, was the son of Sir Edmund Oldhall (d. 1417) of Narford, Bodney, East Dereham, and Little Fransham, Norfolk, and either his first wife, Mary, daughter and coheir of Henry English of Wood Ditton, Cambridgeshire, or his second, Alice, daughter of Geoffrey Fransham of Norfolk. As an esquire he indented on 1 May 1415 to serve with three archers under Thomas Beaufort, earl of Dorset (d. 1426), but his actual presence on the Agincourt campaign is not proven. In the following year he served as a mounted man-at-arms at Harfleur under Beaufort, and was present at the siege of Rouen in 1418–19. Oldhall had to resist efforts to deprive him of part of his inheritance when his father died intestate in 1417, but achieved this through a petition to parliament in 1421.

Oldhall served in France with Beaufort in 1421 and 1423, and was present at the battle of Cravant, where he was knighted. He was probably also present at the battle of Verneuil in the following year. By Michaelmas 1424 he had been appointed seneschal of Normandy (although he seems to have held the office only for one year), and participated in campaigns into Anjou and Maine (1424–8). He held a series of captaincies in Lower Normandy: Essay (September 1424 to about August 1429); Fresnay (December 1429 to September 1430); Alençon (March 1430 to early in 1431). He also served on an embassy to Burgundy in August 1426. Present at a great council in England in the late spring of 1434, he crossed again to France as captain of Essay and *bailli* of Alençon, posts he held from 9 September 1434 to 30 March 1438. By December 1436 he was member of the royal council in Normandy, and was lieutenant of Bayeux in 1438–9.

When the duke of York began his second term as lieutenant-general in France in March 1441, Oldhall, as well as holding a number of further captaincies in Normandy (Regneville from 1442 to at least August 1444; Coutances from October 1441 to December 1443, when he was replaced by Sir Thibault Gorges; and briefly Pont-l'Évêque, Lisieux, and Orbec in 1445), became one of the duke's closest advisers; by 1445 he was his chamberlain as well as overseer of his lands in Normandy, helping to maintain York's interests in the duchy after the latter returned to England. But he became increasingly involved with York's English interests, and may have crossed with the duke to

Ireland in July 1449. He sat as MP for Hertfordshire in the parliament of November 1450, and was elected speaker, clear proof of support for the duke in the Commons, but when York's fortunes began to wane Oldhall found himself vulnerable, and in November 1451 he was forced to take sanctuary in St Martin's-le-Grand, London, accused of stealing the duke of Somerset's goods. There he remained, twice indicted of treason in 1452, outlawed in March 1453 for not appearing for trial, and attainted by parliament on 22 June 1453. When York became protector in 1454 Oldhall obtained a writ of error, but the reversal of his attainder and his liberty were only achieved in July 1455, following York's victory at St Albans. His connection with York persisted. He was with the duke at Ludford Bridge on 12 October 1459, was attainted again in December 1459, and may then have gone to Ireland with York; both were back in London in October 1460, when Oldhall's attainder was again reversed.

Oldhall had married, probably by 1423, Margaret, daughter of William, Lord Willoughby of Eresby (d. 1410) and widow of Sir Thomas Skipwith (d. 1418). They had a daughter, Mary, who married Walter Gorges, son of Sir Thibault Gorges of Wraxall, Somerset. Margaret was still alive in 1450, but probably died within the next four years. John Paston failed to secure Oldhall's marriage to his sister Elizabeth. Oldhall had been granted several estates in France, in addition to the English lands inherited from his father. His wife brought him lands in the West Riding of Yorkshire and Lincolnshire which had been the property of her first husband, although some were held only until his stepson came of age, and he himself purchased estates in south-east Hertfordshire, including the manor of Hunsdon, which he bought from York in 1447 and where he built a fine house. He had further grants made to him by the duke of York of lands in Ireland, Hertfordshire, Kent, and Buckinghamshire. Oldhall died in London between 17 and 20 November 1460 and was buried in the church of St Michael Paternoster Royal.   ANNE CURRY

Sources J. S. Roskell, 'Sir William Oldhall, speaker in the parliament of 1450–1451', *Nottingham Medieval Studies*, 5 (1961), 87–112 · *Chancery records* · PRO, French or treaty rolls, C 76 · PRO, E 163 · accounts various, PRO, E 101 · PRO, KB 27 · will, PRO, PROB 11/4, sig. 21 · Bibliothèque Nationale, Collection Clairambault, manuscrits français, nouvelles acquisitions françaises · Archives Nationales, séries K, JJ · Archives Nationales, Dom lenoir, série Mi 204 · N. H. Nicolas, ed., *Proceedings and ordinances of the privy council of England*, 7 vols., RC, 26 (1834–7) · *RotP* · *Itineraries [of] William Worcestre*, ed. J. H. Harvey, OMT (1969) · C. T. Allmand and C. A. J. Armstrong, eds., *English suits before the Parlement of Paris, 1420–1436*, CS, 4th ser., 26 (1982) · N. Davis, ed., *Paston letters and papers of the fifteenth century*, 2 vols. (1971–6) · 'Oldhall, Edmund', HoP, *Commons* · R. A. Griffiths, *The reign of King Henry VI: the exercise of royal authority, 1422–1461* (1981)

Archives BL, Egerton roll 8354

Wealth at death £216 taxes in 1436; also bequests and moveable goods: will, PRO, PROB 11/4, sig. 21; PRO, E 163/7/31

Oldham, Alice (1850–1907), promoter of women's education, born at 15 Percy Place, Dublin, on 24 June 1850, was the second of twelve children of Eldred Oldham (1816–1880), linen draper, and his wife, Anne Alker. Her brother

Charles Hubert Oldham was professor of national economics at University College, Dublin, 1917–26. She came from a Church of Ireland family noted for its 'very large noses and iron wills' and it was this latter trait which was to prove most useful in her long campaign to gain equality of access to higher education for women.

Alice Oldham's initial experience of the women's movement came in the late 1870s when she became a committee member of the first suffrage group founded in Dublin, the Dublin Women's Suffrage Association. She joined a deputation in July 1878, headed by Isabella Tod and Margaret Byers of Belfast, which persuaded Lord Chancellor Cairns to extend the benefits of the Intermediate Education (Ireland) Bill (1878) to girls' schools as well as boys'. This imposed a new permanent role for the state in girls' secondary education, ensuring uniformity of provision. The major benefits were that subjects such as maths, Latin, and even Greek were now included in the curriculum of girls' schools, opening the way for university entry, while the accomplishments of music, singing, drawing, and dancing were no longer deemed the essential part of a lady's education. But the inclusion of girls' schools in the 1878 act without proper financial provision led to the threat that the intermediate education board would introduce a separate examination for girls, which would have placed them at a disadvantage in relation to girls at English schools, and would have involved dropping subjects compulsory for entry to the Royal University of Ireland. Alice Oldham's response to this threat was to found the Association of Irish Schoolmistresses and other Ladies interested in Education, later the Central Association of Irish Schoolmistresses (CAISM), in January 1882, acting as honorary secretary from 1883 to 1905. The association succeeded in preserving the position of girls as envisaged in 1878, an achievement which was the more remarkable in view of the public apathy on the subject and the relative smallness of its numbers, as it represented only protestant girls' schools in Ireland.

In 1884 Alice Oldham graduated BA in logic, metaphysics, history of philosophy, and ethics, one of the first nine women graduates of the Royal University of Ireland, founded in 1879 mainly as an examining body. She had received most of her teaching from the Alexandra College, Dublin, founded in 1866. It was the first women's college in Ireland to provide higher education for women in Ireland, and was the centre of the reform movement for girls' secondary and university education. Like many of the other early women university students Alice had to support herself by teaching in the morning while attending lectures in the afternoon. She joined the staff of Alexandra College in 1886, and subsequently taught and lectured there to both its secondary and university students in a wide range of subjects, including English language and literature, history, logic, ethics, Latin, and botany. Her interest in the college extended also to extra-curricular activities: she founded the Students' Union, a debating society, in 1887. She wrote three articles on the history of socialism in the *National Review* (1890–91). In the period 1904–6 she gave a series of post-graduate lectures on philosophy in Alexandra College, which were published posthumously as *An Introduction to the Study of Philosophy* in 1909.

As secretary of CAISM, Alice Oldham, who had published an article, 'Women and the Irish university question', in the *New Ireland Review* (January 1897), gave evidence before the intermediate education inquiry commission of 1898–9, and the royal commission on university education in Ireland, 1901–3. The latter evidence proved controversial. She favoured the opening of all university lectures and teaching to women on the same basis as men, and this brought her into conflict with Henrietta White, principal of Alexandra College, who wanted women to be taught separately from men in their own colleges, while sitting for the same examinations and degrees. Alice Oldham believed that this would deprive women of the opportunity to receive the best teaching, and would be 'in opposition to what women have so long painfully worked for, and at last achieved in almost every country—equal education' (Oldham to White, 24 Sept 1901, Alice Oldham MSS). A questionnaire to women graduates in Ireland revealed that the majority favoured equality of access to teaching and degrees, the women's colleges being transformed into residential halls. A new organization to represent these opinions, the Irish Association of Women Graduates, was founded by Alice Oldham in March 1902, reflecting the views of both protestant and Catholic graduates more accurately than the CAISM had been able to do. She became its first president and was a committee member until her death. She was also, despite failing health, Irish correspondent for the *Journal of Education*. In private life she was reserved, courteous, unfailingly kind, and considerate of others. Alice Oldham, who never married, died at her home, 2 Anglesea Villas, Ballsbridge, Dublin, on 21 January 1907 and was buried two days later at Dean's Grange cemetery.

A. V. O'CONNOR

Sources *Journal of Education*, new ser., 29 (1907), 126–7 · *Alexandra College Magazine* (June 1907), 3–9 · Minute-books of the Association of Irish Schoolmistresses, 1882–1906, priv. coll. · Reports of the Association of Irish Schoolmistresses, 1882–1969, priv. coll. · W. G. Brooke, *Statement of the proceedings, 1892–1895, in connexion with the movement for the admission of women to TCD* (1895) · 'Appendix to the first report: minutes of evidence', *Parl. papers* (1901), 31.218, Cd 826 [commission on university education, Ireland] · 'Appendix to the final report of the commissioners: minutes of evidence', *Parl. papers* (1899), 23.456, C. 9512 [intermediate education (Ireland) commission] · Alexandra College council minute books, 1866–1902, Alexandra College, Dublin · M. O'Neill, 'The Dublin Women's Suffrage Association and its successors', *Dublin Historical Record*, 38 (1984–5), 126–40 · private information (2004) · baptismal cert., RCB Library, Dublin · d. cert. · Alexandra College, Dublin, Alice Oldham MSS · *Thom's directory* · *Irish Times* (22 Jan 1907)

Archives Alexandra College, Dublin · TCD, board of TCD minute book · TCD, council of TCD minute book, University of Dublin · TCD, papers on admission of women to TCD | priv. coll., minute books of the Association of Irish Schoolmistresses · priv. coll., reports of the Association of Irish Schoolmistresses

Likenesses group portrait, 1884 (with the first nine women graduates of the Royal University of Ireland), Alexandra College Library, Dublin

Wealth at death £534 5s.: probate, 9 March 1907, *CGPLA Ire.*

Oldham, Charles James (1843–1907). *See under* Oldham, Henry (1815–1902).

Oldham, Henry (1815–1902), obstetric physician, was born in Balham, Surrey, on 31 January 1815, the sixth son and ninth child of Adam Oldham (1781–1839), solicitor, and his wife, Ann Lane Penny, daughter of William Stubbington Penny. His father's family claimed descent from Hugh Oldham, bishop of Exeter, the founder of Corpus Christi College, Oxford, and of the Manchester grammar school, and another forebear, Francis Penny, was at one time the editor of the *Gentleman's Magazine*. One of Oldham's nephews, **Charles James Oldham** (1843–1907), son of James Oldham (1817–1881), who, like his father, practised as a surgeon in Brighton, invented a refracting ophthalmoscope, and bequeathed £50,000 to public institutions, including the Manchester grammar school, Corpus Christi College, Oxford, and the universities of both Oxford and Cambridge, for the foundation of Charles Oldham scholarships and prizes for classical and Shakespearian study. He died in Brighton on 24 January 1907.

After education at Mr Balaam's school at Clapham (1824–31) and at London University, Henry Oldham entered Guy's Hospital medical school in 1834. In May 1837 he became MRCS and the following September a licentiate of the Society of Apothecaries. In 1843 he took the LRCP and in 1857 he became FRCP; he graduated MD at St Andrews in 1858. In 1849, with Dr J. C. W. Lever, he was appointed physician accoucheur and lecturer on midwifery and diseases of women at Guy's Hospital; after twenty years' service he became consulting obstetric physician.

Oldham was an excellent teacher and an impressive lecturer. He was a regular contributor to the *Guy's Hospital Reports*, and published four papers in the *Transactions of the Obstetrical Society of London*, of which he was one of the founders, an original trustee, and subsequently president (1863–5). He invented the term 'missed labour' to describe those cases where the child dies in the womb and labour fails to come on, though the specimen on which he had based his view was subsequently differently interpreted; he also advanced the hypothesis that menstruation was due to periodic excitation of the ovaries, and gave his name to an obstetric instrument, the Oldham perforator. Before his appointment to Guy's Hospital, Oldham had studied embryology in the developing chick by means of coloured injections and the microscope and he subsequently introduced the use of the microscope at Guy's, where he pursued his interest in morbid anatomy. He did not believe in the extensive use of drugs, placing greater emphasis on diet and hygiene as the means to restore health. He was a great walker, an extremely simple eater, and for the last fifteen years of his life he was a vegetarian.

In 1838 Oldham married Sophia (*d.* 1885), eldest daughter of James Smith of Peckham; they had four daughters and two sons, of whom one died in infancy and the other was Colonel Sir Henry Hugh Oldham CVO, lieutenant of the Honourable Corps of Gentlemen-at-Arms. Oldham had an extensive and lucrative practice in the City of London, first at 13 Devonshire Square, Bishopsgate Street, and then at 25 Finsbury Square; about 1870 he moved to 4 Cavendish Place and in 1899 he retired to Bournemouth. Oldham died at Boscombe, Bournemouth, on 19 November 1902, of heart failure, and was buried in Bournemouth cemetery.   H. D. ROLLESTON, *rev.* ORNELLA MOSCUCCI

Sources *Transactions of the Obstetrical Society of London*, 45 (1903), 71 · *Guy's Hospital Gazette*, [3rd ser.], 16 (1902), 505 · private information (1912) [H. H. Oldham and F. Taylor] · *CGPLA Eng. & Wales* (1902); (1907) · Munk, *Roll*
Likenesses Maull & Polyblank, photograph, Wellcome L. · photograph, Wellcome L.
Wealth at death £203,018 4s. 7d.: probate, 8 Dec 1902, *CGPLA Eng. & Wales* · £77,959 16s. 11d.—Charles James Oldham: probate, 1907, *CGPLA Eng. & Wales*

Oldham, Hugh (*c.*1450–1519), bishop of Exeter, was a younger son of Roger and Margery Oldham, apparently minor gentry with property at Ancoats in Salford, Lancashire. His brother Bernard (*d.* 1515) also became a cleric, rising, by his brother's gift, to be archdeacon of Cornwall and treasurer of Exeter Cathedral. Hugh Oldham is first mentioned as a 'clerk, of Durham' in 1475, which suggests that he was born about 1450 and brought up or given early employment in the household of Laurence Booth, bishop of Durham (*d.* 1480), whose own family came from Barton, near Eccles, which was close to Ancoats. By 1488 he was rector of Lanivet, Cornwall, and servant to William Smith (*d.* 1514), keeper of the hanaper in the royal chancery. He also attended university, although it is not clear when. In 1493, on a claim of having studied arts for four years and canon and civil law for four, at Oxford in each case, he was granted a grace to enter in law at Cambridge, evidently as a bachelor of civil (and perhaps canon) law, not as a doctor. There is no contemporary evidence to support Thomas Fuller's assertion of 1662 that he was a member of Queens' College, Cambridge.

By 1492 Oldham had entered the service of Lady Margaret Beaufort, countess of Richmond and Derby (*d.* 1509)—a relationship that seems to have begun in his maturity, rather than through his being educated by her as used to be supposed. He was receiver of her west country estates in that year and rose to be chancellor of her household by 1503, a position he resigned on becoming a bishop. Another of his patrons was his old employer William Smith, now bishop of Lichfield, who in 1496 made Oldham master of the hospital of St John, Lichfield, which Smith had recently reformed to include a free grammar school and almshouse; the post did not require residence. During the 1490s Oldham gained a large amount of church preferment, including cathedral canonries at Exeter, Lichfield, Lincoln, St Paul's, Salisbury, and York, several parochial benefices, the deanery of Wimborne, Dorset in 1499, and the archdeaconry of Exeter about 1502. By 24 January 1503 he was important enough to be included in the group of leading clergy and laity who laid the foundation stone of Henry VII's chapel in Westminster Abbey. On 27 November 1504 he was provided by the pope to be bishop of Exeter and was consecrated on 12 January 1505.

Later tradition at Exeter attributed this promotion to Lady Margaret's influence.

Oldham's episcopal register, though informative, is only a selective record of his activities, but he seems to have been a conscientious bishop. He anticipated the Reformation by annexing the decayed hospitals of Clyst Gabriel and Warland, Devon, to the vicars-choral of Exeter Cathedral to provide common meals in their college (1508–9). He issued statutes for the cathedral in 1511, regulating a wide variety of matters, and joined with Sir John Speke, a local knight, in adding two new chapels to the east end of the building. His closure of Warland Hospital in 1509 involved a successful struggle with the Trinitarian friars of Hounslow, Middlesex, who claimed the place as their house, but his attempts to exert authority over the Benedictine abbey of Tavistock, Devon, were frustrated in 1517 when the abbey gained papal exemption from episcopal jurisdiction. The Exeter historian John Hooker, who collected memories of Oldham in the later sixteenth century, wrote that 'albeit he was not very much learned, yet [he was] a great favourer and a friend both to learning and to learned men' (Exeter City Archives, bk 51, fol. 337r). This is supported by evidence of an examination system for ordination candidates during his reign, and by his choice of university graduates for most of the diocesan officers and cathedral clergy whom he appointed. Like William Smith and Richard Fox (d. 1528), bishop of Durham and Winchester, with whom he had close relationships, he developed a strong interest in promoting education. At Exeter he ordered the adolescent clerks of the cathedral choir to attend the city high school, while at Manchester, near his place of origin, he played a major role in establishing the free grammar school, a project which had begun in 1508. Oldham gave money and property to the school, and its statutes (1515, revised in 1525), which adopted practices from the school foundations of William Smith at Banbury, Oxfordshire, and John Colet at St Paul's, London, probably reflect his influence.

Oldham also patronized higher education. According to Hooker, he thought of assisting Exeter College, Oxford, and William Smith's new college of Brasenose there, but was rebuffed in both cases—an assertion untrue in the case of Brasenose, where Oldham's coat of arms formerly appeared in a library window. His chief university benefaction, however, was directed to Richard Fox's Oxford foundation, Corpus Christi College. Oldham gave £4000 and land in Chelsea towards the project, was officially recognized as a benefactor, and was commemorated in daily prayers. Fox's first known scheme for this college, dated 1513, envisaged a foundation for monks and secular scholars, but in 1517, when the first statutes were issued, the monks were omitted. The Exeter tradition collected by Hooker attributed this change to Oldham, who allegedly counselled Fox that 'monks were but a sort of bussing [buzzing] flies, and whose state could not long endure' (Vowell, fol. h2), or, as another version of the story put it, 'What, my lord, shall we build houses and provide livelihoods for a company of bussing monks, whose end

and fall we ourselves may live to see?' (Holinshed's Chronicles, 3.617). The anecdote probably takes some of its colour from post-Reformation hindsight.

Hooker summarized Oldham as 'a man having more zeal than knowledge and more devotion than learning; somewhat rough in speeches but friendly in doings' (Vowell, fol. h2). The bishop made his will on 16 December 1518. He died on 25 June 1519, and was buried in the chapel he had built in Exeter Cathedral and dedicated to St Saviour. His tomb includes a painted effigy and there is a portrait of him at Corpus Christi College.

NICHOLAS ORME

Sources Emden, *Oxf.* • Emden, *Cam.* • A. A. Mumford, *Hugh Oldham, 1452[?]–1519* (1936) • J. Hooker [J. Vowell], *A catalog of the bishops of Excester* (1584), fol. h.ij r–v • *Holinshed's chronicles of England, Scotland and Ireland*, ed. H. Ellis, 3 (1808), 617 • *VCH Lancashire*, 4.239 • M. K. Jones and M. G. Underwood, *The king's mother: Lady Margaret Beaufort, countess of Richmond and Derby* (1992), 279–80 • *Fasti Angl., 1300–1541*, [Exeter] • G. Oliver, *Lives of the bishops of Exeter, and a history of the cathedral* (1861), 465–9 • N. Orme, 'The medieval clergy of Exeter Cathedral, 1: the vicars and annuellars', *Report and Transactions of the Devonshire Association*, 113 (1981), 79–102, esp. 88–9 • N. Orme, 'Warland Hospital, Totnes, and the Trinitarian friars in Devon', *Devon and Cornwall Notes and Queries*, 36 (1987–91), 41–8 • N. Orme, 'The witch, the clock and the bishop', *Annual Report* [Friends of Exeter Cathedral], 65 (1995), 9–13 • G. Oliver, *Monasticon dioecesis Exoniensis* (1846), 92, 103–4 • T. Fowler, *The history of Corpus Christi College*, OHS, 25 (1893) • S. Hibbert and W. R. Whatton, *History of the foundations in Manchester of Christ's College, Chetham's Hospital and the free grammar school*, 4 vols. (1828–48), vol.3, pp. 3–33 • Devon RO, Exeter city archives, book 51, fols. 336v–337

Archives Devon RO, episcopal register, Charter XIII | Devon RO, Exeter city archives, book 51, fols. 336v–337

Likenesses effigy on tomb, Exeter Cathedral • oils, CCC Oxf.

Oldham, John (*bap.* 1592, *d.* 1636), trader and colonist in America, was baptized at All Saints', Derby, Derbyshire, on 14 July 1592, the son of William Oldham. Nothing else is known of his early life until he sailed to Plymouth, New England, in 1623 on the *Anne*, with his wife (the widow of one Bridges), his stepson William Bridges, and at least seven other associates. Although his sister Lucretia married, at Plymouth, Jonathan Brewster, son of the separatist leader William *Brewster, Oldham was one of the early Plymouth residents who were not associated with the Leiden congregation, and had no interest in promoting the religious activities of that group. Instead, he allied himself in 1624 with the newly arrived John Lyford, a Church of England clergyman and not a separatist. Oldham, Lyford, and others were soon banished from Plymouth, settled briefly at Nantasket, and then dispersed. By 1628 Oldham had redeemed himself sufficiently in the eyes of the Plymouth authorities that he was assigned the job of escorting back to England in 1628 the troublemaker Thomas Morton of Merrymount. While in England in 1629 Oldham approached the Council for New England and obtained a grant of land in Massachusetts Bay, which conflicted with the grant made by the king to the Massachusetts Bay Company. This led, not surprisingly, to disputes between Oldham and the Massachusetts Bay Company. The company got the better of the argument but Oldham did end up with a grant of 500 acres of land within the boundaries of the town of Watertown. He settled there in 1630 and embarked on a career of coastal trading.

By 1636 Oldham had made useful contacts with the Narragansetts, and had received a grant from their leader, Canonicus, of Prudence Island in Narragansett Bay. In July that year he was trading in the area of Block Island and Fisher's Island with 'two English boys, and two Indians of Narragansett' (Bradford, 166) when another coastal trader discovered Oldham's boat, containing his mutilated body. This incident was but one of the many episodes of conflict between the Narragansetts and the Pequots which led up to the Pequot War of 1637.

At the time of Oldham's death he was still considered a member of the Watertown congregation, but had apparently moved his residence, or at least the base of his trading activities, to Hartford, for his will was proved there, and showed £504 9s. 3d. in debts, against £136 66s. 21d. [sic] in assets. In 1644 his stepson William Bridges unsuccessfully petitioned the Massachusetts Bay general court for a grant of land in consideration of Oldham's services to the colony.   ROBERT CHARLES ANDERSON

Sources R. C. Anderson, *The great migration begins: immigrants to New England, 1620–1633*, vol. 2 (1995) · W. Bradford, *Of Plymouth Plantation, 1620–1647*, ed. S. E. Morison (1952) · C. W. Manwaring, 'Haynes, John', *A digest of the early Connecticut probate records*, 1 (1904), 25–8 · parish register, All Saints', 14 July 1592 [baptism]
Wealth at death £133 66s. 21d. in assets and £504 9s. 3d. in debts: Manwaring, *Digest*

Oldham, John (1653–1683), poet, was born on 9 August 1653 at Shipton Moyne, Gloucestershire, where his grandfather, also John (1594–1657), was rector. The poet's father, another John (1629–1716), was rector of the adjoining parish of Long Newton, Wiltshire, from which he was ejected in 1662, but he survived on the proceeds of a small estate and a school. He took charge of his son's early education before sending him to Tetbury grammar school for two years, and thence to Oxford, where Oldham matriculated at St Edmund Hall on 17 June 1670. In 1674 his BA was granted subject to the performance of certain public exercises, but Oldham did not complete these, and returned home without a degree, probably to teach in his father's school for a year or two.

Thereafter, while Oldham developed his poetic skills, he earned his living as a schoolmaster and private tutor, first as usher at Whitgift School, Croydon (1676–9), then in the household of Sir Edward Thurland at Reigate. At one or more points in his life he seems to have made a bid for independence, and 'An allusion to Martial' (c.1681) recounts that the author is living in a garret at the far end of Clerkenwell—though this need not be autobiographical. But (as several of his poems make clear) poetry did not pay, and he soon took another tutorship, this time in the family of Sir William Hickes, of Low Leyton, Essex. Here he studied medicine with the distinguished physician Dr Robert Lower. In June 1682 William Pierrepont, fourth earl of Kingston, became his patron.

Oldham's early poems were addressed to friends and neighbours, with some love poems and Pindaric imitations of Cowley, notably a long ode in memory of his close

friend Charles Morwent (1675), and another on the death of the Croydon worthy Harman Atwood (1677). In 1677 he published a Pindaric poem on the marriage of Prince William of Orange and Princess Mary, which was his first work to appear in print. Cowley would remain a principal influence, and the Pindaric ode a favourite form. But at some point Oldham grew acquainted with the poetry and reputation of the earl of Rochester, and then with the earl himself. His first poem to achieve renown was 'Aude aliquid. Ode' (written in 1676 at Croydon), which circulated in manuscript and appeared in a pirated printed edition in 1679 under the misleading title *A Satyr Against Vertue*. This was imagined to be Rochester's speech on smashing the phallic glass sundials in the king's privy garden in 1675, and its satirical impersonation of Rochester's libertine stance drew an appreciative visit from the earl and his entourage. The 'Dithyrambique on Drinking: Suppos'd to be Spoken by Rochester at the Guinny-Club' and 'Sardanapalus', an erotic heroic extravaganza too obscene for publication, completed a trio of poems satirically mimicking libertine attitudes with such bravura that some readers failed to see their ironic purpose. 'Upon the Author of the Play call'd *Sodom*' (the pornographic drama often attributed to Rochester, and certainly from his circle) is itself characterized by obscenity, and it too remained in manuscript until it was printed in the unauthorized *Poems on Several Occasions by the Right Honourable the E. of R—* (1680). Sir William Soame criticized Oldham's penchant for obscenity in manuscript verses addressed 'To the author of *Sardanapalus*, upon that and his other writings', urging him to refine his verse through the study of Horace and Boileau—which in due course Oldham did.

Oldham's first substantial volume was *Satyrs upon the Jesuits* (written in 1679, published anonymously in 1680, dated 1681). Prompted by the Popish Plot, and informed by extensive reading, these anti-Catholic satires attacked the Jesuits' equivocation, murderous plotting, and gulling of the populace. The first of them, *Garnet's Ghost*, appeared as a pirated publication in 1679, and its evident popularity may have prompted Oldham to complete the set of four satires and to add a prologue. They are robust, vigorous work, rough in versification, coarse in vocabulary, and unsparing in their vilification of Catholic beliefs. They demonstrate Oldham's mastery of the couplet form, and his continuing interest in heroic satirical modes. To many readers these have been the poems by which Oldham has been known, but they are unedifying, and better work would follow. The volume was rounded out by 'Aude aliquid. Ode', 'A Satyr upon a Woman, who by her Falshood and Scorn was the Death of my Friend', and a translation of 'The Passion of Byblis' from Ovid's *Metamorphoses*, the latter prompted by the appearance in 1680 of John Dryden's *Ovid's Epistles*. Of these, 'Byblis' still deserves attention (and was admired at the time) for its portrayal of the psychology of sexual desire, and shows more variety of tone and a subtler handling of verse than the rest of the collection.

As if to demonstrate that he was more than a purveyor

of rough satire and near pornography, Oldham's next volume, *Some New Pieces* (1681), also anonymous, featured a range of translations from the classics. Here Oldham found his true métier, developing the art of 'imitation' or the free transposition of Latin originals into contemporary English dress. The collection starts with a version of Horace's *Ars poetica* which breathes Oldham's characteristic devotion to poetry as a vocation, followed by his *Serm.*, i.9 ('the bore'), in which the scene is transferred to London and Oldham shows his genius for catching conversational idiom in verse. Imitations of Horace's *Odes*, i.31 and ii.14, have a more meditative tone. Among the finest of Oldham's poems is 'A letter from the country to a friend in town, giving an account of the author's inclinations to poetry' (written in 1678), which expresses his passionate commitment to the life of a poet despite its lack of financial rewards, and includes a remarkable passage imagining the emergence of poetry from the author's unconscious into his conscious mind:

> When at first search I traverse o're my mind,
> Nought but a dark and empty Void I find:
> Some little hints at length, like sparks, break thence,
> And glimm'ring Thoughts just dawning into sence:
> Confus'd a while the mixt Idea's lie,
> With nought of mark to be discover'd by,
> Like colours undistinguish't in the night,
> Till the dusk images, mov'd to the light,
> Teach the discerning Faculty to chuse,
> Which it had best adopt, and which refuse.
> (ll. 168–77)

Besides a Pindaric 'Praise of Homer', and a pair of religious poems, the volume also includes a beautiful, mellifluous elegy for Rochester (praised by Ezra Pound in his *ABC of Reading*, 1934, for its cantabile qualities) in the form of a translation of Moschus's pastoral lament for Bion. This fine collection demonstrated Oldham's range of voices, and staked a claim for him as a leading figure among those poets such as Dryden and Roscommon who were fashioning a distinctively English form of classicism.

Poems and Translations (1683) continued the trend established by *Some New Pieces*, and indicated that Oldham had been studying the recent satires of Nicolas Boileau-Despréaux. An unfinished manuscript translation of *Le lutrin* written in 1678 shows that he had been experimenting with Boileau in his attempts to catch the right tone for heroic or mock heroic satire, and this new volume included versions of Boileau's *Satires* 5 and 8. It was Boileau's transposition of Juvenal's *Satire 3* from Rome to Paris that inspired Oldham to his own vigorous imitation of the same original, a vivid evocation of the hazards of life in Restoration London, rendered with a fair imitation of Juvenal's overheated indignation. Other classical translations broaden the collection in style and subject: verses from Anacreon, Catullus, Horace, Martial, Petronius. Two other satires attest to Oldham's fiercely proud independence. 'A Satyr: the Person of Spenser is Brought in, Dissuading the Author from the Study of Poetry' denounces the contemporary neglect of poets and poetry. 'A Satyr addressed to a friend that is about to leave the university and come abroad in the world' includes sharp passages on

the humiliations of life as a chaplain or tutor in great houses, and concludes with an eloquent version of the fable of the wolf and the dog. The wolf envies the dog's comfortable condition, until he notices the scar of the collar round his neck, and proudly embraces freedom with poverty rather than luxury with servitude.

Oldham died of smallpox in the earl of Kingston's house at Holme Pierrepont, Nottinghamshire, where he was buried in the local church on 7 December 1683, aged only thirty. A fine memorial was erected over his grave in the style of Grinling Gibbons. After his death, a volume of *Remains* (1684, 2nd edn 1687) collected up some minor pieces, but is chiefly remarkable for the commemorative poems with which it begins, headed by Dryden's 'To the Memory of Mr Oldham', and continuing with tributes by Thomas D'Urfey, Thomas Flatman, and Nahum Tate among others. Dryden sees him as a kindred spirit:

> Farewell, too little and too lately known,
> Whom I began to think and call my own:
> For sure our Souls were near ally'd; and thine
> Cast in the same poetic mould with mine.
> (ll. 1–4)

It is possible that the *Satyrs upon the Jesuits* helped stimulate Dryden to write *Absalom and Achitophel*, and that Oldham's classical imitations of the early 1680s encouraged Dryden to embark on the succession of magnificent translations which appeared from 1685 onwards. To Dryden, Oldham's verse was rough, but that was appropriate for satire, for

> Wit will shine
> Through the harsh cadence of a rugged line.
> A noble Error, and but seldom made,
> When Poets are by too much force betray'd.
> (ll. 15–18)

Oldham's four volumes were gathered together with a new title-page to constitute his *Works* (1684) and frequently reprinted into the early eighteenth century. Pope read him carefully, but thought him 'too much like Billingsgate' (Spence, 1.202), and he was not included among Johnson's poets. A corrupt and bowdlerized selection appeared in 1854. With renewed interest in Restoration satire and in the history of the classical imitation, his reputation grew somewhat in the twentieth century, thanks largely to the scholarly and critical labours of Harold F. Brooks, which culminated in his edition of 1987. This adds a number of poems printed from manuscript, including material from Oldham's rough drafts and fair copies which are preserved in the Bodleian Library (MS Rawlinson poet. 123).

Though uneven, and in places scatological and obscene, Oldham's work has passion and power; his range is wider than is commonly supposed, he shows great versatility in his handling of the couplet, and adopts an attractive variety of conversational voices. Liberty and poetry are his most cherished themes. Dryden thought of him as the great classical poet whom England never had—the heir who died before his time, the lost hero of Augustan England. It is in these terms that Dryden takes leave of Oldham, in moving lines which conclude what is perhaps the finest elegy in the language:

Once more, hail and farewel; farewel thou young,
But ah too short, *Marcellus* of our Tongue;
Thy Brows with Ivy, and with Laurels bound;
But Fate and gloomy Night encompass thee around.
(ll. 22–25)

PAUL HAMMOND

Sources *The poems of John Oldham*, ed. H. F. Brooks and R. Selden (1987) · *The poems of John Dryden*, ed. J. Kinsley, 4 vols. (1958) · J. Spence, *Observations, anecdotes, and characters, of books and men*, ed. J. M. Osborn, new edn, 2 vols. (1966)
Archives Bodl. Oxf., rough drafts and fair copies, MS Rawlinson poet. 123
Likenesses M. Vandergucht, line engraving, BM, NPG; repro. in Oldham, *Works* (1703) · oils, priv. coll.

Oldham, John (1779–1840), artist and mechanical inventor, was born in Dublin. He served an apprenticeship to an engraver at a calico printing works in Dublin but subsequently pursued a career as an artist. While based at Newry he also developed his interest in mechanics. He invented a machine for individually numbering banknotes to prevent forgery and, in 1812, laid his plans before the Bank of Ireland. In 1814 he was appointed as full-time artist to the bank, and signed over his rights to the invention. His son Thomas Oldham [*see below*] became his apprentice and assistant in 1816, succeeding to his father's position in 1836. Between 1836 and 1840, in the service of the Bank of England, John Oldham made further improvements to the machinery for printing and numbering banknotes, which effected considerable savings in manpower. The machinery continued in use until 1852–3, when a system of surface printing was adopted.

Oldham took a keen interest in marine propulsion, obtaining in 1817 a patent for propelling ships by means of paddles worked by steam engine, an attempt to imitate the normal motion of a paddle. In 1820 he patented an improvement, the paddles being revolved about a shaft placed across the ship and feathered by an adaptation of the gearing used in the original patent. Though very imperfect, the contrivance was used in the *Aaron Manby*, the first seagoing iron ship to be constructed. A further development of the idea resulted in the construction of a feathering paddle-wheel, patented in 1827. His combined system of warming and ventilating buildings, by circulating preheated, filtered, and purified air through the space to be heated, was introduced into both the Bank of Ireland and the Bank of England.

Enjoying a large salary, with the right of a reversion of a portion to his son, Oldham was celebrated for his convivial powers. He died, of an internal haemorrhage, at his house in Montague Street, Russell Square, London, on 14 February 1840.

Thomas Oldham (1801–1851), the eldest of John Oldham's seventeen children, succeeded to his father's position as artist to the Bank of Ireland, where he became involved with the engineering aspects of the machinery employed to print banknotes. He was elected associate of the Institution of Civil Engineers in March 1841. In 1842 he read a paper to the institution 'On the introduction of letterpress printing for numbering and dating the notes of the Bank of England', and the following year one entitled

'A description of the automatic balance at the Bank of England invented by W. Cotton', for which he received a Telford medal. He died at Brussels on 7 November 1851.

R. B. PROSSER, *rev.* R. C. COX

Sources Court of Directors minute books, 1812–37, Bank of Ireland, Dublin · *Mechanics' Magazine*, 32 (1840), 400 · *PICE*, 1 (1841), 14–15 · J. Francis, *History of the Bank of England* (1847), 232 · C. W. Williams, 'Mr Oldham's system of warming and ventilating', *Civil Engineer and Architect's Journal*, 2 (1839), 96–7 · W. G. Strickland, *A dictionary of Irish artists*, 2 (1913); facs. edn with introduction by T. J. Snoddy (1969), 193–5 · *GM*, 2nd ser., 13 (1840), 670

Oldham, Joseph Houldsworth (1874–1969), missionary, was born in Girgaum, Bombay, India, on 10 October 1874, the eldest son of Lieutenant-Colonel George Wingate Oldham RE (1840–1923), and his wife, Eliza (Lillah) Houldsworth (*d.* 1890). George Oldham retired early from his successful career to take his delicate wife home. Oldham attended the Edinburgh Academy and, passing out dux in 1892, entered Trinity College, Oxford, where he obtained a second class in both honour moderations (1894) and *literae humaniores* (1896), with a career in the Indian Civil Service in mind. His plans changed as the result of a religious conversion under the influence of D. L. Moody, the American evangelist. Having signed the pledge of the Student Volunteer Missionary Union, and after working as the first secretary to the Student Christian Mission (1896–7), he went to India in 1897 under the auspices of the Scottish YMCA to work among students and government employees in Lahore. The following year he married Mary (*d.* 1965), only daughter of Sir Andrew Fraser, later governor of Bengal. They had no children.

Oldham spent three years in India, almost entirely in the company of Indians, and became very sensitive to their aspirations. After catching typhoid he was invalided home and in 1901 entered New College, Edinburgh, where he completed his theological studies with distinction. He then went to the University of Halle, Germany, to study missionary theory and practice under Gustav Warneck. Although never ordained, Oldham became a ministerial assistant at Free St George's, Edinburgh, and worked to promote the study of missions among students and in Scottish congregations. Throughout his life he saw the work of the laity and the involvement of youth as everywhere crucial to the future of the church and its mission. In 1908 he was appointed full-time organizing secretary for the Edinburgh World Missionary Conference of 1910. The conference included not only all shades of Anglican opinion but also members of the younger churches, as Oldham had hoped, and can be regarded as the start of the modern ecumenical movement. His own remarkable administrative success led the conference to appoint him secretary to a proposed 'Edinburgh continuation committee' under the chairmanship of his close friend John R. Mott, the American evangelist.

In the brief period before the First World War Oldham managed to meet the main mission boards on the continent, in Great Britain, and in America. Most significant among the committee's ventures was the *International*

Review of Missions, established in 1912 with Oldham as editor. He created a distinguished quarterly by his editorials and comprehensive reviews of the year, and by enlisting as contributors not only outstanding missionaries but scientists and administrators. He won Roman Catholic co-operation and continued as editor until 1927.

Although the continuation committee foundered, Oldham, as the servant of all missions and especially of those hardest hit by the war, tried to keep the spirit of internationalism alive. Working through both the Conference of British Missionary Societies (CBMS) and the committee on missions and governments, Oldham approached heads of government departments on delicate matters such as the internment of German missionaries in India and their expulsion from their African spheres. He was successful in preventing the confiscation of German mission properties; he negotiated the terms for the ultimate return of German missionaries and, with Archbishop Randall Davidson, secured the inclusion in the peace treaty of a clause guaranteeing freedom for missions in former German colonies. In 1920 Joe Oldham, as he was commonly and affectionately known, prepared proposals for a new departure in international missionary co-operation, with the result that in 1921 he became secretary of a new International Missionary Council (IMC), its membership comprising national or regional councils of churches and missions. To further his plans he visited India, China, and Canada (1922–3), and played a crucial role in securing strong Indian representation in the National Christian Council there. The government's recognition of Oldham's unique position as spokesman for so many missions, his mastery of facts, and his recognition that 'governments must govern', established him as a trusted adviser.

Occasionally Oldham was an equally effective critic of government policies. His writings included *The World and the Gospel* (1916) which sold more than 20,000 copies in Britain alone and helped to lift the sights of war-engrossed Christians to the world beyond Europe, above all to Africa.

> Shall the African peoples be enabled to develop their latent powers, to cultivate their peculiar gifts and so enrich the life of humanity by their distinctive contributions? Or shall they be depressed and degraded and made the tool of others?
> (Bliss, 576)

For Oldham this was 'one of the great issues of history' (ibid.) and, as he told Colin Leys, required for him 'the throwing of the weight of missionary influence more definitely and explicitly on the side of justice and the treatment of native populations' (Cell, 145). Soon after the war he joined forces with Bishop Frank Weston, among others, in opposition to forced labour in Kenya. Unable to obtain satisfaction from the secretary of state for the colonies, Oldham organized a massive and highly successful protest by politicians of all parties, humanitarians such as the Anti-Slavery Society, religious leaders, academics, and editors of the national press. In general, however, he preferred quietly to pursue the art of the possible. After Edinburgh, his move to London, the IMC's office in Chelsea,

and membership of the Athenaeum, were positively conducive to constructive compromises behind the scenes. His knowledge of both the Kenyan and the Indian scenes thrust him unexpectedly in 1922–3 into the role of mediator between Europeans and Indians in Kenya. His own principle that, whatever the claims of white settlers or Indians, native African interests should be paramount was eventually spelt out in July 1923 in the imperial government's important statement of policy known as the 'Devonshire declaration'.

Oldham's lifelong interest in education centred at first on India, but his main achievement was in relation to Africa. Despite official reluctance he set out to persuade the Colonial Office in close co-operation with the missions to play a more positive role. Having visited institutions for the education of black people in the southern United States as early as 1912, Oldham worked closely with the Phelps–Stokes Fund on its visits to east Africa in the early 1920s and its recommendations to the British government. With support from several colonial governors and missionary societies he developed proposals that led to the establishment in 1923 of the advisory committee on native education in tropical Africa. Oldham was an active member from its inception until 1936 and, with Sir Frederick Lugard, drafted what became an important statement of policy ('Memorandum on native education in British tropical Africa', *Parl. papers*, 1924–5, 21, Cmd 2374).

From his base in the international missionary movement Oldham thus contributed enormously to the postwar definition of concepts of imperial 'trusteeship'. Very soon his work was given institutional form. In 1926 he organized at High Legh the first conference of missionary educators and colonial administrators, and seized on a suggestion made there for an international institute of African languages and cultures. His links with the Colonial Offices of European governments, his access to Rockefeller funds, and the aid of helpers such as Edwin Smith and Diedrich Westermann enabled him to bring the idea into effect. Lugard became its chairman. From 1931 to 1938 Oldham was administrative director, promoting a research and publications programme which included the distinguished journal *Africa*, Professor B. Malinowski's seminars for young anthropologists, and Lord Hailey's influential *An African Survey* (1938). In 1924 Oldham had published his most influential book, *Christianity and the Race Problem*. As its author he was invited to visit southern and east Africa in 1926. In South Africa he was appalled by the 'colour bar' act, for 'doctrines of racial domination', he was convinced, would lead the world 'directly and inevitably to catastrophe' (*Christianity and the Race Problem*, 9). In east Africa, however, he saw more hope and seriously considered becoming research director to Kenya's governor, Sir Edward Grigg (later Lord Altrincham). Instead he accepted appointment to the commission on closer union between the east African territories, chaired by Sir E. Hilton Young (later Lord Kennet). Oldham and Sir George Schuster wrote its intricate and carefully argued report. Vociferous opposition from the Kenya settlers, coupled with the chairman's refusal to sign, seemed to incline the imperial government towards handing over control to the settlers. Once more Oldham, with the support of the CBMS and again in partnership with Lugard, organized successful pressure and secured reference of the issue to a joint select committee of both houses of parliament (1931). *What is at Stake in East Africa* and *White and Black in Africa* both appeared in 1930, each in its own way attacking that 'most dangerous doctrine' (Oldham to Mott, 21 Nov 1929, J. R. Mott MSS) of 'white Christian settler civilization' as Africa's best hope.

The need for broader missionary perspectives and closer co-operation between missions and state if African interests were to be served in the modern world were themes central to the conference Oldham organized at Le Zoute, Belgium, in 1926. They also influenced his own decision in 1928 to go with Hilton Young to east Africa rather than join the missions at the Jerusalem world conference, and informed the many speeches he made on both sides of the Atlantic which were summarized in *The New Christian Adventure* (1929). Its theological justification Oldham saw in the need for a new missionary approach to engage effectively with a worldwide secular culture, one in which the 'field' and the 'base' of such a mission were everywhere and its chief agents the Christian laity. To supplement the mastery of nature and control of the future which science was progressively achieving there must be an attitude to life based on relationship—man with nature, man with man, and man with God. He introduced the thought of Eberhard Grisebach and Martin Buber to English-speaking audiences, and this 'relational' philosophy informed his later books, *Real Life is Meeting* (1941) and *Life is Commitment* (1953).

Oldham's donnish earnestness and infinite capacity for taking pains bred impatience with inward-looking missionary conferences that failed to seek clear or practical answers to well defined questions. This was heightened by his engagement with governments and public policy, as well as by his mounting deafness in middle life and the logistics of managing his vast hearing aid. Mott and the IMC, however, several times refused his resignation, preferring instead to appoint an additional secretary and to allow Oldham leeway for his own preoccupations. These lay not with ecclesiastical organization but with other forms of support for the laity, trying to live out their faith in the world. In 1934, therefore, Oldham became chairman of the research committee for the Universal Christian Council for Life and Work, and began preparations for the world conference of church, community, and state. Racist philosophies, the growth of totalitarian states, and the church policies of the German government all gave particular point to Oldham's sustained attempt to arouse Christians and others to the issues at stake. This was perhaps his most successful educative campaign, helping to shape Christian thinking for a generation. Before and after the conference, held at Oxford in 1937, essential steps were also taken to bring existing ecumenical movements into a single world council whose members would be individual churches. Archbishop William Temple provided the leadership, Oldham the agenda,

looking forward to the World Council of Churches in 1948.

On retirement in 1938 from the IMC and the International Institute, Oldham remained as active as ever. To carry on the ideas of the life and work conference, he founded the fortnightly *Christian News Letter* in 1939 and edited it throughout the war. The Christian Frontier Council, founded in 1942 as a lay movement bringing together lay expertise and Christian insight, was also his conception. His great capacity for friendship, his eye for issues of the moment, and his management of small discussion groups were legendary. Some of these (for example, *The Era of Atomic Power*, 1947) produced corporate findings. Others, such as the 'Moot', a group of intellectuals drawn to Oldham who included T. S. Eliot and Karl Mannheim, had their outcome in the thought and writings of the members.

Public recognition also came with the degrees of DD conferred on Oldham by Edinburgh (1931) and Oxford (1937) and a CBE in 1951. In 1952 he moved to Dunford House, near Midhurst, where he not only walked in the Sussex countryside but also wrote his last book. As the affairs of east and central Africa again became critical, his *New Hope in Africa* (1955) was a warm but ill judged response to the multiracial enthusiasms of a new generation represented by the Capricorn Africa Society. He died on 16 May 1969 at St Leonards, Sussex.

KATHLEEN BLISS, rev. ANDREW PORTER

Sources K. Bliss, 'J. H. Oldham, 1874–1969: from "Edinburgh 1910" to the World Council of Churches', *Mission legacies*, ed. G. H. Anderson and others (1994) [incl. work list] · Yale U., divinity school, Mott papers, MS Group 45 · *By Kenya possessed: the correspondence of Norman Leys and J. H. Oldham, 1918–1926*, ed. J. W. Cell (1976) · C. H. Hopkins, *John R. Mott, 1865–1955: a biography* (1974) · *The Edinburgh Academy register: a record of all those who have entered the school since its foundation in 1824* (1914) · *The Edinburgh Academy list, 1888–1964* (1965) · *DNB* · *WWW* · T. W. J. Conolly and R. F. Edwards, eds., *Roll of officers of the corps of royal engineers from 1660 to 1898* (1898) · *Army List (1882–1924)* [sel. vols.] · K. Clements, *Faith on the frontier: a life of J. H. Oldham* (1999)

Archives Bodl. RH, corresp. and MSS, MSS Afr. s. 1829 · U. Edin., New Coll. L., corresp. and MSS | Archives of the World Council of Churches, Geneva · BLPES, corresp. with Violet Markham · Bodl. Oxf., corresp. with L. G. Curtis, MSS Eng. Hist. b. 224 and c. 776–877 · Bodl. RH, corresp. with Lord Lugard · Bodl. RH, corresp. with Margery Perham · International Missionary Council and Council of British Missionary Societies, London · JRL, letters to the *Manchester Guardian* · NL Wales, corresp. with Thomas Jones · NRA, priv. coll., corresp. with Sir Geoffrey Vickers · U. Lond., Institute of Education, papers relating to the Moot · Yale U. divinity school, John R. Mott MSS | SOUND BL NSA, 'Out of the wilderness', xx(1822084.1)

Likenesses photograph, repro. in Cell, ed., *By Kenya possessed* · photographs, repro. in Clements, *Faith on the frontier*, esp. 17, 268, 464

Wealth at death £30,508: probate, 13 Aug 1969, CGPLA Eng. & Wales

Oldham, Nathaniel (*fl.* 1728–*c.*1747), virtuoso, was the son of a dissenting minister. Early in life he went to India, where he served in the army. He returned to England on inheriting a fortune estimated at £100,000 from a near relation. From 1728 to 1735 he lived at Ealing House, Middlesex, the former residence of Sir James Montague

(1666–1723), baron of the exchequer. He also had a house at Witton, near Hounslow, Essex, and a third in Southampton Row, Bloomsbury, Middlesex. Oldham was a close friend of Sir Hans Sloane, Dr Richard Mead, and other celebrated collectors. He too began to collect natural and artificial curiosities, although apparently with little taste or discernment. Among his acquisitions was a 'choice collection of butterflies'. He spent a great deal of time at Don Saltero's coffee house at Chelsea in the company of Sloane and others, comparing shells, insects, and plants. Oldham, who collected paintings, was a good friend of the artist Joseph Highmore, from whom he commissioned a full-length portrait of himself, dressed in a green velvet hunting-coat. The painting, dating from about 1740 and untraced, was engraved by J. Faber. Highmore also painted for him a celebrated informal group portrait, *Mr Oldham and his Guests* (Tate collection), based upon a real-life incident when Oldham had returned home late for supper at his home in Ealing to find his friends already well wined and dined. He was also a devotee of horse-racing. His lavish spending, notably on his collections, eventually forced him to take refuge from his creditors within the sanctuary of the court of St James's. There he frequented the refreshment room on Duck Island, in St James's Park, attired in an eccentric costume and regaling friends with performances on a variety of musical instruments. Compelled to sell his collection, he put a sign over the door, 'Oldham's last shift'. At the same time he was arrested by a creditor and sent to the king's bench prison, where he is supposed to have died. He was probably still alive when the *Entire collection of prints, books of prints and drawings of Nathaniel Oldham Esq., of Southampton Row, Bloomsbury* was sold at Cox's auction room on 25–8 February 1747. Oldham was godfather to Nathaniel Smith, the printseller, whose son J. T. Smith was the author of *Nollekens and his Times* (1828) and keeper at the British Museum. Smith contributed an account of Oldham to James Caulfield's *Portraits, Memoirs, &c., of Remarkable Persons* (2 vols., 1794–5; 4 vols., 1819–20).

W. W. WROTH, *rev.* MARTIN POSTLE

Sources J. Caulfield, *Portraits, memoirs, &c. of remarkable persons*, 2 vols. (1819), vol. 2, p. 133 • J. T. Smith, *Nollekens and his times*, 2 vols. (1828), vol. 2, pp. 217–20 • *DNB* • E. Einberg and J. Egerton, *The age of Hogarth: British painters born 1675–1709* (1988), 47–50

Likenesses J. Highmore, group portrait, oils, c.1735–1745 (*Mr Oldham and his guests*), Tate collection • J. Faber, engraving (after J. Highmore, c.1740), BM

Oldham, Richard Dixon (1858–1936), geologist and seismologist, was born on 30 or 31 July 1858 in Dublin, the third of the five sons (there was also a daughter) of Thomas *Oldham (1816–1878), later superintendent of the geological survey of India, and his wife, Louisa Matilda, daughter of William Dixon of Liverpool. He was educated at Rugby School and the Royal School of Mines, London. He refused a science scholarship at Emmanuel College, Cambridge, on account of his father's death in 1878, and was appointed a third-grade assistant geologist to the geological survey of India, taking up his post on 17 December 1879. After his first season working in the Godavari valley he commenced important work on the geology of the outer Himalaya. Subsequently he accompanied the Manipur–Burma boundary commission in 1881–2 and visited the Andaman Islands in 1885. Further fieldwork included Rajputana, the Salt range, Baluchistan, Upper Burma, and the Son valley. He was promoted to superintendent on 1 October 1891, and from 8 May 1896 to 23 November 1897 he officiated as director of the survey in the absence of C. L. Griesbach.

Although he was a versatile geologist with wide interests Oldham's greatest achievements were undoubtedly in the field of seismology. His interest in this field was probably stimulated by his editing of his father's unfinished works on the Cachar earthquake of 1869 (*Memoirs of the Geological Survey of India*, 19, 1882, 1–98) and his 'A catalogue of Indian earthquakes' (*Memoirs of the Geological Survey of India*, 19, 1883, 163–215). Following his own detailed study of the great Assam earthquake of 1897, he was the first to distinguish, in 1900, the three distinct forms of wave-motion recorded by seismographs—primary (P), secondary (S), and tertiary (surface) waves—and in 1906 he provided the first clear evidence for the presence of the earth's central core.

Oldham retired at the early age of forty-five on 2 May 1904, partly because of ill-health—he had contracted the tropical disease sprue—but also perhaps because in 1903 he had been passed over for promotion to director in favour of Thomas Holland (1868–1947). Following a winter spent in Burma as an independent consultant to an oil company he returned to England. He resided firstly on the Isle of Wight near the home of his close friend and fellow seismologist John Milne (1850–1913), and afterwards at Kew with his unmarried sister. On her death he divided his time between Hyères, in the south of France, during the winter, and Llandrindod Wells, Wales, during the summer. From Hyères he made a study of the Rhône delta since Roman times, the subject of his final published papers. He died on 15 July 1936 at the Wingfield Nursing Home, Llandrindod Wells. He never married. Oldham was described by one contemporary as 'an original and independent thinker—a little too independent sometimes for those in authority' (*Nature*).

Oldham was elected a fellow of the Geological Society of London in 1886 (receiving its Lyell medal in 1908, and serving as its president from 1920 to 1922) and of the Royal Society in 1911 (serving on its council in 1920–21). He was also a fellow of the Royal Geographical Society. From 1879 to 1903 he was a fellow of Calcutta University and in 1931 he was elected an honorary fellow of the Imperial College of Science, London.

Oldham was a prolific writer, having over ninety publications to his credit. Fifty of these appeared under the auspices of the geological survey of India, mainly in the *Memoirs* and *Records*, but they also included his *A Bibliography of Indian Geology* (Calcutta, 1888), the first attempted bibliography of its kind, and his major revision of H. B. Medlicott and W. T. Blanford, *A Manual of the Geology of India* (2nd edn, Calcutta, 1893). In addition, he published some thirty-five papers in various British and European journals and four in the *Journal* and *Proceedings of the Asiatic Society of Bengal*. Many of his works were abstracted, reviewed, and reprinted widely throughout Europe.

ANDREW GROUT

Sources A. M. Heron, 'Richard Dixon Oldham', *Records of the Geological Survey of India*, 71 (1937), 347–9 · C. S. M., *Quarterly Journal of the Geological Society of London*, 93 (1937), ciii–cvi · C. Davison, *Obits. FRS*, 2 (1936–8), 111–13 · C. Davison, 'Founders of seismology, IV', *Geological Magazine*, 74 (1937), 529–34 · P. L., *Nature*, 138 (1936), 316–17 · L. Leigh Fermor, *First twenty-five years of the Geological Survey of India* (New Delhi, 1976) · R. D. Oldham, four letters to A. Geikie, 1878–1900, U. Edin. L., MS Gen 526/7 · R. D. Oldham to T. H. D. La Touche, letters, 1897–8, BL OIOC, MS Eur. C. 258/54 · T. H. D. La Touche, *A bibliography of Indian geology and physical geography*, 5 vols. (1917–26) · d. cert. · *CGPLA Eng. & Wales* (1936)
Archives BL OIOC, La Touche MSS, MS Eur. C 258/54 · U. Edin. L., Geikie corresp.
Likenesses photograph, *c*.1910–1920, repro. in Davison, *Obits. FRS*, facing p.111
Wealth at death £4559 18*s*. 10*d*.: probate, 7 Sept 1936, *CGPLA Eng. & Wales*

Oldham, Thomas (1801–1851). *See under* Oldham, John (1779–1840).

Oldham, Thomas (1816–1878), geologist, was born on 4 May 1816 at Dublin, the eldest son of Thomas Oldham, a broker with the Grand Canal Company, and his wife, Margaret Boyd. He was educated at a private school in Dublin and when he was fifteen entered Trinity College, Dublin, where he received his BA in 1836. Following graduation he went to Edinburgh in order to study civil engineering. While there he attended a number of classes at the university, including those on geology given by Robert Jameson. He also worked on civil engineering projects in the city.

On Oldham's return to Ireland in March 1838 he was appointed principal geological assistant to the geological department of the Ordnance Survey of Ireland under Joseph Portlock (1794–1864) and undertook extensive field mapping in the counties of Londonderry and Tyrone. In 1840 he made the important discovery of trace fossils in the Cambrian rocks of the Bray group, co. Wicklow, forms which, in 1848, Edward Forbes (1815–1854) named *Oldhamia* in his honour. In June 1843, following the disbandment of Portlock's geological department, Oldham was appointed curator of the museum of the Geological Society of Dublin, a post which he held until January 1845. From 1848 to 1850 he served as president of that society. In November 1844 he became assistant professor of civil engineering in Trinity College under Sir John MacNeill (1793–1880). In April 1845 Oldham was appointed professor of geology in Dublin University, and on 1 July the following year he was made local director for Ireland of the newly formed Geological Survey of Great Britain and Ireland. He also proceeded MA in 1846. Oldham's work in Ireland was much praised by his superiors, but he was a stern critic of any mapping which he considered unsatisfactory, in particular that by Frederick McCoy (1823–1899).

Oldham married in late 1850 Louisa Matilda, daughter of William Dixon of Liverpool. They had five sons (including

the Indian geologist and seismologist Richard Dixon *Oldham), and one daughter. On 14 November of that year, following the recommendation of Henry De la Beche (1796–1855), Oldham was appointed to the post of geological surveyor to the East India Company, a position which offered him the substantially increased salary of £1000 per annum. He and his wife arrived in Calcutta in March 1851. Here he immediately styled himself 'superintendent of the geological survey of India', and for the next twenty-five years worked tirelessly to build up the staff of the survey and to improve its scientific competency. A large proportion of India was mapped geologically during this time, enabling the publication of the first official geological map of the sub-continent in 1877. Attention was also directed to economic geology, particularly in mapping the coalfields of Bengal. In 1856, as part of a major reorganization of the survey, Oldham established a new Calcutta headquarters where he built up a fine library and museum. He initiated the modern scientific study of earthquakes in India, and organized a collection of meteorites which by his death had become one of the world's finest. He was also instrumental in the establishment of the Indian Museum in 1866. A keen supporter of geological education in India, he instituted a system of geological apprenticeships for Indians in the survey in 1873.

Oldham was elected a member of the Royal Irish Academy in 1842, and a fellow of the Geological Society of London in 1843 and of the Royal Society in 1848, receiving the latter's royal medal in 1875. In India he was elected a member of the Asiatic Society of Bengal in 1857 and served as its president four times between 1868 and 1876. A bearded, patriarchal figure in later life, he commanded great respect for his scientific rigour and administrative dynamism, and is justly remembered as the 'architect' of the geological survey of India. Over 120 publications are attributed to Oldham. In Ireland, in addition to official reports, he published some twenty-nine papers mainly in the *Journal of the Geological Society of Dublin*. As superintendent he inaugurated three important high-quality series of geological survey of India publications—the *Records*, *Memoirs*, and *Palaeontologia Indica*. To the former two he made over fifty contributions. The series of annual reports was also begun by him in 1859. Other papers appeared mainly in the *Journal of the Asiatic Society of Bengal* and in *Nature*.

Following his retirement from the survey owing to ill health, in March 1876 Oldham returned to England and lived at Eldon Place, Rugby. During this time he was appointed an examiner in geology to the University of London, a post which he had also held in respect of the Royal Indian Engineering College, Cooper's Hill. He died at 18 Hillmorton Road, Rugby, after a brief illness, on 17 July 1878; his wife survived him.

ANDREW GROUT

Sources G. L. Herries Davies, *Sheets of many colours: the mapping of Ireland's rocks, 1750–1890* (1983) · *Geological Magazine*, new ser., 2nd decade, 5 (1878), 382–4 · H. C. Sorby, *Quarterly Journal of the Geological Society*, 35 (1879), 46–8 · L. Leigh Fermor, *First twenty-five years of the Geological Survey of India* (New Delhi, 1976) · *A short history of the first hundred years*, Geological Survey of India (Calcutta, 1951) · H. De la Beche to J. Shepherd, 27 June 1850, BGS, MS 1/5 · 'The retirement of

Dr Oldham', *Records of the Geological Survey of India*, 9 (1876), 27 • private information (1894) • *Journal of the Asiatic Society of Bengal* (1877), 71, 203 • T. H. D. La Touche, *A bibliography of Indian geology and physical geography*, 5 vols. (1917–26) • d. cert. • *CGPLA Eng. & Wales* (1878) **Archives** BGS • Geological Survey of India, Calcutta [presumed] • Geological Survey of Ireland, Dublin | ICL, letters to Sir Andrew Ramsay • NMG Wales, De la Beche MSS **Likenesses** group portraits, photographs, *c*.1870, Geological Survey of India, Calcutta, India; repro. in Geological Survey of India, *Short history*, 5, 20 • photograph, *c*.1876, Geological Survey of India, Calcutta, India; repro. in Davies, *Sheets of many colours*, 139 • Geflowski, bust, 1877, Asiatic Society of Bengal, Calcutta, India • group portrait, photograph, BGS • photograph, BGS **Wealth at death** under £2000: administration with will, 28 Oct 1878, *CGPLA Eng. & Wales*

Oldisworth, Giles (1619/20–1678), Church of England clergyman, was born at Coln Rogers, Gloucestershire, in 1619 or the first quarter of 1620, a younger son of Robert Oldisworth of that parish and his wife, Merial, daughter of Sir Nicholas Overbury. His mother was the sister of Sir Thomas *Overbury, whose notorious murder in the Tower of London in 1613 hung over the family. Giles's elder brother, Nicholas *Oldisworth, wrote a manuscript life of Sir Thomas which, he recorded, 'I wrote from dictation, and read over to my old grandfather Sir Nicholas Overbury, on Thursday, 1 Oct. 1637' (BL, Add. MS 15476, fol. 1).

Oldisworth was educated at Westminster School, and must often have listened to the sermons of the dean of St Paul's, John Donne. Admitted as a pensioner at Trinity College, Cambridge, on 17 May 1639, he was elected to a scholarship there on 17 April 1640, and graduated BA in 1643. In 1644 he was deprived of his scholarship on account of his royalist sympathies, and proceeded to Oxford, where, by virtue of a letter written on 29 January 1646 on his behalf by the chancellor of the university, the marquess of Hertford, he was created MA on 20 July 1646. Oldisworth had just been presented by his grandfather Sir Nicholas Overbury to the living of Bourton on the Hill, Gloucestershire, where he succeeded his elder brother as rector.

Giles Oldisworth was able to retain his living at Bourton throughout the interregnum. He married Margaret Warren, who did not survive him, and they had at least five children. He was the owner of a copy of the 1639 edition of John Donne's *Poems by J.D. with Elegies on the Author's Death*. His annotations have helped to identify some of the elegists; they show that Oldisworth studied the work with 'scrupulous care' and that he was 'in close touch with well-informed views upon literary and other topics of the day' (Sampson, 83–4). Oldisworth was himself a published author. In 1663 he issued *The stone rolled away, and life more abundant: an apologie urging self-denyall, new-obedience, faith, and thankfulnesse*, prefaced with a laudatory epistle to the king, dated 5 November. This was reissued the following year with a new title, *The holy royalist, or, The secret discontents of church & kingdom, reduced unto self-denial, moderation and thankfulnes*, and with a portrait of the king as frontispiece. In 1673 he made his own contribution to family piety by publishing an edition of Sir Thomas Overbury's poem, 'The Wife', as *The illustrious wife, viz that excellent poem, Sir Thomas Overburie's wife, illustrated by Giles Oldisworth, nephew to the same Sir T.O.* Oldisworth himself wrote,

under the pseudonym of Sketlius, a manuscript poem entitled 'A Westminster Scholar, or, The Patterne of Pietie'. It is a narrative, written in five books, in high-flown language, describing members of the families of Oldisworth and Overbury under fictitious names, with some explanatory notes in the margin.

On 11 May 1665 Oldisworth preached a sermon at the chapel of the Mercers' Company in London. Before its publication, as *The Race Set before Us*, the following year at Oxford, he had entered the employment of Herbert Croft, bishop of Hereford, signing the dedicatory epistle as 'Your lordship's most obliged servant and devoted chaplain', 'from my study 7 Nov 1665'; a preface to Lady Croft in *The Father of the Faithfull* suggests that he may have retained that position in 1674. Giles Oldisworth died at Bourton on the Hill on 24 November 1678, and was buried in the chancel of the church on 27 November. By his will, dated the day before his death, Oldisworth divided his property equally among four children, of whom Giles (born in 1650 and by now a citizen of London) and Mary were of age; he appointed his brother William guardian to Thomas (*bap.* 10 April 1659) and Hester. STEPHEN WRIGHT

Sources J. Sampson, 'Contemporary light upon John Donne', *Essays and Studies by Members of the English Association*, 7 (1921), 82–107 • Venn, *Alum. Cant.* • Wood, *Ath. Oxon.: Fasti* (1820) • will, PRO, PROB 11/360, fols. 58–9, sig. 73 • G. Oldisworth, *The father of the faithfull tempted as was more concisely shewed August 31 1674, at a solemne funeral in the church at Wotton under Edge, in the countie of Gloucester*, 1674 [MS notes at front of BL copy incl. transcript of note commending Oldisworth as one of those Cambridge students forced out for allegiance to the king and recommending him to be awarded MA; dated from Oxon 29 Jan 1645] • *Gloucestershire Notes and Queries*, 1 (1881), 270 • G. Oldisworth, *The race set before us, showing the necessity laid upon gospel believers, to run with diligence through all gospel duties: a sermon preached in London, May 11 1665 at Mercers chapel* (1666) • *DNB* • *VCH Gloucestershire*, vol. 6 • *Old Westminsters*

Oldisworth, Michael (*b.* 1590/91, *d.* in or after 1659), politician, was baptized on 17 January 1591 at St Martin-in-the-Fields, Westminster, the second son of Arnold Oldisworth (*b.* 1561) of Bradley in Gloucestershire and Lucy, daughter of Francis Barty of Antwerp. He matriculated from Queen's College, Oxford, on 21 November 1606, aged fifteen, and graduated BA from Magdalen College on 10 June 1611. Elected a fellow of Magdalen in the following year, he proceeded MA on 5 July 1614. A man of some literary ability, he was nominated in 1617 as one of eighty-four key people in Edmund Bolton's proposals for a national academy and was later praised as a most accomplished gentleman by Robert Herrick in *Hesperides*. Also in 1617 Oldisworth married Susan (*b.* 1599), daughter of Thomas Poyntz and his wife, Jane.

Oldisworth inherited a lasting interest in politics from his father, who had been MP for Tregony in 1593 and Cirencester in 1640, keeper of the hanaper in chancery, and receiver of fines in king's bench. After leaving university he was appointed secretary to William Herbert, third earl of Pembroke, who was both chancellor of Oxford University and lord chamberlain. Pembroke used his influence to secure Oldisworth's election as MP for Old Sarum in Wiltshire in 1624, 1625, 1626, and 1628. Representing a pocket or nomination borough such as Old Sarum meant that Oldisworth owed no allegiance other than that demanded by his patron. He was one of a number of 'gentleman-servants' in the Commons (*VCH Wiltshire*, 5.119), whose status would not normally have secured for them a seat but who now became members of personal factions.

After the third earl's death in 1630 Oldisworth was eventually appointed, in 1637, as secretary to the fourth earl of Pembroke (brother of the third earl and his successor as lord chamberlain). In 1640 Pembroke succeeded, with the support of the puritan majority on the corporation, in securing the election of Oldisworth for the borough of Salisbury in both the Short and the Long parliaments. Apart from his patron's interests, Oldisworth had no personal connection with Wiltshire, but he generously repaid them for their promotion of his political career. He largely organized the Pembrokes' electoral influence in the county, which the third earl had systematically built up between 1612 and 1630, particularly in Wilton, Downton, and Old Sarum. He managed their patronage and operated as their agent in the Commons, where they had a personal following of about twelve members. In 1639 he supported the fourth earl, who was captain-general of the king's bodyguard, as an officer of the army in the north. Oldisworth also benefited personally from the Herbert influence at court. In 1629 he was granted leases on royal land, including a manor in Kent for which he paid £1200, and in 1639 he was granted income from the western stannaries.

In politics Oldisworth identified with the parliamentarian party, became a friend of Sir John Eliot, and when civil war broke out in 1642 contributed one horse and £30 for the defence of the country. On 5 July 1644 he was a witness at the trial of William Laud, accusing the archbishop of attempting to deprive the current Lord Pembroke of his right, as lord chamberlain, to appoint royal chaplains. At the time, Oldisworth was attributed with credit for securing Pembroke's allegiance to the parliamentarian cause. According to Anthony Wood, 'Tho' in the grand rebellion he was no colonel, yet he was governor of old Pembroke and Montgomery, led him by the nose (as he pleased) to serve both their turns' (Wood, *Ath. Oxon.* 2.356). Contemporary satirists published pamphlets, often with the pretence that they were written by Oldisworth himself, ridiculing Pembroke's vulgar tastes and his total dependence on Oldisworth. In one of these the latter was described as 'Pembrochian Oldisworth that made the Earl, his master's, wise speeches' (*England's Confusion*, 1659, 10).

After the end of the second civil war, Oldisworth became frustrated by parliament's continued negotiations with the king and therefore made few appearances in the Commons during 1648. When, however, matters were brought to a head by the army's intervention and the decision to bring the king to trial, he became an active revolutionary. On 20 December 1648 he registered his dissent to the vote of 5 December that called for further negotiations with the king. His zeal is confirmed by the fact that he was listed, shortly after Pride's Purge, as being one of the radical ultras in the Commons. One of only eight out of twenty-six active Wiltshire MPs who were allowed to remain as members, he served the Rump loyally and, as a pious puritan, became a keen member of its various committees on religious reform, favouring a presbyterian settlement. Although Pembroke died in 1650, his role as Oldisworth's patron had already been taken over by the new government in recognition of his service to the state. In July 1649 Oldisworth was given a lucrative appointment as one of two masters of the prerogative office (renewed by the council of state in 1653); in 1650 he succeeded Pembroke as keeper of Windsor Great Park; and in 1651 he was appointed commissioner to investigate a rising in south Wales. He was still a member of the Rump when it was expelled by Cromwell in April 1653. Although he did not serve in the protectorate parliaments, he resumed his seat for Salisbury when the Rump was restored in May 1659.

Oldisworth's successful political career had almost entirely been dependent on the patronage of the Herberts and his own opportunism. Although it is estimated that he would still have been classed as a member of the lesser gentry in 1649, with an income of under £500 a year, his later appointments would have secured for him a comfortable standard of living. His exact date of death is unknown. JOHN WROUGHTON

Sources 'Oldsworth (or Oldisworth), Michael', Greaves & Zaller, *BDBR*, 2.274–5 • Keeler, *Long Parliament* • Foster, *Alum. Oxon.* • *VCH Wiltshire*, vol. 5 • *DNB* • D. Underdown, *Pride's Purge: politics in the puritan revolution* (1971) • B. Worden, *The Rump Parliament, 1648–1653* (1974) • *The works of the most reverend father in God, William Laud*, 4, ed. J. Bliss (1854) • V. A. Rowe, 'The influence of the earls of Pembroke on parliamentary elections, 1625–41', *EngHR*, 50 (1935), 242–56, esp. 251–2 • Wood, *Ath. Oxon.: Fasti* (1815), 356–7 • R. C. Hoare, *The history of modern Wiltshire*, 1 (1822) • *JHC*, 2 (1640–42) • *CSP dom.*, 1629–31; 1639; 1645–7; 1651 • *IGI*

Oldisworth, Nicholas (*bap.* 1611, *d.* 1645), Church of England clergyman and poet, was born at the home of his grandfather Sir Nicholas Overbury in Bourton on the Hill, Gloucestershire, and baptized in the parish church on 14 July 1611, the elder son of Robert Oldisworth of Coln Rogers, Gloucestershire, and his wife, Merial, sister of Sir Thomas Overbury.

Oldisworth was educated at Westminster School under the headship of Lambert Osbaldeston, who encouraged his verse writing. While at Westminster he developed a close friendship with Richard Bacon, who proceeded as a king's scholar to Trinity College, Cambridge, in 1628 but left after a year for training at Douai. Oldisworth kept up his contact with his friend, addressing many poems to him and to his siblings; he was deeply affected by Bacon's death from the plague in 1636.

From Westminster Oldisworth moved, as a king's scholar, to Christ Church, Oxford, in July 1628. He matriculated on 24 February 1632, in time to take his BA on 24 April and to be incorporated at Cambridge University. His MA followed in 1635, by which time he had already been presented with the living at Bourton on the Hill by his grandfather.

Most if not all of Oldisworth's more than 120 poems

were written while he was at Christ Church. Only two were published in his lifetime, in university commemorative volumes in 1633: *Solis Britannici Perigaeum* and *Vitis Carolinae gemma altera*. A poem to Ben Jonson, paying tribute to his influence, appeared in *Wit Restor'd* (1658), an anthology by Sir John Mennes. Few of the poems display the brittle wittiness valued by Oldisworth's contemporaries but, with an often engaging awkwardness, the collection as a whole evinces an unexpected sensitivity to personal, domestic, and familial relationships.

The fate of Sir Thomas Overbury appears to have haunted the family; Oldisworth himself gathered material relating to the trial of his uncle's murderers. He records reading the manuscript to his aged grandfather, Sir Nicholas Overbury, on 9 October 1637 and includes the old man's comments. Oldisworth also kept a manuscript fair copy of his moderately Laudian sermons (Bodl. Oxf., MS Eng. th. f. 20). Because he used sermons more than once he meticulously recorded when and where he preached them.

Oldisworth married in 1640. He and his wife, Mary (*d.* 1684), had three daughters: Mary (*bap.* 6 Jan 1641), Frances (*bap.* 11 June 1642, *bur.* 28 Nov 1643), and Margaret (*bap.* 8 Feb 1644). Mary married a Londoner, and became Mistress Sherwood; Margaret married John Mann of Tewkesbury.

As a moderate royalist Oldisworth expressed his bewilderment at the course of public events and their effects on people's lives. During the plague of 1644 and 1645 he appears to have moved his family to Willington in Warwickshire, near Shipston-on-Stour and about 11 miles from Bourton on the Hill. He occupied himself with preparing a manuscript fair copy of his poems, entitled 'A Recollection of Certain Scattered Poems', for presentation to his wife; the dedicatory epistle is dated 24 February 1645. (The volume—Bodl. Oxf., MS Don. c. 24—was inherited by his daughter Margaret, who used it to record recipes.)

Oldisworth continued with his pastoral duties, preaching perhaps for the last time in Burmington, Warwickshire, on 16 March 1645. He died at Willington, of the plague, on 25 March 1645 and was buried the next day in the chancel of the nearby church at Barcheston. The church having been refurbished, there is now no trace of his grave. His death is recorded in Barcheston parish register and, more fulsomely, by his brother, Giles, in Bourton on the Hill parish register.   JOHN GOUWS

Sources Bodl. Oxf., MS Don. c. 24 · Folger, MS V. a. 170 · matriculation book, Christ Church Oxf., MS O. P. c. a. 1 · buttery book, Christ Church Oxf., MS (x) c. 62 · parish register, Glos. RO, PFG 59 in 1/1 · Bodl. Oxf., MS Eng. th. f. 20 · BL, Add. MS 15476
Archives Bodl. Oxf., MS Don. c. 24 · Folger, MS V. a. 170

Oldisworth, William (1680–1734), writer and translator, was the son of the Revd William Oldisworth, vicar of Itchen Stoke, Hampshire, and prebendary of Middleton, in Winchester. The family was traditionally royalist, and came from Gloucestershire, where many of Oldisworth's relations had been Anglican clergymen and country squires. Oldisworth matriculated at Hart Hall, Oxford, on

4 April 1698. During his time at university he was associated with the Christ Church wits, and came into contact with the poet Edmund Smith, and with Francis Atterbury, later bishop of Rochester. After leaving Oxford, without having taken his degree, he worked as a clerk for his uncle, a JP in Hampshire, and then moved to London about 1706, where he began his writing career. His first significant publication was his three-volume *A Dialogue between Timothy and Philatheus* (1709–11), a response to Matthew Tindal's assault on revealed religion in *The Rights of the Christian Church Asserted* (1706). In the *Dialogue*, Oldisworth linked Tindal with other notorious freethinkers. He continued this engagement in religious controversy with another pamphlet, *A Vindication of the Right Reverend the Lord Bishop of Exeter* (1709), in which he defended the high-church Bishop Blackall against attacks by Benjamin Hoadly.

Oldisworth was reputed to be a fine translator, and in 1712, he, along with William Broome, contributed to John Ozell's five-volume translation of the *Iliad*. This was followed, in 1712–13, by a parodic version of Horace's odes, in which he translated Richard Bentley's edition of Horace, providing satirical notes on Bentley's lengthy annotations to his edition. However, he is most famous for his role in the continuation of the tory periodical *The Examiner*. Between 1711 and 1714, he was the main contributor to the publication, which had previously been edited by Jonathan Swift and Delarivier Manley. *The Examiner* brought him financial stability, and support from prominent tories, including Robert Harley. However, following the death of Queen Anne this involvement ceased, and Oldisworth adopted a more direct form of political action, travelling north in the autumn of 1715 to join the Scottish Jacobites at the battle of Preston. Although contemporary reports claimed that he was killed in action, Oldisworth survived the battle, and may have then gone to seek refuge in Paris along with other Jacobites. His whereabouts for the next five years are unknown, but he appears to have returned to Oxford at some point in the early 1720s, where he took up antiquarian scholarship. He assisted Richard Fiddes in his life of Cardinal Wolsey, and studied various Middle English texts, including *Piers Plowman*. At this time, between 1723 and 1724, he also seems to have been a contributor to the duke of Wharton's tory paper, the *True Briton*. His last serious piece of writing was his translation of a sixteenth-century Latin work by Wawrzyniec Goslicki, bishop of Posen, *The Accomplished Senator* (1733), in which he emphasized the moderation and independence of his own political position, in order to counter his reputation as a political extremist. Although Oldisworth had achieved financial security through his writing, he was rendered destitute in the early 1730s, apparently by the sudden bankruptcy of a relative. He was imprisoned for debt and he died on 15 September 1734 in the king's bench prison, London.

ABIGAIL WILLIAMS

Sources *DNB* · R. J. Allen, 'William Oldisworth, the author of the tory *Examiner*', *Philological Quarterly*, 26 (1947), 159–80 · A. Chalmers, ed., *The general biographical dictionary*, new edn, 32 vols. (1812–17) · G. Sherburn, *The early career of Alexander Pope* (1934)

Wealth at death bankrupt: *DNB*

Oldknow, Samuel (1756–1828), cotton manufacturer, was born on 5 October 1756 at Anderton, Lancashire, the eldest in the family of two sons and one daughter of Samuel Oldknow, a muslin manufacturer originally from Nottingham, and his wife, Margaret, daughter of Thomas Foster, a small landowner of Anderton. After his father's early death his mother married a local farmer, John Clayton, and had three more children. Educated at Rivington grammar school, Lancashire, Oldknow was apprenticed to his uncle Thomas Oldknow, a draper in Nottingham, and then returned to Anderton in 1781 as his uncle's partner in rebuilding the Anderton muslin business.

The invention of the spinning mule in 1779 made high-quality cotton yarn possible, and it was a propitious moment to compete with the Indian muslins which monopolized the quality market. Oldknow, with his important family contacts, and his delight in technical detail, together with a strong sense of ambition and immense energy, was well placed to exploit this opportunity. Within three years he had become the most successful muslin manufacturer in Britain. By 1789 he produced sales of between £80,000 and £90,000 per annum, 90 per cent of them fine muslins, which now found customers as distant as Botany Bay. Oldknow's costly portrait by Joseph Wright depicts the successful Enlightenment man of business, reason, and science, equal to any in status, talent, and attainment.

Oldknow initially based his enterprise on his warehouse in Anderton. Yarn purchased from Nottingham or from the Arkwrights, the leading firm in the cotton industry, was turned into cloth by numerous hand-loom weavers organized by Oldknow's talented managers. By 1784 a new pool of weavers and a new warehouse in Stockport had been added. Here Oldknow centralized warping and winding, with some weaving, while at nearby Heaton Mersey he established a sizeable finishing works under the control of his brother, Thomas. His ambitions now centred on adding fine spinning to manufacturing. He turned down offers of partnership with the Peels and the Arkwrights, and in 1790 erected the first steam-powered mill in Stockport, during a boom period. Oldknow seems to have had in mind a great combined enterprise, with 1000 factory workers and 1000 weavers, and was on the way to becoming one of England's greatest cotton lords, to rank with the Peels, Arkwrights, and Strutts. Yet his business limitations and overblown ambitions were now exposed. He had already become dependent on Richard Arkwright for funds (a loan of £10,000 in 1788), but the prosperity of muslins now evaporated, while Oldknow failed to achieve the same mastery of technical perfection in fine-cotton spinning. The economic crisis of 1792 ended this phase of his career, forcing him to sell or let all his works in Stockport and Anderton. His future now rested, as it did until his death, on the forbearance of his main creditors, the Arkwrights. He owed Richard Arkwright £205,000 by his death.

Samuel Oldknow (1756–1828), by Joseph Wright of Derby, *c.*1790–92

In 1787 Oldknow had purchased a landed estate at Mellor in Derbyshire, the security for his debts and now the focus for his industrial aspirations. Even before his Stockport vision had collapsed, Oldknow developed a consuming preoccupation with this largely rural community. He had begun building a water-powered factory and consolidating his landed estate by purchase. He now built an intricate series of reservoirs, together with houses for himself, workers, and apprentices. The mill was never to be in the forefront of industry. It produced coarse yarn and employed at its peak only about 550 workers, including many parish apprentices. Yet Oldknow's historical reputation largely derives from the community which he created in this rural setting. He dominated both Mellor and Marple, setting up diverse enterprises: limekilns, coal-shafts, building bridges, and turnpike roads. He was also the mainstay of the Peak Forest Canal. Oldknow the man of Romantic sensibility came to the fore. His limekilns were designed to resemble medieval fortresses. Uniting industry and the countryside, he emerged as one of Derbyshire's leading high-farmers during the Napoleonic wars.

Oldknow joined the county élite as lieutenant-colonel in the volunteers, high sheriff of Derbyshire (1824), and chairman of the Agricultural Society (1828), and he rebuilt the parish church in Mellor, renting 325 pews for his workers. Oldknow died in Mellor on 18 September 1828, and was buried there on the 24th. He had never married. His obituarist in the *Gentleman's Magazine* said of him: 'In private life he had not an equal in the courteous urbanity of his manners. An unvarying, cheerful and benevolent countenance, with which the heart kept pace, accompanied and supported him through every vicissitude of life'.

A. C. HOWE, *rev.*

Sources Oldknow letters and apprenticeship papers, JRL, ENG MSS 751–840 · Oldknow letters and apprenticeship papers, Col. U., Seligman collection, NUC 62–556 · G. Unwin and others, *Samuel Oldknow and the Arkwrights*, 2nd edn (1968) · *GM*, 1st ser., 98/2 (1828), 469–70 · J. Wainwright, *Memories of Marple* (1899) · D. J. Hodgkins, 'Samuel Oldknow and the Peak Forest Canal', *Derbyshire Archaeological Journal*, 97 (1977) **Archives** Col. U., corresp. and papers · Johns Hopkins University, Baltimore, business and estate papers · JRL, corresp. and papers | Man. CL, Manchester Archives and Local Studies, corresp. with London Friendly Hospital about employment of apprentices [microfilm] **Likenesses** J. Wright of Derby, oils, *c.*1790–1792, Temple Newsam House, Leeds [*see illus.*] **Wealth at death** owed creditor £205,000; insolvent: will, PRO, PROB 11/1751; PRO, death duty registers, IR 26/1204, fols. 198–9

Oldman, Cecil Bernard (1894–1969), bibliographer, was born on 2 April 1894 in London, the only child of Frederick James Oldman, a builder and contractor with a business in New Cross Road, south-east London, and his wife, Agnes Barnes Nightingale. From City of London School he won a scholarship to Exeter College, Oxford, where he graduated in 1917 with second-class honours in *literae humaniores*.

After some war service in the Honourable Artillery Company, in 1920 Oldman entered the department of printed books in the British Museum as an assistant (he later became assistant keeper). Having mastered all aspects of the department's work, Oldman rose rapidly through its senior ranks during and just after the Second World War. Promoted a deputy keeper in 1943, he became a keeper in 1946, under Sir Henry Thomas as principal keeper. When the latter retired in 1948, Oldman succeeded him and held office with great distinction until his own retirement in 1959.

Oldman continued to tackle the difficulties of post-war reconstruction. He also faced the increasingly urgent problem posed by the slow progress of the scholarly revision of the general catalogue of printed books, which, seriously disrupted by the war, had only reached a point early in the letter D. When reporting the matter to the trustees in 1953, Oldman had to recommend one of two courses: either, having attempted to secure more staff, to press on with revision, or (as was vigorously advocated by F. C. Francis, the senior of the two keepers serving under Oldman), to terminate the work and then reprint volumes photolithographically together with the unrevised remainder, but with accessions from 1905 to 1955 intercalated. It was a bitter blow when the trustees preferred the reprint.

Oldman was totally dedicated to the department and was highly regarded by his colleagues. Throughout his career he was noted for the calm, far-sighted judgement which, combined with appreciation of scholarship, made him such an outstanding administrator. Of medium stature and with strong, sensitive features, he was reserved by nature and a man of few words, but had a delightful, dry sense of humour. In 1933 he married Sigrid, daughter of Vice-Admiral Adolf Sobieczky, formerly of the Austrian navy, and his wife, Adele, Baroness Potier des Echelles. They had no children.

Oldman specialized in the bibliography of the music of Haydn, Mozart, and Beethoven. His study *Musical First Editions* (1934) is a classic for its lucid exposition of new ideas. He was also by far the finest English Mozart scholar of his generation. Though he published little under his sole name, the best testimony to his erudition is to be found in the prefaces of numerous books on Mozart by both British and foreign authors who readily acknowledged his guidance. His pioneering work, with O. E. Deutsch, *Mozart Drucke: eine bibliographische Ergänzung zu Köchels Werkverzeichnis* (1931–2), became invaluable. Oldman's own Mozart collection included the unique letters written by Constanze Mozart to the publisher J. A. André which first appeared in his English translation within volume 3 of Emily Anderson's *The Letters of Mozart and his Family* (1938). Oldman also owned the so-called Attwood manuscript, which contains the musical exercises written by Thomas Attwood under Mozart's supervision in 1785 and 1786. In collaboration with others Oldman published this source (originally published in 1925) as part of the *Neue Mozart-Ausgabe* in 1965. He was awarded the silver medal of the Mozarteum in 1950.

Oldman was appointed CB in 1952 and CVO in 1958 (the latter in recognition of his services as honorary curator of the queen's music library). He served as president of the Library Association in 1954. In 1956 he received an honorary DMus from the University of Edinburgh and was elected an honorary fellow of Exeter College, Oxford. Oldman died at his home, Flat 3, 37 Gower Street, London, on 7 October 1969.

ALEC HYATT KING, *rev.*

Sources *The Times* (9 Oct 1969) · personal knowledge (2004) · *WWW* · *CGPLA Eng. & Wales* (1970) · A. Hyatt King, 'Oldman, C(ecil) B(ernard)', *New Grove* **Archives** BL **Wealth at death** £28,026: probate, 13 Aug 1970, *CGPLA Eng. & Wales*

Oldmixon, Mrs. *See* George, Georgina (d. 1835).

Oldmixon, John (1672/3–1742), historian and political pamphleteer, was the son of John Oldmixon, merchant, and Elinor Bawden (d. 1689). He belonged to an ancient Somerset family who held the manor of Oldmixon in the parish of Hutton, near Weston-super-Mare. The place and date of his birth are unknown: he described himself as a native of Bridgwater, although there is no entry in the registers of St Mary's Church in that town, where many members of his family can be traced.

Background and early works Oldmixon's father, who was described as a gentleman in his will, which was dated 8

June 1675 and proved on 16 April 1679 by his daughters Hannah and Sarah (d. 1689), bequeathed to his son 'my best cabinet in the little parlour, wherein my writings are now lodged'. His mother's will, proved on 28 December 1689, was administered by her daughter Hannah (b. 1664/5) who had married Richard Legg in 1682, and by John. The older Oldmixon had been involved in bankruptcy proceedings in 1676, probably owing to losses in the Virginia trade, as emerges from a chancery suit later brought by his son. As a result the younger John was forced to mortgage the family estate of Oldmixon in 1696; later he failed to exercise a redemption option and the manor passed into other hands.

As a boy Oldmixon lived with Humphrey Blake, brother of Bridgwater's best-known native, Admiral Robert Blake. Humphrey was led by religious persecution to emigrate to Carolina, but Oldmixon continued to board in the home of his daughter and son-in-law, John Norman, a schoolmaster. In 1685 the boy witnessed the preliminaries to the battle of Sedgmoor as the duke of Monmouth climbed the church tower to reconnoitre the ground. Soon afterwards Oldmixon went to live with his maternal uncle Sir John Bawden, a prominent West Indies merchant who in 1669 had married Letetia Popham: she was the daughter of Edward Popham, Admiral Blake's principal lieutenant in the navy under the Commonwealth. Bawden, who lived in Stoke Newington, was an alderman of Aldersgate ward and a member of the council for Jamaica. He was knighted on 31 October 1687, as a Presbyterian willing to accept James II's declaration of indulgence. However, he died in the following year, leaving a small legacy to his sister Elinor Oldmixon, who was already in debt to him. John Oldmixon probably entered the family business while living with his uncle, but no details are known. More important was the protestant and whig inheritance he received from the Bawdens, Blakes, Pophams, and more distant kinsfolk such as Thomas, Lord Wharton. In addition he acquired enough specialist knowledge to compile an account of Robert Blake for *Lives English and Forein* (1704), which would be the principal source for Samuel Johnson's life of Blake (1740), and a fuller *History and Life of Robert Blake* in 1741. His book *The British Empire in America* (2 vols., 1708; 2nd edn, considerably augmented, 1741) draws on information from relatives and contacts in the family business, especially with regard to Barbados.

Oldmixon first appeared in print with poems in the *Gentleman's Journal* in 1692 and 1693. His collection *Poems on Several Occasions* (1696) was dedicated to Lord Ashley, later third earl of Shaftesbury: it consists mainly of lyric pieces, and several items were included in vocal miscellanies published by Henry Playford and others. In 1697 Oldmixon produced *An Idyll on the Peace* to celebrate the settlement at Rijswijk. It was the first of at least eight works of whig panegyric verse on topical themes, addressed to prominent patrons such as the duchess of Marlborough and the duke of Newcastle, which Oldmixon would issue until his poetic career effectively came to an end in 1714. A more original item appeared in 1703 as *Amores Britannici: Epistles Heroical and Gallant, in English Heroic Verse*. This anticipated the vogue for Ovidian epistles which was to blossom in the following decade, and in fact it is closer to Drayton's *Englands Heroicall Epistles* in conception and execution than to Ovid. In this period Oldmixon contributed prologues, epilogues, and miscellany verse to volumes by friends such as John Dennis and Charles Gildon. His phase as primarily a creative writer ended with his monthly journal *The Muses Mercury*, which lasted for thirteen issues in 1707–8. Although Samuel Garth and John Dennis were regular contributors, and Rowe, Steele, and Wycherley appeared occasionally, Oldmixon had to cobble together much of the material himself. His greatest coup was to garner a contribution from Addison and to publish an appreciative essay on the old poem 'The Nut Brown Maid', which was to prove a pioneering study in the ballad revival.

At the same time Oldmixon was active in the theatre, with a short pastoral forming the first act of *The Novelty* (1697) by Peter Motteux and others, and then a full-length play taken from Tasso, *Amintas: a Pastoral* (1698). In 1700 he wrote the libretto for an opera by Daniel Purcell, *The Grove, or, Love's Paradice*: songs from this work were published by John Walsh. His last contribution to the stage came with a tragedy entitled *The Governour of Cyprus* (1703). None of these works seems to have enjoyed any great success in the playhouse. However, Oldmixon also kept his name before the public when he intervened in the Collier controversy with *Reflections on the Stage* (1699), dedicated to the future Lord Halifax. In January 1712 Oldmixon tried to enlist Halifax's support when, he claimed, John Ozell attempted to steal the credit for a translation of Boileau's works, published by Curll, and also dedicated to Halifax. According to Oldmixon, most of the volume had been his own doing. Oldmixon, described as a bachelor, was granted a licence to marry Elizabeth Parry, spinster, the daughter of George Parry, at Knightsbridge Chapel in March 1703. His wife was still apparently living in 1728. There are many casual references to a double family, and suggestions that Oldmixon may have had as many as six children. His known family consists of two sons and two daughters. John became a writer for Bengal in 1716, serving at Dacca for some years, and rose to be a senior merchant in the East India Company; he died in 1735. George worked in East India House, as chief of the department of the auditor of India accompts, and was a friend of the author John Hoole. He also wrote the English libretto for a 'serenata', *Parnasso in festa*, set by Handel in 1734. George died in 1779 aged sixty-six, leaving bequests to his two sisters, of whom the elder was Hannah (c.1705–1789). The younger, Eleanora (b. 1721), became a singer and married John Marella. Her son John Marella Oldmixon had a play produced, was knighted in 1782, and subsequently emigrated to the United States, where he died c.1816.

Whig pamphleteer From the time of the change of ministry in 1710 Oldmixon became a full-time polemicist on behalf of the whigs. He had already written the first part of *The History of Addresses* (2 vols., 1709–11), and a flood of journalism and pamphleteering followed. He helped his friend Arthur Maynwaring to set up *The Medley*, a weekly paper which ran for forty-five issues from 5 October 1710 to 6 August 1711. This period coincided almost exactly with Swift's editorship of *The Examiner*, which provided the main target and subject matter for the paper. Oldmixon served as managing editor, contributed to most issues, and wrote at least twelve issues single-handedly. The entire run was reprinted in May 1712, but the edition proved unsuccessful and Oldmixon was forced to bear the loss. Meanwhile he kept up his attack on Swift in a succession of pamphlets, including items responding to *The Conduct of the Allies*, *Some Remarks on the Barrier Treaty*, and *A Proposal for Correcting the English Tongue*, which is treated as a politically motivated project. An almost equally virulent barrage of pamphlets identified Defoe as a turncoat and lackey of the tory administration.

In 1716 Oldmixon claimed that since he had been diverted by Maynwaring from the study of history and poetry to politics, he had published more than a hundred tracts in defence of the whig cause through the booksellers Curll and Pemberton. Some twenty of these can be identified with certainty, usually issued under the imprint of the trade publisher James Roberts. These include *The Secret History of Europe* (4 vols., 1712–15); *Arcana Gallica* and *The False Steps of the Ministry* (both 1714); *Memoirs of North-Britain* (1715); and *Memoirs of Ireland* (1716). Oldmixon also specialized in lives of the recently deceased, with biographies of Maynwaring, dedicated to Walpole (1715); Wharton, a kinsman by marriage (1715); and Somers (1716). He also compiled *The Conduct of the Earl of Nottingham* for Curll in 1716, but the earl's relatives got wind of the book when it was printed and caused publication to be suspended.

Pope somehow heard of this episode and mentioned it in one of his satiric pamphlets concerning Edmund Curll. Oldmixon had committed his first major offence against Pope when he reprinted an epigram entitled 'Two or Three', suppressed by Pope after its first anonymous appearance: this occurred in a miscellany edited by Oldmixon, *Poems and Translations*, which was published by Curll in April 1714. The pamphleteer compounded his offence when he helped the scandalous bookseller to issue *Court Poems* in March 1716, as the volume contained unauthorized printings of work by Pope's friends and attributed one item to Pope himself. A month later Oldmixon was responsible for a satire in verse called *The Catholick Poet*, which retailed familiar accusations regarding Pope's Jacobitism and his lack of Greek scholarship. Thereafter Oldmixon remained on Pope's list, with the result that he earned a niche in *Peri Bathous* and in successive recensions of *The Dunciad*, with a damaging note appended to the text of this poem. Oldmixon responded with hostile comments in the *Flying Post* in 1728, as well as a number of barbed references in his critical works, the most prominent of which were *An Essay on Criticism* (1728) and *The Arts of Logick and Rhetorick* (1728). The latter, dedicated to George Bubb Dodington, is chiefly based on *La manière de bien penser dans les ouvrages d'esprit* (1687) by the Jesuit priest Dominique Bouhours.

Oldmixon must have expected that his life would flow more smoothly after the Hanoverian accession, but the opposite proved true. He was in trouble with the authorities again in April 1716, when he assisted in the publication of an unofficial account of the trial of the Jacobite Lord Wintoun, which resulted in punishment for Curll and Pemberton at the bar of the House of Lords. Efforts to gain the post of consul at Madeira for Richard Miles, who was probably the son of his half-sister Elizabeth, proved unavailing, despite petitions to the customs commissioners and an imploring letter to Addison when the latter became secretary of state.

On 11 June 1716 Oldmixon finally obtained his only, belated reward for his loyalty, when he was appointed customs collector for the port of Bridgwater. His tenure lasted twenty years, but it was soon dogged by reverses. According to his *Memoirs of the Press* (published posthumously in 1742), he found the post unprofitable from the start, and in later years he claimed that his salary of £100 was often in arrears. The strongly tory corporation harried him, and in 1718 he was compelled to appear before the mayor along with his friend Dr John Allen (c.1660–1741) to explain riots in the street, while the parish clerk and sexton laid information that he was among those who had attended Presbyterian and Anabaptist conventicles. Oldmixon attempted to gain official favour by reporting on suspicious activities in the neighbourhood, as was no doubt expected of him by the ministry. In 1719 he sent long reports of a mysterious Swede who arrived in the estuary of the Axe near Uphill, and was examined as a possible agent implicated in the invasion mounted that year by the duke of Ormond with Spanish support. Two years later he sent news of the 'insolence and disloyalty' of Jacobites on the birthday of the Pretender, James Stuart (PRO, SP 35/27/23).

Meanwhile Oldmixon attempted to maintain his literary career. In 1714 he had contributed a version of 'Dejanira to Hercules' to a new edition of *Ovid's Epistles*, originally published by Jacob Tonson with Dryden's collaboration in 1680. Now Oldmixon sought to interest Tonson in new work, including translations of the *Amores*, *De tristibus*, and the *Fasti* which ran to thousands of lines, along with extensive compilations on the history of Somerset and other counties, which occupied hundreds of sheets. None of this was published. Oldmixon complained to the Tonsons about difficulties and poor payment in relation to the index which he had compiled for Humphrey Prideaux's *Old and New Testament Connected* and volume 2 of Laurence Echard's *History of England*, both published in 1718. In December of that year Oldmixon wrote pathetically to Jacob Tonson sen., saying that he was 'banished in a corner of the country, surrounded with Jacobites, vilified, insulted and not having a minute's ease'. He asked Tonson to make representations to the duke of Newcastle 'that I may succeed Mr Rowe in the laureate's place which I was to have had before, had it not been for him as Sir Samuel Garth knows' (BL, Add. MS 28275, fol. 46). The application was unsuccessful, as Laurence Eusden was very shortly appointed poet laureate. Oldmixon continued to hound the Tonsons with complaints about the treatment he received, his monetary troubles, and personal isolation in Somerset—his wife was living in London all the while.

In 1724 Oldmixon became involved with James Brydges, duke of Chandos, who was pursuing land and business interests in Bridgwater. The main area of development lay in Castle Street, and Oldmixon rented one of the largest buildings in the street as the customs house. He also acted as agent for the duke's varied projects, and was invited to become a nominal partner in a glasshouse which Chandos had set up. The business connection survived, although under increasing strain, until 1731, by which time the duke had grown impatient with Oldmixon's financial management and had refused to pay sums which were the responsibility of the customs commissioners.

Historical writings During the 1720s Oldmixon shifted his principal concern as a writer to historiography. He had in fact taken a leading share with John Hughes in the compilation of *A Complete History of England* (1706), a cento of older sources supplemented by a section on recent history by White Kennet. He now began a series of strongly whig narratives which focused chiefly on the seventeenth century and singled out Clarendon's *History of the Rebellion* for particular reprobation, with Echard a secondary target. The prime documents are *The Critical History of England* (2 vols., 1724-6); *A Review of Dr Zachary Grey's Defence of our Ancient and Modern Historians* (1725); and *Clarendon and Whitlock Compar'd* (1727). It was in 1729 that controversy really flared, with the appearance of Oldmixon's massive *History of England, during the Reigns of the Royal House of Stuart*. In this he expanded earlier hints and accused Clarendon's editors—Francis Atterbury, Henry Aldrich, and George Smalridge—of falsifying the text of the *History*. He printed an anonymous letter, written by George Duckett, which supported this contention, on the basis of statements made to Duckett by Edmund Smith in 1710. An extensive debate was set off by these charges, with contributions by Atterbury himself and others, as well as three further interventions by Oldmixon himself. The *History of the Stuarts* also provoked the elderly tory Lord Lansdowne into vindicating his ancestors General Monk and Sir Richard Grenville. This in turn prompted a pamphlet in response from Oldmixon. A decisive rebuttal of all the charges against the editors was made by John Burton in *The Genuineness of Lord Clarendon's 'History of the Rebellion'* (1744). Later scholarship has confirmed Burton's position.

Oldmixon was now in his sixties and suffering poor health, but he still kept up a frenzied pace. His gigantic history of England was completed with two long folios devoted respectively to the reigns of William and Mary, Anne, and George I (1735), and to the Tudors (1739). There were new editions of several of his works, including the long popular work of political soothsaying, *Nixon's Cheshire Prophecy* (c.1715), which celebrated the Hanoverian accession, and reached its 'fifteenth' edition by Curll in 1744—it was still being published into the nineteenth century. Meanwhile Oldmixon had been forced to relinquish

his customs post in 1736, and soon afterwards lost a royal bounty paid at the instance of Queen Caroline until her death in 1737. He was saddled with a large debt to the crown, incurred as he claimed by his deputy, and petitioned the Treasury for relief in 1740. More efficacious was a personal letter of appeal to the duke of Newcastle in the following year, which resulted in a grant of £50 from the royal bounty. He told the duke that he had been dragged 'to a place I cannot mention in the midst of all the infirmities of old age, sickness, lameness and almost blindness', a poor reward for his services for 'that good cause I have all my life long laboured to serve in the worst of times' (BL, Add. MS 32697, fol. 308).

After many years of ill health, Oldmixon died at his home in Great Pulteney Street, London, on 9 July 1742, with his age listed in the press as sixty-nine. He was buried three days later at St Mary's, Ealing, near an unidentified son and daughter. Later that month there appeared Oldmixon's most vivid and arresting book, his posthumous *Memoirs of the Press*, which sets out in detail the calamities of authorship as he had experienced them. It is a record of ingratitude and disregard suffered at the hands of those such as Walpole whom Oldmixon had expected to reward him for his services to the whig cause.   PAT ROGERS

Sources P. Rogers, 'The whig controversialist as dunce: a study of John Oldmixon', PhD diss., U. Cam., 1968 · C. H. C. Baker and M. I. Baker, *The life and circumstances of James Brydges, first duke of Chandos, patron of the liberal arts* (1949) · F. H. Ellis, *Swift vs Mainwaring: The Examiner and The Medley* (1985) · P. Rogers, 'John Oldmixon in Bridgwater, 1716–30', *Transactions of Somersetshire Archaeological and Natural History Society*, 93 (1969), 16–30 · P. Rogers, 'Two notes on John Oldmixon and his family', *N&Q*, 215 (1970), 293–300 · P. Rogers, 'John Oldmixon and the family of Admiral Blake', *Notes and Queries for Somerset and Dorset*, 29 (1968–73), 185–8 · P. Rogers, 'Oldmixon, Francis Gwynn and the Prideaux family', *Notes and Queries for Somerset and Dorset*, 29 (1968–73), 54–7 · P. Rogers, 'Sir John Bawden, John Oldmixon's uncle', *Notes and Queries for Somerset and Dorset*, 30 (1974–9), 357–62 · P. Rogers, 'The Catholick poet (1716): John Oldmixon's attack on Pope', *Bodleian Library Record*, 8 (1967–72), 277–84 · P. Rogers, 'The memoirs of Somers and Wharton', *Bulletin of the New York Public Library*, 77 (1974), 224–35 · P. Rogers, 'The conduct of the earl of Nottingham: Curll, Oldmixon and the Finch family', *Review of English Studies*, new ser., 21 (1970), 175–81 · P. Rogers, 'An early colonial historian', *Journal of American Studies*, 7 (1973), 113–23

Archives PRO, letters | BL, Add. MSS 28275, 32697 · BL OIOC · PRO, CII chancery proceedings · PRO, petitions and memoranda · U. Edin., Laing MSS

Wealth at death indigent; annual bounty from Queen Caroline ceased at her death (1737); £50 bounty in 1741, after petition to Treasury and appeal to duke of Newcastle

Old Pretender, the. *See* James Francis Edward (1688–1766).

Oldroyd, Sir Mark (1843-1927), woollen manufacturer and politician, was born on 30 May 1843 at Spinkwell, Dewsbury, Yorkshire, the youngest of the three sons and two daughters of Mark Oldroyd (1797–1874) and his wife, Rachel, the daughter of Marmaduke Fox, of Soothill, Dewsbury. He was educated, to the age of thirteen, in the small local school in Dewsbury of Jesse Smith, then at Batley grammar school, and lastly at New College, St

John's Wood, London, a theological college for Congregationalists, where he trained for the ministry. But his religious vocation was not pursued and he returned to Dewsbury in 1862 to enter the family woollen firm.

The family firm had been established by Oldroyd's father in 1818, after he moved from Hanging Heaton, near Dewsbury, and relinquished his interest in an early local joint-stock company woollen mill. Mark senior was joined in the business by his eldest son, George, and his second son, John, establishing the name of the firm as M. Oldroyd & Sons. The father retired in 1859, leaving the running of the business to George and John, who agreed in 1862 to their father's request to admit Mark junior. As was common at the time, the new junior member of the firm received experience in the various departments of the business. John, however, remained firmly in control of the enterprise, providing the main business mind and taking responsibility for formulating policy. Mark Oldroyd married Maria Tew Mewburn, the daughter of William Mewburn of Wykham Park, Banbury, but previously of Halifax, in 1871. They lived at Hyrstlands in Batley. There were no children.

In 1874 the firm became one of the earliest in the woollen industry to be formed into a limited liability company. By that date George had retired and John and Mark carried on the business as life directors, within the articles of association of the company. The company was floated with a capital of £750,000 in £10 shares, and it amalgamated with the blanket-making business of Blakeley and Latta of Hunslet Mills, Leeds, with which it had previously had a co-partnership.

In 1877 John Oldroyd got into serious personal financial difficulties and was forced to relinquish his connection with the firm. Mark Oldroyd was left with the responsibility of rebuilding and managing the family business. This he did with rapid and great success, creating one of the major enterprises of the British woollen industry in the late nineteenth century. It was a giant in an industry where firms were typically very small. By the 1880s the business had a blanket works near Leeds which could make 1000 pairs of blankets a day, and four large factories in Dewsbury with a peak output of 7000 to 8000 yards of heavy broadcloth a day. By 1888 the business employed over 2000 workers on 18 acres of mill floor space and had substantial interests in two collieries at Castleford, which supplied coal for the textile works.

In the closing decades of the nineteenth century the British woollen industry was holding its own against competition from the continental powers. Its ability to do so was largely the result of its skill in the use of raw materials, particularly the incorporation of shoddy and mungo (wool recovered from rags) in new cloth. Shoddy provided a cheap and effective raw material for the Yorkshire woollen industry, allowing costs and prices to be kept low and products to be adapted rapidly to price fluctuations. Oldroyd had a central role in this trade, not through any major technical contribution, but through the scale of his enterprise and its significance within the local economy of the Dewsbury district. He had a reputation as an independent businessman of high moral standards who paid attention to the well-being of his workforce and recognized its value to the business. He was reputed to have paid above average wages and to have maintained a very loyal and reliable labour force. He was described as being a solitary, aloof, and rather brusque figure. However, many contemporary reports indicate particular respect for him among his workforce and within the neighbourhood. His legacy to the industry and the local community was more significant than that of many of his peers. He championed the cause of woollen manufacture in national debate on industrial and commercial matters, providing evidence to the royal commission on depression of trade and industry in 1886, serving the local chamber of commerce, and acting as president of the Heavy Woollen District Manufacturers' Association from its inception in 1912 until his retirement in 1920. He extolled free trade as a major supporter of the West Riding Free Trade Federation.

Oldroyd was associated with the Congregational church throughout his life. For sixty-three years he was a member of the United Congregational Church in Dewsbury, and he became its senior deacon. On occasions he addressed the annual meeting of the Congregational Union of England and Wales. He supported missionary work and many local charities, including the local Guild of Help and the Dewsbury Day Nursery. In 1919 he donated £10,000 towards the establishment of a children's ward at Dewsbury and District Infirmary. He remained a staunch advocate of temperance and of personal and religious freedom. His political commitment was as a stalwart Liberal, of the Gladstonian persuasion, and from 1868 he was active in the local Liberal Party organization. He served Dewsbury as a councillor, alderman, and mayor and was the first chairman of the Non-County Boroughs Association. He was made the first honorary freeman of Dewsbury in 1919. As the member of parliament for the Dewsbury constituency for thirteen years (from the by-election of 1888) he spoke infrequently in the House of Commons, but had an active involvement in committees concerned with trade and factory legislation. He was knighted in 1909.

Oldroyd's local and national commitments gradually diverted his energies away from the day-to-day management of the woollen business, which was left to the other directors, but he remained firmly in control of the policy of the firm until his retirement. He resigned his life directorship in 1913, but continued as chairman until 1920. His wife died in 1919, and the following year he married Annie Jane, the daughter of a Gainsborough merchant, Richard Pattison; she died in 1926. Oldroyd died suddenly from a seizure on 5 July 1927 at the home in Goathland, Yorkshire, to which he had retired. He was buried in Batley on 8 July. His surprisingly small estate of £93,124 was left mainly for the benefit of the workpeople, past, present, and future, of his firm.   D. T. JENKINS

Sources *Dewsbury Reporter* (9 July 1927) · *Industries of Yorkshire* (1888) · D. T. Jenkins, 'Oldroyd, Sir Mark', *DBB* · *Wool Record and Textile World* (9 July 1927) · *Textile Manufacturer* (Aug–Nov 1877) · C. J.

James, *M.P. for Dewsbury: one hundred years of parliamentary representation* (1970) · *WWW*, 1981–90
Archives U. Newcastle
Likenesses F. Watt, portrait, Kirklees District Council
Wealth at death £93,124: Jenkins, 'Oldroyd, Sir Mark'; *The Times* (1 Oct 1927)

Oldys, Valentine (1620–1685), poet, was born in Oxford, the son of Valentine Oldis, a London merchant. He went to school in Newport, Shropshire, and was admitted pensioner at Sidney Sussex College, Cambridge, on 19 September 1650.

Oldys published *A Poem on the Restoration of King Charles* in 1660, and was a patron of literature and men of letters. He is among the contributors of commendatory verses to Henry Bold's *Poems Lyrique, Macaronique, Heroique, &c.* (1664) and one of the poems in the volume is addressed to him. He also contributed to Alexander Brome's *Songs, and other Poems* (1664). John Phillips dedicated to Oldys his *Macaronides, or, Virgil Travesty* (1673).

Oldys was made MD of Cambridge *per literas regias* on 6 October 1671, and honorary member of the College of Physicians on 30 September 1680. He died in 1685, and was buried near his father in St Helen, Bishopsgate, by St Mary Axe. RONALD BAYNE, *rev.* JOANNA MOODY

Sources Watt, *Bibl. Brit.* · W. T. Lowndes, *The bibliographer's manual of English literature*, ed. H. G. Bohn, [new edn], 3 (1864), 2384 · Munk, *Roll* · Venn, *Alum. Cant.* · BL, Birch MS 4240 [memoirs of the Oldys family]

Oldys, William (1591?–1644?). *See under* Oldys, William (1696–1761).

Oldys, William (1636–1708), civil lawyer and advocate of the Admiralty, was born in Adderbury, Oxfordshire, on 19 October 1636. He was one of eleven surviving children of William *Oldys (1591?–1644?) [*see under* Oldys, William (1696–1761)], vicar of Adderbury, who was killed in a skirmish with parliamentary soldiers, and Margaret (*d.* 1705), daughter of Ambrose Sacheverall. At the age of twelve he entered Winchester College. He then studied civil law at New College, Oxford (BCL, 1661; DCL, 1667), where he was a fellow from 1655 to 1671. In 1670 Oldys was admitted an advocate of Doctors' Commons, the society of civil lawyers who practised in the ecclesiastical and Admiralty courts. He was made chancellor of the diocese of Lincoln in 1683 and held that office until his death. In 1685 he stood unsuccessfully for parliament for Oxford, for what Wood says was the third time (Wood, *Ath. Oxon.: Fasti*, 2.54). Oldys was named advocate of the Admiralty by the royal warrant of James II in July 1686. Within two months, however, he was one of the counsel for Bishop Compton, who had been brought before the ecclesiastical commission for refusing the king's orders to suppress anti-Catholic preaching. At about this time Oldys contributed the life of Pompey to a new translation of Plutarch's *Lives* (*Plutarch's 'Lives', Translated from the Greek by Several Hands*, 4, 1685).

Oldys maintained his place at the Admiralty after the revolution of 1688. In November 1692, however, he refused to prosecute as pirates the Irish captains and officers of vessels who were acting under letters of marque issued by King James from his court in France. In September 1693 Oldys was called before the council to defend his position. He explained that, under the law of nations, even deposed monarchs, when fighting to regain their thrones, had the authority to grant commissions to privateers. It was a dangerous response, since the ruling explanation of the revolution was that James had not been deposed but had 'abdicated'. Sir John Trenchard, the northern secretary, denounced such reasons as 'amount[ing] to high treason' and demanded to know 'what do you think of the abdication?' Oldys replied that he accepted it 'since it was voted', but that the defendants might reasonably have believed otherwise. Not surprisingly, this failed to satisfy and he was removed from his position and replaced with Fisher Littleton, who, at the same meeting, assured the council that the men in question were 'not enemies but rogues' (*State trials*, 12.1270–75). The defendants were tried and several hanged. Oldys's arguments were attacked the next year in a pamphlet by Matthew Tindal, titled *An Essay Concerning the Law of Nations, and the Rights of Soveraigns* (1694).

Oldys continued to practise law and in 1696 found himself representing two privateers (these commissioned by the king of France) who were being prosecuted for treason. His career prospered and by the time of his death in 1708 he had a successful practice and had accumulated a considerable estate. This included a library of more than 1000 volumes that was promptly acquired by Doctors' Commons. 'As a scholar, he was respectable; as a civilian, he was learned; as a pleader, eloquent and judicious' (Coote, 95).

The specifics of Oldys's domestic life are less than clear. Some material suggests he married Theodosia Lovett, the widow of Robert Lovett of Liscombe, Buckinghamshire, and daughter of Sir John Halsey of Great Gaddesden, Hertfordshire, some time after 1686 and that she survived his death. She is not, however, mentioned in his will, executed in 1701. The principal beneficiary of that will was the testator's 'loving cozen', Ann Oldys (1671–1711), the daughter of Oldys's first cousin and assumed to be his mistress (Yeowell, v–vi). Besides some token bequests to his mother and siblings, Ann Oldys inherited all of the estate, including two houses in Kensington said to be already in her possession. Oldys is also said to have fathered his only child, William *Oldys (1696–1761), the well-known antiquary and bibliographer, in that relationship. He inherited Oldys's property from his mother in 1711.

RICHARD S. KAY

Sources [W. Oldys], Family memoirs, BL, Add. MS 4240 · *A literary antiquary: memoir of William Oldys ... together with his diary*, ed. J. Yeowell (1862), v–vii · *State trials*, 12.1270–79 · *DNB* · [C. Coote], *Sketches of the lives and characters of eminent English civilians, with an historical introduction relative to the College of Advocates* (1804), 93–5 · Wood, *Ath. Oxon.: Fasti* · *The life and times of Anthony Wood*, ed. A. Clark, 3, OHS, 26 (1894), 171 · *Remarks and collections of Thomas Hearne*, ed. C. E. Doble and others, 1, OHS, 2 (1885), 83–4 · will, PRO, PROB 11/501, sig. 97 · J. C. Sainty, ed., *Admiralty officials, 1660–1870* (1975), 98, 142 · J. S. Bromley, *Corsairs and navies, 1660–1760* (1987), 157 · PRO, HCA1/13 pts 1 & 2

Oldys, William (1696–1761), herald and antiquary, was born on 14 July 1696, probably in London, the son of the civil lawyer William *Oldys (1636–1708) and his mistress, Ann (1671–1711).

Family background Oldys's grandfather, also **William Oldys** (1591?–1644?), matriculated at New College, Oxford, in 1610, graduated BA in 1614 and MA in 1618, and was a proctor of the university in 1623. He was vicar of Adderbury in Oxfordshire from 1627 and was created DD on 16 January 1643. A staunch supporter of Charles I during the civil war, Oldys went into hiding in Banbury, but was betrayed while conducting his wife, Margaret (*née* Sacheverall, *d.* 1705), and his third son, William, on the road to Winchester. Pursued by parliamentary forces, his horse refused to pass his own house at Adderbury and he was shot and killed by one of the soldiers. A long inscription from the monument in Adderbury church was published in 1785 in the *Gentleman's Magazine* (volume 55, pp. 106–7). His son William was married to Theodosia Lovett, and kept a mistress, Ann, who took the name of Oldys and whom he maintained 'very privately, and probably very meanly', sending her leftover food from taverns on the excuse that it was for his cat (Noble, 419). He died in 1708, and whereas his library was bought by Doctors' Commons, he left two houses in Kensington and the residue of his estate to his 'loving cozen Mrs. Ann Oldys'; she died in 1711, leaving her property to 'her loving friend' Benjamin Jackman, 'for the benefit of her son William Oldys', the future herald, who always claimed Dr Oldys for his father. She further left 'the tuition and guardianship of her son … during his minority' to Jackman (Yeowell, vi).

Early studies Although the young William Oldys was left money for his education, nothing is known of it. He lost money in the South Sea Bubble of 1720, and involved himself in protracted litigation. In 1722–3 he collaborated with Pierre des Maizeaux on a biography of Richard Carew, for a new edition of his *Survey of Cornwall*, but his literary studies were otherwise concentrated upon an interleaved, annotated copy of Langbaine's *Account of the Early Dramatic Poets* (1691). In 1724 Oldys left his London lodgings, in the house of a Mr Burridge, and went to Yorkshire, where he lived, principally at the seat of the first earl of Malton, until 1730. In 1725 he visited the museum of the recently deceased Ralph Thoresby in Leeds. In 1729 he wrote 'An essay on epistolary writings, with respect to the grand collection of Thomas, earl of Strafford', dedicating it to the earl of Malton (it is now in the Beinecke Library, c476). He was unable to prevent the destruction of the manuscript collections of the antiquary Richard Gascoigne by Thomas Wentworth, Baron Malton, in 1728. He was, however, compiling collections of his own, such as the 200 volumes he bought from the library of the earl of Stamford, the earl of Clarendon's collections of historical

William Oldys (1696–1761), by E. Balston, pubd 1795

and political manuscripts, other state papers, and 'a very large collection of English heads in sculpture' (Yeowell, xii).

Oldys is credited with *A Collection of Epigrams* (1727). Between 1728 and 1731 he wrote some twenty papers for Henry Baker's *Universal Spectator*. On his return to London in 1730 he found his books had been dispersed, including the annotated Langbaine, which had been bought by Thomas Coxeter, who would not return it. On Coxeter's death his books were bought by Thomas Osborne, and they were sold again in 1748; Oldys's notes and Coxeter's additions were heavily used by Theophilus Cibber and Robert Shiels in *Lives of the Poets* (5 vols., 1753). About 1730 Oldys compiled a manuscript case (now in the British Library) for a projected edition of *The Negotiations of Sir Thomas Roe*, one volume of which eventually appeared in 1740. About 1731 Oldys became friendly with Edward Harley, the second earl of Oxford, who visited him in Gray's Inn in London and paid £40 for his collections. Oldys used Harley's library for his *Dissertation upon Pamphlets* of 1731 (reprinted with another contribution in Morgan's *Phoenix Britannicus* of 1732) and other bibliographical work. He contributed songs such as 'Busy, Curious, Thirsty Fly!' (later translated into Latin by Samuel Johnson) to *The Scarborough Miscellany* between 1732 and 1734, while working on his first major publication, an edition of Sir Walter Ralegh's *History of the World* (2 vols., 1736). This was prefaced by a colossal 'Life of the author, newly compil'd, from materials more ample and authentick than have yet been publish'd'. A surviving letter to Sir Hans Sloane, dated 29

September 1735, indicates that Oldys was using the baronet's collection for research alongside Harley's. Gibbon was so impressed by Oldys's work that he abandoned his own plans to write a biography of Ralegh.

Grose records that the booksellers were sufficiently impressed by the success of the Ralegh volume to offer to pay Oldys for the use of his name in selling a different work, and that Oldys indignantly refused the offer, despite his insecure financial position. He was generous in assisting editors and booksellers with information, furnishing the importunate Edmund Curll with some notes on Nell Gwyn for a *History of the Stage* (1741), and giving biographical notices on scarce authors to Elizabeth Cooper (for *The Muses Library*, 1737) and Thomas Haywood (for *The British Muse*, 3 vols., 1738, which had a dedication to Lady Mary Wortley Montagu written by Oldys). Mrs Cooper, whose anthology was dedicated to the Honourable Society for the Encouragement of Learning and contained passages of Langland, Lydgate, and Hoccleve, as well as later writers, also borrowed many of Oldys's rare books for a proposed continuation, which failed to appear. In 1737 Oldys began publishing his own researches in *The British Librarian*, a miscellaneous bibliographical compilation of rare books and manuscripts. It was published in six monthly numbers, from January to June 1737, and was thereafter issued as a composite volume with an index of subjects in 1738. It was designed to bring to light 'curious' publications and to offer a bibliographical record for early books: three William Caxton items, from the collection of Peter Thompson, are described, together with works by St Gildas, Thomas More, Richard Hakluyt, Thomas Elyot, William Prynne, Elias Ashmole, and Robert Plot. Each number contained at least one manuscript item. Oldys had used the libraries of the duke of Montagu, John Anstis, Thomas Ames, and some of his neighbours in Gray's Inn—Nathaniel Booth and Charles Grimes. The book was prefaced by an optimistic statement of editorial intention, but in the postscript (from Gray's Inn, dated 18 February [1738]) Oldys cites the 'vast and unseen Mass of Reading' needed to produce the comparatively 'small Quantity of Writing' (W. Oldys, *The British Librarian*, 1738, 375) as a reason for discontinuing the project for the time being. A surviving diary for the period from 1737 to 1738 contains little personal information but records conversations with scholars such as Joseph Ames, Thomas Birch, John Strype, Hans Sloane, George Vertue, and John Christopher Pepusch. Oldys records sales, visits to scientific exhibitions, curious events, and scraps of information, with reminders to himself to check particular sources. He makes many complaints about poor treatment by patrons, collectors, and scholars, and expresses his displeasure at the way his prefatory essay to Hayward's *British Muse*, containing a history of anthologies, had been hastily abridged.

Harley's literary secretary Oldys's diary ends with the arrival of some money from Harley. On reading *The British Librarian*, Harley promised Oldys more remunerative employment and dissuaded him from applying to Sir Robert Walpole, about whose ancestors Oldys had collected

some deeds. In 1738 Oldys, having detached himself from all other patronage, became Harley's literary secretary (and drinking companion), a position which allowed him free use of the library and an introduction to Oxford's circle, which included Alexander Pope. Pope told him Thomas Betterton's story that Sir William Davenant was the natural son of Shakespeare, and Oldys claims to have given Pope (via Oxford) some hints on Shakespeare. His duties for the earl prevented him from completing several biographical contributions to Birch's *General Dictionary, Historical and Critical* (1734–1741), a deprivation of income he later resented. For Harley he attended auctions and sales and transcribed manuscripts for the collection, and had received some £150 by 1739. He also organized Harley's vast collection of manuscript letters for binding, with abstracts and tables of contents. For these services he was paid a further £200 a year until Harley's death in June 1741, a return which he seems to have regarded as inadequate, while acknowledging that he lived on exceptionally good terms with him:

> For the profit of about 500l. I devoted the best part of ten years' service to, and in his lordship's library; impoverished my own stores to enrich the same; disabled myself in my studies, and the advantages they might have produced from the publick; deserted the pursuits which might have obtained me a permanent accommodation; and procured the prejudice and misconceit of his lordship's surviving relations. (Yeowell, xx)

Oldys's *British Librarian* had been published by Thomas Osborne, and it was Osborne who bought for £13,000 Harley's collection of printed books, intending to dispose of them through an elaborate bibliographical catalogue to be edited by Samuel Johnson and Oldys. The first two volumes of *Catalogus Bibliothecae Harleianae* appeared on 12 March 1743, after some six months' work; the third and fourth volumes were published on 4 January 1744. The contributions of Johnson and Oldys are difficult to distinguish. Meanwhile, Osborne proposed (in terms provided by Johnson) a weekly subscription serial known as *The Harleian Miscellany*, which reprinted some of the scarcer tracts from the collection and which commenced in March 1744 with Oldys as its supervisory editor. It eventually ran to eight volumes (1744–6). Alongside the *Miscellany* Oldys edited *A Copious and Exact Catalogue of Pamphlets in the Harleian Library*, which appeared piecemeal but eventually constituted a quarto volume of 168 pages, offering bibliographical descriptions of almost 550 items. Like many of Oldys's publications, this was valued highly by collectors and scholars, and several annotated copies exist.

Oldys provided a life of Thomas Moufet for a new edition of his *Health's Improvement*, published in 1745 by Osborne, but thereafter terminated their connection. He wrote the 'Historical essay' which prefaces the edition of Michael Drayton's *Works* of 1748, and between 1747 and 1760 wrote some twenty-two articles for the first edition of the *Biographia Britannica*, including lives of Edward Alleyn, Drayton, Sir George Etherege, and George Farquhar. His substantial accounts of Caxton, based on extensive examination of his output as a printer, of Sir John Fastolf (enlarged from an earlier contribution to the *General Dictionary*), and of Richard Hakluyt, were regarded as especially illuminating. Some authorities credit him with the co-editorship, with Joseph Towers, of the project as a whole. Oldys's manuscript notes on other figures (notably Arabella Stuart, John Barclay, Mary Beale, and Samuel Butler) were later bought by Thomas Cadell, one of the publishers of the second edition of *Biographia Britannica*, and heavily mined (with acknowledgement) by the editor, Andrew Kippis.

Norroy king-at-arms and final years Despite his labours Oldys was unable to pay his rent in Gray's Inn and was confined to the Fleet prison. Surviving letters to Thomas Birch, dated 22 July 1751 and 23 August 1751, acknowledge helpful sums of money from Birch himself and from 'the Hon. Mr. Yorke' through the agency of Mr Southwell, brother of the second Lord Southwell. His 'loitering, lingering, useless condition' (Yeowell, xxxiii) was ended when his debts were paid by his friends. One account states that Oldys wrote to the duke of Norfolk (Edward Howard, a friend of Harley's), who received the letter at dinner, read it out, and dispatched a messenger to give Oldys money and pay off his debts. Another version relates that the debts were paid by Southwell. The duke of Norfolk was certainly responsible for obtaining for Oldys the post of Norroy king-at-arms, to which he was appointed by patent on 5 May 1755, having previously, on 15 April, been created Norfolk herald-extraordinary at the College of Arms by the earl of Effingham in order to qualify for the office of Norroy. Oldys appointed Edward Orme of Chester as his deputy, and took up residence in the west wing of the College of Arms. There was apparently some resentment among the heralds at Oldys's rapid promotion to a provincial kingship, and malicious rumours were spread to the effect that Oldys was a Roman Catholic.

Two anecdotes indicate something of Oldys's duties during this period. In one story he tells how, having observed another herald correct himself during the reading of a proclamation and thus appear clumsy, when his own turn came 'he read on through thick and thin, never stopping a moment to correct his errors, and thereby excited the applause of the people', despite making more mistakes than his predecessor (Taylor, 1.26). In the other, which apparently first appeared in the colourful sketch of Oldys in the *Olio* (1796) of the Richmond herald, Captain Francis Grose, Oldys is said to have been 'rarely sober in the afternoon, and never after supper' and to have been so drunk at the funeral of Princess Caroline that the crown, which he was holding on a cushion, nearly fell off (Noble, 420). Noble disputes this story on the grounds that at a royal funeral the crown should have been borne by Clarenceux, not Norroy, and Clarenceux is identified as the bearer in *The London Journal* of 5 January 1758 and in *Reed's Weekly Journal* of 7 January. Norroy had been the officer responsible at the funeral of Queen Caroline in 1737, however. Aside from official duties Oldys continued to collect and study books and manuscripts, furnishing a large upstairs room as a library. At one stage he reckoned his collection of historical and political pamphlets amounted to 5000

items. He wrote out scraps of information on slips of paper, classifying and sorting them into parchment bags for each biographical subject. Among these was Shakespeare, whose biography he had agreed to write for Walker, a bookseller, for 20 guineas (later reclaimed from his friend Taylor); his materials were used by Isaac Reed. He also made notes on Sir John Suckling, Aphra Behn (whose biography he had written in the *General Dictionary*), Edmund Spenser, John Milton, and John Dryden, including a memorandum to 'search the old papers in one of my large deal boxes for Mr. Dryden's letter of thanks to my father, for some communications relating to Plutarch' (Yeowell, 32). He visited archives and libraries throughout the capital, making notes on the provenance, prices, and fate of notable collections.

In 1753 Oldys had published *Observations on the Cure of William Taylor, the Blind Boy of Igtham, in Kent*, in collaboration with John Taylor, an oculist in London's Hatton Garden, who performed the cure. Taylor became Oldys's chief friend, and Oldys frequently passed evenings at Taylor's house. Oldys is said to have preferred the quiet of the fireside in the kitchen to more formal social gatherings, and Taylor's son records that he was so particular in his habits that he could not smoke his pipe with ease until his chair was fixed close to a particular crack in the floor. Oldys would not meet Taylor's father, Chevalier Taylor, until the latter sought him out, and spoke to him in Latin, whereupon the two men talked for several hours in that language. Grose relates, however, that Oldys had imbibed a taste for the company to be found in the Fleet prison, formed a 'Dragon Club', and used to drink with his companions 'the Rulers' (because they lived within the rules of the prison) at The Bell in the Old Bailey, near the College of Arms, employing a watchman to get him home before midnight to avoid paying a fine. Grose says that Oldys's favourite drink was porter, washed down with gin.

Oldys's last biographical work was a life of Charles Cotton, prefixed to Sir John Hawkins's edition of Izaak Walton's *Compleat Angler* (1760). Oldys is praised by Grose for his 'great good-nature, honour, and integrity, particularly in his character as an historian', in which respect Grose thought him absolutely incorruptible (Noble, 420). He appears to have had a loose connection with the Society of Antiquaries. He did not marry. He died at his rooms in the College of Arms at about 5 a.m. on 15 April 1761 and was buried on 19 April in the parish church of St Benet Paul's Wharf, towards the upper end of the north aisle. His age was given as seventy-two on the coffin, but he was actually not quite sixty-five. He died intestate. Administration of his property was granted to John Taylor, his friend and major creditor; Taylor paid for the funeral and took possession of Oldys's regalia, books, and manuscripts. Taylor was the owner of a painting of Oldys (looking well-fed and well-dressed), later engraved by Balston, with Oldys's own punning motto beneath:

In word and *Will I am* a friend to you,
And one friend *Old is* worth a hundred new.

Oldys's printed books, including many with his habitual

copious annotation, were sold with some of the manuscripts (and two other libraries) by Thomas Davies, beginning on 12 April 1762. Oldys had bought a second copy of Langbaine's *Account of the English Dramatick Poets* (1691) in 1727, and continued to annotate it marginally and interlinearly until he died; this copy was bought by Thomas Birch, who loaned it to Thomas Percy, who copied the notes into a further interleaved copy of Langbaine, from which Joseph Haslewood annotated his own copy. Steevens, Malone, and Reed also made copies of Oldys's notes. Birch eventually left the volume to the British Museum. Other annotated books included copies of *England's Parnassus*, Butler's *Hudibras*, John Philips's *Life of Milton*, William Nicolson's *English Scotch and Irish Historical Libraries*, and Thomas Fuller's *Worthies of England*, which Steevens bought. Among his manuscript collections were: a catalogue of materials relating to the history of London (used by Richard Gough in his *British Topography* of 1780); a series of remarks on the major institutional and private libraries in London and their catalogues (extending an earlier manuscript by John Bagford, and now in the Hunterian Collection, Glasgow); a catalogue of engraved portraits of national figures; 'Memoirs relating to the family of Oldys' (BL, Add. MS 4240), of which a substantial portion relating to his father was published in the *Gentleman's Magazine* in 1784 (volume 54); collections of data on English poets; commonplace books; and many observations on aspects of natural history. Taylor retained some manuscripts until Thomas Percy requested the loan of them; many were used by literary scholars and were gradually dispersed or acquired by institutions. While Oldys's own attempts at systematic study and publication petered out because of the magnitude of the tasks, his work was thus harnessed by writers such as Thomas Warton (in his *History of English Poetry*) and Johnson (*Lives of the English Poets*) into more literary and comprehensive form. Among more personal manuscript items are: his diary; a collection of poems; and materials for a work called *The patron, or, A portraiture of patronage and dependency, more especially as they appear in their domestick light and attitudes*, which perhaps indicates something of Oldys's feelings regarding his subservient position.   PAUL BAINES

Sources *A literary antiquary: memoir of William Oldys … together with his diary*, ed. J. Yeowell (1862) · *GM*, 1st ser., 7 (1737) · *GM*, 1st ser., 36 (1761), 189 · *GM*, 1st ser., 54 (1784), 32, 161, 260, 329–32 · *GM*, 1st ser., 55 (1785), 106–7 · M. Noble, *A history of the College of Arms* (1805), 419–22 · J. Taylor, *Records of my life*, 2 vols. (1832), 1.25–9 · I. D'Israeli, *A second series of curiosities of literature*, 3 vols. (1824), 3.448–88 · B. Corney, *Facts relative to W. Oldys* (1837) · J. Walker, *An attempt towards recovering an account of the numbers and sufferings of the clergy of the Church of England*, pt 2 (1714), 323 · L. Lipking, *The ordering of the arts in the eighteenth century* (1970), 66–85 · T. Kaminsky, 'Johnson and Oldys as bibliographers: an introduction to the Harleian Catalogue', *Philological Quarterly*, 60 (1981), 439–53 · A. Chalmers, ed., *The general biographical dictionary*, new edn, 32 vols. (1812–17) · *N&Q*, 3rd ser., 2 (1862), 376 · Foster, *Alum. Oxon.* · J. Evans, *A history of the Society of Antiquaries* (1956), 100, 325 · A. Beesley, *The history of Banbury* (1841), 396, 523, 620 · administration, 20 June 1761, PRO, PROB 6/137, fol. 260v

Archives BL, commonplace books, Add. MSS 12522–12523 · BL, notes on trees, birds, and on Langbaine's *English Dramatick Poets*, Add. MSS 20724–20725, 22592–22595 · BL, printed works with MS notes and additions · S. Antiquaries, Lond., annotations to a MS copy of Edward Bolton's petition to James I for a royal academy · U. Glas., MS of London libraries · Yale U., Beinecke L., essay on epistolary writings with respect to the Grand Collection of Thomas, Earl of Strafford [copy]

Likenesses E. Balston, stipple, pubd 1795 (after unknown artist), BM, NPG [*see illus.*]

Wealth at death minimal; left MSS, books, herald's regalia: administration, PRO, PROB 6/137, fol. 260v

O'Leary, Arthur (1729–1802), Roman Catholic priest and religious controversialist, was born at Acres, a townland in the parish of Fanlobbus, near Dunmanway, co. Cork, to a tenant farming couple about whom nothing is known. Having been provided with the rudiments of a classical education at a local 'hedge school' O'Leary was obliged by the prohibition on Catholic education to leave Ireland for France to train for the priesthood. He entered the Capuchin college at St Malo in 1747 and was admitted to orders some time later. One of his first duties was as chaplain to the prisons and hospitals in St Malo during the Seven Years' War, when he ministered to British and Irish prisoners of war. Invited by the duc de Choiseul to encourage the Catholics among their number to transfer their allegiance to France, O'Leary declined because, he later maintained, he 'thought it a crime to engage the king of England's soldiers and sailors in the service of a Catholic monarch against their Protestant sovereign' (Buckley, 18). It was an emblematic moment in O'Leary's life and a pointer to his later advocacy of religious toleration.

Emergence as a public figure O'Leary returned to Ireland in 1771, having spent twenty-four years in France. Following his return he ministered for a number of years in Cork, where he was an energetic addition to the local Capuchin community. His most notable achievement was the construction of a small place of worship, long known as Father O'Leary's chapel, on a site adjoining Blackamoor Lane friary but he also attracted large congregations on account of his preaching, which was chiefly remarkable for strong moral reasoning, bold figure, and scriptural allusion. In 1775 Patrick Blair, a Scottish physician resident at Cork, published a tract entitled *Thoughts on Nature and Religion*, in which he challenged several key articles of Christianity, including the divinity of Christ; O'Leary responded with a combative defence of the doctrinal foundations of religion, entitled *A Defence of the Divinity of Christ and the Immortality of the Soul* (1776). Though it was unusual for Catholic priests, especially regulars, to engage in public disputation O'Leary tactfully informed the Church of Ireland ordinary of his intentions prior to entering into print. He also attempted to bring all believers on side by affirming general Christian principles as distinct from specifically Catholic principles, against the negative observations of sceptics, deists, and freethinkers. He was helped by his lucid writing style and a capacity for argument, and his work earned him applause from all quarters. Encouraged by this he turned his attention to the disagreement between Catholics as to whether the oath of allegiance approved by the Irish parliament in 1774 was doctrinally sound. He had no doubts of this and, eager to promote religious toleration, he disregarded the reservations of the archbishop of Dublin, Dr John Carpenter, and produced a pamphlet entitled *Loyalty Asserted, or, The New Test Oath Vindicated*. For the first time he averred that it was the duty of Irish Catholic subjects not to engage in 'conspiracies and treasonable practices' against their protestant king. He was sharply critical of the Stuarts, whose restoration would, he forecast, result in the 'aggravation of our yoke and new calamities'. More daringly still he claimed that if Christians focused on that on which they were in agreement rather than on their differences, and emphasized charity as opposed to 'religious inflammation' and 'evangelical spleen', it would ensure a welcome diminution in interdenominational dissension (Buckley, 65–9).

This advocacy of toleration was a radical message, given the depth of religious polarization in Ireland, and it enhanced O'Leary's reputation with Gallican Catholics and liberal protestants who were eager to foster interdenominational concord. However it was not until 1779, when the kingdom was gripped by rumours of a French invasion, that O'Leary achieved national renown, with *An Address to the Common People of the Roman Catholic Religion*, in which he urged Catholics to follow the example of their bishops and clergy and support the crown. A French invasion, O'Leary warned, would worsen the condition of the population and, if it brought about a reopening of the seventeenth-century land settlement, would threaten the 'free exercise of religion' and the diminution of 'the unhappy spirit of persecution' (A. O'Leary, *Miscellaneous Tracts*, 1781, 104). The warm welcome afforded this address stood him in good stead in 1780 in his dispute with John Wesley over the latter's claim that 'an open toleration of the Popish religion is inconsistent with the safety of a free people and a Protestant government'. Wesley justified his contention on the traditional ground that, since it was Catholic doctrine that 'no faith is to be kept with heretics', a protestant government could not safely 'tolerate or encourage Roman Catholics' so long as they adhered to 'their intolerant, persecuting principles' (ibid., 4–7). This restatement of traditional protestant anxieties concerning Roman Catholicism struck at the heart of the principles of toleration that O'Leary championed, and he responded combatively to what he denominated Wesley's 'false assertions'. In a series of letters, first published in the *Freeman's Journal* in March 1780, he accused Wesley of seeking to 'haunt the living with the images of the dead' (ibid., 77–8) before embarking on a measured but persuasive appeal for Christian toleration. It was an approach that served O'Leary well as it was he rather than Wesley that emerged from the dispute with an enhanced reputation. This gave his case for the repeal of the remainder of the penal laws against Catholics greater authority but, more significantly, it encouraged him to prepare a fuller statement of his views on religious toleration.

Apostle of toleration O'Leary's *Essay on Toleration, or, Plea for Liberty of Conscience* (1780) was one of the most radical and compelling statements in favour of religious and political forbearance published in late eighteenth-century Ireland.

Positing the thesis that reason as well as religion enjoined humanity to observe moderation O'Leary described the multiplicity of instances of persecution in history that were responsible for the premature death of 'fifty millions of human beings' as a blight on humanity when 'true religion' worked to mitigate and not to justify abuse. He went on to argue that the practice of 'true religion' should be preserved and perpetuated by the same means that established it—by preaching the Word of God, attended with prudence and discretion, the practice of all Christian virtues, boundless peace and charity' (A. O'Leary, *Miscellaneous Tracts*, 1781, 39). Indeed he cited Montesquieu in support of his contention that 'when many religions have got a footing in the state, they are to be tolerated'. His willingness to criticize the leaders of the Christian churches who failed to conduct themselves according to these principles added weight to his argument, particularly in the Irish context, where his plea for the extension of 'all social benefits to ... loyal subjects of every denomination' stood out (ibid., 80). The response to the tract was overwhelmingly positive, although by no means all its admirers embraced its radical implications. The high esteem with which O'Leary was regarded by liberal protestants is vividly illustrated by the decision of the patriot club, the Monks of St Patrick, to admit him to honorary membership. Catholics were also pleased, as is demonstrated by the willingness of the Irish Catholic Committee to provide £40 in 1781 to defray the cost of publishing a collected edition of O'Leary's writings and of the English Committee to distribute 100 copies gratis.

There was considerable speculation that O'Leary's allegiance to the Catholic church was less than secure because it was very unusual for Catholic priests to express publicly controversial opinions. His involvement with the campaign to safeguard the regular clergy against the threat of the imposition of new—or the enforcement of existing legal—restrictions in the early 1780s gave the lie to this suspicion; he was neither tempted to forsake the Catholic church nor interested in doing so. Indeed he looked with particular optimism to the future as the volunteer corps throughout most of the country admitted Catholics to membership; he became honorary chaplain of the radical Irish brigade, and the Ulster Volunteers pronounced publicly in favour of Catholic relief. His confidence in the volunteers was underlined by his presence at the opening of the grand national convention of volunteer delegates in Dublin in November 1783. However, the refusal of the delegates to promote Catholic enfranchisement, combined with allegations that the radicals who took control of the reform movement in 1784 sought to involve France, compelled him to rethink his attitude. He decided to yield to official blandishments and agreed to report on the activities of the Catholic advocates of parliamentary reform in return for pecuniary reward.

Controversialist More than any other event in his life O'Leary's acceptance of government remuneration in 1784 shaped his posthumous reputation and prompted allegations that he was a 'Castle Catholic'. It is indisputable that officials at Dublin Castle identified him as the means by which 'the real designs of the Catholics' (PRO, 100/14, fols. 123–4) could be established and that he apparently agreed to do so in return for an annual payment of £100. His motives are less clear. It is possible that he was drawn by the allure of financial security, since he was dependent on his position as a teacher of rhetoric at the Brunswick Street Academy in Cork, which he took up in 1783. If so it was not a prudent decision, as his failure to produce the required evidence caused officials quickly to lose confidence in him. O'Leary for his part appears to have concluded that what was asked of him was contrary to his commitment to the advancement of toleration. His relationship with Dublin Castle was both less consequential and less personally advantageous than has been suggested. More importantly the strong resistance shown by the Irish administration during the mid-1780s to further relief for Catholics convinced him that his hopes for early implementation of full religious toleration were unfounded. It took the public controversy generated by the Rightboy agrarian movement in Munster in the mid-1780s to disabuse him of the illusion that it was at all attainable.

Given the success of his inspirational appeal for calm in the face of a threatened French invasion in 1779 it was hardly surprising that O'Leary was invited by friends from co. Cork to make another appeal in 1786 as agrarian unrest gripped the southern half of the country. He responded with two addresses 'to the Common people', published in the *Cork Hibernian Chronicle* in February 1786, in which he appealed to the Rightboys to obey the law and to desist from violence. However, his observation that the Rightboys' actions were 'founded on poverty', that their mode of proceeding was 'moderate', that the manner in which the tithe was collected was 'oppressive', and that the Church of Ireland clergy were not free of responsibility was incautious (A. O'Leary, *Mr O'Leary's Defence*, 1787, appx). And instead of a repetition of the warm welcome that greeted his 1779 intervention he was plunged into controversy as supporters of the Church of Ireland rushed to defend their church. O'Leary was disturbed by the vehemence of the criticism directed at him, since he had not set out to criticize the Church of Ireland. Moreover his remarks convinced many protestants that the Rightboys were part of a wider Catholic conspiracy to undermine the protestant constitution in church and state, and he was a prime target for the neo-conservative voices that were raised in support of a law and order response. His most passionate critic was Patrick Duigenan, who identified O'Leary—'the Fryar *with the barbarous surname*'—as the 'instructor of the peasantry in religion and politicks' (Theophilus, 17). This was both offensive and gratuitous but it struck home. Realizing that his hopes for religious toleration as well as his reputation had been severely set back O'Leary prepared a detailed response in which he amply defended himself against the allegations of his accusers. The most striking feature of his defence is his assertion that his critics were intolerant, because it bears witness to

his disappointment at the palpable rise in interdenominational antagonism that took place in the mid-1780s. Liberal protestants, well disposed towards tithe reform, were more supportive but this was not enough to ease O'Leary's concerns. Dispirited by the rejection of his vision of a tolerant future he chose to leave Ireland in 1789 for the more congenial atmosphere of England, and he spent the remainder of his life in London.

London O'Leary served as a chaplain to the Spanish embassy on his arrival in London. One of his colleagues was Thomas Hussey, later bishop of Waterford, but their relationship was difficult and was the subject of *Narrative of the Misunderstanding between the Rev. A. O'Leary and Rev Mr. Hussey* in 1791. O'Leary meanwhile was introduced by Edmund Burke to whig society. His natural bonhomie, abundance of anecdote, and skill as a conversationalist meant that he was a welcome guest even of the prince of Wales for reasons other than his reputation as an apostle of religious toleration. He attended meetings of the English Catholic Committee, although he was less than impressed by their readiness to describe themselves as 'Catholic Dissenters'. His residence in London prompted further speculation in Ireland that he had accepted a pension of £200 per annum from the government 'upon the secret condition that he should for the future withhold his pen, and reside no more in Ireland' (Buckley, 351). Successive biographers have argued that this was not so and, while the absence of a clear documentary trail would bear them out, one cannot entirely discount the fact that he was paid from the secret service list. There were also reports in the Irish press in 1790 that he had embraced protestantism, which he vigorously denied, since he never wavered in his belief that the Catholic church represented 'the right road to eternal life' (ibid., 326). Indeed his recognition that the Catholics of London were poorly served for churches prompted him to convert a large hall on Sutton Street, Soho Square, into a chapel that he named after St Patrick and from which he ministered for the remainder of his life. He was a popular preacher who, even when affirming the doctrines of the Catholic church, declined to criticize others. He was encouraged to take this line as much by his alarm at current events in France as by his continuing belief in the merits of religious toleration. His sympathies with the victims of the French Revolution prompted him to support and to promote the cause of émigré loyalists in Great Britain and to warn against the example of France in his sermons. Persuaded that the revolutionaries were driven by 'irreligion and licentiousness' he was induced by the mistreatment of Pope Pius VI to make a powerful attack, on 8 March 1797, on the 'licentious infidels' whom he held responsible (ibid., 341). This consolidated his reputation in England, which was affirmed further in 1799 when he offered an equally powerful panegyric to Pius VI on his death.

Understandably O'Leary was no less disturbed by the impact of the French Revolution on Ireland. He maintained that both the Catholic and protestant churches had 'everything to dread from the disciples of the New Philosophy, which has made rapid progress amongst their respective flocks' (Buckley, 375) and he was encouraged by this fact to welcome an Anglo-Irish legislative union when Pitt proposed it in 1799. In *Address to the Lords Spiritual and Temporal of Great Britain*, published in June 1800, he pronounced himself 'a friend to the Union' because he believed it would 'close the tumultary scenes which have distracted my ill-fated country for ages, and make the natives, of every religious description, happy' (ibid., 372). His expectation, encouraged by Pitt, was that the early concession of Catholic emancipation would help, and he can only have been encouraged in this conviction by the criticism directed at him by Sir Richard Musgrave in his influential *Memoirs of Different Rebellions*. Though prompted by this experience to gather materials for a history of his own he was never to write such a work. He made his notes available to Francis Plowden shortly before his death, after a short illness, on 8 January 1802 at 45 Great Portland Street, London. The publication of the funeral oration and the erection of an impressive monument over his grave in St Pancras churchyard, where he was buried on 14 January, provided a final testament to the benign impact of a man who, throughout his life, believed that true religion 'instead of inspiring hatred and rancour, commands us to love' (ibid., 374).   JAMES KELLY

Sources J. Kelly, '"A wild Capuchin of Cork": Arthur O'Leary, 1729–1802', *Radical Irish priests, 1660–1970*, ed. G. Moran (Dublin, 1998), 37–59 · T. R. England, *The life of the Reverend Arthur O'Leary* (1822) · M. B. Buckley, *The life and writings of the Rev. Arthur O'Leary* (1868) · J. Kelly, 'Interdenominational relations and religious toleration in late eighteenth-century Ireland: the paper war of 1786–88', *Eighteenth-Century Ireland*, 3 (1988), 39–67 · T. J. Walsh, 'Fr Arthur O'Leary: a Capuchin of Blackamoor Lane', *Journal of the Cork Historical and Archaeological Society*, 2nd ser., 53 (1948), 88–94 · W. J. Fitzpatrick, *Secret service under Pitt* (1892) · PRO, HO 100/14, fols. 123–4 · H. Fenning, *The Irish Dominican province, 1698–1797* (1990) · Theophilus [P. Duigenan], *An address to the nobility and gentry of the Church of Ireland* (1786) · *DNB*

Likenesses W. Bond, stipple, pubd 1822 (after engraving by Murphy), NPG · T. H. Ellis, engraving (after portrait by E. Shiel), repro. in Buckley, *Life and writings of Rev. Arthur O'Leary*

O'Leary, Daniel Florencio (1801–1854), soldier, diplomatist, and author, was born in late January or early February 1801 in Cook Street, Cork, the eighth of the ten children of Jeremiah O'Leary (1757–1830), merchant, and his wife, Caroline, *née* Burke (d. 1837). He was baptized a Catholic on 4 February. Little is known of his school years, but meeting the Irish nationalist Daniel O'Connell, his father's close friend, was an early formative experience.

O'Connell's admiration for Simón Bolívar, leader of South America's struggle for independence from Spain, may have inspired Daniel in 1817 to enlist in the army Bolívar's London agent was recruiting. O'Leary was commissioned cornet and sailed for Venezuela in December 1817. Soon promoted to the rank of captain, in June 1819 he marched with Bolívar over the eastern range of the Andes to attack Spanish forces in New Granada. He fought with distinction and was wounded. In August he was with the patriot forces which defeated Spanish troops at Boyacá, liberating New Granada. He then rode as Bolívar's aide-de-camp into Venezuela for the decisive battle of Carabobo.

In December 1821 Bolívar ordered O'Leary to Panama to arrange reinforcements and transport ships to help liberate Ecuador and Peru. O'Leary subsequently sailed to Ecuador to fight at the crucial battle of Pichincha in May 1822, and was promoted lieutenant-colonel. Bolívar next sent him to persuade the Chilean government to contribute troops and money for the war in Peru. He returned to Lima in February 1825 and accompanied Bolívar on his triumphal march to Upper Peru, soon to become the republic of Bolivia.

By early 1826 the union, formalized by the 1821 constitution, which joined Venezuela, New Granada, and Ecuador into the nation of Colombia, was threatened by the rival separatist ambitions of vice-president General Francisco de Paula Santander and Venezuela's General José Antonio Páez. Bolívar, president of the new nation of Colombia, dispatched the faithful O'Leary from Lima to Venezuela on a fruitless mission to persuade Páez to submit to Santander's authority.

While acting as Bolívar's chief aide in Bogota, O'Leary married, on 20 February 1828, Soledad Soublette (d. 1883), the sister of General Carlos Soublette. Two weeks after the wedding O'Leary was sent by Bolívar as observer to the conference at Ocaña, convened to consider constitutional amendments. Bolívar believed the 1821 constitution gave the legislature too much power and advocated instead a strong central government. Santander favoured a looser federal system. After the conference disbanded inconclusively, Bolívar assumed dictatorial powers. This encouraged Peru to declare war on Colombia. In August 1828 Bolívar dispatched O'Leary to Lima to negotiate a peaceful settlement. This proved impossible. O'Leary then helped rout a Peruvian invasion force and was promoted to the rank of brigadier-general.

O'Leary rejoined Soledad in April 1829. During his absence the couple's first child, a daughter, Mimi, had been born. Soon thereafter he was offered the post of minister-plenipotentiary to the United States. He was not yet destined for a diplomatic career, however, for in September he was ordered to put down a military rebellion in northern Colombia, which he quickly accomplished.

In late 1829 Páez declared Venezuela's independence. In Bogota separatists urged New Granada to follow. Bolívar resigned and in May 1830 departed for the coast and exile. O'Leary and Soledad followed with Mimi and their newborn son, Simón Bolívar O'Leary. In Cartagena another daughter, Bolivia, arrived. Bolívar died of tuberculosis in December 1830 and O'Leary attended his funeral in the cathedral at Santa Marta, Colombia.

The government now revoked O'Leary's diplomatic appointment and banished him and other Bolívar supporters in April 1831. The O'Learys spent the next two years in Jamaica, where Daniel resumed work on a life of Bolívar which he had begun in Cartagena. Because Bolívar, shortly before dying, had stated that he wished O'Leary to write his biography, his executors sent his personal papers to O'Leary in Jamaica.

In 1833 Carlos Soublette, then Venezuelan minister of war, invited O'Leary to Caracas. During the voyage the O'Learys' fourth child, Carlos, was born. The family arrived in late June and in December O'Leary was appointed to a mission to Europe headed by General Mariano Montilla. In May 1834 O'Leary arrived in London where he and Montilla persuaded Lord Palmerston to acknowledge Venezuelan independence; in August he returned to Ireland for the first time in seventeen years to visit his mother and family.

In February 1835 Montilla was replaced by Carlos Soublette. The two brothers-in-law journeyed to Madrid where the Spanish refused to recognize Venezuelan independence except in return for a substantial indemnity. This being unacceptable, O'Leary and Soublette returned to London in January 1837. After Soublette sailed home O'Leary was appointed chargé d'affaires to negotiate a concordat with the Holy See. The pope rejected the Venezuelan proposal, so O'Leary returned to Caracas in January 1840. In November the British consul-general in Caracas, Sir Robert Ker Porter, went on leave to England and suggested O'Leary as a replacement. Lord Palmerston agreed and in January 1841 O'Leary assumed Ker Porter's duties.

When in 1842 Bolívar's remains were transferred to Caracas from Santa Marta, acting consul O'Leary was able to obtain a British corvette to join French, Dutch, and Danish warships as an escort and applied for Ker Porter's position after his death in May 1842. The British government, however, appointed Belford Hinton Wilson, another former Bolívar aide. O'Leary then went to Puerto Cabello as British consul until informed, in January 1844, that he had been made British chargé d'affaires and consul-general at Bogota. By now the political passions of 1830 had abated. Consequently the O'Learys were warmly welcomed in Bogota, where they spent the following ten years, during which Daniel continued revising Bolívar's biography.

In 1852 O'Leary's health began to deteriorate so he sailed to Europe with two daughters to seek medical advice. In Paris he placed the girls in boarding-school and passed the winter in Italy. His health apparently restored, in December 1853 he returned home. However, early in the morning of 24 February 1854 he died, apparently of a stroke. He was buried the following day in Bogota Cathedral, where the president and vice-president gave the funeral orations. His wife and nine children survived him. In April 1882 his remains were brought to Caracas and interred close to those of Bolívar in the Panteon Nacional. Soledad died the following year.

O'Leary was of medium height, clean shaven, with brown hair, a tall forehead, a long nose, and a slender build. Between 1879 and 1888, with Venezuelan government support, O'Leary's son Simón edited and published his father's manuscripts as *Memorias del General O'Leary publicados por su hijo Simón B. O'Leary* in thirty-two volumes. The first two covered Bolívar's life to 1829; the third supplied supporting documents and personal observations, while the other volumes contained Bolívar's correspondence and documents from his personal archives. The *Memorias* remain an indispensable source for scholars and a lasting monument to General O'Leary, their author and compiler.   FRANK GRIFFITH DAWSON

Sources M. P. Vila, *Vida de Daniel Florencio O'Leary* (1957) · D. Carbonell, ed., *General O'Leary intimo* (1937) · N. Navarro, *Actividades diplomáticas del General Daniel Florencio O'Leary en Europa, años 1834 a 1839* (1939) · The 'Detached recollections' of General D. F. O'Leary, ed. R. A. Humphreys (1969)
Archives NRA, priv. coll. | Casa Natal, Caracas, Archivo del Libertador · Casa Natal, Caracas, Archivo de José Rafael Revenga · PRO, FO archives · Caracas, Archivo General de la Nación · Bogota, Archivo Nacional de Colombia
Likenesses portrait, priv. coll. · portrait, priv. coll. · sculptures, Columbia · sculptures, Venezuela

O'Leary, Ellen (1831–1889), poet and Irish nationalist, was born on 23 October 1831 at 16 West Main Street, Tipperary, the second child of John O'Leary (d. 1848), shopkeeper and landlord, and his second wife, Margaret, *née* Ryan. Her elder brother was John *O'Leary (1830–1907), and she also had a younger brother, Arthur (1833–1861). Margaret O'Leary died in the mid-1830s and this affected Ellen O'Leary severely. Her father remarried and had a third family, and an aunt, who helped to rear her and her brothers, encouraged nationalist feelings in the children.

Ellen O'Leary contributed patriotic ballads and songs to the Young Ireland paper, *The Nation*, then to her brother's Fenian paper, the *Irish People*, writing as Eily and Lenel. She also contributed to the *Irish Monthly*, *The Shamrock*, and *The Irishman*. She was closely involved in the affairs of the Irish Republican Brotherhood of which her brother John was a prominent member; in 1864 she handled Irish Republican Brotherhood funds in her brother's absence and in 1866 she raised £200 on her house property in Tipperary, to help finance James Stephens's escape to France. When John O'Leary was tried for treason-felony in 1865, she sat by the dock and she visited him during his five years in Portland prison. On O'Leary's return to Ireland from exile in Paris in 1885 she came to live with him at 40 Leinster Road, Dublin: brother and sister became the centre of a cultural and nationalist circle which included W. B. Yeats, to whom she had a maternal attitude, Maud Gonne, Rose Kavanagh, Rosa Mulholland, Dora Sigerson, and Katharine Tynan. Yeats recalled her as being, like her brother:

> of Plutarch's people. She told me of her brother's life, of the foundation of the Fenian movement, and of the arrests that followed (I believe that her own sweetheart had somehow fallen among the wreckage), of sentences of death pronounced upon false evidence amid a public panic, and told it all without bitterness. No fanaticism could thrive amid such gentleness. She never found it hard to believe that an opponent had as high a motive as her own, and needed upon her difficult road no spur of hate. (Yeats, *Autobiographies*, 95)

In the early 1880s Ellen O'Leary developed breast cancer. John O'Leary remained unaware of her illness and was abroad when she died at 9 Castle Street, Cork, on 15 October 1889, while on a visit to a nephew. She was buried in Tipperary. O'Leary was devastated, writing to Yeats: 'A horrible calamity has come, and the light of my life has gone out' (*Collected Letters of W. B. Yeats*, 1.192). O'Leary later summed up their relationship: 'She was everything to me as I was everything to her' (O'Leary, 2.97). In his *Boston Pilot* obituary Yeats described her verse as having 'mingled austerity and tenderness … like a rivulet flowing from mountain snows' (Yeats, *Letters to the New Island*, 25). Her *Lays of Country, Home and Friends*, with some verses by Arthur O'Leary appended, was published in 1890 with prefatory material by T. W. Rolleston and Sir Charles Gavan Duffy. Yeats selected four poems by Ellen O'Leary for *The Poets and the Poetry of the Century* (Miles), emphasizing the traditional nature of her verse and its closeness to popular sentiment, recalling that her songs had been sung in the streets of Tipperary 'by the ballad-singers from their little strips of fluttering paper' (p. 449). Yeats included her 'To God and Ireland True' in his *A Book of Irish Verse* (1895). Ellen O'Leary is not represented in *The New Spirit of the Nation* (ed. Martin MacDermott, 1894), presumably because her best political verse was given to the *Irish People*, yet poems such as 'The Felon's Last Wish' compare favourably with verse by Eva (Mary Kelly) or Mary (Ellen Downing).

DEIRDRE TOOMEY

Sources M. Bourke, *John O'Leary: a study in Irish separatism* (1967) · T. W. Rolleston, 'Introductory notice', in E. O'Leary, *Lays of country, home and friends* (1890), xi–xxiv · *The collected letters of W. B. Yeats*, 1, ed. J. Kelly and E. Domville (1986) · W. B. Yeats, *Autobiographies* (1955), 94–5, 98 · K. Tynan, *Memories* (1924), 93–109 · *W. B. Yeats: letters to the new island*, new edn, ed. G. Bornstein and H. Witemeyer (1989) · R. Garnett, 'Memoir', *The poets and the poetry of the century*, ed. A. H. Miles, 7 (1892), 189–90 · J. O'Leary, *Recollections of Fenians and Fenianism* (1896) · M. G. MacBride, *A servant of the queen*, ed. A. N. Jeffares and A. M. White (1994), 90–92

Archives City of Belfast Public Libraries, corresp. · NL Ire., letters

O'Leary, John (1830–1907), Irish nationalist and journalist, was born in Tipperary town, Ireland, on 23 July 1830, the eldest child of John O'Leary (d. 1848), merchant, and Margaret Ryan (d. c.1835), the second of his three wives. He was educated at the fashionable protestant Tipperary grammar school and at the age of fifteen entered the Catholic boarding-school Carlow College. A tall, austere, imposing figure, he was admired for his intellect, integrity, and loyalty. In summer 1846 he met James Stephens, the future leader of the Fenians. In common with other young liberal-minded Catholics he identified with the views advocated by Thomas Davis, and after entering Trinity College, Dublin, in 1847 to study law, he attended meetings of the Grattan Club presided over by Thomas Francis Meagher and supported the policies of John Mitchel in 1848. In November 1848 he was detained for two or three weeks as a suspect in the plot to rescue William Smith O'Brien. At this time he made the acquaintance of Thomas Clarke Luby, who like Stephens became a lifelong friend. O'Leary's characteristic political creed—contempt for Irish politicians' agitation at Westminster; dislike of clerical influence in politics; a wish to convert wealthy protestants to nationalism; and a belief in Irish separatism—were formed between mid-1847 and the end of 1849.

On the death of his father O'Leary inherited property in Tipperary town, yielding approximately £200 per year. At the beginning of the same year he had entered the new Queen's College, Cork, to study medicine. In autumn 1850 he moved to the Queen's College, Galway, on being awarded a scholarship, remaining there until 1853 when he proceeded to Dublin in order to attend surgery classes at Meath Hospital. In 1854 he went to study medicine in London and then in 1855 migrated to Paris where he continued his medical education. In Paris, O'Leary established a circle of friends which included the American painter James McNeill Whistler. Late in 1856 he returned to London and then went to Dublin in summer 1857, spending the next year at the Meath Hospital once more. In March 1859 he was again in Paris, having probably given up his intention to practise medicine around this time, though he later claimed that it was only when he became editor of the *Irish People* (in 1863) that he finally abandoned the profession.

During 1858, O'Leary established, via Stephens, his 'first direct connection with Fenianism' (O'Leary, 1.85). This close link led Stephens to persuade a reluctant O'Leary, who was not a republican, to visit the United States in order to secure funds for the Irish Republican Brotherhood. He sailed in April 1859, returning to Europe in September. While in New York, he turned his hand to journalism with the *Phoenix* and travelled extensively. Between 1860 and 1863 he took little part in politics, but then Stephens induced him to come to Dublin and become editor of the *Irish People*, the new Fenian weekly newspaper, at a salary of £150 per annum. In this venture he was closely associated with Luby, Charles J. Kickham, and Jeremiah O'Donovan Rossa among others. During this time O'Leary was the chief financial officer to the revolutionary movement. This, politically and personally his most satisfying period, is described at length in *Recollections of Fenians and Fenianism* (1896).

The newspaper was suppressed after ninety-five issues on 16 September 1865. O'Leary was convicted in December of treason-felony by a special commission and sentenced to twenty years' penal servitude. Most of his confinement was spent in Portland prison, where he was obliged to work in the quarries. He regarded the notorious protests of his fellow inmate O'Donovan Rossa against the prison regime as undignified for a political prisoner. On 21 January 1871 he was released, but he was not allowed to return to the United Kingdom, and except for short trips to the United States and one brief sojourn in Tipperary he lived in Paris until 1885. During his long residence there O'Leary acquired a reputation as a letter writer. He continued to uphold the separatist cause, opposing the 'skirmishing fund' to promote terrorist acts in Great Britain, rejecting the 'new departure' between the militant wing of the Home Rule Party and the Fenians, and also criticizing the land war (1879–82). The land war (and later the Plan of Campaign, from 1886 to 1891, which he opposed) caused a drop in his rental income, and for considerable periods thereafter he faced financial stringency.

Following passage of the amnesty act O'Leary returned to Dublin on 21 January 1885 where, for all but brief periods, he remained for the rest of his life, living with his sister Ellen *O'Leary until her death in 1889. After his release he was active in promoting the separatist ideal and also played a prominent role in literary circles. At this time William Butler Yeats came under his spell, seeing himself later as 'a nationalist of the school of John O'Leary' (Bourke, 187). O'Leary raised funds for the publication of Yeats's *The Wanderings of Oisin* (1888). He was a founder of the Contemporary Club (1885/6), became a patron of the Gaelic Athletic Association (1886), helped form the Pan-Celtic literary group (1888), regularly visited the Southwark Literary Club, and accepted the presidency of the National Literary Society of Ireland. Although he favoured an Irish literature that was Irish in content, he was apathetic towards the Irish language, and ignored the Gaelic League.

Always a fierce critic of parliamentarianism, O'Leary nevertheless admired Charles Stewart Parnell, whom he had first met in the late 1870s; he supported the fallen leader during the Irish party split of 1890 to 1891, and was co-opted onto the Parnell Leadership Committee. In spite of being a bookish man and having engaged in journalism for periods, O'Leary wrote little (authoring only three pamphlets between 1885 and 1895), until during the early 1890s he prepared his *Recollections of Fenians and Fenianism*, published in 1896. He helped form the Young Ireland League in 1895, was active in the '98 celebrations, and was president of the Irish Transvaal Committee during the Second South African War. His last half-sibling died in 1898 and his own health deteriorated from 1901. He continued to support the old causes until he died on 16 March 1907, virtually penniless. He was buried in Glasnevin cemetery with a Celtic cross placed over his grave, beside his old friend James Stephens. In 1913 Yeats penned what remains O'Leary's epitaph:

Romantic Ireland's dead and gone,
It's with O'Leary in the grave.
(*Collected Letters*, 1.503)

A bachelor, he bequeathed an extensive collection of books and pictures to the National Literary Society.

ALAN O'DAY

Sources J. O'Leary, *Recollections of Fenians and Fenianism* (1896) · M. Bourke, *John O'Leary: a study in Irish separatism* (1967) · J. Denieffe, *A personal narrative of the Irish Revolutionary Brotherhood* (New York, 1906); facs. edn (Shannon, 1969) · W. O'Brien and D. Ryan, eds., *Devoy's post bag, 1871–1928*, 2 vols. (1948–53) · R. V. Comerford, *Charles J. Kickham: a study in Irish nationalism and literature* (1979) · R. V. Comerford, *The Fenians in context: Irish politics and society, 1848–82* (1985) · R. Pigott, *Personal recollections of an Irish national journalist* (1882); repr. (Cork, 1979) · A. M. Sullivan, *New Ireland*, [new edn] (1877) · T. W. Moody, *Davitt and Irish revolution* (1982) · *The collected letters of W. B. Yeats*, ed. J. Kelly and others, [3 vols.] (1986–) · R. F. Foster, *The apprentice mage, 1865–1914* (1997), vol. 1 of *W. B. Yeats: a life* · *Some letters from W. B. Yeats to John O'Leary and his sister*, ed. A. Wade (1953)
Archives NA Ire., Fenian reports · NL Ire., John Devoy MSS · NYPL, J. O'Donovan Rossa MSS · NYPL, W. B. Yeats MSS · priv. coll., W. B. Yeats MSS
Likenesses J. B. Yeats, oils, 1904, NG Ire. · O. Sheppard, bronze bust, Hugh Lane Gallery of Modern Art, Dublin · O. Sheppard, plaster bust, Hugh Lane Gallery of Modern Art, Dublin · J. B. Yeats, pencil drawing, NG Ire. · portrait, repro. in Bourke, *John O'Leary* · portrait, repro. in Comerford, *Fenians in context* · portrait, repro. in O'Brien and Ryan, eds., *Devoy's post bag* · portrait, repro. in Kelly and others, eds., *Collected letters of W. B. Yeats*, vol. 1 · portrait, repro. in Denieffe, *Personal narrative*
Wealth at death virtually none; possessed books and pictures

O'Leary, Joseph (1792–1857). *See under* O'Leary, Joseph (*c.*1795–*c.*1845).

O'Leary, Joseph (*c.*1795–*c.*1845), songwriter and journalist, was born in Cork. In his youth, possibly after the death of his father, he joined a company of strolling players, but his theatrical experience was short, as the manager was insolvent. About 1818 he started to write for the Cork papers—notably, *The Freeholder*, a scurrilous sheet which was edited by John Boyle, and lasted until 1842. O'Leary's contributions were considered very powerful; he was likened to Swift by Denny Lane, and it was in its columns that his famous Bacchanalian song 'Whiskey, drink divine', appeared. About 1818 he also wrote for *The Bagatelle*, a short-lived Cork periodical; and for a time he edited the *Cork Mercantile Reporter*. Between 1825 and 1828 he wrote for *Bolster's Cork Quarterly*, and contributed poems under the pseudonyms 'O' and 'O'L', and sketches as Denis Murphy, to two London periodicals, the *Dublin and London Magazine*, and *Captain Rock in London*. In 1825 he contributed to the *Dublin and London Magazine* an anonymous article, 'Bettheen-a-Vryne'; the song 'Glenfinnishk', which concludes it, appeared in several anthologies of Irish poetry. Richard Ryan, the Irish biographer, who seems to have known him, says that he was, in 1826, preparing a translation of Tibullus. In 1830 O'Leary published a pamphlet *On the Late Election in Cork*, under the signature of 'A Reporter'. There are also some poems by him in Patrick O'Kelly's *Hippocrene* (1831); and in 1833 a small collection of his poems and sketches appeared at Cork in an anonymous, possibly autobiographical, volume, entitled *The Tribute*. In 1834 he went to London and joined the staff of the *Morning Herald* as parliamentary reporter. After this date little about O'Leary's life can be verified. It is said that he was one of the earliest writers for *Punch*. But despite praise for his 'racy sketches' he seems to have met with little material success in London, and it is conjectured that he drowned himself in the Regent's Canal about 1845. It is also possible that he returned to Cork and died there.

O'Leary has been confused with the 'Irish whiskey-drinker', John Sheehan, who translated 'Whiskey, drink divine', into Latin.

Another contemporary **Joseph O'Leary** (1792–1857), barrister, was born in Dublin, the eldest son of Jeremiah O'Leary of Cork. He was admitted to Gray's Inn in 1820 and published in Dublin the standard legal works *Law Tithes in Ireland* (1835), *Rent Charges in Lieu of Tithes* (1840), and *Dispositions for Religious and Charitable Uses in Ireland* (1847). He died in 1857.

D. J. O'DONOGHUE, rev. CLARE L. TAYLOR

Sources R. Ryan, *Poetry and poets: a collection of anecdotes relative to the poets of every age and nation*, 3 vols. (1826), vol. 2 · D. J. O'Donoghue, *The poets of Ireland: a biographical and bibliographical dictionary* (1912) · J. Sheehan, ed., *The Bentley ballads* (1869)

Oley, Barnabas (*bap.* 1602, *d.* 1686), Church of England clergyman, was born at Kirkthorpe, Yorkshire, and was baptized on 27 December 1602 in the parish church at Wakefield, the son of Francis Oley (*d.* 1643?), clergyman, and his wife, Mary Watterhouse. From 1602 to 1619 his father was vicar of Penistone, in the same county, and in

1607 Oley entered Wakefield grammar school. In 1617 he was admitted to Clare College, Cambridge, probably as Cave's exhibitioner from his school, and he graduated BA in 1621. Having been elected a probationer fellow of the foundation of Lady Clare at the college on 28 November 1623, he proceeded MA in 1625 and was elected a senior fellow in 1627. Among his students was Peter Gunning, later bishop of Ely.

In 1633 Oley was appointed to the college living of Great Gransden, Huntingdonshire, which he held for the rest of his life, but continuing the duties of his fellowship for several years he continued to live in Cambridge. In 1634–5 he served as taxor, or price regulator, for the university, and in 1635–6 as proctor. The first steps for the rebuilding of Clare College, which was begun on 19 May 1638, although not finished until 1715, were taken under his diligent and careful direction; he was called by Thomas Fuller its 'Master of the fabrick' (T. Fuller, *The History of the University of Cambridge*, 1655, 38).

In the summer of 1642 Oley was an evidently zealous loyalist, and it was to him, according to standard royalist accounts, that the university entrusted the task of taking its plate to the king to be converted into money for his use. Oley, it was said, brought it safely to Charles's headquarters 'at Nottingham' in August (Varley, 80). He was also said to have lent a considerable sum of money on the communion plate of Clare College, which was of solid gold and very valuable. This he later restored to the college on repayment of part of his loan in 1660; there is a college tradition that its three other very old pieces of plate were also preserved by his care. There are, however, flaws in this version of events: there was no 'university plate' as such; the king was not at this date at Nottingham; Oley was not, as described, 'president' of Clare; only relatively insignificant amounts of plate and money from a handful of colleges are recorded as having reached Charles at Oxford. If Oley acted as an agent then he did so secretly the night before Oliver Cromwell and Valentine Walton successfully blocked a major convoy of plate, and took with him only a fraction of what the royalists received— perhaps, indeed, plate from Clare. On 8 April 1644 Oley was ejected from his fellowship by the earl of Manchester on the grounds of non-residence in Cambridge and failure to appear before the commission of visitors. He was also plundered of his personal and landed property, and although not sequestered, was forced to leave Great Gransden, where his curate, Nathaniel Jury, deputized for him.

In the later 1640s Oley led a wandering and impoverished life. In 1643 and 1646 he was in Oxford. During the sieges of Pontefract in 1644 and 1645 he preached to the royalist garrison defending the castle. By 1647 he had been sequestered from the impropriate rectory of Warmfield, Yorkshire, which his father had resigned in 1643. Having helped Sir Marmaduke Langdale to escape in 1648 from prison and a death sentence, the following year Oley had to compound for delinquency in assisting the forces against parliament, and was fined £30. A further £50 was added in 1652, in lieu of which he was required to settle £5

a year on the minister of Warmfield. For some time he had lived at Heath, near Wakefield, but in 1652 and 1653 he stayed 'in the north privately, near the place of Lady Savil's demolished habitation' (J. E. B. Mayor, *Cambridge in the Seventeenth Century, pt 1: Nicholas Ferrar*, 1855, 303–4).

By the 1650s Oley had both the leisure and the resources to prepare manuscripts for publication. In 1652 he edited *Herbert's Remains, or, Sundry Pieces of that Sweet Singer of the Temple, Mr George Herbert*, containing *A Priest to the Temple, or, The Country Parson* and *Jacula prudentum*. Prefixed was an unsigned 'prefatory View of the Life and Vertues of the Author, and Excellencies of this Book', which was written by Oley. The second edition was to appear in 1671 as *A Priest to the Temple, or, The Country Parson*, with a new preface, signed Barnabas Oley. Both prefaces, often polemical in tone, reflect his commitment to a Laudian ideal of the Church of England. The manuscript of 'The Country Parson' was the property of Oley's friend Edmund Duncon: in the 1671 preface Oley corrects Isaac Walton's story that Arthur Woodnoth gave it to him. Walton in turn drew on Oley's prefaces for parts of his own life of Herbert.

Between 1653 and 1657 Oley edited three volumes of the works of Thomas Jackson, the late president of Corpus Christi College, Oxford. In the prefatory epistles he extolled Jackson's merits and begged for the return of borrowed manuscripts of his works. In the third volume, dedicated to Gilbert Sheldon, Oley explained that 'God, by convincing me of disabilitie, hath taken away all hopes and desires of publishing any work of mine own'. Devoting himself to the works of others, he was probably also the historian who collected, but never published, information on Nicholas Ferrar.

In 1659 Oley returned to Great Gransden, where Sir John Hewett of Waresley in Huntingdonshire gave him some furniture, and on 9 July 1660 he was restored to his fellowship by order of the same earl of Manchester. Through the 'voluntary mediation' of Gilbert Sheldon, now bishop of London, he was presented on 3 August 1660 to the third prebendal stall of Worcester Cathedral. Now financially secure, he was able to leave his fellowship in 1663 and to be generous. In 1664 he was the leading benefactor of the brick school house at Gransden, which he endowed with £20 a year. He built brick houses for six poor people on his own freehold land, leasing them for one thousand years to the churchwardens for the time being at a peppercorn rent, and he erected a vicarage. To King's College, Cambridge, he gave £100 for putting up canopies and pillars for stalls in the chapel. Having given a pulpit to Gransden church in the first months of his incumbency in 1633, in 1681 he provided wainscot seats for the chancel.

When Oley's edition of Jackson's works was reissued in 1673, again with a dedication to Sheldon, much was made in the preface of the feebleness of the editor's memory 'by the suddain ingruence of a Lethargy or Apoplexy' (*A Collection of the Works of … T. Jackson*). None the less, in 1678, despite his age, Oley was first choice of the fellows at Clare to replace Theophilus Dillingham as master, although he was not elected because he could not be contacted in time. On 8 November 1679 Oley was collated on the nomination of Bishop Gunning, his old pupil, to the archdeaconry of Ely, but the following year he resigned this preferment because of doubts of his ability to discharge its duties. However, he retained the stall at Worcester until his death, being then 'the senior Prebendary of venerable Memory' (G. Hickes, *Seventeen Sermons of the Reverend and Learned Dr William Hopkins*, 1708, xiii). He established a weekly celebration of the eucharist in the cathedral.

Oley died at Great Gransden on 20 February 1686, and in accordance with his will was buried there on the night of 22 February. The will, dated between 23 May 1684 and 18 October 1685, was considered noteworthy for its generosity to church causes. One feature was its provision of books for poor parishes: records of borrowing by parishioners exist into the eighteenth century. To the dean and chapter of Worcester Oley gave £200 for buttresses for the choir and the chapel at the east end of the cathedral; to Clare College he left 100 marks (£67) for building a library, and £10 to the descendants of John Westley, the builder of the college. The junior fellows of King's College received £50 for the construction of a walkway for their recreation. A charity was set up in his name, with assets in Warmfield, Kirkthorpe, and Great Gransden, overseen by the fellows of Clare College and still operating with limited resources in the late twentieth century.　　ELIZABETH R. CLARKE

Sources Venn, *Alum. Cant.* • Wakefield bishops' transcripts, Borth. Inst. • A. J. Edmonds, *A history of Great Gransden*, 24 pts (1892–5) • J. Walker, *An attempt towards recovering an account of the numbers and sufferings of the clergy of the Church of England*, 2 pts in 1 (1714) • P. Barwick, *The life of … Dr John Barwick*, ed. and trans. H. Bedford (1724) • T. Hearne, *Thomae Caii vindiciae* (1730) • J. Bentham, *The history and antiquities of the conventual and cathedral church of Ely* (1771) • *DNB* • Walker rev., 208 • F. J. Varley, *Cambridge during the civil war, 1642–1646* (1935), 77–83 • J. Twigg, *The University of Cambridge and the English Revolution, 1625–1688* (1990) • *Fasti Angl., 1541–1857*, [Ely] • *Fasti Angl., 1541–1857*, [Canterbury]

Archives Clare College, Cambridge, letters • Worcester Cathedral Library, corresp., D55, 57, 59–62

Wealth at death £600; incl. bequests involving selling lease of Warmfield tithes: will, 1686, PRO

Oliphant [Olifard] **family** (*per.* 1141–*c*.1500), nobility, was important in the history of Perthshire, as well as, from time to time, in national politics. The original form of their name was Olifard. The family, which may have been of Flemish origin, first came to Scotland in 1141 in somewhat romantic circumstances: young David Oliphant of Lilford in Northamptonshire was able to save his godfather, David, king of Scots (*d*. 1153), from King Stephen's army after the siege of Winchester. They fled to Scotland where Oliphant was rewarded with lands in Roxburghshire and East Lothian. Succeeding generations continued to serve the Scottish crown to good effect, most particularly as justiciars of Lothian. David's son and heir, Walter, was married to Christian, daughter of Earl Ferteth of Strathearn, an example of a Celtic–Norman marriage not uncommon in this period. Through this marriage the Oliphants gained a foothold in Perthshire, where they had become well established by the middle of the thirteenth century, along with the Ruthvens, Grahams, Murrays, and

Drummonds. All these families would play a dominant role in local politics during succeeding centuries.

Although the Oliphants were prominent in royal circles before the fourteenth century, the most famous member of the family, by virtue of the part he played in the wars with England, was **Sir William Oliphant** (*d*. 1313?). Unfortunately, his activities are easily confused with those of his cousin, also William Oliphant of Dupplin and Aberdalgie. Both were captured at the battle of Dunbar in 1296: Sir William was sent to Devizes and his cousin, still an esquire, to Rochester. They received their freedom in the following year, on condition that they served Edward I on his campaign against France. As a result of this service, Sir William's lands were restored to him on 12 September 1297. On his return to Scotland, however, he rejoined the fight against Edward; following the success of the Scots in taking Stirling Castle at the beginning of 1300, he was appointed its constable by the Scottish guardian, Sir John Soulis (*d*. before 1310). However, four years later most Scots had submitted to Edward I; only Stirling Castle and a few notables, including Sir William Wallace and Sir Simon Fraser, held out for King John. Oliphant tried to postpone the imminent siege by requesting that he be able to approach Soules for fresh orders; given that the former guardian was now in France, Edward rather naturally refused. A combined English–Scottish army besieged the castle for ninety days, whereafter Sir William and the rest of the garrison, which included his cousin, now also Sir William, were led off again to captivity in England.

Oliphant was finally released in May 1308 on Edward II's orders and returned to Scotland in the latter's service to serve, from 1311 at least, as commander of Perth. Given the confusing references of subsequent years, it seems likely that his cousin also went north in Edward's service. On the night of 7–8 January 1313, believing that the Scottish siege had been lifted, the garrison of Perth let its guard down and the town was duly captured by a force, led by King Robert himself, which scaled the walls. Despite the claims of later chroniclers, the garrison was most likely allowed to go free; however, Sir William seems to have died without known heirs soon afterwards, and subsequent references relate to **Sir William Oliphant of Dupplin and Aberdalgie** (*d*. 1329).

This Sir William now swore allegiance to King Robert, perhaps in the aftermath of the Scottish victory at Bannockburn. He received a number of grants of land throughout the reign and put his seal (three crescents) to the declaration of Arbroath of 1320. In the final years of the reign he also performed the office of escheator. On his death the family had substantial properties, variously acquired through inheritance, marriage, and grants from Robert I. Their landed interests were based on Perthshire and Forfarshire, with their principal residence at Aberdalgie, south-west of Perth, but they also had estates in Fife, Kincardineshire, and Midlothian. Some of these lands were later used to endow younger sons and create different branches of the family. Sir William died in 1329, some four months before the king himself. He was buried at Aberdalgie, where a magnificent tomb was constructed by his family in the following century.

Despite their service to Edward II, the Oliphants certainly seem to have endeared themselves to the Bruces, as the grants of land demonstrate. Even more significantly, Sir William of Aberdalgie's son and heir, **Sir Walter Oliphant of Aberdalgie** (d. in or after 1378), married Elizabeth Bruce, illegitimate daughter of the king and thus half-sister to *David II (1324–1371) and step-aunt to *Robert II (r. 1371–1390). In February 1365 Oliphant surrendered to the king his principal estates in Perthshire—including Aberdalgie—Forfarshire, and Kincardineshire, and received them back in a sequence of grants made to himself and his wife jointly, with an entail securing them for their heirs. The family continued to expand their territorial holdings, receiving, among others, the lands of Kelly, resigned by his cousin, Helen Maxwell, from King David. Although Walter was not particularly active in national politics, he is recorded in 1368 as entrusted with the keeping of Stirling Castle. His wife was also remembered by her half-brother throughout his reign, receiving £3 from wine escheated by a certain William Clapham by the king's gift as late as 1365. The last reference to Sir Walter occurs in 1378. The couple had three sons: Sir John, who inherited most of the family's extensive landed interests; Sir Walter, who was the ancestor of the Oliphants of Pittotter, Kellie, Murdocairnie, and Prinlaws; and Malcolm, who founded the Ayrshire branch of the family.

Despite their royal connections, the Oliphants effectively retired from the national scene for over a century after 1329; it is not even known whether or not representatives of the family were present at Halidon Hill or Nevilles Cross, though it seems very likely. Subsequent events suggest that they preferred to play a greater role in local politics. Sir Walter's son, Sir John, makes little mark on the national record. In 1424, however, John's son and heir, Sir William Oliphant of Aberdalgie, was chosen as one of the hostages sent to England as part of the ransom agreement for the return of James I. He was still there in 1425, and probably died in prison. William's son, Sir John, had the misfortune to become involved in a local dispute through his marriage to Isabel, daughter of Sir Walter Ogilvy of Auchterhouse. The Ogilvys were at feud with the Lindsays, and when their quarrel took a particularly violent turn, in what has sometimes been called the battle of Arbroath, on 23 January 1446, Sir John was among those killed. His son, **Laurence Oliphant**, first Lord Oliphant (d. 1500?), was still a boy at the time of his father's death, and was put under the tutelage of Sir David Hay of Yester. In 1450 Laurence went on pilgrimage to Rome in the magnificent entourage of the ninth earl of Douglas; nevertheless, when James II embarked on his violent struggle with the Douglases a few years later, young Oliphant sided with the king and was rewarded with elevation to the peerage some time before 1458. His marriage, about 1463, to Isobel, daughter of William *Hay, first earl of Erroll (d. 1462) [see under Hay family], constable of Scotland, perhaps also reflects the king's gratitude. Lord Oliphant continued his

service to the crown, holding the office of sheriff of Perthshire. Nevertheless, he was also involved in a number of violent feuds, including one with the earl of Buchan which in 1491 claimed the life of his brother, James. The other side of that coin was the numerous bonds of manrent into which he entered with a number of lairds, including many of his neighbours.

James III, too, seems to have found Oliphant's services useful, sending him as a commissioner to negotiate the marriage of James Stewart, duke of Rothesay (the future James IV), to Anne de la Pole, niece of Richard III of England, in 1484. Unfortunately, the king's alienation of the earl of Argyll, his former chancellor, ensured that Oliphant, whose son was engaged to marry Argyll's daughter, also fought against James, on behalf of the latter's son, at Sauchieburn in 1488. This decision naturally meant that Laurence continued his involvement in affairs of state under James IV, acting, among other things, as a lord of the articles and as Scottish ambassador on the continent. Lord Oliphant also found time to found a Franciscan friary at Perth, perhaps about 1460. Unfortunately, he was also engaged in a dispute with the burgesses of Perth, which resulted in the destruction of his house at Aberdalgie. His eventful life seems to have come to an end before April 1500.

The Oliphants provide a striking and illuminating example of the rise and rise of a Norman family. Originally maintaining their political importance and expanding their landed wealth explicitly through loyal service to the crown, the family had reached sufficient rank, socially and politically, to play a prominent role in the wars with England. The habit of loyalty to the Scottish crown, despite a brief adherence to Edward II, brought them very definite favours from Robert I. Coincidentally or otherwise, this permitted the Oliphants to concentrate on building up power at a local level, based on their main estates in Perthshire; their absence from the national scene throughout most of the fourteenth century may well thus reflect not inactivity, but a preference for local affairs of which their later involvement in feuding and bonds of manrent perhaps provides proof. The maintenance of a local power base, together with continuing loyalty to the crown, brought the Oliphants into the peerage under James II. The activities of Laurence, first Lord Oliphant, are perhaps largely typical of that rank of nobility to which the family now belonged. FIONA WATSON

Sources E. Maxtone Graham, ed., *The Oliphants of Gask* (1910) · *Scots peerage*, vol. 6 · G. W. S. Barrow and others, eds., *Regesta regum Scottorum*, 5, ed. A. A. M. Duncan (1988) · J. Wormald, *Court, kirk, and community: Scotland 1470–1625* (1981) · G. Burnett and others, eds., *The exchequer rolls of Scotland*, 1–6 (1878–83) · J. M. Thomson and others, eds., *Registrum magni sigilli regum Scotorum / The register of the great seal of Scotland*, 2nd edn, 1, ed. T. Thomson (1912) · G. W. S. Barrow and others, eds., *Regesta regum Scottorum*, 6, ed. B. Webster (1982) · G. W. S. Barrow, *The Anglo-Norman era in Scottish history* (1980)
Archives Gask charter chest at Ardblair

Oliphant, Carolina, Lady Nairne (1766–1845), songwriter, was born at the 'Auld Hoose' of Gask, Perthshire, on 16 August 1766, and baptized Carolina in honour of the

Carolina Oliphant, Lady Nairne (1766-1845), by Sir John Watson-Gordon [with her son, William Murray Nairne]

exiled Prince Charles Edward Stuart. She was the fourth child of the three sons and four daughters of Laurence Oliphant (1724-1792), laird of Gask, and his wife, Margaret (1739-1774), the eldest daughter of Duncan Robertson of Struan, the chief of clan Donnachie. Her parents were cousins, grandchildren of the Lord Nairne who had narrowly escaped execution after the Jacobite rising of 1715, and were married at Versailles on 9 June 1755 during nineteen years of political exile following the failure of the Jacobite rising of 1745. The Oliphants, the Robertsons, and the Nairnes had all been attainted for high treason and lost their estates. A part of Gask was bought back from the government and her parents were able to return two years before Carolina's birth.

Laurence Oliphant was active in Jacobite politics throughout his life and the children were carefully reared to 'keep them loyal' (Rogers, 20). In their prayer books the names of the Stuarts were pasted over those of the house of Hanover. The girls had a governess who taught English, since it was felt that their 'very broad Scots … will not be gracefull in a young lady' (Graham, 290), a tutor who was also family chaplain, and a dancing-master whose teaching was supported by regular visits from a traditional fiddle-player. Carolina's younger brother Charles, writing in 1784, gives a glimpse of the resulting musical ethos: 'Carolina is just now playing, "*My wife's lying sick I wish she ne'er may rise again, I'll put on my tartan trews And court another wife again*". It is a very good tune …' (Graham, 322). This song was one of the 'Bonny Highland Laddie' group which

had distinctly licentious connotations. But the days of the old free song-culture, in which daughters of gentlefolk could bound about waving 'gully knives' and singing 'geld him, lassies, geld him' (Crawford, 127) were passing. An evangelical revival was steadily making its way among the Scottish gentry, which would banish the high-kilted muses to the byre and the kitchen and transform the blithe and musical Carolina Oliphant into the prim and pietistic Lady Nairne.

In eighteenth-century Scotland, popular art-song was the dominant literary form and it enjoyed a rich interrelationship with the surrounding oral culture. But performance of much of the traditional repertoire was becoming problematic in polite society because of its explicitly sexual content and the decline in the social segregation of men and women. Carolina Oliphant followed Robert Burns's work with intense interest, particularly his gift for fashioning new words to new tunes, and his editing of existing material beginning to be considered unsuitable for mixed assemblies. One of her earliest pieces was a bowdlerized version of 'The Pleughman' (Randall, 58–9; Rogers, 179–80), for her brother to sing to his tenants at their annual dinner. Many of her songs were set to classic traditional tunes in this way, including 'The Land o' the Leal' (Rogers, 163–4) which was written for her friend Mary Erskine (Mrs Campbell Colquhoun), on the death of her first child in 1797. Sometimes only the tune was used and new lyrics were written for it; sometimes the verbal text was a creative collage of existing versions. Contemporary song-making was often a collective process, making individual attribution difficult. Since anonymity also was the rule (strengthened in Carolina's case by the urge to be taken seriously, which she felt might be compromised if her songs were known to be by a woman), the exact extent of her work and its links with the rest of the tradition have never been clearly established. There is no reliable critical edition.

Jacobite songs probably make up the largest thematic group. The genre had emerged during the later seventeenth century, and by 1820 it was second in importance only to love song in the traditional canon, attracting the attention of major songwriters such as Robert Burns and James Hogg, and acting as a symbolic code for continuing Scottish opposition to the Union. Hence, perhaps, the sense of contemporary relevance that informs her song 'Wha'll be King but Charlie?':

> Come thro' the heather, around him gather,
> Ye're a' the welcomer early;
> Around him cling wi' a' your kin;
> For wha'll be king but Charlie?
> (Rogers, 199–200)

The social life of the Perthshire gentry is another prominent theme. The best of her songs in this vein, 'The Laird o' Cockpen', retains the outstanding old tune but takes no more than a hint from the words traditionally associated with it, which show the central male character forsake the daughter of a lord to go with a collier lassie (Burns and Johnson, no. 353). The morganatic motif survives, but is cleverly reversed in the curt negative response of a 'penniless lass wi' a lang pedigree' to a casual proposal of marriage from a pompous *arriviste*. But not all the tunes were old, and not all the verses adaptations of existing material. The circle of balls and entertainments in the country houses of Perthshire brought Carolina the acquaintance of the master traditional fiddler Niel Gow and his gifted son Nathaniel who furnished her with beautiful new airs which she matched with fresh and inventive verses:

> Wha'll buy my caller herrin'?
> They're bonnie fish and halesome farin';
> Wha'll buy my caller herrin',
> New drawn frae the Forth?
> (Rogers, 165)

Carolina's engagement to her now landless cousin, William Murray Nairne (1757–1830), was lengthy, but they were married at Gask on 2 June 1806, following his appointment as assistant inspector-general of barracks in Scotland. They settled in Edinburgh where their only child, William Murray Nairne (1808–1837), was born two years later.

Carolina's extensive knowledge of Scottish music and song led to contact with the publisher Robert Purdie who was planning 'a collection of the national airs, with words suited for refined circles' (Rogers, 43), which later appeared as *The Scotish Minstrel* (six vols., 1821–4) edited by Robert A. Smith (1780–1829), precentor of St George's, and the leading church musician in Scotland. Since such work was considered incompatible with her status as a gentlewoman, elaborate steps were taken to conceal her identity. Contributions were sent through intermediaries, either anonymously or as coming from the fictitious Mrs Bogan of Bogan. When obliged to visit her publisher she did so in disguise. Only in the posthumous volume, *Lays from Strathearn* (1846), were they eventually avowed.

In 1824, after George IV's visit to Scotland, William Nairne's title was restored. On his death in 1830 Carolina lived with her son in Ireland and on the continent. He died at Brussels in 1837. Thereafter her main interests were charitable and devotional. Lady Nairne became poet laureate of the aspiring and respectable in Victorian Scotland but her efforts to chasten the merry muses with the rod of moral rectitude (at one stage she even contemplated a bowdlerized edition of Burns) began with the passage of time to seem merely quaint. Of the more than eighty songs she made or re-made only a handful—'The Hundred Pipers', 'Wha'll be King but Charlie?', 'The Rowan Tree', 'The Auld Hoose', 'The Laird o' Cockpen' and 'Caller Herrin' '—were to continue as part of the common stock of Scottish expression during the following century.

Lady Nairne's life illuminates the cultural transformation which overtook the Scottish gentry in the century after the Jacobite rising of 1745. 'I sometimes say to myself,' she wrote in 1840, '"This is no me," so greatly have my feelings and trains of thought changed since "auld lang syne" …' (Wilson, 2.428). Lady Nairne died at Gask on 26 October 1845, and was buried in the family chapel.

WILLIAM DONALDSON

Sources C. Rogers, *Life and songs of the Baroness Nairne*, first published 1869 (1905) [Rogers is by default the 'standard' edn, but his work is flawed in several respects: biographical details are described as inaccurate by both Kington Oliphant and Simpson, nor are the texts or attributions entirely reliable] • T. L. Kington-Oliphant, *The Jacobite lairds of Gask* (1870) • E. M. Graham, *The Oliphants of Gask: records of a Jacobite family* (1910) • S. Tytler and J. L. Watson, *The songstresses of Scotland*, 2 vols. (1871) • R. Burns and others, *The Scots musical museum*, ed. J. Johnson, 6 vols. (1787–1803) • G. F. Graham, *The songs of Scotland*, 3 vols. (1861) • M. S. Simpson, *The Scottish songstress* (1894) • J. G. Wilson, ed., *The poets and poetry of Scotland*, 2 vols. in 4 (1876–7) • R. Forbes, *The lyon in mourning, or, A collection of speeches, letters, journals … relative to … Prince Charles Edward Stuart*, ed. H. Paton, 3 vols., Scottish History Society, 20–22 (1895–6) • T. Crawford, *Society and the lyric* (1979) • E. L. Randall, *The merry muses* (1966) • W. Donaldson, *The Jacobite song* (1988) • G. Henderson, *Lady Nairne and her songs* (1901) • journals, 1789–1845, NL Scot., MS 981

Archives NL Scot., corresp. • NL Scot., corresp., journals, and songs • NRA Scotland, priv. coll., corresp. and verses

Likenesses J. Watson-Gordon, oils, *c*.1815, Scot. NPG • British school, four miniatures, priv. coll. • British school, silhouette, priv. coll. • J. Watson-Gordon, double portrait, oils (with her son, William Murray Nairne), Scot. NPG [*see illus.*] • photographic reproduction (after portrait of Lady Nairne as a young woman), repro. in Simpson, *Scottish songstress*

Oliphant, Francis Wilson [Frank] (1818–1859), painter and designer of stained glass, was born on 28 September 1818 at Gateshead, co. Durham, and baptized at St Mary's Church there on 15 September 1819, the son of Thomas Oliphant (*c*.1787–1856), a glass cutter, and his wife, Margery. He studied drawing at the Trustees' Academy, Edinburgh, under Sir William Allan and was involved from an early age in the stained-glass industry, which was undergoing rapid expansion. The revival of Gothic style and ornament led him to make a profound study of ecclesiastical art, visiting many of the great northern European cathedrals. He worked first for the firm of Ballantine and Allan, Edinburgh, and then as chief designer for William Wailes, Newcastle, who supplied glass to Augustus Welby Pugin. About 1847 he moved to London and worked as Pugin's second designer, especially upon the painted windows in the new houses of parliament. He also sent in a cartoon to the competition for the decoration of Westminster Hall, which was not successful. During this period Oliphant exhibited several pictures in the Royal Academy, the chief being a large Shakespearian study of the interview between Richard II and John of Gaunt, and a striking picture of the prodigal son, *Nearing Home*. On 4 May 1852 he married his cousin, Margaret Oliphant Wilson (1828–1897) [*see* Oliphant, Margaret Oliphant Wilson], who was beginning to be known as a writer. They seem to have had a troubled relationship, and the couple soon became dependent on her earnings.

By his mid-thirties Oliphant was able to write, 'the number of windows that have been executed from my designs is past counting and are in nearly every county and cathedral in England' (Letter to Major William Blackwood, 26 March 1856, NL Scot., Blackwood MS 4119). But he was not satisfied with the way his designs were carried out. In 1854 he set up a small stained-glass workshop, hoping to create better quality windows, and also to have more time for his painting. This workshop produced the windows in the ante-chapel of King's College, Cambridge, those in the chancel of Aylesbury church, Buckinghamshire, and several in Ely Cathedral. The famous choristers' window at Ely was the joint work of Oliphant and William Dyce RA, the former being responsible for the original design.

But owing to Oliphant's lack of business sense, the project made heavy losses. In 1857 he developed tuberculosis and was eventually forced to give up work. He left England in January 1859 with his family to seek a warmer climate and died at via Babuino 56 in Rome on 20 October 1859, and was buried in the English cemetery there. He left a daughter and two sons, one born after his death.

Mrs Oliphant was always reserved about her husband. His friend William Bell Scott thought that he became 'an idle and aimless man' (*Autobiographical Notes of the Life of William Bell Scott*, ed. W. Minto, 1892, 1.188). 'He had the ability and the knowledge to imitate the medieval glass of the successive periods of architecture, and yet his ambition was to be a painter of history, which ambition was fatal to him' (ibid.). His only book, *A Plea for Painted Glass* (1855), shows him to have been an idealist who dreamed of competing with the great artists of the middle ages. He was capable of generous but reckless acts, like presenting a window to Aylesbury church when no one could be found to pay for it. None of his paintings is known to have survived, but his stained glass is excellent.

[ANON.], *rev.* MERRYN WILLIAMS

Sources *The autobiography and letters of Mrs M. O. W. Oliphant*, ed. Mrs H. Coghill (1899) · *The autobiography of Margaret Oliphant: the complete text*, ed. E. Jay (1990) · F. W. Oliphant, *A plea for painted glass* (1855) · NL Scot., Oliphant MSS · NL Scot., Blackwood MS 4119 · *Autobiographical notes of the life of William Bell Scott: and notices of his artistic and poetic circle of friends, 1830 to 1882*, ed. W. Minto, 1 (1892), 188 · M. Harrison, *Victorian stained glass* (1980) · CGPLA Eng. & Wales (1860) · IGI · baptism cert., Gateshead, St Mary's Church
Archives Eton, MSS · Hunt. L. · NL Scot. · NRA, priv. coll. · Princeton University, New Jersey, corresp. | BL, corresp. with Bentley, Add. MS 46616 · BL, corresp. with Bryce, Add. MS 42576 · BL, corresp. with MacMillans, Add. MS 54919 · NL Scot., corresp. with *Blackwood's* · NL Scot., Margaret Oliphant archive
Wealth at death under £800: probate, 11 Feb 1860, CGPLA Eng. & Wales

Oliphant, James (1734–1818), Church of Scotland minister, was born in Stirling, the second son of William Oliphant. He entered the University of Glasgow in 1753 and earned an MA three years later. In 1757 Oliphant matriculated at the Associate Burgher Hall, the seceders' divinity school at Glasgow, but he attended only four sessions before leaving the secession movement because of differences with some of the professors at the school. He subsequently joined the Church of Scotland, receiving his licence to preach from the presbytery of Kintyre on 19 May 1760. He was admitted to the Gorbals Chapel of Ease, Glasgow, in 1763, and on 17 May 1764 was ordained to the chapel of ease in Kilmarnock, Ayrshire. Six months later, on 27 November, he married Elizabeth Hay (d. 1780). In October 1773 Oliphant was presented to Dumbarton by its town council, acting on the request of the inhabitants, and he was settled there on 23 December. He also served as

clerk of the presbytery of Dumbarton from 1783 to 1817. Following the death of his first wife, on 29 March 1780 shortly after giving birth to their seventh child, he married, on 27 April 1784, Janet (d. 1805), daughter of Humphrey Colquhoun of Barnhill and Margaret Williamson, with whom he had five more children.

Although Oliphant was described by J. W. Taylor as 'a sound and racy theologian, and an interesting and highly accomplished preacher', he also provoked considerable opposition, even ridicule. In *The Ordination* (1786), Robert Burns, who had heard Oliphant preach at Kilmarnock, lampooned him for his booming voice, as well as the opposition to common sense of Oliphant and his Kilmarnock colleague, John Russell:

> Curst Common-sense, that imp o' h-ll,
> Cam' in wi' Maggie Lauder;
> But O[liphant] aft made her yell,
> An' R[ussell] sair misca'd her.
> (*Poems and Songs*, 2.213, ll. 10–14)

Oliphant's high Calvinism also inspired the hostility of clergymen whose theological views emphasized the role of free will in religious life. In 1773 his Kilmarnock opponents even hired a man to walk the streets of Dumbarton, purporting to sell 'the whole works of the Rev. James Oliphant, presentee to this parish, for the small charge of two pence'.

Oliphant compiled strict Calvinist catechisms for the use of schools and young communicants, and they attracted the greatest attention during his ministry. His *Mother's Catechism* (1770) went through more than twenty editions, and his *Sacramental Catechism* (1772) was also immensely popular. He also wrote the account of the parish of Dumbarton in Sir John Sinclair's *Statistical Account of Scotland* (1792).

Oliphant lost his eyesight several years before his death, which occurred on 10 April 1818.   MICHAEL JINKINS

Sources *Fasti Scot.*, new edn, vol. 3 · DNB · *The poems and songs of Robert Burns*, ed. J. Kinsley, 3 vols. (1968)

Oliphant, Sir Lancelot (1881–1965), diplomatist, was born on 8 October 1881 at 2 Stanhope Street, Kensington, London, the youngest of the three sons (there were no daughters) of Arthur Craigie Oliphant (1840–1920), formerly private secretary to Sir Salar Jung, minister to the nizam of Hyderabad, and his second wife, Agnes Mary (d. 1928), daughter of Rear-Admiral William Horton, and granddaughter of Admiral Joshua Sydney Horton. The younger of his two brothers, Laurence Richard (b. 1877), was captain-superintendent of the Royal Hospital school, Greenwich, from 1922 to 1933, and retired from the Royal Navy with the rank of rear-admiral. Oliphant was educated privately, and joined the Foreign Office as a clerk in August 1903, having passed the examination second out of sixteen. He passed an examination in public law in June 1905, and was appointed third secretary at Constantinople in September of that year. In August 1906 he returned to the Foreign Office, to work in the eastern department. He was third secretary at Tehran, with responsibility for commercial matters, from March 1909 to October 1911, when he again returned to London to work in the Foreign

Office's eastern department. During the First World War he worked in the war department, dealing with political rather than contraband affairs, and in June 1917 was made a CMG.

After the war Oliphant was employed briefly in the Foreign Office's central department, with the rank of assistant secretary and acting counsellor from December 1920. He returned to the eastern department with the rank of counsellor in September 1923. He was promoted acting assistant under-secretary of state in February 1928 and substantive assistant under-secretary of state in April 1929, and was appointed CB in March 1929 and KCMG in January 1931. He was promoted deputy under-secretary of state in March 1936. With Sir Alexander Cadogan, he was thus at the centre of hectic political and diplomatic activity during the years when Neville Chamberlain and Lord Halifax attempted to negotiate a settlement with Hitler. He never lost his interest in Persia and from 1908 to 1939 managed an unusual consistency by retaining a direct or indirect influence over Persian affairs for all that time. While he was in the central department, this meant that Persia had to be declared a part of central Europe. On 6 November 1939 Oliphant married Christine McRae Isham (1895–1972), daughter of William Sinclair; she was the widow of Victor Albert Francis Charles Spencer, first Viscount Churchill (1890–1934), and the divorced wife of Lieutenant-Colonel Ralph Heyward Isham (d. 1955). Oliphant became stepfather to the two children by her first marriage, Sarah Faith Georgina Spencer (b. 1931) and Victor George Spencer (b. 1934), who in 1973 succeeded a half-brother as third Viscount Churchill.

In December 1939 Oliphant was appointed ambassador at Brussels and minister-plenipotentiary to Luxembourg. He then entered on an unusually turbulent period when, after he had spent an extremely tense seven months in Brussels, Belgium was invaded by Germany in May 1940. In attempting to join the exiled Belgian government in France, Oliphant was captured by German forces at Port Mahon, near the mouth of the River Somme. He then endured a long odyssey through different parts of Germany in the hands of the Gestapo, and was sometimes treated less well than the rules of diplomatic immunity demanded, though he readily acknowledged how much he was helped by American missions in Germany. Negotiations for his release in exchange for Germans interned on the Isle of Man took a long time, but eventually he arrived in Spain and reached Britain via Lisbon on 29 September 1941. Two days later he resumed his duties as ambassador to the governments of Belgium and Luxembourg in exile. Oliphant retired when the embassy returned to Brussels, in September 1944, and was succeeded by Sir Hughe Knatchbull-Hugessen; he retired from the Foreign Office in November 1944. He then lived in London until he died of bronchopneumonia, chronic bronchitis, and emphysema at the Middlesex Hospital, St Marylebone, London, on 2 October 1965. He was survived by his wife and stepchildren.　　　RICHARD LANGHORNE

Sources L. Oliphant, *An ambassador in bonds* (1946) · L. S. Frey and M. L. Frey, *The history of diplomatic immunity* (1999) · *WWW*, *1961–70* · Burke, *Peerage* · Burke, *Gen. GB* · *FO List* · Foreign Office Historical Branch records · b. cert. · d. cert.
Archives priv. coll. · PRO, corresp., FO 800 | Bodl. Oxf., corresp. with Rumbold · PRO, corresp. with Sir Percy Loraine, FO 1011
Likenesses W. Stoneman, photographs, 1931–48, NPG · photographs, 1940–41, repro. in Oliphant, *Ambassador in bonds*

Oliphant, Laurence, first Lord Oliphant (d. 1500?). *See under* Oliphant family (*per.* 1141–c.1500).

Oliphant, Laurence, third Lord Oliphant (d. 1566), landowner, was the son of Colin, master of Oliphant, and Lady Elizabeth Keith, second daughter of the third Earl Marischal. Colin was killed at Flodden in 1513, and so it was as a minor that Laurence succeeded his grandfather, John, second Lord Oliphant, some time before 18 November 1516. He married Margaret, eldest daughter of Sir James Sandilands of Calder and widow of Robert Bruce of Auchenbowie, before 10 July 1525, and had come of age by 30 March 1526. He and Margaret had three sons and four daughters; the eldest son, Laurence *Oliphant, was born in 1529.

The core of Oliphant's estates lay in Perthshire, with extensive lands in Aberdalgie, Dupplin, and their environs. In 1533 his right to hold the three-quarter lands of Pitcaithly, south of Perth, by feu-ferme from the crown, was challenged by the king's lawyers, and it was not until 1538 that he and his wife were jointly infeft in this property. He also added substantially to his properties by acquiring lands in Caithness from a cousin. Closer to home, he owned property on the east side of the watergate in Perth. There is no record of his having been entered as a burgess there, nor do the burgh records indicate that he took any part in the affairs of the town. Indeed, he remained so aloof from them that he did not accompany the large contingent from Perth and its environs which went to the aid of the earl of Lennox in 1544.

In 1542 Oliphant had, however, accompanied the Scottish army to Solway Moss, and was there captured by the English. He found the subsequent march to London arduous and was still awaiting a pledge to relieve him from captivity on 19 January 1543. In the meantime, he signed Cassillis's pledge to support King Henry's aims in Scotland and had received a gift of money from the English monarch. Oliphant was back in Edinburgh by early June 1543 and sitting with the council, but in the following March his ransom (set at 800 merks) was still unpaid and his son, acting as his pledge for payment, remained in England. None the less, Oliphant ignored his 'assurance' and did nothing significant to forward King Henry's designs in Scotland.

Oliphant was engaged in a legal dispute early in 1544 but refused to appear in Perth sheriff court and had the case removed to Edinburgh and the lords of council. A contract for the marriage of his daughter Jean to William Moncrieff of that ilk was arranged in May 1550, but at the height of the Reformation crisis, ten years later, the two lairds were engaged in a quarrel which precluded Oliphant's attendance on the affairs of the lords of the congregation. His absence was a cause of annoyance to his peers, but the English ambassador Thomas Randolph noted that Oliphant's influence was of little significance, and that in any case he was most likely to follow the dictates of the earl of Huntly. Oliphant did not sit in the Reformation Parliament in August 1560, and probably opposed the religious reformation. He died at Old Wick on 29 March 1566. His son was served heir to his father on 2 May 1566, and well before that date had become a prominent member of Queen Mary's party.

MARY BLACK VERSCHUUR

Sources CSP Scot., 1547–1603 · J. Bain, ed., The Hamilton papers: letters and papers illustrating the political relations of England and Scotland in the XVIth century, 2, Scottish RO, 12 (1892) · LP Henry VIII, vols. 17–18 · CSP for., 1560–61 · CSP for., 1561–2 · J. M. Thomson and others, eds., Registrum magni sigilli regum Scotorum / The register of the great seal of Scotland, 11 vols. (1882–1914), vols. 4–5 · Reg. PCS, 1st ser. · M. Livingstone, D. Hay Fleming, and others, eds., Registrum secreti sigilli regum Scotorum / The register of the privy seal of Scotland, 1–6 (1908–63) · Scots peerage, 6.544–6 · J. Anderson, The Oliphants in Scotland (1879) · Perth burgh records, A. K. Bell Library, Perth, B59 · sheriff court book of Perth, NA Scot., SC49/1 · I. H. Shearer, Acta dominorum concilii et sessionis, Stair Society, 14 (1951) · GEC, Peerage, new edn, 10.51–2

Oliphant, Laurence, fourth Lord Oliphant (1529–1593),

nobleman, was the eldest son of Laurence *Oliphant, third Lord Oliphant (d. 1566), and Margaret, daughter of Sir James Sandilands of Calder. He succeeded his father on 2 May 1566 having in March 1551 married Margaret (d. c.1594), daughter of George Hay, seventh earl of Erroll. They had six children: Laurence, master of Oliphant, John, William, Elizabeth, whose first husband was William Douglas, tenth earl of Angus, Jean, who married Alexander Bruce of Cultmalindie, and Euphame, wife of James Johnston of Westraw.

Oliphant was seldom a significant figure in public affairs during his relatively long life. His family had important estates in Caithness, and he was appointed justiciar there on 14 March 1557. Appointed a privy councillor in 1567, he attended infrequently. In the disorders of Mary's reign he initially sided with the queen, supporting her marriage to Bothwell, attending their wedding, and subsequently fighting on Mary's side at Langside on 13 May 1568. For this he was denounced as a rebel by the queen's enemies and put to the horn. Thereafter his allegiance wavered. On 6 January 1569 Mary named him as one of her counsellors, but by April he had moved into the regent Moray's camp, and at the convention held at Perth in July voted with the majority which rejected proceedings to divorce the queen from Bothwell, as a prelude to her marriage to the duke of Norfolk and possible restoration. After Moray's murder on 23 January 1570 Oliphant rejoined the queen's followers, and in April, following a meeting with some of the queen's adherents at Linlithgow, was a signatory to a letter on Mary's behalf to Queen Elizabeth requesting that she 'enter into such conditions with the Queen's Highness in Scotland as may be honourable for all parties' (Calderwood, 2.550). But he does not appear to have been otherwise active on Mary's behalf, and by the end of 1572 was said to be favourable to the

king's party. He seems to have supported Morton throughout the latter's regency. In the 1560s Oliphant may have been a sympathizer with Catholicism, but in July 1585 he voted in favour of a league with England in defence of protestantism. In April 1589 he took part in James VI's campaign against the earl of Huntly, and attended a meeting of the privy council for the last time in February 1591.

Oliphant may not have taken a leading role in Scottish politics, but he undeniably achieved prominence through his involvement in a series of bitter feuds between his own and various other noble houses. In July 1569, for example, there was an attack on him and his servants by the earl of Caithness, highlighting a dispute with the contentious Sinclairs, earls of Caithness, which persisted through his lifetime. But the most spectacular and celebrated episode in which Oliphant was concerned was the one in November 1580, involving the powerful Ruthven family. The two families were near neighbours, both having substantial estates in Perthshire, and on this occasion, a disagreement over the right to certain teinds, a common cause of friction, resulted in the fourth lord's eldest son, the master of Oliphant, and his followers making an attack near Dupplin, a few miles south-west of Perth, on a party of Ruthvens and Stewarts as they returned from the marriage of the earl of Mar. In the violent exchanges which ensued, Alexander Stewart of Schutingleyis was struck by a bullet and killed. The upshot of this fracas was Oliphant's arrest followed by his trial for the murder of Stewart. The trial itself was a curious affair, with allegations at one point of the use of a poisoned bullet, but helped by Morton's backing Oliphant was eventually acquitted.

Rather surprisingly this verdict did not create a permanent breach with the Ruthvens and shortly afterwards the master of Oliphant was one of the participants in the Ruthven raid, the seizure of James VI in 1582 by the earl of Gowrie and his supporters. In 1584, as a result of his involvement in these events, Oliphant's son was exiled abroad where he met an uncertain fate. According to one account, following his capture by North Sea pirates 'he was hanged upon the mast of the ship' (Calderwood, 4.46), but another source has him incarcerated in Algiers, a prisoner of the Turks. Oliphant himself, still feuding with the Sinclairs, died in Wick, Caithness, on 16 January 1593, and was buried in Wick church.

G. R. HEWITT

Sources Scots peerage · Reg. PCS, 1st ser., vols. 1–4 · R. Pitcairn, ed., Ancient criminal trials in Scotland, 1, Bannatyne Club, 42 (1833) · D. Calderwood, The history of the Kirk of Scotland, ed. T. Thomson and D. Laing, 8 vols., Wodrow Society, 7 (1842–9), vols. 2, 4 · CSP Scot., 1563–9; 1571–4 · D. Moysie, Memoirs of the affairs of Scotland, 1577–1603, ed. J. Dennistoun, Bannatyne Club, 39 (1830) · G. R. Hewitt, Scotland under Morton, 1572–80 (1982) · K. Brown, Blood feud in Scotland (1986) · GEC, Peerage, new edn, 10.52–4 · G. Donaldson, All the queen's men (1983)

Oliphant, Laurence, of Gask, styled ninth Lord Oliphant

(1691–1767), Jacobite army officer, son of James Oliphant (d. 1732), laird of Gask, and Janet (d. 1729), daughter of the Revd Anthony Murray of Woodend, Perthshire, was born on 29 December 1691 at Williamston, Perthshire. The

Gask branch of the Oliphants descended from William Oliphant of Newton, Perthshire, second son of Colin, master of Oliphant, slain at Flodden. Some of their lands were traditionally 'held on the tenure of a yearly gift of White Roses' (Lang, 129); the Gask estate itself came into their hands in 1625. Oliphant married Amelia (or Amélie) Anne Sophia Murray (1698–1774), second daughter of William *Nairne, styled second Lord Nairne, in 1719; they had one son, also Laurence, the father of the poet Carolina, who fittingly married back into the Nairnes in time for the restoration of their title in 1824. The Oliphants were a strongly royalist and Jacobite family, and in the rising of 1715 Laurence was commissioned as a lieutenant in Lord Rollo's Perthshire horse, in which capacity he was present at the battle of Sheriffmuir; subsequently he acted as adjutant while James VIII and III (James Francis Edward Stuart, Jacobite claimant to the throne) was at Scone. After the failure of the rising he lay low for a while, but was back at Gask by March 1718 at the latest. The Gasks received a call for support from the Jacobite leadership in Scotland in 1719, but the rising was over too rapidly for anything to transpire. On the death of his father on 18 April 1732, Oliphant succeeded to the Gask estates. His political outlook led to the appointment of the Jacobite poet William Meston to be young Laurence's tutor in 1736. The family continued to display its support for the exiled Stuarts, and in the early 1740s (possibly for Charles Edward Stuart's twenty-first birthday in 1741) Ebenezer Oliphant, Gask's younger brother and an Edinburgh silversmith, gave Prince Charles a 'beautiful rococo canteen of silver-gilt travelling cutlery' (Lenman, 106). In 1745 Gask was asked to subscribe 'for a new edition of Fordun's Scotichronicon' (Oliphant, 102): later, in exile, Gask's antiquarian interests would find solace in the holdings of the Scots College in Paris.

By 9 August 1745 Gask had heard of the rising, and he and his son took long walks 'along the upper terrace of the old garden' (Anderson, lxxx) to decide which of them would fight. In the end both did, joining the prince at Blair Atholl on 31 August: the next day, Oliphant made his wife factor over his estate, and brought a letter from the prince to Lord George Murray requesting his support. His own tenants were unwilling to follow, and Gask appears to have inhibited them from harvesting their corn, a prohibition gracefully removed by a cut of Prince Charles's sword. In September the Gasks, together with Viscount Strathallan, raised two troops of the Perthshire horse, the first cavalry of the Jacobite army; Strathallan was overall commander, while Gask served as lieutenant-colonel. The horse were present at the battle of Prestonpans, but took no part in the action. While the prince's army was in England, Gask acted as lieutenant-governor of Perth: in this capacity, he held the council house with only nineteen men against an infuriated Hanoverian mob on 30 November. Eventually relief arrived, and Gask remained in post until 6 February, when he reluctantly retreated in the face of overwhelming force. Besides personal bravery, he also displayed guile: after the battle of Falkirk, he accompanied Viscount Strathallan in the guise of a peasant to secure information concerning the extent of the Jacobite victory. At Culloden, after Viscount Strathallan's death, Gask led the horse out of action to final dispersal at Ruthven. He was in hiding thereafter for seven months at Moy, Birkhall, Glenisla, and Strathdee together with his son, who touchingly recalled their experiences many years later. On one occasion, they were close enough to government troops for their servant to hear one soldier say 'That's Oliphant', but Gask's potential attacker was bought off with an opportune gold piece (Graham, 209).

On the death of Charles, seventh Lord Oliphant, on 19 April 1748, Gask laid claim to the title, which was, however, assumed by William Oliphant. On his death on 3 June 1751, he apparently named Gask his heir, but David Oliphant of Bachilton succeeded instead, and indeed Gask may not have been entitled to the honour in law; however, the peerage was emptily confirmed to him by James VIII and III on 14 July 1760. His estate, under the management of the barons of the exchequer, was purchased by his kinsman Oliphant of Condie in 1753, and Gask took a lively interest in its affairs. In exile, he took the alias John Whytt, and lived in considerable poverty, moving from Versailles to Corbeil in 1755 'in hopes of having everything Cheaper' (Tayler, 212); his grandson apparently died from malnutrition in 1757. None the less, in 1759 he could still gather with other Scots and Irish exiles in Paris on 10 June, James's birthday. In 1763 Gask's wife was granted a pension of £111 by George III, and Oliphant 'returned to his ancestral home, apparently with the tacit consent of the government' (Smith, 12), although the attainder remained. He died at Gask on 1 April 1767. His son went on to become one of the last Jacobites: when the larger part of the Scottish Episcopal church finally accepted the inevitable and disowned Jacobitism on Charles's death in 1788, young Laurence sacked his (now juring) episcopal chaplain. With Lord Ogilvie, the Gasks were 'perhaps the last partisans of the alliance between France and Scotland' (Oliphant, 428), ideological episcopalian Jacobites of undiluted vigour and a distinctly Scottish world view.   MURRAY G. H. PITTOCK

Sources DNB · J. Anderson, ed., *The Oliphants in Scotland* (1879) · E. M. Graham [E. B. Oliphant], *The Oliphants of Gask* (1910) · T. L. Kington-Oliphant, *The Jacobite lairds of Gask* (1870) · A. M. Smith, *Jacobite estates of the Forty-Five* (1982) · A. Lang, *Prince Charles Edward Stuart*, new edn (1903) · *A Jacobite source list: list of documents in the Scottish Record Office relating to the Jacobites* (1995) · F. J. McLynn, *Charles Edward Stuart: a tragedy in many acts* (1988) · B. Lenman, *The Jacobite cause* (1986) · A. Livingstone, C. W. H. Aikman, and B. S. Hart, eds., *Muster roll of Prince Charles Edward Stuart's army, 1745–46* (1984) · G. Dalgleish and D. Mechan, '*I am come home': treasures of Prince Charles Edward Stuart* (1985) [exhibition catalogue, National Museum of Antiquities of Scotland, Edinburgh, 26 June–3 Nov 1985] · D. Dobson, *Jacobites of the '15* (1993) · B. G. Seton and J. G. Arnot, eds., *The prisoners of the '45*, Scottish History Society, 3rd ser., 13–15 (1928–9) · H. Tayler, ed., *Jacobite epilogue* (1941) · *Scots peerage*

Archives NA Scot., diary · NA Scot., annexed estate papers, E 750 · NL Scot., corresp. and MSS

Likenesses portrait, repro. in Graham, *Oliphants of Gask*, facing p. 120

Oliphant, Laurence (1829–1888), diplomatist, traveller, and mystic, the only child of Sir Anthony Oliphant (1793–

Laurence Oliphant (1829–1888), by Thomas Rodger

1859) and his wife, Maria (*d*. 1881), daughter of Colonel Campbell of the 72nd highlanders, was born at Cape Town. Thomas Oliphant, the musician, was his uncle.

Family background and early life Oliphant's father, who was third son of Ebenezer Oliphant of Condie and Newton, Perthshire, and Mary, daughter of Sir William Stirling of Ardoch, had been called to the bar at Lincoln's Inn in 1821, and practised for a time in London as an equity draftsman, but just before his son's birth he was appointed attorney-general at the Cape. Oliphant's father and mother were both fervent evangelicals. His mother returned to Europe on account of her health, and took her son with her. He was sent to the school of a Mr Parr at Durnford Manor, Salisbury, but spent part of his holidays with his mother at Condie, an ancestral home of the Oliphant family.

In 1839 Oliphant's father was made chief justice of Ceylon, and was knighted. Lady Oliphant rejoined her husband in Ceylon in 1841, and Oliphant followed in the winter of the same year, in the charge of a private tutor, who continued to teach him in Ceylon; but despite this his education was much interrupted. His father returned on two years' leave about 1846, and spent the time in a continental tour. He was allowed to accompany his parents instead of going to Cambridge, as had been intended. The family

spent the winter of 1846–7 in Paris, travelled through Germany and the Tyrol during 1847, and at the end of the year crossed the Alps to Italy, where Oliphant witnessed some of the popular disturbances in the beginning of 1848. He went with his parents to Greece, and then accompanied them back to Ceylon, where he acted as his father's private secretary.

The law, diplomacy, and journalism Oliphant was called to the colonial bar in Ceylon. He said that by the age of twenty-two he had been engaged in twenty-three murder cases. In December 1851 he was invited by Jang Bahadur (the prime minister of Nepal, who was in Ceylon on a return voyage from England) to join a hunting excursion in Nepal and he reached Katmandu before returning to Ceylon. A few months later he went to England with his mother, and at the end of 1851 began to keep terms at Lincoln's Inn. Besides studying law, he took an interest in the work of Lord Shaftesbury and others among the London poor. In the spring of 1852 he published an account of his tour in Nepal, called *A Journey to Khatmandu*. He resolved to be called to the Scottish as well as the English bar, and began studies at Edinburgh in the summer of 1852, but these were never completed.

In August 1852 Oliphant set out with Oswald Smith for a visit to St Petersburg, thence to Nizhniy Novgorod, and ultimately to the Crimea, where they entered Sevastopol in disguise and mapped its fortifications. He published an account of part of the journey, *The Russian Shores of the Black Sea in the Autumn of 1852* (1853). The approach of the Crimean War gave special interest to this book, which soon reached a fourth edition. Lord Raglan applied to him for information, and he was engaged to write for the *Daily News*. While keenly interested in this he received an offer of an appointment from James Bruce, eighth earl of Elgin, then governor-in-chief of British North America, with whose family Lady Oliphant was intimate. Oliphant acted as secretary to Lord Elgin during the negotiation at Washington of the reciprocity treaty with Canada, whose economy was in ruins as a result of the repeal of the corn laws in 1846. Elgin's success in achieving free trade between Canada and the USA saved what had been a desperate situation. Oliphant afterwards accompanied Elgin to Quebec. He was soon appointed 'superintendent of Indian affairs', and made a journey to Lake Superior and back by the headwaters of the Mississippi and Chicago, described soon afterwards in *Minnesota and the Far West* (1855). Dancing, travelling, and political business filled up his time agreeably; but on Lord Elgin's retirement at the end of 1854, he declined offers of an appointment under Sir Edmund Head, Elgin's successor. He went back to England (whither his father had now finally returned) and put forward a plan, suggested by his previous journeys, which is described in a pamphlet called *The Trans-Caucasian Provinces, the Proper Field of Operation for a Christian Army* (1855). While the main allied force was bogged down around Sevastopol, Russian troops were besieging Kars in northeast Turkey; its fall would not only be a severe blow to the

Porte, but would renew the Russian threat to Persia, Mesopotamia, and Afghanistan. Oliphant proposed an expedition to relieve Kars through Circassia and the Trans-Caucasian provinces. Privately he asked the foreign secretary, Lord Clarendon, to send him on a personal mission to Schamyl, the Muslim guerrilla leader in the Caucasus, whose aid against the Russians he hoped to secure by the offer of British troops. Clarendon would only go so far as to give Oliphant a recommendation to the British ambassador in Constantinople, Lord Stratford de Redcliffe. Oliphant's father accompanied him to Constantinople, where they found Lord Stratford de Redcliffe about to visit the Crimea; they accompanied him thither and Oliphant had a glimpse of the siege of Sevastopol. He could not obtain an authorization for his scheme, but Stratford allowed him to accompany a member of the embassy on a reconnaissance of the Circassian coast. At Trebizond they fell in with the Turkish commander, Omar Pasha. Oliphant, who got on well with Omar Pasha, joined his force and was present at the battle of the Ingour. The fall of Kars made the expedition fruitless; and after much suffering, and a consequent illness during the retreat, Oliphant returned to England at the end of 1855. *The Trans-Caucasian Campaign … under Omar Pasha* (1856) describes his experiences.

Oliphant had been acting as correspondent of *The Times* during his recent expedition, and in 1856 he was invited by the editor, John Delane, to accompany him on a visit to the United States. He travelled through the southern states to New Orleans, and there was invited to join the filibuster William Walker in his audacious attempt to seize Nicaragua and rule it as a private fief. Oliphant said he accepted for the sake of the book he could write; privately he had been charged by Lord Palmerston to find out what was going on so close to the British protectorate of the Mosquito Coast. However, the expedition fell in with HMS *Cossack* at the mouth of the St Juan River; and when her captain came on board to inspect the 'emigrants', he recognized Oliphant as a British subject in a place where no British subject ought to be, and removed him. An account of this adventure and of his first trip in Circassia is given in *Patriots and Filibusters, or, Incidents of Political and Exploratory Travel* (1860).

In 1857 Oliphant became private secretary to Lord Elgin on his visit to China. He accompanied Elgin to Hong Kong, was present at the bombardment of Canton (Guangzhou), and helped to storm Tientsin (Tianjin). He was employed in several minor missions, and visited Japan with the expedition barely eighteen months after the American Townsend Harris had been accredited as the first foreign diplomat to the shogun's government; he published *Narrative of Elgin's Mission to China and Japan* in 1859. On his return to England, Oliphant found that his father (with whom he was always on very affectionate terms) had recently died. He was without formal employment for a time, but in 1860 ostensibly amused himself by a visit to Italy, where the drive for unification under the Piedmontese leader, Count Cavour, was entering its last phase. Oliphant was granted an interview with Cavour at the

moment when the convention he had agreed with the emperor Napoleon the previous year was about to be made democratically respectable. France had undertaken to help Piedmont drive the Austrians from the Italian peninsula in return for Savoy and Nice. Garibaldi, who was born in Nice, objected to this bargain, and mounted a plot, in which Oliphant became involved, to break up the ballot boxes in Nice on the occasion of the vote for annexation to France. Oliphant gave his view of the value of a plebiscite in a pamphlet called *Universal Suffrage and Napoleon the Third* (1860), and as before the Foreign Office benefited from his private observations. Garibaldi's expedition to Sicily broke up the Nice scheme. In 1861 Oliphant travelled in Montenegro and elsewhere, and soon afterwards accepted his first official appointment, as first secretary of legation in Japan. He arrived at Yeddo at the end of June 1861. On the evening of 5 July a night attack was made on the embassy. Oliphant rushed out with a hunting-whip, and was attacked by a Japanese with a heavy two-handed sword. A beam, invisible in the darkness, interfered with the blows, but Oliphant was severely wounded, and sent on board ship to recover. He had to return to England after a visit to the island of Tsushima, strategically placed between Russia and Japan, where a Russian naval force was discovered, and persuaded to retreat.

Oliphant's first invitation on arriving home was to stay with Lord Palmerston at Broadlands. The rest of 1862 was occupied with visits to Corfu (with the prince of Wales, then on his way to Palestine), and afterwards to Herzegovina and the Abruzzi. The Foreign Office chose to announce that 'family considerations' obliged Oliphant to retire from the diplomatic service, thus providing cover for a series of unofficial missions. Early in 1863 he visited Poland to look at the insurrection there, and later in the year made another attempt, but was turned back. He then travelled in Moldavia, and went northwards to report the Prussian-Danish War. He was now disposed to settle down. He had already once or twice canvassed Stirling burghs, and made himself popular with the electors. In 1864 he joined Sir Algernon Borthwick and some other friends in starting a journal called *The Owl*, of which Thomas Onwhyn was the publisher. It was suggested at a dinner party in fun, and was intended to be partly a mystification, supported by an affected knowledge of profound political secrets. Sir Algernon Borthwick undertook to print it, and it caused much amusement to the initiated. Oliphant contributed only to the first ten numbers, retiring when it was taken up more seriously. In the following year he published the hugely popular 'Piccadilly: a fragment of contemporary biography', in *Blackwood's Edinburgh Magazine* (republished, with illustrations by R. Doyle, in 1870).

Oliphant and Thomas Lake Harris In 1865 Oliphant was elected as Liberal MP for Stirling burghs. He did little in parliament but annoy his own side. Passionately in favour of reform, in 1867, when his leader, Gladstone, tried to amend Conservative proposals for the extension of the franchise, Oliphant encouraged fellow Liberals to vote for Disraeli's bill. A singular change now took place in his life. His rambling and adventurous career had given him much experience, but had not made up for a desultory education. He loved excitement, was a universal favourite in society, and had had flirtations in every quarter of the globe. He was a clear-headed man of business, was familiar with official life, and was a brilliant journalist. From his earliest years, however, he had also strong religious impressions, and in his letters to his mother speculations upon his own state of mind and the various phenomena of religions of all varieties had alternated with sparkling descriptions of adventure and society. He had been interested successively in many of the books which reflected contemporary movements of thought. He had read Theodore Parker, W. Smith's *Thorndale*, Maurice's writings, and Morell's *History of Philosophy*. His lack of a secure belief, however, left him at the mercy of any pretender to inspiration. His official and social experience had dispersed many illusions, and his *Piccadilly*, very brightly written, is not a novel proper, but a satire directed against the various hypocrisies and corruptions of society. In it he had come, he said, to think that the world at large was a lunatic asylum (*Piccadilly*, 1870, 262). He referred to 'the greatest poet of the age, Thomas Lake Harris', author of 'The Great Republic: a Poem of the Sun', and typified him in a mysterious prophet who meets the hero; Harris was the head of a community in America called the Brotherhood of the New Life. The creed was a mixture of philosophy and science, which identified 'physical sensations' caused by the life of Christ in man, and held that marriage should be a Platonic relationship. Oliphant had also some belief in spiritualism, though he came to regard it as rather diabolical than divine.

In 1867 Oliphant resigned his seat in parliament, and joined Harris's community at Brocton, or 'Salem-on-Erie', in New York state, where the leader was in the habit of casting out devils and forming magnetic circles among his disciples. Oliphant was renamed Woodbine by Harris and became his spiritual slave. He was set to work on the farm, was ordered to drive teams and 'cadge strawberries on the railway', and, after walking all day, was sent out at night to draw water 'till his fingers were almost frost-bitten'. He made over all his money to the community. Oliphant's mother also joined the community in 1868, and, though living at the same place, was not allowed to hold any confidential communication with her son. After going through this probation the disciples were to regenerate the world, and mother and son are said to have 'found perfect peace and contentment'. In 1870 Oliphant returned to London under Harris's orders, and was supported by a small allowance from Brocton. He resumed his former occupation by becoming correspondent for *The Times* in the Franco-Prussian War. He was with the French and afterwards with the German armies, but suddenly returned to America, in obedience, it was said, to a sign prescribed by Harris—namely, a bullet's grazing his hair. He was soon back, however, and was again correspondent for *The Times* in Paris towards the end of 1871. His mother was permitted to join him, and it was there that he met Alice (1846?–1887), daughter of Henry le Strange of Hunstanton, Norfolk. All who knew her spoke of her singular attractiveness. She

was twenty-six, and had been much admired in society, but she shared some of Oliphant's dissatisfaction with the world. She adopted his creed, and they were engaged at the beginning of 1872. However, the consent of Harris was required and he made one condition: that the marriage was not to be consummated. The genuine 'human sentiment' was to be considered as an 'abstract and spiritual passion', a text upon which Oliphant discoursed in letters quoted by his biographer. Alice's family were naturally displeased at the financial arrangements, as the 'whole of her property was placed unreservedly in the hands' of Harris (Oliphant, 115). This was her own decision: Oliphant refused to enter into a marriage contract, insisting that his wife must retain control of her own money and do with it as she saw fit. They were married on 8 June 1872 at St George's, Hanover Square, London. In 1873 Oliphant returned to Brocton by Harris's orders, with his wife and mother, who were there employed in menial offices. Oliphant himself was directed to take part in various commercial enterprises for the benefit, apparently, of the community. He was in New York and Canada, and was occasionally sent to England. In 1874 he joined the Direct United States Cable Company, and was 'coaching a bill through the Dominion Legislature'. He learned the secrets of commercial 'rings', and was kindly treated by Jay Gould, the successful American financier and railway entrepreneur. In 1876 he contributed to *Blackwood's Edinburgh Magazine* the 'Autobiography of a joint-stock company', revealing some mysteries of commercial jugglery. He is said to have shown much financial ability in these transactions.

Meanwhile Harris had migrated to Santa Rosa, near San Francisco, and taken Oliphant's wife with him. In the beginning of 1878 Oliphant went to San Francisco, to the office of J. D. Walker, a wealthy businessman of San Rafael, whose friendship he had won by an act of kindness. His purpose was to see his wife, but permission was refused, and he returned to Brocton. In the following autumn Alice Oliphant left Santa Rosa, though still under Harris's rule, and supported herself for a time, first at Vallego and then at Benicia, by keeping a school. She was warmly appreciated by the Californians, and Mrs Walker was able to see her occasionally. It seems that about this time Harris had discovered not only that the marriage was not a marriage of 'counterparts', but that Oliphant had a spiritual 'counterpart' in the other world, who inspired him with rhymed communications, and was therefore an obstacle to union with his earthly wife. Oliphant's belief in these communications struck his first biographer, Margaret Oliphant, as the 'only sign of mental aberration' she ever noticed. Meanwhile, Oliphant took up a scheme for colonizing Palestine with Jews, and early in 1879 went to the East to examine the country, and to endeavour to obtain a concession from the Turkish government. An account of his journey was given in *The Land of Gilead, with Excursions in the Lebanon* (1880). The approach to the Turkish government failed, and the scheme broke down. Oliphant returned to England, and there, in the early winter of 1880, he was rejoined by his wife in answer to an appeal from him: he was depressed and ill. They made a journey to Egypt in the winter, described by him in *The Land of Khemi: Up and Down the Middle Nile* (1882). An accidental difficulty at Cairo prevented them from formally making over to Harris their right in the land at Brocton.

The break with Harris In May 1881 Oliphant returned to America to see his mother, who was still at Brocton. He found her both ill and troubled by doubts as to the Harris creed. They went to Santa Rosa, where the sight of a 'valuable ring' of Lady Oliphant's upon the finger of one of Harris's household staggered their faith. In spite of orders from Harris, Oliphant took his mother to a village, where she died, in the presence of her son and their kind friend Mrs Walker. Oliphant himself now became sceptical as to the prophet's inspiration, and, with the help of Mr Walker, recovered his land at Brocton by legal proceedings. Harris and his disciples took a different view of these transactions. Alice Oliphant had received a telegram from Santa Rosa during her husband's absence requesting her sanction to placing him in confinement as mentally unbalanced. This appears to have ended her allegiance to the prophet.

Oliphant was again in England in January 1882, and prepared the volume called *Traits and Travesties* (1882), consisting chiefly of reprints from *Blackwood's Edinburgh Magazine*. He now took up the Palestine colonization scheme again, and travelled with his wife to Constantinople in the summer of 1882, settling for some time at Therapia. At the end of the year they moved to Haifa in the Bay of Acre, in the neighbourhood of various Jewish colonies. He wrote there his story *Altiora Peto* (1883), in the *Piccadilly* style, the name being derived from a motto of his branch of the Oliphant family. At Haifa they collected a number of sympathizers, though they did not exactly form a community. Oliphant was now regarded as a 'sort of head of affairs at Brocton', which was no longer in connection with Harris. Visitors from Brocton, as well as local people and Jewish immigrants, gathered around them. They built a small house at Daliyyah, on Mount Carmel, and endeavoured to carry out their ideal of life, giving expositions of their views to various enquirers. A strange book, called *Sympneumata, or, Evolutionary Forces Now Active in Man*, was written by the Oliphants in concert and, as they thought, by a kind of common inspiration. The power they called 'sympneuma' was the faculty of superhuman vision, hearing, strength, and resistance to disease and death given to a very few beings. It was the duty of these beings to impart the sympneuma to their fellows through physical contact, thereby leading to the regeneration of the human race. Men and women would be restored to their happy condition before the fall when male and female had been joined in one being and sexual love was pure. The doctrine was too explicit for many who had previously sympathized; some were alienated in fear of social ostracism, others in disgust; others regarded it as harmless nonsense. Oliphant also wrote *Masollam* (1886), which finally rejected Harris's claim to prophetic power but was silent as to the reason why Oliphant had submitted to his domination.

During a trip to the Lake of Tiberias, at the end of 1886,

Alice Oliphant caught a fever; she died on 2 January 1887. Oliphant believed that she soon came back to him in spirit, and sent messages through him to her friends. Her presence was thought to be shown by his strange convulsive movements. He returned to England to carry out a tour which they had planned to take together. He was much broken, though he could still often talk with his old brightness. He wrote a series of papers in *Blackwood's* published in 1887 as *Episodes in a Life of Adventure, or, Moss from a Rolling Stone*, which described his early career with great spirit. He also published at Haifa a description of Palestine, and *Fashionable Philosophy* (1887), a collection of various stories. In 1887 he returned to Haifa, and wrote a pamphlet called *The Star in the East*, directed towards Muslims. It is said to have made one Arab convert, who was 'not much credit to his leader'. Oliphant returned to England and finished his last book, *Scientific Religion, or, The Higher Possibilities of Life* (1888). This professed to be the revelation of a new religion based on the power of 'pure' sexual love, and in it he assumed the mantle of a spiritual leader. It helped to bring about him a crowd of spiritualists and people easily swayed by pseudo-philosophical pronouncements. He visited America in 1888, and returned with Rosamond Dale Owen, daughter of Robert Dale Owen, to whom he was married at Malvern on 16 August. A few days later he was seized with illness, the effects of lung cancer, at the house of his old friends, the Walkers, at Surbiton. Thence he was moved to York House, Twickenham, to be the guest of his friend Sir Mountstuart Grant Duff. His case was hopeless from the first, though he was flattered by faith in a miraculous cure. He was cheerful and even witty to the last, and died peacefully on 23 December 1888.

Character The charm of Oliphant's alert and versatile intellect and sympathetic character was recognized by a wide circle of friends. It was felt not least by those who most regretted the strange religious developments which led to the waste of his powers and his enslavement to such a prophet as Harris, whose claims extended to the ability to rid his followers of disease. Oliphant was loved for his boyish simplicity and the warmth of heart which appeared through all his illusions. Suggestions of insanity were made, but apparently without definite reasons, and Oliphant was most remarkable for his combination of two apparently inconsistent careers. Until his last years, at any rate, his religious mysticism did not disqualify him for being also a shrewd financier, a charming man of the world, and a brilliant writer.

LESLIE STEPHEN, rev. ANNE TAYLOR

Sources M. O. W. Oliphant, *Memoir of the life of Laurence Oliphant and of Alice Oliphant, his wife*, 2nd edn, 2 vols. (1891) · L. Liesching, *Personal reminiscences of Laurence Oliphant* [1891] · P. Henderson, *Laurence Oliphant* (1956) · A. Taylor, *Laurence Oliphant* (1982) · H. W. Schneider and G. Lawton, *A prophet and a pilgrim: being the incredible history of Thomas Lake Harris and Laurence Oliphant* (1942) · d. cert.
Archives FM Cam., letters; family letters · RGS, file · RGS, travel notes and essays; letters | BL, letters to Mrs Ashley, Add. MS 39168 · Col. U., Rare Book and Manuscript Library, Harris/Oliphant MSS · FM Cam., Guy le Strange bequest · Hants. RO, Broadlands MSS, letters to Lord Mount Temple and Lady Mount Temple · News

Int. RO, *The Times* corresp. • NL Scot., corresp. with *Blackwood's* and literary MSS • NL Scot., letters to Jane Welsh Carlyle • PRO, letters to Lord Ampthill, FO918/78 • U. Southampton L., letters to Lord Mount Temple and Lady Mount Temple • UCL, letters to Moses Gaster • W. Sussex RO, letters to F. A. Maxse [copies]
Likenesses daguerreotype, 1854, priv. coll. • photograph, 1858, BL • photograph, 1870, Col. U. • T. Rodger, carte-de-visite, NPG [*see illus.*] • R. Taylor, wood-engraving (after photograph by the Autotype Co.), NPG; repro. in *ILN* (5 Jan 1889)
Wealth at death £1442 13s. 2d.: probate, 24 Jan 1889, *CGPLA Eng. & Wales*

Oliphant, Sir Marcus Laurence Elwin [Mark] (1901–2000), physicist, was born on 8 October 1901 in Kent Town, near Adelaide, South Australia, the eldest of the five sons of Harold George Oliphant, a clerk on the water board, and his wife, Beatrice Fanny, *née* Tucker, a former schoolteacher. The family was always poor, and young Mark was soon found to be short-sighted and completely deaf in one ear. He went to school at Unley and Adelaide high schools, and though his most inspiring teacher was a classicist he had ambitions to become a doctor. Increasingly, however, he became interested in experimental science; for some time he inclined towards chemistry, and then turned to physics, and his talent for constructing scientific apparatus won him a place at Adelaide University. He was hired as a 'cadet', a laboratory technician receiving free tuition plus 10s. a week in return for looking after the instruments in the physics laboratory. He gained the reputation of being an unusually quick and skilful constructor of apparatus; in later life this resulted in his underestimating the time which others would take to build similar equipment.

At Adelaide University, Oliphant had the good fortune to have an excellent teacher, Dr R. S. Burdon; he also learned some geology from the explorer Sir Douglas Mawson. As a technician he managed to take a degree in his spare time, in 1921, and he then became an assistant to Professor Kerr Grant, who had recently visited the Cavendish Laboratory in Cambridge and who encouraged Oliphant to join the laboratory by telling him that the atmosphere there was more lively than at any other physics laboratory in England. A visit from the Rutherfords in 1925 provided further encouragement, and Oliphant decided he would try for Cambridge. Financed by an award from the Royal Commission for the Exhibition of 1851, he became a postgraduate student at Trinity College, Cambridge, in 1927. In the Cavendish Laboratory he was genially greeted by Ernest Rutherford, who immediately invited Oliphant and his wife to tea on the following Sunday. Oliphant had married Rosa Louise Wilbraham (d. 1987), daughter of F. Wilbraham, of Glenelg, South Australia, in 1925; they had two sons (one of whom died in 1933) and a daughter.

Oliphant spent the next ten years on research in Cambridge. He received his Cambridge PhD degree in 1929, and became a Messel research fellow of the Royal Society two years later. He was elected a fellow and lecturer at St John's College in 1934. The following year, after the departure of James Chadwick to be professor of physics at Liverpool, he was appointed assistant director of research at the Cavendish Laboratory.

Oliphant's consummate ability in designing and constructing apparatus with high vacua greatly improved the standards of such techniques at the Cavendish Laboratory. He also improved the accelerator built by John Cockcroft and Ernest Walton by designing ion sources of much greater intensity. The increased accuracy thus obtained for the masses of light elements stimulated F. W. Aston to make fresh measurements with his mass spectrograph. Soon Oliphant was invited to collaborate directly with Rutherford on the artificial disintegration of nuclei. With a simplified form of the accelerator designed by Cockcroft and Walton, beams of protons were used to bombard the light elements lithium, boron, and beryllium. Although the voltage of 250 keV was much lower than the original 600 keV, greater precision was achieved and many uncertainties resolved.

At the end of 1933 the chemist G. N. Lewis from the University of California at Berkeley brought the first two drops of heavy water to England. They were entrusted to Oliphant for use in an accelerator. By reaction with metallic potassium, the hydrogen atoms were released from the heavy water and mixed with helium. Bombardment of deuterium with deuterons led to some remarkable results, including a very large release of several particles—protons, alpha particles, and neutrons. One problem was the surprising number of neutrons, the neutral particle discovered in 1932 by James Chadwick. The most important discovery in 1934 was tritium, a new hydrogen isotope of mass three. Normally Rutherford believed that the evenings should be devoted to thought or relaxation rather than experiment, but one evening he came into Oliphant's laboratory at about a quarter to six and picked out a photographic record from the hypo solution. He insisted that it should be examined that night. The results were exciting. At 11 p.m. Rutherford telephoned Oliphant to talk about it; again at 3 a.m. he rang: 'I've got it. They are particles of helium-3' (Bleaney). This was a new isotope, formed in the decay of tritium.

At this time Oliphant began to wonder if heavy hydrogen might provide a useful source of power, though Rutherford thought that the idea of producing useful energy from nuclear reactions was 'moonshine' (Bleaney), arguing that to initiate a reaction needed such large amounts of energy that less would always be got back than was put in. To avoid his displeasure Oliphant waited until Rutherford was away before attempting another experiment. With the help of his chief laboratory assistant, equipment was hurriedly lashed together. Heavy water vapour was bombarded with deuterons in a first experimental attempt to produce energy by nuclear fusion. It was unsuccessful, and earned Oliphant a stinging reprimand from Rutherford. It was perhaps this which convinced Oliphant that it was time to be in charge of a laboratory of his own.

Oliphant next accepted appointment to the Poynting chair of physics at Birmingham in 1936. He took up his post in 1937, the year that he was elected a fellow of the

Royal Society. It was through his influence that Rudolf Peierls was appointed professor of mathematical physics at Birmingham, also in 1937. Peierls recalled Oliphant as a 'warm, informal, and direct person with a great zest for life, a loud voice, and a hearty laugh':

> He was happiest when he could roll up his sleeves and get to work on a piece of equipment. His instrumentation showed the influence of Rutherford's string-and-sealing-wax approach. Because of the developing needs of the experiments, Oliphant's projects were much more ambitious pieces of engineering than Rutherford would ever have contemplated. Even though they were sophisticated, he liked his machines homemade as far as possible, which made them more ingenious in design and cheaper than others; but they also took longer to build and had more teething troubles.   (Peierls, 133)

At Birmingham, Oliphant had to spend much of his time finding support for equipping his nuclear physics laboratory. He succeeded in securing a gift from Lord Nuffield to cover a new building and a 60 inch cyclotron, but construction was interrupted by the outbreak of the Second World War in 1939. Two projects more urgent and vital for the war effort came to occupy Oliphant's mind for the next six years. One was radio-location, now better known by the American name 'radar'; the other was the atom bomb.

In 1935 an array of radio-location stations had been built around the British coast, starting at Orfordness, Essex. In August–September 1939, most physicists from British universities were sent to various stations to learn about the system; Oliphant took his team to Ventnor on the Isle of Wight, and they were there when war was declared on 3 September. The original wavelength used by this chain of stations was 50 metres, but it was later reduced to 1.5 metres. The major breakthrough came under Oliphant's direction at Birmingham University in February 1940 when H. A. H. (Harry) Boot and J. T. (John) Randall developed the cavity magnetron, with output powers of 10 kW, first for a wavelength of 10 cm, and then for 3 cm. This enabled British (and later American) radar to locate aircraft, ships, and submarines with much greater accuracy.

Also in 1940 Otto Frisch, who was temporarily based at Birmingham, and Rudolph Peierls showed Oliphant their memorandum about the possibility of an atomic bomb. With their warning that scientists in Germany might also be working on it, Oliphant forwarded the memo to the British government, who set up the Maud committee. This produced a report which in 1941 was taken by Chadwick and Oliphant to the United States. Once the Manhattan project had started Oliphant, again in the United States, worked at Berkeley, from 1943, on electromagnetic separation of the uranium isotopes.

In 1945 Oliphant returned to Birmingham. On 21 October that year he published a long article in the *News of the World*, prophesying that 'If war ever developed between the USA and Russia, England is bound to be obliterated whichever side she is on.' For the next fifty years he was prominent in warning about the dangers of nuclear proliferation, though he was also an energetic advocate of the peaceful use of nuclear energy. In 1946 he became the first

scientific adviser to the United Nations Atomic Energy Commission. While at Birmingham he secured £150,000 from the British government to build a new type of accelerator, a proton synchrotron. He left for Australia before it was completed, but it remained in operation for many years.

In 1950 Oliphant was appointed the first director of the research school of physical sciences at the Australian National University, Canberra, having (with Howard Florey and Keith Hancock) been a leading member of the council setting up the new university. He then started to build the world's most powerful accelerator for nuclear particle physics, but it suffered from lack of resources and engineering problems, and was in some quarters known as 'the white Oliphant'. In 1963 Oliphant resigned as director of the research school to become professor of the physics of ionized gases at the Institute of Advanced Studies of the university. From 1964 to 1967 he led his team there in an attempt to achieve a thermonuclear reaction in gases at very high temperatures. This followed a line of research in direct succession to his early efforts in Cambridge, and he recorded his debt to Rutherford and Chadwick for their interest in his work there. Oliphant was also closely involved with the creation of the Australian Academy of Science in Canberra, modelled on the Royal Society of London. Sir Otto Frankel chaired the design committee for the Becker building, which was overseen by him with Oliphant and Sir Sydney Sutherland. During the visit of Queen Elizabeth II in 1954, the queen had handed Oliphant the royal charter for the academy, of which he had become the founding president; he filled the office until 1957. Oliphant was appointed KBE in 1959.

Deeply interested in the ecological problems of Australia, Oliphant believed that solar energy should be used to produce hydrogen from water for use as fuel. As the scientific representative for Australia on the United Nations Atomic Energy Commission he advocated international control of nuclear energy, and he was a founder member of the Pugwash movement. Disliking the slaughter of animals, he also became a vegetarian.

Still vigorous at the age of seventy, Oliphant served as governor of South Australia from 1971 to 1976. In this post he was noted for the outspokenness of his views, including his opposition to racism, violence, drink-driving, single-sex schools, and French nuclear testing in the Pacific. He died at his home, 28 Carstensz Street, Griffith, ACT, Australia, on 14 July 2000, after a short illness, and was cremated in Canberra three days later. He was survived by his daughter Vivian (b. 1938), his wife and his second son, Michael (1935–1971), having predeceased him. A memorial ceremony was held at Adelaide University on 18 August 2000, and a public commemoration of his life was held at the Australian National University on 25 August 2000.   BREBIS BLEANEY

Sources B. Bleaney, 'Sir Mark Oliphant', *Notes and Records of the Royal Society*, 47 (1993) · M. Oliphant, *Rutherford: recollections of the Cambridge days* (1972) · R. Peierls, *Bird of passage: recollections of a physicist* (1983) · E. G. Bowen, *Radar days* (1987) · S. Cockburn, *The patriarchs* (1983) · A. Moyal, *Portraits in science* (1994) · S. Cockburn

and D. Ellyard, *Oliphant: the life and times of Sir Mark Oliphant* (1981) ·
The Times (18 July 2000) · *Daily Telegraph* (18 July 2000) · *The Guardian*
(18 July 2000) · *The Independent* (19 July 2000) · *WWW* · Burke, *Peerage* · personal knowledge (2004) · private information (2004)
Archives Adelaide University, photographs, newspaper cuttings,
and MSS | CAC Cam., corresp. with Sir James Chadwick · IWM,
corresp. with Sir Henry Tizard · RS, corresp. with Lord Blackett ·
Trinity Cam., corresp. with Egon Bretscher · U. Birm. L., corresp.
with P. B. Moon | SOUND NL Aus.
Likenesses photograph, 1976, repro. in *Daily Telegraph* · photograph, 1997, repro. in *The Times* · photograph, repro. in *Guardian* ·
photographs, University of Adelaide, Australia, Oliphant papers

Oliphant, Margaret Oliphant Wilson (1828–1897), novelist and biographer, was born in Wallyford, Midlothian,
on 4 April 1828, the only daughter and youngest surviving
child of Francis W. Wilson (*c*.1788–1858), a clerk, and his
wife, Margaret Oliphant (*c*.1789–1854). During the first ten
years of her life the family moved first to Lasswade, near
Edinburgh, and then in 1834 to Glasgow, where her father
worked at the Royal Bank. In 1838 her father became
excise clerk in the custom house at Liverpool. The Wilsons
changed house in Everton at least five times before moving to Grosvenor Road in Birkenhead in 1850. Her reclusive father remained a shadowy figure. Her mother, who
educated her daughter at home, was the driving force in
the family; she kept abreast of the serious periodicals of
the day and counted David Macbeth Moir, contributor to
Blackwood's Edinburgh Magazine under the pseudonym
Delta, among her friends. Her mother's repertory of tales
of Fife and the Oliphant ancestry fostered a lasting pride
in Margaret's Scottish heritage and in the name to which
she eventually became doubly entitled. Middle-class
accomplishments such as music and art played no part in
this regime. The family was, however, politically, religiously, and socially committed; her mother and elder
brother, Frank Wilson (*c*.1816–1875), were fervent radicals,
and as a teenager Margaret collected signatories for an
anti-cornlaw petition. Her parents had joined the breakaway Free Church of Scotland after the Disruption of 1843
and had imbibed the views of its leader, Dr Thomas Chalmers, on the need to practise philanthropy at the local and
individual level. Her father was treasurer for the Scottish
church's charitable relief work in the fluctuating trade
conditions of Liverpool in the late 1840s, and Margaret's
early fiction preached the importance of a Christocentric
charitable philosophy; it also made use of the seafaring
tales of Fife and of the Liverpool docks, and of the lives of
the newly arrived workers in the terraced streets of a large
city.

Early writings Margaret Oliphant's first novel, *Christian
Melville*, was subsequently published in 1856 without her
permission by her middle brother, Willie Wilson (*c*.1819–
1885). It had been written, when she was seventeen, to
provide herself with 'some amusement and occupation'
(*Autobiography*, 1990, 24) during her mother's serious illness and the heartache of a broken engagement. The
home-instilled puritan work ethic and view of the
woman's role as an uncomplainingly sacrificial moral
exemplar produced in Margaret a lifelong ambivalence
about her professional life as a writer. She was permitted

Margaret Oliphant Wilson Oliphant (1828–1897), by Frederick
Sandys, 1881

to write 'at the corner of the family-table' where the activity could be seen as the equivalent of her mother's sewing,
making no claim to the exceptional demand of time and
space justified by 'genius'. Pride and pleasure in the work
could only be justified in the face of constant reminders
that women had more obvious domestic obligations to
fulfil.

Margaret Oliphant's first published novel, *Passages in the
Life of Margaret Maitland* (1849), attracted the attention of
both Charles Dickens and Charlotte Brontë, but jubilation
was overshadowed by anxiety over her brother Willie,
who had succumbed to his besetting sins of drink and
debt while training for the Presbyterian ministry in London. Margaret was sent to watch over his final three
months in London, where they shared lodgings with their
Oliphant cousins, Frank and Tom. The miseries suffered
by women required to shed a moral influence on male
relatives over whom they had no other authority was to
become a regular motif in her fiction.

Marriage and children Early in 1851 Frank Oliphant, Margaret's cousin, proposed to her and was refused. In the
spring her mother decided to launch her daughter on literary Edinburgh. Mobilizing such connections as Delta
and her husband's second cousins Daniel Wilson (1816–
1892) and George Wilson (1818–1859), she secured Margaret a coveted introduction to the prestigious publishing
firm of Blackwoods. By the autumn of 1851 Margaret had
decided to accept Frank. Possibly the alternative of living

with her alcoholic brother, Willie, who had been precipitately removed from his first post as minister of Etal in Northumberland before the church took disciplinary action, tipped the balance. On 4 May 1852 she married Francis Wilson (Frank) *Oliphant (1818–1859), a painter and stained-glass window artist; their honeymoon was spent in Germany. In August her parents, accompanied by Willie, retired to London to be near her. Willie was paid 10 per cent of her profits for making fair copies of her manuscripts. He was to write five novels of his own but also managed to have four of his sister's attributed to his name—*John Drayton* (1851), *The Melvilles* (1852), *Ailieford* (1853), and *Christian Melville* (1856).

Margaret's marriage felt the competing strains of her mother's need for her, her husband's consequent resentment, and the demands of two baby daughters, Maggie and Marjorie, who were born on 21 May 1853 and 22 May 1854 respectively. Motherhood had become her absorbing passion. Her adored mother's death on 17 September 1854, and the subsequent departure of Willie and her father, was swiftly overshadowed by the death of Marjorie on 8 February 1855, and that of a day-old son in November of that year. A fourth child, Cyril Francis, known as Tids (or Tiddy), was born on 16 November 1856. In the period between the birth of her daughters she traded upon the success of her first serialized novel, *Katie Stewart* (July to November 1852), to obtain regular employment as a reviewer from its publisher, *Blackwood's Edinburgh Magazine*, and effect her escape from 'the Scylla and Charybdis of the novel craft' formed by those commercially exploitative publishers, Bentley and Colburn. In her own self-deprecating terminology she became the 'general utility woman' (Oliphant, *William Blackwood and his Sons*, 2.349, 475) at Blackwoods, in some months contributing as much as one-third of their periodical. She adopted a male persona and the common reader's perspective; only politics, science, and philosophy remained outside her range.

Margaret's writing had become an important addition to the family's income. Her husband, the son of Thomas Oliphant, a glass cutter, frequented the minor artistic and literary circles of London and had an idealistic view of his artistic calling. He set up a workshop to execute his window designs and finance his ambition as a painter of the large historical and biblical pictures then in vogue, but in mid-1857 his tubercular condition first appeared. He disbanded the business and in January 1859 the family set out for the curative climate of Italy. When Margaret finally discovered that Frank had not told her his specialist's grim prognosis she was 'angry and wounded beyond measure' (*Autobiography*, 1990, 65). Pregnant and buoyed up by laudanum, she nursed him until his death on 20 October. She had to await the birth of her last child, Francis Romano (Cecco), in Rome on 12 December, before travelling home in February 1860 with an insurance policy of £200 on her husband's life, her furniture in store, and £1000 in debt. The only worthwhile legacy of the sojourn in Rome was the friendship of a bohemian couple, Robert and Geraldine Macpherson, to whom, in the early 1860s,

she entrusted her alcoholic brother Willie. She contributed to his support for a further twenty-five years.

Further publications Margaret moved restlessly between friends and relations while John Blackwood, her banker–publisher, found her translation work on Comte Charles de Montalembert's *Les moines d'Occident*. In her despair at the refusal of Blackwoods to publish several of the articles which she submitted at this period, she began a story, in the spring of 1861, which was to inaugurate the provincial saga that made her famous: *The Chronicles of Carlingford*. These were published in *Blackwood's Edinburgh Magazine* as follows: *The Executor* (May 1861), *The Rector* and *The Doctor's Family* (September 1861–January 1862), *Salem Chapel* (February 1862–January 1863), *The Perpetual Curate* (June 1863–September 1864), *Miss Marjoribanks* (February 1865–May 1866). (*Phoebe Junior: a Last Chronicle of Carlingford* was published separately in 1876.) Research for a biography of Edward Irving (1862), commissioned by his family, introduced her to what was to become her favourite genre: she wrote lives of the Comte de Montalembert (1872), Richard Brinsley Sheridan (1883), John Tulloch (1888), Laurence Oliphant (1891)—a distant relative—Thomas Chalmers (1893), and Queen Victoria (1890). Research trips also created new friendships, notably with Thomas Carlyle and his wife; John Tulloch, principal of St Andrews, and his family; and Robert Herbert Story, minister of the lochside parish of Rosneath, Dunbartonshire, who probably proposed to her around this time.

Margaret Oliphant settled in Ealing in October 1861, but it was with Mrs Tulloch that she led a large contingent of mothers and children to Rome in November 1863. Here, on 27 January 1864, after four days' fever, Maggie, her only surviving daughter, died. Although she commissioned a memorial window in the church at Rosneath, she avoided all mention of her daughter's name and never revisited Rome. For nineteen months she tried an expatriate peripatetic life, but her sons' need for regular schooling, and perhaps the need to live closer to the source material of her domestic novels, if she were to achieve the goal, that John Blackwood assured her was within her grasp, of joining the first rank of novelists (*Autobiography and Letters*, 198), led her to return to England in September 1865. Blackwood's payment of £1500 for *The Perpetual Curate* (1864), the largest sum she was ever paid for a novel, allowed her to choose Windsor as a base from which to send her sons as day boys to Eton College. Her habit of starting work as others went to bed enabled her to be available as a welcoming mother or gracious hostess over the tea or dinner table.

Increasing financial responsibilities A settled, solvent household attracted dependants: a distant cousin, Annie Louisa Walker, soon became Margaret Oliphant's secretary–housekeeper at 6 Clarence Crescent, in Windsor. In 1868, just as Margaret was granted a civil-list pension of £100, her brother Frank was bankrupted; she took in his two older children, while enabling the two youngest, Margaret (or Madge; 1863–1897) and Janet Mary (Denny; 1865–1954), to join their parents abroad. In mid-1870 Frank, now widowed and psychologically incapable of work, and his younger daughters looked to his sister for a home. She provided her nephew, Frank Wilson, with an education at Eton and training for an engineering career in India. After their father's death in 1875, Madge and Denny soon became 'the unquestioned daughters of the house', receiving schooling in Germany and artistic training, as an engraver and portrait painter respectively, at their aunt's expense.

Margaret perceived 1870, the year in which she became sole breadwinner for two families, as a watershed in her career. Since her brother Willie had negotiated her first contract with Henry Colburn, she had, unusually for a woman of this period, conducted her own business. Dependent always on advances against the next book, but seemingly blessed with astounding literary fecundity, she had not adopted an economic lifestyle; women travelling companions were reputedly shocked by her habit of ordering revivifying champagne and meat for dinner and, despite proclaiming herself 'a fat, little commonplace woman, rather tongue-tied' (*Autobiography*, 1990), portraits of her reveal her love of fine clothes. Now, however, she needed a regular income. She blamed a male-dominated publishing world for her failure to secure an editorship of a periodical such as those achieved by Dickens, Anthony Trollope, or Thackeray; but her loyalty to the Blackwoods, for whom editorships were a matter of family succession, her determination only to consider the top periodicals, and the tartness of speech, of which even her closest friends such as Annie Thackeray accused her, may also have stood in her way. Blackwoods did make her editor of their Foreign Classic series. She financed holidays by obtaining sizable advances from Macmillans for a sporadic but infinitely extendible series of books which purveyed cultural history through biographical sketches: *The Makers of Florence* (1876) was followed by books on Venice (1887), Edinburgh (1890), Jerusalem (1891), and Rome (1896). Finding tenants for their house, or paying members to swell their travelling party, and managing the complex postal arrangements for receiving and dispatching material also fell to her lot.

In 1878, having obtained advances from both Blackwoods and Macmillans, Margaret bought 8–9 Clarence Crescent, Windsor, which she had rented since 1872, for £1600. In the late 1870s she could still command £750 for a three-decker novel, but in the next decade her expenses always exceeded her income and she found herself forced to work incessantly, always in fear of flooding her own market, and without the time necessary for driving harder bargains with publishers. In the 1880s she claimed, 'my anxieties were sometimes almost more than I could bear' (*Autobiography*, 1990, 151). Her son Cyril, who had already displayed propensities to drink and debt as an Oxford undergraduate, showed little enthusiasm for work as a barrister. After a spell as private secretary to the governor of Ceylon in 1884 (which proved threatening to his health), he returned to England to become a dependant of his mother, who tried, with little success, to interest him

in literary work. Cecco, her younger son, was sent abroad to acquire German after a disappointing degree at Oxford, and in July 1889 he acquired a part-time post in the library at Windsor Castle. He was cited by his mother as her co-author for *The Victorian Age of Literature* (1892), but his health and temperament prevented his finding permanent employment.

Spirituality and writing During her despair over her sons' indolence Margaret experienced one important source of comfort: the occasional gift of 'a great quiet and calm' that she identified with 'the peace that passeth all understanding' (*Autobiography*, 1990, 53). This spiritual consolation fed itself into her tales of the supernatural, which undoubtedly responded to a contemporary vogue for such literary antidotes to the age's perceived materialism but also provided her with a genre in which to explore deep-seated preoccupations with family relationships and gender construction. She felt that these tales were 'given' to her and took unusual pains with them. She was particularly proud of *A Beleaguered City* (1879), an experiment in multiple narrative. Robert Louis Stevenson confessed that he had been moved to tears by this tale of a French city taken over by the spirits of the dead. *The Wizard's Son* (1884) was her only novel in this vein. Her popular Little Pilgrim series of tales, designed to console the bereaved, respond to a Victorian obsession with eschatology (21,000 copies of the first of the series had been printed within five years), but some of her tales of the afterlife, such as her dystopia, 'The Land of Darkness' (1888), still hold interest because of her conviction that such a thin veil separates the earthly life from the continuum beyond. Her religious position could best be described as dogmatic Christian unorthodoxy; her sympathies were with those passionate 'outsiders'—Montalembert, Irving, or Laurence Oliphant—who seemed, like her, to combine worldly shrewdness with a naïve enthusiasm for the supernatural. Friendship with the eminent Scottish churchmen Tulloch and Story won her back to the established church but reinforced her sceptical attitude to clerical spiritual authority. The eclecticism of Anglicanism made it an appropriate haven, and Margaret's political radicalism had also disappeared: in 1886 she and Queen Victoria discussed their mutual detestation of Gladstone.

Final years and death In 1889 medical expenses mounted: Cecco was repeatedly sent abroad for his health and Cyril had a seizure in a railway station in Paris. Both sons and Madge accompanied Margaret on the Easter 1890 research expedition for her book on Jerusalem. On 8 November Cyril died, after only four days' illness: there could be no consolation from a life well spent. As the century waned Margaret's only wish was to survive long enough to provide secure futures for Cecco and her nieces. Madge married William Harris Valentine, a Dundee jute manufacturer, in July 1893. Margaret returned from the birth of their daughter and her namesake to find Cecco suffering from 'exhaustion after inflammation of the throat and tongue'. He died on 1 October 1894, and within hours his mother was recording the event in her autobiography. By the end of her life she had worn a hole in her forefinger which would not heal.

In April 1896, accompanied by Denny (who had changed her surname to Oliphant by deed poll) and their almost permanent guest, John Tulloch's daughter, Fanny, Margaret moved to The Hermitage, Wimbledon Common. The invitation by Blackwoods to write *Annals of a Publishing House* yielded £500 p.a. Despite her sense of being 'on the ebb-tide' (Oliphant, *The Ways of Life*), the last three years witnessed a novel, *Old Mr Tredgold*; a tale of the unseen, 'The Library Window'; and the opening chapters of *The Makers of Rome*, which were entirely characteristic of her finest work. In April 1897, commissioned by a new publisher, J. M. Dent, she undertook a research trip to Siena but recognized that she was suffering from more than her chronic rheumatism. She died at The Hermitage on 25 June 1897 from cancer of the colon and exhaustion, and was buried on the 29th alongside her sons in the cemetery at Eton. On 16 July 1908 her friend and admirer, the writer J. M. Barrie, who had edited *A Widow's Tale and other Stories* (1898), unveiled a memorial tablet in St Giles's Church, Edinburgh. Windsor's tributary plaque at 8–9 Clarence Crescent was unveiled on 25 June 1997, the centenary of her death.

Assessing her own achievement, this bereft mother remarked 'I shall not leave anything behind me that will live' (*Autobiography*, 1990, 136). Her death amid the swiftly changing literary preoccupations of the end of the century made Margaret Oliphant a convenient symbol for the outdated female romancers of domestic fiction who had too often been prepared to sacrifice artistic integrity to financial need. Furthermore the reshaping of her autobiography by her literary executors contrived to transform this passionate, witty, wryly self-aware, and immensely energetic author into a model of quietly suffering Victorian femininity. The herculean fictional output of some ninety-eight novels and fifty or more short stories undoubtedly shows her ability to gauge changing fashion: the novels span social concern, Scottish tales, the Gothic, the sensational, the historical, provincial sagas, and quieter psychological studies. They equally reveal her as creator as much as creation of her literary milieu: the voracious reading involved in her twenty-five works of non-fiction and over three hundred periodical articles fuelled the disconcerting questions repeatedly raised in her fiction as to the age's accepted ideologies of marriage, family, religion, and gender. In her obituary Henry James asserted that 'no woman had ever, for half a century, had her personal "say" so publicly'; contemporary writers flinched at the whiplash cracks of epigrammatic wit sometimes woven into her reviews. It seems likely that Anthony Trollope's Lady Carbury in *The Way we Live now* (1875) and James's Mrs Stormer in 'Greville Fane' (1892) were vitriolic responses to the power her voice carried. Despite her well-known asperity about male failings, her distinctive voice, which encompassed both irony and pathos within its deceptively 'artless' cadences, appealed as much to male as female readers: Tennyson, Gladstone, and Darwin all praised her work. Feminist criticism has been slow to recognize her virtues, largely because her thoroughly feminist analysis often resulted in anti-feminist conclusions.   ELISABETH JAY

Sources *The autobiography of Margaret Oliphant: the complete text*, ed. E. Jay (1990) · E. Jay, *Mrs Oliphant: 'a fiction to herself'. A literary life* (1995) · Mrs Oliphant, *William Blackwood and his sons* (1897), vols. 1–2 of *Annals of a publishing house* (1897–8) · Mrs G. Porter, *The life of John Blackwood* (1898) · M. O. W. Oliphant, 'On the ebb-tide', *The ways of life* (1897), preface · *The autobiography and letters of Mrs Margaret Oliphant*, ed. Mrs H. Coghill (1899); repr. as *Autobiography and letters of Mrs M. O. W. Oliphant* (1974) [with introduction by Q. D. Leavis] · H. James, 'London notes', *Harper's Weekly*, 41 (1897); repr. in *Notes on novelists, with some other notes* (1914), 357–60 · *DNB* · m. cert. · d. cert. · *Windsor and Eton Express* (July 1897)
Archives Harvard U., Houghton L., papers · Hunt. L., letters · NL Scot., corresp., literary MSS, and papers · priv. coll. | BL, letters to Francis Bennoch, RP1314 [copies] · BL, letters to Bentley and Bryce, Add. MSS 46616, 42576 · BL, corresp. with Macmillans, Add. MS 54919 · Eton, letters to Lady Anne Ritchie · NL Scot., corresp. with Blackwoods and literary MSS; letters to Isabella Blackwood · NL Scot., letters to Jane Welsh Carlyle · Princeton University Library, New Jersey, letters to William Isbister, Mrs Mapes Dodge, James Payn, and Scribner's
Likenesses photograph, c.1853 (with her mother), NL Scot.; repro. in M. Williams, *Margaret Oliphant: a critical biography* (1986), pl. 1 · group portrait, photograph, 1874, repro. in Jay, *Mrs Oliphant*, pl. 5a; priv. coll. · F. A. Sandys, drawing, 1881, NPG [*see illus.*] · photograph, 1883, NL Scot.; repro. in M. Williams, *Margaret Oliphant: a critical biography* (1986), pl. 9 · J. M. W. Oliphant, pencil and chalk drawing, 1895, NG Scot.; repro. in M. Williams, *Margaret Oliphant: a critical biography* (1986), pl. 10 · group portrait, photograph, 1896, repro. in Jay, *Mrs Oliphant*, pl. 7a; priv. coll. · photograph (in her early thirties), repro. in *The Bookman* (Aug 1897), 114 · woodcut (after photograph by H. S. Mendelssohn), NPG; repro. in *Harper's Magazine* (June 1888)
Wealth at death £4932 14s. 11d.: probate, 30 Oct 1897, *CGPLA Eng. & Wales*

Oliphant, Thomas (1799–1873), music editor and cataloguer, was born on 25 December 1799 at Condie, Perthshire, in the house of his father, Ebenezer Oliphant. His mother, Mary, was the third daughter of Sir William Stirling, bt, of Ardoch, Perthshire. After being educated at Winchester College and by private tutors, he became for a short time a member of the London stock exchange, but soon relinquished commerce to devote himself to literature and music. In 1830 he was admitted to the Madrigal Society and remained an active member until his death, becoming honorary secretary in 1832, vice-president in 1871, and president in 1872. He adapted English words to a considerable number of Italian madrigals (in some cases writing his own verses, in others by merely translating the original texts) for the use of the society's members; his work amounted to some fifty English and Italian works in popular editions as well as several compilations.

In 1834 Oliphant took part in the chorus, as a bass, in the great Handel festival held in Westminster Abbey, and in the same year published, under the pseudonym Solomon Sackbut, *Comments of a Chorus Singer at the Royal Musical Festival in Westminster Abbey*. He also published *A Brief Account of the Madrigal Society* (1835), *A Short Account of Madrigals*

(1836), and *La musa madrigalesca* (1837), a volume containing the words of nearly 400 'madrigals, ballets, roundelays &c. chiefly of the Elizabethan age'. In 1837 he composed the words and music of a madrigal, 'Stay one moment, gentle sires', which he produced as the work of an unknown seventeenth-century composer, Blasio Tomasi. It was performed as such at the anniversary festival of the Madrigal Society. He wrote English versions of Beethoven's *Fidelio* and *The Mount of Olives*, and the words for numerous songs by John Hatton and other composers.

Oliphant was employed from November 1841 to July 1850 as a temporary assistant cataloguing the music in the British Museum. There was initial criticism of his appointment, but during his time there he cleared the backlog of uncatalogued music and also laid the foundations for the collection's expansion. He completed a catalogue of the manuscript music in 1842 and then, with the support of Antonio Panizzi, the keeper of printed books, began the process of providing a comprehensive catalogue of printed music. He resigned in 1850 following the rejection by the trustees of his memorandum for the development of music in the collections.

Oliphant occasionally lectured in public on musical subjects, and was requested by the directors of the Philharmonic Society to translate portions of Wagner's opera *Lohengrin*, which were performed by the society's orchestra and chorus, the composer conducting, at the Hanover Square Rooms in March 1855. Oliphant died, unmarried, on 9 March 1873, at his home, 35 Great Marlborough Street, London, and the following month his valuable private music library, which included many first and early editions of madrigals, was auctioned by Puttick and Simpson.   W. H. CUMMINGS, *rev.* DAVID J. GOLBY

Sources A. H. King, 'Oliphant, Thomas', *New Grove* · A. H. King, 'The music room of the British Museum, 1753–1953', *Proceedings of the Royal Musical Association*, 79 (1952–3), 65 · personal knowledge (1894)

Archives BL, music collections, index to songs, Egerton MS 2422 | BL, Panizzi MSS

Wealth at death under £4000: probate, 10 May 1873, *CGPLA Eng. & Wales*

Oliphant, Sir Walter, of Aberdalgie (*d.* in or after **1378**). *See under* Oliphant family (*per.* 1141–c.1500).

Oliphant, Sir William (*d.* 1313?). *See under* Oliphant family (*per.* 1141–c.1500).

Oliphant, Sir William, of Dupplin and Aberdalgie (*d.* **1329**). *See under* Oliphant family (*per.* 1141–c.1500).

Oliphant, Sir William, Lord Newton (1550–1628), judge, was the second son of Thomas Oliphant of Freeland, Perthshire. He himself married Katherine Blair and they had at least six children: James, who became an advocate; William; John (a future advocate-depute); Helen; Jean; and Elizabeth. There may also have been another daughter, Margaret. After Katherine's death he married Marjory Graham.

Prior to his admission as an advocate in October 1577, Oliphant had studied in France, and before that probably

at St Andrews. He made his first appearance before the privy council on 23 October 1577. Five years later he was appointed a justice-depute, on 14 October 1582, and later he acted as depute for Sir Thomas Hamilton, king's advocate. Oliphant was one of several justices-depute from this generation who proceeded to the bench. Having acted with colleagues as an advocate for Laurence, fourth Lord Oliphant, in February 1593 he was granted the ward and marriage of the latter's grandson and heir by James VI.

According to David Calderwood, in 1599 Oliphant gave advice to members of the kirk in Edinburgh in a dispute with the king over whether a visiting troupe of English actors should be permitted to perform comedies in the burgh. In the following year his 363 appearances before the court of session made him the second busiest advocate appearing before that court. His predominance led to his appointment in 1604 to a commission to discuss proposals for union with England, as one 'best affected and fittest for that eirand' (Burton and Masson, 1604–7, 457). In December 1605 he was selected by Aberdeen burgh council to choose other advocates to join him in acting on their behalf, while on 14 May 1606 he was admitted burgess and guild brother of Edinburgh. He had acted as one of Edinburgh's assessors from at least October 1593 and he also acted as advocate for the burgh.

When in January 1606 six ministers were summoned to appear before the privy council charged with convening a general assembly without royal licence, Oliphant was one of the advocates appointed to defend them. However, he and Thomas Craig advised the ministers that they had no defence and declined to appear for them, leaving the much less experienced Thomas Hope and Thomas Gray to represent them. In August 1607 Oliphant was appointed a commissioner for reforming the teaching of grammar in schools, and in 1608 he was named in the testament of William, tenth earl of Douglas, as tutor to the earl's daughter, Frances.

In December 1610 Oliphant was involved in overseeing the making of desks and seats for advocates in Edinburgh's tolbooth, where the court of session normally sat. In January 1611 he was appointed an ordinary lord of session in succession to Sir David Lindsay of Edzell, whereupon the privy council wrote to the king remarking on the popularity of his elevation to the bench. He took the style Lord Newton. On 19 June 1612 he was nominated king's advocate in succession to Thomas Hamilton, who had been appointed clerk register, which in turn led on 9 July to Oliphant's admission to the privy council and his being knighted by the chancellor. Parliament ratified the appointment in October and granted Oliphant a pension of £1000 Scots for life, as the king had recommended to the council in a letter of 8 April 1611. Oliphant first appeared as king's advocate in a criminal cause on 11 July 1612. Later that year he was appointed to a commission of privy councillors charged with deciding controversies between justices of the peace in the burghs and those in 'landwart'.

Oliphant was heavily involved in public affairs during the latter half of James VI's reign. He regularly attended privy council meetings, and acted as a commissioner for the trials of the Jesuits Robert Philip (August 1613), John Ogilvie (February 1615), and James Moffat (June 1615). In December 1615 he was appointed a member of the reconstructed court of high commission, and in May 1616 he became one of the committee to report on the treatise *God and the King*, a defence of the oath of allegiance, which James had resolved should be circulated and taught in Scotland as it had been in England and Ireland. On 17 December 1616 Oliphant was elected a member of the financial committee of the council known as the commissioners for the king's rents. However, in February 1626 he was compelled to relinquish his place on the bench, following a proclamation by Charles I which prohibited the holding of ordinary seats in the court of session by officers of state and nobles. On 29 May the same year, Thomas Hope was appointed king's advocate to act in conjunction with Oliphant; they operated conjointly until the latter's death, on 13 April 1628. Oliphant was buried in Greyfriars churchyard, Edinburgh. No record of his testament survives.　　　　　　　　　G. G. SMITH, *rev.* JOHN FINLAY

Sources books of sederunt, NA Scot., CS1 · C. B. B. Watson, ed., *Roll of Edinburgh burgesses and guild-brethren, 1406–1700*, Scottish RS, 59 (1929) · M. Wood and R. K. Hannay, eds., *Extracts from the records of the burgh of Edinburgh, 1589–1603* (1916); *1604–1626* (1927); *1626–1641* (1936) · *Reg. PCS*, 1st ser. · A. I. Dunlop, ed., *Acta facultatis artium universitatis Sanctiandree, 1413–1588*, 2, Scottish History Society, 3rd ser., 55 (1964) · G. Brunton and D. Haig, *An historical account of the senators of the college of justice, from its institution in MDXXXII* (1832) · F. J. Grant, ed., *The Faculty of Advocates in Scotland, 1532–1943*, Scottish RS, 145 (1944) · R. K. Hannay, *The college of justice*, Stair Society, supplementary vol. 1 (1990) · D. Calderwood, *The history of the Kirk of Scotland*, ed. T. Thomson and D. Laing, 8 vols., Wodrow Society, 7 (1842–9) · J. Anderson, ed., *The Oliphants in Scotland* (1899) · W. Fraser, ed., *The Douglas book*, 4 vols. (1885) · *The correspondence of the Rev. Robert Wodrow*, ed. T. M'Crie, 3 vols., Wodrow Society, [3] (1842–3) · S. A. Gillon, ed., *Selected justiciary cases*, Stair Society, 16 (1953) · J. A. Clyde, ed., *Hope's major practicks, 1608–1633*, 2 vols., Stair Society, 3–4 (1937–8) · R. Pitcairn, ed., *Ancient criminal trials in Scotland*, 7 pts in 3, Bannatyne Club, 42 (1833) · W. K. Coutts, 'The business of the college of justice in 1600: how it reflects the economic and social life of Scots men and women', PhD diss., U. Edin., 1999

Oliver [Oliver fitz Regis] (*d.* **1218/19**), soldier, was the illegitimate son of King *John and of Hawise, almost certainly the sister of Eve de Tracy and Fulk Fitzwarine. He was probably born before John came to the throne. Very little is known of him until he is found fighting on the royalist side during the civil war of 1215–17. In June 1216 he was one of those besieged in the bishop of Winchester's castle of Wolvesey, situated in Winchester itself, by Prince Louis of France and English rebels. His most important action occurred during the critical siege of Dover. Louis, who had unsuccessfully attempted to take the castle in 1216, sailed from Calais on 22 April 1217 with the intention of landing at Dover itself. But just as his ships drew near a force led by Oliver and William of Kensham (Willikin of the Weald) descended upon the small force left by Louis in 1216, killing some, burning their huts, and gaining control of the cliff tops. This rendered any landing by the French extremely hazardous and obliged Louis to make instead for Sandwich. Dover remained in royal hands.

For his services Oliver was well rewarded, first by his father and then by the regency council of Henry III, chiefly in the form of properties confiscated from rebels. John's confidence in his son is shown by the grant made to him of the castle and honour of Tonge, Kent, in November 1215, which was confirmed in June 1217. Following the end of the civil war Oliver sailed with other English crusaders to join the forces of the fifth crusade assembled in Egypt. They landed at Damietta in August or September 1218, and it was there, later that year, or early in 1219, that Oliver died. It appears that his remains were brought back to England, since William Camden recorded their burial place in Westminster Abbey. Oliver does not appear to have married.　　　　　　　　　　　　SIMON LLOYD

Sources *Feudalism and liberty: articles and addresses of Sidney Painter*, ed. F. A. Cazel (1961), 240–3 · *Chancery records* · Oliver of Paderborn, *The capture of Damietta*, ed. and trans. J. J. Gavigan (1948) · [W. Camden], *Reges, reginae, nobiles* (1600)

Oliver of Malmesbury. *See* Eilmer (*b. c.*985, *d.* after 1066).

Oliver, Andrew (1706–1774), public servant and merchant in America, was born in Boston, Massachusetts, on 28 March 1706, the son of Daniel Oliver (1663–1732), merchant, and Elizabeth Belcher (1677–1735). Oliver was born into one of the élite colonial Boston families. After graduating from Harvard (AB 1724, MA 1727), Oliver entered his father's successful merchant firm, and was soon joined by his younger brother Peter. Andrew Oliver married Mary Fitch (1706–1732) on 20 June 1728, receiving a substantial tract of land outside Boston as part of her dowry. She died four years later, leaving Oliver with their one surviving son, also named Andrew. On 19 December 1734 he remarried; his second wife was Mary Sanford (1712–1773), also from an élite Boston family, with whom he had fourteen children. He believed strongly that one of the principal duties of his station was to serve his country and community in a public capacity. He assumed his first post in 1737, as Boston's town auditor. This proved to be the beginning of a long and active career. Other positions for Boston included overseer of the poor, tax collector, justice of the peace, and town meeting moderator. He was equally active in the Congregationalist church. A lifetime member of the Old South Church in Boston, he was treasurer and later secretary of the Congregationalist missionary arm, the Society for the Propagation of the Gospel in New England and Adjacent Parts. After 1743 he was increasingly active in Massachusetts politics, serving first as a representative in the colony's house of representatives (1743–6) and then as the province's executive secretary (1756–71). The Oliver family was firmly interconnected with the Hutchinsons, another Boston élite family. Thomas Hutchinson, governor of Massachusetts in 1771–4, was the brother-in-law of Oliver's wife. His nephew was married to Hutchinson's daughter, and his own son was married to another of Hutchinson's daughters.

Together, the Hutchinson–Oliver faction dominated late colonial Massachusetts politics. Thomas Hutchinson, appointed lieutenant-governor in 1758, helped to secure

Andrew Oliver's position as secretary, and when Hutchinson became governor in 1771, he saw to it that Oliver was appointed lieutenant-governor and that Peter Oliver was made chief justice of the colony. The Hutchinson–Oliver faction suffered substantially during Boston's road to revolution, with Andrew enduring the most. In 1765 he was appointed, without his knowledge, to the position of stamp distributor for the ill-fated Stamp Act of 1765, which was a direct taxation by the British crown on its American subjects and is traditionally marked by historians as the opening of the Anglo-American rift. When riots broke out in Boston in response to the act, Oliver was the prime target. He was hanged in effigy on 14 August from Deacon Eliot's tree. That evening the protesters dismantled what was rumoured to be the new stamp office and burned Oliver's effigy in a bonfire, using his fence for kindling. Afterwards the more brazen members of the protesters descended on Oliver's house, vandalizing it and the garden. Oliver escaped unharmed, but publicly resigned his position as stamp distributor the following day. In 1773 Oliver and Hutchinson suffered a public humiliation when several of their letters, which expressed support for a number of parliament's unpopular colonial acts, were sent to the speaker of the Massachusetts house of representatives by Benjamin Franklin. The letters were first distributed privately and then given to the press. The popular outrage undermined any remaining authority of the Hutchinson–Oliver faction. Andrew died from a stroke on 3 March 1774, which his family and friends blamed on the stress of the recent events. His funeral on 8 March was hounded by an abusive crowd, which shouted insults at the procession. His brother Peter did not attend for fear of his own safety. Thomas Hutchinson departed for London three months later, having been replaced by a military governor. TROY O. BICKHAM

Sources B. Bailyn, *The ordeal of Thomas Hutchinson* (1974) • R. M. Calhoun, 'Oliver, Andrew', *ANB* • A. S. Walmsley, *Thomas Hutchinson and the origins of the American Revolution* (1999) • J. Hosner, *The life of Thomas Hutchinson: royal governor* (1896) • B. W. Labarree, *Colonial Massachusetts: a history* (1979) • Andrew Oliver's letter-book, 1767–74, BL, Egerton MS 2670 • *The diary and letters of His Excellency Thomas Hutchinson*, ed. P. O. Hutchinson, 2 vols. (1883–6) • *IGI*
Archives BL, letter-book, Egerton MS 2670 | BL, Egerton MSS 2659–2674 • Massachusetts Archives, Boston, Hutchinson–Oliver MSS
Likenesses J. Singleton Copley, oils, repro. in Bailyn, *Ordeal of Thomas Hutchinson*, p. 17 • portrait, repro. in *Diary and letters of Thomas Hutchinson*, ed. Hutchinson, pp. 128–9

Oliver, Archer James (*bap.* 1774, *d.* 1842), portrait painter, was baptized on 3 October 1774 at St Mary, Whitechapel, London, the son of John Oliver and his wife, Anna Maria. On 13 August 1790 he was admitted to the Royal Academy Schools, aged sixteen. Between 1791 and 1842 he was a regular contributor to both the Royal Academy and the British Institution, exhibiting 210 works at the former and 62 at the latter. In his early years Oliver worked chiefly as a portrait painter. He built a large, fashionable practice and occupied a studio in New Bond Street. His portraits at this time include *George Children* (1806; NPG), and in 1807 he was elected an associate of the Royal Academy. In later life

his practice declined owing to ill health. From 1830 onwards he exhibited mostly still lifes or historical groups. In 1835 he was appointed curator of the painting school of the Royal Academy, and it was to the academy that he again turned for financial support in his last years. Oliver died, possibly in Bond Street, London, on 16 March 1842. L. H. CUST, *rev.* TINA FISKE

Sources W. Sandby, *The history of the Royal Academy of Arts*, 2 vols. (1862) • J. E. Hodgson and F. A. Eaton, *The Royal Academy and its members, 1768–1830* (1905) • D. Foskett, *A dictionary of British miniature painters*, 2 vols. (1972) • S. C. Hutchison, 'The Royal Academy Schools, 1768–1830', *Walpole Society*, 38 (1960–62), 123–91, esp. 151 • B. Stewart and M. Cutten, *The dictionary of portrait painters in Britain up to 1920* (1997) • Graves, *RA exhibitors* • Bryan, *Painters* • Redgrave, *Artists* • K. K. Yung, *National Portrait Gallery: complete illustrated catalogue, 1856–1979*, ed. M. Pettman (1981) • *Engraved Brit. ports.* • Waterhouse, *18c painters* • W. G. Strickland, *A dictionary of Irish artists*, 2 vols. (1913) • *IGI* • G. Popp and H. Valentine, *Royal Academy of Arts directory of membership: from the foundation in 1768 to 1995, including honorary members* (1996)
Likenesses A. J. Oliver, self-portrait, exh. RA 1791 • G. Chinnery, portrait, exh. RA 1792 • J. Varley, black chalk, 1812, V&A
Wealth at death died in poverty; repossession of property at death: Hodgson and Eaton, *Royal Academy*

Oliver [*née* Joseph], **Dame Beryl Carnegy** (1882–1972), charity worker and administrator, was born Beryl Carnegy Joseph on 20 August 1882 in Australia. She was the only daughter of Francis Edward Joseph, gentleman, who later adopted the surname of his wife, Isabella Eliza Butter Carnegy (*b.* 1862), the daughter of Patrick Carnegy of Lour, Angus (Forfarshire), Scotland, after she succeeded to her father's estates in 1915. Very little is known about Beryl's early life, except that she was educated privately in England and France, as befitted a young lady in society. What is certain is that she embarked upon her lifetime of voluntary service in 1910, when, aged twenty-seven, she joined the St John Ambulance Brigade. By then the brigade was operating under the auspices of the Volunteer Aid Detachment (VAD) training scheme, established in 1909 soon after the passing of the Territorial and Reserve Forces Act of 1907, and combined the resources of the order of St John of Jerusalem and the British Red Cross Society (BRCS).

Bespectacled and small in stature, with organizational and training skills of particular note, Beryl quickly earned a reputation as a dedicated and hard-working volunteer. On 10 June 1914, in London, she married Sir Henry Francis *Oliver (1865–1965), then a rear admiral in the Royal Navy and later admiral of the fleet, the son of Robert Oliver, a landed proprietor of Lochside, Kelso. Her marriage barely interrupted her career: the couple had no children, and while her husband's naval duties regularly took him abroad, Beryl remained in London, devoting herself to her voluntary work. The outbreak of the First World War created a huge demand for trained volunteers to supplement nursing staff, and she was given responsibility for the military section of the joint VADs, organizing work in hospitals. In 1916 her contribution to the war effort was acknowledged when she was awarded the Royal Red Cross, first class—the decoration instituted by Queen Victoria in 1883, in recognition of special services rendered in

Dame Beryl Carnegy Oliver (1882–1972), by Bassano, 1938

service medal. In 1948 she was invested with the insignia of dame grand cross in the Order of the British Empire (civil division).

After the war Dame Beryl took up the post of director of education to the Red Cross, and on her retirement in 1956 was appointed the society's archivist. Her comprehensive history of the BRCS from its inception, *The British Red Cross in Action*, was published in 1966, a year after the death of her husband. The BRCS considered the completion of this book to be a fitting moment to honour her with its highest award, the certificate of honour, class 1. Her other work, *The Church of Saint Mary the Virgin, Aldermanbury*, was published in 1969. Dame Beryl died at her home, 20 South Eaton Place, Westminster, London, on 13 July 1972. In her will she asked for a requiem mass to be held in her memory at the Anglican church of St Mary, Bourne Street, London, and for her ashes to be interred on the Hill of Lour, Angus.   SUSAN L. COHEN

Sources personnel file, Order of the hospital of St John of Jerusalem archives, St Johns Gate, London · *WWW* · personnel index, joint war committee, British Red Cross Society archives, 9 Grosvenor Crescent, London · personalities file, British Red Cross Society archives, 9 Grosvenor Crescent, London · *Cross Talk* (Sept 1972), 4 · *The Times* (15 July 1972), 16 · B. Oliver, *The British Red Cross in action* (1966) · P. G. Cambray and G. G. Briggs, eds., *Red Cross & St. John: the official record of the humanitarian services of the war organization of the British Red Cross Society and order of St. John of Jerusalem, 1939–1947* (1949), 628 · J. Magill, *The Red Cross: the idea and the development* (1926), 85 · *British Red Cross Society News* (Aug 1966), 186–7 · *Scottish biographies* (1938), 123 · m. cert. · d. cert. · will, 24 May 1968 · *WWW, 1961–70* [H. F. Oliver]

Archives Order of the Hospital of St John of Jerusalem, archives, MSS

Likenesses photograph, 1914–18, British Red Cross Society, pl. 2 · photographs, 1930–39, British Red Cross Society, plates 129, 130 · Bassano, three photographs, 1938, NPG [*see illus.*] · photograph, repro. in *Cross Talk*

Wealth at death £182,241: probate, 14 Aug 1972, *CGPLA Eng. & Wales*

nursing the sick and wounded of the army and navy—and St John's honoured her by making her a lady of justice. Further honours followed: she was created CBE in 1919 and DBE in March 1920.

After the First World War, Dame Beryl continued working at VAD headquarters, but soon became embroiled in the debate concerning the proposed disbandment of the VADs. Her vehement opposition to this plan brought her into direct conflict with a number of her St John's colleagues on the War Office committee, and in 1922, when the War Office confirmed its decision to form a new scheme, she expressed her displeasure by resigning from St John's. Her subsequent affiliation to the BRCS was in some respects a defiant action, but, as she admitted, her work as head of the VAD department with responsibility for the promotion and training of detachments nationwide remained much the same; only the uniform changed.

In 1938 Dame Beryl assisted with the planning and implementation of the International Red Cross Conference in London, and the following year, with the outbreak of the Second World War, she was once again able to demonstrate her organizational and supervisory skills. As a member of the war organization executive committee she was responsible for meeting the huge demand for Red Cross personnel overseas. Her membership of the selection committee also involved her in the first posting of service hospital welfare officers to north Africa and the Middle East in 1943. In recognition of her wartime service, in 1945 she received, among other awards, the silver medal of the French Red Cross and the voluntary medical

Oliver, Daniel (1830–1916), botanist, was born on 6 February 1830 at Newcastle upon Tyne, the first of the nine children of Daniel Oliver (1806–1878), a grocer, and his wife, Ann (1804–1878), daughter of Thomas and Ann Noble of Brockerby, near Carlisle. Since both his parents were members of the Society of Friends, Daniel attended the Friends' school at Wigton (1839–44). Partly on account of shyness he did not flourish academically, but his early interest in natural history developed considerably and he played a leading role in a school society largely devoted to natural history. Returning to Newcastle in 1844 he worked in the family business but, finding this employment 'utterly distasteful' (*Annual Monitor*, 94), he paid increasing attention to natural history, publishing his first paper in *The Phytologist* in 1847. His enthusiasm for natural history was further encouraged by fellow members of the Tyneside Naturalists' Field Club, including John Hancock and Sir Walter Trevelyan, and by several local Quakers. In his early twenties he was elected to the Edinburgh Botanical Society (1851) and the Linnean Society (1853). He also joined the Askesian Society (founded 1853) at which a number of scientifically able young Quakers from the

Newcastle area, including George Stewardson Brady, Henry Bowman Brady, Robert Calvert Clapham, and David Richardson, read and discussed scientific papers. For six years, beginning in the 1851–2 session, Oliver lectured in botany at Durham medical school.

Oliver's career took a dramatic turn in 1858 when, after writing to Sir William Hooker about the possibility of joining a surveying expedition, he was invited to join the staff of the herbarium at the Royal Botanic Gardens, Kew. In 1864 he was appointed keeper of the herbarium and library, a position he held until his retirement in 1890. During this period of over thirty years he worked tirelessly tending, studying, and classifying the botanical collections sent to Kew from all parts of the world. As one contemporary noted, 'Probably no one man ever knew so much as he of those aberrant types which puzzle the most experienced botanists' (Britten, 91). He published approximately fifty papers in scientific journals, mostly descriptions of new and interesting species that he curated at Kew. His main publications, which included the first three volumes of the *Flora of Tropical Africa* (8 vols., 1868–1934) and the *First Book of Indian Botany* (1869), likewise contained an abundance of detailed botanical descriptions. He also wrote an official guide to the museum at Kew (1861) and a new and considerably extended edition of the *Guide to the Royal Botanic Gardens and Pleasure Grounds, Kew* (1868).

Soon after Oliver's arrival at Kew, Joseph Dalton Hooker, the assistant director, asked him to perform crossing experiments on Darwin's behalf. Darwin was clearly impressed by Oliver's abilities as an experimenter and by the wealth of information he possessed on botanical subjects. Soon they were both carrying out experiments on the physiological processes of the insectivorous plants such as *Drosera*, and regularly exchanging notes and specimens. When the chair of botany fell vacant at University College, London, Darwin strongly recommended Oliver for the post, praising 'the range of his knowledge of facts buried in all sorts of foreign publications', his 'philosophical caution' as an experimenter, and the 'high philosophical order' of his mind (Darwin, 7.48). Oliver was appointed to the professorship in 1860, a position he held until his retirement in 1888.

Initially Oliver's main duty at University College was delivering annually a fifty-lecture course on general botany, principally to medical students. To enable him to spend much of the day at Kew, his class was scheduled during the summer months from 8 a.m. to 9 a.m., five days a week. In order to arrive in time, he arranged for the night-constable to rap at the window of his bedroom at 5 a.m. and an hour later a cab collected him from his home in Kew. Each lecture was illustrated by six specimens he brought with him and microscopes were used for demonstrations. Oliver's textbook, *Lessons in Elementary Botany* (1864), passed through many editions and is said to have sold some 70,000 copies. In 1880 the scope of botanical education at University College was extended with the opening of a botanical laboratory and the appointment of an assistant. From 1859 to 1874 Oliver also lectured to the

staff at Kew and in the 1870s he delivered lectures for women at the South Kensington Museum.

Oliver was in close contact with most of the eminent botanists of his generation, including Darwin and Asa Gray, many of whom visited him at Kew. He was particularly close to John Gilbert Baker, a fellow Quaker, who was appointed his assistant at Kew in 1866 and became his near neighbour. When Oliver was elected to the Royal Society of London in 1863 his certificate was signed by Sir William Hooker, George Bentham, Charles Daubeny, George Busk, and three others. In 1884 Oliver received the society's royal medal for 'his Investigations in the Classification of Plants, and for the great services which he has rendered to Taxonomic Botany' (RS, council minutes, 6 November 1884). Other honours included the Linnean Society's gold medal (1892) and honorary degrees from the universities of Edinburgh and Aberdeen.

From 1861 Oliver was one of the editors of the newly constituted editorial board of the *Natural History Review* and compiled much bibliographical material for that journal. Like many systematists Oliver does not appear to have sided publicly either for or against Darwin's theory of evolution. One of his more sophisticated discussions was his informed criticism in 1862 of Oswald Heer's 'Atlantis hypothesis' which postulated that Europe and America were joined during the Miocene epoch.

In 1861 Oliver married Hannah Hobson Wall (1833/4–1919), daughter of James Wall of Sheffield. They had three surviving children, including Francis Wall *Oliver (1864–1951) who succeeded his father at University College, becoming Quain professor of botany in 1890. Although Daniel Oliver had earlier been a rather strict Quaker, in his middle years he dispensed with the more rigid aspects of Quakerism, although always remaining true to its essential teachings. A man of broad cultural interests, following his retirement Oliver had time to read extensively, listen to music, and develop his artistic talents. He collected English watercolours, Pre-Raphaelite art, and botanical illustrations, counting several artists, Ruskin included, among his friends. Possessing a 'decidedly nervous temperament' (*Annual Monitor*, 95), possibly due to having suffered both a dog-bite and cholera during childhood, he had a tendency to retire from company. Oliver was not a charismatic lecturer and many contemporaries found him outwardly abrupt and somewhat forbidding. However, his many friends considered him an upright, modest man who was compassionate, companionable, well informed, and intellectually lively. He was blessed with good health which only deserted him during his short final illness. Following his death at his home, 10 Kew Gardens Road, on 21 December 1916, he was buried two days later in the burial-ground attached to Isleworth Friends' meeting-house. GEOFFREY CANTOR

Sources J. Britten, *Journal of Botany, British and Foreign*, 50 (1917), 89–95 • *Annual Monitor* (1918), 94–100 • F. W. Oliver and T. G. Hill, *An outline of the history of the botanical department of University College, London* (1927) • J. W. Steel and others, *A historical sketch of the Society of Friends … in Newcastle and Gateshead, 1653–1898* (1899) • *The Friend*, new ser., 57 (1917), 28 • D. W. Reed, ed., *Friends' school Wigton* (1954) • D. Embleton, *The history of the medical school, afterwards the Durham*

College of Medicine (1890) · The correspondence of Charles Darwin, ed. F. Burkhardt and S. Smith, [13 vols.] (1985–) · CGPLA Eng. & Wales (1917) · Newcastle Meeting records, RS Friends, Lond.
Archives RBG Kew, corresp. and papers | CUL, corresp. with Charles Darwin · Harvard U., Arnold Arboretum, letters to Asa Gray · Royal Pharmaceutical Society, London, corresp. with Daniel Hanbury
Likenesses photograph, UCL; repro. in N. Harte and J. North, *The world of UCL, 1828–1990* (1991) · photographs, UCL · two photographs, RS
Wealth at death £5117 5s. 3d.: probate, 15 Feb 1917, CGPLA Eng. & Wales

Oliver, David Thomas (1863–1947), lawyer, was born at Pontypridd on 8 February 1863, the fifth of twelve children of the Revd Henry Oliver, a Congregationalist minister, and his wife, Catharine, daughter of the Revd Joshua Thomas, Congregationalist minister, of Aberdâr. Educated at Caterham School, he first entered the civil service, from which he resigned after being called to the bar by the Middle Temple in 1888. In the meantime he had served in Ireland and had graduated BA at the Royal University of Ireland, proceeding MA (1886), LLB (1888), and LLD (1898). In 1898 he also took the LLB degree of the University of London with first class honours. In 1900 he entered Trinity Hall, Cambridge, as an advanced student, taking the degrees of LLB in 1902 and LLM in 1908.

By this time Oliver had found that his heart was in academic work and he became lecturer in law in his own college and supervisor of legal studies for several other colleges, gradually relinquishing his practice in the Temple. In 1920 he became a fellow of Trinity Hall, a position which he retained until his death. His particular interest in Roman law led him to the study of Roman-Dutch law, in which subject he was appointed to the Monro lecturership which was founded for him by the master and fellows of Gonville and Caius College at the end of 1920 to provide for the needs of the students from South Africa who went to read law in Cambridge. This successful enterprise was eventually taken over by the university and thereafter Oliver carried on the course as university lecturer; and although he was compelled to retire officially from this post in 1928 on reaching the statutory age limit he continued to conduct the teaching of the subject for a number of years until a successor could be found.

Oliver's renown as a teacher was founded on an encyclopaedic knowledge of his field and great sympathy with those he taught. Although somewhat slow in speech, he had a penetrating mind. In 1891 he married Lavinia Mary Harrison, who died in 1917; there were no children of the marriage. In 1918 he married Alice Maud, daughter of George Kirby, of Watford; they had two sons, both of whom studied law at Trinity Hall.

Oliver's writings included reviews and articles on Roman law in the *Cambridge Law Journal*, and 'Roman law in modern cases in English courts' in the volume *Cambridge Legal Essays* (1926) edited by P. H. Winfield and A. D. McNair. One of his earliest works, with W. A. Willis, was *The Roman Law Examination Test for Bar and University* (1897). He also published a translation, with commentary, of portions of books xii and xiii of Justinian's *Digest* (De

conditionibus) (1937). He produced the seventh edition of L. A. Goodeve's *Modern Law of Personal Property* (1930), and was also responsible for three editions of B. R. Wise's *Outlines of Jurisprudence* (3rd edn, 1918; 4th edn, 1925; 5th edn, 1930). Oliver died at his home, Woodview, 18 Girton Road, Cambridge, on 18 January 1947. He was survived by his second wife. J. W. C. TURNER, rev. ROBERT BROWN

Sources The Times (21 Jan 1947) · private information (1959) · CGPLA Eng. & Wales (1947) · WWW · personal knowledge (1959)
Likenesses E. O. D. Hoole, portrait, priv. coll.
Wealth at death £12,939 13s. 11d.: probate, 24 April 1947, CGPLA Eng. & Wales

Oliver, Emma Sophia (1819–1885). *See under* Oliver, William (c.1804–1853).

Oliver, Francis Wall (1864–1951), palaeobotanist and ecologist, was born on 10 May 1864 at Richmond, Surrey, the only son of Daniel *Oliver (1830–1916), from 1864 keeper at Kew, and Hannah, daughter of James Wall, of Sheffield. Oliver's father was a member of the Society of Friends and sent his son at the age of nine to the Friends' school at Kendal. There, Oliver developed a passion and skill for mountaineering which persisted; in later years he climbed the Alps with J. Norman Collie and E. J. Garwood. He went next to Bootham School, York, where he was given charge of their 4½ inch telescope and, but for his early love of botany, might have adopted astronomy as a career. After a year at University College, London, he went to Trinity College, Cambridge, where he obtained a foundation scholarship and first-class honours in both parts of the natural sciences tripos (1885–6). He spent vacations studying at Bonn and Tübingen, where he met many leading botanists of the day.

In 1888 Oliver took his father's place at University College, London, first as lecturer, then in 1890 as Quain professor of botany, a chair which he held until 1929. Oliver's earliest papers were mostly of a physiological character and mention should be made of his pioneer investigations of the effect of fog on vegetation at the time when 'London particulars' could turn daylight into darkness (*Journal of the Royal Horticultural Society*, 1891). In 1894–5, with the help of others, he translated the *Pflanzenleben* of Kerner von Marilaun, under the title of *The Natural History of Plants*, which was a great success financially and further stimulated the ecological bias that had been aroused in Oliver by his contacts at Bonn. In 1896 Oliver married Mildred Alice (d. 1932), daughter of Charles Robert Thompson, surgeon, of Westerham, whom he encountered when climbing in the Alps. They had one daughter and two sons, both of whom attained distinction in the navy. The elder son was Sir Geoffrey Nigel *Oliver.

In 1892 Oliver became associated with the newly appointed honorary keeper of the Jodrell Laboratory, D. H. Scott. Oliver induced Scott to give the famous lectures on fossil plants at University College in 1896. Soon afterwards Oliver began his researches, which might best be described as meticulous palaeobotanical detection, on fossil seeds. They led to the recognition of *Lagenostoma lomaxi* as the seed of a woody, fern-like plant, the well-known fossil, *Lyginopteris oldhamia* (*Philosophical Transactions of the Royal Society*, 1905). Oliver thus established the existence of a group, the Pteridosperms, with fern-like habits but bearing seeds, as an important feature of the Coal-Measure vegetation. Apart from this, his chief contributions to the subject were a detailed account of a primitive type (*Physostoma elegans*) of *Stephanospermum* and, with E. J. Salisbury, an account of the seeds of the genus *Conostoma* (*Annals of Botany*, 1911). For his contributions to palaeobotany Oliver was elected FRS in 1905.

From 1904 to 1908 Oliver organized September visits to the Brittany coast to study salt-marsh vegetation, and after 1910 he annually took his honours students for a fortnight to Blakeney Point, Norfolk, to study plant life in relation to habitat conditions and raised the funds to erect the field laboratory there. In his later years Oliver turned his attention increasingly towards the dynamic aspects of ecology, studying in particular the physiography of shingle beaches and salt marsh development in relation to their vegetation. As an outcome he became interested in the value of cord grass (*Spartina townsendii*) as a reclaimer of mud flats and subsequently in collaboration with a marine engineer, A. E. Carey, published a book on *Tidal Lands* (1918) which emphasized the role that plants could play in coastal conservation.

From 1929 until 1935 Oliver was professor at Cairo University. In the latter year he went to live on the edge of the desert and studied the changing aspects of its vegetation. He returned finally to England in 1950. Robust physically, with a strikingly well-cut physiognomy, Oliver had only one serious illness. He was fundamentally shy and reserved, with a marked capacity for silence, but he evoked the affection of his close associates. His sense of humour was reflected in his *Who's Who* entry, where he listed his recreations as 'once mountaineering, now washing up'. He died at his home, Ballards Barn, Limpsfield, Surrey, on 14 September 1951.

E. J. SALISBURY, rev. PETER OSBORNE

Sources E. J. Salisbury, *Obits. FRS*, 8 (1952–3), 229–40 • personal knowledge (1971) • *WWW* • *The Times* (18 Sept 1951) • Desmond, *Botanists*, rev. edn • Venn, *Alum. Cant.* • *CGPLA Eng. & Wales* (1952)
Archives BL, corresp. with Marie Stopes, Add. MS 58468 • CAC Cam., corresp. with A. V. Hill • U. Glas., letters to F. O. Bower • UCL, corresp. with Karl Pearson
Likenesses F. De Biden Footner, crayon drawing, UCL
Wealth at death £18,369 3s. 11d.: probate, 1 Jan 1952, *CGPLA Eng. & Wales*

Oliver, Frederick Scott (1864–1934), draper and polemicist, was born on 20 February 1864 in Edinburgh, elder son of John Scott Oliver, merchant, and Catherine (d. 1869), daughter of Duncan *McLaren. Nephew of John *McLaren, Lord McLaren, and Charles *McLaren, first Baron Aberconway, he was educated in Edinburgh at George Watson's College, before going on first to Edinburgh University and then to Trinity College, Cambridge. He was called to the bar at the Inner Temple in 1889, but found that on a barrister's earnings he could not afford to marry, as he wished, Lord McLaren's daughter Katherine Augusta.

Oliver therefore accepted an offer from his Cambridge contemporary Ernest Debenham, and in 1892 entered the firm of Debenham and Freebody, drapers with a shop in Marylebone, and also wholesalers, manufacturers, and shippers. He trained for business by spending a year with a firm of chartered accountants, and having equipped himself on the financial side, entered the shop, and worked in each of the departments before taking on its general management. In 1893 he was able to marry his cousin, with whom he had two sons and a daughter. He was a superb organizer and delegator whose orderly intelligence was never overstretched by Debenhams's highly ramified retail, wholesale, agency, and commission business. He and Ernest Debenham were successful modernizers who became joint managing directors when the firm was reconstructed as Debenhams Ltd in 1905. The store was rebuilt in 1906–7, and in 1908 the company's capital was increased to £1 million. The profit earned in 1910 alone exceeded £100,000, and by 1914 both partners were rich men.

After the war Oliver and Debenham launched a policy of expansion. In 1919 Debenhams merged with Marshall and Snelgrove, Oxford Street drapers, and the firm also bought the Knightsbridge department store Harvey Nichols for £217,040. Oliver retired as managing director in 1920 and as deputy chairman in 1926. He was also a member of the committee of the Hudson's Bay Company (1917–25).

Reared in a radical household, Oliver espoused the policies of Joseph Chamberlain, and became a brilliant, provocative correspondent of imperial-minded politicians, editors, and officials. He delighted in close, compact argument, and after the publication in 1904 (under the pseudonym of John Draper) of *The Statesman and the Bishop*, he was regarded as the ablest pamphleteer in Britain. His first book, *Alexander Hamilton* (1906), had an influence comparable to Burke's *Thoughts on the Present Discontents* or Disraeli's *Lord George Bentinck*. It described the advent of organic unity into the newly fledged United States, and presented a model for British imperial federation. Oliver was a founder of the Compatriots' Club in 1904, and after 1909 was an active member of the Round Table movement. During the constitutional crisis in 1910 he wrote eight letters to *The Times*, printed under the alias Pacificus, successfully calling for an inter-party conference to break the deadlock and, less successfully, for a federalist convention. He published three cognate books between 1913 and 1917.

An ally of Lord Milner, Oliver disdained what he considered to be the drowsy comforts and factious corruption of parliamentary democracy; he refused to seek a candidature. Though as a great-nephew of John Bright he had been forbidden as a child to play with toy soldiers, he became a fierce supporter of Field Marshal Roberts in his campaign for compulsory military service. He extolled Roberts as a man of plain, unerring instincts; for Oliver hated what he described as the gibbering pedantic subtleties of intellectuals or the grovelling of peacemakers. '*Nothing* will save us except the sight of red blood running pretty freely; but whether British *and* German blood, or only British, I don't know—nor do I think it much matters', he wrote to Milner. 'Blood is the necessity.' (letter of 31 March 1911, Bodl. Oxf., MS Milner 13). He thought British public life mired in cowardice and indolence, and greeted the declaration of war in 1914 with relief. The excuse for these ebullitions must be that Oliver contracted tuberculosis around 1906; ill health made him excitable and induced an extravagant admiration of manly fortitude. 'He was very, very clever and very, very superior, and very spoilt—and he was a dilettante in finance' (Crow, 76–7) according to George Macaulay Booth who tried to recruit him in 1914 to an official committee on wartime supplies. Oliver declined Booth's approach, and instead wrote *The Ordeal of Battle* (1915), a critical examination of the origin and conduct of the war comparable to Swift's *Conduct of the Allies*. He treated war as an eternal human necessity, and contended that under modern conditions the whole nation rather than the armed forces must be conscripted.

Oliver described his choices in 1913 as 'to be a third-rate sermonising litterateur; an officious, mischievous and ignorant puller of wires; or a moderately efficient journalist' (letter to Lord Milner, 1 March 1913, Bodl. Oxf., MS Milner 13). He resembled a seer—imaginative, intuitive, transfiguring facts into visions—and was by turns satirical, farcical, vehement, seductive, and debonair. G. M. Trevelyan wrote of his 'matchless conversation' that 'its intellectual power was tempered with a quaint, sweet humour, testifying to the breadth and kindliness that underlay his revolt against sentiment' (*The Times*, 6 June 1934). He also had a roving eye for pretty women.

From 1905 until 1928 Oliver owned Checkendon Court in the Chiltern hills, but latterly settled on estates which he had bought in 1916 in the Cheviots. His reflections on statecraft in *The Endless Adventure*, a three-volume study of the parliamentary system in the age of Walpole (1930–35), influenced Conservative leaders of the period, particularly Stanley Baldwin. A selection of his wartime letters was posthumously published as *The Anvil of War* (1936). Oliver died on 3 June 1934 at Edgerston, Jedburgh, Roxburghshire, and was buried at Edgerston churchyard on 6 June. He was survived by his wife.

RICHARD DAVENPORT-HINES

Sources J. Draper [F. S. Oliver], *The statesman and the bishop: a letter to a gentleman in the diocese of Hereford, and other papers* (1904) · F. S. Oliver, *Alexander Hamilton* (1906) · F. S. Oliver, *Ordeal by battle* (1915) · F. S. Oliver, *The endless adventure* (1930–35) · *The anvil of war: letters between F. S. Oliver and his brother, 1914–1918*, ed. S. Gwynn (1936) · NL Scot., Oliver MSS · S. Gwynn, introduction, in *The anvil of war: letters between F. S. Oliver and his brother, 1914–1918*, ed. S. Gwynn (1936) · [J. Buchan], *The Times* (5 June 1934); repr. in J. Buchan, Baron Tweedsmuir, *Memory hold-the-door* (1940), 208–11 · G. M. Trevelyan, *The Times* (6 June 1934) · F. S. Oliver, letter to Lord Milner, 31 March 1911, Bodl. Oxf., MS Milner 13 · F. S. Oliver, letter to Lord Milner, 1 March 1913, Bodl. Oxf., MS Milner 13 · D. Crow, *A man of push and go: George Macaulay Booth* (1965), 76–7 · *The crisis of British unionism: the domestic political papers of the second earl of Selborne, 1885–1922*, ed. D. G. Boyce (1987) · D. G. Boyce and J. O. Stubbs, 'F. S. Oliver, Lord Selborne and federalism', *Journal of Imperial and Commonwealth History*, 5 (1976–7), 53–81 · J. E. Kendle, *The Round Table movement and imperial union* (1975) · A. M. Gollin, *The Observer and J. L. Garvin, 1908–1914* (1960) · P. Kennedy and A. Nicholls, eds., *Nationalist and racialist movements in Britain and Germany before 1914* (1981) · L. S. Amery, *My political life*, 1–2 (1953–4) · M. Corina, *Fine silks and oak counters: Debenhams, 1778–1978* (1978)

Archives NL Scot., corresp. and papers | BL, corresp. with Lord Cecil, Add. MS 51090 · BL, corresp. with Macmillans, Add. MSS 55027–55028 · BL, corresp. with Lord Northcliffe, Add. MS 62165 · BL, letters to Shaw Sparrow, Add. MSS 48203, 48207 · Bodl. Oxf., corresp. with L. G. Curtis · Glos. RO, letters to Geoffrey Dawson · IWM, corresp. with Sir Henry Wilson · NA Scot., Lord Lothian MSS · NA Scot., Sir A. Steel Maitland MSS · Plunkett Foundation, Long Hanborough, Oxfordshire, corresp. with Sir Horace Plunkett · PRO NIre., corresp. with Edward Carson · U. Birm. L., special collections department, corresp. with Sir Austen Chamberlain · W. Sussex RO, Leo Maxse MSS

Likenesses C. W. Furse, oils, 1903, repro. in Oliver, *Anvil of war*, frontispiece · O. Wallace, bust; formerly at Edgerston, 1949

Wealth at death £140,833 7s. 5d.: confirmation, 16 Oct 1934, *CCI*

Oliver, Sir Geoffrey Nigel (1898–1980), naval officer, was born in London on 22 January 1898, the eldest of the two sons and three children of Francis Wall *Oliver (1864–1951), a distinguished palaeobotanist and ecologist who held the Quain chair in botany at London University in succession to his father and was a fellow of the Royal Society, and his wife, Mildred Alice, daughter of Charles Robert Thompson, a surgeon who advanced the technique of the trepanning operation.

Oliver was educated at a preparatory school in Dorset and at Rugby School, from which he entered the navy as a 'special entry' cadet in 1915. His first ships were the famous but then elderly battleship *Dreadnought* and the new battle cruiser *Renown*, both of which took part in the First World War but in which Oliver saw no actual fighting.

After that war Oliver, in common with all officers whose education had been cut short, went to Cambridge University for two terms but did not take a degree. Courses for the rank of lieutenant followed, in which he obtained first class certificates in all five subjects and won the Goodenough medal for the best results in the gunnery examination. In 1921 he was selected to specialize in that subject and did brilliantly in both the technical and theoretical sections of the course. He was placed first of his class and awarded the Commander Egerton prize. In 1924 he joined the experimental department of HMS *Excellent*, the navy's premier gunnery school at Portsmouth.

In 1925–7 Oliver served as gunnery officer of the light cruiser *Carlisle* on the China station, after which he was reappointed to the *Excellent*'s experimental department in a higher capacity. His next ship (1930) was the fairly new battleship *Rodney* in which he attracted the attention of Captain A. B. Cunningham (later Viscount Cunningham of Hyndhope). He received money awards from the Admiralty for improvements to the ship's armaments, and was promoted commander in January 1932. In 1933 he married Barbara, daughter of Sir Francis Adolphus Jones KBE, legal adviser to the board of agriculture. They had two sons and a daughter; but the younger son died while a child and the daughter was lost in a bathing accident while on holiday on the east coast.

Oliver returned to the *Excellent* in 1932 as head of the

experimental department with the rank of commander, and after two years he was selected for command of destroyers; from 1934 to 1936 he served in ships of that class on the China and Mediterranean stations. He was next appointed to the *Excellent* for the fourth time but as the executive officer and second in command of the establishment. In June 1937 he was promoted captain at the early age of thirty-nine, and for the first year of the Second World War he served on the naval staff's tactical and training and staff duties divisions.

Late in 1940 Oliver took command of the new light cruiser *Hermione*, in which he took part in the *Bismarck* operation (May 1941) and in Malta convoys. The latter brought him the first of his three gazettes as companion of the DSO. He then took his ship round the Cape of Good Hope to join the Mediterranean Fleet, playing a part in the capture of Madagascar (May 1942) on the way. On 16 June the *Hermione*, which had just taken part in the last and abortive attempt to supply Malta from the east, was torpedoed and sunk off Tobruk by *U-205*; but Oliver was among the survivors and stayed on the station, initially for liaison duties with the army.

Oliver was next selected for the important but shore-based post of director of naval ordnance; but Admiral Cunningham, who was to be allied naval commander-in-chief for the invasion of north Africa, got the appointment cancelled and put him in charge of the enormous number of small craft then assembling at Gibraltar for the attacks on Algiers and Oran (November 1942). After the initial assaults had succeeded Oliver played an important part in the naval side of the operations for the clearance of the Germans from north Africa by developing an advanced base at Bône and in the capture of the key port of Bizerte in Tunisia (7 May 1943). For these services he received a bar to his DSO and the American Legion of Merit. He then took command of the inshore squadron which was to support the army's invasion of Sicily (10 July 1943). The next major operation was the invasion of the Italian mainland, and for the landings at Salerno (September 1943) Oliver was appointed naval commander of the British assault force in the rank of commodore 1st class. In that capacity he was instrumental in getting cancelled the plan proposed by the American General Mark Clark, the commander of the whole Fifth Army, to withdraw the American assault force, which had run into serious difficulties, and re-land it in the British sector or to transfer the British force to the American sector—which Oliver realized would be a recipe for disaster. For his part in this critical operation he was appointed CB (1944).

For the invasion of Normandy (June 1944) Oliver was given command of one of the three British naval assault forces, and the success he achieved brought him a third bar to his DSO. He was next given command of a squadron of escort carriers which took part in the liberation and relief of Greece and then transferred to the Eastern Fleet in time to join in the recapture of Rangoon (May 1945). He was promoted rear-admiral in the following July.

In 1946 Oliver was appointed admiral (air) and hoisted his flag at the naval air station of Lee-on-Solent. Later that year he returned to the Admiralty as assistant chief of naval staff, which then carried membership of the board. In 1948 he became president of the Royal Naval College, Greenwich, where he was promoted vice-admiral in 1949. In 1950–52 he was commander-in-chief, East Indies. He was created KCB in 1951 and was promoted admiral in the following year. He had not expected further employment but an unexpected vacancy for the important post of commander-in-chief, the Nore, brought him his final appointment in 1953–5. On retiring in 1955 he was created GBE and took up farming in Sussex.

Oliver was not only a man of outstanding integrity and inviolable modesty but that very rare officer in any fighting service, having not only a first-class technical brain but also great gifts of leadership in war. He died at Henfield, Sussex, on 26 May 1980.

STEPHEN W. ROSKILL, *rev.*

Sources S. W. Roskill, *The war at sea, 1939–1945*, 3 vols. in 4 (1954–61) · A. Cunningham [first Viscount Cunningham], *A sailor's odyssey: the autobiography of admiral of the fleet, Viscount Cunningham of Hyndhope* (1951) · *Naval Review*, 69/1 (1981) · *The Times* (28 May 1980) · *The Times* (31 May 1980) · personal knowledge (1986) · *CGPLA Eng. & Wales* (1980)
Archives CAC Cam., corresp. and papers
Wealth at death £59,538: probate, 22 Aug 1980, *CGPLA Eng. & Wales*

Oliver, George (1781–1861), Roman Catholic priest and historian, was born at Newington, Surrey, on 9 February 1781, the son of James and Anne Oliver. He was educated at Sedgley Park in Staffordshire from 1789 and at Stonyhurst College from 1796 to 1802. He remained at Stonyhurst for a further five years teaching humanities. In May 1806 he was ordained priest at Durham. He did not become a Jesuit but maintained a close and cordial relationship with the order, and in 1807 was appointed by Marmaduke Stone, president of Stonyhurst, to take charge of the chapel and mission at Exeter, St Nicholas's Priory, which was formerly served by the Jesuits. As a young man he had shown interest in, and appreciation of, antiquities and had come to the notice of John Milner, vicar apostolic of the western district. At Exeter, where he was to stay for the fifty-four remaining years of his life, he found abundant scope for his antiquarian interests, as T. N. Brushfield's bibliography of his published works shows. His missionary duties, which included visiting two prisons and a hospital, left him time for research and also for public charitable activities. His services during a cholera epidemic were long remembered.

Oliver's main works became standard authorities. His first important work, published at Exeter (as were most of his works) in 1820, was *Historic Collections Relating to the Monasteries in Devon*, and in the following year appeared *The History of Exeter*, of which there was a second edition in 1861; an index to this was printed in 1884. In 1828 he published *Ecclesiastical Antiquities of Devon, being Observations on many Churches in Devonshire*, which originally appeared in the *Exeter and Plymouth Gazette* with a letter on the preservation and restoration of churches. The *Ecclesiastical Antiquities* was written in conjunction with the Revd John Pike

Jones of North Bovey who, however, contributed only the introduction and the description of twelve churches. Between 1839 and 1842 there was published at Exeter Oliver's three-volume *Ecclesiastical Antiquities of Devon, being Observations on Several Churches in Devonshire with some Memoranda for the History of Cornwall*. Although professedly a second edition of the former work, it possesses claims to be considered an entirely new one. The introduction to the first edition was the only contribution by Jones to be retained in the second. In 1838 he published *Collections illustrating the biography of the Scotch, English and Irish members of the Society of Jesus*. A second, limited edition was published in London in 1845. These notices appeared originally in the *London and Dublin Weekly Orthodox Journal* (vols. 2–4, 1836–7). The *Description of the Guildhall, Exeter*, written in conjunction with Pitman Jones, was published in 1845 and a second edition followed in 1853. In 1845 he published, again in conjunction with Pitman Jones, *A View of Devonshire in MDCXXX, with a Pedigree of some of its Gentry by Thomas Westcote*. In 1846 there appeared *Monasticon diocesis Exoniensis*, with a supplement, and an *Additional supplement … with a map of the diocese, deaneries, and sites of religious houses* was published in 1854; 'without these additions, the edition of Dugdale's "Monasticon" by [Caley] Ellis and Bandinel must be considered incomplete' (*DNB*). *Collections illustrating the history of the Catholic religion in the counties of Cornwall, Devon, Dorset, Somerset, Wilts, and Gloucester* was published in London in 1857. Oliver presented the copyright to his friend F. C. Husenbeth, together with very copious additions and several corrections for a second edition. In 1861, the year of his death, there was published his *Lives of the Bishops of Exeter and a History of the Cathedral*.

Among Oliver's minor works were a translation of Father John Gerard's Latin autobiography, various articles on the Clifford family and Ugbrooke Park, and a historical novel *Merrye Englaunde, or, The Goldene Daies of Good Queene Besse* (1841). He had the principal share in preparing for publication the *Liber pontificalis* of Edmund Lacy, bishop of Exeter (1847). He wrote over a period of nine years many letters on ecclesiastical and parochial antiquities, family history, and biography, communicated under the signature of Curiosus to local newspapers, principally the *Exeter Flying Post*. He also contributed to the English Catholic periodicals of his time articles on Catholic biography, history, and antiquities.

'Few names,' declared the *Gentleman's Magazine* in an obituary notice, 'will remain more pleasingly connected with the past history of Exeter than that of George Oliver.' It described his publications as 'monuments of painstaking research and practical ability', and Brushfield wrote of 'our great ecclesiastical antiquary' (p. 286). Early in the twentieth century the view was expressed that some of his conclusions were no longer accepted, but that 'his researches considering the limited sources of knowledge available to him showed both industry and judgement' (Ward, 244). Oliver himself wrote, 'I have spared no time or labor [sic] to arrive at the Truth. But still it is but a beginning, a groundwork for something much better. The only title I can claim is that of Gleaner' (letter to Richard Norris, January 1857). Contemporaries and near contemporaries commended his scholarship and indefatigable research; later writers might qualify this view while still acknowledging the value of the immense amount of work that he accomplished.

In recognition of his skill as a researcher Oliver was elected an honorary member of the Historical Society of Boston on 30 March 1843, and on 15 September 1844 he was (without his knowledge, as he said) created DD by Pope Gregory XVI. In 1852 he was appointed provost of the newly erected chapter of the diocese of Plymouth. He became a trustee of the General Charities of Exeter in 1837 and was elected chairman for the year in 1842.

Oliver retired from active duty in 1851 but continued to live at St Nicholas's Priory, where he died on 23 March 1861. He was buried on 2 April near the high altar in the chapel in which he had served so long. A lithograph, presumably taken towards the end of his life, shows a somewhat sharp-featured face with the eyes of an enthusiast.

GEOFFREY HOLT

Sources Gillow, *Lit. biog. hist.*, 5.213–17 • T. N. Brushfield, 'The bibliography of the Rev. George Oliver', *Report and Transactions of the Devonshire Association*, 17 (1885), 266–76 • T. G. Holt, 'George Oliver, antiquary, from his letters', *Report and Transactions of the Devonshire Association*, 119 (1987), 53–65 • *Catholic Miscellany*, 9 (1828), 148 • B. Ward, 'Oliver, George', *The Catholic encyclopedia*, ed. C. G. Herbermann and others, 11 (1911) • F. C. Husenbeth, *The life of … John Milner* (1862), 121 • H. Foley, ed., *Records of the English province of the Society of Jesus*, 7 (1882–3), 559 • *GM*, 3rd ser., 10 (1861), 575–7 • G. Oliver, *Collections illustrating the history of the Catholic religion in the counties of Cornwall, Devon, Dorset, Somerset, Wilts, and Gloucester* (1857), 368–9 • *The Tablet* (13 April 1861), 235 • *The Tablet* (20 April 1861), 251 • *N&Q*, 2nd ser., 9 (1860), 404, 514 • *N&Q*, 3rd ser., 5 (1864), 137, 202 • *N&Q*, 6th ser., 5 (1882), 396 • *N&Q*, 7th ser., 1 (1886), 467, 514 • *Stonyhurst lists, 1794–1886, Stonyhurst College*, 3 vols. in 1 (1886–1905), 43 • *DNB*

Archives Archives of the British Province of the Society of Jesus, London, corresp. and papers • CUL, collections relating to history of Catholicism in the west country • Stonyhurst College, Lancashire, collections | BL, copy of Richard Polwhele's *History of Devonshire* with his copious notes and additions • Bodl. Oxf., corresp. with Sir Thomas Phillipps • Devon RO, letters to Sir Thomas Dyke Acland • Exeter Cathedral, corresp. about cathedral library and archives • Exeter Cathedral, chapter clerk's corresp. • Exeter Central Library, Westcountry Studies Library, notes, and pedigrees mainly relating to Devon families • Inner Temple, London, Monasticon diocesis Exoniensis • Lincs. Arch., letters to John Ross • Ushaw College, Durham, corresp. with John Lingard

Likenesses lithograph, repro. in Brushfield, 'Bibliography of the Rev. George Oliver', 266 • statuette

Wealth at death £450: probate, 27 April 1861, *CGPLA Eng. & Wales*

Oliver, George (1782–1867), antiquary and writer on freemasonry, was born on 5 November 1782 at Papplewick, Nottinghamshire, the eldest son of Samuel Oliver (1756–1847), schoolmaster and, after 1842, rector of Lambley, Nottinghamshire. His mother was Elizabeth, daughter of George Whitehead of Blyth Spital in the same county. He had eight siblings. The family claimed descent from an ancient Scottish family, some members of which moved to England in the reign of James I and later settled at Clipstone Park, Nottinghamshire. Oliver attended his

George Oliver (1782–1867), by unknown engraver

father's school in Lutterworth, Leicestershire, and perhaps another in Nottingham. In 1803 he became usher of the grammar school at Caistor, Lincolnshire. In 1805 he married Mary Ann (1785/6–1856), daughter of Thomas Beverley. They had three sons and two daughters.

From 1809 to 1826 Oliver was headmaster of King Edward's Grammar School at Great Grimsby and, after being ordained deacon in 1812 and priest in 1813, was curate of Grimsby from 1815 to 1831. In addition he had the living of Clee, but never lived there. As a young man, probably in 1802, he became a freemason, joining the Peterborough lodge of which his father was member and chaplain. In Grimsby he started a new lodge, of which he was master for ten years. In 1831, having lost the curacy at Grimsby, he became rector of Scopwick, Lincolnshire, which he held until his death. He was happy there and energetically rebuilt the vicarage, restored the church, and started a school. In 1814 he entered Trinity College, Cambridge, as a 'ten year man', but never took a degree there, though he was awarded a Lambeth DD in 1835. From 1834 to 1846 he was perpetual curate of St Peter's collegiate church, Wolverhampton. He intended to divide his time between Wolverhampton and Scopwick, but after bitter disputes with his churchwardens in Wolverhampton, particularly over church rates, he left the church in the care of a curate after 1841. He was also domestic chaplain to Lord Kensington and, in 1846, was made rector of South Hykeham, Lincolnshire.

From early life Oliver was a prolific author; he wrote mainly on topographical subjects and freemasonry, but also published some religious works. His most important topographical work was his History and Antiquities of the Town and Minster of Beverley (1829), which incorporated material collected earlier by the publisher Matthew Turner. It was, however, remaindered in 1839 after the publication of a rival history, George Poulson's Beverlac (1829 or 1830), which was thought to be superior. Oliver produced other works on the monuments and histories of the places in which he lived and worked, namely Grimsby (1825, 1829), Wolverhampton (1836), and Sleaford and Lincoln (1837, 1846).

Oliver also published more than thirty works on freemasonry, of which he considered The Symbol of Glory (1850) his best; it was as a freemason that he achieved greatest prominence. He regarded masonry as a universal moral code instituted by God at the creation, and his life's work, or 'grand design', was to prove that masonry was necessarily Christian, or rather protestant. This was a concern that he had inherited from his father and on which he expounded in contorted books and regular contributions to the Freemasons' Quarterly Review, which attracted wide notice and earned him the name the Sage of Masonry. In 1833 he became deputy provincial grand master of Lincolnshire. He was dismissed from this post in 1842 after public support for Robert Crucefix, editor of the Review, who had come into conflict with the masonic hierarchy over support for a new charity. It is likely, however, that Oliver's dismissal reflected the opposition of the duke of Sussex, the grand master, who, in an effort to unify the movement, was working to make masonic rites less Christian. Oliver attracted considerable sympathy in the row that ensued, and in 1846 supporters elected him honorary member of the grand lodge of Massachusetts, with the rank of past deputy grand master. Oliver and Crucefix subsequently organized the ancient and accepted rite of freemasons as a Christian body.

In 1854, as his health began to fail, Oliver left his parishes in the hands of curates and retired to Lincoln, where he died on 3 March 1867. He was buried on 7 March with masonic rites in the cemetery attached to the church of St Swithin, Lincoln.   ELIZABETH BAIGENT

Sources R. S. E. Sandbach, Priest and freemason: the life of George Oliver (1993) · C. R. J. Currie and C. P. Lewis, eds., English county histories: a guide (1994) · Venn, Alum. Cant. · DNB
Archives Freemasons' Hall, London
Likenesses J. Harris, lithograph, BM · stipple and line engraving, NPG [see illus.] · three portraits, repro. in Sandbach, Priest and freemason
Wealth at death under £1500: resworn probate, Feb 1868, CGPLA Eng. & Wales (1867)

Oliver, George Augustus. See Conquest, George Augustus (1837–1901).

Oliver, Harry Mander (1855–1918), athletics administrator and journalist, was born at 17 John Street West, Hemingford Road, Islington, on 28 February 1855, one of at least four sons of Henry Oliver (d. 1916) and his wife, Sarah Jane, formerly Mander. His father, a clerk at the Railway Clearing House, was the compiler from 1862 of a Hand Book of the Stations and Sidings on the Railways in the United Kingdom, but was also a keen athlete and one of the original members of the North London rowing club. Oliver was educated from 1867 at Framlingham College, Suffolk, where he made his mark as an athlete; at fourteen he finished fourth in a cross-country race that included boys four and five years older. At eighteen he was a founder member of Spartan Harriers, a club which operated from the Railway inn, Hornsey, and of which his father was president. He subsequently developed into a successful cross-country runner and steeplechaser in senior competition, finishing third in the English cross-country championship in 1878 and winning the steeplechase at the Amateur Athletic Club's meeting in 1879, an event that was effectively the championship of England.

When he moved to Birmingham in May 1876 to take a job with the Birmingham Banking Company, Oliver joined Moseley Harriers. For at least three years he was simultaneously a member of three clubs—the Spartan and Moseley Harriers clubs and Birmingham athletic club—but his chief interest was Moseley. He became the club secretary, retired from running and set out to make Moseley the top cross-country team in the country. This branch of the sport provided the first national inter-club championship in British athletics and Oliver's ambitions for his club were given added impetus when Birchfield Harriers, another Birmingham club, won the prestigious team championship in 1880, the first provincial club to do so. He responded by forming a strong Moseley team that won the title in four successive years from 1881 to 1884. The team included Walter George, William Snook, and other leading runners of the day from outside the Birmingham area. This was criticized as unsporting by Walter Rye, who commented on Oliver:

> Whether his administrative ability operated for the general benefit of the sport is … an open question among those who know anything about the subject, the general impression being that the eagerness with which men are caught up into clubs and imported into crack teams has spoiled the old feeling of *bona fide* competition. (M. Shearman, *Athletics and Football*, 1887, 376)

The organization of athletics in the midlands was developing quickly at this time and Oliver was determined to be involved at all levels. Showing remarkable energy and ambition, he was the first secretary of both the Midland Counties Cross Country Association (from 1879) and the Midland Counties Amateur Athletic Association (from 1880), the moving force behind the formation (in 1883) of the English Cross Country Union, of which he also became secretary, and editor and part owner (1879–1886) of the weekly magazine *Midland Athlete*. He was also official handicapper, timekeeper, and judge at the summer track meetings in the midlands. A man achieving so much power and influence was bound to have detractors and Oliver's chief adversary was W. W. Alexander of Birchfield Harriers. The two men were driven by an ambition to make their respective clubs the most successful in the midlands, and the Moseley–Birchfield rivalry was a feature of the early years of club athletics. 'In constitution, composition and character they were diametrically opposite,' Edward Lawrence Levy later commented:

'Moseley Harriers were a "Sassiety" [*sic*] club, the Birchfield Harriers were typical of the "fierce democracy"' (*Autobiography of an Athlete*, 1913, 119–20.) The likely inference was that Moseley members were 'white collar' and Birchfield's 'blue collar'.

Moseley's standing as the top cross-country club ended in 1885 when George turned professional and Snook joined Birchfield. Oliver's position as the most influential man in midlands athletics came to an end on 7 January 1887, when he went to prison for three months for embezzling money from the bank at which he worked in order to pay debts incurred in financing the *Midland Athlete*. The magazine was discontinued, Moseley Harriers disbanded, and he played no further part in athletics. Oliver, who was married and had children, died at the New Inn, Market Place, Lechlade, Gloucestershire, of which he was proprietor, on 9 March 1918.   WILFRED MORGAN

Sources 'H. M. Oliver', *Sporting Mirror*, 2/7 (1881), 8–11 · *Sport and Play* (10 Jan 1887) · 'A gallant old sportsman', *Sport and Play and Wheel Life*, 578 (29 April 1916) · *Midland Athlete* (1879–86)
Likenesses photograph, Wenlock Olympian Society, Shropshire
Wealth at death £787 17s. 9d.: probate, 11 Sept 1918, CGPLA Eng. & Wales

Oliver, Sir Henry Francis (1865–1965), naval officer, born in Lochside, near Kelso, on 22 January 1865, was the fifth child in a family of seven sons and three daughters of Robert Oliver and his wife, Margaret Strickland. To his father, who came from sound yeoman stock and farmed 2000 acres of good border land, and to his talented mother, he owed a strong constitution and a vigorous approach to life.

Entering the *Britannia* in 1878 Oliver joined a navy in which sail, still dying hard, developed fine seamen. More than once his quick reactions averted disaster. On promotion to lieutenant in 1888 he volunteered for surveying. This service offered better pay and unusual activities abroad, but slender prospects, and in 1894 he returned to general service and qualified as a navigator.

After varied service in cruisers Oliver was promoted to commander in 1899. As navigating commander of the *Majestic*, wearing the flag of Vice-Admiral A. K. Wilson, he became widely known when they took the squadron at high speed from Northern Ireland to the Isles of Scilly in thick fog—a severe test of skill and nerve with the navigational aids then available. He was promoted to captain in June 1903, unusually early for a navigator.

Selected by Sir John Fisher, second sea lord, to improve the training and status of navigation specialists, Oliver established a school first in the *Mercury*, an old cruiser, and then in the old Royal Naval College in Portsmouth Dockyard, with the torpedo gunboat *Dryad* as name ship and floating tender. In 1905 he was appointed MVO, and in 1907, in the new armoured cruiser *Achilles*, led the navy in gunnery skill. Fisher, now first sea lord, summoned him to become his naval assistant, a strenuous post which he retained when Wilson succeeded Fisher in 1910. Returning to sea, Oliver again made gunnery history in the new battleship *Thunderer* in 1912.

Appointed director of naval intelligence and soon promoted to rear-admiral in 1913, Oliver faced increasing responsibilities as war approached. On the outbreak of war, he established wireless interception stations, staffed to decipher enemy messages. In September he preceded Winston Churchill to Antwerp to prevent the advancing enemy from making use of German ships moored there. Working long hours with a small Belgian staff he personally disabled the engines of thirty-eight ships with explosive charges.

He was Churchill's naval secretary for a short while, but on Fisher's return as first sea lord in November Oliver became chief of Admiralty war staff with the acting rank of vice-admiral. In this capacity he favoured the Dardanelles operations, introduced taut-wire measuring gear which greatly improved mine-laying accuracy, and was a general source of sound advice. In June 1916 he was prompted KCB, having been appointed CB in 1913. In January 1917 Sir John Jellicoe assumed the dual role of first sea lord and chief of naval staff and Oliver became deputy chief of naval staff, with board status.

Like many of his senior contemporaries Oliver was temperamentally unable to delegate responsibility, even in detail—a major difficulty in creating an effective naval staff—and his 'extraordinary power of continuous mental toil', remarked on by Churchill, was now becoming strained. He was relieved in January 1918, whereupon he was appointed KCMG. In March he became rear-admiral commanding the 1st battle-cruiser squadron, Grand Fleet, in the *Repulse*, and saw the German fleet surrender off the Firth of Forth in November. When the Grand Fleet dispersed in 1919 he became commander-in-chief, Home Fleet, as a vice-admiral in the *King George V*. The Reserve Fleet was later merged with his force.

In 1920 Oliver received an honorary LLD (Edinburgh) and became second sea lord and chief of naval personnel, which gave him the painful task of reducing the navy list to peacetime needs. The drastic measures taken in 1922 were generally considered as fair and liberal as might be. Promoted to admiral in 1923, in 1924 he declined the Portsmouth command in favour of the Atlantic Fleet, which he commanded with customary efficiency until 1927. He was promoted to admiral of the fleet and to the GCB in 1928 and retired in 1933. He was restored to the active list in 1940 but was denied wartime employment.

Oliver had married in June 1914 Beryl Carnegy White (1882–1972) [*see* Oliver, Dame Beryl], the only daughter of Francis Edward Joseph Carnegy, of Lour in Forfarshire. In the Second World War, Dame Beryl's Red Cross work kept the Olivers much in London, but the admiral regularly visited Scotland for shooting and fishing, his main recreations, together with carpentry. Among his other interests, the foremost was the Royal National Lifeboat Institution, of which he became deputy chairman. The verbal economy which gave him the nickname Dummy (derived presumably from 'Dumby') Oliver did not conceal his solid worth from those who served him. His integrity, justice, foresight, judgement, and seamanship were evident throughout his career. He died at his home, 20 South Eaton Place, London, on 15 October 1965.

A portrait painted by J. Blair Leighton, presented by the officers of the Navigation School to mark his seventieth birthday, was hung in a later *Dryad*, home of the School of Maritime Operations, the successor to Oliver's school.

P. W. BROCK, rev.

Sources *The Times* (18 Oct 1965) • W. James, *A great seaman, Admiral of the Fleet Sir H. F. Oliver* (1956) • A. J. Marder, *Portrait of an admiral: the life and papers of Sir Herbert Richmond* (1952) • personal knowledge (1981) • private information (1981) • *WWW* • *CGPLA Eng. & Wales* (1966)
Archives NMM, corresp. and papers • Royal Naval Museum, Portsmouth, journals | FILM IWM FVA, actuality footage
Likenesses F. Dodd, charcoal and watercolour drawing, 1917, IWM • W. G. Burn-Murdoch, lithograph, c.1923, IWM • W. Stoneman, photograph, 1928, NPG • J. B. Leighton, oils, c.1935, Royal Naval Navigation School, Portsmouth
Wealth at death £15,089 9s.: confirmation, 25 Jan 1965, CCI

Oliver, Isaac (*c*.1565–1617), miniature painter, was apparently the only child of Pierre Olivier, goldsmith of Rouen in Normandy, and his wife, Epiphane. Olivier was among a group of Huguenot refugees from Paris and Rouen, many of them goldsmiths, who were admitted to Geneva on 15 October 1557. Many English protestants had fled to the continent for safety during the reign of the Roman Catholic Queen Mary I (daughter of Henry VIII); one group arrived in Geneva somewhat earlier than the Frenchmen, and in June 1557 were admitted to the English congregation there. Among them was Nicholas Hilliard, then about ten years old, who would soon have met and learned from the French artists. The English exiles returned home in 1559, soon after the accession of the protestant Elizabeth I, and at some unknown date Pierre Olivier returned to Rouen. It was presumably there that he met and married Epiphane (about whom nothing is known), and Isaac was born there. In the eighteenth century George Vertue and Horace Walpole tried, but failed, to establish Oliver's date of birth, and it remains unknown.

Early years in London: instruction by Hilliard The earliest information about the Oliviers' presence in London appears in aliens' returns, which were made at irregular intervals. Two (of 1571) say that they had arrived about three years earlier. Oliver is entered as 'chylde', perhaps indicating a very young one, so that *c*.1565 seems to be a reasonable suggested date of birth. Since he always remained firmly within the large community of immigrant artists in London details of his early life are elusive and have been sketched mainly from incomplete manuscript sources and by way of informed guesswork. From *c*.1568 the Oliviers lodged with a pewterer called Harrison in Fleet Lane, just to the east of the Fleet River, close to its confluence with the Thames, and to Blackfriars, where Isaac was to spend much of his professional life. Pierre no doubt soon sought out Hilliard, whom he had known as a boy in Geneva and who, in 1568, was nearing the end of his apprenticeship. Olivier would have noted the quality of his work, as both limner and goldsmith, and probably then discussed the possibility of instruction for Isaac

Isaac Oliver (*c*.1565–1617), self-portrait, *c*.1590

when he was old enough. They could converse in French, which Hilliard had learned during his continental exile.

The wills, dated 1570 and 1588, of two members of a Netherlandish family from Breda called Matheeusen or Matheeus (soon Anglicized to Mathewe) contain references to the Olivier family. Jacob (James) Matheeusen, painter, settled in Holborn and became a parishioner of St Sepulchre without Newgate. This area was always popular with immigrants; being outside the city wall it escaped the jurisdiction of the authorities and it provided more space for those who needed studios and workshops. On 12 June 1562 Matheeusen became a denizen, and by 1564 he was living in Seacoal Lane. He would have been buried at St Sepulchre's and his only son, Pieter, baptized there. Dates are unknown since the early registers were lost in the great fire of 1666. Pieter was very young when his father died. He had hoped to become an artist but in 1588, when he was apparently lodging in the city parish of St Helen, Bishopsgate, he became seriously ill. He made his will on 17 October and was buried at St Helen's on 6 November. He was a youth of means, having inherited property in Breda from his father, and he left sums ranging from £3 to £10 to many Dutch relatives and friends who had looked after him; his cousin Adrian Van Son, painter to James VI of Scotland, was to have three 'pictures', probably miniatures, of Pieter's late parents and himself (his two sisters had predeceased him). There were also bequests of £3 each to 'Isac Olivier' and his mother, Epiphane (Pierre is not mentioned and had presumably died); his 'bookes of Artes and that which concerneth the

same arte' were left to 'my twoe fellowes Isac Olivyer and Rouland Lacq'. The will seems to imply that the three young men were still being instructed by Hilliard in the autumn of 1588. 'Rouland Lacq' (Rowland Lockey) certainly was; he had started an eight-year apprenticeship under Hilliard on 29 September 1581 and would probably have become free some time in 1589. By sore mischance the Goldsmiths' court minute book covering 1579 to 1592, which might have answered some questions, was lost in a fire—not that of 1666, which badly damaged the company's hall, but a much smaller one in 1681, when repair work was going on. The fragments of information now assembled establish that the three young 'fellows' had been very near neighbours from boyhood. Pieter was born in Seacoal Lane *c*.1569 (Seacoal Lane ran down to Fleet Lane, where the Oliviers lodged from *c*.1568) and Rowland was born *c*.1567 at the south end of Fleet Lane, the only part of it within his family parish of St Bride, Fleet Street, for which registers do not survive so far back.

Maturity: rival to Hilliard Hilliard and his celebrated pupil Isaac Oliver probably began their professional careers at the age of about twenty-two. Oliver's first known portrait miniature is of a twenty-year-old middle-class woman, and is of unusual three-quarters length; it looks experimental and is dated 1587. In 1588 Oliver emerged as an assured and accomplished artist, with miniatures *A Youth Aged 19* (priv. coll.), *A Man of 71* (AM Oxf.), and of a fifty-nine-year-old Dutchman, now known to be Colonel Diederik Sonoy (Royal Collection, the Netherlands). Oliver was always responsive to Netherlandish, French, and Italian influences and it has sometimes been suggested that he had returned to the continent during his youth and that the Sonoy miniature was done there. However, there is compelling evidence that Sonoy sat for him in London. Sonoy was a prominent protestant and anglophile, and in 1588 he was permitted to take refuge in England from the Spanish Netherlands. A letter from Sir William Russell, governor of Flushing, commending him to the queen's principal secretary, Sir Francis Walsingham, is endorsed '17 October 1588 … by Colonel Sonoy', meaning that he delivered it himself (state papers, SP 84/27/122*v*, Netherlands). Hilliard had spent two years and more in Geneva as a boy and two years in France in the 1570s but there is as yet no hard evidence either way about Oliver. Unlike Hilliard he did not practise as a jeweller, goldsmith, or engraver; he did do a number of drawings but he could have learnt techniques and styles from members of the immigrant community in London.

Oliver continued to do small oval portrait miniatures from time to time during his career but he employed the techniques learnt from Hilliard in very different ways. Hilliard favoured daylight for his sitter and was against shadowing the face; if necessary, he used a deeper tone of the same basic flesh colour—'limning is but a shadowing of the same colour your ground is of', as he writes in his *Treatise Concerning the Arte of Limning* (1981, p. 7). Oliver chose a restricted source of light, casting deep shadows, for which he used darker pigments. In 1590 he did a fine limning *Unknown Man, Aged 27* (V&A); similar in handling, and probably of about the same date, is a self-portrait in the Royal Collection, showing the artist at three-quarters length, bearded and wearing a tall hat. Limnings of girls aged four and five (V&A), dated 1590, display Oliver's marked talent, rare at the time, for depicting young children as sentient humans rather than as wooden dolls. During the decade his renown steadily increased and with it the status of the patrons he could attract. His talent and comparative youth appealed to the avant-garde. Robert Devereux, second earl of Essex, who had succeeded Lord Leicester as the queen's favourite, sought out the younger man in 1596 on his return from the expedition to Cadiz. He had grown a beard during his absence; a fine limning by Oliver resulted (Royal Collection) and was much copied. A miniature of an unidentified Sir Arundel Talbot (V&A) provides evidence that Oliver visited Italy in the same year; on the reverse he inscribed: '13. Magio. 1596./In Venetia./Fecit m. Isacq Oliŭiero/Francese' with his monogram (resembling the Greek phi). Larger miniatures include one often called *Unknown Melancholy Young Man* (Royal Collection), at one time wrongly identified as of Sir Philip Sidney, and a striking work, dated 1598, *The Three Brothers Browne* (priv. coll.), portraying the grandsons of the first Viscount Montague, dressed identically in black and with arms entwined.

Oliver benefited at this period from an absence of competition; Queen Elizabeth had never liked the second great seal of the realm, designed by Hilliard, which came into use in 1586, and in 1591 she required him to try again. This caused Hilliard much trouble and expense—ultimately to no avail—and on 2 June 1599 he told Sir Robert Cecil that only one instalment of a £40 annuity, promised in 1591, had been paid: 'throughe missing of so many sutes [commissions] as I have had Wthin this 8. yeres', he wrote, he was now in 'great extremes' (Cecil MSS, Hatfield House, Hertfordshire, 70/76). A striking unfinished and undated limning of the queen (V&A) was probably intended for the guidance of foreign engravers; it is an uncompromising portrayal of an ageing woman and is confidently attributed to Isaac Oliver. Hilliard's monopoly status as the sovereign's limner was reaffirmed by warrant dated 17 August 1599, probably thanks to pressure from Cecil; it is very difficult to believe that Elizabeth would actually have granted a sitting to anyone else. It has been suggested that the unfinished limning of her was a copy done from a Hilliard.

First and second wives and son Peter Isaac Oliver married three times. His first wife, known only as Elizabeth, was buried, aged twenty-eight, at St Peter, Cornhill (near the French church in Threadneedle Street), on 6 September 1599. It was common practice for a man to marry soon after completing an apprenticeship or other training and Oliver may well have married towards the end of 1588, when Elizabeth would have been seventeen or eighteen, at that time a popular age for brides. Thus their son Peter *Oliver could have been born in 1589. If Elizabeth was French, as is probable, the marriage would have been at the French church, for which no registers survive before 1600, and Peter would have been baptized there (as was

Isaac's eldest son by his third marriage, also to a young bride of seventeen).

On 9 February 1602, at the Dutch church, Austin Friars, Oliver married, second, Sara Gheeraerts (*bap.* 1575, *d.* 1605), thereby involving himself with the intricate network of leading families of portrait painters from the Netherlands: specifically, Gheeraerts from Bruges and de Critz from Antwerp. Sara had been baptized at the Dutch church on 12 May 1575 and was a daughter of the portrait painter Marcus Gheeraerts I, who had arrived in London from Bruges in 1567–8; on 9 September 1571, at the same church, Gheeraerts had married, as his second wife, Susanna de Critz, elder sister of John de Critz, who became serjeant-painter at court in 1605. Sara Oliver was half-sister to Marcus Gheeraerts II, the most fashionable portrait painter in England from *c.*1590; he was a son—born in Bruges—of Marcus Gheeraerts I and his first wife. To add to the complexities Isaac Oliver became briefly a brother-in-law of the sculptor Maximilian Colt, from Arras in northern France; Colt married Sara Oliver's younger sister Susanna Gheeraerts in 1604 and was appointed master sculptor at court in 1608.

Limner to Queen Anne of Denmark Nicholas Hilliard retained the monopoly as sovereign's limner on the accession of King James VI of Scotland to the English throne in 1603. His queen, Anne of Denmark—who was genuinely interested in the visual arts—soon had her own household at Somerset House in the Strand (renamed Denmark House during her lifetime); on 22 June 1605 she appointed Isaac Oliver her limner, again at £40 a year. Her elder son, Prince Henry, a precocious and gifted youth, began to employ Oliver in 1608, when he was only fourteen, but these moves should not be seen as a rejection of Hilliard; his official appointment was to the monarch, and he and his assistants (including his son Laurence Hilliard) were fully engaged in providing portrait miniatures and gold presentation medals. It has to be remembered, too, that Hilliard reached the then advanced age of sixty about 1607.

The Olivers had no children and, a month after Isaac's royal appointment, Sara died; she was buried on 27 July 1605 at St Anne Blackfriars. The couple had probably settled in the parish at their marriage. St Anne's still enjoyed certain privileges as a 'precinct' or 'liberty', surviving from the days of its monastic status, and it was much favoured by successful immigrant artists with court connections. It was easy to travel by water from Blackfriars Stairs, upstream to Westminster or downstream to Greenwich Palace. (Van Dyck spent his last years in a house on the riverbank with a garden.)

Third marriage In 1606 Isaac Oliver married for the third and last time; his bride, Elizabeth (*bap.* 1589, *d.* 1628x40), was a daughter of Jacques or James Harden or Harding, a court flautist and composer of French origin. The Hardings were parishioners of Holy Trinity Minories near the Tower of London, and also had a country place at the then fashionable riverside village of Isleworth. Eight children of James Harding and his wife, Ann, were baptized at the

Minories between 1579 and 1591; most of them were very shortlived. The seventh, Elizabeth, survived to become the wife of Isaac Oliver. (The ninth and last, Anne, future wife of Isaac's eldest son, Peter, was baptized at Isleworth on 11 April 1593; the family had probably moved out of London because of the major outbreak of plague in 1592–4.) All Saints, Isleworth, and its registers were badly damaged in a fire in 1943 but it is just possible to make out that 'Isaac Oliver and Elizabeth Hardinge' were married on 23 (or 29) July 1606. A charmingly informal limning of Elizabeth by her husband (priv. coll.), probably a family possession, portrays her half smiling; she wears a winged cap, a white smock with the collar open and turned down, and a jacket embroidered with flowers.

It must now have become clear to Oliver that his future lay in England, and at the end of 1606—on 6 December—he secured the right of denization, thirty-eight years after his arrival as a child. Four sons and two daughters of Isaac and Elizabeth were baptized at Blackfriars between 1608 and 1617, and their grandmother Epiphane was buried there on 6 March 1610. Two sons survived: the first, James—baptized at Blackfriars on 18 December 1608 and on the following 8 January at the French church—married Alice Thurston on 25 November 1634, and they had at least two sons, William (*b.* 1635) and John (*b.* 1636). Isaac junior, baptized on 11 December 1610, was still living in 1672 in the house at Isleworth of his aunt Anne, Peter's widow, and she made careful provision for him in her will.

Isaac Oliver did many limnings of Queen Anne of Denmark, including a profile in masque costume (Royal Collection); she was a leading promoter of these lavish court entertainments, in which she and her ladies sometimes took part. The main focus was on the heir to the throne, Prince Henry, who was well on the way to becoming a major patron of the arts at his untimely death in November 1612, aged eighteen. He had his household at St James's Palace, to which Oliver was attached; one of his finest limnings portrays the prince in gilt armour against a background of an encampment (Royal Collection), of which many copies and variants were produced. Roy Strong suggests a link with his appearance as a chivalric champion in the court entertainment *The Barriers*, put on in 1610, the year of Henry's creation as prince of Wales. 'Mr Isacke' attended the prince's funeral on 7 December 1612.

In general Oliver's works show a remarkable diversity of subjects and styles. He was responsive to the dictates of his patrons; in 1616, the year before his death, he did both a small, austere oval of John Donne (Royal Collection), poet and theologian, in the style of the early 1590s, and a large, highly-coloured full-length of Richard Sackville, third earl of Dorset (V&A), every detail of his extravagant dress painstakingly portrayed. There is no certainty about identities of sitters in two fine and unusually large, 5 inch diameter roundels of exquisitely dressed ladies, and suggested dates have ranged from 1595 to 1613. One (Fitzwilliam Museum, Cambridge) is of a lady, formerly called 'Lucy Harington, countess of Bedford'; the other is of a lady, formerly called 'Frances Howard, countess of Essex and Somerset' (V&A). Also impossible to date are a number of complex limnings and drawings ranging from an erotic *Nymphs and Satyrs* (Royal Collection) to religious subjects. The most ambitious limning, *Entombment*, or *Burial of Christ*, was completed by Peter Oliver after his father's death; a carefully finished preliminary drawing in ink and black chalk is in the British Museum.

Oliver probably died at the end of September 1617, since he was buried at St Anne Blackfriars on 2 October. He bequeathed to Peter Oliver all his finished and unfinished drawings, and his unfinished limnings—historical scenes and narratives as well as portraits. St Anne Blackfriars and all its contents, including the artist's monument and marble bust, were destroyed in the fire of 1666.

Elizabeth Oliver married, second, Pierce Morgan, a gentleman of Blackfriars and Isleworth and a freeman of the premier city livery company, the Mercers. He was a wealthy widower with five daughters, and he and Elizabeth had a sixth, called Jane; a seventh, Katherine, was baptized at Blackfriars on 6 April 1628 and buried six days later. Elizabeth predeceased her husband and was presumably buried at Isleworth, a fact obliterated in the fire of 1943.

A licence was secured on 30 May 1636 for Jane, daughter of Pierce and Elizabeth, to be married to a young nephew of Pierce, and the marriage took place at Twickenham on 1 June. This was evidently a close and affectionate family group, and Pierce Morgan—who was buried at Blackfriars on 9 April 1640—left a will with many references to Olivers. He had built a 'new brick howse' at Isleworth, and he bequeathed to his daughter Jane a 'little dwelling house' there, with grounds, orchards, stable, and coach house; also two pictures at the family home in Blackfriars of her grandfather and grandmother, presumably Isaac Oliver's in-laws, the Hardings. Morgan bequeathed to his 'sonne in law [stepson] Mr Isaack Oliver his Fathers picture in liewe of a silver Cupp he had given him by his godfather or one of his Witnesses … this being his desire' (Edmond, *Walpole Society*, 47.81–3 and pedigree 74).

A major exhibition, entitled 'Nicholas Hilliard and Isaac Oliver', was mounted at the Victoria and Albert Museum, London, in 1947, marking the quatercentenary of Hilliard's probable date of birth; one of its main aims was to establish a clear line of demarcation between the works of the two men, which had become much confused. They were brilliantly gifted but utterly different—Hilliard English, Oliver determinedly French (although he spent most of his life in England)—and they were divided in age by almost a generation. Hilliard believed that the portrait miniature was the highest form of art, although he also practised as a goldsmith, engraver, jeweller, and calligrapher; Oliver used limning for a much wider range of subjects and, unlike Hilliard, was a prolific draughtsman. Judging from the self-portraits each had a good conceit of himself. Oliver left no writings so there is nothing to set beside Hilliard's remarkably self-revealing *Treatise*.

MARY EDMOND

Sources M. Edmond, 'Limners and picturemakers', *Walpole Society*, 47 (1978–80), 60–242, esp. 74, 86, 135, 151 [*pedigrees*; see pt I for

Olivers, their circle etc., pt III for other connections] · M. Edmond, 'An Isaac Oliver sitter identified', *Burlington Magazine*, 124 (1982), 496–501 · M. Edmond, *Hilliard & Oliver* (1983) · E. Auerbach, *Nicholas Hilliard* (1961), 232–54 · G. Reynolds, *Nicholas Hilliard and Isaac Oliver: an exhibition to commemorate the 400th anniversary of the birth of Nicholas Hilliard* (1947) [exhibition catalogue, V&A, 1947] · G. Reynolds, *Nicholas Hilliard and Isaac Oliver: an exhibition to commemorate the 400th anniversary of the birth of Nicholas Hilliard*, 2nd edn (1971) [exhibition catalogue, V&A, 1947] · G. Reynolds, *English portrait miniatures* (1952); rev. edn (1988), 21–9 · G. Reynolds, 'Oliver (1) Isaac Oliver', *The dictionary of art*, ed. J. Turner (1996) · J. Murdoch and others, *The English miniature* (1981) · R. Strong and V. J. Murrell, *Artists of the Tudor court: the portrait miniature rediscovered, 1520–1620* (1983) [exhibition catalogue, V&A, 9 July – 6 Nov 1983] · R. Strong, *The English Renaissance miniature* (1983) · K. Hearn, ed., *Dynasties: painting in Tudor and Jacobean England, 1530–1630* (1995) [exhibition catalogue, Tate Gallery, London, 12 Oct 1995 – 7 Jan 1996] · C. Lloyd and V. Remington, *Masterpieces in little* (1996), 80–95 [exhibition catalogue, Queen's Gallery, Buckingham Palace, 23 July – 5 Oct 1997] · James Matheeusen will, PRO, PROB 11/52/27 · Pieter Mattheus will, PRO, PROB 11/73/15 · Rowland Lockey will, 1616, PRO, PROB 11/127/26 [*Walpole Society*, 47.95–7] · will, PRO, PROB 11/130/93; PROB 10/346 · Pierce Morgan will, PRO, PROB 11/183/65 [*Walpole Society*, 47.81–3] · will, LMA, AM/PW/1672/38 [Anne Oliver; ref. to Isaac Oliver's surviving son, Isaac Jr., *Walpole Society*, 47.93–5] · G. Reynolds, *The sixteenth- and seventeenth-century miniatures in the collection of her majesty the queen* (1999), 84–101 · parish register, St Peter Cornhill, GL, MS 8820 [repr. in Harleian Society, 1, 149] · parish registers, Bishopsgate, St Helen and St Ann Blackfriars, GL, MSS 4508/1; 4509/1; 4510/1 [baptism, marriage, and burial; repr. in Harleian Society, 31, 256] · parish register, Holy Trinity Minories, GL, MS 9238 · parish register, All Saints Isleworth, Hounslow Public Library [remains salvaged from fire] · parish register, Dutch church, Austin Friars, 1571–1601 and 1602–1874, GL, MSS 7381 and 7382 [baptism and marriage; W. J. C. Moens' printed transcripts (1884) not always accurate] · *Huguenot Society* (*Quarto series*), vol. 18 (denizations, England, 1603–1700), 11; in Fleet Lane, 10.1.425, 10.2.8. for James Matheeusen, vol. 8, 163 & 10.3.340) (vol. 10 – 3 pts & index – covers aliens resident in London, Henry VIII to James I.) vol. 9, French church regs., 1600–1636 · Goldsmiths' Company, MS records, Goldsmiths' Hall, London

Likenesses I. Oliver, self-portrait, miniature, *c*.1590, NPG [*see illus.*] · H. Hondius, line engraving (after I. Oliver), BM, NPG · I. Oliver, self-portrait, miniature, Royal Collection · I. Oliver, self-portrait, miniature, V&A

Wealth at death exact sum unknown; works bequeathed to son: will, proved 30 Oct 1617, PRO, PROB 11/130/93

Oliver, John (*d.* 1552), civil lawyer, was sometimes called 'Oliver alias Smith'. His birth date, family, and early education are unknown, but he took the Oxford degrees of BCL on 30 June 1516, BCnL on 23 June 1522, and DCL on 11 October 1522. He probably began his collection of ecclesiastical benefices with the prebend of Norton, Herefordshire, in 1512: some benefices were brief staging posts, but he was vicar of Ross in Herefordshire (1520–49), rector of Pembridge in Herefordshire (1527–51), vicar of Minster in Kent (1528–46), and prebendary of Teynton Regis in Salisbury diocese from 1531 until his death. On 22 April 1533 he was appointed dean of King Henry VIII College in Oxford, but on 20 May 1545 he signed the surrender of the college prior to its refoundation as Christ Church, in return for a pension of £70 per annum. He was sometimes referred to as a clerk or chaplain, but he seems never to have been ordained priest: from 1536 he was given a series of three-year dispensations to hold benefices in plurality without taking holy orders.

Oliver was a busy civil lawyer: a member of Doctors' Commons from 1522, master in chancery by February 1532, and a judge-delegate in the admiralty court by 1539. He was often employed on official business. He served as one of Wolsey's commissaries (1527–9), as collector of the clerical subsidy for the province of York in 1531, and as one of Henry VIII's proctors in the Aragon divorce suit (1531–3). In 1533–5 he sat with other senior lawyers on an informal committee advising the king and Thomas Cromwell on the break with Rome and the relationship between canon and common law. He seems not to have been used on sensitive business between 1535 and 1540, which suggests that Cromwell may have disapproved of him. In 1540 he was involved in the annulment of the king's marriage to Anne of Cleves, and thereafter was commissioned to deal with a number of lesser marriage disputes; on 21 January 1543 he was elected prolocutor of the lower house of the Canterbury convocation, and in 1543 he took part in various heresy investigations relating to the prebendaries' plot against Archbishop Cranmer. As a master in chancery he was appointed to commissions to determine cases while the chancellor was ill or otherwise occupied in October 1544, February 1547, August 1548, October 1551, and January 1552.

Oliver seems to have been favoured by Richard, Lord Rich, chancellor from 1547 to 1551, and he sat on a number of major legal commissions: early in 1550 he was one of those who heard Bishop Bonner's appeal against deprivation, on 18 January 1551 he was appointed to a commission against heresy, and on 27 September 1551 he was named on the commission to hear the charges against bishops Day and Heath. On 12 December 1550 he was put on the commission which tried and deprived Bishop Gardiner; he was the most assiduous of the judges, missing only one out of twenty-two sessions and sitting alone on three occasions. On 20 May 1551 Oliver was appointed to serve with the marquess of Northampton on a special embassy to France to conclude an alliance and seek a royal wife for Edward VI; he brought back some gilt standing cups as souvenirs, and in his will bequeathed one of them to Lord Chancellor Goodrich.

Oliver died in London in 1552; he had made his will on 27 May, and it was proved on 3 July. It was the testament of a prosperous, bachelor lawyer with mildly conservative views. He made bequests to the inmates of all the London prisons and the Bedlam (Bethlem) Hospital, to the widows and orphans of the parishes where he had been incumbent longest, to his poor neighbours in Westminster, to his godchildren, to various servants and tradesmen, and to the politicians and lawyers with whom he had worked: three chancellors, the chief justice of common pleas, a justice of king's bench, and half a dozen civil lawyers. He charged his executors 'in the way of charity, to do for me therein as they would be done for themselves afore Almighty God in that behalf' (PRO, PROB 11/35, fol. 129*v*), which probably means he expected them to seek prayers for his soul. Oliver was a minor agent of the Reformation in England, but it looks as if he did not like it.

CHRISTOPHER HAIGH

Sources Emden, *Oxf.*, 4.425 · *LP Henry VIII* · *CSP dom.*, rev. edn, 1547–53 · *CPR*, 1547–53 · *CSP for.*, 1547–53 · J. Strype, *Ecclesiastical memorials*, 3 vols. (1822) · D. S. Chambers, ed., *Faculty office registers, 1534–1549* (1966) · will, PRO, PROB 11/35, sig. 17 · A. T. Bannister, ed., *Registrum Caroli Bothe, episcopi Herefordensis*, CYS, 28 (1921) · *The acts and monuments of John Foxe*, ed. S. R. Cattley, 8 vols. (1837–41) · R. G. Marsden, ed., *Select pleas in the court of admiralty*, 2, SeldS, 11 (1897) · *Fasti Angl., 1300–1541*, [Hereford] · *Fasti Angl., 1300–1541*, [Salisbury] · *Fasti Angl., 1300–1541*, [Introduction] · *Reg. Oxf.*, 1.99
Wealth at death probably substantial; many bequests

Oliver, John (1600/01–1661), college head, was possibly born in Kent, although his father may have been the John Oliver (d. *c*.1627) who was rector of Little Laver in Essex from April 1599 to May 1607, for it was to this rectory that Oliver himself was later presented. He matriculated from Merton College, Oxford, on 26 January 1616 aged fifteen, graduated BA from Magdalen in 1619, became a fellow in 1621, proceeded MA in 1622, and became tutor to Edward Hyde, later earl of Clarendon. He was incorporated MA at Cambridge in 1626, and was awarded the Oxford degree of BD in 1631. That year he was instituted to Eastmanstead Chenies, Buckinghamshire, on the presentation of the earl of Bedford, and between 1632 and 1638 he held Broughton Poges, Oxfordshire.

Oliver remained a fellow of Magdalen until about 1639, and it was probably towards the end of his tenure that 'his eminence in learning, and orthodox principles in religion being conspicuous', he was appointed a domestic chaplain to Archbishop William Laud (Wood, *Ath. Oxon.: Fasti*, 1.510). Gilbert Burnet stated that Laud sponsored his promotion in the church, and about this time more lucrative benefices came into Oliver's possession. In 1637 he acquired Little Laver, Essex, from 1638 to 1639 he was rector of Monks Eleigh, Suffolk, and in 1639 of Adisham in Kent. Also in 1639 he was awarded his doctorate. Collated on 19 August 1638 and installed on 21 September as canon of the twelfth prebend of Winchester Cathedral, he held the dignity for the next twenty-three years, though for most of that period its income was denied him. On 25 September 1640 Laud wrote from Lambeth to the earl of Pembroke recommending him for a chaplaincy-in-ordinary to the king, vacant through the death of Thomas Jackson. Oliver had 'preached twice to his Majesty with great approbation. I will be answerable for him every way' (*Works*, 6.583). Oliver was by this time well acquainted with Michael Oldsworth, secretary to Pembroke in his post of earl chamberlain. Five years later Laud bequeathed a watch to John Oliver.

On 28 May 1644, following the resignation of Accepted Frewen on 11 May, Oliver, nominated by all the fellows, and with Laud's backing, was admitted to the presidency of Magdalen College, Oxford. The day following, as Charles and his entourage watched from Magdalen tower on the eastern extremity of the city, the army of the earl of Essex moved towards them, drawing up on Bullingdon Green. The attack on Oxford was delayed for over two years, but when it came the fall of the royalists' military headquarters threatened also their control of the university. In May 1647 Oliver was one of the delegates elected by

the university convocation which sought to delay on legal and procedural grounds the purge expected in the wake of the parliamentary visitors, but on 14 December 1647 the committee of the two houses declared several university figures, including the vice-chancellor and John Oliver, guilty of a 'high contempt of authority of Parliament'. On 6 January 1648 they declared Oliver's removal from his place as president, and on 17 March, as he had not removed, sent an order demanding obedience on pain of arrest. By this time, however, Oliver had left Oxford, though retaining the keys to the presidential lodgings. On 12 April the earl of Pembroke arrived in the city; the doors of Magdalen were broken down and John Wilkinson, appointee of the visitors, was admitted as president of the college.

Nothing is certainly known about Oliver's activities during the 1650s, but he may have been the John Oliver who was vicar of St Margaret at Cliffe in Kent from 1655 to 1658. After the Restoration Oliver was readmitted to his prebend of Winchester. On 7 July 1660, through the influence of Edward Hyde, Oliver received the royal patent for the deanery of Worcester, subscribing to the articles before his installation on 12 September 1660. Oliver's chief concern in that year, however, was to reclaim his place as president at Magdalen. He petitioned as early as 18 May 1660, and was readmitted soon after. Named to two commissions of inquiry set up to visit the university, he appears not to have been very active in either. The restoration to their places at Magdalen of all living unmarried fellows and scholars led to tensions between this group and the Independent and presbyterian members who continued in residence. Oliver made it his business to try to keep the peace, and seems to have enjoyed considerable success. But the work seems not to have been to his taste. 'This most learned, meek, and pious person', reports Wood, 'was strangely desirous to leave this world, though few alive had then such temptations to stay in it' (Wood, *Ath. Oxon.: Fasti*, 1.510). Oliver died on 27 October 1661 and was buried in Magdalen College chapel three days later; the funeral sermon was preached by Edmund Diggle. Oliver left money to the poor of several Oxfordshire and Kentish parishes and bequests for maintenance to the cathedrals of Worcester and St Paul's and Westminster Abbey.

STEPHEN WRIGHT

Sources J. R. Bloxam, *A register of the presidents, fellows … of Saint Mary Magdalen College*, 8 vols. (1853–85) · H. A. Wilson, *Magdalen* (1899) · *Walker rev.* · G. Harriss, 'A loyal but troublesome college, 1458–1672', *Magdalen College and the crown: essays for the tercentenary of the restoration of the college, 1688*, ed. L. Brockliss, G. Harriss, and A. Macintyre (1988), 9–30 · Foster, *Alum. Oxon.* · J. Walker, *An attempt towards recovering an account of the numbers and sufferings of the clergy of the Church of England*, 2 pts in 1 (1714) · Wood, *Ath. Oxon.: Fasti* (1815), 1.510 · *The works of the most reverend father in God, William Laud*, ed. J. Bliss and W. Scott, 7 vols. (1847–60) · *Fasti Angl., 1541–1857*, [Canterbury] · will, PRO, PROB 11/306, fols. 246–7 · R. Newcourt, *Repertorium ecclesiasticum parochiale Londinense*, 1 (1708) · J. C. C. Smith, *Some additions to Newcourt's Repertorium*, vol. II (1899) · W. D. Macray, *A register of the members of St Mary Magdalen College, Oxford*, 8 vols. (1894–1915), vol. 3, p. iii · BL, Lansdowne MS 986, fol. 1

Oliver, John (1616/17–1701), glass painter and master mason, who was born presumably in London, was supposed to have been related to the miniature painters Isaac and Peter Oliver and to John Oliver, master mason to James I, but there is no known evidence to support this assertion recorded in Redgrave (Redgrave, *Artists*, 301). A panel formerly at Christ Church, Oxford, *St Peter Delivered from Prison* (lost), inscribed 'J. Oliver, aetat. suae lxxxiv, anno 1700', establishes the year of his birth as 1616 or 1617.

Glass painting appears to have been Oliver's trade, as a small legacy to the Glaziers' Company in his will suggests, and most of his glass seems to have been heraldic work, a feature typical of post-Restoration England. The extant window at Northill, Bedfordshire (*c*.1664), showing the arms of the Grocers' Company, with royal arms, is on a monumental scale, painted in enamel colours, similar to the works of Henry Gyles. Other recorded works include sundials at the Northill rectory and Lambeth Palace and armorial panels at Petworth, Sussex (lost?). Oliver also held the office of master mason to the crown from 1685/6. He was involved as a surveyor in the rebuilding of the City of London from 1667. He is frequently mentioned in connection with the rebuilding of the City's churches. He seems to have been resident in the parish of St Michael Queenhithe. Most of his architectural works appear to have been carried out for City companies (for example the Mercers' hall and chapel, after 1668) and Christ's Hospital (from 1673), of which he was a governor.

Oliver was also active as a cartographer and was the author of *A mapp of the cityes of London & Westminster & burrough of Southwark, with their suburbs as it is now rebuilt since the late dreadfull fire* (*c*.1680). He is recorded to have been in possession of Inigo Jones's papers and drawings (*Brief Lives*, 2.10). He died, presumably in London, before 18 November 1701, when his will was proved. In this he made provision for his wife, Susanna, his daughter Grace Shaw, and his son-in-law George Seagood and for his burial in St Paul's Cathedral. He also left a small legacy to the Glaziers' Company, and money for an annual dinner of roast meat for the boys of Christ's Hospital.

L. H. CUST, *rev.* ALEXANDER KOLLER

Sources Colvin, *Archs.* · Redgrave, *Artists* · P. Cowen, *A guide to stained glass in Britain* (1985) · 'A chronological list of English glass-paintings', *Journal of the British Society of Master-Glass-Painters*, 6 (1935–6), 56, 165 · Vertue, *Note books*, 2.60 · D. Knoop and G. P. Jones, *The London mason in the seventeenth century* (1938), 6 · *Brief lives, chiefly of contemporaries, set down by John Aubrey, between the years 1669 and 1696*, ed. A. Clark, 2 (1898), 10 · will, PRO, PROB 11/462, sig. 157
Likenesses W. Faithorne, crayon
Wealth at death property in Ironmonger Lane and other City locations: will, PRO, PROB 11/462, sig. 157

Oliver, John [*pseud.* Cerddi Cystudd] (**1838–1866**), Welsh-language poet, the son of John Oliver and his wife, Sarah Thomas, was born on 7 November 1838 at Whitehall, Llanfynydd, a small village in Carmarthenshire, where his parents kept a shop. He spent seven years (1843–50) at the village school and nearly four at a Carmarthen school. Before

he was sixteen he was admitted to the Presbyterian college in the same town. Here he made great progress with the regular studies, and read widely, on his own account, in English and German literature. He was soon able to preach with equal facility in Welsh and English. He left college in his twenty-first year, and abandoned an intention of continuing his studies at Glasgow, owing to failing health.

Subsequently Oliver preached occasionally and devoted himself to Welsh poetry. Most of his Welsh poems were written during his enforced retirement. His most ambitious poem is 'Dafydd, ty wysog yr ar glwydd' ('David, the Prince of the Lord'). Other long poems are 'Prydferthwchanian' ('The Beauties of Nature'), 'Mab y weddw o Nain' ('The Widow of Nain'), and 'Drylliad y "royal charter"' ('The Wreck of the Royal Charter'), all showing great promise. His shorter poems, however, are his best, particularly 'Myfyrdod', a meditation or soliloquy. Of his English poems, 'Life' and 'When I die' can be singled out for attention but, being his earliest productions, they are inferior to his Welsh poems.

Oliver died on 24 June 1866 at Mountpleasant, Llanfynydd, of consumption, and his remains were interred in the parish churchyard of Llanfynydd, of which he had sung so sweetly. In 1867 his collected works (Welsh and English) were published under the name Cerddi Cystudd by his brother, the Revd Henry Oliver.

R. M. J. JONES, *rev.* CLARE L. TAYLOR

Sources *Cerddi Cystudd, sef gweddillion barddonol y diweddar John Oliver o Lanfynydd, ynghyd a byr-gofiant gan ei frawd, H. Oliver* (1867) · b. cert. · d. cert.
Likenesses portrait, repro. in *Cerddi Cystudd* · vignetted bust, PRO

Oliver, Martha Cranmer [Pattie] (**1834–1880**), actress, the daughter of John Oliver, a scene painter, was born at Salisbury, and appeared on the stage there when she was only six years old. Here and at Southampton her performances of children's parts attracted attention. In 1847 she made her London début under Mary Warner's management at the Marylebone Theatre. Madame Vestris then employed her at the Lyceum from 1849 to 1855. In 1855 she went to Drury Lane, where on 10 October she played Matilda in *Married for Money* and on 4 September 1856 Celia in *As You Like It*. Her performance as Helen in Sheridan Knowles's *The Hunchback* won such praise from the critics that J. B. Buckstone offered her an engagement at the Haymarket, where she was seen in Francis Talfourd's burlesque *Atalanta* on 14 April 1857. Having accepted an offer from Ada Swanborough, she became the leading actress in comedy and burlesque for several seasons at the Strand Theatre, where her parts included Amy Robsart in *Ye Queen, ye Earl, and ye Maiden* (December 1858), Pauline in H. J. Byron's burlesque *The Lady of Lyons* (June 1859), and the Prince in Byron's burlesque *Cinderella* (December 1860). On E. A. Sothern's first appearance as Lord Dundreary in London, at the Haymarket (16 November 1861), she played Mary Meredith in Tom Taylor's *Our American Cousin*. In April 1863

Martha Cranmer Oliver (1834–1880), by Herbert Watkins, late 1850s

she took the title role in Byron's burlesque *Beautiful Haidee* at the Princess's.

Pattie Oliver became manager of the New Royalty Theatre on 31 March 1866 and opened with a revival of Taylor's *The Ticket-of-Leave Man* and Robert Reece's burlesque *Ulf the Minstrel*. In a clever and successful piece by H. T. Craven, entitled *Meg's Diversion*, which was produced on 17 October, she acted Meg, the author played Jasper Pidgeon, and F. Dewar took the part of Roland. On 29 November 1866 she put on the stage F. C. Burnand's burlesque *The Latest Edition of Black-Eyed Susan, or, The Little Bill that was Taken Up*. The piece failed to please the critics, but succeeded with audiences, and had an unprecedented run of some 400 performances; on its production at the Royalty on 23 September 1868, it was said that Pattie Oliver had sung *Pretty See-usan, Don't Say No* no fewer than 1775 times. During the run of this burlesque she produced as a first piece Andrew Halliday's drama *Daddy Gray* (February 1868), and on 26 November 1868 a serio-comic drama by the same author entitled *The Loving Cup*. Other burlesques were introduced with less success.

On 3 March 1870 *Black-Eyed Susan* was revived; the last night of Pattie Oliver's lesseeship was 30 April 1870 when the burlesque was given for the 490th time. After this period she was seldom seen on the stage. She married by licence at the register office, Marylebone, on 26 December 1876, William Charles Phillips, an auctioneer aged thirty-one, the son of the auctioneer William Phillips of Bond

Street, London. She was a general favourite with the public, and gave liberal aid to the aged and unfortunate members of her profession. She died at her home, 5 Grove End Road, St John's Wood, London, on 20 December 1880.

G. C. BOASE, *rev.* J. GILLILAND

Sources *The life and reminiscences of E. L. Blanchard, with notes from the diary of Wm. Blanchard*, ed. C. W. Scott and C. Howard, 2 vols. (1891) · Boase, *Mod. Eng. biog.* · *The Players*, 1 (1860), 97–8 · *The Theatre*, 3rd ser., 3 (1881), 127–8 · Hall, *Dramatic ports.* · *The Era* (1 Jan 1881), 8
Archives Theatre Museum, London, letters
Likenesses H. Watkins, photograph, 1856–9, NPG [*see illus.*] · lithograph, Harvard TC · portrait, repro. in *The Players* · print, Harvard TC

Oliver, Percy Lane (1878–1944), founder of the first voluntary blood donor service, was born on 11 April 1878 at the home of his maternal grandparents in Fish Street, St Ives, Cornwall, the son of Edward Lane Oliver and his wife, Jane Hosking Curnow. His parents were teachers in Maidenhead, and in 1883 the family moved to south-east London, where he attended the Wesleyan school, Camberwell. In 1893 he passed first out of 450 entrants for the civil service examination but was rejected on medical grounds, so took a librarianship with Camberwell borough council, transferring to town hall staff in 1901. He married Ethel Grace (1879–1973) at St Giles's Church, Camberwell, in July 1905. They had two sons (Edward and John) and a daughter (Marjorie).

Oliver helped found the Camberwell division of the British Red Cross Society, becoming its honorary secretary in 1910. During the First World War he and his wife undertook care and resettlement of Belgian refugees. In 1916 the family moved into rooms over the division's headquarters in Talfourd Road, London, and Oliver joined the Royal Naval Air Service, stationed at Crystal Palace. The Camberwell Red Cross division helped rescue the injured following an explosion at Silvertown munitions factory in 1917. For their war work Oliver and his wife received the Order of the British Empire in 1918.

Blood transfusion, which had been used mainly in military situations, began to enter civilian medicine after the First World War. Two major technical advances had been the recognition of blood types by Karl Landsteiner in Vienna in 1900 and the use of syringes replacing arm-to-arm (direct) transfusion. Surgeons who wished to transfuse blood needed to have a donor on hand. Oliver conceived the idea of forming a panel of donors in 1921, after four members of his Red Cross division responded to a call from King's College Hospital for a blood donor; one of these was of a suitable blood group. Following this episode, he asked for volunteers to have their blood group tested and be ready to attend a hospital whenever a call came through, day or night. Word of this service spread rapidly. In 1922, its first year of operation, the panel responded to thirteen calls from hospitals, by 1927 almost 1300 calls, and by 1938 around 6000 calls. By then, numbers of donors on the panel had risen to about 2700.

The essential characteristic of the service was that donors were not paid. Initially, costs were covered by donations and the collection and sale of tinfoil. Dr Geoffrey Keynes (brother of the economist), medical adviser to Oliver's service, insisted that donors should not be regarded as heroes. This was to counteract press reports that exaggerated the risks of giving blood. Oliver devised a system of rewarding donors with certificates and medals.

In view of the increasing scale and complexity of the work, from 1926 a joint committee of doctors, donors, and Red Cross headquarters personnel supervised the Greater London Red Cross Blood Transfusion Service. Oliver and his wife continued to run the service from their home at 210 Peckham Rye, with notable assistance from Frank Hanley of the Rover Scouts. According to most accounts Oliver worked seven days a week, phoning volunteers (it could take eight phone calls to get hold of the right donor; most did not have a phone at home) and dealing with paperwork. By 1928 the Olivers had to move to larger premises at 5 Colyton Road, London, where the family remained.

Oliver supported the formation in 1932 of the Voluntary Blood Donors Association, the first such voluntary body. In 1933 he took early retirement from Camberwell borough council in order to devote his time entirely to running the service and travelling around the country to lecture. Panels were established in many cities, and the pattern was adopted in other countries, although in the United States payment remained the norm.

Wider use of stored blood (with sodium citrate added) grew out of the Spanish Civil War. Oliver helped to organize multiple donor sessions at hospitals. Thus at the outbreak of the Second World War, the move from panels providing donors on call to blood banks had already begun. The wartime Emergency Blood Transfusion Service capitalized on previous experience to organize mass appeals and build up large blood banks; a million people made about two million donations. After the war, the Ministry of Health developed a National Blood Transfusion Service.

Oliver died at St George's Hospital, Westminster, on 16 April 1944 following a heart attack. His work did not immediately receive public recognition, but the Voluntary Blood Donors Association set up a fund in his name to award work in the field. In 1972 a memorial to Oliver was unveiled in King's College Hospital haematology department, which has a ward named after him. In 1979 the Greater London council placed a blue plaque on 5 Colyton Road, and in 1992 his birthplace in St Ives was similarly marked. J. M. STANTON

Sources G. W. G. Bird, 'Percy Lane Oliver, OBE (1878–1944): founder of the first voluntary blood donor panel', *Transfusion Medicine*, 2 (1992), 159–60 • H. Dodsworth, 'Blood transfusion services in the UK', *Journal of the Royal College of Physicians of London*, 30 (1996), 457–64 • H. H. Gunson and H. Dodsworth, 'Fifty years of blood transfusion', *Transfusion Medicine*, 6/suppl. 1 (1996), 1–88 • F. Hanley, *The honour is due: a personal memoir of the Blood Transfusion Service now known as the Greater London Red Cross Blood Transfusion Service, 1921–1986* (1998) • G. Keynes, ed., *Blood transfusion* (1949), 346–66 • J. Massey, 'The story of blood transfusion', *King's College Hospital Gazette*, 38 (summer 1959), 101–10 • F. W. Mills, 'Percy Lane Oliver, 1878–1944', *British Red Cross Society Greater London Blood Transfusion Service Quarterly Circular*, 1 (Oct 1949) • *Percy Lane Oliver OBE, the Voluntary Blood Donor Service, and the Oliver Memorial Fund* (1996) [Oliver Memorial Fund leaflet] • P. L. Oliver, 'British Red Cross blood transfusion service', *Guy's Hospital Gazette*, 49 (1935), 108–13 • P. L. Oliver, 'Plea for national blood transfusion conference', *BMJ* (21 Nov 1936), 1032–3 • V. Horsley Riddell, *Blood transfusion* (1939), 339–56 • D. Starr, *Blood: an epic history of medicine and commerce* (1998), 53–7 • J. Woodhams, '"Very nearly an armful!": a history of developments that led to the creation of the National Blood Transfusion Service in 1946; with particular reference to the first half of the twentieth century', BSc diss., Wellcome Institute for the History of Medicine, 1995 • private information (2004) [Marion Cayless, granddaughter]

Archives British Red Cross Museum and Archives, London, records

Likenesses double portrait, photograph, *c.*1934 (with his wife), British Red Cross Archives, London • oils (after photograph), King's College Hospital, London • photograph, British Red Cross Archives, London

Wealth at death £764 3*s.* 1*d.*: administration, 1944, *CGPLA Eng. & Wales*

Oliver, Peter [Pierre] (1589–1647), miniature painter, was the eldest son of the miniaturist Isaac *Oliver and his first wife, Elizabeth (*b.* 1570/71), whom he had possibly met and married in the Low Countries about 1588. She died and was buried, aged twenty-eight, on 6 September 1599. The Olivers were Huguenot refugees from Rouen who settled in Blackfriars, a district of London much favoured by immigrant artists and craftsmen because of its traditional freedom from the restrictions on trade maintained by the City livery companies. Through Isaac Oliver's second marriage, in 1602, to Sara Gheeraerts the Olivers became related to the Gheeraerts dynasty of painters and to the close community of Netherlandish artists working in London. Through his third wife, Elizabeth Harding (*b.* 1589, *d.* before 1640), whom Isaac married in 1606 and with whom he had six children, they acquired connections with the Huguenot families of Harding and Lanier, musicians at court, and with the Thames village of Isleworth, Middlesex, in which the Olivers also acquired property. Soon afterwards Peter Oliver also married a Harding, Anne (1593–1672), who was the younger sister of his father's third wife, probably as she reached the age of seventeen, in 1610. Both families continued to live principally in London, Peter Oliver apparently in the north part of the parish of Blackfriars, but they maintained strong connections with Isleworth, where Anne had been born. Ultimately, in his will, Peter would describe himself as a 'gentleman of Isleworth'.

Peter Oliver was brought up to the art of miniature by his father, and through the early part of his career his work is virtually indistinguishable from that of Isaac, except by signature. This was doubtless deliberate and a way of maintaining the stylistic integrity of the family studio, which was in effect bequeathed to Peter as a going concern, together with all work in progress. Among the latter was an apparently original composition of the 'burial of our Lord and saviour Jesus X, done upon a large table of fine abortive parchment & paisted upon a well seasoned & smooth board, as it is thought of Peartree' (Cordellier), which had been begun by his father and

Peter Oliver (1589–1647), self-portrait, c.1625–30

which he finished (and which is now in the Musée d'Angers).

Peter Oliver also succeeded to his father's place at court, continuing the production of official images of Charles as prince of Wales and as king, and perhaps especially of Princess Elizabeth, wife of the elector palatine and 'winter queen' of Bohemia, together with members of her court. Three versions of a miniature portrait of Elizabeth, current c.1623–6, one of which remains in its original enamel locket, are in the Victoria and Albert Museum, London. As a member of the royal household Peter Oliver attended the funeral of Anne of Denmark in 1619 and that of the king in 1625, when he was listed by the lord chamberlain, together with Laurence Hilliard, as an officer of the chamber of the new king, Charles I.

The painting of 'histories' now became an increasingly important aspect of Peter Oliver's work, involving especially miniature copies of paintings in the Royal Collection. According to Edward Norgate:

> Histories in Lymning are strangers to us in England till of late Yeares it pleased a most excellent King to comand the Copieing of some of his owne peeces, of Titian, to be translated into English Lymning, which indeed were admirably performed by his Servant, Mr Peter Oliver. (Norgate, ed. Muller and Murrell, 89)

Seventeenth-century European connoisseurs placed a high value on the accurate copying and, hence, comprehension of famous images; compare for example the series of small oil copies by David Teniers after paintings in the collection of Archduke Leopold Wilhelm commissioned in the 1650s for engraving and publication in one of the earliest published catalogues of great paintings, the *Theatrum pictorium* (1660; fourteen of these are now in the Courtauld Institute). Peter Oliver was undoubtedly the greatest such copyist working in England.

Technically Peter Oliver was the first regular professional miniaturist to adopt the practice, apparently pioneered by Balthasar Gerbier, of using pre-prepared gessoed leaves from commercial 'table books' to support his vellum (Murdoch, 10). Stylistically his work in portraiture evolved from the firm stipple of his father's studio towards a broader and softer touch, the effect of which was none the less always firm and clear in the delineation of features. In his miniature copies of history paintings, however, the evolution towards softness was much more extreme, especially when the intention was evidently to emulate the *sfumato* and *chiaroscuro* of the great north Italian pictures in the Royal Collection. Examples of these histories, made originally for Charles I and dispersed under the Commonwealth, are in the Victoria and Albert Museum, but the most important group, recovered for the Royal Collection after the Restoration, is at Windsor Castle. The most important of Peter Oliver's royal portraits also remain at Windsor. In the light of the increasingly soft focus of his work in miniature it is perhaps significant that he is authoritatively said by Norgate, a cousin, to have taken up the fashionable medium of pastel, which would have been highly suitable for delicate effects of light and shade. Norgate also recorded that he painted landscapes. However, neither pastels nor landscapes are known to survive.

Peter Oliver died at Isleworth and was buried on 22 December 1647 beside his father at the church of St Anne Blackfriars 'in the vault with a stone laid over him'. The church, together with the tomb of the Olivers, was destroyed in the great fire of London in 1666. He had no children, and left his estate, including many miniatures by himself and his father, to his widow. She continued to live a solidly respectable life in Isleworth and died soon after her will was made on 27 July 1672. Vertue records the family tale that at the Restoration Charles II visited her, evidently trying to reconstruct what he could of the *ante bellum* court culture and see what remained of the Oliver inheritance. He chose the miniatures he wanted, offering Anne either £1000 in cash or an annuity of £300 a year. She chose the latter, wrongly, for when she later heard that he had given some of the miniatures to his court ladies she let it be known that she would never have sold them had she known that he would give them to 'whores, bastards and strumpets'. The king stopped the annuity. In her will she directed that the remaining miniatures were to be sold.

A profile drawing identified as a self-portrait by Peter Oliver and a three-quarters full-face drawing identified as Anne are in the National Portrait Gallery, London.

JOHN MURDOCH

Sources E. Norgate, *Miniatura, or, The art of limning*, ed. M. Hardie (1919) · E. Norgate, *Miniatura, or, The art of limning*, ed. J. M. Muller and J. Murrell (1997) · M. Edmond, *Hilliard and Oliver: the lives and works of two great miniaturists* (1983) · J. Murdoch, *Seventeenth-century*

English miniatures in the collection of the Victoria and Albert Museum (1997) · D. Cordellier, 'La mise au tombeau d'Isaac Oliver au Musée d'Angers', *Revue du Louvre*, 33/3 (1983), 178–87

Likenesses P. Oliver, self-portrait, miniature, *c*.1625–1630, NPG [*see illus.*] · A. Hanneman, oils, *c*.1632–1635, Royal Collection

Oliver, Richard (*bap.* 1735, *d.* 1784), politician, the only surviving son of Rowland Oliver, a puisne judge of the court of common pleas of the Leeward Islands, and the grandson of Richard Oliver, speaker of the house of assembly in Antigua, was baptized in St John's, Antigua, on 7 January 1735. At an early age he was sent to London, where he entered the office of an uncle, Richard Oliver, of Low Leyton, Essex, who was a draper and West India merchant. On 2 February 1758 he married Mary Oliver, the daughter of his uncle; they had no children. He succeeded to his father's estates in Antigua in July 1767.

Oliver took up his freedom in the Drapers' Company on 29 June 1770, and on 4 July following was elected alderman of Billingsgate ward. He was a radical and a founder member of the Society of Supporters of the Bill of Rights, which pressed for reform of government and redress to Wilkite grievances. The radicals controlled the City of London at this time, and when a by-election was called in July 1770 Oliver was elected MP, after the original radical candidate, his brother-in-law Thomas Oliver, had withdrawn from the contest because of ill health. He continued to represent the City until the dissolution of parliament in September 1780, and used his platform in the house to support reforming measures, such as Serjeant Glynn's motion for a committee to inquire into the administration of criminal justice.

Oliver's most notable appearance in the House of Commons came in March 1771, during the celebrated *Printers' case* and the subsequent struggle between the City and the Commons. In a deliberate attempt at confrontation, Lord Mayor Crosby and aldermen Wilkes and Oliver arrested a messenger of the Commons. The Commons sought to punish Crosby and Oliver, both MPs, choosing to ignore Wilkes. Due to the illness of Crosby, much of the house's attention was focused on Oliver, who declined to defend himself and defied the Commons, stating that he had acted according to his conscience. An angry Lord North moved for his commitment to the Tower of London, which was carried by a large majority in the house, after midnight in the debate of 25 March 1771. When the parliamentary session closed on 8 May, Oliver and Crosby were released from the Tower and conducted in a triumphal procession to the Mansion House. The City showed its gratitude to Oliver by presenting him with a silver-gilt cup in March 1772, and he was elected a general of the Honourable Artillery Company in August 1773.

Soon after the *Printers' case*, Oliver split with Wilkes, having already refused to serve as sheriff with him in April 1771. Oliver was elected to that office with Watkin Lewes on 1 July 1772. He joined the faction of radicals led by Home and Townshend, who formed the Constitutional Society in opposition to Wilkes. The friends of Wilkes were so enraged at the election of Townshend as lord mayor in 1772 that they appear to have accused Oliver 'of

having taken the vote of the court before their party had arrived' (*Life*, ed. Fitzmaurice, 2.289). Oliver, however, continued to speak in opposition to the government and in favour of reform. He supported Sawbridge's motion to shorten the duration of parliaments and opposed the administration's policies towards the American colonies. By September 1778 he had decided to retire from parliament at the next general election, and he declined to stand for the mayoralty. He resigned his gown at a court of aldermen held at the Guildhall on 25 November 1778, and shortly afterwards sailed to Antigua in order to look after his West Indian estates. He died on 16 April 1784, on board the packet-boat *Sandwich*, while returning to England from Antigua.   G. F. R. BARKER, *rev.* IAN K. R. ARCHER

Sources HoP, *Commons* · P. D. G. Thomas, *John Wilkes: a friend to liberty* (1996) · G. Rudé, *Wilkes and liberty: a social study of 1763 to 1774* (1962) · I. R. Christie, *Wilkes, Wyvill and reform: the parliamentary reform movement in British politics, 1760–1785* (1962) · parliamentary diary of Henry Cavendish, 1768–74, BL, Egerton MSS 215–263, 3711 · Cobbett, *Parl. hist.*, vol. 16 · *GM*, 1st ser., 28 (1758), 94 · *GM*, 1st ser., 40 (1770), 339–41 · *GM*, 1st ser., 41 (1771), 139–41, 188, 233–4, 284, 330 · *GM*, 1st ser., 42 (1772), 294, 338, 489, 492 · *GM*, 1st ser., 46 (1776), 147–8 · *GM*, 1st ser., 48 (1778), 434–5, 549, 605 · *GM*, 1st ser., 54 (1784), 395 · *Life of William, earl of Shelburne … with extracts from his papers and correspondence*, ed. E. G. P. Fitzmaurice, 2nd edn, 2 vols. (1912) · J. Oldmixon, *The British empire in America*, 2nd edn, 2 vols. (1741) · *N&Q*, 8th ser., 4 (1893), 67, 217 · H. Walpole, *Memoirs of the reign of King George the Third*, ed. G. F. R. Barker, 4 vols. (1894) · *Correspondence of William Pitt, earl of Chatham*, ed. W. S. Taylor and J. H. Pringle, 4 vols. (1838–40) · *The letters of Junius, including letters by the same writer under other signatures*, ed. J. Wade, new edn, 2 vols. (1850–60) · *Memoir of Brass Crosby* (1829) · A. Highmore, *The history of the Honourable Artillery Company of the City of London, from its earliest annals to the reign of the present day of 1802* (1804) · B. B. Orridge, *Some account of the citizens of London and their rulers, from 1060 to 1867* (1867)

Likenesses F. Aliamet, lithograph, pubd 1771 (after R. E. Pine), BM, NPG · W. Dickinson, mezzotint, pubd 1773 (after R. E. Pine), BM · double portrait, stipple and line engraving (with the lord mayor of London), NPG

Oliver, Robert Dudley (1766–1850), naval officer, was born on 31 October 1766. He entered the navy in May 1779, on the *Prince George*, flagship of Rear-Admiral Robert Digby, and in her, during the early months of 1780, was shipmate of Prince William, later William IV. Remaining in the *Prince George*, Oliver went to North America in 1781, and later to the West Indies, where he was present in the operations before St Kitts in January 1782 and at the defeat of the French fleet off Dominica on 12 April. After further service in North America and in the channel, Oliver was promoted lieutenant on 21 September 1790, and in 1793 was lieutenant of the *Active* in the North Sea; in 1794 he was in the *Artois* with Captain Edmund Nagle, and after the capture of the *Révolutionnaire* on 21 October he was promoted commander, taking seniority from the date of the action. In 1795 he commanded the sloop *Hazard* on the coast of Ireland, and on 30 April 1796 was posted to the *Nonsuch*, guardship in the Humber, which he commanded until February 1798, when he was appointed to the *Nemesis* (28 guns), going out to Quebec with a large convoy. In March 1799 he joined the *Mermaid* (32 guns), in which he went to the Mediterranean, and after a successful commission brought home Lord Hutchinson from Egypt in July

1802. On the renewal of the war he was appointed in March 1803 to the *Melpomene* (38 guns), which, during the next two years, was on the coast of France.

Oliver married, on 19 June 1805, Mary, daughter of Sir Charles Saxton bt, for many years resident commissioner of the navy at Portsmouth. They had five sons and one daughter. The *Melpomene* joined the fleet off Trafalgar the day after the battle, and helped to tow off the prizes. Oliver was then appointed to the *Mars* (74 guns), made vacant by the death of Captain Duff; he commanded the ship on the coast of France until September 1806. In May 1810 he commissioned the *Valiant* (74 guns), in which, in 1813–14, he took part in the operations on the coast of the United States. He resigned the command in July 1814, and had no further service, though promoted rear-admiral on 12 August 1819, vice-admiral on 22 July 1830, and admiral on 23 November 1841. He was an active member of the Bible Society and other religious societies in Dublin. He died at his residence, Barnhill, Dalkey, near Dublin, on 1 September 1850.   J. K. LAUGHTON, *rev.* ANDREW LAMBERT

Sources D. Syrett and R. L. DiNardo, *The commissioned sea officers of the Royal Navy, 1660–1815*, rev. edn, Occasional Publications of the Navy RS, 1 (1994) • O'Byrne, *Naval biog. dict.* • *GM*, 2nd ser., 34 (1850), 547 • J. Marshall, *Royal naval biography*, 1/2 (1823), 725–6 • return of services, naval records, PRO
Archives NMM, commonplace book; order books and letters received

Oliver, Samuel Pasfield (1838–1907), geographer and antiquary, born at the rectory, Bovinger, Ongar, on 30 October 1838, was the eldest and only surviving son of William Macjanley Oliver, rector of Bovinger, and his wife, Jane Weldon. He entered Eton College in 1853, and after passing through the Royal Military Academy, Woolwich, he received a commission in the Royal Artillery on 1 April 1859. In 1860 he went out to China, where he served at Canton (Guangzhou) before visiting Peking (Beijing) and touring Japan. In the following year he was transferred to Mauritius, and went thence to Madagascar, where he spent some months exploring. The history and ethnology of the island interested him, and he made a close study of them. On his return to Mauritius he studied the flora and fauna of the Mascarene Islands. Oliver married on 10 September 1863 at Port Louis, Mauritius, Clara Georgina, second daughter of the Hon. Frederic Mylius Dick, councillor of Mauritius, with whom he had five sons and four daughters. In 1864 the volcanic eruption on the island of Réunion gave him the opportunity of recording some interesting geological phenomena.

Oliver returned to England with his battery in 1865; but his love of adventure led him in 1867 to join Captain Pym's expedition to Central America. A route was cut and levelled across Nicaragua from Monkey Point to Port Realejo; and at a meeting of the British Association at Dundee on 5 September 1867 Oliver argued that this route might be more practicable than the one projected by M. Ferdinand de Lesseps for the Panama Canal. His adventures in Nicaragua were included in his reminiscences, entitled *On and Off Duty* (1881).

Oliver now turned to archaeology. From Guernsey,

where he was appointed adjutant in 1868, he visited Brittany, and drew up a valuable report on the prehistoric remains at Carnac and other sites (*Proceedings of the Ethnological Society*, 1871). His visits in 1872 to archaeological sites in Asia Minor, Greece, and Sardinia were recorded in *Nuragghi Sardi, and other Non-Historic Stone Structures of the Mediterranean* (1875). Meanwhile Oliver, who had been promoted captain in 1871, was appointed superintendent of fortifications on the Cornish coast in 1873, and there he wrote the history of two castles, *Pendennis and St Mawes* (1875).

After serving on the staff of the intelligence branch of the quartermaster-general's department Oliver was sent to St Helena on garrison duty. There he made a valuable collection of ferns, which he presented to the Royal Botanic Gardens, Kew. Impatience of professional routine induced him to resign his commission in 1878. For a time he acted as special artist and correspondent of the *Illustrated London News* in Cyprus and Syria, but his health had been seriously affected by his travels in malarial countries, and he soon settled down to write, first at Gosport and later at Worthing. He was elected FRGS in 1866, became fellow of the Ethnological Society in 1869, and FSA in 1874. He died at his home, Bovinger, Byron Road, Worthing, on 31 July 1907, and was buried at Findon.

Oliver's sympathetic volumes about Madagascar long remained important English sources on the subject. His works included *Madagascar and the Malagasy* (1866); an ethnological study in French, *Les Hovas et les autres tribus caractéristiques de Madagascar* (1869); *The True Story of the French Dispute in Madagascar* (1885), in which he criticized the treatment of the Malagasy by French colonial officials; and *Madagascar* (2 vols., 1886).

Oliver also edited accounts of the travels of Robert Drury (1890), François Leguat (1891), the Count de Benyowsky (1893), and the Sieur Dubois (1897). In addition he helped to prepare *The Life of Sir Charles MacGregor*, published by MacGregor's widow in 1888, and from notes and documents collected by MacGregor he compiled the abridged official account of *The Second Afghan War, 1878–80* (1908). His *Life of Philibert Commerson*, published posthumously (1909), was edited by G. F. Scott Elliot and prefaced with a memoir of Oliver. To the *Dictionary of National Biography* Oliver contributed articles on François Leguat and Sir Charles MacGregor. Oliver's interests were too varied for him to achieve eminence in any one, but his many works were carefully compiled, often from personal experience, and were valued in his lifetime and beyond.

G. S. WOODS, *rev.* ELIZABETH BAIGENT

Sources G. F. S. Elliot, 'Memoir of Captain Oliver', in S. P. Oliver, *Life of Philibert Commerson* (1909) • *The Athenaeum* (17 Aug 1907), 181 • *Worthing Gazette* (14 Aug 1907) • private information (1912) • *CGPLA Eng. & Wales* (1907) • *The Eton register*, 2 (privately printed, Eton, 1905)
Archives RGS, ornithological notes | BL, corresp. with E. F. Jodrell, Add. MS 40027 • NL Scot., corresp. with Blackwoods
Wealth at death £2839 18s. 6d.: probate, 22 Aug 1907, *CGPLA Eng. & Wales*

Oliver, Stephen. *See* Chatto, William Andrew (1799–1864).

Oliver, Stephen Michael Harding (1950–1992), composer, was born on 10 March 1950 at Chester Nursing Home, the last of the three children of Osborne George Oliver (*b.* 1903), an electricity board official, and his wife, (Charlotte) Hester, *née* Girdlestone (*b.* 1911), an adviser in religious education. Although Oliver became an agnostic the Christian ethic informed everything he did, and he was to write much sacred music. While a chorister at St Paul's choir school he discovered, in *The Mikado*, his empathy with secular music drama. He wrote his first opera at the age of twelve and never stopped. Works, including his earliest oratorio, followed at Ardingly College. But it was his opera *The Duchess of Malfi* (1972), performed while he was at Worcester College, Oxford (from which he graduated BA in 1971 and BMus in 1972), that told the outside world of the arrival of a new theatre composer to be reckoned with. His successful output was such that, after two years spent teaching composition and music history at Huddersfield Polytechnic, he was able to move to London, proud to be a full-time professional.

Oliver regarded himself as a craftsman—someone in the line of eighteenth-century composers who would undertake any commissioned work. He wrote fast, with a facility for inventing the widest ranges of sounds, from pastiche of any century's characteristics to his personal contemporary 'squeaky-gate' music, with anything from Messiaen-scale orchestration to miniatures for lute and viola da gamba, or simply a tray of wine glasses. He composed for every facet of entertainment: film (*Lady Jane Grey*), dance (*La bella Rosina*), radio (incidental music for *The Lord of the Rings*), television (much of the BBC Shakespeare series), and straight theatre (some ninety plays, many for the Royal Shakespeare Company, including scores for *Nicholas Nickleby* and *Peter Pan*). *Blondel*, the musical he wrote with Tim Rice, was not quite a success, though it ran in London for a year, and one song, 'Running Back for More', reached the pop charts. The Thatcherite certainties of Rice's lyrics did not blend happily with Oliver's angst.

It was in opera that Oliver found his most rewarding outlet. Although occasionally he devised his own storyline (*Il giardino*, 1977, *Exposition of a Picture*, 1986, and his version of Mozart's *L'oca del Cairo*, 1991), usually the texts Oliver wrote, and set to music, were drawn from his dauntingly deep knowledge of literature: Webster, Dickens (*Perseverance*, 1974), Beckett (*Past Tense*, 1974), Fielding (*Tom Jones*, 1976), Yeats (*The Dreaming of the Bones*, 1979), Schnitzler (*A Man of Feeling*, 1980), Ostrovsky (*Sasha*, 1984), de Beaumont (*La bella e la bestia*, 1984), Mann (*Mario ed il mago*, 1988), and Shakespeare (*Timon of Athens*, 1991). The theatrical effectiveness of these operas was perfectly judged. They enjoyed naturalistic word-setting, melody in tonal but contemporary idiom, and audacious orchestration, frequently making use of the marimba and a battery of other percussion instruments. The smaller scale works were particularly successful, the clarity and delicacy of chamber music bringing out the best in Oliver. Many of them used an uneasy, tentative 3/4 time to suggest the malaise of the principal characters. Although he was at ease with his homosexuality and did not see himself as an outsider,

the composer's own (quite unjustified) feelings of inadequacy were put to good use in some of the best roles he created: the Beast, Cipolla, and Timon. The need for friendship was a theme that ran through his work, and he was the first to see that the hero's relationship with Smike should be at the core of *Nicholas Nickleby*.

Oliver was the acknowledged star of the *South Bank Show* on the making of *Nicholas Nickleby*, that great Royal Shakespeare Company success; the television public met for the first time the brilliant conversationalist and (occasionally) caustic wit. This was followed by *Understanding Opera*, a slightly didactic series he wrote and presented for BBC2 television. He had dexterity with words both written and spoken. His translations of other men's operas included *Euridice*, *Orlando*, *Le coq d'or*, and *The King Goes Forth*. He would review a concert for the BBC in rhyming couplets, and frequently had his listeners in stitches on Radio 4's *Stop the Week*. He was also an excellent actor. But the dazzling exterior hid a serious, public-spirited man who served on many committees, among them the boards of English National Opera (where he brought commission fees up to date) and the Performing Right Society (where he led the campaign to give lyricists parity with composers). Privately he led an almost (but not quite) monk-like existence, preferring to live undisturbed and alone, spending little on himself and, instead, redirecting his earnings to small, struggling opera companies and a variety of charities. He had, in the fullest measure, the gift of unassailable friendship, and was always ready with advice, help, and, often, hard cash where it was needed. A typical act of sacrifice, despite his need of privacy for composing, was to give a final home to a close friend dying of AIDS.

In the last year of his life, before he was stricken by the same virus, Oliver achieved an astounding compositional *tour de force* which included an oratorio (*The Vessel*), new recitatives for the Glyndebourne production of *La clemenza di Tito*, and two operas (*Timon of Athens* for the English National Opera and *L'oca del Cairo* for the Batignano festival), all in 1991. He bore his last illness with exemplary courage and optimism, and died at his home, Flat B, 44 Queensgate, London, on 29 April 1992. His ashes were scattered at his request in the olive grove of the ex-monastery of Santa Croce, Batignano, Italy, where four of his works were first staged. He left the bulk of his estate in trust to further new opera.   ADAM POLLOCK

Sources personal knowledge (2004) · private information (2004) [Hester Oliver] · records, Novello's Ltd, London · *The Times* (1 May 1992) · *The Independent* (1 May 1992) · *The Times* (4 May 1992) · *The Times* (6 May 1992) · *The Times* (7 May 1992) · *The Independent* (13 May 1992)
Archives Novello's Ltd, London · priv. coll. | SOUND BL NSA, interview, B8293/01 · BL NSA, 'Tribute to Stephen Oliver', H2089/02 · BL NSA, performance recording
Likenesses photograph, repro. in *The Independent* (1 May 1992)
Wealth at death £167,419: probate, 17 Aug 1992, *CGPLA Eng. & Wales*

Oliver, Thomas (*d.* 1610?), mathematician and physician, was perhaps the Thomas Oliver who entered Christ's College, Cambridge, in November 1569. He may have gained a medical degree since, by 1597, he was working as a physician in Bury St Edmunds. He numbered among his patrons both Lord Petre of Ingatestone and Henry Howard, earl of Northampton.

Oliver showed his extensive mathematical knowledge in a work on astronomy which he published in 1601. This was entitled *A New Handling of the Planisphere* and was intended as a means for solving astronomical problems by the use of ruler and compass, thus obviating the need for expensive instruments. The instrument of the title was simply a circular piece of brass with circular scales for degrees, the zodiac, and the hours of the day, and fitted with sights and a plummet. It could be used for various astronomical observations and was obviously designed as an alternative to the astrolabe. The book includes a clear exposition of cosmography but the use of the instrument is rather more convoluted, involving a great many geometrical constructions. In the preface Oliver acknowledged his debt to Christopher Clavius for his writing on the astrolabe.

Oliver's only other published work was a set of four tracts bound in a single volume and printed in Cambridge. These were written between 1597 and 1603 on a wide range of subjects. The first was a treatise on Aristotelian philosophy, the second addressed various geometrical problems, the third was a medical paper, and the fourth considered the question of squaring the circle. These were dedicated to various academics in both Cambridge and Würzburg, including Lancelot Browne and William Butler. There are also two manuscript treatises of his in the British Library entitled 'Tabula longitudinum et latitudinum locorum memorabilium in Europa' and 'Mechanica circuli quadratura cum equatione cubi et sphaerae'.

Oliver remained in Bury St Edmunds until the end of his life. His will was proved in 1610, suggesting that he died in that year.   H. K. HIGTON

Sources E. G. R. Taylor, *The mathematical practitioners of Tudor and Stuart England* (1954) · Venn, *Alum. Cant.* · T. Oliver, *A new handling of the planisphere* (1601) · T. Oliver, *De sophismatum praestigiis cavendis admonitio* (1604)

Oliver, Thomas (1731/2–1815), colonial official, was born in Dorchester, Massachusetts, the son of Robert Oliver and Ann, daughter of James Brown of Antigua. His father was living in Antigua in 1738, but had settled at Dorchester before 1747. Thomas was educated at Harvard University, where he graduated in 1753. He probably resided at Dorchester until 1766, when he purchased an estate on Elmwood Avenue, near Mount Auburn, Cambridge, Massachusetts, and erected the mansion which was afterwards the residence of Governor Elbridge Gerry, and later the author and diplomatist James Russell Lowell. A man of fortune, he did not take much part in public affairs until March 1774, when he accepted the office of lieutenant-governor of Massachusetts. In addition he became the president of a council appointed by George III in a manner especially galling to popular feeling. Prior to Oliver's

appointment existing councillors had been visited by bands of Middlesex freeholders, and one after another forced to renounce their offices. When royal troops seized the militia's stock of powder, the yeomen of the neighbouring towns marched to Cambridge, some of them bringing arms. Governor-General Thomas Gage prepared to send troops against them. After vainly endeavouring to persuade the yeomen to turn back, Oliver hastened to Boston and prevailed on Gage to refrain from military action. On his return the resignation of his seat on the council board was demanded. He urgently requested delay, inasmuch as he could not renounce that office while lieutenant-governor. A threatening multitude outside his residence on the morning of 2 September forced him to step down and to swear his commitment not to take any further part in the 'present novel and oppressive plan of the government'. He left Cambridge immediately and never returned. He was accompanied by his wife, Elizabeth, daughter of Colonel John Vassall, whom he had married in 1760; the couple had several daughters. In 1775 he accompanied the British forces from Boston, and soon afterwards took passage from Halifax to England. He was proscribed in 1778 and his estate confiscated. Oliver died aged eighty-three at Bristol on 29 November 1815.

GORDON GOODWIN, *rev.* PHILIP CARTER

Sources L. R. Paige, ed., *History of Cambridge, Massachusetts, 1630–1877* (1877) · *GM*, 1st ser., 85/2 (1815), 641 · A. French, *The first year of the American Revolution* (1934) · J. Winsor, *The memorial history of Boston, including Suffolk County, Massachusetts, 1630–1880*, 4 vols. (1880–81)

Likenesses J. Blackburn, oils, Museum of Fine Arts, Boston

Oliver, Thomas (1791–1857), architect and surveyor, was born on 14 January 1791 at Over Crailing, near Jedburgh, Roxburghshire, the second son of Adam Oliver (1749–1793), weaver, and his wife, Elizabeth Bell (1762–1829). He was educated at Jedburgh School before working for his future father-in-law, James Lorimer (or Lorrimer), a Kelso stonemason. He moved to Newcastle in or just before 1814, when he married Margaret Lorimer (d. 1838), with whom he had two daughters and four sons. He married secondly, in 1840, Elizabeth Best, with whom he had a son, Charles William (1847–1855). In 1821 he began independent practice as a 'land surveyor and architect'; this was after six years as pupil and assistant to his more illustrious and slightly older contemporary John Dobson, by whom Oliver tended to be overshadowed throughout his career.

In fact, the number of buildings which can be ascribed to Oliver is comparatively small. His principal contribution is perhaps the series of superb engraved maps of Newcastle which he issued in 1830, 1844, 1849, 1851, and (posthumously) 1858, and his topographical works *A New Picture of Newcastle upon Tyne* (1831) and *The Topographical Conductor: a Descriptive Guide to Newcastle and Gateshead* (1851). In addition, he undertook a number of more specific surveys for the corporation and between 1824 and 1825 worked as a surveyor for the Liverpool and Manchester Railway Company.

Oliver was also a noteworthy planner in his own right. He put forward several unexecuted schemes for new streets which would have considerably improved Newcastle's inadequate communication routes; some of these are indicated on his 1830 *Plan of Newcastle upon Tyne*. However, claims that he was the real author of the entrepreneur Richard Grainger's redevelopment of central Newcastle between 1834 and 1839 cannot be sustained. Oliver's ideas were concerned mainly with the periphery of the town, and his *Plan of Building Ground, Together with Proposed and Projected Improvements in Newcastle upon Tyne* of July 1834 indicates that he was summarizing rather than initiating events; it shows not only Grainger's proposals but also those of other developers (including one planned by Dobson) and was almost certainly produced for public sale rather than for Grainger himself.

Oliver's architecture lies within the classical tradition of late Georgian and early Victorian Newcastle. Here his main work was Leazes Terrace, an extended stone-faced block, built for Grainger between 1829 and 1834, together with the elegant but more modest Leazes Crescent; he also designed the West Clayton Street Congregational Chapel (1850–51; dem.). Earlier he had designed for Dr John Baird in 1824 a pair of fashionably stone-fronted houses on the west side of Northumberland Street (dem.), and prepared for the corporation plans for Blackett Street and Eldon Square. The latter two developments were, however, ultimately financed by Grainger and built (1824 and 1825–31 respectively; now mostly dem.) largely to the designs of Dobson. Between 1836 and 1848 he laid out for George Tallantire Gibson a development of neat two- and three-storey streets 'suited to the wants of the humble yet respectable classes of the community' (J. Collingwood Bruce, *Handbook to Newcastle upon Tyne*, 1863, 116). It contained the Gibson Street Methodist (New Connexion) Chapel of 1837 and the Victoria Bazaar (1836–7), a triangular shopping arcade at the junction of Buxton, Gibson, and Melbourne streets which was possibly the prototype for Grainger's prestigious central arcade (*c*.1836–8) in Grey Street. 'Gibson Town' (dem. 1962–8) would, with additional parts of east Newcastle, have been conveniently linked to the quayside had an improvement scheme by Oliver of 1855 been implemented. Oliver died on 9 December 1857, at his home, 3 Picton Place, Newcastle, and was buried in Jesmond (formerly Newcastle general) cemetery. Of his sons by his first marriage, two were civil engineers, while Thomas jun. (1824–1902) became a noted architect in Sunderland and, after his father's death, founded in 1881 the Newcastle partnership of Oliver and Leeson (later Oliver, Leeson, and Wood). T. E. FAULKNER

Sources M. E. Jones and H. L. Honeyman, 'Thomas Oliver and his plans for central Newcastle', *Archaeologia Aeliana*, 4th ser., 29 (1951), 239–52 · R. D. Giddings, 'Thomas Oliver, 1791–1857, architect and surveyor, and the 19th century development of Newcastle upon Tyne', BArch diss., U. Newcastle, 1981 · T. E. Faulkner, 'The early nineteenth century planning of Newcastle upon Tyne', *Planning Perspectives*, 5 (1990), 149–67 · *Northern Worthies*, 5 (1857), 212 · *Newcastle Chronicle* (18 Dec 1857) · J. Noddings, 'Thomas Oliver, 1791–1857', BA diss., U. Newcastle, 1971

Likenesses pair of miniatures, 1814?, repro. in Jones and Honeyman, 'Thomas Oliver and his plans for central Newcastle' · portrait (in middle age), repro. in Jones and Honeyman, 'Thomas Oliver and his plans for central Newcastle'; probably priv. coll.
Wealth at death under £300: probate, 1858

Oliver, Sir Thomas (1853–1942), physician and authority on industrial hygiene, was born at St Quivox, Ayrshire, on 2 March 1853, the second of the nine children of James Oliver (1824?–1904), grocer, and his wife, Margaret, daughter of Thomas McMurtrie. He was educated at Ayr Academy and at Glasgow University, where he graduated MB, CM, with commendation (1874), and MD with honours (1880). He visited Paris for postgraduate study and worked under Jean Martin Charcot, whose lectures on disseminated sclerosis he edited and translated for publication in the *Edinburgh Medical Journal* in 1876. He acted for a short period as assistant pathologist at the Glasgow Royal Infirmary, but in 1875 he set up in practice at Preston, Lancashire. Here he remained until 1879 when he moved to Newcastle upon Tyne. He was elected physician to the Royal Victoria Infirmary and to the Princess Mary Maternity Hospital. In 1880 he was appointed lecturer in physiology in the medical school at Newcastle, which was attached to the University of Durham. He was promoted to a chair in 1889, which he held until 1911 when he became professor of medicine. Oliver married first, in November 1881, Edith Rosina (1852–1888), daughter of William Jenkins, of Consett Hall, co. Durham; and second, in 1893, Emily Octavia (1853/4–1912), daughter of John Anthony Woods, of Benton Hall, Newcastle upon Tyne. There were three daughters and a son from the first marriage and a daughter and a son from the second marriage.

At Newcastle, Oliver came into practical contact with industrial disease and developed an abiding interest in this area of medicine. He was elected FRCP in 1890 and his Goulstonian lectures in the following year were devoted to the subject of lead poisoning. He soon became closely involved in the investigation, exposure, and regulation not only of occupational lead poisoning, but also of a variety of health hazards in the so-called dangerous trades. Oliver served on a number of official inquiries, the first of which was the departmental committee on white lead in 1893, which successfully recommended restrictions on female employment. In 1898 he was appointed with T. E. Thorpe to inquire into the extensive poisoning from the glazes used in various industries in the Potteries, an inquiry which necessitated visits to similar industrial bases in France and Germany. In spite of much opposition from pottery manufacturers, their recommendations helped to bring about reforms which materially reduced the danger to operatives. Also in 1898 Oliver represented the Home Office at the Madrid International Congress on Hygiene. He was the medical expert during the Home Office inquiry on the use of phosphorus in the manufacture of lucifer matches in 1898–9, and a member of the important dangerous trades committee from 1896 to 1899. The extent of Oliver's participation in official inquiries was such that he deserves to be seen as a pioneer figure in the creation of a healthier workplace.

Oliver's most important publications were *Lead Poisoning in its Acute and Chronic Forms* (Goulstonian lectures, 1891); a translation of work by Charles Jacques Bouchard, *Lectures on Auto-Intoxication in Disease* (1894); *Dangerous Trades*, a valuable survey which he edited in 1902; *Diseases of Occupation from the Legislative, Social, and Medical Points of View* (1908); *Occupations from the Social, Hygienic and Medical Points of View* (1916); *The Health of the Workers* (1925); and *The Health of the Child of School Age*, which he edited in 1927. He also published extensively in the medical press.

Oliver's work for the improvement of industrial conditions took him to the United States, where he received the freedom of the city of Boston (1923); to France, where he was made a chevalier of the Légion d'honneur (1929) and was given the gold medal of the Assistance Publique (1924); and to Belgium, where he was given a medal of honour by the University of Brussels (1920). In 1921 he was a delegate of the Australian commonwealth to the International Labour Conference at Geneva. In 1931 at Geneva he was honorary president of the International Congress of Accidents and Industrial Diseases. He was president of the Royal Institute of Public Health and Hygiene from 1937 to 1942. Oliver, who was knighted in 1908, was a JP for Newcastle upon Tyne and a deputy lieutenant for Northumberland. He was awarded the honorary degrees of LLD, Glasgow (1903), DSc, Sheffield (1908), and DCL, Durham (1921). During the First World War he helped to raise the Tyneside Scottish brigade of which he became honorary colonel.

Oliver retired from the chair of medicine in 1927, but he continued as president of the Durham College of Medicine (1926–34). He was vice-chancellor of the University of Durham from 1928 to 1930. At the age of eighty-six he had a leg amputated. Although he made a good recovery, with the help of an artificial limb, he spent much of his final years in a wheelchair. Oliver was a serious and dignified man who cut an imposing figure. His main leisure activities were fishing and shooting. He was chairman of the Tyneside Geographical Society for over thirty years and for many years he was also president of the Tyneside Sunday Lecture Society. He died at his home at 7 Ellison Place, Newcastle upon Tyne, on 15 May 1942, and was buried on 19 May at Jesmond old cemetery.

W. J. BISHOP, rev. P. W. J. BARTRIP

Sources *BMJ* (30 May 1942), 681–2 • *The Lancet* (30 May 1942) • Munk, *Roll* • *Journal of the Royal Institute of Public Health and Hygiene* (June 1942) • *WWW* • *The medical who's who* (1914) • H. H. Stephenson, *Who's who in science* (1913) • A. T. C. Pratt, ed., *People of the period: being a collection of the biographies of upwards of six thousand living celebrities*, 2 vols. (1897) • *The Times* (18 May 1942) • *Annual Register* (1943) • private information (2004)
Likenesses C. K. Robertson, group portrait, oils, 1893, U. Newcastle, Medical School • T. B. Garvie, oils, 1935, U. Newcastle, Medical School • photograph, repro. in *The Lancet* • photograph, repro. in *BMJ*
Wealth at death £91,631 10s. 8d.: probate, 22 Sept 1942, *CGPLA Eng. & Wales*

Oliver, Tom (1788–1864), pugilist, was born at Bledlow in Buckinghamshire on 18 July 1788, the son of William Oliver and his wife, Ann. He left his native place as a boy, and entered the service of Mr Baker, a gardener, at Millbank, London. A visit to a prize-fight in 1811 fired his ambition to enter the ring. The same year he fought Kimber, a stonemason, at Tothill Fields and beat him in an hour and forty minutes. He at once became known as the Chelsea Gardener, a title that stuck to him throughout his career until replaced by that of the Commissary. After several minor fights, on 15 May 1813 he beat George Cooper at Moulsey Hurst, Surrey, in seventeen minutes. On 17 May 1814 he met Ned Painter at Shepperton Range, Middlesex, for a purse of £50 given by the Pugilistic Club, to be contended for in a 24 foot ring. In the second round Oliver received a blow that all but disabled him; but, after coming up to time and adopting Tom Cribb's system of milling on the retreat, he won the battle after fifty-one minutes by a lucky blow. He now became the landlord of the Duke's Head, 31 Peter Street, Westminster, a house which 'the fancy' of the Westminster district made their headquarters. On 4 October 1816 he met Jack Carter, the Lancashire Hero, at Gretna Green, for 100 guineas a side. The spectators numbered about thirty thousand, and the marquess of Queensberry and Captain Barclay acted as the umpires. In the thirty-second round, at the end of forty-six minutes, Oliver was taken out of the ring in a state of stupor, and completely unable to see.

On 10 July 1818 Oliver encountered Bill Neat of Bristol at Gerrards Cross, but the authorities interfered, and the ring was moved to Rickmansworth, Hertfordshire, where Lord Yarmouth, Sir Henry Smith, and other celebrities were present. After one hour had elapsed, and twenty-eight rounds had been fought, Oliver was knocked senseless, and could not come up to time. However, on 28 May 1819 he completely defeated the black fighter Kendrick. He next, on 21 July 1819, encountered Dan Donnelly, the champion of Ireland, at Crawley Hurst, Sussex, for 100 guineas a side. Intense interest was manifested in this affair in both countries, and bets amounting to more than £100,000 were made on the result. Oliver fought with his accustomed bravery, but in the thirty-fourth round he met with his increasingly customary defeat. On 13 January 1820 Oliver defeated Tom Shelton at Sawbridgeworth, Hertfordshire; but in a fight with his former opponent Ned Painter at North Walsham, Norfolk, on 17 July 1820, he lost the battle. He was then matched to fight Tom Spring on 20 February 1821 at Hayes, Middlesex. Spring was too much for him; but he showed great forbearance in the fight, and allowed Oliver much latitude. He also lost to T. Hickman, the gas-lightman, on 12 June 1821, and to Bill Abbott on 6 November 1821.

Oliver was now appointed to take charge of the ropes and stakes of the prize-ring, and he was a constant attendant at the ringside as commissary. His last fight was with Ben Burn at Hampton, Middlesex, on 28 January 1834, when he won in twenty-five minutes. On 15 July 1846 he was sentenced at the Oxford assizes to three weeks' imprisonment for being present at a fight between Gill and Norley. During his latter years he was a fruiterer and greengrocer at Portman Market and 27 New Church

Street, Chelsea. He died in London in June 1864, leaving a son, Frederick Oliver, also a pugilist and a commissary of the ring, who died on 30 January 1870.

G. C. BOASE, *rev.* JULIAN LOCK

Sources H. D. Miles, *Pugilistica: being one hundred and forty-four years of the history of British boxing*, 3 vols. (1880–81), vol. 2, pp. 89–103 · P. Egan, *Boxiana, or, Sketches of ancient and modern pugilism*, 5 vols. (1812–29), vol. 2, pp. 95–107; vol. 3, pp. 262–72; vol. 4, p. 233 · [F. Dowling], *Fistiana* (1868) · [F. Dowling], *Fights for the championship; and celebrated prize battles* (1855) · Boase, *Mod. Eng. biog.* · 'An operator', *The Fancy* (1826), 1.609–16 · *The Post Office London directory* (1846) · parish register, Bledlow, Bucks. RLSS
Likenesses portrait, repro. in 'An operator' · portraits, repro. in Egan, *Boxiana* · portraits (after drawing by Wageman), repro. in Miles, *Pugilistica*, vol. 2, facing p. 90 · woodcut, NPG

Oliver, William (*bap.* **1658**, *d.* **1716**), physician, born at Launceston, Cornwall, was the son of William Oliver (1627–1681), rector of Launceston, and his wife, Alice Middleton; he was baptized on 31 July 1658. He was entered in the physic line at Leiden University on 17 December 1683 when aged twenty-five, but his medical studies were interrupted by his joining the duke of Monmouth's expedition to England, and serving with the troops as one of their three surgeons. Some years later Oliver told Oldmixon that after Monmouth's defeat he rode off the field with the duke, Lord Grey, and a few others. When they had ridden about 20 miles he proposed to the duke to turn off to the sea coast of Somerset, seize a passage boat at Uphill, and cross to Wales. The advice was not taken and Oliver rode away to Bristol, about 12 miles distant. There he concealed himself with friends, and after the 'bloody assizes' travelled to London with the clerk of Judge Jeffreys, to whom he had been recommended as a tory. He then escaped to the continent and made his way to the Netherlands. In 1685 he was at Königsberg in Prussia, and he spent one winter in the most northern part of Poland, but his name appears again in the list of the students at Leiden on 17 February 1688. He accompanied William III to England in 1688 as an officer in his army, and was soon rewarded for his services.

On 30 September 1692 Oliver qualified as a licentiate of the Royal College of Physicians at London, and from 27 April 1693 to 1702 he held the post of physician to the Red squadron. He served with the fleet at Cadiz in 1694, and spent two summers in the Mediterranean, during which period he eagerly pursued his inquiries in medicine and natural philosophy. Extracts from two letters written by Oliver when with the fleet were communicated by Walter Moyle to the *Philosophical Transactions* (17.908–12), and a third letter, written at the same period, was published in the same *Transactions* (24.1562–4). A letter 'on his late journey into Denmark and Holland', about 1701, also appeared in the *Philosophical Transactions* (23.1400–10).

Oliver was elected FRS on 5 January 1704. From 1702 to 1709 he lived in London and Bath, his *Practical Essay* being dated from 'Red Lion Court in Fleet Street, July 10, 1704', but it is doubtful whether he ever practised at Bath. From 1709 to 1714 he was physician to the hospital at Chatham for sick and wounded seamen, and from 1714 to 1716 he was physician to the Royal Hospital at Greenwich. He died unmarried at Greenwich on 4 April 1716, and was buried there. A monument was erected to his memory in the abbey church at Bath.

Oliver published in 1704 *A practical essay on fevers, containing remarks on the hot and cold methods of their cure*, at page 202 of which began 'a dissertation on the hot waters of Bathe', the first draft of his subsequent work. The essay, through its author's references to Dr John Radcliffe, was attacked in *A letter to Dr. Oliver, desiring him to reconcile some few of the contradictory assertions in his Essay on Feavers*, dated from Tunbridge Wells, 25 July 1704. The treatise on Bath was expanded into *A practical dissertation on Bath waters; to which is added a relation of a very extraordinary sleeper near Bath* (1707, 1719; 5th edn, 1764). This account of the sleeper, Samuel Chilton, a 25-year-old labourer at Timsbury, is also in the *Philosophical Transactions* (24.2177–82), and was issued separately in 1707 and 1719. A further communication by Oliver is in the same *Transactions* (24.1596). Oliver's discourse, 'Christian and politike reasons' why England and Holland should not go to war with each other, with other manuscripts, is in the British Library (Sloane MS 1770), as is a letter from him to James Petiver (Sloane MS 4054).

W. P. COURTNEY, *rev.* S. GLASER

Sources Munk, *Roll* · Boase & Courtney, *Bibl. Corn.*, vol. 1 · parish register, Launceston church, Cornwall, 31 July 1658 [baptism] · J. Oldmixon, *The history of England during the reigns of the royal house of Stuart* (1730) · G. Robert, *The life progress and rebellion of James duke of Monmouth*, 2 vols. (1884), vol. 2 · J. F. Meehan, *The Beacon* (April 1906), 39 · R. E. M. Peach, *Historic houses of Bath and their associations*, 2 (1884)
Archives BL, Sloane MSS

Oliver, William (**1695–1764**), physician and philanthropist, born at Ludgvan, Cornwall, on 4 August 1695, was baptized on 27 August 1695, and described as the son of John Oliver. The suggestion that he was the illegitimate child of William *Oliver (*bap.* 1658, *d.* 1716) may be discounted. Oliver's family originally lived at Trevarnoe in Sithney, and later in Ludgvan; the estate of Treneere in Madron, which belonged to him, was sold after his death in 1768. When he decided to erect a monument in Sithney churchyard to the memory of his parents, Alexander Pope wrote the epitaph and drew the design of the pillar (*Quarterly Review*, 139, 1875, 367–95). Oliver was admitted a pensioner of Pembroke College, Cambridge, on 17 September 1714, graduated MB in 1720 and MD in 1725, and, to complete his medical training, entered Leiden University on 15 November 1720. On 8 July 1756 Oliver was incorporated at Oxford, and was elected FRS on 22 January 1730. He is, however, most renowned as the inventor of the Bath Oliver biscuit.

On returning from Leiden, Oliver practised for a time at Plymouth, where he introduced smallpox inoculation. About 1725 he settled in Bath and remained there for the rest of his life, obtaining in a very short time the leading practice of the city. His medical skill is mentioned by Mrs Anne Pitt (*Suffolk Letters*, 1824, 2.246–50) and by Mrs Delany (*Autobiography*, 2.17; 3.625); and he also attended Ralph Allen in his last illness, receiving a complimentary legacy of £100. However, his popularity was mainly due to his friendship with Ralph Allen, a fellow Cornishman, who introduced him to Pope, William Warburton, and the rest of the guests at his house, Prior Park; and with William Borlase, his 'friend and relation', who, after being his patient in 1730, recommended him to the gentry of the west country. Oliver took great pains to obtain subscriptions for the building of the Water or General Hospital, later the Royal Mineral Water Hospital, at Bath, and in 1737 made an offer of some land for its site, which was at first accepted, but afterwards declined. The following year he was appointed one of the treasurers to the hospital fund, and in July 1739 he became a deputy president. On 1 May 1740 he was appointed physician to the hospital, the same day that Jeremiah Peirce became the surgeon. The regulations for the admission and discharge of English patients were drawn up by Oliver; and in 1756 he compiled a comparable set of rules for patients from Scotland and Ireland. A dominant and even domineering man, Oliver played a major role in the government of the institution until both he and Peirce resigned in 1761; he attended over 600 (more than half) of the meetings of the weekly management committee between 1739 and his death (minute books, Bath General Hospital).

It has been suggested that Oliver's whig politics made him vulnerable to tory attacks, but the medical conflicts in which he became embroiled were rather a product of professional conservatism and commercial self-interest. In 1743 Oliver was actively involved in the prosecution of Archibald Cleland, one of the surgeons of the hospital, who was dismissed following a charge that he had sexually assaulted female patients. An outsider, Cleland had been engaged in a long and threatening campaign to improve the spa facilities; therefore the allegations offered an excellent pretext for discrediting a competitor. The hospital governors commended Oliver's conduct in

the affair. Cleland, on the other hand, was scathing of his anatomical competence (and that of a fellow physician, Alexander Rayner): 'I could not have believed that these two learned doctors … could have been so little versed in these matters, if they had not in their *Vindication* thus publicly exposed themselves to the censure of every judicious reader' (A. Cleland, *A Full Vindication of Mr Cleland's Appeal to the Public*, 1744, 42). Oliver was at the centre of controversy again in 1757, when he and some other physicians in the city declined to attend any consultations with William Baylies and Charles Lucas, because they had disputed the sulphur content of the waters to which clinical efficacy was traditionally attributed, and criticized the behaviour of the physicians at the hospital. The voluminous correspondence which ensued was published by Lucas in a bid to demonstrate the existence of a physical confederacy in Bath (*Letters of Doctor Lucas and Doctor Oliver Occasioned by a Physical Confederacy Discovered in Bath*, 1757).

Oliver was not a prolific medical writer. In 1723 and 1755 he contributed brief papers to the *Philosophical Transactions*; in 1751 his *Practical Essay on the Use and Abuse of Warm Water Bathing in Gouty Cases* appeared; and in 1760 he put together a collection of *Cases of the Persons Admitted into the Infirmary at Bath under the Care of Doctor Oliver*. Stimulated by the goading of Lucas and Baylies, this last text was republished in 1774 as one of Rice Charleton's *Three Tracts on Bath Water*. But Oliver had interests besides medicine. Contemporaries recognized him as a 'civilized personality' (Boyce, 87, 243), well connected with the leading figures who frequented Bath, and fascinated by books, painting, and architecture.

Oliver applied to Dr Borlase for minerals for Pope's grotto, and his name frequently occurs in the letters of Pope and Borlase at Castle Horneck, near Penzance. In the

William Oliver (1695–1764), by William Hoare, exh. Society of Artists 1761 [right, examining patients with Mr Peirce]

summer of 1743 he wrote to Pope to free himself from all knowledge of John Tillard's attack on Bishop William Warburton, which was dedicated to him without his knowledge (*Works of Alexander Pope*, 9.233). Oliver was also a correspondent of Warburton himself, Philip Doddridge, and Stephen Duck; and he wrote to Dr Wood on the subject of two Roman altars discovered at Bath. Oliver's literary works included several poems, but most famous was the anonymously published *A Faint Sketch of the Life, Character, and Manners of the Late Mr Nash*. It was praised by Oliver Goldsmith as 'written with much good sense and still more good nature', and he embodied it within his *Life of Richard Nash* (1762). It also appeared in the *Public Ledger* of 12 March 1761, and in the Revd Richard Warner's *History of Bath* (1801).

Legend has it that towards the end of his life Oliver confided the recipe for the Bath Oliver, a savoury biscuit invented for patients, to his coachman Atkins, giving him at the same time £100 in money and ten sacks of the finest wheat flour. The fortunate recipient is said to have opened a shop in Green Street and acquired a large fortune. Although Atkins did not feature in Oliver's will, the story was told to successive generations of the Oliver family. Fortt & Son of Bath, who were manufacturing the biscuit in the 1960s, lost any documents relating to the origins of the recipe when their premises were bombed in 1941. The Bath Oliver is still well known today. Its creator was commemorated in other ways. A plate in the *Antiquities of Cornwall* (1769), engraved at his expense, was inscribed to him by Borlase; and the later impressions of Mary Chandler's *Description of Bath* (1736) contained some verses to him (pages 21–3), acknowledging that he had corrected her poem, and that 'ev'n Pope approv'd when you had tun'd my Lyre'.

However, it is the hospital which stands as the greatest memorial to Oliver's philanthropy. About 1761 he and Peirce were painted together by William Hoare, in the act of examining three candidates for admission: a splendid picture, which still hangs in the hospital. In 1935, moreover, a plaque was unveiled at Oliver's former town house in Queen Square, Bath, marking his association with the institution.

Oliver purchased in 1746, as a vacation residence, a small farmhouse 2 miles from Box, near Bath, and called it Trevarnoe, after the scene of his childhood and the abode of his fathers. His own son, the third William Oliver, matriculated from Christ Church, Oxford, on 20 January 1749, aged eighteen, and his name appears on the books at Leiden on 21 September 1753. Oliver's eldest daughter married a son of the Revd John Acland, rector of Broadclyst, Devon; his second daughter, Charlotte, married Sir John Pringle on 14 April 1752.

For many years before his death Oliver was subject to the gout. He died at Bath on 17 March 1764, and was buried in the church of Weston, near that city, where an inscription 'on a white tablet, supported by palm-branches' was erected to his memory. There is also a plain mural tablet to his memory in the abbey church. The statement in *The Life*

and Times of Selina, Countess of Huntingdon (ed. A. C. H. Seymour, 1, 1839, 450–51), that he remained 'a most inveterate infidel till a short time before his death', is probably an exaggeration. He was generally admitted to have been an eminently sensible man, with a compassionate and benevolent nature.

ANNE BORSAY

Sources J. Murch, *Biographical sketches of Bath celebrities, ancient and modern* (1893), 123–5 · R. W. Falconer, *History of the Royal Mineral Water Hospital, Bath* (1888), 18–40 · J. Wood, *A description of Bath*, 2nd edn (1765), 275–303 · M. R. Neve, 'Natural philosophy, medicine and the culture of science in provincial England', PhD diss., U. Lond., 1984, 75–93 · B. B. Schnorrenberg, 'Medical men of Bath', *Studies in Eighteenth-Century Culture*, 13 (1984), 191–3 · T. Smollett, *An essay on the external use of water*, ed. C. E. Jones (1935), 70–81 · T. Fawcett, 'Selling the Bath waters: medical propaganda at an eighteenth-century spa', *Somerset Archaeology and Natural History*, 134 (1990), 198–201 · R. Rolls, *The hospital of the nation: the story of spa medicine and the Mineral Water Hospital at Bath* (1988) · R. Warner, *The history of Bath* (1801), 289–302, 370–71 · J. Collinson, *The history and antiquities of the county of Somerset*, ed. R. Dunning (1983), 45–50 · D. Harley, 'Religious and professional interests in northern spa literature, 1625–1775', *Bulletin of the Society for the Social History of Medicine*, 35 (1984), 15 · *The works of Alexander Pope*, ed. W. Elwin and W. J. Courthope, 10 vols. (1871–89), vol. 9, p. 233 · B. Boyce, *The benevolent man: a life of Ralph Allen of Bath* (1967) · *DNB* · minute books, Bath RO, Bath General Hospital MSS

Archives Bath and North East Somerset RO, Bath General Hospital MSS · Bath Central Library, local history collection · BL, letters to duke of Newcastle and others

Likenesses W. Hoare, oils, exh. Society of Artists 1761, Royal National Hospital for Rheumatic Diseases, Bath [*see illus.*] · T. Hudson, oils, Royal National Hospital for Rheumatic Diseases, Bath · T. Hudson, portrait, priv. coll. · portrait, biscuits (Bath Olivers)

Oliver, William. *See* Richards, W. J. (1774?–1827).

Oliver, William (c.1804–1853), landscape painter, the son of William Oliver, is first recorded as an artist in 1829 when he exhibited the first of thirty-six paintings at the Society of British Artists in Suffolk Street, London. In 1834 he was elected a member of the New Society of Painters in Water Colours, and his drawings appeared annually at its exhibitions until 1854. He also exhibited twenty-nine landscapes in oils, mainly views in France and Italy, at the Royal Academy between 1835 and 1853, and fifty-four at the British Institution from 1836. In 1843 he published a folio volume, *Scenery of the Pyrenees*, lithographed by George Barnard, Thomas Shotter Boys, and Carl Hughe, among others.

On 21 September 1840 Oliver married Emma Eburne [*see below*], whom he had first met when she was fifteen, when he encouraged her to take drawing lessons. They had one son and one daughter. After their marriage they travelled every autumn, painting the landscape scenery of England, Wales, and Germany. Oliver died on 2 November 1853 at Langley Mill House, Halstead, Essex. His oil painting *Foligno* and a watercolour of the city of Strasbourg are in the Victoria and Albert Museum, London.

Emma Sophia Oliver [*née* Eburne] (1819–1885), landscape painter, was born on 15 August 1819, the daughter of William Eburne (d. c.1831), a coach-builder, and his wife, Mary, of Rathbone Place, London. Emma Oliver was elected a member of the New Society of Painters in Water

Colours in 1849, and exhibited landscapes in watercolours and oils at the Royal Academy, British Institution, Society of British Artists, and at various provincial galleries.

About 1856, following the death of William Oliver in 1853, Emma Oliver married John Sedgwick (1812–1882), a solicitor, of Watford, Hertfordshire, but continued to paint under her first husband's name. Many of her later landscapes were painted in Venice, and along the Rhine. She died on 15 March 1885 at the Brewery House, Great Berkhamsted, Hertfordshire. One of her landscapes, *Vale of Dedham, Essex* (1876), is in the Victoria and Albert Museum.   R. E. GRAVES, rev. ANNE PIMLOTT BAKER

Sources E. C. Clayton, *English female artists*, 2 (1876), 227–9 · L. Lambourne and J. Hamilton, eds., *British watercolours in the Victoria and Albert Museum* (1980) · Graves, *RA exhibitors* · Mallalieu, *Watercolour artists* · Wood, *Vic. painters*, 3rd edn · *Art Journal*, 15 (1853), 311 · m. cert.

Olivers, Thomas (*bap.* 1725, *d.* 1799), Methodist preacher and hymn writer, was the son of Thomas Olivers (*d.* 1729) and his wife, Penelope (*d.* 1730). The parish register of Tregynon, Montgomeryshire, shows that he was baptized on 8 September 1725. After his father and his mother died, he was entrusted to the care of a great-uncle, who, however, did not long survive Olivers's parents, but left him a small legacy. The interest was to be employed in the child's upbringing, and the principal paid to him when he came of age. He received 'such learning as was thought necessary' at Forden, Montgomeryshire, but became a wild and reckless young man, much given to cursing and swearing, and who became known as 'the worst boy who had been in those parts for the last twenty or thirty years' (Jackson, 2.49). At the age of eighteen he was apprenticed to a cobbler, but continued in his violent and careless ways, so much so that (following a scandal over his ill-treatment of a girl) he was forced to leave Wales. He went to Shrewsbury, and from there he wandered through the Welsh border counties until he reached Bristol. There he heard George Whitefield preach on the text 'is not this a brand plucked from the fire?' and was converted. He joined the Methodists at Bradford in Wiltshire, and became a conspicuously reformed character, preaching and also repaying those whom he had cheated in previous years.

In 1753 John Wesley, who later summed up Olivers as having 'good in him' but also as 'a rough stick of wood', chose Olivers to be one of his itinerant preachers. He was sent to Devon, and then to Cornwall; from there he went to Norfolk, where he was attacked by a mob when attempting to preach at Yarmouth, and then to London, Ireland, Leeds, Lancashire, York, Newcastle, and other places in quick succession. He married, probably in 1757 or 1758, a Miss Green, 'noted through all the north of England for her extraordinary piety' (Jackson, 2.80). In 1773 he became for a year Wesley's companion on his preaching tours: the minutes of the Methodist conference recorded that 'Thomas Olivers travels with Mr Wesley'. In 1775 he was appointed supervisor of the Methodist press, a position which he held until 1789, when Wesley removed him

for making too many mistakes: 'I cannot, dare not, will not suffer Thomas Olivers to murder the *Arminian Magazine* any longer. The errata are intolerable and innumerable' (J. Wesley to T. Bradshaw, 15 Aug 1789, *Letters*, 8.160). Despite his errors, the quick-tempered Olivers was a formidable pamphleteer, who engaged in fierce controversies with the Calvinists of his day, such as Augustus Montagu Toplady and Rowland Hill, who attacked Olivers on the grounds that he had once been 'a journeyman shoemaker'. His ferocity in the pamphlet wars of the early Methodist years earned him from Toplady the sobriquet of Wesley's Bully in Chief. 'Mr Wesley', wrote Toplady, 'skulks for shelter under a cobbler's apron'.

In spite of this expenditure of energy on pamphleteering, Olivers is best known for writing a great hymn of the early Methodist years, 'The God of Abrah'm praise'. He is said to have been inspired to write it by hearing the Hebrew *Yigdal* sung by Meyer Lyon, cantor at the Great Synagogue in London, about 1770. Olivers asked Lyon to write down the tune and composed the hymn to fit it. He was the author of other strong hymns, such as 'Come, immortal king of glory', and of a poem entitled 'A Descriptive and Plaintive Elegy on the Death of the Late Reverend John Wesley', written on Wesley's death in 1791. He is also thought to be the composer of the hymn tune 'Helmsley' (printed with the name 'Olivers' in a Wesleyan hymnbook of 1765), used for 'Lo, he comes with clouds descending'. His pamphlets were numerous and polemical, although the posthumously published *A Defence of Methodism* (1818) is a record of a debate held in 1785 ('Have the Methodists done most good or evil?') which shows his skill in reasoned argument. After his dismissal from the *Arminian Magazine* Olivers spent the remainder of his life in retirement in London, where he died on 7 March 1799, in Hoxton. He was regarded by the early Methodists as one of the foremost disciples of John Wesley, and was buried in Wesley's tomb in the grounds of the New Chapel, City Road, London.   J. R. WATSON

Sources *Thomas Olivers of Tregynon*, ed. G. T. Hughes (1979) · T. Jackson, ed., *The lives of early Methodist preachers, chiefly written by themselves*, 3rd edn, 6 vols. (1865–6) · L. Tyerman, *The life and times of the Rev. John Wesley*, 3 vols. (1870–71) · R. Southey, *The life of Wesley*, 2 (1820) · J. Kirk, *Hymns, and an elegy on the death of the Rev. John Wesley, by Thomas Olivers, reprinted from the originals, with a biographical sketch of the author by the Rev. John Kirk* (1868) · *DNB* · *The letters of the Rev. John Wesley*, ed. J. Telford, 8 vols. (1931) · J. Julian, ed., *A dictionary of hymnology*, rev. edn (1907); repr. in 2 vols. (1957)
Likenesses engraving, 1778, repro. in G. T. Hughes, ed., *Thomas Olivers* · portrait (*Old Dundee Exhibition, 1892–3*)

Olivier. For this title name *see* individual entries under Olivier; *see also* Leigh, Vivien [Vivian Mary Olivier, Lady Olivier] (1913–1967).

Olivier, Edith Maud (1872–1948), writer, was born on 31 December 1872 at the rectory, Wilton, Wiltshire, the eighth of the ten children of Canon Dacres Olivier (1831–1919), rector of Wilton, and his second wife, Emma Selina (1836–1908), daughter of Bishop Robert Eden, of Moray,

Ross, and Caithness. The Olivier family was of Huguenot descent, settling in England in the early eighteenth century. Edith's grandfather Henry Stephen Olivier lived at Potterne, Wiltshire, from about 1830, and was high sheriff of the county in 1843. His eldest son, Henry Arnold, was the grandfather of Laurence Olivier, the actor. Educated at home, Edith attended St Hugh's College, Oxford, for four terms only (1895–6) owing to bronchial asthma. Her early years were dominated by her father, with whom she and her younger sister Mildred lived until his death in 1919. From 1922 Edith lived in the Daye House, on the Wilton estate. In 1916 she was asked by Wiltshire county agricultural committee to form the Women's Land Army, for which she was appointed MBE in 1920. She was a member of the Conservative Party, was involved in parliamentary elections, and held local and county offices in the Women's Institute. A devout Christian all her life, she attended the Anglican church regularly and was secretary to the Bishop's Women's Diocesan Council. In 1934 she became the first woman councillor on Wilton town council and was mayor of the borough from 1938 to 1941. During the Second World War her many extra duties as mayor included being president of the local St John Ambulance Brigade.

After the death of Mildred in 1924 Edith's friendship widened to the younger generation and included much of the artistic circle of the day. She was close to the artist Rex Whistler and frequent hostess to Cecil Beaton, Siegfried Sassoon, William Walton, and many others, but she remained fully involved in the local community. Her books include *The Love Child* (1927) and *Four Victorian Ladies of Wiltshire* (1945) (the only ones to be republished), *Dwarf's Blood* (1931), *The Triumphant Footman* (1930), *The Seraphim Room* (1932), *Night Thoughts of a Country Landlady* (1943), a biography of Alexander Cruden (1934), a book on Wiltshire, and an autobiography, *Without Knowing Mr Walkley* (1938). She died on 10 May 1948 following three strokes, and was buried on 14 May in Wilton churchyard, a few yards from where she was born. Cecil Beaton described Edith's funeral thus: 'The dignity of Church and Government was there to pay her honour, as was fitting. But that was only part of what was in our hearts. There was honour, indeed, for what she had done; but there was love for what she was and is' (*Salisbury Journal*).

BERYL HURLEY

Sources E. Olivier, diaries, Wilts. & Swindon RO · E. Olivier, *Without knowing Mr Walkley* (1938) · private information (2004) · *Edith Olivier: from her journals, 1924–48*, ed. P. Middelboe (1989) · parish register, Wilton, Wiltshire, 3 Feb 1873 [baptism] · parish register, Wilton, Wiltshire, 14 May 1948 [burial] · town council minutes, Wilton, Wiltshire, Wilts. & Swindon RO, G23/100, 4 and 6 · GL, Huguenot MSS · *Salisbury Journal* (May 1948) · Central Chancery of the Orders of Knighthood · Crockford (1898) · *Men of the time* (1887)
Archives Wilts. & Swindon RO, corresp. and papers, incl. diaries | BL, corresp. with Society of Authors, Add. MS 63312
Likenesses C. Beaton, photographs · R. Whistler, oils, Wilton Town Council, Wiltshire
Wealth at death £7916 11s. 1d.: probate, 10 Aug 1948, CGPLA Eng. & Wales

Olivier, Giorgio Borg (1911–1980), prime minister of Malta, was born on 5 July 1911 at Valletta, Malta, the youngest of seven sons of Oliviero Borg Olivier, an architect and civil engineer, and his wife, Rosa Amato. Commonly known by his Maltese name, Ġorġ, he officially retained the name Giorgio. This was in accordance with the well-tested Nationalist tradition which had upheld Malta's Latin Mediterranean identity ever since party mobilization had begun in the 1880s over Anglicization policy. He was educated at the Lyceum, Valletta (1925–30), and then studied law at the Royal University of Malta at Valletta (1930–37). He grew up in a family steeped in Nationalist politics. His uncle Salvatore was speaker of the house and then a senator, and led the opposition to Lord Strickland's Imperialist Party in the 1920s before becoming a cabinet minister during the premiership of Ugo Mifsud in the early 1930s. Ġorġ followed in this uncle's footsteps by becoming, like him, a notary. He was active in Nationalist politics, and was president of the students' representative council. After completing his law studies Borg Olivier became an elected member of the council of government, at the age of twenty-eight. At the age of thirty-one in 1942, in wartime, he was the only Maltese representative in the council of government to oppose and vote against the deportation to Uganda of fellow Maltese, without charge or trial, on the suspicion that as Nationalists they might be disloyal to the British crown. Of the two other Nationalist councillors, one, Ugo Mifsud, suffered a heart attack during his speech against the deportation ordinance and died shortly afterwards. The other, Enrico (Nerik) Mizzi, later prime minister, had already been interned, which left Borg Olivier the sole Partit Nazzionalista (PN) standard-bearer on the elected bench.

Throughout his long political career Borg Olivier was almost everything in the vocabulary of political office-holding: minister of education, of justice, of public works and reconstruction; he was deputy leader and subsequently (after Dr Mizzi's death in 1950) leader of his party, a position he held for twenty-seven years. He served as leader of the opposition in the 1950s and 1970s, when Dominic Mintoff's Malta Labour Party (MLP) held office. He became prime minister in all five times and held office in that capacity for fourteen years in total (1950–55, 1962–71). In 1943 Borg Olivier married Alexandra Mattei, the daughter of a business administrator. They had two sons and a daughter.

Borg Olivier's party opposed Mintoff's plan for Malta's integration with Britain in the mid-1950s but the issue failed to win sufficient support. The PN had called officially for dominion status as early as 1932, and was committed to a greater political autonomy for Malta as a national entity. By 1956 the Mediterranean situation had changed dramatically, but in Anglo-Maltese relations too many difficulties seemed unsurmountable, especially financial ones and the uncertain future of the royal dockyard in Valletta's Grand Harbour. In December 1957 the political positions of the PN and of the MLP converged to such an extent that, in a historic move pregnant with national significance and future prospects, Borg Olivier readily seconded in parliament Mintoff's 'Break with Britain' resolution, which practically called for independence. Early in 1958 Mintoff resigned in a huff and his supporters took to the streets. Borg Olivier refused to form a government and called for fresh elections but, in the circumstances, a state of emergency was declared, the constitution suspended, and no elections took place before 1962.

The local situation meanwhile became embroiled in a so-called 'politico-religious' dispute, comparable in some ways to that of thirty years earlier, in Strickland's time. To some extent this was a personality clash between Archbishop Gonzi and Mintoff himself, but other issues of power and jurisdiction were clearly evident in growing tension between, on the one hand, the religious and ecclesiastical, and on the other hand, the secular and statist. Mass hysteria and campaigns of almost sectarian proportions ensued, with Mintoff (whose invective knew no bounds) and several of his colleagues being denied the sacraments and demonized. Borg Olivier, who was no religious fanatic, took the politically correct side against his main adversary and rode on the *religio et patria* wave, although privately he would have argued that by rallying or at least encouraging third parties to enter the political fray from both the Nationalist and the Labour camps, the church was hindering rather than helping him. This referred in particular to the church-linked Nationalist faction led by Dr Herbert Ganado, which returned four MPs in the 1962 elections on a ticket against political independence before economic viability; one of these, however, crossed over to Borg Olivier's side, giving his party an absolute majority in the house. Three other 'pro-church' small parties, two of which returned MPs, were similarly opposed to independence under one guise or another. Gonzi wanted to check Mintoff, but also Borg Olivier, lest under a new political order the established church might lose its guarded status. Both the main political parties, the PN and the MLP, had independence from Britain prominently included in their electoral manifestos. On taking office in 1962, Borg Olivier did not waste time in demanding just that. He tried rather unsuccessfully to get Britain to increase its aid to Malta in an effort to protect against the seemingly inevitable and seemingly ruinous consequences of the planned 'run down' of British service establishments in Malta in line with disengagement policy. After talks which did not yield much, Borg Olivier retorted that he had not gone to London 'to make a silver collection' (Frendo, *Maltese Statehood*, 86). From his London hotel on 20 August 1962 he addressed to the secretary of state for the colonies a formal and urgent request for Malta's independence. The main British concern was of course defence, but also security. The violence of 1958 and subsequent events, including manifestations of support for 'neutrality and non-alignment', had rather dented regard for Mintoff and his party generally, not only among tories; the Malta Labour Party tended to be perceived now as departing from or sidelining the Western camp. It was ironically the Nationalists under Borg Olivier who were now seen by the British as the better able to reassure the West and to offer the best chances for democracy, security, and stability in an independent state.

The demand for independence was put on the table quickly enough and preliminary discussions began almost immediately. After a controversial referendum in May 1964, in which a majority of the votes cast approved the proposed independence constitution, in July a full round of talks with all the five political parties concerned, led by Borg Olivier as prime minister, was held at Marlborough House in London. The minority view against immediate independence was dismissed. The majority view was hindered by disagreements as to constitutional form, mainly concerning civil and secular entitlements against traditional Roman Catholic presumptions and fears, but one of Mintoff's six points also endorsed the potential justification of violence. The MLP also seemed unenthusiastic about Malta's staying in the Commonwealth, or retaining the George Cross in the national colours.

The mild-mannered, soft-spoken Borg Olivier, patiently, persistently, perseveringly, once again had his way. On 21 September 1964 Malta became an independent state within the Commonwealth. This was undoubtedly Borg Olivier's outstanding achievement, and yet more so was the fact that in subsequent years he supervised a reasonably smooth, peaceful, and democratic transition to statehood. In such a context investment was forthcoming, so that even economically, in spite of many difficulties, the country prospered markedly, putting paid to wild fears of mass unemployment and chaos. Independence was part of a package which included retaining British defence facilities for ten years and financial aid to the tune of £51 million. NATO's Mediterranean branch headquarters, just outside Valletta, was also retained, ensuring that Malta would continue to have a Western shield, while British and NATO forces would continue to benefit from this strategic outpost for their general purposes.

Those in Britain who had been impressed by Mintoff's more confident and charismatic posture were surprised when Borg Olivier carried the first elections to be held after independence, in 1966. An article in the *Daily Mirror* early in 1967 warned Harold Wilson that

> Dr Borg Olivier is a hard nut to crack—especially at night. The dapper doctor has already worn out several teams of British negotiators who have tangled with him on the present Malta problem and other issues. Dr Olivier starts the day slowly, but when the sun goes down he begins his work—and his working day becomes a long hard night. … Dr Olivier—a solicitor by profession, a politician by birth and a statesman by force of circumstances—is one of the most persistent and stubborn negotiators Mr Wilson will ever come up against.   (*Daily Mirror*, 24 Feb 1967)

By this time tourism, industry, and even agriculture had benefited considerably from infrastructural readjustments, unemployment had generally decreased, and by 1969 emigration had almost ceased. Rising costs and expectations were problematic in a creeping 'neo-colonial' atmosphere, especially in housing and land speculation. Borg Olivier was sometimes slow and vacillating in his decisions, giving the impression that government was sliding or unduly tolerant in the face of Labour-supported union militancy. Notwithstanding the taint of clericalism, it was in these years that Maltese society began to open up at a fast pace. The secularizing process took various forms, from greater travel and contact with foreigners, to a casino and bikinis on the beach, which the church opposed, and a changing sociological stratification in the workforce, for example with many women for the first time finding jobs in new factories set up under the 'aid to industry' schemes. Still, with the advantage of hindsight, Borg Olivier should perhaps have bowed out of active politics some years after getting independence for Malta, possibly in 1969, to make way for a younger post-war, post-colonial successor, but he would not budge. After narrowly losing two general elections in 1971 and 1976 he was forced to step down as party leader, although he continued to be a main attraction in independence-day festivities. In 1974 he and a handful of other Nationalist MPs opposed the proposals engineered by Mintoff through parliament, without a referendum, to change Malta from a constitutional monarchy to a republic, but a two-thirds majority was obtained none the less.

Borg Olivier died at his home in Sliema on 29 October 1980 and received a state funeral which the then prime minister, Mintoff, personally attended on foot among the thronging crowds. He was buried at Addolorata cemetery, Tarxien, Malta. His wife survived him. On regaining office in 1987, the Nationalist administration had a monument erected to Borg Olivier at the entrance to Valletta near the imposing Auberge de Castille, used from the early 1970s as the office of the prime minister.   HENRY FRENDO

Sources H. Frendo, *The origins of Maltese statehood: a case study of decolonization in the Mediterranean*, 2nd edn (2000) · H. Frendo, *Maltese political development, 1798–1964: a documentary history* (1993) · H. Frendo, *Malta's quest for independence: reflections on the course of Maltese history* (1989) · H. Frendo, *Party politics in a fortress colony: the Maltese experience*, 2nd edn (1991) [esp. epilogue and for backgrounds] · *Lejn stat sovran: Liżvilupp kostituzzjonali tal gżejjer Maltin* (1989) · H. Frendo, 'Storja ta' fiduċja u kuraġġ', *Il-Poplu* (14 Sept 1989), 5–44 · H. Frendo, 'Borg Olivier's legacy', *The popular movement for a new beginning* (1981), 59–65 · H. Frendo, 'Intervista ma' Borg Olivier', *Il-Hajja* (June 1971) · J. M. Pirotta, *Fortress colony: the final act* (1987) · b. cert.

Archives FILM 2 videos showing mainly footage of Independence in Sept 1964

Likenesses bust, National Party Headquarters, Picta, Malta · monument, Castille Place, Valletta, Malta · portrait, the Palace, Valletta, Malta

Olivier, Laurence Kerr, Baron Olivier (1907–1989), actor and director, was born at 26 Wathen Road, Dorking, Surrey, on 22 May 1907, the younger son and youngest of the three children of the Revd Gerard Kerr Olivier (1869–1939) and his first wife, Agnes Louise, *née* Crookenden (1871–1920). His father, a High Anglican, was then serving as assistant priest at St Martin's, Dorking. He was noted for his vocal resonance, athletic prowess, histrionic pulpit manner, and single-minded devotion to his calling. He was also something of a domestic tyrant. Olivier's mother, who came from a family of teachers, was more conspicuous for her intuitive intelligence and emotional sympathy. Out of the melding of these two genetic strains was to come a great actor who succeeded in a wider range of

Laurence Kerr Olivier, Baron Olivier (1907–1989), by Yousuf Karsh, 1954

parts than any of his contemporaries, proved the natural successor to Garrick, Kean, Macready, and Irving, established a national theatre through his exemplary leadership, and made Shakespeare available to a mass audience through the cinema.

Early career 'I believe that I was born to be an actor', Olivier once said (Findlater, 206), and his talent certainly manifested itself early. At ten, while attending the West End choir school at All Saints, Margaret Street, London, he appeared in a production of *Julius Caesar*; it was seen by Irving's former theatrical partner, Ellen Terry, who noted in her diary: 'The small boy who played Brutus is already a great actor' (Holden, 20). Five years later, while a student at St Edward's School, Oxford, he played Kate in *The Taming of the Shrew* (1922) in a school production invited to the Shakespeare Memorial Theatre in Stratford upon Avon. W. A. Darlington wrote in the *Daily Telegraph* that 'The boy who took the part of Kate made a fine, bold, black-eyed hussy badly in need of taming. I cannot remember seeing any actress in the part who looked it better' (ibid., 25).

Despite this early proclamation of his talent the young Olivier imagined he might be forced to follow his father into the church or his elder brother into life as an Indian rubber planter. Instead, his father told him he was going on the stage; and in 1924 he spent a year training under Elsie Fogerty at the Central School of Speech and Drama, situated in the labyrinthine interior of the Royal Albert Hall. Peggy *Ashcroft, a contemporary, recalled him as 'rather uncouth in that his sleeves were too short and his hair stood on end but he was intensely lively and great fun' (Billington, 19). That hectic youthful vitality was spotted by Sir Barry Jackson, who engaged Olivier for two seasons at the Birmingham repertory theatre from 1926 to 1928. This became Olivier's university, enabling him to play a wide variety of lead roles, including Tony Lumpkin, Uncle Vanya, and Parolles in *All's Well that Ends Well*, and leading to a lifelong friendship with his fellow actor Ralph *Richardson that was to have a decisive effect on the British theatre. Olivier also benefited from Jackson's policy of establishing London outlets for Birmingham productions. At the Royal Court, Olivier played the hero in Tennyson's archaic verse-drama, *Harold* (1926), and a flannel-suited Malcolm in *Macbeth* (1928), which engendered a belief in Shakespearian realism. And it was at the Royalty, while playing in John Drinkwater's *Bird in Hand* in 1928, that he met a rising young actress, Jill Esmond Moore Jack (stage name Jill Esmond; 1907–1990), daughter of the actor and playwright Harry Esmond Jack (Henry Vernon *Esmond). They married on 25 July 1930.

Olivier's early years were marked by an impatient hunger for fame, one endorsed by his dashing good looks, fashionable Ronald Colman moustache, and matinée idol presence. But his poor judgement was revealed when he foolishly forsook R. C. Sheriff's *Journey's End* (1928), in which he scored a great success as the war weary commander in a single Sunday night performance, in order to play the foreign legion hero in P. C. Wren's *Beau Geste* (1929). The former turned into a commercial hit: the latter proved a spectacular flop. There followed a period of short runs in bad choices—no fewer than seven plays in 1929— from which he was rescued only by Noël Coward, who cast him as the priggish Victor Prynne in *Private Lives* in 1930. Olivier detested the part but later acknowledged the huge personal influence of Coward, who cured his tendency to giggle on stage, opened his mind to great literature, and 'gave me a sense of balance, right and wrong' (Holden, 63). Coward did not, however, cure Olivier of his insatiable star hunger. During the Broadway run of *Private Lives* (1931), Olivier was spotted by a talent scout and whisked off to Hollywood. Despite Coward's finger-wagging warnings ('you've got no artistic integrity, that's your trouble'; Holden, 165), Olivier headed west, accompanied by his young wife, with reckless enthusiasm.

That enthusiasm was quickly dampened by the American studio system, which led to Olivier being cast in forgettable roles in forgotten pictures such as *Friends and Lovers* (1931) and *The Yellow Passport* (1931). After returning to London disenchanted he was once again seduced by Hollywood in 1933 with what sounded like an irresistible offer: starring opposite Greta Garbo in *Queen Christina* as the lovestruck Spanish envoy. Two weeks into shooting, however, Olivier was fired and replaced by John Gilbert. The official studio line was that Olivier was 'not tall enough': the reality was that he was petrified by his dauntingly unresponsive Swedish co-star. However humiliating at the time, the episode at least saved Olivier from the enervating prospect of a long-term studio contract. It also enabled him first to return to the Broadway stage, playing

a submissive homosexual in *The Green Bay Tree* (1933), directed by the ferociously demonic Jed Harris (later a model both for Disney's Big Bad Wolf and Olivier's Richard III), and then to resume his matinée idol career in London. One particular performance in George S. Kaufman and Edna Ferber's thinly veiled satire on the Barrymore family, *Theatre Royal* (1934), required an 8 foot leap over a balcony that enthralled West End audiences and set the standard for the bravura athleticism that defined Olivier's style throughout his career.

Rescued by Gielgud After ten years as an actor Olivier's early promise remained unfulfilled. He had won some admiring notices and had been marked out as a potentially distinguished romantic actor. But he had also appeared in a string of commercial flops, had flirted unrewardingly with Hollywood, and had largely avoided the classics. His career seemed directionless and his marriage was increasingly unhappy. If anyone redefined his erratic professional life it was John *Gielgud, who by the mid-1930s was already an established Shakespearian master. The two men, though polar opposites in temperament, became twin pillars of the British stage. They first worked together in 1934 when Olivier played Bothwell ('more Hollywood than Holyrood', said one critic) in Gielgud's production of Gordon Daviot's *Queen of Scots* at the New Theatre: a production that led to the forging of important lifelong friendships with George Devine and Glen Byam Shaw. When Gielgud staged *Romeo and Juliet* at the New Theatre in 1935 he audaciously invited Olivier to join him in alternating the roles of Romeo and Mercutio (though Robert Donat had been his first choice), with Peggy Ashcroft as their Juliet.

For Olivier, who opened as Romeo, it was his first major classical role in London, and at first it seemed to have disastrously misfired. Olivier's naturalistic approach to the verse so shocked traditionalist critics that he immediately offered to resign the role; the offer was rejected and during the run Olivier's treatment of Romeo as an impetuous adolescent who, in J. C. Trewin's words, 'entered straight from the high Renaissance' (O'Connor, *Olivier*, 32), won increasingly vocal admirers. When Olivier took over as Mercutio he was widely praised for his athleticism, fire, and swagger. There was little doubt that Gielgud had the superior vocal technique. But Olivier brought to British classical acting a 'muscularity'—in Tyrone Guthrie's phrase—that had long been missing. Olivier and Gielgud never acted together again on stage. But from now on they were regarded as amicable rivals. It was Olivier himself who, in a 1967 television interview, best summed up the vital difference between them:

> I've always thought that we were reverses of the same coin: the top half John, all spirituality, all beauty, all abstract things and myself as all earth, blood, humanity; if you like, the baser part of that humanity without the beauty. (Holden, 94)

Whatever their temperamental differences, Gielgud helped transform Olivier from romantic matinée idol and modest movie star to major classical actor. Olivier's Romeo, in spite of critical hostility, also became an important calling card: not least in cinema. It led Elizabeth Bergner to insist that he play Orlando to her Rosalind in a film of *As You Like It* (1936) that earned him glowing notices. Alexander Korda also engaged him in summer 1936 to play the lead in a costume romance, *Fire over England* (1937), opposite the darkly beautiful Vivien *Leigh. Their off-screen relationship prospered in spite of the birth of the Oliviers' son in August that year.

Impressed by Olivier's athletically romantic stage presence, Tyrone Guthrie invited him to join the Old Vic, initially to play a full-text *Hamlet* (1937). It was a crucial moment. At this stage of his rejuvenated career Olivier could have become a West End actor–manager (having in 1936 made his first venture into producing, in tandem with Ralph Richardson, with a J. B. Priestley play, *Bees on the Boat-Deck*) or a highly paid film actor. Instead, his youthful fame worship now tempered by a growing shrewdness, he plumped for a classical season at the Old Vic for £20 a week boosted by movie work whenever time allowed.

Hamlet opened the season in 1937 and once again Olivier left the critics hopelessly divided, sometimes within the same review. The influential James Agate of the *Sunday Times* flatly asserted: 'Mr Olivier does not speak poetry badly. He does not speak it at all.' At the same time Agate wrote of his 'pulsating vitality and excitement' (Agate, 273). That excitement was evidenced by a famous leap, after the play scene, from the perched up throne to the mimic stage below, and thence down to the footlights: a typical piece of Olivier bravura almost designed to highlight the difference between himself and the nobly lyric but more physically inhibited Gielgud. Again in stark contrast to Gielgud, who rarely stooped to impersonation, Olivier followed Hamlet with an elaborately disguised Toby Belch and then a cool, calculating Henry V. At first Olivier resisted Shakespeare's king because of the play's apparent glorification of war and what he saw as the monarch's scoutmaster ethos. It was Ralph Richardson who persuaded him that Henry V was 'the exaltation of scoutmasters' (Holden, 122). Eventually Olivier inhabited the character with such panache that Charles Laughton came backstage one night to pose the question why he was so good and to give him the exact answer: 'because', said Laughton, 'you are England' (ibid., 123).

No one claimed that Olivier was the embodiment of Scotland in a heavily stylized Michel Saint-Denis production of *Macbeth* (1937). But his intuitive intelligence and quest for psychological realism were demonstrated by the way he and his director, Tyrone Guthrie, turned to Freud's biographer, Ernest Jones, for help in explaining the character of Iago when they came to present *Othello* (1938). Unfortunately they failed to communicate to Ralph Richardson, the Othello, their excited discovery that the ensign had a subconscious homosexual love for the Moor and the production misfired. It was Olivier's Coriolanus, at the end of the 1938 Old Vic season, that marked a turning point and proved his greatest classical success so far. 'Of a stature to come within the line of the great tradition' wrote Alan Dent (Findlater, 215). 'A pillar of fire on a plinth

of marble', enthused J. C. Trewin (O'Connor, *Olivier*, 35). Olivier found in the proudly martial Roman a perfect vehicle for his vocal incisiveness, savage irony, and physical heroism; it helped that he did a spectacular death fall in which, characteristically, he threw himself down a staircase in a somersault and came to a dead halt just short of the footlights.

Success in cinema At the very point, however, when Olivier was being hailed as a great classical actor—worthy to be mentioned in the same breath as Macready or Irving— he disappeared from the London stage, not to be seen again for six years. Partly this was because of the Second World War. But it was also because Olivier became increasingly preoccupied by film. Although suspicious of Hollywood after the fiasco over *Queen Christina*, Olivier was persuaded to return there in 1938 to play Heathcliff in William Wyler's film of *Wuthering Heights* (1939). The process of making the film was well-documented agony: Wyler was a directorial tyrant, Olivier was snobbish about cinema and was coldly hostile to his co-star, Merle Oberon, since he longed for Vivien Leigh, with whom he was engaged in a passionate affair, to play Cathy. But the film was a turning point for Olivier in his movie career: the carapace of theatricality that surrounded his earlier screen performances was replaced by a palpable reality. Sam Goldwyn, the film's producer, threatened to fire Olivier on the grounds that his Heathcliff was ugly and dirty. But the mud and dirt to which Goldwyn objected was part of the attentive physicality of Olivier's performance: it was visible, as Roger Lewis points out, in 'the way he pats the dogs or saddles the horses or frowns into the sunshine when he's lying down in the heather or the way he stands before the fireplace staring into the coals' (Lewis, 26). Thanks to Wyler's remorseless tuition and his own willingness to learn Olivier became a first-rate screen actor. He quickly applied the lessons he had learned on *Wuthering Heights*: his Maxim de Winter in Hitchcock's film of *Rebecca* (1940) and his D'Arcy in *Pride and Prejudice* (1940) both suggest hidden fires lurking underneath an outward grace and civility.

In 1940 Olivier's first marriage was dissolved and on 30 August he was finally married to Vivien Leigh—Vivian Mary Holman (1913–1967), daughter of Ernest Richard Hartley, exchange broker, and former wife of Herbert Leigh Holman, barrister—after a long, semi-public, and faintly scandalous liaison. But, marooned in Hollywood since the outbreak of war, Olivier grew increasingly guilty and fretful at his isolation from the war effort. In California he conquered his fear of flying by taking lessons to prepare himself for active service as a pilot. As a contribution to the war effort, and at the direct suggestion of Winston Churchill, the newly married Oliviers also made a film, *Lady Hamilton* (1941), intended as a morale-boosting effort to show Britain's historic role as the scourge of megalomaniac warmongers. The film achieved its purpose, though it nearly fell foul of the American censor, who protested vigorously about its apparent endorsement of the adulterous liaison of Nelson and Lady Hamilton.

Finally back in England in 1941 Olivier pulled strings to

join the Fleet Air Arm and, to his delight, joined his old friend Ralph Richardson at a naval air station near Winchester. But his swashbuckling heroics on stage and screen were not matched by similar gifts as a pilot: on one occasion, in making an emergency landing, he managed to wreck three stationary aircraft at the base at Worthy Down. Olivier, at the age of thirty-four, realized his chances of seeing active service were limited. It was a relief to all concerned when the Ministry of Information, again at Winston Churchill's suggestion, approached him with the idea of filming *Henry V* as a contribution to the war effort. Initially Olivier's role was that of co-producer and leading actor, but when William Wyler and Carol Reed turned down the chance to direct the film Olivier took over behind the cameras as well.

Although Olivier removed much of the ambiguity from Shakespeare's complex drama of kingship—excising Henry's threats of genocide to the citizens of Harfleur— the film emerged as infinitely more than a piece of patriotic propaganda. Olivier showed genuine directorial flair in his framing device, whereby the action starts with a crane shot over a model of Shakespeare's London and eventually moves from the Globe Theatre into the fields of France. The battle scenes—including a famous moment when English arrows are heard whistling through the air—were also brilliantly filmed. Olivier's own performance was a beautifully poised characterization, balancing a rueful kingly reflectiveness with spine-tingling clarion cries as Henry exhorted his troops on the eve of battle. Released in Britain in 1944 and in America two years later—where it won Olivier a special Academy award— the film not only transcended its immediate propagandist purpose, it proved, to a generation of doubters, that Shakespeare was essentially filmable and could command a popular audience.

The Old Vic While Olivier was completing *Henry V* at Denham Studios, he was persuaded by Ralph Richardson to join himself and a former BBC drama producer, John Burrell, as part of a triumvirate to run the Old Vic company. Since the bombing of its Waterloo Road base in 1941 the Old Vic had been kept alive by Tyrone Guthrie, who turned it, with great success, into an itinerant provincial company. Now the intention was to give it a London base at the New Theatre and to create an ambitious classical repertory: to make it, in all but name, an embryonic national theatre. With his highly competitive actor's instinct Olivier was not overjoyed at his initial allocation of roles. He loathed the part of the gallant Ruritanian soldier, Sergius, in Shaw's *Arms and the Man*, and when the production opened on tour in Manchester in 1944 he was so dispirited he felt tempted to go back to the navy. But, *en route* from the theatre back to the Midland Hotel after the second performance, Tyrone Guthrie responded to Olivier's fierce denunciation of the character by saying, 'Well, of course, if you can't love him, you'll never be any good in him, will you' (Holden, 188). According to Olivier the scales fell from his eyes and Guthrie's shrewd, well-timed observation 'changed the course of my actor's thinking for the rest of my life' (Olivier, 110).

Olivier's versatility and technique were, at this stage of his career, beyond question. But his ability to love a character, to enter totally into his being and to achieve the transubstantiation that is the hallmark of great acting, was conclusively proved by his triumph as Richard III in the third play of the Old Vic London season in 1944. In building the character Olivier used various elements, including the voice of Henry Irving and the malign temperament of the New York director Jed Harris. But the finished article was entirely his own and confirmation of his interpretative originality. In place of downright transpontine villainy Olivier offered a spellbinding mixture of the inner strategist and the outward hypocrite. 'Here indeed', wrote J. C. Trewin after the first night on 13 September,

> we have the double Gloucester, thinker and doer, mind and mask … no other player in recent memory has made us so conscious of the usurper's intellect, made so plausible every move on the board from the great opening challenge to the last despair and death. (Holden, 191)

Irony was the quality seized on by the young Kenneth Tynan:

> I remember the deep concern, as of a bustling spinster, with which Olivier grips his brother George and says, with sardonic, effeminate intentness 'We are not safe, Clarence, we are *not* safe'; while, even as he speaks, the plot is laid which will kill the man. (Tynan, 35)

Olivier's triumph as Richard III was absolute: so much so that it became his most frequently imitated performance and one whose supremacy went unchallenged until Antony Sher played the role forty years later. But if it was Richard III that fully released Olivier's dark genius it may be because the character's blend of outward bonhomie and inner demonism accorded more closely than even he realized with his own, strangely driven private nature.

The Old Vic seasons at the New from 1944 to 1946 quickly became the stuff of theatrical legend. They showed the potential of a permanent classical company. They influenced a whole generation of young theatregoers, including a teenage Peter Hall. And they showed Olivier's infinite versatility. In the two parts of Shakespeare's *Henry IV* (1945) he moved from a ginger wigged, stammering, fiercely virile Hotspur to a shrill, spinsterly, scarecrow-like Justice Shallow. In one tumultuous evening he also played Sophocles' Oedipus and Mr Puff in Sheridan's *The Critic* (1945). In the former, Olivier, avoiding the marble chill associated with Greek tragedy, achieved a bloodshot realism climaxing in a cry of echoing anguish and terror. It says a lot about the retentive memory of the great actor that it was based on the tormented sound made by an ermine when its tongue is trapped by salt scattered upon hard snow. But although the instant transition to Mr Puff, hoisted into the flies on a painted cloud and clinging desperately to the curtain as it came down, was virtuosic, it did Sheridan few favours and seemed designed mainly to exhibit Olivier's showmanship.

Olivier, as the Old Vic seasons proved, held all the court cards as an actor: an incisive voice that could eat like acid into metal, an electrifying physicality, an interpretative originality, and a restless curiosity about humanity that gave everything he did an emotional reality. If there were any lingering doubts they concerned his capacity for tragic grandeur, and they resurfaced when he played King Lear in 1946. Some observers thought it a great performance. Tynan, however, felt 'it merely introduced us to a few wholly unexpected facets of the private life of Mr Justice Shallow' (Tynan, 59). Agate, while applauding its pathos and stillness, astutely observed: 'I have the conviction that Olivier is a comedian by instinct and a tragedian by art' (Findlater, 236).

In 1947 Olivier was knighted 'for services to stage and films'. He was, and throughout the twentieth century remained, the youngest actor ever to have been so honoured, though it says much about his innate competitiveness that he deeply resented Ralph Richardson's prior elevation. But, although Olivier was by now the acknowledged leader of his profession, his film *Hamlet* (1948) was an oddly inert affair. Half the text was cut, including two of Hamlet's greatest soliloquies. The camera endlessly tracked up and down the corridors of Roger Furse's Elsinore. And, despite a prodigiously athletic leap from a 15 foot high platform in order to kill Claudius, Olivier's own performance lacked the fiery energy he had displayed at the Old Vic ten years previously. Even though it was the least interesting of Olivier's screen Shakespeares, the film was a popular commercial success and won four Hollywood Oscars, including those for best film and best actor.

Olivier's fortunes were in the ascendant. And if there was surprise that at the height of his fame he should decide to lead the Old Vic company on a ten-month tour of Australia and New Zealand in 1948 there were good reasons for the move. Olivier and Richardson had been approached by the prospective National Theatre Board with a scheme to incorporate the Old Vic into the finished building: for Olivier an international tour would be a means of forging a wholly new company with a national identity. Cultural diplomacy also played its part: the British Council felt that a display of excellence would be a means of softening antipodean anti-imperialistic sentiment. For Olivier himself there were also private motives for undertaking the trip: his total absorption in his career had put strains on his marriage to the increasingly manic-depressive Vivien and he felt that the tour, in which she was to play three leading roles, would reignite their passion and confirm her theatrical status. The irony is that, although the tour achieved its diplomatic aims and increased the Oliviers' world fame, it led to the unravelling of their marriage and saw the dissolution of the Old Vic partnership.

The three plays chosen were *Richard III*, Thornton Wilder's *The Skin of our Teeth*, and Sheridan's *The School for Scandal*, in which the Oliviers played Sir Peter and Lady Teazle. The schedule, with Olivier appearing in all three plays and directing two of them, was incredibly gruelling. On top of that he was expected to fulfil a quasi-ambassadorial role: he was asked to inspect troops, take salutes, and even, on one occasion, make a speech on monarchy and empire to an audience of 3000 in Melbourne town hall. On one level the tour was a triumphant success: 179 performances were given to more than 300,000 people, a sizeable profit accrued, and any residual anti-British sentiment was overcome by the Oliviers' joint glamour. But the tour also marked a watershed in Olivier's professional and personal fortunes. Physically he sustained a severe cartilage injury which led to his playing the final performances of Richard III on morphine. That, however, was a minor problem compared to the realization that his marriage, as Vivien carried on an open liaison with a member of the company, was little more than a hollow ritual sustained for the benefit of an adoring public.

The biggest blow, however, came half-way through the tour when Olivier received a letter from Lord Esher, the chairman of the Old Vic, announcing that the board of governors planned to dispense with the services of Olivier, Richardson, and John Burrell as directors at the end of their five-year contracts. The move, already prophesied by Richardson, was partly a result of the politicking over a planned national theatre. Some also saw the hand of Tyrone Guthrie in the sacking: he had been critical of recent Old Vic policy and saw Olivier and Richardson as absentee landlords who wanted 'to have their cake and eat it' (Holden, 239). Whatever the motives the timing was cruel and the manner brutal. Far from advancing the cause of the national theatre, it delayed it by many years. With Olivier and Richardson at the helm the Old Vic might have become the basis for a national company; instead the sacking of both actors ensured they returned to the private sector and the pursuit of their individual careers.

Mid-life crisis Although Olivier returned to do a final season with the Old Vic in 1949, adding his own production of Anouilh's *Antigone* to *Richard III* and *The School for Scandal*, the antipodean tour marked a decisive moment in his career. The veteran actor Harcourt Williams noted: 'Larry had lost the basic need that propels every actor. He was leaning more and more towards directing and producing because he no longer had the drive for attention … his attitude to life was almost world-weary' (Holden, 246). Increasingly, in fact, he became an impresario, taking a four-year lease on the St James's Theatre in 1949 where he staged plays by Christopher Fry and Dennis Cannan as well as starring, with Vivien Leigh, in a Festival of Britain pairing of Shaw's *Caesar and Cleopatra* and Shakespeare's *Antony and Cleopatra* (1951). He also played to the hilt the role of country squire at Notley Abbey, the twelfth-century, 22-room Buckinghamshire manor house that he had bought in 1945. Apparently accepting that his marriage was something of a sham he turned a benevolently blind eye on Vivien's affair with Peter Finch, a young actor whom Olivier had talent-spotted in Australia and whose British career he actively promoted.

If Olivier's theatrical career lost much of its dynamism in the early 1950s, he made one film that contains one of his finest, most underrated screen performances: as the doomed George Hurstwood in William Wyler's *Carrie* (1952). Once a rich restaurateur, Hurstwood sacrifices his marriage for a grand passion and ends up destitute, tubercular, and desperately craving a handout from the lover who has abandoned him. It was a total reversal of Olivier's previously heroic screen presence. But, as always, he invested the character with a microscopically accurate realism: he counted the banknotes and handled the keys in the precise manner of a midwestern restaurant owner. In the final scenes, when he begged Jennifer Jones's Carrie for money for a night's lodging, Olivier also touched rare emotional depths: his voice thick with illness, his eyes closed in exhaustion, he gave the lie to the familiar canard that he was an exclusively technical actor. The film was a commercial failure. But William Wyler accurately described it as 'the truest and best portrayal on film of an American by an Englishman' (Holden, 261).

If *Carrie* was a flop *d'estime*, the film of *The Beggar's Opera* (1952), in which Olivier played Macheath, was an unmitigated disaster. Olivier's lightweight baritone was judged inadequate. There were on-set disagreements with the director, Peter Brook, and the film opened to derisive reviews. Olivier's reputation was also scarcely enhanced by his appearance, opposite Vivien Leigh, in Terence Rattigan's *The Sleeping Prince* (1953). He was not only accused of wasting his talent on commercial froth, the play renewed critical speculation, which first surfaced during the season of dual Cleopatras at the St James's, that he was increasingly scaling down his own heroic individualism to accommodate the porcelain prettiness of his co-star. Trapped inside a public showbiz marriage Olivier seemed more concerned with propping up his wife's career and ensuring her mental stability than with scaling the lonely, classical peaks.

It was with some relief that Olivier turned in the winter of 1954 to the filming of *Richard III* (1955). In some ways, it was the hardest of his three Shakespearian films to accomplish: the original text is dynastically complex and studded with references to past events and unseen characters. But Alan Dent's adaptation clarified it admirably for a cinema audience, and Olivier brilliantly used the camera as a co-conspirator, confiding to it—and to the audience—his plans to achieve the throne by giving murder the cloak of constitutional legality. What particularly emerges on screen is Olivier's sly, feminine roguishness; his performance has the twinkling malevolence of a maiden aunt with disturbing psychopathic tendencies. With Ralph Richardson as a Buckingham wittily described by Paul Dehn as 'a Mr Baldwin who has read Machiavelli' (Dehn, 76) and John Gielgud as an exquisitely lyrical Clarence, the film also had a star power impossible to achieve at the Old Vic.

A classical recovery After his return from the antipodes Olivier's own career had seemed to be subordinated to the fabled showbiz construct of 'the Oliviers'. A major turning point, however, came in 1955 with Olivier's return—for the first time since his schoolboy Katharine—to the Shakespeare Memorial Theatre in Stratford upon Avon, then, under the directorship of Anthony Quayle and Glen Byam Shaw, enjoying an artistic prosperity that completely eclipsed the dowdy Old Vic. Olivier's chosen roles for the season were Malvolio, Macbeth, and Titus Andronicus. But, while Vivien Leigh played opposite him in all the productions, there was no sense of Olivier diminishing his blowtorch ebullience to accommodate his wife. After a

modest start with Malvolio, played as a bumptious arriviste with severe vowel problems, Olivier enjoyed a total triumph as Macbeth: a role that, in the annals of British theatre, had traditionally defeated even the greatest actors. Olivier convincingly reconciled the soldier, the poet, and the hero–villain. Above all he invested the character with a brooding inwardness in the early scenes as if he had been living with bloody thoughts for a long time past. But there was also a savage comic irony—not least in the scene with the two murderers—and at the end a heart wrenching despair. When Macbeth lists the consolations of age that he has forever sacrificed, Olivier's voice soared on '*troops* of friends' as if summoning up an eternal, echoing loneliness.

Even more remarkably, Olivier's conquest of Macbeth was followed by his total reclamation of Titus Andronicus as a tragic hero in Peter Brook's starkly ritualistic production. Elizabethan grand guignol was transformed into great art, and Olivier discovered in Titus premonitions of Lear. His cry of 'I am the sea' was accompanied by a sound like waves beating on a distant shore; the on-stage severance of his hand transcended stage trickery through his long withheld howl of pain; and when he leant against a pillar to ask 'When will this fearful slumber have an end?' he became the epitome of antique pathos. Whatever accusations critics made against Olivier in the course of his long career he eventually rebutted. To Agate's claim that he was an instinctive comedian rather than a tragedian or to Tynan's assertion that he was an essentially active player incapable of great suffering, his Stratford Macbeth and Titus provided a definitive riposte.

Olivier's reassertion of his classical supremacy, endorsed by the release of the cinematic *Richard III*, still left him with a gnawing dissatisfaction. His private life, with Peter Finch moving into Notley Abbey to form a *ménage à trois*, was an unholy mess. His mooted film of *Macbeth* was capsized by the death in 1956 of its putative producer, Alexander Korda. And Olivier's experience of directing Marilyn Monroe in *The Prince and the Showgirl* (1957), though it generated prurient showbiz headlines, was a protracted nightmare. By his own admission Olivier was 'going mad, desperately searching for something suddenly fresh and thrillingly exciting' (Holden, 315), when a second courtesy visit to the Royal Court to see *Look Back in Anger*, which he cordially detested, led to an encounter with its author, John Osborne. However much he disliked Osborne's first play Olivier was shrewd enough to see that the theatrical power centre was gradually shifting from Shaftesbury Avenue to Sloane Square, and cannily enquired if Osborne's new play might have a role for him. It was a defining moment both for Olivier in his professional and private life and for the future of British theatre. While Gielgud, Richardson, and Guinness had all rejected the chance to appear in *Waiting for Godot*, Olivier actively embraced the new. The result was a breathtaking performance in *The Entertainer*, which finally opened at the Royal Court in 1957. Not only did Olivier capture the surface detail of Osborne's third-rate, broken-down music-hall comedian, Archie Rice—the cheap grey suit, the fake bonhomie, the leering innuendo, the bent-wristed camp were all exactly observed—but beyond that Olivier conveyed the total desolation of a man aware of his own essential hollowness and atrophied emotions. It was a world away from Macbeth, and yet Olivier invested the role with a similar arc of despair leading to the ultimate revelation of the character's terminal solitude.

Olivier's performance in *The Entertainer* reanimated his career and marked a symbolic union between the theatrical establishment and the radical pioneers: here was the embodiment of theatrical glamour appearing in a play that treated the music-hall as a metaphor for a decaying, post-Suez Britain. The play also introduced Olivier to a young actress, Joan Plowright, who played his daughter in the production's West End transfer and who, after the protracted breakup of his marriage to Vivien Leigh (they were divorced in December 1960), was eventually to become his third wife.

Olivier's renewed zest for work, and eagerness to ally himself with a new generation, was confirmed by his towering 1959 Stratford upon Avon performance as Coriolanus under the direction of the 28-year-old Peter Hall. In his return to a role he had first played at the Old Vic in 1938 Olivier emphasized the character's emotional immaturity, loathing of civilian humbug, and smouldering irony. But, as Laurence Kitchin noted, it was Olivier's 'interpretative intelligence' (Kitchin, 136) that stood out. It was symbolized not just by his sulky pride in the presence of public acclamation or by his spoilt-boy behaviour with his mother, but by the spontaneous joy that greeted any mention of the Volscian leader, Aufidius: a clear indication of the underlying sexuality of martial conflict. Yet there was a bruising virility and fierce athleticism to his performance, culminating in a death fall that led to his being suspended by his ankles from a 12 foot promontory: an athleticism all the more astonishing when set against the fact that he was regularly commuting from Stratford to Morecambe to film *The Entertainer*.

New directions Olivier's appetite for the new led him back to the Royal Court in 1960 to play Berenger, the insignificant little man who stays defiantly human when everyone else turns into a rhino, in Ionesco's absurdist parable *Rhinoceros*. This was a play that hardly stretched his talents and it led to a bitter quarrel with the play's director, Orson Welles, whose role Olivier summarily usurped in the final stages of rehearsal. But although he busily shuttled between London and Broadway, where he played first the title role and then Henry II in Anouilh's *Becket* (1960–61), and although he finally achieved domestic happiness and stability with his marriage to Joan Ann Plowright (*b.* 1929)—the daughter of William Ernest Plowright, a Lincolnshire newspaper editor, and former wife of Roger Gage—on 17 March 1961, his public career still lacked a visible destination.

The focus Olivier desperately needed came almost by accident. A Sussex optician, Leslie Evershed-Martin, had chanced to watch a television programme by Tyrone Guthrie hymning the virtues of the open stage at Stratford, Ontario: ironically a theatrical form that Guthrie

had discovered during an improvised indoor restaging of the Olivier *Hamlet* at Elsinore in 1937. Evershed-Martin decided that the town of Chichester had parallels with the Canadian Stratford and could sustain a similar theatre. Via Guthrie he was put in touch with Olivier and offered him the directorship of the brand new, still unfinished hexagonal theatre. Everything conspired to make Olivier accept: his paternalistic love of companies, his relish for the new, and the fact that he and his wife had decided to settle in nearby Brighton.

Accepting a modest salary of £3000 Olivier threw himself into the Chichester enterprise wholeheartedly, and, after a shaky start with two obscure period plays, the opening season in 1962 sprang to life with his own near definitive production of *Uncle Vanya*. It was a reminder of Olivier's underestimated gifts as a director; everything about the production, from the distant sound of barking dogs to the intrusive peals of thunder, was perfectly orchestrated. It also proved that the open sided Chichester stage was perfectly suited to proscenium arch naturalistic drama. Above all, it was a company achievement dominated by luminous performances from Michael Redgrave as a shrill, pigeon-toed, self-deceiving Vanya, from Olivier himself as a visionary Astrov maimed by self-knowledge, and from Joan Plowright as a defiant, unbearably moving Sonya. *Vanya* performances in that first Chichester season acquired such intensity that backstage they were dubbed 'holy nights'.

The National Theatre Just as Chichester was preparing to open, plans for a national theatre were coming to a head. As far back as 1957 Olivier had been sounded out about the directorship by Lord Chandos (formerly Oliver Lyttelton), chairman of the various groups working towards establishment of a national theatre. Given that the National seemed a distant prospect, Olivier was wary. But in 1961 the Labour-led London county council forced the government's hand and the Conservative chancellor, Selwyn Lloyd, announced the release of £1 million towards the creation of a national theatre: initially an umbrella organization intended to incorporate the Old Vic, Stratford, and the Sadler's Wells opera and ballet companies. Stratford's eventual withdrawal led to the removal of Sadler's Wells from the equation and confirmed the idea of a national theatre as a separate entity. In July 1962 Selwyn Lloyd gave the green light to the revised scheme: the Old Vic would become the temporary home of the National Theatre Company pending the construction of a theatre on the south bank of the Thames. Lord Chandos became the first chairman of the National Theatre Board. Olivier was formally asked to become the theatre's founder-director and had no hesitation in accepting. It was the fulfilment of a lifelong dream and one that would capitalize on his gifts as actor, director, producer, company leader, and rallier of the troops. He could even use Chichester as a means of building a new company.

Olivier's shrewdest move in setting up the National Theatre was to invite two of the brightest young directors from the Royal Court, John Dexter and William Gaskill, to join him as associates. He also cannily acceded to Kenneth

*Tynan's wish to become literary manager, thereby capitalizing on his vast theatrical knowledge while neutralizing him as a critic. His most ungenerous decisions were his failure to recruit Richardson and Gielgud, and his miscasting, and eventually sacking, of Michael Redgrave, seemingly unaware of his disabling illness. But the absence of the older stars paved the way for the emergence of new ones; and under Olivier's tutelage Maggie Smith, Robert Stephens, Colin Blakely, Derek Jacobi, and Anthony Hopkins all developed into major classical performers. In its early years the new National Theatre Company seemed equally adept at all styles: period classics such as *The Recruiting Officer* and *Trelawny of the Wells*, established warhorses such as *Hobson's Choice* and *Hay Fever*, and even new plays such as *The Royal Hunt of the Sun* and, famously, *Rosencrantz and Guildenstern are Dead*.

Olivier himself also led the company from the front. His Astrov, repeated from Chichester, was followed by Captain Brazen in *The Recruiting Officer* (1963), an exact study in controlled flamboyance, and a magisterial and still controversial Othello (1964). With his rolling, loose-limbed gait, his oscillating hips, his rotating palms, Olivier conveyed the vanity, pride, and self-dramatizing narcissism of an Othello who was natural prey to Iago's wiles. His voice, deepened by an octave through rigorous training, also matched the character's mellifluous rhetoric. And his disintegration, under Iago's poison, was truly awesome, leading, as he tore a crucifix from his neck, to an atavistic obeisance to the barbaric gods. But while Harold Hobson spoke for the majority in acclaiming 'the power, passion, verisimilitude and pathos of Sir Laurence's performance' (Holden, 379), doubting voices were raised. Jonathan Miller, while admiring Olivier's bravura and energy, was stolidly unimpressed. The critic of *The Times* argued that the downgrading of Iago seriously impoverished the play, in that 'Othello needs an adversary, not an accomplice' (Elsom, 142).

Olivier's finest performance in the National Theatre's early years was as Captain Edgar, locked in a love and death struggle with his wife, in Strindberg's *The Dance of Death* (1967). As Richard Findlater wrote, he looked and sounded magnificently right: 'close-cropped Prussian head, hooded stony eyes, aggressively jutting jaw, a choleric red face which went purple in his fits and seemed to blanch when he was on the point of doing something particularly nasty' (Findlater, 232). Beyond that, Olivier combined monstrosity and humour in a way that seemed quintessentially Strindbergian and was especially brilliant in the mimetic passages: executing the Boyars' dance with a brutal grace or stamping on his wife's photograph and shooting at her piano with Dionysiac fury. It took Olivier's interpretative zest to remind audiences that Strindberg was not a morbid misogynist but a blackly comic writer.

Under Olivier's leadership the National Theatre enjoyed several years of unstinted glory: there may not have been any discernible house style, as at the rival Royal Shakespeare Company, but there was an ability to adapt to the demands of a particular play. Without creating an inflexible ensemble on European lines, Olivier also succeeded in building up a fiercely loyal company which he led with bulldog tenacity. But after four golden years the National began to seem a troubled organization in the late 1960s. Olivier himself suffered a series of debilitating illnesses, starting with cancer of the prostate. His two directorial associates, Dexter and Gaskill, who had given the company much of its early impetus, decided to leave. There was also a furious public row in 1968 over the National Theatre Board's refusal to sanction a production of Rolf Hochhuth's *Soldiers*: a play which debated the blanket bombing of Dresden and parenthetically branded Churchill a war criminal. The play was enthusiastically championed by Kenneth Tynan and equally firmly rejected by Lord Chandos, who had been a member of Churchill's wartime cabinet. Olivier found himself caught in the middle: he believed strongly in the idea of directorial independence and valued Tynan's literary knowledge but was not, in the end, prepared to resign over a play whose arguments about Churchill were and remained unproven. What was surprising, to an outsider, was Chandos's privately expressed contempt for Olivier's judgement and his belief that he was being manipulated not just by Tynan but by his wife, Joan Plowright, whom Chandos described as 'a Red' (personal knowledge).

By the late 1960s Olivier was suffering increasingly from stage fright, world weariness, and an increasing number of side-effects from his cancer treatment. But he returned to the stage in 1970 as Shylock in Jonathan Miller's production of *The Merchant of Venice*: a performance that, when stripped of the Hebraic accoutrements Olivier had originally planned, poignantly revealed the contradictions in Shylock's character. The contradictions in Olivier's own character were exposed by his ambivalent acceptance of a life peerage (as Baron Olivier, of Brighton) in the same year. The establishment side of him recognized that it was the first ennoblement of an actor in the history of his profession and, as such, must be dutifully accepted: the subversive, pub entertainer side of him was frightened it would cut him off from his colleagues. On the day of his elevation he dispatched a circular to the National Theatre staff suggesting that the first person to address him as 'Your Lordship' would be fired on the spot.

Inevitably there was a twilit quality to Olivier's final years at the National, but one illuminated by periodic bursts of theatrical lightning. One struck in December 1971 at a time when the National, having opened a second front at the New Theatre and come up with a string of duds, was under severe pressure. Olivier's James Tyrone in Michael Blakemore's production of *Long Day's Journey into Night* was both an individual triumph and a symbol of the National's renewed confidence. What was startling was Olivier's ability to play an ageing, miserly, cantankerous American matinée idol who, totally unlike himself, had put commercial safety before artistic adventure. Olivier's genius was to suggest that inside this New England ham lurked an unrealized talent. When he sweetly crooned 'We are such stuff as dreams are made on', he both evoked a vanished acting style and made the audience believe for a moment that Tyrone might once have been an American Kean. For a genuinely great actor to play a nearly great one was a technical feat of extraordinary skill.

Later years Even as Olivier was enjoying a success that would herald a period of renewed energy at the National Theatre, plans were under way to appoint his successor. Informal approaches to Peter Hall had been made by Sir Max Rayne, the National's new chairman, as early as the summer of 1971. Hall was sworn to secrecy, and when Olivier indicated to Rayne in February 1972 that he wished gradually to phase himself out he had no knowledge of the backroom negotiations. Only on 24 March was he formally told of the board's decision that he was to be replaced by Peter Hall. For the second time in his life he felt a deep sense of betrayal by a board, but on this occasion the wounds never healed and to his dying day he was aggrieved at the failure to consult him over his eventual successor. At one stage he wanted an actor—Joan Plowright, Richard Burton, or Richard Attenborough—to take over the reins: at other times, he plumped for Michael Blakemore.

Although Olivier made life difficult for Peter Hall—who finally succeeded him in November 1973 with the intention of leading the company into the new building on the south bank—and prevaricated about the date of his departure, he was still treated with a dismal lack of dignity and respect by the National Theatre Board. It says much about his appetite for the unconventional that his final appearance at the National—or indeed on any stage—was in December 1973 as a tough Glaswegian Trotskyite in Trevor Griffiths's *The Party*. Olivier phrased his climactic twenty-minute speech with a musical command of tempi, and with a vivid ability to clarify the complex argument through the use of his bunched and muscular hands. It was a granite hard performance, possibly imbued with something of Olivier's own growing detestation of unearned authority.

Freed from the shackles of running the National Theatre, Olivier devoted himself in the last fifteen years of his life to capitalizing on his fame and earning a tidy fortune for the benefit of his wife and their three children. He earned $1 million making a Polaroid commercial for American television. He made cameo appearances in a number of often undistinguished films. His best performance, by far, was as a sadistic Nazi dentist in John Schlesinger's *Marathon Man* (1976), for which he was nominated, in the Oscars, as best supporting actor.

It was in television, a medium he initially despised, that Olivier made his greatest impact in his later years. In the 1970s he co-produced (with Derek Granger) and starred in two series of adaptations for Granada of well-known stage plays. It gave him the chance to repeat his brilliant performance as the fetishistic, hat-thieving grandfather in *Saturday, Sunday, Monday* and to essay roles, such as Tennessee Williams's Big Daddy, that he had never played on stage. Most surprising of all was his performance as the muscular homosexual Harry Kane, in Pinter's *The Collection* (1976): listening to Olivier's callous description of his

working-class lover, Bill, as a 'slum-slug' and watching his brutal finesse one could only dream of the many other Pinter roles he might have played. It was also for Granada that Olivier played the dying, guilt-haunted patriarch Lord Marchmain in *Brideshead Revisited* (1981), and for whom in 1983 he played a final, valedictory King Lear. Given an endless series of illnesses that would have destroyed a lesser man, the vocal thunder was inevitably missing but Lear's irascibility and suffering were sharply etched and in the confrontation with Gloucester on Dover cliffs Olivier achieved a lucid pathos that echoed his former glories.

Olivier was awarded an honorary Oscar in 1979, and was appointed OM in 1981. He held honorary degrees from Tufts, Massachusetts (1946), Oxford (1957), Edinburgh (1964), London (1968), Manchester (1968), and Sussex (1978). He continued working until three years before his death of renal failure at his home at The Malthouse, Horsebridge Green, near Steyning, Sussex, on 11 July 1989. He was survived by his wife, their three children, and the son of his first marriage.

Olivier crammed numerous careers into a single lifetime: classical actor, Hollywood star, theatrical and television producer, West End impresario, National Theatre director. His *Confessions of an Actor* (1982) gives the strong impression of a man driven by an overpowering sense of private guilt inherited from his religious upbringing and fuelled by his single-minded career worship, marital failures, and professional jealousies. But what stood out, both in public interviews and in personal encounters, was his magpie memory and insatiable curiosity. It was typical of Olivier that, in the National Theatre *Othello*, a sly, ironic aside to the duke of Venice about the 'Anthropophagi'—implying a complicity of knowledge—was based on an encounter twenty-five years previously with a pseudo-intellectual who, in talking about stimulants, quickly changed the word to 'stimuli'. Olivier's career was studded with examples of gestures, intonations, even pieces of theatrical business retrieved at will from the vast storehouse of his memory. But there was in Olivier a prodigious fascination with humanity at large. His omnivorous actor's observation was akin to that of a great novelist or poet.

Partly because of the lack of discrimination in his later choice of film it became fashionable to downgrade Olivier and to suggest, especially in comparison with Gielgud and Richardson, that he lacked some essential inner richness. But that was to overlook the protean nature of his achievements. Only a man of Olivier's iron determination, political skill, and instinctive leadership could have translated the National Theatre from a platonic idea into a living reality. It took a similar mixture of tenacity, energy, and endurance to make no fewer than three Shakespeare films that proved, against all the intellectual odds, that it was possible to transfer the greatest poetic drama to the screen.

For all Olivier's multiple achievements, it is as an actor that he will live longest in the collective memory. 'He is greatest', wrote G. H. Lewes, 'who is greatest in the highest reaches of his art.' No other actor before Olivier conquered so many of the commanding theatrical heights: not just Macbeth, Hamlet, Lear, and Othello, but Titus, Coriolanus, Henry V, Hotspur, Romeo, Shylock, Sophocles' Oedipus, Ibsen's Halvard Solness, Chekhov's Astrov, Strindberg's Captain Edgar. Olivier was no less adept in comedy, whether as Tony Cavendish in *Theatre Royal*, Sheridan's Mr Puff and Sir Peter Teazle, Congreve's Tattle in *Love for Love*, or Farquhar's Captain Brazen in *The Recruiting Officer*. Even if there were occasional failures in modern drama—such as his performance as a devious midlands insurance agent in David Turner's *Semi-Detached* (1962)—they were made up for by the complex richness of his Archie Rice in *The Entertainer*.

Conscious of his status as a national icon Olivier would have thought it entirely fitting that, after his death, his vast professional and personal archive should be acquired by the British Library with the help of a grant from the Heritage Lottery Fund. But, although the establishment side of Olivier relished honours and acclaim, he saw himself primarily as a practical man of the theatre. And, if he elevated the art of acting in the twentieth century, it was principally by the overwhelming force of his example. Like Garrick, Kean, and Irving before him, he lent glamour and excitement to acting so that, in any theatre in the world, an Olivier night raised the level of expectation and sent spectators out into the darkness a little more aware of themselves and having experienced a transcendent touch of ecstasy. That, in the end, was the true measure of his greatness.　MICHAEL BILLINGTON

Sources L. Olivier, *Confessions of an actor* (1982) · A. Holden, *Olivier* (1988) · D. Spoto, *Laurence Olivier* (1991) · R. Findlater, *The player kings* (1971) · R. Lewis, *The real life of Laurence Olivier* (1997) · G. O'Connor, *Darlings of the gods* (1984) · G. O'Connor, ed., *Olivier: in celebration* (1987) · K. Tynan, *He that plays the king* (1950) · J. Agate, *Brief chronicles* (1943) · M. Billington, *Peggy Ashcroft* (1988) · J. Elsom, ed., *Post-war British theatre criticism* (1981) · P. Dehn, *For love and money* (1956) · I. Herbert, ed., *Who's who in the theatre*, 1 (1981) · *WWW, 1981–90* · Burke, *Peerage* · personal knowledge (2004) · *CGPLA Eng. & Wales* (1989) · L. Kitchin, *Mid-century drama* (1960)
Archives BL, corresp. and papers | Bodl. Oxf., letters to J. W. Lambert · JRL, corresp. with Robert Donat · King's AC Cam., letters to G. H. W. Rylands · NL Wales, corresp. with Emlyn Williams · Tate collection, corresp. with Lord Clark · Theatre Museum, London, corresp. with Christopher Fry
Likenesses photographs, 1922–80, Hult. Arch. · L. Willinger, photograph, 1940, NPG · P. Lambda, two busts, 1950, NPG · Y. Karsh, three photographs, 1954, NPG [*see illus.*] · I. Penn, photograph, 1962, NPG · A. Newman, photograph, 1978, NPG · E. Sergeant, oils, 1982, NPG · A. Morrison, photograph, 1987, NPG · R. Spear, portrait, Royal Shakespeare Company Gallery, Stratford upon Avon · A. Wysard, double portrait, pencil and watercolour drawing (with Vivien Leigh), NPG
Wealth at death £1,352,383: probate, 25 Oct 1989, *CGPLA Eng. & Wales*

Olivier, Sydney Haldane, Baron Olivier (1859–1943), civil servant, politician, and author, was born at Colchester on 16 April 1859, the second son and the sixth of the ten children of Henry Arnold Olivier (*d.* 1912), then curate of All Saints, Colchester, and his wife, Anne Elizabeth Hardcastle (*d.* 1912), the daughter of Joseph Arnould MD, of Whitecross, Wallingford, Berkshire, and the sister of Sir Joseph

Sydney Haldane Olivier, Baron Olivier (1859–1943), by Walter Stoneman, 1924

Arnould. He was descended from a family of French Huguenots. One of his younger brothers was the painter Herbert Arnould Olivier; another brother, the Revd Gerard Kerr Olivier, was the father of the actor Laurence Olivier.

Olivier was educated at Tonbridge School and at Corpus Christi College, Oxford, where he was an exhibitioner and was awarded a second class in *literae humaniores* in 1881. There he became a close friend of Graham Wallas. With another undergraduate friend, Hubert Campion, he wrote a volume of light verse, *Poems and Parodies*, published in 1880. After leaving Oxford he read for the civil service competitive examination, and in 1882, having headed the list of successful competitors, he entered the Colonial Office. On 21 May 1885 he married Margaret (*c.*1862–1953), the eldest daughter of Homersham *Cox, a county court judge, and the sister of Harold *Cox; they had four daughters.

In London Olivier became seriously interested in politics and reform, and in 1885 he joined the Fabian Society, serving as its honorary secretary from 1886 to 1889. Sidney Webb, then a colleague in the Colonial Office, George Bernard Shaw, and Graham Wallas joined about the same time, and it was mainly under the influence of the four friends that the Fabians made their distinctive contribution to the development of modern socialism. In *Fabian Essays in Socialism* (1889), perhaps the most important of the society's publications, Olivier wrote on the moral basis of socialism. He came to socialism through Auguste

Comte, and remained a socialist during the rest of his life.

Olivier was colonial secretary of British Honduras in 1890–91, auditor-general of the Leeward Islands in 1895–6, and secretary to the royal commission on the West Indies in 1896–7. In 1898 he was appointed CMG and spent five months in Washington, DC, assisting on behalf of the West Indian colonies in reciprocity negotiations with the United States. From 1900 to 1904 he was colonial secretary of Jamaica, on three occasions acting as governor. In 1907 he was appointed captain-general and governor-in-chief of Jamaica and advanced to KCMG. His most urgent task was to repair the havoc caused by earthquake and fire a few months earlier, the work including the reconstruction of Kingston on a new plan, in which he obtained the services of his brother-in-law Sir Charles Nicholson. He was a highly popular governor. His six years of office formed a memorable period of development in the island's history, one of his many reforms being the introduction of Jamaica's first comprehensive sanitary code.

Olivier returned to England in 1913 as permanent secretary to the Board of Agriculture and Fisheries and entered the Treasury in 1917 as assistant comptroller and auditor of the exchequer; he was appointed CB the same year. He retired from the civil service in 1920. In 1924 he joined Ramsay MacDonald's first Labour government as secretary of state for India, was sworn of the privy council, and created Baron Olivier of Ramsden. Ten months later his tenure of office was ended by the resignation of the government, the prime minister having, so Olivier told him, needlessly thrown in the sponge.

Olivier proved to be an uncomfortable and unsatisfactory cabinet minister. He was an advocate of peasant self-sufficiency, and his open criticism of Labour's colonial policies, coupled with his inability to defend the party line, precluded his participation in the 1929 Labour government. However, MacDonald's second administration did find ways to employ his expertise in colonial economic affairs, and in 1929–30, as chairman of the West Indian sugar commission, he paid his last official visit to Jamaica.

Olivier was a member of a remarkable generation who came of age in the 1880s imbued with a spirit of humane reform. Often they were, as was Olivier himself, the children of clergymen. In his case the spirit manifested itself in imperial reform, and he displayed a keen insight in issues of race and ethnicity within the empire. His deep interest in these problems found expression chiefly in two books of international repute: *The Anatomy of African Misery* (1927) and *White Capital and Coloured Labour* (2nd edn 1929); he discussed such questions also in contributions to periodicals and in two later books: *The Myth of Governor Eyre* (1933) and *Jamaica: the Blessed Island* (1936). His studies led him to reject what he called 'the short-sighted theory that the dividing habits of race are permanently stronger than the unifying power of humanity'.

Tall and handsome, Olivier was a striking figure in any assembly, 'looking', wrote Shaw, 'like a Spanish grandee in any sort of clothes, however unconventional'. He was a

man of great energy and commanding intellect, and he could, and did, 'labour terribly', demanding a high standard of performance from himself and those who worked with him. He had a remarkable literary talent and was a frequent contributor to periodical literature. His philosophical articles and his short story, *The Empire Builder*, won the admiration of William James, whose guest he was on one of his visits to America. His prose style was distinguished and individual, and he had a felicitous turn for light verse. His writings include three plays, one of which, *Mrs Maxwell's Marriage*, was performed by the Stage Society in January 1900. In 1911 the honorary degree of LLD was conferred upon him by the University of Edinburgh. Baron Olivier died at his home, Wychwood, Selsey Avenue, Bognor Regis, on 15 February 1943, when his peerage became extinct.

G. F. McCleary, *rev.* George Mariz

Sources *Sydney Olivier: letters and selected writings*, ed. M. Olivier (1948) · J. Cerullo, *The secularization of the soul: psychical research in modern Britain* (1982) · F. Lee, *Fabianism and colonialism: the life and thought of Lord Sydney Olivier* (1988) · GEC, *Peerage* · m. cert. · d. cert. · private information (1959) · personal knowledge (1959)

Archives Bodl. RH, corresp., draft memoranda, and chapters of a book never finished | BL, letters to A. R. Dryhurst, Add. MS 46362 · BL, letters to G. B. Shaw, Add. MS 50543 · BL OIOC, corresp. with Lord Goschen, MS Eur. D 595 · BL OIOC, corresp. with second earl of Lytton, MS Eur. F 160 · BL OIOC, letters to Lord Reading, MSS Eur. E 238, F 118 · BL OIOC, corresp. with Lord Willingdon, MS Eur. F 93 · BLPES, letters to Fabian Society · BLPES, notes and papers relating to International Socialist Workers Conference · Bodl. Oxf., Gilbert Murray MSS · Bodl. RH, corresp. with Arthur Creech Jones · CKS, Hardinge MSS · CUL, corresp. with Lord Hardinge · JRL, letters to *Manchester Guardian* · Nuffield Oxf., Fabian Society MSS · Plunkett Foundation, Long Hanborough, Oxfordshire, corresp. with Sir Horace Plunkett · PRO, corresp. with Ramsay MacDonald, 30/69/1/199

Likenesses W. Stoneman, photograph, 1924, NPG [*see illus.*] · photograph, c.1925, repro. in Olivier, ed., *Sydney Olivier* · N. Heath, portrait · H. Olivier, two portraits

Wealth at death £937 16s. 2d.: probate, 22 June 1943, CGPLA Eng. & Wales

Ollier, Charles (1788–1859), publisher, writer, and editor, was born on 4 May 1788 in the parish of St James, Bath, the second among the five or six sons of Charles Ollier (1746/7–1827), a haberdasher and registrar at Bath General Hospital, and Sarah Tuttell (1757/8–1829), a milliner and haberdasher. It is thought that he was descended from a French protestant family which migrated to England at the time of the revocation of the edict of Nantes in 1685.

At fourteen Ollier moved from Bath to London and became a junior clerk in a banking house, and by 1810 he was employed by Coutts's Bank. In 1812 he was indentured to Philip Drake, a notary public and scrivener, and as late as 1816 he worked for the banks of Alexander Davison and of Coutts. During these early years in London he was drawn to literary, theatrical, and musical circles. In 1810 he wrote his first letter to and theatrical criticism for Leigh Hunt's *Examiner*. As a good friend of Hunt and, by 1812, of Charles Cowden Clarke, he became acquainted with others in the arts, including the Novellos, Henry Robertson (later treasurer of Covent Garden Theatre), the painter William Havell, and the four or five musical and theatrical brothers Gattie (including Henry and John Thomas Byng). Ollier was an accomplished flautist who played at Novello and Hunt musical evenings and at annual celebrations of Shakespeare's birthday.

On 13 May 1814, while living at Devonshire Place, Marylebone, London, Ollier married Maria Gattie (1786–1878); they had six children. His second son, Charles (1821–1906), co-founded the booking and opera agency of Lacon and Ollier with George Lacon. His fourth and youngest son, Edmund *Ollier (1826–1886), attained some fame as a journalist and historian.

Between 1817 and 1823 Charles Ollier engaged in business with his younger brother James (1795/6–1851) as a publisher, retail bookseller, stationer, and owner of a circulating library, first at 3 Welbeck Street, Cavendish Square, and then, after May 1818, at Vere Street, Bond Street. The first two publications with an imprint C. and J. Ollier were John Keats's *Poems* and Percy B. Shelley's *Proposal for Putting Reform to the Vote throughout the Kingdom*, both appearing early in March 1817, and both apparently published by commission on the author's own account (that is, an author would pay the printing and advertising costs). Keats soon became dissatisfied with the Olliers, to whom his brother George wrote a letter of complaint less than eight weeks after publication. In their defence of the poor sales, the Olliers (who had advertised the volume in London and Bath newspapers) responded on 29 April that many who had purchased the volume 'found fault with it' and were offered their money back: one customer actually considered *Poems* 'no better than a take in'. Most of the remaining copies of *Poems* were then transferred to Taylor and Hessey, who continued to sell the volume as late as 1824. On the other hand, Shelley continued to publish almost all his works with the Olliers, notwithstanding poor sales and other problems. In December 1817, for example, Charles Ollier wanted to withdraw from publishing Shelley's epic *Laon and Cythna* when customers complained of the incest and anti-Christian expressions therein. After Shelley reluctantly agreed to remove or alter the offending passages, the epic was republished as *The Revolt of Islam* in January 1818. Between 1820 and his death in July 1822 Shelley frequently complained that Charles Ollier was ignoring his many requests and commissions (Robinson, 187–8, 190–92, 199–206).

The fifty titles that the Olliers published in 1817–23 also included Charles Lamb's *Works*, William Hazlitt's *Characters of Shakespear's Plays*, and several volumes by both Leigh Hunt and Bryan Waller Procter (Barry Cornwall). Julius Charles Hare was associated with two of Ollier's periodicals, supplying lists of authors to the *Literary Pocket-Book* (1819–23), and suggesting to Ollier the idea of the short-lived *Olliers Literary Miscellany* (1820), in which appeared pieces by Allan Cunningham, Hare, Lamb, Ollier himself, and Thomas Love Peacock (whose 'Four ages of poetry' prompted Shelley to write his 'Defence of poetry', intended for the second number of the *Miscellany*, which never appeared). During these same years Ollier was very active in the Paddington vestry (at meetings also frequented by the publishers John Hunt and John Joseph

Stockdale) and was elected overseer of the poor for the parish of Paddington.

Ollier went bankrupt in the winter of 1822–3 and sold his complete inventory (including bookshelves, fancy stationery, and 288 unsold copies of *Prometheus Unbound* in quires) on 5–11 March 1823. For some time he continued business as a stationer at his residence in Maida Hill, Paddington, and by the autumn of 1825 he returned to the publishing trade as the chief literary reader and adviser to Henry Colburn in New Burlington Street, then to Colburn and Richard Bentley during their merger of 1829–32, and then to Bentley, who retained Ollier at the annual salary of £300 until the autumn of 1839. During these years his brother James continued as a bookseller in Welbeck Street and occasionally worked for Bentley as a transcriber, translator, and editor, acted as a publisher of *Le chaperon noir* (1835), and also wrote the prose for *The Pictorial Album, or, Cabinet of Paintings, for the Year 1837*. James, whose later career is uncertain, died walking across the isthmus of Darien in 1851.

After leaving Bentley there is evidence that Charles Ollier (or his son Charles) began another ill-fated periodical, *Ollier's Concert Journal and Weekly Register of Musical Entertainments*. He became a publisher again at Southampton Street, Strand (1846–9), his first published volume being Richard Henry Horne's *Ballad Romances*. He also published volumes by Charlton Carew, John James Halls, G. P. R. James, Harriet Kearney, Mary Molesworth Kindersley, the Mackinnons (Daniel Henry, Lauchlan Bellingham, and William Alexander), and John Edmund Reade—certainly less distinguished authors than those from the years 1817–23. To his credit, however, Ollier was one of the first critics in England to celebrate the genius of Walt Whitman; he lectured on the achievements of Henry Fielding; and he delighted in the plays and poetry of Shakespeare, Ben Jonson, Robert Herrick, and Abraham Cowley.

During his long and varied career Ollier wrote and had published a number of his own works: *Altham and his Wife: a Domestic Tale* (1818), which Shelley thought was 'most unaffectedly told … in a strain of very pure & powerful English' (*Letters*, 117); *Inesilla, or, The Tempter, a Romance: with other Tales* (1824), which was delayed owing to the death of his first child, Lucy Frances (1816–1820); *Ferrers: a Romance of the Reign of George the Second* (3 vols., 1842; 2nd edn, 1843), for whose copyright he received £150; the historical and descriptive letterpress for Thomas Boy's *Original Views of London* (1842) and William Delamotte's *Original Views of Oxford* (1843); and *Fallacy of Ghosts, Dreams, and Omens; with Stories of Witchcraft, Life-in-Death, and Monomania* (1848). He also published tales and articles and reviews in a number of periodicals, including *Ainsworth's Magazine* (1842–5), *Bentley's Miscellany* (1837, 1841), *Blackwood's Edinburgh Magazine* (1822), Hunt's *Examiner* (1810), *Leigh Hunt's Journal* (1850), and *Naval and Military Gazette* (1854–5).

Equally significant was Ollier's presence behind the scenes: for example, he was responsible for Colburn publishing Bulwer's *Pelham*, finished the last chapters of William Maginn's *John Manesty* (1844) after the novelist died, offered himself as a ghost writer to Bulwer, and served as the literary agent for a number of writers, including G. P. R. James. As early as 1829 Ollier was frequently asked by James to make certain that his novels were being properly advertised and reviewed and sent to his friends—and he would seek Ollier's editorial advice on novels in manuscript. By the late 1840s, Ollier was paid by James to correct the proofs of his novels, advise him on his contracts and accounts with other publishers, and negotiate the sale of his copyrights. After James moved his family to America in 1850, Ollier saw some of James's last works through the press and arranged that his novels published by Harper in New York were published on the same day by T. C. Newby in London—and he was also commissioned to seek copyrights for James's novels in Germany and France.

Ollier's second publishing business had failed by January 1849. According to his son Edmund, his father 'was not well adapted to making a trade of the sale of books' (Ollier, 'Literary publisher', 248). Suffering from debts of £300, from his chronic respiratory illnesses (his mother and two of his brothers died of asthma), and from the financial strain of supporting his eldest son, Francis (1820–1872), who was committed to a lunatic asylum for most of his life, Ollier was forced to apply to the Royal Literary Fund for grants of £60 each in 1849, 1854, and 1857. In the second application he wrote that he had 'No salary, annuity or pension. I have no other means than working for publishers' (Royal Literary Fund case files, Charles Ollier, 3 May 1854). According to his obituary in the *Annual Register for 1859*, for

> many of his latter years Mr. Ollier was a kind of 'consulting physician' on the merits of works offered to the London publishers, and was much engaged in putting into a readable form works of value by authors whose experience in the journey-work of literature was crude or non-existent.

Ollier died after a long respiratory illness on 5 June 1859 at his home—6 Bute Street, Old Brompton, London—and he was buried on 11 June at Brompton cemetery, where the remainder of his family was eventually interred. His widow, who also received a Royal Literary Fund grant of £60 in 1859–60, died on 8 January 1878 at 154 Oakley Street, Chelsea, London, the home of her son Edmund. Leigh Hunt, Ollier's dearest friend for fifty years, memorialized him in *The Spectator* (18 June 1859, 640) as 'a devoted husband and father' and as a modest man whose religious beliefs were 'equally removed from atheistical hopelessness … and every cruelty of superstition'. The *Morning Chronicle* (10 June 1859) observed that 'Ollier has exercised a considerable influence over the course of literature, although an almost jealous diffidence of himself always kept him in the background'. Ollier was a 'great keeper of things', and many of the autograph letters written to him by the more famous were sold at two Puttick and Simpson sales in 1877 and 1878. No photograph or portrait of Charles Ollier seems to exist.   CHARLES E. ROBINSON

Sources C. E. Robinson, 'Percy Bysshe Shelley, Charles Ollier, and William Blackwood', *Shelley revalued*, ed. K. Everest (1983), 183–226 · [E. Ollier], 'A literary publisher', *Temple Bar*, 58 (1880), 243–52 · S. B. T. Mayer, 'Leigh Hunt and Charles Ollier (chiefly from unpublished sources)', *The St. James Magazine and United Empire Review*, new ser., 14 (1875), 387–413 · L. Hunt, 'The late Mr. Ollier', *The Spectator* (18 Jan 1859), 640 · *Archives of Richard Bentley & Son, 1829–1898*, 1976 [microfilm] · *Archives of the Royal Literary Fund, 1790–1918*, 1982–3 [microfilm] · *The letters of Percy Bysshe Shelley*, ed. F. L. Jones, 2 (1964) · *A catalogue of the miscellaneous bound and quire stock of a publisher, including a well chosen circulating library* [sale catalogue, 5–11 March 1823, Saunders, Poet's Gallery, 1823] · *Catalogue of a fine collection of autograph letters* [sale catalogue, 19 July 1877, Puttick and Simpson, 1877] · *Catalogue of an interesting collection of autograph letters … addressed to the late Charles Ollier* [sale catalogue, 22 July 1878, Puttick and Simpson, 1878] · correspondence of Charles Ollier and Leigh Hunt, University of Iowa Libraries, Iowa City · correspondence of G. P. R. James and Charles Ollier, Princeton University · indenture of Charles Ollier, Keats House, London · 'appendix to chronicle', *Annual Register* (1859), 467 · parish register, Bath, St James, 4 May 1788 [baptism] · private information (2004)

Archives University of Iowa Libraries, Iowa City, corresp. | Bath Central Library, Bath newspapers and directories · BL, archives of Royal Literary Fund, loan 96 · BL, letters to Leigh Hunt and Marianne Hunt, Add. MSS 38108–38111, 38524 · Duke U., Perkins L., letters to J. Philippart · Herts. ALS, letters to Lord Lytton · Marylebone Central Library, London, Paddington vestry records · NL Scot., Blackwood MSS, letters to Blackwoods · U. Cal., Richard Bentley & Son archives · University of Illinois, Richard Bentley & Son archives · Warneford Hospital, Oxford

Ollier, Edmund (1826–1886), journalist and historian, was born on 26 November 1826 in Maida Hill, Paddington, Middlesex, the sixth of the six children of Charles *Ollier (1788–1859), publisher, writer, and editor, and his wife, Maria Gattie (1786–1878). He was uncertain of his genealogy, remarking in his memoir on his father that the name Ollier 'seems to betoken a French origin … possibly … of Huguenot descent' and that his own ancestors were 'connected for some generations with the north-west and west of England', his father having been born in Bath ([Ollier], 'Literary publisher', 243–4). Because his father had been a publisher (1817–23) of works by Shelley, Keats, Hazlitt, Lamb, and Leigh Hunt, Edmund Ollier had an affection for these romantic writers and in the memoir he wrote for the edition of Lamb's *Essays of Elia* that he published in 1867 he remarked that he had 'beheld [Charles Lamb] with infantine eyes' and 'sat in the lap of poor Mary Lamb' (Ollier, 'Memoir', *Essays*, vi). As a boy, he also met many of the authors associated with the publishers Henry Colburn and Richard Bentley (for both of whom his father was chief literary adviser from 1825 to 1840), and he listened to the stories of B. R. Haydon and Leigh Hunt. Ollier, a good friend of Hunt until the latter's death in 1859, later joined with others to raise funds for a monument to Hunt in Kensal Green cemetery in London, and in 1869 he edited and wrote a memoir for Hunt's *A Tale for a Chimney Corner* (1849). His many other correspondents included Richard Henry Horne (Hengist) and Charles and Mary Cowden Clarke.

Ollier published numerous poems, stories, and articles in such periodicals as *Ainsworth's Magazine* (1844–6), *Household Words* (1853–7), and *All the Year Round* (1860–70), also publishing occasionally in *The Athenaeum*, *Magazine of Art*, *Mirror of Literature*, *The Spectator*, and *The Sun*. He was sub-editor of *The Leader* (1855–8), editor of *The Atlas* (1859–60), and literary editor of the *London Review* (1864–6). He was an occasional writer in the *Daily News* from 1853 to 1877. He republished his earlier verses in *Poems from the Greek Mythology, and Miscellaneous Poems* (1867).

Ollier made his literary début in *Ainsworth's Magazine* in 1844 and was very active in the periodical press until 1877. He was the most prolific historian working for Cassell, Petter, and Galpin, the publishers with whom he began his association by writing a biographical and critical study of Gustave Doré in 1870 and a highly successful *Cassell's History of the War between France and Germany*, in two volumes, issued in weekly and monthly parts in 1871–2 (reserialized in 1873–4 and again in 1883–4). His other works include *Our British Portrait Painters* (1873), volume 9 (1874) of *Cassell's Illustrated History of England*, *Cassell's History of the United States* (3 vols., 1874–7), and *Cassell's Illustrated History of the Russo-Turkish War* (2 vols., 1878–9). His writing of *Cassell's Illustrated Universal History* (4 vols., 1881–5) meant that he had to decline Leslie Stephen's invitation of 9 December 1882 to become a sub-editor for the *Dictionary of National Biography*. His last project was *The Life and Times of Queen Victoria*, for which he wrote the first eleven chapters before illness caused him to resign his commission. The work was completed by Robert Wilson in 1887.

With the exception of a few holiday jaunts, Ollier passed all of his life in London. He did not marry until later in life. On 2 October 1875 he wed Emily Jane Dorrell (1833–1917); they had no children. Although baptized and married in the Anglican church, Ollier (like his father) was 'neither in religion nor in politics … a Conservative'. He 'never strove for party position, for honours or distinctions', but in 1867 he received from King Victor Emmanuel 'the cross of the order of Saint Maurice and Saint Lazarus, in recognition of his literary advocacy of the cause of Italian independence' (Oswald, 309–10). Ollier died on 19 April 1886 at his residence, 154 Oakley Street, Chelsea, London. He was buried on 22 April in Brompton cemetery in the same grave as his father, mother, and brother Francis (1820–1872)—a grave in which were later interred his unmarried sister Clara Elizabeth (1818–1898) and, in 1917, his widow.　　　　　　　　　　CHARLES E. ROBINSON

Sources E. Oswald, *The Academy* (1 May 1886), 309–10 · C. E. Robinson, 'Percy Bysshe Shelley, Charles Ollier, and William Blackwood', *Shelley revalued*, ed. K. Everest (1983), 183–226 · [E. Ollier], 'A literary publisher', *Temple Bar*, 58 (1880), 243–52 · S. Nowell-Smith, *The house of Cassell, 1848–1958* (1958) · E. Ollier, letter to L. Stephen, 11 Dec 1882, Bodl. Oxf., MS Don. e. 121 · E. Ollier, 'Charles Lamb', in C. Lamb and E. Ollier, *The essays of Elia* (1867); another edn (1875), i–viii · Leigh Hunt memorial fund circulars, 1866–7, University of Delaware · E. Ollier, 'Memoir', in J. H. L. Hunt, *A tale for a chimney corner*, ed. E. Ollier (1869) · Edmund Ollier–Richard Henry Horne correspondence, University of Iowa · E. Ollier, correspondence with Cowden Clarke, U. Leeds, Brotherton L. · private information (2004) · *The Athenaeum* (1 May 1886), 583 · *The Times* (23 April 1886) · *DNB* · d. cert. · Royal Literary Fund files · parish register (baptism), London, St James's, Paddington, vol. P87-JS-7, 46 · entry of marriage, ALF files, General Register Office for England · register, Brompton cemetery, London

Archives BL, letters to Royal Literary Fund, loan 96 · U. Leeds, Brotherton L., corresp. with Charles Cowden Clarke and Mary Cowden Clarke · University of Iowa, Iowa City, corresp. with Richard Henry Horne

Likenesses photograph, 1864, Keats House, Hampstead, London

Wealth at death £1690 17s. 4d.: probate, 8 June 1886, *CGPLA Eng. & Wales*

Olliffe, Sir Joseph Francis (1808–1869), physician, son of Joseph Olliffe, merchant, of Cork, and Elizabeth, daughter of Charles McCarthy of Sunville, co. Limerick, was born at Cork. He was educated in Paris, and there graduated MA at the university in 1829, and MD in 1840. For some time he acted as tutor in the family of the Count de Cresnoi, but in 1840 he began to practise medicine in Paris. He married Laura (*d*. 1898), the second daughter of Sir William *Cubitt, in 1841, a marriage which gave him access to a considerable fortune. Olliffe was a fellow of the Anatomical Society of Paris, and at one time served as president of the Paris Medical Society. Louis-Philippe in 1846 appointed him a knight of the Légion d'honneur, and he was promoted to the rank of officer in 1855 by Napoleon III.

In March 1852 Olliffe became physician to the British embassy, and on 13 June 1853 he was knighted at Buckingham Palace. The Board of Trade nominated him a juror for hygiene, pharmacy, surgery, and medicine in the French international exhibition in April 1855, and in 1861 he was appointed one of the committee for sanitary appliances in the international exhibition of 1862. He became a fellow of the Royal College of Physicians of London in 1859.

With his friend and patient the Count de Morny, Olliffe invested in extensive building at Deauville near Trouville, a watering-place which they effectively created. This proved an unremunerative speculation. Olliffe died at his home, 12 Chichester Terrace, Brighton, on 14 March 1869.　　　　　　　G. C. BOASE, *rev.* JAMES MILLS

Sources *BMJ* (20 March 1869), 274 · *The Register and Magazine of Biography* (April 1869), 296 · Munk, *Roll* · *CGPLA Eng. & Wales* (1869)

Wealth at death under £16,000: probate, 7 April 1869, *CGPLA Eng. & Wales*

Ollivant, Alfred (1798–1882), bishop of Llandaff, was born on 16 August 1798 in Manchester, the younger son of William Ollivant and his wife, Elizabeth, daughter of Sir Stephen Langston of Great Horwood, Buckinghamshire. The family moved to London when the father became a clerk in the Navy Office and lived at 11 Smith Street, Northampton Square. Educated at St Paul's School (1809–16), he was admitted as a sizar to Trinity College, Cambridge, on 11 June 1816 and matriculated at Easter 1817. He was the Craven scholar in 1820, graduated sixth wrangler in 1821, and gained the chancellor's medal for classics. He won the Tyrwhitt Hebrew scholarship in 1822 and was elected to a fellowship at Trinity College.

In 1827 Ollivant was appointed vice-principal of the newly founded St David's College, Lampeter. While in Cardiganshire he found time to learn Welsh and he preached regularly in that language at Llangeler, of which he was vicar as well as sinecure rector. He returned to Cambridge in 1843 as regius professor of divinity. In 1849 he was nominated to the see of Llandaff, his knowledge of Wales and

Alfred Ollivant (1798–1882), by Lock & Whitfield, pubd 1878

of the Welsh language being the chief reasons for his elevation. In 1831 he married Alicia Olivia Spencer (1801–1886) of Bramley Grange, Yorkshire. Three sons survived them, one of whom, Joseph Earle, was chancellor of the dioceses of Llandaff and St David's.

The diocese of Llandaff had long been impoverished and neglected, served by a long line of absentee bishops. The cathedral was a so-called Italian temple, a partial restoration dating from 1736, set in the medieval ruin. In 1849 the ecclesiastical commissioners augmented the bishop's stipend by £3150 to bring it up to the minimum level of £4500 and bought an official residence in Llandaff. Ollivant was therefore able to live in the diocese and attend to its pressing needs. Industrialization had changed the face of the south Wales valleys, and the church in the erstwhile rural diocese had been overtaken by the rapid growth of nonconformity. The Church Extension Society, which he founded in 1850, undertook a massive programme of church and school building; over 170 churches were built or restored. Ollivant also saw the complete restoration of the cathedral, under the direction of a local architect, John Prichard. He was much concerned about the education of the clergy and the needs of the Welsh-speaking areas of the diocese.

As a young man at Cambridge, Ollivant had been influenced by the famous evangelical Charles Simeon, and he was to retain that influence throughout his life. As a theologian, the former professor was cautious and conservative, fearful of the development of biblical criticism. His *Charge* of 1857 was devoted to a detailed, if now unconvincing, refutation of the works of Rowland Williams, then

vice-principal at Lampeter and an advocate of the still tentative views of the German critics. Ollivant was equally suspicious of the activities of the Anglo-Catholic clergy who began to appear in the diocese after 1870. He inhibited Arthur Stanton, the long-serving curate of St Alban the Martyr, Holborn, from officiating anywhere in the diocese, even though Stanton was a frequent visitor to the home of the powerful Talbot family at Margam. He rebuked the vicar of St Mary's, Cardiff, for wearing a surplice with a large cross on it. It turned out to be a white chasuble borrowed from the parish of Margam.

In person tall and spare with features said by some to resemble the duke of Wellington, but more refined, Ollivant became increasingly deaf. This hindered him in his work for the panel producing the Revised Version of the Bible in 1870. He finally died on 16 December 1882 at Bishop's Court, Llandaff. He was buried on 21 December in the cathedral grounds, his grave marked by a large Celtic cross in a local red stone. A monument with his effigy was placed in the chancel, near the high altar, as befits one who was the second founder of the cathedral. Apart from a chip off the nose it escaped damage when the cathedral was bombed in 1941.

Besides a large number of minor publications, his triennial charges from 1851 onwards are still useful sources for the conditions in the diocese, as is his *Some Account of the Fabric of Llandaff Cathedral* (1857, 1860) for the state of that building. His library, donated to the cathedral, is now housed at St Michael's College, Llandaff, the books amply annotated by his handwritten comments in the margins.

O. W. JONES

Sources Venn, *Alum. Cant.* · J. Morgan, *Four biographical sketches* (1892) · E. T. Davies, *Religion in the industrial revolution in south Wales* (1965), 97–140 · O. W. Jones, *Rowland Williams* (1991), 49–53 · A. Ollivant, *A charge delivered to the clergy of the diocese of Llandaff, at his primary visitation* (1851) · A. Ollivant, *A charge delivered to the clergy of the diocese of Llandaff, at his third visitation* (1857) · Llandaff parish registers

Archives NL Wales, corresp. and papers | LPL, corresp. with A. C. Tait

Likenesses Lock & Whitfield, photograph, pubd 1878, NPG [*see illus.*] · W. W. Ouless, oils, 1882, St Michael's College, Llandaff · photograph, 1882, St Michael's College, Llandaff · H. H. Armitstead, marble effigy on monument, 1883, Llandaff Cathedral · woodcut, NPG

Wealth at death £35,633 11s. 6d.: resworn probate, Nov 1883, *CGPLA Eng. & Wales*

Ollyffe, John (1647/8–1717), Church of England clergyman, was born in Arundel, Sussex. He and his brother Thomas were the sons of John Ollyffe (d. 1667), during the interregnum vicar of Ringmer and curate of Wivelsfield in Sussex, and an ejected minister at the Restoration. Having studied philosophy and logic at St Catharine's College, Cambridge (which he entered on 16 June 1665), Ollyffe migrated to Queen's College, Oxford, where he matriculated, aged twenty, on 7 February 1668. He proceeded BCL from New Inn Hall in 1672, and was ordained. He served the remainder of his life in two rectories: West Almer, Dorset (1673–93), and Dunton, Buckinghamshire (1693–1717).

Ollyffe was a reformer who worked through the established church to restore social order and morality. These efforts he directed mainly at his own parishioners: guiding them in practical matters, in *A Minister's Last Advice to his People* (1694); steering them clear of error, in *A Brief Defence of Infant-Baptism* (1694); and indoctrinating them, in *A Practical Exposition of the Church-Catechism* (1710). Ollyffe encouraged local societies in this effort, as in his *A Sermon Preach'd … before the Society for Reformation of Manners* (1702). Politically outspoken, he preached before local assizes in 1709 and 1715 and published sermons supportive of such whig causes as the union of England and Scotland (*A Sermon … upon Occasion of the Late Day of Thanksgiving for the Union*, 1707) and allegiance to limited, constitutional monarchy (*England's Call to Thankfulness*, 1689), which latter, to many high-churchmen's dismay, he reiterated at the accession of George I (*An Exhortation to Faithful and True Allegiance*, 1715). His concept of order included protestant solidarity against popery, beginning with his oft repeated plan for readmitting moderate dissenters to the church (*An Essay towards a Comprehension*, 1701; 3rd edn, 1718). Just as Ollyffe asserted 'I am no Dissenter, but I love and honour Dissenters that are good Men', he equally disdained shallow formalism and bigotry in his own church (Ollyffe, preface).

Ollyffe earned a reputation as a polemicist with his *Defence of Ministerial Conformity* (1702–5) in which he challenged the claim of Edmund Calamy, made in his *Abridgement of Mr Baxter's History of his Life* and expanded upon in debate with Ollyffe and Benjamin Hoadly in *A Defence of Moderate Non-Conformity* (1703–6), that dissenting principles were still viable. But he managed this temperately, with genuine concern for restoring fellowship. Even Calamy admitted Ollyffe's approach was respectful and moderate, and that they were 'far from differing' in their desire for reformation.

Ollyffe died at Dunton on 24 June 1717, leaving three sons in the ministry: John (*b.* 1676), rector of Hedgerley (1699–1743); George (*b.* 1682), vicar of Kemble in Wiltshire (and the only one of Ollyffe's sons' livings not in Buckinghamshire) in 1707 and of Wendover in 1715; and Thomas, vicar of Dunton and Eyworth (1712–42) and rector of Denham (1742–8).   JIM SPIVEY

Sources E. Calamy, *An historical account of my own life, with some reflections on the times I have lived in, 1671–1731*, ed. J. T. Rutt, 2 vols. (1829) · E. Calamy, ed., *An abridgement of Mr. Baxter's history of his life and times, with an account of the ministers, &c., who were ejected after the Restauration of King Charles II*, 2nd edn, 2 vols. (1713) · *DNB* · Foster, *Alum. Oxon.* · Wood, *Ath. Oxon.*, new edn, vol. 4 · Venn, *Alum. Cant.* · W. Wilson, *The history and antiquities of the dissenting churches and meeting houses in London, Westminster and Southwark*, 4 vols. (1808–14), vols. 1, 4 · J. Ollyffe, *The blessedness of good men after death* (1699), preface · Calamy rev.

Olmius, John Luttrell- (*c.*1740–1829). *See under* Luttrell, James (*c.*1751–1788).

Olney, Sarah Allen (1842–1915), headmistress, was born at Saltash, Cornwall, on 12 May 1842, the daughter of Henry Allen Olney, solicitor, and his wife, Jane Ann, *née* Carpenter, who became the proprietress of a successful private school in the west of England. She had at least three sisters and two brothers. She spent much of her early life abroad, studying in Italy, France, and Germany, and became an excellent linguist. On returning to England she passed the higher local examinations and the external LLA examination of the University of St Andrews. In 1879 she became assistant mistress at the Girls' Public Day School Company (GPDSC) School at St John's Wood, where her sister Rebecca Allen Olney (1846/7–1927) was headmistress. The company appointed her the first headmistress of Blackheath high school, which opened in 1880 with sixty-eight pupils, a figure which was to quadruple during her period of office. She taught both mathematics and English, encouraging an enthusiasm for Shakespeare and Milton. While she ensured that academic standards were high (girls won scholarships at Oxford and Cambridge), her ideas of a rounded education included an insistence on neatness, and she instilled a certain feminine style and elegance among her pupils, whose social skills she carefully scrutinized. Both she and her sister were among the signatories to the petition to the House of Lords in 1885 in favour of the Women's Suffrage Bill.

In 1886 Sarah Allen Olney resigned from Blackheath and with her sister, who also gave up her headship, set up a private school, The Elms, at Hampstead, which met a demand among better-off parents for a more socially exclusive type of school. The success of this venture, which had about 100 pupils, both day girls and boarders, illustrated the continuing vitality of privately run schools for girls at the end of the century, despite the challenge from the movement which backed public day schools for girls. Indeed, the new school caused defections from the St John's Wood School (renamed South Hampstead high school), alienating the Allen Olney sisters from the friendship of the GPDSC. In July 1894 Sarah Allen Olney gave evidence on behalf of the Private Schools Association to the royal commission on secondary education (the Bryce commission), having visited sixty-nine such schools in twenty-nine towns to gather information. She cited the views of parents who considered that schools made dependent on public provision and subject to state control 'would entail the loss of the originality, vitality, and stimulating force of schools carried on by private enterprise' ('Royal commission on secondary education', 15.1). In describing her own school, she emphasized the high standards which were maintained by entering girls for the Cambridge local and London matriculation examinations, but pointed out that the wealthier class of parents remained 'much averse to allowing their daughters to work for examinations' (ibid.). She was personally a strong supporter of teacher registration.

After their retirement the Allen Olney sisters divided their time between their home at 18 Buckland Crescent, Hampstead, and travels abroad. Sarah Allen Olney, who never married, died at Ormea, Cuneo, Italy, on 10 September 1915.   TRIONA ADAMS

Sources M. C. Malim and H. C. Escreet, eds., *The book of the Blackheath High School* (1927) · Minutes of the Girls' Public Day School Company, 1875–86, GPDST Archives · letters from Sarah Allen Olney, Blackheath School · *CGPLA Eng. & Wales* (1915) · *Blackheath School Magazines* · 'Royal commission on secondary education',

Parl. papers (1895), 45.1 · J. Roach, *Secondary education in England, 1870–1902* (1991) · b. cert. · census returns, 1881 **Likenesses** photograph, repro. in Malim and Escreet, eds., *Book of the Blackheath high school*, 37 **Wealth at death** £1145 19s. 4d.: probate, 25 Nov 1915, CGPLA Eng. & Wales

O'Lochlainn, Domhnall. *See* Ua Lochlainn, Domnall (1048–1121).

O'Lochlainn, Muircheartach. *See* Mac Lochlainn, Muirchertach (d. 1166).

O'Loghlen, Sir Colman Michael, second baronet (1819–1877), judge and politician, eldest son of Sir Michael *O'Loghlen, first baronet (1789–1842), master of the rolls in Ireland, and Bidelia, daughter of Daniel Kelly of Dublin, was born on 20 September 1819. He was educated at private schools in England and at University College, London, and graduated BA at London University. He had entered the Middle Temple in 1837, and in 1840 he was called to the Irish bar and went on the Munster circuit. As a junior he took a number of briefs in the state trials at Dublin and Clonmel in 1848, at which a number of Young Irelanders were tried in the wake of their failed insurrection. His performances drew compliments from bench and bar alike, and as one of his clients was to write, 'He resolutely refuses fees. In fact he spends money in our behalf instead of making money by us.'

O'Loghlen took silk in 1852. From 1856 to 1859 he was chairman of Carlow quarter sessions, and from 1859 to 1861 he held the same position in co. Mayo. In 1863, standing as a Liberal, he was elected MP for County Clare, and he held the seat until his death. In 1865 he was made a third serjeant-at-law for Ireland, and he became second serjeant in the following year. He was appointed judge-advocate-general in Gladstone's ministry and a member of the privy council in December 1868; he held the former office until November 1870. O'Loghlen also introduced and carried the bill of 1867 which enabled Roman Catholics to obtain the position of lord chancellor of Ireland.

A member of the Stephen's Green Club (Dublin) and the Reform Club (London), O'Loghlen's unassuming manner and good nature made him universally popular. He died suddenly, on 22 July 1877, on board the mailboat while crossing from Holyhead to Kingstown. He was buried in the family vault in co. Clare. He was unmarried, and his brother Bryan succeeded to the title.

D. J. O'DONOGHUE, *rev.* NATHAN WELLS

Sources *Thom's directory* (1876) · *The Times* (23 July 1877) · *The Times* (27 July 1877) · E. Keane, P. Beryl Phair, and T. U. Sadleir, eds., *King's Inns admission papers, 1607–1867*, IMC (1982) · diary of John Martin, a Young Irelander, Oct–Nov 1848, PRO NIre., D 560/1 · V. T. H. Delany, *Christopher Palles* (1960)
Archives Bodl. Oxf., corresp. with Lord Kimberley
Likenesses J. P. Haverty, group portrait, lithograph with watercolour, pubd 1845 (after his earlier drawing *The monster meeting of the 20th September 1843, at Clifden in the Irish highlands*), NG Ire. · A. Cecioni, caricature, watercolour study, NPG; repro. in *VF* (28 Sept 1872)

O'Loghlen, Sir Michael, first baronet (1789–1842), judge, born in Port, co. Clare, in October 1789, was the third son of Colman O'Loghlen (1745–1810), of Port, and his second wife, Susannah, daughter of Michael Finucane MD, of Ennis. He was educated at the Erasmus Smith School, Ennis, and at Trinity College, Dublin, where he was admitted in 1805 and graduated BA in 1809. He entered the Middle Temple, London, in the same year and was called to the Irish bar in Michaelmas term 1811, after which he joined the Munster circuit. On 3 September 1817 he married Bidelia, daughter of Daniel Kelly of Dublin.

O'Loghlen's first distinction as an advocate was gained in 1815, in a case involving important questions of law in which he was Daniel O'Connell's junior. The case came on for argument in the king's bench the day after the fatal duel between O'Connell and Captain J. N. D'Esterre, and O'Connell was in consequence absent. O'Loghlen asked for a postponement, but, the other side objecting, he argued the case alone, obtained judgment in his favour, and was specially complimented by the court on the ability and learning of his argument. He became a favourite with O'Connell, was constantly employed as his junior, and succeeded to a large part of his practice when O'Connell became absorbed in politics.

In a sketch by R. L. Sheil, written in 1828, O'Loghlen is described as an excellent lawyer, a master of the practice of the courts, in receipt of an immense income, and a great favourite with the judges because of the brevity, simplicity, and clearness with which his points were put. His custom was on receipt of a fee to take the shilling from each guinea and put it in a box for his wife, and at the end of one term Mrs O'Loghlen is said to have received 1500 shillings. On the passing of the Catholic Emancipation Act (April 1829), the leading Roman Catholic barristers expected to be made king's counsel. The honour was somewhat unfairly deferred until Trinity term 1830, when, at the instance of Lord Francis Leveson-Gower (Lord Egerton), then chief secretary, O'Loghlen, Sheil, and two other Catholics were called within the bar.

In January 1831 O'Loghlen was appointed third serjeant, and in 1832 he was elected a bencher of King's Inns. In the same year he was made second serjeant, and stood unsuccessfully as the Liberal candidate for the city of Dublin. On 21 October 1834 he was appointed solicitor-general for Ireland in Lord Melbourne's first government. At the general election in January 1835 he was returned for Dungarvan, and on April 29 of that year, on the formation of Lord Melbourne's second government, he was again appointed solicitor-general for Ireland. On 31 August 1835 he was appointed attorney-general. In November 1836 he was appointed a baron of the court of exchequer in Ireland, and in the following January he succeeded Sir William McMahon as master of the rolls. He was the first Catholic law officer and the first Catholic judge in Ireland since the reign of James II. On 16 July 1838, on the coronation of the queen, he was created a baronet. O'Loghlen died in George Street, Hanover Square, London, on 28 September 1842, and was buried at Recan, co. Clare.

Both at the bar and on the bench O'Loghlen enjoyed a high reputation. O'Connell, writing to Lord Duncannon in October 1834, said:

Than O'Loghlen, a more amiable man never lived—a more learned lawyer, a more sensible, discreet, and, at the same time, a more powerful advocate never belonged to the Irish bar. He never made an enemy, he never lost a friend .... He possesses in an eminent degree all the best judicial qualities. (*Correspondence*, 490)

On the bench O'Loghlen justified O'Connell's forecast of his judicial powers. 'There never was a judge who gave more entire satisfaction to both the suitors and the profession; perhaps never one sitting alone and deciding so many cases of whose decisions there were fewer reversals' (*Irish Equity Reports*, 5.130). He was very courteous, carried patience almost to a fault, and was especially kind and considerate to young men appearing before him. Of his family of four sons and four daughters, three sons followed their father to the bar: the eldest son, Sir Colman Michael *O'Loghlen (1819–1877), became judge-advocate-general; his third son, Sir Bryan O'Loghlen (1828–1905), had a political career in Australia and was premier of Victoria (1881–3). J. D. FitzGerald, rev. Nathan Wells

Sources *The Times* (3 Oct 1842) · *GM*, 2nd ser., 19 (1843), 90 · *Dublin Evening Post* (1 Oct 1842) · F. E. Ball, *The judges in Ireland, 1221–1921*, 2 (1926) · J. R. O'Flanagan, *The Irish bar*, 2nd edn (1879) · R. L. Sheil, *Sketches, legal and political*, ed. M. W. Savage, 2 vols. (1855) · *Correspondence of Daniel O'Connell, the liberator*, ed. W. J. Fitzpatrick, 2 vols. (1888) · W. T. McCullagh, *Memoirs of the Right Honourable Richard Lalor Sheil*, 2 vols. (1855) · *Irish equity reports*, 13 vols. (1839–51), vol. 5, p. 130; facs. edn (1976) · E. Keane, P. Beryl Phair, and T. U. Sadleir, eds., *King's Inns admission papers, 1607–1867*, IMC (1982) · Burke, *Peerage*

Likenesses G. Mulvaney, oils, 1843, NG Ire.

O'Lothchain, Cuan. *See* Cuán ua Lothcháin (d. 1024).

Olpherts, Sir William (1822–1902), army officer, was born on 8 March 1822 at Dartry, near Armagh, the third son of William Olpherts (d. 1876) of Dartry House, Blackwatertown, co. Armagh, and his wife, Rosanna, daughter of Dr Macartney. He was educated at Gracehill School and Dungannon Royal School, and then at Addiscombe College, from which he passed out as a cadet in 1839. He joined the headquarters of the Bengal artillery at Dum-Dum on 24 December 1839. Following the outbreak of disturbances in the province of Tenasserim in Burma, he was sent with four guns to Moulmein in October 1841. Nine months later he returned and immediately went on field service to subdue an insurrection that had broken out near Saugor. For his conduct during an engagement at Jhirna Ghat on 12 November 1842 he was mentioned in the dispatch written by the officer commanding the artillery. Olpherts qualified as an interpreter in Indian languages, and in April 1843 was given command of the 16th Bengal light field battery stationed at Nowgong in Bundelkhand. Later that year he joined General Sir Hugh Gough's expedition against Gwalior in north central India. His battery formed part of the wing of the army commanded by General Gray; it was heavily engaged in the fighting at Punniar on 29 December 1843, and Olpherts was mentioned in dispatches.

For his services in the Gwalior campaign Olpherts received the bronze decoration, and was selected by Lord Ellenborough, the governor-general, to raise and command a battery of horse artillery for the Bundelkhand Legion. He was at once detached with the newly raised battery to form part of Sir Charles Napier's army in Sind, which he joined after an arduous march of 1260 miles across India. He then participated in several engagements with the warlike tribes inhabiting the hills bordering Sind. In 1846 he took part in the capture of the hill fort at Kot Kangra during the First Anglo-Sikh War, attracting the attention of Sir Henry Lawrence, and was later appointed to raise a battery of artillery from the men of the disbanded Sikh army. He then commanded a battery of artillery in the service of the nizam of Hyderabad in the Deccan, but was soon recalled in February 1845 to take the lucrative post of commandant of artillery with the Gwalior contingent. In 1851 he joined the Peshawar garrison, under the command of Sir Colin Campbell, and participated in an expedition against the trans-border Pathan tribes, for which he was later awarded the frontier medal. Olpherts returned to England on furlough in May 1852 and was appointed an orderly officer at Addiscombe College.

Following the outbreak of the Crimean War, Olpherts volunteered in January 1855 to fight against the Russians and was selected to join Sir William Fenwick Williams at Kars. He visited the Crimea *en route* for Kars, and then travelled via the Black Sea and the Zigana Mountains to join his new command. He escaped capture at Kars as he was placed in command of a force of 7000 Turkish troops detached to guard against a possible Russian advance from Erivan by the Araxes River. He was recalled to the Crimea and took command of a brigade of Bashi-Bazoukhs serving in the Turkish contingent. When hostilities ended in 1856 he returned to India and took command of a horse artillery battery at Benares.

Olpherts served throughout the suppression of the Indian mutiny (1857–9) and was heavily involved in the fighting in northern India. On 4 June 1857 his battery, acting under the orders of General James Neill, opened fire on the 37th native infantry regiment which mutinied while being disarmed at Benares. Olpherts's battery was charged on three occasions during the confused fighting which ended with the complete rout of the sepoys. He then accompanied Sir Henry Havelock's column during the advance on Cawnpore and in the relief of the city of Lucknow, when he greatly distinguished himself in action. On 25 September he fought on horseback with the 90th regiment when it entered the city of Lucknow during a difficult engagement in which two guns were captured from the enemy. Despite intense musketry fire, Olpherts displayed great gallantry when he succeeded in bringing up horses and limbers to carry off the captured ordnance. Two days later he once again demonstrated his considerable personal bravery when, along with Colonel Robert Napier, he led a small party which rescued the wounded with the embattled rearguard and brought several guns into the security of the residency. Sir James Outram, commanding the residency at Lucknow, wrote: 'My dear Heroic Olpherts, bravery is a poor and insufficient epithet to apply to a valour such as yours'. Until Sir Colin Campbell relieved the defenders on 21 November 1857 Olpherts acted as brigadier of artillery, and following the evacuation of the residency shared, under Outram, in the defence of the advance position at the Alambagh. In March 1858 he took part in the siege and capture of Lucknow by Campbell, and was once again mentioned in dispatches for conspicuous bravery. Following the end of the campaign he received the brevets of major and lieutenant-colonel, was awarded the Victoria Cross for his distinguished conduct on 25 September 1857, and was made a CB. His dash and valour in action had also earned him the sobriquet of Hell-Fire Jack from the men under his command.

Olpherts volunteered to serve under Brigadier Sir Neville Chamberlain during the 1859–60 punitive expedition against the Wazirs on the north-west frontier, completing twenty years of continuous active service. He married Alice Maria, eldest daughter of Major-General George Cautley of the 5th Bengal European light cavalry, on 3 June 1861; they had one son, William Cautley, and three daughters; Lady Olpherts survived her husband. Between 1861 and 1868 he commanded the artillery at Peshawar and Rawalpindi, and then returned home on furlough; while there he was presented with a sword of honour by the city and county of Armagh. In 1872 he returned to India and commanded successively the Gwalior, Ambala, and Lucknow brigades. He finally left the subcontinent in 1875, on attaining the rank of major-general. He was promoted lieutenant-general on 1 October 1877, general on 31 March 1883, and in 1888 became colonel commandant of the Royal Artillery. He was made KCB in 1886 and GCB in 1900. Olpherts died at his residence, Wood House, Hamlet Road, Upper Norwood, London, on 30 April 1902, and was buried with full military honours at Richmond cemetery, Surrey.   T. R. MOREMAN

Sources P. Collister, 'Hellfire Jack' VC: the life and times of General Sir William Olpherts VC, GCB, 1822–1902 (1989) • The Times (3 May 1902) • DNB • H. M. Vibart, Addiscombe: its heroes and men of note (1894) • Lord Roberts [F. S. Roberts], Forty-one years in India, 2 vols. (1897) • W. Lee-Warner, Memoirs of Field Marshal Sir Henry Wylie Norman (1908) • CGPLA Eng. & Wales (1902)
Archives Bodl. Oxf., corresp. with Lord Kimberley
Likenesses portrait, repro. in Collister, 'Hellfire Jack' VC
Wealth at death £210: probate, 3 July 1902, CGPLA Eng. & Wales

Olschanesky, Sonia (1923–1944). *See under* Women agents on active service in France (*act.* 1942–1945).

Olson, Stanley Bernard (1947–1989), biographer, was born on 8 June 1947 in Akron, Ohio, the youngest of the three children of Sidney Olson, a printer, and his wife, Miriam Klein. Both parents were children of émigré Jewish families: the Kleins were from Hungary, while Sidney's father, Frank Olshanitsky, left Russia to escape conscription, changing his name to Olson and settling in Akron, where he made a living as a printer. His sons Sidney and Irving started a radio repair business which eventually evolved into the vast Olson electronics company.

Olson was unhappy at school, where his grades were abysmal and his behaviour disruptive; at the age of twelve

he was sent to the Culver military academy in Indiana, which he loathed, graduating after five years 149th out of a class of 182. In 1965 he enrolled at Boston University, where he came under the influence of the distinguished Henry James scholar Millicent Bell. It was she who inspired his fascination with Virginia Woolf and Bloomsbury, recommending him as a graduate student at Royal Holloway College, University of London, where he arrived in the autumn of 1968 to write a doctoral thesis on the history of the Hogarth Press, 1917–23. During the course of his research he met Lytton Strachey's biographer Michael Holroyd, as well as surviving members of the Bloomsbury group, and through these contacts he soon established his own circle of friends. Frances Partridge, translator and diarist, the widow of Ralph Partridge, became a particularly close and affectionate mentor.

In 1971 Olson was commissioned to write the life of the poet Elinor Wylie, published in the United States by the Dial Press in 1979. The reviews were respectable, although the book was never issued in paperback or in a British edition. This was followed by the editing of an abridged version of the *Letters and Diaries of Harold Nicolson* (Collins, 1980), a project which, largely owing to an uneasy relationship with Nicolson's son Nigel, Olson came to detest. With his next undertaking, however, he was completely in sympathy: a life of the painter John Singer Sargent, with whose flamboyant work, elusive character, and elegant style of living Olson wholeheartedly identified. 'I do so adore every aspect of his life. His painting, rather like his life, is all surface and not depth', he wrote in a letter (Hatfield, 137). The book was published to considerable acclaim in 1986, by Macmillan in London and St Martin's Press in New York.

Next was to have come a life of Rebecca West—Olson, who had befriended Dame Rebecca in her old age, was named in her will as one of two biographers—but on 18 July 1986 he suffered a severe stroke. Although surviving with great courage for another three and a half years, he remained unable to read and almost speechless, and died of a second stroke at his flat, 1E Montagu Mews North, London, on 9 December 1989. His remains were cremated at Golders Green crematorium on 17 December.

Not least of Stanley Olson's achievements was his re-creation of himself as a Henry James Englishman. Small and thickset, with a large, handsome head and glossy black hair, he transformed himself into a dandy: his beautifully tailored suits were lined in red silk, his shoes in red leather; he wrote on hand-cut, custom-made grey paper. His beloved spaniel, Wuzzo, rode in a carriage-tricycle bought at Harrods, eating off a porcelain bowl manufactured for him in Limoges.

Olson was a generous and affectionate man with a great talent for friendship, although sexual relationships were for him a closed book. Both gourmet and gourmand, he loved to entertain, treating his friends to rich and elaborate meals, often sent in from Claridges or Le Gavroche. (His extravagance was a constant source of complaint from his long-suffering family.) But although a lover of gossip and social life, Olson was essentially a loner, intensely private, often deeply melancholic, contradictions in his character which he felt were treated more kindly by English reserve than by the invasive manners of his compatriots. SELINA HASTINGS

Sources P. Hatfield, *Pencil me in: a memoir of Stanley Olson* (1994) · personal knowledge (2004) · private information (2004)
Likenesses F. von der Schulenberg, photograph · photographs, repro. in Hatfield, *Pencil me in*

Olsson, Julius (1864–1942), marine painter, was born in Islington, London, on 1 February 1864, the third son of Martin Olsson, a Swedish timber agent, and his English wife, Elizabeth Henrietta Tucker. He should not be confused with the Swedish-born painter Bror Julius Olsson (1878–1955), who became a pioneer of post-impressionism in Chicago and changed his surname to that of his mother, Nordfelst. Julius Olsson grew up in Sweden, at Varmland and Karlstrand, and in his childhood he often crossed the North Sea between Gotenberg and Milwall with his father. He was twice married: first, in 1885, to Catherine Mary (d. 1923), daughter of Charles Butt, timber merchant, of Hull; second, in 1925, to Edith Mary, daughter of Charles Luke Ellison, a horse breeder from Castlereagh. There were no children of either marriage. According to his nephew H. William Olsson he was self-taught as a painter. He first painted landscapes in Sweden but settled in St Ives, in Cornwall, in 1888. He was among the first artists of what became the St Ives school, and his place as its founder was secured by the popularity of his paintings of that area and by his teaching of several painters of the next generation who remained in St Ives. He was typical of one strand of the great inundation of sea painting in Britain in the 1880s in that he concentrated on the romantic mood of the sea itself, as subject, rather than the work of fishermen, and in this he was distinct from the rival art colony at Newlyn. His heavily textured oil technique allowed dramatic effects of light and shade, and he specialized in painting nocturnal scenes under moonlight. The titles of his seascapes, for example *Moonlit Shore*, purchased in 1911 for the Chantrey collection at the Tate Gallery, record Olsson's interest in a certain effect of light on the sea. He painted the coast also in Dorset, the Channel Islands, the Mediterranean, and especially in Ireland. His pupils included the Canadian modernist Emily Carr (1871–1945), about 1900, and the artists who became the leaders of the St Ives school in the 1920s, R. Borlase Smart (1881–1947) and John Anthony Park (1878–1962).

Olsson exhibited, plentifully and with success, at the Royal Academy from 1890 to 1940. He joined the Royal Institution of Painters in Oils in 1897 and was its president from 1919 until his death. He twice won gold medals at the Paris Salon, where he exhibited from 1910, and twice served on the committee of the Carnegie International Exhibition in Pittsburgh. He was appointed an associate of the Royal Academy in 1914 and Royal Academician in 1920. In Cornwall he became a justice of the peace and was captain of the West Cornwall Golf Club.

From about 1912 Olsson lived in London, and during the First World War he advised the Admiralty on ship camouflage. He was nevertheless included in the opening exhibition in 1927 of the St Ives Society of Artists, and the first exhibition at the Porthmeor Gallery, where the members showed, was officially opened by Olsson in 1928. After his London home was damaged by bombing he moved to Dalkey, near Dublin, where he died on 8 September 1942. H. B. GRIMSDITCH, rev. DAVID FRASER JENKINS

Sources H. W. Olsson, 'A painter of the sea', *Anglo-Swedish Review* (July 1952) · *Emily Carr in France / Emily Carr en France* (1991) [exhibition catalogue, Vancouver Art Gallery, 22 June – 22 Sept 1991] · P. Davies, 'The sea, St Ives, and the seeing eye', *Artscribe*, 37 (Oct 1982), 68–9 · *St Ives, 1939–64: twenty-five years of painting, sculpture, and pottery* (1985) [exhibition catalogue, Tate Gallery, London]
Likenesses Elliott & Fry, photograph, c.1915, NPG · J. Russell & Sons, photograph, c.1915, NPG · W. Stoneman, photograph, 1931, NPG

O'Maelchonaire, Fearfeasa. *See* Ó Maoilchonaire, Fearfeasa (*fl.* 1630–1646).

Ó Máelmuaid, Ailbe [Albinus O'Molloy] (*d.* 1223), abbot of Baltinglass and bishop of Ferns, had a close association with King John, with whom he probably first came into contact when John, on his visit to Ireland in 1185, issued a confirmation charter to the Cistercian Baltinglass Abbey, where Ó Máelmuaid was abbot. The surname Ó Máelmuaid is associated with kings of Fir Cell (in Offaly), on the northern boundary of which was located the Cistercian monastery of Kilbeggan, which lends support to Ailbe's connection with that area. On 22 March 1186, at a provincial synod at Dublin, Ó Máelmuaid preached a sermon denouncing the incontinence of Welsh and English clergy in Ireland which provoked a response from Gerald of Wales. Shortly thereafter he was made bishop of Ferns (the form 'bishop of Wexford' also occurs), probably with the assent of John, son of Henry II, as lord of Ireland (who, according to Gerald, previously had offered him the see). He was present at the coronation of Richard I on 3 September 1189 and at the council at Pipewell on the 15th. He attended the consecration of St Patrick's Cathedral, Dublin, on 17 March 1192 and was with John, count of Mortain, at Nottingham on 27 December of that year.

On 5 November 1203 Pope Innocent III appointed Ó Máelmuaid, along with the archbishop of Tuam and the bishop of Kilmacduagh, to proclaim the ecclesiastical censure laid on Robert, bishop of Waterford, for despoiling Malachias, bishop of Lismore. On 3 April 1206 he was recommended to the electoral body of the archiepiscopal see of Cashel by King John, as his nominee, and on 6 April received 10 marks as the king's gift. On 2 October 1207 Pope Innocent replied to his queries concerning the ordination of clerics by bishops other than their own. In the same year Ó Máelmuaid provided testimony to Innocent in support of the canonization of Lorcán Ua Tuathail, archbishop of Dublin. On 19 June 1208, along with Meiler fitz Henry, the justiciar, and Philip of Worcester, he was appointed as King John's representative to the king of Connacht and other kings and magnates of Ireland. On 15 September 1215 he was given royal protection while attending the Fourth Lateran Council at Rome.

Evidence for Ó Máelmuaid's long-running dispute with William (I) Marshal, earl of Pembroke and Striguil, over lands of the see of Ferns, first appears on 30 May 1216, when Innocent III, doubtless in response to personal representations made to him by Ó Máelmuaid at the Lateran Council, instructed the archbishops of Dublin and Tuam, as papal judges delegate, to command William Marshal and others to restore the disputed property; an interdict had been placed on the earl's land in Ireland and the bishop of Ferns, then in England, had been ordered to excommunicate the Marshal and his accomplices. On 5 September 1216 King John gave Ó Máelmuaid custody of the vacant see of Killaloe until such time as he could be appointed bishop; but he was not promoted, probably because of the death of John a few weeks later. Early in 1218 he brought a case against William Marshal in an ecclesiastical court presided over by the archbishops of Dublin and Tuam; but on 18 April a royal writ was issued prohibiting the case from being heard until such time as Henry III came of age. Further letters on 20 April directed Geoffrey de Marisco, the justiciar, to see that the judges did not hear a plea regarding a lay fee in an ecclesiastical court. The Marshal took advantage of his position as regent to prevent pursuit of the claim on the grounds that the disputed land was a lay fee held of the king, who would warrant it to the Marshal when he came of age. On 25 June 1218 Pope Honorius III, possibly in response to representations from William Marshal, sent letters to Ó Máelmuaid, to the Marshal, and to Henry, archbishop of Dublin, requesting them to come to some agreement. The Marshal died excommunicate on 14 May 1219, having refused to restore the disputed property to the see of Ferns. According to Matthew Paris, after the Marshal's death Ó Máelmuaid petitioned the crown for restoration of the lands, but the earl's heir, William (II), and his brothers withheld their consent, whereupon he foretold the extinction of the family in the male line. Ironically, Ó Máelmuaid had co-operated with the Marshal in the foundation of the Cistercian abbey of Duiske (Graiguenamanagh), dedicating its cemetery in 1204 and witnessing the Marshal's charter to Duiske about 1207.

Ó Máelmuaid acted as suffragan in the diocese of Winchester, consecrating a chapel at the Cistercian abbey of Waverley on 6 November 1201 and dedicating five altars there on 10 July 1214. The Benedictine community of the cathedral priory of St Swithun's, Winchester, made him a member of their fraternity. He died in 1223. He may have been the author of an extant Latin life of St Abbán.

M. T. FLANAGAN

Sources M. P. Sheehy, ed., *Pontificia Hibernica: medieval papal chancery documents concerning Ireland, 640–1261*, 1 (1962), 125–6, 139–40, 180–81, 199–201 · H. S. Sweetman and G. F. Handcock, eds., *Calendar of documents relating to Ireland*, 5 vols., PRO (1875–86), vol. 1, nos. 258, 291, 385, 658, 721, 818, 823, 825, 1787 · *Gir. Camb. opera*, 1.66–71 · W. Stubbs, ed., *Gesta regis Henrici secundi Benedicti abbatis: the chronicle of the reigns of Henry II and Richard I, AD 1169–1192*, 2 vols., Rolls Series, 49 (1867); vol. 2, p. 79 · *Chronica magistri Rogeri de Hovedene*, ed. W. Stubbs, 3, Rolls Series, 51 (1870), 8, 15 · *Paris, Chron.*, 4.492–524 · *Ann. mon.*, 2.253, 282 · W. M. Hennessy and B. MacCarthy, eds., *Annals of Ulster, otherwise, annals of Senat*, 4 vols. (1887–1901), vol. 2, p. 271 · W. M. Hennessy, ed. and trans., *The annals of Loch Cé: a chronicle of Irish affairs from AD 1014 to AD 1590*, 1, Rolls Series, 54 (1871), 267 · C. M. Butler and J. H. Bernard, eds., 'The charters of the Cistercian abbey of Duiske in the county of Kilkenny', *Proceedings of the Royal Irish Academy*, 35C (1918–20), 1–188, esp. 19, 23–4 · Archbishop Marsh's Library, Dublin, MS Z4.2.7, fol. 65 [Dudley Loftus's collection of annals] · J. Baigent, 'On the abbey of the Blessed Mary of Waverley, in the county of Surrey', *Surrey Archaeological Collections*, 8 (1883), 157–210 · G. Mac Niocaill, 'Charters of John, lord of Ireland, to the see of Dublin', *Reportorium Novum*, 3 (1963–4), 301 · M. V. Ronan, 'St Laurentius, archbishop of Dublin: original testimonies for canonisation', *Irish Ecclesiastical Record*, 5th ser., 27 (1926), 347–64, esp. 350 · R. Sharpe, *Medieval Irish saints' lives: an introduction to Vitae sanctorum Hiberniae* (1991), 349–63, 385 · Register of St Swithun's Priory, BL, Add. MS 29436, fol. 46

O'Mahony [Mahony, Mahun, Marullus], **Connor** [Constantine; *name in religion* Cornelius a Sancto Patricio] (1594–1656), Jesuit and political controversialist, was born in Muskerry, co. Cork. On 17 March 1621 he entered the Society of Jesus in Portugal; Cornelius a Sancto Patricio was the name by which he was known in the society. He was professor of theology at Évora (about 100 kilometres east of Lisbon), and he appears to have been a noted moral theologian in Lisbon, where he was associated with the Jesuit church of São Roque (hence his additional subsidiary name, de Rocha). Acquaintances described him as brave and pious, and he is said to have rendered great services during an earthquake and volcanic eruption on the island of St Michael in the Azores.

Patrick Plunkett, titular bishop of Ardagh and subsequently of Meath, made O'Mahony's acquaintance in Lisbon between 1651 and 1660, as did John Serjeant, an English secular priest who studied at Lisbon. O'Mahony claimed to both Plunkett and Serjeant that he was the author of a controversial book on Ireland, and to the former he gave a copy. The volume contains two texts: 'Disputatio apologetica de jure regni Hiberniae pro Catholicis Hibernis adversus haereticos Anglos' and 'Accessit ejusdem authoris ad eosdem Catholicos exhortatio'. Although the book purports to have been published in Frankfurt, it is clear that Lisbon is the actual place of publication. The date of publication is 1645. The book was a conscious, and partisan, intervention in the Irish civil unrest initiated by the Irish rising of 1641. In these two treatises O'Mahony argued that the four main arguments adduced in support of English rights over Ireland—conquest, papal gift, submission, and prescription—were all false. Even if they were true, the fact that the kings of England were now protestant heretics meant that their claims were null and void. He urged the Catholics of Ireland to continue killing all the protestants in their midst, as well as any Catholics who refused to abandon their allegiance to the English throne, and to establish a new Catholic monarch who should be a 'vernacular or natural' Irishman. In 1647, or perhaps earlier, some copies of this inflammatory book reached Ireland through France or direct from Portugal. Its presence served to highlight deep divisions between the main political forces in Ireland. Stuart partisans were outraged by its assumptions, landowners felt that it undermined the basis of their property rights, while its call for a native king was interpreted both as support for the putative regal ambitions of Owen Roe O'Neill, and as questioning the legitimacy of the Anglo-Norman ('Old English') position in Ireland (though in fact O'Mahony wished to overcome ethnic differences between Irish Catholics). A copy was found with John Bane, parish priest of Athlone, and the nuncio Rinuccini was called upon by the confederate Catholics at Kilkenny to punish him: the nuncio refused to do this, but the book was burned by the common hangman, and rigorous search was made for copies at Galway. Peter Walsh, by the command of the supreme council, preached nine sermons against it at Kilkenny Castle. The book also ran into trouble in Portugal. O'Mahony had drawn a parallel between Portugal's recent rejection of its Castilian overlord in favour of a native prince and the situation in Ireland. Complaints of O'Mahony's book were lodged at Lisbon by an English priest (perhaps John Sergeant). King John IV, incensed by its attack on a fellow monarch, condemned it in December 1647, and it was made penal to possess a copy. O'Mahony died in Lisbon on 28 February 1656.   RICHARD BAGWELL, *rev.* VINCENT GEOGHEGAN

Sources P. Walsh, *The history and vindication of the loyal formulary, or Irish remonstrance* (1674), first treatise, pt 2, no. 22 · J. P. Conlan, 'Some notes on the "Disputatio Apologetica"', *Bibliographical Society of Ireland*, 6/5 (1955), 69–77 · E. Hogan, 'Chronological catalogue of the Irish members of the Society of Jesus, from the year 1550 to 1814', *Records of the English province of the Society of Jesus*, ed. H. Foley, 7/2 (1883), 1–96 [esp. 29] · G. Aiazzi, *The embassy in Ireland of Monsignor G. B. Rinuccini*, trans. A. Hutton (1873) · T. Ó hAnnracháin, '"Though hereticks and politicians should misinterpret their goode zeal": political ideology and Catholicism in early modern Ireland', *Political thought in seventeenth-century Ireland*, ed. J. H. Ohlmeyer (2000)

O'Mahony, Daniel, Count O'Mahony in the Castilian nobility (d. **1714**), army officer in the French and Spanish services, colloquially known as 'le Fameux Mahoni', was the son of John O'Mahony of Coolcorkerane, Killarney, co. Kerry, and Mary Joan Moriarty, the daughter of Thady Moriarty of Castle Drum, Dingle, co. Kerry. His brother Dermod attained the rank of colonel in James II's Irish army, distinguishing himself at the Boyne and at Aughrim before being killed in Italy while serving with the Limerick regiment about 1706. Daniel O'Mahony, having attained the rank of captain in the Royal Irish foot guards during the Williamite wars, went to France in 1692, becoming major in the Limerick and Dillon regiments successively.

O'Mahony served under Villeroy in northern Italy in late 1701, having command of Dillon's regiment during the absence of its colonel in January 1702, the regiment then being part of the 7000 strong garrison of the heavily fortified city of Cremona. In the early hours of 1 February O'Mahony awoke to find the Austrians under Prince Eugène had gained entrance to Cremona by a sewer and captured Villeroy and many French officers in their beds. Despite Austrian cavalry charging through the dark streets, he managed to rally a detachment of his regiment and held the Po gate. Over the next ten hours, although the surviving garrison was scattered in small bodies, mostly half dressed in the freezing winter weather and

with few officers, this position formed the nucleus of an effective resistance to Eugène's occupation of the town. As O'Mahony obtained reinforcements he spread them along the ramparts, and kept up a galling fusillade on the enemy. This diversion gave the comte de Revel time to concentrate and reanimate French troops in the neighbourhood of the Mantua gate, and Eugène, finding himself between two fires, was forced into a precipitate retreat from the city. On account of O'Mahony's crucial service at Cremona, he was selected to carry the dispatch to Paris. Louis XIV accorded him an hour's private conference at Versailles, later relating to De Chamillart that he had never before known a person give such a fair and balanced account, yet display a personality that was both spirited yet agreeable. Saint-Simon confirmed this assessment, describing him as a man of wit and valour. Louis rewarded O'Mahony with the brevet of colonel, a pension of 1000 livres, and a present of 1000 louis d'or. From Versailles he proceeded to St Germain, where the Pretender, James III (James Francis Edward Stuart), knighted him.

O'Mahony continued to serve in northern Italy under Vendôme; he was appointed governor of Brescello upon its surrender on 28 July 1703, and in January 1704 he took part in Vendôme's successes at San Sebastián and Castel de Bormida before leaving Italy. Efficient officers were urgently needed in the Spanish service, and Louis XIV had recommended O'Mahony to his nephew Philip V. He was appointed colonel of his own regiment of Irish dragoons (composed largely of deserters from the British expedition to Cadiz), and during the remainder of 1704 and the whole of 1705 served with distinction under Count Tilly. While placed at Murviedro in January 1706 to block the advance of Lord Peterborough's English relief column to Valencia, O'Mahony, being heavily outnumbered, was obliged to surrender, allowing Peterborough to pass. Despite this failure, Philip appointed him maréchal-de-camp shortly thereafter. After his promotion he stormed and sacked Enguera, and in June defended Alicante for twenty-eight days against Sir John Leake despite an inadequate garrison, ramparts requiring constant repairs, and a severe wound of his own. Although obliged to surrender on 8 September, his troops marched out with the honours of war, being transported to Cadiz without loss of service. Early in 1707 he resumed his command in Valencia, and captured several towns from the allies. At the battle of Almanza on 25 April 1707 he performed distinguished service in command of a brigade of horse that included his own regiment of Irish dragoons. On 7 July he was again badly wounded at the siege of Denia. However, by December 1707 he was again in command of some 6000 regular troops in Valencia, capturing the important town of Alcoy on 2 January 1708.

Appointed viceroy of Sicily in March 1709, with 3000 Spanish troops, including his own regiment of Irish dragoons, O'Mahony reached Messina in April. He suppressed several Austrian conspiracies, and his precautionary measures prevented the English fleet from landing any allied force. He returned to Spain in 1710 to command the cavalry of Philip's army, the king promoting him lieutenant-general; he had already, in 1706, been made a Castilian count. He subsequently served in the campaign of Ivaris, and on 20 August 1710 commanded the Spanish cavalry at the battle of Saragossa. Placed upon the extreme right, he opposed the Portuguese horse, which he utterly broke and drove into the Ebro. The Spanish cavalry, however, proved ill-disciplined and despite his best endeavours impetuously charged, riding over the enemy's artillery and far into their rear. In the meantime the main body of Philip's army had been defeated and was in retreat. O'Mahony rejoined it with the utmost difficulty. Although criticized for losing control of his men at Saragossa, he gained distinction at the head of Vendôme's cavalry at the battle of Villaviciosa on 10 December 1710, Philip rewarding him by appointing him commander of the military order of St Iago. He led the pursuit into Aragon, capturing the stronghold of Illueca and Lieutenant-General Dom Antonio de Villaröel with a detachment of 660 men. He continued to act in Spain under Vendôme until the cessation of hostilities in 1712, when he returned to France, where Louis XIV ennobled him. Before the end of that year O'Mahony, whose first wife, Cecily (Cecilia), daughter of George Weld of the old Catholic family of Lulworth Castle, Dorset, had died about 1708, married Charlotte, widow of Charles O'Brien, fifth Viscount Clare, and a sister of the duchess of Berwick, at St Germain. He did not, however, long survive his second marriage, dying at Ocana in Spain in January 1714. By his first marriage he left two sons, the elder being John Joseph, second count of Castile, whose career included positions as lieutenant-general in the army of the Two Sicilies, inspector-general of cavalry and dragoons, governor of San Elmo, and commander of the order of Saint Januarius. His granddaughter Cecilia, styled Countess Mahony, married in May 1757 Benedetto, Prince Giustiniani. The younger son, Demetrius, became Spain's ambassador to Austria, dying at Vienna in 1776. Neither son left male descendants.

P. J. C. ELLIOT-WRIGHT

Sources DNB · J. C. O'Callaghan, History of the Irish brigades in the service of France, [new edn] (1870), 204–21, 231–5, 241–51, 273–8 · J. A. C. Hugill, No peace without Spain (1991), 56, 64, 71, 124, 139, 177, 195–7, 199–200, 230, 242, 264, 308–9, 313–14, 331–2 · D. Carney, 'General Count Daniel O'Mahony, hero of Cremona', Irish Sword, 14 (1980–81), 95–8 · Burke, Peerage (1999) · Burke, Gen. Ire. (1976), 774–5 · A. E. C. Bredin, A history of the Irish soldier (1987), 141–2, 148, 153, 155, 159–60, 389 · J. O'Mahony, History of the O'Mahony septs of Kinelmeky and Ivagha and the Kerry branch (1912), 162–3 · C. Dalton, ed., English army lists and commission registers, 1661–1714, 2 (1894), 256 · M. O'Conor, Military history of the Irish nation (1885), 245, 254, 329, 336, 356

O'Mahony, John (1815–1877), Irish nationalist, born at Clonkilla, co. Cork, on 12 January 1815, was the son of Daniel O'Mahony and his wife. The family was one of minor Roman Catholic gentry, reputedly in long-standing conflict with the neighbouring magnates of Mitchelstown Castle, the earls of Kingston.

O'Mahony was sent early in life to Dr Hamblin's school in Midleton, co. Cork, and entered Trinity College, Dublin, in 1833, but never took a degree. He was a good Greek and

John O'Mahony (1815–1877), by unknown photographer

Latin scholar, and always more or less devoted to linguistic and philological pursuits, especially in connection with the Irish language. In 1857 he published *The history of Ireland from the earliest times to the English invasion, by Geoffrey Keating, D.D., translated from the original Gaelic, and copiously annotated*. It was at that time the best translation to have been published but was taken from a very imperfect text, and had evidently been executed (as O'Mahony himself confessed) in great haste. O'Mahony contributed to various Irish-American newspapers. His articles were mostly political, and generally somewhat ponderous in style.

In the 1840s O'Mahony took up residence on a substantial family holding near Carrick-on-Suir, co. Tipperary. This was in the region where William Smith O'Brien and his associates attempted to start an insurrection in July 1848, and O'Mahony was one of the few local men of substance who rallied to them. For several weeks after the débâcle at Ballingarry ended Smith O'Brien's venture, O'Mahony and some scores of followers remained under arms on the Tipperary–Kilkenny border near Ahenny. With the authorities offering a reward for his capture, O'Mahony eventually escaped on a schooner from Dungarvan to Newport in Wales and from there to France. For five years from late 1848 he lived in Paris, sharing impoverished lodgings with James Stephens. O'Mahony arrived in New York in January 1854 and quickly became involved in Irish-American revolutionary endeavours.

The Emmet Monument Association was founded in 1855 by Michael Doheny, O'Mahony, and others, but it failed to effect anything. In late 1857, however, an envoy was sent, from a committee in New York composed of O'Mahony and his friends, to James Stephens in Dublin, with proposals for the foundation of a new secret organization in Ireland, with the object of overthrowing English rule and establishing an Irish republic. Stephens consented, under certain conditions, notably the sending over of definite sums of money at stated times. He founded the Irish Republican Brotherhood in Dublin in March 1858, and early in 1859 on a visit to New York he saw to the formation by his American allies of the Fenian Brotherhood. 'Fenian' is derived from the *fianna*, a legendary band of ancient Irish warriors, and the derivation was O'Mahony's. He is thus the author of the term which came in time to designate revolutionary Irish nationalism on both sides of the Atlantic. From the beginning O'Mahony was 'head centre' of the Fenian Brotherhood. In late 1860 he travelled to Ireland and, after visiting his relations, proceeded to Dublin, where in early 1861 he and Stephens met to review their plans.

The American Civil War boosted the movement on both sides of the Atlantic, but expansion rendered the Fenian Brotherhood less amenable to O'Mahony's control. He could not resist the momentum that led to the summoning of a congress of the brotherhood at Chicago in November 1863. Here a representative form of government was adopted and, although O'Mahony was elected head centre, his authority was circumscribed. It was further diminished by the intrigues of James Stephens, who made a fund-raising visit in 1864. O'Mahony survived a second congress, at Cincinnati in January 1865, but a third, at Philadelphia in October 1865, saw him overthrown by a majority which put all power in the hands of a 'senate', from which he was excluded.

In January 1866 O'Mahony was once again head centre but now of a splinter group. The senate wing called for an attack on British power in Canada, a policy denounced by the O'Mahony wing as a diversion. But in April 1866, in an attempt to upstage their opponents, O'Mahony's supporters set out to occupy the small island of Campobello, belonging to New Brunswick but situated close to the coast of Maine. The attempt was prevented by the American navy, and it cost those involved dearly in terms of resources, morale, and prestige. After arriving in America in May 1866, James Stephens took control of the O'Mahony wing, promising an invasion of Ireland by the year's end. When this failed to materialize, morale and prestige were further undermined. The Fenian Brotherhood dragged on in a precarious existence. For several years O'Mahony remained head centre, but neither he nor it thenceforward had any appreciable influence on Irish or Irish-American politics.

O'Mahony was physically a very powerful and handsome man. Although he took part in no action, O'Mahony was briefly in charge of the 99th regiment of the New York national guard during the civil war and so acquired the title of colonel. Before leaving Ireland in 1848, O'Mahony had made over his property to his sister Mrs Jane Mandeville. For most of his subsequent career he depended precariously on politics and journalism for a living. He never married. A friend found him sick and in great poverty a few days before he died in New York on 7 February 1877. His remains, which were brought back to Ireland, were followed to Glasnevin cemetery on 4 March 1877 by a great concourse of people. R. V. COMERFORD

Sources B. Ó Cathaoir, 'John O'Mahony, 1815–77', *Capuchin Annual* (1977), 180–93 · J. Devoy, *Recollections of an Irish rebel* (1929) · J. Maher, ed., *Chief of the Comeraghs: a John O'Mahony anthology* (1957) · W. D'Arcy, *The Fenian movement in the United States, 1858–86* (1947) · R. V. Comerford, *The Fenians in context: Irish politics and society, 1848–82* (1985) · R. V. Comerford, *Charles J. Kickham: a study in Irish nationalism and literature* (1979)
Archives Presbyterian Library, Philadelphia | Catholic University of America, Washington, DC, Fenian MSS
Likenesses oils, 1868, Municipal Gallery, Dublin · photograph (in uniform), repro. in Devoy, *Recollections of an Irish rebel* · photograph, Gill & Macmillan Publishers, Dublin [*see illus.*]

Omai (*c*.1753–*c*.1780), first Tahitian to visit England, was taken to England in July 1774 by Captain Furneaux, commander of the *Adventure* (sister ship of Cook's *Resolution*), and returned by Cook in November 1777, having left England the previous July. He appears to have been born about 1753 on the island of Raiatea, part of the Society Islands of which the main island is Tahiti. His father was not of the chiefly class but was a considerable landowner. However, some twelve years before Omai set out for England, the island was attacked by invaders from the island of Borabora and his father was killed and his lands confiscated. Thereafter, Omai harboured hopes of revenge in which he vainly attempted to involve his English friends.

Omai (or, as he was known by his family, Mai) fled to Tahiti and was there when, on 26 June 1767, Wallis's *Dolphin* arrived. This first encounter between Tahitians and Europeans led to conflict and the use by Wallis of firearms, as a result of which Omai was wounded. When the *Endeavour* arrived in April 1769 Omai was still in Tahiti but soon afterwards he left for Huahine, another of the Society Islands. It was there that Cook and Furneaux encountered him in September 1773, when he enrolled as supernumerary on board Furneaux's *Adventure* under the pseudonym of Tetuby Homey. Though Cook was ultimately to acknowledge that Omai acquitted himself very well while in England he at first regarded him with disfavour, describing him as 'dark, ugly and a downright blackguard' (*Journals*, 2.222). By contrast, James Burney, an officer on the *Adventure*, who came to know Omai well, regarded him as 'a fellow of quick parts … possessed of many good qualities' (*Early Diary*, 70).

When the *Adventure* arrived in England Omai was taken under the wing of Joseph Banks who, along with Solander, presented him at court on 17 July 1774. He was received with such favour that he was granted a royal pension while in England. Shortly afterwards (possibly at the king's urging) he was taken by Banks and Solander to Baron Dimsdale in Hertfordshire to be inoculated against

Omai (c.1753–c.1780), by Sir Joshua Reynolds, c.1776

smallpox. (The disease had killed Omai's compatriot Aoutourou, the first Tahitian to visit Europe, who had been taken to France in 1769 by Bougainville.) While in England, thanks to the connections made possible by Banks, Lord Sandwich, and the Burneys, Omai came to know many of the most prominent members of aristocratic and literary society. When Dr Johnson met him in April 1776 he was 'struck with the elegance of his behaviour', accounting for it on the grounds that 'he had passed his time, while in England, only in the best company; so that all that he had acquired of our manners was genteel' (Boswell, *Life*, 3.8). Under the tutelage of the free-thinking Banks and Lord Sandwich he received no religious tuition, an omission which Granville Sharp attempted to remedy a few months before his return. But he found him a slow pupil in regard to both the English language and Christian morality, responding to Sharp's discussion of adultery with the remark: 'two wives—very good; three wives—very, very good' (McCormick, 167).

In the course of his third and fatal Pacific voyage Cook dropped Omai off on Huahine on 2 November 1777. With his store of European goods Omai purchased land and, at least for a time, the goodwill of the chiefs. His muskets made him particularly useful in the islanders' battles.

However, he appears to have died of natural causes some thirty months after Cook left.

During his two years in England Omai provided élite society with a living example of the 'noble savage' and a focus for discussions about the virtues of natural man as against the artificiality produced by civilization. Fanny Burney, for example, unfavourably compared that 'pedantic Booby', Mr Stanhope, trained by his natural father, Lord Chesterfield, to comply with the manners of polite society, with the natural grace of Omai who 'appears in a *new world* like a man [who] all his life studied *the Graces* … I think this shews how much more *Nature* can do without art, than *art* with all her refinement, unassisted by Nature' (*Early Diary*, 63). He was painted by a number of major artists, most notably Sir Joshua Reynolds, whose celebrated portrait of Omai (exh. RA, 1776) is now in the Tate collection. JOHN GASCOIGNE

Sources E. H. McCormick, *Omai, Pacific envoy* (1977) · 'Genuine account of Omiah, a native of Otaheite … lately brought over to England by Capt. Fourneaux', *London Magazine*, 43 (1774), 363–4 · *Daniel Solander: collected correspondence, 1753–1782*, ed. and trans. E. Duyker and P. Tingbrand (1995) · *The early journals and letters of Fanny Burney*, ed. L. E. Troide, 2: 1774–1777 (1990) · *The journals of Captain James Cook*, ed. J. C. Beaglehole, 4 vols. in 5, Hakluyt Society, extra ser., 34a, 35, 36a–b, 37 (1955–74) · Boswell, *Life*, vol. 3 · *With Captain James Cook in the Antarctic and Pacific: the private journal of James Burney … 1772–3*, ed. B. Hooper (1975)
Likenesses N. Dance, pencil drawing, 1774, National Archives of Canada, Ottawa · engraving, 1774, NL Aus., Rex Van Kivell Collection · J. Reynolds, oil sketch, c.1775, Yale U. Art Gallery · J. Reynolds, oils, c.1776, Tate collection [*see illus.*] · Williams Parry, group portrait, oils, c.1776 (with Banks and Solander), Parham Park, Sussex · J. Jacobi, mezzotint, 1780 (after J. Reynolds), NPG · W. Hodges, drawing, repro. in J. Cook, *Voyage towards South Pole*, pl. 57 · J. Reynolds, pencil drawing, NL Aus., Rex Van Kivell Collection

O Máille, Earnán. *See* O'Malley, Ernest Bernard (1897–1957).

O'Malley, Ernest Bernard [Ernie; Earnán O Máille] (1897–1957), Irish revolutionary and writer, was born on 26 May 1897 in Ellison Street, Castlebar, co. Mayo, the second of eleven children of Luke Malley (*b.* 1861), solicitor's clerk, and his wife, Marion (*b.* 1873), daughter of Bernard Kearney and his wife, Mary Anne. His parents were both Irish, though he later commented upon their lack of 'national faith' and ignorance of 'a national tradition' (*Prisoners: the Civil War Letters*, 70). Baptized Ernest Bernard Malley, his later variations to his name (Earnán O Máille, Earnán O'Malley, and—most commonly—Ernie O'Malley) reflected his adoption of a more aggressively distinctive Irish identity than theirs.

In early childhood O'Malley developed a lasting attachment to the west of Ireland, but in 1906 his family moved to Dublin, where Ernie attended the Christian Brothers' school, North Richmond Street. In 1915 he began studying medicine at the (Catholic) University College, Dublin. O'Malley initially intended to follow his elder brother into the British army but, partly inspired by the 1916 Easter rising, he was to join instead the Irish Republican Army (IRA). He joined the Irish Volunteers in the wake of 1916, and was to become a leading republican zealot during the

Irish revolution. In 1918, having twice failed his second-year university examination, he left home; he was an IRA staff captain in 1919, and in 1921 took up the post of commandant-general of the IRA's second southern division.

Family expectations of respectable, professional employment combined with religious background and an enthusiasm for soldiership provide some of the foundations for O'Malley's republican career: in IRA officership he found professional, military expression for a visceral Catholic nationalism. He also found excitement, liberation from the dullness of life at home, defiant rebellion against his parents, an alternative to his stumbling undergraduate career, and—in cultural and political Irish separatism—a decisive resolution of the tension between his Anglocentrism and his Anglophobia.

A significant IRA figure in the 1919–21 Anglo-Irish War, O'Malley then rejected as an unacceptable compromise the 1921 Anglo-Irish treaty under which the Irish Free State was established, and he was a leading anti-treatyite in the 1922–3 civil war. He was badly wounded in his dramatic Dublin capture by Free State forces in November 1922, and was imprisoned until July 1924, when he returned home to live with his parents at 7 Iona Drive, Dublin. Despite serious injuries, he had stoically spent forty-one days on hunger strike for release from prison in 1923; earlier in the same year he had been elected a republican member of the Dublin parliament, the Dáil. But his politics had always been those of the soldier, and he declined post-revolutionary opportunities to pursue a political career. He twice attempted, unsuccessfully, to complete his medical studies at University College, Dublin (1926–8, 1936–7), but his post-1924 energies were most fully directed towards life as a bohemian writer. He spent much of 1925–6 on a recuperative journey through France, Spain, and Italy—'I learned to walk again in the Pyrénées' (English, 28)—and 1928–35 travelling widely in North America. The years 1929–32 were divided between New Mexico and Mexico City, and in Taos, New Mexico, he mixed with writers and artists and worked extensively on what were to become classic autobiographies of the Irish revolution: *On Another Man's Wound* (1936) and *The Singing Flame* (1978).

O'Malley met Helen Huntington Hooker (1905–1993) in Connecticut in 1933; she was a sculptor, and the daughter of Elon Huntington Hooker, chemical manufacturer. They married in London on 27 September 1935, settling first at 229 Upper Rathmines Road, Dublin; but they enthused over Ireland's rural west and moved in 1937 to co. Mayo where, in the following year, they settled in Burrishoole Lodge, near Newport. This remained O'Malley's primary base until 1954, when he moved to 52 Mespil House Flats, Dublin. Three children were born to the O'Malleys: Cahal (10 July 1936), Etáin (8 August 1940), and Cormac (20 July 1942). Sharing enthusiasm for the arts, and each representing an escape from the other's past, Ernie and Helen had several years of enjoyable intimacy. But by the mid-1940s their love had cooled, and in March 1950 Helen kidnapped (the word was used by both parents

and all three children) Cahal and Etáin, taking them with her to the United States. From there she divorced O'Malley in 1952. Cormac remained with his father.

O'Malley's post-American years in Ireland were devoted to numerous projects. He wrote extensively, including work for *Horizon*, *The Bell*, and the *Sunday Press*. He was technical adviser to the film director John Ford on the making of Irish films, including *The Quiet Man* (1952). He did radio broadcasts, on Mexican painting for the BBC's Third Programme (1947) and on his IRA days for Radio Éireann (1953). In the latter year he suffered a heart attack, and his remaining years were marred by ill health. He died of heart failure on 25 March 1957, in Howth, co. Dublin, at the house of his sister Kathleen. Two days later he was given a state funeral with full military honours and was buried in the Malley family plot in Glasnevin cemetery, Dublin.

Literary, intellectual, and defiantly dissident, O'Malley was the classic bohemian revolutionary. His significance lies in his having been both a leading Irish revolutionary and the author of impressive autobiographical accounts of those crucial years in Irish history. His memoirs are distinguished from their rivals by striking subtlety, self-consciousness, and literary sophistication; in particular, O'Malley's preparedness to seek causes for revolutionary action beyond the realm of ostensible revolutionary purpose renders his work invaluable to the historian.

RICHARD ENGLISH

Sources E. O'Malley, *On another man's wound* (1936) · E. O'Malley, *The singing flame* (1978) · E. O'Malley, *Raids and rallies* (1982) · *Prisoners: the civil war letters of Ernie O'Malley*, ed. R. English and C. O'Malley (1991) · R. English, *Ernie O'Malley: IRA intellectual* (1998) · m. cert.
Archives NL Ire., MSS · University College, Dublin, MSS
Likenesses S. O'Sullivan, charcoal, 1941, NG Ire. · E. Weston, six photographs, Center for Creative Photography, Tucson, Arizona
Wealth at death £5640: probate, 29 July 1957, *CGPLA Éire*

O'Malley, George (1780–1843), army officer, was the son of George O'Malley and Elizabeth, *née* Clarke. He was a volunteer in the Castlebar yeomanry during the attack on the town by the French on 27 August 1798, and was present when it was attacked a fortnight later by a strong Irish rebel force, which was defeated by the yeomanry and a company of Fraser fencibles. O'Malley was confirmed as a lieutenant in the Castlebar yeomanry by Lord Cornwallis in recognition of his services, and soon after joined the North Mayo militia, from which he brought volunteers to the 13th regiment. He was appointed ensign on 23 February 1800, serving with the 13th at Ferrol and in Egypt, where he was severely wounded in the action of 13 March 1801, and afterwards at Malta and Gibraltar. For his success in recruiting in Ireland he received a company in the new 2nd battalion 89th regiment on 25 April 1805, and served with it until Colonel Henry Augustus Dillon raised the 101st regiment, in which O'Malley was appointed major. In Mayo he assisted in forming the regiment. He served with it in Ireland and Jersey, and was dispatched with 300 men to Saint John, New Brunswick, in 1808, when war with the United States was imminent, and the Americans were reportedly collecting a large force near that place. For his services in command of the garrison, and the exemplary conduct of the troops under his command, he received the freedom of the city on 19 July 1809. As major, he commanded the regiment for four years in Jamaica, obtaining the brevet rank of lieutenant-colonel on 4 June 1813. (The regiment was disbanded as the 100th in 1817.)

O'Malley's applications for employment in Europe were initially unsuccessful, but on 12 June 1815 he was appointed to the 2nd battalion 44th foot, and commanded it in Picton's division at Quatre Bras and Waterloo. On 18 June the battalion lost very heavily, being reduced to five officers and 200 men. O'Malley was twice wounded and had two horses shot under him, but he remained in command, for which he was made CB. He commanded the battalion in France until it was disbanded in 1816, when he was placed on half pay. He was appointed major 38th regiment on 12 August 1819 and lieutenant-colonel 88th Connaught Rangers on 2 June 1825. He commanded that regiment, which he brought to a fine state of discipline, until promoted major-general on 23 November 1841. He died in London on 16 May 1843, and was buried at Murisk Abbey, co. Mayo, Ireland. A statue was erected to him at Castletown, Isle of Man.

H. M. CHICHESTER, rev. JAMES FALKNER

Sources *Army List* · *Naval and Military Gazette* (20 May 1843) · private information (2004)
Likenesses oils, c.1810, priv. coll. · W. Salter, group portrait, oils (*Waterloo banquet at Apsley House, London*), Wellington Museum, Apsley House, London · W. Salter, pencil study, NPG · statue, Castletown, Isle of Man

O'Malley, Gráinne [Grace] (*fl.* 1577–1597), chieftain's wife and pirate, was the daughter of Owen Dubhdara O'Malley, chief, lord of Umhall Uachtarach or Upper Owle in the barony of Murrisk, co. Mayo, and his wife, Margaret, daughter of Conchobhar Óg Mac Conchobhair O'Malley of Moher, co. Mayo. The Anglicized version of her Gaelic name, Gráinne, became the basis for her name in folklore, Granuaile. The O'Malleys were a seafaring family with a reputation for piracy off the north and west coast of Ireland.

Very little is known of O'Malley's early life. She was probably brought up in the heart of her family's territory in co. Mayo. Her first husband was Dónal O'Flaherty, chief, son of Gilldubh O'Flaherty, and lord of a sept of the O'Flahertys, based in Connemara, co. Galway. They had a son, Owen. By the time of the first recorded references to O'Malley in the late 1570s, Dónal had died and she was married to Richard an Iarainn Burke (*d.* 1583), chief *tánaiste* (designated successor) to the MacWilliam Burke, chief of the Burkes of lower Connaught, co. Mayo. They had one son, Theobald (*d.* 1629). Richard an Iarainn's territory lay in the barony of Burrishoole, adjacent to the O'Malley lands in Murrisk. When Sir Henry Sidney, lord deputy, visited Galway in 1577 he recorded meeting O'Malley, whom he described as 'a most famous femynyne sea captain'. She offered him the service of her three galleys and 200 men. According to Sidney, O'Malley 'brought with her her husband, for she was aswell by sea as by land well

more than Mrs Mate with him' (LPL, Carew MS 601, fol. 111). Sidney did not avail himself of O'Malley's overtures of assistance and shortly after their encounter she was arrested by Gerald Fitzgerald, fourteenth earl of Desmond, and spent almost two years in prison in Limerick and Dublin. Her crime was not recorded, but it is likely that her arrest was motivated more by Desmond's desire to demonstrate his loyalty to the government than by any serious threat represented by O'Malley.

In the spring of 1579 O'Malley was released, and later that year Richard an Iarainn raided the Galway region, partly as a means of dividing crown forces which were concentrated on controlling the outbreak of Desmond's rebellion in Munster and partly to bolster his own military standing among the Burkes. Through O'Malley's intercession he submitted to the president of Connaught, Sir Nicholas Malby, in 1580, and at the end of the year he succeeded to the position of MacWilliam Burke with government support. He was knighted in 1581. There were, however, limits to Burke's and O'Malley's co-operation with the crown authorities, and over the next two years she is recorded helping him to resist further interference by government officials in the Burke lordship. Richard an Iarainn died in 1583. On her husband's death, O'Malley, according to her own account, 'gathered together all her own followers and with 1000 head of cows and mares' (PRO, SP 63/170, no. 63) went to live in Carraighowley Castle, co. Mayo, on part of her late husband's territory, where she continued to 'maintain herself and her people by sea and land' (ibid., no. 64). She may initially have established friendly relations with the new president of Connaught, Sir Richard Bingham, but she and her sons soon fell out with his regime. Owen was killed by the president's brother George Bingham in 1586 and O'Malley was imprisoned and threatened with death. Theobald was maintained in the president's household for some time as a pledge.

O'Malley was implicated in the Burke rebellions of 1586 and 1588 by Sir Richard Bingham, who accused her of drawing Scottish mercenary soldiers into co. Mayo. Her actions suggest, however, that she was primarily concerned to protect the interests of her immediate family and particularly those of Theobald. By 1591 Theobald had emerged as the leading Burke and the strongest contender for the position of MacWilliam but despite submitting to the government he was still regarded with suspicion. Her son's arrest precipitated O'Malley's visit to Elizabeth I in the summer of 1593. A remarkable aspect of O'Malley's petitions was that she acted as spokesperson for the men in her family. She asked the queen for the release of her son and of her brother, who had also been arrested by Bingham. She also requested that her two sons and two other male members of the Burke family be given letters patent for their lands. As a widow under English common law, O'Malley also laid claim to dower from the land of the O'Malleys and of the O'Flahertys. In a much quoted passage she explained that a widow under Gaelic law had no right to her husband's land. The royal visit was a success from O'Malley's point of view. Bingham was ordered by Elizabeth to release Theobald and to grant O'Malley maintenance from her husbands' lands. As a demonstration of loyalty, O'Malley claimed that she had 'procured all her sons, cousins and followers of the O'Malleys', with a number of galleys (some newly built on her return from London) to assist the Elizabethan forces in the Mayo area (PRO, SP 63/177, no. 36). The Irish administration was, none the less, slow to implement the queen's instructions and in 1595 O'Malley made another visit to London, renewing her requests for herself and her male relatives.

The London administration's endorsement of O'Malley's requests was rooted in the absence of substantial evidence that she had participated in rebellion against the crown despite the strong assertions of Bingham that she, or at least her sons, had done so. Crown support for O'Malley was vindicated during the 1590s when her son and she assisted the government with their galleys. In 1597 Theobald made an agreement with the English administration which granted him the lands of MacWilliam in return for his support for government troops. With the exception of the Bingham era of the late 1580s, the strategy of O'Malley, Richard an Iarainn, and Theobald appears to have been one of negotiated co-operation with the English administration in Ireland. This was successful in the sense that Theobald emerged at the end of the sixteenth century as the greatest landowner in co. Mayo and was created Viscount Mayo in 1627.

The date of O'Malley's death is not recorded, but it was probably in the first decade of the seventeenth century. She is remarkable as being the only woman from sixteenth-century Gaelic Ireland who is recorded as taking a leadership role within her sept. Despite her notoriety among English officials, however, there are no references to her in Gaelic historical sources, a reflection, perhaps, of her relatively minor status within the politics of the north-west of the late sixteenth century. Apart from her two sons, O'Malley had a daughter, Margaret, although it is not known which husband was the father. In later centuries O'Malley's life became the topic of folklore stories which celebrated her piratical and military achievements.   MARY O'DOWD

Sources A. Chambers, *Granuaile: the life and times of Grace O'Malley, c.1530–1603*, rev. edn (Dublin, 1998) · H. T. Knox, *The history of the county of Mayo* (Dublin, 1908); facs. edn (1982) · *CSP Ire., 1574–96* · PRO, SP 63/170, nos. 63, 64; SP 63/171, nos. 18, 35, 37; SP 63/177, nos. 36, 70 · LPL, Carew MS 601, fol. 111

O'Malley [*née* Sanders], **Mary Dolling**, Lady O'Malley [*pseud.* Ann Bridge] (**1889–1974**), novelist, was born on 11 September 1889 at Porters, near Shenley, Hertfordshire, the daughter of James Harris Sanders (1844–1916), a businessman who sold rail and rolling stock, and his American wife, Marie Louise Day (1852–1922), whom he had met on a business trip to New Orleans. Mary Anne, as she was known, was the seventh of nine children, none of whom except her later had their own children. Educated at home, she lived in the country until 1904 and then in London. In 1911 her father was financially ruined; each of his six daughters was allowed £50 a year, their previous dress

allowance, and Mary Anne worked at the Chelsea branch of the Charity Organization Society, earning 23*s.* a week.

Mary Anne was an excellent mountain climber ('climbing was really the greatest thing in my life at that time'; Bridge, *Moments of Knowing*, 15) and by 1910, having had four good seasons, with guides, in the Alps, was made a member of the Ladies' Alpine Club. On 25 October 1913 she married Owen St Clair *O'Malley (1887–1974), the younger son of Sir Edward O'Malley, a distinguished Irish lawyer who had been chief judge of the supreme consular court for the Ottoman empire. Owen had joined the Foreign Office in 1911 and remained there during the war; meanwhile Mary Anne worked at the Admiralty breaking German ciphers—this was while her first child (*b.* 1914) was a baby. In 1919 they moved to a fifteenth-century house at Bridge End, Ockham, Surrey, and took up poultry farming in a small way, two more children being born in 1918 and 1921.

In 1926 Owen was posted to Peking (Beijing) as counsellor. However, on the O'Malleys' return to England he was accused of illegal currency dealing and was given permission to resign; he was reinstated but with five years' loss of seniority. His wife's persuasive arguments that he had been unwise but not criminal helped to exonerate him. She wrote about this injustice much later in *Permission to Resign* (1971). Meanwhile, she had begun writing articles, poems, and short stories and very soon was making between £150 and £200 a year (using a pseudonym because of her husband's profession). She had a great success in 1932 with her first novel, *Peking Picnic*, which the following year won the £3500 *Atlantic Monthly* prize. Sometimes compared to *A Passage to India*, this was to be the first of many novels drawing on her experiences as the wife of a diplomat and mixing history, romance, travelogue, and psychology. *The Ginger Griffin* (1934), the first of her four books that were Book Society choices, and *Four-Part Setting* (1939) again drew on the life of the foreign legations in Peking (the latter being in part based on the story of Mary Anne's unhappy marriage and her decision to make the best of it: the philandering Charles in the book is based on Owen). *Illyrian Spring* (1935) was set on the coast of Yugoslavia—and was in part the reason for its tourist industry, including the prince of Wales's notorious Adriatic cruise with Wallis Simpson.

Enchanter's Nightshade (1937) had an Italian background, then came

> the first of several novels ... dealing with historical events that have taken place in our life-time, of which I have come to have first-hand knowledge; fiction but made as factual as possible ... If any of my work comes to have permanent value, I feel it will be these books: *Frontier Passage* (1942), *The Dark Moment* (1952), *A Place to Stand* (1953) and *The Tightening String* (1962). (Bridge, *Facts and Fictions*, 59)

Frontier Passage, for example, was about Spain in 1938; she had been there only briefly but, as usual, her research was meticulous. Her work was translated into sixteen languages. Its mixture of rigorous observation and romantic comedy, and deep understanding of human nature, make her an outstanding novelist.

In 1940, having given up Bridge End two years earlier, Mary Anne joined Owen in Hungary, where he was British minister; a year later she fled via Russia and the Pacific to the United States east coast and stayed there until 1942. Lady O'Malley, as she became in 1943, was described at this time as

a tall, brown-haired woman who says she is 'very strong, physically and nervously,' and whose personality is positive, energetic, and self-confident. She is immensely interested in people, talks to everyone from cab drivers to waiters, and is constantly on the go. She is a devotee of sailing, skiing, and swimming; speaks fluent French, German, Italian, and Chinese, and a smattering of other languages, including Mongolian; and habitually sends telegrams in Latin. 'I don't in the least mind work,' she says, 'but … I am wife and mother first, and a writer only afterwards.' (Kunitz and Colby)

Singing Waters, published in 1945, had an Albanian background; *The Dark Moment* was about Atatürk's national revolution; these two novels, as well as *The Portuguese Escape* (1958), were choices of the Literary Guild of America. In 1944 Owen went as ambassador to Lisbon; Mary Anne collaborated with Susan Belloc-Lowndes to write a guide to Portugal, published in 1949. After Owen's retirement in 1947 the O'Malleys lived at Rockfleet, co. Mayo, Ireland, then moved to 27 Charlbury Road, Oxford, ten years later. In 1948 Mary Anne was received into the Roman Catholic church. *Facts and Fictions* (1968) and *Moments of Knowing* (1970) were both autobiographical; the latter touched on her interest in the supernatural, for example anticipating events in dreams and reading handwriting intuitively. The last of her twenty-six books, *Julia in Ireland* (1973), the final volume of her popular and profitable Julia Probyn series, was rejected by her long-term fiction publisher, Chatto and Windus, but was published in America. This rejection, and the death of her son from heart failure, clouded her final years. Mary Anne O'Malley died on 9 March 1974 at her house in Oxford, of bronchial pneumonia. At her request her ashes were placed in the O'Malley grave at Cuddesdon, Oxfordshire.　NICOLA BEAUMAN

Sources A. Bridge, *Facts and fictions* (1968) · A. Bridge [M. D. O'Malley], *Moments of knowing: some personal experiences beyond normal knowledge* (1970) · A. Bridge, *Portrait of my mother* (1955) · private information (2004) [J. O'Malley, B. Stoney] · S. J. Kunitz and H. Haycraft, *Twentieth century authors: a biographical dictionary of modern literature* (1942); 1st suppl. (1955) · K. Kellaway, 'Introduction', in A. Bridge, *Peking picnic* (1989) · J. Uglow, 'Introduction', in A. Bridge, *Illyrian spring* (1989) · d. cert.
Archives Ransom HRC, papers | U. Reading L., letters to Herberth Herlitschka and Marlys Herlitschka
Likenesses photograph, repro. in Kunitz and Haycroft, *Twentieth century authors* (1942) · photograph, repro. in A. Bridge, *Permission to resign* (1971), 58
Wealth at death £6847: probate, 20 Aug 1974, *CGPLA Eng. & Wales*

O'Malley, Sir Owen St Clair (1887–1974), diplomatist, was born on 4 May 1887 at 8 Burlington Place, Eastbourne, the third son and youngest of five children of Sir Edward Loughlin O'Malley (1842–1932), barrister and judge, and his wife, Emma Winnifred (d. 1927), daughter of Joseph Alfred Hardcastle, Liberal MP for Colchester (1847–52) and

Bury St Edmunds (1857–74 and 1880–85). His father's family originated from co. Mayo in the west of Ireland. His grandfather Peter Frederick O'Malley was born there but sought his fortune in England. He was admitted to the London bar in 1834, took silk in 1850, and rose to become recorder of Norwich. He married Emily Rodwell, whose family constituted part of the commercial and professional aristocracy of East Anglia. O'Malley's father was educated at Trinity College, Cambridge, graduated in 1864 with a first-class degree in maths, and was subsequently called to the bar. He practised only briefly before entering the colonial legal service, which he served with increasing distinction in a variety of posts as attorney-general and chief justice throughout the empire and its dependencies until his retirement from the bench in 1903.

For Owen O'Malley this background contributed one important influence in forming his character: he was always immensely proud of his Irish ancestry. Although southern protestants, his O'Malley forebears were not unionists; his paternal grandfather had sympathized strongly with the Young Ireland movement, and his father, before marriage and family intervened, had considered putting his name forward as a home-rule candidate for an Irish seat. O'Malley himself, when the centre failed to hold and opinion over Ireland polarized in 1918, made it clear within the Foreign Office that he should be counted as a Sinn Féiner; and in 1947 upon his retirement he chose to settle in the west of Ireland, and returned to England only to be nearer his surviving relatives and reliable medical care as his health declined.

Until the age of eleven O'Malley was educated at home by his mother at Denton, a hamlet of the village of Cuddesdon, a few miles to the south-east of Oxford. There he acquired a lifelong love of natural history and country life, together with a taste for solitude. He went to Hillbrow preparatory school, Rugby, in 1899, and then, in 1902, after a false start at Harrow, to Radley School, which he endured rather than enjoyed. His distaste for the philistinism, the enforced intimacy, and the compulsory games of public school meant that when he went in 1906 to Magdalen College, Oxford, he revelled in the civilized freedom that university life offered, without distinguishing himself socially or academically. He graduated with a second-class degree in modern history in 1909. After Oxford he determined on a diplomatic career and in 1911, at his second attempt, passed in first place in the Foreign Office entrance examination.

In October 1911 O'Malley began work as a clerk in the western department of the Foreign Office under the direction of its head, Sir Eyre Crowe. Crowe became O'Malley's great idol and to some extent the regard was mutual. Having settled in his chosen career O'Malley married, on 25 October 1913, Mary Dolling Sanders [see O'Malley, Mary Dolling (1889–1974)], the seventh of nine children of James Harris Sanders, businessman, and his American wife, Marie Louise, née Day. The marriage proved happy and successful and produced three children: one boy, (John) Patrick Loughlin (b. 1918), and two daughters, (Diana) Jane Sabina (b. 1914) and Helena Grania Kathleen

Clare (Kate; *b.* 1921). Later in life Lady O'Malley, writing under the name Ann Bridge, became a prolific and successful romantic novelist and travel writer, drawing on the scene and social environment of her husband's various diplomatic appointments for her novels.

During the First World War O'Malley served in the contraband department of the Foreign Office, enforcing the blockade against Germany, and from January 1918 to January 1919 he was private secretary to Frederick Leverton Harris, under-secretary of state for blockade. He was promoted first secretary in March 1920. In December 1925 he was sent as acting counsellor to Peking (Beijing) and subsequently, in the absence of an ambassador, was made chargé d'affaires. In this capacity he was directly responsible for the successful negotiations with the nationalist authorities over the administration of the British concessions in Hankow (Hankou) and Kiukiang (Jiujiang), activities which earned him appointment as CMG in June 1927. Upon his return to England in August 1927, nemesis immediately threatened as he found himself named in the Francs case of alleged currency speculation by a group of senior Foreign Office officials. Most damaged by the findings of the subsequent board of inquiry was J. D. Gregory, but O'Malley himself was given 'permission to resign'. This was a devastating sentence, and O'Malley's diplomatic career would have ended then had it not been for a remarkable and successful campaign fought by his wife. Under its impact the board revised its verdict on O'Malley and he was allowed, after one year's 'unemployment', to resume his diplomatic career.

O'Malley spent the early 1930s in Whitehall, and was made counsellor in August 1933. In October 1937 he was appointed minister-plenipotentiary at Mexico city, arriving just in time to confront a first-class diplomatic crisis over the Mexican government's expropriation of the Mexican Eagle Oil Company. O'Malley's brusque delivery of a peremptory note from the Foreign Office, drawing tactless reference to the financial record of the Mexican government, resulted in a mutual withdrawal of ambassadors, and O'Malley found himself unexpectedly back in London in May 1938. Brief service in the British mission to Spain at Hendaye, and subsequently at St Jean de Luz, from July 1938, was followed by his appointment as minister-plenipotentiary at Budapest in May 1939. As German pressure on the Horthy regime intensified, O'Malley was withdrawn from this position, in April 1941. There then followed a hiatus in his diplomatic career until February 1943, when he was appointed ambassador to the Polish government-in-exile in London.

Within weeks of his appointment O'Malley found himself at the flashpoint of one of the greatest diplomatic crises of the Second World War. On 13 April 1943 German radio reported the discovery of mass graves of thousands of massacred Polish officers near Katyn, and alleged Soviet guilt. On 17 April the Polish government requested an International Red Cross investigation, not knowing that the Germans had done the same the previous day. On 19 April *Pravda* denounced 'Hitler's Polish Collaborators', and on 26 April Russia suspended diplomatic relations

with the Poles. Churchill immediately intervened with both the Poles and the Russians to retrieve the situation. At the same time he ordered that O'Malley be instructed to draw up a confidential report on Katyn, assessing likely responsibility. Working at great speed, O'Malley delivered his report on 24 May 1943. Within the Foreign Office it was immediately seen as a brilliant but unorthodox dispatch. Its brilliance lay in the way it dismantled the Soviet claim of innocence and pointed to the overwhelming evidence of Russian guilt. Its unorthodoxy lay in the long disquisition on the need, even in the most difficult of times, to retain an ethical dimension in foreign policy. In language only slightly coded, O'Malley reminded the policy makers that the Soviet alliance was simply a matter of grim necessity: they should not deceive themselves or others that it was built on anything more fundamental, such as shared values. This was, in the circumstances prevailing in 1943, a highly inconvenient message for all concerned. If O'Malley is to be remembered beyond the ranks of professional diplomatic historians it will be above all for this celebrated dispatch. At the time it had no discernible effect on British policy nor, by reason of its secrecy, upon British public opinion. Nevertheless, the Foreign Office was alarmed to learn that it was being talked about in élite London circles, and suspected (correctly, it would appear) that O'Malley himself was doing some of the talking. These suspicions notwithstanding, O'Malley was promoted KCMG in the king's birthday honours in June 1943.

As the position of the London Poles steadily deteriorated after Katyn, O'Malley found himself in the uncongenial role of chief conduit of a British policy of pressing the Poles to make ever more concessions in order to win back Stalin's favour. This distasteful role came to an end when, on 6 July 1945, in concert with the United States, Britain transferred diplomatic recognition from the London Poles to the authorities in Warsaw. Disenchanted as he already was with the course of public policy in regard to eastern Europe, O'Malley now experienced a further, professional, disappointment. Having had hopes of Madrid, or some equivalent embassy, he found himself offered Lisbon instead, just as Lisbon was about to be officially relegated by the Foreign Office to third-class status from its previous second-class grading. O'Malley took it for fear, if he hesitated, of being offered something worse. He assumed this post in July 1945, but retired on reaching the age of sixty in May 1947. As long planned, he then settled in his restored ancestral home, Rockfleet, in Clew Bay, co. Mayo.

In retirement O'Malley devoted his time to his house, his family, ancestral history, and the preparation of a volume of memoirs, the latter being published in 1954, after the usual vetting by the Foreign Office, under the title *The Phantom Caravan*. In many ways these memoirs were typical of their kind, telling historians little or nothing about British foreign policy that they would not have known from already published sources. In one or two ways, however, they were distinctive. O'Malley repeatedly appealed for a more ethical approach to foreign policy than had been the case in his time in Whitehall. He also made it clear that subsequent events since 1945 had vindicated the Poles' view of Stalin's real intentions in 1943–5, and not that of the British or the Americans. Finally he invited the reader to judge whether he, O'Malley, thought any differently about the Russians in 1943–5 than he did in 1954. The tragedy of the Poles was that they were too right too soon—as indeed, on a much more minor note, was O'Malley himself. He lived long enough to witness the publication (in 1973) of his report on the Katyn massacre. He died on 16 April 1974 at 27 Charlbury Road, Oxford, his wife having died some five weeks earlier, on 9 March. He was survived by his two daughters, his son having also predeceased him.   ALAN J. FOSTER

Sources O. O'Malley, *The phantom caravan* (1954) · NL Ire., O. O'Malley MSS · A. Bridge, *Permission to resign* (1971) · L. Fitzgibbon, *Katyn Massacre*, 3rd edn (1984) · PRO, FO 371 series · *The diaries of Sir Alexander Cadogan*, ed. D. Dilks (1971) · WWW · FO List · *The Times* (17 April 1974)
Archives NL Ire., corresp. and family papers · St Ant. Oxf., Middle East Centre, corresp. and family papers | CAC Cam., corresp. with Baron Strong · PRO, FO MSS, FO 371 series
Likenesses W. Stoneman, photograph, 1945, NPG · photographs, repro. in O'Malley, *Phantom caravan*, ii, and facing p. 246
Wealth at death £54,010: probate, 20 Aug 1974, CGPLA Eng. & Wales

O'Malley, Thaddeus (1796–1877), Roman Catholic priest and political writer, was born at Garryowen, near Limerick. At the age of twenty-three he completed his training for the Roman Catholic priesthood and obtained a post in America. In 1827 he was suspended by his ecclesiastical superior, the Rt Revd John England, bishop of Charleston, for difficulties caused by his independence of spirit. On his return to Ireland, he was attached to the cathedral in Marlborough Street, Dublin, where he officiated as an assistant priest under Archbishop Daniel Murray.

After the death of the bishop of Kildare and Leighlin, James Warren Doyle (1786–1834), who had been a powerful advocate for the Irish poor, O'Malley took up the demand for a poor law for Ireland in a series of public letters. He also supported a system of national education, but was suspended by Archbishop Murray for sending an intemperate and caustic letter to Archbishop MacHale in defence of Murray's own views on national schools; he was restored to his position as priest after a short time. He then published a further tract in favour of state education entitled *A Sketch of the State of Popular Education in Holland, Prussia, Belgium, and France* (1840).

O'Malley was appointed rector of the Catholic University of Malta by the British government, but was rebuked for introducing reforms to student discipline there. When he asserted that protestant laymen did not have the right to interfere in a Catholic ecclesiastical institution, he was dismissed from his post. He returned to Dublin, where in 1845 he started a newspaper called the *Social Economist*, which soon fell into disfavour with the Catholic church because of some articles which challenged the enforced celibacy of clerics and advocated marriage for the priesthood. It was a lively and irreverent periodical, one column being headed 'Sips of Punch'. Differing with Daniel

O'Connell on the question of the complete repeal of the Act of Union, he urged the establishment of a federal parliament for Ireland. The differences of opinion between the two men were publicly debated, and many came over to O'Malley's point of view, which was further publicized in the new newspaper which he set up, *The Federalist*. He then turned his attention to an attempt to unite Old and Young Ireland. Old Ireland as represented by O'Connell advocated public pressure, whereas Young Ireland supported armed conflict as the means to liberate Ireland. From about 1850 to 1870, O'Malley retired from controversy, and lived privately in a back lane of Dublin.

O'Malley returned to public debate in 1870 with the inauguration by Isaac Butt of the home-rule movement, which he supported with enthusiasm, speaking and writing in its defence. He also published the anonymous *Harmony in Religion*, which urged changes in ecclesiastical discipline within the Catholic church and alleged that there was a breach between the head of the Catholic church in England, Cardinal H. E. Manning, and its head in Ireland, Cardinal Paul Cullen. For this O'Malley was strongly rebuked by Cullen. His last publication, *Home Rule on the Basis of Federalism* (1873), went into a second edition, and was inscribed 'To the Irish Conservative Party'.

O'Malley was a controversial figure whose taste for polemic made him an exasperating priest to his ecclesiastical superiors, and whose consistent urging for change within the discipline of the priesthood was out of step with prevailing Catholic emphases. But he was also capable of rousing popular opinion to his side, and was entirely orthodox in matters of Catholic doctrine. He died at his lodgings at 1 Henrietta Street, Dublin, on 2 January 1877, leaving possessions worth less than £50, and was buried in Glasnevin cemetery.

W. J. FITZPATRICK, *rev.* DAVID HUDDLESTON

Sources A. J. Webb, *A compendium of Irish biography* (1878), 403–4 · *The works of the Right Rev. John England, first bishop of Charleston*, ed. I. A. Reynolds, 5 (1849), 187–202 · W. J. Fitzpatrick, *The life, times and contemporaries of Lord Cloncurry* (1855) · personal knowledge (1894) · CGPLA Ire. (1877)
Wealth at death under £50: probate, 7 Feb 1877, CGPLA Eng. & Wales

Oman, Sir Charles William Chadwick (1860–1946), historian, was born on 12 January 1860 at Mozaffarpur, India, the only child of Charles Philip Austin Oman (1825–1876), indigo planter, and his wife, Anne (1832–1907), daughter of William Chadwick, railway constructor. The family returned to England almost immediately, and by 1866 had settled in Cheltenham. Charles was sent to public school at Winchester, where he held a scholarship. As an only child, he was anyway solitary, and at 6 feet tall, he stood out awkwardly among his peers, both of which traits led to difficulties. He seems to have taken to academic studies as something of a refuge from bullying and sports, although even then he was conscious that his classical scholarship fell somewhat short of the purest linguistic and philosophical standards. He therefore specialized in ancient history, with modern history as its natural auxiliary, although in the course of his career that relationship would gradually be reversed. In both fields he excelled, winning first place in the scholarship election to New College, Oxford (1878), and then taking a first in *literae humaniores* (1882) and in modern history (1883). Yet he did not fit into the liberal and modernist senior common room at New College, and was not appointed to the fellowship there that he had hoped for. He felt the rejection keenly, but quickly bounced back by winning a still more prestigious fellowship at All Souls, Oxford, to which he devoted the remainder of his life. He divided his time between teaching, writing, and a variety of university activities such as the union, the Non Placet Society, the Kriegspiel Club, the Phantasmagorical Society (an early exercise in the classification of paranormal events), and frequent attendance at church services and sermons, preferably high Anglican. On 16 December 1905 he became Chichele professor of modern history, having been the deputy since 1900. Also in All Souls he was instrumental in setting up the Chichele chair of military history in 1909, and was active as the Codrington's librarian for some thirty years.

Oman worked as a member of only the second generation of professional British historians, and so there were still great swathes of general history that stood in need of elementary school and undergraduate textbooks, or 'manuals' as he called them. His production of such works was as prolific as it was influential. His most successful included *A History of Greece from the Earliest Times to the Macedonian Conquest* (1890), *The Byzantine Empire* (1892), *Europe, 476–918* (1893), *A History of England* (1895), *England and the Hundred Years' War* (1898), *England in the Nineteenth Century* (1899), and *Seven Roman Statesmen of the Later Republic* (1902). If he had written nothing beyond these, his reputation would already have been secure. However, it was in what he called his 'research' books, which included *Warwick the Kingmaker* (1891), *The Great Revolt of 1381* (1906), and his military histories, that he felt most free to pursue his many and diverse personal interests.

Unlike a more meticulous or plodding type of scholar, Oman flitted freely from one arcane subject to another with a rapidity that would suggest shallowness, but which he was normally able to sustain by the liveliness and force of his scrutiny. He was apparently as much at home describing the politics of the Roman senate for his manuals as the design of medieval castles for the Great Western Railway, or of wallpapers and silverware for the Victoria and Albert Museum. Having collected Roman coins as a boy, he had a lifelong interest in numismatics, which he saw as an essential archaeological underpinning for all historical studies, and he would eventually serve as president of both the Royal Numismatic Society and the Royal Archaeological Institute. Still more formative was his early exposure to military history, first through his father's memories of life under siege during the Indian mutiny, then through attending military parades, visiting battlefields, and reading such works as Napier's *History of the War in the Peninsula*. He was already making his mark in military studies as early as his seminal Lothian prize-winning essay, 'The art of war in the middle ages' (1884).

This was expanded into a book in 1885, with further developments and revisions in 1898 and (in two volumes) 1924. It held the field with few serious competitors until the 1960s, and was later complemented by an article, 'The art of war in the fifteenth century' (1936), and a particularly valuable book, *A History of the Art of War in the Sixteenth Century* (1937). However, Oman's greatest achievement was to supersede Sir William Napier with his own *History of the Peninsular War* (7 vols., 1902–30), together with many associated essays—notably those collected as *Wellington's Army* (1913) and *Studies in the Napoleonic Wars* (1929). His *History of the Peninsular War* is unlikely ever to be displaced as the fullest basic military narrative of that conflict, even though a few of the facts and many of the opinions may be revised in the light of more recent research. Its first volume is excessively compressed and prejudiced; but the remaining six volumes show Oman as a mature post-Victorian historian, diligent in his researches, robust in his nationalist convictions, and lucidly assured in his exposition. The work conveys a great sense of clarity and completeness, notably by its full account of the Spanish operations, which had been skimmed over by Napier, and by its innovative compilation of statistics for manpower and casualties. However, it is perhaps unsurprising that the scholarly apparatus lags sadly behind the most advanced practice of his day, since Oman's militant conservatism gave him a strong aversion to all new-fangled 'theories' or 'philosophies' of historiography. He was content to remain a middlebrow historian of 'kings and battles', but as such he was unsurpassed.

Outside All Souls Oman's long, lanky, white-haired figure, his 'rogue-elephant look' (Rowse, 49), and his ever discursive conversation quickly became well known, if not notorious, in many different locales. He helped to organize historical pageants and war games, and he loved to travel, especially to Scotland, Italy, and Paris. For long he was active in Oxford University politics, firmly opposing innovation, and from 1919 to 1935 he sat as a Conservative burgess for the University of Oxford in the House of Commons, where he was nicknamed 'Stone Age Man' (ibid., 52). During the First World War he worked for the press bureau and the Foreign Office, for which he was knighted (KBE) in 1920. This experience also led him to conduct a most exhaustive study, 'The German losses on the Somme, July–December 1916', which was published in 1927 (G. S. Clarke [Lord Sydenham] and others, *The World Crisis, by Winston Churchill: a Criticism*). This showed that the British official historian had set the enemy's losses too high, while W. S. Churchill had set them too low. Oman was elected FBA in 1905, served as president of the Royal Historical Society, and advised on the library of the Imperial War Museum. He became an honorary fellow of New College in 1936, and received honorary degrees of DCL (Oxford, 1926) and LLD (Edinburgh, 1911; Cambridge, 1927).

In 1892 Oman married Mary Mabel (1866–1950), the sixth and youngest child of General Robert Maclagan RE. They had three children: Dulce Roberta (*b.* 1894), Carola Mary Anima (*b.* 1897, later a noted biographer), and

Charles Chichele (*b.* 1901, later a noted antiquary), who all knew him first as C.O. and then, after he had secured his chair, as the Prof. In 1908 they moved round the corner from their central Oxford house next to the Ashmolean Museum into the grandeur of Frewin Hall, off the Cornmarket. Sir Charles Oman died at Frewin Hall on 23 June 1946.　　　PADDY GRIFFITH

Sources *DNB* · C. W. C. Oman, *Memories of Victorian Oxford and of some early years* (1941) · C. Oman, *An Oxford childhood* (1976) · A. L. Rowse, *Historians I have known* (1995) · P. Griffith, 'The life of Sir Charles Oman', *Modern studies of the war in Spain and Portugal, 1808–1814*, ed. P. Griffith (1999), vol. 9 of C. W. C. Oman, *A history of the Peninsular War* (1902–99) · C. W. C. Oman, *Things I have seen* (1933) · *The new Cambridge bibliography of English literature*, [2nd edn], 4, ed. I. R. Willison (1972), 1200–1201 · *CGPLA Eng. & Wales* (1946)
Archives All Souls Oxf., letters to Sir William Anson, warden of All Souls · King's AC Cam., letters to Oscar Browning · NRA, priv. coll., letters to his wife
Likenesses W. Stoneman, photograph, 1938, NPG · F. Dodd, drawing, All Souls Oxf. · J.B. Souter, drawing, All Souls Oxf.
Wealth at death £42,760 0s. 10d.: probate, 10 Oct 1946, *CGPLA Eng. & Wales*

Oman, John Wood (1860–1939), theologian, was born on the farm of Biggins in the parish of Stenness, Orkney, on 23 July 1860, the second son of Simon Rust Oman, a farmer who in earlier years had been master of a sailing vessel, and his wife, Isabella Irvine Rendall. He owed his early education mainly to a tutor engaged for a neighbouring family and shared by a few other boys. Many references in Oman's works reveal how deeply his mind was shaped by the freedom and simplicity of his boyhood—its close contacts with the soil and the sea, and with the hardy and vigorous folk who gained their living from them. He himself described his father, in the dedication of his Kerr lectures, as 'a scholar only of life and action, but my best teacher'. He entered Edinburgh University in 1877, graduating in 1882 with first-class honours in philosophy and winning the Gray and Rhind scholarships. Thence he proceeded to the theological college of the United Presbyterian church in Edinburgh, and at the conclusion of the course there he studied at the universities of Erlangen, Heidelberg, and Neuchâtel. On his return to Scotland he served for a brief period as assistant minister at St James's Church, Paisley. In 1889 he accepted a call to be minister of Clayport Street Church, Alnwick, thus passing into the Presbyterian Church of England, in the service of which he remained to the end of his life. While at Alnwick he married in 1897 Mary Hannah, daughter of Henry Hunter Blair JP of Gosforth, a very happy union broken only by her death in 1936. They had four daughters.

It was during his ministry at Alnwick that Oman's quality as an unusually learned, powerful, and original thinker in the field of theology—already known to his intimates—began to be more widely known, mainly through the publication in 1902 of *Vision and Authority, or, The Throne of St Peter* (rev. edn, 1928), and in 1906 of his Kerr lectures, *The Problem of Faith and Freedom in the Last Two Centuries*. The former revealed a mind singularly able to keep profound and informed theological reflection in close

John Wood Oman (1860–1939), by unknown photographer

relation with the religious life and its problems; the latter showed an easy, firsthand mastery, issuing in penetrating and original judgements, of the works of every relevant writer of importance from Pascal to Albrecht Ritschl. Before the publication of these two works he had produced in 1893 the first translation into English of F. E. D. Schleiermacher's epoch-making *Reden über die Religion*.

In 1907 Oman was appointed professor of systematic theology and apologetics in Westminster College, Cambridge, the theological college of the Presbyterian Church of England, where he remained until his retirement in 1935, having become principal in 1922. At Westminster College he was one of a remarkably distinguished teaching staff, his colleagues being John Skinner, Charles Anderson Scott, and Patrick Carnegie Simpson. During this time Oman came to be recognized, first in Cambridge and later more widely, as one of the most learned and original minds at work in theology. He was thrice (1913–16, 1919–22, 1929–31) appointed Stanton lecturer in the philosophy of religion in the University of Cambridge, and served for many years on the board of the faculty of divinity and on its degree committee. In 1909 he became a member of Queens' College and in 1935 an honorary fellow of Jesus College; the honorary degree of DD was conferred upon him by the universities of Edinburgh and Oxford. In 1938 he was elected a fellow of the British Academy. His own church honoured him by electing him moderator of the general assembly in 1931. He died at Cambridge on 7 May 1939.

Oman's eminent position as a thinker was achieved

partly through his work as a teacher, which greatly influenced all his students, but more through his published writings, among which, besides those already named, should be mentioned *The Church and the Divine Order* (1911), *Grace and Personality* (1917), *The Paradox of the World* (1921), *The Natural and the Supernatural* (1931), *Concerning the Ministry* (1936), and *Honest Religion* (published posthumously in 1941 with a memoir of the author by George Alexander and Herbert Henry Farmer). Of these *Grace and Personality* and *The Natural and the Supernatural* were the most important, both as affording insight into Oman's characteristic teaching and as permanent enrichments of theological literature. Oman's theology was built round a strongly personalistic doctrine of man and of God's dealings with man. Man's true end can only be achieved through a reverence which never subordinates sacred values to expediency or profit, a freedom which accepts all the risks of freedom, a sincerity which walks steadfastly by its own insight. All these needs and prerogatives of personality God himself unwaveringly respects, having himself created and bestowed them. In *Grace and Personality* this theme is worked out in relation to the central Christian doctrines of grace and forgiveness with a thoroughness, consistency, and power which made it, in the words of a critic, 'one of the major treasures of theological literature'. In *The Natural and the Supernatural* the same basic thoughts were made the clue to the understanding of the nature and history of religion, and of the processes of knowledge, evolution, and the natural order, the whole constituting a sustained argument to justify the contention that there is direct awareness of the supernatural which leads on to fuller knowledge of God only as men live in loyalty to those sacred values through which he discloses himself to their souls.

Oman's writing is not always easy to follow, demanding close attention and a willingness to weigh every sentence with care; but it rises at times to real, if restrained, eloquence, is interspersed with apt illustration, and always rests on a vast knowledge which is masked from the uninformed by a refusal to adorn his pages with references to other authors. His character, in its massive and at times almost formidable integrity, was an impressive embodiment of his own teaching. Physically also he was impressive, being tall and with a noble head.

H. H. FARMER, *rev.*

Sources F. R. Tennant, 'John Wood Oman, 1860–1939', *PBA*, 25 (1939), 333–8 · G. Alexander and H. H. Farmer, 'Memoir', in J. W. Oman, *Honest religion* (1941) · private information (1949) · personal knowledge (1949) · *The Times* (18 May 1939) · *CGPLA Eng. & Wales* (1939)
Archives Westminster College, Cambridge, Cheshunt Foundation, lectures, papers, and sermons
Likenesses H. Riviere, oils, *c*.1934, Westminster College, Cambridge; repro. in Tennant, *PBA* · W. Stoneman, photograph, 1938, NPG · photograph, Westminster College, Cambridge [*see illus.*]
Wealth at death £27,165 7*s.* 7*d.*: resworn probate, 21 July 1939, *CGPLA Eng. & Wales*

Ó Maoilchonaire [O' Maelchonaire], **Fearfeasa** (*fl.* 1630–1646), antiquary and poet, was born some time in the late sixteenth century in Cluain Plocáin (Cluain Bolcáin) or Ballymulconry, in the parish of Kiltrustan, co. Roscommon, the chief place of the Uí Mhaoilchonaire family. He was the son of Lochlann Ó Maoilchonaire, a member of the younger branch of a family which from antiquity had been hereditary bards and chroniclers to the kings of Connaught. Almost nothing is known of his career beyond his collaboration between 1630 and 1633 with Míchéal Ó Cléirigh OFM, Cúcoigcríche Ó Duibhgennáin, and Cúcoigcríche Ó Cléirigh on a series of major historical enterprises, including a compilation of the genealogies of the kings and saints of Ireland, an edition of an eleventh-century pseudo-historical account of the successive prehistoric invasions of Ireland known as *Leabhar gabhála*, and, above all, a history of Ireland from the creation up to their own time traditionally known as the annals of the four masters. The last work constitutes the largest single collection of annalistic material relating to Ireland. Because it is largely a copy of older manuscript material no longer extant, it now preserves a unique record of events over considerable spans of time. Ó Maoilchonaire collaborated with Míchéal Ó Cléirigh and the other chroniclers on the first part only of this multi-volume work, covering events to 1333, the transcription of which was completed in 1632 in the Franciscan convent of Drowes or Bundrowes on Donegal Bay, co. Donegal. He states that he checked the old manuscripts of the martyrology of Gormán, of which a transcript had been made by Brother Míchéal. It is now the only copy remaining of this liturgical calendar. Since Ó Maoilchonaire was descended from a family of hereditary antiquaries it is very likely that he not only gave his services as scribe and chronicler but also contributed some source material to the enterprise, including a 'Book of Cluain Plocáin', referred to in a number of sources. Moreover, his name appears three times after Ó Cléirigh's in the dedications and prefaces to the works mentioned above, which preceded the compilation of the annals, indicating his importance to the scholarly enterprise, but in third place in the dedicatory preface to the annals. His handwriting has not yet been identified in the original manuscripts.

When Tuileagna Ó Maoilchonaire, also a Franciscan author and a kinsman of Fearfeasa Ó Maoilchonaire, tried over a number of years, between 1638 and 1646, to prevent publication of the works compiled by Ó Cléirigh and his collaborators, Fearfeasa was the chief respondent, since Ó Cléirigh was dead. He appeared before a provincial chapter of Irish Franciscans at Multyfarnam in August 1641, where the decision went against Tuileagna. The latter's persistence finally elicited two responses from Fearfeasa in Irish, the first in an open letter entitled 'To the reader—a reply' (printed in Walsh's edition of the *Genealogiae*, 6.150–53), the second a long reply in verse entitled 'Beag táirthear [do]n tagra mbaoith' ('Foolish debate achieves nothing'; Mhag Craith, no. 39). Both were penned in 1646, and nothing further is heard of Fearfeasa after that date. The annals and other compilations were not published until the nineteenth century, not because of Tuileagna's objections, but because of the extreme poverty of the Louvain community. Notwithstanding his long association with the Franciscan order and this enterprise, Fearfeasa Ó Maoilchonaire was a layman. His son Peadar was poet to the Ó Rodaighe family of co. Leitrim, specifically to Tadhg Ó Rodaighe. About six poems by him are extant.

The Ó Maoilchonaire family was one of the most distinguished learned families in Ireland, supplying a long line of important poets, chroniclers, and ecclesiastics. O'Reilly's *Catalogue of Irish Writers* lists fourteen poets of that name from 1310 onwards. Fearfeasa's kinsman Flaithrí Ó Maoilchonaire (Florence Conry, as he is more usually known), archbishop of Tuam, in 1607 founded St Anthony's College, Louvain, where Míchéal Ó Cléirigh and his collaborators sought to publish their work. Muirghes mac Páidín Ó Maoilchonaire copied the Book of Fenagh from an earlier exemplar for the Ó Rodaighe family, under whose patronage Fearfeasa's son Peadar later worked. It is written in both prose and verse and purports to be a statement of the dues owing to the high king of Ireland from his sub-kings and of his reciprocal duties to them. The name Ó Maoilchonaire is of frequent occurrence in the fiants. In particular, a fiant of Elizabeth I in 1585 names a 'Ferfesse O Mulconry of same' (that is of Clonpluckane, or Ballymulconry, co. Roscommon), who must have been a kinsman of Fearfeasa. A poem attributed to 'Ferfesa mac Lochlainn Uí Mhaoilchonaire' written in honour of Calvach Rua Ó Domhnaill of Connaught and entitled 'Mo chean do chuairt a Chalbhaigh', now preserved in an eighteenth-century manuscript in the National Library of Ireland, is almost certainly Fearfeasa's. Nothing further is known of him beyond these scraps of biography. Because of the appalling events brought on by the rising of 1641 and its aftermath, the earliest copies of the four masters' works survived for many years on the continent and were only brought back to Ireland in the nineteenth century and published. Ó Maoilchonaire's works are preserved in manuscripts in the libraries of the Royal Irish Academy and Trinity College, Dublin, in the Franciscan library at Killiney, the Bibliothèque Royale, Brussels, and the National Library of Ireland.   AIDAN BREEN

Sources P. Walsh, *Irish men of learning*, ed. C. O Lochlainn (1947), 34–48 · [M. O'Clery], 'Genealogiae regum et sanctorum Hiberniae', ed. P. Walsh, *Archivium Hibernicum*, 5 (1916), appx, pp. 1–96; 6 (1917), appx, pp. 97–164, esp. 142–53 · M. J. Connellan, 'Ballymulconry and the Mulconrys', *Irish Ecclesiastical Record*, 5th ser., 90 (1958), 322–30 · B. Jennings, *Michael O Cleirigh, chief of the four masters, and his associates* (1936), 70, 101, 120, 136, 148, 162–3 · B. Millett, *The Irish Franciscans, 1651–1665* (1964) · C. Mhág Craith, ed., *Dán na mBráthar Mionúr*, 2 vols. (1967–80), no. 39 · P. Breathnach, 'What we know of Cuchoigriche O Cleirigh', *Irish Book Lover*, 23 (1935), 60–66 · *The 'Book of Fenagh' in Irish and English*, ed. W. M. Hennessy and D. H. Kelly (1875) · L. Ó Cléirigh, *The life of Aodh Ruadh Ó Domhnaill*, ed. P. Walsh and C. Ó Lochlainn, 1, ITS, 42 (1948) · L. Ó Cléirigh, *The life of Aodh Ruadh Ó Domhnaill*, ed. P. Walsh and C. Ó Lochlainn, 2, ITS, 45 (1957) · E. Curtis, ed., 'The O'Maolconaire family: unpublished letters from Sir Edward Conry, Bart., to H. F. Hore, esq., 1864', *Galway Archaeological and Historical Society*, 19 (1941), 118–46 · P. Ó Maoilchonaire, 'Díol toile caoinmheas Cormaic', *Leabhar Cloinne Aodha Buidhe*, ed. T. Ó Donnchadha (1931), 272–8 · N. Ní Shéaghdha, *Catalogue of Irish manuscripts in the national library of Ireland*, 5 (1979), 14 · H. R. McAdoo, 'Three poems by Peadar Ó Maolchonaire', *Éigse*, 1 (1939–40), 160–66 · E. O'Reilly, *A chronological account of … four hundred Irish writers … down to … 1750, with a descriptive catalogue of … their works* (1820)

Ó Maoil Chonaire, Flaithri. *See* Conry, Florence (*d.* 1629).

Ó Maolmhuaidh, Froinsias [Francis O'Molloy or Molloy] (*c.*1606–1677?), theologian and grammarian, was born in the diocese of Meath, most probably in the traditional O'Molloy territory of Fercall, in the King's county portion of that diocese. His precise position within the O'Molloy kin group is not known. In old age he recorded stories he had heard from eyewitnesses in his youth of a great Christmas banquet for 960 people, lasting twelve days, held by Calvagh O'Molloy, chief of his name, at the end of the sixteenth century (O'Molloy, *Grammatica*, 180). It is likely that he was also related to the O'Daly family from the same neighbourhood. The Revd John Daly (Seán Ó Dálaigh), who studied at St Isidore's College, Rome, was evidently his nephew, and may have been the person of that name who acted as censor for his *Grammatica*.

Ó Maolmhuaidh was accepted into the order of Friars Minor of Strict Observance on 2 August 1632 in the College of St Isidore, Rome. He was appointed lecturer in philosophy at Klosterneuberg, close to Vienna, in 1642, aged about thirty-six, and was professor of theology at Gratz in 1645. There he published his only strictly theological work, *Disputatio theologica de incarnatione verbi ad mentem Joannis Duns Scoti* (1645), probably prepared as a thesis. He was in Mantua on 4 May 1647 when he was instructed to go to the Irish Franciscan College of St Isidore, Rome, to teach philosophy, and he was teaching theology in that college in 1652, a position he still held in 1677. There is no evidence that he became guardian of the college on Luke Wadding's death in 1657, but he was president (*praeses*) for a time in 1671.

Ó Maolmhuaidh was in Rome in 1658 when his *Iubilatio genethliaca in honorem Prosperi Balthasaris Philippi Hispaniarum principis* was published there. By 1663 he was preparing a course on philosophy for publication. The first part of his *Philosophia … tomus primus dialecticae breviarum complectens* was published at Rome in 1666, but no further part was published.

A general chapter of the Franciscan order was convened at Rome in 1664, which Ó Maolmhuaidh attended on behalf of the Irish provincial. He had been working on behalf of his fellow Irish Franciscans for a number of years and was respected by them. In May 1670 he was appointed procurator of the Irish Franciscan province at the Roman curia. In 1671 he was recommended to the Congregatio de Propaganda Fide for appointment as bishop of Kildare, with Signora Maria Altieri, sister of Pope Clement X, among his supporters. The opposition of Oliver Plunket, archbishop of Armagh, may have been enough to ensure he was not appointed, and he did not return to Ireland.

Ó Maolmhuaidh's best-known work, an Irish-language catechism of the doctrines of the Catholic church, *Lucerna fidelium, seu, Fasciculus decerptus ab authoribus magis versatis qui tractarunt de doctrina Christiana* (*Lochrann na* gCreidmheach), was published at Rome in 1676. It was the first book in Irish issued from the press of the Congregatio de Propaganda Fide. The project had been initiated by the secretary of the Propaganda Fide in 1670. Monsignor Baldeschi, secretary of the Propaganda Fide, and Cardinal Altieri were among Ó Maolmhuaidh's influential contacts in Rome. His last published work was the first printed grammar of the Irish language, *Grammatica Latino-Hibernica nunc compendiata* (1677). Written in Latin, it consisted of twenty-five chapters: nine on the letters of the alphabet, three on etymology, one on contractions and cryptic writings, and twelve on prosody and versification. It, too, was issued by the press of the Congregatio de Propaganda Fide, and included, at the end, an Irish poem composed by the author on the neglect of the Irish language and the prospects for its revival.

Although a commemorative stone in St Isidore's College, Rome, erected in the early twentieth century, mentions 1684 as the date of Ó Maolmhuaidh's death, it has been more reliably asserted, on the basis of Roman archival sources, that he died in the last quarter of 1677, while travelling through France *en route* for Ireland in the company of John Daly. 　　　BERNADETTE CUNNINGHAM

Sources F. Ó Maolmhuaidh, *Lucerna fidelium*, ed. P. Ó Súilleabháin (1962) · B. Jennings, ed., 'Miscellaneous documents, 1588–1715 [pt 2]', *Archivium Hibernicum*, 14 (1949), 1–49 · E. Hogan, 'Father Francis O'Molloy', *Irisleabhar na Gaedhilge*, 8 (1897), 75–6 · B. Millett, *The Irish Franciscans, 1651–1665* (1964) · G. Cleary, *Father Luke Wadding and St Isidore's College, Rome* (1925), 104–8 · C. Giblin, 'The Processus datariae and the appointment of Irish bishops in the 17th century', *Father Luke Wadding: commemorative volume*, ed. Franciscan Fathers dún Mhuire, Killiney (1957), 508–616 · F. O'Molloy, *Grammatica Latino-Hibernica nunc compendiata* (1677)

Omar Ali Saifuddin III (1914–1986), sultan of Brunei, was born on 23 September 1914 at Istana Kota (Kota Palace), Kampong Sultan Lama, Brunei Town, the seventh of ten children of Sultan Muhammad Jamalul Alam II (*d.* 1924) and Fatimah binti Pengiran Tua Omar Ali (*d.* 1947). Ruler of the sparsely populated, British-protected Bornean ministate from 6 June 1950 until his abdication on 4 October 1967, he was widely regarded as the architect of modern Brunei and remained the real power in the land even after he had abdicated. He lived long enough to witness his country's return to full independence (as Negara Brunei Darussalam) on 1 January 1984.

Educated at Malay College, Kuala Kangsar, Federated Malay States (1932–6), Omar Ali Saifuddin gained administrative experience before and during the war. In 1947 he was promoted to vizier rank as *pengiran bendahara*. His succession to the throne three years later was briefly contested on behalf of Princess Ehsan, daughter of his brother and predecessor, Sultan Ahmad Tajuddin (1913–1950).

The key problems facing the new monarch, who was crowned on 31 May 1951, were to modernize his sultanate and manage the process of decolonization. Sultan Omar aimed to wrest power from the British into his own hands, while preventing it from falling into those of the left-leaning Brunei People's Party, founded in 1956 by Sheikh A. M. Azahari. Sultan Omar also had to ward off the possible absorption of his sultanate within either a Bornean federation or a 'Greater Malaysia'. Whether by accident or design, he succeeded brilliantly.

Burgeoning oil revenues in the 1950s facilitated the implementation of wide-ranging development programmes, and after prolonged negotiations with the British, a written constitution was introduced in September 1959. The post of resident was abolished, thereby eliminating Whitehall interference in Brunei's internal affairs and snapping the detested administrative link with British-ruled Sarawak. The constitution strengthened the position of the Malay language and of the Islamic religion; and it enshrined the dominant role of the monarchy while making vague promises on 'democratization'. London retained responsibility only for defence and foreign affairs.

The years immediately following were not happy, governmental unpopularity being exacerbated by an economic downturn and international instability. The People's Party, which had been in the doldrums, gained strength in 1961–2 as it voiced popular dismay at Brunei's possible incorporation within a 'Greater Malaysia', as proposed by Tunku Abdul Rahman in May 1961. The party won a landslide victory at the general election of August 1962 but, finding its voice ignored, launched an uprising in the following December. Following the swift suppression of the revolt by British forces, Sultan Omar suspended the constitution and ruled by decree. He opted to remain outside Malaysia, partly to prevent Kuala Lumpur securing control of Brunei's finances.

After Sultan Omar's abdication in 1967, after which he was officially known as the seri begawan sultan, he ruled jointly with his son Sultan Hassanal Bolkiah II, taking particular responsibility for relations with the British. Latterly, as the father weakened and the son asserted himself, tensions began to emerge; but the fundamental mutual regard between the co-regnant monarchs was never in doubt.

Despite the vast wealth of his country, Sultan Omar's own lifestyle was always frugal. A pious Muslim, he performed the pilgrimage to Mecca in September 1951 and in May 1962. He instituted a religious affairs department (1954) and an Islamic religious council (1955), appointed a government mufti (1962), and expanded religious education. In 1991 he was posthumously proclaimed a *tokoh agama* (doctor of religion).

In May 1961 Sultan Omar founded the Brunei Malay regiment, which developed into a well-rounded fighting force by the time of independence. His final post was minister of defence (1984–6), and he was raised to the rank of general in September 1984.

Short in stature and softly spoken, Omar married three times. First, as a young man, he married Amin binti Awang Hashim, in a union which produced no children. On 6 September 1941 he married his distant cousin Pengiran Anak Damit binti Pengiran Bendahara Pengiran Anak Abdul Rahman (1924–1979); they had four sons and six daughters, and at least one other child died in infancy.

In old age he married Yang Amat Mulia Pengiran Bini Hajjah Salhah, sister of his deceased second wife.

A patron of the Malaysian branch of the Royal Asiatic Society (1980–86), Sultan Omar was an accomplished poet who published several literary works and a collection of speeches. He founded the Brunei Museum.

Sultan Omar was created CMG in 1951, promoted KCMG in 1953 and GCVO in 1972. Further decorations were bestowed upon him by his fellow sultans in Malaya. He instituted several Brunei orders of chivalry.

Having suffered from diabetes for several years, Sultan Omar died on 7 September 1986 at Istana Darussalam (Abode of Peace Palace), Kampong Sumbiling, in Brunei Town, which in 1970 had been renamed Bandar Seri Begawan in his honour. His funeral followed two days later and he was buried at the royal mausoleum in Bandar Seri Begawan. After his death the Brunei government decreed that he was to be known as the late Sultan Haji Omar Ali Saifuddien Sa'adul Khairi Waddien. The anniversary of his birth has been marked every year since 1991 as *Hari Guru* (Teachers' Day). A. V. M. HORTON

Sources B. A. Hussainmiya, *Sultan Omar Ali Saifuddin III and Britain: the making of Brunei Darussalam* (Kuala Lumpur, 1995) · Mohd Jamil Al-Sufri, *Penyair diraja: Sultan Haji Omar Ali Saifuddien Sa'adul Khairi Waddien* (Bandar Seri Begawan, Brunei, 1989) [Penyair diraja: Royal poet] · Mohd Jamil Al-Sufri, *Liku-liku perjuangan pencapaian kemerdekaan Negara Brunei Darussalam* [Ups and downs in the struggle for the achievement of the independence of the State of Brunei, abode of peace] (Bandar Seri Begawan, Brunei, 1992) · G. E. Saunders, *A history of modern Brunei* (Kuala Lumpur, 1994) · Lord Chalfont, *By God's will: a portrait of the Sultan of Brunei* (1989) · K. U. Menon, 'Brunei Darussalam in 1986: in search of the political kingdom', *Southeast Asian Affairs* (1987), 85–101 [Singapore] · *Pelita Brunei* (21 Jan 1997) · *Borneo Bulletin* (13 Sept 1986) · *Borneo Bulletin* (23 Sept 1972), 10–12 · *Borneo Bulletin* (30 Sept 1972), 9–10 · *Borneo Bulletin* (7 Oct 1972), 10–11 · Brunei Annual Reports (1914–86) [esp. 1922, 1951] · P. M. Shariffuddin, *Journal of the Malaysian Branch of the Royal Asiatic Society*, 59/2 (1986), 1–3 · Suhaini Aznam, 'The seri begawan: power behind the throne', *Far Eastern Economic Review* (18 Sept 1986)
Archives Negara Brunei Darussalam, corresp., MSS, government papers, etc | National Archives and Records Administration, Washington, DC, record group no. 59 · National Archives of Brunei, Bandar Seri Begawan, records of the state secretary's office · PRO, Colonial Office files, CO 943, CO 954, CO 1030 · PRO, Foreign Office files, FO 371
Likenesses double portrait, photograph, 1951 (with Raja Isteri Pengiran Anak Damit), repro. in Hussainmiya, *Sultan Omar Ali Saifuddin III and Britain*, following p. 194 · photographs, 1968–86, repro. in Shariffuddin, 'In memoriam: al Marhum Sultan Sir Muda Omar', p. 3 · photograph, repro. in Hussainmiya, *Sultan Omar Ali Saifuddin III and Britain*, frontispiece

O'Meara, Barry Edward (*b.* in or after **1770**?, *d.* **1836**), surgeon, was born in Ireland, the son of Jeremiah O'Meara, variously described as an army officer and a member of the legal profession, and a Miss Murphy, sister of Edmund Murphy MA of Trinity College, Dublin. Different sources give the year of his birth as 1770, 1778, and 1786. He is said to have been a member of the Irish medical family of whom Dermod Meara was a member. He is also said to have been educated at Trinity College, Dublin, and to have

been a member of the Royal College of Surgeons in Ireland, but there is no record of his affiliation to either institution, and his granddaughter's religion and particularly his ready acceptance into Napoleon's household suggest that he may have been a Roman Catholic, in which case his attendance at Trinity College would have been impossible. It is similarly impossible to substantiate the suggestion that he trained in surgery in London. He joined the 62nd regiment in 1804 as an assistant surgeon and served in Sicily, Egypt, and Calabria, but was cashiered after acting as second in a duel while in Sicily. He joined the navy as an assistant surgeon and served initially on the *Victorious* off Sicily in 1810. After further service on the *Espiègle* and the *Goliath* (58 guns) he chanced to be on the *Bellerophon* (74 guns) on 7 August 1815 when Napoleon came on board to surrender himself. O'Meara's professional skill and knowledge of Italian commended him to Napoleon, whom he agreed to accompany to the island of St Helena as his personal surgeon, once he had official permission to undertake this duty while remaining officially in naval service. The party arrived at St Helena on board the *Northumberland* on 15 October 1815. They were housed at Longwood House, on the Deadwood plain, where O'Meara became not only Napoleon's medical adviser but also his confidant.

Relations between Napoleon's household and the British authorities were initially fairly cordial, though Napoleon's domestic arrangements were uncomfortable and solitary residence on the remote and inhospitable island was hardly the outcome he had had in mind when he surrendered himself. However, with the arrival in April 1816 of Sir Hudson *Lowe, who in 1815 had been appointed governor of the island, matters deteriorated markedly. Some see Lowe's restrictions on Napoleon's household as petty and arbitrary; others see them as evidence that he was dutifully if over-assiduously fulfilling his charge of guarding Napoleon. Personal relations between Napoleon and Lowe were always poor and when they collapsed completely O'Meara initially acted as a channel for information between Plantation House and Longwood House. Eventually however relations between O'Meara and Lowe also broke down. Lowe confined O'Meara to Longwood House. At this O'Meara resigned, whereon Lowe ordered him off the island with little notice. He left the island in July 1818 and returned to England. Some have interpreted O'Meara's actions as part of the systematic and deliberate irritation of the authorities by Napoleon's household, while others have interpreted them as the result of a genuine feeling that the British authorities had acted at least shabbily and at worst deceitfully in their treatment of Napoleon.

Back in England on 28 October 1818 O'Meara wrote to the Admiralty alleging that Napoleon's life was not safe while Lowe remained governor. The Admiralty thereon removed his name from the navy list. O'Meara then set himself to continue his attacks on Lowe in print. These had begun with the anonymous *Letters from the Cape of Good Hope* (1817) and continued with *Exposition of some of the* transactions that have taken place at St Helena since the appointment of Sir Hudson Lowe as governor (1819) and *Napoleon in Exile: a Voice from St Helena* (2 vols., 1822), both works being published over his own name. The latter was generally critical of the way in which Napoleon had been treated after his surrender and in particular portrayed Lowe as spiteful, arbitrary, and vindictive. It was received with scepticism, not least because of inconsistencies between it and earlier accounts by O'Meara. These inconsistencies were detailed by John Wilson Croker in the *Quarterly Review* for October 1822 (28.219–64) and the book was savagely reviewed by Christopher North in *Blackwood's Magazine* (14.172) but defended in the *Edinburgh Review* for June 1822 (37.164–204). The book rapidly went through five editions and was issued in translation in France. Lowe obtained a rule *nisi* for criminal information against O'Meara in Hilary term 1823, but it was afterwards discharged on technical grounds. Following legal advice that the onus was now on O'Meara to accuse Lowe of perjury if he wanted to challenge the veracity of Lowe's denials, Lowe decided not to proceed further with this action.

Napoleon had in the meantime died on 5 May 1821 at Longwood, St Helena. He had been in poor health from shortly after his arrival on the island and O'Meara had attempted unsuccessfully to treat him for insomnia, pain in the region of the liver, and swelling of the legs. An autopsy, performed at the house by Napoleon's Italian surgeon Francesco Antommarchi, failed to establish unambiguously the cause of death but cast doubt on the hypothesis that he suffered from liver disease, since that organ, unlike his kidneys, heart, and particularly his stomach, was found to be healthy. Antommarchi secretly removed a piece of the ulcerated lining of the stomach which he later gave to O'Meara. Suggestions that Napoleon was poisoned with arsenic stimulated much writing, including that by O'Meara, about his illness, as did the feeling that his physical and psychological health had been harmed by the circumstances of his exile in a damp, lonely, isolated place. In fact, however, although he was described as 'the confidential medical attendant of the Emperor Napoleon in his last days' (*Gentleman's Magazine*, 1836, 219), O'Meara had had no influence on Napoleon's last illness since he left the island nearly three years before he died.

O'Meara married on 10 February 1823 at her house by special licence Theodosia-Beauchamp (*d.* 1830), daughter of Sir Edward Boughton, sixth baronet, of Lawford, Warwickshire, and his second wife, Anna Maria Beauchamp. Theodosia-Beauchamp was the widow of Captain John Donellan (*d.* 1781) and of Sir Egerton Leigh, bt (*d.* 1818). At the time of the marriage O'Meara was being prosecuted by Lowe. The marriage made his personal circumstances very easy, his new wife enjoying the fortune gained by her first husband by murdering her brother. O'Meara is said to have been twice married, but the details of his other marriage are not known. O'Meara became a follower of Daniel O'Connell. He died at his home on the Edgware Road, London, on 3 June 1836, according to the *Gentleman's Magazine* (1836, 219) of erysipelas in the head caught at one of O'Connell's meetings. The sale of his effects on 18 and 19

July attracted considerable attention since it included several relics of Napoleon. The eldest surviving daughter of his son Dennis O'Meara of Tipperary was Kathleen *O'Meara, the novelist, biographer, and Roman Catholic writer.   ELIZABETH BAIGENT

Sources B. E. O'Meara, *An exposition of some of the transactions that have taken place at St Helena* (1819) · B. E. O'Meara, *Napoleon in exile*, 2 vols. (1822) · Allibone, *Dict.* · *GM*, 2nd ser., 6 (1836), 219, 434 · *GM*, 1st ser., 100/2 (1830), 179–80 [death notice of wife] · *DNB* · J. Blackburn, *The emperor's last island* (1991)
Archives BL, corresp. with Sir Hudson Lowe, etc., Add. MSS 20115–20232

O'Meara [Meara], **Dermot** [Dermod] (*fl. c.*1614–1642), physician and author, was, according to the title-page of his 1615 work *Ormonius*, born in Ormond, co. Tipperary. He was a member of the family of the O'Mearas who were closely connected with the earls of Ormond and may have been the son of Domhnail of Lisaniskey, the most prominent O'Meara of the time, and the brother of William O'Meara, sheriff of the county palatine of Ormond in 1616. About 1614 O'Meara's son, Edmund *O'Meara, was born in Ormond.

O'Meara studied at Oxford University, although Wood could later find no record of his matriculation, and styled himself 'insignissimae Oxoniensis Academiae quondam alumnus' ('erstwhile student of the outstanding academy of Oxford') in his 1615 panegyric on Thomas Butler, tenth earl of Ormond. The work, published in London, was entitled *Ormonius, sive, Illustrissimi herois ac domini D. Thomae Butleri, Ormoniae et Ossoriae comitis commemoratio*, and has been described as 'perhaps the most complete account of Thomas's life in existence' (Carney, 173). With it were printed two other pieces: *Anagramaticon, acrosticon, & chronologicon in eundem Thomae Butler* and *Epicedion in obitum Thomae Butler Ormoniae & Ossoriae comitis*.

Walter Harris notes that O'Meara became a physician of 'great repute' in Ireland; he was physician to both the tenth and eleventh earls of Ormond. In 1619 he published *Pathologia haereditaria generalis*. In the dedication, to Sir Oliver St John, lord deputy of Ireland, he wrote on the need for the regulation of medical practice in Ireland:

> There are certainly more persons in Dublin at the present day practising the Art of Medicine than any other art, yet there are very few of them who have the six qualifications which Hippocrates requires in a Medical Doctor. Here, not only cursed Mountebanks … but also persons of every other craft whatsoever … all have free leave to profane the holy temple of Asculapius.   (translation in Fleetwood, 23–4)

The book was reprinted in a work by Edmund O'Meara in London in 1665 (*Examen diatribae Thomae Willisy*), and again in Amsterdam the following year.

About 1620 O'Meara may have been a teacher in Carrick-on-Suir, co. Tipperary, owing to the imprisonment of his patron Walter Butler, eleventh earl of Ormond. An affidavit of one Captain Edmund Corcoran, dated 26 April 1653 (now in the National Library in Prague), states, 'Col. Walter Butler of Roscrea was able to speak Latin fluently because in his youth he had studied Logic and Humanities under Doctor Dermot Meara in Carrick' (Logan, 313). No more is known about him for the next two decades.

O'Meara was a Catholic and a supporter of the Irish party of the confederation of Kilkenny. On 12 October 1642 a letter from the lords justices of Ireland to the principal secretary of state in London stated 'We hear that Dr. Dermot O'Meara the elder a doctor in physick is now or was lately at the court. He stands indicted here of high treason which we hold fit to make known to his majesty' (Logan, 313). The letter is signed by James Butler, twelfth earl of Ormond, among others, and so it seems O'Meara had lost his position with that family. The last that is known of him is this report by Walter Enos of a letter that O'Meara sent to a friend in Dublin, in which he refers to James Butler, twelfth earl of Ormond: 'his will is that the dismembered parliament there [in Dublin] continue, and [he] prayed the king to turn the Irish over unto him and he would draw them to what condition he pleased' (ibid.). No record of Dermot O'Meara's death, nor of any will, has been found.   JOHN BARRY

Sources P. Logan, 'Dermot and Edmund O'Meara, father and son', *Journal of the Irish Medical Association*, 43 (1958), 312–17 · *The whole works of Sir James Ware concerning Ireland*, ed. and trans. W. Harris, 2/2 (1746) · J. Carney, *Poems on the Butlers* (1945) · J. F. Fleetwood, *The history of medicine in Ireland*, 2nd edn (1983) · *History of the Irish confederation and the war in Ireland … by Richard Bellings*, ed. J. T. Gilbert, 7 vols. (1882–91) · *DNB* · Mr Graves, 'Report', *Transactions of the Kilkenny Archaeological Society*, 2 (1852–3), 387 · J. D'Alton, *King James's Irish Army List* (1689), repr. 1997 · D. F. Gleeson, 'The priory of St John at Nenagh', *Journal of the Royal Society of Antiquaries of Ireland*, 7th ser., 8 (1938), 201–18 · D. F. Gleeson, ed., 'The annals of Nenagh', *Analecta Hibernica*, 12 (1943), 155–64, esp. 157–8 · S. H. O'Grady, ed., *Catalogue of Irish manuscripts in the British Museum*, 2, ed. R. Flower (1926) · K. T. Hoppen, *The common scientist in the seventeenth century: a study of the Dublin Philosophical Society, 1683–1708* (1970) · W. R. Le Fanu, 'Two Irish doctors in England in the seventeenth century', *Irish Journal of Medical Science*, 463 (1964), 303–9 · Wood, *Ath. Oxon.*, new edn, 2.225

O'Meara [Meara], **Edmund** (c.1614–1681), physician, son of Dermot *O'Meara (*fl.* c.1614–1642*), physician to the earls of Ormond, was born in Ormond, co. Tipperary, Ireland. Educated at Oxford and abroad Edmund became MD of Rheims (1636); he may have been a member of the Dublin Fraternity of Physicians established in 1654, a forerunner of the Royal College of Physicians of Ireland, but the roll for the period in question is incomplete. He was elected honorary fellow of the College of Physicians, London (1664). He was medical adviser to the earl of Clanricarde. Like his father, Edmund O'Meara had a talent for Latin verses: he exchanged epigrams with Rinnucini, the papal nuncio, and wrote epitaphs for two archbishops of Tuam. The Cromwellian plantation obliged him to leave Ireland and practise medicine in London; he moved later to Bath and Bristol. After the Restoration he initiated a petition for the return of his confiscated estates in co. Wicklow. Prospects for a successful decision seemed favourable provided he could prove good title to the lands, and that these had not been given to adventurers or soldiers. Contrary to his expectations his claim was dismissed on 28 February 1663 by the commissioners of settlement. Leave to appeal was granted, and it is believed by Patrick Logan that the second petition was successful.

O'Meara's *Examen diatribae Thomae Willisy* (1665), dedicated to Sir Kenelm Digby, was reprinted in Amsterdam (1666). Additional to its attack on Willis's *De febribus* it contains 'medicae rariores', descriptions of nineteen unusual cases which he had seen in Bristol, and includes a reprint of his father's *Pathologia haereditaria generalis*, the first medical book printed in Dublin (1619). The engraved frontispiece of Edmund's *Examen* displays a glow-worm in sunlight and a motto, 'Useless in the light'; below, the same little creature is seen 'shining in the dark'. The polemic against Willis evoked the displeasure of Richard Lower, an Oxford physiologist, who responded so quickly with *Vindicatio diatribae Willisii* (1665) that Kenneth Dewhurst, its translator, suggested that Lower, prone to mood swings, may have been then in a hypomanic state. Later, in his *Tractatus corde*, Lower, still incensed, referred to ignoramuses who obstructed scientific progress with inept criticisms, among whom he included 'Meara quidam Hybernus'. The motivation of O'Meara's attack on Willis is unclear, but may represent the disturbed feelings of a traditionalist who followed doctrines advocated by Galen. His animadversions were supported by his fellow-countryman Conlis Cassin MD, whose book bore a title which may be translated: 'Willis badly vindicated, or an Oxford doctor found out in untruthfulness and ignorance'.

O'Meara returned to Dublin in 1666 and was in demand as a consultant. The association between the O'Mearas and the Butlers of Ormond was re-established in 1674 when Edmund was called as second opinion in an illness of James, duke of Ormond. He expressed the opinion that diet and exercise alone would be insufficient—bleeding in early spring was an absolute necessity, and mineral waters might be taken in either England or Ireland. He also advised that the patient be given 'the spleen broth used by my Lady of Thurles by Dr. Fennell's direction' (Logan, 315). He believed that the underlying disorder emanated from the spleen, and was unlikely to be fully relieved in one season.

O'Meara died in Dublin in 1681, survived by his wife, Cathleen, his daughter, Martha, and three sons—William, who was also a physician and prefixed Latin verses to the 1666 edition of his father's *Examen*; Edmund, a Jesuit; and Francis. The latter, who was the second son, was named a burgess in James II's charter of 1687 to the town of Wicklow, and was granted a commission of horse in Tyrconnel's regiment in the same year. He was sheriff of co. Wicklow in 1688, and was killed at the battle of the Boyne, being then a major, on 1 July 1690.   J. B. LYONS

Sources P. Logan, 'Dermot and Edmund O'Meara, father and son', *Journal of the Irish Medical Association*, 43 (1958), 312–17 · W. R. Le Fanu, 'Two Irish doctors in England in the seventeenth century', *Irish Journal of Medical Science*, 463 (1964), 303–9 · K. Dewhurst, ed., *Richard Lower's 'Vindicatio': a defence of the experimental method* (1983) · *DNB*

O'Meara, Kathleen [pseud. Grace Ramsay] (1839–1888), writer, was born in Dublin, the eldest daughter of Dennis O'Meara of Tipperary. Shortly after her birth her parents moved to Paris and she did not return to Ireland again. Her mother (d. 1887) received a pension under the second empire because she was directly related to Barry Edward O'Meara, Napoleon's physician in his last years.

O'Meara wrote for a period under the pseudonym of Grace Ramsay. Her English publishers suggested the *nom de plume* believing, as she noted, that 'the Irish and Catholic ring of my real name would indispose the liberal British public' (*Irish Monthly*, 531). She wrote stridently Catholic books and her first published novel was *A Woman's Trials* (1867), in which the central incident is the conversion of an English girl to Catholicism. *The Battle of Connemara* (1878), set in Paris and the west of Ireland, features a similar theme. Lady Peggy Blake, an Englishwoman, marries an Irish protestant landlord and settles in Connemara. So inspired is she by her tenants' faith and their acceptance of their lot, that she converts to Catholicism. Other novels include *Are you my Wife?* (1878), *The Old House in Picardy* (1887), and *Narka, a Story of Russian Life* (1888).

O'Meara also wrote a number of biographies such as *Life and Times of Thomas Grant, First Bishop of Southwark* (1874), *Frederick Ozanam, Professor at the Sorbonne, his Life and Works* (1876), *One of God's Heroines: a Biographical Sketch of Mother Mary Teresa Kelly* (1878), and *Madame Mohl, her Salon, and her Friends* (1885). Her short stories appeared in the *Irish Monthly*, *Harper's New Monthly Magazine*, the *Atlantic Monthly*, the *Catholic World*, and *The Tablet*. She appears to have travelled widely in Europe and visited America, and was Paris correspondent for *The Tablet* for many years. She never married. Kathleen O'Meara died of pneumonia at her home, 15 rue Washington, Paris, on 10 November 1888. Her last work, *The Venerable John Baptiste Vianney, Curé d'Ars*, was published posthumously in 1891.

THOMPSON COOPER, rev. MARIA LUDDY

Sources *Irish Monthly* (Oct 1889), 527–36 · *The Tablet* (17 Nov 1888) · *The Times* (13–14 Nov 1888) · A. Ulry Coleman, *A dictionary of nineteenth-century Irish women poets* (1996) · S. J. Brown, SJ, *Ireland in fiction* (1915) · Blain, Clements & Grundy, *Feminist comp.* · R. Welch, ed., *The Oxford companion to Irish literature* (1996) · *CGPLA Eng. & Wales* (1889)

Archives NL Scot., letters to Blackwoods

Wealth at death £3110 17s. 4d.: probate, 8 March 1889, *CGPLA Eng. & Wales*

Omichund. *See* Amir Chand (d. 1758).

Ommanney, Sir Erasmus (1814–1904), naval officer, born in London on 22 May 1814, was the seventh son, in a family of eight sons and three daughters, of Sir Francis Molyneux Ommanney (1774?–1840), a naval agent and from 1818 to 1826 MP for Barnstaple, and his wife, Georgiana Frances, daughter of Joshua Hawkes. The Ommanneys had long distinguished themselves in the navy: Erasmus's grandfather was Rear-Admiral Cornthwaite Ommanney (d. 1801), and his uncles were Admiral Sir John Acworth *Ommanney and Admiral Henry Manaton Ommanney. Major-General Edward Lacon Ommanney RE was his eldest brother and Prebendary George Druce Wynne *Ommanney was a younger brother. Ommanney entered the navy in August 1826 under his uncle, John Ommanney, then captain of the *Albion* (74 guns), which in December

convoyed to Lisbon the troops sent to protect Portugal against the Spanish invasion. The ship then went to the Mediterranean, and on 20 October 1827 took part in the battle of Navarino. The captured flag of the Turkish commander-in-chief was handed down by seniority among the surviving officers until 1890, when Ommanney, the sole survivor, presented it to the king of Greece.

In 1833 Ommanney passed his examination, after which he served for a short time as mate in the brig *Pantaloon*. On 10 December 1835 he was promoted lieutenant, and in the same month was appointed to the transport *Cove* (Captain Clark Ross), which was ordered to Baffin's Bay to release a number of whalers caught in the ice. He received the special commendation of the Admiralty for this dangerous service. In October 1836 he joined the frigate *Pique* (Captain Henry John Rous), and a year later was appointed to the *Donegal* (78 guns), as flag-lieutenant to his uncle, now Sir John Ommanney, commander-in-chief on the Lisbon and Mediterranean stations. He was promoted commander on 9 October 1840, and from August 1841 to the end of 1844 served on board the steam sloop *Vesuvius* in the Mediterranean. Here he was employed on the coast of Morocco for the protection of British subjects during the French hostilities, which included the bombardment of Tangier by the Prince de Joinville's squadron. He married, on 27 February 1844, Emily Mary (d. 1857), daughter of Samuel Smith of HM Dockyard, Malta. Their son, Erasmus Austin Ommanney, entered the navy in 1863, retired with the rank of commander in 1879, took orders in 1883, and was vicar of St Michael's, Southsea, from 1892 to 1911. Ommanney was promoted captain on 9 November 1846, and in 1847–8 was employed under the government commission during the famine in Ireland, carrying into effect relief measures and the new poor law.

When Captain Horatio Austin was appointed to the *Resolute* for the command of the Franklin search expedition in February 1850 he chose his friend Ommanney as second in command. The *Resolute* and Ommanney's ship, the *Assistance*, each had a steam tender, this being the first occasion on which steam was used for Arctic navigation. This expedition was also the first to organize an extensive system of sledge journeys, by means of which the coast of Prince of Wales Land was surveyed. On 25 August 1850 Ommanney discovered the first traces of the fate of Sir John Franklin; these proved that his ships had wintered at Beechey Island. The expedition returned to England in October 1851.

In December 1851 Ommanney was appointed deputy controller-general of the coastguard, and held this post until 1854, when, on the outbreak of the Russian war, he commissioned the *Eurydice* as senior officer of a small squadron for the White Sea, where he blockaded Archangel, stopped the coasting trade, and destroyed government property. His White Sea service culminated in a battle between his squadron and a Russian monastery at Archangel. In 1855 he was appointed to the *Hawke*, blockship for the Baltic, and was employed chiefly as senior officer in the Gulf of Riga, where the service was one of rigid blockade, varied by occasional skirmishes with the

Russian gunboats and batteries. Ommanney's period in the Baltic was marked by his aggressive operations against Russian shore positions and gunboats, summoning defenceless towns to surrender, and his exaggerated reports of successes.

In October 1857 Ommanney was appointed to the *Brunswick* (80 guns), going out to the West Indies, and was senior officer at Colón when the filibuster William Walker attempted to invade Nicaragua. The *Brunswick* afterwards joined the Channel Fleet, and she was sent as a reinforcement to the Mediterranean during the Franco-Austrian War of 1859. Ommanney was not again afloat after being paid off in 1860, but was senior officer at Gibraltar from 1862 until he was promoted to flag rank on 12 November 1864.

In 1862 Ommanney married Mary, daughter of Thomas A. Stone of Curzon Street, London; she died on 1 September 1906, aged eighty-one. In March 1867 he was created CB; on 14 July 1871 he was promoted to vice-admiral, and he accepted retirement on 1 January 1875. He was advanced to admiral on the retired list on 1 August 1877, in which year he was knighted for his scientific work in the Arctic. He had been elected FRS in 1868 for the same reason, and to the end of his life continued to take a great interest in geographical work and service subjects. He attended meetings of the Royal Geographical Society and the Royal United Service Institution (he was for many years a councillor of both bodies) and of the British Association. He was also a JP for Hampshire and a member of the Thames conservancy. In June 1902 he was made KCB.

An officer of some distinction in Arctic exploration, Ommanney died on 21 December 1904 at his son's home, St Michael's vicarage, St Michael's Road, Southsea, Hampshire, and was buried in Mortlake cemetery.

L. G. C. LAUGHTON, rev. ANDREW LAMBERT

Sources G. S. Ritchie, *The Admiralty chart: British naval hydrography in the nineteenth century* (1967) · R. S. Dundas, *Russian war, 1855, Baltic: official correspondence*, ed. D. Bonner-Smith, Navy RS, 84 (1944) · BL, Wood MSS · A. D. Lambert, *The Crimean War: British grand strategy, 1853–56* (1990) · I. R. Stone, 'The Crimean War in the Arctic', *Polar Record*, 21 (1982–3), 577–81 · P. A. Symonds and L. Taylor, 'Ommanney, Francis Molyneux', HoP, *Commons* · O'Byrne, *Naval biog. dict.* · *CGPLA Eng. & Wales* (1905)
Archives Gennadius Library, Athens, Greece, log of HMS *Albion* · Glenbow Alberta Institute, Calgary, journals of HMS *Assistance* and HM Sledge *Reliance* · RGS, corresp. and papers | BL, Wood MSS · RGS, corresp. with Royal Geographical Society
Likenesses S. Pearce, oils, exh. 1861, NPG
Wealth at death £20,395 14s. 4d.: probate, 3 Feb 1905, *CGPLA Eng. & Wales*

Ommanney, George Druce Wynne (1819–1902), Church of England clergyman and theologian, born in Norfolk Street, Strand, London, on 12 April 1819, was the eighth and youngest son of Sir Francis Molyneux Ommanney (1774?–1840), naval agent and politician, and his wife, Georgiana Frances Hawkes, and the younger brother of Sir Erasmus *Ommanney. After education at Harrow School (1831–8), where in 1838 he won the Robert Peel gold medal and the Lyon scholarship, he matriculated as

scholar from Trinity College, Cambridge, in 1838, graduated BA as senior optime and second-class classic in 1842, and proceeded MA in 1845. Taking holy orders in 1842, he was curate of Edwinstone, Nottinghamshire (1843–9), of Cameley, Somerset (1849–52), of Oldbourne, Wiltshire (1852–3), and of Woodborough, Wiltshire (1853–8); vicar of Queen Charlton, near Bristol (1858–62); curate in charge of Whitchurch, Somerset (1862–75); and vicar of Draycot, Somerset (1875–88). He was made prebendary of Whitchurch in Wells Cathedral in 1884. He married Ellen Ricketts of Brislington, Bristol; they had no children. Ommanney died on 20 April 1902 at 29 Beaumont Street, Oxford, where he had lived in retirement since 1888, and was buried at St Sepulchre's cemetery, Oxford.

Ommanney was a voluminous and lucid writer on the Athanasian creed, to which he devoted a large portion of his later life, studying Arabic and visiting the chief European libraries for purposes of research. He was a vigorous champion of the retention of the creed in the Church of England services. He supported its claims to authenticity against the critics who ascribed its composition to the eighth and ninth centuries. His published works include: *The Athanasian Creed: Examination of Recent Theories Respecting its Date and Origin* (1875), *Early History of the Athanasian Creed* (1880), *The SPCK and the Creed of St Athanasius* (1884), and *Critical dissertation on the Athanasian creed, its original language, date, authorship, titles, text, reception, and use* (1897).

W. B. OWEN, rev. H. C. G. MATTHEW

Sources *The Times* (22 April 1902) · *The Guardian* (23 April 1902) · Crockford (1902) · private information (1912)
Wealth at death £10,173 5s. 5d.: probate, 11 June 1902, *CGPLA Eng. & Wales*

Ommanney, Sir John Acworth (1773–1855), naval officer, eldest son of Rear-Admiral Cornthwaite Ommanney (d. 1801), entered the navy in 1786 on board the frigate *Rose* (Captain Henry Harvey) on the Newfoundland station. He afterwards served from 1788 to 1792 in the Mediterranean, and in July 1792 was appointed to the *Lion* (Sir Erasmus Gower), which took Lord Macartney to China. On 20 May 1793 Ommanney was promoted lieutenant, and, on returning to England in October 1794, he was appointed to the frigate *Aquilon*, cruising in the channel. In March 1795 he was moved into the *Queen Charlotte*, one of the ships with Lord Bridport in the engagement off Lorient on 23 June. On 6 December 1796 he was promoted commander. During the mutiny at the Nore he commanded gun-brig no. 28 for the defence of the Thames, and in December 1797 was appointed to the brig *Busy* in the North Sea, with considerable success. In August 1799, in company with the brig *Speedwell*, he stopped a fleet of Swedish merchant ships under the convoy of a frigate. Ommanney had intelligence that some of these ships were laden with contraband of war and were bound for French ports, and, as the frigate refused to allow them to be searched, he sent the whole fleet into the Downs, off the Kent coast, for examination. His tact and determination received the particular approval of the Admiralty.

In January 1800 Ommanney went to the West Indies, but was obliged by the state of his health to return in July. On

16 October he was advanced to post rank, and during 1801 commanded, in rapid succession, the frigate *Hussar*, the *Robust*, and the *Barfleur*, bearing the flag of Rear-Admiral Collingwood, in the Channel Fleet. Ommanney married, in October 1803, Frances, daughter of Richard Ayling, of Slidham, in Sussex; they had four daughters. From 1804 to 1806 he was flag captain to Sir Erasmus Gower on the Newfoundland station. He did not serve at sea again for nineteen years, a period that can be explained only by his whig politics. In 1825 he was appointed to the *Albion*, which, after some time at Lisbon, joined Sir Edward Codrington in the Mediterranean and had an important part in the battle of Navarino on 20 October 1827. Ommanney received the CB and French, Russian, and Greek decorations for this service.

On 22 July 1830 Ommanney was promoted rear-admiral; he was knighted on 23 May 1835, and nominated a KCB on 20 July 1838. From 1837 to 1840, with his flag in the *Donegal*, he had command of the Lisbon station, and from September 1840 to October 1841 he commanded at Malta, during the prolonged absence of the commander-in-chief, Sir Robert Stopford. He became a vice-admiral on 23 November 1841, and admiral on 4 May 1849. He was commander-in-chief at Devonport from 1851 to 1854, during the latter part of which time the fitting out of the fleet for the Baltic put severe strain on nerves enfeebled by age. He died at Warblington House, Havant, Hampshire, on 8 July 1855. Lady Ommanney died a few weeks after her husband, on 17 August. Sir Francis Molyneux Ommanney, the navy agent and MP for Barnstaple, who acted as banker and agent for Lord Collingwood, was Ommanney's brother.

Politically, Ommanney was closely linked to Palmerston, and through him to Lord Minto and Sir Charles Adam, a fact of some significance during his service at Lisbon and in the Syrian crisis of 1840. Palmerston thought highly of his good sense, and valued his political support in Portsmouth.

J. K. LAUGHTON, *rev.* ANDREW LAMBERT

Sources J. H. Boteler, *Recollections of my sea life from 1808–1830* (1883); repr. D. Bonner-Smith, ed., Navy RS, 82 (1942) · U. Southampton L., Palmerston MSS · *The private correspondence of Admiral Lord Collingwood*, ed. E. Hughes, Navy RS, 98 (1957) · C. M. Woodhouse, *The battle of Navarino* (1965) · Boase, *Mod. Eng. biog.* · O'Byrne, *Naval biog. dict.*
Archives NMM, corresp. with Lord Minto · NRA, priv. coll., letters to Sir Charles Adam · U. Southampton L., Palmerston MSS
Likenesses R. J. Lane, lithograph, 1851 (after B. R. Faulkner), BM, NPG

Ommanney, **Sir Montagu Frederick** (1842–1925), civil servant, was born on 4 April 1842, the only child of Francis Ommanney of Worcester Park, Surrey, banker and naval agent, and his wife, Julia, daughter of Thomas Metcalfe. On leaving Cheltenham College in 1861 Ommanney entered the Royal Military Academy, Woolwich, and in 1864 received a commission in the Royal Engineers. In 1867 he married his cousin Charlotte Helen Ommanney, daughter of Octavius Ommanney JP, of Bloxham. They had three sons and four daughters. Bored with his duties as a royal engineer, he applied for and obtained special duties, first at the War Office and then at the Admiralty,

where he worked largely as an architect. Appointed private secretary to the colonial secretary of state, Lord Carnarvon, he assisted Carnarvon's campaign to bring about South African federation. In 1878 Carnarvon appointed him third agent at the office of the crown agents for the colonies, a quasi-government department that acted as the UK commercial and financial agent of the crown colonies and protectorates.

Ommanney's career in the agency started inauspiciously. Persuaded by the senior agent, Sir Penrose Julyan, to become a loan agent to the New Zealand government in direct contradiction of Colonial Office instructions, he was severely reprimanded when, in 1881, the office discovered the appointment. After the retirement of Julyan, however, he prospered, spending much of his time supervising the construction of colonial infrastructure and designing colonial public buildings, many of which, such as Lagos prison, were much admired. On the death of Sir William Sargeaunt in 1888 Ommanney took over the post of senior agent, gave up his design work, and began to concentrate on the financial aspects of the crown agents' duties. These involved the public and private issue on the London market of crown colony loans, the provision of short-term advances obtained from banks and surplus colonial UK balances, and the investment of colonial funds lodged with the agency. By 1900 he had organized the issue of loans worth over £8 million, most of which were fully subscribed and sold at a relatively high price, and managed approximately £9 million of colonial UK funds. In 1888, in addition to his work as a crown agent, he acted as a commissioner of the Royal Colonial Exhibition, and from 1899 to 1900 was a member of the royal commission on the Paris Exhibition. He was created KCMG in 1900 and KCB in 1901.

Like many of the senior agents Ommanney used his position for his own gain. He employed as the agents' solicitor the firm of Sutton and Ommanney, the partners in which included his uncle and cousin. Frederic Shelford, the agents' railway consulting engineer for West African Railways, was his son-in-law. Many of the agency staff were relatives or friends. From 1899 to 1901 Ommanney was a paid director of the agency's insurance company, the London Assurance Corporation.

The arrival of Joseph Chamberlain at the Colonial Office and the implementation of his policy of colonial development greatly increased the work of the agents. Ommanney fully supported Chamberlain's policy, and played a large part in persuading the Treasury to pass the 1900 Colonial Stocks Act which, through its recognition of colonial stocks as trustee investments, allowed the smaller and newer colonies to issue loans in the open market. Impressed by his initiative and engineering and financial knowledge Chamberlain invited him to succeed Sir Edward Wingfield as permanent under-secretary at the Colonial Office in 1901. Although Chamberlain's third choice for the job, after Alfred Milner and Sir George Goldie, Ommanney accepted the offer and took early retirement from the agency. In his new position he managed the work of the Colonial Office, a role in which his 'even temper and great kindliness of heart' (*The Times*, 25 Aug 1925, 13) allowed him to excel, and supervised the activities of crown agents, whom he strongly defended from colonial and Colonial Office criticism. He also contributed to all the major policy decisions of the office, particularly concentrating on the construction of West African Railways. Suspicious of the private sector, he strongly supported the adoption of the 'department' system of construction, under which projects were built by the crown agents' consulting engineers, largely his son-in-law, and which he claimed led to the rapid construction of good quality, low-cost lines. In the event most of the railways built exceeded their estimated cost and construction deadlines, and few earned sufficient receipts to cover loan and debt charges. In 1904 he was made GCMG.

On his retirement from the Colonial Office in 1907 Ommanney entered the business world, becoming a director of the British North Borneo Company, the Union Castle Mail Steamship Company Ltd, the Kimanis Rubber Company, and chairman of Anglo-East African Rubber Plantations Ltd. He was honorary treasurer and vice-president elect of the Royal Colonial Institute and king of arms for the Order of St Michael and St George. Soon after his wife's death in 1913, he married, on 21 March 1914, Winifred Rose, daughter of Charles Edward Harris St John of Finchampstead. Ommanney died at his home, Knowles Lodge, Cuckfield, Sussex, on 19 August 1925.

DAVID SUNDERLAND

Sources D. Sunderland, 'Agents and principals: the crown agents for the colonies, 1880–1914', DPhil diss., U. Oxf., 1996 · F. Shelford, album and press cuttings, Bodl. RH · R. V. Kubicek, *The administration of imperialism: Joseph Chamberlain at the colonial office* (1969) · *Directory of Directors* · *The Times* (22 Aug 1925), 5 · *The Times* (25 Aug 1925), 13 · Burke, *Peerage*
Archives Duke U., Perkins L., corresp. | BL, corresp. with Florence Nightingale, Add. MSS 45801–45802 · Bodl. RH, corresp. with Sir Graham Bower · CUL, letters to Lord Hardinge
Likenesses photographs, Crown Agents' archive, St Nicholas House, St Nicholas Road, Sutton, Surrey
Wealth at death £13,329 10s. 1d.: probate, 4 Nov 1925, *CGPLA Eng. & Wales*

O'Molloy, Francis. See Ó Maolmhuaidh, Froinsias (*c*.1606–1677?).

Omond, George William Thomson (1846–1929), historian, was born on 13 September 1846 at Craigentor, Monzie, near Crieff, Perthshire, the only son and second of the five children of John Reid Omond (1804–1892), minister of the Free Church of Scotland in Monzie, and his wife, Margaret Jane Thomson (*d*. 1887), daughter of William Aird Thomson, minister, of Perth. His parents were both Scottish; his father, the former parish minister of Monzie, 'came out' at the Disruption in 1843. He was baptized 'George William' in the parish church on 11 October 1846, but it was in accordance with the forms of the Free Church of Scotland that he married Margaret Isabella Alice Wright (*c*.1849–1932), daughter of James Wright, foreign merchant, on 23 July 1878. They had one son and three daughters.

Omond was educated at Edinburgh Academy (1857–64) and at Edinburgh University (1864–8); he graduated MA with a first in classics and a second in philosophy. In his second year he matriculated as 'George William Thomson Omond'. He was admitted to the Faculty of Advocates in 1871 but had no extensive practice, though he was appointed as an advocate-depute in 1885. In 1886 he stood as a Liberal for West Perthshire. He was not elected and instead pursued his career in writing, particularly historical writing, rather than the law or politics, though he continued to designate himself advocate of the Scots bar. His first book, *The Merchant Shipping Acts 1854 to 1876* (1877), indicated some early interest in shipping law; but it was his historical interest in the law of the sea, as it affected neutral merchant ships in time of war, which was apparent in two later works, *The Law of the Sea* (1916) and *A Documentary History of the Armed Neutralities 1780 and 1800* (1919), in which he collaborated with Sir F. Piggott.

Undoubtedly Omond's best-known historical work is *The Lord Advocates of Scotland* (2 vols., 1883), which deals with the office of lord advocate and the careers of the holders of it from the fifteenth century to the passing of the Scottish Reform Act (1832). In part it was overtaken by later studies but it remained a valuable source. *The Lord Advocates of Scotland: Second Series, 1834–1880* (1914), less well known and sometimes overlooked, updated the story to 1880. Other contributions to Scottish history are *The Arniston Memoirs … 1571–1838* (1887), an account of the remarkable legal family and dynasty, the Dundases of Arniston; and studies concerning the history of attempts to unite Scotland and England, *Fletcher of Saltoun* (1897) and *The Early History of the Scottish Union Question* (1897). In the 1890s Omond tried his hand at fiction with three novels which were later forgotten. *The Boers in Europe* (1903) was a patriotic piece on continental support for the Boer cause. In 1917 Omond was elected FRHistS. He served on the society's council from 1919 to 1922 and as vice-president from 1922 to 1925.

One of Omond's major interests was the Low Countries and their history, an interest focused principally on Belgium, where Omond lived for a considerable period. This led to a number of publications between 1906 and 1928, including guide books, with some recycled material and illustrated mainly by Amédée Forestier. Omond also produced a popular history, *Belgium and Luxembourg* (1923), and was responsible for the chapter 'Belgium, 1830–1839' in the second volume, published in 1923, of the *Cambridge History of British Foreign Policy*, edited by A. W. Ward and G. P. Gooch. He wrote various articles on questions relating to Belgium and for his contributions to Anglo-Belgian relations he was made a chevalier of the order of the Crown (Belgium).

Omond was said to have a kind and genial personality. In the latter part of his life he lived in England, in Essex, Kent, and Surrey. He died on 18 June 1929 at Knaphill, Surrey, survived by his wife.   W. M. GORDON

Sources *The Times* (19 June 1929) · E. Cammaerts, *The Times* (21 June 1929) · *WWW* · records, Royal Historical Society · D. M. Walter, *The Scottish jurists* (1985), 384–418 · Parish registers, 1846, Monzie, Perthshire · [T. Henderson and P. F. Hamilton-Grierson], eds., *The Edinburgh Academy register* (1914)
Archives Duke U., Perkins L., political corresp.

Omoniyi, Bandele (1884–1913), nationalist and writer on African politics, was born on 6 November 1884 in Lagos in the British colony of Nigeria, the son of Aina Omoniyi. Both his father, said to be headman of a gang of day labourers at the Lagos customs and his mother originated from the Yoruba town of Modakeke, near Ife, in south-western Nigeria. Bandele Omoniyi often styled himself Prince, especially in his political writings and activities in Britain, and claimed to be the nephew of King Lupono of Modakeke. He had also used the name John B. Samuel while in Lagos. Omoniyi was educated at Lagos CMS grammar school, where he also taught, at Edinburgh tutorial college (1906), and at Edinburgh University (1906–7).

Omoniyi first visited Britain in 1905, the cost borne by his father who, despite his humble circumstances, had received sufficient funds for this purpose through the compulsory purchase of his land by the Lagos government. He arrived in Liverpool and may have intended to study in that city. It seems that while there he came into contact with the newly formed Ethiopian Progressive Society (EPA), an early student pan-African organization with members from west Africa and the Caribbean. It was from Liverpool that he wrote to the editor of the *Lagos Standard*, complaining about the lack of support the EPA received from west Africa, the undemocratic nature of British rule, and, unusually for this period, the condition and treatment of 'the working classes' in west Africa.

In 1906 Omoniyi moved to Edinburgh and until 1907 was enrolled as a student in the faculty of medicine at Edinburgh University. He then decided to study law, but in the middle of the academic session he gave up his classes in order to concentrate on writing in support of the political demands of his compatriots. Throughout 1906 he continued his political activities, sending a series of letters to the British prime minister, Henry Campbell-Bannerman, and one to his compatriots, which were all published in the *Lagos Standard*. He took up the case for colonial reform and political representation for Africans and opposed the military campaigns that were still being conducted in west Africa. He also called on his compatriots to organize themselves to petition parliament in support of their rights. In the same year he sent another twelve letters demanding an end to discrimination in employment in west Africa to the colonial secretary, Lord Elgin.

In 1907 Omoniyi wrote a series of articles for the *Edinburgh Magazine* criticizing colonial rule. In the same year he became the first African to write for the Independent Labour Party's *Labour Leader*. He had already shown an interest in the working classes and with socialism, which he associated with 'the equality of freedom and opportunity to all coloured races' (Adi, 595 n. 40). There is even some evidence to suggest that he wrote a book, which has not yet come to light, entitled *Socialism Examined*. An article in the *Labour Leader*, 'The regeneration of Africa', which was well received by the press in west Africa, showed his concern with pan-African issues. It defended the 1906 Zulu uprising in Natal as well as presenting an 'African Programme' of 'urgent reforms which we Africans demand' (Adi, 593).

In March 1908, at the age of twenty-three, Omoniyi published in Edinburgh his major work, *A Defence of the Ethiopian Movement*, which was dedicated 'to The Right Honourable and Honourable Members of the British Parliament'. Here he again defended the Natal rebellion and Ethiopianism, an early form of pan-Africanism particularly evident in South Africa; criticized British colonial rule and 'brute force imperialism'; and devoted a chapter to 'inter-marriage' and 'a vindication of the Half-Castes or Coloured Men' (Adi, 595). His main concern was to urge colonial reforms, and he warned that without them a revolution might take place in Africa that would bring an end to British rule. His writing and correspondence with members of the government brought Omoniyi to the attention of the Colonial Office. In 1908 he began to correspond with the future Labour Party leader Ramsay MacDonald, requesting him to ask a parliamentary question concerning what he believed was an attack on the town of Modakeke by the colonial authorities. MacDonald contacted the Colonial Office, which had already begun to collect damaging but unsubstantiated information about Omoniyi.

Little more is known of Omoniyi's life until in 1912 he again contacted the Colonial Office, this time from Pará-Belém, Brazil. According to his own account he had been selling gold-mining concessions in Brazil for some eighteen months but was also involved in Brazilian politics. In addition he had written a manifesto, one of the first political documents written by an African in Nigeria's history, concerned with the 'elevation of the mass of the Nigerians to a position of respect and honour' (Langley, 181), the need for a political party to represent their interests, and the demand for a federal, semi-autonomous Nigeria. Omoniyi was in contact with the Colonial Office again following his arrest and temporary imprisonment for taking an active part in political disturbances.

Omoniyi's intervention in Brazilian politics was his last political act. A few months later, on 2 January 1913, he died, at the age of twenty-eight, from acute beri-beri in the Hospital da Caridade in Pará-Belém. It was reported that 'he left no estate, and his effects were seized in lieu of rent; his interment provided by the hospital authorities' (Adi, 604).   HAKIM ADI

Sources H. Adi, 'Bandele Omoniyi: a neglected Nigerian nationalist', *African Affairs*, 90 (1991), 581–605 · J. A. Langley, *Ideologies of liberation in black Africa* (1979), 173–87 · Colonial Office records
Likenesses photograph, repro. in *Edinburgh Magazine*, 4 (7 March 1908)

O'Moran, James (1735–1794), army officer in the French service, was born and baptized on 1 May 1735 in the parish of Ross, near Elphin, co. Roscommon, Ireland, allegedly the son of a shoemaker. He was educated at the Irish College at Tournai, Belgium, of which his uncle was rector. On 15 November 1752 he entered the Dillon infantry regiment of the Franco-Irish brigade as a cadet, and was commissioned *lieutenant en second* on 14 January 1759. He served with distinction in the campaigns of 1760–61 in Germany. Although without wealth or obvious influence he was steadily promoted and received the cross of St Louis in

1778. In 1779 he crossed the Atlantic with his regiment to serve at the capture of Grenada and in D'Estaing's subsequent naval victory over the English. His regiment joined the Americans at the siege of Savannah, during which he suffered a leg wound which troubled him for the rest of his life. After recuperating in France he returned to America in 1780 and participated in an expedition to Jamaica in 1782. He became a member of the Society of the Cincinnati in 1783 and was awarded a pension on his return to France. In 1785 he married Patience Singleton (d. 1785), who died within months of their marriage. He later married Eleanor King (b. 1760), a native of Scotland; they had two children, Eleanor (b. 1788) and William (b. 1789).

Unlike many compatriots, O'Moran accepted the French Revolution and on 25 August 1791 he was appointed colonel of the regiment of Dillon, by then the 87th regiment. He was made *maréchal de camp* on 6 February 1792. He served under Dumouriez in Champagne and Belgium and was promoted general of division on 3 October. His headquarters, which was at Tournai, he governed with prudence and firmness. While there he was a witness at the wedding of Lord Edward Fitzgerald, the Irish radical, to Pamela, the adopted daughter of the duc d'Orléans. After Dumouriez's retreat from Belgium and subsequent treason O'Moran came under suspicion. He was removed from command and arrested in 1793. Arraigned before the revolutionary tribunal in Paris, he strongly maintained his innocence but was guillotined there on 6 March 1794. The night before his trial he wrote of his stainless, unbroken service to France and of his cherished dream of liberating Ireland. The latter ideal was probably rooted in his Irish brigade background, but was refined by his experience of the American and French revolutions. A brave and able soldier, O'Moran was noted for his fine manners, bonhomie, and Catholic faith. His son, William O'Moran, served in Napoleon's Irish legion.

HARMAN MURTAGH

Sources R. Hayes, *Irish swordsmen of France* (1934), 39–109 · R. Hayes, *Biographical dictionary of Irishmen in France* (1949), 246–8 · E. Ó Hannracháin, 'Un cadeau pour un général: réflexions sur la vie du Général Jacques O Moran', *Valentiana*, 7 (1991), 29–42 · W. S. Murphy, 'The Irish brigade of France at the siege of Savannah, 1779', *Irish Sword*, 2 (1954–6), 95–102
Archives Service Historique de l'Armée de Terre, France, dossier

O'More, Owny MacRory [Uaithne MacRuaidhri ua Mordha] (b. in or before 1577, d. 1600), chieftain and rebel, was born in Gallen, co. Leix (Laois), a son of Rory Oge *O'More (c.1540–1578), chieftain and rebel, and his wife, Margaret (d. 1577), daughter of Hugh MacShane O'Byrne, chieftain of the Gabhal Raghnaill branch of the O'Byrne clan, and his first wife, Sadhbh. Owny's career was conditioned by two factors: the government's elimination of his parents and four brothers during Rory Oge's rebellion in 1571–8, and the dismemberment of the O'More lordship and replacement with an English plantation. Owny's career, like his father's, oscillated between pursuing lands within the plantation or securing its overthrow. Beyond the fact that he was raised in Wicklow under the fosterage of his uncle Fiach MacHugh *O'Byrne (c.1544–1597), little

is known about Owny's earliest years, save that the government feared him greatly. They believed that the scattered O'Mores were merely 'waiting for Rorie Oge's son, who hath already taken in hande weappon, and is of styrring spirit', before seeking 'to kyll and spoyle the present possesors of that whych they take to be theyr right' (PRO, SP 63/132/8). To forestall this, successive lord deputies attempted to capture Owny, but Fiach MacHugh's protection ensured that he reached maturity safely.

It was not until May 1596, while the government was preoccupied with the Nine Years' War, that Owny made his mark, successfully attacking the Cosbys of Stradbally, Leix. This was an attempt to have his claims to lands within Leix recognized because during the next month he sought pardon, protection, and 'to have lande at a reasonable rennt in Gallyn where his preedecesors and hym self werr borne'. The government's indifference persuaded him to escalate the violence. Thereafter, he harassed the settlers so vigorously that 'Leix was totally ravaged by him, both its crops, corn and dwellings, so that there was nothing in the territory outside the lock of a gate or a bawn which was not in his power' (AFM, s.a. 1597). These martial endeavours saw a corresponding increase in Owny's standing in Leix and in October 1597 he was described as the 'chiefest of the Moores' (PRO, SP 63/201/22). Whereas he was initially willing to accept the plantation if granted land, his ambitions grew during 1597, perhaps as a result of his understanding with Hugh O'Neill, second earl of Tyrone.

The link between Owny and Tyrone was established either through Fiach MacHugh or through Owny's brother Brian Reagh O'More, who served the earl in Ulster. Its terms appear to have been that, in return for military support and inclusion in any peace negotiations, Owny would open a front against the government in Leinster. Thereafter, Owny frequently received mercenaries and munitions from Tyrone, which he used to wreak havoc in Leinster and increase his regional influence: his assistance to junior branches of the Butler family who sought to escape the authority of Thomas Butler, tenth earl of Ormond, dates from this time. After 1597 Owny was the means by which men like Edmund Butler, second Viscount Mountgarret, sought Tyrone's favour in Leinster.

Tyrone's support allowed Owny to transform his strategy. Rather than just waging a guerrilla campaign like his father, he was capable of engaging substantial English contingents in the field, as he illustrated in December 1597 when he decimated two English companies near Maryborough Fort, Leix. In September 1598 he attacked a relief column of 'twenty-four companies of foot and two hundred horse', led by Ormond and bound for Maryborough Fort. In this engagement Ormond 'lost more than the value of the provisions in men, horses, and arms' (AFM, s.a. 1598). Immediately after this success Owny, on Tyrone's orders, marched into Munster at the head of 2000 men. He established Tyrone's nominee, James Fitzgerald, as fifteenth earl of Desmond and destroyed the Munster plantation.

Owny's reputation as 'a gentleman [skilled] in the arts of

war' was well established and enhanced further by his attack on Robert Devereux, second earl of Essex, the lord lieutenant, at the Pass of the Plumes (Bearna na gCleti) in May 1599. As Essex marched south through Leix with 7000 foot and 900 horse he discovered Owny's forces behind prepared ground. In the ensuing battle Owny's men 'made fierce and desperate assaults, and furious, irresistible onsets on him [Essex], in intricate ways and narrow passes, in which both parties came in collision with each other, so that great numbers of the Earl's people were cut off' (*AFM*, s.a. 1597, 1599). This engagement exacerbated the lord lieutenant's difficulties, coming as it did at the same time as Fiach MacHugh's great victory at Deputy's Pass near Wicklow on 29 May.

Owny had been a thorn in the English administration's side since 1596, but his influence was mainly based on support from Ulster. His survival was due to the fact that the government's army was constantly preoccupied elsewhere until 1600. He might have survived until the end of the war but for his most famous and ill-advised exploit—capturing Elizabeth I's Irish favourite, Ormond, in April 1600—which marked him out for elimination. Ormond's abduction caused considerable consternation in certain government circles because it was feared that 'therle wilbe passed over by Owny McRory to the traitor Tyrone'. However, Sir Geoffrey Fenton informed Sir Robert Cecil, the principal secretary, that he believed Owny would 'reserve him in his owne possession, to thend to make his deliverie proffitable to hymself'. Others wondered 'how farr this sodden trecherous action might alter some of the Butlers'. Owny initially planned to use Ormond as a bargaining tool to get Leix and Offaly restored to the O'Mores and the O'Connors but he was forced to abandon this course when it became apparent that many of his allies and supporters sought to dissociate themselves from the earl's abduction. The predictions by Fenton and Sir George Carew that Ormond's captivity would create breaches among Owny's supporters proved correct. Forced to move Ormond 'every night from one cabin to another', Owny appeared at a loss as to how best to use his prisoner. The rumour that the queen resolved to send large numbers of soldiers into the midlands to find Ormond 'brede such alteration in most of the Irishry' that they swore 'to be at open deffiance with him [Owny]'. Consequently, Owny was forced to release Ormond early in June.

With Ormond's liberation the new lord deputy, Charles Blount, eighth Baron Mountjoy, could move safely against Owny. On 15 August 1600 his forces began to ravage Leix, cutting down the ripening wheat and laying waste to the country. Recognizing that Mountjoy was uninterested in concession, Owny engaged the government's forces on 17 August in the Douglas valley in 'an overwhelming and fierce battle', during which he was fatally wounded (*AFM*, s.a. 1600). Fearing that Mountjoy would display Owny's head on Dublin Castle, Owny 'wyled it to be cutt of after his death and burried'. Mountjoy continued his policy of killing and displacing the O'Mores and the O'Connors until mid-1601, when the midlands had been pacified.

Owny's death and Mountjoy's elimination of his followers meant that all the leading O'Mores were removed from Leix and finally ended the resistance of the sept or clan to the plantation scheme. The Gaelic lordship of Leix was shattered, ensuring that the planter community could return and face the seventeenth century with a reasonable degree of confidence—a fact not lost on the annalists, who bitterly lamented the death of 'an illustrious, renowned and celebrated gentleman', who:

> had wrested the government of his patrimony, by the prowess of his hand and the resoluteness of his heart, from the hands of foreigners … until he brought it under his own sway and jurisdiction, and under the government of his stewards and bonnaghts, according to Irish usage. (*AFM*, s.a. 1600)

DAVID FINNEGAN

Sources state papers Ireland, Elizabeth, PRO, SP 63 · *AFM* · J. Graves, 'The taking of the earl of Ormond, 1600', *Proceedings and Papers of the Kilkenny and South-East Ireland Archaeological Society*, 2nd ser. (1862–5) · V. P. Carey, 'Gaelic reaction to plantation: the case of the O'More and O'Connor lordships of Leix and Offaly, 1570–1603', MA diss., National University of Ireland (Maynooth), 1985 · F. Moryson, *An itinerary containing his ten yeeres travell through the twelve dominions*, 4 vols. (1907–8)

O'More, Rory [Roger Moore] (*b. c.*1592, *d.* in or after 1666), conspirator, was the son of Calvach O'More (*d.* 1618) and Margaret Sherlock or Scurlog. Calvach's father had been recognized by the Tudors as chieftain of Laois, but the territory was subsequently shired as Queen's county, and planted with an English colony. In 1567 Queen Elizabeth granted Calvach, in partial recompense, escheated lands amounting to 1078 acres in the barony of Carbury, in the north-west corner of co. Kildare, and former church lands in the parish of Kilmainham Wood in the north of co. Meath. During the plantation of Ulster (1609–10) James I granted him about 7000 acres, in south-east co. Armagh, originally assigned to Art Mac Baron O'Neill, the father of Owen Roe O'Neill.

Rory O'More inherited these scattered estates on the death of his father in 1618. According to a family memoir, he sold the Kilmainham Wood estate because of scruples about owning land which originally belonged to the church, and bought, rather than inherited, the Armagh estate with the proceeds. By 1641 he had married a daughter of Sir Patrick Barnewall, of whom little is known.

In February 1641 O'More approached Conor, Lord Maguire, then attending the parliament in Dublin. He urged that the Anglo-Scottish crisis offered the Irish a chance to regain lost estates by force. He also drew attention to Maguire's own debts and claimed to have secured support for his plan in Leinster and Connaught. The latter claim, while probably untrue, was doubtless given credence by O'More's marital connections to some of the leading families of the pale, including Viscount Gormanstown, the earl of Fingal, and Luke Netterville, the three individuals who would ultimately assume local leadership of the insurgency. When parliament resumed sitting in May, O'More had a second meeting with Maguire and other Ulster conspirators drawn in by the latter. O'More's motives for plotting are not as clear-cut as those of Maguire and Phelim O'Neill, both of whom were deeply in debt. O'More either borrowed heavily or was, in fact, quite wealthy, to judge from the dowries, amounting in aggregate to £4000, that he paid to marry off his daughters. The most likely explanation for his involvement was not immediate financial pressure but that he was 'Piqued by the loss of his ancient patrimony' in co. Laois (Plunkett, fol. 5). That he may have seen himself as the leader of a revived O'More clan is suggested by his recall of the 'several septs that were banished from Leix' to serve him as soldiers ('Examination of Lewis O'Moore', fol. 128).

Having initiated the plot, O'More played a subordinate role as it was transformed from vague scheming into a purposeful movement based on confident and reasonably effective planning. In September 1641 the conspirators decided on a two-pronged rising, involving the seizure of Dublin Castle on 23 October in concert with an uprising in Ulster. O'More was one of the leaders entrusted with taking the castle. The plot was, however, betrayed by Owen O'Connolly on the night of 22 October. O'More, suspicious of O'Connolly, had changed his lodgings that night: he evaded arrest and was ferried upriver towards Lucan, where he took shelter with his daughter and her husband, Patrick Sarsfield of co. Dublin, the parents of Patrick *Sarsfield, the Jacobite leader in the 1689–91 war.

As the insurgents reached the limits of their territorial gains in Ulster it was to the south that the momentum of the insurgency was maintained. O'More probably played a role in this strategic reorientation. At any rate he was one of the three leaders of an insurgent column that routed government forces at Julianstown on 29 November 1641, and cut off Drogheda from the south. Some 500 government soldiers were killed in this demoralizing reverse which, if not 'very considerable' (Plunkett, fol. 5), hastened the alliance of the pale nobility with the Ulster insurgents.

While the alliance would probably have been forced on the pale nobility by government hostility, it was certainly facilitated by 'the trust they reposed in Roger Moore, who by his marriage to Sir Patrick Barnwall's daughter, was allied to most of them' (*Irish Confederation*, ed. Gilbert, 1.34–5). In early December they met the insurgents at Knockcrofty, where they were asked 'wherefore they came armed into the pale' (ibid., 36). O'More's masterful reply played on the palesmen's grievances, fears, and aspirations: 'We are the sole subjects, who, being much the more numerous and powerful, are made incapable of raising our fortunes by serving our King in any place of honour, profit or trust, in that country wherein we were born'. He reminded them that the English parliament and the Scottish covenanters would not discriminate between Old English and Gaelic Irish Catholics: 'you are marked forth for destruction as well as we'. He concluded with a powerful appeal to the nascent sense of common Irish identity: 'We are of the same religion and the same nation; our interest and our sufferings are the same; the bonds of friendship and alliance are mutual between us; and, from the highest to the lowest, we affect you dearly'

(ibid., 36). On this showing O'More has been justifiably called 'the most skilful politician among the Irish leaders' (Perceval-Maxwell, 245).

The period from December 1641 to March 1642 saw the insurgents besiege Drogheda, while trying to prevent relief from Dublin by encircling the capital with insurgent encampments. Shortly after the Knockcrofty meeting in early December, O'More set about instigating an insurgent military organization in co. Kildare. Here, as elsewhere, the original *coup d'état* was in danger of being subsumed within a popular revolt characterized by attacks on British civilians. O'More's directions that 'no man should be wronged in goods or body' ('Deposition of William Pilsworth', TCD, MS 813, fol. 3) were typical of the attempts by the insurgent leadership to rein in their followers. This policy was only moderately successful, as evidenced by his followers' killing three household servants after capturing Castle Carbury.

O'More was nominated as one of seven colonels raised from co. Kildare, and served with his regiment at Newcastle, west of Dublin, in January 1642. The following month this force was pushed back from Dublin, and he shifted his attention to the north of Dublin and to Drogheda. In early March 1642 O'More met with Viscount Gormanstown, the leader of the pale nobility, to compose an appeal for help to Mountgarret, the insurgent leader in south Leinster, and to adopt a draft national 'model of government' (*Irish Confederation*, ed. Gilbert, 1.36–7). The plan for a national government ultimately came to fruition in June 1642 with the creation of the supreme council of the confederate Catholics. However, Mountgarret did not respond to the appeal and, shortly afterwards, Ormond relieved Drogheda.

During the spring of 1642, with government forces launching attacks deep into Catholic territory, O'More was placed in command of King's county and the adjacent half of Queen's county. On 15 April the insurgents attempted to intercept the royalist governor, Ormond, on his return march from Athy towards Dublin at Kilrush in co. Kildare. In the subsequent battle O'More, commanding one of the three Irish divisions, repulsed the initial cavalry charge. A subsequent charge, however, scattered the entire insurgent army.

Between July and September 1642 'General Moore' commanded the unsuccessful siege of Birr, King's county (*Irish Confederation*, ed. Gilbert, 1.lxxvii–lxxix). In a letter written from Wexford on 20 September 1642 he complained of the 'troublesome charge of generalship cast on me in upper Leinster' (Meehan, 334). He styled himself Ruri de O'Mora and expressed his intention to set up a school of Irish and acquire a printing press in Irish type. Soon afterwards he was relieved of this 'troublesome charge', being among several officers cashiered during the pruning and reorganization of the Leinster army into six field infantry regiments on regular lines. However, on 14 January 1643 O'More assisted Thomas Preston, the newly appointed general of Leinster, in capturing Birr, using recently acquired siege artillery.

Thereafter, O'More was a marginal figure in the Catholic confederation. In May 1644 he embroiled himself in attempts by Randal Mac Donnell, earl of Antrim, to wrest command of expeditionary forces to attack the Scottish covenanters in Ulster and in Scotland. Antrim had secured the support of many of the cashiered officers. The supreme council, baulking at confronting Antrim, instead arrested O'More and Philip Mac Maolmhuire O'Reilly for inciting the earl. The council described them as 'men of their own disposition turbulent and much taken … with the condition of troublesome times' (cited in Ohlmeyer, 141).

There is a gap in the record of O'More's activities for the years 1645–7, which, intriguingly, corresponds to the service of the confederate Catholic expeditionary force in Scotland, led by Alasdair Mac Colla Mac Donnell. O'More offered to lead a regiment of 1500 men to Scotland, but his name is not included in the list of officers who embarked.

By 1648 the confederate Catholics had split into opposing Ormondist and clericalist parties, supporting and opposing, respectively, a royalist alliance. Owen Roe O'Neill opposed the alliance and employed O'More on his 'cabinet council' (Gilbert, 2.21) and as an envoy. In early 1649 O'More fell out of favour with O'Neill after acting as an intermediary with Ormond. According to the rabidly clericalist author of the *Aphorismical Discovery*, O'More, 'a well spoken gentleman … though no martial man' (ibid.), seized the opportunity to curry favour with Ormond by giving unfounded assurances to both parties of the other's willingness to seek an accommodation.

In August 1650 the Catholic synod of Jamestown repudiated royalist authority and attempted to reassert control over the faltering Irish resistance to the Cromwellian reconquest. O'More was chosen as one of three Leinster representatives on a proposed new Catholic confederation, and also served as a colonel in the reconstituted Leinster army. In June 1651 the army moved to Connaught belatedly to defend the Shannon line. Between November and December 1652 O'More was serving in one of the last royalist outposts, Inishbofin. He escaped to co. Donegal before the final surrender of the island early in 1653.

O'More was exempted from pardon for life or estate by the 1652 Cromwellian Act of Settlement, and, if apprehended, he would certainly have been executed. However, the authorities believed that he had escaped abroad and died. According to a family memoir, he worked in co. Donegal as a herd for a time, under an assumed identity, until his employer caught him reading a book behind a hedge and dismissed him, saying that he needed a herd, not a scholar. From there he moved to south co. Armagh. Corroboration that he lived for some years afterwards comes from the affidavits of two Irishmen in Madrid in September and October 1666, when Daniel O'Neill (husband of O'More's daughter Leonor) was made knight of the military order of Calatrava. The later of the two affidavits stated that the deponent 'receives letters regularly from Leonor's father, Rory O Moore, who is at present living in Ireland' (Walsh, 137). After the Restoration, Rory O'More's eldest son, Charles, recovered most of the Carbury estate through the court of claims. PÁDRAIG LENIHAN

Sources J. T. Gilbert, ed., *A contemporary history of affairs in Ireland from 1641 to 1652*, 1 (1879), 41, 605, 652, 747, 751; 2 (1879), 21, 114, 158; 3 (1879), 143 · *History of the Irish confederation and the war in Ireland … by Richard Bellings*, ed. J. T. Gilbert, 1 (1882), 34–7, 79–80 · E. O'Leary, 'The O'More family of Balyna in the county Kildare, by James More of Balyna circa 1774', *Journal of the Kildare Archaeological and Historical Society*, 9 (1918–22), 277–91 · [N. Plunkett (?)], 'An account of the war in Ireland since 1641', NL Ire., MS 345, fols. 2–5, 9 · B. O'Ferrall and D. O'Connell, *Commentarius Rinuccinianus de sedis apostolicae legatione ad foederatos Hiberniae Catholicos per annos 1645–1649*, ed. J. Kavanagh, 6 vols., IMC (1932–49), vol. 3, p. 509; vol. 4, pp. 592, 603; vol. 5, pp. 38, 50, 64 · M. Walsh, 'Further notes towards a history of the womenfolk of the wild geese', *Irish Sword*, 5 (1961–2), 133–45 · M. Perceval-Maxwell, *The outbreak of the Irish rebellion of 1641* (1994), 46, 199, 205–11, 245 · A. Clarke, *The Old English in Ireland, 1625–1642* (New York, 1966), 156, 158, 160, 177, 179–82, 191, 211, 225, 227 · D. Cregan, 'The confederate Catholics in Ireland: the personnel of the confederation, 1642–49', *Irish Historical Studies*, 29 (1994–5), esp. 495, 507 · C. P. Meehan, *The rise and fall of the Irish Franciscan monasteries, and memoirs of the Irish hierarchy in the seventeenth century*, 4th edn (1872), 334 · J. H. Ohlmeyer, *Civil war and Restoration in the three Stuart kingdoms: the career of Randal MacDonnell, marquis of Antrim, 1609–1683* (1993), 141 · examination of Lewis O'Moore, TCD, MS 813, fols. 99, 128

O'More, Rory Caoch MacConnell (d. 1545). See under O'More, Rory Oge (c.1540–1578).

O'More, Rory Oge [Ruaidhri Óg Ua Mordha] (c.1540–1578), chieftain and rebel, was the eldest son of Rory Caoch Mac-Connell O'More [*see below*] and his first wife, Margaret, daughter of Thomas Butler and granddaughter of Piers Butler, eighth earl of Ormond. **Rory Caoch MacConnell O'More** [Ruaidhrí Caoch Ua Mordha] (d. 1545), chieftain, was the son of Connell O'More (d. 1537), chieftain, of Leix (Laois) and succeeded his father as chieftain of Leix in 1537. Rory Caoch ('the one-eyed' or 'the blind') was captain of Leix. The O'More family was one of the most important of the minor Irish septs, or clans, and among the most implacable opponents of the government's policy of plantation because their lands, along with the O'Connor lands, were the first to be appropriated for this scheme. Rory Caoch's elder brother Kedagh succeeded Connell after much internal fighting. Kedagh died early in 1542 and was succeeded by Rory Caoch.

The government's botched attempts to protect the pale against raids by outlying septs after Kildare's rebellion (1534–5) engendered anarchy in the midlands. Sir Anthony St Leger, the lord deputy, opted for a policy of conciliation through the conclusion of a surrender and regrant arrangement with Rory Caoch on 13 May 1542. However, this failed to stabilize the pale because Rory Caoch was deposed and murdered by his younger brother Giollaphádraig in 1545. Following the prosecution of that usurper the government, weary of Irish raids against the pale, decided to plant soldier–settlers in Leix and Offaly (later renamed Queen's county and King's county) to contain the native population. In 1549 the first contingents of these colonists arrived in Leix-Offaly to take up their grants, but it was not until 1556 that the colony was officially established. The O'Mores, now under the leadership of Connell Oge MacConnell (d. 1557), refused to acquiesce in the scheme, and began to raid the settlements from hideaways in the impenetrable Gallen woods of western Leix after 1556. As native resistance hardened, Thomas Radcliffe, third earl of Sussex, the lord deputy, resorted increasingly to martial law to maintain order. Connell Oge was hanged in chains from Leighlin Bridge, co. Carlow, in 1557, but resistance continued sporadically until 1564, by which time thirty-five of the leading O'Mores had been killed by the colonists, who quickly earned a reputation for high-handedness among the Irish: 'If it were ones spoken of a … captens mouthe it was a sufficient quarell for the capten to rob, pray and kill the person … and all his tenantes withowt other attoryte or commiscon then the captens owne allegacon' (PRO, SP 63/1/84).

Rory Oge O'More's early years, c.1540-1571 Sir Henry Sidney, the lord deputy, described Rory Oge as an 'obscure and base varlet', despite the importance of the O'More sept. Rory Oge was the most vigorous and most notorious leader of the midland septs opposed to the government's expropriation of their lands. His main significance was that he came to typify the incorrigibility of the Gaelic élite in the eyes of the New English. Little is known of his formative years. He was fostered with the O'Byrnes for a time, probably with Hugh MacShane O'Byrne, chief of the Gabhal Raghnaill branch of the O'Byrne clan, given the extent of Rory Oge's attachment to his family. He was close to Hugh MacShane's son Fiach MacHugh *O'Byrne (c.1544–1597), and married Margaret (d. 1577), daughter of Hugh MacShane O'Byrne and his first wife, Sadhbh, about 1573. Among their children was Owny MacRory *O'More (b. in or before 1577, d. 1600). Rory Oge's sept, the MacRorys, was left landless as a result of the reorganization of landholding in Leix in 1564. Rory Oge was forced to enter the service of Sir John Fitzgerald of Desmond, the younger brother of Gerald fitz James Fitzgerald, fourteenth earl of Desmond, as a swordsman. He returned to Leix by 1570 and began negotiations with the government for a grant of lands, similar to those granted to his cousins Laoighseach and Cathaoir MacKedagh in 1566.

How Rory Oge emerged as leader of the O'Mores in rebellion against the government less than a year later is somewhat unclear. The decisive factor may have been Sidney's arbitrary execution of Laoighseach and Cathaoir MacKedagh, who were both implicated in the Butler revolt in 1569–70. Sidney subsequently decided to 'bare such a hand upon the whole name of the OMores as I trust the Quenes countye shalbe a quiet countye' (PRO, SP 63/30/52). Rory Oge survived the 1570 purge only because he was in the service of Francis Cosby, seneschal of Queen's county, and occupant of Stradbally, his paternal inheritance in co. Leix (now Laois). He was suspicious of Sidney's intentions and refused to meet government officials. In February 1571 Sir William Fitzwilliam, Sidney's successor as lord deputy, observed that Rory Oge was gathering men from among the disgruntled midland septs, and appeared about to 'go out' (PRO, SP 63/31/8). Rory Oge

secured election as chief of his sept in April and rebelled in May.

First rebellion, 1571–1577 That Rory Oge rebelled in order to avenge his kin was suggested by a number of sources, and also by his own indictment of the government's policy towards the leading O'Mores: 'farr betters of his name submytted them selves to the late Lord Deputy and sarved him and that they were after taken and executed'. He refused to disperse his men for this reason, claiming he 'hath no other assurance of his lyfe'. Yet the hidden intention of Rory Oge's rebellion, as Thomas Butler, tenth earl of Ormond, and Gerald Fitzgerald, eleventh earl of Kildare, with whom he parleyed in August 1572, surmised, was to put pressure on the government to grant him the barony of 'Gallen … which he sought afore' (PRO, SP 63/37/37). Rory Oge subsequently submitted and was pardoned after this, while his claim was sent for government arbitration.

In December 1572, having received no response to his petitions, Rory Oge resumed hostilities in order to hasten consideration of his claim. His use of guerrilla warfare against the settlers proved impossible to contain, especially because he adopted the brutal methods of the midlands planters, using them against the same, which won him much support from the region's dispossessed Gaelic élite. Supported by the O'Connors, O'Byrnes, and O'Kavanaghs, Rory Oge used the densely wooded area of Gallen as a base. In 'smalle companies or grete, as ocascon requireth or as the turn is best sarved, the rebel issueth into the heart of the Queens Countye and thence into every parte of the Pale spoylinge the same at pleasure' (PRO, SP 63/38/41). Indeed, by February 1573 so effective had Rory Oge's campaign proved that the government was considering methods 'of so manie circumstances, as it cannot be so comitted to writing but it will admit matters disputable', to end his rebellion (PRO, SP 63/39/27). In another effort to advance his petitions he again submitted (November 1573) but immediately aided the earl of Desmond's escape from Dublin later that month, providing a 400-strong escort for the fugitive through the midlands.

No resolution had been achieved by 1575, when Sidney, again lord deputy, observed that Rory Oge 'hath that Possession, and Settling Place' in Leix, and 'listeth and wasteth what he will'. Recognizing that the devastated midlands would continue to suffer unless Rory Oge was given a living, Sidney offered him lands, provided he accepted the plantation. Rory Oge submitted in St Canice's Cathedral, Kilkenny, 'repenting (as he said) his former Fawltes, and promisinge hereafter, to lyve in better Sorte (for woorsse than he hath ben he cannot be)'. He was, however, more ambitious than before and Sidney warned him that unless he abandoned his 'aspiringe imagination of tytle to the countrie' he would lose 'lyffe, land and all' (PRO, SP 63/54/17). Although Rory Oge was pardoned on 4 June 1576, Sidney, disquieted by his continuing claim to authority over Leix, did not settle his demands.

Second rebellion, 1577–1578 In March 1577, after ten months of peace, Rory Oge broke the stalemate through a devastating raid, and burnt to the ground the town of Naas, co. Kildare. This sealed his fate. Sidney decided drastic action was required and Cosby received an extensive commission of martial law authorizing him to eradicate 'with fire and sword Rory Oge … and all other traitors and rebels in any place where they may be found' (*Irish Fiants*, no. 2997). By August 150 O'Mores had been killed. As his programme and reputation were subjected to unprecedented criticism, Sidney's frustration with Rory Oge, whom he made a paradigm of the opposition he was encountering in Ireland, clearly boiled over. Infuriated by mounting costs and constant resistance, he decided to wage 'as actuall and as cunning warre' upon Rory Oge as possible (Sidney, 1860, 185). A sea change in governmental attitudes to the Irish population occurred, and some New English officials were already articulating the view that normal ethical restraints did not apply when dealing with the native Irish. A rare contemporary Gaelic source states that Rory Oge was subjected to unprecedented attention, relating how his wife, Margaret, was killed on government orders, 'and with her have been killed women, and boys, and humble folk, and people young and old, who, according to all seeming, deserved not to be put to the sword' ('agus mna agus macaim agus mindaoine oga agus arsaidhi do marbhadh maille ria nach ar thuill a marbhadh do fer bharamhla'; Royal Irish Academy, MS 24.14.170).

As the hunt for Rory Oge intensified, the authorities were confounded by their continued failure to apprehend him: 'for never Wretche, beinge so longe and earnestlye followed, hath continued on Foote so longe'. His frequent narrow escapes from his pursuers were attributed to 'Sorcerie or Enchauntement', as he assumed the guise of bogeyman for the English soldiers and administrators (PRO, SP 63/61/29). Sir Nicholas Malby, governor of Connaught, described Rory Oge as the only Robin Hood of Ireland, while John Derricke characterized him as a wolf. In 1599 his reputation as a demonic force was confirmed when Sir John Harington, the courtier and author, wrote that he had escaped his pursuers 'by dint of witchery, and had by magic compelled them not to touch him' (Harington, 2.23–4).

In November 1577 Rory Oge captured two leading figures of the midland garrison, Alexander Cosby and Henry Harington, Sidney's nephew, whom he paraded in chains 'like a slave'. Thereafter the dispute with Sidney assumed an even more personal edge because the lord deputy was outraged by the slight on his family's honour. Even when trapped by Sidney's forces in a cabin, Rory Oge managed to break Harington's arm, to 'cutt off the little finger of one of his handes' and to inflict serious head injuries, before 'miraculously' escaping through the legs of his besiegers. Sidney's forces then proceeded to massacre the cabin's remaining occupants, including Rory Oge's wife and two young sons (Sidney, 1860, 185–6). Rory Oge responded in kind, burning Leighlin and Carlow and beheading those soldiers he could capture.

In March 1578 the government's frustration was revealed when its forces, including Cosby, massacred some of Rory Oge's supporters at Mullaghmast, co. Kildare. Since the O'Mores had convened there under a protection for parley, the Irish annalists were prompted to claim that 'no uglier deed than that was ever committed in Ireland' ('ní dhearnadh in Éirinn riamh gníomh ba ghránna ná sin'; Hennessy, vol. 2, s.a. 1567 [*sic*]). By this point the noose around Rory Oge was tightening. Attempting to ease the pressure, on 30 June he tried to entice one of his most dogged pursuers, Barnaby Fitzpatrick, second baron of Upper Ossory, into an ambush. Anticipating treachery, Upper Ossory concealed the kerne (light foot soldiers) he had with him, and, when Rory Oge appeared:

> the Lord of Upperosseries Kerne, gave the chardge upon hym, and at their Reencounter one of theim light upon hym, and thrust hym presentlye thorough the Boddie with his Swoorde, which was no soner donne, but twoe or three more likewise hacked upon hym at once, and gave hym soch mortall Woundes, as downe he fell: and this was the Ende of this rancke Rebell.   (Collins, 1.263–5)

Despite attempts by Upper Ossory's men to seize it, Rory Oge's body was carried off by his own followers; however, the head was attained soon after and delivered to Sidney, who had it mounted on Dublin Castle. The annalists recorded of Rory Oge that 'there was not in Ireland a greater destroyer against foreigners than that man: and he was a very great loss' ('agus ní raibh a nEirinn fear millte ar Ghaill bá mhó ná fear sin agus fá ro mór'; Hennessy, vol. 2, s.a. 1578).

Rory Oge's death marked the end of O'More efforts to restore the old order of Gaelic lordship, or at least to secure a stake in the plantation. Although his son Owny MacRory O'More managed to raise the O'More banner again in the 1590s, it was only with the support of Hugh O'Neill, second earl of Tyrone. Never again were the O'Mores capable of threatening either the pale or the midlands plantation. On a wider plane Rory Oge's career was critical in the breakdown of the conciliation strategy. Derricke's *Image of Irelande* (1581) reveals the role Rory Oge played in the changing New English mentality. Rory Oge was characterized as a savage wood kerne addicted by nature to rapine and rebellion and depicted as 'a lively image and pattern of rebellion', rather than as a dispossessed member of the Irish élite fighting for his lands. He was cast as the leader of a 'crooked generation', whose 'ireful hearts' were 'bent to every kind of ill' (*Image of Irelande*, 183–8, 199–205). Both contemporary Gaelic commentators and critics of the New English administration identified in the period 1549–78 an increasing breakdown in the rules of war in the midlands. This affected the conduct of New English settlers in their dealings with the disaffected Irish élite. Rory Oge's significance is that he provided the most potent symbol of Irish opposition to the government's reform effort. The government's solution to his vigorous and determined campaign was extermination. Some 725 O'Mores were killed by 1578 and this departure from normal ethical conventions provided the ideological conditions for the wars of extermination in Munster and Ulster which completed the conquest of Ireland at the close of the sixteenth century.

DAVID FINNEGAN

Sources AFM · St Edmund Campion, *Two bokes of the histories of Ireland*, ed. A. F. Vossen (Assen, 1963) · V. P. Carey, 'Gaelic reaction to plantation: the case of the O'More and O'Connor lordships of Leix and Offaly', MA diss., St Patrick's College, 1982 · V. P. Carey, 'The end of the Gaelic political order: the O'More lordship of Laois, 1536–1603', *Laois history and society*, ed. P. Lane (Dublin, 1999) · H. Sydney and others, *Letters and memorials of state*, ed. A. Collins, 2 vols. (1746) · J. Derricke, *The image of Irelande*, ed. D. B. Quinn (1985) · R. Dunlop, 'The plantation of Leix and Offaly', *EngHR*, 6 (1891), 61–96 · J. Harington, *Nugae antiquae*, ed. T. Park and H. Harington, 2 vols. (1804) · W. M. Hennessy, ed. and trans., *The annals of Loch Cé: a chronicle of Irish affairs from AD 1014 to AD 1590*, 2 vols., Rolls Series, 54 (1871) · *Holinshed's Irish chronicle*, ed. L. Miller and E. Power, new edn (1979) · *The Irish fiants of the Tudor sovereigns*, 4 vols. (1994) · *DNB* · Royal Irish Acad., MS 24.14.170 · H. Sidney, 'Memoir of government in Ireland', *Ulster Journal of Archaeology*, 1st ser., 3 (1855), 33–44, 85–90, 336–57 · H. Sidney, 'Memoir of government in Ireland', *Ulster Journal of Archaeology*, 1st ser., 5 (1857), 299–315 · H. Sidney, 'Memoir of government in Ireland', *Ulster Journal of Archaeology*, 1st ser., 8 (1860), 179–95 · state papers Ireland, Henry VIII, PRO, SP 60 · state papers Ireland, Edward VI, PRO, SP 61 · state papers Ireland, Philip and Mary, PRO, SP 62 · state papers Ireland, Elizabeth, PRO, SP 63 · 'The submission of Rory Caech O'More, chief of Leix, 1542', *Kildare Archaeological Society Journal*, 6 (1909–11), 79 · 'A map of the King's and Queen's counties alias Leix and Offaly', 1563, TCD, MS 1209, 9

Ó Neachtain, Seán [John Naughton] (1645×50?–1729), poet and writer, was born at Cluain Oileáin in co. Roscommon, near Athlone and Ballinasloe, probably between 1645 and 1650. He went to Dublin as a young man, perhaps as early as 1670 and certainly before 1690. In the early 1700s he was teaching at a school in co. Meath, probably near Trim; he was certainly there in 1715. He married twice and both his wives were named Úna. The first was Úna Nagle (or Nangle), who died about 1703, and the second was Úna Byrne, who may have been a relative of the Catholic archbishop of Dublin, Edmund Byrne. Ó Neachtain is known to have had three children: Tadhg *Ó Neachtain, who himself became an Irish scholar, and Luke and Anna.

Samples of Ó Neachtain's handwriting show him to have been a capable scribe, but his reputation in his own day and the present rests on his achievements as a poet and as a writer of stories in Irish. He composed political Jacobite poems, love poems, elegies, and literary burlesques. One of the last, called *Cath Bhearna na croise Bríde* ('The Battle at the Gap at Bridget's Cross', probably near Blessington, co. Wicklow), is an amusing tale of a rustic row between the potato growers of the hills and the corn growers of the plains and it is derivative of similar satirical works composed in the early seventeenth century. It is full of literary and topical allusions, some of which are now obscure. Ó Neachtain composed a poetic invitation to his wife, probably Úna Nagle, 'Rachainn fón choill leat' ('I would go into the wood with you'), in which he promises her that if she comes with him they will be accompanied by the joyous music of nature. Such invitations are sometimes refused, but in this case she gladly accepts. It is not surprising that another of his best poems is an elegy, probably for the same lady, in which he raises a common lament to a high personal plane by repeating a line in which he expresses the desire that he should die and be buried with her. However, there is little originality in his poetry and it is his prose that is most innovative. Unfortunately this literature has circulated only in manuscript apart from one of his prose stories *Stair Éamainn Uí Chléire* ('The Story of Eamonn O'Clery'), which was edited by Eoghan Ó Neachtain in 1918. This is an allegorical tale, probably based on the author's own life, in which he tells how the eponymous hero travels from Roscommon to Dublin, struggles to overcome his penchant for drink and debauchery, and is finally saved by the advice of a friend, 'Aogán Feartach' ('miraculous Egan'), probably Seán's good friend the Franciscan friar and fellow poet Paul Egan. The tale, which is like an embryonic novel in Irish, is notable for its bilingual punning and other word play. His other prose works include *Jacobides agus Carina* (an imaginary story about the Jacobite hero, James, duke of Berwick, and his wife), *An gleacaí géaglonnach* ('The Stout-limbed Champion'), and *Imtheachta an chúigir* ('The Adventures of the Five'), the last two being pseudo-romantic heroic tales. These works circulated in manuscript among the coterie of Irish language scholars in Dublin in the early eighteenth century, promoted mainly by the efforts of Ó Neachtain's son Tadhg, and earned him the reputation of being 'the shining light of the scholars' (*niamh na scol*). The lack of proper editions of his poetry and prose has confined Ó Neachtain's reputation to those who are acquainted with the manuscript tradition.

A colophon in a manuscript written by his son Tadhg says that Ó Neachtain died in Tadhg's house in Earl Street in the Dublin liberties on Sunday 9 March 1729, at nine o'clock in the morning.

ALAN HARRISON

Sources A. Harrison, *The dean's friend: Anthony Raymond, 1675–1726, Jonathan Swift, and the Irish language* (1999) · A. Harrison, *Ag cruinniú meala: Anthony Raymond (1675–1726)* (Baile Átha Cliath, 1988) · S. H. O'Grady, ed., *Catalogue of Irish manuscripts in the British Museum*, 2, ed. R. Flower (1926) · N. Ní Shéaghdha, 'Irish scholars and scribes in eighteenth-century Dublin', *Eighteenth-Century Ireland*, 4 (1989), 41–54 · C. Ó Háinle, 'Ar bhás Sheáin Uí Neachtain', *Éigse*, 19 (1982–3), 384–94 · M. H. Risk, 'Seán Ó Neachtain', *Studia Hibernica*, 15 (1975), 47–60 · E. Ó Neachtain, *Stair Éamainn Uí Chléire* (1918) · N. J. A. Williams, 'Cath Bearna na croise Brighde', *Zeitschrift für Celtische Philologie*, 38 (1981), 269–337 · A. Harrison, 'Literature in Irish, 1600–1800', *The field day anthology of Irish literature*, ed. S. Deane, A. Carpenter, and J. Williams (1991), 324 · T. F. O'Rahilly, 'Poem on Dublin scholars', *Gadelica* (1913), 154–62

Archives BL, MSS · King's Inns, Dublin, MSS · NL Ire., MSS · Royal Irish Acad., MSS · TCD, MSS · University College, Dublin, MSS

Ó Neachtain, Tadhg [Thady Naughton or Norton] (*c.*1670–*c.*1752), scribe and lexicographer, was probably the eldest son of Seán *Ó Neachtain (1645×50?–1729) and his first wife, Úna Nagle (*d. c.*1703), and was born about 1670, maybe even in Dublin itself. He spent most of his adult life in the liberties of the capital city. With his father's reputation as a writer and his own interest and diligence as a scribe he became the fulcrum of the coterie of Irish language scholars who were working in Dublin in the early years of the eighteenth century. Between 1726 and 1728 he wrote a poem in Irish in which he named twenty-six such scholars of his acquaintance. He himself was patronized by Anthony Raymond, vicar of Trim, and friend of Jonathan Swift, by Francis Stoughton Sullivan, professor of law at Trinity College, Dublin, and by Charles O'Conor of Belanagare. Ó Neachtain's own function in the circle seems to have been that of intermediary between the scribes and the patrons and encourager and collaborator with them. Two entries in one of his manuscripts indicate that he had a collection of books and manuscripts and that he had lent some of them to his friends. The scribal activity associated with this group resulted in more than a hundred manuscripts which are now extant and there seems to be a direct connection between Ó Neachtain and more than thirty of these.

Ó Neachtain is recorded as teaching a 'popish' school during the 1720s and 1730s, first of all in Coll Alley and later in Earl Street, both within the Dublin liberties. Some or most of this teaching may have been carried out through the medium of Irish. This would explain his translation, or version, of *Geography Anatomized* by Patrick Gordon (1699) and his tendency to translate interesting items from the Dublin daily and weekly prints. He was a natural lexicographer, many of his manuscripts containing word-lists, and texts that he copied into his own manuscripts are often glossed in the margins. When the Franciscan Francis Walsh died in 1724 without completing his Latin–English–Irish dictionary, Ó Neachtain finished it. He then compiled an Irish–English dictionary, completed about 1743, which still has its uses. It is likely that the manuscript copy of this, now in the library of Trinity College, Dublin, was prepared either for a patron or for publication.

Ó Neachtain married four times. His first wife was Caitríona Nic Fheorais (Catherine Corish), and a son of this marriage, Peter, became a Jesuit and visited Spain in the mid-1730s, taking one of his father's manuscripts with him which he signed 'Santiago, Spain, Dr Pedro Norton' (the common Anglicization of Ó Neachtain). Tadhg celebrated his son's birth in 1709 by a colophon in a manuscript and the trip to Spain with a long poem. Caitríona died in 1714 and soon after Ó Neachtain married Máire Ní Chomáin, who died in childbirth towards the end of 1715. The next year he married Máire Ní Reachtagáin (Rhatigan), who lived until 1733. His last marriage was to Isabel Ní Lárrach and she survived until 1745. Ó Neachtain travelled in Ireland, probably in the service of his patrons. Thus in other colophons he tells of his being on the road to Trim, co. Meath, presumably to visit Anthony Raymond and, perhaps, his father, and also of going to Roscommon to visit Charles O'Conor. Other manuscript notes imply that in 1727 he visited France to seek out Irish books and manuscripts that had been taken there, probably by the 'wild geese' after 1691. He may have wished to make copies of these for himself or for a patron, or indeed to buy them. He often mentions his failing eyesight, but

although it may have slowed up his scribal output there are manuscript items from his hand until his death, in Earl Street, Dublin, where he lived, about 1752.

ALAN HARRISON

Sources A. Harrison, *The dean's friend: Anthony Raymond, 1675–1726, Jonathan Swift, and the Irish language* (1999) • A. Harrison, *Ag cruinniú meala: Anthony Raymond (1675–1726)* (Baile Átha Cliath, 1988) • S. H. O'Grady, ed., *Catalogue of Irish manuscripts in the British Museum*, 2, ed. R. Flower (1926) • N. Ní Shéaghdha, *Catalogue of Irish manuscripts in the National Library of Ireland*, 9 vols. (1961–) • N. Ní Shéaghdha, 'Irish scholars and scribes in eighteenth-century Dublin', *Eighteenth-Century Ireland*, 4 (1989), 41–54 • C. N. Buttimer, 'An Irish text on the "War of Jenkin's Ear"', *Celtica*, 21 (1990), 75–98 • C. Ó Háinle, 'Ar bhás Sheáin Uí Neachtain', *Éigse*, 19 (1982–3), 384–94 • TCD, Irish MSS, H.1.6, H.4.20, H.2.6, H.5.27 • Royal Irish Acad., MS 24. P. 41 • T. Ó Cléirigh, 'A student's voyage', *Éigse*, 1 (1939–40), 103–15 • C. Ó Háinle, 'A life in eighteenth-century Dublin: Tadhg Ó Neachtain', *Feile Zozimus* [Dublin, 1991], ed. V. Uibh Eachach (1992), 10–28
Archives BL, MSS • King's Inns, Dublin, MSS • NL Scot., MSS • Royal Irish Acad., MSS • TCD, MSS

O'Neal, Jeffrey Hamet (*fl.* 1766–1772), miniature painter, was a native of Ireland. He practised for many years in London and exhibited occasionally with the Incorporated Society of Artists, of which he was a fellow and whose declaration roll he signed in 1766. He is also stated to have painted landscapes, natural history, and 'Japan' pieces, the last for Smith, a printseller in Cheapside. In addition he worked for a porcelain factory at Worcester, where he painted 'incorrect but very charming figure, animal and landscape subjects' (Foskett, 611). In 1772 O'Neal was living in Lawrence Street, Chelsea.

L. H. CUST, *rev.* ANNETTE PEACH

Sources W. G. Strickland, *A dictionary of Irish artists*, 2 vols. (1913) • D. Foskett, *Miniatures: dictionary and guide* (1987)

O'Neil, Henry Nelson (1817–1880), historical genre painter, was born on 7 January 1817 in St Petersburg, Russia, of British parents. Of his early life nothing is known, except that at the age of six, in 1823, O'Neil went to England with his family. By 1836 he was enrolled at the Royal Academy Schools and there O'Neil met Alfred Elmore, who became a close friend. In the late 1830s they were founding members of The Clique, a sketching club, together with Richard Dadd, Augustus Egg, William Powell Frith, and John Phillip. All were diligent students with differing views on art, who wished to depict modern subjects with a strong emotional element, as a rebellion against the authority of the Royal Academy. They sought to paint better and met every week to draw on a theme, later discussing, comparing, and judging their sketches. O'Neil, in particular, wanted his work to appeal to the viewers' emotions. In 1838 he exhibited his first pictures: at the Royal Academy *A Student* and at the Society of British Artists in Suffolk Street *A Jewish Doctor*, but his work did not receive much notice until after his return from a trip to Italy with Elmore in 1840. O'Neil exhibited fourteen paintings at the Suffolk Street gallery from 1838 until 1843, and thirty-four pictures at the British Institution from 1839 until 1861. All his major works were shown at the Royal Academy, including more than ninety paintings between 1838 and 1879.

The two works for which O'Neil is best-known were *Eastward Ho! August 1857* (exh. RA, 1858; priv. coll.) and *Home Again, 1858* (exh. RA, 1859; priv. coll.). The subject of *Eastward Ho!* was the Indian mutiny of August 1857, when the greatest number of British troops departed for India to suppress the mutiny of the Bengal army. When the Royal Academy exhibition opened in May 1858, news of the massacres and reprisals still dominated the news. The picture's appeal to patriotic fervour and its focus on the domestic side of military life ensured that it was an immediate success: the picture drew huge crowds, exceeded only by those looking at W. P. Frith's *Derby Day*. The success of O'Neil's embarkation painting led to its sequel in the following year, *Home Again, 1858*, where several of the same figures are shown receiving the returning soldiers, a picture that was only slightly less successful in drawing the crowds. Both paintings are examples of the depiction of current events as narratives that are particularly moving because of their implied themes of separation and family loss. Both pictures, like others of O'Neil's paintings, were engraved and widely distributed, and gained great popularity. These two paintings were so much sought after that O'Neil painted several versions in varying sizes, as well as copies of details of some of the main figures. On the basis of their success O'Neil was elected an associate of the Royal Academy in 1860, although he never became a Royal Academician. His pictorial pageants also include *The Landing of her Royal Highness the Princess Alexandra at Gravesend, 7th March 1863* (exh. RA, 1864; NPG).

In the 1860s O'Neil also began to produce portraits, scenes of famous artists, and landscapes. He also played the violin, and wrote on art. O'Neil's published works include *Modern Art in England and France* (1869) and *The Age of Stucco: a Satire in Three Cantos* (1871). He also published the lectures on painting he gave at the Royal Academy. The quality of his art declined in later years. He was a member of the Garrick Club and counted among his friends Elmore, Frith, Frederic Leighton, John Everett Millais, and the novelists Charles Reade and Anthony Trollope. O'Neil died at his home—7 Victoria Road, Kensington, London—on 13 March 1880, leaving a widow, Claudia Anne Greatorex. He was buried at Kensal Green. The contents of his studio were sold by Christie, Manson, and Wood on 18 June 1880. Anthony Trollope in an obituary describes him as 'one who was simple, just, and affectionate as a child' (*The Times*). DELLA CLASON SPERLING

Sources *Men of the time* (1875), 774–5 · A. Trollope, *The Times* (15 March 1880), 6 · *Art Journal*, 42 (1880), 171 · Graves, *RA exhibitors* · Graves, *Brit. Inst.* · Graves, *Artists* · J. Imray, 'A reminiscence of sixty years ago', *Art Journal*, new ser., 18 (1898), 202 · C. Forbes, *The Royal Academy (1837–1901) revisited: Victorian paintings from the Forbes collection* (New York, 1975), 114–15, 176–7 · S. West, 'Henry Nelson O'Neil', *The dictionary of art*, ed. J. Turner (1996), 442 · *DNB* · *CGPLA Eng. & Wales* (1880)
Likenesses H. N. O'Neil, self-portrait, group portrait, 1864 (*The landing of HRH the Princess Alexandra at Gravesend, 7th March 1863*), NPG · H. N. O'Neil, self-portrait, oils, 1864, NPG · H. N. O'Neil, group portrait, oils, 1869 (*The billiard room of the Garrick Club*), Garr. Club · H. N. O'Neil, self-portrait, oils, 1873, Garr. Club · Window & Bridge, carte-de-visite, NPG
Wealth at death under £3000: probate, 31 March 1880, *CGPLA Eng. & Wales*

O'Neill. *See also* O'Neal, O'Neil, Ó Néill, Ua Néill.

O'Neill. For this title name *see* individual entries under O'Neill; *see also* Fleming, Ann Geraldine Mary [Ann Geraldine Mary O'Neill, Lady O'Neill] (1913–1981).

Ó Néill, Aodh [Hugh O'Neill, Aodh Méith] (d. **1230**), king of Tír Eoghain, was the son of Áed an Macaem Tóinlesc (the 'Lazy-Rumped Lad'; d. 1177), who is said to have earned his unusual sobriquet by refusing to rise respectfully to greet his rival kinsman, the high-king Muirchertach Mac Lochlainn (d. 1166). The accession of Ruaidrí Ó Conchobair (d. 1198) to the high-kingship of Ireland in 1166 weakened the Mac Lochlainn family, and Áed an Macaem Tóinlesc Ó Néill shared the kingship of Tír Eoghain with a Mac Lochlainn in 1167–9, enjoyed a brief spell in sole power c.1170–1174, but was deposed before his death, which took place in the same year as the Anglo-Norman invasion of Ulster under John de Courcy.

Aodh Méith (the epithet means 'the Fat') is first recorded in 1199 leading a fleet of five ships to harry the Larne district of Antrim in retaliation for a raid by Courcy on Derry and Inishowen. His successful wars against Tír Conaill (the Donegal area) and Ó hEignigh of Fermanagh that year show Ó Néill leading men from Inishowen and Mag Íotha, or the west bank of the Foyle, traditional homelands of the Mac Lochlainn family. Perhaps it was after this campaign that he married Bean Midhe (d. 1215), the daughter of Ó hEignigh. In 1200–01 Ó Néill repelled a series of Anglo-Norman raids on southern Tír Eoghain, then joined Ó hEignigh on an expedition into Connacht, to support Cathal Croibhdhearg Ó Conchobair (d. 1224) against Cathal Carrach Ó Conchobair and William de Burgh (d. 1206). The annals say the northern Irish were taken unawares by the presence of Anglo-Normans in Cathal Carrach's army and were withdrawing when they were overtaken and defeated, Ó hEignigh being killed and Ó Néill forced to submit and give hostages. On his return home Ó Néill was briefly deposed in favour of Conchobhar Beag Mac Lochlainn, who was, however, slain the same year when Éigneachán, the first Ó Domhnaill king of Tír Conaill (d. 1208), raided Inishowen.

After some years' struggle against both Mac Lochlainn and Ó Domhnaill claims on Derry and Inishowen, Ó Néill concluded a truce c.1208–9 with Domhnall Mór Ó Domhnaill (d. 1241) which the four masters call 'an alliance against such of the English or Irish as should oppose them'. Meanwhile John de Courcy, deposed from the lordship of Ulster in 1205, sought refuge in Tír Eoghain, drawing down punitive raids in 1207 from his successor, Earl Hugh de Lacy (d. c.1243), who failed to exact submission or hostages from Ó Néill. Aodh Méith also refused hostages when he met King John at the siege of Carrickfergus in 1210, during that monarch's expedition to Ireland to expel the rebellious Lacy. However, after the English king departed, his officials exacted a fine of 293 cows from Ó Néill and 321 cows as rent for Tír Eoghain, the earldom of

Ulster being now in the king's hands. The northern coastline was granted away to King John's Scottish allies, Alan Fitzroland and Thomas of Galloway, who mounted a series of raids and built a castle at Coleraine, while the justiciar, Bishop John de Gray of Norwich, built three castles along Ó Néill's southern borders at Belleek, Clones, and Newry, all of which Aodh Méith destroyed in 1213–14, with the assistance of the other Ulster chiefs. He burnt the town of Carlingford in 1214 and raided the Anglo-Normans of eastern Ulster the following year.

The English chancery addressed Ó Néill as one among many Irish vassal kings in a circular letter of 1221, but he soon defied the Anglo-Irish government again, in support of the dispossessed Hugh de Lacy, destroying the castle of Coleraine in 1222 and blocking William (II) Marshal's attempt to enter Ulster with the royal army in 1224. He made destructive king-making expeditions into Connacht in 1225 and 1226, with only temporary success, though he did exact hostages from Tír Conaill on the same campaign. To the surprise of the annalist, this warlike chief died a natural death in 1230, leaving his son Domhnall (d. c.1235), ancestor of the Clann Aodha Buidhe, or Clandeboye O'Neills, to dispute his kingship with Domhnall Mac Lochlainn (d. 1241).   KATHARINE SIMMS

Sources W. M. Hennessy and B. MacCarthy, eds., *Annals of Ulster, otherwise, annals of Senat*, 4 vols. (1887–1901), vol. 2 · W. M. Hennessy, ed. and trans., *The annals of Loch Cé: a chronicle of Irish affairs from AD 1014 to AD 1590*, 1, Rolls Series, 54 (1871) · G. H. Orpen, *Ireland under the Normans*, 4 vols. (1911–20), vols. 2–3 · K. Simms, 'Tír Eoghain north of the Mountain', *Derry and Londonderry: history and society*, ed. G. O'Brien (1999) · *AFM*, vol. 3 · A. M. Freeman, ed. and trans., *Annála Connacht / The annals of Connacht* (1944); repr. (1970) · H. S. Sweetman and G. F. Handcock, eds., *Calendar of documents relating to Ireland*, 5 vols., PRO (1875–86) · O. Davies and D. B. Quinn, eds., 'Irish pipe roll of 14 John, 1211–1212', *Ulster Journal of Archaeology*, 3rd ser., 4 (1941), 16–19, 34–5 [suppl.]

O Néill, Aodh. *See* O'Neill, Hugh, second earl of Tyrone (c.1550–1616).

O'Neill, Arthur George (1819–1896), reformer and minister of religion, was born in Chelmsford, Essex, in September 1819. His father, Arthur O'Neill, a coachmaker, was an Irish protestant refugee, and his mother, Ann, claimed descent from John Rogers, a protestant martyr in Mary Tudor's reign. The father died three months before Arthur's birth, and the mother married an army quartermaster named Cooper. Destined for the army, O'Neill was employed by the 73rd regiment as a hospital dresser and compounder, during which time he attended the University of Malta and the college at Corfu. In 1835 he entered Glasgow University to study medicine but experienced a religious conversion and took up divinity.

As a student, O'Neill was influenced by J. A. Roebuck's defence of the Canadians who rebelled in 1837; in his own words, he became 'a peace man and a Chartist unchanged through nearly half a century' (*Birmingham Post*, 24 Nov 1885). During the late 1830s he supported himself as a public lecturer and Chartist lay preacher. He was one of the leaders of the Christian Chartist movement which developed in Scotland. In 1840 he settled in Birmingham as the minister of a Christian Chartist chapel in Newhall Street. O'Neill's insistence that Christianity should be 'the sole standard of government, commerce, education, and of every other pursuit of man' (*National Association Gazette*, 12 Feb 1842) offended many Chartists. William Lovett attacked his 'cant and sentimentality' (ibid., 18 June 1842), and Feargus O'Connor denounced Christian Chartism as a divisive force. His closest collaborators were John Collins and Henry Vincent, who shared his religiosity. He co-operated with Joseph Sturge and the 'moral radical' dissenters who devised a complete suffrage bill that incorporated the six points of the People's Charter. After Lovett and O'Connor rejected the bill at a conference in Birmingham in December 1842, O'Neill continued to associate with Sturge and was increasingly identified with him. In the meanwhile O'Neill had become involved in the strikes that swept across the midlands in mid-1842. He was prosecuted for sedition and conspiracy, tried in August 1843, and gaoled for nearly twelve months.

Imprisonment deepened O'Neill's religious commitment, and he wrote that henceforward he would work for 'the speedy appearance of the kingdom of Christ' (letter from A. G. O'Neill, 3 Feb 1844, Sturge MSS, priv. coll.), as revealed by scripture prophecy. On his release he resumed his Christian Chartist ministry in Birmingham, but the development of his religious beliefs convinced him of the need for adult baptism by immersion, and in 1846 he became a Baptist minister. The new status did not abate his political fervour. He had joined the Peace Society before his imprisonment, and from the mid-1840s, together with Joseph Sturge, Henry Richard, Elihu Burritt, and Richard Cobden, he promoted arbitration as a means of resolving international disputes. Late in life he attended peace congresses in European cities between 1889 and 1893. True to the ideals that had led to his imprisonment, he helped to set up trade unions and became a member of the Reform League during the 1860s. Towards the end of his life he was calling, not only for the full implementation of the People's Charter, but also for parliamentary suffrage for women ratepayers and a version of home rule that would devolve legislative powers on parliaments elected in all the regions of the British Isles including the midlands. He also opposed slavery, the Contagious Diseases Acts, and the regulations governing the religious aspects of public education. As a teetaller for over half a century, he advocated temperance as part of a programme of working-class self-help.

A strong, burly man, O'Neill had 'soft and tender-looking blue eyes' (*Birmingham Faces and Places*) and a mellifluous voice. Until very late in life he enjoyed excellent health. He married on 17 June 1845 Esther Piddock Fallows, who predeceased him by sixteen years. O'Neill died at his home, 55 Hall Road, Handsworth, Staffordshire, on 14 May 1896 of 'a valvular trouble of the heart and a serious liver disorder' (*Handsworth Herald*). He was buried in Handsworth Old Church beside his wife. Two daughters and a son survived him.   ALEX TYRRELL

Sources *Handsworth Herald and North Birmingham News* (16 May 1896) · *Birmingham Faces and Places*, 2 (1889–90), 152–5 · *National*

Association Gazette (8 Jan 1842) · *National Association Gazette* (12 Feb 1842) · *National Association Gazette* (18 June 1842) · A. Wilson, *Scottish chartist portraits* (1965) · A. Wilson, *The chartist movement in Scotland* (1970) · A. Tyrrell, *Joseph Sturge and the 'moral radical party' in early Victorian Britain* (c.1987) · *DLB* · *CGPLA Eng. & Wales* (1896)

Likenesses J. Pratt, portrait, 1885, Birmingham Museums and Art Gallery · R. Flamank, photograph, 1896, repro. in *The Owl* (22 May 1896) · H. J. Whitlock, photograph, 1896, repro. in *Handsworth Herald* (June 1896)

Wealth at death £2721 3s. 5d.: probate, 3 July 1896, *CGPLA Eng. & Wales*

O'Neill, Brian mac Phelim, lord of Clandeboye (d. 1574), landowner, was the son of Phelim O'Neill (Feidhlimidh Bacach Ó Néill), lord of Clandeboye between 1529 and his death in 1533. Clandeboye was an extensive lordship in south Antrim and north Down. The O'Neills of Clann Aodh Buidhe had come to dominate the region following the disintegration of the earldom of Ulster from the mid-thirteenth century. By the early sixteenth century the English presence in the earldom had been reduced to a small pocket around Carrickfergus, and enclaves in Lecale and southern Ards. However, Brian's grandfather Hugh or Aodh (d. 1524) was the last great lord of Clandeboye. Following Hugh's death the lordship was undermined by the succession of a series of short-lived lords, including Brian's father. Internecine struggles for power left Clandeboye effectively divided by 1555 between Phelim's sons Brian and Hugh and their cousin Conn.

Brian and his brother travelled to Dublin in May 1556 and promised to serve the English crown 'like as by report they have done a long time since' (*Haliday MSS*, 2). The English administration in Dublin decided to formalize the division of Clandeboye as a means of making it more amenable to English influence. However, Brian mac Phelim won to his side William Piers, captain of Carrickfergus Castle, and, to his great benefit, his brother Hugh and cousin Conn were detained in the castle while Brian ruled as lord of all Clandeboye. Brian mac Phelim married twice: first, a daughter of Art Magennis, Viscount Iveagh, who died before 1568; and second Anne, daughter of Brian Carragh MacDonnell, captain of Glenconkoyne, who died with her husband.

In 1565 Piers composed his 'Opinion', advocating the colonization of Ulster east of the River Bann, including Clandeboye. Subsequently, however, he formed a close relationship with Brian mac Phelim O'Neill, based primarily on their common interest in containing the expansion of Scottish power in north Antrim and the ambitions of the O'Neills of Tyrone east of the Bann. O'Neill allowed Piers to exact a levy on part of Clandeboye to supplement the meagre resources allocated to the Carrickfergus garrison by the English crown. In 1570 O'Neill undertook responsibility for victualling the garrison. For his part, Piers helped to bolster O'Neill's authority throughout Clandeboye. He regularly reported Brian's good service and he promoted his suit to have his lordship of Clandeboye formally recognized by Elizabeth, holder of the title to the defunct earldom of Ulster. Brian mac Phelim received a letter of thanks in July 1567 and was subsequently knighted in recognition of his services against the rebellious Seán O'Neill, but the queen would not legitimize his lordship because of plans to colonize eastern Ulster to England's benefit.

On 16 November 1571 Sir Thomas Smith, the English privy councillor, received a royal grant of an extensive portion of Clandeboye in Ards and lands adjoining it south of Belfast. Forewarned, perhaps by Piers, O'Neill protested his loyalty and service to the English crown. When the planters arrived on 30 August 1572 he drove them off. They subsequently returned to establish a foothold at Newtownards but their leader, Thomas Smith junior, was killed by some Irishmen who boiled his body and fed it to their dogs. Despite two attempts by Sir Thomas Smith to reinforce the colony it fizzled out.

In August 1573 Walter Devereux, earl of Essex, landed at Carrickfergus. He had received a royal grant of all of the recently created county of Antrim, excepting only Carrickfergus and its immediate environs, with no regard for the rights of Irish landowners like O'Neill of Clandeboye. O'Neill formed an alliance with Turlough Luineach O'Neill, lord of Tyrone, and, together with the Scots in Antrim, succeeded in thwarting Essex's grandiose plantation plans. Essex had mortgaged much of his estate to finance this venture and, as his wealth was dissipated to no effect, he became increasingly frustrated and vicious. He arrested William Piers and sought his execution for allegedly passing on intelligence to Brian O'Neill for use against him. Essex bitterly resented O'Neill for outwitting him, and for dashing his dreams of winning fame and fortune in Ulster. By 13 May 1574 Essex had the Irish lord proclaimed a traitor and put a bounty of £200 on his head.

O'Neill secured a pardon from the crown on 17 June and left his sons in Dublin as pledges for his good faith. He also agreed to assist Essex in fortifying Belfast. He seems to have been assured, wrongly, that it was possible to effect a reconciliation with Essex. Early in November 1574 O'Neill, accompanied by his wife, his brother Rory Oge, and an entourage of about 200 persons, attended a parley with Essex in Belfast. However, after a banquet, English soldiers massacred O'Neill's entourage. O'Neill, his wife, and brother were taken to Dublin. Between 14 and 24 November they were tried for treason, executed, and quartered, notwithstanding the royal pardon and Essex's own guarantees.

Essex died in 1576 and Brian's son Seán eventually established a title to Belfast Castle and three-quarters of north Clandeboye, while his uncle Hugh's son Niall held the remaining quarter. Brian mac Phelim's cousin Conn, after many years of detention in Carrickfergus Castle, was established at Castlereagh as chief captain in south Clandeboye. The judicial murder of Brian mac Phelim O'Neill, together with his wife and brother, and the slaughter of his entourage, was long remembered as one of the worst acts of English infamy perpetrated in Ireland. Its significance was magnified by the fact that O'Neill was one of those Irish lords who sought an accommodation with the English crown. His demise suggested that the Irish nobility, however accommodating, were expendable should they dare to resist English ambitions.

HENRY A. JEFFERIES

Sources T. P. J. McCall, 'The Gaelic background to the settlement of Down and Antrim', MA diss., Queen's University, Belfast, 1983 · *CSP Ire.*, 1509–85 · *AFM* · J. S. Brewer and W. Bullen, eds., *Calendar of the Carew manuscripts*, 1: 1515–1574, PRO (1867) · *The Irish fiants of the Tudor sovereigns*, 4 vols. (1994), vol. 2 · *The Montgomery manuscripts, 1603–1706*, ed. G. Hill (1869) · N. P. Canny, *The Elizabethan conquest of Ireland: a pattern established, 1565–76* (1976) · D. B. Quinn, 'Sir Thomas Smith (1513–1577) and the beginnings of English colonial theory', *Proceedings of the American Philosophical Society*, 89 (1945), 543–60 · *The manuscripts of Charles Haliday … Acts of the privy council in Ireland, 1556–1571*, HMC, 40 (1897)

O'Neill, Charles Henry St John, Earl O'Neill (1779–1841). *See under* O'Neill, John, first Viscount O'Neill (1740–1798).

O'Neill, Sir Con Douglas Walter (1912–1988), diplomatist, was born in London on 3 June 1912, the second of the three surviving sons (there were no daughters) of Sir (Robert William) Hugh O'Neill (later first Baron Rathcavan), privy councillor and politician, and his wife, Sylvia Irene, daughter of Walter Albert Sandeman, of Morden House, Royston. He attended Eton College and achieved early academic distinction with a scholarship from Eton to Balliol College, Oxford, a first class in English in 1934, and a law fellowship of All Souls College, Oxford, the following year (held until 1946). In 1936 he was called to the bar (Inner Temple) and in the same year entered the diplomatic service.

O'Neill was posted to Berlin as third secretary in 1938; he resigned in 1939 because he disagreed with Neville Chamberlain's policy of appeasement. He served in the army intelligence corps from 1940 to 1943 and was then employed in the Foreign Office. In 1946 he left to become a leader writer on *The Times* but returned to the Foreign Office the following year. From then on he rose steadily in the hierarchy; posts in Frankfurt am Main and Bonn were followed by a period as head of the news department in 1954–5, chargé d'affaires in Beijing (1955–7), a return to the Foreign Office as assistant under-secretary in 1957, and posts as ambassador to Finland (1961–3) and ambassador to the European Communities in Brussels (1963–5). He returned to the Foreign Office as deputy under-secretary, and hoped in 1968 to go to Bonn as ambassador. Germany had been his first post; his German was impeccable and he would have carried considerable weight. But the foreign secretary, George Brown, vetoed this proposal; it was a question of temperamental incompatibility. O'Neill did not dispute his right to do so but resigned to start a career in the City with Hill Samuel.

In 1969 O'Neill was recalled to the Foreign Office to head the team which would negotiate Britain's entry into the European Community. This task successfully accomplished, he left the Foreign Office for the last time in 1972, after writing the official history of the negotiations. From 1972 to 1974 he was chairman of the Intervention Board for Agricultural Produce; and he was a director of Unigate

from 1974 to 1983. In 1974 and in 1975, the year of the referendum, he performed a last service to the European cause as director of the Britain in Europe campaign.

O'Neill was one of the outstanding diplomats of his generation. His intellect was impressive, his reasoning always a masterpiece of logic, and his analysis of any situation penetrating and accurate. To this he brought a lucidity of expression which served him well as a leader writer on *The Times*; some felt that he could have edited the newspaper with distinction. In appearance he resembled one of Anthony Trollope's elders of the church: bald, bespectacled, with an air of measured dignity, and with a voice distinctly canonical. His manner had something of the formality of a previous generation, but those who dealt with him rapidly found that underneath there lurked a delightful sense of humour and a seemingly inexhaustible fund of Irish stories.

O'Neill was also a man of unbending principle. If he thought a policy was wrong he said so in clear and measured terms without any thought of the consequences for his career. It was most unusual for a diplomat to leave the Foreign Office three times before retirement and yet rise to posts of the highest distinction. His greatest accomplishment was the British entry into the European Community. On this the country was bitterly divided and the complexities of the negotiation vast. In addition he had to carry with him the senior officials on the team who vigorously defended the interests of their departments. Through all these hazards he steered his team with imperturbable patience and skill, gaining the confidence and respect of all he dealt with, whether among Britain's European partners or in Whitehall. The success of the negotiations was one of the great achievements in the history of British diplomacy; it owed much to his efforts.

O'Neill was appointed CMG in 1953, KCMG in 1962, and GCMG in 1972. He was married three times, first in 1940 to Rosemary Margaret, daughter of Harold Pritchard MD. They had a son, and a daughter, Onora, who became principal of Newnham College, Cambridge. The marriage was dissolved in 1954 (his wife subsequently became Lady Garvey) and in that year he married Baroness Carola Hertha Adolphine Emma Harriet Luise (Mädy) Marschall von Bieberstein, a widow, and the daughter of Baron Max Reinhard August von Holzing-Berstett. She died in 1960 and in 1961 he married Anne-Marie Lindberg of Helsinki, daughter of Bertil Jungström, civil engineer, of Stockholm. O'Neill died on 11 January 1988 at St Stephen's Hospital, London.

ROY DENMAN, rev.

Sources FO List · WW · *The Independent* (14 Jan 1988) · *The Times* (12 Jan 1988) · personal knowledge (1996) · CGPLA Eng. & Wales (1988)
Archives IWM
Wealth at death £825,881: probate, 30 June 1988, CGPLA Eng. & Wales

O'Neill, Conn Bacach, first earl of Tyrone (*c*.1482–1559), chieftain and magnate, was the youngest son of Conn More O'Neill (*d*. 1493), chieftain, lord of Tyrone, and his wife, Eleanor (*d*. 1497), daughter of Thomas *Fitzgerald, seventh earl of Kildare, and his wife, Joan. Rival O'Neill factions had been fighting for decades to exert control over Tyrone, the unwieldy O'Neill lordship which stretched across much of Ulster. Conn More's marriage to Eleanor Fitzgerald in 1480 secured for him a powerful ally in Kildare and prompted the Irish parliament to recognize Conn More and his issue as English subjects. Subsequently the earls of Kildare intervened periodically in O'Neill politics to install candidates more sympathetic to their position. Following the death in 1519 of his elder brother Art Oge O'Neill, Conn Bacach ('the lame'), supported by Gerald *Fitzgerald, ninth earl of Kildare (1487–1534), succeeded to the chieftaincy. He subsequently married his cousin Alice, fourth daughter of Gerald *Fitzgerald, eighth earl of Kildare, cementing an alliance with the Geraldines.

Lord of Tyrone, 1519–1534 Conn's accession, however, had not gone unopposed; the sons of Art Oge O'Neill, led by Niall Conallach (d. 1544), allied with the neighbouring O'Donnells, who were receptive to any interest capable of destabilizing the O'Neill lordship, mounted consistent opposition. The replacement of the ninth earl of Kildare as lord lieutenant by Thomas Howard, earl of Surrey, in 1520 prompted Conn to threaten the pale's northern marches. However, the O'Donnell–O'Neill alliance 'behind' Tyrone raised the prospect of a two-front war as Surrey marched northwards. In a letter to Conn, John Kite, archbishop of Armagh, urged that he:

> should cultivate a mind worthy of your abilities and character, and no longer take delight in wild and barbarous manners ... It is much better to live in a civilized fashion, than to seek a living by arms and rapine, and to have no thought beyond pleasure and the belly. (Brewer and Bullen, 1515–74, no. 8)

Conn submitted and Henry VIII, eager to win his allegiance inexpensively, sent him gifts and authorized Surrey to grant him a knighthood and to induce him to repair to court. Conn, however, could not offer the lord lieutenant, or the king, his full attention while Sir Hugh O'Donnell threatened, and in summer 1522 he invaded Tyrconnell.

Rumours of Conn's alliance with Colin Campbell, third earl of Argyll, in summer 1521 caused consternation among English officials. Their fear was misplaced as Scottish aid represented only a part of a greater confederacy formed by Conn to crush O'Donnell the following year. Conn brought to the field an impressive array of preponderantly Gaelic clans from across Ireland in what was a battle to confirm traditional O'Neill hegemony in Ulster. After several initial successes, however, the greatly outnumbered forces of O'Donnell inflicted a sharp defeat on Conn at Cnoc Buidhbh near Strabane, in Tyrone, in mid-August 1522. The confederacy disintegrated; and though fighting between Conn and O'Donnell continued intermittently for the rest of the decade, neither could secure a decisive advantage. With his ambitions in Ulster cooled, Conn concentrated on his alliance with his brother-in-law the newly restored ninth earl of Kildare, attending his installation in 1524: 'and so O'Neill, being in the council house with them, bare the sword before the deputy till

they went to Thomas Court and there dined, and after dinner had a goodly banquet' (TCD, MS 543/2, s.a. 1524). He subsequently accompanied Kildare on a hosting against O'Donnell, and in 1526 attended a council held by him in Dublin. This close association with Kildare continued despite Conn's marriage to Sorcha (d. 1530), daughter of Hugh Oge O'Neill, chief of the Clandeboye O'Neills; among their children was Shane *O'Neill (c.1530–1567).

During Kildare's absence at court, Conn did his best to obstruct the stop-gap government of Richard Nugent, third Baron Delvin, which had superseded that of Kildare's brother Sir Thomas Fitzgerald of Leixlip. In May 1528 Conn complained to Cardinal Thomas Wolsey that Delvin withheld his traditional blackrent and requested Kildare's return. Sir William Skeffington, however, was appointed lord deputy on 22 June 1530. In an effort to demonstrate his loyalty, Kildare accompanied Skeffington on a campaign against Conn in 1531. The campaign, carried out with the assistance of both the O'Donnells and the rival O'Neill faction, dealt Conn a devastating blow. The following year the weakened O'Neills underwent a second assault that saw their enemies penetrate the heart of Tyrone. The annals of Ulster note:'do impoadur Gaidhil Letha Cuind uile ar Ó Neill 'munn am sa, achtmadh becc' ('the Gaidhil of all the half of Conn, except a few, turned on O'Neill about that time'; Hennessy and MacCarthy, vol. 3, s.a. 1532). However, Conn's chieftaincy survived the onslaught. Kildare's restoration in 1532 ushered in more peaceful conditions which allowed Conn to re-establish his power base.

Rebel, 1534–1542 Like many Kildare clients Conn initially supported the rebellion of Thomas Fitzgerald, Baron Offaly, in 1534, but abandoned the Geraldines as the rebellion faltered. In July 1535 he entered into a detailed submission with Skeffington at Drogheda. The terms of submission were renewed the following year, although the new lord deputy, Leonard Grey, Viscount Graney, complained of Conn's refusal to give hostages. Unable to predict the government's future alignment in the wake of the rebellion of Offaly, now tenth earl of Kildare, and weakened by the invasions of 1531–2, Conn doubtless hoped to secure his lands and position through formal submission. He had also been engaged in a *rapprochement* with certain O'Donnells since 1535. Sir Hugh O'Donnell's son Manus was particularly receptive to Conn's overtures and their friendship grew into a solid alliance. Shortly before 29 November 1538 Conn married Mary (d. in or after 1560), daughter of Alexander MacRandal Boy MacDonald. By 1539 Graney's aggressive behaviour prompted Conn and Manus O'Donnell to form a confederacy against the government, the so-called Geraldine league, whose nominal aim was Kildare's restoration. They were encouraged by Conn's receipt of a letter from Paul III in June, which revoked the bull *Laudabiliter* and styled Conn 'King of Our Realme of Ireland'. Conn and O'Donnell invaded Meath in August, but failed to press their advantage and on their return to Ulster were routed by Graney at Bellahoe, on the border of Meath and co. Monaghan. This rare mustering of

Gaelic strength was a worrying development for the government and demanded a change of tack. Graney was replaced by Sir Anthony St Leger, who shortly after his arrival in August 1540 embarked on a markedly more conciliatory initiative to defuse the confederacy.

St Leger's conciliatory strategy succeeded gradually in detaching Conn's allies from the confederacy. Yet despite O'Donnell's submission in July 1541 and St Leger's diplomatic advances towards him in March and June 1541, Conn remained unmoved. Two campaigns launched into Tyrone that autumn also failed in securing his submission. A devastating third invasion launched in December left the already isolated Conn with little choice but to surrender unconditionally, condescending at last to offer his son as hostage for his loyalty. His submission marked the confederacy's end and exercised a profound effect on powerful chiefs such as Murrough O'Brien, who subsequently consented to terms offered by St Leger. In January 1542 Conn acknowledged Henry VIII's laws and sovereignty, agreeing to renounce the pope and attend parliament. His submission was formalized at Drogheda on 29 May and the following month he attended St Leger's parliament at Trim. The king baulked at offering the earldom of Ulster, for which Conn petitioned, but offered instead the earldom of Tyrone. Conn accepted and, with his expenses borne by St Leger, afterwards repaired to England to submit formally to Henry.

Earl of Tyrone, 1542–1559 Following his submission to Henry at Greenwich Palace on 24 September 1542, Conn was created earl of Tyrone for life on 1 October. The title was to revert to his illegitimate son and heir with Alison Kelly, Mathew (d. 1558), who was concurrently created baron of Dungannon. The significance of the occasion was not lost on St Leger, who reminded the privy council that: 'yt can not be knowen that ever any Oneile repaired in person before this in to England to any of his noble progenytours, but hitherto usurped to call them selffes Prynces of Ulster' (*State Papers, Henry VIII*, 3.417). Conn surrendered both his kingdom and his Gaelic title to the crown in exchange for an earldom, incurring the wrath of a Gaelic poet as a result: 'Ó Néill Oiligh is Eamhna, rí Teamhrach agus Tailtean, tugsad ar iarlacht Uladh ríoghacht go humhal aimhghlic' ('O'Neill of Oileach and Eamhain (Macha), the king of Tara and Tailte, has exchanged in foolish submission his kingship for the Ulster earldom'; Ó Cuív, 273). The promise of immediate stability and hereditary succession, however, doubtless appealed to Conn, whose tanist, prior to the indenture, was his rival Niall Conallach. With the succession assured and his enemies outmanoeuvred, Tyrone returned to Ireland.

On 7 May 1543 Tyrone was admitted to the Irish privy council and received a grant of lands in Dublin on 9 July. He subsequently set about reaffirming his traditional suzerainty in Ulster both by bringing pressure to bear upon lesser Ulster chiefs and by rekindling hostilities with O'Donnell. His neighbours, however, had very different expectations from St Leger's negotiations: the former understood their tenurial independence, guaranteed by their respective submissions, as tantamount to exoneration from traditional obligations to Tyrone, while O'Donnell withheld payment for lands in the Inishowen peninsula from which the new earl had withdrawn his claim as part of his submission. Detailed judgement on the rights and status of lesser Ulster chiefs was postponed, but St Leger recognized the potential danger posed by an O'Neill–O'Donnell feud at this juncture and brokered a mutually acceptable compromise, finalized by August 1545. Tyrone enjoyed relative stability in the following years, and in 1544–5 he readily provided ninety kerne for the king's war with France and Scotland. Niall Conallach's death in 1544, moreover, removed any immediate internal threat to Tyrone's leadership.

The tanist's death, however, threatened a conflict between English and Gaelic succession laws. Dungannon, heir to the earldom, was indeed Tyrone's eldest son, but appears to have been illegitimate or a 'named' son, born to the wife of a Dundalk blacksmith. Tyrone, a much married man, fathered many children. Four identifiable male children, however, were eligible for the chieftaincy under Gaelic law: Turlough, Brian, Conn, and Shane. Conflict was averted owing principally to Tyrone's strong presence and his continued support of Dungannon. But St Leger's recall and the more aggressive policies introduced by Edward VI's regime placed Tyrone's leadership under considerable strain. The deployment of an English garrison at Newry led to disputes between the earl and its captain, Nicholas Bagenal, who proceeded to raid Tyrone with impunity. The English, moreover, began assisting Dungannon against Tyrone in a premature succession dispute. In January 1551 Tyrone repaired to Dublin to seek redress from the Irish privy council, but Andrew Brereton, constable in Lecale, accused him of complicity with the French. He returned home and commenced hostilities against Dungannon and his other sons who had exploited their father's weakness in pursuit of their own interests. In May 1552 the new lord deputy, Sir James Croft, lured Tyrone into the pale, where he was detained.

During the earl's absence, the earldom of Tyrone descended further into civil war. The earl's younger sons struggled with Dungannon, whom many held responsible for Tyrone's imprisonment, for control of the region. It was, however, his youngest son, Shane, who rose to prominence, emerging as the lordship's defender and Tyrone's likely successor. A desperate attempt to restore the earl was made in December 1552. He was now an old man but nevertheless set about reasserting his authority. He was reconciled with Dungannon and assembled an army to attack the Scots in Clandeboye in 1554. Shane, however, supported the Scots and easily defeated Tyrone and Dungannon. Tyrone was powerless against his enemies, who later imprisoned his wife, son, and grandson in Scotland. Shane was now the dominant force among the O'Neills; his orchestration of Dungannon's assassination in 1558 merely confirmed to the government what had long been apparent in Tyrone. Tyrone himself escaped to the pale, residing with William Walsh, bishop of Meath. He died before 16 July 1559 and was survived by his last wife, Mary.

Shane was proclaimed O'Neill under Gaelic law, and subsequently petitioned for recognition as earl of Tyrone. The annals of the four masters note: 'Conn ... décc iar ccaitheamh a aoisi agus aimsire gan oilbeaim gan imdhearccadh, agus ro ba doilígh do Chenél Eóchain a éccsidhe munbhadh a sheandataidh agus a sheanórdhacht, agus a dhíol doidhre dfaccbháil ina ionadh .i. Seaan' ('Conn ... died after having spent his age and time without blemish or reproach. His death would have been a great cause of great grief to the Kinel-Owen but for his great age and infirmity, and that left an heir worthy of him, i.e. John'; *AFM*, s.a. 1559). Conn's successful transition from Gaelic chief to English earl had a profound influence on the Gaelic order's perceptions of Tudor England. However, the government's inability to prevent Shane from undermining his father's authority exposed both the weakness and impermanence of Conn's transition.

CHRISTOPHER MAGINN

Sources State papers published under ... Henry VIII, 11 vols. (1830–52) · chronicle of Dublin, TCD, MS 543/2 · LP Henry VIII · AFM, 2nd edn · W. M. Hennessy and B. MacCarthy, eds., Annals of Ulster, otherwise, annals of Senat, 4 vols. (1887–1901) · J. S. Brewer and W. Bullen, eds., Calendar of the Carew manuscripts, 6 vols., PRO (1867–73) · J. Morrin, ed., Calendar of the patent and close rolls of chancery in Ireland for the reigns of Henry VIII, Edward VI, Mary, and Elizabeth, 2 vols. (1861–2) · C. McNeill, 'Reports on the Rawlinson collection', Analecta Hibernica, 1 (1930), 12–178 · B. Ó Cuív, ed., 'A sixteenth century political poem', Éisge, 15 (1973–4), 261–76 · The Irish fiants of the Tudor sovereigns, 4 vols. (1994) · J. Hogan, 'The Irish law of kingship, with special reference to Aileach and Cenel Eóghain', Proceedings of the Royal Irish Academy, 40C (1931–2), 186–254 · T. Mathews, The O'Neills of Ulster: their history and genealogy, 3 vols. (1907) · T. B. Lyons, 'Shane O'Neill: a biography', MA diss., University College, Cork, 1998 · C. Brady, Shane O'Neill (Dundalk, 1996) · D. Bryan, Gerald Fitzgerald, the great earl of Kildare (1933) · GEC, Peerage
Archives BL, grant of patent, Cotton MS Titus B. XI, p. 381 · LPL, indenture, MS 603

O'Neill, Daniel (*c*.1612–1664), royalist army officer and courtier, was the eldest son of Con MacNiall MacBrian Faghartach O'Neill (*d*. 1619), lord of Clandeboye in co. Antrim, and his wife, Eilis, the daughter of Art MacBaron O'Neill, the older, base-born brother of Hugh *O'Neill, second earl of Tyrone. Born at the ancestral seat of his father's family at Castlereagh, co. Down, Daniel's life was charted by the political dexterity of his grandfather Niall MacBrian O'Neill and the intemperance of his father. The former owed his position to the crown's favour, which was threatened by the native ascendancy of Tyrone and the upheavals of the Nine Years' War. Playing off the fortunes of the conflict, Niall MacBrian, shortly before his death in February 1601, resecured his estates under the queen. His son Con wasted this recognition by going over to Tyrone's side before the battle of Kinsale. Captured and imprisoned after his 'perfidious revolt' (Chichester to Cecil, 8 Oct 1601, *CSP Ire.*, *1601–3*, 110–11), Con escaped the government's wrath, but squandered his reprieve by inciting trouble over a petty disagreement with local authorities. Reconfined, he made a bargain with Hugh Montgomery, afterwards viscount of the Ards, for a royal pardon in

return for half of his holdings. Recognizing an opportunity for advancement, James Hamilton, later Viscount Claneboye, persuaded the king to reward his service by including him in the Montgomery settlement. On 5 November 1605 the tripartite grant was passed by letters patent under the great seal of Ireland. Over the next fourteen years, until his death in 1619, Con O'Neill sold, mortgaged, and leased his remaining holdings. His eldest son and heir, Daniel, inherited little of an estate once valued at about £12,000 a year.

An aspiring career The prospects for Con O'Neill's surviving family were not encouraging. One son, Hugh Buidhe, died as a youngster, while another, Con, pursued a career in the Spanish Netherlands as an officer in the Irish regiment of his uncle Owen Roe *O'Neill. A daughter, Catherine, married her cousin Thady O'Hara of Crebilly, co. Antrim, and had five children. It was Daniel O'Neill who carried the burden of restoring what his father had dissipated. The government, recognizing the importance of this native Irish heir, made him a ward of chancery and raised him in England as a protestant. This background and the circumstances of his upbringing produced a striving and resourceful young man. Quick-witted and charming by nature, Daniel was described by Clarendon as 'in subtlety and understanding much superior to the whole nation of the old Irish', a 'great observer and discerner of man's natures and humours, and ... very dextrous in compliance where he found it useful' (Clarendon, *Hist. rebellion*, 3.513).

As the recognized head of the Upper Clandeboye O'Neills, much of Daniel O'Neill's status and initial well-being revolved around the fate of his father's forsaken estates. In an inquisition delivered into chancery in June 1624, he and his assigns held only twenty-seven townlands about Castlereagh. By 1635 these lands were conveyed by the king to Viscount Montgomery of the Ards. This decision left O'Neill and his brother with a joint annuity of £160. Without immediate prospects in his homeland, O'Neill entered his majority by serving under Lord Conway in the Low Countries. Here he gained military experience and prominent friends. Until the late 1630s O'Neill divided his time between the English court and the states general—'the winter seasons in the one and the summer always in the army of the other; which was as good an education towards advancement in the world as that age knew' (Clarendon, *Hist. rebellion*, 3.513). On the continent he became well acquainted with Elizabeth, the titular queen of Bohemia and sister of Charles I, and her husband, the elector palatine. Using these connections, in 1635 he redoubled his efforts to regain parts of his father's former estates. These undertakings coloured his politics and ambitions for the rest of his life.

O'Neill's petitions were supported by such noteworthies as Archbishop Laud, Thomas Howard, earl of Arundel, Charles Lewis, the new elector palatine, and Lord Conway, all of whom addressed the Irish lord deputy, Thomas Wentworth, on O'Neill's behalf. Arundel recommended him for master of the Irish mint and Laud urged Wentworth 'to help him to a subsistence' and restore to 'this gentleman that [which] is lost without his own fault' (Laud to Wentworth, 16 Jan 1636, *Works of … Laud*, 7.266–7). O'Neill was also armed with addresses from the king. But his suit never had the lord deputy's support. Wentworth's inactivity was personal. He did not appreciate O'Neill's importunity or the persistent pressures from a well-connected supplicant with, his own protestantism not-withstanding, strong Irish Catholic associations. Went-worth saw O'Neill as a desperate suitor seeking leverage from any opportune source. He was especially troubled by his close relationship with his influential cousin Randal MacDonnell, second earl of Antrim. The lord deputy dis-trusted Antrim, grandson of the late earl of Tyrone, and his ambitions in north-east Ulster and the western isles of Scotland. In particular, Wentworth had misgivings over Antrim's appointment of O'Neill to a royal commission in Scotland. He was wary of arming either man and described O'Neill 'to be in his Heart and affection a Traytor, bred no other, Egg and Bird as they say' (Went-worth to Windebank, 2 March 1639, *Works of … Laud*, 7.297). This estrangement set O'Neill against the lord dep-uty, which prejudiced him with the king.

Pre-civil war plotting Waiting for his claims to be sorted out, O'Neill returned to the Low Countries in 1637 and par-ticipated in the siege of Breda. He distinguished himself and was severely wounded in the primary assault. Follow-ing his recovery, he found himself caught up in the cam-paigns of the erupting bishops' wars with Scotland. He was given command of a troop of horse, 'having had good experience in the most active armies of that time, and courage very notorious' (Clarendon, *Hist. rebellion*, 3.513). After the peace of Berwick he retired to the Netherlands with dispatches for the queen of Bohemia. When hostil-ities renewed, he went back to command a regiment of horse and distinguished himself with his gallant defence at Newburn (28 August 1640), where he was badly wounded and captured. Reported to be dead, he was taken to Newcastle, where he was well treated by captors he knew from the continent. He was released during the Ripon negotiations.

Over the next two years O'Neill took advantage of the evolving crisis between the crown and parliament to enhance his options. He conspired for the overthrow of Thomas Wentworth, now the earl of Strafford, and par-ticipated in a series of plots representing a variety of roy-alist interests. Two of these schemes, the army plots (March–May 1641), were linked to deploying the support of the northern English army officers for the king. For his services, the debt-ridden O'Neill got a royal annuity and the promise of an appointment as groom to the royal bed-chamber. These intrigues were followed by a shrouded conspiracy involving his brother Con, an agent from his uncle Colonel Owen Roe O'Neill, to northern Irish Cath-olic malcontents. Con's initial mission, when he met up with Daniel, was to get recruiting licences for soldiers in Strafford's soon to be disbanded Irish army. Hoping to cap-italize on Daniel's royalist connections, Con believed he could get the king's desperate assent to put these soldiers

under beholden Catholic commanders. In what is some-times called the 'colonels' plot', Con moved between Eng-land and the continent trying to co-ordinate plans through his older and well-connected sibling. In the coded correspondence that ensued, Daniel O'Neill was termed Lewis Lanois. This machination was derailed in mid-June when O'Neill fled to the continent to escape parliament's attempt to arrest him for his role in the original army plots.

When he was questioned about his complicity, there was initially insufficient evidence to convict O'Neill. It was only after incriminating testimony surfaced that he fled to the continent. In September, hoping for immunity under a negotiated act of oblivion, he returned to England and surrendered to John Pym. O'Neill was sent to the Gate-house prison in Westminster to await his trial, declining to respond to the initial indictment. But new revelations about the second plot saw the charges changed to high treason. While he was in custody, his health began to suf-fer and he successfully petitioned in January 1642 for bet-ter treatment. He was moved to the Tower and afforded greater personal liberty. On 5 May he escaped by tying sheets and a tablecloth together. He went over the wall and avoided detection by dressing as a woman. Searches were ordered with descriptions of him 'being of sanguine complection, a middle stature, light brown hair, about the age of thirty, and little or no beard, and of late hath been sickly' (*JHL*, 5.48). His flight gained considerable notoriety in a provocative tract detailing his breakout. It confirmed him 'a consanguinean to that rebellious family [O'Neills] in Ireland' (*Oneales Escape out of the Tower of London*). This association seemed appropriate after the outbreak in October 1641 of the Irish rising.

An agent of the crown The upheaval in Ireland stoked the deteriorating English political crisis which brought an Irish royalist like Daniel O'Neill to the forefront. From Brussels, where he had fled, he raised arms and ammuni-tion for the anticipated royalist campaigns of the civil war. Back in England he became a major in Colonel Osborne's regiment before taking a commission as a lieutenant-colonel of a regiment of horse under Prince Rupert of the Rhine. He participated in the battles of Edge-hill, Chalgrove, and the first Newbury encounter, and was wounded at the failed relief of Reading. Soon after, he learned that his brother Con had been killed in Ireland after quarter had been granted at the skirmish of Clones. But, grief aside, most of O'Neill's attention was given to serving at the royal court in Oxford, where he could have 'access to all those of the best credit in this state of the world' (Trevor to Ormond, 9 Dec 1643, T. Carte, *A Collection of Original Letters and Papers, Concerning the Affairs of England*, 1.26). Through his former services and connections he appeared to be the right person to help the crown deflect parliament's alliance with the covenanting Scots.

The royalist camp knew that a military diversion in Scot-land was necessary to obstruct the new accord. In a scheme similar to that suggested by Antrim during Straf-ford's deputyship, it was hoped that Scottish royalists sup-ported by Irish soldiers would foil the king's enemies. The plan called for Antrim to raise 10,000 troops in northern Ireland to serve under the earl of Montrose in Scotland. Unfortunately, Antrim lacked credibility and was not on good terms with the marquess of Ormond, the lord lieutenant of Ireland, who had just signed a cessation of arms with the ruling Irish Catholic confederacy. To facilitate these negotiations, Lord Digby proposed his good friend the well-trusted Daniel O'Neill. Getting him appointed, Digby had to overcome the king's wariness about Daniel's role in Strafford's overthrow. He also extracted O'Neill's long-promised appointment to be a groom to the royal bedchamber. Digby advised Charles that this post gave O'Neill stature as an emissary. He then mollified his majesty by suggesting that having an Irishman so near 'to the person of the king' would not be a factor, since O'Neill would be taken up with services elsewhere (Clarendon, *Hist. rebellion*, 3.513–21).

O'Neill and Antrim arrived on 23 February 1644 at the confederate capital of Kilkenny and addressed the supreme council, urging that their support would help the confederate peace commissioners get favourable terms from the king. From here O'Neill met Ormond in Dublin, before proceeding with Antrim to Ulster. By the end of June, 1600 soldiers were raised and shipped to Scotland for service in Montrose's army. Departing soon after, O'Neill returned to England too late to join his regiment at the battle of Marston Moor. He did participate in the western campaigns against Essex's forces and took part in the second battle of Newbury. But his value was his royalism and his ties to his uncle Owen Roe, the native military leader and protector of the clerical party.

For most of the next five years O'Neill's primary tasks were to secure aid from the native Irish and bring his uncle over to the king's side. These dealings were frustrating and often futile because he could not offset the suspicions of the papal nuncio Rinuccini and his faction. At stake were religious and landed guarantees that were often neither negotiable nor enforceable. With Owen Roe and Ormond difficult and contrary bargainers, O'Neill's efforts faltered in the kaleidoscopic arena of confederate politics. By 1647 he spoke of quitting his homeland and entering the French service. Digby persuaded him to reconsider, despite their disappointment over Ormond's surrender of Dublin to parliament. Another set-back was the opposition of the clerical party to O'Neill's appointment to be general of the confederacy's Connaught army. With failing prospects, he accompanied Digby to France, where he again was caught up in a variety of enterprises involving the recruitment of Irish soldiers. Not until October 1648 did he return to Ireland with Ormond to resume his royalist representations.

Daniel O'Neill reopened talks with Owen Roe, but the terms of the treaty did not satisfy Rinuccini and the clergy. When the nuncio left Ireland in February 1649, O'Neill again failed to secure a pact because the intentions and good faith of Ormond's party were still suspect. The treaty's urgency was soon redoubled by the changing military climate of Ireland. Parliamentarian forces had defeated Ormond at Rathmines (2 August 1649), Oliver

Cromwell had landed in Dublin (15 August 1649), and truces with Owen Roe proved fruitless. The gravity of these events weighed heavily on O'Neill, who busily tried to revive talks with his terminally ill uncle. On 20 October a peace accord was finally reached between Owen Roe O'Neill and Ormond, and seventeen days later General O'Neill died.

Following the settlement, O'Neill accompanied his cousin Major-General Hugh Dubh *O'Neill and 2200 men south to try to repel Cromwell's forces. Too late to be effective, O'Neill got some satisfaction when the new English king Charles II appointed him to the Irish privy council. But the important selection for O'Neill was the contest over who would succeed Owen Roe as the commander of the northern army. Ormond and his supporters favoured O'Neill's election. Unfortunately, the clerical party led by the bishop of Clogher resisted his candidacy. O'Neill pleaded ill health and proposed Hugh Dubh to lead his uncle's army. He also accused the clergy of looking 'more to their reputations at Rome than their preservation at home' (D. O'Neill to Ormond, 9 Jan 1649–50, Bodl. Oxf., MS Carte 26, fol. 332). After a great deal of scheming, Clogher prevailed by suggesting that if elected he would turn the command over to Daniel O'Neill on the inconceivable condition of his conversion to Catholicism. Three months later the bishop-led army was decimated at the battle of Scariffhollis. Having no other recourse, O'Neill got the permission of Henry Ireton to enlist 5000 men for the service of Spain or the states general, and returned to the continent.

Royalist exile For the next decade Daniel O'Neill's attention was focused on survival. Firmly attached to the fortunes of the exiled court, he risked his life on many occasions for the Stuart cause. He gathered intelligence about conditions in England, reconciled royalist factions, carried dispatches, and acted as a commissariat to Charles and his court. Some of his most important tasks were mediations between the Sealed Knot and Action parties over the ill-fated royalist insurrections in England. But O'Neill and his fellow émigrés suffered for their devotion. They were often debt-ridden and sometimes lived from hand to mouth. Looking for maintenance, O'Neill even offered to raise 3000 soldiers for Spain in return for the position of colonel-general of all Irish in the Spanish service. His proposal rejected, he depended on his position as groom to the royal bedchamber and his ties to Lord Heenvliet and his wife, who cared for Charles II's sister, Princess Mary of Orange. He used his influence at the Dutch court to favour friends such as Ormond and Edward Hyde, who once addressed O'Neill as the 'Infallible Subtle' (Hyde to O'Neill, 31 Oct 1653, Bodl. Oxf., MS Clarendon 46, fol. 361). In one instance O'Neill recommended Hyde's daughter Anne to be a lady-in-waiting to the princess, putting her on a course to become a future duchess of York.

Restoration and reward With the restoration of the Stuarts on 29 May 1660, O'Neill's devotion and friendship were well rewarded by an appreciative monarch. He never received a peerage, but he accumulated money-making positions and sinecures to make him one of the richest men in England. He held numerous lucrative land grants in London and Ireland and built Belsize House in Hampstead. Having married in September 1660 Heenvliet's widow, Katherine, *née* Wotton (*d.* 1667), who had been created countess of Chesterfield as widow of her first husband, Henry Stanhope, in May of that year, he enjoyed her country home at Boughton Malherbe in Kent. O'Neill continued as groom to the bedchamber, was made captain of the King's horse guards, became a member of parliament for St Ives in 1662, was admitted to Gray's Inn, and sat as an absentee representative in the Irish parliament of 1661. He also was granted extensive mining rights and privileges, held the coveted monopoly of sole manufacturer of gunpowder to the crown, was appointed surveyor of the petty customs and tonnage, and was the accountant for the regulation of ale houses. And for the payment of £21,000 annually he became the postmaster-general of all the king's dominions, with the monopoly of carrying all letters to the colonies with power to make contacts with his continental counterparts. Still in the king's service, he worked as the warden of St James's Palace and park, served as building commissioner in London, and co-ordinated the recovery of the royal family's heirlooms. He did not neglect his friends. He helped to restore Antrim to his Irish estates, assisted Sir Henry Bennet in becoming secretary of state, and looked after the well-being of his niece and nephew and three stepchildren. When O'Neill died in his Whitehall lodgings, on 24 October 1664, the king wrote, 'Poor Oneale died … of an ulcer in his guts; he was an honest man as ever lived; I am sure I have lost a very good servant' (Charles II to the duchess of Orléans, 24 Oct 166[4], Dalrymple, 2.2.27). The diarist Samuel Pepys commented that 'This day the great O'Neale died; I believe, to the content of all the protestants in Ireland' (*The Diary of Samuel Pepys*, ed. H. B. Wheatley, vol. 4, 1894, 273–4). O'Neill was buried at Boughton Malherbe parish church. His wife was the major beneficiary of his accumulated wealth.

Historical summary O'Neill's inscripted epitaph lauding how he 'added new lustre by his own merit' to his honorable ancestry (Cregan, 5.73) is also appropriate for his life and career. His accomplishments were considerable, given his father's disappointing bequest and the family's situation in post-plantation Ulster. From early on he appreciated how his fortune was tied to royal favour. Even in desperate times he knew there was no alternative to the crown's goodwill. Raised as a protestant, he never made an issue of religion. He tolerated the old faith and used protestantism as a badge of his political correctness. He endured by using his nurtured charm to gain influential friends and manipulate circumstances to his advantage. His personal dexterity was a major factor in his broad appeal. An experienced soldier, he was also the ultimate courtier, an intimate of the royal family, and confidant to policy makers. His activities during the decades of war and exile were remarkable testimonies to his endurance and political acumen. His post-Restoration awards,

together with his magnanimity, speak to the quality of his character and the success of his endeavours. All told, he was probably a better royalist than an Irishman.

JERROLD I. CASWAY

Sources *The works of the most reverend father in God, William Laud*, 7, ed. J. Bliss (1860) • *CSP dom.*, *1625–49* • *CSP Ire.*, *1596–1670* • Bodl. Oxf., MSS Carte 1–70 • T. Carte, *An history of the life of James, duke of Ormonde*, 3 vols. (1735–6) • J. Casway, 'Belturbet council and election of March 1650', *Clogher Record*, 12 (1986), 159–70 • J. Casway, *Owen Roe O'Neill and the struggle for Catholic Ireland* (1984) • D. Cregan, 'An Irish cavalier: Daniel O'Neill', *Studia Hibernica*, 3 (1963), 60–100; 4 (1964), 104–33; 5 (1965), 42–77 • Bodl. Oxf., MSS Clarendon 7–98 • J. Dalrymple, *Memoirs of Great Britain and Ireland*, 2 vols. (1771–3) • J. T. Gilbert, ed., *A contemporary history of affairs in Ireland from 1641 to 1652*, 3 vols. (1879–80) • *History of the Irish confederation and the war in Ireland … by Richard Bellings*, ed. J. T. Gilbert, 7 vols. (1882–91) • R. Gillespie, *Colonial Ulster: the settlement of East Ulster, 1600–1641* (1985) • T. K. Lowry, ed., *The Hamilton manuscripts* (1867) • *The Montgomery manuscripts, 1603–1706*, ed. G. Hill (1869) • Clarendon, *Hist. rebellion* • G. Radcliffe, *The earl of Strafforde's letters and dispatches, with an essay towards his life*, ed. W. Knowler, 2 vols. (1739) • B. O'Ferrall and D. O'Connell, *Commentarius Rinuccinianus de sedis apostolicae legatione ad foederatos Hiberniae Catholicos per annos 1645–1649*, ed. J. Kavanagh, 6 vols., IMC (1932–49) • J. H. Ohlmeyer, *Civil war and Restoration in the three Stuart kingdoms: the career of Randal MacDonnell, marquis of Antrim, 1609–1683* (1993) • *Oneales escape out of the Tower of London* (1642) • Bodl. Oxf., MSS Rawl. • Strafford papers, Sheff. Arch., Wentworth Woodhouse muniments • *Treason discovered, or, The impeachment of Daniel Oneale* (1641) • D. Underdown, *Royalist conspiracy in England, 1649–1660* (1960); repr. (1971) • GEC, *Peerage*, new edn, 3.180–81 [countess of Chesterfield] • *JHL*, 5 (1642–3)
Archives Berks. RO, letters to Prince Rupert • Bodl. Oxf., Carte MSS • Bodl. Oxf., Clarendon MSS • Bodl. Oxf., Rawlinson MSS • PRO, state papers domestic; Ireland • University of Sheffield Library, Strafford papers
Wealth at death two houses; much property in London and Ireland; generated income from numerous royal appointments, particularly postmaster-general: Cregan, 'An Irish cavalier' (1965), 64–73, 76–7

O'Neill, Edward Francis [Teddy] (1890–1972), headmaster, was born on 28 September 1890 at 22 York Street, Pendleton, Salford, the son of Edward Henry O'Neill, journeyman butcher, and his wife, Louisa Esther (formerly Higginbottom, *née* High), from Mobberley, Cheshire. He was brought up by his mother, who kept a succession of pubs and off-licence shops; his parents had separated, and his father died early of tuberculosis. He attended elementary school, gained a scholarship, and at the age of sixteen became a pupil teacher at Ordsall Lane School, Salford, where he stayed until 1910. He developed his own reading through Everyman Library editions, including Shakespeare, taught himself to play the piano, and worked in his mother's pubs, singing and adulterating the beer. He signed a temperance pledge with the Band of Hope. He returned to school as an uncertificated assistant and enlivened his lessons by the introduction of aquariums and vivariums into the classroom; his talent as a teacher was recognized by an inspector, who arranged for him to enter Crewe Training College in 1911. In 1913 he married Isabel Dick Hutchison (1893/4–1957), who was a great support and stabilizing influence throughout his work. They had a daughter, Margaret, and a son, Alec.

As a certificated teacher in two Salford schools from

1913 O'Neill took children on visits to shops and markets, art galleries and museums, and to his own home for singing and dancing. He was appointed a temporary headmaster in Oswaldtwistle, where he bought tools for children from his own pocket and encouraged them in handiwork. Once again his innovative methods brought him to the attention of the inspectors of schools, whose glowing reports resulted in an invitation from Lord Lytton to address the New Ideals in Education conference in August 1918 in Oxford.

Thereafter O'Neill took up a headship at Prestolee, near Farnworth, Lancashire, where he remained for thirty-four years, gaining national recognition and some notoriety for his innovations and practices. From 1918 to 1923 he was joined on his staff by Commander R. G. A. Holmes, who at first worked in an unpaid capacity out of interest in O'Neill's methods. Holmes was well connected as nephew of Edmond Holmes, former chief inspector and promoter of progressive education, and as cousin of Maurice Holmes, a senior civil servant at the Board of Education, and he later publicized the work of O'Neill in a book, *The Idiot Teacher*, published in 1952. In 1951 O'Neill was made MBE in the new year honours list.

O'Neill's innovations included the use of school premises in the evenings, exotically landscaped school gardens and illuminations, camping holidays and even foreign travel with pupils, and the establishment of a permanent school camp at Plumbley, Cheshire. The contravention of regulations and unconventional interpretation of the teacher's role which these innovations entailed initially aroused local controversy and discontent, and even questions in parliament, which led to investigations and inquiries. O'Neill, however, persisted in realizing his dream of 'making the whole school that centre of day-long animation, learning and beauty, which, through its interests, facilities and generous provision of stimulating apparatus, it has become for the whole of the village community' (Holmes, 99). His maverick work thus paralleled the more orderly contemporary development of community education by Henry Morris in Cambridgeshire. It attracted popular press coverage of Prestolee, and a feature in *Picture Post* recorded great affection and enthusiasm but also criticism from former pupils.

O'Neill's educational philosophy was practical, down-to-earth, conveyed mostly through his practice, and summarized in proverbs displayed around the school, such as 'The best way to learn is to live' and 'Uniformity is death to character'; other proverbs conveyed his loathing for Lancashire's industrialism, but he encouraged children to take control of their environment and to qualify themselves for employment. After his first wife, Isabel, died in May 1957 he married again. Teddy O'Neill died of heart failure on 22 March 1972 at his home, Hurstwood, Clarke's Hill, Whitefield, Lancashire, and left a widow, Clara Irlam Bertha. PETER CUNNINGHAM

Sources G. Holmes, *The idiot teacher, a book about Prestolee School and its headmaster E.F. O'Neill* (1952) • E. F. O'Neill and K. Howarth, interview, 1972, North-West Sound Archive and Bolton Libraries and Arts • *Farnworth Journal* (6 April 1972) • J. Cooper, 'Teddy O'Neill'

(Bolton Workers' Educational Association, 1988) • S. Hicklin, 'Is the "progressive" school a success?', *Picture Post* (3 May 1952) • *Farnworth Journal* (5 Jan 1951) • *Farnworth Journal* (22 May 1953) • *Manchester Evening News* (9 March 1977) • H. Middleton, 'Developments in self-activity in an elementary school: Knuzden, Blackburn', *The new era in education*, ed. E. Young (1920) • b. cert. • d. cert.

Archives Farnworth Library, Bolton | FILM Pathé film 1947 | SOUND North-West Sound Archive, Clitheroe Castle, Clitheroe, Lancashire

Likenesses photograph, 1951, repro. in *Farnworth Journal* (5 Jan 1951) • E. Chat, photograph, 1952, repro. in *Picture Post* (3 May 1952) • photograph, repro. in *Manchester Evening News*

Wealth at death £7600: administration, 1 Nov 1974, *CGPLA Eng. & Wales*

Ó Néill, Éinrí [Henry O'Neill, Éinrí Aimhréidh, Harry Avery] (d. 1392), nobleman, was a younger son of Niall Mór *Ó Néill (d. 1397), king or chief of Tír Eoghain, and his wife, Beanmidhe (d. 1385), daughter of a Mac Mathghamhna chief. He was nicknamed Éinrí Aimhréidh (Henry the Turbulent or Henry the Contentious) and was long remembered in Ulster folklore as Harry Avery. Evidence that his sobriquet was not bestowed on him, as the annals of Connacht flatteringly allege, *per antiphrasim*, comes in a letter to his father, Niall Mór, dated 18 July 1375, in which Milo Sweteman, archbishop of Armagh, complained: 'your degenerate sons Henricus and Catholicus [Cú Uladh Ruadh], hunters ordained by the devil, are raping the wives of divers husbands and their handmaidens with them' (register of Milo Sweteman, fol. 27r), causing the citizens and tenants of Armagh to threaten emigration.

Subsequently Éinrí Ó Néill is found in western Tír Eoghain, on the borders of Fermanagh and Tír Conaill (the Donegal area). In 1379 he inflicted a defeat on the men of Fermanagh and in 1380 intervened in the succession struggles of Tír Conaill to enable his brother-in-law, Toirdhealbhach an Fhíona Ó Domhnaill (d. 1423), to become king there. He appears to have exercised authority over the area around the modern Newtownstewart, in Tyrone, where his sons and grandsons, known as the Sliocht Éinrí ('descendants of Henry') or Slughte Henry Avery O'Neill, held sway subsequently and where the ruin called Harry Avery's Castle is traditionally associated with his rule (the implied date being accepted as possible by modern archaeologists). Ó Néill married a kinswoman, Aiffric (d. 1389), the daughter of Aodh Ó Néill. The year of her death saw the first recorded raid by one of their sons against a vassal of Ó Domhnaill.

In contrast to his sons, who turned against both Ó Domhnaill and Niall Mór, Éinrí Ó Néill was a loyal supporter of his father and of his elder brother Niall Óg *Ó Néill (d. 1403) [see under Ó Néill, Niall Mór]. In March 1390 he yielded his second son as a hostage for the release of Niall Óg, captured in battle by the Anglo-Irish the previous year. This son, soon ransomed, may be identical with Domhnall Bog Ó Néill (d. 1432), the future king of Tír Eoghain, who, after the death of his brother Briain Mór in 1402, emerged as the leader of Éinrí Ó Néill's descendants, and seized the kingship from Eoghan *Ó Néill (d. 1456), son of Niall Óg Ó Néill. Other sons of Éinrí Ó Néill are named as Aodh (*fl.* 1412), Niall Ruadh (*d.* 1430/1432), Seán, Ruaidhrí, and Éinrí Óg. Éinrí Aimhréidh Ó Néill died on 16 May 1392. Described by most annalists as worthy to succeed his brother in the kingship and praised for his extravagant generosity, he was criticized by Aughuistín Magraidhin (*d.* 1405) as 'an unjust, wicked and sinful man' (Ó hInnse, no. 8, 147).   KATHARINE SIMMS

Sources K. Simms, 'The archbishops of Armagh and the O'Neills, 1347–1471', *Irish Historical Studies*, 19 (1974–5), 38–55 · D. Murphy, ed., *The annals of Clonmacnoise*, trans. C. Mageoghagan (1896); facs. edn (1993), 306–7, 315 · T. E. McNeill, *Anglo-Norman Ulster: the history and archaeology of an Irish barony, 1177–1400* (1980), 75, 114, pl. 4B · T. Mathews, *The O'Neills of Ulster*, 3 vols. (1907), 2.248 · AFM, vols. 3, 4 · W. M. Hennessy and B. MacCarthy, eds., *Annals of Ulster, otherwise, annals of Senat*, 4 vols. (1887–1901), vol. 3 · A. M. Freeman, ed. and trans., *Annála Connacht / The annals of Connacht* (1944); repr. (1970) · S. Ó hInnse, ed. and trans., *Miscellaneous Irish annals, AD 1114–1437* (1947) · K. Simms, 'Niall Garbh II O'Donnell, king of Tír Conaill', *Donegal Annual*, 12 (1977), 7–21 · T. Ó Donnchadha, ed., *Leabhar Cloinne Aodha Buidhe* (1931), 34–5 · [M. Sweteman], *The register of Milo Sweteman*, ed. B. Smith, IMC (1996), no. 141, pp. 139–40

Ó Néill, Éinrí [Henry O'Neill] (*d.* **1489**), king or lord of Tír Eoghain, was the eldest son of Eoghan *Ó Néill (*d.* 1456), chief of Tír Eoghain, and of his wife, Caitríona (*d.* 1427), daughter of Ardghal Mac Mathghamhna. Since Eoghan was ransomed in 1422 from Ó Néill of Clandeboye by his own wife and sons, Éinrí and his next brother, Aodh of the Fews, were probably born not long after *c.*1400. In 1431 Éinrí was briefly captured in a frontier conflict by Neachtain Ó Domhnaill, brother of the king of Tír Conaill. In 1432 the hostility was renewed as a 'great war' between the chiefs Eoghan Ó Néill (officially inaugurated in that year) and Neachtain's brother, Niall Garbh Ó Domhnaill (*d.* 1439). Éinrí negotiated with Ó Domhnaill's enemies, the Ó Conchobhair chieftains of Sligo; then in 1433 he joined his father in invading Ulster east of the Bann, where Ó Domhnaill had brought his army to ally with Robert Savage and MacQuillin, leaders of the vestigial Anglo-Irish colony there, who, like Ó Néill and Ó Domhnaill themselves, were nominal subjects of Richard, duke of York, the absentee earl of Ulster.

With the aid of a fleet commanded by Mac Domhnaill, the Scottish lord of the Isles, Éinrí Ó Néill and his father burnt the port of Ardglass and drove Ó Domhnaill and MacQuillin into Louth, to seek the ineffective assistance of the chief governor of Ireland, who joined them in an unsuccessful raid on Armagh but could not prevent the submission of Ó Domhnaill to Ó Néill before the end of the year. As the Anglo-Irish seem to have anticipated, this consolidation of authority in the north resulted in the invasion of Meath and Louth in 1434 by all the Ulster chiefs, during which campaign Ó Domhnaill was captured, but Éinrí Ó Néill and his brother Aodh distinguished themselves by covering the retreat of their troops after burning Nobber.

The annals credit the brothers with similar prowess at the camp-assault of the Rosses and the battle of Slíab Truim on Eoghan Ó Néill's expedition in 1435 against Neachtain Ó Domhnaill, deputy leader of Tír Conaill, and his own hostile kinsman, Brian Óg (a grandson of the Éinrí

*Ó Néill who died in 1392). When Brian Óg deserted Neachtain, coming in to parley under the safe conduct of Ó Néill's court poet, Éinrí and his brothers violated the poet's guarantee by imprisoning and maiming Brian Óg and his two sons, one of whom died in consequence. The poet, having vigorously satirized Ó Néill's sons, was disinherited and exiled to Connacht for eighteen years, as he later lamented in an apologetic address to Éinrí, 'Cionnas do roichfinn rí Oiligh?' ('How shall I reach the king of Oileach?'; Killiney, Franciscan House of Studies, MS A25, p. 149).

Éinrí Ó Néill became increasingly prominent. In 1438 he intervened in Fermanagh to negotiate the release of the chief Mág Uidhir, imprisoned by rival kinsmen. Following his father's submission to the Dublin government in the spring of 1441, Éinrí brought an Anglo-Irish army to the borders of Tír Conaill in 1442 to assist Eoghan in subduing Neachtain Ó Domhnaill, when he annexed the disputed borderland of Cineál Moáin and left a garrison in Neachtain's castle on the River Finn. He dominated Tír Conaill politically thereafter until his appointment of Aodh Ruadh Ó Domhnaill (*d.* 1505) as chief in 1461.

The repeated attempts by Éinrí Ó Néill and his father to force submission from Ó Néill of Clandeboye were less successful. In 1444 they ended in the surrender of nineteen hostages, including a son of Éinrí, to secure a safe retreat. However, Éinrí's presence at Ardglass in company with the chiefs of the Ulster colonists on 9 December 1448 suggests an alliance with these, verified in 1450 when he aided MacQuillin to attack Ó Néill of Clandeboye. At Drogheda on 27 August 1449 Éinrí Ó Néill, having full powers from his father, family, and subjects, ratified an indenture with the duke of York (as earl of Ulster and also king's lieutenant). He undertook, in exchange for the duke's aid and protection: to return any formerly conquered lands; to render the ancient services, including the 'bonnacht of Ulster' (a former right of the earls of Ulster to billet fixed quotas of mercenary soldiers on each of the Ulster chiefs); to war against the duke's enemies; and to serve him whenever summoned with 500 men-at-arms and 500 foot soldiers. In May 1452 Éinrí brought about the death of Neachtain Ó Domhnaill and married his widow, the daughter of MacWilliam Burke, lord of Mayo, although he was already married to Gormlaith (*d.* 1465), mother of his son Éinrí Óg and daughter of Mac Murchadha Caomhánach and of the sister of James Butler, fourth earl of Ormond. That July the dying Ormond brought an army northwards and forced Éinrí to dismiss Ó Domhnaill's widow and take back Gormlaith, the earl's niece.

In 1455 Éinrí Ó Néill was inaugurated chief in place of his father, Eoghan, in July and confirmed in office by Archbishop John Mey of Armagh on 4 August; he drew up a concordat with Mey on 14 November following. Styled in 1474 'the king's friend', Ó Néill brought an Anglo-Irish army on an unsuccessful siege of his own brother Art's castle of Omagh in 1459, and in 1463 received a livery of scarlet and a golden chain from Edward IV, who, as the son of Richard duke of York, was now earl of Ulster. Ó Néill's expeditions to eastern Ulster in 1469, 1470, and 1476 in support of the

White family and MacQuillin against the Savages and Ó Néill of Clandeboye, and his capture of Omagh after a six-month siege in 1470, mark a high point in his career. In 1480 his son and heir, Conn Mór (who married Eleanor, sister of Gerald Fitzgerald, eighth earl of Kildare), received a grant of English law, the earl joining Conn that year in an unsuccessful siege of the castle at Caledon, stronghold of Éinrí Ó Néill's brother, Seán Buidhe. Besides family rivalry, Ó Néill was threatened by Ó Domhnaill and Ó Néill of Clandeboye, who combined in 1481 to capture Conn. After ransoming Conn in 1483, Éinrí Ó Néill handed over the precarious chieftaincy to him, and eventually died on 15 June 1489. KATHARINE SIMMS

Sources K. Simms, '"The king's friend": O'Neill, the crown and the earldom of Ulster', *England and Ireland in the later middle ages: essays in honour of Jocelyn Otway-Ruthven*, ed. J. Lydon (1981), 214–36 · K. Simms, 'The concordat between primate John Mey and Henry O'Neill (1455)', *Archivium Hibernicum*, 34 (1976–7), 71–82 · W. M. Hennessy and B. MacCarthy, eds., *Annals of Ulster, otherwise, annals of Senat*, 4 vols. (1887–1901), vol. 3 · W. G. H. Quigley and E. F. D. Roberts, eds., *Registrum Iohannis Mey: the register of John Mey, archbishop of Armagh, 1443–1456* (1972) · E. Curtis, ed., 'The "bonnacht" of Ulster', *Hermathena*, 46 (1931), 87–105 · E. Curtis, 'Richard, duke of York, as viceroy of Ireland', *Journal of the Royal Society of Antiquaries of Ireland*, 7th ser., 2 (1932), 158–86 · H. F. Berry and J. F. Morrissey, eds., *Statute rolls of the parliament of Ireland*, 4 vols. (1907–39), vol. 4, pt 2 · *AFM* · A. M. Freeman, ed. and trans., *Annála Connacht / The annals of Connacht* (1944); repr. (1970) · W. M. Hennessy, ed. and trans., *The annals of Loch Cé: a chronicle of Irish affairs from AD 1014 to AD 1590*, 2 vols., Rolls Series, 54 (1871), vol. 2 · J. F. O'Donovan, ed., 'The Annals of Ireland 1443–1468, translated by … Duald MacFirbis', *Miscellany of the Irish Archaeological Society* (1846), 198–302 · L. McKenna, ed., *Aithdioghluim Dána*, 2 vols. (1939–40), no. 17 · S. Ó hInnse, ed. and trans., *Miscellaneous Irish annals, AD 1114–1437* (1947) · D. A. Chart, ed., *The register of John Swayne, archbishop of Armagh and primate of Ireland, 1418–1439* (1935) · Franciscan House of Studies, Killiney, co. Dublin, MS A25

O'Neill, Elizabeth [Eliza; *married name* Elizabeth Wrixon-Becher, Lady Wrixon-Becher] (**1791–1872**), actress, was the daughter of an Irish actor, John O'Neill, stage manager of the Drogheda Theatre, and his wife, a Miss Featherstone. She went on to the stage in Drogheda as a young child, and later spent two years in Belfast before going to Dublin, where she rapidly became popular in such roles as Juliet and Jane Shore, and as Ellen in a version of *The Lady of the Lake*. Other parts included the title role in Richard Lalor Sheil's *Adelaide, or, The Emigrants* at the Crow Street Theatre (19 February 1814). She was then engaged by Thomas Harris for Covent Garden, where she made her début as Juliet to William Conway's Romeo and had an immediate triumph. She was hailed as Sarah Siddons's successor as a tragedienne, and stories were told of men borne fainting from the theatre after witnessing her performances. W. C. Macready considered her Juliet to be definitive and praised her for the 'artlessness' of her 'look, voice and manner' (*Macready's Reminiscences*, 1.97). The musicality of her voice was widely admired, as was her 'classical' beauty. Hazlitt commented that her acting was 'smooth, round, polished, and classical, like a marble statue' (West, 91). For five years, in parts including Belvidera (in *Venice Preserv'd*), Mrs Haller (in *The Stranger*), and Jane Shore, she dominated the London stage. Her

attempt at Lady Randolph in Home's *Douglas* was one of her failures: Sir Walter Scott had noted that she 'excels rather in those feminine & soft characters than in those where force & dignity are required' (*Letters*, 4.57), and even the admiring Macready was obliged to admit that Lady Randolph was 'unsuited alike to her juvenile appearance and her style of acting' (*Macready's Reminiscences*, 1.167). She was accepted in comedies, for example as Lady Teazle and Widow Cheerly, but it was in tragedy that she made her reputation.

On 3 July 1819 Eliza O'Neill made what was announced as her last appearance before Christmas, as Mrs Haller; it was her last appearance on the stage. On 18 December 1819 she married William Wrixon-Becher (1780–1850), MP for the Irish constituency of Mallow. Her reputation for virtue and propriety was fierce: it was later reported that when the under-age Lord Normanby [see Phipps, Constantine Henry, first marquess of Normanby] had proposed marriage to her she had sent the letter to his father. The *Gentleman's Magazine* reported the wedding, informing its readers that 'Mr B. settles 1000l a year on the lady; and refuses to take a shilling of her fortune' (*GM*, 635). Wrixon-Becher was a considerable landowner at Ballygiblin, co. Cork, and was created a baronet in 1831; the couple had three sons and two daughters. Lady Wrixon-Becher died on 29 October 1872 at Ballygiblin. K. D. REYNOLDS

Sources *DNB* · *Macready's reminiscences, and selections from his diaries and letters*, ed. F. Pollock, 2 vols. (1875) · *The letters of Sir Walter Scott*, ed. H. J. C. Grierson and others, centenary edn, 12 vols. (1932–79) · *GM*, 1st ser., 89/2 (1819), 635 · Burke, *Peerage* · S. West, *The image of the actor* (1991) · M. Booth, *Theatre in the Victorian age* (1991) · *CGPLA Eng. & Wales* (1873)

Likenesses R. Cooper, line and stipple print, pubd 1811 (after A. W. Devis), NG Ire. · J. J. Masquerier, oils, *c*.1815, NPG · W. Say, mezzotint, pubd 1815 (after J. J. Masquerier), NG Ire. · A. W. Davis, oils, 1816, Wolverhampton Art Gallery · F. C. Lewis, stipple, pubd 1816 (after G. Dawe), NG Ire. · T. Blood, stipple (after S. Drummond), BM, NPG; repro. in *European Magazine* (1814) · H. Dawe, mezzotint (as Juliet in *Romeo and Juliet*), BM · G. F. Joseph, oils (as 'the tragic muse'), Garr. Club · W. J. Newton, miniature, NG Ire.

Wealth at death under £25,000: resworn probate, June 1873, *CGPLA Eng. & Wales*

Ó Néill, Eoghan [Owen or Eugene O'Neill] (*d.* 1456), king or lord of Tír Eoghain, was a younger son of Niall Óg *Ó Néill (*d.* 1403) [*see under* Ó Néill, Niall Mór] and his wife, Úna (*d.* 1417), the daughter of Domhnall Ó Néill. He had clearly reached military age by 21 July 1399 when he slew Cathal, son of Ruaidhrí Mág Uidhir at a time when Niall Óg was forcing submission from all Ulster apart from Ó Domhnaill, the lord of Tír Conaill. However, by 1403 Niall Óg faced rebellion from his nephews, the sons of Éinrí *Ó Néill (*d.* 1392). A matter of months after Niall Óg's death, his eldest son and heir, Brian Óg, died from smallpox and the kingship of Tír Eoghain was seized by Domhnall Bog ('Donal the Soft' or 'the Generous'; *d.* 1432), son of Éinrí Aimhréidh, who was inaugurated as Ó Néill in 1404. Eoghan, however, retained influence over Mág Uidhir of Fermanagh, and was married to Caitríona (*d.* 1427), the daughter of Ardghal Mac Mathghamhna (king of the

Monaghan area from 1403 to 1411), and mother of his eldest son, Éinrí *Ó Néill (d. 1489).

In 1410 Eoghan Ó Néill's brother-in-law, Brian, captured Domhnall Bog, precipitating civil war in Tír Eoghain. Eoghan himself was imprisoned by the sons of his uncle, Éinrí Aimhréidh, in 1414 and released only in exchange for the reinstatement of their leader, Domhnall Bog. In 1419–20, however, Eoghan, in alliance with Ó Domhnaill, Mág Uidhir, and Brian Mac Mathghamhna ignominiously drove Domhnall Bog out of Tír Eoghain to seek refuge with the English settlers of Down. Within a year peace was patched up again. Domhnall Bog retained his title as the Great Ó Néill (as he was known in the English pale), but became politically insignificant thereafter. During the prolonged struggle both Ó Domhnaill in the west and the Anglo-Irish government in the east had expanded their influence.

In 1421 Eoghan Ó Néill was on his way to meet James Butler, fourth earl of Ormond, at Dundalk when he was captured by Ó Néill of Clandeboye. When ransomed a year later by his wife and sons, Eoghan allied with Niall Garbh Ó Domhnaill, the new king of Tír Conaill, to ravage Ó Néill of Clandeboye, forcing him to submit and join a general federation of Ulster chiefs who invaded northern Connacht in 1422 and the English of Meath and Louth in 1423, defeated the justiciar's army, and imposed 'black-rent' (protection money which subsequently developed into a customary annual payment) on the town of Dundalk. This brought Edmund (V) Mortimer, fifth earl of March and Ulster, to Ireland as lieutenant in the autumn of 1424. The Ulster chiefs came to Trim Castle that Christmas to submit, but Mortimer died suddenly on 18 January 1425 and the visitors were promptly arrested by Sir John Talbot, though subsequently released by the new lieutenant, the earl of Ormond, in exchange for ransom and hostages. In his indenture with Ormond on 23 July 1425, Eoghan Ó Néill acknowledged himself vassal to the duke of York, Mortimer's heir, and significantly undertook to desert and inform on any treasonable confederation. Once home he allied with Domhnall Bog to recover land lost to Ó Domhnaill during their contentions. He rebuilt his father's authority over the province, adding the allegiance of Ó Raighilligh of East Bréifne in 1429. In 1430 he once again harried Louth, took black-rent from Dundalk, then received submissions from the Irish chieftains of Longford and Westmeath, Baron Nugent of Delvin (an ally of Ormond), and the Plunkets and Herberts, before making war on the other English in Meath.

In 1432 Eoghan Ó Néill at last succeeded Domhnall Bog as the Great Ó Néill. He then forced Ó Domhnaill to submit, and in the course of a joint raid into Louth in 1434 the latter was conveniently captured by the English. After submitting to Ormond once more in 1441, Ó Néill next year used English troops to win a crushing victory against the new Ó Domhnaill. However, he made war on Louth in 1444, in 1449 just before the duke of York's visit, and again in 1452; and he and his then wife, Evelina Baret, incurred archiepiscopal censure for infringing the property rights of Armagh. In 1455 Archbishop John Mey sanctioned a transfer of the chieftainship from Eoghan to his eldest son, Éinrí, on grounds of infirmity, though the annals speak of forcible deposition, and the retired chief died the following year.

KATHARINE SIMMS

Sources K. Simms, '"The king's friend": O'Neill, the crown and the earldom of Ulster', *England and Ireland in the later middle ages: essays in honour of Jocelyn Otway-Ruthven*, ed. J. Lydon (1981), 214–36 · K. Simms, 'Niall Garbh II O Donnell, king of Tír Conaill', *Donegal Annual*, 12 (1977), 7–21 · W. M. Hennessy and B. MacCarthy, eds., *Annals of Ulster, otherwise, annals of Senat*, 4 vols. (1887–1901) · Irish Record Commission, *Reports from the Commissioners … respecting the public records of Ireland*, 1 (1815), 54–6 · W. G. H. Quigley and E. F. D. Roberts, eds., *Registrum Iohannis Mey: the register of John Mey, archbishop of Armagh, 1443–1456* (1972) · E. Tresham, ed., *Rotulorum patentium et clausorum cancellariae Hiberniae calendarium*, Irish Record Commission (1828) · *AFM*, vol. 4 · A. M. Freeman, ed. and trans., *Annála Connacht / The annals of Connacht* (1944); repr. (1970) · A. J. Otway-Ruthven, *A history of medieval Ireland* (1968)

O'Neill, Flaithbheartach. See Ua Néill, Flaithbertach (d. 1036).

O'Neill, (Daniel) Francis (1848–1936), collector of Irish folk music, was born on 28 August 1848 (often given wrongly as 1849) at Tralibane, co. Cork, the fourth son and youngest of the seven children of John O'Neill (c.1801–1867), a farmer, and his wife, Catherine O'Mahoney (c.1812–1900), from Castlemahon. He was a bright pupil at Bantry national school. In March 1865 he left home for adventure and to escape his elder brother's financial demands. He became a sailor, and over the next three years travelled the world, surviving a shipwreck on Baker Island in the Pacific. In 1869 he settled in Edina, Missouri, gained a teaching qualification, and taught in the local school. After a brief spell in Chicago he returned to Edina, and in November 1870 married Anna Rogers in Bloomington, Illinois. In 1871 he moved to Chicago and on 12 July 1873 was sworn in as a policeman. He rose through the ranks until on 30 April 1901 he was appointed general superintendent of the Chicago police, retiring on 25 July 1905. While he was in post, however, his enduring achievement was to assemble the largest collection of Irish music yet published.

O'Neill's family was musical and he had learned the flute in childhood. On his travels he assimilated tunes at every opportunity. At Edina he boarded with the school director, a flautist from Galway, at whose Irish dances O'Neill learned tunes while sitting at the rear. In Chicago he patrolled the largely Irish Deering Street district, acquiring tunes and participating in impromptu music sessions in the police station. In the 1890s he began the systematic transcription of the tunes he had learned and any others he could find. Despite being the driving force behind the compilation, he was musically barely literate, relying on his fellow policeman James O'Neill for the transcriptions. The result was the publication in 1903 of *O'Neill's Music of Ireland*, containing 1850 tunes. O'Neill, as a practitioner of his art, collected for practical use, not for scholarly analysis. He had no hesitation in supplying or correcting missing or 'wrong' notes, and interpreted the remit of his title broadly. As a result his work was dismissed by some of the luminaries of folk-music scholarship in Ireland. Such disregard was, however, in sharp contrast with its immediate acceptance by practising musicians: it has become the touchstone of Irish musicians everywhere, when they ask of any tune, 'Is it in the book?' O'Neill followed this publication with others, extracting from *O'Neill's Music of Ireland* and adding to it from continued collecting, acquisition of printed and manuscript sources, and transcription from others' manuscripts. In later life he became disillusioned at the low esteem which Irish music commanded in its native land.

O'Neill was a man of medium height, with a military bearing. He had a robust constitution, but his personal happiness was marred by the early deaths of all five of his sons and one of his five daughters. In 1931 he gave his library to the University of Notre Dame, Indiana. His wife died in 1934, and he died from heart failure at his home, 5448 Drexel Boulevard, Chicago, on 28 January 1936. He was buried on 30 January at Mount Olivet, Chicago, after a funeral service at the church of St Thomas Apostle.

MICHAEL HEANEY

Sources N. Carolan, *A harvest saved: Francis O'Neill and Irish music in Chicago* (1997) • F. O'Neill, *Irish folk music: a fascinating hobby* (1910) • C. ffrench, 'Francis O'Neill', *Biographical history of the American Irish in Chicago* (1897), 308–15 • B. Breathnach, 'Francis O'Neill, collector of Irish music', *Dal gCais* (1977), 111–19 • *Chicago Daily Tribune* (29 Jan 1936) • 'Chicago leads Ireland as a storehouse of Irish music', *Chicago Sunday Tribune* (2 March 1902) • L. S. Fuderer, *Music mad: Captain Francis O'Neill and traditional Irish music, an exhibition…* (1990)
Archives University of Notre Dame, Indiana | SOUND University College, Dublin, Folk Music Division, 938b, 939b • University College, Cork, Music Department, 30 cylinders
Likenesses Binner Wells Co., photograph, *c*.1901–1905, repro. in O'Neill, *Irish folk music*, frontispiece • photograph, 1902, repro. in 'Chicago leads Ireland as a storehouse of Irish music' • photograph, *c*.1915, repro. in *Chicago Daily Tribune*

O'Neill, Gordon (*c*.1652–1705). *See under* O'Neill, Sir Phelim Roe (1603–1653).

O'Neill [*née* Boyle]**, Henrietta** (1757/8–1793), poet and patron of the arts, was the only child of Charles Boyle, Lord Dungarvan (1728/9–1759), son of John *Boyle, fifth earl of Cork and Orrery, and Susanna (1732–1783), daughter of Henry *Hoare (1705–1785), a banker who created the gardens at Stourhead, Wiltshire. After Charles's death, Susanna married Thomas Brudenell Bruce, later first earl of Ailesbury (1729–1814). O'Neill was close to her maternal grandfather and followed his example in supporting the arts. Two portraits of O'Neill by one of the painters he patronized, William Hoare (no relation), survive at Stourhead (the attribution of one is uncertain).

Henrietta married John *O'Neill (1740–1798) of Shane's Castle, co. Antrim, on 18 October 1777. Their homes included a London residence in Henrietta Street, Cavendish Square. A nationalist politician who became an Irish peer shortly after his wife's death, John O'Neill was killed in 1798, acting to suppress the Irish rising. Among the rebels was Lord Edward Fitzgerald, who had appeared in 1785 with the O'Neills in a production of *Cymbeline*, in

their private theatre at Shane's Castle. After performing the role of the Queen, O'Neill reappeared as a sylph to deliver an epilogue, written by her, in which she praises the play's setting:

> This favour'd spot a thousand Sylphs engage
> To dress the banquet, and adorn the stage.

Sarah Siddons recalled of Shane's Castle: 'It is scarce possible to conceive the splendour of this almost Royal Establishment, except by recollecting the circumstances of an Arabian Nights entertainment' (*The Reminiscences of Sarah Kemble Siddons, 1773–1785*, ed. W. van Lennep, 1942, 27). On the same bill O'Neill appeared as Termagant in Arthur Murphy's *The Upholsterer*.

Siddons credits O'Neill with launching her acting career. In 1774 O'Neill attended a performance of Thomas Otway's *Venice Preserv'd* in Cheltenham. So moved was she by Siddons's Belvidera, that she not only befriended the actor and became her patron, but also supervised her wardrobe, contributing to it and even taking up the needle. O'Neill's stepfather was a member of the party that evening, and afterward he alerted David Garrick to the appearance of a talented new actor.

O'Neill also befriended and supported Charlotte Smith, who in turn published O'Neill's 'Ode to the Poppy' in *Desmond* (1792). The poem praises the flower for its 'potent charm' that 'Can agonizing Pain disarm'. After O'Neill's death Smith reprinted the poem along with O'Neill's 'Written on Seeing her Two Sons at Play' in volume 2 of *Elegiac Sonnets* (1797). The latter poem recasts Thomas Gray's 'Eton Ode' from the perspective of a mother, who laments,

> Even now, a mother's fond prophetic fear
> Sees the dark train of human ills appear.

Her two sons, Charles Henry St John and John Bruce Richard, attended Eton College. Her other poems include 'To a Lady who Requested the Description of a Gentleman' and 'Ambrosia breathes in every sigh'.

When her health began to fail, O'Neill travelled to Portugal. In 1791 the remedy seemed successful, but did not lead to recovery. O'Neill returned to Portugal and died at Caldas de Rainha, outside Lisbon, on 3 September 1793. She was buried in the English cemetery in Lisbon, near Henry Fielding's grave. Although she lived a mostly private life—her position in prominent families limited her appearances on stage and in print—O'Neill's death was memorialized as a public event. Her friendships with and patronage of Siddons and Smith enhanced her reputation as a contributor to the arts. In its obituary in October 1793 *Anthologia Hibernica* recalls that 'uniting with the polish of courts the brilliancy of genius, she shone preeminent in the fashionable world'. In the periodical's next issue 'Ode to the Poppy' was reprinted alongside an elegy by the poet Thomas Dermody, who eulogized O'Neill as a poet who

> Could o'er the humble poppy's purple bloom,
> Pour a fresh tincture, breathe a new perfume.

SARAH M. ZIMMERMAN

Sources *Anthologia Hibernica*, 2 (Oct 1793), 319–20 · *Anthologia Hibernica*, 2 (Nov 1793), 383–5 · *GM*, 1st ser., 103/2 (1833), 130–32 · D. J. O'Donoghue, *The poets of Ireland: a biographical and bibliographical dictionary* (1912) · R. Power, *The private theatre of Kilkenny* (1825) · W. Withering, *Miscellaneous tracts of the late William Withering*, 2 vols. (1822), 1.137 · Burke, *Peerage* (1862) · GEC, *Peerage* · *DNB* · K. Woodbridge, *Landscape and antiquity: aspects of English culture at Stourhead, 1718–1838* (1970) · L. Fletcher, *Charlotte Smith: a critical biography* (1998)

Likenesses J. R. Smith, mezzotint, pubd 1778 (after M. W. Peters), NG Ire. · W. Hoare?, oils, Stourhead, Wiltshire

O'Neill, Henry

O'Neill, Henry (1798–1880), artist and antiquary, was born at Clonmel, co. Tipperary, the only child of Henry O'Neill and his wife, the daughter of Samuel Watson, a bookseller. After the early death of his parents, he was brought up by his paternal aunt Sarah O'Neill, a Dublin haberdasher. His artistic talent was recognized and he attended the Dublin Society school from 1815. The society awarded him a silver medal for 'industry and talents' in 1825. From 1835 he exhibited regularly at the Royal Hibernian Academy, of which he became an associate in 1837 but from which he resigned in 1844.

Despite his assertions to the contrary, it was financial need that drove O'Neill to London in 1847; he fared little better in England and joined the army, but his friends bought him out shortly thereafter. He returned to Dublin, and dedicated his life to travelling around the country to record the antiquities of Ireland. He is best known for two books, *The most Interesting of the Sculptured Crosses of Ancient Ireland* (1857) and *The Fine Arts and Civilisation of Ancient Ireland* (1863). Both works collected O'Neill's drawings of the antiquities, while the latter work sought to demonstrate the existence of an advanced civilization in Ireland in prehistoric times, and to refute the conclusions of George Petrie in his *Ecclesiastical Architecture of Ireland* (1845). O'Neill's argument that the round towers were of pagan origin was soon discredited, and his other arguments did not carry lasting weight.

O'Neill was a member of Daniel O'Connell's Repeal Association and wrote a pamphlet attacking landlordism, *Ireland for the Irish* (1868). His portrait of O'Connell and his fellow prisoners in Richmond gaol in 1843 was well received. John Ruskin was said to have paid 50 guineas for a small collection of O'Neill's drawings; his 1874 portrait of John Cornelius O'Callaghan, the historian, hangs in the National Gallery in Dublin. He died at 109 Lower Gardiner Street, Dublin, on 21 December 1880, leaving a widow (his second wife) and four children in straitened circumstances.   MARIE-LOUISE LEGG

Sources J. Sheehy, *The rediscovery of Ireland's past: the Celtic revival, 1830–1930* (1980) · *Saunder's News-Letter* (29 Dec 1877) · *The Athenaeum* (1 Jan 1881), 27 · W. G. Strickland, *A dictionary of Irish artists*, 2 vols. (1913) · Bénézit, *Dict.* · Wood, *Vic. painters*, 3rd edn

Likenesses H. O'Neill, self-portrait, drawing, 1913, NG Ire. · H. O'Neill, self-portrait, black and red chalk, NG Ire.

O'Neill, Hugh

O'Neill, Hugh [Aodh Ó Néill], **second earl of Tyrone** (*c*.1550–1616), magnate and rebel, was born in the lordship of Tyrone, in the province of Ulster, the second son of Matthew O'Neill (Feardorcha), first baron of Dungannon (d. 1558), landowner, and his wife, Siobhán (Joan), daughter of Constantine Maguire.

Early years and education, c.1550–1568 Matthew was heir designate, under English law, to the earldom of Tyrone, created in 1542 by Henry VIII for Conn Bacach *O'Neill, Gaelic lord of Tyrone. His eldest son, Brian O'Neill (d. 1562), was his heir in turn. As a younger son, Hugh O'Neill had but limited prospects, and these were further dimmed when an uncle, Shane *O'Neill, forcibly opposed the succession arrangement, contending, among other matters, that Matthew was no O'Neill but the illegitimate son of a blacksmith named Kelly. Shane's opposition led successively to the death of Matthew in 1558 and of Brian O'Neill in 1562. Moreover, following Tyrone's death in 1559, Shane became head of the O'Neills by Gaelic procedures, and forcefully opposed successive government efforts to impose a division of the lordship. The crown, at various points, considered meeting his demands, especially in 1562, when he visited Elizabeth I's court. However, these overtures came to nothing because Shane would not agree to any segmentation of the traditional O'Neill lordship, or to relinquishing authority over the *uir ríthe* ('subsidiary lords'), who customarily paid a head rent to the ruling O'Neill. Thus, as negotiations failed, the crown decided the issue should be settled by force, and in 1567 Shane was killed. This outcome benefited the young Hugh O'Neill, who was recognized as third baron of Dungannon and prospective heir to the earldom.

It is unclear where Dungannon spent his childhood, but any fosterage with the O'Hagans and O'Quinns would have been brief since each of these septs identified with Shane O'Neill in the internecine struggle. It is probable that Hugh spent some of the time from 1556 to 1559 in the Dublin household of Sir Henry Sidney, which seems to have been followed by a period with the family of Giles Hovendon, an English soldier and settler in the Irish midlands, who leased property at Balgriffen, co. Dublin, assigned in 1542 to Tyrone to meet the costs of educating his heirs in English customs. This sequence is consistent with Sidney's claim of 1583 that he had 'bred' Dungannon in his house 'from a little boy, then very poor of goods and full feebly friended' (Brewer and Bullen, 1575–88, 339) and with the fact that Hovendon's sons were regularly described as foster brothers of Dungannon and remained among his most loyal supporters. Hovendon's tutelage had obviously ended by 1567 when Sidney brought Dungannon, together with the heirs of several Irish noble houses, to court.

Dungannon was necessary to this delegation, because Sidney sought authority to restructure the province of Ulster following Shane's death. This is probably the occasion that Thomas Gainsford had in mind when he described how Dungannon 'in his younger time trooped in the streets of London, with sufficient equipage and orderly respect' (Gainsford, 14). The crown probably met his expenses and enabled him to sue out his livery as baron of Dungannon. This installation indicates that the government saw a place for his brother Cormac Mac

Baron and him in a remodelled Ulster. The primary objective was to expel the Scottish MacDonalds from the lands that they had occupied in the province, and to replace them with trustworthy English, Old English, and Gaelic proprietors. Then, to further assure stability, it was intended that the great O'Neill lordship should be parcelled out between various members of the ruling O'Neill family, the principal *uir-ríthe* whose territories lay on the perimeter of the lordship, and the heads of the principal septs within the lordship on whose support O'Neill power was based. Dungannon stood to benefit from this scheme, although clearly the government did not intend to grant him all his grandfather's estates.

Baron of Dungannon, 1568–1587 These various plans for Ulster explain why, after 1568, it made sense for crown officials, including Sir Nicholas Bagenal, marshal of the army, and his son, Henry Bagenal, who were settled at Newry, co. Down, to enable Dungannon to acquire further lands in south Armagh commensurate with his status as baron. Yet Dungannon lacked sufficient support because Sidney, who might have assisted him, was detained in England. When Sidney returned to his post in 1568 his scheme for the reform of Ulster had been compromised both because, in 1567, Turlough Luineach *O'Neill succeeded Shane as the ruling O'Neill, and because the queen demurred at the prospective cost. It was not until 1572, after Sidney's departure, having surrendered the governorship to Sir William Fitzwilliam, that a systematic reform scheme for Ulster was launched. What emerged was fundamentally different both in theory and practice from anything previously contemplated, and these alterations involved a correspondingly different role for Dungannon. The theory underpinning the new scheme was the crown's ancient claim to all Ulster between the River Bann and the sea. It was now also asserted that the crown had title to the entire lordship of Tyrone through the attainder of Shane in the Irish parliament of 1569–71. This put paid to Dungannon's hopes of claiming his grandfather's entire estates by hereditary right. Yet he now had the opportunity to extend his landholdings as this revised reform scheme for Ulster unfolded.

The essence of this scheme was that private individuals would restructure the eastern sector of the province along predetermined lines at their own expense, being compensated with grants of land and office. The two principal adventurers attracted by this opportunity were Sir Thomas Smith, principal secretary, and Walter Devereux, first earl of Essex. Essex hoped to secure control with a fort on the River Blackwater, just east of the customary centre of O'Neill power at Dungannon, and he anticipated that the garrison there would be provisioned by Lord Dungannon himself. The campaigns associated with Smith and Essex were among the bloodiest and most futile undertaken by English planters in early modern Ireland, but they were important to Dungannon because he became indispensable to them and his actions attracted the government's attention. He received favourable mention in dispatches sent by the colonizers to England. Essex placed him in charge of a company of cavalry, and was

soon commending him for his forwardness in 'service' as 'the only man of Ulster … meet to be trusted and used' (W. B. Devereux, ed., *Lives and Letters of the Devereux Earls of Essex … 1540–1642*, 2 vols., 1853, 1.40–42). Continued military exertions, including efforts to ensnare, or kill, Turlough Luineach O'Neill, earned Dungannon further commendation at a time when Essex was complaining of English gentlemen who deserted his cause, and of Old English landowners who refused to support it with either men or money. In return for his services he received military support from Essex to extend the lands he already held in Ulster, and was appointed captain of troops in government pay. These men were available to him for both private and official purposes, but he was called upon regularly between 1575 and the early 1590s to further various government missions with them, including providing assistance to Lord Grey in the suppression of the Desmond revolt.

These various actions helped Dungannon to familiarize himself both with English modes of warfare and with the methods by which impecunious crown captains advanced themselves in Ireland. During these years he also established lasting bonds with several English captains, while, in 1574, the queen advised Essex 'to use all good means to nourish the Baron of Dungannon's and [Calvagh] O'Donnell's good devotion towards us'. This directive was taken by William Cecil, first Baron Burghley, lord treasurer, to mean that Dungannon 'be admitted to be earl of Tyrone according to his right' (*CSP Ire.*, 1571–5, 508), although he also directed that this elevation be linked to a division of the previous Tyrone earldom among several claimants to royal favour. Probably Elizabeth and Dungannon both had this intervention in mind when she later described him as 'a creature of our own', and when he admitted to having been 'raised from nothing by her Majesty' (Morgan, 85, 94).

Despite Dungannon's good reputation in official circles, no specific lands were assigned to him beyond those he had seized with government connivance. However officials tolerated his further aggrandizements provided that they were at the expense either of Turlough Luineach O'Neill, whose power they wished to curb, or the Mac-Shanes (the sons of Shane O'Neill), whose potential they feared. Concurrently, he received several appointments as lieutenant of areas of Ulster bordering the pale which were analogous to the seneschalships held by several army captains occupying Gaelic land beyond the pale's southern marches. If Dungannon's position then resembled that of the many English captains serving in Ireland, he was more adept in advancing his interests because his Ulster origins allowed him to operate within two competing worlds. Thus, besides seizing, with official support, larger parts of the O'Neill lordship, he was able to weaken his O'Neill rivals by inducing the subordinate septs to occupy the lands which he possessed and secured with soldiers under his command. This increased support from within the lordship then permitted Dungannon to aim still higher. Thus on successive occasions in 1579, 1583, and 1585, when Turlough Luineach O'Neill seemed about to die, Dungannon moved to succeed him as O'Neill, and subsequently justified his actions on the grounds that he wished to prevent the title, and the moral authority that it enjoyed, from falling to the crown's enemies. During these, and subsequent, years he also employed marriage as a device to forge, and break, alliances. He first married a daughter (probably called Katherine) of Brian Mac Phelim O'Neill of Clandeboye, a man whom he later alienated by supporting Essex's attempt to seize Clandeboye. This marriage produced several children but, at Dungannon's request in 1574, it was annulled on grounds of consanguinity. This left him free to marry, also in 1574, Siobhán (or Joanna; d. 1591), daughter of Sir Hugh O'Donnell and his first wife. She, in turn, was repudiated in 1579, when Dungannon briefly contemplated marriage with a daughter of Turlough Luineach O'Neill, since restored to health, who then seemed agreeable to Dungannon's nomination as his successor. However, this alliance proved short-lived, and Dungannon welcomed back Siobhán.They had two sons, Hugh (1585–1609) and Henry O'Neill (1586?–1617x21). Dungannon formed further strategic alliances within Gaelic Ulster by negotiating marriages for his sisters, and later, as they grew up, for his various daughters and sons, sometimes also taking hostages as sureties.

Dungannon's bids to claim the O'Neill lordship raised fears in Dublin that their intended agent in Ulster was less malleable than anticipated. However, some senior officials in Dublin and London were convinced by Dungannon's protestations of loyalty. He began his negotiation to secure the title and estate granted in 1542 to Conn O'Neill. His first move was to assume his place as Lord Dungannon in the Irish parliament of 1569–71. His authority was increased further when Arthur Grey, fourteenth Baron Grey of Wilton, lord deputy (1580–82), granted him additional powers of martial law. Dungannon's good standing in official circles earned him commendation. Such praise seemed to presage reward, but not until Sir John Perrot became lord deputy (1584–8) was serious thought given to satisfying Dungannon's ultimate ambition, and then within the context of a plan for an enduring settlement in Ulster. Therefore, while Perrot agreed that Dungannon should be recognized as earl of Tyrone in the Irish parliament of 1585–6, he also had Turlough Luineach O'Neill, whom he knighted, lead the procession when parliament convened. The letters patent confirming Dungannon as earl of Tyrone were issued on 10 May 1587.

Earl of Tyrone, 1587–1595 Perrot intended to segment the former O'Neill lordship between separate proprietors holding their land in chief, with each landowner being required to reallocate his property among tenants-in-chief, and to support the appointment of sheriffs as a preliminary to the extension of English common law to all inhabitants. This implied that provincial administration would, as in Munster and Connaught, be supervised by a president maintained, together with supporting troops, by a composition rent imposed upon the lands of the new proprietors. This conflicted with Tyrone's plans. Although he probably saw himself as a loyal subject at this point, he

argued persistently that he was entitled to everything held by his grandfather. Disagreement over this point delayed any final settlement, and in 1587 Tyrone was granted an audience at court to ventilate his views. These disclosed that his ambition cut across the intentions of both Perrot and Sir William Fitzwilliam, who dedicated himself to shiring Ulster during his final term as lord deputy (1588–94). Perrot ultimately sought to divide the core O'Neill lordship into two units, with the earl excluded from the western portion granted to Turlough Luineach O'Neill, who was to become either earl of Omagh or earl of Clanoneill.

Before visiting court in 1587, Tyrone worked assiduously to pre-empt Perrot's plan by seizing lands intended for Turlough Luineach O'Neill and by undermining his authority and credibility as a ruler, usually in association with his O'Donnell allies to the west. Concurrently, he demonstrated his indispensability to the government: he opposed the MacShanes, who sometimes allied with Turlough Luineach O'Neill and frequently imported Scottish mercenaries, and he screened the pale by frequent proclamations of martial law. This fostered an uneasy relationship with the Irish privy council and, still more, with the various English captains and minor officials who hoped to benefit from Perrot's scheme. However Tyrone did succeed in consolidating his position within the O'Neill lordship, principally at the expense of Turlough Luineach O'Neill (now Sir Turlough O'Neill). Tyrone's court visit proved a spectacular success, principally because the Irish privy council was in turmoil, due to antagonism towards Perrot. Accordingly Elizabeth listened to the advice of her kinsman Thomas Butler, tenth earl of Ormond, who supported Tyrone. As a result, Tyrone's grant of land reflected his grandfather's grant in 1542 rather than circumstances following Shane's attainder.

The English government accepted Tyrone as their leading servant in Ulster, and this grant implied that his lordship would remain outside the authority of any new provincial president or minor official. What he obtained was little short of palatine jurisdiction such as Ormond enjoyed in co. Tipperary, and a further victory followed when an ensuing commission ruled that the country of Rory O'Cahan, principal *uir-rí* to the ruling O'Neill, was part of Tyrone's inheritance, and that the Fews in Armagh was integral to his lordship. Tyrone reciprocated in 1588 by executing many (perhaps over 500) survivors of the Spanish Armada. He maintained order in his lordship's southern marches and the pale borders; was relentless in pursuing and incarcerating the MacShanes who were still importing Scottish mercenaries into Ulster; and he justified fresh forays against Sir Turlough O'Neill on the grounds that he was conspiring with these enemies of the crown. He systematically increased his authority in Tyrone between 1587 and 1595.

If Tyrone was gaining ground against his traditional opponents he was incurring the resentment of an increasing number of officials in Ireland, especially in Ulster. Several of them voiced concern at his growing strength. Sir

Henry Bagenal took the lead in trying to check and ultimately undermine Tyrone's power by forcing him to defend his position against officials more often than against his dynastic rivals. Bagenal succeeded his father as an Irish privy councillor and marshal of the army in 1590, and aspired to become the first president of Ulster. He was active in shiring the province, and also strove to exploit for his own ends and those of the captains and officials posted there the several commissions concerning Ulster affairs. Having failed to limit Tyrone's power he sought to convince successive lord deputies, senior administrators in England, and, ultimately, the queen, of the earl's treasonable intent. The first charge, endorsed by one of the MacShanes, was that Tyrone had in 1588 assisted, and sought help from, some of the Spaniards shipwrecked off the Ulster coast. He was then accused of importing Scottish mercenaries (which he never denied), and of treasonable correspondence with Philip II and James VI against the queen. Concurrently he was charged with pursuing a private vendetta against Sir Turlough O'Neill and the MacShanes contrary to the public interest.

When these various charges and insinuations failed, Bagenal sought Tyrone's conviction for treason on the grounds that he had had Hugh Geimleach O'Neill, the most forceful of the MacShanes, executed by martial law, against Fitzwilliam's specific instructions. Consequently, Tyrone was again called before the privy council in 1590, this time to clear his reputation. Burghley, advised by the disgraced Perrot, now believed that the privy council had an opportunity to reverse, or curtail, the grant of 1587. However, his fellow privy councillors remained unconvinced of Tyrone's treason, and some approved of Hugh Geimleach O'Neill's execution, if not of its manner. Therefore, in June 1590, the earl was permitted to return to Ireland, having agreed to divide his lordship into freeholds to facilitate the introduction of English common law. These developments show that traditional alliances were reversed, with officials now supporting Sir Turlough O'Neill, and the surviving MacShanes, against Tyrone. In desperation Tyrone sought a new alliance by marrying Mabel (1570/71–1595), daughter of Sir Nicholas Bagenal of Newry, co. Down, and Carlingford, co. Louth, and his wife, Eleanor, and Sir Henry Bagenal's sister. Then, when this overture was spurned, Tyrone persuaded Mabel to elope with him. The two were married on 3 August 1591 by Thomas Jones, bishop of Meath, in the house of William Warren of Drumcondra, co. Dublin. An outraged Bagenal interpreted this as an affront to family honour: Tyrone had never been properly separated from his first wife, he contended, and he refused to pay his sister's dowry. This intensified the rivalry between the two men. However, just when Bagenal, with Fitzwilliam's apparent support, seemed to have restrained his rival, Tyrone's position was transformed by the unexpected escape of Hugh Roe O'Donnell from confinement in Dublin Castle.

O'Donnell—Tyrone's former brother-in-law—had been held hostage since 1587, and power within the O'Donnell lordship had slipped away to his O'Donnell rivals, who supported Sir Turlough O'Neill. However, following his return to Tyrconnell he quickly recovered control. Thereafter the ageing Turlough O'Neill remained friendless and a pensioner of Tyrone until his death in 1595. By 1592 Tyrone was master within his own lordship and, enjoying the support of the ruling O'Donnell, was, therefore, the most powerful man in Ulster.

If Tyrone had prevailed over Bagenal he was careful not to provide him with grounds for fresh charges. He complied with the terms agreed with the privy council in 1590, as he interpreted them. While claiming to have consented under duress, he none the less chose freeholders, and recommended his brother Cormac Mac Baron as sheriff of the entire jurisdiction. Officials welcomed these developments, but still demanded that two sheriffs be appointed, one for western Tyrone, to be styled co. Tyrone, where Cormac Mac Baron would serve, the other for co. Armagh. Tyrone's rooted objection to this could have been construed as unreasonable, but communal reaction to sheriffs—usually rapacious military men—in recently constituted counties in Ulster and north Connaught, suggests that he would have faced discord within his own lordship had he permitted officials from outside his control. However, while he defended his independence, marauding bands of English soldiers were imposed upon contiguous lordships, including those of his allies O'Donnell and Hugh Maguire, who confronted them. The resulting conflict rendered Tyrone's position more precarious, especially when some subordinates, including kinsmen, joined in what had become a popular cause. His professions of non-involvement were mocked by minor officials, who also alleged that he, with other Ulster lords, conspired with recently appointed Counter-Reformation Irish bishops to secure Spanish military support and to switch allegiance from Elizabeth to Philip. Senior officials were more circumspect, accepting Tyrone's protestations of good faith provided he induced those in arms to sue for pardon. Tyrone performed this service on two occasions—an especially difficult assignment given the understandable distrust among Ulster lords about meetings with officials—but received little gratitude. His loyalty was further tested when, in 1593, the lord deputy commanded him to accompany, and provide military assistance to, Bagenal in bringing Maguire to order. Once again Tyrone complied, so confounding the sceptics, was injured in the ensuing conflict, and received no praise, with Bagenal taking all the credit. This, and other snubs from Bagenal and Fitzwilliam, provoked Tyrone to complain that officials were bent on discrediting all Irish noblemen, that bribery was rampant within the political process, and that Bagenal was determined to trap him. These charges won Ormond's sympathy, and raised fears in London that Tyrone was about to join his kinsmen in rebellion. Therefore Bagenal was directed not to interfere in co. Tyrone, a commission was appointed to investigate the earl's grievances, and Fitzwilliam was replaced as lord deputy in 1594 by Sir William Russell. The English garrison at Enniskillen, co. Fermanagh, was attacked and routed by a force led by Maguire and Mac Baron. Undeterred, Tyrone, in August 1594, again demonstrated his loyalty by attending, without invitation, upon Russell in Dublin.

Obedience was no longer unconditional, however, and in 1595 Tyrone relayed a petition from O'Donnell and neighbouring Ulster lords that their lordships be exempted from recent innovations, including the stationing of garrisons, in return for payment of crown rent. Affronted by this, Elizabeth directed Russell to reclaim and consolidate government outposts in Ulster. Concurrently, the rebels laid siege to English garrisons, including Blackwater Fort within Tyrone's own lordship, forcing the government to send relief. Finally, Bagenal, with 1750 men, was attacked at Clontibret, co. Monaghan, and forced into retreat on his return journey from a relief expedition by a large, well-armed force commanded by Tyrone himself.

Reluctant rebel, 1595–1600 Tyrone was proclaimed a traitor in English and Irish on 24 June 1595 at Dundalk, co. Louth. The issue of his father's questionable ancestry was now revived, this time by officials, but Tyrone gained alternate authority when, in September, he was chosen to succeed Sir Turlough O'Neill as ruling O'Neill. This supported Bagenal's contention that Tyrone had long conspired, along with his Ulster neighbours, with continental powers, and had orchestrated all recent disturbances. The evidence rather suggests that before 1595 Tyrone strove to work with the government, and was earnest in his demands for palatine jurisdiction to counteract a possible communal challenge to his authority mobilized around his brother Cormac Mac Baron. Also, he restrained his more impetuous associates, possibly on the understanding that he could negotiate a similar autonomy for their territories. Having failed in this, he was forced to choose between assisting Bagenal against his own supporters, or leading them against the marshal. He recognized that, without access to the queen, loyal service no longer won him favour and his statement that 'the Knight Marshal was the only man that urged' him to his 'troubles' seems convincing (Meehan, 125).

Immediately before his break with the government Tyrone, like his associates, worked to strengthen his military capability. He did so by raising and training men from within his lordship, sometimes aided by the English soldiers serving with him, by hiring mercenaries from Scotland, and by purchasing weapons and munitions. His real achievement was in using the English 'butter captains' to train his men in the 'perfect use of firearms' with the result that those who previously were such 'rude soldiers' that 'two or three of them were required to fire one piece' were 'grown ready in managing their pieces and bold to skirmish in boggy and woody places' (Moryson, 12). Consequently, the government was taken by surprise when Tyrone first confronted them. He was cautious because he knew that he could not defeat a large, professional army under an able commander. Therefore, he endorsed the petitions, which O'Donnell, Maguire, and Cormac Mac Baron had previously made to Philip, asking him for a Spanish army of 6000 or 7000 men to pursue what was

now described as a war to preserve Catholicism. Meanwhile Tyrone continued to isolate the crown garrisons in Ulster, and, as at Clontibret, occasionally attacked relief expeditions at carefully chosen sites.

Tyrone proceeded more cautiously than O'Donnell and negotiated with the government while seeking Spanish support. This suggests that he would still have settled for palatine status for himself and his neighbours. Doubtless he felt that Elizabeth could ill afford to confront him because of the war with Spain. He also seemed less enthusiastic than his confederates about proclaiming the Ulster insurrection a religious crusade and was suspicious of continentally educated Catholic bishops bent on recovering church property. He wanted to keep his options open and sought to strengthen his military position, while fighting a defensive war. Consequently, the years 1595–8 were characterized by intermittent war, punctuated by truces and pardons, the spread of insurgency outwards from Ulster in 1596, when help from Spain was expected, and an intensification of government activity in 1597 after an anticipated Spanish force was destroyed by storm off Brittany. By then Thomas Burgh, fifth Baron Burgh, had succeeded Russell as lord deputy, with Sir Conyers Clifford becoming president of Connaught, following Richard Bingham's death. These commanders launched a joint offensive and recovered some Ulster positions, including Blackwater Fort. Seemingly, luck also favoured the government when another Spanish expedition was lost at sea in October 1597. However this was offset by the unexpected death of the government's most accomplished military leaders, Burgh and Sir John Norris. Tyrone's third wife died shortly before 30 December 1595. He married Katherine (d. 1618), daughter of Sir Hugh Magennis of Iveagh, co. Down, before 6 June 1597.

The Irish privy council was initially divided between suing for peace or continuing with the war, but eventually chose the latter: in August 1598 Bagenal received command of 4000 foot and 300 horse sent to relieve the Blackwater garrison, then besieged by Tyrone. On approaching the fort their way was blocked by a confederate army, under Tyrone's command, standing behind prepared ground. In the ensuing battle at Yellow Ford on 14 August the crown forces lost most of their cavalry and munitions while Bagenal and hundreds of his men were killed. Victory transformed both Tyrone's attitude and the character of the conflict. His reticence about religion and his caution were now cast aside for several reasons. First, the government position seemed precarious; second, his victory increased the possibility of tangible assistance from Spain, and many other dissidents in Ireland were now willing to accept his leadership. An indication of his enhanced reputation within Ulster is the appearance of a eulogy in verse, 'Cumam croinic Clainne Néill' ('Let us compose a chronicle on Niall's descendants'), by Dubhtach Ó Duibhgeannáin, which praised Tyrone for his victory. The confederates overran most of Ireland, except for the pale, the walled towns, and fortified positions (which they could never capture without artillery), and parts of some lordships, notably those of Ormond, Thomond, and Clanricarde, whose earls remained loyal. Most spectacularly, the recently established Munster plantation collapsed before the assault of an expeditionary force sent by Tyrone. Concurrently the confederates increased their military capability, meeting the increased cost largely by revenues extracted from territories outside Ulster on which they now encroached. With the Catholic bishops, they also renewed their appeals to Spain, hoping that their victory would convince the new Spanish king, Philip III, that support for them would benefit his wider ambitions. Philip was sympathetic.

Even without Spanish support, the victory of Yellow Ford prompted a reorientation of English military priorities that was symbolized by the appointment in April 1599 of Elizabeth's favourite Robert Devereux, second earl of Essex, as lord lieutenant, with 17,300 troops—the largest army to leave England during her reign. Before assuming his post Essex won endorsement for his strategy of establishing a chain of fortified positions along the eastern and western entries to Ulster, plus a fort on Loughfoyle which could be provisioned by sea. It was intended to attack the confederates from three sides simultaneously, and to destroy the crops and to kill the civilian population that sustained the Ulster war effort. This was delayed and, on arrival in Dublin, Essex was persuaded by the Irish privy council to relieve those outposts that remained loyal in Leinster and Munster before launching an attack on Ulster. He became embroiled in Leinster and Munster while awaiting the marine support needed to execute his Ulster strategy, instead of confronting the confederates as ordered. When Essex eventually headed for Ulster, in September 1599, this support had not yet arrived and the season for fighting was already past. Thus he had no option but to temporize. This explains the famous parley between Tyrone and Essex at a river ford north of Dundalk. There the unarmed Tyrone, 'putting his horse up to the belly in water, with all humbleness' explained to his former patron's son, 'standing on the other bank', that he sought peace with the queen. What Tyrone demanded, besides the usual immunity from direct government supervision, is unclear: his subsequent assertion that he gave priority to religion was categorically denied by Essex, who testified that 'toleration in religion' was 'mentioned in deed, but never yielded unto by him, nor yet stood upon by the Traitor, to whom the earl had said plainly Hang thee up, thou carest for religion as much as my horse' (Moryson, pt 2, bk 2, 38).

Essex's enemies at court used his alleged capitulation to Tyrone to destroy him and Elizabeth resolved not to offer Tyrone pardon. Charles Blount, eighth Baron Mountjoy, was appointed lord deputy in February 1600 essentially to complete Essex's military agenda, but with the resources formerly denied to his predecessor. Tyrone was quickly hemmed in and thrown back on the limited resources available to him in Ulster. Recognizing that confrontation was now inevitable, he offered his associates unqualified support, declaring a religious war. He apparently also cultivated a closer relationship with Catholic clerics, while continuing to represent himself as an upholder of English civility. This is suggested by Sir John Harington's encounter, when visiting Tyrone in 1599. Then the earl's two sons, Hugh and Henry, were both 'dressed in English clothes, with velvet jerkins and gold lace … acquainted with the English tongue' and able to recite from an English translation of Ariosto, but tutored by Aodh Mac Aingil, a Counter-Reformation priest and future activist for the cause at St Anthony's College, Louvain (Meehan, 27).

Counter-Reformation champion, 1600–1603 One of Tyrone's hopes in declaring his religious war was to win support from those people in Ireland who had remained obedient. This prospect faded in 1600 when Sir George Carew, given charge of 3000 men in Munster, succeeded in recovering government authority outside Ulster. Thereafter it was apparent that Tyrone had no hope of fresh adherents unless he could confront and defeat Mountjoy's army, and for that military reinforcements from the continent were essential. Therefore, as prospects of substantial help from Spain increased in 1601, Tyrone avoided conflicts with the crown forces pressing in upon his home territory. The confederacy had to ward against defections, which became ever more frequent, while Tyrone had to guard against assassination attempts prompted by Mountjoy. He maintained discipline and trained his men in the pike warfare that would follow once Spanish assistance arrived. Fynes Moryson acknowledged Tyrone's efforts to meet this challenge but noted with satisfaction that the confederates were not yet ready to confront drilled opponents in the field: they were no sooner exposed to 'some volleys' from field guns than 'their puppets bravery suddenly vanished, and according to their wonted manner, they hid themselves in the woods' (Moryson, pt 2, bk 2, 113). Such inadequacy gave added urgency to the confederate appeals for Spanish support, so as to secure a backbone of seasoned pikemen for the army confronting Mountjoy.

Strategy dictated that any sizeable Spanish force should disembark south of Ulster because of the need for provisions, and Limerick or Galway seemed best, but the force of 3000 men, under Juan del Águila, which reached Ireland in September 1601, disappointed the insurgents, first because it was half the expected size and second because it disembarked at Kinsale, co. Cork, far distant from Ulster. There they were immediately besieged by Carew, president of Munster, while Mountjoy rushed to take command of a larger assault force, 7000 strong. The harsh winter of 1601—with snow, frost, and swollen rivers—both helped and hindered the extraordinary feat of leading from Ulster to Kinsale two armies, Hugh O'Donnell's passing through Connaught, Tyrone's via the pale: it enabled them to follow normally impassable routes, thus evading the English forces sent to cut them off. The two armies also merged successfully and approached the Spanish force, now but 2400 strong. Tyrone hoped to avoid battle and to deny food and fodder to the English army, which was suffering more severely from disease and exposure than the Spaniards were. This plan was rejected by the Spaniards, by the Irish clerics accompanying them, and by O'Donnell, who all wanted to join the two forces, despite confusion. As this difficult manoeuvre was proceeding, Tyrone's ill-prepared forces broke ranks when exposed to an English cavalry charge, O'Donnell's army then fled, and the Spaniards had no opportunity to engage. The battle of Kinsale (24 December 1601) shattered whatever prospect Tyrone ever had of dictating terms to the English crown. The confederates were decimated and demoralized, their weapons mostly abandoned, and the Spaniards surrendered to Mountjoy and were permitted to return home. Tyrone was isolated.

Even in defeat Tyrone remained determined to fight for terms from a government initially fixed on massive confiscation of property and an Ulster plantation. He held out in his Ulster fastnesses even as government troops pillaged his core territories and destroyed the crops that sustained the war effort. Officials were astonished to find that his closest followers would not desert him and speculated that only Tyrone's death, capture, or flight would end what became a war of attrition. Two factors in his favour were the mounting cost to the government and Elizabeth's failing health. Furthermore, if he managed to escape to Spain, Tyrone could complicate the peace overtures under way to end the Spanish war. He remained in arms until Mountjoy and Carew won permission to reach an accommodation. In February 1603 Mountjoy was authorized by Sir Robert Cecil, principal secretary of state, to receive Tyrone to mercy.

The generosity of the terms ultimately conceded to Tyrone by the so-called treaty of Mellifont (30 March) is explained both by Mountjoy's concern to settle before the earl learned of Elizabeth's death and by his determination to attend James VI and I. Tyrone's doggedness was thus rewarded: in return for abjuring the name and title of O'Neill and promising to sever all contact with Spain, he was assured of his earldom in perpetuity, with the promise of new letters patent on condition that his 'country' pay composition rent to the crown. This agreement seemingly left Tyrone in much the same position as he had enjoyed in 1587, albeit as ruler of a lordship devastated by prolonged warfare. In addition, he was without rivals within his lordship, and further strengthened his position by persuading Mountjoy to have the entire O'Donnell lordship granted to Rury O'Donnell, who became first earl of Tyrconnell. Tyrone and O'Donnell accompanied Mountjoy to meet James in England in 1603, with the intention of having 'one assured in Tyrconnell and another in Tyrone' each 'able utterly to suppress' his local opponents (N. Canny, 'The treaty of Mellifont, 1603', *Irish Sword*, 9, 1970, 380–99).

An earl restored, 1603–1607 This outcome represented a diplomatic victory for Tyrone. Army captains, crown officials, and even the English public were dismayed, while lesser lords in Ulster who had deserted the earl during the war had most reason to feel betrayed. Consequently between 1603 and 1607 Tyrone was preoccupied on one level with consolidating his position within his devastated lordship and on another with defending himself against those who resented his success. This attack was many-faceted, involving co-operation between servitors

who held positions or property in Ulster, officials in Dublin, churchmen eager to make the established church a reality in Ulster, and former subordinates of Tyrone who wanted the government to honour its promises to make them independent of a vengeful lord. Collectively these enemies set about identifying concealed land within the two lordships which might be claimed as crown property, especially fishing rights on lakes and rivers and church property. A series of legal challenges and investigations ensued, leading ultimately to the suggestion that title to the disputed properties should be established by an inquisition. This decision produced the apparently reasonable demand that the lordships of Tyrone and Tyrconnell should become shire ground, a task delegated to Sir John Davies, solicitor-general. Davies enjoyed fulsome support from Sir Arthur Chichester, lord deputy, but made little initial progress because the earl of Devonshire (Mountjoy) defended the arrangement on which he had staked his reputation. His influence, however, waned by 1605 and the subsequent struggle between Tyrone and Davies was every bit as personal as that previously fought between Tyrone and Bagenal. Davies held that the patents devised for Tyrone and Tyrconnell were unjust because the earls had been granted outright ownership of their entire lordships irrespective of the rights of the other O'Neills, the lesser lords, and the church. Davies wished to segment the Tyrone and Tyrconnell lordships to reflect the wider claims to property within them, while Tyrone held rigidly to the view that his grandfather in 1542 and he in both 1587 and 1603 had been granted outright ownership of the entire lordship of Tyrone. His position, therefore, was that the only others who had property rights within the lordship were those appointed by him after 1590 and again in 1605 as tenants-in-chief. To counter this Davies encouraged Tyrone's estranged son-in-law, Sir Donnell Ballagh *O'Cahan, to bring an action against him before the Dublin courts contending that since, under the Gaelic dispensation, the ruling O'Cahan had been a sovereign lord, a major injustice had been perpetrated by the passing of Tyrone's patent. Davies hoped, if successful, to establish a precedent which would result in the dismemberment of the Tyrone lordship among several claimants, all of whom, including Tyrone himself, would then be ruled by a provincial president. Confronted with this challenge, Tyrone petitioned James for support. The king's agreement to resolve the dispute in person represented a major concession to Tyrone, who commented that if he were dissatisfied with the outcome he would 'choose' to live in England rather than be 'governed by any other than your Majesty and your deputy general of this realm' (PRO, SP 63/218/71). In this event Tyrone probably intended to play the part of a 'British' courtier at the Jacobean court, leaving his heir, Hugh O'Neill, fourth baron of Dungannon, to handle his Irish affairs. Dungannon would probably be better suited to a rigidly monitored life and, since his father was finalizing a marriage for him with a daughter of Archibald Campbell, seventh earl of Argyll, and his first wife, Anne—thus linking 'Mac O'Neill with the daughter of McKallym, for so the Scottish Irish call the earl of

Argyll' (Meehan, 101)—would also be better placed to receive royal favour.

Following James's decision Tyrone and Davies each spent much of 1607 preparing for the anticipated royal hearing, which would have implications for all Ulster lordships. Yet it seemed of little consequence when Tyrconnell and Cuconnaught Maguire openly admitted their inability to manage their lordships, lamenting that economic circumstances would force them to join their fellow countrymen as soldiers in Spanish service. Nobody thought, for a moment, that Tyrone would also leave, because of his age, his dedication to countering Davies's every move, his involvement with his son's prospective marriage, and his seeming resolve to plead his case before the king. Therefore officials were astonished when they learned on 7 September that Tyrone, as well as Tyrconnell and several family members and retainers of both lords, had taken ship three days previously for an unknown destination. Once Spain emerged as their intended landfall, officials asked why Tyrone decided to participate in this dramatic exit, known in Irish historiography as the 'flight of the earls'. Two points were put forward, and are still being debated by historians; first, whether Tyrone, like Tyrconnell, had long contemplated this move or was panicked into joining the expedition only on hearing that the ship commissioned by Maguire had landed at Lough Swilly, and, second, whether Tyrone was resigned to losing everything or had left in the hope of returning with Spanish military support.

On the first point, the evidence suggests that Tyrone's action was not premeditated: he was at Slane, co. Meath, in the lord deputy's company, and seemingly preparing both for his impending visit to the king and for the marriage of his son when word reached him of the ship's arrival at Lough Swilly. This news would not have surprised him and cannot alone have startled him into abandoning the country. Government officials concluded that Christopher St Lawrence, ninth Baron Howth, then put 'buzzes' in Tyrone's ear convincing him that 'if he went into England he should either be perpetual prisoner in the Tower of London or else lose his head and members'. Tyrone would unquestionably have been alert to this possibility, as on all previous visits to the English court, but in his own version of his meeting at Slane, the fresh information causing him disquiet was that Chichester had persuaded the king, through the procurement of Cecil, the earl of Salisbury, to overlook in favour of himself Tyrone's request to be appointed president of Ulster. This, according to Tyrone, convinced him that the king would similarly dismiss his other petitions and that life in exile would be preferable to 'the misery he saw sustained by others through the oppression of the like government' (Meehan, 126).

The exile, 1607–1616 Tyrone's explanation of his departure suggests that he entertained no hopes in September 1607 of Spanish military support. He was an astute politician who accepted, unlike his lay and clerical associates, that the calamity at Kinsale had ended any realistic prospects of further substantial military support from Spain. His flight was an act of desperation, an interpretation that fits the known details of his final actions in Ireland—the sad farewell to his friends, the desperate effort to gather up his three sons by his fourth wife (ultimately, he was forced to leave one behind), and his seemingly brutal effort to compel his reluctant countess to accompany him. Moreover his subsequent 'articles' addressed to James from the continent (which probably derived from the statement of grievance originally intended for presentation to the king) suggests a belated recognition that he had acted rashly and that his best hope of receiving succour lay in London rather than Madrid. These 'articles' gave priority to religious grievances, and, in correspondence with the Spanish court, Tyrone also emphasized his loss and sufferings for the sake of Catholicism, whose defence had always been his prime concern. This was the only argument to advance once he had placed his trust in Spain, and the only position that his clerical correspondents with the court in Madrid would countenance. Perhaps he became convinced by his own rhetoric, especially as Fearghal Óg Mac an Bhaird, in *Mór do mhill aoibhneas Éirinn* ('Greatly has it destroyed the beauty of Ireland'), sought further to convince him that his failure to return with an invading force meant that the trials of the Nine Years' War had been endured in vain.

Returning to Ireland was not an option for Tyrone, but exile became especially bitter as Philip's embarrassment with his guests became apparent. The exiles intended to disembark at Corunna and to proceed to Madrid in the hope of an audience with the king. They landed, however, in Normandy and were granted safe passage to Spanish Flanders. There they were welcomed by the Irish military and clerical community, including Tyrone's second son, Henry, a colonel in the Spanish army. Despite the honours and entertainment enumerated by Tadhg Ó Cianáin, the dutiful narrator of the flight, the harsh reality was that those declared rebels by James were neither welcome in Flanders nor in Spain lest their presence compromise the peace. Instead, Tyrone and his companions were dispatched along 'the Spanish road' towards Milan and eventually to Rome where they were assigned a residence by Pope Paul V as pensioners of Philip. The correspondence of Tyrone and his companions concerns the early deaths of some of the exiles, the survivors' supplications for continued support, and their futile pleas to the Spanish government—oscillating between demands for a fresh invasion of Ireland and requests for intercession with James for restoration of their estates and of Catholicism as the religion of Ulster. Thomas Gainsford witnessed Tyrone's company making its way to Rome and noted that the earl stayed in a 'common inn' while in Milan and became 'the subject of charity and had only a poor supplement from some special cardinals' during his final years in Rome (Gainsford, 1, 6, 14). Tyrone's health deteriorated and he became almost blind. He died of fever on 20 July 1616 in Rome and was buried there after a fairly elaborate funeral ceremony in the Spanish church of San Pietro Montorio. The countess of Tyrone is believed to have died on 15 March 1618 in Rome.

Conclusion For Gainsford, Tyrone's 'dejection' provided 'exemplary' proof of his maxim that subjects who were 'seduced' from their 'faithfulness' by the promises of foreign princes would be 'made the tennis ball of fortune' and forced 'to fly to foreign princes for refuge' (Gainsford, 1, 6, 14). He believed that Tyrone had been hoodwinked by survivors of the Spanish Armada into allying with Spain and that all his actions after 1588 were motivated by this fact. Ironically, the Counter-Reformation historian Philip O'Sullivan Beare took this story up but used it for a different purpose. Like Gainsford, he saw Tyrone's life largely in terms of prevarication and deception but regarded him as cleverly disguising his intentions from the government before allying with Spain to strike a blow for Catholicism. O'Sullivan saw him as an exemplar to Irish Catholics and wanted to refute the denigration of Moryson and Gainsford and the work of other Irish Catholic historians, including Lughaidh Ó Cléirigh, who remained in Ireland and argued that Hugh Roe O'Donnell was the heroic figure, not Tyrone. In the short term O'Sullivan's version of events proved the more appealing and when Giovanni Battista Rinuccini, archbishop of Fermo, the papal nuncio to Ireland, presented Tyrone's sword to his nephew, Owen Roe *O'Neill, in 1646 it was regarded as identifying the latter as the possible king of a Catholic Ireland.

The evidence concerning Tyrone's career hardly accords with the accounts of Gainsford and O'Sullivan, or the succession of writers following in their respective traditions. Tyrone has been employed to support different causes through selective use of the evidence. More careful attention to each phase of his career and to the explanations that he offered to justify his actions reveals a less charismatic or attractive man, who was committed to few causes other than his own survival and the preservation of his family. However, he was caught in something of a bind between the fears and expectations of the government and the hopes of his Gaelic Irish supporters. He was proud of the achievements of his sons, but displayed a utilitarian attitude towards his wives and children and could be brutal to kinsmen. He was loyal to those of his English and Irish adherents who remained loyal to him, but exacted harsh revenge on any he regarded as having betrayed him. He tried to remain loyal to the crown for as long as possible and to his political allies and was amenable to aspects of royal policy in Ulster. He only championed the cause of Spanish intervention and the Counter-Reformation when he recognized that he could not reconcile loyalty to Elizabeth with acceptance of increased circumscription of his power and of his room to manoeuvre. However, he was a pragmatist, who was conscious of his strengths and weaknesses as a military commander and of the limitations of his forces. Moryson, although biased, made what is perhaps the shrewdest observation of Tyrone, when he met him, describing him as a man:

> of mean stature, but of a strong body, able to endure labours, watching, and hard fare, being withall industrious, and active, valiant, affable, and apt to manage great affairs, and of a high, dissembling, subtle and profound wit. So as many

deemed him born either for the great good or ill of his country. (Moryson, pt 2, chap. 1.7)

NICHOLAS CANNY

Sources PRO, SP 63 · AFM · LPL, Carew MSS · M. Kerney-Walsh, 'Destruction by peace': Hugh O'Neill after Kinsale (1986) · P. O'Sullivan Beare, Historiae Catholicae Iberniae compendium (1621); later edn, ed. M. Kelly (1850) · F. Moryson, An itinerary … containing his ten yeeres travell through the twelve dominions, 3 vols. (1617); facs. edn (Amsterdam, 1971) · C. P. Meehan, The fate and fortunes of Hugh O'Neill, earl of Tyrone, and Rory O'Donel, earl of Tyrconnel, 3rd edn (1886) · T. Gainsford, The true, exemplary, and remarkable history of the earl of Tyrone (1619) · CSP Ire., 1509–1608 · H. Morgan, Tyrone's rebellion: the outbreak of the Nine Years' War in Tudor Ireland, Royal Historical Society Studies in History, 67 (1993) · S. Mitchel, The life and times of Aodh O'Neill, prince of Ulster; called by the English Hugh, earl of Tyrone (1874) · Beatha Aodha Ruaidh Uí Dhomnaill as Leabhar Lughaidh uí Chléirigh, ed. P. Walsh (1957) · T. Ó Cianáin, The flight of the earls, ed. P. Walsh (1916) · J. J. Silke, Kinsale: the Spanish intervention in Ireland at the end of the Elizabethan wars (1970) · P. C. Allen, Philip III and the pax Hispanica, 1598–1621: the failure of grand strategy (New Haven, CT, 2000) · N. Canny, Making Ireland British, 1580–1650 (2001) · G. A. Hayes-McCoy, Irish battles (1969) · P. Walsh, The will and family of Hugh O'Neill, earl of Tyrone (1930) · H. A. Jefferies, 'Hugh O'Neill, earl of Tyrone', Tyrone: history and society, ed. C. Dillon and H. A. Jefferies (Dublin, 2000), 181–231 · Royal Irish Acad., MS D 5, fols. 175–85; MS 23 F, fols. 70–73 · J. S. Brewer and W. Bullen, eds., Calendar of the Carew manuscripts, 6 vols., PRO (1867–73) · DNB · GEC, Peerage · J. K. Graham, 'The birth date of Hugh O'Neill, second earl of Tyrone', Irish Historical Studies, 1 (1938–9), 58–9 · CSP Ire., 1571–5

Archives PRO, state papers Ireland, and calendars, letters

Likenesses print, 17th cent. (Tyrone's submission to Mountjoy, 1603), repro. in G. Carleton, A thankfull remembrance of God's mercy (1627) · engraving (probably of O'Neill), repro. in P. Damaschino, La Spada d'Orione stellata nel cielo di Marte (1980) · oils (reputedly of O'Neill; after portrait in the V&A), Harbour Commissioners, Belfast; repro. in C. R. L. Fletcher, Historical portraits (1909) · portrait (reputedly of O'Neill), V&A

Wealth at death died in exile: Walsh, Will and family; Kerney-Walsh, 'Destruction'

O'Neill, Hugh, styled sixth earl of Tyrone (d. 1660/61), army officer, was born in the Spanish Netherlands the son of Art Oge O'Neill, who was the elder brother of Owen Roe O'Neill and nephew of Hugh O'Neill, the great earl of Tyrone; his mother was Helen (or Evelina) Mac Carthy. He served as a captain in the regiment of Tyrone, in the Spanish service, and had most recently been engaged in fighting Catalan rebels, before coming to Ireland in 1642 to serve in the Ulster army of the confederate Catholics. He was known as Hugh Dubh or Buí because of his black hair and sallow complexion, respectively.

O'Neill was captured when local British forces routed the Ulster Irish army and creaghts at Clones in 1643. Ormond declined Owen Roe O'Neill's offer of an exchange and Hugh O'Neill remained a prisoner until released through exchange after the battle of Benburb in 1646. The following year he was appointed major-general of the Irish forces in Ulster, and they were partly under his direction during the illness of his uncle, General Owen Roe O'Neill, whose confidence he enjoyed, and by whom he was dispatched with 2000 soldiers to aid the marquess of Ormond against the Cromwellian forces. After Owen O'Neill's death, in November 1649, Hugh was, like his cousin Daniel O'Neill, one of the numerous unsuccessful candidates for the command of the Ulster army.

In February 1650 Ormond appointed O'Neill governor of Clonmel. He had under his command some 1200 men, of whom all but fifty-two were infantry, and with these forces he pursued an aggressive defence, mounting frequent sallies to cut off isolated parties of the besiegers. On 27 April Cromwell sited his siege batteries, prompting O'Neill to demand urgent relief from Ormond. The relief did not arrive and on 9 May, after opening a breach, Cromwell's soldiers stormed in: 'never was seen so hot a storm of so long continuance and so gallantly defended, neither in England nor in Ireland' (Whitelocke, 41). On pouring through the breach the attackers were canalized by newly erected embankments into a lane covered by two artillery guns. The gunners fired chain shot while other defenders raked the attackers with musket fire and missiles from the surrounding embankments and houses. Constricted and pushed forward by the press of bodies, some 2000 of the storming party were killed over the ensuing four hours before Cromwell finally called off the attack.

Nevertheless, the garrison could not prolong the struggle, and in the dead of night O'Neill and his followers slipped away in the direction of Waterford, leaving instructions with the mayor to come to terms. On 10 May Cromwell received a deputation, and granted them terms. It was not until he got within the walls that he learned of the escape of the garrison. He kept his word, but sent in pursuit of O'Neill, and, according to Ludlow, killed 200 stragglers.

O'Neill subsequently commanded in Limerick during the siege by Ireton which lasted from May to October 1651. Again, he conducted an active defence, most notably when he annihilated a landing party which tried to establish a beachhead on King's Island preparatory to a general assault. By October, however, about a fifth of the townspeople and garrison had perished owing to the combined effects of famine and pestilence, and the demoralized citizenry sued for peace. In the articles for the surrender of Limerick, dated in October 1651, the governor, Major-General Hugh O'Neill, was excepted from quarter, and excluded from any benefit, on the ground that he had largely contributed to 'the long and obstinate holding out of the place'. In conformity with them, O'Neill, as governor, on 29 October 1651 surrendered the city to Ireton, and was committed to prison. A council of war on the same day voted that O'Neill and others should be executed. In his defence, O'Neill insisted that he had not been guilty of any base or dishonourable act, having only discharged his duty as a soldier, and appealed to the justice of the lord deputy, Ireton. On 1 November, after reconsideration, the vote for the death of O'Neill was revoked, and it was determined to send him as a prisoner to be dealt with by the authorities of the parliament at London. This course, it would appear, was adopted mainly in consequence of his rights as a subject of the king of Spain (having been born in Flanders) and his numerous influential connections.

As a prisoner in the Tower of London, where he arrived on 10 January 1652, O'Neill was treated with consideration by the government, and allowed 20s. a week for his maintenance; he was also granted the privilege of having 'the liberty of the Tower'. In July 1652 Cardenas, the Spanish ambassador at London, applied officially for his discharge from the Tower, on the grounds that he was a subject of the king of Spain, that he had not been guilty of excesses in Ireland, and that his liberation would promote the bringing together of the Irish soldiers then about to be levied for the Spanish service.

O'Neill was released in 1653 and made his way to Madrid. There, in December, he was tasked with mustering the many thousands of recently landed Irish scattered across Galicia and Cantabria and marching them to Aragon to fight the French. In October 1660 on the death of Hugh O'Neill, titular earl of Tyrone, Hugh Dubh succeeded to the title. In that same month he addressed a letter from Madrid to Charles II and the marquess of Ormond asking that his family be 'restored … to a possibility of deserving well of the crown', though he admitted that, because of ill health, he would not live to enjoy such royal grace (Gilbert, 3.xlvii). His pessimism was justified and he died within the following five months.

O'Neill is mainly remembered for his defence of Clonmel and Limerick. While he was, doubtless, a competent practitioner of siege warfare, his reputation was inflated by the amateurish siege tactics of Cromwell and Ireton.

J. T. GILBERT, rev. PÁDRAIG LENIHAN

Sources B. O'Ferrall and D. O'Connell, *Commentarius Rinuccinianus de sedis apostolicae legatione ad foederatos Hiberniae Catholicos per annos 1645–1649*, ed. J. Kavanagh, IMC, 2 (1936), 652, 687; 3 (1939), 462; 4 (1941), 390, 394, 445, 460, 553, 639, 643, 645, 647; 5 (1944), 38, 105, 308, 414 · J. T. Gilbert, ed., *A contemporary history of affairs in Ireland from 1641 to 1652*, 3 vols. (1879–80), vol. 1, p. 149; vol. 2, pp. 70, 75–80, 158–9; vol. 3 p. xlvii · D. Murphy, *Cromwell in Ireland: a history of Cromwell's Irish campaign* (1883), 328–40, 383–5 · R. A. Stradling, *The Spanish monarchy and Irish mercenaries: the wild geese in Spain, 1618–1668* (1994), 81, 96, 106, 125, 146 · T. Ó Donnchadha, ed., 'Cín Lae Ó Mealláin', *Analecta Hibernica*, 3 (1931), 1–61, esp. 21 · [B. Whitelocke], *Memorials of the English affairs* (1682) · M. Walsh, 'O'Neills in exile', *Seanchas Ardmhacha*, 8 (1975–7), 59 · GEC, *Peerage* · J. G. Simms, 'Hugh Dubh O'Neill's defence of Limerick, 1650–1651', *Irish Sword*, 3 (1957–8), 115–23 · *The memoirs of Edmund Ludlow*, ed. C. H. Firth, 2 vols. (1894)

O'Neill, Hugh (1784–1824), architectural draughtsman, was born in Bloomsbury, London, on 20 April 1784, the son of an architect who designed a portion of Portland Place. Nothing is known of his early training but he won a silver palette from the Society of Artists in 1803, and exhibited at the Royal Academy from 1800 to 1804. From 1813 he taught drawing in Oxford and later worked in Edinburgh, Bath, and Bristol, where he settled in 1821. He was a prolific draughtsman, and made over 500 drawings of Bristol alone. Generally he retained his carefully finished originals and disposed only of copies. Many of his drawings were published; for example, his sketches of the ruins of Christ Church, Oxford, after the fire of 3 March 1809, were engraved by W. Crotch and published in Oxford in 1809. Skelton engraved a number of O'Neill's drawings of Oxford and its surroundings for the second volume of his *Oxonia antiqua restaurata* (1823) and O'Neill's work also appears in Skelton's *Antiquities of Bristol* (1820, 1826). Drawings of St Peter's Church and of Balliol, Magdalen, Exeter, and All Souls colleges (engraved by J. Basire and J. S. Storer) were published in the *Oxford Almanack* for 1809, 1810, 1812, 1813, and 1828. O'Neill also made an interesting collection of fossils, minerals, and other curiosities.

O'Neill died in poverty, in Princes Street, Bristol, where he was living, on 7 April 1824. He is represented in the collections of the British Museum, the Victoria and Albert Museum, the Victoria Art Gallery in Bath, the Whitworth Art Gallery in Manchester, and Reading Art Gallery.

M. A. GOODALL

Sources Redgrave, *Artists* · *GM*, 1st ser., 94/1 (1824), 381 · Bryan, *Painters* · *Bristol scenery, 1714–1858: thirty-three drawings and water colours from the City Art Gallery, Bristol*, Bristol City Art Gallery (1962) · Mallalieu, *Watercolour artists*
Wealth at death died in poverty: *DNB*

O'Neill, John, first Viscount O'Neill (1740–1798), politician and landowner, was born on 16 January 1740 at Shane's Castle, co. Antrim, the eldest son of Charles O'Neill (*d.* 1769), MP and landowner, and Catherine Alice (*d.* 1790), third daughter of St John Brodrick MP. He was educated at Trinity College, Dublin, which he entered on 21 April 1757, and Christ Church, Oxford, where he matriculated on 14 April 1762 and graduated MA on 15 June of the same year. The extent of the O'Neill family influence in co. Antrim was reflected in his appointment as high sheriff of the county in 1772, and subsequently as deputy governor, then as governor (1792–8). He entered the Irish parliament in 1761 as representative for the borough of Randalstown, which the O'Neill family controlled. In 1783 and 1790 he was elected as one of the MPs for the county, but preferred to continue sitting for the borough. On 18 October 1777 he married Henrietta (*d.* 1793), only daughter and heir of Charles Boyle, later styled Lord Dungarvan, and Susanna Hoare. They had two sons, who are noted below, and a daughter, who married George Hartwell on 20 June 1792.

O'Neill was regarded as a moderate in politics, a great landowner who was a good and considerate landlord, an amiable and much respected man in public and private. He entered with enthusiasm into the volunteer movement which developed after 1778, when Ireland was denuded of troops during the American war, and became colonel of the first regiment raised in Antrim in 1781. In parliament he aligned himself with the whig and 'patriot' interest on popular issues, but without losing the respect of government. He was a warm supporter of the reform of parliament, and, after some initial hesitation, Catholic emancipation. Early in his parliamentary career he temporarily lost the goodwill of the Presbyterians (who predominated in Antrim and eastern Ulster) by introducing in 1774 a Vestry Bill which would have infringed their customary rights, enabling vestries consisting of Church of Ireland members alone to impose taxes for the repair of churches on dissenting residents of the parish, but the bill was defeated. Almost all of O'Neill's tenants were Presbyterians and henceforward he tended to support measures which had the broad approval of the dissenters.

O'Neill attended the first great volunteer convention in

John O'Neill, first Viscount O'Neill (1740–1798), by Samuel William Reynolds senior (after James Dowling Herbert, after Matthew William Peters, in or after 1778)

Dungannon on 15 February 1782, as a delegate for co. Antrim, in the historic closing stages of the agitation which helped to bring about the independence of the Irish parliament. He was one of the four delegates appointed by the Irish House of Commons to present a petition to the prince of Wales in 1789 requesting him to assume the regency in Ireland without conditions. O'Neill spoke seldom in the house, but when he did he acquitted himself effectively. He was tall and well-proportioned, his voice well-toned and harmonious, though 'somewhat hurt by a tendency to a lisp' (Johnston-Liik). He was described by a contemporary as addicted to the interests of Ireland and acting as the independent representative of a free people, shunning alike 'the meanness of factious opposition and the servile subserviency of the hireling tribe' (ibid.). Although the borough of Randalstown had been in the control of the O'Neill family 'from time immemorial', he insisted on the inhabitants having the uninfluenced choice of their representatives. He was one of the founders of the Northern Whig Club in 1790, his name appearing alongside those of radicals and United Irishmen such as Archibald Hamilton Rowan, Samuel McTier, and Theobald Wolfe Tone, but O'Neill's loyalty was never in doubt, and this was recognized by his elevation to the rank of Baron O'Neill in 1793 and Viscount O'Neill in 1795. During his viceregal tour of the north of Ireland in 1787 the lord lieutenant, the duke of Rutland, visited him at Shane's Castle, and like other guests expressed admiration for the residence and its magnificent setting on the shore of

Lough Neagh. To indulge his wife's enthusiasm for the acting of Sarah Siddons, O'Neill built a private theatre there, and persuaded the celebrated actress to give a performance in it; Siddons wrote of her enchantment on the occasion in her memoirs.

Although sympathetic to the cause of reform, Lord O'Neill was totally opposed to the United Irishmen, who by the late 1790s were planning insurrection. From 1793 he had been colonel of the Antrim militia, and he was active in helping to raise and train the yeomanry. When the Irish rising broke out on 23 May 1798 the north at first remained quiet, but early in June O'Neill, who was in Dublin, had reports of an imminent rising in Antrim. As governor of the county he summoned a meeting of the magistrates for 7 June in Antrim town, a decision which precipitated the calamity he wished to avert, for Henry Joy McCracken, the leader of the Presbyterian insurgents in the county, planned to attack the town on that day and seize the magistrates as hostages. Hastening towards Antrim, O'Neill passed through Lisburn without stopping, and so failed to receive an urgent warning from General Nugent, the army commander in the north. He arrived in the town to find the battle in progress, and at the moment when Colonel Lumley's dragoons were hastily retreating after their disastrous charge along the main street. Accounts of what followed are conflicting, but it is clear that Lord O'Neill found himself alone on horseback near the market house. He fired his pistols at the advancing rebels and one of them drove a pike into his side, probably without recognizing him. After a sortie from the wall of the Massereene estate by the defenders, he was carried into Lord Massereene's residence. When the rebels abandoned the town, Colonel Durham of the Fife fencibles, learning of Lord O'Neill's injuries, went to see him, and sent for two of the army surgeons to dress his wounds. They told Durham that O'Neill 'could not live, as the pike had pierced his stomach' (Dundas MS). That night the exhausted soldiers slept on the benches of O'Neill's private theatre at Shane's Castle, while he lay dying in the house of his neighbour, scarcely a mile away. Against all expectations, he survived for almost two weeks, conscious and able to communicate with family and friends. His death, on 18 June at Massereene House, co. Antrim, was greatly mourned, not least by the United Irishmen themselves. It was widely believed that his assailant had been one of his own tenants.

Charles Henry St John O'Neill, Earl O'Neill (1779–1841), landowner, elder son of the first Viscount O'Neill, was born on 22 January 1779. He was educated at Eton College and Christ Church, Oxford, matriculating on 23 November 1795. On his father's death in 1798 he became second Viscount O'Neill. At the time of the passing of the Act of Union in 1800 Lord Cornwallis, in a letter to the duke of Portland (3 June 1800), recommended that O'Neill and Lord Bandon should have precedence in the creation of Irish earls then contemplated. On 7 August 1800 O'Neill accordingly became first Viscount Raymond and first Earl O'Neill of Shane's Castle. His borough of Randalstown was disfranchised. In September 1800 he was elected one of the first Irish representative peers in the Westminster parliament. In 1807 he was appointed joint postmaster-general of Ireland with the earl of Rosse. This was a comparatively new appointment, and in practice the Post Office was run by the secretary, Sir Edward Lees. The postmasters-general appeared rarely in the office, and never together. On 13 February 1809 O'Neill was created a knight of the Order of St Patrick. In 1831 he was appointed lord lieutenant of the county of Antrim. Understandably, perhaps, he did not share his father's political views and could not bring himself to travel through the town of Antrim. He was a strong supporter of the union and became grand master of the Orange order in Ireland until the union of the Irish and English bodies under the duke of Cumberland. He died unmarried at the Bilton Hotel, Sackville Street, Dublin, on 25 March 1841. The earldom then became extinct and the viscountcy devolved on his younger brother, **John Bruce Richard O'Neill**, third Viscount O'Neill (1780–1855), army officer and politician, who was born on 30 December 1780 at Shane's Castle. After being educated at Eton, he entered the army as an ensign in the Coldstream Guards on 10 October 1799, saw much active service, and attained the rank of major-general on 27 May 1825, lieutenant-general on 28 June 1838, and general on 28 June 1854. He represented the county of Antrim from 19 July 1802 until his succession to the peerage on the death of his brother in 1841. In 1811 he was appointed constable of Dublin Castle. He took little part in politics, though he supported the Reform Bill. In February 1842 he was elected a representative peer of Ireland in the House of Lords at Westminster. Among his honorary appointments was that of vice-admiral of the coast of Ulster. He died unmarried of a complication of gout and influenza at Shane's Castle on 12 February 1855. His title became extinct but the name of O'Neill was assumed by the inheritor of the estates, the Revd William Chichester [see O'Neill, William Chichester, first Baron O'Neill (1813–1883)]. A. T. Q. STEWART

Sources PRO NIre., O'Neill MS, D 1470/6 • *The manuscripts and correspondence of James, first earl of Charlemont*, 2 vols., HMC, 28 (1891–4), vol. 1, pp. 165–6; vol. 2, pp. 31–4, 129, 225, 296, 325–6 • *The manuscripts of his grace the duke of Rutland*, 4 vols., HMC, 24 (1888–1905), vol. 3, p. 401 • MS autobiography of General Durham of Largo, NA Scot., Dundas MS, TD 80/70/24 • E. M. Johnston-Liik, *History of the Irish parliament, 1692–1800*, 6 vols. (2002) • G. Hill, *An historical account of the MacDonnells of Antrim* (1873), 348–50 • *GM*, 1st ser., 68 (1798), 544 • GEC, *Peerage* • E. Malins and the Knight of Glin [D. Fitzgerald], *Lost demesnes: Irish landscape gardening, 1660–1845* (1976), 81 • W. McComb, *Guide to Belfast, the Giant's Causeway, and the adjoining districts of the counties of Antrim and Down* (Belfast, 1861), 54 • *Belfast News-Letter* (18 June–7 Aug 1798) • *Annual Register* (1841) • R. B. McDowell, *The Irish administration, 1692–1800* (1964), 83–4 • *Annual Register* (1855), 251 • *Correspondence of Charles, first Marquis Cornwallis*, ed. C. Ross, 3 vols. (1859), vol. 3, pp. 245, 319, 323 • *DNB*

Archives PRO NIre., MS | BL, corresp. with Lord Hardwicke, Add. MSS 35733–35765 [Charles Henry St John O'Neill] • BL, corresp. with Sir Robert Peel, Add. MSS 40224–40406 [Charles Henry St John O'Neill] • Lpool RO, letters to E. G. Stanley [Charles Henry St John O'Neill] • W. Sussex RO, letters to duke of Richmond [Charles Henry St John O'Neill] • W. Sussex RO, letters to duke of Richmond [John Bruce Richard O'Neill]

Likenesses J. Brown, stipple (Charles Henry St John O'Neill, second Viscount O'Neill; after J. Phillips), BM, NPG • P. Jean, oils (Charles Henry St John O'Neill, second Viscount O'Neill), Eton • P. Maguire, engraving, NG Ire. • S. W. Reynolds senior, engraving (after J. D. Herbert, after M. W. Peters, in or after 1778), NG Ire. [*see illus.*] • portrait (after P. Maguire), repro. in *Ulster Journal of Archaeology*, 1/2 (Jan 1895), 138

Wealth at death considerable; in 1796 rental for Shane's Castle was £11,402; estate in Co. Meath added £500; £15,000 paid in compensation for the borough of Randalstown in 1800; in 1811 estates forming two-thirds of the family property had rental of £18,000: Johnston-Liik, *History*

O'Neill, John (1778–1858), shoemaker and writer, was born in Waterford city, Ireland, on 8 January 1778, the second son of Thomas O'Neill (*d. c.*1810), a poor shoemaker, and his wife, Jane, *née* English (1756/7–*c.*1828). John O'Neill finished his formal schooling at the age of nine and was largely self-educated. He worked as a shoemaker in Ireland, and married Mary Dollard (*c.*1780–1823) in Carrick-on-Suir, co. Tipperary, about 1800. He began to try his hand at writing while working at the boot and shoe trade, and while he dreamed of literary success, after emigrating to London in 1808, he quickly joined the capital's community of shoemakers and successfully tracked down his father, who had deserted the family some thirty years earlier. After the death of his first wife O'Neill married Ann Bass, *née* Lester (*c.*1795–1864), the widow of David Bass, on 30 January 1824 in St Anne's Church, Soho.

O'Neill managed to combine his trade with literary activity and was known in his lifetime primarily as a writer of temperance poetry, especially *The Drunkard*, which he wrote soon after becoming a teetotaller in 1840 (although he had never been an especially heavy drinker). The poem was dedicated to Father Mathew, the foremost teetotaller of his day, and it earned O'Neill the unofficial title of the laureate of the temperance movement; many reformers saw it as a vividly memorable account by a labouring-class author of the ruin brought by drink to a young working man and his family. The edition of 1842 was illustrated by George Cruikshank, who later produced his own series of popular illustrations on the same topic, entitled *The Bottle*. Robert Cruikshank, brother of the illustrator, produced a portrait of O'Neill which was engraved by Charles Wagstaff to form a frontispiece to *The Drunkard*, later renamed *The Blessings of Temperance*.

O'Neill was also the author of 'Fifty years' experience of an Irish shoemaker in London'. This memoir was published eleven years after his death in forty-one weekly instalments (8 May 1869–19 February 1870) in *St Crispin*, a weekly journal for the boot and shoe trade. Its proposed publication in a volume entitled *Struggling through Life* had been announced in 1856, but it remained unpublished in book form at the end of the twentieth century. The text describes O'Neill's struggle to survive when the shoemaking trade went into decline, telling of how he coped with injury and illness, letting rooms, and attempting to run a business of his own. All such enterprises were failures: O'Neill remained poor all his life. He also depicted family life in slum rooms at numerous addresses (especially around Clare Market and Drury Lane, but also in the

John O'Neill (1778–1858), by unknown engraver, *c.*1842

Waterloo area), diet, clothing, entertainment in public houses and other places, parish relief, and finding work for his children. The death of his wife after giving birth to their thirteenth child is described, as is his second marriage, and the resultant six more children, as well as his responsibility for two stepchildren. He tells of how he wrote songs (including a popular drinking piece 'Trim the lamp; fill the bowl'), occasional articles and poems, and an English stage version (published, but not performed) of the Spanish novel *Alva*. Folk-tales remembered from his youth were published in 1854 as *Handerahan, the Irish Fairyman; and Legends of Carrick*, with an introduction by Anna Maria Hall. Such work, in addition to *The Drunkard*, meant that his applications to the Royal Literary Society for loans and grants were generally successful.

John Bedford Leno, editor of *St Crispin*, singled out the importance of the memoirs when he noted in an editorial: 'To the historian of the future, the Reminiscences will be of immense value. Hitherto history has been too much confined and hence in searching for the records of a nation we find merely the history of its kings' (*St Crispin*, 19 Feb 1870, 85–6). O'Neill died at his home, 20 White Horse Yard, Drury Lane, on 3 February 1858 and was buried in the St Pancras cemetery, Finchley, on 7 February.

JOHN EGAN

Sources J. O'Neill, 'Fifty years' experience of an Irish shoemaker in London', *St Crispin* [trade paper] (1869–70) [41 weekly parts] • I. Doxsey, 'Introduction', in J. O'Neill, *The blessings of temperance*, 4th edn (1851) • Mrs S. C. Hall [A. M. Hall], introduction, in J. O'Neill, *Handerahan, the Irish fairyman; and legends of Carrick* (1854) • BL, Archives of the Royal Literary Fund, loan 96, case no. 998, 58 entries • census of Carrick-on-Suir, co. Tipperary, 1799, BL, MS 11.722 • census returns for St Clement Dane's, 1851, PRO, HO 107/1512 • parish register, St Anne, Westminster, 1824, City Westm. AC [marriage] • parish register (baptism), St Patrick (St Olaf), 1783–90 • parish register, St Nicholas, Carrick-on-Suir, co. Tipperary [baptism] • Waterford heritage and genealogical survey, St Patrick's, Waterford • private information (2004) [Linda Dawson, great-great-great-

great-granddaughter] · parish registers, St John the Evangelist, Waterloo, LMA · J. B. Leno, 'Editorial', *St Crispin*, 3 (19 Feb 1870), 85–6 · J. Blackman, *St Crispin* (20 Feb 1869) [unsigned biography of O'Neill] · J. D. Devlin, *The guide to trade: the shoemaker* (1839) · R. L. Patten, *George Cruikshank's life, times, and art*, 2 (1996) · burial register, London, Finchley, St Pancras cemetery, order book no. 5, no. 7084

Likenesses stipple, *c.*1842 (after unknown artist), NPG [*see illus.*] · C. Wagstaff, engraving (after R. Cruikshank, 1841–2), repro. in O'Neill, *Blessings of temperance* (1851)

O'Neill, John Bruce Richard, **third Viscount O'Neill** (**1780–1855**). *See under* O'Neill, John, first Viscount O'Neill (1740–1798).

O'Neill, Maire (**1887–1952**). *See under* Allgood, Sara (1883–1950).

O'Neill, Moira. *See* Skrine, (Agnes) Nesta Shakespear (1865–1955), *under* Keane, Mary Nesta (1904–1996).

O'Neill, Sir Neil [Niall], **second baronet** (**1657/8–1690**), army officer, was born late in December 1657 or early in 1658, and was the eldest son of Sir Henry O'Neill (*b.* 1625) of Shane's Castle, co. Antrim, who was created baronet, of Killelagh, on 23 February 1666, and his wife, Eleanor Talbot, sister of Richard Talbot, earl of Tyrconnell. O'Neill married in January 1677 Frances Molyneux (*d.* 1732), eldest daughter of Caryll *Molyneux, third Viscount Molyneux of Maryborough, with whom he had four or five daughters.

When Tyrconnell became lord deputy of Ireland in 1687, O'Neill received from his uncle first a captain's commission taken from Lord Kingston, and then the colonelcy of a regiment of dragoons. He was in France at the time of the revolution in England. In March 1689 he sailed with the French fleet that brought King James to Ireland. He was present at the siege of Londonderry, where on 13 July he was one of the six commissioners chosen to treat with the garrison. The siege was raised before any agreement was reached. He was appointed lord lieutenant of Armagh, a county then under Williamite occupation, and his regiment served under Patrick Sarsfield in the expedition to Sligo in October 1689. At the end of that year O'Neill tried unsuccessfully to muster recruits to go to France in a proposed Irish brigade.

At the battle of the Boyne (1 July 1690) O'Neill was placed with his dragoons on the extreme left of King James's army to guard the ford at Rosnaree. With his 500 men he 'did wonders' (Gilbert, 100) in preventing the 10,000 commanded by Meinhard, Count Schomberg from crossing for an hour. O'Neill was forced to withdraw by the arrival of the enemy's artillery and during the fighting he was shot in the thigh. The wound proved fatal. He died in Waterford eight days later and was buried in the Franciscan convent there.

He was succeeded to the baronetcy by his brother Sir Daniel O'Neill, who had been one of the members for Belfast in the Irish parliament of 1689. The title and estates became forfeit by a posthumous act of attainder in 1691. On petitioning the government, Sir Neil's widow was granted a forty-one-year lease on the Killelagh estate in 1700, which she sold the following year. Lady O'Neill died in 1732.

A. F. POLLARD, rev. PIERS WAUCHOPE

Sources GEC, *Peerage* · *The life of James the Second, king of England*, ed. J. S. Clarke, 2 vols. (1816) · *Calendar of the manuscripts of the marquess of Ormonde*, new ser., 8 vols., HMC, 36 (1902–20), vol. 8 · W. King, *The state of the protestants of Ireland under the late King James's government*, another edn (1692) · J. T. Gilbert, ed., *A Jacobite narrative of the war in Ireland, 1688–1691* (1892) · J. Macpherson, ed., *Original papers: containing the secret history of Great Britain*, 2 vols. (1775) · T. Ash, *A circumstantial journal of the siege of Londonderry* (1792)

Likenesses J. G. Wright, oils, 1680, Tate collection · G. Morphey, oils, *c.*1689

Ó Néill, Niall Mór (*d.* 1397), king of Tír Eoghain, was known as 'prince of the Irish of Ulster', that is, ruler of Tír Eoghain and overlord of most of the other Irish chiefs in the province. He was a son of Aodh Mór (Hugh the Great), also known as Aodh Reamhar (Hugh the Fat), Ó Néill (*d.* 1364) and grandson of the Domhnall Ó Néill (*d.* 1325) who sent a famous 'Remonstrance of the Irish princes' to Pope John XXII during the Bruce invasion of Ireland (1315–18). For six years after his father's death, Niall Mór (Niall the Elder) contested the kingship with his two brothers, Domhnall and Toirdhealbhach Ó Néill; but in 1370 Domhnall submitted to Niall and they divided Tír Eoghain between them. A bardic poem *Bean ar n-aithéirghe Éire* ('Ireland is a woman risen again'), addressed to Niall Mór, which pleads for an end to fraternal conflict, may celebrate this treaty. The marriage between Úna (*d.* 1417), daughter of Domhnall Ó Néill and her first cousin Niall Óg [*see below*], the eldest son of Niall Mór and his wife, Beanmidhe (*d.* 1385), daughter of a Mac Mathghamhna chief of Airgialla in the Monaghan area, may also relate to this time of reconciliation.

Having achieved sole power in Tír Eoghain, Niall Mór Ó Néill inflicted a crushing defeat on Brian Mac Mathghamhna, chief of Airgialla between 1365 and 1372. On 15 July 1373 the latter's son and heir, Pilib Ruadh Mac Mathghamhna, joined Ó Néill and his brother Toirdhealbhach, Art Mág Aonghusa, chief of Iveagh, Down, and the head of the Mac Domhnaill galloglass troops in a peace treaty with the Anglo-Irish gentry of Louth under the justiciar, Robert Ashton. The following November Ó Néill complained to the archbishop of Armagh of a breach of this peace by some citizens of Dundalk; and the next year he abandoned diplomacy in favour of a claim to province-wide kingship. He threatened to transfer his residence to the Iron Age royal site of Eamhain Macha, now archiepiscopal property, where he did indeed erect a token building in 1387; and he supported Mág Aonghusa in his war against the Ulster colonists, killing the escheator of Ireland, Sir James de la Hyde, at the battle of Downpatrick in 1374. However, when the absentee earl of March and Ulster, Edmund (III) Mortimer (*d.* 1381) arrived in Ireland as king's lieutenant in 1380, Ó Néill was prominent among the chiefs submitting to him as their mesne lord. Mortimer treacherously used the occasion to arrest Art Mág Aonghusa and, after the earl's premature death in 1381, Niall Mór and his sons renewed their war on the Ulster settlements, burning Carrickfergus on 10 April 1384 and acquiring 'great power' over the English there.

Ó Néill's six sons were Niall Óg, Éinrí *Ó Néill (d. 1392), Cú Uladh Ruadh, Aodh Óg, Seán Súileach, and Maoileachlainn. His two daughters, Gormlaith (d. 1416) and Gráinne (d. 1429), were both married to Ó Domhnaill chieftains. His eldest son and heir, **Niall Óg Ó Néill** (d. 1403), became a prisoner of war in 1389, but to the outrage of the Mortimer party was released by the justiciar, Sir John Stanley, on 20 February 1390 in return for ransom, hostages, an oath of fealty, and a promise 'to yield back and not to intermeddle with the bonnaght of Ulster' (Brewer and Bullen, 288)—this was the earls' traditional right to billet mercenary troops in fixed quotas on the Ulster chiefs, now utilized by Niall Mór Ó Néill to support his Mac Domhnaill galloglass.

After his release, Niall Óg (Niall the Younger) became the real chief. His father remained an honoured figurehead, writing as 'prince of the Irish of Ulster' to welcome Richard II to Ireland in 1394, explaining his warfare as arising from a failure to obtain justice from the Anglo-Irish administration, and doing homage to the English king on 19 or 20 January 1395. Nevertheless, extant letters from Niall Óg to the justiciar and archbishop of Armagh, John Colton, show that it was the former who led the submission to Richard, and that when he took the oath to the king, he did so on Colton's advice, and, he claimed, against the wishes of many chiefs in Munster and Connacht. Niall Óg himself did homage to Richard on 16 March, and was knighted by him, along with three other chiefs, probably on 25 March. Niall Mór Ó Néill died two years later, praised as 'high-king of Ulster and a contender [for the kingship] of all Ireland' (Hennessy and MacCarthy, 3.38). Niall Óg died in 1403, survived by his wife, Una (d. 1417). The death of his eldest son, Brian, in the same year, allowed the kingship to pass to Niall Óg's nephew, Domhnall, who in turn contested the kingship with his uncle's younger son, Eoghan *Ó Néill (d. 1456).

KATHARINE SIMMS

Sources K. Simms, 'The archbishops of Armagh and the O'Neills, 1347–1471', *Irish Historical Studies*, 19 (1974–5), 38–55 · E. Curtis, ed., *Richard II in Ireland, 1394–1395, and submissions of the Irish chiefs* (1927) · W. M. Hennessy and B. MacCarthy, eds., *Annals of Ulster, otherwise, annals of Senat*, 4 vols. (1887–1901), vols. 2–3 · E. Tresham, ed., *Rotulorum patentium et clausorum cancellariae Hiberniae calendarium*, Irish Record Commission (1828) · C. Mhág Craith, ed., *Dán na mBráthar Mionúr*, 2 vols. (1967–80) [vol. 1, texts; vol. 2, Eng. trans.] · J. S. Brewer and W. Bullen, eds., *Calendar of the Carew manuscripts, 1: 1515–1574*, PRO (1867), 288 · M. D. Legge, ed., *Anglo-Norman letters and petitions from All Souls MS 182*, Anglo-Norman Texts, 3 (1941) · *AFM*, 2nd edn, vols. 3–4 · A. M. Freeman, ed. and trans., *Annála Connacht / The annals of Connacht* (1944); repr. (1970) · D. Murphy, ed., *The annals of Clonmacnoise*, trans. C. Mageoghagan (1896); facs. edn (1993) · D. Johnston, 'Richard II and the submission of Gaelic Ireland', *Irish Historical Studies*, 22 (1980–81), 1–20

Ó Néill, Niall Óg (d. 1403). *See under* Ó Néill, Niall Mór (d. 1397).

O'Neill, Owen Roe [Eoghan Ruadh O'Neill] (*c.*1583–1649), army officer, was the son of Art MacBaron O'Neill (*c.*1548–1618), the older 'base-born' brother of Hugh O'Neill, earl of Tyrone. Art MacBaron had at least nine sons and four daughters from three marriages. Owen O'Neill's mother was the second wife, an unidentified daughter of Hugh Conallach O'Reilly, lord of Breifne. The birthplace of Owen Roe—or Ruadh, the red or ruddy complexioned—was the scenic lake district in Armagh near his father's 'chief house and holde' at Loughall in the barony of Oneilland. Well educated by continental-trained Franciscans, he was brought up in troubled times and much of his early training involved traditional skirmishing tactics. 'Bred in a nursery of arms since a boy' (Gilbert, *Contemporary history*, 1/1.72), Owen, after the death of six older brothers, served with his uncle, father, and surviving brothers in the campaigns of the Nine Years' War.

Spanish service, 1605–1642 Seeking opportunities that no longer existed in war-ravaged Ulster, O'Neill and his older brothers, Art Oge and Cormack, went to the Spanish Netherlands some time after his uncle's submission to the English crown. They enlisted and received commissions as captains in an Irish regiment led by their cousin, Tyrone's son Henry O'Neill. In this 'vulcanian forge' he and his fellow expatriates learned Spanish military tactics and the politics of survival. In the Spanish army he distinguished himself in the campaigns against the rebellious Dutch states, particularly at the successful siege of Rheinberg. The presence of these young Irish soldiers troubled the English as conditions in post-Elizabethan Ulster deteriorated. When Owen Roe's uncle the earl of Tyrone, together with Rory O'Donnell, the earl of Tyrconnell, succumbed to their failing prospects and fled in September 1607 to the continent, they undermined native Irish resistance and the fortunes of Owen O'Neill's family.

In the wake of this intemperate exodus, native leadership floundered and confiscation and plantation followed. O'Neill's father lost his estates, a recalcitrant older brother was executed, and many of the native northern Irish exiles were reduced to dependants of Catholic Europe. The only reliable vehicle of native Irish restitution was the Irish regiment. In English eyes it was 'a cloud hanging in the sky prepared to break forth upon the realm upon the first offer of a fit time' (PRO, SP 63/22/136, 122). The untimely deaths of Tyrone's sons, including the regiment's colonel, thrust Owen Roe O'Neill into a prominent role. During the minority of Tyrone's sole surviving son, John, the Louvain Franciscans under Florence Conry, titular archbishop of Tuam, chose Owen O'Neill to be the sergeant-major and tacit commander of this invaluable regiment. In this wilderness of exile, he and his Franciscan patrons evolved a crusading attitude directed at recovering their homeland and promoting their faith. The basis of their ideology was Tyrone's vision of *et libertate patriae*, grounded in a shared Catholic fatherland binding the fervour of the Counter-Reformation with the ambitions of provincial and traditional native resistance.

England understood what the Irish regiment meant to a

new generation of displaced Irishmen and fomented discord among the fractious native and Anglicized (Old English) Catholic soldiers. O'Neill and the ever-present Franciscans did everything to deflect this animosity. Their efforts kept the regiment together, but they stirred life-long rivalries between O'Neill and Old English officers like Thomas Preston. Strengthening O'Neill's position in the depleted exiled community was his marriage to Rosa O'Dogherty (c.1588–1660). The sister of Sir Cahir O'Dogherty of Inishowen, the leader of a short-lived post-flight Ulster insurrection, Rosa went to the continent with her first husband, Cathbar O'Donnell, the brother of the earl of Tyrconnell. Widowed in September 1609, she married O'Neill about 1613 and had one son, Henry Roe, with him. Many of O'Neill's duties after his marriage revolved around his obligations in the Spanish army. He served as military governor of the city of Rheinberg and Oloonzel, and with the outbreak of the Thirty Years' War he and the regiment were active in the Palatinate campaigns against the Dutch. He distinguished himself at the sieges of Bergen-op-Zoom and Breda. The outbreak of hostilities with England in 1625 refocused his attention on Ireland. Fearing an invasion through her Irish 'back door', England redoubled her efforts to undermine the regiment's unity. O'Neill and the Franciscans responded with invasion schemes that tried to reconcile the splintered Irish community.

In November 1627 O'Neill and archbishop Conry presented the Spanish king with an elaborate enterprise that became the basis of O'Neill's political philosophy. It called for the liberation of Ireland and its oppressed religion. They proposed the establishment of a unifying 'republic and kingdom' where jurisdiction would be divided among the different provinces. Each jurisdiction would send deputies to the headquarters of the occupying army to vote measures and assessments. In this Catholic commonwealth the interim captain-generals would be advised and counselled by experienced officers and agents without regard to race. The pope and Catholic Europe were expected to recognize and sustain this governing experiment until an integrating Catholic monarch was selected. This extraordinary proposition never passed the drafting stage, but the experience taught O'Neill and his cohorts that the fate of their envisaged Catholic *patria* depended on their own ingenuity and resourcefulness.

Spain's peace with England in 1630 and the expansion of hostilities on the continent increased the need and demand for Irish soldiers. One of the five new Irish regiments formed in the 1630s was led by Colonel Owen O'Neill, known in the Spanish territories as Don Eugenio O'Neill. In his quest for recruits, he bolstered his Irish ties and gathered intelligence about conditions in Ireland. The lord deputy of Ireland, Thomas Wentworth, fearful of strengthening the regiments of disenfranchised native Irishmen, obstructed their recruiting efforts. O'Neill never lost his focus despite the new distraction of France's entry into the European war. His actions in the border province of Artois led in June 1640 to his military governorship of Arras. Outnumbered by fifty to one, for two

months he held off three French armies. His celebrated defence was the apex of his career in the Spanish service.

While O'Neill was combating French offensives, sectarian strife in the three Stuart kingdoms drew the Catholic communities of Ireland together. Fearful that Wentworth's disbanded Irish Catholic army, raised to support the king, would be dispersed overseas, a pro-monarchy conspiracy in 1641 unfolded that attracted a desperate and accommodating O'Neill. To his way of thinking a troubled king could resolve the landed and religious grievances of the disenfranchised Irish. Through the efforts of his nephews, Con and Daniel O'Neill, he was drawn into the evolving intrigue and was granted recruiting licences that had been so vigorously denied him in the past. But the plot was stillborn when Charles I believed he had instead found non-Catholic allies in Scotland for his campaign against the parliament of England.

Return to Ireland The collapse of the plot did not deter O'Neill and his fellow northern plotters. They continued their efforts and proclaimed that their rebellion in October 1641 was not against the king, but 'in defense and liberty of ourselves and the Irish natives of this kingdom' (proclamation of 24 Oct 1641, PRO, SP 63/206/27, 135). The 1641 conspirators rebelled to rescue, or in some cases preserve, their estates and religious rights under the king, or without him, in his name. After planning and supplying the insurrection, O'Neill became intent on leaving the Spanish service and returning to a homeland he had not seen in thirty-five years. Dependent on a new generation of Franciscans, he strove for continual Catholic support and did what he could to elude English surveillance and appease ethnic dissensions. Those wary of his leadership and imagined ambitions were reminded that he was not going to Ireland to command 'but to receive what they [insurgents] may be minded to accord him … as he claims only the right to serve God and enjoy the portion that falls to him of his father's inheritance' (H. Bourke to L. Wadding, 12 April 1642, Franciscan library, Killiney, MS D. IV, 327–9). After taking leave of the Spanish service, he secretly went to Ostend and about 29 June 1642 left for Ireland. With soldiers and supplies on board, his frigate hoisted a green flag with a large Irish harp. After skirting the northern coast of Scotland, he landed on 8 July at Doe Castle in Sheep Haven on the coast of Donegal.

The news of O'Neill's arrival excited the despairing insurgents and on 29 August at the Ulster provincial assembly at Clones he was proclaimed 'lord general'. His cousin Sir Phelim O'Neill, a major conspirator of 1641 and rival claimant for the leadership of Ulster, reluctantly stepped down as the province's leader. With the issue of authority settled for the moment, Owen O'Neill faced the immediate problems of Ulster's deteriorating condition and the insurrection's disarray. He described the war-ravaged countryside 'like a hell if there could be a hell on earth'. The people were so crude and barbarous 'that many are little better off than the most remote Indians'. He lamented how there was no obedience among the soldiers 'if one can call men soldiers who behave nothing better than criminals'. Suffering also from a lack of military supplies, native resistance was disheartened (Jennings, 507–9). He and his young continental-trained officers, his would-be 'Maccabees', strove to put the northern native forces in order while containing the threat of English and Scottish protestant troops under the command of Robert Monro and Alexander Leslie. Chances for a more enduring effort revolved around the new Irish Catholic confederation meeting in Kilkenny.

O'Neill and the confederation of Kilkenny The Kilkenny confederation was a conciliatory vehicle for native and Old English Catholic interests. A rapprochement model was not unfamiliar to the Louvain Franciscans or to O'Neill. In May 1642 an embryonic commonwealth of the desperate native Irish and the legalistic Old English created a government of 'his majesty's Roman Catholic subjects of the kingdom of Ireland' whose motto declared 'pro Deo, rege, et patria Hibernia unanimis' ('United for God, king and the Irish fatherland'). But the problem was whether this consensual experiment could lay the foundation for a Catholic *patria* in a provincial-minded and religiously fractious society. At the opening sessions of the new general assembly in Kilkenny, O'Neill took the confederate oath of association. Unfortunately he was unprepared for the machinations in Kilkenny. Not a subtle politician, his causes—the restoration of estates and the acceptance of his Franciscan-inspired faith—ran counter to the interests of the confederation's dominant Old English constituency. Unlike O'Neill and his supporters, the Old English with their parliamentary traditions viewed the confederation as a temporary expedient for resolving their religious concerns with a struggling protestant king. In no way did they want to jeopardize their leverage and advantages on diffusive natives and their irreconcilable issues. Unwilling to empower a man of O'Neill's stature and ability, the confederate executive, the supreme council, refused to trust a unified military command to the foreign-trained Ulsterman. O'Neill became one of four regional commanders. The Leinster command went to his continental rival, Thomas Preston, whose daughter married O'Neill's Ulster antagonist, Sir Phelim O'Neill. He countered by marrying his son, Henry Roe, into the family of Preston's Leinster competitor, Sir Luke Fitzgerald.

After the session O'Neill returned to the north and briefed his officers and provincial leaders about the events at Kilkenny. He also worked to establish an effective fighting force and defend his vulnerable province. He adapted his considerable military skills to the skirmishing tactics of his adversaries and began by instilling discipline and an organized command to a rabble fighting-force. This task was made difficult by the constant attacks from the Scottish forces under Monro and the incursions of local protestant forces led by Sir William Stewart and Sir Robert Stewart. Not anxious to expose his inexperienced forces to these threats, O'Neill directed his men to less turbulent southern counties. On 13 June, near the town of Clones in co. Monaghan, his scattered forces stumbled into a fatal ambush. He lost many veteran commanders in this embarrassing setback. Afterwards he

vowed never to 'give field upon any man's bidding, other than advantage' (Gilbert, *Contemporary history*, 1/1.49).

O'Neill redeemed himself a few months later when the supreme council ordered the recovering northern army to relieve the embattled county of Meath. At Portlester Castle, 6 miles west of Trim, he defeated English troops under Lord Moore. Once secured, however, the Old English landowners grew anxious to rid themselves of O'Neill's northern army. His eventual withdrawal back to the desperate confines of Ulster was tied to a cessation of arms between the confederates and the king's lord deputy, James Butler, marquess of Ormond. The youthful head of a leading Old English family, Ormond was a devout royalist and protestant convert. His mission, as he saw it, was to pacify the country and provide Irish support for Charles I. These difficult priorities made Ormond, like O'Neill, a hostage to his ethnicity and religious politics. In the peace negotiations following the cessation, the protestant New English community decried concessions to papist rebels, and Old English and native factions bickered over their landed-religious agendas. Complicating the settlement also was the hard line of the new papal envoy, Pierfrancesco Scarampi. He put his faith in the military leadership of General O'Neill and cautioned confederate Catholics about negotiating away their anticipated leverage.

However, O'Neill's situation was precarious. Encamped again in war-torn Ulster, he did not benefit from the cessation. The long-suffering protestant settler communities of the north turned away from the cessation and their failing monarch and joined the English parliament and the Scots in the solemn league and covenant. This decision led to renewed conflict and breaches in the weakened cessation. In November 1643 O'Neill brought his grievances to the confederate general assembly. He warned the delegates about diluting their military power and cautioned the assembly that he would move his troops to Leinster if his native north was denied relief. The delegates responded by raising a confederate army to check the actions of General Robert Monro. The Old English majority did not trust this relieving army to O'Neill, and, with Preston pushing for the command, the assembly compromised and gave it to the inexperienced 'pseudo-general' James Touchet, the earl of Castlehaven. This appointment doomed the summer expedition of 1644. The earl's timid leadership never overcame the campaign's inadequate strategies or O'Neill's illness and disdain. No battle was ever fought; Monro, after wasting the countryside, retired to co. Antrim. In the months that followed, O'Neill's frustration and discontent moved him to consider returning to the Spanish Netherlands.

O'Neill never acted on this threat. Instead he was encouraged that the king's weakening position and growing need for Irish soldiers, together with the accession of a more energetic pope, Innocent X, might evoke significant concessions from the king's new representative, the Catholic Edward Somerset, earl of Glamorgan. But neither Glamorgan's accord nor subsequent proposals from

Ormond satisfied the newly arrived papal nuncio, Archbishop Rinuccini. Disillusioned by the confederate leadership's tempered objectives, O'Neill saw the nuncio as a source of military succour and supporter for his coveted Irish Catholic commonwealth. Bolstered by Rinuccini's aid, he restructured his army and drilled them on the co-ordination of musket and the short pike. Able to defend Ulster, on 5 June 1646 he lured a protestant army led by Monro to a site near the town of Benburb in co. Armagh. Before he decisively defeated Monro in a pitched battle, he aroused his soldiers by telling them how 'All Christendom knows your quarrel is good—to fight for your native birthright and the religion of your forefathers' (Gilbert, *Contemporary history*, 1/1.111–13). Uncontested in the field, he never followed up on his victory. Many of his soldiers dispersed with their booty, and without cannon his victorious army was incapable of capturing the north's walled garrison towns. In Waterford, Rinuccini and the assembled clergy, believing the Catholic position was strengthened, looked unfavourably on the new Ormond settlement negotiated with the supreme council. Courted by both sides, O'Neill proclaimed the guarantees of the 'vile treaty' obstructed 'the propagation of the Catholic religion' and 'the restoration of our country's freedom' (O'Ferrall and O'Connell, 2.322, 2.297).

The confederate schism By the end of August 1646 O'Neill had directed his forces to Kilkenny to support the position of the nuncio and the Catholic clergy. With his backing the council was purged, and a new executive, led by Rinuccini, took control of the confederation. Fissures in this new government erupted over the continuing negotiations with Ormond and the appointment of a confederate commander for an attack on Dublin. Unwilling to alienate the Old English clergy or their vacillating champion, Preston, the command was jointly entrusted to O'Neill and his irresolute rival. Operating under threat of excommunication and lacking sufficient ordnance, the Dublin campaign was troubled from the beginning. The latent distrust between the two generals, Preston's vulnerability to royalist pleadings, and O'Neill's concern for conserving his precious army undermined the enterprise and the momentum of the clerical coup.

Over the next seven months, while O'Neill secured key garrison towns in the confederate heartland, events at Kilkenny and Dublin worked against native Catholic aspirations. As each side jockeyed for power, fateful decisions undercut O'Neill's position. Ormond turned Dublin and the nearby posts over to the parliament of England in summer 1647, while the newly elected supreme council continued to splinter the confederate military command by relegating O'Neill to Connaught. By removing their undesirable protector, the council put their well-being in the hands of Preston's Leinster army, who were badly defeated at Dungan's Hill, near Trim, on 8 August by the new parliamentarian governor of Dublin, Colonel Michael Jones. The council responded by asking Rinuccini to invite the northern army back to Leinster.

O'Neill was distressed by these circumstances, but he recognized the alarming vulnerability of the midlands. His troops were less accommodating to these new directives. At their campsite near Kilbeggan monastery, O'Neill told his dissatisfied officers that he had returned to Ireland to serve the king, the nation, and his native province. He reminded them of their duty and declared that their timely relief would 'endear and create a better understanding between you and the rest of your countrymen' (Gilbert, *Contemporary history*, 1/1.158; 3/2.206–7). Despite the defection of some regiments he led his men to Kilkenny, where he protected the capital and southern Leinster from the Irish protestant general Murrough O'Brien, Lord Inchiquin, who had defeated the confederate Munster forces at Knockanoss in November 1647. Some time after Inchiquin's withdrawal the council directed O'Neill to King's county. Restrained by confederate directives, it was only after Jones returned to Dublin that O'Neill was ordered to move out and waste the countryside north of the city. He reluctantly carried out this mission and unsuccessfully endeavoured to engage Jones and his supporters.

O'Neill's support and service did not deter the supreme council. Wary of his power, the council and its Old English cadre did what it could to discredit the Ulster general and weakened the nuncio and his clerical supporters. As for O'Neill's ill-provisioned and unappreciated troops, they were racked by mutinies and the machinations of recalcitrant leaders like Sir Phelim O'Neill. The situation deteriorated to the point where O'Neill and Rinuccini felt unsafe in the confederate capital, but the fateful breach erupted after the council signed a cessation of arms with Inchiquin on 20 May 1648. They believed that the Munster leader would provide a defender less controversial than O'Neill and hoped that Inchiquin's royalism might rekindle negotiations with Ormond. Put off by their choice of allies, O'Neill supported Rinuccini's condemnation of the cessation with its censure of excommunication. The supreme council responded by rescinding his military command. O'Neill and his officers countered that they had stood by their oath of association for the defence of religion and the king. They accused the 'malignant party' of treachery and 'private advantage even at the cost of the ruin of the kingdom, the violation of their oath and the extinction of the faith' (O'Ferrall and O'Connell, 3.293–5; Bodl. Oxf., MS Carte 68, fols. 156–8). Appreciating that the clerical party depended on O'Neill, the council retaliated, and by the end of June Inchiquin, Preston, and all the confederate forces moved against his ill-succoured army. Throughout the summer months he adeptly manoeuvred his forces against adversaries who were bent on his disarray or defeat. When no advantage for battle presented itself, he cautioned his aroused forces and took the position of the Roman consul Fabius the Delayer. Why risk all in one battle, he asked:

> to purchase the sweet fruits of revenge ... with the hazard of our whole body, the only one in Ireland for religion, king and kingdom, as long as we hold in a body, though we never give a blow: the enemy will fear us.   (O'Ferrall and O'Connell, 3.516–18; Gilbert, *Contemporary history*, 1/1.268)

When he failed at combat, the supreme council and the new general assembly declared O'Neill a traitor, a rebel against the king and the fundamental laws of the land, and a 'manifest opposer of the established government of the Confederation' (proclamation, 30 Sept 1648, Bodl. Oxf., MS Carte 22, fol. 177). At this juncture Ormond returned to Ireland with a commission to conclude a peace treaty. Still preferring to settle things with the crown, O'Neill welcomed Ormond. Unfortunately the reliability of royal agents was fading in proportion to the ascendancy of the English parliament.

Desperation and death O'Neill's position deteriorated rapidly after Ormond and the confederates concluded a treaty on 17 January 1649. It was followed by Charles I's execution and Rinuccini's departure. Ostracized and without dependable benefactors, O'Neill was thrown upon his own devices. Unable to obtain necessary guarantees from Ormond, he unwillingly made desperate accommodations to survive. He opened negotiations with parliamentarian commanders in Ireland and on 8 May signed a cessation of hostilities with George Monck for three months. The benefits of the cessation were short-lived. Monck was secured against O'Neill's attachment to Ormond and O'Neill received much-needed provisions after supporting the parliamentarian garrison at Dundalk. In the end, parliament dissociated itself from Monck's pact and refused openly to deal with O'Neill and his party. Anxious to keep his army in the field, O'Neill also signed a truce with Sir Charles Coote and came to his relief when the Scots besieged Londonderry. Within a few weeks his bargaining position increased when Jones defeated Ormond at Rathmines and Oliver Cromwell landed in Ireland. Despite these desperate conditions, it was almost the middle of October before the parties signed the articles of peace. The accord gave O'Neill most of the secular and religious guarantees he coveted. It also provided him and his followers with the promise of an act of oblivion and assured the native leader land and political considerations in any final peace settlement. Unfortunately the pact was made with a king whose promises no longer had the weight of law. O'Neill was also terminally ill and was carried about on a horse litter. He dispatched his forces to Ormond's service, while he retired to Cloughoughter Castle, about 6 miles west of Cavan. In his last letters to Ormond he asked the lord lieutenant to be patient and not risk his men needlessly. He also requested that Ormond take care of his son, Colonel Henry O'Neill, and see to it that he benefited from 'such conditions, concessions and creations, as his Majesty intended for me' (O'Neill to Ormond, 1 Nov 1649, Bodl. Oxf., MS Carte 26, fol. 49). On Tuesday 6 November 1649, he died at Cloughoughter Castle; he was buried in an unmarked grave in the Franciscan priory in Cavan.

Appraisal O'Neill's unfolding story was first attempted in an unsigned, sentimental article in the *Ulster Journal of Archaeology* in 1856. Towards the end of the nineteenth century the availability of J. T. Gilbert's multi-volume editions of contemporary accounts and correspondence provided a published basis for setting O'Neill in a more full

and balanced historical framework, and S. R. Gardiner drew upon it in his treatment of O'Neill for the *Dictionary of National Biography* in 1894. Two years later J. F. Taylor published the first biography of the Ulster leader, a small popular nationalist account concentrating on his career after 1642. In 1914 Diarmid Coffey contrasted O'Neill to Ormond's royalist dealings, while over the next half-century at least four brief biographies appeared, each of them an abridged adaptation of Taylor's work. No new light was shed either by the work produced for the tercentenary of O'Neill's death or by T. S. O'Cahan's romantic 1969 biography. The first complete historical treatment of O'Neill, detailing both his early life and his civil war career, was published by the present writer in 1984. O'Neill's values and motivations were subsequently evaluated by Raymond Gillespie in a brief biographical article, while further specialized studies of aspects of O'Neill's career and opinions were undertaken by Casway.

In retrospect O'Neill appears a skilled and resourceful military leader who with proper ordnance and support might have made gains commensurate with his abilities. But knowing how to assemble a fighting force and keeping it in the field were fruitless if a general could not affect the maintenance and politics of a campaign. It is also sometimes overlooked that his power rested on his military prowess and not on his hereditary position in the society of the Ulster clans. Never the master of his fate, he remained dependent on myopic and declining powers. Spain, Rome, and the confederate leadership utilized his skills and profited from his service. But these powers never had the capacity or willingness to reorder the protestant landed settlement of Ulster or the resources to restore the privileges of the Irish Catholic church. O'Neill's hope that a liberated Catholic fatherland could ameliorate the ethnic and provincial divisions of Ireland never stood a chance in a realm ruled by a religiously contentious protestant monarch in an age of Calvinist ascendancy. Nor could his efforts and sacrifices move his Old English confederates to tie their threatened well-being to the eclipsed world of native Irish Ulster.

JERROLD I. CASWAY

Sources J. T. Gilbert, ed., *A contemporary history of affairs in Ireland from 1641 to 1652*, 3 vols. (1879–80) · Bodl. Oxf., MSS Carte 17–39 · J. I. Casway, 'George Monck and the controversial Catholic truce of 1649', *Studia Hibernica*, 16 (1976), 54–76 · J. I. Casway, *Owen Roe O'Neill and the struggle for Catholic Ireland* (1984) · J. I. Casway, 'Owen Roe O'Neill's return to Ireland in 1642: the diplomatic background', *Studia Hibernica*, 9 (1969), 48–64 · J. I. Casway, 'Rosa O'Dogherty: a Gaelic woman', *Seanchas Ardmhacha*, 10 (1980–82), 42–62 · J. I. Casway, 'The unpublished letters and papers of Owen Roe O'Neill', *Analecta Hibernica*, 29 (1980), 222–82 · B. Fitzpatrick, *Seventeenth-century Ireland: the war of religions* (1988); repr. (1989) · Franciscan letters, Franciscan House of Studies, Killiney, Ireland, A & D series · *DNB* · *History of the Irish confederation and the war in Ireland … by Richard Bellings*, ed. J. T. Gilbert, 7 vols. (1882–91) · R. Gillespie, 'Owen Roe O'Neill: soldier and politician', *Nine Ulster lives*, ed. G. O. O'Brien and P. Roebuck (1992), 150–68 · B. Jennings, ed., *Wild geese in Spanish Flanders, 1582–1700*, IMC (1964) · B. O'Ferrall and D. O'Connell, *Commentarius Rinuccinianus de sedis apostolicae legatione ad foederatos Hiberniae Catholicos per annos 1645–1649*, ed. J. Kavanagh, 6 vols., IMC (1932–49) · J. H. Ohlmeyer, *Civil war and Restoration in the three Stuart kingdoms: the career of Randal MacDonnell, marquis of Antrim, 1609–*

1683 (1993) • secretario de estado, negociones de Flandes, Archivo General, Simancas, Spain • state papers, Ireland, PRO, SP 63/200–282 • state papers, Flanders, PRO, SP 77/7–31 • D. Stevenson, *Scottish covenanters and Irish confederates: Scottish-Irish relations in the mid-seventeenth century* (1981) • J. I. Casway, 'Gaelic Maccabeanism: the politics of reconciliation', *Political thought in seventeenth-century Ireland: kingdom or colony*, ed. J. H. Ohlmeyer (2000)

Archives BL, Stowe MSS • BL, Egerton MSS • BL, Harleian MSS • NL Ire., Barberini Latini MSS • NL Ire., Borghese MSS • NL Ire., Ormond MSS

Likenesses Van Brugens, oils (after engraving), repro. in *Ulster Journal of Archaeology* (1856)

Wealth at death the peace of 12 Oct 1649 recognized his Ulster land claims; he was also granted consideration for earldom of Tyrone, but accord was nullified by Cromwell's conquest

O'Neill, Sir Phelim Roe [Felim Ruadh] **(1603–1653)**, landowner and insurgent, was the eldest son of Tirlough Oge O'Neill (*d.* 1608), landowner and heir to Sir Henry Oge O'Neill of Kinnard from co. Tyrone, and Catherine, daughter of Tirlough McHenry O'Neill of the Fews. This parentage reflected the intra-sept rivalries that consumed the northern O'Neills.

Origins, early life, and career Sir Henry Oge O'Neill's marriage to Catherine, daughter of Hugh O'Neill, earl of Tyrone, fed the pretensions of the family. Towards the end of the Nine Years' War, Henry Oge, sometimes called 'the queen's O'Neill', deserted Tyrone in the hope of holding his estates directly from the crown. This strategy was shared by Tirlough McHenry O'Neill of the Fews. Drawn together by their shared post-war ambitions, Henry Oge's son married Tirlough McHenry's daughter Catherine. This lineage provided Phelim Roe and his brother with autonomy in the unsettled native north, but Henry Oge paid a high price for his prominence and the schism it provoked. On 20 June 1608 both Henry Oge and his son Tirlough Oge were killed in the king's service during the ill-fated O'Dogherty revolt. The crown, reacting to the troubled condition of Ulster, attempted to reassert control by nurturing the northern Irish who had remained loyal. Towards this end, the lord deputy, Sir Arthur Chichester, violated the laws of succession and turned over parts of Henry Oge's estate to Phelim's uncles and cousins who otherwise threatened to be 'thorns in our feet and pricks in our side' (Chichester to Davies, 31 March 1609, PRO, SP 63/226/58, 154). In March 1609 an inquisition resolved the inheritance issue by recognizing the five and a half-year-old Phelim Roe as the heir to his grandfather's remaining lands. In 1613 his mother was granted a patent for custody of the newly created manor of Kinnard during Phelim's minority.

Raised as a royal ward in conformity with the principles of 'piety and civility' (*APC, 1615–16*, 346), in 1618 O'Neill and his brother Tirlough Oge enrolled at Lincoln's Inn, London, the former staying there for three years. His return to Ireland coincided with the expiration of his mother's patent and his coming of age. Although he took the oath of supremacy, he lapsed back to his native Catholicism after the 1628 'graces', or religious concessions, modified the oath to one of allegiance. He also petitioned for a new grant for his grandfather's estates. On 6 May

Sir Phelim Roe O'Neill (1603–1653), by unknown engraver

1629 the king's council, anxious to sustain O'Neill's loyalty during England's war with Spain, ordered a new patent for much of Sir Henry's lands, estimated at 4500 acres. That same year O'Neill enhanced his standing in Ulster by marrying the daughter of Arthur Magennis, Viscount Magennis of Iveagh. But he lacked the discretion to conduct himself properly, and 'ran into all the follies and extravagances of youth' (Carte, 1.158). His intemperate lifestyle, 'as free and generous as could be desired' (Hogan, 148), could not keep pace with the inflationary age. Moreover, the purchase of his knighthood, a wartime assessment, and the settlement to the crown of the value of his wardship and marriage were unavoidable expenditures. His only recourse was to heavily mortgage his estates. A 1661 inquisition stated that by 1640 he owed over £12,000 to Dublin and London creditors.

This not uncommon plight did not detract from O'Neill's regional prominence. A Tyrone–Armagh notable, he served as a local JP, sat in the Irish parliament for Dungannon in 1641, and through his brother's marriage had ties to the MacDonnells of Antrim. It was through the earl of Antrim's influence in 1639 that he gained his knighthood. Like many others in Ireland, O'Neill was alarmed by the uncompromising policies of the lord deputy, Thomas Wentworth, earl of Strafford, whose regime exposed the vulnerability of Irish tenurial, legal, and religious rights. His assault on traditional sources of Irish power moved O'Neill and others like him to fear that an ascendant English protestant parliament would use Strafford's policies to undermine their place in the post-plantation north. To protect their positions and redress former grievances, O'Neill and other Catholic landholders sought ways to preserve, not overthrow, the colonial system that gave them status and influence.

Conspiracies, 1641 Having attempted to use the Irish parliament to work out constitutional safeguards, Irish politicians failed to resolve their grievances and, moved by the success of the insurgents in Scotland, turned to more militant remedies. Initially O'Neill kept his distance from the conspirators, wary of risking his fragile position on the early plots of Lord Maguire and Rory O'More, although his brother informed him of the progress of their machinations. But his rank among the Ulster O'Neills made his support essential for any action in the native north. It was not until the spring of 1641 that he stepped up his role, as witnessed by his contacts with native commanders and kinsmen in the Spanish service. The key factor for the plotters was the fate of Strafford's Irish Catholic army that was raised to support the king against the covenanting Scots.

With the death of John O'Neill, earl of Tyrone, in 1641, Sir Phelim, identified in the plotters' codes as 'President Rosse' (Gilbert, *A Contemporary History*, 1/2.397), increased his communications with his cousin Colonel Owen Roe *O'Neill in the Spanish Netherlands. This urgency came after the disbandment on 25 May 1641 of Strafford's Catholic army. With parliament unwilling to tolerate unemployed Catholic troops in Ireland, the king directed the earl of Antrim to issue licences to designated Catholic recruiter-colonels for the purpose of maintaining the Irish army. In this context, a royalist conspiracy, termed the 'Antrim plot' or 'colonels' plot' evolved. O'Neill was not an immediate participant. Having worked in the Irish parliament to keep the soldiers together, he already had contact with Owen Roe and native officers on the continent. It was natural that he would attach himself to the original O'More and Maguire conspirators who at this point were plotting with the colonels to seize Dublin Castle and overthrow the pro-parliament regime.

O'Neill was briefed about the conspiracy at his wife's funeral in 1641. With assurances from Owen Roe's agents, he followed his confederates to Dublin to meet spokesmen from the colonels. The colonels, however, 'were fallen from their resolution' (Hickson, 2.349) because of the crown's accommodations with the Scots. Undeterred by the loss of the colonels, 'the fools', as Antrim described the native plotters, 'would not accept our time and manner for ordering the work; but fell upon it without us and sooner and otherwise than we should have done' (Cox, appx, xlix). O'Neill and the original plotters professed that they were acting in the king's best interest and planned an attack on Dublin Castle for 23 October 1641. O'Neill, preferring a contained provincial rising, concentrated his forces in Ulster. On the day preceding the general insurrection he took Charlemont Castle and a host of other fortifications. Always conscious of justifying his actions and

broadening his support, he later asserted that the Ulster rising was for the 'liberty of religion and for the recovery of those lands which should appear by the law of the land to be unjustly held from the native Irish' (TCD, MS 839, fol. 3). This justification was anticipated in his Dungannon proclamation of 24 October, which professed that the uprising was not directed against the king and that no harm would come to the Scots Irish. The sole motive, O'Neill said, was the 'defense and liberty of ourselves and the Irish natives of this kingdom' (proclamation, 24 Oct 1641, PRO, SP 63/260/27, 135). A few weeks later he published a forged royal commission authorizing him to rise up against parliament in support of Irish liberties. None of these validations won over the Scottish settlers, nor did they pacify the outbreak of long-suffering discontent.

Despite his provincial prominence, O'Neill was neither a trained military commander nor a conciliatory leader. He had envisaged a limited rising, not a rebellion that vented popular grievances. He based his actions on a network of kinship groups and affiliates who failed him when local authority broke down. In the anarchic wake, his misconceived expectations suffered from factional self-interests and the disparagement of his intentions. Branded a traitor with a £1000 reward on his head, he was often held responsible for many of the post-rising excesses. He did try to establish military order in the chaotic north, but with few resources and untrained troops his successes were limited. He took the town of Lurgan and ventured into west Tyrone and seized Strabane Castle, wasting the countryside, before being repulsed by Sir William Stewart and his protestant Lagan forces. O'Neill's greatest effort was the attempted capture of Drogheda in early 1642. The county of Meath made him general of the forces and gave him governing authority during the campaign, but neither these efforts nor his forays against the Scots in counties Down and Antrim were successful. He narrowly escaped capture and later eluded the veteran Scottish commander Robert Monro, who had landed with a Scottish army in the spring of 1642, by burning Armagh and fleeing to Charlemont. By the early summer he had lost possession of Fort Mountjoy, Dungannon, Strabane, and Kinnard and was soundly defeated by the Lagan forces at Glenamaquin, near Raphoe. With his resources and leadership waning, he attended a provincial council meeting at Glaslough. It was here on 18 July that a courier announced that Owen Roe O'Neill had arrived on the coast of Donegal with men and supplies from the continent.

Owen Roe O'Neill and the confederate Catholics O'Neill set out with a large contingent to meet and escort Owen Roe O'Neill to Charlemont. They arrived on 13 August to a great celebration. According to an eyewitness, everyone received Owen Roe with bare heads except Sir Phelim. This response portended a leadership struggle between the deposed natives and 'deserving' Irish at a general assembly convened at Clones on 29 August 1642. At this gathering, the delegates, particularly the dispossessed Irish, rallied around and acknowledged Owen Roe as their commander; they conferred upon him the title of lord-general. No reference was made to the earldom of Tyrone, to which Sir Phelim allegedly aspired. Facing up to the north's dire condition and the popular appeal of Owen's generalship, Phelim hesitantly stepped aside and was appeased with the perfunctory title of lord president of Ulster. After the assembly he accompanied Owen Roe to Kilkenny to attend the inauguration of the new Catholic confederation. Representing Ulster on the supreme council, O'Neill, 'puffed by emulation' and caught up by the intrigue at the capital, pursued opportunities to strengthen his deflated position. He not only opposed his kinsman's selection as the chief commander of the confederate forces, he also tried to outmanoeuvre him by marrying, in October 1642, Louise (1623/4–c.1649), the eighteen-year-old daughter of Owen's lifelong military adversary Thomas *Preston. The marriage strengthened him with a dowry of muskets, arms, and £3000. The Franciscan Hugh Bourke, writing to Rome, warned that the Irish cause would suffer unless the differences between Sir Phelim and Owen Roe were healed.

In the years and campaigns that followed, O'Neill busied himself with affairs in Kilkenny and Charlemont. He consolidated his military position and promoted himself as an alternative to his cousin. Lacking siege weaponry, he posed no threat to the north's fortified places, but venturing into Meath with Owen Roe's army he occupied the well-situated castles. During the failed confederate campaign of 1644 against the covenanting armies of Ulster, he remained in Kilkenny and took the confederate government's side against Owen Roe by turning Charlemont over to the campaign's commander, the earl of Castlehaven. His political connivances were eventually constrained in October 1645 by the arrival of a papal nuncio, Giovanni Rinuccini. Concerned about the confederate Catholics' lack of success, particularly in Ulster, Rinuccini focused his attention on the 'irreconcilable enmity' between Owen and Phelim. Owen Roe and his clerical adviser, Ever MacMahon, bishop of Clogher, lost no time accepting the nuncio's mediation. Sir Phelim, not wanting to lose the church's support, followed suit and was granted an all-embracing pardon for his actions. After the reconciliation the northern army received papal succour that allowed them to move against the covenanters. At the battle of Benburb, on 5 June 1646, Sir Phelim's ten-company regiment followed the command of Owen Roe. He and his forces gave a good account of themselves and settled old scores, taking no prisoners.

O'Neill used the Benburb triumph to accumulate provisions and expand his holdings. He also accompanied Owen Roe to Kilkenny to support a clerical-led coup against the confederate government, who had accepted peace terms considered to include unsatisfactory religious guarantees from the king's lord lieutenant, the marquess of Ormond. Unable to withstand Rinuccini's censure or Owen Roe's power, O'Neill righted himself by serving on a reconstituted supreme council more amenable to clerical aims. Operating under clerical duress, he took over the strategic garrison at Maryborough, as Owen Roe and the coerced Thomas Preston marched against Dublin,

held by Ormond. The deposed Old English supporters of the peace with Ormond countered this offensive with divisive appeals to the royalism of Thomas Preston and the ambitions of 'deserving' Irishmen such as O'Neill.

The failure of the 1647 Dublin campaign, the overthrow of the clerical regime, and the discrediting of Owen Roe O'Neill allowed Sir Phelim O'Neill to make amends with the crown's representatives. He knew his advancement was tied to the royalist cause and was not willing to jeopardize his rank and estates for the desperate politics of dispossessed natives or the hard-line expectations of Tridentine continental clergy. Back in the good graces of the king, he dissembled against Owen Roe and drew away key officers such as Lord Iveagh, Myles O'Reilly, and Alexander MacDonnell. By the summer of 1648 he was in a position to ignore Owen Roe's military directives and resisted his call to arms. In the early autumn he settled his differences with Ormond and was appointed a peace commissioner. He was promised a title and an expansion of his estates and was made governor of Charlemont and commander of a regiment of foot. Hoping to rekindle his primacy under a royal–confederate settlement, he continued to disparage Owen Roe and obstruct the general's negotiations with Ormond and the king. About this time he married Lady Jean (d. in or after 1668), daughter of George *Gordon, first marquess of Huntly, and widow of Claud Hamilton, first Lord Hamilton, baron of Strabane. Their younger son was named Gordon [see below].

Disaster, death, and reputation O'Neill's last hope for command occurred after Owen Roe's death (6 November 1649), when the northern leaders assembled at Belturbet in March 1650 to elect a new general of the northern army. However, not only did Sir Phelim lack the respect of Owen Roe's followers, but also a proviso in the articles of peace excluded the candidacy of any officer who had deserted the northern army in 1648. In the end, his old nemesis, Ever MacMahon, bishop of Clogher, was selected bishop-general. A week later, after acts of penance, O'Neill and his compatriots made a formal submission to MacMahon. Unfortunately, the inexperienced bishop-general led the northern army into a disastrous defeat at Scarifhollis on 21 June 1651. O'Neill escaped to co. Tyrone, where he defended Charlemont Castle against the forces of parliament. After surrendering the fortress he fled, leaving his pregnant wife behind for her own safety. He was branded a traitor and criminal, and in August 1652 the Cromwellian regime offered a £300 reward for his apprehension. Six months later O'Neill's hiding place on an island on Lough Roughan in Tyrone was betrayed. He was taken to Dublin, and on 5 March 1653 was put on trial before the high court of justice. Offered a pardon if he admitted the authenticity of the bogus 1641 royal commission, O'Neill refused to implicate the executed Charles I, knowing it might later be held against his wife or heirs. Five days later, in Dublin, on 10 March 1653, he was found guilty and was hanged, drawn, and quartered. His remains were impaled on the gates of Lisnegarvy, Dundalk, Drogheda, and Dublin.

O'Neill has been made the scapegoat for the 1641 rebellion. The sectarian propaganda of the civil war era portrayed him as a villainous rebel, the man behind the undisciplined fury of the Ulster uprising. He was also stigmatized by the clerical party who rallied around Owen Roe O'Neill. His agenda and survival tactics were hardly ever accepted or respected by them. On the other hand, his aspirations to land and status were better appreciated by royalist and Old English confederate parties as a counterforce against the native and religious militants. In the end, he became a vilified and maligned historical figure, a casualty of his post-plantation ambitions.

Contemporary accounts of the rebellion and the civil war did little to redeem O'Neill's reputation. His ambitions and intentions suffered further in the depositions taken after the Ulster rising. In many cases, he was blamed for the revolt's excesses and was accused of being a particularly vengeful leader. Historians of the later twentieth century have proved more objective in their treatments, but are still obliged to draw their conclusions from the same critical sources. For O'Neill, the problem will always be one of appreciating his circuitous and unrelenting struggle to secure his position in the unstable kaleidoscope that was colonial Ulster.

Gordon O'Neill (c.1652–1705), army officer, the younger son of Sir Phelim Roe O'Neill and his third wife, Jean, was named for his mother's family, but lived in the shadow of his father's 1641 infamy. The capture and subsequent execution of his father by the Cromwellians came about when he attempted to communicate with his wife, who was caring for the infant Gordon in their confinement at Charlemont Castle. His fate was also affected by the actions of his older half-brother, James Hamilton, baron of Strabane. Hamilton had joined Phelim Roe and the Catholic royalists in 1649 and as a Roman Catholic recusant forfeited his land to the Commonwealth in June 1655. With declining prospects, Gordon O'Neill and his mother made the necessary accommodations. Gordon was raised outside his faith, never learned the Irish language (P. Walsh, 92), and married 'a Protestant lady' (DNB) from the city of Derry with whom he had at least two children, Catherine and Gordon. Eventually the young O'Neill returned to Catholicism, lived in Derry, and served as a captain of grenadiers in the infantry regiment of William Stewart, Lord Mountjoy. A favoured officer, he was made lord lieutenant of Tyrone and sat for the county in the parliament of 1689. Fighting for the Jacobite Catholic-royalist cause in the Williamite Wars, he led a regiment of foot in many critical campaigns. He participated in the siege and blockade of Derry and was wounded in the thigh. O'Neill and his regiment were reassigned to Drogheda and fought on 12 July 1690 in the battle of the Boyne. Afterwards, he fell back with the Jacobite forces towards the Shannon River and defended the city of Limerick. A year later he was with the French commander St Ruth, near Athlone, when the Dutch General Ginkel soundly defeated the Jacobite forces at the battle of Aughrim. O'Neill and his regiment fought well, but he was severely wounded and was left for dead on the battlefield.

Fortunately, he was recognized by Scottish relatives among the Williamite soldiers and was taken to Dublin.

After his recovery O'Neill took advantage of the treaty of Limerick and joined thousands of Irish soldiers who departed for France. He became a colonel of the Irish Charlemont regiment. They were part of the Irish brigade, wearing British uniforms and serving the kings of France. From 1692 to 1697 he fought with distinction in the French service. Following the treaty of Ryswick, the remnant of his regiment was re-formed and reassembled into an infantry regiment under Pierce Butler, styled Viscount Galmoye. O'Neill rose to the rank of brigadier-general, but before his death in France in early 1705, he was negotiating to raise a regiment for the service of Spain.

O'Neill's daughter Catherine married John Bourke, styled fourth Baron Bourke of Brittas and eighth Baron Bourke of Castle Connell. His son Gordon fought in the Spanish service as a captain in an Irish regiment of dragoons. His older stepbrother Phelim, son of Phelim Roe and Louise Preston, became a Franciscan and returned to Ireland in 1671–2. He was appointed guardian of the convent of Armagh and visitor in Ulster. A controversial figure, he returned to the continent and actively served the church on political missions.   JERROLD I. CASWAY

Sources G. Aiazzi, *The embassy in Ireland of Monsignor G. B. Rinuccini*, trans. A. Hutton (1873) · C. Brady and R. Gillespie, eds., *Native and newcomers: essays on the making of Irish colonial society, 1534–1641* (1986) · Bodl. Oxf., MSS Carte 17–39 · T. Carte, *An history of the life of James, duke of Ormonde*, 3 vols. (1735–6) · J. Casway, 'The Belturbet council and election of March 1650', *Clogher Record*, 12 (1986), 159–70 · J. Casway, *Owen Roe O'Neill and the struggle for Catholic Ireland* (1984) · J. Casway, 'Two Phelim O'Neills', *Seanchas Ardmhacha*, 10 (1985), 331–41 · A. Clarke, 'The genesis of the Ulster rising of 1641', *Plantation and partition*, ed. P. Roebuck (1981), 29–45 · A. Clarke, *The Old English in Ireland, 1625–1642* (1966) · R. Cox, *Hibernia Anglicana* (1690) · depositions, TCD, MS 839 · J. T. Dolen, 'An Irish diary of the confederate wars', *Journal of the County Louth Archaeological Society*, vols. 5–7 · R. Dunlop, 'The forged commission of 1641', *EngHR*, 2 (1887), 527–33 · B. Fitzpatrick, *Seventeenth-century Ireland: the war of religions* (1988); repr. (1989) · J. T. Gilbert, ed., *A contemporary history of affairs in Ireland from 1641 to 1652*, 3 vols. (1879–80) · *History of the Irish confederation and the war in Ireland … by Richard Bellings*, ed. J. T. Gilbert, 7 vols. (1882–91) · J. Hardimann, *Inquisitionum in officio rotulorum cancellariae Hiberniae asservatarum repertorium* (1826–9) · [E. Hogan], *The history of the warr of Ireland from 1641 to 1653* (1873) · B. Mac Cuarta, ed., *Ulster 1641: aspects of the rising* (1993) · B. O'Ferrall and D. O'Connell, *Commentarius Rinuccinianus de sedis apostolicae legatione ad foederatos Hiberniae Catholicos per annos 1645–1649*, ed. J. Kavanagh, 6 vols., IMC (1932–49) · T. O'Fiaich, 'The son of Phelim O'Neill', *Seanchas Ardmhacha*, 1 (1955), 38–71 · J. H. Ohlmeyer, *Civil war and Restoration in the three Stuart kingdoms: the career of Randal MacDonnell, marquis of Antrim, 1609–1683* (1993) · M. O'Siochru, *Confederate Ireland, 1642–1649* (1999) · M. Perceval-Maxwell, *The outbreak of the Irish rebellion of 1641* (1994) · 'The relation of Lord Maguire', *Ireland in the seventeenth century*, ed. M. Hickson, 2 (1884), 341–54 · *The Second Book of the Warre of Ireland*, NL Ire., MS 2257 · state papers, Ireland, PRO, SP 63/200–282 · D. Stevenson, *Scottish covenanters and Irish confederates, Scottish-Irish relations in the mid-seventeenth-century* (1981) · W. P. Baildon, ed., *The records of the Honorable Society of Lincoln's Inn: admissions*, 1 (1896), 188 · K. Danaher and J. G. Simms, eds., *The Danish force in Ireland, 1690–91* (1962) · R. Doherty, *The Williamite war in Ireland* (1998) · *Négociations de M. le Comte d'Avaux en Irlande, 1689–90*, ed. J. Hogan, 1, IMC (1934) · S. Mulloy, ed., *Franco-Irish correspondence, Dec. 1688–Feb. 1692*, 1–3

(1983–4) • J. C. O'Callaghan, *History of the Irish brigades in the service of France*, [new edn] (1870); facs. edn (1969) • J. G. Simms, *Jacobite Ireland, 1685–1691* (1969) • M. Walsh, 'O'Neills in exile', *Seanchas Ardmhacha*, 8 (1975–6), 55–68 • P. Walsh, ed., 'Versos Hibernici D. Gordono O'Neil pro linga Hibernica', *Gleanings from Irish manuscripts* (1933), 88–95 • *DNB*

Archives Hunt. L., corresp. | Bodl. Oxf., MSS Carte • PRO, state papers, Ireland • TCD, depositions
Likenesses line engraving, BM, NPG [*see illus.*]
Wealth at death estates confiscated as a rebel

O'Neill, Shane [Sean O'Neill] (*c.*1530–1567), chieftain, was the youngest son of Conn Bacach *O'Neill, first earl of Tyrone (*c.*1482–1559), chieftain, and his second wife, Sorcha (*d.* 1530), daughter of Hugh Oge O'Neill, chief of the Clandeboye O'Neills. Upon his mother's death in 1530 Shane was fostered out to the O'Donnellys, the hereditary marshals to the O'Neills. Conn's decision to foster Shane out to a lesser dependent family, rather than to an existing or potential ally, was probably due to the fact that he had at least five much older sons. Yet neither Shane's supernumerary status nor his infancy prevented his abduction in 1531 by Niall Conallach, Conn's principal rival for the O'Neill chieftaincy. Conn survived the leadership challenge and Shane was returned to his foster family, with whom he remained until reaching adulthood. During this time the O'Neill lordship underwent rapid change culminating in the surrender by Conn in 1542 of both his kingdom and his Gaelic title in exchange for the earldom of Tyrone; his eldest son, Mathew O'Neill (*d.* 1557), was concurrently created baron of Dungannon, with right of succession to the earldom. But Shane, still in adolescence, remained a discounted quantity, wholly excluded from both the detailed negotiations preceding the settlement and the formal indenture with the crown.

Shane's rise within the O'Neill lordship, 1548–1558 Shane led an army against the Clandeboye O'Neills in 1548 and in the course of the action killed the chief's son. The attack was part of Tyrone's effort to exert control over the failing Clandeboye lordship, which was being gradually undermined by the MacDonalds, the so-called 'Scots', who were emigrating from the western isles. The government shared his desire to arrest the advancing MacDonalds and deployed a garrison at Newry, co. Down, against them. But disputes soon arose between the earl and several aggressive English captains who began raiding Tyrone with impunity. The English had, moreover, begun elevating Dungannon at his father's expense in a premature succession dispute. As the region descended into a triangular war between the earl and Dungannon and his brothers, who exploited their father's weakness in pursuit of their own interests, Tyrone came increasingly to rely on Shane, whose victory in Clandeboye had proved his ability and assured his popularity among the O'Neills. Tyrone's arrest and detention in Dublin in May 1551 provided Shane with an opportunity to assert his independence while nominally defending his father's interests.

Tyrone's removal simplified the situation by uniting Shane and his older brothers against Dungannon, upon whom the blame for their father's imprisonment was squarely placed. It was Shane, however, who rose to prominence, assuming responsibility for Tyrone in his father's absence. Recognizing this, Dungannon and Nicholas Bagenal, marshal of the army, attempted to negotiate or, if possible, capture him in October 1551. Following Dungannon's failure to accomplish this, Shane agreed to talk, revealing that he had been acting on 'instructions receavyd from his father sithens his laste repayre to Dublin' and that 'he shulde submit him sellfe to no man tylle his father returne' (PRO, SP 61/3/56). Shane, however, accepted a truce and agreed to acknowledge Dungannon's authority. But Dungannon's credibility among the O'Neills was in ruin, and in spring 1552 Shane marched into Dungannon, in Tyrone, unopposed taking £800 worth of treasure which, he claimed, belonged to his father. He subsequently sought support for his actions among other Irish chiefs and even made peaceful overtures towards the MacDonalds. Hearing of this, Sir Thomas Cusack, lord chancellor, travelled to Dungannon to learn of Shane's intentions. He perceived in him 'but pryde, stubbornes, and all bent to do what he coulde to distroy the pore countrey' (PRO, SP 61/4/43). Upon Cusack's departure Shane exercised his independence by defiantly burning the earl's house. In December the government released the aged Tyrone in the hope that Shane would acknowledge his father's authority and that the O'Neills would assist in expelling the Scots from Ulster.

Tyrone's restoration, however, failed to achieve either objective because it neglected to address the principal cause of instability in the region: the discrepancy between English and Gaelic laws of succession. Shane's efforts to achieve recognition as *tánaiste* were misinterpreted as simple recalcitrance and the earl's reconciliation with Dungannon upon his return, coupled with his adherence to the English law of succession by primogeniture, reinforced his youngest son's belief that his only means of redress was by the sword. Thus a dangerous situation developed where two successors existed concurrently, one by Gaelic right, the other by English. Upon his reappointment as deputy in November 1553 Sir Anthony St Leger, the architect of the settlement of 1542, lent tacit recognition to Shane's position by awarding him a generous royal pension. The support of Gerald Fitzgerald, eleventh earl of Kildare, for Shane against a rival O'Neill faction in 1554 clouded the question of legitimacy further while echoing an earlier Geraldine–O'Neill alliance. In the same year Tyrone and Dungannon assembled an army to attack the Scots in Clandeboye and to demonstrate their collective strength, but Shane, who by this time had married James MacDonald's daughter, Katherine, maintained his alliance with the MacDonalds and the attacking army was routed. Shane was now the dominant force among the O'Neills. Yet the government failed either to recognize his Gaelic right to the chieftaincy or to uphold vigorously Dungannon's English claim to the earldom. The new lord deputy, Thomas Radcliffe, Lord Fitzwalter, pardoned Shane in 1556 for his recent confederation with the Scots, but similarly ignored the question of succession. This hesitation created a power vacuum that Shane exploited to his advantage.

In 1557 Shane assembled a large army and attacked Tyrconnell. He hoped to re-establish traditional O'Neill suzerainty throughout Ulster by compelling the O'Donnells to submit to his authority 'so that there should be but one king in Ulster for the future' (*AFM*, s.a. 1557). A victory, moreover, would make his position impossible for the government to ignore. The expedition, however, ended in disaster when Shane's army was defeated at Cnoc Buidhbh, near Strabane in Tyrone, ironically the place where his father met with a similar discomfiture, in pursuit of the same goal in 1522. However, a serious challenge to Shane's leadership failed to materialize: the O'Donnells were wracked by internal dissension and were unable to consolidate their victory, the earl was old and sickly and Dungannon lacked support among the O'Neills. The government of Mary I, moreover, failed to pursue any consistent policy towards O'Neill or Ulster save a resolution to expel the Scots. When in 1557 the third earl of Sussex (Fitzwalter) called upon the O'Neills to aid in a campaign against the Scots, Shane was conveniently absent. In October Sussex twice burned Armagh in search of Shane, but failed on both occasions to engage him. Shane—having secured another pardon in December—was sufficiently confident in his position and at last moved against Dungannon, orchestrating his assassination in 1558. Tyrone subsequently escaped to the pale, where he died the following year. Dungannon's young son Brian O'Neill (*d.* 1562) inherited the title second baron of Dungannon, but because of his youth and Shane's strength he did not accede to the earldom to which he was entitled by English law.

Shane's chieftaincy: the pursuit of the earldom of Tyrone, 1558–1562 Tyrone died by 16 July 1559 and Shane was elected O'Neill. This Gaelic distinction, however, did not abrogate or supersede the vacant English title and Shane immediately sought recognition as his father's legitimate successor to the earldom. Elizabeth I was keen to avoid conflict and did not have a viable alternative. She proved receptive to his claim and in July authorized Sussex to recognize him as earl. Yet the absence of trust between Shane and Sussex, coupled with the former's refusal to allow English arbiters to settle his disputes with lesser Ulster chiefs, made the subsequent negotiations impossible. In an effort to circumvent Sussex, Shane, through his trusted foster brother Terence Donnelly, dean of Armagh, petitioned the queen for recognition of his position, noting that the 'rude uncyvill and disobedient people' of his lordship 'will fall to cyvilite and here after be faithfull obedyent and trew subjectes' if his requests were granted (PRO, SP 63/1/79). Sussex, however, vilified Shane, convincing Elizabeth to rescind her offer of the earldom and pursue a more aggressive policy. Within a year any hope of peace was lost as Shane resumed raiding the pale's northern marches and the queen authorized Sussex to 'practise with such other subjects as be neighbours unto him, by reward or otherwise, by whom ye may most probably

reform the said Shane, or otherwise by our force to compel him to stand to your order and governance' (Brewer and Bullen, 1.292). In summer 1560 Sussex, now lord lieutenant, made a feeble attempt to form an English-backed alliance of Ulster chiefs to challenge Shane's authority. However, in August Shane, demonstrating his impressive military capabilities, marched through Ulster intimidating Sussex's would-be allies. Elizabeth subsequently authorized his subjugation and the restitution of Dungannon's rights to the barony.

Sussex, with a reinforced English army, was at last free to wage war openly against Shane. But militarily this presented him with several problems: Shane was master of a sprawling lordship in Ireland's most Gaelic province which had remained consistently militarized for over a decade, he employed thousands of Scottish mercenaries, and was continually surrounded by hundreds of fiercely loyal bodyguards. Sussex was forced to rely on another hastily constructed alliance of Ulster chiefs to maintain a decisive advantage. The most important of these chiefs was Calvagh O'Donnell, who alone was capable of opening up a second front to the north-west of Shane's lordship. In June 1561 Sussex printed a proclamation detailing Shane's offences since 1556 as a public declaration of war. Shane, however, had already struck, capturing O'Donnell and his wife, Katherine *née* MacLean (*d.* 1588), dowager countess of Argyll, in late May. This wrong-footed the lord lieutenant, denying him his second front, and allowed Shane to extend his influence into Tyrconnell. Shane established a firmer foothold in Tyrconnell about 1560 when he divorced his wife and married Calvagh and Katherine O'Donnell's daughter, Mary, who, according to the four masters, 'died of horror, loathing, grief and deep anguish, in consequence of the severity of the imprisonment inflicted on her father' in May 1561 (*AFM*, s.a. 1561). With O'Donnell as a bargaining tool and the freedom to retreat into the fastness of Tyrconnell, Shane became an elusive enemy for the increasingly frustrated Sussex.

Sussex staked his political reputation in Ireland on effectively dealing with Shane. In early 1561 he favoured Shane's repair to England to submit to Elizabeth. However, by summer he had become convinced that English rule in Ireland hinged on Shane's subjugation. For Sussex, Shane's imprisonment of O'Donnell—to whom the government had lately offered an earldom—and his retention of Katherine O'Donnell as his mistress were merely the latest in a series of outrages which demanded an overwhelming military response. Shane, however, was not without allies and they continued to hold out the more conciliatory option of a visit to court. Through Kildare and the under-treasurer, Sir Henry Sidney, who stood as godfather to Shane's child in 1559, he sought to obtain money and sureties for his safe conduct to England. His repeated efforts to plead his case to the queen in person stemmed from his worsening relationship with Sussex which had, by 1561, degenerated into little more than bitter accusations and counter-accusations. In a letter to Sussex in June Shane wrote:

You began with a conquest in my land without cause, and so long as ther be any Englysh man in my contre against my wyll, I wyll not send agreement nor message unto you from hence forthe, but wyll send my complaint in another way to the Quenes Majestie to declare unto her Grace howe youe interupted my going. (PRO, SP 63/4/22 viii)

But Sussex was determined to eliminate Shane before he could secure an audience with Elizabeth, and, in July, he marched into Tyrone. Shane withdrew to Tyrconnell and waited until the advancing army's supplies grew low; and upon their return towards Armagh mounted a successful attack on the rearguard. A failed effort to have Shane assassinated in August and an expensive, but ultimately ineffectual, campaign in September undermined further support for Sussex's coercive policy in Ulster. The queen, her confidence in Sussex's methods shaken, authorized Kildare to treat with Shane in August. Kildare brokered a settlement by October. Yet it was Shane who dictated its terms, receiving £2000 to defray the expenses of a journey to court, a pardon, and a safe conduct signed by five Irish earls. Aware of the dangers of leaving his country, but confident in the guarantees he had painstakingly procured, he consented to go to England. Sussex warned 'yf Shane be overthrowen all is settled, yf Shane settell all is overthrowen' but was defeated and humiliated (PRO, SP 63/4/37). He followed Shane to court to defend his conduct and salvage his reputation.

Shane's submission: the legacy of surrender and regrant, 1562
Shane made his formal submission to Elizabeth on 6 January 1562. Unlike his father, who appeared at court in October 1542 in English dress and flanked by English nobility, Shane wore his native costume and was surrounded by a retinue of elaborately adorned galloglass. The scene, given added effect by Shane's Gaelic speech and his prostration before the queen, created a stir at court and was described, some years later, by William Camden:

Shane O'Neill came out of Ireland that year as promised, surrounded by Galloglass for security, with bare heads, ash-coloured hanging curls, golden saffron undershirts, if not the colour of infected human urine, loose sleeves, short tunics, and shaggy lace: the English nobility followed with as much wonderment as if they had come from China or America. (Camden, 69)

Shane's presence at court, however, went beyond mere ceremony. Accompanied by advisers intimately familiar both with Gaelic and English law and administration, he put forward his case for the earldom. The main point of contention was the settlement of 1542, which Shane held to be invalid on account of Dungannon's illegitimacy. He alleged that his half-brother was not an O'Neill, but rather the son of a Dundalk blacksmith adopted in adolescence by his father. He pressed for renegotiation of the settlement on account of his own legitimacy and his status as the O'Neills' elected leader. Sussex, who arrived in February, however, insisted that the settlement of 1542 was a submission rather than a contract and that the sovereign alone had the authority to revoke its terms. Dungannon, he contended, was Tyrone's accepted heir and he dismissed his illegitimacy as irrelevant to Shane's case. To this Shane replied that his father was merely an 'officer' of

his people incapable of being made owner of his country or investing the succession in an illegitimate child. Sussex replied that Gaelic political custom had no standing in English law.

The argument was familiar; it dated back to 1560, when a number of questions were put to Shane concerning his right to the earldom. His answers and counter-questions, however, exposed more fundamental questions concerning crown rights in Ulster and the legitimacy of Gaelic custom *vis-à-vis* English custom in Ireland. His argument could be applied to every Gaelic lordship and, if successful, threatened to undo painstakingly negotiated submissions. Shane's case placed the entire policy of surrender and regrant under examination and revealed that many Gaelic and English legal customs were simply irreconcilable. Yet the crown could not ignore the reality of his Gaelic lordship in Ulster, and over the following months continued negotiating towards an acceptable settlement without addressing these irreconcilable differences that lay at the heart of the problem. Elizabeth's decision in March to postpone her judgment on the matter of the earldom until Dungannon was interviewed convinced Shane that the negotiations were futile. Dungannon's murder on 12 April 1562 by his cousin Turlough Luineach *O'Neill, amid rumours of a coup in Tyrone, however, delivered the final blow to negotiations as Shane sought immediate licence to return to Ireland. But before his departure Shane hastily agreed to an indenture that acknowledged his 'captaincy' of the O'Neills, but circumscribed his traditional suzerainty in Ulster.

On another level, the failure of Shane's visit can be attributed to court politics. Sussex was concerned that Shane's intimacy with Kildare would unite Old English and Gaelic Irish in opposition to his government in Ireland. Kildare's successful bid to induce Shane to repair to court, moreover, was a humiliating defeat for Sussex and was perceived by many palesmen as vindication of Kildare's more conciliatory methods for the governance of Ireland. Sir Robert Dudley, Elizabeth's favourite, was alive to Kildare's ascendancy and the opportunities for patronage in Ireland; but his lavish entertainment of the earl and Shane during their stay at court aroused the attention of his rival for the queen's attention, Sir William Cecil, principal secretary. Cecil was determined to frustrate Dudley's efforts to establish an affinity in Ireland and used his own influence with Elizabeth to ensure Sussex's arguments were greeted favourably. Shane, moreover, was an obstacle to Cecil's ongoing negotiations with Archibald Campbell, fifth earl of Argyll. Cecil had, for several years, been urging Argyll to employ his forces to bring pressure to bear on Shane and dislodge the Scots from Ulster, but Shane's capture of Argyll's stepmother, Katherine O'Donnell, in 1561 frustrated Cecil's plans. Ultimately it was Cecil who supported Sussex's arguments, delayed Shane's stay for four months, and convinced the queen to suspend judgment on Shane's right to the earldom. Shane's treatment reveals how far court politics obstructed consistent crown policy under Elizabeth. Dungannon's murder coupled with rumours of Shane's intrigues with Alvaro de la Quadra, the Spanish ambassador in England, however, forced Cecil to discontinue his strategy and expedite Shane's bid to return to Ireland.

Shane's hegemony in Ulster, 1562–1566 Upon his return to Ireland on 26 May 1562, Shane proceeded directly to Tyrone where he quickly reasserted his authority, having heard that Turlough Luineach had proclaimed himself O'Neill on 23 May. He subsequently rounded on the neighbouring Ulster chiefs who had, in his absence, pledged to resist his authority. This behaviour clearly violated the terms of his indenture, which stated that grievances between Shane and other Ulster chiefs should be subject to English arbitration. But Sussex, who returned as deputy in July, found the indenture's terms impossible to enforce without resorting to full-scale war. Elizabeth—loath to expend her limited resources on war in Ulster only months after Shane's submission—vacillated. Shane, meanwhile, tightened his grip on Ulster through raiding the pale, attacking the English garrison at Armagh, and opening a second front against the O'Donnells. In September Sussex called for Shane and the Ulster chiefs to attend him at Dundalk, co. Louth, but Shane, whose distrust of the lord lieutenant had not been diluted, refused. Sussex's continued presence made war a certainty and in spring 1563 he launched a campaign against Shane. However, it was poorly organized and under-funded. Despite Sussex's ostensibly successful efforts to detach Shane's most ardent supporters, the operation collapsed having accomplished nothing. By July Elizabeth, influenced by Dudley and his supporters at court, decided to change tack and pursue an inexpensive conciliatory strategy.

Cusack and Kildare met Shane at Drumcree, co. Meath, in September and negotiated a treaty. This granted Shane nearly all the demands that he had failed to secure at court and nullified the indenture that he had signed in April, exempted him from attending the queen's governor in Ireland, and acknowledged him 'to have all the pre-eminence, jurisdiction, and dominions which his predecessors had, and particularly over the Lords subject to him' (Brewer and Bullen, 1.239). This last clause gave tacit recognition to the Gaelic tract known as *Ceart Uí Néill*, the customary right of O'Neill over the province of Ulster. The tract obliged the many lesser Ulster chiefs to join O'Neill in a hosting, to provide billets for his troops, and to pay fixed tributes. Cusack and Kildare, however, went too far in their conciliatory efforts, virtually establishing Shane as an independent entity in Ulster. Elizabeth modified the treaty, insisting that Shane attend her governor, provided assurances were given for his safety, and that differences between him and the government be referred to arbitration. None the less this reflected a volte-face in crown policy towards Shane and, in the final draft, acknowledged his right to accede to the earldom following an examination at the next Irish parliament of the letters patent granted in 1542. The treaty confirmed Sussex's eclipse and Shane—'ever ready to change his wife to suit his policies'—added insult to injury by resuming his efforts to wed Sussex's sister as proof of his willingness to embrace English civility (Hogan, 'Shane O'Neill', 168). A favourable

settlement with the government concluded, Shane confidently turned his attention to the governance of Ulster.

In spring 1564 Shane released O'Donnell from captivity on condition that he relinquish his claim to Lifford Castle and the Inishowen peninsula, co. Donegal. O'Donnell agreed, but, once freed, refused to honour his word and fled to Dublin to reveal the enormity of Shane's cruelty and to appeal for assistance. During his absence Shane invaded Tyrconnell and wasted much of the country. The government, however, was not prepared to risk a confrontation with him following Drumcree and ignored O'Donnell's pleas. Shane had, moreover, offered to aid the government in the expulsion of the Scots. His motivation for such a gesture was twofold: first, it demonstrated his loyalty to the crown and would, he hoped, expedite the settlement of the earldom in his favour; second, it would remove the final obstacle to his goal of achieving O'Neill hegemony across Ulster. A letter from the earl of Leicester (Dudley) in late summer urging Shane to do something to merit Elizabeth's favour pushed him into action. Shane, denied the English aid for which he petitioned, marched against the Scots in September, but following an encounter near Coleraine was defeated. The defeat revealed weaknesses in Shane's military machine—particularly when acting in the offensive in an open confrontation—and forced him to invade Tyrconnell in October to replenish supplies and boost morale. He was capable of holding the O'Neills and their septs together through his standing and his personality but he was a poor commander. The invasion also saw the occupation of certain castles, raising the ominous prospect of permanent O'Neill settlements in Tyrconnell.

By spring 1565 Shane had grown impatient with Elizabeth's failure to call the parliament that would ratify the Drumcree treaty and assure his accession to the earldom. The earldom and the right of Dungannon and his sons to the succession hung over Shane's head like the sword of Damocles for over a decade and he was determined to force a resolution of the matter. In April he assembled a large force and marched towards Clandeboye, co. Antrim. With the support of the local chiefs, he cut passes in the woods and surprised the MacDonalds in the Glens and the Route, forcing them back upon their fortress at Red Bay. Shane destroyed the fortress and marched to Ballycastle, where he overwhelmed a newly reinforced Scottish contingent in the valley of Glenshesk, both in co. Antrim, on 2 May. Two powerful chiefs, James and Sorley Boy MacDonald, were captured and Shane proceeded to destroy every vestige of Scottish occupation along the Antrim coast. His victory was complete. He did not withdraw, however, and, in an unprecedented move by a Gaelic chief, began colonizing the Glens, the Route, and Clandeboye with his own people to maintain his influence and dissuade future Scottish encroachment. That summer he unexpectedly attacked the English garrisons at Newry and Dundrum, co. Down, before invading northern Connaught in the autumn to reassert traditional O'Neill suzerainty. Shane's power reached its apogee and his refusal to release his MacDonald captives won him the attention of Mary, queen of Scots, and Argyll, who saw him as a powerful potential ally against Elizabeth.

Running concurrently with Shane's aggressive military strategy was an effective diplomatic offensive waged with allies to influence the government's political policy towards Ulster. Chief among these allies was Donnelly who, following Drumcree, repeatedly pointed out Shane's conformity and willingness to serve the crown. Shane dispatched him to England to relate the manner of his victory over the Scots and press his claims for the earldom. Together with Robert Fleming, he portrayed Shane as a dutiful subject even as his actions grew bolder late in 1565. Cusack, who tied his reputation and political career to the conciliatory measures embodied in Drumcree, joined Shane's allies in convincing the government of the latter's loyalty. Leicester also contributed to Shane's diplomatic offensive by preserving his reputation at court. It was Shane, however, who maintained the preponderance of correspondence with the government, firmly setting out his demands and proposals to the queen, the privy council, and the Irish privy council. But his diplomatic offensive went beyond England. Rumours of his negotiations with Mary or Argyll abounded towards the close of 1565 and in the previous summer Shane had entertained David Wolfe, the papal nuncio, in Tyrone. Moreover, he hoped to elevate Donnelly to the see of Armagh and denied the bishopric of Down and Connor to the crown's choice, James Mac Caghwell, in May, retaining instead his brother, who held the position through a grant procured from Rome. By 1566 his military aggressions coupled with his wide-ranging diplomatic efforts cost him the support of his allies in Dublin and at court, and convinced the crown to abandon its conciliatory policy in Ulster and to seek his destruction. Reports filtered back to England that he was deeply critical of the queen when drunk.

Shane's incompatibility with the Tudor state, 1566–1567 Sidney was appointed lord deputy on 13 October 1565 and arrived in Ireland on 20 January 1566. He had been convinced for months of the necessity for Shane's destruction, but was unable to persuade Elizabeth to commit to all-out war. Following Shane's refusal to meet him on several occasions, Sidney wrote to Leicester:

> I believe Lucifer was never puft up with more pryde nor ambytyon than that Onelr [O'Neill] ys … he continually kepyth 600 armed men … about him, he ys able to bring to the field a thousand horsmen and 4,000 footmen; he hath already in Dundrum, as I am credibly advertysed 200 toon of wyne and mutch more he lokyth for; he ys the only strong man of Ireland; hys cuntre was never so rytch nor so inhabited; he armyth and weaponnyth all the peasantes of his cuntre, the first that ever so dyd of an Iryshman; he hath agentys continually in the coor [court] of Scotland and with dyvers potentates of the Irysh Scottes. (PRO, SP 63/16/29)

The letter found its way to Elizabeth and the privy council, who recognized the need for Shane's extirpation; but an independent observer, Sir Francis Knollys, was dispatched to conduct a review of the state of Ulster before any resources were released. Knollys's report eventually concluded that war was unavoidable and Shane was proclaimed a traitor in August. Shane, meanwhile, exploited

the delay by making preparations for war. He tightened his grip over his septs, resumed raids on the pale, and evacuated Dungannon and Benburb, co. Armagh. His diplomatic intrigues, moreover, stretched from Munster to Scotland as he sought support both from Sir John Fitzgerald, the brother of Gerald fitz James Fitzgerald, fourteenth earl of Desmond, and at Mary's court. He even approached the Scots offering to 'put away' Katherine O'Donnell, whom he married in 1565, and marry James MacDonald's widow. Most remarkably, however, Shane donned the mantle of defender of Catholicism against English heresy and appealed to Charles IX for 5000 French troops. Foreign or domestic aid, however, was not forthcoming and his military capability was no match for Sidney's professional army, which marched north. Sidney's army traversed Tyrone unopposed leaving a garrison at Derry and restoring O'Donnell. In December Shane sued for peace, but his efforts were rejected.

In spring 1567 Shane marched a large force into Tyrconnell to reassert his authority. The O'Donnells, however, laid aside their differences and, in a concerted effort to repel the invader, attacked his encampment at Farsetmore. Shane's men were forced back upon the swollen River Swilly, which carried hundreds to their deaths. He narrowly escaped, but the battle claimed many of his leading officers. The defeat was disastrous and, sensing his vulnerability, his followers and allies proceeded to abandon him. As Sidney marched north contenders for the chieftaincy and the earldom began to emerge. The Scots, moreover, resumed their settlements in Antrim and pushed west. In desperation Shane considered surrendering unconditionally to the lord deputy, but decided instead to seek reconciliation with the MacDonalds, whose chief, Sorley Boy, remained his captive. Shane travelled to Cushendun, co. Antrim, on 31 May to parley with the MacDonalds. The negotiations—conducted in an open field far removed from their respective forces—continued for two days with Shane hoping to secure much needed reinforcements in exchange for Sorley Boy's release. On 2 June the Scots fell upon him, perhaps provoked by his intemperate speech, killing him by cutting his throat before hacking him to pieces along with five advisers accompanying him. The Scots had no shortage of reasons to seek Shane's murder, but it was his weakness and desperation that afforded them such a golden opportunity. Edmund Campion noted: 'Thus the wretched man ended, who might have lived like a Prince, had he not quenched the sparkes of grace that appeared in him, with arrogancy and contempt against his prince' (Campion, 130). The annals of Loch Cé recorded that Shane was 'Lord of the Ultonian province, and royal heir of Erinn without dispute' (*Annals of Loch Cé*, s.a. 1567). Shane's body, hastily buried at Glenarm and wrapped in a kerne's shirt, was later exhumed and his head was sent 'pickled in a pipkin' to Sidney, who had it placed on a pole over Dublin Castle (*DNB*). He was attainted, his lands declared forfeit, and the title of O'Neill extinguished in 1569 by act of the very parliament which was, according to the Drumcree treaty, to have formalized his accession to the earldom. He was succeeded by Turlough Luineach and was survived by Katherine O'Donnell and at least ten identifiable sons. His sons were too young in 1567 to challenge Turlough Luineach but within a decade emerged as a political faction among the O'Neills known as the MacShanes.

Historical interpretations of Shane's career have, until recently, been inextricably linked with the myth surrounding his character: 'Shane the Proud', a quintessentially Gaelic chief whose overweening ambition and pride upset the balance of power in Ulster and plunged the province into unprecedented chaos for fifteen years. His ascendancy, motivated only by pride and maintained through cruelty, was a fluke leaving no tangible legacy save destruction. Accordingly, detailed studies of Shane and the complicated social and political world he inhabited have been deemed unnecessary. This interpretation was advanced during his lifetime primarily by English politicians and continued by near contemporary English historians like Campion and John Hooker. To the Tudor mind Shane's savagery exemplified the depths to which an unrestrained and uncivilized Gaelic chief might sink. Nineteenth-century English historians—drawing on these contemporary and near contemporary sources—accepted this interpretation without question. Robert Dunlop concluded: 'judged even by the lax standard of his age, he was a bad man—a glutton, a drunkard, a coward, a bully, an adulterer, and a murderer' (*DNB*). Irish nationalist historians, keen to revise hostile English histories of Gaelic chiefs, found it difficult to accommodate Shane within their historical tradition. When they scratched the surface of the standing English interpretation, they found instances of Shane's sexual indiscretion, an ambivalent attitude towards his fellow Gael, and his avid pursuit of English civility. Thus the majority of nationalist historians ignored him, accepting the traditional interpretation of his character and career. Only recently have historians begun to offer a reappraisal of his significance in the Tudor period and to dispel the myths surrounding his character. Shane is re-emerging as an innovative and highly organized leader who transformed his lordship into an often effective military machine, the most powerful force Gaelic Ireland had yet witnessed. That he was ambitious cannot be disputed, but little else can be said about him as an individual. It was his ambition, however, that was most crucial. Shane's aggressive ambition, pursued in the periphery of both the English and Gaelic worlds, frustrated the cultural and political advance of an increasingly centralized Tudor state and made his destruction inevitable.   CHRISTOPHER MAGINN

Sources state papers, Ireland, Elizabeth, PRO, SP 63 · *AFM* · J. S. Brewer and W. Bullen, eds., *Calendar of the Carew manuscripts*, 6 vols., PRO (1867–73) · *The Irish fiants of the Tudor sovereigns*, 4 vols. (1994) · E. Campion, *Two bokes of the histories of Ireland*, ed. A. F. Vossen (Assen, 1963) · J. Hooker, 'A chronicle of Ireland, 1547–86', *The first volume of the chronicles of England, Scotlande, and Irelande*, ed. R. Holinshed, 3 vols. (1587) · 'Original letters of Shane O'Neill in Irish and Latin', ed. J. O'Donovan, *Ulster Journal of Archaeology*, 5 (1857), 259–74 · E. Ó Doibhlin, ed., 'Ceart Uí Néill', *Seanchas Ardmhacha*, 5 (1970), 324–58 · W. Camden, *Rerum Anglicarum et Hibernicarum annales, regnante Elisabetha* (1649) · *CSP for.*, 1561–2 · T. B. Lyons, 'Shane O'Neill: a biography', MA diss., University College, Cork, 1948 · C. Brady, *Shane O'Neill* (Dundalk, 1996) · J. Hogan, 'The Irish law of kingship, with special reference to Aileach and Cenel Eóghain', *Proceedings of the Royal Irish Academy*, 40C (1931–2), 186–254 · J. Hogan, 'Shane O'Neill comes to the court of Elizabeth', *Féilscríbhinn Tórna*, ed. S. Pender (Cork, 1947) · N. P. Canny, *The Elizabethan conquest of Ireland: a pattern established, 1565–76* (1976) · C. Brady, 'The killing of Shane O'Neill: some new evidence', *Irish Sword*, 15 (1983), 116–23 · T. Mathews, *The O'Neills of Ulster: their history and genealogy*, 3 vols. (1907) · G. Hill, *An historical account of the MacDonnells of Antrim* (1873) · C. Breathnach, 'The murder of Shane O'Neill: Oidheadh Chuinn Cheadchathaigh', *Ériu*, 43 (1992), 159–76 · M. Dillon, 'Ceart Uí Néill', *Studia Celtica*, 1 (1966), 1–18 · *DNB* · W. M. Hennessy, ed. and trans., *The annals of Loch Cé: a chronicle of Irish affairs from AD 1014 to AD 1590*, 2 vols., Rolls Series, 54 (1871), s.a. 1567
Archives BL, submission, Cotton MS Titus B.xii · LPL, abstract of Act of Attainder, MS 613 · Royal Irish Acad., papers relating to his being 'outlawed'
Likenesses portrait, Linen Hall Library, Belfast; repro. in Brady, *Shane O'Neill*, cover · portrait (after J. Speed, 1600)

O'Neill, Terence Marne, Baron O'Neill of the Maine (1914–1990), prime minister of Northern Ireland, was born on 10 September 1914 at 29 Ennismore Gardens, Hyde Park, London, the third son and youngest of the five children of Captain Arthur Edward Bruce O'Neill (1876–1914), of Shane's Castle, Randalstown, co. Antrim, Unionist MP for Mid-Antrim, and his wife, Lady Annabel Hungerford Crewe-Milnes (1881–1948), the eldest daughter of Robert Offley Ashburton Crewe-*Milnes, marquess of Crewe, politician. His maternal grandfather was of Liberal stock, and was appointed viceroy of Ireland in 1892 by Gladstone's pro-home rule administration. His paternal grandfather, Edward Chichester, later O'Neill, second Baron O'Neill, was Conservative MP for co. Antrim from 1863 to 1880. O'Neill was less than two months old when his father became the first MP to be killed in action in the First World War, on 6 November 1914. His mother married, second, on 9 February 1922, Major James Hugh Hamilton Dodds, later Crewe (d. 1956), a consular official.

After quitting active politics, O'Neill made much of his Gaelic heritage, both out of pride in lineage and to indicate a special rapport with Northern Ireland's Catholics. Indeed, the dynasty of O'Neill could be traced back to a Tyrone prince killed in battle in 1283, and by tradition the line included Niall of the Nine Hostages, high king of Ireland from c.379 to c.409. O'Neill, however, was indirectly descended from a protestant settler branch of O'Neills founded by a nominee of the English after the 'flight of the earls' in 1607.

O'Neill spent his youth in London and the British consulate in Addis Ababa. He was educated at West Downs School, in Winchester, and at Eton College. Thereafter he spent a year in France and Germany, and then found work in the City of London and, briefly, South Australia. Only summer holidays were spent in Shane's Castle, the family home in Ulster. In May 1940 O'Neill received his commission at Sandhurst and joined the 2nd battalion of the Irish Guards. While waiting for the invasion of Europe, on 4 February 1944 he married (Katharine) Jean (b. 1914/15), the daughter of (William) Ingham Whitaker, of Pylewell Park,

Terence Marne O'Neill, Baron O'Neill of the Maine (1914–1990), by unknown photographer

Lymington, Hampshire. They had one son, Patrick (*b.* 1945), and one daughter, Penelope (*b.* 1947). Once in Europe O'Neill served as intelligence officer of the 2nd battalion. In September 1944, near Nijmegen in the Netherlands, he was injured during shelling and evacuated back to England. Friends close to him died in action, including David Peel, best man at his wedding, as well as both his brothers, Shane Edward Robert O'Neill, third Baron O'Neill (1907–1944), and Brian Arthur O'Neill (1911–1940).

At the end of 1945 O'Neill and his family finally went to live in Northern Ireland, in Glebe House, a converted Regency rectory near Ahoghill, co. Antrim. He would have preferred a Westminster seat, but settled for the Stormont constituency of Bannside, to which he was returned unopposed in October 1946. In February 1948 the prime minister, Lord Brookeborough, appointed him parliamentary secretary to the minister of health. In 1953 he was moved to the post of chairman of ways and means (leader of the house), then in 1955 he became a joint parliamentary secretary to the minister of home affairs and dealt with a controversial rent de-restriction bill. He showed his facility in negotiating the timetable of the bill with his opposite number at Westminster, Enoch Powell. Following a ministerial reshuffle in 1956 he finally reached cabinet level as minister of home affairs and was sworn of the privy council (Northern Ireland). Six months later he took on the finance portfolio, and shortly afterwards he divested himself of home affairs.

O'Neill's tenure as minister of finance coincided with a severe economic crisis. Employment in the Belfast shipyards, for example, contracted by 40 per cent between 1961 and 1964. This was reflected in a swing towards the Northern Ireland Labour Party (NILP), particularly in Belfast. The government's policy was to seek support from Britain for the traditional, though declining, industries of textiles and heavy engineering. However, a joint exchequer working party, chaired by Sir Robert Hall, published a report in October 1962 that seemed decisively to reject throwing good money after bad. O'Neill at first had little idea how to approach the crisis. However, the Northern Ireland civil service autonomously developed a scheme of infrastructural development, concentrating on road building and the promotion of new towns. The Matthew plan, published in February 1963, thus made a more positive case for British subvention. O'Neill was quick to realize the significance of this new approach. It chimed in with his familiar refrain, at first born of Treasury cheeseparing, that Northern Ireland should rely upon self-help. Now he argued, notably in a speech to the Pottinger Unionist Association, Belfast, in February 1963, for generous pump-priming with British funds.

When Lord Brookeborough, by now seen as excessively rigid in his approach to the economy, retired in March 1963, O'Neill was well placed to don the mantle of technocratic modernization. His support, however, was not overwhelming in the parliamentary Unionist Party at Stormont. There was discontentment that he was not elected prime minister by the party, but appointed by the governor. He immediately set about modernizing the administration of devolution in Northern Ireland with some vigour. A series of schemes to rationalize railways, build motorways, encourage growth points, clear slums, reorganize ministries, establish a new university, create a new city, and reach a concordat with the trade unions to facilitate quasi-corporate planning were all designed to wring funds from Britain. Public investment per head of population doubled between 1958 and 1969, with particularly large increases in housing stock, roads, education, and training. Per capita public expenditure in Northern Ireland rose from 88 to 118 per cent of per capita public expenditure in England in the same period. Nevertheless, the economy continued to suffer from the pressures of chronic dependence on declining industries, and resumed a pattern of crisis in the 1970s.

O'Neill's stated ambition to change the face of Ulster had the effect of stealing the thunder of the NILP. Though economic planning was largely cosmetic, it was sufficient to secure a swing to the Unionist Party in the Stormont general election of 1965, and the NILP lost two of its four seats in Belfast. Nevertheless, modernization brought its own political problems, notably by making the economy seem amenable to government manipulation, and thereby convincing Catholics that their relative socio-economic disadvantage was a consequence of deliberate government discrimination. Indeed, there is something to this. A cabal of Unionist leaders in Londonderry, the second city of Northern Ireland, with a Catholic majority but a Unionist corporation, lobbied against the new university coming to the city for fear of upsetting delicately gerrymandered constituencies. Instead it went to the safely protestant town of Larne. Similarly, the new city of Craigavon was planned with an eye to maintaining the integrity of Unionist electorates. The Labour government in Britain, led by Harold Wilson since 1964 and increasingly conscious of the cost of the rising economic subsidy to the province, was anxious to see such abuses reformed.

O'Neill, however, feared that substantive reform would serve only to provoke the ultra-loyalists, who possessed an able leader in waiting in the clerical politician Ian Paisley, and was well aware of the potential for disorder. During the Westminster general election of October 1964 there were three days of rioting on the Falls Road in Belfast, the worst disorder since 1935. O'Neill preferred carefully symbolic gestures. These included visiting Catholic schools and, more dramatically, meeting with the taoiseach of the Irish Republic, Sean Lemass, at Stormont on 14 January 1964. By such a dramatic gesture, made in his own name since he had not consulted his cabinet, O'Neill hoped not only to encourage Catholic acceptance of the state, but also to outflank ambitious rivals within the Unionist Party. Brian Faulkner, the able minister of commerce, was chief of these. O'Neill's poor interpersonal skills and evident distaste for his colleagues, however, meant that his every move tended to aggravate factional opposition within the parliamentary Unionist Party.

Republican commemorations in 1966 of the fiftieth anniversary of the Easter 1916 rising were handled deftly; though illegal, they were allowed to go ahead under the watchful eyes of the Royal Ulster Constabulary (RUC). However, an increasingly large protestant constituency was concerned that O'Neill was weak on the constitution. The very grandeur of his modernization of the economic infrastructure further generated tensions from those who felt excluded from government largesse. In September 1966 it emerged that at least twelve out of thirty-six Unionist back-bench MPs at Stormont had signed a petition demanding his removal as prime minister. It was testimony to his political skills that he rode out this conspiracy. He did this by accentuating his already presidential status and appealing to moderate opinion outside the party. The Ulster Unionists, traditionally assertive in the middle ranks, felt ill-handled.

1967 appeared to be a lull before the storm, though O'Neill himself was notably weary of the burdens of office and ill at ease with his party. Catholic demands for full civil rights were increasingly heard, and, though O'Neill did his best to keep his counsel, gently pushing for mild reform behind the scenes, the issue became increasingly politicized. He hoped to generate local pride to divert attention from polarizing issues of state, and thus encouraged civic weeks.

When, on 5 October 1968, a civil-rights march was attacked by the RUC in Londonderry, a mass movement erupted, primarily of Catholics, demanding civil rights. Under pressure from the British government, O'Neill rushed to convince his cabinet colleagues of the need for concessions, even in the face of street demonstrations. On 22 November he unveiled a programme of reforms, notably the closing down of the gerrymandered Londonderry corporation. However, the local government rate-based franchise was for the time untouched. In a famous television broadcast on the night of 9 December 1968 O'Neill warned that Northern Ireland stood at the crossroads. He condemned those Unionists who would defy the pro-reform British government and demanded an end to street demonstrations. Subsequently he sacked his right-wing minister of home affairs, William Craig. O'Neill enjoyed a massive surge of public support, but the fragile peace was broken by a radical civil-rights march from Belfast to Londonderry, attacked by loyalists at Burntollet Bridge on 4 January 1969. In the following week a civil-rights march in Newry degenerated into violence.

The seeming inability of O'Neill to maintain Unionist authority led to ministerial resignations, most significantly that of Brian Faulkner on 24 January 1969. A coterie of hard-line Unionist MPs was increasingly vocal for O'Neill's resignation. To bolster his position he called an election for 24 February. Dramatically, he refused to campaign for official Unionist candidates opposed to his leadership and lent his support to independent candidates undertaking to support him personally. For the first time, a Unionist leader explicitly called for Catholic votes, to be deployed to overwhelm protestant ultras. This gambit produced confused results, but no clear-cut victory for O'Neill. Most significantly, there was little evidence of Catholics voting in great number for pro-O'Neill Unionists. This fatally undermined the promise of O'Neillism: that economic progress and ameliorative rhetoric would win Catholics from their traditional nationalist loyalties. O'Neill soldiered on as prime minister until, amid a renewal of street violence and a campaign of bombing by loyalist *agents provocateurs*, he announced his resignation on 28 April 1969. He employed the last of his political capital in securing one person, one vote, in place of the rate-payers' franchise in local elections. His casting vote ensured that he was succeeded by the relatively loyal, though hardly adequate, James Chichester-Clark rather than Brian Faulkner.

O'Neill rapidly faded from political view. He was made a life peer, as Baron O'Neill of the Maine, in 1970 and moved to Lisle Court, Lymington, Hampshire, though he continued to speak on the problems of Northern Ireland in the House of Lords, where he sat as a cross-bencher. He was also a trustee of the Winston Churchill Memorial Trust. He died at his home, Lisle Court, of cancer on 12 June 1990, survived by his wife, son, and daughter.

O'Neill worked better with civil servants, notably James Malley and Sir Kenneth Bloomfield, than with politicians. His attempts to reform Northern Irish politics depended upon administrative reform and quasi-presidential rhetoric rather than refashioning the party he led. Himself distinctly Anglo-Irish, he underestimated the fierce identity politics of both Catholic and protestant communities. He viewed popular protestant opinion warily, suspecting it of atavistic sectarianism, and regarded Catholics patronizingly as degraded with a slave mentality. He assumed that his natural supporters were the middle classes and thought them capable of pioneering enlightened public opinion. His final, disillusioned, conclusion was that the 'good men' of politics preferred 'playing golf' to confronting the 'wild men'. His efforts to subsume ethnic passions within a constructive civic society were gratingly patrician, though decent in motivation and sincere.

MARC MULHOLLAND

Sources DNB · T. O'Neill, *The autobiography of Terence O'Neill* (1972) · A. Gailey, ed., *John Sayers: a liberal editor* (1993) · P. Bew and H. Patterson, *The British state and the Ulster crisis* (1985) · M. Mulholland, 'Assimilation versus segregation: Unionist strategy in the 1960s', *Twentieth Century British History*, 2/3 (2000), 284–300 · M. Mulholland, *Northern Ireland at the crossroads: Ulster Unionism in the O'Neill years, 1960–69* (2000) · P. Bew, P. Gibbon, and H. Patterson, *Northern Ireland, 1921–1996: political forces and social classes* (1996) · *The Times* (14 June 1990) · *The Independent* (14 June 1990) · Burke, *Peerage* · WWW · m. cert. · d. cert.
Archives NRA, priv. coll., papers
Likenesses T. McGrath, photograph, 1968, Hult. Arch. · photograph, repro. in *The Independent* · photograph, News International Syndication, London [*see illus.*]
Wealth at death £443,043: probate, 28 Aug 1990, *CGPLA Eng. & Wales*

O'Neill, Sir Turlough Luineach (*c.*1530–1595), chieftain, was the son of Niall Connallach O'Neill (*d.* 1544), whose sobriquet reflects the fact that he was fostered among the ruling O'Donnells of Tyrconnell. His mother was, almost certainly, Rose O'Donnell, sister to Manus O'Donnell, lord of Tyrconnell between 1537 and 1555, and wife of Niall Connallach, though a late pedigree from Lord Justice Drury, a hostile source, claimed that Turlough Luineach was a 'bastard'.

Origins Turlough's grandfather, Art Óg O'Neill, held the title Ó Néill or lord of Tyrone, the greatest lordship in late medieval Ulster, between 1513 and 1519; Turlough Luineach would also rise to be Ó Néill between 1567 and 1595. Art Óg's power base had been on the fertile Lough Neagh basin around Dungannon in east Tyrone. However, to enhance his authority across the Sperrin Mountains, where the Sliocht Airt Uí Néill were dominant, he established his sons in Slewisse in north-western Tyrone. On his death Art Óg was succeeded by his half-brother, Conn Bacach O'Neill (1519–1559), as Ó Néill. Yet one of Art Óg's sons, Niall Connallach O'Neill, father of Turlough Luineach, became Conn Bacach's *tánaiste* (nominated successor). Niall Connallach died in 1544 in unexplained circumstances.

Turlough Luineach O'Neill's cognomen has been taken as an indication that he was fostered by the Muintir Luinigh, though it seems more likely that it simply reflected his control of that district. Joseph Costello has proposed that Turlough Luineach was actually fostered by the Flemings, a gentry family of English descent on the northern borders of the pale.

Rise to prominence Turlough Luineach's rise to provincial prominence is not well documented. After his father's death he secured possession of his demesne lands in Slewisse. He extended his authority to Strabane, where he built an important castle across the river from Lifford Castle, a major stronghold of O'Donnell, lord of the powerful lordship of Tyrconnell in north-west Ulster. He fostered the development of a small but important town at Strabane. This resource base was too slender, and too marginal geographically, for Turlough Luineach O'Neill to have any realistic prospect of emulating his grandfather Art Óg and becoming Ó Néill. Yet that is precisely the goal that he set himself from an early date.

Turlough Luineach built up a formidable power base in western Tyrone by developing the economy of his lordship and by forming alliances with the heads of collateral branches of the O'Neills in western Tyrone, most notably with Hugh mac Niall O'Neill, lord of Omagh and head of Sliocht Airt. He also formed an alliance with his uncle, Manus O'Donnell, lord of Tyrconnell, and in the late 1540s joined O'Donnell in attacking Conn Bacach O'Neill, who had become earl of Tyrone through a compact with Henry VIII in 1542. Turlough Luineach's pretensions might have been crushed quickly were it not for the ageing earl's faltering grasp on his lordship and the consequent contest for power that broke out between the earl and his own sons. Turlough Luineach took advantage of the internecine warfare among the ruling O'Neills to assert a claim to the office of *tánaiste*, but he did not have the strength to realize his ambition. In the event, Conn Bacach's youngest legitimate son, Shane (alias Seán) O'Neill, succeeded in taking control of Tyrone from his father, despite the claims of the baron of Dungannon, the earl's nominated successor. Shane appointed Turlough Luineach as his *tánaiste* in recognition of his influence in western Tyrone.

While Shane O'Neill dominated Tyrone and most of Ulster from the mid-1550s, there was little scope for Turlough Luineach O'Neill to pursue his ambitions. On 12 April 1562, while Shane was engaged in delicate negotiations with Queen Elizabeth at the English court, Turlough Luineach killed Brian O'Neill, the young baron of Dungannon, whom the crown acknowledged as the heir to the earldom of Tyrone. Shane O'Neill claimed that Turlough Luineach acted rebelliously in killing the baron, though it was suspected that Shane had sanctioned the murder to clear the way for the crown to recognize his own claims to succeed his father as Ó Néill and as earl of Tyrone. Certainty on this matter is impossible, though Shane's claim may well have been correct: some weeks later, in May 1562, during Shane's continued absence in England, Turlough Luineach had himself proclaimed as Ó Néill at the traditional inauguration site at Tullyhogue. However, Turlough Luineach O'Neill failed to establish his authority among the leading families of eastern Tyrone, most particularly among the O'Donnellys, who held the hereditary office of marshal of Ó Néill's army and were completely loyal to Shane O'Neill, whom they had fostered in his childhood. Turlough Luineach briefly supported the English viceroy in Ireland, the earl of Sussex, against Shane but soon came to terms with Ó Néill.

Shane O'Neill's decision not to crush Turlough Luineach

for his audacity may be seen as an indication that he did not perceive his cousin from north-west Tyrone as a serious rival for power. Over the subsequent years Shane O'Neill's fortunes were in the ascendant in Tyrone and across Ulster generally. Not until Shane's army suffered a catastrophic defeat at the hands of O'Donnell in the battle of Farsetmore on 8 May 1567 did Turlough Luineach dare to rebel again. The killing of Shane O'Neill by the Scots with whom he was negotiating at Cushendun in north Antrim on 2 June 1567 cleared the way for Turlough Luineach O'Neill to become Ó Néill.

Master of Tyrone Turlough Luineach's accession to the lordship was as much a result of the power vacuum left by the death of Shane O'Neill as of his own political strength and skills. Shane had eliminated his own brothers as contestants for the lordship, while his sons were still too young to take their father's place. None the less, Turlough Luineach needed time to consolidate his authority as Ó Néill. To that end he neutralized the alliance that had brought about the downfall of his predecessor. He contracted a new alliance with O'Donnell, lord of Tyrconnell. He made overtures to the Scots in north Antrim. He gave one of his daughters in marriage to Rory Oge MacQuillan to pacify that Irish lord in north Antrim. The English viceroy, Lord Deputy Sidney, underestimated the new Ó Néill and was readily reassured by Turlough Luineach's submission on 18 June 1567. Sidney departed from Dublin on 9 October 1567 and remained at the court of Elizabeth for almost a year to devise a new programme of reform for Ireland. Turlough Luineach O'Neill used that time very effectively to establish himself in the demesne lands pertaining to his new office around Dungannon, and to win the confidence of Ó Néill's household families (*lucht tighe*) in eastern Tyrone.

The new Ó Néill hoped to secure the English crown's recognition of his authority in Tyrone. However, Elizabeth's ministers envisaged the breakup of Ó Néill's overlordship. Inevitably, the negotiations between Lord Deputy Sidney and Ó Néill in September and October 1568 achieved very little. Ó Néill was obliged to acquiesce in Sidney's establishment of the teenaged Hugh O'Neill, baron of Dungannon and brother of the previous baron whom Turlough Luineach had murdered, in Oneilland, a lordship south of Lough Neagh. In effect, Ó Néill was forced to accept the Blackwater River as the southern boundary of his lordship. Yet Ó Néill was determined not to cede any more ground.

Turlough Luineach entered into negotiations with Scotland's clan Donald South, a junior branch of which had settled in north Antrim, to marry as his second wife Lady Agnes *Campbell (*d.* in or after 1590), widow of James MacDonald, and by February 1569 had contracted to marry her in return for a dowry of more than 1000 Scottish mercenaries. The nuptials were celebrated in August 1569, and it was reported shortly afterwards that Ó Néill had 3000 Scottish mercenaries in his employ, in addition to thousands of local kerne and galloglass. This military establishment proved to be too large for Ó Néill to sustain indefinitely, but it succeeded in discouraging English military

or colonial adventures west of the River Bann. On 20 January 1571 Ó Néill and Sidney agreed to a truce whereby the Irish lord was to dismiss his Scottish mercenaries in return for the opportunity to submit his proposals for a political settlement to Queen Elizabeth. However, Ó Néill's willingness to reach an accommodation with the English crown was not reciprocated.

The younger Sir Thomas Smith's pilot scheme for private colonization in east Ulster, which got under way on 30 August 1572, was stoutly resisted by Sir Brian mac Phelim Ó Néill, lord of Clandeboye, with support from Ó Néill. Smith's death in August 1573 effectively aborted that colonization scheme, but it was succeeded by another of grander scale and ambition devised by Walter Devereux, earl of Essex. Ó Néill again supported Sir Brian ÓNéill, and also worked with the MacDonalds in north Antrim to thwart the English colonists. Despite Essex's considerable investment in the project he ultimately failed ignominiously.

Following Essex's death Sidney was restored as lord deputy on 5 August 1575. He travelled to Ulster to restore some semblance of English order after the turmoil generated by the plantation projects. He met Ó Néill at Armagh, and the two men concluded a formal treaty in which the crown accepted Turlough Luineach's claims to overlordship to a limited degree, while the Irish lord agreed to dismiss his Scottish mercenaries, with the exception of a bodyguard composed of Campbells, his wife's clan. Sidney committed himself to securing Ó Néill a peerage from the crown. Subsequently, in May 1578, a patent was passed to make Turlough Luineach O'Neill earl of Clanoneill and baron of Clogher, albeit only for life, which Sidney reckoned would not be for long given Ó Néill's age, his bullet wound, his poor diet, and his constant over-indulgence in alcohol. However, with Sidney's retirement from office in September 1578 that initiative fell through. Ó Néill, for his part, was unable to observe his side of the agreement made with Sidney, for he was heavily dependent upon his Scottish mercenaries to maintain his authority across Tyrone and among his *uirrithe* ('vassal-chiefs'), the subordinate lords outside Tyrone. Ó Néill also employed his mercenaries to deter English incursions into Ulster, and to exert leverage on the crown to concede formal recognition of his overlordship.

Sir James Fitzmaurice returned to Ireland in July 1579 proclaiming a papally sponsored crusade for Catholicism. He appealed to Ó Néill for support, and informed him of Pope Gregory XIII's offer to make him king. However, while in less sober moments Ó Néill expressed romantic desires for an Ireland free of English interference, he did not commit himself to Fitzmaurice's 'faith and fatherland' ideology. He was conservative in religion, but not imbued with Counter-Reformation zeal despite the promptings of local churchmen such as Raymond O'Gallagher, bishop of Derry (1569–1601). None the less, Ó Néill maintained contacts with the Catholic rebels, and particularly with Viscount Baltinglass after Fitzmaurice's death in August 1579. He made some promises to assist Baltinglass, and he offered himself as a foster father to

James VI, the young king of Scotland, to draw the Scots into the conspiracy. Yet Turlough Luineach, pragmatic as he was, did not employ his considerable military resources to promote the Catholic cause. He waited for the military support that was supposed to arrive from Spain and Scotland, and meanwhile took advantage of the English crown's difficulties with the rebels to extend his own authority in Ulster. In August 1581 he abandoned Baltinglass and made peace with the crown in return for official recognition of his authority over his *uirrithe*.

The challenge from Hugh O'Neill Crown ministers rested their hopes for a settlement in Ulster congruent with English interests on Hugh O'Neill, baron of Dungannon. Hugh O'Neill had assisted Essex's plantation project in Clandeboye, and was well paid for his efforts. Essex's fort and bridge at the Blackwater River remained as a bulwark against Ó Néill behind which the baron was free to establish a dominant position in the region north of the pale. Hugh O'Neill emerged from Essex's débâcle with his personal standing greatly enhanced in both Irish and English eyes. One reflection of his status in Ulster is the fact that he was able to marry Siobhán, a daughter of O'Donnell of Tyrconnell. That alliance gave the baron a provincial profile and had the effect of putting Turlough Luineach under pressure from the west as well as from the south-east. Ó Néill, however, responded with a master stroke: in 1579 he named Hugh O'Neill as his *tánaiste* or nominated successor, gave the baron the hand of his daughter in marriage, and had Siobhán sent back to her father. Without his alliance with O'Donnell, though, Hugh O'Neill lost much of his leverage over Ó Néill, and he soon found himself deposed from the office of *tánaiste*. Turlough Luineach had taught his young rival a humiliating lesson in *realpolitik*.

Lord Deputy Grey promoted Hugh O'Neill with a joint commission alongside Sir Nicholas Bagenal to defend the pale against incursions from Ulster. He subsequently made him a royal lieutenant for south-east Ulster, alongside Ó Néill for the lordship of Tyrone and Bagenal for Antrim and Down. These commissions enhanced the baron's increasing power in southern Ulster *vis à vis* Ó Néill. When, in 1583, Turlough Luineach fell into a coma and was widely presumed to be dead, Hugh O'Neill crossed the Blackwater River with a large force and took possession of Ó Néill's inauguration site at Tullyhogue. However, after a severe hangover, Turlough Luineach made a full recovery and the baron was obliged to retire back across the Blackwater. Hugh O'Neill may have been Turlough Luineach's most likely successor, but the old lord was still predominant within Tyrone.

On 1 August 1584 an estimated 2000–3000 Scottish fighters landed in Tyrconnell with the intention of establishing one of the sons of Shane O'Neill, whose mother was a MacLean from Scotland, in control of Tyrone. The O'Donnellys, who had fostered Shane, and O'Cahan, one of Ó Néill's leading *uirrithe*, defected to the MacShanes (literally the 'sons of Shane'). Turlough Luineach O'Neill was left virtually powerless. His own son, Art O'Neill, forsook him and joined with Hugh O'Neill, his father-in-law, to salvage something of his inheritance. Hugh O'Neill came to an agreement with Turlough Luineach whereby the latter retained the title of Ó Néill but had his authority restricted to western Tyrone, his original power base. The baron, on the other hand, took control of eastern Tyrone and promised to pay Ó Néill 1000 marks per annum. Though this arrangement took the form of a seven-year lease which was revocable by Ó Néill at the end of three years, it left Hugh O'Neill as the predominant figure in Ulster, and Ó Néill was powerless to compel the baron to abide by the terms agreed. Unfortunately for Ó Néill, the baron was very antipathetic towards him, perhaps because he had murdered the baron's elder brother in 1562.

Lord Deputy Perrot sent English soldiers into Ulster to expel the MacLeans. With Perrot's approval, the Irish parliament of 1585, whose opening Turlough Luineach attended, recognized Hugh O'Neill as earl of Tyrone. This was seen as necessary by the crown to prevent the MacShanes taking advantage of any power vacuum which might otherwise have formed in the wake of Ó Néill's loss of authority. None the less, Perrot was concerned lest the earl of Tyrone should become an over-mighty subject. Consequently he endorsed the division of Tyrone agreed between Turlough Luineach and Hugh O'Neill, and sent 300 English soldiers to prop up Ó Néill's position in western Tyrone. Turlough Luineach petitioned the crown for the title of earl of Omagh, to hold western Tyrone as a perpetual inheritance, and for his son, Art, to be legitimated and made baron of Strabane. His petition was not granted. The earl of Tyrone persuaded Queen Elizabeth in 1587 that he was entitled to hold all of Tyrone on Ó Néill's death. None the less, Ó Néill proved to be more resilient than anyone had anticipated. Strengthened by a renewed alliance with the Scots in north Antrim—in October 1588 Ó Néill had one of his daughters marry Sorley Boy MacDonnell at Strabane—and the employment of English and Scottish mercenaries, Turlough Luineach was able to put the earl of Tyrone under real pressure, even to the extent of defeating him in a significant battle at Carricklea on 1 May 1588. Ó Néill also nurtured the ambitions of the MacShanes against the earl, despite an agreement to the contrary in October 1589.

Twilight In April 1592 Red Hugh O'Donnell succeeded his father as lord of Tyrconnell. He was a son-in-law of the earl of Tyrone, and was indebted to the earl for his escape from English custody in Dublin Castle earlier in the year. Together the young O'Donnell and the earl of Tyrone waged war on Ó Néill from east and west. Early in May 1593 Turlough Luineach O'Neill surrendered his rights of lordship in Tyrone in return for an annual pension of £2000. He retained his demesne lands, together with the town of Strabane and the land surrounding it. This agreement was formally ratified by the English administration in Dublin on 28 June 1593. Turlough Luineach retained his title as Ó Néill. It seems unlikely, though, that the earl of Tyrone abided by this agreement any better than with the last made with Turlough Luineach, for in May 1594 Ó Néill offered to assure Ulster to the crown against the increasingly rebellious earl. In June 1595 the English ship

Poppinjay was sent to Strabane to convey Ó Néill to Dublin, but the earl of Tyrone received prior warning and razed Ó Néill's castle at Strabane. Turlough Luineach O'Neill took shelter in a neighbouring ruin until his death in early September 1595. He was buried at Ardstraw in west Tyrone.

Assessment Turlough Luineach O'Neill has been eclipsed in Irish historiography by his more flamboyant predecessor and successor, Shane and Hugh O'Neill. Yet he was a man of very considerable political skill. He became Ó Néill despite the handicap of the peripheral location of his power base within Tyrone, and held on to the office for twenty-eight turbulent years. Like Shane and Hugh, he harboured thoughts of an Ireland free of English rule, but he was pragmatic enough to accept the reality that he had to reach some form of accommodation with the English crown or risk annihilation. The failure to achieve a durable settlement for Ulster cannot be ascribed to Turlough Luineach; it owed more to his rivals within Ulster, and to the crown.   HENRY A. JEFFERIES

Sources CSP Ire., 1509–95 · J. S. Brewer and W. Bullen, eds., *Calendar of the Carew manuscripts*, 1: 1515–1574, PRO (1867) · L. Ó Cléirigh, *The life of Aodh Ruadh Ó Domhnaill*, ed. P. Walsh and C. Ó Lochlainn, 1, ITS, 42 (1948) · AFM · 'Sir Henry Sidney's memoir of his government in Ireland, 1583', *Ulster Journal of Archaeology*, 3 (1855), 33–52, 85–109, 336–57; 5 (1857), 299–315; 8 (1860), 179–95 · T. Ó Laidhin, ed., *Sidney state papers, 1565–70*, IMC (1962) · G. A. Hayes-McCoy, *Scots mercenary forces in Ireland (1565–1603)* (1937); repr. (1996) · H. Morgan, *Tyrone's rebellion: the outbreak of the Nine Years' War in Tudor Ireland*, Royal Historical Society Studies in History, 67 (1993) · C. Brady, *Shane O'Neill* (Dundalk, 1996) · N. P. Canny, *The Elizabethan conquest of Ireland: a pattern established, 1565–76* (1976) · J. Costello, 'Turlough Luineach O'Neill', MA diss., University College Dublin, 1973
Archives Royal Irish Acad., papers
Likenesses B. Gooch, pen-and-ink drawing, state papers, Ireland · portrait, repro. in J. Derricke, *The image of Irelande* (1581)

O'Neill, William Chichester, first Baron O'Neill (1813–1883), Church of Ireland clergyman and composer, was born on 4 March 1813 at Culdaff House, co. Donegal, the son of Edward Chichester (d. 1840), rector of Kilmore, Armagh, and his wife, Catherine, *née* Young. He was educated at Foyle College, Londonderry, and, from 1829 to 1830, at Shrewsbury School. He graduated from Trinity College, Dublin, in 1836 and was ordained in 1837. On 3 January 1839 he married Henrietta (d. 1857), eldest daughter of Robert Torrens, a judge of the common pleas in Ireland. They had three sons and a daughter. In 1848 he was appointed to a prebendal stall in Christ Church, Dublin, which he retained until 1859.

By the death in 1855 of John Bruce O'Neill, third Viscount O'Neill, he came into possession of the great estates of the O'Neill family, to whom he was related by the marriage of his great-grandfather, and took the surname O'Neill. In 1868 the peerage, originally conferred in 1793, and extinct on the death of the third Viscount O'Neill, was restored, and he became Baron O'Neill of Shane's Castle. His first wife having died in 1857, he married Elizabeth Grace (d. 1905), daughter of John Torrens, archdeacon of Dublin, on 8 April 1858.

O'Neill was a talented performer on the violin and organ, especially the latter instrument; he was also a skilled singer and composer. He frequently officiated as organist in the Dublin cathedrals, and wrote church music, glees, and songs, all remarkable for purity of style and grammatical accuracy, some of which were published.

A Conservative in politics, O'Neill contributed to the debate on the disestablishment of the Church of Ireland with a sermon published in 1867 in a volume entitled *The Church in Ireland*. His other publications were principally sermons and addresses, and a response to Herbert Spencer's *First Principles*, which he published as *A Description of Christianity Criticised* (1883). A further volume of his sermons, with a memoir of his life, appeared in 1885, edited by E. J. Hamilton. He died on 18 April 1883, at Shane's Castle, and was buried at Drumaul, co. Antrim.

W. H. CUMMINGS, *rev.* K. D. REYNOLDS

Sources E. J. Hamilton, 'Memoir', *Sermons of the late Rev. Lord O'Neill* (1885) · GEC, *Peerage* · private information (1894)
Wealth at death £38,686 1s. in England: Irish probate sealed in England, 28 July 1883, CGPLA Eng. & Wales · £117,687 18s. 3d.: probate, 6 July 1883, CGPLA Ire.

Oninga. See Radisson, Pierre-Esprit (1639/40?–1710).

Onions, Charles Talbut (1873–1965), lexicographer and grammarian, was born at 40 Spring Street, Edgbaston, Birmingham, on 10 September 1873, the eldest son of Ralph John Onions and his wife, Harriet, daughter of John Talbut, locksmith. Although the traditional occupation of the family had been bellows making, his father was a designer and embosser in metal; the name is of Welsh origin, being based on the form Einion. Charles Talbut Onions was grounded in grammar, first at a board school and later at the Camp Hill branch of King Edward VI's foundation at Birmingham. There he came under the influence of the Revd A. J. Smith, a headmaster of sterling character and scholarly outlook, to whom he owed the very means of entering academic life as well as his first contact with lexicography: Smith kept Littré's French dictionary in his classroom, together with fascicules of the *New English Dictionary* as they appeared. At school, too, Onions was much influenced by a Tractarian organist and choirmaster, John Heywood: his religious sympathies and affiliations were thus permanently established.

With a leaving exhibition Onions entered Mason College, Birmingham, where he studied for the London BA degree, which he gained in 1892 with third-class honours in French, followed in 1895 by his MA degree. Under E. A. Sonnenschein he learned *inter alia* to scan Plautus and to write Greek prose, and he contributed *An Advanced English Syntax* (1904; frequently reprinted) to a Parallel Grammar Series published by Sonnenschein. The professor of English at Birmingham at this time was Edward Arber, who introduced Onions to J. A. H. Murray when the latter was examining at Birmingham in the Oxford local examinations. Shortly after, in September 1895, Murray invited Onions to join the small staff of the English dictionary at Oxford, and at Oxford he lived, except for one short interval, for the rest of his life. There he was soon joined by

Henry Bradley; in later years he spoke of passing from Murray to Bradley as a remarkable experience: 'It was to pass from the practical, professional teacher to the philosophical exponent.' On 17 April 1907 he married Angela (1883/4–1941), youngest daughter of the Revd Arthur Blythman, rector of Shenington; they had seven sons and three daughters.

From 1906 to 1913 Onions was entrusted with the special preparation of various portions of the dictionary under the supervision of Bradley and W. A. Craigie, and then began independent editorial work on the section Su–Sz; he was also responsible for Wh–Worling and the volumes containing X, Y, and Z, and so contributed the very last entry to the whole work in the form of a cross-reference—'Zyxt, obs. (Kentish) 2nd sing. ind. pres. of SEE v.'—which he liked to mention as it was taken, because of its position, as a brand name for a soap. But it was by no means Onions's last word.

In 1922, after the death of William Little, the Clarendon Press commissioned Onions to revise and complete Little's work on the *Shorter Oxford English Dictionary*. This appeared in 1933, and was continually revised and augmented by him until 1959: in the twenty pages of addenda in the 1944 edition he dealt with 1500 words, mostly the product of war. Onions shared with Craigie the preparation of the supplement to the main work (1933), which includes a list of books cited therein that constituted the fullest bibliography of English literature yet made. An equally valuable by-product was his *Shakespeare Glossary* (1911), the introduction to which provides a notable survey of Shakespearian usage; throughout the work he was able to draw on his knowledge of the Warwickshire dialect. On the death of Sir Sidney Lee he completed the editing of *Shakespeare's England* (1916), contributing to the articles on alchemy and on animals, as well as providing a glossary of musical terms. Henceforth the Clarendon Press constantly called on him for advice and help, and many Oxford books owe improvements to him. For many years he was the only visitor allowed into the Walton Street office at 'the sacred hour of 9.30' when the day's work was being planned. The files of the press are rich in his scholarly jottings.

In 1918 Onions donned uniform and went to the naval intelligence division of the Admiralty (where his knowledge of German was put to good use) with the rank of honorary captain, Royal Marines. On his return to Oxford he became university lecturer in English (1920) and later reader in English philology (1927–49). In 1922 he revised for the Clarendon Press the *Anglo-Saxon Reader* originally compiled by Henry Sweet, though 'reverence for the opinion of a great master' restrained the correcting hand. On Bradley's death in 1923 Magdalen elected Onions to fill the vacant fellowship; when the statutes were revised shortly afterwards he chose to remain under the old regulations, and so remained a stipendiary fellow until the day of his death. In 1940–55 he was librarian of the college, and undergraduates and others profited from his constant presence in the dictionary bay of the library; he was equally at home in the senior common room, where his astringent rejoinders to questions on etymology and English usage were much relished.

Onions was president of the Philological Society from 1929 to 1933, and was elected FBA in 1938. Oxford, Leeds, and Birmingham conferred honorary degrees upon him on the completion of the dictionary, and he was appointed CBE in 1934. In 1945 he succeeded R. W. Chambers as honorary director of the Early English Text Society, and, partly by enlisting the help of several former pupils at Oxford, he did much in the following twelve years to extend its publishing programme. He was editor of *Medium Aevum*, the journal of the Society for the Study of Medieval Languages and Literature, from its inception in 1932 to 1956. But the preoccupation of his last twenty years was the *Oxford Dictionary of English Etymology* (1966), which went to press before he died. It treats over 38,000 words and is likely to be his enduring monument.

Onions had an almost personal pride in his mother tongue, which he once described as 'a rum go—but jolly good'. His lifelong study of it bore fruit in the masterly chapter on the English language which he contributed to *The Character of England* (1947), edited by Sir Ernest Barker. His training in the scriptorium of the dictionary taught him the art of conciseness, as is demonstrated in his tracts for the Society for Pure English and in his article 'Grammar' in *Chambers's cyclopaedia*. As a lexicographer his strength lay in etymology: he delighted in teasing out the history of such words as 'syllabus' or 'acne' or Shakespeare's 'dildos and fadings'. His grasp of idiom and his analytical power are well evidenced in the articles in the *Oxford English Dictionary* on 'set', 'shall', 'will', and the interrogative pronouns. To dialectal usages, medieval and modern, he was particularly sensitive. His approach to linguistic and lexical problems was essentially pragmatic. There was something Johnsonian in his attitudes and character (as well as in his early struggles). For much of his life he was handicapped by a stammer and he always had a fellow feeling for other stammerers; but he was undemonstrative in his likings as in his religion. He died at the Radcliffe Infirmary, Oxford, on 8 January 1965, and was buried on 13 January. J. A. W. BENNETT, rev.

Sources J. A. W. Bennett, 'Charles Talbut Onions, 1873–1965', *PBA*, 65 (1979), 743–58 · *A list of the published writings of Charles Talbut Onions* (1948) · *The Times* (12 Jan 1965), 11c · *The Times* (14 Jan 1965), 12b · personal knowledge (1981) · *WWW*, 1961–70 · b. cert. · m. cert. · d. cert.

Archives U. Birm. L., corresp. | Bodl. Oxf., corresp. with R. W. Chapman · NL Scot., corresp. with Sir William Craigie

Likenesses W. Dring, pastel drawing, 1948, Magd. Oxf. · photograph, NPG · photographs, Magd. Oxf.

Wealth at death £26,310: probate, 4 Jan 1966, *CGPLA Eng. & Wales*

Onions, (George) Oliver (1873–1961), novelist, was born on 29 July 1873 at 37 Ripon Street, Bradford, Yorkshire, the eldest child of at least three children of George Frederick Onions, a cashier, and his wife, Emily Alice, *née* Fearnley. His interest in art took him to London and Paris to study, and he tried to make a living at posters, book designing, and similar work. It was poorly paid, so he turned to writing for periodicals. Sketches and other pieces were collected in *The Complete Bachelor* (1900), and short stories of Yorkshire written for magazines were collected in *Tales from a Far Riding* (1902) before he leapt, as he said, from the frying pan of journalism into the 'fire of authorship' with the autobiographical novel *The Odd Job Man* (1903).

The Odd Job Man was followed by a string of mostly realistic fictions: *The Drakestone* and *Back o' the Moon* (both 1906), *Admiral Eddy* (1907), *Pedlar's Pack* (1908), *Draw in your Stool* and *Little Devil Doubt* (both 1909). On 10 June 1909 Onions married the novelist Amy Roberta (Berta) *Ruck (1878–1978). *The Exception*, a tale of blackmail, was published in 1910, and the supernatural work *Widdershins* followed in 1911. *Widdershins* gained him critical approval—he always maintained an uncritical popular readership by following the fashions—which the weakness of his next novel, *Good Boy Seldom* (1911), could not destroy.

Good Boy Seldom, like *Little Devil Doubt*, concerned an ambitious and not over-scrupulous young man, a favourite theme of Onions. He used it again in *In Accordance with the Evidence* (1912), a popular book that was followed by two more along the same rather sensational lines: *The Debit Account* (1913) and *The Story of Louie* (1914). They were successful in Britain, from Secker in London, and from Doran in New York. Frank Swinnerton and others liked their 'veracity', a term which at the time covered a multitude of sins (and exculpated some sinners, too).

The readership this trilogy established stuck with Onions through the rest of his busy career as he moderated his early preachiness (J. B. Priestley had complained of intrusive 'author's remarks' in a *London Mercury* review; Ashley, 233), embraced topicality, titillated with somewhat sordid relationships, introduced new women and fellow authors as characters, toyed with psychological analysis, and entertained with historical novels and ghosts and misty moors. In 1918 Onions changed his name by deed poll to George Oliver, but by then he had established himself as a popular writer and all his work was signed both before and after that date Oliver Onions. Ever striving for success, he remained inventive—and industrious, although it was said that he 'wrote with difficulty, even with anguish', perhaps over-sensitive to adverse criticism of his work (*The Times*). Yet Onions published some forty books, including collections of short stories, ending with the posthumous *A Shilling to Spend* (1965).

A reviewer in *The Atlantic* hailed Onions in 1914 as 'the cleverest' and 'the most advanced of the younger English novelists' (Ashley, 233), but in the event, Onions had to compete with Conrad, Galsworthy, Joyce, Woolf, and D. H. Lawrence, among others. However, he entertained a public who did not read such giants of literature. When Onions died on 9 April 1961 at Bronglais Hospital, Aberystwyth, British fiction had left him behind. *The Poor Man's Tapestry* (1946) is his best historical novel. *The Collected Ghost Stories of Oliver Onions* (1935) is his work most likely to last.

LEONARD R. N. ASHLEY

Sources J. Gawsworth [T. I. Fytton Armstrong] and others, *Ten contemporaries: notes toward their definitive bibliographies* [1933] · F. Swinnerton, *The Georgian literary scene* (1935) · H. Walpole, *Joseph Conrad* (1916) · L. R. N. Ashley, 'George Oliver Onions', *Late-Victorian and Edwardian British novelists: first series*, ed. G. M. Johnson, DLitB, 153 (1995), 228–33 · *The Times* (10 April 1961) · b. cert. · m. cert. **Archives** Indiana University, Bloomington, Lilly Library, corresp. with Society of Authors **Likenesses** J. Russell & Sons, photograph, *c*.1915, NPG · portrait (in middle age), Hult. Arch. **Wealth at death** £7208 1*s*. 7*d*.: probate, 7 June 1961, CGPLA Eng. & Wales

Onslow, Arthur (1691–1768), speaker of the House of Commons, born at Kensington, London, on 1 October 1691, was the elder son of Foote Onslow (1655–1710), first commissioner of excise, and his wife, Susannah, the daughter and heir of Thomas Anlaby of Etton, in the East Riding of Yorkshire, and the widow of Arnold Colwall of Woodford, Essex. His great-grandfather was the politician Sir Richard Onslow (1601–1664). He was educated at Winchester College and matriculated at Wadham College, Oxford, as a fellow commoner on 12 October 1708, but took no degree. He was called to the bar at the Middle Temple in 1713. However, he made little headway in the practice of law. He became a bencher of the Inner Temple in 1728 and served as recorder of Guildford and high steward of Kingston in 1737.

On 8 October 1720 he married Anne (1703–1763), the daughter of John Bridges of Thames Ditton, Surrey, and the niece and coheir of Henry Bridges of Ember Court in the same parish. They had a son, George *Onslow, first earl of Onslow (1731–1814), and a daughter, Anne, who died unmarried on 20 December 1751. Onslow had not been a wealthy man, but his marriage greatly improved his financial circumstances.

At a by-election in February 1720 Onslow had been returned to the House of Commons as a whig MP for the borough of Guildford, which he continued to represent until the dissolution of parliament in July 1727. Only three references to his speeches during the period he was a private member are known. He took part in the debate in November 1722 on the proposal for raising £100,000 upon the real and personal estates of the Roman Catholics, and 'declared his abhorrence of persecuting anybody on account of their opinions in religion' (Cobbett, *Parl. hist.*, 8.52). In April 1725 he strenuously opposed the motion for the reversal of Bolingbroke's attainder, and in March 1726 he supported Richard Hampden's petition on behalf of the latter's great-grandfather, who had opposed Charles I's ship-money levy in 1637. In 1726 he was one of the Commons managers at the trial before the House of Lords of Lord Chancellor Macclesfield, who had been impeached for embezzlement. At the general election in August 1727 he was returned for both Guildford and Surrey. He elected to serve for Surrey, and continued to represent that county until his retirement from the Commons at the dissolution in March 1761.

At the opening of the new parliament, on 23 January 1728, Onslow was unanimously elected speaker. He was

Arthur Onslow (1691–1768), by John Faber junior, 1728 (after Hans Hysing, 1728)

the third member of his family to hold this office, to which he was unanimously re-elected in 1735, 1741, 1747, and 1754. His speakership spanned the entire reign of George II, and by the end of the twentieth century he still held the record for length of service in the office. He was sworn of the privy council at Hampton Court on 25 July 1728, and on 13 May 1729 accepted the post of chancellor and keeper of the great seal to Queen Caroline (who was godmother to his son).

Onslow was a man of rare integrity in an age of corruption, and he realized that the stability of parliament was being undermined by the sordid political intrigues of the day. He was the first speaker to recognize the crucial importance of distancing the chair from all such discreditable activity and of asserting its independence and authority. It was a task for which he was eminently suited, and his renown rests exclusively on his greatness as a speaker. Onslow set the pattern for the impartiality of the chair, but it would be misleading to suggest that he shed his party associations: the total political detachment of the office was to await a later era. He regularly exercised his right to speak and vote in committee, he was known to attend ministerial meetings, and his close friendship with Sir Robert Walpole undoubtedly assisted the furtherance of his early career. But he did not hesitate to oppose government policy when he felt strongly about an issue, and he spoke out against measures he disliked, such as the Regency Bill of 1751 and the Marriage Bill of 1753. Above all other considerations he saw the speaker's role as to protect the institution of parliament and the constitution established by the revolution of 1688.

Onslow insisted on the strict observance of the procedure and practice of the house, a discipline which he saw as an indispensable protection against assaults on the integrity of parliament, whether by bullying ministers or intriguing factions. He had a special regard for the rights of independent members, representing the minority, who were beyond the influence of factions. For him, no procedural detail was too trivial to be enforced, and his rulings amounted to a massive codification of contemporary parliamentary practice. Some regarded this insistence on detail as a tiresome obsession, but John Hatsell, who became a clerk-at-the-table during Onslow's tenure of office, confirmed the speaker's view

> that the forms of proceedings, as instituted by our ancestors, operated as a check and controul on the actions of ministers; and that they were, in many instances, a shelter and protection to the minority, against the attempts of power. (Hatsell, 2.230)

His rigid attachment to precedent probably explains his reactionary stand on the question of the reporting of parliamentary debates. In Onslow's day this was held to be a breach of privilege, and on 13 April 1738 he brought the matter to the attention of the house. A debate ensued which led to a resolution condemning the practice.

Onslow insisted that members show proper respect for the dignity of his office and 'never permitted a member to come in, or go out of the House, whilst he was in the Chair, without calling him, if he observed, that the member did not make his obeysance to the Chair' (Hatsell, 2.232). In his relations with the House of Lords he was ever protective of the privileges of the Commons and swift to protest against attempted encroachments on the part of the peers. To protect his own independence he did not hesitate to sacrifice financial advantage. On 20 April 1734 he was appointed to the lucrative office of treasurer of the navy, but he resigned it eight years later, the day after giving his casting vote on a highly political issue, in order to refute the assertion that he was influenced by personal interest. Thereafter he contented himself with the emoluments attached to the speaker's office, which included the fees from private bills. Onslow introduced important administrative reforms in the House of Commons, and it was due to his influence that in 1742 the house first ordered its journals to be printed.

In consequence of failing health Onslow resolved to retire from parliamentary life, and on 18 March 1761 the thanks of the House of Commons were unanimously voted to him 'for his constant and unwearied attendance in the chair during the course of above thirty-three years in five successive parliaments'. In returning thanks Onslow was deeply affected, and in a moving speech he expressed all that his life's work had meant to him. A further resolution for an address to the king, that he would be 'graciously pleased to confer some signal mark of his royal favour' upon the retiring speaker, was also unanimously carried. Accordingly the king, by letters patent dated 20 April 1761, granted Onslow an annuity of £3000 for the lives of himself and his son George, a provision which was further secured to him by an act of parliament passed in the following year. This was the first occasion when a pension was granted to a retiring speaker. The freedom of the city was voted to Onslow at a court of common council on 5 May 1761 'as a grateful and lasting testimony of the respectful love and veneration which the citizens of London entertain of his person and distinguished virtue'. He was the first speaker to be so honoured. He was admitted to the freedom on 11 June following, but declined, 'on account of his official position', to accept the gold box of the value of 100 guineas which had also been voted by the court. Shortly after his retirement he was elected a trustee of the British Museum. He died at his home in Great Russell Street, London, on 17 February 1768, aged seventy-six. He was buried at Thames Ditton, but his body and that of his wife, who had died in 1763, were afterwards removed to the burial-place of the Onslow family in Merrow church, Surrey.

PHILIP LAUNDY

Sources J. Hatsell, ed., *Precedents of proceedings in the House of Commons*, 4th edn, 2 (1818), vi–vii, 236–8, 241, 354, 384, 393–7 • C. E. Vulliamy, *The Onslow family* (1953), 87–133, 149–54 • P. D. G. Thomas, *The House of Commons in the 18th century* (1971), 212–364 • P. A. C. Laundy, *The office of speaker* (1964), 261–73 • A. I. Dasent, *The speakers of the House of Commons* (1911), 251–74 • E. Porritt, *The unreformed House of Commons*, 1 (1903), 432–81 • M. MacDonagh, *The speaker of the House* (1921), 271–7 • J. S. Watson, 'Arthur Onslow and party politics', *Essays in British history presented to Sir Keith Feiling*, ed. H. R. Trevor-Roper (1964), 139–71 • Cobbett, *Parl. hist.*, vols. 7–16
Archives Clandon Park, Surrey | BM, MSS collection • Bodl. Oxf., corresp. with Thomas Edwards, MSS 1007–1012 • HLRO, precedent books
Likenesses J. Faber junior, mezzotint, 1728 (after H. Hysing, 1728), BM, NPG [*see illus.*] • H. Hysing, oils, *c*.1728, Palace of Westminster, London; version, NPG, Clandon Park, Surrey • J. Thornhill and W. Hogarth, group portrait, oils, 1730, Clandon Park, Surrey • J. Highmore, oils, 1735, Palace of Westminster, London • G. Townsend, caricature, 1751–8, NPG • P. Scheemakers?, tomb effigy, Holy Trinity Church, Guildford, Surrey

Onslow, George (1731–1792), politician, the elder son of the four children of Lieutenant-General Richard Onslow (*c*.1697–1760), politician, and his second wife, Pooley, the daughter of Charles Walton of Little Burstead, Essex, was born on 28 April 1731 in Guildford, Surrey. He entered the army as ensign in the 1st foot guards on 27 February 1748, became captain in Guise's regiment, afterwards the 6th foot, on 12 January 1751, and was promoted major in the 57th regiment on 3 August 1757. He returned to his first regiment as captain-lieutenant on 27 March 1759 and was promoted lieutenant-colonel in the 1st foot guards on 7 November of the same year. On 29 July 1752 he married Jane, the daughter of the Revd Thomas Thorpe, of Chillingham, Northumberland. They had four sons and one daughter: Richard (*b*. 1754), Pooley (*b*. 1758), George (*b*. 1764), George Walton (1768–1844), and Arthur (1773–1851).

On the death of his father in March 1760, Onslow succeeded him as one of the members of parliament for Guildford, and he retired from the army on 10 February 1762. He represented the borough until March 1784 and became known as Colonel Onslow to distinguish him from his first cousin and fellow MP George *Onslow (1731–

1814), the only son of the speaker of the Commons, Arthur Onslow (1691–1768). At the outset of his parliamentary career Onslow followed his cousin's lead and was one of Rockingham's supporters. In the debate on the *North Briton* no. 45 case on 19 January 1764 he was conspicuous as 'the single member who said that No. 45 was not a libel', and he voted against the expulsion of Wilkes (*Cavendish's Debates*, 1.124–5). The Rockingham administration rewarded him in 1765 by granting him the office of outranger of Windsor Forest for life and an increased salary. He voted for the repeal of the Stamp Act in 1766. Later he changed his views, and became an adherent of first the duke of Grafton and then Lord North. On 8 May 1770 he stoutly defended North's American policy when he opposed Burke's resolutions relating to the recent disorders in North America, and called upon him 'to found the censure upon established truth, not upon vague and general declamation'.

Onslow took a leading part in initiating the *Printer's Case* when on 5 February 1771 he moved to have the appropriate regulations read on restricting the printing of debates so as to warn off the newspapers. In one newspaper report of this debate he was offensively described as 'little cocking George', which alluded to his penchant for cockfighting (*Middlesex Journal*, 7 Feb 1771). In the ensuing days he moved for the printers of these reports, John Wheble and Roger Thompson, to be summoned before the Commons for 'misrepresenting the speeches and reflecting on several members of the House' (BL, Egerton MS 224, fols. 181–7). On 12 March he called for six more printers to be summoned before the house for continuing to print debates. This sparked off the Commons' confrontation with the City of London, which cost North's ministry much prestige. Onslow made himself so unpopular that he was hanged in effigy on Tower Hill, on the same gibbet with the speaker.

Onslow proved to be uncompromising in his support for the war in the American colonies. Even after Burgoyne's surrender at Saratoga he protested strongly against peace, insisting in December 1777 that 'it was better to lose America by arms than by treaty', and asserting that the rebellion had been 'fomented, nourished, and supported by the inflammatory speeches and other means used by the incendiaries in that house' (Cobbett, *Parl. hist.*, 19.546–7). He also opposed the petitions for economical reform which were debated in the house in February 1780 and spoke against the Contractors' Bill in March 1781. Above all else, Onslow was an unwavering supporter of North, and he opposed Sir John Rous's motion of want of confidence in North's ministry in March 1782. Having followed North into opposition, he defended him from a personal attack made by Thomas Pitt in February 1783. He continued to support North in the coalition government with Fox, but retired from the Commons at the general election in March 1784.

Onslow, who was 'a short, round man', was aptly described by Walpole as

one of those burlesque orators who are favoured in all public assemblies, and to whom one or two happy sallies of impudence secure a constant attention, though their voice and manner are often their only patents, and who, being laughed at for absurdity as frequently as for humour, obtain a license for what they please.   (Walpole, 2.286)

He died on 12 November 1792, at Dunsborough House, Ripley, Surrey, from the effects of a carriage accident. He was survived by three of his children: George Walton and Arthur, who both became clergymen, and his daughter, Pooley, who married, first, on 23 January 1788, Rear-Admiral Sir Francis Samuel Drake (d. 1789) and secondly, on 13 June 1801, Arthur Onslow (1759–1833), who became MP for Guildford in 1812.

G. F. R. BARKER, rev. IAN K. R. ARCHER

Sources HoP, *Commons* · P. D. G. Thomas, *John Wilkes: a friend to liberty* (1996) · parliamentary diary of Henry Cavendish, 1768–74, BL, Egerton MSS 215–263, 3711 · PRO, War Office, succession books 25/209, p. 73 · *Sir Henry Cavendish's Debates of the House of Commons during the thirteenth parliament of Great Britain*, ed. J. Wright, 2 vols. (1841–3) · Cobbett, *Parl. hist.* · H. Walpole, *Memoirs of the reign of King George the Third*, ed. G. F. R. Barker, 4 vols. (1894) · N. W. Wraxall, *Historical memoirs of his own time*, new edn, 4 vols. (1836) · N. W. Wraxall, *Posthumous memoirs of his own time*, 2nd edn, 3 vols. (1836) · G. O. Trevelyan, *The early history of Charles James Fox* (1889) · *GM*, 1st ser., 58 (1788), 82 · *GM*, 1st ser., 62 (1792), 1060 · *GM*, 1st ser., 71 (1801), 571 · *GM*, 2nd ser., 1 (1834), 227 · *GM*, 2nd ser., 22 (1844), 659 · *GM*, 2nd ser., 37 (1852), 105 · A. Collins, *The peerage of England: containing a genealogical and historical account of all the peers of England* · J. Foster, *The peerage, baronetage, and knightage of the British Empire for 1883*, 1 [1883] · *N&Q*, 8th ser., 3 (1893), 360 · *IGI*
Archives BL, letters to the duke of Newcastle, Add. MSS 32686–33072
Likenesses J. Sayers, caricature, etching, 1782, NPG · J. Sayers, etching, pubd 1782, NPG · J. S. Copley, group portrait, oils (*The collapse of the Earl of Chatham in the House of Lords, 7 July 1778*), Tate collection · J. Field, silhouette, NPG · T. Stewardson, oils, Clandon Park, Surrey

Onslow, George, first earl of Onslow (1731–1814), politician, was born on 13 September 1731, and baptized on 20 October 1731 at St Anne's, Soho, London, the only son of Arthur *Onslow (1691–1768), speaker of the House of Commons, and his wife, Anne (1703–1763), the daughter of John Bridges of Thames Ditton, Surrey. He was educated at Westminster School (from 1739) and Peterhouse, Cambridge (from 1749). On 26 June 1753 at Thames Ditton he married Henrietta (1731–1809), the eldest daughter of Sir John Shelley (1692–1771), of Michelgrove, Surrey, and his second wife, Margaret Pelham, the youngest daughter of Thomas Pelham, first Baron Pelham. They had four sons and one daughter.

Onslow was brought into parliament for Rye, a Treasury borough, in April 1754 by the duke of Newcastle, who was his uncle by marriage. He declared that his election cost him 'not a single shilling save my moiety of the entertainment' (*Buckinghamshire MSS*, 520). At the general election in April 1761 he was returned for his father's seat of Surrey, which he continued to represent until his accession to the House of Lords. Newcastle had already provided him with the sinecure of outranger of Windsor Forest, worth £400 a year, and in 1761 he was given the office of surveyor of the king's gardens and waters, which he described as 'a very

genteel office'. He lost both posts in 1763 during the 'massacre' of Newcastle's followers, and he became an enthusiastic supporter of Pitt and Temple in opposition. He also supported Wilkes, presenting the latter's petition to the Commons in November 1763, and was active in opposition to the Regency Bill in May 1765, when he seconded Rose Fuller's motion for making the queen regent and opposed Morton's motion for reinstating the name of the princess dowager. In June 1765 he urged Temple to accept the Treasury 'for the sake of the country', but a month later he took on the post of a lord of the Treasury on the formation of Lord Rockingham's first administration. He remained in office, however, on Rockingham's split with Chatham in November 1766, and thereby became one of Newcastle's men who placed their loyalty to government above loyalty to the whig party. He was admitted to the privy council on 23 December 1767.

In spite of his former friendship with Wilkes, on 14 April 1769 Onslow moved that Wilkes's fourth election for Middlesex was null and void, and on the following day he carried a resolution by a majority of fifty-four that Colonel Luttrell 'ought to have been returned' (*Cavendish's Debates*, 1.386). On 14 July 1769 he was accused in the *Public Advertiser* by Horne Tooke of having accepted £1000 to procure a place for a person in America. Onslow denounced the story as 'a gross and infamous lie from beginning to end', brought an action for libel against Tooke, and obtained damages for £400, but judgment was arrested by the court of common pleas in Easter term 1771 on technical grounds.

Onslow became a prominent defender of the rights and privileges of the House of Commons, and on 25 January 1770 he opposed Dowdeswell's resolution that the house was bound on matters of election 'to judge according to the law of the land and the known and established law and custom of parliament' (Cobbett, *Parl. hist.*, 16.790–91). In the same session he introduced a bill taking away all privileges of parliament from the servants of members, which, with the aid of Lord Mansfield in the House of Lords, became law (10 Geo. III, c. 50). When the members of the House of Commons were turned out of the House of Lords on 10 December 1770, Onslow, in retaliation, immediately proposed that the Commons should be 'cleared of strangers, members of the House of Lords, and all', but he voted against Dunning's motion for a committee to inspect the journals of the House of Lords. On 7 February 1771 he opposed Sir George Savile's attempt to bring in a bill for 'more effectually securing the rights' of electors. In the same session he took an active part with his cousin and fellow MP George *Onslow (1731–1792) in excluding strangers from the gallery of the House of Commons, and in calling the printers of newspapers to the bar of the house for publishing the debates. In April 1772 he supported a motion for leave to bring in a bill for the relief of protestant dissenters, and strongly advocated the propriety of granting them relief from subscription. On 8 July 1773 he was created DCL of Oxford University.

As his part in the Middlesex election controversy had made him unpopular with the county electors, Onslow retired from the seat for Surrey in 1774, though he retained his place at the Treasury until 1777. He was created Baron Cranley, in the county of Surrey, on 20 May 1776, and took his seat in the House of Lords on the following day. On 8 October of the same year he succeeded his cousin Richard as fourth Baron Onslow, and on 30 October was sworn in as lord lieutenant of Surrey. He spoke for the first time in the House of Lords on 16 April 1777, when he urged that some provision should be made for the discharge of the king's debts, and 'launched into encomiums of the personal and political virtues of the sovereign' (Cobbett, *Parl. hist.*, 19.163–4). On 13 May 1778 he voted against the attendance of the House of Lords at Chatham's funeral, though he 'formerly used to wait in the lobby to help him on with his great-coat' (*Letters of Horace Walpole*, 7.65). It was not surprising that Junius called him 'a false, silly fellow' (Junius, 1.198). He spent the rest of his career as a courtier. He was appointed comptroller of the household on 1 December 1777 and became treasurer of the household in December 1779 until his appointment as a lord of the bedchamber in September 1780, a post which he retained until his death.

During his father's lifetime Onslow had been heavily dependent on his official salary of £1000 per annum and was reportedly in financial difficulties, but in 1768 he inherited his father's pension of £3000, which he kept secret from his creditors. On succeeding to the Onslow title in 1776, he acquired estates reputed to be worth £18,000 a year. He supported the Fox–North India Bill at first, but, on discovering the king's wishes, voted against it when it was defeated in the Lords. He appears to have spoken for the last time in the Lords on 19 March 1788, when he supported the third reading of Pitt's East India Declaratory Bill.

Onslow was in the royal coach, in his capacity of lord-in-waiting, when the king was mobbed on his way to open parliament on 29 October 1795. The king calmed him down and gave him a stone thrown into the carriage on their return. Onslow served as colonel of the Surrey regiment of fencible cavalry from 23 May 1794 to 27 March 1800. In 1798 Tierney moved in the House of Commons for an inquiry into Onslow's conduct with regard to the manner in which the act to provide for the defence of the realm had been carried into effect in the county of Surrey, but the motion was lost by 141 votes to 22. Onslow, whom Walpole described as 'a noisy, indiscreet man' (Walpole, *Memoirs*, 4.218), was created Viscount Cranley and earl of Onslow on 19 June 1801. His wife died on 27 May 1809, and Onslow himself died at his seat, Clandon Park, Surrey, on 17 May 1814, aged eighty-two. He was buried in Merrow church, near Guildford, on 22 May.

Onslow was succeeded by his eldest son, **Thomas Onslow**, second earl of Onslow (1754–1827), politician and eccentric, who was born on 15 March 1754 at Imber Court, Surrey. Commonly known as Tom Onslow, he was MP for Rye from 1775 to 1784, and for Guildford from 1784 to 1806. He married first, on 30 December 1776, Arabella (d. 1782), the third daughter and coheir of Eaton Mainwaring-Ellerker of Risby Park, Yorkshire, and his wife, Barbara;

they had three sons and one daughter. Following Arabella's death, aged twenty-six, on 11 April 1782, he married, on 13 February 1783, Charlotte (d. 1819), the daughter of William and Elizabeth Hale of King's Walden, Hertfordshire, and the widow of Thomas Duncombe of Duncombe Park, Yorkshire; they had only one child, a daughter.

Onslow was a crony of the prince of Wales and shared his passion for driving four-in-hand, which is commemorated in one of Gillray's caricatures and in the lines:

> What can little T. O. do?
> Why, drive a phaeton and two!!
> Can little T. O. do no more?
> Yes, drive a phaeton and four!!!!
> (T. Wright and R. H. Evans, *Historical and Descriptive Account of the Caricatures of James Gillray*, 1851, 463)

Wraxall commented that he was short in stature, and 'destitute of any elegance or grace' and that 'he passed the whole day in his phaeton, and sacrificed every object to the gratification of that "ignoble ambition", as he himself called it' (*Historical and Posthumous Memoirs*, 5.309–10). Gronow recalled that he possessed 'four of the finest black horses in England [and] … his carriage was painted black, and the whole turn-out had more the appearance of belonging to an undertaker' (*Reminiscences*, 2.113).

Onslow supported the Foxites, but rose in the Commons on very few occasions; in 1781 he presented a petition of 'a numerous body of the innholders of England', complaining of the billeting of soldiers on them. His most notorious service to the prince was his mission to Mrs Fitzherbert in 1784 to tell her that the prince had attempted suicide and that she must go to him to save his life. In December 1785 he accompanied the prince to Mrs Fitzherbert's house and stood guard, with a drawn sword, at the door while they were married in secret. Later, for reasons which are unknown, he fell out with the prince; he voted for Pitt's regency proposals in 1789, and against the abolition of the slave trade in 1796. He died on 22 February 1827, aged seventy-two, at Clandon Park.

G. F. R. Barker, rev. E. A. Smith

Sources The manuscripts of the earl of Buckinghamshire, the earl of Lindsey … and James Round, HMC, 38 (1895), 458–524 [Onslow MSS] · J. Brooke, 'Onslow, George', HoP, Commons · HoP, Commons · C. E. Vulliamy, The Onslow family (1953) · The Grenville papers: being the correspondence of Richard Grenville … and … George Grenville, ed. W. J. Smith, 4 vols. (1852–3) · Correspondence of William Pitt, earl of Chatham, ed. W. S. Taylor and J. H. Pringle, 4 vols. (1838–40) · Sir Henry Cavendish's Debates of the House of Commons during the thirteenth parliament of Great Britain, ed. J. Wright, 2 vols. (1841–3) · Cobbett, Parl. hist. · H. Walpole, Memoirs of the reign of King George the Third, ed. G. F. R. Barker, 4 vols. (1894) · The letters of Horace Walpole, earl of Orford, ed. P. Cunningham, 4 (1857); 7 (1858) · The later correspondence of George III, ed. A. Aspinall, 5 vols. (1962–70), vols. 1–3 · The correspondence of George, prince of Wales, 1770–1812, ed. A. Aspinall, 1: 1770–1789 (1963) · The historical and the posthumous memoirs of Sir Nathaniel William Wraxall, 1772–1784, ed. H. B. Wheatley, 5 vols. (1884), vol. 5, pp. 308–10 · The diary and correspondence of Charles Abbot, Lord Colchester, ed. Charles, Lord Colchester, 1 (1861) · The reminiscences and recollections of Captain Gronow, 1810–1860, 2 (1889) · Georgiana: extracts from the correspondence of Georgiana, duchess of Devonshire, ed. E. Ponsonby, earl of Bessborough [1955] · Junius: including letters by the same writer, under other signatures, ed. J. M. Good, 2nd edn, 3 vols. (1814) · GEC, Peerage · IGI · G. Wilson, Reports of cases

*argued and adjudged in the king's courts at Westminster … from Michael-
mas term 1769, until Easter term … 1774*, 3rd edn, 3 vols. (1770–75) ·
GM, 1st ser., 56 (1786), 483 · *GM*, 1st ser., 84/1 (1814), 525, 703–4 · *GM*,
1st ser., 97/1 (1827), 269, 488 · PRO, Chatham MSS, PRO 30/8/164
Archives Surrey HC, family, manorial, and estate papers | BL,
corresp. with duke of Newcastle, etc., Add. MSS 32889–33090 ·
Bodl. Oxf., corresp. with Thomas Edwards · PRO, Chatham MSS,
PRO 30/8/164 · U. Nott. L., letters to second duke of Newcastle; let-
ters to third duke of Portland
Likenesses J. Russell, pastel, exh. Grosvenor Gallery 1889 · J. S.
Copley, group portrait, oils (*The collapse of the earl of Chatham in the
House of Lords, 7 July 1778*), Tate collection; on loan to NPG · J. Field,
silhouette, NPG · T. Stewardson, oils, Clandon Park, Surrey ·
W. Ward, mezzotint

Onslow, (André) George Louis (1784–1853), composer,
was born on 27 July 1784 at Clermont-Ferrand, Auvergne,
France, the son of Edward Onslow (1758–1829), youngest
son of the first earl of Onslow, and his wife, Marie Rosalie
de Bourdeilles de Brantôme (*d.* 1842), a renowned beauty
from a local aristocratic family. There is much conflicting
detail concerning Onslow's youth, but the most accurate
accounts suggest that he was sent to London while a
young boy to be educated under the watchful eye of his
paternal grandfather, and there he received piano lessons
from N.-J. Hüllmandel and Jan Ladislav Dussek. He was
then sent to Germany for two years (1799–1800), where he
took piano lessons from Hüllmandel, Dussek, and J. B.
Cramer as part of the education which befitted an aristocrat, although he apparently remained unmoved by the
great music of his day. On returning to the Auvergne, taking with him the piano he had used in London, which was
the first known in that area of France, he became friendly
with a group of local musicians. This, according to some
sources, prompted him to learn the cello, and thus it was
that he became familiar with the chamber works of
Haydn, Mozart, and Boccherini.

It was when Onslow was in Paris in 1801 that, according
to an autobiographical note, the overture to Méhul's
opera *Stratonice* awakened his sensibilities to the profound
effect music could have on the emotions. The idea of composition came some while later and led to the writing of
his first three string quintets (op. 1) and three quartets (op.
4) in 1807, and their publication in Paris at his own
expense, before he had received so much as one formal
lesson in composition. F.-J. Fétis, damning with faint
praise, writes that Onslow had no real idea of the labour of
composing, but that, as a man of independent means, he
had all the leisure necessary to overcome these obstacles.
Onslow recognized his shortcomings and sought lessons
with Antoine Reicha, who had recently settled in Paris.
Some sources say that it was about now that he learned to
play the cello in order to become better acquainted with
the chamber music of Beethoven, Haydn, and Mozart. In
the same year (1808), on 23 June, he married Charlotte
Françoise Delphine de Fontanges, the daughter of a rich
Aurillac landowner. They had two daughters and a son.

From this time on Onslow produced a steady series of
works for publication. His attempts at opera, the most
highly favoured genre at the time, were limited. *L'Alcalde*

de la vega and *Le colporteur* were both produced at the Thé-
âtre Feydeau, in 1824 and 1827 respectively, and both
achieved a *succès d'estime*. His third and final effort, which
appeared ten years later, was *Guise*. *Le colporteur* also found
modest success in Germany under the titles *Der Hausirer*
and *Der Spion*, and was given in an adaptation by Barham
Livius as *The Emissary, or, The Revolt of Moscow* at Drury Lane,
London, on 13 May 1831.

In 1829 Onslow was injured when out boar-hunting
while taking a rest to jot down a musical idea. His ear was
damaged by a spent ball, leaving him unable to play the
cello, and his hearing was impaired for the rest of his life.
One of his most famous quintets, the fifteenth, was written as a result of this misfortune, being developed out of
the theme he was sketching at the time of the accident: he
charted his pain in the minuet ('Dolore'), convalescence in
the andante ('Convalescenza'), and recovery in the finale
('Guarigione'). Having maintained his English connections, he was elected the second honorary member of the
newly founded Philharmonic Society of London in 1830,
Mendelssohn having been the first. His first symphony
was performed at the Paris conservatory on 10 April 1831.

In 1842 the death of his father-in-law, the marquis de
Fontanges, left Onslow in possession of a large fortune. In
the same year, coincidentally or not, he entered the Institut de France, replacing Cherubini in the chair of the
Académie des Beaux-Arts, having gained more votes than,
among others, Adam, Auber, and Berlioz. When he visited
Paris for the last time in summer 1853 his health had
deteriorated. He died suddenly at Clermont-Ferrand on 3
October 1853, after a morning walk.

For about forty years Onslow had produced a succession
of works, the international publication of which was
awaited eagerly by his appreciative following. By the
1830s Breitkopf and Härtel were producing collected editions of scores and parts, which, in the case of chamber
music, were adaptable to various combinations of instruments and eventually numbered some thirty-four string
quintets, thirty-five string quartets, and twenty-six works
for other combinations. Onslow was highly regarded as an
amateur composer, although some contemporary commentators saw his chamber music as worthy to stand
alongside that of Haydn, Mozart, and Beethoven, which
accounted for his popularity in England and Germany.
Many top French performers of the day also devoted much
of their time and talent to playing Onslow's music, among
them Pierre Baillot, Chrétien Urhan, Théophile Tilmant,
and Auguste Franchomme. But by 1880 his music was
largely forgotten. He is credited, however, as being a 'modest, but legitimate' precursor, influencing several highly
regarded French composers of the day, including Saint-
Saëns, Massenet, Lalo, and Franck, although his music is
not French in style. The quartets and quintets, irrespective of any influence they may or may not have had, are of
exceptional quality. From the standpoint of the late twentieth century his musical language shows parallels with
that of Beethoven, Schubert, and Mendelssohn, along
with a semblance to the style of the later Brahms.

DIANA BICKLEY

Sources J. F. Halévy, 'Académie des Beaux-Arts: notice historique sur la vie et les travaux de M. George Onslow', *Revue et Gazette Musicale* (Nov 1855), 307–12; repr. in J. F. Halévy, *Souvenirs et portraits* (1861) • F. Stoepel, 'Galerie des artistes célèbres: George Onslow', *Gazette Musicale de Paris* (11 May 1834), 149–53 • G. Onslow, F-Pn Lettres autographes, vol. 81, no. 316 • F.-J. Fétis, *Biographie universelle des musiciens, et bibliographie générale de la musique*, 2nd edn, 6 (Paris, 1864), 369 • J. d'Ortigue, 'Une visite à George Onslow en 1832', *Le Ménestral*, 31 (1861), 113 • *New Grove* • *DNB* • Burke, *Peerage* • C. Nobach, *Untersuchungen zu George Onslow Kammermusik* (1985) • V. Niaux, 'Les quatuors à cordes de George Onslow, 1784–1853: étude des sources, analyse et catalogue thématique', PhD diss., Tours • C. E. Vulliamy, *The Onslow family* (1953)
Archives Bibliothèque Nationale, Paris
Likenesses Vigneron, lithograph, NPG • lithograph (after portrait), repro. in Stoepel, 'George Onslow', 148

Onslow, Gwendolen Florence Mary. *See* Guinness, Gwendolen Florence Mary, countess of Iveagh (1881–1966).

Onslow, Muriel Wheldale (1880–1932), plant biochemist, was born on 31 March 1880 at Round Hills, Aston Manor, Warwickshire, the only child of John Wheldale, solicitor, and his wife, Fannie (*née* Hayward). From King Edward VI High School for Girls, Birmingham, she entered Newnham College, Cambridge, in 1900, and, exceptionally well prepared, took a first class in part one of the natural sciences tripos in 1902 and a first class in part two (botany) in 1904.

Wheldale's early research was strongly influenced by the Cambridge geneticist William Bateson. Supported first by a Bathurst fellowship and then by a six-year Newnham College research fellowship (or 'N' fellowship), she investigated inheritance of flower colour in the snapdragon, *Antirrhinum majus*; the work led her directly into the biochemistry (particularly the biosynthesis) of the pigments involved, the anthocyanins. Her isolation and chemical examination of these compounds about 1913–14 was pioneering and preceded the publication of the classic work in this area by German chemist Richard Willstätter. The application of chemical and physical methods to the unravelling of the complexities of biological systems was then in its infancy, and she was one of the first to offer an acceptable discussion of the factors of inheritance from a chemical point of view. Her monograph *The Anthocyanin Pigments of Plants* (1916; rev. edn, 1925), an account of current research on these compounds, their distribution, and theories about their biological function, solidly established her reputation in the field. From about 1919 she concentrated on investigations of the nature of oxidizing enzymes present in higher plants, particularly oxidase, a catalyst involved in pigment production. In addition, she worked with the Food Investigation Board; from 1922 she supervised a team carrying out research on cold storage problems of apples at the Cambridge Low Temperature Research Station.

From 1911 to 1914 Wheldale was a member of the Bateson genetics group at the John Innes Horticultural Institution in Merton, Surrey, but most of her career was spent at Cambridge, in the botany school and in the biochemical department, which, under the leadership of F. G. Hopkins, afforded opportunities for a remarkable number of women at a time when few positions permitting independent research in the chemical sciences were within their reach. She taught at Newnham in 1911–12 and held an assistantship in the university physiological (later biochemical) laboratory from 1918 to 1926. Among the most distinguished of early women biochemists, she was one of the first women appointed to a Cambridge University lectureship (in biochemistry, 1926). She was an inspiring teacher with a gift for clear exposition; her class in plant biochemistry was an important unit in the advanced botany curriculum.

On 3 February 1919 she married a colleague, Victor Alexander Herbert Huia Onslow (1890–1922), second son of William Hillier *Onslow, fourth earl of Onslow, governor of New Zealand; there were no children. Despite formidable physical disability, her husband was active in biochemical research, and she collaborated with him closely from about 1917 until his death, concentrating largely on the problem of colour and iridescence in insect scales.

In addition to *Anthocyanin Pigments* and about twenty original papers on plant pigments and oxidase systems, Wheldale Onslow wrote two textbooks, *Practical Plant Biochemistry* (1920), a general survey of problems in the chemistry of plant life, solidly grounded in organic chemistry, and *Principles of Plant Biochemistry* (1931), the first volume of a projected two-volume work whose second volume was not completed before her death.

Though somewhat critical and self-contained by nature Wheldale Onslow was, to those who passed through her reserve, a pleasant and witty companion and a constant friend. She much enjoyed travel, and during her last years explored many of the more inaccessible parts of central Europe. Her Cambridge home was shared with her widowed mother, whose sole companion she was for a number of years. She died at the height of her professional success at her home, 1 Clare Road, Cambridge, on 19 May 1932. Her funeral service was held on the 23rd at Madingley church. A Newnham prize and research fellowship commemorate her name. MARY R. S. CREESE

Sources M. S., *Biochemical Journal*, 26 (1932), 915–16 • *Nature*, 129 (1932), 859 • *Newnham College Roll Letter* (1933), 59–61 • [A. B. White and others], eds., *Newnham College register, 1871–1971*, 2nd edn, 1 (1979) • Desmond, *Botanists*, rev. edn, 472 • J. C. Poggendorff and others, eds., *Biographisch-literarisches Handwörterbuch zur Geschichte der exacten Naturwissenschaften*, 7b, pt 5 (Berlin, 1978), 3733 • M. Onslow, *Huia Onslow. A memoir* (1924) • *The Times* (20 May 1932) • *The Times* (21 May 1932) • Newnham College, Cambridge, archive • b. cert.
Likenesses group portraits, photographs (of Onslow?), Newnham College, Cambridge
Wealth at death £2116 15s. 5d.: probate, 11 Aug 1932, CGPLA Eng. & Wales

Onslow, Richard (1527/8–1571), lawyer and speaker of the House of Commons, was a younger son of Roger Onslow of Shrewsbury, Shropshire, and his first wife, Margaret, daughter of Thomas Poyner. His elder brother, Fulk (d. 1602), was clerk of the parliaments in the reign of Elizabeth I. He was admitted to the Inner Temple in 1545, aged seventeen, at the instance of Sir Nicholas Hare, and called to the bar some time before 1554. Although he was expelled from the inn in 1556, with seven others, after an outbreak of disorder, this did not prevent him from being elected a bencher in 1559 in advance of reading. Several copies survive of his first reading, given in the autumn of 1562 on the Henrician statute concerning final concords (32 Hen. VIII c. 36). By this time he was a member of parliament, having been elected for Steyning in 1558 and Aldeburgh in 1559. In 1559 he married Katherine (d. 1599), daughter and heir of William Harding of Knowle, Surrey; they would have seven children. In 1560 he became a member of the council in the marches of Wales, in 1561 clerk of the council to the duchy of Lancaster, and in 1562 a justice of the quorum for his home county. These positions, which he retained until his, did not prevent his practice at the bar, and in 1561 he argued successfully for the plaintiff in the earliest known reported case on the doctrine of consideration, when it was held by the queen's bench that an exchange of conditional promises could constitute a binding contract.

In 1563 Onslow was chosen recorder of London, and occupied that office until he became solicitor-general in 1566. In 1563 he was again elected member for Steyning, and in 1566 for the city of London as well as for Steyning, serving for the latter. It was in this last parliament that he was elected speaker of the House of Commons, though not without difficulty. Onslow attempted to disqualify himself on the grounds that the speakership was incompatible with his office as solicitor-general, which bound him not only to the queen but also to attendance on the Lords; but he was elected after a division (eighty-two against seventy). Well might he seek to be excused, for it proved to be a turbulent session, during which the burning issues were the succession to the crown and the queen's marriage. On 25 November 1566, after the suppression of a Bill for Regulating the Succession, Onslow read to the house the queen's command to stay all proceedings touching the crown, which she considered 'very unmeet for the time and place, and certainly very dangerous to the common quietness of all her good subjects now here assembled' (*Lost Notebooks*, 125–6). This interference with freedom of speech—a liberty that Onslow, perhaps with deliberate circumspection, had omitted to claim at the beginning of the session—had been approved by a meeting of judges, and (according to Dyer) was observed by the house. Nevertheless, on 2 January 1567, when the parliament ended, Onslow made a two-hour speech during which he eulogized hereditary monarchy and daringly urged the queen to marry without delay. This earned a further royal rebuke to the Commons for busying themselves in matters that did not concern them. The incident did not harm Onslow's career, for in 1569 he was promoted from the office of solicitor-general to the lucrative attorneyship of the court of wards and liveries.

Onslow is said to be the author of 'Arguments proving the queene's majestie's propertye in the sea landes and salt shores', which survives in several manuscripts and was edited for publication by J. W. Pycroft in 1855. However, his promising career was cut short by the plague. He died on 2 April 1571, still in his early forties, from a pestilential fever caught while visiting his uncle at Shrewsbury, and was buried in St Chad's, Shrewsbury, on 7 April. His will mentions lands in Buckinghamshire, Gloucestershire, Kent, Middlesex, Shropshire, Surrey, Sussex, Warwickshire, and Wiltshire, and a house in the Blackfriars, London, which his widow had as part of her jointure. Among his bequests were a standing cup and cover for the earl of Leicester, to whom he was 'most bounden', and a gilt bowl for Lord Burghley. His second son (and eventual heir), Sir Edward Onslow (d. 1615), was the father of Sir Richard *Onslow (d. 1664) and ancestor of the earls of Onslow.

J. H. BAKER

Sources HoP, *Commons, 1509–58*, 3.32 · HoP, *Commons, 1558–1603*, 3.153–5 · R. Somerville, *History of the duchy of Lancaster, 1265–1603* (1953), 414–15 · G. R. Elton, *The parliament of England, 1559–1581* (1986), 341–9 · F. A. Inderwick and R. A. Roberts, eds., *A calendar of the Inner Temple records*, 1 (1896) · J. H. Baker, *Readers and readings in the inns of court and chancery*, SeldS, suppl. ser., 13 (2000) · J. H. Baker and S. F. C. Milsom, eds., *Sources of English legal history: private law to 1750* (1986), 487 · *Reports from the lost notebooks of Sir James Dyer*, ed. J. H. Baker, 1, SeldS, 109 (1994), lvi, 123, 125–6 · J. W. Pycroft, ed., *Arguments relating to sea landes and salt shores* (1855) · will, PRO, PROB 11/53, sig. 14

Likenesses alabaster? effigy on monument, 1571, St Chad's Church, Shrewsbury, Shropshire · oils, Clandon Park, Surrey; copy, Palace of Westminster, London

Onslow, Sir Richard (*bap.* 1601, *d.* 1664), politician, was baptized on 30 July 1601, the second son of Sir Edward Onslow (d. 1615) of Knoll in Cranley, Surrey, and Isabel Shirley (d. 1630), daughter of Sir Thomas Shirley of Wiston, Sussex. Richard succeeded to the family estates on the death in December 1616 of his elder brother, Sir Thomas Onslow. He matriculated at Jesus College, Cambridge, in 1617 and entered Lincoln's Inn on 8 November 1618. In 1620 he married Elizabeth (d. 1679), daughter and heir of Arthur Strangways of Holborn Bridge, London; they had six daughters and eight sons. He was knighted on 2 June 1624, was colonel of horse in Surrey by July 1626, a Surrey JP by December of that year, and a deputy lieutenant by the following March.

Onslow served as knight of the shire for Surrey in the parliament of 1628 and in both the Short and Long parliaments. In January 1642 he was one of the commissioners who met at Guildford to determine the bounds of Windsor Forest in Surrey, following representations from local residents who were anxious to free the parishes of northwest Surrey from forest law. The commission, which sat in contravention of an order of the House of Lords for the meeting to be postponed owing to the prevailing conditions of political instability, found that no part of Surrey except Guildford Park lay within the bounds of the forest.

Onslow was removed from the commission of the peace on 19 July 1642, but he attended the assizes at Kingston in August in order to serve parliament's arrest warrant on Justice Mallet. In September and October he was active in raising forces in the county for parliament. His house was plundered when the king's army entered Surrey in November. Following the death in December of Anthony

Sir Richard Onslow (*bap.* 1601, *d.* 1664), by John Michael Wright

Fane, Onslow emerged as the dominant figure among Surrey's parliamentarians, and was chiefly responsible for the moderate and conciliatory policies adopted by the county's parliamentarian administration. He was later praised by one Surrey royalist for striving 'to prevent and stop (to his utmost capacity) the rapines and oppressions of those times of Blood and Violence' (E. Andrews, *Gratitude in Season*, 1661, 6), while the poet George Wither was to accuse him of being 'the greatest Favourer of Delinquents, and the most implacable Enemy to them, who are eminently Well-affected to the Parliament, of any man in Surrey' (G. Wither, *Justitiarius justificatus*, 1646, 11). Although Onslow was a committed presbyterian, and was instrumental in attempts to establish a classical system in Surrey, he gained a reputation for protecting ministers who faced ejection, including the rector of Albury, William Oughtred, who dedicated the 1647 edition of his *The Key of the Mathematicks New Forged and Filed* to Sir Richard and his son Arthur. Onslow was also active, as a trustee for the earls of Arundel, in protecting the Howards' property interests in Surrey during the civil war.

Onslow's authority in Surrey was challenged in mid-1643 by rival parliamentarians, led by Sir John Maynard, who sought to increase the county's contribution to the war effort. Maynard and his allies gained temporary control of the Surrey county committee in July 1644, while Onslow was absent from the county as commander of the Surrey regiments at the siege of Basing, but their attempt to place George Wither in command of the militia forces of Surrey's east and middle divisions proved unsuccessful. Maynard was removed from the county committee at the end of August, and in March 1645 his

kinsman Colonel Samuel Jones was forced to relinquish his command of Farnham Castle. An ordinance of parliament of 1 July 1645 led to the creation of a new committee dominated by Sir Richard and his supporters. The successful outcome of these disputes owed much to the support that Onslow obtained from the earl of Northumberland, the county's lord lieutenant, and from the middle group in parliament.

In April 1646 George Wither's belated attack on Onslow in *Justitiarius justificatus* included the accusation that Sir Richard had sought to betray the parliamentarian cause. The pamphlet was voted false and scandalous in the House of Commons on 7 August, and Wither was fined £500 and imprisoned, but a subsidiary charge relating to his claim that Onslow had sent £500 to the king at Oxford went unpunished.

Onslow was named to the revived committee of safety on 11 June 1647, and again on 30 July, but it is doubtful whether he played any significant part in its activities. On 1 June 1648 he was appointed a member of the Derby House committee, and later that month he was nominated by the Commons to the joint committee to consider terms for a personal treaty with the king. He was imprisoned briefly at Pride's Purge, but he remained on the Surrey bench and continued to attend meetings of the county committee. Although he was said in April 1651 to be 'fierce upon the Presbyterian score and also upon the King's' (*Portland MSS*, 1.582), he was active as a militia commissioner and commanded the Surrey regiment which was raised in July 1651 to resist the Scottish invasion.

Sir Richard Onslow sat for the county of Surrey in both the first and second protectorate parliaments. In April 1657 he was prominent in moves to persuade Cromwell to accept the crown, arguing that a king was more accountable than a protector, and in December he was made a member of Cromwell's upper house. He withdrew from national affairs following the fall of Richard Cromwell, but remained active as a JP until the autumn. At the recall of the secluded members of the Long Parliament in February 1660 he was appointed a member of the new council of state. He stood with his son Arthur for the county seats at the elections to the Convention Parliament in April, but lost, partly as a result of local hostility to presbyterians and partly, as his kinsman Denzil Holles suggested, 'by his owne fault, for he was offred one place, but he desired them both, for himself and his sonne, and so hath lost both' (BL, Add. MS 32679, fol. 9v). The Onslows were able to sit instead for the town of Guildford.

By July 1660 Sir Richard had been removed from the commission of the peace in Surrey, and attempts were made to exclude him from the Act of Indemnity. The reasons given for this included his involvement in the arrest of Judge Mallet in 1642, his military activities during the civil war and in 1651, and his having compared Charles I to a hedgehog. He succeeded in obtaining a pardon on 5 November 1660. In May 1661 he was elected, again as burgess for Guildford, to the Cavalier Parliament, of which he became an active member. He was restored to the Surrey bench and attended quarter sessions regularly between April 1662 and his death in 1664.

Onslow's great-grandson, Speaker Arthur Onslow, was to describe him as 'a man of high spirit, of a large fortune and great parts, knowledge and courage, with the gravity and sobriety of the times'. He 'had a sort of art and cunning about him' which could, he suggested, 'only be justified by the uncertainty and confusion of the times he lived in, which made it very difficult for a man to act in them, whose principles did not lead him to the extremes of any party' (*Buckinghamshire MSS*, 476, 482). Onslow died on 19 May 1664 at Arundel House, the Strand, Middlesex. Although William Mountague believed that the cause of death was a gangrene brought on 'by the relics of an ague, which settled in his thigh' (*Buccleuch MSS*, 1.315), most accounts suggest that he died after being hit by lightning. In his will, which was completed in March 1664, he described himself as of West Clandon, Surrey, where the seat he had purchased from Sir Richard Weston in 1642—subsequently his main residence—was situated. The bequests in his will included £2500 to his unmarried daughter Elizabeth, and £1000 each to his sons Richard and Denzill and granddaughter Mary. He was buried in Cranley church and was succeeded by his eldest son, Arthur Onslow. JOHN GURNEY

Sources J. Gurney, 'The county of Surrey and the English revolution', DPhil diss., U. Sussex, 1991 · *HoP, Commons, 1660–90* (1983) · Earl of Onslow, 'Sir Richard Onslow, 1603–1664', *Surrey Archaeological Collections*, 36 (1925), 58–79 · *The manuscripts of the earl of Buckinghamshire, the earl of Lindsey … and James Round*, HMC, 38 (1895), 476–84 · J. Gurney, 'George Wither and Surrey politics, 1642–1649', *Southern History*, 19 (1997), 74–98 · Surrey HC, Onslow papers · PRO, PROB 11/34, fols. 286–287v · W. Scott, ed., *A collection of scarce and valuable tracts … Lord Somers*, 2nd edn, 13 vols. (1809–15), vol. 6, pp. 351, 376–8 · H. Jenkinson and D. L. Powell, eds., *Surrey quarter sessions records: order book and sessions rolls*, 3 vols., Surrey RS, 35–6, 39 (1934–8) · O. Manning and W. Bray, *The history and antiquities of the county of Surrey*, 3 vols. (1804–14) · Venn, *Alum. Cant.*, 1/3.281 · W. P. Baildon, ed., *The records of the Honorable Society of Lincoln's Inn: admissions*, 1 (1896), 181 · *The manuscripts of his grace the duke of Portland*, 10 vols., HMC, 29 (1891–1931), vol. 1 · *Report on the manuscripts of his grace the duke of Buccleuch and Queensberry … preserved at Montagu House*, 3 vols. in 4, HMC, 45 (1899–1926), vol. 1 · *DNB*

Archives HLRO, main papers series · PRO, Commonwealth Exchequer MSS, SP 28 · Surrey HC, Onslow MSS; Godwin–Austen MSS

Likenesses J. M. Wright, portrait, Clandon Park, Surrey [*see illus.*] · portrait, Clandon Park, Surrey; repro. in Onslow, 'Sir Richard Onslow', facing p. 58

Wealth at death considerable: will, PRO, PROB 11/34, fols. 286–287v

Onslow, Richard, first Baron Onslow (1654–1717), speaker of the House of Commons, was born on 23 June 1654, the eldest son of Sir Arthur Onslow, second baronet (1622–1688), politician, of Knowle and West Clandon, Surrey, and his wife, Mary, second daughter and coheir of Sir Thomas Foot, first baronet, mayor of London. He matriculated from St Edmund Hall, Oxford, on 7 June 1671, and was admitted to the Inner Temple three years later, but was never called to the bar. He married Elizabeth (*bap.* 1661, *d.* 1718), the daughter and heir of Sir Henry Tulse, grocer, of Lothbury, London, on 31 August 1676.

They had three sons and one daughter. The Onslow family were well established in the political life of Surrey and Sir Richard's career benefited from these foundations. On 1 March 1679 he entered parliament for the borough of Guildford and supported attempts to exclude the Roman Catholic duke of York from the throne, voting for the first Exclusion Bill. Despite the later tory reaction he retained his seat in 1685. Following his father's death, on 21 July 1688, he succeeded to the baronetcy and as a mark of his new status was returned for one of the Surrey county seats in the Convention Parliament of 1689.

Onslow was later described by his nephew, Sir Arthur Onslow, as

a person of great probity, courage and honour … tall and very thin, not well shaped and with a face exceeding plain, yet there was a certain sweetness with a dignity in his countenance and so much of life and spirit in it that no one who saw him ever thought him of a disagreeable aspect. (*Buckinghamshire MSS*, 489)

His staunch and consistent country whig sympathies made him the victim of some mockery. The first earl of Dartmouth, a moderate tory, described Onslow as a 'vain trifling man of a ridiculous figure, full of party zeal' (*Bishop Burnet's History*, 5.395n.). He also gained the unwelcome sobriquet Stiff Dick as a result of his rigorous devotion to principle.

He was an active back-bencher during the 1690s and served as one of the commissioners of the Admiralty from May 1690 to February 1693. Onslow's political activity was frequently related to commercial affairs and country issues such as disbandment of the armed forces, regulation of elections, and the number of placemen in the Commons. As a consequence of this activity he was nominated as a moderate whig candidate for the speakership in February 1701, but was defeated by Robert Harley. The same year, in another indication of his increasing status, he became high steward of Guildford.

Onslow gained the speaker's chair in the 1708 parliament. Unfortunately his whiggish zeal was unabated and his inability to pretend any kind of neutrality in the chair lost him the goodwill of moderates and tories alike. He was diligent, even pedantic, as a speaker, and very conscious of his role as a defender of the rights of the Commons. He played a significant part in the trial of the high-church clergyman Dr Henry Sacheverell, and on 23 March 1710 led the Commons to the House of Lords to hear the judgment in the case. This resulted in Onslow's successfully challenging black rod on a matter of privilege which, although it increased his unpopularity with the tories, did not prevent his elevation to the privy council on 15 June 1710. The tide of tory support proved so strong in the 1710 election that Onslow lost his Surrey seat and was forced to sit for St Mawes, Cornwall, on Godolphin's recommendation. The tories 'thought there could not be a greater mark of an universal disaffection to the Whig cause' (*Buckinghamshire MSS*, 492).

On the death of Queen Anne, Onslow supported the protestant succession and gained a strong position at court. In October 1714 he became chancellor of the exchequer and after resigning from office a year later he was given a tellership of the exchequer on 4 November 1715 for life. On 19 June 1716 he was elevated to the peerage as Baron Onslow of Onslow, Shropshire, and of Clandon, Surrey, and the following month (6 July) he was appointed lord lieutenant of Surrey.

Onslow died of fever on 5 December 1717 at Soho Square, London, and was buried on 13 December at Merrow, Surrey. His estate passed to his eldest son, Thomas.　　　　　　　　　　　　　　KATHRYN ELLIS

Sources 'Onslow, Sir Richard, 3rd bt', HoP, Commons, 1690–1715 [draft] · GEC, Peerage · The manuscripts of the earl of Buckinghamshire, the earl of Lindsey … and James Round, HMC, 38 (1895) · C. E. Vulliamy, The Onslow family, 1528–1874: with some account of their times (1953) · J. S. Crossette, 'Onslow, Richard', HoP, Commons, 1660–90 · Bishop Burnet's History, vol. 5 · O. Manning and W. Bray, The history and antiquities of the county of Surrey, 1 (1804) · O. Manning and W. Bray, The history and antiquities of the county of Surrey, 3 (1814) · A. Boyer, The political state of Great Britain, 14 (1717), 622–3 · Le Neve's Pedigrees of the knights, ed. G. W. Marshall, Harleian Society, 8 (1873) · IGI · Historical Register [with] the Chronological Register, 3 (1718) · Foster, Alum. Oxon. · M. W. Helms and J. S. Crossette, 'Onslow, Arthur', HoP, Commons, 1660–90

Likenesses attrib. G. Kneller, oils, Clandon Park, Surrey · attrib. G. Kneller, oils, Clandon Park, Surrey · G. Kneller, portrait, priv. coll.; repro. in Vulliamy, Onslow family · oils, Gov. Art Coll.; repro. in A. I. Dasent, Speakers of the House of Commons (1911)

Onslow, Sir Richard, first baronet (1741–1817), naval officer, was born on 23 June 1741, the younger son of Lieutenant-General Richard Onslow (c.1697–1760) and Pooley, daughter of Charles Walton of Little Burstead, Essex; his elder brother was George *Onslow (1731–1792). Arthur *Onslow, speaker of the House of Commons, was his uncle, and this 'interest' brought the young Richard rapid promotion. In the East Indies, Vice-Admiral George Pocock made him fourth lieutenant of the Sunderland on 17 December 1758; fifth of the Grafton on 3 March 1759 and, on 17 March 1760, fourth of the Yarmouth, Pocock's flagship, in which he returned to England. On 11 February 1761 he became commander of the Martin cruising the Skagerrak, until promoted on 14 April 1762 to captain of the Humber (40 guns), which he joined in June. The Humber was wrecked off Flamborough Head on her return from the Baltic in September, but Onslow was acquitted at a court martial (the pilot being blamed) and was appointed to the Phoenix on 29 November.

As a founder member in 1765 of the Navy Society dining club Onslow indulged 'a nautical predilection for conviviality' (Franks, 328). From 18 January 1766 to 1769 he commanded the frigate Aquilon in the Mediterranean and, from 12 October 1770, the Diana in the West Indies. On 18 January 1773 George Rodney gave him the Achilles, in which he returned to England, where he acquired an estate. In the same year he married Anne Michell, daughter of Commodore Matthew Michell, with whom he had three sons and four daughters.

After three years ashore Onslow was appointed to the St Albans (64 guns) on 31 October 1776, and in April 1777 took a convoy to New York, joining Howe's fleet in time to take part in the frustration of D'Estaing at Sandy Hook on 22 July. On 4 November 1778 he sailed for the West Indies with Commodore William Hotham, and was involved in both the capture of St Lucia and its subsequent defence against D'Estaing's attempt to retake the island in the Cul-de-Sac (15–29 December).

In August 1779 Onslow arrived at Spithead with a convoy from St Kitts, and in February 1780 joined Admiral Francis Geary's Channel Fleet in the Bellona (74 guns), capturing the Dutch Prinses Carolina (54 guns) on 30 December. Onslow was next involved in the relief of Gibraltar by Admiral George Darby in April 1781, and again under Howe in October 1782, when he took part in the night action of the 21st. Later, the Bellona captured La Solitaire in the West Indies, before Onslow returned to England and peacetime half pay in June 1783. Early in 1789 he was appointed to the Magnificent (74 guns) at Portsmouth, and during that summer, while at Weymouth, the royal family apparently made some short cruises in her. Unemployed again from September 1791 to 1796 (but promoted rear-admiral of the white on 1 February 1793 and vice-admiral on 4 July 1794), he became port admiral at Portsmouth in 1796, and then in November, in the Nassau, second-in-command of the North Sea Fleet under Admiral Adam Duncan.

During the mutinies of 1797, when the fleet was at Yarmouth, Duncan reported on 1 May that 'a rising in the Nassau was suppressed by Admiral Onslow', and on the 14th that he 'had sent Onslow to quell the Adamant' (Franks, 332). On 26 May the Nassau refused to sail, so Onslow shifted his flag to the Adamant, and from 30 May to 17 June, when the mutiny ended, Duncan in the Venerable and Onslow in the Adamant were alone off the Texel, keeping up an elaborate ruse of signals to an imaginary fleet over the horizon. On 25 July Onslow moved to the Monarch (74 guns), in which he took a leading role in the battle of Camperdown on 11 October 1797. Reputedly, his flag captain, Edward O'Bryen, observed that the enemy ships were too close together for him to get between. Onslow is supposed to have replied 'The Monarch will make a passage' (Vulliamy, 242), and certainly she was the first to cut through the Dutch line and luff up alongside the Jupiter (72 guns), flagship of Vice-Admiral Reyntjes, whose surrender Onslow took. In appreciation, Onslow was created a baronet, and the corporation of London presented him with the freedom of the City and a 100 guinea sword.

Granted sick leave on 10 December 1798, Onslow retired from the sea. Admiral of the red on 9 November 1805, and a GCB in 1815, he died at Southampton on 27 December 1817, leaving directions that no more than £20 was to be spent on his funeral 'to prevent any unnecessary ostentation; the funeral of a brave and honest sailor costs a much less sum' (Franks, 337).　　　　　　　RANDOLPH COCK

Sources R. D. Franks, 'Admiral Sir Richard Onslow', Mariner's Mirror, 67 (1981), 327–37 · C. E. Vulliamy, The Onslow family, 1528–1874 (1953) · Naval Chronicle, 4 (1801), 94–7 · Naval Chronicle, 13 (1805), 249 · commission and warrant books, PRO, ADM 6/19, 20, 21 · captain's letters, PRO, ADM 1/2246 · W. L. Clowes, The Royal Navy: a history from the earliest times to the present, 7 vols. (1897–1903); repr. (1996–7)

Archives PRO, ADM 1/2246; 6/19, 20, 21

Likenesses attrib. T. Phillips, oils, 1797–9, NMM · D. Orme, stipple, pubd 1799, BM, NPG · P. Roberts, group portrait, stipple, pubd 1800 (*British admirals*), BM · G. Noble and J. Parker, group portrait, line engraving, pubd 1803 (*Commemoration of 11th Oct 1797*; after J. Smart, *Naval victories*), BM, NPG · J. Russell, oils, Guildhall, Guildford

Wealth at death under £1000: Vulliamy, *Onslow family*, 243

Onslow, Sir Richard George (1904–1975), naval officer, was born at Garmston, Shropshire, on 15 April 1904, the second child and eldest son in the family of four sons and four daughters of Major George Arthur Onslow, farmer, and his first wife, Charlotte Riou, daughter of the Revd Riou George Benson. He came of a family which had provided the Royal Navy with many distinguished officers since the late eighteenth century. Destroyers which took part in both world wars bore his family's name. He joined the navy as a cadet in 1918 and was educated at the Royal Naval College at Osborne and Dartmouth.

After two years as midshipman in the battleship *Warspite*, Onslow underwent the usual courses for the rank of lieutenant, in which he obtained first-class certificates in all five subjects; but contrary to the practice of most officers who achieved that distinction he declined to specialize in a technical branch and decided to make his career in destroyers. After serving a successful apprenticeship in a number of ships of that class he obtained his first command at an early age and quickly proved a fine leader and a superb ship handler. He was promoted commander when in command of the destroyer *Gypsy* in 1938 and then served two years in the plans division of the naval staff—punctuated by an adventurous but unsuccessful journey to Bordeaux on the fall of France in 1940 to try to rescue the Belgian government and its gold reserves, a trip in which Onslow narrowly escaped being taken prisoner by the Germans.

In May 1941 Onslow took command of the Tribal class destroyer *Ashanti*, in which he took part in some of the most arduous Arctic and Malta convoys. His service in the former brought him appointment as a companion of the DSO (1942), as well as the Soviet order of the Red Banner; while the part he played in later convoy operations in the same theatres, including the 'Pedestal' convoy to Malta which saved the besieged island (August 1942), brought him two bars to his DSO. Perhaps his most famous exploit was his attempt to tow a very badly damaged sister ship 700 miles to safety through stormy Arctic waters.

In 1944 Onslow was promoted captain (D) and given command of a destroyer flotilla which joined the Eastern Fleet as part of the reinforcements being sent out to take the offensive against Japan. For his part in the attack on Sabang, Sumatra (25 July 1944), he received a third bar to his DSO. He then took his flotilla to join the British Pacific Fleet and played a distinguished part in all that fleet's operations during the final stage of the war against Japan.

After the war Onslow first took the Imperial Defence College course in 1946 and the following year became naval officer in charge, Londonderry, and director of the Joint Anti-Submarine School, after which he returned in 1947 to the naval staff as director of the tactics and staff duties division. His next sea appointment (1951) was in command of the cadet training cruiser *Devonshire*—in which one of his sons was undergoing training. He was promoted rear-admiral in July 1952 and became naval secretary to the first lord of the Admiralty, J. P. L. Thomas, after which he hoisted his flag afloat as flag officer (flotillas) and second in command of the Home Fleet (1955–6). He was promoted vice-admiral while holding that appointment and at the end of the usual term he was given command of the Reserve Fleet (1956–7). In 1958 he was promoted admiral and hoisted his flag as commander-in-chief, Plymouth. While holding that appointment an unexpected vacancy occurred in the command of the Mediterranean Fleet and it was offered to Onslow. Despite the fact that to hold that key appointment might have led to his becoming first sea lord he tactfully declined it—possibly because the rigours of his war service had begun to take toll of his health.

In 1932 Onslow married Kathleen Meriel, daughter of Edmund Coston Taylor, cotton merchant, of Longnor Bank House, Shrewsbury. They had two sons. In 1958 he was appointed KCB (having been created CB in 1954) and retired two years later, returning to the county where his family's roots spread so deeply. He was appointed deputy lieutenant of Shropshire in 1960 and gave much time to local and naval charitable organizations.

The outstanding feature of Onslow's career was the profound respect and affection which he inspired in the officers and men of all the ships which he commanded. Under the most taxing circumstances he invariably showed the greatest gift of leadership, as well as a sense of humour which made him one of the best-loved officers of his generation. Onslow died at Dorrington, Shropshire, on 16 December 1975.   STEPHEN W. ROSKILL, *rev.*

Sources S. W. Roskill, *The war at sea, 1939–1945*, 3 vols. in 4 (1954–61) · *Naval Review*, 68/2 (April 1980) · *The Times* (18 Dec 1975) · personal knowledge (1986) · *CGPLA Eng. & Wales* (1976)

Archives FILM IWM FVA, actuality footage · IWM FVA, news footage

Wealth at death £93,174: probate, 27 Jan 1976, *CGPLA Eng. & Wales*

Onslow, Thomas (1754–1827). *See under* Onslow, George, first earl of Onslow (1731–1814).

Onslow, William Hillier, fourth earl of Onslow (1853–1911), politician and colonial governor, was born at Alresford, Hampshire, on 7 March 1853, the only child of George Augustus Cranley Onslow (1813–13 April 1855) of Alresford, Hampshire, who was the nephew of Arthur George, third earl, and grandson of Thomas, second earl. The mother of the fourth earl was Mary Harriet Ann, eldest daughter of Lieutenant-General William Fraser Bentinck Loftus of Kilbride, co. Wicklow, Ireland; she died on 7 November 1880. William Hillier Onslow succeeded his great-uncle as fourth earl in October 1870, and thus, at the age of seventeen, inherited an estate of 13,488 acres (worth nearly £11,000 p.a.), chiefly in Surrey and Essex. He was educated at Eton College, and entered Exeter College, Oxford, in 1871 but left after a year without taking a

William Hillier Onslow, fourth earl of Onslow (1853–1911), by Bassano, 1895

degree. On 3 February 1875 he married the Hon. Florence Coulston Gardner, elder daughter of Alan Legge, third Baron Gardner; she died on 8 August 1934.

While still in his mid-twenties, Onslow was appointed a lord-in-waiting in February 1880 in Lord Beaconsfield's Conservative administration, holding office until the government was dissolved two months later; he represented the Local Government Board in the House of Lords. He held no office in the brief tory government of 1885–6, but was again appointed a lord-in-waiting after Salisbury's sweeping win at the 1886 election, holding office from 5 August 1886 until 21 February 1887. He then held the positions of parliamentary under-secretary of state for the colonies (from 16 February 1887 until 20 February 1888) and parliamentary secretary to the Board of Trade (from 21 February 1888 until 1 January 1889). While at the former office, in April 1887, Onslow served as vice-president of the first Colonial Conference and was a delegate to the Sugar Bounties Conference in 1887–8.

In November 1888, at the age of only thirty-five, Onslow was appointed governor of New Zealand, assuming office on 2 May 1889 and holding it until 24 February 1892. Historians concur that he was a successful governor, businesslike and frank in character, who was, nevertheless, unpopular and unhappy in his political dealings. When the government of Sir Harry Atkinson was defeated at the polls in December 1890, it recommended to Onslow that he approve several appointments to the legislative council (the appointed upper house). He refused to make more

than six and these only on assurance that they were needed to strengthen the chamber and not to reward party services. His decision did not please the incoming government of John Ballance, who protested to the governor against the appointments on the grounds that they were unconstitutional. Onslow's reply was the brusque one that they had already been made and that he was responsible only to the Colonial Office. He was also instrumental in achieving a clarification, throughout the empire, of the responsibility of the governor and ministers in regard to the exercise of the prerogative of mercy. In a particular case, in February 1891, the New Zealand cabinet had asserted its right to advise the governor upon this subject as upon all others. Onslow accepted this advice, but asked that the matter should be made clear in royal instructions. This received the agreement of all other colonies and it was regularized accordingly.

In New Zealand, Onslow took a considerable interest in the Maori people, giving his second son, who was born there, the middle name of 'Huia' and presenting him for adoption to the Ngati-Huia tribe in September 1891. He also encouraged acclimatization societies, and established preserves for native New Zealand birds. Nevertheless, he was also regarded as aloof from New Zealand society and became embroiled, at the time of his departure in February 1892, in another quarrel over appointments to the legislative council. On this occasion, in contrast to his previous stance, he refused to sanction the appointment of new nominees to the upper house.

When the Conservatives returned to power in 1895 Onslow again held office, as under-secretary of state for India (5 July 1895–26 November 1901) and under-secretary of state for the colonies (26 November 1900–20 May 1903). He took part in the Colonial Conference of 1902 and served as acting secretary of state during the visit of Joseph Chamberlain, the colonial secretary, to South Africa. On 20 May 1903 he at last obtained cabinet rank, serving as president of the Board of Agriculture and Fisheries until 14 March 1905. He was well-suited to appointment to this office, for agriculture and farming in Britain were subjects in which he had long taken a great interest. As secretary of state he set up a number of departmental committees, established a national network of correspondents to inform his department on local conditions, and travelled around Britain's agricultural areas taking an interest in the effect of the railway rates question upon farmers. His responsibilities as secretary were also strengthened by the Board of Agriculture and Fisheries Act of 1903, which transferred control of the fishery industry from the Board of Trade to his portfolio.

While secretary of state, however, Onslow had become convinced that even the Conservative government took no real interest in agriculture, noting that Arthur Balfour, the prime minister, was 'indifferent' to the subject. When the Liberals came to power in December 1905, Onslow became convinced of the extreme 'dangers ahead' to the landed interest from the new radical government. He immediately set out to form an active back-bench organization of Unionist peers, which had never existed before.

He hired a barrister as secretary and expert adviser to this group and established sub-committees to consider legislation introduced by the Liberal government. Dubbed the Apaches by Lord Lansdowne, this group had seventy-five members by 1910, eventually becoming the Association of Independent and Unionist Peers. Onslow's organization was thus perhaps the first of the 'die-hard' tory groups which became so notable a part of the right-wing resistance to the advanced legislation of the Edwardian Liberal government. Onslow held a number of other government posts as well: in 1905 he succeeded Albert Edmund Parker, third earl of Morley, as chairman of committees and deputy speaker of the House of Lords, holding this post until the Easter recess of 1911; he was also chairman of the small-holdings committee appointed by the Board of Agriculture and Fisheries in 1905. For many years he was an advocate of the creation of life peerages to enhance the power of the House of Lords, and also wished them to be awarded to notable colonial figures. Outside government, he was president (in 1905–6) of the Royal Statistical Society and chairman of the Central Land Association.

Onslow also made his mark in local politics, serving as an alderman of the London county council (LCC) (1896) and for a time as leader of the moderate (that is, conservative) party in the LCC. He was also an alderman of the City of Westminster (1900–03). In January 1896, as leader of the LCC's moderates, he led a deputation of vestrymen to see the chancellor of the exchequer to plead for a fairer distribution of exchequer grants—part of Onslow's longstanding concern for the unfair burden of taxation falling on the landed interest.

Although Onslow was forced to sell much of his Surrey land in 1905, he was happiest in agricultural pursuits and as a country gentleman at his home at Clandon Park, near Guildford, Surrey. A bearded, balding man in mature life, he served as high steward of Guildford and was a deputy lieutenant of Surrey. Always a keen sportsman, he was a member of the Coaching and Four in Hand Club. He was created a KCMG in 1887, a GCMG in 1889 (on becoming governor of New Zealand), and was sworn of the privy council in 1903. He died on 23 October 1911 at his son's house, Beechworth, Hampstead, and was buried at Merrow near Guildford. He was survived by two sons and two daughters; his eldest son, Richard William Alan, fifth earl of Onslow (1876–1945), held a variety of ministerial offices, including paymaster-general (1928–9), and was chairman of committees in the House of Lords in 1931–44. His elder daughter was MP for Southend under her married name, Gwendolen *Guinness, countess of Iveagh.

W. D. RUBINSTEIN

Sources M. Fforde, Conservatism and collectivism, 1886–1914 (1990) · G. H. Scholefield, ed., A dictionary of New Zealand biography, 2 vols. (1940) · A. Offer, Property and politics, 1870–1914 (1981) · Pall Mall Gazette guide to the House of Lords (1907) · The Times (24 Oct 1911) · GEC, Peerage · J. Davis, Reforming London (1988) · DNB
Archives Surrey HC, corresp., diaries, and papers | BL, corresp. with Lord Northcliffe, Add. MS 62154 · NL Scot., corresp. with Lord Rosebery · U. Birm. L., corresp. with A. Chamberlain · U. Leeds, Brotherton L., letters to L. H. Hayter

Likenesses Bassano, photograph, 1895, NPG [see illus.] · J. Collier, oils, 1903, Clandon Park, Surrey · Spy [L. Ward], watercolour, before 1905, NPG · J. Brown, stipple (after photograph), BM, NPG; repro. in Baily's Magazine (1882) · Lafayette, photograph, NPG; repro. in Our conservative and unionist statesmen, 1 (1897) · Spy [L. Ward], caricature, chromolithograph, NPG; repro. in VF (18 Aug 1883), pl. 430 · engraving (after J. Collier); formerly at Grillian's Club, 1912 · print (after H. J. Haley), NPG
Wealth at death £74,772 5s. 3d.: probate, 5 June 1912, CGPLA Eng. & Wales

Onuist son of Uurguist. See Oengus mac Forgusso (d. 761).

Onwhyn, Thomas (1814–1886), illustrator, was born in Clerkenwell, London, the eldest son of Joseph Onwhyn, a bookseller and newsagent at 3 Catherine Street, the Strand, London, and his wife, Fanny. In the 1830s and 1840s Joseph Onwhyn published a number of guides for tourists—to the highlands, Killarney, Wales, and the Lakes—chiefly compiled from his own notes and observations. Founded in 1864, The Owl (a society newspaper) was published by Joseph Onwhyn, though its success afterwards affected his mind.

Thomas Onwhyn came to public notice by his contribution of a series of 'illegitimate' illustrations to works by Charles Dickens. He executed twenty-one of the whole series of thirty-two plates to The Pickwick Papers, which were issued in eight (though intended to be in ten) monthly parts by E. Grattan, 51 Paternoster Row, London, in 1837; they are for the most part signed with the pseudonym Samuel Weller, but some bear Onwhyn's initials. From June 1838 to October 1839 Grattan issued a series of forty etchings by Onwhyn, illustrating Nicholas Nickleby. In a letter of 13 July 1838 Dickens referred to 'the singular Vileness of the Illustrations' (Letters of Charles Dickens, 1.414). He objected to piracy but not to imitation and was friendly with Charles Selby, the author of Maximums and Specimens of William Muggins (1841), which was also illustrated by Onwhyn (ibid., 2.332). After his death an additional set of illustrations to The Pickwick Papers made by Onwhyn in 1847 was discovered and they were published in 1893 by Albert Jackson of Great Portland Street, London.

Onwhyn's most lasting contribution was to the ephemeral end of the book trade in the 1840s and 1850s, illustrating the comic side of everyday life. Undertaken for shadowy publishers such as Rock Bros and Payne, and Kershaw & Son, he produced a score of pull-out or panorama books, coloured and plain, lithographed or etched for the popular market. Satirizing tourism, teetotalism, and fashion, they included Etiquette Illustrated (1849), A New Matrimonial Ladder (c.1850), What I Saw at the World's Fair (1851), Mr and Mrs Brown's Visit to the Exhibition (1851), A Glass of Grog Drawn from the Bottle … (1853), Cupid's Crinoline (1858), Nothing to Wear (1858), and Scenes on the Sands (c.1860). He signed his work T. O., O., or with the pseudonym Peter Palette, as in Peter Palette's Tales and Pictures in Short Words for Young Folks (1856). He sometimes etched the designs of others—for example, Oakleigh, or, The Minor of Great Expectations by W. H. Holmes (1843). He was an indifferent draughtsman but showed real humour in his designs. His talent was somewhat overshadowed by those of his most eminent contemporaries such as George Cruikshank and Hablot K. Browne (Phiz). Onwhyn, who also drew views of scenery for guidebooks and illustrated six novels by Henry Cockton, abandoned artistic work, becoming a newsagent for the last twenty or thirty years of his life. He died on 21 January 1886, at his home, 9 Great Mays Buildings, St Martin's Lane, London. He was survived by his wife, Maria.

SIMON HOUFE

Sources M. H. Spielmann, *The history of 'Punch'* (1895) · *The letters of Charles Dickens*, ed. M. House, G. Storey, and others, 1–2 (1965–9) · J. Grego, ed., *Pictorial Pickwickiana: Charles Dickens and his illustrators*, 2 vols. (1899) · *CGPLA Eng. & Wales* (1886) · *DNB* · private information (1894) [G. C. Boase, G. S. Layard, and M. H. Spielmann] · *IGI* · census returns for London, 1881
Wealth at death £235: administration with will, 9 March 1886, *CGPLA Eng. & Wales*

Opdebeck [*née* Douglas-Hamilton], **Lady Susan Harriet Catherine** [*other married name* Susan Harriet Catherine Pelham-Clinton, countess of Lincoln] **(1814–1889)**, figure of scandal, was born on 9 June 1814, the only daughter of Alexander Douglas-*Hamilton, tenth duke of Hamilton (1767–1852), and his wife, Susan Euphemia (1786–1859), daughter of William *Beckford of Fonthill. Her only brother, William Alexander Anthony Archibald Douglas-*Hamilton, succeeded as eleventh duke. Her childhood was spent on the family estates in Scotland and in France, where her father sought (unsuccessfully) to claim the dukedom of Chatelherault. She was a much-indulged, attractive child, with chestnut hair and slightly protruding teeth, calling herself 'Toosey'. She soon learned to manipulate her close-knit family by resorting to illness to avoid the consequences of her actions.

On 27 November 1832 she married Henry Pelham Fiennes Pelham-*Clinton (1811–1864), then Lord Lincoln, the eldest son of the fourth duke of Newcastle. The marriage initially produced two sons—Henry (*b.* 1834) and Edward (*b.* 1836)—but rapidly began to break down, Lady Lincoln alleging that her husband forced sexual relations on her too soon after the births of her children. She began an affair with one of her brothers-in-law, or so her maid claimed in 1837. Lady Lincoln was removed by her indulgent parents to Paris where she became very ill, with what appears to have been the mixture of hysterical and physical ailments which were the pattern of her response to criticism. She was treated with homoeopathic cures, hypnosis, and laudanum, to which she became addicted. A reconciliation was effected, and the Lincolns travelled for some months in Germany and Italy. A daughter, also Susan, was born in 1839, and a son, Arthur, in 1840, but the marriage remained unstable. She had a series of affairs, during which she left her husband and children, but again returned to Lincoln and bore another son, Albert, in 1845. Society was divided in its response to Lady Lincoln, but Prince Albert stood sponsor for this last child, suggesting a surprising degree of ignorance or tolerance from the prudish court circle.

In 1848 Lady Lincoln went alone to Baden, ostensibly to seek medical attention for her deteriorating health, but in

Lady Susan Harriet Catherine Opdebeck (1814–1889), by Jan Frans Portaels, 1859 [detail]

fact to join her latest lover, Horatio, Lord Walpole (1813–1894), eldest son of the third earl of Orford, and a notorious rake. They travelled together to Italy, sometimes claiming to be cousins, sometimes brother and sister. Lincoln instituted discussions with his friends Sir Robert Peel, Henry Manning, and William Gladstone, as to how to persuade 'the errant Suzie' to return, despite the scandal now attached to her name. Gladstone agreed to go to Italy, armed with letters of forgiveness; his diary records in detail the 3000 mile journey which he completed in twenty-seven days. Finding that the lady who called herself Mrs Laurence (or Laurance or Laurentz) was heavily pregnant, and having satisfied himself that she was really Lady Lincoln, Gladstone returned home without her. The baby, registered as Horatio, son of Horatio Walpole Laurent and Harriet, was born on 2 August 1849 in Verona. Lincoln finally sued for a parliamentary divorce, the bill first being heard in the House of Lords in May 1850. Many witnesses to Lady Lincoln's behaviour were called, and the divorce was finally granted on 14 August 1850.

Lady Lincoln, meanwhile, remained in Italy, and resumed the name Lady Susan Hamilton. Walpole soon deserted her, and she turned their son over to the care of Italian nuns. She employed a number of couriers on her various travels, and on 2 January 1860 she married the last of these, Jean Alexis Opdebeck, the son of a Belgian farmer. The marriage, which was apparently re-solemnized in 1862, was, according to Lady Susan, a happy one. By 1880 she was back in England, living at Burgess Hill, Sussex. Money had run short, despite her income from her parents' families (Opdebeck was rumoured to be a gambler); through Gladstone, one of the trustees of the Newcastle estates, her grandson, the seventh duke, was persuaded to make her an allowance of £400 a year.

Lady Susan Opdebeck died at Burgess Hill on 28 November 1889; Jean Opdebeck, her husband of nearly thirty years, reported her death. She was buried at Burgess Hill. Her small estate was wiped out by her creditors. Of her five legitimate children, none but Lord Edward Pelham-Clinton either survived her or enjoyed a reputable career. He was eventually master of the queen's household. Her only daughter, Lady Susan (1839–1875), had a marital career as turbulent as that of her mother, marrying, against her father's wishes, Lord Adolphus Vane-Tempest (1825–1864), second son of the third marquess of Londonderry, who was insane and physically violent, and having an illegitimate child by Edward VII. J. GILLILAND

Sources C. C. Eldridge, 'The Lincoln divorce case', *Trivium*, 2 (1976) · Gladstone, *Diaries* · *The letters and memories of Sir William Hardman ... second series, 1863–1865*, ed. S. M. Ellis (1925) · F. D. Munsell, *The unfortunate duke* (1985) · V. Surtees, *A Beckford inheritance: the Lady Lincoln scandal* (1977) · H. C. G. Matthew, *Gladstone, 1809–1874* (1986) · J. Gilliland, *Gladstone's 'dear spirit', Laura Thistlethwayte* (privately printed, Oxford, 1994) · d. cert. · GEC, *Peerage* · Burke, *Peerage*

Archives BL, Gladstone MSS · Clwyd RO, Newcastle, Glynne-Gladstone MSS · LPL, Gladstone MSS · Sandon Hall, Staffordshire, Harrowby MSS · U. Nott., Newcastle MSS · Lennox Love, East Lothian, Hamilton MSS

Likenesses J. F. Portaels, portrait, 1859; Christies, 27 July 1967, lot 173 [*see illus.*] · J. Swinton, portrait, Brodick Castle, Garden and Country Park, Isle of Arran

Wealth at death none: resworn administration with will, March 1891, *CGPLA Eng. & Wales* (1890)

Opechancanough (*d. c.*1646), leader of the Pamunkey Indians, was born of unknown parentage but was according to tradition the second eldest brother of *Powhatan, principal Pamunkey (Virginia Algonquin) leader, and, therefore, the uncle of *Pocahontas, and was thought by colonists to have lived to be a hundred years old. He is most famous for leading the Virginia Indian uprisings of 1622 and 1644 against English colonization.

Opechancanough, 'a Man of large Stature, noble Presence ... perfectly skill'd in the Art of Governing' (Beverley, 61), was the supreme war leader of the largest and most dominant of the thirty Powhatan tribes, the Pamunkeys. Three centuries of speculations about his foreign origins or education in New Spain cannot be substantiated and divert attention from the more important evolution of his justifiable hostility to the English invaders.

After Captain John Smith invaded his home village near present-day West Point, Virginia, in January 1609—seizing 800 bushels of maize and threatening him at gunpoint—Opechancanough assumed a vengeful militancy that influenced intercultural relations for the next four decades. In the First Anglo-Powhatan War (August 1609–April 1614) Opechancanough's Pamunkeys so intimidated the English that they negotiated a peace rather than attack the Pamunkeys' well-defended capital. When Powhatan abdicated in 1617, Opechancanough assumed his powers and revitalized the Powhatan tribes both culturally and militarily, rejecting Christianity but converting to the use of English firearms.

Opechancanough launched the 'great massacre' on 22 March 1622, slaughtering about 25 per cent of all Virginia colonists in a single day, in order to preserve the traditional beliefs and territories of his people. During the ensuing Second Anglo-Powhatan War (1622–32), his Pamunkeys were formidable foes, wearing armour and firing muskets in open field combat, but they were increasingly isolated when former native allies and old enemies supported the colonists. After several failed attempts to assassinate Opechancanough, the English agreed to another treaty in 1632. But because the English only grew stronger in peacetime at the expense of American Indian lives and lands, Opechancanough orchestrated a third major Powhatan uprising on 18 April 1644, which killed 500 colonists, but only 6 per cent of their population.

Ending a manhunt that had lasted intermittently for a quarter of a century, Virginia's governor, Sir William Berkeley, finally captured the 'Great generall of the Savages' (*Good Newes*, 354) in late 1645 or early 1646, with cavalry trained in frontier fighting. According to Beverley's 1705 account, Opechancanough was an aged, blind invalid when Berkeley transported him to Jamestown, where he was placed on public display. Within two weeks of Opechancanough's capture an English guard shot the old warrior in the back, because of 'the Calammities the Colony had suffer'd by this Prince's Means' (Beverley, 62).

Following the death of one of the earliest and most representative patriot chiefs—the last Powhatan leader who remembered a free American Indian Virginia prior to English colonization—Opechancanough's people suffered confinement on reservations in their own homeland, surrounded by foreign enemies they had understood only too well. J. FREDERICK FAUSZ

Sources *The complete works of Captain John Smith (1580–1631)*, ed. P. L. Barbour, 3 vols. (1986) · P. L. Barbour, ed., *The Jamestown voyages under the first charter, 1606–1609*, 2 vols., Hakluyt Society, 2nd ser., 136–7 (1969) · R. Hamor, *A true discourse of the present state of Virginia* (1615); repr. with an introduction by A. L. Rowse (1957) · S. M. Kingsbury, ed., *Records of the Virginia Company of London*, 4 vols. (1906–35) · *Good newes from Virginia* (1623) · *A description of the province of New Albion* (1648) · *A perfect description of Virginia* (1649) · R. Beverley, *The history and present state of Virginia*, ed. L. B. Wright (1947) · J. F. Fausz, 'Opechancanough: Indian resistance leader', *Struggle and survival in colonial America*, ed. D. G. Sweet and G. B. Nash (1981) · C. Bridenbaugh, *Jamestown, 1544–1699* (1980), chap. 2 · C. Bridenbaugh, *Early Americans* (1981), chap. 1 · P. L. Barbour, *Pocahontas and her world* (1969) · J. F. Fausz, 'Opechancanough', *ANB*

Likenesses engraving, 1624, repro. in J. Smith, *Generall historie of Virginia, New-England, and the summer isles*, pp. 20–21

Opicius, Johannes (*fl.* 1492–1493), poet, is known only by his works, which are unusually uninformative about their author. Evidently, he (or at least his family) was of Italian origin, though nothing is known of his birthplace or training. He may possibly have belonged to the family of John de Opiczis or Opizis, papal collector in England in 1429, and prebendary of York in 1432.

Opicius's poems, five in number, are contained in a humanist, Italianate illuminated manuscript now in the Cottonian collection (Vespasian B.iv) in the British Library. They are: a heroic poem in Latin hexameters on Henry VII's French campaign of 1492, likening it to the epic struggles of antiquity; a pastoral dialogue between Mopsus and Meliboeus in praise of Henry's political settlement in England, using 'Tudor rose' symbolism; an exhortation to mortals to celebrate Christmas, which is likened to an ancient triumph, Christ being repeatedly called 'the Thunderer'; a prayer, in Sapphic stanzas, for the preservation of the Tudor dynasty, mentioning the king's mother, his wife, and their children, in addition to Henry himself; and lines on the presentation of his book to the king, which would have taken place at new year 1493.

These stylish, affectedly humanist poems are the work of a learned, accomplished writer, who was well informed about his English circumstances. In the first of them, Opicius speaks familiarly of Henry VII's 'blind poet' Bernard André, but no other contributions from Opicius to the work of Henry's literary establishment, of which André was the central figure, are known.

DAVID R. CARLSON

Sources BL, Cotton MS Vespasian B.iv · W. F. Schirmer, *Der englische Frühhumanismus*, 2nd edn (Tübingen, 1963) · B. André, *Historia regis Henrici septimi*, ed. J. Gairdner, Rolls Series, 10 (1858) · W. Nelson, *John Skelton, laureate* (1939) · *DNB*

Opie [*née* Alderson], **Amelia** (1769–1853), novelist and poet, was born on 12 November 1769 in the parish of St George, Norwich. She was the only child of James Alderson (*d.* 1825), physician—son of James Alderson, dissenting minister of Lowestoft—and his wife, Amelia, *née* Briggs (*d.* 1784), daughter of Mary Worrell Briggs, from an established Norwich family, and Joseph Briggs, descended from an old Norfolk family but then on East India Company service at Cossambaza, Bengal.

As a child Amelia Alderson was high spirited and impetuous, traits which her mother, who was 'as firm from principle, as she was gentle in disposition' (Brightwell, 12), tried to restrain. Mrs Alderson was 'somewhat of a disciplinarian' (ibid., 6) and forced her daughter to overcome girlish fears of beetles and frogs by holding them in her hand. She was also taught to replace fear of the socially marginalized with philanthropic sympathy. She was fascinated by extremes of human experience, as exemplified by inmates of the local insane asylum, women who disguised themselves as men to follow lovers, and those tried at the local assizes. By her own account, interest in French, dancing, and other accomplishments considered appropriate for a lady began to displace these fascinations by the time she was in her early teens.

Upon her mother's death (31 December 1784), and in accordance with contemporary social convention, Amelia Alderson became her father's housekeeper and hostess. She was later described by a friend as 'universally loved and respected' for uniting 'manly wisdom', 'feminine

Amelia Opie (1769–1853), by John Opie, 1798

gentleness', and 'attractive manners' (Brightwell, 32). She had a flair for dramatic performance and a taste for music. She wrote part of a play based on Roman history and at least part of a Gothic drama. She also completed a tragedy, 'Adelaide', which revolved around family conflict caused by a socially unequal marriage (Macgregor, 12, 14). With her father's sanction, it was staged at Norwich on 4 and 6 January 1791 in Mr Plumptre's private theatre, with herself in the title role and the Plumptre sisters taking other parts (*Ladies' Monthly Museum*, 5, 1817, 62). In 1790 she had published anonymously *The Dangers of Coquetry* (2 vols.). She was vivacious, attractive, interested in fine clothes, educated in genteel accomplishments, and had several admirers.

Political interests Amelia Alderson also had strong intellectual and political interests, which were soon fully engaged. Norwich was then a town of almost 40,000, with a large number of weavers and an influential community of religious dissenters; the Aldersons attended the Octagon Presbyterian Chapel, which had a cultivated and well-to-do congregation, many of whom were Unitarians. Norwich had a relatively large electorate of over 2400; political opinion was divided between supporters of government and whig reformists, and municipal and parliamentary elections were strongly contested. The outbreak of the French Revolution intensified these contests. Alderson's father and his friends were active in Norwich reform movements, then among the most vocal in England. They supported parliamentary reform and repeal of the Test and Corporation Acts, which imposed second-class citizenship on religious dissenters. The Aldersons visited London circles of liberal dissenters and met other reformists at such places as the bookshop of Daniel Isaac Eaton.

In September 1794 some Norwich reformers began a periodical of their own, *The Cabinet*, and Amelia Alderson contributed fifteen poems to the first three issues. Increasing revolutionary violence and warfare polarized public opinion, however, and a large show trial of leading 'English Jacobins', including the Aldersons' acquaintances Thomas Holcroft and John Horne Tooke, was scheduled for November 1794. A month earlier Amelia Alderson had told Susannah Taylor that she was pessimistic at the outcome, that *The Cabinet* was considered a 'dangerous' publication, and that the Aldersons and their friends would emigrate to the United States should the trial have a 'fatal' result (Brightwell, 45–6). Horne Tooke was acquitted, and the government abandoned the other prosecutions; Amelia Opie later denied indignantly William Beloe's story that in her joy she had climbed over benches to kiss Horne Tooke.

Amelia Alderson associated with the controversial literary and political Godwin circle, which included such prominent writers as Thomas Holcroft, Elizabeth Inchbald, and Mary Wollstonecraft, and saw such friends as Sarah Siddons, Anna Letitia Barbauld, and French Girondin refugees. She wrote a tragedy with a view to London production, and submitted it for criticism by William Godwin and others. She attracted the romantic interest of several men, including Holcroft, John *Opie (1761–1807), and perhaps Godwin. Opie was a carpenter's son from Cornwall and a self-taught artist married to a woman Wollstonecraft found 'too much of a flirt to be a proper companion for him'; he divorced her in 1796 (*Collected Letters*, 210). After a courtship of some months, he and Amelia Alderson were married at Marylebone church, London, on 8 May 1798, and then lived at 8 Berners Street. In December 1800 Amelia Opie indicated to Susannah Taylor that she thought herself pregnant, but despite their wish the Opies had no children. Self-conscious about his lower-class origins and culture, John Opie preferred literary and artistic friends to the fashionable circles that his wife enjoyed. Writing to Robert Garnham in 1801 Amelia Opie described herself as 'more a wife of the *old*, than *new* school' (Crabb Robinson MSS). To support their household John left the more prestigious historical and mythological painting for the more lucrative portraiture. He encouraged his wife's writing, and she later declared,

> On no subject did Mr. Opie evince more generosity, and liberality of mind, than in his opinions respecting women of talents, especially those who had dared to cultivate the powers which their Maker had bestowed on them, and to become candidates for the pleasures, the pangs, the rewards, and the penalties of authorship. (memoir in J. Opie, *Lectures on Painting*, 1809, 2.25)

His professionalism, diligence, and independence inspired her, and her literary career developed rapidly.

Poems and novels Amelia Opie published five poems in the *Annual Anthology* (1799 and 1800), edited by Robert Southey and including contributions by many English Jacobins. In 1801 she published more poems with her first acknowledged fiction, *The Father and Daughter*, which her preface asserts is not a novel but 'a simple, moral tale'. This distinction rejects the novel of manners, the dominant form of prose fiction, with its complex plots and numerous characters set in fashionable society, which was often criticized for encouraging middle-class emulation of decadent upper-class life. By contrast, the tale was to be simply structured, appealing to readers' moral feelings with post-revolutionary emphasis on common humanity and sentimentalized criticism of social differences that produce inequality and suffering.

The tale recounts the seduction and abandonment of a naïve young woman by an aristocratic rake, the ensuing grief and madness of her father, the later remorse of the rake, and the reconciliation of father and daughter at death. Such fictionalized social protest was popular with reformists and liberals, and Opie's tale went through numerous editions. Fifteen years later Walter Scott told her 'he had cried over it more than he ever cried over such things' (Brightwell, 175). On it Maria Theresa Kemble based her play *Smiles and Tears* (1815) and W. T. Moncrieff his 'domestic drama' *The Lear of Private Life*; Filippo Casari turned it into a 'serio-comic drama' with a happy ending, later adapted by Luigi Buonavoglia, set to music by Ferdinando Paër (1817); and there was a Russian version to music by I. Svechinsky (1823). As late as 1837 *Blackwood's Magazine* predicted that *The Father and Daughter* 'will endure "till pity's self be dead"' (*Blackwood*, 41, 1837, 409).

In August 1802 the Opies joined other British tourists flocking to Paris during the brief peace of Amiens. There they met the whig hero Charles James Fox, Benjamin West, the Polish patriot Kościuszko, the painter David, the actor Talma, and Helen Maria Williams, and they viewed the Louvre and sites of revolutionary history. After watching Bonaparte at a military review Amelia Opie was left shaking with excitement. In 1802 Amelia Opie also published two books of poetry. *An Elegy to the Memory of the Late Duke of Bedford* celebrates in heroic couplets a leading reformist whig of the 1790s, representing him as a virtuous aristocrat uniting different classes around a patriotic ideology of merit. *Poems* includes pieces published with *The Father and Daughter*. Subjects include 'The Dying Daughter to her Mother', 'The Maid of Corinth to her Lover', 'The Negro Boy's Tale', 'Lines respectfully inscribed to the Society for the Relief of Persons imprisoned for Small Debts', and 'The Orphan Boy's Tale' and 'Address of a Felon to his Child', described in 1894 as 'the most popular of all her poems' (*DNB*). There is the same combination of moral sentiment and social criticism that made Opie's fiction popular and respected, and *Poems* went through six editions in nine years. She was now a public figure, and accounts of her began to appear in magazines. In 1803 the *European Magazine* praised her 'great sweetness of countenance', 'eyes beaming with intelligence and good humour', 'unaffected, affable, and engaging' manners, fascinating conversation, and a singing style that 'reaches the heart' (*European Magazine*, 43, 1803, 323).

Despite such adulation Opie maintained her pace of

publication with *Adeline Mowbray, or, The Mother and Daughter* (3 vols., 1804). It fictionalizes Wollstonecraft's and Godwin's attempt to counter the sexism and female subordination within conventional marriage. The heroine holds similar ideas and refuses to marry, living openly with her lover, until a series of disasters force her to repent of such free-thinking. Though the novel was read as a *roman-à-clef*, Opie generalizes her material as did the novelists of Godwin's circle, links the domestic and the public political sphere, and develops the pre-revolutionary literature of sensibility for post-revolutionary liberalism. Such fiction appealed to many in the reading public, and a third edition appeared in 1810. P. B. Shelley who, like Godwin, objected to marriage on philosophical and political grounds, later claimed to have been persuaded otherwise by Opie's novel, though James Mackintosh thought that it could as easily be read as 'a satire on our prejudices in favour of marriage, as on the paradoxes of sophists [such as Godwin] against it' (*Memoirs of … Mackintosh*, 1.255).

Meanwhile Opie continued her pursuit of music. From the 1790s to the 1820s she published songs to music by composers including E. S. Biggs, Thomas Wright, William Horsley, T. Traetta, James Hook, F. H. Jones, Frances Alsop, Sir Henry Bishop, and Bianchi Lacy. Now she sacrificed attendance at the opera in order to take singing lessons; Susannah Taylor commented, in another magazine portrait of Opie, that she

> created a style of singing of her own, which though polished and improved by art and cultivation, was founded on that power which she appears so pre-eminently to possess, of awakening the tender sympathies, and pathetic feelings of the mind. (*The Cabinet*, 1, 1807, 218)

Opie continued to exercise this power in her writing. In 1806 she published *Simple Tales* (4 vols.), first of several collections of stories varying in length and narrative methods, themes, characters, plots, and modes, from a few pages to a full volume, from common life to high society, from the comic to the pathetic, from the historical to the contemporary, from the sentimental to the Gothic. There followed *Tales of Real Life* (1813), *New Tales* (1818), and *Tales of the Heart* (1820). These collections were interspersed with triple-decker novels, really tales of greater length, including *Temper, or, Domestic Scenes: a Tale* (1812), *Valentine's Eve* (1816), and *Madeline: a Tale* (1822). An anonymously published novel entitled *Self-Delusion* (1823) was attributed to her by the *Ladies' Monthly Museum* (18, 1823, 284), but there is no other evidence it is hers. Her story 'The Ruffian Boy' was turned into a chapbook by the indefatigable Sarah Wilkinson, and dramatized by Thomas Dibdin and Edward Fitzball (1820), and her tale 'Love and Duty' was turned into a melodrama by Isaac Pocock.

In their time, her tales and novels made Opie the most respected woman fiction writer of the 1800s and 1810s after Maria Edgeworth. Francis Jeffrey, leading liberal critic in Britain, reviewed *Simple Tales* emphasizing Opie's ability to represent feelings in 'common' life so as 'to reach the heart of every reader' (*Edinburgh Review*, 8, July 1806, 465). Implicitly, this was a democratic art, uniting readers of different classes in a common sympathy, and

this judgement was echoed through the nineteenth century. In her fiction, as in her poetry, Opie repeatedly links the conditions of common life to those in the public and political sphere; this was a central element in nineteenth-century liberal literature, and kept her fiction in print. The tales and novels, singly and in various collections, were reprinted through the nineteenth century, especially in the United States, with translations of individual works in France, Spain, and Sweden.

Widowhood and society After John Opie's unexpected death on 9 April 1807 his widow returned to her father's home in Norwich. In a preface to Opie's *Lectures on Painting* (1809) she eulogized her late husband in that Romantic genre, the bereaved spouse's memoir connecting intellectual or artistic achievement to private and domestic character. She visited London often, frequenting fashionable and literary society, and meeting such figures as Richard Brinsley Sheridan, Germaine de Staël, Lord Byron, and Walter Scott. *The Warrior's Return, and other Poems* (1808) comprises pieces written earlier expressing sentimental humanitarianism and opposing war ('The Warrior's Return'; 'Lines on the Opening of a Spring Campaign'), slavery ('The Lucayan's Song'), political violence ('Lines on the Place de la Concorde at Paris'), and courtly decadence ('To Lothario' and numerous songs). She had suitors, and Mary Mitford later insisted that Opie had engaged to marry Lord Herbert Stuart. She also corresponded and visited with William Hayley.

Opie renewed friendship with the Gurneys, a prominent Norwich Quaker family, and especially Joseph John Gurney. She addressed him as her 'monitor' (letters of Opie to Gurney, RS Friends, Lond.), and he repeatedly advised her to resist worldly pleasures, in 1817 anxiously inquiring in verse,

> Shall fashion's lure, shall flattery's heartless smile,
> Thy higher, better, safer hope beguile?
> (Braithwaite, 1.241)

She gradually abandoned her family's Unitarianism but continued to enjoy society and admiration. The young dramatist Edward Fitzball saw that 'she was worshipped in society, not only for her great talent and her polished manners, but for her peculiar beauty', which reminded him 'of a lovely Bacchante, it was so voluptuous, yet so delicate and feminine, especially when she sang' (E. Fitzball, *Thirty-Five Years of a Dramatic Author's Life*, 2 vols., 1859, 2.61). The young Anna Eliza Bray met her at Norwich in 1819 and later declared she had rarely encountered a woman 'of such fascinating powers of conversation' (J. A. Kempe, ed., *Autobiography of A. E. Bray*, 1884, 138).

Opie also continued to write. In 1815 she edited her late friend Margaret (Wade) Roberts's *Duty: a Novel* (3 vols.), with a prefatory memoir representing Roberts 'as a wife, that character which is best calculated to call forth the virtues of a woman, and in which the heart and the temper are most tried and most displayed to view' (p. 1.5). In 1818 she told a friend that she was writing eight or ten hours a day. She also tried magazine writing, publishing several pieces in the *European Magazine* (1823): a series of verse letters supposedly written by Mary, queen of Scots, at that time regarded as a victim of religious and political conflicts resembling those of Europe in the early 1820s; a memoir of Henry Bathurst, bishop of Norwich, advocate of religious toleration and champion of Catholic emancipation; and two stories, 'False or True' and 'The Shipwreck', anticipating Opie's contributions to the newly fashionable literary annuals. She also continued to socialize, to follow events and literature of the day, and to enjoy material things such as fine clothes, though frequently reproaching herself for doing so. She admitted to enjoying Byron's *Don Juan*, though she was disappointed to find its reputed wickedness over-rated.

From 1820 Opie's father's health declined. She had attended Quaker services since 1814, and with her father's approval she was admitted to the Society of Friends in August 1825, after close questioning about her willingness to relinquish 'the world' (Opie to Arthur Corder, 4 July 1825, Gurney MSS). Her father died two months later, and at his wish was buried in the Friends' cemetery, Gildencroft, Norwich. Years later, someone's dinner-table reference to a father's affection for an only child caused Opie to burst into tears and flee the room.

Philanthropic work It had taken Opie some years to commit herself fully to the Friends, partly because of the linguistic and sartorial distinctness practised by Quakers, and she told Joseph John Gurney 'of the agony of her mind in the view of changing her dress, and of addressing her numerous friends and acquaintances by their plain names, and with the humbling simplicity of "thee" and "thou"' (Braithwaite, 1.242). At the time Mary Mitford heard that Opie 'is all over Quakerized', though 'just as kind and good-humoured as ever' and after 'about a quarter of an hour's chat' able to forget 'her *thee's* and *thou's*' and 'altogether as merry as she used to be' (L'Estrange, 2.198–9). Opie plunged into the kind of philanthropic work promoted by Quakers. She visited workhouses, hospitals, prisons, and the poor; promoted a refuge for reformed prostitutes; supported the Norwich branches of the Bible Society and the Anti-Slavery Society; and in 1840 represented Norwich at the national anti-slavery convention.

Opie claimed that joining the Friends meant abandoning fiction, which Quakers considered a form of lying, and thus sinful. In December 1823 she told Elizabeth Fry that a novel by her entitled 'The Painter and his Wife' was advertised and several hundred copies had been ordered, but she now intended to abandon it, declaring, 'I have felt the sacrifice, but I do not repent of it' (Brightwell, 190). It would have comprised letters and narration, and presented two women both in love with the same man. In 1827 Mrs S. C. Hall requested a short story for a literary annual, and Opie replied that

> since I became a Friend I am not free to what is called 'make a story,' but I will write a *fact* for thy annual, or any little matter of history, or truth, or a poem if thou wishest, but I must not write pure fiction; I must not *lye*, and say, 'so and so occurred,' or 'such and such a thing took place,' when it did not. (Hall, *Memories*, 169n.)

Opie did however publish fiction of explicitly didactic

and ethical purpose; as she wrote to Gurney years later, defending a new, revised edition of *Adeline Mowbray* and some tales, 'I believe simple moral tales the very best mode of instructing the young and *the poor*' (23 Feb 1844, Gurney MSS). Harvey and Darton, leading publisher of books for children, issued *The Negro Boy's Tale* (1824; reprinted from *Poems*, 1802); the prose *Tales of the Pemberton Family* (1825), resembling 'tales for youth' by the prolific Barbara Hofland; and another anti-slavery poem, *The Black Man's Lament, or, How to Make Sugar* (1826). *Illustrations of Lying in All its Branches* (1825) presents moralistic social philosophy with a taxonomy of lies, particularly those kinds used for social competition and self-interest, and each illustrated by a tale, with the declared purpose of national reform designed to avoid social rebellion.

From 1824 to 1834 Opie contributed thirty-nine poems and prose pieces to literary annuals. In 1828 she published *Detraction Displayed*, a combination of conduct book and social analysis attacking social emulation and competition and defending such frequent objects of detraction as 'authoresses', bluestockings, and 'converts to serious religion', groups in which she included herself. *Lays for the Dead* (1834), her last collection of poems and last book, follows Felicia Hemans's popular treatment of Romantic death, but also resumes central themes of Opie's earlier poems, such as opposition to war, and incorporates expressly religious resignation to divine providence.

Travels and later years Opie continued to take a great interest in public affairs and to compare them to the heady 1790s. She visited Paris in 1829 and felt ambivalent about the restored monarchy and awe-struck at the sight of a guillotine once more erected in public, though to execute a wife-murderer (the only case in which she thought she might support the death penalty). When she heard of the July Revolution in the following year she rushed to Paris and

> was in such a state of uncontrollable enthusiasm, all the visions of human perfectibility which the friends of her childhood had associated with the French Revolution rushing on her brain, that while sitting in the boulevards she sang in her clear, brilliant soprano, Fall, tyrants, fall! (G. T. Mayer, *Women of Letters*, 2 vols., 1894, 2.82)

In her own account, Opie placed the July Revolution in the light of eternity and divine wisdom ('A morning at Paris in 1829', *Aurora Borealis*, 1833, 234–40). She also met the French queen, who claimed to have read her works.

In 1832 Opie gave up her Norwich house for freedom to travel. She toured the Scottish highlands in 1834, went from Belgium up the Rhine to Switzerland in 1835, visited Keswick in 1836, and stayed in London often. In 1851 she went around the Great Exhibition in a wheelchair and, meeting Mary Berry in a similar vehicle, challenged her to a race. She indulged her passion for prisms and for flowers: 'Light, heat, and fragrance were three indispensables for her' (Brightwell, 334). She wrote letters constantly, estimating in 1849 that she averaged six a day plus notes, and she maintained the custom of sending anonymous Valentines. She holidayed at Cromer on the Norfolk coast, spring and autumn, as she had done all her life. She continued to attend trials at London and Norwich.

From 1842 to 1846 Opie looked after an ageing aunt. She herself aged well. In 1842 Caroline Fox reported, 'She is having her swing of London excitement' (Fox, 1.263), and in 1843 found her 'in great force and really jolly'; she 'reads Dickens voraciously, takes to Carlyle, but thinks his appearance against him; talks much and of great spirit of people, but never ill-naturedly' (ibid., 2.24). In 1851 S. C. Hall found her 'a charming picture of what goodness of heart and cheerfulness of disposition can do to make age lovely to the last' (Retrospect, 2.185). In later life she was described as of average height for a woman, with fine hair, fair complexion, expressive eyes, and very fine clothes. Enjoying life almost to the end, she died at Norwich at midnight on 2 December 1853, after a few months of declining health and memory. She was buried in her father's grave.

In 1830 the Edinburgh Review placed Opie with Maria Edgeworth and Jane Austen among the major women novelists of the previous three decades, and defined her particular 'province' as 'the passions' and 'the exhibition of their workings' (EdinR, 51, July 1830, 450). Opie's Quakerism, stressed by her Victorian biographers, obscured the political motive in her fiction, derived from the English dissenting and provincial Enlightenment and contributing to international Romantic liberalism. Well into the nineteenth century critics acknowledged what the Edinburgh Review called her ability 'to interest the feelings of her readers in a powerful degree'. As with Felicia Hemans, this sentimentalism was philosophically grounded, politically mobilized, and essential to her feminized social criticism. By century's end, however, the Dictionary of National Biography could declare that 'Her novels, which were among the first to treat exclusively of domestic life, possess pathos and some gracefulness of style, but belong essentially to the lachrymose type of fiction, and are all written to point a moral.' Such traits were rejected by early twentieth-century literary modernism and remained a problem for the later feminist criticism that retrieved other women writers from oblivion. Late twentieth-century historical and contextual research has initiated new understanding of the complexity and originality of her fiction and poetry. GARY KELLY

Sources J. B. Braithwaite, Memoirs of Joseph John Gurney, 2 vols. (1854) • C. L. Brightwell, Memorials of the life of Amelia Opie, 2nd edn (1854) • C. Fox, Memories of old friends, ed. H. N. Pym, 2 vols. (1882) • S. C. Hall, A book of memories of great men and women of the age, 2nd edn (1877) • S. C. Hall, Retrospect of a long life, from 1815 to 1883, 2 vols. (1883) • C. B. Jewson, The Jacobin city: a portrait of Norwich in its reaction to the French Revolution, 1788–1802 (1975) • F. A. Kemble, Record of a girlhood, 3 vols. (1878) • A. G. L'Estrange, The life of Mary Russell Mitford, 3 vols. (1870) • M. L. Macgregor, Amelia Alderson Opie, worldling and Friend, Smith College Studies in Modern Languages, 14/1, 2 (1932–3) • Memoirs of the life of the Right Honourable Sir James Mackintosh, ed. R. J. Mackintosh, 2 vols. (1835) • M. R. Mitford, Letters of Mary Russell Mitford, ed. H. Chorley, 2nd series, 2 vols. (1872) • A. Opie, correspondence, Hunt. L. • A. Opie, correspondence, RS Friends, Lond., Gurney papers • C. Kegan Paul, William Godwin: his friends and contemporaries, 2 vols. (1876) • DWL, Crabb Robinson MSS • A. Thackeray Ritchie, A book of sibyls: Mrs Barbauld, Miss Edgeworth, Mrs Opie, Miss Austen (1883) • J. Ross, Three generations of English women, rev. and enlarged edn (1893) • W. St Clair, The Godwins and the Shelleys (1990) • Collected letters of Mary Wollstonecraft, ed. R. M. Wardle (1979)

Archives Knox College, Galesbury, Illinois, papers • Norfolk RO, letters • Swarthmore College, Swarthmore, Pennsylvania, Friends Historical Library, papers • Women's Library, London, letters | BL, letters to George Thomson, Add. MSS 35263–35264 • Bodl. Oxf., letters to C. S. Edgeworth • Bodl. Oxf., letters to William Godwin and Mary Wollstonecraft • FM Cam., letters to William Hayley • Hunt. L., letters, mainly to the Briggs family • Norfolk RO, letters to Sir John Boileau and Lady Boileau • Norfolk RO, letters to Josiah Fletcher and Sarah Fletcher • Norfolk RO, letters to Simon Wilkin • RS Friends, Lond., letters to J. J. Gurney and Eliza Gurney, and others • Trinity Cam., letters to Dawson Turner • U. Leeds, Brotherton L., letters to Archibald Constable and the Longmans • U. Nott. L., letters to countess of Charleville • UCL, letters to Lord Brougham • Wellcome L., letters to the Hodgkin family, and poems

Likenesses J. Opie, oils, 1798, NPG [see illus.] • stipple, 1807 (after J. Opie), repro. in The Cabinet (1807) • P. D. D'Angers, bronze medallion, 1829, NPG • medallion, 1829; in possession of Mrs Grosvenor Woods in 1894 • H. P. Briggs, drawing, 1834, Staatliche Kunstsammlungen, Dresden • H. P. Briggs, 1835; formerly priv. coll. • P. D. D'Angers, bust, 1836; in possession of Mrs Grosvenor Woods in 1894 • B. R. Haydon, group portrait, oils (The Anti-Slavery Society convention, 1840), NPG • W. Ridley, stipple (after J. Opie), BM, NPG; repro. in European Magazine (1803)

Opie, John (1761–1807), portrait and history painter, was born in May 1761 at Blowing House, Mithian, St Agnes, near Truro, Cornwall. He was the son of Edward Opie (pronounced Oppy in Cornwall and sometimes so spelled), a mine carpenter, and Mary Tonkin (1713–1805), of the Tonkin family of Trevaunance. (The house, renamed Harmony Cot by Opie's first wife, survives.) He was educated at the village school where he proved precocious, not least in mathematics, which he was teaching to other children by the age of twelve. By ten years old, he had already shown skill in drawing and painting, beginning with a copy of a landscape hanging in Mithian, the house of Benjamin Nankivell in the same parish, and a portrait of his own father. His father, however, disapproved both of this pursuit and of his studying, and early on bound him as his own apprentice and subsequently to a sawyer called Wheeler.

'Discovered' When he was fourteen or fifteen, Opie was 'discovered' by Dr John Wolcot (pseudonym Peter Pindar), an amateur artist and critic who was both a pupil and a friend of Richard Wilson, and who had valuable acquaintances in the artistic world (a portrait of him by Opie is in the National Portrait Gallery, London). Wolcot proved to possess something of genius as a publicist and he and Opie went into partnership in the promotion of Opie's career. To begin with Wolcot took Opie into his own house in Truro, where he evidently coached him to some extent: 'I want to polish him … he is an unlicked cub yet, I want to make him respect himself' (Earland, 14). It became important, however, that he should not become too polished, as Wolcot perceived that Opie's greatest chance of swift success in London was to cultivate the impression of a kind of 'noble savage', 'a wild animal of St. Agnes,

John Opie (1761–1807), self-portrait, 1785

caught among the tin-works', as the Revd Richard Pol-whele put it (Earland, 15). Opie's incapacity to change assisted this impression, and he remained (allowing for the animosity which he sometimes incurred) 'a man of invincible vulgarity'. Opie's first exhibit at the Society of Artists in 1780 was duly billed as 'Master Oppy, Penryn, A Boy's Head, an instance of Genius, not having seen a picture' (ibid., 25). This was nothing like the truth, and by this date Opie had been working for about four years as an itinerant portrait painter in Cornwall, producing works which have been described as having 'unaffected virtues of a high order' (Waterhouse, 263).

Wolcot had attempted in a letter of 25 October 1777 to get Ozias Humphry to take his protégé on as an assistant, without success. In 1779 the two moved to Coinage Hall Street, Helston, and Opie worked there and in Falmouth, with a brief interlude at Exeter and then at Plymouth in 1780, until they both arrived in London in autumn 1781. Wolcot and Opie took lodgings at Mr Ricardo's in Orange Court, Castle Street, Leicester Fields (behind what is now the site of the National Gallery), living at the top of the house, with an agreement that they should share all expenses between them. Opie was now launched as the 'Cornish wonder', and he can certainly not have had any more training than Wolcot was able to give him. His unpromising personal appearance, carefully preserved and touched up by Wolcot, gave credence to the near-fiction created, and he was described at this time by Thomas Hearne, the engraver and publisher, in unflattering terms as 'a rude, clownish boy with lank, dark hair, and a green feather' (Earland, 28), the latter detail presumably being Wolcot's hint at 'savagery'. Sir Martin Archer Shee, who became a friend and wrote valedictory verse in

Opie's praise (published in the preface to Opie's Royal Academy lectures, 1809) described him in 1789 as 'in manners and appearance, as great a clown and as stupid a looking fellow as ever I set my eyes on' (Earland, 73).

Wolcot's stratagem was successful and Opie was immediately inundated with visitors and sitters. As a fashionable curiosity he was presented to George III and Queen Charlotte at the end of 1781 or beginning of 1782. He took with him four or five pictures to the Queen's House (Buckingham House, now Palace), of which the king bought two: *A Beggar and his Dog*, and a portrait of Mrs Delany (Royal Collection), apparently commissioned earlier by the king. Hanoverian parsimony meant that Opie was not well rewarded, a point made by John Williams (pseudonym Anthony Pasquin): 'the zealous youth … carried [his payment] triumphantly home that he might ruminate upon the bounty of his sovereign: he arrived, and, unfolding the paper with a panting heart, saw nine guineas and a half and sixpence!' (Earland, 37). The tale is substantiated by a letter from William Mason to Lord Harcourt (Whitley, 1.378). A second version of *Mrs Delany* (NPG) was commissioned by Lady Bute and originally had a frame designed by none other than the exacting Horace Walpole, who approved of the picture: '*Oui vraiment*, it is pronounced [i.e. striking] like Rembrandt' (letter of 14 Feb 1782 to the Revd William Mason, Earland, 36).

Solid patronage Wolcot introduced Opie to Sir Joshua Reynolds, who was very much impressed and rather crushed his former pupil James Northcote, who was then trying once again to establish himself in London: 'You have no chance here', Northcote recorded Reynolds as saying to him, 'There is such a young man come out of Cornwall … Like Caravaggio, but finer' (Leslie and Taylor, 2.341–2). Northcote nevertheless became a lifelong friend of Opie, for whom he retained the highest regard, remarking to Hazlitt, 'He was a true genius' (Earland, 31), and Opie's portrait of Northcote dates from about 1799 (priv. coll.; see Peter, no. 60).

On 4 December 1782, at St Martin-in-the-Fields, Opie married, unhappily as it turned out, Mary, daughter of Benjamin Bunn, a solicitor and moneylender of St Botolph's, Aldgate. Her father was described as 'a Jew broker to whom Opie used to sell his pictures' (Earland, 46). Alfred Bunn, the tyrannical theatre manager, was apparently a relation of his wife's with whom Opie stayed in touch.

The marriage led to Opie's parting from Wolcot. Opie was earning more than Wolcot, but now had a wife to support. Wolcot, on his side, was later wont to point out that he had given up his medical practice and £300 or £400 a year in order to promote Opie. While they were in partnership Wolcot earned some money with his Peter Pindar satires, which also provided a useful vehicle for favourable publicity on Opie's behalf as, for example, with one of two portraits of the organist and composer William Jackson, exhibited at the Royal Academy in 1783. This was the year after Wolcot had written:

Speak, Muse, who form'd that matchless head,
The Cornish boy, in tin-mines bred;

Whose native genius, like his diamonds, shone
In secret, till chance gave him to the sun?
'Tis Jackson's portrait—put the laurel on it,
Whilst to that tuneful swan I pour a sonnet.
(*Lyric Odes to the Royal Academicians for 1782*, Ode III)

The break with Wolcot was not final at this stage: Opie and his wife together with Wolcot visited Wales in 1783 or 1784, and Wolcot and he toured the south-west in 1783–4, for example, but in 1783 Opie was set up independently by a patron, Richard Wyatt (1730–1813) of Egham, Surrey, in a house in Great Queen Street. His first early success as a curiosity to the fashionable *beau monde* was thus succeeded by solid patronage, and for Wyatt he painted a number of portraits of the Hoare and Burrell families (Wyatt was the nephew of Sir Merrick Burrell, bt, whose portrait by Opie remains with the family (Peter, no. 16). Opie's particular gift for child portraiture was demonstrated at this time (*c*.1784), with paintings of the children of the fifth duke of Argyll and his famously beautiful duchess, the former Elizabeth Gunning (priv. coll.). One of Opie's finest fancy pictures, *A Peasant's Family* (Tate collection) is also of children and was painted *c*.1783–5, while Opie further demonstrated his range in a groundbreaking genre group showing a schoolmistress and her varied pupils (priv. coll.). It was exhibited at the Royal Academy in 1784 under the title *A School* and drew Walpole's approving note, 'Great nature, the best of his works yet' (Earland, 54). At the same time in his more original portraits, for example, *Thomas Daniell and Captain Morcom, with Polperro Mine, St. Agnes, in the Background* (1786; Truro, County Museum and Art Gallery; another version ex Sothebys, London, 13 July 1994, no. 66), Opie developed this same rare seam of realistic genre, of a kind which seems to reach back to John Riley's portraits in the preceding century.

Opie was also attracted, however, by that chimera of the British school, history painting on a large scale. By the winter of 1786 he was signed up to create a substantial number of canvases for Alderman John Boydell's Shakspeare Gallery, a commission mentioned in a letter to the Revd John Owen (Earland, 62–4). This commission followed close upon Opie's dramatic success with his first large history picture, *The Assassination of James I of Scotland*, when it was exhibited at the Royal Academy that year. It was bought by Boydell, as was its successor at the next year's academy exhibition, *The Assassination of Rizzio*, which itself features prominently on the left wall of the engraving by Pietro Martini after J. H. Ramberg of *The Exhibition of the Royal Academy, 1787*. Boydell gave both paintings to the Guildhall in the City of London but they were destroyed in the Second World War. Photographs of them, and the surviving smaller-scale oil replica (on panel) of *Rizzio* (ex Sothebys, London, 25 November 1998, lot 88), referred to by John Jope Rogers as 'the beautiful reduction … which Opie himself made' (Rogers, 56), reveal the influence of Caravaggio, not only in the lighting but also in the gestures, although contemporary reference was more often made to the influence of Lo Spagnoletto (Jusepe Ribera).

One can only speculate about how these influences came to bear upon Opie, since the tracks of his artistic education were so carefully covered by Wolcot, but prints after Caravaggio were certainly in circulation in eighteenth-century Britain. At the time, however, Opie was even more widely talked of as an 'English Rembrandt' and Caravaggio's influence would have been mediated through the many works of Rembrandt which Opie could have come across in English collections. He also gained firsthand knowledge of Rembrandt in summer 1786 with a trip to the Low Countries in the company of his father-in-law and 'Mr Gardner, a painter' (possibly Daniel Gardner, *c*.1750–1805). They took in Bruges, Ghent, Brussels, Antwerp, Rotterdam, Amsterdam, and The Hague, and Opie particularly remarked in a letter to Owen upon Rembrandt: 'We saw some fine Rembrandts—he was wonderfully simple in his heads, & his compositions singularly grand, with prodigious force and roundness, & his colouring sometimes exquisitely true' (Earland, 63).

Royal Academician and second marriage The success of Opie's history pictures assisted his election as associate of the Royal Academy in 1786 and as Royal Academician in 1787, at an early age, although he had failed to become an associate at his first attempt, even earlier in his career, in 1782. From 1791 he lived at 8 Berners Street. His career is one of more or less unbroken success from then onwards but was interrupted by his wife's leaving him in 1795. Opie had apparently been too absorbed in his work, which also included, however, teaching the attractive young Jane Beetham. His wife went out of the house on 20 May 1795, saying she was going to dine with her father, and never came back, having run away to Clifton, Bristol, with a Major Edwards. The marriage was dissolved by act of parliament in 1796, leaving both free to marry again. Mary married Edwards; Opie did not marry Miss Beetham, despite rumours in the press. In 1796, also, he wished to marry another of his pupils, Elizabeth Mary, the daughter of Benjamin Booth (whose portrait by Opie of about 1790 is in a private collection) but in 1797 Booth refused to allow the match. Opie's name was also linked with that of Mary Wollstonecraft in 1796 according to Joseph Farington, but she married Opie's friend William Godwin in March 1797. (Opie's portrait of her, *c*.1797, is in the National Portrait Gallery.) Instead, on 8 May 1798, at Marylebone Church, Opie married Amelia (1769–1853) [*see* Opie, Amelia], the daughter of a Norwich doctor, James Alderson. One of Opie's several portraits of her dates from this year (NPG).

His second marriage was successful, although Opie became more highly strung (or just difficult) as he got older, and, with his encouragement, Amelia became a successful novelist, her first book, *Father and Daughter*, appearing in 1801. She for her part championed Opie, almost to a fault, but Wolcot she refused to tolerate. The break in 1798 between Opie and Wolcot was never explicit, but clear enough for Wolcot to grumble about ingratitude. Following his second marriage the number and size of Opie's fancy pictures at first increased, perhaps reflecting the influence of his wife. In 1802 the two of them went to

Paris, a hard-won holiday on Amelia's part, since Opie was inclined to be careful about money. For him it was primarily a chance to study the huge number of paintings looted by Napoleon from all over Europe, and then displayed in the Louvre. Opie was thus able to see Raphael's *Transfiguration* without travelling to Rome, and Raphael forms a touchstone in Opie's lectures to the Royal Academy, where he became professor of painting in 1805. While in Paris the couple dined with Charles James Fox, in the company of Benjamin West (Opie painted Fox in 1804, a picture exhibited at the Royal Academy in 1805; priv. coll.); visited the studio of J. L. David; caught a glimpse of Napoleon; and met Maria Cosway, and went with her and West to look at the fabled collection of the then Archbishop (later Cardinal) Fesch.

Like many another English artist, Opie was frustrated by having to paint portraits for a living rather than grander history paintings, and his income was also augmented by a few pupils: Henry Thomson RA; Theophilus Clarke ARA; Thomas William Stewardson; Jane Beetham; William Chamberlain; John Cawse; and the amateurs Elizabeth Mary Booth and the Revd John Owen (both referred to above) and Katherine St Aubyn. However, despite his yearning for fancy pictures and histories, and his skill at them, Opie exhibited his last historical painting at the academy in 1804, a scene from *Gil Blas*, and thereafter painted only portraits. The focus and freshness of his vision in portraiture gave way in his last years to imitative eclecticism, picking up a hint of Gainsborough here or a touch of Hoppner there.

Opie's further ambition to become professor of painting at the Royal Academy began unpromisingly with a course of lectures at the British Institution in 1804–5 which he failed to finish. Nevertheless, when, on his becoming keeper, Henry Fuseli resigned the professorship at the academy in 1805, Opie was elected to the post, and the four lectures he managed to deliver in February and March 1807 were both better written and better presented than his earlier series. They were published as *Lectures on Painting* (1809). The last lecture was given on 9 March and, after a visit to Henry Tresham a few days later, Opie caught cold and subsequently a fever. He died in London on Thursday 9 April 1807. Opie's death, which followed the intense preparation of these lectures, and his customary incessant painting, has been partly at least attributed to overwork.

Reputation Opie enjoyed a remarkable reputation in his lifetime, although his own (and his second wife's) high estimation of his achievement has not lasted. He had genuine, if often sarcastic, wit and real talent and produced a handful of striking and original images. He struck a distinctive note among his contemporaries which can still be recognized. Technical shortcomings in drawing and in creating coherent figures, of a kind not unknown among his peers, made him inconsistent as a portraitist, but his fancy pictures and portraits of children can be better than those of almost any British artist of his time. He was not congenial and was liked and disliked in almost equal measure, not always for the right reasons in either

case. It was noticeable at the time, for instance, that he was reluctant to stay long with his second wife's relations on visits to Norwich, and it may be that they did not heartily approve of him. A story told of Amelia's cousin Robert Alderson after the funeral on 20 April (a lavish affair at St Paul's Cathedral, where Opie was interred in the same vault as Reynolds) suggests this family mistrust, and also Opie's idiosyncratic character. The undertaker apologized to Alderson for putting the coffin the wrong way round (with Opie's feet towards the west rather than the east). 'Shall we change it?' he asked. 'Oh, Lord, no!' replied Alderson. 'Leave him alone! If I meet him in the next world walking about on his head, I shall know him' (Earland, 234).   ROBIN SIMON

Sources A. Earland, *Opie and his circle* (1911) · J. J. Rogers, *Opie and his works: being a catalogue of 760 pictures by John Opie ... preceded by a biographical sketch* (1878) · W. T. Whitley, *Artists and their friends in England, 1700–1799*, 2 vols. (1928) · J. Wilson, *The dictionary of art* (1996) · M. Peter, *John Opie, 1761–1807*, Arts Council (1962) [exhibition catalogue, Arts Council, 1962–3] · Waterhouse, *18c painters* · J. Northcote, *Memoirs of Sir Joshua Reynolds*, 2 vols. (1813–15) · C. R. Leslie and T. Taylor, *Life and times of Sir Joshua Reynolds*, 2 vols. (1865)
Archives V&A NAL, notes for a catalogue of his paintings
Likenesses J. Opie, self-portrait, oils, 1785, NPG [*see illus.*] · J. Opie, self-portrait, oils, 1789, NG Scot. · J. Opie, self-portrait, oils, *c.*1790, Tate collection · J. Opie, self-portrait, oils, *c.*1790, Royal Institute of Cornwall, Truro · J. Opie, self-portrait, oils, exh. RA 1801–2, RA · S. W. Reynolds, mezzotint, pubd 1802 (after J. Opie), BM, NPG · S. W. Reynolds, mezzotint, pubd 1809 (after J. Opie), BM, NPG · G. Dance, drawing, RA · H. Singleton, group portrait, oils (*The Royal Academicians*, 1793), RA · pen and ink over pencil (after J. Opie), NPG

Opie, Peter Mason (1918–1982), book collector and historian of the lore of childhood, the only child of Major Philip Adams Opie, of the Royal Army Medical Corps, and his wife, Margaret Collett-Mason, was born on 25 November 1918 in Cairo, Egypt, where his father was serving as an army doctor and where his mother had been a volunteer nurse. His father was later posted to India and died there from a fall while horse-racing. Peter was educated at Eton College, and his schooldays and life in India are recalled in *I Want to be a Success* (1939), written when he was eighteen, which opens: '[This story] is about a boy who dreamed of success ... [but] he could not conceive how the Neon lights were to be induced to take notice of him.' He had also stated: 'I wanted to *do something real now*, not just drift on for a further three years at a University'; in the event the 'something real' was the army.

At the outbreak of the Second World War, Opie joined the Royal Fusiliers, was commissioned in the Royal Sussex regiment in 1940, and after a fall during an assault course was invalided out in 1941. He took up work with the BBC and then, after marrying in 1943 Iona Margaret Balfour Archibald (*b.* 13 Oct 1923), daughter of Sir Robert George Archibald, a specialist in tropical diseases, he joined a firm of reference book publishers (Todd Publishing). Iona's mother was Olive Chapman, the only child of Arthur Cant of Claremont House, Colchester. Iona was educated at Sandecotes School, Parkstone, and had joined the meteorological section of the Women's Auxiliary Air Force.

Opie was still ambitious to be a professional writer; a

volume of impressions of wartime life, *Having Held the Nettle* (1945) and a second instalment of autobiography, *The Case of being a Young Man* (1946) were written during those years. The latter won the Chosen Book competition, and with the proceeds, £337 10s., Opie decided to abandon his job and settle down in partnership with Iona to study the lore of childhood, a subject suggested by the birth of their first child in 1944. The first fruit of this was *I Saw Esau* (1947), a small compilation of rhymes of British schoolchildren, but their sights were set on something far more ambitious: a definitive study of nursery rhymes, their histories, and variants. The Bodleian Library's keeper of western manuscripts, seeing them at work in 1946, suggested that Oxford University Press might be interested in the projected work, and thus initiated the Opies' lifelong connection with Oxford. *The Oxford Dictionary of Nursery Rhymes* finally appeared in 1951 and had instant popular success as well as the approval of scholars. 'Unprecedented in the care which it devoted to printed sources', said the *Times* obituary, 'it nonetheless carried its factual burden with an appropriate cheerfulness and a constant awareness that it was dealing with a living subject'. *The Oxford Nursery Rhyme Book*, a collection for the use of children, followed in 1955 and *The Puffin Book of Nursery Rhymes* in 1963.

From the outset the Opies realized that children's own lore and their games was a subject separate from nursery rhymes, and three books finally came out of this: *The Lore and Language of Schoolchildren* (1959), *Children's Games in Street and Playground* (1969), and *The Singing Game* (1985), completed by Iona after Peter Opie's death. In all these Iona was the field worker, standing in playgrounds taking notes which her husband subsequently wrote up, and later taking over the research work at the libraries. Even in the early lean years they, and particularly Peter, were avid collectors of children's books and all objects connected with childhood, from toys and games to baby clothes and feeding bottles. They amassed one of the most important collections of children's books in private hands; in 1988 it was secured for the Bodleian Library by a public appeal. They had two sons and one daughter. Both the sons inherited the collecting instinct: James became a leading expert on toy soldiers and Robert founded his own museum of packaging in Gloucester. From their historical children's books were derived the Opies' *Oxford Book of Children's Verse* (1973); *The Classic Fairy Tales* (1974), which contains the earliest published English texts of the twenty-four selected stories together with notes on their history; *A Nursery Companion* (1980), a compilation of some thirty facsimiles of early nineteenth-century picture books; and *The Oxford Book of Narrative Verse* (1983). Oxford University made both Opies honorary MAs in 1962.

Opie died at his home, Westerfield House, West Liss, Hampshire, on 5 February 1982, with many books still projected. Among the works he had in mind was a dictionary of folklore (this became *A Dictionary of Superstitions*, edited by Iona Opie and Moira Tatem, 1989), for his interests extended well beyond the study of childhood. He had been president of the anthropology section of the British Association in 1962–3 and president of the Folklore Society in 1963–4, and always hoped that when he and Iona had completed their work on childhood they would be able to return to folklore studies.

Slight and boyish in appearance, Opie was a compulsive and dedicated worker who saw friends and recreation as interrupting his life's purpose. Although in *Who's Who* he gave blackberry picking (with book collecting) as his hobby, latterly he could rarely be persuaded to leave the house in West Liss, Hampshire, which he and Iona bought in 1959 (and had chosen for the space it provided to accommodate their books). Indeed, it is recorded that he only once perambulated the boundaries of the house's grounds.   GILLIAN AVERY

Sources *The Times* (8 Feb 1982) · *The Times* (16 Feb 1982) · *New Yorker* (4 April 1983) · H. Carpenter and M. Prichard, *The Oxford companion to children's literature* (1984) · P. Opie, *I want to be a success* (1939) · *Something about the author*, Gale Research Inc., Detroit, Michigan, vol. 6 · personal knowledge (2004) · private information (1990) **Archives** Bodl. Oxf., MSS · University of Bristol Library, corresp. and statements relating to the trial of *Lady Chatterley's lover* | SOUND BL NSA, performance recording **Wealth at death** £239,861: probate, 3 Aug 1982, *CGPLA Eng. & Wales*

Opobo, Ja Ja of. *See* Ja Ja of Opobo (*c*.1821–1891).

Oppé, Adolph Paul (1878–1957), art historian and art collector, was born at 157 The Grove, Camberwell, London, on 22 September 1878, the third son of Siegmund Armin Oppé, a silk merchant, and his wife, Pauline Jaffé. His birth certificate gives his name as Adolphus Oppé. He was educated at Charterhouse School, at St Andrews University, and at New College, Oxford, where he took first classes in classical moderations (1899) and *literae humaniores* (1901). In 1902 Oppé was appointed assistant to the professor of Greek and then lecturer at St Andrews, and in 1904 lecturer in ancient history at Edinburgh University. In 1905 he entered the Board of Education. Except for two periods of secondment to the Victoria and Albert Museum (1906–7 and 1910–13) as deputy director, and war service in the Ministry of Munitions, he remained there until his retirement in 1938. He served the board as head of the branch dealing with the training of teachers and was appointed CB in 1937.

Apart from essays on classical subjects published while he was at St Andrews and Edinburgh, Oppé's first writings were studies in Italian art: *Raphael* (1909; rev. edn 1970) and *Botticelli* (1911). After these, he wrote almost entirely on British subjects and helped to establish the study of British drawings on a sound and scholarly basis. He had collected drawings, both British and foreign, since 1904, starting with a beautiful early work by J. S. Cotman, and his interest had soon been caught by the then almost unstudied British watercolours of the eighteenth and early nineteenth centuries. In 1910 he made the most remarkable of his discoveries in this field: he acquired for 25s. a lot of seventeen drawings by Francis Towne, including the artist's two masterpieces of the *Source of the Arveyron*. At that time they could be compared only with a practically unseen collection at the British Museum; but some years later a chance remark led Oppé to the Devon home of the Merivales who still owned the mass of Towne's drawings, which the artist himself had left to the family. These and some Merivale papers enabled Oppé in 1920 to establish this forgotten artist's position with an article in a Walpole Society volume.

In 1919, in the *Burlington Magazine*, Oppé had demolished the legend that Alexander Cozens was the son of Peter the Great. Under his iconoclastic pen many similar legends about British artists were to be shattered. It was typical of his painstaking quest for finality that he did not publish any book on Alexander Cozens until 1952 when his *Alexander and John Robert Cozens* embodied the researches of over forty years. In this, as in all his books, his criticism was enriched by his extensive knowledge of the art of other countries and by his classical scholarship. In addition to these works, Oppé published *Rowlandson* (1923), *Cotman* (1923), *Turner, Cox and de Wint* (1925), *The Drawings of Paul and Thomas Sandby at Windsor Castle* (1947), *Hogarth* (1948), and *English Drawings at Windsor Castle* (1950). He also wrote the section on art in *Early Victorian England* (1934), edited by G. M. Young. All these publications exhibited his terse style and exacting and uncompromising scholarship.

Oppé was a born collector. With a perceptive eye, he bought regardless of fashion at a time when drawings were still relatively cheap. His collection included, besides its British treasures, drawings by such masters as Fra Bartolommeo, Giovanni da Udine, Barocci, Veronese, Poussin, and Claude Lorrain. Over 3000 of the British drawings and watercolours from the collection were acquired by the Tate Gallery, London, in 1996. Oppé's judgement of drawings was widely respected, and for the last twenty years of his life he acted as adviser to the department of drawings of the National Gallery of Canada, Ottawa.

In appearance, Oppé had a 'slight, rather stooping figure, sallow complexion, black curling hair, almost unsilvered to the end' (*The Times*, 1 April 1957, 14). The critical faculties which distinguished him as a scholar were reflected in his temperament: shallow learning and slovenly writing quickly irritated him and provoked displays of caustic wit. It was reserved for his friends to appreciate the humour and humanity which complemented his rigorous intellect and to enjoy his 'curious likes and prejudices: he liked long walks and the picaresque novel; he disliked halfpennies and afternoon tea' (*The Times*, 3 April 1957, 13).

On 23 February 1909 Oppé married Lyonetta Edith Regina Valentine (1886/7–1951), known as Valentine, daughter of the Revd Ralph William Lyonel *Tollemache; they had a son and a daughter. Oppé was elected FBA in 1952 and made an honorary LLD of Glasgow in 1953. He died at his home, 17 Cheyne Walk, Chelsea, London, on 29 March 1957. BRINSLEY FORD, rev.

Sources *The Times* (1 April 1957), 14 · *The Times* (3 April 1957), 13 · B. Ford, *Burlington Magazine*, 99 (1957), 207–8 · *Exhibition of works from the Paul Oppé collection* (1958) [exhibition catalogue, RA] · *DNB* · b. cert. · m. cert. · d. cert. · C. Mitchell, 'Introduction', in A. P. Oppé, *Raphael* (1970) · R. Hamlyn, 'In pursuit of the abstract and the practical: A. P. Oppé and the collecting of British watercolours and drawings in the early 1900s', in A. Lyles and R. Hamlyn, *British watercolours from the Oppé collection* (1997), 9–18 [exhibition catalogue, Tate Gallery, London, 10 Sept – 30 Nov 1997, and elsewhere] · J. B. Shaw, 'Paul Oppé, 1878–1957', *PBA*, 64 (1978), 459–65

Archives NRA, priv. coll., diary and notebooks | Vaughan Williams Memorial Library, London, corresp. with Cecil Sharp

Likenesses U. Nimptsch, bronze bust, 1949, BM · W. Stoneman, photograph, 1954, NPG · photograph, NPG

Wealth at death £89,409 4s. 3d.: probate, 3 July 1957, CGPLA Eng. & Wales

Oppenheim, Edward Phillips (1866–1946), writer, was born in London on 22 October 1866, the son of a leather merchant, Edward John Oppenheim, and his wife, Henrietta Susannah Temperley Budd. His father's business was located in Leicester, where Oppy (as he was always called) attended Wyggeston grammar school, gaining a history prize but no other distinctions. In 1882 he was removed from school by his father, on the claim that the family business was in difficulties. However, that action was probably designed to deter Oppenheim from becoming a full-time writer, as was his desire. In part it succeeded, for he worked in the leather business for almost twenty years, travelling to London, Norwich, and the continent and even, in 1892, to the United States, where he met and married Elsie Clara Hopkins of Easthampton, Massachusetts. Theirs was to be a lifelong partnership, little disturbed by Oppenheim's numerous and notorious affairs with other women. They had one daughter, Geraldine, and lived initially in a house 8 miles from Leicester, Oppenheim playing cricket for the village and serving as sidesman in the local parish church.

However, Oppenheim had no desire to settle into placid business life. He had visited Monaco and gained what was to be a lifelong fascination with the opulent life of wealthy British expatriates in the Côte d'Azur. Moreover, his writing ambitions had not been deterred by the indifferent reception to his first novel, *Expiation* (1887), 'a novel of England and Canada'. Instead, after a full day of work, he would spend long evenings in writing. His second novel, *A Monk of Cruta*, did not appear until 1894 but, after that, a growing flood of writings poured from his pen.

Following his father's death (probably in 1898), Oppenheim was able progressively to sever his connections with the leather trade. In 1905 the family moved to Sheringham in Norfolk, where he followed for a while the comfortable life of a country squire. Even so, he did not cease to write. Quite the contrary; his productivity increased. By the end of 1906 he had published thirty novels, notably *The World's Great Snare* (1896), *The Mysterious Mr. Sabin* (1898), *The Man and his Kingdom* (1899), and *A Millionaire of Yesterday* (1900). His work during this period established the genre of romantic intrigue in high places that was to please his public so much.

In several of his early novels, Oppenheim had dealt with the menace of German militarism. When the First World War broke out in 1914, this gained him an appointment with the Ministry of Information in London. A particular responsibility was to take neutral journalists on tours of the front in France—a task he performed better than the writing of propaganda, even on one occasion unmasking a German spy who was posing as a journalist.

During the war and afterwards, the Oppenheims lived in rented houses in London, Devon, and Surrey; then there was a return to Norfolk, with the purchase of Reepham House. Yet Oppenheim was not contented; the lure of the French Riviera was too strong, and his income from his writings growing fast. It was boosted especially by two excellent novels of espionage—*The Kingdom of the Blind* (1917) and *The Great Impersonation* (1920). In 1921 Oppenheim abruptly sold Reepham House and transported his family and possessions to France. After renting several furnished villas, he purchased the Villa Deveron, a house standing by a golf course—golf was a passion—at Cagnes-sur-Mer, about half-way between Cannes and Nice. In that house they remained for almost thirteen years. Those years brought unbroken literary success, Oppenheim's novels and short stories mostly being sold for large sums to American magazines in advance of book publication. His life was one of writing (or rather, dictating to his secretary, for Oppenheim wrote no synopses, building the plot as his ideas flowed), entertaining, gambling (though never for large sums), and romantic affairs, the latter most often conducted discreetly on his yacht, *Echo I*.

In 1934 the Villa Deveron was sold. The Oppenheims moved to Guernsey, buying a house called Le Vauquiédor at St Peter Port. However, this was merely a device to evade French death duties; they continued to spend much time on the Riviera. Oppenheim's writing pace was unabated; his eventual publishing record consisted of 118 novels (five initially under the pseudonym Anthony Partridge), forty-four collections of short stories, four plays, a travel book, and a remarkably uninformative autobiography, *The Pool of Memory* (1941). He was also a skilled illustrator of his own work.

Although he had perceived the German threat that caused the First World War, Oppenheim could not believe that there would be another. In 1938 he purchased the Domaine des Rouguets, near Grasse, and after an unwise return from Guernsey in the summer of 1939, he and Elsie found themselves trapped there by the collapse of France, only managing to escape via Spain and Portugal to England in early 1941. Before such an action was officially permitted, they hired a yacht and were landed back on Guernsey in September 1945—a brave venture, when Oppenheim was seventy-nine and both he and his wife were in poor health. After further conflicts with the authorities, they succeeded in repossessing Le Vauquiédor, and Oppenheim died there on 3 February 1946, his wife soon following him.

Between the two world wars, Oppenheim's novels were rivalled in popularity only by those of Edgar Wallace. They are, as Robert Standish notes, the product of an 'unending battle between the hedonist and the Puritan, the playboy libertine and the hard-headed man of affairs' (Standish). Though romance is rife, bedroom scenes do not figure and children scarcely gain mention. The women are always desirable, the men—though sometimes initially dissolute—always prove, under test, to be of sterling worth. Such novels furnished an escape for readers from their own drab lives into a dream world of adventure, wealth, and luxury. In his time, Oppenheim was called 'the Prince of Storytellers'. Although some of his writings have dated beyond recall and all are now out of fashion, they remain highly readable.   WILLIAM A. S. SARJEANT

Sources R. Standish, *The prince of storytellers: the life of E. Phillips Oppenheim* (1957) · E. P. Oppenheim, *The pool of memory* (1941) · B. Hayne, 'Oppenheim, E. Phillips', *Twentieth-century crime and mystery writers*, 3rd edn, ed. L. Henderson (1991), 819–23 · *The Times* (4 Feb 1946) · J. Barzun and W. H. Taylor, *A catalogue of crime* (1971) · G. Overton, 'A great impersonation', *Cargoes for Crusoes* (1924) · P. G. Wodehouse, *Performing flea* (1953), 130 · C. Steinbrunner and O. Penzler, eds., *Encyclopedia of mystery and detection* (1976) · D. McCormick, 'E. Phillips Oppenheim', *Who's who in spy fiction* (1977), 174–7 · J. Symons, 'Bloody murder', *From the detective story to the crime novel: a history* (1972), 217
Archives Boston University, Mugar Memorial Library, MSS | BL, corresp. with Society of Authors, Add. MS 56767
Likenesses O. Edis, group portrait, photograph, *c.*1900, NPG · H. Coster, photographs, 1929, NPG · B. Pares, drawing, repro. in Oppenheim, *Pool of memory* (1941), dust jacket · Topical Press Agency, photograph, repro. in Oppenheim, *Pool of memory* (1941)

Oppenheim, Lassa Francis Lawrence (1858–1919), jurist, was born in Germany on 30 March 1858 at Windekken, near Frankfurt am Main, the third son of Aaron Oppenheim and his wife, Adelheid (*née* Nossbaum). He was educated at the Frankfurt Gymnasium and at the universities of Göttingen, Berlin, Heidelberg, and Leipzig, where he studied law, philosophy, medicine, and theology. At Göttingen he studied Roman law under the great Romanist Von Jhering, and it was here that he took his doctorate, having written his thesis on a highly specialized area of German commercial law.

Having chosen to devote himself to the study and teaching of law, Oppenheim obtained a lectureship in 1885 at the University of Freiburg im Breisgau, where he was appointed extraordinary professor in 1889. Two years later he moved to Basel, again as a professor of law. He lectured on criminal law, philosophy of law, constitutional law, and international law, but throughout his teaching career in mainland Europe he concentrated his area of further study on criminal law. During this time he wrote numerous works on the subject and thereby acquired a considerable academic reputation.

In 1895, however, Oppenheim moved to England for health reasons. His was not a strong constitution, and he felt that the English climate and mode of life would suit him. It was also convenient in that his brother had been living in London for some time. As a German, Oppenheim had been educated in a civil law system, whereas England was the birthplace of the common law, and since he could not hope to continue his criminal-law studies in a common-law system, he instead turned his attentions to the universal topic of international law, which transcended all common- or civil-law boundaries. It was in this branch of legal study that he was to acquire a much wider reputation.

In 1898 Oppenheim was appointed to a lectureship at the London School of Economics, where he remained for ten years. In 1902 he married Elizabeth Alexandra, daughter of Lieutenant-Colonel Phineas Cowan. She took a strong interest in her husband's work. They had one daughter, Mary. During this time Oppenheim published his *magnum opus—International Law: a Treatise*. The first volume, *Peace*, was published in 1905, and the second, *War and Neutrality*, in 1906. This constituted the most complete and systematic account of contemporary public international law yet published, and it placed Oppenheim among the foremost international jurists of his time. Belonging to the positive school of international jurists he derived the rules of legal science from custom and from the quasi-legal international conventions, and he regarded it as the function of the jurist to ascertain and give precision to those rules—to criticize and suggest improvements, but not to create them, nor to select as valid only those of which he approved. Oppenheim protested against the tendency to deduce the law from phrases, too often uncritically accepted as self-evident truths; and he pleaded for the development among jurists of that wider sympathy with other nations which can only come from a study of their juristic systems and from the cultivation of an international outlook.

In recognition of his standing as an international lawyer, Oppenheim was subsequently elected a member of the Institut de Droit International, in 1911, and an honorary member of the Royal Academy of Jurisprudence at Madrid.

In 1908 John Westlake resigned the Whewell chair of international law at Cambridge, and he insisted that a reluctant Oppenheim stand for election as his successor. Oppenheim did so, and was duly appointed to the chair. At Cambridge he continued to add to his considerable list of legal publications, and in joint authorship with Colonel J. E. Edmonds he wrote the official *Manual of Military Law* (1912). He also made frequent trips to London, to give advice at the Foreign Office and at other public departments on questions of international law.

Oppenheim had taken British citizenship in 1900, and when the First World War broke out he staunchly supported the British war effort. Being a moderate liberal he had always disliked the prevalence in the recently unified Germany of Prussian militarism and bureaucracy, and he denounced the German attack on Belgium as 'the greatest international crime since Napoleon I' (*The Times*, 19 May 1915).

During the war Oppenheim became a corresponding member of the American Institute of International Law. He also prepared useful manuals on international legal subjects for the Foreign Office, to be used by the British delegates at the Versailles peace conference. It was about this time, too, that Oppenheim played a principal role in establishing the *British Yearbook of International Law*. Ironically its very first article was to be his obituary. The European situation also led Oppenheim to advocate strongly the foundation of a league of nations.

The strain of the war overtaxed Oppenheim, and in the summer of 1919 his health declined sharply. He was soon to be awarded an honorary doctorate of letters from the University of Cambridge when, on 7 October 1919, he died

at his home, Whewell House, in Cambridge; he was survived by his wife. He was cremated at Golders Green, Middlesex, on 10 October. As an international lawyer Oppenheim had the very highest reputation, while in his private life he was noted for his personal charm and his great enthusiasm in anything he undertook.

J. L. BRIERLY, *rev.* NATHAN WELLS

Sources *The Times* (9 Oct 1919) · R. F. Roxburgh, 'preface', in L. F. L. Oppenheim, *International law: a treatise*, 3rd edn (1920–21) · E. A. Whittuck, 'Professor Oppenheim', *British Yearbook of International Law* (1920–21)
Archives Trinity Cam., notebooks
Wealth at death £16,765 5s. 7d.: probate, 13 Dec 1919, *CGPLA Eng. & Wales*

Oppenheimer, Sir Ernest (1880–1957), diamond merchant and financier, was born in Friedberg, Germany, on 22 May 1880, the fifth son and eighth child of Eduard Oppenheimer (1841–1924), cigar merchant, and his wife, Nanny Hirschhorn (1841–1912). From the age of ten he was educated in French and classics at the Augustinerschule in Friedberg, before following his brothers Bernard and Louis in 1896 into a clerkship with the London diamond merchants A. Dunkelsbuhler & Co.

Oppenheimer's apprenticeship gave him a detailed insight into the valuation and marketing of diamonds through the London diamond syndicate which handled the bulk of world production, as well as valuable contacts through relatives and friends with many of the leading investors in South African mining. After naturalization as a British subject in 1901, he was sent to Kimberley as Dunkelsbuhlers's representative and served on the De Beers Consolidated Mines Ltd diamond committee which negotiated sales and contracts with the London syndicate—an exceptional position of trust for a young man still in his twenties. His business status was complemented socially by his marriage on 19 June 1906 to Mary Lina (1890–1934), daughter of Joseph Pollack, a wealthy London stockbroker. Her sister married Oppenheimer's brother Louis. From that date Oppenheimer became resident in South Africa on behalf of his firm and immersed himself in Kimberley local government following his election to its town council in 1908 and appointment as mayor (1912–15).

In 1914, with the manager of De Beers, Oppenheimer made a detailed survey of the diamond mines of South-West Africa. When these assets came under South African control during the military occupation of the German colony, Oppenheimer was well informed on their value and production potential. Despite his own contribution to this campaign by helping to raise the Kimberley regiment and organizing a labour force to construct a strategic railway, he resigned his position as mayor in the face of anti-German demonstrations in South Africa. He returned temporarily to Dunkelsbuhlers in London in 1915 to learn the business of gold-mining finance in his firm's subsidiary Consolidated Mines Selection Company (CMS), directed by his brother Louis and the American mining engineer William Lincoln Honnold.

Sir Ernest Oppenheimer (1880–1957), by unknown photographer

By acquiring mining property rights in Far East Rand as a basis for a contract with CMS, Oppenheimer became effectively a co-partner and used this position to found and capitalize a new mining house backed by Honnold and American trusts. With the blessing of General J. C. Smuts, the Anglo American Corporation was registered on 25 September 1917 and Oppenheimer ceded his contract with CMS to the new corporation and became its chairman. From this base Oppenheimer was in a position to organize financial backing for the acquisition of South-West African diamond companies from a Cape Town syndicate which had bought out German owners in early September 1919. The formation of Consolidated Diamond Mines of South West Africa Ltd (CDM) by Anglo satisfied the Smuts–Botha government's concern to keep these assets under South African control and Oppenheimer's personal ambition to secure for Anglo a significant quota of sales through the London diamond syndicate. The coup also boosted Oppenheimer's standing with Smuts, who had come to appreciate his qualities in the south-western mine negotiations and at the Versailles peace conference, at which Oppenheimer was an observer. For his wartime services behind the scenes he was created a knight bachelor on 31 December 1920. Oppenheimer remained a supporter of the South African Party and at Smuts's behest represented Kimberley as a member of the house of assembly from 1924 to 1938 in a safe seat supported by mining interests.

As relations between diamond producers, the department of mines, and the Nationalist government deteriorated in the 1920s, Oppenheimer exploited CDM's participation in the system of contracts by offering in January 1925 to set up an alternative sales outlet for South-West African production on very favourable terms. This, he intimated, would head off the threat of government legislation for greater state control, assure revenue for South-West Africa, and manage through other contracts production by 'outside' producers in Angola, the Congo, west Africa, and British Guiana. For this initiative Anglo and Dunkelsbuhlers were expelled from the existing syndicate and, with government approval, became the nucleus for a rival purchasing organization which was financially strong enough to guarantee production quotas at a period of falling demand. Oppenheimer's triumph in forcing this reorganization on De Beers and other companies was marked by his chairmanship of the De Beers board from 1929.

By then, far greater problems of world recession and over-production from uncontrolled claims in South Africa had to be faced in co-operation with government by purchase of alluvial sites to hold in reserve, by deploying funds to buy up diamonds produced by alluvial diggers, by control of production in Nama Land, and, ultimately, by totally restructuring the syndicate to meet its obligations to producers. This was achieved by ensuring high levels of producer investment in the Diamond Corporation which replaced the old syndicate in 1930, and by setting new quotas which guaranteed a share of sales to state alluvial diggings in Nama Land. To further restore confidence, De Beers mines were closed for a period, while 'outside' production in Africa continued. Oppenheimer accepted the creation by government of a statutory body of miners and officials—the Diamond Producers' Association—in 1934 to oversee all contracts and quotas.

As sales of rough diamonds recovered in the late 1930s, Oppenheimer refined the classification and resale mechanisms of the 'central selling organisation' in London and South Africa, invested in the technology and marketing of industrial diamonds, and centralized the joint ownership of the Diamond Corporation and its subsidiaries under Anglo and De Beers who increased their share earnings and reinvested in other areas of South African industry and agriculture. By 1939 Oppenheimer was sufficiently confident of the continued viability of the worldwide diamond cartel to plan for shifting stocks and sales from London to the United States, closer to the main market for cut and industrial stones, a move which was stopped by wartime controls and the British Board of Trade. A further part of his plan to centre classification in Johannesburg and Kimberley was, however, implemented in the 1950s and 1960s, when government and diamond interests co-operated actively for tax advantages and investment in South African industrial expansion.

The innovative techniques of group organization with common financial and technical services which characterized Oppenheimer's restructuring of diamond mining in South Africa owed much to his experience of gold mining through Anglo's investments in Far East Rand which were developed more profitably after 1932 and expanded into Orange Free State goldfields, as deep-level methods were applied. Less successfully, Anglo acquired interests in the Rhodesian copperbelt in 1924, consolidating them as Rhodesian Anglo American in 1928 and acting as consultants to the British South Africa Company (BSA). By co-operation with American financial interests centred on A. Chester Beatty's Selection Trust, Oppenheimer safeguarded Anglo and BSA concessions and weathered the 1930s fall in metal prices into more prosperous expansion and support for Northern Rhodesian power supplies, railways, and mining through Rhodesia Anglo Services Ltd (1952) and the incorporation of Bancroft Mines Ltd in 1953.

Similarly in post-war South Africa, Oppenheimer worked for industrial and manufacturing investment on the basis of mineral wealth and improved the country's financial services by founding a finance corporation, a merchant bank, and a discount house. By the 1950s, therefore, his contribution to the economic development of South Africa and Rhodesia rested on his restructuring and relocation of the diamond cartel in South African hands, his successful long-term investment in deep-level gold mining, and his spread of holdings in manufacturing and services. His firmly paternalistic view of the social and political advancement of African employees allowed considerable scope for the improvement of workers' housing and training, but little for political representation.

Like Cecil Rhodes, philanthropy rather than social or political reform provided an outlet for Oppenheimer's keen sense of the innovative power of great wealth. Unlike Rhodes, Oppenheimer's bequests had no commanding focus and included chairs in international affairs, Portuguese studies at the University of the Witwatersrand, a faculty of engineering at Stellenbosch and grants for medical research, Commonwealth studies at Oxford, and a science laboratory at Cambridge. Nevertheless, for his generous bequests and in recognition of his contribution to South African and Rhodesian development he was awarded the honorary degree of DCL at Oxford University in 1952. His benefactions were continued after his death through the Ernest Oppenheimer Memorial Trust.

With an acerbic and forceful side to his public character, Oppenheimer was most at his ease among family and friends. He handled business rivals and political enemies with subtlety and ruthlessness, but was capable of enduring loyalties. He narrowly escaped death on the *Galway Castle*, sunk by torpedo on 12 September 1918, and he suffered the loss of his first wife, Mary, in 1934, followed by his younger son's death by drowning in 1935. He drew comfort from deep religious convictions, marked by his baptism in the Christian faith on 18 April 1935; and he found personal strength in his second marriage, to Caroline Magdalen (*née* Harvey), Lady Oppenheimer (1899–1971), the widow of his nephew Sir Michael Oppenheimer, whom he married on 1 June 1935. The future of Oppenheimer's business empire was secured by the ability of his second son, Harry Frederick, to take up the management of his complex estate with its core family company, E. Oppenheimer & Son, created in 1935 to hold a personal fortune and help finance the founder's public companies.

When Oppenheimer died in Johannesburg on 25 November 1957 there was national mourning and flags were flown at half-mast on all government buildings throughout South Africa. He was buried three days later at St George's Church, Parktown.   COLIN NEWBURY

Sources J. Dagut, 'Oppenheimer, Sir Ernest', *DSAB* • A. Hocking, *Oppenheimer and Son* (1973) • E. Jessup, *Ernest Oppenheimer: a study in power* (1979) • T. E. Gregory, *Ernest Oppenheimer and the economic development of southern Africa* (1962) • State Archives of South Africa, Pretoria, Central Archives Depot • Brenthurst Library, Parktown, Johannesburg, South Africa • C. Newbury, *The diamond ring: business, politics and precious stones in South Africa, 1867–1947* (1989) • C. Newbury, 'South Africa and the international diamond trade, Part One: Sir Ernest Oppenheimer, De Beers and the evolution of central selling 1920–1950', *The South African Journal of Economic History*, 10/2 (1995), 1–22 • *DNB* • *The Times* (26 Nov 1957) • *The Times* (29 Nov 1957) • *Cape Times* (26 Nov 1957) • m. cert.

Archives Brenthurst Library, Johannesburg, MSS | De Beers, Kimberley, South Africa • National Archives of South Africa, Pretoria, Transvaal archives depot | FILM BFI NFTVA, documentary footage • BFI NFTVA, news footage

Likenesses W. Bartis, portrait, 1913, Kimberley Municipality • T. Epstein, portrait, 1936, Anglo American Corporation, Johannesburg • T. Cuneo, portrait, 1954, priv. coll. • R. Tollast, portrait, 1957, Anglo American Corporation, Johannesburg • G. A. Campbell, portrait, 1960, South African Institute of International Affairs • R. Stern, bust, Memorial Garden, Kimberley • photograph, De Beers Consolidated Mines, South Africa [*see illus.*]

Wealth at death £3,600,000: *DNB*; Dagut, 'Oppenheimer'

Oppenheimer, Sir Francis Charles (1870–1961), diplomatist, was born on 17 December 1870 at 1a Russell Square, Bloomsbury, London, the oldest of seven children of Sir Charles Oppenheimer (1836–1900), City merchant and later British consul-general at Frankfurt am Main, and Bertha (d. 1919), daughter of Leopold Goldbeck, a Frankfurt cloth merchant. Francis Oppenheimer (he adopted the middle name Charles on being baptized into the Church of England in November 1892) was educated at the *Gymnasium* at Frankfurt, to which city his father had returned in 1875 for health reasons. In 1890 he went to Balliol College, Oxford, graduating with a second-class degree in jurisprudence in 1893. He was then articled to the chambers of Rufus Isaacs, later the marquess of Reading, and was called to the bar by the Middle Temple in 1895, though he never intended to pursue a legal career. From 1896 he spent four years in Paris as a painter.

On his father's death in June 1900, Oppenheimer succeeded him to the unsalaried post of consul-general for the Prussian provinces of Hesse-Nassau and the grand duchy of Hesse and by Rhine, residing at Frankfurt. Between 1905 and 1912 he established for himself, through his commercial reports, a niche within the consular service which enabled him ultimately to transfer to the more prestigious diplomatic service. His friendship with his Oxford contemporary Arthur Ponsonby, then private secretary to the prime minister, and Sir Eyre Crowe,

Sir Francis Charles Oppenheimer (1870–1961), by unknown photographer, 1900

the Foreign Office's leading expert on German affairs, opened to him a direct channel of communication with Whitehall. The link with Crowe was particularly important for Oppenheimer's further career. The former appreciated the potential value of commercial reporting and the bearing of economic developments on politics. Having established a direct channel to the senior officials in Whitehall, it was the wide range and quality of the assiduously culled 'hard' data in his commercial reports, skilfully combined with political and diplomatic gossip, that established Oppenheimer's high reputation. Though largely and ostensibly concerned with economic, commercial, and financial matters, these reports were remarkable because of the link that Oppenheimer was able to make between economic developments and German domestic and foreign politics—and their diplomatic and strategic implications for Britain. In September 1909, in response to an Admiralty enquiry, he submitted a lengthy memorandum on the efficacy of a naval blockade of the German coastline in a war with Germany, which reinforced the recommendation of the committee of imperial defence to dispatch an expeditionary force to France rather than to rely on blockading the enemy. He also reported on German preparations for financial mobilization for war and concluded with the strong recommendation that Britain should be equally well prepared.

In the period between 1905 and 1912 Oppenheimer became known to a wider public. His printed commercial reports were frequently quoted in the press and in parliament; and David Lloyd George drew on Oppenheimer's memoranda on German social legislation when framing his own national insurance scheme. In October 1911 he

praised Oppenheimer as 'one of the ablest consuls of the British empire' (*The Times*, 16 Oct 1911). Nevertheless, it was also during this period that Oppenheimer found himself the target of a press campaign against Britain's representatives in Germany, whose loyalty was impugned because of their German names. Although he was born a British subject, to many of his contemporaries Oppenheimer cut a somewhat 'outlandish' figure and his German education had 'tinged [his] speech with a foreign accent' (Oppenheimer, 72). He took the unusual step of defending himself in a letter to *The Times*:

> As I was born in London, took my degrees at Oxford, and am a member of the English bar, it is hardly correct to count me among 'the foreigners'. If my family name does not sound English, I need hardly remind you that I share this disadvantage with a large proportion of the oldest families in England. (*Times Commercial Supplement*, 23 Oct 1908)

His German-Jewish name was indeed a profound handicap for Oppenheimer. In 1911 the Foreign Office refrained from appointing him to the Paris consul-generalship for this very reason. These were ominous signs of what lay ahead of him.

In January 1912 Oppenheimer unprecedentedly secured promotion to a post in the diplomatic service with his appointment as commercial attaché for north-western Europe, with the rank of counsellor at the Berlin embassy. The outbreak of war in August 1914 marked a turning point in his career, cutting him off from the sources of information upon which his authority on German affairs had rested. In October 1914 he was sent as commercial attaché to The Hague. It was symptomatic of his ambiguous position in the wartime diplomatic service that he was posted to the Dutch capital without any specific instructions. He decided to devise a system to disrupt the flow of contraband goods through the Netherlands to the central powers. His initiative led to the establishment in November 1914 of the Netherlands Overseas Trust, an ostensibly private company which, in the course of the war, became one of the cornerstones of Britain's blockade policy. In early 1915 he was transferred to Bern, where he helped to establish the Société Suisse de Surveillance Économique on similar lines. By November 1915 Oppenheimer was back at The Hague, where he spent the remainder of the war.

If in previous years Oppenheimer was sensitive about his German-Jewish family background, he now had good reason to be so. Throughout the war, and from January 1917 with increasing frequency, the Northcliffe press poured its vitriol over Britain's 'German' representative in the Netherlands, apparently with the connivance of some members of the diplomatic service. Lord Robert Cecil's defence of the beleaguered Oppenheimer as 'a public official who had served this country during the war with great efficiency and experience' (*The Times*, 9 Nov 1917) helped to put an end to internal intrigues, but it could not silence the Northcliffe press. Lord Hardinge, the permanent under-secretary, evidently intimidated by the press campaign, used a minor dispute between Oppenheimer and the Dutch government as a pretext for his recall in September 1918. On his return to London he was told that in view of the growing prejudice against 'persons in the service with German names or German parentage' it had been decided to send him on extended leave (diary, 21 Oct 1918, Oppenheimer MSS, box 5). He was now only occasionally employed. A special mission to Vienna in 1919 to investigate the financial position of Austria provided a rare break from his involuntary indolence. Symptomatically, his recommendation of lenient financial terms to be imposed upon Austria was disregarded. The economic turmoil into which the Austrian republic was consequently thrown vindicated Oppenheimer. But by that time he had already decided to leave the diplomatic service. In his final interview with Lord Curzon he made no secret of the fact that 'in the service I had always been made to feel … an outsider' (memorandum, 15 Oct 1919, Oppenheimer MSS, box 6/2). In February 1920 Oppenheimer finally tendered his resignation, thus bringing to an end his short but notable diplomatic career.

Oppenheimer spent the remainder of his life entirely devoted to artistic pursuits, although he was actively involved in helping German-Jewish refugees to resettle in England in the 1930s. He had been knighted in 1907, and in 1919 he was also created KCMG. On 2 September 1931 he married Jane Shillaber, second daughter of Colonel Cunliffe Martin of the Bengal lancers, and divorcée of Sir Ernest Burford Horlick, second baronet. She had three children from her previous marriage; there were no children from her marriage to Oppenheimer. The latter published his memoirs, *Stranger Within*, in 1960. He died at his London home, 20 Lowndes Square, on 25 June 1961.

T. G. OTTE

Sources Bodl. Oxf., Oppenheimer MSS 1–21 · PRO, FO 368 and 371 · F. Oppenheimer, *Stranger within* (1960) · *The Times* (27 June 1961) · J. McDermott, 'Sir Francis Oppenheimer: "stranger within" the foreign office', *History*, new ser., 66 (1981), 199–207 · T. G. Otte, '"Alien diplomatist": anti-semitism and anti-Germanism in the career of Sir Francis Oppenheimer', priv. coll. · T. G. Otte, 'Eyre Crowe and British foreign policy', *Personalities, war and diplomacy: essays in international history*, ed. T. G. Otte and C. A. Pagedas (1997), 14–37 · *The Times* (16 Oct 1911) · *The Times* (9 Nov 1917) · *Times Commercial Supplement* (23 Oct 1908) · b. cert. · d. cert.

Archives Balliol Oxf., MSS relating to India · Bodl. Oxf., corresp. and papers | BL OIOC, letters to Lord Reading, MSS Eur. E 238, F 118 · Bodl. Oxf., Crowe MSS · PRO, Crowe MSS · PRO, Foreign Office archives, FO 244, 368, 371

Likenesses photograph, 1900, repro. in Oppenheimer, *Stranger within* [*see illus.*] · drawings, repro. in Oppenheimer, *Stranger within* · photographs, repro. in Oppenheimer, *Stranger within*

O'Quinn, Jeremiah [Diarmaid Ó Cuinn] (*d.* 1657), Presbyterian minister, was born at Templepatrick, co. Antrim, of parents whose names are unknown but who were Roman Catholic in faith. A native Irish speaker, he converted to protestantism about 1635 and was sent to university by Arthur Upton, the proprietor of Templepatrick, with a view to becoming a preacher to the Irish-speaking population. O'Quinn subsequently attended Glasgow University, where he studied arts and theology, and graduated MA in 1644. Shortly afterwards he was licensed by the army presbytery, the first presbytery in Ireland. With the Church of Ireland then in disarray and suffering a shortage of clergy,

Presbyterian ministers could be inducted to parishes, and O'Quinn was ordained at Billy (near Bushmills), co. Antrim, in 1646. He was the first native Irishman to be ordained to the Presbyterian ministry in Ireland, as before the 1640s Presbyterian ministers were brought over from Scotland.

Although O'Quinn had the support of most of the Billy parish, there were a handful of dissidents who opposed his installation, in particular Daniel McNeill, the Church of Ireland vicar who had been ejected to make way for O'Quinn, and Archibald Stewart of Ballintoy. After a thorough examination of their evidence against O'Quinn their accusations of unsoundness of doctrine were rejected by the presbytery. O'Quinn had strength of character, was forthright in public, and had an appetite for debate which resulted in controversy with his own presbytery. In February 1649 he, along with the Revd James Ker of Ballymoney, opposed the presbytery's 'representation'. This strongly condemned the execution of Charles I, putting the fledgeling Presbyterian church on the wrong side of the new military government. O'Quinn's refusal to read the 'representation' in church and his subscription to the engagement of loyalty to the Commonwealth resulted in an order to suspend him from his office as minister. His refusal to recognize his suspension created strained relations with the presbytery. He continued to minister in Billy with the support of his congregation and also of the Cromwellian government, which before long had either imprisoned or forced most other Presbyterian clergy into hiding. However, O'Quinn eventually tired of his exclusion from the presbytery and, acting as mediator, succeeded through his moderating influence in effecting a reconciliation between the Presbyterians and the Cromwellian government in Ireland. Nevertheless, the personal cost to him was great, and he was looked on with suspicion by both sides. His own brethren refused to shake hands with him at the treaty interview in Antrim church, and in a letter dated 13 November 1651 to Colonel Robert Venables, the Cromwellian government commissioners said they had heard that O'Quinn 'is somewhat embittered against the interest of England and hath of late publicly expressed the same in prayers and other public exercises' (*DNB*). They asked Venables to confirm this and suggested that, if true, O'Quinn might be sent away for a while to Dublin or other places where he could preach to those with no knowledge of the English language. By 1652, however, circumstances had changed and he was in harmony with both sides.

By 1654 O'Quinn was a Commonwealth minister receiving an annual income of £100. On grounds of his fluency in Irish he was frequently sent on preaching missions throughout Ireland, for each of which he usually received the sum of £20 for expenses, and some of the written invitations to him to preach survive. In 1654 he was sent to preach in the Irish-speaking west of Ireland, for which he received expenses of £40 from the government. In June of the following year Colonel Thomas Herbert, clerk of the council, wrote a letter to O'Quinn and James Wallis of Manor-Cunningham, co. Donegal, requesting them to travel to Dublin and Connaught, where they were to preach the gospel in Irish. On O'Quinn's return he continued with his ministry at Billy, where he died on 31 January 1657 and was buried. The executor of his will, Teig O'Mooney, received a grant of £25 from the government to pay for his funeral expenses. Part of this was spent on a fine Latin memorial. The present stone in the graveyard at Billy is a copy of the original and is still clearly legible.

Some fifty-three years after the death of O'Quinn his work among the Irish-speaking population was praised at meetings of the Presbyterian synod of Ulster. He and Gabriel Cornwall gained special mention because of their remarkable success in communicating with Irish speakers. Their good example, and the large number of Irish-speaking ministers, encouraged the synod in 1710 to undertake a programme of preaching to be supplemented by the use of bibles, confessions of faith, and catechisms, all then available in Irish. ROGER BLANEY

Sources P. Adair, *A true narrative of the rise and progress of the Presbyterian church in Ireland (1623–1670)*, ed. W. D. Killen (1866), 124, 135, 165–6, 184, 194 · R. Dunlop, ed., *Ireland under the Commonwealth* (1913), 78, 517 · J. S. Reid, *The history of the Presbyterian church in Ireland* (1837), vol. 2., pp.129, 198–200, 250, 253, 264, 320, 499; vol. 3., p.140 · 'Churchyard notes: Billy', *North Antrim Standard* (31 Dec 1891) · H. B. Wallace, *Bushmills Presbyterian Church, 1646–1996: a short history* (1996), 2–4 · J. E. Mullin, *A history of Dunluce Presbyterian Church* (1995), 11–12 · *Records of the General Synod of Ulster, from 1691 to 1820*, 1 (1890), 211 · J. B. Leslie, *Clergy of Connor* (1993), 534 · *DNB* · R. Blaney, *Presbyterians and the Irish language* (1996), 8, 10–12, 21

Orage, Alfred Richard (1873–1934), journal editor and advocate of social credit, was born on 22 January 1873 at Dacre, near Bradford, Yorkshire, the last of four children of William Steverson Orage (d. c.1875), farmer and later head teacher at his own school at Dacre, and his wife, Sarah Anne McQuire (d. 1895). Soon after his father's death the young Orage and his brother and sisters moved with their mother to Fenstanton, near Huntingdon, where her family lived. Raised in simple circumstances, Orage was educated at the local village school, at Fenstanton, where he later taught as a pupil teacher, before entering a teacher training college at Culham, Oxfordshire. In 1893 he took up a post as a teacher in an elementary school in Leeds, and in 1896 married Jean Walker (*fl.* 1875–1927), a skilled craftswoman in the William Morris tradition, who shared his interest in theosophy and the arts.

Even as a young man Orage had wide-ranging personal and social concerns, including not only education, but philosophy, painting, public speaking, literature, Fabian socialism, and religious belief. With the journalist Holbrook Jackson, whom he met in 1900, he founded the Leeds Arts Club, a thriving civic organization. His early passion for theosophy and Plato soon gave way to an interest in psychoanalysis and the mystical tradition, and he and his wife decided to live apart. In 1906 he left teaching for journalism and moved to London.

In 1907, encouraged by George Bernard Shaw, Orage and Jackson bought the *New Age*, a weekly review whose character quickly came to reflect Orage's principles and tastes.

Alfred Richard Orage (1873–1934), by Francis Ernest Jackson, c.1900–01

Eager to encourage young writers as well as to print established names of the period, Orage became the journal's sole editor in 1909. Helped in his work by a number of friends, Orage was especially close at this time to Beatrice Hastings, his partner from 1907 until 1915, whose angry memoir nevertheless reveals her deep feeling for a man of great energy and generosity. Of middle height, with a prominent nose, full lips, and intense, direct eyes under hair invariably combed boyishly to one side, Orage impressed colleagues and strangers as a personally compelling presence, a vibrant and informed lecturer, and a reflective and perceptive mind.

Among the contributors to the *New Age* were such established authors as Shaw and Henry James, yet the journal also included work by new and modernist writers, among them A. E., Richard Aldington, Michael Arlen, Clifford Bax, Hilaire Belloc, G. D. H. Cole, Eric Gill, T. E. Hulme, Storm Jameson, Augustus John, Ezra Pound, Llewellyn Powys, and Herbert Read. In addition to current developments in art and writing, the editor's personal enthusiasms included Russian literature, French philosophy, guild socialism, and English economic theory. Orage printed Paul Selver's translations of Nietzsche's letters to Strindberg; Aldington's translations of selected Latin Renaissance poets; and a translation of Chekhov's 'The chemist's wife'. The *New Age* also published essays on current medical matters (such as 'The psychical treatment of insanity'), on feminist issues ('The male suffragist'), and on social credit ('The nemesis of capitalist production'). Orage's sense of an intellectual world community was also reflected in the journal's articles on such topics as French literary movements, Polish poetry, and Islam, as well as in regular features on foreign affairs. Orage wrote his own column, 'Readers and writers', signed with a pseudonym like many of the pieces in the journal. A book of his essays appeared under the same title in 1922.

The *New Age* had a small but influential circulation, and both before and during the First World War reflected and helped to shape the climate of artistic experimentation in the capital. After the war Orage became interested in Clifford Douglas's economic system of social credit, a theory he advocated in his journal from 1918 onwards. At this time, influenced first by the Serbian mystic Dimiti Mitrinović and then by the occultist P. D. Ouspensky, he also developed a particular interest in spiritualism, and soon became a disciple of the Russian mystic George Gurdjieff. In October 1922 Orage gave up his editorial position at the *New Age*, and spent a year at Gurdjieff's institute, Le Prieuré, at Fontainebleau. There, with a community of followers, he engaged in both manual farm labour and philosophic study. Orage left France in 1923 and spent the next seven years primarily in New York, but travelled and lectured throughout the United States. He had already written extensively on literary and economic subjects, not only in the *New Age* but in such books as *Nietzsche in Outline and Aphorism* (1907) and *An Alphabet of Economics* (1917); now Orage focused his attention on religious and psychological issues. In the course of his tireless lecturing, he formed a relationship with an American woman, Jessie Dwight (*fl.* 1907–1949), who became his secretary. After securing a divorce from his first wife, Orage married Dwight in 1927. With occasional visits to London and to Fontainebleau, Orage remained in America, lecturing primarily on Gurdjieff's philosophy and raising funds for Le Prieuré. Orage's love for his new wife and son, however, forced him to re-examine his involvement with Gurdjieff, with whom he finally broke in 1930. Orage decided to come back to England, and settled first near Rye in Sussex, then in Hampstead, London, with his family, which soon included a daughter.

Returning during the last years of his life to his earlier interests in literature and economics, Orage once more focused his energies on journalism. In 1932, at the depths of the depression, he founded the *New English Weekly*, championing social credit and publishing the work of both established and newly discovered authors, among them the young Dylan Thomas. Ardent, socially committed, and hopeful, Orage remained, in Philip Mairet's words, a lifelong seeker of 'a light that never was on sea or land' (Mairet, v). Orage told Mairet that he found England 'a deadly country: a heaven for the rich, but purgatory for the talented and hell for the poor' (ibid., 116). T. S. Eliot referred to Orage, again according to Mairet, as 'the finest critical intelligence of our days' (ibid., 121). Indeed, Orage worked tirelessly for both the social and the spiritual causes in which he believed, until his sudden death at his home, 4 The Mount, Heath Street, Hampstead, London, in all likelihood from heart disease, on 6 November 1934. His funeral service was conducted by the dean of Canterbury at the Hampstead parish church, after which Orage was buried in the local churchyard under a gravestone carved by Eric Gill.   CAROLINE ZILBOORG

Sources P. A. Mairet, *A. R. Orage: a memoir*, rev. edn (New York, 1966) · P. Selver, *Orage and the 'New Age' circle: reminiscences and reflections* (1959) · L. Welch, *Orage with Gurdjieff in America* (1982) · W. Martin, *The 'New Age' under Orage* (1967) · J. Carswell, *Lives and letters* (1978) · B. Hastings, *The old 'New Age': Orage, and others* (1936) · T. H. Gibbons, *Rooms in the Darwin Hotel: studies in English literary criticism and ideas, 1880–1920* (1973) · D. Milburn, *The Deutschlandbild of A. R. Orage and the New Age circle* (1996) · A. R. Orage, *Selected essays and critical writings*, ed. D. Saurat and H. Read (1935) · *Orage as critic*, ed. W. Martin (1974) · T. Steele, *Alfred Orage and the Leeds Arts Club, 1893–1923* (1990) · C. S. Nott, *Teachings of Gurdjieff: the journal of a pupil* (1961) · C. S. Nott, *Journey through this world: the second journal of a pupil* (1969) · S. G. Hobson, *Pilgrim to the left: memoirs of a modern revolutionist* (1938) · N. Mackenzie and J. Mackenzie, *The first Fabians* (1977) · L. P. Carpenter, *G. D. H. Cole: an intellectual biography* (1973) · *The Times* (7 Nov 1934) · *The Times* (11 Nov 1934) · *CGPLA Eng. & Wales* (1935)

Archives BL, letters to G. K. Chesterton · BL, letters to G. B. Shaw · NL Scot., letters to Patrick Geddes · Ransom HRC, letters to Holbrook Jackson | SOUND BL NSA

Likenesses F. E. Jackson, drawing, *c*.1900–1901, priv. coll. [*see illus.*] · photograph, 1928, repro. in Mairet, *A. R. Orage* · T. C. Dugdale, oils, 1932, repro. in Mairet, *A. R. Orage* · photograph, 1933, repro. in Mairet, *A. R. Orage*

Wealth at death £2161 15*s.* 8*d.*: probate, 14 March 1935, *CGPLA Eng. & Wales*

Ó Raghallaigh, Aodh. *See* O'Reilly, Hugh (*c*.1581–1653).

Oram, Edward (*d.* in or after **1799**). *See under* Oram, William (*d.* 1777).

Oram, Sir Henry John (1858–1939), naval officer, was born at Plymouth on 19 June 1858, the eldest son of John Joseph Oram, of Plymouth, and his wife, Jane Hall. He was educated at private schools in Plymouth and went, in 1873, to the Royal Naval Engineering College at Keyham, Devonport, entering the navy in 1879 as assistant engineer. Subsequently, his three years' higher engineering course at the Royal Naval College, Greenwich, culminated in his graduating top of his year, with a first, in 1882. He then served as junior engineer in the troopships *Crocodile* and *Malabar*, becoming engineer in 1884. He returned to London on his appointment as assistant engineer in the department of the engineer-in-chief at the Admiralty, where he was to spend thirty-three years.

Oram married, on 12 July 1881, Emily Kate (*d.* 1928), only daughter of John Bardens, of Plymouth; they had two sons and two daughters. Promotion came very rapidly to Oram: in 1889 he became chief engineer, in 1893 staff engineer, and in 1897 fleet engineer. In that year he was specially promoted to inspector of machinery. With Richard Sennett he was author of *The Marine Steam Engine* (1898), long the authorized textbook for naval engineers. Oram became chief inspector in 1901 (the title being changed to engineer rear-admiral in 1903); in 1902 he was made deputy engineer-in-chief, and in 1907 he succeeded Engineer Vice-Admiral Sir Albert John Durston as engineer-in-chief of the fleet, with the rank of engineer vice-admiral.

There were problems with early water tube boilers and it was largely due to Oram's tenacity and skill that by 1902 the vessels fitted with these boilers had reached a satisfactory standard of performance. He was a member of the technical committee formed in 1903 to report on the designs for the machinery of the subsidized liners *Mauretania* and *Lusitania*, and he was responsible for the detailed investigations which enabled Durston to recommend the use of steam turbines in 1905 for the *Dreadnought*. While he was engineer-in-chief he introduced geared drive which enabled the rotational speed of the propeller and turbine each to be optimized, with great improvement in economy. He also served on the royal commission on oil fuel and engines under the chairmanship of Lord Fisher.

Oram was appointed CB in 1906 and was president of the Junior Institution of Engineers in 1908–9. He was knighted in 1910, and was elected FRS in 1912. He was president of the Institute of Metals, of which he was a founder member, in 1914. For his collaboration with the United States Navy during the First World War he received the American Distinguished Service Medal. He retired as engineer-in-chief of the fleet in June 1917. He died at his home, Kilmory, Cranleigh, Surrey, on 5 May 1939.

W. M. WHAYMAN and H. A. BROWN, *rev.*
DAVID K. BROWN

Sources D. K. Brown, 'Marine engineering in the RN, 1860–1909', *Journal of Naval Engineering* (1993–4) · private information (2004) · *WWW* · *Dod's Peerage* (1918) · *CGPLA Eng. & Wales* (1939)
Likenesses portrait, repro. in *Obits. FRS* (8 Jan 1940)
Wealth at death £17,302 17s. 9d.: resworn probate, 20 July 1939, *CGPLA Eng. & Wales*

Oram, William (d. 1777), painter and architect, was educated as an architect, and, through the patronage of Sir Edward Walpole, obtained the position in 1748 of master carpenter in the office of works, a post he held until his death. He designed a triumphal arch in Westminster Hall for the coronation of George III, of which he published an engraving by Anthony Walker. His posthumously published *Precepts and Observations on the Art of Colouring in Landscape-Painting* (1810) records only one building designed by Oram, a house in Lancashire. Walpole noted that he 'was bred an architect, but taking to landscape painting arrived at great merit in that branch' (cited in Colvin, *Archs.*, 716). He painted in the style of Gaspar Poussin and also of John Wootton, under whom he may have studied. His works were often applied to decorative purposes and inserted over doors and mantelpieces. He designed and painted the staircase at Buckingham House, and was employed to repair the paintings on the staircase at Hampton Court. He published an etching of Datchet Bridge in 1745. In the same year he proposed a similar set of eight views in Yorkshire and Derbyshire, one of which, *Knaresborough*, engraved by Edward Rooker, was published by Oram in 1745 (Clayton, 159, plate 174). Clayton records that in advertising his views Oram had taken great pains:

> in the Choice of Prospects as well as in the Points of View, in order to render them the most Picturesque that have hitherto appeared: the whole not considered with Respect only to any one Object, as a Town, Bridge or River; but to such only as would make beautiful Pictures. (*General Advertiser*, 19 March 1745, 12 Aug 1745)

'Thus', Clayton observes, 'fifteen years before Gilpin first

examined "the face of the country by the rules of picturesque beauty", Oram was explaining the rules of picturesque composition to subscribers' (Clayton, 158).

In 1765 Oram was elected a member of the Florentine Academy. In 1766 he exhibited three landscapes at the Society of Artists exhibition. Oram, who was generally known as Old Oram, to distinguish him from his son, had died by 17 March 1777, leaving a widow and a son, Edward Oram [*see below*]. In his will, dated 4 January 1776, and proved on 17 March 1777, Oram describes himself as of St John's, Hampstead, and leaves everything to his wife, Elizabeth. His widow gave Oram's manuscripts to his near relative, Charles Clarke FSA, subsequently published as *Precepts and Observations on the Art of Colouring in Landscape-Painting*.

Edward Oram (d. in or after 1799), son of the above, also practised as a landscape painter. He exhibited landscapes at the Royal Academy from 1775 to 1790, and again in 1798 and 1799. He was also engaged in scene-painting as assistant to Philip James de Loutherbourgh, and painted scenery for the Royalty Theatre in Wellclose Square. He was one of the artists patronized, like John Flaxman and William Blake, by the Revd Henry and Mrs Mathew, and he assisted Flaxman in decorating their house in Rathbone Place, London. In 1799 Oram was residing in Gresse Street, Rathbone Place. All later trace of him is lost.

ANNETTE PEACH

Sources *DNB* · Colvin, *Archs.* · T. Clayton, *The English print, 1688–1802* (1997) · E. Croft-Murray, *Decorative painting in England, 1537–1837*, 2 (1970), 251 · Waterhouse, *18c painters* · will, PROB 11/1029, fol. 217r–217v
Wealth at death left leasehold estates, goods, chattels, pictures, plate, jewels and all other personal estate to wife: will, PRO, PROB 11/1029, fol. 217r–217v

Ó Rathaille, Aodhagán (d. 1729), Gaelic poet, was born in Sliabh Luachra, co. Kerry, where his family leased lands from the MacCarthy family at Scrahanaveele, a little over 10 miles east of Killarney. Nothing is known of his parents, but it is suggested that his father may have been from co. Cavan and that he married a woman from the Sliabh Luachra area. The MacCarthys were an old Gaelic family who were, at the time of Ó Rathaille's birth, subtenants of Sir Nicholas Browne, viscount of Kenmare. It would appear that Ó Rathaille was born into a position of privilege and that he was educated at Captain Eoghan MacCarthy's house at Headford, where he would have been tutored in the manner of the Gaelic professional poets of previous centuries. It seems certain that he would also have spent a good deal of time in Glenflesk, at the castle of the O'Donoghues, themselves a notable literary family, and in the big houses of the remaining Gaelic aristocracy in east Kerry and west Cork. As well as giving him training as a poet, this privileged background gave Ó Rathaille a knowledge of English, Latin, perhaps a little Greek, and a familiarity with the literature of post-Renaissance Europe.

Ó Rathaille's world was to collapse into chaos, however, after the battle of the Boyne in 1690. Sir Nicholas Browne, who had supported the Jacobite cause and the Catholic

King James in the Williamite wars, had his estate confiscated and tenants such as the MacCarthys and the Ó Rathailles were evicted from their homes. In his poem 'Créachta Chrích Fódla' ('The wounds of the Land of Fódla'), Ó Rathaille laments the demise of the MacCarthy family and beseeches God to come to the assistance of 'majestic gentle-mannered Erin' who is portrayed as being ravished by 'foreign churls'. Another poem *An Milleadh d'imthigh ar Mhór-shleachtaibh na hÉireann* ('The ruin that befell the great families of Erin') portrays Ireland 'As a land which wolves have spitefully devoured, a land placed in misfortune and subjection, beneath the tyranny of mercenaries and robbers'. It was against this background of upheaval that, about 1708, Ó Rathaille found himself and his family having to move to the area of Corca Dhuibhne in west Kerry where he wrote his great lyric *Is Fada Liom Oíche Fhírfhliuch* ('The drenching night drags on'). Here, he portrays himself as being reduced to eating 'dogfish and periwinkles' and he rages against the sound of the waves which crash below him at night during a storm, crying at the end: 'Were Help to come again to fair Erin, I would thrust thy discordant clamour down thy throat.' In this poem he equates his own desperate plight with the plight of the Gaelic nation as a whole and this is echoed in his later work. It should be noted, however, that the autobiographical reading of this poem, and of Ó Rathaille's work as a whole, has recently been questioned by B. Ó Buachalla and it is probable that Ó Rathaille was never reduced to anything like the grinding poverty suggested here.

In the years that followed Ó Rathaille, then moving between counties Kerry, Cork, and Limerick, composed a number of *aisling* or vision poems. Typically in *aisling* poetry the poet encounters a beautiful but distressed woman-queen who awaits the return of the rightful Stuart king to free her from bondage and, often, she leaves the poet with a message that help is imminent. The *aisling* was to become the most popular form among eighteenth-century Gaelic poets, but Ó Rathaille was perhaps the greatest practitioner of the genre, transcending as he did what, in the hands of lesser poets, was often a repetitious formula. One of his earliest *aislingí* was *Gile na Gile* ('Brightness most bright'), a remarkable poem in which the beautiful maiden tells the poet 'of one returning by royal right', later referred to as 'a man most fine, thrice over, of Scottish blood' who will free her from 'that black, horned, foreign, hate crested crew'. The overall atmosphere of the poem, however, is one of despair and there is a feeling of great anxiety throughout the poem which does not indicate any great hope on the part of Ó Rathaille that the Pretender was in fact about to come to Ireland's aid. By way of contrast, *Tionól na bhFear Muimhneach* ('The assembly of the men of Munster') tells of the poet's vision of the nobles of Munster preparing for the Jacobite invasion and the return of 'the wanderer without a blemish … to his rightful place in his full power and pure beauty'. In *Maidin sul smaoin Titan a chosa do luadhaill* ('One morning ere yet Titan had thought to stir his feet') the poet encounters a group of other-worldly women who light three candles 'of indescribable light' on a hilltop to guide the return of the Stuart pretender to 'rule and defend the triple realm' of Ireland, England, and Scotland forever. *Mac an Cheannaí* ('The redeemer's son') is perhaps his best-known *aisling* and it may date from as late as 1722. It is also the only one of his *aisling* poems in which he adheres quite rigidly to the usual formula and it is written in a more popular metrical form. In this *aisling ghéar* or 'bitter vision', however, there seems to be no hope of the Pretender returning to the aid of 'the maiden mild whose name was Éire' and, indeed, at the end of the poem the poet himself informs the maiden that her 'redeemer' is in fact dead at which she herself is seen to expire. It has been suggested by Owen Dudley Edwards that the Mac an Cheannaí referred to here was James FitzJames, duke of Berwick, who undermined the Jacobite cause by refusing to join the 1715 rising and by vanquishing Spanish arms during the War of the Spanish Succession. This would undoubtedly explain Ó Rathaille's disillusionment in Mac an Cheannaí and it also indicates that, as well as having a deep knowledge of Jacobite popular culture, he had a fine awareness of contemporary European politics and the Jacobite cause.

Ó Rathaille wrote one prose work, some time about 1713, a satire on the upstarts who had made good in the wake of the dispossession of the MacCarthys and of Ó Rathaille's own people. This work is entitled *Eachtra Thaidhg Dhuibh Uí Chróinín* ('The adventure of Tadhg Dubh Ó Cróinín') and purports to describe a gathering of upstarts in Kerry to discuss the repression of the remaining Gaelic nobility of the area which, in the end, descends into violence and bloodshed. The *Eachtra* is heavily indebted to a famous seventeenth-century prose satire entitled *Pairlement Chloinne Tomáis* and it provides interesting insights into Ó Rathaille's view of those who were making good under the new order.

In 1720 Sir Valentine Browne inherited the lands of his father and Ó Rathaille was furious to find that he was not treated with any more favour by Valentine than he was by upstarts such as Tadhg Dubh Ó Cróinín. He wrote of his feelings towards Valentine in *Vailintín Brún* in which he accused Sir Valentine of having 'usurped the rights of the noble MacCarthy'.

Ó Rathaille seems to have ended his days in the Sliabh Luachra area of his youth, and his great valedictory poem is entitled *Cabhair Ní Ghairfead* ('I will not call for help'), popularly known as *An File ar Leaba a Bháis* ('The poet on his deathbed'). Here he portrays himself as close to death and states that he will no longer ask Valentine Browne or anyone else for help but will follow his beloved MacCarthys, who were his people's princes 'since before the death of Christ', to the grave. Ó Rathaille died in 1729 and was buried in Muckross Abbey in Killarney, burial place of the MacCarthys.

BREANDÁN Ó CRÓINÍN

Sources P. Dineen and T. O'Donoghue, *The poems of Egan O'Rahilly* (1911) · D. Corkery, *The hidden Ireland* (1924) · S. Ó Tuama, *Filí Faoi Sceimhle* (1978) · S. Ó Tuama, *Repossessions* (1995) · B. Ó Buachalla, *Aisling Ghéar* (1996) · B. Ó Buachalla, 'In a hovel by the sea', *Irish Review*,

14 (1993), 48–55 · O. Dudley Edwards, 'Who was Mac an Cheannaí?', *North Munster Antiquarian Journal*, 32 (1991), 55–77

Orchard, William (d. **1504**), master mason, was undoubtedly the foremost master mason active in Oxford during the late fifteenth century. From 1468 he had charge of the building of Magdalen College, newly founded by Bishop William Waynflete of Winchester (d. 1486). After the erection of the wall surrounding the site and the laying out of the buildings in 1473, the progress of the works was rapid. In 1474 the college paid Orchard £1 in compensation for the hindering of his own work due to his diligence in supervising the inception of its buildings, and its grant of a rent in 1475 mentions his laudable service and advice. The design of the great quadrangle of Magdalen evinces a determination to outstrip New College, hitherto a yardstick of ambition for Oxford collegiate architecture. Apart from a generally richer treatment, the main innovations are an approach to symmetry, matched at this time only by Henry Janyns's work at St George's Chapel, Windsor, and the integration of the cloister into the lodgings ranges, a feature clearly derived from the cloister court built at Eton College in the 1440s.

The identity of Orchard's other buildings is not revealed by surviving documentation. Nevertheless, there are several mutually reinforcing pieces of circumstantial evidence which indicate that he was responsible for the completion during the early 1480s of the Divinity School. Begun some sixty years earlier, this was the single most ambitious architectural project in hand in fifteenth-century Oxford. It has been suggested that the initials 'W O' carved on five of the vault-bosses commemorate Orchard, and if so, this would be one of the very few instances known from medieval England of according public recognition to an architect.

In wills dated 20 August 1490 and 21 January 1504, Orchard asks to be buried in the church of the Augustinian priory of St Frideswide's (now Christ Church Cathedral). Parallels with the wills of other leading late medieval master masons suggest that this privilege was given because Orchard had executed some notable work, in this case the vault added to the choir, c.1478–1503, and the reconstruction of the cloister, c.1489–99. Stylistic evidence favouring an attribution of the choir vault to Orchard is its similarity in respect of its very flattened profile and its prominent bosses to those of the small fan vault in the founder's oratory at Magdalen. In overall conception the St Frideswide's choir vault is an ingenious variation on that of the Divinity School. That it was regarded by Orchard's peers as an outstanding work in its own right is suggested by the important influence it exerted on the most ambitious vault built in late medieval England, that over the central span of Henry VII's chapel at Westminster (begun 1503).

Orchard was a contractor and quarryman, activities often more profitable than the architect's essential designing and supervisory functions. He fulfilled all these roles at Magdalen, and also at the Cistercian college of St Bernard (now St John's College), where work began in 1502. In 1479 he supplied stone for Bishop Waynflete's works at Eton College from a quarry at Headington which he leased from the king. He himself owned rights in another Headington quarry of 2½ acres which he bequeathed to a son referred to as 'John the younger', who was presumably intended to follow his father's line of work. William Orchard married twice. His first wife, Agnes, mentioned in the 1470s and also in the will of 1490, would have been the mother of an elder son John, who was a chorister at Magdalen, studied there in 1485–7 with the support of an exhibition provided by his father, and took the BCL degree. The younger John was probably the son of Orchard's second wife, Katherine, who survived her husband. William Orchard also had a daughter, named Isabella or Elizabeth.   CHRISTOPHER WILSON

Sources J. Harvey and A. Oswald, *English mediaeval architects: a biographical dictionary down to 1550*, 2nd edn (1984), 220–23 · J. N. L. Myres, 'Recent discoveries in the Bodleian Library', *Archaeologia*, 101 (1967), 151–68 · J. H. Harvey, *The Perpendicular style, 1330–1485* (1978), 174, 183 · W. H. St J. Hope, 'The heraldry and sculptures at the Divinity School vault at Oxford', *Archaeological Journal*, 71 (1914), 217–60 · *Snappe's formulary and other records*, ed. H. E. Salter, OHS, 80 (1924), 217–18, 253–4 [20 Aug]

Orchard, William Edwin (1877–1955), minister of the Presbyterian Church of England and Roman Catholic priest, was born on 20 November 1877 at Wing Road, Linslade, Buckinghamshire, the eldest child of John Orchard (d. 1899) and his wife, Fanny, née Braggins (d. 1900). John Orchard's employment as a goods agent on the railways accounted for the family moves to Rugby and then to Willesden, north London, during Orchard's childhood. Orchard's early formal education finished when he left elementary school at the age of twelve, and followed his father into railway employment at Euston Station. Through the family's attendance at the Presbyterian Church of England in Willesden, Orchard met the minister, Charles Anderson Scott, whose influence, combined with a powerful conversion experience during a mission, led him to thoughts of Christian ministry. He read voraciously and began to study biblical languages in his spare time. When an opportunity arose to work as a lay minister at St Paul's Presbyterian Church on the Isle of Dogs he gave up his job on the railway and, after a further two years, was accepted for ministerial training at Westminster College, Cambridge.

In June 1904 Orchard was ordained within the North London presbytery to the ministry of St Paul's Presbyterian Church, Enfield. On 3 August the same year he married Annie Maria Hewitt (1864–1920), the widow of Ellis Hewitt, a Presbyterian minister, and daughter of Joseph Davies Lelean, a farmer; she had a teenage son. They had met in Millwall, where Annie Hewitt, who was older than Orchard, had been guide and counsellor to him.

At Enfield, Orchard's reputation as a preacher of unusual power and conviction was widely recognized. His attempts to interpret Christian faith in terms of contemporary thought led him first to the 'new theology' movement. His continuing studies led to his being awarded the degrees of BD and DD from London University, the latter with a thesis published in 1909 as *Modern Theories of Sin*.

By 1910 Orchard was turning away from the new theology movement and discovering spiritual traditions hitherto unfamiliar to him. Sacramental worship became more important to him, and he began to experiment with liturgical forms of worship. In 1913 his published book of prayers, *The Temple*, revealed the depth of his personal spirituality; it was much used and remained in print for almost half a century.

In summer 1914 Orchard accepted a call to be minister at the Congregational King's Weigh House in Mayfair, London, a church with a distinguished history which had recently gone through a difficult period. Two things he made clear from the beginning: firstly, that he would not conceal his condemnation of the war which had just broken out, and, secondly, that he intended to draw on Catholic as well as the reformed traditions in ordering worship. Through the ecumenical Society of Free Catholics, of which he was a leading member, he was exploring the devotional and liturgical practices of all Christian traditions. His desire to exercise a more Catholic form of priesthood led him in 1916 to something he later regretted—a second ordination by an 'irregular' bishop. In 1917 he presided at the first ordination of a woman (Constance Todd) to Christian ministry in the United Kingdom.

The Weigh House congregations steadily increased. Some were drawn by the pacifist preaching, others by the increasingly Catholic liturgical practice. Several books of Orchard's sermons were published, and in 1919 the Oxford University Press published his *Order of Divine Service for Public Worship* (a second, more Catholic, version appeared in 1926), a compilation of the orders of service used regularly at the Weigh House. It drew on a wide range of sources, including the Book of Common Prayer, the Roman missal, and Eastern liturgies.

In 1920 Annie Orchard died, leaving her husband without the psychological anchorage she had provided. He longed to reconcile Catholic and evangelical worship, and while he was drawn more and more to Catholic traditions of worship, he never abandoned evangelical preaching. The music, vestments, prayers, and sacramental practice at the Weigh House were increasingly indistinguishable from Catholic practice. Orchard believed that the Lambeth 'Appeal to all Christian people' of 1920 offered an opportunity for the Weigh House to become a 'bridge church' in the quest for Christian unity, and was devastated when several years of negotiations finally broke down in 1931.

Orchard was now in crisis, and conversion to Rome seemed the only way forward. Early in 1932 he resigned from the Weigh House and on 2 June was received into the Roman Catholic church, in Rome. One of the first tasks he was given was to write an account of his conversion, published as *From Faith to Faith* in 1933. He continued in correspondence with members of his former congregation, many of whom followed him to Rome.

Orchard was now fifty-five, and tired after his long period of spiritual struggle. He was ordained as a Roman Catholic priest in 1935, and henceforward was engaged in writing, in conducting missions and retreats, and in personal counselling both in Britain and America. He did not change his mind on the pacifist issue, but was forbidden to teach, write, or broadcast on the subject by his superiors. In 1943 he was invited to act as a chaplain at a small religious community in Brownshill, near Stroud in Gloucestershire. Here he found peace and the opportunity to study, pray, and write.

Orchard died of cancer on 12 June 1955 at Brownshill. A requiem mass was offered three days later in the chapel at Brownshill and he was buried in the cemetery attached to the Dominican priory, Woodchester. ELAINE KAYE

Sources W. E. Orchard, *From faith to faith: an autobiography of religious development* (1933) · E. Kaye and R. Mackenzie, *W. E. Orchard: a study in Christian exploration* (1990) · DWL, King's Weigh House Church MSS · E. Kaye, *History of the King's Weigh House Church* (1968) · H. Davies, *Worship and theology in England, 1900–65* (1965) · b. cert. · m. cert. · d. cert. · *CGPLA Eng. & Wales* (1955)
Archives Bodl. Oxf., corresp. with J. Dawson and R. Dawson · Bodl. Oxf., letters to Sir James Marchant · DWL, King's Weigh House Church archive
Likenesses A. P. Cole, oils, 1941, NPG
Wealth at death £1347 15s. 4d.: probate, 27 Sept 1955, *CGPLA Eng. & Wales*

Orchardson, **Sir William Quiller** (1832–1910), artist, born in Edinburgh on 27 March 1832, was the only surviving son of Abram Orchardson, a tailor, and his wife, Elizabeth Quiller, whose family was of Austrian origin. His father was descended from a branch of a highland clan or sept named Urquartson, from the Loch Ness region in Inverness-shire.

Orchardson entered the Trustees' Academy, Edinburgh, on 1 October 1845, aged thirteen. The master of the academy, Alexander Christie ARSA, taught ornament and design, and John Ballantyne RSA, who was a competent teacher, took the antique and life classes. Although the academy's reputation had declined, it produced a number of notable artists around this time, including, among those slightly older than Orchardson, James Archer, Thomas Faed, and Erskine Nicol—all of whom, like Orchardson and his friends, were to contribute significantly to the genre tradition already established by their great countryman Sir David Wilkie.

From the start, Orchardson himself showed a remarkable degree of facility. His friends recorded that 'he mastered … in weeks' (Armstrong, *W. Q. Orchardson*, 13) feats possible to them only after months of labour, and he carried off first prizes for all three academic sessions between 1849 and 1852. He was also noted for his independence. Orchardson claimed that on his first day at the academy he refused to draw from the antique, politely insisting that he preferred to work from nature, and the quality of his work was such that he was allowed to have his way.

In February 1852 the mediocre Christie was replaced by Robert Scott Lauder, a change which persuaded Orchardson, who had completed the course, to return to the academy and remain as a mature student until 1855. Orchardson recalled with approval the system of 'wise neglect'

Sir William Quiller Orchardson (1832–1910), by Henry Weigall, c.1878–81

(Gray, 25) which Lauder adopted, allowing students to develop their individual talents unconstrained. Lauder was an inspirational teacher with 'a contagious enthusiasm for all that was beautiful' (Caw, 230), and under his tutelage the school regained its former prestige. Despite the stylistic affinities which would always identify his students, Lauder did not teach a particular method, but in the life classes he communicated his enthusiasm for the great Venetian painters whom he had studied first-hand for many years. His painterly approach, and his emphasis on tonal values and on the unification of the subject through a subtle play of light and atmosphere, provided a welcome alternative to the conventions of traditional academic training. Other younger pupils much influenced by Lauder were William McTaggart, Peter Graham, and two who were to remain Orchardson's lifelong friends, Thomas Alexander Graham and John Pettie.

In 1848, at the age of sixteen, Orchardson began to exhibit at the Royal Scottish Academy. Of his more ambitious subjects, *George Wishart's Last Exultation* (1852, exh. 1853; University of St Andrews), a multi-figure scene from the last days in the life of the Scottish martyr, is a most impressive achievement for so young an artist. Painted in only three days, it owes much to Wilkie's *John Knox*, which Orchardson had seen, unfinished, at the Royal Scottish Academy exhibition of 1842. In 1854 the first of a long line of Orchardson's portraits appeared at the academy, and, in the years following, subjects from Dickens, Shakespeare, and Walter Scott—*Little Nell* (1855), *Claudio and Isabel* (1856), *Jennie Deans and the Laird o' Dumbiedykes* (1860;

priv. coll.)—signified the beginnings of a lifelong interest in literary subjects.

In 1862 Orchardson, Pettie, and Tom Graham moved to London, initially staying at various addresses in Pimlico before sharing a home together at 37 Fitzroy Square in 1863–5. From 1863 Orchardson exhibited annually at the Royal Academy; in the first five years these were mainly literary subjects, including *An Old English Song* (1863), *The Flowers o' the Forest* (1864; Southampton Art Gallery) and two Shakespearian subjects, *Hamlet and Ophelia* (1865) and *Talbot and the Countess of Auvergne* (1867). A historical genre scene, *The Challenge* (1865), showing a confrontation between a cavalier and a puritan, won a prize from the dealer Henry Wallis, and was exhibited in his French Gallery in Pall Mall. It also earned considerable acclaim when it appeared at the Paris Universal Exhibition two years later. By this date Orchardson's reputation was well established, and in 1867 he was elected an associate of the Royal Academy.

The next decade was to mark a considerable advance in Orchardson's career. In 1870 he made the one extended continental visit of his life, to Venice, and in the years following he exhibited several Venetian figurative subjects and townscapes. It was, however, a literary subject that marked his full maturity as an artist. *The Queen of the Swords* (exh. RA, 1877; Forbes Magazine collection), was inspired by a description of a Shetland sword dance in Walter Scott's novel *The Pirate* (1821); but Orchardson's subtle elaboration of the scene, his evident delight in exploiting its formal elements, and his restrained but convincing characterization showed a significant advance in his work and ensured his election as Royal Academician that year. Significantly, this was the last of his Scottish subjects and the last subject from Scott. Orchardson now began to concentrate on the ballroom and drawing-room subjects for which he is best known, and which were suited to the tastes of a great 'metropolitan centre of wealth and fashion' such as London (Errington, 41).

Like Pettie, Orchardson was especially attracted to the elegant décor and fashions of the later eighteenth and early nineteenth centuries. He was an enthusiastic collector of the decorative arts of this period, so that his scenes of high society are authentic as well as glamorous; but what most distinguishes them is their psychological realism. His major exhibit of the following year, *A Social Eddy; Left by the Tide* (1878; Aberdeen Art Gallery), exemplifies the original touch which he brought to this genre, sympathetically suggesting the anxieties and embarrassments attendant on grand social events. On a similar theme, *Her First Dance* (1884; Tate collection) convincingly portrays the shyness and timidity of a young girl in contrast to the egotistical self-confidence of her partner; while in *The Rivals* (1895; NG Scot.), a bored young woman is obliged to suffer the presence of three persistent suitors, each silently angling for her attention.

Orchardson scored his first real sensation with his portrayal of a historical event based on an eyewitness account: *Napoleon on Board the 'Bellerophon'* (1880; Tate collection)—the ship which transported the emperor to his final exile on the island of St Helena. A lone figure, the deposed Napoleon stands brooding on deck, oblivious to the group of officers (all individual portraits) closely observing him as the shores of France recede in the distance. *The Times* described it as 'by common consent, the cynosure of the exhibition' (*The Times*, 3 May 1880, 9), and Walter Armstrong defined it as the occasion when the artist 'first blazed out into popularity' (Armstrong, *W. Q. Orchardson*, 45). Its importance was widely recognized, not least by the trustees of the Chantrey Bequest, who purchased it for £2000. Other French subjects from this later period, both real and imaginary, include *Voltaire* (1883; Kunsthalle, Hamburg; version NG Scot.); *The Salon of Mme Recamier* (1885), and *The Young Duke* (1889; Lady Lever Art Gallery, Port Sunlight), which was rapturously received on its exhibition at the Royal Academy. Orchardson returned to his hero in *St Helena, 1816; Napoleon Dictating the Account of his Campaigns* (1892; Lady Lever Art Gallery).

Orchardson's gifts for restrained composition, economical story telling, and subtle characterization found a new outlet in a series of edgy domestic dramas which focused on the emotional tensions between sophisticated married couples. Although few in number, their modern context gives them added significance, and it is these which have secured his reputation as an innovator. *Mariage de convenance; Before* (1884; Glasgow Art Gallery and Museum) and *After!* (1886; Aberdeen Art Gallery), portray the predictable consequences of an alliance between a rich, elderly husband and a pretty young wife. In the first, the husband anxiously observes her as she sits, bored and resentful, at the opposite end of a long table. In the second, he sits alone at the fireside, the table set only for one. *The First Cloud* (1887; replica, Tate collection) depicts signs of growing conflict between another affluent couple; while in *Trouble* (exh. RA, 1898) some unspecified revelation has evidently initiated a serious rift between husband and wife.

Orchardson maintained a judicious balance between the demands of narrative on the one hand and aesthetics on the other. He insisted that a worthy subject, and in particular 'the dramatic moment' (Gray, 273) were essential to him; indeed, his generous disposition of elegant figures in space and his exploitation of artificial light invite comparison with the stage, but his scenes are never theatrical in the pejorative sense of the word. The restraint and economy of his work and, in particular, his recognition of the value of empty space and its pictorial function—the sense of isolation and alienation which it achieves—won universal favour. Orchardson's respect for the formal elements of painting was such that contemporary critics discussed his work in largely technical terms. Of his 'society' pictures, Gleeson White concluded that it is 'not so much their subject as their "painting" which entitles [them] … to rank with the most important of our time' (White, 3.20); and James Little perceived Orchardson's compositions as primarily 'decorations … alluring patterns' (Little, 9). It is understandable that Degas, Walter Sickert, and J. A. M. Whistler were among the artists who admired his technique.

Orchardson married, on 6 April 1873, at St Mary Abbots, Kensington, Ellen, the daughter of the London publisher Charles Moxon, with whom he had four sons and two daughters. His own favourite among his paintings was a double portrait of his wife and his son Gordon, *Master Baby* (1886; NG Scot.), and this was Sickert's choice also. Orchardson had received portrait commissions from his first years in Edinburgh. In later life the demand was such that, from 1894, portraiture made up the bulk of his work. In 1902 *The Bystander* singled out Orchardson's *Mrs Mosscockle* as 'the finest portrait in the Academy' and talked of the artist as a 'subtle psychologist. No shade of character', the critic wrote, 'is too fine for his acute analysis' (Gray, 295). Orchardson's sitters included Queen Victoria, Albert Edward, prince of Wales (later Edward VII), and George V. He was appointed master of the Society of Portrait Painters in 1897.

Orchardson's kindness, affability, and sociable disposition won him universal popularity. From his youth he was a keen sportsman; although he gave up hunting on his marriage, he remained a keen angler and tennis player, and he was also adept at billiards. At his house in Westgate-on-Sea, Kent, he had his own tennis court constructed, and in his later years he took up golf. Orchardson's urbanity and success led T. H. Escott to name him—with Marcus Stone and G. D. Leslie—as one of the artists who typified this affluent period: 'finished and prosperous men of the world in social request everywhere' (Gillett, 34)—men who had contributed materially to raising both the status and fortunes of their profession.

Orchardson was made an honorary member of the Royal Scottish Academy in 1871; a DCL of Oxford in 1890; a chevalier of the Légion d'honneur in 1895; and an honorary member of the Royal Society of Miniature Painters in 1900; he was knighted in 1907. He died at his home, 13 Portland Place, St Marylebone, London, of heart disease on 13 April 1910, only a fortnight after completing, with some difficulty, the portrait of Lord Blyth which was exhibited at the Royal Academy in the same year. A modern ballroom subject, *The Last Dance*, remained unfinished. A retrospective exhibition of sixty-eight of Orchardson's works was held at the Royal Academy in the winter of 1911. His widow was granted a civil-list pension of £80 in 1912.

MARY COWLING

Sources H. O. Gray, *W. Q. Orchardson* (1930) • W. Armstrong, *The art of W. Q. Orchardson* (1895) • J. S. Little, *W. Q. Orchardson: his life and work*, Art Annual (1897) • W. Meynell, *The modern school of art*, 1 [n.d.] • J. L. Caw, *Scottish painting past and present, 1620–1908* (1908) • L. Errington, *Master class: Robert Scott Lauder and his pupils* (1983) [exhibition catalogue, NG Scot., 15 July – 2 Oct 1983, and Aberdeen Art Gallery, 15 Oct – 12 Nov 1983] • *Art Journal*, 30 (1910), 192 • *Edinburgh Evening News* (14 April 1910), 12 • G. White, *Master painters of Britain*, 3 (1898) • W. Armstrong, 'The art harvest of the year', *National Review*, 1 (1884), 667–79 • J. B. Atkinson, 'The decline of art', *Blackwood*, 138 (1885), 1–25 • W. Sickert, *A free house*, ed. O. Sitwell (1947) • P. Gillett, *The Victorian painter's world* (1990) • m. cert. • d. cert. • CGPLA Eng. & Wales (1910) • *The Times* (15 April 1910)

Archives Mitchell L., Glas.

Likenesses H. Weigall, oils, c.1878–1881, NPG [*see illus.*] • Lock & Whitfield, photograph, 1882, NPG • A. Mongin, etching, 1882, BM,

NPG · T. Graham, oils, exh. Royal Scot. Acad. 1890 · W. Q. Orchardson, self-portrait, oils, 1890, Uffizi Gallery, Florence · E. O. Ford,
bronze bust, 1891, Scot. NPG · R. W. Robinson, photograph, 1891,
NPG · J. H. Lorimer, pencil drawing, 1892, Scot. NPG · E. O. Ford,
bronze bust, exh. RA 1895, Tate collection · J. Archer, oils, Scot.
NPG · H. J. Brooks, group portrait, oils, NPG · R. Cleaver, group portrait, pen-and-ink drawing, NPG · Elliott & Fry, two photographs,
NPG · T. Graham, oils, Aberdeen Art Gallery · J. Hutchinson, plaster bust, Scot. NPG · J. Hutchison, plaster bust, NPG · G. G. Manton,
group portrait, watercolour drawing, NPG · E. K. Mills, photograph, NPG · W. Q. Orchardson, self-portrait, charcoal drawing,
Aberdeen Art Gallery · W. Q. Orchardson, self-portrait, oils, Aberdeen Art Gallery, Macdonald collection · W. Q. Orchardson, self-
portrait, oils, Castle Museum, Nottingham · J. Pettie, two oil paintings, Scot. NPG · Spy [L. Ward], watercolour caricature, NPG;
repro. in *VF* (24 March 1898) · woodcuts, BM, NPG
Wealth at death £7501 9s. 5d.: probate, 16 June 1910, *CGPLA Eng. &*
Wales

Orczy [*married name* Barstow], **Baroness Emma Magdalena Rosalia Maria Josefa Barbara** [*known as* Baroness
Orczy] (**1865–1947**), novelist, was born on 23 September
1865 at Tarnaörs, near Jászberény, about 75 kilometres
west of Budapest in Hungary, the younger of the two
daughters of Baron Bódog (translated as Felix) Orczy
(1835–1892), landowner, and his wife, Emma, daughter of
Count Wass. The Hungarian form of Baroness Orczy's first
name, by which she was called and which she preferred,
was Emmuska. Her father was a great-grandson of the
noted Hungarian poet Lórinc Orczy (1718–1789). Her paternal grandfather lived in considerable state at Tarnaörs
with his Viennese wife, who never allowed Hungarian to
be spoken in her presence. Some time after her birth
Emmuska's father was given the estate of Tisza-Abád, to
which they moved, and to which he sought to bring modern agricultural machinery and methods, which resulted,
when she was about three, in a revolt by the peasants, who
burnt the crops and the machinery. Because of this, and
because of the agricultural depression and the Viennese
banking crisis, her family moved to Budapest; here Felix
Orczy, who was deeply interested in music, was *Intendant*
of the national theatres (1870–73), where he championed
the music of Richard Wagner against some opposition,
and appointed Hans Richter (1843–1916) as *Kapellmeister*.
This again involved him in controversy, and he resigned
and moved to Brussels, where he taught music. There the
girls spent a year at the convent of the Visitation, and
there the elder, Madeleine, died, aged about twelve.
Emmuska subsequently went to another convent in Paris.
She spoke Hungarian with her father, and French with her
mother, but disliked having to speak German to her
grandmother. However, she spoke not a word of English
when, aged fifteen, she moved with her parents to London, and went for a while to a small day school kept by a
German couple near their home, 23 Wimpole Street. In
London several of Felix Orczy's compositions were performed, including the operas *The Renegade* (1881) and *Sisy-
phus* (1882) and the family frequented musical circles.

Emmuska Orczy decided she wanted to be an artist, and
went to the West London School of Art and then to Hea-
therley's. In the latter school she met her future husband,
Henry George Montague Maclean Barstow (1862/3–1943),

Baroness Emma Magdalena Rosalia Maria Josefa Barbara
Orczy (1865–1947), by Elliott & Fry, 1920s

son of the Revd Michael William Barstow (curate of
Thornton Watlass, Yorkshire, *c.*1854–1866); they married
in London on 7 November 1894. Their only child, John
Montagu Orczy Barstow, who wrote novels under the
name John Blakeney, was born in 1899. They set up home
in a studio flat in Holland Park Road and earned their living doing book and magazine illustrations. He illustrated
and she translated *Old Hungarian Fairy Tales* (1895).

Just before the turn of the century, when Orczy was in
her mid-thirties, she began a second career as a writer. A
series of mystery stories for the *Royal Magazine* featured
the Old Man in the Corner, who solves murders by pure
deduction while sitting in an ABC teashop playing with
pieces of string; historians of the genre regard him as one
of the first armchair detectives. The Barstows wanted to
visit the Paris Exhibition of 1900 and arranged journalistic
commissions to pay for their trip. Inspired by the visit to
Paris, Orczy wrote *The Scarlet Pimpernel* in five weeks. It was
rejected by a dozen publishers, and she nearly accepted
£30 for all rights in it. But in 1903 she and her husband succeeded in getting a dramatized version they had written
accepted for production by Fred Terry (1863–1933). It was
produced that autumn in Nottingham, with no great success, and the Barstows rewrote the last act, so that Terry
would not be in a hideous disguise for his final bow. It was
finally produced in London in 1905 and after a shaky start
became very popular.

An instant best-seller when published as a novel in 1905,
the story also became the subject of several film versions:
the earliest, a silent film of 1928, was called *The Triumph of*

the *Scarlet Pimpernel*; the most famous, *The Scarlet Pimpernel* (1935), starred Leslie Howard and was directed by Harold Young; a 1982 version starred Anthony Andrews and was directed by Clive Donner. Television adaptations range from the BBC television series of 1950, starring James Carney, to a British–American co-production, starring Richard E. Grant and directed by Patrick Lau, screened in 1999. The plot was a peculiarly potent mixture of the familiar ingredients of historical fiction. During the French Revolution a secret band of daring Englishmen in disguise rescue French aristocrats from the reign of terror. They are led by Sir Percy Blakeney, who appears to the world a fool and a fop, but is in reality a master of disguise and a brilliant leader of men. As Orczy emphasized in later years, he is the typical English gentleman. This symbol of British foreign policy repeatedly outwits the bungling French bureaucrat Chauvelin; like *The Four Just Men* (1905) by Edgar Wallace, the novel pits a group of self-selected upper-class amateurs against the power of the state. Sir Percy is also the soul of honour; he is temporarily estranged from his beautiful French wife, Marguerite, because she has betrayed an enemy of hers to the revolutionaries, recalling the romantic vision of personal integrity in other novels of the period such as *The Four Feathers* (1902) by A. E. W. Mason. Much historical fiction expresses nostalgia for aristocratic glamour, but *The Scarlet Pimpernel* is remarkable in that its plot literally enacts the desire of its readers to snatch the survivors of the *ancien régime* to safety as they journey towards the guillotine. They are brought to the security of England, which thus figures as a bulwark of conservatism against foreign revolution, and as a model of peaceable class relations in contrast to the class warfare abroad.

Baroness Orczy published eleven more Scarlet Pimpernel adventures between 1908 and 1940, many other novels, mostly historical fiction, and a biography (1935) of the duchesse de Berri. The most notable of her other volumes of fiction, which had a steady sale without ever achieving the same amazing success as *The Scarlet Pimpernel*, is probably the volume of stories called *Lady Molly of Scotland Yard* (1910), whose heroine is an early example of a female detective with official status.

In 1908 the Barstows moved out of London, first to Minster in Thanet and then to Snowfield, at Bearsted, Kent. In 1906 Orczy inherited from an uncle the property of Tarnaörs and a private income, which she was later to lose in the crash which followed the First World War. After the war, partly because Barstow had a weak chest, they bought the Villa Bijou at Monte Carlo, Monaco, a place to which they had taken a liking when she had convalesced there after a nervous breakdown in 1915. There they were instrumental in bringing about the construction of an Anglican church. Their decision to move abroad may have been influenced by the xenophobia current in England at the time; Orczy's widowed mother, who had returned to Hungary in the 1890s but escaped during the war to live near them in Kent, returned home (where she became a captive of the bolsheviks) in 1918 because she thought that her presence as an enemy alien was doing them

harm. Like many Hungarians, Orczy resented the partition of her country under the terms of the 1919 treaty of Trianon; her novel *Pimpernel and Rosemary* (1924) depicts from that point of view the events following the annexation of Transylvania (her mother's home province) by Romania. During the 1920s, as Monte Carlo became built up, the Barstows also bought a house in Italy, La Padula, at Rezzola on the Gulf of Spezia, but, finding life in Mussolini's Italy increasingly disagreeable, they sold it in 1933.

Orczy spent the duration of the Second World War in Monte Carlo, in circumstances of some difficulty. Barstow died in February 1943 (in Switzerland, according to *The Times* of 27 February 1943, but this may be an error). After the war she returned to England, where she published her memoirs and died, in Brown's Hotel, Dover Street, Mayfair, London, of kidney failure and senility, on 12 November 1947.   CHARLOTTE MITCHELL

Sources Ágnes Kenyeres, ed., *Magyar Életrajzi lexikon*, 3 vols. (1967–81) · E. Orczy, *Links in the chain of life* [1947] · Iván Nagy, ed., *Magyarország Családai czimerekkel és nemzékrendi táblákkal*, 8 vols. (1857–68) · *The Times* (23 Jan 1892) · *The Times* (27 Feb 1943) · *The Times* (13 Nov 1947) · private information (2004) [P. Sherwood] · K. Staples, 'Emma, Baroness Orczy', *British mystery writers, 1860–1919*, ed. B. Benstock and T. F. Staley, DLitB, 70 (1988) · BFI · m. cert. · d. cert. · *CGPLA Eng. & Wales* (1948)
Archives U. Birm. L., letters | BL, corresp. with Society of Authors, Add. MS 56767
Likenesses Elliott & Fry, photograph, 1920–29, NPG [*see illus.*] · photographs, repro. in Orczy, *Links*
Wealth at death £35,275 6s. 6d.: administration, 24 July 1948, *CGPLA Eng. & Wales*

Ord, Bernhard [Boris] (1897–1961), musician, was born on 9 July 1897 at Bristol, the youngest of the five children of Clement Ord, a Quaker and head of the German department at Bristol University, and his wife, Johanna, daughter of Hofprediger G. Anthes, who came of a musical German family. Bernhard was educated from 1907 to 1914 at Clifton College, of which he was a scholar and, later, a governor. He took his ARCO diploma while still at school and won a scholarship to the Royal College of Music, London, where he studied the organ under Sir Walter Parratt and also excelled at the pianoforte. He was already a devotee of opera, and his familiar name Boris, by which he became universally known, arose from his enthusiasm for Rimsky-Korsakov's *Boris Godunov*, introduced to London in 1913 by Thomas Beecham. After war service from 1916 to 1918, first with the Artists' Rifles and then as a pilot in the Royal Flying Corps, during which he was twice wounded, he returned to the Royal College of Music, where he took up choir training.

It was as organ scholar of Corpus Christi College that Ord went to Cambridge, in 1919. The next year he founded the Cambridge University Madrigal Society, later to be known for its May week concerts in massed punts on the river. He became MusB in 1922, and the following year was elected to a fellowship at King's, his father's college, within which as a bachelor he spent the rest of his life. As a freelance musician he was much in demand. Sometimes it was as a continuo player on the piano or harpsichord, as for the staging of works by Purcell and Handel produced by Camille Prior and Cyril Rootham, the organist of St John's College; sometimes as a conductor, as for the Greek play committee's revival in 1921 of Aristophanes' *The Birds* with the music of Sir (Charles) Hubert Parry and of Aeschylus' *Oresteia* with Cecil Armstrong Gibbs's music (1924). He also conducted a remarkable performance (1928) of Stravinsky's *The Soldier's Tale* in which Lydia Lopokova, the wife of the economist J. M. Keynes, was the princess, Michael Redgrave the soldier, and Dennis Arundell the narrator. In 1927 he gained valuable experience by working at Cologne opera house.

On the death of A. H. Mann in 1929 Ord was appointed organist of King's College and also of the university. At King's he joined forces with the dean, the Revd Eric Milner-White, in his policy of broadening the repertory of the chapel music, especially by strengthening the sixteenth-century element. In 1936 he became a university lecturer in music, and in 1938 he succeeded Rootham as conductor of the Cambridge University Musical Society. His work for the society greatly broadened his scope and also revealed the range of his musical sympathies. Continuing Rootham's tradition, he conducted a highly successful stage performance of Handel's *Saul* in the Guildhall, with David Franklin in the title role.

The outbreak of war inevitably reduced the number of chapel services at King's. In 1941 Ord handed them over to Dr Harold Darke for the duration and rejoined the air force as a flight lieutenant; he eventually participated in the Normandy landings and the ensuing campaign. Back at Cambridge, he resumed his duties in 1946. His Cambridge University Musical Society concerts included Beethoven's ninth symphony and Stravinsky's *Symphony of Psalms*. On the Guildhall stage there were performances of Handel's *Solomon* and of *The Pilgrim's Progress* by Vaughan Williams, and at the Arts Theatre of Purcell's *Dioclesian* and *King Arthur*. But early in the 1950s Ord's health weakened, and eventually disseminated sclerosis was diagnosed. He retired from the Cambridge University Musical Society in 1954, but for some time continued to conduct concerts at the Festival Hall, including works for varying numbers of harpsichords. It was a great comfort to him that his former organ scholar and assistant David Willcocks returned from Worcester Cathedral to take over from him in 1957–8. He then resigned his university lectureship also. He was created CBE in 1958. His last public appearance, in a wheelchair, was in the Senate House in June 1960, to receive the honorary doctorate of music. He died at Cambridge on 30 December 1961.

As a musician Ord had exacting professional standards. His score-reading classes were a bracing test. As a choir trainer he inspired a mixture of affection and wholesome fear. Under him the King's choir established, by broadcasting and foreign tours, its international reputation. Durham University made him an honorary MusD in 1955. His abundant geniality was shown in many less serious musical productions, in his generous hospitality, and in his quick sense of humour. L. P. WILKINSON, *rev.*

Sources P. F. Radcliffe, *Bernhard (Boris) Ord, 1897–1961* (privately printed, 1962) · personal knowledge (2004) · private information (2004) · *The Times* (1 Jan 1962)
Likenesses P. Horton, drawing, 1957, King's Cam. · H. Bass, oils (aged twenty-nine), King's Cam.
Wealth at death £13,542 7s. 5d.: administration, 14 March 1962, *CGPLA Eng. & Wales*

Ord, Craven (*bap.* 1755, *d.* 1832), antiquary and brass-rubber, was born in London and baptized at the Temple Church on 6 August 1755, the younger son of Harry Ord, of the king's remembrancer's office of the exchequer, and his wife, Anne, daughter of Francis Hutchinson of Barnard Castle, co. Durham. His uncle Robert *Ord (1700–1778) was chief baron of the Scottish exchequer.

Ord's schooling seems to be undocumented and he did not matriculate from either of the English universities. He was, however, a competent classicist, and he developed a strong interest in the middle ages. He was elected a fellow of the Society of Antiquaries on 26 January 1775, when his tastes were probably already formed, and there he found congenial companions. In June 1784 he married Mary Smith, daughter of John Redman of Greenstead Hall, in Greenstead by Ongar, Essex. They had five sons and a daughter, most of whom were born at Greenstead Hall, where Ord lived until the last few years of his life.

Ord's marriage probably accounted for a substantial part of his fortune but it evidently did not make him idle. He was a purposeful and energetic student of history whose works are mainly to be found in other men's books. He made several contributions to *Archaeologia*, the first of which (1790) was an edition of the inventory of the crown jewels made in 1329–30. His interests were not narrowly focused. He ranged over southern England in search of antiquities, in and out of churches, and he read in manuscripts and printed books even more widely. He gave substantial assistance to John Nichols (1745–1826), the geologist Gideon Algernon Mantell (1790–1852), and George Ormerod (1785–1873) in their respective histories of Leicestershire, Surrey, and Cheshire.

Mantell and Ormerod were younger men but Nichols, the master printer and antiquary, was of Ord's own generation. Ord was also a friend of Richard Gough, and worked with him closely and harmoniously. Gough's *Anecdotes of British Topography* appeared in 1768 and in an enlarged edition, of two volumes, in 1780. It led on to his celebrated edition of Camden's *Britannia* (3 vols., 1789; 4 vols., 1806) but its wide array of material also suggested a more detailed study, which was warmly encouraged by Sir John Cullum, of Hardwick, Suffolk, another learned enthusiast, and Ord. Gough had always made sketches of subjects that interested him, and he came to recognize the exceptional value of tombs and memorials as records of costume and other features of medieval life. The outcome was his *Sepulchral monuments of Great Britain applied to illustrate the history of families, manners, habits, and arts from the Norman conquest* (1786–99), a carefully documented survey extending to the end of the fifteenth century. Ord in the meantime had been taken by the lure of medieval brasses. The three friends made a particularly successful tour of the great parish churches of the Lincolnshire and Norfolk marshland in 1780, which began in Wisbech and ended in King's Lynn, proving rich in architectural wonders, and yielding a splendid crop of brasses in Lynn.

Ord's concern, besides assisting Gough, was to further the detailed and comparative study of brasses, which lent themselves to accurate reproduction at a time when other artefacts could only be, with whatsoever pains, drawn and engraved. Instead of taking a simple rubbing from the surface of the brass he took a reverse impression with equipment of his own devising. Its only disadvantage, trifling to the enthusiast, was that inscriptions appeared in mirror-writing. His operations required large sheets of French paper kept damp in a specially commissioned case, a supply of printer's ink, some lengths of cloth, and an abundance of rags. The paraphernalia were clearly such as a gentleman might use for his own dedicated purposes, but probably not such as he might himself carry. He inked the surface of the brass, then wiped it clean with the rags, leaving ink only in the incisions, as though it were an engraver's plate. He then arranged the paper over the brass, covered it with an adequate thickness of cloth, and trampled on it to take an even impression. For intricate images he wetted the paper more thoroughly, on one occasion at least in the neighbouring Thames. At home he cut out the figures and any accompanying features, mounted them, and finally bound them in enormous volumes in deal boards more than 6 feet high. They were acquired after his death by the British Museum and have since been transferred to the British Library (BL, Add. MSS 32478–32479).

Ord collected manuscripts, printed books, drawings, and engravings. He assembled and indexed some twenty volumes of material relating to Suffolk but he also acquired fine manuscripts for their own sake, and large numbers of medieval deeds. He took a close interest in the business of the Society of Antiquaries, and served for several years as its vice-president. He was elected a fellow of the Royal Society in 1787. He began to sell his collections in 1829, when he travelled abroad for his health, and Francis Douce and Sir Thomas Phillipps bought extensively at his sales.

Ord died at Woolwich Common in January 1832. Of his children, his eldest son, Craven Ord (1786–1836), a prebendary of Lincoln, succeeded him at Greenstead and married a niece of Sir John Cullum. Three other sons, Sir Robert Hutchinson Ord, William Redman Ord, and Harry Gough Ord, served in the army, the artillery, and the engineers. Harry Gough's son Sir Harry St George *Ord (1819–1885) became a major-general of the engineers and a colonial governor. Ord's fourth son, John, practised as a physician in Hertford, and his daughter, Harriot Mary, married the Revd George Hughes of Stamford Rivers, Essex.   G. H. MARTIN

Sources DNB · Nichols, *Lit. anecdotes* · Nichols, *Illustrations* · GM, 1st ser., 102/1 (1832), 469–70 · J. Page-Phillips, *Macklin's monumental brasses*, 2nd edn (1972) · IGI

Archives BL, Suffolk collections, journal of tours of East Anglia, brass rubbings, antiquarian notes, and papers, Add. MSS 6391,

7101–7102, 7965–7967, 8986–8987, 14823, 25340, 32478–32479, 39852 · BL, notes and annotations made to the wardrobe accompt of Sir Andrew Wyndsore, Egerton MS 3025 · BL, annotated copy of Edmund Carter's *History of the University of Cambridge*, shelf mark 731.i.12 · Bodl. Oxf., collections and papers · Bodl. Oxf., copy of John Kirby's *Suffolk traveller* interleaved and annotated by Ord (and other antiquaries) · Lincs. Arch., calendar of Lincolnshire charters · LUL, papers relating to English coinage and the mint · Man. CL, Manchester Archives and Local Studies, copy made by Ord of the household book of Lord Thomas, earl of Lancaster · Suffolk RO, Ipswich, collections, notes, and papers relating to Suffolk, incl. notes by Peter Le Neve and Thomas Martin · Suffolk RO, Ipswich, commonplace book · Suffolk RO, Ipswich, pedigrees and arms of Suffolk families with earlier notes by Peter Le Neve, Thomas Martin, and others | Bodl. Oxf., letters to Richard Gough · Norfolk RO, corresp.

Ord, Sir Harry St George (1819–1885), army officer and colonial governor, the son of Captain Harry Gough Ord, Royal Artillery, and his wife, Louisa Latham of Bexley, Kent, was born at North Cray, Kent, on 17 June 1819. He was educated privately at Woolwich, and entered the Royal Military Academy there in 1835. He received a commission as second lieutenant in the corps of Royal Engineers on 14 December 1837, and was trained at Chatham. Having been promoted lieutenant on 27 May 1839, he was quartered at Woolwich and afterwards in Ireland. In January 1840 he was sent to the West Indies, where he remained for the next six years. He returned home in December 1845. On 28 May 1846 he married Julia Graham, the daughter of Admiral James Carpenter RN, and on 29 October he was promoted second captain.

In December 1849 Ord was sent on special duty to the west coast of Africa and Ascension Island. Following his return in September 1850 he received the thanks of the Board of Admiralty for his report and recommendations on naval works at Ascension Island. On 1 January 1852 he was appointed adjutant of the Royal Engineers at Chatham. He was promoted first captain on 17 February 1854, but continued as adjutant until July, when he was appointed brigade major of the Royal Engineers under Brigadier-General Harry David Jones in the combined French and English expedition to the Baltic. Ord was present at the siege and capture of Bomarsund, and was mentioned in dispatches. He received the war medal and was promoted brevet major on 8 September 1854. On his return to England he was quartered at Sheerness.

In November 1855 Ord entered the Colonial Office, and until May 1856 served as a commissioner on a special mission to the Gold Coast. From June to October 1856, and again from February to May 1857, he assisted the British minister at The Hague and the British ambassador in Paris in negotiations respecting the Netherlands' and French possessions on the west coast of Africa.

On 2 September 1857 Ord was appointed lieutenant-governor of the island of Dominica in the West Indies. He was promoted lieutenant-colonel on 28 November 1859. In April 1860 he accepted the governorship of Bermuda, and assumed the position in March 1861. In January 1864 he returned home on leave of absence, and on 28 November was promoted brevet colonel. He was then sent to the west coast of Africa as commissioner on special service under the Colonial Office in connection with the Asante disturbances. On 9 October 1865 he was made a CB, and the same month he resumed the government of Bermuda, which he finally left in November 1866.

On 5 February 1867 Ord was appointed the first colonial governor of the Straits Settlements, these possessions having previously been administered by the government of India. He was knighted, assumed the government on 1 April 1867, and was promoted major-general on 16 April 1869. His tenure of the government was, by request of the Colonial Office, extended beyond the usual time, and he remained at Singapore until November 1873, continuing to promote colonial trade and financial reforms. His administration was the subject of a court of inquiry after his departure.

Ord's health had suffered from the tropical climate, and for the next four years he remained unemployed. He was made a KCMG in 1877, and was offered the governorship of South Australia, which he declined. However, in November 1877 he became governor of Western Australia. Here he opposed demands for responsible government, and sought, with only limited success, to resolve some of the colony's economic difficulties. Having completed the term of office, he retired on full pension in 1880 and returned to England, where he resided at Fornham House, Fornham St Martin, near Bury St Edmunds, Suffolk. The following year he was made a GCMG. He was an honorary fellow of the London Zoological Society, and presented it with many animals from his various postings.

Ord died suddenly of heart disease at Homburg, Germany, on 20 August 1885. He was buried in the churchyard of Fornham St Martin. A village institute was erected at Fornham St Martin in his memory by his friend the sultan of Johore.

Ord was survived by his three sons: Harry St George, who settled in Australia; William St George, a retired captain of the Royal Engineers, of Fornham; and St John St George, a retired major of the Royal Artillery.

R. H. VETCH, rev. LYNN MILNE

Sources D. P. Henige, *Colonial governors from the fifteenth century to the present* (1970) · P. Boyce, 'Ord, Sir Harry St George', *AusDB*, vol. 5 · Royal Engineers Corps' Records · PRO, War Office MSS · **Archives** National Archives of Singapore · **Likenesses** oils; formerly in Singapore, 1894; for the Chinese merchants of the Straits settlements · oils; formerly at the Chamber of Legislative Council, Bermuda, 1894 · **Wealth at death** £31,553 7s. 11d.: probate, 10 Oct 1885, *CGPLA Eng. & Wales*

Ord, John (bap. **1729**, d. **1814**). See under Ord, Robert (1700–1778).

Ord, John Walker (1811–1853), poet and journalist, was born at Guisborough, Yorkshire, on 5 March 1811, the son of Richard Ord, principal partner in the firm of Richard Ord & Son, tanners and leather merchants of that place, and his wife, Ann, *née* Ovington. He entered the University of Edinburgh, and, being intended for the medical profession, was apprenticed to Robert Knox, the lecturer on anatomy who employed the body snatchers Burke and Hare. While at Edinburgh he was friendly with John Wilson, the essayist, and James Hogg, the 'Ettrick Shepherd'. Eventually he abandoned the study of medicine, and, moving to London in 1834, he started, two years later, the *Metropolitan Conservative Journal*, a paper which was afterwards merged with *The Britannia*. His literary labours brought him into contact with Thomas Campbell, Sheridan Knowles, Douglas Jerrold, the countess of Blessington, and other eminent literary figures of the day.

Ord's first publication was *England: a Historical Poem* (2 vols., 1834–5). This was followed by *Remarks on the sympathetic condition existing between the body and the mind, especially during disease* (1836), forming a supplement to the *Metropolitan Literary Journal*; *The Bard, and Minor Poems* (1841); *Rural Sketches and Poems, Chiefly Relating to Cleveland* (1845); and *The History and Antiquities of Cleveland* (1846). The varied nature of his interests is also reflected in the positions he held, including member of the council of the British Archaeological Association, fellow of the Genealogical Society of London, and president of the Charing Cross Medical and Scientific Society. In his later years Ord also edited the *Northern Times* and a poem by Thomas Pierson, *Roseberry Topping*, published in 1847. He retired to his native county and began work on *The Bible Oracles*, which was left unfinished when he died at Guisborough on 29 August 1853. He was buried in the churchyard at Guisborough.

THOMPSON COOPER, rev. NILANJANA BANERJI

Sources H. Schroeder, *The annals of Yorkshire*, 2 (1851), 388 · *History and topography of the city of York, and the North Riding of Yorkshire*, T. Whellan & Co., 2 vols. (1857–9) · *N&Q*, 2nd ser., 10 (1860), 140 · *N&Q*, 2nd ser., 8 (1859), 531 · Allibone, *Dict.* · Boase, *Mod. Eng. biog.* · **Archives** Bodl. Oxf., corresp. with Sir Thomas Phillipps · **Likenesses** B. F. Lloyd & Co, portrait, repro. in J. W. Ord, *The history and antiquities of Cleveland* (1846)

Ord, Robert (1700–1778), politician, baptized on 27 March 1701 at Newcastle upon Tyne, was one of the three sons and a daughter to survive from the thirteen children born to John Ord (d. 1721), solicitor, and his second wife, Anne Hutchinson. John Ord was under-sheriff for Newcastle from 1685 to 1703; his second wife brought a considerable fortune, with which he purchased Fenham, Newminster Abbey, and Hunstanworth. He also founded St John's School, Newcastle, for forty boys.

Robert Ord was educated at Lincoln's Inn in 1718, and called to the bar in 1724, having been elected a fellow of the Royal Society in 1723. He inherited Hunstanworth at his father's death. He married in October 1727 Mary, daughter of Sir John Darnell, with whom he raised a son, John Ord [*see below*], and five daughters.

In the election of 1734 Ord secured the Cornish seat of Mitchell, which he held until 1745, after which he sat for Morpeth, Northumberland, representing the interests of Henry Howard, fourth earl of Carlisle. He held, successively, the offices of secretary to the chancellor of the exchequer and deputy cofferer of the household. In 1755, supported by Carlisle and Hardwicke, he vacated his seat in the house to become chief baron of the Scottish exchequer. He thereupon moved north, where Boswell remarked on him: 'This respectable English judge will be long remembered in Scotland, where he built an elegant house, and lived in it magnificently. His own ample fortune, with the addition of his salary, enabled him to be splendidly hospitable' (*Boswell's Life of Johnson*, 5.28). Ord retired in 1775 and died in Edinburgh on 12 February 1778.

His son **John Ord** (*bap.* 1729, *d.* 1814), also a politician, was baptized on 11 October 1729. He went to school at Hackney and entered Trinity College, Cambridge, in 1746, graduating BA in 1751, holding a fellowship from 1752, proceeding MA in 1755, and meanwhile enrolling at Lincoln's Inn in 1747. In 1761 his father arranged for him to stand for parliament at Morpeth as the second candidate in Carlisle's interest, but he was rejected, the electorate preferring a second candidate unconnected with the Carlisle interests. He married, on 30 October 1762, Eleanor (1741–1818), daughter of John Simpson of Bradley, co. Durham; there were no children of the marriage.

Ord next stood for parliament in 1774 when he was returned unopposed for Midhurst in Sussex. He supported the administration until the fall of Lord North. He transferred to the Hastings seat from 1780 to 1784, and served as chairman of the ways and means committee until the dismissal of the coalition. In 1783 he had voted for the second earl of Shelburne's peace preliminaries, and for Charles James Fox's East India Bill; by 1874 he was being classed as 'opposition'. In the general election of 1784 he stood for Wendover, voting with the opposition, and he retired from parliament in 1790.

For many years Ord lived at Purser's Cross, near Fulham, where, according to the gardener John Loudon, his garden in 1756 'contains a greater number of fine specimens in a very limited space than any garden we know of in the neighbourhood of London' (Loudon, 1.72–3). This interest in horticulture led to his election as a member of the Horticultural Society, and in 1780 as a fellow of the Royal Society. He died at Purser's Cross on 6 June 1814 and was buried in Fulham churchyard.

[ANON.], *rev.* ANITA MCCONNELL

Sources J. B. Owen, 'Ord, Robert', HoP, *Commons, 1715–54* • M. M. Drummond, 'Ord, John', HoP, *Commons, 1754–90* • J. C. Loudon, *Arboretum et fruticetum Britannicarum*, 8 vols. (1838), 1.72–3 • *GM*, 1st ser., 84/2 (1814), 405–6 • *GM*, 1st ser., 48 (1778), 94 • *N&Q*, 4th ser., 7 (1871), 389 • Burke, *Gen. GB* (1846) • W. P. Baildon, ed., *The records of the Honorable Society of Lincoln's Inn: the black books*, 3 (1899) • *Scots Magazine*, 40 (1778), 111 • R. Welford, *Men of mark 'twixt Tyne and Tweed*, 3 vols. (1895) • *Boswell's Life of Johnson*, ed. G. B. Hill, 5 (1955) • Venn, *Alum. Cant.* [John Ord] • IGI

Archives NL Scot., discharges of bonds | NL Scot., letters to his daughter Anne MacDonald • NL Scot., letters to John MacKenzie

Ord, William Miller (1834–1902), physician and medical administrator, was born on 23 September 1834 at Brixton Hill, Surrey, the elder of two sons of George Ord FRCS and his wife, Harriet, the daughter of Sir James Clark, a London merchant. Educated at King's College School, Ord entered St Thomas's Hospital in 1852 and gained his MB from London University in 1855 and his MD in 1877. Following a brief period in general practice with his father at Streatham Hill, Ord remained associated with St

Thomas's for the rest of his career as house surgeon, surgical registrar, demonstrator of anatomy, and, from 1870, assistant physician and joint lecturer in physiology. He was dean of the medical school from 1876 until 1887. Ord was appointed physician in 1877, a post which he held until 1898, when he became consulting physician.

Ord married on 12 April 1859 Julia, daughter of Joseph Rainbow of Norwood; they had two daughters and a son. It was in the year of his marriage that Ord made his name as an exceptionally youthful member of the pioneering circle of medical men and epidemiologists associated with John Simon at the medical office of the privy council. Simon later recalled that he had looked upon his precocious collaborator as one of his 'brightest and most trustworthy students' (Brockington, 287). In the summer of 1858 the foully polluted River Thames, which had long threatened the environmental stability of the capital, had generated a 'great stink' which closed down the law courts and forced members of parliament to flee, halfnauseous, from the debating chamber. Miasmatic theory predicted that the death-rate would soar as a result of a dramatic increase in gastrointestinal infection and that, intermixed with the prevailing 'epidemic atmosphere', the stench from the river would inevitably precipitate yet another outbreak of cholera—there had been severe epidemics in 1848–9 and 1853–4. However, Ord's assiduous analysis of the health of boatmen, wharfingers, and dockers cast serious doubt on this hypothesis and revealed that, in itself, the stinking river was unlikely to generate dysenteric or diarrhoeal disease.

During the next five years Ord undertook investigations into localized outbreaks of typhoid fever on behalf of the medical office of the privy council and produced a classic paper, 'The sanitary circumstances of dressmakers and other needlewomen in London'. This meticulous account of the relationship between the fashionable demands of the London social season and its impact on the lives of 'thousands of women ... [who were] pursuing their occupation under conditions which constantly undermine their vital and physical powers, and contract, with fatal certainty ... their measure of years' ('Medical officer ... sixth report', 28.371) was nevertheless qualified by a cautious conservatism. Eschewing criticism of prevailing economic orthodoxy, Ord remained convinced that market forces would eventually exclude mercilessly exploitative employers and subcontractors.

Following the tragically premature death of his wife in 1864 Ord gradually withdrew from epidemiological and social investigation and, undertaking detailed observations of cretinoid elderly women on the wards at St Thomas's, began to formulate novel ideas on the origins and nature of what he would later term myxoedema. Endemic cretinism had been observed and described in detail by Paracelsus in the duchy of Salzburg. In its sporadic form, however, it was not recognized until C. H. Fogge's account in the early 1870s. This prepared the way for Sir William Gull's authoritative report on the condition among adults in 1873. Building on this work Ord presented a seminal paper in 1877 in which he claimed the essential cause of the disease to be atrophy or fibrosis of the thyroid gland. In 1888 Ord chaired a special committee for the Clinical Society of London and produced 'a remarkable review of the subjects of cretinism and myxoedema' (Ingbar and Braverman, 4). A decade later this was complemented by the synoptic Bradshaw lecture at the Royal College of Physicians, 'On myxoedema and allied conditions'.

On his retirement in 1900 Ord moved to the village of Hurstborne Tarrant, near Andover, to 'enjoy the country life for which he yearned' (*BMJ*, 1315). However, in 1902 he was stricken with what the journal termed 'brain fever' and was moved to the house of his son, The Hall, New Street, Salisbury, where he died on 14 May 1902. He was buried at London Road cemetery, Salisbury. He was survived by his second wife, Jane, daughter of Sir James Arndell Youl, with whom he had two daughters. Ord was a gregarious and life enhancing man, and his London house in Upper Brook Street reflected the 'cultured tastes of its owner' (*Leading Men of London*). Exceptionally well versed in the classics, Ord 'could read his Ovid with ease [and] put his finger immediately on some quotation from Horace or Virgil which exactly fitted the subject under discussion' (*BMJ*, 1316). If he ultimately failed to fulfil his very great potential as a creative medical scientist it was predominantly the result of his dedication to the tasks of teaching and administration at St Thomas's.   BILL LUCKIN

Sources R. Lambert, *Sir John Simon, 1816–1904, and English social administration* (1963) · C. F. Brockington, 'Public health at the privy council, 1858–71', *Medical Officer*, 101 (1959) · W. Luckin, *Pollution and control: a social history of the Thames in C19* (1986) · *St Thomas's Hospital Reports*, new ser., 31 (1904), 349–56 · *The Lancet* (24 May 1902), 1494 · *BMJ* (24 May 1902), 1315–17 · *Leading men of London: a collection of biographical sketches* (1895) · 'Medical officer of the privy council: sixth report', *Parl. papers* (1864), 28.362–82, no. 3416 [sanitary circumstances of dressmakers in London] · S. H. Ingbar and L. E. Braverman, eds., *Werner's Thethyroid: a fundamental and clinical text*, 5th edn (1986) · *Medical Directory* (1880) · *WWW* · m. cert. [Julia Rainbow] · d. cert.
Likenesses wood-engraving, NPG; repro. in *ILN* (27 March 1886)
Wealth at death £36,200 5s.: resworn probate, May 1903, *CGPLA Eng. & Wales* (1902)

Orde, Cuthbert Julian (1888–1968), painter, was born in Great Yarmouth, Norfolk, on 18 December 1888, the second son in the family of three sons and two daughters of Sir Julian Walter Orde (1861–1929), secretary for twenty years and galvanizing force of the Royal Automobile Club, and his wife, Alice Georgiana, daughter of Frederick Archdale of Baldock, Hertfordshire. Educated at Framlingham College, Suffolk, from the 1920s he was a regular exhibitor at the Royal Academy and the Royal Society of Portrait Painters in addition to showing at the Paris Salon and in commercial London galleries.

Orde served throughout the First World War. Commissioned into the Royal Army Service Corps as a second lieutenant on 15 August 1914, he was sent almost immediately to France and was awarded the 1914 Mons star. He transferred to the Royal Flying Corps in October of the following year, and served as an observer in France and Egypt, and as a test pilot at Martlesham Heath, Suffolk, reaching the war substantive rank of major. He relinquished his commission on 15 January 1919 on the grounds of ill health.

Between the wars Orde exhibited portraits, landscapes, and flower paintings, but with the outbreak of the Second World War his twin interests in art and the air force found a common focus. He began painting aircraft at RAF stations and four of his drawings, and a painting of a Wellington 'bombing up', were acquired by the War Artists' Advisory Committee and exhibited at the National Gallery in August 1940. The following month he embarked on a project proposed by the director of public relations at the Air Ministry to draw portraits of the pilots of Fighter Command. Beginning at the height of the battle of Britain in September 1940, he visited almost every operational station in the country, in his element as an airman among airmen, drawing the pilots selected for him by the station commanders. Affectionately known as Turps, Uncle Orde, or the Captain, he worked in makeshift studios, generally set up in the ladies' room in the mess, producing in all a series of some 160 drawings. A selection published by Harraps in 1942 remains of documentary interest and, formulaic as they are, these portraits show Orde at his best, conveying a real sympathy for the men and the ethos of Fighter Command.

A substantial number of these drawings, together with various of Orde's paintings, are in the collections of the Imperial War Museum and the RAF Museum. Others are in the National Portrait Gallery, London. Portraits were also commissioned from him for the Senior United Services Club, the RAF Club, the Royal Aeronautical Society, and the Staff College at Camberley, and among his sitters were Sir Winston Churchill (Royal Airforce College, Cranwell), Air Chief Marshal Sir John Salmond (RAF Club), and Group Captain Sir Douglas Bader (RAF Museum). His modest talent, however, fell far short of securing him a lucrative career.

Tall, dashing, and seeming youthful even in his later years, Orde was a man of ready friendship and devoted family loyalty. On 11 September 1916 he married Lady Eileen Wellesley (1887–1952), younger daughter of Arthur Charles Wellesley, fourth duke of Wellington. Also a painter, she fell victim to Parkinson's disease not long after the First World War and lived a virtual invalid until her death in 1952. They had two daughters. In 1953 Orde married Alexandra (*née* Dalziel), former wife of Sir Alexander Davenport Kinloch, twelfth baronet, and daughter of Frederick Dalziel, of New York. She had two daughters from her former marriage. As his friend Group Captain Douglas Bader wrote of him in *The Times* on 28 December 1968, Orde died at his home, 1 Durham Place, London, 'charmingly and without fuss', a few hours after celebrating his eightieth birthday, on 19 December 1968. His funeral was held at Christ Church, Chelsea, where he was buried on 23 December. His second wife survived him.

                                                                            HONOR CLERK

Sources C. J. Orde, *Pilots of fighter command: sixty-four portraits* (1942) · *DNB* · *The Times* (20 Dec 1968) · *The Times* (27 Dec 1968) · *The Times* (28 Dec 1968) · *Debrett's Peerage* · *Who's who in art* (1934) · *The*

Times (4 Nov 1952) • *The Times* (7 Nov 1952) • *The Times* (19 June 1929) • archival material, IWM • Graves, *RA exhibitors* • *Catalogue*, Royal Society of Portrait Painters (1925–62) [annual exhibition catalogues, London] • [J. P. M. Reid], *Some of the few* (1960) [portraits by Cuthbert Orde]

Archives IWM, letters relating to War Artists' Advisory Committee work

Likenesses C. Morris, double portrait, oils, *c*.1925 (with Lady Eileen) • N. Hepple, oils, exh. Royal Society of Portrait Painters 1958 • H. Carr, oils, exh. RA 1959

Wealth at death £26,548: probate, 14 March 1969, *CGPLA Eng. & Wales*

Orde, Sir John, first baronet (1751–1824), naval officer and politician, was born on 22 December 1751 at Nunnykirk, Morpeth, the youngest of three sons of John Orde (*c*.1704–*c*.1786) of East Orde and Morpeth. Thomas Orde-*Powlett, first Lord Bolton, was young John's brother, both being the sons of Anne (*d*. 1788), their father's second wife, daughter of Ralph Marr of Morpeth and widow of the Revd Pye.

Orde is thought to have attended grammar school at Morpeth before entering the navy in 1766 on the *Jersey*, bearing the broad pennant of Commodore Richard Spry, officer commanding the Mediterranean station. After further service on the Newfoundland and Jamaica stations he was promoted lieutenant of the sloop *Ferret* in 1773 by Sir George Rodney before returning home in the *Rainbow* the following year. After travel in France, in 1775 he sailed for America at the outbreak of the American War of Independence in the *Roebuck* with Captain Andrew Snape Hamond.

In early 1776 Orde was captured and held for a short period during the evacuation of the governor of Virginia, the earl of Dunmore, to Gwynn Island. At the time of his capture Orde had been leading an advance party under a flag of truce onto Gwynn Island to deliver a proclamation and negotiate a ceasefire and surrender. He became first lieutenant in August 1776 after that officer, M. S. Leake, was killed in the combined offensive launched on New York when a squadron, including the *Roebuck*, ran the gauntlet of a barrage of fire from onshore batteries. Early in 1777 Lord Howe appointed Orde first lieutenant of his flagship, the *Eagle*, and soon afterwards he promoted him commander of the sloop *Zebra*, in which command he assisted in the reduction of both Philadelphia and the forts of Delaware, for which, in May 1778, he was made post captain with command of the frigate *Virginia*. In the summer of 1779 the *Virginia* led Sir George Collier's squadron up the Penobscot River in pursuit of Commodore Saltonstall's expeditionary force which was advancing on Fort MacLean. When caught, the Americans ran for the shore and there set fire to all but one of their ships.

In 1780 Orde took part in the reduction of Charlestown. In a combined naval and military offensive Admiral Marriot Arbuthnot's squadron, including the *Virginia*, succeeded in clearing the estuary by forcing a passage through the gut guarded by the well-defended Fort Moultrie, the chief defence of the town. Arbuthnot afterwards singled out six officers for commendation, including Orde, who had taken Mount Pleasant with a contingent of 500 seamen, after which Fort Moultrie had quickly capitulated. At the close of the campaign he was given command of the *Chatham*, in which he captured the *General Washington*, and then, on 14 April 1781, the *Confederacy*. In July he sailed for London as Arbuthnot's flag-captain. In April of that year he had married Margaret Emma (1759–1790), daughter of Richard Stevens of St Helena, Charlestown; the couple had one child who died in infancy.

On his return to England, Orde remained first in the North Sea and then off the coast of France, until, in February 1783, he was appointed governor of Dominica, restored to Great Britain under the peace of Versailles. There his primary objectives were to develop the harbour in Prince Rupert's Bay, restore law and order among the quarrelsome white, black, and Carib population, and retain the island for the British. In all this he was largely successful, so much so that he was rewarded with a baronetcy in 1790, though proceedings were later taken against him by the colonial assembly over his plans for funding improvements to the harbour and fortifications. The privy council dismissed the allegation as 'frivolous'. With the onset of the war with France in 1793 Orde returned to naval duties. He served in the *Victorious*, the *Venerable*, and the *Prince George*, and then, on 1 June 1795, moved out of the *Prince George* on being raised to the rank of rear-admiral of the white in a general promotion. William Dillon described him at this time as 'tall, well-limbed [and] … of a haughty disposition' (Dillon, 1.188, 191), while James Ralfe assessed him as 'firm, cool, kind, dignified, with a noble prepossessing appearance finished by high good breeding' (Ralfe, 2.78–80).

Orde was appointed to temporary command at Plymouth in March 1797, but then, in recognition of his success in suppressing mutinous elements there, he was moved to Portsmouth to preside over the courts martial of the more serious mutineers at the Nore. That autumn he hoisted his flag in the *Princess Royal* and joined the Mediterranean Fleet standing off the Tagus as third in command to Lord St Vincent. After a winter of successful blockade duty at Cadiz, Orde was bitterly disappointed to learn that the more junior Horatio Nelson had been given command of an independent squadron to hunt down and destroy Napoleon's expeditionary force. This was followed on 24 May 1798 by the arrival of reinforcements under Sir Roger Curtis. Orde was thus relegated to fourth in command. A childish squabble then arose between himself and St Vincent concerning a complaint written to St Vincent which he wrongly attributed to Orde and which permanently soured their relationship. St Vincent ordered Orde to strike his flag and return to England in the *Blenheim*. On his return Orde's request that St Vincent be court-martialled was refused; however, the Admiralty gave St Vincent a written reprimand. Orde turned down an offer of employment with the Channel Fleet. Rather, he chose to wait for the arrival of St Vincent in October 1799 and demand satisfaction. However, word of Orde's intention reached Lord Spencer and both Orde and St Vincent were bound over to keep the peace and then forbidden by the king to accept any challenge.

Orde was promoted vice-admiral on 14 February 1799, but remained unemployed until St Vincent's removal as first lord. In the autumn of 1804 he was given command of a squadron formed to strengthen the British presence off Cadiz now that Spain had entered the war. However, although he mounted a most efficient blockade which kept the Spanish fleet in harbour throughout that winter, many complaints emanated from Nelson in the Mediterranean about Orde's policing of the strait and Nelson's lost opportunity to obtain prize money. Weary of his task, Orde made a written request that he should be allowed to retire home. However, soon afterwards Villeneuve escaped through the Strait of Gibraltar and sailed for Cadiz, where Orde's squadron lay at anchor. Outnumbered, and complying with standing orders, Orde skilfully withdrew to join the Channel Fleet off Ushant. His dispatches to London were the first to divine Napoleon's plan that Villeneuve should draw off the Channel Fleet by sailing west and then return to escort his army of invasion across the channel.

On 9 November 1805 Orde was promoted admiral of the blue, in October 1809 of the white, and in June 1814 of the red. A professed admirer of Nelson, his admiration was probably not reciprocated although he acted as a pall-bearer at Nelson's funeral. After the death of his first wife in 1790 Orde married Jane (c.1773–1829), daughter of John Frere; the couple had five children, including a son, John Powlett Orde, who was to inherit the baronetcy on his father's death. In 1807 Orde became MP for the Yarmouth division of the Isle of Wight. This followed the death of his brother Lord Bolton and the elevation of Bolton's son, the then sitting MP, to the peerage. Orde represented the seat until 1812. He died at his home, 20 Gloucester Place, Portman Square, London, on 19 February 1824 after a long and painful illness. He was buried at Hanwell parish church, Middlesex, and was survived by his wife, who died on 16 September 1829.   DENIS A. ORDE

Sources DNB · NMM, Orde MSS · Naval Chronicle, 2 (1799), 440 · 'Biographical memoirs of Sir John Orde', Naval Chronicle, 11 (1804), 177–207 · J. Marshall, Royal naval biography, 1/1 (1823), 69–73 · GM, 1st ser., 94/1 (1824), 276 · J. Ralfe, The naval biography of Great Britain, 2 (1828), 57 · E. P. Brenton, Life and correspondence of John, earl of St Vincent, 1 (1838), 393 · The dispatches and letters of Vice-Admiral Lord Viscount Nelson, ed. N. H. Nicolas, 7 vols. (1844–6) · R. Welford, Men of mark 'twixt Tyne and Tweed, 3 (1895), 239 · W. C. Dawson, Lloyd's Nelson collection (1932) · J. S. Corbett, The campaign of Trafalgar (1910) · D. Orde, Nelson's Mediterranean command (1997) · Letters and papers of Charles, Lord Barham, ed. J. K. Laughton, 3 vols., Navy RS, 32, 38–9 (1907–11) · Private papers of George, second Earl Spencer, ed. J. S. Corbett and H. W. Richmond, 4 vols., Navy RS, 46, 48, 58–9 (1913–24) · J. Leyland, ed., Dispatches and letters relating to the blockade of Brest, 1803–1805, 2 vols., Navy RS, 14, 21 (1899–1902) · W. H. Dillon, A narrative of my professional adventures (1790–1839), ed. M. A. Lewis, 2 vols., Navy RS, 93, 97 (1953–6)
Archives NMM, corresp. and papers
Likenesses S. W. Reynolds, mezzotint (after G. Romney), BM

Orde, Thomas. See Powlett, Thomas Orde-, first Baron Bolton (1746–1807).

Orderic Vitalis (1075–c.1142), Benedictine monk and historian, was the son of Odelerius d'Orléans, son of Constantius, and of an English mother. His childhood was passed in or near Shrewsbury, but he was sent aged ten to become an oblate monk in the Norman monastery of St Evroult where he spent the rest of his life, and where he was given the name of Vitalis. He ordinarily referred to himself as Vitalis the Englishman, though he is known to historians as Orderic Vitalis. His great work, the Ecclesiastical History, completed in 1141, is of exceptional value for the history of the Anglo-Norman world.

Orderic was born near Shrewsbury on 16 February 1075 and was baptized at Atcham, on 4 April 1075, by a priest who gave the child his own name, Orderic. His father, Odelerius, had come to England as a chaplain influential in the service of Roger de Montgomery, earl of Shrewsbury from 1074 to 1194, and successfully urged on his master the foundation of Shrewsbury Abbey. Odelerius was firmly committed to the cause of Benedictine monasticism. He gave generously to the new abbey, and both his second son, Benedict, and Odelerius himself became monks there, while his third son, Everard, was a tenant of the abbey. At the age of five Orderic, the eldest son, was sent to school in Shrewsbury to be taught by an English priest, Siward, and then, aged ten, was sent by his father in 1085 to the monastery of St Evroult, which had been refounded in 1050. In the deeply felt epilogue to his Ecclesiastical History Orderic wrote of never having seen his father again and having left his country, family, and friends for exile, ignorant of French. He never mentioned his mother, presumably because he was troubled by his father's having been a married clerk.

Orderic was tonsured on 21 September 1075, ordained subdeacon on 15 March 1091, deacon on 26 March 1093, and priest on 21 December 1107. When he laid down his pen in 1141 he had spent fifty-six years in St Evroult, never holding administrative office, though he probably came to be in charge of the library. He made occasional journeys, on one occasion to Crowland where he spent five weeks, and it may have been then that he visited Thorney and Worcester. He visited Cambrai, was almost certainly present at the Council of Rheims in 1119, and attended the general chapter at Cluny in 1132. The chief formative influences on Orderic were the teaching of Jean de Rheims, his master in the abbey school whom he so deeply respected, and above all his own extensive reading and work as an accomplished scribe copying manuscripts. From 1095 to c.1114 he was learning his craft as a historian. He compiled the annals of St Evroult from 1095, and he made his own copy of the Gesta Normannorum ducum of William of Jumièges, revising it, adding an account of the Normans in southern Italy, and virtually rewriting the narrative of the Norman conquest of England, quietly correcting the bias of a work that had originally been dedicated to William the Conqueror. Orderic also made his own copy of Bede's Ecclesiastical History of the English People, a work that had the deepest influence on Orderic's outlook and ambitions as a historian, and which may well have led Orderic to call his own major work the Ecclesiastical History.

In its final form the Ecclesiastical History consists of thirteen books which occupied Orderic for over quarter of a century, from *c.*1114 to 1141. Its structure is complex. It began as what Orderic called 'a little work' on the history of St Evroult from its refoundation *c.*1050, commissioned by Roger du Sap, abbot from 1091 to 1123. It was designed, like so many such works, to provide a record of the founders, benefactors, abbots, and properties of the house. At an early point Orderic glanced at the possibility of a great history centred on William the Conqueror and his family, regretfully dismissing it as unsuitable for a cloistered monk. But even within book 3, the first to be written, Orderic suddenly took up the story of the Norman conquest without apology or explanation. Orderic spent at least ten years on book 3, but under Abbot Warin des Essarts (1123–37) the pace of his work was quickened and its scope widened. By *c.*1130, in books 4, 5, and 6, Orderic had combined the history of his abbey with the story of Norman achievements down to 1083. In seven further books he dealt with events of his own lifetime down to 1141, writing rapidly and at times in a mood of exhilaration, as when he described himself as having left the subject of St Evroult and having 'surveyed the wide kingdoms of the world as one caught up in a trance, flying hither and thither' (Ordericus Vitalis, *Eccl. hist.*, 4.337). Elsewhere he described his own part of the world, as distinct from the kingdom of Jerusalem, as Italy, Gaul, Spain, England, and Flanders. The structure of the history was further modified and sometimes enlivened by digressions such as that on the history of the archbishops of Rouen, the legend of the Turkish princess who organized the release of Bohemond from captivity, the prophecies of Merlin, Spanish history, and a judicious treatise on the new monastic orders. At a late stage books 1 and 2 were compiled in order to convert the whole work into a universal history beginning with the birth of Christ.

Orderic's expressed aims were unexceptionable and sincere. He was, he told his readers, concerned with the simple truth, impartial between English and Normans, looking for no rewards from victors or vanquished, and while he would have preferred edifying subject matter, he had to recognize that miracles had ceased and that his task was to describe the follies, fashions, and disputes of men as they were and not as he would have had them be. It is easy to criticize his practice. He copied earlier writers extensively, had no consistent principles of selection or arrangement, and was remarkably careless of chronology, even of events in his own lifetime. But his history remains of inestimable value for the range, variety, and volume of the information he acquired, and above all for his knowledge and understanding of the lay aristocracy of his day, often expressed in the many imaginary speeches and dialogues he composed.

When Orderic wrote the very moving epilogue to his work in 1141, shortly before he died, his ordered Anglo-Norman world had disintegrated after the death of his hero, Henry I, the architect of peace and justice. He had been unable to bring himself to record what he regarded as the useless proceedings of the Lateran Council of 1139. Perhaps this sense of the end of an era partly explains the virtual neglect of Orderic's history until it was printed by

Duchesne in 1619. But if Orderic was unlucky in failing to attract the readers for whom he had hoped, he was fortunate in the survival of his own autograph manuscripts for all but books 7 and 8, for which there is an incomplete twelfth-century transcript by a Caen scribe. In the mid-nineteenth century justice was at last done in the great edition of the *Ecclesiastical History* by A. Le Prévost, assisted by L. Delisle. In the second half of the twentieth century M. Chibnall made this the basis of her own edition, a definitive work of outstanding scholarship, especially effective in relating Orderic to the varied beliefs, prejudices, and passions of his age. One result of the revival of interest in Orderic was the erection of a statue to him in 1912 on the site of the church in St Evroult. Another, some scholars have suggested, was that Orderic has been allowed too much influence on the interpretation of the past, since he had almost single-handedly created a Norman 'myth', imposing on the evidence his thesis of the unity of the Normans and their destiny as a conquering and colonizing people. Orderic himself, it may be surmised, would have been gratified by the statue, but dismayed by the charge that he, an Englishman and a conservative of a compassionate temperament, had been a propagandist for men whose cruelties and oppressions he had so often condemned. J. O. PRESTWICH

Sources Ordericus Vitalis, *Eccl. hist.* · M. Chibnall, *The world of Orderic Vitalis* (1984) · *The Gesta Normannorum ducum of William of Jumièges, Orderic Vitalis, and Robert of Torigni*, ed. and trans. E. M. C. van Houts, 1, OMT (1992) · A. Gransden, *Historical writing in England*, 1 (1974) · R. H. C. Davis, *The Normans and their myth* (1976) · G. A. Loud, 'The *Gens Normannorum*—myth or reality?', *Anglo-Norman Studies*, 4 (1981), 104–16

Ordgar (*d.* 971), magnate, was a prominent landowner in the west country in the middle of the tenth century and maternal grandfather of King *Æthelred II. Although apparently without any official position at the court of King Eadwig (*r.* 955–9), he was clearly a figure of some importance, because in 956 his daughter *Ælfthryth married Æthelwold (II), eldest son of Ealdorman *Æthelstan Half-King. He witnessed King *Edgar's charters as a thegn from 962. Ælfthryth was widowed in 962 or 963, and in 964 married the king. The charter by which Edgar endowed his new wife with an estate in Berkshire was the last which his new father-in-law witnessed as a mere thegn, since Edgar made him an ealdorman later in 964. Later tradition called him ealdorman of Dumnonia, probably meaning Devon and Cornwall, and a connection with the latter shire is evident from the fact that he is known to have freed one of his slaves at the altar of St Petroc in Bodmin. As a thegn, Ordgar had witnessed only a handful of Edgar's charters between 962 and 964; as an ealdorman he was named on almost all of those issued between 964 and 970, a period when he must have been among the king's closest advisers. Ordgar died in 971 and was buried at Exeter. In the twelfth century William of Malmesbury claimed that he had founded and been buried at Tavistock Abbey, through a confusion with his son Ordwulf, the real founder of Tavistock, and with a later Ordgar who was buried there. Although Ordwulf did not become an ealdorman, he was a figure of great importance in the reign of Æthelred.

Ealdorman Ordgar featured as a rich widower with lands in every town and village between Frome and Exeter in a tale elaborated by Geoffrey Gaimar in the twelfth century, which centred on Ordgar's beautiful daughter Ælfthryth, King Edgar, and the deceitful knight Æthelwold, who wooed the girl for himself. In Gaimar's version the story begins with Ælfthryth and her doting father, Ordgar, playing chess when Æthelwold arrives. Ælfthryth's two marriages clearly formed a foundation for the story, though it adds nothing credible to knowledge of Ordgar or anyone else.   C. P. LEWIS

Sources H. P. R. Finberg, 'The house of Ordgar and the foundation of Tavistock Abbey', *EngHR*, 58 (1943), 190–201, esp. 190–91 · H. P. R. Finberg, 'Childe's tomb', *Lucerna: studies of some problems in the early history of England* (1964), 186–203, at 190–92, 198 · C. Hart, 'Athelstan "half king" and his family', *The Danelaw* (1992), 569–604, esp. 582–6, 589–91, 601–3 · John of Worcester, *Chron.*, 2.414–17, 420–21 · *Willelmi Malmesbiriensis monachi de gestis pontificum Anglorum libri quinque*, ed. N. E. S. A. Hamilton, Rolls Series, 52 (1870), 202–3 · *L'estoire des Engleis by Geffrei Gaimar*, ed. A. Bell, Anglo-Norman Texts, 14–16 (1960)

Ordgar (*d.* 1094?), landholder and soldier, was apparently an Englishman who served William II as a household knight. The story of his duel with Edgar Ætheling's champion is told in John Fordun's fourteenth-century history of Scotland from an unknown source, though it may well have taken place and Ordgar's opponent certainly seems to have existed. Fordun related the episode after the death of Malcolm III of Scotland and the consequent flight of his children with Edgar to England in late 1093, and before Duncan's invasion of Scotland in 1094, though it could have taken place later in William II's reign. Ordgar, wishing to win favour with the king, accused Edgar of treachery; the challenge was taken up by Edgar's knight Godwine of Winchester (very likely the Godwine who was Edgar's tenant in Hertfordshire in 1086); Godwine won the duel, killed Ordgar, vindicated Edgar's loyalty, and was awarded Ordgar's lands. Ordgar was a common enough name in the later eleventh century and it is impossible to be certain about the knight's identity; but he may have been the Ordgar who in 1086 held one small Oxfordshire manor as a king's thegn and two others as Miles Crispin's tenant, claiming that he ought to have them as the king's man because he and his father and uncle had held them freely before 1066. The Godwine who had formerly held the first manor is therefore more likely to have been Ordgar's father or uncle, rather than the combatant in 1094 as Freeman suggested.   C. P. LEWIS

Sources *Johannis de Fordun Chronica gentis Scotorum / John of Fordun's Chronicle of the Scottish nation*, ed. W. F. Skene, trans. F. J. H. Skene, 2 vols. (1871–2), vol. 1, pp. 220–22; vol. 2, pp. 210–12 · A. Farley, ed., *Domesday Book*, 2 vols. (1783), fols. 159v, 161 · E. A. Freeman, *The reign of William Rufus*, 2 (1882), 115–18, 615–17

Ordgar (*fl.* 1066), landowner, was sheriff of Cambridgeshire before 1066. He was typical of Edward the Confessor's sheriffs in being a thegn with a moderate landed estate. He certainly owned manors at Chippenham and Isleham in east Cambridgeshire, on the edge of the Isle of Ely, and was presumably the same Ordgar who had land and men in the south of the county and near by in north Essex. Harston in south Cambridgeshire might have been part of his official endowment as it passed to the Norman sheriff Picot, and Ordgar held Sawston as a tenant of Earl Harold. In all Ordgar's estate amounted to six manors assessed at 20 hides and worth almost £40 a year. Probably after the battle of Hastings, Ordgar placed himself under the protection of Asgar the Staller, one of the great English magnates of the south-east midlands. The sheriff can perhaps be identified as the Ordgar who joined Hereward the Wake as a leader of the outlaws and rebels based at Ely in 1070–71. The traditions preserved about the rebellion were that Ordgar was a rich thegn (*procer*), and that a monk of Ely who was presumably his son, Alwine son of Ordgar, slipped out of the abbey to warn Hereward when the other monks decided to surrender to King William, and then persuaded the rebels not to burn Ely in revenge. Conversely, there is no reason to identify sheriff Ordgar with any of the other eight or so Ordgars who were minor landowners in other shires in 1066.   C. P. LEWIS

Sources A. Farley, ed., *Domesday Book*, 2 vols. (1783) · E. O. Blake, ed., *Liber Eliensis*, CS, 3rd ser., 92 (1962), 179 · 'Gesta Herwardi incliti exulis et militis', *Lestorie des Engles solum la translacion Maistre Geffrei Gaimar*, ed. T. D. Hardy and C. T. Martin, 1 (1888), 339–404, 379, 391

Ordish, Rowland Mason (1824–1886), engineer, was born at Melbourne, Derbyshire, on 11 April 1824, the son of John Ordish, land agent and surveyor. Nothing is known about his education prior to his arrival in London in his twenties. After some time in an architect's office, in 1847 he went to work as an assistant in the office of the engineer R. E. Brounger. He was engaged on the design of structures and is said to have soon showed particular promise for this work. He was sent to survey the proposed route for a railway in Denmark, a country to which he returned for a short while in 1855. While involved in preparing drawings for a bridge at Windsor he obtained permission from his employer to submit a scheme of his own. This was selected by the queen and the bridge was constructed to his design. At about this time he worked on the caisson foundations of the Black Potts Bridge on the South Western Railway.

In the summer of 1850 Ordish was working for Fox Henderson as a draughtsman, helping with the preparation of the working drawings for the 1851 Exhibition building in Hyde Park. These were prepared by Charles Fox and Ordish in London and sent to foundries in Smethwick and Dudley. Ordish is reported to have carried out his work so efficiently that more and more important tasks were entrusted to him. In late 1850 he was sent to Birmingham to work with Charles Fox and E. A. Cowper on the details for the roof of New Street Station, Birmingham. This roof and the 1851 Exhibition building were both structures that involved innovative uses of cast and wrought iron and working on them provided useful experience. In 1853–4 he was at Sydenham supervising the re-erection and extension of the Exhibition building, even though he had expressed doubts about the suitability of this use of columns and beams for glass and iron roofs. His work with

Charles Fox on these schemes was the basis for a lasting friendship and working relationship that continued for many years.

From January 1856 to March or April 1858 Ordish was employed as a draughtsman in the works department of the Admiralty, where Colonel G. T. Greene was director and William Scamp was the civil engineer. This again was an office where innovative ideas were developed, especially during 1857 when the rigid iron frame structure for the Sheerness boat shed was being designed. In 1858 he resigned from the works department and set up in practice at 18 Great George Street, Westminster, first in partnership with a Mr Dawdney and very soon after with W. H. Le Feuvre. In April 1858 he took out a patent for improvements in the design and construction of suspension bridges, which involved a rigid road girder suspended on rigid straight chains, which became known as 'Ordish's rigid chain suspension system'. He proposed a low-level bridge of this type across the Thames at the Tower of London in 1862 but the system was not used until 1868 when the Franz Joseph Bridge over the Moldau at Prague was constructed using a chain of steel link bars. For this scheme he received the Austrian gold medal for Arts and Sciences. Another bridge on the same principle was shortly constructed nearby, and later one in Singapore, and one in the USA.

In 1872 a scheme for a bridge at Chelsea was authorized in parliament with, it is said, the promoters insisting that it be designed by Ordish. The Albert Bridge was constructed to his design, but the owners substituted steel wires in place of the link chains he proposed. These were later replaced with the steel link chains he had recommended. He prepared three schemes for other bridges that were not built: in 1872 for a twin-span toll bridge and four tunnels at the Tower; in 1874 with Max am Ende, his chief assistant, for one across the Neva at St Petersburg (for which he received a prize of £300); and, with Ewing Matheson of Andrew Handyside Ltd, in 1885 for a scheme on the site of the present Tower Bridge.

In 1866 Ordish obtained a bill for an underground railway from Charing Cross to Euston, running under Tottenham Court Road, which included a new street through Seven Dials. His skill and experience in the design and detailing of iron structures was much admired and his assistance and expertise were sought and used by many engineers in the sixties and seventies. When the domes of the 1862 Exhibition building in South Kensington were found to be unstable he was asked to prepare a scheme for a form of internal bracing. In 1863–4 he assisted Charles Fox with schemes for the series of bridges south of the Thames and the bridge over it at Pimlico for the London, Chatham, and Dover Railway. Again with Fox he worked on the design for a railway bridge across the River Bremer, Queensland, Australia.

The roof over the train shed at St Pancras Station, commenced in 1865, clearly demonstrates his ability and skill in designing and detailing aesthetically pleasing, practical, and economic wrought-iron structures. With its clear arched span of 240 ft it attracted wide attention in both the technical and lay press and Ordish's contribution was publicly acknowledged by W. H. Barlow at a meeting of the Institution of Civil Engineers in 1870.

Ordish collaborated with Owen Jones on an 80 ft by 40 ft kiosk in India made of cast iron. To stabilize the bases of the columns he used a beam extending into the building below floor level. A similar device was used in 1876 for the bases of the arched roof of St Enoch's Station, Glasgow. This roof was of much the same form as St Pancras and the roof of Cape Town Station, on which Ordish worked. In 1868 he designed, for G. G. Scott, a rectangular dome of iron ribs and glass for the Leeds Infirmary winter gardens. For the next ten years Scott consulted Ordish about the structural ironwork on his schemes and, at Westminster Abbey, Ordish designed for him a polygonal iron framework in the roof space of the chapter house to support the stone vault.

In 1863, with his partner Le Feuvre, Ordish designed and constructed the Dutch-Rhenish railway station at Amsterdam. This was constructed with many cast-iron components, a material that Ordish, unlike many of his contemporaries, considered to be suitable for a variety of structures. His connection with iron founders like Fox Henderson, Handyside, and Heywoods (for whom he designed a cast-iron fronted house) provided him with opportunities to exploit the material. One of his cast-iron bridges is that over Farringdon Street, on the Holborn Viaduct, designed in 1863.

Between 1860 and 1875 Ordish worked on the details of numerous structures, including the Amsterdam Crystal Palace, the Dublin Exhibition building (later re-erected as the Albert Palace at Battersea), the Holloway College at Egham, and another all cast-iron building, the Watson's Hotel at Bombay. In 1869, in conjunction with J. W. Grover, a former Fox Henderson employee, and W. Fairbairn, he designed and detailed the oval, shallow domed roof at the Albert Hall, South Kensington. In 1876, with Perry F. Nursey, he published a scheme for a double cast-iron tube tunnel to be laid on the bed of the channel between Dover and Calais. In addition to the patent he took out for suspension bridges in 1858 he obtained other patents for various devices. One, an elastic chair and rail fixing taken out in 1859, was used on the Stratford upon Avon Railway but was not widely adopted.

Ordish became a member of the Society of Engineers in 1857 (when it was still the Putney Club) and its president in 1860. In September 1857 he gave a paper on suspension bridges and another in May 1858 on the forms and strength of beams, girders, and trusses. He was a member of the Society of Arts, but although asked to join other professional organizations never did. He was a talented designer of structural details with a facility for making rapid mental estimates of the cost of structural ironwork. At the time of his death contemporaries commented that he did not appear to take advantage of the numerous opportunities for advancement that had presented themselves, and that he had little interest in society, which he shunned rather than courted. His death was regretted by the large number of pupils who had been trained in his office and who were in posts all over the world.

In 1881 Ordish became engineer to Dennet and Ingle of Whitehall, and he was inspecting work in progress on their behalf the day before he died. He had suffered from oedema and heart disease for some time and died in his sleep at his home, 19 Stratford Place, Kentish Town, on 12 September 1886. He was buried in the Old Ground, Highgate cemetery, on 17 September 1886.

STANLEY SMITH

Sources *The Engineer* (17 Sept 1886), 232–3 · *Engineering* (17 Sept 1886), 298 · *The Builder*, 51 (1886), 412 · *Iron*, 28 (17 Sept 1886), 265 [obituary] · Boase, *Mod. Eng. biog.* · d. cert.
Likenesses lithograph, Society of Engineers, London

O'Reilly, Alexander, Count O'Reilly in the Spanish nobility (*bap.* **1723**, *d.* **1794**), army officer in the Spanish service, was baptized on 24 October 1723 at the parish church, Baltrasna, co. Meath, Ireland, the son of Thomas O'Reilly. His father, a Roman Catholic, took the family to Spain and O'Reilly was schooled in Saragossa at the Colegio de Padres de las Escuelas Pias. At the age of eleven he entered the Spanish army and by 1739 he was stationed in Catalonia. He served in the Hibernia infantry regiment in the campaigns against Austria in Italy and in 1741 he travelled to Naples in the army of the duke of Montemar, who promoted him to lieutenant. At the battle of Campo Santo in February 1743 he was shot in the boot and lamed for life.

In 1757 O'Reilly volunteered to join the Austrian army in the war against Prussia so that he could study the new infantry tactics introduced into the Prussian army by Frederick the Great, and he took part in two campaigns against the Prussians commanded by his countryman Count Maurice Francis Lacy. His reports on the Prussian infantry were well received by the Spanish high command and O'Reilly was promoted brigadier in 1759. He served in the war with Portugal from 1761 onwards and gained the reputation of being one of the best officers in Spanish service. At the peace of 1763 he was promoted major-general and appointed governor of Havana in Cuba, where he arrived later that year. By 1764 he was advising the Spanish government to encourage Irish immigration to Cuba as a means of improving the local economy and strengthening the island's defences; in 1765 he was transferred as governor to San Juan in Puerto Rico. In the following year he returned to Spain, where, as inspector-general of the Spanish infantry, he was responsible for introducing Prussian tactics to the whole of the Spanish infantry. Rewarded with the order of Alcantara and the rank of lieutenant-general, O'Reilly was sent to restore Spanish rule in Louisiana in 1769 after the previous governor had been thrown out by the largely French population.

O'Reilly benefited greatly from the personal patronage of Charles III, who created him Count O'Reilly in 1772 and selected him to command the Spanish expedition against Algiers in 1775. The king's choice of a foreigner, however, provoked jealousy among the Spanish officers. His fleet of 40 ships of the lane and 350 other vessels carried a force of 22,000 infantrymen, but the ships failed to arrive at Algiers at the same time and the flat-bottomed boats for landing the troops never materialized. Fearing that his ships would run aground, O'Reilly prepared to land and on 8 July put ashore some 10,000 troops under the command of the marqués de La Romana to cover the landing of the rest. The Moroccan counterattack surprised the second landing of Spanish infantrymen, entrenched behind the hedges of prickly pears and aloes, and the Spanish suffered an appalling defeat. 2000 infantrymen were killed, including Romana, and many more were wounded; O'Reilly took full responsibility for the disaster and was exiled to the Chafarinas Islands.

O'Reilly was soon allowed to return to Spain by Charles III, who placed him at the head of the military school, established first at Avila and then at Port Sta Maria in Cadiz Bay. He later became commander-in-chief in Andalusia and governor of Cadiz, but after the death of Charles III he fell into disgrace and was stripped of his military offices and appointments. He retired to Galicia on a small pension, yet his military career was not over for good. Following the outbreak of war with France in 1793 he was restored to his old rank and appointed commander of the naval base at Toulon to help the French monarchists against Bonaparte. The death of General Antonio Ricardos on 11 March 1794 led to his final appointment as commander of the Spanish army in the east Pyrenees. On his way to his troops in Alicante, O'Reilly died from a stroke at a small village, Bonete, in Murcia, Spain, on 23 March 1794. He was married and was survived by his son, Alesandro O'Reilly y Casas (1769–1832), who married a rich Cuban heiress and became commander of the central region of Cuba.

H. M. CHICHESTER, *rev.* D. M. BEAUMONT

Sources E. Beerman, 'Alexander O'Reilly: an Irish soldier in the service of Spain', *Irish Sword*, 15 (1982–3), 101–4 · [J. C. F. Hoefer], ed., *Nouvelle biographie générale*, 31 (1870) · B. O'Connell, 'Reply to a query on three Irish soldiers', *Irish Sword*, 2 (1954–6), 378–9 · F. Carroll, 'Reply to a query on three Irish soldiers', *Irish Sword*, 3 (1957–8), 71–2 · *Report on American manuscripts in the Royal Institution of Great Britain*, 4 vols., HMC, 59 (1904–9), vol. 3, pp. 367–8 · G. de C. Ireland, 'General Alexander O'Reilly and the Spanish attack on Algiers', 12 (1975), 131–8
Archives Archives du Ministère des Affaires Etrangères, Paris, military corresp. · Barcelona Biblioteca Central, military corresp. · Biblioteca Nacional, Madrid, MSS · Musée Condé, Paris, military corresp. · TCD, MSS
Likenesses portrait, Louisiana State Museum, New Orleans; repro. in Beerman, 'Alexander O'Reilly', facing p. 104

O'Reilly, Andrew, Count O'Reilly in the Austrian nobility (**1742–1832**), army officer in the Austrian service, was born at Ballinlough, co. Roscommon, on 3 August 1742, the second son of James O'Reilly of Ballinlough and his wife, Barbara, the daughter of Andrew Nugent and his wife, Catherine. The O'Reillys traced their ancestry back to Rufus Gelasius, a thirteenth-century Irish petty prince. Andrew O'Reilly entered the Austrian service as a cadet in the 54th infantry regiment (Sincère, later Callenberg) on 1 November 1763. He was promoted lieutenant on 7 November 1764 and advanced to first lieutenant on 1 October 1767 and to captain on 1 December 1768. On 5 July 1778, now a major, he was transferred to the general staff, and he served as an aide-de-camp during the War of the Bavarian Succession (1778–9). On 17 June 1779 O'Reilly was transferred to the 2nd regiment of Carabiniers (Erzherzog Franz); he was nominated first major on 22 December 1781 and lieutenant-colonel on 24 April 1784. He married, in 1786, Countess Maria Barbara von Sweerts-Spork (1760–1834). Together they owned considerable property in Bohemia and Galicia.

In the summer of 1787 O'Reilly killed the major of his regiment in a duel but was acquitted by a court martial. He was elevated to the rank of count (Graf) on 8 October 1787. From December 1787 he served with the Hohenzollern cuirassiers, and from 1789 to 1794 he was commanding colonel of the Modena chevauxlegers. He was present at the taking of Belgrade in 1789 during the Turkish War. In the war against revolutionary France he fought in the Low Countries (1792–4) and was promoted major-general (22 July 1794). While serving with the Austrian army in Germany he distinguished himself repeatedly during the campaigns of 1796–7, but he was wounded and made prisoner in April 1797.

After being promoted Feldmarschall-Leutnant on 6 March 1800 O'Reilly served with the Austrian army in Italy during the campaign of 1800. On 18 August 1801 he received the knight's cross of the military order of Maria Theresa, and the same year he was made imperial chamberlain. He was promoted colonel-proprietor of the 3rd regiment of chevauxlegers on 2 October 1803. In the campaign of 1805 he fought at the head of a division at the battle of Caldiero (29–31 October 1805). His personal bravery won him the commander's cross of the order of Maria Theresa (April 1806). From February to May 1809 he was vice-commander of Lower Austria and in charge of the provincial militia forces, but he was then ordered back to Vienna to help organize the defence of the Austrian capital against the approaching French forces. After two days of heavy bombardment Vienna surrendered on 13 May 1809; the garrison escaped across the Danube. The thankless task of signing the capitulation fell to O'Reilly, who retired with the rank of General der Kavallerie on 7 January 1810. He died at Vienna on 5 July 1832 and was buried at the cemetery of Matzleinsdorf in Vienna. As he had no children O'Reilly had adopted as his heir John O'Reilly (b. 1800), the son of his elder brother Sir Hugh O'Reilly and his wife, Catherine Mary Anne Matthew; John served until 1850 as a major of hussars in the Austrian service. Andrew O'Reilly's younger brother James also entered the Austrian army.   MICHAEL HOCHEDLINGER

Sources Österreichisches Staatsarchiv, Vienna, Haus-, Hof- und Staatsarchiv, Oberstkämmereramt, Ahnenproben 48 · Österreichisches Staatsarchiv, Vienna, Allgemeines Verwaltungsarchiv, Adelsakt O'Reilly, 8 Oct 1787 · Österreichisches Staatsarchiv, Vienna, Kriegsarchiv, Hofkriegsrat Akten 1787-62-1096, Direktionsakten 143/1915 · *Genealogisches Taschenbuch der deutschen gräflichen Häuser* (1835), 352 · J. Hirtenfeld, *Der Militär-Maria-Theresien-Orden und seine Mitglieder* (1857), vol. 1, p. 631; vol. 2, p. 765–7 · *DNB* · C. von Wurzbach, *Biographisches Lexikon des Kaiserthums Österreich*, 60 vols. (Vienna, 1856–91), vol. 21, pp. 86–9 · Sch., 'O'Reilly, Andreas', *Allgemeine deutsche Biographie*, ed. R. von Liliencron and others, 24 (Leipzig, 1887), 409–11 · A. von Wrede,

Geschichte der k. und k. Wehrmacht, 5 vols. (Vienna, 1898–1905) · E. Schmidhofer, 'Das irische, schottische und englische Element im kaiserlichen Heer', PhD diss., University of Vienna, 1971

O'Reilly, Edmund (1598–1669), Roman Catholic archbishop of Armagh, was born, according to his own account, on 2 or 3 January 1598, almost certainly in south co. Dublin. His father, perhaps Garret O'Reilly, seems to have belonged to a line not far removed from the main stem of what was the principal family of East Breifne (now co. Cavan), but no reliable personal detail concerning his parents has survived. He received his classical education in Dublin city, probably in one of the schools the Jesuits and Franciscans were able to maintain there at this time. About 1620 he went to the Irish seminary in Douai in the Spanish Netherlands, and may also have spent some time in the Irish College very recently opened in Antwerp. He was ordained priest by the exiled Archbishop Florence Conry of Tuam, though no official record of this has been located.

O'Reilly set out for Ireland in 1626, but on his way through England was arrested and imprisoned for almost two years. On his release in March 1628 he went to Ireland and took up duty in Dublin, where a pragmatic and political toleration succeeded a show of force by the government in 1629. He commended himself to the archbishop, Thomas Fleming, who decided to appoint him his vicar-general, though it is uncertain whether this appointment was made before O'Reilly went to the University of Louvain for further studies about 1637 or after his return in 1641. From 1641 onwards he was, in practice, in charge of ecclesiastical affairs in the diocese because the archbishop was in Kilkenny engaged in the political affairs of the confederate Catholics.

In 1648 the confederates were finally divided: on the one side the supporters of the papal nuncio Rinuccini, who demanded a complete repeal of the penal laws, and on the other side the party, largely Old English in composition, that was ready to accept from the lord lieutenant, the marquess of Ormond, the kind of practical toleration they had grown accustomed to. O'Reilly was a committed supporter of the nuncio's party, and was the chief intermediary in negotiations between the old Irish military leader, Owen Roe O'Neill, and Michael Jones, commander of the parliamentarian forces in Dublin. Rumour even attributed to him responsibility for Ormond's defeat by Jones at Rathmines (August 1649) through his betraying Ormond's position. The rift between the two confederate factions was patched up after the arrival of Oliver Cromwell, but over the course of a few years the country was conquered. O'Reilly had joined the resistance in the mountains of Wicklow, but when this collapsed in 1652 he was arrested. In September 1653 he was put on trial on the charge of having approved of murders at the capture of Wicklow Castle in December 1642. The military court found him guilty, but after more than two years in prison he was deported.

On 16 April 1657 O'Reilly was appointed archbishop of Armagh, principally, it would appear, on the recommendation of Dionisio Massari, who had been Rinuccini's chief assistant in Ireland, and had returned to become secretary of the Roman Congregatio de Propaganda Fide. His appointment was resisted by the English court in exile, but he was consecrated quietly in Brussels on 26 May 1658. He made his way to London, where in the political uncertainties of the Commonwealth he made hostile contact with his future opponent the Irish Franciscan Peter Walsh. He was expelled to France, but he now sailed directly to Ireland, where he arrived at the beginning of October 1658. He found a church that had barely survived the persecutions of the 1650s, but his own position worsened with the Restoration in May 1660. The Roman authorities ordered his recall and the government ordered his arrest, and he was deported in April 1661.

In Ireland the Restoration revived the bitter controversies of the 1640s. By 1663 there were reports that O'Reilly was acting to produce a conjunction between former supporters of the nuncio and exiled English republican opponents of the new regime. By contrast, in Ireland a party loyal to the monarchy and to Ormond felt it necessary to make a dramatic display of loyalty if they were to have any hope of dislodging those who had benefited from the confiscation of their landed property. Under the theological guidance of Peter Walsh, a declaration of loyalty emerged that drew heavily on the Gallican ideas now maturing in France, with the additional complication in Ireland that the monarch was protestant. Ormond, once again lord lieutenant, insisted that it be signed by the clergy, but when Walsh convened a meeting in Dublin he got little support.

Ormond kept up the pressure, however, and Walsh managed to convoke a national synod for Dublin for June 1666. O'Reilly was anxious to attend, and in seeking permission to return he was so obsequious to Ormond and Walsh that they assumed he would support them. The Roman authorities had been warning the Irish clergy, against a background of French developments that had already led to a serious clash, and the nuncio in Brussels personally advised him not to attend. But he arrived in Dublin on 12 June, and the next day made it clear to the synod that he could not accept the proposed formula.

It was decided that O'Reilly be again deported. He left Ireland late in the summer of 1666. He went first to the Netherlands, where he found the nuncio hostile. He then went to Paris, living in poverty there. Early in 1669 he set out for Nantes, apparently because he considered it would be cheaper to live there. He died on the journey, at Saumur, and was buried in the Oratorian church of Notre Dame. Lynch gives 8 March as the date of his death (Lynch, 1.145), but this cannot be quite accurate, for a surviving parish register notes his burial on 17 March.

PATRICK J. CORISH

Sources T. O. Fiaich, 'Edmund O'Reilly archbishop of Armagh, 1657–1669', *Father Luke Wadding: commemorative volume*, ed. Franciscan Fathers dún Mhuire, Killiney (1957), 171–228 • B. O'Ferrall and D. O'Connell, *Commentarius Rinuccinianus de sedis apostolicae legatione ad foederatos Hiberniae Catholicos per annos 1645–1649*, ed. J. Kavanagh, 6 vols., IMC (1932–49) • Thurloe, *State papers* • C. Giblin, ed., 'Catalogue of material of Irish interest in the collection *Nunziatura di Fiandra*, Vatican archives [pt 1]', *Collectanea Hibernica*, 1 (1958), 7–134 • C. Giblin, ed., 'Catalogue of material of Irish interest in the collection *Nunziatura di Fiandra*, Vatican archives [pt 2]', *Collectanea Hibernica*, 3 (1960), 7–144 • J. Linchaeo [J. Lynch], *De praesulibus Hiberniae*, ed. J. F. O'Doherty, 2 vols., IMC (1944) • P. Walsh, *The history and vindication of the loyal formulary, or Irish remonstrance* (1674) • T. Carte, *An history of the life of James, duke of Ormonde*, 3 vols. (1735–6) • L. F. Renehan, *Collections on Irish church history*, ed. D. McCarthy, 1 (1861) • S. J. Connolly, *Religion, law, and power: the making of protestant Ireland, 1660–1760* (1992)
Archives Archivio Vaticano, Vatican City, MSS • Sacra Congregazione di Propaganda Fide, Rome, MSS

O'Reilly, Edmund Joseph (1811–1878), Jesuit and theologian, was born in London on 30 April 1811. His mother was a daughter of Edmund O'Callaghan of Killegorey, co. Clare. In 1817 the family moved to Mount Catherine, near Limerick, where the father soon died, and after receiving private tuition O'Reilly was sent to the Jesuit school at Clongoweswood, near Kildare. He later studied metaphysics at Maynooth College, co. Kildare. About 1830 he entered the Irish College, Rome, where Paul Cullen (1803–1878) (later archbishop of Dublin) was rector; they became lifelong friends. He graduated as a doctor in theology in 1835 and, after acting as assistant to Cullen, was ordained in 1838. Soon afterwards he returned to Ireland, where he was appointed professor of theology at Maynooth, a position which he held until 1850.

In August 1850 O'Reilly acted as theological adviser (at the Synod of Thurles) to Cullen, who had just been appointed archbishop of Armagh. He performed the same service for Bishop James Brown of Shrewsbury at the provincial synod of the English Catholic bishops held at Oscott, and for Bishop Furlong of Ferns at the Synod of Maynooth. In the summer of 1851 he applied for admission to the Society of Jesus; he undertook his noviciate at the Jesuit house in Naples, and during his time there published a revised *Catechism of Scripture History* (1852) which had been compiled by the Sisters of Mercy at Limerick. After completing his noviciate and taking his final vows he was appointed to teach theology at the Jesuit college of St Beuno's, near St Asaph, north Wales. His lectures there attracted attention, and in the summer of 1858 he was selected by J. H. Newman and the Irish bishops to teach divinity at the newly founded Catholic University in Dublin. Early in 1859 he was withdrawn from his university post and appointed superior of a new Jesuit retreat at Milltown Park, near Dublin, where he remained for the rest of his life. From 1863 to 1870 he was Irish provincial of the Society of Jesus.

Newman, in his *Letter to the Duke of Norfolk* during the Vatican controversy, mentioned O'Reilly as 'one of the first theologians of the day'; and W. G. Ward, writing in the *Dublin Review* in praise of his essays, regretted that he had published so little. O'Reilly's knowledge of patristic theology was especially extensive, and he was continually referred to by the Irish bishops and clergy as a high authority. Even in questions of civil law his opinion was thought to be of value. He was scrupulously truthful in controversy, and in private life he was well known for his courtesy and geniality.

In 1873–4 O'Reilly contributed one essay to the *Illustrated*

Monitor, and others to the *Irish Monthly*, and from 1875 he assisted Matthew Russell, the editor of the *Irish Monthly*, to revise accepted articles. O'Reilly's essays, which included four on the question of papal infallibility, three on church legislation, and a number of others on papal obedience, the clergy, the temporal power, Catholic education, and the Council of Constance (in reply to W. E. Gladstone's *Vatican Decrees*), were posthumously published by Russell as *The Relations of the Church to Society* (1892). O'Reilly died at Milltown Park on 10 November 1878, in the same year as his friend, Cardinal Cullen, and was buried at Glasnevin cemetery, Dublin.

G. LE G. NORGATE, *rev.* DAVID HUDDLESTON

Sources 'In memoriam R.P. Edmund J. O'Reilly, S.J.', *Irish Monthly*, 6 (1878), 695–700 · M. Russell, 'Preface', in E. J. O'Reilly, *The relations of the church to society* (1892), i–viii · E. Larkin, *The consolidation of the Roman Catholic church in Ireland, 1860–1870* (1987) · BL cat.

O'Reilly, Edward (*c*.1770–1829), lexicographer, was born either in Harold's Cross, near Dublin, or in co. Cavan, and was a member of a branch of an Irish sept which had dominated Cavan in ancient times. It is known, however, that he settled in Dublin about 1790, and there began to learn Irish. After the death of the translator and grammarian William Haliday in 1812, O'Reilly received Haliday's extensive lexicographic collections. Combining these with materials of his own, O'Reilly arranged the whole to form the first Irish-language dictionary. O'Reilly initially met with little encouragement, but eventually succeeded in raising enough subscriptions to enable him to print the work in Dublin in 1817, entitling it *Sanas Gaoidhilge/sagsbhéarl*. The dictionary contained more than 20,000 words that had never before appeared in any Irish lexicon, along with illustrative quotations from a wide variety of ancient and modern writers, and numerous comparisons of the Irish words with those of similar orthography, sense, or sound in Welsh and Hebrew. The work was something of a *tour de force*, also containing a concise Irish grammar and the Irish names of various indigenous plants alongside their English and Latin names. O'Reilly's dictionary was reissued in 1821, and again in 1864 with a supplement by John O'Donovan.

Not content with this mammoth lexicographic feat, O'Reilly founded the Iberno-Celtic Society in Dublin in 1818, for which he also acted as assistant secretary. The society was primarily a historical and cultural organization, principally formed to preserve and publish the numerous fragments of the laws, history, topography, poetry, and music of ancient Ireland. Through it, O'Reilly published, in Dublin in 1820, *A Chronological Account of Irish Writers*, composed of nearly 400 entries, and with a descriptive catalogue of those prose and verse works which were still extant. The book, written in traditional annals form, was the first of its kind and although the dating is often erroneous, O'Reilly's familiarity with the manuscript sources was unprecedented. He had planned a second volume, this time of anonymous manuscripts, but it was never finished.

O'Reilly's commitment to Irish history and culture continued unabated throughout the 1820s. In 1824 he received a prize from the Dublin Royal Irish Academy for an essay on the nature and influence of the ancient Brehon laws, containing useful information on the number and authenticity of the various available documents, accompanied by translations of some of the most interesting sections. The academy awarded O'Reilly a second prize five years later, this time for an essay questioning the authenticity of Macpherson's Ossian poems, which had been published in Gaelic in 1807, under the sanction of the Gaelic Society of London. In the same period, O'Reilly prepared catalogues of Irish-language manuscripts in Dublin libraries, and also assisted Sir William Betham in his genealogical and antiquarian research. Towards the end of his life, O'Reilly was employed to help with Irish nomenclature for the Ordnance Survey maps of Ireland. He was still at work on this project when he died in Dublin in August 1829.

In the second half of the nineteenth century O'Reilly's reputation began to decline following an inaccurate 1864 Dublin reprint of the dictionary, and his grammatical and lexicographic skills were also brought into question by later Victorian linguists and historians. Eugene O'Curry, for instance, drew attention to his inaccuracies in *On the Manners and Customs of the Ancient Irish* (3 vols., 1873).

J. T. GILBERT, *rev.* JASON EDWARDS

Sources R. Welch, ed., *The Oxford companion to Irish literature* (1996) · J. O'Donovan, *A grammar of the Irish language* (1845) · *On the life and labours of John O'Donovan* (1862) · W. Betham, *Irish antiquarian researches* (1827) · J. Warburton, J. Whitelaw, and R. Walsh, *History of the city of Dublin*, 2 vols. (1818) · *GM*, 1st ser., 99 (1829)

Archives University College, Dublin, corresp. relating to Irish dictionary | NL Ire., letters to Sir William Betham

O'Reilly, Hugh [Aodh Ó Raghallaigh] (*c*.1581–1653), Roman Catholic archbishop of Armagh, was born in co. Cavan in Ireland, the son of Maolmórdha Mac Aodh Ó Raghallaigh and his wife, Mór. He was sufficiently closely related to the principal family of the Ó Raghallaigh or O'Reillys of east Breifne to have been eligible for election to the chieftainship under the Gaelic system of *deirbhfhine*. Until 1611 his father lived at Ballintemple in the barony of Clonmahon in central co. Cavan. These lands became part of the Ulster plantation, and the family was moved to 300 acres of poorer land in Tullyhaw in the west of the county. Aodh's early education was in co. Cavan, possibly under Franciscan auspices in the convent of St Mary in Cavan town. He was ordained a priest in Ireland and then went to continue his education on the continent. In 1618 he was studying philosophy at Rouen, and he later studied theology at Paris before going to Rome. Irish was his first language, and he knew Latin well. He probably learned English only as an adult.

O'Reilly's appointment as Roman Catholic bishop of his native diocese of Kilmore was provided for on 30 May 1625, and he was consecrated in July 1626 at the church of St Peter, Drogheda, by Thomas Fleming, archbishop of Dublin. He was transferred to the archiepiscopal see of Armagh on 11 August 1628. Even as primate, he continued to live in the Lough Uachtair district, close to Kilmore, in the neighbourhood in which he had spent his youth. The first resident primate of Ireland for almost two generations, he was well regarded by Rome and maintained cordial relations with both the hierarchy and the religious orders at home. He maintained a particularly close working relationship with prominent members of the Franciscan order. He was a supporter of the researches of the Irish Franciscans at Louvain into the lives of Irish saints, and in 1645 financed the publication of the first volume of John Colgan's *Acta sanctorum Hiberniae*. The work is dedicated to him.

O'Reilly was a reforming prelate anxious to implement the decrees of the Council of Trent. He has been judged a zealous churchman working in the interests of the Catholic church in Ireland. He presided at synods in his diocese in July 1632 and in 1637. After the outbreak of the uprising in 1641 he presided at the synod held at Kells in 1642 at which the foundations were laid for the Catholic confederation of Kilkenny. He spent time in Kilkenny, particularly in 1643, while serving on the supreme council of the confederation. He was among the influential members of the council until the first Ormond peace treaty of 1646, but was not politically active thereafter. At the time of his death on Trinity Island, co. Cavan, near his lifelong home, in February 1653 when he was said to be in his seventy-second year, O'Reilly was the only resident Roman Catholic bishop in Ireland.

BERNADETTE CUNNINGHAM

Sources S. P. Ó Mórdha, 'Hugh O'Reilly (1581?–1653): a reforming primate', *Breifne*, 4/13 (1970), 1–42; 4/15 (1972), 345–69 · J. Linchaeo [J. Lynch], *De praesulibus Hiberniae*, ed. J. F. O'Doherty, IMC, 2 (1944), 142–4 · D. F. Cregan, 'The social and cultural background of a Counter-Reformation episcopate, 1618–60', *Studies in Irish history presented to R. Dudley Edwards*, ed. A. Cosgrove and D. McCartney (1979), 85–117 · P. O'Connell, *The diocese of Kilmore, its history and antiquities* (1937), xxviii–xxx, 405–21 · J. Carney, ed., *A genealogical history of the O'Reillys* (1959), 41 · T. W. Moody and others, eds., *A new history of Ireland*, 9: *Maps, genealogies, lists* (1984) · B. Jennings, ed., *Wadding papers, 1614–38* (1953) · *History of the Irish confederation and the war in Ireland … by Richard Bellings*, ed. J. T. Gilbert, 7 vols. (1882–91) · W. M. Brady, *The episcopal succession in England, Scotland, and Ireland, AD 1400 to 1875*, 1 (1876), 282 · G. Burnett, *Life of William Bedell*, 2nd edn (1736), 35 · P. F. Moran, ed., *Spicilegium Ossoriense*, 1 (1874), 171

O'Reilly, John Boyle (1844–1890), Irish nationalist and writer, was born on 28 June 1844 at Dowth Castle, co. Meath, 4 miles from Drogheda, second of three sons and five daughters of William David O'Reilly (d. 1871), who for thirty-five years was master of the national school attached to the Netterville institution for widows and orphans there, and Eliza Boyle (d. 1869/70), daughter of a Dublin tradesman. He was educated by his father, and in 1854 became an apprentice compositor on *The Argus* newspaper in Drogheda, replacing an older brother, William, in order to ensure that the premium of £50 would not be lost.

The apprenticeship terminated when the proprietor of the newspaper died in 1858. In late summer 1859 O'Reilly went to Preston, England, where an aunt resided, becoming a compositor on *The Guardian*, a local newspaper. After mastering shorthand he was elevated to reporter. In early 1863 O'Reilly returned to Ireland, enlisting in May as a

trooper in the 10th hussars. A moderately built man of 5 feet 7½ inches, but athletically inclined, O'Reilly was regarded as a model soldier. Whether he joined the Fenian movement before or after enlisting in the army is uncertain but he became an active recruiter for it only from October 1865 after meeting John Devoy, who in spite of later differences in political outlook remained a lifelong friend. According to Devoy's later account, he then enlisted as many as eighty other Irish soldiers (Devoy, 152–9). On 13 February 1866 O'Reilly was arrested and on 9 July condemned by a military court martial to death, a sentence that was quickly commuted to twenty years' imprisonment. After brief incarceration in Mountjoy gaol, Dublin, then in English prisons, O'Reilly was transported to Western Australia, arriving on 10 January 1868. After a short and fairly comfortable confinement in Freemantle as an assistant in the library he was sent to Bunbury. There he soon became a constable in the convict colony but unlike the political prisoners of 1848 O'Reilly was subjected to ordinary regulations. With the aid of Father Patrick McCabe he absconded on 18 February 1869 to an American whaler. Following a perilous journey, during which he narrowly evaded capture, he reached Philadelphia on 23 November 1869 where he immediately took out his first American naturalization papers. He quickly decamped for New York before travelling onwards to Boston, which he reached on 2 January 1870. Fenian connections obtained him a clerkship in a shipping office, and in spring 1870 he joined *The Pilot*. O'Reilly remained associated with this Catholic newspaper for the rest of his life. One of his first assignments as a correspondent was to accompany the Fenian raid on Canada in June, an escapade about which he expressed frank reservations. O'Reilly's mother had died while he fled to America; on 17 February 1871 his father also passed away. On 15 August 1872 O'Reilly married Mary Murphy of Charlestown, Massachusetts, who was the daughter of Irish immigrants. They had four daughters between 1873 and 1880.

O'Reilly began writing while being held for court martial at Arbour Hill, Dublin. His poem 'The Old School Clock' dates from then. He continued writing while in Western Australia, and by the time of his arrival in Boston was known for his daring escape and as 'the poet'. With Devoy and others in 1876 he helped organize the escape of six Fenians prisoners from Western Australia. In the same year he and the Roman Catholic archbishop of Boston purchased *The Pilot*, which O'Reilly edited until his death. He was a committed supporter of the American Democratic Party and advocated advanced positions, championing the cause of southern black people and the toleration of Jews while emphasizing the duties of American citizenship. O'Reilly rapidly established himself in literary, intellectual, and political circles to an extent unusual among recently arrived Irish immigrants. He helped found the literary society the Paphyus Club in 1873, becoming its president in 1879. O'Reilly was prominent in the formation of the Catholic Union of Boston in March 1873, serving as recording secretary. He became a friend of Wendell Phillips. In 1873 he committed himself to the new demand for home rule in Ireland, urging Fenians to give the new movement a fair trial. In 1875 O'Reilly was chosen as the poet for the celebration of Daniel O'Connell's centenary celebration in Boston. In 1878 he promoted the American lecture tour of Michael Davitt, recently released Fenian prisoner. At the close of the decade O'Reilly endorsed the 'new departure' which linked Fenianism and the 'active' section of Irish parliamentarians headed by Charles Stewart Parnell. A regular lecturer, he also published *Songs from the Southern Seas* (1873), *Songs, Legends and Ballads* (1878), and *Moondyne* (1879) during his initial decade in Boston. This last, a portrayal of convict life in Western Australia, was particularly popular, running through numerous editions. In 1879 he was president of the Boston Press Club and in the following year helped form the Cribb Club, dedicated to boxing. This sport fascinated O'Reilly, who was a proponent of 'muscular Christianity'. In 1888 he authored *The Ethics of Boxing and Manly Sport* to 'bring into consideration the high value, moral and intellectual as well as physical, of those exercises that develop healthy constitutions, cheerful minds, manly self-confidence, and appreciation of the beauties of nature and natural enjoyment' (p. xi).

During the 1880s O'Reilly's hectic work schedule continued. His voice was by then a prop to the constitutional home-rule movement. He assisted Parnell's tour of North America at the beginning of 1880 and helped found the Irish National Land League of America in March, chairing its first national convention in May. During the imprisonment of Parnell and others in Ireland (1881–2), O'Reilly was at the forefront in urging that home rule should supplant the land agitation as the chief plank in the national programme. He was present in an unofficial capacity when in April 1883 the Irish National League of America was inaugurated in Philadelphia. Identifying with the conservative wing of Irish-American nationalism, he worked to break the influence of the radical Patrick Ford of the *Irish World*, and he eschewed the dispute between Alexander Sullivan of Chicago who controlled the Irish National League and Devoy. His writing won acclaim as well, and O'Reilly was selected to write odes in commemoration for many celebrations such as the reunion of the army of the Potomac at Detroit in 1881, and in 1888 for the dedication of the monument to Crispus Attucks in Boston. O'Reilly received several major recognitions. In 1881 Notre Dame University (Indiana) awarded him an honorary doctor of laws and Dartmouth College (New Hampshire) made O'Reilly an honorary Phi Beta Kappa. In 1889 Georgetown University (Washington, DC) gave him an honorary doctorate.

O'Reilly was a workaholic who suffered from chronic insomnia. To Devoy on 3 May 1886 he complained, 'I am terribly overworked and cannot go to sleep' (O'Brien and Ryan, 2.281). His work schedule was hectic and the health of his wife, who had been an invalid for several years, was a strain. On 3 March 1890 he began a strenuous lecture tour of the American west, returning exhausted to Boston on 5 May. He died there on 10 August 1890 from a self-administered overdose of chloral for insomnia. His funeral on 12 August in Boston was hugely attended; he was interred in Holyhood cemetery, Brookline, Massachusetts. Subsequently memorials were erected in his native Dowth and in Western Australia, and a park was named in his honour in Charlestown, Boston. The final stanza of 'The Feast of the Gael' written for St Patrick's day epitomized O'Reilly's vision of an inclusive Irish people, something increasingly out of fashion in the militant nationalism sweeping over his native land, revealing why his appeal stretched far beyond his own community:

> Then drink, all her sons—be they Keltic or Danish,
> Or Norman or Saxon—one mantle was o'er us;
> Let race lines, and creed lines, and every line, vanish—
> We drink as the Gael: 'To the Mother that bore us!'
> (Roche, 555)

ALAN O'DAY

Sources J. J. Roche, *Life of John Boyle O'Reilly together with his complete poems and speeches* (1891) · W. O'Brien and D. Ryan, eds., *Devoy's post bag, 1871–1928*, 2 vols. (1948–53) · J. Devoy, *Recollections of an Irish rebel* (1929); repr. (1969) · T. N. Brown, *Irish-American nationalism, 1870–90* (1966) · C. C. Tansill, *America and the fight for Irish freedom, 1866–1922* (1957) · M. Davitt, *Life and progress in Australasia* (1898) · J. O'Leary, *Recollections of Fenians and Fenianism* (1896) · J. Denieffe, *A personal narrative of the Irish Revolutionary Brotherhood* (New York, 1906); facs. edn (Shannon, 1969) · *DAB* · F. R. Walsh, 'The *Boston Pilot*: a newspaper for Irish immigrants, 1829–1908', PhD diss., Boston University, 1968 · T. W. Moody, *Davitt and Irish revolution* (1982) · *United Ireland* (16 Aug 1890) · *United Ireland* (30 Aug 1890) · *The Nation* (16 Aug 1890) · *DNB*
Archives Boston College, Massachusetts, MSS | NL Ire., John Devoy MSS
Likenesses D. C. French, bronze sculpture, 1896, Back Bay Fens, Boston, Massachusetts; related bust, Art Institute of Chicago · portrait, repro. in Roche, *Life of John Boyle O'Reilly* · portrait, repro. in *The Nation* · portrait, repro. in *United Ireland* (30 Aug 1890)

O'Reilly, Myles William Patrick (1825–1880), soldier and politician, was born in Dublin, the son of William O'Reilly of Knock Abbey, co. Louth, and Margaret, daughter of Dowell O'Reilly of The Heath, Queen's county. He was educated at St Cuthbert's College, Ushaw, near Durham, and at the University of London, where he graduated BA in 1845; subsequently he took the degree of LLD at Rome. In 1859 he married Ida (d. 1878), daughter of Edward Jerningham.

A gentleman farmer who bred prize cattle and kept racehorses, O'Reilly joined the Louth rifles militia, in which he held a captain's commission. Invited to Rome by Pius IX he entered the pontifical service, with the rank of major, and was appointed to the command of the Irish brigade, and rose to the challenge of training an undisciplined body of men under very difficult circumstances. In September 1860 the battalion of St Patrick gallantly defended Spoleto against Piedmontese troops, who were repeatedly repulsed. O'Reilly's wife was with him until the women were granted safe conduct by the Piedmontese; O'Reilly himself surrendered only when his position had become untenable.

After his return to Ireland, O'Reilly was elected MP, in March 1862, for the county of Longford, and for many years he was prominent in the House of Commons among the debaters on Irish and military subjects. He was a member of Archbishop Cullen's National Association, urging Catholic causes in the Commons, especially the issue of Catholic education, and of Isaac Butt's Home Rule Party. He was also a magistrate for the counties of Louth and Dublin. Besides occasional pamphlets and articles, he published *Memorials of those who suffered for the Catholic faith in Ireland in the 16th, 17th, and 18th centuries* (1868), reissued in New York in 1869 and reprinted there in 1878 under the title *Lives of the Irish martyrs and confessors, with additions, including a history of the penal laws, by [the] Rev. Richard Brennan, A.M.*. On at least one occasion he acted as examiner in classics at the Catholic University, Dublin, at the time when John Henry Newman was at its head. In 1878 his wife died, and in April 1879 he vacated his seat in parliament, when he accepted the post of assistant commissioner of intermediate education in Ireland.

O'Reilly died at 14 Fitzwilliam Place, Dublin, on 6 February 1880, and was interred in the family burial-place at Philipstown, near Knock Abbey.

THOMPSON COOPER, *rev.* BRIGITTE ANTON

Sources *DNB* · G. F.-H. Berkeley, *The Irish battalion in the papal army of 1860* (1929) · T. W. Moody and others, eds., *A new history of Ireland, 5: Ireland under the Union, 1801–1870* (1989) · C. P. Crean, 'The Irish battalion of St Patrick at the defence of Spoleto, September, 1860', *Irish Sword*, 4 (1959–60), 52–60, 99–108 · R. J. Hayes, ed., *Manuscript sources for the history of Irish civilisation*, 3 (1965) · R. J. Hayes, ed., *Manuscript sources for the history of Irish civilisation: first supplement, 1965–1975*, 1 (1979) · R. J. Hayes, ed., *Sources for the history of Irish civilisation: articles in Irish periodicals*, 4 (1970) · *CGPLA Ire.* (1880) · L. J. McCaffrey, *Ireland from colony to nation state* (1979) · E. Larkin, *The Roman Catholic church and the emergence of the modern Irish political system, 1874–1878* (1996) · E. Larkin, *The Roman Catholic church and the home rule movement in Ireland, 1870–1874* (1990) · E. R. Norman, *The Catholic church and Ireland in the age of rebellion, 1859–1873* (1965)

Likenesses photograph, repro. in *Irish Sword*, 4/15 (winter 1959), 105; in possession of his daughter, in 1929

Wealth at death under £6000: probate, 27 April 1880, *CGPLA Ire.*

O'Reilly, Phillip McHugh (*b.* 1599, *d.* in or after 1664), Irish rebel, was the second son of Hugh O'Reilly of Ballynacargy in co. Cavan, chief of the O'Reillys, and Katherine Mac Mahon, a sister of Hugh *Mac Mahon. His father had supported the English during the Nine Years' War and received land under the Ulster plantation. Despite being a younger son, Phillip succeeded to the family lands upon his father's death in 1629 and to the chieftainship of the O'Reillys in 1635. He was a commissioner of the peace for Cavan in 1625, sheriff of Cavan in 1629, and was elected MP for co. Cavan in 1640. Although he sat on the committee which drew up charges against leading government ministers in February 1641, he did not play a prominent role in the opposition to the government within the Irish parliament.

Indeed that very month O'Reilly met with other leading Gaelic landowners Rory O'More, Rory, Lord Maguire, Turlough O'Neill, and Colonel Brian McMahon to discuss plans to rebel against the government. The conspirators were alarmed by the anti-Catholic rhetoric emanating from the English parliament and hoped to take advantage of the political deadlock in England between the king and parliament. O'Reilly played a key role in the preparations

for the rebellion owing to his connections with exiled Irish on the continent. By 1628 he had married Rose, sister of Owen Roe *O'Neill, commander of the Irish regiment in the Spanish Netherlands. O'Reilly was in constant contact with O'Neill during summer 1641. The plotters originally planned to act in concert with Old English Catholic officers in the Irish army. However, by the start of September the Old English officers had cancelled their plans. Undeterred, the Gaelic plotters decided to go ahead with their rebellion on 21 October 1641, which would involve the seizure of Dublin Castle and of key fortifications in Ulster.

O'Reilly led the rebellion in Cavan and, owing to his clever tactics and good organization, soon achieved complete control over the county. On 23 October, O'Reilly's nephew and sheriff of Cavan, Myles Mulmore O'Reilly, visited many of the British protestant settlers in the county and asked for their weapons so that he could arm his forces to fight the rebels. The ruse worked and most of the settlers were peaceably disarmed. The O'Reillys then assembled 3000 men, prompting the English garrison at Belturbet to flee and that at Cavan Town to surrender. Phillip had also divided his enemies by declaring that his rebellion was aimed only against the English, and he made no attempt to take the less important Scottish garrisons at Kelagh and Croaghan. By 29 October Cavan was more or less under rebel control with virtually no bloodshed. At this point many of O'Reilly's men and the Catholic population generally began robbing and assaulting the local protestants. He did his utmost to preserve the protestants' lives and property, but it is apparent that O'Reilly was struggling to maintain his authority over his own troops. Indeed, he even had to rebuke his own wife for inciting the murder of protestants. He arranged for the protestant inhabitants of Belturbet to be convoyed out of the county, but they were robbed and roughly handled by O'Reilly's men as they left.

During November 1641 O'Reilly mustered about 3000 men and, linking up with other rebels from Monaghan and Fermanagh, swept into Meath, capturing a number of towns. After some debate the rebels decided to march on Drogheda instead of Dublin and crossed the Boyne at Trim, intending to complete the encirclement of Drogheda from the south. Hearing of the approach of an English force of 600 foot and 50 horse sent to relieve Drogheda, O'Reilly and his men ambushed them on 29 November at Julianstown, 5 miles south of Drogheda, taking advantage of the morning mist to rout their enemies. This victory had a major bearing on the decision of the Old English Catholics of the pale to join the rebellion. O'Reilly participated in the rebels' unsuccessful siege of Drogheda in the winter of 1641–2 and returned about March 1642 to Cavan, where the two Scottish garrisons continued to hold out. A tight siege was thrown up around the two castles, which surrendered on 15 June.

O'Reilly was based mainly in Cavan for the rest of the war and served as a colonel in the Ulster army of the Catholic confederation under the command of his brother-in-law, Owen Roe O'Neill. He was also appointed to the first supreme council of the Catholic confederation in November 1642 and attended a number of general assemblies in Kilkenny. However, he was usually preoccupied with his military responsibilities. During the political infighting that slowly ripped the confederation apart in 1646–9, O'Reilly remained a staunch supporter of O'Neill. When O'Neill's troops mutinied at Kilbeggan, co. Westmeath, in 1647, O'Neill relied on O'Reilly's regiment to restore order. During the 1648 civil war within the confederation, O'Reilly was the only important Ulster landowner to support O'Neill. Following the destruction of the Ulster forces at the battle of Scarrifhollis in co. Donegal on 21 June 1650, O'Reilly became the main leader of resistance to the parliamentarians, prosecuting an increasingly futile guerrilla war for the next three years. His surrender on 27 April 1653 at Cloughouter in co. Cavan marked the formal end of the wars in Ireland.

Under the terms of his surrender, O'Reilly and 1000 of his men were transported out of Ireland to join the Spanish army, landing in August 1653 in Corunna, where they were garrisoned. This proved an unhappy posting. Relations between the Irish soldiers and the local populace deteriorated rapidly and O'Reilly was furious that Hugh Dubh O'Neill was appointed commander of the Irish forces in Spain instead of him. Eventually, at O'Reilly's insistence, his garrison was transferred to the Spanish Netherlands in August 1654. There his troops mutinied at Armentières in early April 1655, but they were quickly appeased. In 1658 O'Reilly was arrested and imprisoned by the Spanish authorities on suspicion of conspiring to defect with his regiment to the French in order to win the favour of the English and recover his lands in Ireland. His regiment was also disbanded. On 20 March 1660 he received a pension from the Spanish government, although he seems to have had problems in getting it paid. His last years were spent in some poverty as part of a company of Irish infantry in the Spanish Netherlands. He was still alive in October 1664.　　　　　　　　　　　　　　TERRY CLAVIN

Sources M. Perceval-Maxwell, *The outbreak of the Irish rebellion of 1641* (1994), 135–8, 205, 207, 209, 219 · J. T. Gilbert, ed., *A contemporary history of affairs in Ireland from 1641 to 1652*, 3 vols. (1879–80) · H. Jones, *A remonstrance of divers remarkable passages* (1642) · R. A. Stirling, *The Spanish monarchy and Irish mercenaries* (1994), 90–96, 132 · B. Jennings, ed., *Wild geese in Spanish Flanders, 1582–1700* (1964), 400, 423, 440–42, 446, 452, 458, 461, 463 · *History of the Irish confederation and the war in Ireland … by Richard Bellings*, ed. J. T. Gilbert, 7 vols. (1882–91), vol. 1, pp. 34–6, 45; vol. 2, pp. 47, 86, 94; vol. 3, p. 216; vol. 5, p. 208; vol. 7, p. 367 · R. Dunlop, *Ireland under the Commonwealth* (1913), 48–9, 247, 263, 280–82, 336 · J. I. Casway, *Eoghan Roe O'Neill and the struggle for Catholic Ireland* (1984), 44–5, 48–9, 190, 262, 264 · M. Hickson, *Ireland in the 17th century* (1884), vol. 1, pp. 218–23, 303–12; vol. 2, pp. 341–54, 388–96 · *Collectanea Hibernica*, 1 (1958), 104 · *Trial of Conor, Lord Maguire* (1645)

Orem, Thomas (*d.* 1730), historian, is of unknown background. He was married on 23 July 1693 in Kemnay parish, Aberdeenshire, to Katherine Gordon (*d.* 1732), widow of Robert Keith, minister of Ballantrae, Ayrshire. Orem lived in the burgh of Old Aberdeen from 1698 until his death, apparently without paid employment, and was made an honorary burgess of the burgh on 12 September 1702. He

compiled his manuscript 'A description of the chanonry of Old Aberdeen' in 1725. This account of the history and topography of St Machar's Cathedral and its precincts was later combined with similar accounts of the burgh of Old Aberdeen and of King's College. He died in Old Aberdeen on 9 July 1730, and was buried in St Machar's Cathedral, The Chanonry, Old Aberdeen, on 11 July. His works are based heavily on primary sources, and include extracts from key documents. They also provide a detailed description of Old Aberdeen in the early eighteenth century and remain a major resource for local historians. Copies of the accounts were circulating in manuscript in the eighteenth century, one of which was purchased by Richard Gough in 1771. In *British Topography* (1780) Gough attributed the manuscript to **William Orem** (*d.* 1692), town clerk of Old Aberdeen. This mistake was then repeated in the four editions of the manuscript that were published between 1782 and 1832.　　　　　　　　　IAIN GRAY

Sources T. Orem, 'A description of the chanonry in Old Aberdeen', NL Scot., Adv. MS 33.5.23 · Old Machar old parochial register, General Register Office for Scotland, Edinburgh, OPR 168B/1, 2, 9 · Burgh of Old Aberdeen minutes, accounts, and miscellaneous papers, Aberdeen City Archives · R. G. [R. Gough], *British topography*, [new edn], 2 vols. (1780) · A. Keith, *A view of the diocese of Aberdeen*, NL Scot., Adv. MS 31.2.12 · Kemnay old parochial register, General Register Office for Scotland, Edinburgh, OPR 207/1 · manuscripts relating to Glasgowego, Kinellar, U. Aberdeen L., special libraries and archives, MS 2559 · *DNB*

Orem, William (*d.* **1692**). *See under* Orem, Thomas (*d.* 1730).

Orford. For this title name *see* Russell, Edward, earl of Orford (1652–1727); Walpole, Robert, first earl of Orford (1676–1745); Walpole, Horatio, fourth earl of Orford (1717–1797).

Orford, Robert (*d.* 1310), bishop of Ely, presumably originated from Orford, Suffolk. Ely Cathedral priory had lands there, and Orford became a monk, and eventually prior, of that house. Following the death of Ralph Walpole on 20 March 1302, Orford was elected bishop by the convent by the way of compromise on 14 April, and gained royal assent on 6 May, but the election was quashed on 16 July by Archbishop Robert Winchelsey, on the grounds of the elect's inadequate learning. Orford immediately appealed to Rome, pleading his own case before Pope Boniface VIII. He displayed skill and learning in expounding the hostile hearing he had been given by Winchelsey, and caused pope and cardinals to burst into laughter by describing how, having countered the first two of the archbishop's arguments, he had dealt with the difficult third by answering not theologically but logically, so as to avoid a conclusion. Boniface, deciding that Orford was not, as Winchelsey had described him, an empty vessel, confirmed the election on 22 October, and ordered Orford's consecration, which took place in Rome on the 28th. The temporalities were restored on 4 February 1303, and the new bishop then rebutted Winchelsey's claim to the right to enthrone him, on the grounds that the throne had already been granted by apostolic authority.

As bishop, Orford succeeded in completing the gift made to the priory by his predecessor John Kirkby (*d.* 1290)

of property in Holborn, Middlesex, and Hadham, Hertfordshire, and negotiated with the crown a confirmation of the priory's liberties. He subsequently made gifts to the convent of fine vestments, and also of a precious breviary which was assigned to the priory chapel (Prior Crauden's chapel, in the cathedral precinct). The monastery was in some financial trouble, and Orford, by his injunctions of 1307, made some effort to remedy this: thus the prior was instructed to make customary payments due to the obedientiaries, who in turn were to pay off their predecessors' debts as soon as possible; the accounts of the obedientaries were to be audited; and restrictions were placed on the prior's giving of hospitality. Orford himself, by his journey to Rome, was said to have incurred a debt of £15,000. Despite these difficulties, the building work that beautified the cathedral in the first thirty years of the fourteenth century has led to Orford's episcopate being described as part of 'the flowering time of genius' at Ely (Evans, ix). Orford died at Little Downham, Cambridgeshire, on 21 January 1310 and was buried in Ely Cathedral before the high altar, next to Ralph Walpole.

DOROTHY M. OWEN

Sources 'Monachi Eliensis continuatio historiae Eliensis', *Anglia sacra*, ed. [H. Wharton], 1 (1691), 631–74, esp. 641–2 · J. Bentham, *The history and antiquities of the conventual and cathedral church of Ely*, ed. J. Bentham, 2nd edn (1812), 154–5 · S. J. A. Evans, ed., 'Ely chapter ordinances and visitation records, 1241–1515', *Camden miscellany, XVII*, CS, 3rd ser., 64 (1940), v–xx, 1–74 · *Fasti Angl., 1300–1541*, [Monastic cathedrals], 13 · *Ann. mon.*, 4.552
Archives CUL, Ely dean and chapter, charters and deeds, EDC

Orford, Robert [Robert of Oxford] (*fl. c.*1280–*c.*1293), Dominican friar and theologian, also known as Robertus de Colletorto or Guillelmus de Torto Collo in the manuscript tradition and as Robert of Oxford by English bibliographers, is known almost entirely through his surviving works. He was a member of a group of English Dominican friars at Oxford who defended the teachings of Thomas Aquinas after the condemnation of certain of them by the archbishop of Canterbury, Robert Kilwardby, in 1277.

Orford's *Correctorium corruptorii 'Sciendum'* was among the responses issued before 1284 to the Franciscan William de la Mare's *Correctorium* of Aquinas's alleged errors. *Sciendum* is a hurried work, noted for the mildness of its polemic. A chief cause of controversy was the question whether there was only one substantial form (the rational soul) in man, or a plurality. Orford argues against de la Mare for unicity of form, while rejecting Averroist arguments in favour of it; the influences of Giles of Rome and of Thomas Sutton can be detected. Sutton, the most distinguished of Orford's group, was possibly himself already influenced against Averroist arguments by Orford, if Orford wrote the *De natura materiae* formerly attributed to Aquinas.

Orford and his circle continued to defend Thomism after the renewal of the prohibition in 1284 by Kilwardby's successor, Archbishop John Pecham. From *c.*1284 to *c.*1286 he was responding as a bachelor of the *Sentences* to Richard Clive, fellow of Merton, and to the Franciscan Alan de Wakerfeld. It was not he, however, but his fellow Dominican Richard Knapwell (with whom Orford would have agreed on unicity of form while dissenting from his Averroist arguments) who was the main target of the condemnation of unicity as heretical, and of the excommunication of unicity's defenders, which were issued by Pecham in 1286.

Orford probably incepted as a master some time after 1285, when his group's concerns were broadening in response to the alternative metaphysics being developed in Paris by Giles of Rome and by Henri de Gand. In his *Contra dicta Fr. Aegidii Romani* (1288–92) he manifests his irritation at Giles's apparent change of heart concerning Aquinas. However, his attack on Henri over the real distinction between essence and existence in the *Contra dicta Magistri Henrici de Gandavo* (1289–93) still shows Giles's influence. Orford also criticized Henri on the soul and its faculties and on the creation of matter without form, but his work was overshadowed by Sutton's superior critique.

Though Orford's interest in Parisian theologians was common to his Oxford circle, it has suggested to some that he was in Paris at about the time of these writings or perhaps studied there earlier in life. It has also been suggested that he studied in Cambridge, but there is no evidence for this. He is last heard of preaching a university sermon in the Dominican church at Oxford on 22 February 1293, the second Sunday of Lent.

SIMON FRANCIS GAINE

Sources F. E. Kelley, 'The Thomists and their opponents at Oxford in the last part of the thirteenth century', DPhil diss., U. Oxf., 1977 · A. P. Vella, 'Robert of Orford and his place in the scholastic controversies at Oxford in the late thirteenth century', BLitt diss., U. Oxf., 1946 · F. J. Roensch, *Early Thomistic school* (1964) · W. A. Hinnebusch, *The early English Friars Preachers* (1951) · J. I. Catto, 'Theology and theologians, 1220–1320', *Hist. U. Oxf.* 1: *Early Oxf. schools*, 471–517 · Emden, *Oxf.* · R. Orford, *Reprobationes dictorum a fratre Egidio in primo Sententiarum*, ed. A. P. Vella, Bibliothèque Thomiste, 38 (1968) · [Robert of Orford], *Le Correctorium corruptorii 'Sciendum'*, ed. P. Glorieux (Paris, 1956)

Orger [née Ivers], **Mary Ann** (1788–1849), actress, was born in London on 25 February 1788, one of the three daughters of William Ivers, a musician in a provincial company. Her mother was occasionally seen on the stage with her husband in Henry Thornton's company, and carried her infant daughter on as the child in *King Henry VIII*. The first record of Mary Ann performing is on a bill of the Newbury Theatre when she was five, as the Boy in *Children in the Wood*, although she had probably already acted several other parts under her father's instruction. She played this role for several years. When she was about nine years old she sang in concerts in Brighton and at about eleven was the Gypsy at a fête given by Queen Charlotte at Frogmore. She then acted with Thornton, and appeared in Croydon, Reading, Windsor, Gosport, Newbury, and Chelmsford. George III was a frequent visitor to the Windsor theatre at this time. When she was fifteen, in 1803, Thomas Orger, the son of George Orger of High Wycombe, and a man of literary tastes, fell in love with her. He was a Quaker and had to renounce this affiliation when he married her in July 1804. He agreed to her returning to the stage, and she played in 1805 in Glasgow with Master Betty and in Edinburgh, where her benefit on the last night of the season, 7 May 1806, brought her £78. She also performed in other Scottish towns. In Glasgow in the summer of 1807 she appeared as Caroline Sedley in James Kenney's *False Alarm* at Rosoman Mountain's benefit.

Mrs Orger met John Bannister in Aberdeen in the summer of 1808 and played Nell to his Jobson in *The Devil to Pay* and Ann Lovely to his Colonel Feignwell in *A Bold Stroke for a Wife*. He recommended her for Drury Lane, and she made her first appearance there as Lydia Languish in *The Rivals* on 4 October 1808. She remained at Drury Lane until 1831, while also taking engagements at minor theatres during the summer months. After the destruction of the theatre by fire on 24 February 1809 she went with the company to the Lyceum, where she played an original part in *Temper, or, The Domestic Tyrant*. On 20 November 1809 she was the original Mrs Lovell in *Not at Home*, and she had another original part, as Madge in S. J. Arnold's comic opera *Up All Night, or, The Smuggler's Cave*. She distinguished herself as Patty Larkins in *The Highgate Tunnel* in 1812. A dispute then arose between her and the management of Drury Lane, who prohibited her from appearing at the Lyceum; her correspondence with Arnold and Douglas Kinnaird MP of the management was published. When the Victoria Theatre opened Mrs Orger performed there, but at the same time continued at Drury Lane and at the Haymarket, where she was the original Mrs Sophia Smith in *Mrs Smith, or, The Wife and the Widow*. On leaving Drury Lane she was engaged by Madame Vestris for the Olympic, where she was, in 1832, Mrs Deputy Butts in Dance's farce *The Water Party*. She remained there during Madame Vestris's management, playing with complete success a series of parts suited to her talents, which included a capacity for imitating various local accents. She moved with Madame Vestris to Covent Garden, and just before the sudden closing of the theatre in 1843 she attempted what was for her a new type of character, Old Lady Lambert in Isaac Bickerstaff's *The Hypocrite*.

When the Strand Theatre opened under Maywood, Mrs Orger accepted an engagement which she was prevented by illness from fulfilling, and shortly afterwards, in 1845, her physician recommended that she retire from the stage. The Drury Lane Theatrical Fund provided her with a pension of £120 a year, which enabled her to enjoy in comfort the company of her numerous circle of friends and literary men of the day. She was herself the author of a farce, *Change Partners*, which was produced at Drury Lane on 10 March 1825. She died on 1 October 1849. She left one daughter, Caroline [*see* Reinagle, Caroline], a pianist and composer. Mary Ann Orger was very pretty, above medium height, with a fair complexion, light brown hair, and hazel eyes.   JOSEPH KNIGHT, *rev.* J. GILLILAND

Sources *GM*, 2nd ser., 32 (1849) · J. C. Dibdin, *The annals of the Edinburgh stage* (1888) · Mrs C. Baron-Wilson, *Our actresses*, 2 vols. (1844) · [J. Roach], *Authentic memoirs of the green-room* [1814] · *The biography of the British stage, being correct narratives of the lives of all the principal actors and actresses* (1824) · *Oxberry's Dramatic Biography*, 2/22 (1825) · W. Beckett, *A universal biography*, 3 vols. (1835-6) · J. Pollock, *Macready as I knew him* (1884) · Genest, *Eng. stage* · *The Era* (21 Oct 1849) ·

Hall, *Dramatic ports.* · A. Davies and E. Kilmurray, *Dictionary of British portraiture*, 4 vols. (1979–81)
Likenesses G. Clint, group portrait, oils, 1820, Garr. Club · G. Clint, group portrait, exh. RA 1821, Garr. Club · H. R. Cook, stipple (as Lorenzo; after Walton), NPG; repro. in *Theatrical Inquisitor* (1815) · R. W. Sievier, stipple and line engraving (as Mrs. Loremore in Murphy's *The way to keep him*; after M. Haughton), BM, NPG; repro. in W. Oxberry, *New English drama*, 20 vols. (1819–25) · engraving (as Audrey), repro. in *Oxberry's Dramatic Biography* · prints, BM · six engravings, Harvard TC · stipple, NPG

Oriel. For this title name *see* Foster, John, first Baron Oriel (1740–1828).

Orival [Orivalle], **Hugh de** (d. 1085), bishop of London, was consecrated by Archbishop Lanfranc in 1075, being the first bishop appointed to that see by William I and probably previously a royal chaplain. Although nothing is known of his background, it is pretty certain that, like William's other bishops, he was a Norman. He was afflicted with leprosy and resorted to the drastic cure of castration, but without effect. He died of the disease on 12 January 1085. The location of his burial is unknown.

EDMUND VENABLES, *rev.* MARIOS COSTAMBEYS

Sources *Willelmi Malmesbiriensis monachi de gestis pontificum Anglorum libri quinque*, ed. N. E. S. A. Hamilton, Rolls Series, 52 (1870) · F. Barlow, *The English church, 1066–1154: a history of the Anglo-Norman church* (1979) · E. B. Fryde and others, eds., *Handbook of British chronology*, 3rd edn, Royal Historical Society Guides and Handbooks, 2 (1986)

Orkney. For this title name *see* Einarr, earl of Orkney (*fl.* early 890s–930s); Sigurd (II) Hlödvisson (d. 1014); Rögnvald (II) Brúsason (d. 1046) [*see under* Thorfinn (II) Sigurdson (*c.*1009–*c.*1065)]; Thorfinn (II) Sigurdson (*c.*1009–*c.*1065); Erlend (d. 1098/9) [*see under* Paul (d. 1098/9)]; Paul (d. 1098/9); Magnús Erlendsson, earl of Orkney (1075/6–1116?); Harald Maddadson, earl of Caithness and earl of Orkney (1133/4–1206); Macheth, Hvarflod, countess of Orkney and Caithness (*fl.* 1196) [*see under* Macheth family (*per. c.*1124–1215)]; Magnus, earl of Caithness and earl of Orkney (*c.*1290–1320/21); Sinclair, William, third earl of Orkney and first earl of Caithness (*b.* after 1407, d. 1480) [*see under* Sinclair family (*per.* 1280–*c.*1500)]; Stewart, Robert, first earl of Orkney (1533–1593); Hepburn, James, fourth earl of Bothwell and duke of Orkney (1534/5–1578); Stewart, Patrick, second earl of Orkney (*c.*1566/7–1615); Villiers, Elizabeth, countess of Orkney (*c.*1657–1733); Hamilton, George, first earl of Orkney (*bap.* 1666, d. 1737).

Orléans. For this title name *see* Henriette Anne, Princess, duchess of Orléans (1644–1670).

Orleton [Hereford], **Adam** (*c.*1275–1345), diplomat, politician, and bishop, was probably born not in Orleton but in nearby Hereford, where there were several Orletons, including William who was bailiff or mayor. The brothers John and Thomas Trillek, who both became bishops, are believed to have been his nephews. That Adam Orleton was the Mortimers' protégé remains unproven, but in 1302 he was in the *familia* of Robert Lewyse of Gloucester, chancellor of Hereford (d. 1322). Evidence suggests that he studied at Oxford. He was MA by 1302, and two years later was licensed to leave his rectory of Wotton for three years to enable him to study in England or abroad. By 1307 he is termed *utriusque iuris peritus* and by 1310 doctor of canon law.

First designated king's clerk in 1307, Orleton appears two years later in the entourage of Bishop Walter Reynolds of Worcester (d. 1327), then treasurer. Between 1312 and 1315 he was official of Winchester, although often absent. Thus in 1313 he was proctor of Bishop Richard Swinfield of Hereford (d. 1317) at a provincial council at St Paul's, and in November of that year acted for Gilbert Middleton, who was an arbitrator in a dispute between the Dominican friars and Oxford University. Much later, as conservator of the Franciscans' privileges, Orleton was to warn the chancellor of the renewed conflict between secular and regular masters. Doubtless he came to papal notice at the Council of Vienne (1311). About that time Clement V (r. 1305–14) appointed him papal chaplain. John XXII (r. 1316–34), himself a lawyer, made him an auditor in the Sacred Palace.

Orleton's diplomatic career began in 1307 with a mission to promote the canonization of Thomas de Cantilupe (d. 1282) at the curia, where he could have had a hand in the provision of Reynolds to Worcester (February 1308). A junior member of the embassy sent in 1309 to procure the rescinding of the excommunication of Piers Gaveston (d. 1312), he was subsequently engaged in housing the English delegation at Vienne, and given the task of persuading Pope Clement to annul the ordinances. Abroad again from 1314 he functioned as the king's resident agent at the curia, and in March 1317 helped a royal embassy to secure loans for Edward II from the sexennial tenth levied for a crusade, postpone the king's crusading obligation, and ventilate other matters, including the Scottish truce and the ordinances of 1311.

Up to this point Orleton had been dispensed to hold two rectories, Wotton (Worcester diocese) and Acle (Norwich diocese) with canonries and prebends of Wells and Hereford—moderate plurality by the standard of the time. By bulls dated 15 May 1317 he was provided to Hereford and consecrated bishop on the 22nd at Avignon. The king was furious but restored the temporalities on 24 July. Papal favour was later to bring translation to Worcester (28 September 1327), during the regime of Isabella and Mortimer, who issued a royal prohibition. The temporalities were not released until 2 March 1328. A further translation, by bulls of 1 December 1333, secured for him the wealthy see of Winchester, despite Edward III's resistance. Livery of the temporalities was delayed until 23 September 1334.

Restored to royal favour Orleton went to France in June 1318 on an unsuccessful mission to perform the king's oath of fealty to Philippe V for Aquitaine. On his return he sealed the treaty of Leake between Edward II and Thomas of Lancaster (d. 1322) on 9 August. The following year he was again at Avignon urging Cantilupe's sainthood. He returned in February 1320 with eight papal bulls, including two for the pronouncement of sentences against Robert I by the cardinal–arbitrators. Back at the curia in April he at last secured Cantilupe's canonization, and on the return journey joined Edward and Isabella at Amiens for the homage ceremony. In 1321 he revisited the French court on Gascon affairs, but on returning to London in April found no one to whom he could report, as civil war loomed.

Orleton's career in diplomacy was interrupted when, in January 1322, the king upbraided him at Hereford for assisting the insurgent barons in the Welsh marches. Then the escape from the Tower of London in August 1323 of Roger Mortimer, whom Orleton had earlier been accused of abetting, led to the bishop's arraignment in the Westminster parliament of the following February. In March 1324 his temporalities were confiscated and retained by the king for the duration of the reign. However, the documents that Orleton assembled for his defence do much to call the charges against him into question. With Isabella's landing in September 1326 he delivered a sermon in her interest at Oxford. Having collected the great seal from the captured Edward II he joined the queen at Hereford for the younger Despenser's condemnation, though he claimed the chancellor, Robert Baldock (d. 1327), as a clerk and later took him to his London house. In January 1327 he was a member of a delegation sent to Edward II at Kenilworth to solicit his abdication, and was prominent in the proceedings that led to the king's replacement by his son, though irreconcilable differences among the sources make it impossible to assess the exact extent of his responsibility. On 28 January he was appointed treasurer and attended Edward III's coronation on 1 February. But his treasurership was curtailed in March by a mission to France and Avignon to explain the political changes in England.

In May 1328, following Philippe VI's accession, Orleton was sent with Bishop Roger Northburgh of Lichfield (d. 1358) to claim the French crown for Edward III. On his return he was enthroned as bishop of Worcester (19 June). Two years later, in January 1330, he returned to France, this time with Bishop William Airmyn of Norwich (d. 1336). He was there again in April for marriage negotiations with the French court, and sealed the convention of Bois de Vincennes on 8 May. Mortimer's fall did not end Orleton's activities, for he returned to France in 1331 where in March the treaty of Paris was concluded, Edward III agreeing to perform homage. He was a prominent member of the prestigious embassy that left London for the French court in November 1332 to try in vain to arrange a crusade, establish an alliance, and conclude a marriage settlement. He remained in France until 22 February of the following year, when he proceeded to Avignon. He returned to England in January 1334. His provision to Winchester so irritated the king that he did not summon him to parliament until March 1336, when a summons signalled his rehabilitation. Orleton left London on 21 July and travelled to Paris on his final diplomatic mission. It proved nugatory; the French king was aiding the Scots, and war with France appeared imminent.

Orleton's reputation has been besmirched by the fabrications of the chronicler Geoffrey Baker, who reviled him as the moving spirit behind a supposed long-term plot to dethrone Edward II, invented the story of an ambiguous letter sent by him to Berkeley that sealed Edward's fate, and suggested his connivance at Baldock's death. An antipathy arose between Orleton and Archbishop John Stratford (d. 1348) who—despite his role in the king's abdication—attracted no blame from Baker. The calumnious appeal to the curia against Orleton's advancement to Winchester mirrors Baker's views, but was rebutted by Orleton in the *Responsiones* which he drew up to defend himself. In 1340–41, when Stratford was under attack from Edward III, the chronicler Stephen Birchington implied that Orleton was author of the scurrilous attack on the archbishop contained in the so-called *Libellus famosus*. This too is unlikely, although the aged bishop certainly harboured a grudge against his old rival.

Despite political and diplomatic activities, analysis of Orleton's three registers suggests that he was a conscientious administrator, anxious to perform his duties in person whenever feasible, until old age and blindness prevented him. Able, ambitious, and determined, he was recognized as exceptionally worthy by Pope John XXII. He has been unduly maligned, not least for accepting papal rather than royal directives in matters of episcopal preferment—scarcely surprising for a canon lawyer. With Stratford he was largely responsible for the orderliness of the change of kingship in 1327. He died on 18 July 1345 in Farnham Castle, Surrey.   ROY MARTIN HAINES

Sources BL, letter of Orleton to John XXII, Cotton Vitellius E.iv.9 · *Historia de archiepiscopis*, LPL, MSS 99 · B. G. Charles and H. D. Emanuel, *A calendar of the earlier Hereford Cathedral muniments*, 3 vols. [1955] · A. Orleton, bishop's register, Hants. RO, Winchester diocesan records · A. T. Bannister, ed., *Registrum Ade de Orleton, episcopi Herefordensis*, CYS, 5 (1908) · R. M. Haines, *A calendar of the register of Adam de Orleton, bishop of Worcester, 1327–1333*, Worcestershire Historical Society, 10 (1979) · G. A. Usher, 'The career of a political bishop: Adam de Orleton (c. 1279–1345)', *TRHS*, 5th ser., 22 (1972), 33–47 · G. A. Usher, 'Adam de Orleton', MA diss., U. Wales, 1953 · R. M. Haines, 'Adam Orleton and the diocese of Winchester', *Journal of Ecclesiastical History*, 23 (1972), 1–30 · R. M. Haines, 'A defence brief for Bishop Adam Orleton', *BIHR*, 50 (1977), 232–42 · R. M. Haines, *The church and politics in fourteenth-century England: the career of Adam Orleton, c. 1275–1345*, Cambridge Studies in Medieval Life and Thought, 3rd ser., 10 (1978) · Emden, *Oxf.*, 2.1402–4 · J. H. Parry, ed., *Registrum Johannis de Trillek*, CYS, 8 (1912)

Archives BL, Cotton MS Vitellius E.iv.9 · Hants. RO, register

Orm [Ormin] (*fl. c.*1175), homilist and Augustinian canon, is known by one work only, the *Ormulum*, in the dedication to which he indicates the order of which he was a member. The Augustinian house to which he belonged cannot be definitely identified; but Orm's dialect of English has been localized in south Lincolnshire, and it is possible that the *Ormulum* was written in the Arrouaisian abbey at Bourne, a house of Augustinian canons founded in 1138. The name Orm (or Orrm, as he himself spells it in the dedication) is Scandinavian in origin, and its variant Ormin may have been formed by analogy with names such as Austin.

The *Ormulum*, preserved in Bodl. Oxf., MS Junius 1, is a collection of homilies in English, in which paraphrases of passages from the gospels are followed by exegetical commentary. Its title was given by Orm himself, who may have modelled the name on Latin *speculum* ('mirror') used in the title of works such as *Speculum ecclesiae*. In the dedication Orm states that he was enjoined to undertake the work by Walter, his brother both physically and in God, for Walter too was an Augustinian canon; and Orm sets out his purpose as the elucidation of the gospel for the laity. The homilies of the *Ormulum* were based on gospel readings for mass, arranged to follow the chronological order of the life of Christ. The table of contents lists 242 homilies, and the dedication refers to the work as having been *brohht till ende* ('brought to an end'; Bodl. Oxf., MS Junius 1, line 28), though as it survives in MS Junius 1 the *Ormulum* contains only homilies 1 to 32 (the last of which is a fragment). It is certain that more was written than now survives in MS Junius 1, since Jan van Vliet, who owned the manuscript in the seventeenth century, left copies of some passages no longer present in Junius 1, which itself shows clear evidence of the loss of leaves. As well as having suffered damage the manuscript is irregular in form and untidy in layout, containing many corrections and alterations made during the process of copying; it is plainly not the work of a professional scribe, and is likely to have been written by Orm himself. On palaeographical grounds the completion of Junius 1 is dated early in the last quarter of the twelfth century, though its writing may have extended over a number of years.

The *Ormulum* is the first substantial cycle of homilies in English known to have been composed since the works of Ælfric, written about the end of the tenth century. Orm's exposition of scripture, like that of Ælfric, is allegorical in method, and the Latin sources on which he drew for his exegesis included the *Glossa ordinaria* to the Bible, Bede's commentary on Luke, and the *Enarrationes in Matthœi Evangelium*, a twelfth-century compilation. The homilies are composed in an unrhymed metrical form based on the Latin iambic septenarius, and in the dedication Orm acknowledges that his phrasing has often been influenced by the need to fill out the verse. Orm's literary style is repetitive and wordy, and its effect is not enhanced by the monotony of his invariably regular metre; but in its scope the work is ambitious, and it testifies to the role of the vernacular in the spiritual education of the laity.

The most remarkable feature of the *Ormulum*, however, is not its substance but its distinctive spelling system. This was probably intended as an aid to preachers who would read the work aloud, and it was evidently designed to represent speech sounds in a clearer and more consistent way than conventional orthography achieved. Orm's chief innovation was the use of double consonants to signify that the preceding vowel was short; in his system the first syllable of *Crisstenndom* ('Christendom'), for instance, was spelt with double s since its vowel was short, whereas single s was used after the long vowel of *Crist* ('Christ'). This method of denoting vowel length could not be extended to all words, since by its nature it was inapplicable to syllables that did not end in a consonant, and it was supplemented by the occasional use of accents to indicate long or short vowels. Orm's concern with the exact representation of sounds is shown also by his introduction of a new form of the letter g, which he used for the initial sound of words such as *Godd* ('God'), while reserving inherited forms of g for the sounds now represented by y in 'yet' and dg in 'bridge'. As well as adopting innovations in orthography, Orm showed an exceptional concern to achieve consistency in spelling, best illustrated by his treatment of words which in Old English had been written with eo, such as *beon* ('be') and *cneow* ('knew'). In approximately the first 13,000 of the 20,000 lines of the *Ormulum* that survive, such words were often spelt with eo, though in some instances with e; but after about line 13,000 Orm ceased to use eo, and o was then systematically erased from the words that had originally been written with eo in the preceding part of the manuscript. The magnitude of this labour of correction reveals the extraordinary care expended by Orm upon details of orthography. By virtue of its special system of spelling the *Ormulum* is highly revealing about the pronunciation of the time, and it provides a major source of evidence for the linguistic study of early Middle English.　　　　　　　　　　GEORGE JACK

Sources R. M. White and R. Holt, eds., *The 'Ormulum'*, 2 vols. (1878) · N. R. Ker, 'Unpublished parts of the *Ormulum* printed from MS Lambeth 783', *Medium Ævum*, 9 (1940), 1–22 · M. B. Parkes, 'On the presumed date and possible origin of the manuscript of the *Orrmulum*: Oxford, Bodleian Library, MS Junius 1', *Five hundred years of words and sounds: a Festschrift for Eric Dobson*, ed. E. G. Stanley and D. Gray (1983), 115–27 · J. E. Turville-Petre, 'Studies on the *Ormulum* MS', *Journal of English and Germanic Philology*, 46 (1947), 1–27 · R. W. Burchfield, 'The language and orthography of the *Ormulum* MS', *Transactions of the Philological Society* (1956), 56–87 · K. Sisam, *Studies in the history of Old English literature* (1953), 188–95 · S. Morrison, 'Sources for the *Ormulum*: a re-examination', *Neuphilologische Mitteilungen*, 84 (1983), 419–36 · H. C. Matthes, *Die Einheitlichkeit des 'Orrmulum': Studien zur Textkritik, zu den Quellen und zur sprachlichen Form von Orrmins Evangelienbuch* (1933) · S. Morrison, 'New sources for the *Ormulum*', *Neophilologus*, 68 (1984), 444–50 · S. Morrison, 'Orm's English sources', *Archiv für das Studium der Neueren Sprachen und Literaturen*, 221 (1984), 54–64 · S. Holm, *Corrections and additions in the 'Ormulum' manuscript* (1922) · J. A. W. Bennett, *Middle English literature*, ed. D. Gray (1986), vol. 1, pt 2 of *The Oxford history of English literature*, 30–33
Archives Bodl. Oxf., MS Junius 1

Ormathwaite. For this title name *see* Walsh, John Benn-, first Baron Ormathwaite (1798–1881).

Orme, Daniel (1766–1837), painter and engraver, was born in Manchester on 25 August 1766, the son of Aaron Orme (1707–1782), a fustian manufacturer, and his third wife, Margaret Walmsley (*bap.* 1739, *d.* 1808). He was an older brother of the artist and publisher Edward *Orme and also of the portrait painter William Orme (1771–1850). He entered the Royal Academy Schools on 7 March 1785 and was noted as being '18 years old, 25th last August' (Hutchison, 148). In 1787 he married Ann Barr, and the following year he reputedly competed for the Royal Academy's gold medal. He continued to live in London, where he practised as a portrait painter in oil and in miniature and also as an engraver, working closely in particular with the American-born artist Mather Brown (1761–1831). From 1792 to about 1797 Brown and Orme formed a partnership

to exhibit large history paintings as a loss-leader for the sale of subscription prints after Brown's paintings. The pair concentrated on scenes from contemporary history—similar to those popularized by the American artist John Singleton Copley (1737–1815)—especially recent naval events. One instance of such collaboration between painter and engraver centred on the painting by Mather (now in the National Maritime Museum, Greenwich) of Lord Howe on the quarter-deck of the *Queen Charlotte* with 'the affecting death of the amiable Captain Neville of the queen's regiment'. The picture was advertised as being nautically accurate and also 'entirely novel', as, it was claimed, it was the first naval and portrait subject painted for this type of exhibition. It was exhibited—apparently without charge—in Orme's premises at 14 Old Bond Street from January to April 1795. Orme's large print (943 cm × 58 cm), for which the oil was effectively the advance publicity, was issued on 1 October 1795, at 1 guinea to subscribers. Interestingly, Orme also produced separate small prints of individual portraits from the scene, as well as an informative key to the whole identifying the ships and the personnel shown (copies of the large print and of the key are also in the National Maritime Museum). Another of Orme's naval subjects has been immortalized on Sunderland pottery; the moment when John (Jack) Crawford, a sailor, 'heroically nailed Admiral Duncan's flag to the main top gallant mast of the Venerable after it had been shot away by Admiral de Winter in the glorious action off Camperdown Oct. 11th 1797' (inscription on pottery cited in Baker, cat. no. 51). Orme's engraving is after a sketch he is said to have made on board the flagship *Venerable* and was published on 21 November 1797. It is notable that Orme exhibited at the Royal Academy only for five years, from 1797 to 1801; he showed nearly forty miniatures, many with a marked naval association, such as his portrait of Lady Nelson exhibited in 1799.

Orme also engraved his own works—subject pictures such as *Alexander and Thais*—as well as portraits after other artists, such as *Admiral the Earl of St Vincent* after Daniel Gardner. He was appointed engraver to George III, and in 1814 he styled himself artist to his majesty and the prince regent. In October 1814 he returned to Manchester and resided at 40 Piccadilly, where he gave lessons in oil painting, drawing, and etching and continued his portrait painting both in oil and in miniature. He was represented in the first exhibition of the Royal Manchester Institution in 1827 by one portrait, *William Butterworth, the Oldham Hermit*. He died at Buxton, Derbyshire, in 1837. There is a small drawing, slightly washed in colour—*New Pier, Margate*—in the Victoria and Albert Museum, London. A self-portrait in oil by Orme showing him with his sketchbook is still in the collection at Althorp, Northamptonshire. Other paintings and prints by him are in the National Maritime Museum.　　　　　KATHERINE COOMBS

Sources *DNB* · P. van der Merwe, 'The glorious first of June: a battle of art and theatre', *The glorious first of June, 1794: a naval battle and its aftermath*, ed. M. Duffy and R. Morriss (2001), 132–58 · J. C. Baker, *Sunderland pottery* (1984) · S. C. Hutchison, 'The Royal Academy

Schools, 1768–1830', *Walpole Society*, 38 (1960–62), 123–91, esp. 148 · Orme family tree, Man. CL, Owen MSS

Likenesses D. Orme, self-portrait, oils, Althorp, Northamptonshire

Orme, Edward (1775–1848), engraver and property developer, was born in Manchester, the thirteenth child of Aaron Orme (1707–1782), fustian manufacturer of Manchester, and his third wife, Margaret Walmsley (*bap.* 1739, *d.* 1808). One brother, Robert (1767–1827), became solicitor to the East India Company at Madras, and two other brothers, Daniel *Orme (1766–1837) and William (1771–1850), were professional artists. Edward moved to London, and in 1794 his first engraving was published by his brother Daniel. Orme was married on 22 June 1802 at St George's, Hanover Square, London, to Hester (Etty) Edmonds (1781–1864). Three sons and two daughters are mentioned in his will. On 21 January 1799 Orme was appointed printseller in ordinary to George III and on 5 April 1820 editor of prints in ordinary to George IV. In May 1800 he had a shop in Conduit Street, London (at the corner of George Street), and in 1801 exhibited a portrait at the Royal Academy. In the same year he established himself at 59 New Bond Street, London, at the corner of Brook Street, and published *Rudiments of Landscape*, a volume of uncoloured etchings after his brother William's drawings. He advertised that he stocked 'Books of Instruction in every Branch of Drawing, and Drawing Materials'. Then began the publication of a series of coloured aquatint books, ending in 1819 with *Historic, Military, and Naval Anecdotes*. Some separate engravings of London markets were issued in 1822, but in 1824 the shop was closed, and he concentrated on his new career.

In 1809 Edward Orme had begun buying land and property in Bayswater, London. He exploited the gravel deposits, built houses, and in 1818 added a chapel of ease. Orme Square, developed between 1823 and 1826, was named after him, and Moscow Road and St Petersburgh Place nearby may have commemorated the state visit of Tsar Alexander I in June 1814. In the following year he published a volume of twenty coloured aquatint views of St Petersburg, and the reference in his will to jewellery presented to him by the emperor of Russia may be connected with these events.

Edward Orme was, after Rudolph Ackermann, the most important publisher of illustrated books during the short golden age of the coloured aquatint, but there is no evidence that he followed Ackermann's move into lithography. The only reference to co-operation between the two firms is on the original printed wrappers of *An Historical Account of the Campaign in the Netherlands* (1817) by William Mudford, where both names appear in the imprint. Orme's output totalled some 700 illustrations, but his monument is his *British Field Sports* of 1807, described by C. F. G. R. Schwerdt (1928) as 'the finest and most important sporting book of the last two centuries'. Orme died at his home, 6 Fitzroy Square, London, on 28 September 1848, and was interred initially in the family vault at St Mary's, Paddington, Middlesex. When Etty died on 11 April 1864, the graveyard had been closed. She was buried in the new cemetery 2 miles away at Kensal Green, and Edward's remains were moved to be with her.

JOHN MAGGS, *rev.*

Sources J. R. Abbey, *Life in England in aquatint and lithography*, 4 vols. (1952–6) · *VCH Middlesex*, vol. 9 · Owen's genealogy, Manchester County Library, MS Misc 687/1 · tombstone inscription for Edward Orme

Orme, Eliza (1848–1937), social activist and lawyer, was born on 25 December 1848 at 16 Regent Villas, Avenue Road, London, the seventh of eight children of Charles Orme (*c.*1807–1893), distiller, of Southwark, and his wife, Eliza (1816–1892), eldest daughter of the Revd Edward Andrews of Walworth and eldest sister of Emily Patmore. She attended Bedford College for Women and entered University College, London, in 1871, where she studied law and political economy, winning in 1876 first prize in Roman law and the Hume scholarship in jurisprudence. Among her mentors were John Elliot Cairnes (1823–1875), W. Leonard Courtney (1850–1928), and W. A. Hunter (1844–1898), from whom she learned an attachment to *laissez-faire* economics and Liberal political principles. She went to Lincoln's Inn in 1873, to read in the chambers of Savill Vaizey, but as a woman was refused admittance to the ranks of conveyancers under the bar.

In 1888, when Orme earned the degree of LLB from the University of London, she was already established in the Chancery Lane office out of which, from 1875 until about 1904, she conducted a prosperous business, 'devilling' for lawyers as a conveyancer and patent agent. She became a public figure, writing and lecturing about feminist and other contemporary issues. She was a member of the London National Society for Women's Suffrage and of the Society for Promoting the Employment of Women, and was a founding member of the Women's Liberal Federation (WLF) in 1887, editing their *Women's Gazette and Weekly News* from 1889 to 1891. When the WLF split in 1892 she joined the Women's National Liberal Federation (WNLF), and later wrote the life of the founder (*Lady Fry of Darlington*, 1898). The WNLF disagreed with the WLF policy of giving priority to women's suffrage in the face of opposition from the Liberal Party. In Orme's words, 'the great Liberal organization … was not available for the promotion of reforms about which Liberals are in disagreement, and which are in fact not part of an accepted party programme' (E. Orme, *Lady Fry of Darlington*, 1898). In 1892 she was chosen over Beatrice Potter to be senior lady assistant commissioner to the royal commission on labour, supervising the work of three junior investigators and herself examining women's work in Ireland, in the Black Country iron industry, and in London public houses. She opposed protective labour legislation for women workers and her reports demonstrate a conviction that women should not be excluded from any workplace, even the blacksmith's shop. In 1894 she was a member of the departmental committee on prison conditions, examining the situations of female prison staff and inmates. She stated her views in the *Fortnightly Review*: 'The real fact is that women, instead of being reformed by prison treatment, are dragged down by it, and that our system, planned carefully, with the best intentions, is really calculated to manufacture habitual criminals and drunkards' (*Fortnightly Review*, 69, 1898, 790–96).

Orme remained unmarried, living with her parents until their deaths and then with her sister Beatrice at Tulse Hill from the early 1890s. No portrait or personal papers have survived, and little is known about her private life, but she was regarded as a formidable person by Beatrice and Sidney Webb, George Gissing, and George Bernard Shaw. In an article in *The Examiner* (1 August 1874) she was critical of what she called 'strong-minded women', who went in for stridency and useless eccentricity, preferring the 'sound-minded women … who can take a journey by railway without an escort, who can stand by a friend through a surgical operation, and who yet wear ordinary bonnets and carry medium-sized umbrellas'. A distinctly pragmatic attitude coloured her approach to women's issues: writing in 1897 about the need for higher education and independent careers, rather than charity, for unmarried women she debunked 'the fallacy of supposing a woman keeps other women in employment by living economically on a small income instead of earning and spending a larger one' (E. Orme, 'How poor ladies live: a reply', *Nineteenth Century*, 41, 1897, 613–19). Eliza Orme died of old age and heart failure on 22 June 1937 at Fenstanton, Christchurch Road, Streatham, in London. LESLIE HOWSAM

Sources L. Howsam, '"Sound-minded women": Eliza Orme and the study and practice of law in late-Victorian England', *Atlantis*, 15/1 (1989), 44–55 · *Law Journal* (12 Dec 1903), 620 · *Englishwoman's Review* (1873–1904) · C. Hirschfield, 'Liberal women's organizations and the war against the Boers, 1899–1902', *Albion*, 14 (1982), 27–49 · *The Post Office directory* (1851–1935) · *Royal blue book* (1851–1902) [annuals] · *Court Directory* (1851–1902) · b. cert. · d. cert.
Wealth at death £787 15s. 8d.: probate, 8 Nov 1937, CGPLA Eng. & Wales

Orme, Robert (1728–1801), historian of India and East India Company servant, was born on 25 December 1728 at Anjengo in Travancore, India. One of four children, he was the second son of Alexander Orme (*d*. 1736), chief of the settlement at Anjengo, a physician and surgeon in the service of the East India Company. At the age of two Orme was sent to England to be brought up by his aunt Mrs Adams, at her home in Cavendish Square, London. From 1734 to 1741 he was educated at Harrow School, where he showed considerable promise as a scholar and excelled himself at classics. Destined for a career in India, he was withdrawn early from Harrow and placed in a private academy in London to learn the business of trade and commerce.

In 1742, aged thirteen, Orme was sent to Calcutta. Upon his arrival he was engaged to a private English mercantile concern, Jackson and Wedderburn. Two years later, in 1744, he was appointed a writer in the East India Company service. Not content with performing his daily duties, Orme devoted himself to improving and educating himself, reading and studying as widely as he could. His efforts earned him the affectionate nickname of Cicero and he

Robert Orme (1728–1801), by Joseph Nollekens, 1774

acquired a reputation for his knowledge of Indian affairs. In 1752 he produced a study of Indian society entitled 'A general idea of the government and people of Indostan', eventually published in the new edition of his *Historical Fragments of the Mogul Empire* (1805). At the same time he began work on his *magnum opus*, his history of the Anglo-French conflict in southern India. In 1753 he visited England in the company of his close friend Robert Clive. During this brief stay he used his writings to good effect, making several influential friends in the government and among the directors of the company. These new connections secured him an immediate and unprecedented promotion to the senior ranks of the Madras council.

Orme arrived at Madras on 12 September 1754 as export warehouse keeper and seventh member in council. Despite an aloofness and arrogance which made him extremely unpopular, he proved himself a highly competent bureaucrat and administrator. Always conscious of his superior talents, Orme's besetting sins were his over-riding ambition and impatience. In March 1756 he was appointed third in council, and in September 1758 he became next in line to the governor. However, not content with rapid promotion, he had begun sending home confidential reports to the directors, criticizing his seniors on the council. News of his activities leaked back to Madras, and Orme found himself completely ostracized. Within days of his final promotion he was indicted by the council, charged with extortion and with deserting his post. Finding his position quite untenable, Orme made no attempt to defend himself. By October 1758 he had already left India, his reputation in tatters and his career in ruins. He finally reached London in October 1760, having returned by way of France. He bought a house at 11 Harley Street, London, where he lived for the next thirty years. He had not had the chance to make his fortune and he returned with an estate of only £5597. For a man with his tastes and aspirations this proved a quite inadequate sum, and for the rest of his life Orme was beset by persistent financial difficulties.

In 1761 Orme wrote another dissertation, 'The effeminacy of the inhabitants of Indostan', which analysed the effects of climate on the peoples of India (also published posthumously in *Fragments*, 1805). Then in August 1763 he published the first volume of his *History of the Military Transactions of the British Nation in Indostan*. A work of military history, it narrated the battle for supremacy in southern India which had been waged from 1750 to 1754 between the English, the French, and their Indian allies. It was received with great critical acclaim: Orme was applauded on all sides for his style and accuracy, was hailed as a historian in the true classical tradition, and achieved renown and recognition. In 1769 he was created the first official historiographer of the East India Company, at a salary of £400 a year. In 1770 he was elected a fellow of the Society of Antiquaries.

A cultured and very learned man, with a wide range of interests, Orme was well known and respected in the intellectual and social circles of the day. Described by Boswell as 'that able and elegant historian of Indostan' (Boswell, *Life*, 3.284), he was highly esteemed by his peers, who included the historian Dr William Robertson and the orientalist Sir William Jones. He became particularly close to Jones, with whom he forged a lifelong friendship. A passionate collector of books, Orme was also a great lover of art and beauty. Among his friends were the painter Joshua Reynolds and the sculptor Joseph Nollekens, who in 1774 made a bust of Orme at the age of forty-five, which shows a highly intelligent and very refined face, with finely drawn, sensitive features.

In 1778, after an interval of fifteen years, Orme finally published the second volume of the *History of the Military Transactions*. This recounted the third and final phase of the Anglo-French struggle in India, from 1756 to 1761. Critically this too was very well received, but once again sales were slow and rather poor, although the *History* was to be reprinted four times between 1763 and 1803. Considered as something of a landmark in the history of writing on India, it made a substantial impression on the next generation of British historians. Macaulay later described it as one of the most authentic and finely written in the English language, although he found its attention to detail 'minute to the point of tediousness' (Macaulay, 3.110).

As its title indicates, the *History* was intended to commemorate Britain's military successes in India. It highlighted the stirring deeds of Orme's contemporaries, especially those of his great friend Clive, whom he made the hero of his first volume. Despite this, the *History* was never meant to be a celebration of either conquest or empire. Orme regarded the sweeping conquests which had been made since 1753 with deep dismay. He believed that trade and commerce should remain the East India Company's primary objective. Conquest and empire only brought corruption and decay, which threatened to ruin all the benefits of trade. The saga of bribery and corruption which had followed the conquest of Bengal left Orme bitterly disillusioned with his subject and with Clive, his hero. Rather than continue to chronicle what he saw as an increasingly sordid story he turned elsewhere.

In 1782 Orme published his last major work, *Historical Fragments of the Mogul Empire*, which described the reign of Aurangzeb, the last Mughal emperor, and the rise of Maratha power in India. Although dependent on secondary materials, the *Fragments* was highly valued for its accuracy and information. James Grant Duff, writing almost half a century later in his *History of the Mahrattas* (1826), was full of praise for Orme's efforts to open up such a difficult and uncharted field.

The strain of so much work took its toll on Orme's health, which had always been fragile. By 1781 it had deteriorated very sharply, forcing him to retire to the countryside. He leased a house at Colney in Hertfordshire, and finally, in 1793, retired permanently to Ealing. In 1796 he gave up his house in Harley Street and, finding he was beginning to go blind, sold off part of his beloved library: 2000 items fetched the considerable sum of £1179 16*s*. 3*d*. Orme died at Ealing, aged seventy-two, on 13 January 1801, and was buried in the churchyard of St Mary's, Ealing. He left behind his mistress, whom he appears to have eventually married in secret. In his will he bequeathed £1000 and all his remaining possessions to 'my friend Mrs Mary Dixon who now lives with me'.

SINHARAJA TAMMITA-DELGODA

Sources BL OIOC, MS Eur. Orme · R. Orme, 'An account of the life and writings of the author', *Historical fragments of the Mogul empire* (1805) · Boswell, *Life*, vol. 3 · *Annual Register* (1764), 256 · T. B. Macaulay, *Critical and historical essays* (1843) · J. G. Duff, *A history of the Mahrattas*, 1 (1826) · *GM*, 1st ser., 73 (1803), 517–18 · will, PRO, PROB 11/1356, fols. 303–5
Archives BL OIOC, MSS Eur. Orme | BL, Leeds MSS, Egerton MSS 3488–3489 · BL OIOC, Clive MSS, MS Eur. G37
Likenesses J. Nollekens, marble effigy, 1774, BL OIOC [*see illus.*] · line engraving, BM, NPG; repro. in *European Magazine* (1801)
Wealth at death £2500: will, PRO, PROB 11/1356, fols. 303–5

Orme, William (1787–1830), Congregational minister, was born on 3 February 1787 at Falkirk, Stirlingshire. His parents moved to Edinburgh, and in 1792 he began his education under a schoolmaster named Waugh. On 1 July 1800 he was apprenticed to a wheelwright and turner. He disliked the work, but completed his five years. His father died in October 1803, and about this time he became a protégé of James Alexander Haldane, whom he had heard preach at the tabernacle in Leith Walk, Edinburgh. In October 1805 he was admitted by Robert Haldane as a student for the ministry under George Cowie in Edinburgh. The usual period of study was two years, but Orme's periods of study, interrupted by a spell of preaching in Fife during 1806, amounted to little more than a year in all.

On 11 March 1807 Orme became pastor of the Congregational Tabernacle at Perth, where he was ordained. About

1808 he was married, but his wife died following child-birth, and he later remarried. In 1809 Robert Haldane adopted Baptist views and evicted Orme's Congregationalists in favour of those in his congregation who became Baptists. Orme refused an offer to move to the Congregational church in Dundee, and spent many years searching for a suitable place of worship. He played a leading part in the development of Scottish Congregationalism as one of the twelve who met in September 1812 to draw up a scheme for a Congregational Union of Scotland, which was formed in 1813, and as one of the founders of the Glasgow Theological Academy in 1814.

On 7 October 1824 Orme moved to the Congregational church at Camberwell Green, Surrey, and soon afterwards was elected foreign secretary of the London Missionary Society. In 1827 he was one of a deputation to MPs known to be sympathetic to the repeal of the Test and Corporation Acts, and he also played an important part in the founding of a college in Gower Street, in 1828, which led to the granting of a charter founding the University of London in 1836.

Orme was a leading biographer of seventeenth-century puritans, and his *The Works of John Owen, with Memoirs of his Life* (1820) and *Life and Times of Richard Baxter* (1830) were particularly influential. Other works included *A Catechism of the Constitution and Ordinances of the Kingdom of Christ* (1817), which was regarded by the Scottish Congregational churches as an authentic statement of their views of church membership, *Remarkable Passages in the Life of William Kiffin* (1823), and *Memoirs of John Urquhart* (1827). Orme died on 8 May 1830 at his home in Camberwell, and was buried on 17 May at Bunhill Fields. He was survived by his second wife.

ALEXANDER GORDON, *rev.* ANNE PIMLOTT BAKER

Sources H. Escott, *A history of Scottish Congregationalism* (1960), 278–9 · 'Memoir of the late Rev. William Orme', *Evangelical Magazine and Missionary Chronicle*, new ser., 8 (1830), 253–6, 289–95 · J. Waddington, *Surrey Congregational history* (1866), 115–17, 171–2 **Likenesses** J. Thomson, stipple (after J. R. Wildman), BM; repro. in *Evangelical Magazine* (1830) · portrait, repro. in W. Orme, *Memoirs of the life, writings, and religious connections of John Owen* (1820) · portrait, repro. in W. Orme, *Passages in the life of William Kiffin* (1823)

Ormerod, Edward Latham (1819–1873), physician, sixth son of George *Ormerod (1785–1873), historian of Cheshire, and his wife, Sarah (1784–1860), eldest daughter of John *Latham (1761–1843), physician and president of the Royal College of Physicians, and his wife, Mary Mayer, was born in Welbeck Street, London, on 27 August 1819. The anatomist William Piers *Ormerod (1818–1860) and the geologist George Wareing *Ormerod (1810–1891) were his brothers. He was educated first at Laleham School, and afterwards at Rugby School, which he left in 1838. He was next a medical student at St Bartholomew's Hospital, London, remaining there until October 1841, when he entered Gonville and Caius College, Cambridge. At Caius he held both classical and science scholarships. He graduated MB in 1846 and MD in 1851, and he was elected a fellow of the Royal College of Physicians in 1850.

At St Bartholomew's Hospital, Ormerod worked as demonstrator of morbid anatomy during 1846 and 1847, and he became the first registrar of the hospital. However, in the latter year his health broke down, and he left London and went to practise as a physician at Brighton. In 1848 he published *Clinical Observations on Continued Fever*. He was elected physician to the Brighton and Hove Dispensary in 1850, and three years later he became physician to the Sussex County Hospital. He married, on 12 April 1853, Mary Olivia Porter, daughter of Edward Robert Porter of Brighton, who died three months later; on 29 March 1856 he married Maria Millett (*b.* 1831/2), daughter of Frederick Millett of Woodhill, Surrey, with whom he had six children.

Ormerod published several papers on medical subjects, taking diseases of the heart as his main interest. He delivered the Goulstonian lectures to the Royal College of Physicians and gave an address to the British Medical Association at its 1864 annual meeting. In 1867 and 1868 he was an examiner for the MB degree at Cambridge. Like his sister, the renowned entomologist Eleanor Anne *Ormerod (1828–1901), Edward Ormerod had a great interest in the study of insects. In 1868 he published a natural history, *British Social Wasps*, a work well regarded by contemporary entomologists, and in 1872 he was elected FRS. At the time of his death he was working on the change of colour observable in gurnards, fish of brilliant hues.

Ormerod died at his home, 14 Old Steyne, Brighton, on 17 March 1873, of malignant disease of the bladder. A modest, shy, and sensitive man, his personal character and pathological attainments had won him the respect of a wide circle of professional colleagues.

NORMAN MOORE, *rev.* PATRICK WALLIS

Sources Foster, *Alum. Oxon.* · Venn, *Alum. Cant.* · Munk, *Roll* · *BMJ* (22 March 1873), 319 · *The Lancet* (22 March 1873) · V. C. Medvei and J. L. Thornton, eds., *The royal hospital of Saint Bartholomew, 1123–1973* (1974) · *Eleanor Ormerod, LL.D., economic entomologist: autobiography and correspondence*, ed. R. Wallace (1904) · m. certs. · *GM*, 1st ser., 89/2 (1819), 177 · *CGPLA Eng. & Wales* (1873) **Wealth at death** under £25,000: probate, 19 April 1873, *CGPLA Eng. & Wales*

Ormerod, Eleanor Anne (1828–1901), economic entomologist, was born on 11 May 1828 at Sedbury Park, Gloucestershire, the youngest of the ten children of George *Ormerod (1785–1873), historian and antiquary, and his wife, Sarah (1784–1860), eldest daughter of John *Latham (1761–1843), a president of the Royal College of Physicians. Although he also owned a property, Tyldesley, and its attendant coalmines in Lancashire, George Ormerod's sole residence was Sedbury Park, from 1828, soon after the time of its purchase (1825), until his death in 1873. Consequently, Eleanor Ormerod spent more than half her life on the family's 800 acre estate, between the Severn and Wye rivers, opposite Chepstow.

Although her brothers received instruction from Thomas Arnold, Eleanor Ormerod was educated at home by her mother. Consisting principally of biblical knowledge, moral precepts, and French, her education

Eleanor Anne Ormerod (1828–1901), by Elliott & Fry, c.1900

equipped her with society skills. These were rounded off with private tuition in music and painting. She received the latter from William Holman Hunt, when the family made their annual pilgrimage to London. In addition, Eleanor and her elder sister Georgiana honed their philanthropic skills through the execution of a book-lending scheme for their deserving fellow parishioners of St Mary the Virgin, Tidenham, Gloucestershire. Throughout her life, Eleanor Ormerod dispensed philanthropy through each of her local Anglican parishes. Despite her education and training, however, she participated little in society before the death of her parents. Although her father attended to his duties as magistrate for the counties of Cheshire, Monmouth, and Gloucester, he did not care for society. An amateur historian, he occupied himself with topographical and literary interests, and led a reclusive life. According to a niece, Diana Latham, George Ormerod was an autocrat, who maintained a strict family discipline. This behaviour bore significant repercussions for his entire family: none of his three daughters and only three of his seven sons married.

Within the confines of this insular family setting, the children were encouraged to engage in various intellectual pursuits and hobbies. Two of Eleanor's elder brothers, William Piers *Ormerod (1818–1860) and Edward Latham *Ormerod (1819–1873), who studied medicine, took an interest in botany and entomology. However, the pervasive patriarchy of the family precluded Eleanor from gaining encouragement or approval from her elder male siblings. For this, she drew upon her sister and lifelong companion, Georgiana.

By her own account, Eleanor began her intensive study of entomology in March 1852, when she assiduously pored over a copy of James F. Stephens's *Manual of British Coleoptera or Beetles* (1839). Her entomological contributions to a wider audience began after the death of her mother in 1860, and in the final years of her father's protracted illness. In 1868 she responded to a published plea from the Royal Horticultural Society to contribute to a collection illustrative of insects beneficial and baneful to British agriculturists and horticulturists. For slightly less than a decade, she submitted insect specimens, which either she or the estate's agricultural labourers had procured. Her contributions were acknowledged in 1870, when the Royal Horticultural Society awarded her their silver medal. But this was merely a prelude to her future efforts, because her entomological endeavours 'were not approved of nor taken seriously by some of her elders, and could not have been carried out until the break up of the home on the death of Mr. Ormerod' (*Eleanor Ormerod*, 19). The death of her father in 1873 released Eleanor Ormerod from the confines of familial privacy. Perhaps unsurprisingly, her first published papers appeared in the *Linnean Society Journal*, the *Entomologist's Monthly Magazine*, and the *Gardeners' Chronicle* in the same year as her father's death.

Supported by an inheritance, Eleanor and her sister Georgiana relocated to Torquay to be near an uncle and his family. After three years, the two sisters moved to Dunster Lodge, Spring Grove, Isleworth, where they could be closer to London, and to Joseph D. Hooker, director of Kew Gardens, and his wife. Until she and her sister made their final move to Torrington House, St Albans, Hertfordshire, in September 1887, Eleanor used her intimacy with the Hookers to continue her entomological investigations in the gardens at Kew. These were in addition to her daily recorded observations for the Meteorological Society, to which she was elected a fellow in 1878, the first woman to be so. Two years later, she edited Caroline Molesworth's *Cobham Journals* of meteorological and phenological observations. Her introductory description of Caroline Molesworth (1794–1872) could easily have been an autobiographical statement of Eleanor Ormerod, economic entomologist.

In the last quarter of the nineteenth century, there were numerous unheeded calls for the creation of a post of government entomologist in Britain. At the behest of the prominent agriculturists Maxwell Masters and John Chalmers Morton, Eleanor Ormerod responded to these calls and issued a seven-page questionnaire, entitled *Notes for Observations of Injurious Insects*, in early 1877. Later that year she published and distributed a compilation of the information that she had gleaned from various correspondents in the form of her first 'semi-official' annual report. Compiled in the same manner each year, these reports ran continuously until 1901, and established Ormerod as Britain's *de facto* government entomologist.

Following in John Curtis's footsteps, Eleanor Ormerod constructed a large portion of her entomological career on an association with the Royal Agricultural Society of England (RASE). In May 1882, she became honorary consulting entomologist to the RASE. This followed her election to the Entomological Society of London in 1878, and the publication of her *Manual of Injurious Insects, with Methods of Prevention and Remedy* (1881), and a special report on the turnip fly (1882). As honorary consulting entomologist, she prepared annual and periodic monthly reports, and responded to queries from members. She received no remuneration for her efforts. Charles Whitehead, a member of the RASE, recalled that Ormerod:

> frequently produced from the depths of the pocket in her handsome black silk dress 'strange beasts' as a member … termed them … On two occasions some of these escaped from the box and crawled over the table, much to the discomfiture of the aforesaid member.   (Whitehead, 47)

While returning home from her first RASE meeting, Ormerod suffered a blow to her knee that resulted in partial lameness and periodic pain in one leg. Fittingly, she used the pretence of her troubled leg to resign from the RASE ten years later. The real reasons for her resignation lay in a dispute with Charles Whitehead that had boiled over in 1891. At issue was the 'unacknowledged' work that she did for the RASE and Whitehead, who took up the salaried position of 'agricultural adviser' when the Board of Agriculture was established in 1889.

Eleanor Ormerod was largely responsible for promulgation of the discipline of economic entomology in Great Britain. Between October 1881 and June 1884, she delivered six lectures, as special lecturer on economic entomology, at the Royal Agricultural College, Cirencester. In 1883 she spread her message to schoolteachers by delivering ten lectures at South Kensington's Institute of Agriculture. The latter effort resulted in the publication of her *Guide to the Methods of Insect Life* (1884), which metamorphosed into *A Text-Book of Agricultural Entomology* (1892). In addition, she contributed 'suggestions and revisions' to the relevant parts of William Fream's enduring *Elements of Agriculture* (1892). Between 1882 and 1886 she was a member of a committee, which included T. H. Huxley and J. O. Westwood, appointed by the government to advise on the management of collections relating to economic entomology in the South Kensington and Bethnal Green museums. In 1889–90, she successfully introduced agricultural entomology as a voluntary subject for the senior examination of the RASE, and as a compulsory examination subject at the Royal Agricultural College. And from 1896 to 1899 she acted as an examiner in agricultural entomology for the University of Edinburgh. As part of an unsuccessful lobby to have agricultural science established as a degree subject, she offered the University of Oxford £100 in 1897. By the terms of her will, she bequeathed the University of Edinburgh £5000. Through lectures, textbooks, and examinations, Eleanor Ormerod played a pivotal role in the institutionalization of economic entomology.

As she admitted to one of her numerous foreign correspondents, Eleanor Ormerod stopped 'entirely at home like a limpet on a rock' (*Eleanor Ormerod*, 198). Although she entertained James Fletcher, William Saunders, C. V. Riley, John Smith, and Ritzema Bos when they visited Britain, she never left Britain on professional business. Nevertheless, the versatility of her correspondence networks

allowed her to engage in colonial entomological research. For instance, she became involved with South African economic entomology when a British emigrant, and former contributor to her annual reports, contacted her to identify the Australian bug (the cottony cushion scale, *Icerya purchasi*) for the Eastern Province Naturalists' Society. This work resulted in the publication of her *Notes on the Australian Bug (Icerya purchasi) in South Africa* (1887), and her *Notes and Descriptions of a Few Injurious Farm & Fruit Insects of South Africa* (1887). Similarly, a direct appeal from the government of New Zealand resulted in her publication of a small pamphlet on the Hessian fly. And after the Barbados Agricultural Society requested her services in 1892, she produced a booklet on the sugar-cane shot-borer beetle (*Xyleborus perforans*).

Eleanor Ormerod spread her entomological word with an evangelical fervour. Three of her campaigns, in particular, reached a broad audience and attracted controversy. In each case producing and distributing special booklets, she offered instruction and guidance on the ox-warble fly (*Œstrus bovis*), Paris-green (an acetoarsenite insecticide), and the extermination of the house sparrow. She was intensely aware that she was addressing 'things that might involve discussion unbecoming of a lady writer' (*Eleanor Ormerod*, 272–3). Perhaps perceiving Eleanor Ormerod as the embodiment of her androgynous ideal, Virginia Woolf celebrated her as a 'pioneer of purity even more than of Paris Green' in her short story 'Miss Ormerod' of 1924 (Woolf, 471). Throughout her career, Ormerod remained rather ambivalent about the limitations imposed by her gender. She publicly rebuffed attempts to make her a model for the feminist cause; and she deftly acknowledged the support she received from male colleagues. Often, she used the names of recognized male experts, such as J. O. Westwood, to bolster or legitimate her message. But within the domestic sphere, where she produced all her work, she carefully guarded against any male intrusions. Consequently, she vehemently rejected the suggestion that Professor Allen Harker become her assistant in 1889. After all, she argued, she had her sister and Anne Hartwell, her 'lady amanuensis', who had joined the household in May of the previous year.

By the turn of the twentieth century, Eleanor Ormerod had achieved a pre-eminent position in her chosen field of economic entomology. The Société Nationale d'Acclimatation de France awarded her their silver medal in 1899, and the Royal Horticultural Society awarded her their gold medal the following year. On 14 April 1900, however, she received her greatest honour, when she became the first female recipient of an honorary LLD degree from the University of Edinburgh. She deeply regretted that her sister Georgiana, who had died on 19 August 1896, had not lived to witness the event. Unfortunately, Eleanor Ormerod's own physical decline followed rather rapidly. In early 1901, she suffered a combination of rheumatism and a 'painful and exhausting illness', that often left her bedridden. Originally diagnosed as the 'after effects of influenza', the origins of her illness were later suspected to lie in a diseased liver. By May, Eleanor Ormerod admitted: 'I believe myself the end may come any time' (*Eleanor Ormerod*, 325). On 19 July 1901, she died of cancer of the liver at Torrington House, St Albans, Hertfordshire. After a small and unostentatious funeral at St Albans cemetery, Eleanor Ormerod was buried in the same grave as Georgiana on 23 July 1901.   J. F. M. CLARK

Sources *The Entomologist*, 34 (1901) · *Entomologist's Record*, 13 (1901) · *Canadian Entomologist*, 33 (1901) · *Entomologist's Monthly Magazine*, 37 (1901) · *Nature*, 64 (1901), 330 · *The Times* (20 July 1901) · *Eleanor Ormerod, LL.D., economic entomologist: autobiography and correspondence*, ed. R. Wallace (1904) · J. F. M. Clark, 'Eleanor Ormerod (1828–1901) as an economic entomologist: "pioneer of purity even more than of Paris Green"', *British Journal for the History of Science*, 25 (1992), 431–52 · V. Woolf, 'Miss Ormerod', *The Dial*, 77 (1924), 466–74 · S. A. Neave, *The centenary history of the Entomological Society of London, 1833–1933* (1933) · C. Whitehead, *Retrospections* (1908) · J. F. M. Clark, D. Mabberly, J. Pickering, and S. Raphael, *Women and natural history: artists, collectors, patrons, scientists* (1996) · *ILN* (12 Sept 1891), 334 · G. Ordish, *The constant pest: a short history of pests and their control* (1976) · L. O. Howard, *A history of applied entomology (somewhat anecdotal)* (1930) · N. Goddard, *Harvests of change: the Royal Agricultural Society of England, 1838–1988* (1988) · H. R. Fletcher, *The story of the Royal Horticultural Society, 1804–1968* (1969) · d. cert.

Archives BL, corresp. · Oxf. U. Mus. NH, Hope Library, corresp., specimens · Royal Entomological Society of London, corresp. · U. Edin. L., corresp. | Bodl. Oxf., letters to G. W. Ormerod · Oxf. U. Mus. NH, corresp. with F. S. Crawford; letters to J. O. Westwood · Rothamsted Experimental Station Library, Harpenden, letters to W. Parlour and J. Willis

Likenesses silhouette, 1835 (*Miss Ormerod in childhood*), repro. in Wallace, ed., *Eleanor Ormerod*, facing p. 324 · Elliott & Fry, photogravure, *c*.1900, NPG [*see illus.*] · photograph, *c*.1900, U. Edin. · R. T. [R. Taylor], engraving, repro. in *ILN* (12 Sept 1891), 334 · oils (after photograph by Elliott & Fry), U. Edin. · photograph, repro. in Wallace, ed., *Eleanor Ormerod*, frontispiece · photograph, repro. in *Canadian Entomologist*, pl. 5 · photograph, repro. in *The British Naturalist: an Illustrated Magazine of Natural History* (April 1892), facing p. 60 · photograph, repro. in *ILN* (27 July 1901), 122

Wealth at death £51,921 9*s*.: resworn probate, March 1902, CGPLA Eng. & Wales (1901)

Ormerod, George (1785–1873), county historian, was born in High Street, Manchester, on 20 October 1785, the only (and posthumous) son of George Ormerod (1757–1785) of Bury, Lancashire, who had died thirteen days earlier. His mother was Elizabeth (1752–1822), daughter of Thomas Johnson of Manchester and Tyldesley and his wife, Susanna Wareing of Bury. He was initially educated privately, probably at Ardwick Green, Manchester, but in July 1798 was sent to King's School, Chester, of which a family friend, the Revd Thomas Bancroft, was a former headmaster. From 1793 Bancroft had been vicar of Bolton, Lancashire, and in 1799 he agreed to take Ormerod as a private pupil. Ormerod remained at Bolton vicarage until midsummer 1803, receiving a thorough classical education. He matriculated from Brasenose College, Oxford, on 21 April 1803, graduated BA in 1806, received the honorary degree of MA in 1807 and that of DCL in 1818, the last being in recognition of his recently published history of Cheshire.

On his twenty-first birthday Ormerod came into his inheritance, including the extensive estates in south Lancashire left by his paternal grandparents and his

George Ormerod (1785–1873), by John Jackson, 1817

mother's family. On 2 August 1808 he married, at Sandbach, Cheshire, Sarah (1784–1860), daughter of Dr John Latham MD, and his wife, Mary Mayer; Sarah was the sister of John Latham, a college friend. Between 1809 and 1828 the couple had seven sons, including the anatomist William Piers *Ormerod, and three daughters; the youngest child, Eleanor Anne *Ormerod (1828–1901), became a distinguished entomologist.

During 1808 the Ormerods lived at Rawtenstall, but in 1809 they moved to Great Missenden, Buckinghamshire. By this time Ormerod—who had had a passion for genealogy and an interest in local history from his schooldays—was involved in extensive research for his history of Cheshire. To make the task easier, he decided to move back north, and in 1811 he bought the 83 acre Chorlton House estate, 4 miles from Chester. From then until 1817 the family spent the summers there, living in London during the winter so that Ormerod could conduct research in the British Museum. In Chester Castle he made use of a large collection of original documents, and a valuable loan of books and documents was made to him by Hugh Cholmondeley, dean of Chester, whose assistance and sympathy Ormerod warmly acknowledged. Ormerod also borrowed material extensively from leading county families, using introductions from Cholmondeley as well as his own social connections. Although he supervised the research, and was self-taught in palaeography, most of the transcribing was undertaken by his research assistant the Revd J. Eaton, and by Faithful Thomas, the deputy keeper of the records at Chester Castle. Ormerod himself made lengthy tours of the county and claimed to have visited every township at least once, and to have made copious notes on the spot.

The resulting work was entitled *The history of the county palatine and city of Chester … incorporated with a republication of King's Vale Royal and Leycester's Cheshire antiquities*, and it appeared in ten parts, forming three volumes, between 1816 and 1819. A second edition, revised and enlarged by Thomas Helsby, wholly independently of Ormerod's family, was published in parts during 1875–82.

Ormerod's history of Cheshire is a classic antiquarian county history. He wrote only between a quarter and a third of each volume, the remainder being lengthy transcripts of documents, and reprinted portions of earlier printed works. The *History* was very enthusiastically received at the time, and was well regarded for many years afterwards, although some doubting voices were heard at an early stage. The great Yorkshire historian Joseph Hunter described it in 1822 as 'a succession of facts detached, a rope of sand' (Hess, 62), while the editor of the second edition of the work, Thomas Helsby, felt that 'the swelling stems of genealogy were permitted to have all their own way' (Helsby, xvi). Ormerod himself deliberately excluded all reference to commerce, industry, and urbanization as being outside the scope of his work, and his emphasis was thus heavily towards family history, manorial history, and antiquarian topography.

After the completion of the work on Cheshire, in the autumn of 1817, Ormerod immediately left the county and never again lived in the north of England. In 1823 Chorlton House was sold and in the same year Ormerod inherited important property, mining, and financial interests from his uncle Thomas Johnson. With this increased wealth he was able, in 1825, to buy the 208 acre Barnesville estate at Sedbury, Gloucestershire, on the narrow peninsula between the Severn and Wye estuaries. He renamed the property Sedbury Park, and lived there from 1828 until his death. He was appointed a JP for Gloucestershire in 1827 and for Monmouthshire in 1830, and served as deputy lieutenant for the former in 1861, but otherwise his role in county administration was limited.

As a leading county historian, Ormerod was a founder member of the Historic Society of Lancashire and Cheshire (1848) and of the Chester Archaeological Society (1849). He was a council member of the Chetham Society from its foundation in 1843 until 1846. For this society he edited, among other works, *Lancashire Civil War Tracts* (1844), which is probably of more lasting value than his history of Cheshire. After 1819, with the exception of the *Lancashire Civil War Tracts*, Ormerod's output was drastically diminished and, although he made a number of contributions to the transactions of learned societies in the north-west, little of significance emerged. After his move to Gloucestershire he became particularly interested in the antiquities and Roman history of the Sedbury area, and in Offa's Dyke, which has its southern end close to Sedbury Park. He published a series of books and papers on these subjects between 1850 and 1861, culminating in *Strigulensia* (1861), a volume on the archaeology of the district between the Severn and the Wye.

Ormerod was thus a prosperous leisured gentleman with a genuine and abiding interest in antiquarian history and archaeology: his researches were undertaken in part to 'avert the irksomeness of superabundant leisure' but also because of a 'decided predilection' for the subject. His character was remembered by his niece Dorothy Latham: 'an autocrat in his own family and intolerant of any shortcomings or failings that came under his notice … The family discipline was strict, the younger children were expected to yield obedience to the elders' (Latham, 14). As he grew old his sight began to fail, and for the last few years of his life he was blind. He died on 9 October 1873 at Sedbury Park, Beachley, and was buried with his wife at Tidenham, Gloucestershire, on 15 October.

ALAN G. CROSBY

Sources J. P. Hess, *George Ormerod: historian of Cheshire* (1989) · T. Helsby, introduction, in G. Ormerod, *The history of the county palatine and city of Chester*, 2nd edn, ed. T. Helsby, 1 (1882), xi–xviii · A. G. Crosby, *A society with no equal: the Chetham Society, 1843–1993* (1993) · D. J. Clayton, 'An early Cheshire archivist: Faithful Thomas (*c.*1772–1884) and the records of the palatinate of Chester', *Archives*, 17 (1985–6), 3–26 · D. Latham, 'Reminiscences of Sedbury', in *Eleanor Ormerod, LL.D., economic entomologist: autobiography and correspondence*, ed. R. Wallace (1904), 14 · CGPLA *Eng. & Wales* (1873)

Archives BL, corresp., Add. MSS 24873, 34568–34569, 38514; Egerton MS 2840 · Bodl. Oxf. · Glos. RO · NRA, notes and papers relating to Cheshire, Lancashire, etc. · NRA, priv. coll., notes and papers relating to Gloucestershire and Monmouthshire · U. Edin. L. | Bodl. Oxf., corresp. with Thomas Phillips · Bolton Central Library, corresp. and papers relating to genealogy of Crompton family · Ches. & Chester ALSS, letters to Thomas Hughes; corresp. with Peter Leigh

Likenesses J. Jackson, watercolour drawing, 1817, Bodl. Oxf. [*see illus.*] · J. Jackson, oils, 1819, probably RCP Lond. · J. Jackson, watercolour, 1819, repro. in G. Ormerod, *History*, 1st edn · engraving (after watercolour by J. Jackson, 1819), repro. in G. Ormerod, *History*, ed. T. Helsby, 2nd edn

Wealth at death under £50,000: probate, 29 Nov 1873, CGPLA *Eng. & Wales*

Ormerod, George Wareing (1810–1891), geologist, was born on 12 October 1810 at The Damhouse, Tyldesley, Lancashire, the second son of George *Ormerod (1785–1873), local historian, and his wife, Sarah (1784–1860), the eldest daughter of John Latham (1761–1843), physician, and his wife, Mary. He was educated at private schools and by a private tutor at Harborne, near Birmingham, matriculated in 1829 at Brasenose College, Oxford, and graduated BA in 1833 and MA in 1836. He was admitted a solicitor in 1836 and practised in Manchester until 1855. Ormerod became a fellow of the Geological Society of London in 1833, and studied the Cheshire salt deposits, the Permian of Lancashire, and the drainage and subsidence of Chat Moss, publishing eight papers on these subjects between 1842 and 1853. He was a member of the Manchester Literary and Philosophical Society, and became treasurer in 1854.

In 1855 Ormerod moved to Devon, where he spent the rest of his life. He practised in Chagford until 1869, when he moved to Teignmouth. He continued his geological studies, publishing papers on the northern edge of the Dartmoor granite, on minerals from the Trias, on fossils from Kent's cavern, and on the geology of south Devon.

Ormerod joined the Devonshire Association in 1862 and served on the council and as a local secretary. He published a classified index to the association's publications in 1886, and a similar index to the Geological Society's publications in 1858, with later supplements. In addition to his geological work, Ormerod published papers on prehistoric and later antiquities in Devon, and on local history, including the *Annals of the Teignmouth Cricket Club* (1888). Ormerod, who never married, died at Bonnicliff, East Teignmouth, on 6 January 1891.

JOHN C. THACKRAY

Sources A. Geikie, presidential address, *Quarterly Journal of the Geological Society*, 47 (1891), 61 · *Report and Transactions of the Devonshire Association*, 23 (1891), 108–10 · d. cert. · *CGPLA Eng. & Wales* (1891)
Archives Bodl. Oxf., family corresp. · U. Birm. L., diary | BGS, geological register · GS Lond., letters to L. Horner and drawings
Likenesses D. R. Everest & Co., photograph, 1887, GS Lond. · Hennah & Kent, photograph, GS Lond.
Wealth at death £15,599 15s. 5d.: probate, 3 Feb 1891, *CGPLA Eng. & Wales*

Ormerod, Oliver (*d.* 1626), Church of England clergyman and religious controversialist, was the second son of Oliver Ormerod of Ormerod, Lancashire, and his wife, Sibill Hargrave. He was admitted to Emmanuel College, Cambridge, on 6 June 1596, and graduated BA in 1600. In 1605–6 he was rector of Little Wenham, Suffolk.

Ormerod was the author of two works of religious controversy, attacking puritans and Roman Catholics respectively. *The Picture of a Puritane* (1605) is written 'in a most plaine and familiar manner', designed (as Ormerod states in the preface) to 'bring yourselves, your wives, your children and your servants, to a full detestation of the Puritanfaction'. It consists of two sets of dialogues: the first between an 'Englishman' and a 'Germaine', showing the doctrinal similarities between English puritans and German anabaptists, with examples drawn from the Marprelate tracts and the writings of Thomas Cartwright, 'which many nowadays doe make as great account of as Oracles'; the second between a 'Protestant' and a 'Puritane', including a report of the Hampton Court conference, in which the puritans were 'vanquished in open disputation ... and driven to confess that their opinions were mere novelties and new devised fancies'. In the final dialogue Ormerod criticized the episcopal toleration of moderate puritan ministers, arguing that 'it does not stand with equitie, that some Ministers should be bound to shew their conformitie, and others be dispensed with'.

The success of the work led Ormerod to publish a companion-piece entitled *The Picture of a Papist* (1606), written in similar style as a set of dialogues between a 'Minister' and a 'Recusant'. The work was entered in the Stationers' register on 9 December 1605, only a month after the discovery of the Gunpowder Plot, and violently denounces the conspirators, expressing the hope:

that their privities might be cut off, and thrown into the fire ... that their bellies might be ripped up, and their hearts torn out ... and that their quarters might be fixed upon the gates of our Cities, and exposed to the eyes of men.

In the preface Ormerod denied any connection with

Thomas Dekker's pamphlet *The Double PP* (1605), 'which some in London have reported to be of my drawing', and declared that it was 'a greate disgrace to our Religion' that 'histrionicall jesters and stage players should be suffered to write books of such matters'.

Both these works provoked indignant responses from other writers. In his *Short Dialogue* (1605) the puritan minister Samuel Hieron challenged the accuracy of Ormerod's account 'of a man in Oxfordshire who as the Pamphletter saith, being one of the puritan faction, when his Father's ribs were broken, would not ride for a bonesetter on the Saboth day'. According to Hieron, 'the Father's ribb was never broken; he had a bruise indeede with a fall, and the meanes was seasonably used, and he soone recovered'; however, the story was repeated without alteration in the second edition (1605) of *The Picture of a Puritane*, 'newly corrected and enlarged'. The anonymous Roman Catholic author of *The Image of Bothe Churches* (1623) also criticized 'Ormerode, the picturemaker, who upon erroneous misconceaving, condemned that singular and renowned Doctor Allen, for affirming that princes might be slayne by their subjects'.

On 20 March 1610 Ormerod was presented to the rectory of Norton Fitzwarren, Somerset, resigning on 31 March 1617 when he was presented to the rectory of Huntspill, Somerset, where he remained until his death; the patron of both livings was William Bourchier, third earl of Bath. In or before 1619 he married Joan (or Johanna; *d.* 1638/9), daughter of Richard Hinkson, possibly from Kent. Ormerod's will, dated 17 January 1626, shows him to have been a wealthy man: it bequeathes the sum of £100 to his son Richard, £300 to his eldest daughter, Anne, and £200 each to his younger daughters Jane and Elizabeth. He charged his widow 'to be careful in the tutoring and well bringing up of my children', and left their legacies to be managed by her, 'because my said children are young and not of themselves able to govern their estates'. Ormerod died soon afterwards; his will was proved on 28 June.

ARNOLD HUNT

Sources G. Ormerod, *Parentalia* (1851) · Venn, *Alum. Cant.* · F. T. Colby, ed., *The visitation of the county of Somerset in the year 1623*, Harleian Society, 11 (1876) · F. W. Weaver, ed., *Somerset incumbents* (privately printed, Bristol, 1889) · will, PRO, PROB 11/149 (90 Hele) · will, PRO, PROB 11/179 (21 Harvey) [Joan Ormerod] · [S. Hieron], *A short dialogue* (1605) · P. D. M., *The image of bothe churches* (1623)
Wealth at death £800 in major bequests: will, PRO, PROB 11/149. sig. 90

Ormerod, William Piers (1818–1860), anatomist and surgeon, was born in London on 14 May 1818, the fifth son of the historian George *Ormerod (1785–1873), of Sedbury Park, Tidenham, Gloucestershire, and Sarah (1784–1860), daughter of John *Latham MD (1761–1843); George Wareing *Ormerod and Edward Latham *Ormerod were his brothers, Eleanor Anne *Ormerod his sister. He was sent to a private school at Laleham, Middlesex, together with his younger brother, Edward, and afterwards (in 1832) to Rugby School, where three of his elder brothers had been educated. In 1835 he went to St Bartholomew's Hospital where, on the advice of his uncle, Dr Peter Mere *Latham, he was articled to Edward Stanley, and was helped by James Paget. He was a quiet and diligent student, and did well in examinations.

In 1840–41 Ormerod was house surgeon to William Lawrence, and in 1842 he gained the Jacksonian prize of the Royal College of Surgeons for his 'Essay on the comparative merits of mercury and iodine in the treatment of syphilis'. In 1843 he was appointed demonstrator of anatomy, and in the following year he printed, for the use of the students of the hospital, a collection of *Questions in Practical Anatomy* (1844). He became a member of the Royal College of Surgeons in 1843, and afterwards a fellow (1845); he also belonged to the Royal Medical and Chirurgical Society. His health began to fail from overwork, and in 1844 he left London and retired to his father's house at Sedbury Park. Here he arranged the surgical materials that he had collected in the hospital between 1835 and 1844. He published them in 1846, together with the substance of his 1842 Jacksonian prize essay, under the title *Clinical Collections*.

In the summer of 1846 Ormerod returned to work and went to Oxford. He was elected a surgeon to the Radcliffe Infirmary, and in 1848 he published an essay, *On the Sanatory [sic] Condition of Oxford*, based on the annual reports of the registrar-general for 1844–6; this paid special attention to the sanitary condition of the different places in which deaths from infectious diseases had occurred. But in December 1848, 'after a period of great hurry and anxiety', he suffered from epileptic fits and retired from practice altogether. He never married. He left Oxford in 1849, and in 1850 settled at Canterbury. He hoped to be strong enough to train as a missionary. However, his mind failed gradually, and he died at his home, 33 St Peter's, Westgate, Canterbury, on 10 June 1860, having fractured the base of his skull from a fall during an epileptic seizure. He was buried in the churchyard of St Martin's, Canterbury.

W. A. GREENHILL, *rev.* JEAN LOUDON

Sources V. G. Plarr, *Plarr's Lives of the fellows of the Royal College of Surgeons of England*, rev. D'A. Power, 2 vols. (1930) · *GM*, 3rd ser., 9 (1860), 106 · J. Paget, 'William and Edward Ormerod', *St Bartholomew's Hospital Reports*, 9 (1873), vii–xxi, esp. vii–xiii · private information (1894) · *GM*, 3rd ser., 8 (1860), 534 · personal knowledge (1894) · *CGPLA Eng. & Wales* (1860)

Archives Bodl. Oxf., letters to H. W. Acland

Wealth at death under £1500: probate, 11 July 1860, *CGPLA Eng. & Wales*

Ormesby, Sir William (*d.* 1317), justice, probably derived his name from one of two adjacent villages of Ormesby (St Michael and St Margaret) in south-east Norfolk, about 5 miles north of Great Yarmouth. Nothing else is known of his origins and, if he inherited any property from his parents, it seems only to have been of very modest extent. His first appearance in the records is probably in 1275 when a William of Ormesby, who is probably to be identified with the future judge (although he had at least one contemporary namesake), made a bid to farm three hundreds in south-east Norfolk. By 1283 Ormesby was being paid a retainer, probably for his professional legal services, by the prior of Norwich. He acted as a serjeant on the Norfolk

eyre of 1286 and in the Norfolk assizes at Norwich in 1288, although there is no evidence of his acting as a serjeant in the Westminster bench, either then or later. By 1291 he had entered the service of the earl of Norfolk, subsequently receiving a grant of the contested Yorkshire manor of Thornton in Pickeringlithe from the earl, and he continued to witness the earl's charters for at least a decade after he had entered the king's service. This happened in 1292 when he was appointed a junior justice of the northern eyre circuit led by Hugh Cressingham, who also came from Norfolk. Ormesby was particularly associated with the hearing of crown pleas, and he was also commissioned to hold gaol deliveries to try those who surrendered to justice after the eyres had left the counties concerned. Surviving law reports indicate, however, that he also played a part in the hearing of civil pleas.

Ormesby remained in the king's service after the eyre circuits were suspended in June 1294 and was henceforth regularly appointed both to oyer and terminer commissions and to deliver gaols, mainly in East Anglia but also on occasion elsewhere in the country. He was summoned to the August parliament of 1295, and was sent as a messenger to the king of the Romans later that month. It was also apparently at about this time that he became a knight. At the end of 1295 or early in 1296 he became a justice of the king's bench. He had served there for no more than a year when he was appointed a justice in the newly conquered Scotland, at about the same time that his erstwhile judicial colleague Cressingham was appointed treasurer of Scotland. The beginning of a general revolt of the Scots against the English occupation regime was marked by an attack led by William Wallace against Ormesby while he was holding a session at Scone in May 1297. Ormesby lost all his personal possessions and was lucky to escape with his life. He seems to have fled to England but returned later that summer to Scotland. He had, however, been removed from office in Scotland before the débâcle at Stirling Bridge at which Cressingham was killed, and was commissioned in October 1297 to levy foot soldiers in the northern counties for service against the Scots.

Late in 1297 or early in 1298 Ormesby was reappointed to the court of the king's bench, and was paid as one of its justices until Michaelmas term 1303, although he left the court to act as one of the justices of the eyres for Cambridgeshire and the Isle of Ely in 1299, and to act as a justice in the liberty of Durham while it was in the hands of the king in 1302–3. In 1305 and 1306 he was appointed leader of the groups of trailbaston justices who held sessions in his own home county of Norfolk and in Suffolk, and in 1307 he served briefly as justice of Chester. By September 1308 he had been appointed as the senior assize justice for Norfolk and Suffolk and retained that position, although apparently with some intermissions and with Cambridgeshire and Huntingdonshire later being added to the circuit, until the time of his death. He also continued to be appointed to a variety of other judicial commissions, mainly but not exclusively in the same counties. These included commissions for the enforcement of the Statute of Winchester and commissions to punish the wrongdoing of local officials. He was appointed a justice both of the abortive Durham eyre of 1311 and of the Kent eyre of 1313–14, where he heard both civil and crown pleas.

William Ormesby was married twice. By 1286 he had married his first wife, Agnes, the heir to a considerable landed estate in Norfolk which included lands in Ormesby. He was almost certainly her second husband. If, as seems probable, she was the mother of Ormesby's son John, the marriage must have taken place some years before 1286, for in 1294 William and Agnes settled two Norfolk manors belonging to Agnes on John and his wife, Katherine, and in 1296 and 1297 John accompanied his father to Scotland. Agnes died not long before Michaelmas term 1306. Between 1306 and 1308 Ormesby married as his second wife Sibyl, the widow of the royal justice Roger Loveday who had died in 1287. She brought him a life interest in extensive lands in Cambridgeshire and Suffolk, which had either been settled jointly on Roger and herself or which she held in dower. Ormesby was still alive and capable of transacting business with judicial colleagues on 28 April 1317, but was dead by 12 June 1317, when his executors were instructed to send in to the exchequer his assize and other plea rolls. He was buried in the abbey of St Benet of Hulme, not far from Ormesby, a house of which he had been a benefactor during his lifetime.

PAUL BRAND

Sources *Chancery records* · PRO · G. O. Sayles, ed., *Select cases in the court of king's bench*, 1, SeldS, 55 (1936)

Ormidale. For this title name *see* Macfarlane, Robert, Lord Ormidale (1802–1880).

Ormiston. For this title name *see* Cockburn, Adam, of Ormiston, Lord Ormiston (*c*.1656–1735).

Ormiston, Thomas (1826–1882), civil engineer, was born in Edinburgh on 28 July 1826, one of at least two sons of John Ormiston and his wife, Margaret Lindsay. The family subsequently moved to Glasgow, where Thomas received a rudimentary education before leaving school early to enter the business of his father and uncle, who were builders in Glasgow. With them he acquired a knowledge of carpentry, masonry, and surveying. In 1846 he entered the engineers' department of the River Clyde Improvement Trust; shortly afterwards he became chief assistant and from 1852 he was acting engineer to the trust for a short period on the death of David Bremner. Three years later James Walker, a past president of the Institution of Civil Engineers, appointed him principal assistant in his London office, where he remained until the beginning of 1862.

From early in his career Ormiston was interested in the practical side of engineering. While working for the Clyde trustees he designed works himself at Ormidale pier, Port Glasgow, and Ayr harbour, where he developed his own design for a dredger. Further south he worked on the design of docks and harbours in the Isle of Man, the River Mersey, and Cardiff. He also worked on many of the Trinity House lighthouses and in 1856–7 was entrusted with the entire charge of the erection of the lighthouse on The Needles in the Isle of Wight. In addition he was involved in the preparation of designs for the Plymouth breakwater fort, and from 1862 he served as engineer in charge of the fort works. In 1857 Ormiston married Charlotte, daughter of William Lane of Freshwater, Isle of Wight; they had three sons and four daughters.

At the end of 1864 Ormiston went to Bombay to superintend a large land reclamation scheme adjacent to the harbour for the Elphinstone Land and Press Company of Bombay. This he did so successfully that in 1870 the government of India took the company over, retaining Ormiston's services. In 1873 this led to the establishment of the Bombay Port Trust with Ormiston as chief engineer. Ormiston foresaw the large expansion in Bombay's trade that took place in the 1870s and 1880s, to which the facilities of the Prince's Dock, constructed to his design from 1875 to 1880, made a great contribution. On the occasion of its opening in January 1880 he was appointed CIE. He had previously relinquished his post to his brother George E. Ormiston in 1874 and became consulting engineer to the Bombay Port Trust in London.

Ormiston was for many years a JP for Bombay, and he took a keen interest in municipal affairs. He gave much time and energy to advising the government on engineering projects throughout India, and in 1879 he visited Cyprus to report on the harbour at Famagusta. He was a fellow of the University of Bombay, and was elected dean of the faculty of engineering in 1879.

In 1880 Ormiston's health began to fail and early in 1882 he retired to the Isle of Wight, where he died at Neston Farm, Freshwater, on 9 July 1882. He was survived by his wife. RONALD M. BIRSE, *rev.* MIKE CHRIMES

Sources *PICE*, 71 (1882–3), 409–15 · Boase, *Mod. Eng. biog.*
Archives BL OIOC | Inst. CE, membership records
Wealth at death £49,629 0s. 3d.: probate, 9 Oct 1882, *CGPLA Eng. & Wales*

Ormond. For this title name *see* Butler, James, first earl of Ormond (*c*.1305–1338); Butler, James, second earl of Ormond (1331–1382); Butler, James, third earl of Ormond (*c*.1360–1405); Butler, James, fourth earl of Ormond (1390–1452); Butler, James, first earl of Wiltshire and fifth earl of Ormond (1420–1461); Butler, John, sixth earl of Ormond (*d*. 1476/7); Butler, Piers, first earl of Ossory and eighth earl of Ormond (*b*. in or after 1467, *d*. 1539); Boleyn, Thomas, earl of Wiltshire and earl of Ormond (1476/7–1539); Butler, Margaret, countess of Ossory and Ormond (*d*. 1542); Butler, James, ninth earl of Ormond and second earl of Ossory (*b*. in or after 1496, *d*. 1546); Butler, Thomas, tenth earl of Ormond and third earl of Ossory (1531–1614); Butler, Walter, eleventh earl of Ormond and fourth earl of Ossory (1559–1633); Butler, James, first duke of Ormond (1610–1688); Butler, Elizabeth, duchess of Ormond and *suo jure* Lady Dingwall (1615–1684); Butler, James, second duke of Ormond (1665–1745).

Ormond [Butler], **Sir James** (d. 1497), administrator, was the illegitimate son of John *Butler, sixth earl of Ormond (d. 1476/7), and Raynalda O'Brien. Ambitious and quarrelsome, he was apparently raised at court by his uncle, Thomas, the seventh earl. He became expert in arms and entered Lincoln's Inn in June 1486. In 1487, Earl Thomas appointed Ormond as his deputy in Ireland in succession to Sir James Butler of Dunboyne. Yet this appointment was contested by the latter's son, Piers, son-in-law to Gerald Fitzgerald, eighth earl of Kildare (d. 1513), and to whom Butler had bequeathed the office. Ormond did not return to Ireland until December 1491, when, as squire for the king's body, he was sent with Thomas Garth and 200 soldiers to defend the Ormond region against Perkin Warbeck, being appointed captain and governor of Kilkenny and Tipperary. In June 1492, now king's councillor, he was appointed joint governor of Ireland with Archbishop Walter Fitzsimons of Dublin, the deputy lieutenant, after the earl of Kildare's dismissal. Ormond also succeeded Lord Portlester as lord treasurer and apparently had primary responsibility for the rule of the southern shires. The new Butler-dominated administration gradually strengthened central government control over the outlying shires, as the proceedings of the 1493 parliament show; and supported by his mother's relatives, the Gaelic Ó Briain family, Ormond also consolidated his authority over his uncle's estates. Yet Kildare's dismissal also stoked the old Butler–Fitzgerald feud: clashes followed in Dublin between rival bands of retainers, Ship Street was burned, a former mayor was murdered, and in early summer 1493 there occurred Ormond's famous reconciliation with Kildare when Sir James, having taken refuge in St Patrick's Cathedral, shook hands with Kildare through a hole cut in the chapter house door.

Probably fearing that these disturbances would encourage another invasion by Warbeck, Henry VII dispatched reinforcements and in September 1493 replaced Ormond and Fitzsimons with Viscount Gormanston as caretaker governor. Ormond sailed for England soon after, to be joined shortly at court by other prominent magnates and officials. Over the winter, old quarrels were composed and a new initiative prepared to hold Ireland against Warbeck. This resulted in the appointment of an experienced captain, Sir Edward Poynings, as deputy lieutenant, with 653 soldiers and five or six experienced administrators and lawyers, one of whom, Sir Hugh Conway, replaced Ormond as treasurer. On his return to Ireland in June 1494, Ormond received a grant of manors in Meath, Kilkenny, and Tipperary in compensation, and was also appointed constable of Limerick Castle to keep an eye on Maurice Fitzgerald (d. 1520), the unreliable ninth earl of Desmond. He remained closely associated with Poynings, accompanying the deputy and Kildare on an expedition into Ulster in November; and after Poynings's breach with Kildare, the deputy became even more reliant on Ormond's troops and local connections. Following Kildare's arrest for treason in February 1495, his brother seized Carlow Castle. Poynings and Ormond besieged it during the spring, retaking it in July; but by then Warbeck

and Desmond were besieging Waterford. Ormond had to organize the defence of the Butler territories against Desmond's raiding parties and bring troops to raise the siege. After this, support for Warbeck collapsed and Poynings was recalled; and with the departure of many of Poynings's troops, Ormond's military role expanded still further.

In the spring of 1496, however, Ormond's leading position was jeopardized by the king's decision to rehabilitate and restore as governor the earl of Kildare. Sir James was summoned to court in July for a formal reconciliation between the earls of Ormond and Kildare and their supporters, but his role and prospects were now greatly reduced: the English troops he had commanded were withdrawn and Kildare favoured Ormond's rival, Sir Piers Butler. He became aloof and aggressive, mobilizing support in the Butler territories in alliance with the Ó Briain chief and, according to Sir Piers, intriguing with Warbeck and claiming to be rightful earl of Ormond. Reports of his behaviour drew a royal summons early in 1497, and a second in May, both of which he ignored. Finally, he was attacked and killed by Sir Piers on 17 July 1497 in a kind of impromptu duel near Kilkenny, shortly before Warbeck's last visit to Ireland.   STEVEN G. ELLIS

Sources A. Conway and E. Curtis, *Henry VII's relations with Scotland and Ireland, 1485–1498* (1932) · S. G. Ellis, 'Henry VII and Ireland, 1491–1496', *England and Ireland in the later middle ages: essays in honour of Jocelyn Otway-Ruthven*, ed. J. Lydon (1981), 237–54 · D. B. Quinn, 'Guide to English financial records for Irish history, 1461–1558', *Analecta Hibernica*, 10 (1941), 1–69 · *CPR, 1485–94* · J. Graves and J. G. A. Prim, *History of St Canice's Cathedral, Kilkenny* (1857) · E. Curtis, ed., *Calendar of Ormond deeds*, 6 vols., IMC (1932–43) · J. Gairdner, ed., *Letters and papers illustrative of the reigns of Richard III and Henry VII*, 2 vols., Rolls Series, 24 (1861–3) · S. G. Ellis, *Ireland in the age of the Tudors* (1998) · I. Arthurson, *The Perkin Warbeck conspiracy, 1491–1499* (1994) · T. W. Moody and others, eds., *A new history of Ireland*, 2: *Medieval Ireland, 1169–1534* (1987); repr. with corrections (1993)
Archives NL Ire., papers

Ormond, John [*formerly* John Ormond Thomas] (1923–1990), poet and film-maker, was born on 3 April 1923 at 2 Bridge Terrace, Dunvant, Swansea, the only child of Arthur Thomas (1892–1950), shoemaker, and his wife, Elsie (1894–1965). He was educated at Dunvant elementary school and Swansea grammar school, and his early upbringing in a cultivated working-class community, centred on the local Welsh Independent chapel, made him a lifelong believer in art's power to speak to every social class and to address the spiritual dimensions of human existence. As a young man, he reacted against the anti-aestheticism of orthodox nonconformity (and later abandoned religion) but was thwarted in his wish to emulate his distinguished fellow villager Ceri Richards by training as an artist. Instead, he took a wartime degree in English and philosophy at University College, Swansea, having been exempted from military service as a conscientious objector. In blitzed Swansea (1941) he first read the poetry of Dylan Thomas, whose father had taught him at Swansea grammar school. Excited into poetry, he began to write prolifically in the sub-Thomasian style in which he was to be trapped for some time. His work quickly appeared in minor magazines and (with that of two others) in *Indications* (1943).

John Ormond Thomas left college in 1945, and on 21 September 1946 married Glenys (*b.* 1924), daughter of Evan Roderick, outfitter, a local girl he had met at university. They settled in Datchet, Buckinghamshire, since he had, on the strength of his youthful writing, been recruited to the staff of the celebrated photo-journal *Picture Post*. It was there that, between 1946 and 1949, he developed skills that were to be invaluable to him as film-maker and mature poet. Working closely with gifted photographers, he learned the grammar of visual experience and the art of relating word to image. On returning to Swansea as sub-editor of the *South Wales Evening Post* (1949–55), he renewed acquaintance with the talented pre-war set of Swansea artists, including Dylan Thomas. In 1955 he joined the BBC in Cardiff, and about this time he adopted his middle name as a surname, because of the great number of Thomases working in the Welsh BBC at this time. He began work as television news assistant, where he expanded the news service before being appointed founding head of the documentary film unit in 1957 and subsequently operating as an increasingly distinguished documentary film producer (1963–90). His classic early success, *Borrowed Pasture* (1960), a lyrical evocation of the struggle of two gnarled old Polish former servicemen to fashion a new life farming in west Wales, set the poetic tone and the standard for his later productions. Outstanding among these were his series of filmic portraits of distinguished poets and artists, including Dylan Thomas, R. S. Thomas, Vernon Watkins, Kyffin Williams, Ceri Richards, and Graham Sutherland.

Ormond's verse commentary for *Borrowed Pasture* also bore signs of his slow move away from the emotionally charged and densely symbolical poetry of his younger self. However, having taken to heart Vernon Watkins's early advice to burn most of his early poems, Ormond did not reappear as a poet until the mid-sixties, when his mature work began suddenly to appear in the newly established magazine *Poetry Wales*. He liked to date his recovery from the moment when his poem 'Cathedral builders' came to him seemingly all at once, but many other factors—including his return in imagination to his early Dunvant background—were doubtless involved. Flexible in tone and subtly nuanced, his new style was very accessible and yet richly suggestive. Always an uncompromising craftsman, Ormond slowly accumulated enough poetry for only three collections, containing a handful of poems of enduring interest. The 142 pages of his *Selected Poems* (1987) include most of his work, and demonstrate his distinctive mixture of ebullience, elegantly equivocating wit, and emotional plangency. These were also prominent characteristics of a man who is recalled as notably convivial, a peerless raconteur, and a joyfully fierce inquisitor of ideas. Tending to speak in mesmeric spurts, Ormond was given to thrusting 'his head out in emphasis, like a tortoise approaching the truth of a lettuce leaf' (Smith, 14).

Two childhood bouts of rheumatic fever had weakened Ormond's constitution, which was further undermined by the Lyme disease he contracted in his beloved Tuscany in 1983–4. After a short illness he died of cerebral haemorrhage on 4 May 1990 at the University Hospital of Wales, Cardiff, and was cremated at Thornhill, Cardiff, on 11 May. He was survived by his wife, one son, and two daughters.

M. WYNN THOMAS

Sources private information (2004) [family] · M. Wynn Thomas, *John Ormond* (1997) · J. Harris and E. J. Davies, *A bibliographical guide to twenty-four modern Anglo-Welsh writers* (1994) · D. Smith, 'A cannon off the cush', *Arcade* (14 Nov 1980), 13–14
Archives NL Wales, drafts of poems | NL Wales, letters to Kyffin Williams | FILM BBC Archive Library, Cardiff | SOUND BBC Archive Library, Cardiff · BL NSA
Likenesses K. Hutton, photograph, 1948, Hult. Arch. · K. Williams, oils, 1980, priv. coll. · J. Elwyn, oils, 1987, priv. coll. · photographs, Welsh Arts Council, Cardiff

Ormonde, Sir James. *See* Ormond, Sir James (*d.* 1497).

Ormrod, Sir Roger Fray Greenwood (1911–1992), judge, was born in Whitehaven, Cumberland, on 20 October 1911, the son of Oliver Fray Ormrod, a solicitor, and his wife, Edith Muriel, *née* Pim. He was educated at Shrewsbury School (1924–9), and the Queen's College, Oxford (1930–33), where he read medicine and jurisprudence, obtaining his degree in the latter. He was called to the bar in 1936, when he joined the busy chambers of Edward (later Lord) Pearce in the Temple. On 9 April 1938 he married (Doris) Anne Lush (*b.* 1905/6), a magistrate and marriage guidance counsellor.

On the outbreak of war in 1939 Ormrod completed his medical training at the Radcliffe Infirmary, Oxford, where he became house physician in 1941. In 1942 he joined the Royal Army Medical Corps and served in Normandy and north-west Europe. He returned to the bar in 1945, became a QC in 1958, and was appointed a judge of the High Court (Probate, Divorce, and Admiralty Division) in 1961, in which year he also received a knighthood. His medical background influenced his career in the law, and he retained links with medicine through his active membership of several medical institutions. He was elected FRCP in 1969 and an honorary FRCPsych in 1975.

For his first ten years on the bench Ormrod administered the unreformed divorce laws, which required proof of a 'matrimonial offence' before a divorce could be granted. In 1969 he tried the nullity case of *Corbett* v. *Corbett* ([1971] P83), in which he held that marriage in England involved the union of persons of the opposite sex, and consequently where one party had undergone a sex change the marriage was a nullity, since the wife was 'not a woman for the purposes of marriage but a biological male and had been since birth'.

Ormrod welcomed the reform of the divorce laws in 1971, which replaced the matrimonial offence as the sole ground of divorce with the breakdown of the marriage, and when the Probate, Divorce, and Admiralty Division became the Family Division. Unlike some of his judicial brethren Ormrod took the view that this was a radical change in the law, and for the next eleven years, both at first instance and as a lord justice of the Court of Appeal, to which he was appointed in 1974, he was responsible, practically single-handedly, for the development of family law following the 1971 legislation. An early example of his approach was the case of *Wachtel* v. *Wachtel* ([1973] Fam 72), when he said: 'Shares in responsibility for breakdown cannot be properly assessed without a meticulous examination and understanding of the spouses concerned, the more thorough the investigation the more the shares will in most cases approach equality.' He concluded that, in financial proceedings, conduct usually proved to be a marginal issue 'unless it is both obvious and gross'.

Nowhere was Ormrod's influence more decisive than in cases relating to children. Although since 1925 judges had paid lip-service to the statutory requirement that the welfare of the child was the 'first and paramount consideration', attempts were made to modify the consequences of this rule by considerations of the conduct of the parents, weight being given to the wishes of an 'unimpeachable spouse'. In *S* v. *S* ([1977] 1AER 656), Ormrod said: 'The phrase unimpeachable cannot mean a parent who is beyond criticism because there is no such thing.'

Some, who had not had Ormrod's experience of trying long, defended divorce cases directed to the respective blameworthiness of the spouses, thought that the pendulum had swung too far in disregarding matrimonial conduct, causing injustice to the 'innocent' spouse, especially husbands and fathers. Ormrod defended his approach in his presidential address to the Holdsworth Club in 1980, when he said: 'In the great majority of cases, the closer the investigation the clearer it becomes that the practicalities point to the mother as the parent who should have the care of the children; and consequently the person who will need the house.' And he went on to refer to one of his favourite dicta: 'It takes three to commit adultery. I always ask what has the "innocent" party done or failed to do?'

Ormrod was, in his own field of family law, one of the great reforming judges of the twentieth century whose influence on that branch of the law was profound and extended over more than thirty years. He was not concerned with the past history of a marriage, but always looked ahead to the future and the consequence of a divorce, above all to the welfare of the children and the financial support of the mother. His approach was essentially pragmatic and practical. He refused to allow the Family Division to become a court of morals. Ormrod had perhaps the most original mind of any of his contemporaries in the Court of Appeal except Lord Denning. His mind worked with astonishing rapidity, and he was a fluent and rapid speaker. On the bench, when dealing with matrimonial cases, he often appeared impatient and intolerant of what he regarded as irrelevancies, but this was on account of his profound knowledge of his subject, the speed and clarity with which he saw the nub of the problem, and, above all, his anxiety that he might not be able to do justice within the constraints of the law.

After his retirement in 1982 Ormrod threw himself into his many extramural activities, including the Notting Hill Housing Trust, of which he was chairman for twenty years, and was able to spend more time on Exmoor, where he had a house. He died at his home, 4 Aubrey Road, Kensington, on 6 January 1992, and was cremated. He left his widow, an adopted daughter, and several young people who had benefited from the kindness and generosity of him and his wife.   ROBIN DUNN

Sources personal knowledge (2004) · *WW* (1992) · *The Times* (9 Jan 1992) · *The Independent* (15 Jan 1992) · private information (2004) [Jeffery Jowell] · *BMJ* (17 Nov 1979) · R. Dunn, *Sword and wig* (1993), 201–3 · private information (2004) [Edward Cazalet] · private information (2004) [Roger Henderson] · m. cert. · d. cert.
Likenesses photograph, repro. in *The Independent* · photograph, repro. in *The Times*
Wealth at death £503,473: probate, 11 May 1992, *CGPLA Eng. & Wales*

Ormsby [*née* Rodwell Jones], **Hilda** (1877–1973), geographer, was born on 1 November 1877 at 44 Charles Street, Hanley, Staffordshire, one of the large family of the Revd W. Rodwell Jones (1834–1914), a Welsh Wesleyan Methodist minister, and Sarah Ann Cuthbertson. There is no known record of her early life, but the family is known to have moved seven times by the time Hilda was twenty-one, owing to the peripatetic nature of the Methodist ministry. She took the certificate in geography at the London School of Economics and Political Science (LSE) in 1908–9 and was a teacher in England and France, studying at the École Normale de Melun in France (probably 1909–11). There she studied mostly French and German languages, fitting a three-year course into two. She graduated BSc (Econ) in 1918 while assistant lecturer at the LSE and was one of the few geographers to proceed to the degree of DSc (Econ) (1931).

Hilda Rodwell Jones initially came into contact with Halford Mackinder's work through his Saturday lectures for schoolteachers at the LSE, which she attended with her brother Llewellyn in 1911. She was appointed as demonstrator in geography at the LSE in 1912 and having been the mainstay of the geography department during the First World War was promoted lecturer in geography at the LSE in 1918, taking on responsibility for organizing the diploma and honours BSc (Econ) under Professor A. J. Sargent. In 1919 Llewellyn Rodwell Jones joined his sister in the LSE department, having previously been lecturer in geography at the University of Leeds and having completed distinguished war service. Theirs was a sister–brother partnership unique in United Kingdom geography departments, and included shared responsibility for some courses. In 1920 she became a recognized teacher in the University of London at the London School of Economics. In the same period ('five glorious weeks', according to Harrison Church; *Geography*, 423) she was promoted to lecturer in commerce with special reference to commercial geography, appointed assistant to Mackinder (replacing her brother), and on 26 June 1920 married George V. Ormsby (1885–1950), a fellow LSE student and Reuters journalist who went on to become chief of the London bureau of the *Wall Street Journal*. Her key period of research and lecturing followed and she was subsequently promoted to reader in 1932. Her brother Llewellyn succeeded Mackinder as professor in 1925.

Intellectually, Hilda was much influenced by Mackinder, and recounted how she had sat on the unfinished foundations of an LSE building while Mackinder read to her the manuscript of his *Democratic Ideals and Reality* (1919). Mackinder's influence was explicitly acknowledged in her introduction to *France* (1931) but his influence pervades her texts, with their great emphasis on the physical patterns and processes underlying patterns of human activity, the historical development of those patterns, and the need to use maps to understand the region being studied. Ormsby invariably worked as a regional geographer, producing *London on the Thames* (1924) and *France* (1931), drawing as much as possible on field observation (conducted independently or with the Le Play Society). However, although profound, Mackinder's influence was not undiluted. Hers was an approach to the region that bore the mark of her tutor Professor A. J. Sargent and the French geographer Vidal de la Blache as much as Mackinder. Vidal believed that the physical environment did not determine the character of a particular region but rather presented opportunities for the inhabitants and this approach characterized Ormsby's work as seen clearly in her opening sentences to *France* (p. 3).

London on the Thames is thought to be the first geographical text on London and one which was used as a basis for class and field study and was acclaimed for its original contour map of London. Both books were rich in maps and other illustration and were well received. *France*, organized around the geographical regions defined by drainage basins, was not always accessible to the general reader, but despite this, it remained Ormsby's abiding contribution which, although she described it as a stop gap at the time of publication, continued to be a standard undergraduate text into the 1960s and was still in print at the time of her death. Other European regional studies focused on issues of contemporary topical interest, notably her *Mitteleuropa* (1935) which examined the concepts of central Europe, Deutschland, and Germany. Sadly the manuscript for a long-researched book on Germany was destroyed in an air raid during the Second World War.

While remembered more for her tutorials and map classes than for clarity in lecturing style, Ormsby was a successful teacher and extremely competent departmental organizer. She gave memorable courses on Europe, inspired students to study France, and ran a celebrated seminar on London given in the late 1920s and early 1930s, enlivening lectures with her zest and sense of fun. Known as Dr O. or simply Hilda to staff and students alike, Ormsby earned 'high praise from those under whom she worked' (*Geography*, 423) and was a lively conversationalist and hostess. She was an attractive woman, remembered for her generosity, vivacity, candour, and sometimes unconventional behaviour.

Ormsby, along with her brother, was one of the thirteen founder members of the Institute of British Geographers formed in 1933 to meet the needs of the emerging community of academic geographers of Britain, at a time when the Royal Geographical Society was considered to be concerned primarily with exploration. Ormsby was the only woman in the founding group (although joined by eleven others within the year) and the first woman to serve on the council of the institute, as an ordinary member in 1936–8. In 1962, at the age of eighty-five, Ormsby was created an honorary fellow of both the London School of Economics and the Royal Geographical Society.

Ormsby worked on maps for the naval intelligence division of the Admiralty during the First and Second World Wars and was deeply concerned that British soldiers in the First World War suffered at the hands of cartographers more concerned with aesthetics than accuracy. She and her husband also served as wardens in the air raid precaution service from the beginning of the battle of Britain onwards.

After retiring, Ormsby lived at Water End, an Elizabethan cottage in Hertfordshire, which (like her London homes at Fetter Lane and Clifford's Inn before) became a meeting place for students. Her husband died in March 1950 and she outlived him by twenty-three years, dying on 23 October 1973 within a few days of her ninety-sixth birthday at a nursing home in Althorne, Essex. Her body was cremated on 30 October at Chelmsford. A student bursary at the LSE was endowed by Hilda and George Ormsby.　　　　　　AVRIL M. C. MADDRELL

Sources R. J. H. Church, 'Hilda Ormsby, 1877–1973', ed. T. W. Freeman, *Geographer's Bibliographical Studies* (1981), 95–7 · *Geographical Magazine*, 46 (1973–4), 218 · *GJ*, 140 (1974), 177–8 · *LSE Magazine*, 48 (Nov 1974), 14–15 · *Daily Telegraph* (24 Oct 1973) · H. Ormsby, 'Halford Mackinder', BLPES, H. Ormsby MSS · 'Birthday greetings', *Geography*, 52 (1967), 423 · A. J. Sargent, 'Copy of testimonial from Prof. A. J. Sargent', 1923, BLPES, H. Ormsby MSS · H. R. Jones, 'Geographical training', *Claremarket Review*, 12/1 (1916), 7–9 · H. J. F. [H. J. Fleure], review of H. Ormsby, *France: a regional and economic geography* (1931), *GJ*, 79 (1932), 511–12 · M. J. Wise, 'The department of geography at LSE: a short history' · senate minutes, June 1920, U. Lond., SM 3724 · senate minutes, July 1932, U. Lond., SM 3662 · *Minutes of the Methodist conference* (1915), 129–30 [obit. of W. Rodwell Jones] · *New York Herald Tribune* (6 March 1950) [obit. of George V. Ormsby] · M. J. Wise, 'Llewellyn Rodwell Jones, 1881–1947', *Geographer's Bibliographical Series* [ed. T. W. Freeman and P. Pinchemel] (1980), 49–51 · R. W. Steel, *The Institute of British Geographers: the first fifty years* (1984) · private information (2004) [M. J. Wise, W. R. Mead]

Archives BLPES, MSS

Likenesses photograph, repro. in Church, 'Hilda Ormsby, 1877–1973'

Ormsby, John (1829–1895), writer and translator, was born at Gortner Abbey, co. Mayo, on 25 April 1829, the eldest child and only son of George Ormsby (d. 1836), of the 3rd dragoon guards, who had fought in the Peninsula and became high sheriff of co. Mayo in 1827, and his wife, Marianne (b. 1801), third daughter of Humphrey Jones of Mullinabro, co. Kilkenny. He was a direct descendant of the Ormsby family which migrated from Lincolnshire to co. Mayo in the reign of Elizabeth I, and, on his mother's side, of Catherine Cromwell, eldest sister of Oliver Cromwell. On the death of both parents during his childhood, he was made the ward of Denis Browne, dean of Emly, sent to Dr Homan's private school at Seapoint, near Dublin, and subsequently educated at Trinity College, Dublin, which he entered as a pensioner in 1845. In 1850 he was admitted at the Middle Temple, and kept his terms, but he was never called to the bar. However, the distinguished Hispanist and friend of Ormsby, James Fitzmaurice-Kelly, observed that 'Mr Ormsby took with him into letters an intelligence trained in logical methods, an exact appreciation of the value of evidence' (*Revue Hispanique*, 2, 1895, 364). Leslie Stephen recalled him living amid a book-stacked confusion at 7 King's Bench Walk in the Temple, a 'denizen of [...] the cultivated and scholarlike Bohemia' of London (*Alpine Journal*, 34). He had prints of Hogarth and was very well read in eighteenth-century English literature, especially Defoe and Fielding. T. E. Kebbel remembered him as a convivial and much appreciated fellow-member of the tory Rambler Club, a kindly man with wide sympathies 'whom it was refreshing even to look at and [who] had a humour of his own, which was always finding vent, no matter what the subject' (Kebbel, 198–9).

Ormsby joined the Alpine Club in the first year of its existence—1858—and contributed a vivid account, 'The ascent of the Grivola', about a climb that he made with others in August 1859 to *Peaks, Passes, and Glaciers* (1862). In 1864 he published *Autumn Rambles in North Africa*, travel sketches illustrated by himself and previously brought out in *Fraser's Magazine* recounting 'two seasons' wanderings' starting at Constantine and ending at Tunis. Here a sharp perception of visual detail (as in his account of the Tunis bazaars) and a sympathetic but realistic response to places and people are conveyed with considerable narrative skill. In 1876 he published a volume of pieces (*Stray Papers*) he had contributed to the *Saturday Review*, the *Pall Mall Gazette*, and other journals, where his amused eye is turned mainly towards London and features of English life and culture. He also contributed articles to *Chambers' Encyclopaedia* and the *Dictionary of National Biography*.

It is not clear when or how Ormsby first took an interest in Spain, its language, and its literature. He is plausibly credited with publishing, in 1872, a work entitled *Mountains of Spain*. In any case, it was after an extensive ramble in Spain, following the scenes of the exploits of that country's medieval hero El Cid in Valencia, Aragon, and Castile, with Sánchez's edition of the epic recounting that hero's story as his only book, that he undertook its translation, published in 1879. It is a much reduced version of the original, the greater part of it rendered into prose and only those passages that Ormsby judged to be the most vivid and dramatic put into English rhyming couplets. Here, however, his concern was 'to render [...] line for line and as literally as was compatible with justice to the original' (*The Poem of the Cid*, ed. and trans. J. Ormsby, 1879, 6). The text is preceded by a lengthy and well-informed introduction based on wide scholarly reading and offering an alert examination of the issues that have continued to preoccupy Cidian scholars. The work is dedicated to the eminent Spanish scholar Gayangos.

In 1885 Ormsby's four-volume translation of *Don Quixote* appeared, rounded off with annotated bibliographies of Spanish romances of chivalry and of editions and translations of the *Quixote*, where he displays his interests and learning as a literary scholar, and finally with a list of the proverbs contained in that work. U. R. Burke acknowledged his indebtedness to this list in the third edition (p. viii) of his own *Sancho Panza's Proverbs* (1892). He also rightly judged Ormsby's translation of the *Quixote* to be the best to have been produced in English, an estimate that may be held to remain valid down to the 1990s. The translation is introduced by a discerning evaluation of earlier English versions, an account of Cervantes' life that seeks 'to separate what is a matter of fact from what is a matter of conjecture', and a literary examination of the work itself, written in vigorous reaction against the Romantic idealization of Don Quixote (including 'Byron's melodious nonsense' on the subject) that represents a highly perceptive and in some respects remarkable contribution in its time to Cervantine criticism. According to Palau, the 'notable edition' of the *Quixote* in Spanish published at Edinburgh and London in 1898–9 was the outcome of a scholarly collaboration between Ormsby and Fitzmaurice-Kelly. The latter's edition of 1901 uses Ormsby's 1885 translation as revised in Ormsby's own MS annotations; Fitzmaurice-Kelly comments that 'I have known no man who was a sterner critic of himself and of his own writings' (Cervantes, *Don Quixote*, 1.xxxvi). Ormsby lived out his later years much isolated by deafness and died, unmarried, at 19 Nelson Crescent, Ramsgate on 30 October 1895.   R. W. TRUMAN

Sources Burke, *Gen. Ire.* (1899) • H. A. C. Sturgess, ed., *Register of admissions to the Honourable Society of the Middle Temple, from the fifteenth century to the year 1944*, 2 (1949), 514 • Burtchaell & Sadleir, *Alum. Dubl.* • *The Athenaeum* (9 Nov 1895), 645 • *The Times* (8 Nov 1895) • T. E. Kebbel, *Lord Beaconsfield and other Tory memories* (1907), 195–200 • L. Stephen, 'In memoriam: John Ormsby', *Alpine Journal*, 18 (1896), 33–6 • U. R. Burke, *Sancho Panza's proverbs* (1892), viii, xvii • A. Palau y Dulcet, *Manual del librero hispano-americano*, 2nd edn, 11 (1958), 486a • J. Ormsby, 'The ascent of the Grivola', *Peaks, Passes and Glaciers*, 2nd ser., 2 (1862), 318–38 • J. Fitzmaurice-Kelly, *Revue Hispanique*, 2 (1895), 363–6 • M. de Cervantes, *Don Quixote*, trans. J. Ormsby (1901), vol. 3 of *The complete works of Miguel de Cervantes Saavedra*, ed. J. Fitzmaurice-Kelly (1901–2), xxxvi
Archives NL Scot., letters to *Blackwood's*
Wealth at death £4724 17s. 4d.—in England: administration with will, 1896, *CGPLA Eng. & Wales* • £6297 6s. 4d.: resworn administration, 1896, *CGPLA Ire.*

Ornsby, George (1809–1886), antiquary, born on 9 March 1809 at Darlington, co. Durham, was the eldest son of George Ornsby (1772–1823), a solicitor, of The Lodge, Lanchester, and his wife, Margaret Askwith. Robert *Ornsby (1820–1889) was his younger brother. His father, an accomplished scholar, instructed his sons at home until his death in 1823; George was then sent to Durham grammar school (1823–6). After practising as a solicitor in Durham, he entered University College, Durham, as a theological student in 1839. In 1841 he was ordained, and held in succession the curacies of Newburn, Northumberland (1841–3); Sedgefield, co. Durham (1843–4); and Whickham, in the same county (1845–50). On 1 May 1843 he married Anne (d. 1872), eldest daughter of John Wilson JP and deputy lieutenant, of The Hill, Brigham, Cumberland; they had two sons and two daughters.

In July 1850, on the presentation of the dean and chapter

of Durham, Ornsby was inducted to the vicarage of Fishlake, West Riding of Yorkshire; the charge of this small parish left him ample opportunity for literary pursuits. In 1872 the University of Durham conferred on him the honorary degree of MA, and on 29 May 1873 he was elected a fellow of the Society of Antiquaries. In 1879 he was preferred to the prebendal stall of Ampleforth at York. He was also a JP and deputy lieutenant.

Ornsby was a model parish priest and an accurate, painstaking antiquary. He was the lifelong friend of James Raine, the historian of north Durham. In 1846 he published a valuable little topographical work entitled *Sketches of Durham*, still a sought-after volume at the end of the twentieth century. For the Surtees Society he edited Dean Granville's *Remains*, (2 vols., 1861 and 1865), Bishop John Cosin's *Correspondence* (2 vols., 1869–72), and *Selections from the Household Books of Lord William Howard of Naworth* (1878). He also undertook for the same society an edition of Dean Thomas Comber's *Correspondence*, but never finished it. In 1877 he wrote the historical introduction to the volume of sermons preached at the reopening of Durham Cathedral, and in 1882 his *Diocesan History of York* was published. Ornsby died at his home in Fishlake on 17 April 1886.   GORDON GOODWIN, rev. C. M. FRASER

Sources J. T. Fowler, *Durham University Journal* (29 May 1886), 52–3 · W. H. D. Longstaffe, *The history and antiquities of the parish of Darlington*, new edn (1909), 484–5 · Crockford (1885) · C. S. Earle and L. A. Body, eds., *Durham School register: to June, 1912*, 2nd edn (1912), 88 · *CGPLA Eng. & Wales* (1886)
Wealth at death £3508 4s. 9d.: probate, 22 June 1886, *CGPLA Eng. & Wales*

Ornsby, Robert (1820–1889), classical scholar and biographer, was the third son of George Ornsby of Lanchester, Durham. George *Ornsby was his eldest brother. He matriculated in 1836 at Lincoln College, Oxford, where he became a friend of Mark Pattison. Obtaining one of Lord Crewe's exhibitions, he graduated BA in 1840, after gaining a first class in *literae humaniores*. In 1843 he was elected to a fellowship at Trinity College, and graduated MA. Thereafter he held the college office of lecturer in rhetoric and the university office of master of the schools, and for four or five years was actively engaged in private tuition. For a time he was curate of St Olave's, Chichester, but he seceded from the Church of England, and was received into the Roman Catholic communion in May 1847. In 1846 he married Elizabeth, daughter of William Dalgairns and sister of Newman's close associate, J. D. Dalgairns. She became a Roman Catholic in 1848.

For some years after this Ornsby assisted Frederick Lucas in conducting *The Tablet* newspaper while it was published in Dublin. When Newman undertook the task of founding a Catholic university for Ireland in 1854, Ornsby accepted his invitation to become professor of Greek and Latin literature in the new institution. Later on he became private tutor to the future duke of Norfolk and his brother, whom he accompanied on a short tour through southern and eastern Europe. He was subsequently for a short time librarian at Arundel Castle, but he returned to his old post at the Catholic university in 1874, at the request of the Irish bishops. In 1882, when the senate of the Royal University of Ireland were forming their first staff of examiners, Ornsby was elected a fellow of the university and an examiner in Greek. He died at Earlsfort Terrace, Dublin, on 21 April 1889. He published a life of St Francis of Sales (1856), an edition with notes of the Greek Testament (1860), and *Memoirs of James Robert Hope-Scott, Q.C.* (2 vols., 1884), which involved him in correspondence with W. E. Gladstone.

THOMPSON COOPER, rev. RICHARD SMAIL

Sources Foster, *Alum. Oxon.* · *The Tablet* (27 April 1889) · *The Times* (24 April 1889) · Gillow, *Lit. biog. hist.* · I. Ker, *John Henry Newman* (1988) · Gladstone, *Diaries* · Boase, *Mod. Eng. biog.*
Archives Birmingham Oratory, letters to J. H. Newman · BL, corresp. with W. E. Gladstone, Add. MSS 44444–44486 · Bodl. Oxf., letters to Mark Pattison · CUL, letters to Lord Acton
Wealth at death £515 19s.: probate, 23 May 1889, *CGPLA Eng. & Wales*

O'Rourke, Sir Brian [Briain Ó Ruairc; *known as* Brian-na-Múrtha] (*d.* **1591**), chieftain and rebel, was a younger son of Brian Ballagh O'Rourke (*d.* 1562), chieftain, and his wife, Grainne (*d.* 1551), daughter of Manus *O'Donnell (*d.* 1563), chieftain. Brian Ballagh is considered to have been the last king of West Breifne, co. Leitrim.

Early years as chieftain, 1562–1580 Following the death of Brian Ballagh in 1562 his son Aodh Gallda was declared chief of the O'Rourkes of Breifne, but was murdered in Leitrim in 1564. Contemporaries suspected that this was done on Brian O'Rourke's behalf. Brian Ballagh's next eldest son, Aodh Buidhe, declared himself chief, but he was killed in 1566, again possibly at Brian O'Rourke's instigation—at which point O'Rourke was declared chief. The remainder of O'Rourke's life was characterized by resistance to the English occupation of Connaught, interspersed with battles with his nephews. During the 1570s the Irish administration increased its efforts to bring Connaught under royal control by pressuring the Irish chieftains to surrender their lands, receiving them back again on English tenures, and allow sheriffs into the province. Like many Irish chieftains, O'Rourke was opposed to this interference; consequently, he maintained a large host of galloglass, and often led raids within the province.

Brehon law in Ireland allowed for multiple marriages, and O'Rourke had more than one wife. The first of whom there is record is Annably ni Crean (*d.* after 1582). He seems to have been married to his second wife, Mary (*d.* in or before 1589), daughter of Richard Burke, second earl of Clanricarde, and widow of Theobald Burke, while still married to Annably. However, the English government, opposed to multiple marriages, recognized only Mary as O'Rourke's legitimate wife. O'Rourke married her some time after 1582. While he wrote of the death of his wife in 1589, he was probably referring to a later wife, Eleanor (*d.* 1589), daughter of James fitz John *Fitzgerald, thirteenth earl of Desmond, nobleman, and his fourth wife, Ellen. Eleanor O'Rourke's death is recorded in the Irish annals under 1589. Brian O'Rourke had at least six children by his various wives, the eldest two being Brian Oge [*see below*] and Owen (d. 1589), from his marriage to Annably; however, the English considered only Tadhg, the son of Mary, legitimate.

By 1576 O'Rourke was among the growing number of chieftains who had agreed to submit, meeting the lord deputy, Sir Henry Sidney, in Dublin in June. By October 1577 O'Rourke had made an agreement with Sir Nicholas Malby, governor of Connaught, to pay rent to the crown. Despite these agreements, Malby suspected Hugh O'Donnell and O'Rourke of conspiring to revolt in 1578. Malby's men seized O'Rourke's castle at Leitrim. O'Rourke met Sidney shortly after and Leitrim was returned to him; it is likely at this point that he was knighted. If a knighthood was meant to pacify him, it had little effect, for he took advantage of the rebellions that had spread under his brothers-in-law Gerald fitz James *Fitzgerald, fourteenth earl of Desmond, and James fitz Maurice *Fitzgerald, and rejoined the resistance in Connaught against the government. However, he twice agreed to give Brian Oge to Malby as a pledge, but failed to deliver him.

Rebel, 1580–1591 In summer 1580 O'Rourke hired 500 galloglass to support O'Donnell, and fought Malby over control of Leitrim. In 1581 O'Donnell ended his rebellion and, along with Donough O'Conor Sligo, agreed to guarantee O'Rourke's good behaviour on 3 October. The following year O'Rourke agreed to a one-year truce. Nevertheless, in 1583 he attacked Sligo; it was probably during this raid that he captured his nephew, Tadhg, who later died in his custody. In January 1585 another of O'Rourke's nephews, Brian O'Rourke, sheriff of Sligo, made an incursion into Dartry; O'Rourke came to the aid of Dartry. His men then took his nephew under their own protection, but they killed him three days later. O'Rourke was blamed for being involved in 'this unbecoming deed' (*AFM*, 5.1826–7).

Increasingly preoccupied with the threat from Spain, Elizabeth I charged the new lord deputy, Sir John Perrot, with the task of bringing order to Connaught. Along with the new governor of Connaught, Sir Richard Bingham, Perrot began taking inquests in 1585 to determine the ownership of all the lands in the province and the rent due from each chieftain to the crown. These inquests were to form the basis of the composition of Connaught. On 27 September O'Rourke signed an indenture which identified his lands from which rent was due to the crown. He did well under the composition and was granted the castles of Dromahair, Leitrim, and Newtown rent-free. Despite these favourable terms, he refused to pay the rent he did owe. By 1586 Bingham had pressured him to agree to make payments, to give up his galloglass, and to surrender his eldest son, Brian Oge, as a pledge. In turn, Brian Oge was sent to study at Oxford.

Following the defeat of the Spanish Armada in summer 1588, a portion of the remaining Spanish fleet was wrecked off the coast of Ireland. Fearing a Catholic alliance, Elizabeth ordered Bingham to execute all Spanish survivors captured in Ireland, and declared it treason to offer them aid. The remaining Spanish, starving and destitute, had to rely on the help of the Irish. Faced with such a stark choice, many of the Irish chieftains who found Spanish survivors handed them over to the English authorities; O'Rourke did not. Captain Francisco de Cuellar, one of the survivors to whom he offered comfort, later wrote to Philip II of his ordeal. Cuellar described O'Rourke as 'a very good Christian and an enemy to the heretics, and always fights against them' (*Letter*, trans. Sedgwick, 59). Philip wrote to O'Rourke, thanking him for his support.

Once the Spanish threat had receded, Bingham redoubled his efforts to subdue Connaught, but his brutal approach prompted another revolt in 1589. The chieftains, including O'Rourke, cited Bingham's harassment as the cause of their revolt. O'Rourke complained specifically about Bingham's attacks on him, of his son Owen's death at the hand of William Taaf, and of Dromahair having been burnt. Bingham, it seems, had also attempted in spring 1589 to exact payments from O'Rourke for Brian Oge's board at Oxford. He responded to O'Rourke's complaints, declared 'how naughtily O'Rourke hath always carried himself', and accused him of having defiled an effigy of the queen (*CSP Ire.*, 1588–92, 141). According to the lord deputy, Sir William Fitzwilliam, O'Rourke apparently made an effigy of Elizabeth which his galloglass hacked with axes, before tying it to a horse's tail and dragging it along the ground. These complaints aside, it is also quite possible that O'Rourke was stirred to revolt through the machinations of the chief justice of the common pleas, Sir Robert Dillon. Bingham had many enemies, including Dillon, who may have wished to oust him by fomenting revolt in Connaught. There is evidence that Dillon and O'Rourke corresponded.

After smuggling Brian Oge back from Oxford, O'Rourke renewed his revolt. Despite half-hearted attempts at pacification by Fitzwilliam, the fighting continued. However, the situation deteriorated to the point where, on 14 March 1590, Fitzwilliam ordered Bingham to attack O'Rourke. Bingham, aided by O'Rourke's nephews, Donnell and Hugh Oge (Aodh Óg), drove O'Rourke out of Breifne within the month. Brian Oge returned to his father's territory and continued the fight against Bingham. With the tide in their favour, the government now determined to remove O'Rourke permanently. Confident, Bingham described him as 'more like a beggar than a king, for above a king he esteemed himself, and assuredly the proud beggar held that opinion of his own greatness, as he thought all the force Her Majesty had, durst not meddle with him; but I hope this journey will end his kingdom, if not himself, and haply they may get his head' (*CSP Ire.*, 1588–92, 329). On 30 April the privy council informed Fitzwilliam that they wanted additional forces for Bingham's attack on O'Rourke, considering that 'the subduying of whom wee thought allmost as needefull as the defence against the Spaniardes' (*APC*, 1590, 77). O'Rourke fled to Tyrconnell in late May, sending word that he would consider surrendering if he was promised an 'indifferent' trial. Bingham responded by calling him 'the veriest beggar and wretch, whose demeanour is most odious to all good subjects' (*CSP Ire.*, 1588–92, 231). In December Sir George Carew, president of Munster, informed the privy council that

O'Rourke was expected to return to his territory with galloglass in support.

Instead, O'Rourke fled to Scotland in 1591, possibly to raise Scottish troops, although he professed that it was to receive protection from James VI. After reaching Glasgow in February, he wrote to James, complaining of his rough treatment and asking for royal protection. James informed Robert Bowes, the English ambassador. Keen to have him captured, Elizabeth asked that O'Rourke be kept waiting in Glasgow until he could be apprehended, and James complied. On 16 March the king ordered O'Rourke's arrest in Glasgow, which caused a riot among the townspeople, who feared that their trade with Ireland would be disrupted.

O'Rourke was sent to the Tower of London by May and the privy council instructed Fitzwilliam and Bingham to supply evidence of treason. On 28 October, O'Rourke was tried in Westminster Hall on eight counts of treason, including trying to depose the queen, abusing an effigy of her, offering protection to survivors of the Armada, and receiving letters of thanks from Philip. When he refused to honour the privy council by kneeling before it, the privy councillors asked why he was willing to kneel before Catholic images but not before them. He is reported to have replied, 'because between God and his saints, whose images I respect, and you, I have ever thought there was a great difference' (*Ireland under Elizabeth*, 63). Through an interpreter, John Ly, he informed the judge that he would not consent to be tried by the jury without being given access to a lawyer and a week to prepare his defence. O'Rourke also asked for Elizabeth to be one of the jurors. He refused to enter a plea, but was found guilty none the less. When he was told that he would suffer a traitor's death, he remained unmoved.

O'Rourke was hanged, drawn, and quartered at Tyburn on or soon after 3 November (he was certainly dead by 23 November). On his way to the scaffold, his interpreter asked him to beg forgiveness of the queen, to which he replied that if she had given him the time to defend himself or spared his life he would have asked her forgiveness and promised to serve her. He also remarked that he had not expected James to hand him over to Elizabeth without any protection. His death was described by the four masters as 'one of the mournful stories of the Irish' (*AFM*, 6.1906–7).

O'Rourke was the subject of poems by a number of Gaelic bards. Sean MacTorna Ó Maelchonaire composed a poem for him when he became lord of Breifne in 1566. Tadhg Dall Ó hUiginn, who wrote for various families in Ulster, Connaught, and Leinster, composed a poem to him about 1580. In 1589 Conaire Ó Maoil Chonaire was accused of writing a poem for O'Rourke; however, in a letter he urged Donough O'Brien, fourth earl of Thomond, to intervene on his behalf, pointing out that the charge was groundless, since his family wrote chronicles, not poetry.

O'Rourke's rebel son **Brian Oge O'Rourke** [*known as* Brian-na-Samhthach] (*c.*1569–1604), chieftain and rebel, was the elder of two known sons of Sir Brian O'Rourke and Annably ni Crean. He was educated at New College,

Oxford, from 1584 to 1588. In 1588 his father arranged his escape, and he was back in Ireland by 1589, taking part in O'Rourke's revolts of 1589–90. Following his father's execution his lands were assessed, and the government considered whether to divide the territory among his heirs, or to take control of it. The chief lords, including Brian Oge, wanted the seignory divided among them, and his ensuing battle with his brother Tadhg for the patrimony lasted for the rest of their lives.

During the 1590s Brian Oge's own problems became linked to the Nine Years' War. Unable to return to Breifne, in 1592 he stayed with the MacSweenys and the Maguires, joining the developing confederacy of Irish chiefs under Hugh Roe O'Donnell. According to Philip O'Sullivan Beare, a contemporary who wrote his own history of the period, Brian Oge was committed to the confederacy, losing 'no opportunity of avenging the death of his father, who was killed by the Queen' (*Ireland under Elizabeth*, 69). Brian Oge also had more immediate reasons for revolt. In 1593 Clement VIII acknowledged him as O'Rourke's legitimate heir. However, he was still not allowed to occupy his land, despite the fact that the government demanded that he continue to pay rent on it.

Elizabeth knew that the confederacy was in contact with Philip and that he had promised to send Spanish troops to Ireland. Consequently, Brian Oge, Hugh O'Neill, second earl of Tyrone, Hugh Roe *O'Donnell (1572–1602), Hugh Maguire, and Hugh Roe MacMahon were declared traitors on 23 June 1595. Despite his position, Brian Oge was declared chief of the O'Rourkes by his clansmen in 1595. In 1596, as the rebellion spread, Bingham was dismissed as governor of Connaught and replaced by Sir Conyers Clifford, who took a more conciliatory approach. He sent envoys to Tyrone and O'Donnell to negotiate a peace. Loath to trust the government, Tyrone and O'Donnell rejected the offer, and Elizabeth sent a stronger force to Connaught under Sir John Norreys. Upon his arrival Norreys marched towards the territory of Theobald MacWilliam Burke, who in turn sent to O'Donnell for help. O'Donnell summoned his supporters, among whom Brian Oge was the first to arrive. After some sporadic fighting the two sides met at the Robe River, co. Mayo, to negotiate. Norreys promised O'Donnell, Brian Oge, and others consideration if they returned to the queen's allegiance, but after several attempts by both sides to spy on each other, he ran out of provisions and had to leave.

In summer 1597 the new lord justice, Thomas Burgh, fifth Baron Burgh, removed Norreys and took over as general himself. Brian Oge and Maguire joined O'Donnell against Burgh and Clifford, but little fighting occurred over the summer. In the autumn O'Donnell decided to attack the government forces as well as Hugh O'Conor Roe, who had defected from the rebels. However, Brian Oge had promised O'Conor that he would inform him if O'Donnell planned to attack him. To thwart this, O'Donnell sent for Brian Oge to meet him at his camp, but headed himself for O'Conor's territory, which he plundered and then left. About this time Brian Oge married

Mary, daughter of Cúchonnacht Maguire and his wife, Nuala, and sister of Sir Hugh *Maguire (d. 1600).

Following a dispute with O'Donnell, Brian Oge requested a royal pardon in late 1597, asking that he be restored to his father's lands. About a month later he presented the terms for his submission: he requested both a pardon, and to have his land given back to himself and his heirs; both were granted. He also asked that Bingham not be allowed to arrest him without order from the queen, stating, 'it is openly known how the Binghams maliciously urged [Brian Oge's] father to go into exile' (Brewer and Bullen, 3.279). In May 1598 Brian Oge surrendered hostages to Clifford and the two men promised to support each other, which served only to antagonize O'Donnell further. Nevertheless O'Donnell was loath to attack Brian Oge, since they were related, and tried instead to pressure him into rejoining the rebellion. Brian Oge's retainers feared an attack from O'Donnell more than one from the government and persuaded him to return to O'Donnell.

On 5 August 1599 Brian Oge joined O'Donnell in the battle of the Curlews (in Gaelic, Coirrshliabh). In the continuous warfare, O'Conor Sligo had been stripped of almost all his castles, and joined up with Clifford in order to recoup his losses. He also stole some of O'Donnell's cattle, which O'Donnell used as a pretext and attacked him, causing Clifford to come to O'Conor's aid. Clifford was killed during the battle, and Brian Oge ordered his corpse to be beheaded. Brian Oge himself was shot in the hand and leg. As a result, O'Conor submitted to O'Donnell and the chieftaincy of Sligo was restored to him.

In summer 1600 Charles Blount, eighth Baron Mountjoy, the new lord deputy, appointed Sir Oliver Lambert governor of Connaught. In September 1601 a Spanish force sent by Philip III arrived at Kinsale, co. Cork, to assist the Irish. Mountjoy immediately made for Kinsale, as did Carew and his forces. Tyrone and O'Donnell summoned their supporters, including Brian Oge, to aid the Spanish. The rebels arrived, and besieged the garrison, but on 24 December they were routed, and the Spanish left on 2 January 1602. Kinsale was a disaster and heralded the end of the Nine Years' War. In January 1602, O'Donnell went to Spain to seek help from Philip, but died there, and support ebbed away. O'Donnell's brother Rury *O'Donnell (1574/5–1608) sought Brian Oge's continued backing, but Brian Oge refused, instead returning to Breifne to fight his brother Tadhg, who was attempting to seize the chieftaincy.

On his accession as James I in 1603, the new king offered a pardon to all those involved in the rebellion willing to submit. Most of the chiefs, including Tyrone, accepted. On 9 January Mountjoy informed the privy council that only the 'proud, insolent, and faithless rebel' Brian Oge had not submitted, but while it would be difficult to hunt him down, the lord deputy would eventually be able to overcome his 'pride and contempt' (CSP Ire., 1601–3, 554). In March 1603 Lambert launched an attack on Brian Oge but was driven back. However, Brian Oge's victory was short-lived, for Lambert's attack was followed by another from Brian Oge's brother Tadhg, who succeeded in capturing

most of Breifne. Tadhg then went to Mountjoy who planned to give him the territory and aid him in banishing Brian Oge.

On 4 May Brian Oge wrote to James reminding him of how his father had fled to Scotland and been turned over to Elizabeth, at whose hands he had been unjustly killed. He asked the king that he be restored to O'Rourke's lands as his rightful heir. James was unmoved, for he wrote to Mountjoy (now earl of Devonshire) on 11 September in support of Tadhg, who was subsequently granted the entire territory. Brian Oge's situation turned from bad to worse. He was attacked by Rury O'Donnell, who was still angry with him for his refusal to support him after the defeat at Kinsale. He plundered Breifne and seized Dromahair, driving Brian Oge into the woods. Without his lands, and deprived of his patrimony, Brian Oge died in co. Galway on 28 January 1604 and was buried in the monastery of Rosserilly, co. Galway. According to O'Sullivan Beare, he died of a fever, 'deserted by those to whom he had entrusted his government'; however, at least one more recent historian suspects that he was poisoned by Lambert (Ireland under Elizabeth, 177; MacDermot, 118).

ELIZABETH SCHOALES

Sources CSP Ire., 1574–96; 1600; 1603–6 • CSP Scot., 1589–93 • J. S. Brewer and W. Bullen, eds., Calendar of the Carew manuscripts, 6 vols., PRO (1867–73), vols. 2–3 • M. A. S. Hume, ed., Calendar of letters and state papers relating to English affairs, preserved principally in the archives of Simancas, 4, PRO (1899) • APC, 1590, 1597–8 • P. O'Sullivan Beare, Ireland under Elizabeth: chapters towards a history of Ireland in the reign of Elizabeth, ed. and trans. M. J. Byrne (1903); repr. (Port Washington, NY, 1970) • A letter written on October 4, 1589 by Captain Cuellar of the Spanish Armada to His Majesty King Philip II recounting his misadventures in Ireland and elsewhere after the wreck of his ship, trans. H. D. Sedgwick (New York, 1896) • D. Gallogly, 'Brian of the Ramparts O'Rourke (1566–1591)', Journal of Cumann Seanchais Bhreifne, 2 (1962), 50–79 • B. MacDermot, O Ruairc of Breifne (Nure, 1990) • H. Morgan, 'Extradition and treason: the trial of a Gaelic lord: the case of Brian O'Rourke', Irish Jurist, 22 (1987), 285–301 • J. Carney, 'A tract on the O'Rourkes', Celtica, 1 (1950), 238–79 • DNB • S. G. Ellis, Ireland in the age of the Tudors (1998) • J. McGurk, The Elizabethan conquest of Ireland: the 1590s crisis (1997) • H. Morgan, Tyrone's rebellion: the outbreak of the Nine Years' War in Tudor Ireland, Royal Historical Society Studies in History, 67 (1993) • T. W. Moody and others, eds., A new history of Ireland, 3: Early modern Ireland, 1534–1691 (1976) • N. Canny, Making Ireland British: 1580–1650 (2001) • AFM

O'Rourke, Brian Oge (c.1569–1604). See under O'Rourke, Sir Brian (d. 1591).

O'Rourke, Edmund [pseud. Edmund Falconer] (c.1814–1879), actor and playwright, was born in Dublin about 1814, and entered the theatrical profession in 1835, playing utility parts for many years in the provinces. In 1850 he undertook the lead role in the Worcester circuit, and his last provincial engagement was in the autumn of 1854 at the Adelphi Theatre, Liverpool, where he acted Hamlet and Three-fingered Jack on the same night. While working in the country, he published a volume of poems, Man's Mission (1852).

Falconer's career as a London dramatist began with Heart for Heart, his first full-length verse play, which was brought out at the Lyceum Theatre under Charles Dillon's management on 6 December 1856, with much success. The

Athenaeum commented 'the dialogue is remarkable for noble sentiment, although the verse is not always correct' (13 Dec 1856). His next piece was *A Husband for an Hour*, produced at the Haymarket on 1 June 1857.

Falconer had translated Victor Hugo's *Ruy Blas*, which was performed at the Princess Theatre late in 1858. During that year, he began his profitable collaboration with Michael Balfe by writing the libretto for Balfe's much-loved opera *The Rose of Castile*. He was later to write librettos for several of Balfe's most successful productions, including *Satanella, or, The Power of Love*, first produced at Covent Garden on 20 December 1858, and the popular song 'Killarney', which remained a concert-hall favourite well into the twentieth century. During this period, his first marriage was dissolved and he married secondly a daughter of John Neville, the widow of Weston the actor. On 26 August 1858, in partnership with Webster, he opened the Lyceum, and put on the stage his own play, *Extremes*, a comedy of manners. *The Times* commented 'The characters are sharply defined and exactly of a kind to be perfectly intelligible to a large audience' (27 Aug 1858). He followed this with another piece, *Francesca*, on 31 March 1859.

Later that year Falconer moved to the Princess's Theatre, London, writing *The Master Passion*, first played on 2 November 1859. In the first production of Boucicault's *The Colleen Bawn*, at the Adelphi on 18 July 1860, Falconer played Danny Man, which he continued to perform throughout the original run of the piece, a period of 231 nights.

In 1861 Falconer resumed the management of the Lyceum, and brought out on 19 August his comedy *Woman, or, Love Against the World*. His most popular play, *Peep o' Day*, first acted in London on 9 November 1861, which was adapted from John Banim's novellas *John Doe* and *The Nolans*, enjoyed an uninterrupted run until December 1862. Meanwhile, he contributed two comedies to the Haymarket, *Family Wills*, and *Does He Love Me?*, both starring Amy Sedgwick. In 1862 Falconer invested the £13,000 he had made at the Lyceum in a joint lease with Frederick Balsir Chatterton of the Drury Lane Theatre, for which between 1863 and 1865 he wrote and produced *Bonnie Dundee*, *Nature's above Art*, *Night and Morning*, and *Love's Ordeal, or, The Old and New Régime*. In addition he wrote *The O'Flahertys* and *Galway-go-bragh*, a dramatization of Lever's *Charles O'Malley*, in which he took the part of Mickey Free. As the lessee of Drury Lane, and later as the manager of the Haymarket from 1866, Falconer attempted to popularize Shakespeare, and he directed productions of *Macbeth*, *Cymbeline*, *As You Like It*, *Henry IV*, and *Romeo and Juliet*, among others. Although he employed the best contemporary actors, his Shakespeare revival was not popular, and audiences were small. 'Nothing drew good houses', remarked Edward Stirling (p. 274). In June 1864 Falconer's second wife died. By September 1866, he had lost all his investment, and resigned the lease to his partner Chatterton, who discharged his own and Falconer's liabilities.

While at Drury Lane, Falconer had attempted to establish himself as a poet, publishing *Memories, the Bequest of My Boyhood* in 1863, and *O'Ruark's Bride: the Blood Speck in the Emerald* in 1865. Both collections drew heavily on his childhood in Ireland, and on traditional Irish legends, but they did not meet with any great success. After the Drury Lane disaster, Falconer attempted to revive his fortunes with his five-act drama *Oonagh, or, The Lovers of Lisnamona*, which was performed at Her Majesty's Theatre on 19 November 1866, but was such a failure that its season suddenly terminated ten days later.

Falconer then went to America, where his play *Peep o' Day* had won him a popular following. He toured the continent, finding special success in New York and Boston, where publications of his plays went through several editions. He remained in America for about three years, marrying an American wife and writing three new dramas. During his absence, *A Wife Well Won* was successful at the Haymarket, which encouraged him to return to London about 1871. On his return, he produced at the Princess Theatre *Eileen Oge*, an adaptation of Balfe's light opera *Inisfallen* on which Falconer had collaborated, and which was otherwise known as *Killarney* from its most popular song. It was his swansong: shortly after its success, Falconer retired. He died at his home, 28 Keppel Street, Russell Square, London, on 29 September 1879, and was buried in Kensal Green cemetery. KATHERINE MULLIN

Sources DNB · E. Stirling, *Old Drury Lane*, 1 (1881), 273–4 · C. E. Pascoe, ed., *The dramatic list*, 2nd edn (1880) · G. Biddlescombe, *English opera from 1834 to 1864* (1994) · Ward, *Men of the reign* · Allibone, *Dict.*, suppl. · Boase, *Mod. Eng. biog.* · Adams, *Drama* · D. J. O'Donoghue, *The poets of Ireland: a biographical dictionary with bibliographical particulars*, 1 vol. in 3 pts (1892–3) · *Illustrated Sporting and Dramatic News* (4 Dec 1875), 233–4 · *Era Almanack and Annual* (1868), 21 · *The Era* (5 Oct 1879), 6 · d. cert.

Wealth at death under £100: administration, 1879

O'Rourke, Tiernan. *See* Ua Ruairc, Tigernán (*d.* 1172).

Orpen, Sir William Newenham Montague (1878–1931), painter, was born on 27 November 1878 at Oriel, Blackrock, co. Dublin, the fifth and youngest child of Arthur Herbert Orpen, a solicitor, and Anne Caulfeild, a member of the earl of Charlemont's family. Orpen's grandfather Sir Richard Orpen had been knighted for services to the legal profession and had established a successful legal practice which became the family firm. The home in Blackrock was comfortable; Orpen's childhood there was happy, and he wrote about it in *Stories of Old Ireland and Myself* (1924) with warm affection and not without a hint of nostalgia, indicating that subsequently his personal life proved less satisfactory, as was indeed the case.

Early years Orpen's own interest in painting, demonstrated from an early age, was indulged by his mother, who supported his wish to go to art school against her husband's desire that he should study law and enter the family firm. Orpen entered the Metropolitan School of Art, Dublin, in 1891 at the age of thirteen and showed exceptional talent from the very beginning. Large and well run, the school had benefited from reforms in art teaching in the second half of the nineteenth century, and was linked to the South Kensington schools of art. The headmaster, James Brenan, recognized Orpen's remarkable talent

Sir William Newenham Montague Orpen (1878–1931), self-portrait, 1916 [*The Man from Aran*]

him. Orpen won prizes at the Slade, most notably the £40 painting prize for *The Play Scene from 'Hamlet'* (priv. coll.), and his success led others to turn to him for leadership and example. From his final year, 1899, he exhibited at the New English Art Club (NEAC), which shared the Slade's desire for realism in painting incorporating technical skill in paint, good draughtsmanship, and naturalness of subject. These values gave Orpen a clear sense of purpose and direction to which he applied himself with energy and an enormously rich and varied talent. His earliest oils, notably *The Mirror* (Tate collection), were acclaimed at the club's twice-yearly exhibitions, and Orpen forged a practice for himself as a portrait painter, earning enough from commissions to maintain himself. He moved in a group which included William and Albert Rothenstein (later Albert Rutherston), and through them he met the Knewstub sisters and their brother Jack. On 8 August 1901 he married Grace Knewstub, whose sister Alice had married William Rothenstein. They settled in a house in Royal Hospital Road, Chelsea.

Professional beginnings Orpen travelled quite widely in the British Isles, fulfilling portrait commissions. Twice yearly from 1902 onwards he spent short periods in Dublin, teaching at the Metropolitan School of Art, and seeing his family and former student friends. He became a friend of Hugh Lane, a distant cousin on his mother's side, who was then an art dealer and the promoter of a modern art gallery for Dublin. The two travelled together in Europe in the summer of 1904, arriving first in Paris, where Orpen witnessed Lane's purchase of several impressionist masterpieces and experienced French art, so different stylistically from the teaching he had received at the Slade. They went on to Madrid, where Orpen 'discovered' Velázquez, visiting again and again the collection of his work in the Prado while Lane went off to buy more works of art.

The impact of Velázquez was profound. Before the Madrid trip Orpen had displayed enormous versatility. The great Spanish master focused his mind on economy in painting, and on the simple, grand gesture which produces drama from depiction of realistic and everyday subjects. His *The Wash House* (NG Ire.), *The Idle Girl* (priv. coll.), and *Resting* (Ulster Museum, Belfast) from the series of paintings 'Lottie of Paradise Walk' (others in National Gallery of Canada, Ottawa, and Leeds City Art Gallery) and his nudes of 1905–7 attest to the impact of this encounter. So, too, do the portraits which Lane persuaded Orpen to paint of Irish figures from the period for his new modern art gallery in Dublin. These have the same bold simplicity of statement, and reflect a cultural revival in Ireland. They include paintings of the landscape painter Nathaniel Hone (1907) and the politician Timothy Healy (both Hugh Lane Municipal Gallery of Modern Art, Dublin).

Orpen himself remained detached. While he painted these subjects well, he did not become engaged in the slightly feverish determination to support the nationalist movement. Irish art schools and exhibitions in any case were less committed to the nationalism which inspired writers like W. B. Yeats and Augusta Gregory, another of Orpen's cousins. Orpen could be said to have sided with

early on, and encouraged him. During his years at the school Orpen won every major prize, gold, silver, and bronze medals, scholarships, and an enduring reputation among his fellow students. In his last year he took the British Isles gold medal for life drawing, and then enrolled at the Slade School of Fine Art, London, in 1897.

Orpen enjoyed similar success at the Slade, where he was taught by Frederick Brown, Henry Tonks, and Philip Wilson Steer. Among his fellow students were Augustus John, Spencer Gore, Michel Salaman, Edna Waugh, Herbert Everett, the marine artist, and his mother, the eccentric Augusta Everett, and Orpen lived among a bohemian colony in Fitzroy Street which included John, who was probably closer to him than the others. Tonks in particular put his students under considerable pressure, made them look at great draughtsmanship, and master it as the basis for art. Tonks's exceptional talent as a draughtsman impressed Orpen, who with a brilliant student's ability to imitate and learn produced a number of wonderful early drawings (priv. coll.) with echoes in them of the old masters. Tonks encouraged his students to study old masters, including Chardin, Watteau, and Rembrandt, whose works were exhibited at the Royal Academy and elsewhere. Orpen combined his authority, as probably the finest draughtsman of his generation at the Slade, with a wry, mocking sense of humour which he softened by characterizing himself as an outsider. He was physically small and supposed himself ugly but had boundless ambition, almost to the point where it intimidated those closest to the more cynical view of events held by George Moore, an expressive, experienced, and caustic critic of cultural revolution. Orpen was more interested in the lighter side of Irish life, in sport and entertainment, gossip and drinking. Occasionally he expressed scepticism, as did Moore, about the very possibility of Ireland as an independent entity, either culturally or politically, and this remained his view. His constant self-examination, represented in a remarkable number of self-portraits—probably more numerous than those by any other major figure in the British Isles of the last 200 years—attests to his need to understand himself through the only 'language' which gave him meaning, paint. Nevertheless, in 1906 he began a major work, *Homage to Manet* (Manchester City Art Gallery), in which he attempted, in a conversation piece, to bring together in a group portrait the significant figures in British art at the time: Steer, Sickert, D. S. McColl, Moore, Lane, and Tonks. A parallel work, *The Selecting Jury of the N.E.A.C.*, known only in the form of a study (NPG) and showing the jury of the NEAC, turned into a caricature.

Early successes Orpen and Grace had a daughter, Mary, in 1902, and a second daughter, Kit, in 1906, and this meant that Grace spent more time at home in London, while Orpen, increasingly successful and gregarious, enjoyed himself away from home. Through his mother's interest in seeing him get on, Orpen was asked to paint a portrait of a wealthy American, Mrs Evelyn St George, who was married to another of Orpen's cousins, a land agent. The commission became a liaison, and Mrs St George an important influence; she encouraged Orpen to see himself as a great artist, and to paint appropriately. This advice resulted in a number of portraits, including the double portrait of his parents (NG Ire.; Arnold, 278), which she thought every great painter should attempt, and portraits of herself, large and dramatic treatments of a larger-than-life woman. (See, for example, *Mrs St George*, priv. coll.; Arnold, facing p. 256, plate 12.) Orpen now moved on from genre scenes, and small, intimate portraits in the Dutch manner, to a cycle of commissions from landowners and titled figures in British society. He first exhibited at the Royal Academy in 1904, and regularly from 1908 until his death in 1931, showing over 100 works, mainly portraits. He became an associate of the Royal Academy in 1910, and the following year was a founder member of the National Portrait Society. He became a Royal Academician in 1919. He also exhibited with the Society of Portrait Painters and in a number of international exhibitions, including those which promoted Irish art.

Irishness Orpen's involvement in Irish life was irregular, but through his friendship with Lane he contributed to the collection of portraits commissioned for the new Municipal Gallery of Modern Art, Dublin, painting Anthony McDonald and the provost of Trinity College, J. P. Mahaffy, and remained supportive of Lane's efforts to make the visual arts part of the Irish cultural revival. Even so, he continued to feel ill at ease with the portentousness of much of the activity surrounding W. B. Yeats and Lady Gregory, preferring the irreverence of men like the Dublin throat surgeon Oliver St John Gogarty. Most of all he enjoyed the company of students, notably several future Irish painters of distinction, Sean Keating, Patrick Tuohy, Beatrice Elvery, and James Sleator. Two of these, Sleator and Keating, worked as Orpen's studio assistants as his portrait practice grew. Orpen's increasing unease with his Irishness is reflected in three allegorical works painted in 1913–16, *Sowing New Seed* (Mildura Art Centre, Victoria, Australia), *The Western Wedding* (1914; Arnold, 292), and *The Holy Well* (1915; NG Ire.), which seek to show the country and its people in terms of religious, moral, social, and economic circumstances. Stylistically innovative, and using a tempera technique on large canvases, they failed, however, to capture the developing nationalism in art and culture, and Orpen made no further efforts to contribute to his country's identity, though he painted an outstanding portrait of his closest Irish associate and former student, Sean Keating, depicting him as *A Man of the West* (priv. coll.; Arnold, 164).

Orpen was rapidly becoming the most successful artist of his generation, taking the place in English portrait painting of John Singer Sargent, and arguably challenging Walter Sickert in the field of genre painting. His crowded professional life was matched by his vigorous and hedonistic private pursuit of pleasure and entertainment. The combination of the public and private realms of his life is expressed in the periodic interruption of his list of portrait sitters by individual genre works such as *The Café Royal* (1912; Musée d'Orsay, Paris), in which he brought together artists and writers he knew in a composite interior with figures. An inhabitant first of the Edwardian era, and then of the glittering era of power and prestige which preceded the First World War, he epitomized artistic and social success. A brief reconciliation with his wife, Grace, resulted in a third child, a daughter, Diana, born in 1914.

War artist With the coming of war, Orpen's life changed. He was slow to commit himself, but once the War Artists' Scheme was inaugurated, he saw a role for himself, and he characterized it in terms of repaying England for all it had done for him. He parted company with his Irish studio assistant, Sean Keating, who returned to conscription-free Ireland, and joined up as a war artist, being commissioned as a major. He left for France in April 1917, and for the next four years was totally immersed in the war and its aftermath. His output, and its overall excellence, makes him the outstanding war artist of that period, possibly the greatest war artist produced in Britain. Analysis of his war work, the major part of which is in the Imperial War Museum, London, shows a development in style and understanding, from the idealism which inspired him when he first arrived at the front to the disillusionment with the terrible ending to the war, and then the further dismay he and many felt at the direction taken by the peace deliberations. His paintings of the Somme battlefields are haunting recollections of anguish and chaos, of ruined landscapes baked in the summer sun, the torn ground white and rocky, the debris of the dead scattered and ignored.

With these works, all large and accomplished landscapes, are naturally grouped fine portraits of fighting men: officers and men in action, wounded figures haunting in their distress, German prisoners who are nevertheless noble in appearance and attitude, at odds with the war propaganda which Orpen was meant to support. His war portraits capture, in numerous variations, the expression of fear, shock, resignation, pride, and courage. In tandem with his work at the front, which had an immediacy reinforced by the artist's skill and his compassion, Orpen engaged in a series of formal portraits of the leaders such as Field Marshal Haig, Air Marshal Trenchard, and General Foch. Like many others, they sat to Orpen in the field of action, often breathless with the demands of their military duties, yet still acknowledging the demands of the military record.

Orpen's exhibition 'War' at Thomas Agnews in Bond Street, London, in the spring of 1918 was followed by his gift to the British nation of all his war paintings. In that same year he received a knighthood. But public recognition left him increasingly isolated and sad about the tragedy he had witnessed and recorded. His last war paintings, such as *The Mad Woman of Douai* (IWM), *Bombfire in Picardy*, and *The Harvest*, convey the stress and anguish he certainly felt about the war and its aftermath. With the end of war he was free to leave but instead remained in France, painting portraits and scenes of the peace conference in Paris and Versailles. One, a highly contentious tribute, *To the Unknown British Soldier in France* (IWM), includes a flag-draped coffin with two shell-shocked soldiers flanking it. Under pressure, he painted out the soldiers, their shadowy forms remaining as ghostly *pentimento*.

Orpen wrote vividly of his experiences in *An Onlooker in France* (1921), an irreverent account of his life at the front that included moving tributes to the British soldiers and airmen who had been his companions and the subjects of his paintings. His outspokenness became controversial. His standing as a painter gave him the ear of many people in power, and he took risks, confronting what he saw as foolishness. This made him unpopular, though he survived it well enough. He also invented the persona of a mysterious and beautiful woman spy, portrayed in a number of paintings he did of the French woman he loved, Yvonne Aubicq. British officialdom took a poor view of this, but Orpen survived on the strength of his contacts. His own personality had developed with the war; his early idealism became a form of sombre realistic recognition of the terrible path of war through the lives of a whole generation. He came to love the fighting man, and to despise the politicians, with their glib words and their self-interested carve-up of Europe which was subsequently to prove so disastrous.

Later years During the immediate post-war period Orpen had a studio in Paris as well as in London. Through the intervention of her father, Mrs St George ended their relationship during the war; by then, Orpen had met Yvonne Aubicq. He travelled regularly between the two cities, and spent time in coastal resorts like Dieppe, to which he was frequently driven in his chauffeured Rolls Royce, Yvonne

beside him. To some extent he lost his way, and in the early 1920s he drank heavily, but this did not interfere with his portrait-painting practice, which was prodigious in scope and earned him a huge income, often as much as £45,000 a year in the mid-1920s. Some of this work was inevitably superficial; he did not become involved with his sitters, as he had done before the war. He painted two ravishing nudes of Yvonne, *The Disappointing Letter* (1921; J. B. Speed Art Museum, Kentucky) and *Early Morning* (priv. coll.; Arnold, facing p. 353, plate 18), and a powerful diploma work for the Royal Academy, *The chef de l'Hôtel Chatham, Paris* (RA). This picture clearly did not qualify (as Orpen initially hoped) for acquisition for the nation under the terms of the Chantrey bequest, which requires that works submitted under the scheme to the Royal Academy have to be painted within Great Britain. Orpen treated quite mischievously the obvious fact that the work was painted largely in Paris, and it led to a rancorous controversy.

Orpen was the titular editor of *An Outline of Art* (1923), a large and prodigiously illustrated history of art, and in 1924 published his second book, *Stories of Old Ireland and Myself*. In this mocking and regretful account he seems to be looking for an alternative to the mixture of success and ill health which shaped his existence in his final years. He had a huge and splendid studio in The Boltons, south-west London, but his friendships were made among drinking companions and the many people who sought to benefit from his wealth. Owing to a sense of shame he felt at his physical decline his children had difficulty in getting to see him. And his peers, some of whom had been envious of his success, were now indifferent towards him. Orpen's death, from liver and heart failure on 29 September 1931 at 2 Clareville Grove, South Kensington, was followed by a small tribute exhibition in the Royal Academy. He was buried at Putney cemetery.   BRUCE ARNOLD

Sources B. Arnold, *Orpen: mirror to an age* (1981) · S. Dark and P. G. Konody, *Sir William Orpen: artist and man* (1932) · *War: paintings and drawings executed on the western front by Sir W. Orpen* (1918) [exhibition catalogue, Agnews, London] · CGPLA Eng. & Wales (1931) · R. Cork, *A bitter truth: avant-garde art and the Great War* (1994)

Archives IWM, corresp. · NG Ire., corresp. · NYPL, corresp. · priv. coll., corresp. · priv. coll., studio book · RA, reports · Tate collection, letters relating to a campaign against the mosaic decorations beneath the dome of St Paul's · U. Texas, corresp. | Harvard U., Houghton L., letters to Sir William Rothenstein · HLRO, corresp. with Lord Beaverbrook · priv. coll., MS catalogue of Orpen's works by Miss Cara Copeland · RA, letters to the Royal Academy · Tate collection, letters to Anita Bartle · Tate collection, letters to John Lavery · Tate collection, letters to Sir William McCormick and sketches of McCormick · TCD, corresp. with Thomas Bodkin · University of Victoria, British Columbia, McPherson Library, letters to Beatrice Elvery

Likenesses W. Orpen, self-portrait, oils, 1891, AM Oxf. · W. Orpen, self-portrait, pencil drawing, c.1898, NPG · W. Orpen, self-portraits, 1898–1912 · W. Orpen, self-portrait, ink drawing, c.1899, Scottish National Gallery of Modern Art, Edinburgh · W. Orpen, self-portrait, oils, c.1901, Art Gallery and Museum, Glasgow · G. C. Beresford, photographs, 1902, NPG · W. Orpen, self-portrait, oils, 1903, Ulster Museum, Belfast · W. Orpen, self-portrait, pencil and watercolour drawing, 1903, AM Oxf. · C. Conder, oils, c.1907, NG Ire. · A. L. Coburn, photograph, 1908,

NPG · W. Orpen, self-portrait, oils, 1908, Laing Art Gallery, Newcastle upon Tyne · W. Orpen, self-portrait, oils, c.1908, Hugh Lane Gallery of Modern Art, Dublin · W. Orpen, group portrait, oils, 1909 (*The selecting jury of the N.E.A.C.*), NPG · W. Orpen, self-portrait, oils, c.1909 (*The dead ptarmigan*), NG Ire. · W. Orpen, self-portrait, oils, 1910 (*Myself and Venus*), Carnegie Institute, Pittsburgh · W. Orpen, self-portrait, oils, 1910 (*The jockey*), National Museum, Stockholm · W. Orpen, self-portrait, oils, c.1910, NPG · W. Orpen, self-portrait, pencil and wash drawing, 1910, NPG · W. Orpen, group portrait, oils, 1911–12 (*Group in the Café Royal*), Musée d'Art Moderne, Paris; copy, Café Royal, London · W. Orpen, two self-portraits, ink and wash caricatures, 1912, Birmingham Museum and Art Gallery · F. Lion, charcoal drawing, 1913, NG Ire. · M. Beerbohm, caricature, 1914 (*Bravura*), Tate collection · W. Orpen, self-portrait, oils, 1914 (*Leading the life in the west*), Metropolitan Museum of Art, New York · W. Orpen, self-portrait, 1916 (*The man from Aran*); Christies, 20 May 1999, lot 24 [*see illus.*] · W. Orpen, two self-portraits, oils, 1917 (*Ready to start*), IWM · W. Stoneman, photograph, 1921, NPG · W. Orpen, four self-portraits, oils, c.1923–1924, FM Cam. · W. Orpen, self-portrait, oils, 1925 (*The man with the brush*), Uffizi Gallery, Florence · H. Coster, photographs, 1927, NPG · J. Sleator, oils, c.1937–1938, Hugh Lane Gallery of Modern Art, Dublin · W. Orpen, self-portrait, repro. in Arnold, *Orpen* · W. Orpen, self-portrait, ink drawing, Scot. NPG · W. Orpen, self-portraits, drawings, NG Ire. · W. Orpen, self-portrait, watercolour drawing (*Orpsie boy*), Oldham Art Galleries, Manchester · A. P. F. Ritchie, print, NPG · A. R. Thomson, ink caricature, Athenaeum, London

Wealth at death £159,174 10s. 8d.: probate, 9 Dec 1931, *CGPLA Eng. & Wales*

Orr [*née* Leighton], **Alexandra** [*known as* Mrs Sutherland Orr] (**1828–1903**), biographer, was born on 23 December 1828 at St Petersburg, where her grandfather, Sir James Boniface Leighton, was court physician to her godmother, Alexandra empress of Russia. She was the eldest of the three surviving children of Frederic Septimus Leighton (1800–1892), a medical doctor, and his wife, Augusta Susan (c.1800–1865), daughter of George Augustus Nash of Edmonton, Middlesex. Frederic *Leighton, Lord Leighton (1830–1896), was her only brother. The family travelled extensively in Europe, and Alexandra was educated privately abroad, in Italy, Germany, and Switzerland, and at a girls' boarding-school at Frankfurt am Main. When she was sixteen she had a serious attack of rheumatic fever in Florence which left her partly blind, and she spent more than seven years recovering in Hampstead, Middlesex, with her mother. On account of her near blindness, most of her very considerable knowledge was acquired by listening to books read aloud to her.

On 7 March 1857 Alexandra Leighton married a widower, Sutherland George Gordon Orr of the Madras service, commandant of the 3rd regiment of cavalry, Hyderabad contingent, and she went with him to India. They arrived during the Indian mutiny, and Alexandra had a narrow escape from Aurangabad, having been saved by the fidelity to the English of Sheikh Baran Bukh. Her husband died there on 19 June 1858, worn out by the war. He was gazetted captain and brevet major and CB on the day of his death. Alexandra then returned to England and rejoined her parents, who were sojourning in Bath and Scarborough. It was about this time, in 1860, that Lord Leighton painted her portrait as a beautiful young widow. It was exhibited at the Royal Academy in 1861, and Leighton wrote that it was more admired than anything else.

(Previously Alexandra had sat for the figure of the Moor's wife in *Othello and Desdemona*.) However, she did not settle in London until she moved there with her father in 1869, after her mother's death four years earlier.

Alexandra Orr's main interests were in art, music, and literature. In the winter of 1855–6 she had met in Paris Robert Browning, with whom her brother was close. Browning renewed his acquaintance with her at intervals until 1869, when, both residing in London, they became good friends. For many years he read books to her twice a week, and they used to meet in her brother's studio. She joined the Browning Society shortly after its formation in 1881, became a member of the committee which wrote notes on various difficult points in Browning's poems, and was generous in financial support. The most important result of this connection was *A Handbook to the Works of Robert Browning* (1885; 3rd edn, 1887), which she wrote at the request of the society. It contains ample contributions by Browning, who wrote many of the notes and indices himself, and is a kind of descriptive catalogue, based partly on the historical order and partly on the natural classification of the poems, owing something to the suggestions of the painter and author John Trivett Nettleship. The sixth edition, incorporating her final corrections, was often reprinted.

Alexandra Orr's most important work, however, was her *Life and Letters of Robert Browning*, published in 1891, largely based on material supplied by Browning's sister. Many new letters by the poet have come to light during the twentieth century—and countless more studies and biographies have been written—but Orr's retains the value of a book written by a personal friend. Her estimate of Browning's religious opinions, particularly his views on spiritualism and on the Theosophical Society, caused considerable controversy, and she answered her critics in an article in the December 1891 issue of the *Contemporary Review*. To that and other periodicals she contributed occasional articles on art and literature, as well as on women's suffrage, of which she was a strong opponent. Her last literary efforts were two editions of her brother's *Addresses Delivered to the Students of the Royal Academy by the Late Lord Leighton* (1896; 1897). All her works were dictated, as her vision was too weak to allow her to write or read.

After her father's death in 1892, Alexandra Orr continued to live in their mansion at 11 Kensington Park Gardens, London, until her own death, from a lingering pulmonary disease, on 23 August 1903. She was buried on 29 August in Locksbrook cemetery, Bath, alongside her parents. She had no children.

ELIZABETH LEE, rev. KATHARINE CHUBBUCK

Sources Mrs R. Barrington, *Life, letters and work of Frederic Leighton*, 2 vols. (1906) · W. Gaunt, *Victorian Olympus* (1952) · A. Corkran, *Frederic Leighton* (1904) · E. Rhys, *Frederic, Lord Leighton* (1900) · *The Times* (26 Aug 1903) · *The Times* (31 Aug 1903) · A. Orr, *A handbook to the works of Robert Browning*, 3rd edn (1887) · F. Kenyon and A. Orr, *Life and letters of Robert Browning*, rev. edn (1908) · m. cert. · d. cert. · *CGPLA Eng. & Wales* (1903)

Likenesses F. Leighton, chalk drawing, c.1845–1850, NPG · F. Leighton, oils, exh. RA 1861, Leighton House, Kensington ·

F. Leighton, oils, *c*.1889 (after his portrait), Victoria Art Gallery, Bath

Wealth at death £27,032 4*s*. 3*d*.: probate, 6 Oct 1903, *CGPLA Eng. & Wales*

Orr, Hugh (1715–1798), toolmaker and textile manufacturer in America, was born probably on 2 January 1715 (other sources give 13 January 1717) at Lochwinnoch, Renfrewshire, the son of Robert Orr. Trained as a gunsmith and door-lock filer he emigrated to America in 1740, in his twenties, and settled at Bridgewater, Plymouth county, Massachusetts, where he manufactured scythes and edge-tools. He set up the first trip-hammer ever constructed in Massachusetts, and he succeeded in spreading the manufacture of edge-tools through the states of Massachusetts, Rhode Island, and Connecticut. He married, on 4 August 1742, Mary Bass; they had ten children. In 1748 Orr made 500 muskets for the province of Massachusetts Bay, believed to have been the first weapons of the kind produced in the country. During the American Revolution he engaged in casting iron and brass cannon and cannon balls, for which, in association with a Frenchman, he constructed a foundry. He also cultivated and marketed flax seed for which he invented a cleaning machine.

After the revolution, Orr became a senator for Plymouth county in the Massachusetts legislature. In this position he expressed a strong interest in acquiring Britain's new labour-saving cotton-spinning machinery. In 1786 he recruited the brothers Robert and Alexander Barr from Scotland to Bridgewater to set up carding, roving, and spinning machinery and thus introduce Arkwright's system to the USA. Their work was supported by a £200 grant from the Massachusetts legislature and the machines were completed in 1787. Placed in the custody of Orr, and publicly exhibited in order to encourage replication, they were known as the 'state models'. Copies were made by Rhode Island artisans and then purchased by Moses Brown, the Quaker merchant of Providence, who employed Samuel Slater a few months after he arrived in New York in 1789, fresh from Jedediah Strutt's Derbyshire mills. When Slater (who subsequently pioneered Arkwright technology in the USA) saw the 'state models' he condemned them as worthless. Orr died at Bridgewater on 6 December 1798. His son Robert (1786–1876), a colonel in the Anglo-American War of 1812–14, was armourer of the United States arsenal at Springfield and a congressman, 1817–20.   GEORGE STRONACH, *rev.* DAVID J. JEREMY

Sources *DNB* · W. R. Bagnall, *The textile industries of the United States* (1893) · D. J. Jeremy, *Transatlantic industrial revolution: the diffusion of textile technologies between Britain and America, 1790–1830s* (1981) · P. E. Rivard, 'Textile experiments in Rhode Island, 1788–1789', *Rhode Island History*, 33 (1974) · *Who was who in American: historical volume, 1607–1896* (1963), 459

Orr, James [*called* the Bard of Ballycarry] (1770–1816), radical and poet, born in the parish of Templecorran, co. Antrim, was the only child of James Orr, a linen weaver, who also farmed a few acres of land near Ballycarry. The family, like most of its neighbours, was of Scots descent and Presbyterian. The younger Orr never attended school, but was taught by his parents to read and write. He joined his father in weaving, and like several of his contemporaries began at an early age to write verse. This was locally popular, and many of his poems appeared in the Belfast *Northern Star*. Orr's political beliefs were influenced by millennial hopes for the amelioration of mankind; these, and enthusiasm for education and freemasonry, are all found in his writing. He came to be known as the Bard of Ballycarry. He took part in the battle of Antrim on 7 June 1798, and is credited with having saved some lives on that occasion, by dissuading his fellow insurgents from unnecessary violence. After the failure of the uprising he escaped to America and published poetry in newspapers there. He returned to Ireland in a very short time, and came into possession of the tenancy of the farm on his father's death. His application in 1800 to join the yeomanry was rejected; his radical sympathies were still too obvious. In 1804 he issued a small collection of his poems by subscription at Belfast. Some of his later poems, originally published in newspapers, including the once well-known 'The Irishman', were collected after his death and at his request published for the benefit of the poor of Ballycarry. Several newspaper essays on morality, in prose, may have been by Orr, but have not been republished. His best writing is in the Ulster-Scots language of his own area; the poems have considerable fluency, charm, and power, and the accuracy of his observation of the linguistic and social characteristics of his community partly accounts for Orr's contemporary and continuing popularity in Ulster. His ambitious and often accomplished poems in the standard language, more accessible for a modern audience, provide evidence of the balance between local involvements and wider interests which is represented in Orr's personality as well as in his verse. Orr is probably Ulster's most important eighteenth-century poet; his work is increasingly recognized by scholars as of more than local significance. A sketch of his life by his friend A. McDowell prefaces the posthumous poems, published in 1817, and also appears in a collected edition published by Ballycarry people in 1935; a selection of his poems appeared in 1977 and another in 1992.

Despite or perhaps partly because of his popularity and literary success, Orr drank heavily in the years after the deaths of his parents; this is said to have caused his own death at Ballycarry, co. Antrim, on 24 April 1816. He was unmarried. He was buried in Templecorran churchyard, and a large monument with masonic motifs was erected over his grave.   LINDE LUNNEY

Sources A. McDowell, 'Sketch of the author's life', in *The posthumous works of James Orr of Ballycarry*, ed. A. McDowell (1817) · P. Robinson, 'Introduction', in *The country rhymes of James Orr, the Bard of Ballycarry, 1770–1816* (1992) · D. H. Akenson and W. H. Crawford, *James Orr, Bard of Ballycarry* (1977) · L. C. Lunney, 'Attitudes to life and death in the poetry of James Orr, an eighteenth-century Ulster weaver', *Ulster Folklife*, 31 (1985), 1–12 · gravestone, Templecorran churchyard
Archives TCD, letter-book of S. Thomson

Orr, James (1844–1913), theologian, was born in Glasgow on 11 April 1844, the son of Robert Orr, an engineer, and his wife, Montgomery (*née* Hunter). He began school in

Manchester and Leeds before, when he was about nine, both his parents died. Living with Glasgow relatives, he became an apprentice bookbinder. In 1865 he entered Glasgow University to prepare for the United Presbyterian ministry. He was moulded in philosophy by John Veitch, the last representative of the Scottish common-sense school, and in lesser degree by John and Edward Caird, early advocates of idealism. He graduated MA with first-class honours in mental philosophy in 1870, winning a Ferguson scholarship that enabled him to remain at Glasgow for two further years. In 1872 he graduated BD and shared in the lord rector's prize for a penetrating critique of David Hume that he later published in revised form (1903). From 1868 to 1872 he also attended the United Presbyterian Divinity Hall in Edinburgh and during most of 1873 preached as a probationer at Trinity Church, Irvine, Ayrshire.

From 1874 to 1891 Orr was minister of East Bank United Presbyterian Church, Hawick, Roxburghshire. On 7 April 1874 he married Hannah Fraser, the daughter of James Gibb, a shoemaker from Glasgow; she was to survive him. He became chairman of Hawick school board, campaigned for the reduction of liquor licences, and was known as a Liberal, one of his four sons being named William Gladstone. He helped to draft the United Presbyterian declaratory statement that in 1879 repudiated any total endorsement of Calvinism. Six years later he obtained a Glasgow DD by examination. In 1891 he delivered his church's Kerr lectures, published two years later as *The Christian View of God and the World*, which showed originality in teaching the coherence of an incarnation-centred world-view. The book remained influential a century later.

The lectures secured Orr's appointment in 1891 to the United Presbyterian college in Edinburgh as professor of church history. In 1894 he published one of three replies to the anti-supernaturalist Gifford lectures given by Otto Pfleiderer of Berlin, and in 1895 and 1897 lectured in North America. The resulting books, especially *The Ritschlian Theology and the Evangelical Faith* (1897) and *The Progress of Dogma* (1901) criticizing Adolf Harnack, the German theologian and church historian, cautioned against the subjectivist trend in German theology. In 1896, when the Free Church approached the United Presbyterian church with a proposal of co-operation, Orr urged merger instead and became joint convenor of the United Presbyterian union committee. At the eventual creation of the United Free Church in 1900 Orr was transferred to the chair of systematic theology and apologetics at its Glasgow college but, perhaps partly because of hostility to his pro-Boer stance during the Second South African War, he failed to secure its principalship two years later. He edited the *United Presbyterian Magazine* (1896–1900) and with his friend and Glasgow colleague James Denney co-edited the *Union Magazine* (1901–4) and the *United Free Church Magazine* (1904–6).

In 1902 Orr seconded Robert Rainy's general assembly motion not to proceed against another colleague, George Adam Smith, for his advocacy of higher criticism. Yet, as Orr explained in *The Problem of the Old Testament* (1905), he dissented from the growing acceptance of that approach. In the same year *God's Image in Man*, based on the 1903 Stone lectures at Princeton Seminary, argued that supernatural interruptions of the evolutionary process were essential to account for the emergence of humanity. From 1906 Orr's prolific writings became more popular in tone, a tendency culminating in the republication of four of his articles in *The Fundamentals* (1910–15). His *Revelation and Inspiration* (1910), though explicitly repudiating biblical inerrancy, cogently defended a high estimate of scripture. His final years were spent chiefly as general editor of the conservative *International Standard Bible Encyclopaedia* (5 vols., 1915). After illness caused by a weak heart, he died at his home, 4 Hampton Court Terrace, Glasgow, on 6 September 1913 and was buried in Cathcart cemetery, Glasgow, on 9 September.

Tall and broad-shouldered, Orr was tolerant of opponents and, though sometimes abrupt, markedly kind to students. He swam against the tide of contemporary British theological opinion, but his influence was more widely felt in North America. D. W. BEBBINGTON

Sources G. G. Scorgie, *A call for continuity: the theological contribution of James Orr* (1988) · A. P. F. Sell, *Defending and declaring the faith: some Scottish examples, 1860–1920* (1987) · *Glasgow Herald* (8 Sept 1913), 11 · *The Scotsman* (8 Sept 1913), 7 · *British Weekly* (9 Jan 1913), 390 · *Letters of Principal James Denney to W. Robertson Nicoll, 1893–1917*, ed. W. R. Nicoll (1920) · *CCI* (1913) · m. cert. · *Glasgow Herald* (10 Sept 1913), 8
Archives U. Glas.
Likenesses T. & R. Annan, photograph, c.1885, repro. in Scorgie, *Call for continuity*, p. x · photograph, c.1905, Southwestern Baptist Theological Seminary, Fort Worth, Texas, Texas Baptist historical collection; repro. in Scorgie, *Call for continuity*, p. xi · photograph, 1913, priv. coll.; repro. in Scorgie, *Call for continuity*, p. xiv
Wealth at death £3816 15s. 6d.: confirmation, 20 Dec 1913, *CCI*

Orr, John (c.1760–1835), army officer in the East India Company, became a cadet in the Madras army, and arrived in India in 1777. On 18 August 1777 he was appointed ensign in the 21st Madras native infantry, and served with them in 1778 at the siege of Pondicherry, during which, the adjutant of the 2nd battalion of the 2nd Madras European regiment having been killed, Orr was transferred to that corps. After the siege he served for some time as brigade-major to a detachment under Colonel Hopkins. Towards the end of 1780 he was appointed to command a mixed flying column, to escort supplies to Sir Eyre Coote's army and to various forts, many of which were blockaded. This was very onerous: it was impossible to carry tents and there was much exposure as well as fatigue, and Orr's health suffered. He was constantly in battle, and on one occasion was repeatedly charged by up to 2000 enemy cavalry. He was promoted lieutenant on 12 August 1781, and captain on 20 May 1785. At the end of the war in 1784 Orr, highly commended, was rewarded by being transferred to the cavalry, and appointed to the prestigious command of the governor's bodyguard. He held this appointment until 1787, when he had to go on sick-leave to England.

Orr returned to India in 1789 and, joining the 1st native cavalry as second in command, took part in the Anglo-Mysore War of 1790–92. His regiment in March 1791 formed part of the force which, under Colonel Floyd, when close to Bangalore, was lured into an ambush. A sudden attack by a superior force followed, and nearly resulted in their destruction. Eventually Floyd was relieved by a supporting brigade of Indian infantry which came up to his support and made possible his retreat. His command consisted of the 19th light dragoons and five corps of Indian cavalry; 271 horses were lost, and 71 men killed, wounded, or missing, Floyd himself being among the wounded. In April 1791 Orr became major, and at the head of the 1st native cavalry took part in Floyd's charge on the Mysore army when it was retreating, shortly before the battle outside Seringapatam, in May 1791. In this charge Orr captured two standards with his own hand. In July of the same year he was transferred to the 5th native cavalry. In November 1798 he became lieutenant-colonel, and in January 1799, after transferring to the 3rd native cavalry, proceeded to England on leave. In April 1802 he became full colonel, and in December 1802, being still in England, was transferred to the command of the 7th native cavalry. In 1805 he obtained his regiment (that is, received colonel's allowances or off-reckonings). He became major-general in October 1809, and lieutenant-general in June 1814. He died in London on 26 November 1835.   W. W. KNOLLYS, *rev.* JAMES FALKNER

Sources *East-India Register* · BL OIOC

Orr, John Boyd, Baron Boyd Orr (1880–1971), nutritional physiologist, was born on 23 September 1880 at Kilmaurs, Ayrshire, the middle child in the family of seven (a sister and two brothers were older and two brothers and a sister younger) of Robert Clark Orr, a quarry owner, and his wife, Annie Boyd, daughter of a quarry master. His father was widely read and a man of deep religious convictions, being an earnest and practising member of a sect of the Free Church of Scotland. John Orr was educated first at the local school in West Kilbride, where the family had moved when his father's business had suffered a misfortune, and, after winning a bursary, at Kilmarnock Academy. He returned to West Kilbride as a pupil teacher and in 1899 won a queen's scholarship to enable him to train at Glasgow University as a teacher, graduating MA in 1902. After teaching for three years he had saved enough to enable him to re-enter Glasgow University, where he graduated BSc in 1910 and MB, ChB, in 1912. After a brief period as a ship's surgeon he received a Carnegie research fellowship to enable him to work with E. P. Cathcart, head of physiological chemistry in the Institute of Physiology at Glasgow University. He graduated MD with honours in 1914, being awarded the Bellahouston gold medal for his thesis. In 1915 he married Elizabeth Pearson, daughter of John Callum, businessman, of West Kilbride. They had two daughters and a son, who was killed on active service in 1942.

A committee of the University of Aberdeen and the North of Scotland College of Agriculture planned to establish an institute of nutrition at Aberdeen and Orr was appointed director. He began work in Aberdeen in 1913

John Boyd Orr, Baron Boyd Orr (1880–1971), by Lida Moser, 1949

and some new laboratories were built before war broke out.

During the First World War Orr was first attached to the Royal Army Medical Corps and was later medical officer to the 1st battalion, Sherwood Foresters. He was at the battle of the Somme in 1916, where he won the MC, and at the battle of Passchendaele, where he was appointed to the DSO. He resigned his army commission in 1918 to join the navy, serving at Chatham Naval Hospital and on HMS *Furious*. In the same year he was seconded to the army at the request of the Royal Society to study food resource allocation, and having completed this returned to Aberdeen in 1919.

Orr did not regard the laboratory building he had started in 1914 as sufficient for the new institute, and went on to build the Rowett Institute, opened in 1923. The Reid Library, the Duthie Farm, and Strathcona House also owed much to his active fund-raising.

At the Rowett Institute Orr turned his attention to the nutrition of farm animals and of human populations. In 1927 he showed by experiments the value of milk in the health and growth of British children. This led Orr's lifelong friend, Walter Elliot, then under-secretary of state for Scotland, to introduce legislation to provide milk for children in Scottish schools. Orr continued to draw attention to the poor state of health and nutrition of the British people and advocated a national food policy. Elliot, by then minister of agriculture, asked Orr to report on the matter, but the political implications of his findings were such that they were not published by the government. Orr published them himself in 1936 under the title *Food, Health and Income*, and continued to advocate national and indeed international action. His contribution to scientific thought was recognized when he was elected FRS in 1932 and knighted in 1935.

Orr's views were at the base of national food policy during the Second World War. He advised Lord Woolton, then minister of food, and the relevant cabinet committee. He was not, however, a UK delegate to the Hot Springs conference of 1943, where it was agreed that the international Food and Agriculture Organization (FAO) should be established, and he attended the Quebec conference of 1945 only as an unofficial adviser. In his Quebec address he pleaded that the new agency should be granted executive power, to deal with human undernutrition. He was then asked to become its first director-general. At this time Orr had retired from directing the Rowett Institute and was farming in Angus. He was professor of agriculture in the University of Aberdeen from 1942 to 1945. He was also MP for the Scottish universities from 1945 to 1946 and rector of the University of Glasgow in 1945 (he became its chancellor in 1946). He nevertheless accepted the invitation and was the first director-general of FAO from 1945 to 1948.

Orr began gathering statistics on population, agricultural production, and trade, and planning a world food board, a supra-national body with powers to buy and hold food stocks, provide funds for technical development of agriculture, and finance the supply of food to needy countries. However, his supra-national body was not supported by the major world powers, and his world food plan was rejected in September 1947.

Orr was bitterly disappointed and resigned from FAO a few months later. He took an active part in world peace organizations and travelled widely. Within the developing countries he advised on food and agricultural problems. He was created Baron Boyd Orr in 1949. In the same year he also received the Nobel peace prize and was made a commander of the Légion d'honneur. He was appointed CH in 1968.

Orr received honorary degrees from twelve universities in Britain and abroad, and honorary memberships of the New York Academy of Sciences and of the American Public Health Association. He was a hard worker and expected his staff to show a similar commitment. He never lost his strong west of Scotland accent, and while he spoke well, he convinced people by his sincerity and his own conviction rather than by oratory. He had eyebrows like eaves above penetrating blue eyes; he had a spare physique, and was a confirmed pipe smoker. Orr died on 25 June 1971 at his home at Brechin and was survived by his wife and two daughters. His barony became extinct.

K. L. BLAXTER, rev.

Sources *The Times* (26 June 1971) · H. D. Kay, *Memoirs FRS*, 18 (1972), 43–81 · J. B. Orr, *As I recall* (1966) · D. P. Cuthbertson, *British Journal of Nutrition*, 27 (1972), 1–5 · personal knowledge (1986)

Archives NL Scot., corresp. and papers · PRO, reports on Germany, MH79/358 | NA Scot., corresp. with Lord Lothian · Rowett Research Institute, Aberdeenshire, corresp. and papers relating to Rowett Research Institute
Likenesses L. Moser, photograph, 1949, NPG [*see illus.*] · B. Schotz, bronze head, 1950, Hunterian Museum and Art Gallery, Glasgow · W. Stoneman, photograph, 1953, NPG · photograph, repro. in Kay, *Memoirs FRS*

Orr, William (1766–1797), Irish nationalist, was probably born in Kilbegs, co. Antrim, to where his father, Samuel Orr, had moved his young family from Coleraine. They were New Light Presbyterians and settled at Farranshane, where William Orr was brought up. The Orrs were small farmers involved in flax-growing, horse-trading, and the operation of a linen-bleaching green at Rathbeg, which provided them with a comfortable income and high-quality accommodation. In 1788 at Duneane Orr married Isabella Greer, with whom he had six children.

Several of William Orr's brothers, uncles, and cousins had joined the revolutionary Society of United Irishmen by 1796 and he was evidently an early and popular member. Well known in the community from his service as a volunteer, sportsman, and an Antrim town freemason, Orr was voted that year on to the United Irish baronial committee which met near Carrickfergus. He contributed articles to the United Irish paper *Northern Star* and his name reached the ears of Newry informer Samuel Turner. Orr was arrested at his father's Milltown home on 17 September 1796 on a warrant issued by local magistrate, the Revd George Macartney, vicar of Antrim and Templepatrick. The arrest was made by Macartney's son, Arthur Chichester Macartney, a student at Trinity College, Dublin. Orr was detained in Carrickfergus gaol along with several other prominent United Irishmen seized during a crackdown on the organization's middle ranks. It was alleged that he had administered the United Irish oath to Scottish privates Hugh Wheatly and John Lindsay of the Fifeshire fencibles on 24–25 April 1796. Doubt was later cast on whether the two men were actually soldiers, and both were advanced considerable sums from secret service funds by the crown solicitor, John Pollock. Wheatly was subsequently revealed to be suicidal and a suspected murderer.

The recently enacted Insurrection Act (36 George III) had reclassified the offence of administering an illegal oath from a transportable to a capital felony and this served to focus unusual attention on the Orr case. His lawyers, John Philpot Curran and William Sampson, were confident of acquittal given that their client's innocence was widely accepted. James Hope, a key Ulster organizer, apprised historian R. R. Madden many years later that William McKeever, a Derry city delegate, had made the approach to Wheatly and Lindsay at Jack Gourlay's barn in Farranshane. Orr had been present but had not trusted the two strangers in uniform.

Orr was held on remand in Carrickfergus gaol with many other United Irish prisoners and wore a green necktie as a sign of his radical politics. He was not brought to trial, however, until 17 September 1797 when judges Barry

Yelverton and William Tankerville Chamberlain considered the case presented by prosecuting counsel Arthur Wolfe (later Lord Kilwarden). The jury deliberated all night and, having consulted the judges on a point of law, recommended that Orr be found guilty but worthy of clemency. He was brought up for sentencing the following day, at which time Chamberlain refused to consider Curran's protest at the inebriated state of the jury. In accordance with the law Yelverton had no option but to pronounce sentence of death, a task he performed with, reputedly, great emotion and reluctance. Orr made a statement protesting his innocence while his supporters prepared an appeal.

Orr's wife enlisted the support of Lady Londonderry who, according to Mary Ann McCracken, presented the appeal to her powerful brother, Lord Castlereagh. McCracken also ascertained that the elderly Alexander Thompson of Cushendall, foreman of the jury, had been threatened with violence and financial ruin if he failed to convict. Two other jury members claimed they had erred in their deliberations owing to drunkenness. More remarkable was Wheatly's admission that he had perjured himself in his affidavit against Orr and during the trial. The cumulative effect of the revelations suggested that Orr had been framed by the authorities to ensure the smooth running of a potentially vital test case. Several loyalists were convinced that a miscarriage of justice had occurred, but the lord lieutenant, Lord Camden, refused to intercede.

James Orr, brother of the prisoner, claimed in a letter to *The Press* of 28 October 1797 to have received assurances that clemency would be granted if William acknowledged his crime. This course was flatly rejected by William Orr, and James decided to forge a declaration of guilt which was seized upon by those wishing to uphold the verdict. An attempt to bribe the gaoler failed and the execution date, twice postponed, arrived without compromise. Orr wore his green ribbon to the gallows green outside Carrickfergus on 14 October 1797. He was buried at Templepatrick after a funeral procession viewed by thousands who defied a heavy military presence.

Orr became the first major martyr of the United Irishmen and the slogan 'Remember Orr' soon replaced 'Remember Armagh' in their toasts, propaganda, and memorabilia. William Drennan's poem, 'Wake of William Orr', was immediately popular, as was William Sampson's suppressed trial account. The case precipitated an action for seditious libel against *The Press* for the assertion by 'Marcus' (Deane Swift) that Orr should have been pardoned. The printer, Peter Finnerty, was convicted, imprisoned for two years, fined £20, and obliged to find a large security. Orr was survived by his wife, but his family was burnt out of their home by the military in the aftermath of the battle of Antrim in June 1798.

RUÁN O'DONNELL

Sources F. J. Bigger, *The northern leaders of '98, 'Remember Orr'*, repr. (Dublin, 1998) · R. R. Madden, *The United Irishmen: their lives and times*, 2nd edn, 4 vols. (1857–60) · N. J. Curtin, *The United Irishmen: popular politics in Ulster and Dublin, 1791–1798* (1994) · C. Dickson, *Revolt in the north: Antrim and Down in 1798* (1960) · M. McNeill, *The life and times of Mary Ann McCracken, 1770–1866: a Belfast panorama* (1960) · A. T. Q. Stewart, *The summer soldiers: the 1798 rebellion in Antrim and Down* (1995) · DNB

Archives CKS, corresp. and papers
Likenesses E. A. Morrow, oils, repro. in Bigger, *Northern leaders of '98* · E. A. Morrow, sketch, repro. in Bigger, *Northern leaders of '98*

Orr, William McFadden (1866–1934), mathematician, was born at Ballystockart, Comber, co. Down, on 2 May 1866, the eldest son of Fletcher Blakeley Orr, a farmer who owned corn and flax mills, of Ballystockart, and his wife, Elizabeth, daughter of David Lowry, farmer, of Ballymachashan, Killinchy, co. Down. He received his early training in mathematics at the local national school. After spending two years at an intermediate school in Newtownards, he entered the Methodist college, Belfast, where he came under the mathematical direction of James Adams McNeill, afterwards headmaster of Campbell College, Belfast. He obtained a scholarship in mathematics at the Royal University of Ireland in 1883, and graduated in 1885 from Queen's College, Belfast, then a constituent college of the Royal University. He then moved to St John's College, Cambridge, in April 1885, was senior wrangler in 1888, and obtained the first place in part two of the mathematical tripos of 1889. In 1891 he was both elected to a fellowship at St John's and appointed professor of applied mathematics at the Royal College of Science for Ireland, Dublin. When in 1926 this institution was absorbed by University College, Dublin, he was offered and accepted an equivalent position in that college as professor of pure and applied mathematics, from which he retired in 1933. In 1909 he was elected FRS, and he received the honorary degree of DSc from Queen's University, Belfast, in 1919. In 1892, shortly after he obtained the post in the Royal College of Science, Orr married Elizabeth Campbell (*d*. 1926), daughter of Samuel Watson Campbell, of Melbourne, Australia, who originally came from co. Down. They had three daughters, the eldest of whom died in Orr's lifetime.

His contemporaries at the Royal College of Science record that Orr's teaching was characterized by accurate definition, logical rigour, and clear statements of underlying assumptions. The scrupulous style of his teaching is shown in his *Notes on Thermodynamics for Students* (1909), which is a model of precision in the formulation of principles. He always endeavoured to provide his students with the mathematical tools needed to deal with the physical, chemical, and engineering problems that they met in the laboratories, where he was frequently to be seen modestly deploring his own lack of experimental knowledge. Mathematics under his inspiring influence became, for staff and students alike, an integrating subject in the small college.

Orr's role model was McNeill, of whom he wrote an appreciation containing an unconscious self-portrait, in which he described the persistence with which his teacher would repeatedly attack a difficult mathematical problem and expressed the view that this trait was a moral one, an attempt to live 'the strenuous life' of which he approved. Combined with this stoical austerity, Orr exercised quick and effective generosity towards students and teachers in difficulties.

Orr's mathematical outlook was moulded in the Cambridge tradition of Lord Rayleigh, A. E. H. Love, and Sir Joseph Larmor, with whom he carried on an active correspondence. He was best known for his work on the stability of the steady motions of a liquid. He also worked on the problems arising from the whirling of shafts in his 'Note on Mr. Lees' paper on the whirling of an overhung shaft' (*Philosophical Magazine*, 45, 1923), which was supplemented by correspondence and discussion with his colleagues, and he wrote papers on several issues in mathematical physics. He felt very strongly that clear thinking in applied science rests upon a solid grasp of fundamental principles. He therefore aimed at the best possible exposition in all his work, and especially in textbooks. The climate of the quantum and relativity physics of the twentieth century was not congenial to him, but he never ceased to take an interest in these developments and to look forward to a reconciling synthesis with classical dynamics. Orr died at Nobles Hospital, Douglas, Isle of Man, on 14 August 1934.

F. E. HACKETT, *rev.* JULIA TOMPSON

Sources A. W. Conway, *Obits. FRS*, 1 (1932–5), 559–62 · *The Campbellian* (Nov 1907) · Venn, *Alum. Cant.* · *CGPLA Eng. & Wales* (1935)
Archives Air Force Research Laboratories, Cambridge, Massachusetts, Strutt MSS · St John Cam., letters to Sir Joseph Larmor
Likenesses photograph, repro. in Conway, *Obits. FRS*, 558–9 · photograph, RS
Wealth at death £5014 3s. 6d. in England: administration with will, 25 Feb 1935, *CGPLA Eng. & Wales*

Orrery. For this title name *see* Boyle, Roger, first earl of Orrery (1621–1679); Boyle, Charles, fourth earl of Orrery (1674–1731); Boyle, John, fifth earl of Cork and fifth earl of Orrery (1707–1762); Boyle, Mary, countess of Cork and Orrery (1746–1840); Boyle, William Henry Dudley, twelfth earl of Cork and twelfth earl of Orrery (1873–1967).

Orridge, Benjamin Brogden (1814–1870), antiquary, set up in business in London as a medical agent and valuer. From 1863 until 1869 he was an active member of the court of common council for the ward of Cheap. As chairman of the committee of the Guildhall Library, he distinguished himself by his exertions for the preservation and investigation of the mass of records belonging to the corporation.

Orridge was a fellow of the Geological Society, and a member of the London and Middlesex Archaeological Society. To the *Transactions* of the latter he contributed some valuable papers, including the 'City friends of Shakespeare' (3.578–80) and an 'Account of some eminent members of the Mercers' Company', read at the general meeting held at Mercers' Hall on 21 April 1869. In 1867 Orridge published his most substantial work, *Some Account of the Citizens of London and their Rulers, from 1060 to 1867* (1867), a useful summary of the biography of the lord mayors, accompanied by pedigrees of the more distinguished of their descendants among the aristocracy. Among his

other publications were a *Letter* (1866) on civic records, *Some Particulars of Alderman Philip Malpas and Alderman Sir Thomas Cooke, KB* (1868), and *Illustrations of Jack Cade's rebellion, from researches in the Guildhall records; together with some newly found letters of Lord Bacon* (1869). Orridge died, after a long illness, at his home, 33 St John's Wood Park, London, on 17 July 1870.

GORDON GOODWIN, *rev.* H. C. G. MATTHEW

Sources J. G. Nichols, review, *Transactions of the London and Middlesex Archaeological Society*, 4 (1871–4), 70 · *City Press* (23 July 1870) · *N&Q*, 4th ser., 6 (1870), 106 · *Catalogue of the Guildhall Library* (1889)
Wealth at death under £5000: probate, 2 Aug 1870, *CGPLA Eng. & Wales*

Orrock, James (1829–1913), painter and art collector, was born in Edinburgh, the elder son of the four children of James Orrock, a successful chemist and surgeon-dentist, and his first wife. His mother encouraged his lifelong passion for music and painting; as a boy he collected prints and drawings and his portfolio became his most cherished toy. At the age of eight he went as a boarder to the Revd George Corson's Irvine Academy in Ayrshire. There he received his first formal lessons in art from Mr White, an old-fashioned drawing-master who taught him to copy engravings by Landseer and Lawrence; so he developed the accurate if imitative skills which were to distinguish his future output as an artist. He went to Edinburgh to study medicine and decided on a course of surgeon-dentistry while taking tuition in oil painting from James Ferguson. In order to perfect the mechanical branch of dentistry Orrock moved to Leicester as a pupil assistant to Mr Williamson, dividing his time between private practice and the Leicester dispensary. In all available free time he travelled about the midlands filling sketchbooks, and he sent drawings to various exhibitions to supplement his income. During this time he became a pupil of John Burgess RWS, of Leamington, a respected watercolour painter and art collector who did much to improve his watercolour technique and wider appreciation of art. After returning to Edinburgh to finish his medical studies he won the senior gold medal in anatomy. He also resumed lessons with Ferguson and produced his first pictures for exhibition at the Royal Scottish Academy. In 1853 he married Susan (*d.* 1911), the daughter of Charles Gould of Leicester, and established himself in dental practice in Nottingham, where he entered the school of design run by the Fussell brothers and took instruction from Stewart Smith. This period in Nottingham gave him enough time to exploit a sound but unspectacular talent for painting and sufficient increase in wealth to build a significant collection of English pictures, blue and white porcelain, and fine Chippendale and Adam furniture.

In 1866 Orrock gave up dentistry to become a professional painter and moved to London to Bedford Square, where he shared studio space, and then to 43 Bloomsbury Square. In 1870 he took lessons from William Leighton Leitch, and in the following year he was elected to the New Watercolour Society (later the Royal Institute of Painters in Water Colours), proposed by Leitch and supported by the president, Louis Haag. Thereafter he was influential and active in affairs of the society, and he was mainly responsible for building their fine new gallery in Piccadilly, reconstituting the institute, and gaining the royal charter. He was both skilled and prolific in producing mainly watercolours in an early nineteenth-century style and possessed a confident gift for self-promotion. With his powerful proselytizing personality he took up a public stance for the English watercolour tradition exemplified by J. M. W. Turner, David Cox, Peter DeWint, and William Henry Hunt. The essential collector's instinct enabled him to fill his beautiful Adam house at 48 Bedford Square with the best of these and other great artists from which his own *œuvre* derived. Their merits and, as Orrock perceived it, their lack of recognition by the museum world were argued in an outpouring of pamphlets and impassioned articles in the fashionable and influential magazines of the day; most famous was a lecture to the Society of Arts on 11 March 1890, 'On the claims of the British school of painting to a thorough representation in the National Gallery'.

Orrock's persuasive zeal in turn brought him recognition of his own work and acquisitions, and in his fine domestic setting evolved his lucrative secondary career as an art dealer. This high-profile connoisseurship inevitably gave him acceptance within a wealthy Victorian society and access to rich friends and clients. Lord Leverhulme, the industrial soap tycoon and serial collector, was one notable disciple in taste, and between 1904 and 1912 he bought almost all of Orrock's art collection, as well as sixty oils and more than 1000 watercolours by the artist himself. Most of the last decade of Orrock's life was spent as an invalid at Shepperton-on-Thames, Middlesex, where he died at The Chestnuts on 10 May 1913. He was buried at Watford cemetery.   CHRISTOPHER BEETLES

Sources B. Webber, *James Orrock, R.I.: painter, connoisseur, collector*, 2 vols. (1903) · *The Times* (14 May 1913) · *The Leverhulme collection, Thornton Manor, Wirral, Merseyside* (2001) [sale catalogue, Sothebys, 26–28 June 2001] · *CGPLA Eng. & Wales* (1913) · *WWW*, 1897–1915
Likenesses W. W. Ouless, oils, 1870–79, repro. in Webber, *James Orrock*, frontispiece · Walker and Cockrell, photograph (after W. W. Ouless), repro. in Webber, *James Orrock*, frontispiece
Wealth at death £51,449 11s. 6d.: probate, 20 June 1913, *CGPLA Eng. & Wales*

Ortelius, Abraham (1527–1598), map maker, was born at Antwerp on 4 April 1527, the eldest of the three children of Leonard Ortels (1500–1537), a merchant who probably dealt in antiques; his grandfather Wilhelm Ortels had migrated in 1460 from Augsburg to Antwerp, where he died in 1511. When Leonard died in 1537 he left a widow, Anne Herwayers (*fl.* 1527–1581), and three small children, Abraham, Anne (*d.* 1600), and Elizabeth (*d.* 1594). Little is known about Ortelius's education, but his father had started to teach him Latin and he must have studied mathematics on his own. After his father's death he came under the care of his uncle Jacob van Meteren, who had returned from England after spending several years there to escape persecution for his Reformation sympathies. Ortelius became a lifelong friend of his cousin Emanuel van Meteren, who would later settle in London. Ortelius's sister

Abraham Ortelius (1527–1598), by unknown engraver, pubd 1584

Elizabeth also moved to London following her marriage to Jacob Cole in 1562. Their eldest son, Jacobus Colius Ortelianus or Jacob *Cool (1563–1628), was to be an important figure in Ortelius's later years, not least as a correspondent. Ortelius remained unmarried and spent his life in Antwerp, living with his unmarried sister Anne and his mother.

In 1547 Ortelius was admitted to Antwerp's Guild of Saint Luke as an illuminator of maps. Besides colouring maps, assisted by his sisters, he soon traded in books, prints, and maps. He went to the Frankfurt book fairs, where he made contact with Gerardus Mercator in 1554. Business evidently went well, permitting Ortelius to accumulate a library of many volumes and an extensive collection including coins (represented by his *Deorum dearumque capita*, 1573), medals, and objects of natural history. He travelled widely in the Low Countries (reflected in the *Itinerarium per nonnullas Galliae Belgicae partes*, which he published with Joannes Vivianus in 1584), to France, Italy, Germany, and, in 1577, to England and Ireland. Next to his native Dutch (Flemish), he was reported to be versed in French, German, Italian, and Spanish. Ortelius became one of the leading humanists of the Low Countries, acquainted with many European intellectuals of his time. His extensive correspondence and his *Album amicorum*, which constitute the primary sources for his life and work, provide detailed evidence of his extensive network of correspondents. In England his numerous contacts included William Camden, whose *Britannia* was first undertaken at Ortelius's urging, Richard Hakluyt the elder, the naturalist Thomas Penny, the puritan controversialist William Charke, and Humphrey Llwyd, who provided Ortelius with the map of England and Wales published in the 1573 edition of the latter's *Theatrum*.

Having started his professional career as an illuminator of maps, and then become a dealer and collector of maps, Ortelius eventually started making maps himself. His first map, a wall map of the world, was published in 1564 and was followed by a map of ancient Egypt (1565), a wall map of Asia (1567), a wall map of Spain (1570), and a map of the Roman empire (1571). He had already acquired some renown and means when in 1570 he published his *Theatrum orbis terrarum*, considered to be the first modern atlas, being a handy collection of maps of the same dimensions providing a survey of the world as known up to that moment. The first edition contained 53 map sheets and a list of 87 map makers (*Catalogus auctorum tabularum geographicarum*) used as sources for the maps. The *Theatrum* was an instant success, although it was the most expensive book produced in the second half of the sixteenth century. Altogether twenty-one enlarged editions and thirteen supplements (*Additamenta*) appeared during Ortelius's lifetime, followed by another thirteen enlarged editions after his death, the last one in 1641. The original Latin text of the geographical descriptions was translated into German, French, Spanish, Dutch, Italian, and English (1606). Filips Galle issued a popular version of the *Theatrum* as *Spieghel der Werelt* ('Mirror of the world', 1577). Most editions of this pocket atlas are known under the name *Epitome*.

Ortelius was more of a map editor than an original cartographer. He obtained maps and information from the best authorities for the compilation of his atlas. At heart, he was less a 'cosmographus' than a humanist, obsessed by antiquity, and he was a pioneer in the construction of historical maps related to the ancient world. From 1579 onwards, historical maps were added to the *Theatrum* as an appendix (*Parergon*). Unlike the modern *Theatrum* maps, the *Parergon* maps were designed by Ortelius himself. The latest edition of 1624, the only separate *Parergon* edition, consisted of forty-four historical maps. Ortelius also compiled a catalogue of all place names listed by classical authors, along with their modern forms. Initially part of his *Theatrum*, the list assumed such dimensions that it was published separately (*Synonymia geographica*, 1578; reworked as *Thesaurus geographicus*, 1587). Another list of classical place names, devoted exclusively to Ptolemy, continued to be included in the *Theatrum* as *Nomenclator Ptolemaicus*. Finally, Ortelius published a charming booklet devoted to the life and customs of the ancient Germans (*Aurei saeculi imago*, 1596).

Ortelius is depicted by his biographers as a pious, broad-minded, and tolerant man, highly regarded by his contemporaries. It has been suggested that he might have been in contact with the Family of Love, a heterodox sect,

through his friend Christophe Plantin. Nevertheless his Catholic faith does not seem to have been questioned at any time by the agents of the Spanish crown, and he obtained the title of 'his majesty's geographer' from Philip II in 1573. From 1579 onwards an engraved portrait by Filips Galle was incorporated in the *Theatrum*. Most later portraits, such as the one by Rubens (in the Museum Plantin-Moretus in Antwerp), are derived from Galle's engraving.

Ortelius died in Antwerp on 28 June 1598. He was buried on 1 July in the church of St Michael in Antwerp, where a memorial stone and a funeral monument were erected to his remembrance. The monument was destroyed in 1796, and only its medallions were saved, one of them carved with Ortelius's effigy and another with his device around a globe (*Contemno et orno, mente, manu*; 'I scorn and adorn with mind and hand'); these remain today at the Nationaal Scheepvaartmuseum in Antwerp. The gravestone was transferred to Antwerp Cathedral in 1803.

JOOST DEPUYDT

Sources J. H. Hessels, ed., *Ecclesiae Londino-Batavae archivum*, 1: *Abrahami Ortelii at virorum eruditorum ad eundem et ad Jacobum Colium Ortelianum epistulae* (1887) · *Album amicorum Abraham Ortelius*, ed. and trans. J. Puraye and others (Amsterdam, 1969) · F. Sweertius, ed., *Insignium huius aevi poetarum lacrymae in obitum Cl. V. Abrahami Ortelii Antverpiani* (1601) [incl. first biography of Ortelius by Sweertius] · M. van den Broecke, P. van der Krogt, and P. Meurer, eds., *Abraham Ortelius and the first atlas: essays commemorating the quadricentennial of his death, 1598–1998* (1998) [incl. bibliography] · R. W. Karrow and others, *Abraham Ortelius (1527–1598): cartograaf en humanist* (1998) · J. Denucé, *Oud-Nederlandsche kaartmakers in betrekking met Plantijn*, 2 vols. (1912) · R. W. Karrow, *Mapmakers of the sixteenth century and their maps: bio-bibliographies of the cartographers of Abraham Ortelius, 1570* (1993) · M. P. R. van den Broecke, *Ortelius atlas maps: an illustrated guide* (1996) · P. H. Meurer, *Fontes cartographici Orteliani: das 'Theatrum orbis terrarum' von Abraham Ortelius und seine Kartenquellen* (1991) · C. Koeman, *The history of Abraham Ortelius and his 'Theatrum orbus terrarum'* (1964) · H. Wallis, 'Intercourse with the peaceful muses', *Across the narrow seas: studies in the history and bibliography of Britain and the Low Countries presented to Anna E. C. Simoni*, ed. S. Roach (1991), 31–54 · T. M. Chotzen, 'Some sidelights on Cambro-Dutch relations (with special reference to Humphrey Llwyd and Abrahamus Ortelius)', *Transactions of the Honourable Society of Cymmrodorion* (1937), 101–44 · M. McKisack, *Medieval history in the Tudor age* (1971) · R. Boumans, 'The religious views of Abraham Ortelius', *Journal of the Warburg and Courtauld Institutes*, 17 (1954), 374–7 · P. Génard, 'La génealogie du géographe Abraham Ortelius', *Bulletin de la Société de Géographie d'Anvers*, 5 (1880), 312–56 · A. Rouzet, M. Colin-Boon, and others, *Dictionnaire des imprimeurs, libraires et éditeurs des XVe et XVIe siècles dans les limites géographiques de la Belgique actuelle* (Nieuwkoop, 1975), 165–6 · P. van der Krogt, ed., *Koeman's Atlantes Neerlandici*, new edn, 3 [forthcoming]

Archives Koninklijke Bibliotheek, The Hague, letters · Ransom HRC, letters · University of Leiden, letters | Pembroke Cam., Album amicorum Ortelius

Likenesses F. Galle, engraving, 1572, repro. in *Virorum doctorum de disciplinis benemerentium effigies XLIIII* (1572) · J. Jonghelinck, effigy on gold medal, 1578, Rubens Huis, Antwerp · silver medal, 1578, Koninklijk Penningkabinet, The Hague · engraving, pubd 1584, NPG [*see illus.*] · F. Galle, engraving, *c*.1586 (after H. Goltzius), Stedelijk Prentenkabinet, Antwerp · effigy on funeral monument, 1598, Nationaal Scheepvaartmuseum, Antwerp · P. P. Rubens, oils, *c*.1630, Museum Plantin-Moretus, Antwerp · F. Galle, engraving, repro. in *Theatrum orbis terrarum* (1579)

Orton, Arthur (*b.* **1834**). *See under* Tichborne claimant (*d.* 1898).

Orton, Charles William Previté- (1877–1947), historian, was born at Arnesby in Leicestershire on 16 January 1877. He was the younger son of the vicar there, the Revd William Previté-Orton (1837–1912), and his wife, Eliza Swaffield Orton. The latter, whose maiden surname of Orton was adopted by her husband in 1870 when they married, was of Sicilian descent; but the future historian showed few traces of his Italian ancestry in either appearance or temperament. Shy and diffident by nature, he was forced to terminate his school career at Franklin's Preparatory School, Leicester, at the age of fourteen after chronic sight problems led to the removal of his left eye; he was afterwards taught at home. Only in 1905, when he was twenty-eight, did Previté-Orton's health recover sufficiently to enable him to enter his father's old college of St John's, Cambridge. His academic career there was one of unbroken success. After obtaining a first class in both parts of the historical tripos (1907, 1908) and being awarded the Gladstone and members' prizes in the same years, he was elected a fellow of St John's in 1911. He was devoted to the welfare of his college for the rest of his life. In 1913 Previté-Orton married his first cousin, Ellery Swaffield, daughter of the Revd John Swaffield Orton. Throughout their long married life the couple lived in a large house, 55 Bateman Street, Cambridge; and for over thirty years it was there that Previté (as he was universally known) was most often to be found, vigorously engaged in a ceaseless round of writing, teaching, and—above all—editing the work of other medieval historians.

Although little read now, Previté-Orton's first book, *The Early History of the House of Savoy* (1912), immediately established his reputation as a leading English exponent of the exact scholarship and exhaustive attention to sources exemplified by the influential German historical scholarship of the period. Though not a deeply imaginative historian himself, he displayed an exceptional range of detailed knowledge. Somewhat surprisingly, perhaps, his essays on Marsiglio of Padua and his critical edition of the latter's *Defensor pacis* (1928) have proved to be the most enduringly important of his works. Inevitably the more popular and general historical enterprises to which Previté devoted so much of his formidable industry and editorial skills now seem considerably more ephemeral. In sometimes slightly uneasy partnership with his Cambridge colleague Zachary Brooke, he was responsible for supervising the later stages of the most ambitious and demanding English collaborative venture yet attempted in the field of medieval European history: only in 1937 were the eight volumes of *The Cambridge Medieval History* finally brought to a more or less satisfactory close—to Previté's own intense relief. However, Previté-Orton's own historical influence was greatest among the many readers of his three general textbooks. Only after the 1950s did his *Outlines of Medieval History* (1916), his Methuens textbook *A History of Europe, 1198–1378* (1937),

and his posthumously published *Shorter Cambridge Medieval History* (2 vols., 1952) gradually cease to hold their place among the most widely read of all popular introductions to medieval European history.

Previté-Orton's wide erudition and extraordinary editorial energies naturally received recognition outside Cambridge. In 1925 he was invited to become joint editor, and from January 1927 to January 1938 sole editor, of the *English Historical Review*. After receiving the degree of LittD from his own university in 1928, he was elected FBA in 1929. When a chair of medieval history was at last founded in Cambridge in 1937, he was a natural choice as the first professor. Most unfortunately, a haemorrhage in his remaining eye during the Christmas vacation of 1937–8 caused him temporary blindness; he was obliged to resign the editorship of the *English Historical Review* and to relinquish many of his other responsibilities. However, he continued to work strenuously to the very end. Even after his retirement from his chair in September 1942, he agreed to undertake a certain amount of supervision for St John's. It was while teaching a student at his home on 11 March 1947 that he died suddenly of a heart attack. In the opinion of those who knew him personally, as a scholar Previté was lucid and accurate but passionless rather than original. As an editor, however, he was critical, shrewd, painstaking, and generous: few scholars made so sustained a contribution to the reputation of medieval studies at Cambridge during the first half of the twentieth century.   R. B. Dobson

Sources *DNB* · M. D. Knowles, 'C. W. Previté-Orton, 1877–1947', *PBA*, 33 (1947), 351–60 · P. Grierson, 'Bibliography of Professor C. W. Previté-Orton', *Cambridge Historical Journal*, 9 (1947–9), 118–19 · E. A. Benians, *The Eagle*, 53 (1948–9), 54–6 · F. M. Powicke, *Modern historians and the study of history* (1955), 127–41 · P. A. Linehan, 'The making of the *Cambridge Medieval History*', *Speculum*, 57 (1982), 463–94 · C. N. L. Brooke, *A history of the University of Cambridge*, 4: *1870–1990*, ed. C. N. L. Brooke and others (1993)
Archives Cambridge University Press, records · St John Cam., corresp., mainly with J. R. Tanner, relating to *Cambridge medieval history*
Likenesses W. Stoneman, photograph, 1945, NPG · photograph, repro. in Knowles, 'C. W. Previté-Orton', facing p. 351
Wealth at death £20,391 12s. 2d.: probate, 5 Sept 1947, *CGPLA Eng. & Wales*

Orton, Harold (1898–1975), university teacher and dialectologist, was born on 23 October 1898 in the village of Byers Green, co. Durham, younger son of the village schoolmaster, Thomas Orton (*d.* 1942), and his wife, Emily, *née* Blair. He attended King James I Grammar School, Bishop Auckland, and in 1916 went on to Hatfield College, University of Durham, from where he enlisted in the Durham light infantry. He served as a lieutenant from 1917 to 1919. Having been wounded twice on the same day in 1918 he was under threat of the amputation of his right arm, which he refused to allow. He made himself a left-handed writer and invariably offered his left hand to shake hands, as using the right arm caused great pain.

After demobilization Orton studied at Merton College, Oxford, under Professor H. C. Wyld. Another of his tutors was Joseph Wright, editor of the *English Dialect Dictionary*.

He gained the degrees of BA in 1921, BLitt in 1923, and MA in 1924. He became lektor at Uppsala, Sweden, from 1924 to 1928. On 16 December 1925 he married (Dorothy) Joan (1902–1985), the youngest daughter of the Revd R. Burnham, rector of Trimley St Mary's, Suffolk; they had one daughter, Betty Jean.

In 1928 Orton was appointed to lecture at King's College, Newcastle, then a college of the University of Durham. He published in 1933 *The Phonology of a South Durham Dialect*, written following the tradition of Joseph Wright, outlining the historical development of local speech of his native village. At Newcastle he continued to develop his interest in collecting local speech and inaugurated a Northumbrian dialect survey. He used a portable disc-cutting machine to record local voices in homes and hostelries, and material from as early as 1935 survives, copied digitally to tape.

In September 1939 Orton was appointed lecturer in charge of English language at Sheffield University but was very soon seconded as a wartime post to the British Council, where he was assistant education director, later acting education officer. After his return to Sheffield when the war ended he renewed a friendship with Professor Eugen Dieth of Zürich University, and the two began collaboration on a questionnaire to be used in a dialect survey. He was appointed to the chair of English language and medieval English literature at Leeds University in 1946, and he continued through several summer vacations with Dieth, preparing a series of versions of a *Questionnaire for a Linguistic Atlas of England*, which was published by the Leeds Philosophical and Literary Society in 1951.

An English dialect survey became Orton's life's work, and he combined teaching and research tirelessly to promote interest in dialectology. The whole staff of his department was newly appointed in 1946 and he collected around him a distinguished team of academics in the various fields of Old and Middle English literature, philology, phonetics, and Scandinavian, Celtic, and Germanic language studies. He resurrected 'Leeds Studies in English' publications in 1952 and was editor from 1952 until 1964. During his time at Leeds a school of English was formed by merging his own department and that of English literature. He served on many of the governing bodies of organizations promoting English studies. Orton was well remembered by students for his stimulating teaching. He promoted undergraduate and postgraduate dissertations by students on living local dialects.

Orton was a great raconteur and his benevolent manner made him a popular companion over lunch in the senior common room. His highly successful attempts at describing individuals' linguistic backgrounds established his fame as a local Professor Higgins, the character in Shaw's *Pygmalion*. He was an adept administrator and served with skill on senate and its committees during the complex post-war period of expansion of the university. He served for periods as dean of arts and as chairman of the board of arts.

Money for research support was extremely scarce during those years and Orton was determined in his efforts to augment the university's financial support for the establishment and the running of the dialect survey. In addition to obtaining help from private individuals and foundations, he also persuaded the university to appoint qualified research assistants for field work which continued for over ten years. By the time the collection was complete there was material in phonetic script of answers to the more than 1300 questions of the *Questionnaire* from a total of 313 localities. Mobile tape recorders became available about the time the collection began, and a recorded archive was made under his direction. He worked tirelessly at editing the twelve volumes of basic material, and the publication, *Survey of English Dialects, 1962–72*, was achieved at considerable sacrifice of family life and leisure time. The sheer volume of the editorial work he undertook gave rise to the phrase, famous among his collaborators, 'yawn and bash on'. He was unsparing of himself and encouraged those working with him to be the same. His personal energy and his absolute determination to see the *Survey* completed made this massive research survey the sole major language project to be completed in those difficult post-war years.

On retiring from his chair Orton became professor emeritus in 1964. An institute of dialect and folk life studies was founded at Leeds University, and there followed years working with scholars from Britain and abroad. He visited many American universities after his retirement, promoting dialect studies, and collaborated with Nathalia Wright at the University of Tennessee in the publication of *A Word Geography of England* (1974). *The Linguistic Atlas of England* was published after his death.

Among honours bestowed on Orton were the degrees of honorary LittD in 1969 from the University of Durham and doctor of philosophy *honoris causa* in 1970 from the University of Uppsala. He died on 7 March 1975 at Harrowby Crescent, Leeds, having continued to work until a few weeks earlier, when he suffered a stroke. At his funeral at Lawnswood, Leeds, on 12 March 1975 Stewart Sanderson, director of the institute, said friends who mourned Harold would still have a sense of gratitude at the privilege of having known him, which would far outweigh their sense of loss.   STANLEY ELLIS

Sources *WW* · S. F. Sanderson, funeral memorial tribute, 12 March 1975 · C. Fees, *The imperilled inheritance: dialect and folklife studies at the University of Leeds, 1946–1962*, 1: *Harold Orton and the English dialect survey* (1991) · S. Ellis, ed., *Studies in honour of Harold Orton on the occasion of his seventieth birthday* (1969) · K. Wales and C. Upton, 'Celebrating variation: Harold Orton and dialectology, 1898–1998', *English Today*, 14 (1998), 27 · personal knowledge (2004) · private information (2004) [B. Borthwick, daughter] · *CGPLA Eng. & Wales* (1975)

Archives U. Leeds, Brotherton L., fieldwork records and editorial corresp.

Likenesses photograph, c.1964, U. Leeds, school of English

Wealth at death £19,434: probate, 12 May 1975, *CGPLA Eng. & Wales*

Orton, Job (1717–1783), dissenting minister and theologian, the elder son of Job Orton (d. 1741) and Mary Perkins (d. 1762), was born on 4 September 1717 in Shrewsbury, where both his father and grandfather were in trade as

Job Orton (1717–1783), by unknown engraver

grocers and where the family owned substantial property. He received his early education at the grammar school in Shrewsbury, where he remained for eight years until May 1733, when he left for Warrington. There he was under the care of Charles Owen, a dissenting minister of considerable learning; his sole fellow pupil was John Ashworth, eldest brother of Caleb Ashworth of Daventry. Orton remained at Warrington for a year, then spent the month of June 1734 with the family of Thomas Colthurst, Presbyterian minister at Whitchurch in Shropshire. Here it appears that Orton resolved to devote himself to the ministry.

Orton entered the academy of Philip Doddridge at Northampton in August 1734, where he rapidly mastered the style of shorthand used by Doddridge and his pupils, and within a few weeks he was able to take down entire sermons. His ability and diligence evidently endeared him to Doddridge, who described him as '*omni laude major* … the darling of our congregation' and 'perhaps one of the best of preachers and men' (Nuttall, letters 575 and 663). In March 1739 Doddridge appointed him his assistant at the academy, and he began to lecture in the classics and geography; this position was later supported by a grant from the Coward Trust. He preached his first sermon the following month at Welford, Northamptonshire, and continued to preach regularly in the neighbouring villages

and at Doddridge's own church of Castle Hill, Northampton; he was licensed as a minister later the same year.

Orton's talents as a preacher brought him several invitations from dissenting congregations to settle with them as minister. Approaches were made by the nearby congregations at Welford and Rothwell, Northamptonshire, and by Salters' Hall, London, but Doddridge was reluctant to lose the valuable services of his able assistant, and in response to the deacons of Market Harborough in October 1740 wrote that he would not oppose the church's invitation, but neither could he support it. Eventually a vacancy arose in April 1741 through the death of Charles Berry, the minister of a Presbyterian meeting in Shrewsbury. At about the same time the smaller King's Head Independent society, which numbered among its members Orton's mother and father, also lost its pastor, John Dobson, who moved to Walsall. Thus a joint invitation from the united Presbyterian and Independent congregations presented Orton with an opportunity both to consolidate the new union and to return as minister to his family. In 1777 he wrote to Samuel Palmer, 'It was with much regret that I left Northampton. I should like to have lived and died in that post, but for the circumstances of uniting the congregation at Shrewsbury' (J. Orton, *Letters to Dissenting Ministers*, 2 vols., 1806, 2.187, 18 July 1777). Doddridge was resigned to his departure and Orton returned to Shrewsbury, where he preached his first sermon on 18 October 1741; he was ordained the following year.

Within a month of his return, however, Orton's father died. He was greatly affected by the loss, which caused his health to deteriorate; he received treatment from Dr Cheney Hart, and in September 1742 retired to Bath to convalesce. An assistant was sought to ease Orton's burden and Francis Boult was appointed, remaining until the end of 1745, when he moved to Wrexham. Boult was succeeded by Moses Carter, a former student of Orton and Doddridge, but one who had disagreed with Doddridge and incurred his displeasure. Carter was highly regarded in Shrewsbury, but he died suddenly in 1747, and a third assistant, Joseph Fownes, was appointed in 1748. Fownes was to remain a lifelong friend.

In December 1750 Philip Doddridge contracted a severe chill which further aggravated his already consumptive condition. His health continued to decline in 1751, and in July he left Northampton on his final itinerary. Together with his wife he stayed with the devoted Orton in Shrewsbury from 22 July to 21 August before embarking for Falmouth for Lisbon, where he died on 26 October. Orton preached his funeral sermon, 'The Christian triumph over death', on the text of 1 Corinthians 15: 54, a duty that he regarded as 'a signal honour' ('Memoir', viii). In his will Doddridge bequeathed his personal Bible, formerly owned by Samuel Clark, to his loyal pupil and friend and appointed him his literary executor. In this capacity Orton first published in 1755 a volume of Doddridge's hymns, which he presented 'with a chearful Hope, that they will promote and diffuse a Spirit of Devotion' (P. Doddridge, *Hyms Founded on Various Texts in the Holy Scripture*, 1755, preface, iv). He then oversaw the publication of the final three volumes of Doddridge's *magnum opus*, the *Family expositor*, which was completed in 1756.

According to the terms of Doddridge's amended will, Caleb Ashworth was appointed his successor at the academy which, thereupon, moved to Daventry. The succession at Castle Hill, however, remained unresolved, and Orton was approached in March 1752 to fill the vacancy. Alarmed at the prospect of losing him, the Shrewsbury congregation sent Orton a unanimous address entreating him to stay, and Orton eventually declined the offer. Other attempts were made to entice him away from Shrewsbury, including an invitation from a large congregation at Westminster seeking a replacement for its recently deceased pastor, Obadiah Hughes. Orton showed no inclination for London, which he never visited, and he refused on the grounds of his health. The vacancy was eventually filled in 1753 by Andrew Kippis, another of Doddridge's pupils and, subsequently, Orton's biographer.

Orton remained at Shrewsbury, seemingly comfortable with the assistance and companionship of Joseph Fownes, and his ministry passed uneventfully. In 1765, however, his health, never robust, had declined to the point where he reluctantly decided to resign his ministry. He preached his final sermon on 15 September 1765, his forty-eighth birthday as he continued to observe it in the new calendar. Shortly after, he completed his *Memoirs of Doddridge*, eventually published in 1766, attributing the long delay to 'A deep conviction of my own Incapacity for executing it in the most desirable Manner … my ill State of Health and the necessary Duties of my Station' (*Memoirs of Doddridge*, xiii).

The appointment of Orton's successor resulted in an unfortunate secession from the church in Shrewsbury, and Orton found it necessary to seek retirement elsewhere. On 26 October 1766 he duly set up house in Kidderminster, where Benjamin Fawcett, a near contemporary and fellow pupil at Northampton, had been minister since 1745. In retirement he settled into the role of dissenters' patriarch. Kippis remarked on Orton's 'considerable resemblance, in certain respects, to that famous divine' (Kippis, 314), referring to Richard Baxter, his great dissenting predecessor at Kidderminster. He became a prolific correspondent and, despite his lack of a formal university education, was offered an honorary DD by New Jersey College in 1773. He declined the honour; however, in later years he styled himself STP (Sanctae Theologiae Professor).

Orton remained in Kidderminster for the rest of his life and was able to devote more attention to his own writings, which before his retirement had been confined to a few sermons and anonymous tracts. In 1769 he published a series of sermons, *Religious Exercises Recommended*, followed in 1771 by *Discourses to the Aged*, works which, according to Kippis, showed 'an earnest desire in the writer to advance the interests of genuine piety and practical religion' (Kippis, 311). He published three discourses entitled *Christian Worship* in 1775, and a further series of sermons, *Discourses on Practical Subjects*, the following year.

His final work, published in 1777, *Sacramental Meditations*, was a series of fifty reflections on the administration of the sacrament as practised by dissenters.

Between 1744 and 1765 Orton had already compiled what would become his greatest work, a commentary on the Old Testament that was eventually published posthumously as *A Short and Plain Exposition of the Old Testament* in six volumes from 1788 to 1791. Publication was finally overseen by Robert Gentleman, another former student at Daventry academy, Orton's own successor at Shrewsbury, and later Fawcett's replacement at Kidderminster. It was mostly well received; Samuel Palmer, Orton's original choice as editor, thought it 'somewhat similar to Dr. Doddridge's *Family Expositor*', and Kippis described it as 'calculated for general utility' (Kippis, 311) and conveying valuable instruction.

Orton's ecumenical appeal and tolerance of the established church are apparent in the volumes of his correspondence that also appeared posthumously, *Letters to a Young Clergyman* (1791), addressed to Thomas Stedman, a friend of long standing and vicar of St Chad's, Shrewsbury, and *Letters to Dissenting Ministers* (1806), edited by Samuel Palmer. His collected works were eventually published in two volumes, *The Practical Works*, in 1842.

During his years at Kidderminster Orton was fortunate to have the services of a very able physician, Dr James Johnstone, whose care evidently alleviated his sufferings but could not halt the continued decline in his health. By 1783 his condition had deteriorated beyond recovery, and he died at Kidderminster on 19 July, in his sixty-sixth year. According to his wishes, he was buried on 25 July in the chancel of St Chad's, Shrewsbury, in the grave of a former vicar, John Bryan, who had been ejected from St Chad's in 1662. Funeral sermons were delivered by Joseph Fownes and Samuel Lucas. However Orton had directed them to make no reference to himself but only 'exhibit the glory of the gospel and the honour of the Christian ministry'; the first was published later the same year.

Orton had never married, and after a number of small bequests to his doctor and to fellow dissenting ministers the bulk of his estate passed to his nephews. Appropriately, he left a number of books, including the Bible bequeathed by Doddridge, to Thomas Robins, another of Doddridge's former pupils, 'for the use of the Library belonging to the Academy in Daventry'.

It is not easy to place Orton within the complex context of eighteenth-century dissent. His background was Presbyterian but he thought himself 'quite an Independent'. Like his mentor, Doddridge, his view of the Trinity was essentially Sabellian, and, again like Doddridge, his teaching found wide acceptance within other nonconformist traditions and he embraced a large circle of friends and correspondents within both the established and dissenting churches. He evidently regarded his own achievements as something of a disappointment, particularly the period of his ministry at Shrewsbury, although it was almost certainly his perpetual poor health that prevented his being more active. It was as a preacher that he was most successful: Fownes described his style as 'practical, serious and affectionate' (Kippis, 314).

Orton was fiercely protective of what he saw as the traditions of the old dissent. When Lady Huntingdon's preachers came to Kidderminster, he criticized Benjamin Fawcett for encouraging 'strolling preachers' and he later berated him for allowing a drum-major of the Northamptonshire militia to preach from his pulpit. He was deeply suspicious of the spread of Methodism and saw Methodist preachers 'propagating their Antinomian notions' as a threat. Baptists, he considered, had also done much injury.

Although a distinguished minister and theologian in his own right, Orton made no great contribution to nonconformist theology and is now chiefly remembered through his association with Philip Doddridge, first as pupil and protégé, later as assistant, and finally as biographer and literary editor.   DAVID L. BATES

Sources A. Kippis and others, eds., *Biographia Britannica, or, The lives of the most eminent persons who have flourished in Great Britain and Ireland*, 2nd edn, 5 vols. (1778–93), vol. 5, pp. 308–15 · 'Memoir of the Rev. Job Orton', J. Orton, *The practical works of the Rev. Job Orton*, 2 vols. (1842), v–xiv · *DNB* · M. Deacon, *Philip Doddridge of Northampton* (1980) · *Calendar of the correspondence of Philip Doddridge*, ed. G. F. Nuttall, HMC, JP 26 (1979) · R. F. Skinner, *Nonconformity in Shropshire, 1662–1816* (1964) · will, PRO, PROB 11/1107, fols. 239r–241v

Archives BL, sermons, Add. MSS 32007–32009 · DWL, letters and papers | Bodl. Oxf., letters mainly to Thomas Stedman [copies]
Likenesses engraving, repro. in J. Orton, *A short and plain exposition of the Old Testament*, ed. R. Gentleman, 6 vols. (1791) · line engraving, BM, NPG [*see illus.*]
Wealth at death not known: will, PRO, PROB 11/1107, fols. 239r–241v

Orton, John Kingsley [Joe] (1933–1967), playwright, was born on 1 January 1933 in the Maternity Hospital, Leicester, the eldest of four children of William Orton (1905–1978), gardener, and his wife, Elsie Mary Bentley (1904–1966), machinist and charwoman. Their seaside-postcard personae of dissatisfied, domineering wife and frail, henpecked husband later resurfaced in their son's plays. Orton was educated at Marriots Road primary school and, after failing his eleven-plus, at Clark's College, where his mother enrolled him privately on a secretarial course. He was determined to improve both mind and body: the former with a process of self-education (he had read the whole of Shakespeare by the age of fifteen); the latter with a Charles Atlas chest-expander. He found escape from a series of badly paid, boring office jobs in the world of amateur dramatics. Then, after reading an article by Laurence Olivier on the availability of scholarships, and paying for elocution lessons to eradicate his east midlands vowels, he applied to the Royal Academy of Dramatic Art (RADA), and was accepted for 1951.

Orton was proficient enough to gain his diploma when he graduated from RADA in 1953, but his most dramatic encounter took place off-stage, with his fellow student Kenneth Leith Halliwell (1926–1967). Halliwell was seven years older than Orton and affected an air of superiority in both dress and manner. He had an impressive breadth of

John Kingsley Orton (1933–1967), by Lewis Morley, 1965

knowledge and a disconcerting physical presence. Whereas Orton felt alienated from his family, Halliwell was a genuine orphan. Whereas Orton had a puckish, round face, impeccable skin, and smouldering eyes, Halliwell was prematurely bald, heavy, and clammy. Nevertheless, unlike his fellow students, Orton did not dismiss Halliwell as a misfit. Instead, in his first term, he accepted Halliwell's offer to move into his West Hampstead flat. They lived together for the next sixteen years.

In the first years of their relationship Orton was happy to defer to the more experienced Halliwell. After a miserable four-month stint as an assistant stage manager at Ipswich Repertory Theatre, he willingly fell in with Halliwell's plan that they should devote their energies to writing. They lived a modest, almost monastic, existence, eking out Halliwell's small inheritance with a variety of odd jobs, rising at dawn and going to bed at dusk to save on electricity. They collaborated on a series of novels: 'The Silver Bucket' (1953), 'Lord Cucumber' (1954), 'The Mechanical Womb' (1955), 'The Last Days of Sodom' (1955), and 'The Boy Hairdresser' (1956). Each also wrote separately, with Halliwell producing 'Priapus in the Shrubbery' (1959), and Orton 'Between Us Girls' (1957) and 'The Vision of Gombold Proval' (1961).

None of the novels was published in Orton's lifetime, but 'The Vision of Gombold Proval' appeared posthumously as *Head to Toe* in 1971, and *The Boy Hairdresser* and *Lord Cucumber* were published in 1999. While each contains passages of comic invention, the overall effect is laboured, artificial, and monotonous. *Between Us Girls*, however, the diary of would-be actress Susan Hope, published in 1998, constitutes Orton's first exercise in literary ventriloquism which, paradoxically, led to the discovery of his own voice.

The turning point in the development of that voice took place in 1962, when both Orton and Halliwell received six-month prison sentences for stealing and defacing books from Islington Public Library. Orton later recalled their practice of doctoring covers and authors' photographs:

> I once pasted a picture of a naked tattooed man over the photograph of John Betjeman; I think the book was *Summoned by Bells*. And another time I pasted a picture of a female nude over a photograph of Lady Lewisham. It was some book on etiquette.   (Fox, 72)

With an irony he would have relished, the contentious covers were later exhibited in the very library that originally brought the prosecution.

The two men responded to prison very differently: Halliwell attempted suicide, while Orton found it gave him a perspective he had hitherto lacked.

> Being in the nick brought detachment to my writing. I wasn't involved any more and it worked. Before, I had been vaguely conscious of something rotting somewhere: prison crystallised this. The old whore society really lifted up her skirts and the stench was pretty foul.   (Fox, 72)

The experience fired him. After two unperformed apprentice plays, *Fred and Madge* and *The Visitors*, his breakthrough came in 1963 when the BBC Third Programme accepted *Ruffian on the Stair*. By the time it was broadcast, *Entertaining Mr Sloane* had been produced at the Arts Theatre (1964), and audiences had been given their first taste of Orton's singular brand of sexual subversion, Oedipal outrage, and epigrammatic wit. Aspects of the plot were derivative of Pinter—though Orton himself considered the influence to flow in the other direction, claiming that Pinter could never have written *The Homecoming* without the example of *Entertaining Mr Sloane*. The language, however, was all Orton's own, a style that John Mortimer neatly dubbed 'South Ruislip Mandarin' (Lahr, 56).

In order to distinguish himself from John Osborne, John Orton became Joe. And, in the three years before his premature death, Joe Orton enjoyed all the success that John had lacked. Largely because of the enthusiasm and financial support of Terence Rattigan, *Entertaining Mr Sloane* transferred, first to the West End, where it ran successfully for five months, and then to Broadway, where critical hostility killed it. Its West End run was curtailed by the concerted efforts of ticket-sales chief Peter Cadbury and impresario Emile Littler, who led a backlash against the rash of so-called 'dirty plays'.

Orton was astute enough to realize that his career would not be harmed by scandal (indeed, he fostered it himself in letters to the press from his female *alter ego*, Edna Welthorpe). He continued his project of comic sedition in *The Good and Faithful Servant* (1964) and *Loot* (1966), the latter of which underlined his disdain for taboos, with its farcical antics involving a corrupt police inspector, a murderous nurse, a devout Catholic widower, two sexually ambivalent youths, and a corpse. Many would argue with the attitudes that his drama embodied; few could dispute the force of the laughter it generated. Orton wrote the part of Inspector Truscott for his close friend Kenneth Williams,

but Williams's baroque comic style, together with Peter Wood's ornate production, scuppered the play's chances, confirming Orton's instincts that 'unless *Loot* is directed and acted perfectly seriously, the play will fail' (Lahr, 241). Its London première, the following year, fared better, winning Orton the 1966 *Evening Standard* best play award and establishing its enduring place in the repertoire.

Loot's success sparked Orton's creativity. In the ten months between its London opening and his murder, he wrote one one-act play, 'Funeral Games', and revised two others, 'Ruffian on the Stair' and 'The Erpingham Camp', which were presented as the double bill *Crimes of Passion* (1967). He also completed a film script for the Beatles, 'Up Against It', which was never produced (though his work was later represented on screen by indifferent versions of *Entertaining Mr Sloane*, 1969, and *Loot*, 1970). His final play was the madcap farce *What the Butler Saw*. Like *Loot* it received an unsatisfactory première, in a star-studded production at the Haymarket (1969), and its rehabilitation had to wait until Lindsay Anderson's 1975 revival at the Royal Court.

What the Butler Saw, set in a psychiatric clinic where the doctors are far madder than any of the (unseen) patients, culminates in the descent of a Dionysiac figure, Sergeant Match, drugged and dressed in a woman's gown. In the diary that Orton had begun to keep at the instigation of his agent, Margaret (Peggy) Ramsay, he noted with approval Halliwell's recognition of his classical devices. But the couple's intellectual empathy was no longer mirrored elsewhere, and Halliwell felt increasingly sidelined in Orton's life. While Orton's artistic endeavours triumphed, his own exhibition of collages in a King's Road basement failed. While Orton was socially and sexually desirable (as witnessed by the diary record of his fervidly priapic adventures), Halliwell thought himself unloved. Finally, on 9 August 1967, he battered Orton to death at their home, 25 Noel Road, London, and swallowed a fatal dose of sleeping-pills. Orton was cremated at Golders Green on 18 August.

Halliwell's hammer-blows ended Orton's life and established his legend. After seeing *Loot* the critic Ronald Bryden dubbed its author 'the Oscar Wilde of Welfare State gentility' (Lahr, 268). Although, unlike Wilde, Orton would never have claimed to have put his genius into his life and his talent into his works, he has, like Wilde, threatened to become more celebrated for his life (in particular for his sex life) than for his plays. John Lahr's edition of *The Orton Diaries* (1986) and his earlier biography, *Prick up your Ears* (1978), which was adapted by Alan Bennett for the screen in 1987, have combined to create an indelible image of the rough-trade playwright whose private life was largely conducted in public lavatories. Nevertheless, it is as a stylist so unique that he furnished a new critical term, Ortonesque, that he will be remembered. The playwright and critic Frank Marcus put it most pertinently when he wrote of *What the Butler Saw* 'I think it will survive and tell people more about what it felt to be alive in the sixties than anything else of that period' (Fox, 67).

MICHAEL ARDITTI

Sources J. Lahr, *Prick up your ears* (1978) · *The Orton diaries: including the correspondence of Edna Welthorpe and others*, ed. J. Lahr (1986) · J. Fox, 'The life and death of Joe Orton', *Theatre 71*, ed. S. Morley (1971) · S. Shepherd, *Because we're queers: the life and crimes of Kenneth Halliwell and Joe Orton* (1989) · C. Chambers and M. Prior, *Playwrights' progress* (1987) · N. De Jongh, *Not in front of the audience* (1992) · D. Shellard, *British theatre since the war* (1999) · A. Sinfield, *Out on stage* (1999) · b. cert.
Archives University of Leicester, corresp. and papers | SOUND BL NSA, recording of interview of J. Orton by Alan Brien, 044R
Likenesses L. Morley, photograph, 1965, NPG [*see illus.*]
Wealth at death £20,266: administration with will, 29 March 1968, *CGPLA Eng. & Wales*

Orton, Reginald (1810–1862), surgeon, born at Surat, near Bombay, on 27 January 1810, was the only son of James Orton (d. 1857), a surgeon in the East India Company's service and inspector-general of Bombay hospitals, and the grandson of Reginald Orton, rector of Hawksworth, near Richmond, Yorkshire. Reginald was educated at the grammar school, Richmond, under James Tate. He afterwards returned to Bombay, where he was apprenticed to his father. On the completion of his apprenticeship he returned to England and entered St Thomas's Hospital as a medical student. He was admitted a member of the Royal College of Surgeons of England in 1833 and a licentiate of the Society of Apothecaries the following year.

In 1834 Orton became a partner in a Mr Fothergill's practice in Sunderland. On 4 October 1836 he married Agnes Caroline, the second daughter of Orton Bradley of Westmorland. They had one son and two daughters. Agnes died on 31 January 1840, and on 25 March 1841 Orton married Mary Isabella, the eldest daughter of Turner Thompson, a shipowner of Sunderland. They had four children.

Orton lived in Sunderland until shortly before his death, when he took a farm at Bishopwearmouth. He was surgeon to the Sunderland Eye Infirmary and consulting surgeon to the Seaham Infirmary. Throughout his life he was a busy medical practitioner and an active reformer. Sunderland owed to his initiative its system of gas lighting, its water supply, its public baths, its library, and its institute. Orton was one of the leading campaigners against the duty on glass and windows, which was repealed in 1845. He suggested to the government that, if light was still to be taxed, the duty should be regulated by the size of the panes, so that those who could afford large sheets of plate glass should pay more than their poorer neighbours. If it were to be found that the duty could be entirely abolished, however, he advocated the imposition of a moderate house duty, commencing at a certain rental, to make good the loss of revenue. This scheme was eventually adopted.

Orton also took a lively interest in maritime matters, and turned his attention to appliances for saving life at sea. He projected a new form of reel lifebuoy, and invented a lifeboat which was light, low in the water, open so that the sea passed through it (the crew being encased in waterproof bags), and practically incapable of being capsized; for these he took out a patent in 1845. The boat was used on one or two occasions.

Orton died on 1 September 1862 at Ford North Farm, Bishopwearmouth, and was buried in the town cemetery.

He wrote no books (the *Essay on the Epidemic Cholera of India* (1831) is by his uncle of the same name) but did publish two medical papers.

D'A. POWER, *rev.* MARK CLEMENT

Sources *GM*, 3rd ser., 13 (1862), 644–6 · *Sunderland Times* (10 Sept 1862) · d. cert.
Wealth at death under £3000: administration, 25 Oct 1862, *CGPLA Eng. & Wales*

Ó Ruairc, Briain. *See* O'Rourke, Sir Brian (d. 1591).

Orum, John (b. in or before 1364, d. 1436), ecclesiastic and theologian, was probably a member of a Wells merchant family, who by 1388 had begun his career relatively humbly as a vicar-choral of Wells Cathedral. In 1388 and 1391 the chapter granted him absence for study at Oxford University, where by 1406 he had graduated with a doctorate in theology. While at Oxford he made useful connections, gaining access to royal patronage, and serving as the university chancellor's commissary in 1406–7. From 1398 to 1414 his career advanced steadily through a succession of benefices, the most important of which were cathedral appointments: the archdeaconry of Barnstaple, held from 1400 to 1429, canonries at Wells from 1407 to 1431 and Exeter from 1414 to 1436, and the chancellorship of Exeter from 1429 to 1436. On leaving Oxford Orum became a residentiary canon, first at Wells from 1407 to 1422, and later, from 1414 until his death, at Exeter, unusually combining simultaneous residence at two cathedrals.

Orum's principal activity in both chapters was as a scholar rather than administrator. He belonged to a post-Wycliffite generation of highly orthodox theologians promoted by reforming bishops to defend the church against Lollardy: he was active against heresy in the diocese of Wells in 1417. His theological reputation rests on a series of lectures on the Apocalypse delivered to the clergy at Wells Cathedral about 1407–29 (Bodl. Oxf., MS Bodley 859). They concern aspects of clerical office, including church unity, heresy, avarice, and music. Orum owned theological works by Anselm, Aquinas, and Duns Scotus and was interested in mysticism, possessing a copy of the *Revelations* of the Swedish mystic St Bridget. As chancellor of Exeter he was expected to give theology lectures and is known to have preached in the diocese. It may be a reflection of his interest in music that he endowed the singing of an antiphon near his tomb, which in his will he asked should be in the north porch of Exeter Cathedral. Orum exemplified the educated resident clergy advocated by conciliar reformers of the early fifteenth century like Richard Ullerston (d. 1423). He died at Exeter in September 1436.

D. N. LEPINE

Sources Emden, *Oxf.* · J. I. Catto, 'Wyclif and Wycliffism at Oxford, 1356–1430', *Hist. U. Oxf. 2: Late med. Oxf.*, 175–261 · L. S. Colchester, ed., *Wells Cathedral communars accounts, 1327–1600* (1984) · refections accounts, Exeter Cathedral, dean and chapter archives · *Chancery records* · T. S. Holmes, ed., *The register of Nicholas Bubwith, bishop of Bath and Wells, 1407–1424*, 2 vols., Somerset RS, 29–30 (1914) · *The register of Edmund Lacy, bishop of Exeter*, ed. G. R. Dunstan, 5 vols., CYS, 60–63, 66 (1963–72), vol. 4, pp. 24–6
Archives Bodl. Oxf., MS Bodley 859
Wealth at death £239 16s. 9d.: will, *The register of Edmund Lacy*, vol. 4, pp. 24–6

Orundellico. *See* Jemmy Button (*b*. 1815/16, *d*. in or after 1855) *under* Exotic visitors (*act. c.*1500–*c.*1855).

Orwell, George. *See* Blair, Eric Arthur (1903–1950).

Orwell, Sonia. *See* Brownell, Sonia Mary (1918–1980).

Orwin, Charles Stewart (1876–1955), agricultural economist and historian, was born on 26 September 1876 at Horsham, Sussex, the only son of Frederick James Orwin and Elizabeth, daughter of Robert Campbell Stewart, of Blackheath, and niece of George Gawler, governor of South Australia (1838–41). Born into a medical family with a reputation for independent, radical thinking, from his earliest days Orwin wanted to be a farmer and, on leaving Dulwich College, he obtained a county scholarship and entered the South Eastern Agricultural College at Wye. There he established a lasting friendship with the principal, Daniel Hall. He left Wye with a college diploma, and went on to receive another from Cambridge—there was no degree in agriculture at this time—and an associateship of the Surveyors' Institution.

As his family could not afford to establish him in farming, Orwin decided on a career as land agent and joined a house agent in the West End of London; a year later, when the firm opened a country office, he found himself in charge of it. On 18 October 1903 he married Elise Cécile (*d*. 1929), daughter of Edward Renault, of Cognac; they had three sons and three daughters. Also in 1903 Orwin accepted a lectureship at his old college at Wye, of which he later became an honorary fellow. In 1906 he was recommended as agent to Christopher Turnor (1873–1940), who had recently inherited some 24,000 acres in Lincolnshire. Orwin accepted the post, which enabled him to utilize his comprehensive knowledge of the country and to develop his aptitude for far-sighted administration. He was also active in local government and, then and later, in the affairs of the church. This did not prevent him from finding time to work out a system of cost accounting which enabled farmers to exercise the same control over their affairs as industrialists had over their factories, and which would also provide a reliable basis for sound agricultural policy, a contribution soon to be given an added significance by war.

When Daniel Hall, representing the Development Commission, persuaded the University of Oxford to sponsor a research institute in agricultural economics, Orwin became its first director in 1913. Hitherto the subject had not been recognized as one for academic study. Orwin's appointment enabled him to be the architect in this new field, to introduce the subject to a rather suspicious public, to attract promising young students, and to lead the way with his own pioneering researches. He was the first to use surveys, first by county, then by topic, in the study of agricultural economics. When he retired in 1945 nearly every university in England, Scotland, and Wales had a department of agricultural economics, and the Ministry of Agriculture had an economics branch; most of these departments were led or staffed by men who had had their

initial training at the Oxford Institute for Research in Agricultural Economics. Orwin's energy and capacity for original thinking appealed to the young, whom he went out of his way to encourage.

Early in his career at Oxford Orwin became connected with Balliol College, of which he was a fellow (1922), estates bursar (1926–46), and honorary fellow (1946). In 1939 he became the first DLitt in the Oxford school of social studies. As a research worker in land problems, he did not lose sight of practical issues. He served on the council of the Land Agents' Society and of the Royal Institution of Chartered Surveyors; as editor of the *Journal of the Royal Agricultural Society* from 1912 to 1927 he was in touch with the more prominent landowners and farmers in England; and he was a member of the first Agricultural Wages Board (1917–21). He was also president of the agricultural section of the British Association (1921) and assessor to the agricultural tribunal of investigation (1922–4). On 3 January 1931, following the death of his first wife two years earlier, he married Christabel Susan, daughter of Charles Lowry, headmaster of Tonbridge School. They wrote a number of books together, but she was also a prolific author in her own right, particularly after Orwin's death. The coincidence that they shared common initials has led to some confusion in this respect.

Orwin was best known to the general public for his work as an agricultural historian. His first work of this kind was the *History of Wye Church and College*, followed sixteen years later with the *Reclamation of Exmoor Forest* (1929, 2nd edn revised with additional material by R. J. Sellick, 1970). His outstanding contribution to agricultural history was *The Open Fields* (1938; 2nd edn, 1954; 3rd edn, 1967 with preface by Joan Thirsk), written in collaboration with his second wife, Christabel. This provided a detailed reappraisal of the conventional view of the egalitarian nature of traditional strip farming. Utilizing the records of the only surviving open-field system, of Laxton in Nottinghamshire, it showed how the traditional system was primarily a pragmatic response to the prevailing agricultural conditions, rather than, as traditionally claimed, a means of catering for the social needs of the community.

Orwin's other books were aimed at farmers and landowners, and dealt with accounting and legal matters. Orwin also produced articles on farming matters and agricultural policy for the *Manchester Guardian* and the *Yorkshire Post*. His contribution to agricultural economics through articles in professional journals was less significant.

Besides a substantial contribution to teaching and research, as director of the Agricultural Economics Institute, Orwin played a key role in enhancing the role and status of the institute during its difficult embryonic stage. Although the institute was temporarily disbanded during the Second World War, Orwin remained as director until A. W. Ashby was appointed in 1946.

Orwin was very tall, his appearance most impressive, and his face handsome and leonine. Generous in his affections and opinions, he could be easily hurt, for he was a deeply sensitive man. He gave short shrift to the sillinesses of cleverer men, but to the young he reached out with an especial and characteristic courtesy. Orwin died at his home, the Red House in Blewbury, Berkshire, on 30 June 1955.   JOHN CRIPPS, *rev.* JOHN MARTIN

Sources E. H. Whetham, *Agricultural economists in Britain, 1900–1940* (1981) · *The Countryman*, 34 (autumn 1946) · *The Countryman*, 34 (winter 1946) · R. Dixey, *The Countryman*, 52 (1955), 55–8 · *The Times* (1 July 1955), 13 · m. certs. · d. cert. · *CGPLA Eng. & Wales* (1955)
Archives Bodl. Oxf. | BL, memoranda and corresp. with Sir W. J. Ashley, Add. MSS 42255–42256 · JRL, letters to the *Manchester Guardian*
Likenesses R. Murray, oils, Institute of Agricultural Economics, Oxford · photograph, repro. in *The Countryman* (autumn 1946), 36 · photograph, repro. in Whetham, *Agricultural economists in Britain*, 1
Wealth at death £1704 18s. 8d.: probate, 26 Aug 1955, *CGPLA Eng. & Wales*

Osbald (*d.* 799), king of Northumbria, may be identical with the ealdorman (*dux*) of that name who in 780 (the date 779 given by the Anglo-Saxon Chronicle is probably incorrect) gathered an army with another ealdorman called Æthelheard and burned King Ælfwald I's patrician (*patricius*) Bearn at an unidentified place called 'Seletune'. The burning happened on 24 December, so presumably Bearn was incinerated in his house while celebrating Christmas. At some time after 793, Alcuin wrote to King Æthelred I (*d.* 796) and Osbald, now designated as his patrician, and warned them against following those kings and princes who 'perished because of their injustices, rapines, and uncleanliness of life' (Dümmler, no. 18). In 796, following the murder of Æthelred I, certain nobles (presumably those responsible for the murder) made Osbald king, but after only twenty-seven days he was 'deprived of the society of the royal household and of the princes' (Symeon of Durham, *Opera*, 2.57) and forced into flight, first to Lindisfarne and then, in company with some of the monks, by sea to Pictland. Following his deposition, perhaps in the same year but possibly in 798, Alcuin again wrote to him reminding him that more than two years previously he had sworn a vow to give up secular life and enter religion and urging him to fulfil that vow. Apparently he did so, for he died an abbot in 799, when he was buried in St Peter's Minster, York. Osbald's origins are unknown, but his family had clearly been ruthless contenders for royal power, since Alcuin urges him to 'think how much blood of kings, princes and people has been shed through you and your family' (Dümmler, no. 109; *English Historical Documents*, 1, no. 200).

DAVID ROLLASON

Sources E. Dümmler, ed., *Epistolae Karolini aevi*, MGH Epistolae [quarto], 4 (Berlin, 1895); trans. in *English historical documents*, ed. D. Whitelock, 1 (1955), no. 200 · Symeon of Durham, *Opera*, vol. 2 · ASC, s.a.779 [texts D, E] · E. Classen and F. E. Harmer, eds., *An Anglo-Saxon chronicle from British Museum, Cotton MS Tiberius B. IV* (1926) · D. P. Kirby, *The earliest English kings* (1991)

Osbaldeston, George (1786–1866), sportsman, was born on 26 December 1786 at Welbeck Street, London, the only son of the five children of George Osbaldeston (1753–1793), previously Wickins, landowner and MP for Scarborough, and his wife, Jane (*d.* 1821), daughter of Sir Thomas Head. His parents, who were from ecclesiastical,

academic, and political families, were from the south of England, but in 1770 Osbaldeston's grandfather had inherited half the Yorkshire estates of his wife's uncle Fountayne Wentworth Osbaldeston (1694–1770), on condition that he took the Osbaldeston name. The family lived in the Osbaldeston house at Hutton Buscel, near Scarborough. When his father died, the estate was left in trust for six-year-old George, whose mother squandered much of it.

Osbaldeston lived at Hutton Buscel until he was nine years old, from which time he attended successively the schools run by the Revd Carr and the Revd Wallington, both at Ealing, London, and then Eton College (1802–3), where sport was his sole interest. Following a wild spell at Brighton (1803–4), he went to Brasenose College, Oxford, where he matriculated in 1805, but sport took precedence over study and he left in 1807 without a degree. His wealth qualified him to be commissioned lieutenant-colonel of the 5th regiment North Riding local militia from 1809 to 1811, and family connections enabled him to be elected as a whig MP for East Retford, Lincolnshire, from 1812 to 1818, although he rarely attended parliament. The appointment as high sheriff for Yorkshire, in 1829, was more to his taste, as it involved much socializing.

Osbaldeston's obsession was to be the best at competitive sports; he was skilled at billiards, cricket, shooting, rowing, tennis, horse-racing, carriage-racing, and especially fox-hunting. He was sixteen when he first bought hounds; they were Southern hounds, and were too slow for him, so he bought Lord Jersey's dwarf foxhounds and built kennels, to Beckford's design, at Hutton Buscel. In 1810, when a fire destroyed Hutton Buscel Hall, he rented a house with his mother, the Palace, Lincoln, where she could entertain, and he hunted the local Burton country, after purchasing the late Lord Monson's pack. He was reputed to have a son, by a Miss Green, a Lincoln prostitute, but the child was sent abroad. For the next twenty-four years he was an itinerant master of foxhounds, serving nine hunts, including the Atherstone (1815–17), the Quorn (1817–21 and 1823–7), and the Pytchley (1827–34), usually subsidizing the cost; he may have been tolerated only for this reason, as he antagonized all ranks of society by his self-centred, arrogant attitudes and his persistent belief that people cheated him. W. Sparrow has suggested that Osbaldeston's great reputation as a huntsman and hound-breeder was mainly due to the skill of his whipper-in, Tom Sebright: after they parted company, Osbaldeston's hunt declined considerably, and he overworked his hounds (Sparrow, xviii). At cricket, he first played at Lord's in 1808 and bowled and batted for the All England team. He rowed competitively, with success from boyhood to middle age. He was a famous shot, both at game birds and at live pigeons, released from traps, at the Old Hat and Red House clubs, although the bore of his gun was 1½ inches, so he may not have been particularly skilful.

Horse-racing was an obsession that Osbaldeston pursued in many forms. Nicknamed the Squire by the press, he was only 5 feet 6 inches tall but weighed 11 stone and was a powerful man, who rode well as a gentleman jockey in horse races and steeplechases, as well as carriage races with the Four-in-hand Club and trotting races. He rode at least one horse to death. He also bred racehorses at his new seat at Ebberston Hall, Scarborough, Yorkshire, where he desperately prospected for coal, hoping to solve his financial problems. In 1831 he rode an endurance horse race against time, covering 200 miles in ten hours, for a bet of 1000 guineas, which he won easily. The same year he fought a duel on Wormwood Scrubs with Lord George Bentinck over a gambling debt, following a race in which Osbaldeston probably bent the rules; neither was hurt, and the two men later became reconciled.

Gambling was Osbaldeston's downfall; he lost about £200,000 on horses, and was forced to sell his estates in 1848 for £190,000 to pay his debts of £167,000. This sale allowed the purchase of an annuity for £10,500, and provided a safe income for life. On 29 July 1851 he married a widow, Elizabeth Williams, *née* Cornes; they lived in her houses in Regent's Park, London, and in the south of England, where he kept a few racehorses, without success, until his death; he rode his last race in 1855. Osbaldeston, whose exploits made him a folk-hero of the hunting classes, died intestate and virtually penniless at his home, 2 Grove Road, St John's Wood, London, on 1 August 1866, and was buried in Highgate cemetery.

THOMAS SECCOMBE, *rev.* IRIS M. MIDDLETON

Sources E. D. Cuming, ed., *Squire Osbaldeston: his autobiography* (1926) · *DNB* · *The Times* (4 Aug 1866) · *ILN* (11 Aug 1866) · *GM*, 4th ser., 1 (1866), 417 · W. S. Sparrow, introduction, in C. Apperley, *Nimrod's hunting reminiscences*, ed. W. S. Sparrow, new edn (1926) · HoP, *Commons* · J. Kent, *Racing life of Lord George Cavendish Bentinck, and other reminiscences*, ed. F. Lawley (1892), 402–8 · W. Day, *Reminiscences of the turf*, 2nd edn (1886), 84–5
Archives N. Yorks. CRO, corresp. and papers | NRA, priv. coll., letters to E. J. Shirley · U. Hull, Brynmor Jones L., documents deposited by the Baines family of Bell Hall, Naburn, Yorkshire
Likenesses photograph, 1865–6, priv. coll. · J. Brown, stipple (after photograph by J. Watkins), NPG · J. Dighton, watercolour, priv. coll. · J. E. Ferneley, oils (*The Quorn hunt, 1805*), priv. coll. · B. Marshall, oils, priv. coll. · P. W. Mayking, print, Marylebone Cricket Club, Lord's, London · Roffe, stipple (after Woodhouse), NPG · T. C. Wilson, lithograph, BM, NPG; repro. in G. Tattersall, *The cracks of the day*, ed. Wildrake (1841)
Wealth at death virtually penniless

Osbaldeston, Lambert (1594–1659), schoolmaster, was the second son of Lambert Osbaldeston, haberdasher, of London, and his wife, Martha Banks, and brother of William *Osbaldeston. Lambert was educated at Westminster School, where he was a scholar by 1609, and he was elected to a scholarship at Christ Church, Oxford, in 1612. He matriculated as the son of a gentleman on 20 October 1615, and was admitted to Gray's Inn on 25 October. He graduated BA at Oxford on 13 June 1616 and proceeded MA on 27 April 1619.

On 7 December 1621 Osbaldeston had with John Wilson a joint patent from the dean and chapter of Westminster of the headmastership of Westminster School, which was granted to him alone on 4 December 1622. He was incorporated MA at Cambridge in 1628. Having been promised by 13 August 1628 the next vacant canonry of Westminster, he was on 22 July 1629 presented to the tenth stall. In July 1629 he was collated by his friend Bishop John Williams (also dean of Westminster) to the prebend of Biggleswade in Lincoln Cathedral. In 1637 he was presented to the rectory of Wheathampstead, with the chapel of Harpenden, Hertfordshire. Osbaldeston's close association with Williams made him a target for those in the Westminster chapter, led by Peter Heylyn, who wanted to oust the dean. Osbaldeston was accused of charging fees in what ought to have been a 'free' school, of being 'given to company, good fellowship, and muche gadding abrode', and even of pilfering cups and spoons.

In 1638 letters written by Osbaldeston were found in Williams's house at Buckden referring to 'the little urchin' and 'the little medling hocus-pocus' (Rushworth, 2.803). Laud naturally assumed this referred to him. Williams and Osbaldeston were brought to trial in Star Chamber on 14 February 1639, and the latter was condemned to lose all his spiritualities, to pay a fine of £5000 to the king and a like sum to Laud, and to have his ears nailed to the pillory, one in Palace Yard, Westminster, the other outside the school. While the lord keeper was giving judgment Osbaldeston, who was in court but not in custody, hurried home, burnt some documents, and wrote on a paper left on his desk: 'If the Arch-bishop inquire after me, tell him, I am gone beyond Canterbury' (ibid., 2.817). This simple ruse outwitted his pursuers, who searched the Kent ports in vain. It was to be alleged that the archbishop had been prepared to intercede for remission of the corporal punishment and to forbear 'anything done in order to his apprehension' (Heylyn, 221). Osbaldeston hid in Drury Lane until parliament met in November 1640.

Meanwhile Osbaldeston had been deprived of his mastership and his church preferments, but he was restored to the latter by the Long Parliament in 1641 after he had petitioned the Lords through the earl of Bedford (BL, Harleian MS 6424, fol. 8, cited in C. S. R. Russell, *The Fall of the British Monarchies*, 1991, 249). He was pardoned by the king on 28 May 1641 and restored to his Westminster canonry. On 2 November following he was collated to the prebend of Ilton in Wells Cathedral, being installed on 8 November. Subsequently his parochial living was again sequestered. In 1645 an ordinance of parliament for the college of Westminster named him as the only canon who had not deserted his charge. By the act of 1649 which continued the school (following the abolition of deans and chapters) he was given an annuity of £100, which he received until his death.

As headmaster Osbaldeston promoted the study of English composition and of geography. He fostered the school's dramatic tradition, though he may have discontinued the play briefly in sympathy for his friend William Prynne, punished in 1634 for writing against the stage. Osbaldeston's pupils included the future Archbishop John Dolben and future politicians Henry Bennet, later earl of Arlington, and Heneage Finch, later earl of Nottingham, as well as Abraham Cowley, whose *Pyramus and Thisbe*, written at the age of ten, was dedicated to his headmaster. Osbaldeston received a poetic dedication from another

Westminster, Thomas Randolph. The only known composition by Osbaldeston himself is a poem presented to Charles I on the king's recovery from smallpox in 1632. Osbaldeston was buried on 7 October 1659 in the south aisle of Westminster Abbey, without any memorial.

THOMPSON COOPER, *rev.* C. S. KNIGHTON

Sources *Reg. Oxf.*, 2/2.341; 2/3.346 · *Fasti Angl.* (Hardy), 2.112 · *Fasti Angl., 1541–1857*, [Salisbury], 70 · *Fasti Angl., 1541–1857*, [Ely], 81 · *Fasti Angl., 1541–1857*, [Lincoln], 41 · J. Foster, *The register of admissions to Gray's Inn, 1521–1889, together with the register of marriages in Gray's Inn chapel, 1695–1754* (privately printed, London, 1889), 138 · Chapter Act Book 2, Westminster Abbey Muniments, fols. 30v, 32v · BL, Add. MS 5884, fol. 86v · BL, Add. MS 24489, fol. 91 · BL, Add. MS 24492, fol. 62v · BL, Harleian MS 1476, fol. 100v · J. Rushworth, *Historical collections*, new edn, 2 (1721), 803–17 · P. Heylyn, *Examen historicum* (1659), 221 · J. Hacket, *Scrinia reserata: a memorial offer'd to the great deservings of John Williams*, 2 pts (1693), pt. 2, pp. 130–32 · *CSP dom.*, 1628–9, 255; 1638–9, 491 · J. L. Chester, ed., *The marriage, baptismal, and burial registers of the collegiate church or abbey of St Peter, Westminster*, Harleian Society, 10 (1876), 151, n. 4 · J. Sargeaunt, *Annals of Westminster School* (1898), 66–72 · J. D. Carleton, *Westminster School* (1965), 149 · *Letters of John Holles, 1587–1637*, ed. P. R. Seddon, 3, Thoroton Society Record Series, 36 (1986), 476

Osbaldeston, Richard (1691–1764), bishop of London, was born on 6 January 1691, and baptized on 13 January at Hunmanby, Yorkshire, the second son of Sir Richard Osbaldeston (1665–1728) of Havercroft, Yorkshire, and his second wife, Elizabeth (d. 1697), daughter and coheir of John Fountaine, of Melton, Yorkshire. He was educated at Mr Lambert's school at Beverley before being admitted a pensioner at St John's College, Cambridge, on 2 June 1707. He graduated BA in 1711, as 16th on the tripos list, and proceeded MA in 1714 and DD in 1726. He was elected fellow of Peterhouse on the Park foundation on 26 July 1714, which he resigned on 22 March 1715. He was ordained deacon by Sir William Dawes, archbishop of York, in September 1714 and priest early the next year.

Osbaldeston was an ambitious and wealthy whig cleric in Yorkshire. In 1715 he was favoured by William Henry Bentinck, second earl of Portland, with the rich living of Hinderwell, which he resigned in 1747; the same year he was appointed vicar of Hunmanby, the large parish where the Osbaldestons held the manor, a living that he retained until 1762 and where he built a new rectory. While a chaplain to both George I and George II (appointed 23 February 1725, reappointed 1727) he was made rector of Folkton in 1727 (a sinecure worth nearly £900 p.a. and held until 1762), and was dean of York from 19 September 1728. His main achievement at York was collecting the money for a new pavement in the minster and having Richard Boyle, third earl of Burlington, and William Kent lay it; he also officiated at the marriage of Laurence Sterne. He himself married, at Hutton Buscel, Yorkshire, on 30 July 1733, Elizabeth (*bap.* 1694, *d.* 1748), daughter of Thomas and Elizabeth Farside of that parish. She was buried on 10 April 1748, having been known, apparently, for her piety. In the words of William Coates:

> Smooth as the gentle stream her passions flow'd,
> Her Lord, her Love, her only Rapture GOD.
> (Coates, 61)

On 4 October 1747 Osbaldeston was consecrated bishop of Carlisle. He remained in this manageable diocese for fifteen years and ran it with a modest efficiency, thanks to the assistance of the Revd Dr John Waugh, chancellor of the diocese and dean of Worcester, and his chaplains John Brown and Gustavus Thompson. Though he acted as one of George III's first tutors, Osbaldeston spent most of his summers in Carlisle. The sharp exchange of letters with his successor, Bishop Charles Lyttleton, about the decrepit state of the main episcopal residence, Rose Castle, should not count too much against him; Osbaldeston had an interest in building and had spent £1000 on the repair of the castle, selling timber from the park to reimburse himself. It seems likely that the castle was starting to fall into disrepair only in the last few years of Osbaldeston's episcopate as age and ambition for a translation made him opt to spend more time on his estate at Hutton Buscel, where two ordinations were conducted. Until then his pastoral concern is undeniable. In 1753 he conducted an episcopal visitation of the cathedral and made several recommendations for improvements. He attended the coronation of George III as bishop of Carlisle and held the Bible.

As a Pelhamite loyalist Osbaldeston set his hopes on a return to York as archbishop. He applied to the duke of Newcastle for the northern primacy twice, on neither occasion with success. On 13 March 1757 he stressed his 'many connexions' in Yorkshire (BL, Add. MS 32870, fol. 271); on 14 August 1761 the best he could say was that 'my family and I for many years past have never failed to do all in our power for the service of the present government' (BL, Add. MS 32927, fol. 30). He finally achieved promotion the following year, when on the death of Bishop Hayter he was translated to London as his replacement, 'to nobody's joy that I know of', as Richard Hurd waspishly remarked (*Works of William Warburton*, ed. R. Hurd, 7 vols., 1788–94, 1.84). He was in possession for only two years but managed to leave his mark on the diocese, principally by holding a visitation in 1763. Osbaldeston was a discerning patron. He recommended Hurd for preferment, made the historian John Jortin first his domestic chaplain and then archdeacon of London, and in 1762 nominated César de Missy one of the French chaplains to the king. He took an immediate interest in the see of London's supervisory role over the British colonies in North America, where he attempted to uphold church and crown interests, for instance recommending to the Board of Trade in May 1762 that all vestrymen in North Carolina declare their conformity to the liturgy of the Church of England. Osbaldeston had already become involved in colonial Anglicanism before his elevation as bishop of London. Acting for Bishop Thomas Sherlock he had ordained Samuel Seabury as priest on 23 November 1753. As bishop, Osbaldeston lived in Frith Street while putting in hand plans for the rebuilding of Fulham Palace.

Osbaldeston died on 15 May 1764 and was buried in Hutton Buscel church on 29 May. His second wife, Lucy Digby (1723/4–1793), daughter of John and Jane Digby of Mansfield Woodhouse, Nottinghamshire, died on 11 April 1793, aged sixty-nine. He had no children with either wife and his estate at Hutton Buscel passed to his brother Fountayne Wentworth Osbaldeston (1696–1770). He presented communion plate to most of the parishes where he had been incumbent. Osbaldeston's only publications were three sermons, his papers having been burnt on his instructions, and this has not helped his posthumous reputation. Archbishop Thomas Secker was reported to have considered him in 'every way unequal to the situation' of running the London diocese (Chandler, 197). One of his archdeacons, Charles Moss, was in no doubt, however, of Osbaldeston's merit: 'a general knowledge of the world, and of business, a gentlemanly address and deportment, a just sense of his own dignity and a becoming zeal for the interests of religion, are valuable qualities in a Christian Bishop' (Moss, 20). NIGEL ASTON

Sources Dugdale's visitation of Yorkshire, with additions, ed. J. W. Clay, 1 (1899) · J. Hunter, South Yorkshire, 2 vols. (1828–31), 2.413 · Venn, Alum. Cant., 1/3.284 · T. Baker, History of the college of St John the Evangelist, Cambridge, ed. J. E. B. Mayor, 2 (1869), 706 · VCH Yorkshire East Riding, 2.175, 231, 242 · G. Lawton, Collectio rerum ecclesiasticarum de diocesi Eboracensi (1840), 2.291, 296 · PRO, LC 3/64 [47, 108, 167] · G. Aylmer and R. Cobb, eds., York Minster (1977), 257 · T. Friedman, 'The transformation of York Minster, 1726–1742', Architectural History, 38 (1995), 76–81 · C. M. L. Bouch, Prelates and people of the lake counties: a history of the diocese of Carlisle, 1133–1933 (1948), 356–62 · Cumbria AS, Carlisle, DRC 1/8 · R. S. Ferguson, Diocesan history of Carlisle (1889), 172 · W. Roberts, The contribution of John Brown to eighteenth-century thought and literature (1996) · N&Q, 4th ser., 4 (1869), 149–52 · W. Coates, A collection of original miscellaneous poems and translations (1770), 59–64 · J. D. Legard, The legends of Ancaby and Ganton (1926) · Fasti Angl., 1541–1857, [St Paul's, London] · Nichols, Lit. anecdotes, 1.569; 5.405 · Nichols, Illustrations, 3.719 · T. B. Chandler, The life of Samuel Johnson, D.D., the first president of King's College, in New York (1824), 197 · The works of the Right Reverend Thomas Newton (1782), 1.108 · C. Moss, A charge to the clergy of the archdeaconry of Colchester, May 1764, occasioned by the uncommon mortality and quick succession of bishops in the see of London (1764) · private information (2004) [H. Stapleton] · parish register, Hutton Buscel, 22 Aug 1694 [baptism: Elizabeth Farside, wife] · parish register, Hutton Buscel, 10 April 1748 [burial: Elizabeth Farside, wife] · parish register, Hutton Buscel, 29 May 1764 [burial]

Archives East Riding of Yorkshire Archives Service, Beverley, family papers · LPL, corresp. and papers as bishop of London, vols. 1 and 2 · N. Yorks. CRO, papers and letters | BL, letters to T. Birch, Add. MS 4316, fols. 94, 96 · BL, letters to George Grenville, Add. MS 57819, fol. 12 · BL, letters to duke of Newcastle, Add. MSS 32702, fol. 292; 32712, fol. 223; 32870, fol. 271; 32927, fol. 30; 32933, fol. 250 · LPL, bishop of London's jurisdiction in America, pp. 64–6, 74–7, MS 2589 · LPL, Fulham papers, Colonial Section, vi. 290–3; xvi. 226–7, 228–9 · LPL, Fulham papers/Terrick papers, vol. 19

Likenesses T. Hudson, oils, 1752, Jesus College, Cambridge; version, Fulham Palace, London · J. Macardell, mezzotint (after T. Hudson), BM · portrait (aged eighteen), repro. in D. Singh, Portraits in Norfolk houses, 2 vols., ed. E. Farrar (1928)

Wealth at death £500 for support and maintenance of a bishop (or bishops) in America

Osbaldeston, William (c.1578–1645×7), Church of England clergyman and university professor, eldest son of Lambert Osbaldeston, haberdasher, of London, and his wife, Martha Banks, and brother of Lambert *Osbaldeston, attended Westminster School before election to Christ Church, Oxford. Having matriculated early in 1598, aged nineteen, he graduated BA on 24 October 1601 and proceeded MA on 4 July 1604. He resided at Oxford for some years after taking his bachelor's degree, and contributed to poems written at Christ Church on the visit of James I in 1605.

In 1610, having become rector of Great Parndon, Essex, on 13 December Osbaldeston also succeeded George Montaigne as divinity professor at Gresham College. Although he proceeded BD on 19 June 1611 he resigned his Gresham post that year, and in 1612 unsuccessfully sought to return to the college as rhetoric professor. Meanwhile, on 12 May 1612, he was licensed to preach. On 21 January 1617 he became rector of East Hanningfield, again in Essex.

In 1643 Osbaldeston was deprived of Great Parndon, having been charged with preaching against frequent sermons, of encouraging football, and of saying he would cut his throat rather than contribute to the parliamentary cause. On 24 May 1645 he was further summoned before the committee for plundered ministers, which on 5 August deprived him of his other living. His will, made on 3 November 1629 and proved on 25 February 1647, mentions his wife, Mary, and brothers Lambert and Robert. Robert's son, also Robert, was rector of Great Parndon between 1662 and 1680.

C. W. SUTTON, rev. C. S. KNIGHTON

Sources Old Westminsters, 2.705 · Reg. Oxf., 2/2.225; 2/3.228 · J. Foster, The register of admissions to Gray's Inn, 1521–1889, together with the register of marriages in Gray's Inn chapel, 1695–1754 (privately printed, London, 1889), 154 · J. Ward, The lives of the professors of Gresham College (1740), 52–3 · Walker rev., 160–61 · BL, Add. MS 15669, fols. 77v, 91v, 101v, 132 · BL, Harleian MS 1476, fol. 100v · GL, MS 9531/14, fols. 223v–224 · PRO, PROB 11/199, fols. 318v–319

Osberht (d. 867), king of Northumbria, is an extremely obscure figure, owing to the lack of contemporary annals for ninth-century Northumbria. Writing in the thirteenth century, Roger of Wendover represented him as succeeding to the throne in 848, reigning for eighteen years, and being deposed (presumably in 866) in favour of Ælle. Symeon of Durham's Libellus de exordio … Dunhelmensis ecclesie suggests that his reign lasted from 849 to 862, and this is consistent with the length of thirteen years assigned to the reign by other twelfth-century sources associated with Durham. Numismatic evidence, however, indicates that the reign was shorter than either of these spans, perhaps only five years in length; combined with the apparent contemporaneity between coins issued by Osberht and those of Archbishop Wulfhere (elected 854), this suggests that the king's reign in fact extended from c.862 to his death. Little is known about him. According to the eleventh-century Historia de sancto Cuthberto, he alienated Warkworth and Tillmouth from the church of St Cuthbert. The same source agrees broadly with the Anglo-Saxon Chronicle, and Asser, in describing how Osberht and Ælle were in conflict for the throne, but united in face of the first viking assault on York, on 1 November 866. They successfully retook the city, only to be killed in a fresh viking assault on 21 March 867. In the twelfth century Geffrei Gaimar told a story about how Osberht had raped the wife of a Northumbrian called Buern, who took revenge by having Osberht deposed in favour of Ælle and calling in the vikings to kill Osberht.

DAVID ROLLASON

Sources Symeon of Durham, *Opera* · *Rogeri de Wendover chronica, sive, Flores historiarum*, ed. H. O. Coxe, 4 vols., EHS (1841–2) · Symeon of Durham, *Libellus de exordio atque procursu istius, hoc est Dunhelmensis, ecclesie / Tract on the origins and progress of this the church of Durham*, ed. and trans. D. W. Rollason, OMT (2000) · *Asser's Life of King Alfred: together with the 'Annals of Saint Neots' erroneously ascribed to Asser*, ed. W. H. Stevenson (1904) · H. E. Pagan, 'Northumbrian numismatic chronology in the ninth century', *British Numismatic Journal*, 38 (1969), 1–15 · *L'estoire des Engleis by Geffrei Gaimar*, ed. A. Bell, Anglo-Norman Texts, 14–16 (1960) · ASC, s.a. 867 (texts A, E)

Osbern (*d.* 1094?), Benedictine monk, hagiographer, and musician, was precentor of Christ Church, Canterbury, whose life centred around the saints and relics of his priory. The earliest information concerning him comes from his *Miracula S. Dunstani*, where he describes how as a boy he was witness to two of the saint's miracles. It is also known that he visited Dunstan's cell at Glastonbury, perhaps as a pilgrim, and that later in life he experienced directly the saint's miraculous powers when Dunstan enabled him to win an apparently hopeless legal battle.

This love for Christ Church's saints perhaps brought Osbern into conflict with Archbishop Lanfranc, who seems initially to have played down the role of relics in monastic devotion. The first indication of trouble between the two appears about 1076, when, as a disciplinary action, Osbern was sent to Bec to study with Anselm, at that time prior. The exact character of the problem is unknown, but in a letter to Prior Henry, Anselm begs indulgence for Osbern 'who knows himself to have sinned not through pride but through imprudence' (*Anselmi opera omnia*, letters 58, 66). Disobedience to Prior Henry was in fact to be a recurring theme in Osbern's life.

Another of Anselm's letters on Osbern's behalf, written to Lanfranc, provides a surprisingly intimate picture of the monk. He was possessed of a quick mind and a tenacious memory, one who had 'grown venerably fat' under Anselm's tutelage (*Anselmi opera omnia*, letter 39). He also suffered from a recurrent and debilitating illness which manifested itself in a variety of symptoms, making Osbern perhaps especially dependent upon the aid of the saints. Anselm concludes the letter with a request for a life of St Dunstan and for the *Regularis concordia*, which demonstrates that Osbern was not without influence on Anselm, and that his thoughts were never far from the Canterbury saints.

In 1080 Osbern returned to Canterbury, perhaps with Anselm during the latter's first visit to Christ Church. During that visit Anselm convinced a sceptical Archbishop Lanfranc of the validity of St Ælfheah's martyrdom. Lanfranc then embraced the cult with some enthusiasm and commissioned a verse *passio* of the martyr from Osbern. Later, apparently under his own initiative, Osbern composed a prose life and an account of the saint's translation from London to Canterbury during the reign of Cnut. Almost nothing seems to have been known about

Ælfheah's career, but Osbern expanded freely on the few details that he did have. At least one event—Ælfheah's reception of two pallia at Rome, one of them belonging to the pope himself—he took from the career of Lanfranc.

Osbern wrote his other book, the *Vita et miracula S. Dunstani*, during the vacancy after Lanfranc's death. Two earlier lives of Dunstan existed which Osbern used, but again he expanded freely upon the information he had to hand. Some of the details that he added—such as the story of the saint's catching the devil's face in hot tongs, or the description of Dunstan's deathbed rising towards the ceiling in anticipation of his ascension towards heaven—became the most well-known events associated with Dunstan's life. Osbern's was also the first life to state repeatedly and explicitly Dunstan's position of leadership in the tenth-century monastic revival. Earlier lives had made only oblique references to Dunstan's role as a reformer, but Osbern characterized the archbishop as one who directly and forcefully expelled secular canons from their churches. This portrait is undoubtedly inaccurate. But it must have seemed an important claim to make if, as Eadmer suggests in his *Historia novorum*, Christ Church's monastic status was under attack during Lanfranc's archiepiscopate.

The full extent of the authority enjoyed by Osbern within the Christ Church community is indicated by two letters he wrote to Anselm in 1093, enjoining the abbot of Bec to accept the office of archbishop to which he had been elected. He also urges Anselm to take no action towards his consecration or in regard to any ecclesiastical issue without first consulting Osbern himself. This sense of authority must have brought him into further conflict with Prior Henry, and in fact Eadmer does say that, during the vacancy, Osbern led a search of Christ Church's relics without first seeking permission from the prior, as monastic obedience required.

The last extant reference to Osbern is in one of Anselm's first letters as archbishop, addressed to Prior Henry, Osbern, and to certain other monks. The letter concerns disorder at the monastery because of the reluctance of some of the brethren to obey Henry's commands. Whether Anselm addressed Osbern as a respected member of the community who could restore order or as a possible source of the turmoil itself must remain uncertain. Osbern may have been the disobedient monk whose death in 1094 is reported by Goscelin.

Osbern was also a renowned musician. None of his musical compositions has been identified, which is unfortunate, since William of Malmesbury described Osbern as 'taking the prize' in music.

J. C. RUBENSTEIN

Sources Osbern of Canterbury, 'Vita Sancti Dunstani', *Memorials of St Dunstan, archbishop of Canterbury*, ed. W. Stubbs, Rolls Series, 63 (1874), 68–164 · Osberno, 'Vita s. Alphegi archiepiscopi Cantuariensis', *Anglia sacra*, ed. [H. Wharton], 2 (1691), 122–48 · *Willelmi Malmesbiriensis monachi de gestis regum Anglorum*, ed. W. Stubbs, 2 vols., Rolls Series (1887–9) · *S. Anselmi Cantuariensis archiepiscopi opera omnia*, ed. F. S. Schmitt, 6 vols. (1938–61) · *Eadmeri Historia novorum in Anglia*, ed. M. Rule, Rolls Series, 81 (1884) · 'Edmeri Cantuarensis cantoris nova opuscula de sanctorum veneratione et obsecratione', ed. A. Wilmart, *Revue des Sciences Religieuses*, 15 (1935),

184–219, 354–79 · J. C. Rubenstein, 'The life and writings of Osbern of Canterbury', *Canterbury and the Norman conquest: churches, saints and scholars, 1066–1109*, ed. R. Eales and R. Sharpe (1995), 27–40 · M. L. Colker, 'A hagiographic polemic', *Mediaeval Studies*, 39 (1977), 60–108, esp. 68–96

Osbern (*d.* 1103), bishop of Exeter, was the son of Osbern the seneschal, who was guardian of Normandy for the then Duke William. He was therefore brother of William Fitz Osbern, earl of Hereford. He went to England during the reign of Edward the Confessor, and was one of the king's chaplains, holding land at Stratton, Cornwall, at the time of Edward's death. As a royal chaplain he was present at the dedication of Westminster Abbey on 28 December 1065, and retained that position after the conquest, when he witnessed a charter to St Martin's, London, in 1068. The suggestion that he became the king's chancellor depends entirely upon a charter to St Augustine's, Canterbury, which is largely spurious.

Osbern was consecrated bishop of Exeter at St Paul's, London, on 27 May 1072, by Archbishop Lanfranc. He was present as bishop at the councils held at Windsor in 1072 and London in 1075. A dispute arose between Osbern and the monks of St Nicholas's, Exeter, which he seems to have resolved after prompting from Pope Paschal II. William of Malmesbury relates with approval Osbern's preference for English rather than Norman customs. He seems to have made little impact at Exeter, since, according to Malmesbury, 'after the manner of ancient prelates, he was content with old buildings'. The earliest building work there dates from the time of his successor. Osbern was blind for some years before his death and for this reason William of Warelwast, who eventually succeeded him, may have tried to have him deprived of his bishopric. Osbern died in the latter part of 1103, before the scheme could take effect.

C. L. KINGSFORD, *rev.* MARIOS COSTAMBEYS

Sources *Willelmi Malmesbiriensis monachi de gestis pontificum Anglorum libri quinque*, ed. N. E. S. A. Hamilton, Rolls Series, 52 (1870) · A. Farley, ed., *Domesday Book*, 2 vols. (1783), fol. 121b · *Reg. RAN*, 1.22 · D. Wilkins, ed., *Concilia Magnae Britanniae et Hiberniae*, 1 (1737) · G. Oliver, *Lives of the bishops of Exeter, and a history of the cathedral* (1861) · F. Barlow, *The English church, 1066–1154: a history of the Anglo-Norman church* (1979)

Osbern fitz Richard (*fl. c.*1066–1088). *See under* Richard Scrob (*fl.* 1052–1066).

Osborn, Elias (*bap.* 1643, *d.* 1720), Quaker minister, was born at Chillington, Somerset, where he was baptized on 24 June 1643, the son of Timothy Osborn; his mother, whose name is unknown, died when he was two years old. Osborn records in his autobiography that his parents 'were religious people, of those who were then called Puritans' (Osborn, 16), and that his father kept him at school and made him attend weekly lectures and repeat the substance of the sermon on the way home. Elias was, as he recalled, 'inclined to religion' when he was thirteen, but also loved 'pleasure and vanity' (ibid., 18). At about fifteen he left school and was employed in the clothing trade. At the Restoration he records how 'I tried the common

prayer, but was very soon weary of it, and indeed of all other religions that I then knew' (ibid., 19).

At the age of nineteen Osborn first heard of the Quakers, and after reading some of their books finally became 'convinced of the truth' (Osborn, 19). His father and other puritan relatives strongly opposed his conversion, and Osborn left home and began working in the clothing trade for a widow with two daughters, all of whom were Quakers. On 1 October 1665, at the age of twenty-two, Osborn married Mary Horte (*d.* 1675), the younger of the daughters. His father, though strongly objecting to this Quaker daughter-in-law, afterwards 'loved her dearly', and desired her to be buried by his side (ibid., 21). Indeed, he eventually accepted his son's beliefs and 'came to have a love for Friends, and would sometimes go to meetings, which was a great comfort to me' (ibid., 29).

Osborn and his family entertained many travelling Friends at their home in Chillington, but began to feel the brunt of persecution in the 1670s. In 1670 Osborn and his mother-in-law were imprisoned at the suit of Lord Paulet's steward for non-payment of tithes, and their goods were seized more than once for the same cause. After the passage of the 1670 Conventicle Act, Osborn remembered, 'the nation seemed all of a flame' and the 'worst of men let loose to ruin honest neighbours by a law' (Osborn, 23). A large monthly meeting at Stoke Gregory was the first in the area to be broken up, and other meetings were disturbed, chiefly by Henry Waldron, a JP and militia captain who employed informers and illegally consigned numbers of Quakers from meetings as 'rioters' and 'conventiclers' (ibid., 25). Osborn and some others procured a counsel to plead their case and defeated Waldron at quarter sessions. Some land was then bought and a large meeting-house built at Ilminster, 3 miles from Chillington, mainly at the expense of Osborn and his family.

In 1673 Osborn moved to Chard, where he continued to suffer frequently from distraints on his property. On 12 July 1675 his wife died, leaving four children. About three years later, in 1678, he married Mary Smith, with whom he had a further three children. Of the seven children, the eldest son, Elias, born at Chillington on 15 June 1668, settled at Bristol and died there on 3 August 1703, and the second son, Timothy, born on 30 April 1670, died at Ilminster on 15 November 1704.

On 23 September 1680, the day appointed for the Somerset quarterly meeting at Ilchester, the Friends met in the house of an innkeeper named Abbott, as the house usually rented by them from the gaolkeeper was full of prisoners. After the meeting for worship they had divided as usual for separate business meetings—women upstairs, men below—when Captain Waldron appeared with his troop, took down many names, and, treating the assembly as two conventicles, fined Abbott £40. Assisted by Osborn and other Quakers, the innkeeper brought an action at common law against Waldron at Wells assizes, but without success. A month later Waldron went to Ilminster while Osborn was preaching, and carried him and sixty-nine others before Sir Edward Phillips. The group included Osborn's wife, who suffered a miscarriage as a result of the turmoil. Phillips fortunately allowed Osborn time to explain the case, so that only he and a few others were committed to prison. They appeared at Bath and were remanded until the next sessions, but through the influence of Lord Fitzhardinge, who represented that the Quakers were clothiers and large employers of labour, were released. Osborn was returned to prison, but allowed considerable liberty and discharged at the next sessions. On 28 April 1685 Osborn and three Somerset Quakers drew up an address to the county MPs in which they outlined the ill treatment of Friends, quoting the declaration of Breda as a guarantee for liberty of conscience, apparently to no effect.

After his release Osborn continued preaching around the villages of Somerset, whose inhabitants joined the Quakers in large numbers. He held a meeting of 500 people in the market-house of Wellington, and in Devon at Spiceland, Collumpton, Okehampton, and Crediton. He was prominent in the local business meetings of the Society of Friends as well as in the quarterly meeting, and he was often chosen to represent his county at the yearly meeting in London. He was evidently well liked in these circles, for a testimony by the quarterly meeting written after his death described him as 'a great and good man', who was 'well gifted in the ministry' and 'of good service' in meetings for business (Osborn, 4–7).

On 26 October 1711, aged sixty-eight, Osborn completed his autobiography, published after his death as *A Brief Narrative of the Life, Labours and Sufferings of Elias Osborn* (1723). On 13 December 1718 he wrote of his inability through age and deafness to be present at the funeral of William Penn, of whom he said, 'I can truly say, that I never loved any man better on a religious or civil account' (Osborn, 121). Osborn died on 29 June 1720 in his own house at Chard, and was buried in the Quaker burial-ground there on 5 July.

CHARLOTTE FELL-SMITH, *rev.* CAROLINE L. LEACHMAN

Sources E. Osborn, *A brief narrative of the life, labours, and sufferings of Elias Osborn* (1723) · J. Kendall, ed., *Letters on religious subjects written by divers Friends deceased*, 2 (1805), vol. 2 · J. Besse, *A collection of the sufferings of the people called Quakers*, 1 (1753) · W. Tanner, *Three lectures on the early history of the Society of Friends in Bristol and Somersetshire* (1858) · S. C. Morland, ed., *The Somersetshire quarterly meeting of the Society of Friends, 1668–1699*, Somerset RS, 75 (1978) · J. Smith, ed., *A descriptive catalogue of Friends' books*, 2 (1867) · digest registers of births, marriages, and burials, RS Friends, Lond. · will of Timothy Osborn, PRO, PROB 11/480, sig. 35, fols. 261v–262r · PRO, PROB 11/577, sig. 259, fols. 111r–112r
Wealth at death approximately £300; plus household goods; also £1367 of deceased son Timothy's money ('for the use and benefit of the … surviving children of … Timothy Osborn'): will, PRO, PROB 11/577, sig. 259

Osborn, Emily Mary (1828–1925), genre and portrait painter, was born in Kentish Town, London, and was baptized on 19 March 1828 at Old Church, St Pancras, the eldest of the nine children of the Revd Edward Osborn (*c.*1794–1859), clergyman, and his wife, Mary Bolland (*c.*1806–1868). Emily Osborn's childhood was spent in Kent and at West Tilbury, Essex, until 1842 when the family moved to London, where Edward Osborn had obtained a curacy. Her mother had herself wanted to study art professionally and so it was presumably with her encouragement that Emily Osborn entered Mr Dickinson's academy in Maddox Street in 1848, receiving three months' instruction from John Mogford and James Matthew Leigh. Her father then wishing to withdraw her from the school, she studied privately with Leigh at his home before spending a year learning to paint in oils at Leigh's General Practical School of Art in Newman Street. Emily Osborn lived with her family at 37 Bernard Street, Bloomsbury (by 1851 until 1855) and at 30 Upper Gower Street, renamed 133 Gower Street in 1864 (1855 until about 1865).

Osborn's portraits and genre paintings—their titles often embellished with poetical quotations from Tennyson, Collins, Longfellow, Byron, and her brother, Edward Haydon Osborn—were exhibited widely during these years at the Royal Academy, the British Institution, the Birmingham Society of Artists (BSA), the Society of British Artists (SBA), the Liverpool Academy (LA), the Royal Manchester Institution, and also at Mr Wallis's French Gallery in Pall Mall and at the Crystal Palace Picture Gallery. In 1854 Charles James Mitchell, a member of the stock exchange and friend of the Osborns, bought *Pickles and Preserves* (exh. RA, 1854) and his brother, William Mitchell, commissioned a life-sized portrait of *Mrs. Sturgis and Children* (exh. RA, 1855; priv. coll., Chicago) for £210. Queen Victoria having purchased *My Cottage Door* (exh. RA, 1855; the Royal Collection) Emily Osborn added a studio to the family house and over the next ten years enjoyed considerable success in her career. A small number of her most highly acclaimed early works represent 'a sort of protest in favour of the afflicted and down-trodden classes' (*Queen*, 4 Dec 1880, 501): *Nameless and Friendless* (exh. RA, 1857, and International Exh. 1862; priv. coll., studies in York City Art Gallery and Ashmolean Museum, Oxford), purchased for £250 by Lady Chetwynd, draws attention to the difficulties faced by women artists struggling to earn a living. Other examples include *The Governess* (exh. RA, 1860, Liverpool Academy, 1860, sketch, Royal Manchester Institution, RMI, 1861, Liverpool Society of Fine Arts, LSFA, 1862, sketch; the Royal Collection), her second painting bought by Queen Victoria, which was engraved, and *Half the world knows not how the other half lives*, awarded £63 at Crystal Palace in 1864 as the best historical or figure subject in oil by a British artist (exh. Liverpool Institute of Fine Arts, LIFA, 1864, sketch, RMI, 1865, and Royal Scottish Academy, 1877).

The effect of death is the subject of several other works such as *For the Last Time* (exh. RA, 1864, and LIFA, 1864, sketch; priv. coll.) and *God's Acre* (exh. Mr Wallis's French Gallery, Pall Mall, 1866; exh. Christies, 7 November 1997), which was engraved for the *Art Journal* in 1868. Other acclaimed paintings include *The Escape of Lord Nithisdale from the Tower, 1716* (exh. RA, and RMI, 1861, and LIFA, 1863; exh. Sothebys, New York, 26 May 1994), priced at £315 in Manchester and also engraved for the *Art Journal*, and *Tough and Tender* (exh. RA, and LA, 1859, BSA, 1860, and

SBA, 1862) which was awarded a silver medal by the Society for the Encouragement of the Fine Arts in 1862 and bought by William Mitchell.

About 1861 Emily Osborn travelled to southern Germany visiting Hesse, Württemberg, and Munich. In 1865 or 1866 she left England again and in 1866 spent some months in Venice studying at the Accademia with Karl Theodor von Piloty (1826–1886). She then returned to Munich, where she continued to receive Piloty's advice. Following her mother's death in 1868 and the destruction by fire in 1869 of a painting measuring 9 feet and with fifteen figures depicting Württemberg peasants returning from a festival—executed in 1866 for Mr Wallis's gallery in Pall Mall (the French Gallery)—Emily Osborn painted little for two years. During the Franco-Prussian War she and a sister spent six months nursing the wounded in Heidelberg. From 1870 to 1873 she exhibited in London from 9 Amalien Street, Munich.

On her return to England in 1873 Emily Osborn lived and worked in London (at 58 Charlotte Street in 1873 and 12 Buckland Villas, Belsize Park, in 1875) and in Glasgow (4 West Regent Street in 1876). In 1877 she settled in the studio formerly occupied by Thomas Landseer—10A Cunningham Place, St John's Wood, London—where Emily Davies, pioneer of higher education for women, was a close neighbour and where she remained until the end of her life. Her paintings continued to appear at the Royal Academy, the Birmingham Society of Artists, and the Royal Manchester Institution and she also exhibited intermittently at the Dudley Gallery, Society of Lady Artists, Royal Scottish Academy, Atkinson Art Gallery, Southport, and the Paris Salon from the 1870s and at the Grosvenor Gallery, New Gallery, and Crystal Palace Picture Gallery from the 1880s. Despite this comprehensive exhibiting programme Emily Osborn did not maintain her previous reputation—a result, possibly, of Germanic influence on her style. She did, however, receive silver medals for *Hero Worship in the 18th Century* (exh. RA, 1873, RMI, 1875, and Society of Women Artists, 1900) and for a painting called *For Ever* depicting a young nun seated in her cell. *Cornish Balmaidens Going to Work* (exh. RMI, 1873), depicting surface workers at a Cornish tin mine, entered the National Museum of Wales, Cardiff, in 1881.

Following a visit or visits to north Africa in the early 1880s—where she may have stayed with the artist and campaigner for women's rights, Barbara Leigh Smith Bodichon—Emily Osborn devoted herself mainly to landscape, her exhibited work from that time comprising not only Algerian subjects (1881–1907) but also subjects from the Norfolk broads (1886–1906), Venice (1890–1902), Devon (1900–04), and Moret-sur-Loing, near Paris (1902–6). Two exhibitions of her Norfolk landscapes were held at the Goupil Gallery (GG), London, in 1886 and 1887. Among occasional portraits were at least two of Barbara Leigh Smith Bodichon; a large oil of 1884 (exh. GG, 1884, and BSA, 1885), presented to Girton College, Cambridge, has since disappeared; a smaller picture, currently at Girton, may be one or both of the portraits exhibited at the Society of Women Artists in 1899 and 1913. She also portrayed

another feminist, Jane Cobden (exh. National Gallery, London, 1890; SWA, 1891; and Whitechapel Loan Exh., 1891). Emily Osborn's own interest in the position of women is attested by her signing of the petition for the admission of women to the Royal Academy Schools (1859) and the declaration in favour of women's suffrage (1889). By 1886 she was sharing her home with her 'great friend' (*The Lady*, 2 Sept 1886, 183), Mary E. Dunn, whose portrait she exhibited at the Society of Women Artists in 1893.

Emily Osborn died, unmarried, at the age of ninety-seven, on 14 April 1925 at her home, 10A Cunningham Place, St John's Wood. Further examples of her work are in the Yale Center for British Art, New Haven, Connecticut. CHARLOTTE YELDHAM

Sources J. Dafforne, 'British artists: their style and character, no. LXXV, Emily Mary Osborn', *Art Journal*, 26 (1864), 261–3 · *Art Journal*, 30 (1868), 148 · *Art Journal*, 34 (1872), 10 · *The Queen* (4 Dec 1880), 501 · *The Queen* (5 Oct 1889), 465 · *The Lady* (2 Sept 1886), 183 · Graves, *RA exhibitors* · Graves, *Brit. Inst.* · A. Graves, *A century of loan exhibitions, 1813–1912*, 1 (1913); repr. (1970) · J. Johnson, ed., *Works exhibited at the Royal Society of British Artists, 1824–1893, and the New English Art Club, 1888–1917*, 2 vols. (1975) · C. B. de Laperriere, ed., *The Royal Scottish Academy exhibitors, 1826–1990*, 4 vols. (1991) · J. Soden and C. Baile de Laperrière, eds., *The Society of Women Artists exhibitors, 1855–1996*, 4 vols. (1996) · E. Morris and E. Roberts, *The Liverpool Academy and other exhibitions of contemporary art in Liverpool, 1774–1867* (1998) · D. Cherry, *Painting women: Victorian women artists* (1987) [exhibition catalogue, Rochdale Art Gallery, Manchester, 4 April – 30 May 1987] · P. Nunn, *Victorian women artists* (1987) · L. Nochlin, 'Some women realists', *Women, art and power, and other essays* (1988) · exhibition catalogues (1852–98) [Birmingham Society of Arts] · exhibition catalogues (1861–92) [Royal Manchester Institution] · exhibition catalogues (1872); (1877); (1889) [Dudley Gallery, London] · exhibition catalogue (1879); (1881) [Paris Salon] · exhibition catalogue (1879) [Atkinson Art Gallery, Southport] · exhibition catalogues (1882–90) [Grosvenor Gallery, London] · exhibition catalogues (1888–1907) [New Gallery, London] · exhibition catalogues (1895–9) [Crystal Palace Picture Gallery] · artist's file, archive material, Courtauld Inst., Witt Library · CGPLA Eng. & Wales (1925) · IGI · census returns, 1851 · d. cert.

Likenesses Fradelle & Young, photograph, repro. in *Queen* (5 Oct 1889), p. 465 · T. G. Stowers, engraving, repro. in *The Lady*

Wealth at death £569 18s. 4d.: probate, 8 June 1925, CGPLA Eng. & Wales

Osborn, Sir Frederic James (1885–1978), town planner and writer, was born on 26 May 1885 in Kennington, London, the eldest in the family of the two sons and one daughter of Thomas Frederick Osborn (d. 1913), mercantile clerk of Kennington, and his wife, Edith Paull (d. 1925). He was educated at dame and council schools, and left Hackford Road board school, Brixton, at fifteen for an office boy's job with a firm of City importers. This was the first of several clerking jobs over the next twelve years which, although demanding little of him, allowed plenty of time to read and lay the foundations of his lifelong enthusiasm for literature. His free time was largely devoted to the Fabian Society and the Independent Labour Party, to evening classes, and to numerous amateur literary, dramatic, debating, and cricket clubs in south London. With G. B. Shaw and H. G. Wells his idols, he became a typical self-educated, lower middle-class, metropolitan intellectual, developed an enthusiasm for socialism, and discovered in himself an above-average talent as a writer and behind-the-scenes organizer.

In 1912, almost fortuitously and knowing nothing of Sir Ebenezer Howard and his proposals for garden cities, Osborn successfully applied for the post of secretary to the Howard Cottage Society in Letchworth Garden city, Hertfordshire. Letchworth, then nine years old and with 8000 inhabitants, was a revelation. Overnight he found himself in a gracious, planned town which combined healthy housing with town and countryside. Letchworth embodied a radical form of land ownership and control, which offered a rich, do-it-yourself culture, and had been founded as a model for the reconstruction of urban society. Together with Howard's ideals it provided a focus, a practical outlet, for Osborn's reforming enthusiasms: he became an ardent convert to the garden city movement and discovered in the ideal of planned towns a lifetime's cause.

As Howard's disciple and friend, Osborn became an accomplished, nationally known exponent of the garden city case and an influential figure in Letchworth life. With Howard, C. B. Purdom, and W. G. Taylor he founded the New Townsmen to rescue garden city principles from garden suburb deviations. Under its auspices he published *New Towns after the War* (1918), an argument for 100 government-sponsored new towns; he wrote it in the British Museum while declining military service on political grounds. When Howard purchased land for a second garden city in 1919, it was no surprise that Osborn moved with him to become company secretary and later estate manager of Welwyn Garden City Ltd. On 30 August 1916 he married Margaret Paterson (1889–1970), a teacher, and daughter of Andrew Robb, a commercial traveller, of Glasgow; her wisdom and strength were an essential part of his achievements. They had a son and a daughter.

At Welwyn, one of a brilliant team working in difficult circumstances, Osborn learned the skills and experienced the problems of town building; he contributed to most aspects of the town's planning and development, and played a full part in its social and political life. He held parish and urban district council offices from 1921 to 1931, was a founder of the local Labour Party and Fabian Society, founded the Welwyn Drama Festival with Flora Robson in 1929, and was prominent in business and cultural life. It was, therefore, something of a bombshell when he was abruptly dismissed from his job in 1936, when the Welwyn Company was restructured. Within the year, however, he was appointed financial director to the local Murphy Radio Ltd and became honorary secretary to the Garden Cities and Town Planning Association (subsequently the Town and Country Planning Association).

For the next forty years, variously as honorary secretary, chairman of the executive committee, editor of *Town and Country Planning*, chairman of the association, president or *éminence grise*, Osborn worked with astonishing energy, single-mindedness, and political acumen to further the association's policies for limiting the size of cities, industrial relocation, low-density housing, green belts, and planned decentralization to new towns. The report of the royal commission on the distribution of the industrial population (1940), for which he had prepared and argued evidence and whose findings were something of a triumph for him, marked the beginning of seven intense years which proved also to be his most active and effective. He sat on the government's panel of physical reconstruction, was on the Labour Party post-war reconstruction committee (while advising the Conservative and Liberal Party equivalents), advised Patrick Abercrombie over the county of London and greater London plans, and as member or lobbyist was involved with innumerable committees and organizations concerned with planning or the environment. He became particularly identified as an advocate of low-density housing—one who, on the basis of his first-hand knowledge of ordinary people's housing preferences, vigorously contested prevailing architectural fashions for urbanity and multi-storey flats. His labours were crowned by membership of the 1946 new towns committee, chaired by Lord Reith, which in nine arduous months produced the blueprints for establishing and administering new towns. These Lewis Silkin embodied in his historic New Towns Act (1946) and Town and Country Planning Act (1947).

During these years Osborn also revised *New Towns after the War* (1942), produced a new edition of Howard's *Garden Cities of To-morrow* (1946), wrote *Green-Belt Cities* (1946, 1969), and edited and contributed to the Rebuilding of Britain series. Through journalism, pamphlets, correspondence, lectures, and broadcasts he incessantly bombarded politicians, planners, and public with propaganda for dispersal and new-town policies.

The war years had offered Osborn a unique opportunity to affect future events and were undoubtedly the period of his greatest influence. The new towns committee marked the high point of these endeavours, for to his regret he did not play an official part in developing the new towns, although he was offered the chairmanship of Bracknell. He remained active as a writer and propagandist, becoming the conscience of the movement against the vicissitudes and fashions of governments, planners, and architects—a force within the association into his eighties. With Arnold Whittick he wrote *The New Towns: the Answer to Megalopolis* (1963, 1969, 1977), the standard work on the British experience, while his *Can Man Plan?* (1959) recorded his lifelong devotion to writing light verse. *The Letters of Lewis Mumford and Frederic J. Osborn, 1939–70* (1971) give a rounded picture of a literate 'specialist on things in general', a man for whom new towns were but one of many interests.

Osborn received many honours and was knighted in 1956. He was particularly proud of receiving the Ebenezer Howard memorial medal (1968) and the gold medal of the Royal Town Planning Institute (1963). He took mischievous delight, as scourge of architectural fashions, in his honorary fellowship of RIBA. His election as vice-president and honorary member of the International Federation for Housing and Planning recognized his worldwide influence. On 16 August 1974 he married Shirley

Catherine (b. 1934/5), daughter of musician Brinley Stephens, and fifty years his junior. Osborn died at Queen Elizabeth II Hospital, Welwyn Garden City, on 1 November 1978 after suffering a stroke. He was cremated at the West Hertfordshire crematorium six days later. He was survived by his second wife.   MICHAEL HUGHES

Sources Welwyn Garden City Public Library, Sir Frederic Osborn archive · A. Whittick, *F. J. O.—practical idealist* (1987) · private information (2004) [family] · personal knowledge (2004) · m. cert. [Shirley Stephens]
Archives Welwyn Garden City Central Library, corresp. and MSS | University of Strathclyde, Glasgow, corresp. with G. L. Pepler
Likenesses K. Jonzen, bronze head, 1965–9, Sir Frederic Osborn School, Welwyn Garden City; copy, public library, Welwyn Garden City
Wealth at death £47,173: probate, 2 Feb 1979, *CGPLA Eng. & Wales*

Osborn, George (1808–1891), Wesleyan Methodist minister, was born at Rochester, Kent, on 29 March 1808, the eldest of ten children of George Osborn (1764–1836) and his wife, Hannah (*née* Lambly). His father was a draper in the town, a class leader among the Methodists for twenty-one years, and a member for over fifty. George junior was educated at Dr Hulett's school at Brompton. He married Elizabeth Chubb, with whom he had eleven children, one of his sons entering the Wesleyan ministry and another becoming headmaster of the New Kingswood School, Bath.

Osborn entered the Wesleyan ministry in 1828, and was initially appointed to the St Albans circuit. Thereafter he had nine more appointments in Brighton (1829–31), Liverpool (1831 and 1845–8), Deptford (1832), Stockport (1833–6), London (1836–42), and Manchester (1842–5 and 1848–51). He was conspicuous as a debater very early in life, and rose rapidly in the estimation of his co-religionists, being elected in 1849 into the legal hundred, the governing body of the conference. In 1851 he was nominated one of the Wesleyan foreign missionary secretaries, and retained that office for seventeen years. The jubilee of the foreign missions took place in 1863. In the same year Osborn was elected president of the conference, albeit by the narrowest of majorities, and rendered great service to the missions by his advocacy of their claims in the large towns in England. On the retirement of the Revd Thomas Jackson in 1868 he was elected theological tutor at Richmond College, the institution for training Wesleyan missionaries, and continued to reside there until 1885. He was invited to deliver the first Fernley lecture in 1870, on the work and mission of the Holy Spirit. In 1881, in the year of the first ecumenical Methodist conference, he was for the second time elected to the chair of the conference, on this occasion by a large majority. From 1885 he was a supernumerary minister, and died at his home, 24 Cambrian Road, Richmond, Surrey, on 18 April 1891.

In his approach to theology and church polity Osborn was emphatically on the conservative wing of Wesleyan Methodism, regarded by many as carrying the torch of Jabez Bunting, to whom he largely owed his own elevation in the connexion. Indeed, he himself once declared that in

resisting any attempt to alter the principles of Methodism he would spend his last sixpence and breathe his last breath. He therefore became an implacable opponent of all significant reformist tendencies in Wesleyanism, passionately defending the conference line during the secessions in the 1830s and 1840s, and resisting the admission of lay representatives to the conference in 1875–6. At the same time, his commitment to Methodist tradition resulted in two major and long-enduring pieces of historical scholarship, a thirteen-volume edition of *The Poetical Works of John and Charles Wesley* (1868–72) and his *Outlines of Wesleyan Bibliography* (1869). He also wrote or edited eleven other books and pamphlets, furnished prefaces or introductions to at least seven works, and contributed articles to the *Wesleyan Methodist Magazine* and *London Quarterly Review*.   G. C. BOASE, *rev.* CLIVE D. FIELD

Sources G. J. Stevenson, *Methodist worthies: characteristic sketches of Methodist preachers of the several denominations*, 3 (1885), 360–8 · [B. Gregory], 'George Osborn, D.D.', *Wesleyan Methodist Magazine*, 114 (1891), 468–78 · H. D. Osborn, 'Two Methodist families', *Proceedings of the Wesley Historical Society*, 46 (1987–8), 93–6 · G. Osborn, 'Memoir of the late Mr George Osborn, of Rochester', *Wesleyan Methodist Magazine*, 62 (1839), 785–803 · d. cert.
Archives JRL, Methodist Archives and Research Centre, corresp. · Wesley's Chapel, London, letters
Likenesses portrait, repro. in *ILN* (2 May 1891), 563 · wood-engraving (after photograph by Appleton & Co.), NPG; repro. in *ILN* (6 Aug 1881), 124
Wealth at death £1706 2s. 3d.: probate, 27 May 1891, *CGPLA Eng. & Wales*

Osborn, Henry (*bap.* 1694, *d.* 1771), naval officer, was baptized on 27 August 1694 at Campton, Bedfordshire, the second son of Sir John Osborn, second baronet (1659–1720), of Chicksands, Bedfordshire, and his second wife, Martha (*c.*1665–1713), daughter of Sir John Kelynge, serjeant-at-law. His parents were both from the Bedfordshire gentry. Following the example of his elder brother, Peter, Henry chose a naval career, entering as a volunteer per order in the *Superb* (Captain James Moneypenny), on 20 December 1710, and proceeding to the Mediterranean. Rated as midshipman, he later joined the *Lion* (Captain Robert Bouler, or Bowler), before passing for lieutenant on 8 March 1717. On 3 July 1717 he was promoted lieutenant in the *Barfleur* by Sir George Byng, commanding the fleet in the Baltic (Byng's daughter Sarah had married his half-brother John). His subsequent service as lieutenant is not clear, as a Henry Osborne also passed for lieutenant a year later, and many conflicting appointments are found in 1720–21. It seems that the future admiral was in the *Experiment* in 1719 on the north African coast and then in the *Yarmouth* between 1722 and 1725. He was certainly in the *Leopard* early in 1726, exchanging into the *Bredah* on 22 June, the flagship of the fleet then in the West Indies. On 12 October 1727 he was appointed commander of the sloop *Weazle*, in which he returned to England, and was immediately appointed captain of the *Squirrel* on 4 January 1728; while in command of her he was appointed governor of Newfoundland, a position he held until 1731. The post was at that time normally held by a sea officer who went there for each season. In 1734 he commanded the *Portland* in the channel and in 1738 took the *Salisbury* to the Mediterranean with Sir Chaloner Ogle. Later he was sent to the West Indies to join Edward Vernon's fleet and returned in the *Chichester* (80 guns) in 1741. About 1740 he married Mary Hughes, daughter of the commissioner of Portsmouth Dockyard; they had two sons and three daughters.

Osborn was next appointed to the *Princess Caroline* (80 guns), and joined Thomas Mathews's fleet in the Mediterranean. He therefore participated in the unsuccessful battle off Toulon on 11 February 1744, where he was in the van division, next astern of Rear-Admiral William Rowley, and was closely engaged, despite his ship having her lower deck awash. In the subsequent courts martial, he deposed that he considered Vice-Admiral Richard Lestock's neglect to get into station in the day and night before to be a principal cause of the miscarriage. After the battle Osborn, now a senior captain, gained considerable experience in command of detached squadrons, being sent to escort a convoy of victuallers and storeships with the supplies urgently needed by the Mediterranean fleet. He was, however, blockaded in the Tagus for a time by a French squadron, but eventually brought the convoy to Gibraltar. He then operated against Franco-Spanish supplies on the Italian coast and made an unsuccessful attempt to intercept a French Levant convoy. During 1745, now a commodore, he commanded a force cruising between capes Spartel and St Vincent to intercept ships arriving at Cadiz. He returned to England later in 1745, and declined an offer of the governorship of Louisbourg, apparently for financial reasons.

Osborn reached flag rank on 15 July 1747, and for a time commanded at the Nore, before being appointed commander-in-chief at the Leeward Islands on 5 February 1748. Reaching Barbados at the end of April, he arranged the homeward bound convoys and precautions against privateers, and initiated a programme of repairs for the dockyard at English Harbour, Antigua. However, the coming of peace cut short his command, and he left Barbados in December. Before sailing Osborn had to initiate proceedings against the first lieutenant of the *Chesterfield* who had seized the ship off Cape Coast Castle, west Africa, before being overpowered and imprisoned by other members of the crew who then sailed on to Barbados.

In early 1756 with the approach of the Seven Years' War, Osborn took a squadron to escort convoys and then reconnoitre Brest. He then commanded at Portsmouth for a time, until on 2 May 1757, as a full admiral since 2 February, he was appointed commander-in-chief, Mediterranean, Rear-Admiral Charles Saunders being second-in-command. Osborn's task of watching the French Toulon fleet and protecting British trade proved particularly difficult after the loss of Minorca. None the less he successfully performed this role with, it seems, aid from Augustus Hervey. The Toulon fleet emerged, but was obliged to take refuge in Cartagena, so Osborn based his force on Gibraltar to prevent their escape into the Atlantic. In 1758 rumours of a reinforcement coming from Toulon were prevalent, and Osborn took his squadron east in the hope

of intercepting them. On 28 February the French squadron was sighted and Osborn ordered general chase, his ships separating after the four French ships. Two were captured, one was driven ashore, the smallest escaped. One of the captures was the *Foudroyant* after a remarkable action by a ship of its size, the *Monmouth* (Captain Arthur Gardiner). This success disposed of the threat and the squadron in Cartagena returned to Toulon. Osborn, however, soon afterwards suffered a stroke and was obliged to resign his command, though he recovered quite well. He received the thanks of the House of Commons, and by the influence of the duke of Bedford, was MP for Bedfordshire from December 1758 until 1761, though he is not known to have spoken or voted. In 1763 he succeeded Lord Anson as vice-admiral of England, and later he received a pension. Osborn died on 4 February 1771 at his home in Hill Street, Berkeley Square, Westminster; he was survived by his wife.

Although John Charnock gives a very unflattering character to Osborn, other evidence does not fully support him. Augustus Hervey refers to him as a 'worthy good man' (*Hervey's Journal*, 243), and while he puzzled Edward Boscawen, he made it clear that they were on good terms. Osborn seems to have cared for the seaman, for several sought to go with him to the Leeward Islands (PRO, ADM 1/306) and he was dismayed by the frequent arrests for desertion and proposed a 'rambling area' round Portsmouth to give seamen some freedom (Rodger, 191). His ability and humanity are further evident in his correspondence while commander-in-chief at Portsmouth (PRO, ADM 1/920–4). Although he may have had interest in Bedfordshire, from which county both Byng and the duke (first lord of the Admiralty, 1744–8) came, it is evident from his appointments that he was considered reliable, even if his principal action was a chase which did not require tactical skill.   A. W. H. PEARSALL

Sources *DNB* · 'Boscawen's letters to his wife, 1755–1756', ed. P. K. Kemp, *The naval miscellany*, ed. C. Lloyd, 4, Navy RS, 92 (1952), 163–256 · J. S. Corbett, *England in the Seven Years' War: a study in combined strategy*, 2 vols. (1907) · J. Gwyn, ed., *The Royal Navy and North America: the Warren papers, 1736–52* (1973) · [earl of Bristol], *Augustus Hervey's journal*, ed. D. Erskine (1953) · R. Pares, *War and trade in the West Indies, 1739–1763* (1936) · H. W. Richmond, *The navy in the war of 1739–48*, 3 vols. (1920) · N. A. M. Rodger, *The wooden world: an anatomy of the Georgian navy* (1986) · R. Beatson, *Naval and military memoirs of Great Britain*, 2nd edn, 6 vols. (1804) · J. Charnock, ed., *Biographia navalis*, 4 (1796), 197 · GEC, *Baronetage* · M. M. Drummond, 'Osborn, Henry', HoP, *Commons, 1754–90* · letters, PRO, ADM 1/306, 384, 924, 2242 · muster books, PRO, ADM 36/299 (*Experiment*), 304 (*Bredah*), 1737 (*Leopard*), 4072 (*Superb*), 4522 (*Weazle*), 4695 (*Yarmouth*) · passing certificates, PRO, ADM 107/3, pp. 50, 62 · *GM*, 1st ser., 41 (1771), 95 · *IGI* · *Political and social letters of a lady of the eighteenth century, 1721–1771*, ed. E. F. D. Osborn [1890] · will, PRO, PROB 11/964, fol. 187

Archives NMM, logbooks and order books
Likenesses attrib. C. Arnulphy, oils, *c.*1744, NMM

Osborn, John (*c.*1580–*c.*1634), worker in pressed horn and whalebone, was born in Worcestershire, where he appears to have been engaged in making cases, sheaths, or small boxes in horn and other material. About 1600 he emigrated to the Netherlands, possibly for religious reasons, and settled at Amsterdam. There, on 2 June 1607, he married Frances Cotton of Berkshire, then living at Uilenburg in the Netherlands. Osborn became one of the principal workers in horn and whalebone in Amsterdam, and his works appear to have been highly valued. When the Northern Company of Amsterdam was granted a monopoly of Dutch whaling in 1614, it sought to market its products, and in 1618 John Osborn was granted an exclusive patent to prepare and supply baleen. This was disputed in 1620 by a Dutch cabinet-maker, and in that year Osborn obtained a second exclusive patent. This was disputed by Osborn's brother, Richard, in 1624, when John Osborn obtained a third patent giving him the exclusive right to work baleen. Osborn specialized in pressing portrait medallions in horn and baleen, using copper stamps made from models provided by the goldsmith Jan Lutma the elder (c.1584–1669). The reliefs were made by pressing the prepared baleen between pairs of positive and negative copper stamps, and were finished by being blackened to imitate ebony, then a fashionable and expensive import. Twelve surviving reliefs in public collections can be attributed to Osborn on the basis of four signed and dated portrait medallions of Frederick Henry, prince of Orange, and his wife, Amalia von Solms (a pair in the British Museum, London, and single portraits of Amalia von Solms in the Koninklijk Penningkabinet, Leiden, and the Kunstgewerbe Museum, Berlin). Osborn died about 1634 in Amsterdam. L. H. CUST, rev. DORA THORNTON

Sources P. J. J. van Thiel, 'Hollandse lijsten van balein, Bekends en onbekends over Jan Osborn en zijn octrooi', *Miscellanea T. Q van Regteren Altena* (Amsterdam, 1969), 104–10 • N. de Roever, 'Johannes Osborn, kunstig baleinwerker', *Oud Holland*, 5 (1887), 309–11 • D. S. van Zuiden, 'Johannes Osborn', *Oud Holland*, 33 (1915), 87–90 • S. Muller, 'John Osborn', *Oud Holland*, 33 (1915), 199–206 • H. E. van Gelder, 'Naschrift op het artikel van S. Muller', *Oud Holland*, 33 (1915), 206–7 • F. A. Dreier, 'Ein Fischbeinmedaillon mit Bildnisder Amalia von Solms', *Berliner Museen*, 18 (1968), 59–64 • B. T. Hill, 'Baleen bacchanal', *Kendall Whaling Museum Newsletter*, 4/1 (1986), 10–11 • S. Vandenberghe, 'Portretten in walvisbalein prins Maurits (1567–1625) en koning Hendrik IV van Bourbon (1553–1610)', *Antiek* (Nov 1994), 12–16 • A. Schaverien, 'Horn, medals and straw', *The Medal*, 32 (1998), 31–8

Osborn, Robert Durie (1835–1889), army officer, was born at Agra, India, on 6 August 1835, the son of Henry Roche Osborn (*bap.* 1798, *d.* 1849) and his wife, Charlotte (1808/9–22 Sept 1894), third daughter of Major Robert Durie, 11th light dragoons. Henry Roche Osborn was baptized at Swanage on 29 June 1798, entered the East India Company's service in May 1819, and served mostly with the 54th native infantry, but latterly was lieutenant-colonel of the 13th native infantry; he died at Ferozepore on 10 March 1849. Robert was educated for a cadet at Dr Greig's school at Walthamstow, and was appointed ensign of the 26th Bengal native infantry on 16 August 1854, becoming lieutenant on 31 July 1857. He served throughout the Indian Mutiny War of 1857–9, and was present in the actions of Bulandshahr on 27 September and of Aligarh on 5 October 1857. He commanded a detachment of the 4th Punjab infantry at the actions of Gungaree and Puttiallee, was present in various operations against the rebels in the Agra district, served with Colonel Troup's column in Oudh in November 1858, and took part in the action at Biswan. From January to May 1859 he was with the Saugor field force under General Whitelock; he afterwards commanded a field detachment in the Ooraie district, and later on defeated a rebel force at Tudhoorkee. In 1859–60 he was with the Bundelkhand field force under Brigadier Wheeler. He was lieutenant in the Bengal staff corps (30 July 1857) and captain (20 December 1865). On 25 August 1859 he became adjutant of the 2nd regiment of Sikh irregular cavalry, converted into the 12th regiment of Bengal cavalry in 1861, in which Osborn was third squad officer from 4 November 1865 to 17 May 1866. He was captain in his regiment from 8 June 1868 to 1872. In the latter year he was appointed tutor to the Paikharah wards, became major on 20 December 1873, and retired with the honorary rank of lieutenant-colonel on 1 May 1879. He served through the Afghan campaign of that year, but retired after the signature of the treaty of Gundamuk.

Osborn was a serious thinker on both religious and political topics. As a young man he enjoyed the friendship of F. D. Maurice and of Charles Kingsley, and occasionally wrote papers in the magazines on Maurice's religious position and influence. While in India he studied oriental religions, and spent fourteen years on the complex materials for his two works, *Islam under the Arabs* (1876) and *Islam under the Khalifs of Baghdad* (1877), which were highly valued by serious students. Osborn was a zealous advocate of Indian rights, and his retirement from the army was largely due to his dissatisfaction with Lord Lytton's policy which, in his opinion, outraged Indian sentiment and needlessly provoked the Anglo-Afghan War of 1879. On his return from India he settled at Hampstead, and mainly devoted himself to journalistic and literary work. He became London correspondent of the Calcutta *Statesman*, and took a leading part in the conduct of the London *Statesman*, which was published for a few months in 1879 and 1880 to oppose Disraeli's Indian policy. In the *Scotsman*, the New York *Nation*, and the *Contemporary Review* he also wrote much on India and on native claims to popular government. He also wrote *Friends of the Foreigner in the Nineteenth Century: a Critique* (1879) and *Lawn Tennis: its Players and How to Play* (1881). Osborn married at Trinity Church, Bayswater, on 12 November 1864, Edith, daughter of the Revd Gregory Rhodes; they had two daughters and she survived him. A keen lawn-tennis player, Osborn collapsed from syncope on Good Friday, 19 April 1889, while playing Ernest Renshaw, the champion of all England, at the Hyde Park tennis court, London, and died that day at 3 Porchester House, Porchester Road, Bayswater, London.

G. C. BOASE, rev. ROGER T. STEARN

Sources *The Times* (25 April 1889) • F. E. Barnes, *Records of Hampstead* (1890) • *The Athenaeum* (27 April 1889), 538 • *Statesman* [Calcutta] (May 1889) • private information (1894) • C. Hibbert, *The great mutiny, India, 1857* (1978) • B. Robson, *The road to Kabul: the Second Afghan War, 1878–1881* (1986) • V. C. P. Hodson, *List of officers of the Bengal army, 1758–1834*, 3 (1946)
Likenesses J. R. Hodgson, oils, exh. RA 1877, priv. coll.
Wealth at death £400 1s. 1d.: administration, 28 May 1889, *CGPLA Eng. & Wales*

Osborn [*née* Byng], **Sarah** (1693–1775), letter writer, was born in October 1693 at Southill, Bedfordshire. She was the eldest and only surviving daughter of George *Byng, first Viscount Torrington (1663–1733), the eminent naval officer, and his wife, Margaret (1670–1756), daughter of James Master of East Langden, Kent. She had six surviving brothers, including Admiral John *Byng (*bap.* 1704, *d.* 1757). Presumably educated at home, Sarah was married in August 1710 to John Osborn (1683–1719), eldest son of Sir John Osborn, bt, of Chicksands Priory, Bedfordshire, and his first wife, Elizabeth Strode. John Osborn died in January 1719, a few months before his thirty-sixth birthday, leaving his wife with two children: Danvers, born in 1715, and John, born in 1718. Three other sons and a daughter predeceased their father; the infant John died in the summer of 1719. Danvers became the third baronet on the death of his grandfather in April 1720.

Only a few months after her twenty-fifth birthday Sarah Osborn became the guardian of her son, with responsibility for maintaining his inheritance. The earliest of her published letters are primarily concerned with settling the estate and collecting all the rents and other income owed to her son. She depended on the help of her brother Robert (1703–1740) in dealing with the lawyers and the courts, for 'When they see a man appear for one they will not delay so, but a poor woman is made nothing of—she may live upon air seven year if she can' (*Letters of Sarah Byng Osborn*, 9). Nevertheless, hers was the guiding force in managing her son's inheritance and seeing to the upkeep of his houses and lands.

In 1740 Danvers Osborn married Lady Mary Montagu, fourth daughter of George, first earl of Halifax. She died in 1743 after the birth of her second son, John. Greatly distressed by his wife's death, Danvers withdrew from his family, travelling and serving with the Bedfordshire regiment during the Jacobite rising of 1745. He died in North America as governor of New York in 1753. Once again Sarah was left with small children to bring up and an estate to manage. Not only was she once again supervising the Osborn family interest, but as the senior surviving member of the Byng family, with her only brother an admiral often absent in the Mediterranean, she was concerned with that family as well. She played an active part in trying to secure mercy for her brother John Byng after he was sentenced to death on 22 January 1757 for failing to engage the French fleet at Minorca the previous year. Osborn, based not at Chicksands but at a town house in Charles Street, Berkeley Square, sought the help of John Russell, fourth duke of Bedford, a member of the cabinet and the most powerful neighbour of the Byngs and the Osborns. In her letter she emphasized both the justice of her cause and her status as 'a distressed sister, surrounded only by weeping females, and helpless boys' (*Letters of Sarah Byng Osborn*, 85). This was followed by a cogently argued letter to the lords of the Admiralty questioning the procedure and principles under which Byng had been sentenced. Despite her efforts Byng was executed on 14 March; his last letter to Osborn, dated two days before his death, told her that 'All has proved fruitless, but nothing

wanting in you that could be done' (ibid., 89). Osborn continued to maintain her connections with the duke of Bedford, and her letters to her younger grandson John, written while he was a fledgeling diplomat in Italy from 1766 to 1768, kept him informed of political issues and ministerial changes at home with the family's links to the Bedford whigs in mind. Her elder grandson Sir George Osborn, fourth baronet (1742–1818), married in 1771; she welcomed the birth of his son John in 1773.

Sarah Osborn, born and married into families widely connected among the gentry and nobility of Bedfordshire and surrounding counties, lived a typical life for one of her time and class. She visited country houses, travelled on the continent, went to Bath, spent the season in London, attended court. Her family and friends were active in county politics. A number of family members held government appointments. However, she also had to assume responsibilities which few women would have expected to bear. Nearly forty years of her life were spent as guardian of her son and grandsons and in caring for the Osborn family inheritance. She learned to deal with lawyers, bankers, tenants, servants, and tradesmen. She carried on through family tragedies both great and small. She died in November 1775 and was buried on 22 November at Campton, Bedfordshire.

The challenges that Sarah Osborn faced are remembered because at least some of her letters survived and were published by a descendant in 1890 and republished with a new commentary in 1930. Although this collection contains only ninety-three letters and has doubtless been edited, it is sufficient to provide a picture of her life. The cost of housekeeping, the difficulties of renovation at Chicksands, and problems with livestock during her years of guardianship take up as much space as politics. Accounts of local elections and marriage arrangements, especially when these involved acquaintances, are frequently reported. Osborn's letters contain little about literature, art, or music. What has been published, however, is valuable for the reader who wants to know more about the life and responsibilities of aristocratic women in the eighteenth century. Osborn surely wrote many more letters than this small number, and it is to be hoped that more of her correspondence has survived. Perhaps other family members were not so ruthless as Osborn herself; she wrote to Danvers in 1739 that 'I have amused myself with cleaning away drawers full of old letters and papers, to save you the trouble of making a bonfire of them' (*Letters of Sarah Byng Osborn*, 43). This was, alas, often the fate of women's letters.

BARBARA BRANDON SCHNORRENBERG

Sources *Letters of Sarah Byng Osborn, 1721–1773*, ed. J. McClelland (1930) · *Political and social letters of a lady of the eighteenth century, 1721–1771*, ed. E. F. D. Osborn [1890] · *DNB* · Burke, *Peerage* (1999) · GEC, *Baronetage*

Osborn, Sherard (1822–1875), naval officer, son of Colonel Edward Osborn of the Madras army, was born on 25 April 1822. In September 1837 he was entered by Commander William Warren as a first-class volunteer on board the sloop *Hyacinth*, fitting for the East Indies. The *Hyacinth* arrived at Singapore in May 1838, and in September was ordered to blockade Kedah, then in a state of revolt. Osborn was appointed to command a tender and so from December 1838 to March 1839 he was 'captain of his own ship'. The responsibility thrust on him at such an early age went far to strengthen and mature his character. Parts of his journal during the time were published in 1857 as *Quedah, or, Stray Leaves from a Journal in Malayan Waters*. In 1840 the *Hyacinth* went to China, and took part in the operations in the Canton River. In 1842 Osborn was moved into the *Clio* with Commander Troubridge, and in her was present at the capture of Woosung (Wusong) on 16 June. He was afterwards transferred to the *Volage*, and came home in the *Columbine* in 1843. He passed his examination in December, and, after going through the gunnery course in the *Excellent*, was appointed gunnery mate of the *Collingwood*, fitting out for the Pacific as flagship of Sir George Seymour.

On 4 May 1846 Osborn was promoted lieutenant of the *Collingwood*, in which he returned to England in the summer of 1848. He then had command of the *Dwarf*, a small screw-steamer, employed during the disturbances of the year on the coast of Ireland. In 1849, when public attention was turned to the fate of Sir John Franklin, Osborn entered into the question with enthusiasm and energy, and in 1850 was appointed to command the steam tender *Pioneer*, in the Arctic expedition under Captain Austin in the *Resolute*. Considered as a surveying expedition, it was eminently successful, and proved that Franklin's ships had not been lost in Baffin's Bay. Much of the success of the voyage was due to the steam tenders, which, during the summers of 1850 and 1851, held out new prospects for Arctic navigation. The way in which the *Pioneer* or *Intrepid* cut through rotten ice, or steamed through the loose pack in a calm, led directly to the employment of powerful screw-steamers in the whaling fleet. On his return to England in 1851, Osborn urged the renewal of the search for Franklin.

Osborn married, in January 1852, Helen, daughter of John Hinksman of Queen Anne Street, London, who survived him; they had two daughters. In February 1852 he published an account of the two previous years' work, *Stray Leaves from an Arctic Journal*, which further stimulated public interest; and early in the year he joined another expedition under Sir Edward Belcher in the *Assistance*, Osborn again going in command of the *Pioneer*, to which he was formally promoted on 30 October. By what Osborn considered a most serious error of judgement, the *Pioneer*, with the other ships of the expedition, was abandoned on 20 August 1854, the officers and men being brought to England on 28 September. His Arctic service, including five summers and three winters, had severely tried Osborn's health, and for some time he had charge of the coastguard in Norfolk.

Early in 1855 Osborn was sent out to take command of the *Vesuvius* in the Black Sea, where he took part in the capture of Kerch, and, after the death of Captain Lyons, he remained as senior officer in the Sea of Azov, in command of a large squadron of gunboats, with which he destroyed many depots of provisions and stores destined for Sevastopol. On 18 August he was advanced to the rank of captain, but, by Sir Edmund Lyons's desire, was appointed to the *Medusa*, a small steamer, in which he remained as senior officer in the Sea of Azov until the conclusion of the war, for his conduct in which he received the CB, the cross of the Légion d'honneur, and the Mejidiye of the fourth class. The occupation of the Sea of Azov destroyed the Russian logistics' support for its Crimean army, and led directly to the fall of Sevastopol. Osborn was consulted by the Admiralty on the strategy to be followed in 1856.

In the spring of 1857 Osborn was appointed to the paddle-frigate *Furious* and ordered to escort fifteen gunboats to China, a duty considered at the time one of serious difficulty. The gunboats, however, arrived safely at Hong Kong where they contributed to the success of the attack on Canton, in which Osborn was actively engaged. In December 1857 the *Furious* was appointed for the use of the plenipotentiary, Lord Elgin, and in the following year took him to Shanghai and the Gulf of Po Hai (Bohai). After the signing of the treaty of Tientsin, Lord Elgin, still in the *Furious*, went to Tokyo, where he concluded a treaty which largely opened Japan to relations with the West; and in September 1858 he went up the Yangtze (Yangzi) River as far as Hangchow (Hangzhou), a piece of difficult and intricate navigation.

In 1859 Osborn returned to England in bad health, and, while on leave, contributed many articles to *Blackwood's Edinburgh Magazine*, mostly on naval or Chinese topics. In 1861 he was appointed to the *Donegal*, which he commanded in the Gulf of Mexico during the Mexican war, and was paid off in the beginning of 1862. In the following June he agreed to the Chinese government's request to take command of a squadron fitted out in England for the suppression of piracy on the Chinese coast. In 1863 he went out with six specially built steamers. It had been expressly stipulated that Osborn was to receive his orders from the imperial government alone, independent of the local authorities; but on his arrival in China he found that the government had determined that the squadron was to be under the command of the mandarins at the several ports. Osborn refused to accept this, resigned, and returned to England. In 1864 Osborn commanded the *Royal Sovereign*, a ship fitted with turrets on the plan proposed by his friend Captain Cowper Phipps Coles. In this experimental command, Osborn demonstrated the value of the turret system of mounting heavy guns, and, despite his well-known connection with Coles, advised the Admiralty on the adoption of the system. The *Royal Sovereign* was the prototype of the first-class coast assault battleships which were a feature of the navy for the next thirty years. On the 1871 Admiralty committee on designs he stressed the need for first-class ships to be capable of breaking into defended bases, specifically Brest and Cherbourg.

In 1865 Osborn accepted an appointment as agent to the Great Indian Peninsula Railway, the traffic organization of which he remodelled and improved. Ill health compelled him to resign in 1866, and in 1867 he became managing director of the Telegraph Construction and Maintenance Company, an office which he held until 1873. In 1871 he commanded the *Hercules* in the channel for a few months, and on 29 May 1873 attained the rank of rear-admiral. He continued to take great interest in Arctic exploration, and in 1873 suggested to Commander Albert Markham that he examine for himself the new conditions of the work under steam, which Markham did by a summer voyage in a whaler. Markham's favourable report strongly influenced public opinion. An expedition was determined on, and an advising committee of experts, of whom Osborn was one, was appointed. On Monday, 3 May 1875, when the ships were on the point of sailing, Osborn went down to Portsmouth to wish the officers farewell. He died suddenly at his home, 33 Charles Street, Berkeley Square, London, on 6 May, and was buried in Highgate cemetery on the 10th.

Osborn's more important works, including *The Discovery of a North-West Passage by Captain M'Clure*, *Arctic Journal*, and *Last Voyage and Fate of Sir John Franklin*, were published in a collective edition of three volumes in 1865. He also published many articles in *Blackwood's Edinburgh Magazine* and in the *Journal* or *Proceedings of the Royal Geographical Society*. Osborn was an intelligent and resourceful officer, better suited to independent command than the restrictions of peacetime squadron service. He held strong views on a number of issues and was never behindhand in setting them before the public. His services in the Sea of Azov were the highlight of a brilliant, if unconventional, career, largely devoted to the projection of power from the sea against the shore.

J. K. LAUGHTON, *rev.* ANDREW LAMBERT

Sources G. S. Graham, *The China station: war and diplomacy, 1830–1860* (1978) · A. D. Lambert, *The Crimean War: British grand strategy, 1853–56* (1990) · S. Sandler, *The emergence of the modern capital ship* (1979) · A. C. Dewar, ed., *Russian war, 1855, Black Sea: official correspondence*, Navy RS, 85 (1945) · D. Bonner-Smith and E. W. R. Lumby, eds., *The Second China War, 1856–1860*, Navy RS, 95 (1954) · S. M. Eardley-Wilmot, *Life of Vice-Admiral Edmund, Lord Lyons* (1898) · 'Committee on designs for ships of war', *Parl. papers* (1872), 14.501, C. 477; 14.581, C. 477-I · G. S. Ritchie, *The Admiralty chart: British naval hydrography in the nineteenth century* (1967) · private information (1894) · *CGPLA Eng. & Wales* (1875)

Archives NMM, letters and papers | BL, letters to Sir R. I. Murchison, Add. MS 46127 · NL Scot., corresp. with Blackwoods · Scott Polar RI, letters to William Penny

Likenesses S. Pearce, oils, 1857, NPG; replica, NPG · R. & E. Taylor, wood-engraving, NPG; repro. in *ILN* (22 May 1875)

Wealth at death under £35,000: probate, 24 May 1875, *CGPLA Eng. & Wales*

Osborn, William (1736–1808), man-midwife, was born in London, and received his medical education at St George's Hospital, London. He practised for some years as a surgeon, and was elected man-midwife to the lying-in hospital in Store Street, London. On 10 October 1777 he obtained the degree of MD from St Andrews University and was admitted a licentiate in midwifery of the Royal College of Physicians on 22 December 1783. Osborn was one of only eight *accoucheurs* to acquire this title, which was discontinued in 1800. With Thomas Denman, Osborn set up a private school of midwifery, and they taught together from about 1770 to 1782. Following a rift with Denman, Osborn lectured alone, and then with John Clarke (1761–1815). Together Denman and Osborn were believed to have educated more than 1200 practitioners in midwifery. In 1783 Osborn published *An essay on laborious parturition: in which the division of the symphysis pubis is particularly considered*. Sigault and other Frenchmen had advocated the use of this operation, and in England William Hunter (1718–1783) had expressed a favourable opinion on it. Osborn thought it useless and dangerous. In this volume Osborn advocated the use of the crochet in cases where the pelvis was abnormally small, citing the case he had attended of Elizabeth Sherwood, who was 3 feet 6 inches tall, and unable to stand erect without a crutch. She became pregnant at the age of twenty-seven and was in labour for four days. Many well-known London *accoucheurs* were called to the labour by Osborn, who delivered her after a long and complicated embryotomy. Elizabeth Sherwood survived. In 1792 Osborn published *Essays on the Practice of Midwifery, in Natural and Difficult Labours*, which was an expansion of his former book. He was strongly opposed to caesarean section. Osborn advocated the use of forceps, but with prudence, and in general supported non-intervention in midwifery. His preference for the forceps over the vectis led him into controversy with Denman in the 1780s, when Denman announced his conversion from the forceps to the vectis. This began a public debate which continued up to the late nineteenth century, when the forceps finally displaced the vectis. Osborn developed his own modification of the obstetric forceps, which was depicted in his *Essays on the Practice of Midwifery*. A second edition of this, which is believed to have been surreptitious, appeared in 1795. Osborn attained considerable wealth, and died at his residence, at Old Park, near Dover, on 15 August 1808.

HILARY MARLAND

Sources Munk, *Roll* · W. Osborn, *An essay on laborious parturition* (1783) · W. Osborn, *Essays on the practice of midwifery, in natural and difficult labours* (1792) · I. Loudon, *Death in childbirth: an international study of maternal care and maternal mortality, 1800–1950* (1992) · W. Radcliffe, *Milestones in midwifery and the secret instrument* (1989) · A. Wilson, *The making of man-midwifery: childbirth in England, 1660–1770* (1995) · *GM*, 1st ser., 78 (1808), 854 · *DNB*

Likenesses J. Jones, engraving, 1791 (after portrait by T. Hardy), repro. in R. Burgess, *Portraits of doctors and scientists in the Wellcome Institute of the History of Medicine* (1973), pl. 2189.1

PICTURE CREDITS

Norie, John William (1772–1843)—
© National Portrait Gallery, London

Norman, Sir Henry Wylie (1826–
1904)—© National Portrait Gallery,
London

Norman, Montagu Collet, Baron
Norman (1871–1950)—© The
Governor and Company of the Bank
of England

Norman, Sir Richard Oswald Chandler
(1932–1993)—© News International
Newspapers Ltd

Normanton, Helena Florence (1882–
1957)—© National Portrait Gallery,
London

Norrington, Sir Arthur Lionel Pugh
(1899–1982)—The President and
Fellows of Trinity College, Oxford

Norris, Thomas (bap. 1742, d. 1790)—
© National Portrait Gallery, London

North, Brownlow (1741–1820)—All
Souls College, Oxford

North, Brownlow (1810–1875)—
© National Portrait Gallery, London

North, Dudley, fourth Baron North
(1602–1677)—© National Portrait
Gallery, London

North, Sir Dudley (1641–1691)—
© National Portrait Gallery, London

North, Francis, first Baron Guilford
(1637–1685)—© National Portrait
Gallery, London

North, Frederick, second earl of
Guilford [Lord North] (1732–1792)—
© National Portrait Gallery, London

North, Frederick, fifth earl of Guilford
(1766–1827)—Jean-Auguste-
Dominique Ingres, Gift of James
Fairfax 1992, Art Gallery of New
South Wales, photograph: Ray
Woodbury for AGNSW

North, Marianne (1830–1890)—© Royal
Botanic Gardens, Kew: reproduced
by kind permission of the Director
and the Board of Trustees

North, Roger (1651–1734)—© reserved

Northcote, James (1746–1831)—
© National Portrait Gallery, London

Northcote, Stafford Henry, first earl of
Iddesleigh (1818–1887)—© National
Portrait Gallery, London

Northwood, John, first Lord
Northwood (1254–1319)—reproduced
by courtesy of H. M. Stutchfield,
F.S.A., Hon. Secretary of the
Monumental Brass Society

Norton, Caroline Elizabeth Sarah
(1808–1877)—© National Portrait
Gallery, London

Norton, Edward Felix (1884–1954)—
The Royal Geographical Society,
London

Norton, Fletcher, first Baron Grantley
(1716–1789)—Palace of Westminster
Collection

Norton, John (1770–1831?)—Collection
of the Duke of Northumberland.
Photograph: Photographic Survey,
Courtauld Institute of Art, London

Norton, (Kathleen) Mary (1903–1992)—
private collection

Norwood, Sir Cyril (1875–1956)—
© National Portrait Gallery, London

Notari, Angelo (1566–1663)—
© Fitzwilliam Museum, University of
Cambridge

Nott, Sir William (1782–1845)—
Oriental Club; photograph National
Portrait Gallery, London

Nove, Alexander (1915–1994)—© James
L. Millar

Novello, (Joseph) Alfred (1810–1896)—
© National Portrait Gallery, London

Novello, Clara Anastasia (1818–1908)—
© National Portrait Gallery, London

Novello, Ivor (1893–1951)—© Estate of
Paul Tanqueray; collection National
Portrait Gallery, London

Novello, Vincent (1781–1861)—
© National Portrait Gallery, London

Novikov, Olga (1840–1925)—© National
Portrait Gallery, London

Nowell, Alexander (c.1516/17–1602)—
Principal and Fellows of Brasenose
College, Oxford

Noyce, (Cuthbert) Wilfrid Francis
(1917–1962)—© National Portrait
Gallery, London

Noyes, Alfred (1880–1958)—© National
Portrait Gallery, London

Nugent, Robert Craggs, Earl Nugent
(1709–1788)—private collection;
photograph courtesy of the
Holburne Museum of Art, Bath

Nureyev, Rudolf Hametovich (1938–
1993)—© Cecil Beaton Archive,
Sotheby's

Nuthall, Thomas (d. 1775)—© Tate,
London, 2004

Nyerere, Julius Kambarage (1922–
1999)—Getty Images – Hulton
Archive

Oakeley, Sir Charles, first baronet
(1751–1826)—Christie's Images Ltd.
(2004)

Oakeley, Sir Herbert Stanley (1830–
1903)—© National Portrait Gallery,
London

Oakeshott, Michael Joseph (1901–
1990)—reproduced by kind
permission of the Master and
Fellows of Gonville and Caius
College, Cambridge; photograph:
Christopher Hurst

Oakley, Kenneth Page (1911–1981)—
© National Portrait Gallery, London

Oastler, Richard (1789–1861)—
© National Portrait Gallery, London

Oates, Lawrence Edward Grace (1880–
1912)—© Popperfoto; collection
National Portrait Gallery, London

Oates, Titus (1649–1705)—© National
Portrait Gallery, London

O'Beirne, Thomas Lewis (1749–1823)—
National Gallery of Ireland

Oberon, Merle (1911–1979)—© National
Portrait Gallery, London

Obolensky, Alexander (1916–1940)—
© National Portrait Gallery, London

O'Brien, Cornelius (1843–1906)—
© National Portrait Gallery, London

O'Brien, James [Bronterre O'Brien]
(1804–1864)—© National Portrait
Gallery, London

O'Brien, James Francis Xavier (1828–
1905)—© National Portrait Gallery,
London

O'Brien, Murrough, first earl of
Inchiquin (c.1614–1674)—
© Manchester City Art Galleries

O'Brien, William (1852–1928)—
Crawford Municipal Art Gallery,
Cork / Bridgeman Art Library

O'Brien, William Smith (1803–1864)—
National Gallery of Ireland

O'Callaghan, John Cornelius (1805–
1883)—National Gallery of Ireland

O'Casey, Sean (1880–1964)—National
Gallery of Ireland

Occom, Samson (1723–1792)—
© National Portrait Gallery, London

Ochterlony, Sir David, first baronet
(1758–1825)—© National Portrait
Gallery, London

O'Connell, Daniel (1775–1847)—by
courtesy of the National Gallery of
Ireland

O'Connor, Arthur (1763–1852)—
© National Portrait Gallery, London

O'Connor, Feargus Edward (1796?–
1855)—National Gallery of Ireland

O'Connor, Thomas Power (1848–
1929)—© National Portrait Gallery,
London

O'Conor, Charles (1710–1791)—
Ashmolean Museum, Oxford

O'Conor, Sir Nicholas Roderick (1843–
1908)—© National Portrait Gallery,
London

Odger, George (1813–1877)—© National
Portrait Gallery, London

Odo, earl of Kent (d. 1097)—by special
permission of the City of Bayeux

O'Donnell, Patrick (1856–1927)—
photograph National Portrait
Gallery, London

O'Donovan, Michael Francis Xavier
(1903–1966)—© reserved;
photograph National Portrait
Gallery, London

O'Duffy, Eimar Ultan (1893–1935)—
© National Portrait Gallery, London

O'Duffy, Eoin (1890–1944)—Getty
Images

Offa (d. 796)—© Copyright The British
Museum

Ogden, Samuel (1716–1778)—
© National Portrait Gallery, London

Ogdon, John Andrew Howard (1937–
1989)—© Godfrey Argent Studios;
collection National Portrait Gallery,
London

Ogilby, John (1600–1676)—© National
Portrait Gallery, London

Ogilvie, Sir Frederick Wolff (1893–
1949)—BBC Picture Archives

Ogilvie, John (1732–1813)—© National
Portrait Gallery, London

Ogilvy, James, fourth earl of Findlater
and first earl of Seafield (1663–
1730)—in a private Scottish
collection; photograph courtesy the
Scottish National Portrait Gallery

Ogilvy, Mabell Frances Elizabeth,
countess of Airlie (1866–1956)—in a
private Scottish collection

Ogle, Sir Chaloner (1680/81–1750)—
© National Maritime Museum,
London, Greenwich Hospital
Collection

Ogle, George (1742–1814)—National
Gallery of Ireland

Ogle, James Adey (1792–1857)—The
President and Fellows of Trinity
College, Oxford

Oglethorpe, James Edward (1696–
1785)—© Copyright The British
Museum

O'Grady, Sir James (1866–1934)—
© reserved

O'Grady, Standish James (1846–1928)—
National Gallery of Ireland

O'Hagan, Thomas, first Baron O'Hagan
(1812–1885)—National Gallery of
Ireland

Oldenburg, Henry (c.1619–1677)—
© The Royal Society

Oldfield, Anne (1683–1730)—
© National Portrait Gallery, London

Oldfield, Joshua (1656–1729)—by
permission of Dr Williams's Library

Oldknow, Samuel (1756–1828)—private
collection; photograph National
Portrait Gallery, London

Oldys, William (1696–1761)—
© National Portrait Gallery, London

Oliphant, Carolina, Lady Nairne (1766–
1845)—Scottish National Portrait
Gallery

Oliphant, Laurence (1829–1888)—
© National Portrait Gallery, London

Oliphant, Margaret Oliphant Wilson
(1828–1897)—© National Portrait
Gallery, London

Oliver, Dame Beryl Carnegy (1882–
1972)—© National Portrait Gallery,
London

Oliver, George (1782–1867)—
© National Portrait Gallery, London

Oliver, Isaac (c.1565–1617)—© National
Portrait Gallery, London

Oliver, Martha Cranmer (1834–1880)—
© National Portrait Gallery, London

Oliver, Peter (1589–1647)—© National
Portrait Gallery, London

Oliver, William (1695–1764)—Royal
National Hospital for Rheumatic
Diseases, Bath; photograph © Clive
Quinnel

Olivier, Laurence Kerr, Baron Olivier
(1907–1989)—© Karsh / Camera
Press; collection National Portrait
Gallery, London

Olivier, Sydney Haldane, Baron Olivier
(1859–1943)—© National Portrait
Gallery, London

Ollivant, Alfred (1798–1882)—
© National Portrait Gallery, London

O'Mahony, John (1815–1877)—Gill &
Macmillan Ltd

Omai (c.1753–c.1780)—© reserved

Oman, John Wood (1860–1939)—
photograph reproduced by

Oxford dictionary of
national biography